CONTRACT

CASES AND MATERIALS

FIFTH EDITION

H G BEALE QC (Hon), BA, FBA

Honorary Bencher of Lincoln's Inn;
Professor of Law, University of Warwick

W BISHOP   MA, BCL, PHD

Charles River Associates

M P FURMSTON   TD, BCL, MA, LLM

Bencher of Gray's Inn;
Emeritus Professor and Senior Research Fellow,
University of Bristol;
Professor of Law, Singapore Management University

OXFORD

UNIVERSITY PRESS

OXFORD
UNIVERSITY PRESS

Great Clarendon Street, Oxford OX2 6DP

Oxford University Press is a department of the University of Oxford.
It furthers the University's objective of excellence in research, scholarship,
and education by publishing worldwide in

Oxford New York

Auckland Cape Town Dar es Salaam Hong Kong Karachi
Kuala Lumpur Madrid Melbourne Mexico City Nairobi
New Delhi Shanghai Taipei Toronto

With offices in

Argentina Austria Brazil Chile Czech Republic France Greece
Guatemala Hungary Italy Japan Poland Portugal Singapore
South Korea Switzerland Thailand Turkey Ukraine Vietnam

Oxford is a registered trade mark of Oxford University Press
in the UK and in certain other countries

Published in the United States
by Oxford University Press Inc., New York

© Oxford University Press 2008

British Library Cataloguing in Publication Data

Data available

Library of Congress Cataloging in Publication Data

Data available

Typeset by Newgen Imaging Systems (P) Ltd., Chennai, India
Printed in Great Britain on acid-free paper by
Antony Rowe Ltd., Chippennam

ISBN 978–0–19–928736–9

10 9 8 7 6 5 4 3 2 1

PREFACE

This is the first edition of this book to be published by Oxford University Press. The translation from Butterworths has been happy and harmonious and everyone at the Press has been most helpful.

We remarked in the Preface to the fourth edition on the wide variety of ways in which Contract is now taught in Law Schools. This tendency has become, if anything, wider still. Our strategy continues to be to offer students and their teachers a broad range of choice. We do not expect that many will read the whole book, although we would hope that anyone who did would learn a good deal.

There has continued to be a broad range of interesting new cases. These include the decisions of the House of Lords in *Actionstrength* v *International Glass*; *Shogun Finance* v *Hudson*; *HIH Casualty* v *Chase Manhattan Bank*; *Sirius International Insurance* v *FAI*; *The Starsin*; *AIB Group* v *Martin*; *Hilton Barker* v *Eastwood*; *Wilson* v *First County Trust*; *Jackson* v *Royal Bank of Scotland*; *Farley* v *Skinner*; *Royal Bank of Scotland* v *Etridge*; *Jindal Iron and Steel* v *Islamic Solidarity*; *DG of Fair Trading* v *First National Bank*; and *The Golden Victory* (decided in February 2007 while the book was in the press). Among the many decisions of other courts, attention should perhaps be directed to the decision of the Privy Council in *Pratt Contractors* v *Transit New Zealand*; of the Court of Appeal in *Baird Textile* v *Marks and Spencer* and *The Great Peace*; and of the Singapore Court of Appeal in *Chwee Kin Keong* v *Digilandmall*.

MPF
HGB
WDB

In this edition, Bill Bishop's participation has been largely confined to the economic readings and linked material. All three take joint responsibility for the book but, as with the last edition, the major burden of the work has fallen on Michael Furmston. The other editors are most grateful to him.

HGB
WB

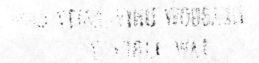

CONTENTS

Preface   v
Suggested 'core' readings for first-year students   xv
Acknowledgements   xvii
Table of statutes   xxiii
Table of cases   xxix

SECTION ONE INTRODUCTION

  1 Contracts and contract law   3
   I   The scope of contract law   3
  II   The function of contract law   5
  III   Contract as a dynamic body of rules   8
  IV   Different approaches to contract law   10
  V   Economic and empirical analysis   11
  VI   Plan of the book   12
  VII   Using the book   12

  2 Contract, tort and restitution   13
   I   Contract   13
  II   Tort and contract   24
  III   Restitution and contract   39

  3 The functions of contract law   46

  4 Economic analysis of contract law   73

  5 Empirical work   81

SECTION TWO ENFORCEABLE TYPES OF PROMISE

  6 Consideration   97
   I   Definitions of consideration   97
  II   Sufficient consideration   99
  III   Exchange   123
  IV   Gratuitous promises and bargains   129

V   Moral obligation   139

VI   Formal requirements   143

VII Reliance on non-bargain promises   146

7   **Intention to create legal relations**   175

SECTION THREE HAS AN AGREEMENT BEEN REACHED?

8   **Offer and acceptance**   191

I   The objective principle   192

II   Offer or preliminary negotiations   195

III Acceptance in bilateral contracts   204

IV   Acceptance in unilateral contracts   215

V   Bilateral or unilateral?   221

VI   Differing proposals   222

VII Postal communications   230

VIII Exchange of contracts   240

IX   Tenders   242

9   **Uncertainty and incompleteness**   258

I   Uncertainty   259

II   Incompleteness   263

III Preliminary contracts   271

IV   Work done and steps taken before a contract has been agreed   281

10   **Communication mistakes**   289

I   Mistakes as to the terms   289

II   Rectification   296

III Misunderstanding as to terms   301

IV   Mistaken expectations   303

V   Mistakes as to identity   309

VI   *Non est factum*   318

SECTION FOUR OBLIGATIONS AND RISKS

11   **Express terms in oral agreements**   323

I   Terms, representations and puffs   323

II   What was being promised?   328

III Incorporation of written terms into an oral contract   332

12	Contents of written contracts	345
I	Effect of signature	345
II	Parol evidence rule	349

13	Inaccurate information and misrepresentation	354
I	Rescission for misrepresentation	355
II	Limits to rescission for misrepresentation	363
III	Rescission and consequential loss	369
IV	Damages for misrepresentation	370
V	Attempts to exclude or restrict liability for misrepresentation	386

14	Gap-filling by interpretation	389
I	Introduction	389
II	Interpretation	397

15	Implied terms	411
I	Terms implied by custom	411
II	Terms implied by statute	412
III	Terms implied at common law	413
IV	Contracts for the sale or supply of goods	425
V	Contracts for services	446
VI	Contracts of employment	449
VII	Justifications for implied terms	456

16	Discharge by frustration	459
I	The juristic basis of frustration	463
II	Should one party bear the risk?	467
III	Frustration of purpose	473
IV	Foreseen events	479
V	Effect of frustration	481
VI	Relief in cases of hardship	493

17	Expectation mistakes	499

18	Discharge by construction	521

19	Duties of disclosure	529
I	Undue influence	530
II	Contracts *uberrimae fidei*	530
III	Information wrongfully obtained	531
IV	Statutory duties of disclosure	532
V	A general duty of disclosure?	532

SECTION FIVE REMEDIES

20   Some preliminary questions   547
  I   The distinction between rights and remedies   547
  II   Self-help and judicial remedies   549
  III   Off-the-shelf remedies and expressly planned remedies   549

21   Withholding performance and termination for default   550
  I   The notion of conditions   551
  II   Conditions and the order of performance   553
  III   Entire and severable obligations   556
  IV   Effect of partial performance of an entire obligation   559
  V   Conditions and warranties   564
  VI   A more flexible approach   566
  VII   Time stipulations   573
  VIII   Conditions in unilateral contracts and options   581
  IX   Anticipatory breach   581
  X   Relief against forfeiture   588
  XI   Reprise: flexibility or certainty?   592
  XII   Agreed rights of termination   599
  XIII   The nature of termination   611
  XIV   Loss of the right to terminate   615
  XV   Consumer Remedies   620

22   Damages   623
  I   The basic measure of recovery   623
  II   Remoteness of damage   644
  III   Mitigation   651
  IV   Quantification, markets and other contracts   662
  V   Problem cases   671
  VI   Agreed damages, deposits and forfeitures   689
  VII   Reprise: liability for consequential damages   706

23   Literal enforcement   709
  I   Specific performance and injunction   709
  II   Action for sums due under the contract   732

24   Restitutionary remedies   742
  I   Unjust enrichment by subtraction   742
  II   Unjust enrichment by wrongdoing   745

SECTION SIX CONTRACT THEORY

25 Why are promises binding?   757

26 Economic analysis of contract law   784

27 The impact of the empirical studies   786

28 Critical approaches to contract   791

29 Developing the relational contract notion   807

30 Fairness and distributive justice   813

31 Transformation thesis   838

SECTION SEVEN CHANGING THE BARGAIN

32 Rescission, variation, waiver and promissory estoppel   845
 I The setting   845
 II Basic concepts   846
 III Discharge or variation by contract   847
 IV Waiver   860

33 Adjustments in longer term contracts   881

SECTION EIGHT POLICING THE BARGAIN

34 Duress   901

35 Undue pressure and undue influence   917

36 Unconscionable bargains   938
 I Mortgages   938
 II Poor and ignorant persons and expectant heirs   939
 III The insane   945
 IV Salvage agreements   948
 V Consumer credit   949
 VI Minors   951
 VII Restraint of trade   952

37 A general principle? 954

I Is there a general principle? 954

II Possible advantages of a general doctrine 958

38 Standard-form contracts 964

39 Exclusion clauses 975

I The common law approach to exclusion clauses: interpretation 977

II Statutory controls 995

40 Unfair terms in consumer contracts 1035

41 Regulated contracts 1055

I 'Necessities' in short supply 1055

II Intractable problems of inadequate information 1056

III Problems with transactions costs 1058

IV Vulnerability to exploitation in long-term relationships 1058

V Private enforcement costs are too high 1059

VI Monopolies, oligopolies and anti-competitive arrangements 1061

VII Paternalism 1061

VIII Human rights 1065

SECTION NINE ILLEGALITY

42 Contracts contrary to public policy 1069

I The heads of public policy 1072

II Policy issues 1078

43 Contracts involving the commission of a crime or a tort 1079

I Contracts requiring the deliberate commission of a crime or a tort 1079

II Contracts involving other unlawful acts 1081

III Benefits from deliberate illegal acts 1088

IV Summary so far 1092

V Collateral contracts 1092

VI Recovery of payments or property 1094

VII Severance 1104

44 Contracts in restraint of trade 1105

SECTION TEN INTERMEDIARIES, THIRD PARTIES AND ASSIGNMENT

45	**Agency**	1127
I	Intermediary or party?	1127
II	Types of authority	1128
III	The unauthorised agent	1130
IV	The undisclosed principal	1132
46	**Privity and the benefit of a contract between others**	1136
I	The basic rule	1136
II	Damages on behalf of another	1143
III	Qualifications to the privity rule	1150
IV	Negative benefits, or vicarious immunity	1153
V	Privity of contract and liability in tort	1162
VI	Circles of indemnity	1174
VII	Reform	1178
VIII	Agency and privity	1194
47	**Subsequent assignment of the benefit of a contract**	1195
I	Assignment	1195
II	Negotiable instruments	1197
48	**Privity and burdens**	1200
I	Undisclosed principals	1200
II	Bailment	1200
III	Tort	1204
IV	Property	1204
49	**Assignment and the burden of a contract**	1207
	Appendix Specimen contracts	1209
	Index	1249

SUGGESTED 'CORE' READINGS FOR FIRST-YEAR STUDENTS

The aim of this list is to provide a core of readings around which a course suitable for first-year students can be constructed. It includes a certain amount of critical material and economic analysis. Teachers will no doubt wish to add to this list; they may also decide to omit some topics.

   Please note that this selection assumes that the readings from this book will be supplemented by either full lectures or quite wide reading in a textbook.

1. *Introductory readings*: Chapter 2 plus pp 57–63 Adams & Brownsword); Chapter 4 (economic analysis); pp 81–83 (Beale and Dugdale); pp 91–92 (questions).

2. *Consideration*: pp 97–100 (introduction to consideration); pp 105–116 (performance of existing duty, requirements contracts); pp 122–123 (adequacy); pp 123–129 (exchange); pp 173–174 (questions).

3. *Gratuitous promises; Reliance; Intention*: pp 129, 135, 139–146 (gratuitous promises and formal requirements); pp 148–158 (estoppel), 165–169 (Atiyah), 175–179 (intention); p 187 (questions).

4. *Offer and acceptance*: pp 191–200 (offers in correspondence; advertisements and displays of goods); pp 208–220 (acceptance by conduct, silence, unilateral contracts); pp 222–227 (differing proposals); pp 256–257 (questions).

5. *Postal rules; Uncertainty*: pp 230–238, 258–259, 263, 266; pp 271–275, 279–280 (preliminary contracts); pp 281–283 (contracts which do not materialise); p 288 (questions).

6. *Communication mistakes*: pp 288–295; pp 299–300 (rectification); pp 301–302 (mutual mistake); pp 303–306 (mistaken expectations); pp 309–318 (mistaken identity); p 323 (questions).

7. *Express terms*: pp 323–330 (term or representation); pp 332–341 (ticket cases); p 345 (signature).

8. *Misrepresentation*: pp 354–358; pp 363–369 (limits to rescission); pp 369–372, 377–379 (damages); pp 386–387 (clauses restricting liability); pp 387–388 (questions).

9. *Interpretation; Implied terms*: pp 389–392; pp 397–408; pp 412–413, 418 note 1 (implied terms); pp 427–431 (description and quality under SGA); pp 457–458 (questions).

10. *Frustration*: pp 459–465, 467–471 (self-induced frustration); pp 474–479 (frustration of purpose); pp 481–485 (LR (FC) Act 1943); pp 497–498 (questions).

11. *Expectation mistake; Duty to disclose*: pp 499–500, 503–507, 517 note 4, 524–525 (discharge by construction); pp 529–532 (duty to disclose); p 541 (summary table); p 543 (questions).

12. *Express and constructive conditions*: pp 550–554, 559–564, 555–560 (substantial performance), 564–573 (conditions, warranties and innominate terms); pp 599–611 (agreed rights of termination); p 619 (questions 1–5).

13. *Termination:* pp 581–588 (anticipatory repudiation); pp 611–615 (nature of termination); pp 615–619 (loss of right to terminate); p 622 (questions).

14. *Damages:* pp 623–630, 633–644 (economic analysis); pp 644–646 (remoteness); pp 671–679 (problem cases); pp 683–689 (consumer surplus); p 708 (questions 1–5).

15. *Liquidated damages; Other remedies:* pp 689–692, 703–705, 709–711 (specific performance); pp 713–716 (economic analysis); pp 733–738 (action for price); p 708 and 741 (questions).

16. *Contract theory:* pp 626–628, 765–768 (Fuller); pp 771–777 (Atiyah); pp 784–785 (Leff); pp 63–66, 807–812 (relational); pp 66–72, 838–841 (Collins).

17. *Changing the bargain:* pp 846–857 (consideration); pp 861–875 (promissory estoppel); pp 875–877 (economic analysis); pp 879–880 (questions).

18. *Duress, etc:* pp 905–915, (economic duress); pp 917–923 (undue influence); pp 939–945 (poor and ignorant persons); pp 954–959 (a general doctrine?); pp 963–964 (questions).

19. *Standard forms; Exclusion clauses at common law:* pp 964–967, 975–980, 981–988 (interpretation); pp 986–990 (substantive doctrine); p 1000 (questions).

20. *UCTA 1977:* pp 995–1013; pp 1033–1034 (questions).

21. *Unfair terms in consumer contracts:* pp 1035–1045; p 1054 (questions).

22. *Contracts involving commission of crime or tort:* pp 1069–1078 (public policy); pp 1079–1099, 1122–1123 (questions 3 and 5–9).

23. *Contracts in restraint of trade:* pp 1105–1116, 1120–1122; pp 1122–1123 (questions).

24. *Privity:* pp 1126–1150, 1153–1162; pp 1127–1130 (agency); pp 1174–1178 (indemnities); pp 1187–1194 (Contracts (Rights of Third Parties) Act); pp 1200–1204 (burdens).

ACKNOWLEDGEMENTS

We are grateful to all authors and publishers of copyright material used in this book and in particular to the following for permission to reprint from the sources indicated:

Extracts from Law Commission Reports, Working Papers, and Consultation Papers, are Crown copyright material and are reproduced under the terms of the Click-Use Licence Number C2006010631 with the permission of the Controller of Her Majesty's Stationery Office and the Queen's Printer for Scotland.

Parliamentary copyright material from House of Lords judgments is reproduced with the permission of the Controller of Her Majesty's Stationery Office on behalf of Parliament.

V A Aivazian for extracts from V A Aivazian, M J Trebilcock and M Penny: 'The Law of Contract Modifications: The Uncertain Quest for a Benchmark of Enforceability', (1984) 22 *Osgoode Hall Law Journal* 173.

Aspen Publishers, Wolters Kluwer Law & Business for extracts from A T Kronman & Richard A Posner: *Economics of Contract Law* (Aspen, 1979); and Richard A Posner: *Economic Analysis of Law* (6e, Aspen, 2002)

P S Atiyah for extracts from *Sale of Goods* (8e, Pitman, 1990) and from 'Freedom of Contract and the New Right' in P S Atiyah: *Essays on Contract* (OUP, 1990).

AgustaWestland for Westland Helicopters Ltd Order form with conditions of purchase and indemnity clause from Sales Contract, and for Weslake Aeromarine Engines Ltd Sales Quotation with conditions of sale, specimen documents. The Sales Quotation form is no longer in use and AgustaWestland now use bespoke terms for their sales.

Baltic and International Maritime Council (BIMCO) for BALTIME 1939 (revised 2001) Time Charter Party, and GENCON 1994 Voyage Charter Party specimen documents.

Bancroft-Whitney for extract from *California Appeals Reports* [Cal App].

Basic Books, a member of the Perseus Books Group for extracts from Peter Gabel and Jay M Feinman: 'Contract Law as Ideology', in *The Politics of Law: a progressive critique* edited by David Kairys (5e, Basic Books, 1998), copyright © David Kairys 1988.

Blackwell Publishing for extracts from Robert Nozick: *Anarchy, State and Utopia*; from Brian Napier: 'The contract of employment' in *Labour Law in Britain* edited by Roy Lewis (Blackwell, 1986); from *British Journal of Law and Society*: H G Beale & A Dugdale: 'Contracts Between Businessmen', (1975) 2 *BJLS* 45; Richard Lewis: 'Contracts between Businessmen: Reform of the law of Firm Offers', (1982) 9 *BJLS* 153; and Robert B Ferguson: 'The adjudication of Commercial Disputes and the legal system in modern England', (1980) 7 *BJLS* 14; from *Modern Law Review*: B Coote: 'Another look at Bowmakers', (1972) 35 *MLR* 38; G Teubner: 'Legal Irritants: Good Faith in British Law or How Unifying Law Ends Up in New Divergences', (1998) 61 *MLR* 11; and G H Treitel: 'Some problems of Breach of Contract', (1967) 30 *MLR* 139; from *Law and Society Review*: Stewart Macaulay: 'Elegant Models, Empirical Pictures, and the Complexities of Contracts', (1977) 11 *LSR* 507; and from *Legal Studies*: J N Adams and R Brownsword: 'The Ideologies of Contract Law', (1987) 7 *LS* 205, and 'Privity and the concept of a network contract', (1990) 10 *LS* 112.

Roger Brownsword for extracts from *Contract Law: Themes for the Twenty-First Century* (Butterworths, 2000).

Andrew Burrows for extract from *The Law of Restitution* (Butterworths, 1993).

Cambridge Law Journal and the authors for extracts from *Cambridge Law Journal*: C J Hamson: 'Illegal Contracts and Limited Interests', (1949) 10 *CLJ* 249; I M Jackman: (1989) 48 *CLJ* 302; John Shand: 'Unblinkering the Unruly Horse: Public Policy in the Law of Contract', (1972A) *CLJ* 144; and John Spencer: 'Signature, Consent and the Rule in *L'Estrange v Graucob*, (1973) *CLJ* 103.

Cambridge University Press for extracts from M Eisenberg: 'The Theory of Contracts', in P Benson: *The Theory of Contract Law* (CUP, 2001); and from Hugh Collins: *The Law of Contract* (4e, LexisNexis, 2003).

Canada Law Book, a Division of The Cartwright Group Ltd (1–800–263–3269, www.canadalawbook.ca) for extracts from *Dominion Law Reports* (DLR).

Hugh Collins for extracts from *Law of Contract* (4e, LexisNexis, 2003).

Construction Plant-Hire Association for Model Conditions for the Hiring of Plant (July 2001), specimen document.

Consumer Credit Trade Association (CCTA) for Hire Purchase Agreement, and Guarantee and Indemnity Form, specimen documents.

CSBC Ltd for Carbolic Smoke Ball advertisement.

Duke University School of Law and the author for extract from T J Muris: 'The Costs of Freely Granting Specific Performance', *Duke Law Journal* (1982) 1053.

Faber & Faber Ltd for extracts from Lord Radcliffe: *The Law and Its Compass* (Faber, 1961).

Fordham Law Review for extracts from Jay M Feinman: 'The Last Promissory Estoppel Article', (1992) 61 *Fordham Law Review* 303.

Grain and Free Trade Association (GAFTA) for Sales Contract No 119, specimen document.

Harvard Law Review Association and William S Hein Company for extracts from *Harvard Law Review*: D Charny: 'Nonlegal Sanctions in Commercial Relationships', (1990) 104 *Harvard LR* 373; Morris R Cohen: 'The Basis of Contract', (1933) 46 *Harvard LR* 553; M Eisenberg: 'The Bargaining Principle and its Limits', (1982) 95 *Harvard LR* 741; D Kennedy: 'Form and Substance in Private Law Adjudication', (1976) 89 *Harvard LR* 1685: George L Priest: 'Breach and Remedy for the Tender of Non-conforming Goods under the Uniform Commercial Code: An Economic Approach', (1978) 91 *Harvard LR* 960; and Percy Winfield: 'Public Policy in the English Common Law', (1929) 42 *Harvard LR* 76.

Harvard University Press for extracts from Charles Fried: *Contract as Promise: A Theory of Contractual Obligations* (Cambridge, Mass.: Harvard University Press, 1981), © 1981 by the President and Fellows of Harvard College.

The Institution of Civil Engineers for Form of Tender, and other extracts from ICE Conditions.

The Incorporated Council of Law Reporting for extracts from *Appeal Court Reports* (AC), *Chancery Reports* (Ch), *Industrial Cases Reports* (ICR), *King's Bench Reports* (K), *Queen's Bench Reports* (QB), and *Weekly Law Reports* (WLR).

Indiana University School of Law for extract from A Schwartz: 'The Private Law Treatment of Defective Products in Sales Situations', (1973) 49 *Indiana Law Journal* 8, © 1973 by the Trustees of Indiana University.

Informa Professional, a trading division of T & F Informa UK Ltd, Informa House, 30–32 Mortimer Street, London W1W 7RE, for extracts from *Lloyds Law Reports* (LLR) and from *Building Law Reports* (BLR).

Duncan Kennedy for extracts from D Kennedy: 'Distributive and Paternalist Motives in Contract and Tort Law', (1982) 41 *Maryland Law Journal* 563.

Kluwer Academic Publishers for extracts from Wilhelmmson: 'Social *Force Majeure*: a New Approach', (1990) 13 *Journal of Consumer Policy* 1.

Koninklijke Brill NV for extracts from Stewart Macaulay: 'The Standardised Contracts of United States Automobile Manufacturers' in *International Encyclopedia of Comparative Law*. Vol VII, Ch 3 'Contracts in General' S3–21/29 (M Nijhoff, 1974).

Law Book Co for extracts from *Commonwealth Law Reports* (CLR), © Law Book Co, part of Thomson Legal and Regulatory Ltd, http://thomson.co.au.

LexisNexis Canada Inc for extracts from Michael J Trebilcock: 'An Econmic Approach to the Doctrine of Unconscionability' in *Studies in Contract Law* edited by Barry J Reiter and John Swan (Butterworths, Toronto, 1980).

LexisNexis Pty Ltd and the authors for extracts from *Journal of Contract Law*: M P Ellinghaus: 'An Australian Contract Law', (1989) *J of Contract Law* 13; and P Drahos and S Parker: 'Critical Contract Law in Australia', (1990) 3 *J of Contract Law* 30.

McGill Law Journal for extracts from Philip Slayton: 'The Unequal Bargain Doctrine: Lord Denning in *Lloyds Bank v Bundy*', (1976) 22 *McGill Law Journal* 94.

Ian Macneil for extract from Ian Macneil: 'Relational Contract Theory as Sociology', (1987) 143 *Journal of Institutional and Theoretical Economics* 272.

Mohr Siebeck GmbH & Co for extracts from Stewart Macaulay: 'The Standardised Contracts of United States Automobile Manufacturers' in *International Encyclopedia of Comparative Law*, Vol VII, Ch 3 'Contracts in General' S3–21/29 (M Nijhoff, 1974).

Northwestern University School of Law for extracts from Ian Macneil: 'Contracts: 'Adjustment of Long Term Economic Relations under Classical, Neo-Classical and Relational Contract Law', (1978) 72(6) *Northwestern University Law Review* 854.

Ohio State University for extract from Grant Gilmore: *The Death of Contract* (Ohio State U P, 1974).

Oxford University Press for extracts from W R Anson: *Law of Contracts* edited by A G Guest (26e, OUP, 1984); P S Atiyah: *The Rise and Fall of Freedom of Contract* (OUP, 1979); P S Atiyah: *Essays on Contract* (OUP, 1986, rev. 1990); F H Lawson and B Rudden: *Law of Property* (2e, OUP, 1982); and Richard O'Dair: in *Legal Ethics in Current Legal Problems* edited by R D A Freeman (OUP, 1993) Vol. 46, part 2.

Oxford University Press and the authors for extracts from *Oxford Journal of Legal Studies*: H Collins: 'Good Faith in European Contract Law', (1994) 14 *OJLS* 229, B J Reiter: 'The Control of Contract Power', (1981) 1 *OJLS* 347, and C A Riley: 'Designing Default Rules in Contract Law', (2000) 20 *OJLS* 367.

Pearson Education, Inc. for extracts from Robert Cooter and Thomas Ulen: *Law and Economics* 3e, (Addison-Wesley, 2003), © 2004, 2000, 1997 Pearson Education, Inc. All rights reserved.

Reed Elsevier (UK) Ltd trading as LexisNexis Butterworths for extracts from *All England Law Reports* (ALL ER).

Sweet & Maxwell Ltd for extracts from *Law Quarterly Review*: P S Atiyah: 'Promises, Obligations, and the Law of Contract', (1978) *LQR* 193; P Birks: 'Profit of Breach of Contract', (1993) 1209 *LQR* 518; Donald Harris, Anthony Ogus & Jennifer Phillips: 'Contract Remedies and the Consumer Surplus', (1979) 95 *LQR* 581; J K Grodecki: 'In Pari Delicto', (1995) 71 *LQR* 254; F M B Reynolds: 'Warranty, Condition and Fundamental Term', (1963) 79 *LQR* 534; A W B Simpson: 'Innovation in Nineteenth Century Contract Law', (1975) 91 *LQR* 247; S Smith: 'Contracts—Mistake, Frustration and Implied Terms', (1994) 110 *LQR* 400; and Stephen A Smith: 'In Defence of Substantive Unfairness', (1996) 112 *LQR* 138; and from *Civil Justice Quarterly*: Peter Vincent-Jones: 'Contract Litigation in England and Wales 1975–1991—A Transformation in Business Disputing', (1993) *CJQ* 337; and from *Property Planning and Compensation Reports* (P & CR).

M J Trebilcock for extracts from V A Aivazian, M J Trebilcock and M Penny: 'The Law of Contract Modifications: The Uncertain Quest for a Benchmark of Enforceability', (1984) 22 *Osgoode Hall Law Journal* 173.

Thomson West for extracts from *West's National Reporter System*: *Federal Reporter*, © 1946 Thomson/West; *Atlantic Reporter* © 1969 Thomson/West; *North Eastern Reporter* © 1891 Thomson/West and © 1917 Thomson/West; *North Western Reporter* © 1965 Thomson/West; and *Pacific Reporter* © 1958 Thomson/West and © 1960 Thomson/West. All rights reserved.

University of Bristol Alumni Foundation for Deed of Covenant form formally used for gift promises and donations.

University of California Berkeley and the authors for extracts from *California Law Review*: James Gordley: 'Equality in Exchange', (1981) 69 *Calif Law Rev* 1587, © 1981 by the California Law Review; and Justin Sweet: 'Liquidated Damages in California', (1972) 60 *Calif Law Rev* 86, © 1972 by the California Law Review.

University of Chicago Law School and the authors for extracts from *Journal of Law and Economics*: Richard A Epstein: 'Unconscionability: A Critical Re-appraisal' (1975) 18 *J Law & Econ* 293; and Victor P Goldberg: 'Institutional change and the quasi-invisible hand' (1974) 17 *J Law & Econ* 461; and extracts from *Journal of Legal Studies*: William Bishop: 'The Contract-Tort Boundary and the Economics of Insurance', (1983) 12 *J Legal Stud* 241; Richard Danzig: Hadley v Baxendale: a study in the Industrialization of the Law', (1975) 4 *J Legal Stud* 249; Richard A Epstein: 'Beyond Foreseeability', (1989) 18 *J Legal Stud* 105; Daniel Friedmann: (1989) 18 *J Legal Stud* 1; Anthony T Kronman: 'Mistake, Disclosure Information and the Law of Contracts', (1978) 7 *J Legal Stud* 1; Richard A Posner: 'Gratuitous Promises in Economics and Law', (1977) 6 *J Legal Stud* 411; Richard A Posner and Andrew M Rosenfeld: 'Impossibility and Related Doctrines in Contract Law: An Economic Analysis', (1977) 6 *J Legal Stud* 83; and Samuel A Rea: 'Efficiency, Implications of Penalties and Liquidated Damages', (1984) 13 *J Legal Stud* 147.

University of Chicago Law School via Copyright Clearance Center for extracts from *University of Chicago Law Review*: A T Kronman: 'Specific Performance', 44 *U Chi Law Rev* (1978), and Richard Craswell : 'Against Fuller and Pendue', 67 *U Chi Law Rev* 99 (2000).

University of Toronto Press for extracts from *University of Toronto Law Journal*: M P Furmston: 'The Analysis of Illegal Contracts', (1966) 16 *U Toronto LJ* 267; and Iain Ramsay: 'Consumer Redress Mechanisms for Poor-Quality and Defective Products', (1981) 21 *U Toronto LJ* 117.

University of Wisconsin Press for extracts from Lawrence M Friedmann: *Contract Law in America* (1965), © 1965.

Virginia Law Review Association via Copyright Clearance Center for extracts from *Virginia Law Review*: Ian Macneil: 'Efficient Breach of Contract: Circles in the Sky', (1982) 68 *VLR* 947; Ian Macneil: 'Restatement (Second) of Contracts and Presentation', (1974) 60 *VLR* 589; and Arthur Alan Leff: 'Economic Analysis of Law: Some Realism about Nominalism', (1974) 60 *VLR* 451.

Yale Law Journal Company and William S Hein Company for extracts from *Yale Law Journal*: Arthur L Corbin: 'Conditions in the Law of Contract', 28 *Yale LJ* 739; Clare Dalton: 'An Essay on the Deconstruction of Contract Doctrine', (1985) 94 *Yale LJ* 997; L L Fuller and William R Perdue Jr: 'The Reliance Interest in Contract Damages', (1936) 46 *Yale LJ* 52; Anthony T Kronman: 'Paternalism and the Law of Contracts', 92 *Yale LJ* 763, and 'Contract Law and Distributive Justice', (1980), 89 *Yale LJ* 472; Alan Schwartz: 'The case for Specific Performance', (1980) 89 *Yale LJ* 271; and William C Whitford: 'Comment on a Theory of the Consumer Product Warranty', 91 *Yale LJ* 1371.

Every effort has been made to trace and contact copyright holders but this has not been possible in every case. If notified, the publisher will undertake to rectify any errors or omissions at the earliest opportunity.

TABLE OF STATUTES

Page references in bold type indicate where the section of the Act is set out in part or in full

A

Administration of Justice Act 1970
  s 4 ... 89
  s 36 ... 496
Administration of Justice Act 1982
  s 15 ... 672
Apportionment Act 1870
  s 2 ... **557**
  s 5 ... **557**
Arbitration Act 1889 ... 89, 258, 259
Arbitration Act 1979 ... 90, 1073
Arbitration Act 1996
  s 69 ... 1073

B

Bankruptcy Act 1869
  s 4 ... 140
Betting and Loans (Infants) Act 1892
  s 5 ... 140
Bills of Exchange Act 1882
  s 62 ... 856
  s 3(1) ... 144
  s 17(2) ... 144
Bills of Lading Act 1855 ... 1168
  s 1 ... 1159
Bills of Sale (1878) Amendment Act 1882 ... 144
Builder's Licensing Act 1971
  s 45 ... 45
Building Societies Act 1962
  s 32 ... 1085

C

Canals and Railways Act 1854 ... 995
Carriage of Goods by Sea Act 1924 ... 1058
Carriage of Goods by Sea Act 1971 ... 1032, 1058, 1172
Carriage of Goods by Sea Act 1992
  s 1(3) ... 1220
  s 2 ... 1220
  s 3 ... 1220
Chancery Procedure Amendment Act 1858 (Lord Cairns Act) ... 381, 382, 634, 635, 686
Common Law Procedure Act 1852
  ss 210–212 ... 496, 590
Companies Act 1985
  s 56 ... 532
  s 57 ... 532
  s 66 ... 532
  s 67 ... 532
Consumer Credit Act 1974 ... 146, 955, 1026, 1063
  s 60 ... 950
  s 67 ... **949, 950**
  s 68 ... **949, 950**
  s 87 ... **589**

s 88 ... **589**
s 89 ... **589**
s 90 ... **589–590**
s 91 ... **590**
s 129 ... **495–496**
ss 140A–140B ... 947
Consumer Credit Act 2006
  ss 19–20 ... 949
Consumer Protection Act 1987 ... 36, 494, 1061
  s 4(1)(e) ... 26
  s 5(2) ... 36
  s 7 ... **1033**
  s 20 ... 202
  s 20(1) ... 202
Consumer Safety Act 1978 ... 957
Contract (Rights of Third Parties) Act 1999
  ... 26, 1136
  s 1 ... **1187–1188**
  s 1(1)(a) ... 1192
  s 1(1)(b) ... 1192
  s 1(2) ... 1192
  s 1(3) ... 1192
  s 2 ... 1188
  s 3 ... 1188
  s 4 ... 1188
  s 5 ... 1188
  s 6 ... **1188–1190**
  s 7 ... 1190
  s 8 ... **1190–1191**
  s 9 ... 1191
  s 10 ... 1191
Copyright Act 1956
  s 8 ... 126
Criminal Law Act 1967
  s 5 ... 1073

D

Defective Premises Act 1972
  s 1 ... 27, 1032–1033
  s 1(1) ... 1152
  s 6 ... 1033

E

Enterprise Act 2002 ... 1003
  Part 8 ... 1059
  s 211 ... 1059
  s 211 ... 1059
European Communities Act 1972 ... 1035, 1180

F

Factors Act 1889 ... 262
Fair Trading Act 1973 ... 1003
  Pt II ... 1043, 1059
  Pt III ... 1043
Fatal Accidents Act 1976 ... 1151

Financial Services Act 1986
s 132 . . . 1086
Food Act 1984 . . . 1085

H

Hallmarking Act 1973 . . . 532
Hire-Purchase Act 1938 . . . 262
Housing Act 1961
s 32(1) . . . 413, 416
Housing Act 1988 . . . 1055, 1056
Housing Act 1996
s 193 . . . 1036
Housing Act 2005
Part 5 . . . 541
Human Rights Act 1998 . . . 1065

I

Increase of Rent and Mortgage Interest (Restrictions)
Act 1920
s 2(1) . . . 510
Indian Contract Act 1872
s 16(3) . . . 921
Industrial Relations Act 1971 . . . 728
Infants Relief Act 1874
s 2 . . . 140
Insurance Companies Act 1974 . . . 1085, 1086
Insurance Companies Act 1982 . . . 957
Interpretation Act 1978 . . . 1059

J

Judicature Act 1873 . . . 355
s 25(1) . . . 575
s 25(6) . . . 1195

L

Land Charges Act 1925 . . . 635
Late Payment of Commercial Debts (Interest) Act
1998 . . . 672
Law of Property Act 1925 . . . 145
s 40 . . . 196, 218
s 40(1) . . . 144
s 41 . . . 575
s 47(1) . . . 1152
s 49 . . . 591, 703
s 49(2) . . . 703
s 53(1)(c) . . . 1196
s 56(1) . . . 1139, 1141, 1153
s 136 . . . 1195–1196
s 136(1) . . . 1195
s 146 . . . 496, 590
s 205 . . . 1153
s 205(1) . . . 1153
Law of Property (Miscellaneous Provisions)
Act 1989
s 3 . . . 673
s 1 . . . **132**
Law Reform (Contributory Negligence) Act 1945
s 1 . . . 375, **656–657**
s 4 . . . 376, **657**
Law Reform (Enforcement of Contracts) Act
1954 . . . 146

Law Reform (Frustrated Contracts) Act
1943 . . . 483–486, 498, 558, 568
s 1 . . . **483–484**
s 1(2) . . . 483, 486, **487–488**, 490, 491
s 1(3) . . . 483, 486–487, **488–489**, 490, 491, 492
s 1(3)(a) . . . 488, 489
s 1(3)(b) . . . 488, 492
s 2 . . . **484–485**
s 2(3) . . . 491
s 2(5) . . . 485
Law Reform (Miscellaneous Provisions) Act 1989 . . . 144
s 3 . . . 672
s 2(1) . . . 143
Limitation Act 1939 . . . 153
Limitation Act 1980 . . . 139
s 29(7) . . . 140
Lord Cairns Act *see* Chancery Procedure Amendment
Act 1858 (Lord Cairns Act)

M

Marine Insurance Act 1906 . . . 424
s 14(2) . . . 1152
s 18 . . . 531
s 18(2) . . . 357
Married Women's Property Act 1882
s 11 . . . 1152
Matrimonial Causes Act 1973
s 34 . . . 107
Medicines Act 1968 . . . 532
Merchant Shipping Act 1844 . . . 452
Merchant Shipping Act 1854 . . . 452
Merchant Shipping (Safety and Load Line Conventions)
Act 1932 . . . 1081
Minors' Contracts Act 1987
s 1 . . . 140
Misrepresentation Act 1967 . . . 329, 370, 673
s 1 . . . 357, 363, 368, **369**
s 2 . . . **369**, **372**, 380
s 2(1) . . . 38, 372, **377–381**, 382, 538
s 2(2) . . . 369, **381–384**, 948
s 2(3) . . . 382
s 3 . . . **386–387**, 1009, 1010, 1023
s 4 . . . 381
Misrepresentation Act (Northern Ireland) 1967
s 3 . . . 1010

N

National Minimum Wage Act 1998 . . . 182

O

Occupiers' Liability Act 1957 . . . 413, 1004
Occupiers' Liability Act (Northern Ireland) 1957 . . . 1004

P

Partnership Act 1890
s 35(d) . . . 615
s 40 . . . 483
Pharmacy and Poisons Act 1933
s 17(1) . . . 199
s 18(1) . . . 200
Police Act 1964
s 15(1) . . . 105

Purchase Tax Act 1963
  s 2(1) ... 183

R

Railway and Canal Traffic Act 1854 ... 1024
Rent and Mortgage Interest Restrictions Act 1939
  Sch 1 ... 510
Road and Rail Traffic Act 1933
  s 1 ... 1084
Road Traffic Act 1930 ... 179
Road Traffic Act 1960 ... 995
  s 151 ... 1175, 1176, 1177
  s 207 ... 1090
Road Traffic Act 1988
  s 148(7) ... 1152

S

Sale and Supply of Goods Act 1994 ... 4, 412, 430
  s 2 ... 617
  s 2B(a) ... 432
  s 3 ... 617
  s 4 ... 559, 598
  s 14(2) ... 430, 431
  ss 14(2)–(2C) ... 439
  s 14(2A) ... 430
  s 14(2A)–(2C) ... 430
  s 14(2B) ... 431
  s 14(2B)(a) ... 430
  s 14(2D) ... 430
  s 14(2D)–(2F) ... 430
  s 14(2E) ... 430
  s 14(3) ... 431
  s 14(3)(b) ... 431
  s 61 ... 598
  Sch 2 ... 598
Sale of Goods Act 1893 ... 258–259, 412, 430, 500,
  569, 600, 612
  s 4 ... 144, 145, 308
  s 6 ... 503
  s 7 ... 485, 501
  s 8 ... 268
  s 11(1)(c) ... 366
  s 14(1) ... 572
  s 14(2) ... 441, 572
  s 35 ... 366
  s 50 ... 666, 667, 668
  s 51 ... 654
  s 52 ... 710
  s 53(3) ... 665
Sale of Goods Act 1979 ... 365, 412, 424, 462, 571
  s 2(1) ... 425
  s 3 ... **945**
  s 3(3) ... 559
  s 6 ... **500**
  s 7 ... **463**
  s 8 ... **258**
  s 8(2) ... 259
  s 9 ... **263**
  s 10 ... 574–575
  s 11 ... **565**
  s 11(1) ... 572
  s 12 ... 412, **426**, 431
  s 12(3) ... 426

ss 12–15 ... 413
s 13 ... 412, **427**, 429, 430, 431, 529, 567, 598, 996
ss 13–15 ... 413, 566, 594, 596, 597, 598, 619
s 14 ... 412, **428**, 529, 598, 996
s 14(2) ... 430, 431, 439, 998
s 14(2A) ... 428
s 14(2B) ... 428
s 14(2C) ... 428
ss 14(2D)–(2F) ... 430
s 14(3) ... 428, 430
s 14(6) ... 430
s 15 ... 412, **428–429**, 598, 996
s 17 ... 731
s 18 ... 731
s 20 ... 412, 462
s 28 ... **554**
s 29 ... **439–440**
s 29(3) ... 412
s 30 ... **558**, 597, 598
s 30(1) ... 559
s 30(2) ... 559
s 30(2A) ... 559
s 30(2B) ... 559
s 30(4) ... 559
s 31 ... **558–559**
s 31(2) ... 587
s 34 ... **617**, 617, 618
s 35 ... **617**, 617, 618, 619
s 35(4) ... 618
s 35A ... 559, **617–618**
s 41 ... **587–588**
ss 48A–48F ... 619, 709
s 49 ... **733**
s 50 ... **624**
s 50(3) ... 629, 654
s 51 ... **624**
s 51(3) ... 654
s 52 ... **711**
s 53(1) ... 1147
s 53(2) ... 665
s 53(3) ... 665
s 55 ... **413**, 1014, 1015, 1017
s 55(4) ... 1014, 1016
s 55(5) ... 1014, 1016
  paras (a) to (e) ... 1017
s 55(5)(c) ... 1015
s 57 ... 202
s 57(2) ... 202
s 59 ... 618
Sch 1 ... 1014
Seeds Act 1920 ... 1087
South Staffordshire Waterworks Act 1909 ... 521
Statute of Frauds 1677 ... 168
  s 4 ... 98–99, 144, 145
  s 17 ... 144, 145
Statute of Frauds 1950
  s 4 ... 43
Supply of Goods and Services Act 1982 ... 425, 957
  s 2 ... 426
  ss 3–5 ... 429
  s 5A ... 598
  s 7(1) ... 427
  ss 11A–11F ... 619

s 12 ... **446–447**
s 12(2) ... 447
s 13 ... **447**
s 14 ... **447**
s 15 ... 447
Supply of Goods (Implied Terms) Act 1973 ... 413, 425, 430, 957, 995, 1011, 1014
s 8 ... 413, 426
s 9 ... 995
ss 9–11 ... 429
s 10 ... 995
s 11 ... 995
ss 12–15 ... 413
Supreme Court Act 1981
s 35A ... 672
Supreme Court of Judicature Act 1873 ... 1176, 1177
Supreme Court of Judicature (Consolidation) Act 1925 ... 1175
s 41 ... 1176

T

Trade Descriptions Act 1968 ... 997, 1176
s 14(1)(b) ... 361
Trade Union and Labour Relations Act 1974
s 13 ... 910
s 13(1) ... 912
s 29 ... 912
s 29(1) ... 912

U

Unfair Contract Terms Act 1977 ... 329, 413, 443, 446, 912, 967, 976, 980, 992, 994, 1015, 1028, 1029, 1035, 1043, 1167, 1215
Part I ... 598
s 1 ... 995, 1004
s 1(1) ... 1004
s 1(2) ... 1032
s 1(3) ... 998, 1004
s 2 ... 995, 998, **1005**, 1010
s 2(1) ... 443, 444
s 2(1)–(3) ... 1004
s 2(2) ... 1005, 1018
ss 2–7 ... 1004
s 3 ... 996, **1007**, 1008, 1012, 1042
s 3(2)(b) ... 1008
s 3(2)(b)(i) ... 1009
s 3(2)(b)(ii) ... 610, 1009
s 4 ... 996
s 5 ... 996, **1003**, 1004
s 5(3) ... 1004
ss 5–7 ... 998
s 6 ... 413, 995, **996**, 996, 998, 1003, 1004, 1011, 1012
s 6(1) ... 998
s 6(2) ... 996, 999
s 6(3) ... 346, 996, 998, 1011
s 6(4) ... 998, 1004
s 7 ... **996**, 997, 1004, 1011, 1012
s 7(1) ... 996
s 7(2) ... 996
s 7(3) ... 996, 1011

s 7(3A) ... 997
s 7(4) ... 997, 1011
s 8 ... 386, 996, 1009
s 9 ... 996
s 10 ... 996, **1032**
s 11 ... 996, **1011**, 1016, 1017, 1035
s 11(1) ... 387, 413, 1010, 1011, 1012, 1019, 1043
s 11(2) ... 1011, 1012
s 11(3) ... 1010
s 11(5) ... 1010, 1013, 1019
s 12 ... 996, 997, 998, 1042
s 13 ... 996, 998, 999, 1008
s 13(1) ... 998, 999, 1005
s 14 ... 996, 998
s 14(3) ... 997
s 26 ... 1032
s 27 ... 1032
s 31 ... 1032
Sch 1 ... 1032
Sch 2 ... 1011, 1012, 1030
   para (c) ... 346
Unsolicited Goods and Services Act 1971
s 1 ... 210
s 2 ... **211**
s 3A ... 210

V

Victorian Goods Act 1928
s 11 ... 503

Statutory Instruments

Air Corporations (Dissolution) Order 1973 ... 361
Auction Regulations 1976 ... 1122

Consumer Protection (Distance Selling) Regulations 2000 ... **210**
Consumer Transactions (Restrictions on Statements) Order 1976 (SI 1976/1813, as amended by SI 1978/127) ... 1003

Food Labelling Regulations 1996 ... 532

Package Travel, Package Holidays and Package Tours Regulations 1992 (SI 1992/3288)
   reg 4 ... 358
Public Works Contracts Regulations 1991 (SI 1991/2680) ... 247

Sale and Supply of Goods to Consumers Regulations 2002 (SI 2002/3025) ... 430, 619
Sale and Supply of Goods to Consumers Regulations 2002 (SI 2002/3045)
   reg 3(2) ... 430

Unfair Terms in Consumer Contracts Regulations 1994 (SI 1994/3159) ... 1036, 1043, 1044
   reg 4(3) ... 1043
   reg 8 ... 1043
   Sch 2 ... 1043

Unfair Terms in Consumer Contracts Regulations 1999
(SI 1999/2083) ... 10, 287, 353, 610, 996, 1036
reg 2(1) ... 1042
reg 3 ... 1040
reg 3(1) ... 1036–1037
reg 3(2) ... 1037
reg 4(1) ... 1037
reg 4(2) ... 1037
reg 5(1) ... 1037
reg 5(2) ... 1037, 1042
reg 5(3) ... 1037, 1042
reg 5(4) ... 1037, 1042
reg 5(5) ... 1037, 1040
reg 6(1) ... 1037
reg 6(2) ... 1037, 1042, 1043
reg 7(1) ... 1038
reg 7(2) ... 1038
reg 8(1) ... 1038
reg 8(2) ... 1038
reg 9 ... 1038
reg 10(1) ... 1038
reg 10(2) ... 1038
reg 10(3) ... 1038
reg 11(1) ... 1038
reg 11(2) ... 1038
reg 12(1) ... 1038
reg 12(2) ... 1038
reg 12(3) ... 1038
reg 12(4) ... 1039
reg 13(1) ... 1039
reg 13(2) ... 1039
reg 13(3) ... 1039
reg 13(4) ... 1039
reg 13(5) ... 1039
reg 13(6) ... 1039
reg 14 ... 1039
reg 15(1) ... 1039–1040
reg 15(2) ... 1040
Sch 1 ... 1040, 1045
Sch 2 ... 1040
Unsolicited Goods and Services (Northern Ireland) Order
1976 ... 210

International Legislation

Australia

Builder's Licensing Act 1971
Insurance Contracts Act 1984 ... 1180
Queensland
    Property Law Act 1974
        s 55(1) ... 1180
        s 55(6)(c)(ii) ... 1180
Victoria
    Goods Act 1928
        s 11
Western Australia
    Property Law Act 1969

Canada

Fisheries Act
    s 69a ... 467–468

Finland

    Act on Interest

Consumer Protection Act
Person Registration Decree ... 494

Germany

AGBG (Unfair Terms in Standard Contracts) 1976 ... 10
AGB-Gesetz (Standard Form Contracts Act) ... 1043
Civil Code (BGB)
    δ242 ... 9
Standard Business Terms Act 1976
    Art 9 ... 1029

India

Contract Act 1872

Kenya

Central Bank of Kenya Act 1966

New Zealand

Contracts (Privity) Act 1982
    s 4 ... 1180
    s 8 ... 1180
Mercantile Law Act 1908
    s 13 ... 1159

Sweden

Consumer Insurance Act
    s 25 ... 494

Uganda

Rent Restriction Ordinance ... 1094

United States of America

Carriage of Goods by Sea Act 1936 ... 1154
    s 1(a) ... 1154
The Restatement ... 769, 807
    s 45 ... 249
    s 69(1)(c) ... 213
    s 75 ... 807
    s 90 ... 170, 171, 249, 282, 629,
        807, 808, 809
Restatement (Second) of Contracts ... 432, 808
Restatement 2d ... 98, 99, 147, 794
    s 30 ... 221
    s 32 ... 221
    s 54 ... 221, 222
    s 58 ... 221
    s 62 ... 221
    s 69 ... 213
    s 71 ... 97–98, 170
    s 75 ... 132
    s 86 ... 143
    s 90 ... 171, 173
    s 234 ... 554
    s 302 ... 1182
    s 304 ... 1182
    s 307 ... 1182
    s 311 ... 1182
    s 315 ... 1183
Uniform Commercial Code ... 433, 435, 1026
    s 2–103 ... 879
    s 2–201 ... 878
    s 2–204 ... 270
    s 2–204(3) ... 270

s 2–206 ... 222
s 2–207 ... 228, 229
s 2–207(1) ... 229
s 2–207(3) ... 229
s 2–209 ... 878, 879, 914–915
s 2–209(2) ... 878
s 2–209(4) ... 878
s 2–305 ... 270–271
s 2–305(2) ... 271
s 2–609 ... 588

European Legislation

Directives
Certain Aspects of the Sale of Consumer Goods and
   Associated Guarantees (1999/44/EC)
   Art 2(2)(d) ... 430
   Art 2(4) ... 430
Consumer Credit 1987 (87/102/EEC)
   Art 3 ... 1047
   Art 4 ... 1047
Contracts Negotiated Away from Business Premises
   1985 (85/577/EEC) ... 1047
Misleading Advertising 1984 (84/450/EEC) ... 1047
Procurement (71/305) ... 247
Procurement (89/440) ... 247
Unfair Business-to-Consumer Commercial Practices in
   the Internal Market 2005 (2005/29/EC)
   Art 3(2) ... 1059
   Art 5 ... 1059
   Art 6 ... 1060
   Art 7 ... 1060

Art 8 ... 1060
Art 9 ... 1060
Unfair Terms in Consumer Contracts (93/13/EEC)
   ... 4, 336, 967, 977, 1035, 1045, 1047
Art 3(1) ... 1043
Art 3(2) ... 1042
Art 4(2) ... 1042, 1047–1048
Art 7 ... 1044
Art 8 ... 1035
Recital 6 ... 1048
Recital 7 ... 1048
Recital 9 ... 1048
Recital 11 ... 1048
Recital 12 ... 1048
Recital 13 ... 1048
Recital 16 ... 1043
Recital 19 ... 1043

International Instruments

Hague-Visby Rules ... 1032, 1058, 1172
Treaty of Rome
   Art 100A ... 1035, 1047
   Art 129A ... 1047
UNIDROIT General Principles for International
   Commercial Contracts
   Art 2.22 ... 229
   Art 6.2.1 ... 895–896
   Art 6.2.2 ... 896
   Art 6.2.3 ... 897
   Art 6
      s 2 ... 493, 898

TABLE OF CASES

A

A & M Produce Co v FMC Corpn 135 Cal App 3d 473 (1982) ... 1025–1026

A C Controls Ltd v British Broadcasting Corporation (2002) 89 Con LR 52 ... 281

A Roberts & Co, Ltd v Leicestershire County Council [1961] Ch 555 ... 299–300

Aberfoyle Plantations Ltd v Khaw Bian Cheng [1960] AC 115 ... 279

Actionstrength Ltd v International Glass Engineering [2003] UKHL 17 [2003] 2 AC 541 (2003) 2 All ER 615 ... 146, 163

Adams v Lindsell (1818) 1 B & Ald 681, 106 ER 250 ... 230–231, 233

Addis v Gramophone Co Ltd [1909] AC 488, 78 LJKB 1122, [1908–10] All ER Rep 1, 101 LT 466, HL ... 673, 677, 678

AEG (UK) Ltd v Logic Resource Ltd [1996] CLC 265, CA ... 339

Affréteurs Réunis SA v Leopold Walford (London) Ltd [1919] AC 801, 88 LJKB 861, 14 Asp MLC 451, 24 Com Cas 268, 121 LT 393, 35 TLR 542, HL ... 1151, 1191

Agip SpA v Navigazione Alta Italia SpA, The Nai Genova and Nai Superba [1984] 1 Lloyd's Rep 353, CA ... 300

AIB Group (UK) plc v Martin [2002] 1 All ER 353 ... 403

Ailion v Spierkermann [1976] Ch 158, [1976] 1 All ER 497, [1976] 2 WLR 556, 31 P & CR 369, 120 Sol Jo 9, 238 Estates Gazette 48 ... 1104

Ailsa Craig Fishing Co Ltd v Malvern Fishing Co Ltd and Securicor (Scotland) Ltd [1983] 1 All ER 101, [1983] 1 WLR 964, [1983] 1 Lloyd's Rep 183n, 127 Sol Jo 508, [1983] LS Gaz R 2156, 1982 SLT 377, HL ... 995, 1016

Ajayi (t/a Colony Carrier Co) v RT Briscoe (Nigeria) Ltd [1964] 3 All ER 556, [1964] 1 WLR 1326, 108 Sol Jo 857, PC ... 159, 866–867

Akerblom v Price (1881) 7 QBD 129 ... 956

Alan (WJ) & Co Ltd v El Nasr Export and Import Co [1972] 2 QB 189, [1972] 2 All ER 127, [1972] 2 WLR 800, [1972] 1 Lloyd's Rep 313, 116 Sol Jo 139, CA ... 868–875

Alaska Packers' Association v Domenico (1902) 117 F 99 ... 845, 859, 860, 878

Alaskan Trader (Clea Shipping Corpn v Bulk Oil International Ltd, The Alaskan Trader Albacruz (Cargo Owners), The Albazero [1977] AC 774, [1976] 3 All ER 129, [1976] 3 WLR 419, [1976] 2 Lloyd's Rep 467, 120 Sol Jo 570, 126 NLJ 953, HL). *See* Clea Shipping Corpn v Bulk Oil International Ltd, The Alaskan Trader [1984] 1 All ER 129, [1983] 2 Lloyd's Rep 645

Albacruz (Cargo Owners) v Albazero (owners), The Albazero [1977] AC 774 ... 1144, 1145, 1146, 1147, 1148, 1149

Albert (L) & Son v Armstrong Rubber Co (1949) 178 F 2d 182 ... 632, 633

Albert v Motor Insurers' Bureau [1972] AC 301, [1971] 2 All ER 1345, [1971] 3 WLR 291, [1972] RTR 230, [1971] 2 Lloyd's Rep 229, 115 Sol Jo 588, HL ... 179–180

Alderslade v Hendon Laundry Ltd (1945) 1 KB 189 ... 978, 980

Alec Lobb (Garages) Ltd v Total Oil (GB) Ltd [1985] 1 All ER 303, CA ... 1114

Alexander v Railway Executive [1951] 2 KB 882 ... 985

Alexander v Rayson [1936] 1 KB 169, 105 LJKB 148, [1935] All ER Rep 185, 80 Sol Jo 15, 154 LT 205, 52 TLR 131, CA ... 1097

Alexander v Standard Telephones and Cables plc (No 2) [1990] ICR 291, [1990] IRLR 55 ... 183

Alford v West Bromwich Building Society [1998] 1 All ER 98, [1998] 1 BCLC 493, HL ... 849

Aliakmon, The (Leigh and Sillavan Ltd v Aliakmon Shipping Co Ltd, The Aliakmon Allcard v Skinner (1887) 36 Ch D 145, 56 LJ Ch 1052, 36 WR 251, [1886–90] All ER Rep 90, 57 LT 61, 3 TLR 751, CA ... 1167, 1168, 1172, 1240

Allcard v Skinner (1887) 36 Ch D 145 ... 917, 921, 930, 932, 955, 956, 957

Allen v Robles (Compagnie Parisienne de Garantie third party) [1969] 3 All ER 154, [1969] 1 WLR 1193, [1969] 2 Lloyd's Rep 61, 113 Sol Jo 484, CA ... 615–617

Allied Maples Group Ltd v Simmons & Simmons (a firm) [1995] 4 All ER 907, [1995] 1 WLR 1602, [1995] NLJR 1646, CA ... 670

Allied Marine Transport Ltd v Vale do Rio Doce Navegacao SA, The Leonidas D [1983] 3 All ER 737, [1984] 1 WLR 1, [1983] 2 Lloyd's Rep 411, 127 Sol Jo 729; revsd [1985] 2 All ER 796, [1985] 2 Lloyd's Rep 18, 129 Sol Jo 431, [1985] LS Gaz R 2160, CA ... 194, 212, 213, 847, 848

Aluminium Co of America v Essex Group 499 F Supp 53 (WD Pa 1980) ... 895

Aluminium Industrie Vaassen BV v Romalpa Aluminium Ltd [1976] 2 All ER 552, [1976] 1 WLR 676, [1976] 1 Lloyd's Rep 443, 120 Sol Jo 95, CA ... 733

Amalgamated Investment and Property Co Ltd (in liquidation) v Texas Commerce International Bank Ltd [1982] QB 84, [1981] 1 All ER 923, [1981] 2 WLR 554, 125 Sol Jo 133; affd [1982] QB 84, [1981] 3 All ER 577, [1981] 3 WLR 565, [1982] 1 Lloyd's Rep 27, 125 ... 149, 408–409

Ammons v Wilson 170 So 227, 176 Miss 645 (1936) ... 213

Amoco Australia Pty Ltd v Rocca Bros Motor Engineering Co Pty Ltd [1975] AC 561, [1975] 1 All ER 968, [1975] 2 WLR 779, 119 Sol Jo 301, PC ... 1114

Amsprop Trading Ltd v Harris Distribution Ltd [1997] 2 All ER 990, [1997] 1 WLR 1025, [1997] 47 EG 127 ... 1153

Anderson Ltd v Daniel ... 1087

André et Cie v Marine Transocean Ltd, The Splendid Sun [1981] QB 964, [1981] 2 All ER 993, [1981] 3 WLR 43, [1981] 2 Lloyd's Rep 29, [1981] Com LR 95, 125 Sol Jo 395, CA ... 213

Andrews Bros (Bournemouth) Ltd v Singer & Co Ltd [1934] 1 KB 17, 103 LJKB 90, [1933] All ER Rep 479, 150 LT 172, 50 TLR 33, CA ... 345, 566, 977, 986

Angel v Jay [1911] 1 KB 666, 80 LNKB 458, [1908–10] All ER Rep 470, 55 So Jo 140, 103 LT 809 ... 365, 368

Angelia, Trade and Transport Inc v Lino Kaiun Kaisha Ltd [1973] 1 WLR 210 ... 993

Anglia Television Ltd v Reed [1972] 1 QB 60, [1971] 3 All ER 690, [1971] 3 WLR 528, 115 Sol Jo 723, CA ... 629–631, 633, 635

Anglo-Continental Holidays Ltd v Typaldos (London) Ltd [1967] 2 Lloyd's Rep 61, 111 Sol Jo 599, CA ... 975, 1009

Anns v Merton London Borough Council [1978] AC 728, [1977] 2 All ER 492, [1977] 2 WLR 1024, 75 LGR 555, 141 JP 526, 121 Sol Jo 377, 5 BLR 1, 243 Estates Gazette 523, 591, [1977] JPL 514, HL ... 31, 32, 35, 36, 1163, 1166, 1169

Antaois Cia Naviera SA v Salen Rederierna AB, The Antaois [1983] 3 All ER 777, [1983] 1 WLR 1362, [1983] 2 Lloyd's Rep 473, 127 Sol Jo 730, CA; affd [1985] AC 191, [1984] 3 All ER 229, [1984] 3 WLR 592, [1984] 2 Lloyd's Rep 235, 128 Sol Jo 564, [1984] LS Gaz R 2776, HL ... 400, 616

Appleby v Myers (1867) LR 2 CP 651, 36 LJCP 331, [1861–73] All ER Rep 452, 16 LT 669, Ex Ch ... 483, 560, 744

Arcadian Phosphates Inc v Arcadian Corpn 884 F 2d 69 (USCA 2d Circ 1989) ... 278

Archbolds (Freightage) Ltd v S Spanglett Ltd (Randall, third party) [1961] 1 QB 374, [1961] 1 All ER 417, [1961] 2 WLR 170, 105 Sol Jo 149, CA ... 1083–1087

Archer v Cutler [1980] 1 NZLR 386 ... 944, 945

Arcos Ltd v EA Ronaasen & Son [1933] AC 470, 102 LJKB 346, 38 Com Cas 166, [1933] All ER Rep 646, 77 Sol Jo 99, 149 LT 98, 49 TLR 231, 45 Ll L Rep 33, HL ... 429, 566–567

Argy Trading Development Co Ltd v Lapid Developments Ltd [1977] 3 All ER 785, [1977] 1 WLR 444, [1977] 1 Lloyds Rep 67, 120 Sol Jo 677 ... 154

Armitage v West Bromwich Building Society [1998] 1 All ER 98, [1998] 1 BCLC 493, HL ... 849

Armour v Thyssen Edelstahlwerke AG [1991] 2 AC 339, [1990] 3 All ER 481, [1990] 3 WLR 810, [1991] 1 Lloyd's Rep 95, [1991] BCLC 28, [1990] BCC 925, 134 Sol Jo 1337, 1990 SLT 891, HL ... 733

Arocs Ltd v EA Ronaasen & Son [1933] AC 470, 102 LJKB 346, 38 Com Cas 166, [1933] All ER Rep 646, 77 Sol Jo 99, 149 LT 98, 49 TLR 231, 45 Ll L Rep 33, HL ... 429

Aron (J) & Co Inc v Comptoir Wegimont [1921] 3 KB 435, 90 LJKB 1233, 26 Com Cas 303, 37 TLR 879 ... 975

Arrale v Costain Civil Engineering Ltd [1976] 1 Lloyd's Rep 98, 119 Sol Jo 527, CA ... 102, 405

Ashdown v Samuel Williams & Sons Ltd [1957] 1 QB 409, [1957] 1 All ER 35, [1956] 3 WLR 1104, 100 Sol Jo 945, CA ... 1005

Ashington Piggeries Ltd v Christopher Hill Ltd [1972] AC 441, [1971] 1 All ER 847, [1971] 2 WLR 1051, [1971] 1 Lloyd's Rep 245, 115 Sol Jo 223, HL ... 431

Ashmore Benson Pease & Co Ltd v AV Dawson Ltd [1973] 2 All ER 856, [1973] 1 WLR 828, [1973] RTR 473, [1973] 2 Lloyd's Rep 21, 117 Sol Jo 203, CA ... 1088

ASLEF ... 453

Associated Japanese Bank (International) Ltd v Crédit du Nord SA [1988] 3 All ER 902, [1989] 1 WLR 255, 133 Sol Jo 81, [1989] 8 LS Gaz R 43, [1988] NLJR 109 ... 513–520, 543

Astley v Reynolds 2 Strange 915 ... 907, 954

Aswan Engineering Establishment Co v Lupdine Ltd (Thurgar Bolle, third party) [1987] 1 All ER 135, [1987] 1 WLR 1, [1986] 2 Lloyd's Rep 347, [1986] BTLC 293, 130 Sol Jo 712, [1986] LS Gaz R 2661, CA ... 430

Atlantic Baron, The. *See* North Ocean Shipping Co Ltd v Hyundai Construction Co Ltd, The Atlantic Baron [1979] QB 705, [1978] 3 All ER 1170, [1979] 3 WLR 419, [1979] 1 Lloyd's Rep 89, 123 Sol Jo 352

Atlantic Lines & Navigation Co Inc v Hallam Ltd, The Lucy [1983] 1 Lloyd's Rep 188 ... 383

Atlas Express Ltd v Kafco (Importers and Distributors) Ltd [1989] QB 833, [1989] 1 All ER 641, [1989] 3 WLR 389, 133 Sol Jo 977, [1989] NLJR 111 ... 913

Attica Sea Carriers Corpn v Ferrostaal Poseidon Bulk Reederei GmbH, The Puerto Buitago [1976] 1 Lloyd's Rep 250, CA ... 737, 739

Attorney General of Commonwealth of Australia v Adelaide Steamship Co Ltd [1913] AC 781, 83 LJPC 84, 12 Asp MLC 361, [1911–13] All ER Rep 1120, 109 LT 258, 28 TLR 743, PC ... 1071, 1113

Attorney General of Hong Kong v Humphreys Estate (Queen's Gardens) Ltd [1987] AC 114, [1987] 2 All ER 387, [1987] 2 WLR 343, 54 P & CR 96, 131 Sol Jo 194, [1987] LS Gaz R 574, PC ... 160, 163, 799

Attorney General v Blake (Jonathan Cape Ltd third party) [1998] Ch 439, [1998] 1 All ER 833, [1998] 2 WLR 805, [1998] NLJR 15, [1998] EMLR 309, sub nom Attorney General v Blake [1998] 04 LS Gaz R 33, 142 Sol Jo LB 35, CA; affd sub nom Attorney General v Blake (Jonathan Cape Ltd third party) [2001] 1 AC 268, [2000] 4 All ER 385, [2000] 3 WLR 625, [2000] NLJR 1230, [2000] EMLR 949, [2000] 2 All ER (Comm) 487, sub norm Attorney General v Blake [2001] IRLR 36, [2000] 32 LS Gaz R 37, 144 Sol Jo LB 242, HL ... 44, 548, 639, 750, 753

Attorney-General to His Royal Highness the Prince of Wales v Collom ... 156

Attwood v Lamont [1920] 3 KB 571, 90 LJKB 121, [1920] All ER Rep 55, 65 Sol Jo 25, 124 LT 108, 36 TLR 895, CA ... 730, 1121–1122

Attwood v Small (1838) 6 Cl & Fin 232, [1835–42] All ER Rep 258, sub nom Small v Attwood 2 Jur 226, 246, HL ... 356

Avery v Bowden (1855) 5 E & B 714, 25 LJQB 49; affd 6 E & B 953, 26 LJBQ 3, 3 Jur NS 238, 5 WR 45, 28 LTOS 145, Ex Ch ... 584

Avon Finance Co Ltd v Bridger [1985] 2 All ER 281, 123
Sol Jo 705, [1984] CCLR 27, CA ... 923, 928

Awilco A/S v Fulvia SpA di Navigazione, The Chikuma
[1981] 1 All ER 652, [1981] 1 WLR 314, [1981] 1
Lloyd's Rep 371, [1981] Com LR 64, 125 Sol Jo 184,
HL ... 602

Aylesford (Earl) v Morris (1873) 8 Ch App 484, 37 JP
227, 42 LJ Ch 546, 21 WR 424, [1861–73] All ER Rep
300, 28 LT 541 ... 944

B

B & B Viennese Fashions v Losane [1952] 1 All ER
909 ... 1087

B & S Contracts and Design Ltd v Victor Green
Publications Ltd [1984] ICR 419, 128 Sol Jo 279,
[1984] LS Gaz R 893, CA ... 913

Backhouse v Backhouse [1978] 1 All ER 1158, [1978] 1
WLR 243, 121 Sol Jo 710 ... 942, 944

Bacon v Cooper (Metals) Ltd [1982] 1 All ER 397 ... 659

Bagot v Stevens, Scanlon & Co [1966] 1 QB 197 ... 371

Baily v De Crespigny (1869) LR 4 QB ... 475

Bain v Fothergill (1874) LR 7 HL 158, 39 JP 228, 43 LJ Ex
243, 23 WR 261, [1874–80] All ER Rep 83, 31 LT
387 ... 672, 673

Bainbrigge v Brown (1881) 18 Ch D 188, 50 LJ 522, 29
WR 782, 44 LT 705 ... 926, 930, 936

Baird (James) Co v Gimbel Bros Bros Inc 64 F 2d 344
(2d Circ, 1933) ... 249

Baird Textile Holdings Ltd v Marks and Spencer plc
[2001] EWCA Civ 274 [2002] 1 All ER (Comm)
737 ... 282–283

Balfour Beatty Construction (Scotland) Ltd v Scottish
Power plc 1993 SLT 1005; on appeal 71 BLR 20, 1994
SC 20, 1994 SLT 807, HL ... 647

Balfour v Balfour [1919] 2 KB 571, 88 LJKB 1054,
[1918–19] All ER Rep 860, 63 Sol Jo 661, 121 LT 346,
35 TLR 609, CA ... 175–176, 177

Bank Line Ltd v A. Capel & Co [1919] AC 435 ... 464,
468

Bank of Australasia v Palmer [1897] AC 540 ... 351

Bank of Boston Connecticut v European Grain and
Shipping Ltd, The Dominique [1989] AC 1056, sub
nom Colonial Bank v European Grain and Shipping
Ltd, The Dominique [1988] 3 All ER 233, [1988] 3
WLR 60, [1988] 1 Lloyd's Rep 215, 132 Sol Jo 896,
[1988] 7 LS Gaz R 39, CA; revsd sub nom Bank of
Boston Connecticut v European Grain and Shipping
Ltd, The Dominique [1989] AC 1056, [1989] 1 All ER
545, [1989] 2 WLR 440, [1989] 1 Lloyd's Rep 431,
133 Sol Jo 219, [1989] 10 LS Gaz R 43,
HL ... 615, 1147

Bank of Credit and Commerce International SA (In
liquidation) v Ali (No 2) [1999] 4 All ER 83, [2000] ICR
1354, [1999] IRLR 508, [1999] 30 LS Gaz R
28 ... 848–851

Bank of Credit and Commerce International SA v
Aboody [1990] 1 QB 923, [1992] 4 All ER 955, [1989]
2 WLR 759, [1990] 1 FLR 354, [1989] Fam Law 435,
132 Sol Jo 1754, [1989] 2 LS Gaz R 37, CA ... 917,
922, 926, 931

Bank of Credit and Commerce International SA v Ali
[1999] 2 All ER 1005, [1999] ICR 1068, [1999] IRLR

226, [1999] NLJR 53; revsd [2000] 3 All ER 51, [2000]
ICR 1410, [2000] IRLR 398, [2000] IRLR 398, sub nom
Naeem v Bank of Credit and Commerce
International ... 848–851

Bank of Montreal v Stuart [1911] AC 120, 80 LJPC 75,
103 Lt 641, 27 TLR 117 ... 921, 924, 932

Bannerman v White (1861) 10 CBNS 844, 31 LJCP 28, 8
Jur NS 282, 9 WR 784, 4 LT 740 ... 323–324

Banque Financière de la Cité SA v Westgate Insurance
Co Ltd [1989] 2 All ER 952 ... 531, 538

Barclays Bank plc v Coleman [2001] QB 20, [2000] 1 All
ER 385, [2000] 3 WLR 405, [2000] 1 FCR 398, [2000]
1 FLR 343, [2000] Fam Law 245, 33 HLR 86, [2000]
03 LS Gaz R 37, [2000] EGCS 4, 144 Sol Jo LB 42, 79
P & CR D28, [2000] Lloyd's Rep Bank 67, CA ... 932

Barclays Bank plc v Fairclough Building Ltd [1995] QB
214, [1995] 1 All ER 289, [1994] 3 WLR 1057, 39
Con LR 86, [1995] PIQR P 152, 68 BLR 1, [1994] BLM
(June) 1, CA ... 657

Barclays Bank plc v O'Brien [1993] QB 109, [1992] 4 All
ER 983, [1992] 3 WLR 593, 66 P & CR 135, [1993] 1
FCR 97, [1993] 1 FLR 124, [1993] Fam Law 62, 25
HLR 7, [1992] 27 LS Gaz R 34, [1992] NLJR 1040, 136
Sol Jo LB 175, CA; affd [1994] 1 AC 180, [1993] 4 All
ER 417, [1993] 3 WLR 786, [1994] 1 FCR 357, [1994]
1 FLR 1, [1994] Fam Law 78, 26 HLR 75, [1993] 46 LS
Gaz R 37, [1993] NLJR 1511, 137 Sol Jo LB 240,
HL ... 917, 923–937, 933, 934, 935, 936

Barr v Gibson (1838) 3 M & W 390 ... 503

Barry v Heathcote Ball & Co (Commercial Auctions) Ltd
[2001] 1 All ER 944, [2000] 1 WLR 1962, [2000] 39
LS Gaz R 41, [2000] NLJR 1377, [2000] EG 178, 144
Sol Jo LB 249, CA ... 203

Bartenstein, The. *See* Damon Cia Naviera SA v Hapag-
Lloyd International SA, The Blankestein, The
Bartenstein, The Birkenstein

Barton, Thompson & Co Ltd v Stapling Machines Co
[1966] Ch 499, [1966] 2 All ER 222, [1966] 2 WLR
1429, 110 Sol Jo 313 ... 592

Barton v Armstrong [1976] AC 104, [1975] 2 All ER 465,
[1975] 2 WLR 1050, 119 Sol Jo 286, 3 ALR 355,
[1973] 2 NSWLR 598, PC ... 904, 909, 910, 911, 912

Basham, Re [1987] 1 All ER 405, [1986] 1 WLR 1498,
[1987] 2 FLR 264, [1987] Fam Law 310, 130 Sol Jo
986, [1987] LS Gaz R 112 ... 164

Bates (Thomas) & Son Ltd v Wyndham's (Lingerie) Ltd
[1981] 1 All ER 1077, [1981] 1 WLR 505, 41 P & CR
345, 125 Sol Jo 32, 257 Estates Gazette 381,
CA ... 299–301, 319–320

Beale v Taylor [1967] 3 All ER 253, [1967] 1 WLR 1193,
111 Sol Jo 668, CA ... 430

Beck & Co v Szymanowski & Co [1924] AC 43, 93 LJKB
25, 29 Com Cas 50, [1923] All ER Rep 244, 130 LT
387, HL ... 975, 977

Beckett v Cohen [1972] 1 WLR 1593 ... 361

Beckett v Nurse [1948] 1 KB 535, [1948] 1 All ER 81,
[1948] LJR 450, 92 Sol Jo 54, 64 TLR 95, CA ... 350

Bedford Insurance Co Ltd v Instituto de Resseguros do
Brasil [1985] QB 966, [1984] 3 All ER 766, [1984] 3
WLR 726, [1984] 1 Lloyd's Rep 210, 218n, [1985] FLR
49, 128 Sol Jo 701, [1985] LS Gaz R 37, 134 NLJ
34 ... 1085, 1086

Behnke v Bede Shipping Co Ltd [1927] 1 KB 649 ... 710, 711

Behzadi v Shaftesbury Hotels Ltd [1992] Ch 1, [1991] 2 All ER 477, [1991] 2 WLR 1251, 62 P & CR 163, [1990] NLJR 1385, CA ... 575

Bell v Lever Bros Ltd [1932] AC 161, 101 LJKB 129, 37 Com Cas 98, [1931] All ER Rep 1, 76 Sol Jo 50, 146 LT 258, 48 TLR 133, HL ... 501, 503–509, 510, 514, 515, 516, 517, 518, 519, 520, 540, 541

Belvoir Finance Co Ltd v Stapleton [1971] 1 QB 210, [1970] 3 All ER 664, [1970] 3 WLR 530, 114 Sol Jo 719, CA ... 1094

Bence Graphics International Ltd v Fasson UK Ltd [1988] QB 87, [1997] 1 All ER 979, [1997] 3 WLR 205, [1996] 40 LS Gaz R 25, [1996] NLJR 1577, 140 Sol Jo LB 227, CA ... 664

Bennett v Bennett [1952] 1 KB 249, CA ... 107, 1070, 1119

Bentley (Dick) Productions Ltd v Harold Smith (Motors) Ltd [1965] 2 All ER 65, [1965] 1 WLR 623, 109 Sol Jo 329, CA. *See* Dick Bentley Productions Ltd v Harold Smith (Motors) Ltd [1965] 2 All ER 65, CA

Bentsen v Taylor Sons & Co (No 2) [1893] 2 QB 274, 63 LJQB 15, 7 Asp MLC 385, 4 R 510, 42 WR 8, 69 LT 487, 9 TLR 552, CA ... 566, 569

Beresford v Royal Insurance Co Ltd [1938] AC 586 [1938] 2 All ER 602, 107 LJKB 464, 82 Sol Jo 431, 158 LT 459, 54 TLR 789, HL ... 1082, 1088–1090, 1091

Berger & Co Inc v Gill & Duffus SA [1984] AC 382, [1984] 2 WLR 95, 128 Sol Jo 47, [1984] LS Gaz R 429, sub nom Gill & Duffus SA v Berger & Co Inc [1984] 1 All ER 438, [1984] 1 Lloyd's Rep 227, HL ... 574

Berkley-Freeman v Bishop (1740) 2 Atk 39 ... 940

Berkshire, The [1974] 1 Lloyd's Rep 185 ... 402

Bernstein v Pamson Motors (Golders Green) Ltd [1987] 2 All ER 220, [1987] RTR 384, [1987] BTLC 37 ... 618, 619

Berry v Berry (16 April 1999) 978 P 2d 93 ... 151

Beseler, Waechter, Glover & Co v South Derwent Coal Co Ltd ... 861

Beswick v Beswick [1968] AC 58, [1967] 2 All ER 1197, [1967] 3 WLR 932, 111 Sol Jo 540, HL ... 1139–1144, 1153, 1178

Bettini v Gye (1876) 1 QBD 183 ... 600

Beynon v Cook ... 940

BICC plc v Burndy Corpn [1985] Ch 232, [1985] 1 All ER 417, [1985] 2 WLR 132, [1985] RPC 273, 128 Sol Jo 750, [1984] LS Gaz R 3011, CA ... 592

Bilton (Percy) Ltd v Greater London Council [1982] 2 All ER 623, [1982] 1 WLR 794, 80 LGR 617, 126 Sol Jo 397, 20 BLR 1, HL ... 1165

Binions v Evans [1972] 1 Ch *359* ... 21

Birch v Paramount Estates Ltd (1956) 167 EG 196 ... 325, 326

Birmingham and District Land Co v London & North Western Rly Co (1888) 40 ChD 268 ... 151, 153, 156, 864, 866, 871

Bishop v Kitchen ... 1120

Bisset v Wilkinson [1927] AC 177, 96 LJPC 12, [1926] All ER Rep 343, 136 LT 97, 42 TLR 727, PC ... 358–360, 507

Blackburn Bobbin Co Ltd v TW Allen & Sons Ltd [1918] 2 KB 467, 87 LJKB 1085, 119 LT 215, 34 TLR 508, CA ... 472–473, 526

Blackpool and Fylde Aero Club Ltd v Blackpool Borough Council [1990] 3 All ER 25, [1990] 1 WLR 1195, 88 LGR, [1990] 26 LS Gaz R 37, CA ... 147, 244–249, 256

Bliss v South East Thames Regional Health Authority (1983), *Times*, 13 December ... 675

Blomley v Ryan (1956) 99 CLR 362 ... 943

Bolton v Mahadeva [1972] 2 All ER 1322, [1972] 1 WLR 1009, 116 Sol Jo 564, CA ... 563

Boomer v Muir 24 P 2d 570 (1933) ... 744, 745

Boot (Henry) & Sons Ltd v LCC [1959] 1 All ER 77, [1959] 1 WLR 133, 57 LGR 15, 123 JP 101, 103 Sol Jo 90, CA; revsd sub nom LCC v Henry Boot & Sons Ltd [1959] 3 All ER 636, [1959] 1 WLR 1069, 59 LGR 357, 103 Sol Jo 918, HL ... 404

Boothby v Boothby ... 940

Borrowman, Phillips & Co v Free and Hollis (1878) 4 QBD 500, 48 LJQB 65, 40 LT 25, CA ... 573–574

Boston Deep Sea Fishing and Ice Co Ltd v Ansell (1888) 39 Ch D 339 ... 993

Boustany v Pigott (1993) 69 P & CR 298, [1993] NPC 75, PC ... 942

Bower v Bantam Investments Ltd [1972] 3 All ER 349, [1972] 1 WLR 1120, 116 Sol Jo 633 ... 732

Bowerman v Association of British Travel Agents Ltd [1995] NLJR 1815, [1996] CLC 451, CA ... 19

Bowlay Logging Ltd v Domtar Ltd [1982] 6 WWR 528 ... 632

Bowmakers Ltd v Barnet Instruments Ltd [1945] KB 65, [1944] 2 All ER 579, 114 LJKB 41, 89 Sol Jo 22, 172 LT 1, 61 TLR 62, CA ... 1099–1100, 1101, 1102

Bowman v Secular Society Ltd [1917] AC 406, 86 LJ Ch 568, [1916–17] All ER Rep 1, 61 Sol Jo 478, 117 LT 161, 33 TLR 376, HL ... 1075

BP Exploration Co (Libya) Ltd v Hunt (No 2) [1982] 1 All ER 925, [1979] 1 WLR 783, 123 Sol Jo 455; affd [1982] 1 All ER 925, [1981] 1 WLR 232, 125 Sol Jo 165, CA; affd [1983] 2 AC 352, [1982] 1 All ER 925, [1982] 2 WLR 253, 126 Sol Jo 116, HL ... 486–492

Bracewell v Appleby [1975] Ch 408, [1975] 1 All 993, [1975] 2 WLR 282, 29 P & CR 204, 119 Sol Jo 114 ... 637, 681, 686

Bradley v Carritt [1903] AC 253, 72 LJKB 471, 51 WR 636, [1900–3] All ER Rep 633, 47 Sol Jo 534, 88 LT 633, 19 TLR 466, HL ... 939

Brady v St Margaret's Trust Ltd [1963] 3 WLR 1162 ... 609

Brandt v Liverpool [1924] 1 KB 575 ... 1157

Branwhite v Worcester Works Finance Ltd [1968] 3 All ER 104, [1969] 1 AC 552 ... 318

Brazil and River Plate Steam Navigation Co Ltd ... 1159

Bremer Handelsgesellschaft mbH v Continental Grain Co New York [1983] 1 Lloyd's Rep 269, CA ... 470

Bret v JS (1600) Cro Eliz 756 ... 100

Bridge v Campbell Discount Co Ltd [1962] AC 600, [1962] 1 All ER 385, [1962] 2 WLR 439, 106 Sol Jo 94, HL ... 700

Brikom Investments Ltd v Carr [1979] QB 467, [1979] 2 All ER 753, [1979] 2 WLR 737, 39 P & CR 326, 123 Sol Jo 182, 251 Estates Gazette 359, CA ... 874, 875

Brimnes, The. *See* Tenaz Steamship Co Ltd v Reinante Transoeania Navegacion SA, The Brimnes

Brinkibon Ltd v Stahag Stahl und Stahlwarenhandel GmbH [1983] 2 AC 34, [1982] 1 All ER 293, [1982] 2 WLR 264, [1982] 1 Lloyd's Rep 217, [1982] Com LR 72, 126 Sol Jo 116, HL ... 236

British Airways Board v Taylor [1976] 1 All ER 65, [1976] 1 WLR 13, [1976] 1 Lloyd's Rep 167, 140 JP 96, [1977] 120 Sol Jo 7, HL ... 361

British Bank for Foreign Trade Ltd v Novinex Ltd [1949] 1 KB 623, [1949] 1 All ER 155, [1949] LJR 658, 93 Sol Jo 146, CA ... 266–267

British Columbia and Vancouver's Island Spar, Lumber and Sawmill Co Ltd v Nettleship (1868) LR 3 CP 499, 37 LJCP 235, 3 Mar LC 65, 16 WR 1046, [1861–73] All ER Rep 339, 18 LT 604 ... 646, 650

British Crane Hire Corpn Ltd v Ipswich Plant Hire Ltd [1975] QB 303, [1974] 1 All ER 1059, [1974] 2 WLR 856, 118 Sol Jo 387, CA ... 340–341

British Eagle International Airlines Ltd v Compagnie Nationale Air France [1975] 2 All ER 390, [1975] 1 WLR 758, [1975] 2 Lloyd's Rep 43, 119 Sol Jo 368, HL ... 1208

British Motor Trade Association v Salvadori [1949] Ch 556, [1949] 1 All ER 208, [1949] LJR 1304, 65 TLR 44 ... 1204

British Movieonews Ltd v London and District Cinemas Ltd [1951] 1 KB 190, CA; [1952] AC 166, [1951] 2 All ER 617, 95 Sol Jo 499, [1951] 2 TLR 571, HL ... 464–465, 522

British Road Services Ltd v Arthur V Crutchley & Co Ltd ... 227

British Steel Corpn v Cleveland Bridge and Engineering Co Ltd [1984] 1 All ER 504, [1982] Com LR 54, 24 BLR 94 ... 39–45, 180, 230, 281–283

British Transport Commission v Gourley [1956] AC 185, [1955] 3 All ER 796, [1956] 2 WLR 41, [1955] 2 Lloyd's Rep 475, 34 ATC 305, 49 R & IT 11, [1955] TR 303, 100 Sol Jo 12, HL ... 659

British Westinghouse Electric and Manufacturing Co Ltd v Underground Electric Railways Co of London Ltd [1912] AC 673, 81 LJKB 1132, [1911–13] All ER Rep 63, 56 Sol Jo 734, 107 LT 325, HL ... 623, 651–652, 660–661, 666

Brogden v Metropolitan Rly Co (1877) 2 App Cas 666, HL ... 196, 208–209, 211, 271, 1134

Brown, Jenkinson & Co Ltd v Percy Dalton (London) Ltd [1957] 2 QB 621, [1957] 2 All ER 844, [1957] 3 WLR 403, [1957] 2 Lloyd's Rep 1, 101 Sol Jo 610, CA ... 1078, 1080

Brown v KMR Services Ltd [1995] 4 All ER 598, [1995] 2 Lloyd's Rep 513, [1995] 32 LS Gaz R 29, CA ... 649

Brown v Raphael [1958] Ch 636, [1958] 2 All ER 79, [1958] 2 WLR 647, 102 Sol Jo 269, CA ... 359

Browning v Morris (1778) 2 Cowp 790 ... 1093

Bryan v Maloney (1995) 51 Con LR 29, 182 CLR 609, 74 BLR 35, 128 ALR 163, 69 ALJR 375, Aust Torts Reports 81–320, HC of A ... 36

Bunge Corpn v Tradax Sa [1981] 2 All ER 513, [1980] 1 Lloyd's Rep 294, CA; affd [1981] 2 All ER 513, [1981] 1 WLR 711, [1981] 2 Lloyd's Rep 1, 125 Sol Jo 373, HL ... 570, 572, 576–580, 602, 607, 613

Burke (Raymond) Motors Ltd v Mersey Docks and Harbour Co [1986] 1 Lloyd's Rep 155 ... 1160

Burmah Oil Co Ltd v Governor of the Bank of England (1981) 125 Sol Jo 528, *Times*, 4 July ... 957

Bushwall Properties Ltd v Vortex Properties Ltd [1976] 2 All ER 283, [1976] 1 WLR 591, 120 Sol Jo 183, CA ... 262

Butler Machine Tool Co Ltd v Ex-Cell-O Corpn (England) Ltd [1979] 1 All ER 965, [1979] 1 WLR 401, 121 Sol Jo 406, CA ... 225–230, 523

Butterworth v Kingsway Motors Ltd [1954] 2 All ER 694, [1954] 1 WLR 1286, 98 Sol Jo 717 ... 427

Buttery v Pickard ... 151

Bywater, Re ... 181

C

C (a debtor), Re (1994) *Times*, 11 May, CA ... 856

C & P Haulage (a firm) v Middleton [1983] 3 All ER 94, [1983] 1 WLR 1461, 127 Sol Jo 730, CA ... 631–633

Campbell Discount Co v Bridge [1962] 1 All ER 385 ... 591

Campbell v Campbell & Worthington ... 669

Canada Steamship Lines Ltd v R [1952] AC 192 ... 1016

Canadian Dyers Association Ltd v Burton (1920) 47 OLR 259 ... 198

Candler v Crane Christmas & Co [1951] 2 KB 164, [1951] 1 All ER 426 ... 371

Candlewood Navigation Corpn Ltd v Misui OSK Lines Ltd, The Mineral Transporter, The Ibaraki Maru [1986] AC 1, [1985] 2 All ER 935, [1985] 3 WLR 381, [1985] 2 Lloyd's Rep 303, 129 Sol Jo 506, PC ... 30

Caparo Industries plc v Dickman [1990] 2 AC 605, [1990] 1 All ER 568, [1990] 2 WLR 358, [1990] BCLC 273, [1990] BCC 164, 134 Sol Jo 494, [1990] 12 LS Gaz R 42, [1990] NLJR 248, HL ... 29, 30, 32, 1162, 1166

Capital Finance Co Ltd v Donati ... 609

Capital Motors Ltd v Beecham [1975] 1 NZLR 576 ... 371

Captain Gregos (No. 2), The (Cia Portorafti Commerciale SA v Ultramar Panama Inc, The Captain Gregos (No 2) Car and Universal Finance Co Ltd v Caldwell [1965] 1 QB 525, [1963] 2 All ER 547, [1964] 2 WLR 600, 107 Sol Jo 738; affd [1965] 1 QB 525, [1964] 1 All ER 290, [1964] 2 WLR 600, 108 Sol Jo 15, CA ... 311, 1201

Carle v Montanari Inc v American Export Isbrandtsen Lines Inc [1968] 1 Lloyd's Rep 260 ... 1159

Carlill v Carbolic Smoke Ball Co [1893] 1 QB 256, 57 JP 325, 62 LJQB 257, 4 R 176, 41 WR 210, 67 LT 837, 9 TLR 124, CA ... 14–16, 19, 109, 184, 199, 201, 211, 214, 215, 216, 245, 1159, 1247

Carpenters Estates Ltd v Davies [1940] Ch 160, [1940] 1 All ER 13, 109 LJ Ch 92, 83 Sol Jo 960, 162 LT 76, 56 TLR 269 ... 727–728

Carr v J A Berriman Pty Ltd (1953) 89 CLR 327, 27 ALJ 273, HC of A ... 883

Carter v Boehm (1766) 3 Burr 1905 ... 540

Carter v Sullivan [1957] 2 QB 117, [1957] 1 All ER 809, [1957] 2 WLR 528, 101 Sol Jo 265, CA ... 668

Cartwright v Rowley ... 954

Casey's Patents, Re (Stewart v Casey) [1892] 1 Ch 104 ... 127–128

Cassidy v Ministry of Health [1951] 2 KB 598 ... 371

Catt v Tourle (1869) 4 Ch App 654 ... 732

CBS Songs Ltd v Amstrad Consumer Electronics plc [1988] AC 1013, [1988] 2 All ER 484, [1988] 2 WLR 1191, [1988] RPC 567, 132 Sol Jo 789, HL ... 245

CCC Films (London) Ltd v Impact Quadrant Films Ltd [1985] QB 16, [1984] 3 All ER 298, [1984] 3 WLR 245, 128 Sol Jo 297 ... 633

Cehave NV v Bremer Handelsgesellschaft mbH, The Hansa Nord [1976] QB 44, [1975] 3 All ER 739, [1975] 3 WLR 447, [1975] 2 Lloyd's Rep 445, 119 Sol Jo 678, Ca ... 566 ... 570–571, 572, 577, 594

Cellulose Acetate Silk Co Ltd v Widnes Foundry (1925) Ltd [1933] AC 20, 101 LJKB 694, 38 Com Cas 61, [1932] All ER Rep 567, 147 LT 401, 48 TLR 595, HL ... 692

Central London Property Trust Ltd v High Trees House Ltd [1947] KB 130, [1956] 1 All ER 256n, [1947] LJR 77, 175 LT 332, 62 TLR 557 ... 150–152, 153, 154, 156, 159, 187, 193, 860, 861, 862, 864, 865, 866, 867, 868, 869, 871, 872, 873

Centrovincial Estates plc v Merchant Investors Assurance Co Ltd [1983] Com LR 158, CA ... 194, 292, 294

Chandelor v Lopus (1603) 79 Eng Rep 3 Cro Jac 4 Eng Ct Exch ... 324, 326

Chandler v Webster [1904] 1 KB 493, 73 LJKB 401, 52 WR 290, 48 Sol Jo 245, 90 LT 217, 20 TLR 222, CA ... 481, 482

Chandris v Isbrandtsen-Moller Co Inc [1950] 1 All ER 768, [1951] 1 KB 240 ... 402

Channel Home Centers Division of Grace Retail Corpn v Grossman 795 F 2d 291 (1986) ... 274

Chapelton v Barry UDC [1940] 1 KB 532, [1940] 1 All ER 356, 38 LGR 149, 104 JP 165, 109 LJKB 213, 84 Sol Jo 185, 162 LT 169, 56 TLR 331, CA ... 334

Chaplin v Hicks [1911] 2 KB 786, 80 LJKB 1292, [1911–13] All ER Rep 224, 55 Sol Jo 580, 105 LT 285, 27 TLR 458, CA ... 276, 670

Chappel & Co v Nestlé Co Ltd [1960] AC 87, [1959] 2 All ER 701, [1959] 3 WLR 168, 103 Sol Jo 561, HL ... 126

Chappell v Times Newspapers Ltd [1975] 2 All ER 233, [1975] 1 WLR 482, [1975] ICR 145, [1975] IRLR 90, 119 Sol Jo 82, CA ... 728

Charles Hunt v Palmer ... 1024

Charles Rickards Ltd v Oppenheim [1950] 1 All ER 420, CA ... 575, 861–862, 869

Charnock v Liverpool Corpn [1968] 3 All ER 473, [1968] 1 WLR 1498, [1968] 2 Lloyd's Rep 113, 112 Sol Jo 781, CA ... 99

Charterhouse Credit Co Ltd v Tolly [1963] 2 QB 683 320n ... 609, 994

Chess (Oscar) Ltd v Williams [1957] 1 All ER 325, [1957] 1 WLR 370, 101 Sol Jo 186, CA ... 324–326, 327

Chester Grosvenor Hotel Ltd v Alfred McAlpine Management Ltd (1991) 56 BLR 115 ... 1008

Chikuma, The (Awilco A/S v Fulvia SpA di Navigazione, The Chikuma Christie, Owen and Davies Ltd v Rapacioli [1974] QB 781, [1974] 2 All ER 311, [1974] 2 WLR 723, 118 Sol Jo 167, CA) ... 602

Christie, Owen & Davies Ltd v Rapacioli [1974] QB 781 ... 220

Christopher Moran Holdings v Bairstow [2000] 2 AC 172, sub nom Park Air Services, Re, Christopher Moran Holdings Ltd v Bairstow [1999] 1 All ER 673, [1999] 1 BCLC 155, [1999] NLJR 195, sub nom Christopher Moran Holdings Ltd v Bairstow [1999] 2 WLR 396, [1999] 14 EG 149, [1999] EGCS 17, HL ... 614

Chwee Kin Keong v Digilandmall Com Pte Ltd [2005] 1 SLR 502 ... 296, 300

Cia Portorafti Commerciale SA v Ultramar Panama Inc, The Captain Gregos (No 2) [1990] 2 Lloyd's Rep 395 ... 311, 1201

CIBC Mortgages plc v Pitt [1994] 1 AC 200, [1993] 4 All ER 433, [1993] 3 WLR 802, [1994] 1 FCR 374, [1994] 1 FLR 17, [1994] Fam Law 79, 26 HLR 90, [1993] 46 LS Gaz R 37, [1993] NLJR 1514, HL ... 922, 925, 929

City and Westminster Properties (1934) Ltd v Mudd [1959] Ch 129, [1958] 2 All ER 733, [1958] 3 WLR 312, 102 Sol Jo 582 ... 350, 352

Clark v Kirby Smith [1964] Ch. 506 ... 371

Clark v Urquhart [1930] AC 28, 99 LJPC 1, 141 LT 641, HL ... 374

Clarke v Dickson (1858) EB & E 148, 27 LJQB 223, 4 Jur NS 832, 31 LTOS 97 ... 367–368

Clarkson Booker Ltd v Andjel [1964] 2 QB 775, [1964] 3 All ER 260, [1964] 3 WLR 466, 108 Sol Jo 580, CA ... 1135

Clay v Yates (1856) 1 H & N 73, 25 LJ Ex 237, 2 Jur NS 908, 4 WR 557, 27 LTOS 126 ... 1086

Clayton (Herbert) and Jack Waller Ltd v Oliver [1930] AC 209, 99 LJKB 165, [1930] All ER Rep 414, 74 Sol Jo 187, 142 LT 585, 46 TLR 230, HL ... 678

Clea Shipping Corpn v Bulk Oil International Ltd, The Alaskan Trader [1984] 1 All ER 129, [1983] 2 Lloyd's Rep 645 ... 738–740, 1144, 1145, 1146, 1147, 1148, 1149

Clef Aquitaine SARL v Laporte Materials (Barrow) Ltd [2001] QB 488, [2000] 3 All ER 493, [2000] 3 WLR 1760, CA ... 377

Clegg v Anderson [2003] EWCA Civ 320, [2003] 2 Lloyd's Rep 32 ... 619

Cleveland Petroleum Co Ltd v Dartstone Ltd [1969] 1 All ER 201, [1969] 1 WLR 116, 20 P & CR 235, 112 Sol Jo 962, CA ... 1114

Clough Mill Ltd v Martin [1984] 3 All ER 982, [1985] 1 WLR 111, [1985] BCLC 64, 128 Sol Jo 850, [1985] LS Gaz R 116, CA ... 733

Clough v London and North Western Rly Co [1871] LR 7 Exch 26 ... 615

Clydebank Engineering and Shipbuilding Co Ltd v Don Jose Ramos Yzquierdo y Castaneda [1905] AC 6, 74 LJPC 1, [1904–7] All ER Rep 251, 91 LT 666, 21 TLR 58, 7 F 77, HL ... 690, 691, 694

Codelfa Construction Pty Ltd v State Rail Authority of New South Wales (1982) 149 CLR 337, 41 ALR 367, 56 ALJR 459; on appeal sub nom State Rail Authority of New South Wales v Codelfa Construction Pty Ltd 150 CLR 29, 42 ALR 289, 56 ALJR 800 . . . 415, 496–497

Coldunell Ltd v Gallon [1986] QB 1184, [1986] 1 All ER 429, [1986] 2 WLR 466, 130 Sol Jo 88, CA . . . 923

Collen v Wright (1857) 8 E & B 647 . . . 1131, 1132

Colley v Overseas Exporters [1921] 3 KB 302, 90 LJKB 1301, 26 Com Cas 325, [1921] All ER Rep 596, 126 LT 58, 37 TLR 797 . . . 733

Collins v Blantern (1767) 2 Wilson 347 . . . 1096

Collins v Godefroy (1831) 1 B & Ad 950, 1 Dowl 326, 9 LJOS 158 . . . 105

Collins v Uniroyal Inc 315 A 2d 16, 64 NJ 260 (1974) . . . 1004

Colonial Bank v European Grain and Shipping Ltd, The Dominique [1989] AC 1056 . . . 614–615, 1147

Combe v Combe (1951) 2 KB 215, [1951] 1 All ER 767, 95 Sol Jo 317, [1951] 1 TLR 811, CA . . . 147, 152–155, 159, 160, 161, 164, 165, 167, 170, 187, 860, 865–866

Commercial Bank of Australia Ltd v Amadio (1983) 151 CLR 447, 46 ALR 402, 57 ALJR 358, HC of A . . . 942, 943

Commerciale SA v Ultramar Panama Inc, The Captain Gregos (No 2) [1990] 2 Lloyd's Rep 395, CA . . . 311, 1201

Commission for the New Towns v Cooper (Great Britain) Ltd [1995] Ch 259, [1995] 2 All ER 929, [1995] 2 WLR 677, 72 P & CR 270, [1995] NPC 34, [1995] 2 EGLR 113, [1995] 26 EG 129, 139 Sol Jo LB 87, CA . . . 300

Commonwealth of Australia v Amann Aviation Pty Ltd (1991) 174 CLR 64, 104 ALR 1, 66 ALJR 123, HC of A . . . 633

Commonwealth of Australia v Verwayen (1990) 170 CLR 394, 95 ALR 321, 64 ALJR 540 . . . 162–163

Commonwealth v Scituate Savings Bank (1884) 137 Mass 301 . . . 160

Compagnie Noga D'Importationet D'Exportation Sa v Abacha [2003] EWCA Civ 1100 [2003] 2 All ER (Comm) 915 . . . 851

Conemsco Ltd v Contrapol Ltd . . . 1015

Conquest v Ebbetts [1896] AC 490, 65 LJ Ch 808, 45 WR 50, [1895–9] All ER Rep 622, 40 Sol Jo 700, 75 LT 36, 12 TLR 599, HL . . . 681

Constantine (Joseph) Steamship Line Ltd v Imperial Smelting Corpn Ltd, The Kingswood [1942] AC 154, [1941] 2 All ER 165, 110 LJKB 433, 46 Com Cas 258, 165 LT 27, 57 TLR 485, 70 Ll L Rep 1, HL . . . 472

Continental Forest Products Inc v Chandler Supply Co 518 P 2d 121, 95 Idaho 739 (1974) . . . 310

Cooden Engineering Co v Stanford [1953] 1 QB 86 . . . 604

Cook v Wright (1861) 1 B & S 559, 30 LJQB 321, 7 Jur NS 1121, 121 ER 822, 4 LT 704 . . . 103–105

Cooper v Micklefield Coal & Lime Co Ltd (1912) 56 Sol Jo 706, 107 LT 457 . . . 1196

Cooper v Parker . . . 854

Cooper v Phibbs (1867) LR 2 HL 149 . . . 504, 511, 512, 518, 519

Co-operative Insurance Society Ltd v Argyll Stores (Holdings) Ltd [1998] AC 1, [1997] 3 All ER 297, [1997] 2 WLR 898, [1997] 1 EGKR 52, [1997] 26 LS Gaz R 30, [1997] NLJR 845, [1997] 23 EG 141, 141 Sol Jo LB 131, HL . . . 723

Cope v Rowlands (1836) 2 Mees & Wels 149 . . . 608

Cornelius v Philips . . . 1085

Cory v Thames Ironworks Co (1868) LR 3 QB 181, 37 LJQB 68, 16 WR 456, [1861–73] All ER Rep 597, 17 LT 495 . . . 615

Cosgrove v Horsfall (1946) 62 TLR 140 . . . 1160

Couchman v Hill [1947] KB 554, [1947] 1 All ER 103, [1948] LJR 295, 176 LT 278, 63 TLR 81, CA . . . 325, 342–344

Coulls v Bagot's Executor and Trustee Co Ltd (1967) 119 CLR 460, [1967] ALR 385, 40 ALJR 471, HC of A . . . 1141, 1142

Courtney and Fairbairn Ltd v Tolaini Brothers (Hotels) Ltd [1975] 1 All ER 716, CA . . . 263–265, 274

Couturier v Hastie (1856) 5 HL Cas 673, 25 LJ Ex 253, 2 JR NS 1241, 10 ER 1065, [1843–60] All ER Rep 280, 28 LTOS 240 . . . 499–500, 501, 503

Cowan v Milbourn (1867) LR 2 Exch 230, 31 JP 423, 36 LJ Ex 124, 15 WR 750, 16 LT 290 . . . 1075

Coward v Motor Insurers' Bureau [1963] 1 QB 259, [1962] 1 All ER 531, [1962] 2 WLR 663, [1962] 1 Lloyd's Rep 1, 106 Sol Jo 34, CA . . . 179

Cox v Philips Industries Ltd [1976] 3 All ER 161, [1976] 1 WLR 638, [1976] ICR 138, [1975] IRLR 344, 119 Sol Jo 760 . . . 675

Cox v Smail (1912) VLR 274 . . . 903

Crabb v Arun District Council [1976] Ch 179, [1975] 3 All ER 865, [1975] 3 WLR 847, 119 Sol Jo 711, CA . . . 155–158, 163, 164, 169, 282, 811

Craig (decd), Re [1970] 2 All ER 390, [1971] Ch 95 . . . 936

Crane v Hegeman-Harris Co Inc [1939] 1 All ER 662 . . . 297, 307

Crédit Lyonnais Bank Nederland NV v Burch [1997] 1 All ER 144, 74 P & CR 384, [1997] 2 FCR 1, [1997] 1 FLR 11, [1997] Fam Law 168, 29 HLR 513, [1996] 5 Bank I R 233, [1996] 32 LS Gaz R 33, [1996] NLJR 1421, 140 Sol Jo LB 158, CA . . . 935, 936, 937, 944

Cremdean Properties Ltd v Nash (1977) 244 Estates Gazette 547, [1977] EGD 63, CA . . . 387

Cresswell v Potter [1978] 1 WLR 255n . . . 941–945, 942, 944

CTN Cash and Carry Ltd v Gallagher Ltd [1994] 4 All ER 714, CA . . . 914

Cullinane v British Rema Manufacturing Co Ltd [1954] 1 QB 292, [1953] 2 All ER 1257, [1953] 3 WLR 923, 97 Sol Jo 811, CA . . . 630–631

Cumber v Wane (1721) 1 Stra 426, 93 ER 613 . . . 853, 857

Cundy v Lindsay (1878) 3 App Cas 459 . . . 311, 316, 317, 318

Curlewis v Clark (1887) 31 Fed. 71 . . . 853, 857

Currie v Misa (1875) LR 10 Exch 153, 44 LJ Ex 94, 23 WR 450; affd sub nom Misa v Currie 1 App Cas 554, 45

LJQB 852, 24 WR 1049, [1874–80] All ER Rep 686, 35 LT 414, HL . . . 97, 98

Curtis v Chemical Cleaning and Dyeing Co Ltd [1951] 1 KB 805, [1951] 1 All ER 631, 95 Sol Jo 253, [1951] 1 TLR 452, CA . . . 346

Cutter v Powell (1795) 6 Term Rep 320, [1775–1802] All ER Rep 159 . . . 556–557, 558, 560, 561, 744

Czarnikow v Ruth, Schmidt & Co [1922] 2 KB 478, 92 LJKB 81, 28 Com Cas 29, [1922] All ER Rep 45, 127 LT 824, 38 TLR 797, CA . . . 89, 1073, 1120

D

D & C Builders Ltd v Rees [1966] 2 QB 617, [1965] 3 All ER 837, [1966] 2 WLR 288, 109 Sol Jo 971, CA . . . 856–857, 867, 877, 906, 913, 915, 960

D & F Estates Ltd v Church Comrs for England [1989] AC 177, [1988] 2 All ER 992, [1988] 3 WLR 368, 15 Con LR 35, 132 Sol Jo 35, 132 Sol Jo 1092, [1988] 2 EGLR 262, [1988] NLJR 210, 41 BLR 1, HL . . . 34, 420, 1165

Dagenham (Thames) Dock Co, Re, ex p Hulse (1873) 8 Ch App 1022, 38 JP 180, 43 LJ 261, 21 WR 898 . . . 591

Dahl v Nelson, Donkin & Co (1953) 56 NW 2d 757 . . . 465

Damodar General TJ Park and King Theras, The (Mosvolds Rederi A/S v Food Corpn of India, The Damodar General TJ Park and King Theras Damon Cia Naviera SA v Hapag-Lloyd International SA, The Blankenstein, The Bartenstein, The Birkenstein [1985] 1 All ER 475, [1985] 1 WLR 435, [1985] 1 Lloyd's Rep 93, 129 Sol Jo 218, CA . . . 702

Darlington Borough Council v Wiltshier Northern Ltd [1995] 3 All ER 895, [1995] 1 WLR 68, [1994] 37 LS Gaz R 49, 69 BLR 1, 11 Const LJ 36, 138 Sol Jo LB 161, CA . . . 1149

Darlington Futures Ltd v Delco Australia Pty Ltd (1986) 161 CLR 500, 68 ALR 385, 5 ACLC 132, 61 ALJR 76, HC of A . . . 995, 1149, 1179

Daulia Ltd v Four Millbank Nominees Ltd [1978] Ch 231, [1978] Ch 231, [1978] 2 All ER 557, [1978] 2 WLR 621, 36 P & CR 244, 121 Sol Jo 851, CA . . . 217–218, 220

Davis Contractors v Fareham UDC [1956] AC 696, [1956] 2 All ER 145, [1956] 3 WLR 37, 54 LGR 289, 100 Sol Jo 378, HL . . . 463–467, 473, 480, 493, 523

Davis v Duke of Marlborough (1818) 1 Swan 74, 36 ER 303 . . . 940

Davis v Garrett (1830) 6 Bing 716 . . . 984

Dawood (Ebrahim) Ltd v Heath (East 1927) Ltd [1961] 2 Lloyd's Rep 512 . . . 483, 743

Dawson v Helicopter Exploration Co Ltd [1955] SCR 868, [1955] 5 DLR 404 . . . 221

De La Bere v Pearson Ltd [1908] 1 KB 280, 77 LJKB 380, [1904–7] All ER Rep 755, 98 LT 71, 24 TLR 120, CA . . . 7, 147

De Lassalle v Guildford [1901] 2 KB 215, 70 LJKB 533, 49 WR 467, [1900–3] All ER 495, 84 LT 549, 17 TLR 384, CA . . . 350

De Mattos v Gibson (1858) 4 De G & J 276, 28 LJ Ch 165, 5 Jr NS 347, 7 WR 152, LTOS 268; on appeal 4 De G & J 284, 28 LJ Ch 498, 5 Jur NS 555, 7 WR 514, LTOS 193 . . . 1206

De Molestina v Ponton [2002] EWHC 2413 (Comm) [2002] 1 All ER (Comm) 587 . . . 368

Deacon v Transport Regulation Board [1958] VR 458 . . . 908

Dean v MacDowell (1878) 8 Ch D 345, 42 JP 580, 47 LJ Ch 537, 26 WR 486, 38 LT 862, CA . . . 455

Decro-Wall International SA v Practitioners in Marketing Ltd [1971] 2 All ER 216, [1971] 1 WLR 361, 115 Sol Jo 171, CA . . . 586, 587, 732

Deepak Fertilisers and Petrochemicals Ltd v Davy McKee (London) Ltd [1999] 1 Lloyd's Rep 387, 62 Con LR 86, [1999] BLR 41, CA . . . 353

Deglman v Guaranty Trust Co of Canada and Constantineau [1954] 3 DLR 785 . . . 43

Demerara Bauxite Co v Hubbard [1923] AC 673, 92 LJPC 148, 129 LT 517 . . . 922

Denney v Reppert 432 SW 2d 647 (1968) . . . 105

Dennis's case . . . 1084

Denny, Mott & Dickson Ltd v James B. Fraser & Co Ltd . . . 464, 465

Denton v Great Northern Railway Co (1856) 20 JP 483, 5 E & B 860, 25 LJQB 129, 2 Jur NS 185, Saund & M 128, 4 WLR 240, 26 LTOS 216 . . . 203, 204

Derry v Peek (1887) 37 Ch D 541, 57 LJ Ch 347, 36 WR 899, 59 LT 78, 4 TLR 84, CA; 14 App Cas 337, 54 JP 148, 58 LJ Ch 864, 1 Meg 292, 38 WR 33 [1886–90] All ER Rep 1, 61 LT 265, 5 TLR 625, HL . . . 356, 370

Diamond v British Columbia Thoroughbred Breeders' Society and Boyd (1965) 52 DLR (2d) 146 (BC) . . . 507

Dick Bentley Productions Ltd v Harold Smith (Motors) Ltd [1965] 2 All ER 65, CA . . . 326–328, 329, 357, 426

Dickinson (Inspector of Taxes) v Abel [1969] 1 All ER 484, [1969] 1 WLR 295, 45 TC 353, 47 ATC 441, [1968] TR 419, 112 Sol Jo 967 . . . 100

Dickinson v Dodds (1876) 2 Ch D 463, 40 JP 532, 45 LJ Ch 777, 24 WR 594, 34 LT 607, CA . . . 238–240, 248

Dies v British and International Mining and Finance Corpn Ltd [1939] 1 KB 724, 108 LJKB 398, 160 LT 563 . . . 700

Dillwyn v Llewelyn (1862) 4 De GF & J 517, 31 LJ Ch 658, 8 Jur NS 1068, 10 WR 742, [1861–73] All ER Rep 384, 6 LT 878 . . . 155, 167, 168, 169

Dimsdale Developments (South East) Ltd v De Haan (1983) 47 P & CR 1 . . . 703

Director General of Fair Trading v First National Bank [2000] QB 672, [2000] 2 All ER 759, [2000] 2 WLR 1353, [2000] 07 LS Gaz R 39, [2000] 1 All ER (Comm) 371, CA . . . 1044

Dodd v Churton [1897] 1 QB 562, 66 LJQB 477, 45 WR 490, 41 Sol Jo 383, 76 LT 438, 13 TLR 305, CA . . . 695

Doherty v Allman (or Allen) (1878) 3 App Cas 709, 42 JP 788, 26 WR 513, 39 LT 129, HL . . . 731–732

Domb v Isoz [1980] Ch 548, [1980] 1 All ER 942, [1980] 2 WLR 565, 40 P & CR . . . 242

Don King Productions Inc v Warren [1999] 2 All ER 218 . . . 1196

Donnell v Bennett (1883) LR 22 Ch Div 835 . . . 732

Donoghue (or M'Alister) v Stevenson [1932] AC 562, 101 LJPC 119, 37 Com CAS 350, 48 TLR 494, 1932 SC (HL) 31, [1932] All ER Rep 1, 1932 SLT 317, 76 Sol Jo 396, 147 LT 281 ... 24–28, 30–31, 33, 34, 35, 39, 442, 797, 1162, 1169, 1170

Down v Hatcher ... 854

Doyle v Olby (Ironmongers) Ltd [1969] 2 QB 158, [1969] 2 All ER 119, [1969] 2 WLR 673, 113 Sol Jo 128, CA ... 38, 373–374, 375, 376, 377, 378, 383

DPP for Northern Ireland v Lynch [1975] AC 653, [1975] 2 WLR 641, 61 Cr App Rep 6, 119 Sol 233, sub nom Lynch v DPP for Northern Ireland [1975] NI 35, [1975] 1 All ER 913, 139 JP 312, [1975] Crim LR 707, HL ... 910

Drennan v Star Paving Co 51 Cal 2d 409, 333 P 2d 757 (1958) ... 249

Drimmie v Davies [1899] 1 IR 176 ... 1141

Drive Yourself Hire Co (London) Ltd v Strutt [1954] 1 QB 250 ... 1153

Duke of Beaufort v Patrick (1853) 17 Beav 60 ... 157

Dunkirk Colliery Co v Lever [1878] 9 Ch D 20 ... 652, 667

Dunlop Pneumatic Tyre Co Ltd v New Garage and Motor Co Ltd [1915] AC 79, 83 LJKB 1574, [1914–15] All ER Rep 739, 111 LT 862, 30 TLR 625, HL ... 689–692

Dunlop Pneumatic Tyre Co Ltd v Selfridge & Co Ltd [1915] AC 847, 84 LJKB 1680, [1914–15] All ER Rep 333, 59 Sol Jo 439, 113 LT 386, 31 TLR 399, HL ... 1136–1139, 1155

Dunlop v Lambert (1839) 6 Cl & Fin 600, Macl & R 663, HL ... 1148, 1149

Dunnachie v Kingston upon Hull City Council [2004] UKHL 36 [2004] 3 All ER 1011 ... 678

Dutton v Bognor Regis UDC [1972] 1 QB 373, [1972] 2 WLR 299, 70 LGR 57, [1972] 1 Lloyd's Rep 227, 136 JP 201, 116 Sol Jo 16, 3 BLR 11, sub nom Dutton v Bognor Regis United Building Co Ltd [1972] 1 All ER 462, CA ... 31, 34, 35

Dyster v Randall & Sons [1926] Ch 932, 95 LJ Ch 504, [1926] B & CR 113, [1926] All Rep 151, 70 Sol Jo 797, 135 LT 596 ... 1133

E

Earl Beauchamp v Winn (1873) LR 6 HL 223 ... 511

Earl of Aldborough v Trye (1840) 7 Cl & F, 436 7 ER 136 ... 940

Earl of Aylesford v Morris (1873) 8 Ch App 484 ... 940, 944, 946–947

Earl of Chesterfield v Jansen (1751) 2 Ves Sen 125 ... 943

Earl of Portmore v Taylor (1831) 4 Sim 182 ... 940

East Ham Borough Council (or Corpn) v Bernard Sunley & Sons Ltd [1966] AC 406, [1965] 3 All ER 619, [1965] 3 WLR 1096, 64 LGR 43, [1965] 2 Lloyd's Rep 425, 109 Sol Jo 874, HL ... 1144, 1146

East v Maurer [1991] 2 All ER 733, [1991] 1 WLR 461, CA ... 372–377, 628

Eastham v Newcastle United Football Club Ltd [1964] Ch 413, [1963] 3 All ER 139, [1963] 3 WLR 574, 107 Sol Jo 574 ... 1072

Eastwood v Kenyon (1840) 11 Ad & El 438, 9 LJQB 409, 4 Jur 1081, 3 Per & Dav 276, 113 ER 482, [1835–42] All ER Rep 133 ... 130, 141–142

Eastwood v Magnax Electric plc [2004] UKHL 35 [2004] 3 All ER 991 ... 678

Ebrahim Dawood Ltd v Heath (Est 1927) Ltd [1961] 2 Lloyd's Rep 512 ... 483, 743

Eccles v Bryant and Pollock [1948] Ch 93, [1947] 2 All ER 865, [1948] LJR 418, 92 Sol Jo 53, CA ... 240–242

Edgington v Fitzmaurice (1885) 29 Ch D 459, 50 JP 52, 55 LJ Ch 650, 33 WR 911, 53 LT 369, 1 TLR 326, CA ... 359

Edmonds v Lawson [2000] QB 501 ... 182

Edmunds v Bushell (1865) LR 1 QB 97 ... 1135

Edmunds v Merchants' Despatch Transportation Co (1883) 135 Mass 283 ... 316

Edwards v Mallan [1908] 1 KB 1002, 77 LJKB 608, 52 Sol Jo 316, 98 LT 824, 24 TLR 376, CA ... 38

Ee v Kakar (1979) 40 P & CR 223, 124 Sol Jo 327, [1980] 2 EGLR 137, 255 Estates Gazette 879 ... 279–280

Elacy & Co Ltd v Hyde ... 604

Elder, Dempster and Co Ltd v Paterson, Zochonis and Co Ltd [1924] AC 522, 93 LJKB 625, 16 Asp MLC 351, 29 Com Cas 340, [1924] All ER Rep 135, 68 Sol Jo 497, 131 LT 449, 40 TLR 464, HL ... 1153–1154, 1155, 1156, 1157, 1181, 1201

Elderton v Emmens (1847) 4 CB 479, 136 ER 594 ... 582

Elliot v Boynton ... 1087

Elphinstone (Lord) v Monkland Iron and Coal Co ... 690, 691

Emmanuel Ayodeji Ajayi v R T Briscoe (Nigeria) Ltd [1964] 3 AU ER 556 ... 869

Empire Jamaica, The. *See* Western Steamship Co Ltd v NV Koninklijke Rotterdamsche Lloyd, The Empire Jamaica

Empress Towers Ltd and Bank of Nova Scotia, Re (1991) 73 DLR (4th) 400 ... 276–277

Engelbach's Estate, Re [1924] 2 Ch 348 ... 1139

England v Davidson (1840) 11 Ad & El 856, 9 LJQB 287, 4 Jur 1032, 3 Per & Dav 594 ... 105

Enrico Furst & Co v W E Fischer Ltd [1960] 2 Lloyd's Rep 340 ... 868, 869

Entores Ltd v Miles Far East Corpn [1955] 2 QB 327, [1955] 2 All ER 493, [1955] 3 WLR 48, [1955] 1 Lloyd's Rep 511, 99 Sol Jo 384, CA ... 234–236

Equitable Life Assurance Society v Hyman [2000] 3 All ER 961, [2000] 3 WLR 529, 144 Sol Jo LB 239, [2001] Lloyd's Rep IR 99, HL ... 424

Erlanger v New Sombrero Phosphate Co (1878) 3 App Cas 1218, 27 WR 65, [1874–80] All ER Rep 271, 39 LT 269, sub nom New Sombrero Phosphate Co v Erlanger 48 LJ Ch 73, HL ... 367–368

Errington v Errington and Woods [1952] 1 KB 290, [1952] 1 All ER 149, 96 Sol Jo 119, [1952] 1 TLR 231, CA ... 216–217

Esso Petroleum Co Ltd v Customs and Excise Comrs [1976] 1 All ER 117, [1976] 1 WLR 1, 120 Sol Jo 49, HL ... 19

Esso Petroleum Co Ltd v Harper's Garage (Stourport) Ltd [1968] AC 269, [1967] 1 All ER 699, [1967] 2 WLR

871, 111 Sol Jo 174, 201 Estates Gazette 1043, HL ... 1111–1114

Esso Petroleum Co Ltd v Mardon [1976] QB 801, [1976] 2 All ER 5, [1976] 2 WLR 583, [1976] 2 Lloyd's Rep 305, 120 Sol Jo 131, 2 BLR 85, CA ... 17, 183–185, 327, 328–332, 370–372, 375

Eugenia, The. *See* Ocean Tramp Tankers Corpn v V/O Sovfracht, The Eugenia

Evans (J) & Son (Portsmouth) Ltd v Andrea Merzario Ltd [1976] 2 All ER 930, [1976] 1 WLR 1078, [1976] 2 Lloyd's Rep 165, 120 Sol Jo 734, CA ... 185–187, 323, 980–981

Evans & Co v Heathcote [1918] 1 KB 418 ... 1119

Evans Marshall & Co v Bertola SA [1973] 1 All ER 992, [1973] 1 WLR 349, [1973] 1 Lloyds' Rep 453, 117 Sol Jo 225, CA ... 712

Evans v Llewellin (1787) 1 Cox Eq Cas 333, 2 Bro CC 150 ... 939, 941, 955, 1001

Evanson v Crooks ... 1095

Experience Hendrix LLC v PPX Enterprises Inc [2003] EWCA Civ 323 [2003] 1 All ER (Comm) 830 ... 753

Export Credits Guarantee Department v Universal Oil Products Co [1983] 2 All ER 205, [1983] 1 WLR 399, [1983] 2 Lloyd's Rep 152, 127 Sol Jo 408, 23 BLR 106, 133 NLJ 662, HL ... 700

Eyre v Measday [1986] 1 All ER 488, [1986] NLJ Rep 91, CA ... 332

F

Fairclough v Swan Brewery Co Ltd [1912] AC 565, 81 LJPC 207, [1911–13] All ER Rep 397, 106 LT 931, 28 TLR 450 ... 248, 938

Fairline Shipping Corpn v Adamson [1975] QB 180, [1974] 2 All ER 967, [1974] 2 WLR 824, [1974] 1 Lloyd's Rep 133, 118 Sol Jo 406 ... 212–213

Falck v Williams [1900] AC 176, 69 LJPC 17, 16 NSWWN 152, 21 LRNSW 78 ... 303

Falcke v Gray (1849) 4 Drew 651, 29 LJ Ch 28, 5 Jur NS 645, 7 WR 535, 33 LTOS 297 ... 709–710

Falcke v Scottish Imperial Insurance Co (1886) 34 Ch D 234, 56 LJ Ch 707, 35 WR 143, 56 LT 220, 3 TLR 141, CA ... 44

Farley v Skinner [2001] UKHL 49 [2001] 4 All ER 801 ... 675

Farnworth Finance Facilities Ltd v Attryde [1970] 2 All 774, [1970] 1 WLR 1053, [1970] RTR 352, 114 Sol Jo 354, CA ... 365

Fawcett and Holmes' Contract, Re (1889) 42 Ch D 150, 58 LJ Ch 763, 61 LT 105, 5 TLR 515, CA ... 562

Feather (Thomas) & Co (Bradford) Ltd v Keighley Corpn (1953) 52 LGR 30 ... 605

Federal Commerce and Navigation Co Ltd v Molena Alpha Inc, The Nanfri [1979] AC 757, [1979] 1 All ER 307, [1978] 3 WLR 991, [1979] 1 Lloyd's Rep 201, 122 Sol Jo 843, HL ... 585

Federal Commerce and Navigation Co Ltd v Molena Gamma inc, The Lorfri [1979] AC 757, [1979] 1 All ER 307, [1978] 3 WLR 991, [1979] 1 Lloyd's Rep 201, 122 Sol Jo 843, HL ... 585

Felthouse v Bindley (1862) 11 CBNS 869, 31 LJCP 204, 10 WR 423; affd 1 New Rep 401, 11 WR 429, 7 LT 835 ... 211, 212

Fender v St John-Mildmay [1938] AC 1, 81 Sol Jo 549, 53 TLR 885, sub nom Fender v Mildmay [1937] 3 All ER 402, 106 LJKB 641, 157 LT 340, HL ... 1073, 1075

Fenner v Blake [1900] 1 QB 426 ... 151

Fercometal SARL v Mediterranean Shipping Co SA, The Simona [1989] AC 788, [1988] 2 All ER 742, [1988] 2 Lloyd's Rep 199, 132 Sol Jo 966, [1988] 27 LS Gaz R 41, [1988] NLJR 178, HL ... 584

Ferguson v Davies [1997] 1 All ER 315, CA ... 855

Fetim BV v Oceanspeed Shipping Ltd, The Flecha [1999] 1 Lloyd's Rep 612 ... 402

Fibrosa Spolka Akcynja v Fairbairn Lawson Combe Barbour Ltd [1943] AC 32, [1942] 2 All ER 122, 111 LJKB 433, 86 Sol Jo 232, 167 LT 101, 58 TLR 308, HL ... 481, 483, 485, 701

Financings Ltd v Baldock [1963] 2 QB 104, [1963] 1 All ER 443, [1963] 2 WLR 359, 107 Sol Jo 15, CA ... 604, 609, 610, 611

Financings Ltd v Stimson [1962] 3 All ER 386, [1962] 1 WLR 1184, CA ... 524–526

Finelli v Dee (1968) 76 DLR (2d) 393, [1968] 1 OR 676 ... 737

Firestone Tyre & Rubber Co Ltd v Vokins & Co Ltd [1951] 1 KB 32 ... 981

First National Bank plc v Syed [1991] 2 All ER 250, [1991] CCLR 37, 10 Tr LR 154, CA ... 496

Fisher v Bell [1961] 1 QB 394, [1960] 3 All ER 731, [1960] 3 WLR 919, 125 JP 101, 104 Sol Jo 981 ... 201

Fitch v Sutton ... 854

Floods of Queensferry Ltd v Shand Construction Ltd [2000] BLR 81 ... 369

Foakes v Beer (1884) 9 App Cas 605, 54 LJQB 130, 33 WR 233, [1881–5] All ER Rep 106, 51 LT 833, HL ... 852–855, 856, 857, 863, 864

Foley v Classique Coaches Ltd [1934] 2 KB 1, 103 LJKB 550, [1934] All ER Rep 88, 151 LT 242, CA ... 267–268, 270

Ford Motor Co Ltd v Amalgamated Union of Engineering and Foundry Workers [1969] 2 QB 303, [1969] 2 All ER 481, [1969] 1 WLR 339, 113 Sol Jo 203 ... 182–183

Ford v Tiley 6 B & C 325 ... 582

Forsikringsaktieselskapet Vesta v Butcher, Bain Dawles Ltd and Aquacultural Insurance Services Ltd [1989] AC 852, [1988] 2 All ER 43, [1988] 3 WLR 565, [1988] 1 Lloyd's Rep 19, 132 Sol Jo 1181, CA; affd [1989] AC 852, [1989] 1 All ER 402, [1989] 2 WLR 290, [1989] 1 Lloyd's Rep 331, 133 Sol Jo 184, [1989] 11 LS Gaz R 42, HL ... 380, 657

Fortescue v Lostwithiel and Fowey Railway Co (1894) 3 Ch 621 ... 726

Foster v Driscoll [1929] 1 KB 470, 98 LJKB 282, [1928] All ER Rep 130, 140 LT 479, 45 TLR 185, CA ... 1073

Foster v Roberts ... 940

Fothergill v Phillips (1871) 6 Ch App 770 ... 635

Fraser River Pile & Dredge Ltd v Can-Dive Services Ltd [2000] 1 Lloyd's Rep 199, 176 DLR (4th) 257 ... 1182

Frederick E Rose (London) Ltd v W H Pm. *See* Rose (Frederick E) (London) Ltd v William H Pim Jnr & Co

Ltd [1953] 2 QB 450, [1953] 2 All ER 739, [1953] 3
WLR 497, [1953] 2 Lloyd's Rep 238, 97 Sol Jo
556, CA

Freeman v Cooke (1848) 2 Exch 554, 6 Dow & L
187 . . . 305

Freeth v Burr (1874) LR 9 CP 208, 43 LJCP 91, 22 WR
370, [1874–80] All ER Rep 750, 29 LT 773 . . . 585,
586

Fry, Re, Whittet v Bush (1888) 40 Ch D 312, 58 LJ Ch
113, 37 WR 135, [1886–90] All ER Rep 1084, 60 LT
12, 5 TLR 45 . . . 944

Fry v Lane (1888) 40 Ch D 312, 58 LJ 113, 37 WR 135,
[1886–90] All ER Rep 1084, 60 LT 12, 5 TLR
45 . . . 23, 940–941, 952, 955

G

G Percy Trentham Ltd v Archital Luxfer Ltd [1992] Lloyd's
Rep 07/20 . . . 230, 266

Gadd v Houghton and another 35 Law Times R (NS) 222
(Eng 1876) 1 Exch Div 357 . . . 1127

Gaisberg v Storr [1950] 1 KB 107 . . . 153

Gallie v Lee [1969] 2 Ch 17, [1969] 1 All ER 1062, [1969] 2
WLR 901, 20 P & CR 310, 113 Sol Jo 187, 209 Estates
Gazette 1435, CA; affd sub nom Saunders (Executrix of
Will of Gallie) v Anglia Building Society [1971] AC
1004, [1970] 3 All ER 961, [1970] 3 W . . . 319

Gamerco SA v ICM/Fair Warning (Agency) Ltd [1995] 1
WLR 1226, [1995] EMLR 263 . . . 485

Garrard v Frankel . . . 299

Gator Shipping Corpn v Trans-Asiatic Oil Ltd SA and
Occidental Shipping Establishment, The Odenfeld
[1978] 2 Lloyd's Rep 357 . . . 738, 739, 740

Gebrüder Metelmann GmbH & Co KG v NBR (London)
Ltd [1984] 1 Lloyd's Rep 614, CA . . . 653

Gibaud v Great Eastern Rly Co [1921] 2 KB 426, 90 LJKB
535, [1921] All ER Rep 35,65 Sol Jo 454, 125 LT 76,
37 TLR 422, CA . . . 983–984

Gibson v Manchester City Council [1979] 1 All ER 972,
[1979] 1 WLR 294, 77 LGR 405, 123 Sol Jo 201,
HL . . . 60, 195–198

Gilbert & Partners (a firm) v Knight [1968] 2 All ER 248,
112 Sol Jo 155, 4 BLR 9, 205 Estates Gazette 993,
CA . . . 129

Gilbert-Ash (Northern) Ltd v Modern Engineering
(Bristol) Ltd [1974] AC 689, [1973] 3 All ER 195,
[1973] 3 WLR 421, 72 LGR 1, 117 Sol Jo 745, 1 BLR
75, HL . . . 1147

Gilchrist, Watt and Sanderson Pty Ltd v York Products Pty
Ltd [1970] 3 All ER 825, [1970] 1 WLR 1262, 114 Sol
Jo 571, sub nom York Products Pty Ltd v Gilchrist
Watt and Sanderson Pty Ltd [1970] 2 Lloyd's Rep 1,
[1970] 2 NSWR 156, PC . . . 1201, 1202, 1203

Giles (C H) & Co Ltd v Morris [1972] 1 All ER 960, [1972]
1 WLR 307, 116 Sol Jo 176 . . . 725–729

Gill (Stewart) Ltd v Horatio Myer & Co Ltd [1992] QB 600,
[1992] 2 All ER 257, [1992] 2 WLR 721, CA . . . 1012

Gillatt v Sky Television Ltd [2000] 1 All ER (Comm)
461 . . . 270

Gillespie Bros & Co v Cheney, Eggar & Co [1896] 2 QB
59, 65 LJQB 552, 1 Com Cas 373, 40 Sol Jo 354, 12
TLR 274 . . . 350

GKN Centrax Gears Ltd v Matbro Ltd [1976] 2 Lloyd's
Rep 555, 120 Sol Jo 401, CA . . . 646

Glasbrook Bros Ld v Glamorgan County Council [1925]
AC 270, 23 LGR 61, 89 JP 29, 94 LJKB 272, [1924]
All ER Rep 579, 69 Sol Jo 212, 132 LT 611, 41 TLR
213, HL . . . 105

Gloucestershire County Council v Richardson (t/a W J
Richardson & Son) [1969] 1 AC 480, [1968] 2 All ER
1181, [1968] 3 WLR 645, 67 LGR 15, 112 Sol Jo 759,
207 Estates Gazette 797, HL . . . 442, 443, 1165

Glynn v Margetson & Co [1893] AC 351, 62 LJQB 466, 7
Asp MLC 366, 1 R 193, 69 LT 1, 9 TLR 437,
HL . . . 401, 402, 981–983

Goddard v O'Brian . . . 853, 857

Goebel v Linn (47 Mich 489, 11 NW 484) . . . 858, 859,
860

Goff v Gauthier (1991) 62 P & CR 388 . . . 360–361

Golden Strait Corp v Nippon Yusen Kubishika Kaisha,
The Golden Victory [2007] UKHL, [2007] 3 All ER
1 . . . 655, 656

Golden Victory. See Golden Strait Corp v Nippon Yusen
Kubishika Kaisha, The Golden Victory [2007] UKHL,
[2007] 3 All ER 1

Golding v London & Edinburgh Insurance Co
Ltd . . . 736

Goldsoll v Goldman [1915] 1 Ch 292, 84 LJ Ch 228,
[1914–15] All ER Rep 257, 59 Sol Jo 188, 112 LT 494,
CA . . . 1120–1121

Gompertz v Bartlett (1853) 2 El & Bl 849 . . . 501

Goodinson v Goodinson [1954] 2 QB 118, [1954] 2 All
ER 255, [1954] 2 WLR 1121, 98 Sol Jo 369,
CA . . . 106, 1070–1071

Goods v Cheesman (1831) 2 B & Ad 328 . . . 856

Goods v Cheesman (1831) 2 B & Ad 328, 9 LJOS
234 . . . 856

Gordon v Gordon (1821) 3 Swan 400 530 . . . 531

Gore v Van der Lann [1967] 2 QB 31, [1967] 1 All ER
360, [1967] 2 WLR 358, 65 LGR 94, [1967] 1 Lloyd's
Rep 145, 110 Sol Jo 928, CA . . . 1174–1178

Gosling v Anderson (1972) 223 Estates Gazette 1743,
[1972] EGD 709, 122 NLJ 152, CA . . . 378

Gove District Council v Power Co Ltd [1996] 1 NZLR
58 . . . 523

Grainger & Son v Gough (Surveyor of Taxes) [1896] AC
325, 3 TC 462, 60 JP 692, 65 LJQB 410, 44 WR 561,
74 LT 435, 12 TLR 364, HL . . . 199

Gran Gelato Ltd v Richcliff (Group) Ltd [1992] Ch 560,
[1992] 1 All ER 865, [1992] 2 WLR 867, [1992] 1
EGLR 297, [1992] 18 LS Gaz R 36, [1992] NLJR
51 . . . 380–381

Grant v John Grant & Sons Pty Ltd (1954) 91 CLR 112,
[1954] ALR 517, 28 ALJ 217, HC of A . . . 849

Granville v Betts . . . 726

Gray v Barr [1971] 2 QB 554, [1971] 2 All ER 949, [1971]
2 WLR 1334, [1971] 2 Lloyd's Rep 1, 115 Sol Jo 364,
CA . . . 1089, 1091, 1092

Great Northern Rly Co v Witham (1873) LR 9 CP 16, 43
LJCP 1, 22 WR 48, 29 LT 471 . . . 109, 116

Great Peace Shipping Ltd v Tsavliris, The Great Peace
[2002] 4 All ER 689 . . . 517, 518, 520

Great Western Rly Co v Redmayne . . . 662

Greater Nottingham Co-operative Society Ltd v Cementation Piling and Foundations Ltd [1989] QB 71, [1988] 2 All ER 971, [1988] 3 WLR 396, 17 Con LR 43, 132 Sol Jo 754, [1988] 16 LS Gaz R 41, [1988] NLJR 112, 41 BLR 43, CA . . . 421, 1166

Greaves & Co (Contractors) Ltd v Baynham Meikle and Partners [1975] 3 All ER 99, [1975] 1 WLR 1095, [1975] 2 Lloyd's Rep 325, 119 Sol Jo 372, 4 BLR 56, CA . . . 447–448, 449

Green v Duckett (1883) 11 QBD 275 . . . 954

Green v Russell [1959] 2 QB 226, [1959] 2 All ER 525, [1959] 3 WLR 17, 103 Sol Jo 489, CA . . . 1151

Gregg v Scott [2005] UKHL 2 [2005] 4 All ER 812 . . . 671

Grimston v Cuningham [1894] 1 QB 125 . . . 731

Grist v Bailey [1967] Ch 532, [1966] 2 All ER 875, [1966] 3 WLR 618, 110 Sol Jo 791 . . . 515, 517, 527

Groom v Crocker [1939] 1 KB 94 . . . 371

Grover & Grover Ltd v Mathews [1910] 2 KB 401, 79 LJKB 1025, 15 Com Cas 249, 102 LT 650, 26 TLR 411 . . . 1130

Grundt v Great Boulder Pty Gold Mines Ltd (1937) 59 CLR 641, 11 ALJ 272 . . . 148, 871

GUS Property Management Ltd v Littlewoods Mail Order Stores Ltd 1982 SC 157, 1982 SLT 533, HL . . . 1146

H

H Dakin & Co Ltd v Lee [1916] 1 KB 566 . . . 560, 561

Hadley v Baxendale (1854) 23 LJ Ex 179, 9 Exch 341, 18 Jur 358, 2 WR 302, 156 ER 145, [1843–60] All ER Rep 461, 2 CLR 517, 23 LTOS 69 . . . 78, 87, 625–626, 635, 643, 644–645, 646, 648, 649, 650, 651, 672, 692

Haigh v Brooks (1839) 10 Ad & El 309, 9 LJQB 99, 2 Per & Dav 477, 113 ER 119; affd sub nom Brooks v Haigh 10 Ad & El 323, 4 Per & Dav 288, Ex Ch . . . 102

Hain Steamship Co Ltd v Tate and Lyle Ltd [1936] 2 All ER 597, 19 Asp MLC 62, 41 Com Cas 350, 80 Sol Jo 68, 155 LT 177, 52 TLR 617, 55 Ll L Rep 159, HL . . . 987, 994

Hall (R & H) Ltd & W H Pim Jnr & Co's Arbitration, Re (1928) 33 Com Cas 324, [1928] All ER Rep 763, 139 LT 50, 30 Ll L Rep 159, HL . . . 664

Hall v Wright . . . 460, 461

Hamer v Sidway 124 NY 538, 27 NE 256, (1891) . . . 101–102

Hamilton v Mendes (1761) 2 Burr 1198 . . . 401

Hamlyn & Co v Wood & Co [1891] 2 QB 488 . . . 476

Hamzeh Malas & Sons v British Imex Industries Ltd [1958] 2 QB 127 . . . 122

Hannah Blumenthal, The (Wilson (Paal) & Co A/S v Partenreederi Hannah Blumenthal, The Hannah Blumenthal) . . . 192–195, 212, 213, 616, 847–848

Hansa Nord, The. *See* Cehave NV v Bremer Handelsgesellschaft mbH, The Hansa Nord

Hansen-Tangen v Sanko Steamship Co [1976] 3 All ER 570, [1976] 1 WLR 989, 120 Sol Jo 719, HL . . . 399

Harbutt's Plasticine Ltd v Wayne Tank and Pump Co Ltd [1970] 1 QB 447, [1970] 1 All ER 225, [1970] 2 WLR 198, [1970] 1 Lloyd's Rep 15, 114 Sol Jo 29, CA . . . 661, 975, 990, 991, 993, 994

Hardman v Booth (1863) 1 H & C 803, 158 ER 1107 . . . 317

Hardwick Game Farm v Suffolk v Suffolk Agricultural and Poultry Producers Association Ltd [1966] 1 All ER 309, [1966] 1 WLR 287, [1966] 1 Lloyd's Rep 197, 111 Sol Jo 11, CA; affd sub nom Kendall (Henry) & Sons (a firm) v William Lillico & Sons Ltd [1969] 2 AC 31, [1968] 2 All ER 444, [1968] 3 WLR 110, [1968] 1 Lloyd's Rep 547, 112 Sol Jo 562, HL . . . 339

Hardy v Motor Insurers' Bureau [1964] 2 QB 745, [1964] 2 All ER 742, [1964] 3 WLR 433, [1964] 1 Lloyd's Rep 397, 108 Sol Jo 422, CA . . . 1090, 1091

Hargreaves Transport Ltd v Lynch [1969] 1 All ER 455, [1969] 1 WLR 215, 20 P & CR 143, 112 Sol Jo 54 . . . 280

Harling v Eddy [1951] 2 KB 739 . . . 325

Harlingdon & Leinster Enterprises Ltd v Christopher Hull Fine Art Ltd [1991] 1 QB 564, [1990] 1 All ER 737, [1990] 3 WLR 13, [1990] NLJR 90, CA . . . 429–430, 507

Harmon CFEM Façades (UK) Ltd v Corporate Officer of the House of Commons (2000) 72 Con LR 21 . . . 248, 276

Harnett v Yeilding (1805) 2 Sch & Lef 549 . . . 709

Harrington v Taylor 36 SE 2d 227, 225 NC 690 (1945) . . . 141, 142

Harris v Nickerson (1873) LR 8 QB 286, 37 JP 536, 42 LJQB 171, 21 WR 635, 28 LT 410 . . . 203–204, 245

Harris v Pepperell LR 5 Eq 1 25 . . . 299

Harris v Sheffield United Football Club Ltd [1988] QB 77, [1987] 2 All ER 838, [1987] 3 WLR 305, 85 LGR 696, 131 Sol Jo 540, [1987] LS Gaz R 1327, CA . . . 105

Harris v Watson (1791) Peake 102, 170 ER 94 . . . 109–110, 114

Harrison (T & J) v Knowles and Foster [1918] 1 KB 608, 87 LJKB 680, 14 Asp MLC 249, 23 Com Cas 282, [1918–19] All ER Rep 306, 118 LT 566, CA . . . 429

Harse v Pearl Life Assurance Co [1904] 1 KB 558 . . . 1095

Hart v A R Marshall & Sons (Bulwell) Ltd [1978] 2 All ER 413, [1977] 1 WLR 1067, [1977] ICR 539, [1977] IRLR 51, 12 ITR 190, 121 Sol Jo 677, EAT . . . 467

Hart v Hart . . . 1141

Hart v O'Connor [1985] AC 1000, [1985] 2 All ER 880, [1985] 3 WLR 214, 129 Sol Jo 484, [1985] LS Gaz R 2658, PC . . . 942, 945–948

Hartley v Hymans [1920] 3 KB 475, 90 LJKB 14, 25 Com Cas 365, [1920] All ER Rep 328, 124 LT 31, 36 TLR 805 . . . 574, 862

Hartog v Colin and Shields [1939] 3 All ER 566 . . . 291–292, 294, 295, 296, 300, 320

Harvela Investments Ltd v Royal Trust Co of Canada (CI) Ltd [1985] Ch 103, [1984] All ER 65, [1984] 2 WLR 884, 128 Sol Jo 348, [1984] LS Gaz R 1837; on appeal [1985] Ch 103, [1985] 1 All ER 261, [1984] 3 WLR 1280, 128 Sol Jo 701, [1984] LS Gaz R 2850, CA . . . 244

Harvey v Facey [1893] AC 552, 62 LJPC 127, 1 R 428, 42 WR 129, 69 LT 504, 9 TLR 612, PC . . . 198

Hawkes v Saunders (1782) 1 Cowp 289 . . . 139

Hawkins (George) v Chrysler (UK) Ltd and Burne Associates (1986) 38 BLR 36, CA . . . 449

Haygarth v Wearing . . . 941

Hayn v Culliford . . . 1154

Heather & Son v Webb (1876) 2 CPD 1, 46 LJQB 89, 25 WR 253 . . . 140

Heaven v Pender (1883) 11 QBD 503 . . . 798

Hedley Byrne & Co Ltd v Heller & Partners Ltd [1964] AC 465, [1963] 2 All ER 575, [1963] 3 WLR 101, [1963] 1 Lloyd's Rep 485, 107 Sol Jo 454, HL . . . 28–29, 30–31, 33, 35, 37, 38, 147, 149, 370, 371, 381, 420, 503, 538, 539, 1005, 1160, 1162, 1164, 1165, 1166, 1167

Heilbut, Symons & Co v Buckleton [1913] AC 30, 82 LJKB 245, 20 Mans 54, [1911–13] All ER 83, 107 LT 769, HL . . . 184, 245, 325, 326, 327, 402

Helstan Securities Ltd v Hertfordshire County Council [1978] 3 All ER 262, 76 LGR 735 . . . 1196

Henderson v Merrett Syndicates Ltd [1995] 2 AC 145, [1994] 3 All ER 506, [1994] 3 WLR 761, [1994] NLJR 1204, HL . . . 29, 38, 1172

Henningsen v Bloomfield Motors Inc (1960) 32 NJ 358, 161 A 2d 69 . . . 706, 1117

Henry Boot & Sons Ltd v LCC [1959] 1 All ER 77 . . . 404

Henry Kendall & Sons v William Lillico & Sons Ltd . . . 339

Henthorn v Fraser [1892] 2 Ch 27, 61 LJ Ch 373, 40 WR 433, [1891–4] All ER Rep 908, 36 Sol Jo 380, 66 LT 439, 8 TLR 459, CA . . . 231–233

Hepburn v A Tomlinson (Hauliers) Ltd (Tomlinson (A) (Hauliers) Ltd v Hepburn Hermann v Charlesworth [1905] 2 KB 123, 74 LJKB 620, 54 WR 22, 93 LT 284, 21 TLR 368, CA) . . . 1144, 1151

Herbert Morris Ltd v Saxelby [1916] 1 AC 688, HL . . . 1108–1111

Hermann v Charlesworth [1905] 2 KB 123 . . . 1073

Herne Bay Steam Boat Co v Hutton [1903] 2 KB 683, 72 LJKB 879, 9 Asp MLC 472, 52 WR 183, [1900–3] All ER Rep 627, 47 Sol Jo 768, 89 LT 422, 19 TLR 680, CA . . . 477–479

Heron Garage Properties Ltd v Moss [1974] 1 All ER 421, [1974] 1 WLR 148, 28 P & CR 54, 117 Sol Jo 697, 229 Estates Gazette 439 . . . 280

Heron II. See Koufos v C Czarnikow Ltd, The Heron II

Hertzog v Hertzog 29 Pa 465 (1857) . . . 794, 795

Heyman v Darwins Ltd [1942] AC 356, [1942] 1 All ER 337, 111 LJKB 241, 166 LT 306, 58 TLR 169, HL . . . 583, 987, 993, 994

Heywood v Wellers [1976] QB 446, [1976] 1 All ER 300, [1976] 2 WLR 101, [1976] 2 Lloyd's Rep 88, 120 Sol Jo 9, CA . . . 674–675

Hick v Raymond and Reid [1893] AC 22, 62 LJQB 98, 7 Asp MLC 233, 1 R 125, 41 WR 384, [1891–4] All ER Rep 491, 37 Sol Jo 145, 68 LT 175, 9 TLR 141, HL . . . 440, 861

Hickman & Co v Roberts [1913] AC 229, 82 LJKB 678, 108 LT 436n, [1911–13] All ER Rep Ext 1485, sub nom Roberts v Hickman & Co 2 Hudson's BC (4th Edn) 426, (10th Edn) 463, 468, HL . . . 884

Hickman v Haynes (1875) LR 10 CP 598, 44 LJCP 358, 23 WR 872, 32 LT 873 . . . 860

High Trees case. See Central London Property Trust Ltd v High Trees House Ltd [1947] KB 130, [1956] 1 All ER 256n, [1947] LJR 77, 175 LT 332, 62 TLR 557

Highwayman's case . . . 1078

HIH Casualty and General Insurance Ltd v Chase Manhattan Bank [2003] 1 All ER (Comm) 349 [2003] 2 Lloyd's Rep 61 . . . 386

Hill v CA Parsons & Co Ltd [1972] Ch 305, [1971] 3 All ER 1345, [1971] 3 WLR 995, 12 KIR 135, 115 Sol Jo 868, CA . . . 728

Hill v Chief Constable of West Yorkshire [1989] AC 53, [1988] 2 All ER 238, [1988] 2 WLR 1049, 132 Sol Jo 700, [1988] NLJR 126, HL . . . 32

Hillas & Co Ltd v Arcos Ltd (1932) 38 Com Cas 23, [1932] All ER Rep 494, 147 LT 503, HL . . . 259–261, 262, 265, 268, 402

Hilton v Barker Booth and Eastwood [2005] UKHL 8, [2005] 1 All ER 651 . . . 530, 1123, 1128

Hirachand Punamchand v Temple [1911] 2 KB 330, 80 LJKB 1155, 55 Sol Jo 519, 105 LT 277, 27 TLR 430, [1911–13] All ER Rep Ext 1597, CA . . . 856

Hirji Mulji v Cheong Yue Steamship Co Ltd [1926] AC 497, 95 LJPC 121, 17 Asp MLC 8, 31 Com Cas 199, [1926] All ER Rep 51, 134 LT 737, 42 TLR 359, PC . . . 465, 466

Hispanica de Petroleos SA v Vencedora Oceanica Navegacion SA, The Kapetan Markos NL (No 2) [1987] 2 Lloyd's Rep 321, CA . . . 246

Hochster v De La Tour (1853) 2 E & B 678, 22 LJQB 455, 17 Jur 972, 1 WR 469, [1843–60] All ER Rep 12, 1 CLR 846, 22 LTOS 171 . . . 581–587

Hoenig v Isaacs [1952] 2 All ER 176, [1952] 1 TLR 1360, CA . . . 563

Hoffman v Red Owl Stores Inc 26 Wis 2d 683, 133 NW 2d 267 (1965) . . . 281–282, 283, 810

Holland Hannen & Cubitts (Northern) Ltd v Welsh Health Technical Services Organisation (1981) 18 BLR 80; affd 7 Con LR 1, 35 BLR 1, [1985] CILL 217, CA . . . 883

Hollier v Rambler Motors (AMC) Ltd [1972] 2 QB 71, [1972] 1 All ER 399, [1972] 2 WLR 401, [1972] RTR 190, 116 Sol Jo 158, CA . . . 340, 978

Holman v James . . . 1098

Holme v Guppy (1838) 3 M & W 387 . . . 695

Holwell Securities Ltd v Hughes [1974] 1 All ER 161, [1974] 1 WLR 155, 26 P & CR 544, 117 sol Jo 912, CA . . . 233–234

Homburg Housimport Bv v Agroisin Private Ltd, The Starsin [2003] UKHL 12 [2004] 1 AC 715 [2003] 2 All ER 785 . . . 401

Home Office v Dorset Yacht Co Ltd [1970] AC 1004, [1970] 2 All ER 294, [1970] 2 WLR 1140, [1970] 1 Lloyd's Rep 453, 114 Sol Jo 375, HL . . . 27, 31, 35, 1171

Hong Kong Fir Shipping Co Ltd v Kawasaki Kisen Kaisha Ltd [1962] 2 QB 26, [1962] 1 All ER 474, [1962] 2 WLR 474, [1961] 2 Lloyd's Rep 478, 106 Sol Jo 35, CA . . . 565, 567–573, 574, 577, 578, 579, 580, 586

Hooper and Grass' Contract, Re [1949] VLB 269 . . . 906

Horne v Midland Rly Co (1873) LR 8 CP 131 . . . 662, 664

Horsley v MacLaren, The Ogopogo [1971] 2 Lloyd's Rep 410, [1972] SCR 441, 22 DLR (3rd) 545 . . . 143

Horton v Horton (No 2) [1961] 1 QB 215, [1960] 3 All ER 649, [1960] 3 WLR 914, 104 Sol Jo 955, CA . . . 102

Hotson v East Berkshire Area Health Authority [1987] AC 750, [1987] 1 All ER 210, [1987] 2 WLR 287, 130 Sol Jo 925, [1987] LS Gaz R 37, [1986] NLJ Rep 1163, CA; revsd [1987] AC 750, [1987] 2 All ER 909, [1987] 3 WLR 232, 131 Sol Jo 975, [1987] LS Gaz R 23 . . . 671

Hounslow London Borough Council v Twickenham Garden Developments Ltd [1971] Ch 233, [1970] 3 All ER 326, [1970] 3 WLR 538, 69 LGR 109, 114 Sol Jo 603, 7 BLR 81 . . . 736

Household Fire and Carriage Accident Insurance Co Ltd v Grant (1879) 4 Ex D 216, 44 JP 152, 48 LJQB 577, 27 WR 858, 41 LT 298, CA . . . 232

Howard Marine and Dredging Co Ltd v A Ogden & sons (Excavations) Ltd [1978] QB 574, [1978] 2 All ER 1134, [1978] 2 WLR 515, [1978] 1 Lloyd's Rep 334, 122 Sol Jo 48, 9 BLR 34, CA . . . 371–372, 1024

Howard v Harris (1683) 1 Eq Cas Abr 312, 2 Cas in Ch 147, Freem Ch 86, 1 Vern 190, [1558–1774] All ER Rep 609 . . . 938

Howard v Pickford Tool Co Ltd [1951] 1 KB 417 . . . 736

Howe v Smith (1884) 27 Ch D 89, 48 JP 773, 53 LJ Ch 1055, 32 WR 802, [1881–5] All Rep 201, 50 LT 573, CA . . . 702, 703

Howes v Bishop [1909] 2 KB 390, 78 LJKB 796, 100 LT 826, 25 TLR 533, [1908–10] All ER Rep Ext 1299, CA . . . 925

Howie v Anderson . . . 736

HR & S Sainsbury Ltd v Street [1972] 3 All ER 1127, [1972] 1 WLR 834, 116 Sol Jo 483 . . . 524

Huddersfield Banking Co Ltd v Lister (Henry) & Son Ltd [1895] 2 Ch 273 . . . 511

Hudson, Re, Creed v Henderson (1885) 54 LJ Ch 811, 33 WR 319, 1 TLR 447 . . . 22–24, 164, 170

Hughes Aircraft Systems International v Airservices Australia (1997) 146 ALR 1 . . . 247, 276

Hughes v Metropolitan Rly Co (1877) 2 App Cas 439, 42 JP 421, 46 LJQB 583, 25 WR 680, [1874–80] All ER Rep 187, 36 LT 932, HL . . . 151, 152, 153, 159, 863–864, 866, 867, 868, 870, 874, 875

Huguenin v Baseley (1807) 14 Ves Jun 273, [1803–13] All Rep 1 . . . 921, 930

Hummingbird Motors Ltd v Hobbs [1986] RTR 276, [1986] BTLC 245, CA . . . 359

Hurst v Bryk [2000] 2 All ER 193, [2000] 2 WLR 740, [2000] 2 BCLC 117, [2000] 17 LS Gaz R 35, [2000] NLJR 511, [2000] EGCS 49, 144 Sol Jo LB 189, HL . . . 613

Hutton v Warren (1836) 5 LJ Ex 234, 2 Gale 71, 1 M & W 466, Tyr & Gr 646, [1835–42] All ER Rep 151 . . . 411–412

Hyde v The Dean of Windsor . . . 461

Hyde v Wrench (1840) 3 Beav 334, 4 Jur 1106 . . . 222, 226, 227

Hydraulic Engineering Co Ltd v McHaffie, Goslett & Co (1878) 4 QBD 670, 27 WR 221, CA . . . 626

Hyman v Hyman [1929] AC 601 . . . 153

Hyundai Heavy Industries Co Ltd v Papadopoulos [1980] 2 All ER 29, [1980] 1 WLR 1129, [1980] 2 Lloyd's Rep 1, 124 Sol Jo 592, HL . . . 700, 701

I

Ibaraki Maru, The. *See* Candlewood Navigation Corpn Ltd v Misui OSK Lines Ltd, The Mineral Transporter, The Ibaraki Maru

ICS case . . . 407

Imperial Glass Ltd v Consolidated Supplies Ltd (1960) 22 DLR (2d) 759, CA . . . 306

Inche Noriah v Shaik Allie Bin Omar [1929] AC 127, [1928] All ER Rep 189 . . . 936

Independent Broadcasting Authority v EMI Electronics Ltd and BICC Construction Ltd (1980) 14 BLR 1, HL . . . 186

Ingram v Little [1961] 1 QB 31, [1960] 1 QB 31, [1960] 3 All ER 332, [1960] 3 WLR 504, 104 Sol Jo 704, CA . . . 60, 312–314, 315, 316, 317, 318, 320

Inntrepreneur Pub Co v East Crown Ltd [2000] 2 Lloyd's Rep 611, [2000] 41 EG 209 356 Interfoto Picture Library Ltd v Stiletto Visual Programmes Ltd [1989] QB 433, [1988] 1 All ER 348, [1988] 2 WLR 615, [1988] BTLC 39, 132 Sol Jo 460, [1988] 9 LS Gaz R 45, [1987] NLJ Rep 1159, CA . . . 10, 284, 336–339, 348

Inntrepreneur Pub Co v East Crown Ltd [2000] 2 Lloyd's Rep 611, [2000] 41 EG 209 356 Interfoto Picture Library Ltd v Stiletto Visual Programmes Ltd [1989] QB 433, [1988] 1 All ER 348, [1988] 2 WLR 615, [1988] BTLC 39, 132 Sol Jo 460, [1988] 9 LS Gaz R . . . 353

Interfoto Picture Library v Stiletto Visual Programmes Ltd [1988] 1 All ER 348, CA . . . 10, 284, 336–339, 348

Intertradex SA v Lesieur-Tourteaux SARL [1977] 2 Lloyd's Rep 146; affd [1978] 2 Lloyd's Rep 509, CA . . . 470

Investors Compensation Scheme Ltd v Hopkin & Sons (a firm) [1988] 1 All ER 98, [1998] 1 WLR 896, [1988] 1 BCLC 493, HL . . . 849

Investors Compensation Scheme Ltd v West Bromwich Building Society [1988] 1 All ER 98, [1998] 1 WLR 896, [1998] 1 BCLC 531, [1997] NLJR 989, [1997] PNLR 541, [1997] CLC 1243, HL . . . 399, 849

Inwards v Baker [1965] 2 QB 29, [1965] 1 All ER 446, [1965] 2 WLR 212, 109 Sol Jo 75, CA . . . 155, 157, 158

IRC v National Federation of Self Employed and Small Businesses [1982] AC 617, [1981] 2 All ER 93, [1981] 2 WLR 722, [1981] STC 260, 55 TC 133, 125 Sol Jo 325, HL . . . 547

Iron and Steel Holding and Realisation Agency v Compensation Appeal Tribunal [1966] 1 All ER 769, 1 WLR 480 . . . 379

Istros, SS (Owner) v F W Dahlstroem & Co [1931] 1 KB 247, 100 LJKB 141, 18 Asp MLC 177, 36 Com Cas 65, 144 LT 124 . . . 981

J

J & H Ritchie Ltd v Lloyd Ltd [2007] UKHL 9, [2007] 2 All ER 353 . . . 618

J Evans & Son (Portsmouth) Ltd v Andrea Merzario Ltd [1976] 2 All ER 930. *See* Evans (J) & Son (Portsmouth) Ltd v Andrea Merzario Ltd [1976] 2 All ER 930, [1976] 1 WLR 1078, [1976] 2 Lloyd's Rep 165, 120 Sol Jo 734, CA

Jackson v Horizon Holidays Ltd [1975] 3 All ER 92,
[1975] 1 WLR 1468, 119 Sol Jo 759, CA ... 1143,
1144, 1147

Jackson v Royal Bank of Scotland [2005] UKHL 3 [2005]
2 All ER 71 ... 670

Jackson v Union Marine Insurance Co (1874) LR 10 CP
125 ... 476, 569

Jacobs v Batavia and General Plantations Trust Ltd
[1924] 1 Ch 287; affd [1924] 2 Ch 329, 93 LJ Ch
520, 68 Sol Jo 630, 131 LT 617, 40 TLR 616,
CA ... 349, 353

Jajbhay v Cassim (1939) AD 537 ... 1101, 1102

James Archdale & Co Ltd v Comservices Ltd [1954] 1
WLR 459 ... 1168, 1170

James Baird Co v Gimbel Bros, Inc 64 F 2d 344 (2d Cir,
1933) ... 249

James Miller and Partners Ltd v Whitworth Street Estates
(Manchester) Ltd [1970] 1 ELR 796 ... 409

James Morrison & Co v Shaw, Savill & Albion Co [1916]
2 KB 783 ... 984

James Nelson & Sons Ltd v Nelson Line (Liverpool) Ltd
[1908] AC 16 ... 402

Janson v Driefontein Consolidated Mines Ltd [1902] AC
484, HL ... 1074, 1075

Jarvis v Swans Tours Ltd [1973] QB 233, [1973] 1 All ER
71, [1972] 3 WLR 954, 116 Sol Jo 822, CA ... 378,
673, 679, 686

Jennings v Ward (1705) 2 Vern 520 ... 938

Jindal Iron and Steel Co Ltd v Islamic Solidarity Co Jordan
Inc [2005] 1 All ER 175 ... 983

Jobson v Johnson [1989] 1 All ER 621, [1989] 1 WLR
1026, 4 BCC 488, CA ... 592, 692

Johnson Matthey & Co Ltd v Constantine Terminals Ltd
[1976] 2 Lloyd's Rep 215 ... 1201, 1202, 1204

Johnson v Agnew [1980] AC 367, [1979] 1 All ER 883,
[1979] 2 WLR 487, 39 P & CR 424, 123 Sol Jo 217,
251 Estates Gazette 1167, HL ... 614, 636, 654, 993

Johnson v Calvert 851 P 2d 776 (Cal SC,
1993) ... 1076–1077

Johnson v Unisys [2001] 2 All ER 801 ... 678

Johnstone v Bloomsbury Health Authority [1992] QB
333, [1991] 2 All ER 293, [1991] 2 WLR 1362, [1991]
ICR 269, [1991] IRLR 118, [1991] 2 Med LR 38,
CA ... 443–446

Jones v Bright (1829) 5 Bing 533, 7 LJOSCP 213, 3 Moo
& P 155, Dan & Ll 304 ... 1006

Jones v Gallagher [2004] EWCA Civ 10 ... 619

Jones v Herxheimer [1950] 2 KB 106 ... 681

Jones v Padavatton [1969] 2 All ER 616, [1969] 1 WLR
328, 112 Sol Jo 965, CA ... 165, 176, 177–181

Jones v Stroud District Council [1988] 1 All ER 5, [1986]
1 WLR 1141, 84 LGR 886, 8 Con LR 23, 130 Sol Jo
469, [1987] 2 EGLR 133, [1986] LS Gaz R 1810, 34
BLR 27, 279 Estates Gazette 213, 2 Const LJ 185,
CA ... 1145

Jorden v Money (1854) 5 HL Cas 185, 23 LJ Ch 865, 101
RR 116, 10 ER 868, [1843–60] All ER Rep 350, 24
LTOS 160 ... 149–150, 151, 168, 169, 860,
863, 872

Joscelyne v Nissen [1970] 2 QB 86, [1970] 1 All ER 1213,
[1970] 2 WLR 509, 114 Sol Jo 55, CA ... 296–298

Joseph Constantine Steamship Line Ltd v Imperial
Smelting Corpn Ltd, The Kingswood [1942] AC 154,
[1941] 2 All ER 165, 110 LJKB 433, 46 Com Cas 258,
165 LT 27, 57 TLR 485, 70 Ll L Rep 1, HL ... 472

Joseph Thorley Ltd v Orchis Steamship Co Ltd [1907]
1 KB 660, 76 LJKB 595, 10 Asp MLC 431, 12 Com
Cas 251, 51 Sol Jo 289, 96 LT 488, 23 TLR 338,
CA ... 987

Joyner v Weeks [1891] 2 QB 31 ... 679

JT Developments Ltd v Quinn (1990) 62 P & CR 33,
[1991] 2 EGLR 257, CA ... 163

Junior Books Ltd v Veitchi Co Ltd [1983] 1 AC 520,
[1982] 3 All ER 201, [1982] 3 WLR 477, [1982] Com
LR 221, 126 Sol Jo 538, [1982] LS Gaz R 1413, 21
BLR 66, 1982 SLT 492, HL ... 32–33, 36, 1163–1167

K

Kaines (UK) Ltd v Osterreichische
Warrenhandelsgesellschaft Austrowaren Gesellschaft
mbH (formerly CGL Handelsgesellschaft mbH) [1993]
2 Lloyd's Rep 1, CA ... 656

Kanchenjunga, The. *See* Motor Oil Hellas (Corinth)
Refineries SA v Shipping Corpn of India, The
Kanchenjunga

Kapetan Markos NL (No 2), The. *See* Hispanica de
Petroleos SA v Vencedora Oceanica Navegacion SA,
The Kapetan Markos NL (No 2) [1987] 2 Lloyd's Rep
321, CA

Karen Oltmann, The. *See* Partenreederei MS Karen
Oltmann v Scarsdale Shipping Co Ltd, The Karen
Oltmann

Karsales (Harrow) Ltd v Wallis [1956] 2 All ER 866,
[1956] 1 WLR 936, 100 Sol Jo 548, CA ... 975, 984,
985–990

Kearley v Thomson (1890) 24 QBD 742, 54 JP 804, 59
LJQB 288, 38 WR 614, [1886–90] All ER Rep 1055,
63 LT 150, 6 TLR 267, CA ... 1096–1097

Kearney v Whitehaven Colliery Co [1893] 1 QB
700 ... 1120

Keighley, Maxsted & Co v Durant [1901] AC 240, 70
LJKB 662, [1900–3] All ER Rep 40, 45 Sol Jo 536, 84
LT 777, 17 TLR 527, HL ... 1133–1135

Kelner v Baxter (1866) LR 2 CP 174, 36 LJCP 94, 12 Jur
NS 1016, 15 WR 278, 15 LT 213, [1861–73] All ER
Rep Ext 2009 ... 1130

Kemp v Intasun Holidays Ltd [1987] BTLC 353, [1987] 2
FTLR 234, 6 Tr L Rep, CA ... 648

Kennedy v Panama New Zealand and Australian Royal
Mail Co Ltd (1867) LR 2 QB 580, 8 B & S 571, 36
LJQB 260, 15 WR 1039, 17 LT 62, [1861–73] All ER
Rep Ext 2094 ... 500, 505

Keppell v Bailey (1834) 2 My & K 517, Coop temp
Brough 298, [1824–34] All ER Rep 10 ... 1205

Ketley (A) Ltd v Scott [1981] ICR 241, [1980] CCLR
37 ... 951

KH Enterprise v Pioneer Container, The Pioneer
Container [1994] 2 AC 324, [1994] 2 All ER 250,
[1994] 3 WLR 1, [1994] 1 Lloyd's Rep 593, [1994] 18
LS Gaz R 37, PC ... 1161, 1200–1202, 1204

King Construction Company v Smith Electric
Co ... 906

King v Wilkinson [1995] NZ Law Journal 196 . . . 363

King's Norton Metal Co Ltd v Edridge, Merrett & Co Ltd (1897) 14 TLR 98, CA . . . 311, 315, 318, 510

Kingston v Preston (1773) 2 Doug KB 689, sub nom Anon Lofft 194 . . . 553–554, 555

Kingswood, The. *See* Constantine (Joseph) Steamship Line Ltd v Imperial Smelting Corpn Ltd, The Kingswood [1942] AC 154, [1941] 2 All ER 165, 110 LJKB 433, 46 Com Cas 258, 165 LT 27, 57 TLR 485, 70 Ll L Rep 1, HL The Kingswood Kiriri Cotton Co Ltd v Dewani [1960] AC 192, [1960] 1 All ER 177, [1960] 2 WLR 127, 104 Sol Jo 49, PC . . . 1055, 1094

Kiriri Cotton Ltd v Dewani. *See* The Kingswood Kiriri Cotton Co Ltd v Dewani [1960] AC 192, [1960] 1 All ER 177, [1960] 2 WLR 127, 104 Sol Jo 49, PC

Kleinwort Benson Ltd v Malaysia Mining Corpn Bhd [1989] 1 All ER 785, [1989] 1 WLR 379, [1989] 1 Lloyd's Rep 556, 5 BCC 337, 133 Sol Jo 262, [1989] 16 LS Gaz R 35, [1989] NLJR 221, CA . . . 16–18

Knightsbridge Estates Trust Ltd v Byrne [1989] Ch 441, [1938] 4 All ER 618, 108 LJ Ch 105, 82 Sol Jo 989, 160 LT 989, 160 Lt 68, 55 TLR 196, CA; affd [1940] AC 613, [1940] 2 All ER 401, 109 LJ Ch 200, 84 Sol Jo 488, 162 LT 388, 56 TKR 652, HL . . . 939

Knupp v Bell (1968) 67 DLR 2d 256 (Canada) 135 . . . 955

Knutson v Bourkes Syndicate [1941] SCR 419 . . . 906

Koninklijke Rotterdamsche Lloyd (NV) v Western Steamship Co Ltd, The Empire Jamaica. *See* Western Steamship Co Ltd v NV Koninklijke Rotterdamsche Lloyd, The Empire Jamaica

Koufos v C Czarnikow Ltd, The Heron II [1969] 1 AC 350, [1967] 3 All ER 686, [1967] 3 WLR 1491, [1967] 2 Lloyd's Rep 457, 111 Sol Jo 848, HL . . . 648

Kreglinger v New Patagonia Meat and Cold Storage Co Ltd [1914] AC 25, 83 LJ Ch 79, [1911–13] All ER Rep 970, 58 Sol Jo 97, 109 LT 802, 30 TLR 114, HL . . . 939

Krell v Henry [1903] 2 KB 740, 72 LJKB 794, 52 WR 246, [1900–3] All ER Rep 20, 89 LT 328, 19 TLR 711, CA . . . 474–476, 479

Kum v Wah Tat Bank Ltd [1971] 1 Lloyd's Rep 439, PC . . . 341

L

Lacey (William) (Hounslow) Ltd v Davis [1957] 2 All ER 712, [1957] 1 WLR 932, 101 Sol Jo 629 . . . 41, 281

The Laemthong Glory (No 2) [2005] EWCA Civ 519, [2005] 1 Lloyd's Rep 632 . . . 1193

Laidlaw v Organ (2 Wheat) 178 (1815) . . . 536

Lake v Simmons [1927] AC 487, [1927] All ER Rep 49 . . . 317

Lambert v Co-operative Insurance Society Ltd [1975] 2 Lloyd's Rep 485, CA . . . 530–531

Lambert v Lewis. *See* Lexmead (Basingstoke) Ltd v Lewis

Lampleigh v Brathwait . . . 127

Lancashire County Council v Municipal Mutual Insurance Ltd [1997] QB 897, [1996] 3 All ER 545, [1996] 3 WLR 493, 95 LGR 234, [1996] 21 LS Gaz R 27, 140 Sol Jo LB 108, CA . . . 1075

Langen and Wind Ltd v Bell [1972] Ch 685, [1972] 1 All ER 296, [1972] 2 WLR 170, 115 Sol Jo 966 . . . 729

Langford & Co Ltd v Dutch [1952] SC 15 . . . 734, 739

Laters v Min Ltd 412 Mass 64, 587 NE 2d 231 . . . 958

Laurelgates Ltd v Lombard North Central Ltd (1983) 133 NLJ 720 . . . 619

Lauritzen (J) AS v Wijsmuller BV, The Super Servant Two [1989] 1 Lloyd's Rep 148; affd [1990] 1 Lloyd's Rep 1, CA . . . 469–472, 498

Lauritzencool AB v Lady Navigation Inc [2006] 1 All ER 860 . . . 592

Lavarack v Woods of Colchester Ltrd [1967] 1 QB 278, [1966] 3 All ER 683, [1966] 3 WLR 706, 1 KIR 312, 110 Sol Jo 770, CA . . . 245

Lawrence v Fox 20 NY 268 (1859) . . . 1182

Lazenby Garages Ltd v Wright [1976] 2 All ER 770, [1976] 1 WLR 459, 120 Sol Jo 146, CA . . . 668–671

Leaf v International Galleries [1950] 2 KB 86, [1950] 1 All ER 693, 66 (pt 1) TLR 1031, CA . . . 365–366, 368, 507

Lee v Muggeridge (1813) 128 Eng Rep 599 . . . 141

Leeds Industrial Co-operative Society Ltd v Slack [1924] AC 851, 93 LJ 436, [1924] All ER Rep 259, 68 Sol Jo 715, 131 LT 710, 40 TLR 745, HL . . . 381

Lee-Parker v Izzet (No 2) [1972] 2 All ER 800, [1972] 1 WLR 775, 23 P & CR 301, 116 Sol Jo 446 . . . 279, 280

Lefkowitz v Great Minneapolis Surplus Store 251 Minn 188, 86 NW 2d 689 (1957) . . . 201

Legione v Hateley (1983) 152 CLR 406, 46 ALR 1 . . . 159, 591

Leigh and Sillavan Ltd v Aliakmon Shipping Co Ltd, The Aliakmon [1985] QB 350, [1985] 2 All ER 44, [1985] 2 WLR 289, [1985] 1 Lloyd's Rep 199, 129 Sol Jo 69, [1985] LS Gaz R 203, [1985] NLJ Rep 285, CA; affd [1986] AC 785, [1986] 2 All ER 145, [1986] 2 WLR 902, [1986] 2 Lloyd's Rep 1, 130 Sol Jo 357, [1986] LS Gaz R 1810, [1986] NLJ Rep 415, HL . . . 1165, 1168, 1172, 1240

Leonidas D, The. *See* Allied Marine Transport Ltd v Vale do Rio Doce Navegacao SA, The Leonidas D [1983] 3 All ER 737, [1984] 1 WLR 1, [1983] 2 Lloyd's Rep 411, 127 Sol Jo 729; revsd [1985] 2 All ER 796, [1985] 2 Lloyd's Rep 18, 129 Sol Jo 431, [1985] LS Gaz R 2160, CA

Lesters Leather and Skin Co Ltd v Home and Overseas Brokers Ltd [1948] WN 437, 92 Sol Jo 646, 64 TLR 569, 82 Ll L Rep 202, CA . . . 652

L'Estrange v F Graucob Ltd [1934] 2 KB 394, 103 LJKB 730, [1934] All Rep 16, 152 LT 164, DC . . . 284, 285, 308–309, 345, 346

Lever v Goodwin (1887) 36 Ch D 1, [1887] WN 107, 4 RPC 492, 36 WR 177, [1886–90] All ER Rep 427, 57 LT 583, 3 TLR 650, CA . . . 635

Levison v Patent Steam Carpet Cleaning Co Ltd [1978] QB 69, [1977] 3 All ER 498, [1977] 3 WLR 90, 121 Sol Jo 406, CA . . . 994, 1013, 1024

Lewis v Averay [1972] 1 QB 198, [1971] 3 All ER 907, [1971] 3 WLR 603, 115 Sol Jo 755, CA . . . 314–318, 363

Lexmead (Basingstoke) Ltd v Lewis [1982] AC 225, sub nom Lambert v Lewis [1980] 1 All ER 978, [1980] 2 WLR 299, [1980] RTR 152, [1980] 1 Lloyd's Rep 311, 124 Sol Jo 50, CA; revsd sub nom Lexmead (Basingstoke) Ltd v Lewis [1982] AC 225, 268, [1981] 2 WLR 713, [1981] RTR 346, [1981] 2 Lloyd's Rep 17, 125 Sol Jo 310, sub nom Lambert v Lewis [1981] 1 All ER 1185, HL ... 19, 658, 1162

Lilley v Doubleday (1881) 7 QBD 510 ... 983, 984

Limland v Stephen (1801) 3 Esp 269, 170 ER 611 KB ... 451

Linden Gardens Trust Ltd v Lenesta Sludge Disposals Ltd [1994] 1 AC 85, [1993] 3 All ER 417, [1993] 3 WLR 408, 36 Con LR 1, [1993] 45 LS Gaz R 39, [1993] NLJR 1152, 137 Sol Jo LB 183, HL ... 1144–1150, 1149–1150, 1196

Lindsay v Cundy (1876) 1 QBD 348, 45 LJQB 381, 13 Cox CC 162, 24 WR 730, 34 Lt 314; revsd 2 QBD 96, 46 LJQB 481, 25 WR 417, 36 LT 345, CA; on appeal sub nom Cundy v Lindsay 3 App Cas 459, 42 JP 483, 42 JP 483, 14 Cox CC 93, 26 WR 406, [1874–80] All ER Rep 1149, 38 LT 573, sub nom Lindsay & Co v Cundy 47 LJQB 481, HL ... 311, 511

Lister v Romford Ice and Cold Storage Co Ltd [1957] AC 555, [1957] 1 All ER 125, [1957] 2 WLR 158, [1956] 2 Lloyd's Rep 505, 121 JP 98, 101 Sol Jo 106, HL ... 417, 418, 419, 421, 423

Little v Spreadbury ... 1129

Littlefield v Shee (1831) 2 B & Ad 811 ... 141

Liverpool City Council v Irwin [1977] AC 239, [1976] 2 WLR 562, 74 LGR 392, 32 P & CR 43, 13 HLR 38, 120 Sol Jo 267, 238 Estates Gazette 879, 963, HL ... 245, 415–420, 423

Livingstone v Rawyards Coal Co (1880) 5 App Cas 25, 44 JP 392, 28 WR 357, 42 LT 334, HL ... 1146

Lloyds Bank Ltd, Bomze v Bomze, Re [1931] 1 Ch 289 ... 931

Lloyds Bank Ltd v Bundy [1975] QB 326, [1974] 3 All ER 757, [1974] 3 WLR 501, [1974] 2 Lloyd's Rep 366, 118 Sol Jo 714, CA ... 918–923, 944, 954–958, 959

Lloyd's Bank plc v Waterhouse (1991) 10 Tr LR 161, CA ... 319

Lloyds v Harper [1888] 16 CD 290 ... 1140–1141, 1143

Lobb (Alec) (Garages) Ltd v Total Oil GB Ltd [1985] 1 All ER 303, [1985] 1 WLR 173, 129 Sol Jo 83, [1985] 1 EGLR 33, [1985] LS Gaz R 45, 273 Estates Gazette 659, CA ... 1114

Lock v Bell [1931] 1 Ch 35, 100 LJ Ch 22, [1930] All ER Rep 635, 144 LT 108 ... 705

Lombard North Central plc v Butterworth [1987] QB 527, [1987] 1 All ER 267, [1987] 2 WLR 7, [1986] BTLC 382, 130 Sol Jo 681, [1986] LS Gaz R 2750, CA ... 607–613, 692, 1009

Lombard Tricity Finance Ltd v Paton [1989] 1 All ER 918 ... 271

London, Chatham and Dover Rly Co v South Eastern Rly Co [1893] AC 429, 58 JP 36, 63 LJ Ch 93, 1 R 275, 69 LT 637, HL ... 671

London Drugs Ltd v Kuehne and Nagel International Ltd [1992] 3 SCR 299, [1993] 1 WWR 1, [1993] 4 LRC 415, 97 DLR (4th) 261, Can SC ... 1181

London Holeproof Hosiery Co Ltd v Padmore (1928) 44 TLR 499, CA ... 303

Long v Lloyd [1958] 2 All ER 402, [1958] 753, 102 Sol Jo 488, CA ... 363–365

Lorfri, The (Federal Commerce and Navigation Co Ltd v Molena Gamma Inc, The Lorfri Lovell and Christmas Ltd v Wall (1911) 104 LT 85, 27 TLR 236, CA) ... 297, 307, 398–399, 412

Lovell and Christmas. *See* Lorfri, The (Federal Commerce and Navigation Co Ltd v Molena Gamma Inc, The Lorfri Lovell and Christmas Ltd v Wall (1911) 104 LT 85, 27 TLR 236, CA)

Loyd v Lee (1718) 1 Str 94 ... 141

Lucy, The. *See* Atlantic Lines & Navigation Co Inc v Hallam Ltd, The Lucy [1983] 1 Lloyd's Rep 188

Lumley v Gye (1853) 2 E & B 216, 22 LJQB 463, 17 Jur 827, 1 WR 432, [1843–60] All ER Rep 208 ... 1204, 1206

Lumley v Wagner (1852) 1 De GM & G 604, 42 ER 687 ... 730

Luong Dinh Luu v Sovereign Development Pty Ltd [2006] NSWCA 40 ... 703

Luxor (Eastbourne) Ltd v Cooper [1941] AC 108, [1941] 1 All ER 33, 110 LJKB 131, 46 Com Cas 120, 85 Sol Jo 105, 164 LT 313, 57 TLR 213, HL ... 219–220, 220, 419, 424

Lynch v DPP v Northern Ireland [1975] 1 All ER 913, 910

Lynch v Thorne [1956] 1 All ER 744, [1956] 1 WLR 303, 100 Sol Jo 225, 167 Estates Gazette 233, CA ... 445

M

MacKenzie v Royal Bank of Canada [1934] AC 468 ... 511

Maclaine v Gatty [1921] 1 AC 376, 90 LJPC 73, 26 Com Cas 148, [1920] All ER Rep 70, 124 LT 385, 37 TLR 139, HL ... 148

Maclaine Watson & Co Ltd v Department of Trade and Industry [1989] Ch 72, [1988] 3 All ER 257, [1988] 3 WLR 1033, [1988] BCLC 404, 4 BCC 559, 563, 132 Sol Jo 1494, CA; affd [1990] 2 AC 418, [1989] 3 All ER 523, [1989] 3 WLR 969, [1990] BCLC 102, 5 BCC 872, 133 Sol Jo 1485, HL ... 17

Maddison v Alderson (1883) 8 App Cas 467, 47 JP 821, 52 LJQB 737, 31 WR 820, [1881–5] All ER Rep 742, 49 LT 303, HL ... 19–20

Magee v Pennine Insurance Co Ltd [1969] 2 QB 507, [1969] 2 All ER 891, [1969] 2 WLR 1278, [1969] 2 Lloyd's Rep 378, 113 Sol Jo 303, CA ... 515, 517, 519

Mahkutai, The [1996] AC 650, [1996] 3 All ER 502, [1996] 3 WLR 1, [1996] 2 Lloyd's Rep 1, [1996] NLJR 677, 140 Sol Jo LB 107, PC ... 1161

Mahmoud and Ispahani, Re [1921] 2 KB 716, 90 LJKB 821, 26 Com Cas 215, [1921] All ER Rep 217, 125 LT 161, 37 TLR 489, CA ... 1083, 1084, 1085, 1093

Mahmud v Bank of Credit and Commerce International SA (in compulsory liquidation) [1998] AC 20, [1997] 3 All ER 1, [1997] 3 WLR 95, [1997] ICR 606, [1997] IRLR 462, [1997] 94 LS Gaz R 33, HL ... 850–851

Maira and Maira (No 3), The (National Bank of Greece SA v Pinios Shipping Co, The Maira and Maira (No 3)

Malas (Hamzeh) & Sons v British Imex Industries Ltd [1958] 2 QB 127, [1958] 1 All ER 262, [1958] 2 WLR 100, [1957] 2 Lloyd's Rep 549, 102 Sol Jo 68, CA . . . 122

Malhotra v Choudhury [1980] Ch 52, [1979] 1 All ER 186, [1978] 3 WLR 825, 122 Sol Jo 681, CA . . . 673

Malik v Bank of Credit and Commerce International SA (in liquidation) [1998] AC 20, [1997] 3 All ER 1, [1997] 3 WLR 95, [1997] ICR 606, [1997] IRLR 462, [1997] 94 LS Gaz R 33, [1997] NLJR 917, HL . . . 676–677, 848, 850–851

M'Alister (or Donoghue) v Stevenson. *See* Donoghue (or M'Alister) v Stevenson [1932] AC 562, 101 LJPC 119, 37 Com CAS 350, 48 TLR 494, 1932 SC (HL) 31, [1932] All ER Rep 1, 1932 SLT 317, 76 Sol Jo 396, 147 LT 281

Manchester Diocesan Council for Education v Commercial and General Investments Ltd [1969] 3 All ER 1593, [1970] 1 WLR 241, 21 P & CR 38, 114 Sol Jo 70 . . . 236–238

Mannai Investment Co Ltd v Eagle Star Life Assurance Co Ltd [1997] AC 749, [1997] 3 All ER 352, [1997] 2 WLR 945, [1997] 1 EGLR 57, [1997] 30 LS Gaz R 30, [1997] NLJR 846, [1997] 24 EG 122, 141 Sol Jo LB 130, HL . . . 400–401

Maple Flock Co Ltd v Universal Furniture Products (Wembley) Ltd [1934] 1 KB 148, 103 LJKB 513, 39 Com Cas 89, [1933] All ER Rep 15, 150 LT 69, 50 TLR 58, CA . . . 587

Marbé v George Edwardes (Daly's Theatre) Ltd [1928] 1 KB 269, 96 LJKB 980, [1927] All ER Rep 253, 138 LT 51, 43 TLR 809, CA . . . 678

Marc Rich & Co AG v Bishop Rock Marine Co Ltd [1995] 3 All ER 307, HL. *See* Rich (Marc) & Co AG v Bishop Rock Marine Co Ltd, Bethmarine Co Ltd and Nippon Kaiji Kyoki, The 686, [1994] 1 WLR 1071, [1994] 1 Lloyd's Rep 492, CA; aff'd sub nom Rich (Marc) & Co AG v Bishop Rock

Maredelanto Cia Naviera SA v Bergbau-Handel GmbH, The Mihalis Angelos [1971] 1 QB 164, [1970] 3 All ER 125, [1970] 3 WLR 601, [1970] 2 Lloyd's Rep 43, 114 Sol Jo 548, CA . . . 572

Marine Diesel Service (Grimsby) Ltd v The Swan (Owner), The Swan [1968] 1 Lloyd's Rep 5 . . . 1125, 1126

Maritime National Fish Ltd v Ocean Trawlers Ltd [1935] AC 524, 104 LJPC 88, 18 Asp MLC 551, [1935] All ER Rep 86, 79 Sol Jo 320, 153 LT 425 . . . 467–469, 470, 471, 479

Mark Rowlands v Berni Inns [1986] 1 QB 211 . . . 1168

Marks v Board . . . 279

Marleasing SA v La Comercial Internacional de Alimentación SA: C-106/89 [1990] ECR I-4135, [1992] 1 CMLR 305, [1993] BCC 421, 135 Sol Jo 15, ECJ . . . 1042

Marles v Philip Trant & Sons Ltd (No 2) [1954] 1 QB 29, [1953] 1 All ER 651, [1953] 2 WLR 564, 97 Sol Jo 189, CA . . . 1082, 1087–1088, 1091

Marley v Forward Trust Group Ltd [1986] ICR 891, [1986] ICR 891, [1986] IRLR 369, CA . . . 344

Marshall v Broadhurst (1 Tyr 348) . . . 461

Martin v Great Indian Peninsula Rly Co . . . 1154

Maskell v Horner [1915] 3 KB 106, 13 LGR 808, 79 JP 406, 84 LJKB 1752, [1914–15] All ER Rep 595, 59 Sol 429, 113 LT 126, 31 TLR 332, CA . . . 904–905, 905, 909, 911, 954

Mason & Risch Ltd v Christner . . . 669

Mason v Provident Clothing and Supply Co Ltd [1913] AC 724, 82 LJKB 1153, [1911–13] All ER Rep 400, 57 Sol Jo 739, 109 Lt 449, 29 TLR 727, HL . . . 1107–1108, 1120

Matheson v Smiley [1932] 2 DLR 787, [1932] 1 WWR 758 . . . 44

May and Butcher v R [1934] 2 KB 17n, 103 LJKB 556n, 151 LT 246n, HL . . . 258–259, 268, 269

May v Platt . . . 299

Mayson v Clouet [1924] AC 980, 93 LJPC 237, 131 LT 645, 40 TLR 678, PC . . . 702

MB Pyramid Sound MV v Briese Schiffahrts GmbH, The Ines [1995] 2 Lloyd's Rep 144 . . . 402

McConnel v Wright (2006) 280 Ga. App 546 (634 SE 2d 495) . . . 38

McCutcheon v David MacBrayne Ltd [1964] 1 All ER 430, [1964] 1 WLR 125, [1964] 1 Lloyd's Rep 16, 108 Sol Jo 93, 1964 SC (HL) 28 . . . 340, 341

McDonald v Dennys Lascelles Ltd (1933) 48 CLR 457, 39 ALR 381, 7 ALJ 95, HC of A . . . 615, 700

McEllistrim v Ballymacelligott Co-operative Agricultural and Dairy Society Ltd [1919] AC 548, 88 LJPC 59, 120 LT 613, 35 TLR 354, HL . . . 1110

McEvoy v Belfast Co Ltd [1935] AC 24, 103 LJPC 137, 40 Com Cas 1, [1934] All ER Rep 800, 151 LT 501, HL . . . 1142

McFadden & Co v Blue Star Line [1905] 1 KB 697, 74 LJKB 423, 10 Asp MLC 55, 10 Com Cas 123, 53 WR 576, 93 LT 52, 21 TLR 345 . . . 580

McGregor . . . 383

McGruther v Pitcher [1904] 2 Ch 306, 73 LJ Ch 653, 53 WR 138, 48 Sol Jo 639, 91 LT 678, 20 TLR 652, CA . . . 1205

McLaughlin v Daily Telegraph Newspaper Ltd (1904) 1 CLR 243 . . . 946

McMaster University v Wilchar Construction Ltd (1971) 22 DLR (3d) 9, [1971] 3 OR 801; affd 69 DLR (3d) 400 . . . 292, 306

McRae v Commonwealth Disposals Commission (1951) 84 CLR 377, [1951] ALR 771, 25 ALJ 425, HC of A . . . 500–503, 516, 629

Meehan v Jones (1982) 149 CLR 571, 42 ALR 463, 56 ALJR 813, HC of A . . . 280

Mendelssohn v Normand Ltd (1970) 1 QB 177 . . . 981

Merritt v Merritt [1970] 2 All ER 760, [1970] 1 WLR 1211, 114 Sol Jo 455, 214 Estates Gazette 1355, CA . . . 176–177

Mersey Docks Trustees v Gibbs (1866) LR 11 HLC 686, 11 ER 1500 . . . 414

Mersey Steel and Iron Co v Naylor, Benzon & Co (1884) 9 App Cas 434, 53 LJQB 497, 32 WR 989, [1881–5] All ER Rep 365, 51 LT 637, HL . . . 586, 1207

Metropolitan Electric Supply Co Ltd v Ginder [1901] 2 Ch. 799 . . . 732

Meux v Great Eastern Rly Co [1895] 2 QB 387 . . . 1154

Midland Bank Trust Co Ltd v Hett, Stubbs & Kemp (a firm) [1979] Ch 384, [1978] 3 All ER 571, [1978] 3 WLR 167, 121 Sol Jo 830 . . . 37–38

Midland Silicones. *See* Scruttons Ltd v Midland Silocones Ltd [1962] AC 446, [1962] 1 All ER 1, [1962] 2 WLR 186, 106 Sol Jo 34, sub nom Midland Silicones Ltd v Scruttons Ltd [1961] 2 Lloyd's Rep 365, HL

Mihalis Angelos, The (Maredelanto Cia Naviera SA v Berbau-Handel GmbH, The Mihalis Angelos Miles v Wakefield Metropolitan District Council [1987] AC 539, [1987] 1 All ER 1089, [1987] 2 WLR 795, 85 LGR 649, [1987] ICR 368, [1987] IRLR 193, 131 Sol Jo 408, [1987] LS Gaz R 1239, [1987] Rep 266, HL . . . 572

Miles v Wakefield Metropolitan District Council [1987] 1 All ER 1089 . . . 550

Millar's Karri and Jarrah Co (1902) v Weddel, Turner & Co (1908) 11 Asp MLC 184, 14 Com Cas 25, 100 LT 128, [1908–10] All ER Rep Ext 1274 . . . 587

Miller v Karlinski (1945) 62 TLR 85, CA . . . 1074, 1104

Mineral Transporter, The (Candlewood Navigation Corpn Ltd v Mitsui OSK Lines Ltd, The Mineral Transporter, The Ibaraki Maru Minnevitch v Café de Paris (Londres) Ltd [1936] 1 All ER 884, 80 Sol Jo 425, 52 TLR 413 . . . 30

Minnevitch v Café de Paris (Londres) Ltd [1936] 1 All ER 884, 52 TLR 413 . . . 524

Minter (FG) Ltd v Welsh Health Technical Services Organisation (1980) 13 BLR 1, CA . . . 672

Mitchell (George) (Chesterhall) Ltd v Finney Lock Seeds Ltd [1983] QB 284, [1983] 1 All ER 108, [1982] 3 WLR 1036, [1983] 1 Lloyd's Rep 168, 126 Sol Jo 689, [1982] LS Gaz R 1144, CA; affd [1983] 2 AC 803, [1983] 2 All ER 737, [1983] 3 WLR 163, [1983] 2 Lloyd's Rep 272, [1983] Com LR 209, HL . . . 985, 1011, 1014–1017, 1019, 1023, 1025, 1030, 1053

MJB Enterprises Ltd v Defence Construction (1951) Ltd (1999) 170 DLR (4th) 577 . . . 244

Modern Engineering (Bristol) Ltd v Gilbert-Ash (Northern) Ltd [1974] AC 689, [1973] 3 All ER 195, [1973] 3 WLR 421, 72 LGR 1, 117 Sol Jo 745, 1 BLR 75 . . . 1147

Mogul Steamship Co v McGregor, Gow & Co [1892] AC 25, 56 JP 101, 61 LJQB 295, 7 Asp MLC 120, 40 WR 337, [1891–4] All ER Rep 263, 66 LT 1, 8 TLR 182, HL . . . 1071, 1072

Monarch Steamship Co Ltd v A/B Karlshamns Oljefrabriker [1949] AC 196 . . . 645

Mondel v Steel (1841) 1 Dowl NS 1, 10 LJ Ex 426, 8 M & W 858, 151 ER 1288, [1835–42] All ER Rep 511, 1 BLR 108 . . . 561, 1147

Moody v Cox and Hatt [1917] 2 Ch 71, 86 Lj 424, 61 Sol Jo 398, 116 LT 740, CA . . . 529–530, 922

Moorcock, The (1889) 14 PD 64, 58 LJP 73, 6 Asp MLC 373, 37 WR 439, [1886–90] All ER Rep 530, 60 LT 654, 5 TLR 316, CA . . . 413–415, 414, 417, 418, 419, 444, 476

Moorgate Mercantile Co Ltd v Twitchings . . . 156

Morgan Crucible Co plc v Hill Samuel & Co Ltd [1991] Ch 295, [1991] 2 WLR 655, [1991] BCC 82, [1900] NLJR 1605, sub nom Morgan Crucible Co plc v Hill Samuel Bank Ltd [1991] 1 All ER 148, [1991] BCLC 178, CA . . . 30

Morgan Munitions Supply Co v Studebaker Corpn (1919) 123 NE 146 . . . 317

Morley v Boothby (1825) 3 Bing 107, 3 LJOSCP 177, 10 Moore CP 395 . . . 23

Morris (Herbert) Ltd v Saxelby [1916] 1 AC 688, 85 LJ Ch 210, [1916–17] All ER Rep 305, 60 Sol Jo 305, 114 LT 618, 32 TLR 297, HL . . . 1108–1111

Morris v Baron & Co [1918] AC 1, 87 LJKB 145, 118 LT 34, HL . . . 851

Morris v CW Martin & Sons Ltd [1966] 1 QB 716, [1965] 2 All ER 725, [1965] 3 WLR 276, [1965] 2 Lloyd's Rep 63, 109 Sol Jo 451, CA . . . 994, 1201, 1202, 1203

Morrison v Coast Finance Ltd (1965) 55 DLR (2d) 710, 54 WWR 257 . . . 942, 955

Mortgage Express Ltd v Bowerman & Partners [1995] QB 375, [1996] 2 All ER 836, [1995] 2 WLR 607, [1995] NPC 129, [1996] 1 EGLR 129, [1995] 12 LS Gaz R 34, [1996] 04 EG 126, [1996] PNLR 62, CA . . . 1128

Moschi v Lep Air Services Ltd [1973] AC 331 . . . 993–994

Moses v Macferlan (1760) 2 Burr 1005, 1 Wm Bl 219, [1558–1774] All Rep 581 . . . 44

Mosvolds Rederi A/S v Food Corpn of India, The Damodar General TJ Park and King Theras [1986] 2 Lloyd's Rep 68 . . . 415

Motor Oil Hellas (Corinth) Refineries SA v Shipping Corpn of India, The Kanchenjunga [1990] 1 Lloyd's Rep 391, HL . . . 616

Mountford v Scott . . . 265

Muirhead v Industrial Tank Specialities Ltd [1986] QB 507, [1985] 3 All ER 705, [1985] 3 WLR 993, 129 Sol Jo 855, [1986] LS Gaz R 116, CA . . . 1166

Multiservice Bookbinding Ltd v Marden [1979] Ch 84, [1978] 2 All ER 489, [1978] 2 WLR 535, 35 P & CR 201, 122 Sol Jo 210 . . . 522, 523, 939

Murphy v Brentwood District Council [1991] 1 AC 398, [1990] 2 All ER 908, [1990] 3 WLR 414, 89 LGR 24, [1990] 2 Lloyd's Rep 467, 22 HLR 502, 21 Con LR 1, 134 Sol Jo 1076, [1990] NLJR 1111, 50 BLR 1, HL . . . 32, 33–39, 1004, 1162, 1166

Murphy v Wexford County Council [1921] 2 IR 230 . . . 681

Mutual Life and Citizens' Assurance v Evatt [1971] 1 All ER 150 . . . 371

N

Nagle v Feilden [1966] 2 QB 633, [1966] 1 All ER 689, [1966] 2 WLR 1027, 110 Sol Jo 286, CA . . . 1072, 1074

Nai Genova and Nai Superba, The. *See* Agip SpA v Navigazione Alta Italia SpA, The Nai Genova and Nai Superba [1984] 1 Lloyd's Rep 353, CA

Nanfri, The. *See* Federal Commerce and Navigation Co Ltd v Molena Gamma Inc, The Lorfri [1979] AC 757, [1979] 1 All ER 307, [1978] 3 WLR 991, [1979] 1 Lloyd's Rep 201, 122 Sol Jo 843, HL

Nash v Halifax Building Society [1979] Ch 584, [1979] 2 All ER 19, [1979] 2 WLR 184, 37 P & CR 490, 122 Sol Jo 744 . . . 1085

National Assistance Board v Parkes . . . 106

National Bank of Greece SA v Pinios Shipping Co, The Maira [1990] 1 AC 637, [1989] 1 All ER 213, [1989] 3 WLR 185, 133 Sol Jo 817, sub nom National Bank of Greece SA v Pinios Shipping Co and George Dionysios Tsitsilianis, The Maira (No 3) [1988] 2 Lloyd's Rep 126, CA; on appeal sub nom National Bank of Greece v Pinios Shipping Co [1990] 1 AC 637, [1990] 1 All ER 78, [1989] 3 WLR 1330, 134 Sol Jo 261, [1990] 3 LS Gaz R 33, sub nom National Bank of Greece SA v Pinios Shipping Co and George Dionysios Tsitsilianis, The Maira (No 3) [1990] 1 Lloyd's Rep 225, HL . . . 420

National Coffee Palace Co, Re ex p Panmure (1883) 24 Ch D 367, 53 LJ Ch 57, 32 WR 236, 50 LT 38, CA . . . 1132

National Westminster Bank plc v Morgan [1983] 3 All ER 85, 133 NLJ 378, CA; revsd [1985] AC 686, [1985] 1 All ER 821, [1985] 2 WLR 588, [1985] FLR 266, 17 HLR 360, 129 Sol Jo 205, [1985] LS Gaz R 1485, [1985] NLJ Rep 254, HL . . . 923

National Westminster Bank v Morgan [1985] 1 All ER 821, [1985] AC 686 . . . 922, 923, 931, 957

Nema, The. *See* Pioneer Shipping Ltd v BTP Tioxide Ltd

Neville v Dominion of Canada News Co Ltd [1915] 3 KB 556, 84 LJKB 2105, [1914–15] All ER Rep 979, 113 LT 979, 31 TLR 542, CA . . . 1074

New York Star, The. *See* Port Jackson Stevedoring Pty Ltd v Salmond & Spraggon (Australia) Pty Ltd, The New York Star

New Zealand Shipping Co Ltd v AM Satterthwaite & Co Ltd [1975] AC 154, [1974] 1 All ER 1015, [1974] 2 WLR 865, 118 Sol Jo 387, sub nom The Eurymedon [1974] 1 Lloyd's Rep 534, PC . . . 62, 108, 226, 255, 908, 1143, 1157–1162, 1174

Newbigging v Adam (1886) 34 Ch D 582, 56 LJ 275, 35 WR 597, [1886–90] All ER Rep 975, 55 LT 794, 3 TLR 259, CA; on appeal sub nom Adam v Newbigging 13 App Cas 308, 57 LJ Ch 1066, 37 WR 97, [1886–90] All ER Rep 975, 59 LT 267, [1886–90] All ER Rep Ext 1465 . . . 370

Newcomb v De Roos (1859) 2 E & E 271, 29 LJQB 4, 6 Jur NS 68, 8 WR 5, 1 LT 6 . . . 234

Nicholas, H, The. *See* Rich (Marc) & Co AG v Bishop Rock Marine Co Ltd, Bethmarine Co Ltd and Nippon Kaiji Kyoki, The Nicholas H

Nicholson and Venn v Smith-Marriott (1947) 177 LT 189 171 . . . 511

Nickol and Knight v Ashton, Edridge & Co . . . 476

Nicolene Ltd v Simmonds [1953] 1 QB 543, [1953] 1 All ER 822, [1953] 2 WLR 717, [1953] 1 Lloyd's Rep 189, 97 Sol Jo 247, CA . . . 263, 405

Nisshin Shipping Co v Cleaves & Co [2003] EWHC 2602 [2004] 1 All ER (Comm) 481 . . . 1193

Nixon v Furphy (1926) 26 SR (NSW) 161 . . . 906

Nocton v Lord Ashburton [1914] AC 932, 83 LJ Ch 784, [1914–15] All ER Rep 45, 111 Lt 641, HL . . . 29, 370, 371

Nordenfelt v Maxim Nordenfelt Gunds and Ammunition Co Ltd [1894] AC 535, 63 LJ Ch 908, 11 R 1, [1891–4] All ER Rep 1, 71 LT 489, 10 TLR 636, HL . . . 1105–1107, 1113

North Ocean Shipping Co Ltd v Hyundai Construction

Co Ltd, The Atlantic Baron [1979] QB 705, [1978] 3 All ER 1170, [1979] 3 WLR 419, [1979] 1 Lloyd's Rep 89, 123 Sol Jo 352 . . . 100, 112, 905–908, 910, 911, 913, 915

North West Metropolitan Regional Hospital Board v T A Bickerton & Son Ltd [1970] 1 All ER 1039, [1970] 1 WLR 607, 68 LGR 447, 114 Sol Jo 243, 214 Estates Gazette 973, HL . . . 1165

North-Western Salt Co Ltd v Electrolytic Alkali Co Ltd [1914] AC 461, 83 LJKB 530, [1914–15] All ER Rep 752, 58 Sol Jo 338, 110 LT 852, 30 TLR 313, HL . . . 1071

Norwich City Council v Harvey [1989] 1 All ER 1180, [1989] 1 WLR 828, 133 Sol Jo 694, [1989] 25 LS Gaz R 45, [1989] NLJR 40, 45 BLR 14, CA . . . 1168–1170

Norwich Union Fire Insurance Society v Price Ltd . . . 511

Nottingham Patent Brick and Tile Co v Butler (1885) 15 QBD 261, (1886) 16 QB 778 . . . 1024

Nunan v Southern Rly Co [1923] 2 KB 703, 92 LJKB 703, 39 TLR 514; affd [1924] 1 KB 223, 93 LJKB 140, [1923] All ER Rep 21, 68 Sol Jo 139, 130 LT 131, 40 TLR 21, CA . . . 335

Nykredit Mortgage Bank plc v Edward Erdman Group Ltd [1996] 3 All ER 365, [1996] 3 WLR 87, [1996] 32 LS Gaz R 33, [1996] 27 EG 125, 140 Sol Jo LB 156, HL . . . 424, 672

Nykredit Mortgage Bank plc v Edward Erdman Group Ltd (No 2) [1998] 1 All Er 305, [1997] 1 WLR 1627, [1998] 01 LS Gaz R 24, [1998] 05 EG 150, 142 Sol Jo LB 29, 75 P & CR D28, HL . . . 385

O

Obde v Schlemeyer 56 Wash 2d 449, 353 P 2d 672 (1960) . . . 532–533

Obestain Inc v National Mineral Development Corpn Ltd, The Sanix Ace [1987] 1 Lloyd's Rep 465 . . . 1146

Occidental Worldwide Investment Corpn v Skibs A/S Avanti, Skibs A/S Glarona, Skibs A/S Navalis, The Siboen and The Sibotre [1976] 1 Lloyd's Rep 293 . . . 909, 910, 913

Ocean Island. See Tito v Waddell (No 2) [1977] Ch 106, [1977] 3 All ER 129, [1977] 2 WLR 496 Sol Jo 10

Ocean Tramp Tankers Corpn v V/O Sovfracht, The Eugenia [1964] 2 QB 226, [1964] 1 All ER 161, [1964] 2 WLR 114, [1963] 2 Lloyd's Rep 381, 107 Sol Jo 931, CA . . . 479–481

Odenfeld, The. *See* Gator Shipping Corpn v Trans-Asiatic Oil Ltd SA and Occidental Shipping Establishment, The Odenfeld [1978] 2 Lloyd's Rep 357

Ogwo v Taylor [1988] AC 431 . . . 143

Okehampton, The [1913] P 173 . . . 402

O'Laoire v Jackel International Ltd (No 2) [1991] ICR 718, [1991] IRLR 170, CA . . . 677, 678

Oliver v Davis . . . 154

Olley v Marlborough Court Ltd [1949] 1 KB 532, [1949] 1 All ER 127, [1949] LJR 360, 93 Sol Jo 40, 65 TLR 95, CA . . . 335

On Demand Information plc v Michael Gerson (Finance) plc [2002] UKHL 13, [2003] 1 AC 368 . . . 592

Ormes v Beadel (1860) 2 Giff 166, 9 WR 25; affd 2 De
  GF & J 333, 30 LJ Ch 1, 6 Jur NS 1103, 9 WR 25, 3 LT
  344, CA ... 921, 922

Oscar Chess Ltd v Williams [1957] 1 All ER 325,
  CA ... 324–326, 327

OTM Ltd v Hydranautics ... 41

Overbrooke Estates Ltd v Glencombe Properties Ltd
  [1974] 3 All ER 511, [1974] 1 WLR 1335, 118 Sol Jo
  775 ... 387

Overseas Tankship (UK) Ltd v Morts Dock and
  Engineering Co Ltd, The Wagon Mound [1961] AC
  388, [1961] 1 All ER 404, [1961] 2 WLR 126, [1961] 1
  Lloyd's Rep 1, 105 Sol Jo 85, [1961] ALR 569,
  PC ... 377

Overstone Ltd v Shipway [1962] 1 All ER 52, [1962] 1
  WLR 117, 106 Sol Jo 14, CA ... 601 ... 604

P

Pacific Associates Inc v Baxter [1990] 1 QB 993, [1989] 2
  All ER 159, [1989] 3 WLR 1150, 16 Con LR 90, 133
  Sol Jo 123, [1989] 6 LS Gax R 44, [1989] NLJR 41, 44
  BLR 33, CA ... 1173

Pacific Gas and Electric Co v G W Thomas Drayage and
  Rigging Co 69 Cal 2d 33, 69 Cal Rptr 561, 442 P 2d
  641 (1968) ... 399, 403

Pacoe v Turner [1979] 2 All ER 945 ... 164

Page One Records Ltd v Britton (t/a The Troggs) [1967] 3
  All ER 822, [1968] 1 WLR 157, 111 Sol Jo
  944 ... 731

Paget v Marshall ... 299

Panatown Ltd v Alfred McAlpine Construction Ltd
  (McAlpine (Alfred) Construction Ltd v Panatown Ltd
  Panoutsos v Raymond Hadley Corpn of New York
  [1917] 2 KB 473, 86 LJKB 1325, 22 Com Cas 308,
  [1916–17] All ER Rep 448, 61 Sol Jo 590, 117 LT 330,
  33 TLR 436, CA) ... 861, 862, 868, 869, 1149–1150

Pao On v Lau Yiu Long [1980] AC 614, [1979] 3 All ER
  65, [1979] 3 WLR 435, 123 Sol Jo 319, PC ... 108,
  112, 126–129, 908–910, 911, 913, 914

Paradine v Jane (1647) Mich 23 Car Banco Regis Hil 22
  Car Rot 1178, Aleyn 26 ER 897 ... 569

Paragon Finance plc v Staunton [2001] EWCA Civ 1466
  [2002] 2 All ER 248 ... 271

Paris v Stepney Borough Council [1951] AC 367, [1951]
  1 All ER 42, 49 LGR 293, 115 JP 22, 94 Sol Jo 837,
  [1951] 1 TLR 25, 84 Ll L Rep 525, HL ... 444

Parker v Bristol and Exeter Railway Co (1862) 11 CBNS
  787 ... 954

Parker v South Eastern Rly Co (1877) 2 CPD 416, 41 JP
  644, 46 LJQB 768, 25 WR 564, [1874–80] All ER Rep
  166, 36 LT 540, CA ... 332–336, 337

Parkinson (Sir Lindsay) & Co Ltd v Comrs of Works and
  Public Buildings [1949] 2 KB 632, [1950] 1 All ER
  208, CA ... 883

Parkinson v College of Ambulance Ltd and Harrison
  [1925] 2 KB 1, 93 LJKB 1066, [1924] All ER Rep 325,
  69 Sol Jo 107, 133 LT 135, 40 TLR 886 ... 1073

Parsons (H) (Livestock) Ltd v Uttley Ingham & Co Ltd
  [1978] QB 791, [1978] 1 All ER 525, [1977] 3 WLR
  990, [1977] 2 Lloyd's Rep 522, 121 Sol Jo 811,
  CA ... 649

Parsons v BNM Laboratories Ltd [1964] 1 QB 95, [1963]
  2 All ER 658, [1963] 2 WLR 1273, 42 ATC 200,
  [1963] TR 183, 107 Sol Jo 294, CA ... 659

Partenreederei MS Karen Oltmann v Scarsdale Shipping
  Co Ltd, The Karen Oltmann [1976] 2 Lloyd's Rep
  708 ... 405–406

Partridge v Crittenden [1968] 2 All ER 421, [1968] 1
  WLR 1204, 132 JP 367, 112 Sol Jo 582 ... 201

Pascoe v Turner [1979] 2 All ER 945, [1979] 1 WLR 431,
  123 Sol Jo 164, CA ... 164

Patel v Ali [1984] Ch 283, [1984] 1 All ER 978, [1984] 2
  WLR 960, 48 P & CR 118, 128 Sol Jo 204, [1984] LS
  Gaz R 1285 ... 291, 729

Pavey & Matthews Pty Ltd v Paul (1987) 162 CLR 221,
  69 ALR 577, 61 ALJR 151, HC of A ... 45

Payman v Lanjani [1985] Ch 457, [1984] 3 All ER 703,
  [1985] 2 WLR 48 P & CR 398, 128 Sol Jo 853,
  CA ... 616

Payzu Ltd v Saunders [1919] 2 KB 581, 89 LJKB 17,
  [1918–19] All ER Rep 219, 121 LT 563, 35 TLR 657,
  CA ... 653–656

Peabody Donation Fund (Governors) v Sir Lindsay
  Parkinson & Co Ltd [1985] AC 210, [1983] 3 All ER
  417, [1983] 3 WLR 754, 82 LGR 138, 127 Sol Jo 749,
  25 BLR 108, CA; affd [1985] AC 210, [1984] 3 All ER
  529, [1984] 3 WLR 953, 83 LGR 1, 128 Sol Jo 753,
  [1984] LS Gaz R 3179, 28 BLR 1, [1984] CILL 128,
  HL ... 32, 1168

Peacock v Peacock ... 13

Pearce v Brooks (1866) LR 1 Exch 213, 30 JP 295, 4 H &
  C 358, 35 LJ Ex 134, 12 Jur NS 342, 14 WR 614,
  [1861–73] All ER Rep 102, 14 LT 288 ... 1073, 1080

Pearl Mill Co v Ivy Tannery Co Ltd ... 193

Pearson (S) & Son Ltd v Dublin Corpn [1907] AC 351, 77
  LJPC 1, [1904–7] All ER Rep 255, 97 LT 645, HL ... 386

Pearson v Wheeler (1825) Ry & M 303 ... 374

Peek v Derry (1887) 37 Ch D 541 ... 374

Peek v Gurney (1873) LR 6 HL 377 ... 533

Peek v North Staffordshire Rly Co (1863) 10 HL Cas 473,
  32 LJQB 241, 9 Jur NS 914, 3 New Rep 1, 11 WR
  1023, 8 LT 768 ... 1024

Penarth Dock Engineering Co Ltd v Pounds [1963] 1
  Lloyd's Rep 359 ... 637

Pennsylvania Shipping Co v Compagnie Nationale de
  Navigation [1936] 2 All ER 1167, 42 Com Cas 45, 80
  Sol Jo 722, 155 LT 294, 55 Ll L Rep 271 ... 357

Pepper (Inspector of Taxes) v Hart [1993] AC 593, [1993]
  1 All ER 42, [1992] 3 WLR 1032, [1992] STC 898, 65
  TC 421, [1993] ICR 291, [1993] IRLR 33, [1993] NLJR
  17, [1993] RVR 127, [1993] 2 LRC 153, HL ... 1042

Percy Bilton Ltd v Greater London Council [1982] 2 All
  ER 623 ... 1165

Perera v Vandiyar [1953] 1 All ER 1109, [1953] 1 WLR
  672, 97 Sol Jo 332, CA ... 639

Perini Corpn v Commonwealth of Australia (1969) 12
  BLR 82, [1969] 2 NSWR 530 ... 884

Petterson v Pattberg 248 NY 86, 161 NE 428
  (1928) ... 216

Pettitt v Pettitt [1970] AC 777, [1969] 2 All ER 385,
  [1969] 2 WLR 966, 20 P & CR 991, 113 Sol Jo 344,
  211 Estates Gazette 829, HL ... 177, 180

Pharmaceutical Society of Great Britain v Boots Cash Chemists (Southern) Ltd [1953] 1 QB 401, [1953] 1 All ER 482, [1953] 2 WLR 427, 117 JP 132, 97 Sol Jo 149, CA . . . 199–202

Pharmaceutical Society of Great Britain v Dickson [1970] AC 403, [1968] 2 All ER 686, [1968] 3 WLR 286, 112 Sol Jo 601, HL . . . 1119

Philips Electronique Grand Public SA v British Sky Broadcasting Ltd [1995] EMLR 472 . . . 285, 286

Philips Hong Kong Ltd v Attorney-General of Hong Kong (1993) 61 BLR 41 . . . 694

Philips International BV v British Satellite Broadcasting Ltd [1995] EMLR 472 . . . 285, 286

Phillips Products Ltd v Hyland [1987] 2 All ER 620, [1987] 1 WLR 659n, 129 Sol Jo 47, [1985] LS Gaz R 681, Tr L 98, CA . . . 1005, 1013, 1018–1031

Phillips v Brooks Ltd [1919] 2 KB 243, 88 LJKB 953, 24 Com Cas 263, [1918–19] All ER Rep 246, 121 LT 249, 35 TLR 470 . . . 311–312, 315, 316, 317

Phillips v Homfray, Fothergill v Phillips (1871) 6 Ch App 770 . . . 531, 635

Phoenix General Insurance Co of Greece SA v Administratia Asigurarilor de Stat [1988] QB 216, [1987] 2 All ER 152, [1987] 2 WLR 512, [1986] 2 Lloyd's Rep 552, 131 Sol Jo 257, [1987] LS Gaz R 1055, CA . . . 1085

Photo Production Ltd v Securicor Transport Ltd [1980] AC 827, [1980] 1 All ER 556, [1980] 2 WLR 283, [1980] 1 Lloyd's Rep 545, 124 Sol Jo 147, 130 NLJ 188, HL . . . 611–615, 976, 990–995, 1013

Pinnel's Case (1602) . . . 852, 854, 855, 857

Pinnock Bros v Lewis and Peat Ltd [1923] 1 KB 690, 92 LJKB 695, 28 Com Cas 210, 67 Sol Jo 501, 129 LT 320, 39 TLR 212 . . . 984–985

Pioneer Container, The. *See* KH Enterprise v Pioneer Container, The Pioneer Container [1994] 2 AC 324, [1994] 2 All ER 250, [1994] 3 WLR 1, [1994] 1 Lloyd's Rep 593, [1994] 18 LS Gaz R 37, PC

Pioneer Shipping Ltd v BTP Tioxide Ltd [1982] AC 724, [1981] 2 All ER 1030, [1981] 3 WLR 292, [1981] Com LR 197, 125 Sol Jo 542, sub nom BTP Tioxide Ltd v Pioneer Shipping Ltd and Armada Marine SA, The Nema [1981] 2 Lloyd's Rep 239, HL . . . 466

Pitt v PHH Asset Management Ltd [1993] 4 All ER 961, [1994] 1 WLR 327, 68 P & CR 269, [1993] 2 EGLR 217, [1993] NLJR 1187, [1993] 40 EG 149, [1994] Conv 58, CA . . . 105, 276

Planché v Colburn (1831) & Bing 14, 5 C & P 58, 1 LJCP 7, 1 Moo & S 51, [1824–34] All ER Rep 94 . . . 743, 745

Plasticmoda Societa Per Azioni v Davidsons (Manchester) Ltd [1952] 1 Lloyd's Rep 527 . . . 868

Platform Home Loans Ltd v Oyston Shipways Ltd [1998] Ch 466, [1998] 4 All ER 252, [1998] 3 WLR 94, 13 PN 14, [1998] 01 LS Gaz R 26, [1998] 13 EG 148, 142 Sol Jo LB 46, CA; revsd [2000] 2 AC 190, [1999] 1 All ER 833, [1999] 2 WLR 518, [1999] NLJR 283, [1999] 13 EG 119, [1999] EGCS 26, 143 Sol Jo LB 65, HL . . . 385–386

Platform Home Loans Ltd v Oyston Shipways Ltd [1998] Ch 466, [1998] 4 All ER 252, [1998] 3 WLR 94, 13 PN 14, [1998] 01 LS Gaz R 26, [1998] 13 EG 148, 142

Sol Jo LB 46, CA; revsd [2000] 2 AC 190, [1999] 1 All ER 833, [1999] 2 WLR 518, [1999] NLJR 283, [199 . . . 657

Plevins v Downing [1876] 1 CPD 220 . . . 859

Plimmer v City of Wellington Corpn (1884) 9 App Cas 699, 53 LJPC 105, 51 LT 475, PC . . . 155, 156, 157

Poosathurai v Kannappa Chettiar (1919) LR 47 Ind App 1 . . . 921

Port Caledonia, The and The Anna [1903] P 184, 72 LJP 60, 9 Asp MLC 479, 52 WR 223, 89 LT 216 . . . 948–949, 956

Port Jackson Stevedoring Pty Ltd v Salmond & Spraggon (Australia) Pty Ltd, The New York Star [1980] 3 All ER 257, [1981] 1 WLR 138, [1980] 2 Lloyd's Rep 317, 124 Sol Jo 756, PC . . . 1160–1161

Port Line Ltd v Ben Line Steamers Ltd [1958] 2 QB 146, [1958] 1 All ER 787, [1958] 2 WLR 551, [1958] 1 Lloyd's Rep 290, 102 Sol Jo 232 . . . 1206

Portman Building Society v Dusangh [2000] 2 All ER (Comm) 221, [2000] Lloyd's Rep Bank 197, 80 P & CR D20, CA . . . 945

Posner v Scott-Lewis [1987] Ch 25, [1986] 3 All ER 513, [1986] 3 WLR 531, 130 Sol Jo 14, [1986] 1 EGLR 56, 277 Estates Gazette 859 . . . 727

Post Chaser, The (Société Italo-Belge pour le Commerce et l'Industrie SA v Palm and Vegetable Oils (Malaysia) Sdn Bhd, The Post Chaser Poussard v Spiers and Pond (1876) 1 QBD 410, 40 JP 645, 45 LJQB 621, 24 WR 819, 34 LT 572 . . . 865, 872, 874

Poussard v Spiers and Pond (1876) 1 QBD 410 . . . 524

Powell v Brent London Borough Council [1988] ICR 176, [1987] IRLR 466, CA . . . 728

Powell v Powell [1900] 1 Ch 243 . . . 936

Pratt Contractors Ltd v Transit New Zealand [2004] BLR 143 . . . 248

Prenn v Simmonds [1971] 3 All ER 237, [1971] 1 WLR 1381, 115 Sol Jo 654, HL . . . 399, 403–404, 405, 407, 409

President of India v La Pintada Compania Navigacion SA [1985] AC 104, [1984] 2 All ER 773, [1984] 3 WLR 10, [1984] 2 Lloyd's Rep 9, 128 Sol Jo 414, HL . . . 671, 672

Prestwich v Poley (1865) 18 CBNS 806, 144 Eng Rep 662 . . . 1129

Price v Green . . . 1119

Price v Strange [1978] Ch 337, [1977] 3 All ER 371, [1977] 3 WLR 943, 36 P & CR 59, 121 Sol Jo 816, 243 Estates Gazette 295, CA . . . 729

Priestley v Fowler . . . 450

Printing & Numerical Registering Co v Sampson . . . 47

Proforce Recruit Ltd v The Rugby Group Ltd [2005] EWCA 698 . . . 406

Proodos C, The. *See* Syros Shipping Co SA v Elaghill Trading Co, The Proodos C

Public Works Comr v Hills [1906] AC 368, 75 LJPC 69, 94 LT 833, PC . . . 690, 702

Puerto Buitrago, The. *See* Attica Sea Carriers Corpn v Ferrostaal Poseidon Bulk Reederei GmbH, The Puerto Buitago [1976] 1 Lloyd's Rep 250, CA

Q

Quinn (or Quin) v Burch Bros (Builders) Ltd [1966] 2 QB 370, [1965] 3 All ER 801, [1966] 2 WLR 430, 109 Sol Jo 921; affd [1966] 2 QB 370, [1966] 2 All ER 283, [1966] 2 WLR 1017, 110 Sol Jo 214, CA ... 657, 658

Quinn v Williams Furniture Ltd ... 201, 838

R

R & B Customs Brokers Co Ltd v United Dominions Trust Ltd (Saunders Abbott (1980) Ltd, third party) [1988] 1 All ER 847, [1988] 1 WLR 321, [1988] RTR 134, [1988] BTLC 52, 132 Sol Jo 300, [1988] 11 LS Gaz R 42, CA ... 997, 998

R & H Hall Ltd & WH Pim Jr & Co's Arbitration (1928) 33 Com Cas 324, [1928] All ER Rep 763, 139 LT 50, 30 L1 L Rep 159, HL ... 664

R v Clarke (1927) 40 CLR 227 ... 216

R v Ron Engineering and Construction Eastern Ltd (1981) 119 DLR (3d) 267 ... 243

R W Green Ltd v Cade Bros Farm [1978] 1 Lloyd's Rep 602 ... 1013, 1015

Radford v de Froberville [1978] 1 All ER 33, [1977] 1 WLR 1262, 35 P & CR 316, 121 Sol Jo 319, 7 BLR 35 ... 682, 683, 684

Raffles v Wichelhaus (1864) 2 H & C 906, 33 LJ Ex 160, 159 ER 375 ... 301–302, 303, 405

Raineri v Miles [1981] AC 1050, [1980] 2 All ER 145, [1980] 2 WLR 847, 41 P & CR 71, 124 Sol JO 328, HL ... 575

Ramsden v Dyson (1866) LR 1 HL 129 ... 155, 156, 157

Raymond Burke Motors Ltd v Mersey Docks and Harbour Board Co [1986] 1 Lloyd's Rep 155 ... 1160

Reardon Smith Line Ltd v Hansen-Tangen [1976] 3 All ER 570, [1976] 1 WLR 989, [1976] 2 Lloyd's Rep 621, 120 Sol Jo 719, HL ... 206, 399, 429

Redgrave v Hurd (1881) 20 Ch D 1, 57 LJ Ch 113, 30 WR 251, [1881–5] All ER Rep 77, 45 LT 185, CA ... 355–358, 356, 357, 518, 948

Rees Hough Ltd v Redland Reinforced Plastics Ltd (1984) 2 Con LR 109, 27 BLR 136, [1984] CILL 84, 134 NLJ 706, 1 Const LJ 67 ... 1013

Regalian Properties plc v London Dockland Development Corpn [1995] 1 All ER 1005, [1995] 1 WLR 212, 45 Con LR 37, [1994] NPC 139, [1995] Conv 135 ... 281

Reid v Rush & Tompkins Group plc [1989] 3 All ER 228, [1990] 1 WLR 212, [1990] RTR 144, [1989] 2 Lloyd's Rep 167, [1990] ICR 61, [1989] IRLR 265, CA ... 420–425

Reigate v Union Manufacturing Co (Ramsbottom) Ltd and Elton Cop Dyeing Co Ltd [1918] 1 KB 592, 87 LJKB 724, [1918–19] All ER Rep 143, 118 LT 479, CA ... 415

Renton (GH) & Co Ltd v Palmyra Trading Corpn of Panama [1957] AC 149, [1956] 3 All ER 957, [1957] 2 WLR 45, [1956] 2 Lloyd's Rep 379, 101 Sol Jo 43, HL ... 983

Rewia, The [1991] 2 Lloyd's Rep 325 ... 402

Reynell v Sprye (1852) 1 De GM & G 660 ... 902

Rhodes, Re, Rhodes v Rhodes (1890) 44 Ch D 94, 59 LJ Ch 298, 38 WR 385, [1886–90] All ER Rep 871, 62 LT 342, CA ... 42

Rich (Marc) & Co AG v Bishop Rock Marine Co Ltd, Bethmarine Co Ltd and Nippon Kaiji Kyoki, The Nicholas H [1992] 2 Lloyd's Rep 481; revsd [1994] 3 All ER 686, [1994] 1 WLR 1071, [1994] 1 Lloyd's Rep 492, CA; aff'd sub nom Rich (Marc) & Co AG v Bishop Rock Marine Co Ltd, The Nicholas H [1996] AC 211, [1995] 3 All ER 307, [1995] 3 WLR 227, [1995] 2 Lloyd's Rep 299, [1995] 31 LS Gaz R 34, [1995] NLJR 1033, 139 Sol Jo LB 165, HL ... 1170–1174

Rickards (Charles) Ltd v Oppenhaim (or Oppenheim) [1950] 1 KB 616, [1950] 1 All ER 420, 94 Sol Jo 161, 66 (pt 1) TLR 435, CA ... 156

Ricketts v Pennsylvania Rly Co 153 F 2d 757 (1946) ... 294

Ricketts v Scothorn 77 NW 365, 57 Neb 51 (1898) ... 146, 147–148, 149, 150, 163, 165, 170

River Wear Comrs v Adamson ... 404

Riverlate Properties Ltd v Paul [1975] Ch 133, [1974] 2 All ER 656, [1974] 3 WLR 564, 28 P & CR 220, 118 Sol Jo 644, 231 Estates Gazette 1287, CA ... 298–299, 300–301

Robb v Hammersmith and Fulham London Borough Council [1991] ICR 514, [1991] IRLR 72 ... 728–729

Robertson v British Gas Corpn [1983] ICR 351, [1983] IRLR 302, CA ... 343, 344

Robertson v French (1803) 4 East 130, 102 ER 779 ... 401–402

Robertson v Minister of Pensions [1949] 1 KB 227, [1948] 2 All ER 767 ... 154

Robinson v Harman (1848) 18 LJ Ex 202, 1 Exch 850, [1843–60] All ER 383, 13 LTOS 141 ... 24, 623, 634

Robinson v National Bank of Scotland Ltd ... 28

Robophone Facilities Ltd v Blank [1966] 3 All ER 128, [1966] 1 WLR 1428, 110 Sol Jo 544, CA ... 211, 692

Rodocanachi v Milburn (1886) 18 QBD 67 ... 662, 665

Rogers v Ingham LR 3 Ch D 351 ... 1095

Rogers v Parish (Scarborough) Ltd [1987] QB 933, [1987] 2 All ER 232, [1987] 2 WLR 353, [1987] RTR 312, [1987] BTLC 51, 131 Sol Jo 223, [1987] LS Gaz R 905, CA ... 431, 437, 619

Rose (Frederick E) (London) Ltd v William H Pim Jnr & Co Ltd [1953] 2 QB 450, [1953] 2 All ER 739, [1953] 3 WLR 497, [1953] 2 Lloyd's Rep 238, 97 Sol Jo 556, CA ... 297, 307 308, 309

Rose and Frank Co v JR Crompton and Bros Ltd [1923] 2 KB 261, 92 LJKB 959, 67 Sol Jo 538, 129 LT 610, CA; revsd [1925] AC 445, 94 LJKB 120, 30 Com Cas 163, [1924] All ER Rep 245, 132 LT 641, HL ... 180–183

Routledge v McKay [1954] 1 WLR 615 ... 325

Rover International Ltd v Cannon Film Sales Ltd (No 3) [1989] 3 All ER 423, [1989] 1 WLR 912, [1988] BCLC 710n, CA ... 508, 701, 743

Rowe v Turner, Hopkins & Partners [1980] 2 NZLR 550; revsd [1982] 1 NZLR 178 ... 380, 657

Rowland v Divall [1923] 2 KB 500, 92 LJKB 1041, [1923] All Rep 270, 67 Sol Jo 703, 129 LT 757, CA ... 427

Rowling v Takaro Properties Ltd [1988] AC 473, [1988] 1 All ER 163, [1988] 2 WLR 418, 132 Sol Jo 126, [1988] 4 LS Gaz R 35, PC ... 32

Royal Bank of Scotland plc v Etridge (No 2) [1998] 4 All
ER 705, [1998] 3 FCR 675, [1998] 2 FLR 843, [1998]
Fam Law 665, 31 HLR 575, [1998] 32 LS Gaz R 31,
[1998] NLJR 1390, 76 P & CR D39, CA . . . 929, 931

Royscot Trust Ltd v Rogerson [1991] 2 QB 297, [1991] 3
All ER 294, [1991] 3 WLR 57, 135 Sol Jo 444, [1991]
NLJR 493, CA . . . 377–381

Rugg v Minett (1809) 11 East 210 . . . 461–462

Rutter v Palmer [1922] All ER Rep 367, [1922] 2 KB 87,
91 LJKB 657 . . . 978, 979, 980

Ruxley Electronics and Construction Ltd v Forsyth [1996]
AC 344, [1995] 3 All ER 268, [1995] 3 WLR 118,
[1995] 31 LS Gaz R 33, [1995] NLJR 996, 73 BLR 5,
139 Sol Jo LB 163, HL . . . 676, 689

Ryan v Mutual Tontine Westminster Chambers Association
[1893] 1 Ch 116, 62 LJ Ch 252, 2 R 156, 41 WR 146,
37 Sol Jo 45, 67 LT 820, 9 TLR 72, CA . . . 724, 725

S

Sabemo Pty Ltd v North Sydney Municipal Council
[1977] 2 NSWLR 880 . . . 281

Said v Butt [1920] 3 KB 497, 90 LJKB 239, [1920] All ER
Rep 232, 124 LT 413, 36 TLR 762 . . . 1133

Sainsbury (H R & S) Ltd v Street [1972] 3 All ER 1127,
[1972] 1 WLR 834, 116 Sol Jo 483 . . . 524

Sajan Singh v Sardara Ali [1960] AC 167, [1960] 1 All ER
269, [1960] 2 WLR 180, 104 Sol Jo 84, PC . . . 1094

Salford Corpn v Lever [1891] 1 QB 168 . . . 664

Salisbury (Marquess) v Gilmore [1942] 2 KB 38 . . . 151

Salkeld v Vernon (1758) 1 Eden 64 . . . 849

Salt v Marquess of Northampton [1892] AC 1, 61 LJ Ch
49, 40 WR 529, 36 Sol Jo 150, 65 LT 765, 8 TLR 104,
HL . . . 938

Samuel v Jarrah Timber and Wood Paving Corpn Ltd
[1904] AC 323, 73 LJ Ch 526, 11 Mans 276, 52 WR
673, 90 LT 731, 20 TLR 536, HL . . . 938

Sanders & Forster Ltd v A Monk & Co Ltd . . . 41

Sanix Ace, The. *See* Obestain Inc v National Mineral
Development Corpn Ltd, The Sanix Ace [1987] 1
Lloyd's Rep 465

Santa Carina, The (Vlassopulos (N & J) Ltd v Ney
Shipping Ltd, The Santa Carina Santa Clara, The.
Vitol SA v Norelf Ltd, The Santa Clara Sauter
Automation v H C Goodman (Mechanical Services)
[1986] 2 FTLR 239, 34 BLR 81) . . . 1128

Sauter Automation Ltd v Goodman (Mechanical
Services) Ltd (1986) 34 BLR 81 . . . 228

Sayers v Harlow UDC [1958] 2 All ER 342, [1958] 1 WLR
623, 122 JP 351, 102 Sol Jo 419, CA . . . 657

Scally v Southern Health and Social Services Board
[1992] 1 AC 294, [1991] 4 All ER 563, [1991] 3 WLR
778, [1991] ICR 771, [1991] IRLR 522, 135 Sol Jo LB
172, HL . . . 422, 424

Scammell (G) & Nephew Ltd v Ouston [1941] AC 251,
[1941] 1 All ER 14, 110 LJKB 197, 46 Com Cas 190,
85 Sol Jo 224, 164 Lt 379, 57 TLR 280,
HL . . . 261–262, 405

Scandinavian Trading Tanker Co AB v Flota Petrolera
Ecuatoriana, The Scaptrade [1983] 2 AC 694, [1983]
2 All ER 763, [1983] 3 WLR 203, [1983] 2 Lloyd's Rep
253, 127 Sol Jo 476, HL . . . 591, 592, 739

Scaptrade, The. *See* Scandinavian Trading Tanker Co AB
v Flota Petrolera Ecuatoriana, The Scaptrade [1983] 2
AC 694, [1983] 2 All ER 763, [1983] 3 WLR 203,
[1983] 2 Lloyd's Rep 253, 127 Sol Jo 476, HL

Schaefer v Schuhmann [1972] AC 572, [1972] 1 All ER
621, [1972] 2 WLR 481, 116 Sol Jo 121, [1972–73]
ALR 501, PC . . . 20

Schebsman, Re, ex p Official Receiver, Trustee v Cargo
Superintendents (London) Ltd and Schebsman [1944]
Ch 83, [1943] 2 All ER 768, 113 LJ Ch 33, 88 Sol Jo
17, 170 LT 9, 60 TLR 128, CA . . . 1139, 1151

Schroeder (A) Music Publishing Co Ltd v Macaulay
[1974] 3 All ER 616, [1974] 1 WLR 1308, 118 Sol Jo
734, HL . . . 71, 120–121, 952, 961, 965–966, 1024,
1115–1116, 1117, 1118, 1119

Schuler (L) AG v Wickman Machine Tool Sales Ltd [1974]
AC 235, [1973] 2 All ER 39, [1973] 2 WLR 683,
[1973] 2 Lloyd's Rep 53, 117 Sol Jo 340,
HL . . . 409–410, 571, 599–603, 602

Schwartzreich v Bauman-Basch (1921) 131 NE
887 . . . 860

Scotson v Pegg (1861) 6 H & N 295, 30 LJ Ex 225, 9 WR
280, 3 LT 753 . . . 107–108

Scott v Brown, Doering, McNab & Co [1892] 2 QB 724,
57 JP 213, 61 LJQB 738, 4 R 42, 41 WR 116,
[1891–4] All ER Rep 654, 36 Sol Jo 698, 67 LT 782, 8
TLR 755, CA . . . 1079–1080

Scottish Special Housing Association v Wimpey
Construction Ltd [1986] 1 WLR 995 . . . 1168–1169,
1170

Scriven Bros & Co v Hindley & Co [1913] 3 KB 564, 83
LJKB 40, 109 LT 526 . . . 292–296, 303, 306,
346–347

Scruttons Ltd v Midland Silicones Ltd [1962] AC 446,
[1962] 1 All ER 1, [1962] 2 WLR 186, 106 Sol Jo 34,
sub nom Midland Silicones Ltd v Scruttons Ltd [1961]
2 Lloyd's Rep 365, HL . . . 1154–1157, 1160, 1161,
1174, 1194, 1201, 1204

Sealand of the Pacific Ltd v Ocean Cement Ltd (1973) 33
DLR (3d) 625 . . . 371

Seddon v North Eastern Salt Co Ltd [1905] 1 Ch 326, 74
LJ Ch 199, 53 WR 232, [1904–7] All ER Rep 817, 49
Sol Jo 119, 91 LT 793, 21 TLR 118 . . . 368

Selectmove Ltd, Re [1995] 2 All ER 531, [1995] 1 WLR
474, [1995] STC 406, 66 TC 552, CA . . . 856, 865

Selmer Co v Blakeslee-Midwest Co 704 F 2d 924 (ISCA
7th Circ, 1983) . . . 877

Service Station Association v Berg Bennett (1993) 117
ALR 393 . . . 247

Shadwell v Shadwell (1860) 9 CBNS 159, 30 LJCP 145, 7
Jur NS 311, 9 WR 163, 142 ER 62, 3 LT 628 . . . 107,
124–125, 147, 165

Shamia v Joory [1958] 1 QB 448, [1958] 1 All ER 111,
[1958] 2 WLR 84, 102 Sol Jo 70 . . . 1195

Shanklin Pier Ltd v Detel Products Ltd [1951] 2 KB 854,
[1951] 2 All ER 471, [1951] 2 Lloyd's Rep 187, 95 Sol
Jo 563 . . . 19, 38–39, 442

Sharp Brothers & Knight v Chant [1917] 1 KB
771 . . . 1095

Sharp v Ellis, Re Edward Love & Co Pty Ltd [1972] VR
137 . . . 139–140

Sheikh Bros v Ochsner [1957] AC 136, [1957] 2 WLR 254, 101 Sol Jo 128, PC ... 515

Shell UK Ltd v Lostock Garage Ltd [1977] 1 All ER 481, [1976] 1 WLR 1187, 120 Sol Jo 523, CA ... 418

Shepherd (FC) & Co Ltd v Jerrom [1987] QB 301, [1986] 3 All ER 589, [1986] 3 WLR 801, [1986] ICR 802, [1986] IRLR 358, 130 Sol Jo 665, CA ... 471

Shiloh Spinners Ltd v Harding [1973] AC 691, [1973] 1 All ER 90, [1973] 2 WLR 28, 25 P & CR 48, 117 Sol Jo 34, HL ... 591

Shindler v Northern Raincoat Co Ltd [1960] 2 All ER 239, [1960] 1 WLR 1038, 104 Sol Jo 806 ... 656

Shipley Urban District Council v Bradford Corpn ... 297, 307

Shipton, Anderson & Co v Weil Bros & Co [1912] 1 KB 574, 81 LJKB 910, 17 Com Cas 153, 106 Lt 372, 28 TLR 269 ... 559

Shirlaw v Southern Foundries (1926) Ltd [1939] 2 KB 206, [1939] 2 All ER 113, CA; affd sub nom Southern Foundries (1926) Ltd v Shirlaw [1940] AC 701, [1940] 2 All ER 445, 109 LJKB 461, 84 Sol Jo 464, 164 LT 251, 56 TLR 637, HL ... 415, 514

Shogun Finance Ltd v Hudson [2003] UKHL 62 [2004] 1 AC 919 [2004] 1 All ER 215 ... 316

Short v Stone ... 582

Shove v Downs Surgical plc [1984] 1 All ER 7, [1984] ICR 532, [1984] IRLR 17, 128 Sol Jo 221 ... 659

Siboen and the Sibotre, The (Occidental Worldwide Investment Corpn v Skibs A/S Avanti, Skibs A/S Glarona, Skibs A/S Navalis, The Siboen and The Sibotre Sibree v Tripp (1846) 15 LJ Ex 318, 15 M & W 23) ... 903, 905, 911

Sibree v Tripp 15 M & W 23 ... 853, 854, 857

Simaan General Contracting Co v Pilkington Glass Ltd (No 2) [1988] QB 758, [1988] 1 All ER 791, [1988] 2 WLR 761, 132 Sol Jo 463, [1988] 11 LS Gaz R 44, [1988] NLJR 53, 40 BLR 28, CA ... 1166

Simona, The (Fercometal SARL v Mediterranean Shipping Co SA, The Simona Sinclair v Brougham [1914] AC 398, 83 LJ Ch 465, [1914–15] All ER Rep 622, 58 Sol Jo 302, 111 LT 1, 30 TLR 315, HL) ... 584

Simond v Boydell (1779) 1 Dougl 268, 99 ER 175 ... 402

Simpson v Bloss (1816) 7 Taunt 246 ... 1099

Sinclair v Brougham [1914] AC 398 ... 508, 906

Sindall (William) plc v Cambridgeshire County Council [1994] 3 All ER 932, [1994] 1 WLR 1016, 92 LGR 121, [1993] NPC 82, CA ... 381–384, 527

Singer Co (UK) v Tees and Hartlepool Port Authority [1988] 2 Lloyd's Rep 164, [1988] 1 FTLR 442 ... 1201

Singh (Sajan) v Sardara Ali [1960] AC 167, [1960] 1 All ER 269, [1960] 2 WLR 180, 104 Sol Jo 84, PC ... 1094

Sir Lindsay Parkinson & Co Ltd v Commissioners of Works ... 466, 883

Sirius International Insurance (Publ) v FAI General Insurance Ltd [2005] 1 All ER 191 ... 400

Skeate v Beale 11 A & E 983 ... 905–906

Sky Petroleum Ltd v VIP Petroleum Ltd [1974] 1 All ER 954, [1974] 1 WLR 576, 118 Sol Jo 311 ... 712–713

Slater v Hoyle & Smith Ltd [1920] 2 KB 11, 89 LJKB 401, 25 Com Cas 140, [1918–19] All ER Rep 654, 122 LT 611, 36 TLR 132, CA ... 664, 665, 1147

Slowey v Lodder (1900) 20 NZLR 321; affd sub nom Lodder v Slowey [1904] AC 442, 73 LJPC 82, 53 WR 131, 91 LT 211, 20 TLR 597, PC ... 744–745

Smallman v Smallman [1972] Fam 25 ... 279

Smeaton Hanscomb & Co Ltd v Sassoon I Setty, Son & Co [1953] 2 All ER 1471, [1953] 1 WLR 1468, [1953] 2 Lloyd's Rep 580, 97 Sol Jo 862 ... 985, 986, 987

Smiley v Townshend [1950] 2 KB 311, [1950] 1 All ER 530, 66 (pt 1) TLR 546, CA ... 681

Smith and Snipes Farm Ltd v River Douglas Catchment Board [1949] 2 KB 500 ... 1153

Smith New Court Securities Ltd v Citibank NA [1997] AC 254, [1996] 3 WLR 1051, [1997] 1 BCLC 350, [1996] 46 LS Gaz R 28, [1996] NLJR 1722, 141 Sol Jo LB 5, sub nom Smith New Court Securities Ltd v Scrimgeour Vickers (Asset Management) Ltd [1996] 4 All ER ... 380

Smith v Chadwick (1882) 20 Ch D 20 ... 358–359

Smith v Eric S Bush [1990] 1 AC 831, [1989] 2 All ER 514, [1989] 2 WLR 790, 87 LGR 685, 21 HLR 424, 17 Con LR 1, 133 Sol Jo 597, [1989] 1 EGLR 169, [1989[NLJR 576, [1989] 17 EG 68, 18 EG 99, HL ... 29, 30, 1006, 1021, 1167

Smith v Hughes (1871) LR 6 QB 597, 40 LJQB 221, 19 WR 1059, [1861–73] All ER Rep 632, 25 LT 329 ... 192, 303, 308, 309, 310, 354, 505, 510, 511, 529

Smith v Jeffryes (1846) 14 M & W 561 ... 302, 308

Smith v Land and House Property Corporation (1884) 28 Ch D 7 ... 358

Smith v New Court Securities Ltd v Scrimgeour Vickers (Asset Management) Ltd [1996] 4 All ER 769 ... 376

Smith v William Charlick Ltd [1924] 34 CLR 38 ... 906

Smith v Wilson (1832) 3 B & Ad 728, 1 LJKB 194 ... 412

Smout v Ilbery (1842) O M & W ... 1131

Snelling v John G Snelling Ltd [1973] QB 87, [1972] 1 All ER 79, [1972] 2 WLR 588, 116 Sol Jo 217 ... 856, 1178

Société des Industries Métallurgiques SA v Bronx Engineering Co Ltd [1975] 1 Lloyd's Rep 465, CA ... 710

Société Italo-Belge pour le Commerce et l'Industrie SA v Palm and Vegetable Oils (Malaysia) Sdn Bhd, The Post Chaser [1982] 1 All ER 19, [1981] 2 Lloyd's Rep 695, [1981] Com LR 249 ... 865, 872, 874

Solle v Butcher [1950] 1 KB 671, [1949] 2 All ER 1107, 66 (pt 1) TLR 448, CA ... 309, 509–513, 515, 517, 518, 519, 520

South Australia Asset Management Corpn v York Montague Ltd [1997] AC 191, [1996] 3 All ER 365, [1996] 2 EGLR 93, [1996] LS Gaz R 33, [1996] NLJR 956, 80 BLR 1, [1996] 27 EG 125, 140 Sol Jo LB 156, HL ... 377, 384–386, 424

South Caribbean Trading Co Ltd v Trafigura Beheer [2005] 1 Lloyd's Rep 128 ... 115

Southern Water Authority v Carey [1985] 2 All ER 1077 ... 1161, 1167, 1168

Sowler v Potter [1940] 1 KB 271 ... 314, 510, 511

Spartan Steel and Alloys Ltd v Martin & Co (Contractors) Ltd [1973] QB 27, [1972] 3 All ER 557, [1972] 3 WLR 502, 116 Sol Jo 648, CA . . . 31

Spencer v Harding (1870) LR 5 CP 561, 39 LJCP 332, 19 WR 48, 23 LT 237 . . . 242–243, 245

Spice Girls Ltd v Aprilia World Service BV [2000] EMLR 478 . . . 363

Splendid Sun, The. *See* André et Cie v Marine Transocean Ltd, The Splendid Sun [1981] QB 964, [1981] 2 All ER 993, [1981] 3 WLR 43, [1981] 2 Lloyd's Rep 29, [1981] Com LR 95, 125 Sol Jo 395, CA

Sport International Bussum BV v Inter-Footwear Ltd [1984] 2 All E 321, [1984] 1 WLR 776, 128 Sol Jo 383, [1984] LS Gaz R 1992, 134 NLJ 568, HL . . . 592

Spurgeon v Collier (1758) 1 Eden 55 . . . 938

Spurling (J) Ltd v Bradshaw [1956] 2 All ER 121, [1956] 1 WLR 461, [1956] 1 Lloyd's Rep 392, 100 Sol Jo 317, CA . . . 337, 985, 987

St Albans City and District Council v International Computers Ltd [1996] 4 All ER 481, 95 LGR 592, [1997] FSR 251, 15 Tr LR 444, CA . . . 1008, 1022

St John Shipping Corpn v Joseph Rank Ltd [1957] 1 QB 267, [1956] 3 All ER 683, [1956] 3 WLR 870, [1956] 2 Lloyd's Rep 413, 100 Sol Jo 841 . . . 1081–1083, 1086, 1087, 1092

St John Tugboat Co Ltd v Irving Refinery Ltd [1964] SCR 614, 46 DLR (2d) 1 . . . 213

St Martins Property Corpn Ltd v Sir Robert McAlpine Ltd (formerly Sir Robert McAlpine & Sons Ltd) [1994] 1 AC 85, [1993] 3 WLR 408, 36 Con LR 1, [1993] 45 LS Gaz R 39, 137 Sol Jo LB 183, sub nom Linden Gardens Trust Ltd v Lenesta Sludge Disposals Ltd [1993] 3 All ER 417, HL. *See* Linden Gardens Trust Ltd v Lenesta Sludge Disposals Ltd [1994] 1 AC 85, [1993] 3 All ER 417, [1993] 3 WLR 408, 36 Con LR 1, [1993] 45 LS Gaz R 39, [1993] NLJR 1152, 137 Sol Jo LB 183, HL

Staffordshire Area Health Authority v South Staffordshire Waterworks Co [1978] 3 All ER 769, [1978] 1 WLR 1387, 77 LGR 17, 122 Sol Jo 331, CA . . . 521–524, 895

Stag Line Ltd v Tyne Shiprepair Group Ltd, The Zinnia [1984] 2 Lloyd's Rep 211 . . . 1020, 1023, 1031

Standard Chartered Bank v Pakistan National Shipping Cap (No 2) [2002] UKHL 43 [2003] 1 All ER 173 . . . 375

Staniforth v Lyall 7 Bing 169 . . . 660

Stanton v Richardson (1872) LR 7 CP 421, 41 LJCP 180, 1 Asp MLC 449, 21 WR 71, 27 LT 513; on appeal LR 9 CP 390, 43 LJPC 230, 2 Asp MLC 228, 22 WR 223, 30 LT 643, Ex Ch; affd 45 LJPC 78, 3 Asp MLC 23, 24 WR 324, 33 LT 193, HL . . . 580

Starside Properties Ltd v Mustapha [1974] 2 All ER 567, [1974] 1 WLR 816, 28 P & CR 95, 118 Sol Jo 388, CA . . . 590

Steel Co of Canada Ltd v Willand Management Ltd [1966] SCR 746, 58 DLR (2d) 595 . . . 442

Steel v Williams . . . 954

Stepps Investments Ltd v Security Capital Corpn Ltd (1976) 73 DLR (3d) 351 . . . 301

Stern v McArthur (1988) 165 CLR 489, 81 ALR 463, 62 ALJR 588 . . . 591

Stevenson, Jaques & Co v McLean (1880) 5 QBD 346, 49 LJQB 701, 28 WR 916, 42 LT 897 . . . 222–223

Stevenson v Rogers [1999] QB 1028, [1999] 1 All ER 613, [1999] 2 WLR 1064, [1999] 02 LS Gaz R 29, [1999] NLJR 16, 143 Sol Jo LB 21, CA . . . 998

Stewart Gill Ltd v Horatio Myer & Co Ltd [1992] QB 600, [1992] 2 All ER 257, [1992] 2 WLR 721, CA . . . 1012

Stewart v Casey (Re Casey's Patents) [1892] 1 Ch 104 . . . 127–128

Stewart v Hansen 218 P 959 . . . 669

Stewart v Kennedy (1890) 15 App CAs 75, HL . . . 290

Stickney v Keeble [1915] AC 386, 84 LJ Ch 259, [1914–15] All ER Rep 73, 112 LT 664, HL . . . 575, 862

Stilk v Myrick (1809) 2 Camp 317, 6 Esp 129, 170 ER 851 . . . 110–111, 112, 113, 114, 115, 173, 845, 855, 856

Stirling v Maitland (1864) 5 B & S . . . 732

Stocker v Wedderburn 3 Kay & J 393 . . . 726

Stockloser v Johnson [1954] 1 QB 476, [1954] 1 All ER 630, [1954] 2 WLR 439, 98 . . . 704, 705

Stocznia Gdanska SA v Latvian Shipping Co and Latreefers Inc [1998] 1 All ER 883, [1998] 1 Lloyd's Rep 609, [1998] 15 LS Gaz R 33, [1998] NLJR 330, 142 Sol Jo LB 118, HL . . . 679–703

Storer v Manchester City Council [1974] 3 All ER 824, [1974] 1 WLR 1403, 73 LGR 1, 118 Sol Jo 599, CA . . . 196, 198, 241–242

Stracey v Urquhart [1930] AC 28, 99 LJPC 1, 141 LT 641, HL . . . 374

Strand Electric and Engineering Co Ltd v Brisford Entertainments Ltd [1952] 2 QB 246, [1952] 1 All ER 796, 96 Sol Jo 260, [1952] 1 TLR 939, CA . . . 635

Strathcona (Lord) Steamship Co Ltd v Dominion Coal Co Ltd [1926] AC 108, 95 LJPC 71, 16 Asp MLC 585, 31 Com Cas 80, [1925] All ER Rep 87, 134 LT 227, 42 TLR 86, PC . . . 1206

Strickland v Turner (1852) 7 Exch 208 . . . 501

Strongman (1945) Ltd v Sincock [1955] 2 QB 525, [1955] 3 All ER 90, [1955] 3 WLR 360, 99 Sol Jo 540, CA . . . 1092–1093

Stubbs v Holywell Rail Co LR 2 Exch 311 . . . 476

Sudbrook Trading Estate Ltd v Eggleton [1983] 1 AC 444, [1982] 3 All ER 1, [1982] 3 WLR 315, 44 P & CR 153, 126 Sol Jo 512, 265 Estates Gazette 215, HL . . . 268–271

Suisse Atlantique Société d'Armement Maritime SA v Rotterdamsche Kolen Centrale NV [1967] 1 AC 361, [1966] 1 Lloyd's Rep 529, 110 Sol Jo 367, HL . . . 573, 611, 969, 987, 990, 991, 992, 993, 994, 1234

Sullivan v O'Connor 363 Mass 579, 276 NE 2d 183 (1973) . . . 449

Sumpter v Hedges [1898] 1 QB 673, 67 LJQB 545, 46 WR 454, 42 Sol Jo 362, 78 LT 378, CA . . . 483, 559–560, 562, 574

Sunrise Maritime Inc v Uvisco Ltd, The Hector [1998] 2 Lloyd's Rep 287 . . . 402

Super Servant Two, The (Lauritzen (J) AS v Wijsmuller BV, The Super Servant Two Superior Overseas Development Corpn and Phillips Petroleum (UK) Co Ltd v British Gas Corpn [1982] 1 Lloyd's Rep 262, CA). *See* Lauritzen (J) AS v Wijsmuller BV, The Super

Servant Two [1989] 1 Lloyd's Rep 148; affd [1990] 1 Lloyd's Rep 1, CA

Superior Overseas Development Corpn v British Gas Corpn [1982] 1 Lloyd's Rep 261 ... 894–895

Surrey County Council v Bredero Homes Ltd [1993] 3 All ER 705, [1993] 1 WLR 1361, [1993] 1 EGLR 37, [1993] 25 EG 141, 137 Sol Jo LB 135, CA ... 633–639, 745, 746

Sutherland Shire Council v Heyman (1985) 157 CLR 424, 60 ALR 1, 59 ALJR 564, 2 Const LJ 150, HC of A ... 32, 1169

Svanosio v McNamara (1956) 96 CLR 186, 30 ALR 961, 30 ALJ 372 ... 513

Swan, The. *See* Marine Diesel Service (Grimsby) Ltd v The Swan (Owner), The Swan [1968] 1 Lloyd's Rep 5

Swinton v Whitinsville Savings Bank (1942) 42 NE 2d 808, 311 Mass ... 532

Swiss Bank Corpn v Lloyds Bank Ltd [1979] Ch 548, [1979] 2 All ER 583, [1979] 3 WLR 201, 123 Sol Jo 536; varied [1982] AC 584, [1980] 2 All ER 419, [1980] 3 WLR 457, 124 Sol Jo 741, CA; affd [1982] AC 584, [1981] 2 All ER 449, [1981] 2 WLR 893, 125 Sol Jo ... 1205, 1206

Sykes (F and G) (Wessex) Ltd v Fine Fare Ltd [1967] 1 Lloyd's Rep 53, CA ... 267, 270

Sykes v Sykes (1870) LR 5 CP 113, 39 LJCP 179, 18 WR 551, 22 LT 236 ... 1157

Syros Shipping Co SA v Elaghill Trading Co, The Proodos C [1981] 3 All ER 189, [1980] 2 Lloyd's Rep 390 ... 154–155

T

T & J Harrison v Knowles and Foster [1918] 1 KB 608, 87 LJKB 680, 14 Asp MLC 249, 23 Com Cas 282, [1918–19] All ER Rep 306, 118 LT 566, CA ... 429

T A Sundell & Sons Pty Ltd v Emm Yannoulatos (Overseas) Pty Ltd (1956) Supreme Court NSW Australia ... 906

Taddy & Co v Sterious & Co [1904] 1 Ch 354, 73 LJ Ch 191, 52 WR 152, 48 Sol Jo 117, 89 LT 628, 20 TLR 102 ... 1205

Tai Hing Cotton Mill Ltd v Liu Chong Hing Bank Ltd [1986] AC 80, [1985] 2 All ER 947, [1985] 3 WLR 317, [1985] 2 Lloyd's Rep 313, 129 Sol Jo 503, [1985] LS Gaz R 2995, [1985] NLJ Rep 680, PC ... 37, 38, 421, 423

Talbot v Staniforth ... 940

Tamplin (F A) Steamship Co v Anglo-Mexican Petroleum Products Co [1916] 2 AC 397, 85 LJKB 1389, 21 Com Cas 299, [1916–17] All Rep 104, 32 TLR 677, sub nom Re F A Tamplin Steamship Co Ltd and Anglo-Mexican Petroleum Products Co Ltd 13 Asp MLC 467, 115 LT 315, HL ... 464, 479, 527

Tamplin v James (1880) 15 Ch D 215, 20 WR 311, [1874–80] All ER Rep 560, 43 LT 520, CA ... 289–291, 291, 294

Tanner v Tanner [1975] 3 All ER 776, [1975] 1 WLR 1346, 119 Sol Jo 391, CA ... 7, 20–21, 42

Tanwar Enterprises Pty Ltd v Cauchi (2003) 217 CLR ... 591

Tate v Williamson (1866) 2 Ch App 55, LR 1 Eq 528, 15 WR 321, 15 LT 549, on appeal 2 Ch App 55, CA ... 530, 955

Tatem Ltd v Gamboa [1939] 1 KB 132, [1938] 3 All ER 135, 108 LJKB 34, 19 Asp MLC 216, 43 Com Cas 343, 82 Sol Jo 569, 160 LT 159 ... 480, 481

Taylor v Allon [1966] 1 QB 304 ... 216

Taylor v Bowers (1876) 1 QBD 291, 46 LJQB 39, 24 WR 499, [1874–80] All ER Rep 405, 34 LT 938, CA ... 1095–1096

Taylor v Brewer (1813) 1 M & S 290, 105 ER 108 ... 13

Taylor v Caldwell (1863) 27 JP 710, 3 B & S 826, 32 LJQB 164, 2 New Rep 198, 11 WR 726, 122 ER 826, [1861–73] All ER Rep 24, 8 LT 356 ... 459, 460–463, 476, 477, 478, 492, 500, 569

Taylor v Chester (1869) LR 4 QB 309, 33 JP 709, 10 B & S 237, 38 LJQB 225, [1861–73] All ER Rep 154, 21 LT 359 ... 1099, 1100

Taylor v Johnson (1983) 151 CLR 422, 45 ALR 265, 57 ALJR 197, HC of A ... 295

Taylor v Laird (1856) 1 H & N 266, 25 LJ Ex 329, 27 LTOS 221 ... 557

Taylor v Webb [1937] 2 KB 283, [1936] 2 All ER 763, 2 All ER 763, 80 Sol Jo 288, 52 TLR 339; revsd [1937] 2 KB 283, [1937] 1 All ER 590, 106 LJKB 480, 81 Sol Jo 137, 156 LT 326, 53 TLR 377, CA ... 554

Teachers Insurance and Annuity Association of America v Tribune Co 670 F Supp 491 (USDC, SDNY 1987) ... 277

Tenax Steamship Co Ltd v Reinante Transoceania Navegacion SA, The Brimnes [1975] QB 929, [1974] 3 All ER 88, [1974] 3 WLR 613, [1974] 2 Lloyd's Rep 241, 118 Sol Jo 808, CA ... 235

Thake v Maurice [1986] QB 644, [1984] 2 All ER 513, [1985] 2 WLR 215, 129 Sol Jo 86, [1985] LS Gaz R 871; revsd [1986] QB 644, [1986] 1 All ER 497, [1986] 2 WLR 337, 129 Sol Jo 894, [1986] LS Gaz R 123, [1986] NLJ Rep 92, CA ... 330, 330–331, 449

Thomas Bates & Son Ltd V Wyndham's (Lingerie) Ltd [1981] 1 All ER 1077. *See* Bates (Thomas) & Son Ltd v Wyndham's (Lingerie) Ltd [1981] 1 All ER 1077, [1981] 1 WLR 505, 41 P & CR 345, 125 Sol Jo 32, 257 Estates Gazette 381, CA

Thomas Feather & Co (Bradford) Ltd v Keighley Corpn (1953) 52 LGR 30 ... 605

Thomas v Thomas (1842) 2 QB 851, 11 LJQB 104, 2 Gal & Dav 226, 6 Jur 645 ... 97, 98, 123

Thomas Witter Ltd v TBP Industries [1996] 2 All ER 573, 12 TR LR 145 ... 369

Thompson (W L) Ltd v Robinson (Gunmakers) Ltd [1955] Ch 177, [1955] 1 All ER 154, [1955] 2 WLR 185, 99 Sol Jo 76 ... 666–668, 669

Thompson v London, Midland and Scottish Rly Co [1930] 1 KB 41, 98 LJKB 615, [1929] All ER Rep 474, 141 LT 382, CA ... 335

Thoresen Car Ferries Ltd v Weymouth Portland Borough Council [1977] 2 Lloyd's Rep 614 ... 204–208

Thorley (Joseph) Ltd v Orchis Steamship Co Ltd [1907] 1 KB 660, 76 LJKB 595, 10 Asp MLC 431, 12 Com Cas 251, 51 Sol Jo 289, 96 LT 488, 23 TLR 338, CA ... 987

Thorne v Motor Association [1937] AC 797 ... 912

Thornett v Haines 15 M & W 367 ... 203

Thornton v Shoe Lane Parking Ltd [1971] 2 QB 163, [1971] 1 All ER 686, [1971] 2 WLR 585, [1971] RTR 79, [1971] 1 Lloyd's Rep 289, 115 Sol Jo 75, CA . . . 335, 336, 337, 339

Tilden Rent-a-Car Co v Clendenning (1978) 83 DLR (3d) 400, 18 OR (2d) 601 . . . 347

Timothy v Simpson (1834) 6 C & P 499 . . . 201

Tinline v White Cross Insurance Association Ltd [1921] 3 KB 327, 90 LJKB 1118, 26 Com Cas 347, 125 LT 632, 37 TLR 733 . . . 1090

Tinsley v Milligan [1994] 1 AC 340, [1993] 3 All ER 65, [1993] 3 WLR 126, [1994] 2 FCR 65, [1993] 2 FLR 963, HL . . . 1102–1104

Tito v Waddell (No 2) [1977] Ch 106, [1977] 3 All ER 129, [1977] 2 WLR 496 Sol Jo 10 . . . 637, 679–682, 685, 686, 1208

Tomlinson (A) (Hauliers) Ltd v Hepburn [1966] 1 QB 21, [1965] 1 All ER 284, [1965] 2 WLR 634, [1965] 1 Lloyd's Rep 1, 109 Sol Jo 10, CA; on appeal sub nom Hepburn v A Tomlinson (Hauliers) Ltd [1966] AC 451, [1966] 1 All ER 418, [1966] 2 WLR 453, [1966] 1 Lloyd's Rep 309, 110 Sol Jo 86, HL . . . 1144, 1151

Tool Metal Manufacturing Co Ltd v Tungsten Electric Co Ltd [1955] 2 All ER 657, [1955] 1 WLR 761, 72 RPC 209, 99 Sol Jo 470, HL . . . 865, 866, 868, 869

Torkomian v Russell (1916) 90 Conn 481, 97 Atl 760 . . . 669

Total Gas Marketing Ltd v Arco British Ltd [1998] 2 Lloyd's Rep 209, HL . . . 602

Total Liban SA v Vitol Energy SA [2000] 1 All ER 267, [2000] 3 WLR 1142, [1999] 2 Lloyd's Rep 700, [1999] 2 All ER (Comm) 65 . . . 665

Total Oil Great Britain Ltd v Thompson Garages (Biggin Hill) Ltd [1972] 1 QB 318, [1971] 3 All ER 1226, [1971] 3 WLR 979, 115 Sol Jo 848, 220 Estates Gazette 1591, CA . . . 554

Toteff v Antonas (1952) 87 CLR 647 . . . 374

Trans Trust SPRL v Danubian Trading Co Ltd [1952] 2 QB 297, [1952] 1 All ER 970, [1952] 1 Lloyd's Rep 348, 96 Sol Jo 312, [1952] 1 TLR 1066, CA . . . 551–553, 573, 671, 672

Transag Haulage Ltd v Leyland DAF Finance plc [1994] 2 BCLC 88, [1994] BCC 356, [1994] CCLR 111 . . . 592

Tremills v Benton (1892) 18 VLR 607 . . . 947

Trentham (G Percy) Ltd v Archital Luxfer Ltd [1993] 1 Lloyd's Rep 25, 63 BLR 44, [1992] BLM (December) 5, CA . . . 230, 266

Treseder-Griffin v Co-operative Insurance Society [1956] 2 QB 127 . . . 522

Tribe v Tribe [1996] Ch 107, [1995] 4 All ER 236, [1995] 3 WLR 913, 71 P & CR 503, [1996] 1 FCR 338, [1995] 2 FLR 966, [1996] Fam Law 29, [1995] 32 LS Gaz R 30, [1995] NLJR 1445, 139 Sol Jo LB 203, CA . . . 1103

Trident Center v Connecticut General Life Insurance Co 847 F 2d 564 (US CA 9th Cir 1988) . . . 403

Trident General Insurance Co Ltd v McNiece Bros Pty Ltd (1988) 165 CLR 107, 80 ALR 574, 62 ALJR 508, HC of A . . . 1180

Trollope (George) & Sons v Martyn Bros [1934] 2 KB 436 . . . 219

Trollope & Colls Ltd and Holland & Hannen and Cubitts Ltd (t/a Nuclear Civil Constructors (a firm)) v Atomic Power Constructions Ltd [1962] 3 All ER 1035, [1963] 1 WLR 333, 107 Sol Jo 254 . . . 226, 227, 281

Trollope & Colls Ltd v North West Metropolitan Regional Hospital Board [1973] 2 All ER 260, [1973] 1 WLR 601, 117 Sol Jo 355, 9 BLR 60, HL . . . 419

Tsakiroglou & Co Ltd v Noblee Thorl GmbH [1962] AC 93, [1961] 2 All ER 179, [1961] 2 WLR 633, [1961] 1 Lloyd's Rep 329, 105 Sol Jo 346, HL . . . 473, 480

TSB Bank plc v Camfield [1995] 1 All ER 951 . . . 368

Tudor Grange Holdings Ltd v Citibank NA [1992] Ch 53, [1991] 4 All ER 1, [1991] 3 WLR 750, [1991] BCLC 1009 . . . 850, 1032

Tufton v Sperni (1952) 2 TLR 516 . . . 955

Tulk v Moxhay (1848) 2 Ph 774, 18 LJ Ch 83, 1 H & Tw 105, 13 Jur 89, [1843–60] All ER Rep 9, 13 LTOS 21 . . . 1204, 1206

Turnbull & Co v Duval [1902] AC 429, 71 LJPC 84, 87 LT 154, 18 TLR 521, [1900–3] All ER Rep Ext 1229 . . . 923, 925, 926

Turner v Green [1895] 2 Ch 205, 64 LJ Ch 539, 43 WR 537, 39 Sol Jo 484, 72 LT 763 . . . 362

Turriff Construction Ltd v Regalia Knitting Mills Ltd (1971) 9 BLR 20, 222 Estates Gazette 169 . . . 40, 41

Tweedle v Atkinson (1861) 25 JP 517, 1 B & S 393, 30 LJQB 265, 8 Jur NS 332, 9 WR 781, [1861–73] All Rep 369, 4 LT 468 . . . 113, 1138, 1155

21st century Logistic Solutions Ltd v Madysen Ltd [2004] 2 Lloyds Rep 92 . . . 1097

U

Ultramares Corpn v Touche 255 NY 170 (1931), SC . . . 30

Union Eagle Ltd v Golden Achievement Ltd [1997] AC 514, [1997] 2 All ER 215, [1997] 2 WLR 341, 141 Sol Jo LB 56, PC . . . 590–592, 703

United Bank of Kuwait plc v Prudential Property Services Ltd [1996] 3 All ER 365, [1996] 3 WLR 87, [1996] 32 LS Gaz R 33, [1996] 27 EG 125, 140 Sol Jo LB 156, HL . . . 424

United City Merchants (Investments) Ltd and Glass Fibres and Equipments Ltd v Royal Bank of Canada, Vitrorefuerzos SA and Banco Continental SA (incorporated in Canada) [1983] 1 AC 168, [1982] 2 All ER 720, [1982] 2 WLR 1039, [1982] 2 Lloyd's Rep 1, [1982] Com LR 142, 126 Sol Jo 379, HL . . . 122

United Dominions Corpn (Jamaica) Ltd v Shoucair [1969] 1 AC 340, [1968] 2 All ER 904, [1968] 3 WLR 893, 112 Sol Jo 482, 12 WIR 510, PC . . . 851

United Dominions Trust (Commercial) Ltd v Eagle Aircraft Services Ltd [1968] 1 All ER 104, [1968] 1 WLR 74, 111 Sol Jo 849, CA . . . 581

United Dominions Trust (Commercial) v Ennis [1968] 1 QB 54 . . . 609

United Dominions Trust Ltd v Western [1976] QB 513, [1975] 3 All ER 1017, [1976] 2 WLR 64, 119 Sol Jo 792, CA . . . 319

United Scientific Holdings Ltd v Burnley Borough Council [1978] AC 904, [1977] 2 All ER 62, [1977] 2 WLR 407, 75 LGR 407, 33 P & CR 220, 121 Sol Jo 223, 243 Estates Gazette 43, HL . . . 575, 576, 578

Universal Cargo Carriers Corpn v Citati [1957] 2 QB 401, [1957] 2 All ER 70, [1957] 2 WLR 713, [1957] 1 Lloyd's Rep 174, 101 Sol Jo 320; affd [1957] 3 All ER 234, [1957] 1 WLR 979, [1957] 2 Lloyd's Rep 191, 101 Sol Jo 762, CA . . . 569, 574, 575, 583

Universal Corpn v Five Ways Properties Ltd [1979] 1 All ER 552, 38 P & CR 687, 123 Sol Jo 33, 250 Estates Gazette 447, CA . . . 703

Universal Steam Navigation Company Ltd v James McKelvie & Co [1923] AC 492 . . . 1127

Universe Tankships Inc of Monrovia v International Transport Workers Federation, The Universe Sentinel [1983] 1 AC 366, [1982] 2 All ER 67, [1982] 2 WLR 803, [1982] 1 Lloyd's Rep 537, [1982] ICR 262, [1982] IRLR 200, 126 Sol Jo 275, HL . . . 913

Upton-on-Severn RDC v Powell [1942] 1 All ER 220, CA . . . 22

Urquhart, Lindsay & Co Ltd v Eastern Bank Ltd [1922] 1 KB 318, 91 LJKB 274, 27 Com Cas 124, [1921] All ER Rep 340, 126 LT 534 . . . 122

V

Vancouver Malt and Sake Brewing Co Ltd v Vancouver Breweries Ltd [1934] AC 181, 103 LJPC 58, [1934] All ER Rep 38, 78 Sol Jo 173, 150 LT 503, 50 TLR 253 . . . 1107

Vardasz v Pioneer Concrete (SA) Pty Ltd (1995) 184 CLR 102 . . . 368

Venezuela, The [1980] 1 Lloyd's Rep 393 . . . 402

Vic Mill, Re . . . 666

Victoria Laundry (Windsor) Ltd v Newman Industries Ltd [1949] 2 KB 528, [1949] 1 All ER 997, 93 Sol Jo 371, 65 TLR 274, CA . . . 626, 644, 650

Vine v National Dock Labour Board [1957] AC 488, [1956] 3 All ER 939, [1957] WWLR 106, [1956] 2 Lloyd's Rep 567 . . . 712

Vitol SA v Norelf Ltd, The Santa Clara [1994] 4 All ER 109, [1994] 1 WLR 1390, [1993] 2 Lloyd's Rep 301, [1993] 30 LS Gaz R 36, 137 Sol Jo LB 146; revsd [1996] QB 108, [1995] 3 All ER 971, [1995] 3 WLR 549, [1995] 2 Lloyd's Rep 128, CA; revsd [1996] AC 800, [1996] 3 All ER 193, [1996] 3 WLR 105, [1996] 2 Lloyd's Rep 225, [1996] 26 LS Gaz R 19, [1996] NLJR 957, HL . . . 583, 848

Vlassopulos (N & J) Ltd v Ney Shipping Ltd, The Santa Carina [1977] 1 Lloyd's Rep 478, 121 Sol Jo 10, CA . . . 1128

W

W J Alan & Co v El Nasr Export and Import Co . . . 554

Waddell v Blockey (1879) 4 QBC 678, 48 LJQB 517, 27 WR 931, 41 LT 458, CA . . . 383

Wade v Simeon (1846) 2 CB 548, 135 ER 1061, Court of Common Pleas; 3 Dow & L 587, 15 LJCP 114, 10 Jur 412, 6 LTOS 346 . . . 102–103

Wadsworth v Lydall [1981] 2 All ER 401, [1981] 1 WLR 598, 125 Sol Jo 309, CA . . . 672

Wagon Mound, The. *See* Overseas Tankship (UK) Ltd v Morts Dock and Engineering Co Ltd, The Wagon Mound

Wakefield v Newborn (1844) 6 QB 276 . . . 905

Walford v Miles [1992] 1 All ER 453, HL . . . 10, 271–278, 286, 636

Walker v Boyle [1982] 1 All ER 634, [1982] 1 WLR 495, 44 P & CR 20, 125 Sol Jo 724, [1982] LS Gaz R 954, 261 Estates Gazette 1090 . . . 1023

Wall v Standard Telephones and Cables plc [1990] ICR 291, [1990] IRLR 55 . . . 343

Wallington v Townsend [1939] Ch 588, [1939] 2 All ER 225, 108 LJ Ch 305, 83 Sol Jo 297, 160 LT 537, 55 TLR 531 . . . 635

Wallis, Son and Wells v Pratt and Haynes [1910] 2 KB 1003, 79 LJKB 1013, 103 LT 118, 26 TLR 572, CA; on appeal [1911] AC 394, 80 LJKB 1058, [1911–13] All ER Rep 989, 55 Sol Jo 496, 105 LT 146, 27 TLR 431, HL . . . 309–312, 345, 366, 564

Wallis v Smith (2001) NMCA 17 22 P 3d 682 130 NM 214 . . . 690

Walton Stores (Interstate) Ltd v Maher (1988) 164 CLR 387, 76 ALR 513, 62 ALJR 110, HC of A . . . 158, 163, 170, 282, 283, 422, 800, 801, 802, 811

Walton v Waterhouse (1672) KB 2 Wms Saunders , 421a 6th Edition . . . 460

Ward v Byham [1956] 2 All ER 318, [1956] 1 WLR 496, 100 Sol Jo 341, CA . . . 107, 112

Warlow v Harrison (1859) 1 E & E 309, 29 LJQB 14, 6 Jur NS 66, 8 WR 95, 120 ER 925, [1843–60] All ER Rep 620, 1 LT 211, Ex Ch . . . 147, 203–204

Warner Bros Pictures Inc v Nelson [1937] 1 KB 209, [1936] 3 All ER 160, 106 LJKB 97, 80 Sol Jo 855, 155 LT 538, 53 TLR 14 . . . 729–732

Wathes (Western) Ltd v Austins (Menswear) Ltd [1976] 1 Lloyd's Rep 14, 119 Sol Jo 527, 9 BLR 113, CA . . . 990, 994

Watkin v Watson-Smith [1986] CLY 424, *Times*, 3 July . . . 942

Watteau v Fenwick [1893] 1 QB 346, 56 JP 839, 5 R 143, 41 WR 222, [1891–4] All ER Rep 897, 37 Sol Jo 117, 67 LT 831, 9 TLR 133 . . . 1134–1135, 1200

Watts v Morrow [1991] 4 All ER 937, [1991] 1 WLR 1421, 23 HLR 608, [1991] 2 EGLR 152, [1992] 1 LS Gaz R 33, 54 BLR 86, [1991] 43 EG 121, CA . . . 676

Waugh v HB Clifford & Sons Ltd [1982] Ch 374, [1982] 1 All ER 1095, [1982] 2 WLR 679, 126 Sol Jo 66, CA . . . 1129–1130

Way v Latilla [1937] 3 All ER 759, 81 Sol Jo 786, HL . . . 490

Weatherby v Banham (1832) 5 C & P 228 . . . 209–210

Weaver v American Oil Co 276 NE 2d 144 (1972) . . . 1027

Webb v McGowin 168 So 196, 27 Ala App 82 (1935) . . . 141, 142, 143, 187

Webster v Cecil (1861) 30 Beav 62 . . . 290, 291

Wells (Merstham) Ltd v Buckland Sand and Silica Ltd [1965] 2 QB 170, [1964] 1 All ER 41, [1964] 2 WLR 453, 108 Sol Jo 177 . . . 19, 20, 147

Wennall v Adney (1802) 3 B & P 247 . . . 141

Wentworth v Cock 10 Adol & E 42, 2 Peny & D 251, 3 Williams, Exrs (7th Edn 1723–25) . . . 461

Wertheim v Chicoutimi Pulp Co [1911] AC 301 . . . 663–664, 665, 666

West Sussex Properties Ltd v Chichester District Council (28 June 2000, unreported) . . . 517, 519

Westdeutsche Landesbank Girozentrale v Islington London Borough Council [1994] 4 All ER 890, 91 LGR 323; varied [1994] 4 All ER 890, [1994] 1 WLR 938, [1994] 8 LS Gaz R 38, 138 Sol Jo LB 26, CA; revsed [1996] AC 669, [1996] 2 All ER 961, [1996] 2 WLR 802, 95 LGR 1, [1996] NLJR 877, 140 Sol Jo LB 136, HL . . . 507–508, 509

Western Fish Products Ltd v Penwith District Council [1981] 2 All ER 204, 77 LGR 185, 38 P & CR 7, 122 Sol Jo 471, [1978] JPL 623, CA . . . 164

Western Steamship Co Ltd v NV Koninklijke Rotterdamsche Lloyd, The Empire Jamaica [1955] P 259, [1955] 3 All ER 60, [1955] 3 WLR 385, [1955] 2 Lloyd's Rep 109, 99 Sol Jo 561, CA; affd sub nom Koninklijke Rotterdamsche Lloyd (NV) v Western Steamship Co Ltd, The Empire Jamaica [1957] AC 386, [1956] 3 All ER 144, [1956] 3 WLR 598, [1956] 3 WLR 598, [1956] 2 Lloyd's Rep 119, 100 Sol Jo 618, HL . . . 384

Westminster (Duke) v Swinton [1948] 1 KB 524, [1948] 1 All ER 248, 92 Sol Jo 97 . . . 681

Wetherell v Jones (1832) 3 B & D 221 . . . 1080

Wheeler v White 398 SW 2d 93 (1966) . . . 282

Whincup v Hughes (1871) LR 6 CP 78, 40 LJCP 104, 19 WR 439, 24 LT 76 . . . 483, 742–743

White and Carter (Councils) Ltd v McGregor [1962] AC 413, [1961] 3 All ER 1178, [1962] 2 WLR 17, 105 Sol Jo 1104, 1962 SC (HL) 1, 1962 SLT 9, HL . . . 246, 734–738, 739

White v Bluett (1853) 23 LJ Ex 36, 2 WR 75, 2 CLR 301, 22 LTOS 123 . . . 100, 101–102

White v John Warrick & Co Ltd [1953] 2 All ER 1021, [1953] 1 WLR 1285, 97 Sol Jo 740, CA . . . 977

Whittington v Seale-Hayne (1900) 44 Sol 229, 82 LT 49, 16 TLR 181 . . . 370

Whitwood Chemical Co v Hardman [1891] 2 Ch 416, 60 LJ Ch 428, 39 WR 433, 64 LT 716, 7 TLR 325, CA . . . 732

Wickham, Re . . . 151

Wickman Machine Tool Sales. *See* Schuler (L) AG v Wickman Machine Tool Sales Ltd [1974] AC 235, [1973] 2 All ER 39, [1973] 2 WLR 683, [1973] 2 Lloyd's Rep 53, 117 Sol Jo 340, HL

Wigan v English and Scottish Law Life Assurance Assocn . . . 153

Wigsell v School for Indigent Blind (1882) 8 QB 357 . . . 679–680

Wild v Tucker [1914] 3 KB 36, 83 LJKB 1410, 21 Mans 181, 111 Lt 250, 30 TLR 507 . . . 140

Wilde v Gibson (1848) 1 HL Cas 605, 12 Jur 527, [1843–60] All ER Rep 494 . . . 368

Wilkie v London Passenger Transport Board [1947] 1 All ER 258 . . . 1175, 1176

William Lacey (Hounslow) Ltd v Davis [1957] 2 All ER 712, [1957] 1 WLR 932, 101 Sol Jo 629 . . . 41, 281

William Porter & Co Ltd, Re [1937] 2 All ER 361 . . . 151

William Robinson & Co Ltd v Heuer [1989] 2 Ch 451 . . . 730, 730

William Sindall plc v Cambridgeshire County Council [1994] 3 All ER 932, [1994] 1 WLR 1016, 92 LGR

121, [1993] NPC 82, CA . . . 381–384, 527

William Whiteley Ltd v The King . . . 1095

Williams Bros v E T Agius Ltd [1914] AC 510, 83 LJKB 715, 19 Com Cas 200, [1914–15] All ER Rep 97, 58 Sol Jo 377, 110 LT 865, 30 TLR 351, HL . . . 664, 665, 1147

Williams v Bayley (1866) LR 1 HL 200, 30 JP 500, 35 LJ Ch 717, 12 Jur NS 875, [1861–73] All ER Rep 227, 14 LT 802 . . . 917, 955

Williams v Carwardine (1833) 4 B & Ad 621, 5 C & P 566, 2 LJKB 101, 1 Nev & MKB 418 . . . 15, 216

Williams v Reynolds . . . 662

Williams v Roffey Bros & Nicholls (Contractors) Ltd [1991] 1 QB 1, [1990] 1 All ER 512, [1990] 2 WLR 1153, [1990] 12 LS Gaz R 36, [1989] NLJR 1712, 48 BLR 75, CA . . . 111–115, 152, 173, 256, 856, 865

Williams v Walker-Thomas Furniture Co 121 US App DC 315, 350 F 2d 445 (DC Circ 1965) . . . 814, 1026

Williams v Williams [1957] 1 All ER 305, [1957] 1 WLR 148, 121 JP 93, 101 Sol Jo 108, CA . . . 105–107, 112

Willson v Love [1896] 1 QB 626, 65 LJQB 474, 44 WR 450, [1895–9] All ER Rep 325, 74 LT 580, CA . . . 691

Wilsher v Essex Area Health Authority [1988] AC 1074, [1988] 1 All ER 871, [1988] 2 WLR 557, 132 Sol Jo 418, [1988] 15 LS Gaz R 37, [1988] NLJR 78, HL . . . 671

Wilson (Paal) & Co A/S v Partenreederei Hannah Blumenthal, The Hannah Blumenthal [1983] 1 AC 854, [1983] 1 All ER 34, [1982] 3 WLR 1149, [1983] 1 Lloyd's Rep 103, 126 Sol Jo 835, HL. *See* Hannah Blumenthal, The (Wilson (Paal) & Co A/S v Partenreederi Hannah Blumenthal, The Hannah Blumenthal)

Wilson v Darling Island Stevedoring and Lighterage Co Ltd [1956] 1 Lloyd's Rep 346, 95 CLR 43 . . . 1157, 1201

Wilson v First County Trust [2003] UKHL 40 [2003] 4 All ER 97 . . . 1065

Wilson v Tumman (1843) 6 Man & G, 236 . . . 1134

Wilson v West Hartlepool Railway Co (1865) 2 De GJ & Sm 475, 5 New Rep 289, 34 LJ Ch 241, 11 LT 692, 11 Jur NS 124, 46 ER 459, 44 Digest . . . 725

Wilson v Wilson . . . 726

Winnipeg Condominium Corpn No 36 v Bird Construction Co Ltd (1995) 50 Con LR 124, 74 BLR 5, [1995] 1 SCR 85, [1995] 3 WWR 85, 23 CCLT (2d) 1, 121 DLR (4th) 193, 18 CLR (2d) 1, Can SC . . . 36

Wisconsin Knife Works v National Metal Crafters (1986) 781 F 2d 1280 (USCA 7th Circ, 1986) . . . 878

Wiseman v Beake . . . 940

With v O'Flanagan [1936] Ch 575, [1936] 1 All ER 727, 105 LJ Ch 247, 80 Sol Jo 285, 154 LT 634, CA . . . 362–363

Withers v General Theatre Corpn Ltd [1933] 2 KB 536, 102 LJKB 719, [1933] All ER Rep 385, 149 LT 487, CA . . . 677, 678

Witter (Thomas) Ltd v TBP Industries Ltd [1996] 2 All ER 573, 12 TR LR 145 . . . 369

Wolverhampton and Walsall Railway Co v London and North-Western Railway Co . . . 732

Wolverhampton Corpn v Emmons [1901] 1 KB 515, 70 LJKB 429, 49 WR 553, 45 Sol Jo 256, 84 LT 407, 17 TLR 234, CA ... 727

Wood v Lucy, Lady Duff Gordon 222 NY 88 (NY Ct of Apps 1917) ... 119–121, 220

Wood v Scarth (1855) 2 K & J 33, 1 Jur NS 1107, 4 WR 31, 26 LTOS 87; (1858) 1 F & F 293 ... 290

Woodar Investment Development Ltd v Wimpey Construction UK Ltd [1980] 1 All ER 571, [1980] 1 WLR 277, 124 Sol Jo 184, HL ... 585–586, 1143, 1144, 1147, 1179

Woodhouse AC Israel Cocoa Ltd SA v Nigerian Produce Marketing Co Ltd [1972] AC 741, [1972] 2 All ER 271, [1972] 2 WLR 1090, [1972] 1 Lloyd's Rep 439, 116 Sol Jo 392, HL ... 111, 114, 869, 873

Woodman v Photo Trade Processing Ltd (7 May 1981, unreported) cited in (1981) 131 NLJ 935 ... 1024

Woolcock Street Investments Pty Ltd v CDG Pty Ltd (2004) 205 ALR 522 ... 36

Workers Trust and Merchant Bank Ltd v Dojap Investments Ltd [1993] AC 573, [1993] 2 All ER 370, [1993] 2 WLR 702, 66 P & CR 15, [1993] 1 EGLR 203, [1993] 14 LS Gaz R 44, [1993] NLJR 616, 137 Sol Jo LB 83, PC ... 703–705

Wright v Carter [1903] 1 Ch 27, 72 LJ 138, 51 WR 196, [1900–3] All Rep Rep 706, 87 LT 624, 19 TLR 29, CA ... 923

Wroth v Tyler [1974] Ch 30, [1973] 1 All ER 897, [1973] 2 WLR 405, 25 P & CR 138, 117 Sol Jo 90 ... 673

Wrotham Park Estate Co v Parkside Homes Ltd [1974] 2 All ER 321, [1974] 1 WLR 798, 27 P & CR 296, 118 Sol Jo 420, 229 Estates Gazette 617 ... 634, 636, 637, 638, 681, 687, 753

Y

Yates (1973) 36 MLR 535 ... 673

Yerkey v Jones (1939) 63 CLR 649 ... 926, 931

Yonge v Toynbee [1910] 1 KB 215, 79 LJKB 208, [1908–10] All ER Rep 204, 102 LT 57, 26 TLR 211, CA ... 1130–1132

Young & Marten Ltd v McManus Childs Ltd [1969] 1 AC 454, [1968] 2 All ER 1169, [1968] 3 WLR 630, 67 LGR 1, 112 Sol Jo 744, 9 BLR 77, 207 Estates Gazette 797, HL ... 440–442, 449

Young v Canadian Northern Rly Co [1931] AC 83, 100 LJPC 51, 144 LT 255, PC ... 344

Yuen Kun Yeu v Attorney General of Hong Kong [1988] AC 175, [1987] 2 All ER 705, [1987] 3 WLR 776, 131 Sol Jo 1185, [1987] LS Gaz R 2049, [1987] NLJ Rep 566, PC ... 32, 1169

Z

Zamet v Hyman [1961] 3 All ER 933, [1961] 1 WLR 1442 ... 930

Zanzibar v British Aerospace (Lancaster House) Ltrd [2000] 1 WLR 2333 ... 369

Zinnia, The. *See* Stag Line Ltd v Tyne Shiprepair Group Ltd, The Zinnia [1984] 2 Lloyd's Rep 211

SECTION ONE

INTRODUCTION

CHAPTER ONE

CONTRACTS AND CONTRACT LAW

I. THE SCOPE OF CONTRACT LAW

What is contract law? What is it for? Both questions are of fundamental importance, but it is surprisingly difficult to give a definitive answer to either. Contract law is most obviously the law relating to agreements or promises. As we shall see, it is primarily concerned with agreements that involve one party, or each party, giving an undertaking or promise to the other. It governs such questions as which agreements the law will enforce, what obligations are imposed by the agreement in question and what remedies are available if the obligations are not performed. Thus one answer to the first question might be that contract law is the law based on liability for breach of promise. When a lawyer says that on a particular set of facts contractual liability will arise, she usually means liability in this sense, predicated upon a promise that has been broken. In the next chapter, we will explore the main characteristics of contractual liability and compare it with liability in tort and in restitution. However, 'contract law' is also used to mean the whole collection of rules which apply to contracts, and these include many rules that are not 'contractual' in the sense of being based on a promise to do something. For example, if one party induces the other to enter a contract by fraud or misrepresentation, the innocent party may be able to claim compensation based largely not on contract but on tort or statute. Despite the conceptual differences, the rules on misrepresentation as between contracting parties are 'part of' contract law. There is no precise consensus among lawyers as to just which rules fall into this wider category: for instance, in the next chapter, we will look at some cases that involve tortious not contractual liability, but which are concerned with a series of contracts. The rules stated in these cases are part of the law of tort, but to the extent that they apply in the context of contracts, it can be argued that they are also part of the law of contract in the wider sense.

We shall see that there is even some controversy over the exact scope of contractual liability in the narrow sense. The traditional view is that it is predicated upon breach of a promise that formed part of an agreed exchange between the parties, and that unless there was to be some exchange there cannot be contractual liability. Some commentators now argue that there may also be contractual liability when there was simply a promise by one party to another with nothing in exchange but the other party has relied on the promise in some way. We will explore the extent to which English contract law recognises such 'reliance' liability in Section 2. For the moment, it is enough to think of contractual liability as based on promises forming part of agreed exchanges, but to note that sometimes there is only a rather attenuated form of exchange.

While contract law is primarily concerned with supporting the social institution of exchange, the law is not as broad as the institution. An enormous proportion of our life is carried on on the basis of exchanges that are in some sense agreements, but many of them are not governed by what is usually thought of as contract law. Some are not governed by law at all, such as domestic arrangements over household chores made by spouses or flatmates. Others are so complex that although they are to some extent still governed by contract law, the latter only plays a fairly small part in a scheme governed also by other common law principles and heavily dependent on special rules developed for the particular transactions. These have come to be viewed as legal subjects in their own right. Company law is an example, and to a lesser extent the law of employment.

Even in these cases it would be a mistake to think of contract law as irrelevant. There is no such thing as a contract in the abstract. Every contract is made, or is found by the court to exist, in a particular context—a contract to sell goods to a consumer, a contract to charter the services of a ship, a contract to look after an elderly relative in exchange for a share in his property when he dies: the possibilities are almost endless. Sometimes few other legal rules are relevant. On these occasions, the obligations of the parties fall to be determined almost entirely by purely contractual principles. At other times, there are many other rules, yet contract may still be in the background providing the framework for the transaction and the general principles on which the court or contract drafter can rely.

In this book, we will be studying mainly the general rules of contract, but we will not ignore the special rules governing particular types of contract. There are a number of reasons for this. First, the rules that distinguish between different types of contract are now appearing in areas which previously have been thought of as part of 'general' contract law: eg the Sale and Supply of Goods Act 1994 provides for different remedies for consumers and non-consumers in sales and supply of goods contracts. Second, many of the important legislative developments are dealing with particular contracts, notably the Regulations implementing the EC Directive on Unfair Terms in Consumer Contracts. It is rather early to say what impact this may have on non-consumer contracts: it may be, for example, that the concept of 'good faith' used in the Regulations will come to be applied in other areas. Whether this happens or not, the Regulations have a significant impact on the overall shape and character of English contract law. Third, the needs and difficulties that led to the development of special rules governing particular types of contract can tell us a good deal about the value of the general rules.

We also have to remember that the courts always have to apply even the general rules in the context of the particular contract. Sometimes there is nothing particularly difficult in the context and the general rule is applied straightforwardly. At other times, we shall see that the need to fit the rules to the contexts seems to produce some rather odd results. But usually the courts keep the general rules fairly abstract and then apply these rules rather differently in the various contexts with which they are confronted. We shall see countless examples.

Professor Ian Macneil has suggested a distinction that has excited a good deal of academic interest in the last few years. This is between 'discrete' and 'relational' exchanges. Many simple exchanges are to be completed within a short timescale. What each party is to do can easily be agreed and the exchange will not involve the parties in any longer term relationship to each other, nor involve anyone else. The casual purchase of fruit from a roadside stall is a simple example. Such exchanges can be treated in isolation from any other and there is little relevant background to consider (hence 'discrete'). Other exchanges may be much more complex. Firstly, the parties may expect to be cooperating with each other over a long enough period that it is hard for them to decide at the outset exactly what each of them is to do; they will have to adjust their relationship as it progresses. An employment contract is an example. Secondly, the contract may be made against a background of understandings and expectations that have arisen either through previous dealings between the same parties or through more general custom and habit in the industrial or social context concerned. Thirdly, other people may be involved in the project—for instance, in a large construction project or a distribution chain. The parties may try to deal with these complexities in various ways: for instance, they may enter flexible long-term contracts, perhaps with several parties, or they may make a series of short-term contracts. In either event, the law may have to treat this 'relational' contracting differently, for instance by providing mechanisms for allowing flexibility or by recognising that the short-term contracts need to be considered in the context of the understandings and expectations engendered by the longer term relationship or the background from which they sprang. Whether the modern law of contract caters adequately for relational contracting is an open question that will be explored later (see especially Chapters 29 and 33).

There are so many different contracts and within the area of 'contract law' there are, in fact, so many special rules, both statutory and common law, governing particular contracts that many commentators prefer to speak of a law of *contracts*. One went so far as to describe the idea of a unitary law as the artificial construct of law teachers in the latter part of the nineteenth century (Gilmore, *The Death of Contract*). Whatever the origin of the unitary theory, it seems to have many judges among its adherents (eg, p 571), and although this might be because they have never escaped the baleful influence of their contract(s) teachers, a more plausible hypothesis is that the unitary approach has its uses. If, for instance, the court faces a set of facts for which there is no authority relating to the particular type of contract, it is obviously helpful to be able to fall back on general principles developed in relation to other types of contract. On the other hand, it has to be admitted that sometimes the unitary theory hinders the development of a solution that would be particularly appropriate to one type of contract but which would be inappropriate for the majority of contract types. The fact that there seem to be more rules applying to single contract types derived from eighteenth-century cases (see, eg, p 925) than from modern ones lends some support to Gilmore's thesis. But for the moment it is not necessary to decide on the merits of the singular versus the plural, if indeed there is any one answer; it is sufficient to bear in mind that there are many different contract types and that some do have idiosyncratic rules.

Thus the core of this book is an analysis of the law relating to promises and agreements. The book does not, however, stop there. Firstly, to get a proper picture of what contract law is, it is necessary to see it in the context of other legal rules that are not so closely related as to be thought of as 'part of' the subject. In particular, it is important to compare liability in contract with liability in tort and in restitution, to see how the rules interconnect and how the concepts differ. The materials in the second chapter of this Introduction are chosen for this purpose.

II. THE FUNCTION OF CONTRACT LAW

The book also attempts to answer the second question: what is contract law for? No study of an area of law will be complete without an attempt to analyse the rules in terms of their function: we need to answer such questions as what is the purpose of this rule, does it achieve the desired effect, and might the effect be reached more easily by other means? This type of analysis is much less well developed than the traditional legal one, but it is equally important.

So what is contract law for? By the end of the book, it will become very clear that there is no one answer, because contract law has many 'purposes', but the central one is to support and to control the millions of agreements that collectively make up the 'market economy'.

We live in a 'mixed' economy, one in which the allocation of resources is determined partly by administrative decisions of public officials and partly through the private sector. For instance, for the majority of the population, the provision of education is largely undertaken and controlled by the State, and the division of the myriad tasks involved is a matter of administrative decision; whereas the provision of food is left to private enterprise, to the many individuals and companies who are primarily motivated by the quest for profit. Of course, neither scheme is purely public or private: the education authorities operate through contracts with their suppliers, their employees and quite possibly between different organs of the authorities, while the food market is heavily influenced by subsidies, taxes and regulations. But the mainspring of each system is different, and so is the legal regime. If a person wishes to complain about a failure in the provision of education, any legal remedy will usually be in administrative or perhaps criminal law, whereas failure to provide food will normally give rise to remedies only if a breach of contract is involved.

In order to have a stable capitalist or mixed economy, the law must guarantee the freedom of individuals and the protection of property: real, personal and intellectual. These laws form the link between persons and resources, including labour. The private enterprise system depends, however, on the exchange of resources. Some exchanges can take place simultaneously without any promises being involved, so that one can say simply that resource x, which was A's, is now the property of B; unless A has given some additional undertaking, such as that x is of a particular quality or will last a certain length of time, contract law has nothing to say about such a trade. But for the most part the process of exchange involves a period of time, and the extension of credit by one party to the other—maybe credit in the normal sense of having to wait to be paid, maybe credit in the sense of having to trust that the other will do as he promised or that some assurance he gave about the goods will turn out to be true. It is here that contract law comes in. For instance, the law will support the exchange by enforcing what the parties agreed if one party defaults; it provides a set of rules that apply when something goes wrong and the agreement is silent as to what is to happen. This simultaneously provides a mechanism for deciding existing disputes and provides a set of 'standard terms' for each type of contract, so saving parties contracting in the future the need to negotiate a complete set of terms for themselves.

Contract law operates most obviously in the context of dispute resolution in the courtroom. But it will be apparent that contract law also has an importance outside the courtroom: by empowering the parties to make an agreement that the law will then enforce, it enables them to make exchanges that might otherwise carry too great a risk, whether of disruption by some contingency or of default by the other party. They can arrange matters so that the risk is shared, and they can devise remedies to coerce each other into performance. There are limits to what the law permits in this respect, as we shall see, but the planning function of contract law is an essential one. We shall return frequently to the theme of how proper contract planning can avoid a particular problem.

Thus the book will concentrate on what we see as being the core of contract law: the agreements made between business and business, business and employee, and business and consumer. How is contract law's function in relation to these to be described or assessed? A first step is to look at the agreements that are actually made in commerce. This will not only give context to the disputes in the cases in the book; it will also show how contract draftsmen react to the factual problems and legal rules with which they are confronted, and re-emphasise the 'planning' aspect of contract law. Readers will, of course, be familiar with the many simple contracts each of us makes each day when buying goods in a shop, taking a bus or getting a haircut. They may not be so familiar with more complex commercial transactions, and for this reason the Appendix contains a number of specimen contract documents, with some notes to explain the main features of each one. Each contract is of a type that will feature in some case later in the book. In addition, there will be frequent examples of particular types of contract clause throughout.

A second step is to attempt to analyse the court's decisions not only in terms of logic and consistency with authority, but also in terms of underlying policy. Is the court, consciously or unconsciously, adopting a rule that supports the market, and if so, how does the rule do so? We shall see that a given situation may give rise to several possible approaches. For example, the fact that contract law operates as a dispute resolution mechanism in the courtroom, and at the same time as a device for future contract planning, often gives rise to a tension between 'flexibility' and 'certainty'. The court may have to choose between a solution that will produce an apparently fair solution to the dispute before it, but which will lead to considerable uncertainty in future contracting, and a rule that will be easier to apply but less fair. Which should the court adopt? Some of the policies the courts can pursue are explored in readings contained in Chapter 3.

One of these policies needs separate mention. So far, we have described contract law as supporting the institution of private exchange by creating power in the parties to commit themselves to legally enforceable agreements. It is important to note, however, that at the same time as it creates this power, contract law goes some way to controlling its exercise. In some cases, the control takes the form of frustrating the intentions of the parties for the good of the rest of society: thus contracts that involve the commission of serious crimes or which are for some other reason contrary to public policy may be unenforceable (see Section 9). More frequently, the control is for the supposed benefit of the parties themselves. Contract power can be abused or used unwisely; people are occasionally caught in extreme need, are sometimes rash and are frequently ill-informed. The law may step in to protect them against the consequences of the agreements they made in these circumstances, especially if the other party has contributed to the situation or has taken advantage of it. The most obvious forms of the policing of bargains will be found in Section 8, but the theme of control pervades the whole of contract law. The preliminary readings in Chapter 3 of this Introduction also deal with this aspect of contract law. In the context of private consumers, there are now so many statutory controls over contracting that 'consumer law' is treated as a subject in its own right; we do not see it as conceptually distinct from contract, but for reasons of space, only a selection of the controls will be covered in this book.

We have presented contract law as being primarily concerned with exchanges, and in terms of the number of contracts made and their economic importance this must be correct. However, we want to re-emphasise that contract law is sometimes concerned with situations that involve 'exchanges' of a most marginal nature, if they are exchanges at all. We shall see a number of cases in which family arrangements that were not obviously profit-seeking exchanges were nonetheless enforced as contracts, and a few cases in which liability was imposed on a party and was justified in terms of there being a contract, although it is extremely doubtful whether the parties were thinking in those terms. In other words, contract law is not only the law that is applied to what we normally think of as exchanges; it is also a mode of analysis, a justification for legal intervention, that can be used by a judge in other situations. The book contains several examples of this, eg *Tanner v Tanner* (p 20) and *De la Bere v Pearson* (p 147). Whether it is always an appropriate analysis for the other situations is another question; sometimes contractual liability may be imposed because, for some reason, the court finds itself unable to impose liability on any other basis, yet it may not seem right to impose the full consequences of contractual liability (see, for example, p 170). These marginal cases may seem to take up both the courts' time and space in the book that is out of all proportion to their economic significance, but legally they are very important: they mark the boundaries of the subject, and often illuminate clearly what is understood by contractual liability, as opposed to liability in, say, restitution.

III. CONTRACT AS A DYNAMIC BODY OF RULES

Much of the law of consumer protection mentioned earlier is of fairly recent origin, and this serves to emphasise the point that contract law is dynamic, always developing and sometimes changing rapidly as new problems confront the courts and legislature. Sometimes the problem is an internal legal one: for instance, the growth of the doctrine of consideration as a limitation on what promises will be enforced (see Section 2) seems to have been prompted by the adoption in the sixteenth century of a new form of action, the action of assumpsit, to enforce promises. Before that, promises were actionable in the royal courts only if they were part of one of a recognised type of exchange such as a sale, or were made in a sealed covenant or bond. The new action might have led to the enforceability of any promise, however informal and even if nothing was to be received in return, but it came to be limited by the consideration doctrine. More often, new developments in contract law have been prompted by changes in society; thus, the rules on offer and acceptance (to be discussed in Section 3) seem to have been a response to the growth of contracting between parties at a distance when a reliable postal system was established in the early nineteenth century: many of the rules governing exemption clauses (see Section 8, Chapter 39) are a response to the increased use of preprinted standard form contracts in the late nineteenth and twentieth centuries.

The American writer Horwitz has argued that during the nineteenth century, when much of the framework of modern contract law was established in a recognisable form, the courts were actively transforming the law in order to create the conditions necessary for economic growth and social development (see (1974) 87 Harvard LR 917). The thesis has been doubted. Firstly, it is not clear that there was a transformation; rather, there was very little contract law before the nineteenth century and the courts were developing rules to govern many situations for the first time (see Simpson (1979) 47 Chicago LR 533). Secondly, the relationship between the law and economic development seems to have been much more complex than the theory suggests (see Rubin, GR and Sugarman, D (eds) *Law, Economy and Society, 1750–1914*, pp 3–12). But no one doubts that there is a connection.

There is also a clear connection between the development of contract law and contemporary political thought. In his *Rise and Fall of Freedom of Contract*, Atiyah has traced the influence of notions of *laissez-faire* on the nineteenth-century law and then the gradual increase in controls over contracts as the more collective notions underlying the welfare state emerged. During the last decade, this trend seems to have been reversed again; Atiyah argues that this reflects the thinking of the 'New Right' (see his *Introduction to the Law of Contract*, 6th edn, 2005, pp 16–20. It is very common to describe the nineteenth-century contract law as 'classical' and to note how the modern law has changed. A useful summary may be found in the Introduction, 'From "Classical" to Modern Contract Law' by Beatson and Friedmann (eds) in their book, *Good Faith and Fault in Contract Law*, 1995, especially pp 7–17.

Frequently, the need for a solution to a new problem has made the judges look to other legal systems. During the nineteenth century, the judges were much influenced by Roman law (which many of them would have studied) and by Continental writers such as Pothier. We shall see that the introduction of Continental ideas has not always met with success, because of the conceptual differences between the common law and the civil law, but it is remarkable to what extent the civil law systems do, in fact, reach similar results to the common law. Perhaps this should not surprise us: the needs of an effective legal framework for the use of resources in producing goods and services will be essentially the same in every society of a given type. As Holmes wrote over a century ago (*The Common Law*, 1882, pp 1–2):

The substance of the law at any given time pretty nearly corresponds, so far as it goes, with what is then understood to be convenient; but its form and machinery, and the degree to which it is able to work out desired results, depend very much upon its past.

We will occasionally refer to the civil law's solution to problems, but more often we will compare the devices employed in other common law jurisdictions, notably Australia, Canada and the USA, where the law started from the same base as ours but has in many ways developed rather differently.

In the last twenty years, there has been much more discussion of common problems between common law contract lawyers and their civil law counterparts. Perhaps to the surprise of both sides, it has become clear that although there are significant differences in conceptual structure, there are substantial similarities in practical results. On reflection, this should not have been surprising because the underlying problems facing contract law in any capitalist market-oriented economy must be the same.

One result is the appearance of a book by two German scholars, Kötz and Flessner, on *European Contract Law*, Volume 1 of which appeared in its English translation in 1997 and which treats the differences between, for example, English and German contract law as variations on a theme like those between French and German contract law.

At a practical level, two bodies have been concerned with attempts to produce a workable synthesis of the various systems. The Commission on European Contract Law has been concerned to do this within a European framework (see *Principles of European Contract Law, Parts I and II*, Lando, O and Beale, H (eds), 2000; *Part III*, Lando, O, Clive, E, Pvüm, A and Zimmermann, R (eds), 2003), while a working group set up by UNIDROIT has been concerned to produce a set of principles for international commercial contracts. (See UNIDROIT, *Principles of International Commercial Contracts*, 1994. A second edition was produced in 2004. This was not a revision of the first edition so much as an extension to cover some new topics: agency; assignment; third-party rights. Work has now started on a further extension to produce a third edition.)

On one question, however, there has been considerable debate as to whether English law should adopt a principle found in many continental systems of law, namely the principle of good faith. For instance, § 242 of the German Civil Code (BGB) provides:

The debtor is bound to effect performance according to the requirement of good faith, giving consideration to common usage.

The German courts have used the good faith principle as the basis for developing a number of doctrines to fill gaps in the BGB, and also as the basis of a number of defences and indeed as the basis for reallocating risks in private contracts (see p 524). (See generally Ebke and Steinhauer, 'The Doctrine of Good Faith in German Contract Law', in Beatson and Friedmann (eds), *Good Faith and Fault in Contract Law*, 1995, pp 171–190; and for a very broad survey, Whittaker and Zimmermann, *Good Faith in European Contract Law*, 2000.)

To some extent, the concept of good faith has already entered directly into English law via European legislation. We will see that the Unfair Terms in Consumer Contracts Regulations 1999, which implement a European Directive of 1993, use a test of whether the term is 'contrary to good faith' (p 1043). This appears to be a direct reflection of the German Act on Unfair Terms in Standard Contracts (AGBG) of 1976. The debate, however, is about whether English law already recognises a broader concept of good faith and, if not, whether it should do so. As to the first question, the classic answer is that given by Bingham LJ in the *Interfoto* case (see p 338):

English law has characteristically, committed itself to no such overriding principle but has developed piecemeal solutions in response to demonstrated problems of unfairness.

Other judges have explicitly rejected the application of the notion of good faith in particular contexts: see, for example, the rejection by the House of Lords of a 'duty to negotiate in good faith' in *Walford v Miles* (p 271). Nonetheless there are many modern developments in English contract law by which the law attempts to promote 'good behaviour' by the parties. Examples are the recent cases of public bodies which invite 'tenders' from would-be contracting partners and then fail to give proper consideration to the tender submitted (p 244); and the decisions preventing one party from using a slight breach of contract by the other as a pretext for escaping from a contract that, because of a change in the market, has turned out to be unprofitable (pp 566 ff). It is at least arguable that these cases are based on an underlying principle that, in making or performing a contract, the parties must observe requirements of good faith, in the sense of respecting the legitimate interests and expectations of the other party.

As to the second question, it has been argued persuasively that it would be advantageous were English law to recognise a general principle of good faith openly (see p 283).

IV. DIFFERENT APPROACHES TO CONTRACT LAW

It is not only the history of contract law and its relationship to economic and social change that is debatable. There is much discussion about how best to describe the modern law and about what its role *should* be. In the nineteenth century, the courts seemed to place great emphasis on freedom of contract (see, eg, p 47). During this period, the courts tended to reduce the number of rules controlling contract power (although this was rather undercut by the considerable body of legislation protecting employees and consumers: see pp 54 and 1056). There are still writers, particularly in the USA, who suggest that the law should enforce any agreement that was 'freely made' between the parties provided it has no adverse effect on others (eg p 813). These 'libertarians' see the individual as the best judge of his or her own interest and consider that what was freely agreed is, by definition, fair. Any attempt to use contract law to influence substantive outcomes (eg to try to produce a fairer distribution of wealth in society, or even to maintain the previous distribution) is both illegitimate and misguided (see further pp 813–818).

Others take a less extreme position. They agree that individuals should be free to pursue their own self-interest but they recognise that, in some cases, 'the market' may not operate efficiently. For example, in cases in which there is some kind of monopoly or in which one party does not fully understand the contract, the law may need to intervene (eg pp 959 and 968). Many such writers would say that contract law, like it or not, does affect the distribution of wealth in society and that this should be recognised. This debate is taken up in Section 6.

A few writers go further and argue that it is no longer adequate to describe the law of contract as primarily concerned with supporting voluntary exchange in the market and correcting occasional abuses or market failures. In their view, another transformation has taken place and the modern law's prime concern is with controlling domination and promoting fair exchange and co-operation (eg p 66).

An introductory selection of readings on these themes will be found in Chapter 3 and a broader selection in Section 6.

V. ECONOMIC AND EMPIRICAL ANALYSIS

Looking at specimen contracts certainly gives some idea of the function of contract law, but it is only a starting point, and the fact that a draftsman has confronted a problem in this way or that can only tell us a limited amount: it does not tell us, for instance, whether his device was effective to achieve what he had in mind, even if we are sure what that was. The same is true of court decisions: not only may we be unsure what end the court was pursuing, but we may have little idea beyond instinct as to the results the rule enunciated is likely to produce in future situations. For a more rigorous analysis, we must turn to other academic disciplines. In the context of contract, the most intensively used discipline to date is micro-economics. This by no means provides all the answers, but a limited amount of simple economic analysis can give extremely interesting and valuable insights into the way that contracting parties are likely to react to various rules of law, and into the costs involved in the different legal approaches. The book contains a number of readings from the 'law and economics' literature, and after many of the cases there will be questions designed to prompt an economic analysis of the problems. For those who, like two of your editors, have no training in economics, a basic introduction to the necessary concepts is contained in Chapter 4 of the Introduction.

Even economic analysis gives only theoretical models of the likely impact of a rule of law under certain, often quite limiting, assumptions. Ascertaining the 'real' function of the law requires empirical investigation. Unfortunately, only a very limited amount of work has so far been done in this field: on both sides of the Atlantic, there are fewer than twenty significant empirical pieces on contract law. Extracts from many of the pieces will be found below. They present a sharp contrast to the blackletter law of the contract texts, and even the economists' models: to give the flavour, some extracts are given in Chapter 5 of the Introduction. The extracts show that contract law is not always the answer to the businessman or -woman's prayer; indeed, it sometimes seems an irrelevance. This work is important for at least two reasons. From an academic viewpoint, it is part of the analysis of the function and the limits of law. It is also important from a strictly practical viewpoint. The pieces bring out that 'using' contract law—even just making enforceable contracts—is an expensive business. A lawyer who is consulted about a contract dispute or drafting a contract, and who immediately recommends litigation or the negotiation of a long and complex agreement, will scare clients away. Before giving advice, the lawyer must weigh the costs of litigation or negotiation against the likely benefits, and the more the lawyer knows about the way contract functions in practice, the better his or her advice is likely to be.

VI. PLAN OF THE BOOK

It may be helpful to include in the Introduction a summary of what is to follow in the later sections, so that the reader has some idea of what is to come. Section 2 deals with the question of what agreements or promises are recognised by the law as being contractual and thus prima facie enforceable. Section 3 covers the questions of whether an effective agreement has been reached. The core of the book is then contained in Sections 4 and 5, which cover, respectively, the topics of the liabilities under various agreements and the remedies available when some disruption occurs. Section 6 explores 'contract theory': in many respects, the readings in Section 6 are chosen to develop themes mentioned in this Introduction. Section 7 deals with changes in the agreement, a difficult and important topic given the long-term nature of many contracts. Section 8 is on policing, although as mentioned above this theme crops up regularly in the other sections. Section 9 covers agreements that are unenforceable for reasons of illegality or public policy, and the book ends with a section dealing with contracts involving or affecting more than two parties.

VII. USING THE BOOK

Contract courses vary considerably in their approach. In this book, we try to present the law in a functional way, to get you, the reader, to think about what the rules are designed to achieve and to use a limited amount of economic analysis as one way of assessing their likely impact on parties' behaviour. We have also tried, however, to include enough material to enable you to use it to study the law from other approaches as well, by including a reasonably full coverage of the cases and legislation (some of it in the 'Notes' to the extracts, which we would strongly urge you to read as carefully as the extracts themselves) and by giving a selection of readings on 'other approaches' (we do not personally find all of these completely convincing but the ones we have included seem to be influential enough to deserve study).

The result is that the book is rather long and we recognise that if you are doing contract for the first time you will not be able to read it all. To try to help you select, we give a list of suggested 'core readings' (mainly cases and legislation). Linked to these are sets of questions (roughly one set for each major substantive topic) which, if you do not cover the topic in detail in class, you may find it helpful to work through on your own or preferably with two or three colleagues. They concentrate primarily on the substantive rules, leaving more theoretical and interpretative questions for discussion in class—although notes related to theoretical and interpretative readings will be found after the relevant material.

CHAPTER TWO

CONTRACT, TORT AND RESTITUTION

The aim of this chapter is to introduce some of the basic concepts that underlie the three categories of personal liability recognised by the common law: contract, tort and restitution. It looks at the different ideas on which each type of liability is founded and the remedies available, in particular the way in which compensation is measured.

I. CONTRACT

Contractual liability is based on the defendant's failure to perform an undertaking or 'promise'. We shall see that the promise may be express or the court may infer one from the circumstances, but a promise is one of the essential elements of contractual liability, and if the court finds that the defendant did not promise anything, there can be no contractual liability. (The plaintiff must also have accepted the defendant's promise and have provided 'consideration' for it: see below.)

■ *Taylor v Brewer*
(1813) 1 M&S 290, 105 ER 108, King's Bench

Walsh had worked for a committee, which had been formed to manage the sale of lottery tickets. The committee had, on 4 January 1810, resolved that 'any service to be rendered by Walsh should, after the third lottery, be taken into consideration, and such remuneration be made as should be deemed right'. Walsh had become bankrupt and his debts had been assigned to the plaintiff, who sued the members of the committee for recompense for the work Walsh had done. Lord Ellenborough nonsuited the plaintiff, whose counsel moved to set aside the nonsuit.

Park moved to set aside the nonsuit, on the ground that the bankrupt was entitled to some recompense; inasmuch as an agreement with a person that he should do work, and should have what is right for it, did not import that he should have nothing for his trouble if his employer should be so minded, but that he should have a reasonable reward: it should have been left therefore to the jury to consider what was reasonable, as was done in *Peacock v Peacock*.

Lord Ellenborough CJ

In that case the defendant expressly told the plaintiff that he should have a share in the business, leaving only unsettled what particular share he was to have; but here, I own it struck me, was an engagement accepted by the bankrupt on no definite terms, but only in confidence that if his labour deserved any thing he should be recompensed for it by the defendants. This was throwing himself upon the mercy of those with whom he contracted; and the same thing does not unfrequently happen in contracts with several of the departments of Government.

Grose J

I consider the resolution to import that the committee were to judge whether any or what recompense was right.

Le Blanc J

It seems to me to be merely an engagement of honour.

Bayley J

The fair meaning of the resolution is this, that it was to be in the breast of the committee whether he was to have any thing, and if any thing, then how much.

Rule refused.

NOTE

Lord Ellenborough describes Walsh as 'contracting' with the defendants, but he was probably not using 'contract' to refer to any legal obligation: it seems to have been the court's unanimous view that the committee was promising nothing. Compare the words of Le Blanc J.

Often the question of whether a promise has been made is put in terms of whether an offer has been made by the defendant, or, when the defendant has made some statement that might have been an undertaking, whether the statement was intended as a binding commitment.

■ *Carlill v Carbolic Smoke Ball Co*
[1893] 1 QB 256, Court of Appeal

The defendants inserted in the Pall Mall Gazette and other newspapers the advertisement reproduced on p 1247. The plaintiff, on the faith of this advertisement, bought a smoke ball and used it as directed three times a day from 20 November 1891 to 17 January 1892, when she caught influenza. Hawkins J held that she was entitled to £100, and the defendants appealed.

Lindley LJ

. . . The first observation I will make is that we are not dealing with any inference of fact. We are dealing with an express promise to pay £100 in certain events. Read the advertisement how you will, and twist it about as you will, here is a distinct promise expressed in language which is perfectly unmistakable— '£100 reward will be paid by the Carbolic Smoke Ball Company to any person who contracts the influenza after having used the ball three times daily for two weeks according to the printed directions supplied with each ball.'

We must first consider whether this was intended to be a promise at all, or whether it was a mere puff which meant nothing. Was it a mere puff? My answer to that question is No, and I base my answer upon this passage: '£1000 is deposited with the Alliance Bank, shewing our sincerity in the matter.' Now, for what was that money deposited or that statement made except to negative the suggestion that this was a mere puff and meant nothing at all? The deposit is called in aid by the advertiser as proof of his sincerity in the matter—that is, the sincerity of his promise to pay this £100 in the event which he has specified. I say this for the purpose of giving point to the observation that we are not inferring a promise; there is the promise, as plain as words can make it.

Then it is contended that it is not binding. In the first place, it is said that it is not made with anybody in particular. Now that point is common to the words of this advertisement and to the words of all other advertisements offering rewards. They are offers to anybody who performs the conditions named in the advertisement, and anybody who does perform the condition accepts the offer. In point of law this advertisement is an offer to pay £100 to anybody who will perform these conditions, and the perform-ance of the conditions is the acceptance of the offer. That rests upon a string of authorities, the earliest of which is *Williams v Carwardine*, which has been followed by many other decisions upon advertise-ments offering rewards.

Bowen LJ

. . . We were asked to say that this document was a contract too vague to be enforced.

The first observation which arises is that the document itself is not a contract at all, it is only an offer made to the public. The defendants contend next, that it is an offer the terms of which are too vague to be treated as a definite offer, inasmuch as there is no limit of time fixed for the catching of the influenza, and it cannot be supposed that the advertisers seriously meant to promise to pay money to every person who catches the influenza at any time after the inhaling of the smoke ball. It was urged also, that if you look at this document you will find much vagueness as to the persons with whom the contract was intended to be made—that, in the first place, its terms are wide enough to include persons who may have used the smoke ball before the advertisement was issued; at all events, that it is an offer to the world in general, and, also, that it is unreasonable to suppose it to be a definite offer, because nobody in their senses would contract themselves out of the opportunity of checking the experiment which was going to be made at their own expense. It is also contended that the advertisment is rather in the nature of a puff or a proclamation than a promise or offer intended to mature into a contract when accepted. But the main point seems to be that the vagueness of the document shews that no contract whatever was intended. It seems to me that in order to arrive at a right conclusion we must read this advertise-ment in its plain meaning, as the public would understand it. It was intended to be issued to the public and to be read by the public. How would an ordinary person reading this document construe it? It was intended unquestionably to have some effect, and I think the effect which it was intended to have, was to make people use the smoke ball, because the suggestions and allegations which it contains are directed immediately to the use of the smoke ball as distinct from the purchase of it. It did not follow that the smoke ball was to be purchased from the defendants directly, or even from agents of theirs directly. The intention was that the circulation of the smoke ball should be promoted, and that the use of it should be increased. The advertisement begins by saying that a reward will be paid by the Carbolic Smoke Ball Company to any person who contracts the increasing epidemic after using the ball. It has been said that the words do not apply only to persons who contract the epidemic after the publication of the advertisement, but include persons who had previously contracted the influenza. I cannot so read the advertisement. It is written in colloquial and popular language, and I think that it is equivalent to this; '£100 will be paid to any person who shall contract the increasing epidemic after having used the car-bolic smoke ball three times daily for two weeks'. And it seems to me that the way in which the public would read it would be this, that if anybody, after the advertisement was published, used three times daily for two weeks the carbolic smoke ball, and then caught cold, he would be entitled to the reward. Then again it was said: 'How long is this protection to endure? Is it to go on for ever, or for what limit of time?' . . .

I…have myself no hesitation in saying that I think, on the construction of this advertisement, the protection was to enure during the time that the carbolic smoke ball was being used. My brother, the Lord Justice who preceded me, thinks that the contract would be sufficiently definite if you were to read it in the sense that the protection was to be warranted during a reasonable period after use. I have some difficulty myself on that point; but it is not necessary for me to consider it further, because the disease here was contracted during the use of the carbolic smoke ball.

Was it intended that the £100 should, if the conditions be fulfilled, be paid? The advertisement says that £1000 is lodged at the bank for the purpose. Therefore, it cannot be said that the statement that £100 would be paid was intended to be a mere puff. I think it was intended to be understood by the public as an offer which was to be acted upon.

But it was said there was no check on the part of the persons who issued the advertisement, and that it would be an insensate thing to promise £100 to a person who used the smoke ball unless you could check or superintend his manner of using it. The answer to that argument seems to be that if a person chooses to make extravagant promises of this kind he probably does so because it pays him to make them, and, if he has made them, the extravagance of the promises is no reason in law why he should not be bound by them.

[Further extracts from this case will be found on p 215.]

NOTES

1. At the time, many exaggerated claims were made in advertisements for quack medicine and the case excited a good deal of interest. See Simpson (1985) 14 J Legal Studies 345.

2. The doctrines of intention to create legal relations and offer and acceptance are examined in greater detail in Chapters 7 and 8 respectively.

3. The Carbolic Smoke Ball Company's advertisement contained a promise and the Court held that it was contractually binding. There are many examples of promises that are held not to be intended as legal commitments, especially promises made on social occasions or in domestic contexts: see Chapter 7.

4. You will notice that although the Lord Justices are discussing whether the advertisement was intended as a contract or as a mere puff, they do not consider what the defendants actually intended. Normally, in contract, the subjective intentions of the parties are irrelevant; intention is judged 'objectively', that is, as it would reasonably appear to the other party. It is what you say or do that is important, not what you mean. This is explored in more detail at pp 192–195 and 289 ff.

■ *Kleinwort Benson Ltd v Malaysia Mining Corpn Bhd*

[1989] 1 All ER 785, Court of Appeal

The defendants' wholly owned subsidiary, Metals, had been set up to operate as a ring-dealing member of the London Metal Exchange. This required large sums of money and the plaintiffs granted Metals an acceptance credit/multi-currency cash loan facility to a maximum of £5m. During negotiations, the plaintiffs sought a guarantee of the loan from the defendants, but the defendants refused. Instead the defendants furnished to the plaintiffs two 'letters of comfort', each of which stated, in paragraph 3: 'It is our policy to ensure that the business of [Metals] is at all times in a position to meet its liabilities to you under the loan facility arrangements.' The letters also stated that the defendants would not reduce their current financial interest in Metals until the loans had been repaid.

In 1985, the tin market collapsed (for an account, see *Maclaine Watson & Co Ltd v Department of Trade and Industry* [1988] 3 All ER 257) and Metals went into liquidation without repaying the plaintiffs. The plaintiffs brought an action against the defendants to recover the amount owing and Hirst J upheld their claim.

Ralph Gibson LJ

The central question in this case, in my judgment, is that considered in *Esso Petroleum Co Ltd v Mardon* [1976] QB 801, [1976] 2 All ER 5, on which counsel for the plaintiffs relied in this court but which was not cited to Hirst J. That question is whether the words of para 3, considered in their context, are to be treated as a warranty or contractual promise. Paragraph 3 contains no express words of promise. Paragraph 3 is in its terms a statement of present fact and not a promise as to future conduct. I agree with the submission of counsel for the defendants that, in this regard, the words of para 3 are in sharp contrast with the words of para 2 of the letter: 'We confirm that we will not' etc. The force of this point is not limited, as Hirst J stated it, to the absence from para 3 of the words 'We confirm'. The real contrast is between the words of promise, namely 'We will not' in para 2, and the words of statement of fact, 'It is our policy' in para 3. Hirst J held that, by the words of para 3, the defendants gave an undertaking that now and at all times in the future, so long as Metals should be under any liability to the plaintiffs under the facility arrangements, it is *and will be* the defendants' policy to ensure that Metals is in a position to meet their liabilities. To derive that meaning from the words it is necessary to add the words emphasised, namely 'and will be', which do not appear in para 3. In short, the words of promise as to the future conduct of the defendants were held by Hirst J to be part of the necessary meaning of the words used in para 3. The question is whether that view of the words can be upheld.

The absence of express words of warranty as to present facts or the absence of express words of promise as to future conduct does not conclusively exclude a statement from the status of warranty or promise. . . .

The evidence does not show that the words used in para 3 were intended to be a promise as to the future conduct of the defendants but, in my judgment, it shows the contrary.

The concept of a comfort letter was, as counsel for the defendants acknowledged, not shown to have acquired any particular meaning at the time of the negotiations in this case with reference to the limits of any legal liability to be assumed under its terms by a parent company. A letter, which the parties might have referred to at some stage as a letter of comfort, might, after negotiation, have emerged containing in para 3 in express terms the words used by Hirst J to state the meaning which he gave to para 3. The court would not, merely because the parties had referred to the document as a comfort letter, refuse to give effect to the meaning of the words used. But in this case it is clear, in my judgment, that the concept of a comfort letter, to which the parties had resort when the defendants refused to assume joint and several liability or to give a guarantee, was known by both sides at least to extend to or to include a document under which the defendants would give comfort to the plaintiffs by assuming, not a legal liability to ensure repayment of the liabilities of its subsidiary, but a moral responsibility only. Thus, when the defendants by Mr John Green in June 1984 told the plaintiffs that Mr Green would recommend that credit lines for Metals be covered by a letter of comfort rather than by guarantee, the response of Mr Irwin, before any draft of a comfort letter had been prepared, was '. . . that a letter of comfort would not be a problem, but that [he] would probably have to charge a higher rate'. The comfort letter was drafted in terms which in para 3 do not express any contractual promise and which are consistent with being no more than a representation of fact. If they are treated as no more than a representation of fact, they are in that meaning consistent with the comfort letter containing no more than the assumption of moral responsibility by the defendants in respect of the debts of Metals. There is nothing in the evidence to show that, as a matter of commercial probability or common sense, the parties must have intended para 3 to be a contractual promise, which is not expressly stated, rather than a mere representation of fact which is so stated.

Next, the first draft of the comfort letter was produced by the plaintiffs. Paragraph 1 contained confirmation that the defendants knew of and approved of the granting of the facilities in question by the plaintiffs to Metals, and para 2 contained the express confirmation that the defendants would not reduce their current financial interests in Metals until (in effect) facilities had been paid or the plaintiffs consented. Both are relevant to the present and future moral responsibility of the defendants. If the words of para 3 are to be treated as intended to express a contractual promise by the defendants as to their future policy, which Hirst J held the words to contain, then the recitation of the plaintiffs' approval and the promise now to reduce their current financial interest in Metals, would be of no significance. If the defendants have promised that at all times in the future it will be the defendants' policy to ensure that Metals is in a position to meet its liabilities to the plaintiffs under the facility, it would not matter whether they had approved or disapproved, or whether they had disposed of their shares in Metals. Contracts may, of course, contain statements or promises which are caused to be of no separate commercial importance by the width of a later promise in the same document. Where, however, the court is examining a statement which is by its express words no more than a representation of fact, in order to consider whether it is shown to have been intended to be of the nature of a contractual promise or warranty, it seems to me to be a fact suggesting at least the absence of such intention if, as in this case, to read the statement as a contractual promise is to reduce to no significance two paragraphs included in the plaintiffs' draft, both of which have significance if the statement is read as a representation of fact only.

That point can be made more plainly thus: if para 3 in its original or in its final form was intended to contain a binding legal promise by the defendants to ensure the ability of Metals to pay the sums due under the facility, there was no apparent need or purpose for the plaintiffs, as bankers, to waste ink on paras 1 and 2.

As I have said, the absence of express words of promise does not by itself prevent a statement from being treated as a contractual promise. The example given in argument by counsel for the plaintiffs, namely of the shop stating by a notice that it is its policy to accept, within 14 days of purchase, the return in good condition of any goods bought and to refund the price without question, seems to me to be a case in which a court would be likely to hold that the notice imported a promise that the policy would continue over the 14-day period. It would be difficult on those facts to find any sensible commercial explanation for the notice other than a contractual promise not to change the policy over the 14-day period. It would not be satisfactory or convincing to regard the notice as no more than the assumption of a moral responsibility by the shop giving such a notice to its customers. In such a case, and in the absence of any relevant factual context indicating otherwise, it seems to me that the court would probably hold that the statement was shown to have been intended to be a contractual promise.

In this case, however, the opposite seems to me to be clear. . . .

If my view of this case is correct, the plaintiffs have suffered grave financial loss as a result of the collapse of the tin market and the following decision by the defendant company not to honour a moral responsibility which it assumed in order to gain for its subsidiary the finance necessary for the trading operations which the defendants wished that subsidiary to pursue. The defendants have demonstrated, in my judgment, that they made no relevant contractual promise to the plaintiffs which could support the judgment in favour of the plaintiffs. The consequences of the decision of the defendants to repudiate their moral responsibility are not matters for this court.

I would allow this appeal.

Nicholls and **Fox LJJ** agreed.

Appeal allowed.

NOTES

1.   Ralph Gibson's example of the statement of policy in a shop suggests that similar words may be construed differently in different contexts. To a consumer, a statement of policy may reasonably appear to be a contractual undertaking (although what should the consumer think if the shop had earlier refused to give an explicit promise?). In addition,

as *Carlill's* case illustrates, there is a tendency to treat statements by businesses intended to drum up trade as contractual. See also *Esso Petroleum Ltd v Commissioners of Customs and Excise*, p 183. In *Bowerman v Association of British Travel Agents* [1995] NLJR 1815, the plaintiff booked a holiday with a tour operator who was a member of the defendant association (ABTA). The tour operator displayed on its wall an ABTA notice, which stated that in the event of the financial failure of an ABTA member before commencement of the holiday 'ABTA arranges for you to be reimbursed the money you have paid in respect of your holiday arrangement'. The majority of the Court of Appeal held that this notice could be construed as an offer by ABTA, accepted by the plaintiff booking the holiday.

2. Ralph Gibson refers to a 'warranty'. This word has a number of legal meanings (eg, p 324), but here it is used to mean a contractual undertaking that a statement of fact, eg about goods sold, is or will be true. Thus the seller of a machine may 'warrant' that it is capable of a certain speed of operation and will remain so for a given period of time.

3. Just like statements of 'policy', statements of fact will be construed differently in different contexts. We shall see later (pp 323–330) that when the parties have definitely entered a contract, it is common for important statements made about the subject matter (eg by the seller about the goods sold) to be treated as warranties, so that if the statement is incorrect, the seller is liable for breach of contract. On the other hand, statements made by manufacturers in advertisements for goods that the public can buy through retail outlets are not regarded as contractual promises even though they are clearly designed to induce consumers to buy the goods. The courts have persisted in holding that such statements do not show any 'intention to contract': eg *Lexmead Ltd v Lewis* [1982] AC 225, 262–263. Note that in *Carlill's* case it was the promise to pay £100 if the user caught 'flu that was enforced, not the statement that the ball would cure influenza within 24 hours. Presumably a statement suggesting that a consumer would have a direct right against the advertiser ('Your Bealemobile will not break down for two years—and if it does Beale will give you a new one') might be construed as a contractual promise.

4. The nearest the courts have come to enforcing statements made to induce purchase from a third party are cases in which the plaintiff has individually sought the defendant's advice before buying. In *Wells (Merstham) Ltd v Buckland Sand and Silica Co Ltd* [1965] 2 QB 170, the plaintiffs, who were chrysanthemum growers, asked the defendant sand merchants whether their sand had the low oxide content, necessary for propagating cuttings. When the defendants said it did, the plaintiffs bought some of the defendants' sand from a third party. When the sand turned out to have a high oxide content, the defendants were held liable in contract. See also *Shanklin Pier Ltd v Detel Products Ltd*, noted at, pp 38–39.

5. Whether statements are construed as promises or not may also change over time as judges' perceptions change. In *Maddison v Alderson* (1883) 8 App Cas 467, a woman had for years acted as housekeeper to Alderson and, because of his straitened circumstances, had 'begun to leave wages in his hand'. In 1860, she was thinking of leaving but he persuaded her to stay by indicating that in his will he would leave her a life interest in his farm. He drew up a will to this effect and read it over to her, asking 'whether she was satisfied'; the will was not properly witnessed. She continued to look after him without wages for the rest of his life. After Alderson's death, she brought an action against his personal representative for possession of the farm. The jury found that there was a

contract, but the House of Lords held that she was not entitled to recover. The main reason was that there was not sufficient written evidence to satisfy the Statute of Frauds (which required contracts for the disposition of interests in land to be evidenced in writing; but every member of the House doubted whether Alderson had made a binding promise. Lord Fitzgerald said:

> . . . although Alderson probably made representations to her of the benefits he intended to confer on her if she remained with him during his life, there never was any agreement binding on him to do so.

In *Schaefer v Schuhmann* [1972] AC 572, the facts were almost identical but the Privy Council decided that a contractual promise had been made. Lord Simon dissented on the ground that the two cases were indistinguishable.

6.   The court may infer that the parties were making promises to each other, and thus that there was a contract between them, even though it is extremely improbable that the parties thought they were making a contract. *Wells v Buckland Sand* (above) may be one example; the next case is even clearer.

■ *Tanner v Tanner*
[1975] 3 All ER 776, Court of Appeal

In 1968, the plaintiff, a married man, formed an association with the defendant, a single woman, who took his name. The defendant was the tenant of a rent-controlled flat, where the plaintiff frequently visited her. In 1969, she gave birth to twins of whom the plaintiff was the father. In 1970, the parties decided that it would be best to purchase a house to provide accommodation for the defendant and the twins. The plaintiff made it clear to the defendant, however, that he did not intend to marry her. He purchased a house in his own name and himself provided the purchase price by means of a mortgage. The defendant made no contribution to the purchase. She gave up her rent-controlled tenancy, and brought a good deal of furniture from her flat to the house; she also spent £150 on furnishings for the house. She and the twins moved into the house and occupied the ground floor flat. The rest of the house was let and the defendant managed the lettings for the plaintiff. After the defendant had moved into the house, the plaintiff stopped paying to her the £5 a week maintenance for the twins that he had previously paid and did not pay her anything for herself or the twins. She obtained a social security allowance. The plaintiff formed an association with another woman whom he later married. He wanted to get the defendant and the twins out of the house so that he could live there himself with his new wife and her family. He offered the defendant £4,000 to leave the house—the house was likely to fetch £6,400 if it were sold furnished—but the defendant refused the offer saying that the house was supposed to be for herself and the children until they left school. By letter dated 16 July 1973 the plaintiff purported to terminate forthwith the licence under which he alleged the defendant had been occupying the ground-floor flat. She refused to vacate the house. The plaintiff brought proceedings claiming possession of the house. The judge found that the defendant had made no contribution in cash or kind from which it could be inferred that she was to have any proprietary interest in the house; accordingly he made an order for possession in the plaintiff's favour and the defendant moved out of the house in pursuance of that order. The defendant appealed against the order for possession. She and the children had been rehoused by the local authority and she did not ask to be put back into the house.

Lord Denning MR

...[It] seems to me plain on the evidence that the house was acquired in the contemplation and expectation that it would provide a home for Miss MacDermott and the twin daughters. The babies were only eight months old at the time. She gave up her flat in Steele's Road (where she was protected by the Rent Acts) to move into this house. It was obviously provided for her as a house for herself and the twins for the foreseeable future.

It is said that they were only licensees—bare licensees—under a licence revocable at will; and that he was entitled in law to turn her and the twins out on a moment's notice. I cannot believe that this is the law. This man had a moral duty to provide for the babies of whom he was the father. I would go further. I think he had a legal duty towards them. Not only towards the babies. But also towards their mother. She was looking after them and bringing them up. In order to fulfil his duty towards the babies, he was under a duty to provide for the mother too. She had given up her flat where she was protected by the Rent Acts—at least in regard to rent and it may be in regard also to security of tenure. She had given it up at his instance so as to be able the better to bring up the children. It is impossible to suppose that in that situation she and the babies were bare licensees whom he could turn out at a moment's notice. He recognised this when he offered to pay her £4,000 to get her out. What then was their legal position? She herself said in evidence: 'The house was supposed to be ours until the children left school.' It seems to me that enables an inference to be drawn, namely that in all the circumstances it is to be implied that she had a licence—a contractual licence—to have accommodation in the house for herself and the children so long as they were of school age and the accommodation was reasonably required for her and the children. There was, it is true, no express contract to that effect, but the circumstances are such that the court should imply a contract by him—or, if need be, impose the equivalent of a contract by him—whereby they were entitled to have the use of the house as their home until the girls had finished school. It may be that if circumstances changed—so that the accommodation was not reasonably required—the licence might be determinable. But it was not determinable in the circumstances in which he sought to determine it, namely to turn her out with the children and to bring in his new wife with her family. It was a contractual licence of the kind which is specifically enforceable on her behalf, and which he can be restrained from breaking; and he could not sell the house over her head so as to get her out in that way. That appears from *Binions v Evans*.

If therefore the lady had sought an injunction restraining him from determining the licence, it should have been granted. The order for possession ought not to have been made...

But what is to be done? The judge ordered possession in six weeks. Thereupon the local housing authority (as they usually do when an order for possession is made) provided accommodation for Miss MacDermott and the children. She moved out in pursuance of the order and does not ask to be put back now. Seeing that the order ought not to have been made and we reverse it, what is to be done? It seems to me that this court has ample power, when it reverses an order of the court below, to do what is just and equitable to restore the position as fairly as it can in the circumstances. The plaintiff has obtained an unjust benefit and should make restitution. In the circumstances the courts can and should assess compensation to be payable by him. He has not been paying any maintenance for these children for years—ever since she went into the house. It seems to me a reasonable sum for loss of this licence (which she ought not to have lost) would be £2,000. So I would allow the appeal and say that the order for possession shall be set aside, and as compensation to her for being wrongly turned out, the sum of £2,000 to be payable by Mr Tanner. I would allow the appeal accordingly.

Browne and **Brightman LJJ** delivered judgments to the same effect.

Appeal allowed.

NOTE

It may be legitimate to infer a contract when neither party gave any thought to the legal position, but what if both actually believed at the time that no contract was involved? In *Upton-on-Severn RDC v Powell* [1942] 1 All ER 220, the defendant, who was entitled to free service from the Pershore fire brigade, called the police and asked for 'the fire brigade'. The police thought he lived in the Upton district and sent the Upton brigade, who came thinking 'that they were rendering gratuitous services in their own area'. The defendant also thought he was getting a free service. The court held that he was under a contractual obligation to pay for the service he had received, but the case has been severely criticised (eg Treitel, p 36).

■ *Re Hudson*

(1885) 54 L J Ch 811

Hudson had promised to give £20,000 to the Jubilee Fund of the Congregational Union, in five annual instalments of £4,000 each, for the liquidation of chapel debts. On his death, the last two instalments remained unpaid and unprovided for. His executors sought a declaration that his estate was not liable for the two instalments.

Pearson J

Mr Cookson [counsel for the Congregational Union] admitted very fairly at the beginning that, unless he could shew that there was a legal debt due from the estate of the testator, he had no case at all; and it was therefore necessary for him to shape the case so as to satisfy the Court that there was a positive legal contract entered into by the testator to pay the whole of this sum of 20,000*l*, which rendered the estate of Mr Hudson liable for so much of the 20,000*l* as was not paid by him during his lifetime. I do not mean to go into all the cases that have been cited. The first question is whether or not there is any contract at all to pay—I mean a contract in the legal sense of the word 'contract'; was there any consideration of any sort or description for Mr Hudson's promise to pay 20,000*l*—anything that could be considered a consideration either in this Court or elsewhere? I am utterly at a loss to ascertain that there was any consideration . . .

  Mr Cookson says that there really was a consideration, because the consideration was the risks and liabilities which the parties were to undertake who composed themselves into a committee and became the distributors of the fund. In the first place, there was no duty between themselves and Mr Hudson which they undertook at that time—there was no binding obligation between themselves and Mr Hudson; and I put it to Mr Cookson just now when he was pressing this point: Supposing that at the end of the year, before any more instalments than one had been paid, this committee had chosen to dissolve itself and to relinquish any trouble whatever in the distribution of the fund whether it was gathered in or not, was there any obligation between Mr Hudson and the committee which would have given Mr Hudson any control over the committee, or have made the committee liable to him for not discharging its duty in distributing the fund which is said to be the consideration for the contract? Of course there was none. It was voluntary on the part of both parties—voluntary on the part of Mr Hudson, and voluntary on the part of the committee. The whole thing from beginning to end was nothing more than this: an intention of this gentleman to contribute to the fund, and an intention of the committee, so long as the different members of it remained members of that committee, to dispose of that fund according to the purposes for which it was contributed. There really is in this matter nothing whatever in the shape of a consideration which could form a contract between the parties.

NOTES

1. If Hudson had made his promise in a deed under seal, it would have been enforceable even though there was no consideration for it. In *Morley v Boothby* (1825) 3 Bing 107, at 111–112, Best CJ said:

   The Common law protected men against improvident contracts. If they bound themselves by deed, it was considered that they must have determined upon what they were about to do, before they made so solemn an engagement; and therefore it was not necessary to the validity of the instrument, that any consideration should appear upon it. In all other cases the contract was invalid, unless the party making the promise was to obtain some advantage, or the party to whom it was made, was to suffer some inconvenience in consequence of the one making or the other accepting the promise [ie there was consideration].

   The doctrine of consideration and the function of the deed are considered in more detail in Section 2, Chapter 6.

2. What was the consideration for the Company's promise in *Carlill's* case? Bowen LJ said ([1893] 1 QB 271):

   Inconvenience sustained by one party at the request of the other is enough to create a consideration. I think, therefore, that it is consideration enough that the plaintiff took the trouble of using the smoke ball. But I think also that the defendants received a benefit from this user, for the use of the smoke ball was contemplated by the defendants as being indirectly a benefit to them, because the use of the smoke balls would promote their sale.

3. In *Carlill's* case, the contract was what is termed 'unilateral': there was only an obligation on one side. Mrs Carlill did not promise to use the smoke ball, whereas the Company was held to have promised that if she did use it as prescribed and still caught 'flu, it would pay. A more common example of a unilateral contract is that made between a person wishing to sell a house and an estate agent. The agent does not undertake to sell the house or even to take any particular steps to try to do so; the vendor promises that if the agent does find someone who buys the house, the vendor will pay the agent's commission (see p 219). More usually, a contract will involve obligations on each side. Thus in a contract of sale the seller promises, among other things, to deliver the goods and the buyer promises to accept them and pay for them. Such a contract is termed 'bilateral' and each party's promise is said to be consideration for the other's. (See further p 98.)

4. Lack of consideration will prevent a person who has promised a gift from being sued for it. If the person has done what is legally sufficient actually to complete the gift (for instance, a gift of a chattel may be completed by actually delivering the chattel to the donee), she can't get the gift back just because the donee provided no consideration.

5. If Hudson's promise had been made by deed, or if there had been consideration for it (for instance, if he had asked that in exchange for the money a new chapel be named for him), his estate would have been liable for the full amount promised, not just the amount disbursed by the committee. As his promise was one to pay money, the Congregational Union would have been able to bring an action for the price, at least if they had performed their side of the bargain (see Chapter 23). If the defendant has failed to perform some other kind of promise—eg to convey property or to perform some service—the plaintiff's normal remedy will be to bring an action for damages. The damages should compensate the plaintiff for not getting what was promised, not merely reimburse the amount by which the plaintiff was left worse off than before.

The rule of the common law is, that where a party sustains a loss by reason of a breach of contract, he is, so far as money can do it, to be placed in the same situation, with respect to damages, as if the contract had been performed. (Parke B in *Robinson v Harman* (1848) 1 Exch 850 at 855.)

Sometimes a plaintiff will be able to get an order of specific performance, forcing the defendant to perform on pain of being in contempt of court, but specific performance is treated as an extraordinary remedy in English law. It is only granted routinely in contracts for the sale of land. (See further, Chapter 23.)

This section has attempted to set out the basic elements of contractual liability. A useful discussion will be found in Brownsword, *Contract Law: Themes for the Twenty-First Century*, 2nd edn, 2006, pp 1–45.

II. TORT AND CONTRACT

■ *Donoghue v Stevenson*

[1932] AC 562, House of Lords (Scotland)

The appellant alleged that she and a friend had visited Minchella's cafe in Paisley, where the friend had ordered some ginger beer for the appellant. The ginger beer, which was in an opaque glass bottle, was opened by Minchella, who poured part of it over some ice cream in a tumbler. The appellant drank part of the mixture and then poured out the remaining ginger beer. The decomposed remains of a snail floated out with the ginger beer. The appellant suffered shock and gastric illness as the result of drinking the ginger beer, and sued the manufacturer of the ginger beer for negligence. The respondent manufacturer pleaded that these allegations disclosed no cause of action; his plea was rejected by the Lord Ordinary. On appeal, the Second Division dismissed the appellant's action, holding that a manufacturer does not owe any duty to anyone with whom he does not have a contract, unless the article is inherently dangerous or the manufacturer actually knows that it is in a dangerous condition. The appellant appealed to the House of Lords.

Lord Atkin

... [I]n English law there must be, and is, some general conception of relations giving rise to a duty of care, of which the particular cases found in the books are but instances. The liability for negligence, whether you style it such or treat it as in other systems as a species of 'culpa', is no doubt based upon a general public sentiment of moral wrongdoing for which the offender must pay. But acts or omissions which any moral code would censure cannot in a practical world be treated so as to give a right to every person injured by them to demand relief. In this way rules of law arise which limit the range of complainants and the extent of their remedy. The rule that you are to love your neighbour becomes in law, you must not injure your neighbour; and the lawyer's question, Who is my neighbour? receives a restricted reply. You must take reasonable care to avoid acts or omissions which you can reasonably foresee would be likely to injure your neighbour. Who, then, in law is my neighbour? The answer seems to be—persons who are so closely and directly affected by my act that I ought reasonably to have them in contemplation as being so affected when I am directing my mind to the acts or omissions which are called in question. ...

My Lords, if your Lordships accept the view that this pleading discloses a relevant cause of action you will be affirming the proposition that by Scots and English law alike a manufacturer of products, which he sells in such a form as to show that he intends them to reach the ultimate consumer in the form in which they left him with no reasonable possibility of intermediate examination, and with the knowledge that the absence of reasonable care in the preparation or putting up of the products will result in an injury to the consumer's life or property, owes a duty to the consumer to take that reasonable care.

It is a proposition which I venture to say no one in Scotland or England who was not a lawyer would for one moment doubt. It will be an advantage to make it clear that the law in this matter, as in most others, is in accordance with sound common sense. I think that this appeal should be allowed.

Lord Macmillan

...It humbly appears to me that the diversity of view which is exhibited in [the] cases...is explained by the fact that in the discussion of the topic which now engages your Lordships' attention two rival principles of the law find a meeting place where each has contended for supremacy. On the one hand, there is the well established principle that no one other than a party to a contract can complain of a breach of that contract. On the other hand, there is the equally well established doctrine that negligence apart from contract gives a right of action to the party injured by that negligence—and here I use the term negligence, of course, in its technical legal sense, implying a duty owed and neglected. The fact that there is a contractual relationship between the parties which may give rise to an action for breach of contract, does not exclude the co-existence of a right of action founded on negligence as between the same parties, independently of the contract, though arising out of the relationship in fact brought about by the contract. Of this the best illustration is the right of the injured railway passenger to sue the railway company either for breach of the contract of safe carriage or for negligence in carrying him. And there is no reason why the same set of facts should not give one person a right of action in contract and another person a right of action in tort.

Where, as in cases like the present, so much depends upon the avenue of approach to the question, it is very easy to take the wrong turning. If you begin with the sale by the manufacturer to the retail dealer, then the consumer who purchases from the retailer is at once seen to be a stranger to the contract between the retailer and the manufacturer and so disentitled to sue upon it. There is no contractual relation between the manufacturer and the consumer; and thus the plaintiff, if he is to succeed, is driven to try to bring himself within one or other of the exceptional cases where the strictness of the rule that none but a party to a contract can found on a breach of that contract has been mitigated in the public interest, as it has been in the case of a person who issues a chattel which is inherently dangerous or which he knows to be in a dangerous condition. If, on the other hand, you disregard the fact that the circumstances of the case at one stage include the existence of a contract of sale between the manufacturer and the retailer, and approach the question by asking whether there is evidence of carelessness on the part of the manufacturer, and whether he owed a duty to be careful in a question with the party who has been injured in consequence of his want of care, the circumstance that the injured party was not a party to the incidental contract of sale becomes irrelevant, and his title to sue the manufacturer is unaffected by that circumstance....I have no hesitation in affirming that a person who for gain engages in the business of manufacturing articles of food and drink intended for consumption by members of the public in the form in which he issues them is under a duty to take care in the manufacture of these articles. That duty, in my opinion, he owes to those whom he intends to consume his products. He manufactures his commodities for human consumption; he intends and contemplates that they shall be consumed. By reason of that very fact he places himself in a relationship with all the potential consumers of his commodities, and that relationship which he assumes and desires for his own ends imposes upon him a duty to take care to avoid injuring them. He owes them a duty not to convert by his own carelessness an article which he issues to them as wholesome and innocent into an article which is dangerous to life and health.

Lord Thankerton delivered a judgment to the same effect; **Lords Buckmaster** and **Tomlin** dissented.

Appeal allowed.

NOTES

1.   Why could Donoghue not sue Minchella?

2.   If she had bought the ginger beer herself, would she have been better advised to sue Stevenson in tort or Minchella in contract? Why? (She could, of course, do both, but that might be unnecessarily expensive.)

3.   In the consumer context, the difficulties faced by plaintiffs who have been injured by defective products in proving that the manufacturer or producer was negligent were one of the reasons behind the introduction of 'strict' product liability by the Consumer Protection Act 1987. In fact, the 'development risk defence' contained in s 4(1)(e)

... that the state of scientific and technical knowledge at the relevant time was not such that a producer of products of the same description as the product in question might be expected to have discovered the defect. ...

means that the producer's liability is far from strict, although it is for the producer to show that the defence applies rather than for the consumer to prove negligence. The Act applies where the defective product has caused death or personal injury, or property damage of more than £275. (See generally, Clark, *Product Liability*, 1989; Stapleton, *Product Liability*, 1994; Howells, *The Law of Product Liability*, 2000.)

At the time of *Donoghue v Stevenson* and for many years thereafter it was a rule of English law that contracts only created rights and duties between parties to the contract—the privity of contract doctrine. This doctrine has been the subject of a major amendment by the Contracts (Rights of Third Parties) Act 1999 which broadly permits the contracting parties to confer contractual rights on third parties if they wish to do do. The details of this are discussed in Chapter 46 but it is worth pointing out here that the privity doctrine has a major effect on how English lawyers conceptualise contracts, which will probably have important effects for another generation.

The difficulties created by the privity doctrine were illustrated in previous editions of this book by reference to the position of building contracts. These illustrations can in fact still be used because most building contracts now have clauses excluding the effect of the 1999 Act.

One difficulty is where the employer engages a contractor to do the work and the contractor in turn employs a subcontractor to do part of it. If the work is done badly by the subcontractor, does the employer have a remedy against the subcontractor? The employer will usually have a remedy against the contractor, because the contractor is responsible for ensuring that the work is done properly, whether by itself or by a subcontractor (see p 440, but for some exceptions, pp 442–443 and 1165). In turn, the contractor will have a remedy against the subcontractor, so that the liability will pass along the chain. However, the contractor may have become insolvent, or the employer and the contractor may have reached a final settlement of all claims between them before the defect became apparent. The employer may then want to proceed directly against the subcontractor if it can do so. This problem is discussed in detail on p 1165.

A second situation is that in which a building has been constructed defectively by a builder but, before the defect has become apparent, the employer has sold the building to a purchaser. Usually, the employer/vendor will not be liable to the purchaser for physical defects in the property. She may be able to assign to the purchaser her rights against the builder, or to take action herself against the builder and then to pay what she recovers to the purchaser (on these points see further p 1142 ff); but she may not be able or willing to do either. If the vendor cannot or will not help the purchaser, what rights does the purchaser have against the original builder?

If the building is a private dwelling, the purchaser may have direct rights against the builder without having to resort to the law of tort. Most new homes are now covered by a scheme run by the National House Building Council. This provides a two-year guarantee and then a further eight-year insurance cover against defects. Even if the original owner/vendor has not assigned her rights under this scheme to the purchaser, the scheme forbids the builder to take the privity objection. New homes not covered by the scheme and all other building work done on dwellings are covered by the Defective Premises Act 1972, s 1. Under this Act, the builder will be responsible either to the person who employed it or to any subsequent owner to see that the work is done properly and with proper materials and that as regards the work the dwelling is fit for habitation when completed. This protection lasts for six years from when the building work was completed.

Where the building is not a dwelling, the purchaser's position is much less satisfactory for reasons which are explained below. This has led many employers, particularly developers who plan to resell or lease the building as soon as it is complete, to insist that the contractor and other 'construction professionals' involved give 'collateral warranties' against defective work and materials to subsequent owners or tenants so that the latter also have contractual rights.

The purchaser who cannot sue in contract or under the Defective Premises Act 1972 will have to try to recover from the builder under the law of tort. If because of the builder's negligence the building has actually collapsed, causing damage to the purchaser's property or personal injury, the purchaser will recover on the basis of *Donoghue v Stevenson*. What if it has not yet collapsed but will do so shortly if it is not repaired? Or if it is not dangerous but the defect renders it useless? Can there be liability in tort when there has been no physical injury or damage to property? Recent cases on this issue have raised fundamental issues about the law of tort and its relationship to contract.

Donoghue v Stevenson involved a negligent act leading to physical injury. The original decision was about the liability of manufacturers for defective products but the courts came gradually to accept Lord Atkin's 'neighbour principle' as a guideline to be applied in deciding whether or not there should be a 'duty of care' in novel situations. In *Home Office v Dorset Yacht Co Ltd* [1970] AC 1004, the question was whether the Home Office was responsible for the negligence of its officers in allowing the escape of some young offenders who stole and damaged the plaintiff's yacht. Lord Reid said:

> In later years there has been a steady trend towards regarding the law of negligence as depending on principle so that, when a new point emerges, one should ask not whether it is covered by authority but whether recognised principles apply to it. *Donoghue v Stevenson* may be regarded as a milestone, and the well-known passage in Lord Atkin's speech should I think be regarded as a statement of principle. It is not to be treated as if it were a statutory definition. It will require qualification in new circumstances. But I think that the time has come when we can and should say that it ought to apply unless there is some justification or valid explanation for its exclusion.

It is now generally the case that a defendant who has acted carelessly and has caused physical injury or property damage directly to a plaintiff will be liable, provided, firstly, that it was foreseeable that the plaintiff might be injured in the way that occurred, and secondly, that there is nothing in the relationship between the parties, or in a network of contracts in which they are both taking part, to suggest that the normal duty should not apply (this is discussed in detail at p 1162 ff).

Where the defendant's negligence consisted of a careless statement leading only to financial loss, it was long thought that there was no liability in tort; the plaintiff could only recover if it could be shown that the defendant had broken a contract under which he was obliged to use care in giving information. However, in 1963, the House of Lords held in *Hedley Byrne & Co Ltd v Heller & Partners* that there might be liability in tort for negligent misstatement if there was a sufficiently close relationship between the parties, although in that case the defendants were not liable because they had given the information 'without responsibility'.

■ *Hedley Byrne & Co Ltd v Heller & Partners Ltd*

[1964] AC 465, House of Lords

Hedley Byrne, an advertising agency, asked its bank to obtain a credit reference on Easipower Ltd. The bank enquired of Easipower's bankers, Hellers, and were told, in confidence and 'without responsibility', that Easipower was 'good for its ordinary business engagements'. Relying on this information, Hedley Byrne booked advertising time and space for Easipower on the basis that it was personally responsible to the television and newspaper companies concerned, and when Easipower went into liquidation, Hedley Byrne lost over £17,000 on these contracts. McNair J held Hellers was negligent, but that it owed no duty of care to Hedley Byrne. The Court of Appeal agreed with the latter point. The House of Lords held that it was unnecessary to decide whether Hellers was negligent, because it was not liable in the light of its disclaimer. However, the House of Lords said that, in some circumstances, there might be liability for negligent advice or misrepresentation if responsibility were not disclaimed.

Lord Reid

. . . [A] negligently made article will only cause one accident, and so it is not very difficult to find the necessary degree of proximity or neighbourhood between the negligent manufacturer and the person injured. But words can be broadcast with or without the consent or the foresight of the speaker or writer. It would be one thing to say that the speaker owes a duty to a limited class, but it would be going very far to say that he owes a duty to every ultimate 'consumer' who acts on those words to his detriment. It would be no use to say that a speaker or writer owes a duty but can disclaim responsibility if he wants to. He, like the manufacturer, could make it part of a contract that he is not to be liable for his negligence: but that contract would not protect him in a question with a third party, at least if the third party was unaware of it.

So it seems to me that there is good sense behind our present law that in general an innocent but negligent misrepresentation gives no cause of action. There must be something more than the mere misstatement. I therefore turn to the authorities to see what more is required. The most natural requirement would be that expressly or by implication from the circumstances the speaker or writer has undertaken some responsibility, and that appears to me not to conflict with any authority which is binding on this House. Where there is a contract there is no difficulty as regards the contracting parties: the question is whether there is a warranty. The refusal of English law to recognise any jus quaesitum tertii causes some difficulties, but they are not relevant, here. Then there are cases where a person does not merely make a statement but performs a gratuitous service. I do not intend to examine the cases about that, but at least they show that in some cases that person owes a duty of care apart from any contract, and to that extent they pave the way to holding that there can be a duty of care in making a statement of fact or opinion which is independent of contract . . . [Lord Haldane in *Robinson v National Bank of Scotland Ltd*] did not think that a duty to take care must be limited to cases of fiduciary relationship in the narrow sense of relationships which had been recognised by the Court of Chancery as being of a fiduciary character. He speaks of other special relationships, and I can see no logical stopping place short of all those relationships where it is plain that the party seeking information or advice was trusting the other to exercise such a degree of care as the circumstances required, where it was reasonable for him to do that, and where the other gave the information or advice when he knew or ought to have known that the inquirer was relying on him. I say 'ought to have known' because in questions of negligence we now apply the objective standard of what the reasonable man would have done.

A reasonable man, knowing that he was being trusted or that his skill and judgment were being relied on, would, I think, have three courses open to him. He could keep silent or decline to give the information or advice sought: or he could give an answer with a clear qualification that he accepted no responsibility for it or that it was given without that reflection or inquiry which a careful answer would require: or he could simply answer without any such qualification. If he chooses to adopt the last course he must, I think, be held to have accepted some responsibility for his answer being given carefully, or to have accepted a relationship with the inquirer which requires him to exercise such care as the circumstances require.

Lord Morris, Lord Hodson, Lord Devlin and **Lord Pearce** delivered speeches to the same effect.

Lord Devlin

... I think that there is ample authority to justify your Lordships in saying now that the categories of special relationships which may give rise to a duty to take care in word as well as in deed are not limited to contractual relationships or to relationships of fiduciary duty, but include also relationships which in the words of Lord Shaw in *Nocton v Lord Ashburton* are 'equivalent to contract', that is, where there is an assumption of responsibility in circumstances in which, but for the absence of consideration, there would be a contract.

NOTES

1. Both Lord Reid and Lord Devlin seem to explain the imposition of liability for economic loss caused by a negligent misstatement by the fact that the defendant had assumed responsibility to the plaintiff. In *Smith v Eric S Bush (a firm)* [1989] 2 All ER 514 at 536, Lord Griffiths said that this was 'unlikely to be a helpful or realistic test in most cases'. In that case, a surveyor employed by a building society to value a house as security for a loan should have known that if the loan was granted the purchaser would assume that the surveyor had found no serious defects in the house. The surveyor was held to owe a duty of care to the prospective purchaser even though the report disclaimed responsibility to the purchaser. But in *Henderson v Merrett Syndicates Ltd* [1994] 3 All ER 506 at 520–521, Lord Goff seemed to accept 'assumption of responsibility' as the basis of liability for negligent misstatement in most cases:

    There seems to be no reason why recourse should not be had to the concept, which appears after all to have been adopted, in one form or another, by all of their Lordships in *Hedley Byrne & Co Ltd v Heller & Partners Ltd*... Furthermore, especially in a context concerned with a liability which may arise under a contract or in a situation 'equivalent to contract', it must be expected that an objective test will be applied when asking the question whether, in a particular case, responsibility should be held to have been assumed by the defendant to the plaintiff: see *Caparo Industries plc v Dickman* [1990] 1 All ER 568 at 588–589 per Lord Oliver of Aylmerton. In addition, the concept provides its own explanation why there is no problem in cases of this kind about liability for pure economic loss; for if a person assumes responsibility to another in respect of certain services, there is no reason why he should not be liable in damages for that other in respect of economic loss which flows from the negligent performance of those services. It follows that, once the case is identified as falling within the *Hedley Byrne* principle, there should be no need to embark upon any further inquiry whether it is 'fair, just and reasonable' to impose liability for economic loss—a point which is, I consider, of some importance in the present case. The concept indicates too that in some circumstances, for example where the undertaking to furnish the relevant service is given on an informal occasion, there may be no assumption of responsibility; and likewise that an assumption of responsibility may be negatived by an appropriate disclaimer.

2.   In *Caparo Industries Ltd v Dickman* [1990] 1 All ER 568, it was emphasised that liability will arise only if the defendant gives the incorrect information knowing, at least in general terms, by whom the information will be acted on and for what purpose. It was alleged that auditors who, as required by statute, had audited the annual accounts of a company had negligently allowed the company to appear more profitable than was actually the case. On a preliminary issue, it was held by the House of Lords that the auditors were not under a duty of care either to investors who purchased shares, or to existing shareholders who increased their holdings, in reliance on the accounts. The auditors were responsible only to the company for which the accounts had been audited. Lord Bridge referred to a number of cases including *Hedley Byrne* and *Smith v Eric S Bush* and said (at 576):

The salient feature of all these cases is that the defendant giving advice or information was fully aware of the nature of the transaction which the plaintiff had in contemplation, knew that the advice or information would be communicated to him directly or indirectly and knew that it was very likely that the plaintiff would rely on that advice or information in deciding whether or not to engage in the transaction in contemplation. In these circumstances the defendant could clearly be expected, subject always to the effect of any disclaimer of responsibility, specifically to anticipate that the plaintiff would rely on the advice or information given by the defendant for the very purpose for which he did in the event rely on it. So also the plaintiff, subject again to the effect of any disclaimer, would in that situation reasonably suppose that he was entitled to rely on the advice or information communicated to him for the very purpose for which he required it. The situation is entirely different where a statement is put into more or less general circulation and may foreseeably be relied on by strangers to the maker of the statement for any one of a variety of different purposes which the maker of the statement has no specific reason to anticipate. To hold the maker of the statement to be under a duty of care in respect of the accuracy of the statement to all and sundry for any purpose for which they may choose to rely on it is not only to subject him, in the classic words of Cardozo CJ, to 'liability in an indeterminate amount for an indeterminate time to an indeterminate class' (see *Ultramares Corp v Touche* (1931) 255 NY 170 at 179), it is also to confer on the world at large a quite unwarranted entitlement to appropriate for their own purposes the benefit of the expert knowledge or professional expertise attributed to the maker of the statement. Hence, looking only at the circumstances of these decided cases where a duty of care in respect of negligent statements has been held to exist, I should expect to find that the 'limit or control mechanism ... imposed on the liability of a wrongdoer towards those who have suffered economic damage in consequence of his negligence' (see the *Candlewood* case [1985] 2 All ER 935 at 945, [1986] AC 1 at 25) rested on the necessity to prove, in this category of the tort of negligence, as an essential ingredient of the 'proximity' between the plaintiff and the defendant, that the defendant knew that his statement would be communicated to the plaintiff, either as an individual or as a member of an identifiable class, specifically in connection with a particular transaction or transactions of a particular kind (eg in a prospectus inviting investment) and that the plaintiff would be very likely to rely on it for the purpose of deciding whether or not to enter on that transaction or on a transaction of that kind.

In contrast, in *Morgan Crucible Co plc v Hill Samuel Bank Ltd* [1991] 1 All ER 148, the Court of Appeal held that if financial advisors to a company which was the target of a takeover bid were to make express representations about its affairs to the bidder, it was reasonably arguable that the advisors would be under a duty of care to the bidder.

3.   The differences between *Hedley Byrne* and *Donoghue v Stevenson* are twofold. Firstly, *Hedley Byrne* involved a statement, not an act, and secondly, the plaintiff had not suffered physical injury or damage, only financial loss. In contract, it is immaterial

whether the plaintiff's loss is physical or financial and in *Hedley Byrne* Lord Devlin (at 517) said that he could see no logical distinction between the two. But his has been a lone voice. The courts have treated cases of negligent misstatement as an exception to the rule that pure economic loss is not recoverable in tort and have said that where the negligence consisted of an action, purely economic loss is not normally recoverable: negligent statement apart, tort compensates only for physical harm and any financial consequences flowing directly from it, such as loss of earnings after an injury (see *Spartan Steel and Alloys Ltd v Martin & Co (Contractors) Ltd* [1973] QB 27).

4.   At one time, it appeared that liability was more extensive: in particular, that there would be liability where the plaintiff had bought a house that the defendant had negligently either built itself, or which it had allowed to be built, in a dangerously defective manner. In *Dutton v Bognor Regis UDC* [1972] 1 QB 373, the defendant council had statutory power to inspect the foundations of houses under construction but its surveyors negligently failed to stop a house being built on inadequate foundations. The Court of Appeal allowed a subsequent owner of the house to recover the cost of repair for it from the council. Lord Denning MR and Sachs LJ were prepared to treat the loss as physical damage (see [1972] 1 QB 373, 396, 403–404) and said that the builder would equally have been liable. Stamp LJ agreed that the Council was liable but did not agree that the builder would have been liable. He said (at 414–415):

...[A] distinction has been drawn between constructing a dangerous article and constructing one which is defective or of inferior quality. I may be liable to one who purchases in the market a bottle of ginger beer which I have carelessly manufactured and which is dangerous and causes injury to person or property; but it is not the law that I am liable to him for the loss he suffers because what is found inside the bottle and for which he has paid money is not ginger beer but water. I do not warrant, except to an immediate purchaser, and then by the contract and not in tort, that the thing I manufacture is reasonably fit for its purpose.

...the distinction between the case of the manufacturer of a dangerous thing which causes damage and that of a thing which turns out to be defective and valueless lies I think not in the nature of the injury but in the character of the duty. I have a duty not carelessly to put out a dangerous thing which may cause damage to one who may purchase it, but the duty does not extend to putting out carelessly a defective or useless or valueless thing.

The liability of councils in similar circumstances came before the House of Lords in *Anns v Merton London Borough Council* [1978] AC 728. The House of Lords held that, as the purpose of the statutory powers was to ensure that houses were built in compliance with the bye-laws, the council would be liable for the cost of any repairs necessary to remove any danger to health and safety of the occupants through non-compliance if negligence on the part of the council or its employees were shown. Lord Wilberforce developed Lord Reid's dictum in *Home Office v Dorset Yacht Co Ltd*, saying:

...the position has now been reached that in order to establish that a duty of care arises in a particular situation, it is not necessary to bring the facts of that situation within those of previous situations in which a duty of care has been held to exist. Rather the question has to be approached in two stages. First one has to ask whether, as between the alleged wrongdoer and the person who has suffered damage there is a sufficient relationship of proximity or neighbourhood such that, in the reasonable contemplation of the former, carelessness on his part may be likely to cause damage to the latter—in which case a prima facie duty of care arises. Secondly, if the first question is answered affirmatively, it is necessary to consider whether there are any considerations which ought to negative, or to reduce or limit the scope of the duty or the class of person to whom it is owed or the damages to which a breach of it may give rise: . . .

> However, during the 1980s opinion in the House of Lords and the Privy Council changed. In a number of cases, liability for economic loss was denied and it was said that Lord Wilberforce's two-stage test was not appropriate for such cases. For example, in *Caparo v Dickman* (see p 30), Lord Bridge quoted Lord Wilberforce and said (at 573–574):

But since *Anns's* case a series of decisions of the Privy Council and of your Lordships' House, notably in judgments and speeches delivered by Lord Keith, have emphasised the inability of any single general principle to provide a practical test which can be applied to every situation to determine whether a duty of care is owed and, if so, what is its scope: see *Peabody Donation Fund v Sir Lindsay Parkinson & Co Ltd* [1985] AC 210 at 239–241, *Yuen Kun Yeu v A-G of Hong Kong* [1988] AC 175 at 190–194, *Rowling v Takaro Properties Ltd* [1988] AC 473 at 501 and *Hill v Chief Constable of West Yorkshire* [1989] AC 53 at 60. What emerges is that, in addition to the foreseeability of damage, necessary ingredients in any situation giving rise to a duty of care are that there should exist between the party owing the duty and the party to whom it is owed a relationship characterised by the law as one of 'proximity' or 'neighbourhood' and that the situation should be one in which the court considers it fair, just and reasonable that the law should impose a duty of a given scope on the one party for the benefit of the other. But it is implicit in the passages referred to that the concepts of proximity and fairness embodied in these additional ingredients are not susceptible of any such precise definition as would be necessary to give them utility as practical tests, but amount in effect to little more than convenient labels to attach to the features of different specific situations which, on a detailed examination of all the circumstances, the law recognises pragmatically as giving rise to a duty of care of a given scope. Whilst recognising, of course, the importance of the underlying general principles common to the whole field of negligence, I think the law has now moved in the direction of attaching greater significance to the more traditional categorisation of distinct and recognisable situations as guides to the existence, the scope and the limits of the varied duties of care which the law imposes. We must now, I think, recognise the wisdom of the words of Brennan J in the High Court of Australia in *Sutherland Shire Council v Heyman* (1985) 60 ALR 1 at 43–44, where he said:

> 'It is preferable in my view, that the law should develop novel categories of negligence incrementally and by analogy with established categories, rather than by a massive extension of a prima facie duty of care restrained only by indefinable "considerations which ought to negative, or to reduce or limit the scope of the duty or the class of person to whom it is owed".'

One of the most important distinctions always to be observed lies in the law's essentially different approach to the different kinds of damage which one party may have suffered in consequence of the acts or omissions of another. It is one thing to owe a duty of care to avoid causing injury to the person or property of others. It is quite another to avoid causing others to suffer purely economic loss.

> Ultimately, in *Murphy v Brentwood DC* (below), the House of Lords overruled its own earlier decision in *Anns*.

5.   Before the judicial retrenchment started, the House of Lords decided one case in which liability was imposed even outside the 'dangerously defective' doctrine laid down in *Anns*. In *Junior Books Ltd v Veitchi Co Ltd* [1983] 1 AC 520 (see p 1163), the owners engaged a building company to build a factory for them, under a form of building contract which required the builders to employ for certain tasks subcontractors 'nominated' by the owners. The owners nominated the appellant subcontractors to lay a special concrete floor in the main production area, and the appellants duly entered a subcontract with the builders.

There was no contract between the owners and the nominated subcontractors. Two years after the floor had been laid it developed cracks and, rather than have perpetual maintenance to keep the floor usable, the owners wanted to have it replaced, which they alleged would be cheaper. They brought an action against the subcontractors alleging that the subcontractors had laid the floor negligently, and claiming the cost of replacing the floor and the economic loss that would result from closing the factory and moving the machinery out of it while the work was done. The subcontractors replied that, as there was no allegation that the floor was dangerous, the owners' claim disclosed no cause of action. The House of Lords held that the owners did have a cause of action. However this decision seems to rest on the existence of a special relationship between the owners and the nominated subcontractors similar to the special relationship which, but for the disclaimer, would have existed in *Hedley Byrne*. The implications of *Junior Books* are discussed below (p 1164 ff) but you will see references to it in the next case.

■ *Murphy v Brentwood District Council*
[1990] 2 All ER 908, House of Lords

In 1970, the plaintiff purchased from a construction company one of a pair of semi-detached houses newly constructed on an in-filled site on a concrete raft foundation to prevent damage from settlement. The plans and calculations for the raft foundation were submitted to the local council for building regulation approval prior to the construction of the houses. The council referred the plans and calculations to consulting engineers for checking and on their recommendation approved the design under the building regulations and bye-laws. In 1981, the plaintiff noticed serious cracks in his house and discovered that the raft foundation was defective and that differential settlement beneath it had caused it to distort. The plaintiff was unable to carry out the necessary repairs to the foundation, which would have cost £45,000, and in 1986, the plaintiff sold the house subject to the defects for £35,000 less than its market value in sound condition. He brought an action against the council claiming that it was liable for the consulting engineers' negligence in recommending approval of the plans and alleging that he and his family had suffered an imminent risk to health and safety because gas and soil pipes had broken and there was a risk of further breaks. The judge, who found as a fact that the plaintiff had been exposed to an imminent risk to health and safety, held the council liable for the consulting engineers' negligence and awarded the plaintiff damages of £38,777, being the loss on the sale of the house and expenses. The council appealed to the Court of Appeal, which held, following existing House of Lords authority, that the council owed a duty of care to the plaintiff to see that the house was properly built so that injury to the safety or health of those who lived in it was avoided and that it was in breach of that duty when it approved plans for a defective raft foundation. The court accordingly dismissed the appeal. The council appealed to the House of Lords.

Lord Bridge

...

Dangerous defects and defects of quality

If a manufacturer negligently puts into circulation a chattel containing a latent defect which renders it dangerous to persons or property, the manufacturer, on the well-known principles established by *Donoghue v Stevenson* . . ., will be liable in tort for injury to persons or damage to property which the chattel causes. But if a manufacturer produces and sells a chattel which is merely defective in quality, even to the extent that it is valueless for the purpose for which it is intended, the manufacturer's liability at common law arises only under and by reference to the terms of any contract to which he is a party in relation to the chattel; the common law does not impose on him any liability in tort to persons to whom he owes no duty in contract but who, having acquired the chattel, suffer economic loss because the chattel is defective in quality. If a dangerous defect in a chattel is discovered before it causes any personal injury or damage to property, because the danger is now known and the chattel cannot be safely used unless the defect is repaired, the defect becomes merely a defect in quality. The chattel is either capable of repair at economic cost or it is worthless and must be scrapped. In either case the loss sustained by the owner or hirer of the chattel is purely economic. It is recoverable against any party who owes the loser a relevant contractual duty. But it is not recoverable in tort in the absence of a special relationship of proximity imposing on the tortfeasor a duty of care to safeguard the plaintiff from economic loss. There is no such special relationship between the manufacturer of a chattel and a remote owner or hirer.

I believe that these principles are equally applicable to buildings. If a builder erects a structure containing a latent defect which renders it dangerous to persons or property, he will be liable in tort for injury to persons or damage to property resulting from that dangerous defect. But, if the defect becomes apparent before any injury or damage has been caused, the loss sustained by the building owner is purely economic. If the defect can be repaired at economic cost, that is the measure of the loss. If the building cannot be repaired, it may have to be abandoned as unfit for occupation and therefore valueless. These economic losses are recoverable if they flow from breach of a relevant contractual duty, but, here again, in the absence of a special relationship of proximity they are not recoverable in tort. The only qualification I would make to this is that, if a building stands so close to the boundary of the building owner's land that after discovery of the dangerous defect it remains a potential source of injury to persons or property on neighbouring land or on the highway, the building owner ought, in principle, to be entitled to recover in tort from the negligent builder the cost of obviating the danger, whether by repair or by demolition, so far as that cost is necessarily incurred in order to protect himself from potential liability to third parties.

The fallacy which, in my opinion, vitiates the judgments of Lord Denning MR and Sachs LJ in *Dutton* . . . is that they brush these distinctions aside as of no consequence. Stamp LJ, on the other hand, fully understood and appreciated them and his statement of the applicable principles as between the building owner and the builder seems to me unexceptionable . . . He rested his decision in favour of the plaintiff against the local authority on a wholly distinct principle which will require separate examination.

The complex structure theory

In my speech in the *D & F Estates* case . . . I mooted the possibility that in complex structures or complex chattels one part of a structure or chattel might, when it caused damage to another part of the same structure or chattel, be regarded in the law of tort as having caused damage to 'other property' for the purpose of the application of *Donoghue v Stevenson* principles. I expressed no opinion as to the validity of this theory, but put it forward for consideration as a possible ground on which the facts considered in *Anns* might be distinguishable from the facts which had to be considered in *D & F Estates* itself. I shall call this for convenience 'the complex structure theory' and it is, so far as I can see, only if and to the extent that this theory can be affirmed and applied that there can be any escape from the conclusions I have indicated above under the rubric 'Dangerous defects and defects of quality' . . . The reality is that the structural elements in any building form a single indivisible unit of which the different parts are essentially interdependent. To the extent that there is any defect in one part of the structure it must to a greater or lesser degree necessarily affect all other parts of the structure. Therefore any defect in the structure is a defect in the quality of the whole and it is quite artificial, in order to impose a legal liability which the law would not otherwise impose, to treat a defect in an integral structure, so far as it weakens the structure, as a dangerous defect liable to cause damage to 'other property'.

A critical distinction must be drawn here between some part of a complex structure which is said to be a 'danger' only because it does not perform its proper function in sustaining the other parts and some distinct item incorporated in the structure which positively malfunctions so as to inflict positive damage on the structure in which it is incorporated. Thus, if a defective central heating boiler explodes and damages a house or a defective electrical installation malfunctions and sets the house on fire, I see no reason to doubt that the owner of the house, if he can prove that the damage was due to the negligence of the boiler manufacturer in the one case or the electrical contractor in the other, can recover damages in tort on *Donoghue v Stevenson* principles. But the position in law is entirely different where, by reason of the inadequacy of the foundations of the building to support the weight of the superstructure, differential settlement and consequent cracking occurs. Here, once the first cracks appear, the structure as a whole is seen to be defective and the nature of the defect is known. Even if, contrary to my view, the initial damage could be regarded as damage to other property caused by a latent defect, once the defect is known the situation of the building owner is analogous to that of the car owner who discovers that the car has faulty brakes. He may have a house which, until repairs are effected, is unfit for habitation, but, subject to the reservation I have expressed with respect to ruinous buildings at or near the boundary of the owner's property, the building no longer represents a source of danger and as it deteriorates will only damage itself.

For these reasons the complex structure theory offers no escape from the conclusion that damage to a house itself which is attributable to a defect in the structure of the house is not recoverable in tort on *Donoghue v Stevenson* principles, but represents purely economic loss which is only recoverable in contract or in tort by reason of some special relationship of proximity which imposes on the tortfeasor a duty of care to protect against economic loss.

The relative positions of the builder and the local authority

I have so far been considering the potential liability of a builder for negligent defects in the structure of a building to persons to whom he owes no contractual duty. Since the relevant statutory function of the local authority is directed to no other purpose than securing compliance with building byelaws or regulations by the builder, I agree with the view expressed in *Anns* and by the majority of the Court of Appeal in *Dutton* that a negligent performance of that function can attract no greater liability than attaches to the negligence of the builder whose fault was the primary tort giving rise to any relevant damage. I am content for present purposes to assume, though I am by no means satisfied that the assumption is correct, that where the local authority, as in this case or in *Dutton*, has in fact approved the defective plans or inspected the defective foundations and negligently failed to discover the defect, its potential liability in tort is coextensive with that of the builder.

Only Stamp LJ in *Dutton* was prepared to hold that the law imposed on the local authority a duty of care going beyond that imposed on the builder and extending to protection of the building owner from purely economic loss. I must return later to consider the question of liability for economic loss more generally, but here I need only say that I cannot find in *Hedley Byrne & Co Ltd v Heller & Partners Ltd* . . . or *Home Office v Dorset Yacht Co Ltd* . . . any principle applicable to the circumstances of *Dutton* or the present case that provides support for the conclusion which Stamp LJ sought to derive from those authorities.

Imminent danger to health or safety

A necessary element in the building owner's cause of action against the negligent local authority, which does not appear to have been contemplated in *Dutton* but which, it is said in *Anns*, must be present before the cause of action accrues, is that the state of the building is such that there is present or imminent danger to the health or safety of persons occupying it. Correspondingly the damages recoverable are said to include the amount of expenditure necessary to restore the building to a condition in which it is no longer such a danger, but presumably not any further expenditure incurred in any merely qualitative restoration. I find these features of the *Anns* doctrine very difficult to understand.

As I have already said, since the function of a local authority in approving plans or inspecting buildings in the course of construction is directed to ensuring that the builder complies with building byelaws or regulations, I cannot see how, in principle, the scope of the liability of the authority for a negligent failure to ensure compliance can exceed that of the liability of the builder for his negligent failure to comply.

There may, of course, be situations where, even in the absence of contract, there is a special relationship of proximity between builder and building owner which is sufficiently akin to contract to introduce the element of reliance so that the scope of the duty of care owed by the builder to the owner is wide enough to embrace purely economic loss. The decision in *Junior Books Ltd v Veitchi Co Ltd* [1982] 3 All ER 201, [1983] 1 AC 520 can, I believe, only be understood on this basis.

The other members of the Judicial Committee, **Lord Mackay LC** and **Lords Keith**, **Brandon**, **Ackner**, **Oliver** and **Jauncey** gave speeches to broadly similar effect.

Appeal allowed.

NOTES

1.   Thus it appears that a builder will not be liable in tort for a house that is badly built even if it is dangerous to the owner. Note that in both *Anns v Merton London Borough Council* and *Murphy v Brentwood District Council* the defendants were not, in fact, the builders but the local authority. It is possible to envisage a system in which the builder is liable but the local authority is not, but in England it appears to have been assumed that the two stand in the same position. The Supreme Court of Canada held in *Winnipeg Condominium Corpn No 36 v Bird Construction Co Ltd* (1995) 50 Con LR 124 that the builder was liable where he negligently constructed the building in a way which was dangerous to person or property even though the only loss actually suffered by the plaintiff was the cost of repairing damage to the building or making it safe. The High Court of Australia went a step further in *Bryan v Maloney* (1995) 51 Con LR 29 and held, by a majority, that the negligent builder was liable even if the product of his negligence was a shoddy rather than a dangerous building. However, in the later case of *Woolcock Street Investments Pty Ltd v CDG Pty Ltd* (2004) 205 ALR 522, the High Court refused to extend *Bryan v Maloney* and, indeed, came close to overturning it.

2.   On parallel legal reasoning, in English law a manufacturer will not be liable for defective goods that have not caused any injury or damage to property, unless there is a 'special relationship' between the builder or manufacturer and the owner. Nor will a manufacturer be liable under the 'product liability' provisions of the Consumer Protection Act 1987 merely because a product is defective. Damage to property is recoverable under the Act if the damage exceeds £275, but there is no liability for loss or damage to the product itself: s 5(2).

3.   The circumstances in which a special relationship may exist are explored in more detail below (p 1166), but at this stage it is worth asking a simple question relating to a fact pattern that we have touched on already. Might there be a special relationship between the manufacturer of goods and a consumer who bought the goods from a third party, typically from a retailer? *In Junior Books*, Lord Roskill was definite that there would not be a special relationship in such a case. The 'proximity' required

would not easily be found to exist in the ordinary everyday transaction of purchasing chattels when it is obvious that in truth the real reliance was upon the immediate vendor and not upon the manufacturer.

With respect, this argument is not wholly convincing. Sometimes consumers buy goods from retailers relying entirely on the retailers' reputations, eg when they buy 'own brand' goods. But frequently they rely on the manufacturer's reputation rather than the retailer's choice or advice. (Think about your own experience. Have you ever decided which manufacturer's brand you want to buy and then bought it from whatever retailer is offering it most cheaply or is most convenient to you?) However, denial of a special relationship between the manufacturer of brand-name goods and the consumer is consistent with *Caparo:* the manufacturer will not know who is buying the goods nor for what specific purpose.

4.   Lord Bridge says that there will not be liability just because one part of a structure fails, causing damage to other parts; to regard this as 'damage to other property' would be 'quite artificial'. But he accepts that if a central heating boiler explodes, damaging the rest of the house, the boiler manufacturer may be liable. What is the distinction between the two situations? It seems to rest on who the defendant is. As far as the builder of the house is concerned, a house in which the boiler has exploded is still a defective house. However, if the owner were to sue the manufacturer of the boiler, it might be said that the exploding boiler has damaged 'other property'—the rest of the house. Lord Keith (at 922) and Lord Jauncey made this even clearer. Lord Jauncey said (at 942):

It seems to me that the only context for the complex structure theory in the case of a building would be where one integral component of the structure was built by a separate contractor and where a defect in such a component had caused damage to other parts of the structure, eg a steel frame erected by a specialist contractor which failed to give adequate support to floors or walls. Defects in such ancillary equipment as central heating boilers or electrical installations would be subject to the normal *Donoghue v Stevenson* principle if such defects gave rise to damage to other parts of the building.

5.   Most of the tort cases considered so far have been ones in which the claimant could not have sued the defendant in contract because there was no contract between them. On occasion, a claimant who has a contract with the defendant has tried to use *Hedley Byrne* as the basis for arguing that the defendant has a duty of care in tort that is more extensive that its obligations under the contract. Here, the courts have been reluctant to impose tortious liability. In *Tai Hing Cotton Mill Ltd v Liu Chong Hing Bank Ltd* [1985] 2 All ER 947 at 957, Lord Scarman said:

Their Lordships do not believe that there is anything to the advantage of the law's development in searching for a liability in tort where the parties are in a contractual relationship. This is particularly so in a commercial relationship. Though it is possible as a matter of legal semantics to conduct an analysis of the rights and duties inherent in some contractual relationships including that of banker and customer either as a matter of contract law when the question will be what, if any, terms are to be implied or as a matter of tort law when the task will be to identify a duty arising from the proximity and character of the relationship between the parties, their Lordships believe it to be correct in principle and necessary for the avoidance of confusion in the law to adhere to the contractual analysis: on principle because it is a relationship in which the parties have, subject to a few exceptions, the right to determine their obligations to each other, and for the avoidance of confusion because different consequences do follow according to whether liability arises from contract or tort, eg in the limitation of action.

6.   Sometimes, the same event will result in the defendant being liable in both contract and tort. The claimant may choose which action to bring: for example, the limitation period under one may be more favourable than under the other. This principle is long established in cases of physical injury or property damage. As Oliver J said in *Midland*

Bank & Trust Co Ltd v Hett, Stubbs & Kemp (a firm) [1978] 3 All ER 571 at 578:

There is not and never has been any rule of law that a person having alternative claims must frame his action in one or the other. If I have a contract with my dentist to extract a tooth, I am not thereby precluded from suing him in tort if he negligently shatters my jaw *(Edwards v Mallan* [1908] 1 KB 1002).

In *Henderson v Merrett Syndicates Ltd* [1994] 3 All ER 506, the House of Lords held that the same rule applies to claims under *Hedley Byrne v Heller* and under contract. The fact that there was a claim in contract did not preclude one under *Hedley Byrne*. Lord Goff (at 526), as had Sir Thomas Bingham MR in the Court of Appeal ([1994] 2 Lloyd's Rep at 476), distinguished the *Tai Hing*, case. As Sir Thomas put it, in *Tai Hing*, the argument had been that a duty was owed in tort which was more extensive than that owed in contract. In *Henderson*, the duty contended for was the same, irrespective of its source.

7.   Later we will consider one situation in which liability in tort is regularly imposed between parties to a contract even though there may be no liability under the contract itself. This is when one party has entered the contract relying on incorrect information given her by the other party. If the person who gave the incorrect information (the misrepresentor) was acting fraudulently (eg he knew that what he said was untrue), he will be liable in tort for fraud. If he was not fraudulent but should have known that his statement was incorrect, he may be liable either for negligence under *Hedley Byrne*, if there was a special relationship between the parties, or under the Misrepresentation Act 1967, s 2(1). This subsection makes him liable in damages unless he can disprove negligence. For details, see Chapter 13.

8.   If the claimant does have an action in tort against the defendant, the damages will not be assessed in the same way as they would be if the claimant had an action for breach of contract arising on the same facts. In *Doyle v Olby (Ironmongers) Ltd* [1969] 2 QB 158, a case of fraud, Lord Denning MR said:

Damages for fraud and conspiracy are assessed differently from damages for breach of contract... [In] *McConnel v Wright*, Lord Collins MR pointed out the difference. It was an action for fraudulent statements in a prospectus whereby a man was induced to take up shares. Lord Collins said of the action for fraud:

'It is not an action for breach of contract, and, therefore, no damages in respect of prospective gains which the person contracting was entitled by his contract to expect to come in, but it is an action of tort—it is an action for a wrong done whereby the plaintiff was tricked out of certain money in his pocket, and, therefore, prima facie, the highest limit of his damages is the whole extent of his loss, and that loss is measured by the money which was in his pocket...'

On principle the distinction seems to be this: in contract, the defendant has made a promise and broken it. The object of damages is to put the plaintiff in as good a position, as far as money can do it, as if the promise had been performed. In fraud, the defendant has been guilty of a deliberate wrong by inducing the plaintiff to act to his detriment. The object of damages is to compensate the plaintiff for all the loss he has suffered, so far, again, as money can do it.

It seems that the same would apply if the claimant had an action for negligence under *Hedley Byrne*. In *Shanklin Pier Ltd v Detel Products Ltd* [1951] 2 KB 854, the Pier enquired whether the defendants' paint would be suitable for its pier and was assured by the defendants' representative that it would be suitable and would last seven years. Relying on this, the plaintiffs ordered its painting contractor to buy and use Detel's paint.

The paint was not suitable for the job and peeled off. On such facts, there might nowadays be a special relationship between the plaintiff and the defendants. Suppose the plaintiffs, via the painting contractor, had spent £5,000 for the paint but to buy paint that would last seven years in salt water would cost £7,500. If the claim is in tort, will the plaintiff's recover £5,000 or £7,500? The actual decision in *Shanklin Pier* was that there was a contract between the plaintiffs and the defendants. (Compare *Donoghue*, p 24 above, and see further, p 1166–1167.) How much would the damages be in contract? (The cost of having the painting done again would be recoverable under either tort or contract.)

III. RESTITUTION AND CONTRACT

■ *British Steel Corpn v Cleveland Bridge and Engineering Co Ltd*
[1984] 1 All ER 504

The plaintiffs (BSC) were approached by the defendants (CBE) to supply a number of steel nodes to be used in the construction of a steel-framed building, which CBE were building under another contract. There were extensive discussions as to the specification and the terms on which the nodes were to be supplied, and while the discussion over terms was still continuing, CBE issued a letter of intent requesting BSC to start work, 'pending the preparation and issuing to you of the official form of sub-contract'. By 28 December, all but one of the nodes had been delivered but the parties were still negotiating over the terms, including the question of liability for loss caused by late delivery. Because it had not been paid for any of the nodes delivered so far, BSC withheld delivery of the last node; there was then a steel strike, and the node could not be delivered until 11 April. BSC, claiming that no contract had been made, brought an action for the reasonable value of the nodes, and CBE counterclaimed for damages of a higher amount for late delivery.

Robert Goff J

... I now turn to the first issue in the case, which is concerned with the legal basis for BSC's claim for payment, and in particular whether there was any binding contract between BSC and CBE and, if so, what were its terms. As I have already indicated, it is the contention of CBE that there was such a contract; whereas BSC contends that they are entitled to payment in quasi contract ...

Now the question whether in a case such as the present any contract has come into existence must depend on a true construction of the relevant communications which have passed between the parties and the effect (if any) of their actions pursuant to those communications. There can be no hard and fast answer to the question whether a letter of intent will give rise to a binding agreement: everything must depend on the circumstances of the particular case. In most cases, where work is done pursuant to a request contained in a letter of intent, it will not matter whether a contract did or did not come into existence, because, if the party who has acted on the request is simply claiming payment, his claim will usually be based on a quantum meruit, and it will make no difference whether that claim is contractual or quasi-contractual. Of course, a quantum meruit claim (like the old actions for money had and received and for money paid) straddles the boundaries of what we now call contract and restitution, so the mere framing of a claim as a quantum meruit claim, or a claim for a reasonable sum, does not assist in classifying the claim as contractual or quasi contractual. But where, as here, one party is seeking to claim damages for breach of contract, the question whether any contract came into existence is of crucial importance.

As a matter of analysis the contract (if any) which may come into existence following a letter of intent may take one of two forms: either there may be an ordinary executory contract, under which each party assumes reciprocal obligations to the other; or there may be what is sometimes called an 'if' contract, ie a contract under which A requests B to carry out a certain performance and promises B that, if he does so, he will receive a certain performance in return, usually remuneration for his performance. The latter transaction is really no more than a standing offer which, if acted on before it lapses or is lawfully withdrawn, will result in a binding contract.

The former type of contract was held to exist by Mr Edgar Fay QC, the official Referee, in *Turriff Construction Ltd v Regalia Knitting Mills Ltd*, and it is the type of contract for which counsel for CBE contended in the present case. Of course, as I have already said, everything must depend on the facts of the particular case; but certainly, on the facts of the present case (and, as I imagine, on the facts of most cases), this must be a very difficult submission to maintain. It is only necessary to look at the terms of CBE's letter of intent in the present case to appreciate the difficulties. In that letter, the request to BSC to proceed immediately with the work was stated to be 'pending the preparation and issuing to you of the official form of sub-contract', being a sub-contract which was plainly in a state of negotiation, not least on the issues of price, delivery dates, and the applicable terms and conditions. In these circumstances, it is very difficult to see how BSC, by starting work, bound themselves to any contractual performance. No doubt it was envisaged by CBE at the time they sent the letter that negotiations had reached an advanced stage, and that a formal contract would soon be signed; but, since the parties were still in a stage of negotiation, it is impossible to say with any degree of certainty what the material terms of that contract would be. I find myself quite unable to conclude that, by starting work in these circumstances, BSC bound themselves to complete the work. In the course of argument, I put to counsel for CBE the question whether BSC were free at any time, after starting work, to cease work. His submission was that they were not free to do so, even if negotiations on the terms of the formal contract broke down completely. I find this submission to be so repugnant to common sense and the commercial realities that I am unable to accept it. It is perhaps revealing that, on 4 April 1979, BSC did indeed state that they were not prepared to proceed with the contract until they had an agreed specification, a reaction which, in my judgment, reflected not only the commercial, but also the legal, realities of the situation.

I therefore, reject CBE's submission that a binding executory contract came into existence in this case. There remains the question whether, by reason of BSC carrying out work pursuant to the request contained in CBE's letter of intent, there came into existence a contract by virtue of which BSC were entitled to claim reasonable remuneration; ie whether there was an 'if' contract of the kind I have described. In the course of argument, I was attracted by this alternative (really on the basis that, not only was it analytically possible, but also that it could provide a vehicle for certain contractual obligations of BSC concerning their performance, eg implied terms as to the quality of goods supplied by them). But the more I have considered the case, the less attractive I have found this alternative. The real difficulty is to be found in the factual matrix of the transaction, and in particular the fact that the work was being done pending a formal sub-contract the terms of which were still in a state of negotiation. It is, of course, a notorious fact that, when a contract is made for the supply of goods on a scale and in circumstances such as the present, it will in all probability be subject to standard terms, usually the standard terms of the supplier. Such standard terms will frequently legislate, not only for the liability of the seller for defects, but also for the damages (if any) for which the seller will be liable in the event not only of defects in the goods but also of late delivery. It is a commonplace that a seller of goods may exclude liability for consequential loss, and may agree liquidated damages for delay. In the present case, an unresolved dispute broke out between the parties on the question whether CBE's or BSC's standard terms were to apply, the former providing no limit to the seller's liability for delay and the latter excluding such liability altogether. Accordingly, when, in a case such as the present, the parties are still in a state of negotiation, it is impossible to predicate what liability (if any) will be assumed by the seller for, eg defective goods or late delivery, if a formal contract should be entered into. In these circumstances, if the buyer asks the seller to commence work 'pending' the parties entering into a formal contract, it is difficult to infer from the buyer acting on that request that he is assuming any responsibility for his performance, except such responsibility as will rest on him under the terms of the contract which both parties confidently anticipate they will shortly enter into. It would be an extraordinary result if, by acting on such a request in such circumstances, the buyer were to assume an unlimited liability for his contractual performance, when he would never assume such liability under any contract which he entered into.

For these reasons, I reject the solution of the 'if' contract. In my judgment, the true analysis of the situation is simply this. Both parties confidently expected a formal contract to eventuate. In these circumstances, to expedite performance under that anticipated contract, one requested the other to commence the contract work, and the other complied with that request. If thereafter, as anticipated, a contract was entered into, the work done as requested will be treated as having been performed under that contract; if, contrary to their expectation, no contract was entered into, then the performance of the work is not referable to any contract the terms of which can be ascertained, and the law simply imposes an obligation on the party who made the request, such an obligation sounding in quasi contract or, as we now say, in restitution. Consistently with that solution, the party making the request may find himself liable to pay for work which he would not have had to pay for as such if the anticipated contract had come into existence, eg preparatory work which will, if the contract is made, be allowed for in the price of the finished work (cf *William Lacey (Hounslow) Ltd v Davis*). This solution moreover accords with authority: see the decision in *Lacey v Davis*, the decision of the Court of Appeal in *Sanders & Forster Ltd v A Monk & Co Ltd*, though that decision rested in part on a concession, and the crisp dictum of Parker J in *OTM Ltd v Hydranautics*, when he said of a letter of intent that 'its only effect would be to enable the defendants to recover on a quantum meruit for work done pursuant to the direction' contained in the letter. I only wish to add to this part of my judgment the footnote that, even if I had concluded that in the circumstances of the present case there was a contract between the parties and that that contract was of the kind I have described as an 'if' contract, then I would still have concluded that there was no obligation under that contract on the part of BSC to continue with or complete the contract work, and therefore no obligation on their part to complete the work within a reasonable time. However, my conclusion in the present case is that the parties never entered into any contract at all.

Judgment for the plaintiffs.

NOTES

1. Restitutionary (or quasi-contractual) liability is based on the unjust enrichment of the defendant at the expense of the claimant. Burrows, *Law of Restitution* 2nd ed, 2002); p 15, explains:

   Stripping the unjust enrichment principle down into its component parts, there are four questions to be answered:

   (1) has the defendant been *benefited* (ie enriched)?
   (2) was the enrichment *at the claimant's expense*?
   (3) was the enrichment *unjust*?
   (4) are there any *defences*?

   If the first three questions are answered affirmatively and the fourth negatively the claimant will be entitled to restitution.

2. Restitution is frequently used 'in the contractual context'. The *British Steel* case involved work done in anticipation of a contract that never came into existence. This situation will be discussed in detail later, when we will see that restitutionary liability is only one of the bases on which, depending on the facts of the case, liability might be imposed on one of the parties. Other possibilities include liability on a 'preliminary contract' (as in

Turriff Construction Ltd v Regalia Knitting Mills Ltd, referred to by Robert Goff J) and liability for fraud or negligence.

3.   We will also find that restitutionary liability is relevant when a mistake prevents the formation of a contract (Chapters 10 and 17); when a contract is voidable for misrepresentation (Chapter 13), duress (Chapter 34), undue influence (Chapter 35) or because it falls within one of the categories of unconscionability (Chapter 36); when a contract is discharged for frustration (Chapter 16) or on similar grounds (Chapter 18); where the contract is unenforceable for illegality (Section 9); and in some cases after a contract has been terminated by one party because of a serious breach by the other (Chapter 24).

4.   Restitutionary (or quasi-contractual) liability should be distinguished from liability on an 'implied contract'. The latter is simply a contract that the court infers from the conduct of the parties although they had not made a contract in so many words (eg *Tanner v Tanner*). There may be restitutionary liability even though there could not be a contract. For example, in *Re Rhodes* (1890) 44 Ch D 94, part of the cost of maintaining a woman in a private lunatic asylum had been paid by the plaintiffs, who after her death brought an action against her estate. It was held that, even if she was incapable of making a contract, there might be a claim in restitution, although the claim failed because when they made the payments the plaintiffs had no intention of seeking repayment.

5.   As Robert Goff points out, a *quantum meruit* (a claim for the value of the work) may be a restitutionary claim or a contractual claim. A claimant who claims in restitution for the value of the services rendered to the defendant when there was no contract between them, as the judge held here, will bring a *quantum meruit* claim; but where there is contract to pay a reasonable sum, the sum payable is often also referred to as a *quantum meruit*.

6.   The first element of a restitutionary claim mentioned by Burrows, benefit to the defendant, was present in the *British Steel* case. This seems intuitively obvious but it is worth pausing to analyse precisely why the defendants were benefited. In some cases of restitution, the claimant is simply seeking to recover money he has paid or his property, which has somehow come into the defendant's hands. Then there can be little argument that the defendant is benefited. But in *British Steel* the plaintiffs were not asking for the return of the nodes; they were seeking their price or their value. Thus they must show that the defendants were benefited by having them.

7.   In many cases, showing that the defendant was benefited will be easy: the defendant has received money or property, which has a resale value, and there is what Burrows terms an 'objective benefit'. In *British Steel*, however, the nodes were of a special design and probably had little, if any, resale value in the general market. (Rather similar problems arise if the defendant has received a benefit that cannot simply be resold and which he claims is of no value to him: eg the claimant has landscaped the defendant's garden and the defendant claims that this is of no value to him. This is often called the 'subjective devaluation' argument.) The argument could be countered in one of two ways:

(i)   *Incontrovertible benefit.*

(a)   If Cleveland Bridge had actually been paid for the nodes by its client when they were delivered to the building site or were installed, Cleveland Bridge would not be permitted to argue that they were valueless. As it is sometimes put, it would have been 'incontrovertibly benefited'.

(b)   If Cleveland Bridge had not been paid, it might still be argued that, had it not obtained nodes from BSC, it would have been obliged under its contract with its client to obtain them from another supplier. Thus BSC had saved Cleveland

Bridge expense. This form of negative benefit is just as valuable to the defendant as a realisable gain.

(ii) *The benefit was bargained for.* Cleveland Bridge had asked BSC to produce and deliver the nodes, and this may prevent it from arguing that it received nothing of value. This sort of argument is usually used in cases in which the claimant has performed some service at the defendant's request, but there has been no tangible end product. In such cases, there is some controversy over granting a restitutionary remedy and the question is explored in greater detail on p 492.

8. There are frequently difficulties in valuing the benefit that the defendant has received. Suppose the defendant has requested the claimant to perform a service such as prospecting for minerals and (either without a contract ever being made, or under a contract which is subsequently discharged) the claimant does the prospecting. Should the benefit to the defendant be judged by the cost of providing the services or by the value of the end product—which, according to whether or not minerals are discovered, may be much greater or less than the cost of the services? This is explored on p 486.

9. It is worth emphasising that, when restitution is used in the 'contractual context', recovery will normally be based on the benefit to the defendant. The amount that the claimant may have been promised, or the amount that he has spent, is not directly relevant (see below). In the Canadian case of *Deglman v Guaranty Trust Co of Canada and Constantineau* [1954] 3 DLR 785, the respondent was the nephew of the deceased. When he was aged 20, he lived with his aunt for about six months. She promised him that if he would be good to her and do such services as she might request during her lifetime, she would make adequate provision for him in her will and, in particular, would leave him a house she owned. He drove his aunt on trips to Montreal and elsewhere, did chores about the house and performed other minor services. The Supreme Court of Canada held that the respondent had performed these services in the expectation of receiving the promised reward, but that any contract was unenforceable under the Statute of Frauds (RSO 1950, c 371) s 4, which provided that no action could be brought on a contract concerning land unless the agreement was in writing or there was a written note of it signed by the other party. Nor did the respondent's actions constitute sufficient part performance to take the case out of the statute (the Statute of Frauds is dealt with on p 144). However, the respondent was awarded $3,000 in restitution as the reasonable value of his services.

10. The second element stated by Burrows is that the defendant has received the benefit at the claimant's expense. The majority of restitutionary claims relating to contracts that were never effective or were discharged are based on the transfer of money or property, or the performance of services, by the claimant. Here, the benefit is at the claimant's expense; indeed, the strength of the claimant's claim lies in the fact that there was a loss to him matched by a gain to the defendant (see p 765). But there can be difficulties when the property transferred did not in fact belong to the claimant but to a third person (see p 427).

11. The status of the second element raises important and difficult questions where the defendant breaks the contract in a way that creates a profit for it which exceeds the loss to the claimant. There is no doubt that the general rule is that damages for breach of contract depend on the extent of the claimant's loss. Where the breach of contract involves misuse of the claimant's property, the claimant has been permitted to claim a reasonable sum for the use of the property without having to prove that it has suffered any loss (for example, it does not have to prove that it would have been using the

property itself, or hiring it out to anyone else, at the time). Such compensation has sometimes been termed 'restitutionary damages'. (Somewhat similarly, it is recognised that the victims of certain torts may 'waive the tort' and seek restitution of the gain the defendant has made through the wrong rather than compensation for the loss caused by it.) These misuse of property cases were thought to be exceptional and that in all other cases of breach of contract the claimant could recover compensation only for the amount of any loss suffered. However, in *A-G v Blake* [2000] 4 All ER 385, the House of Lords had held that the rule that damages are only to compensate the claimant for loss is subject to further exceptions (see p 750), although it deprecated the use of the expression 'restitutionary damages' to describe cases of this kind.

12. Burrow's third element is that the enrichment must be unjust. The general principle underlying liability in restitution is, as Lord Mansfield put it in *Moses v Macferlan* (1760) 2 Burr 1005, 1012,

that the defendant, upon the circumstances of the case, is obliged by the ties of natural justice and equity to refund the money.

However, this general principle is not a rule of law: in order to recover, the claimant must show that her case falls within one of a limited number of categories. Leaving aside the cases of restitution on the basis of the defendant's wrongdoing mentioned at the end of the last note, Burrows (at 42) lists the main autonomous unjust factors:

mistake, ignorance, duress, undue influence, exploitation of weakness, legal compulsion, necessity, failure of consideration, illegality, incapacity and ultra vires demands by public authorities.

His category of mistake includes misrepresentation, which may also lead to rescission of the contract and restitution: see Chapter 13.

13. The fourth element listed by Burrows is a negative one: the absence of any defences. The defences that will be of principal concern to us are (i) where a claimant is seeking to recover property, that a third person has bought it in good faith (see p 311); (ii) that the defendant has 'changed her position' (p 491); and (iii) that the claimant's claim rests on an illegal transaction (p 1094).

14. The scope of some of the 'unjust factors' is doubtful. For example, the scope of necessity is far from clear. In *Falcke v Scottish Imperial Insurance Co* (1886) 34 Ch D 234, at 248–249, Bowen LJ said:

The general principle is, beyond all question, that work and labour done or money expended by one man to preserve or benefit the property of another do not according to English law . . . if standing alone, create any obligation to repay the expenditure. Liabilities are not to be forced upon people behind their backs any more than you can confer a benefit upon a man against his will.

There are some cases in which there is liability: one is the supply of necessaries to an insane person. It is thought that another is if essential medical services are supplied to someone who is unconscious. In the Canadian case of *Matheson v Smiley* [1932] 1 WWR 758, the Manitoba Court of Appeals allowed a doctor to claim for services rendered in an unsuccessful attempt to save the life of a man who had shot himself with intent to commit suicide. Do you think the suicide would have welcomed the doctor's attentions?

15. Allowing a party who for one reason or another cannot enforce a contractual claim to claim in restitution instead may raise difficult issues of policy, since it may undercut the

purpose of the rule making the contract unenforceable. One example of this problem, in relation to illegal contracts, is explored on pp 1094 ff. The same difficulty may also arise in relation to other unenforceable contracts. In the Australian case of *Pavey & Matthews Pty Ltd v Paul* (1986) 162 CLR 221, the plaintiff had done building work for the defendant without a written contract for the work. The Builder's Licensing Act 1971, s 45 provided that the contract was not enforceable by the builder

... against the other party to the contract unless the contract is in writing signed by each of the parties ... and sufficiently describes the building work the subject of the contract.

The High Court, by a majority, allowed the builder to recover the value of the work done. Mason and Wilson JJ said:

Once the true basis of the action on a quantum meruit is established, namely execution of work for which the unenforceable contract provided, and its acceptance by the defendant, it is difficult to regard the action as one by which the plaintiff seeks to enforce the oral contract. True it is that proof of the oral contract may be an indispensable element in the plaintiff's success but that is in order to show that (a) the benefits were not intended as a gift, and (b) that the defendant has not rendered the promised exchange value (Fuller and Perdue, 46 Yale LJ at 387 n 125). The purpose of proving the contract is not to enforce it but to make out another cause of action having a different foundation in law.

Brennan J, dissenting, said:

If s 45 were held not to bar such an action to recover a debt due under the contract the section would have had little, if any, practical effect on his obligations to completion (or perhaps to substantial completion). If it were necessary to prove the discharge of the licence-holder's obligations under the unwritten contract in order to establish an enforceable debt recoverable by the plaintiff, litigation arising out of unwritten building contracts would focus on the work which had been agreed upon and the renumeration promised. The effect of s 45 would be to exacerbate the very problem, identified by Samuels and McHugh JJA, which s 45 was intended to overcome. In my opinion, s 45 precludes the arising of an enforceable debt. The contractual promise to pay is clearly unenforceable and there is no room, while the unenforceable contract is subsisting, for a quasi-contractual claim.

In this chapter, we have presented what may be called the orthodox view of the divisions between contract, tort and restitution. On this view, contractual liability is based on promise and leads to damages for loss of expectation; tort is based on negligence and foreseeability of harm (or, where the loss is purely economic, a special relationship 'equivalent to contract') and leads to damages for reliance loss; and restitutionary liability is viewed as based upon unjust enrichment and leading to recovery of the benefit received by the defendant at the claimant's expense. Even on the orthodox view, the divisions are not as neat as this: for instance, we shall see examples of 'contractual liability' that can only be described as based on 'promise' in a highly fictitious sense (eg, pp 413 ff). But the real challenge to the analysis presented here comes from Atiyah, who argues that much of contractual liability is in fact based on the receipt of a benefit by the defendant or reliance by the claimant, and that the element of 'promise' is grossly exaggerated by the traditional view. We will explore this controversy in Section 6.

CHAPTER THREE

THE FUNCTIONS OF CONTRACT LAW

In Chapter 1, we suggested that there are many different approaches to contract law, and differing views as to what the role of contract law is or should be. Not only have views changed over time, but there is still plenty of room for legitimate disagreement. The aim of this chapter is to introduce a variety of these approaches. As you will see, the thrust of several of the pieces is that the law is not committed to any one view and there is a constant tension between different policies and values.

■ Sidgwick, *Elements of Politics* (1879)
p 82

In a summary view of the civil order of society, as constituted in accordance with the individualistic ideal, performance of contract presents itself as the chief positive element, protection of life and property being the chief negative element. Withdraw contract— suppose that no one can count upon the fulfilment of any engagement—and the members of a human community are atoms that cannot effectively combine; the complex cooperation and division of employments that are the essential characteristics of modern industry cannot be introduced among such beings. Suppose contracts freely made and effectively sanctioned, and the most elaborate social organization becomes possible, at least in a society of such human beings as the individualistic theory contemplates: gifted with mature reason, and governed by enlightened self-interest. Of such beings it is prima facie plausible to say that, when once their respective relations to the surrounding material world have been determined so as to prevent mutual encroachment and secure to each the fruits of his industry, the remainder of their positive mutual rights and obligations ought to depend entirely on that coincidence of their free choices, which we call contract.

NOTE

Commenting on this passage, Kessler and Sharp say:

The representatives of this school of thought were firmly convinced, to state it somewhat roughly, of the existence of a natural law according to which, if not in the short run then at least in the long run, the individual serving his own interest was also serving the interest of the community. Profits, under this system, could only be earned by supplying wanted commodities, and freedom of competition would prevent profits from rising unduly. The play of the market, if left to itself, would, therefore, maximize net satisfactions and afford the ideal conditions for the distribution of wealth. Justice within this context has a very definite meaning. It means freedom of property and of contract, of profitmaking and of trade. The 'pre-established harmony' of a social system based on freedom of enterprise and perfect competition sees to it that the private autonomy of contracting parties will be kept within bounds and will work out to the benefit of society as a whole. Freedom of contract, within this cultural framework, like all freedom, is not an end in itself; it is only valuable as a means to an end: 'the liberation of the powers of all men equally for contributions to a common good'.

Small wonder, that freedom of contract, as evolved in the spirit of *laissez faire*, has found repeated expression in Anglo-American case law. '(If) there is one thing which more than another public policy requires,' Sir George Jessel, MR, assures us, 'it is that men of full age and competent understanding shall have the utmost liberty of contracting, and that their contracts entered into freely and voluntarily shall be held sacred and shall be enforced by Courts of Justice.' [*Printing & Numerical Registering Co v Sampson.*] True, fraud and force must be ruled out by the courts in the exercise of their function of making sure that the 'rules of the game' will be adhered to. But this qualification was thought to be of no great moment, owing to the policing force of the competitive market. Except for according protection against force and fraud, it is not the function of courts to make contracts for the parties or to strike down or tamper with improvident bargains. Courts have only to interpret contracts made by the parties; they do not make them. This attitude is in keeping with liberal social and moral philosophy, according to which it pertains to the dignity of man to lead his own life as a reasonable person and to accept responsibility for his own mistakes.

('Contract as a Principle of Order', from *Contracts: Cases and Materials*, 1953.)

■ Atiyah, *The Rise and Fall of Freedom of Contract* (1979)
pp 402–405

The emphasis on contract law as the law of the market was, in England at least, well established by 1870, although in America it may have been a later development. One of its principal characteristics was its abstractness, its lack of particularity, its attempt to treat all contracts as being of the same general character . . .

. . . The emphasis on the fixed rules of contract law, the emphasis on the abstract nature of these rules and of their applicability to all people and all subject-matter alike, has been treated as part of the very nature of certain and predictable rules as opposed to more flexible, but more unpredictable discretionary justice. The rule of the market place is thus equated with the Rule of Law itself. Whatever may be thought of the value-judgments implicit in such an equation in the modern world, there seems little doubt that historically the equation is correct. . . .

In general terms, this equation of general principles of contract law with the free market economy led to an emphasis on the framework within which individuals bargained with each other, and a retreat from interest in substantive justice or fairness. The model of contract theory which implicitly underlay the classical law of contract— for such we may now call it—was thus the model of the market. Essentially this model is based on the following principal features. First, the parties deal with each other 'at arm's length' in the legal phrase; this carries the notion that each relies on his own skill and judgment, and that neither owes any fiduciary obligation to the other. In the market place, no man is his brother's keeper. Secondly, the parties bargain or negotiate, they higgle over the price and terms of the deal. Offers are made, accepted, rejected, or met by counter-offers. Prior to acceptance, offers can be revoked, even though relied upon. Neither party owes any duty to the other until a deal is struck, hence silence is not binding even where a reply might be expected. Third, neither party owes any duty to volunteer information to the other, nor is he entitled to rely on the other except within the narrowest possible limits. Each party must study the situation, examine the subject-matter of the contract, and the general market situation, assess the future probabilities, and rely on his own sources of information. He may take advice, consult experts, buy information from third parties; but if he does not do so, he relies on his own judgment and acts at his peril. The only limitation to this market bargaining is that there must be no fraud or misrepresentation, but even these concepts are narrowly construed. Prima facie a man must rely on his own judgment, and not on what the other party says in the normal process of negotiation. Only if categorical statements of fact are made by one party is the other entitled to rely upon them, and even then, his remedies may be limited if the statement is not made fraudulently. . . . Fourthly, the deal is finally struck when the parties agree, or indicate their agreement. Mistakes and subjective intentions are irrelevant unless they can be said to affect the 'free' and voluntary consent needed to reach agreement. The agreement must be made 'freely' and without 'pressure' but these concepts are very narrowly interpreted, for they must not conflict with the rule of the market place; and in the market place pressures are themselves a normal part of the scene. It is not these pressures, but only abnormal pressures, wholly exceptional pressures, which can be said to affect a party's free consent or free will and hence relieve him of his obligations. Fifthly, the content of the contract, the terms and the price and the subject-matter, are entirely for the parties to settle. It is assumed that the parties know their own minds, that they are the best judges of their own needs and circumstances, that they will calculate the risks and future contingencies that are relevant, and that all these enter into the bargain. It follows that unfairness of the bargain—gross inadequacy or excess of price—is irrelevant, and that once made, the contract is binding. 'The common lawyers hardly recognised the principle of fair dealing as one that needed independent support. For them free dealing was fair dealing.' [Devlin, *The Enforcement of Morals* (Oxford, 1965), p 47.] Finally, this bindingness is, in principle, a matter of pecuniary calculation. Each party is bound; he must therefore perform, or pay damages for his failure to perform.

The Court's function in all this is to ensure procedural fair play: the Court is the umpire to be appealed to when a foul is alleged, but the Court has no substantive function beyond this. It is not the Court's business to ensure that the bargain is fair, or to see that one party does not take undue advantage of another, or impose unreasonable terms by virtue of superior bargaining position. Any superiority in bargaining power is itself a matter for the market to rectify. If there is free competition in the market, mere size or skill should not in any case confer an undue advantage, since the forces of competition will ensure fairness in terms and prices. Nor is it the Court's business to create or impose obligations on anybody from its own sense of justice. It is the task of the parties to fix their liabilities themselves. A person is not to be liable for example, for a benefit received at the hands of another unless he has agreed to pay for it; there is scarcely any room for a law of quasi-contract in the market place. Nor, conversely, is there much room for the protection of reliance unless it has been expressly bargained for. If a party buys advice, for example, from a paid agent, then he is entitled to rely on that advice; or if he buys a warranty from a seller, he is entitled to rely upon the warranty. But unbargained-for reliance is at a man's own risk in the market place. The only justifiable way to protect such reliance is to bring it under the head of tort or Equity; but tort law and Equity, like quasi-contract, have a very limited role in the market place. Their task is the simple one of preventing force and violence and outright fraud.

This theoretical model of contract ideals came to underlie the general principles of contract law during the classical period. But three important qualifications need to be made to this if an accurate picture of the period is to be obtained. The first is that English judges have always been stronger in doing justice in a pragmatic fashion, than they have been in theoretical justifications for what they are doing. While the English judge's sense of justice had been to some degree conditioned by his acceptance of the ideals of a free market economy, there were occasions when it revolted and refused to abide by those ideals. Wherever the rule of the market place seemed to lead to results which outraged the judicial conscience, there was even in the classical period, always the chance that somehow substantive justice would be achieved, for example, by invoking Equity or by implying suitable terms in a contract, or by finding the facts in an appropriate way. The second qualification that needs to be made is to bear in mind the sheer force, at times, of precedent and legal doctrine. Occasions arose, even in the heyday of classical law, when older eighteenth-century principles were adhered to simply because of legal inertia, or the weight of precedent or the conservatism of the particular judges who happened to be hearing an important case. For example, the older rules with regard to the refusal of expectation damages in an action for the sale of land, and again the older rules as to the award of interest on overdue debts, were adhered to throughout the classical period, even though they accorded ill with the law of the market. And thirdly, we must bear in mind the statutory changes which were going on throughout the whole of this period. . . . It must be appreciated that even while the common law of contract was gradually being converted into the law of the market place, statutory erosions of the freedom of the market were taking place. How were these new statutes to be reconciled with the principles of a contract law based on the free market? The answer was largely found in a semantic trick. Statutory changes were excluded from the emerging general law of contract by the simple process of definition. If a statute made particular provision for companies, or for passengers, or for factories, or for prohibiting the payment of wages in truck, or for the protection of the consumer, then these statutory changes were not part of the general law of contract. They were special rules . . .

NOTES

1. Atiyah points out that even in the so-called heyday of *laissez-faire* in the nineteenth century, however, there was very considerable legislative interference with contracts. More detail will be found in *The Rise and Fall of Freedom of Contract*, 1979, pp 523–561; a brief extract can be found at p 1056). Thus the statement by Jessel MR quoted by Kessler and Sharp (see p 47) should not be taken as an accurate description of the law of the nineteenth century, let alone modern law. See the extract from Reiter, p 54.

2. The importance of contract and the free market has been strongly emphasised in recent years by the adherents of economic analysis of contract law (see Chapter 4). This stresses the role of enlightened self-interest in promoting the social good. Some of its adherents seem to assume that, in the absence of such factors as incapacity, fraud or duress, it can be presumed that parties knew what they were doing and they should be held to whatever they agreed (eg, Posner, see p 967). Attempts to interfere with the market are viewed with suspicion (eg by Epstein, see p 813).

The next reading brings out some of the tensions in the law between competing values ('individualism' and 'altruism'). It links these to different types of rule: relatively inflexible 'formal' rules and more flexible 'standards'.

■ Kennedy, 'Form and Substance in Private Law Adjudication'

(1976) 89 Harvard LR 1685, 1687–1691, 1698–1700, 1713–1718, 1738–1740

This article is an inquiry into the nature and interconnection of the different rhetorical modes found in American private law opinions, articles and treatises. I argue that there are two opposed rhetorical modes for dealing with substantive issues, which I will call individualism and altruism. There are also two opposed modes for dealing with questions of the form in which legal solutions to the substantive problems should be cast. One formal mode favors the use of clearly defined, highly administrable, general rules; the other supports the use of equitable standards producing ad hoc decisions with relatively little precedential value.

My purpose is the rational vindication of two common intuitions about these arguments as they apply to private law disputes in which the validity of legislation is not in question. The first is that altruist views on substantive private law issues lead to willingness to resort to standards in administration, while individualism seems to harmonize with an insistence on rigid rules rigidly applied. The second is that substantive and formal conflict in private law cannot be reduced to disagreement about how to apply some neutral calculus that will 'maximize the total satisfaction of valid human wants.' The opposed rhetorical modes lawyers use reflect a deeper level of contradiction. At this deeper level, we are divided, among ourselves and also within ourselves, between irreconcilable visions of humanity and society, and between radically different aspirations for our common future.

I. THE JURISPRUDENCE OF RULES

A. Dimensions of Form

1. Formal Realizability

The first dimension of rules is that of formal realizability. I will use this term, borrowed from Rudolph von Ihering's classic *Spirit of Roman Law*, to describe the degree to which a legal directive has the quality of 'ruleness.' The extreme of formal realizability is a directive to an official that requires him to respond to the presence together of each of a list of easily distinguishable factual aspects of a situation by intervening in a determinate way. Ihering used the determination of legal capacity by sole reference to age as a prime example of a formally realizable definition of liability; on the remedial side, he used the fixing of money fines of definite amounts as a tariff of damages for particular offenses.

At the opposite pole from a formally realizable rule is a standard or principle or policy. (A standard refers directly to one of the substantive objectives of the legal order. Some examples are good faith, due care, fairness, unconscionability, unjust enrichment, and reasonableness. The application of a standard requires the judge both to discover the facts of a particular situation and to assess them in terms of the purposes or social values embodied in the standard.)

It has been common ground, at least since Ihering, that the two great social virtues of formally realizable rules, as opposed to standards or principles, are the restraint of official arbitrariness and certainty...

It has also been common ground, at least since Ihering, that the virtues of formal realizability have a cost. The choice of rules as the mode of intervention involves the sacrifice of precision in the achievement of the objectives lying behind the rules. Suppose that the reason for creating a class of persons who lack capacity is the belief that immature people lack the faculty of free will. Setting the age of majority at 21 years will incapacitate many but not all of those who lack this faculty. And it will incapacitate some who actually possess it.

...

3. Formalities vs. Rules Designed to Deter Wrongful Behavior

...

Formalities are premised on the lawmaker's indifference as to which of a number of alternative relationships the parties decide to enter. Their purpose is to make sure, first, that the parties know what they are doing, and, second, that the judge will know what they did. These are often referred to as the cautionary and evidentiary functions of formalities....

If the rules are clear, people will invest time and energy in finding out what they are. They will then adjust their behavior so that they commit torts only up to the point at which what they gain is equal to what they have to pay in compensation. A regime of standards, on the other hand will 'chill' private activity by making its consequences less certain. At the same time uncertainty reduces the incentive to find out the nature of one's duties and then choose rationally between performing them and paying damages.

B. The Critique of the Argument for Rules

The argument for casting formalities as rules rests on two sets of assumptions, each of which is often challenged in discussions of actual legal institutions. The first set of assumptions concerns the impact on real participants in a real legal system of the demand for formal proficiency. If the argument for rules is to work, we must anticipate that private parties will in fact respond to the threat of the sanction of nullity by learning to operate the system. But real as opposed to hypothetical legal actors may be unwilling or unable to do this.

The contracts of dealers on produce exchanges are likely to use the most exquisite and most precisely manipulable formal language. Poor consumers, by contrast, are likely to be formally illiterate. Somewhere in between lie the businessmen who have a highly developed understanding of the mechanics of their deals, yet persistently—and perfectly rationally, given the money cost of lawyers and the social and business cost of legalism—fail to master legal technicalities that return to plague them when things go wrong. We must take all the particular variations into account. In the end, we may decide that a particular formal system works so smoothly that a refusal to fill the gaps with general rules would be a wanton sacrifice of the parties to a judicial prima donna. But others work so badly that little is lost by riddling them with loopholes.

. . .

In those situations in which some parties are responsive to the legal system, a regime of formally realizable general rules may intensify the disparity in bargaining power in transactions between legally skilled actors who use the legal system constantly, and unskilled actors without lawyers or prior experience. At one extreme there is a kind of fraud that is extremely difficult to police effectively: one party knows that the other party does *not* know that the contract must be in writing if it is to be legally binding. At the other is the bargaining confrontation in which the party with the greater skills legitimately relies on them to obtain a result more favorable than would have occurred if everyone knew that the issue had to be left to the judge's discretion.

The second set of assumptions underlying the argument for rules concerns the practical possibility of maintaining a highly formal regime. A great deal of legal scholarship between the First and Second World Wars went into showing that legal directives that looked general and formally realizable were in fact indeterminate. Take, for example, the 'rule' that a contract will be rescinded for mutual mistake going to the 'substance' or 'essence' of the transaction, but not for mistakes as to a 'mere quality or accident,' even though the quality or accident in question was the whole reason for the transaction. We have come to see legal directives of this kind as in invitations to sub rosa balancing of the equities. Such covert standards may generate more uncertainty than would a frank avowal that the judge is allocating a loss by reference to an open textured notion of good faith and fair dealing.

In other situations, a 'rule' that appears to dispose cleanly of a fact situation is nullified by a counter-rule whose scope of application seems to be almost identical. Agreements that gratuitously increase the obligations of one contractual partner are unenforceable for want of consideration. *But*, such agreements may be binding if the judge can find an implied rescission of the old contract and the formation of a new one incorporating the unilaterally onerous terms. The realists taught us to see this arrangement as a smokescreen hiding the skillful judge's decision as to duress in the process of renegotiation, and as a source of confusion and bad law when skill was lacking.

The critic of the argument for rules can often use this sort of analysis to show that what looks like a rule is really a covert standard.

III. ALTRUISM AND INDIVIDUALISM

A. The content of the ideal of individualism

The essence of individualism is the making of a sharp distinction between one's interests and those of others, combined with the belief that a preference in conduct for one's own interests is legitimate, but that one should be willing to respect the rules that make it possible to coexist with others similarly self-interested. The form of conduct associated with individualism is self-reliance. This means an insistence on defining and achieving objectives without help from others i.e. without being dependent on them or asking sacrifices of them). It means accepting that they will neither share their gains nor one's own losses. And it means a firm conviction that I am entitled to enjoy the benefits of my efforts without an obligation to share or sacrifice them to the interests of others.

. . .

It is important to be clear from the outset that individualism is sharply distinct from pure egotism, or the view that it is impossible and undesirable to set any limits at all to the pursuit of self-interest. The notion of self-reliance has a strong affirmative moral content, the demand for respect for the rights of others....

A pure egotist defends the laws against force on the sole ground that they are necessary to prevent civil war. For the individualist, the rules against the use of force have intrinsic rightness, because they are identified with the ideal of self-reliance, the economic objective of security for individual effort, and the political rhetoric of free will, autonomy, and natural rights. Rules against violence provide a space within which to realize this program rather than a mere bulwark against chaos.

Some level of protection of person and property against non-violent interference (theft, fraud, negligence) is also desirable from the point of view of self-reliance....

Beyond these fundamental legal institutions, the individualist program is much less clear....

B. The content of the ideal of altruism

The rhetoric of individualism so thoroughly dominates legal discourse at present that it is difficult even to identify a counterethic. Nonetheless, I think there is a coherent, pervasive notion that constantly competes with individualism, and I will call it altruism. The essence of altruism is the belief that one ought not to indulge a sharp preference for one's own interest over those of others. Altruism enjoins us to make sacrifices, to share, and to be merciful. It has roots in culture, in religion, ethics and art, that are as deep as those of individualism. (Love thy neighbor as thyself.)

The simplest of the practices that represent altruism are sharing and sacrifice. Sharing is a static concept, suggesting an existing distribution of goods which the sharers rearrange. It means giving up to another gains or wealth that one has produced oneself or that have come to one through some good fortune. It is motivated by a sense of duty or by a sense that the other's satisfaction is a reward at least comparable to the satisfaction one might have derived from consuming the thing oneself. Sharing may also involve participation in another's losses: a spontaneous decision to shift to oneself a part of the ill fortune, deserved or fortuitous, that has befallen someone else. Sacrifice is the dynamic notion of taking action that will change an ongoing course of events, at some expense to oneself, to minimize another's loss or maximize his gain.

The polar opposite concept for sharing and sacrifice is exchange (a crucial individualist notion). The difference is that sharing and sacrifice involve a vulnerability to non-reciprocity. Further, this vulnerability is undergone out of a sense of solidarity: with the hope of a return but with a willingness to accept the possibility that there will be none . . .

There is a strong analogy between the arguments that lawyers make when they are defending a 'strict' interpretation of a rule and those they put forward when they are asking a judge to make a rule that is substantively individualist. Likewise, there is a rhetorical analogy between the arguments lawyers make for 'relaxing the rigor' of a regime of rules and those they offer in support of substantively altruist lawmaking. The simplest of these analogies is at the level of moral argument. Individualist rhetoric in general emphasizes self-reliance as a cardinal virtue. In the substantive debate with altruism, this means claiming that people *ought* to be willing to accept the consequences of their own actions. They ought not to rely on their fellows or on government when things turn out badly for them. They should recognize that they must look to their own efforts to attain their objectives. It is implicit in this idea that they are entitled to put others at arm's length—to refuse to participate in their losses or make sacrifices for them.

. . .

The same argument applies to rules that are designed to enforce substantive policies rather than merely to facilitate choice between equally acceptable alternatives. Like formalities, these rules are concerned with intentional behavior in situations defined in advance. When one enters a perfectly fair contract with an infant, one has no right to complain when the infant voids it for reasons having nothing to do with the law's desire to protect him from his own folly or from overreaching.

The position of the advocate of rule enforcement is unmistakably individualist. It is the sibling if not the twin of the general argument that those who fare ill in the struggle for economic or any other kind of success should shoulder the responsibility, recognize that they deserved what they got, and refrain from demanding state intervention to bail them out. The difference is that the formal argument is interstitial. It presupposes that the state has already intervened to some extent (eg, by enforcing contracts rather than leaving them to business honor and nonlegal sanctions). It asserts that within this context, it is up to the parties to look out for themselves. The fact of altruistic substantive state intervention does not ipso facto wipe out the individual's duty to take care of herself.

The argument of the advocate of 'relaxation,' of converting the rigid rule into a standard, will include an enumeration of all the particular factors in the situation that mitigate the failure to avoid over- or underinclusion. There will be reference to the substantive purpose of the rule in order to show the arbitrariness of the result. But the ultimate point will be that there is a moral duty on the part of the private beneficiary of the over- or underinclusion to forego an advantage that is a result of the other's harmless folly. Those who take an inheritance by course of law because the testator failed to sign his will should hand the property over to those the testator wanted to receive it. A contracting party ought not to employ the statute of frauds to void a contract honestly made but become onerous because of a price break.

This argument smacks as unmistakably of altruism as the argument for rules smacks of individualism. The essential idea is that of mercy, here concretized as sharing or sacrifice. The ethic of self-reliance is rejected in both its branches: the altruist will neither punish the incompetent nor respect the 'right' of the other party to cleave to her own interests. Again, the difference between the substantive and the formal arguments is the area of their application. It may well be that the structure of rules falls far short of requiring the level of altruistic behavior that the altruist would prefer. But within that structure, whatever it may be, there are still duties of sharing and sacrifice evoked by the very operation of the rules.

It is important to note that the altruist demand for mercy will be equally strong whether we are dealing with formalities, or with rules designed to deter substantively undesirable behavior (crimes, unconscionable contracts). The party who tries to get out of a losing contract because of failure to comply with a formality is betraying a contractual partner, someone toward whom he has assumed special duties. The infant who voids the same contract although it was neither foolish nor coerced is behaving equally reprehensibly.

NOTES

1. The 'essential ethic' of contracting is explored by Brownsword, *Contract Law: Themes for the Twenty-First Century* (2000), 2nd edn, 2006, pp 28–37. He concludes that 'the contrast between the ethic of individualism and that of co-operativism is one of the keys to contract doctrine....' For further analysis by Brownsword, see p 57.

2. For an obvious example of the way that English courts have moved between formal rules and flexible standards in an attempt to encourage parties to have greater regard for each other's interests, see the rules on when a contract may be terminated, pp 566–580. You may wish to look for other examples as you work through the book.

3. Kennedy is a member of the 'Critical Legal Studies' movement. For further writings taking a broadly similar approach, see pp 791 and 796. It will be seen that later writers have emphasised among other things the 'indeterminacy' of rules of law—in other words, that even though the courts regularly apply a particular rule in a given situation, other rules reflecting other value choices might be adopted without being demonstrably 'wrong'.

4. Kennedy's message that the law reflects two competing values may be accepted by commentators who do not accept all the 'tenets' of the CLS movement. See, for example, p 57. But it seems that not everyone agrees...

■ Reiter, 'The Control of Contract Power'

(1981) 1 Oxford J of Legal Studies 347, 347–350, 356, 358–361

(NB: Do not worry about the details of the rules mentioned by Reiter; concentrate on his general arguments.)

I. INTRODUCTION

The issue addressed in this article is illustrated by the juxtaposition of two judicial quotations:

'... [If] there is one thing which more than another public policy requires it is that men of full age and competent understanding shall have the utmost liberty of contracting, and that their contracts... entered into freely and voluntarily shall be held sacred...'(Jessel MR)

'... [Is] there any principle which is more familiar or more firmly embedded in the history of Anglo-American law than the basic doctrine that the courts will not permit themselves to be used as instruments of inequity and injustice? Does any principle in our law have more universal application than the doctrine that courts will not enforce transactions in which the relative positions of the parties are such that one has unconscionably taken advantage of the necessities of the other?' (Frankfurter J)

These quotations suggest an apparent conflict of values in contract law. The former indicates a bias favouring free enterprise, the delegation of society's power, and generally, individualism. The latter implies limits on freedom of contract and social concern with the fairness of contracts, an apparently opposite altruistic bias. Kennedy has referred to individualism and altruism as 'two opposed rhetorical modes' that lawyers employ. He said:

'... The substantive and formal conflict in private law cannot be reduced to disagreement about how to apply some neutral calculus that will "maximize the total satisfaction of human wants." The opposed rhetorical modes lawyers use reflect a deeper level of contradiction. At this deeper level we are divided among ourselves and also within ourselves between irreconcilable visions of humanity, and society, and between radically different aspirations for our common future.'

This sort of dualism in legal thought has been noted by many learned observers, from Polanyi to Leff, from Havighurst to Unger.

... [I]t is my thesis that the two tendencies referred to by Jessel, Kennedy and the others, are not, in fact, visible in the law at all. Rather, the view presented as a fact by Jessel MR is simply wrong. We never did have, we do not have, and we never could have a total and unthinking delegation of contract power in society...

My thesis applies at two levels. It applies at what I shall call a 'macro' level. Here, I suggest that contract as an organizing principle in society—the society—the market—has a limited role. The thesis also applies at what I shall call a 'micro' level. Within the area nominally delegated to private individuals' law-making, I assert that 'contract law' contains principles for limiting the ability to exercise contract power. I shall attempt to describe the controls, to assert their legitimacy and necessity, and to examine the institutions fit to impose them.

II. A SOCIETY ORGANIZED ON MARKET PRINCIPLES?

The more important level of the thesis is the macro level, which considers the extent to which society should be organized by the market as opposed to other, and historically more venerable principles. These principles, around which many other societies have been organized, include custom, kinship, authoritarianism, religion, feudalism, and the more modern varieties of socialized power ranging from communism through democracy. It is important to appreciate at the outset the implausibility of a claim that society should be organized on the basis of private contracting behaviour. The claim advocates apparent anarchy and amoralism. Never before the birth of faith in markets had gain been advanced as an inherently worthy motive. Nor had economic structures ever been sharply differentiated from social structures and relations. But in an effort to throw off feudal and religious shackles, to release energy and to give vent to new theories of social justice, a broad coalition was forged over the sixteenth through the nineteenth century. The coalition, including economic liberals, utilitarians, and classes rising in power politically and intellectually, adduced powerful arguments in support of the market. The central benefits they attributed to organization in this form included the following. First, the market would provide powerful incentives motivating individuals to work and to produce wealth in society. The resultant gain would improve the lot of all (or of most, depending on the economist) individuals in society. The notion of incentives could be, and indeed was, pushed to the point of urging the necessity of a substantial level of poverty in society and of starvation as a sharp stick to keep the incentive structure keen. Second, market organization offered promises of efficiency. The consumer would determine what society produced: the cheapest mode of production of the right quantities of goods and an efficient distribution network were explicit outcomes of the model. Third, market organization would allow for innovation. This was a particularly critical attribute given the substantial barriers to innovation that had been erected by the guilds and other local protective arrangements. Fourth, the market meant freedom from imposition by governmental or religious authorities. This freedom offered a consent basis to society, a basis seen both as good in itself and as a legitimating force. Finally, the market promised justice. The entire notion of market rewards and failures could be and was linked to a personal merit principle.

The case was powerful, but it was never wholly accepted. Instead, strange and shifting alliances of intellectual and political power combined to prevent the excesses of the market through the assertion of political power. Society reacted in a 'spontaneous outburst' to assert its primacy over economics. The details of the social reaction and the proof of what I assert about its success are provided in Polanyi's class study, *The Great Transformation* and in Atiyah's interesting and extensive recent work, *The Rise and Fall of Freedom of Contract*. It may suffice to describe the nature of the rejection of market principles in one critical sector only, that of 'the supply of labour'. The commodification of labour was a critical step necessary to establish a market-based economy. Older feudal notions of the relationship between workers and those responsible for them had to give way if mobile labour was to be available to be bought and sold as supply and demand dictated. The commodification of labour was not really achieved even in theory until the repeal of the Poor Laws in 1834. However, as the momentum to turn labour into a commodity grew, the social reaction was already taking shape. It appeared in the form of the reassertion and the continued assertion of values limiting market values in respect of human labour. The force of the social reaction demonstrates that the nineteenth century was anything but an era of *laissez-faire*. The best known reactions involve those associated with the various Factory Acts, dating from 1833. The Acts dealt with employment of children, hours of work and safety matters. Similar legislation regulated other important industrial sectors. A bureaucracy was created, industrial inspection Commissions were established. Reports were issued and legislation followed frequently. Combination laws were enacted early in the nineteenth century and Truck Acts were passed frequently thereafter.

All of this social reaction occurred early in the 'era of market economy'. Today the dimensions of the reaction are even more apparent...

III. CONTRACT AT THE GRASS ROOTS

[At the micro level]...I ask, 'What is the current "law of contract"?', and more specifically, 'Where is that law to be found?' Two competing expressions and sources of the law appear. First, one could refer to the views of Jessel MR and of textwriters who have based their opinions on what he said. Or, alternatively, one could refer to the 'mine run' of cases, to legislation in *pari materia*, to philosophical and other social scientific writing, and to community expectations revealed through sources that may be referred to legitimately by common law judges.

There is little doubt about what Jessel and the textwriters would say. Expressions to the effect that 'the courts enforce contracts as written', that they 'mend no man's bargain', and that 'inadequacy of consideration is of no concern to the law', abound. But are such expressions accurate as descriptions or predictions of what courts do, or will do? Do they state 'the law' correctly?

...[O]ne must appreciate the extent to which the courts have overridden 'contract principles' and have established limits on the exercise of contract power. They have achieved this in a direct and consistent manner through the use of doctrines of public policy and illegality. For instance, well before the classical theory of contract was evolved, and ever since, the courts have exercised control over contracts in restraint of trade in an endeavour to assure their reasonableness. The courts have always asserted a power to find common law illegality or to deny enforcement to contracts found repulsive ...

The courts have also asserted limits to contract power in less open and direct ways. In large areas where judges have felt that contract principles are unsuitable, but that it would be inadvisable to admit the fact, the courts have created 'exceptions', or special bodies of law that are regarded as 'not contract'. More suitable treatment can then be accorded to the 'exceptional cases' without risk to 'contract' generally. Consider, for instance, aspects of the 'law of' mortgages, sureties, insurance, fiduciaries, bailment, or admiralty. Though what may often be involved in each of these fields is a consensual arrangement between two individuals, it is quite clear that the courts pay no attention to what the contract says where judicially ordained limits have been exceeded. In many cases the written contract is neglected completely, and the parties' rights are determined wholly by the court. It would be interesting and, I believe, informative to establish empirically the proportion of the nineteenth century or even of the twentieth century 'contracts docket' represented by these 'exceptional cases'. As well, and even within 'contract' itself, a number of unique spheres have been created where judicial control of contract power is regarded as quite legitimate because the areas are somehow regarded as 'special', rather than as reflective of general principle. Consider, for instance, the 'law of' penalties, forfeitures, expectant heirs, or the various forms of duress (ranging from duress of the person, through duress *colore officii*, practical duress and economic duress). It is only by ignoring the existence of all these various 'pockets' of law that a theory devoid of a notion of limits to contract power could be constructed. Gilmore has argued that the isolation of 'pockets' reflecting such conflicting values was the result of conscious efforts by the classical theory builders.

Courts have asserted limits to contract power in an even more subtle but practically more important manner. Through a great variety of techniques, the courts have paid lip service to contract law in theory, and have ignored it in practice. Consider, for instance, the various interpretation, or more realistically non-interpretation, techniques they have employed in an attempt to make contracts read 'fairly' (from the courts' point of view) rather than as one of the parties undoubtedly intended them to read. Or consider the use of implied terms. While one view of the law is that courts can imply terms only when it is absolutely necessary to do so, it is quite clear that courts have implied terms frequently in an effort to make the parties' obligations appear as the courts think they should. The courts have used notions of 'repugnancy' to exclude undesirable terms. For many years, they manipulated a concept of fundamental breach so that exclusion clauses could not operate to the grave disadvantage of a weaker or a surprised party. (Now, and more realistically, that line is being pursued through notions of unreasonableness and unconscionability.) Courts have found collateral contracts that either serve to import warranties not available in the 'main contract', or that introduce different terms that the court considers preferable to those contained in the 'main contract'. They have limited the scope of contracts through various devices in order to keep undesirable terms at bay. For instance, they have used techniques of characterization to achieve such ends, characterizing an offer and acceptance so that a harsh clause is excluded. The use of these concepts can always be defended as other than manipulative: it *really was* necessary to imply a term in this case; the offer really was made before the ticket came out of the machine; it *really was* the intention of one of the parties to give a collateral warranty. However, I would submit that any but the most biased and blind observer can appreciate the policy orientations lying behind the manipulations of the various techniques. To my mind, the manipulations show what Friedman concluded about what happened to doctrine in the Wisconsin Supreme Court over about 150 years. While the stated doctrine remained the same, there was a fundamental transformation in its role and functions: the effects of its use changed dramatically. I suggest that we in England and in Canada have witnessed a similar transformation in the use of doctrine and that the different devices (varying in availability depending on the legal climate) have been employed in pursuit of values oft-unexpressed but nonetheless readily apparent.

NOTES

1. The reference to Friedman is to Friedman, Contract Law in America, 1965; an extract from this will be found on p 86.

2. Reiter concludes his article with a discussion of the appropriateness of allowing judicial, as opposed to legislative, control of contract power (see (1981) 1 Oxford J Legal Studies 347, 363 367). This is a theme that will recur in various guises throughout the book. There are at least three issues:

    (i) Do the courts have adequate conceptual tools to tackle the problems? (See, eg, p 191.)

    (ii) Is it appropriate for the courts to intervene or should this be left to the legislature, which has a democratic mandate? (See, eg, p 422.)

    (iii) Is judicial control of contracts which are somehow unfair likely to have any significant impact on practices generally, especially in consumer, cases which are rarely brought to court? (See pp 1044 and 1059.)

3. Reiter's thesis, that a tendency towards individualism and allowing the free operation of the market cannot be seen, may seem rather an overstatement at least for English law. You may like to consider this as you read further.

4. Reiter's thesis that, at the 'micro' level, courts have established ways of controlling contract power, implies that judges have some element of choice in the way they 'shape' the law as it develops or in the way they refine or change it as conditions alter. In general terms, how might judges approach their task? The next reading gives one answer.

■ Adams and Brownsword, 'The Ideologies of Contract Law'
(1987) 7 Legal Studies 205, 205–222

Our sketch elaborates two central contentions. First, we contend that it is illuminating to interpret the materials which comprise the contract rule-book (ie the rules and principles which are traditionally taken to represent the law of contract) in the light of two underpinning 'ideologies', which we will term 'Market-Individualism' and 'Consumer-Welfarism'. Secondly, we contend that decisions of the higher courts in contract disputes (or in any tribunal where the dispute hinges on a point of contract law) should be interpreted within a framework in which general judical ideologies (ie general understandings of the judical role) are combined with the specifically contractual market-individualist and consumer-welfarist ideologies. At the price of some over-simplification, we employ just two such general judical ideologies, which we term 'Formalism' and 'Realism'. . . .

[T]hese terms are employed stipulatively: they simply mean what we say they mean. . . .

[These ideologies are] a resource for interpreting the actions of others, or for organising our understanding of some phenomenon. Accordingly, our proposed ideological framework should be read as a resource which enables us both to reinterpret the materials in the contract rule-book and to understand more clearly what is going on when judges resolve contract disputes. . . .

1 Market-Individualism
The ideology of Market-Individualism has both market and individualistic strands. The strands are mutually supportive, but it aids exposition to separate them. We can look first at the market side of this ideology and then at its individualistic aspect.

(1) The market ideology

According to Market-Individualism, the market place is a site for competitive exchange. The function of contract is not simply to facilitate exchange, it is to facilitate *competitive* exchange. Contract establishes the ground rules within which competitive commerce can be conducted. Thus, subject to fraud, mistake, coercion and the like, bargains made in the market must be kept. In many ways, the line drawn between (actionable) misrepresentation and mere non-disclosure, epitomises this view. There are minimal restraints on contractors: the law of the market is not the law of the jungle, and this rules out misrepresentations. However, non-disclosure of some informational advantage is simply prudent bargaining—contractors are involved in a competitive situation and cannot be expected to disclose their hands. In line with these assumptions, the market-individualist philosophy attaches importance to the following considerations.

First, security of transactions is to be promoted. This means that where a party, having entered the market, reasonably assumes that he has concluded a bargain, then that assumption should be protected....

Secondly, it is important for those who enter into the market to know where they stand. This means that the ground rules of contract should be clear. Hence, the restrictions on contracting must not only be minimal (in line with the competitive nature of the market), but also must be clearly defined (in line with the market demand for predictability, calculability etc)...

Thirdly, since contract is concerned essentially with the facilitation of market operations, the law should accommodate commercial practice, rather than the other way round....

(2) The Individualistic Ideology

A persistent theme in Market-Individualism is that judges should play a non-interventionist role with respect to contracts. This distinctive non-interventionism derives from the individualistic side of the ideology. The essential idea is that parties should enter the market, choose their fellow-contractors, set their own terms, strike their bargains and stick to them. The linchpins of this individualistic philosophy are the doctrines of 'freedom of contract' and 'sanctity of contract'.

The emphasis of freedom of contract is on the parties' freedom of choice. First, the parties should be free to choose one another as contractual partners (ie partner-freedom). Like the tango, contract takes two. And, ideally the two should consensually choose one another. Secondly, the parties should be free to choose their own terms (ie term-freedom). Contract is competitive, but the exchange should be consensual. Contract is about unforced choice....

Although the principle of partner-freedom still has some life in it (eg in defending the shopkeeper's choice of customer), it is the principle of term-freedom which is the more vital. Term-freedom can be seen as having two limbs:

(i) The free area within which the parties are permitted, in principle, to set their own terms should be maximised; and,

(ii) Parties should be held to their bargains, ie to their agreed terms (provided that the terms fall within the free area)....

The second limb of term-freedom is none other than the principle of sanctity of contract. By providing that parties should be held to their bargains, the principle of sanctity of contract has a double emphasis. First, if parties must be held to *their* bargains, they should be treated as masters of their own bargains, and the courts should not indulge in *ad hoc* adjustment of terms which strike them as unreasonable or imprudent. Secondly, if parties must be *held* to their bargains, then the courts should not lightly relieve contractors from performance of their agreements. It will be appreciated that, while freedom of contract is the broader of the two principles, it is sanctity of contract which accounts for the distinctive market-individualistic stand against paternalistic intervention in particular cases.

2 Consumer-Welfarism

The consumer-welfarist ideology stands for a policy of consumer-protection, and for principles of fairness and reasonableness in contract. It does not start with the market-individualist premise that all contracts should be minimally regulated. Rather, it presupposes that consumer contracts are to be closely regulated, and that commercial contracts, although still ordinarily to be viewed as competitive transactions, are to be subject to rather more regulation than Market-Individualism would allow. The difficulties with Consumer-Welfarism appear as soon as one attempts to identify its particular guiding principles (ie its operative principles and conceptions of fairness and reasonableness).

Without attempting to draw up an exhaustive list of the particular principles of Consumer-Welfarism, we suggest that the following number amongst its leading ideas:

(1) The principle of constancy: parties should not 'blow hot and cold' in their dealings with one another, even in the absence of a bargain. A person should not encourage another to act in a particular way or to form a particular expectation (or acquiesce in another's so acting or forming an expectation) only then to act inconsistently with that encouragement (or acquiescence)...

(2) The principle of proportionality: an innocent party's remedies for breach should be proportionate to the seriousness of the consequences of the breach...

(3) The principle of bad faith: a party who cites a good legal principle in bad faith should not be allowed to rely on that principle...

(4) The principle that no man should profit from his own wrong...

(5) The principle of unjust enrichment: no party, even though innocent, should be allowed unfairly to enrich himself at the expense of another...

(6) The better loss-bearer principle: where a loss has to be allocated to one of two innocent parties, it is reasonable to allocate it to the party who is better able to carry the loss. As a rule of thumb, commercial parties are deemed to be better loss-bearers than consumers...

(7) The principle of exploitation: a stronger party should not be allowed to exploit the weakness of another's bargaining situation; but parties of equal bargaining strength should be assumed to have a non-exploitative relationship...

(8) The principle of a fair deal for consumers: consumers should be afforded protection against sharp advertising practice, against misleading statements, against false representations, and against restrictions on their ordinary rights. Moreover, consumer disappointment should be properly compensated.

(9) The principle of informational advantage: representors who have special informational advantage must stand by their representations; but representees who have equal informational opportunity present no special case for protection. The positive aspect of the principle of informational advantage is protective, but its negative aspect offers no succour to representees who are judged able to check out statements for themselves.

(10) The principle of responsibility for fault: contractors who are at fault should not be able to avoid responsibility for their fault...

(11) The paternalistic principle: contractors who enter into imprudent agreements may be relieved from their bargains where justice so requires. The case for paternalistic relief is at its most compelling where the party is weak or naïve...

II JUDICIAL DECISIONS IN CONTRACT CASES

Our second contention is that if we are to understand contract decisions we must construct an interpretive framework which links general judicial ideologies with the specifically contractual ideologies.

1 The general judicial ideologies

Although there are no doubt many starting points for constructing a scheme of general judicial ideologies, the black-letter assumption of judicial fidelity to the rule-book give us an obvious cue. Therefore, we take the decisive question to be the judicial attitude towards the materials in the rule-book. Accordingly, in this section, we outline the characteristics of two general judicial ideologies. At one extreme, which we call the ideology of Formalism, the judicial role is defined in terms of applying the materials in the rule-book, irrespective of the result. At the other extreme, which we call the ideology of

Realism, the judicial role is defined in terms of handing down acceptable decisions, irrespective of the dictates of the rule-book. In other words, the formalist approach is rule-book-orientated, the realist approach result-orientated. In between these extremes, of course, there will be many graduations, and to do justice to the complexity of judicial reasoning, it would be essential to construct other categories. However, for our purposes, the crude dichotomy between Formalism and Realism will suffice, for it dramatises the standing tension between rules and results.

(1) Formalism

The formalist view gravitates around the rule-book. Its dominant characteristics are as follows.

First, and foremost, the rule-book governs. Lawton LJ's observations on the problem of the 'Battle of the Forms', are a clear example of this attitude: . . .

The new problem presented by the Battle of the Forms was to be resolved according to the traditional rules. The world may change, but the traditional rules of contract, like 'Ol' Man River', 'jus' keep rollin' along'.

Secondly, the rule-book is viewed as a closed logical system. Rule-book exercises are exercises in the logic of the concepts of contract. Just as one plus one must equal two, formalists view contractual concepts as having a logic of their own. The traditional schematic approach to formation particularly reflects this aspect of Formalism.

Thirdly, the conceptual purity and integrity of the rule-book is to be maintained. Formalists are uncomfortable when they encounter ill-fitting or otherwise deviant doctrines. The attempt to clean up the doctrine of fundamental breach is a good example of a formalist purifying operation.

Fourthly, Formalism tends towards doctrinal conservatism . . .

Fifthly, as Geoffrey Lane L J said in *Gibson v Manchester City Council*, 'sympathy and politics' are not material consideration for formalist judges (unless, of course, the rule-book makes such considerations material). Judges may sympathise with a litigant, but if the rule-book is against that party then that is conclusive. Hard cases make bad law (ie introduce ad hoc distinctions into the rule-book). In the same way, politics, interpreted broadly as judicial values and commitments, must not influence a formalist judge. A judge may regard a particular rule as unfair or inconvenient, but this must not act as an excuse for deviation from the rule-book.

Sixthly, Formalism implies an uncritical acceptance of, and a mechanical application of, the rule-book doctrines . . .

Seventhly, because Formalism favours the routine application of the rule-book it works best with clear general rules, which do not involve the exercise of judicial discretion . . .

Finally, it is also possible to view as corollaries of a formalist outlook, the tendency both to eschew responsibility for major law-reform ('This is best left to Parliament'), and to interpret appeal court jurisdiction narrowly ('Provided that the trial court asked the right legal question, and provided that the answer acted upon was not totally unreasonable, then the ruling must stand'). The former tendency can be seen as a by-product of formalist caution coupled with the formalist belief that the function of judges is to apply, not to make, the rules. The latter tendency is assisted by the formalist detachment from the results of cases. Consequently, when a case comes up on appeal, the question for the appeal court is not whether the trial judge got the right result, but whether the right questions were asked, the right rules applied.

(2) Realism

Realism is the antithesis of Formalism. It follows that each of the formalist tendencies is matched by a realist tendency which pushes in the opposite direction.

First, the rule-book is not decisive. The most important aspects of a dispute are the facts and the decision; rules are a secondary consideration. As we have seen already, if Formalism is rule-orientated, Realism is result-orientated. In many ways, Lord Devlin's observation that 'The true spirit of the common law is to override theoretical distinctions when they stand in the way of doing practical justice' (*Ingram v Little* [1961] 1 QB 31) enshrines the realist articles of faith.

Secondly, the logic of the rule-book concepts is by no means the be-all and end-all. Immediately one thinks here of Lord Denning's criticisms of traditional offer and acceptable analysis, and of his cavalier treatment of consideration . . .

Thirdly, realists do not regard blotting the rule-book as the ultimate sin. If practical justice demands some running repairs, then the elegance or conceptual neatness of the solution hardly matters. What matters is that the repair-job works . . .

Fourthly, Realism tends towards doctrinal and conceptual innovation . . .

Fifthly, for realist judges, 'sympathy and politics' do matter. It is all very well complaining that hard cases make bad law; but, if judges ignore the obvious merits of a case, practical justice goes by the board and the law is rightly accused of being an ass. Likewise, politics, broadly interpreted, *do* count. . . .

Sixthly, for realists, the mechanical and uncritical adoption and application of the rule-book will not do. Rules are laid down for a purpose, to defend some principle or to support some policy. . . .

Seventhly, Realism is not inconvenienced by a rule-book which is replete with discretions. On the contrary, if the rules enjoin judges to decide according to the canons of reasonableness, fairness, conscionability, and the like, this is no problem, for it is precisely how realist judges will want to decide anyway.

Finally, because realists have a passion for results rather than rules, they will tend to take a broad view of appeal court jurisdiction. For realists, the point of an appeal is not to test out whether the trial court applied the right rules, but primarily to assess the result handed down. Accordingly, appeal courts should feel free to overturn trial court rulings where they are judged to have arrived at the wrong result. Similarly, where the rule-book is in obvious and urgent need of reform, realists do not see the sense of simply exhorting the legislature to come to their rescue. If the legislature duly reforms the law, all well and good, but in the meantime, realist judges will think that they have a responsibility to get on with the reforming work themselves. . . .

2 Completing the interpretive framework: the ideological field

The specifically contractual ideologies of Market-Individualism and Consumer-Welfarism feed into the general framework of judicial ideologies at two points. On the one hand, they are fed in by the formalist approach (the particular configuration of the rule-book largely determining which of the contractual ideologies will actually be applied by a judge employing a formalist approach). On the other hand, judges adopting a realist approach will be guided by considerations drawn from the contractual ideologies. Thus, while one brand of realist approach measures the desirability of results by reference to the market-individualist ideology, another takes the consumer-welfarist ideology as its yardstick. This entails that judicial decisions in contract cases should be interpreted against the backcloth of three basic approaches, namely: formalist, realist guided by Market-Individualism, and realist guided by Consumer-Welfarism. Overall, therefore, our interpretive framework can be represented thus:

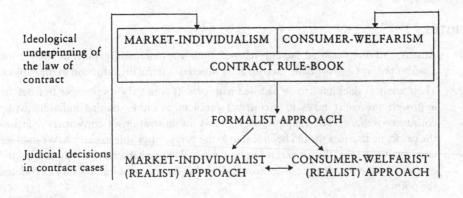

Put rather crudely, this entails that the interpreter must decide whether a judge is concerned in a particular case to apply the rule-book (ie to follow the formalist approach) or to generate desired results (ie to follow a realist approach). In the latter eventuality, the interpreter must consider whether the realist approach followed by the judge is inspired by the ideas of Market-Individualism or Consumer-Welfarism.

Now it is tempting to treat our model as a basis for classifying particular judges as eg formalists, market-individualist realists, and consumer-welfarist realists—schools of judges as it were. Moreover, readers may already believe that they can identify modern leaders of these schools in the persons of, say, Lord Diplock (for Formalism), Lord Wilberforce (for market-individualist Realism), and Lord Denning (for consumer-welfarist Realism). Our intention, however, is not to pigeonhole judges in this way. Our contention, rather, is that judges are caught within the ideological tensions represented by our model, and that their decisions in particular cases will necessarily reflect one of the basic approaches. However, this does not imply that any one judge must necessarily adopt the same approach in every case, although, no doubt, some judges are more consistent than others in this respect. Just how consistent judges are is a matter about which readers must form their own views if and when they attempt to apply our interpretive framework.

The significance of our remark that judges are 'caught within the ideological tensions' should not be lost. It means, that there is no escape for judges, who are necessarily drawn towards one or other opposing ideology, and are likely to be criticised whichever it is. . . .

It is possible, however, to discern certain features of the ideologies which create a natural affinity, on the one hand, between Formalism and Market-Individualism, and, on the other, between Realism and Consumer-Welfarism.

Consider, first, Formalism and Market-Individualism. Market-individualist realists will not shrink from putting the rule-book to one side where it obstructs commercial convenience (see eg in *The Eurymedon*). Nevertheless, they cannot encourage unbridled Realism, for this would be to invite the destruction of certainty and predictability so essential to Market-Individualism. Market-individualist realists, therefore, must exercise their Realism with restraint, departing from the rule-book only where it is judged that the market needs change more than it needs continuity. Now, formalist judges seek a rule-book which has just the sort of clear rules generally favoured by market-individualists. It follows that formalists must find it easier to work with Market-Individualism than with Consumer-Welfarism. There is, therefore, a natural affinity between Formalism and Market-Individualism for, irrespective of the content of the rule-book, both ideologies favour a particular form of rule-book (comprising clear, general, non-discretionary rules) and a particular style of judging (basically directed towards the routine application of general rules).

Converse considerations suggest a natural affinity between Realism and Consumer-Welfarism. Both ideologies favour a flexible rule-book giving judges discretion to accommodate the particular circumstances surrounding a dispute. Naturally, this militates against setting down rules which will settle disputes irrespective of their particular characteristics. In a sense, the whole thrust of Consumer-Welfarism is to point judges in a realist direction, by insisting that decisions should be fair and reasonable in the particular circumstances. . . .

NOTES

1. Adams and Brownsword have developed their approach more fully in their book *Understanding Contract Law*, 4th edn, 2004 which is a useful introduction to the subject.

2. Their analysis does have to be handled with care. It is not always possible to label the approach the court takes to a contract problem as either market-individualist or consumer-welfarist. For example, they give as an illustration of consumer-welfarism the principle that loss should be allocated to the party better able to carry it. We shall see later (pp 393 ff) that the same rule can be explained in market terms, as representing the efficient outcome that the parties would probably have agreed on had they negotiated the point.

3. It can also be difficult to decide whether a court which, without comment on any issues of policy, reaches its decision by straightforward deduction from the previous cases, is being formalist or realist. Does it not consider the practical outcome important, or does it think that the case law embodies the most appropriate solution? See generally, Wightman (1989) 52 MLR 115.

4. Since this piece was written, Brownsword has developed his ideas further. He has analysed in some detail possible meanings of welfarism (see his 'The Philosophy of Welfarism and its Emergence in the Modern Law English Law of Contract' in Brownsword, Howells and Wilhelmssohn (eds), *Welfarism in Contract Law 21*); and he has reclassified some examples of what under the earlier analysis might have been termed 'consumer-welfarism' as 'dynamic market-individualism' (see *Brownsword, Contract Law: Themes for the Twenty-First Century*, 2nd edn, 2006, chapter 7). An extract from the latter will be found at p 254.

5. Nonetheless the extract from Adams and Brownsword provides a helpful framework within which to begin to ask, 'what is going on?' There are writers who make much stronger claims that, since the nineteenth century consumerist notions have transformed the law.

In Chapter 1, we referred to the work of the American writer Macneil, who presents a rather different view and critique of contract law. Macneil points out that classical contract law, and to a lesser extent the modern law (which he terms 'neo-classical'), treats a contract as something that takes place almost in a vacuum. Nothing before the contract and nothing after it is relevant: it is a 'discrete' event. As such, what is to happen between the parties during the duration of the contract must be fully fixed at the outset, or 'presentiated' (for a more detailed description by Macneil of presentation, see p 64). Macneil argues that in fact very few, if any, contracts, are truly discrete. Many are designed to last a long time and it cannot be determined at the outset exactly what each party is to do. But even short-term contracts take place in a social matrix, in a world of relations that give rise to behaviour patterns; these in turn give rise to expectations.

Macneil has stated his theory many times in slightly different versions. Many of the descriptions are lengthy. The extract we have chosen is a summary he made when his theory was fairly well known. This means that he does not always explain his thinking fully, but we think the essence of his message can be gathered more easily from a short piece than from a longer extract.

■ Macneil. 'Relational Contract Theory as Sociology'

(1987) 143 Journal of Institutional and Theoretical Economics 272, 274–277

(1) The world encompassed by relational contract theory is the world of contract, defined as relations among people who have exchanged, are exchanging or expect to be exchanging in the future.

(2) All exchange occurs in relations. *(Note: Even the purest discrete exchange necessarily postulates a social matrix providing at least the following: (1) a means of communication understandable to both parties: (2) a system of order so that the parties exchange instead of killing and stealing: (3) typically, in modern times, a system of money; and (4) in the case of exchanges promised, an effective mechanism to enforce promises.*

This social matrix is, of course, the minimum necessary for exchange; it takes great imagination to produce examples of exchange, in any society, with as few relations as the minimum . . .)

(3) A number of categories of behaviour are required for such relations to exist, two of which, maintaining reciprocity and maintaining solidarity, are first among equals. The others are using roles, planning, consenting flexibility, protecting restitution, reliance, and expectation interest, creating

and restraining power, following accepted ways of doing things, and harmonizing the relation with its internal and external social matrix. Obviously these categories of behavior conflict in many ways, but some minimum level is required of each of them, else the relations will cease to exist.

(4) The behavior patterns give rise to norms, a case of an 'is' creating an 'ought'. The norms parallel the elements of behavior in some cases the behavioral words being satisfactory to describe the norms as well: reciprocity and solidarity, again first among equals, role integrity (requiring consistency, involving internal conflict, and being inherently complex), implementation of planning, effectuation of consent, flexibility, the restitution, reliance, and expectation norms, the power norm justifying both creation and restraint of power, propriety of means, and harmonizing the relation with the internal and external social matrix.

(5) Underlying this structure in my view, but not essential for most of the uses to which it might be put, is the proposition that

> 'Man is both an entirely selfish and an entirely social creature, in that man puts the interests of his fellows ahead of his own interests at the same time that he puts his own interests first . . . Man, being a choosing creature, is easily capable of paralysis when two conflicting desires are in equipoise. Two principles of behavior are essential to the survival of such a creature: solidarity and reciprocity. Getting something back for something given neatly releases, or at least reduces, the tension in a creature desiring to be both selfish and social at the same time; and solidarity—a belief in being able to depend on another—permits the projection of reciprocity though time' (Macneil 348, (1983) 78 Northwestern ULR 340 rearranged).

(6) Exchange occurs in various patterns along a spectrum ranging from highly discrete to highly relational.

(7) Discrete contracts are characterized by short duration, limited personal interactions, and precise party measurements of easily measured objects of exchange. They require a minimum of future cooperation between the parties. No sharing of benefits or burdens occurs, nor is altruism expected. The parties are bound precisely and tightly. The parties view themselves as free of entangling strings. Everything is clearly defined and presentiated. If trouble is anticipated at all, it is anticipated only if someone or something turns out unexpectedly badly.

Discrete behavior of this kind gives rise to an intensification in an exchange relation of two of the common contract norms: implementation of planning and effectuation of consent. When so intensified they may usefully be labeled as the discrete norm: enhancing discreteness and presentiation.

> 'Discreteness and presentiation are themselves not the same phenomenon, in spite of their merger in discrete contracts. Discreteness is the separating of a transaction from all else between the participant at the same time and before and after. Its ideal, never achieved in life, occurs when there is nothing else between the parties, never has been, and never will be. Presentiation, on the other hand, is the bringing of the future into the present. Underlying both is the ideal of 100 percent planning of the future' (Macneil The New Social Contract (1980), p 60).

(8) Relational contracts

> 'are of significant duration (for example, franchising). Close whole persons relations form an integral aspect of the relation (employment). The object of exchange typically includes both easily measured quantities (wages) and quantities not easily measured (the projection of personality by an airline stewardess). Many individuals with individual and collective poles of interest are involved in the relations (industrial relations). Future cooperative behavior is anticipated (the players and management of the Oakland Raiders). The benefits and burdens of the relation are to be shared rather than divided and allocated (a law partnership). The bindingness of the relation is limited (again a law partnership in which in theory each member is free to quit almost at will). *(Note: This sentence is so oversimplified as to be incorrect. It was meant to contrast the discrete transaction, which theoretically is totally binding, with intertwined relations, which can never be.*

But, of course, many intertwined relations are very binding.) The entangling strings of friendship, reputation, interdependence, morality, and altruistic desires are integral parts of the relation (a theatrical agent and his clients). Trouble is expected as a matter of course (a collective bargaining agreement). Finally the participants never intend or expect to see the whole future of the relation as presentiated at any single time, but view the relation as an ongoing integration of behavior which will grow and vary with events in a largely unforeseeable future (a marriage; a family business)' (Macneil (1974) 60 Virginia LR 589, 595).

Just as discrete behavior gives rise to discrete norms, so too, relational behavior gives rise to relational norms. Similarly, these norms are intensifications of particular common contract norms. The norms intensified are primarily solidarity, role integrity, and harmonization with the social matrix, especially the internal social matrix.

'In addition, relational context affects the nature of other common contract norms. For example, flexibility in relations is at least partially an internal, rather than an entirely external norm as it is (in theory) in discrete transactions. Hence, flexibility comes into partial conflict with the planning and consent norms in ways not occurring in discrete transactions. Reciprocity also becomes an important internal matter, lest the relation break down. Power also is an important internal matter in relations' (Macneil (1983) 78 Northwestern ULR 340, 350–351).

This then is the relational contract theory . . . As suggested earlier, however, the foregoing exposition needs some further clarification. The careful reader will have noticed that 'relational' has been used to mean two different things. It is used globally to describe all relations in which exchange occurs, and since all exchange, even the most discrete, occurs in relations, all exchange is thereby 'relational'. But it is also used to mean the opposite of discrete, that is exchange occurring in relatively intertwined patterns, as for example, much of the exchange in nuclear families and within corporations.

Thus the spectrum of exchange relations is ambiguously described when its poles are labeled discrete and relational. This ambiguity may have some bad effects, even apart from simple confusion. It may, for example, contribute to the erroneous, but extremely common, belief that discrete transactions can and do occur free of relations. For that reason, I propose from hereon to describe the poles of this spectrum of exchange relations as discrete at one end and intertwined at the other. Both, of course, are always relative terms; just as seemingly discrete transactions are in fact parts of relations, and hence intertwined, so too, elements of discreteness penetrate all human relations.

Stripping out this ambiguity also helps show the dual elements of relational contract theory as thus far developed. First is the description of behavior and norms which I believe to be universal in exchange relations. Second is the dimension of discreteness, from discrete to intertwined. Of the two, the first is more fundamental in the sense that the second makes no sense without it.

NOTES

1. A selection of Macneil's work, with a critical introduction, can be found in Campbell (ed), *The Relational Theory of Contract: Selected Works of Ian Macneil*, 2001.

2. Macneil sees contract as an outgrowth of the division of labour, which he has described as one of the 'primal roots of contract' (*The New Social Contract*, 1980, pp 1–4). Hence his concentration on exchange relations.

3. His point that all contracts require a minimum social matrix may seem rather obvious, but note what he says in the last sentence of the words in parentheses (a footnote in the original) to (2): almost every exchange requires more than this minimum. The vast majority of transactions take place in a much more sophisticated framework. When you go to buy goods, you nearly always have some idea of who is likely to be willing to supply

you, what their prices and quality are likely to be, how the goods are likely to have been made, how they are likely to have been looked after since, etc. All of these things will be known to you because of the social framework within which you and the other party are operating. (At times, eg during war or famine, these frameworks break down and contracting becomes fraught with danger . . .)

4.   Macneil emphasises the norms to which behavioural patterns give rise. He stresses 'reciprocity'—'something for something'—and solidarity, which he describes as being able to depend on the other. This is often quite independent of the law. Thus you expect the shop to deliver the flowers you have ordered not only because they have a legal obligation to do so but because that's the way responsible businesses behave. Your expectations may well go beyond any legal rights, eg you may expect to be allowed to change goods that you have decided are not right after all, provided the goods are unused and you can produce the receipt.

5.   Given the description Macneil gives of relational contracts in (8), it is not surprising that his work has most frequently been seen as relevant to long-term relationships. (This aspect of it is explored further in Chapter 28). But Macneil points out that even discrete relations (ie ones that do not involve the parties in long-term commitments to each other) take place in relations in a broader sense (see note 4 above). As we shall see later (see Chapter 29), other writers have used this analysis to argue that even a short-term arrangement must be viewed in its relational matrix, and the latter may give rise to expectations which were completely unstated but yet assumed, and to which the law should perhaps give effect.

We began this chapter with an extract emphasising the creative potential of contract (Sidgwick, see p 46) and another describing the market model of contract (Atiyah, see p 47). We noted that some writers even today think that the law should seldom interfere with the operation of the market.

   Most writers today would accept that contract law should go beyond the rather limited forms of control envisaged by the *laissez-faire* approach, at least in consumer cases. This includes many economists who would argue that contract law should not necessarily enforce what the parties agreed when there was a 'market failure' of some kind, caused for instance by a monopoly or one party's lack of understanding. What is fiercely contested is whether the law can or should confine itself to interference designed to promote the better operation of the market or whether it has, or should have, distributional aims—ie to maintain the existing distribution of wealth in society, or even to promote a fairer one. This theme is taken up in Section 6, Chapter 30.

   Some writers claim, as mentioned in Chapter 1, that it is no longer adequate to describe the law as upholding the values of freedom of contract and merely smoothing away the effects of market failures. Collins, for example, argues that the law has been transformed.

■ **Hugh Collins,** *The Law of Contract* (4th edn, 2003)
pp 10–29

D. The market order

Every society creates an order of wealth and power. It establishes rules and institutions which direct the means for the creation and distribution of wealth and allocate power to certain individuals to control others. In modern western societies, market transactions play a central role in establishing the order of wealth and power. Consequently, the law of contract, which regulates these transactions, plays a leading role in determining the order of wealth and power.

Where considerable social division of labour exists in a market economy, wealth is normally created and distributed through the actions of selling, hiring and lending. These transactions tend to move commodities, services and capital towards those persons who value them most and who can exploit these factors of production efficiently. The bulk of most people's assets are purchased with income from contractual productive relations such as employment. Distributive relations reallocate this wealth through trade in commodities, securities and other forms of property. As well as the willingness to take risks with the resource of capital, superior information and expertise permit advantageous trading, resulting in a redistribution of wealth. Since the law of contract regulates both productive and distributive relations, it supplies a key ingredient in the determination of the distribution of wealth, although of course such laws as inheritance, taxation, social security payments and obligations of status (such as a parent's duty to care for a child) alter this pattern.

Not only does the market provide a principal mechanism for the distribution of wealth, it also establishes some of the significant relations of power in modern society. Contracts provide the basis for the construction of many institutional arrangements which operate in the market. These institutions, be they firms, trade unions, or trade associations, can exert power over members of the organization, according to the licence of the contractual constitution. In addition, however, many market transactions that contribute to the system of production create power relations. Employees of a business usually accept the managers' contractual right to direct and control their efforts during working hours in return for the payment of wages. The firm enters into numerous agreements with suppliers of raw materials and components, often in the form of a requirements contract, which obliges the supplier to satisfy the needs of the firm, as determined by the firm, at a fixed price. Similarly, through franchise agreements with retailers and distributorships with wholesalers, a firm tries to secure reliable outlets for its product and the right to control price and exclude competition. Within this production network established by a variety of contractual relations, each party necessarily becomes heavily dependent upon the others for the proper performance of contracts: a distributor can be driven out of business by a refusal to supply the finished product, or a supplier or a group of employees can easily halt production unless alternative raw materials and employees are easily obtainable. Often these arrangements comprise symbiotic contracts, where the economic interests of the parties are closely tied together so that wealth maximization depends upon intensive co-operation. The contractual rights and duties both create and regulate the allocation and legitimate exercise of the powers required for efficient, co-ordinated production. Furthermore, even in a consumer's purchase of goods we can detect opportunities for the exercise of power, such as a retailer's refusal to repair defective goods or offer a replacement, which leaves the consumer in a weak position.

Standing back from these dimensions of power and wealth located in production and distribution relations, we can glimpse the main outlines of the market order. Every stable social system possesses an order of power and wealth but, unlike historically prior distributive schemes, the market order avoids the imposition of a detailed pattern. Instead of a structure of rank and privilege fixing entitlements to wealth and power, the distributive mechanism of the market allocates resources to those persons both able and willing to pay the highest price for them. Thus anyone with sufficient money may purchase a Rolls-Royce, or employ someone as a servant, or set himself or herself up in a country seat. The market order avows blindness to claims of privilege or force, so it recognizes no claims of an inherent right to govern or to possess superior wealth. Each transaction creates its own power relation and exerts an independent effect upon the distribution of wealth. In an employment relation, for instance, the level of wages and the employer's measure of control depend upon many factors, including the type of work, the effectiveness of union organization and the scarcity of labour. Each employment relation potentially differs from the next in its distribution of wealth and the range and oppressiveness of managerial control. Although certain patterns and regularities emerge in the course of the myriad of market transactions, their contingency upon the vector of market forces renders them always subject to renegotiation. The market order lets fly the centrifugal forces of radical individualism, permitting philosophers to celebrate the relative fluidity of its distributive outcome, and to legitimate it by appeals to the impervious mask of market forces. No other social order so successfully disguises the fact that it constitutes an order at all.

In what sense should we regard the market as constituting an order of power and wealth? Under a regime of contract law which facilitates all types of voluntary transactions, it can be argued that individual choices determine distributive outcomes and the law does not impose any particular pattern of distribution of wealth and power. The justice of this distributive scheme can be defended either on the ground that each individual has chosen his or her lot, or on the ground that no justification is called for because the state does not seek to impose any pattern of distribution at all. Both arguments resist the claim that the market constitutes an order of wealth and power in any strong sense. But these arguments are gravely flawed.

Even supposing that the law of contract might permit all voluntary transactions to take place, the effects of such a free market on the distribution of wealth and power are predictable. The decisions of the legislature and the courts to allow those predictable consequences to occur by abstaining from intervention in the market call for justification, just as much as attempts to control distributive outcomes.

Moreover, the law of contract cannot avoid taking a stand on which distributive consequences should be permitted. In the legal rules which determine whether a voluntary transaction has taken place, as opposed to some coercive taking of property, the law necessarily takes a stand on the question of which bargaining chips may be used to a person's advantage in the marketplace. The law must determine what kinds of pressure may be used to secure better terms. It must determine the limits of fair dealing, so that certain types of lying and cheating cannot be used to gain advantage. Although all these rules may be described in the traditional understanding of the law of contract as rules designed to distinguish between voluntary and involuntary transactions, whatever rules may be chosen will inevitably have distributive consequences. They will determine the extent to which natural advantages, such as intelligence, strength and a facility for lying, and acquired advantages, such as ownership of resources and a monopoly position in the market, can be used to win further advantageous transactions and so redistribute wealth. Because the law cannot avoid taking a stand on these questions, the rules of contract law, even if conceived solely in terms of facilitating voluntary choices, have necessary and foreseeable distributive consequences.

. . .

A. The transformation thesis

This chapter briefly describes the interpretation of the law of contract presented in this book. The claim advanced suggests that the modern law of contract differs from the classical tradition in its motivating ideals, in its methods of legal reasoning, and in its sources of law. When these differences are considered together, these developments amount to a transformation of the law of contract.

. . .

I. The justice of exchange

The governing ideal of the nineteenth-century law of contract is usually described as 'freedom of contract'. This slogan was certainly a crucial political banner. It signified both a resistance to state interference in the economy and a desire to augment each individual's freedom of choice. It summarizes well some of the cardinal principles of the law: citizens enjoy a broad discretion to make contracts; the law routinely respects their choice of terms; and the voluntariness of their choices is protected against coercion and fraud. Yet respect for individual liberty comprises only one element in the ideas embedded in the Victorians' interpretation of the market order. In many respects, the ideal of individual liberty plays second fiddle to a deeper faith in the justice of an order of wealth and power established through exchange relations. This faith stems from the belief that the market order establishes both equality in place of social hierarchy and reciprocity instead of exploitation.

(a) EQUALITY

Unlike social orders which distribute wealth and power by reference to such criteria as social status, political power, physical force, or moral worth, the market order claims to respect the ideal of equality. Each person enjoys the same opportunity to enter any kind of transaction, and through trade to improve his or her lot in life. This market order achieves a great social levelling, since the distribution of wealth and power depends upon success in trading under the regime of contract law, not upon social rank or military might. People transfer commodities according to voluntary agreements, not under imposed laws of political fealty. The market mechanism for the allocation of wealth and power is therefore fit for a democratic republic.

The ideal of equality which lies at the root of this conception of the market order is not, of course, one which insists upon an egalitarian distribution of wealth and power. It is not concerned with the ultimate distributive consequences of trade. It is concerned rather with formal equality and a narrow view of equality of opportunity. Formal equality requires that each person enjoys the same set of rights to enter contracts and to own property. The narrow view of equality of opportunity insists that each person in principle should be permitted to enter into any branch of trade and thereby to improve his or her position without limit. The law recognized some exceptions to formal equality with respect to children and the insane, and, more controversially, married women, but in general the rhetoric of the law admitted no distinctions of rank and privilege in determining contractual rights and duties.

Within this perspective there seems to be no serious concern that freedom of contract might be used, in combination with ownership of scarce resources and superior technical knowledge, to achieve relations of domination which subvert the equality of citizens. The belief seems to be that, provided that a person has freely consented to the terms of the contract, there is no danger that the contract establishes unjustifiable positions of power. Under this analysis, for example, an employer's rights to give orders to his employees and demand obedience on pain of dismissal rests upon consent at the moment of hiring and is restricted to the scope of the duties envisaged in the contract. Such a limited, consensual obligation apparently runs little risk of establishing unjustifiable domination. Questions about the effects of inequality of bargaining power upon the terms of contracts, and thus upon the nature of social relations established by contracts, seem to be ignored or suppressed. It is as if positions of unjustifiable power over others simply cannot arise within the framework of freely chosen agreements.

(b) DISTRIBUTIVE JUSTICE

It is often overlooked that the nineteenth-century interpretation of the market order also proclaimed its fairness. The law insisted that only those transactions which involved an exchange could be enforceable. Both parties should give up something of value in return for something which was desired. This requirement of reciprocity, as defined by the doctrine of consideration . . . , established a distinction between, on the one hand, enforceable market transactions which had to be bargains or exchanges, and, on the other hand, instances of expropriation, domination, and exploitation. The nineteenth-century lawyers perceived a vital difference between an employment relation where wages are paid and one where no remuneration is given: the former constitutes a bargain struck between equals from which both parties expect to benefit, whereas the latter smacks of slavery and extortion. From this perspective, the presence of reciprocal rights and duties guarantees the fairness of productive and distributive relations.

This idea of fairness does not ensure an exact equivalence in the value of the performance supplied by each party to the contract. The courts did not believe that it was either possible or desirable to test the balance of the bargain. It was impossible because value depends upon a subjective appreciation by each individual, which differs from one person to the next, so the court could only assume that parties entering a contract had accepted at that time the fairness of the exchange. Any such interference would also be undesirable, for it would undermine the reliability of bargains which had been struck and post a threat to freedom of contract. But above all, such intervention was unnecessary, because the presence of a freely chosen exchange ensured that the bargain was fair. No one enters a transaction voluntarily unless he or she expects to benefit from it, so that every voluntary bargain must be fair, because it should leave each party better off than before.

Some limited intervention was necessary, however, to ensure the preservation of competitive markets. It is readily apparent that someone holding a monopoly over a scarce and valuable item of commerce might use that bargaining position to impose contracts which were scarcely distinguishable from expropriation. Legislation against combinations and cartels, allied with the judges' development of the doctrine of restraint of trade, tried to preserve a competitive market. In addition, some legislation prevented owners of monopolies such as railways from charging unfair prices. But these were limited and necessary interventions in order to uphold the general ideal that contractual exchanges established fair economic relations and distributive outcomes.

Absent from this conception of fairness in the market order is the possibility that the distributive consequences of freely chosen agreements could be unjust in any but a few isolated instances of foolishness and carelessness. The idea that large groups of people entering transactions in competitive markets might all suffer a diminution of their resources from concluding bad bargains is simply dismissed as absurd. Tenants who pay high rents, borrowers who accept exorbitant rates of interest, workers who settle for wages below subsistence levels, all have only themselves to blame for errors of judgement. Nor does this concept of the market order recognize any need for a distribution of wealth which protects people against poverty and hardship. In particular, the classical law of contract believed that it should not concern itself with the ultimate distributive consequences of the market order.

(c) Freedom of contract

The slogan 'freedom of contract' both summarized vital elements of these ideals of equality and fairness, and then added to them an interpretation of the kind of freedom which the state should establish and protect. This idea of freedom insisted that individuals should be given the choice whether to enter contracts or not, which ruled out compulsory contracts and other legally imposed duties, and that individuals should also enjoy the freedom to choose the terms of their agreements. This idea of freedom contains a negative element, which rejects the interference of the state in the terms of market transactions, but also a positive element, for it sees in the general licence to enter binding contracts an enhancement of freedom, because this facility permits new forms of co-operative endeavours which last over a period of time.

The adherence to the negative aspect of liberty could not be absolute without endangering the justice of the market order. Parties entering into contracts had to be protected against threats of violence and fraudulent misrepresentations, but this intervention could be justified as being designed to protect freedom by ensuring the genuineness of the choice to enter the contract. It also seemed possible, although unlikely, that a person might freely choose to enter a contract which permanently circumscribed liberty, as in the example of a contract of slavery, and in such instances the courts insisted that such contracts would be unenforceable. The courts further declined to enforce certain transactions on the grounds that they exhibited gross immorality or criminal behaviour: liberty of contract could not be permitted to become a licence to misbehave. But the limited nature of these exceptions to the general ideal of freedom of contract reveals how strongly this ideal informed interpretations of the just market order in the nineteenth century.

Liberty, equality, and fairness in reciprocity: these ideals make up the conception of the just market order expressed by the law of contract as it was originally conceived in the nineteenth century. For convenience, this interpretation of the market order which informed the values embedded in the law will be called 'the justice of exchange'.

. . .

Most advocates of this economic interpretation of the law of contract do not in fact generally support restrictions on freedom of contract. On the contrary, they use economic analysis to identify certain interventions as undesirable and unjustifiable infringements of the market order, and propose deregulation instead. Price controls, for example, as occur sometimes in rented accommodation and on minimum wages, will normally be rejected on the ground that these do not respond to a market failure, but in fact create a market failure themselves. By artificially lowering the price of rented accommodation, the law will reduce the supply, thereby creating a problem of homelessness. Similarly, by artificially raising the price of wages, the law reduces employers' demand for labour, which in turn creates the market failure represented by unemployment. By analogy, the desirability and justice of many other types of interference in free contracts may be questioned, such as the imposition of compulsory terms in leases and contracts of employment, on the ground that they cause a market failure which in the long run leaves everyone worse off than before. In short, restrictions on freedom of contract, although occasionally justifiable under an economic analysis as a last resort to handle market failures, often create a market failure themselves, so should normally be avoided.

3. The value of autonomy

Like the paradigm of the justice of exchange, the market failure approach shares a disregard for problems of power, distributive fairness, and the need to encourage co-operation in the realization of market opportunities. Its system of understanding the market order confines attention to the process of economic exchange and an assessment of how best to facilitate its efficient operation as a mechanism for the generation of wealth. This view represents a vital perspective on the market order, but this system of understanding seems to me to be impoverished in its appreciation of the issues raised by contractual disputes.

Consider, for example, the case of the unknown songwriter in *Schroeder Music Publishing Co Ltd v Macaulay*. This young composer agreed to give all his songs to a publisher for a period of five years, renewable at the option of the publisher, in return for royalties on published work but no promise to publish the work. The House of Lords declared the agreement void under the doctrine of restraint of trade, arguing that the weak bargaining position of the composer had led to an unfair agreement under which the publisher undertook minimal obligations in return for total commitment by the composer. If one considers this decision from the perspective of market failure, it seems hard to justify. As Trebilcock points out, there seems to have been a competitive market operating in this instance, with many music publishers competing for young talent. Nor can it be seriously suggested that the composer did not understand the terms of the agreement because they were too complex. In the absence of such grounds to suspect market failure, economic analysis suggests that the contract should be enforced, for any interference may disrupt the market opportunities for young composers in the future.

But these arguments, although sound in themselves, miss the real objections to this contract, which concern the dimensions of power, fairness, and co-operation, not the efficiency of the market. Because the composer's career was completely dependent upon the publisher's discretion for a period of up to ten years, his degree of subordination to another represented an unjustifiable form of domination. The absence of an undertaking on the part of the publisher to publish any of his songs rendered the exchange too one-sided to be fair. In addition, because the composer could not terminate the agreement during its fixed period, he had no effective sanction against the publisher to ensure that at least it made reasonable efforts to bring the venture to fruition by publishing and promoting his work.

These three themes—the concern about unjustifiable domination, the equivalence of the exchange, and the need to ensure co-operation—which seem to me to motivate the decision in *Schroeder Music Publishing Co Ltd v Macaulay*, form the core of the interpretation of law of contract presented in this book. The emphasis upon these values in the modern law signifies a new understanding and justification of the market order. The law's endorsement of those values does not represent the adoption of a socialist or communitarian political philosophy or a rejection of the market order. The constitution of the market by reference to these values, as well as the traditional concerns for liberty and competitive markets, merely represents a revised understanding of the market order and its justificatory principles, not a wholesale rejection of markets as the most efficient system for the satisfaction of wants.

The question of what political philosophy underpins this conception of the market order is more troublesome to answer. It cannot be the libertarian philosophies which underpin the justice of exchange paradigm, nor the wealth-maximization goal which seems to provide the main justification for the market failure interpretation. On the other hand, these values do not seem to be incompatible with certain liberal ideals, which it may be sensible to attribute to legislators and judges as the basis for their unarticulated political assumptions.

Perhaps the core principle in this interpretation of the market order consists in a revised notion of liberty or autonomy. Whilst one should celebrate the liberating potential of a market order, because it offers considerable choices of occupation and consumption, we should recognise that not all choices seem so worthwhile and deserving of approbation. For instance, choices to harm the environment, to injure one's own body, to sell one's property at far less than its market value, and to enter into economic relations which give others discretionary power over major aspects of one's well-being, do not seem to be valuable choices which the law should respect and protect. If so, although the law should continue to support the facility of entering into binding commitments by voluntary choice, it should limit this facility to choices which are likely to prove worthwhile ways of pursuing one's life. The law can tolerate a considerable range of economic transactions and give the benefit of the doubt to activities which seem of little worth to most people, but the law sets limits to freedom of contract when the choices made do not appear worthwhile on any reckoning.

NOTES

1. Collins's attempt to restate the law in terms of the prevention of unjustifiable domination, the encouragement of equivalence in exchange and the ensuring of cooperation is a bold one. Whether his case is made out is for you to judge as you read through this book.

2. You will frequently find that, as was noted after the extract from Adams and Brownsword, some rules may equally well be explained from differing viewpoints. It will be obvious from the many law-and-economics readings included in this book (on economic analysis of contract, see the next chapter) that your editors often find the explanation that the rules of law are primarily concerned with assisting the market and preventing market failure an enlightening one. It may not, however, tell the whole story and it seems only right to present the reader with a very carefully developed alternative analysis.

3. You may be interested to see a review of the first edition of Collins by Wightman (1989) 52 MLR 115.

4. Collins develops his ideas further in *Regulating Contracts*, 1999.

CHAPTER FOUR

ECONOMIC ANALYSIS OF CONTRACT LAW

■ **Kronman and Posner,** *Economics of Contract Law* (1979)
pp 1–4

The fundamental economic principle with which we begin is that if voluntary exchanges are permitted—if, in other words, a market is allowed to operate—resources will gravitate toward their most valuable uses. If A owns a good that is worth only $100 to him but $150 to B, both will be made better off by an exchange of A's good for B's money at any price between $100 and $150; and if they realize this, they will make the exchange. By making both of them better off, the exchange will also increase the wealth of the society (of which they are members), assuming the exchange does not reduce the welfare of non-parties more than it increases A's and B's welfare. Before the exchange—which, let us say, takes place at a price of $125—A had a good worth $100 to him and B had $125 in cash, a total of $225. After the exchange, A has $125 in cash and B has a good worth $150 to him, a total of $275. The exchange has increased the wealth of society by $50 (ignoring, as we have done, any possible third-party effects).

The principle is the same whether we are speaking of the purchase of a string of pearls, a lawyer's time, a machine for making shoes, or an ingot of aluminium. The existence of a market—a locus of opportunities for mutually advantageous exchanges—facilitates the allocation of the good or service in question to the use in which it is most valuable, thereby maximizing the wealth of society.

This conclusion may be questioned on various grounds. For example, it may be argued that since 'value' in this analysis is measured by willingness to pay, which in turn is affected by the distribution of income and wealth (one cannot offer to buy a good without having money or the means to obtain it), the maximization of value cannot be regarded as an uncontroversially proper goal for society to pursue. An introductory chapter is not the place to explore the philosophical basis of the economist's concept of value. For our purposes it is enough that the reader understand the technical meaning of the concept. The reader can then decide whether there is any 'value', in an ultimate social sense, to the *economic* concept of value which the system of free exchanges promotes.

The principle that voluntary exchange should be freely permitted in order to maximize value is frequently summarized in the concept (or slogan) of 'freedom of contract'. This is something of a misnomer, for the concept of *contract* typically plays an insignificant role in elucidations and critiques of the principle of voluntary exchange. Many value-maximizing exchanges occur without contracts, or with contracts so rudimentary or transitory as to have little interest for economists studying the phenomenon of voluntary exchange. If A buys the *Chicago Tribune* from B, a news vendor, paying 20c for it on the spot, this is a value-maximizing exchange; but it would be pretentious to speak of a contract between A and B, though technically there is one (if a section of the paper is missing. A can probably rescind the contract and get his 20c back). One can talk about the principle or system of voluntary exchange for quite some time before it becomes necessary to consider the role of contracts and contract law in facilitating the process.

In the newspaper example, the exchange is virtually (though not completely) instantaneous; and this provides a clue to the role of contracts in the process of voluntary exchange. It is true that, although money and good cross at the same moment, the actual *use* of the good—the reading of the newspaper—occurs after the exchange and takes some time; so really the process of exchange is not complete until the paper has been opened and inspected. Only then can the buyer be satisfied that he got what he paid for (that no pages are missing or illegible, etc). Still, the time required to complete the exchange in the newspaper example is quite short. Where the time is long, contracts and contract law become important.

Suppose that A promises to build a house for B, construction to take six months to complete and B to pay either periodically or on completion. With construction so time-consuming, there is a significant likelihood that something will occur to frustrate the exchange—insolvency, changes in the price inputs, labour troubles, etc. Nor is A's performance complete when construction of the house is finished. A durable good like a house by definition yields services to the purchaser over a period of time, a long one in the case of a house; and it is these services rather than the physical structure itself that the purchaser is hoping to acquire. If the house wears out long before the purchaser reasonably believed it would, the exchange will be effectively thwarted long after nominal completion of performance by the promisor.

Economists have pointed out that the cost of an undertaking tends to be inversely related to the time allowed for completion. Stated differently, it is costly to accelerate completion of a time-consuming task. It would also be costly to make goods less durable in order to compress the period in which the full exchange of the goods could be completed. These observations suggest that a system of contract rights, and not merely one of property rights, may be necessary to minimize the cost of production in a market system.

Thus far we have been attempting to elucidate the concept of a contract and explain its economic significance. We have said nothing about the economic function of contract *law*. Its basic function is to provide a sanction for reneging, which, in the absence of sanctions, is sometimes tempting where the parties' performance is not simultaneous. During the process of an extended exchange, a point may be reached where it is in the interest (though perhaps only the very narrow, short-run interest) of one of the parties to terminate performance. If A agrees to build a house for B and B pays him in advance. A can make himself better off, at least if loss of reputation (which, depending on A's particular situation, may be unimportant to him) is ignored, by pocketing B's money and not building the house. The problem arises because the nonsimultaneous character of the exchange offers one of the parties a strategic advantage which he can use to obtain a transfer payment that utterly vitiates the advantages of the contract to the other party. Clearly, if such conduct were permitted, people would be reluctant to enter into contracts and the process of economic exchange would be retarded.

A noninstantaneous or extended exchange creates not only strategic opportunities that parties might try to exploit in the absence of legal sanction, but also uncertainty with regard to the conditions under which performance will occur. This uncertainty exposes the parties to the risk that the costs and benefits of their exchange will turn out to be different from what they expected. An important function of contract law is to enforce the parties' agreed upon allocation of risk.

A related function is to reduce the costs of the exchange process by supplying a standard set of risk-allocation terms for use by contracting parties. Many substantive rules of contract law are simply specifications of the consequences of some contingency for which the contract makes no express provision. If the parties are satisfied with the way in which the rules allocate the risk of that contingency, they have no need to incur the expense of writing their own risk-allocation rule into the contract.

Besides (1) imposing costs on people who try to exploit the other party to the contract by refusing to abide by its terms and (2) providing a stock of standard contractual provisions, the law of contracts (3) imposes costs on, and thereby discourages, *careless* behavior in the contracting process—behavior that unnecessarily increases the costs of the process itself. Suppose A promise to give B a boat if B stops smoking, B complies with this condition (at some cost to himself), but A refuses to give him the boat. A proves that B misunderstood him—he never meant to promise him a boat. B in turn proves that he was reasonably induced by A's words and conduct to believe that A had indeed promised him the boat. If we believe that A did not in fact intend such a promise, then enforcement of the promise cannot be justified as necessary to prevent frustration of a value-maximizing exchange; there is no basis for presuming that an exchange will make the parties better off if one of them never intended to make it. But we may still want to enforce the contract in order to give people in A's position an incentive to avoid carelessly inducing others to incur costs in reliance on the existence of a contract. This problem may seem to belong to the law of torts rather than contracts, since enforcement serves not to promote a mutually beneficial exchange but instead to deter careless behavior. But enforcement does promote the contractual process by discouraging a costly form of carelessness that would tend to impede it.

The foregoing discussion suggests a resolution along economic lines of the old dispute in contract law over whether the basis of contract formation is a 'subjective' or 'objective' one—whether the law requires an actual meeting of minds or whether it is enough that the parties use words or conduct that would signify agreement to an impartial observer. Only a contract that involves an actual meeting of minds satisfies the economist's definition of a value-maximizing exchange; but the economist allows a place for rules designed to prevent people from misleading others into thinking they have a contract with them; hence both the subjective and objective theories have a place in contract law.

NOTES

1. It is worth considering some of the concepts and assumptions that Kronman and Posner use in this piece, together with some of the really quite simple ideas upon which economic analysis is based. These notes should form a sufficient introduction to all of the economic analysis contained in the book.

2. The first assumption is that individuals are rational maximisers of their own self-interest—that is, they will respond to other people and to events in a way that increases their own utility. It is this that lies behind the notion that individuals will trade resources until the resources reach the people who value them most highly.

3. Economists express the idea that something may be worth more to one person than to another by saying that the first will be prepared to pay more for it than the other. However, they use the word 'utility' rather than 'wealth' because the theory does not assume that every one is selfishly pursuing greater personal wealth. Individuals may well like to see other individuals made better off and be prepared to give some of their own wealth to achieve that. An economist fits this into his general theory by saying that the donor's 'utility' is increased by seeing the donee made better off. (See further, p 136.)

4. Exchanges that increase the utility of both the parties increase 'efficiency', in the special sense in which economists use that term. Efficiency will also be increased even if one of the parties is left worse off, provided that the other party is made so much better off that she could compensate the first party for his loss and still gain herself—in other words, if the benefits exceed the costs. A state of affairs will be fully efficient (or 'optimal') if it is not possible to make any further change without finding that the aggregate losses to the losers equal or exceed the aggregate gains to the gainers. When this state has been achieved, wealth has been maximised.

5. In economics, cost also has a special meaning: it is measured by the value of opportunities forgone. Economics is all about understanding what happens when people who are subject to constraints and to incentives make choices, such as the choice between the various ways in which they could use resources. What matters is the value of the resource

in its next best alternative use, not the amount that was spent to acquire or produce it. So if A has spent £3m on a factory to produce CFCs but the government has now banned production of CFCs on environmental grounds, and A now has to decide whether to use it to produce other gases or to knock it down and sell the land, the choice will be between the revenue each of those activities will produce; the £3m spent already is irrelevant. Bygones are always bygones in economics.

6.   On the other hand, cost will include normal profit. The cost of using capital will always include the amount that the capital might earn in alternative risk-free investments, such as government stocks—and if a firm does not offer at least such a return to investors, it will not attract the capital it needs any more than it would be able to employ workers if it didn't offer them wages. (In fact, it will have to offer something extra: a 'risk premium'.)

7.   Kronman and Posner say that the increase in the wealth of the two individuals who trade will increase the overall wealth of society provided that the exchange does not make third parties worse off. The effect on the third party is known as an 'externality'—although there is also an externality if a third party is made better off. The externality problem is not relevant to most contract law problems, which will involve only the parties to the contract. There is one important exception: illegal contracts. Suppose Beale concludes that the only thing standing between him and a highly prestigious chair at the University of Bristol is Furmston. He might be tempted to hire an assassin to poison Furmston for £10,000—which, if the crime were not detected, might leave both Beale and the assassin better off, but would not be value-maximising for Furmston or society at large. Where parties enter into a contract to do something illegal, the general task of the law may be to frustrate their intentions—the exact opposite of the usual purpose of contract law. (We shall see later that the economist's normal assumption that most contracts have no external effects may be made much too easily: see p 784.)

8.   The question the authors raise about whether the maximisation of value is a proper goal to pursue given the unequal distribution of income and wealth is taken up at pp 784 and 813.

9.   Kronman and Posner point out that the provision of legal remedies reduces the likelihood of default in an exchange that extends over a period of time. Without legal remedies, some such exchanges might not take place because they would seem too costly—the risk of default would outweigh the gains to be made. This would discourage what would otherwise be a value-maximising exchange. Posner in his *Economic Analysis of Law* (2nd edn, p 66) gives other examples:

…[T]he absence of legally enforceable rights would, among other consequences, bias investment toward economic activities where the interval in which the contemplated economic activity could be completed was short, and this would reduce the efficiency of resource use. Suppose A wants to sell his cow, and there are two bidders, B and C. The cow is worth $50 to B and $60 to C (and only $30 to A), so efficiency requires that the cow be sold to C rather than to B. However, B has $50 cash in hand while C cannot obtain any cash for a week. C promises to pay $55 to A in a week, and let us assume that the $5 difference would more than compensate A for the costs, in the event of default, of bringing suit for damages or for return of the cow, discounted by the risk of default—if the law made C's promise to A enforceable. But if the law does not enforce such promises A may decide that, since C may fail to raise the money and B in the interim lose interest in the transaction, he is better off selling to B now. If so, the failure of the law to provide a remedy if C breaks his promise will, by discouraging parties from entering into exchanges in which performance by one party is deferred, have induced a suboptimum allocation of resources.

Now suppose that A offers a shirt for sale at $5 and B offers one for $6 which he claims (truthfully) will last three times as long as A's shirt and is therefore better value. But the difference in shirts is not apparent on casual inspection or handling, so while B may be willing to guarantee the superior durability of this shirt, if his promise is not legally enforceable consumers may doubt the honesty of his claim and buy A's shirt instead, again a suboptimum result.

In broad terms, this is an example of how contract law can reduce 'transaction costs'.

10. The idea that if exchanges were riskier or more costly in other ways, fewer of them would take place, is simply an application of a basic economic idea often expressed as 'demand curves slope down'. Anything desirable will be demanded, purchased and consumed more as its price falls and less as its price rises relative to other prices. In elementary textbooks, the idea is captured by a diagram which relates price (on the vertical axis) to quantity demanded (on the horizontal): the demand curve falls as the eye moves from left to right.

11. Not all parties will stop entering a particular type transaction because it becomes more expensive or start entering it when it becomes cheaper. Some people value certain resources so much that they will be willing to pay more to obtain them, but others will not. Conversely, if the price of an item falls, some people for whom it was not previously worthwhile will start to buy, while for others it will remain too expensive. (The degree to which demand is affected by changes in price is referred to as the 'elasticity' of demand.) The people whose behaviour alters in response to the change in price are referred to as the 'marginal' buyers and their behaviour is particularly important—indeed, it can be said that every important quantity in economics is decided 'at the margin'.

12. The risk of the other party defaulting and leaving you out of pocket is just one example of a 'transaction cost'. In the real world, all contracting involves some transactions costs. People need to acquire information, to negotiate terms and conditions, and to monitor the other party's performance, as well to enforce the agreement if there is a breach—and usually all of these are costly. All are examples of transactions costs. As we shall see, economists often start an analysis by assuming that there are no transaction costs, but this 'modelling' should never be assumed to represent the real world. (For an example, see notes 9 and 10.)

13. Kronman and Posner point out that a second way in which the law can reduce transactions costs is by 'supplying a standard set of risk-allocation terms'. If negotiation were to cost nothing, parties would presumably make sure that whatever future events might affect the contract, they had agreed a set of terms that would leave them both as well off as possible. They would continue to negotiate, in other words, until they had reached an optimal arrangement under which any further change could only make one of them better off by making the other one equally worse off. The result would be that the parties had what economists call a 'complete contingent claims contract'—one in which every eventuality was provided for.

14. If all contracts were complete in this sense, the whole law of contract could be reduced to a single sentence: 'whatever the parties have agreed shall be enforced.' But although some contracts are very detailed, none is complete. Nonetheless, the idea is useful, because to an economist the question, 'what should the law be now that such and such has happened' should be answered by asking what the parties would probably have agreed had they negotiated on it. If the court can decide what terms the parties would have negotiated in a hypothetical world in which negotiation was costless, and then 'mimic'

this solution by applying it as a rule of law, that rule can be described as efficient: the parties could not negotiate to any other solution that would leave them jointly better off, so there is no need for them to negotiate (see Coase, 'The Problem of Social Cost' (1960) 3 J Law & Econ 1, 15–16). Thus transactions costs are reduced and more exchanges are encouraged. Of course, if the court chooses a solution that is less than optimal for parties making that type of contract, the law will then be inefficient: the parties will either have to make an express agreement excluding the legal rule and substituting their own preferred solution, or put up with the suboptimal result.

15.   Analysis of legal rules from an economic point of view often leads to what is called 'the economics of the second best'. A simple economic model sometimes suggests a legal rule that, in the real world, would be impracticable, because it would be too difficult to apply. Kronman and Posner's example of misleading the other party into thinking you are contracting provides an example. If you were to make a mistake and did not mean what you said, the resulting exchange would not be a value-maximising exchange, and they suggest that there ought in this case to be tort-like liability to deter such careless behaviour. But we shall see that the law does not distinguish between the person who means what he says and the person who does not: subject to some qualifications (see Chapter 10), the law judges contracting parties objectively, by their words and actions not their thoughts. This decision not to distinguish between genuine bargains and merely misleading conduct can be justified on the basis that to try to distinguish them would be just too costly. Judges and arbitrators do not have privileged access to the workings of the minds of the parties; they cannot always easily discern who is telling the truth. To ask them to do so would increase the length (and therefore the cost) of trials— and also the difficulties of reaching a settlement out of court. Thus it may be sensible to adopt a rule that does not require them to distinguish, as being the best compromise between theoretical efficiency and administrative cost. Such costs are often termed 'adjudication costs'. The converse, of course, is that the law may end up with a solution that is not really appropriate on the facts of the case: this may be termed 'error cost'. The choice of which rule of law to adopt is frequently influenced by the balance between adjudication and error costs.

16.   The assumption that parties will bargain in ways that leave each of them better off assumes that they have information about each other. Information is extremely import-ant to the operation of markets and to contract law, even though the economics of information have been studied only during the last thirty years. Information is often very valuable; it can also be very costly to acquire or produce. If the parties do not have adequate information, they may well misjudge the costs or benefits of the transactions they are contemplating, with inefficient results: see, for example, the discussion of the 'small print' in consumer contracts, see p 967. There are a number of rules that place contractual liability in such a way as to encourage the use of existing information by the party who has access to it (eg the rule in *Hadley v Baxendale*, see p 625).

17.   However, information is a peculiar commodity: once it has been produced, it can be reproduced and passed on to others at very little cost. Thus it is hard for the producer to capture the full benefit of what he produces: he cannot 'sell' the information without revealing it to all and sundry, so that even information of great social benefit may not be produced without special incentives to the producer. It is not worth going to the expense of designing a better mousetrap if, as soon as you put it on the market, your design can be copied by your competitors. It is for this reason that the law creates intellectual

property rights in the form of patents and copyright. We shall see that there are also rules of contract law apparently aimed at encouraging the acquisition of information (eg the rules allowing parties to make contracts without disclosing some types of relevant information to the other party, see p 533).

18.　You will notice that analysis in terms of efficiency looks to see whether a transaction or change will increase the aggregate or joint wealth of the parties, but it is not concerned with how the increase is distributed between them. Thus, to use the example in Kronman and Posner's first paragraph, the exchange would still be efficient if B agreed to buy the good from A at $149.99. Normally, the maximum amount that A can charge B (and, conversely, the minimum amount that B can get A to accept) will be constrained by competition: the presence of other sellers (or buyers) in the market. It is easier to explain this if we first introduce the notion of 'marginal cost'.

19.　Marginal cost is the cost of producing an extra unit of what is on offer. Every producer has limited capacity. If it is operating at below capacity, it will be eager to sell more; but at some point to produce extra units may cost the producer more on average than it has been spending up to that point. For instance, a solicitor handling 30 conveyances a month might well like to see more business come through her door if her staff are not fully occupied. But if the number were to reach 60 a month, she might be rushed, and at 90 a month, she might find that the extra business is costing more in overtime, temps and so on than it is bringing in. In other words, the marginal cost would have risen until it exceeded the 'marginal revenue': the extra income brought in by each conveyance. A producer will not normally want marginal cost to exceed marginal revenue.

20.　Under competition, market price will normally equal marginal cost. If it rises above that, some firms will see a profit opportunity. They will hire more resources and produce more. But eventually this will lead to a significant rise in supply in the total market. Assuming demand does not change, the rise in supply will lead to a lower price, and this will go on until price equals marginal cost again. At that point, no firm sees any further profit opportunity. (Remember that, in economics, cost includes normal profit.) The market has reached a point of stability, an equilibrium, in which P = MC. Conversely, if market price goes below MC, some firms will drop out of this now-unprofitable line of business, and a parallel process will bring the market back to the point of equilibrium P = MC. This is an attractive destination, because at this point, and at no other, the cost of resources (eg the *labour*, earning normal wages, and the *capital*, earning normal profit) needed to produce the good exactly equals its value to the marginal consumer.

21.　Under monopoly, however, price exceeds marginal cost. A monopolist is someone with significant control over the price of a good and the total quantity supplied to the market—eg the sole producer of the product. Such a person will maximise his own profit by putting the price above marginal cost. Then he can make a greater profit than competing businesspeople can normally make. Of course, because demand curves slope down, he will sell less than he would sell at the competitive price P = MC. Therein lies the problem of monopoly. Some marginal consumers would be willing to buy if the price were a little lower than the monopoly price. They are willing to pay enough to 'hire' the resources (eg labour and capital) needed to produce the good, but they cannot because the monopolist stands between them and the hiring of the resources. Thus monopoly leads to a misallocation of resources, ie too few resources flow into the prod uction of the monopolised good. Note that it is *not* the extra profit made by the monopolist that worries economists. That is a distributional question, a 'mere transfer of wealth'.

Customers lose but shareholders in the monopolist firm (the majority of shares nowadays are held by pension funds, which are in turn owned by the individuals in the pension scheme) benefit: nothing to get excited about. But all economists are happy to condemn misallocation of resources. Thus economists and the person in the street both dislike monopoly, but their reasons differ sharply. (Note that economists may accept that temporary monopolies are necessary in order to encourage the development of new products: see note 17 above. A patent is nothing more than a grant of a temporary monopoly.)

CHAPTER FIVE

EMPIRICAL WORK

Kronman and Posner envisage contracts involving a short timeframe being made and performed without reference to the law, but say: 'Where the time is long, contracts and contract law become important.' Their statement contains a vital insight, but it is an oversimplification.

■ Beale and Dugdale 'Contracts between Businessmen' (1975)

2 Brit J Law & Society, 45, 45–48

Contract law may be 'used' in at least two ways. First, use may be made of the remedies which the law provides in the event of something going wrong: for instance, the victim of a breach of contract may be able to bring the contract to an end or to recover damages....

But much more 'use' of contract law is made in a second way... The parties may... 'use' contract law to regulate their relationship, to plan what is to happen in the future. They may plan their primary obligations, for instance in a contract sale the item, the price and the delivery date, and also mechanisms by which these primary obligations may be adjusted; for instance, what is to happen if the cost of materials increases or an unavoidable delay occurs. The agreement may proceed further and set out the rights of the parties in the event of something going seriously wrong. In other words the parties may plan their own remedies. Examples would be an express right to terminate or a 'liquidated damages' clause fixing in advance the amount payable by a party who breaks the contract. At this point the planning use of contract merges with the remedial use, at least if the parties make use of the planned remedies.

...Professor Stewart Macaulay has published the results of some research into this topic done in Wisconsin, where he interviewed representatives of 43 companies and six law firms. He described contract as involving '...two distinct elements: (a) rational planning of the transaction with careful provision for as many future contingencies as can be foreseen, and (b) the existence or use of actual or potential legal sanctions to induce performance of the exchange or to compensate for non-performance'. He divided the types of issue which might be planned into four—description of the primary obligations, contingencies, defective performances and legal sanctions—and concluded that while many business exchanges will involve a high degree of planning about each category, equally many at least 'reflect no planning, or only a minimal amount of it, especially concerning legal sanctions and the effect of defective performances'. He found little use of 'contractual practices' in the later adjustment of relationships, though there was some evidence of tacit reliance on contractual rights; and very little use of the formal dispute-settlement procedures available through the courts.

The picture which emerges from our research is, as will be seen, broadly similar to that drawn by Macaulay, and many of the general explanations of why contract law may or may not be used are the same as his...

We interviewed representatives of nineteen firms of engineering manufacturers, mainly in Bristol, about their firm's contracts of purchase and sale. We talked to 33 persons: five of these were legal staff, and in other cases we normally spoke to at least one senior member of the firm. In some cases we spoke to sales personnel and in other cases to purchasing officers: we have tried where appropriate to contrast the attitudes of the 'two sides'. The interviews varied in length according to the time that could be spared us, from twenty minutes to several hours: in some cases we made more than one visit to a firm. It was therefore not possible to ask the same questions of each representative, and regrettably we obtained no information on some topics from a few firms. We did endeavour to find out however not only what each firm did but what was generally done in the trade. Contracts of sale and purchase by engineering manufacturers were chosen because of their relative simplicity and our findings may have no validity outside that area.

We realize that our sample was small (about half the size of Macaulay's), but we hope it is sufficiently large to show general trends and to confirm Macaulay's picture. On the more detailed issues it will clearly not indicate accurately how common particular practices are, but we think it worthwhile to indicate their existence so that they can be studied in more depth if that is thought worthwhile.

Before dealing with the particular issues on which we concentrated it may be useful to indicate some of the more general factors which may influence engineering manufacturers in their decision on whether to plan a contract in detail, whether to adhere to their contractual rights and duties and whether to employ contractual remedies. For instance the reason why in most exchanges the parties agree expressly only on their primary obligations, and not on the effect of, say, late or defective performances may be that on each of the issues studied there appeared to be a certain amount of 'tacit' planning: within the trade certain terms and certain customs or 'unwritten laws' were widely accepted. For instance it was generally accepted that the seller would not compensate the buyer for certain losses. Thus, although firms would sometimes claim 'unusual' rights the trade custom might provide a basis for settling any dispute. Moreover, most firms traded regularly with the other party, and would know what attitude the other was likely to take. Firms frequently stated that they would take much greater care when contracting with relatively unknown parties, especially those outside the engineering trade.

A second general reason for not planning a transaction in much detail is that such planning is expensive, while the risk of a serious dispute or loss may be low; for instance if orders of low value are sold on credit to a diversity of customers the loss likely to be caused by customers failing to pay may not be great, and may not justify the cost of planning security arrangements. Conversely a high degree of planning was often explained by a high risk—perhaps a customer who would lose heavily if delivery were late or a machine which would cause great loss of life if it were defective. Even then there might be reluctance to do any more than was strictly necessary: there seemed to be a feeling that a carefully negotiated contract might be insufficiently flexible to meet even foreseeable events, and too much negotiation might sour a peaceful relationship.

Even if plans had been made to cover possible disruptions, there was usually thought to be no need to fall back on legal rights if the disruption materialized. It was made very clear to us that, besides there being a common acceptance of certain norms within the trade, there was a considerable degree of trust among firms. This was particularly so among smaller firms who obtained most of their orders locally and who frequently placed great trust in the fairness of one or two very large firms. No doubt belief in mutual fairness was reinforced by the considerable degree of personal contact between officers, usually in the business context but sometimes on social occasions. The firm's general reputation was also at stake. Not only did salesmen stress the need to have a good product and to stand behind it, buyers also emphasized the need to maintain a reputation for the firm as fair and efficient, and both said that any attempt to shelter behind contractual provisions or even frequent citation of contractual terms would destroy the firm's reputation very quickly. But even more important than the general reputation of the firm was the desire to do business again with the other party, or with other firms in the same group of companies. Each side had to be prepared to make concessions and to do so in a spirit of co-operation. The importance of the 'on-going' nature of the relationship will become clear when the individual issues are discussed.

With this need to avoid 'taking sides' and thereby souring the relationship and the time and expense involved in taking legal advice and remedies, it was not surprising to find relatively little use of contractual remedies and almost none of formal dispute-settlement procedures such as a court hearing or an arbitration. It would be a mistake however to assume that contract law has very little relevance. Firstly, it is always in the background: contract law may not be mentioned but the parties probably know in general what the legal position is and may adjust their attitudes accordingly. As one sales manager put it: 'it is an umbrella under which we operate'. But secondly we hope to show that while non-legal factors and extra-contractual devices do commonly reduce the need to use contract law, there are certain problems which for one reason or another are not infrequently dealt with by contract planning and sometimes by the use of contractual remedies . . .

NOTES

1. Although this study suggests that some businesses make only limited use of contract law, it must be remembered that it was studying only a small sample from one industry. Other trades may well demonstrate a much more 'legalistic' approach: for instance, a glance into Lloyd's Reports, which concentrate on commercial cases, suggests that businesses in some commodity trades and in the charter markets litigate much more regularly—frequently taking points that lack any real merit in order to escape unprofitable contracts (see p 566). The contracts seem to have been planned in quite some detail, using forms similar to those reproduced in the Appendix. (Possible explanations for this are explored at p 887).

2. Other parts of this article and other empirical studies, including the seminal one by Macaulay, are extracted on pp 117, 223, 250 and 389. Not a great deal of empirical work on contract has been done. Fairly complete lists of references will be found in the bibliography to Macaulay (1977) 11 Law & Society Rev 507, in Weintraub [1992] Wisconsin LR 1, 4 n 10 and in Vincent-Jones [1993] Civil Justice Q 337, 337 n 2. The articles will themselves repay study.

3. Charny, 'Nonlegal Sanctions in Commercial Relationships' (1990) 104 Harvard LR 373 considers, among other points, how rational transactors decide between legal and nonlegal 'sanctioning systems'. On this, he concludes (at 425):

    It appears that rational transactors would tend to prefer legally enforceable contracts when the commitment is easily understood by courts, so that litigation and error costs are relatively low. Conversely, transactors would prefer commitments to be enforced by nonlegal sanctions in circumstances in which many of the costs of the sanctioning system are 'sunk'—that is, in which the mechanisms for enforcing the bond are already in place because they serve some other social function. Markets of transactors closely monitoring each other and, alternatively, markets of well-informed and highly sophisticated transactors also provide fertile opportunities for developing effective nonlegal sanctioning arrangements. In other markets, however, the use of nonlegal commitments might indicate a mistake by the parties or corrigible defects in the available legal institutions.

    The analysis developed in this Part also supports generalizations about the mix of legal and nonlegal sanctions that rational parties would use to enforce the various commitments made in a particular type of commercial transaction. In corporate bond transactions, covenants to control debtor behavior would be used when the relevant covenant is easily formulated—for example, standard clauses limiting disposition of assets or payment of dividends. Creditors would use nonlegal reputational sanctions to control behavior that would be more costly to prohibit through a contract term, either because the term would be complex and thus open to judicial misconstruction or because no term could realistically capture the complexity of the behavior at issue.

    The easy availability of nonlegal sanctions, the ready coexistence of legal and nonlegal commitments in a transactional setting, and the clear advantages that nonlegal sanctions may confer upon one party suggest that in some cases parties may choose to rely upon nonlegal sanctions when legal sanctions would be preferable. This possibility provides the grounding for the analysis of legal intervention, to which I now turn.

On the question of legal intervention, he summarises (at 467):

[This] Article has identified circumstances in which a rational legal decisionmaker can improve transactors' welfare by regulating transactions in which nonlegal commitments are made. In particular, the analysis emphasized the decisive differences—generally neglected in the contract literature—between two types of transactors: rational transactors, who face information costs but rationally respond to these costs; and poor-judgment transactors, who do not understand the consequences of their own ignorance of how they ought to transact. Regulation of nonlegal commitments can aid rational transactors by providing efficient terms that they do not draft because of high information costs; regulation aids poor-judgment transactors by preventing them from entering contracts that are wasteful or exploitive.

4.   It is commonly said that there has been a 'litigation explosion' in this country in recent years. Vincent-Jones [1993] Civil Justice Q 337 examined the available statistical evidence and concluded (at 355–356):

With regard to breach of contract cases in the Queen's Bench division, there has been a consistent rise in the number and proportion of writs, trial disposals and judgments relative to increases in these categories recorded for the general population of cases over the past 15 years. This is so even though contract cases continue to be a small part of litigation business, accounting in 1989 for only 2.9 per cent. of writs issued and 8 per cent. of trial disposals (10.3 per cent. in 1991) in the Division. Support for the proposition that contract disputes are of increasing importance may be found in the growth in work of the specialist Commercial and Official Referees' jurisdictions. A distinction may be drawn between these breach of contract actions and the recovery cases, particularly recovery of debt (whether by ordinary action or petition for insolvency). Whereas breach of contract cases have increased at a comparatively fast, steady rate, and expanded as a proportion of total cases, recovery actions have been subject to greater fluctuations in the past decade, and have generally maintained a constant proportion of overall litigation business. Whether the dramatic increase in insolvency cases between 1989 and 1991 also applies to the recovery actions is open to speculation, because the change in presentation of data after 1989 does not permit this comparison.

These findings are persuasive, but far from conclusive, evidence of a transformation in business disputing. The major question remaining unanswered, disregarding the general statistical problems identified earlier, concerns the identity of the parties in breach of contract and debt recovery cases. But although a significant proportion of plaintiffs and defendants in these cases in the County Court and Queen's Bench Division must be private individuals, the cases appearing in the specialist Companies, Official Referees and Commercial Courts are a more reliable indicator of business disputing because of the general absence of private individuals in this type of litigation. Overall, it seems reasonable to conclude that businesses are likely to be at least partly responsible for the recorded increases in contract-based litigation.

A good deal of 'contract work' done by the Commercial Court involves foreign litigants who may have no connection with this country other than that their contract is made subject to English law. Vincent-Jones notes that the Civil Justice Review in 1986 considered that the proportion of foreign to domestic work appeared to be constant over time, so that the increase in workload is likely to be due at least in part to an increase in domestic disputing.

5.   There does not seem to have been any systematic study of what contract cases the courts in this country are actually handling. Indeed, the only figures in which the cases are

broken down by subject matter relate to the House of Lords. These show an interesting contrast to the Australian High Court.

■ Ellinghaus 'An Australian Contract Law?' (1989)
1 J of Contract Law 13, 19–20

The *important* differences between one country's law and another's, particularly in a field as ancient as contract law, are not the divergencies of doctrine. Rather, the autonomous quality of a nation's case-law lies in the 'shape' in which it is cast by the particular situations brought before its courts. It will cause no surprise to Australian contract lawyers to learn that by far the most litigated contract before the High Court from its inception to 1986 has been that of sale of land.[1] The most litigated contract before the House of Lords in the same period (1904–86) although by a much smaller margin, was the charterparty.[2] These contracts both continue respectively to lead the field before each tribunal.[3] It must be the case that a law of contract devised by a court most often confronted with one type of contract will differ from that devised by a court most often confronted with another type of contract. A court of ultimate appeal which draws on its own precedents in the development of a particular body of doctrine will naturally be influenced by the data most often placed before it. The recurrence of certain issues and contexts results in corresponding accumulations of doctrine at certain points, the disposition of which determines the 'shape' of the whole. Thus the suggestion has been plausibly made that the Australian High Court has been more inclined to grant equitable relief in contracts than the House of Lords because 'we are not an international commercial or maritime centre'. But the difference in shape between Australian and English contract law can as yet be perceived only dimly, precisely because of the veiling effect of constant reference to English decisions.

Footnotes

1 Of 718 reported High Court cases arising from contract disputes (forming nearly 12% of a total of about 6100 reported cases) an astonishing 493, or 68%, concerned the sale of land. The next most litigated contracts were (percentage of total in brackets): sale of goods (11.5%); construction (6.8%); insurance (6.4%) [marine insurance in 13% of these cases]; employment (4.6%); sale of business (3.9%). Only 2% of High Court cases concerned charterparties; only 2.4% contracts of carriage.

2 Of 593 reported House of Lords cases arising from contract disputes (forming nearly 20% of a total of about 3000 reported cases) 46, or nearly 8% concerned charterparties. The next most litigated contracts were: carriage (7.3%); insurance (6.6%) [marine insurance in 56% of these cases]; sale of goods (5.2%); construction (5.2%); employment (4.4%). Only 1.5% of House of Lords cases concerned the sale of land.

3 In the decade 1975–85 the most litigated contracts were: High Court, sale of land (34%); construction (10%); rent (7.5%); mortgages (7%); insurance (6%); restraints (6%); House of Lords, charterparties (20%); carriage (14%); sale of goods (14%); sale of land (12%); rent (12%).

NOTES

1. There can be little doubt that the nature of the cases coming before the House of Lords and the other superior courts has done much to 'shape' English law (see, eg, p 567). The famous American commercial lawyer Karl Llewellyn said that he never understood English contract law until he opened Lloyd's Reports.

2. The study of the work of the Wisconsin Supreme Court by Friedman has already been mentioned (see p 57). He shows how the cases changed in nature over the three periods he studied.

■ Friedman, *Contract Law in America* (1965)
pp 11–12, 186–187, 189–190, 217

This study explores contract law and contract behavior as revealed in the opinions of the Wisconsin Supreme Court and the work of some other agencies of Wisconsin government, especially the Wisconsin legislature. . . .

The decisions of the Wisconsin Supreme Court on contract questions form the basic material of the study. These cases have been drawn from three periods. Period I covers the time between the organization of Wisconsin Territory (1836) and the outbreak of the Civil War (1861); the study embraces all reported contract decisions during this span of years. This period is significant in that it marks the beginning of Wisconsin's functioning legal system; it also coincides with the 'frontier' period in the state, a period which had just about ended at the time of the Civil War. For Period II, 1905–1915, the cases were drawn from the years 1905–1907, and 1913. This period is equidistant in time between Periods I and III; more important, it provides a sample of legal materials drawn from the age of the Progressives in Wisconsin. This was a time in which the consequences of a maturing economic system and the effects of the post-Civil War industrialization and urbanization of the state had been strongly felt, and had called forth a set of major legal and social responses which reached a kind of climax during the days of the La Follette Progressives. For Period III (the decade of the 1950's), the cases were drawn from the years 1955–1958. The major characteristics of this period, on the threshold of the present, will be known to most readers: the post-World War II economic boom, the growth of the metropolitan areas, the cold war, the continuance of the big government of wartime and depression, and an ever increasing unification of the country through mass communications and transport. In Periods II and III, the volume of decisions of the Court was heavier than in Period I, and reporting was more complete. For these two periods, it was necessary to use a sample (large but limited) in order to examine the materials with the necessary intensity.

Within each period the cases were analyzed and tabulated according to their underlying fact-situations and their use of legal doctrines. The total number of tabulated cases comes to 553. Intensive use was made of the briefs and records of the cases as well. Unfortunately, for Period I most of these have been lost; for Periods II and III the records were full and invaluable. Within each period some examination was also made of non-contract cases, which shed incidental light on major topics and helped place the contract cases in perspective, ie, in relation to the general flow of appellate court business. . . .

In Period I, economic theory was valued as a statement of appropriate means to ends grounded in general notions of the common good. The end which enlisted widest loyalty in nineteenth-century Wisconsin was economic growth. People felt that this end would be best served by legal arrangements which legitimized and encouraged the maximum exercise of private will. But economic growth was the end, rather than some abstract ideal of freedom of private enterprise from public interference. Positive use of law in the economy—land grants to subsidize the building of canals and railroads are a good example—was widely approved where this use of law seemed likely to promote economic development. Abstraction, then, had to give way whenever it interfered with a greater goal.

In general, however, Period I was the age of abstraction. Abstraction was not simply a tool of the law; it also reflected the actual state of the economy. It was fact, not theory, that the land was often bought and sold as a colorless commodity. It was fact, not theory, that the residents of Wisconsin were mobile men, not rooted to a particular community or to ancient customs which fixed persons from birth with a given social status. It was fact, not theory, that the economy was in a state of rapid growth. Opportunities were not limited by all the built-in and conservative values which inhere in a locality of age-old settlement, whose cultural shape has been decisively molded by existing social patterns.

As the economy matured, these factual underpinnings of abstraction weakened; and the weakness of abstraction as a theory was reflected in the work of both the court and the legislature. The decay of the abstract rules of the law of contract has as one of its sources the decay of those conditions which lent strong support to abstraction in pioneer Wisconsin. But the weakening of abstraction cannot be attributed only to the differences within the state between its first age of growth and a more economically mature generation. Nor can the argument be pressed too far that the many derogations from contract abstraction (particularly the legislative derogations) were necessary to maintain the social system presupposed by abstraction. In Period II, the revolt against the full sweep of the competitive system was strong enough to indicate that it must have had broad roots in contemporary ideas and attitudes. It affected all classes of society. The urban workers expressed their opinions through unions, strikes, and boycotts. Big businesses formed 'trusts'. The farmers joined co-operative movements and raised hell along with corn. The middle-class tradesmen, the retailers, and the wholesalers spawned great numbers of national, state, and local 'associations' of one form or another, responding to the same hunger for unity and standardized strength. . . .

The economic struggle, so far as it was viewed by the unsophisticated, now centered not over position in the race to develop the economy, but over the status quo—a struggle to exact a greater share in existing product, existing wealth. If conservatives decided that freedom of contract and laissez faire were God-given rights, it was in order to stave off the urban poor who would storm the citadels of prosperity. The worker and the farmer tended to deny the truth of the free market altogether; it did not give them the fair share they deserved. . . .

The effect of these grand movements of public opinion and of the critical facts of economic life—the interdependence of human relationships, the growth of technology, the increasing industrial cast of economic life—was deeply felt by the law of contract. On the legislative side, the ambit within which the law of contract was allowed to operate was increasingly narrowed. Occupational licensing was only one symptom. Commodity legislation, for example, reflected technological advance, judgments concerning inequality of bargaining power (between producer and consumer), humanitarian impulses toward state action of a kind which presupposed an economically mature community, and not least of all, the attempt of 'reputable' producers forcefully to insure a rationalized and standardized market through invocation of the power of the state. . . .

The number of cases which arose out of personal, non-business situations rather than in pure market transactions also illustrated the increasing use of contract law, not for purposes of policing an abstract system, but for solving disputes of unique particularity. The docket affected deeply the court's mode of handling its cases. The heavy use of such malleable concepts as waiver and estoppel shows how the court, faced with inherited rules, but with facts which looked the other way, was inclined to use these formulae of escape from the rigors of abstraction. Concepts such as fraud and mistake, the doctrine of specific performance, the permutation of the rule of *Hadley v Baxendale*—all these illustrate the court's retreat from abstraction, its growing interest in the precise and particular facts of the immediate case.

The court's interest in the unique situation before it was only heightened in Period III. . . .

Table III. Wisconsin Contract Cases by Fact-Category

	Period I No.	Period II No.	Period III No.	Total
1. Land	54	46	22	122
2. Labor	31	61	34	126
3. Sales	30	32	12	74
4. Merchandise	12	15	4	31
5. Insurance	8	15	9	32
6. Business ventures	11	16	10	37
7. Credit	31	14	8	53
8. Government	15	12	6	33
9. Public utilities	4	5	1	10
10. Arbitration	8	5	3	16
11. Miscellaneous	2	6	3	11
12. Testamentary	—	—	8	8
	206	227	120	553

NOTES

1.   The docket of the Wisconsin Supreme Court is very different to that of the House of Lords, and one would not necessarily expect contract litigation to be performing even broadly similar functions in two legal systems which have developed in very different cultures. But the move that Friedman notes from abstraction to particularity has also been noted in this country: see Atiyah, *From Principles to Pragmatism*, 1978.

2.   Friedman and Ellinghaus look only at the cases in the highest courts. These, of course, are responsible for much of the doctrinal developments in the law, but to get anything like an accurate picture of the ways in which contract disputes are adjudicated it would be necessary to look at all courts—and, of course, at all the cases, whether reported or not. The cases that are selected for reporting because they raise some interesting point of legal principle are not an accurate guide to what the courts are actually handling. In addition, in this country it would also be essential to look at a mass of 'third-party adjudication' that is hidden from public view because it is conducted before arbitrators.

■ **Ferguson, 'The Adjudication of Commercial Disputes and the Legal System in Modern England'** (1980)
7 Brit J Law & Society 141, 142–148, 151–154

The legal system offers participants in commerce a mechanism for the determination of commercial disputes, namely trial. In the mid-nineteenth century that still meant trial by jury.

The most extensive evidence of the commercial community's attitude to jury trial is to be found in the traces left by the tribunals of commerce movement, whose grievances and goals were articulated by the Tribunals of Commerce Association, chambers of commerce and individual businessmen before a House of Commons Select Committee in 1871 and the Judicature Commission in 1874. The movement was an amalgam of businessmen's demands for three things:

(*i*)   A quicker and cheaper administration of justice.
(*ii*) A less capricious decision-making procedure.
(*iii*) The ascription of priority in adjudication to norms based on commercial usage. [Discussion of this point is omitted—eds]

Quicker and cheaper justice. A leading complaint was that litigation for sums just beyond the scope of the County Courts' jurisdiction was not worth the candle, the expenditure risked being disproportionate to the prospective gain. Even in more or less straightforward cases of default the uncertainties of legal process were said to be such that one could not be sure of recouping one's outlay. According to Jacob Behrens, a Bradford export merchant, if a defaulter was pressed

'...the rogue has a very ready answer. He says, "Bring an action." I have myself been dared to bring actions, and my solicitor has said, "It is not worth your while or expense; submit to it." '

Less capricious decision-making. In the hearings before the Judicature Commission in 1874 witness after witness complained about the extreme uncertainty of the jury system. The gist of it was: 'The verdict of a jury in commercial cases is as fair a subject for gambling as horse-racing.' The trouble with juries, according to the proponents of tribunals of commerce, was that they tended to lack the commercial acumen and experience which would enable them to understand the evidence: as a result, verdicts contrary to the weight of the evidence were not unusual....

[I]n the decades after the passage of the Judicature Acts of the mid-1870s the option of doing without the jury was more and more often taken by commercial litigants so that by 1913 their cases were largely tried by judges alone.... So commercial litigants solved the jury problem by voting with their feet.

In some sections of the commercial community however, particularly in the commodity trades, the primary response to the problems which actuated the tribunals of commerce movement has been a resort to non-forensic decision-making procedures—that is, arbitration.

The present-day position is that arbitration is firmly established as the most adjudicative mechanism. Overall it has been estimated that London arbitration bodies handle about 10,000 disputes *per annum*. All the commodity associations have 'long-established arbitration tribunals, both first instance and appellate, to which disputes under commodity contracts are referred.' Such arbitrations are predominantly international in character, reflecting the worldwide currency of the English standard contract forms with their arbitration clauses. The arbitration machinery of the London commodity associations handles about three or four thousand cases annually. In some trades, however, for example, grain, quality disputes no longer predominate. This change reflects modern market conditions: 'the hazards involved in postwar trading, such as the sudden imposition of export restrictions and duties, and violent fluctuations of price, have occasioned...a considerable increase in the number of "technical" arbitrations.' Currency fluctuations and the involvement of state trading companies whose governments are sometimes short of foreign exchange have also played their part.

Arbitration in London is also the usual adjudicative procedure for disputes arising on charterparties made on the Baltic Exchange, the world's leading freight market. Some 70% or 80% of the world's maritime arbitrations, involving shipbroking and chartering disputes, are held in London. The members of the London Maritime Arbitrators' Association thus account for perhaps 4,000 arbitrations each year.

This can be contrasted with the volume of business handled by the forensic alternative to commercial arbitration, the Commercial Court, with its abbreviated procedure and manning by judges whose experience lies on the commercial law side. In the 1950s a couple of dozen or so cases were tried annually in the Commercial Court. In the later 1970s there was a marked increase in its caseload, over 200 actions being brought in 1976 and over 100 annually being tried. Even so, it is clear that in purely quantitative terms the Commercial Court plays a relatively small part in commercial dispute adjudication.

The commercial preference for arbitration over trial in a court of law is obviously attributable to some extent to its speed and cheapness. On the whole arbitration is still quicker and less expensive, although a typical maritime arbitration now costs over £2,000 and takes about a year. But its *decisive* virtue is that arbitrators are chosen for their personal knowledge and experience of the trade in which the dispute has arisen so that they have the requisite technical expertise and a detailed grasp of commercial practice. This point is borne out by the reception given to section 4 of the Administration of Justice Act 1970. The 1970 Act authorised Commercial Court judges to accept appointment as arbitrators in commercial disputes. The idea was that commercial disputants would appreciate the opportunity to dispense with the formality and publicity of an ordinary trial while nevertheless securing the juridical expertise of a Judge. The scheme has not proved attractive, having scarcely been used at all. And yet it is inexpensive to use, the statutory fees being lower than those usual in many ordinary arbitrations. The best explanation is that judge-arbitrators cannot be relied upon to have the intimate familiarity with the trade or the market which characterises the professional or semi-professional arbitrator...

Notwithstanding the developments sketched in previous sections, the English courts occupy ground of strategic importance in the process of commercial dispute adjudication by virtue of their powers of judicial review in relation to arbitrations. Questions of fact are within the exclusive domain of the arbitrators but the Arbitration Act, 1889 and its successor in effect enabled either 'arbitrant' to appeal against the arbitrators' decision on a point of law, by means of the special case procedure. In *Czarnikow v Roth, Schmidt* (1922), a contract incorporating the rules of the Refined Sugar Association came before the Court of Appeal. The Association's rules expressly purported to negate the Courts' power of review. But the judges held that this was legally impossible: their power to review was entrenched.

...The virtue of judicial review for a company like Tradax, one of the world's leading dry-cargo charterers, was recently put thus:

> '[It has been] the essential factor in developing English law into the most sophisticated and highly developed maritime and commercial law in the world. We further consider that the existence of this right of appeal has ensured that English arbitrators decide cases in accordance with law and not in accordance with the necessarily subjective notions of *ex aequo et bono;* [and] that this has led to the certainty and... predictability which is essential to a trading company like our own which must have a solid foundation of clearly fixed rules on which to base its everyday trading decisions and assessment of risks.'

Some businesses at least, therefore, value the exegetical function of judicial review. ...

Nonetheless the circumstances whose conjunction eventuated in the passage of the Arbitration Act 1979 show that judicial review—at any rate while undertaken by means of the special case procedure—cannot be regarded as an unalloyed benefit to commerce. The Act was passed as a response to apprehensions that London's standing as leading centre of international commercial arbitration was endangered by certain modern developments. On the one hand the economic climate of the seventies—high inflation, high interest rates and unstable exchange rates—had made it worthwhile to some companies to mobilise the special case procedure, not to raise *bona fide* points of law, but to postpone the evil day of payment. In the words of one judge, 'success in litigation is no longer measured simply by the decision whether or not a party is liable to pay. The problems of liquidity are such that an immediate judgment, or the ability to stave off the day of reckoning, can make the difference between survival and insolvency.' The point was reached where some major companies began to delete English arbitration clauses. On the other hand there was the fact that the arbitration work from supranational development contracts was not on the whole finding its way to London. One reason was that governments or government agencies are often party to these contracts, and 'their desire to avoid submitting to the jurisdiction of foreign courts is equalled by the private parties' unwillingness to litigate in local courts, in which the local governments may be given a friendlier reception.' But arbitration in London on the basis of English law would have entailed submission to the review jurisidiction of the English courts.

...[A] compromise was enacted in the Arbitration Act 1979. By the Act the special case procedure is abolished, and in its place is substituted a streamlined system of appeals from reasoned awards, which is expected to place 'very grave obstacles in the way of those seeking unmeritoriously to avoid meeting their just obligations.' At the same time, contracting out of judicial review by means of an 'exclusion agreement' is authorised in respect of supranational contracts, but not, broadly speaking in respect of maritime, insurance and commodity contracts. ...

The emphasis so far has been on the use of contracts and contract law by business and commercial interests. Contract law may also be used by employees and by consumers. Although we shall see examples of each succeeding in contract litigation, it is likely that the 'litigation rates' for each category are very low. In 1982–1983, the National Consumer Council conducted a survey, which concluded:

In formal terms, the courts exist to resolve disputes of fact or law or to enable legal rights to be enforced. In real life, however, it is rare for consumers to go to court with disputes about goods. In our Consumer Concerns survey [1979–1980] amongst the population at large, there was not a single case of court action. Our latest survey confirms that very few consumers take this option. The strongest influence appeared to be the policy or resources of the individual advice centre. Out of nine questionnaires returned by clients of one centre, no fewer than three told us they had started proceedings. But this level of activity was quite exceptional... (*Buying problems* (1984), para 3.12.)

■ Ramsay, 'Consumer Redress Mechanisms for Poor-Quality and Defective Products' (1981)

31 U of Toronto LJ 117, 134–136

Recent literature provides depressing reading for those consumers interested in mobilizing the legal system. The reactive nature of legal institutions means that consumers must expend significant transaction costs if they wish to use the court system. It is not surprising to find either that few consumers are willing or able to take their disputes to court or that the great majority of product-quality cases involve automobiles or mobile homes.

Law reformers have concentrated much of their effort on changes within the structure of the existing court system. Greater access to small claims courts and more extensive and effective private law remedies have been advocated and in some cases legislated. The focus has been primarily on dispute resolution and case-by-case adjudication of individual claims. Yet reformers have not adequately solved the fundamental problem of the difference between the competence of one-shotters and repeat-player organizations in effectively using the legal system.

The majority of civil litigation in Canada and the United States involves organizations suing individuals, primarily for default on debts. These cases are part of the bureaucratic process of debt collection, and the judgment (usually by default) of the court provides formal validity to a creditor's claims. Few of these cases could be classified as disputes about legal rules. Many of these organizations use the court system on a continuing basis. They are repeat players and thus have many strategic advantages over the one-shotter. An individual consumer, unless he is a lawyer or a self-appointed consumer advocate, is a one-shotter. Individuals suing organizations account for only 5% of civil litigation in Canada. Among the advantages of the repeat player are the ability to use 'advance intelligence' and 'structure transactions in advance' (the form contract), to develop 'expertise and access to specialists' such as lawyers, and to 'develop continuing relations with institutional incumbents' such as court personnel. They have 'the ability to play for rules as well as for immediate gain. It pays a recurrent litigant to expend resources in influencing the making of the relevant rules and avoiding unfavourable litigation outcomes through settlements.'

There is also a clear dichotomy between legal services provided to organizations and to individuals. This is reflected in the division within the legal profession between those who provide a limited range of services to individuals on an occasional basis and those who provide a far wider range of preventive and counselling services to organizations on a continuing basis.

It is becoming clear, therefore, that the disparity in the use of legal services and recourse to litigation is not simply a question of individual social status or income or of rich and poor individuals but is rather a disparity between organizations and individuals. For example, statistics indicate that organizations as plaintiffs tend to be represented more often by counsel than are individual defendants.

One conclusion from these studies, therefore, is the importance of organization as a strategy for reform if consumers are to become 'effective players of the law game'. Changing the rules either at the legislative or the judicial level may have little effect if there are not competent parties capable of fully taking advantage of the benefit of the rules....

QUESTIONS

1. From the readings on pp 13–24, what do you conclude are the essential elements of a contract?

2. Alan agrees to sell to Beth for £50 a used table tennis table, which Beth tells him she wants to give her children for Christmas. Beth is to collect the table a week before Christmas. When she comes, Alan tells her he has decided not to sell. She discovers that used tables

in similar condition normally sell for about £75, although none are being advertised for sale at present. What remedies do you think Beth would like to have against Alan? Advise her as to what remedy (or remedies) she may actually have against him. (*Hint*: look at p 24.)

3. Would you expect Beth actually to sue Alan? Even if Alan was a second-hand furniture dealer rather than a private seller? If not, why not? (*Hint*: look at the readings in Chapter 5.)

4. From the readings on pp 24–39, what do you see as the principal differences between liability in tort and liability in contract? You may like to think about the following points in relation to each kind of liability:

    (i)   who will be liable?
    (ii) to whom?
    (iii) if there is a duty or an obligation, what needs to be shown to prove that it has been broken?
    (iv) what kinds of loss are recoverable?

    (In relation to tort, your answers to (i) and (ii) may vary according to the kind of loss.)

5. Cathy reads an advertisement for a dishwasher made by Econoclean plc, which describes it as 'reliable and cheap to run: washes a load for less than 20p'. She buys an Econoclean machine by mail order, from Discount Retailers Ltd. With the instructions she finds a card saying: 'This machine is guaranteed by Econoclean for one year.' Six months later, she reads in a consumer magazine that the Econoclean machine actually uses about 50p's worth of electricity at normal rates to wash a load; the figure of 20p had been calculated on the basis of cheap night rates, although (because of a careless error by the typesetter) the advertisement did not state this and even though most consumers (including Cathy) cannot easily obtain such a cheap rate. The next day, the machine suffers a major mechanical breakdown due to a negligently-made part failing. Does Cathy have any remedy against either Discount Retailers Ltd (who Cathy thinks may have gone out of business anyway) or against Econoclean for either (i) the cost of repairing the machine or (ii) the additional electricity costs Cathy will have to pay?

6. Gull is a trustee of a small trust for the benefit of his six aunts. The assets of the trust are managed by Midas Private Bank Ltd, which, every quarter, sends out a 'Client Newsletter'. In January 1995, it is announced that the royal palaces are to be privatised and the public is invited to apply for up to 500 shares each at £5 per share. Midas writes, in its next newsletter:

    The Royal Palaces issue is too good to miss. The properties have been grossly undervalued and the moment trading starts the shares cannot fail to reach twice the price asked now . . . Let us know if you want to apply . . .

    Gull decides to apply for 500 shares in his own name, which he does directly and not through Midas. What was written in the newsletter reflected current thinking in the City but, nearer the closing date, it is discovered that the palaces all have death-watch beetle and the shares do not look at all attractive. Midas' next newsletter is not due for a while and it decides not to bother circulating a withdrawal of its advice. When trading in the shares starts, the price never exceeds £2.50 a share. Instead of making a profit of £5,000, Gull loses £2,500.

Advise Gull whether he might have a claim against Midas in either (i) contract or (ii) tort. Might it make a difference if he had asked Midas to apply on his behalf and it had failed to point out that the palaces were no longer a good investment?

7. From the materials on pp 39–45, what do you think are the principal elements of a claim in restitution?

8. Fred contracts with Gardens Ltd that, while Fred is away on his Easter holiday, Gardens will landscape Fred's garden. By mistake, Gardens' employees do the landscaping not in Fred's garden, but in the garden of Fred's next-door neighbour Hugh, who is also away. Hugh never goes into his garden, which was completely overgrown. When Hugh returns, he refuses to pay Gardens for the work it has done even though he starts using the garden regularly. Does Gardens have a claim against Hugh? Can you think of any slight change of the facts which might make Hugh liable? (*Hint*: suppose Hugh were thinking of selling, or were a short-term tenant . . .)

9. Kate and Larry are a young couple who live in rented accommodation and cannot afford a home of their own, although they have some money saved. Larry's friend Mike tells him that the canal holiday company of which Mike is a director has a used boat that Kate and Larry can buy to live in. He says he will have to get the other directors to agree but that 'that will be a formality'. Kate and Larry are delighted at the prospect and, even before the directors have discussed the sale, give notice to leave the rented accommodation. Mike knows they are doing this. But when they arrive at the yard to collect their new home, he tells them that the other directors would not agree to the sale. Kate and Larry are left homeless.

At this stage, we do not expect you to know for certain whether or not Kate and Larry may have a remedy against either Mike or his company (you should have a better idea after studying Chapters 6 and 9). But we would like you to think about what would be a desirable outcome in a case like this. Leaving aside for the moment the question of whether or not a court might find a remedy for them on the existing authorities, would a court wish to do so:

(i) if it were to take the '*laissez-faire*' approach described on pp 46–49?
(ii) if it were to take the realist, 'market-individualist' approach described on pp 57–58?
(iii) if it were to take the 'consumer-welfarist' approach (pp 58–59)?

ENFORCEABLE TYPES OF PROMISE

CHAPTER SIX

CONSIDERATION

In the first chapter, we saw that contractual liability is based on the breach of a promise, but that not every promise will be enforced even if it was meant as a binding commitment: in particular, the law of contract appears to be concerned with enforcing promised exchanges, and unless the promise is made by deed (see pp 130–132), the promise must be supported by consideration if it is to be enforceable.

I. DEFINITIONS OF CONSIDERATION

■ *Currie v Misa*

(1875) LR 10 Exch 153, 162

A valuable consideration, in the sense of the law, may consist either in some right, interest, profit or benefit accruing to one party or some forbearance, detriment, loss or responsibility, given, suffered or undertaken by the other.

■ *Thomas v Thomas*

(1842) 2 QB 851, per Patteson J

Consideration means something which is of some value in the eye of the law, moving from the plaintiff; it may be some detriment to the plaintiff or some benefit to the defendant, but at all events it must be moving from the plaintiff.

■ Pollock, *Principles of Contract* (13th edn)

p 133, approved by Lord Dunedin in *Dunlop v Selfridge* (1915) (see p 1134)

An act or forbearance of the one party, or the promise thereof, is the price for which the promise of the other is bought, and the promise thus given for value is enforceable.

■ Restatement, *Contracts 2d*, s 71

(1) To constitute consideration, a performance or a return promise must be bargained for.

(2) A performance or return promise is bargained for if it is sought by the promisor in exchange for his promise and is given by the promisee in exchange for that promise.

(3)   The performance may consist of
    (a)   an act other than a promise, or
    (b)   a forbearance, or
    (c)   the creation, modification or destruction of a legal relation.

The Restatement of contract is one of nine Restatements produced by the American Law Institute. In the USA, contracts are governed by state law, so that there is not one law but fifty laws. The Institute was founded in 1923 'to promote the clarification and simplification of the law . . .'; its membership includes judges, practitioners and law professors. The final draft of the first Restatement of contracts was approved in 1932. The Reporter, Williston, stated that 'the endeavour in the Restatement is to restate the law as it is, not as new law' (3 ALI Proceedings 159), but several of its sections were remarkable innovations, as we shall see later. As a statement of law, it has no binding force, but it has been extremely influential, many of its sections being adopted by state courts as representing the law. A revised version was begun in 1962 and was published in final form in 1981 as the Restatement Second; its Reporters were Braucher and later Farnsworth.

NOTES

1.   The descriptions of consideration given in *Currie v Misa* and *Thomas v Thomas* are often quoted but were almost certainly not meant as complete definitions, but only as sufficient to decide the points before the court. The newer definitions, Pollock and Restatement 2d, are more complete. It will be seen that they differ from the older ones in three ways. Firstly, they do not speak of benefit and detriment but of an act or a return promise. Why this change in the formulation? In some types of contract, the promise is not exchanged for any return undertaking by the promisee, but is to operate *if* the promisee performs a certain act, which he may or may not do. As we saw in Chapter 2, this is called a *unilateral* contract. For example a person selling his house usually promises his estate agent, that if the agent introduces a person who buys the house, the seller will pay the agent a commission, but the agent does not (for obvious reasons) promise that he will find a buyer, nor does he necessarily promise that he will even look for one. The consideration for the seller's promise is the agent's act of introducing the purchaser (see further pp 219–220), and here there is no difficulty over describing the act as a benefit to the promisor and a detriment to the promisee. More commonly, however, each party makes promises to perform in the future and the contract is *bilateral*. The consideration for each promise is said to be the promise received in return: thus in a contract to sell a book for £10, the seller's promise to deliver the book is consideration for the buyer's promise to pay the money, and vice versa. The contract is enforceable even if it is wholly 'executory' (ie neither party has yet performed), but is there any benefit or detriment to either party at that stage? See Atiyah, *Essays on Contract*, pp 191–192.

2.   Secondly, the newer definitions stress the act or the return promise, rather than whether this benefits the person making the promise that it is sought to enforce (the promisor) or is detrimental to the person seeking to enforce it (the promisee). The reasons for this change are less easy to explain. It is well established that there may be consideration even though the promisor appears to derive no benefit from the act or the performance of the promise. For instance, if Furmston promises in writing to guarantee a loan that Bishop intends to make to Beale, and on the strength of that promise Bishop lends money to Beale who fails to repay it, Furmston is liable even though he derived no benefit from the arrangement. (The Statute of Frauds 1677, s 4 makes Furmston's promise unenforceable

unless evidenced in writing. See p 144.) Do you see why there might be thought a need to protect the promisor in this situation?

3.   Whether there can be consideration consisting of a benefit to the promisor with no corresponding detriment to the promisee is less clear. Patteson J's definition of consideration stresses that it must move from the plaintiff. Thus there will no consideration for a promise just because the promisor gets some other advantage (eg a reduction in his tax) from having made it (for another example, see below). But if the consideration must stem from something the promisee does, or has promised to do, isn't there always going to be a detriment to the promisee? Perhaps the point is that sometimes a person will do something, or forbear from doing something, which in fact seems to cost him nothing— eg giving up a right that he is not likely ever to exercise. This is almost certainly consideration. It is not easy to think of other examples of consideration without any detriment to the promisee.

4.   The newer definitions try to avoid these difficulties by speaking simply of 'act' or 'promise'. We shall consider whether the attempt is successful in a moment; it seems that there are some acts or promises that are not recognised as 'sufficient' consideration. Whether this is because they involve no benefit to the promisor or detriment to the promisee is more controversial: see p 165.

5.   Thirdly, the newer definitions stress that the promise must be exchanged for the act or return promise. As we shall see, this reflects the language of the English decisions, at least in this century, but whether it reflects the actual outcomes is also controversial.

II. SUFFICIENT CONSIDERATION

Neither Pollock's definition nor Restatement 2d specify what act or forbearance, actual or promised, will suffice. The older definitions' use of 'benefit' and 'detriment' may seem more helpful, but everything depends on what has 'value in the eye of the law'. It is often said that consideration need not be adequate (ie there will be consideration even if the values of the things exchanged are in no way equivalent) but it must have some economic value (eg Treitel, p 83; see further p 122).

It is worth stressing that, in the vast majority of commercial contracts, there is no problem over consideration when the contract is made. This is because the parties will have agreed on an exchange, say of goods or services for money. In the normal course of events, the things to be exchanged will be more or less equivalent in value, but even if they are not—for instance, if goods are sold at much more or much less than their normal price—the doctrine of consideration will be satisfied. Because the consideration does not have to 'adequate', a marginal financial advantage can be good consideration for a promise. Thus in *Charnock v Liverpool Corpn* [1968] 1 WLR 1498, CA, the owner of a car that had been damaged in an accident took it to the defendants for repairs, which were to be paid for by his insurers (thus the contract for repairs was between the defendants and the insurers). The defendants were dilatory in carrying out the repairs. The Court of Appeal held that the defendants had impliedly promised to carry out the repairs in a reasonable time; the consideration for this promise was 'leaving his car with the repairers'.

In family and social arrangements, on the other hand, it is not uncommon for people to make promises seeking nothing in return—so called 'gratuitous' or 'gift' promises. The doctrine of consideration seems to mean that gratuitous promises are not enforceable unless they are made by deed. (We shall see that there are a number of qualifications to this apparently simple rule, eg, pp 129 and 146.)

Occasionally, of course, promises are made even in the commercial world with nothing being asked for in return: for an example, see the tax case of *Dickinson v Abel* [1969] 1 WLR 295. In these cases, the promise will be without consideration and therefore unenforceable unless made by deed. There are also a number of commercial situations that give rise to difficulties over consideration, and we shall examine these shortly. The other great source of difficulties over consideration is cases that are 'marginal' in relation to normal contracts.

1. Intangible returns

The promisor may feel natural love and affection toward the promisee, which will be fulfilled to some extent by the promise. It is firmly established that this is not sufficient consideration: *Bret v JS* (1600) Cro Eliz 756. Nor is the fact that the promisee will feel some moral obligation to the promisor in return.

In *The Atlantic Baron* (see p 905), the builders of a tanker, faced with increased costs because of a currency devaluation, demanded a price increase from the purchasers. The latter were concerned to have the tanker delivered on time and agreed to pay the increase 'in order to maintain an amicable relationship'. Mocatta J held that this could not be consideration.

■ *White v Bluett* (1853)
23 LJ Ex 36, Court of Exchequer

Bluett had given his father a promissory note (see note 1 below) for money his father had lent him. When sued on the note by his father's executor, he pleaded that he had had just grounds to complain about his father's distribution of property among his children, and that his father, admitting this, had promised that if Bluett stopped complaining he would discharge Bluett from liability on the note.

Pollock CB

. . . Looking at the words merely, there is some foundation for the argument, and, following the words only, the conclusion may be arrived at. It is said, the son had a right to an equal distribution of his father's property, and did complain to his father because he had not an equal share, and said to him, I will cease to complain if you will not sue upon this note. Whereupon the father said if you will promise me not to complain I will give up the note. In reality, there was no consideration whatever. . . . The son had no right to complain, for the father might make what distribution of his property he liked; and the son's abstaining from doing what he had no right to do can be no consideration.

Parke and **Alderson BB** also held the plea bad and **Platt B** concurred.

Judgment for the plaintiff.

NOTES

1.   A promissory note is a promise to pay contained in a written document: an example, and a description of its legal characteristics, will be found on p 1198. The main point is that a promissory note is a 'negotiable instrument', that is, it can be passed to a third party by

endorsement, and the third party can then sue on the note. If the note is payable to bearer, delivery to the third party is sufficient: the most common example of a promissory note payable to bearer is a bank note.

2. *White v Bluett* involves the alleged discharge of an existing obligation, rather than the creation of a new contract, but the traditional rule is that a promise to discharge a debt must equally be supported by consideration. See further Chapter 32.

3. The point that it cannot be consideration to promise not to do that which you have no right to do seems sensible enough (and compare the converse, promising to do what you already have a duty to do, see pp 105–115). It would be undesirable to say there was consideration if Furmston promised Beale £10 if Beale would stop stealing Furmston's books. But when Pollock says the son had no right to complain, is he using right in this sense? The son had no right to complain in the sense that the father was not under a duty to take any notice of the complaint but it was not wrong of the son to complain in the sense that the father had any legally enforceable right to stop him. Lawyers use the word 'right' in a number of different senses. That failure to remember this can readily lead to confusion was long ago demonstrated by Hohfeld in two articles in (1913) 23 Yale LJ 16 and (1917) Yale LJ 710, reprinted under the title *Fundamental Legal Conceptions* (ed Cook Yale UP).

■ *Hamer v Sidway*

124 NY 538, 27 NE 256 (Court of Appeals, New York, 1891)

Parker J

The question which provoked the most discussion by counsel on this appeal, and which lies at the foundation of plaintiff's asserted right of recovery, is whether by virtue of a contract defendant's testator, William E. Story, became indebted to his nephew, William E. Story, 2d, on his twenty-first birthday in the sum of $5,000. The trial court found as a fact that 'on the 20th day of March, 1869, . . . William E. Story agreed to and with William E. Story, 2d, that if he would refrain from drinking liquor using tobacco, swearing, and playing cards or billiards for money until [he] should become twenty-one years of age, then he, the said William E. Story would at that time pay him, the said William E. Story, 2d, the sum of $5,000 for such refraining, to which the said William E. Story, 2d, agreed', and that he 'in all things fully performed his part of said agreement'.

[The nephew assigned any right of action he might have to the plaintiff. The defendant was William E Story's executor.]

The defendant contends that the contract was without consideration to support it, and therefore invalid. He asserts that the promisee, by refraining from the use of liquor and tobacco, was not harmed, but benefited; that that which he did was best for him to do, independently of his uncle's promise,—and insists that it follows that, unless the promisor was benefited, the contract was without consideration,— a contention which, if well founded, would seem to leave open for controversy in many cases whether that which the promisee did or omitted to do was in fact of such benefit to him as to leave no consideration to support the enforcement of the promisor's agreement. Such a rule could not be tolerated, and is without foundation in the law.

. . . [T]he promisee used tobacco, occasionally drank liquor, and he had a legal right to do so. That right he abandoned for a period of years upon the strength of the promise of the testator that for such forbearance he would give him $5,000. We need not speculate on the effort which may have been required to give up the use of those stimulants. It is sufficient that he restricted his lawful freedom of action within certain prescribed limits upon the faith of his uncle's agreement, and now, having fully performed the conditions imposed, it is of no moment whether such performance actually proved a benefit to the promisor, and the court will not inquire into it; but, were it a proper subject of inquiry, we see nothing in this record that would permit a determination that the uncle was not benefited in a legal sense.

Judgment for the plaintiff.

NOTES

1.   This American case is not, of course, binding in this country, but it is usually assumed to represent English law (eg Atiyah, *Essays on Contract*, p 195).

2.   Did the nephew suffer any detriment, or the uncle gain any benefit, in *Hamer v Sidway?*

3.   Suppose the nephew in *Hamer* already had religious beliefs that prevented him from indulging in any of the things he agreed to forgo, would the outcome be different? Compare the judgment with *Arrale v Costain Civil Engineering Ltd* [1976] 1 Lloyd's Rep 98, 106: 'It is no consideration to refrain from a course of conduct which it was never intended to pursue.' (This case involved the validity of a 'release' of a claim for compensation for personal injuries signed by a workman. The majority of the Court of Appeal decided that the release did not affect the workman's claim to damages at common law as a matter of construction of the document, but all three judges appear to have agreed on this consideration point. Whether it was fully argued is not clear. How often will it be possible to prove that the relevant course of conduct would not be pursued under any circumstances whatever?)

4.   Of what economic value were the actions in *Hamer*? If the nephew in *Hamer* could not sue, how could uncles persuade their nephews to live lives free of vice?

5.   If there was an action of economic value in *Hamer*, why did the claim in *White v Bluett* fail? Could the court's perception of whether the nephew's or son's forbearance constituted adequate consideration have been influenced by the nature of the conduct forgone? What did Pollock CB mean when he said that the son 'had no right to complain'?

6.   Suppose that performance of a contract between A Ltd and B Ltd unexpectedly becomes much more expensive for A to perform, but B refuses to increase the payment although it is now making a very large profit. A complains publicly that B is a harsh employer and, to protect its reputation, B agrees to pay A 10% extra if A will stop. Is there consideration?

2. Compromise of a claim

If I agree to compromise a valid claim for an uncertain amount, or a genuinely doubtful claim, there is no doubt that the promise to drop the claim is consideration for the promise to pay the sum offered in settlement (see *Haigh v Brooks* (1839) 10 Ad & El 309, and *Horton v Horton (No 2)* [1961] 1 QB 215). What if my claim was demonstrably bound to fail?

■ *Wade v Simeon*

(1846) 2 CB 548, 135 ER 1061, Court of Common Pleas

Tindal CJ

The only question now remaining is upon the demurrer [see note below] to the fourth plea. I am of opinion that the fourth plea is a good and valid plea, on general demurrer. The declaration alleges that the plaintiff had commenced an action against the defendant in the Exchequer, to recover two sums of

£1300 and £700 respectively, which action was about to be tried, and that, in consideration that the plaintiff would forbear proceeding in that action, until the 14th of December then next, the defendant promised the plaintiff that he would on that day pay the money, with interest, and costs; that the plaintiff, confiding in the defendant's promise, forbore prosecuting the action, and stayed the proceedings until the day named; but that the defendant did not pay the money or the costs. The fourth plea states that the plaintiff never had any cause of action against the defendant in respect of the subject-matter of the action in the court of Exchequer, which he, the plaintiff, at the time of the commencement of the said action, and thence until the time of the making of the promise in the first count mentioned, well knew. By demurring to that plea, the plaintiff admits that he had no cause of action against the defendant in the action therein mentioned, and that he knew it. It appears to me, therefore, that he is estopped from saying that there was any valid consideration for the defendant's promise. It is almost contra bonos mores, and certainly contrary to all the principles of natural justice, that a man should institute proceedings against another, when he is conscious that he has no good cause of action. In order to constitute a binding promise, the plaintiff must shew a good consideration, something beneficial to the defendant, or detrimental to the plaintiff. Detrimental to the plaintiff it cannot be, if he has no cause of action: and beneficial to the defendant it cannot be; for, in contemplation of law, the defence upon such an admitted state of facts must be successful, and the defendant will recover costs, which must be assumed to be a full compensation for all the legal damage he may sustain. The consideration, therefore, altogether fails. On the part of the plaintiff it has been urged, that the cases cited for the defendant were not cases where actions had already been brought, but only cases of promises to forbear commencing proceedings. I must, however, confess, that, if that were so, I do not see that it would make any substantial difference . . .

Here, . . . there was no uncertainty: the defendant asserts, and the plaintiff admits, that there never was any cause of action in the original suit, and that the plaintiff knew it. I therefore think the fourth plea affords a very good answer, and that the defendant is entitled to judgment thereon.

Maule, Cresswell and **Erle JJ** also held that the defendant was entitled to judgment on the fourth plea.

NOTE

A demurrer is a plea that accepts the truth of the facts alleged by the other party, but objects that they do not disclose a cause of action, or have the legal effect contended for.

■ *Cook v Wright*

(1861) 1 B & S 559, 121 ER 822, Queen's Bench

After a verdict for the defendant in an action on three promissory notes, the plaintiffs moved that the evidence did not show want of consideration for the notes, and that they were entitled to a verdict.

Blackburn J delivered the judgment of **Cockburn CJ, Wightman J** and himself

. . .

   In this case it appeared on the trial that the defendant was agent for a Mrs Bennett, who was non-resident owner of houses in a district subject to a local Act. Works had been done in the adjoining street by the Commissioners for executing the Act, the expenses of which, under the provisions of their Act, they charged on the owners of the adjoining houses. Notice had been given to the defendant, as if he had himself been owner of the houses, calling on him to pay the proportion chargeable in respect of them. He attended at a Board meeting of the Commissioners, and objected both to the amount and nature of the charge, and also stated that he was not the owner of the houses, and that Mrs Bennett was. He was told that, if he did not pay, he would be treated as one Goble had been. It appeared that

Goble had refused to pay a sum charged against him as owner of some houses, and the Commissioners had taken legal proceedings against him, and he had then submitted and paid, with costs. In the result it was agreed between the Commissioners and the defendant that the amount charged upon him should be reduced, and that time should be given to pay it in three instalments; he gave three promissory notes for the three instalments; the first was duly honoured; the others were not, and were subject of the present action. At the trial it appeared that the defendant was not in fact owner of the houses. As agent for the owner he was not personally liable under the Act. In point of law, therefore, the Commissioners were not entitled to claim the money from him; but no case of deceit was alleged against them. It must be taken that the Commissioners honestly believed that the defendant was personally liable, and really intended to take legal proceedings against him, as they had done against Goble. The defendant, according to his own evidence, never believed that he was liable in law, but signed the notes in order to avoid being sued as Goble was. Under these circumstances the substantial question reserved . . . was whether there was any consideration for the notes. We are of opinion that there was.

. . . Here there was no mistake on the part of the defendant either of law or fact. What he did was not merely the making an erroneous account stated, or promising to pay a debt for which he mistakenly believed himself liable. It appeared on the evidence that he believed himself not to be liable; but he knew that the plaintiffs thought him liable, and would sue him if he did not pay, and in order to avoid the expense and trouble of legal proceedings against himself he agreed to a compromise; and the question is, whether a person who has given a note as a compromise of a claim honestly made on him, and which but for that compromise would have been at once brought to a legal decision, can resist the payment of the note on the ground that the original claim thus compromised might have been successfully resisted . . . it was argued before us that . . . though where the plaintiff has actually issued a writ against a defendant, a compromise honestly made is binding, yet the same compromise, if made before the writ actually issues, though the litigation is impending, is void.

We agree that unless there was a reasonable claim on the one side, which it was bona fide intended to pursue, there would be no ground for a compromise; but we cannot agree that (except as a test of the reality of the claim in fact) the issuing of a writ is essential to the validity of the compromise. The position of the parties must necessarily be altered in every case of compromise, so that, if the question is afterwards opened up, they cannot be replaced as they were before the compromise. The plaintiff may be in a less favourable position for renewing his litigation, he must be at an additional trouble and expense in again getting up his case, and he may no longer be able to produce the evidence which would have proved it originally. Besides, though he may not in point of law be bound to refrain from enforcing his rights against third persons during the continuance of the compromise, to which they are not parties, yet practically the effect of the compromise must be to prevent his doing so. For instance, in the present case, there can be no doubt that the practical effect of the compromise must have been to induce the Commissioners to refrain from taking proceedings against Mrs Bennett, the real owner of the houses, while the notes given by the defendant, her agent, were running; though the compromise might have afforded no ground of defence had such proceedings been resorted to. It is this detriment to the party consenting to a compromise arising from the necessary alteration in his position which, in our opinion, forms the real consideration for the promise, and not the technical and almost illusory consideration arising from the extra costs of litigation. The real consideration therefore depends, not on the actual commencement of a suit, but on the reality of the claim made and the bona fides of the compromise.

In the present case we think that there was sufficient consideration for the notes in the compromise made as it was.

NOTES

1.   What distinction is there between these two cases? Isn't the defendant saved the trouble of legal proceedings irrespective of the good faith of the plaintiff? Is the court's perception again swayed by some policy consideration? What policy?

2. If a person brings a claim that he knows to be false against another who, for some good reason, cannot wait for the action to be heard and so pays up, the latter may be able to recover the money under the doctrine of duress: see p 901.

3. Should giving up a claim be consideration, provided the claim was honest, or should the claim also have to be reasonable? In *Pitt v PHH Asset Management Ltd* [1993] 4 All ER 961, it was held that dropping a claim for an injunction could be consideration although the claim could not have succeeded and thus had only 'nuisance value'.

3. Performance of a duty imposed by law

If the defendant promises to pay the plaintiff for performing an act that the plaintiff is already obliged to do as a matter of general law, it is hard to see that the defendant gets any additional benefit or that the plaintiff suffers any additional detriment. In the USA this approach has often been applied quite rigidly: for example, in *Denney v Reppert* 432 SW2d 647 (Kentucky, 1968), employees of a bank that had been robbed gave information leading to the capture of the robbers, but it was held that they were obliged to give the information and therefore they could not recover a promised reward.

In England, there are some cases taking this line. One example is *Collins v Godefroy* (1831) 1 B & Ad 950, in which it was held that a promise to pay a witness who had been subpoenaed six guineas for his trouble was without consideration. (Nowadays, a subpoenaed witness must be given 'conduct money'.) In *Glasbrook Bros Ltd v Glamorgan County Council* [1925] AC 270, it was assumed that this was the law; the actual decision was that the police had gone beyond the duty imposed on them by law when at a colliery owner's request they provided him with a garrison, and his promise to pay was binding. (See also *Harris v Sheffield United Football Club Ltd* [1988] QB 77, in which it was held that providing police at a football match was 'special police services', within s 15(1) of the Police Act 1964, for which the club was required to pay.)

Other cases take a more flexible line, holding that performance of an existing public duty may be consideration if that would encourage performance of the duty. In *England v Davidson* (1840) 11 Ad & El 856, a police constable was held to be entitled to claim the reward offered for information he had given. Lord Denman CJ said: 'I think there may be services which the constable is not bound to render, and which he may therefore make the ground of a contract. We should not hold a contract to be against the policy of the law unless the grounds for so deciding were very clear.'

What do you think Denman's view would have been if the constable had flatly refused to give the information unless paid the reward—might that have been 'against the policy of the law'? Money that has been paid to an official who, without authority, has refused to perform his duty unless paid is recoverable in restitution: see Burrows, pp 435–438.

■ *Williams v Williams*

[1957] 1 All ER 305, Court of Appeal

Denning LJ

In the present case a wife claims sums due to her under a maintenance agreement. No evidence was called in the court below because the facts are agreed. The parties were married on Apr 25, 1945. They have no children. On Jan 24, 1952, the wife deserted the husband. On Mar 26, 1952, they signed the agreement now sued on, which has three clauses:

'(1) The husband will pay to the wife for her support and maintenance a weekly sum of £1 10s to be paid every four weeks during the joint lives of the parties so long as the wife shall lead a chaste life the first payment hereunder to be made on Apr 15, 1952. (2) The wife will out of the said weekly sum or otherwise support and maintain herself and will indemnify the husband against all debts to be incurred by her and will not in any way at any time hereafter pledge the husband's credit. (3) The wife shall not so long as the husband shall punctually make the payments hereby agreed to commence or prosecute against the husband any matrimonial proceedings other than proceedings for dissolution of marriage but upon the failure of the husband to make the said weekly payments as and when the same become due the wife shall be at full liberty on her election to pursue all and every remedy in this regard either by enforcement of the provisions hereof or as if this agreement had not been made.'

So far as we know, the parties have remained apart ever since. On June 1, 1955, the husband petitioned for divorce, on the ground of his wife's desertion, and so on Oct 12, 1955, a decree nisi was made against her. On Dec 2, 1955, the decree was made absolute. In this action the wife claims maintenance at the rate of £1 10s a week under the agreement for a period from October, 1954, to October, 1955. The sum claimed is £30 5s 9d, which is the appropriate sum after the deduction of tax. The husband disputes the claim, on the ground that there was no consideration for his promise. Clause 2, he says, is worthless and cl 3 is unenforceable.

Let me first deal with cl 3. It is settled law that a wife, despite such a clause as cl 3, can make application to the magistrates or to the High Court for maintenance. If this wife had made such an application, the husband could have set up the fact of desertion as an answer to the claim, but he could not have set up cl 3 as a bar to the proceedings. The clause is void, and as such is no consideration to support the agreement: see *Bennett v Bennett*. Now let me deal with cl 2. The husband relies on the fact that his wife deserted him. If there had been a separation by consent, he agrees that the agreement would have been enforceable. In that case the husband would still be under a duty to maintain, and the sum of 30s a week would be assumed to be a quantification of a reasonable sum for her maintenance having regard to her own earning capacity. The ascertainment of a specific sum in place of an unascertained sum has always been held to be good consideration. So long as circumstances remained unchanged, it would be treated by the courts as binding on her and she could not recover more from him: see *National Assistance Board v Parkes*. In the present case the husband says that, as the wife deserted him, he was under no obligation to maintain her and she was not entitled to pledge his credit in any way. Clause 2 therefore gives him nothing and is valueless to him. The husband says that *Goodinson v Goodinson* is distinguishable because there was no finding in that case that the wife was in desertion, and, moreover, the wife promised to maintain the child as well as herself.

Now I agree that, in promising to maintain herself whilst she was in desertion, the wife was only promising to do that which she was already bound to do. Nevertheless, a promise to perform an existing duty is, I think, sufficient consideration to support a promise, so long as there is nothing in the transaction which is contrary to the public interest. Suppose that this agreement had never been made, and the wife had made no promise to maintain herself and did not do so. She might then have sought and received public assistance or have pledged her husband's credit with tradesmen; in which case the National Assistance Board might have summoned him before the magistrates, or the tradesmen might have sued him in the county court. It is true that he would have an answer to those claims because she was in desertion, but nevertheless he would be put to all the trouble, worry and expense of defending himself against them. By paying her 30s a week and taking this promise from her that she will maintain herself and will not pledge his credit, he has an added safeguard to protect himself from all this worry, trouble and expense. That is a benefit to him which is good consideration for his promise to pay maintenance. That was the view which appealed to the county court judge, and I must say that it appeals to me also.

There is another ground on which good consideration can be found. Although the wife was in desertion, nevertheless it must be remembered that desertion is never irrevocable. It was open to her to come back at any time. Her right to maintenance was not lost by the desertion. It was only suspended. If she made a genuine offer to return which he rejected, she would have been entitled to maintenance from him. She could apply to the magistrates or the High Court for an order in her favour. If she did so, however, whilst this agreement was in force, the 30s would be regarded as prima facie the correct figure. It is a benefit to the husband for it to be so regarded, and that is sufficient consideration to support his promise.

I construe this agreement as a promise by the husband to pay his wife 30s a week in consideration of her promise to maintain herself during the time she is living separate from him, whether due to her own fault or not.

Hodson LJ

[It was argued that, as the wife was in desertion,] she had forfeited all right to be maintained by her husband and so she was giving no consideration at all when she said she would maintain herself, because that is what she would have to do anyway. The short answer to that is, I think, that she had not forfeited her right to be maintained by her husband by being in desertion. She had only suspended her right and not destroyed it. . . .

The wife had deserted the husband and was temporarily wrongfully away from home; but she might at any time return. In those circumstances, if she returned or offered to return her husband's liability to maintain her would revive. So that there was good consideration there to meet that contingency, which was a real contingency and not a fanciful one at that time. It is not affected by the fact that (as we now know, as a matter of history) the parties never have come together again but have been divorced.

It was urged by counsel for the wife that, whether the point which I have just put was or was not good, nevertheless it was a valid consideration even if the wife was in desertion, because it was some benefit to the husband to be protected from the embarrassment of invalid claims against him. For my part, I would prefer not to rest my judgment on that, because, once it is conceded that there is no basis for a claim by a wife, no consideration for giving an indemnity by the wife appears to me to emerge. It is unnecessary to express any concluded opinion on that matter.

Morris LJ delivered a judgment in similar terms to that of Hodson LJ.

Appeal dismissed.

NOTES

1. *Bennett v Bennett* was reversed by the Matrimonial Causes Act 1973, s 34.
2. If the wife had returned to the husband, what would have happened to the agreement?
3. What would have been the position if she had offered to return but he had refused her offer?
4. Denning expressed similar views in *Ward v Byham* [1956] 2 All ER 318, which also involved the performance of an existing duty, in this case the maintenance of an illegitimate child by her mother. Again, the other members of the court found consideration: in return for the father's promise to pay £1 a week, the mother had to keep the child well looked after and happy, and to allow her to decide for herself whether she wished to live with the mother.
5. Do you think the outcome of *Williams v Williams* and *Ward v Byham* was influenced by policy? If so, by what policy?

4. Performance of a duty imposed by contract with a third party

In *Shadwell v Shadwell* (1860) 9 CBNS 159, 30 LJCP 145, an uncle promised his nephew an annual sum if the nephew married his fiancee. Although an engagement to marry was a binding contract (and remained legally enforceable until 1971), the Common Bench held that there was consideration for the uncle's promise. In *Scotson v Pegg* (1861) 6 H & N 295, 30 LJ

Ex 225, the defendant agreed to unload a cargo of coal in consideration of the plaintiff delivering it to him, which the plaintiff was already obliged to do under a contract with a third party. The plaintiff sued the defendant for delay in unloading and succeeded. In neither case does the point seem to have been argued fully. However, the general rule that performance of an existing contractual obligation to a third party may be good consideration was approved by the Privy Council in *New Zealand Shipping Co Ltd v A M Satterthwaite & Co Ltd* (see p 1157) and again in *Pao On v Lau Yiu Long* (see p 126).

The *New Zealand Shipping* case illustrates the complex commercial context in which the 'contractual duty owed to a third party' point is likely to arise. The owners of goods (to keep the parties straight, let us call them A) had contracted with carriers (B) for the goods to be transported by ship to New Zealand under a bill of lading contract. The goods were negligently damaged by stevedores (C) who had been employed (it was assumed) by B to unload them. By this time, the plaintiffs had become holders of the bill and thus stood in A's shoes (see Appendix). In the bill of lading (see Appendix), which contained the terms of the contract, the owners (A) purported to promise the stevedores (C) the benefit of various exemptions and limitations of liability (in fact, the main dispute in the case was whether the terms of the bill of lading were clear enough to constitute such a promise: the majority held they were, see p 1158). The Privy Council held that by unloading the goods the stevedores (C) had provided consideration for this promise. Lord Wilberforce said:

If the choice, and the antithesis, is between a gratuitous promise, and a promise for consideration, as it must be, in the absence of a tertium quid, there can be little doubt which, in commercial reality, this is. The whole contract is of a commercial character, involving service on one side, rates of payment on the other, and qualifying stipulations as to both. The relations of all parties to each other are commercial relations entered into for business reasons of ultimate profit. To describe one set of promises, in this context, as gratuitous, or nudum pactum, seems paradoxical and is prima facie implausible. It is only the precise analysis of this complex of relations into the classical offer and acceptance, with identifiable consideration, that seems to present difficulty, but this same difficulty exists in many situations of daily life, eg sales at auction; supermarket purchases; boarding an omnibus; purchasing a train ticket; tenders for the supply of goods; offers of rewards; acceptance by post; warranties of authority by agents; manufacturers' guarantees; gratuitous bailments; bankers' commercial credits. These are all examples which show that English law, having committed itself to a rather technical and schematic doctrine of contract, in application takes a practical approach, often at the cost of forcing the facts to fit uneasily into the marked slots of offer, acceptance and consideration.

In their Lordships' opinion the present contract presents much less difficulty than many of those above referred to. It is one of carriage from Liverpool to Wellington. The carrier assumes an obligation to transport the goods and to discharge at the port of arrival. The goods are to be carried and discharged, so the transaction is inherently contractual. It is contemplated that a part of this contract, viz discharge, may be performed by independent contractors—viz the stevedore. By cl 1 of the bill of lading the shipper agrees to exempt from liability the carrier, his servants and independent contractors in respect of the performance of this contract of carriage. Thus, if the carriage including the discharge, is wholly carried out by the carrier, he is exempt. If part is carried out by him, and part by his servants, he and they are exempt. If part is carried out by him, and part by an independent contractor, he and the independent contractor are exempt. The exemption is designed to cover the whole carriage from loading to discharge, by whomsoever it is performed: the performance attracts the exemption or immunity in favour of whoever the performer turns out to be.

There is possibly more than one way of analysing this business transaction into the necessary components; that which their Lordships would accept is to say that the bill of lading brought into existence a bargain initially unilateral but capable of becoming mutual, between the shippers and the stevedore, made through the carrier as agent. This became a full contract when the stevedore performed services by discharging the goods. The performance of these services for the benefit of the shipper was the consideration for the agreement by the shipper that the stevedore should have the benefit of the exemptions and limitations contained in the bill of lading. The conception of a 'unilateral contract' of this kind was recognised in *Great Northern Railway Co v Witham* and is well established. This way of regarding the matter is very close to, if not identical to, that accepted by Beattie J in the Supreme Court: he analysed the transaction as one of an offer open to acceptance by action such as was found in *Carlill v Carbolic Smoke Ball Co.*

... In their Lordships' opinion, consideration may quite well be provided by the stevedore, as suggested, even though (or if) it was already under an obligation to discharge to the carrier. (There is no direct evidence of the existence or nature of this obligation, but their Lordships are prepared to assume it.) An agreement to do an act which the promisor is under an existing obligation to a third party to do, may quite well amount to valid consideration and does so in the present case: the promisee obtains the benefit of a direct obligation which he can enforce. This proposition is illustrated and supported by *Scotson v Pegg* ... which their Lordships consider to be good law.

Further extracts from this case will be found at p 1157.

NOTE

It is clear that the majority of the Privy Council wanted if possible to put what the parties appeared to have intended into effect. At the end of his speech, Lord Wilberforce remarked:

In the opinion of their Lordships, to give the stevedore the benefit of the exemptions and limitations contained in the bill of lading is to give effect to the clear intentions of a commercial document, and can be given within existing principles. They see no reason to strain the law or the facts in order to defeat these intentions. It should not be overlooked that the effect of denying validity to the clause would be to encourage actions against servants, agents and independent contractors in order to get round exemptions (which are almost invariable and often compulsory) accepted by shippers against carriers, the existence, and presumed efficacy, of which is reflected in the rates of freight. They see no attraction in this consequence.

What exactly is the extra benefit to A, which constitutes the consideration for its return promise to C? Is making a second promise to perform, or actually performing, the contract with B an additional detriment to C? Remember that if for some reason C does not perform its contract with B, A may suffer a loss, and if C is liable only to B, A may have no remedy.

5. Performance of a contractual duty owed to the promisor

■ *Harris v Watson*

(1791) Peake 102, 170 ER 94, King's Bench

In this case the declaration stated, that the plaintiff being a seaman on board the ship 'Alexander', of which the defendant was master and commander, and which was bound on a voyage to Lisbon: whilst the ship was on her voyage, the defendant, in consideration that the plaintiff would perform some extra work, in navigating the ship, promised to pay him five guineas over and above his common wages. ...

The plaintiff proved that the ship being in danger, the defendant, to induce the seamen to exert themselves, made the promise stated in the first count.

Lord Kenyon

If this action was to be supported, it would materially affect the navigation of this kingdom. It has been long since determined, that when the freight is lost, the wages are also lost. This rule was founded on a principle of policy, for if sailors were in all events to have their wages, and in times of danger entitled to insist on an extra charge on such a promise as this, they would in many cases suffer a ship to sink, unless the captain would pay any extra extravagant demand they might think proper to make. The plaintiff was nonsuited.

■ *Stilk v Myrick*

(1809) 2 Camp 317, 170 ER 851; 6 Esp 129, 170 ER 851, King's Bench

The Espinasse report:

This was an action brought by the plaintiff, a private sailor, to recover the amount of his wages, on a voyage from London to the Baltick and back.

The sum claimed was partly for monthly wages, according to articles which he had signed, and a further sum claimed under these circumstances.

Two sailors, part of the crew, had deserted the ship, and the master (the defendant), not being able to supply their places at Cronstadt, promised to divide among the crew, in addition to their wages, the wages due to the two men who had deserted.

Upon this being claimed, it was objected, That any engagement by the master for a larger sum than was stipulated for by the articles was void, and the case of *Harris v Watson*, cited.

It was answered, that this case was very different from the case cited: that this engagement was made before the ship sailed on her voyage home; it was made under no coercion, from the apprehension of danger, nor extorted from the captain; but a voluntary offer on his part for extraordinary service.

Lord Ellenborough ruled, That the plaintiff could not recover this part of his demand. His Lordship said, That he recognized the principle of the case of *Harris v Watson* as founded on just and proper policy. When the defendant entered on board the ship, he stipulated to do all the work his situation called upon him to do. Here the voyage was to the Baltick and back, not to Cronstadt only; if the voyage had then terminated, the sailors might have made what terms they pleased. If any part of the crew had died, would not the remainder have been forced to work the ship home? If that accident would have left them liable to do the whole work without any extraordinary remuneration, why should not desertion or casualty equally demand it?

Campbell's report:

Lord Ellenborough

I think *Harris v Watson* was rightly decided; but I doubt whether the ground of public policy, upon which Lord Kenyon is stated to have proceeded, be the true principle on which the decision is to be supported. Here, I say, the agreement is void for want of consideration. There was no consideration for the ulterior pay promised to the mariners who remained with the ship. Before they sailed from London they had undertaken to do all that they could under all the emergencies of the voyage. They had sold all their -services till the voyage should be completed. If they had been at liberty to quit the vessel at Cronstadt, the case would have been quite different; or if the captain had capriciously discharged the two men who were wanting, the others might not have been compellable to take the whole duty upon themselves, and their agreeing to do so might have been a sufficient consideration for the promise of an advance of wages. But the desertion of a part of the crew is to be considered an emergency of the voyage as much as their death; and those who remain are bound by the terms of their original contract to exert themselves to the utmost to bring the ship in safety to her destined port. Therefore, without looking to the policy of this agreement, I think it is void for want of consideration, and that the plaintiff can only recover at the rate of £5 a month.

Verdict accordingly.

NOTES

1.   On what ground was this case decided according to Espinasse? And according to Campbell? Campbell's explanation is the one now generally accepted. See Gilmore, *The Death of Contract*, 1974, pp 22–28.

2.   Although one might have expected Espinasse to report accurately the judgment given in a case in which he had appeared as counsel, his reputation as a reporter is poor. Pollock CB is quoted as having said: 'Mr Espinasse was deaf. He heard one half of a case and reported the other.' (See Megarry, *A Second Miscellany-at-law*, 1973, p 118.)

Even if *Stilk v Myrick* reflects a policy of guarding one party to a contract against the other threatening to break the contract unless he is promised an extra payment, on the traditional interpretation, it seemed to lay down a simple rule that performing an existing contractual duty owed to the promisor could not amount to consideration. (See also p 852 for the converse case of a party who agrees that if the other will perform part of his contractual obligation he will be released from the rest of it.) Although the promisor might see a practical advantage in persuading the promisee actually to perform, and even if the promisee would actually have to perform in order to get the promised extra payment, the law appeared to refuse to recognise that there was any 'legal' benefit to the promisor or 'legal' detriment to the promisee.

More recently, however, the courts have developed a separate doctrine to deal with cases in which one party has pressurised the other into giving a promise to pay extra. This is the doctrine of economic duress, which is considered in detail at p 905 ff. Its existence seems to be encouraging a more flexible attitude towards consideration in cases in which, without there having been any coercion, one party has promised the other an extra payment to encourage the other to perform its existing contractual duty. In *Woodhouse AC Israel Cocoa Ltd SA v Nigerian Produce Marketing Co Ltd* [1972] AC 741 (see p 873), Lord Hailsham said:

...I imagine that a modern court would have found no difficulty in discovering consideration for such a promise. Businessmen know their own business best, even when they appear to grant an indulgence...

■ *Williams v Roffey Bros & Nicholls (Contractors) Ltd*
[1990] 1 All ER 512, Court of Appeal

The defendants were building contractors who had agreed to refurbish 27 flats for a housing association under a contract that contained a 'penalty clause' for late completion (ie a clause stating that the defendants would pay so much for every week that they were late). The defendants employed the plaintiff, a carpenter, as a subcontractor to do the necessary carpentry for £20,000. There was nothing in the contract about how the plaintiff was to be paid, but in fact he was paid as the work progressed. By April 1986, he had been paid some £16,000 and he had done some work on all the flats, but he had completed only nine of them and he was in financial difficulties. These were caused partly by his failure to supervise his workmen properly but largely because, as the defendants agreed, the original price for the work was too low. The defendants therefore promised to pay him an extra amount of £10,300, to be paid at the rate of £575 per completed flat. The plaintiff completed work on eight further flats but the defendants paid only £1,500 more and the plaintiff stopped work and brought this action for payment. The Recorder awarded him £3,500 (8 x £575 plus a proportion of the original £20,000 less the £1,500 paid and various deductions for defects). The defendants appealed.

Glidewell LJ

... The Judge quoted and accepted the evidence of [the defendant's surveyor] to the effect that a main contractor who agrees too low a price with a sub-contractor is acting contrary to his own interests. He will never get the job finished without paying more money.

The Judge therefore concluded:

> 'In my view where the original sub-contract price is too low, and the parties subsequently agree that the additional monies shall be paid to the sub-contractor, this agreement is in the interests of both parties. This is what happened in the present case, and in my opinion the agreement of 9 April 1986 does not fail for lack of consideration.'

In his address to us, counsel for the defendants outlined the benefits to his clients the defendant which arose from their agreement to pay the additional £10,300 as:

(i)   seeking to ensure that the plaintiff continued work and did not stop in breach of the sub-contract;
(ii) avoiding the penalty for delay;
(iii) avoiding the trouble and expense of engaging other people to complete the carpentry work.

However, counsel submits that, though his clients may have derived, or hoped to derive, practical benefits from their agreement to pay the 'bonus', they derived no benefit in law, since the plaintiff was promising to do no more than he was already bound to do by his sub-contract, ie continue with the carpentry work and complete it on time. Thus there was no consideration for the agreement.

Counsel relies on the principle of law which, traditionally, is based on the decision in *Stilk v Myrick*....

In *North Ocean Shipping Co Ltd v Hyundai Construction Co Ltd* Mocatta J regarded the general principle of the decision in *Stilk v Myrick* as still being good law. He referred to two earlier decisions of this court, dealing with wholly different subjects, in which Denning LJ, as he then was, sought to escape from the confines of the rule, but was not accompanied in his attempt by the other members of the court.

[Glidewell LJ referred to *Ward v Byham* and *Williams v Williams* and continued:]

There is, however, another legal concept of relatively recent development which is relevant, namely, that of economic duress. Clearly if a sub-contractor has agreed to undertake work at a fixed price, and before he has completed the work declines to continue with it unless the contractor agrees to pay an increased price, the sub-contractor may be held guilty of securing the contractor's promise by taking unfair advantage of the difficulties he will cause if he does not complete the work. In such a case an agreement to pay an increased price may well be voidable because entered into under duress. Thus this concept may provide another answer in law to the question of policy which has troubled the courts since before *Stilk v Myrick*, and no doubt led at the date of that decision to a rigid adherence to the doctrine of consideration.

This possible application of the concept of economic duress was referred to by Lord Scarman, delivering the judgment of the Judicial Committee of the Privy Council in *Pao On v Lau Yiu Long* ...

It is true that *Pao On* is a case of a tripartite relationship, ie a promise by A to perform a pre-existing contractual obligation owed to B, in return for a promise of payment by C. But Lord Scarman's words seem to me to be of general application, equally applicable to a promise made by one of the original two parties to a contract.

Accordingly, following the view of the majority in *Ward v Byham* and of the whole court in *Williams v Williams* and that of the Privy Council in *Pao On* the present state of the law on this subject can be expressed in the following proposition:

(i)   if A has entered into a contract with B to do work for, or to supply goods or services to, B in return for payment by B, and
(ii) at some stage before A has completely performed his obligations under the contract B has reason to doubt whether A will, or will be able to, complete his side of the bargain; and
(iii) B thereupon promises A an additional payment in return for A's promise to perform his contractual obligations on time; and

(iv) as a result of giving his promise, B obtains in practice a benefit, or obviates a disbenefit; and

(v) B's promise is not given as the result of economic duress or fraud on the part of A; then

(vi) the benefit to B is capable of being consideration for B's promise, so that the promise will be legally binding.

As I have said, counsel for the defendants accepted that in the present case by promising to pay the extra £10,300 his client secured benefits. There is no finding, and no suggestion, that in this case the promise was given as a result of fraud or duress.

If it be objected that the propositions above contravene the principle in *Stilk v Myrick*, I answer that in my view they do not; they refine, and limit the application of, that principle, but they leave the principle unscathed, eg where B secures no benefit by his promise. It is not in my view surprising that a principle enunciated in relation to the rigours of seafaring life during the Napoleonic wars should be subjected during the succeeding 180 years to a process of refinement and limitation in its application in the present day.

It is therefore my opinion that on his findings of fact in the present case, the Judge was entitled to hold, as he did, that the defendants' promise to pay the extra £10,300 was supported by valuable consideration, and thus constituted an enforceable agreement.

As a subsidiary argument, Mr Evans submits that on the facts of the present case the consideration, even if otherwise good, did not 'move from the promisee'. This submission is based on the principle illustrated in the decision in *Tweddle v Atkinson*.

My understanding of the meaning of the requirement that 'consideration must move from the promisee' is that such consideration must be provided by the promisee, or arise out of his contractual relationship with the promisor. It is consideration provided by somebody else, not a party to the contract, which does not 'move from the promisee'. This was the situation in *Tweddle v Atkinson*, but it is, of course, not the situation in the present case. Here the benefits to the defendants arose out of their agreement of 9 April 1986 with the plaintiff, the promisee. In this respect I would adopt the following passage from Chitty on Contracts, 25th edition, para 173, and refer to the authorities there cited:

> 'The requirement that consideration must move from the promisee is most generally satisfied where some detriment is suffered by him, eg where he parts with money or goods, or renders services, in exchange for the promise. But the requirement may be equally well satisfied where the promisee confers a benefit on the promisor without *in fact* suffering any detriment.' *(Chitty's* emphasis.)

That is the situation in this case . . . For these reasons I would dismiss this appeal.

Russell LJ

I find [the] argument relating to consideration much more difficult . . . whilst consideration remains a fundamental requirement before a contract not under seal can be enforced, the policy of the law in its search to do justice between the parties has developed considerably since the early nineteenth century when Stilk v Myrick was decided by Lord Ellenborough CJ. In the late twentieth century I do not believe that the rigid approach to the concept of consideration to be found in Stilk v Myrick is either necessary or desirable. Consideration there must still be but in my judgment the courts nowadays should be more ready to find its existence so as to reflect the intention of the parties to the contract where the bargaining powers are not unequal and where the finding of consideration reflects the true intention of the parties.

What was the true intention of the parties when they arrived at the agreement pleaded by the defendants in paragraph 5 of the amended defence. The defendants, through their [surveyor], recognised the price that had been agreed originally with the plaintiff was less than what [the surveyor] himself regarded as a reasonable price. There was a desire on [the surveyor's] part to retain the services of the plaintiff so that the work could be completed without the need to employ another sub-contractor. There was further a need to replace what had hitherto been a haphazard method of payment by a more formalised scheme involving the payment of a specified sum on the completion of each flat. These were all advantages accruing to the defendants which can fairly be said to have been in consideration of their undertaking to pay the additional £10,300. True it was that the plaintiff did not undertake to do any work additional to that which he had originally undertaken to do but the terms upon which he was to carry out the work were varied and, in my judgment, that variation was supported by consideration which a pragmatic approach to the true relationship between the parties readily demonstrates.

For my part I wish to make it plain that I do not base my judgment upon any reservation as to the correctness of the law long ago enunciated in *Stilk v Myrick*. A gratuitous promise, pure and simple, remains unenforceable unless given under seal. But where, as in this case a party undertakes to make a payment because by so doing it will gain an advantage arising out of the continuing relationship with the promisee the new bargain will not fail for want of consideration. As I read the judgment of the assistant recorder this was his true ratio upon that part of the case wherein the absence of consideration was raised in argument. For the reasons that I have endeavoured to outline I think that the assistant recorder came to a correct conclusion and I too would dismiss this appeal.

Purchas LJ

... [T]here were clearly incentives to both parties to make a further arrangement in order to relieve the plaintiff of his financial difficulties and also to ensure that the plaintiff was in a position, or alternatively was willing, to continue with the sub-contract works to a reasonable and timely completion. Against this context the judge found that on the 9th April 1986 a meeting took place between the plaintiff and a man called Hooper, on the one hand, and [the surveyor] and Mr Roffey on the other hand. The arrangement was that the defendants would pay the plaintiff an extra £10,300 by way of increasing the lump sum for the total work. It was further agreed that the sum of £10,300 was to be paid at the rate of £575 per flat on the completion of each flat. This arrangement was beneficial to both sides. By completing one flat at a time rather than half completing all the flats the plaintiff was able to receive moneys on account and the defendants were able to direct their other trades to do work in the completed flats which otherwise would have been held up until the plaintiff had completed his work ...

In my judgment, the rule in *Stilk v Myrick* remains valid as a matter of principle, namely that a contract not under seal must be supported by consideration. Thus, where the agreement upon which reliance is placed provides that an extra payment is to be made for work to be done by the payee which he is already obliged to perform then unless some other consideration is detected to support the agreement to pay the extra sum that agreement will not be enforceable. The two cases *Harris v Watson* and *Stilk v Myrick* involved circumstances of a very special nature, namely the extraordinary conditions existing at the turn of the eighteenth century under which seamen had to serve their contracts of employment on the high seas. There were strong public policy grounds at that time to protect the master and owners of a ship from being held to ransom by disaffected crews. Thus, the decision that the promise to pay extra wages even in the circumstances established in those cases, was not supported by consideration is readily understandable. Of course, conditions today on the high seas have changed dramatically and it is at least questionable, as Mr Makey submitted, whether these cases might not well have been decided differently if they were tried today. The modern cases tend to depend more upon the defence of duress in a commercial context rather than lack of consideration for the second agreement. In the present case the question of duress does not arise. The initiative in coming to the agreement of the 9th April came from [the surveyor] and not from the plaintiff. It would not, therefore, lie in the defendants' mouth to assert a defence of duress. Nevertheless the court is more ready in the presence of this defence being available in the commercial context to look for mutual advantages which would amount to sufficient consideration to support the second agreement under which the extra money is paid.

[Purchas LJ referred to Lord Hailsham's speech in *Woodhouse Cocoa* and continued:]

The question must be posed: What consideration has moved from the plaintiff to support the promise to pay the extra £10,300 added to the lump sum provision? In the particular circumstances, which I have outlined above, there was clearly a commercial advantage to both sides from a pragmatic point of view in reaching the agreement of 9 April. The defendants were on risk that as a result of the bargain they had struck the plaintiff would not or indeed possibly could not comply with his existing obligations without further finance. As a result of the agreement the defendants secured their position commercially. There was, however, no obligation added to the contractual duties imposed upon the plaintiff under the original contract. Prima facie this would appear to be a classic *Stilk v Myrick* case. It was, however, open to the plaintiff to be in deliberate breach of the contract in order to 'cut his losses' commercially. In normal circumstances the suggestion that a contracting party can rely upon his own breach to establish consideration is distinctly unattractive. In many cases it obviously would be and if there was any element of duress brought upon the other contracting party under the modern development of this branch of the law the proposed breaker of the contract would not benefit. With some hesitation and comforted by the passage from the speech of Lord Hailsham, to which I have referred, I consider that the modern approach to the question of consideration would be that where there were benefits derived by each party to a contract of variation even though one party did not suffer a detriment this would not be fatal to establishing sufficient consideration to support the agreement. If both parties benefit from an agreement it is not necessary that each also suffers a detriment. In my judgment, on the facts as found by the judge, he was entitled to reach the conclusion that consideration existed and in those circumstances I would not disturb that finding. This is sufficient to determine the appeal . . .

Appeal dismissed.

NOTES

1. These cases are about purported changes to the terms of existing contracts and we will return to them in Section 7.

2. In all of the 'existing duty' cases, the promisee has done something, that he might not otherwise have done, and the promisor has had the benefit of this performance, which he might not otherwise have got. Isn't the problem the law's reluctance to acknowledge that, but for the extra payment, the promisee might not have performed his legal duty? Or is the courts' main concern that the promisee might refuse to perform as a way of extorting additional payment from the promisor? If so, the decision in *Williams v Roffey Bros* that, when there is no question of extortion, performance of an existing contractual duty owed to the promisor can constitute good consideration seems sensible. It is not clear that consideration should ever have been required in such a case: see p 860.

3. In *Williams v Roffey Bros*, the Court of Appeal stresses the practical benefit to the promisor from the new arrangement. Some commentators point to this as a case in which there is consideration because there is a benefit to the promisor without any corresponding detriment to the promisee (Treitel, p 82; Adams & Brownsword (1990) 55 MLR 536, 541). Is this correct? Although it may seem odd to say that the subcontractors were suffering a detriment through an arrangement that was to their benefit, it is submitted that, if the fact that they were bound to do it already is laid aside, the subcontractors suffered a detriment by having to complete the work. This is just as much a 'detriment' as may be suffered by a seller who is obliged to deliver goods under a contract; he suffers a detriment even if he is to receive a price greater than the goods are worth.

4. We return to the question of whether the consideration must 'move from the promisee' at p 138.

5. For a critical analysis of the *Williams v Roffey* case, see Chen-Wishart, 'Consideration, Practical Benefit and the Emperor's New Clothes' in Beatson and Friedmann (eds), *Good Faith and Fault in Contract Law*, 1995, pp 123–150.

6. The correctness of the reasoning in *Williams v Roffey* was seriously doubted in *South Caribbean Trading Co Ltd v Trafigura Beheer* [2005] 1 Lloyd's Rep 128.

6. Requirements contracts

As we suggested earlier, even in the commercial context there are occasional situations in which there is difficulty about the sufficiency of consideration.

■ *Great Northern Railway Co v Witham* (1873)
LR 9 CP 16, Common Pleas

Keating J

In this case Mr Digby Seymour moved to enter a nonsuit. The circumstances were these:—The Great Northern Railway Company advertised for tenders for the supply of stores. The defendant made a tender in these words,—'I hereby undertake to supply the Great Northern Railway Company, for twelve months, from &c to &c, with such quantities of each or any of the several articles named in the attached specifications as the company's store-keeper may order from time to time, at the price set opposite each article respectively,' &c. Some orders were given by the company, which were duly executed. But the order now in question was not executed; the defendant seeking to excuse himself from the performance of his agreement, because it was unilateral, the company not being bound to give the order. The ground upon which it was put by Mr Seymour was, that there was no consideration for the defendant's promise to supply the goods; in other words, that, inasmuch as there was no obligation on the company to give an order, there was no consideration moving from the company, and therefore no obligation on the defendant to supply the goods. . . . If before the order was given the defendant had given notice to the company that he would not perform the agreement, it might be that he would have been justified in so doing. But here the company had given the order, and had consequently done something which amounted to a consideration for the defendant's promise. I see no ground for doubting that the verdict for the plaintiffs ought to stand.

Brett J delivered a judgment to the same effect. **Grove J** concurred.

NOTES

1. What do you think the position would have been if the defendant had notified the company that he would not accept any further orders? The traditional view is that non-exclusive requirements contracts (ones that do not require the buyer to take all his requirements from the seller) are unenforceable, because there is no consideration for the seller's promise to supply at the stated price if the buyer is not promising to buy from the seller (although for a different view, see Adams, 'Consideration for Requirements Contracts' (1978) 94 LQR 73). The same is true of the converse 'output' contract, whereby a buyer agrees to take a seller's output.

2. If, on the other hand, the contract is 'exclusive', in the sense that the buyer is promising that if he has any requirements for the goods in question he will buy from the seller (or in an output contract, the seller will sell the whole of its output to the buyer), there is consideration.

3. What is the purpose of entering into a requirements contract whereby the buyer agrees to take all his requirements of a particular item from the seller? What advantage does either party get out of the arrangement?

4. Why enter a non-exclusive contract that does not oblige the buyer to take all of his requirements from the seller? Although the latter type of contract is probably unenforceable, it appears that it is not uncommon; if it is unenforceable, what is the point of it?

■ Macaulay, 'The Standardized Contracts of United States Automobile Manufacturers'

International Encyclopedia of Comparative Law, VII, paras 3.21–29

CONTRACTS TO BUILD AND SELL CARS

The manufacturers and their suppliers

Description of the relationship

Although the manufacturers can and do make in their own plants some of almost all of the parts which go into an assembled automobile, they also buy many of these parts from suppliers. There are a number of reasons why they purchase from outside suppliers. First, the manufacturer gets a product without investing additional capital in buildings, machines and a trained work force. Second, the manufacturer gets a yardstick which can be used to measure the efficiency of its own division making the same item. If a division making grease seals can produce them at 2 cents each, but an outsider can make them for 11/2 cents each, the manufacturer knows he must re-examine the efficiency of his internal operation. Third, the manufacturer increases the chance that he may benefit from technological innovation. The supplier's designers and engineers may be able to suggest a different design or an improved manufacturing process. On the other side, most businesses, but not all, that can produce parts for automobiles want to sell their output to the automobile manufacturers because of the possibilities for extremely high volume production which, in an efficiently managed firm, can be highly profitable.

There are three additional factors influencing the course a manufacturer-supplier relationship takes: First, the mass production techniques of American automobile manufacturing require that the assembly line not be stopped. When, for example, a particular Ford sedan arrives at a certain point on the assembly line four hubcaps must be there ready to be installed. It would be extremely costly to the manufacturer if the line had to be stopped because the supplier's machines that stamp out hubcaps broke down, because a supplier's inventory was not great enough to meet the demand or because the parts were lost in shipment. However, demand for automobiles and even for particular types of automobiles fluctuates. To a great extent, this second factor offsets the first. The easiest way to avoid stopping assembly lines would be to produce large quantities of parts far in advance of need. Yet this approach increases costs because of the possibility of waste and the loss of the use of funds thus devoted to inventories. If, for example, the demand for station wagons declines during the year, exhaust pipes that fit only station wagons that will never be produced are mere scrap metal. Third, component parts can be defective, the defect can cause injury to property or person, and in United States law the injured party in such cases has increasingly been gaining rights against manufacturers. Not surprisingly, one finds that manufacturers wish to hold suppliers responsible for such claims, and the suppliers must defend themselves against the costly results of seemingly minor defects in the parts they make.

The blanket order system

The system described

The *manufacturers* have accommodated all of these economic and legal factors in an imaginative piece of transaction architecture which is usually called a 'blanket order'. Coupled with the suppliers' great desire to do business with the automobile manufacturers, the blanket order system almost always insures that parts will arrive at the assembly plants at the right time, that the suppliers will take the risk of scrapped parts caused by fluctuations in demand, and that the suppliers will be responsible for claims caused by defects. Moreover, the system gives the manufacturers great leverage to ward off price increases caused by the suppliers' increased costs.

This is how it works: Some time before the beginning of the model year, the manufacturer will issue a blanket order to a supplier of, for example, tail pipes designed specifically for one of the manufacturer's station wagons. The blanket order states a number of 'agreements'. One of the most important is the price per unit. This price is computed on the basis of an estimated number of units to be ordered, and it will not be increased if fewer are actually ordered. Thus, the manufacturer has made the supplier run the risk that he will not even recover his cost of producing the items actually shipped to the manufacturer in the event that the manufacturer uses substantially fewer than the estimated number. And the blanket order does not oblige the manufacturer to take and pay for *any* of the parts described in it. That obligation comes only when the manufacturer sends the supplier documents called 'releases'. The idea seems to be that the blanket order creates a force which is held back until released little by little.

Each month, sometimes more often, the manufacturer sends the supplier a release, ordering him to manufacture and ship a specified number of the parts each week. On the release form, the manufacturer also will estimate the number of parts he will require for the next two or three months, but this estimate, to quote one manufacturer's form, 'is for planning purposes only and does not constitute a commitment'. Typically, manufacturers do not send releases calling for more parts than they will need in a month since their monthly estimates of sales are fairly accurate. However, sometimes they do order too few or too many parts. If there is an increase in public demand for a particular model, the blanket order allows the manufacturer to send another release form to the supplier calling for increased deliveries. Such sudden increases may be a great strain on the supplier if he does not have unused capacity for production. Moreover, a supplier must always guard against a break-down of his machinery, which temporarily destroys his ability to meet the manufacturer's demands. As a result, the supplier usually makes more than the number of parts ordered by the manufacturer so that the supplier will have an inventory to cover anticipated future demands. He builds this inventory at his own risk since the blanket order clearly provides that 'Seller shall not fabricate any articles covered by this order, or procure materials required therefor, or ship any articles to Purchaser, except to the extent authorized by... written releases... Purchaser will make no payment for finished work, work in process or raw material fabricated or produced by Seller in excess of Purchaser's written releases'.

If a manufacturer has 'released' too many parts in light of a sudden decrease in demand, the blanket order gives it the right to cancel the amount ordered in whole or in part. It then is obligated to pay the contract price for each part finished and 'the cost to Seller (excluding profit or losses) of work in process and raw material based on any audit Purchaser may conduct and generally accepted accounting principles...'

Blanket orders and American contract law

Legal enforceability

...In effect at the manufacturer's request, the supplier makes an offer—a promise to supply certain goods if they are ordered—which the manufacturer accepts every time it sends a release... The large automobile manufacturers try to avoid placing total reliance on any one supplier, and other suppliers usually can increase production so that a manufacturer's assembly line is not stopped for lack of an item. Thus manufacturers tend to avoid injury rather than litigate for compensation. On the other hand, no automobile parts supplier is likely to bring a case against a manufacturer; the loss on any one order is very unlikely to be large enough to justify jeopardizing future business. Of course, the trustee of a bankrupt supplier would be free of this constraint. However, in light of the uncertainty of the supplier's legal position, many trustees would think it unwise to risk the cost of legal action against a manufacturer.

What are the consequences of the legal situation? If we assume that the developing reliance and fairness doctrines would not apply, the parties get legal rights only after the manufacturer has issued a release and only as to the goods ordered in that release. This means that there can be a great deal of reliance by the supplier which is unprotected by contract rights. On the other hand, legally the supplier would be free to refuse to continue the relationship by revoking his outstanding offer to supply the parts as ordered by the release forms. As we have said previously, few suppliers who were not going out of business could afford to exercise such a right; very few situations short of bankruptcy would justify losing the good will of General Motors, Ford, Chrysler or American Motors. Most importantly for the manufacturer, it does get legal rights once a release is issued. As a result, it manages to avoid any question that the supplier will bear liability for injuries caused by defective parts which it ships. Once the parts are ordered by a release there is a contract which the manufacturer has written, and the disclaimers and limitations of remedy so typically found in documents drafted by sellers are thus avoided. As between Chrysler and its suppliers, the responsibility for compliance with federal safety and air pollution regulations is also clearly placed on the supplier.

Remedies

The standard blanket order documents drastically limit the remedies to which a supplier would otherwise be entitled under American contract law once a legally binding contract is created by the issuance of a release. Typically, the manufacturer reserves a right to cancel the goods ordered by its release, either in whole or in part. Under American contract law such a cancellation would be a breach if not authorized by the agreement, and, absent a contract provision to the contrary, the seller would be entitled to recover what he had spent in performance before the buyer's notice of cancellation plus the profit he would have made had he been allowed to complete his performance. Most blanket order cancellation clauses, however, exclude a right to profit except as to those parts which have been completed before cancellation. Thus even when a contract is formed by a release, the supplier's rights in most situations will be minimal. The manufacturer gains a practical commitment from the supplier to meet the demands of its assembly line. It retains maximum flexibility by making no commitment to buy any parts until a release is given and making only a very limited payment if it wishes to cancel after one is sent.

The absence of a reform movement

There are no statutes attempting to regulate this relationship, and no movement seeking such legislation has been discovered. Insofar as statutes in the United States are the result of pluralistic struggle and compromise, one essential element of pluralism seems lacking. It would be hard to form a group of suppliers to seek legislation. Supplying the manufacturers is very profitable for a firm that can accept all the risks allocated to it by the blanket order system . . .

In summary, the manufacturers have tailored a relationship whereby they get most of the advantages of producing parts in a division of their own firms while preserving most of the advantages of dealing with an outside organization. The suppliers are offered a chance to make high profits in exchange for assuming great risks. Most suppliers are eager for the chance to play the blanket order game. The public may get better automobiles at a lower price as a result of the system, but one cannot be sure.

[This paper is based on Macaulay, Law and the Balance of Power (New York 1966); Whitford, Strict Products Liability and the Automobile Industry—Much Ado About Nothing: 1968 Wis L Rev 83, cited Strict Products Liability; idem, Law and the Consumer Transaction—A Case Study of the Automobile Warranty: 1968 Wis L Rev 1006, cited Law; and an unpublished study of the 'blanket order' system by the author.]

NOTE

This is not the only study suggesting that businessmen set considerable store by contracts which they know are legally unenforceable.

■ *Wood v Lucy, Lady Duff–Gordon*
222 NY 88, 118 NE 214 (Court of Appeals, New York, 1917)

Cardozo J

The defendant styles herself 'a creator of fashions'. Her favor helps a sale. Manufacturers of dresses, millinery and like articles are glad to pay for a certificate of her approval. The things which she designs, fabrics, parasols, and what not, have a new value in the public mind when issued in her name. She employed the plaintiff to help her turn this vogue into money. He was to have the exclusive right, subject always to her approval, to place her indorsements on the designs of others. He was also to have the exclusive right, to place her own designs on sale, or to license others to market them. In return, she was to have one-half of 'all profits and revenues' derived from any contracts he might make. The exclusive right was to last at least one year from April 1, 1915, and thereafter from year to year unless terminated by notice of ninety days. The plaintiff says that he kept the contract on his part, and that the defendant broke it. She placed her indorsement on fabrics, dresses and millinery without his knowledge, and withheld the profits. He sues her for the damages, and the case comes here on demurrer.

The agreement of employment is signed by both parties. It has a wealth of recitals. The defendant insists, however, that it lacks the elements of a contract. She says that the plaintiff does not bind himself to anything. It is true that he does not promise in so many words that he will use reasonable efforts to place the defendant's indorsements and market her designs. We think, however, that such a promise is fairly to be implied . . .

The implication of a promise here finds support in many circumstances. The defendant gave an exclusive privilege. She was to have no right for at least a year to place her own indorsements or market her own designs except through the agency of the plaintiff. The acceptance of the exclusive agency was an assumption of its duties. . . . We are not to suppose that one party was to be placed at the mercy of the other. . . . Many other terms of the agreement point the same way. We are told at the outset by way of recital that 'the said Otis F. Wood possesses a business organization adapted to the placing of such indorsements as the said Lucy, Lady Duff–Gordon has approved'. The implication is that the plaintiff's business organization will be used for the purpose for which it is adapted. But the terms of the defendant's compensation are even more significant. Her sole compensation for the grant of an exclusive agency is to be one-half of all the profits resulting from the plaintiff's efforts. Unless he gave his efforts, she could never get anything. Without an implied promise, the transaction cannot have such business 'efficacy as both parties must have intended that at all events it should have' (Bowen LJ, in *The Moorcock)*. But the contract does not stop there. The plaintiff goes on to promise that he will account monthly for all moneys received by him, and that he will take out all such patents and copyrights and trademarks as may in his judgment be necessary to protect the rights and articles affected by the agreement. It is true, of course, as the Appellate Division has said, that if he was under no duty to try to market designs or to place certificates of indorsement, his promise to account for profits or take out copyrights would be valueless. But in determining the intention of the parties, the promise has a value. It helps to enforce the conclusion that the plaintiff had some duties. His promise to pay the defendant one-half of the profits and revenues resulting from the exclusive agency and to render accounts monthly, was a promise to use reasonable efforts to bring profits and revenues into existence. For this conclusion, the authorities are ample. . . .

The judgment of the Appellate Division should be reversed, and the order of the Special Term affirmed, with costs in the Appellate Division and in this court.

Cuddeback, **McLaughlin** and **Andrews JJ**, concur; **Hiscock CJ**, **Chase** and **Crane JJ**, dissent.

Judgment reversed.

NOTES

1. In this case, Cardozo was prepared to imply an obligation on the part of the plaintiff, whereas with non-exclusive requirements contracts, the courts have not implied an obligation on the buyer (for example, to take a reasonable proportion of its requirements from the seller). Is there anything in the nature of the arrangements that justifies this difference in treatment?

2. In *A Schroeder Music Publishing Co Ltd v Macaulay* (see p 1115), the House of Lords held an agreement between a young composer and a music publisher, under which the publisher obtained copyright of any compositions of the composer during the contract period and the composer would be paid royalties on sales, contrary to public policy as being in unreasonable restraint of trade and therefore void. One of the reasons given by Lord Reid was that the publisher was not obliged to publish the songs. It was argued that the publishers had an implied obligation to act in good faith, so that they could not

maliciously refrain from publishing. Lord Reith doubted this but said it would make no difference. Why do you think it was not argued that the publisher was under an implied obligation to use its best efforts to earn royalties for the composer? (You may like to return to this question after you have read the chapter on implied terms.)

7. Irrevocable commercial credits

■ **Atiyah, *The Sale of Goods*** (11th edn, 2005)
pp 439–440

Where a person carrying on business in one country buys goods from seller in another country, it is common practice for the price to be paid by means of a banker's commercial credit. The normal procedure is more or less as follows, although there may frequently be variations of details.

The buyer instructs his own bank (the issuing bank) to open a credit in favour of the seller with a bank in the seller's country (the 'intermediary' or 'correspondent' or 'confirming' banker). Almost; invariably, the buyer instructs the issuing bank that the seller is only to be allowed to draw on the credit on presentation to the paying bank of documents showing that the goods have been shipped and are on their way to the buyer. The shipping documents will comprise (at least) the seller's invoice for the goods, the bill of lading and, frequently (always in c.i.f. contracts), an insurance policy or certificate. The intermediary banker will then notify the seller that instructions have been received to open a credit in his favour and will inform him of the precise terms on which he will be allowed to avail himself of the credit. As soon as the goods are shipped and the seller has received the necessary documents himself from the carriers or their agents and the insurers, he will present these documents together with his invoice to the intermediary banker. The bank will check the documents with the terms of the credit to ensure that the goods shipped are (so far as can be seen from the documents) the contract goods and that everything appears to be in order and, if satisfied that this is the case, will permit the seller to draw against the credit. This may be done by accepting a bill of exchange, or discounting a bill drawn on the buyer, or by making funds available in cash.

The intermediary bank will then transmit the documents to the issuing bank, which will likewise have to check the documents against the terms of the credit, and which will pay the intermediary bank if satisfied that all is in order. The issuing bank will then inform the buyer that the documents have been received, and will be transferred to him against payment. The buyer will also satisfy himself that the documents are in order and will, in due course, pay the issuing bank an amount corresponding to the price paid to the seller, together with the bank's own charges. Of course the issuing bank may be providing credit to the buyer—that is a matter for the contract between them—in which case it will transmit the documents to him before receiving payment. Armed with the documents, the buyer will then be in a position to resell the goods and transfer the documents to a sub-buyer or, alternatively, to take delivery as soon as the goods arrive. The holder of the documents is prima facie the person to whom the carrier will deliver the goods.

Virtually all bankers' credits are today granted on the terms that they are to be governed by the Uniform Customs and Practice for Documentary Credits prepared by the International Chamber of Commerce. The banks of nearly all the countries in the world use this document (hereafter referred to as the Uniform Customs) which is, therefore, to all intents and purposes a part of the law of bankers' commercial credits. But this document is not a statute, and should not be interpreted as such; for instance, reasonable implications can be read into the Uniform Customs.

There are many variations in the forms of commercial credits, the principal distinctions being between revocable and irrevocable credits, and confirmed and unconfirmed credits. Under the Uniform Customs, an irrevocable credit constitutes a definite undertaking by the issuing bank that the credit will be made available if the seller complies with the stipulated conditions. A revocable credit does not constitute a definite undertaking by the issuing bank and may be cancelled or modified without notice until payment is made or documents accepted under the credit. The distinction between a confirmed and an unconfirmed credit turns upon whether or not the intermediary bank accepts a direct obligation to the seller to honour the credit. In the former event, the intermediary bank 'confirms' the credit, that is, undertakes (sometimes for an extra commission payable directly by the seller) to pay, whether or not it is put in funds by the issuing bank; in the latter event, the credit is unconfirmed, the intermediary bank merely informs the seller that the credit has been opened in this favour, and the seller will have no right of recourse against the bank in the event of its refusing to pay.

In the past, doubts have even existed as to whether the seller could sue the bank if it refused to honour a confirmed credit, anyhow prior to shipment, on the ground that there is no contract between seller and bank, owing to the absence of any consideration supplied by the seller. There is no difficulty when the goods have once been shipped, because this is action by the seller in reliance on the bank's undertaking, and that should suffice as a valid consideration by any modern test. But it is theoretically arguable that, if the bank repudiates the credit before shipment the seller may be unable to enforce the letter of credit by direct action against the bank. In practice, banks never take this technical point and judicial pronouncements now seem to have put their liability beyond doubt.*

* See especially *Hamzeh Malas & Sons v British Imex Industries Ltd* [1958] 2 QB 127, 129 per Jenkins, LJ; Urquhart Lindsay & Co v Eastern Bank Ltd [1922] 1 KB 318; *United City Merchants (Investments) Ltd v Royal Bank of Canada* [1983] 1 AC 168, 183, *per* Lord Diplock.

NOTE

It is, as Atiyah says, generally considered that an irrevocable confirmed credit becomes binding on the bank as soon as it has notified the seller that the credit has been opened. Unless the seller has paid the bank an extra commission for the confirmation, what consideration has the seller provided? Suppose (i) the bank only refuses to pay when the seller presents the documents; (ii) the bank revokes the credit when the seller has got the goods ready for shipment but has not yet shipped them; and (iii) the bank revokes the credit soon after it has notified the seller of its opening and before the seller has taken any steps in response? It is strongly arguable that the best course is simply to recognise that credits are an exception to the doctrine of consideration.

8. Why need not consideration be adequate?

■ **Posner, *Economic Analysis of Law*** (2nd edn, 1977)
pp 70–71

...[C]ourts have no comparative advantage in determining at what price goods should be sold. On the contrary, in all but very exceptional cases negotiation between buyer and seller is the more reliable method of determining a reasonable price, ie one at which exchange is mutually beneficial.

Courts inquire only as to the existence, not as to the adequacy, of the consideration for a contract. The distinction is important and economically sound. To ask whether there is consideration is simply to enquire whether the situation is one of exchange and a bargain has been struck. To go further and ask whether the consideration is adequate would require the court to do what we have just said it is less well equipped to do than the parties—decide whether the price (and other essential terms) specified in the contract are reasonable. It does not follow that a court is bound to enforce every contract. We shall see that there are cases where the presumption that the contemplated exchange increases value can be rebutted without inquiry into the reasonableness of particular terms; in such cases enforcement is appropriately refused even though the promise sought to be enforced is supported by consideration.

NOTE

In fact, the rule that consideration need not be adequate can be seriously misleading. It is quite true that a contract in which the consideration is inadequate will not fail for lack of consideration, but as we shall see (in Section 8 especially) there are many situations in which inadequacy of consideration combined with other factors is a ground for relief. Moreover, it can be argued that many rules of contract law that do not explicitly refer to the adequacy of consideration are nonetheless concerned with the fairness of exchanges: see Atiyah, 'Contract and Fair Exchange' in *Essays on Contract*, 1986. We will note some of them as we come to them. Some writers have argued that contracts in which the price deviates significantly from the market price, but in which there was no element of risk-taking and no intention to make a gift, should be avoidable without the need to point to any other factor (see pp 819–823 and 823–829). Whether this would be desirable is a matter of debate; it certainly does not represent present English law. For example, no one doubts that a football team must pay for a player it has 'bought' even if it has paid more than the market price for the player!

III. EXCHANGE

1. Consideration or conditional gift?

If I promise you an outright gift, there is no consideration for my promise. What if my promise is conditional on some event, and the event is your doing something — for instance, I promise you a wedding present if you marry? Is your marriage consideration for my promise, or is my promise merely a conditional gift promise?

It is clear that a promise that is essentially gratuitous may be made enforceable by casting it into the form of a bargain. A case that is probably an example of this is *Thomas v Thomas* (1842) 2 QB 851. The plaintiff, Eleanor Thomas, was the widow of John Thomas. On the eve of his death, John stated that he wished to make further provision for his wife, and the next morning said he wished her to have the house and all that it contained, or £100 instead. His will made no mention of this, but his executors and residuary legatees, hearing of the testator's wishes, executed with the plaintiff an agreement that provided that 'in consideration of such desire', they would convey the premises to her for her life,

... provided nevertheless, and it is hereby further agreed and declared, that the said Eleanor Thomas, or her assigns, shall and will, at all times during which she shall have possession of the said dwelling house, &c, pay to the said Samuel Thomas and Benjamin Thomas, their executors, &c, the sum of 1*l* yearly towards the ground rent payable in respect of the said dwelling house and other premises thereto adjoining, and shall and will keep the said dwelling house and premises in good and tenantable repair.

The plaintiff was allowed possession for some time, but after the death of his fellow executor, the defendant refused to convey the house to her and had her ejected. The plaintiff brought an action, alleging that the defendant had made the promise in consideration of her undertaking to pay the £1 per year and keep the premises in repair. Williams, for the defendant, argued that there was no consideration, or that if there was, that it was the fulfilment of the testator's wishes, and as the plaintiff had not alleged this as the consideration in her declaration, she must fail. The Court of Queen's Bench held that fulfilling the testator's wishes could not be consideration, being merely the motive behind the transaction. Patteson J remarked:

It would be giving to causa too large a construction if we were to adopt the view urged for the defendant: it would be confounding consideration with motive. Motive is not the same thing with consideration. Consideration means something which is of some value in the eye of the law, moving from the plaintiff: it may be some benefit to the plaintiff, or some detriment to the defendant; but at all events it must be moving from the plaintiff. Now that which is suggested as the consideration here, a pious respect for the wishes of the testator, does not in any way move from the plaintiff; it moves from the testator; therefore, legally speaking, it forms no part of the consideration.

However, the undertaking to pay £1 towards the ground rent and to keep the house in repair were consideration. In the words of Denman CJ:

... the stipulation for the payment of it is not a mere proviso, but an express agreement. (His Lordship here read the proviso.) This is in terms an express agreement, and shews a sufficient legal consideration quite independent of the moral feeling which disposed the executors to enter into such a contract.

Would the result have been different if the proviso had merely stated 'provided that the said ET shall ... pay ...'?

■ *Shadwell v Shadwell*

(1860) 9 CBNS 159, 42 ER 62, Common Bench

After his engagement, the plaintiff received the following letter:

11th August, 1838. Gray's Inn. My dear Lancey,—I am glad to hear of your intended marriage with Ellen Nicholl; and, as I promised to assist you at starting. I am happy to tell you that I will pay to you 150*l* yearly during my life and until your annual income derived from your profession of a Chancery barrister shall amount to 600 guineas; of which your own admission will be the only evidence that I shall receive or require. Your ever affectionate uncle, Charles Shadwell.

His uncle, now deceased, had paid 13 yearly sums; the plaintiff claimed the remaining five from his uncle's executors. The plaintiff alleged that this promise was made in consideration of his marriage, and that because his income as a barrister never amounted to 600 guineas he was now entitled to the money. The executors demurred.

Erle CJ

The question raised by the demurrer ... is, whether there is a consideration which will support the action on the promise to pay the annuity of 150*l* per annum

The circumstances are, that the plaintiff had made an engagement to marry one Ellen Nicholl, that his uncle had promised to assist him at starting,—by which, as I understand the words, he meant on commencing his married life. Then the letter containing the promise declared on is sent, to specify what that assistance would be, namely, 150*l* per annum during the uncle's life, and until the plaintiff's professional income should be acknowledged by him to exceed 600 guineas per annum; and the declaration avers, that the plaintiff, relying on this promise, without any revocation on the part of the uncle, did marry Ellen Nicholl.

Now, do these facts shew that the promise was in consideration either of a loss to be sustained by the plaintiff or a benefit to be derived from the plaintiff to the uncle, at his, the uncle's, request? My answer is in the affirmative.

First, do these facts shew a loss sustained by the plaintiff at his uncle's request? When I answer this in the affirmative, I am aware that a man's marriage with the woman of his choice is in one sense a boon, and in that sense the reverse of a loss: yet, as between the plaintiff and the party promising to supply an income to support the marriage, it may well be also a loss. The plaintiff may have made a most material change in his position, and induced the object of his affection to do the same, and may have incurred pecuniary liabilities resulting in embarrassments which would be in every sense a loss if the income which had been promised should be withheld; and, if the promise was made in order to induce the parties to marry, the promise so made would be in legal effect a request to marry.

Secondly, do these facts shew a benefit derived from the plaintiff to the uncle, at his request? In answering again in the affirmative, I am at liberty to consider the relation in which the parties stood and the interest in the settlement of his nephew which the uncle declares. The marriage primarily affects the parties thereto; but in a secondary degree it may be an object of interest to a near relative, and in that sense a benefit to him. This benefit is also derived from the plaintiff at the uncle's request. If the promise of the annuity was intended as an inducement to the marriage, and the averment that the plaintiff, relying on the promise, married, is an averment that the promise was one inducement to the marriage, this is the consideration averred in the declaration; and it appears to me to be expressed in the letter, construed with the surrounding circumstances . . . My judgment is for the plaintiff.

Keating J agreed with **Erle CJ**.

Byles J (dissenting)

I am of opinion that the defendant is entitled to the judgment of the court on the demurrer . . .

The inquiry . . . narrows itself to this question,—Does the letter disclose any consideration for the promise? the consideration relied on by the plaintiff's counsel being the subsequent marriage of the plaintiff. I think the letter discloses no consideration . . .

It is by no means clear that the words 'at starting' mean 'on marriage with Ellen Nicholl', or with any one else. The more natural meaning seems to me to be, 'at starting in the profession'; for, it will be observed that these words are used by testator in reciting a prior promise made when the testator had not heard of the proposed marriage with Ellen Nicholl, or, so far as appears, heard of any proposed marriage. This construction is fortified by the consideration that the annuity is not in terms made to begin from the marriage, but, as it should seem, from the date of the letter: neither is it in terms made defeasible if Ellen Nicholl should die before marriage.

But, even on the assumption that the words 'at starting' mean on marriage, I still think that no consideration appears, sufficient to sustain the promise . . .

Marriage of the plaintiff at the testator's express request would be no doubt an ample consideration. But marriage of the plaintiff without the testator's request is no consideration to the testator. It is true that marriage is or may be a detriment to the plaintiff: but detriment to the plaintiff is not enough, unless it either be a benefit to the testator, or be treated by the testator as such by having been suffered at his request. Suppose a defendant to promise a plaintiff,—'I will give you 500l if you break your leg',—would that detriment to the plaintiff, should it happen, be any consideration? If it be said that such an accident is an involuntary mischief, would it have been a binding promise if the testator had said,—'I will give you 100l a year while you continue in your present chambers?' I conceive that the promise would not be binding, for want of a previous request by the testator.

Now, the testator in the case before the court derived, so far as appears, no personal benefit from the marriage. The question, therefore, is still further narrowed to this point,—Was the marriage at the testator's request? Express request there was none. Can any request be implied? The only words from which it can be contended that it is to be implied, are the words 'I am glad to hear of your intended marriage with Ellen Nicholl.' But it appears . . . that the marriage had already been agreed on, and that the testator knew it. These words, therefore, seem to me to import no more than the satisfaction of the testator at the engagement,—an accomplished fact. No request can, as it seems to me, be inferred from them.

Judgment for the plaintiff.

NOTE

A similar problem of whether an act was consideration or merely a condition occurred in *Chappell & Co Ltd v Nestlé Co Ltd* [1960] AC 87 HL. The defendants offered records, including 'Rockin' Shoes', to anyone sending in a postal order for 1s 6d together with three wrappers from 6d bars of Nestlé's milk chocolate. Section 8 of the Copyright Act 1956 permitted the making of records of a musical work for selling retail, provided the maker gave the owner of the copyright prior notice and paid a royalty of $6\frac{1}{4}$ per cent of the 'ordinary retail selling price'. The plaintiffs, who were exclusive licensees of the copyright of 'Rockin' Shoes', were given notice that the ordinary retail selling price was 1s 6d. They sought an injunction to restrain a breach of copyright, contending that 1s 6d was not the 'ordinary retail selling price' and that the defendants could not avail themselves of s 8, which applied only where the price was solely money. Upjohn J granted the injunction, but it was reversed by the Court of Appeal. The plaintiffs appealed, and the House of Lords held by a majority that the injunction should be granted. Sending in the wrappers was not only a condition that had to be fulfilled before the record could be obtained: the wrappers formed part of the consideration. Perhaps the determining factor was that having to send in the wrappers would increase the sales of chocolate, and so would benefit the sellers. Compare Williston, *Contracts*, 3rd edn, 1953, s 112:

> It is often difficult to decide whether words of condition in a promise indicate a request for consideration or state a mere condition in a gratuitous promise. An aid, though not a conclusive test in determining which interpretation of the promise is more reasonable, is an inquiry whether the happening of the condition will be a benefit to the promisor. If so, it is a fair inference that the happening was requested as a consideration.

2. Past consideration

Suppose Beale misses his train from Oxford back to Warwick, so Bishop takes him there by car. As he gets out of the car, Beale promises to pay Bishop £15 for his trouble. Is there any consideration for the promise?

■ *Pao On v Lau Yiu Long*
[1979] 3 All ER 65, Privy Council

The plaintiffs owned all the shares in a private company, Shing On, whose principal asset was a building. The defendants, 'the Laus', were the majority shareholders in a public company, Fu Chip, which wanted to acquire the building. Rather than SO simply selling the building to FC, the parties agreed in February 1973 that the plaintiffs would transfer their shares in SO to FC and receive in exchange shares in FC. The plaintiffs could then sell these shares, but to avoid depressing the market in FC shares, the plaintiffs also agreed that they would retain 60 per cent of these shares for one year. The plaintiffs wanted some form of guarantee in case the price of the shares fell during the year, so the Laus and the plaintiffs simultaneously entered a subsidiary agreement that the Laus were to buy back 60 per cent of the shares at or before the end of the year at $2.50 each.

The plaintiffs then realised that if the FC shares *rose* in value during the year, the defendants and not the plaintiffs would benefit. They therefore refused to perform the main agreement unless the subsidiary agreement was cancelled and replaced by a guarantee by way of indemnity.

The Laus, fearing delays and loss of public confidence in FC, acceded, and signed a written contract stating that '…in consideration of your having at our request agreed to sell all your shares' in SO, they would indemnify the plaintiffs if at the end of the year the 60 per cent of the shares retained by the plaintiffs were worth less than \$2.50 each. When this occurred, the Laus refused to indemnify the plaintiffs. The plaintiffs brought an action, which succeeded in the High Court, but the decision was reversed on appeal. They then appealed to the Privy Council.

The opinion of their Lordships was delivered by **Lord Scarman:**

The first question

The first question is whether on its true construction the written guarantee of 4th May 1973 states a consideration sufficient in law to support the Laus' promise of indemnity against a fall in value of the Fu Chip shares…

Counsel for the plaintiffs before their Lordships' Board but not below contends that the consideration stated in the agreement is not in reality a past one. It is to be noted that the consideration was not on 4th May 1973 a matter of history only. The instrument by its reference to the main agreement with Fu Chip incorporates as part of the stated consideration the Paos' three promises to Fu Chip: to complete the sale of Shing On, to accept shares as the price for the sale, and not to sell 60% of the shares so accepted before 30th April 1974. Thus, on 4th May 1973 the performance of the main agreement still lay in the future. Performance of these promises was of great importance to the Laus, and it is undeniable that, as the instrument declares, the promises were made to Fu Chip at the request of the Laus. It is equally clear that the instrument also includes a promise by the Paos to the Laus to fulfil their earlier promises given to Fu Chip.

The Board agrees with the submission of counsel for the plaintiffs that the consideration expressly stated in the written guarantee is sufficient in law to support the Laus' promise of indemnity. An act done before the giving of a promise to make a payment or to confer some other benefit can sometimes be consideration for the promise. The act must have been done at the promisor's request, the parties must have understood that the act was to be remunerated either by a payment or the conferment of some other benefit, and payment, or the conferment of a benefit, must have been legally enforceable had it been promised in advance. All three features are present in this case. The promise given to Fu Chip under the main agreement not to sell the shares for a year was at Lau's request. The parties understood at the time of the main agreement that the restriction on selling must be compensated for by the benefit of a guarantee against a drop in price: and such a guarantee would be legally enforceable. The agreed cancellation of the subsidiary agreement left, as the parties knew, the Paos unprotected in a respect in which at the time of the main agreement all were agreed they should be protected.

Counsel's submission for the plaintiffs is based on *Lampleigh v Brathwait*. In that case the judges said:

'First…a mere voluntary curtesie will not have a consideration to uphold an assumpsit. But if that curtesie were moved by a suit or request of the party that gives the assumpsit, it will bind, for the promise, though it follows, yet it is not naked, but couples it self with the suit before, and the merits of the party procured by that suit, which is the difference.'

The modern statement of the law is in the judgment of Bowen LJ in *Re Casey's Patents, Stewart v Casey*. Bowen LJ said:

'Even if it were true, as some scientific students of law believe, that a past service cannot support a future promise, you must look at the document and see if the promise cannot receive a proper effect in some other way. Now, the fact of a past service raises an implication that at the time it was rendered it was to be paid for, and, if it was a service which was to be paid for, when you get in the subsequent document a promise to pay, that promise may be treated either as an admission which evidences or as a positive bargain which fixes the amount of that reasonable remuneration on the faith of which the service was originally rendered. So that here for past services there is ample justification for the promise to give the third share.'

Conferring a benefit is, of course, an equivalent to payment:...

Counsel for the defendants does not dispute the existence of the rule but challenges its application to the facts of this case. He submits that it is not a necessary inference or implication from the terms of the written guarantee that any benefit or protection was to be given to the Paos for their acceptance of the restriction on selling their shares. Their Lordships agree that the mere existence or recital of a prior request is not sufficient in itself to convert what is prima facie past consideration into sufficient consideration in law to support a promise: as they have indicated, it is only the first of three necessary preconditions. As for the second of those preconditions, whether the act done at the request of the promisor raises an implication of promised remuneration or other return is simply one of the construction of the words of the contract in the circumstances of its making. Once it is recognised, as the Board considers it inevitably must be, that the expressed consideration includes a reference to the Paos' promise not to sell the shares before 30th April 1974, a promise to be performed in the future, though given in the past, it is not possible to treat the Laus' promise of indemnity as independent of the Paos' antecedent promise, given at Lau's request, not to sell. The promise of indemnity was given because at the time of the main agreement the parties intended that Lau should confer on the Paos the benefit of his protection against a fall in price. When the subsidiary agreement was cancelled, all were well aware that the Paos were still to have the benefit of his protection as consideration for the restriction on selling. It matters not whether the indemnity thus given be regarded as the best evidence of the benefit intended to be conferred in return for the promise not to sell, or as the positive bargain which fixes the benefit on the faith of which the promise was given, though where, as here, the subject is a written contract, the better analysis is probably that of the 'positive bargain'. Their Lordships, therefore, accept the submission that the contract itself states a valid consideration for the promise of indemnity.

This being their Lordships' conclusion, it is unnecessary to consider the further submission of counsel for the plaintiffs (also raised for the first time before the Board) that the option given the Laus, if called on to fulfil their indemnity, to buy back the shares at $2.50 a share was itself a sufficient consideration for the promise of indemnity. But their Lordships see great force in the contention. The Laus promised to indemnify the plaintiffs if the market price of Fu Chip shares fell below $2.50. However, in the event of the Laus being called on to implement this promise they were given an option to take up the shares themselves at $2.50. This on the face of it imposes on the plaintiffs in the circumstances envisaged, an obligation to transfer the shares to the Laus at the price of $2.50 if called on to do so. The concomitant benefit to the Laus could be a real one, for example, if they thought that the market, after a temporary set-back, would recover to a price above $2.50. The fact that the option is stated in the form of a proviso does not preclude it being a contractual term or one under which consideration moves.

[His Lordship went on to hold that there was good consideration for the promise of indemnity despite the fact that the primary consideration was the promise given by the plaintiffs to the Laus to perform their contract with FC: a promise to perform, or the performance of, a pre-existing contractual obligation to a third party can be valid consideration. See p 108.]

Further extracts from this case will be found on p 908.

NOTES

1.   In what circumstances will it be inferred that the party who later made the promise was originally requesting the service on the understanding that it would be remunerated? To revert to the example of Bishop driving Beale home, suppose that Beale asks for the lift. Do you think the result might differ according to whether Bishop lives in Oxford or just outside Warwick?

2. Suppose the service is provided on the understanding that it is to be paid for, but Beale never makes any promise to pay. Can Bishop recover, and if so, how much?

3. In *Gilbert & Partners v Knight* [1968] 2 All ER 248, the parties agreed that the plaintiff surveyors would plan and supervise some alterations estimated to cost some £600, for a fee of £30. Later, the defendant decided to make the alterations more extensive and the total cost was £2,238. The surveyors supervised the work and claimed an additional fee (in effect, a scale fee) of £105. The Court of Appeal held that given that the defendant knew nothing of scale fees and had not been warned by the plaintiffs that an extra fee would be charged, there was no necessary implication that the defendant was going to pay extra, and she was not liable.

4. What would have been the outcome in *Gilbert v Knight* if the defendant had equally not realised that she would be asked to pay, but when the plaintiffs broached the matter she had said she would pay them £50 extra and had then failed to pay it?

IV. GRATUITOUS PROMISES AND BARGAINS

We have seen that a 'bargain', an agreed exchange of promises or of promise for act, is normally enforceable, but an informal gratuitous promise is not. What are the reasons for this difference? This is one of the questions explored in this part of the chapter. But we must note three preliminary points.

First, not all commentators accept the basic dichotomy between enforceable bargains and unenforceable gift promises. Professor Atiyah has argued that it is incorrect to think of the executory bargain (ie a bargain that has been agreed but which has not yet been acted on in any way by either party) as the central paradigm of contract law. He points out that 'wholly executory contracts are rarer, more ephemeral in practice and somewhat less binding than the Classical model would suggest'. For example, he argues that parties rarely sue for pure loss of profit and that, if they were to, their claims would often be reduced to nominal damages by the doctrine of mitigation. This prevents a party recovering for losses that might have been avoided by taking reasonable steps such as making a substitute contract with someone else. He goes on to ask whether it would not be better to see contractual liability as based not on the enforcement of bargains but on making the defendant pay for benefits he has received from the plaintiff and losses that the plaintiff has suffered in reliance on the contract.

Conversely, Atiyah argues that frequently English courts *do* enforce gratuitous promises that have been relied on in a way that the defendant foresaw might happen. This is explored in detail later in this chapter.

Both arguments are controversial; both are largely matters of interpretation. For what it is worth, it is your authors' view that Atiyah's argument that contractual liability should be seen as based on benefit and reliance gives insufficient weight to the cases in which the courts can, and do, give compensation for 'lost expectations' in addition to, or even in the absence of, benefit received by the defendant or reliance losses suffered by the plaintiff. We find the second argument much more convincing and in the last part of this chapter we will suggest that English law is now very close to recognising two separate bases of liability: consideration and reliance.

Before we do that, however, we would like to explore the apparent dichotomy between executory bargains and informal gift promises on which the promisee has not relied. A bargain is enforceable as soon as it is made; it is not necessary that the plaintiff should have relied on it. Why is the same not true of a gift promise?

This leads to the second point, which is that it is very important to be clear exactly what is being asked. It is easy to confuse the debate by comparing unlike situations. For example, in *Eastwood v Kenyon* (see p 141) Lord Denman gave as a reason for refusing to enforce a gratuitous promises that it would lead to

the frequent preference of voluntary undertakings to claims for just debts . . . voluntary undertakings would also be multiplied, to the prejudice of real creditors.

He seems to be referring to the problem that might well occur if the defendant has incurred two obligations, one under a bargain and the other a gift promise, and cannot pay both. There is then the question of whether one creditor has preference over the other, or whether they should be treated equally. What did Denman CJ have in mind when he spoke of 'just debts' and 'real creditors'? One suspects he had in mind the case of a debtor who is bankrupt and can pay his creditors only part of what is due to them. The creditors include people who have supplied goods and services to the bankrupt and haven't been paid for them. If this is right, it is easy to see that these creditors should be preferred to (ie paid before) one who simply hasn't received some gift the bankrupt promised him. But that isn't comparing like with like, because in the case of the 'normal creditor' there is reliance by the creditor and probably benefit to the debtor, whereas both are absent in the case of the gift promise (assuming, as we are, that the promise has not been relied on). If, however, the contest is between a person who was promised a gift and a bargain creditor who is simply claiming the profit he would have made if the bargain had been carried out, it is rather less clear that one claim is more 'just' or 'real' than the other.

The third preliminary point is that it is very easy to make even a promise to make a gift binding.

Firstly, a gift promise is enforceable if it is made by deed. Traditionally, the deed had to bear a seal, although this came to mean no more than that the document bore some reference to a seal or 'being sealed': a typical example is shown on p 131. In its Working Paper No 93, *Transfer of Land: Formalities for Deeds and Escrows* (1985), the Law Commission said:

4.2 In practice, sealing today is for most individuals a meaningless exercise involving sticking a small circle of red adhesive paper onto the document. It is probably not fixed to the document by the grantor himself, but by his solicitor. As long ago as 1937 it was said that ' . . . a seal nowadays is very much in the nature of a legal fiction . . . It is the party's signature, and not his seal, which in fact authenticates the document . . .' More recently Lord Wilberforce has suggested the removal of 'this medieval doctrine of the seal'. He continued ' . . . sealing is now a completely fictitious matter . . . I would have hoped that we might have got rid of that mumbo-jumbo and aligned ourselves with most other civilised countries.'

4.3 Quite apart from the lack of any reason of substance for requiring a seal, the law as to what constitutes a valid seal is still unclear. The Court of Appeal in *First National Securities Ltd v Jones* held that a document which had no wax or water seal but which had a circle with the letters 'L.S.' printed on it was capable of being a deed. It was sufficient that the document purported to be a deed and indicated where the seal should be.

It proposed instead that deeds should have to be witnessed. Its final recommendations (Report No 163, *Deeds and Escrows*, HC1, 1987) led to legislation.

FORM 2

To be returned with Form 1

University of Bristol
Alumni Foundation

ANNUAL GIFTS

DEED OF COVENANT

Please insert full name and address

I (Professor/Dr/Mr/Mrs/Miss) ....
of ....

hereby covenant with the University of Bristol that for four years from the date hereof or during my life if shorter, I will pay to the University of Bristol on the ..... *day of .... in each year such sum as after deduction of income tax at the standard rate for the time being in force will amount to £. .....†

Signed, sealed and delivered

Donor's signature ....
Date ....

in the presence of
Signature of witness ....
Address of witness ....

Notes: *This date must be the same as or later than the date on which this deed is signed.
†Enter here the actual amount which you wish to give annually.

■ Law of Property (Miscellaneous Provisions) Act 1989

Section 1: Deeds and their execution

(1) Any rule of law which
    (a) restricts the substances on which a deed may be written;
    (b) requires a seal for the valid execution of an instrument as a deed by an individual; or
    (c) requires authority by one person to another to deliver an instrument as a deed on his behalf to be given by deed,
is abolished.

(2) An instrument shall not be a deed unless
    (a) it makes it clear on its face that it is intended to be a deed by the person making it or, as the case may be, by the parties to it (whether by describing itself as a deed or expressing itself to be executed or signed as a deed or otherwise); and
    (b) it is validly executed as a deed by that person or, as the case may be, one or more of those parties.

(3) An instrument is validly executed as a deed by an individual if, and only if
    (a) it is signed
        (i) by him in the presence of a witness who attests the signature; or
        (ii) at his direction and in his presence and the presence of two witnesses who each attest the signature; and
    (b) it is delivered as a deed by him or a person authorised to do so on his behalf.

(4) In subsections (2) and (3) above 'sign', in relation to an instrument, includes making one's mark on the instrument and 'signature' is to be construed accordingly.

. . .

(11) Nothing in this section applies in relation to instruments delivered as deeds before this section comes into force.

It is quite likely that seals will continue to be used; their presence will not invalidate deeds. You will find that some of the readings that follow refer to sealed documents.

Secondly, a gift promise can be made enforceable by employing the device of nominal consideration, so that the promise is ostensibly exchanged for £1 or a peppercorn. The enforcement of promises made for merely nominal consideration may seem to follow from the law's (supposed) refusal to investigate the adequacy of consideration, but it is not a necessary consequence. It would be possible for the law to differentiate between exchanges that were bargains, even though the items exchanged were not apparently of equal value, and 'sham' bargains, gift promises merely cast into the form of bargains. Such distinctions could be very difficult, but just this sort of distinction has to be made frequently in tax cases. This is also the approach taken by Restatement 2d s 75 comment (b): '. . . a mere pretence of bargain does not suffice, as where there is a false recital of consideration or where the consideration is purely nominal.' It remains to be seen whether this lead will be followed by the US courts.

Why are gift promises by deed and promises for merely nominal consideration treated differently from gift promises made without such formalities? Why are bargains normally (but see p 143) enforceable without the need to comply with any formal requirements?

■ Fuller 'Consideration and Form' (1941)

31 Col LR 799 at 800–806, 822–823

THE FUNCTIONS PERFORMED BY LEGAL FORMALITIES

The evidentiary function. The most obvious function of a legal formality is, to use Austin's words, that of providing 'evidence of the existence and purport of the contract, in case of controversy'. The need for evidentiary security may be satisfied in a variety of ways: by requiring a writing, or attestation, or the certification of a notary. It may even be satisfied, to some extent, by such a device as the Roman *stipulatio*, which compelled an oral spelling out of the promise in a manner sufficiently ceremonious to impress its terms on participants and possible bystanders.

The cautionary function. A formality may also perform a cautionary or deterrent function by acting as a check against inconsiderate action. The seal in its original form fulfilled this purpose remarkably well. The affixing and impressing of a wax wafer— symbol in the popular mind of legalism and weightiness— was an excellent device for inducing the circumspective frame of mind appropriate in one pledging his future. To a less extent any requirement of a writing, of course, serves the same purpose, as do requirements of attestation, notarization, etc.

The channeling function. Though most discussions of the purposes served by formalities go no further than the analysis just presented, this analysis stops short of recognizing one of the most important functions of form. That a legal formality may perform a function not yet described can be shown by the seal. The seal not only insures a satisfactory memorial of the promise and induces deliberation in the making of it. It serves also to mark or signalize the enforceable promise; it furnishes a simple and external test of enforceability. This function of form Ihering described as 'the facilitation of judicial diagnosis', and he employed the analogy of coinage in explaining it.

> 'Form is for a legal transaction what the stamp is for a coin. Just as the stamp of the coin relieves us from the necessity of testing the metallic content and weight—in short, the value of the coin (a test which we could not avoid if uncoined metal were offered to us in payment), in the same way legal formalities relieve the judge of an inquiry *whether* a legal transaction was intended, and—in case different forms are fixed for different legal transactions—*which* was intended.'

In this passage it is apparent that Ihering has placed an undue emphasis on the utility of form for the judge, to the neglect of its significance for those transacting business out of court ... To the business man who wishes to make his own or another's promise binding, the seal was at common law available as a device for the accomplishment of his objective. In this aspect form offers a legal framework into which the party may fit his actions, or, to change the figure, it offers channels for the legally effective expression of intention. It is with this aspect of form in mind that I have described the third function of legal formalities, as 'the channeling function'.

Interrelations of the three functions. Though I have stated the three functions of legal form separately, it is obvious that there is an intimate connection between them. Generally speaking, whatever tends to accomplish one of these purposes will also tend to accomplish the other two. He who is compelled to do something which will furnish a satisfactory memorial of his intention will be induced to deliberate. Conversely, devices which induce deliberation will usually have an evidentiary value. Devices which insure evidence or prevent inconsiderateness will normally advance the desideratum of channeling, in two different ways. In the first place, he who is compelled to formulate his intention carefully will tend to fit it into legal and business categories. In this way the party is induced to canalize his own intention. In the second place, wherever the requirement of a formality is backed by the sanction of the invalidity of the informal transaction (and this is the means by which requirements of form are normally made effective), a degree of channeling results automatically. Whatever may be its legislative motive, the formality in such a case tends to effect a categorization of transactions into legal and non-legal.

Just as channeling may result unintentionally from formalities directed toward other ends, so these other ends tend to be satisfied by any device which accomplishes a channeling of expression. There is an evidentiary value in the clarity and definiteness of contour which such a device accomplishes. Anything which effects a neat division between the legal and the non-legal, or between different kinds of legal transactions, will tend also to make apparent to the party the consequences of his action and will suggest deliberation where deliberation is needed. . . .

Despite the close interrelationship of the three functions of form, it is necessary to keep the distinctions between them in mind since the disposition of borderline cases of compliance may turn on our assumptions as to the end primarily sought by a particular formality. . . .

When are formalities needed? The effect of an informal satisfaction of the desiderata underlying the use of formalities. The analysis of the functions of legal form which has just been presented is useful in answering a question which will assume importance in the later portion of this discussion when a detailed treatment of consideration is undertaken. That question is: In what situations does good legislative policy demand the use of a legal formality? One part of the answer to the question is clear at the outset. Forms must be reserved for relatively important transactions. We must preserve a proportion between means and end; it will scarcely do to require a sealed and witnessed document for the effective sale of a loaf of bread.

But assuming that the transaction in question is of sufficient importance to support the use of a form if a form is needed, how is the existence of this need to be determined? A general answer would run somewhat as follows: *The need for investing a particular transaction with some legal formality will depend upon the extent to which the guaranties that the formality would afford are rendered superfluous by forces native to the situation out of which the transaction arises*—including in these 'forces' the habits and conceptions of the transacting parties.

Whether there is any need, for example, to set up a formality designed to induce deliberation will depend upon the degree to which the factual situation, innocent of any legal remolding, tends to bring about the desired circumspective frame of mind. An example from the law of gifts will make this point clear. To accomplish an effective gift of a chattel without resort to the use of documents, delivery of the chattel is ordinarily required and mere donative words are ineffective. It is thought, among other things, that mere words do not sufficiently impress on the donor the significance and seriousness of his act. In an Oregon case, however, the donor declared his intention to give a sum of money to the donee and at the same time disclosed to the donee the secret hiding place where he had placed the money. Though the whole donative act consisted merely of words, the court held the gift to be effective. The words which gave access to the money which the donor had so carefully concealed would presumably be accomplished by the same sense of present deprivation which the act of handing over the money would have produced. The situation contained its own guaranty against inconsiderateness.

So far as the channeling function of a formality is concerned it has no place where men's activities are already divided into definite, clear-cut business categories. Where life has already organized itself effectively, there is no need for the law to intervene. It is for this reason that important transactions on the stock and produce markets can safely be carried on in the most 'informal' manner. At the other extreme we may cite the negotiations between a house-to-house book salesman and the housewife. Here the situation may be such that the housewife is not certain whether she is being presented with a set of books as a gift, whether she is being asked to trade her letter of recommendation for the books, whether the books are being offered to her on approval, or whether—what is, alas, the fact—a simple sale of the books is being proposed. The ambiguity of the situation is, of course, carefully cultivated and exploited by the canvasser. Some 'channeling' here would be highly desirable, though whether a legal form is the most practicable means of bringing it about is, of course, another question.

NOTES

1.   How far are Fuller's three functions fulfilled in the case of:

(1) a witnessed deed promising to pay £100?

(2) a promise in a letter written in the promisor's own handwriting and signed by her?

    (3) a promise by a company to sell some used office equipment to a charitable organisation for £1 when both sides know the equipment is worth at least £1,000?

2.   Fuller argues that sometimes the inherent nature or circumstances of the transaction will ensure that the three functions are adequately fulfilled without need for formalities. To what extent is this the case with:

    (1) a bargain that has been performed on one side, for example a contract for the sale of goods where the goods have been delivered but not paid for?

    (2) a bargain that is wholly executory, neither party having performed yet?

    (3) a promise by a woman to a bank to guarantee her son-in-law's overdraft?

3.   For further reading, see Dawson, *Gifts and Promises*, 1980, especially chapter 4; Hamson, 'The Reform of Consideration' (1938) 54 LQR 233.

Is the doctrine of consideration nothing but a form with which the parties must comply? Or are there substantive reasons for enforcing bargains more readily than gratuitous promises? This is connected with the question of the overall justification for the law of contract. This is treated more fully in Section 6 but it is worth introducing some of the main themes at this point.

Some commentators have suggested that contract is based on the moral duty to keep a promise. The American writer Fried has argued that the basis of contract is the moral obligation to keep promises, or at least those that have been accepted by the promisee. This approach seems to suggest that any promise that was seriously meant and was accepted should be enforceable. Fried does not claim that his theory is consistent with the doctrine of consideration: he rejects it as unnecessary (*Contract as Promise*, chapter 6).

Atiyah's argument that contractual liability may be better seen as grounded on making the defendant pay for benefits received and for losses incurred by the plaintiff in reliance on the contract has already been mentioned. It is related to the argument made in 1936 by Fuller and Perdue that the primary aim of contract law is to facilitate reliance and that compensation for loss of expectation (and thus damages for breach of a purely executory contract) are awarded only because this is easier in administrative terms, and therefore more effective, than compensating for reliance only.

Economists have offered separate rationales for enforcing bargains on the one hand and gratuitous promises on the other.

■ Posner, *Economic Analysis of Law* (2nd edn, 1977)

s 4.2

The principle that a promise, to be enforceable, must be supported by 'consideration' is used to deny liability for breach of a promise mainly in two types of cases. The first is where there is no exchange and where, therefore, enforcement of the promise would not advance the economic purpose of the law of contracts, which is to facilitate exchange. A truly gratuitous promise, nonreciprocal promise is not part of the process by which resources are moved, through a series of exchanges, into successively more valuable

For a further extract from this section of Posner's book, see p 170.

■ **Posner, *'Gratuitous Promises in Economics and Law'*** (1977)
6 JLS 411 at 411–415, 419–420

THE ECONOMICS OF 'GRATUITOUS' PROMISES

Why would 'economic man' ever make a promise without receiving in exchange something of value from the promisee, whether it be money, a promise of future performance beneficial to the promisor, or something else of value to him? It is tempting to answer this question simply by invoking 'interdependent utilities'. Since people may indeed derive utility or welfare from increases in the utility or welfare of family members, or for that matter of strangers, interdependence may explain why (some) gifts or transfers are made. But it cannot explain why a *promise* to make a transfer in the future is made. . . .

[I]f A wanted merely to transfer $25,000 to B (his favourite charity), why would he *promise* B to make the transfer in the future? Why not wait until he is ready to make the transfer and just do it? The purpose of a promise seems to be to induce performance of some sort by the promisee; if reciprocal performance is not desired, there seems no reason to make a promise.

The approach taken here is that a gratuitous promise, to the extent it actually commits the promisor to the promised course of action (an essential qualification), creates utility for the promisor over and above the utility to him of the promised performance. At one level this proposition is a tautology: a promise would not be made unless it conferred utility on the promisor. The interesting question is how it does so. I shall argue that it does so by increasing the present value of an uncertain future stream of transfer payments.

To illustrate, suppose A promises to give $1000 a year for the next 20 years to the B symphony orchestra. The value of the gift to B is the discounted present value of $ 1000 to be paid yearly over a 20-year period in the future. Among the factors that will be used by B in discounting these expected future receipts to present value is the likelihood that at some time during the 20-year period A will discontinue the annual payments. Depending on B's estimation of A's fickleness, income prospects, etc, the present value of the gift of $1000 a year may be quite small; it may not be much more than $1000. But suppose the gift is actually worth more to B because A is certain to continue the payments throughout the entire period, though this fact is not known to B. If A can make a binding promise to continue the payments in accordance with his intention, B will revalue the gift at its true present worth. The size of the gift (in present-value terms) will be increased at no cost to A. Here is a clear case where the enforcement of a gratuitous promise would increase net social welfare.

This can be seen even more clearly by considering A's alternatives if his promise is not enforceable. One possibility would be for A to promise a larger gift, the discounted value of which to B would be equal to the true value as known to A. The higher cost of the gift to A would be a measure of the social cost of the unenforceability of his promise. Another possibility would be for A to substitute for the promised series of future transfers a one-time transfer the present value of which would be the same as that of the series of enforceable future transfers. However, the fact that A preferred making a future gift to a present one suggests that they are not perfect substitutes; there are many reasons (including tax and liquidity considerations) why they might not be. Consequently, if A cannot bind himself to make a series of future gifts, he may be led to substitute a one-time transfer, the present value of which is less than that of the series of future gifts, although greater than that of a declared but unenforceable intention to make a series of future gifts. Thus, nonenforceability of gratuitous promises could tend to bias transfers excessively toward immediacy.

The above analysis rests on the assumption of a symmetry of information between promisor and promisee. Such an assumption may seem implausible: why would not the asymmetry be corrected by a simple communication from A to B, which would make both parties better off? However, because the relevant information concerns A's subjective intentions, the asymmetry is both plausible and difficult to eliminate. A can state his true intentions to B, but how is he to convince B that the statement is correct? One way of making his statement credible is for A to make it costly for himself to lie; embodying the statement in a promise that is legally enforceable does this.

. . . Suppose that A really is fickle and B assesses his fickleness accurately. There is then no asymmetry in the information possessed by the parties. But A may still want to make a gift having a present value that is larger than it would be if B's future receipts had to be discounted by the probability that A would actually make each payment when the time came to do so. A will balance the utility to him of making a larger (in present-value terms) gift now against the disutility of losing the freedom to change his mind in the future. He may decide that the utility of the larger gift now is greater, in which event it will be in his self-interest to make a promise that commits him irrevocably. Once again, enforcement of a gratuitous promise will lead to a net increase in social welfare.

The economic case for enforcing the gratuitous promise, it should be noted, is similar to that for enforcing bilateral promises. The failure to enforce bilateral promises would bias exchanges toward those that take place instantaneously, as distinct from those that are completed only over a period of time, even though the former may often be less valuable (as in our examples), or more costly, than the deferred exchange. But the symmetry between gratuitous and bilateral promises has been obscured in conventional legal analysis by a tendency to view a promise as a pure cost to the promisor, a limitation on his freedom of action and nothing more.

[T]his analysis ignores the fact that being legally bound to make an intended transfer may enhance ex ante the value of the transfer to A and thereby increase the social product, just as in the case of bilateral promises.

One may doubt in light of the foregoing analysis whether the term 'gratuitous' promise is useful or even meaningful. To make a binding promise may, as we have seen, be rational maximizing behavior even in the absence of consideration flowing from the promisee. The *source* of the benefit to the promisor would seem a detail from the standpoint of whether particular promises should be enforced by the law.

OPTIMAL RULES FOR ENFORCING 'GRATUITOUS' PROMISES

The analysis in Part I may seem to imply that *all* promises, whether compensated or 'gratuitous', should be enforced; or at least that enforceability should not depend on whether the promise is one or the other. The second implication has, as we shall see, appeal; but the first is questionable because it ignores the costs to the legal system of enforcing promises. The design of optimal rules of substantive law must always take into account the costs of enforcement. Promises should not be enforced where the enforcement cost—to the extent not borne by the promisor—exceeds the gain from enforcement. The qualification is, of course, essential; if the promisor bore the full costs of enforcement, it would be a matter of indifference to society whether he chose to make enforceable a promise that seemed to confer on him but trivial utility relative to enforcement costs. But it is in fact unlikely—quite apart from the public subsidy of the court system—that such a promisor would bear those costs fully: if he reneged on his promise, and the promisee brought suit against him, the promisor would not be required to defray the promisee's costs of suit. Another category of enforcement costs that are not fully internalized consists of the costs of legal error. Here the focus is not on the promisor but on the mistaken or dishonest 'promisee' who imposes on his 'promisor' the costs of defending a groundless suit, at the same time incurring litigation costs of his own which have no social value either.

The question whether it is economical for society to recognize a promise as legally enforceable thus requires a comparison of the utility of the promise to the promisor with the social cost of enforcing the promise.

. . . The social costs of enforcing the promise depend first of all on the administrative costs of enforcement. These in turn are a function in part of the size of the promised transfer, for expenditures on litigation are an investment in its outcome and therefore tend to be larger, the greater the stakes in the litigation. The social costs of enforcement also depend on the likelihood of an error—eg of finding a promise where none in fact was made. . . .

Promises under seal

Promises under seal are a traditional and, again, an economically appropriate exception to the requirement that an enforceable promise must be supported by consideration. The requirement of the seal eliminates the major administrative costs associated with the enforcement of unilateral promises. The formalities and written character of the promise reduce both the costs of determining the content of the promise and the probability that the promise was not made or was not intended to be binding.

NOTES

1.   Posner is writing of American law, and his point that the promisor who is successfully sued by a promisee does not have to pay the latter's costs of suit refers to the American practice of not awarding costs. Even in England, however, it is rare that the winning party recovers his or her full costs.

2.   If a person covenants to pay a sum of money to a charity but then defaults, how likely is it that the charity will sue? If the answer is 'not at all likely', does that affect Posner's analysis?

3.   Posner's analysis suggests that a person who makes a purely gratuitous promise may well derive a benefit thereby. Yet it is firmly established that a gratuitous promise is without consideration. Is this an example of a benefit to the promisor that does not move from the promisee and therefore does not amount to consideration? (See pp 97–98.)

4.   There is a considerable literature on 'gift' promises. A useful survey will be found in Eisenberg, 'The World of Contract and the World of Gift' (1997) 85 California LR 821. Eisenberg argues that donative promises, promises that are made for 'affective reasons like love . . . or to satisfy moral duties or aspirations like benevolence or generosity', and which are 'not expressly conditioned on a reciprocal exchange', should be distinguished from other gratuitous promises 'which lie in the hard-headed world of contract, like promises to hold an offer open for a fixed period of time' (pp 823–824). (On promises to hold open offers, see pp 249–254.) Eisenberg argues that to enforce simple donative promises

> would move the commodity [promised] rather than the relationship to the forefront, would essentially convert the gift promise into a cash equivalent, and would submerge the affective relationship that the gift was intended to totemise. Simple donative promises would be degraded into bills of exchange . . . the principle that simple donative promises are unenforceable does not show that the law fails to value donative promises. Just the opposite is true. The principle that simple donative promises are unenforceable is justified not because donative promises are less important than bargain promises, but because they are more important. The world of gift is a world of our better selves . . . affective values like love . . . would be undermined if the enforcement of simple affective donative promises were to be mandated by law (pp 848–849). . . . It is also wrong for the promisee [of a donative promise] to insist on performance, because under the morality of aspiration, where a donative promise is made for affective reasons, the donative promisee is normally obliged to release a repenting promisor (p 849).

What are we to make of these various arguments? The 'doctrine' of consideration seems to say that only a bargain is enforceable; yet a gratuitous promise may be enforceable if the device of nominal consideration is employed or if a deed is used. It is hard to come up with a clear rationale for the doctrine.

We noted earlier (p 135) that a simple argument that a promise is morally binding (see, eg, p 778) is very hard to reconcile with the doctrine. Could it be based on a different argument that a promise which has been paid for, in some sense, ought to be performed, whereas a gratuitous one need not? (There might be other reasons also for making gratuitous promises binding, see p 135.) The difficulty is that this does not explain the binding nature of deeds and contracts for nominal consideration.

Fuller (see p 133) suggests that consideration provides similar safeguards as do formal requirements. There is clearly something in this, but it does not seem an adequate explanation. We may be prepared to enforce a gratuitous promise when it is put into a particular form, including the 'form' of giving it nominal consideration, but is the fact that the promisor is to get something, however little, in exchange for the promise an adequate safeguard against a rash promise? Nor does Fuller's explanation seem to fit with the rhetoric of bargain that is found in the cases: this suggests that the question is one of substance, not just one of form.

Conversely, the argument that bargains are part of the process of wealth creation (see p 135) and should be enforced, whereas gift promises are not, also fails to explain deeds and nominal consideration.

Professor Atiyah (see pp 135 and 771; see also a different piece by Fuller, p 765) seems to come close to arguing that the law is really based on the harm principle: that is, that a promise is binding when the promisor has received a benefit from the promisee or the promise has been relied on by the promisee, who would now lose if the promise is broken. But it is clear that a purely executory contract is binding, even if it is relatively rare to find a plaintiff seeking to enforce one. This is not consistent with the harm principle.

Perhaps, at the end of the day, we have to conclude that the ideas underlying consideration are not coherent, or that the doctrine is based on a number of different strands—eg encouraging economically valuable transactions (without checking that each one actually is value-maximising) while at the same time allowing people to commit themselves to gratuitous promises, provided they make it clear what they are doing and (assuming the formal devices are effective in their apparent cautionary purpose) that they think about what they are doing.

V. MORAL OBLIGATION

Before we consider the case of the gratuitous promise that has been relied on, are there other promises that should be enforced without consideration? Suppose a bankrupt who has been discharged promises one of his erstwhile creditors that he will pay the discharged debt; that a minor who obtained goods on credit and was not liable for them because they were not 'necessaries' (see p 951) on coming of age promises to pay the supplier; or that a debtor whose liability is barred under the Limitation Act promises to pay his creditor after all?

At one time, each of these three promises would have been binding in English law. Lord Mansfield held that, in such cases of a liability that was unenforceable because of a technical rule of law, the existence of a moral obligation to pay was sufficient.

Where a man is under a moral obligation, which no Court of Law of Equity can inforce, and promises, the honesty and rectitude of the thing is a consideration. As if a man promises to pay a just debt, the recovery of which is barred by the Statute of Limitations: or if a man, after he comes of age, promises to pay a meritorious debt contracted during his minority, but not for necessaries; or if a bankrupt, in affluent circumstances after his certificate, promises to pay the whole of his debts...In such and many other instances, though the promise gives a compulsory remedy, where there was none before either in law or equity; yet as the promise is only to do what an honest man ought to do, the ties of conscience upon an upright mind are a sufficient consideration. (*Hawkes v Saunders* (1782) 1 Cowp 289, at 290.)

Historically, there was support for this doctrine (see Simpson, *History of the Common Law of Contract*, 1975, p 323). In *Sharp v Ellis, Re Edward Love & Co Pty Ltd* [1972] VR 137, an Australian judge refused to extend it to a case in which a company subsequently promised to pay a debt that when it was contracted, was void by statute because it was ultra vires, but the doctrine enunciated by Mansfield has never formally been overruled. In many of the US states, it is still in force (see Farnsworth, *Contracts*, pp 53–54), and as the next reading suggests, there is something to be said for it.

■ Posner, 'Gratuitous Promises in Economics and Law' (1977)
6 JLS 411, 411–415, 417–418, 421–424, at 418

Past consideration

Among the exceptions to the general principle that gratutitous promises will not be enforced are several which are grouped under the rubric of 'past consideration'. A subsequent promise to pay a debt barred by the statute of limitations, or to pay a debt discharged in bankruptcy, or to pay a debt that is uncollectable because the debtor was a minor at the time the debt was contracted, is legally enforceable even though there is no fresh consideration for the promise. These are classes of promise in which the utility of the promise to the promisor is often great and the costs of enforcement low. First, as regards utility, it should be noted not only that the stakes are often substantial (these are formal debts after all) but that the *incremental* gain in utility from the enforceable character of the promise may be great. The legal promise conveys information (which a mere stated intention to pay would not) about the promisor's attitude toward the payment of debts barred by a technicality. The information conveyed enhances the promisor's reputation for credit-worthiness and may induce people—not necessarily the promisee himself, which is why the promise itself may not be bilateral—to extend credit to him in the future. And enforcement costs are likely to be low or at least no higher than in conventional bilateral-contract cases because the underlying obligation—the original debt—is fully bilateral. The original debt is not directly enforceable only because of a condition which in the case of the statute of limitations slightly, and in the case of discharge in bankruptcy or voidability by reason of minority not at all, increases the likelihood of error compared to what it would have been in a suit on the original bilateral contract that gave rise to the debt.

However, in English law the rule has been changed by a statute in two of the three situations: Bankruptcy Act 1869, s 4, and see *Heather &Son v Webb* (1876) 2 CPD 1; Limitation Act 1980, s 29(7). Now the promisor will only be liable if there is fresh consideration for the promise. Why have these changes been made? Since the changes are statutory, they are unlikely to be the result of a quest for doctrinal purity. What policies underlie the statutes? You may like to consider *Wild v Tucker* [1914] 3 KB 36; Law Reform Committee, 21st Report, *Final Report on Limitation of Actions*, Cmnd 6923 (1977) paras 2.68–2.71.

For many years, promises to perform obligations incurred in infancy were also invalidated by the Infants Relief Act 1874, s 2. This may have given young adults some protection against being pressured into promising to perform, but the restrictions were easily evaded because they did not apply to 'fresh contracts' to perform the previously unenforceable bargains (except for fresh contracts to repay loans incurred in infancy, which were invalidated by the Betting and Loans (Infants) Act 1892, s 5). Thus if the creditor gave some fresh consideration, however small, to the young adult, the latter's promise would be binding. The Law Commission thought it illogical to distinguish between fresh promises and fresh contracts (see Report No 184, *Law of Contract: Minors' Contracts*, 1984) and both the Infants Relief Act 1874, s 2, and the Betting and Loans (Infants) Act 1892, s 5, were repealed by the Minors' Contracts Act 1987, s 1. Thus the old common law, whereby a promise made to perform an obligation incurred in infancy is binding without fresh consideration, was revived.

Could the moral obligation doctrine be broadened to cover the case of a benefit that the promisee has earlier conferred gratuitously on the promisor?

In *Webb v McGowin* 27 Ala App 82, 168 So 196 (1935), Webb was in the act of dropping a pine block from the upper floor of a sawmill (this being the accepted procedure) when McGowin stepped where the block would have fallen. Webb kept hold of the block and fell with it, preventing it hitting McGowin but himself receiving injuries that crippled him for life. A month later, McGowin promised to support Webb for the rest of Webb's life at a rate of $15 every two weeks, but after McGowin's death eight years later, the payments were discontinued. The Court of Appeals of Alabama held that the benefit received by McGowin was sufficient consideration. In contrast, in *Harrington v Taylor* 225 NC 690, 36 SE 2d 227 (1945), the defendant had assaulted his wife, who took refuge in the plaintiff's house. The next day, the defendant gained access to the house and began another assault on his wife. The wife knocked down the defendant with an axe and was on the point of cutting his head open or decapitating him while he lay on the floor when the plaintiff intervened, catching the axe as it descended. The defendant's life was saved but the plaintiff's hand was badly mutilated. The defendant subsequently promised to pay the plaintiff her loss, but after paying a small sum failed to pay any more. The Supreme Court of North Carolina held that the promise was without consideration.

At present, English courts could not achieve the result in *Webb v McGowin* without overruling venerable authority.

■ *Eastwood v Kenyon*

(1840) 11 Ad & El 438, 113 ER 482, Queen's Bench

John Sutcliffe had died, leaving his infant daughter Sarah as his sole heiress. The plaintiff, Sutcliffe's executor, acted as her guardian and spent money on her education and improving her estate, borrowing £140 for these purposes. When she came of age, Sarah promised to pay the plaintiff the amount of the loan, and when she married, her husband, the defendant, made a similar promise. The plaintiff sued on the husband's promise. The Court of Queen's Bench held the promise to be unenforceable. **Lord Denman CJ** said:

Most of the older cases on this subject are collected in a learned note to the case of *Wennall v Adney*, and the conclusion there arrived at seems to be correct in general, 'that an express promise can only revive a good consideration, which might have been enforced at law through the medium of an implied promise, had it not been suspended by some positive rule of law; but can give no original cause of action, if the obligation, on which it is founded, never could have been enforced at law, though not barred by any legal maxim or statute provision'. Instances are given of voidable contracts, as those of infants ratified by an express promise after age, and distinguished from void contracts, as of married women, not capable of ratification by them when widows; *Loyd v Lee;* debts of bankrupts revived by subsequent promise after certificate; and similar cases....

The eminent counsel who argued for the plaintiff in *Lee v Muggeridge*, spoke of Lord Mansfield as having considered the rule of nudum pactum as too narrow, and maintained that all promises deliberately made ought to be held binding. I do not find this language ascribed to him by any reporter, and do not know whether we are to receive it as a traditional report, or as a deduction from what he does appear to have laid down. If the latter, the note to *Wennall v Adney*, shews the deduction to be erroneous. If the former, Lord Tenterden and this Court declared that they could not adopt it in *Littlefield v Shee*. Indeed the doctrine would annihilate the necessity for any consideration at all, inasmuch as the mere fact of giving a promise creates a moral obligation to perform it.

The enforcement of such promises by law, however plausibly reconciled by the desire to effect all conscientious engagements, might be attended with mischievous consequences to society; one of which would be the frequent preference of voluntary undertakings to claims for just debts. Suits would thereby be multiplied, and voluntary undertakings would also be multiplied, to the prejudice of real creditors.

The temptations of executors would be much increased by the prevalence of such a doctrine, and the faithful discharge of their duty be rendered more difficult.

NOTE

Why is this kind of voluntary undertaking less deserving than a 'just debt'? Compare p 137.

■ Posner, 'Gratuitous Promises...' (1977)
6 JLS 411, at 418–419

Another class of 'past consideration' cases, however, is best understood on the premise of the law's (implicit) recognition of the existence of interdependent utility functions. These are cases involving promises to compensate rescuers or others who have rendered an unbargained but valuable service to the promisor. The existence of a promise in such a case is strongly attested by the presence of circumstances likely to induce an act of altruism by the promisor toward the promisee. A sees B about to be run down by a speeding car and pushes him out of the way. He saves him but sustains a serious injury in the process. In economic terms. A rescued B because at the moment of danger B's expected utility or wealth was very low; the rescue was like a gift to a starving man. But after the rescue the wealth positions of the parties are dramatically reversed: now A's wealth is low relative to B's since B is whole and A is injured. Hence it is to be expected that B would promise to reward A. The presence of altruistic motivation makes the promise a more plausible one—ie, one less likely to be a figment of the promisee's imagination—than in the standard unilateral promise case. Stated otherwise, the legal-error costs of enforcing the promise are lower in the rescue case.

The facts of a leading rescue past consideration case, *Webb v McGowin*, illustrate the benefits that may accrue to the promisor in such cases if the promise is legally enforceable, over and above the benefits of the transfer itself. The rescued person promised to pay his rescuer $15 every two weeks for the rest of the rescuer's life. This was a generous gift to the extent that the promise was enforceable but a much less generous one to the extent it was not. Had the promisor believed that such a promise was unenforceable, he might have decided instead to make a one-time transfer that might have had a much lower present value than that of the annuity which he in fact promised. Both parties would have been made worse off by this alternative. Hence, it is not surprising that the court held the promise to be enforceable.

NOTES

1. Posner presents apparently persuasive reasons for enforcing the promise in *Webb v McGowin*, but can you see any reasons against enforcing the promise as if it had been made for consideration? Firstly, suppose McGowin had, immediately after the accident, promised Webb a sum that McGowin could pay only by making himself destitute? Were the circumstances in which McGowin made his promise such that the 'cautionary function' was automatically fulfilled?

2. Secondly, suppose that after McGowin had paid Webb for some months, circumstances changed—perhaps McGowin himself had to stop work because of ill health, or the state introduced a scheme of industrial injury benefits that covered Webb. Should McGowin's promise still be enforced? If it ranked as a normal contract, would it still be enforceable?

3. In the light of the last question, do you think that it may have been significant that in *Webb v McGowin* the defendant was McGowin's executor, whereas in *Harrington v Taylor* the defendant had made the promise himself?

4. If you think it may not be appropriate to impose normal contractual liability in a case such as *Webb v McGowin*, is there some other basis on which it might be done? Sometimes the rescued person was negligent in putting himself into a dangerous situation and should have foreseen that someone might try to rescue him and get injured in the process. In such a case, the rescuer may recover for her injuries in tort, quite irrespective of whether the rescued person has promised her anything (see *Horsley v MacLaren* [1971] 2 Lloyds Rep 410, Sup Ct of Canada; *Ogwo v Taylor* [1988] AC 431).

5. If the rescued person has not been negligent, no tort action will lie. Might the plaintiff recover in restitution? Compare this type of case to the restitution cases considered earlier (p 41). It may well be correct to deny restitution to the 'officious intermeddler' when the defendant has never indicated any willingness to pay for the benefit conferred on him; if he does indicate that he is willing to pay by promising to pay the rescuer something, even if only subsequently, why deny recovery?

You may like to consider Restatement 2d s 86:

Promise for benefit received

(1) A promise made in recognition of a benefit previously received by the promisor from the promisee is binding to the extent necessary to prevent injustice.

(2) A promise is not binding under subsection (1)

  (a) if the promisee conferred the benefit as a gift or for other reasons the promisor has not been unjustly enriched; or

  (b) to the extent that its value is disproportionate to the benefit.

The reporter, the late Professor Robert Braucher, conceded that the section 'bristles with non-specific concepts' (42 ALI Procs 273–274, 1965). For an analysis of the US cases, see Thel and Yorio (1992) 78 Yale L J 1045.

VI. FORMAL REQUIREMENTS

Fuller's three functions of form are, as we have seen, fulfilled to some extent in the case of even a wholly executory bilateral contract, but the safeguards may not be adequate. Many businessmen seem to believe that no contract is binding unless it is in writing, or at least that without writing it is practically unenforceable—witness Samuel Goldwyn's famous aphorism, 'a verbal contract isn't worth the paper it's written on'.

As a matter of law, the general rule is that oral contracts are fully enforceable, but there are certain types of contract that must either be in writing or be evidenced in writing. For example:

(i) *Contracts which must be in writing*. The Law of Property (Miscellaneous Provisions) Act 1989, s 2(1) provides:

A contract for the sale or other disposition of an interest in land can only be made in writing and only by incorporating all the terms which the parties have expressly agreed . . .

Under the Consumer Credit Act 1974, various types of agreement must be in a particular written form if they are to be 'properly executed' and thus fully enforceable (see p 950). Bills of exchange, promissory notes and bills of sale must also be in writing (Bills of Exchange Act 1882, ss 3(1), 17(2); Bills of Sale Act (1878) Amendment Act 1882).

(ii) *Contracts which must be evidenced in writing.* The Statute of Frauds 1677 imposed this requirement on several types of contract.

Section 4

No action shall be brought whereby to charge any executor or administrator upon any special promise to answer damages out of his own estate; or whereby to charge the defendant upon any special promise to answer for the debt, default or miscarriage of another person; or to charge any person upon any agreement made upon consideration of marriage; or upon any contract or sale of lands, tenements or hereditaments, or any interest in or concerning them; or upon any agreement that is not to be performed within the space of one year from the making thereof; unless the agreement upon which such action shall be brought, or some memorandum or note thereof, shall be in writing and signed by the party to be charged therewith or some other person thereunto by him lawfully authorised.

Section 17

No contract for the sale of goods, wares or merchandises for the price of £10 sterling or upwards shall be allowed to be good except the buyer shall accept part of the goods so sold and actually receive the same, or give something in earnest to bind the bargain or in part payment, or that some note or memorandum in writing of the said bargain be made and signed by the parties to be charged by such contract or their agents thereunto lawfully authorised.

(Section 17 was later replaced by s 4, Sale of Goods Act 1893.)

   The part of s 4 relating to land was replaced by the Law of Property Act 1925, s 40(1); this in turn was repealed by the Law of Property (Miscellaneous Provisions) Act 1989. The rest of the list, including the Sale of Goods Act 1893, s 4, was gradually whittled away until now only promises 'to answer for the debt, default or miscarriage of another person' remain. This book will not cover the law on this topic, nor consider why the requirements for contracts for the sale of land were changed recently—that is a complex topic involving the doctrine of 'part performance', which the courts had developed as a qualification to the statutory requirements. (See Law Commission Report No 164, *Formalities for contracts for sale etc of land*, HC2, 1987.) However, it is worth considering why the remainder of ss 4 and 17 of the Statute of Frauds have been repealed, and why it was seen fit to leave the existing requirements.

■ Sixth Interim Report (Statute of Frauds and the Doctrine of Consideration) of the Law Revision Committee, Cmd 5449 (1937)

[I]n 1851 so experienced a common lawyer as Lord Campbell could record the opinion that the Act 'promotes more frauds than it prevents'. Lord Nottingham (who, since the Act was his offspring, may well have felt for it some parental partiality) used to claim that 'every line of it was worth a subsidy'; upon which claim a learned lawyer, nearly two centuries later, commented that 'every line has cost one'.

   Contemporary opinion is almost unanimous in condemning the Statue and favouring its amendment or repeal.

   The main criticisms directed against Section 4 may be summarised under the following heads:-

(1) First and foremost, it is urged that the Act is a product of conditions which have long passed away. At the time when it was passed, essential kinds of evidence were excluded (eg, the parties themselves could not give evidence), and objectionable types of evidence were admitted (eg juries were still in theory entitled to act on their own knowledge of the facts in dispute). It was an improvement on this state of affairs to admit the evidence of the parties, even though only to the

extent that such evidence was in signed writing. To-day, when the parties can freely testify, the provisions of Section 4 are an anachronism. A condition of things which was advanced in relation to 1677 is backward in relation to 1937.

(2) 'The Act', in the words of Lord Campbell already cited 'promotes more frauds than it prevents'. True, it shuts out perjury; but it also and more frequently shuts out the truth. It strikes impartially at the perjurer and at the honest man who has omitted a precaution, sealing the lips of both. Mr Justice FitzJames Stephen (writing of Section 17, but his observation applies equally to Section 4) went so far as to assert that 'in the vast majority of cases its operation is simply to enable a man to break a promise with impunity, because he did not write it down with sufficient formality'.

(3) The classes of contracts to which Section 4 applies seem to be arbitrarily selected and to exhibit no relevant common quality. There is no apparent reason why the requirement of signed writing should apply to these contracts, and to all of them, and to no others.

(4) The Section is out of accord with the way in which business is normally done. Where actual practice and legal requirement diverge, there is always an opening for knaves to exploit the divergence.

(5) The operation of the Section is often lopsided and partial. A and B contract: A has signed a sufficient note or memorandum, but B has not. In these circumstances B can enforce the contract against A, but A cannot enforce it against B.

(6) The Section does not reduce contracts which do not comply with it to mere nullities, but merely makes them unenforceable by action. For other purposes they preserve their efficacy (for *what* other purposes precisely, is doubtful). Anomalous results flow from this: eg in *Morris v Baron* . . . a contract which complied with the Section was superseded by a second contract which did not so comply. It was held that neither contract could be enforced: the first, because it was validly rescinded by the second, the second because, owing to its purely oral character, no action could be brought on it. This was a result which the parties could not possibly have intended.

(7) Apart from its policy the Statute is in point of language obscure and ill-drafted. 'It is universally admitted', observed the original editor of Smith's Leading Cases, 'that no Enactment of the Legislature has become the subject of so much litigation.' This could hardly have been so if its terms had been reasonably lucid.

Most of the above criticisms apply, both to Section 4 and to Section 17 of the Statute of Frauds, and therefore to Section 4 of the Sale of Goods Act, 1893, so far as it reproduces that Section. . . .

RECOMMENDATION BY A MINORITY AS TO GUARANTEES

. . . [I]f oral contracts of guarantee are allowed, we feel that there is a real danger of inexperienced people being led into undertaking obligations that they do not fully understand, and that opportunities will be given to the unscrupulous to assert that credit was given on the faith of a guarantee which in fact the alleged surety had no intention of giving. A guarantee is in any case a special class of contract; it is generally one-sided and disinterested as far as the surety is concerned, and the necessity of writing would at least give the proposed surety an opportunity of pausing and considering, not only the nature of the obligation he is undertaking, but also its terms. The contract often gives rise to many questions, eg whether it is to apply to the whole of the debt or to a portion only, and, if the former, whether it is to be limited in amount or to a certain period. We think these questions ought to be definitely settled and recorded before the contract becomes binding on the surety. Parliament has in the Law of Property Act, 1925, reenacted the requirement of a signed note or memorandum in writing in the case of contracts for the sale of land, and has quite recently enacted that a money-lending contract is invalid unless the exact terms are embodied in a document which must be given to the proposing borrower so that he may see exactly to what he is agreeing, and, while it may be doubted if a needy borrower has ever been deterred from taking a loan by this provision, at least he cannot say that he did not know to what he was consenting. We see nothing unreasonable in putting sureties in a like position and giving them the same opportunity.

It is the 'small man' we desire to protect, the father or father-in-law of the small tradesman who may be pressed to guarantee the account for goods supplied to stock the shop of his son or son-in-law. Moreover, we believe that guarantees are a class of contract that at present most people know quite definitely must be in writing. The lay public know nothing about the Statute of Frauds; but they do, we believe, appreciate that writing is necessary for a guarantee; so our proposal only perpetuates that to which they are accustomed.

Legislation did not follow this report. In 1952, the Law Reform Committee in its First Report (Cmnd 8809) adopted the Interim Report, with the revision that contracts of guarantee should remain subject to the old requirement. The Law Reform (Enforcement of Contracts) Act 1954 put these recommendations into effect.

The requirements of the Consumer Credit Act 1974 also serve evidentiary, cautionary and channelling functions. However, some of the requirements are aimed at more specific problems and they will be considered later (p 949).

In *Actionstrength Ltd v International Glass Engineering* [2003] UKHL 17 [2003] 2 AC 541, the second defendant (Saint Gobain) wished to build a new factory in Yorkshire and the first defendant (Inglen) was the main contractor. The claimant (Actionstrength) entered into an agreement with Inglen to provide workers on the site. The deal was that Actionstrength would pay the workers and Inglen would pay Actionstrength. Inglen fell behind with these payments. There was a meeting on the site, which was attended by representatives of all three parties. Actionstrength's account of the meeting was that it had indicated that it was minded to take its men away and that Saint Gobain had said that if Actionstrength kept its men on site, Saint Gobain would see that they were paid. Relying on this, Actionstrength kept men on site. In due course, Inglen went into liquidation owing Actionstrength a great deal of money.

Saint Gobain argued that even if Actionstength's story was true, its promise was simply a guarantee, which was not enforceable because it was unwritten. The House of Lords upheld this argument.

Do you think that Saint Gobain looks like the sort of person that the legislation is designed to protect? Do you think that this result is fair? Does it make a difference whether Actionstrength knew about this rule? (We do not know whether it did or not.)

VII. RELIANCE ON NON-BARGAIN PROMISES

In the American case of *Ricketts v Scothorn* 57 Neb 51, 77 NW 365 (1898), Katie Scothorn was at work when her grandfather entered and gave her a promissory note, which read:

May 1st 1891. I promise to pay to Katie Scothorn on demand, $2,000, to be at 6 per cent per annum J C Ricketts.

He said: 'I have fixed something that you have not got to work any more. None of my grandchildren work and you don't have to.' Miss Scothorn gave notice to her employer and left her job, although a year and a half later, with her grandfather's consent, she did go back to work. Her grandfather paid her some interest but died without paying all the interest due or any of the principal sum. Miss Scothorn sued his executor.

Is it possible to say that Miss Scothorn's leaving work was consideration for her grandfather's promise? The Supreme Court of Nebraska held not: 'Her right to the money promised in the note was not made to depend on an abandonment of her employment . . . Mr Ricketts made no condition, requirement or request.' The same decision might be reached in English law—indeed, this seems inevitable if, as Pollock and Restatement 2d suggest, the only test of consideration is bargain. Even in more recent years, some commentators have taken this view: for instance, Hamson (1938) 54 LQR 233 and Odgers (1970) 86 LQR 69, 79. On this view, Miss Scothorn's act could not be consideration unless it were requested, or at least specified, by her grandfather as the price of his promise (see Smith (1953) 60 LQR 99; Goodhart, ibid 106; Atiyah, *Essays on Contract*, pp 213–214). There is also judicial support for this view. In *Combe v Combe*, the wife argued that her husband's promise in a separation agreement to pay her £100 a year was supported by consideration in that she never applied to the divorce court for maintenance. The Court of Appeal held that this forbearance could not be consideration because the husband had never requested it, even impliedly.

Other decisions do not seem to fit so easily with the requirement of the bargain. The promisee has done something that is to his or her detriment, and it *might* be inferred that the promisor requested it, but this interpretation seems a bit strained.

In *Shadwell v Shadwell* (see p 124), did Charles bargain for Lancey's marriage to Ellen?

In *De La Bere v Pearson Ltd* [1908] 1 KB 280, CA, a newspaper offered financial advice to readers who wrote asking for it. The advice given to the plaintiff was negligent and he lost money. It was held that the newspaper had a contractual duty to use care, the consideration being that the defendants had the right to publish the reader's letter. Was this bargained for? (Note that tortious liability for negligent advice was not recognised in this type of case until *Hedley Byrne & Co Ltd v Heller & Partners Ltd* [1964] AC 465. In that case, Lord Devlin said (at 528) that 'today the result [in *De la Bere v Pearson*] can and should be reached by application of the law of negligence and . . . it is unnecessary and undesirable to construct an artificial consideration'.)

In *Wells (Merstham) Ltd v Buckland Sand and Silica Co Ltd* (see p 19), D told P that D's sand would conform to a certain chemical analysis, which would make it suitable for propagating chrysanthemum cuttings. P later bought some of this sand from a third party, but the sand did not conform to the analysis and P's cuttings died. It was held that D had given a warranty and that buying the sand from a third party in reliance on D's statement was consideration. Was this bargained for?

In *Warlow v Harrison* (see p 203), an auction was advertised as being 'without reserve', but the auctioneer allowed the owner to bid when the goods seemed to be going for a low price. It was held that the auctioneer was in breach of a contract with the highest bona fide bidder; the consideration was presumably the act of bidding, or perhaps attending the auction. Did the auctioneer bargain for this act?

In *Blackpool and Fylde Aero Club Ltd v Blackpool Borough Council* (see p 244), the defendants issued invitations to a small number of organisations to tender for a concession to operate pleasure flights from the defendant's airport. Tenders had to be submitted by a certain time. The plaintiff's tender was delivered in time but, by mistake, it was recorded as having been received late and it was not considered. It was held that there was a contractual obligation on the defendants to consider tenders that conformed to the conditions of tendering. Is it realistic to say that the plaintiffs' expectation that the council would carry out proper procedures was the result of a 'bargain' to that effect with the council?

In each of these cases, it seems at least equally plausible to say that there was a promise, express or implicit, which was not 'bargained for' by the plaintiff but on which the plaintiff relied.

Returning to *Ricketts v Scothorn*, the court found that there was no consideration, but nonetheless held that Miss Scothorn could enforce the note. Because she had changed her position for the worse in reliance on her grandfather's promise, just as he had intended, he was 'estopped' from 'denying the consideration'.

Would an English court enforce Rickett's promise? The question must be answered in two parts. Firstly, would it employ estoppel as a substitute for consideration? Secondly, would it be prepared to find that there was consideration after all?

1. Estoppel as a substitute for consideration

What is estoppel? The essentials of the traditional version of estoppel were stated by Lord Birkenhead in *Maclaine v Gatty* [1921] 1 AC 376, at 386:

Where A has by his words or conduct justified B in believing that a certain state of facts exists, and B has acted upon such belief to his prejudice, A is not permitted to affirm against B that a different state of facts existed at the same time.

A classic example of estoppel is if one party represents to another that A has authority to contract on his behalf, when in fact he has not so authorised A. If, in reliance on this representation, the other party enters a contract with A as agent, the first party (the principal) is estopped from denying that A had authority to act as his agent, and the contract made through A will be binding on him.

The estoppel is said to arise when B acts on the facts he has assumed to be true to his 'prejudice' or 'detriment'. This appears to mean that B must have acted in such a way that, were A now permitted to assert the true facts, B would be left worse off than before A misled him. In *Grundt v Great Boulder Pty Gold Mines Ltd (1937) 59* CLR 641 at 674–675, Dixon J explained the point as follows:

...[T]he real detriment or harm from which the law seeks to give protection is that which would flow from the change of position if the assumption were deserted that led to it. So long as the assumption is adhered to, the party who altered his situation upon the faith of it cannot complain. His complaint is that when afterwards the other party makes a different state of affairs the basis of an assertion of right against him then, if it is allowed, his own original change of position will operate as a detriment. His action or inaction must be such that, if the assumption upon which he proceeded were shown to be wrong and an inconsistent state of affairs were accepted as the foundation of the rights and duties of himself and the opposite party, the consequence would be to make his original act or failure to act a source of prejudice.

The traditional doctrine of estoppel is limited in two ways. Firstly, it is usually said that estoppel will not create a cause of action; it can be used as a shield but not as a sword. This is apt to be misleading; in the example just given, if an action is brought against the principal, the estoppel plays a crucial role, because without the estoppel the contract would not be binding on him. What seems to be meant is this: if there would be a cause of action against the person who made the statement if only the statement were true, estoppel will operate to provide the missing element; but if there would not be an action against the representor even if the fact stated were true, then estoppel will not create one.

The point may be illustrated by an example. Suppose a customer were to ask her bank what the balance is in an account on which the customer has not drawn in some years, and were told £500. If as a result of this information the customer were to incur a debt for that amount and to pay it by a cheque drawn on the account, the bank would have to honour the cheque even if in fact the bank had made a mistake and the account had less money in it. If the account did contain £500, the bank would be obliged to honour the cheque and the effect of the estoppel is to make it liable. In contrast, if the incorrect balance were stated not to the customer but (with the customer's consent) to a third party seeking information about her credit standing, the bank would not be affected by estoppel. Even if the account did hold £500, the bank would not be liable to the third party and the bank's statement makes no difference to this. (The bank might be liable in tort on the principle of *Hedley Byrne v Heller* (see p 28) if a special relationship with the enquirer were shown.)

As the example shows, estoppel can provide an essential element in a cause of action that would otherwise fail. Take the case in which a principal has held out an agent as having authority that in fact has not been given to the agent. An action against the principal by a third party with whom the agent contracted in the principal's name would fail without the estoppel: the unauthorised action would not be binding on the principal. The estoppel prevents the principal denying that the agent *did* have authority, so the third party's action can succeed. For a fuller discussion, see the judgment of Robert Goff J in *Amalgamated Investment and Property Ltd v Texas Commerce Bank Ltd* [1982] QB 84.

It is presumably with the point that estoppel does not itself create a cause of action in mind that the Supreme Court of Nebraska formulated its judgment in *Ricketts v Scothorn* in terms that the promisor was estopped from denying the consideration—if there had been consideration, he would have been bound.

Secondly, for traditional estoppel, the representation must be one of fact. In a number of situations, the law draws a distinction between a statement of existing fact, such as '*x* is the case' or 'I have done *y*', and a promise for the future, such as 'I will do z'. A promise can only be binding if there is consideration or if it is in a deed, but a statement of fact can give rise to an estoppel.

■ *Jorden v Money*

(1854) 5 HL Cas 185, 10 ER 868, House of Lords

Money had given Charles Marnell a bond and warrant of attorney to secure repayment of a debt of £1,200 that Money owed to Charles's brother. On Charles's death, the defendant Mrs Jorden (then Miss Marnell) took the bond as Charles' executrix. She felt that Money had been badly treated, and frequently stated that she would never enforce the bond, repeating this particularly when Money's prospective parents-in-law expressed concern about Money's position. In reliance on her statements, Money married, and then sought a declaration that the debt had been abandoned, and a release from the bond. The Master of the Rolls granted an injunction to prevent enforcement and this was upheld by the Court of the Lord Justices. Jorden appealed.

Lord Cranworth LC

There are two grounds upon which it is said that the parties have lost their right to enforce the bond. The one is, that previously to William Money's marriage Mrs Jorden, then Miss Marnell, represented that the bond had been abandoned, that she had given up her right upon it, and upon the faith of that representation the marriage was contracted. And then it is said that upon a principle well known in the law, founded upon good faith and equity, a principle equally of law and of equity, if a person makes any false representation to another, and that other acts upon that false representation, the person who has made it shall not afterwards be allowed to set up that what he said was false, and to assert the real truth in place of the falsehood which has so misled the other. That is a principle of universal application, and has been particularly applied to cases where representations have been made as to the state of the property of persons about to contract marriage, and where, upon the faith of such representations, marriage has been contracted. There the person who has made the false representations has in a great many cases been held bound to make his representations good. . . .

I am bound to state my view of the case; I think that that doctrine does not apply to a case where the representation is not a representation of a fact, but a statement of something which the party intends or does not intend to do. In the former case it is a contract, in the latter it is not; what is here contended for, is this, that Mrs Jorden, then Miss Marnell, over and over again represented that she abandoned the debt. Clothe that in any words you please, it means no more than this, that she would never enforce the debt; she does not mean, in saying that she had abandoned it, to say that she had executed a release of the debt so as to preclude her legal right to sue. All that she could mean, was that she positively promised that she never would enforce it. My opinion is, that if all the evidence had come up to the mark, which, for reasons I shall presently state, I do not think it did, that if upon the very eve of the marriage she had said, 'William Money, I never will enforce the bond against you', that would not bring it within these cases. It might be, if all statutable requisites, so far as there are statutable requisites, had been complied with, that it would have been a very good contract whereby she might have bound herself not to enforce the payment. That, however, is not the way in which it is put here; in short, it could not have been, because it must have been a contract reduced into writing and signed; but that is not the way in which this case is put; it is put entirely upon the ground of representation. Now, my Lords, I think that the not adhering to this statement, call it contract or call it representation, is no more a fraud than it would be not adhering to her engagement, if she had said, 'Mr William Money, you may marry; do not be in fear, you will not be in want; I promise to settle £10,000 Consols upon you'. If she does not perform that promise, she is guilty of a breach of contract, in respect of which she may be sued, if it is put into a valid form, but not otherwise; so if she had said, as she did to William Money, 'I mean to give you everything I am worth in the world; I promise to do so' her not doing so, is no fraud in the sense in which these cases speak of fraud; it is no misrepresentation of a fact which the party is afterwards held bound to make good as true; it seems to me that the distinction is founded upon perfectly good sense, and that in truth in the case of what is something future, there is no reason for the application of the rule, because the parties have only to say, 'Enter into a contract', and then all difficulty is removed. It appears to me, therefore, that this which is the ground upon which the Master of the Rolls proceeded, and upon which he thought that the Plaintiff Money had the right to restrain the Jordens from enforcing this bond, fails, for the reasons which I have stated.

Lord Brougham concurred and **Lord St Leonards** dissented.

Appeal allowed.

NOTES

1. In practice, the distinction between a statement of fact and a promise may be a narrow one. What would have been the outcome had Mrs Jorden stated that she *had released* the debt (by release under seal) when in fact she had not?

2. In *Ricketts v Scothorn*, did Mr Ricketts make any false statement of fact?

■ *Central London Property Trust Ltd v High Trees House Ltd*
[1947] KB 130

In 1937, the plaintiff had granted the defendant, a subsidiary of the plaintiff, a 99-year lease of a block of flats at a rent of £2,500 per year. The flats had not been fully sublet at the beginning of the war, and the tenant company could not pay the rent out of the profits of the flats that had been sublet. After discussions, the landlord company agreed that the rent should be reduced to £1,250 per year as from the beginning of the lease, and the tenant company paid accordingly. By the beginning of 1945, the flats were fully let, and the receiver of the landlord company wrote claiming the full arrears. Later, however, he instituted a friendly action to test the legal position, merely claiming the difference between the rent paid and the original full rent as from the third quarter of 1945.

Denning J stated the facts and continued:

If I were to consider this matter without regard to recent developments in the law, there is no doubt that had the plaintiffs claimed it, they would have been entitled to recover ground rent at the rate of 2,500*l* a year from the beginning of the term, since the lease under which it was payable was a lease under seal which, according to the old common law, could not be varied by an agreement by parol (whether in writing or not), but only by deed. Equity, however stepped in, and said that if there has been a variation of a deed by a simple contract (which in the case of a lease required to be in writing would have to be evidenced by writing), the courts may give effect to it as is shown in *Berry v Berry*. That equitable doctrine, however, could hardly apply in the present case because the variation here might be said to have been made without consideration. With regard to estoppel, the representation made in relation to reducing the rent, was not a representation of an existing fact. It was a representation, in effect, as to the future, namely, that payment of the rent would not be enforced at the full rate but only at the reduced rate. Such a representation would not give rise to an estoppel, because, as was said in *Jorden v Money*, a representation as to the future must be embodied as a contract or be nothing.

But what is the position in view of developments in the law in recent years? The law has not been standing still since *Jorden v Money*. There has been a series of decisions over the last fifty years which, although they are said to be cases of estoppel are not really such. They are cases in which a promise was made which was intended to create legal relations and which, to the knowledge of the person making the promise, was going to be acted on by the person to whom it was made, and which was in fact so acted on. In such cases the courts have said that the promise must be honoured. The cases to which I particularly desire to refer are: *Fenner v Blake, In re Wickham, Re William Porter & Co Ld*, and *Buttery v Pickard*. As I have said they are not cases of estoppel in the strict sense. They are really promises— promises intended to be binding, intended to be acted on, and in fact acted on, *Jorden v Money* can be distinguished, because there the promisor made it clear that she did not intend to be legally bound, whereas in the cases to which I refer the proper inference was that the promisor did intend to be bound. In each case the court held the promise to be binding on the party making it, even though under the old common law it might be difficult to find any consideration for it. The courts have not gone so far as to give a cause of action in damages for the breach of such a promise, but they have refused to allow the party making it to act inconsistently with it. It is in that sense, and that sense only, that such a promise gives rise to an estoppel. The decisions are a natural result of the fusion of law and equity. for the cases of *Hughes v Metropolitan Rly Co, Birmingham and District Land Co v London & North Western Rly Co* and *Salisbury (Marquess) v Gilmore*, afford a sufficient basis for saying that a party would not be allowed in equity to go back on such a promise. In my opinion, the time has now come for the validity of such a promise to be recognized. The logical consequence, no doubt is that a promise to accept a smaller sum in discharge of a larger sum, if acted upon, is binding notwithstanding the absence of consideration: and if the fusion of law and equity leads to this result, so much the better. That aspect was not considered in *Foakes v Beer*. At this time of day, however, when law and equity have been joined together for over seventy years, principles must be reconsidered in the light of their combined effect. It is to be noticed that in the Sixth Interim Report of the Law Revision Committee, it is recommended that such a promise as that to which I have referred, should be enforceable in law even though no consideration for it has been given by the promise. It seems to me that, to the extent I have mentioned, that result has now been achieved by the decisions of the courts.

I am satisfied that a promise such as that to which I have referred is binding and the only question remaining for my consideration is the scope of the promise in the present case. I am satisfied on all the evidence that the promise here was that the ground rent should be reduced to £1,250 a year as a temporary expedient while the block of flats was not fully, or substantially fully let, owing to the conditions prevailing. That means that the reduction in the rent applied throughout the years down to the end of 1944, but early in 1945 it is plain that the flats were fully let, and, indeed the rents received from them (many of them not being affected by the Rent Restrictions Acts), were increased beyond the figure at which it was originally contemplated that they would be let. At all events the rent from them must have been very considerable. I find that the conditions prevailing at the time when the reduction in rent was made, had completely passed away by the early months of 1945. I am satisfied that the promise was understood by all parties only to apply under the conditions prevailing at the time when it was made, namely, when the flats were only partially let, and that it did not extend any further than that. When the flats became fully let, early in 1945, the reduction ceased to apply.

In those circumstances, under the law as I hold it, it seems to me that rent is payable at the full rate for the quarters ending September 29 and December 25, 1945.

If the case had been one of estoppel, it might be said that in any event the estoppel would cease when the conditions to which the representation applied came to an end, or it also might be said that it would only come to an end on notice. In either case it is only a way of ascertaining what is the scope of the representation. I prefer to apply the principle that a promise intended to be binding, intended to be acted on and in fact acted on, is binding so far as its terms properly apply. Here it was binding as covering the period down to the early part of 1945, and as from that time full rent is payable.

I therefore give judgment for the plaintiff company for the amount claimed.

Judgment for plaintiffs.

NOTES

1.   The landlords did not claim the unpaid rent for the war years, but Denning J clearly indicates that such a claim would have failed. Was there any consideration for the promise not to exact this rent? (NB: You may need to answer this in two parts: (a) as the law was perceived to be in 1947 and (b) as it might be perceived to be since the decision in *Williams v Roffey Bros* (see p 111). However, the Court of Appeal has recently held that binding authority precludes it from applying the 'practical benefit' approach to a promise to release part of a debt in exchange for payment of the rest: see p 855.)

2.   It is not clear that the tenants had acted to their detriment in the case see p 871.

3.   In support of his dicta, Denning J cited a number of cases including *Hughes v Metropolitan Rly Co*. Whether these cases actually support him will be examined in Section 7.

■ Combe v Combe
[1951] 1 All ER 767, Court of Appeal

After they had been divorced, the husband promised to pay the wife £100 per year maintenance, but he failed to pay. She pressed him for payment, but she did not make any application to the divorce court. Her income was in fact greater than his. Nearly seven years after the decree absolute of divorce had been given, she brought an action for £675, being arrears for six and three-quarter years.

Denning LJ

... Byrne J held that the first three quarterly instalments of £25 were barred by the Limitation Act, 1939, but he gave judgment for £600 in respect of the instalments which accrued within the six years before the action was brought. He held, on the authority of *Gaisberg v Storr*, that there was no consideration for the husband's promise to pay his wife £100, but, nevertheless, he held that the promise was enforceable on the principle stated in *Central London Property Trust Ltd v High Trees House Ltd* and *Robertson v Minister of Pensions*, because it was an unequivocal acceptance of liability, intended to be binding, intended to be acted on, and, in fact, acted on.

Much as I am inclined to favour the principle of the *High Trees* case, it is important that it should not be stretched too far lest it should be endangered. It does not create new causes of action where none existed before. It only prevents a party from insisting on his strict legal rights when it would be unjust to allow him to do so, having regard to the dealings which have taken place between the parties. That is the way it was put in the case in the House of Lords which first stated the principle—*Hughes v Metropolitan Rly Co*—and in the case in the Court of Appeal which enlarged it—*Birmingham and District Land Co v London & North Western Rly Co*. It is also implicit in all the modern cases in which the principle has been developed.

It may be part of a cause of action, but not a cause of action in itself. The principle, as I understand it, is that where one party has, by his words or conduct, made to the other a promise or assurance which was intended to affect the legal relations between them and to be acted on accordingly, then, once the other party has taken him at his word and acted on it, the one who gave the promise or assurance cannot afterwards be allowed to revert to the previous legal relations as if no such promise or assurance had been made by him, but he must accept their legal relations subject to the qualification which he himself has so introduced, even though it is not supported in point of law by any consideration, but only by his word.

Seeing that the principle never stands alone as giving a cause of action in itself, it can never do away with the necessity of consideration when that is an essential part of the cause of action. The doctrine of consideration is too firmly fixed to be overthrown by a side-wind. Its ill effects have been largely mitigated of late, but it still remains a cardinal necessity of the formation of a contract, although not of its modification or discharge. I fear that it was my failure to make this clear in *Central London Property Trust Ltd v High Trees House Ltd* which misled Byrne J in the present case. He held that the wife could sue on the husband's promise as a separate and independent cause of action by itself, although, as he held, there was no consideration for it. That is not correct. The wife can only enforce the promise if there was consideration for it. That is, therefore, the real question in the case: Was there sufficient consideration to support the promise?

If it were suggested that, in return for the husband's promise, the wife expressly or impliedly promised to forbear from applying to the court for maintenance—that is, a promise in return for a promise—there would clearly be no consideration because the wife's promise would not be binding on her and, therefore, would be worth nothing. Notwithstanding her promise, she could always apply to the divorce court for maintenance—perhaps, only with leave—but nevertheless she could apply. No agreement by her could take away that right: *Hyman v Hyman*, as interpreted by this court in *Gaisberg v Storr*. There was, however, clearly no promise by the wife, express or implied, to forbear from applying to the court. All that happened was that she did, in fact, forbear—that is, she did an act in return for a promise. Is that sufficient consideration? Unilateral promises of this kind have long been enforced so long as the act or forbearance is done on the faith of the promise and at the request of the promisor, express or implied. The act done is then in itself sufficient consideration for the promise, even though it arises *ex post facto*, as Parker J pointed out in *Wigan v English and Scottish Law Life Assurance Assocn*. If the findings of Byrne J are accepted, they are sufficient to bring this principle into play. His finding that the husband's promise was intended to be binding, intended to be acted on, and was, in fact, acted on—although expressed to be a finding on the principle of the *High Trees House* case—is equivalent to a finding that there was consideration within this long-settled rule, because it comes to the same thing expressed in different words: see *Oliver v Davis*. My difficulty, however, is to accept the findings of Byrne J that the promise was 'intended to be acted on'. I cannot find any evidence of any intention by the husband that the wife should forbear from applying to the court for maintenance, or, in other words, any request by the husband, express or implied, that the wife should so forbear.

Birkett LJ

... There does not appear any evidence of a request by the husband that the wife should refrain from going to the court, or a promise by the wife that she would not go to the court, or any matter of that kind. It appears simply to have been that after some talk in February, 1943, an agreement was arrived at that the husband would pay £100 a year free of tax. It seems on the first point, therefore, that there was no consideration for this agreement.

With regard to the second point, we have had the great advantage of hearing Denning LJ deal with *Central London Property Trust Ltd v High Trees House Ltd* and *Robertson v Minister of Pensions* which formed such a prominent part of the judgment of the court below. I am bound to say that reading them for myself I think the description which was given by counsel for the husband in this court, namely, that the doctrine there enunciated was, so to speak, a doctrine which would enable a person to use it as a shield and not as a sword, is a very vivid way of stating what, I think, is the principle underlying both those cases.

Asquith LJ

I agree. The learned judge decided that while the husband's promise was unsupported by any valid consideration, yet the principle in *Central London Property Trust Ltd v High Trees House Ltd* entitled the wife to succeed. It is unnecessary to express any view as to the correctness of the decision in the *High Trees* case, although I certainly must not be taken to be questioning it. I would, however, remark in passing that it seems to me a complete misconception to suppose that it struck at the roots of the doctrine of consideration. Assuming, without deciding, that it is good law, I do not think it helps the wife at all. What that case decides is that when a promise is given which (i) is intended to create legal relations, (ii) is intended to be acted on by the promisee, and (iii) is, in fact, so acted on, the promisor cannot bring an action against the promisee which involves the repudiation of his promise or is inconsistent with it. It does not, as I read it, decide that a promisee can sue on the promise. Denning J expressly states the contrary. Neither in the *High Trees* case nor in *Robertson v Minister of Pensions* (another decision of my Lord which is relied on by the plaintiff) was an action brought by the promisee on the promise. In the first of those two cases the plaintiff was, in effect, the promisor or a person standing in the shoes of the promisor, while in the second the action, although brought by the promisee, was brought on a cause of action which was not the promise, but was an alleged statutory right. ...

Finally, I do not think an actual forbearance, as opposed to an agreement to forbear to approach the court, is a good consideration unless it proceeds from a request, express or implied, on the part of the promisor. If not moved by such a request, the forbearance is not in respect of the promise. For these reasons and the others given by my Lords, I agree that the appeal should be allowed.

Appeal allowed.

The doctrine propounded by Denning, often known as the *High Trees* doctrine or the doctrine of promissory estoppel, has been applied in a number of cases in which one party has promised to forgo, or has waived, his rights under an existing contract: these will be examined in Section 7. The limitation imposed or confirmed by *Combe v Combe*, that the doctrine applies only to such a situation and cannot be used as a substitute for consideration to create a fresh contractual right, remains good law in England: see *Argy Trading Development Co Ltd v Lapid Developments Co Ltd* [1977] 3 All ER 785, at 796, and *Syros Shipping Co SA v Elaghill*

Trading Co, The Proodos C [1981] 3 All ER 189. See also Halson, 'The offensive limits of promissory estoppel' [1999] LMCLQ 256.

There is one class of case, however, in which estoppel has come to be used despite the absence of a representation of fact, with a result that looks very much like making estoppel into a cause of action. These cases are often referred to as 'acquiescence' or 'proprietary estoppel'. In *Dillwyn v Llewelyn* (1862) 4 De GF & J 517, a father and son signed a written memorandum by which the father purported to present the son with a farm. There was no consideration for the father's promise, so the memorandum conferred no interest in the land on the son. The son took possession and, with his father's knowledge, built a residence on it at a cost of some £14,000; no conveyance of the land to the son was ever executed. After the father's death, the son sought a declaration of his rights and a conveyance to him. Lord Westbury LC held that the son's expenditure had given him an equitable right to have the incomplete gift completed, and he was entitled to a conveyance in fee simple.

... [T]he subsequent expenditure by the son, with the approbation of the father, supplied a valuable consideration originally wanting ...

It is possible to look at this case as one in which the testator represented that he *had* given the land. In *Plimmer v Wellington Corpn* (1884) 9 App Cas 699, 53 LJPC 105, it was held that where the representor had encouraged the building, a representation that the land *would* be conveyed was sufficient. See also the statement of the principle by Lord Kingsdown in *Ramsden v Dyson* and the more modern case of *Inwards v Baker* [1965] 2 QB 29.

If the person to whom the promise has been made builds on the promisor's land, to allow the promisor to turn the promisee off might result in the promisor getting a house for nothing at the expense of the promisee. What if the element of unjust enrichment is taken away because the plaintiff has not built on the defendant's land, but he has relied on the defendant's representation in some other way and will suffer loss if the defendant does not act as he had indicated he would?

■ *Crabb v Arun District Council*
[1975] 3 All ER 865, Court of Appeal

The plaintiff owned a plot of land adjoining an existing road. Next to the land was a plot owned by the defendants, on which the defendants were to build houses. The defendants built a new road running down the boundary between their property and the plaintiff's. They granted him access onto this road through a gateway (point A) in the front portion of his property, and a right of way over the road. Subsequently, the plaintiff decided to divide his property into two and sell the front portion. He discussed the matter with representatives of the defendants, and was given the impression that he would be given a right of access at a second point (point B), serving the back portion of his property. The defendants later erected a boundary fence, with apparently permanent gates at both access points, but no right of access or easement for the back access point was ever granted. Believing he nonetheless had a right of access to the back portion, the plaintiff sold the front portion without reserving to himself any right of way to either the front access point or the old road. The defendants later blocked the rear access point (B) and offered to grant the plaintiff a right of access for £3,000. The plaintiff refused this offer and was unable to obtain access to his land. He sought a declaration that he was entitled to a right of way from the back part of the land along the new road, and an injunction to restrain the defendants from interfering with this right of way.

Pennycuick V-C dismissed the action on the ground that the defendants' representative had given no definite assurance, so no question of estoppel could arise. The plaintiff appealed.

Lord Denning MR

...In June 1971 Mr Crabb brought this action claiming a right of access at point B and a right of way along the estate road. He had no such right by any deed or conveyance or written agreement. So, in strict law, on the conveyance, the council were entitled to their land, subject only to an easement at point A, but none at point B. To overcome this strict law, Mr Crabb claimed a right of access at B on the ground of equitable estoppel, promissory or proprietary. The judge held that he could not avail himself of any estoppel. He said: 'In the absence of a definite assurance by the representative of the Council, no question of estoppel can arise, and that really concludes the action.' Mr Crabb appeals to this court.

When counsel for Mr Crabb said that he put his case on an estoppel, it shook me a little, because it is commonly supposed that estoppel is not itself a cause of action. But that is because there are estoppels and estoppels. Some do give rise to a cause of action. Some do not. In the species of estoppel called proprietary estoppel, it does give rise to a cause of action... The new rights and interests, so created by estoppel, in or over land, will be protected by the courts and in this way give rise to a cause of action. This was pointed out in Spencer Bower and Turner on Estoppel by Representation.

The basis of this proprietary estoppel—as indeed of promissory estoppel—is the interposition of equity. Equity comes in, true to form, to mitigate the rigours of strict law. The early cases did not speak of it as 'estoppel'. They spoke of it as 'raising an equity'... What then are the dealings which will preclude him from insisting on his strict legal rights? If he makes a binding contract that he will not insist on the strict legal position, a court of equity will hold him to his contract. Short of a binding contract, if he makes a promise that he will not insist on his strict legal rights—even though that promise may be unenforceable in point of law for want of consideration or want of writing—and if he makes the promise knowing or intending that the other will act on it, and he does act on it, then again a court of equity will not allow him to go back on that promise: see *Central London Property Trust v High Trees House, Charles Rickards v Oppenheim*. Short of an actual promise, if he, by his words or conduct, so behaves as to lead another to believe that he will not insist on his strict legal rights—knowing or intending that the other will act on that belief—and he does so act, that again will raise an equity in favour of the other, and it is for a court of equity to say in what way the equity may be satisfied. The cases show that this equity does not depend on agreement but on words or conduct. In *Ramsden v Dyson* Lord Kingsdown spoke of a verbal agreement 'or what amounts to the same thing, an expectation, created or encouraged'. In *Birmingham Land Co v London and North Western Railway* Cotton LJ said that '...what passed did not make a new agreement but what took place...raised an equity against him'. And it was the Privy Council who said that 'the Court must look at the circumstances in each case to decide in what way the equity can be satisfied', giving instances: see *Plimmer v Mayor of Wellington*...

The question then is: were the circumstances here such as to raise an equity in favour of Mr Crabb? True the council on the deeds had the title to their land, free of any access at point B. But they led Mr Crabb to believe that he had or would be granted a right of access at point B. At the meeting of 26th July 1967, Mr Alford and Mr Crabb told the council's representative that Mr Crabb intended to split the two acres into two portions and wanted to have an access at point B for the back portion, and the council's representative agreed that he should have this access. I do not think the council can avoid responsibility by saying that their representative had no authority to agree this. They entrusted him with the task of setting out the line of the fence and the gates: and they must be answerable for his conduct in the course of it: see *Attorney-General to His Royal Highness the Prince of Wales v Collom; Moorgate Mercantile Co Ltd v Twitchings*.

The judge found that there was 'no definite assurance' by the council's representative, and 'no firm commitment', but only an 'agreement in principle', meaning I suppose that, as Mr Alford said, there were 'some further processes' to be gone through before it would become binding. But if there were any such processes in the minds of the parties, the subsequent conduct of the council was such as to dispense with them. The council actually put up the gates at point B at considerable expense. That certainly led Mr Crabb to believe that they had agreed that he should have the right of access through point B without more ado.

The judge also said that, to establish this equity or estoppel, the council must have known that Mr Crabb was selling the front portion without reserving a right of access for the back portion. I do not think this was necessary. The council knew that Mr Crabb *intended* to sell the two portions separately and that he would need an access at point B as well as point A. Seeing that they knew of his intention— and they did nothing to disabuse him, but rather confirmed it by erecting gates at point B—it was their conduct which led him to act as he did; and this raised an equity in favour against them.

In the circumstances it seems to me inequitable that the council should insist on their strict title as they did; and to take the high-handed action of pulling down the gates without a word of warning; and to demand of Mr Crabb £3,000 as the price for the easement. If he had moved at once for an injunction in aid of his equity—to prevent them removing the gates—I think he should have been granted it. But he did not do so. He tried to negotiate terms, but these failing, the action has come for trial. And we have the question: in what way now should the equity be satisfied?

Here equity is displayed at its most flexible: see Snell's Equity and the illustrations there given. If the matter had been finally settled in 1967, I should have thought that, although nothing was said at the meeting in July 1967, nevertheless it would be quite reasonable for the council to ask Mr Crabb to pay something for the access at point B, perhaps—and I am guessing—some hundreds of pounds. But, as counsel for the plaintiff pointed out in the course of the argument, because of the council's conduct, the back land has been landlocked. It has been sterile and rendered useless for five or six years; and Mr Crabb has been unable to deal with it during that time. This loss to him can be taken into account. And at the present time, it seems to me, in order to satisfy the equity, Mr Crabb should have the right of access at point B free of charge without paying anything for it.

I would, therefore, hold that Mr Crabb, as the owner of the back portion, has a right of access at point B over the verge on to Mill Park Road and a right of way along that road to Hook Lane without paying compensation. I would allow the appeal and declare that he has an easement, accordingly.

Scarman LJ

I agree that the appeal should be allowed. . . .

I think it is now well-settled law that the court, having analysed and assessed the conduct and relationship of the parties, has to answer three questions. First, is there an equity established? Secondly, what is the extent of the equity, if one is established? And, thirdly, what is the relief appropriate to satisfy the equity? See *Duke of Beaufort v Patrick*, *Plimmer v Mayor of Wellington* and *Inwards v Baker*, a decision of this court, and particularly the observations of Lord Denning MR. Such therefore I believe to be the nature of the enquiry that the courts have to conduct in a case of this sort. In pursuit of that enquiry I do not find helpful the distinction between promissory and proprietary estoppel. This distinction may indeed be valuable to those who have to teach or expound the law, but I do not think that, in solving the particular problem raised by a particular case, putting the law into categories is of the slightest assistance.

I come now to consider the first of the three questions which I think in a case such as this the court has to consider. What is needed to establish an equity? In the course of an interesting addition to his sub-missions this morning, counsel for the defendants cited *Ramsden v Dyson* to support his proposition that in order to establish an equity by estoppel, there must be a belief by the plaintiff in the existence of a right created or encouraged by the words or actions of the defendant. With respect, I do not think that that is today a correct statement of the law. I think the law has developed so that today it is to be considered as correctly stated by Lord Kingsdown in his dissenting speech in *Ramsden v Dyson*. Like Lord Denning MR, I think that the point of dissent in *Ramsden v Dyson* was not on the law but on the facts. Lord Kingsdown's speech, insofar as it dealt with propositions of law, has been often considered, and recently followed, by this court in *Inwards v Baker*. Lord Kingsdown said:

> 'The rule of law applicable to the case appears to me to be this: If a man, under a verbal agreement with a landlord for a certain interest in land, or what amounts to the same thing, *under an expectation, created or encouraged by the landlord* [my italics], that he shall have a certain interest, takes possession of such land, with the consent of the landlord, and upon the faith of such promise or expectation, with the knowledge of the landlord, and without objection by him, lays out money upon the land, a Court of equity will compel the landlord to give effect to such promise or expectation.'

...I turn now to the other two questions—the extent of the equity and the relief needed to satisfy it. There being no grant, no enforceable contract, no licence, I would analyse the minimum equity to do justice to the plaintiff as a right either to an easement or to a licence on terms to be agreed. I do not think it is necessary to go further than that. Of course, going that far would support the equitable remedy of injunction which is sought in this action. If there is no agreement as to terms, if agreement fails to be obtained, the court can, in my judgment, and must, determine in these proceedings on what terms the plaintiff should be put to enable him to have the benefit of the equitable right which he is held to have....

I am not disposed to consider whether or not the defendants are to be blamed in moral terms for what they did. I just do not know. But the effect of their action has been to sterilise the plaintiff's land; and for the reasons which I have endeavoured to give, such action was an infringement of an equitable right possessed by the plaintiff. It has involved him in loss, which has not been measured; but, since it amounted to sterilisation of an industrial estate for a very considerable period of time, it must surpass any sort of sum of money which the plaintiff ought reasonably, before it was done, to have paid the defendants in order to obtain an enforceable legal right. I think therefore that nothing should now be paid by the plaintiff and that he should receive at the hands of the court the belated protection of the equity that he has established. Reasonable terms, other than money payment, should be agreed: or, if not agreed, determined by the court. For those reasons I also would allow the appeal.

Lawson LJ delivered a concurring judgment.

Appeal allowed.

It thus seems that English law sometimes comes close to enforcing gratuitous promises that have been relied on under the guise of estoppel, but only where the promise was one to convey property. Promissory estoppel extends only to promises not to enforce existing rights. In Australia, the law has developed further than this.

■ *Walton Stores (Interstate) Ltd v Maher*

(1988) 164 CLR 387, High Court of Australia

Mr and Mrs Maher had been negotiating for Waltons to lease property owned by the Mahers. The scheme was that the Mahers would demolish an old building on the site and put up a new building to a specification approved by Waltons.

On 21 October 1983, Waltons' solicitors sent a draft agreement for the lease to the Mahers' solicitors. Certain proposed amendments were discussed and Waltons' solicitor was told that the Mahers had started demolishing the old building. On 7 November, the Mahers' solicitors told Waltons' solicitors that unless the agreement was concluded within the next day or two, it would be impossible to finish the new building by the agreed date of 5 February 1984. It was also said that the Mahers did not want to demolish a new part of the old building until it was clear that there were no problems. On the same day, the Waltons' solicitor sent to the Mahers' solicitor fresh documents incorporating the amendments and stating

We have not yet obtained our client's specific instructions to each amendment requested, but we believe that approval will be forthcoming. We shall let you know tomorrow if any amendments are not agreed to.

On 11 November 1983, the Mahers' solicitor forwarded to Waltons' solicitor 'by way of exchange' the documents executed by the Mahers. The Mahers then began to demolish the new portion of the old building. Waltons became aware of this on 10 December.

As a result of a projected alteration in its retailing policy and having been advised that, as contracts had not been exchanged, it was not bound to proceed, Waltons decided not to commit itself and instructed its solicitors to 'go slow'. In early January, the Mahers began construction of the new building, which was about 40 per cent complete when, on 19 January, Waltons' solicitors informed the Mahers' solicitors that Waltons did not intend to proceed. There had been no earlier indication that Waltons would not exchange contracts.

Kearney J and the New South Wales Court of Appeal held that Waltons were estopped from denying that a contract by way of exchange had been concluded. Waltons appealed to the High Court of Australia. All of the members of the High Court of Australia held in favour of the Mahers. Deane and Gaudron JJ substantially agreed with the lower courts that Waltons had effectively represented that there was a contract (a fact) and were estopped from denying this. The majority of the High Court, Mason CJ, Wilson and Brennan JJ held that Waltons had made no representation of fact but had merely led the Mahers to believe that a contract would be completed in due course. However, they held that this did constitute a promissory estoppel, which gave rise to a cause of action. **Mason CJ** and **Wilson J** said:

Our conclusion that the respondents assumed that exchange of contracts would take place as a matter of course, not that exchange had in fact taken place, undermines the factual foundation for the common law estoppel by representation found by Kearney J and the common law estoppel based on omission to correct a mistake favoured by the Court of Appeal.

Promissory estoppel certainly extends to representations (or promises) as to future conduct: *Legione v Hateley* (1983) 152 CLR 406 at 432. So far the doctrine has been mainly confined to precluding departure from a representation by a person in a pre-existing contractual relationship that he will not enforce his contractual rights, whether they be pre-existing or rights to be acquired as a result of the representation: *Ajayi v R T Briscoe (Nigeria) Ltd*. . . . But Denning J in *Central London Property Trust Ltd v High Trees House Ltd* treated it as a wide-ranging doctrine operating outside the pre-existing contractual relationship; see the discussion in *Legione* at 432–5. In principle there is certainly no reason why the doctrine should not apply so as to preclude departure by a person from a representation that he will not enforce a non-contractual right. . . .

There has been for many years a reluctance to allow promissory estoppel to become the vehicle for the positive enforcement of a representation by a party that he would do something in the future. Promissory estoppel, it has been said, is a defensive equity *(Hughes v Metropolitan Railway* Co; *Combe v Combe)* and the traditional notion has been that estoppel could only be relied upon defensively as a shield and not as a sword. . . . *High Trees* itself was an instance of the defensive use of promissory estoppel. But this does not mean that a plaintiff cannot rely on an estoppel. Even according to traditional orthodoxy, a plaintiff may rely on an estoppel if he has an independent cause of action, where in the words of Denning LJ in *Combe v Combe*, the estoppel 'may be part of a cause of action, but not a cause of action in itself'.

But the respondents ask us to drive promissory estoppel one step further by enforcing directly in the absence of a pre-existing relationship of any kind a non-contractual promise on which the representee has relied to his detriment. For the purposes of discussion, we shall assume that there was such a promise in the present case. The principal objection to the enforcement of such a promise is that it would outflank the principles of the law of contract. Holmes J expressed his objection to the operation of promissory estoppel in this situation when he said 'It would cut up the doctrine of consideration by the roots, if a promisee could make a gratuitous promise binding by subsequently acting in reliance on it': *Commonwealth v Scituate Savings Bank* (1884) 137 Mass 301 at 302. Likewise, Sir Owen Dixon considered that estoppel cut across the principles of the law of contract, notably offer and acceptance and consideration: 'Concerning Judicial Method' (1956) 29 *ALJ* 468 at 475. And Denning LJ in *Combe v Combe*, after noting that 'The doctrine of consideration is too firmly fixed to be overthrown by a side-wind', said that such a promise could only be enforced if it was supported by sufficient consideration.

The foregoing review of the doctrine of promissory estoppel indicates that the doctrine extends to the enforcement of voluntary promises on the footing that a departure from the basic assumptions underlying the transaction between the parties must be unconscionable. As failure to fulfil a promise does not of itself amount to unconscionable conduct, mere reliance on an executory promise to do something, resulting in the promisee changing his position or suffering detriment, does not bring promissory estoppel into play. Something more would be required. *Attorney-General (Hong Kong) v Humphreys Estate Ltd* [1987] AC 114 suggests that this may be found, if at all, in the creation or encouragement by the party estopped in the other party of an assumption that a contract will come into existence or a promise will be performed and that the other party relied on that assumption to his detriment to the knowledge of the first party. . . .

But the crucial question remains: was the appellant entitled to stand by in silence when it must have known that the respondents were proceeding on the assumption that they had an agreement and that completion of the exchange was a formality? The mere exercise of its legal right not to exchange contracts could not be said to amount to unconscionable conduct on the part of the appellant. But there were two other factors present in the situation which require to be taken into consideration. The first was the element of urgency that pervaded the negotiation of the terms of the proposed lease. As we have noted, the appellant was bound to give up possession of its existing commercial premises in Nowra in January 1984; the new building was to be available for fitting out by 15 January and completed by 5 February 1984. The respondents' solicitor had said to the appellant's solicitor on 7 November that it would be impossible for Maher to complete the building within the agreed time unless the agreement were concluded 'within the next day or two'. The outstanding details were agreed within a day or two thereafter, and the work of preparing the site commenced almost immediately.

The second factor of importance is that the respondents executed the counterpart deed and it was forwarded to the appellant's solicitor on 11 November. The assumption on which the respondents acted thereafter was that completion of the necessary exchange was a formality. The next their solicitor heard from the appellant was a letter from its solicitors dated 19 January, informing him that the appellant did not intend to proceed with the matter. It had known, at least since 10 December, that costly work was proceeding on the site.

It seems to us, in the light of these considerations, that the appellant was under an obligation to communicate with the respondents within a reasonable time after receiving the executed counterpart deed and certainly when it learnt on 10 December that demolition was proceeding. It had to choose whether to complete the contract or to warn the respondents that it had not yet decided upon the course it would take. It was not entitled simply to retain the counterpart deed executed by the respondents and do nothing. . . . the appellant's inaction, in all the circumstances, constituted clear encouragement or inducement to the respondents to continue to act on the basis of the assumption which they had made. It was unconscionable for it, knowing that the respondents were exposing themselves to detriment by acting on the basis of a false assumption, to adopt a course of inaction which encouraged them in the course they had adopted. To express the point in the language of promissory estoppel the appellant is estopped in all the circumstances from retreating from its implied promise to complete the contract.

Brennan J said:

...[An] assumption or expectation by one party which does not relate to what the other party is bound to do or not to do gives no foundation for an equitable estoppel, though the assumption or expectation relates to the prospect of the other party conducting himself in a particular way. The risk that the other party who, being free to conduct himself in whatever way he chooses, may choose to conduct himself in a way different from that assumed or expected rests with the party who adopts the assumption or expectation.

Parties who are negotiating a contract may proceed in the expectation that the terms will be agreed and a contract made but, so long as both parties recognise that either party is at liberty to withdraw from the negotiations at any time before the contract is made, it cannot be unconscionable for one party to do so. Of course, the freedom to withdraw may be fettered or extinguished by agreement but, in the absence of agreement, either party ordinarily retains his freedom to withdraw. It is only if a party induces the other party to believe that he, the former party, is already bound and his freedom to withdraw has gone that it could be unconscionable for him subsequently to assert that he is legally free to withdraw.

...

The unconscionable conduct which it is the object of equity to prevent is the failure of a party, who has induced the adoption of the assumption or expectation and who knew or intended that it would be relied on, to fulfil the assumption or expectation or otherwise to avoid the detriment which that failure would occasion. The object of the equity is not to compel the party bound to fulfil the assumption or expectation; it is to avoid the detriment which, if the assumption or expectation goes unfulfilled, will be suffered by the party who has been induced to act or to abstain from acting thereon.

If this object is kept steadily in mind, the concern that a general application of the principle of equitable estoppel would make non-contractual promises enforceable as contractual promises can be allayed. A non-contractual promise can give rise to an equitable estoppel only when the promisor induces the promisee to assume or expect that the promise is intended to affect their legal relations and he knows or intends that the promisee will act or abstain from acting in reliance on the promise, and when the promisee does so act or abstain from acting and the promisee would suffer detriment by his action or inaction if the promisor were not to fulfil the promise. When these elements are present, equitable estoppel almost wears the appearance of contract, for the action or inaction of the promisee looks like consideration for the promise on which, as the promisor knew or intended, the promisee would act or abstain from acting. . . .

If the object of the principle were to make a promise binding in equity, the need to preserve the doctrine of consideration would require a limitation to be placed on the remedy. But there is a logical difficulty in limiting the principle so that it applies only to promises to suspend or extinguish existing rights. If a promise by A not to enforce an existing right against B is to confer an equitable right on B to compel fulfilment of the promise, why should B be denied the same protection in similar circumstances if the promise is intended to create in B a new legal right against A? There is no logical distinction to be drawn between a change in legal relationships effected by a promise which extinguishes a right and a change in legal relationships effected by a promise which creates one. Why should an equity of the kind to which *Combe v Combe* refers be regarded as a shield but not a sword? The want of logic in the limitation on the remedy is well exposed in Mr David Jackson's essay 'Estoppel as a Sword' in (1965) 81 *Law Quarterly Review* 84, 223 at 241–3.

Moreover, unless the cases of proprietary estoppel are attributed to a different equity from that which explains the cases of promissory estoppel, the enforcement of promises to create new proprietary rights cannot be reconciled with a limitation on the enforcement of other promises. If it be unconscionable for an owner of property in certain circumstances to fail to fulfil a non-contractual promise that he will convey an interest in the property to another, is there any reason in principle why it is not unconscionable in similar circumstances for a person to fail to fulfil a non-contractual promise that he will confer a non-proprietary legal right on another? It does not accord with principle to hold that equity, in seeking to avoid detriment occasioned by unconscionable conduct, can give relief in some cases but not in others.

If the object of the principle of equitable estoppel in its application to promises were regarded as their enforcement rather than the prevention of detriment flowing from reliance on promises, the courts would be constrained to limit the application of the principles of equitable estoppel an order to avoid the investing of a non-contractual promise with the legal effect of a contractual promise....

...[T]he better solution of the problem is reached by identifying the unconscionable conduct which gives rise to the equity as the leaving of another to suffer detriment occasioned by the conduct of the party against whom the equity is raised. Then the object of the principle can be seen to be the avoidance of that detriment and the satisfaction of the equity calls for the enforcement of a promise only as a means of avoiding the detriment and only to the extent necessary to achieve that object. So regarded, equitable estoppel does not elevate non-contractual promises to the level of contractual promises and the doctrine of consideration is not blown away by a side wind. Equitable estoppel complements the tortious remedies of damages for negligent misstatement or fraud and enhances the remedies available to a party who acts or abstains from acting in reliance on what another induces him to believe.

...

In my opinion, to establish an equitable estoppel, it is necessary for a plaintiff to prove that (1) the plaintiff assumed or expected that a particular legal relationship exists between the plaintiff and the defendant or that a particular legal relationship will exist between them and, in the latter case, that the defendant is not free to withdraw from the expected legal relationship; (2) the defendant has induced the plaintiff to adopt that assumption or expectation; (3) the plaintiff acts or abstains from acting in reliance on the assumption or expectation; (4) the defendant knew or intended him to do so; (5) the plaintiff's action or inaction will occasion detriment if the assumption or expectation is not fulfilled; and (6) the defendant has failed to act to avoid that detriment whether by fulfilling the assumption or expectation or otherwise. For the purposes of the second element, a defendant who has not actively induced the plaintiff to adopt an assumption or expectation will nevertheless be held to have done so if the assumption or expectation can be fulfilled only by a transfer of the defendant's property, a diminution of his rights or an increase in his obligations and he, knowing that the plaintiff's reliance on the assumption or expectation may cause detriment to the plaintiff if it is not fulfilled, fails to deny to the plaintiff the correctness of the assumption or expectation on which the plaintiff is conducting his affairs....

NOTES

1.   It is clear from reading the judgments that all of the judges who tried this case had a strong intuitive perception that the Mahers should be given a remedy. Is this right? Would it matter what legal advice the Mahers had been given by their lawyers? Would the position be different if the Mahers thought that they had strengthened their bargaining position by pressing ahead with the work?

2.   Granted the desire to give the Mahers a remedy, different remedies could be imagined. Legal systems that impose a duty to negotiate in good faith might easily regard the conduct of Waltons as bad faith. Note the difference of opinion between the majority and minority as to the kind of estoppel to which the circumstances gave rise.

3.   In the later and very difficult case of *Commonwealth of Australia v Verwayen* (1990) 170 CLR 394, the High Court was divided on the application of the doctrine of estoppel. In this case, the plaintiff was injured while a member of the Royal Australian Navy by a ship collision in 1964. In 1984, he started an action against the Commonwealth of Australia for damages for negligence. By its defence, the Commonwealth admitted liability but reserved the quantum of damages. It did not plead that the action was barred by limitation or that because the plaintiff was a serviceman in the middle of combat training there was no duty of care. The question arose whether, in 1986, the Commonwealth could change its mind so as to raise the limitation and absence of duty of care as defences. Deane, Dawson, Toohey

and Gaudron JJ held that the Commonwealth was not free to raise these points; Mason CJ and Brennan and McHugh JJ held essentially that justice did not require the Commonwealth to be barred altogether from raising the defences. The legitimate interests of the plaintiff would be adequately met by indemnifying the plaintiff against any costs wasted by the Commonwealth's change of mind.

4.　In *Walton Stores*, the anticipated contract did not materialise. See further p 281.

5.　For a radical commentary on this case, see p 796.

6.　Can *Walton Stores* be seen as an example of an obligation derived not from a clear promise of contract but from the 'relational background' of what took place? Cf Macneil (p 63) and the commentary by Feinman (p 807).

In *Actionstrength* (see p 146), the claimant sought to get over the difficulty that the guarantee was not in writing by relying on an estoppel argument. This was rejected by the House of Lords.

　Lord Bingham said:

If Saint Gobain were held to be estopped in this case it is hard to see why any oral guarantee, where credit was extended to a debtor on the strength of a guarantee, would not be similarly estopped.

This language may suggest that the case was being approached on the basis that both Actionstrength and Saint Gobain knew the law about oral guarantees at the time of the site meeting, but there does not seem to be any evidence of this.

　Several of the Australian cases were cited to the House of Lords, but these are not discussed in the judgments. Some Australian commentators have thought that a case with the same facts would be decided differently in Australia (see Robertson, 19 JCL 173).

　In many of the US states, promissory estoppel has long been recognised as an alternative basis to consideration for enforcing promises. The idea foreshadowed in *Ricketts v Scothorn* (p 146) was incorporated into s 90 of the Restatement (1932):

A promise which the promisor should reasonably expect to induce action or forbearance of a definite and substantial character on the part of the promisee and which does induce such action or forbearance is binding if injustice can be avoided only by enforcement of the promise.

(The Restatement 2d version will be considered on p 171.)

　Returning to the doctrine of proprietary estoppel as currently recognised under English law, is this enforcement 'contractual'? Atiyah (1976) 92 LQR 174 argued that, in *Crabb*, there was a contract that the Court of Appeal in effect enforced. But as Millett (1976) 92 LQR 342 pointed out in a riposte, the parties had not reached a concluded agreement. Thus one difference between proprietary estoppel and 'contract' is that contract requires a promise, even if only implicit, which has been accepted by the other party; proprietary estoppel can give rise to liability on the basis of less definite representations, provided that these have created a 'belief or expectation' that the proprietary interest has been or will be granted: *A-G of Hong Kong v Humphreys Estate (Queens Gardens) Ltd* [1987] 2 All ER 387.

　In *A-G for Hong Kong v Humphreys Estate*, the negotiations were 'subject to contract' (ie stated to be not binding until a full contract had been negotiated and signed). It was held that both parties fully understood this and that there was no representation that the prospective lessees would not withdraw from the agreement in principle that had been reached between them and the government. Compare the *Walton Stores* case and *JT Developments Ltd v Quinn* (1990) 62 P & CR 33 (tenant told that, unless informed otherwise, he could rely on getting a new lease on the same terms as another tenant).

A second difference appears to be the nature of the remedies available. If there is a contract, the court will normally protect the plaintiff's expectation by granting specific performance (if the contract is for land) or full damages. The proprietary estoppel cases envisage something more flexible—'the minimum equity to do justice to the plaintiff', as Scarman put it. In *Pascoe v Turner* [1979] 2 All ER 945, the plaintiff told the defendant, with whom he had been living, that a house was hers, but no conveyance was ever drawn up. With his encouragement, she spent some of her money on improving the house. When the plaintiff tried to regain possession, the Court of Appeal held that he was estopped. In determining the remedy, it took into account the ruthlessness with which the plaintiff had tried to evict the defendant, and concluded that the defendant could only be properly protected if she were given the fee simple of the house as she had been promised. While this approach suggests that if the plaintiff had been less demanding the defendant might have got less, it amounts to enforcing the promise the plaintiff had made to her. As Cumming-Bruce LJ put it:

Weighing such considerations this court concludes that the equity to which the facts in this case give rise can only be satisfied by compelling the plaintiff to give effect to his promise and her expectations.

Moriarty (1984) 100 LQR 376 argues that, in fact, the courts have consistently used proprietary estoppel to protect the expectations engendered by the party estopped:

Normally...a remedy will be chosen which gives the party precisely what he has been led to expect, but occasionally, where joint rights to land have been represented, he may get money instead.

This would mean that the difference between the remedies for contract and proprietary estoppel is more apparent than real. However, Gardner (1999) 115 LQR 438 points out that the proprietary estoppel cases have not always resulted in the plaintiff's expectation being fulfilled or his loss of expectation compensated.

Proprietary estoppel is confined to rights in or over land or other property: *Western Fish Products Ltd v Penwith District Council* [1981] 2 All ER 204 at 217–218. On the other hand, the belief or expectation created by the defendant does not have to relate to any specific piece of property; in *Re Basham* [1987] 1 All ER 405, the plaintiff was held to be entitled to the residue of an estate. The principle is thus very wide.

Proprietary estoppel will arise when the plaintiff has acted to her detriment on the defendant's representation, but what she did does not have to have been requested or even known to the defendant (see Denning's judgment in *Crabb's* case, p 155 above). At least on the traditional 'bargain' analysis of consideration, an act done by the plaintiff to her detriment will only be consideration if it was requested by the defendant: see *Combe v Combe*, p 152. You may remember that this point also came up in *Re Hudson* (p 22); the risks and liabilities assumed by the committee formed to distribute the fund were not consideration for Hudson's promise. In argument, Pearson J had made the point even more clearly:

If A says 'I will give you, B, £1,000', and B in reliance on that promise spends £1,000 in buying a house, B cannot recover the £1,000 from A. (54 LJCh at 813.)

But whether the bargain analysis is an accurate description of consideration is fiercely contested. We will explore this in the next subsection.

To summarise, it seems that there are two situations in which a gratuitous promise that has been relied on to his detriment by the promisee may become binding by virtue of 'estoppel' acting as a substitute for consideration. One is the 'proprietary estoppel' cases just described; the other is where the promise is that the promisor will not enforce some contractual right against the promisee, a subject that will be dealt with in detail in Section 7. In other cases, a gratuitous promise will be unenforceable unless contained in a deed.

2. An act done in reliance on the promise as consideration

As we saw, the court in *Ricketts v Scothorn* held that there was no consideration for the grandfather's promise because he did not ask anything of Miss Scothorn in return; in other words, there was no bargain. Would the same result be reached in English law? Certainly cases such as *Combe v Combe* seem to suggest so. On the other hand, Atiyah in his *Consideration in Contracts: A Fundamental Restatement* (1971) has denied the validity of most of the 'conventional' statement of the doctrine of consideration. In particular, he denies that benefit to the promisor or detriment to the promisee are either sufficient or necessary, and that the law of contract enforces only bargains. The piece deserves reading in full: the following extracts, which are taken from a revised version published in 1986, are chosen to show his approach, and his views on gratuitous promises, which have been relied on.

■ **Atiyah, 'Consideration: A Restatement' in *Essays on Contract* (1986)**
pp 184–187, 226–230, 232–235, 238–239, 241

At a relatively early date it was established that the courts would enforce a promise if another promise or an act was given in return for it; and also that they would not normally enforce a promise if it was merely intended as a gift with no return of any kind. In the first class of case it came therefore to be said that there was good consideration; there were good reasons for enforcing the promise. In the second class there was no such reason, and therefore no consideration. But it also became clear from a very early time that the whole law could not be reduced to such very simple terms. There were some cases in which a promise was given in return for another promise or an act, in which for one reason or another it was felt unjust or inexpedient that the promise should be enforced. Such cases could be, and sometimes were explained by saying that there was no consideration for the promise; but as the nineteenth century wore on, an alternative approach began to manifest itself. This was to say that there was good consideration (though perhaps the word 'good' would more usually be omitted) but that nevertheless the promise was unenforceable for other reasons, for example, because it had been extorted by duress, or fraud, or because it was illegal. The last type of case was often dealt with by saying that the consideration was unlawful; a judge who formulated his reasons in this way would perhaps, if pressed, have said that there was no 'good' consideration.

More recently still, this alternative approach has hardened so that courts now find nothing inconsistent in holding that there is consideration for a promise, but nevertheless refusing to enforce it because the transaction is illegal. This approach also manifests itself in the relatively modern device of refusing to enforce a promise on the ground that the promisor did not 'intend' to create legal relations by his promise. Where this is done (as it usually is) in a case where there is no express disavowal of the intent to create legal relations, it appears to be merely a legal justification for refusing to enforce a promise which the courts think, for one reason or another, it is unjust or impolitic to enforce. There seems no doubt that a hundred years ago the courts would have dealt with these problems in terms of consideration. Indeed, the comparison between *Shadwell v Shadwell* and *Jones v Padavatton* is striking. . . .

This change of approach is symptomatic of the change which has developed in the way lawyers think about consideration. It is no longer thought that consideration is a compendious word simply indicating whether there are good reasons for enforcing a promise; it is widely assumed that consideration is a technical requirement of the law which has little or nothing to do with the justice or desirability of enforcing a promise. Modern lawyers thus see nothing incongruous in asserting that a promise made for good consideration should nevertheless not be enforced.

Exactly the same development has taken place with regard to those promises which are not normally enforced, that is the promise to make a gift with no return of any kind. Since the courts first decided that such promises were not enforceable, it came to be asserted that gratuitous promises were promises given without consideration. But in course of time, occasions arose when the courts found that there were sometimes very good reasons for enforcing gratuitous promises in certain cases, and they accordingly enforced them. When cases of this kind arose during the first part of the nineteenth century the natural approach of the courts was to say that there *was* consideration—which at that time seems merely to have meant that there were good reasons for enforcing the promise. But here again, as lawyers began to treat consideration as a 'doctrine' whose content was a set of fixed and rigid rules tailored to the typical case, these cases came to seem anomalous. It therefore became fashionable to deny that there was consideration; and yet such promises were and still are quite often enforced. Modern lawyers are thus forced to say that some promises may be enforceable even though there is no consideration for them.

As will be apparent from the above discussion, there has gradually been a hardening of the attitude of the English common lawyer to the whole notion of consideration. . . . Because most contracts are bargains, lawyers have steadfastly refused to recognise the evidence under their very eyes, that courts often enforce promises which are not bargains, and that they do so for reasons of justice and good policy. Because a promise to make a gift is not usually recognised as a sufficient reason for its enforcement, lawyers have refused to acknowledge that in some circumstances it is particularly desirable to enforce a gratuitous promise and that the courts in fact do so. . . .

As we shall see below, the restatement of the law which the actual decisions compel us to adopt, differs from the conventional view principally in recognising the importance of the untypical and marginal cases. It is not, however, merely a question of recognising that there are exceptions to the ordinary rules to which adequate attention has not always been paid. If that were all, there would be little need, or justification, for a fundamental restatement of the law. A restatement will require rather more than that; it will require in particular that lawyers start to think of consideration once again in terms of reasons for enforcing a promise; it will require lawyers to recognise that the presence of factors like benefit, detriment, and bargain is taken into account not because they fit some preconceived plan or definition, but because they are often very material factors in determining whether it is just or desirable to enforce a promise; and this necessarily involves recognition that these are not the only factors to which attention must be, and is in practice paid by the Courts.

The frontier between promissory estoppel and unilateral contracts

Orthodox theory draws a firm line between a promise given for consideration, and a promise enforceable on the ground of promissory estoppel. In the case of a promise for an act, the distinction comes down to a very fine point. If the act is stated or specified (or possibly if it is requested) by the promisor, then the promise is enforceable in the ordinary way; the performance of the act is a good consideration. If the act is done by the promisee in reliance on the promise, but it has not been requested or stated or specified by the promisor, then orthodoxy asserts that there is no consideration, though there is a sufficient reason for giving the promise the limited validity recognised by promissory estoppel. It may help to see this distinction in perspective if the following fact situations are differentiated. . . .

5. The promisor does not state any act which is to be performed by the promisee but it is reasonably implicit that such an act is requested or desired by him, eg A promises additional payment to his creditor without stating that he asks for more time to pay, but it is reasonably implicit in the circumstances that this is what he wants. This promise is enforceable.
6. The promisor does not state any act which is to be performed by the promisee but the promisee does act in reliance on the promise in a way which was the natural and foreseeable result of the promise. This promise is said to be not enforceable as a contract, but enforceable to the limited extent recognised by promissory estoppel.
7. The promisor states the act to be performed by the promisee, and the promisee performs some other act which is a necessary step towards the performance of the act stated by the promisor, but he does not perform the act stated. The promisee cannot enforce the principal promise but may in some circumstances be able to enforce an implied subsidiary promise.

8. The promisor does not state any act which is to be performed by the promisee, but the promisee acts in reliance on the promise in a way which the promisor had no reason to anticipate.

The factual difficulty of defining the frontier

If the law of consideration had been recognised for what I suggest it to be, namely a set of guides for deciding whether there is good reason for the enforcement of a promise, the answer would surely have been clear. There is no natural frontier between Case 5 and Case 6. Indeed, there are frequently great difficulties in drawing the factual distinction between Case 5 and Case 6. . . .

The fineness of this distinction in fact is illustrated by the situation in *Hohler v Aston*. In this case the defendant, Mrs A, promised to give a London house to Mr and Mrs R, her niece and husband. She contracted to acquire the property and Mr and Mrs R gave up the lease of their country property and moved into the London house. The defendant then died before the property had been transferred to her or to Mr and Mrs R. Sargant J was able to decide the case in favour of the plaintiffs without having to consider whether the facts already stated were sufficient to enable Mr and Mrs R to enforce the aunt's promise. But he expressed the view that the promise would probably not have been enforceable, although he acknowledged the hardship which this would have entailed for Mr and Mrs R. If they had given up their country house at Mrs A's request, this would have rendered the promise enforceable, but because this was not actually stated as an act to be performed by them, the promise was (he thought) unenforceable. This distinction is exactly the orthodox doctrine, but the distinction seems so fine as to be virtually unintelligible. It seems most undesirable to decide a case of this kind on such a point because the whole issue would turn on oral evidence as to whether the aunt ever said to Mr and Mrs R that they must give up their country property and come and live in the London house. It is probable that recollection of oral discussions to this degree of accuracy would be impossible, and that the decision would actually turn on findings of fact which are bound to be unreliable. Perhaps if the decision had actually turned on this issue Sargant J would have been prepared to imply a request. It could not be said that this was a *necessary* implication of the defendant's conduct; doubtless Mr and Mrs R could have retained the lease of their country house while going to live in the London house. But the possibility of implying a request where the Court feels it necessary to do justice is another confirmation of the unreality of the factual distinction between Case 5 and Case 6.

Policy arguments for maintaining the frontier

But even if these arguments are not felt to be convincing, it remains to inquire whether there can be any rational ground for distinguishing between Case 5 and Case 6. I have already indicated that this seems to me an impossible line to maintain. So long as it is believed that all contracts are bargains, there is some rational ground for requiring that the act to be performed by the promisee must be stated, if not actually requested, by the promisor; but once it is agreed that many promises are enforced though they are not bargains, it is hard to see what rational purpose is intended to be served by the insistence that the act must be stated. The natural place to draw a line in the above listed cases is not between Case 5 and Case 6 but between Case 7 and Case 8. The difference between an act done by the promisee which is impliedly stated by the promisor, and an act done in natural and foreseeable reliance on the promise seems much less substantial than the distinction between the latter case and an act in reliance which could not have been anticipated by the promisor. That is not to say that even this last case may not, in certain circumstances, be thought to be a promise worthy of enforcement . . .

Once again I feel obliged to depart from orthodox doctrine. I would suggest that, on the contrary, [*Combe v Combe*] decided nothing more than this: that an act (or forbearance) which naturally and foreseeably follows from and in reliance on a promise is not a consideration for the enforcement of the promise *where the justice of the case does not require that it should be*. So viewed the decision is perfectly in line with older cases. Among these cases are the ones to which I have already made reference, namely *Dillwyn v Llewellyn*, and the line of authorities following it, and culminating in

Inwards v Baker. There is no doubt that the principle stated in these cases is flatly inconsistent with orthodox doctrine; for these cases stand for the principle that if a man promises to give another some land, and permits the other to build a property on his land, then even though he has not requested or stated that such building, is the act on which his promise becomes enforceable, the promise will be enforceable.

I do not rely solely on *Dillwyn v Llewellyn* and the cases following it for my view that an act done in reliance on a promise may be a good consideration even though it is not stated or requested by the promisor as an act to be performed by the promisee. These particular cases may be explained away as anomalous or exceptional. I therefore turn to an examination of the House of Lords' decision in *Jorden v Money* which lies at the heart of this whole question. The treatment of this case by lawyers during the past thirty-five years is one of the most extraordinary chapters in the whole law of consideration, and must make one wonder whether lawyers actually read the cases which form the pillars of orthodoxy. . . .

The truth is that there is a very much simpler explanation of *Jorden v Money* which seems to stare in the face anyone who actually reads the report. Discussions of the case all start with the assumption that the plaintiff could not enforce the defendant's promise in contract because he could show no consideration; and it is for this reason that (it is assumed) the plaintiff relied on estoppel. The truth is precisely the opposite. The plaintiff could have proved a good contract; in fact he *did* show a good contract, and that is precisely why he failed. To understand this paradoxical statement it must be recalled that the Statute of Frauds required at this time that a promise in consideration of marriage must be proved in writing. The only act in reliance on the promise which the plaintiff could show was his marriage; *but he had no written note or memorandum signed by the defendant*. His counsel, therefore, deliberately refrained from arguing his case in contract but relied on estoppel. The whole point of the case (at all events as it developed in the House of Lords) was whether the plaintiff was entitled to do this. Could he evade the Statute of Frauds by calling his cause of action estoppel instead of contract? Had this stratagem succeeded, a blow would have been dealt to the Statute of Frauds greater than anything that had gone before; for it would have meant that any plaintiff who could show that he had altered his position in reliance on the defendant's promise could ignore the Statute and rely on estoppel. And since at this time the distinction between estoppel as a cause of action and as a ground of defence was not established, the threatened evasion of the Statute would have seemed even wider than it might today. It is, therefore, quite understandable that the House of Lords should not have sanctioned the plaintiff's claim.

The true view; an unnecessary frontier

It will be seen, therefore, that virtually all modern academic (and much judicial) discussion of promissory estoppel has been entirely beside the point. This discussion invariably takes as its starting point the assumption that the performance of an act in reliance on a promise, not requested or stated by the promisor, cannot be a good consideration. If this assumption is unfounded then there is not, and never has been, any need for promissory estoppel. *Jorden v Money*, far from being (as the new orthodoxy would have it) a difficult obstacle in the way of recognition of promissory estoppel, is a clear indication that promissory estoppel was never necessary at all. The facts of *Jorden v Money* are the clearest possible example of my Case 6 that I have been able to find. The plaintiff undoubtedly married in reliance on the defendant's promise but the defendant never requested the marriage nor did she promise to release the debt if and when the plaintiff married. Her promise was, indeed, originally made before any question of marriage was in contemplation; it was repeated time and again and the plaintiff acted upon it by his marriage. I have myself no doubt that, as the law was then understood, this was a good consideration for the enforcement of the promise which would (apart from the Statute of Frauds) have been enforced by the House of Lords in 1854.

I do not of course, mean to say that nineteenth-century Courts would have held that a promise always becomes enforceable whenever the promisee acts in reliance on it (even though the act is not requested or stated by the promisor). But what I suggest is that the Courts were at that time prepared to enforce such a promise where they felt that the justice of the case required it. If this was so, then there was good reason (or consideration) for enforcement in the promisee's actions in reliance on the promise. Alas, the new orthodoxy has now itself grown so strong and vigorous that it seems too late for the courts to recognise what they have actually done. In *Crabb v Arun District Council* the Court of Appeal actually 'enforced' (by appropriate equitable decrees) an arrangement (to use a neutral term) in a case where one judge insisted that the whole question was whether there was an agreement between the parties. But this 'agreement' though 'enforced' by court decrees was not regarded as a contract, but merely as a set of representations of intention which were enforceable because they had been relied upon to the plaintiff's prejudice. When I protested that if there was an agreement and it was enforced, this must have been a contract, I was rebuked for failing to understand that contracts are designed to enforce agreements, while estoppel is designed to protect reliance. The reader will (I trust) by now know enough of my views to appreciate that I do not assume that because there was (as I think) a 'contract' in this case, it should have been enforceable without any reliance by the plaintiff. I merely protest at the absurdity of a conceptual analysis which states that the agreement in *Crabb v Arun District Council* was not enforceable because the detrimental reliance was not requested, and therefore failed to comply with the requirements of consideration; and then proceeds to add that the 'agreement' was nevertheless enforceable because the element of reliance did satisfy the doctrine of promissory estoppel. Surely, it would be simpler and more sensible if the law made up its mind what kind of detrimental reliance was sufficient to justify the imposition of some kind of obligation without regard to whether the case should be classified as involving consideration or promissory estoppel.

The present position—which I have called the new orthodoxy—might be more defensible if estoppel, or promissory estoppel, was only called upon to protect reliance. . . .

Consideration *means* a reason for the enforcement of a promise.

NOTE

Atiyah's views have not gone unchallenged, in particular his opinion about *Jorden v Money* (although you might like to consider the language used in *Dillwyn v Llewelyn* in this context) and his assertion that there is no doctrine of consideration. See in particular Treitel, *Consideration: A Critical Analysis of Professor Atiyah's Fundamental Restatement* (1976) 50 Austr LJ 439. Moreover, we have seen that it is doubtful whether *Dillwyn* and the other cases of proprietary estoppel are cases of contractual liability at all—the basis and the remedies available seem different. On the other hand, Treitel says that the English doctrine of consideration does not just enforce bargains: the rule adopted in many of the US states that 'Nothing is consideration which is not regarded as such by both parties' (Holmes) 'quite clearly does not represent English law' (p 440). He cites a number of cases to support this, including some of those we noted earlier as being hard to reconcile with a requirement of bargain. Atiyah's riposte (*Essays on Contract*, pp 182–183) is worth noting:

> Professor Treitel's critique of my original essay (and his textbook on the *Law of Contract*) insists that the courts have power to 'invent' consideration, and that this ability is an important phenomenon which I have overlooked and which explains many otherwise puzzling things about the doctrine. I find this a difficult concept to grasp. Is an 'invented' consideration something different from a 'real' consideration or is it the same thing? If it is the same thing, then it is hard to see in what sense it is invented; and if it is not the same thing, then it either violates the rules of law, or it modifies them. Presumably Professor Treitel does not mean to suggest that when judges invent consideration they are defying the law and violating their judicial oaths, but if an invented consideration modifies the rules governing ordinary consideration, then an invented consideration becomes again an ordinary consideration, though the legal significance of the doctrine has now changed. The only other possibility that occurs to me is that the courts might use the concept of 'invented consideration' rather like an equitable or merciful dispensation from the ordinary law, but it is unthinkable that

judges should behave in this way. They have no power to invent a consideration in one case and refuse to do so in a relevantly identical case. Thus an invented consideration must in the end be the same thing as an ordinary consideration. I fear that Professor Treitel has himself invented the concept of an invented consideration because he finds it the only way in which he is able to reconcile many decisions with what he takes to be the 'true' or 'real' doctrine.

Thus the outcome of a case with the same facts as *Ricketts* is somewhat doubtful in English law; although the courts ostensibly enforce only bargains, so that an act done in reliance on a promise but not requested by the promisor cannot be consideration, they sometimes infer a request even though the inference seems a bit strained. Clearly, it would not take much of a reinterpretation of the facts of *Ricketts* to say that the grandfather was impliedly requesting that Miss Scothorn give up her job. Cases such as *Combe v Combe* in which the court refused to imply a request may, as Atiyah says, be explicable on the ground that there were good reasons for not enforcing the promise. It is noteworthy that, in *Re Hudson*, Pearson J followed his decision that there was no consideration with the words:

> I do not know to what extent a contrary decision might open a new form of posthumous charity. Posthumous charity is already bad enough. . . .

A similar 'flexibility' has been shown in some of the US states, not all of which were or are firmly wedded to the bargain principle. However, it was Corbin's insistence that many of the cases did not really involve bargains, but were ones of gratuitous promises that had been relied on, which led the American Law Institute to adopt s 90 of the Restatement.

An account of the events leading up to adoption of s 90 alongside a strict bargain definition of consideration (see Rest 2d s 71) will be found in Gilmore, *The Death of Contract* (1974) pp 62–65; see also Henderson, 'Promissory Estoppel and Traditional Contract Doctrine' (1969) 78 Yale LJ 343.

At this stage, you may like to look again at some of the readings in Chapter 3, especially Atiyah's description of the values underlying the 'classical' law of contract. How far does (i) the present English law or (ii) the *Walton Stores* case represent a departure from the values of the 'classical' law?

3. Should reliance be recognised?

Should a similar principle be adopted by English law? The Law Reform Committee recommended so in 1937 (see Sixth Interim Report, Cmd 5449). On the merits, consider the following extract.

■ **Posner, *Economic Analysis of Law*** (2nd edn, 1977)
pp 67–70

Holding people to their promises is not, however, the only economic function of contract law, as [an] example will illustrate. A wealthy man in an expansive moment promises to pay my way through college. I give up my part-time job, but he then breaks his promise and I am unable to get a new job.

. . . There is no exchange in [this] case: giving up my part-time job confers no advantage on the wealthy promisor. Indeed, he may not even have known that I gave it up. . . .

Yet . . . there is an economic argument for imposing sanctions on the party who fails to perform. The wealthy man's idle promise induced reliance that cost the promisee heavily when it was broken. Such a cost can be avoided for the future by holding such a promisor liable for the promisee's reliance costs. It is, of course, necessary to distinguish the sort of donative promise that is likely to induce reliance from the sort that is not. I promise you a trivial gift and the next day withdraw my promise. I had no reason to expect you to rely, so whether or not you do rely the law will not hold me to my promise.

...

§4.2 CONSIDERATION

The principle that a promise, to be enforceable, must be supported by 'consideration' is used to deny liability for breach of a promise mainly in two types of cases. The first is where there is no exchange and where, therefore, enforcement of the promise would not advance the economic purpose of the law of contracts, which is to facilitate exchange. A truly gratuitous, nonreciprocal promise to confer a benefit is not a part of the process by which resources are moved, through a series of exchanges, into successively more valuable uses. This justification of the doctrine of consideration has been obscured by the characterization of 'detrimental reliance' (my giving up my part-time job, in the first example of the preceding section) as consideration sufficient to support a wholly one-sided promise. There is, as we have seen, a good economic reason for awarding damages to one who has reasonably relied, to his detriment, on another's promise. But it obscures analysis to equate reliance with consideration in circumstances where no exchange is contemplated. A better approach would be to treat the breach of a promise likely to induce reliance as a form of negligence actionable under tort law.

If gratuitous promises were always enforced, however, people would be very cautious about making any statement that could possibly be construed as promissory; they might go to considerable lengths to disclaim promissory intentions whenever there was the slightest ambiguity. Such elaborate forbearance would involve costs not offset by benefits in the form of a more efficient system of exchange. It is uneconomical to require people to be too careful.

NOTES

1. Writers such as Eisenberg, who argues that simple donative promises should not be enforced (see above, p 138), agree that reasonable reliance on a donative promise should give the promisee a remedy: 'A donative promisor's refusal to reimburse the promisee for a diminution in the promisee's wealth resulting from the reliance on the promise takes the relationship out of the affective realm.' (Eisenberg (1997) 85 California LR 821 at 851)

2. If 'reliance' were to be recognised as creating liability, what would be the appropriate measure of damages? This was debated in a famous exchange between Williston and Coudert during the drafting of the first Restatement. Johnny is promised $1,000 by his uncle and on the strength of the promise buys a car for $500. Williston argued that the uncle should be liable for $1,000 (4 ALI Proceedings 98–99; reprinted in (1936) 46 Yale LJ at 64 n 14).

    In their article in 1936 referred to earlier, Fuller and Perdue argued for a reliance measure of damages to be used more broadly in s 90 cases and this became the standard academic approach. The Restatement 2d version of s 90 reads (*emphasis supplied*):

    (1) A promise which the promisor should reasonably expect to induce action or forbearance on the part of the promisee . . . and which does induce such action or forbearance is binding if injustice can be avoided only by enforcement of the promise. *The remedy granted for breach may be limited as justice requires* . . .

    However, a study by Yorio and Thel (1991) 101 Yale LJ 111 argues that the courts have more often used reliance by the plaintiff as a justification for enforcing the defendant's promise in full by granting specific performance or awarding expectation damages measured by the value of the promise. This study is criticised by Eisenberg (1997) 85 California LR 821 at 852–865.

3.   Goetz and Scott, 'Enforcing Promises: An Examination of the Basis of Contract' (1980)
      89 Yale LJ 1261 (extracted in Ogus and Veljanovski (eds), *Readings in the Economics of
      Law and Regulation*, 1984), have propounded a theory of the reasons behind the
      enforcement of promises, including a more developed theory of promissory estoppel.
      Goetz and Scott begin by noting that a promise gives information about the promisor's
      future action. The promisee may, and frequently will, adapt his behaviour in accordance
      with this new information (cf Posner, 'Gratuitous Promises'). If the promisor does act as
      promised, this reliance by the promisee will normally have beneficial effects. If, on the
      other hand, the promise is broken, the promisee's reliance will normally prove detri-
      mental. The aim of the law is to encourage beneficial reliance as well as to discourage
      detrimental reliance (which is the justification put forward by Posner in the last extract).
          There is always some possibility that, when the time comes to perform, the promised
      action will have become unattractive to the promisor. Where the promisor and promisee
      are in a trading relationship (exchanging resources), the price the promisee is willing to
      pay for the promisor's promise can be adjusted to reflect the fact that, the greater the
      likelihood that the promisor will not perform, the less valuable his promise is to the
      promisee. The promisor thus has an incentive to find an appropriate balance between
      making his promise reliable (for instance, not hedging it about with conditions), and
      preserving himself some freedom to choose whether or not to perform if, when the time
      comes, he finds that performance would be very burdensome. But where the promise is
      gratuitous, no such adjustment can be made. If liability is imposed on the promisor, he
      will adjust in a quite different way: he will make fewer and vaguer promises, thus
      conveying less valuable information to the promisee. If liability for the gratuitous
      promise is *not* imposed, the promisee will adopt 'self-protective' measures—perhaps
      simply passing up the opportunity to change his expenditure pattern as he would have
      done if he could have been sure of receiving the promised benefit. What is needed is a
      rule that makes the gratuitous promise binding, and thus encourages reliance by the
      promisee, when the benefits to be gained from the reliance outweigh the costs imposed
      on the promisor. This theory, the authors suggest, can give content to the notion of
      'reasonable reliance' required by s 90. It also suggests, however, that neither a full
      expectation measure of damages, nor a measure based on the actual detriment incurred
      by the promisee, is wholly appropriate. The former would encourage too great a degree
      of reliance by the promisee, the latter too little. At least in an ideal world, the measure of
      damages should be based on the degree of reliance that would be optimal, rather than
      that which has in fact occurred. However, such a measure would be too difficult to apply,
      and use of the traditional 'reliance' measure is a reasonable second-best.

4.   A number of scholars, including Yorio and Thel (see note 2) have argued that the US
      courts have abandoned, or should abandon, the theory that a gratuitous promise
      should be actionable only if relied on by the promisee to her detriment. For a survey, see
      Barnett, 'The Death of Reliance' (1996) 46 J of Legal Education 518. Barnett himself
      argues (at 528):

      [My proposals] distinguish between commercial and noncommercial promises. Commercial promises
      are presumptively enforceable unless the parties, by using formalities, indicate their intention not to
      be legally bound. In contrast, noncommercial promises are presumed to be unenforceable unless the
      parties formally manifest their intention to be legally bound. . . . [The] existence of detrimental
      reliance can manifest to a promisee the promisor's intention to be legally bound.

My proposed doctrinal scheme attempts to facilitate both aspects of freedom of contract— freedom *to* contract and freedom *from* contract—by setting the background presumption in a manner that reflects the tacit understanding of most persons. With commercial promises, freedom *to* contract is facilitated by presuming such contracts to be enforceable, while enforcing the parties' expression of their intention not to be legally bound respects their freedom *from* contract. With non-commercial promises, the parties' freedom *from* contract is facilitated by presuming such contracts to be unenforceable, and enforcing the parties' expression of their intention to be legally bound respects their freedom *to* contract. The differential treatment of promises made in these two distinct contexts reflects the comparative likelihood that parties in each context intend to be legally bound by their promises.

While this doctrinal scheme is far from simple (and I welcome suggestions of its improvement), perhaps the primary source of the weakness of section 90 as a rule of law was the idea (espoused by Gilmore and many others) that the cases embraced by the doctrine of promissory estoppel could be explained simply by the concept of detrimental reliance. Ironically, this sentiment is remarkably similar to the common law's monistic preference for a single criterion of enforceability. Perhaps in this instance—to paraphrase Gilmore—multiplication *is* preferable to division.

QUESTIONS

1. Sarah agrees to sell Bert a car for £2,000. What is the consideration? (NB: Just as there is a promise on each side, there must be consideration on each side.)

2. If consideration is defined in terms of benefit to the promisor and/or detriment to the promisee, do you see an element of circularity in the way the definition is applied to bilateral contracts, at least when neither party has yet performed? How did Pollock's definition of consideration attempt to overcome this?

3. Pollock's definition refers to 'an act or forbearance or the promise thereof'. Will any act or forbearance suffice or are there some that the law does not recognise as 'sufficient' consideration?

4. If you think that some acts or forbearances are not sufficient, are these explicable on the ground that there was neither benefit to the promisor nor detriment to the promisee? You may want to think about the cases on intangible benefits (pp 100–102), compromises (pp 102–105) and performance of existing duties of various kinds (pp 105–115). If you do not think that the cases can be explained in terms of benefit and detriment, what explanations would you give?

5. How would you state the law on whether performance of an existing contractual duty owed to the promisor is consideration if both *Stilk v Myrick* and *Williams v Roffey Bros* are good law? (We will return to this question in Section 7.)

6. A loss-making company, which is part of a group of companies, is put into receivership. The holding company is subjected to adverse criticism for failing to 'stand behind' its failed subsidiary, although it has no legal obligation to do so. After a few days, it writes to all companies who normally do business with its other subsidiaries that, 'in order to maintain the reputation of the group and to encourage trading partners to continue to do business with us in future', it will guarantee that all creditors of the failed company will be paid in full. A number of creditors write 'accepting' this arrangement. Is the holding company bound to them?

7.   Norman has recently inherited a house. In an outbuilding, he finds the remains of an old car. He tells his friend Olly that Olly may have the car if he will come to take it away. Olly turns up to take the car away but Norman has realised that it is a rare model of some value and refuses to let Olly take it. Advise Olly. *(Hint:* see p 126.)

8.   Pauline, a lecturer, knows that Quentin, a student, feels he needs a copy of Treitel but can't afford it. One day, Pauline meets Quentin outside the University bookshop and tells him that she has decided to award a weekly prize of £25 for the best contribution in class, and that Quentin is to be the first recipient for the brilliant critique of the *Smoke Ball* case he gave last week. On the strength of this, Quentin goes and buys a copy of Treitel. At the next lecture, Pauline announces that after all she will not be giving any prize because she has just discovered that her bank account is wildly overdrawn. Advise Quentin.

9.   Rust plc, a steel maker, asks Sinter Ltd to give 'firm prices' for the supply of iron ore for Rust's steel works for the next six months. Sinter sends a list of prices for different quantities.

    (i)   Thereafter, the market price climbs steadily, and after three months, Sinter informs Rust that it will no longer supply at the quoted prices. Advise Rust.

    (ii) Would your answer to (i) differ if, to the knowledge of both parties, steel-making machinery has to be adjusted to take various types of iron ore and Rust could only switch to a different supplier at considerably higher cost?

    (iii) Rust agrees that it will purchase its requirements exclusively from Sinter. The market price climbs steadily and Sinter finds that Rust is ordering larger and larger quantities of ore, almost certainly reselling it to other steel makers. Advise Sinter.

    (Whatever your answer to (ii), you may feel that somehow Sinter should be protected from such opportunism on Rust's part. The courts might be able to do this by interpreting the contract as one to supply at the agreed prices only the iron genuinely needed by Rust for its own production; cf p 883. Is this an example of what Collins refers to as 'the problem of power': see p 66?)

CHAPTER SEVEN
INTENTION TO CREATE LEGAL RELATIONS

■ *Balfour v Balfour*

[1918–1919] All ER Rep 860, Court of Appeal

In 1915, the parties came to England from Ceylon, where the husband had a government post, during the husband's leave. He returned when his leave expired, but the wife remained in England on her doctor's advice, intending to follow when she could. She alleged that just before the husband sailed, they entered an oral contract whereby the husband agreed to pay the wife an allowance of £30 a month. Subsequently, they agreed to live apart. The wife brought an action to recover the money she claimed was due under the agreement. Sargant J gave judgment for the wife, and the husband appealed.

Atkin LJ

The defence to this action on the alleged contract is that the husband says he entered into no contract with his wife, and for the determination of that it is necessary to remember that there are agreements between parties which do not result in contracts within the meaning of that term in our law. The ordinary example is where two parties agree to take a walk together, or where there is an offer and an acceptance of hospitality. Nobody would suggest in ordinary circumstances that those agreements result in what we know as a contract, and one of the most usual forms of agreement which does not constitute a contract appears to me to be the arrangements which are made between husband and wife. It is quite common, and it is the natural and inevitable result of the relationship of husband and wife, that the two spouses should make agreements between themselves, agreements such as are in dispute in this action, agreements for allowances by which the husband agrees that he will pay to his wife a certain sum of money per week or per month or per year to cover either her own expenses or the necessary expenses of the household and of the children, and in which the wife promises either expressly or impliedly to apply the allowance for the purpose for which it is given.

   To my mind those agreements, or many of them, do not result in contracts at all, and they do not result in contracts even though there may be what as between other parties would constitute consideration for the agreement. The consideration, as we know, may consist either in some right, interest, profit, or benefit accruing to one party, or some forbearance, detriment, loss, or responsibility given, suffered, or undertaken by the other. That is a well-known definition, and it constantly happens. I think, that such arrangements made between husband and wife are arrangements in which there are mutual promises, or in which there is consideration in form within the definition that I have mentioned. Nevertheless they are not contracts, and they are not contracts because the parties did not intend that they should be attended by legal consequences. It would be the worst possible example to hold that agreements such as this resulted in legal obligations which could be enforced in the courts. It would mean that when a husband made his wife a promise to give her an allowance of 30s or £2 per week, whatever he could afford to give her for the maintenance of the household and children, and she promised so to apply it, not only could she sue him for his failure in any week to supply the allowance, but he could sue her for non-performance of the obligation, express or implied, which she had undertaken upon her part. The small courts of this country would have to be multiplied one hundredfold if these arrangements did result in fact in legal obligations. They are not sued upon, and the reason that they are not sued upon is not because the parties are reluctant to enforce their legal rights when the agreement is broken, but they are not sued upon because the parties in the inception of the arrangement never intended that they should be sued upon. Agreements such as these, as I say, are outside the realm of contracts altogether. The common law does not regulate the form of agreements between spouses. Their promises are not sealed with seals and sealing wax. The consideration that really obtains for them is that natural love and affection which counts for so little in these cold courts. The terms may be repudiated, varied, or renewed as performance proceeds, or as the disagreements develop, and the principles of the common law as to exoneration and discharge and accord and satisfaction are such as find no place in the domestic code. The parties themselves are advocates, judges, courts, sheriff's officer and reporter. In respect of these promises each house is a domain into which the king's writ does not seek to run, and to which his officers do not seek to be admitted.

The only question in the present case is whether or not this promise was of such a class or not. For the reasons given by my brethren it appears to me to be plain. I think it is plainly established that the promise here was not intended by either party to be attended by legal consequences. I think the onus was upon the wife, and that the wife has not established any contract.

Warrington and **Duke LJJ** delivered judgments to the same effect.

Appeal allowed.

■ *Merritt v Merritt*

[1970] 2 All ER 760, Court of Appeal

The husband left the matrimonial home, which was in the joint names of husband and wife. Later, he met the wife to discuss financial arrangements, and they agreed that he would pay the wife £40 a month, out of which she must pay the outstanding mortgage payments. He gave her the building society book, and at the wife's insistence, signed an agreement, which stated:

In consideration of the fact that you will pay all charges in connection with the house ... until such time as the mortgage repayment has been completed I will agree to transfer the property into your sole ownership.

The wife paid off the mortgage, but the husband refused to transfer the house to the wife.

Lord Denning MR

... The first point taken on his behalf by counsel for the husband was that the agreement was not intended to create legal relations. It was, he says, a family arrangement such as was considered by the court in *Balfour v Balfour* and in *Jones v Padavatton*. So the wife could not sue on it. I do not think that those cases have any application here. The parties there were living together in amity. In such cases their domestic arrangements are ordinarily not intended to create legal relations. It is altogether different when the parties are not living in amity but are separated, or about to separate. They then bargain keenly. They do not rely on honourable understandings. They want everything cut and dried. It may safely be presumed that they intend to create legal relations ...

Widgery and **Karminski LJJ** delivered judgments to the same effect.

NOTES

1. Is the presumption stated by Atkin LJ based on (i) the parties' actual intentions, (ii) what as reasonable people they probably would have agreed had they considered the question, or (iii) a policy of non-intervention? If the last, why should there be such a policy?

2. In *Pettitt v Pettitt* [1970] AC 777, a case in which one spouse had improved the matrimonial home, which was in the other's name, Lord Diplock said (at 822):

    Where the acquisition or improvement is made as a result of contributions in money or money's worth by both spouses acting in concert the proprietary interests in the family asset resulting from their respective contributions depend upon their common intention as to what those interests should be.

    I have used the neutral expression 'acting in concert' because many of the ordinary domestic arrangements between man and wife do not possess the legal characteristics of a contract. So long as they are executory they do not give rise to any chose in action, for neither party intended that non-performance of their mutual promises should be the subject of sanctions in any court (see *Balfour v Balfour*). But this is relevant to non-performance only. If spouses do perform their mutual promises the fact that they could not have been compelled to do so while the promises were executory cannot deprive the acts done by them of all legal consequences upon proprietary rights; for these are within the field of the law of property rather than of the law of contract. It would, in my view, be erroneous to extend the presumption accepted in *Balfour v Balfour* that mutual promises between man and wife in relation to their domestic arrangements are prima facie not intended by either to be legally enforceable to a presumption of a common intention of both spouses that *no* legal consequences should flow from acts done by them in performance of mutual promises with respect to the acquisition, improvement or addition to real or personal property—for this would be to intend what is impossible in law.

3. The decision whether legal relations were intended seems to depend on the circumstances. What factors are relevant? Consider the next case.

■ *Jones v Padavatton*
[1969] 2 All ER 616, Court of Appeal

The daughter, who had a good job in Washington DC, was offered by her mother, who lived in Trinidad, an allowance of $200 a month if she would go to England to study for the Bar, with a view to practising in Trinidad. Although she did not want to leave Washington, the daughter accepted; she also accepted $200 West Indian dollars, which was what the mother had meant, although the daughter had expected $200 US dollars, which were worth considerably more. No written contract was entered, nor was there any agreement as to the duration of the arrangement. The daughter came to England in 1962. In 1964, it was arranged that the mother would buy a house in London for the daughter to live in: she was to rent out some of the rooms and use the income to maintain herself in place of the $200 a month. In 1967, the mother claimed possession of the house; the daughter had not yet passed the Bar examinations.

Danckwerts LJ delivered judgment to the same effect as Fenton Atkinson LJ below.

Salmon LJ

I agree with the conclusion at which Dankwerts LJ has arrived, but I have reached it by a different route. . . .

In the present case the learned county court judge, having had the advantage of seeing the mother and the daughter in the witness box, entirely accepted the daughter's version of the facts. He came to the conclusion that on these very special facts the true inference must be that the arrangements between the parties prior to the daughter's leaving Washington were intended by both to have contractual force. On the facts as found by the learned county court judge this was entirely different from the ordinary case of a mother promising her daughter an allowance whilst the daughter read for the Bar, or a father promising his son an allowance at university if the son passed the necessary examinations to gain admission.

I cannot think that either intended that if, after the daughter had been in London, say, for six months, the mother dishonoured her promise and left her daughter destitute, the daughter would have no legal redress. . . .

The agreement was to last for a reasonable time. The parties cannot have contemplated that the daughter should go on studying for the Bar and draw the allowance until she was seventy, nor on the other hand that the mother could have discontinued the allowance if the daughter did not pass her examinations within, say 18 months. The promise was to pay the allowance until the daughter's studies were completed, and to my mind there was a clear implication that they were to be completed within a reasonable time. Studies are completed either by the student being called to the Bar or giving up the unequal struggle against the examiners. I cannot think that a reasonable time could possibly exceed five years from November 1962, the date when she began her studies.

It follows, therefore, that on no view can she now in November 1968 be entitled to anything further under the contract which the learned county court judge, rightly I think, held that she made with the mother in 1962. She has some of Part I of the Bar examination still to pass, and necessarily the final has not yet even been attemped.

Fenton Atkinson LJ

. . . In my judgment it is the subsequent history which gives the best guide to the parties' intention at the material time. There are three matters which seem to me important: (i) The daughter thought that her mother was promising her $(U.S.) 200, or £70 a month, which she regarded as the minimum necessary for her support. The mother promised $200 but she had in mind $(West Indian) 200. £42 a month, and that was what she in fact paid from November 1962 to December 1964. Those payments were accepted by the daughter without any sort of suggestion at any stage that the mother had legally contracted for the larger sum. (ii) When the arrangements for the purchase of no 181, Highbury Quadrant were being discussed, and the new arrangement was made for maintenance to come out of the rents, many material matters were left open: How much accommodation was the daughter to occupy; how much money was she to have out of the rents: if the rents fell below expectation, was the mother to make up the difference below £42, or £42 less the sum saved by the daughter in rent; for how long was the arrangement to continue, and so on. The whole arrangement was, in my view, far too vague and uncertain to be itself enforceable as a contract; but at no stage did the daughter bring into the discussions her alleged legal right of £42 per month until her studies were completed, and how that right was to be affected by the new arrangement. (iii) It is perhaps not without relevance to look at the daughter's evidence in cross-examination. She was asked about the occasion when the mother visited the house, and she, knowing perfectly well that the mother was there, refused for some hours to open the door. She said:

> 'I didn't open the door because a normal mother doesn't sue her daughter in court. Anybody with normal feelings would feel upset by what was happening.'

Those answers and the daughter's conduct on that occasion provided a strong indication that she had never for a moment contemplated the possibility of the mother or herself going to court to enforce legal obligations, and that she felt it quite intolerable that a purely family arrangement should become the subject of proceedings in a court of law.

At the time when the first arrangement was made, the mother and the daughter were, and always had been, to use the daughter's own words, 'very close'. I am satisfied that neither party at that time intended to enter into a legally binding contract, either then or later when the house was bought. The daughter was prepared to trust the mother to honour her promise of support, just as the mother no doubt trusted the daughter to study for the Bar with diligence, and to get through her examinations as early as she could. It follows that in my view the mother's claim for possession succeeds. . . .

■ *Coward v Motor Insurers' Bureau* [1962]
1 All ER 531, Court of Appeal

Coward was killed in an accident caused by the negligence of Cole, on whose motorbike Coward was a pillion passenger. Cole was also killed. Coward's widow brought an action against Cole's personal representatives and was given judgment, but the judgment was unsatisfied because Cole's insurance did not cover pillion passengers and his estate had no other assets. The widow then sued the MIB, which had an obligation to pay unsatisfied judgments in respect of a 'liability which is required to be covered by a policy...' under the Road Traffic Act 1930, claiming that Cole was bound to insure as he was carrying Coward for 'hire or reward'. The Court of Appeal thought it was necessary to decide whether there was a contract between Cole and Coward (in *Albert v Motor Insurers' Bureau*, below, the House of Lords held by a majority that this question need not be answered after all).

Upjohn LJ, delivering the judgment of the court, said:

On this point, the fact that both parties are dead, we believe matters little, for if the question had been posed to Coward or Cole: 'Did you intend to enter into a legal relationship?' each would probably have answered 'I never gave it a thought'. The practice whereby workmen go to their place of business in the motor car or on the motor cycle of a fellow-workman on the terms of making a contribution to the costs of transport is well known and widespread. In the absence of evidence that the parties intended to be bound contractually, we should be reluctant to conclude that the daily carriage by one of another to work on payment of some weekly (or it may be daily) sum involved them in a legal contractual relationship. The hazards of everyday life, such as temporary indisposition, the incidence of holidays, the possibility of a change of shift or different hours of overtime, or incompatibility arising, make it most unlikely that either contemplated that the one was legally bound to carry and the other to be carried to work. It is made all the more improbable in this case by reason of the fact that alternative means of transport seem to have been available to Coward.

■ *Albert v Motor Insurers' Bureau* [1971]
2 All ER 1345, House of Lords

Quirk had regularly carried other dockers to work in his car, on the understanding that they should pay five to ten shillings each per week. Sometimes he received beer or cigarettes in lieu, and he sometimes did not charge friends who were short of money.

The majority held that a vehicle was used to carry passengers for hire or reward if the carriage was on a systematic basis going beyond acts of social kindness, even if there was no contract between the owner and the passengers: Quirk's vehicle had been so used. Lord Cross, differing from the majority, held it *was* necessary to determine whether there was a contract, and continued:

I think that the judge was wrong in holding that the facts which he found warranted the inference that there were no legally binding agreements between Mr Quirk and any of his passengers. It is not necessary in order that a legally binding contract should arise that the parties should direct their minds to the question and decide in favour of the creation of a legally binding relationship. If I get into a taxi and ask the driver to drive me to Victoria Station it is extremely unlikely that either of us directs his mind to the question whether we are entering into a contract. We enter into a contract not because we form any intention to enter into one but because if our minds were directed to the point we should as reasonable people both agree that we were in fact entering into one. When one passes from the field of transactions of an obviously business character between strangers to arrangements between friends or acquaintances for the payment by the passenger of a contribution towards expenses the fact that the arrangement is not made purely as a matter of business and that if the anticipated payment is not made it would probably never enter into the head of the driver to sue for it disposes one to say that there is no contract; but in fact the answer to the question 'contract' or 'no contract' does not depend on the likelihood of an action being brought to enforce it in case of default.

Suppose that when one of Mr Quirk's fellow workers got in touch with him and asked him whether he could travel in his car to Tilbury and back next day, an 'officious bystander' had asked 'Will you be paying anything for your transport?' the prospective passenger would have answered at once 'Of course I will pay'. If the 'officious bystander' had gone on to ask Mr Quirk whether, if he was not paid, he would sue the the man in the county court, Mr Quirk might well have answered in the words used by the driver in *Connell's* case—'Not bloody likely'. But the fact that if default was made Mr Quirk would not have started legal proceedings but would have resorted to extra-judicial remedies does not mean that an action could not in theory have been brought to recover payment for the carriage. If one imagines such proceedings being brought a plea on the part of the passenger that he never meant to enter into a contract would have received short shrift and so, too, would a plea that the contract was void for uncertainty because no precise sum was mentioned. If the evidence did not establish a regular charge for the Tilbury trip the judge would have fixed the appropriate sum.

NOTE

Are these statements by Upjohn LJ and Lord Cross reconcilable? Could it be that there is no contract for the future, yet there is liability to pay for lifts received (compare *Pettitt v Pettitt*, p 177)? Query, however, whether the liability to pay for the lifts received would be contractual or restitutionary: see *BSC v Cleveland Bridge Engineering* (p 39).

■ *Rose & Frank Co v JR Crompton Bros*

[1924] All ER Rep 245, Court of Appeal; [1925] AC 445, House of Lords

In 1913, the plaintiffs and defendants signed a document expressing their willingness that the existing arrangements between them for goods made by the defendants to be supplied to the plaintiffs should be continued for a specified period, at prices quoted for periods of six months. The document concluded:

This arrangement is not entered into, nor is this memorandum written, as a formal or legal agreement, and shall not be subject to legal jurisdiction in the law courts either of the United States or England, but it is only a definite expression and record of the purpose and intention of the three parties concerned, to which they each honourably pledge themselves with the fullest confidence—based on past business with each other—that it will be carried through by each of the three parties with mutual loyalty and friendly co-operation.

The defendants terminated the agreement without notice, and the plaintiffs sued for breach of the agreement and also for failure to deliver goods they had ordered in accordance with the agreement in 1919, before the termination.

Scrutton LJ

In 1913 the parties concurred in signing a document which gives rise to the present dispute. I agree that if the clause beginning 'This arrangement' were omitted, the courts would treat the rest of the agreement as giving use to legal relations, though of great vagueness. But the clause in question beginning 'This arrangement' is not omitted. Bailhache J thought that by itself this clause 'plain as it is' means that the parties shall not be under any legal obligation to each other at all, but, coming to the conclusion that without this clause the agreement would create legal obligations, he takes the view that the clause must be rejected as repugnant to the rest of the agreement. He also holds that, if the clause merely means to exclude recourse to the law courts as a means of settling disputes, it is contrary to public policy as ousting the jurisdiction of the King's courts.

In my view, the learned judge adopts a wrong canon of construction. He should seek the intention of the parties as shown by the language they use, not in part of that language only, but in the whole of that language. It is true that in deeds and wills where it is impossible from the whole of the contradictory language used to ascertain the true intention of the framers, resort may be had, but only as a last expedient, to what Jessell MR called 'the rule of thumb' in *Re Bywater*, of rejecting clauses as repugnant according to their place in the document, the later clause being rejected in deeds and the earlier in wills. But before this heroic method is adopted of finding out what the parties meant by assuming that they did not mean part of what they have said, it must be clearly impossible to harmonise the whole of the language they have used. It is quite possible for parties to come to an agreement by accepting a proposal with the result that the agreement concluded does not give rise to legal relations. The reason of this is that the parties do not intend that their agreement shall give rise to legal relations. This intention may be implied from the subject-matter of the agreement, but it may also be expressed by the parties. In social and family relations such an intention is readily implied, while in business matters the opposite result would ordinarily follow. But I can see no reason why, even in business matters, the parties should not intend to rely on each other's good faith and honour, and to exclude all idea of settling disputes by any outside intervention with the accompanying necessity of expressing themselves so precisely that outsiders may have no difficulty in understanding what they mean. If they clearly express such an intention I can see no reason in public policy why effect should not be given to their intention. . . .

The remaining question is the claim in the statement of claim for damage for the non-delivery of the whole of the undelivered part of the goods said to be legally due under some thirty-two specified orders. . . .

Messrs Crompton, on Feb 12, 1919, wrote a letter which appears to me fully to carry out the vague arrangements in honour which I have held to be constituted by the arrangements of 1913, but, as made under that arrangement in honour, to give rise to no legal obligation. It runs as follows:

> 'We beg to acknowledge receipt of your favour of the 24th ult, contents of which are duly noted. We also thank you for the twenty-four orders for 286 cases of Messrs Brittains' papers, and eight orders for sixty-four cases of our paper, to all of which we will give our best attention, and Messrs Brittains write us with regard to the orders for their papers that they are endeavouring to let you have deliveries this year up to at least the full 100 per cent for the standard year ending Feb 28, 1918, but that at the moment conditions are particularly uncertain. Nevertheless, they would like us to assure you that they would give their most careful attention to your requirements, and endeavour to let you have the fullest output they possibly can, and they add that time will make the position clearer.'

This I cannot construe as a binding acceptance of a legal proposal. It is, in my opinion, an assurance that the suppliers will do their best to comply with the probable requirements of the agents, but do not bind themselves.

[Atkin LJ agreed in relation to the alleged contract of 1913, but in relation to the specific orders said:]

In this case the defendants by the honourable understanding entered into the vague engagement contained in the document which had as a basis the average turnover for the last three years before the agreement. But whatever the terms of the agreement or understanding, it contemplated, as nearly all such agreements do, that the actual business done under it should be done by particular contracts of purchase and sale upon the terms of the general agreement so far as applicable. The actual business was done in this case, as in countless others, by orders for specific goods given by the 'agent' and accepted by the manufacturer or merchant. To see whether the orders given were accepted the terms of the alleged acceptance have to be regarded. . . .

'We . . . thank you for the twenty-four orders for 286 cases of Messrs Brittains' papers and eight orders for sixty-four cases of our paper, to all of which we will give our best attention.'

Pausing there, this is the common formula of acceptance in the business world which has been treated as acceptance in countless cases since merchants first wrote to one another. It would be understood as an acceptance passing between two merchants while there was no obligation at all on the part of the vendor to accept. Why it should bear a different meaning in a case where there is an honourable understanding by the merchant to accept up to some vague limit, I am unable to understand. The letter continues.

'and Messrs Brittains write us with regard to the orders for their papers that they are endeavouring to let you have deliveries this year up to at least the full 100 per cent for the standard year ending Feb 28, 1918, but that at the moment conditions are particularly uncertain.'

This seems to me to relate to the business likely to be done over the whole year, and particularly to the plaintiff's statement in the letter of Jan 24, 1919, under reply that they had not yet determined the full quantity of paper that they would require, and that they would send on further orders later. I read the whole letter as saying: 'We definitely accept these orders and as to further orders for Brittains' paper we expect to be able to execute them up to the 1918 quantity, but this is not certain.'

The House of Lords agreed with Atkin LJ.

NOTES

1. Compare the cases on whether the defendant made a promise (see pp 13–20). Aren't those cases and many of the 'intention to create legal relations' cases asking the same question?

2. In *Edmonds v Lawson* [2000] QB 501, the claimant accepted an offer from a set of chambers of an unfunded pupillage. Later, she sought to argue that she was a 'worker' within the meaning of the National Minimum Wage Act 1998. The chambers argued that there was no intention to create legal relations and no consideration, and therefore no contract. The Court of Appeal was clear that although no money changed hands, there was both intention to create legal relations and consideration, because the transaction was beneficial to both sides. Chambers had an interest in recruiting a pool of able pupils, and pupils had an interest in the opportunity of developing and displaying skills that might give the chance of a tenancy.

3. In *Ford Motor Co Ltd v Amalgamated Union of Engineering and Foundry Workers* [1969] 2 All ER 481, the question arose whether a series of collective agreements between Ford and the union were legally enforceable contracts. Geoffrey Lane J held that they were not intended to create legal relations. Firstly, in determining the parties' intentions, it was proper to look at the general opinion on the point in industrial circles at the time the agreements were made. The Report of the Royal Commission on Trade Unions (the Donovan Report, Cmd 3623, 1968), and the evidence given to the Commission, showed clearly that collective agreements were generally regarded as legally unenforceable. Both

Ford and the union would have known that. Secondly, many of the clauses were very vague. The judge concluded:

If one applies the subjective test and asks what the intentions of the various parties were, the answer is that, so far as they had any express intentions, they were certainly not to make the agreement enforceable at law. If one applies an objective test and asks what intention must be imputed from all the circumstances of the case the answer is the same. The fact that the agreements prima facie deal with commercial relationships is outweighed by the other considerations, by the wording of the agreements, by the nature of the agreements, and by the climate of opinion voiced and evidenced by the extra-judicial authorities. Agreements such as these, composed largely of optimistic aspirations, presenting grave practical problems of enforcement and reached against a background of opinion adverse to enforceability, are, in my judgment, not contracts in the legal sense and are not enforceable at law. Without clear and express provisions making them amenable to legal action, they remain in the realm of undertakings binding in honour. None of the authorities cited by counsel for Fords dissuades me from this view. In my judgment, the parties, neither of them, had the intention to make these agreements binding at law.

See on this case and the general doctrine, Hepple, 'Intention to create Legal Relations' [1970] CLJ 122.

4.   Terms of collective agreement may become part of individual employee's contracts of employment, either by express reference or by implicit incorporation (see p 343). However, even express reference will only incorporate those terms of the agreement that are 'apt' for incorporation. In *Alexander v Standard Telephones & Cables Ltd (No 2)* [1990] ICR 291, Hobhouse J said (at 297–298):

The principles to be applied can therefore be summarised. The relevant contract is that between the individual employee and his employer; it is the contractual intention of those two parties which must be ascertained. In so far as that intention is to be found in a written document, that document must be construed on ordinary contractual principles. In so far as there is no such document or that document is not complete or conclusive, their contractual intention has to be ascertained by inference from the other available material including collective agreements. The fact that another document is not itself contractual does not prevent it from being incorporated into the contract if that intention is shown as between the employer and the individual employee. Where a document is expressly incorporated by general words it is still necessary to consider, in conjunction with the words of incorporation, whether any particular part of that document is apt to be a term of the contract; if it is inapt, the correct construction of the contract may be that it is not a term of the contract. Where it is not a case of express incorporation, but a matter of inferring the contractual intent, the character of the document and the relevant part of it and whether it is apt to form part of the individual contract is central to the decision whether or not the inference should be drawn.

■ *Esso Petroleum Ltd v Commissioners of Customs and Excise*
[1976] 1 All ER 117, House of Lords

In 1970, Esso devised a sales promotions scheme under which garage owners offered a 'free' 'World Cup Coin' with every four gallons of petrol. The coins had little intrinsic value. The Commissioners claimed that the coins were chargeable to purchase tax under s 2(1) of the Purchase Tax Act 1963, on the ground that they were 'produced in quantity for general sale'.

The House of Lords held, by a majority, that the coins were not being 'sold'. It differed on whether there was any intention to create legal relations.

Lord Simon of Glaisdale

My Lords, I have had the advantage of reading in draft the speech prepared by my noble and learned friend, Lord Russell of Killowen. I beg to take advantage of his explanation of the facts that have led to the appeal and the statutory provisions by which they are to be judged.

I am, however, my Lords, not prepared to accept that the promotion material put out by Esso was not envisaged by them as creating legal relations between the garage proprietors who adopted it and the motorists who yielded to its blandishments. In the first place, Esso and the garage proprietors put the material out for their commercial advantage, and designed it to attract the custom of motorists. The whole transaction took place in a setting of business relations. In the second place, it seems to me in general undesirable to allow a commercial promoter to claim that what he has done is a mere puff, not intended to create legal relations (cf *Carlill v Carbolic Smoke Ball* Co). The coins may have been themselves of little intrinsic value; but all the evidence suggests that Esso contemplated that they would be attractive to motorists and that there would be a large commercial advantage to themselves from the scheme, an advantage in which the garage proprietors also would share. Thirdly, I think that authority supports the view that legal relations were envisaged.

[I]t begs the question to assert that no motorist who bought petrol in consequence of seeing the promotion material prominently displayed in the garage forecourt would be likely to bring an action in the county court if he were refused a coin. He might be a suburb Hampden who was not prepared to forego what he conceived to be his rights or to allow a tradesman to go back on his word.

Believing as I do that Esso envisaged a bargain of some sort between the garage proprietor and the motorist, I must try to analyse the transaction. The analysis that most appeals to me is one of the ways in which Lord Denning MR considered the case, namely a collateral contract of the sort described by Lord Moulton in *Heilbut, Symons & Co v Buckleton*:

> '. . . there may be a contract the consideration for which is the making of some other contract. "If you will make such and such a contract I will give you one hundred pounds", is in every sense of the word a complete legal contract. It is collateral to the main contract . . .'

So here. The law happily matches the reality. The garage proprietor is saying, 'If you will buy four gallons of my petrol. I will give you one of these coins.' None of the reasons which have caused the law to consider advertising or display material as an invitation to treat, rather than an offer, applies here. What the garage proprietor says by his placards is in fact and in law an offer of consideration to the motorist to enter into a contract of sale of petrol. Of course, not every motorist will notice the placard, but nor will every potential offeree of many offers be necessarily conscious that they have been made. However, the motorist who does notice the placard, and in reliance thereon drives in and orders the petrol, is in law doing two things at the same time. First, he is accepting the offer of a coin if he buys four gallons of petrol. Secondly, he is himself offering to buy four gallons of petrol: this offer is accepted by the filling of his tank.

Here the coins were not transferred for a money consideration. They were transferred in consideration of the motorist entering into a contract for the sale of petrol. The coins were therefore not produced for sale, and do not fall within the schedule. They are exempt from purchase tax.

I would therefore dismiss the appeal.

Lord Wilberforce agreed with **Lord Simon's** analysis. **Lord Fraser of Tullybelton** also held that there was intention to create legal relations.

Lord Russell of Killowen

. . . My Lords, it is not in dispute that unless the medals were produced at the instance of Esso for the purpose of, ie with a view to, their being sold by garage proprietors to motorists there cannot be the suggested charge of purchase tax. The first question accordingly is whether, notwithstanding the liberal references in the documents attending the promotion scheme to 'giving', 'gifts', and 'free', that which would and did take place gave rise to a contract, enforceable by a motorist who bought four gallons from a participating proprietor, that he should receive one of these medals. It is to be borne in mind in this connection that the mere facts that Esso and the garage proprietors undoubtedly had a commercial aim in promoting the scheme does not deprive the delivery of a medal of the quality of a gift as distinct from a sale; for benevolence it is not a necessary feature of a gift which may well be motivated by self interest. On the other hand it is trite law that if on analysis a transaction has in law one character, the fact that the parties either accidentally or deliberately frame the transaction in language appropriate to a transaction of a different character will not deny to it its true character.

We have here, my Lords, a promotion scheme initiated by Esso, who procured the production of the medals. Each medal was of negligible intrinsic value, though the incentive to soccer enthusiasts to collect all 30 may have been strong. Plainly it was never in Esso's mind that this negligible intrinsic value should be reflected in an increase in the pump price of petrol, and it never was: indeed the price of a gallon could not be increased by 3/16 of a penny. In my opinion it would have been thought by Esso, and rightly, that there could have been no occasion, in order to ensure success of the scheme, for an outlet proprietor to subject himself to a contractual liability to deliver a coin to a motorist who had bought four gallons. The subject matter was trivial: the proprietor was directly interested in the success of the scheme and would be in the highest degree unlikely to renege on the free gift offer, and indeed there is no suggestion that a motorist who qualified and wanted a medal ever failed to get one; from the motorist's viewpoint, if this had ever happened, I cannot think that he would have considered that he had a legal grievance, though he might have said that he would not patronise that outlet again; similarly in my opinion if a garage advertised 'Free Air' and after buying petrol or oil the motorist was told that the machine was out of order that day. In my opinion, the incentive for the garage proprietor to carry out the scheme was such as to make it quite unnecessary to invest, or for Esso to intend to invest, the transaction with the additional compulsion of a contractual obligation, and in all the circumstances of the case I am unable to regard that which under the scheme was intended by Esso to take place in relation to the medals, and did take place, as something which would be intended to or regarded as creating a legal contractual relationship. In forming that opinion I regard the mimimal intrinsic value of a medal as important. I would not wish it to be thought that my opinion, if correct, would, in other cases in which a sales promotion scheme involves substantial benefits, give carte blanche to participants to renege on 'free' offers. I am simply of opinion, in agreement with the Court of Appeal, though not I fear with the majority of your Lordships, that in the instant case, because of the absence of any contractual element, it should not be said that any medal was produced for general sale.

Suppose however that there was a contractual obligation on the proprietor to deliver a medal to the motorist who had bought four gallons of petrol, the further question arises whether there was a contract of sale of the medal for a price in money.

[Lord Russell went on to hold that the coins were not being 'sold': there was an offer to give a coin to any motorist who purchased four gallons of petrol.

Viscount Dilhorne gave judgment to the same effect as **Lord Russell.**

Appeal dismissed.

■ *J Evans & Son (Portsmouth) Ltd v Andrea Merzario Ltd*
[1976] 2 All ER 930

The plaintiffs, who were importers of machinery, regularly used the defendant forwarding agents to arrange the carriage of the goods to England. The contracts were on the standard conditions of the forwarding trade. The machinery was liable to rust if carried on deck, and, before 1967, the defendant had always arranged for the crates or trailers containing it to be carried below decks. In 1967, in the course of a 'courtesy call' to the plaintiffs, the defendant's representative proposed that in future the plaintiffs' machinery should be carried by container transport. When the plaintiffs expressed concern about rusting, the representative gave an oral assurance that any container used for the plaintiffs' goods would be shipped below decks (many container ships are designed to carry large numbers of containers stacked on the decks). On that basis, the plaintiffs agreed to the change in method. Subsequently, the defendants, arranged for the transport in a container of an injection-moulding machine for the plaintiffs, and by an oversight it was placed on deck. The container was not properly fastened down, and when the ship left port, the container fell overboard and the machine was lost.

At first instance, Kerr J held that the oral assurance made during the courtsey call was not intended to be legally binding. The Court of Appeal disagreed. **Roskill LJ** said:

I unreservedly accept counsel for the defendants' submission that one must not look at one or two isolated answers given in evidence; one should look at the totality of the evidence. When one does that, one finds first, as I have already mentioned, that these parties had been doing business in transporting goods from Milan to England for some time before; secondly, that transportation of goods from Milan to England was always done on trailers which were always under deck; thirdly, that the defendants wanted a change in the practice—they wanted containers used instead of trailers; fourthly, that the plaintiffs were only willing to agree to that change if they were promised by the defendant that those containers would be shipped under deck, and would not have agreed to the change but for that promise. The defendants gave such a promise which to my mind against this background plainly amounted to an enforceable contractual promise. In those circumstances it seems to me that the contract was this: 'If we continue to give you our business, you will ensure that those goods in containers are shipped under deck'; and the defendants agreed that this would be so. Thus there was a breach of that contract by the defendants when this container was shipped on deck; and it seems to me to be plain that the damage which the plaintiffs suffered resulted from that breach.

Lord Denning MR and **Geoffrey Lane LJ** delivered concurring judgments.

Appeal allowed.

Further extracts from this case will be found on p 980.

NOTE

In contrast, in *Independent Broadcasting Authority v EMI Electronics Ltd and BICC Construction Ltd* (1980) 14 BLR 1, EMI was employed as main contractor by the IBA to put up the Elmley Moor television mast, which, at 1,250 feet, was the tallest mast erected on this side of the Atlantic. It was understood that the design of the mast and its construction would be carried out by BIC (now BICC), which was employed as subcontractor: there was no direct contract between IBA and BIC.

The mast was erected, but it collapsed on a day when there was only a light wind but it was very cold. The trial judge found that the collapse was caused by a combination of oscillations set up in the mast by 'vortex shedding', as the light wind blew past the cylindrical part of the mast, and asymmetric icing on the stays of the mast. It appeared that no one had foreseen the dangerous combination of oscillations and icing at wind speeds low enough that the ice was not blown off the stays. The judge held that this failure on BIC's part constituted negligence.

During the course of construction, IBA had questioned the safety of the mast after another, similar mast being built had started to oscillate. However, on 11 November 1964, BIC wrote to EMI that 'we are well satisfied that the structure will not oscillate dangerously', and relying on this, IBA permitted work to go ahead without further investigation of the design.

The House of Lords held that because EMI had tendered for the 'design, supply and erection' of the mast, it was contractually liable for the defective design. However, the House also considered whether BIC was liable to IBA.

The House of Lords, differing from the courts below, held that BIC was not liable in contract to IBA: the letter did not show any intention to contract. BIC was, however, held liable in tort for giving the assurance negligently.

QUESTIONS

1. In 1937, the Law Revision Committee proposed that a promise in writing should be binding even though not supported by consideration (Sixth Interim Report, Cmnd 5449). Do you agree with this proposal?

2. The Committee also proposed that past consideration should be good consideration. This would mean that even a purely oral promise for past consideration would be binding. Do you agree with this proposal? *(Hint:* you may find it useful to think about the types of situation in which such promises might be made (eg *Webb v McGowin,* p 141) and consider what safeguards on the liability of the promisor, if any, should be imposed in such a case.)

3. Was there any consideration for the landlord's promise to reduce the rent in the *High Trees* case? Why was the wife's forbearance from taking proceedings in *Combe v Combe* not consideration?

4. What are the elements of traditional estoppel? What are the differences between traditional estoppel and contract?

5. How does the doctrine of promissory estoppel as stated by Denning J in the *High Trees* case differ from 'traditional' estoppel? (We will explore this in more detail in Section 7.)

6. What is meant by saying that estoppel cannot be a cause of action?

7. What are the essential elements of proprietary estoppel? How does it differ from contract?

8. How do the policies reflected in, or the values underlying, promissory and proprietary estoppel differ from those of 'classical' contract?

9. What is the thrust of Atiyah's argument about consideration (pp 165–169)? Do you think there is a doctrine of consideration? Might the answer depend to some extent on what one means by 'a doctrine'?

10. The Law Revision Committee (see question 1) also proposed that a promise that the promisor knows, or reasonably should know, will be relied on by the promisee and which is acted on by the promisee to his detriment should be binding. How much difference to the practical outcome of cases would this change make? Should the proposal be adopted? If such a reform were to be introduced, what damages should be given?

11. In a case in which an agreement seems to be on the borderline between a contract and a merely social or domestic arrangement, list the factors that may influence the court in one way or the other in deciding whether or not there was 'intention to create legal relations'.

SECTION THREE

HAS AN AGREEMENT BEEN REACHED?

CHAPTER EIGHT
OFFER AND ACCEPTANCE

The traditional method of determining whether the parties have in fact agreed to be bound by a contract is to ask whether one party has made an 'offer' and the other has 'accepted' that offer.

Throughout the materials that follow, it will be seen that the courts are faced with striking a balance between conflicting interests. On the one hand, it is important to preserve the freedom of action of a party seeking to make an exchange. He must be able to disseminate information about his willingness to contract without the risk of being subjected to obligations he cannot meet, and without having to hedge his words so carefully that the process becomes too costly and the information appears too unreliable to the recipient (who may not understand the need for the hedging phrases and be suspicious of them). On the other hand, the recipient may need to be able to rely on the information given her. She may want to be able to 'count on' a contract even though the first party is still not ready to commit himself.

To take an example, a person with goods to sell needs to be able to advertise them widely, but does not want to become committed to more buyers than he can supply; he may need the freedom to negotiate with a number of buyers until he obtains the best price. Clearly, the seller could protect himself by stating that he is reserving the right to refuse any order, but should the seller have to do this in order to prevent himself being bound to a potential buyer who simply sends in an order for the goods? The recipient's position may also be complicated. She may want to rely on the seller being willing and able to supply at a particular price but herself not yet be in a position in which she can commit herself to buying. She could make contracts for the goods with elaborate cancellation clauses, but this is an expensive approach that is seldom adopted unless the risks are very high. Instead, the courts have to construe the facts of what happened during negotiations in a way that seems fair to the parties and workable for the future.

To some extent, the courts' ability to do this has been limited by the tools available: in particular, by the fact that the analysis has traditionally been 'contract or no contract', with no intermediate position. This is not always the case even in English law, because the courts have sometimes been able to provide a solution through restitutionary or even tortious remedies (see pp 281 ff), but English law has not yet followed the US example of manipulating reliance doctrine (see p 170) to impose liability without subjecting the parties to a contract. Whether this is a sensible approach will be discussed later (p 283).

See generally Winfield, 'Some Aspects of Offer and Acceptance' (1939) 55 LQR 499; Kahn (1955) 72 SALJ 246.

I. THE OBJECTIVE PRINCIPLE

As mentioned earlier (**p 17**), it is normally what you say or do that matters in contract, not what you meant. The objective principle is particularly important in cases of mistake about what the proposed terms are (see Chapter 11) and a classic formulation of the principle is found in one of these, *Smith v Hughes* (see p 303). Blackburn J said:

If, whatever a man's real intention may be, he so conducts himself that a reasonable man would believe that he was assenting to the terms proposed by the other party, and that other party upon that belief enters into the contract with him, the man thus conducting himself would be equally bound as if he had intended to agree to the other party's terms.

However, exactly the same principle applies to determine whether an offer has been made or accepted.

■ *The Hannah Blumenthal*
[1983] 1 All ER 34, House of Lords

A contract for the sale of a ship provided that any dispute arising out of the sale should be settled by arbitration in London. In 1972, the buyers commenced arbitration proceedings. There followed a long delay, with letters being exchanged intermittently, until 1980, when the buyers proposed fixing a date for arbitration. The sellers then issued a writ seeking a declaration that the arbitration agreement had been discharged by the buyers' repudiation of it, or by frustration or by mutual rescission arising out of an agreement to abandon the arbitration. The House of Lords held, firstly, that because there were mutual obligations to avoid delay, neither party could rely on the other's conduct as amounting to a repudiation; secondly, that the agreement was not frustrated, because there had been no external change of events affecting the performance of the arbitration agreement, nor had the delay occurred without the fault of either party. On the abandonment point:

Lord Brandon

... I pass now to the further question raised by the cross-appeal. That question is, as I indicated earlier, whether, assuming (contrary to the decisions of the courts below) that the agreement to refer in the present case was not frustrated, the conduct of the parties was nevertheless of such a character as to lead to the inference that they impliedly consented with each other to abandon that agreement.

The question whether a contract has been abandoned or not is one of fact. That being so, it would, I think, be sufficient, for the purposes of the present case, to say that there are concurrent findings of fact by both the courts below against the sellers on that question, that it is not the practice of your Lordships' House to interfere with such concurrent findings of fact save in exceptional circumstances which are not here present, and that the cross-appeal fails on that ground alone.

Because the question of the abandonment of a contract is, however, of some general importance, I consider that it may be helpful to examine the matter, as it arises in the present case, somewhat further. For this purpose it is, I think, necessary to make some additions to the history of the parties' conduct in relation to the reference which I set out earlier. The additional facts which I regard, for reasons which will become apparent later, as necessary to state are these. According to the affidavit of Mr Fitzpatrick, a solicitor employed by Sinclairs, sworn on 16 December 1980, that firm was still seeking to trace, and obtain evidence from, witnesses whom it might be necessary to call on the hearing of the arbitration as late as November 1979, February 1980 and November 1980.

The concept of the implied abandonment of a contract as a result of the conduct of the parties to it is well established in law: see *Chitty on Contracts* (23rd edn, 1968) vol 1, para 1231 and cases there cited. Where A seeks to prove that he and B have abandoned a contract in this way, there are two ways in which A can put his case. The first way is by showing that the conduct of each party, as evinced to the other party and acted on by him, leads necessarily to the inference of an implied agreement between them to abandon the contract. The second method is by showing that the conduct of B, as evinced towards A, has been such as to lead A reasonably to believe that B has abandoned the contract, even though it has not in fact been B's intention to do so, and that A has significantly altered his position in reliance on that belief. The first method involves actual abandonment by both A and B. The second method involves the creation by B of a situation in which he is estopped from asserting, as against A, that he, B, has not abandoned the contract (see *Pearl Mill Co Ltd v Ivy Tannery Co Ltd*).

On whichever of the two bases of abandonment discussed above the sellers seek to reply in the present case, it seems to me that they are bound to fail. As I indicated above, Sinclairs, as the sellers' solicitors, were still, in November 1979, February 1980 and even as late as November 1980, trying to trace, and obtain evidence from witnesses who might be called at the hearing of the arbitration. Even if it could fairly be said (which I do not think that it can) that the buyers' prolonged delays from 1974 onwards were such as to induce in the minds of the sellers or their solicitors a reasonable belief that the buyers had abandoned the agreement to refer, Sinclairs' continuing conduct with regard to tracing, and obtaining evidence from, witnesses referred to above makes it impossible for the sellers to say that they acted on any such belief, or that they altered their position significantly in reliance on it.

For the reasons which I have given I would allow the buyer's original appeal and dismiss the sellers' cross-appeal, with costs against the sellers in either case.

Lord Diplock

. . . Abandonment of a contract (the former contract) which is still executory, ie one in which at least one primary obligation of one or other of the parties remains unperformed, is effected by the parties entering into a new contract (the contract of abandonment) . . .

To the formation of the contract of abandonment, the ordinary principles of the English law of contract apply. To create a contract by exchange of promises between two parties where the promise of each party constitutes the consideration for the promise of the other what is necessary is that the intention of each *as it has been communicated to and understood by the other* (even though that which has been communicated does not represent the actual state of mind of the communicator) should coincide. That is what English lawyers mean when they resort to the latin phrase consensus ad idem and the words that I have italicised are essential to the concept of consensus ad idem, the lack of which prevents the formation of a binding contract in English law.

Thus if A (the offeror) makes a communication to B (the offeree), whether in writing, orally or by conduct, which, in the circumstances at the time the communication was received, (1) B, if he were a reasonable man, would understand as stating A's intention to act or refrain from acting in some specified manner if B will promise on his part to act or refrain from acting in some manner also specified in the offer, and (2) B does in fact understand A's communication to mean this, and in his turn makes to A a communication conveying his willingness so to act or to refrain from acting which mutatis mutandis satisfies the same two conditions as respects A, the consensus ad idem essential to the formation of a contract in English law is complete.

The rule that neither party can rely on his own failure to communicate accurately to the other party his own real intention by what he wrote or said or did, as negativing the consensus ad idem, is an example of a general principle of English law that injurious reliance on what another person did may be a source of legal rights against him. I use the broader expression 'injurious reliance' in preference to 'estoppel' so as to embrace all circumstances in which A can say to B, 'You led me reasonably to believe that you were assuming particular legally enforceable obligations to me', of which promissory or *High Trees* estoppel (see *Central London Property Trust Ltd v High Trees House Ltd* . . .) affords another example, whereas 'estoppel', in the strict sense of the term, is an exclusionary rule of evidence, though it may operate so as to affect substantive legal rights inter partes...

Lord Brightman

The basis of 'tacit abandonment by both parties', to use the phraseology of the sellers' case, is that the primary facts are such that it ought to be inferred that the contract to arbitrate the particular dispute was rescinded by the mutual agreement of the parties. To entitle the sellers to rely on abandonment, they must show that the buyers so conducted themselves as to entitle the sellers to assume, *and that the sellers did assume*, that the contract was agreed to be abandoned sub silentio. The evidence which is relevant to that inquiry will consist of or include: (1) what the buyers did or omitted to do *to the knowledge of the sellers*. Excluded from consideration will be the acts of the buyers of which the sellers were ignorant, because those acts will have signalled nothing to the sellers and cannot have founded or fortified any assumption on the part of the sellers; (2) what the sellers did or omitted to do, *whether or not to the knowledge of the buyers*. These facts evidence the state of mind of the sellers, and therefore the validity of the assertion by the sellers that they assumed that the contract was agreed to be abandoned. The state of mind of the buyers is irrelevant to a consideration of what the sellers were entitled to assume. The state of mind of the sellers is vital to what the sellers in fact assumed.

Lords Roskill and **Keith** concurred.

Appeal allowed. Cross-appeal dismissed.

NOTES

1.   Some commentators have seen significant differences in the way the three members of the House of Lords formulated the objective test. On the one hand, Lord Diplock's words have been interpreted as meaning that the parties (A and B) must actually be in agreement (B must actually think A was making an offer to him and accept in such a way that A actually understands that B is accepting). On the other hand, Lord Brandon's formulation seems to suggest that it is not enough that one party reasonably understood the other to be making an offer and accepted that apparent offer; he seems to suggest that the first party must have acted in reliance on the apparent offer. If this means he must have changed his position (as is required for estoppel, see p 148), this is inconsistent with the normal understanding that it is enough simply to accept the apparent offer (see the *Centrovincial* case, p 294). In *The Leonidas D* (see p 847), Robert Goff LJ said:

Three distinct views were however expressed by their Lordships as to how an implied abandonment of a contract might come about. Lord Brandon, who delivered the leading speech, considered that it could be established 'by showing that the conduct of each party, as evinced to the other party and acted on by him, leads necessarily to the inference of an implied agreement between them to abandon the contract' (see [1983] 1 All ER 34 at 47, [1983] 1 AC 854 at 914). Lord Diplock's formulation appears to us to involve the requirement that the actual intentions of both parties should in fact coincide (see [1983] 1 All ER 34 at 48–49, [1983] 1 AC 854 at 915–916). Lord Brightman, on the other hand, thought that, to enable one party (the sellers) to rely on abandonment, it was enough for them to show 'that the buyers so conducted themselves as to entitle the sellers to assume, *and that the sellers did assume*, that the contract was agreed to be abandoned sub silentio' (see [1983] 1 All ER 34 at 55, [1983] 1 AC 854 at 924) (Lord Brightman's emphasis).

It is apparent that these three approaches are not identical. However, if we have to choose between them, we would respectfully prefer to follow the approach of Lord Brightman. In his speech Lord Brightman was, as we understand it, asserting that if one party (O) so acts that his conduct, objectively considered, constitutes an offer, and the other party (A), believing that the conduct of O represents his actual intention, accepts O's offer, then a contract will come into existence, and on those facts it will make no difference if O did not in fact intend to make an offer, or if he misunderstood A's acceptance, so that O's state of mind is, in such circumstances, irrelevant. With that proposition we very respectfully agree and so, if it is necessary for us to choose, we would prefer to follow the reasoning of Lord Brightman in so far as it differs from the reasoning of Lord Brandon and Lord Diplock.

For further discussion of these points, see Atiyah (1986) 102 LQR 363; Vorster (1987) 103 LQR 274.

2. Why do the courts apply the objective principle when that may mean parties become bound by contracts when they didn't intend to?

3. Classical doctrine bases contractual liability on voluntary assent: I am bound because I agreed to be (see p 47). Yet the effect of the objective principle may be to bind me to a promise I did not, in fact, intend at all. Isn't this imposing a kind of public standard? Some writers have argued that the law is caught in an inescapable conflict between the 'private' and the 'public': see eg Dalton (p 791).

II. OFFER OR PRELIMINARY NEGOTIATIONS

1. Correspondence

■ *Gibson v Manchester City Council*

[1979] 1 All ER 972

In 1970, the city council, then in the control of the Conservative party, adopted a policy of selling council houses to its tenants. It circulated printed forms that tenants could send in to obtain details. The form read in part:

Please inform me of the price of buying my council house. I am interested in obtaining a mortgage from the Corporation to buy the house. Please send me the details.

Gibson sent in a form and received a letter from the city treasurer stating (in part):

The Corporation may be prepared to sell the house to you at the purchase price of £2, 725 less 20% = £2, 180 (freehold).
   Maximum mortgage the Corporation may grant: £2, 177 repayable over 20 years.
   ...
   This letter should not be regarded as a firm offer of a mortgage.
   If you would like to make a formal application to buy your council house, please complete the enclosed application form and return it to me as soon as possible.

(Emphasis supplied.)
   Gibson completed the application form except for the price and returned it; after being told that the Corporation would not lower the price as he had requested, he wrote:

I would be obliged if you will carry on with the purchase as per my application already in your possession.

Thereafter, the house was removed from the council's maintenance list and placed on their house purchase list—but before the contracts had been exchanged, control of the council passed to the Labour party and it was resolved to discontinue sales of council houses except in cases where there was a binding contract to sell. Gibson was notified that the council would not be proceeding with the sale to him, and he brought an action seeking specific performance of the agreement he alleged had been made. The county court judge and, on appeal, the Court of Appeal, held that there was a concluded contract and ordered specific performance. Lord Denning said:

We have had much discussion as to whether Mr Gibson's letter of 18th March 1971 was a new offer or whether it was an acceptance of the previous offer which had been made. I do not like detailed analysis on such a point. To my mind it is a mistake to think that all contracts can be analysed into the form of offer and acceptance. I know in some of the textbooks it has been the custom to do so; but, as I understand the law, there is no need to look for a strict offer and acceptance. You should look at the correspondence as a whole and at the conduct of the parties and see therefrom whether the parties have come to an agreement on everything that was material. If by their correspondence and their conduct you can see an agreement on all material terms, which was intended thenceforward to be binding, then there is a binding contract in law even though all the formalities have not been gone through. For that proposition I would refer to *Brogden v Metropolitan Railway Co*.

It seems to me that on the correspondence I have read (and, I may add, on what happened after) the parties had come to an agreement in the matter which they intended to be binding.

The council appealed.

Lord Diplock

My Lords, this is an action for specific performance of what is claimed to be a contract for the sale of land. The only question in the appeal is of a kind with which the courts are very familiar. It is whether in the correspondence between the parties there can be found a legally enforceable contract for the sale by the Manchester Corporation to Mr Gibson of the dwelling-house of which he was the occupying tenant at the relevant time in 1971. That question is one that, in my view, can be answered by applying to the particular documents relied on by Mr Gibson as constituting the contract, well settled, indeed elementary, principles of English law. This being so, it is not the sort of case in which leave would have been likely to be granted to appeal to your Lordships' House, but for the fact that it is a test case.

...Lord Denning MR rejected what I have described as the conventional approach of looking to see whether on the true construction of the documents relied on there can be discerned an offer and acceptance. One ought, he said, to 'look at the correspondence as a whole and at the conduct of the parties and see therefrom whether the parties have come to an agreement on everything that was material'. This approach, which in referring to the conduct of the parties where there is no allegation of part performance appears to me to overlook the provisions of s 40 of the Law of Property Act 1925, led him however to the conclusion that there should be imported into the agreement to be specifically performed additional conditions, against use except as a private dwelling-house and against advertising and a restriction not to sell or lease the property for five years. These are conditions which would not be implied by law in an open contract for the sale of land. The reason for so varying the county court judge's order was that clauses in these terms were included in the standard form of 'Agreement for Sale of a Council House' which, as appears from the earlier case of *Storer v Manchester City Council*, was entered into by the council and council tenants whose applications to purchase the freehold of their council house reached the stage at which contracts were exchanged. There was, however, no reference to this standard form of agreement in any of the documents said to constitute the contract relied on in the instant case, nor was there any evidence that Mr Gibson had knowledge of its terms at or before the time that the alleged contract was concluded...

My Lords, there may be certain types of contract, though I think they are exceptional, which do not fit easily into the normal analysis of a contract as being constituted by offer and acceptance; but a contract alleged to have been made by an exchange of correspondence between the parties in which the successive communications other than the first are in reply to one another is not one of these. I can see no reason in the instant case for departing from the conventional approach of looking at the handful or documents relied on as constituting the contract sued on and seeing whether on their true construction there is to be found in them a contractual offer by the council to sell the house to Mr Gibson and an acceptance of that offer by Mr Gibson. I venture to think that it was by departing from this conventional approach that the majority of the Court of Appeal was led into error.

My Lords, the words italicised seem to me, as they seemed to Geoffrey Lane LJ, to make it quite impossible to construe this letter as a contractual offer capable of being converted into a legally enforceable open contract for the sale of land by Mr Gibson's written acceptance of it. The words 'may be prepared to sell' are fatal to this; so is the invitation, not, be it noted, to accept the offer, but 'to make formal application to buy' on the enclosed application form. It is, to quote Geoffrey Lane LJ, a letter setting out the financial terms on which it may be the council would be prepared to consider a sale and purchase in due course.

Both Ormrod LJ and the county court judge, in reaching the conclusion that this letter was a firm offer to sell the freehold interest in the house for £2, 180, attached importance to the fact that the second paragraph, dealing with the financial details of the mortgage of which Mr Gibson had asked for particulars, stated expressly, 'This letter should not be regarded as a firm offer of a mortgage'. The necessary implication from this, it is suggested, is that the first paragraph of the letter *is* to be regarded as a firm offer to sell despite the fact that this is plainly inconsistent with the express language of that paragraph. My Lords, with great respect, this surely must be fallacious. If the final sentence had been omitted the wording of the second paragraph, unlike that of the first, with its use of the indicative mood in such expressions as 'the interest rate *will* change', might have been understood by council tenants to whom it was addressed as indicating a firm offer of a mortgage of the amount and on the terms for repayment stated if the council were prepared to sell the house at the stated price. But, whether or not this be the explanation of the presence of the last sentence in the second paragraph, it cannot possibly affect the plain meaning of the words used in the first paragraph.

My Lords, the application form and letter of 18th March 1971 were relied on by Mr Gibson as an unconditional acceptance of the council's offer to sell the house; but this cannot be so unless there was a contractual offer by the council available for acceptance, and, for the reason already given I am of opinion that there was none. It is unnecessary to consider whether the application form and Mr Gibson's letters of 5th and 18th March 1971 are capable of amounting to a contractual offer by him to purchase the freehold interest in the house at a price of £2, 180 on the terms of an open contract, for there is no suggestion that, even if it were, it was ever accepted by the council. Nor would it ever have been even if there had been no change in the political control of the council, as the policy of the council before the change required the incorporation in all agreements for sale of council houses to tenants of the conditions referred by Lord Denning MR in his judgment and other conditions inconsistent with an open contract. I therefore feel compelled to allow the appeal.

Lords Edmund-Davies and **Russell** made speeches allowing the appeal and **Lords Fraser** and **Keith** agreed with Lord Diplock.

Appeal allowed.

NOTES

1. Suppose that the city treasurer's letter had stated that the sale would be on the 'Standard Form of Agreement for Sale of a Council House' referred to. It might then have been said that the parties had agreed what all the material terms should be. Would there then have been a contract, or is something else required?

2.   In *Storer v Manchester City Council* [1974] 3 All ER 824, another case arising from the same change of policy, the town clerk had written to the tenant:

> I understand you wish to purchase your council house and enclose the Agreement for Sale. If you will sign the agreement and return it to me I will send you the agreement signed on behalf of the Corporation in exchange. From the enclosed list of solicitors, who are prepared to act for you and advise you on the purchase, please let me know the name of the firm that you select, as soon as possible.

The letter enclosed an agreement for sale in which were set out details of the mortgage. The date at which the tenancy was to cease and mortgage payments commence was left blank. The form continued:

> . . . *Warning*. As from the date mentioned . . . the property is at your risk. If you are taking a mortgage from the Corporation it will be insured for you but the cost recharged to you. *If you are not taking a Mortgage insure it at once . . .*

The plaintiff signed and returned the agreement, but before it had been signed by the town clerk, the council changed hands. The Court of Appeal held that there was a contract. What distinguishes the two cases? (Note that it was held that the council was, by the language of the town clerk's letter, dispensing with the 'exchange of contracts' by which contracts for the sale of land are usually made. See p 240.)

3.   Apart from the words of the letter from the city treasurer italicised, do you see any other words that suggest the letter did not contain an offer? Remember that if it were an offer that Mr Gibson could accept by completing and sending in the application, the resulting contract would be binding on both parties.

4.   Would it be sensible for the city council to commit itself to selling to an applicant without first deciding on the mortgage? Was the difference in language in the letters to Gibson and to Storer, from whom the council had already received an 'application', fortuitous?

5.   Gibson had already made some alterations to the property. If he had done this in the expectation that he would be buying the house, should this make a difference? Should the law protect (and thus encourage) such a form of reliance in this type of case? See further pp 281 ff.

In *Harvey v Facey* [1893] AC 552, appellants sent a telegram from Kingston to the respondent 'on the train to Porus', asking: 'Will you sell us Bumper Hall Pen? Telegraph lowest cash price.' The respondent telegraphed in reply: 'Lowest price for Bumper Hall Pen £900.' Assuming this to be an offer, the appellants wired an acceptance, but the Privy Council held that no offer had been made that they could accept: the respondent had merely replied to the second of the two questions contained in the appellants' telegram. In *Canadian Dyers Association Ltd v Burton* (1920) 47 OLR 259, the plaintiff company had for some time been negotiating to buy the house next door to its factory from the defendant, who had been a director of the company. In response to an enquiry, the defendant wrote: 'The last price I gave you is the lowest I am prepared to accept. In fact I feel that under present conditions this is exceptionally low and if it were to any other party I would ask more.' The plaintiff accepted. The letter was held to be an offer, especially because the defendant had his solicitor send a draft deed. Are the cases distinguishable? What if the defendant's subsequent conduct is left out of account?

2. Advertisements and displays of goods

■ *Grainger & Son v Gough*

[1896] AC 325, House of Lords

The question was whether a foreign merchant who canvassed for orders through agents in the United Kingdom was exercising a trade in the United Kingdom within the meaning of the Income Tax Acts.

Lord Herschell said in the course of his judgment:

The learned Solicitor-General, in his argument for the Crown, did not contend that any contracts were made in this country by M Roederer either personally or through his agents; indeed, he admitted the contrary. Mr Danckwerts did argue that there were such contracts. His argument was an ingenious one. He called attention to certain price-lists which were distributed by the appellants amongst persons likely to give orders, and contended that as soon as an order was given to them by a person receiving one of those lists a contract to supply the specified quantity at the price named in the list was complete, subject only to a right on the part of Roederer to disavow it. I think it impossible to accede to this contention. In my opinion, this would not be understood by any one in the trade to be the effect of giving an order for goods specified in such a price-list. The transmission of such a price-list does not amount to an offer to supply an unlimited quantity of the wine described at the price named, so that as soon as an order is given there is a binding contract to supply that quantity. If it were so, the merchant might find himself involved in any number of contractual obligations to supply wine of a particular description which he would be quite unable to carry out, his stock of wine of that description being necessarily limited. I entertain, I confess, a very clear opinion that the Solicitor-General was quite right in arguing the case on the assumption that no sales were made in this country.

NOTE

A competitive market requires a full and free flow of information. What might be the effect if advertisements *were* treated as offers—how would potential sellers react (assuming they knew the law)?

■ *Carlill v Carbolic Smoke Ball Co*

[1893] 1 QB 256, Court of Appeal (see above, p 14)

NOTE

If this advertisement had been held not to constitute an offer, what would have been the practical problem facing parties wishing to offer rewards to persons giving information, or coming forward to do some other specified act?

■ *Pharmaceutical Society of GB v Boots Cash Chemists (Southern) Ltd* [1953]

1 QB 401, Court of Appeal

The defendant's 'self-service' shop comprised one room around whose walls were shelves on which were laid out certain drugs and medicines specified in Part I of the Poisons List compiled under s 17(1) of the Pharmacy and Poisons Act 1933. These preparations were wrapped in packages and containers with the prices marked on them. A customer entering the shop took a wire basket, selected any articles he required from the shelves, placed them in the basket, and carried them to a cashier at one of the two exits. The cashier then examined the articles the customer wished to purchase, stated the total price, and accepted payment. At this stage, a registered pharmacist, who was authorised by the chemist to prevent the customer from buying any article if he thought fit, supervised the transaction.

Section 18(1) of the Act provided:

Subject to the provisions of this Part of this Act, it shall not be lawful—(a) for a person to sell any poison included in Part I of the Poisons List, unless . . . (iii) the sale is effected by, or under the supervision of, a registered pharmacist.

Somervell LJ

. . . The point taken by the plaintiffs is this: it is said that the purchase is complete if and when a customer going round the shelves takes an article and puts it in the receptacle which he or she is carrying, and that therefore, if that is right, when the customer comes to the pay desk, having completed the tour of the premises, the registered pharmacist, if so minded, has no power to say: 'This drug ought not to be sold to this customer.' Whether and in what circumstances he would have that power we need not inquire, but one can, of course, see that there is a difference if supervision can only be exercised at a time when the contract is completed.

I agree with the Lord Chief Justice in everything that he said, but I will put the matter shortly in my own words. Whether the view contended for by the plaintiffs is a right view depends on what are the legal implications of this layout—the invitation to the customer. Is a contract to be regarded as being completed when the article is put into the receptacle, or is this to be regarded as a more organized way of doing what is done already in many types of shops—and a bookseller is perhaps the best example—namely, enabling customers to have free access to what is in the shop, to look at the different articles, and then, ultimately, having got the ones which they wish to buy, to come up to the assistant saying 'I want this'? The assistant in *999* times out of 1, 000 says 'That is all right', and the money passes and the transaction is completed. I agree with what the Lord Chief Justice has said, and with the reasons which he has given for his conclusion, that in the case of an ordinary shop, although goods are displayed and it is intended that customers should go and choose what they want, the contract is not completed until, the customer having indicated the articles which he needs, the shopkeeper, or someone on his behalf, accepts that offer. Then the contract is completed. I can see no reason at all, that being clearly the normal position, for drawing any different implication as a result of this layout.

The Lord Chief Justice, I think, expressed one of the most formidable difficulties in the way of the plaintiffs' contention when he pointed out that, if the plaintiffs are right, once an article has been placed in the receptacle the customer himself is bound and would have no right, without paying for the first article, to substitute an article which he saw later of a similar kind and which he perhaps preferred. I can see no reason for implying from this self-service arrangement any implication other than that which the Lord Chief Justice found in it, namely, that it is a convenient method of enabling customers to see what there is and choose, and possibly put back and substitute, articles which they wish to have, and then to go up to the cashier and offer to buy what they have so far chosen. On that conclusion the case fails, because it is admitted that there was supervision in the sense required by the Act and at the appropriate moment of time. For these reasons, in my opinion, the appeal should be dismissed.

Birkett and **Romer LJJ** delivered concurring judgments.

Appeal dismissed.

NOTES

1.   If the display had been treated as an offer, would it necessarily have followed that the customer could not change his mind after putting the goods in his basket? Why not say there is no acceptance until he presents the goods to the cashier? See generally Montrose, 'Contract of Sale in Self-Service Stores' 4 Am J Comp Law 235.

2.   If the display of actual goods in a shop is not an offer, this allows the shopkeeper to refuse to sell to a particular customer. There may be perfectly good reasons for this, eg if a child seeks to buy a medicine that is available 'over the counter' but which is suitable only for adults. Some of the older cases have rather unpleasant overtones, however, eg *Timothy v Simpson* (1834) 6 C & P 499. You may like to compare *Quinn v Williams Furniture Ltd*, described by Collins.

3.   Furmston picks up a bottle of tonic water from the shelves of Beale's Supermarket Ltd, and the bottle bursts injuring his hand. He could attempt to sue Beale or Bishop Ltd, the manufacturer, but because there is no evidence as to whether the defect (a cracked bottle) was caused by the carelessness of Bishop, Beale or another customer who might have dropped the bottle and then put it back onto the shelf, he wishes to know whether he can recover from Beale in contract (on the basis of strict liability for goods not of merchantable quality). Advise him on the basis that the explosion occurred:

   (a)   as he first placed the bottle in his trolley;

   (b)   as he took it out of the trolley and placed it on the checkout desk;

   (c)   as he put it into his shopping bag after the assistant had rung it up, but before all the other items he had selected had been rung up?

4.   Suppose that when all the items Furmston has selected have been rung up, the total is more than he has the cash to pay for?

5.   The 'rules' that advertisements and displays of goods in shops do not amount to offers are so firmly established that it has been held that advertising bramblefinch hens and displaying flickknives do not amount to the crimes of 'offering for sale' those articles (*Partridge v Crittenden* [1968] 2 All ER 421; *Fisher v Bell* [1961] 1 QB 394). But do such advertisements and displays *never* amount to offers? And what problems arise if they are not treated as offers? Consider the American case of *Lefkowitz v Great Minneapolis Surplus Store* 251 Minn 188, 86 NW 2d 689 (1957). The defendants published the following in a newspaper on 6 April:

   Saturday 9 am sharp; 3 Brand new fur coats, worth to $100, First come first served, $1 each.

   On 13 April, they published another similarly worded advertisement in the same newspaper. On each of the Saturdays concerned, the plaintiff was the first to present himself at the appropriate counter of the defendants' store, and demanded the coat, offering to pay the $1. On each occasion, the defendants refused to sell to him, stating on the first occasion that under their house rules the offer was open only to women, and on the second occasion that the plaintiff knew the rules. The Supreme Court of Minnesota held that each of the advertisements amounted to an offer. How do you think an English court would decide this case? You may like to compare it to *Carlill's* case, p 14. (If you think it would hold there to be an offer, could the plaintiff have demanded all three coats?)

6.   The answer to this question and to the questions posed in notes 2 and 3 might well depend on the approach the judge takes to her role. A 'formalist' judge might think that the answer should depend solely on the rules to be derived from close analysis of the

previous authorities. A realist might think that the rules are actually indeterminate in some of these cases (cf Kennedy, p 49) and might start from the desired result. The difficulty is that in each case the judge might think that Furmston should win—yet find it difficult to say that there was a contract in situations (a) and (b) in note 2 but no contract in the situation in note 3. What attitude would you expect the judge to take if in this general area her view is 'market-individualist'? What if it is 'consumer-welfarist'? (Cf Adams & Brownsword, p 57.)

■ Consumer Protection Act 1987
Section 20

(1) Subject to the following provisions of this Part, a person shall be guilty of an offence if, in the course of any business of his, he gives (by any means whatever) to any consumers an indication which is misleading as to the price at which any goods, services, accommodation or facilities are available (whether generally or from particular persons).

(2) Subject as aforesaid, a person shall be guilty of an offence if—
   (a) in the course of any business of his, he has given an indication to any consumers which, after it was given, has become misleading as mentioned in subsection (1) above; and
   (b) some or all of those consumers might reasonably be expected to rely on the indication at a time after it has become misleading and
   (c) he fails to take all such steps as are reasonable to prevent those consumers from relying on the indication.

3. Auctions

■ Sale of Goods Act 1979
Section 57

(1) Where goods are put up for sale by auction in lots, each lot is prima facie deemed to be the subject of a separate contract of sale.

(2) A sale by auction is complete when the auctioneer announces its completion by the fall of the hammer, or in other customary manner; and until the announcement is made any bidder may retract his bid.

(3) A sale by auction may be notified to be subject to a reserve or upset price, and a right to bid may also be reserved expressly by or on behalf of the seller.

(4) Where a sale by auction is not notified to be subject to a right to bid by or on behalf of the seller, it is not lawful for the seller to bid himself or to employ any person to bid at the sale, or for the auctioneer knowingly to take any bid from the seller or any such person.

(5) A sale contravening subsection (4) above may be treated as fraudulent by the buyer.

(6) Where, in respect of a sale by auction, a right to bid is expressly reserved (but not otherwise) the seller or any one person on his behalf may bid at the auction.

NOTES

1. Under s 57(2), who makes the offer, who the acceptance?

2. Auctioneer holds an auction of Beale's horse, and the bidding is between Bishop and Furmston. Bishop outbids Furmston and the horse is knocked down to him. He then discovers that Furmston was employed by Beale as a 'puffer' to drive up the bidding. What rights does Bishop have?

■ *Warlow v Harrison*

(1859) 1 E & E 309, 120 ER 925, Exchequer Chamber

The defendant auctioneer advertised the sale of a horse as 'without reserve' but allowed the owner to bid. The plaintiff, the next highest bidder, was informed of this and refused to bid further, and the horse was knocked down to its owner. The plaintiff claimed it as the highest bona fide bidder. It was held that the plaintiff could not succeed on the pleadings he had entered, but **Martin B**, delivering the judgment of the court, said:

Upon the facts of the case, it seems to us that the plaintiff is entitled to recover. In a sale by auction there are three parties, viz the owner of the property to be sold, the auctioneer, and the portion of the public who attend to bid, which of course includes the highest bidder. In this, as in most cases of sales by auction, the owner's name was not disclosed: he was a concealed principal. The name of the auctioneers, of whom the defendant was one, alone was published; and the sale was announced by them to be 'without reserve'. This, according to all the cases both at law and equity, means that neither the vendor nor any person on his behalf shall bid at the auction, and that the property shall be sold to the highest bidder, whether the sum bid be equivalent to the real value or not; *Thornett v Haines* . . . We cannot distinguish the case of an auctioneer putting up property for sale upon such a condition from the case of the loser of property offering a reward, or that of a railway company publishing a time table stating the times when, and the places to which, the trains run. It has been decided that the person giving the information advertised for, or a passenger taking a ticket, may sue as upon a contract with him; *Denton v Great Northern Railway Company* . . . Upon the same principle, it seems to us that the highest bona fide bidder at an auction may sue the auctioneer as upon a contract that the sale shall be without reserve. We think the auctioneer who puts the property up for sale upon such a condition pledges himself that the sale shall be without reserve; or, in other words, contracts that it shall be so; and that this contract is made with the highest bona fide bidder; and, in case of a breach of it, that he has a right of action against the auctioneer . . . Neither does it seem to us material whether the owner, or person on his behalf, bid with the knowledge or privity of the auctioneer . . . For these reasons, if the plaintiff think fit to amend his declaration, he, in our opinion, is entitled to the judgment of the Court.

Willes J

My brother Bramwell and myself do not dissent from the judgment which has been pronounced. But we prefer to rest our decision, as to the amendment, upon the ground that the defendant undertook to have, and yet there was evidence that he had not, authority to sell without reserve. The result is the same.

Judgment of Court of Queen's Bench to be affirmed; unless the parties elect to enter a stet processus, or the plaintiff amend his declaration; in which latter case, a new trial to be had.

NOTES

1. The opinion of the majority in *Warlow v Harrison* was followed in *Barry v Heathcote Ball & Co (Commercial Auctions) Ltd* [2001] 1 All ER 944. The Court of Appeal upheld the trial judge's decision that there was a collateral contract between the highest bidder and the auctioneer, who had advertised the auction as without reserve but had withdrawn the goods (which were worth some £14, 000) when the highest bid was £200.

2. The difficulties involved in the case of goods advertised as being sold without reserve simply being withdrawn are discussed in Slade, 68 LQR 238; Gower, 68 LQR 457; Slade, 69 LQR 21.

3. In *Harris v Nickerson* (1873) LR 8 QB 286, the defendant, acting in good faith, advertised that certain furniture would be auctioned on a particular day. The plaintiff travelled to

the auction with a commission to buy the furniture, but it was withdrawn from the sale. The judge at first instance allowed the plaintiff's action to recover his loss of time, but the Court of Queen's Bench reversed the decision: *Warlow v Harrison* was no authority for saying that the advertisement of an auction amounted to a contract with everyone attending the sale. What is the distinction between the two cases? Would the potential liability in the case of a cancelled auction be much greater? What difficulties of proof can you envisage?

4.   In *Denton v Great Northern Rly Co* (1856) 5 E & B 860, the plaintiff arrived at the station to catch a train that he had seen advertised in the company's timetable as providing a connecting service to Hull, but discovered that the connecting service (operated by another company) had been withdrawn some time before the timetable had been published. As a result, the plaintiff missed an appointment in Hull and suffered damage amounting to £5 10s. The Queen's Bench held he could recover on the ground of fraud, and (Crompton J dissenting) breach of contract. Lord Campbell CJ remarked:

... It seems to me that the representations made by railway companies in their time tables cannot be treated as mere waste paper; and in the present case I think the plaintiff is entitled to recover, on the ground that there was a contract with him... The consideration is one which is a prejudice to the person who makes his arrangements with a view to the fulfilment of the contract, and comes to the station on the faith of it...

Crompton J disagreed because he doubted 'whether the promise here in fact was in consideration of coming to the station'. How do the privatised railway companies prevent themselves becoming liable for trains that are cancelled?

5.   There are a number of situations in which it has been argued, sometimes successfully, that a party who somehow held out to another the prospect of a contract but who prevented it coming into being has broken an implicit promise. See further pp 271 and 281.

III. ACCEPTANCE IN BILATERAL CONTRACTS

The question of whether an offer has been made is one of fact, to be decided in the light of what was said or written and the circumstances. The question of acceptance is similar; the next case is included to give some idea of the practical difficulties.

1. Acceptance by words

■ *Thoresen Car Ferries Ltd v Weymouth Portland Borough Council*
[1977] 2 Lloyd's Rep 614

Mr Justice Donaldson

Neither of the parties to this action needs any introduction. Their dispute concerns the roll-on/roll-off ferry terminal which was begun in 1972 and completed in 1973, at Weymouth. Thoresen contend that the council contracted to allow them the use of the terminal for one hour a day from the last week of June until the first week of September in 1975. The council denies that the exchanges between the harbour master and Thoresen resulted in any contract. However, if there was a contract, the council admits that it repudiated that contract in the autumn of 1974 . . .

Major Byrne [of Thoresen] had worked out a skeleton schedule for 1975, which assumed an availability for four ships on the Southampton-Le Havre-Cherbourg-Weymouth circuit and a daily trip each way between Weymouth and Cherbourg by different ships. On July 19, 1974, the Board of Thoresen approved this schedule in principle. Following that decision, Major Byrne wrote to the harbour master in the following terms on July 22, 1974:

'Dear Captain Holden,

I thank you for your letter of the 17th July and I am pleased to inform you that we wish to make use of your linkspan and roll-on/roll-off facilities from approximately the last week in June, 1975, to the first week in September, 1975, from 17 30 to 18 30 hours daily.

I have asked our Operations Director, Mr R Kirton, to arrange to pay a visit in the very near future to discuss the matter.

Yours sincerely,
T Byrne
Managing Director.'

Mr Kirton visited Weymouth on Aug 1 and discussed a large number of operational problems, such as facilities for car parking, Customs, immigration control, communications, pilotage, gangways, handling of mooring ropes and the rates and charges to be expected in 1975. So far as Thoresen were concerned, a decision to go ahead had been made on July 19 and the purpose of Mr Kirton's visit was merely to work out how the roll-on/roll-off facility should be used—not whether it should be used. However, the council might not have appreciated this fact.

This situation, however, changed when on the instructions of Major Byrne, Mr Kirton wrote to the harbour master on Aug 7, 1974, saying:—

'Dear Captain Holden,

Further to my letter dated 2nd August, in due course you will be contacted either by our Marine Department or even possibly by one of our Masters with a view to considering any problems to do with docking and manning, etc.

In the meantime, we should be grateful to have your formal reply to Major Byrne's letter dated 22nd July agreeing that we may make use of the facilities from approximately the last week in June 1975 to the first week in September from 17 30 to 18 30 hours daily.

Yours sincerely.'

That letter made the position clear beyond doubt. I quote from my note of the harbour master's evidence—

'I was being asked to give a formal reply agreeing that they could use the facilities. They were asking for a firm booking of the slot. I knew why they wanted a firm commitment—because of taking bookings, arranging advertising, etc.'

On receipt of this letter, the harbour master saw the town clerk to discuss how foot passengers could be embarked . . .

Having resolved the foot passenger problem, the harbour master on Aug 23, 1974, wrote to Thoresen as follows:

'Dear Sir,

Weymouth Harbour-Roll-on/Roll-off Facilities

I refer to your letters dated 2nd and 7th August, 1974, following our meeting in Weymouth.

The situation regarding embarking foot passengers is that facilities for their reception will be available in and through the existing Baggage Hall at No 4 Berth leading directly along the quayside to the car ferry ship at No 2 Berth.

I confirm the availability of the linkspan and ferry terminal for the period from approximately the last week in June, 1975, to the first week in September, 1975, from 17 30 to 18 30 hours daily for a ship not exceeding 113m in length, 20m in beam and 4.3m in draught.

Please let me know in due course when I may expect a visit from a member of your Marine Department, but note I shall be absent from Weymouth between 5th-25th September, 1974.

Yours faithfully,
Harbour Master.'

Mr Kirton acknowledged this letter in the following terms:

'Dear Captain Holden,

Thank you for your letter of the 23rd August confirming the availability of the linkspan and that facilities will be available for foot passengers.

I shall be in contact with you again in the near future concerning a further visit from myself and a member of our Marine Department.

Yours sincerely.'

In fact this further visit never took place, because the harbour master went away on a holiday from Sept 5 to 25 and meanwhile British Rail learnt of Thoresen's intentions. Its reactions were swift and to the point. It informed the council that the existence of a competitive service would threaten the viability of the Sealink service which could not then be continued. The council instructed the harbour master to inform Thoresen that, pending the outcome of negotiations with British Rail, the offer of the use of the ramp would be temporarily withdrawn.

I have not been concerned with these negotiations, but it appears that British Rail offered the council a long term guarantee of the interest charges incurred in building the terminal, if competing operators were excluded and suggested that if Thoresen were allowed to operate, British Rail might well withdraw from Weymouth totally. The council was convinced that its best interests and that of the local citizenry, large numbers of whom were employed by British Rail, lay in agreeing to British Rail's proposals. Accordingly, Thoresen were informed that berthing facilities would not be made available to them. It is not for me to say whether this decision was wise or unwise, or in accordance with the best traditions of commercial morality. My concern is . . . with whether it involved a breach of contract . . .

Let me now return to the issues . . .

Was there a legally binding contract?

Mr Yorke takes two points. First, he submits that on a true analysis of the communications between the parties, there was no intention of creating a binding legal relationship. Second, that even if there was such an intention, the plaintiffs have failed to prove any consideration which could support an obligation on the part of the council.

In *Reardon Smith Line v Hansen-Tangen* [1976] 2 Lloyd's Rep 621; [1976] 1 WLR 989, Lord Wilberforce discussed the duty of a Court which is called upon to construe a commercial contract. His conclusion, at pp 625 and 997, was that the Court must

' . . . place itself in thought in the same factual matrix as that in which the parties were.'

Let me do just that.

The council had built an expensive terminal which was only of use to operators on the short sea crossings to Normandy, Brittany and the Channel Islands. Although there might be benefits to local traders from the passing traffic, the council had to try to service its investment out of the harbour dues and charges payable by operators who made use of the terminal. The idea that British Rail might be prepared to pay the council to keep competitors away had not occurred to anyone. The key to achieving this objective lay in a co-ordinated use of the terminal by several operators, each using different slots.

This necessarily involved planning in the late summer and early autumn for use in the following summer, because operators are bound to prepare their schedules well in advance of the effective dates.

When the exchange of letters was taking place in July and August, 1974, Thoresen needed to know whether they could be certain of having the use of a specific slot in the summer of 1975. They could not publish time-tables and take bookings on the chance that a suitable slot might in the event be available. The council knew this. Equally the council needed to know promptly and for certain that Thoresen would use the slot and thus become liable for and pay the harbour dues and charges in the summer of 1975. If at any later stage Thoresen had decided not to use the slot, it would have been too late to interest any other operator. Thoresen knew this.

Both parties therefore needed a binding commitment at that stage. Mr Yorke says that this is not enough. It is a common place that two commercial men who need mutual commitments will proceed without a contract being content to rely upon an identity in their respective self interests. Indeed, this case contains an illustration of that approach, for Thoresen would not have been prepared to set up a Weymouth service for a single year without the virtual certainty of being able to continue the service in succeeding years. However, they do not suggest that the council ever entered into any legally binding obligation with regard to 1976 and subsequent years. What Thoresen say, and I accept this as the commercial reality, is that once a service has been started and is giving satisfaction, it is in no one's interest to stop it. But setting up a new service is an altogether different matter. No one knows whether it will succeed. The interests of the parties are much more likely to differ or drift apart. The operator may have second thoughts before he has committed himself to much expenditure. The harbour authority may change its mind on the best way to co-ordinate the activities of the various users to the detriment to a particular operator. It follows that neither party would be likely at this stage to rely solely upon an identity of interest although neither might think that a formal agreement was necessary.

It is within this factual matrix that I approach the language used by the parties. Certainly it is commercial rather than legal language and it is to be construed as such. Thoresen's letter of June 28 acknowledged the receipt of information about available slots and sought information about the size of the berth. The reply of July 17 gave information about the berth, but it also indicated that the 16 00–18 00 hours slot still could be the subject of a firm commitment for 1975, although no such commitment had yet been entered into with any rival operator. I do not, however, think that it was an offer which was capable of simple acceptance. Some initiative was called for from Thoresen. This was provided by Thoresen's letters of July 23 and Aug 7 which, read together, were a clear offer to enter into a firm agreement and were so understood by the harbour master. The crucial letter is therefore that of Aug 23, 1974, from the harbour master.

Mr Yorke invites me to construe this letter literally as merely informing the defendants that the foot passenger problem had been solved, that the desired slot had still not been allocated to anyone else and that the size of vessel which could be berthed at the terminal had not changed. No reasonable man could have so construed it and Thoresen did not do so. The harbour master now says that he wrote in this way in order to invite Thoresen to go on talking. If this were true, the harbour master was either naive or seeking to trap Thoresen. In fact, I think that he has thought himself into this untenable explanation and that the truth is that at the time he was intending to commit himself, and thus the council, to making this slot available during 1975, and, even more important, he was intending to commit Thoresen to using it. In the light of later reactions by the council, he has now persuaded himself that this could not have been his intention.

I do however accept that this commitment was subject to one unexpressed qualification, namely that he should be satisfied that Thoresen's vessels would be able to use the berth without detriment to other users of the harbour. In this context he was thinking of the possibility that the vessel might be of excessive draught, might use its bow thrusters in such a way as to create silting problems or might, for a variety of reasons, be unable to effect a turn-round within the time limits set by the slot.

Does this unexpressed qualification affect the matter? It could only do so, if, although unexpressed, it must have been apparent to Thoresen. All or most of the problems which troubled the harbour master were known to Thoresen and, as they told him, they intended that their marine department and possibly one of their masters should discuss them. But in the main they were Thoresen's problems in the sense that if they could not be resolved the use of the slot would be much less economic and might prove unprofitable. Thoresen, as the harbour master knew, were prepared to take their chances on this. Were it otherwise they would not have been seeking a firm agreement at that stage. The council was fully protected either by the terms of the commitment which defined the size of vessel and time on the ramp or by the harbour master's statutory powers to regulate the manner in which vessels use the harbour. I can therefore see no reason why Thoresen should not have acted as they did and treated the harbour master's letter as the acceptance of a legally binding commitment to make the slot available to them in the summer of 1975.

But this will not avail Thoresen if there was no consideration for the council's promise to make the slot available to them. The consideration originally pleaded was a promise to pay the council's 1975 charges. Mr Yorke objects that this is no consideration, since there is a statutory obligation to pay these charges if Thoresen use the berth. In my judgment this is correct. The true consideration, which was eventually pleaded, was an implied promise by Thoresen to use the berth daily and thus make themselves liable to pay the council's charges. Mr Yorke objects that Thoresen, while asserting that the council had undertaken a contractual obligation to make the berth available, never asserted that they were bound to use it. Why should they have done so? When the contract was made Thoresen wanted to use the berth and the council wanted them to do so. No question of obligation was then relevant. After the repudiation, Thoresen still wanted to use the berth. It was the council which objected. The issue was whether the council had to make the berth available not whether Thoresen had to use it. What possible reason was there for Thoresen to assert that if the position of the parties had been reversed, the council could have compelled them to use the berth or pay damages.

A defence of lack of consideration rarely has merit. This case is certainly no exception. The realities of the dispute were always known to both parties and they did not include the question of whether there was consideration for the contract . . .

Judgment for the plaintiffs.

NOTES

1.　This case does not lay down any new principle. It is included in order to show a typical situation in which there may be a dispute about whether or not there has been acceptance, and of how a court may go about resolving the dispute.

2.　Would it have made any difference if, when the harbour master wrote on 23 August, he had *not* intended to commit himself and the council? Compare *The Hannah Blumenthal*, p 192.

3.　Notice that the judge says that the parties' words and actions should be interpreted in the light of the 'factual matrix' of the alleged contract. See further p 403.

4.　The judge considers the likelihood that the parties would be content to rely on non-legal pressures (here, 'self-interest') to protect their interests. Compare p 83.

2. Acceptance by conduct

■ *Brogden v Metropolitan Railway Co*

(1877) 2 App Cas 666, House of Lords

The defendants (the appellants) had, for some years, supplied coal to the plaintiffs. The plaintiffs' agent sent the defendants a draft agreement for 220 tons or, at the plaintiffs' option, up to

350 tons, per week from 1 January 1872, at 20s per ton. The defendants filled in some blanks, wrote 'approved' on the contract, signed it and returned it to the plaintiffs' manager, who put it in his desk. The manager then ordered 250 tons per week from 1 January and these were supplied at 20s per ton; there were delays in delivery, and after some correspondence, the defendants declined to supply further coal.

Lord Blackburn

. . . I have always believed the law to be this, that when an offer is made to another party, and in that offer there is a request express or implied that he must signify his acceptance by doing some particular thing, then as soon as he does that thing, he is bound. If a man sent an offer abroad saying: I wish to know whether you will supply me with goods at such and such a price, and, if you agree to that, you must ship the first cargo as soon as you get this letter, there can be no doubt that as soon as the cargo was shipped the contract would be complete, and if the cargo went to the bottom of the sea, it would go to the bottom of the sea at the risk of the orderer. So again, where, as in the case of *Ex parte Harris*, a person writes a letter and says, I offer to take an allotment of shares, and he expressly or impliedly says, If you agree with me send an answer by the post, there, as soon as he has sent that answer by the post, and put it out of his control, and done an extraneous act which clenches the matter, and shews beyond all doubt that each side is bound, I agree the contract is perfectly plain and clear.

But when you come to the general proposition which [the judge at first instance] seems to have laid down, that a simple acceptance in your own mind without any intimation to the other party, and expressed by a mere private act, such as putting a letter into a drawer, completes a contract, I must say I differ from that . . .

But my Lords, while, as I say, this is so upon the question of law, it is still necessary to consider this case farther upon the question of fact. I agree, and I think every Judge who has considered the case does agree, certainly Lord Chief Justice Cockburn does, that though the parties may have gone no farther than an offer on the one side, saying, Here is the draft, (for that I think is really what this case comes to,)—and the draft so offered by the one side is approved by the other, everything being agreed to except the name of the arbitrator, which the one side has filled in and the other has not yet assented to, if both parties have acted upon that draft and treated it as binding, they will be bound by it.

[His Lordship went on to hold that the subsequent order for and supply of coal at 20s per ton, which was higher than the price had been before, showed that the offer was accepted.]

The **Lord Chancellor** and **Lords Hatherley**, **Selborne** and **Gordon** gave judgment to the same effect.

NOTES

1. Why does 'a mere private act, such as putting a letter into a drawer', not amount to acceptance?

2. If your answer to that question is because the offeror will have no way of knowing whether or not she is bound, then why in the first example given by Lord Blackburn is there a contract as soon as the goods are shipped, even if the offeror does not know that the shipment has taken place?

Suppose that Arts Magazine Ltd, without having been asked to do so, sends Beale a copy of its magazine every week for six weeks. Each copy has printed on the front cover, price £1. There is nothing to indicate that it has been sent as a free sample. Beale reads part of the first copy, decides he is not interested and throws it and all the subsequent copies straight into the dustbin. He then receives a bill from Arts Magazine Ltd for £6 for the copies sent to him. Does he have to pay? At common law, see *Weatherby v Banham* (1832) 5 C & P 228; now see the following.

■ Consumer Protection (Distance Selling) Regulations 2000
Inertia Selling

24.—(1) Paragraphs (2) and (3) apply if:
    (a) unsolicited goods are sent to a person ('the recipient') with a view to his acquiring them;
    (b) the recipient has no reasonable cause to believe that they were sent with a view to their being acquired for the purposes of a business; and
    (c) the recipient has neither agreed to acquire nor agreed to return them.

(2) The recipient may, as between himself and the sender, use, deal with or dispose of the goods as if they were an unconditional gift to him.

(3) The rights of the sender to the goods are extinguished.

(4) A person who, not having reasonable cause to believe there is a right to payment, in the course of any business makes a demand for payment, or asserts a present or prospective right to payment, for what he knows are:
    (a) unsolicited goods sent to another person with a view to his acquiring them for purposes other than those of his business, or
    (b) unsolicited services supplied to another person for purposes other than those of his business, is guilty of an offence and liable, on summary conviction, to a fine not exceeding level 4 on the standard scale.

(5) A person who, not having reasonable cause to believe there is a right to payment, in the course of any business and with a view to obtaining payment for what he knows are unsolicited goods sent or services supplied as mentioned in paragraph (4)—
    (a) threatens to bring any legal proceedings, or
    (b) places or causes to be placed the name of any person on a list of defaulters or debtors or threatens to do so, or
    (c) invokes or causes to be invoked any other collection procedure or threatens to do so,
    is guilty of an offence and liable, on summary conviction, to a fine not exceeding level 5 on the standard scale.

(6) In this regulation—
    'acquire' includes hire;
    'send' includes deliver;
    'sender', in relation to any goods, includes—
    (a) any person on whose behalf or with whose consent the goods are sent;
    (b) any other person claiming through or under the sender or any person mentioned in paragraph (a); and
    (c) any person who delivers the goods; and 'unsolicited' means, in relation to goods sent or services supplied to any person, that they are sent or supplied without any prior request made by or on behalf of the recipient.

(7) For the purposes of this regulation, an invoice or similar document which—
    (a) states the amount of payment, and
    (b) fails to comply with the requirements of regulations made under section 3A of the Unsolicited Goods and Services Act 1971 or, as the case may be, Article 6 of the Unsolicited Goods and Services (Northern Ireland) Order 1976 applicable to it,
    is to be regarded as asserting a right to the payment.

NOTE

This replaces the Unsolicited Goods and Services Act 1971, s 1.

■ *Unsolicited Goods and Services Act 1971*
Section 2

(1) A person who, not having reasonable cause to believe there is a right to payment, in the course of any trade or business makes a demand for payment, or asserts a present or prospective right to payment, for what he knows are unsolicited goods sent (after the commencement of this Act) to another person with a view to his acquiring them for the purposes of his trade or business, shall be guilty of an offence and on summary conviction shall be liable to a fine . . .

(2) A person who, not having reasonable cause to believe there is a right to payment, in the course of any trade or business and with a view to obtaining any payment for what he knows are unsolicited goods sent as aforesaid—

   (a) threatens to bring any legal proceedings; or
   (b) places or causes to be placed the name of any person on a list of defaulters or debtors or threatens to do so; or
   (c) invokes or causes to be invoked any other collection procedure or threatens to do so, shall be guilty of an offence and shall be liable on summary conviction to a fine . . .

3. Communication of acceptance

It is common for large organisations selling on credit to ask would-be buyers to sign an agreement, but not to commit the organisation until it has taken up credit references on the buyer. The form signed by the buyer usually contains a clause such as:

This agreement shall only become binding on the Owners upon acceptance by signature on their behalf and shall be deemed to be made on the date on which it is so signed.

(Taken from a hire-purchase agreement.)

If the agreement is signed by the owners, but before they have communicated this to the other party the latter notifies them that he is withdrawing, what is the position? Consider the *Brogden* case and *Carlill's* case. In *Robophone Facilities Ltd v Blank* [1966] 3 All ER 128, a form for the hire of an answering machine provided: 'This agreement shall become binding upon the [owners] only upon acceptance thereof on their behalf.' The hirer cancelled before the fact of the owner's signature had been communicated to him, but it was held that his offer had been accepted earlier when he was asked by the owners to fill in an application to the post office for permission to use the machine. Lord Denning MR said an uncommunicated signature would not suffice, but Diplock LJ refused to express an opinion and Harman LJ did not do so.

It is generally said that silence is not acceptance, even if the offeror told the offeree that the offeree need not reply. The authority cited is *Felthouse v Bindley* (1862) 11 CBNS 869. Paul Felthouse and his nephew John had been negotiating for Paul to buy one of John's horses, but confusion had arisen over the price. Paul wrote:

Dear Nephew, —Your price, I admit, was 30 guineas. I offered £30—never offered more: and you said the horse was mine. However as there may be a mistake about him, I will split the difference— £30.15s . . . If I hear no more about him, I consider the horse mine at £30.15s . . .

John did not reply, but, on 25 February, instructed Bindley, an auctioneer who was selling John's stock, to keep back the horse because it was already sold. Bindley forgot and sold it. On 27 February, John wrote to Paul explaining what had happened. Paul sued Bindley in conversion, and obtained a verdict for £33, but the verdict was set aside. One ground for the decision, and the ground on which it was upheld in the Court of Exchequer Chamber (1863) 1 New Rep 401, was that Paul had no title to the horse because there was no written evidence of the contract to satisfy the Statute of Frauds (see p 144); in his judgment Willes J also said:

... the uncle had no right to impose upon the nephew a sale of his horse for £30.15s unless he chose to comply with the condition of writing to repudiate the offer... It is clear... that the nephew in his own mind intended his uncle to have the horse at the price which he (the uncle) had named, —£30.15s: but he had not communicated such his intention to his uncle or done anything to bind himself. Nothing therefore had been done to vest the property in the horse in the plaintiff....

The Leonidas D [1985] 2 All ER 796 was another case (see *The Hannah Blumenthal*) on whether a claim in arbitration had implicitly been abandoned. Mustill J held that the charterers, by commencing arbitration but then totally stopping, tacitly represented that they did not intend to pursue the claim, and the owners, whose response (with one exception, which the judge held was neutral) had been a 'complete blank', had accepted the tacit offer of abandonment. The Court of Appeal disagreed. Robert Goff LJ said (at 805):

... We have here to consider an appeal from a decision that a binding agreement should be inferred from silence and inaction. Silence and inaction by both parties are apparently here considered to be capable of giving rise to an offer by one, and to an acceptance by the other communicated in response to that offer. This is most surprising. We have all been brought up to believe it to be axiomatic that acceptance of an offer cannot be inferred from silence, save in the most exceptional circumstances (as to which see, for example, G H Treitel *The Law of Contract* (6th edn, 1983) p 27) [see 11th edn, 2003, pp 31–35]. Yet it is here suggested that silence and inaction can give rise both to an offer and to an acceptance; and there do not appear to be any special circumstances, in the silent abandonment of this reference to arbitration, which could justify any departure from general principle. In the absence of special circumstances, silence and inaction by a party to a reference are, objectively considered, just as consistent with his having inadvertently forgotten about the matter; or with his simply hoping that the matter will die a natural death if he does not stir up the other party; or with his office staff, or his agents, or his insurers, or his solicitors, being appallingly slow. If so, there should, on ordinary principles, be no basis for the inference of an offer. Exactly the same comment can be made of the silence and inaction of the other party, for the same reasons, there appears to be no basis for drawing the inference of an acceptance in response to the supposed offer, still less of the communication of that acceptance of the offeror.

We should add that we see the same difficulty in invoking the principle of equitable estoppel in such circumstances. It is well settled that that principle requires that one party should have made an unequivocal representation that he does not intend to enforce his strict legal rights against the other; yet it is difficult to imagine how silence and inaction can be anything but equivocal.

NOTES

1.   Is it correct that in *Felthouse v Bindley* there was no contract—why was John's instruction to Bindley not acceptance by conduct?

2.   Suppose John had simply put the horse on one side himself, and, relying on what Paul had written, had not replied to Paul. Would John have been able to hold Paul to a contract if the latter were subsequently to try to withdraw?

   Miller, '*Felthouse v Bindley* Revisited' (1972) 35 MLR 489 argues that if the offeror has waived the need for communication of the acceptance, the offeree who remains silent intending to accept should be able to hold the offeror to a contract. In *Fairline Shipping*

Corpn v Adamson [1975] QB 180, Kerr J disagreed:

It seems to me ... that such a result can only flow from an estoppel operating against the offeror and that such facts cannot give rise to any contract or fit into the settled law governing offer and acceptance. The plaintiff's cause of action cannot be founded on an estoppel ...

But is it correct that the offeree would be founding an action on an estoppel? Wouldn't he be founding it on a contract, the estoppel merely preventing the offeror from denying communication of any acceptance? (Cf p 148.)

3. Suppose an offer is made to which the offeree does not reply. If he sees the offeror starting to perform, thinking there is a contract, and he does nothing to correct the offeror's misunderstanding, might he be estopped from denying acceptance? See Restatement 2d s 69 (next note) and *St John Tugboat Co Ltd v Irving Refinery Ltd* [1964] SCR 614 (offeree knew tug being kept 'standing by' for offeree's use and that offeror expected to be paid, but did nothing to dispense with service or complain: held, offer accepted). Compare using unsolicited goods.

4. In many circumstances, it is obviously sensible to have a rule that silence on the part of an offeree who does not want to enter a contract will not amount to acceptance, even if the offeror says he will treat it as acceptance. But is it always sensible? Consider Restatement 2d s 69:

Acceptance by Silence or Exercise of Dominion

(1) Where an offeree fails to reply to an offer, his silence and inaction operate as an acceptance in the following cases only:

    (a) Where an offeree takes the benefit of offered services with reasonable opportunity to reject them and reason to know that they were offered with the expectation of compensation.

    (b) Where the offeror has stated or given the offeree reason to understand that assent may be manifested by silence or inaction, and the offeree in remaining silent or inactive intends to accept the offer.

    (c) Where because of previous dealings or otherwise, it is reasonable that the offeree should notify the offeror if he does not intend to accept.

Between 1981 and 1992, there were a whole series of cases in which it was argued that an agreement to resolve a dispute by arbitration had, by agreement, been abandoned by the parties—the agreement to be deduced from inaction on both sides.

At first sight, it seems odd to hold that silence on both sides can constitute an agreement (see Goff LJ in *The Leonidas D* [1985] 2 All ER 796 at 805, [1985] 1 WLR 925 at 936) but the House of Lords held that this was possible in *The Hannah Blumenthal* [1983] 1 AC 854, [1983] 1 All ER 34 and expressly approved *The Splendid Sun* [1981] QB 694, [1981] 2 All ER 993 as a decision on this ground. One clue here may be that what was agreed was to abandon an existing contract. For further discussion, see Furmston, Norisada and Poole, *Contract Formation and Letters of Intent*, pp 38–49.

The First Restatement version of s 69(1)(c) was applied in the case *of Ammons v Wilson* 176 Miss 645, 170 So 227 (1936). The offeror had regularly ordered shortening from the offeree: he would give the order to the offeree's traveller, who would give him a tentative booking (without legal effect), and transmit the order to head office. Every order had been accepted. On the occasion in question, he was given the booking, but not told until 12 days later (when he enquired when shipment would be made) that his order was not accepted. Meanwhile the price of shortening had risen from 7 1/2 c to 9c a pound. The Supreme Court of Mississippi held a contract had been created.

■ **Richard Craswell, 'Offer, Acceptance and Efficient Reliance'** (1996)
48 Stan L Rev 481

...I focus on the effect of an enforceable commitment on the other party's incentive to rely on the proposed transaction. As Charles Goetz and Robert Scott pointed out in 1980, a legally enforceable commitment may sometimes be the only way to induce the other party to choose an **efficient** level of **reliance**. Building on their insight, I suggest that the legal doctrines governing offer and acceptance can be interpreted to prevent one party from withdrawing in just those cases where an enforceable commitment would have been necessary to induce an **efficient** level of **reliance** by the other party. In those cases, I argue, even the party who now seeks to withdraw would have wanted to be committed (if he or she had been asked that question at the time the other party had to rely), precisely in order to induce **efficient reliance**.

....

A. Finding an Offer

It is standard hornbook law that if S has made an offer to B, B can bind S simply by accepting the offer. By contrast, if S's statements are not interpreted as an offer—for example, if they are instead interpreted as 'mere enquiries'—B has no power to bind S, so S remains free to withdraw at any time. A court's decision to interpret S's statements as an offer will thus affect the extent to which S is committed to B, and the extent to which B's **reliance** on the proposed transaction will be protected.

....

My claim is that courts (sometimes) decide whether to interpret a communication as an offer based on the effect an offer would have on B's **reliance** incentives. Under this approach, a court would interpret a communication as an offer whenever an offer would be likely to induce a more **efficient** level of **reliance** than a 'mere enquiry' would. If an offer would indeed induce a more **efficient** level of **reliance**, then (for the reasons given earlier) it should be in S's interest to give B the higher level of commitment represented by a legal offer. These are the cases where it would make sense to interpret S as having made a legal offer rather than a 'mere enquiry'.

....

The pattern seems even stronger in cases where the consumer's **reliance** goes beyond a visit to the dealer's showroom or store. For example, when an auto dealer's advertisement for end-of-the-year 1954 cars announced that any purchaser would be allowed to trade his purchase "even" for a 1955 car when the new models arrived, a court treated this advertisement as an offer, and held the dealer bound to a consumer who bought a 1954 model with the belief that he would be able to exchange it. The classic case of Carlill v. Carbolic Smoke Ball Co., where the seller advertised a [£]100 reward to anyone who used its product for two weeks but still contracted influenza, also fits into this category. In each case, the party in S's position wanted to induce **reliance** by B, and probably would not have been able to induce that **reliance** if it had reserved the right to withdraw at any time.

....

B. The Duration of the Power of Acceptance

....

Significantly, in at least some cases where courts have held the offer open for a period longer than the bare minimum necessary for the offeree to think it over, the offeror wanted to induce more substantial **reliance** by the offeree. For example, in one case an employee of a state's social services department wanted to take a leave of absence and return to school for a master's degree. Rather than grant a leave, which would have required the department to keep his position vacant, the department instead asked the employee to resign, promising to reappoint him when he returned if there was a vacancy. The employee resigned, took one year to get his master's degree, spent nine or ten months working at two veterans' hospitals to receive further training, and then asked for his old job back. When the department refused to reinstate the employee, in spite of available vacancies, the court held that the ten-month delay was not long enough to cause the department's offer to lapse. Significantly, there was evidence that the department originally made their offer because they wanted to encourage the employee to continue his education, as that would make him a more effective employee on his return. This suggests that the department (a) believed the employee's **reliance to be efficient**, and (b) believed the employee would not have relied in this way without a binding commitment.

...

1. Acceptance by correspondence

The 'mailbox rule' holds that B's acceptance takes effect as soon as B puts his acceptance into the mail (or dispatches it by any other appropriate method), regardless of when S actually receives it. Where the rule is in force, its practical effect is to increase the effective duration of S's offer....

This concern for B's **reliance** makes itself felt in the mailbox rule cases. While it might seem that the mailbox rule gives courts little discretion to adjust B's protection on a case-by-case basis, the rule contains a number of exceptions that permit just this kind of flexibility. For one thing, the mailbox rule applies only when B sends his acceptance by a 'reasonable' medium of communication. What is 'reasonable' normally depends on the facts of each case. For example, in a case where S does not seem to have wanted to induce B's **reliance**, the court held that it was unreasonable for B to post his acceptance by mail, thus depriving B of the benefit of the mailbox rule and permitting S to withdraw.

More important, the mailbox rule applies only if S does not provide otherwise in her offer, and deciding whether S has provided otherwise often gives courts a great deal of flexibility. For example, in one case the offer stated, 'If I do not hear from you [by a certain date]...I shall conclude "No." ' The court interpreted this offer as reversing the mailbox rule, and requiring that S actually receive B's offer in order to be bound. In another case, the offer stated, 'As soon as [your acceptance is] received, we shall send amongst the farmers and secure the first lots...'—but this court ruled that the offer did not reverse the mailbox rule, thus permitting B's acceptance to take effect when mailed. Offers requiring that B "notify" or 'give notice' to S have also received mixed treatment. Some courts have interpreted this language to mean that S must actually receive B's notice of acceptance. Other courts have required only that B put his notice in the mail. Not surprisingly, some courts have regarded the phrase as ambiguous....

NOTE

Professor Crasswell's article cites mainly US cases. As you read through the cases in this subsection and the next, ask yourself whether his model fits the UK cases.

IV. ACCEPTANCE IN UNILATERAL CONTRACTS

In *Carlill v Carbolic Smoke Ball Co* (see p 14), the defendants argued that Mrs Carlill had never accepted any offer they might have made. Bowen LJ said:

Then it was said that there was no notification of the acceptance of the contract. One cannot doubt that, as an ordinary rule of law, an acceptance of an offer made ought to be notified to the person who makes the offer, in order that the two minds may come together. Unless this is done the two minds may be apart, and there is not that consensus which is necessary according to the English law—I say nothing about the laws of other countries—to make a contract. But there is this clear gloss to be made upon that doctrine, that as notification of acceptance is required for the benefit of the person who makes the offer, the person who makes the offer may dispense with notice to himself if he thinks it desirable to do so, and I suppose there can be no doubt that where a person in an offer made by him to another person, expressly or impliedly intimates a particular mode of acceptance as sufficient to make the bargain binding, it is only necessary for the other person to whom such offer is made to follow the indicated method of acceptance; and if the person making the offer, expressly or impliedly intimates in his offer that it will be sufficient to act on the proposal without communicating acceptance of it to himself, performance of the condition is a sufficient acceptance without notification. . . .

Now, if that is the law, how are we to find out whether the person who makes the offer does intimate that notification of acceptance will not be necessary in order to constitute a binding bargain? In many cases you look to the offer itself. In many cases you extract from the character of the transaction that notification is not required, and in the advertisement cases it seems to me to follow as an inference to be drawn from the transaction itself that a person is not to notify his acceptance of the offer before he performs the condition, but that if he performs the condition notification is dispensed with. It seems to me that from the point of view of common sense no other idea could be entertained. If I advertise to the world that my dog is lost, and that anybody who brings the dog to a particular place will be paid some money, are all the police or other persons whose business is to find lost dogs to be expected to sit down and write me a note saying that they have accepted my proposal? Why, of course, they at once look after the dog, and as soon as they find the dog they have performed the condition. The essence of the transaction is that the dog should be found, and it is not necessary under such circumstances, as it seems to me, that in order to make the contract binding there should be any notification of acceptance. It follows from the nature of the thing that the performance of the condition is sufficient acceptance without the notification of it, and a person who makes an offer in an advertisement of that kind makes an offer which must be read by the light of that common sense reflection. He does, therefore, in his offer impliedly indicate that he does not require notification of the acceptance of the offer.

The first point to note is that it is now established that an offer of a unilateral contract is not 'accepted' by doing the required act in ignorance of the offer (see *R v Clarke* (1927) 40 CLR 227; *Taylor v Allon* [1966] 1 QB 304). It is not necessary that the offer is the main motivation for the offeree acting, provided he or she is aware of the offer *(Williams v Carwardine* (1833) 5 C & P 566).

The second and more difficult point concerns the point at which there is an effective acceptance and the offeror becomes bound. Look again at the facts of *Carlill's* case (p 14). Might the company have revoked their offer at any time before Mrs Carlill had completed the required performance, ie using the ball for three weeks? In *Petterson v Pattberg* 248 NY 86, 161NE 428 (1928), Pattberg, who held a mortgage on Petterson's property, told Petterson that he would 'allow' Petterson $780 if the latter paid off the mortgage by 31 May 1924. Before that date, Petterson knocked at Pattberg's door, and when the latter demanded the name of his caller, replied: 'It is Mr Petterson. I have come to pay off the mortgage.' Pattberg replied that he had sold the mortgage. He then partly opened the door but refused to take the case exhibited by Petterson. The Court of Appeals (Kellogg J, Cardozo CJ, Pound, Crane and O'Brien JJ concurring) held that, even though the offeree had approached with the intention of performing, the offer could be withdrawn at any time before an actual tender had been made, and that Pattberg's statement was effective to withdraw it. Lehman J dissented on the ground that the offer of payment was a sufficient tender.

■ *Errington v Errington*

[1952] 1 All ER 149, Court of Appeal

The plaintiff appealed from a refusal to make an order for possession of a house occupied by her daughter-in-law.

Denning LJ

The facts are reasonably clear. In 1936 the father bought the house for his son and daughter-in-law to live in. The father put down £250 in cash and borrowed £500 from a building society on the security of the house, repayable with interest by instalments of 15s a week. He took the house in his own name and made himself responsible for the instalments. The father told the daughter-in-law that the £250 was a present for them, but he left them to pay the building society instalments of 15s a week themselves. He handed the building society book to the daughter-in-law and said to her: 'Don't part with this book. The house will be your property when the mortgage is paid.' He said that when he retired he would transfer it into their names. She has, in fact, paid the building society instalments regularly from that day to this with the result that much of the mortgage has been repaid, but there is a good deal yet to be paid. The rates on the house came to 10s a week. The couple found that they could not pay those as well as the building society instalments so the father said he would pay them and he did so.

It is to be noted that the couple never bound themselves to pay the instalments to the building society, and I see no reason why any such obligation should be implied. It is clear law that the court is not to imply a term unless it is necessary, and I do not see that it is necessary here. Ample content is given to the whole arrangement by holding that the father promised that the house should belong to the couple as soon as they had paid off the mortgage. The parties did not discuss what was to happen if the couple failed to pay the instalments to the building society, but I should have thought it clear that, if they did fail to pay the instalments, the father would not be bound to transfer the house to them. The father's promise was a unilateral contract—a promise of the house in return for their act of paying the instalments. It could not be revoked by him once the couple entered on performance of the act, but it would cease to bind him if they left it incomplete and unperformed, which they have not done. If that was the position during the father's lifetime, so it must be after his death. If the daughter-in-law continues to pay all the building society instalments, the couple will be entitled to have the property transferred to them as soon as the mortgage is paid off, but if she does not do so, then the building society will claim the instalments from the father's estate and the estate will have to pay them. I cannot think that in those circumstances the estate would be bound to transfer the house to them, any more than the father himself would have been. . . .

In the present case it is clear that the father expressly promised the couple that the property should belong to them as soon as the mortgage was paid, and impliedly promised that, so long as they paid the instalments to the building society, they should be allowed to remain in possession. They were not purchasers because they never bound themselves to pay the instalments, but nevertheless they were in a position analogous to purchasers. They have acted on the promise and neither the father nor his widow, his successor in title, can eject them in disregard of it. The result is that, in my opinion, the appeal should be dismissed and no order for possession should be made.

Somervell and **Hodson LJJ** delivered concurring judgments.

Appeal dismissed.

■ *Daulia v Four Milbank Nominees Ltd*
[1978] 2 All ER 557, Court of Appeal

The plaintiffs were keen to buy a portfolio of properties from the defendants, who were mortgagees entitled to sell because the mortgagor was in default. The plaintiffs alleged that, on 21 December, an agent of the defendants had orally promised the plaintiffs that, if the latter attended the defendants' offices at ten o'clock the next morning, and tendered the plaintiffs' part of the contract engrossed and signed together with a banker's draft for the deposit, the defendants would enter a written contract of sale of the properties to the plaintiffs. The plaintiffs duly attended and tendered the documents, but the defendants refused to go ahead (they had, the evening before, received a substantially higher offer and had been advised that their duty as mortgagees required them to accept this and refuse the plaintiffs' offer). The plaintiffs' action was struck out as disclosing no cause of action, and they appealed.

Goff LJ

... The facts pleaded ... give rise to three questions of law: (a) Do they establish a valid unilateral contract? If they do, then there is no question but that they disclose a breach. (b) If the answer to (a) is 'Yes' then is that contract unenforceable for want of a written note or memorandum to satisfy s 40 of the Law of Property Act 1925, unless there be sufficient acts of part performance to take the case out of the statute? (c) If s 40 applies are there such acts? ... Was there a concluded unilateral contract by the defendants to enter into a contract for sale on the agreed terms?

The concept of a unilateral or 'if' contract is somewhat anomalous, because it is clear that, at all events until the offeree starts to perform the condition, there is no contract at all, but merely an offer which the offeror is free to revoke. Doubts have been expressed whether the offeror becomes bound so soon as the offeree starts to perform or satisfy the condition, or only when he has fully done so. In my judgment, however, we are not concerned in this case with any such problem, because in my view the plaintiffs had fully performed or satisfied the condition when they presented themselves at the time and place appointed with a banker's draft for the deposit and their part of the written contract for sale duly engrossed and signed, and there tendered the same, which I understand to mean proferred it for exchange. Actual exchange, which never took place, would not in my view have been part of the satisfaction of the condition but something additional which was inherently necessary to be done by the plaintiffs to enable, not to bind, the defendants to perform the unilateral contract.

Accordingly in my judgment, the answer to the first question must be in the affirmative.

Even if my reasoning so far be wrong the conclusion in my view is still the same for the following reasons. Whilst I think the true view of a unilateral contract must in general be that the offeror is entitled to require full performance of the condition which he has imposed and short of that he is not bound, that must be subject to one important qualification, which stems from the fact that there must be an implied obligation on the part of the offeror not to prevent the condition becoming satisfied, which obligation it seems to me must arise as soon as the offeree starts to perform. Until then the offeror can revoke the whole thing, but once the offeree has embarked on performance it is too late for the offeror to revoke his offer.

[His Lordship went on to hold that the contract was one for the disposition of an interest in land and was unenforceable because there was no memorandum or sufficient act of part performance.]

Buckley and **Orr LJJ** delivered judgments agreeing with Goff LJ, Buckley LJ specifically agreeing with the last excerpt.

Appeal dismissed.

NOTES

1. Another suggested way of reaching a similar result is to say that the offer of a unilateral contract is accepted, and thus can no longer be withdrawn, once the offeree starts performing, although the offeror is not bound to perform his part until the offeree has performed completely (Pollock, *Principles of Contract*, 13th edn, p 19).

2. The explanation given by Goff LJ is based on an implied obligation not to revoke the offer. Implied terms and obligations are supposedly based on the intentions of the parties. Do you think that the offeror actually intends to prevent himself revoking once the offeree has begun to perform? Or is this an example of an obligation 'imposed' on the offeror in order to protect the offeree?

3. Is it always appropriate to prevent the offeror revoking once the offeree has begun to perform? And what does 'perform' mean in this context? On both questions, consider the next case.

■ *Luxor (Eastbourne) Ltd v Cooper*

[1941] AC 108, House of Lords

The two appellant companies (the owners) orally agreed with the respondent (the agent) that if he introduced a party who should buy the appellants' two cinemas for at least £185, 000, each of the appellants would pay the respondent £5, 000 on the completion of the sale. The respondent introduced a party who agreed to pay that price subject to contract and remained willing to pay it, but the appellants did not proceed. The respondent claimed £10, 000 commission, or £10, 000 damages for breach of an implied term that the appellants would not without just cause so act as to prevent the respondent earning his commission. The Court of Appeal, reversing Branson J, had awarded the respondent damages of £8, 000.

Lord Russell of Killowen

. . . A few preliminary observations occur to me. (1) Commission contracts are subject to no peculiar rules or principles of their own. The law which governs them is the law which governs all contracts and all questions of agency. (2) No general rule can be laid down by which the rights of the agent or the liabilities of the principal under commission contracts are to be determined. In each case, these must depend upon the exact terms of the contract in question, and upon the true construction of those terms. (3) Contracts by which owners of property, desiring to dispose of it, put it in the hands of agents on commission terms are not (in default of specific provisions) contracts of employment in the ordinary meaning of those words. No obligation is imposed on the agent to do anything. The contracts are merely promises binding on the principal to pay a sum of money upon the happening of a specified event, which involves the rendering of some service by the agent. There is no real analogy between such contracts and contracts of employment by which one party binds himself to do certain work and the other binds himself to pay remuneration for the doing of it.

I do not assent to the view, which I think, was the view of the majority in *Trollope (George) & Sons v Martyn Bros*, that a mere promise by a property owner to an agent to pay him a commission if he introduces a purchaser for the property at a specified price, or at a minimum price, ties the owner's hands and compels him, as between himself and the agent, to bind himself contractually to sell to the agent's client who offers that price, with the result that, if he refuses the offer, he is liable to pay the agent a sum equal to, or less than, the amount of the commission, either (a) on a *quantum meruit*, or (b) as damages for breach of a term to be implied in the commission contract. As to the claim on a *quantum meruit*, I do not see how this can be justified in the face of the express provision for remuneration which the contract contains. This must necessarily exclude such a claim, unless it can (upon the facts of a particular case) be based upon a contract subsequent to the original contract, and arising from some conduct on the part of the principal. As to the claim for damages, this rests upon the implication of some provision in the commission contract, the exact terms of which were variously stated in the course of the argument, the object always being to bind the principal not to refuse to complete the sale to the client whom the agent has introduced. I can find no safe ground on which to base the introduction of any such implied term. Implied terms, as we all know, can be justified only under the compulsion of some necessity. No such compulsion or necessity exists in the case under consideration. The agent is promised a commission if he introduces a purchaser at a specified or minimum price. The owner is desirous of selling. The chances are largely in favour of the deal going through if a purchaser is introduced. The agent takes the risk in the hope of a substantial remuneration for comparatively small exertion. In the case of the plaintiff, his contract was made on Sept 23, 1935, and his client's offer was made on Oct 2, 1935. A sum of £10, 000, the equivalent of the remuneration of a year's work by a Lord Chancellor, for work done within a period of 8 or 9 days is no mean reward, and is one well worth a risk. There is no lack of business efficacy in such a contract, even though the principal is free to refuse to sell to the agent's client. The position will no doubt be different if the matter has proceeded to the stage of a binding contract having been made between the principal and the agent's client. In that case, it can be said with truth that a 'purchaser' has been introduced by the agent. In other words, the event has happened upon the occurrence of which a right to the promised commission has become vested in the agent. From that moment, no act or commission by the principal can deprive the agent of that vested right. . . .

Lord Thankerton agreed with Lord Russell, and **Viscount Simon LC** and **Lords Wright** and **Romer** delivered speeches in favour of allowing the appeal.

Appeal allowed.

NOTES

1. At what point does an estate agent earn the commission? In *Christie, Owen & Davies Ltd v Rapacioli* [1974] QB 781, the Court of Appeal applied Lord Russell's dictum that it depends on the terms of the contract and held that as the contract provided for a commission in the event of the plaintiffs 'effecting an introduction . . . of a person . . . ready, able and willing to purchase' at an agreed price, and they had done this, the commission was payable even though the vendor later refused to complete. No commission would have been payable had the purchaser withdrawn.

2. Even if it were appropriate to imply into estate agents' contracts a term that the vendors would not unreasonably withdraw once the agent had started to perform, what would count as starting? Does advertising the property count as starting performance, or is the performance actually introducing a buyer, the advertising being merely preparatory? See Murdoch, 'The Nature of Estate Agency' (1975) 91 LQR 357, at 371–373.

3. Murdoch also points out that, if the restriction on the offeror's power to revoke an offer of a unilateral contract is based on an implied term, the case for implying the term is weaker than in some other types of unilateral contract: in many of the unilateral contract cases, the offeror will get no greater personal benefit from complete performance than from partial performance, but a vendor who withdraws a property from the hands of his agent thereby deprives himself of the benefit of a suitable introduction. Presumably most vendors expect to pay the agent out of the proceeds of sale.

4. Suppose an estate agent is promised a commission of £500 if she 'introduces a party who buys the property'. She incurs expenditure of £100 on advertising and expenditure of time, and introduces a buyer who is ready to complete, but the vendor refuses to go ahead. If the agent *were* to be protected on the *Daulia* principle, should she recover £500 or £100? Which would be more appropriate?

5. An estate agent is approached by a vendor wishing to sell an unusual house, which is unlikely to find a ready buyer without widespread and expensive advertising. What form of agreement would you advise the agent to make with the vendor?

6. It may be that much of the foregoing discussion is misconceived, because even in the normal case the contract with the agent is bilateral. It might surprise many clients to discover that the agent is not liable if she does nothing at all to attempt to find a buyer, which seems to be the result of the unilateral contract analysis. Compare *Wood v Duff-Gordon*, above. In the light of *Luxor v Cooper*, however, it might take a bold court to adopt a bilateral contract approach.

V. BILATERAL OR UNILATERAL?

An offer of a bilateral contract may be accepted by an acceptance communicated to the offeror, or by an 'extraneous' act; an offer of a unilateral contract, by commencing, or perhaps completing, performance. It is not always clear which type of contract is involved.

Suppose Ace Manufacturing Ltd telexes Bends Ltd: 'Urgent. Please make us and dispatch as soon as possible by express 100 bends as per previous special order'. Bends Ltd starts manufacturing these bends, which are of a special design, during the night shift that same evening, and next morning a letter is written accepting Ace's order. However, before the letter has been sent, Ace telexes: 'Cancel order of yesterday.' Has Bends accepted Ace's order: (i) if the contract was bilateral; (ii) if it was unilateral? A decision that the offer was for a unilateral contract would protect the offeree, but equally might hamper the offeror, who might be trying to obtain goods from other suppliers at the same time. (For a case involving a choice between unilateral and bilateral, see *Dawson v Helicopter Exploration* Co *Ltd* [1955] 5 DLR 404.)

Some commentators think the distinction between unilateral and bilateral contracts is too rigid: the offeror may be indifferent as to whether the offeree accepts verbally or starts performing. Restatement 2d provides:

§54. Acceptance by performance; necessity of notification to offeror

(1) Where an offer invites an offeree to accept by rendering a performance, no notification is necessary to make such an acceptance effective unless the offer requests such a notification.

(2) If an offeree who accepts by rendering a performance has reason to know that the offeror has no adequate means of learning of the performance with reasonable promptness and certainly, the contractual duty of the offeror is discharged unless

   (a) the offeree exercises reasonable diligence to notify the offeror of acceptance, or

   (b) the offeror learns of the performance within a reasonable time, or

   (c) the offer indicates that notification of acceptance is not required.

§62. Effect of performance by offeree where offer invites either performance or promise

(1) Where an offer invites an offeree to choose between acceptance by promise and acceptance by performance, the tender or beginning of the invited performance or a tender of a beginning of it is an acceptance by performance.

(2) Such an acceptance operates as a promise to render complete performance.

Comment:

a. The offeree's power to choose. The offeror normally invites a promise by the offeree for the purpose of obtaining performance of the promise. Full performance fulfills that purpose more directly than the promise invited, and hence constitutes a reasonable mode of acceptance. The offeror can insist on any mode of acceptance, but ordinarily he invites acceptance in any reasonable manner; in case of doubt, an offer is interpreted as inviting the offeree to choose between acceptance by promise and acceptance by performance. See §§30, 32, 58.

Illustrations:

1. A, a merchant, mails B, a carpenter in the same city, an offer to employ B to fit up A's office in accordance with A's specifications and B's estimate previously submitted, the work to be completed in two weeks. The offer says, 'you may begin at once', and B immediately buys lumber and begins to work on it in his own shop. The next day, before B has sent a notice of acceptance or begun work at A's office or rendered the lumber unfit for other jobs, A revokes the offer. The revocation is timely, since B has not begun to perform.

2. A, a regular customer of B, orders fragile goods from B which B carries in stock and ships in his own trucks. Following his usual practice, B selects the goods ordered, tags them as A's, crates them and loads them on a truck at substantial expense. Performance has begun, and A's offer is irrevocable. See Uniform Commercial Code §§2–206 and Comment 2.

The result in our problem would be that there is a contract, as Bends has begun the stipulated performance, although s 54 would also require him to notify the offeror within a reasonable time of starting, or 'the contractual duty of the offeror is discharged'. Do you think this is a worthwhile approach, or might it be better to treat this type of problem not by holding that there is a contract, but by imposing liability on some other basis? Compare the cases discussed on p 281 ff.

VI. DIFFERING PROPOSALS

■ *Hyde v Wrench*
(1840) 3 Beav 334, 49 ER 132, Rolls Court

The defendant offered to sell a farm to the plaintiff for £1, 000, to which the plaintiff responded by offering (through his agent) £950 for it. The defendant rejected this offer, and the plaintiff then purported to accept the defendant's original offer of £1, 000. The plaintiff brought an action for specific performance, and the defendant filed a general demurrer.

The Master of the Rolls [Lord Langdale]

Under the circumstances stated in this bill, I think there exists no valid binding contract between the parties for the purchase of the property. The Defendant offered to sell it for £1, 000, and if that had been at once unconditionally accepted, there would undoubtedly have been a perfect binding contract; instead of that, the Plaintiff made an offer of his own, to purchase the property for £950, and he thereby rejected the offer previously made by the Defendant. I think that it was not afterwards competent for him to revive the proposal of the Defendant, by tendering an acceptance of it; and that, therefore, there exists no obligation of any sort between the parties; the demurrer must be allowed.

■ *Stevenson, Jacques & Co v McLean* (1880)
5 QBD 346

The defendant wrote to the plaintiffs offering to sell them some iron, represented by a number of delivery warrants, at 40s net cash, and stating that he would hold the offer open until the following Monday. At 9.42 am on the Monday morning, the plaintiffs telegraphed the defendant:

Please wire whether you would accept forty for delivery over two months, or if not, longest limit you could give.

The defendant did not answer this telegram but sold the warrants, and at 1.25 pm telegraphed the plaintiffs to inform them. Meanwhile, the plaintiffs had found a buyer for the iron and, at 1.34 pm (before the defendant's telegram had reached them), they sent a telegram accepting his offer. The plaintiffs sued for breach of contract.

Lush J

... Two objections were relied on by the defendant: first, it was contended that the telegram sent by the plaintiffs on the Monday morning was a rejection of the defendant's offer and a new proposal on the plaintiffs' part, and that the defendant had therefore a right to regard it as putting an end to the original negotiation.

Looking at the form of the telegram, the time when it was sent, and the state of the iron market, I cannot think this is its fair meaning. The plaintiff Stevenson said he meant it only as an inquiry, expecting an answer for his guidance, and this, I think, is the sense in which the defendant ought to have regarded it.

It is apparent throughout the correspondence, that the plaintiffs did not contemplate buying the iron on speculation, but that their acceptance of the defendant's offer depended on their finding some one to take the warrants off their hands. All parties knew that the market was in an unsettled state, and that no one could predict at the early hour when the telegram was sent how the prices would range during the day. It was reasonable that, under these circumstances, they should desire to know before business began whether they were to be at liberty in case of need to make any and what concession as to the time or times of delivery, which would be the time or times of payment, or whether the defendant was determined to adhere to the terms or his letter; and it was highly unreasonable that the plaintiffs should have intended to close the negotiation while it was uncertain whether they could find a buyer or not, having the whole of the business hours of the day to look for one. Then, again, the form of the telegram is one of inquiry. It is not 'I offer forty for delivery over two months', which would have likened the case to *Hyde v Wrench* ...

Here there is no counter proposal. The words are, 'Please wire whether you would accept forty for delivery over two months, or, if not, the longest limit you would give.' There is nothing specific by way of offer or rejection, but a mere inquiry, which should have been answered and not treated as a rejection of the offer. This ground of objection therefore fails.

(The second objection was that the offer had been revoked before it had been accepted: this also failed, see p 231.)

Judgment for the plaintiffs.

NOTE

Why is a counter-offer, but not a mere enquiry, treated as revoking the original offer? Would it be reasonable in either case for the offeree to assume the original offer was still good?

■ **Beale and Dugdale 'Contracts between Businessmen'**
(1975) 2 Br J Law & Soc45, at 48–51

(For another extract from this piece, describing the research upon which it was based, see pp 81–83.)

Formation

The attitudes of firms towards problems of formation provide an indication of their awareness of and concern about the process of contract law, and illustrate the conscious nature of the decision whether or not to plan in detail. The degree of planning is in part likely to be determined by the process of formation adopted. Contracts formed as a result of detailed negotiation were comparatively rare. They were usually to be found only where the goods to be supplied were expensive and complex, for instance complete aircraft, aero engines or machinery worth more than £50, 000, and the risks were thus sufficient to justify the time and trouble, particularly as the sale of a finished product of this type would often be to a customer outside the trade who would not know or accept the usual practices. The negotiated contracts were often many pages in length and contained detailed planning of both the primary obligations and the mechanisms for adjustment. However even in such contracts planning might not be complete. Some details might be left vague, either consciously because the parties had decided that it was not worth negotiating certain areas of conflict, or unconsciously: managing directors might draw up 'heads of agreement' unwittingly leaving many areas vague. Research and development contracts provided a special problem for by their very nature they required some areas to be left unnegotiated in order to provide for future eventualities.

At the other extreme were contracts made informally by telephone or simple exchange of letters. Here only the primary obligations would be planned expressly but the parties to such contracts often held unexpressed assumptions about the way in which obligations would be adjusted or enforced, relying either upon trade custom or a 'gentlemen's agreement' with the other contracting party. The informal formation process was deliberately adopted only by a minority of firms who either were not prepared to create sufficient office capacity to deal with much paper work or who felt able to place faith in the other contracting party because of the market conditions. Often such firms were doing nearly all their business locally and there was close and continuous personal contact with their customers and suppliers; this would be more important to them than safeguarding an individual exchange which was usually of low value anyway.

The majority of firms intended to make their contracts by the use of forms containing standard conditions of sale or purchase. Usually these forms would have the primary obligations (item, price, delivery date and perhaps terms of payment) typed on the front, while terms providing for adjustment, contingencies and so on would be printed on the back—hence they were commonly referred to as 'back of order' conditions.

When one set of conditions has been accepted by both seller and buyer as governing their exchange then in law a contract on the basis of those conditions has been formed. It was common for buyers of component parts or raw materials to accept sellers' conditions; occasionally sellers would accept the buyer's terms. It was clear that this was not done, however, with any conscious aim of ensuring that there would be a legally enforceable, fully-planned contract. It was partly the product of market power: a buyer faced with short supply might be forced to accept the seller's terms while we found sellers accepting buyers' terms only when selling to very powerful concerns such as a nationalized industry. But it may also be explained by the difficulty in drafting uniform purchase conditions to suit a wide variety of different purchases, and the generally greater prestige and time given to sales, for the firm will be known by its product.

More usually each party attempted to get its 'back of order' conditions accepted by the other. Under commercial pressure this system might break down—salesmen trying to meet targets might enter informal contracts without bothering with their terms or engineers more concerned about production than purchasing arrangements might unthinkingly accept the other party's terms. The significance of what was being done was not always appreciated by the officer concerned despite occasional lectures complete with instructive cartoons provided by purchasing officers. Firms seemed to consider that it was difficult to prevent this sort of breakdown but the majority of contracts were made by each party using his 'back of order' conditions.

This meant that in many cases one party's conditions would not be fully accepted by the other, but the parties would instead exchange conditions. Typically the seller would issue to the purchaser a quotation form backed with his standard conditions, the buyer would reply with an order form with his conditions, and the seller would then acknowledge the order and in doing so refer again to his conditions. This stage would normally complete the exchange. Inevitably the seller's and buyer's conditions would conflict and indeed this was contemplated for most forms contained a condition to the effect that in the case of a conflict that set of conditions would override the other.

The legal effect of such an exchange of conflicting forms is not entirely clear but it seems most likely that no enforceable contract results: each communication, providing it refers clearly to the standard conditions, is an offer which is refused and replaced by another on different terms, the last one (the sellers' 'acknowledgment') remaining an unaccepted offer. If however the other party later does something recognizing the existence of a contract, such as telephoning the seller to press for delivery, he may be held to have accepted that offer, so that the last set of conditions sent may win the day.

There was considerable awareness of the fact that in many cases an exchange of conditions would not necessarily lead to an enforceable contract, and some that the last set of conditions might prevail: one legal adviser had prepared a 'confirmation of order' form to be used to 'get his firm's conditions in last' when buying as well as when selling. But most firms seemed unconcerned about the failure to make a contract. They usually tried to ensure that they referred to their conditions in any written communications, which would prevent the letter 'accepting' the other party's terms, but no more, and some were not even concerned with that.

What did concern all the firms who contracted by this method was to reach a clear understanding on particular important points or ones on which any difficulty was anticipated. Of course in every exchange certain items would be agreed expressly, if only the item and the price, and in some cases the 'back of order' would never be looked at. In others however almost every major difference would be followed up and settled, and in the majority of cases at least a few of the more important items dealt with in the standard conditions would be discussed and agreed. Usually these were the same items that would be the subject of detailed discussion if a contract were specifically negotiated, or at the other extreme which would be mentioned if a contract were made formally by 'phone or letter; for instance payment terms or warranty periods, and whether the price was fixed or open.

In commercial terms therefore the result of an exchange of 'back of order' conditions did not offer a complete contrast to a negotiated contract on the one hand or an informal exchange of letters on the other: the number of issues planned would vary enormously, but there would be definite agreement on certain of them. Legal enforceability seemed secondary to reaching a common understanding. But even this was not always considered necessary. Frequently we were told that the other party's 'back of order' conditions would be scrutinized but no objection would be raised unless some unusual term was found: for instance, many sellers did not mind what the buyer order contained on the question of delay provided it did not attempt to impose liquidated damages. The implication seems to be that provided the two sets of conditions contained terms commonly found in the trade a sufficient basis would exist to enable any dispute to be settled without difficulty; even common understanding did not have to be very precise.

As far as the legal enforceability of agreement is concerned, two qualifications should be made to what has been said. First it is possible that enforceable contracts were created by the exchange of standard conditions more frequently than our analysis above suggests. A court faced with a clearly unresolved conflict of terms on the one hand but a clear intention to contract on the other *might* decide that there was a contract containing those terms which had been agreed, and dismiss the remainder of the conditions. Therefore positive planning on particular issues even while using standard terms may have legal as well as commercial significance. Secondly we were told of and saw signs of a gradual change in attitude towards tightening up procedures and creating legally enforceable agreements. For instance we came across several examples of purchasing departments who for years had bought from their main suppliers on 'back of order' conditions now negotiating standing supply contracts to govern future orders. This may be entirely explicable by the recent inflation and economic troubles which make it desirable to have clear agreement on such matters as price increases and delays, but we were told by several representatives that it was the result of a new professionalism among young managers, many of whom have studied contract law.

■ *Butler Machine Tool Co Ltd v Ex-Cell-O Corpn (England) Ltd*
[1979] 1 All ER 965, Court of Appeal

On 23 May 1969, in response to an enquiry by the buyers, the sellers made a quotation offering to sell a machine tool to the buyers for £75, 535, delivery to be in ten months' time. The offer was stated to be subject to certain terms and conditions, which 'shall prevail over any terms and conditions in the Buyer's order'. The conditions included a price variation clause providing for the goods to be charged at the price ruling on the date of delivery. On 27 May, the buyers replied by placing an order for the machine. The order was stated to be subject to certain terms and conditions, which were materially different from those put forward by the sellers and which, in particular, made no provision for a variation in price. At the foot of the buyers' order, there was a tear-off acknowledgement of receipt of the order stating that we 'accept your order on the Terms and Conditions stated thereon'. On 5 June, the sellers completed and signed the acknowledgement and returned it to the buyers with a letter stating that the buyers' order was being entered in accordance with the sellers' quotation of 23 May. When the sellers came to deliver the machine, they claimed that the price had increased by £2, 892. The buyers refused to pay the increase in price and the sellers brought an action claiming that they were entitled to increase the price under the price variation clause contained in their offer.

The judge upheld the sellers' claim and the buyers appealed.

Lord Denning MR

This case is a 'battle of forms'. The suppliers of a machine, Butler Machine Tool Co Ltd ('the sellers'), on 23rd May 1969 quoted a price for a machine tool of £75, 535. Delivery was to be given in ten months. On the back of the quotation there were terms and conditions. One of them was a price variation clause. It provided for an increase in the price if there was an increase in the costs and so forth. The machine tool was not delivered until November 1970. By that time costs had increased so much that the sellers claimed an additional sum of £2, 892 as due to them under the price variation clause.

The buyers, Ex-Cell-O Corpn, rejected the excess charge. They relied on their own terms and conditions. They said: 'We did not accept the sellers' quotation as it was. We gave an order for the self-same machine at the self-same price, but on the back of our order we had our own terms and conditions. Our terms and conditions did not contain any price variation clause.'

... If [the] documents are analysed in our traditional method, the result would seem to me to be this: the quotation of 23rd May 1969 was an offer by the sellers to the buyers containing the terms and conditions on the back. The order of 27th May 1969 purported to be an acceptance of that offer in that it was for the same machine at the same price but it contained such additions as to cost of installation, date of delivery and so forth, that it was in law a rejection of the offer and constituted a counter-offer. That is clear from *Hyde v Wrench*. As Megaw J said in *Trollope & Colls Ltd v Atomic Power Constructions Ltd*: '... the counter-offer kills the original offer'. The letter of the sellers of 5th June 1969 was an acceptance of that counter-offer, as is shown by the acknowledgement which the sellers signed and returned to the buyers. The reference to the quotation of 23rd May 1969 referred only to the price and identity of the machine ...

The judge held that the sellers were entitled to the sum of £2, 892 under the price variation clause. He did not apply the traditional method of an analysis by way of offer and counter-offer. He said that in the quotation of 23rd May 1969 'one finds the price variation clause appearing under a most emphatic heading stating that it is a term or condition that is to prevail'. So he held that it did prevail.

I have much sympathy with the judge's approach to this case. In many of these cases our traditional analysis of offer, counter-offer, rejection, acceptance and so forth is out-of-date. This was observed by Lord Wilberforce in *New Zealand Shipping Co Ltd v A M Satterthwaite*. The better way is to look at all the documents passing between the parties and glean from them, or from the conduct of the parties, whether they have reached agreement on all material points, even though there may be differences between the forms and conditions printed on the back of them

... Applying this guide, it will be found that in most cases when there is a 'battle of forms' there is a contract as soon as the last of the forms is sent and received without objection being taken to it. That is well observed in Benjamin on Sale. The difficulty is to decide which form, or which part of which form, is a term or condition of the contract. In some cases the battle is won by the man who fires the last shot.

He is the man who puts forward the latest terms and conditions: and, if they are not objected to by the other party, he may be taken to have agreed to them. Such was *British Road Services Ltd v Arthur V Crutchley & Co Ltd* per Lord Pearson; and the illustration given by Professor Guest in Anson's Law of Contract where he says that 'the terms of the contract consist of the terms of the offer subject to the modifications contained in the acceptance'. That may however go too far. In some cases, however, the battle is won by the man who gets the blow in first. If he offers to sell at a named price on the terms and conditions stated on the back and the buyer orders the goods purporting to accept the offer on an order form with his own different terms and conditions on the back, then, if the difference is so material that it would affect the price, the buyer ought not to be allowed to take advantage of the difference unless he draws it specifically to the attention of the seller. There are yet other cases where the battle depends on the shots fired on both sides. There is a concluded contract but the forms vary. The terms and conditions of both parties are to be construed together. If they can be reconciled so as to give a harmonious result, all well and good. If differences are irreconcilable, so that they are mutually contradictory, then the conflicting terms may have to be scrapped and replaced by a reasonable implication.

In the present case the judge thought that the sellers in their original quotation got their blow in first; especially by the provision that 'These terms and conditions shall prevail over any terms and conditions in the Buyer's order'. It was so emphatic that the price variation clause continued through all the subsequent dealings and that the buyer must be taken to have agreed to it. I can understand that point of view. But I think that the documents have to be considered as a whole. And, as a matter of construction, I think the acknowledgment of 5th June 1969 is the decisive document. It makes it clear that the contract was on the buyers' terms and not on the sellers' terms: and the buyers' terms did not include a price variation clause.

I would therefore allow the appeal and enter judgment for the buyers.

Lawton LJ

The modern commercial practice of making quotations and placing orders with conditions attached, usually in small print, is indeed likely, as in this case, to produce a battle of forms. The problem is how should that battle be conducted? The view taken by the judge was that the battle should extend over a wide area and the court should do its best to look into the minds of the parties and make certain assumptions. In my judgment, the battle has to be conducted in accordance with set rules. It is a battle more on classical 18th century lines when convention decided who had the right to open fire first rather than in accordance with the modern concept of attrition.

The rules relating to a battle of this kind have been known for the past 130–odd years. They were set out by the then Master of the Rolls, Lord Langdale, in *Hyde v Wrench*, and Lord Denning MR has already referred to them; and, if anyone should have thought they were obsolescent, Megaw J in *Trollope & Colls Ltd v Atomic Power Constructions Ltd* called attention to the fact that those rules are still in force.

When those rules are applied to this case, in my judgment, the answer is obvious . . . the [sellers] completed that tear-off slip and sent it back to the buyers . . . It is true, as counsel for the sellers has reminded us, that the return of that printed slip was accompanied by a letter which had this sentence in it: 'This is being entered in accordance with our revised quotation of 23rd May for delivery in 10/11 months.' I agree with Lord Denning MR that, in a business sense, that refers to the quotation as to the price and the identity of the machine, and it does not bring into the contract the small print conditions on the back of the quotation. Those small print conditions had disappeared from the story. That was when the contract was made. At that date it was a fixed price contract without a price escalation clause. . . .

I agree with Lord Denning MR that this appeal should be allowed.

Bridge LJ also delivered judgment allowing the appeal on the basis of 'the classical doctrine'.

NOTES

1.   Why treat the tear-off slip as the crucial document, and the accompanying letter as merely identifying the relevant papers, rather than the other way round?

2.   Subsequent cases in which there was no tear-off slip have followed Lawton's approach, holding that the last document was a counter-offer only accepted by conduct when the contract was performed: eg *Sauter Automation Ltd v Goodman (Mechanical Services) Ltd* (1986) 34 BLR 81.

3.   Can you draft a clause that, if included in your client's standard conditions, will ensure that any contract he purports to make using those conditions will in fact be on his terms, not the other party's? Was the 'clause paramount' in the sellers' conditions in the *Butler Machine Tool* case of any effect?

4.   If you cannot devise an effective clause paramount, what advice would you give him about buying and selling the routine items he now buys and sells 'on' his standard conditions?

5.   Could the law be improved? Consider Uniform Commercial Code s 2–207*:

2–207. Additional Terms in Acceptance or Confirmation

(1) A definite and seasonable expression of acceptance or a written confirmation which is sent within a reasonable time operates as an acceptance even though it states terms additional to or different from those offered or agreed upon, unless acceptance is expressly made conditional on assent to the additional or different terms.

(2) The additional terms are to be construed as proposals for addition to the contract. Between merchants such terms become part of the contract unless:
   (a) the offer expressly limits acceptance to the terms of the offer;
   (b) they materially alter it; or
   (c) notification of objection to them has already been given or is given within a reasonable time after notice of them is received.

(3) Conduct by both parties which recognizes the existence of a contract is sufficient to establish a contract for sale although the writings of the parties do not otherwise establish a contract. In such case the terms of the particular contract consist of those terms on which the writings of the parties agree, together with any supplementary terms incorporated under any other provisions of this Act.

*   The Uniform Commercial Code is a model statute produced under the joint sponsorship of the American Law Institute and the National Conference of Commissioners on Uniform State Laws. Work began on it in the 1940s, and the first edition was approved in 1952. It covers a wide range of commercial transactions; in this book, we shall examine sections from arts 1 (general) and 2 (sale of goods). The UCC has been adopted in full by all the US states except Louisiana (which was originally a civil law jurisdiction, and has adopted only certain articles of the UCC), and by the District of Columbia. Its stated purpose, 'to simplify, clarify and modernize the law governing commercial transactions; to permit the continued expansion of commercial practices through custom, usage and agreement of the parties; to make uniform the law among the various jurisdictions' (s 1–102(2)), does not reveal the many innovations contained in the code; many of these reflect the ideas of the professor considered to be the code's chief architect, Karl Llewellyn. See Danzig, 'A Comment on the Jurisprudence of the UCC' (1975) 27 Stan LR 621.

If you like the look of s 2–207, try answering the following questions:

B orders goods by a purchase order that describes the goods and states the price on its face and states 'subject to the terms overleaf', one of which is that all contracts are fixed price. S sends back an acknowledgement, 'accepting your order subject to our terms overleaf', one of which is that all prices are subject to cost increases between the date of order and the date of delivery (let us assume, quite unrealistically, that this is the only difference).

(i)   Has there been 'a definite and seasonable expression of acceptance' within s 2–207(1)?

(ii) Is S's 'acceptance' 'expressly made conditional upon an assent to the additional or different terms'?

(iii) If there is a contract, is it fixed price or variable price? Would your answer differ if B's forms were silent on price?

(iv) Suppose S starts manufacturing the goods, which are to be made to B's special design. Is there a contract under s 2–207(3)?

(v)   Suppose the goods are delivered by S and accepted by B before the discrepancy is noticed. Whose terms apply? Is the solution provided by s 2–207(3) any better than the common law solution?

The majority view in the USA seems to be that UCC s 2–207(1) has not been a success and revised wording will be adopted in the second edition.

Another and rather different solution is adopted in the UNIDROIT General Principles for International Commercial Contracts (2004), Art 2.1.22 of which provides:

Where both parties use standard terms and reach agreement except on those terms, a contract is concluded on the basis of the agreed terms and of any standard terms which are common in substance unless one party clearly indicates in advance, or later and without undue delay informs the other party, that it does not intend to be bound by such a contract.

Try to work out some cases in which this leads to a different result from UCC s 2–207(1).

6.   Having gone through those questions, how important or worthwhile do you think law reform on these lines is?

See further Ontario Law Reform Commission, *Sale of Goods Report* (1979) and Scottish Law Commission, Consultation Paper: *Contract Law—Exchange of Standard Forms in Contract Formation* (1981).

7.   Ann orders some goods from Bert, asking Bert to ship them immediately. Bert does so, but while he is preparing an invoice to send to Ann, he receives a fax from her cancelling the order. The goods are still in transit. Is there a contract?

8.   How would you answer question 7 if, when Bert received Ann's fax, he had labelled the goods for dispatch to her but had not yet posted them?

9.   Carrie writes to David: 'I have decided that after all I will sell you my car at the price you suggested last week. I'll bring it round next Saturday. No need to answer.' David does not answer. Is there a contract: (i) which Carrie can enforce against David; (ii) which David could enforce against Carrie?

10. Bertie placed an advertisement in the newspaper reading:

Reward of £5, 000 for precise location (within 1 mile) of yacht Satanita, stolen from Mudhook on 1 Jan 1995, or location of wreck. Information to 0171–234–5678.

Claire, a detective with a nautical bent, began a search for the missing yacht. She discovered that the yacht had been seen on 15 January near Tenerife and, in her excitement, rang Bertie to tell him this. Bertie immediately replied that he was withdrawing his offer, and he flew out to Tenerife and discovered the yacht himself in a harbour on an adjacent island. Claire had incurred expenses of £2, 000 in tracing the yacht. Is she entitled to any compensation and, if so, how much?

11.   Dumbells Ltd asks Export plc to quote for supplying Dumbells with 1, 000 widgets. Export sends a quotation of £4, 000 for the 1, 000 widgets for delivery in February; it uses its standard quotation form with its terms on the back. Dumbells sends back an order form for the widgets, using its standard form, which also has terms on the back. Export writes back on its acceptance form, which contains the same terms as it used before. A month later, the goods are delivered, and three weeks after that, Dumbells pays for them. When is the contract made?

12.   Dumbells's terms allow for a discount of 5 per cent for payment within 30 days of delivery; Export's do not. Whose terms prevail?

13.   Can you devise a way of making sure one party's terms prevail?

14.   What does the fact that business people regularly do business in the way described in question 11 tell us about contract law, or, more precisely, when are businesses likely to rely on the law and when are they likely to rely on non-legal sanctions? (See Chapter 5.)

It is usually assumed that, at the latest, once the goods have been delivered to and accepted by the buyer there will be a contract (see note 2 above and *G Percy Trentham Ltd v Archital Luxfer Ltd*, below, p 266). The question then is, on whose terms is the contract? A buyer who has accepted the goods must be liable to pay for them, but McKendrick (1988) 2 Oxford J Legal Studies 197 has pointed out that an alternative analysis is possible: it might be held that the parties had never reached an agreement and that the buyer is liable not in contract but in restitution, cf *British Steel v Cleveland Bridge* (p 39). An objection to this analysis, noted by McKendrick, concerns the situation if the goods later turned out to be defective. The buyer could argue that goods that were not in accordance with the contract were of no value to it (save insofar as they had a resale value, in which case there would be an objective benefit). However, if the defect caused consequential financial loss (eg a loss of production), the buyer would not have any remedy for this in restitution (or *ex hypothesi* in contract) and there would be difficulties in recovering in tort (cf pp 36–37).

VII. POSTAL COMMUNICATIONS

■ *Adams v Lindsell*

(1818) 1 B & Ald 681, 106 ER 250, King's Bench

Action for non-delivery of wool according to agreement. At the trial at the last Lent Assizes for the county of Worcester, before Burrough J it appeared that the defendants, who were dealers in wool, at St Ives, in the county of Huntingdon, had, on Tuesday the 2nd of September 1817, written the following letter to the plaintiffs, who were woollen manufacturers residing in Bromsgrove, Worcestershire. 'We now offer you eight hundred tods of wether fleeces, of a good fair quality of our country wool at 35s 6d per tod, to be delivered at Leicester, and to be paid for by two months' bill in two months, and to be weighed up by your agent within fourteen days, receiving your answer in course of post.'

This letter was misdirected by the defendants, to Bromsgrove, Leicestershire, in consequence of which it was not received by the plaintiffs in Worcestershire till 7 pm on Friday, September 5th. On that evening the plaintiffs wrote an answer, agreeing to accept the wool on the terms proposed. The course of the post between St Ives and Bromsgrove is through London, and consequently this answer was not received by the defendants till Tuesday, September 9th. On the Monday September 8th, the defendants not having, as they expected, received an answer on Sunday September 7th, (which in case their letter had not been misdirected, would have been in the usual course of the post,) sold the wool in question to another person. Under these circumstances, the learned Judge held, that the delay having been occasioned by the neglect of the defendants, the jury must take it, that the answer did come back in due course of post; and that then the defendants were liable for the loss that had been sustained: and the plaintiffs accordingly recovered a verdict.

[The defendants sought a new trial, arguing that there was no contract until the plaintiffs' acceptance was received.]

The Court said, that if that were so, no contract could ever be completed by the post. For if the defendants were not bound by their offer when accepted by the plaintiffs till the answer was received, then the plaintiffs ought not to be bound till after they had received the notification that the defendants had received their answer and assented to it. And so it might go on ad infinitum. The defendants must be considered in law as making, during every instant of the time their letter was travelling, the same identical offer to the plaintiffs; and then the contract is completed by the acceptance of it by the latter. Then as to the delay in notifying the acceptance, that arises entirely from the mistake of the defendants, and it therefore must be taken as against them, that the plaintiffs' answer was received in course of post.

Rule discharged.

NOTE

On what ground was this case decided, according to the report? Can you see any other ground upon which the same result might have been reached?

■ *Henthorn v Fraser*
[1892] 2 Ch 27, Court of Appeal

The secretary of a land society in Liverpool had handed to Henthorn a written option to purchase some houses belonging to the society at £750. At about midday the next day, the secretary of the society posted a withdrawal of the offer; it did not reach Henthorn's home in Birkenhead until after 5 pm. Meanwhile, at 3.50 pm Henthorn had posted an acceptance of the offer; this was delivered to the society's office after it had closed and was opened by the secretary the next day. Henthorn's action for specific performance was dismissed and he appealed.

Lord Herschell

... If the acceptance by the Plaintiff of the Defendants' offer is to be treated as complete at the time the letter containing it was posted, I can entertain no doubt that the society's attempted revocation of the offer was wholly ineffectual. I think that a person who has made an offer must be considered as continuously making it until he has brought to the knowledge of the person to whom it was made that it is withdrawn ...

The grounds upon which it has been held that the acceptance of an offer is complete when it is posted have, I think, no application to the revocation or modification of an offer. These can be no more effectual than the offer itself, unless brought to the mind of the person to whom the offer is made. But it is contended on behalf of the Defendants that the acceptance was complete only when received by them and not on the letter being posted. It cannot, of course, be denied, after the decision in *Dunlop v Higgins* in the House of Lords, that, where an offer has been made through the medium of the post, the contract is complete as soon as the acceptance of the offer is posted, but that decision is said to be inapplicable here, inasmuch as the letter containing the offer was not sent by post to *Birkenhead*, but handed to the Plaintiff in the Defendants' office at *Liverpool*. The question therefore arises in what circumstances the acceptance of an offer is to be regarded as complete as soon as it is posted. . . .

I am not sure that I should myself have regarded the doctrine that an acceptance is complete as soon as the letter containing it is posted as resting upon an implied authority by the person making the offer to the person receiving it to accept by those means. It strikes me as somewhat artificial to speak of the person to whom the offer is made as having the implied authority of the other party to send his acceptance by post. He needs no authority to transmit the acceptance through any particular channel; he may select what means he pleases, the Post Office no less than any other. The only effect of the supposed authority is to make the acceptance complete so soon as it is posted, and authority will obviously be implied only when the tribunal considers that it is a case in which this result ought to be reached. I should prefer to state the rule thus: Where the circumstances are such that it must have been within the contemplation of the parties that, according to the ordinary usages of mankind, the post might be used as a means of communicating the acceptance of an offer, the acceptance is complete as soon as it is posted. It matters not in which way the proposition be stated, the present case is in either view within it . . .

Lindley and **Kay LJJ** delivered concurring judgments.

Appeal allowed.

NOTES

1.   See Evans, 'The Anglo-American Mailing Rule' 15 ICLQ 553 and, especially on the contemporary background to the cases that developed the 'postal rule', Gardner (1992) 12 Oxford J Legal Studies 170.

2.   Is the 'postal rule' a logical deduction from the rules of offer and acceptance, or a rule of commercial convenience? In *Household Fire and Carriage Accident Insurance Co Ltd v Grant* (1879) 4 Ex D 216, in which it was held that the letter of acceptance was effective even though it never arrived at all, Thesiger LJ said (at 223–224):

> There is no doubt that the implication of a complete, final, and absolutely binding contract being formed, as soon as the acceptance of an offer is posted, may in some cases lead to inconvenience and hardship. But such there must be at times in every view of the law. It is impossible in transactions which pass between parties at a distance, and have to be carried on through the medium of correspondence, to adjust conflicting rights between innocent parties, so as to make the consequences of mistake on the part of a mutual agent fall equally upon the shoulders of both. At the same time I am not prepared to admit that the implication in question will lead to any great or general inconvenience or hardship. An offerer, if he chooses, may always make the formation of the contract which he proposes dependent upon the actual communication to himself of the acceptance. If he trusts to the post he trusts to a means of communication which, as a rule, does not fail, and if no answer to his offer is received by him, and the matter is of importance to him, he can make inquiries of the person to whom his offer was addressed. On the other hand, if the contract is not finally concluded, except in the event of the acceptance actually reaching the offerer, the door would be opened to the perpetration of much fraud, and, putting aside this consideration, considerable delay in commercial transactions, in which despatch is, as a rule, of the greatest consequence, would be occasioned; for the acceptor would never be entirely safe in acting upon his acceptance until he had received notice that his letter of acceptance had reached its destination.

Does the rule enable reliance by one party or the other? Would it cause practical difficulty if the letter of acceptance did have to arrive to be effective? Or if the rule were reversed, so that acceptances had to be communicated but revocations were effective on posting?

3.   What if the offeree posts an acceptance but then changes his mind and sends a rejection of the offer by telex, which arrives before the letter? Should he be allowed to play 'fast and loose' in this manner? Can you see any practical difficulty that might arise if it were held that the acceptance was effective despite the overtaking telex?

4.   What if the offeree carelessly puts the wrong address on the envelope? Should the offeror still have to bear the risk of loss or delay in the post? Compare *Adams v Lindsell*.

5.   In what circumstances will acceptance by post *not* be impliedly authorised?

■ *Holwell Securities Ltd v Hughes*
[1974] 1 All ER 161, Court of Appeal

By cl 1 of an agreement dated 19 October 1971 made between the defendant of the one part and the plaintiffs of the other, the plaintiffs were granted an option to purchase certain freehold property from the defendant. Clause 2 of the agreement provided: 'The said option shall be exercisable by notice in writing to the [defendant] at any time within six months from the date hereof...' On 14 April 1972, the plaintiffs' solicitors wrote a letter to the defendant giving notice of the exercise of the option. The letter was posted, properly addressed and prepaid, on 14 April, but it was never in fact delivered to the defendant or to his address. No other written communication of the exercise of the option was given or sent to the defendant before the expiry of the time limit on 19 April. In an action against the defendant seeking specific performance of the option agreement, the plaintiffs contended that, since a contractual offer could be accepted by posting a letter of acceptance, the time of acceptance being the moment of posting, the option had been validly exercised when their letter of 14 April was posted.

Russell LJ

... It is the law in the first place that prima facie acceptance of an offer must be communicated to the offeror. On this principle the law has engrafted a doctrine that, if in any given case the true view is that the parties contemplated that the postal service might be used for the purpose of forwarding an acceptance of the offer, committal of the acceptance in a regular manner to the postal service will be acceptance of the offer so as to constitute a contract, even if the letter goes astray and is lost. Nor, as was once suggested, are such cases limited to cases in which the offer has been made by post. It suffices I think at this stage to refer to *Henthorn v Fraser*. In the present case, as I read a passage in the judgment below, Templeman J concluded that the parties here contemplated that the postal service might be used to communicate acceptance of the offer (by exercise of the option); and I agree with that.

But that is not and cannot be the end of the matter. In any case, before one can find that the basic principle of the need for communication of acceptance to the offeror is displaced by this artificial concept of communication by the act of posting, it is necessary that the offer is in its terms consistent with such displacement and not one which by its terms points rather in the direction of actual communication...

The relevant language here is, 'The said option shall be exercisable by notice in writing to the Intending Vendor...' a very common phrase in an option agreement. There is, of course, nothing in that phrase to suggest that the notification to the defendant could not be made by post. But the requirement of 'notice . . . to', in my judgment, is language which should be taken expressly to assert the ordinary situation in law that acceptance requires to be communicated or notified to the offeror, and is inconsistent with the theory that acceptance can be constituted by the act of posting, referred to by Anson as 'acceptance *without notification*'.

It is of course true that the instrument could have been differently worded. An option to purchase within a period given for value has the characteristic of an offer that cannot be withdrawn. The instrument might have said 'The offer constituted by this option may be accepted in writing within six months': in which case no doubt the posting would have sufficed to form the contract. But that language was not used, and, as indicated, in my judgment the language used prevents that legal outcome. Under this head of the case hypothetical problems were canvassed to suggest difficulties in the way of that conclusion. What if the letter had been delivered through the letterbox of the house in due time, but the defendant had either deliberately or fortuitously not been there to receive it before the option period expired? This does not persuade me that the artificial posting rule is here applicable. The answer might well be that in the circumstances the defendant had impliedly invited communication by use of an orifice in his front door designed to receive communications. . . .

Accordingly I would dismiss the appeal; and Buckley LJ authorises me to say that he agrees with the judgment I have delivered.

Lawton LJ delivered a concurring judgment. He commented:

A notice is a means of making something known. The Shorter Oxford English Dictionary gives as the primary meanings of the word: 'Intimation, information, intelligence, warning . . . formal intimation or warning of something.' If a notice is to be of any value it must be an intimation to someone. A notice which cannot impinge on anyone's mind is not functioning as such.

■ *Entores Ltd v Miles Far East Corpn*
[1955] 2 All ER 493, Court of Appeal

An English company in London was in communication by telex with a Dutch company in Amsterdam; the Dutch company was acting as agent for an American company in New York. Messages typed in on one telex machine were simultaneously printed out by the other. The English company received an offer of goods from the Dutch company via telex, and made a counter-offer, which the Dutch company accepted by telex. The English company applied for leave to service notice of a writ on the American principal in New York; service out of the jurisdiction is allowed under RSC Ord 11, r 1 if the contract to be enforced was made within the jurisdiction.

Denning LJ
. . . The question for our determination is: Where was the contract made?

When a contract is made by post it is clear law throughout the common law countries that the acceptance is complete as soon as the letter of acceptance is put into the post box, and that is the place where the contract is made. But there is no clear rule about contracts made by telephone or by Telex. Communications by these means are virtually instantaneous and stand on a different footing.

The problem can only be solved by going in stages. Let me first consider a case where two people make a contract by word of mouth in the presence of one another. Suppose, for instance, that I shout an offer to a man across a river or a courtyard but I do not hear his reply because it is drowned by an aircraft flying overhead. There is no contract at that moment. If he wishes to make a contract, he must wait till the aircraft is gone and then shout back his acceptance so that I can hear what he says. Not until I have his answer am I bound. I do not agree with the observations of Hill J in *Newcomb v De* Roos (2E & E at p 275).

Now take a case where two people make a contract by telephone. Suppose, for instance, that I make an offer to a man by telephone and, in the middle of his reply, the line goes 'dead' so that I do not hear his words of acceptance. There is no contract at that moment. The other man may not know the precise moment when the line failed. But he will know that the telephone conversation was abruptly broken off, because people usually say something to signify the end of the conversation. If he wishes to make a contract, he must therefore get through again so as to make sure that I heard. Suppose next that the line does not go dead, but it is nevertheless so indistinct that I do not catch what he says and I ask him to repeat it. He then repeats it and I hear his acceptance. The contract is made, not on the first time when I do not hear, but only the second time when I do hear. If he does not repeat it, there is no contract. The contract is only complete when I have his answer accepting the offer.

Lastly take the Telex. Suppose a clerk in a London office taps out on the teleprinter an offer which is immediately recorded on a teleprinter in a Manchester office, and a clerk at that end taps out an acceptance. If the line goes dead in the middle of the sentence of acceptance, the teleprinter motor will stop. There is then obviously no contract. The clerk at Manchester must get through again and send his complete sentence. But it may happen that the line does not go dead, yet the message does not get through to London. Thus the clerk at Manchester may tap out his message of acceptance and it will not be recorded in London because the ink at the London end fails or something of that kind. In that case the Manchester clerk will not know of the failure but the London clerk will know of it and will immediately send back a message 'not receiving'. Then, when the fault is rectified, the Manchester clerk will repeat his message. Only then is there a contract. If he does not repeat it, there is no contract. It is not until his message is received that the contract is complete.

In all the instances I have taken so far, the man who sends the message of acceptance knows that it has not been received or he has reason to know it. So he must repeat it. But suppose that he does not know that his message did not get home. He thinks it has. This may happen if the listener on the telephone does not catch the words of acceptance, but nevertheless does not trouble to ask for them to be repeated: or if the ink on the teleprinter fails at the receiving end, but the clerk does not ask for the message to be repeated: so that the man who sends an acceptance reasonably believes that his message has been received. The offeror in such circumstances is clearly bound, because he will be estopped from saying that he did not receive the message of acceptance. It is his own fault that he did not get it. But if there should be a case where the offeror without any fault on his part does not receive the message of acceptance—yet the sender of it reasonably believes it has got home when it has not—then I think there is no contract.

My conclusion is that the rule about instantaneous communications between the parties is different from the rule about the post. The contract is only complete when the acceptance is received by the offeror: and the contract is made at the place where the acceptance is received.

Applying the principles which I have stated, I think that the contract in this case was made in London where the acceptance was received. It was therefore a proper case for service out of the jurisdiction.

Birkett and **Parker LJJ** gave judgments to the same effect.

Appeal dismissed.

NOTES

1. In *The Brimnes* [1975] QB 929, a charterparty gave the shipowner the right to withdraw the vessel if the hire was not paid punctually. The trial judge held that a notice of withdrawal that had been sent during office hours was 'received' then although it was apparently not seen by the charterers' staff until the following morning. The Court of Appeal agreed with his conclusion.

2.   *Entores Ltd v Miles Far East Corpn* was approved and applied by the House of Lords in *Brinkibon Ltd v Stahag Stahl* [1983] 2 AC 34, although Lord Wilberforce remarked:

> Since 1955 the use of telex communications has been greatly expanded, and there are many variants on it. The senders and recipients may not be the principals to the contemplated contract. They may be servants or agents with limited authority. The message may not reach, or be intended to reach, the designated recipient immediately: messages may be sent out of office hours, or at night, with the intention, or on the assumption, that they will be read at a later time. There may be some error or fault at the recipient's end which prevents receipt at the time contemplated and believed in by the sender. The message may have been sent and/or received through machines operated by third persons. And many other variations may occur. No universal rule can cover all such cases: they must be resolved by reference to the intentions of the parties, by sound business practice and in some cases by a judgment where the risks should lie.

3.   What rule should apply to acceptance sent by fax?

4.   Many contracts are now made by email. What rules should be applied in this case?

■ *Manchester Diocesan Council for Education v Commercial and General Investments Ltd*
[1969] 3 All ER 1593

Late in 1963, the plaintiff decided to sell property by tender. Particulars and conditions of sale were prepared and these incorporated a form of tender. The conditions required, inter alia, that tenders be sent to the plaintiff's surveyor by 27 August 1964 and stipulated that the sale was subject to the approval of the purchase price by the Secretary of State. Clause 4 provided: 'The person whose tender is accepted shall be the purchaser and shall be informed of the acceptance of his tender by letter sent to him by post addressed to the address given in the tender...' On 25 August 1964, the defendant company completed the form of tender and stated thereon: 'and we agree that in the event of this offer being accepted in accordance with the above conditions... we will pay the said purchase price and carry out and complete the purchase in accordance with the said conditions...' This was sent on the following day to the plaintiff's surveyor. On 1 September, the plaintiff's surveyor informed the defendant company's surveyor that he would recommend acceptance of the defendant company's offer and that he would write again as soon as he had formal instructions. On 14 September, the defendant company's surveyor replied to the effect that he looked forward to receiving formal acceptance of the offer and he named the solicitors acting for the defendant company. This letter was acknowledged by the plaintiff's solicitor on 15 September, when he also stated that the 'sale has now been approved' by the plaintiff and that instructions had been given to obtain the approval of the Secretary of State. The approval of the Secretary of State (in relation to that part of the property in respect of which approval was necessary) was obtained on 18 November. On 23 December, the plaintiff's solicitors wrote to the defendant company's solicitors and, after reciting that the offer by tender had been accepted by the plaintiff subject to the consent of the Secretary of State, added that the consent had been forthcoming and they concluded therefore that the contract was binding on both parties. The defendant company's solicitors replied that they did not agree that there was any subsisting binding contract. On 7 January 1965, the plaintiff's solicitors wrote to the defendant company at the address given by it in the form of tender giving formal notification of acceptance of its offer.

Buckley J

... The offer contained in the tender was to the effect that in the event of its being accepted in accordance with the conditions of sale on or before the day named therein for that purpose (and none was so named) the defendant company would pay the price and complete the purchase. An offerer may by the terms of his offer indicate that it may be accepted in a particular manner. In the present case the conditions included condition 4 which I have read. It is said on the defendant company's behalf that that condition was not complied with until 7th January 1965; that until that date the offer was never accepted in accordance with its terms; and that consequently nothing earlier than that date can be relied on as an acceptance resulting in a binding contract. If an offeror stipulates by the terms of his offer that it may, or that it shall, be accepted in a particular manner a contract results as soon as the offeree does the stipulated act, whether it has come to the notice of the offeror or not. In such a case the offeror conditionally waives either expressly or by implication the normal requirement that acceptance must be communicated to the offeror to conclude a contract. There can be no doubt that in the present case, if the plaintiff or its authorised agent had posted a letter addressed to the defendant company at no. 15, Berkeley Street, on or about 15th September informing the defendant company of the acceptance of its tender, the contract would have been complete at the moment when such letter was posted, but that course was not taken. Condition 4, however, does not say that that shall be the sole permitted method of communicating an acceptance. It may be that an offeror, who by the terms of his offer insists on acceptance in a particular manner, is entitled to insist that he is not bound unless acceptance is effected or communicated in that precise way, although it seems probable that, even so, if the other party communicates his acceptance in some other way, the offeror may by conduct or otherwise waive his right to insist on the prescribed method of acceptance. Where, however, the offeror has prescribed a particular method of acceptance, but not in terms insisting that only acceptance in that mode shall be binding, I am of opinion that acceptance communicated to the offeror by any other mode which is no less advantageous to him will conclude the contract. ... If an offeror intends that he shall be bound only if his offer is accepted in some particular manner, it must be for him to make this clear. Condition 4 in the present case had not, in my judgment, this effect.

Moreover, the inclusion of condition 4 in the defendant company's offer was at the instance of the plaintiff, who framed the conditions and the form of tender. It should not, I think, be regarded as a condition or stipulation imposed by the defendant company as offeror on the plaintiff as offeree, but as a term introduced into the bargain by the plaintiff and presumably considered by the plaintiff as being in some way for the protection or benefit of the plaintiff. It would consequently be a term strict compliance with which the plaintiff could waive, provided the defendant company was not adversely affected. The plaintiff did not take advantage of the condition which would have resulted in a contract being formed as soon as a letter of acceptance complying with the condition was posted, but adopted another course, which could only result in a contract when the plaintiff's acceptance was actually communicated to the defendant company.

For these reasons, I have reached the conclusion that in accordance with the terms of the tender it was open to the plaintiff to conclude a contract by acceptance actually communicated to the defendant company in any way; and, in my judgment, the letter of 15th September constituted such an acceptance. It follows that, in my judgment ... the parties thereupon became contractually bound ....

If I am right in thinking that there was a contract on 15th September 1964 that disposes of the case but, in case I should be held to be wrong in that view, I will now consider the other point in the case and will for this purpose assume that no contract was made at that date. On this basis no contract can have been concluded before 7th January 1965. The defendant company contend that, as the tender stipulated no time within which it must be accepted, it was an implied term of the offer that it must be accepted, if at all, within a reasonable time. It is said that acceptance on 7th January was not within a reasonable time.

It has long been recognised as being the law that, where an offer is made in terms which fix no time limit for acceptance, the offer must be accepted within a reasonable time to make a contract ... There seems, however, to be no reported case in which the reason for this is explained.

There appear to me to be two possible views on methods of approaching the problem. First, it may be said that by implication the offer is made on terms that, if it is not accepted within a reasonable time, it must be treated as withdrawn. Alternatively, it may be said that, if the offeree does not accept the offer within a reasonable time, he must be treated as having refused it. On either view the offer would cease to be a live one on the expiration of what in the circumstances of the particular case should be regarded as a reasonable time for acceptance. The first of these alternatives involves implying a term that if the offer is not accepted within a reasonable time, it shall be treated as withdrawn or lapsing at the end of that period if it has not then been accepted; the second is based on an inference to be drawn from the conduct of the offeree, that is, that having failed to accept the offer within a reasonable time he has manifested an intention to refuse it. If, in the first alternative, the time which the offeror is to be treated as having set for acceptance is to be such a time as is reasonable at the date of the offer, what is reasonable must depend on circumstances then existing and reasonably likely to arise during the continuance of the offer; but it would be not unlikely that the offeror and offeree would make different assessments of what would be reasonable even if, as might quite possibly not be the case, they based those judgments on identical known and anticipated circumstances. No doubt a court could resolve any dispute about this, but this approach clearly involves a certain degree of uncertainty about the precise terms of the offer. If on the other hand the time which the offeror is to be treated as having set for acceptance is to be such as turns out to be reasonable in the light of circumstances then existing and of circumstances arising thereafter during the continuance of the offer, whether foreseeable or not, an additional element of uncertainty is introduced. The second alternative on the other hand involves simply an objective assessment of facts and the determination of the question whether on the facts the offeree should in fairness to both parties be regarded as having refused the offer.

It does not seem to me that either party is in greater need of protection by the law in this respect than the other. Until his offer has been accepted it is open to the offeror at any time to withdraw it or to put a limit on the time for acceptance. On the other hand, the offeree can at any time refuse the offer or, unless he has been guilty of unreasonable delay, accept it. Neither party is at a disadvantage. Unless authority constrains me to do otherwise, I am strongly disposed to prefer the second alternative to the first.

[Buckley J examined the cases, finding them inconclusive.]

. . . I have dealt with this part of the case at some length because, if the first alternative were the correct view of the law and if what is reasonable had to be ascertained as at the time of the offer, the subsequent conduct of the parties would be irrelevant to the question how long the offer should be treated as remaining open. In my opinion, however, the subsequent conduct of the parties is relevant to the question, which I think is the right test, whether the offeree should be held to have refused the offer by his conduct.

In my judgment the letter of 15th September 1964 excludes the possibility of imputing to the plaintiff a refusal of the offer. If that letter does not itself constitute an effective acceptance, it clearly discloses an intention to accept from which there is nothing to suggest a departure before 7th January 1965. Accordingly, if no contract was formed earlier, I am of opinion that it was open to the plaintiff to accept it on 7th January and that the plaintiff's letter of that date was effectual to bind the defendant company contractually.

Order for specific performance.

■ *Dickinson v Dodds*

(1876) 2 Ch D 463, Court of Appeal

On Wednesday 10 June 1874, Dodds gave Dickinson a note which read, in part:

I hereby agree to sell to Mr George Dickinson the whole of the dwelling-houses, garden ground, stabling, and outbuildings thereto belonging, situate at *Croft*, belonging to me, for the sum of £800. As witness my hand this tenth day of June, 1874.

£800   (Signed)   John Dodds.
P.S.—This offer to be left over until Friday, 9 o'clock, am. J D (the twelfth), 12th June, 1874.
                                                        (Signed)   J Dodds.

[It was] alleged that Dodds understood and intended that the Plaintiff should have until Friday 9 am within which to determine whether he would or would not purchase, and that he should absolutely have until that time the refusal of the property at the price of £800, and that the Plaintiff in fact determined to accept the offer on the morning of Thursday, the 11th of June, but did not at once signify his acceptance to Dodds, believing that he had the power to accept it until 9 am on the Friday.

In the afternoon of the Thursday the Plaintiff was informed by a Mr Berry that Dodds had been offering or agreeing to sell the property to Thomas Allan, the other Defendant. Thereupon the Plaintiff, at about half-past seven in the evening, went to the house of Mrs Burgess, the mother-in-law of Dodds, where he was then staying, and left with her a formal acceptance in writing of the offer to sell the property. According to the evidence of Mrs Burgess this document never in fact reached Dodds, she having forgotten to give it to him.

On the following (Friday) morning, at about seven o'clock, Berry, who was acting as agent for Dickinson, found Dodds at the Darlington railway station, and handed to him a duplicate of the acceptance by Dickinson, and explained to Dodds its purport. He replied that it was too late, as he had sold the property. A few minutes later Dickinson himself found Dodds entering a railway carriage, and handed him another duplicate of the notice of acceptance, but Dodds declined to receive it, saying, 'You are too late. I have sold the property.'

It appeared that on the day before, Thursday, the 11th of June, Dodds had signed a formal contract for the sale of the property to the Defendant Allan for £800, and had received from him a deposit of £40. Dickinson brought a bill for specific performance.

James LJ

. . . 'This offer to be left over until Friday, 9 o'clock am, 12th June, 1874.' That shews it was only an offer. There was no consideration given for the undertaking or promise, to whatever extent it may be considered binding, to keep the property unsold until 9 o'clock on Friday morning; but apparently Dickinson was of opinion, and probably Dodds was of the same opinion, that he (Dodds) was bound by that promise, and could not in any way withdraw from it, or retract it, until 9 o'clock on Friday morning, and this probably explains a good deal of what afterwards took place. But it is clear settled law, on one of the clearest principles of law, that this promise, being a mere nudum pactum was not binding, and that at any moment before a complete acceptance by Dickinson of the offer, Dodds was as free as Dickinson himself. Well, that being the state of things, it is said that the only mode in which Dodds could assert that freedom was by actually and distinctly saying to Dickinson, 'Now I withdraw my offer'. It appears to me that there is neither principle nor authority for the proposition that there must be an express and actual withdrawal of the offer, or what is called a retraction. It must, to constitute a contract, appear that the two minds were at one, at the same moment of time, that is, that there was an offer continuing up to the time of the acceptance. If there was not such a continuing offer, then the acceptance comes to nothing. Of course it may well be that the one man is bound in some way or other to let the other man know that his mind with regard to the offer has been changed; but in this case, beyond all question, the Plaintiff knew that Dodds was no longer minded to sell the property to him as plainly and clearly as if Dodds had told him in so many words, 'I withdraw the offer'. This is evident from the Plaintiff's own statements in the bill . . .

Mellish LJ delivered a judgment to the same effect and **Baggallay JA** concurred.

Bill dismissed.

NOTE

Does the offeree have to believe every rumour he hears to the effect that the offer has been withdrawn? Is it enough that she hears that the offeror has *offered* the property to a third person, or must she have heard that it has been *sold*?

VIII. EXCHANGE OF CONTRACTS

In contracts for the sale of land, it is very common for the parties to negotiate over the price, and then to hand the matter over to their solicitors, leaving the agreement 'subject to contract'. Although it depends on the circumstances, this expression is nearly always taken to mean that the parties do not intend to be legally bound until formal contracts have been completed, signed and exchanged. Although contracts for the sale of land must be in writing (See p 139), this requirement can be satisfied by a quite informal writing. Delaying the point at which the contract is binding until formal contracts are exchanged is useful to buyers because it gives them time for pre-contract investigations, surveys of the property and mortgage negotiation; in times when house prices are rising, it gives sellers the chance to withdraw unless the price is increased (called 'gazumping'). This practice is widely disapproved of, but the Law Commission concluded in its report on 'Subject to Contract' (No 65, 1975) that any change in the law would cause more difficulties than it was worth. A purchaser who is particularly afraid of being gazumped can make a conditional contract or take an option. Parties who want additional protection against default by the other but who don't want to enter even a conditionally binding contract to buy and sell can use a device recommended by the Conveyancing Standing Committee *(Pre-Contract Deposits: A Practice Recommendation*, 1987). This involves each side depositing a small sum, say $\frac{1}{2}$ per cent of the purchase price, with a stakeholder; if either party backs out unjustifiably, his deposit will be forfeited and paid to the other party.

■ *Eccles v Bryant*

[1947] 2 All ER 865, Court of Appeal

The vendors had agreed to sell the purchaser a house by correspondence, which was expressly stated to be 'subject to contract'. The vendors' solicitors wrote to the purchaser's solicitors: 'Our clients have now signed their part of the contract herein and we are ready to exchange and shall be glad to hear from you.' A week later, the purchaser's solicitors wrote back: 'We accordingly enclose herewith the contract signed by our client and shall be glad to receive in exchange the part signed by your client.' The vendors changed their minds and did not send their part in exchange. A decree of specific performance was granted to the purchaser, and the vendors appealed.

Lord Greene MR

. . . It is clear that both firms of solicitors, when they were instructed to carry this matter through by their clients, intended to do so in the customary way which is familiar to every firm of solicitors in the country, namely, by preparing the engrossment of the draft contract when agreed in duplicate and exchanging the two parts when signed by their clients. Anyone, I think, would have understood from the language of the earlier correspondence and the words 'subject to contract' that the contract would be brought about by an exchange of the two parts signed by the parties. Vaisey J pointed out that what he called the ceremonial form of exchange, namely, the meeting of solicitors in the offices of one of them— usually the vendor's solicitor's office— and the passing of the two engrossments signed over the table may be taken to have fallen, and, indeed, no doubt it has, into disuse to a certain extent, particularly when the solicitors are in different parts of the country. He recognised that an exchange by post would in many cases take the place of the old more ceremonial exchange, but that an exchange was contemplated by both firms of solicitors appears to me to be clear. I am prepared to assume that their intention was that the exchange should take place by post. When an exchange takes place by post and a contract comes into existence through the act of exchange, the earliest date at which such a contract can come into existence would be the date when the later of the two documents to be put in the post is actually put in the post. Another view might be that the exchange takes place and the contract thereby comes into existence when, and not before, the parties or their solicitors receive from their opposite numbers their parts of the contract. It is not necessary here to choose between those two views. I mention them particularly because counsel for the purchaser tried to suggest an intermediate stage, that where the parties contemplate an exchange by post the contract is completed, not when an exchange takes place, but when one of the parties puts his part into the post. I am afraid I cannot accept that. It seems to me to be a contradiction in terms to speak of that as an exchange . . .

It is said that a contract took place when, in response to an alleged invitation on behalf of the vendors, the purchaser signed his part of the contract and communicated the fact to the vendors. It was argued that there is no necessity in this class of case for an exchange of documents, and that the references which have been made in many judgments in this court and other courts to an exchange are either inaccurate or wrong. The answer to that seems to me to be simple. When parties are proposing to enter into a contract, the manner in which the contract is to be created so as to bind them must be gathered from the intentions of the parties, express or implied. In such a contract as this, there is a well-known common and customary method of dealing, namely, by exchange, and anyone who contemplates that method cannot contemplate the coming into existence of a binding contract before the exchange takes place. It was argued that exchange is a mere matter of machinery, having in itself no particular importance or significance. So far as significance is concerned, it appears to me that not only is it not right to say of exchange that it has no significance, but it is the crucial and vital fact which brings the contract into existence. As for importance, it is of the greatest importance, and that is why in past ages this procedure came to be adopted by everybody as the proper procedure. In dealing with contracts for the sale of land, it is of the greatest importance to the vendor that he should have a document signed by the purchaser and to the purchaser that he should have a document signed by the vendor. It is of the greatest importance that there should be no dispute whether a contract has or has not been made, and that there should be no dispute as to the terms of it. This procedure of exchange ensures that none of those difficulties will arise. Each party has got a document of title, because directly a contract is entered into and that contract is in writing relating to land, it is a document of title. That can be illustrated by the simple case where a purchaser makes a sub-sale. The contract is a vital document for the purpose of the sub-sale. If he had not got the vendor's part, signed by the vendors, to show to the sub-purchaser, the purchaser would not be able to make a good title.

Cohen and **Asquith LJJ** delivered judgments to the same effect.

Appeal allowed.

NOTE

In *Storer v Manchester City Council* (see p 198), the Court of Appeal held that there was a contract despite the fact that contracts had not been exchanged. The instructions given by the council to the town clerk to devise a simple procedure for selling the houses, coupled with the language of the clerk's letter ('If you will sign the Agreement and return it to me, I will send you the Agreement signed on behalf of the [council] in exchange') showed that the parties intended to be bound without an exchange of contracts.

If there is a 'chain' transaction—for example, Furmston selling his cottage to Beale, Beale selling his house to Bishop and Bishop selling his flat to Bentham—exchanging contracts will be too slow and uncertain. Neither Beale nor Bishop will normally be prepared to sell his old property until he has secured his new one, or vice versa. One individual in the chain can safeguard himself by getting possession of signed contracts from both people he is dealing with before accepting either contract by sending off his own parts; because Beale and Bishop have to deal with each other, they cannot both do this: one will have to commit himself in one direction not knowing whether he has a contract in the other. A way of reducing the risks to a minimum is for their solicitors to agree to 'exchange by telephone'. The solicitors on each side get their clients to sign their parts of the contracts but hold on to them. When all of the solicitors for everyone in the chain are ready to exchange on behalf of their clients, they agree by telephone (which will only take a matter of minutes) to hold the signed documents not for their own clients any longer but as agents for the solicitors representing the other party to each transaction. This means that each seller's part of the contract is now in the constructive possession of the buyer's solicitor and vice versa. In *Domb v Isoz* [1980] Ch 548, the Court of Appeal held that this was effective to make the contracts binding.

IX. TENDERS

If tenders are invited for the construction of a project or the purchase of property, what is the process of offer and acceptance?

■ *Spencer v Harding*
(1870) LR 5 CP 561, Common Pleas

Willes J

I am of opinion that the defendants are entitled to judgment. The action is brought against persons who issued a circular offering a stock for sale by tender, to be sold at a discount in one lot. The plaintiffs sent in a tender which turned out to be the highest, but which was not accepted. They now insist that the circular amounts to a contract or promise to sell the goods to the highest bidder, that is, in this case, to the person who should tender for them at the smallest rate of discount; and reliance is placed on the cases as to rewards offered for the discovery of an offender. In those cases, however, there never was any doubt that the advertisement amounted to a promise to pay the money to the person who first gave information. The difficulty suggested was that it was a contract with all the world. But that, of course, was soon overruled. It was an offer to become liable to any person who before the offer should be retracted should happen to be the person to fulfil the contract of which the advertisement was an offer or tender. That is not the sort of difficulty which presents itself here. If the circular had gone on, 'and we undertake to sell to the highest bidder', the reward cases would have applied, and there would have been a good contract in respect of the persons. But the question is, whether there is here any offer to enter into a contract at all, or whether the circular amounts to anything more than a mere proclamation that the defendants are ready to chaffer for the sale of the goods, and to receive offers for the purchase of them. In advertisements for tenders for buildings it is not usual to say that the contract will be given to the lowest bidder, and it is not always that the contract is made with the lowest bidder. Here there is a total absence of any words to intimate that the highest bidder is to be the purchaser. It is a mere attempt to ascertain whether an offer can be obtained within such a margin as the sellers are willing to adopt.

Keating and **Montague Smith JJ** concurred.

Judgment for the defendants.

■ Institution of Civil Engineers Form of Tender (7th edn)

To . . . .
. . . .
. . . .

GENTLEMEN,

Having examined the Drawings, Conditions of Contract, Specification and Bill of Quantities for the construction of the above-mentioned Works (and the matters set out in the Appendix hereto), we offer to construct and complete the whole of the said Works in conformity with the said Drawings, Conditions of Contract, Specification and Bill of Quantities for such sum as may be ascertained in accordance with the said Conditions of Contract.

We undertake to complete and deliver the whole of the Permanent Works comprised in the Contract within the time stated in the Appendix hereto.

If our tender is accepted we will, if required, provide security for the due performance of the Contract as stipulated in the Conditions of Contract and the Appendix hereto.

Unless and until a formal Agreement is prepared and executed this Tender, together with your written acceptance thereof, shall constitute a binding Contract between us.

We understand that you are not bound to accept the lowest or any tender you may receive.

We are, Gentlemen,

Yours faithfully,

Signature . . . .
Address . . . .
. . . .

Date . . . .

NOTE

Tenderers may be required to give a 'bid bond' or guarantee that they will not withdraw. In the Canadian case of *R v Ron Engineering & Construction (Eastern) Ltd* (1981) 119 DLR (3d) 267, the defendants submitted a tender to do building work. One of the clauses of the invitation to tender provided

Except as otherwise herein provided the tenderer guarantees that if his tender is withdrawn before the Commission shall have considered the tenders or before or after he has been notified that his tender has been recommended to the Commission for acceptance or that if the Commission does not for any reason receive within the period of seven days as stipulated and as required herein, the Agreement executed by the tenderer, the Performance Bond and the Payment Bond executed by the tenderer and the surety company and the other documents required herein, the Commission may retain the tender deposit for the use of the Commission and may accept any tender, advertise for new tenders, negotiate a contract or not accept any tender as the Commission may deem advisable.

A representative of the defendants attended the tender evaluation meeting, at which it was revealed that the defendant's tender was some $600,000 less than the next highest tender. The defendant wrote to the plaintiff saying that it now realized that it had made a mistake and that its tender should be some $700, 000 higher, offering to provide substantiation of this claim. The plaintiffs sent the defendants a contract document for the building work at the price in the defendant's tender, which the defendants did not sign in return. The Supreme Court of Canada adopted a two-contract analysis and held that the invitation to tender plus the sub-mission of the tender by the defendants created a contract, which made the stipulation in the invitation to tender binding. There was nothing in the allegations of mistake that would affect the validity of this first contract. (See also *MJB Enterprises Ltd v Defence Construction (1951) Ltd* (1999) 170 DLR (4th) 577, noted in (1999) 115 LQR 583.)

In *Harvela Investments Ltd v Royal Trust* Co *of Canada (CI) Ltd* [1984] 2 All ER 65, trustees of a settlement invited two parties to submit sealed offers or confidential telexes for a parcel of shares that formed part of the settlement property, and they stated in the invitation that 'we bind ourselves to accept the [highest] offer'. Peter Gibson J held that this constituted an offer, which was accepted by the highest genuine bid, the consideration for the promise to accept the highest bid being the act of bidding. He also held that one of the bids was invalid because it was a referential bid ('C$2, 100, 000 or C$101, 000 in excess of any other offer'): he held that it was an implied term of the offer that such bids were excluded. Thus the trustees were bound to accept the other bid, which was for C$2, 175, 000. The Court of Appeal reversed this part of the decision, holding that there was nothing to exclude referential bids, so that there was a contract with the referential bidder [1985] 1 All ER 261; the House of Lords restored the first instance judgment [1985] 2 All ER 966.

■ *Blackpool and Fylde Aero Club Ltd v Blackpool Borough Council*
[1990] 3 All ER 25, Court of Appeal

The council owned and managed an airport, and raised revenue by granting a concession to an air operator to operate pleasure flights from the airport. The plaintiff club was granted the concession in 1975, 1978 and 1980. Shortly before the last concession was due to expire in 1983, the council sent invitations to tender to the club and six other parties, all of whom were connected with the airport. The invitations to tender stated that tenders were to be submitted in the envelope provided and were not to bear any name or mark that would identify the sender, and that tenders received after the date and time specified, namely 12 noon on 17 March 1983, would not be considered. Only the club and two other tenderers responded to the council's invitation. The club's tender was put in the town hall letterbox at 11 am on 17 March, but the letterbox was not cleared by council staff at noon that day as it was supposed to be. The club's tender was recorded as being received late and was not considered. The club brought an action against the council claiming damages for breach of contract, contending that the council had warranted that if a tender was received by the deadline it would be considered and that the council had acted in breach of that warranty. The judge held that the council was liable in damages to the club for breach of contract and negligence. The council appealed.

Bingham LJ

... The judge resolved the contractual issue in favour of the club, holding that an express request for a tender might in appropriate circumstances give rise to an implied obligation to perform the service of considering that tender. Here, the council's stipulation that tenders received after the deadline would not be admitted for consideration gave rise to a contractual obligation (on acceptance by submission of a timely tender) that such tenders would be admitted for consideration.

In attacking the judge's conclusion on this issue, four main submissions were made on behalf of the council. Firstly, it was submitted that an invitation to tender in this form was well established to be no more than a proclamation of willingness to receive offers. Even without the first sentence of the council's invitation to tender in this case, the council would not have been bound to accept the highest or any tender. An invitation to tender in this form was an invitation to treat, and no contract of any kind would come into existence unless or until, if ever, the council chose to accept any tender or other offer. For these propositions reliance was placed on *Spencer v Harding* and *Harris v Nickerson*.

Secondly, counsel submitted that on a reasonable reading of this invitation to tender the council could not be understood to be undertaking to consider all timely tenders submitted. The statement that late tenders would not be considered did not mean that timely tenders would. If the council had meant that it could have said it. There was, although counsel did not put it in these words, no maxim exclusio unius, expressio alterius.

Thirdly, the court should be no less rigorous when asked to imply a contract than when asked to imply a term in an existing contract or to find a collateral contract. A term would not be implied simply because it was reasonable to do so: *Liverpool City Council v Irwin*. In order to establish collateral contracts, 'Not only the terms of such contracts but the existence of an animus contrahendi on the part of all the parties to them must be clearly shewn': see *Heilbut Symons & Co v Buckleton* [1913] AC 30 at 47. No lower standard was applicable here and the standard was not satisfied.

Fourthly, counsel submitted that the warranty contended for by the club was simply a proposition 'tailor-made to produce the desired result' (to quote Lord Templeman in *CBS Songs Ltd v Amstrad Consumer Electronics plc* [1988] 2 All ER 484 at 497) on the facts of this particular case. There was a vital distinction between expectations, however reasonable, and contractual obligations: see *Lavarack v Woods of Colchester Ltd* [1966] 3 All ER 683 at 690 per Diplock LJ. The club here expected its tender to be considered. The council fully intended that it should be. It was in both parties' interests that the club's tender should be considered. There was thus no need for them to contract. The court should not subvert well-understood contractual principles by adopting a woolly pragmatic solution designed to remedy a perceived injustice on the unique facts of this particular case.

In defending the judge's decision counsel for the club accepted that an invitation to tender was normally no more than an offer to receive tenders. But it could, he submitted, in certain circumstances give rise to binding contractual obligations on the part of the invitor, either from the express words of the tender or from the circumstances surrounding the sending out of the invitation to tender or (as here) from both. The circumstances relied on here were that the council approached the club and the other invitees, all of them connected with the airport, that the club had held the concession for eight years, having successfully tendered on three previous occasions, that the council as a local authority was obliged to comply with its standing orders and owed a fiduciary duty to ratepayers to act with reasonable prudence in managing its financial affairs and that there was a clear intention on the part of both parties that all timely tenders would be considered. If in these circumstances one asked of this invitation to tender the question posed by Bowen LJ in *Carlill v Carbolic Smoke Ball Co*. 'How would an ordinary person reading this document construe it?', the answer in the submission of counsel for the club was clear: the council might or might not accept any particular tender; it might accept no tender; it might decide not to award the concession at all; it would not consider any tender received after the advertised deadline; but if it did consider any tender received before the deadline and conforming with the advertised conditions it would consider all such tenders.

I found great force in the submissions made on behalf of the council and agree with much of what was said. Indeed, for much of the hearing I was of opinion that the judge's decision, although fully in accord with the merits as I see them, could not be sustained in principle. But I am in the end persuaded that the argument proves too much. During the hearing the following questions were raised: what if, in a situation such as the present, the council had opened and thereupon accepted the first tender received, even though the deadline had not expired and other invitees had not yet responded? or if the council had considered and accepted a tender admittedly received well after the deadline? Counsel answered that although by so acting the council might breach its own standing orders, and might fairly be accused of discreditable conduct, it would not be in breach of any legal obligation because at that stage there would be none to breach. This is a conclusion I cannot accept, and if it were accepted there would in my view be an unacceptable discrepancy between the law of contract and the confident assumptions of commercial parties, both tenderers (as reflected in the evidence of Mr Bateson) and invitors (as reflected in the immediate reaction of the council when the mishap came to light).

A tendering procedure of this kind is, in many respects, heavily weighted in favour of the invitor. He can invite tenders from as many or as few parties as he chooses. He need not tell any of them who else, or how many others, he has invited. The invitee may often, although not here, be put to considerable labour and expense in preparing a tender, ordinarily without recompense if he is unsuccessful. The invitation to tender may itself, in a complex case, although again not here, involve time and expense to prepare, but the invitor does not commit himself to proceed with the project, whatever it is; he need not accept the highest tender; he need not accept any tender; he need not give reasons to justify his acceptance or rejection of any tender received. The risk to which the tenderer is exposed does not end with the risk that his tender may not be the highest (or, as the case may be, lowest). But where, as here, tenders are solicited from selected parties all of them known to the invitor, and where a local authority's invitation prescribes a clear, orderly and familiar procedure (draft contract conditions available for inspection and plainly not open to negotiation, a prescribed common form of tender, the supply of envelopes designed to preserve the absolute anonymity of tenderers and clearly to identify the tender in question and an absolute deadline) the invitee is in my judgment protected at least to this extent: if he submits a conforming tender before the deadline he is entitled, not as a matter of mere expectation but of contractual right, to be sure that his tender will after the deadline be opened and considered in conjunction with all other conforming tenders or at least that his tender will be considered if others are. Had the club, before tendering, inquired of the council whether it could rely on any timely and conforming tender being considered along with others, I feel quite sure that the answer would have been 'of course'. The law would, I think, be defective if it did not give effect to that.

It is of course true that the invitation to tender does not explicitly state that the council will consider timely and conforming tenders. That is why one is concerned with implication. But the council does not either say that it does not bind itself to do so, and in the context a reasonable invitee would understand the invitation to be saying, quite clearly, that if he submitted a timely and conforming tender it would be considered, at least if any other such tender were considered.

I readily accept that contracts are not to be lightly implied. Having examined what the parties said and did, the court must be able to conclude with confidence both that the parties intended to create contractual relations and that the agreement was to the effect contended for. It must also, in most cases, be able to answer the question posed by Mustill LJ in *Hispanica de Petroleos SA v Vencedora Oceanica Navegacion SA, The Kapetan Markos NL (No 2)* [1987] 2 Lloyd's Rep 321 at 331: 'What was the mechanism for offer and acceptance?' In all the circumstances of this case (and I say nothing about any other) I have no doubt that the parties did intend to create contractual relations to the limited extent contended for. Since it has never been the law that a person is only entitled to enforce his contractual rights in a reasonable way *(White & Carter (Councils) Ltd v McGregor* [below, p 636] per Lord Reid), counsel for the club was in my view right to contend for no more than a contractual duty to consider. I think it plain that the council's invitation to tender was, to this limited extent, an offer, and the club's submission of a timely and conforming tender an acceptance.

Counsel's fourth submission on behalf of the council is a salutary warning, but it is not a free-standing argument: if, as I hold, his first three submissions are to be rejected, no subversion of principle is involved. I am, however, pleased that what seems to me the right legal answer also accords with the merits as I see them. . . .

Stocker LJ gave judgment to the same effect and **Farguharson LJ** agreed.

Appeal dismissed.

NOTES

1. Might an organisation that invites tenders be under further obligations to those firms that submit proper tenders: for example, must the tenders be evaluated carefully or at least in good faith? Evaluating tenders can be extremely complex. For example, in a large construction contract, the contractor will be entitled to be paid a certain proportion of the value of the work, as priced in the 'bills of quantities' submitted with the tender, as the work progresses. It is not uncommon for a contractor to price certain items, which will be done in the early stages of the work, at more than their cost and later items at less, so that, while the price is the same, the contractor receives some of the money earlier (this is called 'front-end loading'). Thus a tender with a lower total but which has a considerable front-end loading may turn out to be more expensive to the employer, which may have to borrow the money to pay, than one with a slightly higher total but no loading. Suppose a tenderer discovers that its bid has been rejected simply because the employer was told by its employee that it was front-end loaded when this was not in fact true, the employee having confused it with another bid? Or suppose a tender is turned down for no reason other than that it comes from a foreign firm? In *Hughes Aircraft Systems International v Airservices Australia* (1997) 146 ALR1, there were in effect two bidders for the Australian advanced air traffic system acquisition contract: the plaintiffs, a Californian corporation, and Thomson Radar Australia Corporation Ltd (Thomson), the Australian subsidiary of a well-known French company. In due course, the defendants awarded the contract to Thomson. In the invitation to tender, the defendant's predecessor, the Civil Aviation Authority (CAA) stated that the parties' best and final offers would be evaluated in accordance with specified major and minor criteria, and prescribed priority rankings for the major criteria. Finn J held that CAA was under a contractual obligation scrupulously to apply the criteria as stated. He considered that a duty of good faith and fair dealing is implied by law in all contracts (at 36–37; declining to follow the contrary views expressed by Gummow J in *Service Station Association Ltd v Berg Bennett & Associates Pty Ltd* (1993) 111 ALR 393, 406). On the possible role of good faith in contract formation, see further p 283.

2. The letting of many forms of public contract is now governed by Regulations implementing EU Directives, which are aimed at strengthening the European Union by encouraging competition and preventing discrimination against firms from other member States. This is to be achieved by increasing the transparency of tendering and award procedures, and giving aggrieved tenderers a remedy if the proper procedures are not used. The contracts concerned include contracts for: public services, supply and works; public procurement in water, energy, transport and communications services; public procurement of construction products. The Public Contracts Regulations (SI 2006/5), which implement EC Directive 2004/18 (replacing earlier Directives), are typical. Contracting authorities must normally use either the *open* procedure, under which any interested person may tender, or the *restricted* procedure, under which only those who have been preselected by the authority may tender. There are rules on what information the authority must consider and may rely on in selecting contractors to tender. The intention to seek offers must be published in the Official Journal of the EU and advertisements may not be published in the national press before a notice has been sent to the OJ—nor may national advertisements contain additional information. Technical specifications and specifications of materials must, except in certain circumstances, be defined by reference to European specifications. The authority is required to award the

contract on the basis either of the lowest or of the 'most economically advantageous' offer. Failure to comply with the Regulations is actionable by an aggrieved tenderer. Only in limited circumstances may a *competitive dialogue* procedure be used to let a contract. In *Harmon CFEM Facades (UK) Ltd v Corporate Officer of the House of Commons* (1999) 67 Con LR 1, the plaintiff, a subsidiary of an American company, was the unsuccessful tenderer for the fenestration contract for the new parliamentary building in Bridge Street, Westminster. The trial judge held that the plaintiff was, in fact, the lowest bidder, but that the bids had been manipulated so as to prefer another bidder, which was a consortium that included a British partner. The judge held that this contravened both the European procurement rules and the common law of contract.

His Honour Judge Humphrey Lloyd QC held:

I consider that it is now clear in English law that in the public sector where competitive tenders are sought and responded to, a contract comes into existence whereby the prospective employer impliedly agrees to consider all tenderers fairly (see the *Blackpool* and *Fairclough* cases).

In later proceedings, the judge made an interim award in favour of the plaintiff of about £1.8m. In effect, this was on the basis that the plaintiff would recover at trial the costs of tendering and a substantial part of the profit it would have made on the contract. Later newspaper reports said the case had been settled for a figure in excess of £5m.

3.   In *Pratt Contractors Ltd v Transit New Zealand* [2004] BLR 143, the defendant was a New Zealand state entity with responsibility for the maintenance and security of state highways. It was required by statute to employ competitive pricing procedures (CFP). CFP provided for two methods: one based solely on lowest price, and the other, the weighted attribute method, in which marks were given not only for price but also for relevant experience, track record, technical skills, resources, management skills and methodology.

The defendant invited tenders for a particular project on the weighted attribute method and the claimant was one of those invited to tender. Its price was the lowest but it was marked down on other factors. In particular, the consultants employed by the defendants regarded the claimants as 'lowballers', that is, as contractors who sought to obtain contracts by quoting low prices and pursuing aggressive claims policies.

In an action brought by the claimants it was accepted that the tendering process was the subject of a preliminary contact that it would be conducted in good faith, but the Privy Council thought that there had been no breach of this contract.

Lord Hoffmann said:

The duty to act fairly meant that all the tenderers had to be treated equally . . . but Transit were not obliged to give tenderers the same mark if it honestly thought their attributes were different.

4.   In the light of these developments, you may like to look again at the extract from Collins, p 66.

On the effect of breaches of other procedural requirements imposed on authorities making contracts, see Arrowsmith, 'The Impact of Public Law on the Private Law of Contract', in Halson (ed), *Exploring the Boundaries of Contract*, 1996, pp 3, 11–17.

A general contractor, wishing to put in a tender for a large project, himself invites tenders from subcontractors for parts of the work. He uses a low bid put in by a subcontractor in calculating his own tender price, and he is awarded the main contract. What if before he has had time to notify the subcontractor, the latter withdraws his bid, perhaps even though he had agreed to keep it open (see *Dickinson v Dodds*, p 238)? In the USA, Learned Hand J held there was no remedy: *James Baird Co v Gimbel Bros, Inc* 64 F 2d 344 (2d Cir, 1933). However, in *Drennan v Star Paving Co* 51 Cal 2d 409, 333 P 2d 757 (1958), the plaintiff general contractor put in a bid for the 'Monte Vista School Job' calculated on the basis of a bid by the defendant subcontractor to do the paving work for $7,132, and naming the defendant as the subcontractor. The plaintiff was awarded the contract, but when he called at the defendant's office, he was immediately told that a mistake had been made and the defendant could not do the work at that price. Ultimately, the plaintiff employed another subcontractor who charged $10,949. The Supreme Court of California affirmed a judgment for the plaintiff.

Traynor J said:

There is no evidence that defendant offered to make its bid irrevocable in exchange for plaintiff's use of its figures in computing his bid. Nor is there evidence that would warrant interpreting plaintiff's use of defendant's bid as the acceptance thereof, binding plaintiff, on condition he received the main contract, to award the subcontract to defendant. In sum, there was neither an option supported by consideration nor a bilateral contract binding on both parties.

Plaintiff contends, however, that he relied to his detriment on defendant's offer and that defendant must therefore answer in damages for its refusal to perform. Thus the question is squarely presented: Did plaintiff's reliance make defendant's offer irrevocable?

. . . Section 90 of the Restatement . . . applies in this state . . . .

Had defendant's bid expressly stated or clearly implied that it was revocable at any time before acceptance we would treat it accordingly. It was silent on revocation, however, and we must therefore determine whether there are conditions to the right of revocation imposed by law or reasonably inferable in fact. In the analogous problem of an offer for a unilateral contract, the theory is now obsolete that the offer is revocable at any time before complete performance. Thus section 45 of the Restatement of Contracts provides: "If an offer for an unilateral contract is made, and part of the consideration requested in the offer is given or tendered by the offeree in response thereto, the offeror is bound by a contract, the duty of immediate performance of which is conditional on the full consideration being given or tendered within the time stated in the offer, or, if no time stated therein, within a reasonable time." In explanation, comment b states that the "main offer includes as a subsidiary promise, necessarily implied, that if part of the requested performance is given, the offeror will not revoke his offer, and that if tender is made it will be accepted. Part performance or tender may thus furnish consideration for the subsidiary promise. Moreover, merely acting in justifiable reliance on an offer may in some cases serve as sufficient reason for making a promise binding (see s 90)."

Whether implied in fact or law, the subsidiary promise serves to preclude the injustice that would result if the offer could be revoked after the offeree had acted in detrimental reliance thereon. Reasonable reliance resulting in a foreseeable prejudical change in position affords a compelling basis also for implying a subsidiary promise not to revoke an offer for a bilateral contract . . .

When plaintiff used defendant's offer in computing his own bid, he bound himself to perform in reliance on defendant's terms. Though defendant did not bargain for this use of its bid neither did defendant make it idly, indifferent to whether it would be used or not . . .

It bears noting that a general contractor is not free to delay acceptance after he has been awarded the general contract in the hope of getting a better price. Nor can he reopen bargaining with the subcontractor and at the same time claim a continuing right to accept the original offer.

■ Law Commission Working Paper No 60, 'Firm Offers' (1975)
Provisional recommendations

55. We have formulated five provisional recommendations on which comments are invited. They will of course only apply to firm offers that are not made under seal and for which no consideration has

been given by the offeree:

(a) An offeror who has promised that he will not revoke his offer for a definite time should be bound by the terms of that promise for a period not exceeding six years, *provided that* the promise has been made 'in the course of a business' as that expression is explained in paragraph 31 above (paras 30–34). (b)Such a promise need not be evidenced in writing (paras 35–38).

(b) It should be capable of applying to land or interests in land (paras 39–40).

(c) A firm offer to which (a) applies should be capable of acceptance by the offeree during the time that the offeror is bound by his promise, notwithstanding his purported revocation of it (paras 41–47).

(d) An offeror who breaks a promise by which he is bound under (a) should be liable in damages to the offeree (paras 48–50).

56. We should, in addition, welcome information on business practices in relation to firm offers and comments on the relevance to those practices of our provisional recommendations.

■ Lewis, 'Contracts between Businessmen: Reform of the Law of Firm Offers' (1982)

9 Brit J Law & Society 153, at 153, 158–160, 162–165, 166, 168–171

This article examines the role of a particular area of the law of contract in a specific commercial context involving the relationship of a general building contractor and a sub-contractor. The focus is upon the formation of agreement through the submission of bids to carry out work put out to tender. An empirical examination of the attitudes of these builders to the tendering procedure has been carried out and is related to a Law Commission proposal to change the law on 'firm offers'. To what extent do those in business rely on legal sanction as a method of guaranteeing the expectations to which a promise may give rise? The aim of the article is to provide a case study for Weber's discussion of the extent the law of contract is required to support the development of commercial relations in a market economy. The article forms a part of but a limited literature empirically examining the use and non-use of law by the business community. It also reflects upon the legitimising force of the general principles of classical contract law and considers the difficulties of those, such as the Law Commission, who continue to refine these principles when faced with the specific circumstances of a particular relationship....

As Macaulay puts it:

'A rough sketch of the classical model of the contract process in western capitalist societies would stress its formal and normative aspects. Formally, it assumes that the rules of contract law will be invoked by the parties and applied by the courts; normatively, it holds that they ought to be.'

...Classical theory has continued to dominate the analysis of the exchange relationship despite studies exposing the non-use of its general principles and their attendant sanctions in certain areas....

The classical model is thus the orthodox picture of contract which has influenced, among others, those whose direct task it is to reform the law...

The...example [of a subcontract bid being revoked] given by the Law Commission carries with it several implications concerning the importance and effectiveness of the general principles of contract and of business attitudes towards legal remedies. In investigating the reform proposals questions such as the following could be asked: What is the overall relationship of the general to the sub-contractor and how do they both view the tendering procedure? Do general contractors find withdrawal by sub-contractors a problem and if so do they do anything about it? To what extent are the parties already influenced by the general principles of law embodied in offer and acceptance? Would general contractors resort to any legal solution to withdrawal rather than more informal and flexible techniques of control found in other business relationships? Are the views of contractors sufficiently cohesive and their practices sufficiently uniform to provide some basis for establishing a rule to affect all bids made? Is the unequal balance in the bidding procedure as illustrated by the Commission the whole story or does the sub-contractor have a tale to tell?

To answer these and other questions this article relies upon two particular sources. The first is the evidence submitted to the Law Commission in response to its appeal for the views of business men upon withdrawal. . . .

The second source of information was a survey by questionnaire of the views of a small number of contractors operating in the Cardiff area. . . .

Withdrawal by a sub and the action a general may take

How common is the problem of withdrawal by the sub after the general has used his bid? Most of the generals noted that at some time they had encountered the problem, and one small firm even remarked that withdrawal 'is the great difficulty with sub-contracting today'. The others, however, doubted whether the problem was very common, one of them commenting 'we have never (in 30 years) known a sub-contractor withdrawing his bid before an award' [of the main contract to the general. This does not exclude withdrawal after the award].

There are certain precautions that could be taken by generals in advance of submitting their own bids to ensure that a sub's bid is reliable. Firstly a general could create an option contract and threaten the use of legal sanction in order to bind the sub to his bid. This would necessitate the general obtaining the sub's agreement that in exchange for a nominal fee the sub's bid would be kept firm for a set period. In the survey this had been considered only by one general, being the exceptional firm which had stated that it had found withdrawal of bids a common practice. Even this small firm had only considered and not actually attempted to use option contracts. Its failure to do so may be related to the inconvenience of building into the tendering system an option procedure, especially when bids are received late. But the difficulties of employing such a technique are not insuperable, especially with regard to those subs from whom it is usual to expect tenders. The reason for the failure of generals to establish a legal sanction to prevent withdrawal of a bid before acceptance must lie elsewhere.

A second method of protection for the general is for him to demand from the sub a sum of money as a guarantee or 'bid bond'. In large international contracts it is common to find a requirement that the tenderer should submit together with his bid a deposit of around one per cent of the contract sum. 'The purpose inherent in this machinery is the protection of the employer against default by the contractor, whom it would be difficult to sue owing to his being outside the jurisdiction of the employer's country. The "bid bond" is forfeit if, upon being offered a contract on the basis of his tender, the tenderer refuses to enter upon the contract.' However the survey revealed that such precautions were not adopted by generals for those domestic contracts with subs which form the basis of the present investigation.

Although withdrawal was uncommon, what would be the attitude of a general towards a sub who did try to revoke his bid? Five of the nine generals believed that before the award of the main contract the sub was free to do as he liked: after all, within certain limits the general was also free to change his bid at this time. However, after the award six generals considered that a sub should be bound to his bid, and only three felt he was free to withdraw. A similar majority of subs agreed that they felt bound to their bid. Eight of the eleven said that after the award they were committed to performing the work at the price quoted. However, their commitment was not influenced by the legal position: they would keep to their bid either because they felt morally bound not to revoke, or because they feared loss of their business reputation. Only two subs considered themselves legally bound to perform, although one of these had gone so far as to ensure that liability would not arise by stating that his bid was only an estimate and did not form a legally binding undertaking to keep his price firm.

What action would a general take against a sub who withdrew his bid? As found in the previous studies in the USA no general mentioned threat of legal action, but nearly all considered that if they had a continuing relationship with a sub they could bring pressure to bear. Persuasion 'might well pay dividends if he is already doing work for you or hopes to in the future'. If the sub could not be persuaded to change his mind 'we would have serious reservations about inviting him to tender for future work', or ultimately, 'we would strike him off our list'. Other action 'would depend a lot upon the size of job, size of subcontractor relative to the size of job, and the difference between the price of the lowest sub's tender and the next lowest. If the financial implications were not much relatively, we would accept the second lowest tender. If they were serious we would approach the clients' Quantity Surveyors and try to reach an agreement with them on a revised tender'. . . .

The use made by generals of the bidding procedure

Withdrawal of a bid by a sub reveals only one side of the problem for the general similarly may be guilty of what some consider unethical or improper practice which in turn can injure the sub. In evidence to the Law Commission it was said of the Commission's example: 'No mention is made of the fact that just as the sub is not bound to the general, neither is the general bound to the sub.' The general can take advantage of the open nature of the tendering procedure and the fact that a contract with a sub is not formed until some time after the award of the main contract. As a result of this delay in the formation of contract the general has the opportunity after receiving a bid to disclose it to other subs and thus put pressure upon them to undercut the price quoted ('bid shopping'). Alternatively the initiative may be taken by the other subs themselves in inquiring of the general as to the lowest bid submitted. If the general provides the information he may be encouraging the subs to make a lower offer ('bid peddling'). Both practices reveal that a general in fact may not rely upon employing the sub whose bid he has used in computing his tender, and it is then more difficult for him to claim that in justice the sub should be bound to his bid whilst he remains free to do as he pleases. To what extent does the general fail to use the sub on whose bid he has relied or to what extent does he try to change that bid? Several questions in the survey were aimed at investigating this aspect of the problem.

After receiving a sub's tender all the generals agreed that sometimes the lack of detail in the bid led to further negotiations taking place and these could continue even after the general had been awarded the main contract. They dealt with such matters as 'work content, extent, areas, sequence of work, timing, phasing, agreement concerning the extent of assistance or services to be provided'. But there could also be discussion of the specifications for the job and of the quality of materials to be used, and in particular, the price to be paid could be re-negotiated. Six of the nine generals admitted that occasionally they had been involved in further negotiations about the price and that this happened both before and after they had been awarded the main contract. This may simply reflect that there were indeed matters which had been left vague in the subs' original bids, but it could also indicate that generals were shopping around for a lower price. The subs confirmed that such shopping was taking place, one of them stating that '[i]t is almost common practice for a larger number of general contractors to request further negotiations regarding the price prior to their placing an order. They are usually trying to obtain a reduction'.

Further evidence of the generals not always relying upon sub's bids came from their admission that even after using a bid they were quite willing to switch subs if necessary. . . .

Further possible 'abuse' of the bidding procedure was admitted by five of the generals. They agreed that sometimes they used a sub's tender to estimate what a part of their job should cost with an eye to doing that part of the work themselves. One of them remarked, 'Why not? The tendering subcontractor is fully aware that this is a general practice and can always decine to submit a quotation if he so desires.' Somewhat less forcefully another said that it was only an occasional practice employed 'if we are not sure if our own men will be free to do the work. We would only ask for a tender if there was some chance that the tenderer would get the work'. The subs, again with the one exception, condemned the practice for, as one said, we cannot afford to be a free estimating service.

The survey's final question to both generals and subs sought their reaction to [binding the general to the sub whose bid he had used] combined with . . . the proposal to make the sub's bid irrevocable for the time it stated it was to be firm. In the survey of generals the form of the question was as follows:

'Would you support a proposal that a contract between you and the sub is formed when you used a sub's tender in submitting your own bid? This contract would only come into operation if you were successful in being awarded the main contract. It would then bind you to employ the subcontractor, but equally, once you have used his tender he could not withdraw.'

The question produced a divided response from both subs and generals, with about half of each group rejecting the proposal and the rest, with varying degrees of enthusiasm, accepting it subject to serious qualifications. . . .

Summary

In a private construction contract withdrawal of a firm bid by a sub is less of a problem than the Law Commission's example implies. It cannot occur where there is direct nomination of a sub, nor where a sub's bid is not stated to be firm as in a third of the cases in the survey. Even where there are firm bids generals do not necessarily rely upon the figures supplied by the lowest tendering sub when computing their own bid. Instead of being troubled by an enforced change of sub resulting from withdrawal, generals are as likely to initiate such a change themselves by encouraging undercutting of original tenders.

The infrequency of the problem of withdrawal undoubtedly influences attitudes towards the introduction of legal sanctions to control it. But it may also be that the informal control methods that already exist make formal legal regulation unnecessary. At least it is important to observe that the potential which exists for making use of the legal system has not been exploited. Generals have either not devised standard tender forms or allow subs to ignore them. They do not use option contracts or bid bonds and they do not close a deal as soon as possible so as to create a contract and threaten legal sanction to prevent withdrawal. Resort to a court to determine rights and liabilities was not mentioned as a possible remedy. Instead the sanctions discussed were informal: re-negotiation and applying economic pressure; arbitration by a third party such as a quantity surveyor or architect; and, as an ultimate deterrent, the severing of trade relations between the respective firms. The same pattern emerged with regard to the sub's attitudes to generals 'misusing' the bidding procedure, although the subs were generally thought to be in a weaker economic position. The final question in the survey was biased in favour of relying upon formal remedies based upon legal rights and it carried with it a balance and appearance of justice which might be thought superficially to appeal to the contractors surveyed. Despite this its legal solutions were rejected either as impractical, easily avoided and difficult to enforce, or as unfair and too inflexible in not making allowance for the several excuses which contractors recognised as good reasons for non-performance. The informal remedies which already existed, whether cost cutting by subs or the use or economic 'muscle' by generals, emerged as more important methods of regulating the commercial relationship. . . .

Conclusion

. . . [I]t may be suggested, for example, that in bringing about reform it may be advisable at times to examine a specific commercial relationship *in toto*, for to change the legal position in relation to certain aspects of a transaction without considering the bargaining strength occasioned by the legal framework as a whole may produce unintended results. To focus upon the potential abuse of power by only one of the parties, as the Law Commission example does, can lead to a mistaken impression as to the nature and extent of reform required. By taking the broader view it is possible to conclude, as Schultz did, that either both general and sub should be bound or neither. However, the present study reveals how difficult it is to decide whether both parties should be bound.

. . . [T]he Law Commission might also wish to reflect upon the attitude of the parties towards legal remedies. The contractors' need of and desire for litigation must be contrasted with their use of other, more informal methods of regulating their relationship as summarised above.

Such a law reform perspective, however, is but incidental to a second level upon which this article may be read. It is intended as a case study of the extent to which commercial people rely on or are interested in legal sanction as a method of guaranteeing the expectations which arise from a promise made in the course of a business. . . .

In addition to the above study this article has suggested that the work of the Law Commission in relation to the general principles of the law of contract may be explained in part as being the product of a particular ideology. The refinement of the general principles of contract has been the concern of lawyers steeped in classical contract theory. The working paper on firm offers rests on an assumption of classical theory that formally available legal opportunities will be exploited in practice. This article together with earlier empirical studies has suggested that in the particular areas investigated such an assumption is not warranted.

NOTE

For an examination of the US courts' approach to offer and acceptance in the light of efficiency, see Craswell, 'Offer, Acceptance and Efficient Reliance' (1996) 48 Stanford LR 481.

At this point, it may be useful to return to a general theme mentioned in the introductory chapters: the ideologies underlying contract decisions.

■ Brownsword, Contract Law: Themes for the Twenty-First Century
(2nd edn, 2006)
pp 137–140, 145–146

The leading doctrines of the English law of contract, whether in legislation or case law, reflect two principal ideologies, 'market-individualism' and 'consumer-welfarism'. Putting the contrast very generally, whereas the former ideology insists upon contractors being held to their freely agreed exchanges, the latter seeks to ensure a fair deal for contractors (particularly consumer contractors) and, more generally, to relieve against harsh or unconscionable bargains. Where we are dealing specifically with the case law of contract, however, we must reckon with a second layer of ideological complexity. All adjudication, in all branches of law, is caught up in a tension between an ideology of 'formalism' (which dictates that the settled law should be applied, the precedents followed, and so on) and an ideology of 'realism' (which, at its most robust, demands that cases should be determined according to their merits, settled law notwithstanding). In practice, this double layering of ideological tensions generates three strands in judicial reasoning— first, a formalist regard for applying the law, secondly a market-individualist brand of realism with an emphasis on calculability and holding contractors to their bargains, and thirdly a consumer-welfarist brand of realism concerned with protecting contractors (particularly consumer contractors) against sharp practice and generally relieving against unconscionable deals.

If we treat the modern law of contract as having two principal divisions, one regulating commercial contracts and the other regulating consumer contracts, then it is fairly clear how the ideas of reasonableness, inequality of bargaining, and the like, have shaped the modern law of consumer protection. Quite simply, the ideology of consumer-welfarism has superseded that of market-individualism. However, it is perhaps less clear what the modernising tendencies are in relation to commercial contracts. In this section, we will seek to clarify the modernisation of the commercial law of contract by drawing a distinction between two versions of market-individualism, which we can term 'static' and 'dynamic' market-individualism. Although both versions of market-individualism take the process of contracting to be an essentially self-interested activity, with a freely agreed exchange as the paradigm, they rest on rather different bases. Static market-individualism is a fully detached or independent ideology: it has a particular vision of the purpose of contract and how transactions should be regulated; it imposes this view on the contracting community; and, in this sense, it 'constitutes' the market. By contrast, the ideology of dynamic market-individualism is to a considerable extent dependent, reflecting the practice and expectations of the contracting community (particularly the business community). It follows that, as the practice and the views of the contracting community change, the ideology of dynamic market-individualism moves to track these changes. To this extent, therefore, dynamic market-individualism is less than fully constitutive of the market.

Static and dynamic market-individualism contrasted

Market-individualism, whether static or dynamic, is an ideology with two aspects, a market and an individualistic aspect. To draw the contrast between static and dynamic market-individualism, we can work first through the market dimension of each version of the ideology and then through their individualistic aspects.

Static market-individualism sees the principal function of contract law as being to establish a clear set of ground rules within which a market can operate. To this extent, contract law is constitutive of the market. Markets, of course, may operate with all sorts of ground rules, customs and practices. In some markets, a nod and a wink may be sufficient to close a deal; in others, the deal is not closed until the sealing wax has dried on the contractual documents. For the static market-individualist, the distinctive contribution of the English law of contract is to declare the conventions in such a way that all those who deal in the contract-constituted market place know exactly where they stand.

Three of the most important ground rules concern formation (ie at what moment the parties are bound), third-party effects, and remedies for breach. Here, static market-individualism develops its rules around two key concepts, exchange and expectation. First, the (formation) rule is that a contract comes into existence when, and only when, the terms of an exchange have been fully specified and freely agreed upon. Secondly, only those who deal as parties to the exchange can take the benefit of the contract (or be burdened by its terms). And, thirdly, the basic remedial rule is that, where there is a breach, the innocent party's expectation of performance (by the contract-breaker) is to be protected—generally speaking, by damages or an action for the agreed price rather than by a decree of specific performance as such. These ground rules have the virtue of drawing bright lines (between situations where a binding contract is in place and where it is not, between those who can sue on a particular contract and those who cannot, and so on). However, the rules do not always generate results that seem entirely reasonable. Examples of such hard cases are legion: for instance, cases where an expected contract does not eventuate and one side incurs significant (anticipatory) reliance costs, cases where an agreed variation of a contract does not qualify as an exchange, cases where an intended third-party beneficiary is unable to enforce a contract, cases where the expectation measure of compensation seems over-generous (or, indeed, inadequate), and so on. Now, although it can be argued in response to such hard cases that the results are simply in line with the constitutive rules, and that these rules are well-known, this does not assist where significant numbers in both the commercial and the legal communities feel uneasy with these outcomes.

Dynamic market-individualism responds to these difficulties by favouring a more flexible approach, guided by the practices and expectations of the contracting community (particularly the commercial community). Accordingly, the paradigms of static market-individualism remain central but they are qualified in significant ways. For example, if the commercial community favours protection in certain situations for pre-contractual reliance, enforcement of agreed variations (even though they might be one-sided), recognition of third-party interests, and the like, then dynamic market-individualism argues that the law should run with the grain of business opinion. A textbook statement of such sentiments can be found in Lord Wilberforce's well-known remarks in *The Eurymedon* (where . . . the point at issue was whether the stevedore third-parties were entitled to rely on protective provisions in the main carriage contract):

'The whole contract is of a commercial character, involving service on one side, rates of payment on the other, and qualifying stipulations as to both. The relations of all parties to each other are commercial relations entered into for business reasons of ultimate profit. To describe one set of promises in this context as gratuitous, or *nudum pactum*, seems paradoxical and is *prima facie* implausible. It is only the precise analysis of this complex of relations into the classical offer and acceptance, with identifiable consideration, that seems to present difficulty, but this same difficulty exists in many situations of daily life, eg sales at auction; supermarket purchases; boarding an omnibus; purchasing a train ticket; tenders for the supply of goods; offers of rewards; acceptance by post; warranties of authority by agents; manufacturers' guarantees; gratuitous bailments; bankers' commercial credits. These are all examples which show that English law, having committed itself to a rather technical and schematic doctrine of contract, in application takes a practical approach, often at the cost of forcing the facts to fit uneasily into the marked slots of offer, acceptance and consideration.'

. . . .

One of the pillars of static market-individualism is the idea that contract is constituted by exchange. Where there is no exchange, there is no contract. From this simple idea, two doctrinal consequences of enormous importance follow. First, it follows that there is no contract where the parties have not yet reached the moment of exchange (even though they are working towards it). And, secondly, it follows that, even though the parties are already joined by an exchange, there is no fresh contract where the terms are modified without there being a fresh exchange. In the modern case law, these consequences (and the central idea itself) have been significantly qualified by two major decisions of the Court of Appeal, the *Blackpool and Fylde Aero Club* case and *Williams v Roffey Bros & Nicholls (Contractors) Ltd*.

In the *Blackpool and Fylde Aero Club* case, it will be recalled, the Court of Appeal held that the club could hold the defendant council to its advertised procedures for the consideration of tenders submitted in relation to a local airport concession. According to Sir Thomas Bingham, the council was not free to ignore its own published tendering guidelines (for example, by accepting a tender well before the deadline for tenders to be submitted had been reached, or by accepting a tender received well after the deadline) otherwise 'there would in my view be an unacceptable discrepancy between the law of contract and the confident assumptions of commercial parties'. Moreover, in holding that the club's understanding of the tendering process raised an entitlement, 'not as a matter of mere expectation but of contractual right', that the council should abide by its own rules, the court followed the line taken in a number of other jurisdictions that the law of contract is capable of giving at least some protection to the interests of commercial parties who are working their way towards an exchange.

If the *Blackpool and Fylde Aero Club* case breaks new ground in relation to pre-contractual reliance and expectation, *Williams v Roffey Bros & Nicholls (Contractors) Ltd* follows suit in relation to reliance and expectation encouraged during the performance of a contract. As is well known, the question in *Williams v Roffey* was whether the main contractors were contractually bound by their promise to pay the carpenter sub-contractors *additional* sums (over and above the agreed contractual price) for the contract work. In holding that the main contractors were so bound, provided that their promise was freely given and procured some practical advantage to the promisors, the Court of Appeal departed from the settled principle that A's promise to perform (or the actual performance of) his existing contractual duty to B is no consideration for a promise by B to pay additional sums to A. Although the decision gives rise to a host of doctrinal concerns, for present purposes, we need not agonise about whether it is better to say that the Court of Appeal revised the traditional concept of an 'exchange' (as embedded in the English doctrine of consideration) or simply that it effectively dispensed with the requirement of an exchange for a binding variation within an existing contractual relationship—for, either way, the court must be seen as taking its lead from the expectations of commercial contractors rather than from the classical rule-book associated with the static form of market-individualism.

QUESTIONS

1.   What is the 'objective principle'? What practical difference does it make whether the approach is subjective or objective?

2.   What does the objective principle tell us about whether contractual liability depends on the voluntary will of the parties?

3. Applying the normal 'rules' of offer and acceptance as laid down in the *Boots* case (p 199), which is the offer and which is the acceptance when you take your car to a filling station and buy petrol: (i) when an attendant fills the tank for you; and (ii) when it is self-service?

4. The general rule is that a display of goods in a shop with an indication of the price does not amount to an offer to supply the goods at that price. Why is that? What practical difference, if any, would it make if the display were to be treated as an offer? Would the change on balance be desirable or not?

5. Will a display of goods with a price attached, or even just a price list, ever amount to an offer? Can you think of an example when it might? (*Hint:* for one example, think about the sign displaying petrol prices at a self-service filling station.)

6. An offer may be accepted by the conduct of the offeree, which the offeror knows about, but can an offer ever be accepted by the offeree's conduct of which the offeror does not know?

CHAPTER NINE

UNCERTAINTY AND INCOMPLETENESS

The parties may leave even fundamental obligations under a contract vague or 'to be agreed'. What is the legal effect?

■ Sale of Goods Act 1979
Section 8

(1) The price in a contract of sale may be fixed by the contract, or may be left to be fixed in a manner agreed by the contract, or may be determined by the course of dealing between the parties.
(2) Where the price is not determined as mentioned in subsection (1) above the buyer must pay a reasonable price.
(3) What is a reasonable price is a question of fact dependent on the circumstances of each particular case.

■ *May & Butcher Ltd v R*
[1934] 2 KB 17n, House of Lords 1929

The plaintiffs (suppliants) alleged that the Controller of the Disposals Board had agreed to sell them tentage on terms contained in a letter, as follows:

(1) The Comission agrees to sell and [the suppliants] agree to purchase the total stock of old tentage...

(3) The price or prices to be paid, and the date or dates on which payment is to be made by the purchasers to the Commission for such old tentage shall be agreed upon from time to time between the Commission and the purchasers as the quantities of the said old tentage become available for disposal, and are offered to the purchasers by the Commission....

(10) It is understood that all disputes with reference to or arising out of this agreement will be submitted to arbitration in accordance with the provisions of the Arbitration Act 1889.

The Disposals Board contended that there was no binding contract, and the House of Lords upheld this view. **Viscount Dunedin** said:

To be a good contract there must be a concluded bargain, and a concluded contract is one which settles everything that is necessary to be settled and leaves nothing to be settled by agreement between the parties. Of course it may leave something which still has to be determined, but then that determination must be a determination which does not depend upon the agreement between the parties... [T]he Sale of Goods Act 1893, says that if the price is not mentioned and settled in the contract it is to be a reasonable price. The simple answer in this case is that the Sale of Goods Act provides for silence on the point and here there is no silence, because there is a provision that the two parties are to agree.... Here there was clearly no contract. There would have been a perfectly good settlement of price if the contract had said that it was to be settled by arbitration by a certain man, or it might have been quite good if it was said that it was to be settled by arbitration under the Arbitration Act so as to bring in a material plan by which a certain person could be put in action. The question then arises, has anything of that sort been done? I think clearly not. The general arbitration clause is one in very common form as to disputes arising out of the arrangements. In no proper meaning of the word can this be described as a dispute arising between the parties: it is a failure to agree, which is a very different thing from a dispute.

NOTES

1. A legal system might provide that certain matters must be agreed for there to be a binding contract. So Roman law provided that in a contract of sale the price must be certain. English law has not adopted this approach.

2. Beale rings up Bishop and orders 100 widgets to be delivered in a month's time; they agree that 'we will fix the price when we meet next week'. Bishop, who is a distributor, rings up Furmston, a manufacturer of widgets, and places an order for 100 widgets for delivery in three weeks: Furmston accepts the order without any discussion about the price. If widgets are a standard item of commerce for which there is an established market, is there a contract between Bishop and Furmston? Is there one between Bishop and Beale before they have met again? If you think there is a contract in one case but not in the other, why do you think the courts treat the two situations differently? Does doing so accord with business reality? (See further p 268.)

3. A comparison of s 8(2) and *May & Butcher v R* suggests that there are two categories: terms left vague or unstated will not prevent the formation of a contract but there will be no contract if something is left 'to be agreed'. Is it quite so simple?

I. UNCERTAINTY

If the parties leave something uncertain, does it matter that in practice they would normally negotiate over it? How far can the courts go in filling in the gaps?

■ *Hillas & Co Ltd v Arcos Ltd*
(1932) 147 LT 503, House of Lords

Arcos were business representatives of the Russian government, which, in 1930, was very anxious to defeat the 'English ring' who were refusing to buy. Hillas, who had left the ring, were therefore given very favourable terms.

The timber was of various kinds, mainly redwood and whitewood, and was cut into many different lengths and scantlings. A price list was issued each year giving prices for wood of each type, length, etc. The wood was shipped at First Open Water (May in Leningrad, June in the White Sea) until the ice closed the ports again (in January and November respectively).

In the 1930 season, Hillas agreed to buy 22,000 standards of 'fair specification' at agreed prices with certain agreed discounts. Clause 6 of the agreement provided: 'Buyers to arrange shipping dates and loading instructions according to the readiness of the goods purchased.' Clause 9 provided: 'Buyers shall also have the option of entering into a contract with sellers for the purchase of 100,000 standards for delivery in 1931. Such contract to stipulate that, whatever the conditions are, buyers shall obtain the goods on conditions and at prices which show to them a reduction of 5% on the f.o.b. value of the official price list at any time ruling during 1931. Such option to be declared before 1st January, 1931.'

Hillas purported to exercise this option on 22 December, 1930, but Arcos had already sold its entire production to the British Isles. Hillas sued for damages for breach of contract.

During cross-examination, Mr Hillas was asked how a specification for the actual parcel of timber would be arrived at. He replied that he would give the sellers a specification: they would never accept it in its entirely but would make a counter proposal, and so on, until a specification was arrived at.

The Court of Appeal held that there was no contract and Hillas appealed.

Lord Tomlin

... In the present case one or two preliminary observations fall to be made.

First, the parties were both intimately acquainted with the course of business in the Russian softwood timber trade and had without difficulty carried out the sale and purchase of 22,000 standards under the first part of the document of the 21st May 1930;

Secondly, although the question here is whether clause 9 of the document of the 21st May 1930, with the letter of the 22nd Dec. 1930, constitutes a contract, the validity of the whole of the document of the 21st May 1930 is really in question so far as the matter depends upon the meaning of the phrase 'of fair specification'; and

Thirdly, it is indisputable, having regard to clause 11, which provides that 'this agreement cancels all previous agreements', that the parties intended by the document of the 21st May 1930 to make, and believed that they had made, some concluded bargain ... it is said that there is in clause 9 no sufficient description of the goods to be sold ... it is plain that something must necessarily be implied in clause 9. The words '100,000 standards' without more do not even indicate that timber is the subject-matter of the clause. The implication at the least of the words 'of softwood goods' is, in my opinion, inevitable, and if this is so I see no reason to separate the words 'of fair specification' from the words 'of softwood goods'. In my opinion there is a necessary implication of the words 'of softwood goods of fair specification' after the words '100,000 standards' in clause 9.

What then is the meaning of '100,000 standards of softwood goods of fair specification for delivery during 1931'?

If the words 'of fair specification' have no meaning which is certain or capable of being made certain, then not only can there be no contract under clause 9 but there cannot have been a contract with regard to the 22,000 standards mentioned at the beginning of the document of the 21st May 1930. This may be the proper conclusion; but before it is reached it is, I think, necessary to exclude as impossible all reasonable meanings which would give certainty to the words. In my opinion this cannot be done.

The parties undoubtedly attributed to the words in connection with the 22,000 standards, some meaning which was precise or capable of being made precise. Scrutton LJ laid stress upon the evidence of Mr Hillas as indicating a different view on the part of the parties. I am unable to think that upon a question of construction such evidence if directed to the intention of the parties was admissible at all. In fact, I think, Mr Hillas's evidence was misunderstood. It really amounted, in my opinion, to nothing more than a statement as to how the parties would in the first instance proceed, just as on a purchase of property at its fair value the parties would no doubt first endeavour to reach agreement as to the fair value.

Reading the document of the 21st May 1930 as a whole, and having regard to the admissible evidence as to the course of the trade, I think that upon their true construction the words 'of fair specification over the season, 1930', used in connection with the 22,000 standards, means that the 22,000 standards are to be satisfied in goods distributed over kinds, qualities, and sizes in the fair proportions having regard to the output of the season 1930, and the classifications of that output in respect of kinds, qualities, and sizes. That is something which if the parties fail to agree can be ascertained just as much as the fair value of a property.

I have already expressed the view that clause 9 must be read as '100,000 standards of fair specification for delivery during 1931' and these words, I think, have the same meaning, *mutatis mutandis*, as the words relating to the 22,000 standards. Thus, there is a description of the goods which if not immediately yet ultimately is capable of being rendered certain. . .

It was also urged as a minor point that there was no provision as to shipment and that this was an essential of such a contract.

. . . [U]pon the true construction of the document the sale conditions in relation to the 22,000 standards are so far as applicable imported into the option for the sale of the 100,000 standards, and in particular that clause 6 relating to shipping dates and loading instructions is so imported.

It was urged on behalf of the respondents before your Lordships that if there was a contract still it was one upon which only nominal damages should have been awarded . . . because the respondents were free to give to other customers an equal or greater reduction in price. . . .

. . . I think the phrase 'the official price list at any time ruling during 1931' makes plain that the reduction given is from the general operative price and not from a merely nominal price which is not being adhered to in actual practice.

Lords Warrington and **Macmillan** concurred with Lord Tomlin; **Lords Thankerton** and **Wright** delivered judgments to similar effect.

Appeal allowed.

■ *Scammell v Ouston*

[1941] 1 All ER 14, House of Lords

The parties agreed that the respondents should buy a new lorry from the appellants, trading in an old lorry and paying the balance of the agreed purchase price 'on hire-purchase terms' over two years. The precise terms of the hire-purchase agreement were not settled. The appellants subsequently refused to go ahead, alleging that there was no contract.

Viscount Maugham

. . . It is a regrettable fact that there are few, if any, topics on which there seems to be a greater difference of judicial opinion than those which relate to the question whether, as the result of informal letters or like documents, a binding contract has been arrived at. Many well-known instances are to be found in the books, the latest being that of *Hillas & Co Ltd v Arcos Ltd*. The reason for these different conclusions is that laymen unassisted by persons with a legal training are not always accustomed to use words or phrases with a precise or definite meaning. In order to constitute a valid contract, the parties must so express themselves that their meaning can be determined with a reasonable degree of certainty. It is plain that, unless this can be done, it would be impossible to hold that the contracting parties had the same intention. In other words the *consensus ad idem* would be a matter of mere conjecture. This general rule, however, applies somewhat differently in different cases. In commercial documents connected with dealings in a trade with which the parties are perfectly familiar, the court is very willing, if satisfied that the parties thought that they made a binding contract, to imply terms, and, in particular, terms as to the method of carrying out the contract, which it would be impossible to supply in other kinds of contract: *Hillas & Co Ltd v Arcos Ltd*. . . .

We come, then, to the question as to the effect of the so-called purchase being on 'hire-purchase terms', and here we are confronted with a strange and confusing circumstance. The term 'hire-purchase' for a good many years past has been understood to mean a contract of hire by the owner of a chattel conferring on the hirer an option to purchase on the performance of certain conditions: *Helby v Matthews*. There is in these contracts—and this is, from a business standpoint, a most important matter—no agreement to buy within the Factors Act, 1889, or the Sale of Goods Act, 1893. There is only an option, and the hirer can confer on a purchaser from him no better title than he himself has, except in the case of sale in market overt. It is inaccurate and misleading to add to an order for goods, as if given by a purchaser, a clause that hire-purchase terms are to apply, without something to explain the apparent contradiction. Moreover, a hire-purchase agreement may assume many forms, and some of the variations in those forms are of the most important character—eg those which relate to termination of the agreement, warranty of fitness, duties as to repair, interest, and so forth.

Bearing these facts in mind, what do the words 'hire-purchase terms' mean in the present case? They may indicate that the hire-purchase agreement was to be granted by the appellants, or, on the other hand, by some finance company acting in collaboration with the appellants. They may contemplate that the appellants were to receive by instalments a sum of £168 spread over a period of 2 years upon delivering the new van and receiving the old car, or, on the other hand, that the appellants were to receive from a third party a lump sum of £168, and that the third party, presumably a finance company, was to receive from the respondents a larger sum than £168, to include interest and profit spread over a period of 2 years. Moreover, nothing is said (except as to the 2-years' period) as to the terms of the hire-purchase agreement—for instance, as to the interest payable, and as to the rights of the letter, whoever he may be, in the event of default by the respondents in payment of the instalments at the due dates. As regards the last matters, there was no evidence to suggest that there are any well-known 'usual terms' in such a contract, and I think that it is common knowledge that in fact many letters, though by no means all of them, insist on terms which the legislature regards as so unfair and unconscionable that it was recently found necessary to deal with the matter in the Hire-Purchase Act, 1938. These, my Lords, are very serious difficulties, and, when we find, as we do, in this curious case, that the trial judge and the three Lords Justices, and even the two counsel who addressed your Lordships for the respondents, were unable to agree upon the true construction of the alleged agreement, it seems to me that it is impossible to conclude that a binding agreement has been established by the respondents.

Viscount Simon LC and **Lords Wright** and **Russell of Killowen** made speeches to the same effect.

Appeal allowed.

NOTES

1.   It is possible that since this case was decided, hire-purchase contracts have become more standardised, and that if it were clear that the supplier was going to grant the hire-purchase agreement in its own name, the case might be decided the other way; there is, however, no certainty about this!

2.   In *Bushwall Properties Ltd v Vortex Properties Ltd* [1976] 1 WLR 591, an agreement for the sale of land by instalments provided for 'a proportionate part' of the land to be conveyed as each instalment was paid. The Court of Appeal rejected suggestions that one party should be allowed to select which parts should be conveyed each time and held the agreement void for uncertainty.

■ *Nicolene Ltd v Simmonds* [1953]

1 All ER 822, Court of Appeal

Denning LJ

This case raises a short, but important, point which can be stated quite simply. There was a contract for the sale of three thousand tons of steel reinforcing bars; the seller broke his contract, and when the buyer claimed damages the seller set up the defence that, owing to a sentence in one of the letters which were alleged to constitute the contract, there was no contract at all. The material words are: 'We are in agreement that the usual conditions of acceptance apply.' There were no usual conditions of acceptance and so it is said that those words are meaningless, that there is nothing to which they can apply, and that, therefore, there was never any contract between the parties.

In my opinion, a distinction must be drawn between a clause which is meaningless and a clause which is yet to be agreed. A clause which is meaningless can often be ignored, while still leaving the contract good, whereas a clause which has yet to be agreed may mean that there is no contract at all, because the parties have not agreed on all the essential terms. I take it to be clear law that, if one of the parties to a contract inserts into it an exempting condition in his own favour which the other side agrees and it afterwards appears that that condition is meaningless or is so ambiguous that no ascertainable meaning can be given to it, that does not render the whole contract a nullity. The only result is that the exempting condition is a nullity and must be rejected. It would be strange, indeed, if a party could escape every one of his obligations by inserting a meaningless exemption from some of them.

…The sentence is meaningless and must be ignored, but the contract, nevertheless, remains good. I agree that the appeal should be dismissed.

Singleton and **Hodson LJJ** delivered judgments to the same effect.

II. INCOMPLETENESS

■ Sale of Goods Act 1979
Section 9

(1) Where there is an agreement to sell goods on the terms that the price is to be fixed by the valuation of a third party, and he cannot or does not make the valuation, the agreement is avoided; but if the goods or any part of them have been delivered to and appropriated by the buyer he must pay a reasonable price for them.
(2) Where the third party is prevented from making the valuation by the fault of the seller or buyer, the party not at fault may maintain an action for damages against the party at fault.

■ *Courtney and Fairbairn Ltd v Tolaini Brothers (Hotels) Ltd*

[1975] 1 All ER 716, Court of Appeal

Lord Denning MR

The question in this case is whether two letters give rise to a concluded contract.

Mr Tolaini wanted to develop a site in Hertfordshire. It was The Thatched Barn Hotel together with five acres of land. He got in touch with a property developer, a Mr Courtney. It appears that Mr Courtney was well placed to obtain finance for building development. He was also a building contractor himself. The two met and discussed ways and means at the office of Mr Sacks, an architect. The proposal was that Mr Courtney should introduce someone to provide the money and lend it to Mr Tolaini. Mr Tolaini was to develop the site by building a motel and other things. But he was to employ Mr Courtney or his company to do the construction work. After the meeting, on 10th April 1969, Mr Courtney wrote to Mr Tolaini this letter:

'... I would be very happy to know that, if my discussions and arrangements with interested parties lead to an introductory meeting, which in turn leads to a financial arrangement acceptable to both parties you will be prepared to instruct your Quantity Surveyor to negotiate fair and reasonable contract sums in respect of each of the three projects as they arise. (These would, incidentally be based upon agreed estimates of the net cost of work and general overheads with a margin for profit of 5%) which, I am sure you will agree, is indeed reasonable.'

... Mr Tolaini [replied] on 28th April 1969, in the terms:

'In reply to your letter of the 10th April, I agree to the terms specified therein, and I look forward to meeting the interested party regarding finance.'

Those are the two letters on which the issue depends. But I will tell the subsequent events quite shortly. Mr Courtney did his best. He found a person interested who provided finance of £200,000 or more for the projects. Mr Tolaini on his side appointed his quantity surveyor with a view to negotiating with Mr Courtney the price for the construction work. But there were differences of opinion about the price. And nothing was agreed. In the end Mr Tolaini did not employ Mr Courtney or his company to do the construction work. Mr Tolaini instructed other contractors and they completed the motel and other works. But then Mr Tolaini took advantage of the finance which Mr Courtney had made possible, but he did not employ Mr Courtney's company to do the work. Naturally enough, Mr Courtney was very upset. He has brought this action in which he says that there was a contract by which his company were to be employed as builders for the work, and it was a breach of contract by Mr Tolaini or his company to go elsewhere and employ somebody else. Mr Courtney's company claimed the loss of profits which they would have made if they had been employed as builders for this motel.

...

I am afraid that I have come to a different view from the judge. The reason is because I can find no agreement on the price or on any method by which the price was to be calculated. The agreement was only an agreement to 'negotiate' fair and reasonable contract sums. The words of the letter are 'your Quantity Surveyor to *negotiate* fair and reasonable contract sums in respect of each of the three projects as they arise'. Then there are words which show that estimates had not yet been agreed, but were yet to be agreed. The words are: 'These [the contract sums] would, incidentally be based upon agreed estimates of the net cost of work and general overheads with a margin for profit of 5%.' Those words show that there were no estimates agreed and no contract sums agreed. All was left to be agreed in the future. It was to be agreed between the parties themselves. If they had left the price to be agreed by a third person such as an arbitrator, it would have been different. But here it was to be agreed between the parties themselves.

Now the price in a building contract is of fundamental importance. It is so essential a term that there is no contract unless the price is agreed or there is an agreed method of ascertaining it, not dependent on the negotiations of the two parties themselves. In a building contract both parties must know at the outset, before the work is started, what the price is to be, or, at all events, what agreed estimates are. No builder and no employer would ever dream of entering into a building contract for over £200,000 without there being an estimate of the cost and an agreed means of ascertaining the price.

In the ordinary course of things the architects and the quantity surveyors get out the specification and the bills of quantities. They are submitted to the contractors. They work out the figures and tender for the work at a named price; and there is a specified means of altering it up or down for extras or omissions and so forth, usually by means of an architect's certificate. In the absence of some such machinery, the only contract which you might find is a contract to do the work for a reasonable sum or for a sum to be fixed by a third party. But here there is no such contract at all. There is no machinery for ascertaining the price except by negotiation. In other words, the price is still to be agreed. Seeing that there is no agreement on so fundamental a matter as the price, there is no contract.

But then this point was raised. Even if there was not a contract actually to build, was not there a contract to negotiate? In this case Mr Toliani did instruct his quantity surveyor to negotiate, but the negotiations broke down. It may be suggested that the quantity surveyor was to blame for the failure of the negotiations. But does that give rise to a cause of action? There is very little guidance in the book about a contract to negotiate. It was touched on by Lord Wright in *Hillas & Co Ltd v Arcos Ltd* where he said: 'There is then no bargain except to negotiate, and negotiations may be fruitless and end without any contract ensuing.' Then he went on:

> '. . . yet even then, in strict theory, there is a contract (if there is good consideration) to negotiate, though in the event of repudiation by one party the damages may be nominal, unless a jury think that the opportunity to negotiate was of some appreciable value to the injured party.'

That tentative opinion by Lord Wright does not seem to me to be well founded. If the law does not recognise a contract to enter a contract (when there is a fundamental term yet to be agreed) it seems to me it cannot recognise a contract to negotiate. The reason is because it is too uncertain to have any binding force. No court could estimate the damages because no one can tell whether the negotiations would be successful or would fall through; or if successful, what the result would be. It seems to me that a contract to negotiate, like a contract to enter into a contract, is not a contract known to the law. We were referred to the recent decision of Brightman J about an option, *Mountford v Scott*, but that does not seem to me to touch this point. I think we must apply the general principle that when there is a fundamental matter left undecided and to be the subject of negotiation, there is no contract. So I would hold that there was not any enforceable agreement in the letters between the plaintiff and the defendants. I would allow the appeal accordingly.

Lord Diplock

I agree and would only add my agreement that the dictum—for it is no more—of Lord Wright in *Hillas & Co Ltd v Arcos Ltd* to which Lord Denning MR has referred, though an attractive theory, should in my view be regarded as bad law.

Lawton LJ

I agree with both the judgments which have been delivered.

Appeal allowed. Action dismissed.

NOTES

1. There are 'going rates' for both building labour and materials. Why then could not the contract be treated as one for a reasonable sum? One explanation is that the 'going rates' are for individual items of work done on their own and probably the total of the items needed would be more than any employer would be willing to pay for a large project as a whole.

2. The decision that English law does not recognise a contract to negotiate has since been upheld by the House of Lords: see p 271.

3. Is there some method by which Courtney could have ensured that Tolaini was committed to him? You may like to return to this question when you have read the rest of the cases in the chapter.

■ *British Bank for Foreign Trade Ltd v Novinex Ltd*
[1949] 1 All ER 155, Court of Appeal

The plaintiffs had arranged for P to supply a consignment of oilskins to the defendants, who had not had any previous contact with P, and the defendants wrote confirming that they had agreed to pay the plaintiffs a commission for this. The letter continued:

We also undertake to cover you with an agreed commission on any other business transacted with your friends [P]. In return for this, you are to put us in direct touch with your friends.

The plaintiffs put the defendants in direct contact with P, and the defendants entered into further transactions with P, but they refused to pay the plaintiffs any commission on them. The plaintiffs' action was dismissed by Denning J, and they appealed.

Cohen LJ

. . . Is this an enforceable agreement? A number of authorities have been cited to us, to which I do not propose to refer in detail, because, in my view, the effect of the authorities is stated correctly in the learned judge's judgment where he said:

'The principle to be deduced from the cases is that, if there is an essential term which has yet to be agreed and there is no express or implied provision for its solution, the result in point of law is that there is no binding contract. In seeing whether there is an implied provision for its solution, however, there is a difference between an arrangement which is wholly executory on both sides, and one which has been executed on one side or the other. In the ordinary way, if there is an arrangement to supply goods at a price "to be agreed", or to perform services on terms "to be agreed", then, although, while the matter is still executory there may be no binding contract, nevertheless, if it is executed on one side, that is, if the one does his part without having come to an agreement as to the price or the terms, then the law will say that there is necessarily implied from the conduct of the parties a contract that, in default of agreement, a reasonable sum is to be paid.'

With that statement of the principle of law I respectfully agree. My difference with the learned judge is only on the question whether he has correctly applied that statement of principle to the facts of this case. . . . Denning J goes on to say that this shows that the agreement is too vague, but this argument involves the proposition that the agreement had not said in terms: 'We also undertake to cover you with a reasonable commission on any other business transacted with your friends.' Denning J regarded that condition as being too vague to be enforceable. I cannot agree with his view. I think that the court should take the view that a jury properly directed would be able to arrive at a proper conclusion as to what in the circumstances of this case is a reasonable commission.

[His Lordship then considered what would be a reasonable commission in respect of the transactions and concluded that it would not exceed $\frac{1}{4}$d per skin.]

Bucknill and **Singleton LJJ** agreed.

NOTES

1. Denning J seems to assume that, once performance has taken place, there must be a contract. Is this a necessary analysis? Compare McKendrick's suggestion of a 'restitutionary analysis' to the battle of the forms problem. However, Denning's approach is the one normally adopted; see *Trentham Ltd v Archital Luxfer* [1993] 1 Lloyd's Rep 25. Steyn LJ said (at 27):

    The fact that the transaction was performed on both sides will often make it unrealistic to argue that there was no intention to enter into legal relations. It will often make it difficult to submit that the contract is void for vagueness or uncertainty. Specifically, the fact that the transaction is executed makes it easier to imply a term resolving any uncertainty, or, alternatively, it may make it possible to treat a matter not finally established in negotiations as inessential.

2.   Suppose Bishop agrees to sell Beale 200 widgets 'at a price to be agreed', delivery to be in two instalments. Bishop delivers and Beale accepts the first instalment without there being any further negotiation on the price. How much does Beale have to pay for the first instalment? Is there a binding contract for the second instalment?

■ *Foley v Classique Coaches Ltd*
[1934] 2 KB 1, Court of Appeal

The defendants agreed to buy from the plaintiff a piece of land adjoining the plaintiff's garage. The defendants intended to use the land for their motor coach business, and the sale was made subject to the defendants entering a second agreement, which was executed on the same day, to purchase all of the petrol they required for their business from the plaintiff 'at a price to be agreed by the parties in writing and from time to time'. Clause 8 provided that: 'If any dispute or difference shall arise on the subject matter or construction of this agreement the same shall be submitted to arbitration . . .' For three years after the conveyance of the land, the defendants obtained all their petrol from the plaintiff, but a dispute arose and they repudiated the second agreement, alleging that it was not binding (i) because no written agreement on the price of petrol had been made, and (ii) because the obligation to take all of the petrol they required from the plaintiff was an unreasonable restraint of trade. The Court of Appeal held that there was a binding agreement and that it was not an unreasonable restraint of trade. On the first point, **Scrutton LJ** said:

> In the present case the parties obviously believed they had a contract and they acted for three years as if they had; they had an arbitration clause which relates to the subject-matter of the agreement as to the supply of petrol, and it seems to me that this arbitration clause applies to any failure to agree as to the price. By analogy to the case of a tied house there is to be implied in this contract a term that the petrol shall be supplied at a reasonable price and shall be of reasonable quality. For these reasons I think the Lord Chief Justice was right in holding that there was an effective and enforceable contract, although as to the future no definite price had been agreed with regard to the petrol.

NOTES

1.   The price of a standard commodity like petrol is easy to fix once it has been determined that the parties originally intended, or in the light of their performance must be taken to intend, that the price shall be a reasonable one. What about other obligations? In *F & G Sykes (Wessex) Ltd v Fine Fare Ltd* [1967] 1 Lloyd's Rep 53, the plaintiffs had agreed with the defendants that the plaintiffs would produce large numbers of day-old chicks, which would then be sold to growers to be reared to a size fit for eating. The growers would then supply the birds to the defendants, who planned to build a new plant to process them. The agreement was to last five years or more. The defendants were to give at least 26 weeks' notice of the number of fowls they would require in each week, and it was agreed that the number would be not less than 30,000 and not more than 80,000 per week for the first year, 'and thereafter such other figures as may be agreed between the parties hereto'. The defendants then discovered that there were problems over water supplies to the proposed site of their new plant, and, after the agreement had run for over a year, they cancelled the arrangements. In an action for damages by the plaintiffs, the Court of

Appeal held that the contract was still binding: given that the parties clearly intended a five-year agreement and had commenced implementing it, the court should strive to uphold it. Lord Denning MR pointed out that, in default of agreement, the number of chicks should be treated as a reasonable one that could be ascertained under the arbitration clause. Danckwerts and Winn LJJ agreed with this approach, pointing out that the reasonable maximum and minimum figures would be the maximum throughput of the factories and the minimum throughput for efficient operation respectively. What if the defendants had shown that the numbers of chicks for the first year were not related to those criteria, but were, for instance, a much narrower band? How would an arbitrator go about determining a reasonable figure for chicks?

2.   If a dispute about the price of petrol or the number of chicks to be supplied could go to arbitration, why couldn't a dispute as to the price of tentage in *May & Butcher's* case?

3.   A price 'to be agreed', with no mechanism for valuation or arbitration, can be treated as an agreement to pay a reasonable price when it forms only a subsidiary part of an agreement that has been partially performed. Why cannot the same be done when it is a major element, but the court thinks the parties nonetheless intended to be bound? In other words, should phrases such as 'price to be negotiated' always be taken literally? In *Hillas v Arcos*, Scrutton LJ in the Court of Appeal said of the case of *May & Butcher v The King*:

I took the view, for the reasons stated in my judgment, that there was a contract; that if no price was agreed, the price under sect. 8 of the Sale of Goods Act 1893 would be a reasonable price, or there would be a dispute arising out of the agreement, which should be settled under the arbitration clause. My brothers Sargant LJ and Eve J took Lord Parker's view that there could not be a contract to make a contract, and that in spite of the language of absolute sale used in the document, there was no enforceable contract. The three members of the House of Lords who heard the appeal thought there was no need to call on the respondents. They said that the price should be agreed and was not agreed, and when the arbitration clause spoke of disputes arising out of the contract, its framers forgot that there was no contract. I refer to the judgment for its terms. I am afraid I remain quite impenitent. I think I was right and that nine out of ten business men would agree with me. But of course I recognise that I am bound as a judge to follow the principles laid down by the House of Lords. But I regret that in many commercial matters the English law and the practice of commercial men are getting wider apart, with the result that commercial business is leaving the courts and is being decided by commercial arbitrators with infrequent reference to the courts.

■ *Sudbrook Trading Estate Ltd v Eggleton*

[1982] 3 All ER 1, House of Lords

Lord Fraser of Tullybelton

My Lords, the appellants (the lessees) are the tenants in four leases, by each of which they were granted an option to purchase the freehold reversion of the leased premises at a valuation. The lessees have exercised the options, but the respondents (the lessors), who are the landlords, contend that the options are unenforceable. The questions now to be determined, therefore, are whether the options are valid and enforceable, and, if so, how they should be enforced.

The leases relate to adjacent industrial premises in Gloucester . . . The clause in the [earliest] lease, cl 11, has been taken as typical of them all. It entitled the lessees to purchase the reversion in fee simple, on certain conditions which were all satisfied—

'at such price not being less than Seventy five thousand pounds as may be agreed upon by two valuers one to be nominated by the Lessor and the other by the Lessee or in default of such agreement by an Umpire appointed by the said Valuers . . . '

The lessors contend that the options are void for uncertainty on the ground that they contain no formula by which the price can be fixed in the event of no agreement being reached, and that they are no more than agreements to agree. The lessors have therefore declined to appoint their valuer. The machinery provided in the leases has accordingly become inoperable.

In these proceedings the lessees seek a declaration that the options are valid, that they have been validly and effectively exercised, and that the contents constituted by the exercise ought to be specifically performed. As regards the mode of performance, the main argument for the lessees is that the court should order such inquiries as are necessary to ascertain the value of each of the properties. Lawson J decided the question of principle in favour of the lessees, but his decision was reversed by the Court of Appeal which held that the options were unenforceable. Templeman LJ, who delivered the judgment of the Court of Appeal, made a full review of the English authorities and the conclusion which he drew from them was, in my opinion inevitably, adverse to the lessees' contentions. The fundamental proposition on which he relied was, in his own words—

> 'that where the agreement on the face of it is incomplete until something else has been done, whether by further agreement between the parties or by the decision of an arbitrator or valuer, the court is powerless, because there is no complete agreement to enforce . . .'

I agree that that is the effect of the earlier decisions but, with the greatest respect, I am of opinion that it is wrong. It appears to me that, on the exercise of the option, the necessary preconditions having been satisfied, as they were in this case, a complete contract of sale and purchase of the freehold reversion was constituted. The price, which was of course an essential term of the contract, was, for reasons which I shall explain, capable of being ascertained and was therefore certain. Certum est quod certum reddi potest: see *May & Butcher Ltd v The King*, per Viscount Dunedin.

The courts have applied clauses such as those in the present case in a strictly literal way and have treated them as making the completion of a contract of sale conditional on agreement between the valuers either on the value of the property or, failing that, on the choice of an umpire. They have further laid down the principle that where parties have agreed on a particular method of ascertaining the price, and that method has for any reason proved ineffective, the court will neither grant an order for specific performance to compel parties to operate the agreed machinery nor substitute its own machinery to ascertain the price, because either of these clauses would be to impose on parties an agreement that they had not made. . . .

While that is the general principle it is equally well established that, where parties have agreed to sell 'at a fair valuation' or 'at a reasonable price' or according to some similar formula, without specifying any machinery for ascertaining the price, the position is different. . . .

I recognise the logic of the reasoning which has led to the courts refusing to substitute their own machinery for the machinery which has been agreed on by the parties. But the result to which it leads is so remote from that which parties normally intend and expect, and is so inconvenient in practice, that there must in my opinion be some defect in the reasoning. I think the defect lies in construing the provisions for the mode of ascertaining the value as an essential part of the agreement. That may have been perfectly true early in the nineteenth century, when the valuer's profession and the rules of valuation were less well established than they are now. But at the present day these provisions are only subsidiary to the main purpose of the agreement, which is for sale and purchase of the property at a fair or reasonable value. In the ordinary case parties do not make any substantial distinction between an agreement to sell at a fair value, without specifying the mode of ascertaining the value, and an agreement to sell at a value to be ascertained by valuers appointed in the way provided in these leases. The true distinction is between those cases where the mode of ascertaining the price is an essential term of the contract and those cases where the mode of ascertainment, though indicated in the contract, is subsidiary and non-essential. . . . The present case falls, in my opinion, into the latter category. Accordingly, when the option was exercised, there was constituted a complete contract for sale, and the clause should be construed as meaning that the price was to be a fair price. On the other hand, where an agreement is made to sell at a price to be fixed by a valuer who is named, or who, by reason of holding some office such as auditor of a company whose shares are to be valued, will have special knowledge relevant to the question of value, the prescribed mode may well be regarded as essential. Where, as here, the machinery consists of valuers and an umpire, none of whom is named or identified, it is in my opinion unrealistic to regard it as an essential term. If it breaks down there is no reason why the court should not substitute other machinery to carry out the main purpose of ascertaining the price in order that the agreement may be carried out.

Lords Diplock, **Scarman** and **Bridge** delivered concurring judgments.

Lord Russell of Killowen [dissenting]

My Lords, it appears to be generally accepted that the law as previously understood since at least the early nineteenth century is in favour of the respondents (the lessors) and of the decision of the Court of Appeal. It is proposed by the majority of your Lordships to assert that that previous understanding was erroneous. I cannot agree.

Basically the assumption is made that the parties intended that the exercise of the option should involve payment of a 'fair price' or a 'fair value'. Of course parties to such a contract could in terms so agree, and I am not concerned to deny that in such a case a court could enforce the contract by ascertainment of a fair price or fair value, treating specific provisions in the contract for methods (which proved to be unworkable) of ascertaining that fair price or valuation as being inessential. But that is not this case. Why should it be thought that potential vendor and purchaser intended the price to be a 'fair'? The former would intend the price to be high, even though 'unfairly' so. And the latter vice versa. Vendors and purchasers are normally greedy. . . .

Appeal allowed.

NOTES

1. The option to purchase the freehold in this case was, of course, part of a contract that had been partly performed, but not a lot of stress seems to have been laid on this.

2. The House of Lords relied on the fact that the price of the reversion was to be fixed by *valuers* as indicating that a fair or reasonable price was to be paid. Arbitrators, on the other hand, are supposed to decide cases in the same way as judges. Was Scrutton correct to lay stress on the arbitration clause in *Foley v Classique Coaches?* Would the case have to be decided the other way if there were no arbitration clause? What about *F & G Sykes (Wessex) Ltd v Fine Fare Ltd?*

3. The reasoning in *Sudbrook* leaves it open to a court in another case to hold that the price-fixing provision is essential and not mere machinery. This is what happened in *Gillatt v Sky Television Ltd* [2000] 1 All ER (Comm) 461, in which the provision was for valuation 'by an independent Chartered Accountant'.

You may like to compare English law to the Uniform Commercial Code:

2–204. Formation in general
 (3) Even though one or more terms are left open a contract for sale does not fail for indefiniteness if the parties have intended to make a contract and there is a reasonably certain basis for giving an appropriate remedy.

2–305. Open price term
 (1) The parties if they so intend can conclude a contract for sale even though the price is not settled. In such a case the price is a reasonable price at the time for delivery if
  (a) nothing is said as to price; or
  (b) the price is left to be agreed by the parties and they fail to agree; or

    (c) the price is to be fixed in terms of some agreed market or other standard as set or
        recorded by a third person or agency and it is not so set or recorded.

(2) A price to be fixed by the seller or by the buyer means a price for him to fix in good faith.

(3) When a price left to be fixed otherwise than by agreement of the parties fails to be fixed
through fault of one party the other may at his option treat the contract as cancelled or himself fix a reasonable price.

(4) Where, however, the parties intend not to be bound unless the price be fixed or agreed and
it is not fixed or agreed there is no contract. In such a case the buyer must return any goods
already received or if unable so to do must pay their reasonable value at the time of delivery
and the seller must return any portion of the price paid on account.

NOTE

Do you think these provisions are an improvement on English law? Or do you think the test
of whether the parties 'intended' there to be a contract causes more problems than it solves?
What sort of evidence do you think a court might appropriately consider when trying to
decide what the parties intended? Should it, for instance, consider evidence as to whether the
seller had instructed its delivery department to package some goods and label them for the
buyer? Whether the buyer had filed away the seller's acknowledgment form in its 'completed
contracts' file? Compare *Brogden v Metropolitan Rly Co*, and see the note on adjudication and
error costs in the Introduction.

The provision in s 2–305(2) does not seem to represent English law. It might seem odd for
anyone to agree to a contract in which the other party can fix the price, but most readers of this
passage will have a credit card, the interest rate of which can be altered upwards or downwards
by the credit card company, and in England (unlike many other countries), most mortgages of
houses provide for interest rates variable at relatively short notice by the lender.

    It used to be assumed that there were no legal controls on this practice (*Lombard Tricity
Finance Ltd v Paton* [1989] 1 All ER 918), but in *Paragon Finance plc v Staunton* [2001] EWCA
Civ 1466 [2002] 2 All ER 248, it was held that the variation of a loan under such a contract
should not be dishonest, capricious or arbitrary. The Court of Appeal was careful not to say
that the variation must be reasonable.

III. PRELIMINARY CONTRACTS

A party may not yet be in a position to finalise the contract it hopes to make, for instance,
because it needs to raise finance, to make further investigations or to secure consents: all three
reasons may lie behind making an agreement for the sale and purchase of land 'subject to
contract'. The effect of using that phrase is that there is no commitment on either side. But
suppose that a party wishes to get some sort of commitment from the other that it will not
back away in the meantime? A number of techniques have been tried.

■ *Walford v Miles*
[1992] 1 All ER 453, House of Lords

The respondents owned a company, together with premises that were let to the company and
in which it carried on a photographic processing business. In 1986, the respondents decided

to sell the business and the premises and received an offer of £1.9m from a third party. In the meantime, the appellants entered into negotiations with the respondents, and on 12 March 1987, the respondents agreed in principle to sell the business and the premises to them for £2m and warranted that the trading profits in the 12 months following completion would be not less than £300,000. On 17 March, it was further agreed in a telephone conversation between the parties that, if the appellants provided a comfort letter from their bank by the close of business on 20 March confirming that the bank had offered them loan facilities to enable them to make the purchase for £2m, the respondents 'would terminate negotiations with any third party or consideration of any alternative with a view to concluding agreements' with the appellants, and that even if the respondents received a satisfactory proposal from any third party before then, they 'would not deal with that third party and nor would [they] give further consideration to any alternative'. The appellants duly provided the comfort letter from their bank in the time specified, and on 25 March, the respondents confirmed that, subject to contract, they agreed to the sale of the property and the shares in the company to the appellants for £2m. On 30 March, the respondents withdrew from the negotiations and decided to sell to the third party because they were concerned that their staff would not get on with the appellants and that a loss of staff would put the warranted £300,000 profit in jeopardy. The appellants brought an action against the respondents for breach of a 'lockout' agreement, under which the appellants had been given an exclusive opportunity to try to come to terms with the respondents and which was collateral to the subject to contract negotiations that were proceeding for the purchase of the business and the premises. The appellants alleged that it was a term of the collateral agreement necessarily to be implied to give business efficacy to it that, so long as the respondents continued to desire to sell the business and the premises, the respondents would continue to negotiate in good faith with the appellants. It was contended that the consideration for the collateral contract was the appellants' agreement to continue negotiations and the provision of the comfort letter from their bank. The judge upheld the claim, but on appeal, the Court of Appeal held that the collateral agreement alleged was no more than an agreement to negotiate and was therefore unenforceable. The appellants appealed to the House of Lords.

Lord Ackner

The pleaded case

The appellants relied upon an oral agreement, collateral to the negotiations which were proceeding to purchase the company and the land it occupied 'subject to contract'. The consideration for this oral agreement was twofold: firstly, the appellants agreeing to continue the negotiations and not to withdraw and, secondly, their providing the comfort letter from their bankers in the terms requested.

For this consideration it was alleged in para 5 of the statement of claim as follows:

> '. . . the [first respondent] on behalf of himself and the [second respondent] would terminate negotiations with any Third Party or consideration of any alternative with a view to concluding an agreement with the [appellants] and further that even if he received a satisfactory proposal from any Third Party prior to the close of business on 20th March 1987, he would not deal with that Third Party or give further consideration to any alternative.'

As thus pleaded, the agreement purported to be what is known as a 'lock-out' agreement, providing the appellants with an exclusive opportunity to try and come to terms with the respondents, but without expressly providing any duration for such an opportunity.

For reasons which will become apparent hereafter, it was decided to amend this paragraph by the following addition:

'It was a term of the said collateral agreement necessarily to be implied to give business efficacy thereto that, so long as they continued to desire to sell the said property and shares, the [first respondent] on behalf of himself and the [second respondent] would continue to negotiate in good faith with the [appellants].'

Thus the statement of claim alleged that, not only were the respondents 'locked out' for some unspecified time from dealing with any third party, but were 'locked in' to dealing with the appellants, also for an unspecified period.

In the statement of claim it was further alleged that, by reason of the wrongful repudiation by the respondents, the appellants lost the opportunity of completing the sale and purchase of the shares and property, and that the true market value of the shares and the property was of the order of £3m. According, the appellants claimed that they lost the difference between the price which they had agreed to pay of £2m and the true market value. In addition to the above, there was a claim for damages for misrepresentation by the respondents in continuing to deal with third parties. This consisted of the expenses incurred in the negotiations and in the preparation of contract documents.

The decision of first instance and the Court of Appeal

...

...The judge held that there was a collateral agreement whereby the respondents undertook to terminate negotiations with any third party or consideration of any alternative and that even if Mr Miles received a satisfactory proposal from any third party before the close of business on the Friday night (20 March) he would not deal with that third party or give further consideration to any alternative, and that this agreement had been repudiated by the respondents. He therefore ordered that the damages for the alleged loss of opportunity be assessed. He further held that the promises of Mr Miles under the collateral agreement were misrepresentations and awarded the appellants £700 on account of special damages, being the agreed wasted expenditure.

In the Court of Appeal, by majority (Dillon and Stocker LJJ), the appeal was allowed (save to the extent of the award of the damages for misrepresentation) on the grounds that the agreement alleged was no more than an agreement to negotiate and was therefore unenforceable. Bingham LJ, who dissented, would have held that the agreement was enforceable on the ground that it could be construed as an agreement by the respondents not to deal with any party other than the appellants and not to entertain any alternative proposal. He would have set aside the award of damages for misrepresentation on the grounds that it was not justified by the evidence or the trial judge's findings. Before your Lordships the respondents were not contesting the £700 award.

The validity of the agreement alleged in para 5 of the statement of claim as amended

The justification for the implied term in para 5 or the amended statement of claim was that, in order to give the collateral agreement 'business efficacy', Mr Miles was obliged to 'continue to negotiate in good faith'. It was submitted to the Court of Appeal and initially to your Lordships that this collateral agreement could not be made to work, unless there was a positive duty imposed upon Mr Miles to negotiate. It was of course conceded that the agreement made no specific provision for the period it was to last. It was however contended, albeit not pleaded, that the obligation to negotiate would endure for a reasonable time, and that such time was the time which was reasonably necessary to reach a binding agreement. It was however accepted that such period of time would not end when negotiations had ceased, because all such negotiations were conducted expressly under the umbrella of 'subject to contract'. The agreement alleged would thus be valueless if the alleged obligation to negotiate ended when negotiations as to the terms of the 'subject to contract' agreement had ended, since at that stage the respondents would have been entitled at their whim to refuse to sign any contract.

Apart from the absence of any term as to the duration of the collateral agreement, it contained no provision for the respondents to determine the negotiations, albeit that such a provision was essential. It was contended by Mr Naughton that a term was to be implied giving the respondents a right to determine the negotiations, but only if they had 'a proper reason'. However, in order to determine whether a given reason was a proper one, he accepted that the test was not an objective one: would a hypothetical reasonable person consider the reason a reasonable one? The test was a subjective one: did the respondents honestly believe in the reason which they gave for the termination of the negotiations? Thus they could be quite irrational, so long as they behaved honestly.

Mr Naughton accepted that as the law now stands and has stood for approaching 20 years an agreement to negotiate is not recognised as an enforceable contract. This was first decided in terms in *Courtney & Fairbairn Ltd v Tolaini Bros (Hotels) Ltd* . . .

Before your Lordships it was sought to argue that the decision in the *Courtney & Fairbairn Ltd* case was wrong. Although the cases in the United States did not speak with one voice your Lordships' attention was drawn to the decision of the United States Court of Appeals, Third Circuit in *Channel Home Centers Division of Grace Retail Corp v Grossman* (1986) 795 F 2d 291 as being 'the clearest example' of the American cases in the appellants' favour. That case raised the issue whether an agreement to negotiate in good faith, if supported by consideration, is an enforceable contract. I do not find the decision of any assistance. While accepting that an agreement to agree is not an enforceable contract, the United States Court of Appeals appears to have proceeded on the basis that an agreement to negotiate in good faith is synonymous with an agreement to use best endeavours and, as the latter is enforceable, so is the former. This appears to me, with respect, to be an unsustainable proposition. The reason why an agreement to negotiate, like an agreement to agree, is unenforceable is simply because it lacks the necessary certainty. The same does not apply to an agreement to use best endeavours. This uncertainty is demonstrated in the instant case by the provision which it is said has to be implied in the agreement for the determination of the negotiations. How can a court be expected to decide whether, *subjectively*, a proper reason existed for the termination of negotiations? The answer suggested depends upon whether the negotiations have been determined 'in good faith'. However, the concept of a duty to carry on negotiations in good faith is inherently repugnant to the adversarial position of the parties when involved in negotiations. Each party to the negotiations is entitled to pursue his (or her) own interest, so long as he avoids making misrepresentations. To advance that interest he must be entitled, if he thinks it appropriate, to threaten to withdraw from further negotiations or to withdraw in fact in the hope that the opposite party may seek to reopen the negotiations by offering him improved terms. Mr Naughton, of course, accepts that the agreement upon which he relies does not contain a duty to complete the negotiations. But that still leaves the vital question: how is a vendor ever to know that he is entitled to withdraw from further negotiations? How is the court to police such an 'agreement'? A duty to negotiate in good faith is as unworkable in practice as it is inherently inconsistent with the position of a negotiating party. It is here that the uncertainty lies. In my judgment, while negotiations are in existence either party is entitled to withdraw from these negotiations, at any time and for any reason, There can be thus no obligation to continue to negotiate until there is a 'proper reason' to withdraw. Accordingly, a bare agreement to negotiate has no legal content.

The validity of the agreement as originally pleaded in the statement of claim

Paragraph 5 of the statement of claim, as unamended, followed the terms of the oral agreement as recorded in the penultimate paragraph of the letter of 18 March. It alleged that for good consideration (and this certainly covered the provision by the appellants of the 'comfort letter') Mr Miles on behalf of himself and his wife agreed that they—

'would terminate negotiations with any Third Party or consideration of any alternative with a view to concluding an agreement with the [appellants] and, further, that even if he received a satisfactory proposal from any Third Party prior to the close of business on 20 March 1987, he would not deal with that Third Party or give further consideration to any alternative.'

Despite the insistence by Mr Naughton upon the implied term pleaded in the amendment involving the obligation to negotiate, Bingham LJ, in his dissenting judgment, considered that that obligation could be severed from the agreement. He concluded that the agreement, as originally pleaded, was a valid and enforceable agreement and entitled the appellants to recover whatever damages they could establish resulted in law from its repudiation.

Before considering the basis of Bingham LJ's judgment, I believe it is helpful to make these observations about a so-called 'lock-out' agreement. There is clearly no reason in English contract law why A, for good consideration, should not achieve an enforceable agreement whereby B agrees for a specified period of time not to negotiate with anyone except A in relation to the sale of his property. There are often good commercial reasons why A should desire to obtain such an agreement from B. B's property which A contemplates purchasing may be such as to require the expenditure of not inconsiderable time and money before A is in a position to assess what he is prepared to offer for its purchase or whether he wishes to make any offer at all. A may well consider that he is not prepared to run the risk of expending such time and money unless there is a worthwhile prospect, should he desire to make an offer to purchase, of B, not only then still owning the property, but of being prepared to consider his offer. A may wish to guard against the risk that, while he is investigating the wisdom of offering to buy B's property, B may have already disposed of it or, alternatively, may be so advanced in negotiations with a third party as to be unwilling or for all practical purposes unable to negotiate with A. But I stress that this is a negative agreement—B, by agreeing not to negotiate for this fixed period with a third party, locks himself out of such negotiations. He has in no legal sense locked himself *into* negotiations with A. What A has achieved is an exclusive opportunity, for a fixed period, to try and come to terms with B, an opportunity for which he has, unless he makes his agreement under seal, to give good consideration. I therefore cannot accept Mr Naughton's proposition, which was the essential reason for his amending para 5 of the statement of claim by the addition of the implied term, that without a positive obligation on B to negotiate with A the lock-out agreement would be futile.

The agreement alleged in para 5 of the unamended statement of claim contains the essential characteristics of a basic valid lock-out agreement, save one. It does not specify for how long it is to last. Bingham LJ sought to cure this deficiency by holding that the obligation upon the respondents not to deal with other parties should continue to bind them 'for such time as is reasonable' in all the circumstances. He said:

> '...the time would end once the parties, acting in good faith, had found themselves unable to come to mutually acceptable terms...The defendants could not...bring the reasonable time to an end by procuring a bogus impasse, since that would involve a breach of the duty of reasonable good faith which parties such as these must, I think, be taken to owe to each other.'

However, as Bingham LJ recognised, such a duty, if it existed, would indirectly impose upon the respondents a duty to negotiate in good faith. Such a duty, for the reasons which I have given above, cannot be imposed. That it should have been thought necessary to assert such a duty helps to explain the reason behind the amendment to para 5 and the insistence of Mr Naughton that without the implied term the agreement, as originally pleaded, was unworkable—unworkable because there was no way of determining for how long the respondents were locked out from negotiating with any third party.

Thus, even if, despite the way in which the Walford's case was pleaded and argued, the severance favoured by Bingham LJ was permissible, the resultant agreement suffered from the same defect (although for different reasons) as the agreement contended for in the amended statement of claim, namely that it too lacked the necessary certainty, and was thus unenforceable.

I would accordingly dismiss this appeal with costs.

The other members of the Judicial Committee agreed with Lord Ackner.

Appeal dismissed.

NOTES

1. How would you categorise Lord Ackner's view of the role the law should play in the bargaining process? (Compare Adams and Brownsword, p 57).

2. Many legal systems, including some common law ones (see Finn J in *Hughes Aircraft Systems International v Air Services Australia* (1997) 146 ALR 1), now recognise that there may be a duty to negotiate in good faith. In one way and another, English law has got closer to this position than is widely recognised. See Furmston, Norisada and Poole, *Contract Formation and Letters of Intent*, chapter 10, which contains references to much of the growing literature in this field; see also the reading at p 283.

3. There are no doubt contract negotiations that are fundamentally adversarial, eg if two commodity traders are haggling over the price of wheat. Do you think this is true of all contract negotiation? Compare the attitudes shown by business people in the empirical surveys described above. If the attitude of the parties is more cooperative than adversarial, should the law try to be more supportive of attempts to create a legal framework for future negotiation? Or do you think that this is best left to non-legal sanctions?

4. Suppose the law were to recognise a contract to negotiate in good faith: would the Miles have been in breach of it? It is not as if they sold to the third party because the third party was going to pay more for the property. They seem rather to have had second thoughts about the wisdom of selling to the Walfords because of concerns about how all their staff would get on with them and because they thought Mr Miles' health might suffer during the year he would have to work with the Walfords. If an unforeseen difficulty arises, is that a good reason for breaking off relations? What if the difficulty is one that they could have foreseen when the agreement was made but which seemed to become ominous as time went on?

5. If a contract to negotiate in good faith were to be recognised, how should the damages be calculated? Should the disappointed party get the full profit it would have made had the contract been concluded? Some proportion of that as damages for 'loss of chance' (compare *Chaplin v Hicks* [1911] 2 KB 786, in which an actress was wrongly prevented from attending the final of a beauty contest and was awarded damages for loss of the chance to win)? The loss of other opportunities for profitable deals passed over in reliance on the agreement? Or just the expenditure wasted in reliance on it? What were the Walfords claiming and what did they in fact recover (on the basis of misrepresentation)? These questions are helpfully discussed in *Harmon CFEM Facades v Corporate Officer of House of Commons* (2000) 72 Con LR 21 (see p 248) although not in a case that was explicitly based on a duty to negotiate in good faith. This case would certainly support a claim for wasted expenditure (cost of tendering) and in appropriate circumstances for loss of the chance of making a profit.

6. Lord Ackner's dictum that a 'lockout' agreement would be enforceable was followed by the Court of Appeal in *Pitt v PHH Asset Management Ltd* [1993] 4 All ER 961.

7. In the Canadian case *of Empress Towers Ltd v Bank of Nova Scotia* (1991) 73 DLR (4th) 400, the parties were respectively landlords and tenants of an office block. The lease provided for periodic rent renewals as follows:

23. Renewal:
The Landlord hereby grants to the Tenant rights of renewal of this Lease for two successive periods of five (5) years each, such rights to be exercisable by three (3) months' written notice from the

Tenant, subject to all the terms and conditions herein contained excepting any right of renewal beyond the second five (5) years period *and excepting the rental for any renewal period, which shall be the market rental prevailing at the commencement of that renewal term as mutually agreed between the Landlord and the Tenant.* If the Landlord and the Tenant do not agree upon the renewal rental within two (2) months following the exercise of a renewal option, then this agreement may be terminated at the option of either party.

> The 1984 lease was due to expire on 31 August 1989. On 25 May 1989, the bank exercised its option to renew for five years and proposed a rental of $5,400 a month. The landlord made no effective response until the last day of the first five-year term, when it asked not only for $5,400 a month but for a premium of $15,000 and a revision of the terms making the lease terminable on 90 days' notice. The majority of the British Columbia Court of Appeal held that the renewal clause did not amount to an agreement to renew at the prevailing market rent. Lambert JA said

In my opinion, the effect of the requirement for mutual agreement must be that the landlord cannot be compelled to enter into a renewal tenancy at a rent which it has not accepted as the market rental. But, in my opinion, that is not the only effect of the requirement of mutual agreement. It also carried with it, first, an implied term that the landlord will negotiate in good faith with the tenant with the objective of reaching an agreement on the market rental rate and, secondly, that agreement on a market rental will not be unreasonably withheld: . . . Those terms are to be implied under the officious bystander and business efficacy principles in order to permit the renewal clause, which was clearly intended to have legal effect, from being struck down as uncertain. The key to implying the terms that I have set out is that the parties agreed that there should be a right of renewal at the prevailing market rental. (I do not have to decide in this case whether a bare right of renewal at a rental to be agreed carries with it an obligation to negotiate in good faith or not to withhold agreement unreasonably.)

8.   In *Teachers Insurance and Annuity Association of America v Tribune Company* 670 F Supp 491 (USDC, SDNY 1987), an action was brought by an institutional lender against a prospective borrower charging the borrower with breach of a commitment letter agreement for a 14-year $76m loan yielding 15.25 per cent. The exchange of letters constituting the commitment agreement stated that the borrower and lender had made a 'binding agreement' to borrow and to lend on the agreed terms, subject to the preparation and execution of final documents satisfactory to both sides and the approval of the borrower's board of directors. Prior to the preparation of final agreements, the borrower broke off negotiations, declining to negotiate further unless the lender agreed that the borrower's obligation to borrow would be contingent on its ability to report the loan on its financial statement by an off-balance-sheet offset. The court held that there was a binding commitment. Pierre N Leval, USDJ said:

Teachers argues that although the commitment letter did not constitute a concluded loan agreement, it was nonetheless a binding commitment which obligated both sides to negotiate in good faith toward a final contract conforming to the agreed terms; it thus committed both sides not to abandon the deal, nor to break it by a demand that was outside the scope of the agreement. . . .

Contractual liability, unlike tort liability, arises from consent to be bound (or in any event from the manifestation of consent). It is fundamental to contract law that mere participation in negotiations and discussions does not create binding obligation, even if agreement is reached on all disputed terms. More is needed than agreement on each detail, which is overall agreement (or offer and acceptance) to enter into the binding contract. Nor is this principle altered by the fact that negotiating parties may have entered into letters of intent or preliminary agreements if those were made with the understanding that neither side would be bound until final agreement was reached . . .

Preliminary contracts with binding force can be of at least two distinct types. One occurs when the parties have reached complete agreement (including the agreement to be bound) on all the issues perceived to require negotiation. Such an agreement is preliminary only in form—only in the sense that the parties desire a more elaborate formalization of the agreement. The second stage is not necessary; it is merely considered desirable . . . The second and different sort of preliminary binding agreement is one that expresses mutual commitment to a contract on agreed major terms, while recognizing the existence of open terms that remain to be negotiated. Although the existence of open terms generally suggests that binding agreement has not been reached, that is not necessarily so. For the parties can bind themselves to a concededly incomplete agreement in the sense that they accept a mutual commitment to negotiate together in good faith in an effort to reach final agreement within the scope that has been settled in the preliminary agreement. To differentiate this sort of preliminary agreement from the first, it might be referred to as a binding preliminary commitment. Its binding obligations are of a different order than those which arise out of the first type discussed above. The first type binds both sides to their ultimate contractual objective in recognition that that contract has been reached, despite the anticipation of further formalities. The second type—the binding preliminary commitment—does not commit the parties to their ultimate contractual objective but rather to the obligation to negotiate the open issues in good faith in an attempt to reach the alternate objective within the agreed framework. In the first type, a party may lawfully demand performance of the transaction even if no further steps have been taken following the making of the 'preliminary' agreement. In the second type, he may not. What he may demand, however, is that his counterparty negotiate the open terms in good faith toward a final contract incorporating the agreed terms. This obligation does not guarantee that the final contract will be concluded if both parties comport with their obligation, as good faith differences in the negotiation of the open issues may prevent a reaching of final contract. It is also possible that the parties will lose interest as circumstances change and will mutually abandon the negotiation. The obligation does, however, bar a party from renouncing the deal, abandoning the negotiations, or insisting on conditions that do not conform to the preliminary agreement . . .

Giving legal recognition to preliminary binding commitments serves a valuable function in the marketplace, particularly for relatively standardized transactions like loans. It permits borrowers and lenders to make plans in reliance upon their preliminary agreements and present market conditions. Without such legal recognition, parties would be obliged to expend enormous sums negotiating every detail of final contract documentation before knowing whether they have an agreement, and if so, on what terms. At the same time, a party that does not wish to be bound at the time of the preliminary exchange of letters can very easily protect itself by not accepting language that indicates a 'firm commitment' or 'binding agreement'.

Upon careful consideration of the circumstances and the express terms of this commitment letter, I conclude that it represented a binding preliminary commitment . . . the reservation of Board approval and the expressed 'contingen[cy] upon the preparation, execution and delivery of documents' did not override and nullify the acknowledgement that a 'binding agreement' had been made on the stated terms . . .

Compare *Arcadian Phosphates, Inc v Arcadian Corpn* 884 F2d 69 (USCA 2d Circuit, 1989), in which it was held that there was no adequate indication that the parties intended to be bound. However, it was said that a promise to negotiate in good faith might raise issues of promissory estoppel. The US law is discussed by Farnsworth (1987) 87 Columbia LR 217, 264ff.

If the further step can be defined with sufficient certainty, a useful device in this context is the conditional contract.

■ *Ee v Kakar* (1979)

40 P & CR 223

The defendant agreed to sell his house to the plaintiff for £14, 250 'subject to survey of the property', but later repudiated the agreement. The plaintiff brought an action for specific performance, claiming that because the condition was in his favour, he could waive it.

Walton J

...[A]t the end of the day there is one and only one crucial question in the case, namely, what is the effect of the words 'subject to survey'. I therefore now turn to that crucial question, which is whether the document of April 1, 1978, is or is not a contract.

It is said that the words 'subject to survey' are in law equivalent to the words 'subject to contract' and produce the same result.

[Walton J referred to *Marks v Board*, in which Rowlatt J had held that an agreement 'subject to surveyor's report' was not binding, and continued:]

The nub of the judgment is contained in the few words 'there was no contract because the buyer was not yet bound and, therefore, the seller was not bound either'.

It appears to me to be well settled that, in order to constitute a contract, there must be consideration on both sides. Consideration consists in the suffering of detriment by the person furnishing the consideration, not necessarily in a benefit to the other party to the contract. I need do no more than refer to *Currie v Misa*.

The oddity of the decision, as I see it, in *Marks v Board* [is that] Rowlatt J recognised, as I should in any event have thought would have been obvious, that as a result of the— I shall use the neutral word— document in question, the purchaser became bound to obtain a surveyor's report. In other words, he was not free simply to say, 'I am not going on with the transaction', although, doubtless subject to a qualification I shall pose hereafter, he was free when he had received the report to come to his own conclusion as to whether he was satisfied with it or not. Looking further ahead, if the purchaser had not obtained such a report within a reasonable time, it would then, I should have thought, have been too late for him to resile from the document. He would have waived this condition completely.

If that be correct, then the purchaser does furnish consideration. He has to obtain a surveyor's report, and that will cost him money, and money which will not be *de minimis* either. He has therefore suffered detriment, and so given consideration. Hence, it appears to me that the inevitable conclusion is that, the document being otherwise on its face intended to take effect as a contract, it will do so.

I can myself see no reason why, although of course retaining the right to be satisfied with any kind of report, a purchaser should not be bound, if presented with a report which is basically a satisfactory one, to have to act bona fide, just as he must, as I take it, in any event, proceed with due diligence. Although the two tests are quite clearly not the same, if a reasonable man would be satisfied with the report. I should have thought that a purchaser would experience some difficulty in persuading a court that his failure to proceed with the contract was bona fide. ...

There is also another possible analysis of the legal situation which can be made, which leads to the same result. In *Lee-Parker v Izzet (No 2)* the contract for sale contained the clause, 'Subject to the purchaser obtaining a satisfactory mortgage.' This clause was, indeed and obviously, held to be void for uncertainty, but it was first analysed as constituting a condition precedent.

Now it is well settled that a contract may be made subject to conditions precedent, for example, *Aberfoyle Plantations Ltd v Cheng, Smallman v Smallman* in both of which cases the condition precedent—in one case fulfilled and the other not—was contained in the contract.

So far as I am aware, it has never been suggested that, provided the condition is not void for uncertainty, its form or any question of consideration is of any materiality. So here, provided that it is a real condition, I see no reason why the condition 'subject to survey' should not represent a simple suspensory condition, suspensory of a contract as to which there can be no question as to the consideration furnished by each side.

Of course I would readily agree that, if the condition was an illusory one, that is to say, the fulfilment of which was wholly at the whim of one party, the case would be different. But the condition as to survey is not, because, at the least, the purchaser must obtain the survey and consider it and, in my judgment, also act bona fide.

So, looked at from this slightly different point of view, it also appears to me that the document of April 1, 1978, was a perfectly valid and binding contract.

I think the only other point in the case which arises, arises from the fact that the statement of claim, somewhat oddly, pleads waiver of the condition rather than fulfilment, which, I gather is what in fact happened. It is of course well settled that a party to a contract can waive a condition wholly in his favour: see, for example, *Heron Garage Properties Ltd v Moss*. This form of the pleadings afford Mr Raffety an opportunity of arguing that the condition in the present case was not one exclusively in favour of the plaintiff, but that, as the defendant was also clearly interested in the condition of the property, it was one in favour of both parties, and hence one which could not be unilaterally waived in this manner. I cannot, I am afraid, accept this submission.

To test it, suppose that the plaintiff had obtained a surveyor's report, which, let us suppose, had stated that the property was in a deplorable condition, but that, as a result of some wholly extraneous factor, plans to build a swimming pool nearby, the property had become an absolute bargain at the contract price. What would there be in the contract to prevent the plaintiff notifying the defendant that the survey was acceptable to him and he was proceeding to go ahead with the transaction? So far as I can see, nothing. There is no provision for disclosure of the report to the defendant under any circumstances at all.

It follows, in my judgment, that the plaintiff in the present action succeeds on all counts.

NOTES

1.   What is the vendor's position if the purchaser (i) fails to get a survey or (ii) refuses to go ahead on the ground that he is dissatisfied with the report even though the report is largely a favourable one?

2.   Walton J referred to *Lee-Parker v Izzet (No 2)* [1972] 2 All ER 800, where an agreement to buy and sell land 'subject to the purchaser obtaining a satisfactory mortgage' was held invalid for uncertainty. There is no doubt that conditions must be sufficiently certain, but whether a condition in such terms passes the test has provoked widespread differences of judicial opinion. See *Meehan v Jones* (1982) 42 ALR 463 (High Court of Australia); Furmston (1983) 3 Oxford J of Legal Studies 438.

3.   In *Heron Garage Properties Ltd v Moss* [1974] 1 All ER 421, land had been sold subject to the purchasers obtaining planning permission for use as a filling station. The vendor had retained adjoining land on which he planned to build a car showroom. Brightman J held that, because having a filling station on the land sold might benefit both the parties, the condition was for the benefit of both, and the purchasers could not waive it and insist on the land being conveyed to them when they failed to get the permission.

The fulfilment of the condition is quite often outside the control of either party, for example, sale of Blackacre 'subject to planning permission being obtained for use as a hotel'. In such a case, one party will commonly be under a subsidiary obligation to make a serious application for permission: see *Hargreaves Transport Ltd v Lynch* [1969] 1 All ER 455.

IV. WORK DONE AND STEPS TAKEN BEFORE A CONTRACT HAS BEEN AGREED

It is quite common for the parties to start work before the contract has been fully negotiated or signed. When the contract is ultimately signed, it will (unless otherwise agreed) 'relate back' so as to apply to what has been done: *Trollope & Colls Ltd v Atomic Power Constructions Ltd* [1962] 3 All ER 1035. What if agreement is never reached?

■ *British Steel Corpn v Cleveland Bridge and Engineering Co Ltd*
[1984] 1 All ER 504, Robert Goff J (see p 38)

NOTES

1. There may still be liability on a *quantum meruit* even if the work done at the defendant's request is ultimately of no use to him, such as the preparation of detailed estimates, as required by the licensing authority, of the cost of converting a building that, ultimately, the defendant sells without converting: *William Lacey (Hounslow) Ltd v Davis* [1957] 2 All ER 712. In *Regalian Properties plc v London Dockland Development Corpn* [1995] 1 All ER 1005, Rattee J held that the plaintiff could not recover for very substantial wasted expenditure in relation to a development that (without fault on either side) was eventually aborted because the plaintiff always knew that payment depended on the development going ahead. The opposite view was taken on very similar facts by Sheppard J in *Sabemo Pty Ltd v North Sydney Municipal Council* [1977] 2 NSWLR 880.

2. The *British Steel* case did not decide that letters of intent never give rise to contracts: it decided that there was no contract on the particular facts of the case. The only safe rule is that one must examine the facts with great care. Sometimes, a letter of intent will be a non-binding expression of goodwill; sometimes, it will be an instruction to start work and to pay for some defined preliminary steps; sometimes, it will be a full-blown contract. A good example is *A C Controls Ltd v British Broadcasting Corporation* (2002) 89 Con LR 52.

3. A full survey of the cases may be found in Jones, 'Claims Arising out of Anticipated Contracts which do not Materialise' (1980) 18 Univ of W Ontario LR 447.

What if one party, to the knowledge of the other and perhaps encouraged by him, takes some steps other than beginning to perform in anticipation of a contract that never materialises? Should he have some remedy, or should he be regarded as having proceeded at his own risk? If there should sometimes be a remedy, under what circumstances should it be available and what form should it take? A problem of this type arose in *Hoffman v Red Owl Stores Inc* 26 Wis 2d 683, 133 NW 2d 267 (1965). Hoffman wanted to obtain a franchise to operate a Red Owl store, and the Red Owl agent encouraged him to take several steps in preparation, such as selling his existing business, moving house and buying a site for the new store. The franchise never materialised. The jury found that Red Owl had represented to Hoffman that if he fulfilled certain conditions he would get a franchise, and that he had fulfilled these conditions when the negotiations broke down because Red Owl unexpectedly increased the amount of capital that Hoffman was required to put into the store to be the subject of the franchise.

Hoffman was awarded his reliance loss. Currie CJ said:

There remains for consideration the question of law raised by defendants that agreement was never reached on essential factors necessary to establish a contract between Hoffman and Red Owl. Among these were the size, cost, design, and layout of the store building; and the terms of the lease with respect to rent, maintenance, renewal, and purchase options. This poses the question of whether the promise necessary to sustain a cause of action for promissory estoppel must embrace all essential details of a proposed transaction between promisor and promisee so as to be the equivalent of an offer that would result in a binding contract between the parties if the promisee were to accept the same.

Originally the doctrine of promissory estoppel was invoked as a substitute for consideration rendering a gratuitous promise enforceable as a contract. See Williston, Contracts (1st ed) p 307, sec 139. In other words, the acts of reliance by the promisee to his detriment provided a substitute for consideration. If promissory estoppel were to be limited to only those situations where the promise giving rise to the cause of action must be so definite with respect to all details that a contract would result were the promise supported by consideration, then the defendants' instant promises to Hoffman would not meet this test. However, sec. 90 of Restatement, 1 Contracts, does not impose the requirement that the promise giving rise to the cause of action must be so comprehensive in scope as to meet the requirements of an offer that would ripen into a contract if accepted by the promisee. Rather the conditions imposed are:

(1) Was the promise one which the promisor should reasonably expect to induce action or forbearance of a definite and substantial character on the part of the promisee?
(2) Did the promise induce such action or forbearance?
(3) Can injustice be avoided only by enforcement of the promise?

We deem it would be a mistake to regard an action grounded on promissory estoppel as the equivalent of a breach of contract action. As Dean Boyer points out, it is desirable that fluidity in the application of the concept be maintained, 98 University of Pennsylvania Law Review (1950), 459, at page 497. While the first two of the above listed three requirements of promissory estoppel present issues of fact which ordinarily will be resolved by a jury, the third requirement, that the remedy can only be invoked where necessary to avoid injustice, is one that involves a policy decision by the court. Such a policy decision necessarily embraces an element of discretion.

We conclude that injustice would result here if plaintiffs were not granted some relief because of the failure of defendants to keep their promises which induced plaintiffs to act to their detriment.

See also *Wheeler v White* 398 SW 2d 93 (Sup Ct of Texas, 1966), in which one party, encouraged by the other, had taken steps in reliance on a contract that the court held was void for uncertainty, and was held to be entitled to recover his reliance loss. The majority said:

. . . [W]here there is actually no contract the promissory estoppel theory may be invoked, thereby supplying a remedy which will enable the injured party to be compensated for his foreseeable, definite and substantial reliance. Where the promisee has failed to bind the promisor to a legally sufficient contract, but where the promisee has acted in reliance upon a promise to his detriment, the promisee is to be allowed to recover no more than reliance damages measured by the detriment sustained.

Could such a result be reached in English law? Where one party has indicated that the other will get an interest in property, similar results have already been reached under the doctrine of proprietary estoppel (see pp 155–158). Note that in one way, *Crabb v Arun District Council* (see p 155) went beyond the US authorities: the council did not actively encourage Crabb to sell his front plot. Their position seems to have been much closer to that of the potential lessees in *Walton Stores* (see p 158). Where that case goes beyond the English authorities is that it did not relate to an indication that the plaintiffs would be given an interest in property.

Perhaps the most significant English case here is *Baird Textile Holdings Ltd v Marks and Spencer plc* [2001] EWCA Civ 274 [2002] 1 All ER (Comm) 737, although it is significant for what the Court of Appeal did *not* do rather than for what it did.

The claimant (Baird) had been one of the principal suppliers of garments to the defendants (M&S) for thirty years. Very substantial orders were placed by M&S, predominantly twice a year, for the summer and winter seasons. These orders clearly gave rise to contracts. There was nothing on paper about the long-term relationship, although there appear to have been extensive informal contacts. It seems that this was the way in which M&S wished to manage its relationships with its suppliers.

In October 1999, M&S told Baird that the relationship would come to an end at the end of the current production season without any previous notice. Baird argued that it was entitled to reasonable notice, which it said would be three years. It put this argument on the basis either that there was a contract or that M&S should be estopped.

The Court of Appeal upheld M&S's application that the proceedings should be struck out on the grounds that they disclosed no reasonable cause of action. This meant that the evidence was not considered and, in particular, that there was no disclosure (that is, the process by which each side has access to the other side's files and papers). This might have revealed internal memoranda discussing policy towards suppliers.

The Court of Appeal thought it clear that there was no contract. It clearly found the estoppel argument more difficult and, in effect, said that if *Waltons v Maher* were English law, the case would have to go to trial, but that it would need a decision of the House of Lords for *Waltons v Maher* to become English law.

Does the decision in *Baird* seem fair to you? Remembering that we generally decide these matters objectively, what do you think Baird should have deduced from M&S's behaviour? What do you think would have happened if it had pressed M&S to state its long-term intentions?

Not all American courts and writers think *Hoffmann v Red Owl* is a great decision. In an important article in (2007) 120 Harvard LR 662, Schwartz and Scott criticise the case (at 668–671), and see discussion on p 808 below.

When the parties are involved in drawn-out negotiations, their situation is to some extent 'relational' (see Macneil, p 63) and it is not surprising to find parties relying on rather unclear indications of intent, informal understandings and on the other party 'not backing out'. With this in mind, you may like to look at the extract from Feinman, on p 805.

At this point, it is worth returning to a question raised several times in the chapters above: should English law recognise a duty of good faith? One writer who has considered this in some detail is Brownsword. The following extract is intended to give the flavour of his thinking.

■ **Brownsword** *Contract Law: Themes for the Twenty-First Century*
(2nd edn, 2006)
pp 114, 119–121, 123–128, 129–131

The sceptical view

The arguments against adopting a general principle of good faith are well-rehearsed. At least five negative themes are recurrent.

...

To sum up, the case against the adoption of a general principle of good faith is that English contract law is premised on adversarial self-interested dealing (rather than other-regarding good faith dealing); that good faith is a vague idea, threatening to import an uncertain discretion into English law; that the implementation of a good faith doctrine would call for difficult inquiries into contracting parties' reasons in particular cases; that good faith represents a challenge to the autonomy of contracting parties; and, that a general doctrine cannot be appropriate when contracting contexts vary so much—in particular, harking back to the first objection, a general doctrine of good faith would make little sense in those contracting contexts in which the participants regulate their dealings in a way that openly tolerates opportunism.

Neutrality and scepticism

In the *Interfoto* case, Sir Thomas Bingham, having noted that many legal systems employ a doctrine of good faith to regulate fair dealing in contract, observed that English law has arrived at much the same position by developing 'piecemeal solutions in response to demonstrated problems of unfairness'. Such remarks might be read as encouraging a pragmatic neutrality towards good faith. According to this view, whilst there is nothing intrinsically objectionable about a good faith doctrine, English law has its own doctrinal tools for achieving the results that are achieved via a good faith doctrine in other jurisdictions. Moreover, Sir Thomas's relatively sanguine assessment seems to be vindicated by both the approach and the outcome of *Interfoto* where, in the context of a commercial contract, the English doctrine of 'reasonable notice' was manipulated to disallow a standard term that had not been adequately disclosed—English piecemeal solutions, in other words, are no less effective than single principle good faith solutions.

The paradigm of neutrality holds: (i) that there is a strict equivalence between a general doctrine of good faith and the piecemeal provisions of English law that regulate fair dealing (we can call this 'the equivalence thesis'); and (ii) that it makes no difference whether English law operates with a general doctrine or with piecemeal provisions (we can call this 'the indifference thesis'). Once we differentiate between the equivalence and the indifference theses, and once we distinguish between holding these theses in the abstract as against in the context of an ongoing legal system, it becomes apparent that the neutral view has a strong bias to slide towards the negative view.

One way in which this bias will reveal itself is if we imagine a neutral, who accepts both the equivalence and the indifference theses *in the abstract*, but who is now asked whether it would be sensible to replace the English piecemeal approach with a general doctrine of good faith. Clearly, since (*ex hypothesi*) nothing is to be gained by replacing one approach with the other, the neutral must take a negative view on this practical question (unless, for some bizarre reason, incurring transaction costs is judged to be a good thing).

...

In his seminal paper ['Good Faith in Contracts' (1956) 9 CLP 16, 26], Raphael Powell argued that the adoption of a good faith doctrine would be beneficial in that it would enable the English courts to avoid having 'to resort to contortions or subterfuges in order to give effect to their sense of the justice of the case'. Moreover, citing the notorious decision in *L'Estrange v Graucob Ltd* and implicitly rejecting a neutral view, Powell argued that a good faith doctrine would sometimes be a more powerful and effective resource than the favoured English tools for dealing with perceived unfairness. Although such a positive view is probably shared by no more than a minority of English contract lawyers, at least four arguments can be offered in its support as follows.

First, to the extent that English law already tries to regulate bad faith dealing, it might be argued that it would be more rational to address the problem directly (rather than indirectly) and openly (rather than covertly) by adopting a general principle of good faith. This is Powell's first line of argument and it is a familiar theme in the North American literature advocating adoption of good faith.

...

Secondly, in the absence of a doctrine of good faith, it may be argued—as Powell contended in relation to English law...—that the law of contract is ill-equipped to achieve fair results, on occasion leaving judges 'unable to do justice at all'. This particular argument in favour of good faith can be developed in several ways. For example, if we imagine good faith as an umbrella principle, covering, unifying, infusing, and filling the gaps between a range of specific doctrines designed to secure fair dealing, then in hard cases (of the kind that supposedly make bad law) judges could appeal to the umbrella principle to justify a one-off decision, or to adumbrate some new principle of fairness, or to extend the range of an already recognised principle (for example, extending the range of equitable estoppel into pre-contractual dealings, or extending the principle of duress to some forms of economic pressure, and so on). So equipped, judges in the *appeal courts*, would have no need *covertly* to stretch and manipulate existing resources; and they would have no excuse for handing down patently unfair decisions—with good faith in play, *L'Estrange v Graucob* becomes *Tilden Rent-A-Car v Clendenning*. Moreover, in the *trial courts*, judges who might otherwise bow to the pressure of precedent, would have the opportunity to avoid declaring that hard cases simply yield hard decisions. With good faith openly adopted as a foundational doctrine, there would be no need for *sub rosa* adjudication; and both trial judges and appeal courts would have the legal support that they require.

Thirdly, turning on its head one of the negative arguments against a general principle of good faith, it might be argued that, with such a principle, the courts are better equipped to respond to the varying expectations encountered in the many different contracting contexts—and, in particular, it might be argued that the courts are better able to detect co-operative dealing where it is taking place. Thus, the argument runs, if English contract law adopted a doctrine of good faith, it would pose questions of contractual interpretation and implication in a context, not only of background standards of fair dealing, but more immediately of the concrete expectations of the parties. Such concrete expectations would be based as much on the way that the parties related to one another (whether they dealt with one another in an adversarial or non-adversarial manner) as on the express provisions of the agreement. As a result, English law would recover the ability to give effect to the spirit of the deal in a way that prioritised the parties' own expectations.

To appreciate the significance of this argument, consider the judgment of the Court of Appeal in the BSkyB case [Philips Electronique Grand Public SA v British Sky Broadcasting Ltd; Philips International BV v British Satellite Broadcasting Ltd [1995] EMLR 472]. The dispute in this case arose out of a number of agreements made in 1989 and 1990 between British Satellite Broadcasting (BSB) and Philips at the time that BSB and Sky were locked in competition to control the satellite television market in the UK. By late 1990, BSB had lost the battle and had merged with Sky. One of the results of this merger was that Philips, who had contracted with BSB to develop and manufacture receivers for the BSB system, were left with unsold stock, surplus manufacturing capacity, and no continuing opportunity to sell the receivers. Philips tried to recoup their losses by arguing that BSB were in breach of various implied terms of their agreements, but particularly an implied term to the effect that BSB 'would not commit any act which would tend to impede or render impossible the marketing of the Receivers and/or to render the Receivers useless or unmarketable'. Although Philips persuaded the trial judge that such an implied term was part of the agreement, they failed before the Court of Appeal. According to Sir Thomas Bingham MR:

> 'Had the parties addressed their minds at the outset to the eventuality that the operation turned out to be a major commercial flop, it is by no means clear how they would have agreed that the risk should be allocated or, if they had agreed that Philips should be protected, what form they would have agreed that that protection should take. It seems likely that there would have been tough negotiation, with Philips seeking maximum protection and BSB conceding the minimum.'

Sir Thomas, however, was not wholly unsympathetic to Philips's position for he indicated that, if it had been material, he would have been prepared to 'imply a term that BSB should act with good faith in the performance of [the] contract'.

In the *BSkyB* case, we find the court willing to speak the language of good faith performance, and yet apparently respecting the orthodox view that only such terms as can be confidently attributed to the parties' unstated intentions are to be implied. Underlying this orthodoxy is an adversarial model of each contracting party seeking to maximise its utility, as in Sir Thomas's picture of tough negotiation, with one side seeking the maximum protection against risk and the other side conceding the minimum. If the adoption of a doctrine of good faith simply adds a rhetorical gloss to this orthodox view, it involves no substantive change to the law.

We need to look more carefully, however, at Sir Thomas's model of the negotiating situation. The classical version of this model is one of tough self-interested bargaining in the context of a discrete contract—it is a model of self-interested dealers converging on a market-place, making their one-off exchanges, and going their separate ways. However, although we can assume that BSB and Philips would meet as self-interested dealers, the classical picture is hardly appropriate. For one thing, the transaction between BSB and Philips was more in the nature of a joint venture than a spot contract and, equally importantly, we must assume that each party would pursue its self-interest in a reasonably enlightened way. With these revisions to the classical picture, we can see that the parties' 'tough negotiation, with Philips seeking maximum protection and BSB conceding the minimum' is potentially constrained in at least three respects. First, prudent would-be contractors must calculate the disutility of failed negotiations (ie no contract) and give ground up to the point where the disutility of concession is less than the disutility of being excluded from the deal. Secondly, where the contractors are involved in long-term dealing, intelligent negotiation will involve smaller (expected) short-term utilities being subordinated to greater (expected) long-term utilities. Thirdly, and linked to the second point, the symbolic utility of a co-operative gesture is one element that must enter into an enlightened contractor's calculations. Of course, the background picture remains one of minimal concession and, even if we assume constraints against the blinkered pursuit of short-term self-interest, this does not demonstrate that, if the question of the venture failing had been raised during negotiations, BSB would have agreed to underwrite some of the risk to which Philips would be exposed. However, once we have transposed the issue from the classical context of the discrete (spot) contract and short-term adversarial dealing to the context of longer term dealing with a willingness to invest in the future, it is a great deal more plausible to imply terms that involve some act of co-operation or sharing of risk—and, what is more, to do this on the basis that such implications are necessary if we are to be faithful to the parties' unex-pressed intentions and expectations. In other words, if a good faith doctrine is adopted there is a substantive change to the law; but it is not so much a rewriting of general principle as a recognition that adversarial dealing is not the only game in town and, concomitantly, a modification to our appreciation of the possible range of transactional settings within which doctrine is to be applied.

This third argument in favour of good faith might be put more directly in terms of the protection of reasonable expectation. Indeed, Lord Steyn has recently couched the argument in precisely this way, taking as his starting point the idea that the principal task for the modern law of contract is to protect the contractors' reasonable expectations. Having outlined the revisionist nature of such a general principle in relation to questions of formation, privity, and the like, Lord Steyn turns to criticise the narrow approach in *Walford v Miles*, claiming that a good faith principle is perfectly practical and workable. However, he continues:

> 'I have no heroic suggestion for the introduction of a general duty of good faith in our contract law. It is not necessary. As long as our courts always respect the reasonable expectations of parties our contract law can satisfactorily be left to develop in accordance with its own pragmatic traditions. And where in specific contexts duties of good faith are imposed on parties our legal system can readily accommodate such a well tried notion. After all, there is not a world of difference between the objective requirement of good faith and the reasonable expectations of parties.' ['Contract Law: Fulfilling the Reasonable Expectations of Honest Men' (1997) 113 LQR 433 at 439]

Although this might be mistaken for the neutral view, it is in fact a quite different position. Lord Steyn's (implicit) premise is that there is no equivalence between the traditional piecemeal approach of English law and a general requirement of good faith. Having rejected the equivalence thesis, his argument is that we should adopt what is in effect a general duty of good faith but that this can be cast in the more familiar form of a general principle that the reasonable expectations of the parties should be respected (and, to this extent, we can be indifferent about our doctrinal terminology). In other words, an overriding principle of reasonable expectation serves the same purpose as a general principle of good faith. The language might be different but the idea is the same.

Finally, it is arguable that the beneficial effects of a good faith doctrine go beyond (reactive) dispute-settlement, for a good faith contractual environment has the potential to give contracting parties greater security and, thus, greater flexibility about the ways in which they are prepared to do business. In a society without any kind of contract law dealing will tend to be very defensive—present (and simultaneous) exchange will be the order of the day, credit being extended only to those who are already known and trusted. Whilst English law goes some way towards meeting the concerns of defensive contractors and, to some extent, liberates practice, it falls short of what is required if the potential synergies of co-operation are to be fully exploited.

. . .

In sum, there are four strands in the positive view of good faith. A good faith doctrine allows problems of bad faith to be addressed in a clean and direct fashion; it enables judges at all levels to deal in a coherent and an effective manner with cases of unfair dealing; it can bring the law much more closely into alignment with the protection of reasonable expectations (which, it must be recognised, vary from one contracting situation to another); and it can contribute to a culture of trust and co-operation that enhances the autonomy of contractors and that, on a larger scale, is an important feature of successful economies.

What are we to make of the arguments for and against adopting a general doctrine of good faith? This rather depends on which model of good faith we have in mind; for, essentially, there are three such models, each of which needs to be made explicit before either the negative or the positive arguments can be evaluated. The first model, 'a good faith requirement' as we can call it, simply acts on the standards of fair dealing that are already recognised in a particular contracting context. These standards may or may not yet have crystallised into express terms commonly used, but they nevertheless represent the informal expectations of those who deal in the particular market. The second model, 'a good faith regime' as we may term it, acts on the standards of fair dealing that are dictated by a critical morality of co-operation. Unlike the first model of good faith, this second model does not track recognised standards (although it may sometimes coincide with them) but, instead, tries to make the market in the sense of prescribing the co-operative ground rules. The third model of good faith is what Michael Bridge evocatively calls 'visceral justice'. Here, judges react impressionistically to the merits of a situation and dispose of cases accordingly—all in the name of good faith. Unlike either the first or the second models of good faith, this third model is judicial licence.

On the face of it, judicial licence has little to recommend it; thus, the third model of good faith does not merit serious consideration. It follows that the only plausible choices are between the status quo and the first or second models of good faith.

. . .

NOTES

1. For further writings by Brownsword on good faith, see, in particular, his 'Good Faith in Contracts Revisited' (1996) 49 Current Legal Problems 111, and Brownsword, Hird and Howells (eds), *Good Faith in Contract: Concept and Context*, 1999.

2. For a view against the adoption of a doctrine of good faith, see Bridge, 'Does Anglo-Canadian Contract Law Need a Doctrine of Good Faith?' (1984) 9 Canadian JBL 385.

3. For the impact of good faith in the context of the Unfair Terms in Consumer Contracts Regulations 1999, see pp 1035 ff.

QUESTIONS

1.   Edgar offers to sell a used computer to Fay for £1,000. His offer is made by letter, and is stated to be 'Irrevocable'. He states in the letter, however, 'you must accept this offer by Friday if you are going to'. Fay sends a letter of acceptance to Edgar by first-class post, posting it on Thursday morning, but it does not arrive until Saturday because Fay put the wrong postcode on the envelope. However, on Friday morning, Fay tells a friend that she has bought Edgar's computer, and George, who overhears the conversation, mentions it to Edgar that afternoon. Edgar thereupon sends a fax to Fay revoking his offer, because he has realised that he could get a lot more than £1,000 for the computer.

2.   What rules apply when a contract that has been negotiated:
     (a) leaves some important term vague or says nothing about it?
     (b) leaves a term 'to be agreed'?

     Does it make any difference whether the parties have started to perform the supposed contract?

3.   Bangers plc, a sausage manufacturer, needs a large and continuous supply of fresh pork for a new factory. It reaches a 'five-year' agreement with Farmer Giles that Giles will raise pigs for Bangers, following strict instructions as to the diet and other conditions, and will supply them to Bangers at numbers and prices to be agreed from month to month. The contract does not contain an arbitration clause. Giles needs to sell an average of at least 5,000 pigs a year at £1.00 a kilo for five years in order to recoup his investment. All goes very well for two years, but then public tastes change and Bangers finds its market for sausages has shrunk. Accordingly, it refuses to take any more pigs from Giles. Giles cannot sell enough pigs elsewhere to recoup his investment. Does he have a claim against Bangers?

4.   Would your answer differ if Bangers and Giles had agreed to 'negotiate numbers and prices in good faith from month to month'?

5.   Would your answer to question 3 differ if Giles had not had to make any new investment in order to fulfil the contract with Bangers?

6.   At the beginning of Chapter 9, we suggested that there may be a tension between pre-serving one party's freedom to negotiate and protecting the other party's reasonable reliance. What examples of this problem have you seen in Chapters 9 and 10? How were they resolved by the courts?

7.   In what circumstances can a party who has acted on the assumption that a contract will be concluded, but then finds that the other party has pulled out, be entitled to a remedy? What losses may be claimed?

8.   How far along the spectrum between 'market-individualism' and 'consumer-welfarism' (see Adams and Brownsword, above p 57) would you place the law applying when an anticipated contract does not materialize:
     (i)   taking account of the doctrine of proprietary estoppel?
     (ii) leaving that doctrine out of account?

CHAPTER TEN

COMMUNICATION MISTAKES

I. MISTAKES AS TO THE TERMS

■ *Tamplin v James*

(1880) 15 ChD 215, Baggallay LJ (for the V-C) and Court of Appeal

The Ship inn and an adjoining saddler's shop were put up for auction. Behind the property, there were two pieces of garden, which for many years had been occupied with the inn and the shop and were hardly fenced off from them. The gardens did not belong to the vendors, and the area of land stated in the particulars as being for sale did not include them; nor were the gardens included in the plans showing the property to be sold. At the auction, the property remained unsold, but immediately afterwards, the defendant offered £750 for it and his offer was accepted. The defendant, who knew the property and that the gardens were occupied along with the inn and shop, had not looked at the plans and bought the property in the belief that he was buying the gardens as well as the inn and shop. When the defendant discovered his mistake, he refused to complete. The vendors sought specific performance.

Baggallay LJ

The Defendant insists in his statement of defence that he signed the memorandum in the reasonable belief that the property comprised therein included the whole of the premises in the occupation of Mrs Knowles and of Mr Samuel Merrick, and not merely the messuages and hereditaments which the Plaintiffs allege to be the only property comprised therein, and that such his belief was induced and confirmed by the acts and words of the auctioneer at the sale. The Defendant has sworn positively that he had such a belief at the time he signed the memorandum, and I see no reason to doubt the statement so made by him; but was such a belief a reasonable belief?

It is doubtless well established that a Court of Equity will refuse specific performance of an agreement when the Defendant has entered into it under a mistake, and where injustice would be done to him were performance to be enforced. The most common instances of such refusal on the ground of mistake are cases in which there has been some unintentional misrepresentation on the part of the Plaintiff (I am not now referring to cases of intentional misrepresentation which would fall rather under the category of fraud), or where from the ambiguity of the agreement different meanings have been given to it by the different parties... But where there has been no misrepresentation, and where there is no ambiguity in the terms of the contract, the Defendant cannot be allowed to evade the performance of it by the simple statement that he has made a mistake. Were such to be the law the performance of a contract could rarely be enforced upon an unwilling party who was also unscrupulous.

A decree for specific performance was therefore made.

The defendant appealed but the Court of Appeal dismissed the appeal.

James LJ

... The defence on the ground of mistake cannot be sustained. It is not enough for a purchaser to swear, 'I thought the farm sold contained twelve fields which I knew, and I find it does not include them all', or, 'I thought it contained 100 acres and it only contains eighty.' It would open the door to fraud if such a defence was to be allowed. Perhaps some of the cases on this subject go too far, but for the most part the cases where a Defendant has escaped on the ground of a mistake not contributed to by the Plaintiff, have been cases where a hardship amounting to injustice would have been inflicted upon him by holding him to his bargain, and it was unreasonable to hold him to it. *Webster v Cecil* is a good instance of that, being a case where a person snapped at an offer which he must have perfectly well-known to be made by mistake, and the only fault I find with the case is that, in my opinion, the bill ought to have been dismissed with costs. It is said that it is hard to hold a man to a bargain entered into under a mistake, but we must consider the hardship on the other side. Here are trustees realizing their testator's estate, and the reckless conduct of the Defendant may have prevented their selling to some-body else. If a man makes a mistake of this kind without any reasonable excuse he ought to be held to his bargain.

Brett and **Cotton LJJ** delivered concurring judgments.

NOTES

1. If there had been any misrepresentation by the plaintiff, even an unintentional one, the defendant would have been entitled to rescind the contract: see pp 354 ff.

2. It was explained earlier that granting specific performance involves forcing the defend-ant to take the land and pay the agreed price for it. In contrast, if the defendant is made liable in damages, he will not have to go through with the purchase but will have to reim-burse the plaintiff's loss, typically the cost of arranging a resale, plus the difference between the price the defendant had agreed to pay and the price obtained on the resale. The remedy of specific performance is discretionary, and is sometimes refused on the ground of hardship to the defendant, even though the contract is valid at common law and so the defendant will be liable in damages if he does not perform. An example is *Wood v Scarth:* a landlord intended to take a premium when he let a public house, but failed to make this clear to the lessee. The lessee's action for specific performance (without premium) was refused ((1855) 2 K & J 33, 3 Eq Rep 385) but an action against the landlord for damages succeeded ((1858) 1 F & F 293). The grounds on which specific performance may be refused were described by Lord Macnaghten in *Stewart v Kennedy* (1890) 15 App Cas 75, 105, thus:

   It cannot be disputed that the Court of Chancery has refused specific performance in cases of mistake when the mistake has been on one side only; and even when the mistake on the part of the defendant resisting specific performance has not been induced or contributed to by any act or omis-sion on the part of the plaintiff. But I do not think it is going too far to say that in all those cases—certainly in all that have occurred in recent times—the Court has thought, rightly or wrongly, that the circumstances of the particular case under consideration were such that (to use a well-known phrase) it would be 'highly unreasonable' to enforce the agreement specifically. The Court will not be active in assisting one party to an agreement who has always his remedy in damages to take advantage of the mistake of the other so as to involve him in serious and unforeseen consequences . . . the remedy of specific performance is an extraordinary remedy. It is a matter of discretion . . .

For a recent example of specific performance being refused on the ground of hardship, see *Patel v Ali* (p 729).

3.   What is the purpose of making the defendant perform a contract that he would not have entered had he realised the truth? Is the exchange value-maximising? Or is the point that the defendant has behaved carelessly and should bear the consequences, so as to provide an incentive to others to exercise more care (see Kronman and Posner's comment, p 74)? If the point is the latter, is it right to force actual performance by the defendant?

4.   James LJ referred to *Webster v Cecil*. In that case, the defendant wrote to the plaintiff offering to sell a piece of land for £1,250. He meant £2,250, and it must have been obvious to the plaintiff that there had been some mistake because the defendant had recently refused the plaintiff's offer of £2,000. The plaintiff wrote accepting, but the court refused his action for specific performance, saying he might 'bring such action at law as he might be advised'. Read the next case and consider how you would advise him.

■ *Hartog v Colin & Shields*
[1939] 3 All ER 566

The defendants offered to sell the plaintiff a quantity of Argentine hare skins at $106\frac{1}{4}$d per lb. This was an error for $10\frac{1}{4}$ d per piece. In the trade, such skins were always sold by the piece; there are about three pieces to the pound, so that the defendants' offer was the equivalent of $3\frac{3}{4}$ d per piece, whereas three weeks earlier the quoted price had been $10\frac{3}{4}$ d per piece. The plaintiff purported to accept the offer and, when the defendants refused to deliver, brought this action.

Singleton J

In this case, the plaintiff, a Belgian subject, claims damages against the defendants because he says they broke a contract into which they entered with him for the sale of Argentine hare skins. The defendants' answer to that claim is: 'There really was no contract, because you knew that the document which went forward to you, in the form of an offer, contained a material mistake. You realised that, and you sought to take advantage of it.'

Counsel for the defendants took upon himself the onus of satisfying me that the plaintiff knew that there was a mistake and sought to take advantage of that mistake. In other words, realising that there was a mistake, the plaintiff did that which James LJ in *Tamplin v James* described as 'snapping up the offer'. It is important, I think, to realise that in the verbal negotiations which took place in this country, and in all the discussions there had ever been, the prices of Argentine hare skins had been discussed per piece, and later, when correspondence took place, the matter was always discussed at the price per piece, and never at a price per pound. . . .

I am satisfied however, from the evidence given to me, that the plaintiff must have realised, and did in fact know, that a mistake had occurred. . . .

There was an absolute difference from anything which had gone before—a difference in the manner of quotation, in that the skins are offered per pound instead of per piece.

I am satisfied that it was a mistake on the part of the defendants or their servants which caused the offer to go forward in that way, and I am satisfied that anyone with any knowledge of the trade must have realised that there was a mistake. . . .

The offer was wrongly expressed, and the defendants by their evidence, and by the correspondence, have satisfied me that the plaintiff could not reasonably have supposed that that offer contained the offerers' real intention. Indeed, I am satisfied to the contrary. That means that there must be judgment for the defendants.

NOTE

Did the plaintiff actually know of the defendants' mistake, or was it that he should have known of it? In *McMaster University v Wilchar Construction Ltd* (1971) 22 DLR (3d) 9 (affd (1973) 69 DLR (3d) 400n), Thompson J said:

In this context, it should be stressed that one is taken to have known that which would have been obvious to a reasonable person in the light of the surrounding circumstances: *see Hartog v Colin & Shields*.

In *Centrovincial Estates plc v Merchant Investors Assurance Co Ltd* [1983] Com LR 158, the English Court of Appeal seemed to imply that this is the correct approach. Slade LJ said:

... [I]t is contrary to the well established principles of contract law to suggest that the offeror under a bilateral contract can withdraw an unambiguous offer, after it has been accepted in the manner contemplated by the offeror, merely because he made a mistake which the offeree neither knew nor could reasonably have known at the time he accepted it.

However, we shall see later that in cases on the rectification of mistakes in written contracts the same court said that relief should not be granted unless one party's mistake was actually known to the other party (see p 300).

■ *Scriven Bros & Co v Hindley & Co*
[1913] 3 KB 564

The plaintiffs instructed an auctioneer, Northcott, to sell a number of bales of hemp and tow. The auctioneer's catalogue described the goods as so many bales in different lots, all bearing the same shipping marks (SL), which was unusual for two different commodities, and the catalogue did not show the difference between the lots bearing the same marks. Samples of the hemp and tow were on view before the auction, marked with the catalogue numbers for the relevant lots: the defendant's manager, Gill, examined the hemp, but not the tow because he did not intend to bid for tow. He was not warned by the auctioneer's foreman, Calman, that the hemp and tow bore the same marks. When the lots, which were in fact tow, were put up for sale, the defendant's buyer, Macgregor, bid on them at a price that was extravagant for tow and they were immediately knocked down to him.

The jury in answer to questions found: (1) that hemp and tow are different commodities in commerce (2) that the auctioneer intended to sell 176 bales of tow (3) that Macgregor intended to bid for 176 bales of hemp (4) that the auctioneer believed that the bid was made under a mistake when he knocked down the lot (5) that the auctioneer had reasonable ground for believing that the mistake was merely one as to value (6) that the form of the catalogue and the conduct of Calman, or one of them, contributed to cause the mistake that occurred (7) that Mr Gill's 'negligence' in not taking his catalogue to Cutler Street and more closely examining and identifying the bales with the lots contributed to cause Macgregor's mistake.

A T Lawrence J

... The jury have found that hemp and tow are different commodities in commerce. I should suppose that no one can doubt the correctness of this finding. The second and third findings of the jury shew that the parties were never ad idem as to the subject-matter of the proposed sale; there was therefore in fact no contract of bargain and sale. The plaintiffs can recover from the defendants only if they can shew that the defendants are estopped from relying upon what is now admittedly the truth. Mr Hume Williams for the plaintiffs argued very ingeniously that the defendants were estopped; for this he relied upon findings

5 and 7, and upon the fact that the defendants had failed to prove the allegation in paragraph 4 of the defence to the effect that Northcott knew at the time he knocked down the lot that Macgregor was bidding for hemp and not for tow.

I must, of course, accept for the purpose of this judgment the findings of the jury, but I do not think they create any estoppel. Question No 7 was put to the jury as a supplementary question, after they had returned into Court with their answers to the other questions, upon the urgent insistence of the learned junior counsel for the plaintiffs. It begs an essential question by using the word 'neligence' and assuming that the purchaser has a duty towards the seller to examine goods that he does not wish to buy, and to correct any latent defect there may be in the sellers' catalogue.

Once it was admitted that Russian hemp was never before known to be consigned or sold with the same shipping marks as Russian tow from the same cargo, it was natural for the person inspecting the 'S.L.' goods and being shewn hemp to suppose that the 'S.L.' bales represented the commodity hemp. Inasmuch as it is admitted that some one had perpetrated a swindle upon the bank which made advances in respect of this shipment of goods it was peculiarly the duty of the auctioneer to make it clear to the bidder either upon the fact of his catalogue or in some other way which lots were hemp and which lots were tow.

. . . In my view it is clear that the findings of the jury upon the sixth question prevents the plaintiffs from being able to insist upon a contract by estoppel. Such a contract cannot arise when the person seeking to enforce it has by his own negligence or by that of those for whom he is responsible caused, or contributed to cause, the mistake.

I am therefore of opinion that judgment should be entered for the defendants.

Judgment for defendants.

NOTES

1. Did the auctioneer know that the buyer was under a mistake as to what was being sold? If not, why was the buyer not held to the contract he had appeared to agree to, when he bid and allowed his bid to be accepted?

2. Do you think the result would have been different if the jury had concluded that there had been some carelessness on the auctioneer's part, but that the predominant fault had been the buyer's, because he should have realised that the bales were tow?

3. If, as in these cases, one party has made some mistake about the terms on which he is prepared to contract, why is he not held bound to what he appeared to agree to, even if the other party knew of the mistake, should have known of it or had caused it by his own misleading conduct? Where the second party has *actual knowledge* of the mistake, does it seem fair to allow him to take advantage of it? He will not have been misled, and he could easily correct the mistaken party's error by pointing it out. Where he *caused* it, it seems equally unfair to allow him to benefit by it, and moreover, of the two parties, it seems sensible to put the loss caused on the party whose negligence was responsible—he is the 'least cost avoider' (see below, and compare liability in tort for negligence). What of the case in which the mistaken party causes his own mistake (by careless typing, for instance), but the other *should have known* of it? Is the point that here also the party who should have realised the mistake on the other's part has become the least cost avoider?

4. We suggested earlier that the reason for holding a party to a contract that he would not have made but for a mistake that was not known to the other party may be that he has misled the other, and that of the two it is right that the mistaken party should bear the consequences (unless the other should have realised the mistake). We also suggested that such a case may be an appropriate one for refusing specific performance and leaving the

non-mistaken party to his remedy in damages. Normally, the damages will include loss of expectation, ie loss of profit. In a case in which the defendant can show that he only entered the contract under a mistake, is it right to make him pay expectation damages? It is likely that his mistake will have led him to pay more than the market value of the property, although it does not have this extra value to him. Where the land is sold at auction, the mistaken party is unlikely to be paying much 'over the odds'—he will normally have bid up the price just 'one notch higher than other bidders were prepared to pay (although note what happened in *Tamplin v James* and in *Scriven v Hindley*, in which Macgregor seems to have been the only bidder). But if the sale had been by private treaty, the mistaken party might make an offer at much more than the market value. Wouldn't the plaintiff be justly compensated if he were given the cost of arranging another sale—or at most the value of some other offer for the land that he passed up because he thought he had a contract with the defendant? Consider the following extract from the judgment of Frank J in *Ricketts v Pennsylvania Rly Co* 153 F2d 757, 766–767(1946):

Two approaches have been suggested which diverge from that of Williston and the Restatement but which perhaps come closer to the realities of business experience. The first utilizes the concept of an assumption of risk: The parties to a contract, it is said, are presumed to undertake the risk that the facts upon the basis of which they entered into the contract might, within a certain margin, prove to be non-existent; accordingly, one who is mistaken about any such fact should not, absent a deliberate assumption by him of that risk, be held for more than the actual expenses caused by his conduct. Otherwise, the other party will receive a windfall to which he is not entitled. The second suggestion runs thus: Business is conducted on the assumption that men who bargain are fully informed as to all vital facts about the transactions in which they engage; a contract based upon a mistake as to any such fact as would have deterred either of the parties from making it, had he known that fact, should therefore be set aside in order to prevent unjust enrichment to him who made the mistake; the other party, on this suggestion also, is entitled to no more than his actual expenses. Each of those suggestions may result in unfairness, if the other party reasonably believing that he has made a binding contract, has lost the benefit of other specific bargains available at that time but no longer open to him.

5.   Is there also a case for allowing the mistaken party to escape the contract if the non-mistaken party has not yet relied on it in any way? The Court of Appeal in *Centrovincial* rejected this approach. After the passage quoted above (p 292), Slade LJ went on to say:

. . . [I]t is nothing to the point that the offeree may not have changed his position beyond giving the promise requested of him.

6.   In *Hartog v Colin & Shields* and *Scriven Bros & Co v Hindley & Co*, the mistake was used as a defence to an action to enforce the contract, and all that the courts had to decide was that the defendant was not liable to perform on the terms that he had mistakenly given his apparent consent to. What would have been the position if he had wanted to enforce the contract, either on those terms, or (more realistically) on the terms that he actually intended? To put the same question another way, in a case like *Hartog v Colin & Shields* is there, as counsel for the defendants argued, no contract? There are at least two other possibilities:

(i)   there is a contract on the terms stated by the seller (ie $10\frac{1}{4}$ d per lb), but it is voidable at the seller's option;

(ii)   there is a contract on the terms actually intended by the seller (ie $10\frac{1}{4}$ d per piece).

There is no clear answer to this question on the present authorities in England, but cases on rectification suggest that, at least where it is obvious what the terms are meant to be, the correct solution is that there is a contract on the terms the mistaken party intended and the other party should have known he intended.

7. It may be helpful at this point to note the distinction between void and voidable contracts. If, for instance, you have entered a contract as the result of a misrepresentation of fact by the other party, you may set the contract aside, or 'rescind' it, if you wish to do so and act quickly enough (see note 1 on p 290 and Chapter 13). The contract is thus 'voidable' at your option; until you rescind it, the contract remains in force. If, on the other hand, you never reach any effective agreement at all (eg what you agree is too uncertain to be enforceable: see Chapter 10), the supposed contract is 'void'—ie there is no contract at all. This was what counsel for the defendants in *Hartog v Colin & Shields* argued was the effect of the mistake. As the last note suggested, it is not completely clear that this is correct. There are certainly some cases in which the existence of a mistake makes the supposed contract void (see the mistaken identity cases, pp 309 ff); but where the mistake is not about who the parties are but about the other terms of the contract, there are, as suggested in the last note, two other possibilities. One is that there is a contract that is voidable at the seller's option (but there is little if any authority for this: see p 320). The other is that there is a contract that is neither void nor voidable, but which is on the terms intended by the mistaken party and which the other party knew (or perhaps should have known) the mistaken party meant.

8. Australian authority seems to suggest that a party's mistake as to terms that is known to the other party will make the contract voidable at the mistaken party's option. In *Taylor v Johnson* (1983) 151 CLR 422, Mrs Johnson granted an option to Mr Taylor or his nominee to purchase two five-acre pieces of land for a total price of $15,000. The option was granted on 27 March 1975 and exercised on 7 May 1975, when Mr Taylor's children, his nominees, entered into a contract of purchase and sale. Mrs Johnson refused to perform that contract on the ground that she believed the price to be $15,000 per acre.

The evidence was that the land was worth in total about $50,000 but that it might increase in value to $95,000 if a proposed rezoning (planning application in English terms) were successful. The trial judge held that Mrs Johnson was indeed mistaken, but that Mr Taylor did not know of this mistake, and therefore granted specific performance to the plaintiffs. The New South Wales Court of Appeal held that Mr Taylor did know of the mistake and that he had taken care once he became aware of the mistake to deflect any steps that might lead to the mistake being clarified. The majority of the High Court of Australia held that the evidence permitted the Court of Appeal to take this view. The majority of the High Court of Australia (Mason A CJ, Murphy and Deane JJ) held that the contract should be set aside and said:

The particular proposition of law which we see as appropriate and adequate for disposing of the present appeal may be narrowly stated. It is that a party who has entered into a written contract under a serious mistake about its contents in relation to a fundamental term will be entitled in equity to an order rescinding the contract if the other party is aware that circumstances exist which indicate that the first party is entering the contract under some serious mistake or misapprehension about either the content or subject matter of that term and deliberately sets out to ensure that the first party does not become aware of the existence of his mistake or misapprehension. What we have said is sufficient to demonstrate the broad basis of support which the authorities provide for that proposition. Moreover, and perhaps more importantly, it is a principle which is best calculated to do justice between the parties to a contract in the situation which it contemplates. In such a situation it is unfair that the mistaken party should be held to the written contract by the other party whose lack of precise knowledge of the first party's actual mistake proceeds from wilful ignorance because, knowing or having reason to know that there is some mistake or misapprehension, he engages deliberately in a course of conduct which is designed to inhibit discovery of it. Our comment can for present purposes, be limited in its application to the case where the second party has not materially altered his position and the rights of strangers have not intervened.

9.   In *Chwee Kin Keong v Digilandmall Com Pte Ltd* [2005] 1 SLR 502, one of the claimants noticed that the defendants were advertising colour laser printers on the Internet at Singapore$66. A normal price would have been between $3,500 and $4,000 (the defendant's list price at the time was $3,854). He alerted a number of his friends and, between them, they placed orders over the Internet for 1,606 printers. The defendant's computer went through the appropriate motions to complete the deal. All of the transactions took place in the early hours of a Singapore morning. When the defendants became aware of the transactions when business opened, they immediately repudiated them and the claimants brought an action for breach of contract.

        The Singapore Court of Appeal held that the action failed. It treated the case as like *Hartog v Colin and Shields*. The claimants knew that the defendants did not intend to sell at $66. At first instance [2004] SLR 594, V K Rajah JC would have been willing to reach the same conclusion on the basis that the claimants ought to have known.

II. RECTIFICATION

▪ *Joscelyne v Nissen*

[1970] 1 All ER 1213, Court of Appeal

The father lived in a house called Martindale from where he carried on a car hire business. In 1960, the father received a notice to quit. The daughter, in order to help her parents, bought Martindale with the help of a mortgage and let her husband's house furnished to pay off the mortgage instalments and moved to Martindale. The parents occupied the ground floor and the daughter and her husband the first floor. In 1963, the daughter's mother became very ill with two successive strokes and was unable to look after herself. The father had to devote a good deal of his time to looking after her with the result that his business was adversely affected. The father and the daughter discussed a scheme, which culminated in the signing by them of a contract dated 18 June 1964. By this contract, the father agreed to transfer his motor car hire business to the daughter on certain terms and conditions, one of which was that, in consideration of the transfer, the daughter would permit the father during his life to have the uncontrolled right to occupy and reside in the ground floor of Martindale 'free of all rent and outgoings of every kind in any event'. In pursuance of this term in the contract, the daughter for a time paid the gas, electricity and coal bills and the cost of home help for the father. Trouble then arose between the daughter and her parents, and the father commenced proceedings in the county court against the daughter. The daughter was apparently advised that the wording of the contract did not require her to pay for the items previously mentioned and she accordingly stopped further payments of those items. The father amended his particulars of claim to raise the point either as a matter of construction or by way of rectification.

        The first instance judge rectified the contract.

Russell LJ

For the daughter it is argued that the law is that the father cannot get rectification of the written instrument save to accord with a complete antecedent concluded oral contract with the daughter, and, as was found by the judge, there was none. For the father it is argued that if in the course of negotiation a firm accord has been expressly reached on a particular term of the proposed contract, and both parties continue minded that the contract should contain appropriate language to embrace that term, it matters not that the accord was not part of a complete antecedent concluded oral contract.

The point of law has a curious judicial history.

[His Lordship considered a number of authorities including *Lovell and Christmas Ltd v Wall* (below, p 398), *Frederick E Rose (London) Ltd v W H Pim Jnr & Co* (below, p 307).]

In *Crane v Hegeman-Harris Co Inc* ... Simonds J said:

'Before I consider the facts and come to a conclusion whether the defendants are right in their contention, it is necessary to say a few words upon the principles which must guide me in this matter. I am clear that I must follow the decision of Clauson J as he then was, in *Shipley Urban District Council v Bradford Corpn.*, the point of which is that, in order that this court may exercise its jurisdiction to rectify a written instrument, it is not necessary to find a concluded and binding contract between the parties antecedent to the agreement which it is sought to rectify. The judge held, and I respectfully concur with his reasoning and his conclusion, that it is sufficient to find a common continuing intention in regard to a particular provision or aspect of the agreements. If one finds that, in regard to a particular point, the parties were in agreement up to the moment when they executed their formal instrument, and the formal instrument does not conform with that common agreement, then this court has jurisdiction to rectify, although it may be that there was, until the formal instrument was executed, no concluded and binding contract between the parties. That is what the judge decided, and, as I say, with his reasoning I wholly concur, and I can add nothing to his authority in the matter, except that I would say that, if it were not so, it would be a strange thing, for the result would be that two parties binding themselves by a mistake to which each had equally contributed, by an instrument which did not express their real intention, would yet be bound by it. That is a state of affairs which I hold is not the law, and, until a higher court tells me it is the law, I shall continue to exercise the jurisdiction which Clauson J as I think rightly, held might be entertained by this court. Secondly, I want to say that upon the principle of the jurisdiction. It is a jurisdiction which is to be exercised only upon convincing proof that the concluded instrument does not represent the common intention of the parties. That is particularly the case where one finds prolonged negotiations between the parties eventually assuming the shape of a formal instrument in which they have been advised by their respective skilled legal advisers. The assumption is very strong in such a case that the instrument does represent their real intention, and it must be only upon proof which Lord Eldon, I think, in a somewhat picturesque phrase described as 'irrefragable' that the court can act. I would rather, I think, say that the court can only act if it is satisfied beyond all reasonable doubt that the instrument does not represent their common intention, and is further satisfied as to what their common intention was. For let it be clear that it is not sufficient to show that the written instrument does not represent their common intention unless positively also one can show what their common intention was. It is in the light of those principles that I must examine the facts of this somewhat complicated case.'

In our judgment the law is as expounded by Simonds J in *Crane's* case with the qualification that some outward expression of accord is required. We do not wish to attempt to state in any different phrases that with which we entirely agree, except to say that it is in our view better to use only the phrase 'convincing proof' without echoing an old fashioned word such as 'irrefragable' and without importing from the criminal law the phrase 'beyond all reasonable doubt'. Remembering always the strong burden of proof that lies on the shoulders of those seeking rectification, and that the requisite accord and continuance of accord of intention may be the more difficult to establish if a complete antecedent concluded contract be not shown, it would be a sorry state of affairs if when that burden is discharged a party to a written contract could, on discovery that the written language chosen for the document did not on its true construction reflect the accord of the parties on a particular point, take advantage of the fact.

The contention in law for the daughter would, we apprehend, involve this proposition, that if all the important terms of an agreement were set out in correspondence with clarity, but expressly 'subject to contract', and the contract by a slip of the copyist unnoticed by either part, departed from what had been 'agreed', there could not be rectification.

Appeal dismissed.

Rectification can be also obtained, however, where the document does not record correctly the intentions of only one of the parties, provided the other knew of this and took advantage of it.

■ *Riverlate Properties Ltd v Paul*

[1974] 2 All ER 656, Court of Appeal

The lessor, the owner of a maisonette on the first and second floors of a building, sent the lessee's solicitor a draft lease, which provided by cl 5(iii) that the lessee covenanted to pay half of the reasonable costs, expenses, outgoings and matters for which the lessor was responsible by virtue of the provisions of cl 6(b), (c) and (d), namely insurance, decoration of the exterior of the building and water rates. This was a drafting error: the lessor intended the reference to be to cl 6(a), (b) and (c), so that the lessee would be responsible for part of the expense of exterior and structural repairs. Neither the lessee nor her solicitor appreciated that a mistake had been made or intended that she should undertake this responsibility. Contracts were exchanged and the lease was executed in the form of the draft. Later, the lessor commenced an action to have the lease set aside or, at the lessee's option, rectified to substitute in cl 5(iii) a reference to cl 6(a), (b) and (c). Templeman J dismissed the action and the lessor appealed.

Russell LJ read the judgment of the court, in which Stamp and Lawton LJJ concurred.

. . . Finally, the proposition is put forward for the plaintiff that there was unilateral mistake by the plaintiff of a character which entitles the plaintiff to rescission or annulment of the lease, subject only to this, that the defendant can escape rescission or annulment by agreeing to retain the lease subject to variation in the manner suggested as appropriate to correct the plaintiff's unilateral mistake—here for example by variation substituting in cl 5(iii) reference to cl 6(a), (b) and (c) for 6(b), (c) and (d). It is to be observed that this contention does not depend in any way on the knowledge or state of mind of the other party at the time of the transaction in question. It is further to be observed that we are not concerned with a case in which a party is seeking an equitable remedy under a contract such as specific performance, where in an appropriate case the court may refuse specific performance if the defendant has made a unilateral mistake. Here the lessee seeks no equitable remedy: she is in possession under a lease.

Is the plaintiff entitled to rescission of the lease on the mere ground that it made a serious mistake in the drafting of the lease which it put forward and subsequently executed when (a) the defendant did not share the mistake, (b) the defendant did not know that the document did not give effect to the plaintiff's intention, and (c) the mistake of the plaintiff was in no way attributable to anything said or done by the defendant? What is there in principle, or in authority binding on this court which requires a person who has acquired a leasehold interest on terms on which he intended to obtain it, and who thought when he obtained it that the lessor intended him to obtain it on those terms either to lose the leasehold interest, or, if he wish to keep it, to submit to keep it only on the terms which the lessor meant to impose but did not? In point of principle we cannot find that this should be so. If reference be made to principles of equity, it operates on conscience. If conscience is clear at the time of the transaction, why should equity disrupt the transaction? If a man may be said to have been fortunate in obtaining a property at a bargain price, or on terms that make it a good bargain, because the other party unknown to him has made a miscalculation or other mistake, some high-minded men might consider it appropriate that he should agree to a fresh bargain to cure the miscalculation or mistake, abandoning his good fortune. But if equity were to enforce the views of those high-minded men, we have no doubt that it would run counter to the attitudes of much the greater part of ordinary mankind (not least the world of commerce), and would be venturing on the field of moral philosophy in which it would soon be in difficulties.

What then of authority? There are a number of authorities at first instance, of some antiquity, to which our attention was drawn, which it was said decided that in cases of mere unilateral mistake rescission could be ordered, but with the opportunity being given to the defendant to retain the benefit of the transaction if he consent to a variation (that is to say, rectification) which will mend the plaintiff's mistake.

[His Lordship then referred to a number of cases, including *Garrard v Frankel, Harris v Pepperell, Paget v Marshall* and *May v Platt.*]

It follows from this review of the authorities cited to us that there is no authority binding on this court which requires us to arrive at a conclusion for which, as we have indicated, there is no justification in principle.

Consequently, since the defendant neither directly nor through her solicitor, Mr Mills, knew of the plaintiff's mistake, and was not guilty of anything approaching sharp practice in relation thereto, it is a case of mere unilateral mistake which cannot entitle the plaintiff to rescission of the lease either with or without the option to the defendant to accept rectification to cure the plaintiff's mistake.

Appeal dismissed.

■ *Thomas Bates & Son Ltd v Wyndham's (Lingerie) Ltd*
[1981] 1 All ER 1077, Court of Appeal

In 1957, the tenants took an assignment of an existing lease, which gave the tenants the option, on the expiration of the lease, to take a further seven or 14 years' lease 'at a rent to be agreed between the landlords and the tenants but in default of such agreement at a rent to be fixed by [an] arbitrator'. The tenants exercised the option and, in 1963, were granted a new seven-year lease containing a similar option for a renewal for seven further years. In 1970, the tenants gave notice exercising that option and negotiations followed. Ultimately, the tenants accepted the landlords' offer of a 14-year lease at £2,350 pa for the first five years and subject to review every five years thereafter. By an oversight, the landlords failed to include a provision for the fixing of the rent by arbitration in the default of agreement. It had not been agreed that this should be omitted; the tenants noticed the omission but did not point it out before executing the new lease. The landlords sought rectification, and the trial judge ordered it. The tenants appealed.

Buckley LJ

... The landlords claim rectification in the present case on the basis of a principle enunciated by Pennycuick J in *A Roberts & Co, Ltd v Leicestershire County Council.* ...

> 'The second ground rests on the principle that a party is entitled to rectification of a contract on proof that he believed a particular term to be included in the contract and that the other party concluded the contract with the omission or a variation of that term in the knowledge that the first party believed the term to be included ... The principle is stated in Snell's Principles of Equity (25th edn, 1960, p 569) as follows: "By what appears to be a species of equitable estoppel, if one party to a transaction knows that the instrument contains a mistake in his favour but does nothing to correct it, he (and those claiming under him) will be precluded from resisting rectification on the ground that the mistake is unilateral and not common".'

Of course if a document is executed in circumstances in which one party realises that in some respect it does not accurately reflect what down to that moment had been the common intention of the parties, it cannot be said that the document is executed under a common mistake, because the party who has realised the mistake is no longer labouring under the mistake.

For this doctrine (that is to say the doctrine of *A Roberts v Leicestershire County Council*) to apply I think it must be shown: first, that one party, A, erroneously believed that the document sought to be rectified contained a particular term or provision, or possibly did not contain a particular term or provision which, mistakenly, it did contain; second, that the other party, B, was aware of the omission or the inclusion and that it was due to a mistake on the part of A; third, that B has omitted to draw the mistake to the notice of A. And I think there must be a fourth element involved, namely that the mistake must be one calculated to benefit B. If these requirements are satisfied, the court may regard it as inequitable to allow B to resist rectification to give effect to A's intention on the ground that the mistake was not, at the time of execution of the document, a common mistake.

[Buckley LJ went on to hold that, on the facts as found by the trial judge, rectification was properly ordered.]

Eveleigh and **Brightman LJJ** delivered concurring judgments.

Appeal dismissed.

NOTES

1. Is there any essential different between this case and *Hartog v Colin & Shields*? If not, doesn't that suggest that, in *Hartog's* case, there must have been a contract at $10\frac{1}{4}$ d per piece and, if necessary, the sellers could have had the documents rectified to reflect this? Does this mean that in *Chwee Kin Keong v Digilandmall* the defendants could have sought rectification, so as to compel the claimants to buy 1,606 printers at $3,854 each?

2. What will be the position if it is obvious to the offeree that the offeror has made a mistake, for instance, because the price offered is far too low, but it is not apparent what the offeror did intend?

3. In *The Nai Genova* [1984] 1 Lloyd's Rep 353, the Court of Appeal pointed out that in none of the cases was it suggested that rectification could properly be granted on account of unilateral mistake unless the defendant had actual knowledge of the existence of the plaintiff's mistake at the time when the contract was signed. Slade LJ said (at 365):

    While it is not necessary to go so far for the purpose of this present decision, I might perhaps add that I strongly incline to the view that in the absence of estoppel, fraud, undue influence or a fiduciary relationship between the parties, the authorities do not in any circumstances permit the rectification of a contract on the grounds of unilateral mistake, unless the defendant had actual knowledge of the existence of the relevant mistaken belief at the time when the mistaken plaintiff signed the contract. In view of the drastic nature of such an order, so far as the non-mistaken defendant is concerned, the consequences of any such conclusion may not appear unduly harsh.

    However, rectification may be ordered if A intended B to be mistaken and diverted B from discovering his mistake, even if A did not actually know B was mistaken: *Commission for the New Towns v Cooper (Great Britain) Ltd* [1995] 2 All ER 929.

4   Why limit relief to cases in which the defendant actually knew of the plaintiff's mistake? Particularly if he suspects that a mistake has been made, is it too much to ask that he check with the plaintiff?

5. In *Riverlate Properties Ltd v Paul*, the Court of Appeal seemed to reject the idea of giving the defendant an option between rectification and rescission of the contract. However, this might be an appropriate remedy when the defendant did not actually know of the

mistake but should have known of it see *Stepps Investments Ltd v Security Capital Corpn Ltd* (1976) 73 DLR (3d) 351 (High Court of Ontario).

6. In the extract in note 3 above, Slade refers to estoppel. An estoppel might arise if the parties had earlier reached an accord including the terms the plaintiff intended, the defendant had represented to the plaintiff that the document gave effect to that accord, and the plaintiff, foreseeably, did not check the document: [1984] 1 Lloyd's Rep 353, 365. For undue influence and fiduciary relationships, see chapter 35 below.

III. MISUNDERSTANDING AS TO TERMS

■ *Raffles v Wichelhaus*
(1864) 2 H & C 906, 159 ER 375, Exchequer

Declaration. For that it was agreed between the plaintiff and the defendants to wit, at Liverpool, that the plaintiff should sell to the defendants, and the defendants buy of the plaintiff, certain goods, to wit, 125 bales of Surat cotton, guaranteed middling fair merchant's Dhollorah, to arrive ex 'Peerless' from Bombay; and that the cotton should be taken from the quay, and that the defendants would pay the plaintiff for the same at a certain rate, to wit, at the rate of $17\frac{1}{4}$d per pound, within a certain time then agreed upon the arrival of the said goods in England. Averments: that the said goods did arrive by the said ship from Bombay in England to wit, at Liverpool, and the plaintiff was then and there ready, and willing and offered to deliver the said goods to the defendants, &c. Breach: that the defendants refused to accept the said goods or pay the plaintiff for them.

Plea. That the said ship mentioned in the said agreement was meant and intended by the defendants to be the ship called the 'Peerless', which sailed from Bombay, to wit, in October; and that the plaintiff was not ready and willing and did not offer to deliver to the defendants any bales of cotton which arrived by the last mentioned ship, but instead thereof was only ready and willing and offered to deliver to the defendants 125 bales of Surat cotton which arrived by another and different ship, which was also called the 'Peerless', and which sailed from Bombay, to wit in December.

Demurrer, and joinder therein.

Milward, in support of the demurrer. The contract was for the sale of a number of bales or cotton of a particular description, which the plaintiff was ready to deliver. It is immaterial by what ship the cotton was to arrive, so that it was a ship called the 'Peerless'. The words 'to arrive ex "Peerless"', only mean than if the vessel is lost on the voyage, the contract is to be at an end. [Pollock CB. It would be a question for the jury whether both parties meant the same ship called the 'Peerless'.] That would be so if the contract was for the sale of a ship called the 'Peerless'; but it is for the sale of cotton on board a ship of that name. [Pollock CB. The defendant only bought that cotton which was to arrive by a particular ship. It may as well be said, that if there is a contract for the purchase of certain goods in warehouse A, that is satisfied by the delivery of goods of the same description in warehouse B.] In that case there would be goods in both warehouses; here it does not appear that the plaintiff had any goods on board the other 'Peerless'. [Martin B. It is imposing on the defendant a contract different from that which he entered into. Pollock CB. It is like a contract for the purchase of wine coming from a particular estate in France or Spain, where there are two estates of that name.] The defendant has no right to contradict by parol evidence a written contract good upon the face of it. He does not impute misrepresentation or fraud, but only says that he fancied the ship was a different one. Intention is of no avail, unless stated at the time of the contract. [Pollock CB. One vessel sailed in October and the other in December.] The time of sailing is no part of the contract.

Mellish (Cohen with him), in support of the plea. There is nothing on the face of the contract to shew that any particular ship called the 'Peerless' was meant; but the moment it appears that two ships called the 'Peerless' were about to sail from Bombay there is a latent ambiguity, and parol evidence may be given for the purpose of shewing that the defendant meant one 'Peerless' and the plaintiff another. That being so, there was no consensus ad idem, and therefore no binding contract. He was then stopped by the Court.

Per Curiam. There must be judgment for the defendants.

Judgment for the defendants.

Pollock CB, Martin and **Pigott BB**.

NOTES

It is far from clear on what ground the court actually decided this case. Clearly, the court did not accept that the ship was immaterial, but it is not clear whether there was a contract to deliver from the earlier ship, or whether, as was argued for the defendants, there was no contract because there was no actual agreement, no *consensus ad idem*. During the nineteenth century, actual agreement was often thought of as an essential ingredient of a contract, although there were competing theories.

■ Simpson, 'Innovation in Nineteenth Century Contract Law' (1975)
91 LQR 247, 268

This case [*Raffles v Wichelhaus*] seems doomed to being misunderstood. The plaintiff sued for failure to accept delivery of goods 'to arrive ex Peerless from Bombay'. The defendants had refused to accept goods arriving on a ship 'Peerless' leaving Bombay in December; they pleaded that the ship *they* had intended was another vessel of the same name. The plaintiffs demurred to this plea and there was join-der in demurrer. The plaintiffs argued that so long as the goods arrived on any ship 'Peerless' from Bombay the express terms of a written contract had been complied with; hence the plea was no answer to the action. The court took the view that the plea was good, and the ground for this view (there being no judgments given) must be gleaned from the arguments and interjections of the judges. From these it seems plain that it was good because the court took the view that it was open to the defendants, once a latent ambiguity appeared, to adduce parol evidence to show what the intention was; the jury would then have to determine whether the parties meant one ship (if so which) or different ships. In the latter case, *counsel* suggested, there would be no *consensus* and no contract, but the decision on the demur-rer does not enable one to say whether the court agreed with this or not and no judicial interjection deals with the suggestion. On the concept of latent ambiguity see *Smith v Jeffryes*.

NOTES

1. For another account of *Raffles v Wichelhaus*, claiming that it was decided on a *consensus ad idem* basis and later 'objectivized', see Gilmore, *The Death of Contract*, 1974, pp 35–44.

    Whatever the original basis of *Raffles v Wichelhaus*, it now seems to be the law that actual agreement is not needed to create a contract: if one party reasonably appears to the other to assent, and the resulting agreement is not hopelessly ambiguous, there will be a contract. Occasionally, the parties will sign a contract conscious that they are not agreed on its meaning, in effect leaving it to the court to establish the proper meaning of the words if necessary: see p 405.

2. When a court is called upon to interpret a contract, it will normally look only at the words of the contract, and not at external ('parol') evidence of what was meant. This case

establishes an exception to the rule, namely that external evidence can be considered to resolve a latent ambiguity—although here it is not at all clear that the parol evidence helped. On interpretation and the parol evidence rule, see p 399.

3. The cases in subsection (a) above are often referred to as cases of unilateral mistake, whereas *Raffles v Wichelhaus* is referred to as mutual mistake. What is the difference?

4. Cases of mutual mistake—ie cases in which there is a misunderstanding that cannot be resolved on the ground that one party knew or should have known what the other meant, so that the contract is void—are rare in the reports, but see *Falck v Williams* [1900] AC 176 and *London Holeproof Hosiery Co Ltd v Padmore* (1928) 44 TLR 499. It is possible that *Scriven Bros & Co v Hindley & Co* is better looked at as a case of mutual mistake than as one of unilateral mistake: it is not clear that there was any reason to prefer one party's version of the transaction to the other's. On the facts, the category did not matter; if the buyers had sued the sellers for failing to deliver hemp, it might have been crucial.

IV. MISTAKEN EXPECTATIONS

■ **Beatson (ed), *Anson's Law of Contract* (28th edn)**
p 324

A sells *X* a piece of china.

(1) *X* thinks that it is Dresden china. *A* thinks it is not. Each takes his chance. *X* may get a better thing than *A* intended to sell, or a worse thing than *X* intended to buy; in neither case is the validity of the contract affected.

(2) *X* thinks that it is Dresden china. *A* knows that *X* thinks so, and knows that it is not. The contract holds. *A* must do nothing to deceive *X*, but she is not bound to prevent *X* from deceiving himself as to the quality of the thing sold. *X*'s error is one of motive alone, and although it is known to *A*, it is insufficient.

(3) *X* thinks that it is Dresden china and thinks that *A* intends to contract to sell it as Dresden china; and *A* knows that it is not Dresden china, but does not know that *X* thinks that A is contracting to sell it as Dresden china. *A* reasonably believes that *X* is assenting to a sale of china in general terms.

The contract holds. The misapprehension by *X* of the extent of *A*'s promise, *if unknown to A*, has no effect, unless, as in *Scriven Bros & Co v Hindley & Co*, *A* has caused or contributed to *X*'s misapprehension.

(4) *X* thinks it is Dresden china, and thinks that A intends to contract to sell it as Dresden china. A knows that *X* *thinks A is contracting to sell it as Dresden china*, but does not mean to, and in fact does not, offer more than china in general terms. There is no contract to sell the particular piece of china. *X*'s error was not one of judgment as to the quality of the china, as in (2), but was an error as to the nature of *A*'s promise, and A, knowing that her promise was misunderstood, nevertheless allowed the mistake to continue. The apparent agreement is not a contract is A knows that X has accepted her offer in terms different from those in which it was in fact made. Moreover, A's knowledge in principle should deprive her of the right to deny the agreement as understood and intended by X, i.e. for Dresden china.

■ *Smith v Hughes*
(1871) LR 6 QB 597, Queen's Bench

The plaintiff, a farmer, offered the defendant, a racehorse trainer, a quantity of oats. The defendant's manager inspected a sample of the oats and the defendant agreed to take the whole quantity. When the first parcel was delivered, the defendant discovered that they were 'green', ie that season's oats, and he refused to pay for them or accept further deliveries, saying that he had been under the impression that the oats were 'old', ie oats of the previous season; he had no use for green oats. The plaintiff brought an action to recover the price of the oats delivered and for damages for the defendant's refusal to take the remainder. At the trial, the plaintiff alleged that he did not know the defendant did not want green oats: the plaintiff had no old oats to sell. On what had been said, there was a conflict of evidence. The plaintiff said he had told the defendant that he 'had some good oats for sale', and the defendant had replied that he was always a buyer of good oats; whereas the defendant claimed the plaintiff had said 'good *old* oats', and he had replied that he was always a buyer of good *old* oats.

In summing up, the judge told the jury that the first question for their consideration was whether the word 'old' had been used by the plaintiff or defendant in making the contract, and that the inclination of his opinion was that the word 'old' had not been so used, but that was a question entirely for their consideration. If they were of opinion that the word 'old' had been so used, they would return a verdict for the defendant. If, however, they thought that the word 'old' had not been used, the second question would be, whether they were of opinion, on the state of the evidence, that the plaintiff believed the defendant to believe, or to be under the impression, that he was contracting for the purchase of old oats. If so, there would be a verdict for the defendant. But if the jury were of opinion that nothing was said as to the oats being old or new, and if they were of opinion that the plaintiff did not believe that the defendant believed or was under the impression that he was contracting for old oats, then they would find for the plaintiff.

The jury found a verdict for the defendant.

The question for the opinion of the Court was whether the direction to the jury as above is or is not correct.

Cockburn CJ

. . . It is to be regretted that the jury were not required to give specific answers to the questions so left to them. For, it is quite possible that their verdict may have been given for the defendant on the first ground; in which case there could, I think, be no doubt as to the propriety of the judge's direction; whereas now, as it is possible that the verdict of the jury—or at all events of some of them—may have proceeded on the second ground, we are called upon to consider and decide whether the ruling of the learned judge with reference to the second question was right.

For this purpose we must assume that nothing was said on the subject of the defendant's manager desiring to buy *old* oats, nor of the oats having been said to be old; while, on the other hand, we must assume that the defendant's manager believed the oats to be old oats, and that the plaintiff was conscious of the existence of such belief, but did nothing, directly or indirectly, to bring it about, simply offering his oats and exhibiting his sample, remaining perfectly passive as to what was passing in the mind of the other party. The question is whether, under such circumstances, the passive acquiescence of the seller in the self-deception of the buyer will entitle the latter to avoid the contract. I am of opinion that it will not . . .

I take the true rule to be, that where a specific article is offered for sale, without express warranty, or without circumstances from which the law will imply a warranty—as where, for instance, an article is ordered for a specific purpose—and the buyer has full opportunity of inspecting and forming his own judgment, if he chooses to act on his own judgment, the rule caveat emptor applies. If he gets the article he contracted to buy, and that article corresponds with what it was sold as, he gets all he is entitled to, and is bound by the contract. Here the defendant agreed to buy a specific parcel of oats. The oats were what they were sold as, namely, good oats according to the sample. The buyer persuaded himself they were old oats, when they were not so; but the seller neither said nor did anything to contribute to his deception. He has himself to blame. The question is not what a man of scrupulous morality or nice honour would do under such circumstances. The case put of the purchase of an estate, in which there is a mine under the surface, but the fact is unknown to the seller, is one in which a man of tender conscience or high honour would be unwilling to take advantage of the ignorance of the seller; but there can be no doubt that the contract for the sale of the estate would be binding...

Now, in this case, there was plainly no legal obligation on the plaintiff in the first instance to state whether the oats were new or old. He offered them for sale according to the sample, as he had a perfect right to do, and gave the buyer the fullest opportunity of inspecting the sample, which practically, was equivalent to an inspection of the oats themselves. What, then, was there to create any trust or confidence between the parties, so as to make it incumbent on the plaintiff to communicate the fact that the oats were not, as the defendant assumed them to be, old oats? If, indeed, the buyer, instead of acting on his own opinion, had asked the question whether the oats were old or new, or had said anything which intimated his understanding that the seller was selling the oats as old oats, the case would have been wholly different; or even if he had said anything which shewed that he was not acting on his own inspection and judgment, but assumed as the foundation of the contract that the oats were old, the silence of the seller, as a means of misleading him, might have amounted to a fraudulent concealment, such as would have entitled the buyer to avoid the contract. Here, however, nothing of the sort occurs. The buyer in no way refers to the seller, but acts entirely on his own judgment....

It only remains to deal with an argument which was pressed upon us, that the defendant in the present case intended to buy old oats, and the plaintiff to sell new, so the two minds were not ad idem; and that consequently there was no contract. This argument proceeds on the fallacy of confounding what was merely a motive operating on the buyer to induce him to buy with one of the essential conditions of the contract. Both parties were agreed as to the sale and purchase of this particular parcel of oats. The defendant believed the oats to be old, and was thus induced to agree to buy them, but he omitted to make their age a condition of the contract. All that can be said is, that the two minds were not ad idem as to the age of the oats; they certainly were ad idem as to the sale and purchase of them. Suppose a person is to buy a horse without a warranty, believing him to be sound, and the horse turns out unsound, could it be contended that it would be open to him to say that, as he had intended to buy a sound horse, and the seller to sell an unsound one, the contract was void, because the seller must have known from the price the buyer was willing to give, or from his general habits as a buyer of horses, that he thought the horse was sound? The cases are exactly parallel.

The result is that, in my opinion, the learned judge of the county court was wrong in leaving the second question to the jury, and that, consequently, the case must go down to a new trial.

Blackburn J

...I have more difficulty about the second point raised in the case. I apprehend that if one of the parties intends to make a contract on one set of terms, and the other intends to make a contract on another set of terms, or, as it is sometimes expressed, if the parties are not ad idem, there is no contract, unless the circumstances are such as to preclude one of the parties from denying that he has agreed to the terms of the other. The rule of law is that stated in *Freeman v Cooke*. If, whatever a man's real intention may be, he so conducts himself that a reasonable man would believe that he was assenting to the terms proposed by the other party, and that other party upon that belief enters into the contract with him, the man thus conducting himself would be equally bound as if he had intended to agree to the other party's terms.

The jury were directed that, if they believed the word 'old' was used, they should find for the defendant—and this was right; for if that was the case, it is obvious that neither did the defendant intend to enter into a contract on the plaintiff's terms, that is, to buy this parcel of oats without any stipulation as to their quality; nor could the plaintiff have been led to believe he was intending to do so.

But the second direction raises the difficulty. I think that, if from that direction the jury would understand that they were first to consider whether they were satisfied that the defendant intended to buy this parcel of oats on the terms that it was part of his contract with the plaintiff that they were old oats, so as to have the warranty of the plaintiff to that effect, they were properly told that, if that was so, the defendant could not be bound to a contract without any such warranty unless the plaintiff was misled. But I doubt whether the direction would bring to the minds of the jury the distinction between agreeing to take the oats under the belief that they were old, and agreeing to take the oats under the belief that the plaintiff contracted that they were old.

The difference is the same as that between buying a horse believed to be sound, and buying one believed to be warranted sound: but I doubt if it was made obvious to the jury, and I doubt this the more because I do not see much evidence to justify a finding for the defendant on this latter ground if the word 'old' was not used. There may have been more evidence than is stated in the case and the demeanour of the witnesses may have strengthened the impression produced by the evidence there was; but it does not seem a very satisfactory verdict if it proceeded on this latter ground. I agree, therefore, in the result that there should be a new trial.

Hannen J

... In order to relieve the defendant it was necessary that the jury should find not merely that the plaintiff believed the defendant to believe that he was buying old oats, but that he believed the defendant to believe that he, the plaintiff, was contracting to sell old oats. ...

Judgment accordingly.

NOTES

1. If the word 'old' was used, on what grounds should judgment be given for the defendant? One ground would be that there was a warranty by the seller that the oats were old, another that he had misrepresented the age of the oats.

2. Even if the sale is in what Anson calls 'general terms' (ie of that piece of China or those oats, rather than of 'a piece of Dresden' or 'so many old oats'), does it seem fair that A should be able to hold X to the contract for the china even if A knows that X thinks it is a piece of Dresden? See further Chapter 20.

3. In *Scriven Bros & Co v Hindley & Co*, was the contract meant to be for 'lots x and y', or was it that the sellers were trying to sell what they were promising was tow and the buyers were trying to buy what they thought was promised to be hemp?

4. In the Canadian case of *Imperial Glass Ltd v Consolidated Supplies Ltd* (1960) 22 DLR (2d) 759 (BC, CA), a glazing subcontractor put in a bid for a job at far too low a figure because an assistant had misplaced a decimal point in calculating the square footage of glass involved. The court held that this was not a mistake about the terms of the contract, but only about the motives for it, so that the offeree could accept the bid even though he knew of the mistake. Do you agree with this reasoning? Do you think the outcome should have been different if the bid had set out the method of calculation, so that the error was 'on the face' of the bid? (Compare *McMaster University v Wilchar Construction Ltd* (1971) 22 DLR (3d) 9 (Ont), in which it was held that an employer could not hold a contractor to a bid that, to the employer's knowledge, omitted an escalation clause.)

5. The same requirement, that the mistake must be about the terms of the contract, seems to apply to rectification as well: see the next case.

■ *Frederick E Rose (London) Ltd v William H Pim Jnr & Co Ltd*
[1953] 2 All ER 739, Court of Appeal

The plaintiffs were asked by an English firm in Egypt if they could supply 'up to five hundred tons of Moroccan horsebeans described here as feveroles', which a customer had asked them for. The plaintiffs did not know what feveroles were, and consulted the defendants, who replied 'feveroles means just horsebeans'. The plaintiffs then agreed to buy five hundred tons of Tunisian horsebeans from the defendants; they also entered a contract with the firm in Egypt in similar terms, and the defendants agreed to buy a like quantity of horsebeans from an Algerian company. When the customer in Egypt ultimately received the beans, he complained that they were not feveroles. There are three sizes of bean, 'feves', 'feveroles' and 'fevettes', all of which in English are known generically as horsebeans, and the beans supplied were the larger and less valuable feves, not feveroles. The customer took the beans but claimed damages. In order to cover themselves against a claim against them by the firm in Egypt, the plaintiffs sought to have their agreement with the defendants rectified to read 'feveroles', so that they would be able to claim damages from the defendants for having delivered the wrong article.

Denning LJ

... The buyers now, after accepting the goods, seek to rectify the contract. Instead of its being a contract for 'horsebeans' simpliciter, they seek to make it a contract of 'horsebeans described in Egypt as feveroles' or, in short, a contract for 'feveroles'. The judge has granted their request. He has found that there was 'a mutual and fundamental mistake' and that the sellers and the buyers, through their respective market clerks, 'intended to deal in horsebeans of the feverole type'. And he has held that, because that was their intention—their continuing common intention—the court could rectify their contract to give effect to it. In this I think he was wrong. Rectification is concerned with contracts and documents, not with intentions. In order to get rectification, it is necessary to show that the parties were in complete agreement on the terms of their contract, but by an error wrote them down wrongly. And in this regard, in order to ascertain the terms of their contract, you do not look into the inner minds of the parties—into their intentions—any more than you do in the formation of any other contract. You look at their outward acts, ie, at what they said or wrote to one another in coming to their agreement, and then compare it with the document which they have signed. If you can predicate with certainty what their contract was, and that it is, by a common mistake, wrongly expressed in the document, then you rectify the document. But nothing less will suffice. It is not necessary that all the formalities of the contract should have been executed so as to make it enforceable at law: see *Shipley Urban District Council v Bradford Corpn;* but, formalities apart, there must have been a concluded contract. There is a passage in *Crane v Hegeman-Harris Co Inc*, which suggests that a continuing common intention alone will suffice, but I am clearly of the opinion that a continuing common intention is not sufficient unless it has found expression in outward agreement. There could be no certainty at all in business transactions if a party who had entered into a firm contract could afterwards turn round and claim to have it rectified on the ground that the parties intended something different. He is allowed to prove, if he can, that they *agreed something different:* see *Lovell & Christmas, Ltd v Wall* . . . , per Lord Cozens-Hardy MR and per Buckley LJ: but not that they *intended* something different.

The present case is a good illustration of the distinction. The parties, no doubt, intended that the goods should satisfy the inquiry of the Egyptian buyers, namely, 'horsebeans described in Egypt as feveroles'. They assumed that they would do so, but they made no contract to that effect. Their agreement, as outwardly expressed, both orally and in writing, was for 'horsebeans'. That is all that the sellers ever committed themselves to supply, and all they should be bound to. There was, no doubt, an erroneous assumption underlying the contract—an assumption for which it might have been set aside on the ground of misrepresentation or mistake—but that is very different from an erroneous expression of the contract, such as to give rise to rectification. The matter can best be tested by asking what would have been the position if the contract between the sellers and the buyers had been for 'feveroles'. Surely, then, the sellers on their side would have stipulated with their Algerian suppliers for the delivery of 'feveroles', and the buyers on their side would have agreed with their sub-buyers to deliver 'feveroles'. It would not be fair to rectify one of the contracts without rectifying all three, a thing which is obviously impossible.

There is one other matter I must mention. In the statement of claim the buyers originally claimed damages for breach of a collateral warranty—a warranty that the horsebeans would be a compliance with a demand for 'feveroles'—but that claim was formally abandoned at the trial. I do not myself quite see why it was abandoned. Section 4 of the Sale of Goods Act 1893, was no bar to it. Nor was such a warranty in anyway in contradiction of the written contract. *(Smith v Jeffryes* was not an action on a collateral warranty.) The only difficulty might be whether it was a contractual warranty or merely an innocent misrepresentation. I should myself have thought that it had a better chance of success than the claim for rectification. It was put forward by the buyers very forcibly in their letter on Mar 12, 1951, but its abandonment at the trial makes it impossible for us to consider it. We have only to consider the question of rectification, and on that I think that the buyers fail. I agree that the appeal should be allowed and judgment entered for the sellers.

Morris LJ

...It seems to me clear beyond doubt that both parties proceeded on the basis that 'feveroles' and 'horsebeans' were the same. Mr Hampson expressed the matter succinctly when he said:

'I had agreed to buy because feveroles were horsebeans and horsebeans were feveroles.'

In that belief the parties came to agreement, and the formal written contracts were prepared and signed. The parties had throughout a clear common intention and purpose of buying and selling horsebeans, and their written agreements faithfully embodied and exactly recorded what they had agreed. In these circumstances it seems to me that no claim for rectification can succeed.

Singleton LJ delivered a concurring judgment.

Appeal allowed.

■ Spencer, 'The Rule in *L'Estrange v Graucob*' [1973]
CLJ 104, 108–113

A rival theory of agreement

The notion behind what has been said so far is that A's words must be judged as they appeared to B, the person to whom they were directed. There is nothing new or original in this: in fact, it has been repeated so often in the past that some readers may wonder why it has been necessary to labour the point. The reason is that in recent years an even more objective theory of agreement has emerged, according to which A's words must be judged, not as they appeared to B, but as they would have appeared to C, a reasonable man eavesdropping on the negotiations. The test is not what the other party would have thought, but how things would have appeared to the reasonable fly on the wall. This rival theory has begun to gain ground at the expense of the more orthodox theory which we have just examined, and it is time we examined it closely to see what its implications are.

In some cases, the two theories produce the same results. Thus according to either theory, the unobservant A will usually be bound to buy the bull he bid for thinking it was a cow; if the *Smith v Hughes* theory is used, this is because A led B to believe A was contracting to buy a bull; if the later theory is used, it is because a reasonable bystander would have thought A was contracting to buy a bull. On these facts, it makes no difference which theory is used—'you pays your money and you takes your choice' . . . .

The dissemination of the 'fly on the wall' theory of agreement appears to be largely the work of Lord Denning MR. In *Solle v Butcher* he said

> 'once a contract has been made, that is to say, once the parties, whatever their inmost states of mind, have to all outward appearances agreed with sufficient certainty in the same terms on the same subject-matter, then the contract is good unless and until it is set aside for failure of some condition on which the existence of the contract depends, or for fraud, or on some equitable ground. Neither party can rely on his own mistake to say it was a nullity from the beginning, no matter that it was a mistake which to his mind was fundamental, *and no matter that the other party knew that he was under a mistake.'*

. . . The 'fly on the wall' theory is . . . open to the objection that it leads to absurd results. What happens if the parties are *inwardly* agreed, but *outwardly* at variance, or agreed on something else? Suppose, for example, that Ali and Benedetto, two immigrants with little knowledge of English, agree on the purchase and sale of a 'bull' both of them intending to deal with a cow, and in the belief that the word 'bull' means the female of the species. According to the 'fly on the wall' theory of agreement, they have made a contract to buy and sell a bull, although A does not want one and B has not got one to sell. This is ridiculous. Yet this is the result reached in the Court of Appeal by Denning LJ in *Rose v Pim*. The facts as interpreted by Denning LJ were that A and B made a written agreement for the purchase and sale of 'horsebeans', by which both A and B meant 'feveroles', which, again according to Denning LJ, are something 'essentially different'. Denning LJ held that although both parties meant to deal with feveroles, they were contractually bound to buy and sell horsebeans, because their agreement as outwardly expressed, both orally and in writing, was for 'horsebeans'. It is a platitude to say that the law of contract exists to enforce agreements, and that agreements are what people have agreed to do, not what officious people with no interest in the matter would think they had agreed to do. It may be acceptable for the law occasionally to force upon *one* of the parties an agreement he did not want; but surely there is something wrong with a theory which forces upon *both* of the parties an agreement which *neither* of them wants. If the 'fly on the wall' theory does this, that is an excellent reason for rejecting it.

NOTE

Is Spencer's analysis of *Rose v Pim* correct? Did the parties mean to deal in feveroles, or did they mean to deal in horsebeans, which they thought were the same thing as feveroles? What would have been the outcome of the case if the parties had known the differences between the various sizes of beans, but had both mistakenly thought the middle-sized beans were called 'feves' and had concluded their contract in these terms; if the buyers had later refused to accept anything but the middle-sized beans properly called feveroles, could the sellers not have obtained rectification? This situation is akin to Spencer's example about the cow and the bull. See Glanville Williams (1954) 17 MLR 154, 155.

V. MISTAKES AS TO IDENTITY

■ *Boulton v Jones*

(1857) 27 LJ Ex 117, Exchequer

The defendant sent a written order for some goods to Brocklehurst, against whom the defendant had a set-off. Unknown to the defendant, Brocklehurst had that day sold his stock-in-trade and assigned his business to the plaintiff. The plaintiff sent the goods to the defendant and only later sent him an invoice showing the change in the business. The defendant refused to pay. At the trial, it was objected that the contract was with Brocklehurst, not the plaintiff, and the Assessor reserved the point.

Pollock CB

. . . Now the rule of law is clear, that if you propose to make a contract with A, then B cannot substitute himself for A without your consent and to your disadvantage, securing to himself all the benefit of the contract. . . .

Martin B

. . . Where the facts prove that the defendant never meant to contract with A alone, B can never force a contract upon him; he has dealt with A, and a contract with no one else can be set up against him.

Bramwell, B

It is an admitted fact, that the defendant supposed he was dealing with Brocklehurst; and the plaintiff misled him by executing the order unknown to him. It is clear also, that if the plaintiff were at liberty to sue, it would be a prejudice to the defendant, because it would deprive him of a set-off, which he would have had if the action had been brought by the party with whom he supposed he was dealing. And upon that my judgment proceeds . . .

As to the difficulty suggested, that if the plaintiff cannot sue for the price of goods, no one else can, I do not feel pressed by it any more than I did in such a case as I may suppose, of work being done to my house, for instance, by a party different from the one with whom I had contracted to do it. The defendant has, it is true, had the goods; but it is also true that he has consumed them and cannot return them. And that is no reason why he should pay money to the plaintiff which he never contracted to pay, but upon some contract which he never made, and the substitution of which for that which he did make would be to his prejudice, and involve a pecuniary loss by depriving him of a set-off.

Channell B delivered a concurring judgment.

Rule absolute for a nonsuit.

NOTES

1. The plaintiff had been Brocklehurst's foreman and may have known of the set-off. If he had been a newcomer, would he have had any reason to think that the offer was not addressed to the current owner of the business?

2. The goods were supplied and appear to have been used by the defendant. Even if there was no contract to sell them to him, shouldn't he still have to pay their value, either in an action for conversion of someone else's property, or by way of restitution? Bramwell 'disliked the whole law of quasi-contract, for he could not understand how a man could be forced to pay for a benefit which he had received but which he had not agreed to pay for': Atiyah, *Rise and Fall of Freedom of Contract*, 1979, p 376.

3. Without accepting Bramwell's extreme view, it can be argued that Jones was not unjustly enriched because he expected to receive the goods without further payment to anyone. If Boulton acted 'officiously' in supplying goods under an order that he should have known was not meant for him, there seems some merit in this argument, particularly if Jones could not recover the credit balance on his running account with Brocklehurst, for instance because the latter had subsequently become insolvent see *Continental Forest Products Inc v Chandler Supply Co* 95 Idaho 739, 518 P2d 121 (1974). A neat solution

would be to require Jones to assign to Boulton the debt owed him by Brocklehurst: if Boulton manages to enforce the debt, he gets paid without Jones being put at risk.

Most of the reported cases of contracts involving mistaken identity have a different and distinctive fact pattern. A would-be seller of goods is tricked by a rogue into believing that the rogue is someone else, and on the strength of that the seller allows the rogue to buy the goods and take them away on credit or against a cheque. Before the seller discovers the fraud or that the cheque is worthless, the rogue resells or pledges the goods to an innocent party (for cash) and disappears. In an attempt to recover the goods (or their value) from the third party, the original seller brings an action of conversion against him. Whether this action will succeed depends on whether the 'property' in the goods has passed to the third party via the rogue. There is no doubt that, if there is any contract between the seller and the rogue, it will be voidable for fraud, and if the seller acts quickly enough he may be able to rescind and revest the property in himself (this normally entails the victim of the fraud giving notice of rescission to the fraudulent party, but it has been held that giving notice to the police and other authorities may suffice if the rogue is deliberately hiding: *Car and Universal Finance Co Ltd v Caldwell* [1965] 1 QB 525). In the cases to be considered here, however, the right to rescind was lost when the innocent third party acquired rights over the goods, ie before the seller discovered that he had been tricked. If, on the other hand, the original seller can show that there was no contract with the rogue, then the rogue never acquired any property in the goods and could not pass any to the innocent third party, so the owner's action in conversion will succeed.

In these cases, therefore, the original seller relies on his mistake about the rogue's identity as preventing the formation of a contract. There are many cases, and not all of them are easy to reconcile. Some of the older ones may have been influenced by the theory mentioned earlier that actual agreement, *consensus ad idem*, is necessary for the formation of a contract. Thus in *Cundy v Lindsay* (1878) 3 App Cas 459, the rogue was named Blenkarn and had an address at 37 Wood Street. A highly respectable firm called Blenkiron & Co carried on business at 123 Wood Street. Blenkarn ordered large numbers of handkerchiefs from the plaintiffs, signing his name so as to look like Blenkiron. The plaintiffs despatched the goods on credit to 'Blenkiron & Co' but at 37 Wood Street; they were received by Blankarn and some were resold to the defendants before the fraud was discovered. Queen's Bench held that there was a contract: '...the intention of the plaintiffs was to contract with the person carrying on business at 37, Wood Street.' (See *Lindsay v Cundy* (1876) 1 QBD 348, 355.) The Court of Appeal and the House of Lords disagreed, the Lord Chancellor (Lord Cairns) saying (at 465):

> ...[H]ow is it possible to imagine that in that state of things any contract could have arisen between the Respondents and Blenkarn the dishonest man? Of him they knew nothing, and of him they never thought. With him they never intended to deal. Their minds never even for an instant of time rested on him, and as between him and them there was no *consensus* of mind which could lead to any agreement or any contract whatsoever.

In *King's Norton Metal Co Ltd v Edridge, Merrett & Co* (1897) 14 TLR 98, CA, the rogue set up business as Hallam & Co and had notepaper printed that suggested that Hallam & Co was a substantial concern with agencies and depots overseas. The plaintiffs supplied goods on credit and the rogue sold them to the defendants. The Court of Appeal held that there was a contract between the plaintiffs and the rogue: *Cundy v Lindsay* was distinguished on the ground that there a confusion of two distinct entities was involved, whereas the plaintiffs had not confused Hallam & Co with anyone else.

In *Phillips v Brooks Ltd* [1919] 2 KB 243, 88 LJKB 953, a man named North entered the plaintiff's jewellery shop and selected some pearls and a ring. As he made out a cheque to pay for them, he said 'You see who I am, I am Sir George Bullough', and gave an address in St James' Square. After checking that Sir George, of whom he had heard, did live at the address given, the plaintiff allowed the rogue to take the ring. The rogue pledged the ring to the defendant, who had no notice of the fraud. Horridge J held that the plaintiff intended to contract with the person present, although he thought that person was Sir George.

■ *Ingram v Little*
[1960] 3 All ER 332, Court of Appeal

The Ingram sisters were joint owners of a car that they advertised for sale. The rogue called on them and agreed with one of the sisters to buy the car for £717. When, however, he offered a cheque in payment, she categorically refused to accept it. He then said he was a PGM Hutchinson of Stanstead House, Stanstead Road, Caterham. While the discussion was going on, the other sister went to the post office and checked this name and address in the telephone directory. The sisters then agreed to let him buy the car and pay by cheque. The cheque was dishonoured and the rogue, who was not PGM Hutchinson, disappeared after having sold it to the defendant, who bought in good faith. The plaintiffs' action for conversion succeeded and the defendant appealed.

Sellers LJ

. . . It does not seem to me to matter whether the right view of the facts is, as the judge has held and as I would agree, that there was no concluded contract before the cheque book was produced and before the vital fraudulent statements were made or that there was a concluded contract which Hutchinson at once repudiated by refusing to pay cash and that this repudiation was accepted by the plaintiffs and the transaction was then and there at an end. The property would not have passed until cash had been paid and it never was paid or intended to be paid.

Was there a contract of sale subsequently made which led to the plaintiffs' taking Hutchinson's cheque and in exchange for it handing over the car and its log book? The judgment holds that there never was a concluded contract, applying, as I understand it, the elementary factors required by law to establish a contract. The learned judge, treating the plaintiffs as the offerors and the rogue Hutchinson as the offeree, finds that the plaintiffs in making their offer to sell the car not for cash but for a cheque (which in the circumstances of the Bank Holiday week-end could not be banked before the following Tuesday, Aug 6) were under the belief that they were dealing with, and therefore making their offer to, the honest Mr P G M Hutchinson, of Caterham, who they had reason to believe was a man of substance and standing. Hutchinson, the offeree, knew precisely what was in the minds of the two ladies, for he had put it there and he knew that their offer was intended for Mr P G M Hutchinson, of Caterham, and that they were making no offer to and had no intention to contract with him, as he was. There was no offer which he, Hutchinson, could accept and therefore there was no contract. The judge pointed out that the offer which the plaintiffs made was one which was capable of being accepted only by the honest Mr P G M Hutchinson, of Caterham, and was incapable of acceptance by the rogue Hutchinson. In all the circumstances of this case I would accept the learned judge's findings. Indeed the conclusion so reached seems self-evident.

Is the conclusion to be held wrong in law? If it is, then, as I see it, it must be on the sole ground that as Hutchinson was present, albeit making fraudulent statements to induce the plaintiffs to part with their car to him in exchange for his worthless cheque and was successful in so doing, then a bargain must have been struck with him personally, however much he deceived the plaintiffs into thinking they were dealing with someone else.

Where two parties are negotiating together and there is no question of one or the other purporting to act as agent for another and an agreement is reached, the normal and obvious conclusion would no doubt be that they are the contracting parties. A contrary finding would not be justified unless very clear evidence demanded it. The unfortunate position of the defendant in this case illustrates how third parties who deal in good faith with the fraudulent person may be prejudiced. The mere presence of an individual cannot, however, be conclusive that an apparent bargain which he may make is made with him. If he were disguised in appearance and in dress to represent someone else and the other party, deceived by the disguise, dealt with him on the basis that he was that person and would not have contracted had he known the truth, then, it seems clear, there would be no contract established. If words are substituted for outward disguise so as to depict a different person from the one physically present, in what circumstances would the result be different?

Whether the person portrayed, by disguise or words, is known to the other party or not is important in considering whether the identity of the person is of any moment or whether it is a matter of indifference....

The question in each case should be solved in my opinion by applying the test which Slade J applied: 'How ought the promisee to have interpreted the promise?' in order to find whether a contract has been entered into. I am in agreement with the learned judge when he quotes, accepts and applies the following passage from Dr Goodhart's article (Law Quarterly Review (1941), Vol 57, at p 231):

> 'It is the interpretation of the *promise* which is the essential thing. This is usually based on the interpretation which a reasonable man, in the promisee's position, would place on it, but in those cases where the promisor knows that the promisee has placed a peculiar interpretation on his words, then this is the binding one. The English law is not concerned with the motives of the parties nor with the reasons which influenced their actions. For practical reasons it has limited itself to the simple questions: what did the promisor promise, and how should... The legal position is, I think, well illustrated by Dr Goodhart in the article already referred to. There is a difference between the case where A makes an offer to B in the belief that B is not B but is someone else and the case where A makes an offer to B in the belief that B is X. In the first case B does in fact receive an offer, even though the offeror does not know that it is to B to whom he is making it, since he believes B to be someone else. In the second case A does not in truth make any offer to B at all; he thinks that B is X, for whom alone the offer is meant. There was an offer intended for and available only to X. B cannot accept it, if he knew or ought to have known that it was not addressed to him...'

If it is the formation of a contract which calls for consideration, as it is here, 'How ought the promisee to have interpreted the promise?' is in my opinion the correct approach, as the judge has held; but I recognise that the correct answer may not always prove as ascertainable as I believe it to be in the present case. I would dismiss the appeal.

Pearce LJ

I agree. The question here is whether there was any contract, whether offer and acceptance met...

An apparent contract made orally inter praesentes raises particular difficulties. The offer is apparently addressed to the physical person present. Prima facie, he, by whatever name he is called, is the person to whom the offer is made. His physical presence identified by sight and hearing preponderates over vagaries of nomenclature. 'Praesentia corporis tollit errorem nominis' said Lord Bacon. Yet clearly, though difficult, it is not impossible to rebut the prima facie presumption that the offer can be accepted by the person to whom it is physically addressed. To take two extreme instances. If a man orally commissions a portrait from some unknown artist who had deliberately passed himself off, whether by disguise or merely by verbal cosmetics, as a famous painter, the imposter could not accept the offer. For, though the offer is made to him physically, it is obviously, as he knows, addressed to the famous painter. The mistake in identity on such facts is clear and the nature of the contract makes it obvious that identity was of vital importance to the offeror. At the other end of the scale, if a shopkeeper sells goods in a normal cash transaction to a man who misrepresents himself as being some well known figure, the transaction will normally be valid. For the shopkeeper was ready to sell goods for cash to the world at large, and the particular identity of the purchaser in such a contract was not of sufficient importance to override the physical presence identified by sight and hearing. Thus the nature of the proposed contract must have a strong bearing on the question whether the intention of the offeror (as understood by his offeree) was to make his offer to some other particular identity rather than to the physical person to whom it was orally offered.

In our case the facts lie in the debatable area between the two extremes...I should hesitate long before interfering with [the learned judge's] finding of fact and I would only do so if compelled by the evidence or by the view that the judge drew some erroneous inference...I am not persuaded that on the evidence he should have found otherwise.

Devlin LJ dissented on the ground that Hutchinson's identity was immaterial to Miss Ingram. She was concerned only with his creditworthiness.

Appeal dismissed.

NOTE

Is an explanation of the test laid down in this case that, in order to prevent a contract coming into existence, the mistake must be one about a term—ie one of the terms of the offer must be that the offer is open only to the person the rogue is thought to be?

■ *Lewis v Averay*
[1971] 3 All ER 907, Court of Appeal

L was the owner of a car that he wanted to sell. He advertised it in a newspaper. In reply, a man rang up; he gave no name but said that he was interested in buying the car at the price advertised. Arrangements were made for him to come to L's flat that evening. He was there shown the car, which was parked outside. The man, who turned out to be a rogue, tested the car and said that he liked it. L and the rogue then went to the flat of L's fiancée, Miss K. There, the rogue introduced himself as 'Richard Green' and made L and Miss K believe that he was the well-known film actor Richard Greene. He said that he would like to buy the car and they agreed a price of £450. The rogue wrote out a cheque for that amount, signing it 'RA Green'. He wanted to take the car at once. L was hesitant and asked for proof of identity. He was shown a special pass of admission to Pinewood Studios with an official stamp on it. It bore the name 'Richard A Green', an address, and a photograph, which was plainly that of the rogue. On seeing this, L was satisfied and let the rogue have the car and log book. A few days later, the bank told L that the cheque was worthless. Meanwhile, the rogue had sold the car to A, who bought it in good faith and without knowledge of the fraud.

L brought an action against A for conversion of the car, and was successful at first instance. On appeal:

Lord Denning MR

...This case therefore raises the question: what is the effect of a mistake by one party as to the identity of the other? It has sometimes been said that, if a party makes a mistake as to the identity of the person with whom he is contracting, there is no contract, or, if there is a contract, it is a nullity and void, so that no property can pass under it. This has been supported by a reference to the French jurist Pothier but I have said before, and I repeat now, his statement is no part of English law. I know that it was quoted by Viscount Haldane in *Lake v Simmons* and, as such, misled Tucker J in *Sowler v Potter* into holding that a lease was void whereas it was really voidable. But the statement by Pothier has given rise to such refinements that it is time it was dead and buried altogether.

For instance, in *Ingram v Little* the majority of the court suggested that the difference between *Phillips v Brooks* and *Ingram v Little* was that in *Phillips v Brooks* the contract of sale was concluded (so as to pass the property to the rogue) before the rogue made the fraudulent misrepresentation, whereas in *Ingram v Little* the rogue made the fraudulent misrepresentation before the contract was concluded. My own view is that in each case the property in the goods did not pass until the seller let the rogue have the goods.

Again it has been suggested that a mistake as to the identity of a person is one thing; and a mistake as to his attributes is another. A mistake as to identity, it is said, avoids a contract; whereas a mistake as to attributes does not. But this is a distinction without a difference. A man's very name is one of his attributes. It is also a key to his identity. If then, he gives a false name, is it a mistake as to his identity? or a mistake as to his attributes? These fine distinctions do no good to the law.

As I listened to the argument in this case, I felt it wrong that an innocent purchaser (who knew nothing of what passed between the seller and the rogue) should have his title depend on such refinements. After all, he has acted with complete circumspection and in entire good faith; whereas it was the seller who let the rogue have the goods and thus enabled him to commit the fraud. I do not, therefore, accept the theory that a mistake as to identity renders a contract void.

I think the true principle is that which underlies the decision of this court in *King's Norton Metal Co Ltd v Eldridge, Merrett & Co Ltd* and of Horridge J in *Phillips v Brooks Ltd*, which has stood for these last 50 years. It is this: when two parties have come to a contract—or rather what appears, on the face of it, to be a contract—the fact that one party is mistaken as to the identity of the other does not mean that there is no contract, or that the contract is a nullity and void from the beginning. It only means that the contract is voidable, that is, liable to be set aside at the instance of the mistaken person, so long as he does so before third parties have in good faith acquired rights under it.

Applied to the cases such as the present, this principle is in full accord with the presumption stated by Pearce LJ and also by Devlin LJ in *Ingram v Little*. When a dealing is had between a seller like Mr Lewis and a person who is actually there present before him, then the presumption in law is that there is a contract, even though there is a fraudulent impersonation by the buyer representing himself as a different man than he is. There is a contract made with the very person there, who is present in person. It is liable no doubt to be avoided for fraud but it is still a good contract under which title will pass unless and until it is avoided. . . .

Megaw LJ

For myself, with very great respect, I find it difficult to understand the basis, either in logic or in practical considerations, of the test laid down by the majority of the court in *Ingram v Little*. That test is I think accurately recorded in the headnote:

> '. . . where a person physically present and negotiating to buy a chattel fraudulently assumed the identity of an existing third person, the test to determine to whom the offer was addressed was how ought the promisee to have interpreted the promise . . .'

The promisee, be it noted, is the rogue. The question of the existence of a contract and therefore the passing of property, and therefore the right of third parties, if the test is correct, is made to depend on the view which some rogue should have formed, presumably knowing that he is a rogue, as to the state of mind of the opposite party, to the negotiation, who does not know that he is dealing with a rogue.

However that may be, and assuming that the test as so stated is indeed valid, in my view this appeal can be decided on a short and simple point. It is the point which was put at the outset of his argument by counsel for the defendant. The well-known textbook on the Law of Contract, *Cheshire and Fifoot* deals with the question of invalidity of a contract by virtue of unilateral mistake, and in particular unilateral mistake relating to mistaken identity. The learned editors describe what in their submission are certain facts that must be established in order to enable one to avoid contract on the basis of unilateral mistake by him as to the identity of the opposite party. The first of those facts is that at the time when he made the offer he regarded the identity of the offeree as a matter of vital importance. To translate that into the facts of the present case, it must be established that at the time of offering to sell his car to the rogue, Mr Lewis regarded the identity of the rogue as a matter of vital importance. In my view, counsel for the defendant is abundantly justified, on the notes of the evidence and on the findings of the learned judge, in his submission that the mistake of Mr Lewis went no further than a mistake as to the attributes of the rogue. It was simply a mistake as to the creditworthiness of the man who was there present and who described himself as Mr Green. . . .

Phillimore LJ also held that a contract had come into existence.

Appeal allowed.

NOTE

These cases were all reconsidered in *Shogun Finance Ltd v Hudson* [2003] UKHL 62 [2004] 1 AC 919 [2004] 1 All ER 215. A man, X, went to a dealers and negotiated to acquire a Mitsubishi Shogun on hire-purchase terms. He was allowed to take the car away and, soon afterwards, sold it to the defendant, Mr Hudson. Under s 27 of the Hire Purchase Act 1964, a non-trade buyer of a car who buys in good faith from a hirer under a hire-purchase agreement becomes the owner. So Mr Hudson would have become the owner if the hire-purchase transaction were valid. In fact, X had told the dealer that his name was Patel and produced Mr Patel's driving licence. The dealer had completed the paperwork, using Mr Patel's name, and sent it to the finance company, who did a credit search on Mr Patel. No other checks were made on X's identity.

If X had been buying on credit from the dealer, this would have been very like *Phillips v Brooks, Ingram v Little* and *Lewis v Averay*. The House of Lords considered these cases and four of their Lordships clearly held that *Phillips v Brooks* and *Lewis v Averay* were correctly decided.

Lords Nicholls and Millett thought that this case should be treated in the same way, but the majority disagreed. They thought the case should be treated like *Cundy v Lindsay*. The hire-purchase contract purported to be with Mr Patel and not with X. There could be no contract with Mr Patel and there was no contract with X, because of the way in which the form was completed.

Lord Walker of Gestingthorpe said:

The objective nature of the enquiry tends to narrow, perhaps close to vanishing-point, the difference (mentioned in the speeches of my noble and learned friends Lord Millett and Lord Phillips of Worth Matravers MR) between the person for whom the offer or acceptance is *intended* and the person to whom it is *directed*. I venture to suggest that the right question to ask, whether the parties to an alleged contract have been negotiating face-to-face or at a distance, is to whom the offer is *made* (or to whom acceptance of an offer is made; but I shall for the sake of simplicity assume that, as in this case, the rogue is the offeror). Posed in that way, the question may be no easier to answer, but it does avoid the sort of pointless speculation which Devlin LJ exposed in *Ingram v Little* [1960] 3 All ER 332 at 346, [1961] 1 QB 31, 65:

'If Miss Ingram had been asked whether she intended to contract with the man in the room or with Mr PGM Hutchinson, the question could have no meaning for her since she believed them both to be one and the same. The reasonable man of the law—if he stood in Miss Ingram's shoes—could not give any better answer.'

The principle to be applied in the case of face-to-face negotiations has sometimes been treated as an exception, but to my mind it is the best starting-point, as it exemplifies the simplest form of oral contract. The principle was first spelled out in England in *Phillips v Brooks Ltd* [1919] 2 KB 243, [1918–19] All ER Rep 246, following the Chief Justice of Massachusetts in *Edmunds v Merchants' Despatch Transportation Co* (1883) 135 Mass 283 at 284:

'The fact that the seller was induced to sell by fraud of the buyer made the sale voidable, but not void. He could not have supposed that he was selling to any other person; his intention was to sell to the person present, and identified by sight and hearing; it does not defeat the sale because the buyer assumed a false name, or practised any other deceit to induce the vendor to sell.'

The only case out of line with the principle is *Ingram v Little*. The reasoning in Devlin LJ's powerful dissenting judgment is in my view unanswerable. I consider that *Ingram v Little* was wrongly decided.

My noble and learned friends Lord Nicholls of Birkenhead and Lord Millett accept the face-to-face principle but consider that it should not be limited to situations where the parties have negotiated face-to-face. Lord Millett also takes the view that the principle should not be regarded as a mere presumption, but as a rule of law (subject, as I understand it, to an exception in cases of agency, such as *Hardman v Booth* (1863) 1 H & C 803, 158 ER 1107, which may be the best explanation of the difficult case of *Lake v Simmons* [1927] AC 487, [1927] All ER Rep 49 (see Sir Jack Beatson's 28th (2002) edition of *Anson's Law of Contract* pp 330–331, which contain an illuminating discussion).

If the principle is no more than a presumption, it is a strong presumption, and exceptions to it would be rare (in *Ingram v Little* Devlin LJ himself ([1960] 3 All ER 332 at 347, [1961] 1 QB 31 at 67) was content to leave this point open). I would hesitate to state it as an inflexible rule (apart from cases of agency) because the notion of one individual impersonating another covers a wide range of factual situations (broadly corresponding to the wide range of meaning conveyed by saying that one person knows, or knows of, another). At one end of the spectrum is the confidence trickster who falsely but convincingly asserts that he is a baronet (or a barrister, or a brain surgeon) in order to inspire confidence and obtain credit. Then there are cases like *Phillips v Brooks Ltd* and *Ingram v Little*, where the rogue falsely gives the name and address of a real person whose existence the other party can and does check (but whom the other party does not actually know by sight, or the deception would fail). The most audacious form of impersonation would be where a rogue (such as the Tichborne claimant was held to be) attempts, face-to-face, to deceive a member of the family of which he claims to be part, or someone else personally acquainted with the individual whom the rogue is impersonating. Impersonation of that sort must be very rare indeed, and probably limited to deception of those whose senses are impaired (as Isaac was when, according to Ch 27 of Genesis, Jacob successfully impersonated his elder twin brother Esau). I would not exclude the possibility that impersonation of that sort might be outside the presumption. Your Lordships were shown the decision of the Court of Appeals of New York in *Morgan Munitions Supply Co v Studebaker Corp* (1919) 123 NE 146, where one brother impersonated his more distinguished brother in order to obtain a contract of employment; but it appears (so far as can be discerned from the report) that the contract was in writing, and that neither brother was personally known to the employer.

I return to the question, which is of central importance to this appeal, whether (as Lord Nicholls and Lord Millett propose) the face-to-face principle should be applied much more generally. It may be that it should apply to an oral contract alleged to have been made on the telephone, where the parties are identified by hearing, although not by sight. An alleged oral contract made by telephone might be a case where the presumption applied, but was rebuttable. But to extend the principle to cases where the only contract was by written communication sent by post or by e-mail would be going far beyond identification by sight and hearing. Where there is an alleged contract reached by correspondence, offer and acceptance must be found, if they are to be found at all, in the terms of the documents. Devlin LJ put it simply and clearly in *Ingram v Little* [1960] 3 All ER 332 at 346, [1961] 1 QB 31 at 64:

'The classic case of *Cundy v Lindsay* was one in which the acceptance was not addressed to the offeror. The offer, as in the instant case, was addressed to a person who held himself out as willing to do business. But the offer was made by Blenkarn and the acceptance addressed to Blenkiron. The fact that there was a real Blenkiron, whom Blenkarn was pretending to be, showed that it was not a case of falsa demonstratio non nocet.'

There was in that case the appearance of a complete contract only because the rogue, Blenkarn, had forged the signature of Blenkiron & Co (Lord Cairns LC said ((1878) 3 App Cas 459 at 456, [1874–80] All ER Rep 1149 at 1151) 'just in the same way as if he had forged the signature'; but the facts as set out in the report appear to amount to nothing less than forgery.) The documentary evidence provided no ground for concluding that the manufacturer (Lindsay & Co) intended to contract with anyone other than Blenkiron & Co as addressee of the manufacturer's acceptance.

King's Norton Metal Co Ltd v Edridge, Merrett & Co Ltd (1897) 14 TLR 98 went the other way because there was no ground for concluding that the manufacturer's offer was made to anyone other than Wallis, trading as Hallam & Co. Wallis, trading as Hallam & Co, had previously placed at least one order with the manufacturer, and had paid with a cheque drawn by 'Hallam & Co'. The judge at first instance described the case as a long firm fraud. So in that case there was no question of the manufacturer being deceived into thinking he was dealing with someone else. The deceit was as to the standing and credit-worthiness of Wallis, who had embellished his writing paper with deceptive material.

In *Cundy v Lindsay* (1878) 3 App Cas 459 at 465, [1874–80] All ER Rep 1149 at 1151 Blenkiron & Co, the firm whose name was misappropriated by the rogue, was described by the Lord Chancellor as 'a well known and solvent house'. The implication is that Lindsay & Co, the manufacturer, would have known of its existence, although that was not a question explicitly put to the jury. What if Lindsay & Co had never heard of Blenkiron & Co? One answer to that question is that the sequence of events would probably have been different, since Lindsay & Co would have been put on enquiry as to what to make of the rogue's deceptive signature, and would probably have acted more cautiously before despatching such a large quantity of goods. There would have been more room for argument about who was the real addressee of the manufacturer's offer. The Latin maxim referred to by Devlin LJ in *Ingram v Little* case means in its full form that misdescription is not fatal when the real subject-matter is common ground. These last words are important. Whether the real subject is common ground depends on all the circumstances, and the old textbooks are full of illustrations, some going one way and some the other (see for instance *Jarman on Wills* (8th edn, 1951) vol 2, pp 1246 ff). The modern approach to construction of documents is much less regimented by detailed rules, but the essential issue remains the same.

However, the present appeal is, as my noble and learned friend Lord Hobhouse of Woodborough has demonstrated, easier to resolve. Shogun Finance had no doubt never heard of the real Mr Patel before the day on which the written contract was signed by the rogue, forging Mr Patel's signature. But by the time it accepted the written offer it had, by efficient information technology, confirmed that Mr Patel existed and had learned a good deal of relevant information about him, including his creditworthiness. The form of contract made quite clear that Shogun Finance's intention was to accept an offer made by the real Mr Patel, and no one else. The appellant's attempt to analyse the matter as a face-to-face contract (effected through the agency of the car salesman) was accepted by Sedley LJ but in my view it must fail, for the reasons stated by Lord Hobhouse. The appellant relied on the decision of this House in *Branwhite v Worcester Works Finance Ltd* [1968] 3 All ER 104, [1969] 1 AC 552, but in my view it is against him: see especially the remarks of Lord Upjohn ([1968] 3 All ER 104 at 116, [1969] 1 AC 552 at 578).

VI. *NON EST FACTUM*

If one party is induced to sign a contract by the other's misrepresenting what the document signed contains, the resulting 'contract' is at least voidable for misrepresentation (see Chapter 13). It may also be that the first party can escape from the contract he has signed on the ground of mistake: the other party may have known that the document did not represent the first party's true intention. As between the original parties, the case should be dealt with as one of misrepresentation or of mistake: *Lloyds Bank plc v Waterhouse* (1991) 10 TrLR 161, 185, 191.

As we have seen, even between the contracting parties the right to rescind for fraud will be lost once an innocent third party's rights have intervened. Moreover, in many cases, the fraud is committed not by the other party to the contract but by a third party. For instance, in *United Dominions Trust Ltd v Western* [1976] QB 513, the defendant signed a hire-purchase proposal in blank and left it with the car dealer, who filled in incorrect figures and forwarded it to the finance company. In such a case, no question of mistake can arise if the other party does not know what has happened.

Equally, no question of mistake can arise if the document signed is not a contract with the fraudulent party but a conveyance to him: the conveyance may be voidable for fraud, but it cannot be void for mistake as offer and acceptance are not required for such a conveyance to be valid (see Russell LJ in *Gallie v Lee* [1969] 2 Ch 17, 41). If a third party has acquired rights over the property conveyed, the right to rescind will have been lost.

In these cases, therefore, the mistaken party's only hope will be to show that the document was totally invalid under the old defence of *non est factum*. This was originally available to illiterate people who signed deeds that had been read over to them incorrectly: at least if they had not been negligent, they could claim that the deed 'was not their deed'. The law of *non est factum* was comprehensively reviewed by the House of Lords in *Gallie v Lee, sub nom Saunders v Anglia Building Society* [1971] AC 1004. A distinction that had grown up between mistakes as to the 'character' and as to the 'contents' of the document was rejected and it was held that the defence is available to a party who signed under a fundamental misapprehension as to the substance of the document in terms of its practical result, provided that the party also proves that he or she took all due care. It was pointed out that the defence will very seldom be available to literate people who are in full possession of their faculties and who sign documents in a language they can understand. On the facts of the case, a widow 78 wanted to help her nephew raise money on the security of her house provided that she could continue to live there. She signed what she was told was a deed of gift of her house to her nephew, but which was actually an assignment on sale to a third party for £3,000 (which was never paid). This scheme had been arranged by the nephew, who did not wish to raise the money in his own name in case this enabled his wife, from whom he was separated, to enforce maintenance payments against him. The third party mortgaged the house to the building society but failed to pay the money over to the nephew. The widow had not read the document because her glasses were broken. It was held that the widow's mistake was not sufficiently serious; the document enabled the nephew to raise the money, although not in the way she had envisaged.

NOTES

1. Why is this defence so restricted? For a full discussion, see Stone, 'The Limits of *Non est Factum* after *Gallie v Lee*' (1972) 88 LQR 190.

2. Should the defence not be abolished altogether?

3. Can it be argued that where a person signs a contract after a fraudulent misrepresentation by the other party as to the contents, no contract results at all, since the misrepresentor knows that the apparent offer made by the signer is not what the signer intends? It was suggested earlier that where the other party (as here, *ex hypothesi*) knows what the signing party thinks the terms of the document to be, the preferable view is that there is a contract on the latter terms and the document can be rectified accordingly, as in *Bates v*

Wyndham's. Rectification is, however, an equitable remedy that will be refused if third-party rights have intervened, so that the mistake will not help the signer. The result seems to be that the law of mistake affects written contracts rather differently to oral ones: if there is an operative unilateral mistake in an oral contract, either there will be no contract or there will be one on the terms actually intended by the mistaken party, whereas if the contract is written it will in *effect* be voidable only, since a third party's reliance on it may defeat the right of the mistaken party to have it rectified. Lord Denning has often said that, in his view, a mistake only makes a contract voidable, not void. Most lawyers regard this as heresy, but perhaps there is something to be said for Lord Denning's view.

QUESTIONS

1.   Normally, the 'objective principle' means that you can take the other party's words at their face value—he is bound by what he said and what he meant to say is not relevant. When does that *not* apply?

2.   I offer to sell you my car for £2,000. You know from previous conversations that I meant to write £5,000. Nonetheless, you simply accept my offer without pointing out my mistake. Is there (i) a contract at £2,000, (ii) a contract at £5,000, or (iii) no contract? What if you know there has been a mistake but you don't know what I meant to write?

3.   What is the position if you did not realise that I had made a mistake but from what you had been told previously, you should have realised? *Should* the law give relief to the mistaken party in such a case?

4.   John Jones receives two letters, both addressed to him by name, one from Porterhouse College offering him a ticket for the Porterhouse College Members' Ball for £20 and the other from a wine merchant offering him, as a member of Porterhouse College, a special discount on a case of wine. He is not a member of the College and it is clear that he has been mistaken for another John Jones who is a member and lives at a similar address. He writes accepting both offers. Is there a contract with either the College or the wine merchant?

5.   Are cases of mistaken offers such as *Hartog v Colin & Shields* or *Ingrams v Little* best explained as part of a doctrine of mistake or as part of the rules of offer and acceptance?

6.   The University of Barchester invites tenders for some building work on campus. Bricks Ltd put in a tender do the work for £5,000. This is very much lower than any of the other tenders and the University accepts it. Bricks then try to withdraw claiming that it had made a mistake. Can it do so if (i) the figures for the various items of work (which are shown in its tender) had been added up incorrectly, or (ii) the mistake was due to the fact that Bricks had seriously underestimated the amount of earth to be excavated before building proper could begin?

7.   Why does the law draw a distinction between a mistake over the terms of the contract (which the other party should point out) and a mistake as to the facts surrounding the contract? (We will return to this question in Section 4.)

8.   When can a party who has signed a contract under a mistake get relief under *non est factum* when there would be relief from mistake or fraud?

OBLIGATIONS AND RISKS

CHAPTER ELEVEN

EXPRESS TERMS IN ORAL AGREEMENTS

When the parties have reached a binding oral agreement, the express terms of that agreement will normally consist of any promises made by either party during the course of negotiations and not withdrawn before final agreement. At least three questions may arise: firstly, did a particular statement amount to a promise; secondly, if the statement was a promise, what was being promised; thirdly, did the oral contract incorporate a set of written terms, printed perhaps on a notice or ticket?

I. TERMS, REPRESENTATIONS AND PUFFS

A promise made by one party, and not withdrawn before final agreement, will be treated as a term of the oral contract (for an example, see *Evans v Merzario*, p 185). At the other extreme, there are the vague commendatory statements known as 'puffs', to which no legal liability attaches—statements that are regarded as unsafe to rely on because they are obviously not to be taken literally ('This car goes like a bomb') or because they are merely vague commendations ('This washing powder washes whiter than white'). In between clear promises and puffs is a 'grey area' of statements that are not on their face promissory, but which are not just puffs either, because the statement is one of fact. The statement of fact may be explicit, or it may be implicit in a statement of opinion. A statement of opinion, which turns out to be incorrect, does not normally give rise to liability, but it may do so where it carries with it an implication that the opinion expressed is a genuine one, or that the speaker has some facts to justify the opinion and this is not true (see p 358 ff).

If such an assertion of fact is made and turns out to be untrue, there will usually be a remedy in misrepresentation (see Chapter 13), but even today this will often be less effective than if it can be shown that the maker of the statement was promising that what he asserted was true, 'guaranteeing' the truth of his statement.

Whether a statement contains a promise that it is true depends on the parties' 'intentions'. This contractual intention is judged objectively. A critical question is what factors a court will take into account in deciding whether a statement was 'intended' to be contractual.

One factor is the importance of the statement. If the statement is about something that is critical to the other party, it is likely to be treated as a term of the contract. Thus in *Bannerman v*

White (1861) 10 CBNS 844, the buyer asked the seller during the negotiations if the hops had been treated with sulphur, adding that if they had, he would not even trouble to ask the price. The seller said they had not been treated with sulphur, which he believed to be the case. It was held that the seller's statement was a term of the contract. If, on the other hand, the statement seems to be about some incidental characteristic of the goods being sold—something that at most affects the price to be paid rather than whether the buyer will buy the goods at all—the statement is probably less likely to be treated as a term: see the next case.

■ *Oscar Chess Ltd v Williams*
[1957] 1 All ER 325, Court of Appeal

In June 1955, the defendant sold to the plaintiffs, who were motor dealers, a second-hand Morris motor car for £290, this sum being credited to the defendant on the purchase of a new car through the dealers. The car sold to the dealers had been obtained by the defendant's mother in 1954 under a hire-purchase contract, and was shown in the registration book to have been first registered in 1948. There had been five changes of ownership between 1948 and 1954. The defendant, who honestly believed that the car was a 1948 model, described it as such to L, the salesman who acted for the plaintiffs in the matter, and showed L the registration book. L, who had frequently been given lifts in the car, also believed that it was a 1948 model, and the purchase price of £290 was calculated on this basis. In January 1956, the plaintiffs sent the chassis and engine numbers of the car to the manufacturers and were informed by them that the car was a 1939 model. If the plaintiffs had known at the time of the purchase that the car was a 1939 model, they would have paid only £175 for it. In an action brought by them against the defendant eight months after the sale, the plaintiffs claimed the sum of £115 as damages for breach of warranty.

[The trial judge held that the assumption that the car was a 1948 model was fundamental and gave judgment for the plaintiffs.]

Denning LJ

... I entirely agree with the judge that both parties assumed that the Morris car was a 1948 model and that this assumption was fundamental to the contract. This does not prove, however, that the representation was a term of the contract. The assumption was based by both of them on the date given in the registration book as the date of first registration. They both believed that the car was a 1948 model, whereas it was only a 1939 one. They were both mistaken and their mistake was of fundamental importance.

The effect of such a mistake is this: It does not make the contract a nullity from the beginning, but it does in some circumstances enable the contract to be set aside in equity. If the buyer had come promptly, he might have succeeded in getting the whole transaction set aside in equity on the ground of this mistake (see *Solle v Butcher*), but he did not do so and it is now too late for him to do it (see *Leaf v International Galleries*). His only remedy is in damages, and to recover these he must prove a warranty.

In saying that he must prove a warranty, I use the word 'warranty' in its ordinary English meaning to denote a binding promise. Everyone knows what a man means when he says, 'I guarantee it', or 'I warrant it', or 'I give you my word on it'. He means that he binds himself to it. That is the meaning which it has borne in English law for three hundred years from the leading case of *Chandelor v Lopus* onwards. During the last hundred years, however, the lawyers have come to use the word 'warranty' in another sense. They use it to denote a subsidiary term in a contract as distinct from a vital term which they call a 'condition'. In so doing they depart from the ordinary meaning, not only of the word 'warranty', but also of the word 'condition'. There is no harm in their doing this, so long as they confine this technical use to its proper sphere, namely to distinguish between a vital term, the breach of which gives the right to treat the contract as at an end, and a subsidiary term which does not.

The material distinction here is between a statement which is a term of the contract and a statement which is only an innocent misrepresentation. This distinction is best expressed by the ruling of Holt CJ, 'Was it intended as a warranty or not?', using the word 'warranty' there in its ordinary English meaning: because it gives the exact shade of meaning that is required. It is something to which a man must be taken to bind himself.

In applying this test, however, some misunderstanding has arisen by the use of the word 'intended'. It is sometimes supposed that the tribunal must look into the minds of the parties to see what they themselves intended. That is a mistake . . . The question whether a warranty was intended depends on the conduct of the parties, on their words and behaviour, rather than on their thoughts. If an intelligent bystander would reasonably infer that a warranty was intended, that will suffice. And this, when the facts are not in dispute, is a question of law . . . .

It is instructive to take some recent instances to show how the courts have approached this question. When the seller states a fact which is or should be within his own knowledge and of which the buyer is ignorant, intending that the buyer should act on it and he does so, it is easy to infer a warranty; see *Couchman v Hill*, where a farmer stated that a heifer was unserved, and *Harling v Eddy*, where he stated that there was nothing wrong with her. So also if the seller makes a promise about something which is or should be within his own control; see *Birch v Paramount Estates, Ltd*, decided on Oct 2, 1956, in this court, where the seller stated that the house would be as good as the show house. If, however, the seller, when he states a fact, makes it clear that he has no knowledge of his own but has got his information elsewhere, and is merely passing it on, it is not so easy to imply a warranty. Such a case was *Routledge v McKay*, where the seller stated that a motor cycle combination was a 1942 model, and pointed to the corroboration of that statement to be found in the registration book, and it was held that there was no warranty.

Turning now to the present case, much depends on the precise words that were used. If the seller says: 'I believe the car is a 1948 Morris. Here is the registration book to prove it', there is clearly no warranty. It is a statement of belief, not a contractual promise. If however, the seller says: 'I guarantee that it is a 1948 Morris. This is borne out by the registration book, but you need not rely solely on that. I give you my own guarantee that it is', there is clearly a warranty. The seller is making himself contractually responsible, even though the registration book is wrong.

In this case much reliance was placed by the judge on the fact that the buyer looked up 'Glass's Guide' and paid £290 on the footing that the car was a 1948 model, but that fact seems to me to be neutral. Both sides believed the car to have been made in 1948 and in that belief the buyer paid £290. That belief can be just as firmly based on the buyer's own inspection of the log-book as on a contractual warranty by the seller.

Once that fact is put on one side, I ask myself: What is the proper inference from the known facts? It must have been obvious to both that the seller had himself no personal knowledge of the year when the car was made. He only became owner after a great number of changes. He must have been relying on the registration book. It is unlikely that such a person would warrant the year of manufacture. The most that he would do would be to state his belief, and then produce the registration book in verification of it. In these circumstances the intelligent bystander would, I suggest, say that the seller did not intend to bind himself so as to warrant that the car was a 1948 model. If the seller was asked to pledge himself to it, he would at once have said 'I cannot do that. I have only the log-book to go by, the same as you.'

The judge seems to have thought that there was a difference between written contracts and oral contracts. He thought that the reason why the buyer failed in *Heilbut, Symons & Co v Buckleton* and *Routledge v McKay* was because the sales were afterwards recorded in writing, and the written contracts contained no reference to the representation. I agree that that was an important factor in those cases. If an oral representation is afterwards recorded in writing, it is good evidence that it was intended as a warranty. If it is not put into writing, it is evidence against a warranty being intended; but it is by no means decisive. There have been many cases, such as *Birch v Paramount Estates, Ltd*, where the courts have found an oral warranty collateral to a written contract. When, however, the purchase is not recorded in writing at all, it must not be supposed that every representation made in the course of the dealing is to be treated as a warranty. The question then is still: Was it intended as a warranty? In the leading case of *Chandelor v Lopus* in 1603 a man by word of mouth sold a precious stone for £100 affirming it to be a bezoar stone whereas it was not. The declaration averred that the seller *affirmed* it to be a bezoar stone, but did not aver that he *warranted* it to be so. The declaration was held to be ill because (Cro Jac 4): '. . . the bare affirmation that it was a bezoar stone, without warranting it to be so, is no cause of action . . . ' That has been the law from that day to this and it was emphatically re-affirmed by the House of Lords in *Heilbut, Symons & Co v Buckleton* . . .

Hodson LJ delivered a judgment to the same effect.

Morris LJ (dissenting)

. . . In the present case, on a consideration of the evidence which he heard, the learned judge came to the conclusion that the statement which he held to have been made by the defendant at the time of the making of the contract was a statement made contractually. It seems to me that the totality of the evidence points to that view. The statement related to a vitally important matter: it described the sub-ject-matter of the contract then being made and directed the parties to, and was the basis of, their agreement as to the price to be paid or credited to the defendant. In the language of Scott LJ, it seems to me that the statement made by the defendant was 'an item in [the] description' of what was being sold and that it constituted a substantial ingredient in the identity of the thing sold. It is with diffidence that I arrive at a conclusion differing from that of my Lords, but I cannot see that the learned judge in any way misdirected himself or misapplied any principle of law, and I see no reason for disturbing his conclusion.

Appeal allowed.

NOTE

Denning LJ's statement that, had the buyer acted promptly, he could have had the transaction set aside for *mistake*, must be doubted. However, if he had acted promptly he could have rescinded for *misrepresentation*. On the facts, he had lost this right and, because the seller had not been fraudulent, as the law stood then, the buyer had no remedy unless he could prove a warranty. Because the court held that the seller had not even been negligent, the same would apply today.

■ Dick Bentley Productions Ltd v Harold Smith (Motors) Ltd
[1965] 2 All ER 65, Court of Appeal

The plaintiff asked the defendant car dealer to find him a 'well vetted' Bentley car. The defend-ant found a car and told the plaintiff that it had been fitted with a replacement engine and gearbox, and that it had since done only 20,000 miles (the mileage shown on the odometer). The plaintiff bought the car but it turned out to be unsatisfactory, and he brought an action against the defendant. The trial judge held that the statement as to the mileage was untrue although not dishonest, and awarded the plaintiff £400 damages for breach of warranty. The defendant appealed.

Lord Denning MR

. . . The first point is whether this representation, namely that the car had done twenty thousand miles only since it had been fitted with a replacement engine and gearbox, was an innocent misrepresentation (which does not give rise to damages), or whether it was a warranty. It was said by Holt CJ and repeated in *Heilbut, Symons & Co v Buckleton:*

'An affirmation at the time of the sale is a warranty, provided it appear on evidence to be so intended.'

But that word 'intended' has given rise to difficulties. I endeavoured to explain in *Oscar Chess Ltd v Williams* that the question whether a warranty was intended depends on the conduct of the parties, on their words and behaviour, rather than on their thoughts. If an intelligent bystander would reasonably infer that a warranty was intended, that will suffice. What conduct, then? What words and behaviour, lead to the inference of a warranty?

Looking at the cases once more, as we have done so often, it seems to me that if a representation is made in the course of dealings for a contract for the very purpose of inducing the other party to act on it, and it actually induces him to act on it by entering into the contract, that is prima facie ground for inferring that the representation was intended as a warranty. It is not necessary to speak of it as being collateral. Suffice it that the representation was intended to be acted on and was in fact acted on. But the maker of the representation can rebut this inference if he can show that it really was an innocent misrepresentation, in that he was in fact innocent of fault in making it, and that it would not be reasonable in the circumstances for him to be bound by it. In the *Oscar Chess* case the inference was rebutted. There a man had bought a second-hand car and received with it a log-book, which stated the year of the car, 1948. He afterwards resold the car. When he resold it he simply repeated what was in the log-book and passed it on to the buyer. He honestly believed on reasonable grounds that it was true. He was completely innocent of any fault. There was no warranty by him but only an innocent misrepresentation. Whereas in the present case it is very different. The inference is not rebutted. Here we have a dealer, Mr Smith, who was in a position to know, or at least to find out, the history of the car. He could get it by writing to the makers. He did not do so. Indeed it was done later. When the history of this car was examined, his statement turned out to be quite wrong. He ought to have known better. There was no reasonable foundation for it....

Danckwerts LJ

I agree with the judgment of Lord Denning MR.

Salmon LJ

I agree. I have no doubt at all that the learned county court judge reached a correct conclusion when he decided that Mr Smith gave a warranty to the second plaintiff Mr Bentley, and that that warranty was broken. Was what Mr Smith said intended and understood as a legally binding promise? If so, it was a warranty and as such may be part of the contract of sale or collateral to it. In effect, Mr Smith said: 'If you will enter into a contract to buy this motor car from me for £1,850, I undertake that you will be getting a motor car which has done no more than twenty thousand miles since it was fitted with a new engine and a new gearbox.' I have no doubt at all that what was said by Mr Smith was so understood and was intended to be so understood by Mr Bentley.

I accordingly agree that the appeal should be dismissed.

Appeal dismissed.

NOTES

1. Normally, when a seller gives a warranty, his liability is strict (although for an exception, see *Esso v Mardon*, below). Denning suggests that the test is whether the seller was actually at fault, but a more suitable test is whether he was in a better position to discover the truth. Suppose he *had* contacted the car's makers but they had misinformed him: should the outcome be different?

2.   Placing the risk that the facts will turn out to be different from what was stated upon the party best able to discover the truth (the 'least cost avoider') has a clear economic rationale. See p 395.

3.   In these two cases, the test of which party was in the better position to discover the truth and the test of whether the statement was critical to the other party seem to have pointed in the same direction: it seems unlikely that Bentley would have bought the car had he known the truth, whereas Oscar Chess Ltd would presumably have bought the Morris for £175. What if the tests point in opposite directions?

4.   Nowadays, the question of whether the statement was contractual or merely a representation is of less practical importance because, as we shall see (pp 372 ff), since 1967, even a misrepresentation will give rise to damages provided it was negligent. However, there is still no liability in damages in the absence of negligence and the measure of damages is sometimes less generous than for breach of contract.

II. WHAT WAS BEING PROMISED?

■ *Esso Petroleum Co Ltd v Mardon*
[1976] 2 All ER 5, Court of Appeal

The plaintiffs ('Esso') were a company engaged in the production and distribution of petroleum. In 1961, Esso acquired a site on a busy main street of a town for development as a petrol filling station. The site was acquired on the basis of calculations, which showed that the estimated annual consumption of petrol at the station would be 200,000 gallons from the third year of operation. After the site had been acquired, the local planning authority required the forecourt and petrol pumps to be placed at the back of the site, which was accessible only from side streets and which was not visible from the busy main road. The station was constructed in compliance with that requirement. The result of that change of plan was to falsify the basis on which Esso had calculated the annual consumption of petrol, but through lack of care, Esso failed to revise its original estimate of 200,000 gallons. Subsequently, Esso opened negotiations with the defendant for the grant to him of a tenancy of the station. During the negotiations, L, an Esso representative who had had forty years' experience in the petrol trade, told the defendant in good faith that Esso had estimated that the throughput of petrol would reach 200,000 gallons a year in the third year of operation of the station. The defendant was aware of the deficiencies of the station and suggested that a lower estimate would be more realistic, but L's greater expertise quelled his doubts, and on the basis of L's representation as to the potential throughput the defendant was induced to enter into a tenancy agreement in April 1963. That agreement was for three years at a rent assessed by Esso in accordance with their estimate of the potential throughput of petrol. The defendant put capital into the station and incurred a bank overdraft to operate it but, despite his hard work, at the end of the first 15 months only 78,000 gallons of petrol had been consumed at the station and the defendant had incurred a loss in running it. In July 1964, he tendered notice to quit the tenancy but Esso wished to retain him as the tenant and granted him a new tenancy agreement, dated 1 September 1964, at a reduced rent. The defendant accepted the new tenancy in an attempt to mitigate the loss already incurred, but continued to lose money in the business, since the site with the pumps situated at the back was only capable of an annual throughput of some 70,000 gallons of petrol. By

August 1966, the defendant was unable to pay Esso for petrol supplied to the station, and in December 1966, Esso issued a writ against him claiming possession of the station, money due for petrol and mesne profits. The defendant continued trading at the station until March 1967 when he gave up possession. He had lost all of the capital he had put into the station and had incurred a substantial overdraft. By his defence and counterclaim, the defendant claimed damages in respect of the representation made by L as to the potential throughput of petrol, alleging (i) that it amounted to a warranty for breach of which the defendant was entitled to damages, and (ii) that it also amounted to negligent misrepresentation in breach of Esso's duty of care to the defendant in advising him as to the potential throughput. The trial judge rejected the claim for breach of warranty, but held that Esso were liable in damages for breach of their duty of care to the defendant. In assessing those damages, the judge limited the recoverable loss to that suffered between April 1963 and September 1964 on the ground that the misrepresentation made in 1963 had not induced the defendant to enter into the tenancy agreement of September 1964. The defendant appealed.

Lord Denning MR

Collateral warranty

Ever since Heilbut, Symons & Co v Buckleton we have had to contend with the law as laid down by the House of Lords that an innocent misrepresentation gives no right to damages. In order to escape from that rule, the pleader used to allege—I often did it myself—that the misrepresentation was fraudulent, or alternatively a collateral warranty. At the trial we nearly always succeeded on collateral warranty. We had to reckon, of course, with the dictum of Lord Moulton that 'such collateral contracts must from their very nature be rare'. But more often than not the court elevated the innocent misrepresentation into a collateral warranty; and thereby did justice—in advance of the Misrepresentation Act 1967. I remember scores of cases of that kind, especially on the sale of a business. A representation as to the profits that had been made in the past was invariably held to be a warranty. Besides that experience, there have been many cases since I have sat in this court where we have readily held a representation—which induces a person to enter into a contract—to be a warranty sounding in damages. I summarised them in Dick Bentley Productions Ltd v Harold Smith (Motors) Ltd.

Counsel for Esso retaliated, however, by citing Bisset v Wilkinson where the Privy Council said that a statement by a New Zealand farmer that an area of land 'would carry 2000 sheep' was only an expression of opinion. He submitted that the forecast here of 200,000 gallons was an expression of opinion and not a statement of fact; and that it could not be interpreted as a warranty or promise.

Now, I would quite agree with counsel for Esso, that it was not a warranty—in this sense—that it did not guarantee that the throughput would be 200,000 gallons. But, nevertheless, it was a forecast made by a party, Esso, who had special knowledge and skill. It was the yardstick (the 'e a c') by which they measured the worth of a filling station. They knew the facts. They knew the traffic in the town. They knew the throughput of comparable stations. They had much experience and expertise at their disposal. They were in a much better position than Mr Mardon to make a forecast. It seems to me that if such a person makes a forecast—intending that the other should act on it and he does act on it—it can well be interpreted as a warranty that the forecast is sound and reliable in this sense that they made it with reasonable care and skill. It is just as if Esso said to Mr Mardon: 'Our forecast of throughput is 200,000 gallons. You can rely on it as being a sound forecast of what the service station should do. The rent is calculated on that footing.' If the forecast turned out to be an unsound forecast, such as no person of skill or experience should have made, there is a breach of warranty. Just as there is a breach of warranty when a forecast is made 'expected to load' by a certain date if the maker has no reasonable grounds for it: see Samuel Sanday v Keighley Maxted & Co: or bunkers 'expected 600/700 tons': see The Pantanassa by Diplock J. It is very different from the New Zealand case where the land had never been used as a sheep farm and both parties were equally able to form an opinion as to its carrying capacity.

In the present case it seems to me that there was a warranty that the forecast was sound, that is that Esso had made it with reasonable care and skill. That warranty was broken. Most negligently Esso made a 'fatal step' in the forecast they stated to Mr Mardon, and on which he took the tenancy. For this they are liable in damages . . . .

Ormrod LJ

. . . A representation of fact is much more likely to be intended to have contractual effect than a statement of opinion; so it is much easier to infer that in the former case it was so intended, and more difficult in the latter. Similarly, where statements of future fact or forecasts are under consideration, it will require much more cogent evidence to justify the conclusion that such statements were intended to be contractual in character. It is, therefore, with respect to counsel for Esso's argument, not an answer to say, simply, that the statement relied on was an expression of opinion or a forecast and therefore cannot be a warranty. In my view, following Lord Moulton in the *Heilbut, Symons* case, the test is whether on the totality of the evidence the parties intended or must be taken to have intended that the representation was to form part of the basis of the contractual relations between them . . . .

I think that Mr Mardon has established the warranty alleged in para 6 of the defence and counterclaim and is entitled to damages for breach of contract . . . .

Shaw LJ

. . . Mr Mardon complained that 'he had been sold a pup'. I think he had; but it was a warranted pup so that Esso are in breach of warranty and liable in damages accordingly . . . .

Appeal allowed.

[Further extracts from this case will be found below, p 978.]

NOTES

1.   In *Esso v Mardon*, the court held that Esso had given a warranty, but it was not a warranty that the station would sell 200,000 gallons a year: that was outside Esso's control (although there is no doubt that Esso could have given Mardon such a warranty if it had used clear enough language). The warranty was only that it had made the forecast with reasonable care and skill.

2.   A point that *Esso v Mardon* did not have to decide was whether Esso's liability was one for negligence only, or a strict one that reasonable care and skill had been taken. If, for instance, unknown to Mardon, the estimated annual consumption (eac) had been prepared by an independent firm of specialists employed by Esso (ie by a third party for whom Esso would not normally be responsible), would Esso still have been liable?

In *Thake v Maurice*, the plaintiffs, who were husband and wife, arranged for the defendant to carry out a vasectomy to sterilise the husband. The defendant made it clear that the operation was irreversible, demonstrating with his arms how the vas is cut and the ends tied back. The plaintiffs signed forms stating that they understood the nature of the operation. Apparently, the defendant did not give them his normal warning that there was a small chance that after the normal sperm tests the operation might reverse itself naturally, or at least he failed to ensure that this risk was conveyed to the plaintiffs. The operation was carried out with all due care and skill and the sperm tests were satisfactory, but the vasectomy reversed itself and the wife became pregnant. She did not realise this until it was too late to have an abortion and she gave birth to a healthy child. At first instance ([1984] 2 All ER 513), Peter Pain J held that the contract was not merely one to carry out a vasectomy but one to render the husband irreversibly sterile. Alternatively, he held the defendant's failure to give an adequate warning was a breach of a contractual duty of care. He awarded damages for the cost of a layette for the baby, the cost of her upkeep to the age of 17 and loss of earnings for the wife, but nothing for pain and distress. The defendant appealed and the plaintiffs cross-appealed on damages. The Court of Appeal ([1986] 1 All ER 497) upheld the finding of negligence and increased the damages to include an element for pain and suffering. Kerr LJ agreed that, on the facts, the plaintiffs could not reasonably have concluded anything other than that the defendant had undertaken to make the husband permanently sterile, but the majority disagreed. Nourse LJ said (at 511):

Would the words and visual demonstrations of the defendant have led a reasonable person standing in the position of the plaintiffs to understand that, come what may, Mr Thake would be rendered sterile and incapable of parenthood?

The function of the court in ascertaining, objectively, the meaning of words used by contracting parties is one of everyday occurrence. But it is often exceedingly difficult to discharge it where the subjective understandings and intentions of the parties are clear and opposed. Here the plaintiffs understood that Mr Thake would be permanently sterile. The defendant himself recognised that they would have been left with that impression. On the other hand, he did not intend, and on the state of his knowledge he could not have intended, to guarantee that that would be the case. Both the understanding and the intention appear to them, as individuals, to have been entirely reasonable, but an objective interpretation must choose between them. In the end the question seems to be reduced to one of determining the extent of the knowledge which is to be attributed to the reasonable person standing in the position of the plaintiffs. Would he have known that the success of the operation, either because it depended on the healing of human tissue, or because in medical science all things, or nearly all things, are uncertain, could not be guaranteed? If he would, the defendant's words could only have been reasonably understood as forecasts of an almost certain, but nevertheless uncertain, outcome and his visual demonstrations as no more than explanations of how the operation would be done. He could not be taken to have given a guarantee of its success.

I do not suppose that a reasonable person standing in the position of the plaintiffs would have known that a vasectomy is an operation whose success depends on a healing of human tissue which cannot be guaranteed. To suppose that would be to credit him with an omniscience beyond all reason. But it does seem to me to be reasonable to credit him with the more general knowledge that in medical science all things, or nearly all things, are uncertain. That knowledge is part of the general experience of mankind, and in my view it makes no difference whether what has to be considered is some form of medical or surgical treatment or the excision, apparently final, of a section of the vas. Doubtless the general experience of mankind will acknowledge the certainty that a limb, once amputated, has gone forever. Such has been the observation from time immemorial of a species to whom the spectacle of war and suffering is commonplace. But where an operation is of modern origin, its effects untried over several generations, would a reasonable person, confronted even with the words and demonstrations of the defendant in this case, believe that there was not one chance in ten thousand that the object would not be achieved? I do not think that he would.

On the measure of damages, Kerr LJ said (at 509):

In the event of the plaintiffs succeeding in contract, the damages for pain and suffering were agreed in the sum of £2,500 . . . without the need for any division between the two plaintiffs. However, in the event of the plaintiffs only succeeding in tort, it was agreed that there should be a reduction of £1,000 for this sum, because credit would have to be given for the fact that Mrs Thake did not have to undergo the distress and suffering of an abortion. Although surprising at first sight, I agree that this must logically follow. If the plaintiffs are only entitled to complain of the defendant's failure to warn them that Mrs Thake might become pregnant again, as she did, then her renewed pregnancy did not in itself amount to a breach on his part, with the result that, but for the events which in fact happened after she had again become pregnant, she would have had to undergo an abortion . . . Since my brethren take the view that the plaintiff's claim in contract fails, the additional award on the cross-appeal will only be £1,500.

See also *Eyre v Measday* [1986] 1 All ER 488 (no implied term that sterilisation operation would render woman absolutely sterile).

III. INCORPORATION OF WRITTEN TERMS INTO AN ORAL CONTRACT

If a set of conditions is contained in a document that has been signed by the parties, the conditions form part of the contract. The problem comes with unsigned documents, such as tickets or notices which purport to state some or all of the terms of the contract. If the parties explicitly agree that the conditions shall apply, the conditions will be 'incorporated by reference' (see further p 346). What if they are not referred to? Most of the cases in which there is a dispute about whether a contract that has been concluded orally incorporates a set of written terms seem to involve exemption clauses (see Section 8, Chapter 39). However, the rules on this point seem equally applicable to other types of clause, and we consider them here.

1. Reasonable notice

■ *Parker v South Eastern Rly Co*
(1877) 2 CPD 416, Court of Appeal

The plaintiff deposited his bag in the cloakroom at the defendants' station. He paid 2d and was given a ticket, on the face of which was printed the times at which the cloakroom was open and the words 'see back'. On the back was a clause stating that the company would not be responsible for any package exceeding the value of £10, and a placard to the same effect hung in the cloakroom. The bag, which was worth more than £10, was lost or stolen, and the plaintiff claimed its value. The trial judge left two questions to the jury: (1) did the plaintiff read or was he aware of the special condition upon which the article was deposited; (2) was the plaintiff, under the circumstances, under any obligation, in the exercise of reasonable and proper caution, to read or make himself aware of the condition? The jury answered both questions in the negative, and judgment was directed for the plaintiff.

Mellish LJ

. . . The question then is, whether the plaintiff was bound by the conditions contained in the ticket. In an ordinary case, where an action is brought on a written agreement which is signed by the defendant, the agreement is proved by proving his signature, and, in the absence of fraud, it is wholly immaterial that he has not read the agreement and does not know its contents. The parties may, however, reduce their agreement into writing, so that the writing constitutes the sole evidence of the agreement, without signing it; but in that case there must be evidence independently of the agreement itself to prove that the defendant has assented to it. In that case, also, if it is proved that the defendant has assented to the writing constituting the agreement between the parties, it is, in the absence of fraud, immaterial that the defendant had not read the agreement and did not know its contents. Now if in the course of making a contract one party delivers to another a paper containing writing, and the party receiving the paper knows that the paper contains conditions which the party delivering it intends to constitute the contract, I have no doubt that the party receiving the paper does, by receiving and keeping it, assent to the conditions contained in it, although he does not read them, and does not know what they are ... [I]f the person receiving the ticket does not know that there is any writing upon the back of the ticket, he is not bound by a condition printed on the back ... the plaintiffs admitted that they knew there was writing on the back of the ticket, [but] they swore not only that they did not read it, but that they did not know or believe that the writing contained conditions ...

Now, I am of opinion that we cannot lay down, as a matter of law, either that the plaintiff was bound or that he was not bound by the conditions printed on the ticket, from the mere fact that he knew there was writing on the ticket, but did not know that the writing contained conditions. I think there may be cases in which a paper containing writing is delivered by one party to another in the course of a business transaction, where it would be quite reasonable that the party receiving it should assume that the writing contained in it no condition, and should put it in his pocket unread. For instance, if a person driving through a turnpike-gate received a ticket upon paying the toll, he might reasonably assume that the object of the ticket was that by producing it he might be free from paying toll at some other turn-pike-gate, and might put it in his pocket unread. On the other hand, if a person who ships goods to be carried on a voyage by sea receives a bill of lading signed by the master, he would plainly be bound by it, although afterwards in an action against the shipowner for the loss of the goods, he might swear that he had never read the bill of lading, and that he did not know that it contained the terms of the contract of carriage, and that the shipowner was protected by the exceptions contained in it. Now the reason why the person receiving the bill of lading would be bound seems to me to be that in the great majority of cases persons shipping goods do know that the bill of lading contains the terms of the contract of carriage, and the shipowner, or the master delivering the bill of lading, is entitled to assume that the person shipping goods has that knowledge. It is, however, quite possible to suppose that a person who is neither a man of business nor a lawyer might on some particular occasion ship goods without the least knowledge of what a bill of lading was, but in my opinion such a person must bear the consequences of his own exceptional ignorance, it being plainly impossible that business could be carried on if every person who delivers a bill of lading had to stop to explain what a bill of lading was.

Now the question we have to consider is whether the railway company were entitled to assume that a person depositing luggage, and receiving a ticket in such a way that he could see that some writing was printed on it, would understand that the writing contained the conditions of contract, and this seems to me to depend upon whether people in general would in fact, and naturally, draw that infer-ence. The railway company, as it seems to me, must be entitled to make some assumptions respecting the person who deposits luggage with them: I think they are entitled to assume that he can read, and that he understands the English language, and that he pays such attention to what he is about as may be reasonably expected from a person in such a transaction as that of depositing luggage in a cloak-room. The railway company must, however, take mankind as they find them, and if what they do is sufficient to inform people in general that the ticket contains conditions. I think that a particular plain-tiff ought not to be in a better position than other persons on account of his exceptional ignorance or stupidity or carelessness. But if what the railway company do is not sufficient to convey to the minds of people in general that the ticket contains conditions, then they have received goods on deposit without obtaining the consent of the persons depositing them to the conditions limiting their liability. I am of opinion, therefore, that the proper direction to leave to the jury in these cases is, that if the person receiv-ing the ticket did not see or know that there was any writing on the ticket, he is not bound by the con-ditions; that if he knew there was writing, and knew or believed that the writing contained conditions, then he is bound by the conditions; that if he knew there was writing on the ticket, but did not know or believe that the writing contained conditions, nevertheless he would be bound, if the delivering of the ticket to him in such a manner that he could see there was writing upon it, was, in the opinion of the jury, reasonable notice that the writing contained conditions.

Baggallay LJ delivered a judgment to the same effect.

Bramwell LJ [dissenting]

... The plaintiffs have sworn that they did not know that the printing was the contract, and we must act as though that was true and we believed it, a least as far as entering the verdict for the defendants is concerned. Does this make any difference? The plaintiffs knew of the printed matter. Both admit they knew it concerned them in some way, though they said they did not know what it was: yet neither pretends that he knew or believed it was not the contract. Neither pretends he thought it had nothing to do with the business in hand; that he thought it was an advertisement or other matter unconnected with his deposit of a parcel at the defendants' cloak-room. They admit that, for anything they knew or believed, it might be, only they did not know or believe it was, the contract. Their evidence is very much that they did not think, or, thinking, did not care about it. Now, they claim to charge the company, and to have the benefit of their own indifference. Is this just? Is it reasonable? Is it the way in which any other business is allowed to be conducted? Is it even allowed to a man to 'think', 'judge', 'guess', 'chance' a matter, without informing himself when he can, and then when his 'thought', 'judgment', 'guess' or 'chance' turns out wrong or unsuccessful, claim to impose a burthen or duty on another which he could not have done had he informed himself as he might?

... Has not the giver of the paper a right to suppose that the receiver is content to deal on the terms in the paper? What more can be done? Must he say, 'Read that?' As I have said, he does so in effect when he puts it into the other's hands. The truth is, people are content to take these things on trust. They know that there is a form which is always used—they are satisfied it is not unreasonable, because people do not usually put unreasonable terms into their contracts. If they did, then dealing would soon be stopped. Besides, unreasonable practices would be known. The very fact of not looking at the paper shews that this confidence exists. It is asked: What if there was some unreasonable condition, as for instance to forfeit 1000l if the goods were not removed in forty-eight hours? Would the depositor be bound? I might content myself by asking: Would he be, if he were told 'our conditions are on this ticket', and he did not read them? In my judgment, he would not be bound in either case. I think there is an implied understanding that there is no condition unreasonable to the knowledge of the party tendering the document and not insisting on its being read—no condition not relevant to the matter in hand. I am of opinion, therefore, that the plaintiffs, having notice of the printing, were in the same situation as though the porter had said, 'Read that, it concerns the matter in hand'; that if the plaintiffs did not read it, they were as much bound as if they had read it and had not objected. The judges should have directed verdicts for the defendants.

Order for a new trial.

NOTES

1.   Bramwell was well known for his strong ideas on self-reliance. See Atiyah, *Rise and Fall of Freedom of Contract*, 1979, pp 374–380.

2.   Mellish's point that some tickets might reasonably be regarded as mere receipts was applied in *Chapelton v Barry UDC* [1940] 1 KB 532. The plaintiff visited a seaside resort and wished to sit in a deckchair on the beach. The defendant council had left a pile of deckchairs near to a notice that indicated that they could be hired for 2d per session of three hours. The notice contained no exempting conditions, but requested the hirer to obtain a ticket from the attendant. The plaintiff took two chairs and gave 4d to the attendant, receiving two tickets in return. The ticket stated:

The council will not be liable for any accident or damage arising from the hire of the chair.

The plaintiff's chair collapsed when he sat on it owing to the negligence of the defendants. The Court of Appeal held that the clause did not protect the defendants: the ticket was 'a mere voucher or receipt'. In the normal case, the person hiring a chair would not receive a ticket until after he had sat on the chair, so it was reasonable to regard the notice as an offer of the terms on which the chairs were to be hired, and the ticket as a mere receipt to show the person had paid; it made no difference that in this case the plaintiff had received his ticket at the outset. The 'mere voucher or receipt' point is sometimes treated as an independent principle, but seems really to be an application of the reasonable notice requirement.

3.   Unless the plaintiff actually knew of the terms, a notice that is given only after the contract has been concluded is of no effect. Thus in *Olley v Marlborough Court Ltd* [1949] 1 KB 532, the plaintiff was not affected by clauses in a notice in her hotel bedroom when she had made the contract earlier at the reception desk.

A graphic illustration of this rule came in *Thornton v Shoe Lane Parking Ltd* [1971] 1 All ER 686. The plaintiff went to park his car at a multi-storey car park owned and operated by the defendants. At the entry to the car park, there was a sign stating the charges and that parking was 'at owner's risk'; the motorist then drove in past a machine that dispensed tickets. The ticket bore the time of entry and, in small print, the words:

This ticket is issued subject to the conditions of issue as displayed on the premises.

Inside the premises were notices displaying the conditions, which purported to exclude liability to customers, not only for damage to cars but for personal injuries. On his return to collect his car, the plaintiff was injured, due partly to his own negligence and partly to that of the defendants. The defendants argued that the conditions excluded their liability, but the Court of Appeal held that the ticket came too late, because by that stage the plaintiff had driven up the entrance ramp and, as Megaw LJ put it, 'it was practically impossible for him to withdraw from his intended entry'. Lord Denning MR said of ticket machines generally (at 689):

The customer pays his money and gets a ticket. He cannot refuse it. He cannot get his money back. He may protest to the machine, even swear at it, but it will remain unmoved. He is committed beyond recall. He was committed at the very moment when he put his money into the machine. The contract was concluded at that time. It can be translated into offer and acceptance in this way. The offer is made when the proprietor of the machine holds it out as being ready to receive the money. The acceptance takes place when the customer puts his money into the slot. The terms of the offer are contained in the notice placed on or near the machine stating what is offered for the money. The Customer is bound by those terms as long as they are sufficiently brought to his notice beforehand, but not otherwise. He is not bound by the terms printed on the ticket if they differ from the notice, because the ticket comes too late. In the present case the offer was contained in the notice at the entrance giving the charges for garaging and saying "at owner's risk", ie at the risk of the owner so far as damage to the car was concerned. The offer was accepted when the plaintiff drove up to the entrance and, by the movement of his car, turned the light from red to green, and the ticket was thrust at him. The contract was then concluded, and it could not be altered by any words printed on the ticket itself.

4.   It is treated as common knowledge that some types of ticket, eg railway tickets, are issued subject to conditions (see *Thompson v London Midland and Scottish Rly Co* [1930] 1 KB 41). Suppose an intending traveller asks for a ticket for London and pays the price demanded by the booking clerk. The clerk then hands her a ticket, which has printed on it that it is subject to some condition (eg a restriction on trains she can take) that she did not know of and does not like. Can she demand her money back? Who makes the offer and when does acceptance take place? See *Nunan v Southern Rly Co* [1923] 2 KB 703 at 707. Does it make any difference whether the railway timetables or advertising refer to the restriction? In the modern system, railways commonly have a number of different

fares for the same journey, depending largely on the times of the outward and return journeys. Booking clerks usually ask questions about the intended time of travel. Does the law of contract require this?

5.   Beale owns a multi-storey car park, which has its entrance on a very busy street where waiting is not permitted and its exit on the other side of the building onto another street. How can he effectively incorporate a set of conditions into the contracts with his customers?

6.   In *Thornton's* case, Denning seemed to suggest that an unreasonable condition might be void. He made the same suggestion in other cases, but it is generally accepted that at common law there is no rule that an unreasonable condition is for that reason invalid. Unreasonable conditions may, however, be ineffective under the Unfair Contract Terms Act 1977 (see pp 995 ff) or the Regulations implementing the EC Directive on Unfair Terms in Consumer Contracts (see p 1035).

■ *Interfoto Picture Library Ltd v Stiletto Visual Programmes Ltd*
[1988] 1 All ER 348, Court of Appeal

The defendant advertising agency required photographs of the 1950s for a presentation for a client. On 5 March 1984, it telephoned the plaintiffs, who ran a library of photographic transparencies and with whom it had not dealt before, inquiring whether the plaintiffs had any photographs of that period that might be suitable for the presentation. On the same day, the plaintiffs dispatched to the defendants 47 transparencies packed in a bag with a delivery note, which clearly specified that the transparencies were to be returned by 19 March and which, under the heading 'Conditions', printed prominently in capitals, set out nine printed conditions in four columns. Condition 2 stated that all transparencies were to be returned within 14 days from the date of delivery and that 'A holding fee of £5.00 plus VAT per day will be charged for each transparency which is retained by you longer than the said period of 14 days'. The defendants accepted delivery of the transparencies but it was unlikely that they read any of the conditions. The defendants did not use the transparencies for their presentation but instead put them to one side and forgot about them. The transparencies were not returned to the plaintiffs until 2 April. The plaintiffs sent the defendants an invoice for £3,783.50 being the holding charge calculated at £5 per transparency per day from 19 March to 2 April. The defendants refused to pay and the plaintiffs brought an action against them claiming the amount of the invoice. The trial judge gave judgment for the plaintiffs and the defendants appealed.

Dillon LJ

. . . The primary point taken in the court below was that condition 2 was not part of the contract between the parties because the delivery note was never supplied to the defendants at all. That the judge rejected on the facts; he found that the delivery note was supplied in the same Jiffy bag with the transparencies, and that finding is not challenged in this court. He made no finding however that Mr Beeching or any other representative of the defendants read condition 2 or any of the other printed conditions, and it is overwhelmingly probable that they did not.

An alternative argument for the defendants, in this court as below, was to the effect that any contract between the parties was made before the defendants knew of the existence of the delivery note, viz either in the course of the preliminary telephone conversation between Mr Beeching and Miss Fraser or when the Jiffy bag containing the transparencies was received in the defendants' premises but before the bag was opened. I regard these submissions as unrealistic and unarguable. The original telephone call was merely a preliminary inquiry and did not give rise to any contract. But the contract came into existence when the plaintiffs sent the transparencies to the defendants and the defendants, after opening the bag, accepted them by Mr Beeching's phone call to the plaintiffs at 3.10 on 5 March. The question is whether condition 2 was a term of that contract.

There was never any oral discussion of terms between the parties before the contract was made. In particular there was no discussion whatever of terms in the original telephone conversation when Mr Beeching made his preliminary inquiry. The question is therefore whether condition 2 was sufficiently brought to the defendant's attention to make it a term of the contract which was only concluded after the defendants had received, and must have known that they had received the transparencies *and* the delivery note.

This sort of question was posed in relation to printed conditions, in the ticket cases, such [as] *Parker v South Eastern Rly Co.* in the last century. At that stage the printed conditions were looked at as a whole and the question considered by the courts was whether the printed conditions as a whole had been sufficiently drawn to a customer's attention to make the whole set of conditions part of the contract: if so the customer was bound by the printed conditions even though he never read them.

More recently the question has been discussed whether it is enough to look at a set of printed conditions as a whole. When for instance one condition in a set is particularly onerous does something special need to be done to draw customer's attention to that particular condition? In an obiter dictum in J *Spurling Ltd v Bradshaw* [1956] 2 All ER 121 at 125, [1956] 1 WLR 461 at 466 (cited in *Chitty on Contracts* (25th edn 1983) vol 1. para 742, p 408) Denning LJ stated:

'Some clauses which I have seen would need to be printed in red ink on the face of the document with a red hand pointing to it before the notice could be held to be sufficient.'

Then in *Thornton v Shoe Lane Parking Ltd* both Lord Denning MR and Megaw LJ held as one of their grounds of decision, as I read their judgments, that where a condition is particularly onerous or unusual the party seeking to enforce it must show that that condition, or an unusual condition of that particular nature, was fairly brought to the notice of the other party . . . .

Counsel for the plaintiffs submits that *Thornton v Shoe Lane Parking Ltd* was a case of an exemption clause and that what their Lordships said must be read as limited to exemption clauses and in particular exemption clauses which would deprive the party on whom they are imposed of statutory rights. But what their Lordships said was said by way of interpretation and application of the general statement of the law by Mellish LJ in *Parker v South Eastern Rly Co* and the logic of it is applicable to any particularly onerous clause in a printed set of conditions of the one contracting party which would not be generally known to the other party.

Condition 2 of these plaintiffs' conditions is in my judgment a very onerous clause. The defendants could not conceivably have known, if their attention was not drawn to the clause, that the plaintiffs were proposing to charge a 'holding fee' for the retention of the transparencies at such a very high and exorbitant rate.

At the time of the ticket cases in the last century it was notorious that people hardly ever troubled to read printed conditions on a ticket or delivery note or similar document. That remains the case now. In the intervening years the printed conditions have tended to become more and more complicated and more and more one-sided in favour of the party who is imposing them, but the other parties, if they notice that there are printed conditions at all, generally still tend to assume that such conditions are only concerned with ancillary matters of form and are not of importance. In the ticket cases the courts held that the common law required that reasonable steps be taken to draw the other parties' attention to the printed conditions or they would not be part of the contract. It is in my judgment a logical development of the common law into modern conditions that it should be held, as it was in *Thornton v Shoe Lane Parking Ltd*, that, if one condition in a set of printed conditions is particularly onerous or unusual, the party seeking to enforce it must show that that particular condition was fairly brought to the attention of the other party.

In the present case, nothing whatever was done by the plaintiffs to draw the defendants' attention particularly to condition 2; it was merely one of four columns' width of conditions printed across the foot of the delivery note. Consequently condition 2 never, in my judgment, became part of the contract between the parties . . . .

Bingham LJ

... In many civil law systems, and perhaps in most legal systems outside the common law world, the law of obligations recognises and enforces an overriding principle that in making and carrying out contracts parties should act in good faith. This does not simply mean that they should not deceive each other, a principle which any legal system must recognise; its effect is perhaps most aptly conveyed by such metaphorical colloquialisms as 'playing fair', 'coming clean' or 'putting one's cards face upwards on the table'. It is in essence a principle of fair and open dealing. In such a forum it might, I think, be held on the facts of this case that the plaintiffs were under a duty in all fairness to draw the defendants' attention specifically to the high price payable if the transparencies were not returned in time and, when the 14 days had expired, to point out to the defendants the high cost of continued failure to return them.

English law has, characteristically, committed itself to no such overriding principle but has developed piecemeal solutions in response to demonstrated problems of unfairness. Many examples could be given. Thus equity has intervened to strike down unconscionable bargains. Parliament has stepped in to regulate the imposition of exemption clauses and the form of certain hire-purchase agreements. The common law also has made its contribution, by holding that certain classes of contract require the utmost good faith, by treating as irrecoverable what purport to be agreed estimates of damage but are in truth a disguised penalty for breach, and in many other ways.

The well-known cases on sufficiency of notice are in my view properly to be read in this context. At one level they are concerned with a question of pure contractual analysis, whether one party has done enough to give the other notice of the incorporation of a term in the contract. At another level they are concerned with a somewhat different question, whether it would in all the circumstances be fair (or reasonable) to hold a party bound by any conditions or by a particular condition of an unusual and stringent nature....

Turning to the present case, I am satisfied for reasons which Dillon LJ has given that no contract was made on the telephone when the defendants made their initial request. I am equally satisfied that no contract was made on delivery of the transparencies to the defendants before the opening of the Jiffy bag in which they were contained. Once the Jiffy bag was opened and the transparencies taken out with the delivery note, it is in my judgment an inescapable inference that the defendants would have recognised the delivery note as a document of a kind likely to contain contractual terms and would have seen that there were conditions printed in small but visible lettering on the face of the document. To the extent that the conditions so displayed were common form or usual terms regularly encountered in this business, I do not think the defendants could successfully contend that they were not incorporated into the contract.

The crucial question in the case is whether the plaintiffs can be said fairly and reasonably to have brought condition 2 to the notice of the defendants. The judge made no finding on the point, but I think that it is open to this court to draw an inference from the primary findings which he did make. In my opinion the plaintiffs did not do so. They delivered 47 transparencies, which was a number the defendant had not specifically asked for. Condition 2 contained a daily rate per transparency after the initial period of 14 days many times greater than was usual or (so far as the evidence shows) heard of. For these 47 transparencies there was to be a charge for each day of delay of £235 plus value added tax. The result would be that a venial period of delay, as here, would lead to an inordinate liability. The defendants are not to be relieved of that liability because they did not read the condition, although doubtless they did not; but in my judgment they are to be relieved because the plaintiffs did not do what was necessary to draw this unreasonable and extortionate clause fairly to their attention. I would accordingly allow the defendants' appeal and substitute for the judge's award the sum which he assessed on the alternative basis of quantum meruit.

In reaching the conclusion I have expressed I would not wish to be taken as deciding that condition 2 was not challengeable as a disguised penalty clause. This point was not argued before the judge nor raised in the notice of appeal. It was accordingly not argued before us. I have accordingly felt bound to assume, somewhat reluctantly, that condition 2 would be enforceable if fully and fairly brought to the defendant's attention.

Appeal allowed.

NOTES

1. By what criteria is it to be decided if conditions are 'unusual'? In an important dissenting judgment in *AEG (UK) Ltd v Logic Resource Ltd* [1996] CLC 265, Hobhouse LJ said:

    The emphasis in those passages which were quoted was to the 'sort' of provision. This was directly germane to the *Interfoto Picture* case where what was fairly described as an extortionate stipulation was introduced which imposed a wholly excessive and unexpected collateral financial obligation upon the hirer in a certain situation. It was a sort of clause that no one would expect to find in the standard terms which were being referred to . . .

    The clause which we are concerned with here is cl. 7. It is a clause which covers a topic which is commonly, and indeed normally, dealt with in the standard conditions of sellers of goods. It is in no way unusual nor is it suggested that it is unusual for standard conditions in some way to qualify the obligations of the sellers under a contract of sale. Nor is it suggested that it is unusual for such clauses to include warranty conditions, which have a limited effect both in time and obligation. In my judgment, the clauses which we find in cl. 7 deal with a topic which one would expect to be dealt with in the conditions of sale of a supplier of manufactured goods and they cover the type of points which would commonly be dealt with.

    The problem in the present case arises from the fact that these clauses have been unreasonably drafted. As is almost inevitable in printed standard terms, they are not related to the particular circumstances of the case and, furthermore, they stipulate for a greater protection of the seller than is reasonable, or anyway is reasonable without some special justification. In my judgment, and this is where I part company from Hirst and Waite LJJ, it is necessary before excluding the incorporation of a clause in limine to consider the type of clause it is. Is it a clause of the type which you would expect to find in the printed conditions? If it is, then it is only in the most exceptional circumstances that a party will be able to say that it was not adequately brought to his notice by standard words of incorporation. If a party wishes to find out precisely how a clause of a normal sort has been worded, he should ask for the actual text of the clause. This case is not analogous to either of the two cases upon which the appellant founds. The *Interfoto* case involved an extortionate clause which did not relate directly to the expected rights and obligations of the parties. In the *Shoe Lane Parking* case, it related to personal injuries and the state of the premises and not to the subject matter of the car parking contract, which would, in the view of the Court of Appeal, have been concerned with damage to property.

    Do you think that the clause in *Interfoto* was one that no one would expect to find? Are you surprised to have to pay for returning library books or hired videos late? Surely what was surprising in *Interfoto* was the amount that had to be paid for late return. But this would put *Interfoto* and *AEG* on the same side of the line.

2. For the rules on penalty clauses, see p 689.

2. Course of dealing

In *Henry Kendall & Sons v William Lillico & Sons Ltd* (appeals from *Hardwick Game Farm v Suffolk Agricultural and Poultry Producers Association*) [1969] 2 AC 31, there had been three or four contracts a month between two of the parties: Grimsdale and SAPPA. The practice had been that, when an oral contract had been made, Grimsdale would send a contract note to SAPPA, either later on the same day or on the following day. On the back of the notes were conditions, including one that 'the buyer ... takes the responsibility for latent defects'. The House of Lords held that it was

... reasonable to hold that when SAPPA placed an order to buy, they did so on the basis and with the knowledge that an acceptance of the order by Grimsdale and their agreement to sell would be on the terms and conditions set out on their contract notes.

In this case, the course of dealings was long, continuous and consistent. In *McCutcheon v David MacBrayne Ltd* [1964] 1 All ER 430, the plaintiff had shipped his car several times on the defendants' ship between Islay and the mainland of Scotland. The evidence was that sometimes he was asked to sign a risk note, containing exempting conditions, and sometimes not. On the relevant voyage, on which the ship sank owing to the defendant's negligence, the plaintiff's brother had arranged the shipment and had not been asked to sign a risk note. It was held by the House of Lords that there was no consistent course of dealings. See MacDonald (1988) 8 Legal Studies 48.

In *Hollier v Rambler Motors (AMC) Ltd*, the plaintiff had taken his car for servicing to the defendants' garage three or four times over a five-year period. On previous occasions, he had been asked to sign a service 'invoice' containing conditions, but on the relevant occasion, this step was omitted. The Court of Appeal held that the previous contracts did not amount to a course of dealings incorporating the defendants' conditions into the oral contract.

3. Common understanding

■ *British Crane Hire Corporation Ltd v Ipswich Plant Hire Ltd*
[1974] 1 All ER 1059, Court of Appeal

The plaintiffs and the defendants were companies engaged in the business of hiring out heavy earth-moving equipment. The defendants were themselves carrying out drainage and other work of a civil engineering nature on marshy ground. They urgently required a dragline crane and so got in touch with the plaintiffs, who agreed to supply one on hire. The agreement was made by telephone. The hiring and transport charges were agreed but nothing was said about the conditions of hire. Soon after the crane had been delivered, the plaintiffs, in accordance with their normal practice, sent the defendants a printed form to be signed by them, which set out the conditions of hire. Before the defendants had signed it, however, an accident occurred in consequence of which the crane sank into the marshy ground. The accident was not caused by any negligence on the part of the defendants. Under the printed conditions, the defendants were liable to indemnify the owner against all expense in connection with the use of the crane. The plaintiffs' conditions were in similar terms to those used by all firms in the plant-hiring business, including the defendants themselves. In an action by the plaintiffs for the cost of recovering the crane, the defendants claimed that they were not liable under the plaintiffs' conditions because they had not been incorporated into the oral contract of hire.

Lord Denning MR

... [H]ere the parties were both in the trade and were of equal bargaining power. Each was a firm of plant hirers who hired out plant. The defendants themselves knew that firms in the plant-hiring trade always imposed conditions in regard to the hiring of plant; and that their conditions were on much the same lines. The defendants' manager, Mr Turner (who knew the crane), was asked about it. He agreed that he had seen these conditions or similar ones in regard to the hiring of plant. He said that most of them were, to one extent or another, variations of a form which he called 'the Contractors' Plant Association form'.

The defendants themselves (when they let out cranes) used the conditions of that form. The conditions on the plaintiffs' form were in rather different words, but nevertheless to much the same effect . . . .

From [the] evidence it is clear that both parties knew quite well that conditions were habitually imposed by the supplier of these machines: and both parties knew the substance of those conditions. In particular that, if the crane sank in soft ground, it was the hirer's job to recover it; and that there was an indemnity clause. In these circumstances, I think the conditions on the form should be regarded as incorporated into the contract. I would not put it so much on the course of dealing, but rather on the common understanding which is to be derived from the conduct of the parties, namely, that the hiring was to be on the terms of the plaintiffs' usual conditions.

As Lord Reid said in *McCutcheon v David MacBrayne Ltd*, quoting from the Scottish textbook Gloag on Contract:

'The judicial task is not to discover the actual intentions of each party: it is to decide what each was reasonably entitled to conclude from the attitude of the other.'

It seems to me that, in view of the relationship of the parties, when the defendants requested this crane urgently and it was supplied at once—before the usual form was received—the plaintiffs were entitled to conclude that the defendants were accepting it on the terms of the plaintiffs' own printed conditions—which would follow in a day or two. It is just as if the plaintiffs had said, 'We will supply it on our usual conditions', and the defendants said 'Of course, that is quite understood'.

Applying the conditions, it is quite clear that conditions 6 and 8 cover the second mishap. The defendants are liable for the costs of recovering the crane from the soft ground.

Megaw LJ and **Sir Eric Sachs** agreed.

NOTES

1. Was the clause incorporated on the basis of a custom in the trade, or on some other basis? For a trade custom to form an implied term of a contract, the custom must be generally accepted by those doing business in the particular trade in the particular place, and be so generally known that an outsider making reasonable enquiries could not fail to discover it (*Kum v Wah Tat Bank Ltd* [1971] 1 Lloyd's Rep 439, 444, PC). It will thus become binding on a newcomer to the trade. Had the hirers in this case been newcomers (eg a building firm that had not hired plant before), do you think the court would have decided the case the same way? If not, what was the basis of the decision?

2. There was evidence of the terms each company used when hiring *to* other people; was there any evidence of the terms either used when hiring *from* others?

3. How is the equality or otherwise of bargaining power relevant to this point? Should the outcome of the case be different if the owners were a large, prosperous company and the hirers a small, struggling one?

4. Suppose A Ltd and B Ltd are engineering firms: A makes castings; B builds machinery using castings made by other firms. B has ordered castings from A three or four times in the last two years and has previously agreed to A's standard conditions of trading, which provide for a price increase or decrease if the market price of copper rises or falls. A similar clause is used by all firms making copper castings. B has its own set of purchasing conditions, which provide for a fixed price. B makes a contract over the telephone to buy from A 1,000 castings at £1.00 each, for delivery in six months' time. No letters are exchanged and no reference is made to A's conditions. After three months, the price of copper doubles and A tells B that he will not deliver unless he is paid the price increase that would be appropriate if A's 'rise and fall' clause applies. Advise B.

4. Negation by circumstances

■ *Couchman v Hill*

[1947] 1 All ER 103, Court of Appeal

The plaintiff bought at an auction sale a heifer belonging to the defendant and described in the sale catalogue as a 'red and white stirk heifer, unserved'. The catalogue contained the following words: 'All lots must be taken subject to all faults or errors of description (if any) and no compensation will be paid for the same.' By No 3 of the conditions of sale: 'The lots are sold with all faults, imperfections, and errors of description, the auctioneers not being responsible for the correct description, genuineness, or authenticity of, or any defect in, any lot, and giving no warranty whatever.' Before the sale and when the heifers were in the ring, the plaintiff asked the defendant and the auctioneer 'Can you confirm heifers unserved?' and received from both the answer, 'Yes.' Between seven and eight weeks after the purchase, the heifer suffered a miscarriage, and three weeks later, died as a result of the strain of carrying a calf at too young an age for breeding. The plaintiff brought an action for damages for breach of warranty.

Scott LJ

. . . The real question is.: What did the parties understand by the question addressed to and the answer received from both the defendant and the auctioneer? It is contended by the defendant that the question meant 'having regard to the onerous stipulations which I know I shall have to put up with if I bid and the lot is knocked down to me, can you give me your honourable assurance that the heifers have in fact not been served? If so, I will risk the penalties of the catalogue'. The alternative meaning is: 'I am frightened of contracting on your published terms, but I will bid if you will tell me by word of mouth that you accept full responsibility for the statement in the catalogue that the heifers have not been served, or, in other words, give me a clean warranty. That is the only condition on which I will bid'. If that was the meaning there was clearly an oral offer of a warranty which over-rode the stultifying condition in the printed terms, that offer was accepted by the plaintiff when he bid, and the contract was made on that basis when the lot was knocked down to him. In some circumstances I concede that such a question might on its face be somewhat ambiguous, but I think in the present case the only inference that could properly be drawn by the judge or jury charged with the duty of finding the facts—and this is a question of fact as to the intention of the parties—is that the question was asked and answered with the alternative meaning indicated. That this is so follows, I think, conclusively from the plaintiff's evidence which was accepted by the judge, taken in conjunction with the admissions of the defendant that the words if used—which he denied—would have bound him. It is obvious that it was the stipulations that prompted the question. The plaintiff was not a lawyer, but he knew what he wanted. So did the defendant, and he got it. What the plaintiff wanted was to know where he stood before he made an offer which the fall of the hammer would turn into a contract.

The county court judge in a careful reserved judgment has found that this oral statement was made, and he refers to it as a warranty, but holds that its value was destroyed by the qualifying stipulations. He has not in terms put the question to himself: 'Did the parties by this question and answer intend to exclude the stipulations from the contract that resulted on the fall of the hammer?' I have, accordingly, felt some doubt whether or not the proper course was to order a new trial. On reading his judgment as a whole I have, however, arrived at the conclusion that it is implicit therein that it was not the intention of the parties to exclude the stipulation. As we are of opinion that on the facts found by him he could not properly arrive at this conclusion, I think we are not compelled to put the parties to the expense of a further trial.

There was a good deal of discussion whether the description 'unserved' constituted a warranty or a condition. I have, in what I have said so far deliberately refrained from expressing a view thereon, but as a matter of law I think every item in a description which constitutes a substantial ingredient in the 'identity' of the thing sold is a condition, although every such condition can be waived by the purchaser who thereon becomes entitled to treat it as a warranty and recover damages.

I think there was here an unqualified condition which, on its breach, the plaintiff was entitled to treat as a warranty and recover the damages claimed. One final word. The printed condition that the vendor will take no responsibility for errors of description of things or animals specifically offered for sale on inspection is reasonable for visible defects, but for qualities or attributes which are invisible it is not reasonable. It may well become a mere trap for the unwary. The point deserves consideration by the Auctioneers' Associations.

The appeal should, therefore, in my opinion be allowed with costs here and below, the latter on Scale B.

Tucker and **Bucknill LJJ** agreed.

Appeal allowed.

NOTES

1. For the distinction between 'condition' and 'warranty', see p 426.

2. A party that has misrepresented the effect of a clause may not be permitted to rely on it: see p 346.

A rather different problem of the incorporation of terms occurs with clauses in collective labour agreements: are they incorporated into individual employees' contracts even if they are not expressly referred to? We saw earlier that even where there is an express reference, only those terms of a collective agreement that are 'appropriate' will be incorporated into the individuals' contracts. Provided the terms are appropriate, however, the courts seem willing to infer that they have been incorporated if the agreement has been acted on. In *Wall v Standard Telephones & Cables Ltd* [1990] ICR 291, the question was whether cl 6 of a collective agreement, providing that, in the case of compulsory redundancy, selection would be made on the basis of length of service with the group, was part of the individuals' contracts. Hobhouse J said (at 297):

The so-called 'normative effect' by which it can be inferred that provisions of collective agreements have become part of individual contracts of employment is now well recognised in employment law (see, for example, *Harvey on Industrial Relations and Employment Law*, vol. 235). However, serious difficulties still arise because the principle still has to be one of incorporation into the individual contracts of employment and the extraction of a recognisable contractual intent as between the individual employee and his employer. The mere existence of collective agreements which are relevant to the employee and his employment does not include a contractual intent (see for example per Ackner LJ. *Robertson v British Gas* [1983] IRLR 302). The contractual intent has to be found in the individual contract of employment and very often the evidence will not be sufficient to establish such an intent in a manner which satisfies accepted contractual criteria and satisfies ordinary criteria of certainty. Where the relevant subject-matter is one of present day-to-day relevance to the employer and employee, as for example wage rates and hours of work, the continuing relationship between employer and employee, the former paying wages and providing work, the latter working and accepting wages, provides a basis for inferring such a contractual intent. Where, as in the case of redundancy, the situation is one which does not have daily implications but only arises occasionally the inference will be more difficult to sustain. Here, there had not previously been any question of compulsory redundancies. There was no previously tested position by which a local custom could be demonstrated, nor was there any previous situation involving any of the relevant individuals, or for that matter any other employees of the defendants from which it could be inferred as a matter of individual contractual intent, that individual contracts of employment were to include as a matter of contractual right and obligation selection for redundancy on the seniority principle. It must be borne in mind that although the present plaintiffs would be the beneficiaries of the application of such a principle, by a parity of reasoning there would be other employees who would be disadvantaged. Similarly, there is no necessity to infer an intention to incorporate since collective agreements have a function and value of their own which exists wholly independently of any individual contract of employment (see, for example, the reasoning of the Judicial Committee in *Young v Canadian Northern Railway* [1931] AC 83 at 88 to 89).

There have been a large number of cases decided the one way or the other on individual issues of incorporation in a variety of circumstances. In the leading case *Robertson v British Gas* (supra) it was held that the terms of an incentive bonus agreement negotiated between the employer and the unions were incorporated into the individual contracts of employment so as to give the individual employees the right to sue for the bonus payments. In both the employees' letters of appointment and the statutory statements, there were references to the bonus scheme; it followed that the employers could not unilaterally vary the individual contracts of employment by failing to renew the collective agreement. The essence of the Court of Appeal's approach is to recognise the primacy of the individual contract of employment and to apply ordinary contractual principles in order to ascertain its content and how it might be varied.

This reasoning was followed and applied by the Court of Appeal in *Marley v Forward Trust Group Ltd* [1986] IRLR 369. In that case, the letter of employment of the relevant employee referred to the company's personnel manual in such a way as to make it clear that the terms and conditions of his employment were as set out in that manual. The manual made express provision for redundancy, including provision for a mobility clause, which gave redundant employees who were relocated at other workplaces the right to opt for redundancy within six months of relocation. The provisions of the manual had been the subject of negotiation between the employers and the unions, and were effectively a collective agreement. However, since they were incorporated into the relevant individual contracts of employment, they became contractually enforceable as between the individual employees and the employer. That case specifically illustrates that there is no objection in principle to the capacity for redundancy provisions to be made contractually enforceable as between employer and employee.

However, on the facts, Hobhouse J held that cl 6 of the agreement was the only one in the collective agreement that might be appropriate for incorporation and that, in the context of the agreement as a whole, its wording was too weak to support the inference of incorporation.

CHAPTER TWELVE

CONTENTS OF WRITTEN CONTRACTS

I. EFFECT OF SIGNATURE

■ *L'Estrange v Graucob Ltd*

[1934] 2 KB 394, Divisional Court

The plaintiff bought an automatic slot machine from the defendants, signing an order form that contained, in small print, a number of conditions, one of which was that 'any express or implied condition, statement, or warranty, statutory or otherwise not stated herein is hereby excluded'. She received in exchange a printed confirmation order. The machine did not work satisfactorily and the plaintiff brought an action in the county court in which she claimed that the machine was not fit for the purpose for which it was sold. The county court judge held that the sellers could not rely on the printed condition, and the defendant appealed. The plaintiff claimed that she had not read the form and did not know what it contained.

Scutton LJ

...A clause of [this] sort has been before the Courts for some time. The first reported case in which it made its appearance seems to be *Wallis, Son & Wells v Pratt & Haynes* where the exclusion clause mentioned only 'warranty' and it was held that it did not exclude conditions. In the more recent case of *Andrews Bros (Bournemouth), Ltd v Singer & Co Ltd* where the draftsman had put into the contract of sale a clause which excluded only implied conditions, warranties and liabilities, it was held that the clause did not apply to an express term describing the article, and did not exempt the seller from liability where he delivered an article of a different description. The clause here in question would seem to have been intended to go further than any of the previous clauses and to include all terms denoting collateral stipulations in order to avoid the result of these decisions.

The main question raised in the present case is whether that clause formed part of the contract. If it did, it clearly excluded any condition or warranty.

In the course of the argument in the county court reference was made to the railway passenger and cloak-room ticket cases...

These cases have no application when the document has been signed. When a document containing contractual terms is signed, then, in the absence of fraud, or, I will add, misrepresentation, the party signing it is bound, and it is wholly immaterial whether he has read the document or not.

Maugham LJ agreed.

Appeal allowed.

NOTES

1.   This decision must now be read in the light of the Unfair Contract Terms Act 1977, s 6(3) and Schedule 2, para (c): see pp 996 and 1011.

2.   A party's signature will bind her not only to the contents of the document signed but also to other documents referred to ('incorporation by reference'). The document referred to may not in itself be legally binding. Thus a contract of employment may incorporate by reference the terms of a collective agreement between the employers and a union (which is not normally legally binding, see p 182), provided that, where the words of incorporation are in general terms, the clauses sought to be incorporated are apt to be part of the individual contract.

3.   When Scrutton says that a party will not be bound when there has been fraud or misrepresentation, he may be referring to the rule that a misrepresentation, whether fraudulent or innocent, may entitle the misrepresentee to rescind the contract (see Chapter 13), or to a misrepresentation about the meaning of the clause itself. In *Curtis v Chemical Cleaning and Dyeing Co Ltd* [1951] 1 All ER 631, the plaintiff took a wedding dress to the defendants for cleaning and was asked to sign a document exempting the defendants from liability 'for any damage howsoever arising'. She asked why she had to sign and was told that it was because the defendants would not accept liability for damage to beads or sequins on the dress. The plaintiff then signed. The dress was returned with a stain on it that had not been there before. The defendants denied liability, relying on the clause. The Court of Appeal held that the statement made to the plaintiff misrepresented the effect of the clause and prevented the defendants from relying on it. Somervell LJ said that the clause 'never became part of the contract', but probably this goes too far: what if the only damage had been to the sequins? Compare estoppel, p 148.

4.   Suppose Graucob Ltd knew that the plaintiff thought she was being given a full and unrestricted warranty?

■ Spencer, 'Signature, Consent and the Rule in *L'Estrange v Graucob*' [1973] CLJ 103 at 114–116

Was [the decision in *L'Estrange v Graucob*] right? When Miss L'Estrange signed the order form on which were written various terms, she gave the appearance of agreeing to everything that was written on the document. To borrow the words from *Smith v Hughes* itself, she so conducted herself 'that a reasonable man would believe that she was assenting to the terms proposed by the other party'. It would usually follow from this that she was bound by her apparent consent to all those terms. However, a person is not bound by apparent consent where the other party knew that his mind did not go with his apparent consent, or where the other party is responsible for the mistake which has been made. Didn't the facts of the case bring Miss L'Estrange within the scope of these exceptions to apparent consent?

   The order form which Graucob Ltd provided seems to have been drawn up in a most confusing way. Maugham LJ said '...I could wish that the contract had been in a simpler and more usual form. It is unfortunate that the important clause excluding conditions and warranties is in such small print'. Not only was this clause printed in small print, but it was also printed on brown paper, which must have made the small print even harder to read. The general layout of the form also appears to have been confusing, too, the exemption clause being in a part of the document where it easily escaped notice. Then was this not one of those cases where although A apparently consented to B's terms, he did so because B had earlier confused him as to what those terms should be? In principle, the case is surely the same as *Scriven v Hindley*, where A was allowed to deny his apparent consent to a contract to buy tow, because the auction catalogue had been confusing, and had contributed to form A's belief that he was offering to buy, not tow, but hemp.

Perhaps Miss L'Estrange could have gone even further than this, and also denied her apparent consent to the exemption clause on the ground that the company either knew or ought to have known that her mind did not go with her apparent consent. Why did Graucob Ltd use order forms printed on brown paper containing obscure exemption clauses in minute print in unexpected places? Was it because it knew that if it said what it meant more plainly, its customers would understand the document they were being asked to sign, and would refuse to do so? ...

The truth is that whatever may have been Graucob Ltd's intentions disreputable companies put harsh exemption clauses in minute print in order to 'put one over' people like Miss L'Estrange. Then why should people in her position not be allowed to deny their apparent consent to the clause because the company either *knew or ought to have known* that their mind did not go with their apparent consent?

NOTES

1. Compare Samek, 'The Objective Theory of Contract and the Rule in *L'Estrange v Graucob*' (1974) 52 Can BR 351; Howarth, 'The Meaning of Objectivity in Contract' (1984) 100 LQR 252; Vorster (1987) 103 LQR 274.

2. If it was clear to Graucob Ltd that Miss L'Estrange thought she was getting a full warranty, one can see Spencer's argument succeeding, but what if she simply 'didn't know what she was signing'?

3. In *Tilden Rent-a-Car Co v Clendenning* (1978) 83 DLR (3d) 400, the Ontario Court of Appeal cited Spencer's article. Clendenning rented a car from the defendant's office at Vancouver airport, as he had often done before. He was asked whether he required additional insurance coverage, and he replied that he did. In fact, the contractual document that he received and signed, while excluding the whole of the driver's liability for damage to the rented car, limited this exclusion to cases in which there was no breach of the conditions of the rental agreement. On the back of the contract, in very small print, there was a clause by which the customer undertook not to drive in violation of any traffic law or ordinance, or after consuming any quantity of intoxicating liquor. Clendenning had an accident while driving after having had a drink, but not so as to be incapable of driving. The majority of the court held that Clendenning was not bound by this 'onerous' provision, as Tilden had not taken steps to alert him to its presence.

Tilden Rent-a-Car cannot rely on provisions of the contract which it had no reason to believe were being assented to by the other contracting party...

4. It may be hard to reconcile this approach with more traditional attitudes to mistake, which at least recently have denied relief unless one party actually knew of the other's mistake: see pp 292 and 300. Is there anything to be said for it in policy terms? Would denying that a customer's signature on a standard form is conclusive evidence of her consent to all the terms of the document be an improper interference with freedom of contract?

■ Atiyah, 'Freedom of Contract and the New Right' (1988)
20 Skriftserien, Juridiska Fakulteten i Stockholm, pp 11–13

The whole point of Freedom of Contract is to reject paternalism and leave the parties to their own bargain. Yet, as all lawyers know, there are many types of circumstances in which for fifty years and more the law has been busy interfering with express contractual terms on grounds of unfairness.

Furthermore, most lawyers brought up in the atmosphere prevailing after the second World War have shown considerable sympathy with these legislative interferences with Freedom of Contract. I myself have often argued (for example in my Cecil Wright Memorial Lecture [see *Essays on Contract*, chap. 11]) that it is impossible to ignore the idea of a fair exchange in contract law. In that lecture I pointed out that there are all sorts of legal doctrines which enable the common law courts to pursue normative criteria of fairness in handling contractual disputes, and I rejected the idea that the express terms of the contract can always be treated as a conclusive and definite decision on what is fair. On the other hand, I must admit to a good deal of sympathy with the ideology of the New Right, so a major problem for those who think as I do is to reconcile much traditional and apparently paternalistic interference with free contract with this new ideology. . . .

To what extent can this sort of interference with contractual freedom be reconciled with the ideology of the New Right?

First, there is surely nothing seriously objectionable about the provisions requiring information to be given to the consumer, nor even about the cooling-off provisions. It is true that even these may seem unnecessarily fussy and over-protective in the more robust market favoured by the New Right, but the main purpose here is to ensure that the contracts do indeed have the full consent and understanding of the consumer. There is nothing contrary to Freedom of Contract ideology in that. In fact, the giving of information about true rates of interest available from suppliers of credit can be justified as an aid to the competitive market.

But I would go much further, and suggest that there is nothing in Freedom of Contract ideology which requires us to accept without question the binding validity of pages of small print, simply because they are signed by contracting parties, whether they are consumers or even commercial organisations. The truth perhaps is that the practical convenience of treating signed printed forms as binding on the parties is so great that we have far too readily accepted these forms as conclusive evidence of what the parties really intended. This may well have been a wrong turning from the beginning, and if modern protective legislation is ever to be challenged by the New Right, some fundamental rethinking on this question will surely be in order. This could be a major gain, because much of our protective legislation, like the Consumer Credit Act itself draws no distinction between the consumer who truly understands the nature and essential terms of the contract he is entering into, and the consumer who does not. Nor will it suffice today to insist blandly that no consumers can understand the essential elements of a credit transaction. Some consumers are well informed, and others may have independent advice.

In this connection it is interesting to note that there are at least some recent judicial decisions which do seem more willing to treat consumers as rational adults, at least where they have been advised by their own lawyers. Of course this is not likely to happen with the purchase of consumer goods, but in two recent cases dealing with mortgage loan transactions, in which consumers were advised by their own lawyers, and fully understood the nature and essential elements of the transactions, the contracts were upheld by the courts even though the terms were arguably harsh or unfair. So here perhaps is a small pointer suggesting that the message of the New Right is being heard in the law courts as well as in the City of London. . . .

NOTES

1. Questions of the provision of information to consumers are explored in more detail at pp 967 ff.

2. Compare the *Interfoto* case, on p 336.

3. As so often seems to be the case, the courts, in an indirect fashion, evade the rule in *L'Estrange v Graucob* by using other doctrines. See in particular the rules on interpretation of exclusion clauses, pp 977 ff.

II. PAROL EVIDENCE RULE

Suppose the parties have signed a written contract (this may be a single document, or the part signed may refer expressly to another document, in which case the contract will include both documents read together). One party then alleges that the writings do not contain the whole contract: there is some other term that was expressly agreed, either orally or in a separate writing, but which is not stated or referred to in the signed writings.

Two points arise. Firstly, if the term was agreed to, why was it left out? Doesn't leaving it out show that it was not 'part of the final deal'? (Compare Fuller's 'channelling function': **p 138**.) Secondly, to allow the party to rely on the unstated term may produce costly uncertainty—uncertainty in court, where it will be more difficult to determine what the contract really was; uncertainty for third parties who may rely on the written contract (eg a bank, which, after seeing a written contract its client has made, lends him money on the strength of it); uncertainty for the parties, who later may not recollect just what was agreed. The last is particularly a problem when a party is a company, because the contract may be made by one officer but administered by another; this may explain why it is common in commercial contracts to find 'merger' or 'integration' clauses, such as:

The parties have negotiated this Agreement and shall enter into any Contract made subject hereto on the basis that the provisions of this Agreement and such Contract represent their entire agreement relating to the matters contained in this Agreement and such Contract.

On the effect of such a clause see further p 353.

An example of the problem is *Jacobs v Batavia and General Plantations Trust Ltd* [1924] 1 Ch 287; affd [1924] 2 Ch 329. The plaintiff applied for and was allotted four £100 deposit notes of the defendant company. He relied on the prospectus issued by the defendants. This stated that, in the event of the sale of the Rio Bravo estates owned by the Trust, the Trust would set aside out of the proceeds of sale a sum sufficient to redeem all the notes then outstanding, and the holders would be given the option of being paid off then in cash at 105 per cent, or of retaining their notes until the normal date for redemption. The notes themselves (which were in the same form as a specimen contained in the prospectus) made no reference to this undertaking. The estates in question were sold and the plaintiff brought an action for an injunction to restrain the Trust from dealing with the proceeds of sale without first setting aside a sum sufficient to pay off the outstanding notes. Was the contract simply what was contained in the notes or what was in the prospectus as well?

At one time, the courts appeared to apply a strict rule, known as the 'parol evidence rule', to this sort of case: 'parol evidence cannot be admitted to add to, vary or contradict a deed or other written instrument.' The rule applied not only to oral promises but also to written promises that were not in or referred to by the written and signed contract (in the strict legal sense, parol means 'not under seal'; here it is used to mean 'extrinsic to the written and signed contract'). When the rule was applied, it prevented the party who would otherwise have relied on the extrinsic promise from adducing any evidence on the point. It was thus not a rule of evidence at all, because it did not govern *how* the extrinsic promise might be proved; it was a rule of substantive law.

Some contracts, particularly contracts for the sale of land, were enforceable only if there was written evidence of their terms (see p 144). A complex body of rules was developed to deal with cases in which this requirement was not complied with, but generally speaking, the contract could only be enforced in the terms set out in the writing—indeed, in some situations, if it were proved that the writing did not contain all the terms, the whole contract might turn out to be unenforceable (eg *Beckett v Nurse* [1948] 1 KB 535). Dicta often seem to suggest that the parol evidence rule applied to other kinds of contract as well. At least by the turn of the century, this was misleading. The rule did not apply to contracts that were partly written and partly oral. Thus it was open to the court to find that, on the facts, the contract was not a 'written contract' within the meaning of the rule, but only partly written, and thus the parol evidence could be admitted. (It is not wholly clear whether this was always implicit in the rule or was a later development.) Although statements of the rule in a strict form continued (eg in *Jacobs'* case), it was openly acknowledged that the rule was really no more than a presumption.

Although when the parties arrive at a definite written contract the implication or presumption is very strong that such contract is intended to contain all the terms of their bargain, it is a presumption only, and it is open to either of the parties to allege that there was, in addition to what appears in the written agreement, an antecedent express stipulation not intended by the parties to be excluded, but intended to continue in force with the express written agreement. (Lord Russell of Killowen CJ in *Gillespie Bros & Co v Cheney, Eggar & Co* [1896] 2 QB 59,62)

In the *Jacobs* case itself, PO Lawrence J held that the deposit notes did not contain the whole contract, but must be read with the prospectus. As Wedderburn put it in 1959:

What the parol evidence rule has bequeathed to modern law is a presumption— namely that a document which *looks* like a contract is to be treated as the whole contract. ([1959] CLJ 58, 62)

Alternatively, the courts would sometimes give effect to the oral promise as an independent or collateral contract, for which the consideration was entering the main contract. In *De Lassalle v Guildford* [1901] 2 KB 215, for example, the tenant had refused to sign the lease until the landlord gave an assurance that the drains were in good order. This assurance was held to be a collateral contract. The majority in the Court of Appeal in the *Jacobs* case upheld the first instance decision on this ground (Pollock MR held that the notes and the prospectus should be read together). A collateral contract has even been found when its terms directly contradict the written contract. In *City and Westminster Properties (1934) Ltd v Mudd* [1959] Ch 129, the defendant had, in 1941, become tenant of premises which included a lock-up shop and a back room in which he slept. In 1947, he was offered a new lease, which contained covenants against using the premises for dwelling or sleeping. He objected to this and only signed after being told that if he would sign the lease in its original form the landlords would make no objection to his residing on the premises. Ten years later, the landlords attempted to forfeit the lease for breach of the convenant but Harman J held that there was 'a clear contract acted upon by the defendant to his detriment and from which the plaintiffs cannot be allowed to resile'. The landlords' action therefore failed.

In 1976, the Law Commission provisionally proposed that what remained of the parol evidence rule should be abolished (Working Paper No 70). However, in 1986, it issued a report stating that legislation is not required because the rule no longer exists.

■ *'Law of Contract: The Parol Evidence Rule' (No 154),*
Law Commission (Cmnd 9700, 1986)
paras. 2.7, 2.10–13, 2.15, 2.17, 2.22–24

2.7. We have now concluded that although a proposition of law can be stated which can be described as the 'parol evidence rule' it is not a rule of law which, correctly applied, could lead to evidence being unjustly excluded. Rather, it is a proposition of law which is no more than a circular statement: *when it is proved or admitted that the parties to a contract intended that all the express terms of their agreement should be as recorded in a particular document or documents, evidence will be inadmissible (because irrelevant) if it is tendered only for the purpose of adding to, varying, subtracting from or contradicting the express terms of that contract.* We have considerable doubts whether such a proposition should properly be characterised as a 'rule' at all, but several leading textbook writers and judges have referred to it as a 'rule' and we are content to adopt their terminology for the purposes of this report . . . .

2.10. The two principal reasons which have led us to our conclusion on the nature of the parol evidence rule are, in substance, two aspects of the same process of reasoning. The first relates to the circumstances in which the rule is to be applied. In our view, some statements of the rule may have given rise to misunderstandings because they have concentrated on the *effect* of the rule rather than *when it is to be applied.* The effect of the rule is to exclude evidence or to cause the judge to ignore the evidence if given. As to the application of the rule, Lord Morris' statement in *Bank of Australasia v Palmer* refers to the inadmissibility of parol evidence to 'contradict, vary, add to or subtract from the terms of a *written contract*' (emphasis added). Thus, the rule can only be applied where the parties have entered into a 'written contract'. Parties can only be said to have entered into a written contract when 'the writing is intended by the parties as a contractual document which is to contain all the terms of their agreement'. When the parties have set down *all* the terms of their contract in writing, extrinsic evidence of other terms must be ignored. If the contract is not entirely in writing, it is not a written contract. There are many authorities and dicta to support this view. . . . If it is proved or admitted that all the terms of the contract have been set out in a particular document or documents, then evidence of other terms must be irrelevant and therefore inadmissible, because inconsistent with the finding that the parties have entered into a written contract.

2.11. The second reason for our conclusion as to the nature of the parol evidence rule is exemplified by the concept of the contract which is made partly orally and partly in writing . . . .

2.12. Because a contract can be made partly orally and partly in writing, the mere production of a contractual document, however complete it may look, cannot as a matter of law exclude evidence of oral terms if the other party asserts that such terms were agreed. If that assertion is proved, evidence of the oral terms cannot be excluded because the court will, by definition, have found that the contractual terms are partly to be found in what was agreed orally as well as in the document in question. No parol evidence rule could apply. On the other hand, if that assertion is not proved, there can be no place for a parol evidence rule because the court will have found that all the terms of the contract were set out in the document in question and, by implication, will thereby have excluded evidence of terms being found elsewhere. The pleadings in the action should normally reveal whether there is an issue as to where the contractual terms are to be found and what those terms are. If there is an issue, it will be an issue of fact for resolution on the balance of probabilities. If there is no issue, neither party will be permitted to adduce evidence of the contractual terms being found elsewhere than as admitted in the pleadings.

2.13. Of course, the more the parties have done to create what appears to be a written contract, the greater are the probabilities that the court will conclude that they did indeed make such a contract.

[The Law Commission referred to Wedderburn's statement above] . . .

[W]e do not think that in this context it is strictly correct to refer to a 'presumption'. In reaching a conclusion as to whether a document which looks like a complete contract was the whole contract, the court does not apply any presumption of law. Rather, it will reach its conclusion on the evidence tendered, applying to its judgment the prima facie probability derived from its experience of how people normally behave in a given situation. For example, if the plaintiff proves that the parties signed a document, such as a complicated lease of a commercial chattel, which document appears to be a complete contract and which is in a form generally adopted for setting out all the contractual terms, it may be difficult in practice for the defendant to prove, on the balance of probabilities, that terms were orally agreed in addition to those set out in the document.

2.15. Sometimes parties may include in their contracts a clause to the effect that the whole contract is contained in the document and that nothing was agreed outside it (sometimes called a 'merger' or 'integration' clause). In particular, it may be provided that nothing said during negotiations is intended to be of any contractual effect unless recorded in the document. Without legislative provision such a clause cannot, we think, have conclusive effect. It may have a very strong persuasive effect but if it were proved that, notwithstanding the clause, the parties actually intended some additional term to be of contractual effect, the court would give effect to that term because such was the intention of the parties....

2.17. The conclusion which emerges from the discussion above is that there is no *rule of law* that evidence is rendered inadmissible or is to be ignored solely because a document exists which looks like a complete contract. Whether it is a complete contract depends upon the intention of the parties, objectively judged, and not on any rule of law.

...

Rectification

2.22. It is the very essence of the parol evidence rule that the parties wrote down all that they had agreed, at least in relation to a particular subject-matter. It is in these circumstances that evidence of anything else which it is alleged they agreed is excluded. However, having agreed orally what had to be written down, the parties might mistakenly have written down something else or mistakenly have omitted something which they intended should be in the contractual document. The writing would not then accurately record their agreement. In these circumstances the party who alleges and is able to prove the error in the written contract can obtain from the court an order of rectification. The effect of the order is retrospectively to amend the document so that it states what it should have stated all the time. Parol evidence is, of course, admissible in support of an application to rectify.

2.23. Rectification may be sought of any written contract or the written part of a contract which is partly oral and partly in writing. The essence of the remedy is that the written agreement does not accurately state what it was intended it should state. If, therefore, the parties agreed a term but also agreed that it should not appear in the written contract, rectification could not be ordered so as to include that term in the document. It is important to note that the factual basis for rectification must be very clearly proved.

2.24. In one sense rectification may be seen as complementary to the parol evidence rule: if the parties made a contract and they intended that all they had agreed should be recorded in writing, effect can be given to omitted terms by rectifying the agreement so as to include them. If the parties did not intend their agreement to be wholly in writing, the parol evidence rule does not exclude evidence of oral terms. The terms would be enforced as terms of a contract made partly orally and partly in writing. Alternatively, they could be enforced as a collateral contract.

NOTES

1.   Not all commentators agree completely with the Law Commission's analysis of the rule, eg Treitel, p 194, who argues that the presumption that a written document is the exclusive record of the terms of the contract goes beyond the normal objective test of the parties' intentions.

2.   If it was always open to the courts to find that a contract was partly oral, partly written, why go to the trouble of treating the oral promise as a collateral contract? There seem to be two answers. One is that if the main contract has to be in writing, or evidenced in writing, treating the oral promise as a separate contract may allow both 'parts' of the contract to be given effect without rendering the whole thing unenforceable because the statutory requirement of writing is not fulfilled. Another is that sometimes the 'two-contract analysis' reflects the intentions of the parties. In *Mudd's* case, the landlords had specifically refused to alter the lease itself to allow the tenant to sleep there for fear that the tenancy would then fall under the Rent Restriction Acts; the concession that the tenant might sleep on the premises was intended to be personal to him, not assignable to

future tenants. Treating it as a separate collateral contract achieved these aims. In other cases, it simply did not matter which analysis is used—witness the judgments in the Court of Appeal in the *Jacobs* case.

3. As mentioned earlier (p 349), in professionally drafted written contracts it is extremely common to find clauses that say that the written contract is the whole contract ('whole contract' or 'entire contract' clauses). These are obviously intended to reintroduce a kind of parol evidence rule by agreement. In a contract between two parties who have both had legal advice, such a clause may well be taken at face value. See *Deepak Fertilisers and Petrochemicals Ltd v Davy McKee (London) Ltd* (1998) 62 Con LR 86; *Inntrepreneur Pub Co Ltd v East Crown Ltd* [2000] 2 Lloyd's Rep 611. On the other hand, if one party is a consumer, the Director General of Fair Trading, in exercising his powers under the Unfair Terms in Consumer Contracts Regulations (see p 1038), has objected vigorously to such clauses.

CHAPTER THIRTEEN

INACCURATE INFORMATION AND MISREPRESENTATION

In this chapter, we will deal with the problems of one party being under a misapprehension as to the facts because he has been misled by the other (we call this the problem of 'inaccurate information'), and we look at the remedies for misrepresentation. We have already seen that, as a rule, a party who is under a self-induced misapprehension as to the facts cannot complain that, the other failed to put him right (*Smith v Hughes*, p 303). We shall consider later cases in which there is an obligation to disclose relevant information; in particular, we shall concentrate on this problem in Chapter 19 of this section, which we have entitled 'Duties of Disclosure'. In fact, however, there are a number of other doctrines that, in effect, impose duties of disclosure, and we shall return to this theme frequently in this section of the book.

What makes it so difficult to mark out boundaries is that the problems caused by one or both parties entering a contract under a misapprehension as to the facts are dealt with by a broad array of doctrines. Some of these have been explained already: the cases on when a representation amounts to a term of the contract clearly involved one party giving the other inaccurate information. Equally, many of the cases in later chapters—those on implied terms, the common mistake cases and most of the frustration cases—involve situations in which the parties had inadequate information about present facts or future developments. We shall have to consider in turn each of these doctrines, and examine the relationship of each to the others. The case in which one party has actively misled the other is perhaps the easiest to visualise and thus the best place to start.

In one way, this chapter is separate from the rest of the section. The doctrine of misrepresentation involves a different legal technique to the cases in the previous chapters and the chapters that follow. The statement is often treated as being something 'outside' the contract. The victim of the misrepresentation, 'the misrepresentee', may be entitled to rescind the contract even though the contract itself has not been broken. In addition or instead, the misrepresentee may be able to recover damages, but they will be damages for fraud or negligence in tort, or damages under statute, not damages for breach of contract.

Before we turn to misrepresentation itself, please look again at Chapter 11 (pp 321–344). If one party makes a statement of fact to the other, and the statement is crucial or he is in a better position to know the truth, he is likely to be treated as promising that the fact stated is true. The cases that follow largely involve situations in which a statement was made that did *not* amount to a promise.

I. RESCISSION FOR MISREPRESENTATION

■ *Redgrave v Hurd*
(1881) 20 ChD 1, Court of Appeal

The plaintiff, an elderly solicitor, advertised for a younger partner, who would not object to buying the plaintiff's suburban residence. The defendant had two interviews with the plaintiff, who told him that the practice brought in about £300 a year. The plaintiff produced summaries for three years showing business of about £200 a year and said the rest was made up by other business not included in the summaries; he showed the defendant a bundle of papers relating to this other business. The defendant did not examine these papers; they, in fact, showed that there was almost no other business. The defendant signed an agreement to purchase the house; at the plaintiff's insistence, this agreement made no reference to the agreement to buy the practice. The defendant discovered the truth and refused to complete. The plaintiff sought specific performance, and the defendant counter claimed for rescission of the agreement and damages. Fry J held that the defendant, having had the opportunity to check the truth of the representations but not having taken it, must be taken not to have relied on them. The Court of Appeal held that the defendant's counterclaim for damages for fraud must fail because he had not pleaded that the plaintiff knew that the statements he was making were untrue; it reversed Fry J's decision and rescinded the contract on the grounds of innocent misrepresentation.

Jessel MR

... As regards the rescission of a contract, there was no doubt a difference between the rules of Courts of Equity and the rules of Courts of Common Law—a difference which of course has now disappeared by the operation of the *Judicature Act*, which makes the rules of equity prevail. According to the decisions of Courts of Equity it was not necessary, in order to set aside a contract obtained by material false representation, to prove that the party who obtained it knew at the time when the representation was made that it was false. It was put in two ways, either of which was sufficient. One way of putting the case was, 'A man is not allowed to get a benefit from a statement which he now admits to be false. He is not allowed to say, for the purpose of civil jurisdiction, that when he made it he did not know it to be false; he ought to have found that out before he made it.' The other way of putting it was this: 'Even assuming that moral fraud must be shewn in order to set aside a contract, you have it where a man, having obtained a beneficial contract by a statement which he now knows to be false, insists upon keeping that contract. To do so is a moral delinquency: no man ought to seek to take advantage of his own false statements.' The rule in equity was settled, and it does not matter on which of the two grounds it was rested. As regards the rule of Common Law there is no doubt it was not quite so wide. There were, indeed, cases in which, even at Common Law, a contract could be rescinded for misrepresentation, although it could not be shewn that the person making it knew the representation to be false. They are variously stated, but I think, according to the later decisions, the statement must have been made recklessly and without care, whether it was true or false, and not with the belief that it was true ...

There is another proposition of law of very great importance which I think it is necessary for me to state, because, with great deference to the very learned Judge from whom this appeal comes, I think it is not quite accurately stated in his judgment. If a man is induced to enter into a contract by a false representation it is not a sufficient answer to him to say, 'If you had used due diligence you would have found out that the statement was untrue. You had the means afforded you of discovering its falsity, and did not choose to avail yourself of them.' I take it to be a settled doctrine of equity, not only as regards specific performance but also as regards rescission, that this is not an answer unless there is such delay as constitutes a defence under the *Statute of Limitations*. That, of course, is quite a different thing. Under the statute delay deprives a man of his right to rescind on the ground of fraud, and the only question to be considered is from what time the delay is to be reckoned. It had been decided, and the rule was adopted by the statute, that the delay counts from the time when by due diligence the fraud might have been discovered. Nothing can be plainer, I take it, on the authorities in equity than that the effect of false representation is not got rid of on the ground that the person to whom it was made has been guilty of negligence. One of the most familiar instances in modern times is where men issue a prospectus in which they make false statements of the contracts made before the formation of a company, and then say that the contracts themselves may be inspected at the offices of the solicitors. It has always been held that those who accepted those false statements as true were not deprived of their remedy merely because they neglected to go and look at the contracts. Another instance with which we are familiar is where a vendor makes a false statement as to the contents of a lease, as, for instance, that it contains no covenant preventing the carrying on of the trade which the purchaser is known by the vendor to be desirous of carrying on upon the property. Although the lease itself might be produced at the sale, or might have been open to the inspection of the purchaser long previously to the sale, it has been repeatedly held that the vendor cannot be allowed to say, 'You were not entitled to give credit to my statement'. It is not sufficient, therefore, to say that the purchaser had the opportunity of investigating the real state of the case, but did not avail himself of that opportunity.

. . . [T]he learned Judge came to the conclusion either that the Defendant did not rely on the statement, or that if he did rely upon it he had shewn such negligence as to deprive him of his title to relief from this Court. As I have already said, the latter proposition is in my opinion not founded in law, and the former part is not founded in fact; I think also it is not founded in law, for when a person makes a material representation to another to induce him to enter into a contract, and the other enters into that contract, it is not sufficient to say that the party to whom the the representation is made does not prove that he entered into the contract, relying upon the representation. If it is a material representation calculated to induce him to enter into the contract, it is an inference of law that he was induced by the representation to enter into it and in order to take away his title to be relieved from the contract on the ground that the representation was untrue, it must be shewn either that he had knowledge of the facts contrary to the representation or that he stated in terms, or shewed clearly by his conduct, that he did not rely on the representation . . . .

Baggallay and **Lush LJJ** concurred.

NOTES

1.   It appears that, even at common law, rescission was available to the victim of a fraudulent misrepresentation. Fraud, however, requires proof that the misrepresentor either knew that his statement was false, or was reckless as to whether or not it was false: *Derry v Peek* (1889) 14 App Cas 337.

2.   What justification does Jessel MR offer for the rule that a contract entered in reliance on an innocent (ie non-fraudulent) misrepresentation should be rescinded? It is interesting to compare this to the approach taken in cases of unconscionability, eg p 940, note 4.

3.   Why is it no answer that the misrepresentee could have discovered the truth for himself?

4.   Suppose that, in *Redgrave v Hurd*, it had been possible to ascertain the true position from the books, and the defendant had examined them, but he had not noticed that the figures in the books did not correspond to those given by the plaintiff (cf *Attwood v Small* (1838) 6 Cl & Fin 232).

5.   If the misrepresentation had been fraudulent, the misrepresentee would have been entitled to claim damages as well as to rescind. The damages would not have been for

breach of contract but for the tort of deceit. The measure of damages in tort does not include compensation for 'loss of expectation', see pp 45 and 372.

6.   Jessel MR states that an innocent misrepresentation must be 'material' if it is to be a ground for relief. This presumably excludes incorrect statements of facts that would not influence the reasonable person. Cf Marine Insurance Act 1906, s 18(2): 'every circumstance is material which would influence the judgment of a prudent insurer in fixing the premium, or determining whether he will take the risk.' In principle, the claimant has to show both that (a) he was in fact induced by the misrepresentation to enter the contract (inducement), and (b) that the misrepresentation would have induced a reasonable person (materiality). In practice, in most modern misrepresentation cases, once the claimant has shown inducement, materiality is assumed. (You may like to compare this with the position about non-disclosure: see p 530.)

7.   The contract for the house in *Redgrave v Hurd* deliberately made no reference to the business, and thus the defendant could not recover for breach of contract. What if it had done? As we saw earlier, some statements of fact do amount to contractual terms: for example, the dealer's statement about the car's mileage in *Dick Bentley Productions Ltd v Harold Smith Motors Ltd* (p 326). Could the buyer in that case have elected to treat the statement as a representation, so as to seek rescission? In *Pennsylvania Shipping Co v Compagnie Nationale de Navigation* [1936] 2 All ER 1167, the plaintiffs had time-chartered the defendants' tanker. During lengthy negotiations, the defendants had made statements, which turned out to be inaccurate, about the pipe lines and heating coils. These statements were embodied as 'Guaranteed' in the charterparty. Branson J held that the pre-contract representations had become merged with the contract terms, so that there could be no question of rescission. This view was reversed by the Misrepresentation Act 1967, s 1, which states that rescission is available even though the representation has *become* a term of the contract (for the text of s 1, see p 369). It is not quite clear whether this applies to a statement such as that in the *Dick Bentley* case, which has been made only once and which is held to constitute a contractual promise. Probably even in this case the representee has the choice of remedies for breach or for misrepresentation. Needless to say, he cannot opt for inconsistent alternatives, such as both rescinding the contract for misrepresentation and recovering damages for breach.

8.   Rescission is normally available only where the misrepresentation was made by another party to the contract (or someone acting as the other party's agent). The only exception to this is where one party had notice that a misrepresention had been made to the other party by a third person. As examples of misrepresentations by third parties, consider the following.

   (i) A husband whose business needs a loan is required by the lender to get a charge over the matrimonial home to secure the loan. This requires the wife's signature. The wife is induced to agree to the charge by misrepresentations made by the husband. (Because, in such cases, there are often also allegations of undue influence, this situation is considered in detail in Chapter 35.)

   (ii) A consumer buys goods from a retailer, relying on information about the goods from the manufacturer, which gave the information either directly to the consumer or advertised it to the public at large. The information is incorrect. In what circumstances will the consumer have a remedy against the retailer? Against the manufacturer? Of course, if the retailer repeats the information, or even passes on the manufacturer's information without disclaiming responsibility for it, the retailer will be held responsible for it. Compare Package Travel, Package Holidays and Package Tours Regulations 1992, SI 1992/3288, reg 4:

(1) No organiser or retailer shall supply to a consumer any descriptive matter concerning a package, the price of a package or any other condition applying to the contract which contains any misleading information.

(2) If an organiser or retailer is is breach of paragraph (1) he shall be liable to compensate the consumer for any loss which the consumer suffers in consequence.

■ *Bisset v Wilkinson*

[1927] AC 177, Privy Council

The respondents had agreed to buy from the plaintiff (the appellant) two blocks of land, called 'Homestead' and 'Hogan's', at Avondale in New Zealand. During the negotiations, the plaintiff had led the respondents to believe that the land would carry 2,000 sheep, but he had never run sheep on anything but a small part of it and that only for a short time. The respondents alleged that the plaintiff's statement was a misrepresentation and refused to proceed.

Lord Merrivale

... Sheep-farming was the purpose for which the respondents purchased the lands of the plaintiff. One of them had no experience of farming. The other had been before the war in charge of sheep on an extensive sheep-farm carried on by his father, who had accompanied and advised him in his negotiation with the appellant and had carefully inspected the lands at Avondale. In the course of coming to his agreement with the respondents the appellant made statements as to the property which, in their defence and counterclaim, the respondents alleged to be misrepresentations ...

In an action for rescission, as in an action for specific performance of an executory contract, when misrepresentation is the alleged ground of relief of the party who repudiates the contract, it is, of course, essential to ascertain whether that which is relied upon is a representation of a specific fact, or a statement of opinion, since an erroneous opinion stated by the party affirming the contract, though it may have been relied upon and have induced the contract on the part of the party who seeks rescission, gives no title to relief unless fraud is established. The application of this rule, however, is not always easy, as is illustrated in a good many reported cases, as well as in this. A representation of fact may be inherent in a statement of opinion and, at any rate, the existence of the opinion in the person stating it is a question of fact. In *Karberg's* case Lindley LJ, in course of testing a representation which might have been, as it was said to be by interested parties, one of opinion or belief, used this inquiry: 'Was the statement of expectation a statement of things not really expected?' The Court of Appeal applied this test and rescinded the contract which was in question. In *Smith v Land and House Property Corporation* there came in question a vendor's description of the tenant of the property sold as 'a most desirable tenant'—a statement of his opinion, as was argued on his behalf in an action to enforce the contract of sale. This description was held by the Court of Appeal to be a misrepresentation of fact, which, without proof of fraud, disentitled the vendor to specific performance of the contract of purchase. 'It is often fallaciously assumed', said Bowen LJ 'that a statement of opinion cannot involve the statement of fact. In a case where the facts are equally well known to both parties, what one of them says to the other is frequently nothing but an expression of opinion. The statement of such opinion is in a sense a statement of fact about the condition of the man's own mind, but only of an irrelevant fact, for it is of no consequence what the opinion is. But if the facts are not equally well known to both sides, then a statement of opinion by one who knows the facts best involves very often a statement of a material fact, for he impliedly states that he knows facts which justify his opinion'. The kind of distinction which is in question is illustrated again in the well known case of *Smith v Chadwick*. There the words under consideration involved the inquiry in relation to the sale of an industrial concern whether a statement of 'the present value of the turnover or output' was of necessity a statement of fact that the produce of the works was of the amount mentioned, or might be, and was a statement that the productive power of the works was estimated at so much. The words were held to be capable of the second of these meanings. The decisive inquiries came to be: what meaning was actually conveyed to the party complaining: was he deceived, and, as the action was based on a charge of fraud, was the statement in question made fraudulently?

In the present case, as in those cited, the material facts of the transaction, the knowledge of the parties respectively, and their relative positions, the words of representation used, and the actual condition of the subject-matter spoken of, are relevant to the two inquiries necessary to be made: What was the meaning of the representation? Was it true?

In ascertaining what meaning was conveyed to the minds of the now respondents by the appellant's statement as to the two thousand sheep, the most material fact to be remembered is that, as both parties were aware, the appellant had not and, so far as appears, no other person had at any time carried on sheep-farming upon the unit of land in question. That land as a distinct holding had never constituted a sheep-farm. The two blocks comprised in it differed substantially in character. Hogan's block was described by one of the respondents' witnesses as 'better land'. 'It might carry', he said, 'one sheep or perhaps two or even three sheep to the acre'. He estimated the carrying capacity of the land generally as little more than half a sheep to the acre. And Hogan's land had been allowed to deteriorate during several years before the respondents purchased. As was said by Sim J: 'In ordinary circumstances, any statement made by an owner who has been occupying his own farm as to its carrying capacity would be regarded as a statement of fact.... This, however, is not such a case. The defendants knew all about Hogan's block and knew also what sheep the farm was carrying when they inspected it. In these circumstances ... the defendants were not justified in regarding anything said by the plaintiff as to the carrying capacity as being anything more than an expression of his opinion on the subject.' In this view of the matter their Lordships concur.

Whether the appellant honestly and in fact held the opinion which he stated remained to be considered. This involved examination of the history and condition of the property. If a reasonable man with the appellant's knowledge could not have come to the conclusion he stated, the description of that conclusion as an opinion would not necessarily protect him against rescission for misrepresentation. But what was actually the capacity in competent hands of the land the respondents purchased had never been, and never was, practically ascertained. The respondents, after two years' trial of sheep-farming, under difficulties caused in part by their inexperience, found themselves confronted by a fall in the values of sheep and wool which would have left them losers if they could have carried three thousand sheep. As is said in the judgment of Ostler J: 'Owing to sheep becoming practically valueless, they reduced their flock and went in for cropping and dairy-farming in order to make a living.'

Appeal allowed. Judgment of Sim J restored

NOTES

1. It is often said that only a statement of fact, not a statement of opinion, can amount to a misrepresentation. This can be misleading.

2. Firstly, if a person states as her opinion something that she does not in fact believe, she is making a misrepresentation about her opinion: compare *Edgington v Fitzmaurice*, below.

3. Secondly, if she states her opinion in circumstances in which she is in a better position than the other party to know the truth, she is likely to be held to be representing that she has some reasonable grounds for her belief: see *Brown v Raphael* [1958] Ch 636 and contrast *Hummingbird Motors Ltd v Hobbs* [1986] RTR 276, in which the private seller of a car, which he had himself bought used, stated that he believed the odometer reading to

be correct; it was held that this was only a statement of opinion because he had no real way of knowing whether or not it was correct.

4.   Thirdly, *Bisset's* case suggests that even if the statement looks like one of fact, if it is made by a person who to the other party's knowledge has no way of knowing whether or not is is correct, the statement will be treated as one of opinion.

5.   The cases here are on whether a statement is one of fact, or one of opinion on which no reliance should be placed. The test that appears to be used, was it reasonable for the other party to rely on the statement, is parallel to the one used to decide whether a statement of fact amounts to a term of the contract: see p 323. The difference is probably that to be a term of the contract, the statement must be both one on which it is reasonable to rely and one that is important to the contract. Thus there seem to be three categories: terms of the contract, representations, and mere statements of opinion.

■ *Edgington v Fitzmaurice*
(1885) 29 ChD 459, Court of Appeal

The directors of a company issued a prospectus that invited subscriptions for debentures, and which stated that the objects for which the money was being raised were to complete some alterations and additions to the buildings, to purchase horses and vans, and to develop the supply of fish. The plaintiff advanced money on the strength of this and other statements. In fact, the money was being raised to meet pressing liabilities. Denman J held the directors liable for deceit.

Bowen LJ

This is an action for deceit, in which the Plaintiff complains that he was induced to take certain debentures by the misrepresentations of the Defendants, and that he sustained damage thereby. The loss which the Plaintiff sustained is not disputed. In order to sustain his action he must first prove that there was a statement as to facts which was false; and secondly, that it was false to the knowledge of the Defendants, or that they made it not caring whether it was true or false . . .

But when we come to the third alleged misstatement I feel that the Plaintiff's case is made out. I mean the statement of the objects for which the money was to be raised. These were stated to be to complete the alterations and additions to the buildings, to purchase horses and vans, and to develop the supply of fish. A mere suggestion of possible purposes to which a portion of the money might be applied would not have formed a basis for an action of deceit. There must be a misstatement of an existing fact: but the state of a man's mind is as much a fact as the state of his digestion. It is true that it is very difficult to prove what the state of a man's mind at a particular time is, but if it can be ascertained it is as much a fact as anything else. A misrepresentation as to the state of a man's mind is, therefore, a misstatement of fact. Having applied as careful consideration to the evidence as I could, I have reluctantly come to the conclusion that the true object of the Defendants in raising the money were not those stated in the circular.

Fry and **Cotton LJJ** were of the same opinion.

Appeal dismissed.

NOTES

1.   In *Goff v Gauthier* (1991) 62 P & CR 388, a purchaser exchanged contracts for a house, even though he had not yet secured finance for the purchase, after the vendor's solicitors had (innocently) told him that, if contracts were not exchanged the next day, the vendor

would call the transaction off. In fact, the vendor did not have any intention of calling off the transaction there and then. The purchaser was permitted to rescind.

2. Suppose the defendant makes a statement as to his intention that is true when he speaks, and it is only after the contract is made that he changes his mind? For instance, a vendor sells a plot of land, telling the purchaser that he intends to keep an adjoining plot (which he is retaining) as an open field, but he later changes his mind and builds on the field. Will the purchaser have any remedy if he does not have one for misrepresentation? (If you do not see the answer, look again at pp 323 and 324.)

3. In *British Airways Board v Taylor* [1976] 1 All ER 65, BOAC had informed a passenger that his reservation on a flight from London to Bermuda was 'confirmed'. BOAC operated a policy of 'overbooking' seats, and although when the confirmation was given there were sufficient seats for the passenger to travel on that flight, it was subsequently overbooked and the passenger was refused a seat on it. An information was laid against British Airways Board (which had subsequently taken over the rights and liabilities of BOAC pursuant to the Air Corporations (Dissolution) Order 1973) that the confirmation had contravened the Trade Descriptions Act 1968, s 14(1)(b), in that it had recklessly made a false statement about the provision of services. The House of Lords held that British Airways Board was not responsible for offences committed by BOAC, but held that there was evidence to entitle the justices in finding that there had been a false statement of fact. Lord Wilberforce said:

My Lords, the distinction in law between a promise as to future action, which may be broken or kept, and a statement as to existing fact, which may be true or false, is clear enough. There may be inherent in a promise an implied statement as to a fact, and where this is really the case, the court can attach appropriate consequences to any falsity in, or recklessness in the making of, that statement. Everyone is familiar with the proposition that a statement of intention may itself be a statement of fact and so capable of being true or false. But this proposition should not be used as a general solvent to transform the one type of assurance with another: the distinction is a real one and requires to be respected particularly where the effect of treating an assurance as a statement is to attract criminal consequences, as in the present case. As Lord Widgery *CJ said in Beckett v Cohen* it was never intended that the 1968 Act should be used so as to make a criminal statement out of what is really a breach of warranty.

Which character—promise or statement—should be attributed to the letter, seems on the face of it to be debatable.

The justices made the following relevant findings:

... (c) The statement contained in the letter was false and made recklessly since in view of the [Board's] admitted policy a reservation on the flight could not be confirmed at the date of the letter as it was always possible that Mr Edmunds would be off-loaded. It followed that no reservation had been made in the sense that an ordinary person would take it to mean ie a certain booking. This was especially so in view of the circumstances in which the letter was written.

In my opinion these were findings which the justices were entitled to make. And the essence of them is that the letter, taken together with the ticket and the Earlybird Certificate, would be taken as a statement that Mr Edmunds had a certain booking, which statement, in view of the overbooking policy, was untrue, since his booking though very likely to be a firm one was exposed to a risk—small but, as events proved, real—that it might not give him a seat on the aircraft. I think that the justices were entitled to find that this would be taken as a statement of a fact, rather than as a mere promise that Mr Edmunds would be flown on the day and at the time specified, and that they did so find.

■ *Turner v Green* [1895]
2 Ch 205

The plaintiff's solicitor, Fowler, met the defendant and his solicitor, and the parties negotiated the compromise of an action, without Fowler revealing that shortly beforehand he had received a telegram to the effect that other proceedings in the action, before the chief clerk in London, had gone in the defendant's favour.

Chitty J

...Ought the Court to decline to enforce this agreement because Fowler, being aware of the circumstance that the chief clerk has expressed his opinion—which however did not amount to a decision—did not disclose that circumstance to the defendant and his solicitors when the terms of this compromise were being settled?

The question thus raised is not one of fraud, but one as to the doctrine of the Court in granting relief against a claim for specific performance, where the Court has a discretion; but that is, of course, a judicial discretion, which cannot be exercised arbitrarily, but only according to settled principles laid down for it by the authorities. I will take the proposition laid down by Sir Edward Fry in his book (3rd ed p 325, para 705) as a good exposition of the law; there he says: 'Mere silence as regards a material fact which the one party is not under an obligation to disclose to the other cannot be a ground for rescission or a defence to specific performance.'

It cannot be contended that Fowler was under any obligation to disclose the result of the telegram: therefore Mr Butcher, who argued his case with skill and ingenuity, was driven to say that it was a shabby trick on Fowler's part not to disclose the information he had received, and that such conduct was not consistent with the usual practice of solicitors of high standing in their dealing with one another, who would ordinarily have disclosed any such circumstance; therefore, he argued that specific performance ought to be refused, because the course adopted in this case would be generally condemned by high-minded men. I find myself unable to act judicially on any such ground. Had there been any overreaching by Fowler, or any misleading conversation with reference to the proceedings in London before the chief clerk, at the time the terms of the compromise were settled, a very different case might have been presented on behalf of the defendant, and in such a case an obligation might have arisen binding Fowler at law or in equity to make a disclosure of all he knew; but I am satisfied on the evidence that no conversation on the subject took place.

■ *With v O'Flanagan*
[1936] Ch 575, Court of Appeal

In January 1934, the vendor of a medical practice had truthfully told the purchasers that the practice took in £200 a year. Before the contract was signed on 1 May, the practice had fallen away to almost nothing because the vendor had been ill, but the change of circumstances was not revealed to the purchasers.

Romer LJ

The only principle invoked by the appellants in this case is as follows. If A with a view to inducing B to enter into a contract makes a representation as to a material fact, then if at a later date and before the contract is actually entered into, owing to a change of circumstances, the representation then made would to the knowledge of A be untrue and B subsequently enters into the contract in ignorance of that change of circumstances and relying upon that representation, A cannot hold B to the bargain. There is ample authority for that statement and, indeed, I doubt myself whether any authority is necessary, it being, it seems to me, so obviously consistent with the plainest principles of equity.

Lord Wright MR and **Clauson J** delivered judgments to the same effect.

Appeal allowed.

NOTE

For a discussion of the reasons for the duty to disclose being so limited, see below.

A misrepresentation may be express or implied. In *Spice Girls Ltd v Aprilla World Service BV* [2000] EMLR 478, ChD, it was held that a pop group had made an implied misrepresentation when they continued with arrangements to publicise the defendant's products when they knew that one member of the group was intending to leave the group shortly, which would prevent the defendants deriving any benefit from the arrangement. In *King v Wilkinson* (NZ High Court, 29 March 1994) unreported (see [1995] NZ Law Journal 196), the vendor of land failed to point out that there was a difference between the boundary of the property and the line of the fence, so the area of the land was smaller than it appeared. It was held there had been a misrepresentation.

II. LIMITS TO RESCISSION FOR MISREPRESENTATION

1. Bars to rescission

To rescind a contract may be rather a drastic step, particularly where the contract has been performed. Equity therefore took the view that the right to rescind could be lost, or 'barred'. So rescission is barred if an innocent third party has in the meantime acquired rights over the property that is the subject of the contract, eg *Lewis v Averay* (p 314).

Other bars are illustrated by the next three cases. It should be noted that, in the first two, the Court of Appeal was also considering a possible bar now removed by the Misrepresentation Act 1967, s 1 (p 369).

■ *Long v Lloyd*
[1958] 2 All ER 402, Court of Appeal

The defendant, a haulage contractor, advertised for sale, at £850, a 1947 motor lorry, which he described as in 'exceptional condition'. The plaintiff, also a haulage contractor, saw the lorry at the defendant's premises on a Saturday; the defendant said that it was capable of a speed of 40 miles per hour. During a trial run on the following Monday, the plaintiff found that the speedometer was not working, that the spring was missing from the accelerator pedal, and that he had difficulty with the top gear. The defendant said that the lorry did 11 miles to the gallon and assured the plaintiff that he had told him all that was wrong with the vehicle. The plaintiff thereupon purchased the lorry for £750, paying £375 and agreeing to pay the balance at a later date. On the following Wednesday, the plaintiff drove from Sevenoaks to Rochester to pick up a load. During the journey, the dynamo ceased to function, and the plaintiff also noticed that an oil seal was leaking, that there was a crack in a wheel and that he had used 8 gallons of petrol on the journey of about 40 miles. That evening the plaintiff told the defendant of these defects and the defendant offered to pay half the cost of a reconstructed dynamo but denied any knowledge of a broken oil seal. The plaintiff accepted the offer. He had a dynamo fitted and on the next day, Thursday, the lorry was driven by the plaintiff's brother on a journey to Middlesbrough. On Friday night, the plaintiff, having heard that the lorry had broken down on its journey, wrote to the defendant pointing out the various defects in the lorry and asking for the return of his money. The lorry was subsequently examined by an expert who was of the opinion that the lorry was not in roadworthy condition. The lorry had, in fact, the defects alleged but the defendant's representations concerning it, although untrue, were honestly made. The plaintiff's action for rescission of the contract on the ground of the defendant's innocent misrepresentations was dismissed and he appealed.

Pearce LJ

. . . Nevertheless, a strict application to the facts of the present case of Denning LJ's view to the effect that the right (if any) to rescind after completion on the ground of innocent misrepresentation is barred by acceptance of the goods must necessarily prove fatal to the plaintiff's case. Apart from special circumstances, the place of delivery is the proper place for examination and for acceptance. It was open to the plaintiff to have the lorry examined by an expert before driving it away, but he chose not to do so. It is true, however, that the truth of certain of the representations, for example, that the lorry would do 11 miles to the gallon—could not be ascertained except by user and, therefore— the plaintiff should have a reasonable time to test it. Until he had had such an opportunity it might well be said that he had not accepted the lorry, always assuming, of course, that he did nothing inconsistent with the ownership of the seller. An examination of the facts, however, shows that on any view he must have accepted the lorry before he purported to reject it.

Thus, to recapitulate the facts, after the trial run the plaintiff drove the lorry home from Hampton Court to Sevenoaks, a not inconsiderable distance. After that experience he took it into use in his business by driving it on the following day to Rochester and back to Sevenoaks with a load. By the time he returned from Rochester he knew that the dynamo was not charging, that there was an oil seal leaking, that he had used 8 gallons of fuel for a journey of 40 miles, and that a wheel was cracked. He must also, as we think, have known by this time that the vehicle was not capable of 40 miles per hour. As to oil consumption, we should have thought that, if it was so excessive that the sump was practically dry after 300 miles, the plaintiff could have reasonably been expected to discover that the rate of consumption was unduly high by the time he had made the journey from Hampton Court to Sevenoaks and thence to Rochester and back.

On his return from Rochester the plaintiff telephoned to the defendant and complained about the dynamo, the excessive fuel consumption, the leaking oil seal and the cracked wheel. The defendant then offered to pay half the cost of the reconstructed dynamo which the plaintiff had been advised to fit, and the plaintiff accepted the defendant's offer. We find this difficult to reconcile with the continuance of any right of rescission which the plaintiff might have had down to that time.

But the matter does not rest there. On the following day the plaintiff, knowing all that he did about the condition and performance of the lorry, dispatched it, driven by his brother, on a business trip to Middlesbrough. That step, at all events, appears to us to have amounted, in all the circumstances of the case, to a final acceptance of the lorry by the plaintiff for better or for worse, and to have conclusively extinguished any right of rescission remaining to the plaintiff after completion of the sale.

Appeal dismissed.

NOTES

1. A misrepresentee will not usually lose her right to rescind by affirmation until after she discovers that there has been a misrepresentation: see p 616.

2.   Pearce suggests that the right to rescind may have been lost as soon as the plaintiff accepted the defendant's offer to repair the defects. Doesn't it seem rather draconian to expect the plaintiff to reject any such compromise out of hand? A possible way out is to treat a claimant's acceptance of repair as merely conditional upon there being no further defects: see *Farnworth Finance Facilities Ltd v Attryde* [1970] 1 WLR 1053. The rules in the Sale of Goods Act 1979 on loss of the right to reject did not always seem very appropriate in the consumer context and have been amended: see pp 618–619.

■ *Leaf v International Galleries* [1950]
2 KB 86, Court of Appeal

The plaintiff, on 8 March 1944, purchased from the defendants, International Galleries, a picture called *Salisbury Cathedral* for 85l. At the time of the purchase, the defendants represented that the picture was painted by John Constable, but when, five years later, the plaintiff tried to sell it, he was informed that it was not by Constable. Thereupon he returned it to the defendants and asked them to refund the 85l that which he had paid for it. The defendants having refused to do so, the plaintiff by this action claimed to rescind the contract and to have repayment of the 85l.

When the hearing began in the county court, the judge suggested that the plaintiff's proper remedy was a claim for damages, and asked if he wished to amend his claim. It was then stated that no such amendment was desired. At the end of the hearing, however, the plaintiff applied for leave to amend and add a claim for damages, but this was refused on the ground that the application had been made too late. The county court judge found that the defendants had made an innocent misrepresentation and that the picture had not been painted by Constable. He gave judgment for them, however, holding, on the authority of *Angel v Jay*, that the equitable remedy of rescission was not available in the case of an executed contract.

The plaintiff appealed.

The Court of Appeal doubted the existence of the rule applied by the judge, at least in contracts for the sale of goods, but declined to decide the point because the case could be decided on another ground.

Jenkins LJ

. . . In those circumstances, it seems to me to be quite out of the question that a court of equity should grant relief by way of rescission. It is perfectly true that the county court judge held that there had been no laches, and, of course, it may be said that the plaintiff had no occasion to obtain any further evidence as to the authorship of the picture until he wanted to sell; but in my judgment contracts such as this cannot be kept open and subject to the possibility of rescission indefinitely. Assuming that completion is not fatal to his claim, I think, that, at all events, it behoves the purchaser either to verify or, as the case may be, to disprove the representation within a reasonable time, or else stand or fall by it. If he is allowed to wait five, ten, or twenty years and then re-open the bargain, there can be no finality at all. I, for my part, do not think that equity will intervene in such a case, more especially as in the present case it cannot be said that, apart from rescission, the plaintiff would have been without remedy. The county court judge was of opinion, and it seems to me that he was clearly right, that the representation that the picture was a Constable amounted to a warranty. If it amounted to a warranty, and that was broken, as on the findings of the county court judge it was, then the plaintiff had a right at law in the shape of damages for breach of warranty. That remedy he did not choose to exercise, and, although he was invited at the hearing to amend his claim so as to include a claim for breach of warranty, he declined that opportunity. That being so, it seems to me that he has no justification at all for now coming to equity five years after the event and claiming rescission. Accordingly, it seems to me that this is not a case in which the equitable remedy of rescission, assuming it to be available in the absence of fraud in respect of a completed sale of chattels, should be allowed to the plaintiff. For these reasons, I agree that the appeal fails and should be dismissed.

Denning LJ

... There was a term in the contract as to the quality of the subject-matter: namely, as to the person by whom the picture was painted—that it was by Constable. That term of the contract was, according to our terminology, either a condition or a warranty. If it was a condition, the buyer could reject the picture for breach of the condition at any time before he accepted it, or is deemed to have accepted it; whereas, if it was only a warranty, he could not reject it at all but was confined to a claim for damages.

I think it right to assume in the buyer's favour that this term was a condition, and that, if he had come in proper time he could have rejected the picture; but the right to reject for breach of condition has always been limited by the rule that, once the buyer has accepted, or is deemed to have accepted, the goods in performance of the contract, then he cannot thereafter reject, but is relegated to his claim for damages: see Sale of Goods Act, 1893, s 11(1)(c) and *Wallis, Son & Wells v Pratt & Haynes.*

The circumstances in which a buyer is deemed to have accepted goods in performance of the contract are set out in s 35 of the Act, which says that the buyer is deemed to have accepted the goods, amongst other things, 'when, after the lapse of a reasonable time, he retains the goods without intimating to the seller that he has rejected them.' In this case the buyer took the picture into his house and, apparently, hung it there, and five years passed before he intimated any rejection at all. That, I need hardly say, is much more than a reasonable time. It is far too late for him at the end of five years to reject this picture for breach of any condition. His remedy after that length of time is for damages only, a claim which he has not brought before the court.

Is it to be said that the buyer is in any better position by relying on the representation, not as a condition, but as an innocent misrepresentation? ...

Although rescission may in some cases be a proper remedy, it is to be remembered that an innocent misrepresentation is much less potent than a breach of condition; and a claim to rescission for innocent misrepresentation must at any rate be barred when a right to reject for breach of condition is barred. A condition is a term of the contract of a most material character, and if a claim to reject on that account is barred, it seems to me a fortiori that a claim to rescission on the ground of innocent misrepresentation is also barred.

So, assuming that a contract for the sale of goods may be rescinded in a proper case for innocent misrepresentation, the claim is barred in this case for the self-same reason as a right to reject is barred. The buyer has accepted the picture. He had ample opportunity for examination in the first few days after he had bought it. Then was the time to see if the condition or representation was fulfilled. Yet he has kept it all this time. Five years have elapsed without any notice of rejection. In my judgment he cannot now claim to rescind. His only claim, if any, as the county court judge said, was one for damages, which he has not made in this action. In my judgment, therefore, the appeal should be dismissed.

Lord Evershed MR delivered a judgment to the same effect.

Appeal dismissed.

NOTE

'Laches' is delay that makes it inequitable for the plaintiff to enforce his or her right.

■ *Clarke v Dickson*

(1858) EB & E 148, Queen's Bench

On the trial, before Lord Campbell CJ, at the London sittings after the Michaelmas term, the statements made by the plaintiff's counsel, in opening his case, were: that, in 1853, the plaintiff was induced, by representations made by the three defendants, to take shares in a company called The Welsh Potosi Lead and Copper Mining Company, which was then formed for working a mine on the cost-book principle, and of which the defendants were directors, and to pay deposits for those shares. The mine was worked by the company during the years 1854, 1855 and 1856; dividends were declared in each of those years. The plaintiff was induced to accept fresh allotments of shares in lieu of the dividends declared. In 1857, the company was in bad circumstances: it was, with the plaintiff's assent, registered as a company with limited liability, and was afterwards wound up under the Winding-up Act. During the process of winding up, the plaintiff for the first time discovered that the representations by which he was induced to make the purchase were false and fraudulent on the part of the defendants, and that the dividends declared were fraudulent dividends. He therefore brought this action to recover back the deposits that he had paid for the shares.

Crompton J

When once it is settled that a contract induced by fraud is not void, but voidable at the option of the party defrauded, it seems to me to follow that, when that party exercises his option to rescind the contract, he must be in a state to rescind; that is, he must be in such a situation as to be able to put the parties into their original state before the contract. Now here I will assume, what is not clear to me, that the plaintiff bought his shares from the defendants and not from the Company, and that he might at one time have had a right to restore the shares to the defendants if he could, and demand the price from them. But then what did he buy? Shares in a partnership with others. He cannot return those; he has become bound to those others. Still stronger, he has changed their nature: what he now has and offers to restore are shares in a quasi corporation now in process of being wound up. That is quite enough to decide this case. The plaintiff must rescind in toto or not at all: he cannot both keep the shares and recover the whole price. That is founded on the plainest principles of justice. If he cannot return the article he must keep it, and sue for his real damage in an action on the deceit. Take the case I put in the argument, of a butcher buying live cattle, killing them, and even selling the meat to his customers. If the rule of law were as the plaintiff contends, that butcher might, upon discovering a fraud on the part of the grazier who sold him the cattle, rescind the contract and get back the whole price: but how could that be consistent with justice? The true doctrine is, that a party can never repudiate a contract after, by his own act, it has become out of his power to restore the parties to their original condition.

Erle J and **Lord Campell CJ** delivered concurring judgments.

NOTES

1. If the property has deteriorated to some extent through use by the misrepresentee but it can still be returned in substantially the same condition, rescission will be permitted provided the misrepresentee makes an allowance for depreciation and accounts for any profits she has made from using the property: *Erlanger v New Sombrero Phosphate Co*

(1878) 3 App Cas 1218. It has been said that the object is to prevent unjust enrichment of the representee at the representor's expense, but the representee may have to make an allowance for depreciation even though she would not be left with a benefit if she were simply allowed to rescind: Burrows, p 178.

2.   The orthodox English position has been that partial rescission is not possible: *De Molestina v Ponton* [2002] EWHC 2413 (Comm) [2002] 1 All ER (Comm) 587; *TSB Bank pls v Camfield* [1995] 1 All ER 951. The High Court of Australia took the opposite view in *Vardasz v Pioneer Concrete (SA) Pty Ltd* (1995) 184 CLR 102. Powerful arguments for reconsidering the English view are advanced by Poole and Keyser 121 LQR 273.

3.   It has been argued that, where third-party rights (see p 363) are not in question, the courts should take a more flexible approach to the requirement that it be possible to restore the benefits received, allowing restitution to be made in the form of money: Birks [1997] IRLR 72.

2. The court's discretion

Originally, rescission was available if there had been any misrepresentation of fact, provided the misrepresentee had relied on it and it was material. As we saw above (p 357), the latter requirement probably means only that the misrepresentation must not be trivial; it does not mean that the misrepresentation needs to be a very serious one. Thus while the misrepresentee might only get damages if he could prove fraud, rescission for misrepresentation was more readily available than is termination when there has been a breach of contract: as we shall see in Chapter 21, termination is often only permitted if the breach deprives the innocent party of the substance of what he was contracting for.

Thus the rather Draconian remedy of rescission might be available, and be the only remedy, for a rather slight misrepresentation—eg a statement that the drains in a house were in good order when, in fact, one drain was broken and needed replacement. No doubt the parties in such a case could bargain their way to a settlement under which the vendor paid the cost of repairs if the purchaser would refrain from rescinding, but the law itself permitted rescission. On the other hand, in cases of the sale or lease of land, the remedy was severely curtailed by a rule that the right to rescind for innocent misrepresentation was lost once the contract had been executed by the conveyance of the land or the grant of the lease (see *Wilde v Gibson* (1848) 1 HL Cas 605; *Angel v Jay* [1911] 1 KB 666). This had the effect of preventing rescission in the most inconvenient case, in which the purchaser has already moved in before discovering the untruth, and the vendor has spent the purchase money on another property. On the other hand, the rule deprived the misrepresentee of an remedy unless fraud could be proved, and, in other contexts in which the rule applied (eg the sale of shares: *Seddon v North Eastern Salt Co Ltd* [1905] 1 Ch 326), it was hard to see any justification for it. It was not clear whether the rule applied to sale of goods (see *Leaf v International Galleries*, above). Despite a recommendation of the Law Reform Committee (Tenth Report (Innocent Misrepresentation), Cmnd 1782, 1962) that the rule should be retained for sale of land and leases for over three years, it was abolished by the Misrepresentation Act 1967, s 1. At the same time, however, power was given to the court to refuse to permit rescission, or to reinstate a contract already rescinded by the misrepresentee and give damages in lieu of rescission if rescission did not seem an appropriate remedy.

■ *Misrepresentation Act* 1967

Section 1

Where a person has entered into a contract after a misrepresentation, has been made to him, and—
(a) the misrepresentation has become a term of the contract; or
(b) the contract has been performed
or both, then, if otherwise he would be entitled to rescind the contract without alleging fraud, he shall be so entitled, subject to the provisions of this Act, notwithstanding the matters mentioned in paragraphs (a) and (b) of this section.

Section 2

(2) Where a person has entered into a contract after a misrepresentation has been made to him otherwise than fraudulently, and he would be entitled, by reason of the misrepresentation, to rescind the contract, then, if it is claimed, in any proceedings arising out of the contract, that the contract ought to be or has been rescinded, the court or arbitrator may declare the contract subsisting and award damages in lieu of rescission, if of opinion that it would be equitable to do so, having regard to the nature of the misrepresentation and the loss that would be caused by it if the contract were upheld, as well as to the loss that rescission would cause to the other party.

NOTES

1.   Section 2(2) refers to the case in which the misrepresentee 'would be entitled... to rescind'. Can the court award damages under this subsection if the misrepresentee has already lost the right to rescind under one of the 'bars'? Most commentators thought that the wording of the section meant that the right to damages was dependent on the continued existence of a right to rescission. This view was rejected by Jacob J in *Thomas Witter Ltd v TBP Industries Ltd* [1996] 2 All ER 573, partly on the ground that such a rule made little sense (since the disappearance of the right to rescind did not necessarily extinguish the plaintiff's loss) and partly on an examination of the legislative history of the clause (see 111 LQR 385). However, in *Zanzibar v British Aerospace (Lancaster House) Ltd* [2000] 1 WLR 2333, Judge Jack QC (sitting as a High Court judge) held that the words of s 2(2) are quite clear: the power to award damages is an alternative to rescission and no longer exists when the right to rescission has been lost. The same conclusion had been reached earlier by Judge Humphrey Lloyd QC in *Floods of Queensferry Ltd v Shand Construction Ltd* [2000] BLR 81, who refused to follow the decision of Jacob J in *Thomas Witter Ltd v TBP Industries Ltd*. See further p 538, note 5.

2.   If the court exercises its discretion under s 2(2) to declare the contract subsisting, it may (or perhaps must—it is not clear on the wording of the section) 'award damages in lieu of rescission'. How these damages might be assessed is discussed pp 381–384.

III. RESCISSION AND CONSEQUENTIAL LOSS

If there has been an innocent misrepresentation, and the misrepresentee rescinds, he will recover any money paid to the other party; but (unless there has been negligence, see p 370) he will not recover damages. What if the contract required the misrepresentee to make some payment to a third party, or to incur liabilities to third parties, and he has done so before discovering the misrepresentation and seeking rescission?

Suppose a student takes a flat under a lease that puts the obligation to pay the rates on her, and she has paid the rates before she discovers that the landlord has made a misrepresentation. If, when she rescinded, she simply got back the rent, the misrepresentor would not have 'given back' all that he received, because the obligation to pay the rates would otherwise have fallen on him; the student's obligation to pay rates is really part of the price the landlord was paid.

To correct this, the court will give the misrepresentee an indemnity against payments made and liabilities incurred as obligations under the contract. Thus in *Newbigging v Adam* (1886) 34 ChD 582, the plaintiff had been induced to join a partnership by false representations. He obtained dissolution of the partnership, the return of the money he had paid to it and an indemnity against the liabilities he had incurred while a partner.

Payments that the misrepresentee made in reliance on the contract but which were not required by it can only be recovered by way of damages. In *Whittington v Seale-Hayne* (1900) 82 LT 49, the plaintiffs, who were breeders of prize poultry, leased premises from the defendant, relying on his statement that the premises were in a sanitary condition. Under the lease, the plaintiffs covenanted to execute all such works as might be required by the local or public authority. The water supply was contaminated due to the insanitary condition of the premises. The plaintiffs' manager and his family became ill, the poultry died or became valueless for breeding, and the local authority required the drains to be put in good order and the house to be made fit for human habitation. The plaintiffs claimed the value of the stock lost, the loss of a breeding season and removal expenses. Farwell J, following *Newbigging v Adam*, held that the plaintiffs were entitled to an indemnity in respect of the repairs they had done under the covenant, but that they could not recover for the other items, which were 'really damages pure and simple'.

IV. DAMAGES FOR MISREPRESENTATION

1. When damages are available

At common law, before 1963, damages were recoverable for misrepresentation only if it had been made fraudulently—ie made in the knowledge of its falsity or recklessly, not caring whether it was true or false—or if a fiduciary relationship existed between the parties (*Derry v Peek* (1889) 14 App Cas 337; *Nocton v Ashburton* [1914] AC 932). The Law Reform Committee recommended in its Report of 1962 that damages should be recoverable from the misrepresentor unless he could show that he believed the representation to be true and had reasonable grounds for his belief.

The following year, the House of Lords held in the *Hedley Byrne* case (see p 28) that there could be liability in tort for negligent misrepresentation; until 1976, it was not clear whether there could be a 'relationship equivalent to contract' between the parties when there actually was a contract between them.

■ *Esso Petroleum Co Ltd v Mardon*

[1976] 2 All ER 5 at 14–16, Court of Appeal

(For the facts of this case, see p 328. Note that the events occurred before the Misrepresentation Act 1967 had come into force.)

Lord Denning MR

Negligent misrepresentation

Assuming that there was no warranty, the question arises whether Esso are liable for negligent mis-statement under the doctrine of *Hedley Byrne & Co Ltd v Heller & Partners Ltd*. It has been suggested that *Hedley Byrne* cannot be used so as to impose liability for negligent pre-contractual statements; and that, in a pre-contract situation, the remedy (at any rate before the 1967 Act) was only in warranty or nothing. Thus in *Hedley Byrne* itself Lord Reid said: 'Where there is a contract there is no difficulty as regards the contracting parties: the question is whether there is a warranty.' ...

In arguing this point, counsel for Esso took his stand in this way. He submitted that, when the negotiations between two parties resulted in a contract between them, their rights and duties were governed by the law of contract and not by the law of tort. There was, therefore, no place in their relationship for *Hedley Byrne*, which was solely a case of liability in tort. He relied particularly on *Clark v Kirby Smith* where Plowman J held that the liability of a solicitor for negligence was a liability in contract and not in tort, following the observations of Greene MR in *Groom v Crocker*. Counsel for Esso might also have cited *Bagot v Stevens, Scanlon & Co* about an architect, and other cases, too. But I venture to suggest that those cases are in conflict with other decisions of high authority which were not cited in them. These decisions show that, in the case of a professional man, the duty to use reasonable care arises not only in contract, but is also imposed by the law apart from contract, and is therefore actionable in tort....

To this there is to be added the high authority of Viscount Haldane LC in *Nocton v Lord Ashburton*: '...the solicitor contracts with his client to be skilful and careful. For failure to perform his obligation he may be made liable at law in contract or even in tort, for negligence in breach of a duty imposed on him.'

That seems to me right. A professional man may give advice under a contract for reward; or without a contract, in pursuance of a voluntary assumption of responsibility, gratuitously without reward. In either case he is under one and the same duty to use reasonable care: see *Cassidy v Ministry of Health*. In the one case it is by reason of a term implied by law. In the other, it is by reason of a duty imposed by law. For a breach of that duty, he is liable in damages; and those damages should be, and are, the same, whether he is sued in contract or in tort.

It follows that I cannot accept counsel for Esso's proposition. It seems to me that *Hedley Byrne* properly understood, covers this particular proposition: if a man, who has or professes to have special knowledge or skill, makes a representation by virtue thereof to another—be it advice, information or opinion—with the intention of inducing him to enter into a contract with him, he is under a duty to use reasonable care to see that the representation is correct, and that the advice, information or opinion is reliable. If he negligently gives unsound advice or misleading information or expresses an erroneous opinion, and thereby induces the other side into a contract with him, he is liable in damages. This proposition is in line with what I said in *Candler v Crane Christmas & Co*, which was approved by the majority of the Privy Council in *Mutual Life and Citizens' Assurance Ltd v Evan*. And the judges of the Commonwealth have shown themselves quite ready to apply *Hedley Byrne* between contracting parties: see, in Canada, *Sealand of the Pacific Ltd v Ocean Cement Ltd* and, in New Zealand, *Capital Motors Ltd v Beecham*.

Applying this principle, it is plain that Esso professed to have—and did in fact have— special knowledge or skill in estimating the throughput of a filling station. They made the representation—they forecast a throughput of 200,000 gallons—intending to induce Mr Mardon to enter into a tenancy on the faith of it. They made it negligently. It was a 'fatal error'. And thereby induced Mr Mardon to enter into a contract of tenancy that was disastrous to him. For this misrepresentation they are liable in damages.

Ormrod and **Shaw LJJ** agreed.

NOTE

It does not follow from this case that there will always be a special relationship within *Hedley Byrne* as between contracting parties: see *Howard Marine and Dredging* Co Ltd v A Ogden &

Sons Ltd [1978] QB 574, in which the majority seems to have considered that the relatively casual nature of the incorrect statement precluded a duty of care. The absence of a duty of care will now be much less important because of the Misrepresentation Act 1967, s 2(1), but it may matter if there was contributory negligence on the part of the representee.

■ Misrepresentation Act 1967

Section 2

(1) Where a person has entered into a contract after a misrepresentation has been made to him by another party thereto and as a result thereof he has suffered loss, then, if the person making the misrepresentation would be liable to damages in respect thereof had the misrepresentation been made fraudulently, that person shall be so liable notwithstanding that the misrepresentation was not made fraudulently, unless he proves that he had reasonable grounds to believe and did believe up to the time the contract was made that the facts represented were true.

NOTES

1.   This subsection contains what has been described as the 'fiction of fraud' (eg Treitel, p 351). Can you see why the subsection has been described in this way? The 'fiction of fraud' seems to mean that liability under the subsection should be subject to the same rules as liability for fraud, which has a number of consequences for the way in which damages under the section are to be assessed: see pp 377–381. Should a misrepresentor who is liable under s 2(1) really be treated just as if he had been fraudulent?

2.   Under this section, is it for the misrepresentee to prove that the misrepresentation was negligent or for the misrepresentor to prove that it was not?

2. The measure of damages for misrepresentation

Damages for deceit

■ East v Maurer

[1991] 2 All ER 733, Court of Appeal

Beldam LJ (giving the first judgment at the invitation of Mustill LJ).

Ever changing style and fashion makes the ability to attract and satisfy intending customers a particularly valuable asset in the proprietor of a ladies' hair styling salon. According to the evidence, it was an attribute possessed by the first defendant who, in 1979, owned two salons in Bournemouth which he carried on under the name of Roger de Paris. One of the salons was at 44 Haven Road, Canford Cliffs. It had only recently been opened under the managership of a Mr Mole. The other salon, at 37 Exeter Road, was closer to the centre of the town. Canford Cliffs, as those who are familiar with the area will know, is an expensive and fashionable area in which to live and the need to keep up with fashion may be more pronounced there. But the salon at 37 Exeter Road was conveniently placed for hotel guests and was close to the central shopping area. It was also much longer established. The first defendant had, by 1979, been there, first as an employee and then as its proprietor since 1958.

The first defendant's experience in styling ladies' hair was cosmopolitan. From time to time he had worked in salons in Hamburg, in Stockholm, in Paris, in Lausanne and in Mayfair. He had also taken part in competitions at international level. According to witnesses he had a personality which reflected his experience and, as the judge found, he had built up at Exeter Road a very good business.

By 1979 he had decided to concentrate his efforts at a smaller and more exclusive salon; he had decided to sell his Exeter Road business and to devote all his energies to Canford Cliffs. The plaintiffs bought the business at Exeter Road from him in September 1979. The second plaintiff, Mrs East, intended to continue the business, but under the style and name of 'Xellance'. The second plaintiff herself had had considerable experience as a ladies' hairdresser and stylist, but it was of a more restricted character. She had run, successfully, several businesses in outlying districts of Oxford, Iffley and Kennington, but she and her husband wanted to have a business in the Bournemouth area and so, for £20,000, they bought the salon at Exeter Road from the first defendant and his company, the second defendant.

In the course of the negotiations for the sale they learnt that the first defendant had another salon at Canford Cliffs, but he deliberately and completely misled the plaintiffs about his intentions. He told them falsely that he had no intention of working at the Canford Cliffs salon unless, for example, a staff emergency arose due to illness or for some other reason. He told them that he intended to open a salon abroad, probably in Switzerland. Such an intention obviously meant that his valuable personal contact with the clientele at Exeter Road could not follow him to the continent and would probably not follow him to the Canford Cliffs salon because he would not be working there. His representations would obviously play a most significant part in inducing the plaintiffs to buy the salon, and so the learned judge held. He found that the representations were false to the first defendant's knowledge, and held that the plaintiffs were entitled to damages. On this aspect of the case there is no appeal against his finding.

Mrs East started to run the salon on 1 September 1979. It was not long before it was apparent to her, and to others who were working in the salon, that the level of business was falling away at an alarming rate. In due course she learnt that the first defendant was working full-time at his Canford Cliffs salon.

For just over three years Mrs East tried to make the salon profitable. In her attempts she spent considerable sums on advertising; she installed a solarium bed and eventually began to combine the hairdressing business with a boutique.

During this period she made several attempts to sell the business and eventually, on 6 February 1989, she succeeded in selling the lease of the premises for £7,500. The learned judge found that the plaintiffs had behaved reasonably throughout; that they could not have sold the business before they actually did. He awarded them damages totalling £33,328; interest on the sums awarded brought the total award to £55,205.

His award was made up in this way. Firstly, he took the capital expenditure by taking the cost price of the business, £20,000, and deducting from it the amount realised on the sale, thus arriving at the figure of £12,500. Secondly, he awarded the plaintiffs the fees and expenses incurred by them in buying and selling the business, and in carrying out improvements in an attempt to make it profitable. The figures awarded there amounted in total to £2,390. Next, he awarded trading losses incurred during the three and a quarter years during which the plaintiffs attempted to run the business. Those amounted to £2,438.

The next head of damages he awarded has led the defendants to appeal to this court against the amount of the damages. In addition to the sums already mentioned, he awarded the plaintiffs loss of profits during the three and a quarter year period arriving at a figure of £15,000. Finally he awarded the figure of £1,000 as general damages for disappointment and inconvenience of the plaintiffs in their attempt to establish this business. It is against the award of £15,000 for loss of profit that the defendants now appeal.

. . .

That the measure of damages for the tort of deceit and for breach of contract are different no longer needs support from authority. Damages for deceit are not awarded on the basis that the plaintiff is to be put in as good a position as if the statement had been true; they are to be assessed on a basis which would compensate the plaintiff for all the loss he has suffered, so far as money can do it.

This was confirmed in *Doyle v Olby (Ironmongers) Ltd:* . . .

The observations of Lord Denning MR, to which I have referred, are supported by an earlier judgment of Dixon J in *Toteff v Antonas* (1952) 87 CLR 647, a decision of the High Court of Australia. In that case Dixon J said (at 650–651):

'In an action of deceit a plaintiff is entitled to recover as damages a sum representing the prejudice or disadvantage he has suffered in consequence of his altering his position under the inducement of the fraudulent misrepresentations made by the defendant. When what he has been induced to do is to make a purchase from the defendant and part with his money to him in payment of the price, then, if the transaction stands and is not disaffirmed or rescinded, what is recoverable is "the difference between the real value of the property, and the sum which the plaintiff was induced to give for it" per *Abbot* L.C.J. *Pearson v Wheeler* ((1825) Ry & M 303 at 304, 171 ER 1028 at 1029). As Sir *James Hannen* P. in *Peek v Derry* ((1887) 37 Ch D 541 at 594) pointed out, the question is how much worse off is the plaintiff than if he had not entered into the transaction. If he had not done so he would have had the purchase money in his pocket. To ascertain his loss you must deduct from the amount he paid the real value of the thing he got . . . .'

Mr Shawcross has pointed out that both in *Doyle v Olby* and in *Toteff v Antonas* none of the judgments referred to loss of profit as a recoverable head of damage; it may well be that the facts of each of those cases and the period involved before the claims were made may not have made loss of profit a considerable head of damage. But, as to the statements of principle to which I have referred, it seems to me clear that there is no basis upon which one could say that loss of profits incurred whilst waiting for an opportunity to realise to its best advantage a business which has been purchased are irrecoverable. It is conceded that losses made in the course of running the business of a company are recoverable. If in fact the plaintiffs lost the profit which they could reasonably have expected from running a business in the area of a kind similar to the business in this case I can I see no reason why those do not fall within the words of Lord Atkin in *Clark v Urquhart, Stracey v Urquhart* [1930] AC 28 at 68: ' . . . actual damage directly flowing from the fraudulent inducement.'

So I consider that on the facts found by the learned judge in the present case, the plaintiffs did establish that they had suffered a loss due to the defendants' misrepresentation which arose from their inability to earn the profits in the business which they hoped to buy in the Bournemouth area.

I would therefore reject the submission of Mr Shawcross that loss of profits is not a recoverable head of damage in cases of this kind.

However, I am not satisfied that in arriving at the figure of £15,000 the learned judge approached the quantification of those damages on the correct basis. It seems to me that he was inclined to base his award on an assessment of the profits which the business actually bought by the plaintiffs might have made if the statement made by the first defendant had amounted to a warranty that customers would continue to patronise the salon in Exeter Road; further, that he left out of account a number of significant factors. What he did was to found his award on an evaluation which he made of the profits of the business at Exeter Road made by the first defendant in the year preceding the purchase of the business by the plaintiffs. Basing himself on figures which had been given to him by an accountant, and making an allowance for inflation he arrived at a figure for the profits which might have been made if the first defendant had continued to run the business at Exeter Road during the three and a quarter years. He then made an allowance only for the fact that the second plaintiff's experience in hair styling and hairdressing was not as extensive or as cosmopolitan as that of the first defendant. Thus he based his award on an assessment of what the profits would have been, less a deduction of 25% for the second plaintiff's lack of experience.

It seems to me that he should have begun by considering the kind of profit which the second plaintiff might have made if the representation which induced her to buy the business at Exeter Road had not been made, and that involved considering the kind of profits which *she* might have expected to make in another hairdressing business bought for a similar sum. Mr Nicholson has argued that on the evidence of Mr Knowles, an experienced accountant, the learned judge could have arrived at the same or an equivalent figure on that basis. I do not agree. The learned judge left out of account the fact that the second plaintiff was moving into an entirely different area and one in which she was, comparatively speaking, a stranger, secondly, that she was going to deal with a different clientele and, thirdly, that there were almost certainly in that area of Bournemouth other smart hairdressing salons which represented competition and which, in any event, if the first defendant had, as he had represented, gone to open a salon on the continent, could have attracted the custom of his former clients.

The learned judge, as Mr Nicholson has pointed out, had two clear starting points: first, that any person investing £20,000 in a business would expect a greater return than if the sum was left safely in the bank or in a building society earning interest, and a reasonable figure for that at the rates then prevailing would have been at least £6,000; secondly, that the salary of a hairdresser's assistant in the usual kind of establishment was at this time £40 per week and that the assistant could expect tips in addition. That would produce a figure of over £2,000, but the proprietor of a salon would clearly expect to earn more, having risked his money in the business. It seems to me that those are valid points from which to start to consider what would be a reasonable sum to award for loss of profits of a business of this kind. As was pointed out by Winn LJ in *Doyle v Olby*, this is not a question which can be considered on a mathematical basis. It has to be considered essentially in the round, making what he described as a 'jury assessment' (see [1969] 2 All ER 119 at 124, [1969] 2 QB 158 at 169).

Taking all the factors into account, I think that the learned judge's figure was too high; for my part I would have awarded a figure of £10,000 for that head of damage, and to this extent I would allow the appeal.

Butler-Sloss LJ agreed; **Mustill LJ** gave judgment to the same effect.

Appeal allowed in part.

NOTES

1. *East v Maurer* was a case of fraud. A similar award to compensate the victim for loss of the profit that could have been made in another business was made in a case of negligent misrepresentation: *Esso v Mardon*, above.

2. This compensation for 'lost opportunity' is regarded as a form of reliance loss. Fuller and Perdue (1936) 46 Yale LJ 52, 60:

    Physicians with an extensive practice often charge their patients the full office fee for broken appointments. Such a charge looks on the fact of things like a claim to the promised fee; it seems to be based on the 'expectation interest'. Yet the physician making the charge will quite justifiably regard it as compensation for the loss of the opportunity to gain a similar fee from a different patient.

3. The decision in *East v Maurer* has been criticised by Marks (1992) 108 LQR 386 on the ground that the award was based on hypothesis, not the passing up of any specific opportunity. See also Chandler (1994) 110 LQR 35.

4. It was held by the House of Lords in *Standard Chartered Bank v Pakistan National Shipping Corp. (No 2)* [2002] UKHL 43 [2003] 1 All ER 173 that, in cases of fraud, the plaintiff's damages cannot be reduced on the ground of contributory negligence under the Law Reform (Contributory Negligence) Act 1945. The Act provides:

    Section 1. Apportionment of liability in case of contributory negligence

    (1) Where any person suffers damage as the result partly of his own fault and partly of the fault of any other person or persons, a claim in respect of that damage shall not be defeated by reason of the fault of the person suffering the damage, but the damages recoverable in respect thereof shall be reduced to such extent as the court thinks just and equitable having regard to the claimant's share in the responsibility for the damage . . .

Section 4. Interpretation

The following expressions have the meanings hereby respectively assigned to them, that is to say—

'fault' means negligence, breach of statutory duty or other act or omission which gives rise to a liability in tort or would, apart from this Act, give rise to the defence of contributory negligence.

The definition of fault in s 4 means that, for the Act to apply, the *claimant's* action must either be one that would gives rise to liability to the *defendant* in tort (which will rarely happen) or be one which would give rise to a defence of contributory negligence. At common law, contributory negligence (which at common law was a complete defence) was not a defence to fraud and therefore the Act does not apply to fraud either.

In *Smith New Court Securities Ltd v Scrimgeour Vickers (Asset Management) Ltd* [1996] 4 All ER 769, the plaintiffs were persuaded to buy a parcel of some 28 million shares in a company called Ferranti by the fraudulent misrepresentation of the defendant that there were other possible purchasers in the market. The price paid by the plaintiffs was $82\frac{1}{4}$ p per share. At the time of the contract, shares were trading on the Stock Exchange at about 78p per share. It is important to understand that there were potentially advantages for both sides in a large deal somewhat above the market rate. If the plaintiffs had gone into the market through their brokers to try to buy 28 million shares in Ferranti all at once, this would have inevitably driven the price up well above $82\frac{1}{4}$ p per share. Conversely, if the defendants had gone into the market to try to sell 28 million shares all at once, this would have driven the price well below the then market level.

The defendant had clearly been guilty of deceit. What was the plaintiff's loss? At first sight, the obvious answer is 28 million $\times$ $4\frac{1}{4}$ p, the premium paid above market price for each share. However, it turned out that the plaintiff's actual loss was much bigger. Unknown to both parties, the shares in Ferranti were greatly overvalued by the market because nobody knew that Ferranti had been the subject of a highly successful fraud by an American gentleman who managed to sell Ferranti a worthless company for a large amount of money. In fact, the plaintiffs managed to sell the shares back on the market over a long period of time before the market discovered this fraud at prices between 49p and 30p a share. When the full truth was discovered, Ferranti was bought by another company for 1p a share. But the question before the court was whether the plaintiff could recover the whole of its loss, which was in excess of £11m, or only 28 million $\times$ $4\frac{1}{4}$ p. The House of Lords had no doubt, reversing the Court of Appeal, that the plaintiff could recover the full amount of its losses owing to it ever having entered into the transaction.

Lord Steyn said:

The logic of the decision in *Doyle v Olby (Ironmongers) Ltd* justifies the following propositions.

(1) The plaintiff in an action for deceit is not entitled to be compensated in accordance with the contractual measure of damage, ie the benefit of the bargain measure. He is not entitled to be protected in respect of his positive interest in the bargain.

(2) The plaintiff in an action for deceit is, however, entitled to be compensated in respect of his negative interest. The aim is to put the plaintiff into the position he would have been in if no false representation had been made.

(3) The practical difference between the two measures was lucidly explained in a contemporary case note on *Doyle v Olby (Ironmongers) Ltd* (see Treitel 'Damages for Deceit' (1969) 32 MLR 558–559). The author said:

'If the plaintiff's bargain would have been a bad one, even on the assumption that the representation was true, he will do best under the tortious measure. If, on the assumption that the representation was true, his bargain would have been a good one, he will do best under the first contractual measure (under which he may recover something even if the actual value of what he has recovered is greater than the price).'

(4) Concentrating on the tort measure, the remoteness test whether the loss was reasonably foreseeable had been authoritatively laid down in *The Wagon Mound* in respect of the tort of negligence a few years before *Doyle v Olby (Ironmongers) Ltd* was decided: *Overseas Tankship (UK) Ltd v Morts Dock and Engineering Co Ltd, The Wagon Mound* [1961] 1 All ER 404, [1961] AC 388. *Doyle v Olby (Ironmongers) Ltd* settled that a wider test applies in an action for deceit.

(5) The dicta in all three judgments, as well as the actual calculation of damages in *Doyle v Olby (Ironmongers) Ltd*, make it clear that the victim of the fraud is entitled to compensation for all the actual loss directly flowing from the transaction induced by the wrongdoer. That includes heads of consequential loss.

(6) Significantly in the present context the rule in the previous paragraph is not tied to any process of valuation at the date of the transaction. It is squarely based on the overriding compensatory principle, widened in view of the fraud to cover all direct consequences. The legal measure is to compare the position of the plaintiff as it was before the fraudulent statement was made to him with his position as it became as a result of his reliance on the fraudulent statement.

NOTE

You will see in a little while that the House of Lords applied a significantly different rule here to that which it applied where the defendant was negligent rather than fraudulent (see *South Australia Asset Management Co v York Montague*, pp 377, 384–386, 424. These two cases are considered by the Court of Appeal in *Clef Aquitaine SARL v Laporte Materials (Barrow) Ltd* [2000] 3 All ER 493. In this case, the first claimant entered into two long-term distributor agreements with the first defendant, undertaking to buy the defendant's products and to market and distribute them in France. The claimants established that the defendants had been guilty of deceit in the negotiation of the contract. The defendants argued that the claimants suffered no loss because the contracts had turned out profitable to them, but the Court of Appeal accepted the argument that, but for the defendant's fraud, the claimants would have entered into a contract that was more profitable than the one they had actually entered into and that, accordingly, they should recover damages to compensate them for this loss.

Damages under the Misrepresentation Act 1967, s 2(1)

■ *Royscot Trust Ltd v Rogerson*

[1991] 3 All ER 294, Court of Appeal

The plaintiff finance company bought a car from a dealer and entered a hire-purchase agreement to hire it to a hirer, after a misrepresentation by the dealer that the purchase price was £8,000 and the hirer had paid a deposit of 20 per cent (£1,600). The plaintiffs paid the balance apparently owing, £6,400, to the dealer. In fact, the price was £7,200 and the hirer had paid a deposit of only £1,200. Although the balance owing was the same as represented, the plaintiffs required a 20 per cent deposit and would not have entered the arrangements had they known the truth. The hirer defaulted after paying £2,775 to the plaintiffs, who sued the dealer for the difference between this and what they had paid out, ie £3,625.

Balcombe LJ

...I turn to the issue on this appeal which the dealer submits raises a pure point of law: where (a) a motor dealer innocently misrepresents to a finance company the amount of the sale price of, and the deposit paid by the intended purchaser of, the car and (b) the finance company is thereby induced to enter into a hire-purchase agreement with the purchaser which it would not have done if it had known the true facts and (c) the purchaser thereafter dishonestly disposes of the car and defaults on the hire-purchase agreement, can the finance company recover all or part of its losses on the hire-purchase agreement from the motor dealer?

The finance company's cause of action against the dealer is based on s 2(1) of the Misrepresentation Act 1967 . . . .

As a result of some dicta by Lord Denning MR in two cases in the Court of Appeal— *Gosling v Anderson* [1972] EGD 709 *and Jarvis v Swans Tours Ltd* [1973] 1 All ER 71 at 73—and the decision at first instance in *Watts v Spence* [1975] 2 All ER 528, there was some doubt whether the measure of damages for an innocent misrepresentation giving rise to a cause of action under the 1967 Act was the tortious measure, so as to put the representee in the position in which he would have been if he had never entered into the contract, or the contractual measure, so as to put the representee in the position in which he would have been if the misrepresentation had been true, and thus in some cases give rise to a claim for damages for loss of bargain . . . .

However, there is now a number of decisions which make it clear that the tortious measure of damages is the true one. Most of these decisions are at first instance and will be found in *Chitty on Contract* (26th edn, 1989) para 439, note 63 . . . In view of the wording of the subsection it is difficult to see how the measure of damages under it could be other than the tortious measure and, despite the initial aberrations referred to above, that is now generally accepted. Indeed counsel before us did not seek to argue the contrary.

The first main issue before us was: accepting that the tortious measure is the right measure, is it the measure where the tort is that of fraudulent misrepresentation, or is it the measure where the tort is negligence at common law? The difference is that in cases of fraud a plaintiff is entitled to any loss which flowed from the defendant's fraud, even if the loss could not have been foreseen: see *Doyle v Olby (Ironmongers) Ltd*. In my judgment the wording of the subsection is clear: the person making the innocent misrepresentation shall be 'so liable', ie liable to damages as if the representation had been made fraudulently . . . . 'By "so liable" I take it to mean liable as he would be if the misrepresentation had been made fraudulently.'

This was also the original view of the academic writers. In Atiyah and Treitel 'Misrepresentation Act 1967' (1967) 30 MLR 369 at 373–374 it says:

> 'The measure of damages in the statutory action will apparently be that in an action of deceit . . . But more probably the damages recoverable in the new action are the same as those recoverable in an action of deceit . . . '

Professor Treitel has since changed his view. In *Law of Contract* (7th edn, 1987) p 278 he says:

> 'Where the action is brought under section 2(1) of the Misrepresentation Act, one possible view is that the deceit rule will be applied by virtue of the fiction of fraud. But the preferable view is that the severity of the deceit rule can only be justified in cases of actual fraud and that remoteness under section 2(1) should depend, as in actions based on negligence, on the test of foreseeability.'

With all respect it seems to me that to suggest that a different measure of damage applies to an action for innocent misrepresentation under the section than that which applies to an action for fraudulent misrepresentation (deceit) at common law is to ignore the plain words of the subsection and is inconsistent with the cases to which I have referred. In my judgment, therefore, the finance company is entitled to recover from the dealer all the losses which it suffered as a result of its entering into the agreements with the dealer and the customer, even if those losses were unforeseeable, provided that they were not otherwise too remote.

If the question of foreseeability had been the only issue in this appeal, the judgment so far would have rendered it unnecessary to decide whether, in the circumstances of the present case, the wrongful sale of the car by the customer was reasonably foreseeable by the dealer. Since the judge did not expressly deal with this point in his judgment, it might have been preferable that we should not do so. Nevertheless there is a separate issue of whether the wrongful sale of the car was novus actus interveniens and thus broke the chain of causation, and the reasonable foreseeability of the event in question is a factor to be taken into account on that issue. Accordingly it is necessary to deal with this matter. Mr Kennedy, for the dealer, submitted that, while a motor car dealer might be expected to foresee that a customer who buys a car on hire purchase may default in payment of his instalments, he cannot be expected to foresee that he will wrongfully dispose of the car. He went on to submit that, in the particular circumstances of this case, where the customer was apparently reputable, being a young married man in employment, it was even less likely that the dealer could have foreseen what might happen. There appears to have been no oral evidence directed to this particular point.

In my judgment this is to ignore both the reality of the transaction and general experience. While in legal theory the car remains the property of the finance company until the last hire-purchase instalment is paid, in practice the purchaser is placed in effective control of the car and treats it as his own. Further, there have been so many cases, both civil and criminal, where persons buying a car on hire purchase have wrongfully disposed of the car that we can take judicial notice that this is an all too frequent occurrence. Accordingly I am satisfied that, at the time when the finance company entered into the agreements with the dealer and the customer, it was reasonably foreseeable that the customer might wrongfully sell the car . . . .

Mr Kennedy's next submission was that the customer's wrongful sale of the car was novus actus interveniens. This issue was considered by the judge, although the brief note of his judgment on this point is corrupt and is not agreed by counsel. It is implicit in his decision to award £1,600 damages to the finance company that the sale was not novus actus interveniens: otherwise on the figures in this case he would have been bound to find that the finance company had suffered no loss. However, the judgment contains no indication of how he came to that conclusion.

In the present case the customer was a free agent and his act in selling the car was unlawful. Nevertheless neither of these facts is conclusive in determining whether the sale of the car was a novus actus sufficient to break the chain of causation: see generally *Clerk and Lindsell on Torts* (16th edn, 1989) paras 1–117, 1–121; *McGregor on Damages* (15th edn, 1988) paras 152–166. However, if the dealer should reasonably have foreseen the possibility of the wrongful sale of the car, then that is a strong indication that the sale did not break the chain of causation. As Winn LJ said in *Iron and Steel Holding and Realisation Agency v Compensation Appeal Tribunal* [1966] 1 All ER 769 at 775, [1966] 1 WLR 480 at 492:

'In my opinion, wherever any intervening factor was itself foreseen or reasonably foreseeable by the actor, the person responsible for the act which initiated the chain of causes leading to the final result, that intervening cause is not itself, in the legal sense, a novus actus interveniens breaking the chain of causation and isolating the initial act from the final result.'

I doubt whether further citation of authority will be helpful: in this field authority is almost too plentiful. For the reasons I have already given, in my judgment the dealer should reasonably have foreseen the possibility that the customer might wrongfully sell the car. In my judgment, therefore, the sale was not novus actus interveniens and did not break the chain of causation.

Ralph Gibson LJ gave judgment to the same effect.

Appeal dismissed. Cross-appeal allowed.

NOTES

1.   It seems rather curious that, after holding that the loss did not have to be foreseeable to be recoverable under s 2(1) because the remoteness rule did not apply, the Court of Appeal held that it was foreseeable so as to prove causation.

2.   Would it be fair to categorise Balcombe LJ's reasoning as formalist? (Compare p 57.) In *Smith New Court Securities Ltd v Scrimgeour Vickers (Asset Management) Ltd* [1996] 4 All ER 769, both Lord Browne-Wilkinson and Lord Steyn went out of their way to say that they were expressing no view about the correctness of *Royscot*. (Translated, this is an open invitation to counsel to argue the point in an appropriate case.)

3.   In *Royscot*, the plaintiffs would not have entered any transaction with the defendants had they known the truth. What if the misrepresentee would have made a contract but at a different price?

4.   Can damages under s 2(1) be reduced because of contributory negligence on the part of the misrepresentee? In *Gran Gelato Ltd v Richcliff (Group) Ltd* [1992] 1 All ER 865, this defence was advanced. Nicholls V-C referred to the Act (see p 375) and said (at 875):

> ...[L]iability under the 1967 Act is essentially founded on negligence, in the sense that the defendant, the representor, did not have reasonable grounds to believe that the facts represented were true. (Of course, if he did not believe the facts represented were true he will be liable for fraud.) This being so, it would be very odd if the defence of contributory negligence were not available to a claim under that Act. It would be very odd if contributory negligence were available as a defence to a claim for damages based on a breach of a duty to take care in and about the making of a particular representation, but not available to a claim for damages under the 1967 Act in respect of the same representation.
>
> In my view, the answer to this point is provided by the decision of the Court of Appeal in *Forsikringsaktieselskapet Vesta v Butcher* [1989] AC 852. There the court held that the 1945 Act applies to a case where there is a claim for damages for negligence at common law even if, in addition, there is a claim in contract to the same effect. O'Connor LJ adopted the view expressed by Prichard J in *Rowe v Turner Hopkins & Partners* [1980] 2 NZLR 550 at 555–556 regarding the equivalent section of the New Zealand legislation:
>
>> 'I therefore conclude, in the absence of any clear authority to the contrary, that the first limb of the definition of s 2 determines the meaning of the word "fault" as it relates to the plaintiff's cause of action: that accordingly, the Contributory Negligence Act cannot apply unless the cause of action is founded on some act or omission on the part of the defendant which gives rise to liability in tort: that if the defendant's conduct meets that criterion, the Act can apply—whether or not the same conduct is also actionable in contract.'
>
> Neill LJ agreed with this approach, and I do not read Sir Roger Ormrod's judgment as differing on this point (see [1989] AC 852 at 866, 875).
>
> In the present case the conduct of which Gran Gelato complains founds a cause of action both in negligence at common law and under the 1967 Act. As already noted, under the 1967 Act liability is essentially founded on negligence. By parity I of reasoning with the conclusion in *Forsikringsaktieselskapet Vesta v Butcher* I regarding concurrent claims in negligence in tort and contract, the 1945 Act applies in the present case where there are concurrent claims against Richcliff in negligence in tort and under the 1967 Act.

However, he held that, on the facts of the case, it would not be just and equitable to reduce the damages when the representor had intended, or should be taken as having intended, that the representee should act in reliance on the answers that had been given to his questions.

5.   It seems that it is not possible for damages under s 2(1) to be reduced because of the claimant's contributory negligence if the case is not one of concurrent liability in negligence. The difficulty follows from the 'fiction of fraud'. The decision in *Gran Gelato*

was based on the fact that there was concurrent liability under s 2(1) and in tort for negligent misrepresentation under the principle of *Hedley Byrne*. There is no doubt that the Act applies to *Hedley Byrne* liability: in terms of the definition of fault in s 4, the plaintiff's contributory negligence is an act that would 'give rise to the defence of contributory negligence' at common law. But the Act seems not to apply to liability solely under s 2(1) without concurrent liability under *Hedley Byrne*, because the defendant's liability under s 2(1) is equated with liability for fraud and, as we saw earlier, contributory negligence is not a defence in an action for fraud (see pp 375–376). Whether this effect was intended may be doubted.

Damages under the Misrepresentation Act 1967, s 2(2)

■ *William Sindall plc v Cambridgeshire County Council*

[1994] 3 All ER 932, Court of Appeal

Builders agreed to buy some land from the council for development purposes for some £5m. Later, it was discovered that there was a foul sewer running under part of the site, which would have a slight impact on the proposed development. The builders alleged that the council had made a misrepresentation as to the effect that there were no such matters affecting the site or alternatively that the contract was voidable for mistake, and claimed a declaration that the contract had been rescinded and repayment of the price. By this time, there had been a general fall in land prices and the value of the land was only some £2.5m. The Court of Appeal, allowing an appeal by the council, held that there had been no operative mistake and no misrepresentation, but the application of s 2(2) was discussed.

Hoffmann LJ

6. DISCRETION

My conclusion that there are no grounds for rescission, either for misrepresentation or mistake, means that it is unnecessary to consider whether the judge correctly exercised his discretion under s 2(2) of the Misrepresentation Act 1967 not to award damages in lieu of rescission. But in case this case goes further, I should say that in my judgment the judge approached this question on a false basis, arising from his mistake about the seriousness of the defect. This vitiated the exercise of the discretion and would have made it necessary, if we thought that Sindall would otherwise have been entitled to rescind for misrepresentation, to exercise our own discretion under s 2(2).

... This provision was adopted as a result of the Tenth Report of the Law Reform Committee *Innocent Misrepresentation* (Cmnd 1782), which also recommended abolishing the bar on rescission after completion. The relevant paragraphs of the report were 11 and 12....

> '12. We recommend that wherever the court has power to order rescission it should, as an alternative, have a discretionary power to award damages if it is satisfied that these would afford adequate compensation to the plaintiff, having regard to the nature of the misrepresentation and the fact that the injury suffered by the plaintiff is small compared with what rescission would involve. The courts were given power to award damages in addition to or in substitution for an injunction or a decree of specific performance by section 2 of Lord Cairns' Act (the Chancery Procedure Amendment Act, 1858), and since the decision of the House of Lords in *Leeds Industrial Co-operative Society Limited v Slack* ([1924] AC 851, this power has been exercised on principles similar to those we have just mentioned.'

The discretion conferred by s 2(2) is a broad one, to do what is equitable. But there are three matters to which the court must in particular have regard.

The first is the nature of the misrepresentation. It is clear from the Law Reform Committee's Report that the court was meant to consider the importance of the representation in relation to the subject matter of the transaction. I have already said that in my view, in the context of a £5m sale of land, a misrepresentation which would have cost £18,000 to put right and was unlikely seriously to have interfered with the development or resale of the property was a matter of relatively minor importance.

The second matter to which the court must have regard is 'the loss that would be caused by it [the misrepresentation] if the contract were upheld'. The section speaks in terms of loss suffered rather than damages recoverable, but clearly contemplates that if the contract is upheld such loss will be compensated by an award of damages. Section 2(2) therefore gives a power to award damages in circumstances in which no damages would previously have been recoverable. Furthermore, such damages will be compensation for loss caused by the misrepresentation, whether it was negligent or not. This is made clear by s 2(3), which reads as follows:

> 'Damages may be awarded under subsection (2) of this section whether or not he is liable to damages under subsection (1) thereof, but where he is so liable any award under subsection (2) shall be taken into account in assessing his liability under the said subsection (1).'

Damages under s 2(2) are therefore damages for the misrepresentation as such. What would be the measure of such damages? This court is not directly concerned with quantum, which would be determined at an inquiry. But since the court, in the exercise of its discretion, needs to know whether damages under s 2(2) would be an adequate remedy and to be able to compare such damages with the loss which rescission would cause to Cambridgeshire, it is necessary to decide in principle how the damages would be calculated.

The Law Reform Committee drew the analogy with Lord Cairns' Act and in some respects this analogy is a good one. But it breaks down when one comes to decide the measure of damages. Under Lord Cairns' Act, the plaintiff who is refused specific performance or an injunction is left to his damages in contract or tort. The measure of such damages is exactly what it would be at common law *(see Johnson v Agnew* [1980] AC 367 at 400). The only change made by the Act was to give a remedy for purely equitable rights, such as breach of a restrictive covenant to which the plaintiff was not a party. But in such cases the common law analogy enabled a suitable measure of damages to be devised. Section 2(2), on the other hand, creates a power to award damages in a wholly new situation.

Under s 2(1), the measure of damages is the same as for fraudulent misrepresentation . . . In my judgment, however, it is clear that this will not necessarily be the measure of damages under s 2(2).

First, s 2(1) provides for damages to be awarded to a person who 'has entered into a contract after a misrepresentation has been made to him by another party and as a result thereof [of having entered into the contract] he has suffered loss'. In contrast s 2(2) speaks of 'the loss which would be caused by it [the misrepresentation] if the contract were upheld'. In my view, s 2(1) is concerned with the damage flowing from having entered into the contract, while s 2(2) is concerned with damage caused by the property not being what it was represented to be.

Secondly, s 2(3) contemplates that damages under s 2(2) may be less than damages under s 2(1) and should be taken into account when assessing damages under the latter subsection. This only makes sense if the measure of damages may be different.

Thirdly, the Law Reform Committee Report makes it clear that s 2(2) was enacted because it was thought that it might be a hardship to the representor to be deprived of the whole benefit of the bargain on account of a minor misrepresentation. It could not possibly have intended the damages in lieu to be assessed on a principle which would invariably have the same effect.

The Law Reform Committee drew attention to the anomaly which already existed by which a minor misrepresentation gave rise to a right of rescission whereas a warranty in the same terms would have grounded no more than a claim for modest damages. It said that this anomaly would be exaggerated if its recommendation for abolition of the bar on rescission after completion were to be implemented. I think that s 2(2) was intended to give the court a power to eliminate this anomaly by upholding the contract and compensating the plaintiff for the loss he has suffered on account of the property not having been what it was represented to be. In other words, damages under s 2(2) should never exceed the sum which would have been awarded if the representation had been a warranty. It is not necessary for present purposes to discuss the circumstances in which they may be less.

If one looks at the matter when Sindall purported to rescind, the loss which would be caused if the contract were upheld was relatively small: the £18,000 it would have cost to divert the sewer, the loss of a plot and interest changes on any consequent delay at the rate of £2,000 a day. If one looks at the matter at the date of trial, the loss would have been nil because the sewer had been diverted.

The third matter to be taken into account under s 2(2) is the loss which would be caused to Cambridgeshire by rescission. This is the loss of the bargain at the top of the market (cf *Atlantic Lines and Navigation Co Inc v Hallam Ltd, The Lucy* [1983] 1 Lloyd's Rep 188) having to return about £8m in purchase price and interest in exchange for land worth less than £2m.

Having regard to these matters, and in particular the gross disparity between the loss which would be caused to Sindall by the misrepresentation and the loss which would be caused to Cambridgeshire by rescission, I would have exercised my discretion to award damages in lieu of rescission.

Evans LJ

...[The] damages contemplated by s 2(2) are damages in lieu of rescission...When there has been a decline in market values since the date of the contract, then one party or the other will suffer that loss, depending on whether rescission is ordered or not. But that loss is not caused by the misrepresentation, except in the sense that the decline has occurred since the representation was made, and it does not measure the loss caused by the misrepresentation either when the representation was acted upon, or when the court decides whether to order rescission or not. The 'loss caused by it', in my judgment, can be measured by the cost of remedying the defect, or alternatively by the reduced market value attributable to the defect, together with additional compensation, if appropriate, of the kind described in the *Cemp Properties* case.... [In] my judgment [the contract measure] becomes the correct measure in circumstances where the plaintiff is entitled to an order for rescission, but rescission is refused under s 2(2) of the Act. This is because the difference in value between what the plaintiff was misled into believing that he was acquiring and the value of what he in fact received seems to me to be the measure of the loss caused to him by the misrepresentation in a case where he cannot rescind the contract and therefore retains the property which he received.

...[The] tortious measure benefits a plaintiff who made a bad bargain, that is to say who agreed to pay more than the market value of the property in the state in which he believed it to be, more so than the contract measure would do. Conversely, it disbenefits one who paid less than the market value, because it disentitles him from recovering the whole of the difference which the contract measure would otherwise produce. Likewise, the right to rescind benefits a plaintiff who has paid, or agreed to pay more than, with hindsight, he should have done. The period of hindsight may be short or long; where it is long, and the value has fallen in line with the market and therefore for reasons unconnected with the misrepresentation, there is no justification, in my view, for holding that the author of the misrepresentation is liable to compensate the plaintiff for that loss, in a case where rescission is refused.

It is unnecessary to explore the wider questions whether a tortious measure should ever include damages for a fall in market values, and whether this measure, as described by Lord Denning MR in *Doyle v Olby (Ironmongers) Ltd* [1969] 2 All ER 119 at 121, [1969] 2 QB 158 at 166, is necessarily exclusive of, or inconsistent with, the contractual measure to the extent which has been suggested. The recovery of such damages in the present case, even if the tortious measure under s 2(2) applies, appears to be barred by the following three obstacles: (1) such damage was caused, not by the misrepresentation, but by the subsequent fall in market values, an extraneous cause; (2) the authorities suggest that the plaintiff's loss has to be assessed at the date when the property was transferred (see *McGregor* para 1727, citing *Waddell v Blockey* (1879) 4 QBD 678); and (3) if a subsequent rise, or fall, in market values is relevant at the date of trial, then a chance element enters into the calculation, whether the contract is rescinded or not.

Russell LJ agreed with both judgments.

Appeal allowed.

NOTES

1.   Can the misrepresentee claim damages for consequential loss under s 2(2) according to Hoffmann LJ? According to Evans LJ?

2.   Are the damages under s 2(2) to be measured by the contract measure (to put the misrepresentee into the same position is if what was stated had been true) or on a measure based on the difference between what the misrepresentee paid and the value of what it received, according to Hoffmann LJ? According to Evans LJ?

3.   Which of those two measures do you think the damages should be assessed by?

■ *South Australia Asset Management Corpn v York Montague Ltd*
[1996] 3 All ER 365, House of Lords

During the 1990s, a large number of cases came before the courts in which lenders, who had lent money for the acquisition of property during the property boom and had suffered losses when the borrowers were unable to repay when the market collapsed, sought to pass the loss on to valuers. Typically, the allegation was that the lenders had only advanced the money because the valuers had negligently valued the property at a higher figure than the property was in fact worth, and as a result, the lenders had entered into a transaction that they would otherwise not have entered into. Of course, if negligence could be proved, then liability would follow, but for what figure? The lenders argued that they could recover the whole of the loss they had suffered, both that flowing from the carelessness of valuation and that flowing from collapse of the market. Different judges expressed different views on this question. Six of these cases were consolidated before the Court of Appeal, which held that, in principle, the lenders could recover the whole of their loss on the basis that they would never have entered into the transaction but for the careless valuation. Three of these cases were taken, on appeal, to the House of Lords in the present case. The House of Lords reversed the Court of Appeal and held that only that loss which foreseeably flowed from the careless valuation was recoverable.

Lord Hoffmann

What therefore should be the extent of the valuer's liability? The Court of Appeal said that he should be liable for the loss which would not have occurred if he had given the correct advice. The lender having, in reliance on the vlauation, embarked upon a transaction which he would not otherwise have undertaken, the valuer should bear all the risks of that transaction, subject only to the limitation that the damage should have been within the reasonable contemplation of the parties.

There is no reason in principle why the law should not penalise wrongful conduct by shifting onto the wrongdoer the whole risk of consequences which would not have happened but for the wrongful act. Hart and Honoré *Causation in the Law* (2nd edn, 1985) p 120 say that it would, for example, be perfectly intelligible to have a rule by which an unlicensed driver was responsible for all the consequences of his having driven, even if they were unconnected with his not having a licence. One might adopt such a rule in the interests of deterring unlicensed driving. But that is not the normal rule. One may compare, for example, *Western Steamship Co Ltd v Konninklijke Rotterdamsche Lloyd, The Empire Jamaica* [1955] 3 All ER 60 at 61 per Evershed MR, in which a collision was caused by a 'blunder in seamanship of . . . a somewhat serious and startling character' by an uncertificated second mate. Although the owners knew that the mate was not certificated and it was certainly the case that the collision would not have happened if he had not been employed, it was held in limitation proceedings that the damage took place without the employer's 'actual fault or privity' because the mate was in fact experienced and (subject to this one aberration) competent (see [1955] 3 All ER 60 at 69). The collision was not, therefore, attributable to his not having a certificate. The owners were not treated as responsible for all the consequences of having employed an uncertificated mate, but only for the consequences of his having been uncertificated.

Rules which make the wrongdoer liable for all the consequences of his wrongful conduct are exceptional and need to be justified by some special policy. Normally the law limits liability to those consequences which are attributable to that which made the act wrongful. In the case of liability in negligence for providing inaccurate information, this would mean liability for the consequences of the information being inaccurate.

I can illustrate the difference between the ordinary principle and that adopted by the Court of Appeal by an example. A mountaineer about to undertake a difficult climb is concerned about the fitness of his knee. He goes to a doctor who negligently makes a superficial examination and pronounces the knee fit. The climber goes on the expedition, which he would not have undertaken if the doctor had told him the true state of his knee. He suffers an injury which is an entirely foreseeable consequence of mountaineering, but has nothing to do with his knee.

...

The other cases cited by the Court of Appeal and counsel for the respondent plaintiffs fall into two categories. The first comprises those cases concerned with the calculation of the loss which the plaintiff has suffered in consequence of having entered into the transaction. They do not address the question of the extent to which that loss is within the scope of the defendant's duty of care. The calculation of loss must, of course, involve comparing what the plaintiff has lost as a result of making the loan with what his position would have been if he had not made it. If, for example, the lender would have lost the same money on some other transaction, then the valuer's negligence has caused him no loss. Likewise, if he has substantially overvalued the property, so that the lender stands to make a loss if he has to sell the security at current values, but a rise in the property market enables him to realise enough to pay off the whole loan, the lender has suffered no loss. But the question of whether the lender has suffered a loss is not the same as the question of how one defines the kind of loss which falls within the scope of the duty of care. The Court of Appeal justified its view on the latter question by an appeal to symmetry: 'if the market moves upwards, the valuer reaps the benefit; if it moves downwards, he stands the loss' (see [1995] 2 All ER 769 at 856). This seems to me to confuse the two questions. If the market moves upwards, it reduces or eliminates the loss which the lender would otherwise have suffered. If it moves downwards, it may result in more loss than is attributable to the valuer's error. There is no contradiction in the symmetry. A plaintiff has to prove both that he has suffered loss and that the loss fell within the scope of the duty. The fact that he cannot recover for loss which he has not suffered does not entitle him to an award of damages for loss which he has suffered, but which does not fall within the scope of the valuer's duty of care.

NOTES

1. It is not easy to find in Lord Hoffmann's judgment a simple exlanation of how the principle he laid down should be applied. However, in *Nykredit Mortgage Bank plc v Edward Erdman Group Ltd* [1997] 1 WLR 1627, 1632, Lord Nicholls said that the measure should be the loss suffered by the lender 'but limited to the extent of the overvaluation'.

2. This test is clearly less favourable to the plaintiffs than that applied by the Court of Appeal in the *South Australia* case. Even so, in one of the three cases combined for the appeal, the plaintiffs still recovered in full. In the title case, the plaintiffs advanced £11m on a property valued at £15m. The trial judge found that the true value at the date of the valuation was £5m. The property was eventually sold for £2,477,000 and the trial judge quantified the plantiffs' loss at £9,753,927.99. Because this was less than the £10m undervaluation, the plaintiff should recover in full. (Of course, the mistake in the valuation was here very large.)

3. Contributory negligence is clearly a possibility here. In *Platform Home Loans Ltd v Oyston Shipways Ltd* [1999] 1 All ER 833, the trial judge held that the lenders lending policy was improvident and made a deduction of 20 per cent for contributory negligence. By the

time the case came to the House of Lords, this finding was not effectively challenged, but there was a problem as to the way in which the sums should be done. Basically, the total out-of-pocket loss of the plaintiffs, ignoring contributory negligence, was £611,748.51 and the negligent overvaluation was £500,000. The Court of Appeal had said that the contributory negligence should be applied first to the overvaluation and so the plaintiffs could not recover more than £400,000. The House of Lords was clear that that was wrong and that the correct course was, first of all, to apply the 20 per cent reduction to the figure of £611,748.51, which produced a figure of £489,398.81. Since this figure was below £500,000, the plaintiffs could recover in full. In other words, the contributory negligence should be applied to the plaintiffs' loss first, and only if that left a figure of above the limits applied by the *South Australia* case should there be a further reduction. Lord Cooke took the opposite view, agreeing with the Court of Appeal.

V. ATTEMPTS TO EXCLUDE OR RESTRICT LIABILITY FOR MISREPRESENTATION

Any clause purporting to exclude or restrict liability for fraudulent misrepresentation is probably ineffective at common law. This was probably the view of the House of Lords in *S Pearson & Son Ltd v Dublin Corp* [1907] AC 351. The matter was considered again by the House of Lords in *HIH Casualty and General Insurance Ltd v Chase Manhattan Bank* [2003] 1 All ER (Comm) 349 [2003] 2 Lloyd's Rep 61.

In this case, the respondent bank was lending money against the receipts from movies to be made in the future. Because no one can tell what movies will do well in cinemas before they are made, this was a highly speculative venture and the bank wished to lay off a substantial part of the risk, which it did by taking out a policy of insurance with the appellant insurance company. The detailed negotiations were in the hands of intermediaries, who knew much more about movie finance than either of the parties.

The insurance contract contained extensive disclaimers on the part of the bank. In due course, the bank made a claim, which was resisted by the appellant. No one suggested any fraud on the part of the bank, but there were allegations of misrepresentations, fraudulent or negligent, by the bank's agents. The House of Lords held that the disclaimers were certainly effective to exclude liability for negligent misrepresentation by the agents, but by a majority, that they did not exclude liability for fraud if fraud were established.

The House thought that it would be possible, by appropriate words, to exclude liability for the fraud of an agent but not for one's own fraud.

Clauses attempting to do the same for non-fraudulent misrepresentations are now governed by the Misrepresentation Act 1967, s 3 (as amended by the Unfair Contract Terms Act 1977, s 8).

■ *Misrepresentation Act* 1967

Section 3

If a contract contains a term which would exclude or restrict—
(a) any liability to which a party to a contract may be subject by reason of any misrepresentation made by him before the contract was made; or

(b) any remedy available to another party to the contract by reason of such a misrepresentation; that term shall be of no effect except in so far as it satisfies the requirement of reasonableness as stated in section 11(1) of the Unfair Contract Terms Act 1977; and it is for those claiming that the term satisfies that requirement to show that it does.

NOTES

1.   Does s 3 apply to any clause that excludes liability for misrepresentation? It certainly covers a straightforward exclusion of liability, such as:

no error, misstatement or omission in any preliminary answer shall annul the sale (National Conditions of Sale for land, 19th edn).

But what about a clause that purports to deny one of the essential elements of misrepresentation, such as by stating that the purchaser does not rely on any statement made to him? In *Cremdean v Nash* (1977) 244 Estates Gazette 547, it was said that, if the purchaser can prove that despite the clause he did in fact rely on the misrepresentation, this clause would also be caught by the Act, since it effectively excluded his remedy.

2.   In contrast, in *Overbrooke Estates Ltd v Glencombe Properties Ltd* [1974] 3 All ER 511, the contract of sale stated:

The vendors do not make or give and neither the Auctioneers nor any person in the employment of the Auctioneers has any authority to make or give any representation or warranty in relation to these premises.

Brightman J held that, even assuming that the auctioneers had made a misrepresentation to the purchaser, the clause prevented the vendor from being responsible for it. Section 3 would not help the purchaser (at [1974] 3 All ER 511, 517):

The section does not . . . in any way qualify the right of a principal publicly to limit the otherwise ostensible authority of his agent.

On the authority of agents, see p 1128 ff.

3.   The requirement of reasonableness under the Unfair Contract Terms Act 1977, s 11(1), including its application to cases under the Misrepresentation Act 1967, s 3, is taken up on p 1023.

QUESTIONS

1.   In what circumstances may a clause that has not been referred to during negotiations nonetheless form part of an oral contract?

2.   For the last ten years, Jane Marple has taken her 30-year-old Morris 1000 car to Poirot's Garage Ltd for its twice-yearly service and for repairs. Normally, Poirot asks her to sign a 'service/repair contract', which contains, among other things, the following clause:

Additional items. If in the course of servicing or repairs, Poirot's find any additional item in need of adjustment, repair or replacement, they will use their best endeavours to contact the customer for authorization to carry out the additional work. The customer agrees that, should Poirot's be unable to contact the customer within two hours of the matter being brought to the attention of management, Poirot's may use complete discretion in carrying out any work it considers necessary or desirable and the customer will pay the full list price for such work.

Such clauses are occasionally found in other garages' contracts. Ms Marple has never bothered to read the contract and Poirot's has always managed to contact her when they have found additional items needing attention.

In February 1999, Ms Marple took her car to Poirot's for a routine service. When she came up to the service desk, she was warmly welcomed by the manager, Hercule. After exchanging pleasantries and writing into a notebook what she wanted done, he said 'You may be interested in our new fixed price scheme for repairs' and he gave her a leaflet with a long list of prices on it. Then the phone rang. While Hercule answered it, Ms Marple wandered away and looked at a used Jaguar XJS, which Poirot's had for sale. She stuffed the slip of paper into her pocket unread. Had she looked at it, she might have noticed that printed on the back and headed 'Terms and conditions' were the terms of Poirot's servicing and repairs contract, including the 'Additional items' clause.

When Hercule had finished on the phone, he quite forgot that he hadn't asked Ms Marple to sign the contract, and he called out to her: 'OK, Ms M, just leave it with us. See you this afternoon.'

Ms Marple, thinking hard about Jaguars, left the building.

While servicing the Morris, Poirot's found that the clutch assembly needed replacement. Hercule tried to contact Ms Marple but she was out pursuing a mass poisoner and, after three hours, Hercule told his mechanic, Hastings, to fit a new clutch assembly.

When Ms Marple, having caught the poisoner, returned to collect the car, she was presented with a bill for servicing and another for £350 for the clutch. She was most unwilling to pay because, earlier in the day, she had decided that, the next time the Morris needed any major repair, she would sell it for scrap and buy a new Jaguar. Advise her whether the 'Additional items' clause formed part of her contract with Poirot Ltd.

3. A seller makes a statement about the goods to be sold, eg that 'this car will do 30 mpg in traffic'. What are various ways in which the statement might be classified?

4. In what circumstances will the statement fall into each category—in other words, what are the basic legal requirements for each? (Give authority.)

5. What difference does it make which way the statement is classified? In other words, what remedies are available in each case should the statement turn out to be untrue? To what extent do the remedies depend upon the fault of the person who made the statement?

6. Frazier, who knows nothing about computers, decides to buy a used one so that he can start using it to write his novel. He sees a used computer advertised for sale by Rebecca and goes to see it. He asks her whether it will run Word for Windows 2000 and she replies 'Certainly, 'though I've never used Windows myself'. Frazier decides to buy the computer for £300 and, at Rebecca's insistence, he signs a contract of sale which states:

The buyer takes this machine as is, relying entirely upon his own skill and judgment.

After about a week, he gets a friend to help him install Windows but they immediately discover that the computer has insufficient memory to handle it. The friend tells him that the computer is only worth £200 at most. To buy one powerful enough to handle Word for Windows 2000 will cost about £400. Advise Frazier.

7. How may the right to rescind for misrepresentation be lost?

8. What are the arguments for and against the rule that a party is under no duty to disclose facts that (s)he knows would make a difference to the other party?

CHAPTER FOURTEEN

GAP-FILLING BY INTERPRETATION

I. INTRODUCTION

The last two chapters dealt with the question of what had expressly been agreed between the parties. This is only the beginning of the process of deciding what the parties' contractual obligations are in a given situation. The terms expressly agreed may not provide a clear answer, or may not cover the situation at all. This frequently happens with even the basic performance obligations: for instance, there may be no express agreement on price or the time for performance. It is even more common for there to be no express agreement on the effect of events that may occur before the contract has been performed and which disrupt it in some way ('contingencies').

■ **Macaulay, 'Non-contractual Relations in Business'** (1963)
28 American Sociological Review 55, 55–60

What good is contract law? who uses it? when and how? Complete answers would require an investigation of almost every type of transaction between individuals and organizations. In this report, research has been confined to exchanges between businesses, and primarily to manufacturers. Furthermore, this report will be limited to a presentation of the findings concerning when contract is and is not used and to a tentative explanation of these findings.

This research is only the first phase in a scientific study. The primary research technique involved interviewing 68 businessmen and lawyers representing 43 companies and six law firms. The interviews ranged from a 30-minute brush-off where not all questions could be asked of a busy and uninterested sales manager to a six-hour discussion with the general counsel of a large corporation. Detailed notes of the interviews were taken and a complete report of each interview was dictated, usually no later than the evening after the interview. All but two of the companies had plants in Wisconsin; 17 were manufacturers of machinery but none made such items as food products, scientific instruments, textiles or petroleum products. Thus the likelihood of error because of sampling bias may be considerable. However, to a great extent, existing knowledge has been inadequate to permit more rigorous procedures—as yet one cannot formulate many precise questions to be asked of a systematically selected sample of 'right people'. Much time has been spent fishing for relevant questions or answers, or both . . . .

Tentative findings

It is difficult to generalize about the use and nonuse of contract by manufacturing industry. However, a number of observations can be made with reasonable accuracy at this time. The use and nonuse of contract in creating exchange relations and in dispute settling will be taken up in turn.

The creation of exchange relationships

In creating exchange relationships, businessmen may plan to a greater or lesser degree in relation to several types of issues. Before reporting the findings as to practices in creating such relationships, it is necessary to describe what one can plan about in a bargain and the degrees of planning which are possible.

People negotiating a contract can make plans concerning several types of issues: (1) They can plan what each is to do or refrain from doing; eg, S might agree to deliver ten 1963 Studebaker four-door sedan automobiles to B on a certain date in exchange for a specified amount of money. (2) They can plan what effect certain contingencies are to have on their duties; eg, what is to happen to S and B's obligations if S cannot deliver the cars because of a strike at the Studebaker factory? (3) They can plan what is to happen if either of them fails to perform; eg, what is to happen if S delivers nine of the cars two weeks late? (4) They can plan their agreement so that it is a legally enforceable contract— that is, so that a legal sanction would be available to provide compensation for injury suffered by B as a result of S's failure to deliver the cars on time.

As to each of these issues, there may be a different degree of planning by the parties. (1) They may carefully and explicitly plan; eg S may agree to deliver ten 1963 Studebaker four-door sedans which have six cylinder engines, automatic transmissions and other specified items of optional equipment and which will perform to a specified standard for a certain time. (2) They may have a mutual but tacit understanding about an issue; eg, although the subject was never mentioned in their negotiations, both S and B may assume that B may cancel his order for the cars before they are delivered if B's taxi-cab business is so curtailed that B can no longer use ten additional cabs. (3) They may have two inconsistent unexpressed assumptions about an issue; eg, S may assume that if any of the cabs fails to perform to the specified standard for a certain time, all S must do is repair or replace it. B may assume S must also compensate B for the profits B would have made if the cab had been in operation. (4) They may never have thought of the issue; eg, neither S nor B planned their agreement so that it would be a legally enforceable contract. Of course, the first and fourth degrees of planning listed are the extreme cases and the second and third are intermediate points. Clearly other intermediate points are possible: eg, S and B neglect to specify whether the cabs should have automatic or conventional transmissions. Their planning is not as careful and explicit as that in the example previously given.

	Definition of Performances	Effect of Contingencies	Effect of Defective Performances	Legal Sanctions
Explicit and careful	X			
Tacit agreement		X		
Unilateral assumptions			X	
Unawareness of the issue				X

The following diagram represents the dimensions of creating an exchange relationship just discussed with 'X's' representing the example of S and B's contract for ten taxi-cabs.

Most larger companies, and many smaller ones, attempt to plan carefully and completely. Important transactions not in the ordinary course of business are handled by a detailed contract. For example, recently the Empire State Building was sold for $65 million. More than 100 attorneys, representing 34 parties, produced a 400 page contract. Another example is found in the agreement of a major rubber company in the United States to give technical assistance to a Japanese firm. Several million dollars were involved and the contract consisted of 88 provisions on 17 pages. The 12 house counsel—lawyers who work for one corporation rather than many clients—interviewed said that all but the smallest business carefully planned most transactions of any significance. Corporations have procedures so that particular types of exchanges will be reviewed by their legal and financial departments.

More routine transactions commonly are handled by what can be called standardized planning. A firm will have a set of terms and conditions for purchases, sales, or both printed on the business documents used in these exchanges. Thus the things to be sold and the price may be planned particularly for each transaction, but standard provisions will further elaborate the performances and cover the other subjects of planning. Typically, these terms and conditions are lengthy and printed in small type on the back of the forms . . . .

While businessmen can and often do carefully and completely plan, it is clear that not all exchanges are neatly rationalized. Although most businessmen think that a clear description of both the seller's and buyer's performances is obvious common sense, they do not always live up to this ideal. The house counsel and the purchasing agent of a medium size manufacturer of automobile parts reported that several times their engineers had committed the company to buy expensive machines without adequate specifications. The engineers had drawn careful specifications as to the type of machine and how it was to be made but had neglected to require that the machine produce specified results. An attorney and an auditor both stated that most contract disputes arise because of ambiguity in the specifications.

Businessmen often prefer to rely on 'a man's word' in a brief letter, a handshake, or 'common honesty and decency'—even when the transaction involves exposure to serious risks. Seven lawyers from law firms with business practices were interviewed. Five thought that businessmen often entered contracts with only a minimal degree of advance planning. They complained that businessmen desire to 'keep it simple and avoid red tape' even where large amounts of money and significant risks are involved. One stated that he was 'sick of being told, "We can trust old Max", when the problem is not one of honesty but one of reaching an agreement that both sides understand'. Another said that businessmen when bargaining often talk only in pleasant generalities, think they have a contract, but fail to reach agreement on any of the hard, unpleasant questions until forced to do so by a lawyer. Two outside lawyers had different views. One thought that large firms usually planned important exchanges, although he conceded that occasionally matters might be left in a fairly vague state. The other dissenter represents a large utility that commonly buys heavy equipment and buildings. The supplier's employees come on the utility's property to install the equipment or construct the buildings, and they may be injured while there. The utility has been sued by such employees so often that it carefully plans purchases with the assistance of a lawyer so that suppliers take this burden . . . .

It is likely that businessmen pay more attention to describing the performances in an exchange than to planning for contingencies or defective performances or to obtaining legal enforceability of their contracts. Even when a purchase order and acknowledgment have conflicting provisions printed on the back, almost always the buyer and seller will be in agreement on what is to be sold and how much is to be paid for it. The lawyers who said businessmen often commit their firms to significant exchanges too casually, stated that the performances would be defined in the brief letter or telephone call; the lawyers objected that nothing else would be covered. Moreover, it is likely that businessmen are least concerned about planning their transactions so that they are legally enforceable contracts. For example, in Wisconsin requirements contracts—contracts to supply a firm's requirements of an item rather than a definite quantity—probably are not legally enforceable. Seven people interviewed reported that their firms regularly used requirements contracts in dealings with Wisconsin. None thought that the lack of legal sanction made any difference. Three of these people were house counsel who knew the Wisconsin law before being interviewed. Another example of a lack of desire for legal sanctions is found in the relationship between automobile manufacturers and their suppliers of parts. The manufacturers draft a carefully planned agreement, but one which is so designed that the supplier will have only minimal, if any, legal rights against the manufacturers. The standard contract used by manufacturers of paper to sell to magazine publishers has a pricing clause which is probably sufficiently vague to make the contract legally unenforceable. The house counsel of one of the largest paper producers said that everyone in the industry is aware of this because of a leading New York case concerning the contract, but that no one cares. Finally, it seems likely that planning for contingencies and defective performances are in-between cases—more likely to occur than planning for a legal sanction, but less likely than a description of performance.

Thus one can conclude that (1) many business exchanges reflect a high degree of planning about the four categories—description, contingencies, defective performances and legal sanction—but (2) many, if not most, exchanges reflect no planning, or only a minimal amount of it, especially concerning legal sanctions and the effect of defective performances. As a result, the opportunity for good faith disputes during the life of the exchange relationship often is present.

NOTE

This study by Macaulay is the one referred to earlier (p 83). If you would like to read more of it but do not have access to the *American Sociological Review*, you will find a slightly abridged version in Aubert (ed), *Sociology of Law*.

In a case in which there is a gap in the terms, the court has to fulfil two functions at once. One is to decide what was the obligation or risk allocation in the present case; the other is, by deciding what the terms mean or what the parties' implied obligations are, to supply a standard set of risk-allocation terms for use by contracting parties in the future. This will save the cost of negotiating over the point in the future, because parties making similar contracts in future will be able to rely on the standard set of terms—provided, of course, that the obligations imposed by the court fit the parties' needs. If they do not, the parties will then have to agree expressly on a different solution, thus increasing the cost of contracting once more.

There are a number of techniques by which the court may 'fill' the gap in the express terms; this chapter and the next concentrate on the two most obvious: the interpretation of the words expressly agreed and the implication of terms. There are other doctrines, however, which are, on their face, very different but in fact involve very similar issues—in particular, the doctrines of common mistake (under which a contract entered under a shared and fundamental mistake as to the facts may be void, or voidable in equity) and frustration (under which a contract may be discharged if without the fault of either party a subsequent event makes it impossible to perform).

The solutions that the doctrines provide are different in their theoretical effect and sometimes in their practical outcome. When the court interprets an express term as applying to the contingency that has occurred, or implies a term covering it, it is normally thought of as 'enforcing' the contract, and the usual outcome will be that one or other of the parties is held to have borne the risk of the loss that the contingency caused. Thus a party may have to perform his part of the contract, even though the contingency has seriously impaired the value to him of the performance he is to receive in exchange, or a party may have to pay compensation because he is held in default, even though his default was unintentional and sometimes without blame on his part. In contrast, if the doctrine of the common mistake or frustration is applied, the contract is not enforced: it is void (or perhaps voidable) for mistake or it is discharged by frustration and neither party will be liable in damages to the other for failing to perform. The result thus appears to be that the loss is divided between the parties, although we shall see that the division is sometimes pretty rough and ready. Occasionally, a similar result (which we shall refer to as 'the discharge solution') is reached via interpretation or the implication of terms (see Chapter 18).

Despite these differences, the various techniques are clearly interrelated. Firstly, when considering one approach, the court will always have to bear in mind the outcome that would be reached under another: thus interpretation of the express terms will be carried out in the light of what implied term would otherwise apply; the question of what terms should be implied will depend in part on the express terms of the contract; the question of whether the contract is discharged by frustration will depend on the express and implied terms; and so on. Secondly, whichever doctrine is applied, it has been traditional to justify the outcome in terms of the presumed intentions of the parties. In recent years, this has often been decried as a mere pretence. For instance, the implication of terms into a contract has often been explained as giving effect to the presumed intention of the parties. This is clearly no longer an acceptable rationale, as some of the terms implied by statute are now compulsory, and will thus apply even when the parties both consciously intend to exclude them. Even before the advent of such compulsory terms, the explanation seemed inadequate: many of the implied terms were so complex and so uniformly applied that it was more accurate to say that each type of contract carried with it a set of 'normal' obligations, which would govern unless it was the intention to exclude them. Similarly with frustration: the older cases explained the discharge of the contract as based on a term implied 'in order to fulfil the intention of those who entered into the contract'. Later courts have baulked at implying a term to cover something the parties 'neither expected nor foresaw', and have preferred to rest the doctrine on so-called construction: the contract does not apply to the new situation.

There is no doubt that in many cases of implied terms or frustration the parties did not have any actual intention on what was to happen in the circumstances, or certainly no common intentions; reference to their intentions was partly a polite fiction by which the court justified its decision. But the fictitious nature of the 'intention' should not be allowed to obscure the fact that the courts, in asking what was the parties' intention, may have been using a justifiable approach. It is arguable that in seeking solutions to particular situations for which the parties have not provided, the single most important guide both is and should be: what would the parties have agreed on if they *had* negotiated a clause on this question? The following extract explores this point further. It is discussing the doctrine of discharge by frustration, but the criteria suggested are equally relevant to what terms should be implied, to cases of mistake and even as a guide to interpretation.

■ Posner and Rosenfield, 'Impossibility and Related Doctrines in Contract Law: An Economic Analysis' (1977)
6 JLS 83, 87–92

There is . . . in the literature some recognition that the problem of discharge is one of allocating risk, since the effect of granting discharge is to place the risk of the event preventing performance on the promisee, while the effect of denying discharge is to place it on the promisor. But thus far the insight has been a sterile one because of a failure to develop any criteria for assigning the risk to one party or the other. Corbin is typical in suggesting both that it is a matter of indifference who bears the risk and that risk allocation is arbitary: 'Where neither custom nor agreement determines the allocation of risk, the court must exercise its equity powers and pray for the wisdom of Solomon.'

We shall try to give content to the concept of risk allocation as applied to the discharge question, first by sketching a theoretical framework that demonstrates why and when it is economically sensible to discharge a contract because of some unexpected event, and then by subjecting the theory to preliminary verification by comparing its implication with prevailing doctrinal positions and typical case holdings.

B. Economic principles

1. *Of contract law in general.* The process by which goods and services are shifted into their most valuable uses is one of voluntary exchange. The distinctive problems of contract law arise when the agreed-upon exchange does not take place instantaneously (for example, A agrees to build a house for B and construction will take several months). The fact that performance is to extend into the future introduces uncertainty, which in turn creates risks. A fundamental purpose of contracts is to allocate these risks between the parties to the exchange.

One purpose of contract *law*, but not a particularly interesting one here, is to assure compliance with the allocation of risks that the parties have agreed upon (that is, to prevent bad faith). A second purpose, central to our subject, is to reduce the costs of contract negotiation by supplying contract terms that the parties would probably have adopted explicitly had they negotiated over them. This purpose has been understood since Bentham's day:

'... [O]bligations may be distinguished into original and adjective. I call those original, of which express mention is made in the contract itself: I call those adjective, which the law thinks proper to add to the first. The first turn upon events which the contracting parties have foreseen; the others upon events which they could not foresee.

It is thus that in every country the law has supplied[?] the shortsightedness of individuals, by doing for them what they would have done for themselves, if their imagination had anticipated the march of nature.'

This function of contract *law* is analogous to that performed by standard or form *contracts*. The form contract economizes on the costs of contract negotiation by providing a set of terms to govern in the absence of explicit negotiations. The parties can of course vary the terms of the form contract, but to the extent that they do not, finding the terms suitable for their needs, contracting costs are reduced. It is much the same with the law of contracts. Judicial decisions, the Uniform Commercial Code, and other sources of contract law operate to define the parties' contractual obligations in the absence of express provisions in the contract. Every contract automatically incorporates a host of (generally) appropriate terms, over which the parties do not have to negotiate explicitly unless they want to vary the standard terms supplied by the law. Incidentally, the role of contract law in supplying contract terms, like the role of the standard or form contract, is less important the larger the stakes in the contract and hence the smaller the ratio of the costs of transacting to the value of the exchange. The larger the stakes, the more it will pay the parties to negotiate contract terms finely adapted to the particular circumstances of their contract.

If the purpose of the law of contracts is to effectuate the desires of the contracting parties, then the proper criterion for evaluating the rules of contract law is surely that of economic efficiency. Since the object of most voluntary exchanges is to increase value or efficiency, contracting parties may be assumed to desire a set of contract terms that will maximize the value of the exchange. It is true that each party is interested only in the value of the contract to it. However, the more efficiently the exchange is structured, the larger is the potential profit of the contract for the parties to divide between them.

The use of economic efficiency as a criterion for legal decision-making is of course controversial. In the area of contract, however, the criterion is well-nigh inevitable once it is conceded that the parties to a contract have the right to vary the terms at will. If the rules of contract law are inefficient, the parties will (save as transaction costs may sometimes outweigh the gains from a more efficient rule) contract around them. A law of contract not based on efficiency considerations will therefore be largely futile. This is a powerful reason for expecting that the law of contract has, in fact, been informed by efficiency considerations, even if judges and lawyers may have found it difficult to articulate the underlying economic premises of the law.

Moreover, the spirit of our analysis is severely positive. We are interested not in whether a contract law based on efficiency is ultimately a good law, but in whether the assumption that contract law has been shaped by a concern with economic efficiency is a fruitful one in explaining the doctrinal positions and typical case outcomes of that law.

(2) *The economics of impossibility.* The typical case in which impossibility or some related doctrine is invoked is one where, by reason of an unforeseen or at least unprovided-for event, performance by one of the parties of his obligations under the contract has become so much more costly than he foresaw at the time the contract was made as to be uneconomical (that is, the costs of performance would be greater than the benefits). The performance promised may have been delivery of a particular cargo by a specified delivery date—but the ship is trapped in the Suez Canal because of a war between Israel and Egypt. Or it may have been a piano recital by Gina Bachauer—and she dies between the signing of the contract and the date of the recital. The law could in each case treat the failure to perform as a breach of contract, thereby in effect assigning to the promisor the risk that war, or death, would prevent performance (or render it uneconomical). Alternatively, invoking impossibility or some related notion, the law could treat the failure to perform as excusable and discharge the contract, thereby in effect assigning the risk to the promisee.

From the standpoint of economics—and disregarding, but only momentarily, administrative costs—discharge should be allowed where the promisee is the superior risk bearer; if the promisor is the superior risk bearer, nonperformance should be treated as a breach of contract. 'Superior risk bearer' is to be understood here as the party that is the more efficient bearer of the particular risk in question, in the particular circumstances of the transaction. Of course, if the parties have expressly assigned the risk to one of them, there is no occasion to inquire which is the superior risk bearer. The inquiry is merely an aid to interpretation.

A party can be a superior risk bearer for one of two reasons. First, he may be in a better position to prevent the risk from materializing. This resembles the economic criterion for assigning liability in tort cases. It is an important criterion in many contract settings, too, but not in this one. Discharge would be inefficient in any case where the promisor could prevent the risk from materializing at a lower cost than the expected cost of the risky event. In such a case efficiency would require that the promisor bear the loss resulting from the occurrence of the event, and hence that occurrence should be treated as precipitating a breach of contract.

But the converse is not necessarily true. It does not necessarily follow from the fact that the promisor could not at any reasonable cost have prevented the risk from materializing that he should be discharged from his contractual obligations. Prevention is only one way of dealing with risk; the other is insurance. The promisor may be the superior insurer. If so, his inability to prevent the risk from materializing should not operate to discharge him from the contract, any more than an insurance company's inability to prevent a fire on the premises of the insured should excuse it from its liability to make good the damage caused by the fire.

To understand how it is that one party to a contract may be the superior (more efficient) risk bearer even though he cannot prevent the risk from materializing, it is necessary to understand the fundamental concept of risk aversion. Compare a 100 percent chance of having to pay $10 with a one percent chance of having to pay $1,000. The expected cost is the same in both cases, yet not everyone would be indifferent as between the two alternatives. Many people would be willing to pay a substantial sum to avoid the uncertain alternative—for example, $15 to avoid having to take a one percent chance of having to pay $1,000. Such people are risk averse. The prevalence of insurance is powerful evidence that risk aversion is extremely common, for insurance is simply trading an uncertain for a certain cost. Because of the administrative expenses of insurance, the certain cost (that is, the insurance premium) is always higher, often much higher, than the uncertain cost that it avoids—the expected cost of the fire, of the automobile accident, or whatever. Only a risk-averse individual would pay more to avoid bearing risk than the expected cost of the risk.

The fact that people are willing to pay to avoid risk shows that risk is a cost. Accordingly, insurance is a method (alternative to prevention) of reducing the costs associated with the risk that performance of a contract may be more costly than anticipated. It is a particularly important method of cost avoidance in the impossibility context because the risks with which that doctrine is concerned are generally not preventable by the party charged with nonperformance. As mentioned, if they were, that would normally afford a compelling reason for treating nonperformance as a breach of contract. (Stated otherwise, a 'moral hazard' problem would be created if the promisor were insured against a hazard that he could have prevented at reasonable cost.)

The factors relevant to determining which party to the contract is the cheaper insurer are (1) risk-appraisal costs and (2) transaction costs. The former comprise the costs of determining (a) the probability that the risk will materialize and (b) the magnitude of the loss if it does materialize. The amount of risk is the product of the probability loss and of the magnitude of the loss if it occurs. Both elements—probability and magnitude—must be known in order for the insurer to know how much to ask from the other party to the contract as compensation for bearing the risk in question.

The relevant transaction costs are the costs involved in eliminating or minimizing the risk through pooling it with other uncertain events, that is, diversifying away the risk. This can be done either through self-insurance or through the purchase of an insurance policy (market insurance). To illustrate, a corporation's shareholders might eliminate the risk associated with some contract the corporation had made by holding a portfolio of securities in which their shares in the corporation were combined with shares in many other corporations whose earnings would not be (adversely) affected if this particular corporation were to default on the contract. This would be an example of self-insurance. Alternatively, the corporation might purchase business-loss or some other form of insurance that would protect it (and, more important, its shareholders) from the consequence of a default on the contract; this would be an example of market insurance. Where good opportunities for diversification exist, self-insurance will often be cheaper than market insurance.

The foregoing discussion indicates the factors that courts and legislatures might consider in devising efficient rules for the discharge of contracts. An easy case for discharge would be one where (1) the promisor asking to be discharged could not reasonably have prevented the event rendering his performance uneconomical, and (2) the promisee could have insured against the occurrence of the event at lower cost than the promisor because the promisee (a) was in a better position to estimate both (i) the probability of the event's occurrence and (ii) the magnitude of the loss if it did occur, and (b) could have self-insured, whereas the promisor would have had to buy more costly market insurance. As we shall see, not all cases are this easy.

NOTES

1.   Posner gives the following explanation of risk aversion (*Economic Analysis of Law*, 2nd edn, pp 75–77):

The theoretical explanation is the principle of diminishing marginal utility of money income. If a person who has one chair buys a second, and then a third, and then a fourth, he will probably derive less utility from the second than from the first, and from the third than from the second, and so on; this illustrates the principle of diminishing marginal utility (notice that his *total* utility increases with every additional purchase, since he would not make a purchase that did not add to his net utility). Although money is a more versatile commodity than chairs, it is plausible to suppose that as an individual acquires more and more money the contribution of each dollar to his total utility or well being diminishes. His last $100 will be worth less than his next-to-last $100, etc, and therefore a $100 insurance premium (or indeed, a substantially larger one) will represent a lesser cost to him than 1 percent of the sum of 99 intramarginal $100 wealth units.

Clearly, then, to the risk-averse risk is a cost, and its elimination a gain. But, it may be asked, how does shifting a risk from the insured to the insurance company reduce or eliminate the risk and thus enhance welfare? The answer is that the insurance company, by pooling the insured's fire risk with many other risks with which the insured's is uncorrelated, is able to transform a risky into a (nearby) certain cost and thus eliminate risk—which is why it is able to charge an insurance premium that covers all its own costs yet is still attractive to the insured, ie, that is lower than his costs including the disutility he attaches to risk. For example, the insurance company might insure 1,000 buildings, each with a 1 percent probability of sustaining $10,000 damage. If these probabilities are independent (can you guess the meaning and significance of this qualification?), then the company can be reasonably certain that it will have to pay out close to $100,000 in insurance claims; the probability that it will have to make good the total loss insured against—$10,000,000—is infinitesimal. In contrast, the probability that, in the absence of insurance, the individual building owner would sustain his maximum loss is, as we know, a nonnegligible 1 percent. Stated otherwise, an expected cost, when incurred repeatedly, becomes a more or less certain average cost.

The purchase of an explicit insurance policy is referred to as 'market insurance'. In some cases 'self-insurance' is possible. A real estate company may own the 1,000 buildings in the previous example; if so, its 'risk' of fire loss is a nearly certain prospect of incurring a $100,000 cost. We shall see . . . that an investor can reduce the risks associated with a particular security by holding a diversified portfolio, ie, a set of securities whose risks are (at least partially) uncorrelated with one another; it is the same principle as illustrated by our fire self-insurance example.

2. For a different analysis of what is happening in cases of interpretation and implied terms, see p 457.

II. INTERPRETATION

When there is a dispute about the obligations of the parties in a given situation, the first task of the court will normally be to apply the express terms of the contract, if any are relevant. It is at this point that interpretation is necessary.

■ **Extract from *Evening Times and Echo*** (Saturday 8 May 1920)

Is a Dog a Workman?

A Problem which Remains Unsolved

Is a dog a workman?

The question has arisen at Bath in consequence of the revision of the tramcar fares owing to the increased running costs. Hitherto dogs have travelled free, but now a fare is charged.

A workman who boarded a car accompanied by his dog tendered the money for two workmen's tickets (says the Daily Express correspondent) whereupon the following dialogue took place:

> *Conductor:* Where is the dog's ticket?
> *Workman:* Oh, the second ticket is for the dog.
> *Conductor:* But he is not a workman.
> *Workman:* Oh, yes he is. I take him to look after my kit.

The problem remains unresolved.

Despite the obvious importance of interpretation, it is very difficult to give a description of the process. There are a few 'rules', but for the most part, the courts proceed case by case. Some of the following cases that state rules; others are put in simply as examples. The only area in which many 'rules' have developed is in the interpretation of exemption clauses. The interpretation of exemption clauses raises rather different issues, relating to the policing of bargains, and it will be dealt with later (p 975 ff).

■ *Lovell & Christmas Ltd v Wall*
(1911) 104 LT 85, Court of Appeal

The defendant had been a director of a company of provision merchants, which had made a substantial part of its profit from the manufacture and sale of margarine by two subsidiaries. When the company amalgamated with the plaintiff company, the defendant agreed to become a director of the plaintiff company, and agreed that for five years he would not, at any time, solely or jointly, directly or indirectly, carry on or be engaged or concerned or interested in the business of a 'provision merchant', within a certain area, save on behalf of the plaintiff company. Before five years had elapsed, the defendant ceased to be a director and threatened to carry on a business of making margarine and selling it wholesale within the prohibited area. The plaintiff company sought an injunction to restrain him.

Cozens-Hardy MR

In this action the plaintiffs claim an injunction against the defendant Charles Tomlinson Wall to restrain him from carrying on a business as a manufacturer of margarine at Liverpool. Their right to such an injunction depends upon the true construction of an agreement under seal dated the 16 June 1906, to the terms of which I must presently refer more particularly. If, however, the document does not bear the construction contended for by the plaintiffs, they claim to have it rectified so as to make it prohibit the defendant from doing the act complained of. Now, it is of the utmost importance to keep those two heads of relief perfectly distinct. The question of construction logically comes first. The question of rectification only arises if and when the plaintiffs have failed on the question of construction. If there is one principle more clearly established than another in English law it is surely this: It is for the court to construe a written document. It is irrelevant and improper to ask what the parties, prior to the execution of the instrument, intended or understood. What is the meaning of the language that they have used therein? That is the problem, and the only problem. In saying that, I do not mean to assert that no evidence can be admitted. Indeed, the contrary is clear. If a deed relates to Black Acre, you may have evidence to show what are the parcels. If a document is in a foreign language, you may have an intepreter. If it contains technical terms, an expert may explain them. If, according to the custom of a trade or the usage of the market, a word has acquired a secondary meaning, evidence may be given to prove it. A well-known instance is where in a particular trade 1,000 rabbits meant 1,200. But unless the case can be brought within some or one of these exceptions, it is the duty of the court, which is presumed to understand the English language, to construe the document according to the ordinary grammatical meaning of the words used therein, and without reference to anything which has previously passed between the parties to it. When we come to the question of rectification, wholly different considerations apply. The essence of rectification is to bring the document which was expressed and intended to be in pursuance of a prior agreement into harmony with that prior agreement.

  . . . in considering clause 13, I am entitled to receive evidence that in the term 'provision merchant' there is a secondary meaning attached to the word 'provision' so as to exclude many articles which in its primary sense would be included, such as bread, fruit, and vegetables, but to include margarine. Such evidence was rightly admitted by Eve J. Enlightened by that evidence, I ask myself whether a margarine manufacturer—as distinguished from a dealer in margarine—falls within the meaning of the words 'provision merchant', and I hold that he does not. Certain evidence was tendered to show that some people in the trade might consider or call a margarine manufacturerer a 'provision merchant'. But when it was admitted—as it was deliberately admitted by the appellant's counsel—that there is no special or secondary meaning attached to the words 'provision mechant', it seems to me to follow that the evidence tendered was properly rejected.

[The discussion of rectification is omitted; it was held that there were no grounds for rectification.]

Appeal dismissed.

NOTES

1. Many courts treat the rule that, when construing a contract, it is not proper to consider what the parties intended, as an aspect of the parol evidence rule (see p 349). The same rule applies, however, to construing the words of a purely oral contract, to which the parol evidence rule proper (if, indeed, there is such a thing) would not apply, and it is probably better to treat them as separate rules.

2. In *Prenn v Simmonds* [1971] 3 All ER 237, Lord Wilberforce claimed that English law was not 'left behind in some island of literal interpretation'. A liberal approach to the problems can be found in the judgment of Traynor J in *Pacific Gas and Electric Co v G W Thomas Drayage and Rigging Co* 69 Cal 2d 33, 69 Cal Rptr 561, 442 P 2d 641 (1968), Supreme Court of California, where he said:

Although extrinsic evidence is not admissible to add to, detract from, or vary the terms of a written contract, these terms must first be determined before it can be decided whether or not extrinsic evidence is being offered for a prohibited purpose. The fact that the terms of an instrument appear clear to a judge does not preclude the possibility that the parties chose the language of the instrument to express different terms. That possibility is not limited to contracts whose terms have acquired a particular meaning by trade usage, but exists whenever the parties' understanding of the words used may have differed from the judge's understanding.

You may like to return to this statement after you have read the remaining cases in this chapter, and consider whether it reflects English law. For an instructive extrajudicial discussion, see Goff, 'The Commercial Court and Commercial Contracts' [1984] Lloyd's MCLQ 382.

3. The leading modern discussion of the process of construction is by Lord Hoffmann in *Investors Compensation Scheme Ltd v West Bromwich Building Society* [1998] 1 All ER 98 (the facts are immaterial for this purpose). Lord Hoffmann said:

My Lords, I will say at once that I prefer the approach of the learned judge. But I think I should preface my explanation of my reasons with some general remarks about the principles by which contractual documents are nowadays construed. I do not think that the fundamental change which has overtaken this branch of the law, particularly as a result of the speeches of Lord Wilberforce in *Prenn v Simmonds* [1971] 3 All ER 237 at 240–242, [1971] 1 WLR 1381 at 1384–1386 and *Reardon Smith Line Ltd v Hansen-Tangen, Hansen-Tangen v Sanko Steamship Co* [1976] 3 All ER 570, [1976] 1 WLR 989, is always sufficiently appreciated. The result has been, subject to one important exception, to assimilate the way in which such documents are interpreted by judges to the common sense principles by which any serious utterance would be interpreted in ordinary life. Almost all the old intellectual baggage of 'legal' interpretation has been discarded. The principles may be summarised as follows.

(1) Interpretation is the ascertainment of the meaning which the document would convey to a reasonable person having all the background knowledge which would reasonably have been available to the parties in the situation in which they were at the time of the contract.

(2) The background was famously referred to by Lord Wilberforce as the 'matrix of fact', but this phrase is, if anything, an understated description of what the background may include. Subject

to the requirement that it should have been reasonably available to the parties and to the exception to be mentioned next, it includes absolutely anything which would have affected the way in which the language of the document would have been understood by a reasonable man.

(3) The law excludes from the admissible background the previous negotiations of the parties and their declarations of subjective intent. They are admissible only in an action for rectification. The law makes this distinction for reasons of practical policy and, in this respect only, legal interpretation differs from the way we would interpret utterances in ordinary life. The boundaries of this exception are in some respects unclear. But this is not the occasion on which to explore them.

(4) The meaning which a document (or any other utterance) would convey to a reasonable man is not the same thing as the meaning of its words. The meaning of words is a matter of dictionaries and grammars; the meaning of the document is what the parties using those words against the relevant background would reasonably have been understood to mean. The background may not merely enable the reasonable man to choose between the possible meanings of words which are ambiguous but even (as occasionally happens in ordinary life) to conclude that the parties must, for whatever reason, have used the wrong words or syntax (see *Mannai Investment Co Ltd v Eagle Star Life Assurance Co Ltd* [1997] 3 All ER 352, [1997] 2 WLR 945).

(5) The 'rule' that words should be given their 'natural and ordinary meaning' reflects the commonsense proposition that we do not easily accept that people have made linguistic mistakes, particularly in formal documents. On the other hand, if one would nevertheless conclude from the background that something must have gone wrong with the language, the law does not require judges to attribute to the parties an intention which they plainly could not have had. Lord Diplock made this point more vigorously when he said in *Antaios Cia Naviera SA v Salen Rederierna AB, The Antaios* [1984] 3 All ER 229 at 233, [1985] AC 191 at 201:

> '. . . if detailed semantic and syntactical analysis of words in a commercial contract is going to lead to a conclusion that flouts business common sense, it must be made to yield to business common sense.'

If one applies these principles, it seems to me that the judge must be right and, as we are dealing with one badly drafted clause which is happily no longer in use, there is little advantage in my repeating his reasons at greater length. The only remark of his which I would respectfully question is when he said that he was 'doing violence' to the natural meaning of the words. This is an over-energetic way to describe the process of interpretation. Many people, including politicians, celebrities and Mrs Malaprop, mangle meanings and syntax but nevertheless communicate tolerably clearly what they are using the words to mean. If anyone is doing violence to natural meanings, it is they rather than their listeners.

4. It is common to contrast the approach set out by Lord Hoffmann with literalism. It is quite hard to find cases that are good examples of literal interpretation of contracts causing bad results (as opposed to construction of statutes or wills). This was discussed by Lord Steyn in *Sirius International Insurance (Publ) v FAI General Insurance Ltd* [2005] 1 All ER 191 at 200:

There has been a shift from literal methods of interpretation towards a more commercial approach. In *Antaios Compania Naviera SA v Salen Rederierna AB, The Antaios* [1984] 3 All ER 229 at 233, [1985] AC 191 at 201, Lord Diplock, in an opinion concurred in by his fellow Law Lords, observed:

> '. . . if detailed semantic and syntactical analysis of a word in a commercial contract is going to lead to a conclusion that flouts business common sense, it must be made to yield to business common sense.'

In *Mannai Investment Co Ltd v Eagle Star Life Assurance Co Ltd* [1997] 3 All ER 352 at 372, [1997] AC 749 at 771, I explained the rationale of this approach as follows:

> 'In determining the meaning of the language of a commercial contract . . . the law . . . generally favours a commercially sensible construction. The reason for this approach is that a commercial

construction is more likely to give effect to the intention of the parties. Words are therefore interpreted in the way in which a reasonable commercial person would construe them. And the standard of the reasonable commercial person is hostile to technical interpretations and undue emphasis on niceties of language.'

The tendency should therefore generally speaking be against literalism. What is literalism? It will depend on the context. But an example is given in *The Works of William Paley* (1838 edn) vol III, p 60. The moral philosophy of Paley influenced thinking on contract in the nineteenth century. The example is as follows. The tyrant Temures promised the garrison of Sebastia that no blood would be shed if they surrendered to him. They surrendered. He shed no blood. He buried them all alive. This is literalism. If possible it should be resisted in the interpretative process. This approach was affirmed by the decisions of the House in the *Mannai Investment* case [1997] 3 All ER 352 at 376, [1997] AC 749 at 775 per Lord Hoffmann . . .

5. It is usual to say that, in construing a contract, one must read the whole contract. Although this is certainly the general rule, there will be cases in which some parts carry more weight than others. So if one has a standard printed contract to which the parties have made handwritten or typed additions or amendments, these will usually carry greater weight because they reflect the desires of the parties in relation to the particular transaction.

In *Homburg Housimport Bv v Agrosin Private Ltd, The Starsin* [2003] UKHL 12 [2004] 1 AC 715 [2003] 2 All ER 785, one of the questions before the House of Lords was whether the bill of lading was issued by the charterers or the shipowners. There was an apparent conflict between the front of the bill, which bore a signature by the charterers' port agent on behalf of the charterer, and small print on the back, which said that the contract was with the shipowner.

Lord Bingham said:

When construing a commercial document in the ordinary way the task of the court is to ascertain and give effect to the intentions of the contracting parties. Here, the task is to ascertain who, on one side, the contracting party was. But a similar approach is appropriate. Mr Milligan urged that the House should not seize on a single canon of construction and give it effect to the exclusion of all others. I am sure that warning is salutary. But there are a number of rules, some of very long standing, which give valuable guidance.

First is the rule to which Lord Halsbury alluded in *Glynn v Margetson & Co* [1893] AC 351 at 359, [1891–4] All ER Rep 693 at 698 'that a business sense will be given to business documents'. The business sense is that which businessmen, in the course of their ordinary dealings, would give the document. It is likely to be a reasonably straightforward sense since, as Lord Mansfield famously observed (*Hamilton v Mendes* (1761) 2 Burr 1198 at 1214, 97 ER 787 at 795):

'The daily negotiations and property of merchants ought not to depend upon subtleties and niceties; but upon rules, easily learned and easily retained, because they are the dictates of common sense, drawn from the truth of the case.'

In the present case, the suggestion that CPS contracted jointly on its own behalf and on behalf of the shipowner loses credibility when one notes that this possibility, although not objectionable in legal principle, first occurred to a member of the Court of Appeal during argument: [2001] 1 All ER (Comm) 455 at 75.

Secondly, it is common sense that greater weight should attach to terms which the particular contracting parties have chosen to include in the contract than to pre-printed terms probably devised to cover very many situations to which the particular contracting parties have never addressed their minds. It is unnecessary to quote the classical statement of this rule by Lord Ellenborough in *Robertson v French* (1803) 4 East 130 at 136, 102 ER 779 at 782, cited with approval by Lord Halsbury in *Glynn v Margetson & Co* [1893] AC 351 at 358, [1891–4] All ER Rep 693 at 697 and by Scrutton LJ in *L Sutro & Co and Heilbut, Symons & Co* [1917] 2 KB 348 at 361–362.

Thirdly, it has long been recognised by very distinguished commercial judges that to seek perfect consistency and economy of draftsmanship in a complex form of contract which has evolved over many years is to pursue a chimera: see, for example, *Simond v Boydell* (1779) 1 Dougl 268, 99 ER 175; *James Nelson & Sons Ltd v Nelson Line (Liverpool) Ltd* [1908] AC 16 at 20–21; *Hillas & Co Ltd v Arcos Ltd* (1932) 43 Ll L Rep 359 at 367; *Chandris v Isbrandtsen-Moller Co Inc* [1950] 1 All ER 768 at 772–773, [1951] 1 KB 240 at 245. The court must of course construe the whole instrument before it in its factual context, and cannot ignore the terms of the contract. But it must seek to give effect to the contract as intended, so as not to frustrate the reasonable expectations of businessmen. If an obviously inappropriate form is used, its language must be adapted to apply to the particular case: *The Okehampton* [1913] P 173 at 180 per Hamilton LJ.

Fourthly:

> 'In all mercantile transactions the great object should be certainty: and therefore, it is of more consequence that a rule should be certain, than whether the rule is established one way or the other. Because speculators in trade then know what ground to go upon.' (See *Vallejo v Wheeler* (1774) 1 Cowp 143 at 153, [1558–1774] All ER Rep 411 at 416.)

This observation is, I suggest, particularly pertinent where the issue is one which, like that now under consideration, has been the subject of repeated litigation over the years in cases which have included *The Berkshire* [1974] 1 Lloyd's Rep 185; *The Venezuela* [1980] 1 Lloyd's Rep 393; *The Rewia* [1991] 2 Lloyd's Rep 325; *MB Pyramid Sound MV v Briese Schiffahrts GmbH, The Ines* [1995] 2 Lloyd's Rep 144; *Sunrise Maritime Inc v Uvisco Ltd, The Hector* [1998] 2 Lloyd's Rep 287; and *Fetim BV v Oceanspeed Shipping Ltd, The Flecha* [1999] 1 Lloyd's Rep 612. In his accomplished extempore judgment in the last of these cases, on a form of bill and on facts indistinguishable from the present, Moore-Bick J concluded that the contract of carriage was made with the owners of the vessel and not with CPS, a decision which Colman J declined to follow in the present case.

Lord Hoffmann said:

How is this conflict to be resolved? The interpretation of a legal document involves ascertaining what meaning it would convey to a reasonable person having all the background knowledge which is reasonably available to the person or class of persons to whom the document is addressed. A written contract is addressed to the parties; a public document like a statute is addressed to the public at large; a patent specification is addressed to persons skilled in the relevant art, and so on.

To whom is a bill of lading addressed? It evidences a contract of carriage but it is also a document of title, drafted with a view to being transferred to third parties either absolutely or by way of security for advances to finance the underlying transaction. It is common general knowledge that such advances are frequently made by letter of credit and that the bill of lading is ordinarily one of the documents which must be presented to the bank before payment can be obtained. The reasonable reader of the bill of lading will therefore know that it is addressed not only to the shipper and consignee named on the bill but to a potentially wide class of third parties including banks which have issued letters of credit.

Since a bill of lading is a legal document, the merchant or banker to whom it is addressed will know that on some questions of interpretation he will need to consult a lawyer. But he will also expect to be able to find out certain essential things for himself. These will include the identity of the carrier. The normal bill of lading recognises this distinction by having some of its terms written or printed on the front, where the businessman or banker can readily find them without a lawyer at his elbow, and the mass of other clauses printed at the back. Of course there will be cases in which the information provided on the front will be too obscure to provide the businessman or banker with the information he expects. In such a case, he may have to ask his lawyer to see whether the question can be elucidated by plunging into the small print at the back, or, if he is a banker offered the bill of lading pursuant to a letter of credit, he may simply reject it on the ground that he cannot be expected to puzzle out the answer by reference to other parts of the document. On the other hand, if the information is clearly stated on the front, the reasonable merchant or banker would go no further. The banker, for example, will accept the bill of lading when tendered against a letter of credit as having been issued by the named carrier without examining the terms on the back.

As it is common general knowledge that a bill of lading is addressed to merchants and bankers as well as lawyers, the meaning which it would be given by such persons will usually also determine the meaning it would be given by any other reasonable person, including the court. The reasonable reader would not think that the bill of lading could have been intended to mean one thing to the merchant or banker and something different to the lawyer or judge.

6.   In some trades and industries, standard contracts are produced that are repeatedly used by many of the players in the game. Books are written, which discuss the meaning of clauses in such contacts, and substantial bodies of case law are built up. Building contracts and contracts for the carriage of goods by sea are important examples: in such cases, the contract must usually have the same meaning irrespective of the identity of the contracting parties.

This was clearly stated by Lord Millett in *AIB Group (UK) plc v Martin* [2002] 1 All ER 353 at 355:

My Lords, your Lordships are concerned with the application of an interpretation clause contained in a standard form. Both features are significant. A standard form is designed for use in a wide variety of different circumstances. It is not context-specific. Its value would be much diminished if it could not be relied upon as having the same meaning on all occasions. Accordingly the relevance of the factual background of a particular case to its interpretation is necessarily limited. The danger, of course, is that a standard form may be employed in circumstances for which it was not designed. Unless the context in a particular case shows that this has happened, however, the interpretation of the form ought not to be affected by the factual background.

7.   Even in the USA there are differing views as to the desirability of allowing the parties to show that words in a contract were not intended to have their normal meaning. In *Trident Center v Connecticut General Life Insurance Co* 847 F 2d 564 (US Court of Appeals, Ninth Circuit, 1988), Kozinski J held that, under California law as established in *Pacific Gas*, even if the words were quite clear, he had to remand the case to enable the plaintiff to give extrinsic evidence as to the intentions of the parties in drafting the contract, but he said:

Under *Pacific Gas*, it matters not how clearly a contract is written, nor how completely it is integrated, nor how carefully it is negotiated, nor how squarely it addresses the issue before the court: the contract cannot be rendered impervious to attack by parol evidence....

Pacific Gas casts a long shadow of uncertainty over all transactions negotiated and executed under the law of California. As this case illustrates, even when the transaction is very sizeable, even if it involves only sophisticated parties, even if it was negotiated with the aid of counsel, even if it results in contract language that is devoid of ambiguity, costly and protracted litigation cannot be avoided if one party has a strong enough motive for challenging the contract. While this rule creates much business for lawyers and an occasional windfall to some clients, it leads only to frustration and delay for most litigants and clogs already overburdened courts.

8.   In *Prenn v Simmonds*, it was argued that, when a word in a contract is vague or ambiguous, the courts should interpret it in the light of prior negotiations. The House of Lords rejected this. Lord Wilberforce said (at 239–241):

In order for the agreement...to be understood, it must be placed in its context. The time has long passed when agreements, even those under seal, were isolated from the matrix of facts in which they were set and interpreted purely on internal linguistic considerations. There is no need to appeal here to any modern, anti-literal, tendencies, for Lord Blackburn's well-known judgment in *River Wear Comrs v Adamson* provides ample warrant for a liberal approach. We must, as he said, enquire beyond the language and see what the circumstances were with reference to which the words were used, and the object, appearing from those circumstances, which the person using them had in view.

Counsel . . . however, contended for even greater extension of the court's interpretative power. They argued that later authorities have gone further and allow prior negotiations to be looked at in aid of the construction of a written document. In my opinion, they did not make good their contention . . . .

The reason for not admitting evidence of these exchanges is not a technical one or even mainly one of convenience (although the attempt to admit it did greatly prolong the case and add to its expense). It is simply that such evidence is unhelpful. By the nature of things, where negotiations are difficult, the parties' positions, with each passing letter, are changing and until the final agreement, although converging, still divergent. It is only the final document which records a consensus. If the previous documents use different expressions, how does construction of those expressions, itself a doubtful process, help on the construction of the contractual words? If the same expressions are used, nothing is gained by looking back; indeed, something may be lost since the relevant surrounding circumstances may be different. And at this stage there is no consensus of the parties to appeal to. It may be said that previous documents may be looked at to explain the aims of the parties. In a limited sense this is true; the commercial, or business object, of the transaction, objectively ascertained, may be a surrounding fact . . . . And if it can be shown that one interpretation completely frustrates that object, to the extent of rendering the contract futile, that may be a strong argument for an alternative interpretation, if that can reasonably be found. But beyond that it may be difficult to go; it may be a matter of degree, or of judgment, how far one interpretation, or another, gives effect to a common intention; the parties, indeed, may be pursuing that intention with differing emphasis, and hoping to achieve it to an extent which may differ, and in different ways. The words used may, and often do, represent a formula which means different things to each side, yet may be accepted because that is the only way to get 'agreement' and in the hope that disputes will not arise. The only course then can be to try to ascertain the 'natural' meaning. Far more, and indeed totally, dangerous is it to admit evidence of one party's objective—even if this is known to the other party. However strongly pursued this may be, the other party may only be willing to give it partial recognition, and in a world of give and take, men often have to be satisfied with less than they want. So, again, it would be a matter of speculation how far the common intention was that the particular objective should be realised.

In my opinion, then, evidence of negotiations, or of the parties' intentions, and a fortiori of Dr Simmonds's intentions, ought not to be received, and evidence should be restricted to evidence of the factual background known to the parties at or before the date of the contract, including evidence of the 'genesis' and objectively the 'aim' of the transaction . . . .

9. In *Prenn v Simmonds*, Wilberforce says that the parties may adopt a formula that they realise means different things to each side because that is the only way to get 'agreement'. In *Henry Boot & Sons Ltd v LCC* [1959] 1 All ER 77, the question was whether a 'rise-and-fall' clause in a building contract, allowing for an adjustment in the price if the 'rates of wages' changed, covered an increase in the amount of 'holiday credits' payable to the contractor's workmen. ('Holiday credits' were sums set aside by employers for each employee and which could be drawn out as a lump sum when the employee went on holiday.) The parties had corresponded on the point before entering the contract, the employer maintaining that holiday credits were not within the clause and the contractor maintaining that they were. The dispute was not resolved. In the Court of Appeal, Lord Somervell said of the employers' letter:

The letter is on the face of it saying: 'This is what we say these words mean'; I think that the contractor was entitled to reply: 'We do not agree with that; we accept your contract, and let the court decide whether you are right, or we are'.

The court held that 'rates of wages' did include holiday credits. This decision was reversed on appeal to the House of Lords [1959] 3 All ER 636, but Lord Somervell's statement on the effect of the pre-contractual discussions was approved. Presumably, if the court found that the phrase adopted was hopelessly ambiguous, it would have either to ignore it as redundant (cf *Nicolene Ltd v Simmonds)* or hold the whole contract void for uncertainty (cf *Scammel v Ouston*, see p 261, and *Raffles v Wichelhaus,* see p 301.)

10.   What if, during negotiations, the parties have clearly settled on one particular meaning of a word, although that meaning is not stated in the contract? See the next case.

■ *The Karen Oltmann*

[1976] 2 Lloyd's Rep 708

The owners of the *Karen Oltmann* let her on a timecharter to the charterers 'for a period of 2 years 14 days more or less'. Clause 26 of the charter provided that:

Charterers to have the option to redeliver the vessel after 12 months trading subject to giving three months' notice.

After the vessel had been in the charterers' service for 19 months, the charterers (on 30 July 1971) gave three months' notice of their intention to redeliver the vessel. The owners protested on the ground that 'after 12 months trading' meant 'on the expiry of 12 months trading', so that notice should have been given about nine months after the vessel had entered the charterers' service; they pleaded an estoppel to the effect that, in a telex sent before the conclusion of the contract, the charterers had represented that 'after 12 months trading':

... involved that the charter would be a period of two years with an option in favour of [the charterers] to keep the vessel for twelve months only instead of the full two years.

The owners sought a declaration that the charterers were not entitled to give notice under cl 26 after 19 months.

Kerr J

... The first question which arose at this point was whether this plea and the submissions founded on it entitled the Court to look at the exchange of telex messages. In my view they do. Take *Prenn v Simmonds*, as an example. The issue in that case was whether the reference to 'profits' in the contract meant the profits of the holding company only or the consolidated profits of the whole group. If in the course of the negotiations one party had made anything in the nature of a representation to the other to the effect that references to 'profits' were to be taken in one of these senses and not in the other, and the other party had thereupon negotiated on this basis, then extrinsic evidence to establish this representation would in my view clearly be admissible. Similarly, if it had been contended that the parties had conducted their negotiations on an agreed basis that the word 'profits' was used in one sense only, although in the contract it was capable of having two senses, and that the contract had been executed on this basis, then I do not think that the Court would be precluded by authority from admitting extrinsic evidence to see whether or not this agreed basis could be established. Both these situations would be a long way from the attempts made in *Prenn v Simmonds* and *Arrale v Costain*, to adduce extrinsic evidence to try to persuade the Court that one interpretation of the contract was in all the circumstances to be preferred to the other.

I think that in such cases the principle can be stated as follows. If a contract contains words which, in their context, are fairly capable of bearing more than one meaning, and if it is alleged that the parties have in effect negotiated on an agreed basis that the words bore only one of the two possible meanings, then it is permissible for the Court to examine the extrinsic evidence relied upon to see whether the parties have in fact used the words in question in one sense only, so that they have in effect given their own dictionary meaning to the words as the result of their common intention. Such cases would not support a claim for rectification of the contract, because the choice of words in the contract would not result from any mistake. The words used in the contract would ex hypothesi reflect the meaning which both parties intended.

In the present case, after some argument about these principles and the limits of the parole evidence rule, I decided to look at the pleaded telex messages, though Counsel for the charterers rightly submitted that I could only do so de bene esse. He was right about this, because if they did not support the owners' arguments on the lines discussed above, then I would have to put them out of mind and fall back on my construction as a matter of first impression.

I therefore turn to consider the pleaded telex exchanges. Although I do not consider that they support the allegation of an estoppel, I think that they clearly show that the words 'after 12 months trading' were used in an agreed sense. From start to finish the owners wanted maximum duration and certainty whereas the charterers wanted minimum duration and maximum flexibility. It is clear that both parties throughout used the word 'after' in the sense of 'on the expiry of' and not 'at any time after the expiry of'.

Judgment for the owners.

NOTES

1. Suppose a buyer contacts a seller saying he needs 'feveroles'. The seller asks what these are and the buyer says he thinks they are just horsebeans. The seller says he thinks so too, and they enter a contract for 'feveroles'. The seller supplies horsebeans. The buyer then discovers that the technical meaning of 'feverole' is a particular kind of bean different to those supplied. Is the seller in breach?

2. Would your answer differ if there had been no discussion between the parties about the meaning of 'feverole', but it can be proved from each party's internal memoranda that neither realised that 'feverole' had this narrower meaning?

In *Proforce Recruit Ltd v The Rugby Group Ltd* [2005] EWCA 698, the claimants ran an employment and recruitment agency in Rugby. On 31 July 2001, the parties made a written agreement under which the claimants would, for a two-year term, provide specific cleaning services. The contract contained a provision that the claimants would have 'preferred supplier status'. This expression was not defined in the contract. The claimants argued that the agreement gave them rights in relation to the provision of non-cleaning personnel, and between July and November 2001, they appear to have enjoyed such rights. They wished to lead evidence as to what was said during the negotiations; Field J said that such evidence was inadmissible but the Court of Appeal disagreed.

Arden LJ said:

This appeal concerns the question whether the appellants ('ProForce') has a real prospect of success as regards its claim for damages for the failure by the respondent ('Rugby') to give it the opportunity to tender for the supply of personnel before engaging contractors through other agencies. As this appeal arises at an interim stage in these proceedings, this court must proceed on the basis that the ProForce's allegations can be proved at trial.

ProForce's case is that the obligation to give that preferential opportunity arises from a service cleaning contract made on 31 July 2001 between ProForce and Rugby. The critical provision in that agreement is as follows:-

'This contract will be a minimum two-year period and will be re-negotiable at the end of that period. During that period ProForce will hold preferred supplier status.'

The principal issue is as to the meaning of the words 'preferred supplier status'. A major plank in ProForce's case is that the meaning of those words for which it contends was in fact the meaning which the parties placed on those words when they were negotiating the agreement. That evidence is disputed. In addition, the effect of clause 9.2 has to be considered. Clause 9.2 provides:

> "This Agreement together with any other document expressed to be incorporated herein constitutes the entire [Contract] between the parties and supersedes all prior representations, agreements, negotiations or understandings whether oral or in writing."

The evidence as to the meaning of the term "preferred supplier status" is set out in the witness statement of Mr Allen Bloor[. A]t paragraph 13 of his witness statement, Mr Bloor states:

> 'Discussions continued in that vein until about May [2001] when Emma Gough offered ProForce 'preferred supplier status' explaining that we would have the opportunity to supply all labour and additional plant at the Rugby site.'

The judge held that Mr Bloor's evidence as to what Miss Gough said in the course of discussions leading to the agreement constituted negotiations and was therefore inadmissible on the interpretation of the agreement (judgment paragraph 21). He further held that, if he was wrong about this, Mr Bloor's evidence was excluded by clause 9.2 of the agreement (judgment, para 22).

. . .

In this case, the parties have used a very unusual combination of words ('preferred supplier status'). These words are undefined and they are not introduced or accompanied by any words of explanation. In those circumstances it is in my judgment reasonably arguable that on their true interpretation those words bear the meaning that the parties in common gave them in their communications leading up to the signing of the agreement. In admitting evidence as to those communications, the court would be hearing that evidence not with a view to taking the parties' subjective intent into account for the purposes of interpretation (a purpose precluded by the principles laid down by Lord Hoffmann in the *ICS* case) but for the purpose of identifying the meaning that the parties in effect incorporated into their agreement in circumstances where the court was satisfied that on their true interpretation the terms of the agreement were to have this effect.

In my judgment, there is a sufficient prospect of success in distinguishing this situation from the usual situation in which, in the course of negotiations, the parties agree a matter which is to become binding on them (only) when a written agreement has been drawn up and signed. In that situation, evidence of the parties' negotiations would in principle not be admissible: see per Lord Hoffmann in the *ICS* case and per Lord Wilberforce in *Prenn v Simmonds* [1971] 1 WLR 1382 at 1314 to 1315. This court cannot, however, at this stage determine the points which I have identified as reasonably arguable because they depend upon the true interpretation of the agreement, and the court cannot determine the true interpretation of the agreement without making findings of fact as to the circumstances surrounding its execution. That cannot be done on a summary application.

Evidence as to negotiations between the parties to a contract leading up to the making of that contract may be admissible for the purposes of interpretation in wider circumstances than I have indicated above, but it is unnecessary for me to go further than those circumstances for the purpose of this appeal. Lord Hoffmann recognises in the *ICS* case that the boundaries of the rule excluding evidence of pre-contractual negotiations on questions of interpretation is unclear. Moreover, Lord Nicholls has argued in the passage cited by Mummery LJ in para 34 of his judgment and elsewhere, that the rule should be relaxed. The exclusion of pre-contractual negotiations is not on the face of it consistent with the general principle that a contract should be interpreted in the light of its context. Nor, on the face of it, is the application of a meaning which is not that which the parties themselves gave to a term consistent with the general approach of contract law, which is to respect party autonomy. The results may be anomalous. If the judge's ruling in this case expresses the general position in law, the result would be that the parties' meaning would be adopted if they defined the term in their written contract but not if they only did so only in the course of pre-contractual negotiations. Moreover, in that latter event, the meaning given to the term by the court would prevail, and (if the court's meaning is one which is different from that on which both parties in fact proceeded) a party would be able to avoid its contractual obligations deriving from the parties' meaning. That may be the law but, if it is, it is not, on the face of it, an attractive result. There are considerations that may go the other way. Lord Hoffmann's holding is that the exclusionary rule is based on reasons of practical policy (see para (3) of the passage cited above from the *ICS* case). That policy would have to be carefully considered if evidence of pre-contractual negotiations is to be admitted in evidence in interpretation questions in the future on any wider basis than the law presently permits. In that sense there may be parallels to be drawn with the use of legislative history in the interpretation of statutes. In addition, careful consideration may have to be given to the aims to be achieved by contractual interpretation and the precise extent to which the law requires an objective interpretation, as set out in para. (1) of the passage cited above from the *ICS* case. It may be appropriate to consider a number of international instruments applying to contracts. It is sufficient to take two examples. The UNIDROIT Principles of International Commercial Contracts give primacy to the common intention of the parties and on questions of interpretation requires regard to be had to all the circumstances, including the pre-contractual negotiations of the parties (article 4.3). The UN Convention on Contracts for the International Sale of Goods (1980) provides that a party's intention is in certain circumstances relevant, and in determining that intention regard is to be had to all relevant circumstances, including preliminary negotiations. Consideration may also have to be given to the question whether some matters outside the text of a contract should be given less weight where (for example) the contract is one to which different persons adhere at different points in time, such as a company's constitution, than in the case of 'one-off' contracts between two persons, as in this case.

(The reference to Lord Nicholls is to a lecture he gave to the Chancery Bar, which was published in (2005) 121 LQR 577 and in which he suggested that the ban on evidence of negotiations might be ripe for relaxation.)

■ *Amalgamated Investment & Property Co Ltd v Texas Commerce International Bank Ltd*
[1981] 3 All ER 577, Court of Appeal

The plaintiff, AIP, had arranged with the defendant bank that the bank should make a loan to a subsidiary of the plaintiffs, ANPP, based in the Bahamas, the loan being guaranteed by the plaintiffs. To avoid Bahamian restrictions on foreign banks trading in the Bahamas, the defendants purchased an 'off-the-shelf' subsidiary company, Portsoken, and lent the money to it; Portsoken then lent the money to the plaintiffs' subsidiary. The guarantee read as follows:

The Guarantor will pay to you on demand all moneys which now are or shall at any time or times hereafter be due or owing or payable to you on any account whatsoever by [ANPP] . . .

In the course of dealings between them, both plaintiff and defendant treated the guarantee as covering the loan by Portsoken to the plaintiff's subsidiary. However, after the plaintiffs got into financial difficulties and were ordered to be compulsorily wound up, the liquidator sought a declaration that the plaintiff was under no liability under the guarantee in respect of the outstanding amount of the loan. Robert Goff J held that, on its wording, the guarantee did not apply to the loan made, but that, as both parties had treated the guarantee as covering the loan and had acted on that assumption, they were estopped 'by convention' from denying that the guarantee covered the loan. In the Court of Appeal, it was held that the judge was wrong on the question of construction: viewed in its factual circumstances, the proper meaning of the guaranee was that it covered loans originating from the defendant bank even if made through a subsidiary.

Eveleigh LJ

. . . Ignoring the existence of the guarantee form, in my opinion the agreement reached between the parties orally and evidenced by or contained in (it matters not) the correspondence was clearly to the effect that Amalgamated would be responsible for seeing that the bank was repaid. The subsequent negotiations between Amalgamated and the bank after the money was made available on 31st December 1970 and up to 1976 in which Amalgamated clearly recognised this obligation provides admissible and strong evidence of this. Are we driven to arrive at a different conclusion because of the existence of the standard guarantee form containing the name of ANPP?

It might have been possible to have approached this case on the basis that the form was not introduced into the final contract. In that case the position would be as I have stated above. However, this case has been argued on the basis that it formed part of the final agreement. In that case the undertaking by the guarantor must be construed in the general setting of the transaction. It was a document that had been used by the bank to secure its own position in relation to the facilities it was affording. I think that the reference to 'all monies . . . payable to you . . . by the Principal' (ie ANPP) can only refer to the facility which the bank was affording. In the context of the whole transaction, it can in my opinion have no other meaning. The fact that the money could be legally demanded in the first instance by Portsoken does not rob it of its character of moneys payable to the bank, and the fact that Portsoken would first receive it and hand it over to the bank does not rob it of the description of moneys payable by ANPP. To deny this result by an analytical examination of the different legal liabilities engendered by the form which the transaction ultimately took is to deprive the words of the guarantee of a wider meaning which they are fully capable of bearing. It runs counter to all principles of construction to give the words a meaning that would defeat the clear intention of the parties as revealed by the rest of the relevant evidence of the agreement. I too am of the opinion that Amalgamated's claim fails on this ground . . . .

■ *Schuler (L) AG v Wickman Machine Tool Sales Ltd*

[1973] 2 All ER 39, House of Lords

This case involved the allegedly wrongful termination of a distributorship agreement. Whether the termination was wrongful depended on the meaning of the word 'condition' in cl 7 of the agreement (a full account of the case will be found at p 599). During argument, the question was raised whether, in deciding the meaning of the word, the court was entitled to take into account the conduct of the parties subsequent to the making of the contract. **Lord Wilberforce** said:

. . . In my opinion, subsequent actions ought not to have been taken into account. The general rule is that extrinsic evidence is not admissible for the construction of a written contract; the parties' intentions must be ascertained, on legal principles of construction, from the words they have used. It is one and the same principle which excludes evidence of statements, or actions, during negotiations, at the time of the contract, or subsequent to the contract, any of which to the lay mind might at first sight seem to be proper to receive. As to statements during negotiations this House has affirmed the rule of exclusion in *Prenn v Simmonds*, and as to subsequent actions (unless evidencing a new agreement or as the basis of an estoppel) in *James Miller and Partners Ltd v Whitworth Street Estates (Manchester) Ltd*.

There are of course exceptions. I attempt no exhaustive list of them. In the case of ancient documents, contemporaneous or subsequent action may be adduced in order to explain words whose contemporary meaning may have become obscure. And evidence may be admitted of surrounding circumstances or in order to explain technical expressions or to identify the subject-matter of an agreement: or (an overlapping exception) to resolve a latent ambiguity. But ambiguity in this context is not to be equated with difficulty of construction, even difficulty to a point where judicial opinion as to meaning has differed. This is, I venture to think, elementary law. On this test there is certainly no ambiguity here . . . .

In my opinion, therefore, the subsequent action relied on should have been left entirely out of account: in saying this I must not be taken to agree that the particular actions relied on are of any assistance whatever towards one or other construction of the contract. Indeed if one were to pursue the matter, the facts of the present case would be found to illustrate, rather vividly, the dangers inherent in entertaining this class of evidence at all.

NOTE

Subsequent conduct may not be taken into account in interpreting the meaning of the words of a contract. It may, however, amount to a *variation* of the terms or give rise to a waiver or an estoppel: see Chapter 32.

CHAPTER FIFTEEN

IMPLIED TERMS

Terms may be implied in a contract as a matter of custom, by statute or by common law. In this chapter, we will consider these three sources of implied terms, before looking briefly at three types of contract—contracts for the supply of goods, contracts for services and contracts of employment—to see how the term that the law implies give a characteristic shape to each one.

I TERMS IMPLIED BY CUSTOM

■ *Hutton v Warren* (1836)

1 M & W 466, Exchequer

By a lease under seal, dated 2 January 1811, the plaintiff became tenant to the defendant's father, the rector of the parish, of a farm consisting of the parsonage house and glebe land for a term of six years, if the lessor continued as incumbent, from the following Lady Day. The lease contained a stipulation that the plaintiff should 'consume three-fourths of the hay and straw on the farm spread the manure arising therefrom, and have such of it as was not so spread for the use of the landlord on receiving a reasonable price for it'. In October 1832, his father, having resigned the living, the defendant became landlord, and in October 1833, served a notice to quit on the plaintiff, who had continued to occupy the farm, paying the same rent. Having first sown the arable land, the plaintiff quitted the farm on Lady Day 1834. In an action in which the plaintiff, as outgoing tenant, claimed compensation for the sowing of the arable land, it was proved that, by the custom of the country, the tenant of a farm, cultivating it according to the course of good husbandry, was entitled, on quitting, to receive from the landlord a reasonable allowance for seeds and labour bestowed on the arable land in the last year of the tenancy; the plaintiff was bound to leave the manure for the landlord if he would purchase it. The defendant contended that the stipulation in the lease excluded the custom of the country as to allowances.

The judgment of the court (Parke and Alderson BB) was delivered by Parke B.

Parke B

...The second question requires some consideration. The custom of the country as to cultivation and the term of quitting with respect to allowances for seed and labour, is clearly applicable to a tenancy from year to year, and, therefore, if this custom was, by implication, imported into the lease, the plaintiff and defendant were bound by it after the lease expired. We are of opinion that this custom was, by implication, imported into the lease. It has long been settled that, in commercial transactions, extrinsic evidence of custom and usage is admissible to annex incidents to written contracts in matters with respect to which they are silent. The same rule has also been applied to contracts in other transactions of life, in which known usages have been established and parties did not mean to express in writing the whole of the contract by which they intended to be bound, but a contract with reference to those known usages. Whether such a relaxation of the strictness of the common law was wisely applied where formal instruments have been entered into, and particularly leases under the seal, may well be doubted; but the contrary has been established by such authority, and the relations between landlord and tenant have been so long regulated on the supposition that all customary obligations not altered by the contract, are to remain in force, that it is too late to pursue a contrary course; and it would be productive of much inconvenience if this practice were now to be disturbed....

We are therefore of opinion that the plaintiff is entitled to recover....

NOTES

1. For the legal definition of a custom, see p 341.

2. A customary term will not be implied if this would be inconsistent with the express terms of the agreement, but it is possible to rely on custom to show that a particular express term has a meaning different to its normal one. See the reference in *Lovell & Christmas Ltd v Wall* (p 402) to the case in which '1,000 rabbits' was held to mean by custom, '1,200 rabbits': *Smith v Wilson* (1832) 3 B & Ad 728, 1 LJKB 194.

II. TERMS IMPLIED BY STATUTE

A contract for the sale of goods is an example of a contract in which the main implied terms are statutory, as the result of the codification of the common law by the Sale of Goods Act 1893. The 1893 Act has been replaced by the Sale of Goods Act 1979, which in turn was amended by the Sale and Supply of Goods Act 1994, but the basic structure and many of the sections remain unchanged.

For example, under the Sale of Goods Act 1979 (as amended), the following terms will normally be implied: that the seller has the right to sell the goods (s 12); that the goods will correspond to their description (s 13); that, if the seller sells in the course of a business, the goods will be of satisfactory quality and, subject to certain conditions, will be reasonably fit for the particular purpose for which the buyer requires them (s 14); that, if the goods were sold by sample, the goods will correspond to the sample (s 15). We will consider these implied terms in more detail later (pp 425 ff).

Curiously, not all of the obligations that the Act imposes are described as implied terms. It seems to make little practical difference, but frequently the Act simply lays down rules that are to apply to the point in question. The rules on who bears the risk of accidental damage to or destruction of the goods (s 20; see p 462) and on the time for delivery when no date has been agreed (s 29(3), see p 439) are examples.

Determining what terms are implied in any particular sale of goods contract is not, however, a simple matter of reading the statute. Firstly, a complex body of case law has developed around some sections of the Act. Secondly, the Sale of Goods Act adopts the same theoretical basis as the common law, that implied terms rest on the 'intentions' of the parties. To a large extent, this is a fiction: it would be idle to pretend that each seller intends, or reasonably appears to intend, the elaborate implied undertakings set out in the Act. But the parties' 'intentions' are still relevant under the Sale of Goods Act in that the terms will not be implied if the contract specifically excludes them or if the terms would be inappropriate in the circumstances of the contract. The Act provides:

Section 55: Exclusion of implied terms

(1) Where a right, duty or liability would arise under a contract for the sale of goods by implication of law, it may (subject to the Unfair Contract Terms Act 1977) be negatived or varied by express agreement, or by the course of dealing between the parties, or by such usage as binds both parties to the contract.

For an example of the normal implied term being excluded by the circumstances, see p 440.

However, the words 'subject to the Unfair Contract Terms Act 1977' are critical. In 1973, the Supply of Goods (Implied Terms) Act, the relevant sections of which were later incorporated into Unfair Contract Terms Act 1977, radically changed the law on sale of goods by making the regime of implied terms in ss 12–15 at least partly mandatory. The details of the Act will be considered in Section 8, but broadly speaking, the Act distinguished between consumer sales (in which a business sells goods of a type ordinarily supplied for private use or consumption to a private purchaser) and non-consumer sales (eg sales by one business to another). In consumer sales, the seller cannot rely on a term of the contract to exclude or restrict its obligations under ss 12–15 of the Sale of Goods Act. In non-consumer sales, the terms implied by ss 13–15 may be excluded or restricted, but only in so far as the clause excluding or restricting them was a fair and reasonable one (see now UCTA 1977, ss 6 and 11(1)).

Even in a consumer sale, the intentions of the parties still seem to have some residual relevance. It is probably the case (although the matter is debated—see pp 996–997) that the usual implied terms will not apply in the first place (and thus the ban on excluding them by a contract term will not bite) if the circumstances of the contract show that, quite apart from the contract term, the normal implied term would not be appropriate. For instance, while a car dealer selling a used car cannot exclude its obligation to deliver a car of satisfactory wuality, is it possible for it to sell an old banger 'as is' or 'for parts' without any obligation as to quality? (See further pp 438–439.)

III. TERMS IMPLIED AT COMMON LAW

There is considerable debate about the conditions that must exist before the court may imply a term adding to or qualifying the express terms of the contract.

■ *The Moorcock*

[1886–90] All ER Rep 530, Court of Appeal

The plaintiffs had agreed with the defendant wharfingers that the plaintiffs' vessel should discharge and load cargo at the defendants' wharf, where both parties knew that the vessel would take the ground at low tide. The vessel was damaged by the unevenness of the river bed, which was not within the defendants' control but the state of which they could have ascertained. The plaintiffs brought an action for damages.

Lord Esher MR held the defendants liable.

Bowen LJ

The defendants in this case are the owners of a wharf and jetty attached in the river Thames, and the only use to which it is put is holding out to ships facilities for loading and unloading alongside of it. There is only one berth where the ships can lie, and that is close alongside the jetty. The question which arises in this case is whether, when a contract is made to let the use of this jetty to a ship which can only use it, as is known to both parties, by her taking the ground, there is any implied warranty on the part of the wharfingers, and if so what is the extent of that warranty.

An implied warranty, or as it is called a covenant in law, as distinguished from an express contract or express warranty, really is in every instance founded on the presumed intention of the parties and upon reason. It is the implication which the law draws from what must obviously have been the intention of the parties, an implication which the law draws with the object of giving efficacy to the transaction and preventing such a failure of consideration as cannot have been within the contemplation of either of the parties. I believe that if one were to take all the instances, which are many, of implied warranties and covenants in law which occur in the earlier cases which deal with real property, passing through the instances which relate to the warranties of title and of quality, and the cases of executory contracts of sale and other classes of implied warranties like the implied authority of an agent to make contracts, it will be seen that in all these cases the law is raising an implication from the presumed intention of the parties with the object of giving to the transaction such efficacy as both parties must have intended it should have. If that is so the reasonable implication which the law draws must differ according to the circumstances of the various transactions, and in business transactions what the law desires to effect by the implication is to give such business efficacy to the transaction as must have been intended by both parties; not to impose on one side all the perils of the transaction or to emancipate one side from all the burdens, but to make each party promise in law as much, at all events, as it must have been in the contemplation of both parties that he should be responsible for.

What did each party in the present case know? because, if we are examining into their presumed intention, we must examine into their minds as to what the transaction was. Both parties knew that the jetty was let for the purpose of profit, and knew that it could only be used by the ship taking the ground and lying on the ground. They must have known that it was by grounding that she would use the jetty. They must have known, both of them, that unless the ground was safe the ship would be simply buying an opportunity of danger and buying no convenience at all, and that all consideration would fail unless the ground was safe. In fact, the business of the jetty could not be carried on unless, I do not say the ground was safe, it was supposed to be safe. The master and crew of the ship could know nothing, whereas the defendants or their servants might, by exercising reasonable care, know everything. The defendants or their servants were on the spot at high and low tide, morning and evening. They must know what had happened to the ships that had used the jetty before, and with the slightest trouble they could satisfy themselves in case of doubt whether the berth was or not safe. The ship's officers, on the other hand, had no means of verifying the state of the berth, because, for aught I know, it might be occupied by another ship at the time the *Moorcock* got there.

The question is how much of the peril or the safety of this berth is it necessary to assume in order to get the minimum of efficacy to the business consideration of the transaction which the ship consented to bear, and which the defendants took upon themselves. Supposing that the berth had been actually under the control of the defendants, they could, of course, have repaired it and made it fit for the purpose of loading and unloading. It seems to me that *Mersey Docks Trustees v Gibbs* shows that those who own a jetty, who take money for its use, and who have under their control the locus in quo, are bound to take all reasonable care to prevent danger to those using the jetty, either to make the berth good or else not to invite ships to go to the jetty, ie either to make it safe or to advise ships not to go there. But there is a distinction between that case and the present. The berth here was not under the actual control of the defendants. . . .

Applying that modification, which is a reasonable modification, to this case, it may well be said that the law will not imply that the defendants, who had not control of the place, ought to have taken reasonable care to make the berth good, but it does not follow that they are relieved from all responsibility, a responsibility which depends not merely on the control of the place, which is one element as to which the law implies a duty, but on other circumstances. The defendants are on the spot. They must know the jetty cannot be safely used unless reasonable care is taken. No one can tell whether reasonable safety has been secured except themselves, and I think that, if they let out their jetty for use, they at all events imply that they have taken reasonable care to see that the berth, which is the essential part of the use of the jetty, is safe, and, if it is not safe, and if they have not taken such reasonable care, it is their duty to warn persons with whom they have dealings that they have not done so. . . .

Fry LJ agreed.

Appeal dismissed.

NOTES

1. Since *The Moorcock*, there have been a number of judicial attempts to describe the test for implying terms. One that is often quoted is that of MacKinnon LJ in *Shirlaw v Southern Foundries (1926) Ltd* [1939] 2 KB 206, 227:

   Prima facie that which in any contract is left to be implied and need not be expressed is something so obvious that it goes without saying.

   Thus, if, while the parties were making their bargain, an officious bystander were to suggest some express provision for it in their agreement, they would testily suppress him with a common: 'Oh, of course.'

   A very similar test had earlier been suggested by Scrutton LJ in *Reigate v Union Manufacturing* Co *(Ramsbottom) Ltd* [1918] 1 KB 592, 605.

2. The 'business efficacy' test used in *The Moorcock* and MacKinnon LJ's 'so obvious that it goes without saying' test are often treated as interchangeable, but in *Mosvolds Rederi A/S v Food Corpn of India* [1986] 2 Lloyd's Rep 68, Steyn J held that a proposed implied term was not necessary to make the contract workable. However, he accepted it on the basis that reasonable men in the same circumstances would undoubtedly have assented to the term if the fact that they had not mentioned it had been drawn to their attention. If you look at the discussion of implied terms by Mason J in the High Court of Australia in *Codelfa Construction Pty Ltd v State Rail Authority of New South Wales* (1982) 149 CLR 337, you will see that he assumed that the tests are cumulative: that is, if they are different, both have to be passed.

■ *Liverpool City Council v Irwin*
[1976] 2 All ER 39, House of Lords

A local corporation was the owner of a tower block, which contained some seventy dwelling units. Access to the various units was provided by a common staircase together with two electrically operated lifts. The tenants were provided with an internal chute into which they could discharge rubbish and garbage. In July 1966, the appellants, who were husband and wife, became the tenants of a maisonette on two floors of the block. The tenancy agreement incorporated a list of obligations imposed on tenants but contained nothing concerning the obligations of the corporation. Over the course of years, the condition of the block deteriorated very badly, partly in consequence of the activities of vandals and the lack of cooperation on the part of tenants. The defects in the common parts of the block included the following: (a) continual failure of the lifts; (b) lack of proper lighting on the stairs; and (c) blockage of the rubbish chutes. In addition, the lavatory cisterns in the block had been designed and constructed so badly that they overflowed, causing damage to the property. The appellants, together with other tenants, protested against the condition of the block by refusing to pay rent to the corporation. The corporation sought an order for possession of the appellants' premises and the appellants counterclaimed against the corporation, alleging, inter alia, a breach on the part of the corporation of its implied covenant for the appellants' quiet enjoyment of the property. The trial judge granted the corporation an order for possession against the appellants, but held (a) that the corporation was under an implied covenant to keep the common parts in repair and properly lighted, (b) that the corporation had been in breach of that implied covenant together with the covenant implied under s 32(1) of the Housing Act 1961, and (c) that accordingly the appellants were entitled to £10 damages on their counterclaim. The Court of Appeal allowed an appeal by the corporation, holding, by a majority, that there was no implied covenant on the part of the corporation to repair the common parts of the block and, unanimously, that the corporation was not in breach of the covenant implied under s 32(1) of the 1961 Act. On appeal to the House of Lords, it was contended, inter alia, for the appellants, that there was an implied obligation on the corporation to keep the staircase and corridors of the block in repair and the lights in working order, and that the corporation was in breach of the obligation.

Lord Wilberforce

. . . . I consider first the appellants' claim insofar as it is based on contract. The first step must be to ascertain what the contract is. This may look elementary, even naive, but it seems to me to be the essential step and to involve, from the start, an approach different, if simpler, from that taken by the members of the Court of Appeal. We look first at documentary material. As is common with council lettings there is no formal demise or lease or tenancy agreement. There is a document headed 'Liverpool Corporation, Liverpool City Housing Department' and described as 'Conditions of Tenancy'. This contains a list of obligations on the tenant—he shall do this, he shall not do that, or he shall not do that without the corporation's consent. This is an amalgam of obligations added to from time to time, no doubt, to meet complaints, emerging situations, or problems as they appear to the council's officers. In particular there have been added special provisions relating to multi-storey flats which are supposed to make the conditions suitable to such dwellings. We may note under 'Further special notes' some obligations not to obstruct staircases and passages, and not to permit children under ten to operate any lifts. I mention these as a recognition of the existence and relevance of these facilities. At the end there is a form for signature by the tenant stating that he accepts the tenancy. On the landlords' side there is nothing, no signature, no demise, no covenant; the contract takes effect as soon as the tenants sign the form and are let into possession.

We have then a contract which is partly, but not wholly, stated in writing. In order to complete it, in particular to give it a bilateral character, it is necessary to take account of the actions of the parties and the circumstances. As actions of the parties, we must note the granting of possession by the corporation and reservation by it of the 'common parts'—stairs, lifts, chutes etc. As circumstances we must include the nature of the premises, viz a maisonette for family use on the ninth floor of a high block, one which is occupied by a large number of other tenants, all using the common parts and dependent on them, none of them having any expressed obligation to maintain or repair them.

To say that the construction of a complete contract out of these elements involves a process of 'implication' may be correct: it would be so if implication means the supplying of what is not expressed. But there are varieties of implications which the courts think fit to make and they do not necessarily involve the same process. Where there is, on the face of it, a complete, bilateral contract, the courts are sometimes willing to add terms to it, as implied terms; this is very common in mercantile contracts where there is an established usage; in that case the courts are spelling out what both parties know and would, if asked, unhesitatingly agree to be part of the bargain. In other cases, where there is an apparently complete bargain, the courts are willing to add a term on the ground that without it the contract will not work—this is the case, if not of *The Moorcock* itself on its facts, at least of the doctrine of *The Moorcock* as usually applied. This is, as was pointed out by the majority in the Court of Appeal, a strict test—though the degree of strictness seems to vary with the current legal trend, and I think that they were right not to accept it as applicable here. There is a third variety of implication, that which I think Lord Denning MR favours, or at least did favour in this case, and that is the implication of reasonable terms. But though I agree with many of his instances, which in fact fall under one or other of the preceding heads, I cannot go so far as to endorse his principle; indeed, it seems to me, with respect, to extend a long, and undesirable, way beyond sound authority.

The present case, in my opinion, represents a fourth category or, I would rather say, a fourth shade on a continuous spectrum. The court here is simply concerned to establish what the contract is, the parties not having themselves fully stated the terms. In this sense, the court is searching for what must be implied.

What then should this contract be held to be? There must first be implied a letting, ie a grant of the right of exclusive possession to the tenants. With this there must, I suppose, be implied a covenant for quiet enjoyment, as a necessary incident of the letting. The difficulty begins when we consider the common parts. We start with the fact that the demise is useless unless access is obtained by the staircase; we can add that, having regard to the height of the block, and the family nature of the dwellings, the demise would be useless without a lift service; we can continue that there being rubbish chutes built in to the structures and no other means of disposing of light rubbish there must be a right to use the chutes. The question to be answered—and it is the only question in this case—is what is to be the legal relationship between landlord and tenant as regards those matters.

There can be no doubt that there must be implied (i) an easement for the tenants and their licensees to use the stairs, (ii) a right in the nature of an easement to use the lifts and (iii) an easement to use the rubbish chutes.

But are these easements to be accompanied by any obligation on the landlord, and what obligation? There seem to be two alternatives. The first, for which the corporation contends, is for an easement coupled with no legal obligation, except such as may arise under the Occupiers' Liability Act 1957 as regards the safety of those using the facilities, and possibly such other liability as might exist under the ordinary law of tort. The alternative is for easements coupled with some obligation on the part of the landlords as regards the maintenance of the subject of them, so that they are available for use.

My Lords, in order to be able to choose between these, it is necessary to define what test is to be applied, and I do not find this difficult. In my opinion such obligation should be read into the contract as the nature of the contract itself implicitly requires, no more, no less; a test in other words of necessity. The relationship accepted by the corporation is that of landlord and tenant; the tenant accepts obligations accordingly, in relation, inter alia, to the stairs, the lifts and the chutes. All these are not just facilities, or conveniences provided at discretion; they are essentials of the tenancy without which life in the dwellings, as a tenant, is not possible. To leave the landlord free of contractual obligation as regards these matters, and subject only to administrative or political pressure, is, in my opinion, totally inconsistent with the nature of this relationship. The subject-matter of the lease (high-rise blocks) and the relationship created by the tenancy demands, of its nature, some contractual obligation on the landlord.

I do not think that this approach involves any innovation as regards the law of contract. The necessity to have regard to the inherent nature of a contract and of the relationship thereby established was stated in this House in *Lister v Romford Ice and Cold Storage Co Ltd*. That was a case between master and servant and of a search for an 'implied term'. Viscount Simonds made a clear distinction between a search for an implied term such as might be necessary to give 'business efficacy' to the particular contract and a search, based on wider considerations, for such a term as the nature of the contract might call for, or as a legal incident of this kind of contract. If the search were for the former, he said: 'I should lose myself in the attempt to formulate it with the necessary precision'. We see an echo of this in the present case, when the majority in the Court of Appeal, considering a 'business efficacy term'. ie *'Moorcock'* term, found themselves faced with five alternative terms and therefore rejected all of them. But that is not, in my opinion, the end, or indeed, the object, of the search . . . .

It remains to define the standard. My Lords, if, as I think, the test of the existence of the term is necessity the standard must surely not exceed what is necessary having regard to the circumstances. To imply an absolute obligation to repair would go beyond what is a necessary legal incident and would indeed be unreasonable. An obligation to take reasonable care to keep in reasonable repair and usability is what fits the requirements of the case. Such a definition involves—and I think rightly—recognition that the tenants themselves have their responsibilities. What it is reasonable to expect of a landlord has a clear relation to what a reasonable set of tenants should do for themselves . . . .

. . . [I]t has not been shown that there was any breach of [the corporation's] obligation . . .

Lord Cross of Chelsea

. . . When it implies a term in a contract the court is sometimes laying down a general rule that in all contracts of a certain type—sale of goods, master and servant, landlord and tenant, and so on—some provision is to be implied unless the parties have expressly excluded it. In deciding whether or not to lay down such a prima facie rule the court will naturally ask itself whether in the general run of such cases the term in question would be one which it would be reasonable to insert. Sometimes, however, there is no question of laying down any prima facie rule applicable to all cases of a defined type but what the court is being in effect asked to do is to rectify a particular—often a very detailed—contract by inserting in it a term which the parties have not expressed. Here it is not enough for the court to say that the suggested term is a reasonable one the presence of which would make the contract a better or fairer one; it must be able to say that the insertion of the term is necessary to give—as it is put— 'business efficacy' to the contract and that if its absence had been pointed out at the time both parties—assuming them to have been reasonable men—would have agreed without hesitation to its insertion. The distinction between the two types of case was pointed out by Viscount Simonds and Lord Tucker in their speeches in *Lister v Romford Ice and Cold Storage Co Ltd*, but I think that Lord Denning MR in proceeding—albeit with some trepidation—to 'kill off' Mackinnon LJ's 'officious bystander' must have overlooked it . . .

Lord Salmon, Lord Edmund-Davies and **Lord Fraser of Tullybelton** delivered speeches to the same effect.

Appeal dismissed.

NOTES

1. In *Shell UK Ltd v Lostock Garage Ltd* [1977] 1 All ER 481, 487–488, Lord Denning MR summarised the effect of *Liverpool City Council v Irwin* as follows:

    As I read the speeches, there are two broad categories of implied terms.

    (i) *The first category*
    The first category comprehends all those relationships which are of common occurrence, such as the relationship of seller and buyer, owner and hirer, master and servant, landlord and tenant, carrier by land or by sea, contractor for building works, and so forth. In all those relationships the courts have imposed obligations on one party or the other, saying they are implied terms. These obligations are not founded on the intention of the parties, actual or presumed, but on more general considerations . . . In such relationships the problem is not solved by asking: what did the parties intend? or, would they have unhesitatingly agreed to it, if asked? It is to be solved by asking; has the law already defined the obligation or the extent of it? If so, let it be followed. If not, look to see what would be reasonable in the general run of such cases (see per Lord Cross of Chelsea) and then say what the obligation shall be. The House in *Liverpool City Council v Irwin* went through that very process. They examined the existing law of landlord and tenant, in particular that relating to easements, to see if it

contained the solution to the problem; and, having found that it did not, they imposed an obligation on the landlord to use reasonable care. In these relationships the parties can exclude or modify the obligation by express words, but unless they do so, the obligation is a legal incident of the relationship which is attached by the law itself and not by reason of any implied term....

(ii) *The second category*

The second category comprehends those cases which are not within the first category. These are cases, not of common occurrence, in which from the particular circumstances a term is to be implied. In these cases the implication is based on an intention imputed to the parties from their actual circumstances: see *Luxor (Eastbourne) Ltd v Cooper* per Lord Wright. Such an imputation is only to be made when it is necessary to imply a term to give efficacy to the contract and make it a workable agreement in such manner as the parties would clearly have done if they had applied their mind to the contingency which has arisen. These are the 'officious bystander' type of case: see *Lister v Romford Ice and Cold Storage Co* per Lord Tucker. In such cases a term is not to be implied on the ground that it would be reasonable, but only when it is necessary and can be formulated with a sufficient degree of precision. This was the test applied by the majority of this court in *Liverpool City Council v Irwin;* and they were emphatically upheld by the House on this point; see per Lord Cross of Chelsea and Lord Edmund-Davies.

There is this point to be noted about *Liverpool City Council v Irwin.* In this court the argument was only about an implication in the second category. In the House of Lords that argument was not pursued. It was only the first category.

2. Those terms that are normally implied in all contracts of a particular type are sometimes called 'terms implied in law', while those implied on a 'one-off' basis in order to give business efficacy to the individual contract are called 'terms implied in fact'.

3. Within the first category, it is fairly clear that the 'officious bystander' test does not have to be satisfied; yet some judges, such as Lord Wilberforce, insist that, in the absence of previous authority, a term will only be implied on the basis of necessity; reasonableness is not sufficient. Is this anything more than judicial reluctance to abandon the pretence that judges will not make a contract for the parties? Doesn't it overlook the point that a decision *not* to imply a maintenance obligation is just as much an allocation of responsibility as the decision to do so?

4. Into which category would you put *The Moorcock?*

5. As Denning suggests, the courts are reluctant to imply 'one-off' terms, and will do so only if both parties would clearly have agreed to the term and the term is capable of precise formulation. An illustration is *Trollope and Colls Ltd v North West Metropolitan Regional Hospital Board* [1973] 2 All ER 260. A building contract, which was to be completed in three phases, provided that phase I was to be completed by 30 April 1969; phase III was to be commenced six months after the completion of phase I, and was to be completed by 30 April 1972. Phase I was completed 59 weeks late, leaving only 16 months in which to build phase III by the stated date. The respondent board was unable to nominate subcontractors who could perform the work that was to be done by nominated subcontractors within the remaining time, and the appellants claimed that they were released from the contract. The respondents argued that a term should be implied that the completion date for phase III should be put back. The House of Lords held that no term could be implied. Two factors were particularly important in the decision.

The first was that the terms of the contract were clear and unambiguous. The possibility that phase I might be late was easily apparent, but the parties had chosen a fixed completion date for phase III, which was independent of the starting point for that phase: it might even be the case that this had been done deliberately to limit the contractor's obligations if phase I were so late that subcontractors could not be nominated for phase III. A second consideration was that, if a term were to be implied to cover the overrun of phase I, it was difficult to say what that term should be. For instance, should the completion date for phase III be set back by the whole period of delay, or only by that part of the delay for which the contractor was not responsible?

■ *Reid v Rush & Tompkins Group plc*

[1989] 3 All ER 228, Court of Appeal

The plaintiff was offered employment by the defendants as a quarry foreman on a project in Ethiopia. In the course of his employment, the plaintiff, while driving along a bush road, was seriously injured when his vehicle collided with a lorry being driven in the opposite direction by an unidentified person. The sole cause of the accident was the negligence of the other driver, but since the driver's identity was unknown, the plaintiff was unable to recover against him and, furthermore, there was no compulsory third-party motor insurance and no scheme to cover uninsured third parties in Ethiopia. The plaintiff brought an action against the defendants alleging that they were in breach of their duty of care as employers in failing either to insure the plaintiff against being injured in a traffic accident as the result of the negligence of a third party or to advise him to obtain such cover for himself. The master struck out the claim on the ground that it disclosed no reasonable cause of action and, on appeal, the judge upheld that decision. The plaintiff appealed to the Court of Appeal.

On the question of whether the plaintiff had a claim in contract:

Ralph Gibson LJ

The implied term to provide insurance cover

. . . I can see no basis in the facts pleaded for holding that the defendants gave an implied undertaking to insure the plaintiff against the risk of uncompensated injury caused to him, while acting in the course of his employment, by third party drivers in Ethiopia. Such a term could not be implied by law under the test of necessity, as applicable to all such contracts of employment; nor could it be implied as a term which the parties must have agreed: see *Liverpool City Council v Irwin* [above, p 369] and per Lloyd LJ in *National Bank of Greece SA v Pinios Shipping Co No 1, The Maira* [1989] 1 All ER 213 at 218. As to treating such a term as implied by law, the arguments in favour of a social policy, which would require employers to provide some level of personal accident insurance for the benefit of men and women working overseas and for their dependants, are obvious but there appears to me to be no way in which the court could 'embody this policy in the law without the assistance of the legislature': see Lord Bridge in *D & F Estates Ltd v Church Comrs for England* [1989] AC 177 at 210. Further, as to treating such a term as one which the parties must have agreed, it seems to me unarguable that the parties would have agreed that any of the various obligations as to the provision of personal accident insurance, as put forward by the plaintiff, was a part of the contract. The written contract contained, as I have said, a number of detailed terms dealing with the economic welfare of the plaintiff, such as the provision of retirement benefits and of medical services, and it is impossible to suppose that the defendants would have acknowledged as obviously included within the contract additional terms with reference to provision by them of personal accident insurance. As to an implied term to the effect that the defendants would inform the plaintiff as to the existence of the special risk and advise the plaintiff to obtain for himself suitable personal accident insurance, I will deal with that part of the case when I came to examine the plaintiff's case based on an implied assumption of responsible by the Partners Ltd defendants on the principle contained in *Hedley Byrne & Co Ltd v Heller & Partners Ltd.*

The plaintiff's case on implied term

The next submission, based on the two cases of *Tai Hing Cotton Mill Ltd v Liu Chong Hing Bank Ltd* and *Greater Nottingham Co-op Society Ltd v Cementation Piling and Foundations Ltd* [1989] QB 71, was that, since there was between the parties the contract of employment, the plaintiff can only recover damages for economic loss if a term in that contract so provides and not in tort. It is necessary first to determine whether there was any implied term in the contract of employment to the effect that the defendants would give to the plaintiff all necessary advice relating to the special risk and would advise the plaintiff that he should himself obtain appropriate insurance cover. The alleged implied assumption of responsibility gave rise, it is alleged, to a similar duty.

In my judgment, it is impossible to hold on the facts pleaded that an implied term arose on the particular relationship of this plaintiff to these defendants as his employers. The only facts are the offer and acceptance of the employment and the defendants' knowledge both of the circumstances in which the plaintiff would in Ethiopia be exposed to the special risk and of the plaintiff's ignorance of that risk. If the parties had been asked what the position was with reference to the risk of the plaintiff suffering injury in the course of his employment by the negligence of another driver, for whom the defendants were not responsible, and from whom the plaintiff could recover no damages, it is impossible to be confident, on the facts pleaded, that either side would have answered that the defendants had undertaken a duty to deal specifically with the matter, whether by advice or otherwise. Both parties must have expected and intended that the plaintiff and the defendants would respectively perform the express terms set out in the contract and would comply with any other obligations arising out of their mutual relationship as master and servant. As in *Lister v Romford Ice and Cold Storage Co Ltd* [1957] AC 555, according to the view of the majority (Viscount Simonds, Lord Morton and Lord Tucker), the term on which the plaintiff in this case claims to rely cannot, in my judgment, be implied as a term agreed between the two individuals and, if it is to be implied at all, must be implied by law. That would mean that it is to be implied in any contract of employment where the master engages the servant to work abroad in a country where, in doing his work, the servant will face a special risk of the nature relied on in this case and the servant is, to the knowledge of the master, ignorant of that risk. It is clear, I think, that a new term can be implied by law into contracts of employment. *Lister v Romford Ice and Cold Storage Co Ltd* is an example of differing opinions held by judges whether a new term should on the facts be held to arise by law; and the majority in the House of Lords gave reasons to explain why on the evidence in that case the term then contended for could not be accepted. It is, however, impossible, in my judgment, to imply in this case a term as a matter of law in the form contended for, namely a specific duty to advise the plaintiff to obtain specific insurance cover. Such a duty seems to me inappropriate for incorporation by law into all contracts of employment in the circumstances alleged. The length of time during which the servant will work abroad and the nature of his work may vary greatly between one job and another and hence the extent to which the servant would be exposed to the special risk. Further, having regard to the many different ways in which a servant working abroad may run the risk of uncompensated injury caused by the wrongdoing of a third party, apart from a traffic accident, it seems to me impossible to formulate the detailed terms in which the law could incorporate into the general relationship of master and servant a contractual obligation to the effect necessary to cover the plaintiff's claim. I have considered whether the implied term could be limited to the risk from injuries in a traffic accident, but then the question is raised whether the obligation should arise on any difference between the total protection provided in this country by compulsory third party insurance and the MIB scheme, on the one hand, and such protection as exists in the foreign country, on the other hand, or only on the total absence of the protection provided in this country. I have also considered whether the term could be expressed as follows: an employer who takes a person into his employment in this country for work to be done in a foreign country shall take reasonable care to provide sufficient information and warning to that servant with reference to any risk of suffering uncompensated injury in the course of his employment in the foreign country, caused through the fault of a third party, which risk would not be suffered in this country and of which a reasonable person would require to be informed before accepting such employment. For my part I am unable to accept that the court could properly incorporate such a term by law into contracts of employment. It seems to me that it would require of employers, many of whom may have no such resources of advice or experience as may be available to these defendants, and who may employ only one or two servants, to discover much information about foreign legal and social systems in order to decide whether such a term requires action on their part. The usefulness of the principle contended for seems to me, in social terms, to be plain enough; but to incorporate the duty by law into contracts of employment would, in my view, require, if it were to work fairly, exemptions and limitation which can only properly be achieved by legislation.

Neill and **May LJ** agreed.

On the question of a cause of action in tort, the Court held that the plaintiff's claim did not disclose one. In the words of Ralph Gibson LJ:

[O]n the facts alleged, it is not open to this court to extend the duty of care owed by these defendants to the plaintiff by imposing a duty in tort which, if I am right, is not contained in any express or implied term of the contract.

Appeal dismissed.

NOTES

1.   This case demonstrates the courts' unwillingness to bypass the law of contract by imposing supplementary duties of care in tort.

2.   What were the principal reasons for refusing to find an implied term that the employer would (i) procure insurance cover or (ii) warn the employee of the risk?

3.   Is the argument that the employer's responsibilities are best left to legislation really relevant? The case raises a question that has to be answered one way or the other: either the employer has an obligation or it doesn't. Does saying that there is a duty usurp the function of Parliament any more than saying that there is not? (Some might argue that the court was deliberately leaving the law in such a bad state that Parliament would have no option but to intervene! But this hardly seems plausible.) Does the case reveal anything about the court's attitude to employer's obligations and to self-reliance by employees?

4.   Is this a case in which the facts might be retold in rather different terms? The 'relational background' might be that employees who have to travel abroad for extended periods rely on their employers for advice, because the employers 'have done it all before'; that the detailed provisions of the contract on other matters might suggest that matters not mentioned were 'not a problem'. You may like to compare the 'reading' of the facts of the *Walton Stores* case in an article extracted on p 794.

5.   You may also find it interesting to contrast the *Reid* case with *Scally v Southern Health and Social Services Board* [1991] 4 All ER 563. The plaintiff medical practitioners had to join a statutory superannuation scheme. An amendment to the scheme was introduced, which allowed members, to purchase 'added years' in order to qualify for the maximum pension. The DHSS issued circulars to the regional health boards requiring them to inform members, but the plaintiffs were never told and missed the chance to exercise their right to buy the added years. The House of Lords held the defendant Health Board liable. Lord Bridge said (at 569–572):

The contractual claim
The central question then is whether the employing boards owed any such duty. Leaving aside the claim based on breach of statutory duty, which turns on the true construction of the 1965 Act, it seems to me that the plaintiffs' common law claims can only succeed if the duty allegedly owed to

them by their employers arose out of the contract of employment. If a duty of the kind in question was not inherent in the contractual relationship, I do not see how it could possibly be derived from the tort of negligence. The observations of Lord Scarman in delivering the advice of the Judicial Committee of the Privy Council in *Tai Hing Cotton Mill Ltd v Liu Chong Hing Bank Ltd* [above, p 36] are here very much in point . . . .

. . . There are three possible views of the legal consequences arising from this situation. The first is that it could be properly be left to individual employees, knowing that they were compulsory contributors to a superannuation scheme, to make enquiries and ascertain the details of the scheme for themselves. In the light of the judge's findings, I think this view can be confidently rejected. There was no reason whatever why young doctors embarking on a career in the health services should appreciate the necessity to enquire into the details of the superannuation scheme to which they were contributors in order to be in a position to enjoy its benefits. The second view is that the law provided no means of ensuring that the intended beneficiaries of the opportunity to buy added years became aware of it, so that it would be a matter of chance whether or not, in relation to any individual employee, the relevant provision of the 1974 regulations achieved its intended purpose. I find this view so unattractive that I would accept it only if driven to the conclusion that there was no other legally tenable alternative. The third view is that there was an obligation on either the employing board or the department to take reasonable steps to bring the relevant provision to the notice of employees in time to avail themselves of the opportunity to buy added years if they so decided.

It was argued for the boards that the responsibility, if there was one, for bringing the matter to the attention of employees lay with the department rather than the boards . . . . it seems to me beyond question that the legal obligation, if there was one, to notify the plaintiffs of their rights in relation to the purchase of added years rested in each case on the board, not on the department.

Will the law then imply a term in the contract of employment imposing such an obligation on the employer? The implication cannot, of course, be justified as necessary to give business efficacy to the contract of employment as a whole. I think there is force in the submission that, since the employee's entitlement to enhance his pension rights by the purchase of added years is of no effect unless he is aware of it and since he cannot be expected to become aware of it unless it is drawn to his attention, it is necessary to imply an obligation on the employer to bring it to his attention to render efficacious the very benefit which the contractual right to purchase added years was intended to confer. But this may be stretching the doctrine of implication for the sake of business efficacy beyond its proper reach. A clear distinction is drawn in the speeches of Viscount Simonds in *Lister v Romford Ice and Cold Storage Co Ltd* [1957] 1 All ER 125 at 132–133, [1957] AC 555 at 576 and Lord Wilberforce in *Liverpool City Council v Irwin* [1976] 2 All ER 39 at 44, [1977] AC 239 at 255 between the search for an implied term necessary to give business efficacy to a particular contract and the search, based on wider considerations, for a term which the law will imply as a necessary incident of a definable category of contractual relationship. If any implication is appropriate here, it is, I think, of this latter type. Carswell J accepted the submission that any formulation of an implied term of this kind which would be effective to sustain the plaintiffs' claims in this case must necessarily be too wide in its ambit to be acceptable as of general application. I believe however that this difficulty is surmounted if the category of contractual relationship in which the implication will arise is defined with sufficient precision. I would define it as the relationship of employer and employee where the following circumstances obtain: (1) the terms of the contract of employment have not been negotiated with the individual employee but result from negotiation with a representative body or are otherwise incorporated by reference; (2) a particular term of the contract makes available to the employee a valuable right contingent upon action being taken by him to avail himself of its benefit; (3) the employee cannot, in all the circumstances, reasonably be expected to be aware of the term unless it is drawn to his attention. I fully appreciate that the criterion to justify an implication of this kind is necessity, not reasonableness. But I take the view that it is not merely reasonable, but necessary, in the circumstances postulated, to imply an obligation on the employer to take reasonable steps to bring the term of the contract in question to the employee's attention, so that he may be in a position to enjoy its benefit. Accordingly I would hold that there was an implied term in each of the plaintiffs' contracts of employment of which the board were in each case in breach.

In *Equitable Life Assurance Society v Hyman* [2000] 3 All ER 961, the appellant issued large numbers of with-profits pension policies. Many of the terms of such policies are, in effect, determined by the tax concessions granted to policies approved by the Inland Revenue. The policy, holder pays contributions, which are invested by the pension provider. On the retirement date, the policy, holder has a fund, part of which he can take in cash and part of which he can use to purchase an annuity. Annuities can usually be bought either from the pension provider or on the open market.

The distinguishing feature of the present policies was that the appellant guaranteed the minimum annuity. At the time the pensions were taken out the guaranteed rate was well below the market rate, but in recent years, annuity rates have fallen as a result of lower interest rates and greater longevity, and by 1993, the guaranteed rate was above the market rate.

The other relevant feature of the policies was that there were bonuses declared by the directors, some each year as a result of the success of the society's investment policy and some (terminal bonuses) at the end of the policy period. The amount of the bonuses were within the directors' discretion.

The directors decided to pay lower terminal bonuses to those policy holders who took advantage of the guaranteed annuities. No express terms forbad this, but the House of Lords implied a term that did so. Lord Steyn said:

It is necessary to distinguish between the processes of interpretation and implication. The purpose of interpretation is to assign to the language of the text the most appropriate meaning which the words can legitimately bear. The language of art 65(1) contains no relevant express restriction on the powers of the directors. It is impossible to assign to the language of art 65(1) by construction a restriction precluding the directors from overriding GARs. To this extent I would uphold the submissions made on behalf of the Society. The critical question is whether a relevant restriction may be implied by art 65(1). It is certainly not a case in which a term can be implied by law in the sense of incidents impliedly annexed to particular forms of contracts. Such standardised implied terms operate as general default rules: see *Scally v Southern Health and Social Services Board (British Medical Association, third party)* [1991] 4 All ER 563, [1992] 1 AC 294. If a term is to be implied, it could only be a term implied from the language of art 65 read in its particular commercial setting. Such implied terms operate as ad hoc gap fillers. In *Luxor (Eastbourne) Ltd v Cooper* [1941] 1 All ER 33 at 52, [1941] AC 108 at 137 Lord Wright explained this distinction as follows:

'The expression "implied term" is used in different senses. Sometimes it denotes some term which does not depend on the actual intention of the parties but on a rule of law, such as the terms, warranties or conditions which, if not expressly excluded, the law imports, as, for instance, under the Sale of Goods Act and the Marine Insurance Act... However, a case like the present is different, because what it is sought to imply is based on an intention imputed to the parties from their actual circumstances.'

It is only an individualised term of the second kind which can arguably arise in the present case. Such a term may be imputed to parties: it is not critically dependent on proof of an actual intention of the parties. The process "is one of construction of the agreement as a whole in its commercial setting": *South Australia Asset Management Corpn v York Montague Ltd, United Bank of Kuwait plc v Prudential Property Services Ltd, Nykredit Mortgage Bank plc v Edward Erdman Group Ltd* [1996] 3 All ER 365 at 371, [1997] AC 191 at 212, per Lord Hoffmann. This principle is sparingly and cautiously used and may never be employed to imply a term in conflict with the express terms of the text. The legal test for the implication of such a term is a standard of strict necessity. This is how I must approach the question whether a term is to be implied into art 65(1) which precludes the directors from adopting a principle which has the effect of overriding or undermining GARs.

The enquiry is entirely constructional in nature: proceeding from the express terms of art 65, viewed against an objective setting, the question is whether the implication is strictly necessary. My Lords, as counsel for the GAR policyholders observed, final bonuses are not bounty. They are a significant part of the consideration for the premiums paid. And the directors' discretions as to the amount and distribution of bonuses are conferred for the benefit of policyholders. In this context the self-evident commercial object of the inclusion of guaranteed rates in the policy is to protect the policyholder against a fall in market annuity rates by ensuring that if the fall occurs he will be better off than he would have been with market rates. The choice is given to the GAR policyholder and not to the Society. It cannot be seriously doubted that the provision for guaranteed annuity rates was a good selling point in the marketing by the Society of the GAR policies. It is also obvious that it would have been a significant attraction for purchasers of GAR policies. The Society points out that no special charge was made for the inclusion in the policy of GAR provisions. So be it. This factor does not alter the reasonable expectations of the parties. The supposition of the parties must be presumed to have been that the directors would not exercise their discretion in conflict with contractual rights. These are the circumstances in which the directors of the Society resolved upon a differential policy which was designed to deprive the relevant guarantees of any substantial value. In my judgment an implication precluding the use of the directors' discretion in this way is strictly necessary. The implication is essential to give effect to the reasonable expectations of the parties. The stringent test applicable to the implication is satisfied.

This is a very important and instructive case. The contract appeared to give the directors an unfettered discretion as to the level of bonuses. There were, of course, commercial pressures on the directors. Insurance companies use the level of past bonuses as a sales tool to encourage the belief that future bonuses will be at the same (high) level. This can encourage insurers to realise profits in order to keep the level of bonuses up, but it can have dangers because next year the market may go down. Prudent insurers have usually, therefore, kept something in hand so as to try to keep bonuses at a steady level. These investment decisions are clearly outside the area of judicial oversight, but the case shows that the discretion is nevertheless not unfettered. In a system that recognised a role for good faith, the result might be explained in this way: see Peden *Good Faith in the Performance of Contracts*, para 7.6.

IV. CONTRACTS FOR THE SALE OR SUPPLY OF GOODS

In this and the next two subsections, we look at the implied terms in three common types of contract. The aim is not to give a complete account of them, but to give some idea of the general nature of the implied obligations under each one.

A contract of sale is one under which the seller transfers, or agrees to transfer, the ownership of goods to the buyer in exchange for money (SGA 1979, s 2(1)). The Sale of Goods Act applies only to such transactions. There are several other types of contract under which goods are supplied. The implied terms in contracts of hire (in which the owner transfers possession but not ownership), contracts of barter (in which goods are exchanged for goods), and contracts for work and materials (in which the element of work is predominant but goods are also supplied, eg a building contract) are governed by the Supply of Goods and Services Act 1982. The implied terms about title and quality in hire-purchase contracts (see p 1078) are governed by Supply of Goods (Implied Terms) Act 1973.

1. Implied terms as to title

■ Sale of Goods Act 1979, s 12: Implied terms about title, etc

Section 12: Implied terms about title, etc

(1) In a contract of sale, other than one to which subsection (3) below applies, there is an implied term on the part of the seller that in the case of a sale he has a right to sell the goods, and in the case of an agreement to sell he will have such a right at the time when the property is to pass.

(2) In a contract of sale, other than one to which subsection (3) below applies, there is also an implied term that
   (a) the goods are free, and will remain free until the time when the property is to pass, from any charge or encumbrance not disclosed or known to the buyer before the contract is made, and
   (b) the buyer will enjoy quiet possession of the goods except so far as it may be disturbed by the owner or other person entitled to the benefit of any charge or encumbrance so disclosed or known.

(3) This subsection applies to a contract of sale in the case of which there appears from the contract or is to be inferred from its circumstances an intention that the seller should transfer only such title as he or a third person may have.

(4) In a contract to which subsection (3) above applies there is an implied term that all charges or encumbrances known to the seller and not known to the buyer have been disclosed to the buyer before the contract is made.

(5) In a contract to which subsection (3) above applies there is also an implied term that none of the following will disturb the buyer's quiet possession of the goods, namely
   (a) the seller;
   (b) in a case where the parties to the contract that the seller should transfer only such title as a third person may have, that person;
   (c) anyone claiming through or under the seller or that third person otherwise than under a charge or encumbrance disclosed or known to the buyer before the contracts is made....

(5A) As regards England and Wales and Northern Ireland, the term implied by subsection (1) above is a condition and the terms implied by subsections (2), (4) and (5) above are warranties.

(Section 8 of the Supply of Goods (Implied Terms) Act provides very similar terms for hire purchase. Section 2 of Supply of Goods and Services Act 1982 provides similar terms for other contracts under which the ownership of goods is to be transferred.)

NOTES

1. It is an implied '*condition*' that the seller has the right to sell but only an implied *warranty* that the goods are free from encumbrances, etc. Here, the word 'condition' is being used in its technical sense, meaning not only 'a term of the contract' (as in the phrase 'conditions of sale') but a term that is so important that, if it is not complied with, the other party may refuse to perform its side of the contract. Equally, 'warranty' here has a technical meaning: a term of the contract that is not sufficiently important that breach of it will justify a refusal to perform; the remedy for a breach of warranty will only be damages. This should be contrasted with the use of 'warranty' to mean an undertaking relating to the quality of goods sold (as in the *Dick Bentley* case. See further pp 565–566 ff). If the seller has no right to sell the goods, the buyer might be dispossessed by the true owner at the time, and so needs the right to reject the goods and recover the money paid. If the goods are found to be encumbered (eg they are subject to a charge in favour of a third party), damages should be a sufficient remedy, because the damages can be used to pay off the charge.

2. Although many goods are bought for the purpose of use for a limited period of time, the seller's obligation to pass title is regarded as so essential in a contract of sale that if the buyer has not received title, the whole of the price is recoverable (on the grounds of 'total failure of consideration': see p 742) even though the buyer has had some use from the goods: *Rowland v Divall* [1923] 2 KB 500. In that case, in which the seller had in good faith sold the buyer a car that later turned out to have been stolen, Atkin LJ (at 506) said:

It seems to me that in this case there has been a total failure of consideration, that is to say that the buyer has not got any part for which he paid the purchase money. He paid the money in order that he might get the property, and he has not got it....

In *Butterworth v Kingsway Motors Ltd* [1954] 1 WLR 1286, the buyer was allowed to recover the whole price even after having used the car for a considerable period and even though, shortly after he had demanded his money, the sellers had obtained the title. Pearson J described the plaintiff's case as somewhat without merit, and several proposals were made to require the buyer to pay for the use that he or she had had (see Law Reform Committee, Twelfth Report (Cmnd 2958, 1966), para 36 ff; Law Commission Working Paper no 65, part IV and Working Paper No 85, paras 6.11–6.21). Ultimately, however, the Law Commission recommended that the law be left unchanged. The benefit to the buyer would be hard to value and, in any event, it was gained at the expense of the true owner rather than that of the seller (see p 43).

3. In a contract of hire purchase, the ultimate object of the buyer is to become owner, so the same rule applies. In a contract of simple hire, the hirer does not normally care about the ownership of the thing provided that the firm that hires it out has the right to do so, so that the hirer can be sure of getting uninterrupted use. Supply of Goods and Services Act 1982 provides:

7.(1) In a contract for the hire of goods there is an implied condition on the part of the bailor that in the case of a bailment he has a right to transfer possession of the goods by way of hire for the period of bailment and in the case of an agreement to bail he will have such a right at the time of bailment.

(A bailment is the relationship created when goods possessed by one person, the 'bailor', are temporarily in the possession of another, the 'bailee'.)

2. Implied terms as to description and quality of goods

■ *Sale of Goods Act* 1979

Section 13: Sale by description

(1) Where there is a contract for the sale of goods by description, there is an implied term that the goods will correspond with the description.

(1A) As regards England and Wales and Northern Ireland, the term implied by subsection

(1) above is a condition.

(2) If the sale is by sample as well as by description it is not sufficient that the bulk of the goods corresponds with the sample if the goods do not also correspond with the description.

(3) A sale of goods is not prevented from being a sale by description by reason only that, being exposed for sale or hire, they are selected by the buyer....

Section 14: Implied terms about quality or fitness

(1) Except as provided by this section and section 15 below and subject to any other enactment, there is no implied term about the quality or fitness for any particular purpose of goods supplied under a contract of sale.

(2) Where the seller sells goods in the course of a business, there is an implied term that the goods supplied under the contract are of satisfactory quality.

   (2A) For the purposes of this Act, goods are of satisfactory quality if they meet the standard that a reasonable person would regard as satisfactory, taking account of any description of the goods, the price (if relevant) and all the other relevant circumstances.

   (2B) For the purposes of this Act, the quality of goods includes their state and condition and the following (among others) are in appropriate cases aspects of the quality of goods—

      (a) fitness for all the purposes for which goods of the kind in question are commonly supplied,

      (b) appearance and finish,

      (c) freedom from minor defects,

      (d) safety, and

      (e) durability.

   (2C) The term implied by subsection (2) above does not extend to any matter making the quality of goods unsatisfactory—

      (a) which is specifically drawn to the buyer's attention before the contract is made,

      (b) where the buyer examines the goods before the contract is made, which that examination ought to reveal, or

      (c) in the case of a contract for sale by sample, which would have been apparent on a reasonable examination of the sample.

(3) Where the seller sells goods in the course of a business and the buyer, expressly or by implication, makes known—

      (a) to the seller, or

      (b) where the purchase price or part of it is payable by instalments and the goods were previously sold by a credit-broker to the seller, to that credit-broker,

any particular purpose for which the goods are being bought, there is an implied term that the goods supplied under the contract are reasonably fit for that purpose, whether or not that is a purpose for which such goods are commonly supplied, except where the circumstances show that the buyer does not rely, or that it is unreasonable for him to rely, on the skill or judgment of the seller or credit-broker.

(4) An implied term about quality or fitness for a particular purpose may be annexed to a contract of sale by usage.

(5) The preceding provisions of this section apply to a sale by a person who in the course of a business is acting as agent for another as they apply to a sale by a principal in the course of a business, except where that other is not selling in the course of a business and either the buyer knows that fact or reasonable steps are taken to bring it to the notice of the buyer before the contract is made.

(6) As regards England and Wales and Northern Ireland, the terms implied by subsections (2) and (3) above are conditions.

...

Section 15: Sale by sample

(1) A contract of sale is a contract for sale by sample where there is an express or implied term to that effect in the contract.

(2) In the case of a contract for sale by sample there is an implied term—

      (a) that the bulk will correspond with the sample in quality;

      (b) (repealed);

      (c) that the goods will be free from any defect, making their quality unsatisfactory, which would not be apparent on reasonable examination of the sample.

(3) As regards England and Wales and Northern Ireland, the term implied by subsection (2) above is a condition.

NOTES

1. Similar terms are implied into hire-purchase contracts by Supply of Goods (Implied Terms) Act 1973, ss 9–11, and into other supply of goods contracts by Supply of Goods and Services Act 1982, ss 3–5.

2. The requirement under s 13 that goods correspond with their description is treated strictly, and apparently trifling non-conformities had been held to entitle the buyer to reject the goods even when the buyer did not appear to be prejudiced by them and was rejecting the goods for other reasons. For example, in *Arcos Ltd v E A Ronaasen & Son* [1933] AC 470, a buyer was permitted to reject barrel staves that did not correspond to the contractual description of half-an-inch thick, even though they were only one-16th of an inch out and were perfectly suitable for the buyer's purpose of making barrels. The probable reason for this strict approach is that, in many of the contracts that have come before the courts on this topic, the goods were being bought for resale and the exact description might be important to some other buyer further down the 'chain'. A non-consumer buyer may no longer reject goods because of breach of s 13 if the breach is so slight that rejection would be unreasonable: see p 598.

3. On the other hand, not every statement about the goods amounts to the 'description' of them within s 13: the description for this purpose only covers those characteristics of the goods that 'identify' what is being sold. Thus if the parties are negotiating for the sale of two specific ships and the seller states their capacity is 460 tons, but this is not a characteristic in which the buyer appeared particularly interested, the statement does not form part of the description and is only a misrepresentation: *T & J Harrison v Knowles and Foster* [1918] 1 KB 608. It would be different if the buyer had asked for ships of that capacity.

4. Even words that in one sense identify the goods do not form part of the description if their purpose is merely to indicate which goods are being sold. In *Reardon Smith Line Ltd v Hansen-Tangen* [1976] 1 WLR 989, a charterparty described the ship to be chartered as 'called Yard no 354 at Osaka', Osaka being the name of the yard responsible for building it; in fact, the building was subcontracted to another yard, Oshima, because the Osaka yard could not handle a tankship of that size. Both parties knew this but the buyers argued that the ship did not correspond with the description. It was held that the words were merely labelling which vessel was involved and there was no breach of s 13: the words either did not form part of the description or were not promissory at all. (If you have difficulty following this, think of this example: if Furmston were to sell his cottage, 'known as Denning's Orchard' to Beale, would Beale be able to get out of the contract on the grounds that the cottage had never belonged to anyone called Denning and didn't have a single fruit tree in the grounds?)

5. The vast majority of sales are by description: either the seller states what it is that it is selling or the buyer states what it is that it wants to buy. Sometimes a specific item may be sold without the seller taking any responsibility as to what the item is. The example that springs immediately to mind is if you were to buy some unidentifiable object in a junk shop, but the same principle may operate even at higher levels of the art market. In *Harlingdon & Leinster Enterprises Ltd v Christopher Hull Fine Art Ltd* [1990] 1 All ER 737, a picture thought to be by the German expressionist Gabrielle Münter, and listed in the

invoice as such, was later found to be a forgery. The seller had made it clear that he knew nothing about the painting and was not expert on expressionist works, whereas the buyers were. By a majority, the Court of Appeal upheld the trial judge's decision that the sale was not one by description. The buyers had relied on their own judgment that the painting was authentic.

6.   The implied term that the goods should correspond with their description applies to all sales, but the implied terms as to quality under s 14(2) and fitness for purpose under s 14(3) apply only if the seller sells in the course of a business. Thus if you buy a 1961 Triumph Herald from a private seller and later discover that it is actually the front and back ends of two cars of different years welded together, you may have a remedy for breach of s 13 *(Beale v Taylor* [1967] 1 WLR 1193), but if the engine blows up after five miles, you won't have any remedy, unless you can prove misrepresentation or breach of an express warranty.

7.   The seller is not responsible for defects drawn to the buyer's attention nor for defects that the buyer's examination ought to have revealed. What if the buyer doesn't bother to examine the goods and so doesn't spot the defect?

8.   The Sale of Goods Act 1893 did not refer to 'satisfactory' quality but to 'merchantable quality'. There was no statutory definition of this before 1973. The courts had developed two tests of whether goods were merchantable. One, perhaps most suited to cases where the goods are of generally lower quality than expected, is whether the goods would be commercially resaleable under the description applied to them to buyers who knew all the facts, without a substantial reduction in price. A statutory definition was first introduced by Supply of Goods (Implied Terms) Act 1973. The requirement was changed to 'satisfactory quality' by Sale and Supply of Goods Act 1994.

9.   By virtue of s 2B(a), the goods must be fit for *all* of the purposes for which such goods are commonly supplied. This was inserted by Sale and Supply of Goods Act 1994 after the decision of the Court of Appeal in *Aswan Engineering Establishment Co v Lupdine Ltd* [1987] 1 WLR 1. The Court had held that

... the goods did not have to be suitable for every purpose for which goods were normally bought under that description. It was sufficient that they were suitable for one or more of such purposes without abatement of price since, if they were, they were commercially saleable under that description. (at p 12)

10.   To save space and complexity, we have not reproduced s 14(2D)–(2F), which were inserted by S.I. 2002/3045, reg. 3(2) in order to implement article 2(2)(d) and (4) of the EC Directive on certain aspects of the sale of consumer goods and associated guarantees (1999/44/EC of 25 May 1999, [1999]OJ L171/12–16.) Section 14 (2D) provides that 'if the buyer deals as consumer ... the relevant circumstances mentioned in subsection (2A) include any public statements on the specific characteristics of the goods made about them by the seller, the producer or his representative, particularly in advertising or on labelling'. S 14(2E) provides the seller with various defences, for example if he could not have been aware of the public statement.

11.   If the buyer wishes to be sure that the goods will be suitable for its particular purpose, which is not one for which such goods are commonly supplied, it must make the purpose known to the seller and rely on the seller's judgment. Unless it is unreasonable for the buyer to rely on the seller, for instance because the seller makes it clear that there may be problems in using the goods for that purpose, the seller is then responsible. It seems

that this is still the law, but now that, under s 14(2B), the goods must be fit for all of the common purposes, the rule is much less significant because the buyer will have to rely on s 14(3) much less frequently.

12. If the buyer indicates a purpose in very general terms, and reasonably relies on the seller, the latter is responsible for the goods being fit for all normal applications within the general purpose indicated. So if the buyer indicates that herring meal is required for making into animal foodstuffs (as opposed to fertiliser) without specifying which animals are to be given it, the meal must be fit for feeding to all animals to which it might normally be fed: *Ashington Piggeries Ltd v Christopher Hill Ltd* [1972] AC 441. (In that case, the food was for mink. This might now be a common purpose under s 14(2).)

13. Section 14(3)(b) is dealing with the case in which the retailer arranges for the buyer to buy the goods on credit—normally under a conditional sale, see Appendix—not from the retailer but from a finance company, to which the retailer sells the goods. Then it is sufficient that the buyer's purpose is made known to the retailer, who is termed the 'credit-broker'.

14. Why shouldn't the buyer take responsibility for deciding whether the goods are fit for some unusual purpose for which he requires them? Is it really right to make the seller liable for some bland assertion by an enthusiastic salesperson, who may not have had a chance to assess properly how the goods will function in the unusual application? Consider this clause from a contract for the sale of axles:

WARRANTY. Except where the buyer has completed an 'Application Recommendation' form and this has been accepted in writing by the seller, the seller does not warrant that the goods are fit for any particular purpose.

15. We have suggested already that the courts' interpretation of the implied terms under the Sale of Goods Act has been influenced by the nature of the cases that come before it. Thus the interpretation of s 13, and perhaps of s 12, seemed affected by cases in which the goods were being bought for resale. Commercial cases have also had a strong influence on the interpretation of the old s 14(2): the notions of 'useable for the common purpose' and 'resaleable' do not seem appropriate to consumer goods such as cars, where the customer will legitimately be concerned with the finish of the vehicle as well as whether it is useable for the common purpose of transportation. This caused considerable concern to consumer organisations, and the matter was referred to the Law Commission. (Subsequently, the Court of Appeal in *Rogers v Parish (Scarborough) Ltd* [1987] QB 933 suggested that the common purposes for which cars are bought include comfort, convenience, ease of handling, reliability and appearance.) It was the Law Commission's Report that led to amendment of s 14(2) in 1994.

English judges, professors and law reformers discuss how the implied terms should be formulated, but they do not, so often, explicitly discuss what they are trying to do.

■ **Ayres and Gertner, 'Filling Gaps in Incomplete Contracts: An Economic Theory of Default Rules'** (1989)
99 Yale LJ 87, 87, 91–100

The legal rules of contracts and corporations can be divided into two distinct classes. The larger class consists of 'default' rules that parties can contract around prior to agreement, while the smaller, but important, class consists of 'immutable' rules that parties cannot change by contractual agreement. Default rules fill the gaps in incomplete contracts; they govern unless the parties contract around them. Immutable rules cannot be contracted around; they govern even if the parties attempt to contract around them. For example, under the Uniform Commercial Code (U.C.C.) the duty to act in good faith is an immutable part of any contract, while the warranty of merchantability is simply a default rule that parties can waive by agreement. . . .

This Article provides a theory of how courts and legislatures should set default rules. We suggest that efficient defaults would take a variety of forms that at times would diverge from the 'what the parties would have contracted for' principle. To this end we introduce the concept of 'penalty defaults'. Penalty defaults are designed to give at least one party to the contract an incentive to contract around the default rule and therefore choose affirmatively the contract provision they prefer. In contrast to the received wisdom, penalty defaults are purposefully set at what the parties would not want—in order to encourage the parties to reveal information to each other or third parties (especially the courts).

This Article also distinguishes between tailored and untailored defaults. A 'tailored default' attempts to provide a contract's parties with precisely 'what they would have contracted for'. An 'untailored default', true to its etymology, provides the parties to all contracts with a single, off-the-rack standard that in some sense represents what the majority of contracting parties would want. *The Restatement (Second) of Contracts'* approach to filling gaps, for example, provides tailored defaults that are 'reasonable in the circumstances'. 'Reasonable' defaults usually entail a tailored determination of what the individual contracting parties would have wanted because courts evaluate reasonableness in relation to the 'circumstances' of the individual contracting parties. In contrast, Charles Goetz and Robert Scott have proposed that courts should set untailored default rules by asking 'what arrangements would *most* bargainers prefer'?

An essential component of our theory of default rules is our explicit consideration of the sources of contractual incompleteness. We distinguish between two basic reasons for incompleteness. Scholars have primarily attributed incompleteness to the costs of contracting. Contracts may be incomplete because the transaction costs of explicitly contracting for a given contingency are greater than the benefits. These transaction costs may include legal fees, negotiation costs, drafting and printing costs, the costs of researching for effects and probability of a contingency, and the costs to the parties and the courts of verifying whether a contingency occurred. Rational parties will weigh these costs against the benefits of contractually addressing a particular contingency. If either the magnitude or the probability of a contingency is sufficiently low, a contract may be insensitive to that contingency even if transaction costs are quite low.

The 'would have wanted' approach to gap filling is a natural outgrowth of the transaction cost explanation of contractual incompleteness. Lawmakers can minimize the costs of contracting by choosing the default that most parties would have wanted. If there are transaction costs of explicitly contracting on a contingency, the parties may prefer to leave the contract incomplete. Indeed, as transaction costs increase, so does the parties' willingness to accept a default that is not exactly what they would have contracted for. Scholars who attribute contractual incompleteness to transaction costs are naturally drawn toward choosing defaults that the majority of contracting parties 'would have wanted' because these majoritarian defaults seem to minimize the costs of contracting.

We show, however, that this majoritarian 'would have wanted' approach to default selection is, for several reasons, incomplete. First, the majoritarian approach fails to account for the possibly disparate costs of contracting and of failing to contract around different defaults. For example, if the majority is more likely to contract around the minority's preferred default rule (than the minority is likely is to contract around the majority's rule), then choosing the minority's default may lead to a larger set of efficient contracts. Second, the received wisdom provides little guidance about how tailored or particularized the 'would have wanted' analysis should be. Finally, the very costs of ex ante bargaining may encourage parties to inefficiently shift the process of gap filling to ex post court determination. If it is costly for the courts to determine what the parties would have wanted, it may be efficient to choose a default rule that induces the parties to contract explicitly. In other words, penalty defaults are appropriate when it is cheaper for the parties to negotiate a term ex ante than for the courts to estimate ex post what the parties would have wanted. Courts, which are publicly subsidized, should give parties incentives to negotiate ex ante by penalizing them for inefficient gaps.

This Article also proposes a second source of contractual incompleteness that is the focus of much of our analysis. We refer to this source of incompleteness as strategic. One party might strategically withhold information that would increase the total gains from contracting (the 'size of the pie') in order to increase her private share of the gains from contracting (her 'share of the pie'). By attempting to contract around a certain default, one party might reveal information to the other party that affects how the contractual pie is split. Thus, for example, the more informed party may prefer to have inefficient precaution rather than pay a higher price for the good. While analysts have previously explained incomplete contracting solely in terms of the costs of writing additional provisions, we argue that contractual gaps can also result from strategic behavior by relatively informed parties. By changing the default rules of the game, lawmakers can importantly reduce the opportunities for this rent-seeking, strategic behavior. In particular, the possibility of strategic incompleteness leads us to suggest that efficiency-minded lawmakers should sometimes choose penalty defaults that induce knowledgeable parties to reveal information by contracting around the default penalty. The strategic behaviors of the parties in forming the contract can justify strategic contractual interpretations by courts. . . .

The Zero-Quantity Default

The diversity of default standards can even be seen in contrasting the law's treatment of the two most basic contractual terms: price and quantity. Although price and quantity are probably the two most essential issues on which to reach agreement, the U.C.C. establishes radically different defaults. If the parties leave out the price, the U.C.C. fills the gap with 'a reasonable price'. If the parties leave out the quantity, the U.C.C. refuses to enforce the contract. In essence, the U.C.C. mandates that the default quantity should be zero.

How can this be? The U.C.C.'s reasonable-price standard can be partly reconciled with the received wisdom that defaults should be set at what the parties would have contracted for. But why doesn't the U.C.C. treat a missing quantity term analogously by filling the gap with the reasonable quantity that the parties would have wanted? Obviously, the parties would not have gone to the expense of contracting with the intention that nothing be exchanged.

We suggest that the zero-quantity default cannot be explained by a 'what the parties would have wanted' principle. Instead, a rationale for the rule can be found by comparing the cost of ex ante contracting to the cost of ex post litigation. The zero-quantity rule can be justified because it is cheaper for the parties to establish the quantity term beforehand than for the courts to determine after the fact what the parties would have wanted.

It is not systematically easier for parties to figure out the quantity than the price ex ante, but it is systematically harder for the courts to figure out the quantity than the price ex post. To estimate a reasonable price, courts can largely rely on market information of the type 'How much were rutabagas selling for on July 3?' But to estimate a reasonable quantity, courts would need to undertake a more costly analysis of the individual litigants of the type 'How much did the buyer and seller value the marginal rutabagas?'

The U.C.C.s zero-quantity default is what we term a 'penalty default'. Because ex ante neither party would want a zero-quantity contract, such a rule penalizes the parties should they fail to affirmatively specify their desired quantity. Because the non-enforcement default potentially penalizes both parties, it encourages both of them to include a quantity term.

Toward a More General Theory of Penalty Defaults

Penalty defaults, by definition, give at least one party to the contract an incentive to contract around the default. From an efficiency perspective, penalty default rules can be justified as a way to encourage the production of information. The very process of 'contracting around' can reveal information to parties inside or outside the contract. Penalty defaults may be justified as (1) giving both contracting parties incentives to reveal information to third parties, especially courts, or (2) giving a more informed contracting party incentives to reveal information to a less informed party.

The zero-quantity default, for instance, gives both contracting parties incentives to reveal their contractual intentions when it would be costly for a court to discover that information ex post. This justification—that ex ante contracting can be cheaper than ex post litigation—can also explain the common law's broader rule that 'for a contract to be binding the terms of the contract must be reasonably certain and definite'. . . .

Lawmakers should select the rule that deters inefficient gaps at the least social cost. When the rationale is to provide information to the courts, the non-enforcement default is likely to be efficient. Non-enforcement defaults are likely to provide least-cost deterrence because they are inexpensive to enforce and give each party incentives to contract around the rule. It might seem that a penalty default set solely against one side of a contract would be sufficient to get both sides to reveal information. For example, a penalty default that makes the seller sell at one-tenth the market price would certainly encourage sellers to affirmatively fill any price gaps. But one side's penalty may be the other side's windfall. One-sided penalties can create incentives for opportunism. The non-penalized buyer in the above example would have incentives to induce sellers to enter indefinite contracts in order to extract the penalty rent. By taking each party back to her ex ante welfare, the non-enforcement default eliminates this potential for opportunism.

In contrast, when the rationale is to inform the relatively uninformed contracting party, the penalty default should be against the relatively informed party. This is especially true when the uninformed party is also uninformed about the default rule itself. If the uninformed party does not know that there is a penalty default, she will have no opportunistic incentives.

In some situations it is reasonable to expect one party to the contract to be systematically informed about the default rule and the probability of the relevant contingency arising. If one side is repeatedly in the relevant contractual setting while the other side rarely is, it is a sensible presumption that the former is better informed than the latter. Consider, for example, the treatment of real estate brokerage commissions when a buyer breaches a purchase contract. Such contracts typically include a clause which obligates the purchaser to forfeit some given amount of 'earnest' money if she breaches the agreement. How should the earnest money be split between the seller and the broker if their agency contract does not address this contingency? Some courts have adopted a 'what the parties would have wanted' approach and have awarded all the earnest money to the seller. We agree with this outcome, but for different reasons. The real estate broker will more likely be informed about the default rule than the seller. Indeed, the seller may not even consider the issue of how to split the earnest money in case of default. Therefore, if the efficient contract would allocate some of the earnest money to the seller, the default rule should be set against the broker to induce her to raise the issue. Otherwise, if the default rule is set to favour the broker, a seller may not raise the issue, and the broker will be happy to take advantage of the seller's ignorance. By setting the default rule in favour of the uninformed party, the courts induce the informed party to reveal information, and, consequently, the efficient contract results.

Although social welfare may be enhanced by forcing parties to reveal information to a subsidized judicial system, it is more problematic to understand why society would have an efficiency interest in inducing a relatively informed party to a transaction to reveal information to the relatively uninformed party. After all, if revealing information is efficient because it increases the value created by the contract, one might initially expect that the informed party will have a sufficient private incentive to reveal information—the incentive of splitting a bigger pie. This argument ignores the possibility, however, that revealing information might simultaneously increase the total size of the pie and decrease the share of the pie that the relatively informed party receives. If the 'share-of-the-pie effect' dominates the 'size-of-the-pie effect', informed parties might rationally choose to withhold relevant information.

Parties may behave strategically not only because they have superior information about the default, but also because they have superior information about other aspects of the contract. We suggest that a party who knows that a particular default rule is inefficient may choose not to negotiate to change it. The knowledgeable party may not wish to reveal her information in negotiations if the information would give a bargaining advantage to the other side.

How can it be that by increasing the total gains from contracting (the size-of-the-pie effect) the informed party can end up with a smaller share of the gains (the share-of-the-pie effect)? This Article demonstrates how relatively informed parties can sometimes benefit by strategically withholding information that, if revealed, would increase the size of the pie. A knowledgeable buyer, for example, may prefer to remain indistinguishable from what the seller wrongly perceives to be the class of similarly situated buyers. By blending in with the larger class of contractors, a buyer or a seller may receive a cross-subsidized price because the other side will bargain as if she is dealing with the average member of the class. A knowledgeable party may prefer to remain in this inefficient, but cross-subsidized, contractual pool rather than move to an efficient, but unsubsidized, pool. If contracting around the default sufficiently reduces this cross-subsidization, the share-of-the-pie effect can exceed the size-of-the-pie effect because the informed party's share of the default pie was in a sense being artificially cross-subsidized by other members of the contractual class. Under this scenario, withholding information appears as a kind of rent-seeking in which the informed party forgoes the additional value attending the revealed information to get a larger piece of the contractual pie. . . .

NOTES

1. English and American law both say that, if the price is unfixed, there is an implied term that the price is a reasonable price. The UCC says that if the parties do not agree the quantity, there is no contract. Do you think this is the English rule? Suppose Beale rings his grocer and says, 'Can you send me some potatoes? and the grocer delivers two 5lb sacks. Is there a contract?

2. For an example of a rule encouraging one party to disclose information to another, see the discussion of remoteness of damage, p 645.

3. A further analysis of 'default rules' will be found in Riley, 'Designing Default Rules in Contract Law' (2000) 20 Oxford J Legal Studies 367. One of the points he makes is that while there is a strong case for choosing rules that will promote efficiency when the rules are to be enacted in statute, the case for them is weaker when it is a court that is promulgating them. Other bases for default terms, such as the subjective consent of the parties or, more importantly, 'conventionalism' (seeking 'to ground defaults in the shared understandings and expectations immanent within the parties' own community') may also be important (although he notes the empirical finding made by Bernstein ((1999) 66 University of Chicago LR 610—that even within specific trades there may be no agreement on precise usages and customs that can simply be used to fill gaps in the contract. Any understanding may be very vague, such as that the parties should act cooperatively or in good faith and thus the court will have to give these content on the facts of each case (p 376).) Riley writes (pp 384–388):

A. *The normative appeal of efficient defaults*

The most familiar criticism levelled against efficiency analysis is a distributional one: that efficiency concerns itself only with the maximization of *aggregate* welfare, without regard to how that welfare is distributed. It is important, however, to be clear just what the complaint here really is. It is not—or should not be—the crude one that aggregatively ('Kaldor-Hicks') efficient defaults will leave some parties worse off. Default rules, as noted, are designed just to identify winners and losers. Condemning *efficient* defaults for leaving some worse off would apply a standard of evaluation that no prescription for default rules could hope to satisfy. Conventionalist norms, as we have seen already, are also likely to create winners and losers, and thus have distributional effects. Rather, the real complaint concerns the criterion by which the principle of efficiency distributes gains and losses and thus determines winners and losers. It requires that gains and losses be distributed just in whatever manner is necessary to maximize aggregate welfare. In fact we can identify two separate criticisms here. First, pursuit of efficiency ignores those 'connecting factors' described above which, it was there argued, rendered fair the enforcement of conventionalist norms. Second, it replaces these connecting factors with a particularly unappealing distributional criterion of its own. For losers must put up with their losses just as the price to be paid for a 'bigger cake', a justification that is at least problematic if there is, as Burton claims, 'no general background political obligation for everyone to act to produce the best social consequences'.

Proponents of economic analysis respond to these two criticisms by invoking the possibility of the parties' knowledge of the law's default rules, and their ability to bargain around those rules, as sufficient to overcome distributional concerns. . . .

How persuasive is this response to the distributional criticism? Certainly it has some force, and provides some reason for overriding the (already limited) case for enforcing conventionalist norms. However, the force of this response varies according to the institution promulgating the default rule, being far stronger in the case of rules promulgated legislatively than those promulgated adjudicatively. The essence of the economic response turns on the parties' awareness of the law's (efficient) defaults at the time they choose to contract. So far as *legislative* defaults are concerned, such rules will typically be promulgated in advance of any particular contract into which they will be implied, and should thus be *discoverable* by the parties before they contract. To be sure, the mere fact a rule is discoverable does not entail that parties will actually be aware of, or understand, the rule. Repeat players may make it their business to learn of the default rules applicable to their contractual relationships; others may remain rationally ignorant. Against this, however, we may think that parties ought to bear some responsibility for learning of those already-promulgated rules by which they will be bound. Moreover, given the costs to the state in promulgating legislative default rules, it seems likely that such defaults will be used in far less remote contingencies, leaving remoter ones to be dealt with, if and when necessary, by a judicially promulgated rule.

Given the discoverability of legislative defaults, the possibility of contracting around those rules in the way described above also seems quite high. . . .

In the case of *adjudicative* defaults, however, the distributional problem remains much more severe. The parties to the case in which such a default is first promulgated can hardly have known of that rule at the time they contracted. Now can all those other parties to any contracts entered into prior to the date of the rule's first promulgation. Such ignorance is the consequence of the 'retroactivity' of judicial rule-making. Of course, once the default has been adjudicatively promulgated, it will be discoverable by those who contract after that date, although how far rules hidden in the depths of law reports are likely to be appreciated by prospective contractors must be doubtful. In any event, this future discoverability is little consolation to the losers in those cases that the courts use to promulgate new defaults in this way.

B. *How much efficiency?*

So far, it has been argued that the 'distributional problem' remains much greater in the case of adjudicative, as opposed to legislative, defaults. However, this is still only half the picture. How seriously the distributional problem undermines the case for efficient defaults depends also on some assessment of the magnitude of the gains which such defaults promise. We might be prepared to trade off, say, the frustration of some parties' reasonable expectations against sizable gains in aggregate welfare. At least two considerations, however, suggest that the ability of defaults to promote welfare maximization will often be rather more modest than proponents of efficient defaults might hope or claim. Importantly, this problem is again likely rather greater in relation to adjudicative than legislative defaults.

First, recall just how some rules manage to be "efficient" in the first place. They do so partly by creating *incentives* to act in appropriately efficient ways. So, for example, a rule might assign a risk to the party who can avoid that risk at the lowest cost. Or, in the case of penalty defaults, a rule might be designed so as to incentivize the parties to disclose their privately held information. However, rules can only have such incentive effects if known in advance. Yet a rule declared by the court cannot work in this way for the particular parties whose dispute the rule is first designed to resolve. To be sure, once the rule has been declared, *other* contractors can learn of its existence and respond to the incentives it creates. But if judicial defaults are chiefly used to deal with less frequently occurring contingencies, then this will likely reduce the number of future occasions on which any efficient judicial default will generate its maximizing consequences.

The second consideration which undermines the ability of default rules to promote efficiency lies in the contestability and complexity inherent in efficiency analysis. There is, recall, a "double-blind" here. Given the possible efficiency of conventionalist norms, the question is whether still greater efficiency can be achieved by the direct application of efficiency analysis. But working that out requires both an evaluation of the likely efficiency of the conventionalist norm, and an ability to come up with a better (more efficient) rule still. Although this problem likely affects both legislatures and courts, once again there is good reason to think it more severe for the latter. For courts look particularly ill-equipped to undertake the sort of sophisticated economic analysis that may well be necessary to discover the appropriately efficient rule. . . .

The reference to Burton is to (1993) 3 S Cal Interdisciplinary LJ 115, 133–139.

■ **Law Commission Report No 160, 'Sale and Supply of Goods'**
(Cm 137, 1987) paras 3.5–3.12 and p 70

2 Should the implied term as to quality be altered at all?

3.5 In the Consultative Document we suggested that the present implied term is not satisfactory. The reasons we gave for this view are set out in Part 2 above, but it may be helpful to summarise them here:

(i)   The word 'merchantable' refers to transactions between merchants and is not suitable for consumer transactions, even in its dictionary meaning. In any event it is also a word of uncertain meaning which is largely obsolete.

(ii) The present definition relies on the fitness of goods for their purpose and not on their other characteristics. Despite the recent Court of Appeal decision in *Rogers v Parish (Scarborough) Ltd*, the exact extent to which minor defects and defects of appearance and finish fall within the definition remains unclear.

(iii) The present definition does not expressly say that the goods must be reasonably durable. There is no doubt that if goods are to be 'merchantable' they must be reasonably durable, but this important point is found only in cases.

3.6 Almost all of those who commented on our proposals in the Consultative Document agreed that the implied term as to merchantable quality needed alteration. While in theory it would be possible to return to the pre-1973 situation and leave the word 'merchantable' (or any replacement word) undefined, we suggested in the Consultative Document that the required quality should continue to be defined. The arguments which led our predecessors to recommend that the required standard of quality be defined still remain and we agreed with them. It would not, we thought, be helpful to ask sellers and buyers to rely once again upon a single word to express the required standard of quality, whatever that word might be. After consultation we are confirmed in that view. It is therefore necessary to consider what new definition of the implied term as to quality is needed. In seeking to answer this question we have had to consider what is the primary function of the implied term itself.

3. In what way should the implied term be re-defined?

(a) The function of the implied term

3.7 The implied term as to quality has to play a very subtle role. As we have seen, the word 'merchantable' was derived from Victorian cases where (putting the matter at its simplest) the question was, 'were the goods of such a quality that one merchant buying them from another, would have regarded them as suitable?' But, as so often happens, although the word had been perfectly apt on the facts of the cases in which it was first used by the judges, when the word became of universal application in the 1893 Act, it was gradually seen not to be suitable for all cases. On its face the word is not suitable for non-mercantile transactions. It became necessary for judges to explain what the word meant. In some cases it was said to mean that the goods had to be fit for their purpose. In other cases it was said that the goods had to be acceptable. In all of these cases what was really at issue was whether the goods were 'up to scratch' in the particular circumstances. But sale transactions may take an almost infinite variety of forms. A sale may be of a new jet aircraft from the manufacturers to a major international carrier, of a washing machine still in its packaging from a department store to a young married couple, of a catapult to a child, of an old motor car from a back-street garage to a student, of a breeding ewe from one farmer to another, of thousands of tons of a primary product, such as wheat, from one trader to another (neither of whom will ever see the goods), or a newspaper or box of matches from a street-vendor to a passer-by. The possible circumstances are so varied that a single formula to describe the required quality is hard to define.

3.8 One way out of this difficulty might be to define the standard differently for, say, different types of goods or different types of transaction. Could there be a different standard for new goods from that applicable to second-hand goods? Could there be a different standard applicable to transactions where one party deals as a consumer? We said in the Consultative Document that we did not think it practical to provide different standards of quality for different types of goods, different types of transaction, or different types of buyer and seller. On consultation there was very little, if any, support for having different quality standards, at least within the framework of existing legislation. The creation of different categories of transaction is likely to give rise to many disputes on the question which side of any given line a particular transaction falls. Further, although it might (for example) seem obvious that 'new' goods should be of a different standard from 'second-hand' goods, is this really always so? A 'second-hand' Rolls Royce motor car, sold after only 300 miles driving, should probably have all the qualities of a brand new car of that marque. On the other hand, 'new' goods may be sold as 'seconds' or their sub-standard quality otherwise indicated. Some 'new' crockery is very cheap and of poor quality. Certainly it is (and would be expected to be) of lower quality than some expensive 'second-hand' crockery. Defining different types of sale for the purposes of implying a different quality for each type of sale did not seem to us in the Consultative Document a promising way out of the difficulties; those we consulted overwhelmingly supported this conclusion and, although we have reconsidered it, we maintain our view that different implied terms for different types of transaction would not be satisfactory.

3.9 It may be suggested that there should, at least, be a special implied quality term for transactions in which the buyer acts as a consumer. As will be seen below, we are suggesting that if the implied term has been broken the buyer's rights should differ according to whether he dealt as a consumer or not. However, our proposals regarding the consumer buyer's rights on a breach of contract by the seller are justified only by an overriding policy consideration that he needs a regime which favours him if he is not to be disadvantaged in his dealings with a seller who has broken the contract. In the case of the implied term as to quality, we can see no special justification for putting the consumer buyer in a different position from other buyers. To do so would carry with it the obvious danger that the shopkeeper would buy from his wholesaler under a contract containing a different implied term from that under which he sells to his customer. The shopkeeper might find that there has been no breach of contract by the wholesaler but that he himself is in breach of contract as against the consumer who bought from him. This is a situation which we wish to avoid as far as possible. We propose below what the remedies available to a consumer on a breach by the seller may differ from those available to a shopkeeper, but we think that the question whether there was a breach of contract at all should be answered in the same way for both.

3.10 A further ground which leads us not to recommend that there should be a special implied term for a buyer who deals as a consumer is that the circumstances in which consumers buy goods vary enormously, just as do the circumstances in which buyers generally buy goods. They can buy low quality as well as high quality goods, new or second-hand, from the manufacturer or from the shop round the corner. Consumer transactions, such as the purchase of a motor car, may involve large sums of money and complicated objects with hundreds of parts which may go wrong. No particular term seemed especially appropriate for consumer transactions, and organisations which represented consumers' interests did not press us for a special implied term relating to consumers. We have decided not to recommend such a term.

3.11 The decision to recommend a single implied term as to the quality of goods to be supplied under all types of contract brings with it certain consequences. There is no one word which we have found or which has been suggested to us by which the appropriate standard can be defined. The term must be sufficiently flexible to be able to apply to all the many types of sale which can take place. Above all, there is no 'magic' formula which will provide an instant answer in every case to the question whether goods meet the standard of quality which they should have. (Even if there were, this would not resolve most disputes about defective goods, since most disputes are not about the law but about the facts.)

3.12 In the Consultative Document we suggested that the new definition of quality should consist of two elements:

(i) a basic principle formulated in language sufficiently general to apply to all kinds of goods and all kinds of transaction; this principle would also refer, as at present, to the description of the goods, their price, and any other relevant circumstances, which are factors which would be taken into account in determining how stringent the quality requirement should be in any particular case; and

(ii) a list of aspects of quality, any of which could be important in a particular case; the list would, however, not be exhaustive.

This approach was generally supported on consultation and is the one which we now recommend. The definition which we shall propose is longer and more complex than the existing one. For the reasons which we have set out, we do not believe this is avoidable. . . .

The Law Commission Report concluded by recommending that s 14(2) be replaced by what are now ss 14(2)-(2C), the only difference being that it suggested 'acceptable quality' rather than 'satisfactory quality'.

3. Time and place for delivery

■ Sale of Goods Act 1979, s 29: Rules about delivery

(1) Whether it is for the buyer to take possession of the goods or for the seller to send them to the buyer is a question depending in each case on the contract, express or implied, between the parties.

(2) Apart from any such contract, express or implied, the place of delivery is the seller's place of business if he has one, and if not, his residence; except that, if the contract is for the sale of specific goods, which to the knowledge of the parties when the contract is made are in some other place, then that place is the place of delivery.

(3) Where under the contract of sale the seller is bound to send the goods to the buyer, but no time for sending them is fixed, the seller is bound to send them within a reasonable time.

(4) Where the goods at the time of sale are in the possession of a third person, there is no delivery by seller to buyer unless and until the third person acknowledges to the buyer that he holds the goods on his behalf; but nothing in this section affects the operation of the issue or transfer of any document of title to goods.

(5) Demand or tender of delivery may be treated as ineffectual unless made at a reasonable hour; and what is a reasonable hour is a question of fact.

(6) Unless otherwise agreed, the expenses of and incidental to putting the goods into a deliverable state must be borne by the seller.

NOTE

If a party undertakes to perform by a particular date, but is delayed by some event, he is liable whether it was his fault or not. If, on the other hand, no date was set for the performance, he must perform within a reasonable time, and unavoidable delays caused by events outside his control may be taken into account. This is so even though the events could not have been anticipated at the time the contract was made *(Hick v Raymond and Reid* [1893] AC 22). Why the difference? Is it just that courts tend to enforce express promises literally, or is there some other factor at work?

In practice, the strict obligation to perform on time is often qualified by a force majeure clause, such as:

> If it becomes apparent that the Works will not be completed by the date for completion . . . (or any extended date . . . in accordance with this sub-clause) for reasons beyond the control of the Contractor, then the Contractor shall so notify the Architect/ Supervising Officer who shall extend the time for completion by a reasonable period. (JCT Minor Works.)

Another example is the following:

> We shall not be held responsible or liable for any loss, damage, retention or delay caused by fire, strike, civil or military authority, insurrection or riot, earthquake, transportation embargo or by any other means beyond our control. (Bendix Westinghouse Ltd)

(See also the specimen conditions of sale in the Appendix, cl 14, and p 469.)
Why should the parties agree to such a term? Is either party in a better position to prevent such delays? If not, is either in a better position than the other to estimate their likelihood, or to insure against them?

4. Standard of liability for quality

■ *Young and Marten Ltd v McManus Childs Ltd*
[1969] 1 AC 454

The respondents, the employers, engaged a contractor to build a number of houses for sale. The contractor subcontracted the roofing to the appellants; the appellants were instructed to use a rather expensive type of tile called a 'Somerset 13', manufactured only by Browne of Bridgwater. The appellants in turn subcontracted the work to Acme, who bought the tiles from Browne. The tiles were defective in a way that could not have been detected by any reasonable examination and the buyers of the houses recovered the cost of reroofing them from the respondents. The respondents then brought in the appellants, arguing that the appellants were liable to them on an implied warranty of quality. (For reasons that are not explained, the case was argued on the basis that the contractor had merely acted as agent for the employers in making the contract with the appellants, so that there was a direct contract between appellant and respondents, and the judgments discuss the situation as if the appellants were the contractors.) The appellants were unable to bring in Acme in turn, as they would normally have done, because the limitation period for their claim against Acme had expired.

Lord Reid

This is a contract for the supply of work and materials and this case raises a general question as to the nature and extent of the warranties which the law implies in such a contract. As regards the contractor's liability for the work done there is no dispute in this case: admittedly it must be done with all proper skill and care. The question at issue relates to his liability in respect of material supplied by him under the contract. The appellants maintain that the warranty in respect of materials is similar to that in respect of work, so that, if the selection of material and of the person to supply it is left to the contractor, he must exercise due skill and care in choosing the material and the person to supply it. But where, as in this case, the material and the supplier were chosen by the respondents, the appellants maintain that there was no warranty as to the fitness or quality of the tiles. The respondents admit that, if it is held that the choice of this type of tile was theirs and theirs alone, there can be no implied warranty that this type of tile was fit for the contract purpose. But they say that there still was a warranty that the tiles would be of good quality and that that warranty must be implied, notwithstanding the fact that they left no choice to the appellants in selecting the person who was to supply the tiles. If that is right, then the respondents must succeed. The loss was not caused by Somerset 13 tiles being unsuitable for the contract purpose: it was caused by the tiles which were supplied being of defective quality.

There is not very much authority on this matter, so it may be well first to consider it as a question of principle.

I take first the general question of the contractor's liability where the material which he is required to use can be obtained from any one of several suppliers and the choice of suppliers is left to him. There is no doubt that in every case he is bound to make a proper inspection of the material before using it, and he will be liable if the loss is caused by the use of material which reasonable inspection would have shown to be defective. The question is whether he warrants the material against latent defects.

There are, in my view, good reasons for implying such a warranty if it is not excluded by the terms of the contract. If the contractor's employer suffers loss by reason of the emergence of the latent defect, he will generally have no redress if he cannot recover damages from the contractor. But, if he can recover damages, the contractor will generally not have to bear the loss: he will have bought the defect-ive material from a seller who will be liable under section 14 (2) of the Sale of Goods Act, 1893, because the material was not of merchantable quality. And, if that seller had in turn bought from someone else, there will again be liability, so that there will be a chain of liability from the employer who suffers the damage back to the author of the defect. Of course, the chain may be broken because the contractor (or an earlier buyer) may have agreed to enter into a contract under which his supplier excluded or limited his ordinary liability under the Sale of Goods Act. But in general that has nothing to do with the employer and should not deprive him of his remedy. If the contractor chooses to buy on such terms, he takes the risk of having to bear the loss himself if the goods prove to be defective.

Moreover, many contracts for work and materials closely resemble contracts of sale: where the employer contracts for the supply and installation of a machine or other article, the supply of the machine may be the main element and the work of installation be a comparatively small matter. If the employer had bought the article and installed it himself, he would have had a warranty under section 14 (2), and it would be strange that the fact that the seller also agreed to instal it should make all the difference.

The specialty in the present case is that these tiles were only made by one manufacturer. So the contractor had to buy them from him or from someone who bought from him. Why should that make any difference? It would make a difference if that manufacturer was only willing to sell on terms which excluded or limited his ordinary liability under the Sale of Goods Act, and that fact was known to the employer and the contractor when they made their contract. For it would be unreasonable to put on the contractor a liability for latent defects when the employer had chosen the supplier with knowledge that the contractor could not have recourse against him. If the manufacturer's disclaimer of liability caused him to supply the goods at a cheaper price, as in theory at least it should, the employer ought not to get the benefit of a cheap price as well as a warranty from the contractor.

A more difficult case would be where the employer and contractor had no reason to suppose, when they made their contract, that the manufacturer would refuse to sell subject to a seller's ordinary liabil-ities in respect of the goods which he sells. But I need not consider that case now because there is no suggestion that Brownes had refused to sell except on terms which limited their ordinary liability in respect of latent defects in their tiles. No doubt there will be some cases where, although the contractor had a right of recourse against the manufacturer, he cannot in fact operate that right. The supplier may have become insolvent, or, as in the present case, the action against the contractor may be so delayed that he has no time left in which to sue his supplier. But these cases must be relatively few and it would seem better that the contractor should occasionally have to suffer than that the employer should very seldom have any remedy at all. It therefore seems to me that general principles point strongly to there being an implied warranty of quality in this case.

There is little assistance to be got from the earlier authorities....

In the present case one must sympathise with the appellants because, through no fault of their own, they have lost their right of ultimate recourse against the makers of these tiles. But, putting that aside, because the existence or non-existence of the warranty must be determined as at the date of the contract, this appears to me to be a clear case in which a warranty of quality must be implied. I would therefore dismiss this appeal.

Lord Pearce

...If the appellants' argument is correct, an employer has no redress for loss arising out of the use of material with latent defects, if he has ordered a particular kind of material. For it was not the employer but the contractor who bought from the manufacturer. The employer therefore cannot sue the manufacturer, unless it is possible to extend *Donoghue v Stevenson* further than it has gone up to the present.

I see great difficulty in extending to an ultimate consumer a right to sue the manufacturer in tort in respect of goods which create no peril or accident but simply result in substandard work under a contract which is unknown to the original manufacturer. And if originally, as a term of his contract, the manufacturer limited his liability for defects, there seems no reason (where there is no peril or accident) why a third party should have better rights than the original purchaser. And, if his rights are the same, there is no need to introduce a rule which would cause various confusions and difficulties, since the same result can be achieved in the normal case by the third party procedure.

If, however, the employer can sue the contractor in respect of the faulty materials, then the contractor can in turn recover from the manufacturer, with whom the ultimate blame lies. This would follow the normal chain of liability which attaches to sales and sub-sales of goods....

Appeal dismissed.

NOTES

1. The question in this case was whether the contractors were liable for the quality of the tiles, not for their fitness for the particular purpose. If the tiles had been of generally satisfactory quality, but had been specified to be used for some unusual purpose and had proved unsuitable for it, would the contractors have been responsible? Compare *Shanklin Pier v Detel* (p 38).

2. If, before finalising the specification, the employer consults the contractor about materials, and the contractor agrees that a particular material can be used even though it is not usual for this purpose, the contractor will be responsible if the material turns out to be unsuitable: *Steel Co of Canada v Will and Management* (1966) 58 DLR (2d) 595. The onus seems to be on the contractor to raise a positive objection.

3. Lord Reid refers to the case in which the contractor is instructed to use a material that is only available from a particular manufacturer who 'was only willing to sell on terms which excluded or limited his ordinary liability under the Sale of Goods Act, and that fact was known to the employer and the contractor when they made their contract'. This is a reference to the case of *Gloucestershire County Council v Richardson* [1968] 2 All ER 1181, which was heard by the House of Lords between the dates of the hearing and of the judgment in *Young & Martens*. The employer had 'nominated' a particular supplier from

which the contractor was then obliged to obtain precast concrete columns for the build-ing. Under the RIBA form of contract used, the contractor had no right to object to the nomination of a supplier (although it did have the right to object to the nomination of a subcontractor), and the supplier would only sell on limited liability terms. The columns were incorporated into the building but then failed, which caused serious losses. It was held that the normal responsibility of the contractor for the quality of the beams was excluded by the particular circumstances.

4.   The *Gloucestershire County Council* case is an example of a situation in which, even if there were to be a clause stating that the contractor is not liable for the quality of goods from the nominated supplier, the provisions of the Unfair Contract Terms Act 1977 restricting the exclusion of the implied terms as to quality (see p 413) might not 'bite', because the contractor would not be liable even apart from the clause.

5.   The *Gloucestershire County Council* case caused a considerable practical difficulty. If the contractor was not responsible, the employer had to bear the loss. Thus the only party with contract rights against the supplier suffered no loss for which it could sue, and the party who had suffered the loss had no right to sue anyone for breach of contract. (Could the employer now sue the supplier in tort? See pp 31–32 and p 1162.) Thus the employer was left without a remedy and the supplier got away free. We will consider difficulties of this kind in more detail p 1155.

6.   The particular problem encountered in the *Gloucestershire County Council* case is not likely to recur because the RIBA contract used in that case has been replaced by the Joint Contract Tribunal form (currently JCT 98). This gives the contractor a right to object to the nomination of a supplier as well as of a subcontractor. If the contractor does not object, it is responsible for the quality of the goods supplied.

7.   Although in the *Gloucestershire County Council* case it was held that the circumstances excluded the normal implied term, the courts are reluctant to reach this result, especially if the term is one that would also be an obligation under the law of tort. See the next case.

■ *Johnstone v Bloomsbury Health Authority*
[1991] 2 All ER 293, Court of Appeal

The plaintiff was employed by the defendant health authority as a junior hospital doctor under a contract of employment that required him, by para 4(b), to work 40 hours per week and to 'be available' for overtime of a further 48 hours per week on average. The plaintiff brought an action against the authority alleging breach of the authority's duty as his employer to take all reasonable care for his safety and well-being and seeking a declaration that the plaintiff could not lawfully be required by the defendant to work under his contract of employment for so many hours in excess of his standard working week as would foreseeably injure his health. The plaintiff alleged that he had been required to work intolerable hours with such deprivation of sleep that his health had been damaged and the safety of his patients put at risk, and that he suffered from stress and depression, had been physically sick from exhaustion and had felt suicidal. The plaintiff also sought declarations that his contract was contrary to s 2(1) of the Unfair Contract Terms Act 1977, which provided that a term of a contract could not exclude or restrict a person's liability for death or personal injury resulting from negligence, and that the contract was void on the grounds of public policy. An application by the authority to strike out the main claim was granted by the master, but an appeal against the striking out was allowed by the judge. An application by the authority to strike out the claims based on the 1977 Act and public policy was granted by another judge. The authority and the plaintiff appealed to the Court of Appeal.

Stuart Smith LJ

There was a duty on the part of the plaintiff to be available for duty for an average of 48 hours each week beyond the basic 40 hours (duty A). There was a duty on the authority to take reasonable care not to injure his health (duty B). It is the interaction or reconciliation of these two duties which is in question here. Mr Beloff [for the Health Authority] submits that duty A must prevail over duty B, because the former is an express term of the contract and the latter is implied. But this is not an implication that arises because it is necessary to give business efficacy to the contract as in *The Moorcock;* it arises by implication of law. While therefore Mr Beloff asks the question, how does duty B cut down or override duty A? One can equally ask how does duty A cut down or override duty B? I can quite see that an express clause in a contract of employment could be so framed as to limit or exclude duty B. If for example the employee agreed to take the risk that his employer would be negligent towards him in requiring him to work so many hours within the contract entitlement although it would foreseeably injure his health, and so waived any right to claim compensation for such negligence. This would be tantamount to an express term of volenti non fit injuria. I am quite unable to construe para 4(b) of the contract as amounting to this; and Mr Beloff did not contend that it should be so construed. Moreover if it can be so construed, it falls to be considered in the light of s 2(1) of the Unfair Contract Terms Act 1977 . . . Mr Beloff submits that para 4(b) of the contract in some way limits the ambit or scope of duty B. I know of no authority that supports this contention and it seems to me to be contrary to principle. A workman whose contract requires him to work in a particular factory is not precluded from claiming damages for breach of duty to take care of him if he is exposed to noxious fumes in the factory and suffers injury as a result. A man who is engaged expressly to work on a particular machine or range of machinery is not thereby precluded from suing his employer if he sustains injury because the machine is dangerous. Take the case of a man whose contract requires him to work a certain number of basic hours and overtime in addition as required: if he is required to work such long hours that he is exhausted and his attention or concentration fail so that he suffers an accident, it is no defence to the employer to say that the workman expressly agreed to work such hours. So much is trite law . . .

It must be remembered that the duty of care is owed to the individual employee and different employees may have different stamina. If the authority in this case knew or ought to have known that by requiring him to work the hours they did, they exposed him to risk of injury to his health, then they should not have required him to work in excess of those hours that he safely could have done.

In my opinion para 4(b) gave the authority the power to require the plaintiff to work up to 88 hours per week on average. But that power had to be exercised in the light of the other contractual terms and in particular their duty to take care for his safety. Mr Beloff submits that the authority cannot be expected to treat their house officers differently according to their physical stamina. But this is not the law. In *Paris v Stepney BC* [1951] 1 All ER 42, [1951] AC 367 the employer owes a duty to take greater care of a one-eyed man than a normal man in respect of risk of injuries to the eyes. If employers know or ought to know that a workman has a vulnerable back they are in breach of duty in requiring him to lift and move weights which are likely to cause him injury even if a normal man can carry them without risk.

Mr Beloff's suggested solution was that if a potential house officer thought that he could not perform the hours required, he should not take the job. Although the principle that if you cannot stand the heat in the kitchen you should get out, or not go in, may often be a sound one, it would have serious implications if applied in these circumstances. Any doctor who wishes to practise has to serve at least one year as a house officer in a hospital; the national health service (NHS) is effectively a monopoly employer. Is the aspiring doctor who has spent many years in training to this point to abandon his chosen profession because the employer may exercise its power to call upon him to work so many hours that his health is undermined? I fail to see why he should not approach the matter on the basis that the employer will only exercise that power consistently with its duty to have proper regard to his health and safety. The fact that one doctor may have less stamina and physical strength than another does not mean that he is any less competent at his profession.

It follows that I would hold that if the pleaded facts are established, and they are of course contested, para 4(b) of the contract does not preclude or limit the plaintiff's claim as contended by Mr Beloff. I therefore have no difficulty in concluding that the prayer in the writ and statement of claim should not be struck out in the manner sought. I would dismiss the main appeal.

Leggatt LJ

Although it is a canon of construction that the terms of a contract will be construed, as far as possible, so as to be compatible with each other, it is axiomatic that the scope of an express term cannot be cut down by an implied term; and that is as true of terms implied by law as it is of terms which depend on the intentions of the parties: see *Chitty on Contracts* (26th edn, 1989) vol 1, para 903 and *Lynch v Thorne* [1956] 1 All ER 744 at 749, [1956] 1 WLR 303 at 310.

In the light of the provisions of para 4(b), which are simple and clear, no implied provision can, as a matter of construction, have the effect directly or indirectly of reducing the number of hours per week which the plaintiff is required to be available. To meet this objection the plaintiff has amended the indorsement on the writ to seek:

> 'A declaration that the Plaintiff could not lawfully have been required by the Defendant to work under his contract of employment for so many hours in excess of his standard working week as would foreseeably injure his health, not withstanding that in consequence the total number of such excess hours worked by him might have amounted on average to fewer than 48 per week.'

But, although that avoids reference to a particular number of hours in excess of which the plaintiff is not to be required to work, it does not get away from the difficulty, even if it conceals it, that it is envisaged that there might be weeks in which the defendants would not be entitled to call upon the plaintiff for as many hours of work as he had contracted to be available for. Then it is said that there may be a difference between the 40 hours basic week, for which there is a mutual commitment, and the 48 hours for which the plaintiff has undertaken to make himself available. It is suggested that during the latter period the defendants may not be entitled to call upon the plaintiff if it is foreseeable that to do so would injure his health. But I am persuaded by Mr Beloff QC that there is no warrant for any distinction between the two periods: the doctor's duty to make himself available has as its correlative a right in the employer to take advantage of his availability by requiring him to work; and there can in principle be no difference in the nature or extent of the duty owed to the employee according to whether he contracts to work or merely to be on call. It is therefore not permissible to argue that the implied duty to look out for an employee's health may cut down the number of hours for which a doctor who is on call may be required to work, even though not the number of hours for which he is required to work in any event. The only difference between the two is that the employer has an option in the one case but not in the other: the employee's duty is the same in both. And the implied duty cannot detract from the employer's right any more than from the employee's duty.

It seems to me that the operation of the regime contemplated by the declaration sought would be fraught with difficulty. The number of hours that a person can work in a week without injuring his health will vary infinitely . . .

Sir Nicolas Browne-Wilkinson VC

. . . [If] there is a term of the contract which is in general terms (eg a duty to take reasonable care not to injure the employee's health) and another term which is precise and detailed (eg an obligation to work on particular tasks notwithstanding that they involve an obvious health risk expressly referred to in the contract) the ambit of the employer's duty of care for the employee's health will be narrower than it would be were there no such express terms. In the absence of such express term, an employer would be in breach of the normal obligation not knowingly to put the employee's health at risk. But the express term postulated would demonstrate that, in that particular contract, the duty was restricted to taking such care of the employee's health as was consistent with the employee working on the specified high risk tasks. The express and the implied terms of the contract have to be capable of coexistence without conflict. (I am of course ignoring the effect of the Unfair Contract Terms Act 1977 or any statutory duties overriding the contract.)

Therefore I agree with Leggatt LJ and disagree with Stuart-Smith LJ that in the present case the scope of the duty of care for the plaintiff's health owed by the authority falls to be determined taking into account the express terms of para 4(b) of the contract. If the contract, on its true construction, were to impose an absolute obligation to work 48 hours' overtime per week on average, it would, in my judgment, preclude an argument by the employee that the employer, in requiring 48 hours per week overtime, was in breach of his implied duty of care for the employee's health.

But this case is not the same as the example I have used above. Although para 4(b) imposes an absolute duty on the plaintiff to work for 40 hours and in addition an obligation 'to be available' for a further 48 hours per week on average, the authority has a discretion as to the number of hours it calls on the plaintiff to work 'overtime'. There is no incompatibility between the plaintiff being under a duty to be available for 48 hours' overtime and the authority having the right, *subject to its ordinary duty not to injure the plaintiff*, to call on him to work up to 48 hours' overtime on average. There is, in the present contract, no incompatibility between the plaintiff's duty on the one hand and the authority's right, subject to the implied duty as to health, on the other. The implied term does not contradict the express term of the contract.

In my judgment there must be some restriction on the authority's rights. In any sphere of employment other than that of junior hospital doctors, an obligation to work up to 88 hours in any one week would be rightly regarded as oppressive and intolerable. But even that is not the limit of what the authority claims. Since the plaintiff's obligation is to be available 'on average' for 48 hours per week, the authority claims to be entitled to require him to work more than 88 hours in some weeks regardless of possible injury to his health. Thus the plaintiff alleges that he was required to work for 100 hours during one week in February 1989 and 105 hours during another week in March 1989. How far can this go? Could the authority demand of the plaintiff that he worked 130 hours (out of the total of 168 hours available) in any one week even if this would manifestly involve injury to his health? In my judgment the authority's right to call for overtime under para 4(b) is not an absolute right but must be limited in some way. There is no technical legal reason why the authority's discretion to call for overtime should not be exercised in conformity with the normal implied duty to take reasonable care not to injure their employee's health . . .

Defendants' appeal dismissed. Plaintiff's appeal allowed in part.

NOTES

1.　Which of the different approaches taken by the three LJJ in this case do you think is the best, and why?

2.　What would have been the result if it had been established that (a) no doctor could safely work 88 hours a week, or (b) that 88 hours a week is safe as long as the doctor gets five hours' unbroken rest in each 24 hours?

V. CONTRACTS FOR SERVICES

■ Supply of Goods and Services Act 1982

Section 12: The contracts concerned

(1) In this Act a 'contract for the supply of a service' means, subject to subsection (2) below, a contract under which a person ('the supplier') agrees to carry out a service.

(2) For the purposes of this Act, a contract of service or apprenticeship is not a contract for the supply of a service.

(3) Subject to subsection (2) above, a contract is a contract for the supply of a service for the purposes of this Act whether or not goods are also—

(a) transferred or to be transferred, or

(b) bailed or to be bailed by way of hire,

under the contract, and whatever is the nature of the consideration for which the service is to be carried out.

(4) The Secretary of State may by order provide that one or more of sections 13 or 15 below shall not apply to services of a description specified in the order, and such an order may make different provision for different circumstances.

(5) The power to make an order under subsection (4) above shall be exercisable by statutory instrument subject to annulment in pursuance of a resolution of either House of Parliament.

Section 13: Implied term about care and skill

In a contract for the supply of a service where the supplier is acting in the course of a business, there is an implied term that the supplier will carry out the service with reasonable care and skill.

Section 14: Implied term about time for performance

(1) Where, under a contract for the supply of a service by a supplier acting in the course of a business, the time for the service to be carried out is not fixed by the contract, left to be fixed in a manner agreed by the contract or determined by the course of dealing between the parties, there is an implied term that the supplier will carry out the service within a reasonable time.

(2) What is a reasonable time is a question of fact.

Section 15: Implied terms about consideration

(1) Where, under a contract for the supply of a service, the consideration for the service is not determined by the contract, left to be determined in a manner agreed by the contract or determined by the course of dealing between the parties, there is an implied term that the party contracting with the supplier will pay a reasonable charge.

(2) What is a reasonable charge is a question of fact.

■ *Greaves & Co (Contractors) Ltd v Baynham Meikle & Partners*
[1975] 3 All ER 99, Court of Appeal

The plaintiffs, who were building contractors, were employed by a company to construct a warehouse under a 'package deal' whereby, in addition to providing the labour and materials, the plaintiffs were to employ the architects and engineers as subcontractors. The warehouse was required by the company as a store for oil drums, which were to be kept on the first floor of the warehouse and, when required for despatch, were to be moved into position by forklift stacker trucks. The plaintiffs knew the purpose for which the warehouse was required and therefore were under a duty to the company to see that the building, when finished, was reasonably fit for that purpose. The plaintiffs employed the defendants, a firm of consultant structural engineers, to design the structure of the warehouse. It was to be built according to a new system of construction that was governed by a British Standards code of practice. A circular had been issued by the British Standards Institution warning designers of the effect of vibrations caused by imposed loadings in such constructions. The plaintiffs made known to the defendants the purpose for which the warehouse was required and, in particular, that the first floor would have to take the weight of loaded forklift trucks moving to and fro. Although the defendants were aware of the circular, they did not read it as a warning against vibrations in general and so did not take measures to deal with the random impulses of forklift trucks. There was evidence that other designers might have taken the same view of the circular. The warehouse was built in accordance with the defendants' design, and the first floor was put into use for storing oil drums and moving them about by forklift trucks. After a time, the floor cracked and became dangerous, and it was found that remedial works costing some £100,000 would have to be carried out to cure structural damage. The plaintiffs became liable to the company to remedy that damage. They brought an action against the defendants for damages for breach of the agreement to design the structure, and claimed a declaration of the defendants' liability for the cost of all work necessary to rectify the damage caused by breach of the agreement and an indemnity against all sums payable by the plaintiffs to the company by reason of breach of the agreement. At the trial of the action, the defendants gave evidence admitting that they had been engaged by the plaintiffs to produce a building, the first floor of which would be fit for use as a store for oil drums and for moving the drums by forklift truck. Further, by the original defence to the statement of claim, the defendants admitted that it was an implied term of the agreement that the defendants' design should be such that the building would be structurally sound, although on the second day of the trial, the defence was amended to strike out that admission. The trial judge found that the cracks in the floor had been caused by vibration produced by movement of loaded forklift trucks, and that the floor had not been designed with sufficient strength to withstand that vibration. He held that, as the design was inadequate for its intended purpose, the defendants were in breach of duty and in breach of an implied term of the agreement that the design would be fit for its purpose; the plaintiffs were therefore entitled to the declaration and indemnity claimed. The defendants appealed.

Lord Denning MR

. . . The law does not usually imply a warranty that [a professional man] will achieve the desired result, but only a term that he will use reasonable care and skill. The surgeon does not warrant that he will cure the patient. Nor does the solicitor warrant that he will win the case. But, when a dentist agrees to make a set of false teeth for a patient, there is an implied warranty that they will fit his gums: see *Samuels v Davis*.

What then is the position when an architect or an engineer is employed to design a house or a bridge? Is he under an implied warranty that, if the work is carried out to his design, it will be reasonably fit for the purpose? Or is he only under a duty to use reasonable care and skill? This question may require to be answered some day as a matter of law. But in the present case I do not think we need answer it. For the evidence shows that both parties were of one mind on the matter. Their common intention was that the engineer should design a warehouse which would be fit for the purpose for which it was required. That common intention gives rise to a term implied *in fact* . . . .

Browne LJ and **Geoffrey Lane LJ** delivered judgments to the same effect.

NOTES

1. Furmston employs Bishop to design a house for him. Bishop's design specifies Beale's tiles, which are of apparently high quality. After a year, however, the tiles disintegrate because of a latent defect. Both Beale and the building contractor are insolvent. Is Bishop liable? Wasn't it the common intention that the house should be watertight?

2. Although this case seemed to suggest that professionals who are given a specification of what is required might now be strictly liable, it has been interpreted as depending on its

special facts, in particular that the contractors who had employed the engineer were themselves employed under a 'package deal' contract under which they may have been obliged to produce a building that was fit for the employers' purposes: see *Hawkins v Chrysler (UK) Ltd and Burne Associates* (1986) 38 BLR 36.

3.   Why are suppliers of goods, builders and other such tradesmen strictly liable, but professional people liable only for negligence? Or is that the wrong question?

4.   Perhaps one explanation for the difference is that suppliers are much more likely to be involved in a 'chain'—ie to have obtained the goods from someone else to whom the liability can be passed back: see the *Young & Marten* case, p 440. Professionals are more likely to be doing the work themselves. However, professionals may also subcontract—and the 'oddball result' in the *Greaves* case cannot be explained on this ground: there was a chain in that case but the engineer was at the end of it.

5.   Are there any circumstances in which it will be inferred that a professional was under-taking to achieve a particular result? Furmston, who already has a fine Roman nose, employs Beale, a plastic surgeon, to give him a 'nose job'. Beale tells Furmston: 'I will turn your nose into a real Sherlock Holmser.' Without any negligence on Beale's part, the operation is a failure and Furmston's nose ends up resembling a squashed tomato. Is Beale liable? (Consider *Thake v Maurice*; you might also like to look at *Sullivan v O'Connor* (363 Mass 579, 296 NE 2d 183 (1973).) (The measure of damages, if any, will be considered on pp 673 ff.)

VI. CONTRACTS OF EMPLOYMENT

■ **Napier, 'The Contract of Employment' in Lewis (ed), Labour Law in Britain** (1986)
pp 327–331, 337–339, 347–348

The content of individual employment law has altered dramatically in the last twenty years, mainly as a result of changes which occurred in the 1970s, the decade in which legislation brought a new frame-work of rights for employees, and created specialised labour courts—the industrial tribunals—before which these rights can be claimed. Important though these rights are, however, it remains true—and this is perhaps one of the leading paradoxes of the contemporary employment law—that they complement rather than oust the common law of the contract. Today the common law fulfils a dual function. It oper-ates as a backcloth, providing a set of rules important in the many situations left unregulated by specific statutory measures, or where the legislative remedies that do exist are either inadequate or restricted in their application. It also has a crucial role to play in the operation of the statutory rights themselves, however, for Parliament has typically incorporated contractual terms and concepts in defining these. Thus, for example, there can be no proper understanding of what amounts to a 'dismissal' for the purposes of unfair dismissal without a knowledge of the common law rules regarding repudiation of contract, and no real grasp of redundancy law without an appreciation of the limits placed on job mobil-ity by the implied terms of the contract of employment.

It follows that the history of the common law of the contract deserves attention too. For, through the system of binding precedent, the response of the courts to problems arising today is conditioned by what their predecessors had to say about similar problems in the past. This account of the modern contract thus begins with an examination of the historical antecedents of the present law.

DEVELOPMENT OF THE CONTRACT OF EMPLOYMENT

Status and Contract

Although there has been systematic legal regulation of the employment relationship since the fourteenth century, it has only been in the last hundred and fifty years or so that this regulation has taken contract as its primary model. Before then the relationship was shaped in part by the criminal law, operating through a line of statutes which imposed compulsory labour and gave magistrates the power to fix wages, in part by the civil law regulating the status of different categories of persons. The great jurist Blackstone, writing in 1795, analysed the relationship of master and servant in ways which, to modern eyes, are both revealing and deficient. For Blackstone, employment was akin to the relationships of husband and wife, parent and child and guardian and ward, and was classed by him alongside these as one of the 'great relations in private life'. Moreover, his world of servants was peopled almost exclusively by workers in domestic service and engaged in agricultural labour. As Kahn-Freund (1977: 508–13) has shown, Blackstone's concept of employment was seriously out of date even against the social conditions of late eighteenth century England. His treatment of the topic tells us not only that the understanding of employment as the product of a free bargain between individuals had not yet been achieved, but also that the leading jurist of the age was little concerned with explaining and classifying the diverse forms of engagement of labour which, from other sources, we know existed in English society of the time. Why did Blackstone ignore the position of the factory labourer, the office clerk, indeed the urban worker in general? Probably for two reasons: the conditions of employment of the new working classes took them outside the terms of the disused but still-venerated Elizabethan and Jacobean criminal statutes, and there was no incentive for lawyers of his time to concern themselves with the details of such employment. The workers did not have the resources to go to law to ascertain the dimensions of their employment obligations, and, if their employers did, they lacked the inclination to do so.

The nineteenth century saw fundamental changes in the legal attitude towards the employment relationship, changes which still underpin many of the assumptions found in the law. To begin with there was, in the first half of the century, a transformation in the basic legal model. Instead of being part of the law dealing with personal status, employment was brought within the fold of the expanding law of contract. Most famously expressed in Maine's dictum that the movement of civilised society was from status to contract and that the status of the slave was superseded by the contractual relations of the servant to his master (cf. Kahn-Freund, 1977: 512), the view that the key to understanding the history of employment in the nineteenth century lies in an appreciation of how contract replaced status has recently been attacked by writers who rightly warn against over-simple explanations of complex phenomena (Merritt, 1982; Foster, 1983). None the less, it would be a mistake to underestimate the impact of the shift towards contract at both theoretical and practical levels. On a theoretical level, the embracing of contractual notions was seen as an important part of the general liberal trend in labour law which, in the second half of the century, led in 1875 to the repeal of the Master and Servant Acts and gave a measure of protection to those engaged in certain trade union activities (Ruegg, 1901: 277–9). To explain the employment relationship as a bargain, the terms of which lay entirely within the control of two independent parties, was to stress the even-handedness of the law, and was a view which accorded well with Benthamite thinking on individualism which, as Dicey (1962: 63–4) noted, exercised such a potent intellectual force in the middle years of the century. But the influence of contract was also felt in the content of specific legal rules with practical consequences.

In the shape of the doctrine of common employment, for example, it was used as a means of developing a particular legal doctrine which had dramatic and disastrous effects for many thousands of working people and their families (Bartrip and Burman, 1983: 103–25). The legal rule that an employee, injured at work by the negligence of a fellow employee, could not hold the common employer liable for the tort originated in the case of *Priestley v Fowler* in 1837. At first the rule was expressed as turning on what, in modern terminology, would be seen as the employer's 'duty of care' to his employees. But, as it was refined and enthusiastically developed by the English courts (in Scotland the courts were far more cautious), it was explained in contractual terms. The employee (or his successors) could not sue because he had bargained away his right to do so as a term (albeit implied) of the contract he had entered into with his employer: 'the negligence of a fellow servant is taken to be one of the risks, which a servant as between himself and his master undertakes, when he enters into the service.' The convenience and plausibility of the contractual analysis was a potent factor in the spread of a doctrine which became one of the most controversial aspects of the law of tort, and which was eventually to provide the impetus for the introduction of workmen's compensation legislation in 1897.

As the example of common employment illustrates, the transition from status to contract was far from being the unqualified improvement it seemed to many Victorian and Edwardian jurists. As the form of the relationship of master and servant changed, so too did its content. The transition from what Fox (1974: 181–90) has called a 'high-trust' to a 'low-trust' relationship brought with it the abandonment of some of the rules which had existed in the earlier law for the protection of the weaker party. In the case of *Limland v Stephen* at the beginning of the century, Lord Kenyon could say there were 'reciprocal duties between masters and servants. From the servant is due obedience and respect; from the master protection and good treatment.' While the principle of employer's control remained largely unaffected under the changing law, except in so far as the duty to obey was now explained as an implied term of the contract and not as an essential part of the relationship of master and servant (Selznick, 1969: 130), the master's obligations in respect of welfare were watered-down in several important respects. For example, the obligation to pay wages and to provide medical assistance to sick servants was cut back by a judiciary increasingly aware of the phenomenon of industrial employment and the appropriateness of linking payment of wages directly with productive effort.

Judges had the opportunity of developing the law in this and other ways because, to an unprecedented extent, cases on the master and servant relationship were coming before them. This was not just due to a change in attitudes as to the desirability of recourse to law as a means of settling disputes, although no doubt the rise of a commercial middle-class did have some influence here, but also to the workings of the poor law. Parish fought parish in the courts over who had the burden of looking after the poor, and often the answer was given by where the unfortunate pauper had previously acquired a 'settlement' of a year's duration. This in turn was largely dependent on the terms of the employment over the period, and thus the courts were brought to consider the terms of service of even the most menial workers.

A range of other developments in the detail of the master and servant relationship are also associated with judicial activity in the nineteenth century (Haines, 1980: 271–84). As tort liability became more important, so too it was increasingly important to distinguish between the acts of servants (for whom the employer was vicariously liable) and those of independent contractors (for whom he was not). So detailed case law also emerged to decide what acts were carried out 'in the scope of employment', and which were not. Gradually, the courts recognised that employment relationships were not governed by rules appropriate to an agricultural economy; periods of hiring, it was accepted, might be terminated by the giving of notice, although the presumption that, unless the contrary was indicated, a hiring was to last for the rotation of the year was not abandoned by English law until 1969. More generally, the nineteenth century saw the development and, in some instances, creation of many of the basic principles within the contract of employment relating to the payment of wages and dismissal which still apply today.

But no account of the many changes in individual employment law in this period should neglect the tension which arose between the standards tolerated by the common law and those laid down by statute. For although the judges, by and large, embraced contractualism and laissez-faire ideas of economic behaviour with energy and enthusiasm—except, it should be noted, in developing the notion of contractual terms unenforceable because they were incompatible with the fundamental principles of freedom of trade—the nineteenth century also saw legislative intervention to maintain minimum standards of civilised conditions of labour. One commentator (Friedmann, 1959: *99)* has concluded from this and other evidence that the judges are incapable of effecting major social adjustment by using the common law device of contract as a social equaliser. The most notable example of statutory intervention is to be found in the history of factory legislation. But mention can also be made of the Truck Acts, which sought to protect the worker's right to payment of wages, and lesser measures such as the Merchant Shipping Acts of 1844 and 1854 which gave close regulation of the terms of employment of sailors (Atiyah, 1979: 543–4). Thus the significance of the nineteenth century from the point of view of the history of employment law is not simply the displacement of status by contract; it is also that during this period English law accepted the propriety of imposing, by legislation, certain protections for workers outside the realm of contract (Hepple, 1982: 399). In so doing, some of the worst effects of unbridled individualism were mitigated, and a pattern for legal intervention was set which was to have profound consequences for the subsequent development of the law.

Characteristics of the Modern Law

The story of the contract of employment during the present century can be more briefly told, notwithstanding the many fundamental changes in society and industrial relations which have taken place in this period. There has been no truly radical alteration in the conception of the individual employment relationship similar to that which occurred in Victorian England. By 1914 most of the great legislative and judicial battles in this field had been fought, and the foundations of social and industrial legislation had been well and truly laid. Thus, in particular, the doctrine of freedom of contract has remained central to the common law's understanding of employment throughout this century, although this understanding has had to be modified in various ways in order to accommodate new phenomena such as the growth in collective bargaining, and different forms of statutory intervention in the employment relationship . . .

THE CONTRACT AS AN AUTHORITATIVE SOURCE OF RULES

Although the parties are free (within the limits imposed by the general law and particular statutory rules) to contract on their own terms, the great majority of contracts of employment share certain common features. The employee undertakes, in exchange for the payment of remuneration, to obey the lawful and reasonable orders of the employer, and to take reasonable care in the carrying out of his employment duties. There is also a duty of fidelity towards the employer, which is translated into particular obligations not to enter into competition with him during working time, not to divulge or improperly use confidential information acquired in the course of his employment, and, within certain limits, to disclose to the employer information harmful to the employer's interests. The employee is, however, under no general duty to disclose personal misconduct, although he may be required to inform the employer of the misbehaviour of fellow employees.

The employer is bound by a duty to take reasonable care for the safety of the employee, to pay wages, and to exercise due respect and consideration in dealings with the employee. This duty of respect may be seen as the counterpart of the employee's duty of fidelity. It is not of recent creation, but it is a duty which, through the operation of the law of unfair dismissal and, in particular, that part of it concerned with 'constructive' dismissal (see below), has acquired a much-increased significance in recent years.

Express and Implied Terms

Although the parties are free to make the bargain of their choice, in practice many of the key features of their relationship are left undefined, and are settled by the courts through the device of the implied term. Implied terms are, in legal theory, of secondary significance in defining the contract, in the sense that they will not override express terms which state the contrary, nor can they be used as a basis for an interpretation having this effect. In reality, however, it would be hard to overemphasise either the contribution made by such terms in building up the content of the contract, or the flexibility and power this operation gives to the judges whose job it is to construe the contract. The importance is only enhanced by the closer link (explained below) between implied contractual terms and the legal effect of collective bargaining.

Implied terms are often divided by lawyers into those implied in fact, and those implied in law. The difference between the two is not as clear in practice as it appears on paper, but its basis is that, in relation to the former category, the courts will seek to justify their findings by reference to the presumed but unexpressed wishes of the parties. As an aid in so doing they will, among other things, have regard to what is established practice in the trade or industry in question, and to what they are sure must have been in the parties' contemplation. In the past, the standards to be met before such a power of implication was exercised were high, and imposed, in theory at least, a limit on judicial creativity. Judges were supposed to imply terms only where it was necessary to do so to give business efficacy to the contract, or where the term was one which would immediately have been accepted by both parties when their attention was drawn to it. Today, although it is going too far to say openly that the judges have power to imply all terms which they think reasonable, the case law has developed in that direction. It has recently been said judicially that 'we can treat as an agreed term a term which would not have been at once assented to by both parties at the time when they made the contract, for example where one party would at once have assented to it and the other would have done so after it had been made clear to him that unless he did so there would be no contract', and it has also been held that the conduct of the parties under the contract is highly relevant to deciding the content of any implied terms which may be contained in it.

In relation to terms implied in law, as opposed to fact, the basis for judicial intervention is a legal requirement that the employment relationship contains a term dealing with a particular matter. Sometimes this will be as a result of statute, but, more often, the legal requirement will arise as a result of judicial interpretation of the rules of the common law. There the judges obviously enjoy a great measure of discretion. The term implied by law is seen as a necessary incident of the constitution of the employment relationship.

One of the best illustrations is to be found in the *ASLEF* case, where the Court of Appeal in an important judgment (Napier, 1972) held that a 'work to rule' on the railways amounted to breach of an implied duty of co-operation, which was a part of the contract of employment. Such a finding could in no sense be justified by reference to the common intentions of the parties, since it was so contrary to the interests of the workers concerned. Nevertheless, the term in question was held, as a matter of law, to form part of the contract. The case provides the clearest evidence of what the judges think are the proper dimensions of the employment bargain, and an object lesson in the discovery and application of one of the most significant implied terms to be found in the contract . . . .

SUBSTANCE OF THE CONTRACT

The following discussion, which is in no sense exhaustive, is intended to illustrate the duties arising in three important areas: the employee's duty of obedience . . . .

Duty of Obedience

As noted above the employee's duty to obey the reasonable orders of his employer constitutes one of the traditional distinguishing features of the contract of employment. In the modern law, the legal basis for this feature is a term implied into the contract as a matter of law. In the past, breach of this duty left the employee open to the sanction of summary dismissal, and this remains true today, although the standards of behaviour expected of employees have been somewhat relaxed in line with changing social attitudes. Some of the most interesting developments, however, have taken place elsewhere. In the past, the ambit of the duty of obedience was explored by the courts only in the context of allegedly wrongful dismissals; not so today, when the existence of the range of statutory employment protection rights directs attention on to what may legitimately or reasonably be required by an employer of his employee. Examples may be drawn from the law of unfair dismissal and redundancy, topics which are discussed in detail in Chapter 15.

In unfair dismissal law the question whether an order falls within the scope of the powers of command given by the contract to the employer may be relevant at the stage of deciding either the reasonableness of a dismissal, or whether or not a dismissal took place. With regard to the former, while the issue whether the employee was contractually bound to obey is not decisive one way or the other as to fairness, this test allows the courts to evaluate and criticise the exercise of managerial prerogative.

The cases show, for example, the courts' readiness to express views on such diverse matters as the scope of the employer's right to specify the details of his employee's dress, and to implement badly thought-out systems for assessing work performance. By contrast, in proving a constructive dismissal—where the employer's improper conduct has allegedly justified the employee in leaving—the test is based on contract. A tribunal will often have to decide whether the giving of orders which the employee has found unacceptable amounts to a serious breach of the employer's implied duty of good and reasonable conduct, and as such warranted the employee's departure.

Another example may be taken from the law of redundancy, where the concept of job mobility has become of fundamental importance. An employee who is dismissed because of refusal to comply with a lawful order to take up another job with the same employer in another part of the country is dismissed for misconduct, not redundancy, and accordingly it is often vital to know the extent to which such a right on the part of the employer to direct movement forms part of the contract.

As these particular examples demonstrate, under the influence of the framework of individual statutory rights, the courts have, to a much greater extent than in the past, been given opportunities of passing judgment on the orders given by an employer to his employees. Under the influence of these rights, the prevailing view which has emerged favours a much more restrictive interpretation of the right to command than was previously found acceptable. The right to command is seen as more limited in scope and is itself subject to the employer's contractual duty to maintain the employee's trust and confidence. Some (for example, Napier, 1977; Elias, 1981) have seen in these changes a movement among the judiciary towards a more pluralistic analysis of the employment relationship, although this argument has not gone unchallenged (Collins, 1982; Glasbeek, 1984).

REFERENCES

Atiyah, P S 1979. *The Rise and Fall of Freedom of Contract.* Oxford: Clarendon Press.

Bartrip, P W J, and S B Burman. 1983. *The Wounded Soldiers of Industry.* Oxford: Clarendon Press.

Collins, H 1982. 'Capitalist Discipline and Corporatist Law'. *Industrial Law Journal*, 11 June (June and September), 78–93, 170–77.

Dicey, A V 1914. *Lectures on the Relation between Law and Public Opinion in England During the Nineteenth Century.* 2nd edn. London: Macmillan. Reissued 1962. London: Macmillan.

Elias, P 1981. 'Fairness in Unfair Dismissal: Trends and Tensions'. *Industrial Law Journal*, 10 (December), 201–17.

Foster, K 1983. 'The Legal Form of Work in the 19th Century: The Myth of Contract?' Paper presented to conference on 'The History of Law, Labour and Crime', University of Warwick, September. (Unpublished).

Fox, A 1974. *Beyond Contract: Work, Power and Trust Relations:* London: Faber.

Friedmann, W 1959. *Law in a Changing Society.* London: Stevens.

Glasbeek, H J 1984. 'The Utility of Model Building—Collins' Capitalist Discipline and Corporatist Law'. *Industrial Law Journal*, 13 (September), 133–52.

Haines, B W 1980. 'English Labour Law and the Separation from Contract'. *Journal of Legal History*, 1 (December), 262–96.

Hepple, B A 1982. 'Labour Law and Public Employees in Great Britain'. *Labour Law and the Community: Perspectives for the 1980s* Eds. Lord Wedderburn and W T Murphy. London: Institute of Advanced Legal Studies, 67, 83.

Kahn-Freund, O 1977. 'Blackstone's Neglected Child: The Contract of Employment'. *Law Quarterly Review*, 93 (October), 508–28.

Merritt, A 1982. 'The Historical Role of Law in the Regulation of Employment—Abstentionist or Interventionist?'. *Australian Journal of Law and Society*, 1 (1), 56–82.

Napier, B W 1972. 'Working to Rule—A Breach of the Contract of Employment?' *Industrial Law Journal*, 1 (September), 125–34.

Napier, BW 1977. 'Judicial Attitudes towards the Employment Relationship—Some Recent Developments'. *Industrial Law Journal*, 6 (March), 1–18.

Ruegg, A H 1901. 'Changes in the Law of England Affecting Labour'. *A Century of Law Reform. Twelve Lectures on the Changes in the Law of England During the Nineteenth Century.* London: Macmillan, 241–79.

Selznick, P 1969. *Law, Society and Industrial Justice*, New York: Russell Sage Foundation.

NOTES

1. The current judicial attitude towards contracts of employment—for instance, the extent to which the judges adopt a pluralist approach by recognising that employers and employees have divergent interests and the need for some sort of partnership between them—is clearly a matter of debate. No attempt to resolve the question need be made here. What is important for our purposes is to realise that neither judge-made law nor statute is 'neutral'—it is premised on particular, although changing, views of the proper relationship between employer and employee.

2. An employment contract is an example of a 'relational' contract (cf Macneil, p 63, and p 884): it will normally last some time and it is usually not possible to specify at the out-set exactly what the employee will be required to do. The 'management prerogative' to give orders to the employee is a response to this. Without suggesting that the current approach is in any way wrong, it is interesting to contrast it with the contract of partnership. This shares many of the employment contract's relational characteristics, but the common law and the Partnership Act 1890, which codified it, take the view that the relationship between parties is not hierarchical but equal. Thus the Partnership Act 1890 s 24 provides:

   (8) Any difference arising as to ordinary matters connected with the partnership business may be decided by a majority of the partners, but no change may be made in the nature of the partnership business without the consent of all existing partners.

   Under the Act, partners owe each other a series of fiduciary duties, derived from the earl-ier common law. In *Dean v MacDowell* (1878) 8 Ch D 345, 350–351, James L J said:

   It is quite clear . . . that in partnership matters there must be the utmost good faith, and that there is to that extent a fiduciary relation between the parties. That is to say, one partner must not directly or indirectly use the partnership assets for his own private benefit. He must not, in anything connected with the partnership, take any profit clandestinely for himself . . . .

   As we shall see, this goes further than the obligations imposed upon employees (p 503); it is completely different to the obligations of an employer.

3. An interesting development of the implied terms in contracts of employment was made by the House of Lords in *Malik v Bank of Credit and Commerce International* [1997] 3 All ER 1. The bank had operated for many years on two fronts. On the surface, it appeared to be a normal bank carrying on normal banking business. Behind this facade, however, it was a complete fraud dedicated to cheating customers and third parties. The plaintiffs were employees of the bank who knew nothing of the dark side of its business. In due course, the bank went into insolvency and the plaintiffs were made redundant.

   The plaintiffs brought an action against the liquidator arguing that the bank was in breach of an implied term and that their careers were blighted because future employers would be reluctant to take on ex-BCCI staff.

It is now an orthodox implied term in a contract of employment that neither party should 'engage in conduct likely to undermine the trust and confidence required if the employment relationship is to continue'. Lord Steyn remarked (at 15–16):

The evolution of the term is a comparatively recent development. The obligation probably has its origin in the general duty of co-operation between contracting parties: Hepple *Employment Law* (4th edn, 1981) paras 291–292, pp 134–135. The reason for this development is part of the history of the development of employment law in this century. The notion of a "master and servant" relationship became obsolete. Lord Slynn of Hadley recently noted in *Spring v Guardian Assurance plc* [1994] 3 All ER 129 at 161, [1995] 2 AC 296 at 335-

'the changes which have taken place in the employer/employee relationship, with far greater duties imposed on the employer than in the past, whether by statute or by judicial decision, to care for the physical, financial and even psychological welfare of the employee.'

A striking illustration of this change is *Scally v Southern Health and Social Services Board* to which I have already referred where the House of Lords implied a term that all employees in a certain category had to be notified by an employer of their entitlement to certain benefits. It was the change in legal culture which made possible the evolution of the implied term of trust and confidence.

There was some debate at the hearing about the possible interaction of the implied obligation of confidence and trust with other more specific terms implied by law. It is true that the implied term adds little to the employee's implied obligations to serve his employer loyally and not to act contrary to his employer's interests. The major importance of the implied duty of trust and confidence lies in its impact on the obligations of the employer: see Douglas Brodie 'The heart of the matter: mutual trust and confidence' (1996) 25 ILJ 121 (recent cases commentary). And the implied obligation as formulated is apt to cover the great diversity of situations in which a balance has to be struck between an employer's interest in managing his business as he sees fit and the employee's interest in not being unfairly and improperly exploited.

The evolution of the implied term of trust and confidence is a fact. It has not yet been indorsed by your Lordships' House. It has proved a workable principle in practice. It has not been the subject of adverse criticism in any decided cases and it has been welcomed in academic writings. I regard the emergence of the implied obligation of mutual trust and confidence as a sound development.

The bank argued that the implied term should not apply:

(a) if the dishonest behaviour of the bank was aimed at customers and not at employees; or

(b) if the employee only became aware of the dishonest conduct after he had ceased to be employed; or

(c) unless the conduct was such as to destroy or seriously damage the relationship between employee and employer.

The House of Lords rejected all three suggested limitations. (For later proceedings, see [1999] 2 All ER 1005, [1999] 4 All ER 83 and [2000] 3 All ER 51.)

VII. JUSTIFICATIONS FOR IMPLIED TERMS

We saw that Posner and Rosenfield (above, p 393) explained 'gap-filling' rules, including implied terms, on the basis that the courts provide default rules reflecting what the parties would have agreed in the absence of transactions costs. Not all commentators accept that this is an adequate description of what is taking place. See also Ayres and Gertner (above, p 431).

■ Collins, *The Law of Contract* (4th edn, 2003)
pp 245–246

4. Justifications for implied terms

How can we explain and justify the above use of implied terms to supplement contractual obligations? In some instances it is apparent that the reference to the joint intention of the parties, as evidenced by the need to give business efficacy to their transaction, supports the implication of terms on grounds which merely complement the traditional justification of contractual obligations based upon the will of the parties. It is true that the will of the parties was never expressed, but the evidence supporting the claim that the term represents a presupposition or necessary implication of the words used can be so overwhelming that few could doubt that the term represents their original intention. But it is clear that the use of implied terms extends beyond any sort of justification of the type that the term merely states expressly what was silently understood by the parties.

Economic analysis of law suggests a good reason why the courts should provide a set of default rules to govern contractual relations in the absence of express terms. Default rules save transaction costs by permitting the parties to avoid the costs of negotiating every detail of their arrangement every time they make a contract, because they know that the courts will fill in the gaps in the usual way. This makes good sense, but it is arguable whether or not participants in the market deliberately avail themselves of this opportunity to save transaction costs. On the contrary, the proliferation of the standard form contract suggests that any party with sufficient resources is likely to devise a standard set of express terms to suit his or her purposes exactly. Many cases we have discussed so far concerning implied terms, such as *Johnstone v Bloomsbury Health Authority* and *Liverpool City Council v Irwin*, comprise instances where the claim that an implied term exists is used to combat the one-sided standard form contract of the other party.

Nor does the economic analysis suggest a satisfactory account of the grounds for the selection of terms by the courts. Under the efficiency analysis, the court should select those implied terms to which the parties would have agreed but for the presence of transaction costs. Although this criterion makes sense for terms which give a contract business efficacy, it is far from clear that it provides an intelligible guide in other cases. Consider the bargaining situation in *Liverpool City Council v Irwin*. The council was presumable reluctant to agree to an obligation to maintain the common premises, so it would have held out against such an obligation, and, depending upon the local forces of supply and demand for tower block local authority housing, it might or might not have been successful. But even if it had agreed to the obligation, it could have insisted upon an increased rent to cover those costs, so to imply a term requiring a maintenance obligation without adjusting the rent produces a contract to which the parties never would have agreed.

. . .

The notion of a default rule is, therefore, a misleading description of the use of implied terms. Through the implication of terms the courts can achieve what they regard as a fair and practical allocation of risks between the contracting parties, a view which may alter over time as illustrated by the changing implied terms inserted into the contract of employment. In this process the courts can seek to equalize the obligations of the parties, even in the teeth of express terms of standard form contracts, and so pursue ideas of fairness. The justification for implied terms therefore rests ultimately not on the intentions of the parties but rather the court's view of the reasonable expectations of the parties to the transaction.

QUESTIONS

1. In interpreting the words of a contract, when will the courts be prepared to depart from the meaning of the words used as given in a dictionary?

2.   What use may be made of evidence of statements as to the meaning of the words made by the parties during negotiations? Is their conduct after the contract has been made relevant for any purpose?

3.   When, in the absence of an express term or a term implied by statute, will the courts imply a term into a contract?

4.   What is the test of whether a term should be implied 'at law'? Why are the judges (eg Lord Wilberforce in *Liverpool City Council v Irwin*) sometimes so coy about the implication of terms?

5.   Can you invent an example of a term that would not be implied into the contract at law, but which would be implied under the 'business efficacy' or 'officious bystander' tests?

6.   A buyer of goods complains that the goods she has received were not what she had expected. Explain to her in broad terms the protection she may have under the implied terms under the Sale of Goods Act 1979 (as amended).

CHAPTER SIXTEEN

DISCHARGE BY FRUSTRATION

In this chapter, we examine the doctrine of frustration, under which a contract may be discharged by some subsequent change of circumstance. As we shall see, the doctrine is dealing with events that are outside the control of either party and which the contract does not provide for—it is perhaps even confined to events that the parties had not foreseen (see p 479). As we noted earlier (p 392), the doctrine is thus concerned with allocating risks, but rather than put the risk wholly on one or other of the parties, the doctrine achieves a very rough-and-ready division of the risks between them. Often this can be justified in terms of efficiency: the parties would probably have agreed something similar had they made a 'complete contingent contract' (see p 77). Often the result can also be justified as promoting fairness. (See Posner and Rosenfield's, 'Impossibility in Contract Law', on p 393.)

■ Allen Sykes, *The New Palgrave Dictionary of Economics and the Law*
pp 264–266

Impossibility Doctrine in Contract Law

Claims of impossibility or impracticability have arisen in a variety of settings. The leading early case on impossibility, *Taylor v. Caldwell*, held that the owner of a concert hall had no liability to the promoters of a concert for lost profits when the hall burned down and the owner was unable to provide the promised concert facility. A number of cases have held that an obligation to deliver crops grown on a particular tract of land is discharged in the event of crop failure. . . .

Impossibility and impracticability decisions have been the focus of considerable economic commentary, much of it from the economic perspective. The earlier writers tended to view the doctrine fairly favourably, although later writers have been more critical.

I. THE RISK-SHARING/DIVERSIFICATION JUSTIFICATION

Sykes (1990) and others have been critical of the proposition that impossibility decisions generally can be justified on these grounds. In particular, nothing in the doctrine is expressly sensitive to the factors that might indicate whether the promisor was a comparatively poor risk bearer in a given case. Rather, the focus is on matters such as the 'unforeseen' nature of the contingency that interferes with performance or the magnitude of the increase in cost of performance (see especially Triantis 1992). As a result, large agribusiness interests have been the beneficiary of the crop-failure doctrine, and non-profit corporations have been the beneficiary of the doctrine in *Taylor v. Caldwell* at the expense of individual performing artists. . . .

Not only is the risk-sharing issue by itself a potentially complicated one depending on the case, but the shifting of risk to the promisee that results from the impossibility doctrine may have unfortunate incentive effects. The benefits of the bargain to the promisee are external to the promisor and will not be considered by the promisor in taking precautions against adverse contingencies (unless those precautions are contractable at reasonable cost). Thus, perhaps the owner of a music hall, as in *Taylor*, may as a result of the impossibility doctrine take inadequate precautions against fire and other events that would put the hall out of service. . . .

Related to these moral hazard concerns, information asymmetries may reduce or eliminate any gains from shifting risk to a less risk-averse promisee, as Posner and Rosenfield (1977) acknowledge. Promisors may often have better information about the likelihood of events that may make their performance 'impossible'. Unless the discharge of the promisor under the impossibility doctrine is made conditional on disclosure of this superior information at the time of contracting, various problems may arise. Promisees may enter into contracts with negative expected value, for example, or may fail to take certain precautions themselves that are valuable. Yet, the cases often seem to pay little attention to these issues . . .

■ *Taylor v Caldwell*

(1863) 3 B & S 826, 122 ER 826, Queen's Bench

Blackburn J

In this case the plaintiffs and defendants had, on the 27th May, 1862, entered into a contract by which the defendants agreed to let the plaintiffs have the use of The Surrey Gardens and Music Hall on four days then to come, viz, the 17th June, 15th July, 5th August and 19th August, for the purpose of giving a series of four grand concerts, and day and night fêtes at the Gardens and Hall on those days respectively; and the plaintiffs agreed to take the Gardens and Hall on those days, and pay 100l for each day.

The parties inaccurately call this a 'letting', and the money to be paid a 'rent'; but the whole agreement is such as to shew that the defendants were to retain the possession of the Hall and Gardens so that there was to be no demise of them, and that the contract was merely to give the plaintiffs the use of them on those days. Nothing however, in our opinion, depends on this. The agreement then proceeds to set out various stipulations between the parties as to what each was to supply for these concerts and entertainments, and as to the manner in which they should be carried on. The effect of the whole is to shew that the existence of the Music Hall in the Surrey Gardens in a state fit for a concert was essential for the fulfilment of the contract,—such entertainments as the parties contemplated in their agreement could not be given without it.

After the making of the agreement, and before the first day on which a concert was to be given, the Hall was destroyed by fire. This destruction, we must take it on the evidence, was without the fault of either party, and was so complete that in consequence the concerts could not be given as intended. And the question we have to decide is whether, under these circumstances, the loss which the plaintiffs have sustained is to fall upon the defendants. The parties when framing their agreement evidently had not present to their minds the possibility of such a disaster, and have made no express stipulation with reference to it, so that the answer to the question must depend upon the general rules of law applicable to such a contract.

There seems no doubt that where there is a positive contract to do a thing, not in itself unlawful, the contractor must perform it or pay damages for not doing it, although in consequence of unforeseen accidents, the performance of his contract has become unexpectedly burthensome or even impossible. The law is so laid down in 1 Roll Abr 450, Condition (G), and in the note to *Walton v Waterhouse*, and is recognised as the general rule by all the Judges in the much discussed case of *Hall v Wright*. But this rule is only applicable when the contract is positive and absolute, and not subject to any condition either express or implied: and there are authorities which, as we think, establish the principle that where, from the nature of the contract, it appears that the parties must from the beginning have known that it could not be fulfilled unless when the time for the fulfilment of the contract arrived some particular specified thing continued to exist, so that, when entering into the contract, they must have contemplated such continuing existence as the foundation of what was to be done; there, in the absence of any express or implied warranty that the thing shall exist, the contract is not to be construed as a positive contract, but as subject to an implied condition that the parties shall be excused in case, before breach, performance becomes impossible from the perishing of the thing without default of the contractor.

There seems little doubt that this implication tends to further the great object of making the legal construction such as to fulfil the intention of those who entered into the contract. For in the course of affairs men in making such contracts in general would, if it were brought to their minds, say that there should be such a condition. . . . There is a class of contracts in which a person binds himself to do something which requires to be performed by him in person; and such promises, eg promises to marry, or promises to serve for a certain time, are never in practice qualified by an express exception of the death of the party; and therefore in such cases the contract is in terms broken if the promisor dies before fulfilment. Yet it was very early determined that, if the performance is personal, the executors are not liable; *Hyde v The Dean of Windsor*. See 2 Wms Exors 1560 5th edn, where a very apt illustration is given. 'Thus', says the learned author, 'if an author undertakes to compose a work, and dies before completing it, his executors are discharged from this contract: for the undertaking is merely personal in its nature, and, by the intervention of the contractor's death, has become impossible to be performed.' For this he cites a dictum of Lord Lyndhurst in *Marshall v Broadhurst*, and a case mentioned by Patteson J in *Wentworth v Cock*. In *Hall v Wright*, Crompton J, in his judgment, puts another case. 'Where a contract depends upon personal skill, and the act of God renders it impossible, as, for instance, in the case of a painter employed to paint a picture who is struck blind, it may be that the performances might be excused.'

It seems that in those cases the only ground on which the parties or their executors, can be excused from the consequences of the breach of the contract is, that from the nature of the contract there is an implied condition of the continued existence of the life of the contractor, and, perhaps in the case of the painter of his eyesight. In the instances just given, the person, the continued existence of whose life is necessary to the fulfilment of the contract, is himself the contractor, but that does not seem in itself to be necessary to the application of the principle; as is illustrated by the following example. In the ordinary form of an apprentice deed the apprentice binds himself in unqualified terms to 'serve until the full end and term of seven years to be fully complete and ended', during which term it is covenanted that the apprentice his master 'faithfully shall serve', and the father of the apprentice in equally unqualified terms binds himself for the performance by the apprentice of all and every covenant on his part. (See the form, 2 Chitty on Pleading, 370, 7th edn by Greening.) It is undeniable that if the apprentice dies within the seven years, the covenant of the father that he shall perform his covenant to serve for seven years is not fulfilled, yet surely it cannot be that an action would lie against the father? Yet the only reason why it would not is that he is excused because of the apprentice's death.

These are instances where the implied condition is of the life of a human being, but there are others in which the same implication is made as to the continued existence of a thing. For example, where a contract of sale is made amounting to a bargain and sale, transferring presently the property in specific chattels, which are to be delivered by the vendor at a future day; there, if the chattels, without the fault of the vendor, perish in the interval, the purchaser must pay the price and the vendor is excused from performing his contract to deliver, which has thus become impossible . . .

That this is the rule of the English law is established by the case of *Rugg v Minett*, where the article that perished before delivery was turpentine, and it was decided that the vendor was bound to refund the price of all those lots in which the property had not passed; but was entitled to retain without deduction the price of those lots in which the property had passed, though they were not delivered, and though in the conditions of sale, which are set out in the report, there was no express qualification of the promise to deliver on payment. It seems in that case rather to have been taken for granted than decided that the destruction of the thing sold before delivery excused the vendor from fulfilling his contract to deliver on payment.

This also is the rule in the Civil law, and it is worth noticing that Pothier, in his celebrated Traité du Contrat de Vente (see Part 4, ss 307 et seq; and Part 2, ch 1, s 1, art 4, s 1) treats this as merely an example of the more general rule that every obligation de certo corpore is extinguished when the thing ceases to exist. See Blackburn on the Contract of Sale, p 173.

It may, we think, be safely asserted to be now English law, that in all contracts of loan of chattels or bailments if the performance of the promise of the borrower or bailee to return the things lent or bailed, becomes impossible because it has perished, this impossibility (if not arising from the fault of the borrower or bailee from some risk which he has taken upon himself) excuses the borrower or bailee from the performance of his promise to redeliver the chattel.

...The principle seems to us to be that, in contracts in which the performance depends on the continued existence of a given person or thing, a condition is implied that the impossibility of performance arising from the perishing of the person or thing shall excuse the performance.

In none of these cases is the promise in words other than positive, nor is there any express stipulation that the destruction of the person or thing shall excuse the performance; but that excuse is by law implied, because from the nature of the contract it is apparent that the parties contracted on the basis of the continued existence of the particular person or chattel. In the present case, looking at the whole contract, we find that the parties contracted on the basis of the continued existence of the Music Hall at the time when the concerts were to be given; that being essential to their performance.

We think, therefore, that the Music Hall having ceased to exist, without fault of either party, both parties are excused, the plaintiffs from taking the gardens and paying the money, the defendants from performing their promise to give the use of the Hall and Gardens and other things. Consequently the rule must be absolute to enter the verdict for the defendants.

Rule absolute.

NOTES

1. In theory, there were three possible outcomes to this case:

   (a) the licensees should pay even though they could not use the Hall (risk on licensee);
   (b) the licensors should be liable for failing to provide the hall even though they were not at fault (risk on licensor);
   (c) both parties were released by discharge of the contract (risk divided).

2. The fire seems to have been treated as purely accidental. If this was really so (see Treitel p 866, n 9), presumably neither party could be singled out as better able to prevent the risk from materialising (see Posner and Rosenfield p 393). Who was in a better position to insure against (a) the licensor's loss of rent and (b) the waste of advertising expenditure by the licensee? In the event, (a) was not argued: the contest was between (b) and (c).

3. Blackburn uses, as an example of a party being excused by impossibility, the case of goods that are destroyed after they have become the buyer's property but before they have been delivered. What he says is still the law but it would probably be analysed rather differently nowadays. Under the Sale of Goods Act, the risk of accidental destruction of or damage to the goods normally passes to the buyer with the property, s 20; once the risk has passed, the buyer will have to pay the price even if there is nothing left for the seller to deliver. Although to that extent the seller is excused, this outcome is usually explained in terms that the seller has performed its side of the contract, rather than the contract being discharged. The other situation mentioned by Blackburn, the destruction of the

turpentine *before* property has passed, *is* considered to be a case of discharge of the contract. The Sale of Goods Act 1979 provides:

Section 7

Where there is an agreement to sell specific goods and subsequently the goods, without any fault on the part of the seller or buyer, perish before the risk passes to the buyer, the agreement is avoided.

The result is that the buyer can recover the price paid, but the seller is not liable for non-delivery. (Note that in some contracts by express agreement or by implication, the risk passes before the property: thus in fob and cif contracts, risk passes as from shipment.)

4.   The doctrine that originated in *Taylor v Caldwell* and which has come to be known as the doctrine of frustration may apply not only where the subject matter of the contract has been destroyed but also in other cases in which one party's obligation has, without either party's fault, become impossible to perform, in which the contract has become illegal, and, but only in very extreme cases, in which the commercial purpose of the contract has been destroyed (see section IV of this chapter).

5.   Although it is usual to think of there being a single doctrine of frustration, in practice it applies rather differently in the various situations. This is particularly clear with contracts that have become illegal. As we shall see, normally there will be no frustration if the parties foresaw the event or provided for it, but neither restriction applies when the contract is frustrated by illegality. This is because, whereas the other rules about frustration are primarily concerned with the allocation of risks of unexpected events, the rules on contracts frustrated by illegality are primarily concerned with matters of 'public policy', see Section 9 . We shall see, however, that the rules do not fit terribly easily into some other contexts, particularly employment contracts (p 467).

I. THE JURISTIC BASIS OF FRUSTRATION

■ *Davis Contractors Ltd v Fareham UDC*

[1956] 2 All ER 145, House of Lords

The appellants agreed to build 78 council houses for the respondent council within a period of eight months. In fact, the work took 22 months. The respondents paid the contract price. The appellants argued that the contract has been frustrated by the long delay, which was due mainly to a shortage of skilled labour. Since the houses had been completed, the purpose of the contention was to argue for payment on a *quantum meruit* basis. The House of Lords held that the contract had not been frustrated.

Lord Reid

. . . Frustration has often been said to depend on adding a term to the contract by implication. . . .
    I may be allowed to note an example of the artificiality of the theory of an implied term given by Lord Sands in *Scott & Sons v Del Sel* . . .

'A tiger has escaped from a travelling menagerie. The milkgirl fails to deliver the milk. Possibly the milkman may be exonerated from any breach of contract; but, even so, it would seem hardly reasonable to base that exoneration on the ground that "tiger days excepted" must be held as if written into the milk contract.'

I think that there is much force in Lord Wright's criticism in *Denny, Mott & Dickson, Ltd v James B. Fraser & Co, Ltd:*

> 'The parties did not anticipate fully and completely, if at all, or provide for what actually happened. It is not possible to my mind to say that, if they had thought of it, they would have said, "Well, if that happens, all is over between us". On the contrary, they would almost certainly on the one side or the other have sought to introduce reservations or qualifications or compensations.'

It appears to me that frustration depends, at least in most cases, not on adding any implied term but on the true construction of the terms which are, in the contract, read in light of the nature of the contract and of the relevant surrounding circumstances when the contract was made....

Lord Radcliffe

... Before I refer to the facts, I must say briefly what I understand to be the legal principle of frustration. It is not always expressed in the same way, but I think that the points which are relevant to the decision of this case are really beyond dispute. The theory of frustration belongs to the law of contract and it is represented by a rule which the courts will apply in certain limited circumstances for the purpose of deciding that contractual obligations, ex facie binding, are no longer enforceable against the parties. The description of the circumstances that justify the application of the rule and, consequently, the decision whether, in a particular case, those circumstances exist are, I think, necessarily questions of law. It has often been pointed out that the descriptions vary from one case of high authority to another. Even as long ago as 1918, Lord Sumner was able to offer an anthology of different tests directed to the factor of delay alone, and delay, though itself a frequent cause of the principle of frustration being invoked, is only one instance of the kind of circumstance to which the law attends (see *Bank Line, Ltd v A. Capel & Co*). A full current anthology would need to be longer yet. But the variety of descriptions is not of any importance, so long as it is recognised that each is only a description and that all are intended to express the same general idea. I do not think that there has been a better expression of that idea than the one offered by Earl Loreburn in *F A Tamplin SS Co. Ltd v Anglo-Mexican Petroleum Products Co. Ltd*. It is shorter to quote than to try to paraphrase it:

> '... a court can and ought to examine the contract and the circumstances in which it was made, not of course to vary, but only to explain it, in order to see whether or not from the nature of it the parties must have made their bargain on the footing that a particular thing or state of things would continue to exist. And if they must have done so, then a term to that effect will be implied, though it be not expressed in the contract ... no court has an absolving power, but it can infer from the nature of the contract and the surrounding circumstances that a condition which is not expressed was a foundation on which the parties contracted.'

So expressed, the principle of frustration, the origin of which seems to lie in the development of commercial law, is seen to be a branch of a wider principle which forms part of the English law of contract as a whole. But, in my opinion, full weight ought to be given to the requirement that the parties 'must have made' their bargain on the particular footing. Frustration is not to be lightly invoked as the dissolvent of a contract.

Lord Loreburn ascribes the dissolution to an implied term of the contract that was actually made. This approach is in line with the tendency of English courts to refer all the consequences of a contract to the will of those who made it. But there is something of a logical difficulty in seeing how the parties could even impliedly have provided for something which, ex hypothesi, they neither expected nor foresaw; and the ascription of frustration to an implied term of the contract has been criticised as obscuring the true action of the court which consists in applying an objective rule of the law of contract to the contractual obligations that the parties have imposed on themselves. So long as each theory produces the same result as the other, as normally it does, it matters little which theory is avowed (see *British*

Movietonews, Ltd v London & District Cinemas, Ltd per Viscount Simon). But it may still be of some importance to recall that, if the matter is to be approached by way of implied term, the solution of any particular case is not to be found by inquiring what the parties themselves would have agreed on had they been, as they were not, forewarned. It is not merely that no one can answer that hypothetical question; it is also that the decision must be given 'irrespective of the individuals concerned, their temperaments and failings, their interest and circumstances' (*Hirji Mulji v Cheong Yue SS Co*). The legal effect of frustration 'does not depend on their intention or their opinions, or even knowledge, as to the event'. On the contrary, it seems that, when the event occurs, the

> 'meaning of the contract must be taken to be, not what the parties did intend (for they had neither thought nor intention regarding it), but that which the parties, as fair and reasonable men, would presumably have agreed upon if, having such possibility in view, they had made express provision as to their several rights and liabilities in the event of its occurrence.'

(*Dahl v Nelson, Donkin & Co*, per Lord Watson.)

By this time, it might seem that the parties themselves have become so far disembodied spirits that their actual persons should be allowed to rest in peace. In their place there rises the figure of the fair and reasonable man. And the spokesman of the fair and reasonable man, who represents after all no more than the anthropomorphic conception of justice, is, and must be, the court itself. So, perhaps, it would be simpler to say at the outset that frustration occurs whenever the law recognises that, without default of either party, a contractual obligation has become incapable of being performed because the circumstances in which performance is called for would render it a thing radically different from that which was undertaken by the contract. Non haec in foedera veni. It was not this that I promised to do. There is, however, no uncertainty as to the materials on which the court must proceed.

> 'The data for decision are, on the one hand, the terms and construction of the contract, read in the light of the surrounding circumstances, and, on the other hand, the events which have occurred.'

(*Denny, Mott & Dickson Ltd v James B Fraser & Co Ltd*, per Lord Wright.)

In the nature of things there is often no room for any elaborate inquiry. The court must act on a general impression of what its rule requires. It is for that reason that special importance is necessarily attached to the occurrence of any unexpected event that, as it were, changes the face of things. But, even so, it is not hardship or inconvenience or material loss itself which calls the principle of frustration into play. There must be as well such a change in the significance of the obligation that the thing undertaken would, if performed, be a different thing from that contracted for.

I am bound to say that, if this is the law, the appellants' case seems to be a long way from a case of frustration. . . .

NOTES

1. Isn't Radcliffe's objection to the implied term theory almost equally applicable to any of the 'usual' implied terms? Doesn't Lord Watson's formulation of the implied term test come closest to what is going on? (Perhaps 'technique' would be a more appropriate word than theory: see Atiyah, *Essays on Contract*, 1986, p 273.)

2. Some view the doctrine as based more on fairness. In *British Movietonenews Ltd v London and District Cinemas Ltd*, Denning LJ in the Court of Appeal said ([1951] 1 KB 190, 200):

    In these frustration cases . . . the court really exercises a qualifying power—a power to qualify the absolute, literal or wide terms of the contract—in order to do what is just and reasonable in the new situation; and it can now by statute make ancillary orders to that end. Until recently the court only exercised this power when there was a frustrating event, that is a supervening event which struck away the foundations of the contract. But in the important decision of *Sir*

Lindsay Parkinson & Co Ltd v Commissioners of Works this court exercised a like power when there was no frustrating event, but only an uncontemplated turn of events. . . .

This does not mean that the courts no longer insist on the binding force of contracts deliberately made. It only means that they will not allow the words, in which they happen to be phrased, to become tyrannical masters. The court qualifies the literal meaning of the words so as to bring them into accord with the true scope of the contract. Even if the contract is absolute in its terms, nevertheless if it is not absolute in intent, it will not be held absolute in effect. The day is done when we can excuse an unforeseen injustice by saying to the sufferer 'It is your own folly. You ought not to have passed that form of words. You ought to have put in a clause to protect yourself.' We no longer credit a party with the foresight of a prophet or his lawyer with the draftsmanship of a Chalmers. We realize that they have their limitations and make allowances accordingly. It is better thus.

> The House of Lords [1952] AC 166 pointed out that the doctrine is still governed by strict rules. Thus Viscount Simon said (at 183):

With all respect to the learning and acumen of the Lord Justice, I do not agree that there has been a recent change as the result of which the courts now exercise a wider power . . .

> The case referred to by Denning is not usually regarded as one of frustration: see p 883.

3.   Why does the doctrine require such a fundamental change of circumstances before the contract is discharged? Why not permit discharge whenever one party satisfies the court that he would never have agreed to the contract on these terms had he foreseen the risk? (Compare force majeure clauses, p 440.) Should it be sufficient for the contract to be frustrated that businessmen in the relevant trade would consider the contract to be at an end in the circumstances that have occurred? Although the rule is that a contract will only be frustrated if events have rendered performance fundamentally different, it is recognised that the decision may follow closely

. . . from a commercial arbitrator's findings as to mercantile usage and the understanding of mercantile men about the significance of the commercial differences between what was promised and what in the changed circumstances would now fall to be performed. (Lord Diplock in *Pioneer Shipping Ltd v BTP Tioxide Ltd, The Nema* [1981] 2 All ER 1030 at 1036)

> In that case, arbitrators had found that a charter was frustrated when strikes at the loading port would probably prevent more than three out of the seven voyages originally contemplated. The House of Lords refused to upset this finding, saying that this should be done only if the arbitrator had not applied the right legal test or had reached a conclusion no reasonable person could have reached (ibid, at 1047).

4.   If a contract is frustrated, the discharge is automatic, rather than depending on a choice by one of the parties: *Hirji Mulji v Cheong Yue Steamship Co Ltd* [1926] AC 497. The parties may think it is still in force when it has been frustrated, and vice versa. When it is clear what the effect of the supervening event is, this may not cause too much uncertainty: one may take the line that they should have realised. But what if the effect of the event is hard to gauge, for instance, if a strike or the illness of one of the parties is preventing performance, but the parties cannot tell how long it will last? In *The Nema* at 1047 Lord Roskill said:

. . . where the effect of [the] event is to cause delay in the performance of contractual obligations, it is often necessary to wait on events in order to see whether the delay already suffered and the prospects of further delay from that cause will make the ultimate performance of the relevant contractual obligations 'radically different', to borrow Lord Radcliffe's phrase, from that which was undertaken by the contract.

As frustration is automatic, it would seem that the parties' conduct should not be taken into account in determining the date of frustration, if any. In the context of employment contracts, this rule does not sit easily. Frequently, when an employee falls ill it is not clear how long the illness will be nor what permanent effects it will have, and often the parties leave matters unresolved. As Phillips J said in *Hart v AR Marshall & Sons (Bulwell) Ltd* [1978] 2 All ER 413:

... if the employer has not dismissed the employee on the ground that he cannot reasonably be expected to wait any longer for his return, why should the court declare that the contract of employment has terminated by operation of law?

It seems to us that considerable importance attaches to the failure of an employer in such circumstances to dismiss the employee. We have wondered whether in truth the doctrine of frustration has anything much to do with short-term periodic contracts of employment, for there is no doubt that the concept is alien to both employers and employees, and is often not matched by the reality of the situation as they see it. The automatic ending of a contract by operation of law in a case where the subject-matter is destroyed is easily understood and matches experience. So is the case where a sudden calamity overtakes an employee which there and then renders any future service by him impossible. But in the case of an illness of uncertain duration the situation is quite different and neither employer nor employee thinks in terms approaching those underlying the concept of frustration.

However, experience shows that in a surprisingly large area of industry formal contracts of employment, and standard terms and conditions, still do not exist or if they do, make no provision for the rights of the parties during a prolonged period of illness of an employee. Very often, as in the present case, no wages are paid during sickness nor are any other formal arrangements made. In such cases the employee is in a sort of limbo. It seems that from the employer's point of view there is a reluctance to dismiss an employee when he is away sick; because to do so may seem harsh. From the employee's point of view it may seem preferable not to be dismissed, albeit that no wages are being paid, because there is a hope that one day he will be able to return to work, though not necessarily to the same job. Experience in such cases shows that the parties very often drift along in this situation for long periods of time during which the employee has ceased to do any work, or to be able to do any work, but has not been formally dismissed. The legal position seems to be that the employee is still employed although he is not in receipt of wages, and that his employment continues until he is dismissed or the contract is frustrated and comes to an end by operation of law. In these circumstances, while we think it right to attach considerable importance in a case of this kind to the failure by the employer to dismiss the employee, it is, we think, impossible to say that unless the employee is dismissed the contract must always be taken to continue. To do so would be tantamount to saying that frustration cannot occur in the case of short-term periodic contracts of employment. ...

In our judgment it comes to this. The failure of the employer to dismiss the employee is a factor, and an important factor, to take into account when considering whether the contract of employment has been frustrated. But it is not conclusive.

II. SHOULD ONE PARTY BEAR THE RISK?

Even if there is a radical change, the contract is not necessarily discharged.

■ *Maritime National Fish Ltd v Ocean Trawlers Ltd*
[1935] AC 524, Privy Council

By s 69a of the Canadian Fisheries Act, it was a punishable offence to leave any port in Canada with intent to fish with a vessel that used an otter trawl, except under licence from the

Minister. The appellants were charterers of the *St C*, a steam trawler belonging to the respondents, which was fitted with, and could only operate as trawler with, an otter trawl. It was expressly agreed that the trawler should be employed in the fishing industry only. The charterparty was dated 23 October 1928, and was to continue from year to year. It was renewed on 25 October for one year. On 11 March 1933, the appellants applied to the Minister of Fisheries for licences for the five trawlers they were operating. The Minister, in his reply, stated that only three licences would be granted, and he requested the appellants to state for which of the five trawlers they desired to have licenses. The appellants gave the names of three trawlers other than the *St C* and licences were issued for those three trawlers. The appellants thereupon claimed that the charterparty had thereby been frustrated and that they were no longer bound by it. In an action brought by the respondents for hire due under the charter, the appellants pleaded that the contract had become impossible of performance, and that they were wholly discharged from it.

The opinion of the Privy Council (Lords Atkin, Tomlin, Macmillan and Wright) was delivered by **Lord Wright:**

In a case such as the present it may be questioned whether the Court should imply a condition resolutive of the contract (which is what is involved in frustration) when the parties might have inserted an express condition to that effect but did not do so, though the possibility that things might happen as they did, was present in their minds when they made the contract.

This was one of the grounds on which the judges of the Supreme Court were prepared to decide this case. Their Lordships did not indicate any dissent from the reasoning of the Supreme Court on this point, but they did not consider it necessary to hear a full argument, or to express any final opinion about it, because in their judgment the case could be properly decided on the simple conclusion that it was the act and election of the appellants which prevented the *St Cuthbert* from being licensed for fishing with an otter trawl. It is clear that the appellants were free to select any three of the five trawlers they were operating and could, had they willed, have selected the *St Cuthbert* as one, in which event a licence would have been granted to her. It is immaterial to speculate why they preferred to put forward for licences the three trawlers which they actually selected. Nor is it material, as between the appellants and the respondents, that the appellants were operating other trawlers to three of which they gave the preference. What matters is that they could have got a licence for the *St Cuthbert* if they had so minded. If the case be figured as one in which the *St Cuthbert* was removed from the category of privileged trawlers, it was by the appellants' hand that she was so removed, because it was their hand that guided the hand of the Minister in placing the licences where he did and thereby excluding the *St Cuthbert*. The essence of 'frustration' is that it should not be due to the act or election of the party. There does not appear to be any authority which has been decided directly on this point. There is, however, a reference to the question in the speech of Lord Sumner in *Bank Line, Ltd v Arthur Capel & Co*. What he says is: 'One matter I mention only to get rid of it. When the shipowners were first applied to by the Admiralty for a ship they named three, of which the *Quitto* was one and intimated that she was the one they preferred to give up. I think it is now well settled that the principle of frustration of an adventure assumes that the frustration arises without blame or fault on either side. Reliance cannot be placed on a self-induced frustration; indeed, such conduct might give the other party the option to treat the contract as repudiated. Nothing, however, was made of this in the courts below, and I will not now pursue it.' . . . their Lordships are of opinion that the loss of the *St Cuthbert's* licence can correctly be described, quoad the appellants, as 'a self induced frustration'.

NOTE

The appellants nominated for licences ships they owned themselves. It seems reasonable that a party should bear the risk of 'impossibility' that came about through its own choice. What would have been the outcome if the five ships they operated had all been chartered to them, so that the only choice was which of the chartered ships should go without licences?

■ *J Lauritzen A S v Wijsmuller B V, The Super Servant II*

[1990] 1 Lloyd's Rep 1, Court of Appeal

By a contract dated 7 July 1980, the defendants (Wijsmuller) agreed to carry the plaintiffs' (Lauritzen's) drilling rig (*Dan King*) from the Hitachi shipyard at Aryake Japan to a delivery location off Rotterdam. The drilling rig was to be delivered between 20 June 1981 and 20 August 1981 and was to be carried by using what the contract described as the 'transportation unit'. The unit was defined as meaning *Super Servant One* or *Super Servant Two*.

The contract provided in cl 17:

17. Cancellation

17.1. Wijsmuller has the right to cancel its performance under this Contract whether the loading has been completed or not, in the event of force majeur (sic), Acts of God, perils or danger and accidents of the sea, acts of war, warlike-operations, acts of public enemies, restraint of princes, rulers or people or seizure under legal process, quarantine restrictions, civil commotions, blockade, strikes, lockout, closure of the Suez or Panama Canal, congestion of harbours or any other circumstances whatsoever, causing extra-ordinary periods of delay and similar events and/or circumstances, abnormal increases in prices and wages, scarcity of fuel and similar events, which reasonably may impede, prevent or delay the performance of this contract.

On Jan. 29, 1981 *Super Servant Two* sank. The defendants had intended to use *Super Servant Two* for this contract; they had entered into other contracts with other persons which they could only perform using *Super Servant One*. On or about Feb. 16, 1981 the defendants informed the plaintiffs that they would not carry out the transportation of the drilling rig with either *Super Servant One* or *Super Servant Two*.

In the event a 'without prejudice' agreement was entered into in April, 1981 under which the rig was transported on a barge towed by a tug.

The plaintiffs claimed the losses they had suffered and the defendants counterclaimed in respect of the increased expenses they had incurred.

The preliminary issues for decision were (1) whether the defendants were entitled to cancel the contract under cl 17 and/or (2) the contract was frustrated (a) if the loss of *Super Servant Two* occurred without the negligence of the defendants and (b) if the loss was caused by the defendants' negligence.

At first instance ([1989] 1 Lloyd's Rep 148), Hobhouse J held for the defendants on issue 1(a) (ie under cl 17, they were entitled to cancel the contract if the loss of the *Super Servant II* occurred without their negligence), but against them on the other issues. The defendants appealed against the decision on questions 1(a) and 2(a) and (b). The Court of Appeal agreed that cl 17 would only protect the defendants if the loss had occurred without their or their servants' negligence. On the issue of frustration:

Bingham LJ

Certain propositions, established by the highest authority are not open to question:

1. The doctrine of frustration was evolved to mitigate the rigour of the common law's insistence on literal performance of absolute promises...The object of the doctrine was to give effect to the demands of justice, to achieve a just and reasonable result, to do what is reasonable and fair, as an expedient to escape from injustice where such would result from enforcement of a contract in its literal terms after a significant change in circumstances...

2. Since the effect of frustration is to kill the contract and discharge the parties from further liability under it, the doctrine is not to be lightly invoked, must be kept within very narrow limits and ought not to be extended . . .
3. Frustration brings the contract to an end forthwith, without more and automatically . . .
4. The essence of frustration is that it should not be due to the act or election of the party seeking to rely on it . . . A frustrating event must be some outside event or extraneous change of situation . . .
5. A frustrating event must take place without blame or fault on the side of the party seeking to rely on it . . . [citations omitted].

Question 2(a)

Mr Clarke for Wijsmuller submitted that the extraneous supervening event necessary to found a plea of frustration occurred when *Super Servant Two* sank on Jan. 29, 1981. The *Dan King* contract was not, however, thereupon frustrated but remained alive until Wijsmuller decided a fortnight later that that contract could not be, or would not be, performed. There was, he submitted, factually, no break in the chain of causation between the supervening event and the non-performance of the contract. He acknowledged that *Maritime National Fish Ltd* sup., contained observations on their face inimical to his argument, but distinguished that as a decision on causation confined to its own peculiar facts and laying down no general rule. For authoritative support Mr Clarke relied on cases dealing with the application of force majeure clauses in commodity contracts, and in particular on an unreported judgment of Mr Justice Robert Goff, as he then was, adopted with approval by the Court of Appeal in *Bremer Handelsgesellschaft mbH v Continental Grain Co* [1983] 1 Lloyd's Rep. 269 at p. 292:

> '. . . the question resolves itself into a question of causation: in my judgment, at least in a case in which a seller can (as in the present case) claim the protection of a clause which protects him where fulfilment is hindered by the excepted peril, subsequent delivery of his available stock to other customers will not be regarded as an independent cause of shortage, provided that in making such delivery the seller acted reasonably in all the circumstances of the case. . . .'

A similar approach was reflected in other cases: see, for example, *Intertradex S.A. v Leisieur—Tourteaux S.A.R.L.*, [1977] 2 Lloyd's Rep. 146 at p 115, per Mr Justice Donaldson as he then was; [1978] 2 Lloyd's Rep. 509 at p 513, per Lord Denning, M.R. Reliance was also placed on passages in The Law of Contract (7th ed) by Professor Treitel, which the Judge quoted in his judgment at p 152. Thus, Mr Clarke urged, this was a case in which Wijsmuller could not perform all their contracts once *Super Servant Two* was lost: they acted reasonably (as we must assume) in treating the *Dan King* contract as one they could not perform; so the sinking had the direct result of making that contract impossible to perform.

   Had the *Dan King* contract provided for carriage by *Super Servant Two* with no alternative, and that vessel had been lost before the time for performance, then assuming no negligence by Wijsmuller (as for purposes of this question we must), I feel sure the contract would have been frustrated. The doctrine must avail a party who contracts to perform a contract of carriage with a vessel which, through no fault of his, no longer exists. But that is not this case. The *Dan King* contract did provide an alternative. When that contract was made one of the contracts eventually performed by *Super Servant One* during the period of contractual carriage of *Dan King* had been made, the other had not, at any rate finally. Wijsmuller have not alleged that when the *Dan King* contract was made either vessel was earmarked for its performance. That, no doubt, is why an option was contracted for. Had it been foreseen when the *Dan King* contract was made that *Super Servant Two* would be unavailable for performance, whether because she had been deliberately sold or accidentally sunk, Lauritzen at least would have thought it no matter since the carriage could be performed with the other. I accordingly accept Mr Legh-Jones' submission that the present case does not fall within the very limited class of cases in which the law will relieve one party from an absolute promise he has chosen to make.

   But I also accept Mr Legh-Jones' submission that Wijsmuller's argument is subject to other fatal flaws. If, as was argued, the contract was frustrated when Wijsmuller made or communicated their decision on

Feb. 16, it deprives language of all meaning to describe the contract as coming to an end automatically. It was, indeed, because the contract did not come to an end automatically on Jan. 29, that Wijsmuller needed a fortnight to review their schedules and their commercial options. I cannot, furthermore, reconcile Wijsmuller's argument with the reasoning or the decision in *Maritime National Fish Ltd* sup. In that case the Privy Council declined to speculate why the charterers selected three of the five vessels to be licensed but, as I understand the case, regarded the interposition of human choice after the allegedly frustrating event as fatal to the plea of frustration. If Wijsmuller are entitled to succeed here, I cannot see why the charterers lost there. The cases on frustrating delay do not, I think, help Wijsmuller since it is actual and prospective delay (whether or not recognized as frustrating by a party at the time) which frustrates the contract, not a party's election or decision to treat the delay as frustrating. I have no doubt that force majeure clauses are, where their terms permit, to be construed and applied as in the commodity cases on which Wijsmuller relied, but it is in my view inconsistent with the doctrine of frustration as previously understood on high authority that its application should depend on any decision, however reasonable and commercial, of the party seeking to rely on it.

I reach the same conclusion as the Judge for the reasons which he lucidly and persuasively gave.

Question 2(b)

The issue between the parties was short and fundamental: what is meant by saying that a frustrating event, to be relied on, must occur without the fault or default, or without blame attaching to, the party relying on it?

Mr Clarke's answer was that a party was precluded from relying on an event only when he had acted deliberately or in breach of an actionable duty in causing it. Those conditions were not met here . . .

Wijsmuller's test would, in my judgment, confine the law in a legalistic strait-jacket and distract attention from the real question, which is whether the frustrating event relied upon is truly an outside event or extraneous change of situation or whether it is an event which the party seeking to rely on it had the means and opportunity to prevent but nevertheless caused or permitted to come about. A fine test of legal duty is inappropriate; what is needed is a pragmatic judgment whether a party seeking to rely on an event as discharging him from a contractual promise was himself responsible for the occurrence of that event.

Lauritzen have pleaded in some detail the grounds on which they say that *Super Servant Two* was lost as a result of the carelessness of Wijsmuller, their servants or agents. If those allegations are made good to any significant extent Wijsmuller would (even if my answer to Question 2(a) is wrong) be precluded from relying on their plea of frustration.

I would answer this question also as the Judge did and would therefore dismiss the appeal.

Dillon LJ gave judgment to the same effect. He remarked that the parallel to *Maritime National Fish:*

. . . seems to be even closer, if, as some of the documents seem to suggest, the defendants, after the loss of the *Super Servant Two*, negotiated extra fees with the parties with whom they had other contracts of carriage before finally allocating the *Super Servant One* to perform those other contracts.

Appeal dismissed.

NOTES

1. Was the defendants' inability to perform the contract in any real sense caused by their choice? Weren't they forced to break either this contract or one for which their second ship was scheduled? See Treitel 907–908. Treitel also notes that frustration is not always automatic: for instance, it has been held that if an employee is imprisoned, the employer may choose to treat the contract as discharged (*FC Shepherd & Co Ltd v Jerrom* [1987] QB 301), but the employee would not be allowed to plead frustration.

2.   Although the decision in *The Super Servant II* may seem hard, it may be justifiable on the grounds that to hold the *Dan King* contract discharged might encourage the defendants to choose which of their contracts to perform on the basis of which would give them the highest profit, rather than on the basis of efficiency. Suppose that the *Super Servant II* has been lost and the defendants are trying to decide whether to say they cannot perform this contract or to redeploy the *Super Servant I* and break another contract. Suppose that, on the *Dan King* contract, their profit would have been £5,000, and on the other £25,000. However, suppose also that the plaintiff's loss if there is a breach of the *Dan King* contract would be £100,000, whereas the party to the other contract would lose only £30,000 if it were broken. Is it economically more efficient to perform the *Dan King* contract or the other? The 'joint gain' to be made from performing the *Dan King* contract is £105,000; that on the other is only £55,000. It would thus be more efficient to perform the *Dan King* contract. If, however, the law allows the defendants to claim frustration, which contract will they choose to perform? (There may have been an element of 'calculation' on the actual facts; note Dillon LJ's remark.)

3.   Will any act of negligence, even completely unconnected to the contract, prevent a party from relying on frustration? Would a concert pianist be allowed to plead frustration if she could not play because of injuries received in a road accident for which she was to blame?

4.   If an event occurs that would normally frustrate the contract, but one party alleges that it was caused by the other's fault so that the doctrine does not apply, it is for the party alleging fault to prove it: *Joseph Constantine Steamship Line Ltd v Imperial Smelting Corpn Ltd* [1942] AC 154.

■ *Blackburn Bobbin Company Ltd v TW Allen & Sons Ltd*

[1918] 2 KB 467, Court of Appeal

Pickford LJ

This is an appeal from a decision of McCardie J, and the point raised is whether an implication is to be read into the contract the performance of which has been interfered with or prevented by matters arising out of the war. The contract, which contained no exceptions, was for the sale by the defendants to the plaintiffs of 70 standards of Finland birch timber at the price of 10/15 s per standard free on rail at Hull. Before the war it was the regular practice to load the timber on vessels at ports in Finland for direct sea carriage to English ports, and not to send it by rail across Scandinavia and ship it from a Scandinavian port to England. When war broke out the Germans declared timber to be contraband, but, even before that declaration, sailings from Finnish ports had entirely ceased, and therefore the ordinary and normal method of supplying Finland timber came to an end. I will assume that it was not possible, at first at any rate, to get Finland birch timber to England at all, although it is true that in 1916 a certain amount was sent across Scandinavia and shipped from ports there. In August, 1914, and the following months some correspondence took place between the plaintiffs and the defendants as to the timber, the former asking for supplies, and the defendants taking up the position that all pre-war contracts had been cancelled by the war.

The defendants contend that the contract was at an end because it was in the contemplation of both parties that the defendants should be able to supply the timber according to the ordinary method of supplying it in the trade, and that when that became impossible both parties were discharged from their obligations.

. . . In my opinion McCardie J was right in saying that the principle of [frustration] did not apply to discharge the defendants in this case. He has found that the plaintiffs were unaware at the time of the contract of the circumstance that the timber from Finland was shipped direct from a Finnish port to Hull, and that they did not know whether the transport was or was not partly by rail across Scandinavia, nor did they know that timber merchants in this country did not hold stocks of Finnish birch. I accept the finding that in fact the method of dispatching this timber was not known to the plaintiffs. But there remains the question, Must they be deemed to have contracted on the basis of the continuance of that method although they did not in fact know of it? I see no reason for saying so. Why should a purchaser of goods, not specific goods, be deemed to concern himself with the way in which the seller is going to fulfil his contract by providing the goods he has agreed to sell? The sellers in this case agreed to deliver the timber free on rail at Hull, and it was no concern of the buyers as to how the sellers intended to get the timber there. I can see no reason for saying—and to free the defendants from liability this would have to be said—that the continuance of the normal mode of shipping the timber from Finland was a matter which both parties contemplated as necessary for the fulfilment of the contract. To dissolve the contract the matter relied on must be something which both parties had in their minds when they entered into the contract, such for instance as the existence of the music hall in *Taylor v Caldwell*, or the continuance of the vessel in readiness to perform the contract, as in *Jackson v Union Marine Insurance Co*. Here there is nothing to show that the plaintiffs contemplated, and there is no reason why they should be deemed to have contemplated, that the sellers should continue to have the ordinary facilities for dispatching the timber from Finland. As I have said, that was a matter which to the plaintiffs was wholly immaterial. It was not a matter forming the basis of the contract they entered into. . . . For the reasons I have given the defendants have failed on the facts to make out their case that the contract was dissolved. The appeal will be dismissed. . . .

Warrington and **Bankes LJJ** delivered concurring judgments.

Appeal dismissed.

NOTES

1. In this case, which party was better able to bear the risk that the goods would be available? (Which would more easily be able to ensure that the birch could be obtained?)

2. Suppose the contract had been for 10,000 standards of Finnish birch *ex Peerless* from Helsinki, and the *Peerless* had been trapped in Helsinki by the enemy ships. Would the result have been different?

3. In *Davis Contractors Ltd v Fareham UDC*, which party was the least cost avoider?

III. FRUSTRATION OF PURPOSE

It is very rare for a contract to be held to have been frustrated by an event that leaves it possible to perform, but which makes it much more burdensome to one party. Thus increased costs in performing did not excuse the contractors in *Davis Contractors Ltd v Fareham UDC*; in *Tsakiroglou & Co Ltd v Noblee Thorl GmbH* [1962] AC 93, it was held that a contract to sell groundnuts cif Hamburg was not frustrated by the blockage of the Suez Canal, even though the nuts were to be loaded at Port Sudan and would normally have been carried through the Canal. The seller could have performed by shipping them via the Cape of Good Hope, even though that would have been more expensive and taken longer. Lord Reid pointed out that it was not a case in which the longer voyage would damage the goods, or one in which the buyers would suffer extraordinary losses as a result of the goods arriving later than anticipated. Similarly, it is rare for the contract to be frustrated by some event that makes the transaction pointless as far as one party is concerned.

■ *Krell v Henry*

[1900–03] All ER Rep 20, Court of Appeal

The plaintiff, Paul Krell, sued the defendant, C S Henry, to recover £50, being the balance of a sum of £75, at which price the defendant had agreed to hire from the plaintiff some rooms at 56A, Pall Mall, London, of which the plaintiff was tenant, on 26 and 27 June, 1902, to view the processions that it had been intended to hold on those days in connection with the coronation of King Edward VII. The defendant denied that he was liable to pay the £50 and counter-claimed for the return of £25, which he had paid as a deposit, on the ground that, the processions not having taken place owing to the illness of the King, there had been a total failure of consideration for the contract entered into by him. On 11 August 1902, the action came on for trial before Darling J, sitting without a jury, when the learned judge gave judgment for the defendant on both claim and counterclaim. The plaintiff appealed.

Vaughan Williams LJ

The real question in this case is the extent of the application in English law of the principle of the Roman law which has been adopted and acted on in many English decisions, and notably in *Taylor v Caldwell*.

. . . English law applies the principle not only to cases where the performance of the contract becomes impossible by the cessation of existence of the thing which is the subject-matter of the contract, but also to cases where the event which renders the contract incapable of performance is the cessation or non-existence of an express condition or state of things, going to the root of the contract, and essential to its performance. It is said, on the one side, that the specified thing, state of things, or condition the continued existence of which is necessary for the fulfilment of the contract, so that the parties entering into the contract must have contemplated the continued existence of that thing, condition, or state of things as the foundation of what was to be done under the contract, is limited to things which are either the subject-matter of the contract, or a condition or state of things, present or anticipated, which are expressly mentioned in the contract. But, on the other side, it is said that the condition or state of things clearly appears by extrinsic evidence to have been assumed by the parties to be the foundation or basis of the contract and the event which causes the impossibility is of such a character that it cannot reasonably be supposed to have been in the contemplation of the contracting parties when the contract was made. In such a case the contracting parties will not be held bound by general words which, though large enough to include, were not used with reference to a possibility of a particular event rendering performance of the contract impossible.

I do not think that the principle of the civil law as introduced into the English law is limited to cases in which the event causing the impossibility of performance is the destruction or non-existence of some thing which is the subject-matter of the contract or of some condition or state of things expressly specified as a condition of it. I think that you first have to ascertain, not necessarily from the terms of the contract, but if necessary from necessary inferences, drawn from surrounding circumstances recognised by both contracting parties, what is the substance of the contract, and then to ask the question whether that substantial contract needs for its foundation the assumption of the existence of a particular state of things. If it does, this will limit the operation of the general words, and in such case if the contract becomes impossible of performance by reason of the non-existence of the state of things assumed by both contracting parties, as the foundation of the contract, there will be no breach of the contract thus limited. What are the facts of the present case? The contract is contained in two letters of June 20, 1902, which passed between the defendant and the plaintiff's agent, Mr Cecil Bisgood. These letters do not mention the coronation, but speak merely of the taking of Mr Krell's chambers, or, rather, of the use of them, in the daytime of June 26 and 27, 1902, for the sum of £75, £25 then paid, balance £50 to be paid on the 24th. But the affidavits, which by agreement between the parties are to be taken as stating the facts of the case, show that the plaintiff exhibited on his premises, third floor, 56A, Pall Mall, an announcement to the effect that windows to view the royal coronation processions were to be let, and that the defendant was induced by that announcement to apply to the housekeeper on the premises, who said that the owner was willing to let the suite of rooms for the purpose of seeing the royal procession for both days, but not nights, of June 26 and 27. In my judgment, the use of the rooms was let and taken for the purpose of seeing the royal processions. It was not a demise of the rooms or even an agreement to let and take the rooms. It was a licence to use rooms for a particular purpose and none other. And in my judgment the taking place of those processions on the days proclaimed along the proclaimed route, which passed 56A, Pall Mall, was regarded by both contracting parties as the foundation of the contract. I think that it cannot reasonably be supposed to have been in the contemplation of the contracting parties, when the contract was made, that the coronation would not be held on the proclaimed days, or the processions not take place on those days along the proclaimed route; and I think that the words imposing on the defendant the obligation to accept and pay for the use of the rooms for the named days, although general and unconditional, were not used with reference to the possibility of the particular contingency which afterwards occurred.

It was suggested in the course of the argument that if the occurrence, on the proclaimed days, of the coronation and the processions in this case were the foundation of the contract, and if the general words are thereby limited or qualified, so that in the event of the non-occurrence of the coronation and processions along the proclaimed route they would discharge both parties from further performance of the contract, it would follow that if a cabman was engaged to take someone to Epsom on Derby-day at a suitable enhanced price for such a journey, both parties to the contract would be discharged in the contingency of the race at Epsom for some reason becoming impossible, but I do not think this follows, for I do not think that in the cab case the happening of the race would be the foundation of the contract. No doubt the purpose of the engager was to go to see the Derby, and that the price was proportionately high; but the cab had no special qualifications for the purpose which led to the selection of the cab for this particular occasion. Any other cab would have done as well. Moreover, I think that, under the cab contract, the hirer, even if the race went off, could have said: 'Drive me to Epsom, I will pay you the agreed sum, you have nothing to do with the purpose for which I hired the cab'—and that if the cabman refused he would have been guilty of a breach of contract, there being nothing to qualify his promise to drive the hirer to Epsom on a particular day, whereas, in the case of the coronation, there is not merely the purpose of the hirer to see the coronation processions, but it is the coronation procession and the relative position of the rooms which is the basis of the contract as much for the lessor as the hirer; and I think that if the King, before the coronation days and after the contract had died, the hirer could not have insisted on having the rooms on the days named. It could not in the cab case be reasonably said that seeing the Derby race was the foundation of the contract, as viewing the processions was of the licence in this case, whereas, in the present case, where the rooms were offered and taken, by reason of their peculiar suitability from the position of the rooms for a view of the coronation processions, surely the view of the coronation processions was the foundation of the contract, which is a very different thing from the purpose of the man who engaged the cab—viz, to see the race—being held to be the foundation of the contract.

Each case must be judged by its own circumstances. In each case one must ask oneself, first: What having regard to all the circumstances, was the foundation of the contract?; secondly: Was the performance of the contract prevented?; and thirdly: Was the event which prevented the performance of the contract of such a character that it cannot reasonably be said to have been in the contemplation of the parties at the date of the contract? I think both parties are discharged from further performance of the contract. I think that the coronation processions were the foundation of this contract, and that the non-happening of them prevented the performance of the contract; and, secondly, I think that the non-happening of the processions, to use the words of Sir James Hannen in *Baily v De Crespigny*, was an event

'of such a character that it cannot reasonably be supposed to have been in the contemplation of the contracting parties when the contract was made, and that they are not to be held bound by general words which, though large enough to include, were not used with reference to the possibility of the particular contingency which afterwards happened'.

The test seems to be, whether the event which causes the impossibility was or might have been anticipated and guarded against. It seems difficult to say, in a case where both parties anticipate the happening of an event, which anticipation is the foundation of the contract, that either party must be taken to have anticipated, and ought to have guarded against, the event which prevented the performance of the contract. In both *Jackson v Union Marine Insurance Co* and *Nickoll and Knight v Ashton, Edridge & Co* the parties might have anticipated as a possibility that perils of the sea might delay the ship and frustrate the commercial venture, in the former case the carriage of the goods to effect which the charter-party was entered into, and in the latter case the sale of the goods which were to be shipped on the steamship which was delayed. But the court held in the former case that the basis of the contract was that the ship would arrive in time to carry out the contemplated commercial venture, and in the latter that the steamship would arrive in time for the loading of the goods the subject of the sale.

I wish to observe that cases of this sort are very different from cases where a contract or warranty or representation is implied, such as was implied in *The Moorcock*, and refused to be implied in *Hamlyn & Co v Wood & Co*. But *The Moorcock* is of importance in the present case as showing that, whatever is the suggested implication—be it condition, as in this case, or warranty or representation—one must, in judging whether the implication ought to be made, look not only at the words of the contract, but also at the surrounding facts and the knowledge of the parties of those facts. There seems to me to be ample authority for this proposition. Thus, in *Jackson v Union Marine Insurance Co* in the Common Pleas, the question whether the object of the voyage had been frustrated by the delay of the ship was left as a question of fact to the jury, although there was nothing in the charterparty defining the time within which the charterers were to supply the cargo of iron rails for San Francisco, and nothing on the face of the charterparty to indicate the importance of time in the venture. That was a case in which, as Bramwell, B, points out in his judgment, *Taylor v Caldwell* was a strong authority to support the conclusion arrived at—that not arriving in time for the voyage contemplated, but at such time that it frustrated the commercial venture, was not only a breach of the contract, but discharged the charterer, though he had such an excuse that no action would lie.

. . . I myself am clearly of opinion that in this case, where we have to ask ourselves whether the object of the contract was frustrated by the non-happening of the coronation and its processions on the days proclaimed, parol evidence is admissible to show that the subject of the contract was seats to view the coronation processions, and was so to the knowledge of both parties.

When once this is established, I see no difficulty whatever in the case. It is not essential to the application of the principle of *Taylor v Caldwell* that the direct subject of the contract should perish or fail to be in existence at the date of performance of the contract. It is sufficient if a state of things or condition expressed in the contract and essential to its performance perishes or fails to be in existence at that time. In the present case the condition which fails and prevents the achievement of that which was, in the contemplation of both parties, the foundation of the contract, is not expressly mentioned either as a condition of the contract or the purpose of it, but I think for the reasons which I have given that the principle of *Taylor v Caldwell* ought to be applied. This disposes of the plaintiff's claim for £50 unpaid balance of the price agreed to be paid for the use of the rooms. The defendant at one time set up a cross-claim for the return of the £25 he paid at the date of the contract. As that claim is now withdrawn it is unnecessary to say anything about it. I have only to add that the facts of this case do not bring it within the principle laid down in *Stubbs v Holywell Rail. Co*, that in the case of contracts falling directly within the rule of *Taylor v Caldwell* the subsequent impossibility does not affect rights already acquired, because the defendant had the whole of June 24 to pay the balance, and the public announcement that the coronation and processions would not take place on the proclaimed days was made early on the morning of the 24th, and no cause of action could accrue till the end of that day. I think this appeal ought to be dismissed.

Romer and **Stirling LJJ** concurred.

Appeal dismissed.

■ *Herne Bay Steam Boat Co v Hutton*

[1900–03] All ER Rep 627, Court of Appeal

The defendant had chartered the steamboat *Cynthia* from the plaintiffs for 28 and 29 June 1902, 'to take out a party . . . for the purpose of viewing the naval review and for a day's cruise around the fleet'. The naval review was cancelled because of the King's illness, but the fleet remained anchored at Spithead. The defendant, who had paid £50 in advance, did not use the *Cynthia*, and the plaintiffs sued for the balance of the price. Grantham J held that they could not recover.

Vaughan Williams LJ

. . . The defendant when hiring this boat had the object in view of taking people to see the Naval Review, and on the next day of taking them round the fleet and also round the Isle of Wight. But it does not seem to me that, because those purposes of the defendant became impossible, it is a legitimate inference that the happening of the Naval Review was contemplated by both parties as the foundation of the contract, so as to bring the case within the doctrine of *Taylor v Caldwell*. On the contrary, when the contract is properly considered, I think that the purposes of the defendant, whether of going to the review or going round the fleet or the Isle of Wight with a party of paying guests, do not make those purposes the foundation of the contract within the meaning of *Taylor v Caldwell*.

Having expressed this view, I do not know that there is any advantage to be gained by in any way defining what are the circumstances which might or might not constitute the happening of a particular contingency the foundation of the contract. I will only say I see nothing to differentiate this contract from a contract by which some person engaged a cab to take him on each of three days to Epsom to see the race, and for some reason, such as the spread of an infectious disease or an anticipation of a riot, the races are prohibited. In such a case it could not be said that he would be relieved of his bargain. So in the present case it is sufficient to say that the happening of the Naval Review was not the foundation of this contract.

Romer LJ

. . . It is really a contract for hiring the ship by the defendant for a certain voyage, though the object of the hirer is stated—viz., to see the Naval Review and the fleet. But that object was one with which the defendant as hirer of the ship was alone concerned, and not the plaintiffs, the owners. This contract cannot, in my opinion, be distinguished from many common cases of the hiring of vessels in which the object of the hiring is stated; very often the contract states the details of the voyage and the nature and details of the cargo to be carried. If the voyage is a pleasure trip it might also state the object in view, which is a matter which concerns the passengers, but this statement of the objects of the hirer would not, in my opinion, make the owner of the ship as much concerned with these objects as the hirer himself. The shipowner would say: 'I am concerned with the ship only as a passenger or cargo carrying machine. It is for the hirer to concern himself with the objects'. In the present case it is suggested that the provision that the plaintiffs were to have the right of having ten persons on board besides the crew changed the nature of the hiring; but there is nothing in that provision to prevent the court treating the transaction as a hiring of the vessel by the defendant. It does not make it in any sense a joint speculation. It only amounts to this, that the defendant, being the hirer, gives the owners a licence to put ten men on board. This view of the general effect of the contract is borne out by this consideration. The ship itself had nothing to do with the review or the fleet. It was only a carrier of passengers to see it, and many other ships would have done just as well. It is similar to the hiring of a cab or other vehicle, on which, though the object of the hirer was stated, that statement would not make the object any less a matter for the hirer alone, and would not affect the person who was letting the vehicle for hire. There was not here, by reason of the review not taking place, a total failure of the consideration, nor anything like a total destruction of the subject-matter of the contract. Nor can I on this contract imply any condition which would relieve the defendant from liability to carry out the contract. Conditions are only implied to carry out the presumed intentions of the parties, and I cannot find any such presumed intention here. It follows that in my opinion, so far as the plaintiffs are concerned, the objects of the passengers on this voyage with regard to sightseeing do not form the subject-matter or essence of the contract. . . .

Stirling LJ

. . . It seems to me that the reference in the contract to the review is explained by the object of the voyage, and I am quite unable to treat the reference to the voyage as the foundation of the contract so as to entitle either party to the benefit of the doctrine in *Taylor v Caldwell*. I come to that conclusion more readily as the object of the voyage was not to see the review only, but included a cruise round the fleet. The fleet was there and the passengers might have been willing to go round it. It seems to me that that was the business of the defendant, whose venture it was. I am therefore unable to agree with the decision of Grantham J, and I think the defendant was not discharged from the performance of the contract. . . .

Appeal allowed.

NOTES

1. These cases may be seen as inconsistent, although they were decided at the same time by the same judges in the Court of Appeal. Certainly, the suitability of the particular ship or room does not seem a relevant distinction. In the *Herne Bay* case, it was still possible to view the fleet at anchor, but only Stirling LJ makes that point. Does the distinction perhaps lie in what it seems likely the parties would have agreed on had they foreseen the problem? The steamboat company, like the driver of the cab to Epsom, was presumably prepared to carry passengers on any day, but is it likely that Krell would have agreed in advance to suffering a crowd of strangers in his flat if there were no procession? It has to be remembered that if Henry had to take the room 'procession or no procession', he would almost certainly not have been prepared to pay as much for it as he would have been if the contract provided that he need not pay at all in the event of cancellation. It is a reasonable guess that Krell would have preferred the higher payment, given the inconvenience of having to move out. (This explanation rests to some extent on the fact that Krell was a private property owner, whereas the Herne Bay Steam Boat Company was a business. Contrast Brownsword (1985) 129 SJ 860, who argues that the distinction is that Henry was a consumer whereas Hutton, who intended to sell tickets for the trip on the *Cynthia*, was not.)

2. A second possible distinction is this. If the coronation procession were cancelled, it would be very likely that it would be rearranged (as indeed happened). If the contract in *Krell v Henry* had not been frustrated, Krell would have been able to profit from his flat all over again, while Henry would have to pay twice to see the procession. Making the reasonable assumption that they were equally risk-averse, it seems unlikely that the parties would have chosen such a result had they foreseen the problem. More probably, they would have provided what some of the other contracts related to the coronation did, namely that Henry should have the use of the room on the rearranged date. The court could not solve the problem by implying that into the agreement—it hardly 'goes without saying'—but by holding the contract frustrated, it permitted the negotiation of a fresh agreement without leaving Krell enriched at Henry's expense. There was no certainty that the naval review would be rearranged, however.

Occasionally, the change in circumstances may make the contract much *more* profitable to one party and the other may claim frustration in an attempt to capture the profit: eg, *F A Tamplin Steamship Co Ltd v Anglo-Mexican Petroleum Products Co Ltd* [1916] 2 AC 397, in which the owner of a chartered ship unsuccessfully claimed frustration when the vessel was requisitioned for a few months, hoping thereby to receive the compensation.

IV. FORESEEN EVENTS

If the parties had foreseen an event but did not provide for it, a possible interpretation is that they intended the contract to continue regardless, with the risk lying where it falls. There are many dicta to the effect that the event must be one that could not have been 'anticipated or guarded against' (Vaughan Williams LJ in *Krell v Henry*) if it is to frustrate a contract. On the other hand, there are a number of situations in which a foreseen event may still frustrate a contract—if the contract becomes illegal because of the outbreak of war, or if an employee dies in service—and it is not clear what the general position is.

■ *Ocean Tramp Tankers Corpn v V/O Sovracht, The Eugenia*
[1964] 1 All ER 161, Court of Appeal

By a charterparty dated 8 September 1956, the *Eugenia*, which was then in Genoa, was let to the charterers 'for a trip out to India via the Black Sea'. Both parties realised at the time of the negotiations that there was a danger of the Suez Canal being closed, but they came to no agreement on that eventuality. On 25 October, the *Eugenia*, having loaded, sailed from Odessa. At that time the customary route to India was still via Suez. By the time the vessel reached the vicinity of the canal, it had become a 'dangerous' zone, but in breach of contract the charterers failed to take steps to prevent the ship entering Port Said. The ship entered the canal on 31 October, and became trapped when the canal was closed. The charterers claimed that the contract had been frustrated by the closure of the canal.

Lord Denning MR

. . . The second question is whether the charterparty was frustrated by what took place. The arbitrator has held that it was not. The judge has held that it was. Which is right? One thing that is obvious is that the charterers cannot rely on the fact that the *Eugenia* was trapped in the canal; for that was their own fault. They were in breach of the war clause in entering it. They cannot rely on a self-induced frustration; see *Maritime National Fish, Ltd v Ocean Trawlers, Ltd*. But they seek to rely on the fact that the canal itself was blocked. They assert that, even if the *Eugenia* had never gone into the canal but had stayed outside (in which case she would not have been in breach of the war clause) nevertheless she would still have had to go round by the Cape; and that, they say, brings about a frustration, for it makes the venture fundamentally different from what they contracted for. The judge has accepted this view. . . . This means that, once again, we have had to consider the authorities on this vexed topic of frustration. But I think that the position is now reasonably clear. It is simply this: If it should happen, in the course of carrying out a contract, that a fundamentally different situation arises for which the parties made no provision—so much so that it would not be just in the new situation to hold them bound to its terms—then the contract is at an end.

It was originally said that the doctrine of frustration was based on an implied term. In short, that the parties, if they had foreseen the new situation, would have said to one another: 'If that happens, of course, it is all over between us'. But the theory of an implied term has now been discarded by everyone, or nearly everyone, for the simple reason that it does not represent the truth. The parties would not have said: 'It is all over between us'. They would have differed about what was to happen. Each would have sought to insert reservations or qualifications of one kind or another. Take this very case. The parties realised that the canal might become impassable. They tried to agree on a clause to provide for the contingency. But they failed to agree. So there is no room for an implied term.

It has frequently been said that the doctrine of frustration only applies when the new situation is 'unforeseen' or 'unexpected' or 'uncontemplated', as if that were an essential feature. But it is not so. It is not so much that it is 'unexpected', but rather that the parties have made no provision for it in their contract. The point about it, however, is this: If the parties did not foresee anything of the kind happening, you can readily infer that they have made no provision for it. Whereas, if they did foresee it, you would expect them to make provision for it. But cases have occurred where the parties have foreseen the danger ahead, and yet made no provision for it in the contract. Such was the case in the Spanish Civil War when a ship was let on charter to the Republican Government. The purpose was to evacuate refugees. The parties foresaw that she might be seized by the Nationalists. But they made no provision for it in their contract. Yet, when she was seized, the contract was frustrated: see *W J Tatem, Ltd v Gamboa*. So, here, the parties foresaw that the canal might become impassable. It was very thing that they feared. But they made no provision for it. So the doctrine may still apply, if it be a proper case for it.

We are thus left with the simple test that a situation must arise which renders performance of the contract 'a thing radically different from that which was undertaken by the contract': see *Davis Contractors, Ltd v Fareham UDC*, per Lord Radcliffe. To see if the doctrine applies, you have first to construe the contract and see whether the parties have themselves provided for the situation that has arisen. If they have provided for it, the contract must govern. There is no frustration. If they have not provided for it, then you have to compare the new situation with the old situation for which they did provide. Then you must see how different it is. The fact that it has become more onerous or more expensive for one party than he thought is not sufficient to bring about a frustration. It must be more than merely more onerous or more expensive. It must be positively unjust to hold the parties bound. It is often difficult to draw the line. But it must be done, and it is for the courts to do it as a matter of law: see *Tsakiroglou & Co. Ltd v Noblee & Thorl GmbH*, per Viscount Simonds and per Lord Reid.

Applying these principles to this case, I have come to the conclusion that the blockage of the canal did not bring about a 'fundamentally different situation' such as to frustrate the venture. My reasons are these: (i) The venture was the *whole* trip from delivery at Genoa, out to the Black Sea, there load cargo, thence to India, unload cargo, and re-delivery. The time for this vessel from Odessa to Vizagapatam via the Suez Canal would be twenty-six days, and via the Cape fifty-six days. But that is not the right comparison. You have to take the whole venture from delivery at Genoa to re-delivery at Madras. We were told that the time for the whole venture via the Suez Canal would be 108 days, and via the Cape 138 days. The difference over the whole voyage is not so radical as to produce a frustration. (ii) The cargo was iron and steel goods which would not be adversely affected by the longer voyage, and there was no special reason for early arrival. The vessel and crew were at all times fit and sufficient to proceed via the Cape, (iii) The cargo was loaded on board at the time of the blockage of the canal. If the contract was frustrated, it would mean, I suppose, that the ship could throw up the charter and unload the cargo wherever she was, without any breach of contract. (iv) The voyage round the Cape made no great difference except that it took a good deal longer and was more expensive for the charterers than a voyage through the canal...

Donovan LJ

...There is clearly no room here for holding that the parties agreed by implication that the blocking of the Suez Canal should end the contract, or that they would have so agreed had the considered this contingency. In fact, they did consider it, and, through their agents, made rival suggestions what should happen in that event. But they came to no conclusion, except to leave the terms of the contract as they were. Should the canal be blocked before the vessel passed through it, the parties were content to have their rights and duties settled on the basis of the terms of the contract which they were signing. In other words, the problem, should it arise, would be left to the lawyers...

Danckwerts LJ concurred in the judgments above.

Appeal allowed.

NOTES

1. In *WJ Tatem Ltd v Gamboa* [1939] 1 KB 132, Goddard J also said that a contract might be frustrated by an event that had been foreseen.

2. Many events are foreseeable, but only as such remote possibilities that it is reasonable to assume that even if the parties foresaw them, they did not take them into account when they made the contract. The more likely the event, the more probable that the parties took it into account and intended that the contract should continue to apply. See Treitel, pp 901–904.

V. EFFECT OF FRUSTRATION

If a contract is frustrated, each party is released from any further obligation to perform. Accrued rights to damages for any breach that may have occurred before the date of frustration are not affected, but neither can be liable in damages to the other for non-performance of the rest of the contract.

What is the position if a party has performed part or all of its contractual obligations before frustration occurs? Firstly, a party may have made an advance payment, eg for goods that were to have been delivered after the date of frustration. Secondly, a party may have delivered some of the goods due or have partially performed some service. Sometimes, parts of the performance are to be paid for separately (see pp 556 ff). Accrued claims for any parts of the price that have been earned by partial performance will not be affected by the subsequent frustration. Often, however, none of the price may be due until all the goods have been delivered or the whole of the services have been performed.

In the absence of a claim that accrued before the contract was frustrated, the remedy at common law was in restitution. Let us take advance payments first. At one time, the rule at common law was that payments made before the date of frustration were not repayable, on the ground that the contract was discharged only from the moment of frustration and accrued rights were not affected: *Chandler v Webster* [1904] 1 KB 493. However, *Chandler's* case was overruled by the House of Lords in *Fibrosa Spolka Akcyjna v Fairbairn Lawson Combe Barbour Ltd* [1943] AC 32. The Lords pointed out that, even under a contract that has not been frustrated, a party who has received no part of the promised performance is entitled to claim in restitution for return of the money paid for total failure of consideration. (Thus the victim of a breach of contract may have a choice between claiming damages and simply reclaiming any money paid: see p 742.) Unless the parties have agreed otherwise, this rule applies also when the contract has been frustrated: the claim in restitution is not affected by the discharge of the contractual obligations. Viscount Simon LC said (of the judgment of Sir Richard

Collins MR in *Chandler v Webster*):

It appears to me that the reasoning . . . is open to two criticisms:

(a) The claim of a party who has paid money under a contract to get the money back, on the ground that the consideration for which he paid it has totally failed, is not based upon any provision contained in the contract, but arises because, in the circumstances which have happened, the law gives a remedy, in quasi-contract to the party who has not got that for which he bargained. It is a claim to recover money to which the defendant has no further right because, in the circumstances which have happened, the money must be regarded as received to the plaintiff's use. It is true that the effect of frustration is that, while the contract can no further be performed, 'it remains a perfectly good contract up to that point, and everything previously done in pursuance of it must be treated as rightly done'; but it by no means follows that the situation existing at the moment of frustration is one which leaves the party that has paid money and has not received the stipulated consideration without any remedy. To claim the return of money paid on the ground of total failure of consideration is not to vary the terms of the contract in any way. The claim arises not because the right to be repaid is one of the stipulated conditions of the contract, but because, in the circumstances which have happened, the law gives the remedy. It is the failure to distinguish between (i) the action of *assumpsit* for money had and received in a case where the consideration has wholly failed, and (ii) an action on the contract itself, which explains the mistake which I think has been made in applying English law to this subject-matter . . . it does not follow that because the plaintiff cannot sue 'on the contract', he cannot sue *dehors* the contract for the recovery of a payment in respect of which consideration has failed.

(b) There is, no doubt, a distinction between cases in which a contract is 'wiped out altogether', eg. because it is void as being illegal from the start, or as being due to fraud which the innocent party has elected to treat as avoiding the contract, and cases in which intervening impossibility 'only releases the parties from further performance of the contract'. Does the distinction between these two classes of case, however, justify the deduction of Sir Richard Collins MR, that 'the doctrine of failure of consideration does not apply' where the contract remains a perfectly good contract up to the date of frustration? This conclusion seems to be derived from the view that, if the contract remains good and valid up to the moment of frustration, money which has already been paid under it cannot be regarded as having been paid for a consideration which has wholly failed. The party who has paid the money has had the advantage, whatever it may be worth, of the promise of the other party. That is true, but it is necessary to draw a distinction. In English law, an enforceable contract may be formed by an exchange of a promise for a promise, or by the exchange of a promise for an act—I am excluding contracts under seal—and thus, in the law relating to the formation of contract, the promise to do a thing may often be the consideration; but, when one is considering the law of failure of consideration and of the quasi-contractual right to recover money on that ground, it is, generally speaking, not the promise which is referred to as the consideration, but the performance of the promise. The money was paid to secure performance and, if performance fails, the inducement which brought about the payment is not fulfilled.

If this were not so, there could never be any recovery of money, for failure of consideration, by the payer of the money in return for a promise of future performance. Yet there are endless examples which show that money can be recovered, as for a complete failure of consideration, in cases where the promise was given but could not be fulfilled:

. . .

Thus in the *Fibrosa* case, the plaintiff buyers had made an advance payment of £1,000 for a machine that was to be delivered cif Gdynia. Before the machine had been shipped, the contract was frustrated by the German occupation of Poland. The buyers were entitled to recover the £1,000. However, as Viscount Simon L C pointed out, neither this rule nor the one it replaced were satisfactory.

While this result obviates the harshness with which the previous view in some instances treated the party who had made a prepayment, it cannot be regarded as dealing fairly between the parties in all cases, and must sometimes have the result of leaving the recipient who has to return the money at a grave disadvantage. He may have incurred expenses in connection with the partial carrying out of the contract which are equivalent, or more than equivalent, to the money which he prudently stipulated should be prepaid, but which he now has to return for reasons which are no fault of his. He may have to repay the money, though he has executed almost the whole of the contractual work, which will be left on his hands. These results follow from the fact that the English common law does not undertake to apportion a prepaid sum in such circumstances—contrast the provision, now contained in the Partnership Act, 1890, s 40, for apportioning a premium if a partnership is prematurely dissolved. It must be for the legislature to decide whether provision should be made for an equitable apportionment of prepaid monies which have to be returned by the recipient in view of the frustration of the contract in respect of which they were paid.

In 1943, the rule was changed by the Law Reform (Frustrated Contracts) Act: see below.

In the *Fibrosa* case, the buyers could recover their advance payment because there had been a total failure of consideration: they had not received anything from the sellers. If the sellers had delivered part of the goods, the failure would have been only partial, and at common law, none of the advance payment would be recoverable: *Whincup v Hughes* (p 742). The only exceptions to this would be if the contract were severable into distinct units, and an advance payment had been made in respect of a unit that remained completely unperformed, or perhaps if the price was clearly apportionable among the units even though the contract was entire (ie the buyer could insist on delivery in full as a condition of his having to accept any of the goods). Thus in *Ebrahim Dawood Ltd v Heath (Est 1927) Ltd* [1961] 2 Lloyd's Rep 512 (a case of breach by the seller, not frustration, but the same rule applied at common law, see p 735) the buyer paid in advance for the steel sheets he was buying at a price per ton, but justifiably rejected four-fifths of them as not conforming to the contract. He was allowed to recover four-fifths of the money he had paid. The basic rule that money can be recovered only if the failure of consideration was total seemed unsatisfactory and was also changed by the Law Reform (Frustrated Contracts) Act 1943, s 1(2) (below).

Turning now to the case in which a party has partly performed in some other way than by paying money, the position at common law depends upon the nature of the performance. If the party has delivered goods to the other party, the latter will have either to return them or to pay for them at the contract rate if the contract is frustrated. In contrast, if the party has performed services so that there is nothing to return, the other party need pay nothing. Thus in *Appleby v Myers* (1867) LR 2 CP 651, a contract to instal machinery in a factory with payment due upon completion was frustrated when the factory was destroyed by fire after only some of the machinery was in place. The contractor was held not to be entitled to any payment—the price had not yet been earned and recovery would not be given on a restitutionary basis either. To do so would be inconsistent with the express terms of the contract stipulating for payment only on completion. (See also *Sumpter v Hedges*, p 559, which applies a similar rule when the contract has been terminated because of a breach by the contractor.) This rule was also altered by the Law Reform (Frustrated Contracts) Act 1943, s 1(3), (below).

■ Law Reform (Frustrated Contracts) Act 1943
Section 1

(1) Where a contract governed by English law has become impossible of performance or been otherwise frustrated, and the parties thereto have for that reason been discharged from the further

performance of the contract, the following provisions of this section shall, subject to the provisions of section two of this Act, have effect in relation thereto.

(2) All sums paid or payable to any party in pursuance of the contract before the time when the parties were so discharged (in this Act referred to as 'the time of discharge') shall, in the case of sums so paid, be recoverable from him as money received by him for the use of the party by whom the sums were paid, and, in the case of sums so payable, cease to be so payable:

Provided that, if the party to whom the sums were so paid or payable incurred expenses before the time of discharge in, or for the purpose of, the performance of the contract, the court may, if it consid s it just to do so having regard to all the circumstances of the case, allow him to retain or, as the case may be, recover the whole or any part of the sums so paid or payable, not being an amount in excess of the expenses so incurred.

(3) Where any party to the contract has, by reason of anything done by any other party thereto in, or for the purpose of, the performance of the contract, obtained a valuable benefit (other than a payment of money to which the last foregoing subsection applies) before the time of discharge, there shall be recoverable from him by the said other party such sum (if any), not exceeding the value of the said benefit to the party obtaining it, as the court considers just, having regard to all the circumstances of the case and, in particular,—

(a) the amount of any expenses incurred before the time of discharge by the benefited party in, or for the purpose of, the performance of the contract, including any sums paid or payable by him to any other party in pursuance of the contract and retained or recoverable by that party under the last foregoing subsection, and

(b) the effect, in relation to the said benefit, of the circumstances giving rise to the frustration of the contract.

(4) In estimating, for the purposes of the foregoing provisions of this section, the amount of any expenses incurred by any party to the contract, the court may, without prejudice to the generality of the said provisions, include such sum as appears to be reasonable in respect of overhead expenses and in respect of any work or services performed personally by the said party.

(5) In considering whether any sum ought to be recovered or retained under the foregoing provisions of this section by any party to the contract, the court shall not take into account any sums which have, by reason of the circumstances giving rise to the frustration of the contract, become payable to that party under any contract of insurance unless there was an obligation to insure imposed by any express term of the frustrated contract or by or under any enactment.

(6) Where any person has assumed obligations under the contract in consideration of the conferring of a benefit by any other party to the contract upon any other person, whether a party to the contract or not, the court may, if in all the circumstances of the case it considers it just to do so, treat for the purposes of sub-section (3) of this section any benefit so conferred as a benefit obtained by the person who has assumed the obligations as aforesaid.

Section 2

(1) This Act shall apply to contracts, whether made before or after the commencement of this Act, as respects which the time of discharge is on or after the first day of July, nineteen hundred and forty-three, but not to contracts as respects which the time of discharge is before the said date.

(2) This Act shall apply to contracts to which the Crown is a party in like manner as to contracts between subjects.

(3) Where any contract to which this Act applies contains any provision which, upon the true construction of the contract, is intended to have effect in the event of circumstances arising which operate, or would but for the said provision operate, to frustrate the contract, or is intended to have effect whether such circumstances arise or not, the court shall give effect to the said provision and shall only give effect to the foregoing section of this Act to such extent, if any, as appears to the court to be consistent with the said provision.

(4) Where it appears to the court that a part of any contract to which this Act applies can properly be severed from the remainder of the contract, being a part wholly performed before the time of discharge, or so performed except for the payment in respect of that part of the contract of sums which are or can be ascertained under the contract, the court shall treat that part of the contract as if it were a separate contract and had not been frustrated and shall treat the foregoing section of this Act as only applicable to the remainder of that contract.

(5) This Act shall not apply—

> (a) to any charterparty, except a time charterparty or a charterparty by way of demise, or to any contract (other than a charterparty) for the carriage of goods by sea; or
>
> (b) to any contract of insurance, save as is provided by subsection (5) of the foregoing section; or
>
> (c) to any contract to which section seven of the Sale of Goods Act, 1893 (which avoids contracts for the sale of specific goods which perish before the risk has passed to the buyer) applies, or to any other contract for the sale, or for the sale and delivery, of specific goods, where the contract is frustrated by reason of the fact that the goods have perished.

NOTES

1. For a detailed account of the Act and the common law that it was intended to change, see Glanville Williams, *Law Reform (Frustrated Contracts) Act 1943* (Stevens, 1944).

2. How would the *Fibrosa* case be decided under the Act? Suppose the sellers had incurred expenses of £600 in starting work on the machine: what would be the maximum and minimum amounts the court could have ordered the sellers to return to the buyers?

3. Suppose the sellers had been paid £1,000 in advance, and had delivered some accessories for the machine that cost £750. In addition, the sellers had spent £600 on starting to build the machine itself. What is the maximum amount that the court could have awarded the seller under the Act? (NB: See s 1(3)(a).)

4. The Act does not cover the case in which the seller has incurred expenditure before the time of discharge but the expenditure is not covered by an advance payment nor results in any benefit to the buyer (see further the next case). Why is no recovery provided for in this case? The Law Revision Committee, on whose Seventh Interim Report (Cmd 6009 of 1939) the Act was based, considered that the seller who does not stipulate for an advance payment must be taken to be incurring such expense at his own risk. Given that frustration occurs only when there is some event that was unforeseen or at least not 'covered' by the contract, how realistic is the Committee's approach? There is still controversy over what the law on this point should be: see the literature cited in Burrows, pp 285–287.

5. Section 2(5) preserves the common law rules in certain cases in which it was felt that the rules were well known and accepted. Williams argues convincingly that cases falling within Sale of Goods Act 1893 (now 1979), s 7 should have been covered by the new rules.

6. Go back to the facts in note 2. How much should the court allow the sellers to retain in respect of their expenditure: the full £600, nothing, or some amount in between? The Law Revision Committee seemed to think the seller should be reimbursed in full, but Williams favoured an equal distribution of the loss (see Williams, pp 35–39). In *Gamerco SA v ICM/Fair Warning (Agency) Ltd* [1995] 1 WLR 1226, the plaintiffs had agreed to promote a rock concert at a stadium in Madrid on 4 July 1992. The plaintiffs had paid $412,000 on account and had contracted to pay a further $362,500. Both sides had incurred expenses: the plaintiffs of about $450,000 and the defendants about $50,000.

There were safety concerns about the stadium because of the use of high alumina cement in its construction. On 1 July 1992, the relevant government body withdrew the permit for the concert and the parties became aware of this on 2 July 1992. It was not possible to find another stadium.

Garland J held that the contract was frustrated by the withdrawal of the permit. (Do you see why it matters that the frustrating event was the withdrawal of the permit rather than the weaknesses of the stadium?) He held that the plaintiffs were entitled to the return of the £412,000 they had paid in advance.

As to the expenses, he held that he had a very broad discretion and held that he would make no deduction in respect of the defendant's expenses from the sum he had ordered them to repay. The most important factor in this decision seems to be the much larger expenses that the plaintiffs had incurred. (For discussion, see Carter and Tolhurst (1996) 10 JCL 264.)

7.   If the plaintiff has conferred some benefit on the defendant and makes a claim under s 1(3), how should the court value the benefit and determine the 'just sum' to award the plaintiff? See the next case.

■ *BP Exploration Co (Libya) Ltd v Hunt (No 2)*
[1982] 1 All ER 925

In December 1957, the then Libyan government granted the defendant a concession to explore for oil and extract oil from a specified area of the Libyan desert. The defendant did not have the resources to exploit the concession himself and, in 1960, entered into what was called a 'farm-in agreement' with the plaintiffs. Essentially, the contract involved a transfer by the defendant to the plaintiffs of a half, share in the concession, in return for which the plaintiffs agreed to explore, develop and operate the whole of the concession entirely from their own resources and to make down payments to the defendant in cash and oil. This put the risk of failure to find oil in commercial quantities on the plaintiffs. However, if oil were discovered, the agreement provided for the repayment of the plaintiffs' expenditure out of the defendant's share of the oil (the precise details were very complex). Oil was discovered in large quantities and the field came on stream in 1967.

In 1971, the then Libyan government expropriated the plaintiffs' share of the concession, and in 1973, the defendant's share. The plaintiffs brought an action claiming that the contract had been frustrated and seeking such sums as the court considered just under s 1(3) of the 1943 Act in respect of benefits obtained by the defendant prior to the frustration by reason of the plaintiffs' performance of the contract.

The whole judgment repays careful study, but for reasons of space, the extracts are limited to the most important points of principle arising under s 1(2) and

Robert Goff J

(1) The principle of recovery

The principle, which is common to both s 1(2) and (3), and indeed is the fundamental principle underlying the Act itself, is prevention of the unjust enrichment of either party to the contract at the other's expense. It was submitted by counsel, on behalf of BP that the principle common to both subsections was one of restitution for net benefits received, the net benefit being the benefit less an appropriate deduction for expenses incurred by the defendant. This is broadly correct so far as s 1(2) is concerned; but under s 1(3) the net benefit of the defendant simply provides an upper limit to the award: it does not measure the amount of the award to be made to the plaintiff. This is because in s 1(3) a distinction is drawn between the plaintiff's performance under the contract, and the benefit which the defendant has obtained by reason of that performance, a distinction about which I shall have more to say later in this judgment; and the net benefit obtained by the defendant from the plaintiff's performance may be more than a just sum payable in respect of such performance, in which event a sum equal to the defendant's net benefit would not be an appropriate sum to award to the plaintiff. I therefore consider it better to state the principle underlying the Act as being the principle of unjust enrichment, which underlies the right of recovery in very many cases in English law, and indeed is the basic principle of the English law of restitution, of which the Act forms part.

Although s 1(2) and (3) is concerned with restitution in respect of different types of benefit, it is right to construe the two subsections as flowing from the same basic principle and therefore, so far as their different subject matters permit, to achieve consistency between them. Even so, it is always necessary to bear in mind the difference between awards of restitution in respect of money payments and awards where the benefit conferred by the plaintiff does not consist of a payment of money. Money has the peculiar character of a universal medium of exchange. By its receipt, the recipient is inevitably benefited: and (subject to problems arising from such matters as inflation, change of position and the time value of money) the loss suffered by the plaintiff is generally equal to the defendant's gain, so that no difficulty arises concerning the amount to be repaid. The same cannot be said of other benefits, such as goods or services. By their nature, services cannot be restored; nor in many cases can goods be restored, for example where they have been consumed or transferred to another. Furthermore the identity and value of the resulting benefit to the recipient may be debatable. From the very nature of things, therefore, the problem of restitution in respect of such benefits is more complex than in cases where the benefit takes the form of a money payment; and the solution of the problem has been made no easier by the form in which the legislature has chosen to draft s 1(3) of the Act.

The Act is *not* designed to do certain things. (i) It is not designed to apportion the loss between the parties. There is no general power under either s 1(2) or s 1(3) to make any allowance for expenses incurred by the plaintiff (except, under the proviso to s 1(2), to enable him to enforce pro tanto payment of a sum payable but unpaid before frustration); and expenses incurred by the defendant are only relevant in so far as they go to reduce the net benefit obtained by him and thereby limit any award to the plaintiff. (ii) It is not concerned to put the parties in the position in which they would have been if the contract had been performed. (iii) It is not concerned to restore the parties to the position they were in before the contract was made. A remedy designed to prevent unjust enrichment may not achieve that result; for expenditure may be incurred by either party under the contract which confers no benefit on the other, and in respect of which no remedy is available under the Act.

An award under the Act may have the effect of rescuing the plaintiff from an unprofitable bargain. This may certainly be true under s 1(2), if the plaintiff has paid the price in advance for an expected return which, if furnished, would have proved unprofitable; if the contract is frustrated before any part of that expected return is received, and before any expenditure is incurred by the defendant, the plaintiff is entitled to the return of the price he has paid, irrespective of the consideration he would have recovered had the contract been performed. Consistently with s 1(2), there is nothing in s 1(3) which necessarily limits an award to the contract consideration. But the contract consideration may nevertheless be highly relevant to the assessment of the just sum to be awarded under s 1(3); this is a matter to which I will revert later in this judgment.

(2) Claims under s 1(2)

Where an award is made under s 1(2), it is, generally speaking, simply an award for the repayment of money which has been paid to the defendant in pursuance of the contract, subject to an allowance in respect of expenses incurred by the defendant. It is not necessary that the consideration for the payment should have wholly failed: claims under s 1(2) are not limited to cases of total failure of consideration, and cases of partial failure of consideration can be catered for by a cross-claim by the defendant under s 1(2) or (3) or both. There is no discretion in the court in respect of a claim under s 1(2), except in respect of the allowance for expenses; subject to such an allowance (and, of course, a cross-claim) the plaintiff is entitled to repayment of the money he has paid. The allowance for expenses is probably best rationalised as a statutory recognition of the defence of change of position. True, the expenses need not have been incurred by reason of the plaintiff's payment; but they must have been incurred in, or for the purpose of, the performance of the contract under which the plaintiff's payment has been made, and for that reason it is just that they should be brought into account. . . .

(3) Claims under s 1(3)

General In contract, where an award is made under s 1(3), the process is more complicated. First, it has to be shown that the defendant has, by reason of something done by the plaintiff in, or for the purpose of, the performance of the contract, obtained a valuable benefit (other than a payment of money) before the time of discharge. That benefit has to be identified, and valued, and such value forms the upper limit of the award. Secondly, the court may award to the plaintiff such sum, not greater than the value to such benefit, as it considers just having regard to all the circumstances of the case, including in particular the matters specified in s 1(3)(a) and (b). In the case of an awarded under s 1(3) there are, therefore, two distinct stages: the identification and valuation of the benefit, and the award of the just sum. The amount to be awarded is the just sum, unless the defendant's benefit is less, in which event the award will be limited to the amount of that benefit. The distinction between the identification and valuation of the defendant's benefit, and the assessment of the just sum, is the most controversial part of the Act. It represents the solution adopted by the legislature of the problem of restitution in cases where the benefit does not consist of a payment of money: but the solution so adopted has been criticised by some commentators as productive of injustice, and it certainly gives rise to considerable problems, to which I shall refer in due course.

Identification of the defendant's benefit In the course of the argument before me, there was much dispute whether, in the case of services, the benefit should be identified as the services themselves, or as the end product of the services. One example canvassed (because it bore some relationship to the facts of the present case) was the example of prospecting for minerals. If minerals are discovered, should the benefit be regarded (as counsel for Mr Hunt contended) simply as the services of prospecting, or (as counsel for BP contended) as the minerals themselves being the end product of the successful exercise? Now, I am satisfied that it was the intention of the legislature, to be derived from s 1(3) as a matter of construction, that the benefit should in an appropriate case be identified as the end product of the services. This appears, in my judgment, not only from the fact that s 1(3) distinguishes between the plaintiff's performance and the defendant's benefit, but also from s 1(3)(b) which clearly relates to the product of the plaintiff's performance. Let me take the example of a building contract. Suppose that a contract for work on a building is frustrated by a fire which destroys the building and which, therefore, also destroys a substantial amount of work already done by the plaintiff. Although it might be thought just to award the plaintiff a sum assessed on a quantum meruit basis, probably a rateable part of the contract price, in respect of the work he has done, the effect of s 1(3)(b) will be to reduce the award to nil, because of the effect, in relation to the defendant's benefit, of the circumstances giving rise to the frustration of the contract. It is quite plain that, in s 1(3)(b), the word 'benefit' is intended to refer, in the example I have given, to the actual improvement to the building, because that is what will be affected by the frustrating event; the subsection therefore contemplates that, in such a case, the benefit is the end product of the plaintiff's services, not the services themselves. This will not be so in every case, since in some cases the services will have no end product; for example, where the services consist of doing such work as surveying, or transporting goods. In each case it is necessary to ask the question: what benefit has the defendant obtained by reason of the plaintiff's contractual performance? But it must not be forgotten that in s 1(3) the relevance of the value of the benefit is to fix a ceiling to the award. If, for example, in a building contract, the building is only partially completed, the value of the partially completed building (ie the product of the services) will fix a ceiling for the award; but the stage of the work may be such that the uncompleted building may be worth less than the value of the work and materials that have gone into it, particularly as completion by another builder may cost more than completion by the original builder would have cost. In other cases, however, the actual benefit to the defendant may be considerably more than the appropriate or just sum to be awarded to the plaintiff, in which event the value of the benefit will not in fact determine the quantum of the award. I should add, however, that, in a case of prospecting, it would usually be wrong to identify the discovered mineral as the benefit. In such a case there is always (whether the prospecting is successful or not) the benefit of the prospecting itself, ie of knowing whether or not the land contains any deposit of the relevant minerals; if the prospecting is successful, the benefit may include also the enhanced value of the land by reason of the discovery; if the prospector's contractual task goes beyond discovery and includes development and production, the benefit will include the further enhancement of the land by reason of the installation of the facilities, and also the benefit of in part transforming a valuable mineral deposit into a marketable commodity.

I add by way of footnote that all these difficulties would have been avoided if the legislature had thought it right to treat the services themselves as the benefit. In the opinion of many commentators it would be more just to do so; after all, the services in question have been requested by the defendant, who normally takes the risk that they may prove worthless, from whatever cause. In the example I have given of the building destroyed by fire, there is much to be said for the view that the builder should be paid for the work he has done, unless he has (for example by agreeing to insure the works) taken on himself the risk of destruction by fire. But my task is to construe the Act as it stands. On the true construction of the Act, it is in my judgment clear that the defendant's benefit must, in an appropriate case, be identifed as the end product of the plaintiff's services, despite the difficulties which this construction creates, difficulties which are met again when one comes to value the benefit. . . .

Valuing the benefit Since the benefit may be identified with the product of the plaintiff's performance, great problems arise in the valuation of the benefit. First, how does one solve the problem which arises from the fact that a small service may confer an enormous benefit, and conversely, a very substantial service may confer only a very small benefit? The answer presumably is that at the stage of valuation of the benefit (as opposed to assessment of the just sum) the task of the court is simply to assess the value of the benefit to the defendant. For example, if a prospector after some very simple prospecting discovers a large and unexpected deposit of a valuable mineral, the benefit to the defendant (namely, the enhancement in the value of the land) may be enormous; it must be valued as such, always bearing in mind that the assessment of a just sum may very well lead to a much smaller amount being awarded to the plaintiff. But conversely, the plaintiff may have undertaken building work for a substantial sum which is, objectively speaking, of little or no value, for example, he may commence the redecoration, to the defendant's execrable taste, of rooms which are in good decorative order. If the contract is frustrated before the work is complete, and the work is unaffected by the frustrating event, it can be argued that the defendant has obtained no benefit, because the defendant's property has been reduced in value by the plaintiff's work; but the partial work must be treated as a benefit to the defendant, since he requested it, and valued as such.

. . .

Other problems can arise from the valuation of the defendants benefit as the end product; I shall come to these later in the consideration of the facts of the present case. But there is a further problem which I should refer to, before leaving this topic. Section 1(3)(a) requires the court to have regard to the amount of any expenditure incurred before the time of discharge by the benefited party in, or for the purpose of, the performance of the contract. The question arises: should this matter be taken into account at the stage of valuation of the benefit, or of assessment of the just sum? Take a simple example. Suppose that the defendant's benefit is valued at £150 and that a just sum is assessed at £100, but that there remains to be taken into account defendant's expenses of £75: is the award to be £75 or £25? The clue to this problem lies, in my judgment, in the fact that the allowance for expenses is a statutory recognition of the defence of change of position. Only to the extent that the position of the defendant has so changed that it would be unjust to award restitution, should the court make an allowance for expenses. Suppose that the plaintiff does work for the defendant which produces no valuable end product or a benefit no greater in value than the just sum to be awarded in respect of the work, there is then no reason why the whole of the relevant expenses should not be set off against the just sum. But suppose that the defendant has reaped a large benefit from the plaintiff's work, far greater in value than the just sum to be awarded for the work. In such circumstances it would be quite wrong to set off the whole of the defendant's expenses against the just sum. The question whether the defendant has suffered a change of position has to be judged in the light of all the circumstances of the case. Accordingly, on the Act as it stands, under s 1(3) the proper course is to deduct the expenses from the value of the benefit, with the effect that only in so far as they reduce the value of the benefit below the amount of the just sum which would otherwise be awarded will they have any practical bearing on the award.

Finally, I should record that the court is required to have regard to the effect, in relation to the defendant's benefit, of the circumstances giving rise to the frustration of the contract. I have already given an example of how this may be relevant, in the case of building contracts; and I have recorded the fact that this provision has been the subject of criticism. There may, however, be circumstances where it would not be just to have regard to this fact or, for example, if, under a building contract, it was expressly agreed that the work in progress should be insured by the building-owner against risks which include the event which had the effect of frustrating the contract and damaging or destroying the work.

Assessment of the just sum The principle underlying the Act is prevention of the unjust enrichment of the defendant at the plaintiff's expense. Where, as in cases under s 1(2), the benefit conferred on the defendant consists of payment of a sum of money, the plaintiff's expense and the defendant's enrichment are generally equal; and, subject to other relevant factors, the award of restitution will consist simply of an order for repayment of a like sum of money. But where the benefit does not consist of money, then the defendant's enrichment will rarely be equal to the plaintiff's expense. In such cases, where (as in the case of a benefit conferred under a contract thereafter frustrated) the benefit has been requested by the defendant, the basic measure of recovery in restitution is the reasonable value of the plaintiff's performance: in a case of services, a quantum meruit or reasonable remuneration, and in a case of goods, a quantum valebat or reasonable price. Such cases are to be contrasted with cases where such a benefit has not been requested by the defendant. In the latter class of case, recovery is rare in restitution; but if the sole basis of recovery was that the defendant had been incontrovertibly benefited, it might be legitimate to limit recovery to the defendant's actual benefit, a limit which has (perhaps inappropriately) been imported by the legislature into s 1(3) of the Act. However, under s 1(3) as it stands, if the defendant's actual benefit is less than the just or reasonable sum which would otherwise be awarded to the plaintiff, the award must be reduced to a sum equal to the amount of the defendant's benefit.

A crucial question, on which the 'Act is surprisingly' silent, is this: what bearing do the terms of the contract, under which the plaintiff has acted, have on the assessment of the just sum? First, the terms on which the work was done may serve to indicate the full scope of the work done, and so be relevant to the sum awarded in respect of such work. For example, if I do work under a contract under which I am to receive a substantial prize if successful, and nothing if I fail, and the contract is frustrated before the work is complete but not before a substantial benefit has been obtained by the defendant, the element of risk taken by the plaintiff may be held to have the effect of enhancing the amount of any sum to be awarded. Secondly, the contract consideration is always relevant as providing some evidence of what will be a reasonable sum to be awarded in respect of the plaintiff's work. Thus if a prospector, employed for a fee, discovers a goldmine before the contract under which he is employed is frustrated (for example, by illegality or by his illness or disablement) at a time when his work was incomplete, the court may think it just to make an award in the nature of a reasonable fee for what he has done (though of course the benefit obtained by the defendant will be far greater), and a rateable part of the contract fee may provide useful evidence of the level of sum to be awarded. If, however, the contract had provided that he was to receive a stake in the concession, then the just sum might be enhanced on the basis that, in all the circumstances, a reasonable sum should take account of such a factor: cf Way v Latilla [1937] 3 All ER 759. Thirdly, however, the contract consideration, or a rateable part of it, may provide a limit to the sum to be awarded. To take a fairly extreme example, a poor householder or a small businessman may obtain a contract for building work to be done to his premises at considerably less than the market price, on the basis that he cannot afford to pay more. In such a case, the court may consider it just to limit the award to a rateable part of the contract price, on the ground that it was the understanding of the parties that in no circumstances (including the circumstances of the contract being frustrated) should the plaintiff recover more than the contract price or a rateable part of it. Such a limit may properly be said to arise by virtue of the operation of s 2(3) of the Act. But it must not be forgotten that, unlike money, services can never be restored, nor usually can goods, since they are likely to have been either consumed or disposed of, or to have depreciated in value; and since, ex hypothesi, the defendant will only have been prepared to contract for the goods or services on the basis that he paid no more than the contract consideration, it may be unjust to compel him, by an award under the Act, to pay more than that consideration, or a rateable part of it, in respect of the services or goods he has received. It is unnecessary for me to decide whether this will always be so; but it is likely that in most cases this will impose an important limit on the sum to be awarded: indeed it may well be the most relevant limit to an award under s 1(3) of the Act. The legal basis of the limit may be s 2(3) of the Act; but even if that subsection is inapplicable, it is open to the court, in an appropriate case, to give effect to such a limit in assessing the just sum to be awarded under s 1(3), because in may cases it would be unjust to impose on the defendant an obligation to make restitution under the subsection at higher than the contract rate.

Applying s 1(3), Robert Goff J awarded the plaintiffs some US $15 m and some £9 m. Subject to a minor variation, his decision was affirmed by the Court of Appeal and the House of Lords, [1982] 1 All ER 925. Delivering the judgment of the Court of Appeal, Lawton LJ noted that Robert Goff J had thought the concept behind the Act was the prevention of unjust enrichment, and remarked: 'We get no help from the use of words which are not in the statute'. He went on to point out that there were various possible approaches to the assessment of a 'just sum' and the Court of Appeal would not be justified in setting aside the judge's method 'merely because we thought there were better ways'.

NOTES

1. Robert Goff J notes that a person who has received money is 'incontrovertibly benefited': see the introductory notes on restitution, p 42. In his judgment, he refers several times to the 'time value of money'. This is important, but for reasons of space, the discussion of it has been omitted.

2. The judge points out several things that the Act is *not* designed to do; see also p 485, note 4.

3. He remarks that the Act may have the effect of rescuing the plaintiff from an unprofitable bargain. This is one of the advantages of using a restitutionary remedy instead of suing for damages when a contract has been terminated because of a serious breach: see below, p 743.

4. The judge notes that the allowance for expenses under s 1(2) 'is probably best rationalised as a statutory recognition of the defence of change of position.' See, however, Burrows, pp 362–364.

5. The judge held that the effect of the frustrating circumstances must be taken into account in assessing the value of the benefit received. Is this what the Act provides, or does it say that the relevant benefit is that received *before* the frustration, and the effect of the frustrating event is to be taken into account when assessing the 'just sum'? It might make a considerable difference. If the contract had been frustrated by expropriation without compensation before any oil had been obtained, it would seem on the judge's approach that Hunt would have received no benefit, so BP could not be awarded anything for its work; whereas on the other approach, the benefit would be the value of the work done before the frustration, and the expropriation without compensation would

merely be a factor tending to reduce the just sum. See Treitel, pp 914–915. Burrows (pp 370–371) notes:

With great respect, it is possible that Robert Goff J took a false step in regarding there as being a crucial difference, so far as restitution is concerned, between the end product of contracted-for services and the services (or performance of the services) themselves. *Even if there is an end product produced by the services the defendant's benefit comprises his saving of expense in paying for the services producing that end product.* And the crucial line between when services constitute mere reliance loss to the performer and when they become objectively beneficial to the other party (and hence, subject to subjective devaluation, belong within restitution) is, it is submitted, when the other party receives the services. Where the purpose of the services is to produce an end product (eg building work) it is true that one regards the owner as receiving the services at the time when he receives part of the end product (eg when the first part of the building is erected). But the same notion of receipt explains why a theatregoer is only objectively benefited when the play begins or why a home owner who engages a gardener to mow the lawn is only objectively benefited when the gardener starts to cut the lawn. On a restitutionary interpretation of s 1(3) the important distinction is therefore between services that are not received and services that are received and not between services and the end product of those services.

Once one excises the distinction between end product and services the acute problems encountered by Robert Goff J in interpreting s 1(3) disappear. For example, there is now no problem of a small service producing very substantial end products and vice versa; there is no need to carve out inconsistent 'exceptions' where there is no end product or an end product of no objective value; there is no reason to confine a true restitutionary analysis to the assessment of the just sum; and, while the same conclusion may be reached by applying 'change of position' reasoning, s 1(3)(b) does not have to be interpreted as meaning that no valuable benefit was obtained where a building under construction is destroyed by fire. Indeed on this last point Treitel's more specific criticisms of Robert Goff J's interpretation of s 1(3)(b) seem irrefutable. His interpretation does contradict the emphasis in s 1(3) on a valuable benefit having been obtained 'before the time of discharge' and also cuts across the natural structure of s 1(3) whereby s 1(3)(b) goes to the exercise of the court's discretion as to what is a just sum to award rather than to the prior non-discretionary question of whether a valuable benefit has been obtained.

In the introduction Chapter 14 (pp 392–397), we noted that the doctrine of frustration seems to enable the court to allocate losses that it feels the contract itself had not allocated between the two parties. How far do its powers under the Act enable it to achieve that end? We have seen one problem already: the wasted expenditure incurred by one party in preparing to perform, when the expenditure does not produce a benefit to the other party and is not covered by an advance payment. Are there other examples? As Robert Goff J points out, the Act does not enable the court to put the parties into the position they would have been in if the contract had been performed (eg no recovery of lost profit), nor to restore them to their pre-contractual position. Thus the licensees in *Taylor v Caldwell* would still get nothing for the wasted advertising, Krell nothing for the cost of arranging to store his valuables away while Henry and company were in his flat, etc. Perhaps this is right: the court has already determined that neither party was better able to prevent the frustrating event, and maybe each is the best insurer of his own expenses, since he alone knows the amount of them.

A different view of what is 'going on' in frustration cases is presented below.

VI. RELIEF IN CASES OF HARDSHIP

We saw earlier that the doctrine of frustration does not release a party simply because its obligations have become much more burdensome (eg *Davis Contractors v Fareham UDC*). One party may give itself protection against difficulties that are outside its control by using a force majeure clause (eg as in *The Super Servant II*, p 469). It is now quite common in sophisticated commercial contracts, particularly those that are to run for a long time, to have a hardship provision, which imposes some duty to renegotiate if events change so as to cause serious hardship to one party.

The UNIDROIT Principles of International Commercial Contracts provide for hardship in Art. 6, s 2. See pp 893 ff.

They provide for force majeure as follows:

7.1.7 . . . . (Force majeure)

(1) Non-performance by a party is excused if that party proves that the non-performance was due to an impediment beyond its control and that it could not reasonably be expected to have taken the impediment into account at the time of the conclusion of the contract or to have avoided or overcome it or its consequences.

(2) When the impediment is only temporary, the excuse shall have effect for such period as is reasonable having regard to the effect of the impediment on the performance of the contract.

(3) The party who fails to perform must give notice to the other party of the impediment and its effect on its ability to perform. If the notice is not received by the other party within a reasonable time after the party who fails to perform knew or ought to have known of the impediment, it is liable for damages resulting from such non-receipt.

(4) Nothing in this article prevents a party from exercising a right to terminate the contract or to withhold performance or request interest on money due.

The Working Group regarded these decisions as representing something akin to best practice in modern international commercial contracts.

Is there any general rule of law that offers relief? It has been argued that, in Nordic law, a general principle is developing in consumer cases.

■ Wilhelmsson ' "Social Force Majeure"—A New Conception Nordic Consumer Law' (1990)
13 Journal of Consumer Policy 1, 2–7, 10–12

In Nordic law, there are a couple of regulations in which illness, unemployment, and other such circumstances are more or less specifically stated as grounds for limiting the sanctions against a debtor in delay.

Hire-Purchase and Consumer Credit

The first example, which has existed for some time, is to be found in the Nordic legislation concerning hire-purchase. The then new legislation on this type of contract, which was prepared jointly by the Nordic countries and was enacted during the 1950s in the other Nordic countries and in 1966 in Finland, contained a provision according to which repossession of goods or the claiming of some other contract-based sanction in case of delayed payment could be waived if the payment difficulties of the debtor were caused by illness, unemployment, or similar circumstances. When the creditor sought the assistance of the bailiff to effect repossession, the bailiff could also grant the debtor relief in these situations.

More recently, the legislation on hire-purchase has been wholly or partly replaced— the Nordic countries have chosen different solutions in this respect—by new legislation on consumer credit or credit sales. In the new Finnish legislation on consumer credit, there is a specific reference to the circumstances dealt with in this paper. According to the Consumer Protection Act ch 7 sec 16.2, the creditor shall not have the right to enforce repossession of the goods, claim an installment that has not otherwise matured, or enforce any other special sanction agreed upon by the parties, if the delay in payment is due to the illness or unemployment of the consumer or to a similar factor that is not the fault of the consumer, unless in view of the length of the delay and other circumstances this would clearly be unreasonable for the creditor.

. . .

Interest on Delayed Payments

In the new Finnish Act on Interest sec 11, there is a provision on adjustment of interest on delayed payments. According to this provision, a consumer may claim adjustment of his liability to pay such interest, if the delay was caused by difficulties in paying which the consumer has encountered mainly through no fault of his own as a consequence of illness, unemployment, or some other special cause. The provision gives the court wide discretion: The interest *may* be adjusted and the adjustment may be effected by a lowering of the interest rate or a postponement of the date from which interest should be paid or both. . .

Delayed Payment of Insurance Premiums

. . .

According to sec 25 of the Swedish Consumer Insurance Act, an insurance contract does not cease on the basis of the general rules on delayed payment of premiums if the delay was caused by severe illness of the policyholder, by his loss of liberty, by the fact that he has not received his pension or salary, or by some other similar unexpected event. . . .

Registration of Delayed Payments

Finally, the obstacles for due payment referred to in this paper may be taken into account in the regulation of credit information registers as well. In the Finnish Person Registration Decree, there is a provision which—according to the *travaux préparatoires*—is intended to prevent registration of some (temporary) defaults caused by illness, unemployment, or other special causes. In this way, one may try to protect the creditworthiness of debtors hit by difficulties of a temporary nature.

TOWARDS A GENERAL PRINCIPLE

. . .

All these fragments of new ideas in Nordic law indicate a social need for new doctrinal thinking too. The legal system seems to be ripe for the discussion of a more general principle of social force majeure which could also be applied in cases which do not directly fall within the sphere of the special provisions mentioned above. . . . The principle of social force majeure could be applied when the following four conditions are fulfilled:

1. The consumer is affected by some *special occurrence* such as an unfavourable change in his health (physical or mental illness, personal injury), work (unemployment, reduced work, strike and lockout), housing (termination of lease) or family (divorce, death or injury of family member). The list is not exhaustive; other occurrences may be relevant, too.
2. There is a *casual connection* between this occurrence and the consumer's difficulties in paying. If the occurrence has not led to economic difficulties for the person concerned—if he is wealthy and has other resources—he may not invoke the principle of social force majeure.
3. If the consumer *foresaw* the special occurrence when he concluded the contract, he cannot rely on it.

4. If the occurrence was caused by the *fault* of the consumer, he is also prevented from invoking the principle of social force majeure.

There are various legal consequences which may be attached to social force majeure. Such consequences have been mentioned above, in the presentation of the concrete legal material. . . .

. . . One may therefore as an argument against a principle of social force majeure make the claim that it is not the responsibility of private parties to finance the supporting of other parties even if those parties are in a socially and economically difficult situation.

In some cases this argument seems very convincing. In relationships between individuals, or even between individuals and small firms, there is obviously often little room for a solution which takes into account the special needs of one party at the expense of the other. The situation is different, however, when one is dealing with a typical relationship in consumer law, that between an individual and a large enterprise. As a matter of fact several of the well-known arguments concerning enterprise liability in the doctrine of private law could easily be used for imposing a 'duty to take into account the other party's needs' on such large enterprises. Such a duty may be based on, eg, the bureaucratic image and economic power of large enterprises and the idea that there should be some tie between power and responsibilities. One may also refer to the well-known possibility of dispersal of risk; an enterprise may often in its price policy be able to arrange for the loss to be borne by a large number of consumers. Finally one could argue, at least in some cases, that liability follows from causing the problem in the first place. If the developing 'credit card society' causes problems for persons not able to function properly in that society, then the finance companies, which have made this development possible, should have some responsibility for taking care of the problems.

The claim has been made that the principle of social force majeure is a rather *ineffective* means of protection with limited practical importance. This is obviously true. Even if the doctrine achieves an undisputed position in Nordic law, this would, of course, solve but a very small portion of the problems connected with the overindebtedness of consumers . . . However, the practical importance of the doctrine may grow if the Consumer Ombudsmen took more frequent steps towards getting social force majeure clauses written into important standard form contracts.

In spite of this possible development, other types of measures, such as informal and easily accessible bankruptcy proceedings resulting in definitive reduction of the debts of the consumer, would, however, still be needed and would certainly also be much more important means of reducing problems connected with the over-indebtedness of consumers. The acceptance of a principle of social force majeure in no way blocks the development of such other measures. The principle should not be seen as the only means of dealing with overindebtedness in connection with illness and unemployment but as one measure complementing other types of measures with the same purpose.

Furthermore, one should not appraise the principle of social force majeure only on the basis of its direct practical effect. The ideological value of the principle should not be overlooked. The principle embodies notions which make it possible to take unemployment and other similar occurrences into account in the legal discourse: it makes these occurrences visible within the realm of private law . . .

NOTES

1.   You may like to compare the Consumer Credit Act 1974, s 129:

Section 129: Time orders

(1) If it appears to the court just to do so—
   (a) on an application for an enforcement order; or
   (b) on an application made by a debtor or hirer under this paragraph after service on him of—
      (i)   a default notice, or
      (ii) a notice under section 76(1) or 98(1); or

> (c) in an action brought by a creditor or owner to enforce a regulated agreement or any security, or recover possession of any goods or land to which a regulated agreement relates, the court may make an order under this section (a 'time order').
>
> (2) A time order shall provide for one or both of the following, as the court considers just—
>
> (a) the payment by the debtor or hirer or any surety of any sum owed under a regulated agreement or a security by such instalments, payable at such times, as the court, having regard to the means of the debtor or hirer and any surety, considers reasonable;
>
> (b) the remedying by the debtor or hirer of any breach of a regulated agreement (other than non-payment of money) within such period as the court may specify.

See also the Administration of Justice Act 1970, s 36, and compare the procedures governing the forfeiture of leases for non-payment of rent (governed by the Common Law Procedure Act 1852, ss 210–212) or other breaches of covenant (Law of Property Act 1925, s 146).

However, the relief that can be given under these provisions is limited, even in cases of inability to pay through, eg, redundancy. In *First National Bank plc v Syed* [1991] 2 All ER 250, it was held that it was not just to make a time order if the instalments would not meet the accruing interest and there is no realistic prospect of the debtor's financial position improving. See also Sayer (1994) 144 NLJ 429.

2. It is frequently possible for debtors taking out consumer credit to take out insurance that will pay the debt if the debtor dies, is prevented by illness from working or is made redundant.

In Australia, relief has been given under the doctrine of frustration when one party's obligations have become more onerous.

■ *Codelfa Construction Pty Ltd v State Rail Authority of New South Wales*
(1982) 149 CLR 337, High Court of Australia

The State Rail Authority engaged Codelfa to excavate tunnels as part of a construction of a railway in the eastern suburbs of Sydney. Codelfa planned to work three shifts a day, seven days a week and this was well known to the rail authority. Local residents, however, obtained an injunction to restrain Codelfa from working a 24-hour, seven-day week and they were not able to work between 10.00 pm in the evening and 6.00 am in the morning or on Sundays at all. Codelfa claimed that the inability to work a seven-day week significantly increased their costs. The dispute was referred to arbitration. The arbitrator, the trial judge and the New South Wales Court of Appeal all agreed that some term to reflect the parties' common understanding as to working hours should be implied. The High Court of Australia disagreed and held that no term could be implied. Mason J said:

To say that the maintenance of three eight hour shifts a day for six days a week was a matter of common contemplation between the parties is not enough in itself to justify the implication of a term. Lord Atkin's example of the sale of a painting believed by both seller and buyer to be the work of an old master [*Bell v Lever Bros*] is a striking illustration. It must appear that the matter of common contemplation was necessary to give the contract business efficacy and that the term sought to be implied is so obvious that it goes without saying.

In this case the problem, as I see it, lies not so much in saying that the implication of a term is necessary to give business efficacy to the contract, as in concluding that the particular term to be implied is so obvious that 'it goes without saying'.

. . .

[T]here remains an insurmountable problem in saying that 'it goes without saying' that had the parties contemplated the possibility that their legal advice was incorrect and that an injunction might be granted to restrain noise or other nuisance, they would have settled upon the term implied by the Court of Appeal or that implied by the Arbitrator and by Ash J at first instance. I doubt whether the fiction of treating the parties as reasonable and fair makes the problem any the less difficult. This is not a case in which an obvious provision was overlooked by the parties and omitted from the contract. Rather it was a case in which the parties made a common assumption which masked the need to explore what provision should be made to cover the event which occurred. In ordinary circumstances negotiation about the matter might have yielded any one of a number of alternative provisions, each being regarded as a reasonable solution.

The High Court went on, however, to hold that the contract had been frustrated. Mason J said:

. . . The submission of the proposed program of work with the tender, its supersession by the revised program pursuant to cl s 6 of the specifications, together with the very provisions of cl s 6 itself dealing with the construction program, provide a link between the contract and the antecedent discussions so as to enable us, subject to a consideration of specific provisions in the specifications, to say that the contract contemplated that completion would be achieved within the time stipulated by the method of work already mentioned, it being assumed that it could not be disturbed by the grant of an injunction.

I come back then to the question whether the performance of the contract in the new situation was fundamentally different from performance in the situation contemplated by the contract. The answer must, I think, be in the affirmative. Paragraphs 14, 15, 16, 18 and 19 of the arbitrator's award go a long way towards establishing this answer. The finding contained in para 16 proceeds on the footing that the contract work could not be carried out as contemplated by the contract once injunctions were granted, the effect of which was to prohibit the continuous three shift a day operations six days a week. Performance by means of a two shift operation, necessitated by the grant of the injunctions, was fundamentally different from that contemplated by the contract . . .

NOTES

1. Is the High Court's decision not to imply a term logically consistent with its decision that the contract was frustrated?

2. The possibility that an injunction might be granted to restrict working hours was well known to the parties at the time they made the contract. They appear to have received legal advice, erroneous as it later appeared, that the contractors would enjoy the immunity that the railway authority would have enjoyed under statute if it had done the work itself. Does this make the case one of mistake, rather than frustration? If so, what kind of mistake was it? Would it matter that it was perhaps a mistake of law? (See p 512.)

QUESTIONS

1. Will a contract ever be frustrated by a subsequent change of circumstances that has not made the contract either physically impossible or illegal?

2. Will a contract that unforeseeably has become physically impossible to perform ever not be frustrated? In what circumstances?

3.   Do you agree or disagree with the outcome of the argument based on frustration in the *Super Servant II* (p 469)?

4.   Can a contract that has become impossible to perform through a foreseeable event ever be frustrated? When?

5.   Before the contract was frustrated, one party has paid money to the other. Can the first party recover any of it? Explain the rules that applied at common law and those that apply under the Law Reform (Frustrated Contracts) Act 1943.

6.   Before the contract was frustrated, one party has incurred expenditure in beginning to perform. Can it recover anything? Explain the rules that applied at common law and those that apply under the Law Reform (Frustrated Contracts) Act 1943.

CHAPTER SEVENTEEN

EXPECTATION MISTAKES

In the previous chapter, we saw that in some cases the courts divide the losses caused by an event not covered by the contract, by holding the contract discharged by frustration. A similar solution is achieved in cases in which the risk in question is not one of a subsequent contingency, but of the facts existing when the contract was made turning out to be different to what the parties believed. In this case of common mistake, however, technically, the contract is not discharged: if the mistake operates it renders the contract either void *ab initio* or voidable in equity.

Suppose that A has agreed to sell to B a particular machine that B is to collect from a disused factory. Unknown to either party, there has just been a fire at the factory, and the machine has been rendered valueless except as scrap. Just as in the case of frustration, three solutions are possible:

(a) A is liable to B for failing to deliver, and will have to compensate B for any consequential loss (eg wasted transport costs);

(b) B must take the remains of the machine and pay the full price;

(c) the contract is void or voidable, so that B does not have to pay but cannot recover damages.

In cases of alleged frustration, the court normally had to choose between holding the contract discharged and holding that its express and implied terms were still enforceable, so that the parties must perform or, if that was impossible, pay damages. In cases of common mistake, the same choice applies, but the position is complicated by the possibility that during the negotiations one party will have stated his understanding of the facts. This may have two effects. Firstly, the courts may treat the statement as a warranty that the facts stated are true (see, p 323). This will automatically lead to the risk of their being untrue being placed on the speaker. Secondly, even if the statement is not a warranty, it may give rise to remedies for misrepresentation if the other party relied on it, and the contract may be avoided on that ground, without the need to argue mistake. As a result, the doctrine of common mistake has a narrow field of practical operation, because it will not normally be needed if one party has stated his version of the facts. It will only apply if the parties were mistaken about unstated assumptions, or each relied on his own understandings rather than on what the other said. This no doubt explains why there are so few cases.

The doctrine of common mistake appears to have been a nineteenth-century importation from civil law (see Simpson (1975) 91 LQR 247, 269). During the first half of the century, various cases, which are now seen as involving common mistake, were decided without invoking any such doctrine. Perhaps the best known is *Couturier v Hastie* (1856) 5 HL Cas

673. A c&f contract (rather like the cif contract described Appendix, but without the insurance element) had been made for a cargo of corn that both parties assumed was in existence. In fact, the corn had begun overheating and the captain of the ship had unloaded and sold it (the normal practice). The sellers argued that the buyers must still take up the shipping documents and pay the price. If it had been the case that the goods had been damaged or lost after the contract had been made, then at least in modern law the buyer would indeed have been obliged to pay—the risk (see p 462) would have passed as from shipment and the buyer would be expected to claim on the insurance, if any. But the House of Lords affirmed the decision of Exchequer Chamber that, on the actual facts, the buyer did not have to pay. The contract was one 'for the sale of a cargo supposed to exist', not 'for goods lost or not lost'. The word mistake does not occur in the judgments, nor is there any discussion of whether the contract was void—the only point decided was that the sellers could not require the buyer to perform.

The most obvious source for the doctrine of mistake is *Kennedy v Panama, New Zealand and Australian Royal Mail* Co Ltd (1867) LR 2 QB 580. The plaintiff had bought some shares relying on a statement that the company had obtained a valuable contract to carry mail for the New Zealand government. This was an innocent misrepresentation, but the case was argued and decided on purely common law grounds, and the question was simply whether there had been a total failure of consideration so that the plaintiff could get his money back (see **p 480**). Again, this is something different from mistake, but in deciding that there had not been a total failure of consideration, Blackburn J drew on Roman law principles (cf his judgment in *Taylor v Caldwell*, p 460). He referred to the Roman doctrine of *error*, under which a mistake as to substance would invalidate a contract but a mistake merely as to quality would not, and said that the misunderstanding about the shares went only to quality, so that there was no total failure of consideration. It is easy to see how this could be interpreted as saying that a mistake as to substance will make the contract void for mistake, as it did in Roman law. At any rate, by the end of the century, *Couturier v Hastie* was considered to have been decided on the ground that the contract was *void*, and this solution was adopted by Sale of Goods Act 1893.

■ Sale of Goods Act 1979
Section 6

Where there is a contract for the sale of specific goods, and the goods without the knowledge of the seller have perished at the time when the contract is made, the contract is void.

■ *McRae v Commonwealth Disposals Commission*
(1950) 84 CLR 377, High Court of Australia

The Commonwealth Disposals Commission, which was authorised to make contracts on behalf of the Commonwealth, invited tenders 'for the purchase of an oil tanker lying on Jourmaund Reef, which is approximately 100 miles north of Samarai. The vessel is said to contain oil'. The Commission notified the plaintiff by letter that his tender had been accepted and that a 'sales advice note' would be sent him within a few days. The plaintiff subsequently received the sales advice note, which described what was sold as 'one (1) oil tanker including contents wrecked on Jourmaund Reef approximately 100 miles north of Samarai. Price £285', and referred to conditions, one of which was that the goods 'are sold as and where they lie with all faults' and no warranty was given as to 'condition description quality or otherwise'. The plaintiff was unable to locate Jourmaund Reef on a map and, on inquiry, was supplied by the Commission with the latitude and longitude at which the tanker was alleged to be lying. At considerable expense, the plaintiff fitted out a salvage expedition and proceeded to the locality given but found no tanker there; in fact, there was none in the locality at any material times.

Dixon and Fullagar JJ

... The first question to be determined is whether a contract was made between the plaintiffs and the Commission. The argument that the contract was void, or, in other words, that there was no contract, was based, as has been observed, on *Couturier v Hastie*. It is true that *Couturier v Hastie* has been commonly treated in the text-books as a case of a contract avoided by mutual mistake, and it is found cited in the company of such cases as *Gompertz v Bartlett* and *Strickland v Turner*. Section 7 [sic] of the English Sale of Goods Act 1893 is generally regarded as expressing the effect of the case. The case has not, however, been universally regarded as resting on mistake...

In considering *Couturier v Hastie* it is necessary to remember that it was, in substance, a case in which a vendor was suing for the price of goods which he was unable to deliver. If there had been nothing more in the case, it would probably never have been reported: indeed the action would probably never have been brought. But the vendor founded his claim on the provision for 'payment upon handing over shipping documents'. He was not called upon to prove a tender of the documents, because the defendant had 'repudiated' the contract, but he was able and willing to hand them over, and his argument was, in effect, that by handing them over he would be doing all that the contract required of him. The question thus raised would seem to depend entirely on the construction of the contract, and it appears really to have been so treated throughout...

The judgment of the Exchequer Chamber was delivered by Coleridge J. The view that the contract was void is probably derived from certain expressions which were used in the course of this judgment. But it does seem clear that again the question of construction was regarded as the fundamental question in the case. In stating the question for decision Coleridge J refers first to the direction of Martin B to the jury, and says that the Lord Chief Baron had agreed with the opinion of Martin B whereas the other learned Barons had differed from him. The judgment below, he says 'turned entirely on the meaning of the contract' and he proceeds to set out its terms in full. 'The question', he says, 'turns entirely upon the terms of the contract'. The argument for the defendant is then put as including the proposition 'that a vendor of goods undertakes that they exist', and the argument for the plaintiff as being 'that this was not a mere contract for the sale of an ascertained cargo, but that the purchaser bought the adventure, and took upon himself all risks from the shipment of the cargo'. The final conclusion reached is expressed at the end of the judgment by saying that 'the basis of the contract in this case was the sale and purchase of goods, and all the other terms in the bought note were dependent upon that, and we cannot give to it the effect of a contract for goods lost or not lost'. In the light of these passages it seems impossible to regard the expressions 'If the contract for the sale of the cargo was valid' and 'the contract failed as to the principal subject-matter of it' as meaning that the contract was treated as being void. All that the passages in which those expressions occur seem in their context to mean is that the principal subject matter of the contract was a cargo of goods, that the purchaser did not buy shipping documents representing non-existent goods, that the consideration to the purchaser had failed, and that he could not therefore be liable to pay the contract price....

The observation of Lord Atkin in *Bell v Lever Bros Ltd* [below, p 504] seems entirely appropriate to *Couturier v Hastie*. In that case there was a failure of consideration, and the purchaser was not bound to pay the price: if he had paid it before the truth was discovered, he could have recovered it back as money had and received. The construction of the contract was the vital thing in the case because, and only because, on the construction of the contract depended the question whether the consideration had really failed, the vendor maintaining that, since he was able to hand over the shipping documents, it had not failed. The truth is that the question whether the contract was void, or the vendor excused from performance by reason of the non-existence of the supposed subject matter, did not arise in *Couturier v Hastie*. It would have arisen if the purchaser had suffered loss through non-delivery of the corn and had sued the vendor for damages. If it had so arisen, we think that the real question would have been whether the contract was subject to an implied condition precedent that the goods were in existence. Prima facie, one would think, there would be no such implied condition precedent, the position being simply that the vendor *promised* that the goods *were* in existence. That is the real meaning of the direction of Martin B to the jury, and so the argument for the defendant, as has already been pointed out, included the proposition that 'a vendor of goods undertakes that they exist and that they are capable of being transferred, although he may not stipulate for their condition'. . . .

If the view so far indicated be correct, as we believe it to be, it seems clear that the case of *Couturier v Hastie* does not compel one to say that the contract in the present case was void. But, even if the view that *Couturier v Hastie* was a case of a void contract be correct, we would still think that it could not govern the present case. . . . [I]t must be true to say that a party cannot rely on mutual mistake where the mistake consists of a belief which is, on the one hand, entertained by him without any reasonable ground, and, on the other hand, deliberately induced by him in the mind of the other party. It does not seem possible on the evidence to say that Bowser or Sheehan was guilty of fraud in the sense that either knew at the date of the contract that the Commission had no tanker to sell. And even at the later stage, after the receipt of the message from Misima, it is difficult to impute to them actual knowledge that there was no tanker at Jomard Entrance. The message should have conveyed to them the fact that the only vessel lying in the vicinity was almost certainly worthless, and ordinary commonsense and decency would have suggested that the contents of the message ought to be communicated to the plaintiffs. But the message referred to a 'barge type tanker', and it is quite possible that this description would fail to bring home to their minds that there was no tanker. A finding of actual knowledge that they had nothing to sell does not seem justified by the evidence, though it is difficult to credit them at the time of the publication of the advertisements with any honest affirmative belief that a tanker existed. The confusion as to locality in the description advertised is almost enough to exclude the inference of any such affirmative belief. But, even if they be credited with a real belief in the existence of a tanker, they were guilty of the grossest negligence. It is impossible to say that they had any reasonable ground for such a belief. Having no reasonable grounds for such a belief, they asserted by their advertisement to the world at large, and by their later specification of locality to the plaintiffs, that they had a tanker to sell. They must have known that any tenderer would rely implicitly on their assertion of the existence of a tanker, and they must have known that the plaintiffs would rely implicitly on their later assertion of the existence of a tanker in the lattitude and longitude given. They took no steps to verify what they were asserting, and any 'mistake' that existed was induced by their own culpable conduct. In these circumstances it seems out of the question that they should be able to assert that no contract was concluded. It is not unfair or inaccurate to say that the only 'mistake' the plaintiffs made was that they believed what the Commission told them.

The position so far, then, may be summed up as follows. It was not decided in *Couturier v Hastie* that the contract in that case was void. The question whether it was void or not did not arise. If it had arisen, as in an action by the purchaser for damages, it would have turned on the ulterior question whether the contract was subject to an implied condition precedent. Whatever might then have been held on the facts of *Couturier v Hastie*, it is impossible in this case to imply any such term. The terms of the contract and the surrounding circumstances clearly exclude any such implication. The buyers relied upon, and acted upon, the assertion of the seller that there was a tanker in existence. It is not a case in which the parties can be seen to have proceeded on the basis of a common assumption of fact so as to justify the conclusion that the correctness of the assumption was intended by both parties to be a condition precedent to the creation of contractual obligations. The officers of the Commission made an assumption, but the plaintiffs did not make an assumption in the same sense. They knew nothing except what the Commission had told them. If they had been asked, they would certainly not have said: 'Of course, if there is no tanker, there is no contract'. They would have said: 'We shall have to go and take possession of the tanker. We simply accept the Commission's assurance that there is a tanker and the Commission's promise to give us that tanker.' The only proper construction of the contract is that it included a promise by the Commission that there was a tanker in the position specified. The Commission contracted that there was a tanker there. 'The sale in this case of a ship implies a contract that the subject of the transfer did exist in the character of a ship' *(Barr v Gibson)*. If, on the other hand, the case of *Couturier v Hastie* and this case ought to be treated as cases raising a question of 'mistake', then the Commission cannot in this case rely on any mistake as avoiding the contract, because any mistake was induced by the serious fault of their own servants, who asserted the existence of a tanker recklessly and without any reasonable ground. There *was* a contract, and the Commission contracted that a tanker existed in the position specified. Since there was no such tanker, there has been a breach of contract, and the plaintiffs are entitled to damages for that breach.

Before proceeding to consider the measure of damages, one other matter should be briefly mentioned. The contract was made in Melbourne, and it would seem that its proper law is Victorian law. Section 11 of the Victorian Goods Act 1928 corresponds to s 6 of the English Sale of Goods Act 1893, and provides that 'where there is a contract for the sale of specific goods, and the goods without the knowledge of the seller have perished at the time when the contract is made the contract is void'. This has been generally supposed to represent the legislature's view of the effect of *Couturier v Hastie*. Whether it correctly represents the effect of the decision in that case or not, it seems clear that the section has no application to the facts of the present case. Here the goods never existed, and the seller ought to have known that they did not exist. . . .

McTiernan J delivered a concurring judgment.

Appeal allowed.

NOTES

1. Suppose that the tanker had been on the reef at one stage but had disintegrated long before the contract was made, and that the Commission should have known this. Could the court have reached the same result, or would s 6 have forced them to hold that the contract was void and so the Commission was not liable? Unlike many sections of the Sale of Goods Act, s 6 seems to impose an absolute rule rather than a rule that applies only in the absence of contrary intention (see Treitel, pp 296–297). Probably the Commission could nowadays be found liable under *Hedley Byrne v Heller* (see p 28), or perhaps the court would discover a collateral contract that the tanker existed. (What could be the consideration for a collateral contract?)

2. Was one of the parties in *McRae's* case able to avoid the loss at less cost than the other? Isn't there a close parallel to self-induced frustration (see p 469)?

■ *Bell v Lever Bros*

[1931] All ER Rep 1, House of Lords

By agreements dated 9 August 1923, 9 October 1923, and 1 July 1926, made between the respondents (plaintiffs in the action) and Bell and Snelling, the appellants (defendants), it was agreed that the appellants should act as chairman and vice-chairman respectively of the Niger Co Ltd, for five years, devoting the whole of their time to the business of the company. The assets of the Niger Co were afterwards transferred to a new company called the United Africa Co Ltd, and in March 1929, the respondents entered into a further agreement with the appellants under which they paid them £50,000 as compensation for the termination of the agreement of 1 July 1926, and in full satisfaction of all claims against the respondents or the Niger Co. Subsequent to this agreement, it was discovered that the appellants had entered into certain dealings on their own account, which they had kept secret from the respondents. The respondents then demanded a return of the £50,000. The appellants admitted they were liable to account for profits on the private dealings, but denied liability to repay the £50,000. The respondents then brought this action claiming damages for fraudulent misrepresentation and breach of contract. The jury, by their findings, negatived the allegation of fraudulent misrepresentation or concealment, but found that the appellants had committed a breach of contract owing to the private transactions, and that the respondents were entitled on this account to terminate the service contract of 1926 and would have elected to do so had they known of the breach in question. The Court of Appeal held that the cancellation agreement was invalidated on the ground of mutual more usually nowadays termed 'common' mistake.

Lord Atkin

... In the view that I take of the whole case it becomes unnecessary to deal finally with the appellants' complaint that the points upon which the plaintiffs succeeded were not open to them. I content myself with saying that much may be said for that contention.

Two points present themselves for decision. (i) Was the agreement of March 19, 1929, void by reason of a mutual mistake of Mr D'Arcy Cooper and Mr Bell? (ii) ... The rules of law dealing with the effect of mistake on contract appear to be established with reasonable clearness. If mistake operates at all it operates so as to negative or in some cases to nullify consent. The parties may be mistaken in the identity of the contracting parties, or in the existence of the subject-matter of the contract at the date of the contract, or in the quality of the subject-matter of the contract. These mistakes may be by one party, or by both, and the legal effect may depend upon the class of mistake above mentioned. Thus a mistaken belief by A that he is contracting with B, whereas in fact he is contracting with C, will negative consent where it is clear that the intention of A was to contract only with B. So the agreement of A and B for the purchase of a specific article is void if in fact the article had perished before the date of sale. In this case, though the parties in fact were agreed about the subject-matter, yet a consent to transfer take or delivery of something not existent is deemed useless, the consent is nullified. As codified in the Sale of Goods Act, 1893, the contract is expressed to be void if the seller was in ignorance of the destruction of the specific chattel. I apprehend that if the seller with knowledge that a chattel was destroyed purported to sell it to a purchaser, the latter might sue for damages for non-delivery though the former could not sue for non-acceptance, but I know of no case where a seller has so committed himself. This is a case where mutual mistake certainly and unilateral mistake by the seller of goods will prevent a contract from arising. Corresponding to mistake as to the existence of the subject-matter is mistake as to title in cases where unknown to the parties the buyer is already the owner of that which the seller purports to sell him. The parties intended to effectuate a transfer of ownership; such a transfer is impossible; the stipulation is naturali ratione inutilis. This is the case of *Cooper v Phibbs*, where A agreed to take a lease of a fishery from B though, contrary to the belief of both parties at the time, A was tenant for life of the fishery and B appears to have had no title at all. To such a case Lord Westbury applied the principle that, if parties contract under a mutual mistake and misapprehension as to their relative and respective rights, the result is that the agreement is liable to be set aside as having proceeded upon a common mistake. Applied to the context the statement is only subject to the criticism that the agreement would appear to be void rather than voidable. Applied to mistake as to rights generally it would appear to be too wide. Even where the vendor has no title, though both parties think he has, the correct view would appear to be that there is a contract, but that the vendor has either committed a breach of a stipulation as to title or is not able to perform his contract. The contract is unenforceable by him, but is not void. Mistake as to quality of the thing contracted for raises more difficult questions. In such a case a mistake will not affect assent unless it is the mistake of both parties and is as to the existence of some quality which makes the thing without the quality essentially different from the thing as it was believed to be. Of course it may appear that the parties contracted that the article should possess the quality which one or other or both mistakenly believed it to possess. But in such a case there is a contract and the inquiry is a different one, being whether the contract as to quality amounts to a condition or a warranty, a different branch of the law. The principles to be applied are to be found in two cases which, so far as my knowledge goes, have always been treated as authoritative expositions of the law.

The first is *Kennedy v Panama, New Zealand and Australian Royal Mail Co*. In that case the plaintiff had applied for shares in the defendant company on the faith of a prospectus which stated falsely but innocently that the company had a binding contract with the government of New Zealand for the carriage of mails. On discovering the true facts the plaintiff brought an action for the recovery of the sums that he had paid on calls. The defendants brought a cross-section for further calls... The court came to the conclusion in that case that, though there was a misapprehension as to that which was a material part of the motive inducing the applicant to ask for the shares, it did not prevent the shares from being in substance those he applied for.

The next case is *Smith v Hughes*, the well-known case as to new and old oats....

The court ordered a new trial. It is not quite clear whether they considered that if the defendant's contention was correct the parties were not ad idem or there was a contractual condition that the oats sold were old oats. In either case the defendant would succeed in defeating the claim.

In these cases I am inclined to think that the true analysis is that there is a contract, but that the one party is not able to supply the very thing, whether goods or services, that the other party contracted to take, and, therefore, the contract is unenforceable by the one if executory, while, if executed, the other can recover back money paid on the ground of failure of the consideration.

We are now in a position to apply to the fact of this case the law as to mistake so far as it has been stated. The agreement which is said to be void is the agreement contained in the letter of March 19, 1929, that Bell would retire from the board of the Niger Co and its subsidiaries, and that in consideration of his doing so Levers would pay him as compensation for the termination of his agreements and consequent loss of office the sum of £30,000 in full satisfaction and discharge of all claims and demands of any kind against Lever Bros, the Niger Co, or its subsidiaries. The agreement which, as part of the contract, was terminated, had been broken so that it could be repudiated. Is an agreement to terminate a broken contract different in kind from an agreement to terminate an unbroken contract, assuming that the breach has given the one party the right to declare the contract at an end? I feel the weight of the respondents' contention that a contract immediately determinable is a different thing from a contract for an unexpired term and that the difference in kind can be illustrated by the immense price of release from the longer contract as compared with the shorter. And I agree that an agreement to take an assignment of a lease for five years is not the same thing as to take an assignment of a lease for three years, still less a term for a few months. But on the whole I have come to the conclusion that it would be wrong to decide that an agreement to terminate a definite specified contract is void if it turns out that the contract had already been broken and could have been terminated otherwise. The contract released is the identical contract in both cases; and the party paying for release gets exactly what he bargains for. It seems immaterial that he could have got the same result in another way: or that, if he had known the true facts, he would not have entered into the bargain. A buys B's horse: he thinks the horse is sound, and he pays the price of a sound horse: he would certainly not have bought the horse if he had known as the fact is that the horse is unsound. If B has made no representation as to soundness and has not contracted that the horse is sound A is bound, and cannot recover back the price. A buys a picture from B: both A and B believe it to be the work of an old master, and a high price is paid. It turns out to be a modern copy. A has no remedy in the absence of representation or warranty. A agrees to take on lease or to buy from B an unfurnished dwelling-house. The house is in fact uninhabitable. A would never have entered into the bargain if he had known the fact. A has no remedy: and the position is the same whether B knew the fact or not, so long as he made no representation or gave no warranty. A buys a roadside garage business from B abutting on a public thoroughfare: unknown to A, but known to B, it has already been decided to construct a by-pass road which will divert substantially the whole of the traffic from passing A's garage. Again A has no remedy. All these cases involve hardship on A, and benefit B, as most people would say, unjustly. They can be supported on the ground that it is of paramount importance that contracts should be observed: and that if parties honestly comply with the essentials of the formation of contracts, ie, agree in the same terms on the same subject-matter they are bound: and must rely on the stipulations of the contract for protection from the effect of facts unknown to them.

This brings the discussion to the alternative mode of expressing the result of a mutual mistake. It is said that in such a case as the present there is to be implied a stipulation in the contract that a condition of its efficacy is that the facts should be as understood by both parties, namely, that the contract would not be terminated till the end of the current term. The question of the existence of conditions express or implied is obviously one that affects not the formation of contract, but the investigation of the terms of the contract when made. A condition derives its efficacy from the consent of the parties express or implied. They have agreed, but on what terms? One term may be that unless the facts are or are not of a particular nature, or unless an event has or has not happened, the contract is not to take effect. With regard to future facts such a condition is obviously contractual. Till the event occurs the parties are bound. Thus the condition (the exact terms of which need not here be investigated) that is generally accepted as underlying the principle of the frustration cases is contractual: an implied condition. Counsel for the respondents formulated for the assistance of your Lordships a proposition which should be recorded: 'Whenever it is to be inferred from the terms of a contract or its surrounding circumstances that the consensus has been reached upon the basis of a particular contractual assumption, and that assumption is not true, the contract is avoided; ie, it is void ab initio if the assumption is of present fact and it ceases to bind if the assumption is of future fact.' I think few would demur to this statement, but its value depends upon the meaning of 'a contractual assumption' and also upon the true meaning to be attached to 'basis', a metaphor which may mislead. When used expressly in contracts—for instance, in policies of insurance which state that the truth of the statements in the proposal is to be the basis of the contract of insurance—the meaning is clear. The truth of the statements is made a condition of the contract which, failing the contract, is void unless the condition is waived. The proposition does not amount to more than this, that, if the contract expressly or impliedly contains a term that a particular assumption is a condition of the contract, the contract is avoided if the assumption is not true. But we have not advanced far on the inquiry how to ascertain whether the contract does contain such a condition. Various words are to be found to define the state of things which makes a condition. 'In the contemplation of both parties fundamental to the continued validity of the contract', 'a foundation essential to its existence', and 'a fundamental reason for making it', are phrases found in the important judgment of Scrutton LJ in the present case. The first two phrases appear to me to be unexceptionable. They cover the case of a contract to serve in a particular place, the existence of which is fundamental to the service, or to procure the services of a professional vocalist whose continued health is essential to performance. But 'a fundamental reason for making a contract' may with respect be misleading. The reason of one party only is presumedly not intended, but in the cases that I have above suggested of the sale of a horse or of a picture, it might be said that the fundamental reason for making the contract was the belief of both parties that the horse was sound or the picture an old master, yet in neither case would the condition as I think exist. Nothing is more dangerous than to allow oneself liberty to construct for the parties contracts which they have not in terms made by importing implications which would appear to make the contracts more business-like or more just. The implications to be made are to be no more than are 'necessary' for giving business efficacy to the transaction; and it appears to me that as to both existing facts and future facts a condition should not be implied unless the new state of facts makes the contract something different in kind from the contract in the original state of facts. . . . We, therefore, get a common standard for mutual mistake, and implied conditions whether as to existing or as to future facts. Does the state of the new facts destroy the identity of the subject-matter as it was in the original state of facts? To apply the principle to the infinite combinations of facts that arise in actual experience will continue to be difficult; but if this case results in establishing order in what has been a somewhat confused and difficult branch of the law it will have served a useful purpose. I have already stated my reasons for deciding that in the present case the identity of the subject-matter was not destroyed by the mutual mistake, if any, and I need not repeat them. . . .

Lord Blanesburgh and **Thankerton** agreed that the plea of mistake must fail; **Viscount Hailsham** and **Lord Warrington of Clyffe** dissented.

Order of the Court of Appeal reversed.

NOTES

1.   Bishop sells Furmston a picture of Salisbury Cathedral, which they both believe to be by Constable. It is, in fact, a modern painting after the style of Constable. Is the identity of the subject matter destroyed? Was the bargain essentially for a picture of Salisbury Cathedral, or for a Constable? See Treitel, pp 293–294.

2.   If the answer to the last question is 'a Constable', the contract might be void. But what if:

  (a) the seller was an art dealer who had told the buyer the picture was a Constable? (See p 324, and *Leaf v International Galleries,* p 365).

  (b) the sale was made by an auctioneer selling off the contents of a country house at an informal auction held at the house, and it was quite obvious that the auctioneer knew nothing about pictures? Cf *Bisset v Wilkinson,* p 358 and *Harlingdon & Leinster Enterprises Ltd v Christopher Hull Fine Art Ltd,* p 429.)

3.   In the Canadian case of *Diamond v British Columbia Thoroughbred Breeders' Society and Boyd* (1965) 52 DLR (2d) 146 (BC), the plaintiff attended an auction and successfully bid on a horse numbered 'Hip No 16'. The sale catalogue identified this horse as Pennate, a full brother of the winner of the Canadian Derby in Alberta in 1961. In fact, the horse had been mislabelled, and was not Pennate but Palloffair, a half-brother to the winner. When the plaintiff discovered the mistake, he sought the return of his purchase money and damages. Aikins J held that the contract was not void for mistake because it was for the horse displayed in the ring. He went on to hold that the plaintiff could have rescinded for misrepresentation had he acted more promptly, but that the plaintiff could also recover damages for breach of contract that the horse had the stated lineage. This case illustrates the possible solutions to the problem in note 2, above; with respect, it seems that the judge was trying to adopt inconsistent solutions at the same time. Either the contract was one to sell Pennate, in which case the seller is liable for breach or the contract was for the horse in the ring. If it was the latter, then there might still be a remedy for misrepresentation, if there had been one; if the mistake was sufficiently fundamental, the contract might be void for mistake. It is hard to see that the mistake in this case was fundamental, but it might have been if the horse were being sold and bought for breeding and turned out to be a nag of no pedigree whatever. If neither mistake nor misrepresentation will assist the buyer, he must accept the horse and cannot claim compensation.

4.   It has been argued that a contract will only be void for common mistake in cases in which goods have perished or the buyer buys his own property, but see p 514.

5.   If a contract is void for mistake, but one or both of the parties have started performing before they realise the mistake, what will happen? Firstly, any money paid will be recoverable for total failure of consideration: see p 481. In *Westdeutsche Landesbank Girozentrale v Islington Borough Council* [1994] 4 All ER 890, the question was whether

the bank could recover sums paid to the local authotity under a 'swap' agreement, which was later found to be ultra vires. It was held that it could. Leggatt LJ said (at 967-969):

The parties believed that they were making an interest swaps contract. They were not, because such a contract was ultra vires the local authority. So they made no contract at all. Islington say that they should receive a windfall because the purpose of the doctrine of ultra vires is to protect council taxpayers whereas restitution would disrupt Islington's finances. They also contend that it would countenance 'unconsidered dealings with local authorities'. If that is the best that can be said for refusing restitution, the sooner it is enforced the better. Protection of council taxpayers from loss is to be distinguished from securing a windfall for them. The disruption of Islington's finances is the result of ill-considered financial dispositions by Islington and its officers. It is not the policy of the law to require others to deal at their peril with local authorities, nor to require others to undertake their own inquiries about whether a local authority has power to make particular contracts or types of contract. Any system of law, and indeed any system of fair dealing, must be expected to ensure that Islington do not profit by the fortuity that when it became known that the contract was ineffective the balance stood in their favour. In other words, in circumstances such as these they should not be unjustly enriched.

It is common ground that the interest swaps and Islington's payments were ultra vires the local authority, and that the contract was therefore void ab initio; that there was no illegality involved; and that the legal property in the money which was paid by the parties to each other under the swap contract passed to the recipient.

Where A has in his possession the money of B under a void transaction, B should be entitled to reimbursement unless some principle of law precludes it. If the transaction was a contract, initially valid, the question will arise whether it has been partially performed. If so, the failure of consideration will not be total. But if the transaction was entered into by both parties in the belief, which proves unfounded, that it was an enforceable contract, in principle the parties ought to be restored to the respective positions from which they started. To achieve that, where there have been mutual payments the recipient of the larger payment has only to repay the net excess over the payment he has himself made.

Hobhouse J said [at first instance, [1994] 4 All ER at p 929]:

'In my judgment the correct analysis is that any payments made under a contract which is void ab initio, in the way that an ultra vires contract is void, are not contractual payments at all. They are payments in which the legal property in the money passes to the recipient but in equity the property in the money remains with the payer. The recipient holds the money as a fiduciary for the payer and is bound to recognise his equity and repay the money to him. This relationship and the consequent obligation have been recognised both by courts applying the common law and by Chancery courts. The principle is the same in both cases: it is unconscionable that the recipient should retain the money. Neither mistake nor the contractual principle of total failure of consideration are the basis for the right of recovery.'

In my judgment that formulation is wholly accurate, provided that the contract in question is not a borrowing contract. If it were a borrowing contract, it would fall foul (as the judge recognised) of the principle in *Sinclair v Brougham* [1914] AC 398 that restitution will not be ordered where to do so would have the effect of enforcing a void contract. That is not the case here. In relation to a contract other than a borrowing contract the effect of restitution is to put the payer into the position in which he would have been if the transaction had never been entered into.

. . . In *Rover International Ltd v Cannon Film Sales Ltd (No 3)* Kerr LJ expressed the test as being 'whether or not the party claiming total failure of consideration has in fact received any part of the benefit bargained for under the contract or purported contract'. That seems to me to be the test to apply here.

As Westdeutsche submitted, the fact that the payer had received a benefit did not mean that there had been no total failure of consideration, if the payer did not get the benefit for which he bargained. What in this case Westdeutsche bargained for were payments which would discharge a contractual obligation and which Westdeutsche were entitled lawfully to receive. What they obtained were payments made under a void agreement, which in equity remained the property of Islington and which even at law they were always entitled to recover back.

Islington criticised this formulation as artificial, contending that if the formulation of counsel for Westdeutsche in the court below, which appears to have been indorsed by Hobhouse J, is that Islington must also show absence of consideration, then the argument is circular. The payments by Westdeutsche were tainted by 'absence of consideration' because they received payments from Islington which were recoverable because Islington received payments from Westdeutsche, which are recoverable by Westdeutsche, and so on. Islington argued that Westdeutsche here did not bargain for the right to receive repayment of their payment to Islington. No doubt it hoped to do so. It bargained for participation in a series of risks on specified days in the future on each of which the prevailing London Inter-Bank Offered Rate would be compared with 7.5% and, if the risk favoured Westdeutsche, a payment would be made by Islington, and vice versa. It bargained for the risk-taking twice a year for ten years. It got two years. There was no total failure of consideration, only partial. It was so held by Hobhouse J.

There can have been no consideration under a contract void ab initio. So it is fallacious to speak of the failure of consideration having been partial. What is meant is that the parties did, in the belief that the contract was enforceable, part of what they would have been required to do if it had been. As it was, they were not performing the contract even in part: they were making payments that had no legal justification, instead of affording each other mutual consideration for an enforceable contract. In my judgment, the payments made are in those circumstances recoverable by Westdeutsche, in so far as they exceed the payments made by Islington, as money had and received to the use of Westdeutsche by which Islington have been unjustly enriched.

The decision of the Court of Appeal was reversed by the House of Lords ([1996] AC 669, [1996] 2 All ER 961) but only on the question of whether compound interest could be awarded. There was no appeal on the question discussed by Leggatt LJ.

6.   Secondly, any other property supposedly transferred under the contract will still belong to the transferor and will be recoverable. Thirdly, if services have been performed or if goods have been transferred and have been consumed, it may be that the person who performed may recover their value on a *quantum meruit* or a *quantum valebat*, at least to the extent that the defendant was 'incontrovertibly benefited': see p 42.

■ *Solle v Butcher*

[1949] 2 All ER 1107, Court of Appeal

In 1947, the landlord acquired a long lease of a war-damaged house that, in 1939, had been let in flats subject to the Rent Restrictions Acts. The landlord carried out repairs and alterations to the house, in the course of which he reconstructed the flat the subject of the present proceedings. The alterations left the outside and cubic capacity of the house and of the flat in question unchanged, the only substantial change made to the flat being the removal of inner walls so as to subtract from a bedroom a space that was then incorporated into the dining room. During the course of the work, the parties discussed whether the flat, when rebuilt, would be subject to the standard rent fixed by the 1939 letting, and they came to the conclusion that it would not, the tenant expressing that opinion. The standard rent of the flat in 1939 was £140 a year, and if the reconstructed flat were the same dwelling, it would have been possible to increase the rent in respect of expenditure on improvements, in accordance with s 2(1) of the Increase of Rent and Mortgage Interest (Restrictions) Act, 1920, as amended by the Rent and Mortgage Interest Restrictions Act, 1939, Sch 1, to approximately £250, by serving the necessary notices of increase. On 29 September 1947, on completion of the work, the landlord let the flat, including a garage that had not formed part of the 1939 demise, to the tenant on a lease for seven years at a rent of £250 a year, but, being under the impression that the rent fixed by the 1939 letting had no application to the reconstructed flat, he served no notice of increase. The tenant paid rent at £250 a year for some time and then took proceedings in the county court for a declaration that the standard rent of the flat was £140 a year and that he was entitled to recover from the landlord the amount overpaid since the commencement of the tenancy. The landlord contended that the alterations were such that the flat had become a new and separate dwelling by reason of change of identity, but the county court judge found as a fact that the flat was not a new and separate dwelling. The landlord further contended that the lease should be rescinded because it had been entered into under a mutual mistake of fact.

Denning LJ

... In this plight the landlord seeks to set aside the lease. He says with truth that it is unfair that the tenant should have the benefit of the lease for the outstanding five years of the term at £140 a year when the proper rent is £250 a year. If he cannot give a notice of increase now, can he not avoid the lease? The only ground on which he can avoid it is on the ground of mistake. It is quite plain that the parties were under a mistake. They thought that the flat was not tied down to a controlled rent, whereas in fact it was. In order to see whether the lease can be avoided for this mistake it is necessary to remember that mistake is of two kinds: first, mistake which renders the contract void, that is, a nullity from the beginning, which is the kind of mistake which was dealt with by the courts of common law, and secondly, mistake which renders the contract not void, but voidable, that is, liable to be set aside on such terms as the court thinks fit, which is the kind of mistake which was dealt with by the courts of equity. Much of the difficulty which has attended this subject has arisen because, before the fusion of law and equity, the courts of common law, in order to do justice in the case in hand, extended this doctrine of mistake beyond its proper limits and held contracts to be void which were really only voidable, a process which was capable of being attended with much injustice to third persons who had bought goods or otherwise committed themselves on the faith that there was a contract. Since the fusion of law and equity there is no reason to continue this process, and it will be found that only those contracts are now held void where the mistake was such as to prevent the formation of any contract at all.

Let me first consider mistakes which render a contract a nullity. All previous decisions on this subject must now be read in the light of *Bell v Lever Bros Ltd*. The correct interpretation of that case, to my mind, is that once a contract has been made, that is to say, once the parties, whatever their inmost states of mind, have to all outward appearances agreed with sufficient certainty in the same terms on the same subject-matter, then the contract is good unless and until it is set aside for breach of some condition expressed or implied in it, or for fraud, or on some equitable ground. Neither party can rely on his own mistake to say it was a nullity from the beginning, no matter that it was a mistake which to his mind was fundamental, and no matter that the other party knew he was under a mistake. *A fortiori* if the other party did not know of the mistake, but shared it. The cases where goods have perished at the time of sale, or belong to the buyer, are not really contracts which are void for mistake, but are void by reason of an implied condition to that effect, and even cases like *Smith v Hughes* turn at law on whether there was a contractual condition or not. So far as cases later than *Bell v Lever Bros Ltd* are concerned, I do not think that *Sowler v Potter* can stand with *King's Norton Metal Co Ltd v Edridge, Merrett & Co Ltd*, which shows that the doctine of French law as enunciated by Pothier is no part of English law. Nor do I think that the contract in *Nicholson and Venn v Smith-Marriott* was void from the beginning. Applying these principles it is clear that here there was a contract. The parties agreed in the same terms on the same subject-matter. It is true that the landlord was under a mistake which was to him fundamental. He would not for one moment have considered letting the flat for seven years if it meant that he could only charge £140 a year for it. He made the fundamental mistake of believing that the rent he could charge was not limited to a controlled rent, but, whether it was his own mistake or a mistake common to both him and the tenant, it is not a ground for saying that the lease was from the beginning a nullity. Any other view would lead to remarkable results, for it would mean that in the many cases where the parties mistakenly think the house is outside the Rent Acts when it is really within them, the tenancy would be a nullity, and the tenant would have to go, with the result that tenants would not dare to seek to have their rents reduced to the permitted amounts lest they should be turned out.

Let me next consider mistakes which render a contract voidable, that is, liable to be set aside on some equitable ground. While presupposing that a contract was good at law, or at any rate not void, the court of equity would often relieve a party from the consequences of his own mistake, so long as it could do so without injustice to third parties. The court had power to set aside the contract whenever it was of opinion that it was unconscientious for the other party to avail himself of the legal advantage which he had obtained: *Torrance v Bolton*. This branch of equity has shown a progressive development. It is now clear that a contract will be set aside if the mistake of the one party has been induced by a material misrepresentation of the other, even though it was not fraudulent or fundamental, or if one party, knowing that the other is mistaken about the terms of an offer, or the identity of the person by whom it is made, lets him remain under his delusion and conclude a contract on the mistaken terms instead of pointing out the mistake, which is, I venture to think, the ground on which the defendant in *Smith v Hughes* would be exempted nowadays, and on which, according to Blackburn J's view of the facts, the contract in *Lindsay v Cundy* was voidable and not void, and on which the lease in *Sowler v Potter* was, in my opinion, voidable and not void. A contract is also liable in equity to be set aside if the parties were under a common misapprehension either as to facts or as to their relative and respective rights, provided that the misapprehension was fundamental and that the party seeking to set it aside was not himself at fault.... [T]he House of Lords in 1867 in the great case of *Cooper v Phibbs* affirmed the doctrine there acted on as perfectly correct doctrine. In that case an uncle had told his nephew, not intending to misrepresent anything but being in fact in error, that he (the uncle) was entitled to a fishery, and the nephew, after the uncle's death, acting in the belief of the truth of what the uncle had told him, entered into an agreement to rent the fishery from the uncle's daughters, whereas it actually belonged to the nephew himself. The mistake there as to the title to the fishery did not render the tenancy agreement a nullity. If it had done so, the contract would have been void at law from the beginning and equity would have had to follow the law. There would have been no contract to set aside and no terms to impose. The House of Lords, however, held that the mistake was only such as to make it voidable, or, in Lord Westbury's words (LR 2 HL 170) 'liable to be set aside' on such terms as the court thought fit to impose, and it was so set aside.

The principle so established by *Cooper v Phibbs* has been repeatedly acted on: see, for instance, *Earl Beauchamp v Winn; Huddersfield Banking Co, Ltd v Lister (Henry) & Son Ltd*. It is in no way impaired by *Bell v Lever Bros Ltd* which was treated in the House of Lords as a case at law depending on whether the contract was a nullity or not. If it had been considered on equitable grounds, the result might have been different. In any case the principle of *Cooper v Phibbs* has been fully restored by *Norwich Union Fire Insurance Society v Price Ltd*.... On the landlord's evidence, which the judge preferred, I should have thought there was a good deal to be said for the view that the lease was induced by an innocent material misrepresentation by the tenant. It seems to me that the tenant was not merely expressing an opinion on the law. He was making an unambiguous statement as to private rights and a misrepresentation as to private rights is equivalent to a misrepresentation of fact for this purpose: *MacKenzie v Royal Bank of Canada*. But it is unnecessary to come to a firm conclusion on this point, because, as Bucknill LJ has said, there was clearly a mutual mistake, or, as I would prefer to describe it, a common misapprehension, which was fundamental and in no way due to any fault of the landlord, and *Cooper v Phibbs* affords ample authority for saying that, by reason of the common misapprehension, this lease can be set aside on such terms as the court thinks fit. . . .

What terms then should be imposed here? If the lease were set aside without any terms being imposed, it would mean that the tenant would have to go out and would have to pay a reasonable sum for his use and occupation. That would, however, not be just to the tenant. It is similar to a case where a long lease is made at the full permitted rent in the common belief that notices of increase have previously been served, whereas in fact they have not. In *Cooper v Phibbs*, as in this, when the lease is set aside, terms must be imposed so as to see that the tenant is not unjustly evicted. . . . If the mistake here had not happened a proper notice of increase would have been given and the lease would have been executed at the full permitted rent. I think this court should follow these examples and should impose terms which will enable the tenant to choose either to stay on at the proper rent or to go out.

In my opinion, therefore, the appeal should be allowed. The declaration that the standard rent of the flat is £140 per annum should stand. An order should be made on the counter-claim that, on the landlord giving the undertakings which I have mentioned, the lease be set aside. An account should be had to determine the sum payable for use and occupation. The tenant's claim for repayment of rent and for breach of covenant should be dismissed. In respect of the tenant's occupation during the rescinded lease and subsequent licence, he will be liable to pay a reasonable sum for use and occupation. That sum should, *prima facie*, be assessed at the full amount permitted by the Acts, not, however, exceeding £250 a year. Mesne profits as against a trespasser are assessed at the full amount permitted by the Acts, even though notices of increase have not been served, because that is the amount lost by the landlord. The same assessment should be made here because the sums payable for use and occupation are not rent, and the statutory provisions about notices of increase do not apply to them. All necessary credits must, of course, be given in respect of past payments, and so forth.

Bucknill LJ delivered a concurring judgment.

Jenkins LJ (dissenting)

. . . The learned county court judge in the passage I have just quoted said that 'both parties for some obscure reason imagined that the Rent Acts did not apply', and that he did not think 'they ever addressed their minds to the material question of identity'. This was criticised as contrary to the evidence. I do not agree. I think the learned county court judge, who had himself formed a clear opinion to the effect that the reconstructed flat was in substance the same dwelling-house as the original flat, described the reason why the parties did not appreciate this and the consequent continued application of the standard rent of £140 as 'obscure', but accounted for it by concluding that the parties formed the view that the alterations and improvements prevented the old standard rent from applying without really directing their minds to the material question whether, notwithstanding all the alterations and improvements, the flat proposed to be let to the tenant was not, after all, substantially the same dwelling-house as the flat formerly let to Mr Howard Taylor. I see nothing in the evidence inconsistent with this explanation of the mistake, but, whether the parties failed to ask themselves the right question or, having asked it, answered it wrongly, I find it impossible to hold that a mutual mistake of the character here involved affords a good ground for rescission. The landlord meant to grant and the tenant meant to take a lease in the terms in which the lease was actually granted of the premises which the lease as granted actually comprised. They knew all the material facts bearing on the effect of the Rent Restrictions Acts on a lease of these premises, but they mutually misapprehended the effect which in that state of facts those Acts would have on such a lease. That is a mistake of law of a kind which, so far as I am aware, has never yet been held to afford good ground for rescission. It is a mistake, not as to the subject-matter, nature or purport of the contract entered into, nor as to any question of private right affecting the basis of the contract entered into: see *Cooper v Phibbs*; but simply a mistake as to the effect of certain public statutes on the contract made, being in all respects precisely the contract the parties intended to make. . . .

NOTE

In *Svanosio v McNamara* (1956) *96* CLR 186 at 196, Dixon CJ and Fullagar J of the High Court of Australia said:

> 'Mistake' might, of course, afford a ground on which equity would refuse specific performance of a contract, and there may be cases of 'mistake' in which it would be so inequitable that a party should be held to his contract that equity would set it aside. No rule can be laid down *a priori* as to such cases: see an article by Professor *R. A. Blackburn* in *Res Judicatae* (1955), vol 7, p 43. But we would agree with Professor *Shatwell* (1955) 33 Can BR 164, at 186–187 that it is difficult to conceive any circumstances in which equity could properly give relief by setting aside the contract unless there has been fraud or misrepresentation or a condition can be found expressed or implied in the contract.

Associated Japanese Bank (International) Ltd v Crédit du Nord SA
[1988] 3 All ER 902

Under a sale and leaseback transaction, the plaintiff bank purchased four specified precision engineering machines from B and then leased them back to him. B received £1,021,000 from the plaintiff bank under the transaction. As a condition of the transaction, B's obligations under the leaseback agreement were guaranteed by the defendant bank. At all times, both banks believed that the four machines existed and were in B's possession. Afer B failed to keep up payments under the lease, it was discovered that the machines did not, in fact, exist and that the transaction was a fraud perpetrated by B. The plaintiff claimed the outstanding balance due under the lease from B but he went bankrupt and the plaintiff then sued the defendant on the guarantee. The defendant refused to pay, contending, inter alia, that the guarantee was subject to an express or implied condition precedent that the machines in fact existed and therefore the guarantee was void *ab initio* for common mistake.

Steyn J

THE CONSTRUCTION POINT

The first question to be considered is whether the guarantee was expressly made subject to a condition precedent that the four machines existed. The factual matrix, which is relevant to this question of construction, is that both parties, the creditor and the guarantor, were induced to commit themselves by information supplied by the lease brokers employed by Mr Bennett. That information included the statement, which was made expressly or by necessary implication, that the four machines existed. . . . Against that contextual scene, CDN provided a guarantee to AJB—

> '. . . in consideration of your leasing 4 Textile Compression Packaging machines to British Consolidated Engineering Company . . . pursuant to a Leasing Contract dated 29th February 1984 . . . '

The only other provision of the guarantee which is relevant to this question of construction is cl 6 of the guarantee. It reads as follows:

> '*This Guarantee and your rights under it shall not be affected or prejudiced* by your holding or taking any other or further securities or by your varying releasing or omitting or neglecting to enforce any such securities or by your giving time for payment or granting any other indulgence to or making any other arrangements with or accepting any composition from the Lessee or *subject to our prior consent to any such variation by your varying the terms of the Leasing Contract made between*

yourselves and the Lessee or by the substitution of any other goods comprised in such contract.' (My emphasis.)

On behalf of AJB it was submitted that the words 'subject to our prior consent' govern only variations of the lease other than variations entailing a substitution of goods. In other words, it was submitted that consent of the guarantor was required for any variation except one of the most important of all variations, viz substitution of goods. That interpretation is not justified by the language of cl 6, and it is a wholly unreasonable interpretation. I reject it. Clause 6 of the guarantee therefore contemplated the existence of the machines, and made provision for a right of substitution only if the guarantor granted consent. Against that background the question is whether it was *expressly* agreed that the guarantee would only become effective if there was a lease of four existing machines. The point is not capable of elaborate analysis. It is a matter of first impression. On balance, my conclusion is that, sensibly construed against its objective setting, the guarantee was subject to an express condition precedent that there was a lease in respect of four existing machines. If this conclusion is right. AJB's claim against CDN as guarantor or as sole or principal debtor under cl 11 fails.

If my conclusion about the construction of the guarantee is wrong, it remains to be considered whether there was an *implied* condition precedent that the lease related to four existing machines. . . . It is possible to imply a term if the court is satisfied that reasonable men, faced with the suggested term which was ex hypothesi not expressed in the contract, would without hesitation say, 'Yes, of course, that is so obvious that it goes without saying': see *Shirlaw v Southern Foundries (1926) Ltd*, per Mackinnon LJ. . . . [A]gainst the contextual background of the fact that both parties were informed that the machines existed, and the express terms of the guarantee, I have come to the firm conclusion that the guarantee contained an implied condition precedent that the lease related to existing machines. Again, if this conclusion is right. AJB's claim against CDN as guarantor or as sole or principal debtor under cl 11 fails. . . .

Notwithstanding these conclusions, which are determinative of the case, I will now consider the arguments as to common or mutual mistake which played such a large part at the hearing of this case.

MISTAKE

The common law regarding mutual or common mistake

There was a lively debate about the common law rules governing a mutual or common mistake of the parties as to some essential quality of the subject matter of the contract. Counsel for CDN submitted that *Bell v Lever Bros Ltd* authoritatively established that a mistake by both parties as to the existence of some quality of the subject matter of the contract, which makes the subject matter of the contract without the quality essentially different from the subject matter as it was believed to be, renders the contract void ab initio. Counsel for AJB contested this proposition. He submitted that at common law a mistake even as to an essential quality of the subject matter of the contract will not affect the contract unless it resulted in a total failure of consideration. It was not clear to me that this formulation left any meaningful and independent scope for the application of common law rules in this area of the law. In any event, it is necessary to examine the legal position in some detail.

The landmark decision is undoubtedly *Bell v Lever Bros Ltd*. . . .

[Steyn J considered the history of common mistake and continued:]

Lord Atkin held:

' . . . a mistake will not affect assent unless it is the mistake of both parties, and is as to the existence of some quality which makes the thing without the quality essentially different from the thing as it was believed to be.'

In my view none of the other passages in Lord Atkin's speech detract from that statement of the law. Lord Thankerton came to a similar conclusion. He held that common mistake 'can only properly relate to something which both must necessarily have accepted in their minds as an essential and integral part of the subject-matter'.

That seems to me exactly the same test as Lord Atkin enunciated. . . .

It seems to me that the better view is that the majority in *Bell v Lever Bros Ltd* had in mind only mistake at common law. That appears to be indicated by the shape of the argument, the proposed amendment placed before the House of Lords (see [1932] AC 161 at 191, [1931] All ER Rep 1 at 15) and the speeches of Lord Atkin and Lord Thankerton. But, if I am wrong on this point, it is nevertheless clear that mistake at common law was in the forefront of the analysis in the speeches of the majority.

The law has not stood still in relation to mistake in equity. Today, it is clear that mistake in equity is not circumscribed by common law definitions. A contract affected by mistake in equity is not void but may be set aside on terms: see *Solle v Butcher; Magee v Pennine Insurance Co Ltd; Grist v Bailey*. It does not follow, however, that *Bell v Lever Bros Ltd* is no longer an authoritative statement of mistake at common law. On the contrary, in my view the principles enunciated in that case clearly still govern mistake at common law. It is true that in *Solle v Butcher* Denning LJ interpreted *Bell v Lever Bros Ltd* differently. He said that a common mistake, even on a most fundamental matter, does not make the contract void at law. That was an individual opinion. . . . With the profoundest respect to the former Master of the Rolls, I am constrained to say that in my view his interpretation of *Bell v Lever Bros* does not do justice to the speeches of the majority.

When Lord Denning MR referred in *Magee v Pennine Insurance Co Ltd* to the views of commentators he may have had in mind comments in Cheshire and Fifoot *Law of Contract* (6th edn, 1964) p 196. In substance the argument was that the actual decision in *Bell v Lever Bros Ltd* contradicts the language of the speeches. If the test was not satisfied there, so the argument runs, it is difficult to see how it could ever be satisfied: see the latest edition of this valuable textbook for the same argument (Cheshire, Fifoot and Furmston *Law of Contract* (11th edn, 1986) pp 225–226). This is a point worth examining because at first glance it may seem persuasive. *Bell v Lever Bros Ltd* was a quite exceptional case; all their Lordships were agreed that common mistake had not been pleaded and would have required an amendment in the House of Lords if it were to succeed. The speeches do not suggest that the employees were entitled to keep both the gains secretly made and the golden handshakes. The former were clearly recoverable from them. Nevertheless, the golden handshakes were very substantial. But there are indications in the speeches that the so-called 'merits' were not all in favour of Lever Bros. The company was most anxious, because of a corporate merger, to terminate the two service agreements. There was apparently a doubt whether voidability of the service agreements if revealed to the company *at the time of the severance contract* would have affected the company's decision. . . .

. . . With due deference to the distinguished authors who have argued that the actual decision in *Bell v Lever Bros Ltd* contradicts the principle enunciated in the speeches it seems to me that their analysis is altogether too simplistic, and that the actual decision was rooted in the particular facts of the case. In my judgment there is no reason to doubt the substantive reasons emerging from the speeches of the majority.

No one could fairly suggest that in this difficult area of the law there is only one correct approach or solution. But a narrow doctrine of common law mistake (as enunciated in *Bell v Lever Bros Ltd*), supplemented by the more flexible doctrine of mistake in equity (as developed in *Solle v Butcher* and later cases), seems to me to be an entirely sensible and satisfactory state of the law: see *Sheikh Bros Ltd v Ochsner* [1957] AC 136. And there ought to be no reason to struggle to avoid its application by artificial interpretations of *Bell v Lever Bros Ltd*.

It might be useful if I now summarised what appears to me to be a satisfactory way of approaching this subject. Logically, before one can turn to the rules as to mistake, whether at common law or in equity, one must first determine whether the contract itself, by express or implied condition precedent or otherwise, provides who bears the risk of the relevant mistake. It is at this hurdle that many pleas of mistake will either fail or prove to have been unnecessary. Only if the contract is silent on the point is there scope for invoking mistake. That brings me to the relationship between common law mistake and mistake in equity. Where common law mistake has been pleaded, the court must first consider this plea. If the contract is held to be void, no question of mistake in equity arises. But, if the contract is held to be valid, a plea of mistake in equity may still have to be considered: see *Grist v Bailey* and the analysis in *Anson's Law of Contract* (26th edn, 1984) pp 290–291. Turning now to the approach to common law mistake, it seems to me that the following propositions are valid although not necessarily all entitled to be dignified as propositions of law.

The first imperative must be that the law ought to uphold rather than destroy apparent contracts. Second, the common law rules as to a mistake regarding the quality of the subject matter, like the common law rules regarding commercial frustration, are designed to cope with the impact of unexpected and wholly exceptional circumstances on apparent contracts. Third, such a mistake in order to attract legal consequences must substantially be shared by both parties, and must relate to facts as they existed at the time the contract was made. Fourth, and this is the point established by *Bell v Lever Bros Ltd*, the mistake must render the subject matter of the contract essentially and radically different from the subject matter which the parties believed to exist. While the civilian distinction between the substance and attributes of the subject matter of a contract has played a role in the development of our law (and was cited in the speeches in *Bell v Lever Bros Ltd*), the principle enunciated in *Bell v Lever Bros Ltd* is markedly narrower in scope than the civilian doctrine. It is therefore no longer useful to invoke the civilian distinction. The principles enunciated by Lord Atkin and Lord Thankerton represent the ratio decidendi of *Bell v Lever Bros Ltd*. Fifth, there is a requirement which was not specifically discussed in *Bell v Lever Bros Ltd*. What happens if the party who is seeking to rely on the mistake had no reasonable grounds for his belief? An extreme example is that of the man who makes a contract with minimal knowledge of the facts to which the mistake relates but is content that it is a good speculative risk. In my judgment a party cannot be allowed to rely on a common mistake where the mistake consists of a belief which is entertained by him without any reasonable gounds for such belief: cf *McRae v Commonweath Disposals Commission*. That is not because principles such as estoppel or negligence require it, but simply because policy and good sense dictate that the positive rules regarding common mistake should be so qualified. Curiously enough this qualification is similar to the civilian concept where the doctrine of error in substantia is tempered by the principles governing culpa in contrahendo. More importantly, a recognition of this qualification is consistent with the approach in equity where fault on the part of the party adversely affected by the mistake will generally preclude the granting of equitable relief: see *Solle v Butcher*.

Applying the law to the facts

It is clear, of course, that in this case both parties, the creditor and the guarantor, acted on the assumption that the lease related to existing machines. If they had been informed that the machines might not exist, neither AJB nor CDN would for one moment have contemplated entering into the transaction. That, by itself, I accept, is not enough to sustain the plea of common law mistake. I am also satisfied that CDN had reasonable grounds for believing that the machines existed. That belief was based on CDN's discussions with Mr Bennett, information supplied by National Leasing, a respectable firm of lease brokers, and the confidence created by the fact that AJB were the lessors.

The real question is whether the subject matter of the guarantee (as opposed to the sale and lease) was essentially different from what it was reasonably believed to be. The real security of the guarantor was the machines. The existence of the machines, being profit-earning chattels, made it more likely that the debtor would be able to service the debt. More importantly, if the debtor defaulted and the creditor repossessed the machines, the creditor had to give credit for 97 1/2 of the value of the machines. If the creditor sued the guarantor first, and the guarantor paid, the guarantor was entitled to be subrogated to the creditor's rights in respect of recovery against the debtor: see Go ff and Jones *Law of Restitution* (3rd edn, 1986) pp 533–536. No doubt the guarantor relied to some extent on the creditworthiness of Mr Bennett. But I find that the prime security to which the guarantor looked was the existence of the four machines as described to both parties. For both parties the guarantee of obligations under a lease with non-existent machines was essentially different from a guarantee of a lease with four machines which both parties at the time of the contract believed to exist. The guarantee is an accessory contract. The non-existence of the subject matter of the principal contract is therefore of fundamental importance. Indeed the analogy of the classic res extincta cases, so much discussed in the authorities, is fairly close. In my judgment, the stringent test of common law mistake is satisfied; the guarantee is void ab initio. . . .

Equitable mistake

Having concluded that the guarantee is void ab initio at common law, it is strictly unnecessary to examine the question of equitable mistake. Equity will give relief against common mistake in cases where the common law will not, and it provides more flexible remedies, including the power to set aside the contract on terms. It is not necessary to repeat my findings of fact save to record again the fundamental nature of the common mistake, and that CDN was not at fault in any way. If I had not decided in favour of CDN on construction and common law mistake, I would have held that the guarantee must be set aside on equitable principles. Unfortunately, and counsel are not to blame for that, the question of the terms (if any) to be imposed (having regard particularly to sums deposited by Mr Bennett with CDN) were not adequately explored in argument. If it becomes necessary to rule on this aspect, I will require further argument. . . .

Claim dismissed.

NOTES

1. The first ground for the decision in this case was that the guarantee was void as a matter of construction. We shall see in the next chapter a number of cases in which the courts have used the 'construction technique' to find contracts void or discharged without ever mentioning mistake or frustration.

2. If, as we have suggested, common law cases on mistake are really exercises in deciding how, given the terms and circumstances of the contract, the risk of what has happened should be allocated, how much difference is there between the 'construction technique' and the 'mistake technique' at common law? In other words, when Steyn J considered first construction and then whether the contract was void for mistake, was he really considering two different questions or the same question twice but dressed up in different language? See further pp 525–526.

3. For a rather different view of what is 'going on' in these cases, see pp 526 ff.

4. In *Solle v Butcher*, the Court of Appeal held that although the parties had made a mistake, it was not a mistake of a kind that made the contract void at common law in the light of *Bell v Lever Bros*. This seems clearly correct. The majority of the Court of Appeal went on to hold, however, that the contract could be set aside in equity. This had the advantage of flexibility because it was said that equity could impose terms on the setting aside.

    Even at the time, some people wondered why this equitable possibility had not been mentioned in *Bell v Lever Bros*, but the equitable doctrine was applied in *Grist v Bailey* [1967] Ch 532 [1966] 2 All ER 875, and in *Magee v Pennine Insurance Co Ltd* [1969] 2 QB 507 [1969] 2 All ER 891 (Winn LJ dissenting), and the Court of Appeal said in *West Sussex Properties Ltd v Chichester District Council* (28 June 2000, unreported) that it was bound by *Solle v Butcher* unless and until it was overruled by the House of Lords.

    However, the Court of Appeal thought differently in *Great Peace Shipping Ltd v Tsavliris, The Great Peace* [2002] 4 All ER 689. In this case, the *Cape Providence* suffered severe structural damage in the South Indian Ocean. The appellants offered their salvage services, which were accepted. A tug was found in Singapore, which would take five or six days to reach the ship. The appellants were anxious to find another ship that was nearer and which could, if necessary, take off the crew. For this purpose, a deal was done to hire the *Great Peace* for five days at US$16,500 a day. At the time of the deal, it was thought that the *Cape Providence* and the *Great Peace* were about 12 hours apart (but not because of anything said by or on behalf of the owners of the *Great Peace*). The ships were, in fact, about 410 miles apart. When the true position was discovered, the appellants looked for another nearer ship and, having found one, purported two hours later to cancel the contract. They argued that the contract was void and they need pay nothing.

Lord Phillips of Worth Matravers said:

We conclude that the two authorities to which Lord Atkin referred provided an insubstantial basis for his formulation of the test of common mistake in relation to the quality of the subject matter of a contract. Lord Atkin advanced an alternative basis for his test: the implication of a term of the same nature as that which was applied under the doctrine of frustration, as it was then understood. In so doing he adopted the analysis of Scrutton LJ in the Court of Appeal. It seems to us that this was a more solid jurisprudential basis for the test of common mistake that Lord Atkin was proposing. At the time of *Bell v Lever Bros Ltd* the law of frustration and common mistake had advanced hand-in-hand on the foundation of a common principle. Thereafter frustration proved a more fertile ground for the development of this principle than common mistake, and consideration of the development of the law of frustration assists with the analysis of the law of common mistake.

. . .

Circumstances where a contract is void as a result of common mistake are likely to be less common than instances of frustration. Supervening events which defeat the contractual adventure will frequently not be the responsibility of either party. Where, however, the parties agree that something shall be done which is impossible at the time of making the agreement, it is much more likely that, on true construction of the agreement, one or other will have undertaken responsibility for the mistaken state of affairs. This may well explain why cases where contracts have been found to be void in consequence of common mistake are few and far between.

Lord Atkin himself gave no examples of cases where a contract was rendered void because of a mistake as to quality which made 'the thing without the quality essentially different from the thing as it was believed to be' (see *Bell v Lever Bros Ltd* [1932] AC 161 at 218, [1931] All ER Rep 1 at 28). He gave a number of examples of mistakes which did not satisfy this test, which served to demonstrate just how narrow he considered the test to be. Indeed this is further demonstrated by the result reached on the facts of *Bell v Lever Bros Ltd* itself.

. . .

The precise circumstances in which the Court of Chancery would permit rescission of a contract were not clearly established in the latter half of the nineteenth century. Thus, not until after the Supreme Court of Judicature Act did the judgment of Jessel MR in *Redgrave v Hurd* (1881) 20 Ch D 1 at 12, [1881–5] All ER Rep 77 at 79 make it clear that equity would order rescission of a contract induced by innocent, as opposed to fraudulent, misrepresentation. In such circumstances both parties would normally be labouring under a common mistake when the contract was concluded, but a significant further step was needed if equity was to grant rescission where a contract was based on a common mistake that was not induced by one of the parties. While a number of eighteenth and nineteenth century cases prior to the decision in *Cooper v Phibbs* (1867) LR 2 HL 149 lend some support to the thesis that equity had taken that step, 'no coherent equitable doctrine of mistake can be spelt from them'—see the discussion in Goff & Jones *The Law of Restitution* (5th edn, 1998) pp 288–289 and *Meagher*, pp 375–376, para 1420. *Cooper v Phibbs* was however the decision primarily relied upon by Denning LJ in *Solle v Butcher*—he described it as 'the great case', and it is necessary to consider it with care. In this task we have been assisted by the analysis in 'A Note on *Cooper v. Phibbs*' (1989) 105 LQR 599 by Paul Matthews which was informed by access to the record of proceedings in the House of Lords.

At the heart of the case was a dispute as to title to a fishery in Ireland. The fishery, together with a cottage, was the subject of an agreement for a three-year lease entered into by Phibbs, the respondent, with Cooper, the appellant. Phibbs was acting as agent for five sisters, who believed that they had inherited the fishery from their father. He, in the belief that he was the owner of the fishery in fee simple, had expended much money in improving it. Cooper contended that, after entering into the lease, he had discovered that the fishery had at all material times been trust property and that, in consequence of a series of events of very great complexity, he was entitled to an equitable life interest. It was ultimately not disputed, however, that the head lease of the cottage was vested in the sisters.

...

These passages demonstrate that the House of Lords in *Bell v Lever Bros Ltd* considered that the intervention of equity, as demonstrated in *Cooper v Phibbs*, took place in circumstances where the common law would have ruled the contract void for mistake. We do not find it conceivable that the House of Lords overlooked an equitable right in *Bell v Lever Bros Ltd* to rescind the agreement, notwithstanding that the agreement was not void for mistake at common law. The jurisprudence established no such right. Lord Atkin's test for common mistake that avoided a contract, while narrow, broadly reflected the circumstances where equity had intervened to excuse performance of a contract assumed to be binding in law.

The effect of Solle v Butcher

The material facts of *Solle v Butcher* [1949] 2 All ER 1107, [1950] 1 KB 671 can shortly be summarised as follows. The defendant agreed to let a flat to the plaintiff for £250 a year. The flat had previously been let at a rent of £140. Substantial work had been done on the flat and both parties believed that this so altered the nature of the premises as to free them from relevant rent control. In this they were mistaken. The defendant would have been able to charge the plaintiff an increased rent of £250 to reflect the work done on the flat had he complied with the requisite formalities but, under the influence of the mistake, he failed to do so. In the result he could not lawfully charge a rent higher than £140. The plaintiff obtained a declaration in the county court that the rent was restricted to £140 and an order for repayment of rent overpaid. The judge rejected the contention that the contract had been concluded under a common mistake of fact, holding that the mistake was one of law.

...

Toulson J ([2001] All ER (D) 152 (Nov) at [69]) described this decision by Lord Denning as one which 'sought to outflank *Bell v Lever Bros Ltd*'. We think that this was fair comment. It was not realistic to treat the House of Lords in *Bell v Lever Bros Ltd* as oblivious to principles of equity, nor to suggest that 'if it had been considered on equitable grounds the result might have been different'. For the reasons that we have given, we do not consider that *Cooper v Phibbs* demonstrated or established an equitable jurisdiction to grant rescission for common mistake in circumstances that fell short of those in which the common law held a contract void. In so far as this was in doubt, the House of Lords in *Bell v Lever Bros Ltd* delimited the ambit of operation of *Cooper v Phibbs* by holding, rightly or wrongly, that on the facts of that case the agreement in question was void at law and by holding that, on the facts in *Bell v Lever Bros Ltd*, the mistake had not had the effect of rendering the contract void.

...

We have been in some doubt as to whether this line of authority goes far enough to permit us to hold that *Solle v Butcher* [1949] 2 All ER 1107, [1950] 1 KB 671 is not good law. We are very conscious that we are not only scrutinising the reasoning of Lord Denning in *Solle v Butcher* and in *Magee v Pennine Insurance Co* [1969] 2 All ER 891, [1969] 2 QB 507, but are also faced with a number of later decisions in which Lord Denning MR's approach has been approved and followed. Further, a division of this court has made it clear in *West Sussex Properties Ltd v Chichester DC* [2000] All ER (D) 887 that they felt bound by *Solle v Butcher*. However, it is to be noticed that while junior counsel in the court below in the *West Sussex Properties* case had sought to challenge the correctness of *Solle v Butcher*, in the Court of Appeal leading counsel accepted that it was good law unless and until overturned by their Lordships' House. In this case we have heard full argument, which has provided what we believe has been the first opportunity in this court for a full and mature consideration of the relation between *Bell v Lever Bros Ltd* and *Solle v Butcher*. In the light of that consideration we can see no way that *Solle v Butcher* can stand with *Bell v Lever Bros Ltd*. In these circumstances we can see no option but so to hold.

It is difficult to do justice to the judgment of Lord Phillips by extracts, however extensive. This is one judgment you should try to read in full.

5.   It seems clear that the mistake was not one of a kind to make the contract void at common law. The *Great Peace* was near enough to offer the *Cape Providence* several days' help before the tug arrived.

6.   It is very doubtful whether Lord Denning would have thought the case one suitable for equitable intervention.

7.   It is not clear by the rules of the precedent game whether *The Great Peace* trumps *Solle v Butcher*. It may be that a third court of appeal could choose between them.

CHAPTER EIGHTEEN

DISCHARGE BY CONSTRUCTION

There are a number of cases in which the court has held that the occurrence of a contingency has the effect of discharging the contract, without relying specifically on either frustration or mistake.

■ *Staffordshire Area Health Authority v South Staffordshire Waterworks Co*
[1978] 3 All ER 769, Court of Appeal

In 1908, a water company proposed to pump water from a well about a mile away from a hospital that had its own well. By the South Staffordshire Waterworks Act 1909, the water company was given statutory authority to pump water from its well, subject to providing the hospital with such water as it required, at the rate it would cost the hospital to operate its own well, if the supply from the hospital's own well was diminished by reason of the water company's operations. Any disputes were to be settled by arbitration. In 1915, the water company began pumping water from its well, and by 1918, this had an adverse effect on the supply from the hospital's well. The water company agreed to make up the deficiency from their mains. In 1927, the hospital authorities decided to abandon their well and commenced taking all the hospital's water from the company's mains. In 1929, the hospital authorities and the water company entered into an agreement under seal whereby 'at all times hereafter' the hospital was to receive 5,000 gallons of water per day free and all the additional water it required at the rate of 7d per 1,000 gallons. When decimal currency was introduced, the rate was changed to 2.9p per 1,000 gallons. By 1975, the normal rate charged by the water company was 45p, and on 30 September 1975, the water company wrote to the hospital authorities giving notice that it intended to terminate the 1929 agreement in six months' time, and that thereafter it would supply 5,000 gallons per day free and any excess at normal rates. The hospital authorities refused to accept the notice as valid and took out an originating summons to establish that it was not. The judge upheld their claim on the ground that the 1929 agreement, being expressed to apply 'at all times hereafter', had been made forever or in perpetuity, and therefore the water company could not resile from it.

Lord Denning MR

. . . I think that the rule of strict construction is now quite out of date. It has been supplanted by the rule that written instruments are to be construed in relation to the circumstances as they were known to or contemplated by the parties; and that even the plainest words may fall to be modified if events occur which the parties never had in mind and in which they cannot have intended the agreement to operate....

As I understand this modern rule, we are no longer to go by the strict construction of the words as judges did in the 19th century. We are to put ourselves in the same situation as the parties were in at the time they drew up the instrument, to sit in their chairs with our minds endowed with the same facts as theirs were, and envisage the future with the same degree of foresight as they did. So placed we have to ask ourselves: what were the circumstances in which the contract was made? Does it apply in the least to the new situation which has developed? If events occur for which they have made no provision, and which were outside the realm of their speculations altogether, or of any reasonable persons sitting in their chairs, then the court itself must take a hand and hold that the contract ceases to bind. Such was the rule which I suggested long ago in *British Movietonews Ltd v London and District Cinemas Ltd* without success at that time: but which seems to have come into its own now....

We were taken through six cases which considered contracts which contained no provision for determination. On going through them, they seem to show that, when a person agrees to supply goods or services continuously over an unlimited period of time in return for a fixed monthly or yearly payment, the courts shrink from holding it to be an agreement in perpetuity. The reason is because it is so unequal. The cost of supply of goods and services goes up with inflation through the rooftops: and the fixed payment goes down to the bottom of the well so that it is worth little or nothing. Rather than tolerate such inequality, the courts will construe the contract so as to hold that it is determinable by reasonable notice. They do this by reference to the modern rule of construction. They say that in the circumstances as they have developed, which the parties never had in mind, the contract ceases to bind the parties forever. It can be determined on reasonable notice.

[His Lordship considered the cases and continued:]

[From these cases] it is possible to detect a new principle emerging as to the effect of inflation and the fall in the value of money. In the ordinary way this does not affect the bargain between the parties. As I said in *Treseder-Griffin v Co-operative Insurance Society*:

> '...in England we have always looked on a pound as a pound whatever its international value...Creditors and debtors have arranged for payment in our sterling currency in the sure knowledge that the sum they fix will be upheld by the law. A man who stipulates for a pound must take a pound, whenever payment is made, whatever the pound is worth at that time.'

But times have changed. We have since had mountainous inflation and the pound dropping to cavernous depths. In the recent case of *Multiservice Bookbinding Ltd v Marden* Browne-Wilkinson J departed from some of the things I said in *Treseder-Griffin* for that very reason, because of 20 years' experience of continuing inflation. The time has come when we may have to revise our views about the principle of nominalism, as it is called. Dr F A Mann in his book, The Legal Aspect of Money, said: 'If the trend of inflation which has clouded the last few decades continues some relief in the case of long-term obligations will become unavoidable.' That was written in 1971. Inflation has been more rampant than ever since that time. Here we have in the present case a striking of a long term obligation entered into 50 years ago. It provided for yearly payments for water supplied at seven old pence a 1,000 gallons. In these 50 years, and especially in the last 10 years, the cost of supplying the water has increased twentyfold. It is likely to increase with every year that passes. Is it right that the hospital should go on forever only paying the old rate of 50 years ago? It seems to me that we have reached the point which Viscount Simon contemplated in *British Movietonews Ltd v London and District Cinemas Ltd*. Speaking apropos of a depreciation of currency, he envisaged a situation where:

> '...a consideration of the terms of the contract, in the light of circumstances existing when it was made, shows that they never agreed to be bound in a fundamentally different situation which has now unexpectedly emerged, [and he went on to say that when such a situation emerges] the contract ceases to bind at that point—not because the court in its discretion thinks it just and reasonable

to qualify the terms of the contract, but because on its true construction it does not apply in that situation.'

That is the forerunner of the modern rule of construction.

So here the situation has changed so radically since the contract was made 50 years ago that the term of the contract 'at all times hereafter' ceases to bind: and it is open to the court to hold that the contract is determined by reasonable notice.

I do not think that the water company could have determined the agreement immediately after it was made. That cannot have been intended by the parties. No rule of construction could sensibly permit such a result. But, in the past 50 years, the whole situation has changed so radically that one can say with confidence: 'The parties never intended that the supply should be continued in these days at that price.' Rather than force such unequal terms on the parties, the court should hold that the agreement could be and was properly determined in 1975 by the reasonable notice of six months.

Cumming-Bruce LJ

...I have come to the conclusion that the words do not carry the meaning that the judge decided but that the words 'at all times hereafter' mean that the obligations granted and accepted by the agreement were only intended to persist during the continuance of the agreement; and the agreement, in my view, was determinable on reasonable notice at any time, so that had there been a change of circumstances which would have afforded either party an opportunity for arbitration under s 23 the agreement could then have been determined on reasonable notice.

Having regard to the cases which were helpfully cited in argument, I agree with the analysis of those cases proposed by Goff LJ and cannot usefully add anything. With all respect to Lord Denning MR, I do not found my decision on the existence of an implied term that the agreement should not continue to bind the parties on the emergence of circumstances which the parties did not then foresee. I find it unnecessary on the view which I have formed about the intention of the parties to be collected from the circumstances to consider that. I am not attracted against the history of fact in this case either by the argument founded on frustration or on an implied term akin to frustration, and I can find no authority which leads me to the view that the changing value of money has the effect in relation to domestic as compared to international contracts of giving rise to the operation of an implied term that the contract should only persist while money maintained the value or more or less the value that it had at the date of the formation of the agreement.

Goff LJ also held that the agreement was determinable by reasonable notice.

Appeal allowed.

NOTES

1. Is it correct that the majority's analysis would have permitted determination for any reason whatever after one or two years? Is that a sensible outcome?

2. In *Gove District Council v Power Co Ltd* [1996] 1 NZLR 58, an agreement to supply power at fixed prices expressed to be binding 'for all time hereafter' was held by the New Zealand Court of Appeal to mean what it said: it could not be terminated on reasonable notice.

3. Are Denning's dicta reconcilable with *Davis Contractors Ltd v Fareham UDC*?

4. What can the parties do to cope with the uncertainties of inflation? One possibility is to agree that the price will be the seller's list price for the item at the date of delivery (see *Butler Machine Tool Co Ltd v Ex-Cell-O Corpn (England) Ltd*, p 225); another, to link the price directly to indices that give the prices of the materials and labour involved. It is also permissible, it seems, to link the price to an 'unrelated' index, such as the value of the Swiss franc: see *Multiservice Bookbinding Ltd v Marden*, (noted, p 939).

5. England has suffered serious inflation, but not hyperinflation. Should hyperinflation occur, should the risk be allocated in the same way as that of 'normal' inflation? You may find it interesting to look at Horn, Kotz and Leser, *German Private and Commercial Law*, 1982, pp 140–143. French law has also developed a doctrine ('imprévision') to permit adjustment of long-term contracts with public authorities that have become too burdensome for the contractor to perform, so that the public interest in performance is at risk: see Nicholas, *French Law of Contract*, 2nd edn, 1992, pp 208–210.

6. Quite different problems are posed by a sharp price increase in only the commodity sold, or only the class from which the commodity comes (eg fuels). A very interesting discussion of the recent difficulties faced by Westinghouse when uranium increased dramatically in price will be found in Joskow, 'Commercial Impossibility, The Uranium Market and the *Westinghouse* Case' (1977) 6 JLS 119. Note that Joskow is discussing American law under UCC 2–615, which is in theory markedly different to English law in allowing a defence of commercial impracticability.

In *HR & S Sainsbury Ltd v Street* [1972] 3 All ER 1127, there was a contract between the plaintiffs and the defendant for the purchase of 275 tons of feed barley to be grown on the defendant's land at East Knoyle in Wiltshire. The harvest was a very poor one and the land produced only 140 tons, which the defendant sold to another corn merchant at a higher price per ton. The plaintiffs claimed damages for failure to deliver the 140 tons produced. MacKenna J decided in favour of the plaintiffs; he was prepared to assume that there was an implied condition that the defendant would be excused if, through no fault of his, the land did not produce the contract quantity, but that did not release him from the obligation to deliver the barley actually produced. Since there was an obligation to deliver the barley grown, the contract was not frustrated (unless there can be frustration pro rata, as to which, see Hudson, 'Prorating in the English Law of Frustrated Contracts' (1968) 31 MLR 535 and Treitel p 878). Presumably, the buyer was equally bound to take the 140 tons? Yet the seller was excused from his obligation to deliver the ungrown portion. For other cases of partial excuse, see *Minnevitch v Café de Paris (Londres) Ltd* [1936] 1 All ER 884, 52 TLR 413; *Poussard v Spiers and Pond* (1876) 1 QBD 410.

■ *Financings Ltd v Stimson*
[1962] 3 All ER 386, Court of Appeal

On 16 March 1961, the defendant saw a motor car on the premises of a dealer and signed a hire purchase form provided by the plaintiff finance company and produced by the dealer. The form contained, amongst others, clauses that the agreement should be binding on the finance company only on acceptance by its signature, that the hirer acknowledged that before he signed the agreement he had examined the goods and satisfied himself was they were in good order and condition, and that the goods should be at the risk of the hirer from the time of purchase by the owner. On 18 March, the defendant paid the first instalment due and was allowed to take possession of the motor car, but on 20 March, being dissatisfied with it, he returned it to the dealer, saying that he did not want it and offering to forfeit the instalment that he had paid. Neither the defendant nor the dealer informed the finance company of the return of the car. On the night of 24–25 March, the car was stolen from the dealer's premises and recovered severely damaged. On 25 March, the finance company signed the agreement. Subsequently, the finance company sold the damaged car and claimed damages from the defendant for breach of the hire-purchase agreement or as bailee on the terms of the agreement.

The majority (Lord Denning MR and Donovan LJ, Pearson LJ dissenting) held that the plaintiffs' claim should be dismissed, and the defendant's counterclaim for the return of his deposit be allowed, on two grounds. Firstly:

... the return of the motor car by the defendant to the dealer on Mar. 20 amounted to revocation of the offer by the defendant, since, on the facts of the case, the dealer had ostensible authority to accept the revocation of the offer on behalf of the finance company ...

On the second point:

Lord Denning MR

[T]here is the second point to be considered which appealed to the county court judge: He said:

'When this offer was made, it was made on the basis that the car was in good condition, or at all events in the condition in which the defendant had seen it, but, before the offer was accepted (it was accepted on Mar 25), on the night of Mar 24/ 25 it suffered this extra damage which cost £44 to repair, having been scratched and dented by the thieves who stole it. Can a man accept an offer when the condition of the goods has deteriorated in a material respect since the date of the offer?'

It seems to me that, on the facts of this case, the offer made by the defendant was a conditional offer. It was conditional on the car remaining in substantially the same condition until the moment of acceptance. Take the case put by Donovan LJ in the course of the argument: Suppose an offer is made to buy a Rolls-Royce car at a high price on one day and, before it is accepted, it suffers the next day severe damage. Can it be accepted and the offeror bound? My answer to that is: No, because the offer is conditional on the goods at the moment of acceptance remaining in substantially the same condition as at the time of the offer. Counsel for the plaintiffs argued that there was an express clause here saying that the goods were to be 'at the risk of the hirer from the time of purchase by the owner'. The time of purchase by the owner, he said, was Mar 18, when the plaintiffs told the dealer orally that they accepted the transaction. Thence-forward, he said, the goods were at the risk of the defendant. This shows, says counsel, that the condition which I have suggested is inconsistent with the express terms, or, at all events, is not to be implied. In my judgment, however, this clause on which counsel relies only comes into operation when a contract is concluded and accepted. Meanwhile the offer is made on the understanding that, so long as it remains an offer, it is conditional on the goods being in substantially the same condition as at the time when the offer was made. I agree, therefore, with the county court judge in thinking that, in view of the damage which occurred to this car before the acceptance was given, the plaintiffs were not in a position to accept the offer, because the condition on which it was made had not been fulfilled. So on that ground also there was no contract.

NOTES

1. Technically, this decision again meant that a contract had never come into existence, but it is included in this chapter because the court achieves a just result by holding that neither party is bound.

2. For a discussion of this case and others using a 'construction' technique to solve a variety of problems, see Atiyah, 'Judicial Techniques and the Law of Contract' in *Essays on Contract*, 1986, chapter 9.

3. If cases in which the parties did not know the true facts when they made the contract can be dealt with as questions of construction, is there any need for a separate doctrine of mistake? Smith, 'Contracts—Mistake, Frustration and Implied Terms' (1994) 110 LQR

400 argues not. He writes (at pp 407 and 419):

... The argument was, and judge's assumption seems to be, that, if there had been no express or implied condition precedent which invalidated the contract, it might still have been held to be void on grounds of mistake . . . . If the first stage is confined to deciding whether either party has given an undertaking as to the matter in issue i.e. if that is what is meant by a provision as to 'who bears the risk of the relevant mistake'), and the answer is that neither has, then there is clearly a second stage when the question is, was there a common and mistaken assumption of such fundamental import-ance that it was the basis of the contract—a condition precedent? But if the first stage includes that second question, it is submitted that there is no room for any second stage at which 'mistake' can be invoked. The test of failure of a 'common fundamental assumption' has been applied and found unsatisfied. There has been no such failure. If a second test is to be applied, what is it? All contracts must have some common fundamental assumption or assumptions and the courts have found that it (or they) is (or are) well founded. To hold the contract to be void in such circumstances would seem to contradict the intention of the parties.

. . .

It is submitted that (1) . . . an apparent contract between A and B may be void because . . . an express or implied condition precedent to the contract is not satisfied; but (2) if there has been a valid offer and acceptance and there is no such express or implied term, the contract is not void for mistake. There is no room for an independent doctrine of mistake rendering a contract void . . .

▪ Collins, *The Law of Contract* (4th edn, 2003)
pp 293–301

D. Judicial revision

During the performance of a contract, the classical rule holds the parties strictly liable for failure to fulfil their obligations. No matter than unexpected events have dramatically altered the costs of one party's performance, the courts have generally insisted upon a principle of strict enforcement of the terms of the contract. In *Blackburn Bobbin Co Ltd v TW Allen & Sons*, for example, the seller of Finland birch timber found it impossible to import the commodity from Finland as he had intended because of the outbreak of war. Even so, he remained liable to the buyer for breach of contract. He had agreed to deliver the timber, and it was of no concern to the buyer where he acquired the timber.

This rule of strict enforcement of the contract is not as harsh as it first appears. It provides an incentive for the parties to plan for risk and contingencies, so that if performance becomes more onerous, the contract will provide for some exception or adjustment of the obligations. . . .

(c) THE RELEVANCE OF FAIRNESS

Although the courts prefer to describe their practices that are analogous to judicial revision as either construction of the contract in order to fulfil the intentions of the parties or as independent rules of law concerned with impossibility, neither of these accounts appears strongly persuasive. If the intervention is described as merely construction of the contract, given that the parties did not foresee and have any clear intentions towards the events which have occurred, we must suspect that the courts use a further criterion for determining the intent of the parties. This criterion may be one which takes fairness in the sense of the preservation of the balance of advantage of the contract as the unacknowledged but vital guide to interpretation. Alternatively, if the intervention is described as the application of a rule about impossibility, again the decision whether an unexpected event renders an obligation impossible seems likely to depend upon a judgment as to whether to continue to insist upon performance would upset the balance of advantage contained in the contract. On this interpretation, the real issue in *Blackburn Bobbin Co Ltd v TW Allen & Sons Ltd* was not whether supplies of Finnish timber could be obtained any longer, but rather whether to impose this obligation upon the seller after the outbreak of war would upset the balance of advantage of the contract. Here the court took the view that the parties to a commercial agreement had allocated the risk of this eventuality in their contract, and that the materialization of the risk did not upset the balance of the obligations.

The relevance of fairness is often betrayed when a courts finds an excuse to deny that a contract has been frustrated on the ground either of attributing the insuperable difficulty to the fault of the party in breach or by denying that performance has become impossible. For example, in *Tamplin Steamship Co Ltd v Anglo-Mexican Petroleum Co*, a ship hired under a five-year time charter was requisitioned by the government during the war in 1915 after three years of the charter. Normally a court would find that the requisitioning of a ship would frustrate a time charter, but in this case the House of Lords declined to hold that the contract had been frustrated on the dubious ground that the was might be over in time to permit further use of the charter. In reality, by this decision the court tried to achieve fairness between the parties, for the person entitled to use the ship would benefit from government compensation which was higher than the charge under the agreed hire. In this case the owner of the ship was attempting unsuccessfully to escape from his contract, so that he would receive the superior level of income from the government.

Although many judges deny that fairness is relevant to the question of whether or not a contract is frustrated, they frequently acknowledge that their interventions are required by the need to do justice between the parties. In a representative description of the doctrine of frustration, Bingham LJ states:

'The object of the doctrine was to give effect to the demands of justice, to achieve a just and reasonable result, to do what is reasonable and fair, as an expedient to escape from injustice where such would result from enforcement of a contract in its literal terms after a significant change in circumstances . . . '

These references to injustice, or as we prefer to say unfairness, require further elucidation.

The process of judicial revision is not so simple as to compare the obligation of one party before and after the unexpected event in order to discover whether the event has substantially increased the cost of performance of his obligation. The criterion of fairness must also be sensitive both the sophistication of the parties when they established their contract and the precise allocation of risks by the contract. Where the parties enjoyed comparable resources for devising a complex commercial transaction and exercised those resources in order to create a contract which attempted to allocate all the risks between the parties, it is unlikely except in calamitous circumstances that the courts will be prepared to accept that unexpected events have created any imbalance in the obligations. If, on the other hand, either one or both parties lack these skills, the terms of the contract are less likely to be regarded as a presumptively fair allocation of the burdens of unforeseen eventualities. In these cases, the courts are more likely to use the techniques of judicial revision such as construction or frustration in order to restore the expectations of the parties with respect to the balance of advantage contained in the contract. But intervention may be rejected, of course, if the court finds that a reconstruction of the contract or the application of the doctrine of frustration would not produce a fairer result. Frustration of the contract is, in truth, a crude device, which is rarely applied by the courts, because it fails usually to satisfy the criterion of restoring the balance of advantage between the parties. Better results can often be achieved by techniques aimed at restoring the viability of the contract for both parties . . .

NOTES

1.   *Grist v Bailey* was a case in which the vendor was given relief under the equitable doctrine of mistake. It effectively placed the risk that the tenant would unexpectedly turn out to be protected on the purchaser. This is contrary to the normal allocation of risk of defects of title in sales of land and the case may have been wrongly decided: see Hoffmann LJ in *William Sindall plc v Cambridgeshire County Council* [1994] 3 All ER 932, 952. It does seem odd to place this risk on the party who was in a less good position to discover the

truth beforehand. The case may even be said to pay insufficient regard to the requirement that the party seeking relief should not be at fault. Although neither the plaintiff nor her solicitor were personally at fault, there had clearly been a slip-up somewhere on their side. But, as Collins shows, there may be other views of the case.

2. How far do you agree with Collins' analysis of what is going on in frustration, mistake and discharge by construction cases? Is it possible to prove that either his explanation or the efficiency explanation put forward earlier is the 'right' one?

CHAPTER NINETEEN
DUTIES OF DISCLOSURE

■ *Smith v Hughes*

(1871) LR 6 QB 597 (see, p 303)

There is no doubt that Cockburn CJ's judgment represents the general law. There are, however, a number of important exceptions. As far as the sale of goods is concerned, the most important are the implied terms under the Sale of Goods Act 1979, ss 13 and 14. These, in effect, require the seller to disclose any defect that would mean that the goods were not of the correct description, of satisfactory quality or fit for the buyer's particular purpose (see p 428). The main difficulties arise in other contracts in which there is no equivalent implied term or, in contracts of sale, if the defect would not result in a breach of one of the implied terms.

■ *Moody v Cox & Hatt*

[1917] 2 Ch 71, Court of Appeal

Hatt, a solicitor, and Cox, his managing clerk, were trustees of some property, which they agreed to sell to Moody. Hatt, through Cox, acted as solicitor for both vendors and purchaser. Cox failed to reveal to Moody that the property was worth much less than Moody was paying for it.

Scrutton LJ

...First of all as to the law. Generally when you have made a legal contract and correctly expressed it in writing, and it has not been obtained by any misstatement of fact, innocent or fraudulent, the contract stands, and the fact that one party or the other knows facts about which he says nothing, which make the contract an unprofitable one to the other party, is of no legal importance. But there are certain relations and certain contracts in which a higher duty is imposed upon the parties, and they must not only tell the truth, but they must tell the whole truth so far as it is material, and they must not only not misrepresent by words, but they must not misrepresent by silence if they know of something that is material. Some of those cases depend on the relation between the parties, and, generally speaking, are cases where the relation is such that you have confidence reposed by one party and influence exercised by the other. In that class of relation of parties you may get the duty, first of all, that the party who has influence must make a full disclosure of everything that he knows material to the contract; secondly, that the party who has the influence must not make a contract with the party over whom he has the influence unless he can satisfy the Court that that contract is an advantageous one to the other party. The second class of cases is one not depending on the relation of the parties, but depending on the nature of the contract; and a typical case of that kind is the contract of insurance, where to an underwriter who knows nothing comes an assured, a man who wants to be insured and who knows everything, and on him is imposed the duty of telling the man who knows nothing all that he knows, so that the underwriter may fix the premium. In the first class of relations that of solicitor and client is one of the obviously and constantly recognized examples. If a man who is in the position of solicitor to a client so that the client has presumably confidence in him, and the solicitor has presumably influence over the client, desires to contract with his client, he must make a full disclosure of every material fact that he knows, and must take upon himself the burden of satisfying the Court that the contract is one of full advantage to his client. . . .

This case was applied by the House of Lords in *Hilton v Barker Booth and Eastwood* [2005] UKHL8, [2005] 1 All ER 651.

I. UNDUE INFLUENCE

In *Tate v Williamson* (1866) 2 Ch App 55, Tate, an extravagant undergraduate hard pressed by his Oxford creditors and anxious to extricate himself from his financial embarrassment, sought the advice of Williamson. Having recommended the sale of Tate's Staffordshire estate, Williamson offered to buy it himself without disclosing that it was worth at least double the amount offered because of minerals under the land. Tate accepted Williamson's offer and conveyed the land, but some years later, after Tate had drunk himself to death, the sale was set aside at the instance of Tate's heir. Similar cases of undue influence will be dealt with in Chapter 35.

II. CONTRACTS *UBERRIMAE FIDEI*

■ *Lambert v Co-operative Insurance Society Ltd*
[1975] 2 Lloyd's Rep 485, Court of Appeal

In 1963, the plaintiff signed a proposal form for one of the defendants' 'All Risks' insurance policies to cover her own and her husband's jewellery. She did not mention that her husband had been convicted some years earlier of receiving 1,730 cigarettes, knowing them to have been stolen, and had been fined £25. The defendants issued a policy. In December 1971, Mr Lambert was convicted of two further offences of dishonesty and was sentenced to 15 months' imprisonment. At the next renewal date in March 1972, Mrs Lambert did not reveal this conviction. In April 1972, a number of items, valued at £311, were lost or stolen. The defendants refused to meet the plaintiff's claim on the ground of her failure to disclose her husband's convictions. The trial judge held for the defendants and the plaintiff appealed.

Mackenna J

. . . Everyone agrees that the assured is under a duty of disclosure and that the duty is the same when he is applying for a renewal as it is when he is applying for the original policy. The extent of that duty is the matter in controversy. There are, at least in theory, four possible rules or tests which I shall state. (1) The duty is to disclose such facts only as the particular assured believes to be material (2) It is to disclose such facts as a reasonable man would believe to be material. (3) It is to disclose such facts as the particular insurer would regard as material. (4) It is also to disclose such facts as a reasonable or prudent insurer might have treated as material.

Section 18 of the Marine Insurance Act, 1906, chooses the fourth...

There is no obvious reason why there should be a rule in marine insurance different from the rules in other forms of insurance and in my opinion, there is no difference...The present case shows the unsatisfactory state of the law. Mrs Lambert is unlikely to have thought that it was necessary to disclose the distressing fact of her husband's recent conviction when she was renewing the policy on her little store of jewellery. She is not an underwriter and has presumably no experience in these matters. The defendant company would act decently if, having established the point of principle, they were to pay her. It might be thought a heartless thing if they did not, but that is their business, not mine. I would dismiss the appeal.

NOTE

The duty to disclose material facts applies to the insurer as well as to the insured. The duty is not founded on an implied term of the contract or on tort but on 'the jurisdiction originally exercised by the Courts of Equity to prevent imposition'. As a result, the remedy for a breach of it is rescission of the contract, and not damages: *Banque Financière de la Cité SA v Westgate Insurance Co Ltd* [1989] 2 All ER 952. (For more on this case, see p 538.)

Family arrangements form another category of contracts *uberrimae fidei*. In *Gordon v Gordon* (1821) 3 Swan 400, a settlement, agreed on the basis that the elder son was probably illegitimate, was set aside upon proof that the younger son had concealed his knowledge of a private ceremony solemnised between his parents in America before the birth of the elder brother. Lord Eldon said:

I think myself justified by the authority of *Cann v Cann* and other decisions, in holding that if a dispute arises relative to the legitimacy of children, and the members of the family, to maintain their character in the world, arrange their rights among themselves, if the matter is fully before them, their arrangement will not be disturbed, because it is founded on a supposition, which imputes the character of legitimacy to the illegitimate, or illegitimacy to the legitimate; but then there must be not only good faith and honest intention, but full disclosure; and without full disclosure honest intention is not sufficient.

III. INFORMATION WRONGFULLY OBTAINED

In *Phillips v Homfray* (1871) 6 Ch App 770, the owners of a colliery entered into a contract with an adjoining landowner to buy his land, without disclosing that they had wrongfully extracted a considerable quantity of coal from under it. It was held by the Lord Chancellor, on appeal from Stuart V-C, that the contract was not enforceable by the purchasers, even though it was not shown to be at an undervalue.

Lord Hatherley LC said:

...I apprehend that in such a case the Court, whatever it might do as to cancelling the contract, certainly would decline to enforce it. The case would, I think, be something analogous to this: Suppose a picture-dealer, employed to clean a picture, scrapes off a part of the picture to see if he can discover a mark which will tell him who is the artist, and thus finds a mark shewing it to be the work of a great artist; that would not be a legitimate mode of acquiring knowledge for the purpose of enabling him to buy the picture at a lower price than the owner would have sold it for had he known it to be the work of that artist. I do not, however, dwell on that point, as it is not satisfactorily established in my mind that the price was inadequate. The ground of my decision is, that the Appellants suppressed the fact of their having wrongfully got a large quantity of the Respondents' coal, and so given the Respondents a heavy pecuniary claim against them.

IV. STATUTORY DUTIES OF DISCLOSURE

There are many statutory duties of disclosure relating to information to which the other party is unlikely to have access. See the Companies Act 1985, ss 56, 57, 66 and 67; Medicines Act 1968; Food Labelling Regulations 1996; Hallmarking Act 1973, etc. Of the statutes listed, only the Companies Act gives rise to civil liability if there is a breach, but nonetheless the buyer is given more information about the product than he might otherwise receive.

V. A GENERAL DUTY OF DISCLOSURE?

Should English law recognise a general duty to disclose facts that one party knows that the other party is ignorant of, and which would influence the other in his decision whether or not to enter the contract? In the USA different courts have reached different solutions in different contexts. Parties who have (without acting wrongfully) discovered minerals under another's land have usually been permitted to take advantage of their knowledge, by being permitted to buy the land without disclosing their information. In contrast, read the next case.

■ *Obde v Schlemeyer*

56 Wash 2d 449, 353 P2d 672 (Supreme Court of Washington, 1960)

The plaintiffs bought a house from the defendants. The house was infested with termites. The trial court found that the defendants knew of the termite infestation and had not revealed it to the plaintiffs. The plaintiffs had asked no question about termites. The plaintiffs claimed damages for fraudulent concealment and the trial court awarded them $3,950. The defendants appealed.

Finley J

...The Schlemeyers urge that, in any event, as sellers, they had no duty to inform the Obdes of the termite condition. They emphasize that it is undisputed that the purchasers asked no questions respecting the possibility of termites. They rely on a Massachusetts case involving a substantially similar factual situation, *Swinton v Whitinsville Savings Bank* (1942)...Applying the traditional doctrine of *caveat emptor*—namely, that, as between parties dealing at arm's length (as vendor and purchaser), there is no duty to speak, in the absence of a request for information—the Massachusetts court held that a vendor of real property has no duty to disclose to a prospective purchaser the fact of a latent termite condition in the premises.

Without doubt, the parties in the instant case were dealing at arm's length. Nevertheless, and notwithstanding the reasoning of the Massachusetts court above noted, we are convinced that the defendants had a duty to inform the plaintiffs of the termite condition. In *Perkins v Marsh* (1934) a case involving parties dealing at arms length as landlord and tenant, we held that,

> 'Where there are concealed defects in demised premises, dangerous to the property, health, or life of the tenant, which defects are known to the landlord when the lease is made, but unknown to the tenant, and which a careful examination on his part would not disclose, it is the landlord's duty to disclose them to the tenant before leasing, and his failure to do so amounts to a fraud.'

We deem this rule to be equally applicable to the vendor-purchaser relationship. See 15 TexLaw Review (December, 1936) 1, 14–16, Keeton: 'Fraud—Concealment and Non-Disclosure'. In this article Professor Keeton also aptly summarized the modern judicial trend away from a strict application of *caveat emptor* by saying:

> 'It is of course apparent that the content of the maxim "caveat emptor", used in its broader meaning of imposing risks on both parties to a transaction, has been greatly limited since its origin. When Lord Cairns stated in *Peek v Gurney* that there was no duty to disclose facts, however morally censurable their non-disclosure may be, he was stating the law as shaped by an individualistic philosophy based upon freedom of contract. It was not concerned with morals. In the present stage of the law, the decisions show a drawing away from this idea, and there can be seen an attempt by many courts to reach a just result in so far as possible, but yet maintaining the degree of certainty which the law must have. The statement may often be found that if either party to a contract of sale conceals or suppresses a material fact which he is in good faith bound to disclose then his silence is fraudulent.
>
> The attitude of the courts toward non-disclosure is undergoing a change and contrary to Lord Cairns' famous remark it would seem that the object of the law in these cases should be to impose on parties to the transaction a duty to speak whenever justice, equity, and fair dealing demand it'. (page 31.)

A termite infestation of a frame building, such as that involved in the instant case, is manifestly a serious and dangerous condition. . . . Further, at the time of the sale of the premises, the condition was clearly latent—not readily observable upon reasonable inspection. As we have noted, all superficial or surface evidence of the condition had been removed by reason of the efforts of Senske, the pest control specialist. Under the circumstances, we are satisfied that 'justice, equity, and fair dealing', to use Professor Keeton's language, demanded that the Schlemeyers speak—that they inform prospective purchasers, such as the Obdes, of the condition, regardless of the latter's failure to ask any questions relative to the possibility of termites.

Weaver CJ, Rosellini, Foster and **Hill JJ** concurred.

Judgment affirmed.

NOTE

To some extent, the opposing results reflect different attitudes to self-reliance, but it has been suggested that there is an underlying economic rationale.

■ Kronman, 'Mistake Disclosure, Information and the Law of Contracts' (1978)
7 JLS 1, 2–5, 13–15, 25

Every contractual agreement is predicated upon a number of factual assumptions about the world. Some of these assumptions are shared by the parties to the contract and some are not. It is always possible that a particular factual assumption is mistaken. From an economic point of view, the risk of such a mistake (whether it be the mistake of only one party or both) represents a cost. It is a cost to the contracting parties themselves and to society as a whole since the actual occurrence of a mistake always (potentially) increases the resources which must be devoted to the process of allocating goods to their highest-valuing users.

There are basically two ways in which this particular cost can be reduced on an optimal level. First, one or both of the parties can take steps to prevent the mistake from occurring. Second, to the extent a mistake cannot be prevented, either party (or both) can insure against the risk of its occurrence.

Information is the antidote to mistake. Although information is costly to produce, one individual may be able to obtain relevant information more cheaply than another. If the parties to a contract are acting rationally, they will minimize the joint costs of a potential mistake by assigning the risk of its occurrence to the party who is the better (cheaper) information-gatherer. Where the parties have actually assigned the risk—whether explicitly, or implicitly through their adherence to trade custom and past patterns of dealing—their own allocation must be respected. Where they have not—and there is a resulting gap in the contract—a court concerned with economic efficiency should impose the risk on the better information-gatherer. This is so for familiar reasons: by allocating the risk in this way, an efficiency-minded court reduced the transaction costs of the contracting process itself.

The most important doctrinal distinction in the law of mistake is the one drawn between 'mutual' and 'unilateral' mistakes. Traditionally, courts have been more reluctant to excuse a mistaken promisor where he alone is mistaken than where the other party is mistaken as to the same fact. Although relief for unilateral mistake has been liberalized during the last half-century (to the point where some commentators have questioned the utility of the distinction between unilateral and mutual mistake and a few have even urged its abolition), it is still 'black-letter' law that a promisor whose mistake is not shared by the other party is less likely to be relieved of his duty to perform than a promisor whose mistake happens to be mutual.

Viewed broadly, the distinction between mutual and unilateral mistake makes sense from an economic point of view. Where both parties to a contract are mistaken about the same fact or state of affairs, deciding which of them would have been better able to prevent the mistake may well require a detailed inquiry regarding the nature of the mistake and the (economic) role or position of each of the parties involved. But where only one party is mistaken, it is reasonable to assume that he is in a better position than the other party to prevent his own error. As we shall see, this is not true in every case, but it provides a useful beginning point for analysis and helps to explain the generic difference between mutual and unilateral mistakes.

Allocative efficiency is promoted by getting information of changed circumstances to the market as quickly as possible. Of course, the information doesn't just 'get' there. Like everything else, it is supplied by individuals (either directly, by being publicized, or indirectly, when it is signalled by an individual's market behavior).

In some cases, the individuals who supply information have obtained it by a deliberate search; in other cases, their information has been acquired casually. A securities analyst, for example, acquires information about a particular corporation in a deliberate fashion by carefully studying evidence of its economic performance. By contrast, a businessman who acquires a valuable piece of information when he accidentally overhears a conversation on a bus acquires the information casually.

As it is used here, the term 'deliberately acquired information' means information whose acquisition entails costs which would not have been incurred but for the likelihood, however great, that the information in question would actually be produced. These costs may include, of course, not only direct search costs (the cost of examining the corporation's annual statement) but the costs of developing an initial expertise as well (for example, the cost of attending business school). If the costs incurred in acquiring the information (the cost of the bus ticket in the second example) would have been incurred in any case—that is, whether or not the information was forthcoming—the information may be said to have been casually acquired. The distinction between deliberately and casually acquired information is a shorthand way of expressing this economic difference. Although in reality it may be difficult to determine whether any particular item of information has been acquired in one way or the other, the distinction between these two types of information has—as I hope to show—considerable analytical usefulness.

If information has been deliberately acquired (in the sense defined above), and its possessor is denied the benefits of having and using it, he will have an incentive to reduce (or curtail entirely) his production of such information in the future. This is in fact merely a consequence of defining deliberately acquired information in the way that I have, since one who acquires information of this sort will by definition have incurred costs which he would have avoided had it not been for the prospect of the benefits he has now been denied. By being denied the same benefits, one who has casually acquired information will not be discouraged from doing what—for independent reasons—he would have done in any case. . . .

One (seldom noticed) way in which the legal system can establish property rights in information is by permitting an informed party to enter—and enforce—contracts which his information suggests are profitable, without disclosing the information to the other party. Imposing a duty to disclose upon the knowledgeable party deprives him of a private advantage which the information would otherwise afford. A duty to disclose is tantamount to a requirement that the benefit of the information be publicly shared and is thus antithetical to the notion of a property right which—whatever else it may entail— always requires the legal protection of private appropriation. . . .

Where the seller actually knows of the defect, and the buyer does not, the seller is clearly the party best able to avoid the buyer's mistake at least cost— unless the seller has made a deliberate investment in acquiring his knowledge which he would not have made had he known he would be required to disclose to purchasers of the property any defects he discovered. A seller, of course, may make a substantial investment in acquiring information concerning a particular defect: for example, he may hire exterminators to check his property for termites. But even so, it is unlikely that his principal aim in acquiring such information is to obtain an advantage over potential purchasers. Typically, homeowners conduct investigations of this sort in order to protect their own investments. In most cases, a homeowner will have an adequate incentive to check for termites even if the law requires him to disclose what he discovers; furthermore, many termite infestations are discovered by simply living in the house— something the owner will do in any event. A disclosure requirement is unlikely to have a substantial effect on the level of investment by homeowners in the detection of termites: the point is not that information regarding termites is costless (it isn't), but that a disclosure requirement would not be likely to reduce the production of such information. This represents an important distinction between cases like *Obde*, on the one hand, and [cases where it was held that relevant information need not be disclosed] . . .

■ Cooter and Ulen, *Law and Economics* (4th edn, 2003)
pp 279–283

. . . We will explain how contract doctrines contribute to the efficient discovery and transmission of information. Economists say that *public* information is known to both parties in a bargain, whereas *private* information is known to one party and unknown to the other. Private information often motivates exchange. To illustrate, assume that someone knows how to get more production from a resource than does its owner. To increase production, knowledge must be united with control. To unite knowledge with control, the owner of the resource must acquire the information, or else the informed person must acquire ownership of the resource. In general, the transmission of information and the sale of goods unites knowledge and control over resources. *Efficiency requires united knowledge and control over resources at least cost, including the transaction costs of transmitting information and selling goods.*

The parties can usually solve the problem of private information through private bargaining. For example, the informed party may offer to buy the resource and pay more than uninformed owner can earn from using it. Or the informed party may offer to share the information with the uninformed owner of the resource in exchange for a proportion of the resulting increase in profits. Private bargaining usually solves the problem of asymmetrical information much better than any alternative, such as having the state dictate a solution. Consequently, the law usually enforces contracts based on asymmetrical information.

Instead of united knowledge and control, however, some contracts separate them. Separating knowledge and control reduces efficiency in the use of resources. Contracts that separate knowledge and control should be suppressed for the sake of efficiency. In subsequent sections, we will discuss three such doctrines: mistake, failure to disclose, and fraud.

1. Unilateral Mistake Each of the parties to a bargain usually knows something that the other does not know. Sometimes one of the parties knows that the other party has a mistaken belief. For example, the seller of a car may think that it is merely old, whereas the buyer may know that it is a classic. Although the seller was mistaken about the car's value, the buyer was not, so mistake was unilateral. When one party to a bargain knows the truth and the other party does not, the exchange is based on a 'unilateral mistake,' according to the language of the law. Courts usually enforce contracts based on unilateral mistakes. For example, if the owner promises to sell a classic car for less than its market value, the law will usually enforce the promise.

When the buyer acquires the classic car in this example, knowledge and control are united, which typically increases efficiency. For example, the buyer will probably take better care of the car because he or she knows its worth. The contract also increased efficiency in another way. Discovering information often requires investing time and resources, which requires a reward. In this example, the buyer may have searched long and hard to find a seller who does not know that he or she owns a classic car. The profit from buying the classic car at a low price rewards the buyer for the search.

We explained above that a mutual mistake about facts or identity is a valid formation defense in common law, whereas unilateral mistake is not. Consequently, a party who seeks performance of a contract may say that mistake was unilateral, and a party who seeks release from a contract may say that mistake was mutual. Economic efficiency provides a criterion for making this distinction. Mutual mistake converts a contract into an involuntary exchange, which can destroy value. In contrast, a contract based on a unilateral mistake usually promotes efficiency by rewarding discovery and uniting knowledge with control. We propose the following principle to improve the legal distinction underlying the doctrines of unilateral and mutual mistake: *Withhold enforcement from contracts involving involuntary exchange, and enforce contracts that reward discovery and unite knowledge with control.*

We apply this principle to the famous case of *Laidlaw v. Organ*, 15 U.S. (2 Wheat.) 178 (1815). During the War of 1812 between Britain and the United States, the British blockaded New Orleans, which depressed the price of export goods like tobacco. Organ, a buyer of tobacco, received private information that the war had ended by treaty, so he called on a representative of the Laidlaw firm and offered to buy tobacco. The representative of the Laidlaw firm was ignorant about the peace treaty, so a contract was concluded between them at the depressed price. The next day public notice was given in New Orleans that peace was concluded, and the price of tobacco soared. The mistake in this contract was obviously unilateral, not mutual—Organ knew about the treaty, and Laidlaw did not. Even so, the contract was apparently set aside by the court after a trial.

This outcome can be defended on economic grounds. According to the preceding principle, the contract should be enforced if doing so rewards discovery and unites knowledge with control. The evidence suggests that Organ discovered fortuitously that peace was concluded, rather than investing time and resources in making the discovery. Furthermore, the contract merely accelerated by one day the uniting of knowledge and control, which did not contribute to production of tobacco. So enforcing the contract would probably not increase efficiency.

To sharpen this analysis, distinguish between *productive* information and *redistributive* information. Productive information can be used to produce more wealth. It is information that allows existing resources to be moved to more productive uses (such as information that farmland contains valuable mineral resources) or discovers new methods of organizing resources for more productive uses (such as double-entry bookkeeping methods). The discovery of a vaccine for polio and the discovery of a water route between Europe and China were productive. Efficiency demands giving people strong incentives to discover productive facts. Transmitting information is so easy that the person who discovers productive information seldom captures its full value. Consequently, the state must take special measures to reward people who discover productive information. For example, the state must subsidize basic scientific research and provide patents to inventors.

In contract, redistributive information creates a bargaining advantage that can be sued to redistribute wealth in favor of the informed party. To illustrate, knowing before anyone else where the state will locate a new highway conveys a powerful advantage in real-estate markets. Investment in discovering redistributive information wastes resources. In addition, investment in redistributive information induces defensive expenditures by people trying not to lose their wealth to better-informed people. Defensive expenditures prevent redistribution, rather than produce something. Thus, investment information wastes resources directly and indirectly.

The state should not create incentives to discover redistributive information. Instead, the state should discourage investment in discovering redistributive information. For example, the state should punish officials who leak information about the location of a new highway prior to the public announcement. Such leaks encourage real-estate dealers to devote resources to gaining privileged information from officials.

To further sharpen this complicated issue, let us also distinguish the methods by which people acquire information. One can acquire information either *actively*—that is, by investing resources in the acquisition of information—or *fortuitously*—that is, by chance. As we argued at some length in Chapter 5, there is a strong social interest in encouraging the investment of resources in acquiring valuable information. That, recall, is the premise upon which intellectual property law rests. Fortuity is different, and there is nothing that society gains from more or less chance occurrences.

We can bring together our concerns about the nature of the information—whether it is productive or redistributive—and about the method by which it was acquired—whether by active investment of fortuity—in order to make a proposal about encouraging the efficient exchange and use of information in contracts. Consider the two-by-two chart shown in Table 7.4.

Table 7.4

Information in Contracts			
		METHOD BY WHICH THE INFORMATION WAS ACQUIRED	
		Acquired by investment	Acquired by fortuity
NATURE OF THE	*Productive*	Enforcement	No enforcement
INFORMATION	*Redistributive*	No enforcement	No enforcement

Note that the only combination of the nature of the information and the method by which it was acquired for which there is a strong efficiency argument for enforcement is the one in the upper left-hand corner of Table 7.4—productive information that is the result of an active investment of resources. There is no efficiency case to be made for enforcing any of the other combinations in the chart. Indeed, we can go further than that and say that there is probably an argument to be made in favor of actively discouraging the investment of resources in acquiring redistributive information, such as investing in eavesdropping or establishing personal connections with powerful people so as to be the first to discover the route of the new major highway.

These considerations prompt another formulation of the economic principle for improving the legal distinction underlying the doctrines of unilateral and mutual mistake: *Contracts based upon one party's knowledge of productive information—especially if that knowledge was the result of active investment—should be enforced, whereas contracts based upon one party's knowledge of purely redistributive information or fortuitously acquired information should not be enforced.* This principle rewards investment in discovering productive information and discourages investment in discovering redistributive information.

In our discussion of information economics in ... , we explained that most information is both productive and redistributive, what we might call 'mixed' information. To illustrate, the invention of the cotton gin in 1792 by Eli Whitney increased cotton production and promoted speculation in land suitable for growing cotton. The example of the informed buyer who purchased a classic car from an uninformed seller also illustrates mixed information, that is, information that is both productive and redistributive. The information was productive because the informed buyer knew that the car deserved special care. The information was redistributive because the informed buyer's gain from buying the car probably exceeded the increase in value from taking special care of it. We argued that private bargains usually succeed in rewarding discovery and uniting knowledge with control. Consequently, most bargains based upon differences in information affecting production and distribution should be enforced. In other words, most bargains based upon mixed information should be enforced.

We have arrived at three economic principles to govern the analysis of contract cases in which the formation defense of mistake is raised:

1. enforce contracts based on differences in productive information, especially if that information was acquired by investment;
2. enforce most contracts based on difference in mixed information (productive and redistributive); and
3. set aside contracts based on differences in purely redistributive information or if the information was acquired fortuitously.

NOTES

1. Is encouraging parties to invest in acquiring information a sufficient justification for allowing, for instance, companies that have discovered minerals under the other party's land to buy the land without disclosing anything and thereby to capture the whole of the increased value of the land? (See further p 829).

2. A comparative survey and an alternative approach will be found in Fabre-Magnan, 'Duties of Disclosure and French Contract Law' in Beatson and Friedmann (eds), *Good Faith and Fault in Contract Law*, 1995, pp 99–120.

There is no sign of any move in English case law towards recognition of a general duty of disclosure—if anything, the indications are negative. Thus we will see below (p 918 ff) that the grounds on which relief will be given after there have been other forms of advantage-taking seem to have been narrowed in the last few years. Moreover, in *Banque Financière de la Cité SA v Westgate Insurance Co Ltd* [1989] 2 All ER 952, the Court of Appeal, having held that a breach of the duty to disclose in an insurance contract does not give any right to damages (see p 531), went on to hold that it did not give a right to damages under s 2(1) of the Misrepresentation Act or under the common law of tort. Section 2(1) did not apply because it refers to a 'misrepresentation' having been 'made', which does not cover mere non-disclosure, and the fact that the parties to an insurance contract are under mutual obligations to disclose material facts does not put them into a special relationship within *Hedley Byrne v Heller* (see p 28). In the *Banque de la Cité* case, a Mr Dungate, who was an employee of the insurers, had become aware that an employee of the insurance brokers, a Mr Lee, was issuing false cover notes on the strength of which the plaintiff banks were advancing loans, but Dungate did not tell either the brokers or the banks of the deception. As a result, the banks could not recover on the insurance itself, but they argued that the insurers were liable to them in damages for failure to disclose Lee's dishonesty. Slade LJ said (at 1007–1012):

Can a mere failure to speak ever give rise to liability in negligence under *Hedley Byrne* principles? On our view it can, but subject to the all-important proviso that there has been on the facts a voluntary assumption of responsibility in the relevant sense and reliance on that assumption. These features may be much more difficult to infer in a case of mere silence that in a case of misrepresentation . . .

[However we] can see no sufficient reason on principle or authority why a failure to speak should not be capable of giving rise to liability under *Hedley Byrne* principles, provided that the two essential conditions are satisfied.

A hypothetical example may illustrate the point. Suppose that a father employs an estate agent for a fee to advise his son on the proposed purchase of a house and the estate agent negligently fails to inform the son that a motorway is shortly to be constructed within a few hundred yards of the property. We would not doubt that in such a case the son, knowing of the estate agent's duty and relying on it, would have a claim in negligence . . .

. . . Did Mr Dungate in fact assume responsibility towards the banks? If so, did the banks rely on that assumption of responsibility? The answer to each part of the question must surely be no.

We can see no justification for holding that Mr Dungate, who made no representation, assumed any responsibility at all in relation to Mr Lee's honesty or dishonesty. Counsel for the banks other [than] Chemical Bank argued that a voluntary assumption of responsibility is to be found in Mr Dungate's voluntary conduct in continuing to deal with Mr Lee. We do not agree. The phrase 'voluntary assumption of responsibility' in this context means what it says: conduct by the party signifying that he assumes responsibility for taking due care in respect of the statement or action. No doubt, in deciding whether there has been such an assumption of responsibility the conduct of the party may be objectively construed. To deal in the ordinary way with an agent without any relevant communication to his principal cannot, we think, be held to be an assumption of responsibility because the party has done nothing which signifies assumption of responsibility in the relevant sense.

Nor is there any evidence that the banks relied on any assumption of responsibility by the insurers in respect of Mr Lee's honesty. . . .

But counsel for the banks other than Chemical Bank had an alternative submission. He argued that, although voluntary assumption of responsibility, coupled with reliance, is a condition for the existence of a duty of care in some cases of pure economic loss, it is not a condition of every such case; a duty of care not to cause economic loss may be owed without it.

. . . [w]e are prepared to accept, for the purposes of this judgment, that in some cases (if rare) of pure economic loss the court may be willing to find the existence of a duty of care owed by a defendant to a plaintiff even in the absence of evidence of any actual voluntary assumption by the defendant of such duty and/or of any reliance on such assumption. We shall accordingly proceed on the basis that, on appropriate facts, the court may be willing to hold that, having regard to the special circumstances and the relationship between the parties, a defendant should be treated *in law* (even though not in fact) as having assumed a responsibility to the plaintiff which is capable of giving rise to a claim for damages for pure economic loss. The remaining question, therefore, is whether Hodge should be so treated in this case.

In this context we attach importance to the distinction to which the judge in our view gave insufficient weight. For better or worse, our law of tort draws a fundamental distinction between the legal effects of acts on the one hand and omissions on the other . . .

The example given by Lord Keith is of a failure to prevent physical harm. But the same reluctance on the part of the courts to give a remedy in tort for pure omission applies, perhaps even more so, when the omission is a failure to prevent economic harm. As will appear below, a corresponding distinction is drawn by the law of contract which in general imposes no liability by virtue of a failure to speak as opposed to a misrepresentation.

In an important passage of his judgment the judge said that he did not regard the present case as 'a case of pure omission'. He gave two reasons (see [1987] 2 All ER 923 at 951, [1987] 2 WLR 1300 at 1338–1339):

'The relationship between the parties involved obligations of good faith and fair dealing. Moreover, the alleged duty arises in the context of insurers who had an established business relationship with the banks, and continued to transact further with the banks (and to make profits) in the knowledge that a risk, viz further dishonesty by Mr Lee, which was obvious to the insurers, was not appreciated by the banks and could not be discovered by them. It is a situation essentially different from pure omission cases. In my judgment the fact that the duty relied on by the banks required affirmative action on the part of the insurers (unless they simply decided in the circumstances not to insure) does not preclude a ruling that such a duty existed.'

We take first his point that there was here an established business relationship with the banks, and the insurers continued to do business with the banks, even though they knew of the risk resulting from Mr Lee's dishonesty, while the banks did not.

In our judgment, to hold that these factors by themselves gave rise to a duty on the part of Mr Dungate to report Mr Lee's dishonesty to the banks, capable of exposing him or his employers to a liability in tort, would undermine basic principles of our law of contract.

Throughout this case it has to be borne in mind that the period in June 1980 in which it is said that Mr Dungate's duty to report arose and continued was one during which he was in the course of conducting contractual negotiations with the banks on behalf of his employers.

The general principle that there is no obligation to speak within the context of negotiations for an ordinary commercial contract (though qualified by the well-known special principles relating to contracts *uberrimae fidei*, fraud, undue influence, fiduciary duty etc) is one of the foundations of our law of contract, and must have been the basis of many decisions over the years. There are countless cases in which one party to a contract has in the course of negotiations failed to disclose a fact known to him which the other party would have regarded as highly material, if it had been revealed. However, ordinarily in the absence of misrepresentation, our law leaves that other party entirely without remedy. Lord Atkin gave some striking examples in *Bell v Lever Bros Ltd*...

...[I]n our judgment, it would be wholly contrary to principle to suggest, at least in the case of an ordinary contract made between persons in an ordinary relationship, that B, having undertaken no relevant contractual obligation to A, should be treated as having assumed a responsibility which could give rise to a liability to A in tort. To reach such a decision as to the effect of a non-disclosure in the course of contractual negotiations would run counter to the general principle of caveat emptor on which our law of contract is founded....

By the same token we would hold that no legal obligation on the part of Mr Dungate to inform the banks of Mr Lee's dishonesty arose, either in contract or in tort, merely because there was an 'established business relationship' between the parties, and because the insurers continued to transact further business with the banks. That factor does not turn a pure omission into a misrepresentation, in tort any more than in contract. It would not justify the court treating Mr Dungate as having assumed a duty or responsibility to speak, in tort, which was not imposed on him by the law of contract.

This brings us to what was, in our view, the most forceful submission made on behalf of the banks. It ran on the following lines. As is common ground the negotiations between Hodge and the banks which resulted in the contract of insurance of 24 June 1980 imported mutual obligations of disclosure...

Why on those facts should the court not treat Hodge as having in law voluntarily assumed responsibility to make full disclosure of all material facts to the banks, not only for the purpose of the principles of *Carter v Boehm*, but also for the purpose of the law of negligence in tort? The very nature of the contract which was being negotiated, it is said, gives rise to a special relationship between the negotiating parties which justifies the imposition of a duty of care....

We do not think that the nature of the contract as one of the utmost good faith can be used as a platform to establish a common law duty of care. Parliament has provided that in the case of marine insurance the consequence of a failure to disclose a material fact, and by inference the *only* consequence, is that the contract may be avoided. It is not suggested that the consequences in non-marine insurance should be different. In those circumstances it is not, we think, open to the court to assist the banks by providing a supplementary remedy in tort. No doubt, on the very unusual facts of the present case, the statutory remedy of rescission seems inadequate. This is unfortunate for the banks. But the banks' misfortune is of the same kind as the misfortune suffered by the injured party in the various instances given by Lord Atkin in *Bell v Lever Bros Ltd* [see p 504 above], where the law affords no remedy at all. What the banks cannot do in our judgment is to invoke the nature of the contract as one of good faith, with its limited contractual remedy, to bridge the gap so as to give them cause of action in tort.

In 1988, the Conveyancing Standing Committee of the Law Commission provisionally recommended that:

A vendor of land should be under a positive duty to disclose all material facts about the property he is selling, providing he is aware of those facts or ought reasonably to be aware of them. *(Caveat Emptor in Sale of Land,* para 4.1)

It appears that this proposal did not meet with favour: the Committee's report, *Let the Buyer be Well Informed* (1990), made much more limited recommendations. But in 1998, the Department of the Environment, Transport and the Regions provisionally proposing that sellers should be encouraged or even required to provide buyers with, among other things, a surveyor's report and Housing Act 2004, Part 5, introduced 'Home Information Packs'.

1. Summary of the rules on inaccurate and inadequate information

At this point, it may be helpful to summarise the various forms of relief and remedies available when one party has entered the contract on the basis of inaccurate or inadequate information.

Basis of relief	Effect on contract	Damages
Breach of express promissory statement	Termination if serious	Contract measure
Breach, undisclosed defect renders goods not in accordance with description or unmerchantable	Termination	Contract measure
Fraudulent misrepresentation	Rescission	Tort measure
Negligent misrepresentation	Rescission, subject to court's discretion	Tort measure
Innocent misrepresentation	Rescission, subject to court's discretion	(only in lieu of rescission, restitutionary measure)
Non-disclosure (if applicable)	Rescission	—
Common mistake at common law	Void	—
Common mistake in equity	?	—

Bishop mentions to Beale that he wants to buy an antique ring for his (Bishop's) wife's birthday. Beale has in his desk an antique ring, which belonged to his mother, and he shows it to Bishop. Bishop offers to buy it at a price that clearly indicates that he thinks it is gold. Beale knows that the ring is made of base metal and is worth much less, but he does nothing to point out Bishop's mistake and accepts Bishop's offer. Bishop later discovers the truth and wants to get his money back. Is he entitled to recover? Would it make any difference if Beale were a dealer in antique jewellery? If Bishop were a dealer? What if Bishop had resold the ring as gold and had incurred liability to his buyer when the truth was discovered? What is the least alteration in the facts that would give Bishop the right to recover the price? To recover damages?

What, if anything, justifies the many subtle distinctions in this area?

NOTES

1. Why is relief given so much more readily when one party has given the other inaccurate information, even if the party giving the information was in no way to blame, than when he knows that the other is acting under some misapprehension?

2. If one party makes an inaccurate statement, why is it sometimes treated as a promise, carrying (normally) strict liability for loss-of-bargain damages, but at other times only as a representation, leading to out-of-pocket damages, and then only if the misrepresentor was at fault? A possible explanation is that when the court holds that a statement amounts to a warranty, it does so because the statement relates to some crucial characteristic of the subject matter, something the buyer was 'bargaining for'. If the characteristic is lacking, the buyer should get at least the cost of purchasing a substitute that does have it—ie expectation damages. If, on the other hand, the statement is about something that is only incidental and merely affects the price paid, for instance, it is sufficient to allow the buyer to rescind or recover her out-of-pocket loss.

3. Why is there no liability for damages if a misrepresentation is purely innocent? Is it because neither party is then the least cost avoider, and each is perhaps the best insurer of his own losses? (Compare Posner and Rosenfield, p 393 we leave damages under s 2(2) for the moment.)

4. Why then allow rescission for innocent misrepresentation? Is it because of the unjust enrichment that might otherwise occur, or for some other reason?

5. In some situations, rescission will be a costly and inappropriate remedy (on this, see p 368). The court is therefore given power to refuse to permit it when the representation was not fraudulent, and in addition, the right to rescission is easily lost under the 'bars'. If the court refuses to permit rescission that would otherwise be justified, it can award damages to remove the unjust enrichment element. It seems that it has no such power when the right to rescind has been lost under one of the bars. Why not?

6. Turning to cases of inadequate information, why is relief granted more readily (in theory, at least) when both parties have made the same mistake than when only one has made the mistake? Kronman argues that if only one party is mistaken, it is reasonable to assume that he was in a better position to prevent his own error than the other party. Do you agree? What if the other party actually knows of the first party's error? (Compare communication mistakes, pp 291–292.)

7. He also argues that when the parties share the mistake it is costly to inquire who was the least cost avoider. What does English law do in such a case? (See p 516.)

8. If one party carelessly makes a false statement to the other, the misrepresentee may recover damages in addition to rescinding. If the parties enter the contract sharing a fundamental false assumption, but they make no statements to each other (or do not rely on what the other said), the party prejudiced may be able to rescind or the contract may be void, but no damages will be available to compensate for any consequential loss she may have suffered. Do you think a mistaken party should be allowed to recover her consequential loss? (Compare p 492.)

QUESTIONS

1. In what circumstances will a contract be void for mistake at common law?

2. A seller purports to sell some goods. Unknown to either party, the goods have been destroyed. The seller should have known this from a fax, which he had received but had not read. Can the seller claim the price of the goods? Can the buyer claim damages for non-delivery? If your answer to the second part of the question is 'yes', why is the contract not void for mistake?

3. In the *Associated Japanese Bank* case, Steyn J held that the first question was whether the contract, as a matter of construction, was subject to an implied condition that the four machines existed. This seems the same as asking whether the contract allocated the risk of what had happened to one party or the other. Once a decision has been made on this point, is it possible that the decision on common law mistake would go the other way? In other words, does the common law doctrine add anything to the law?

4. What is the equitable doctrine of mistake? When will a contract be voidable in equity for common mistake when it would not be void at common law?

5. Why are courts apparently so reluctant to give relief on the ground of common mistake? In your view, is the doctrine one that should be widened, or should it be narrowed down still further?

6. Why is relief only given for mistake when both parties have made the same mistake and not (as happens in many other legal systems) when only one party has made a serious mistake—at least if the other party knows the first party is mistaken? Would you favour the adoption of a duty to disclose? Would you limit the duty in any way?

7. In your view, is what is happening in frustration and mistake cases best explained by the account given by Posner and Rosenfield (see p 393) or by the one given by Collins (p 526)? Or does the latter emphasise a rather different, and perhaps inconsistent, strand in the case law (especially, in England, in relation to mistake)?

REMEDIES

CHAPTER TWENTY

SOME PRELIMINARY QUESTIONS

In this section, we shall be considering the remedies available when one party has broken the contract, or has not yet performed his obligations. It may be helpful to list the main remedies available. Refusing to perform until the other has done so, called here 'withholding performance', and termination of the contract are considered in Chapter 21; Chapter 22 covers damages; Chapter 23 considers the action for sums due under the contract, specific performance and injunction; Chapter 24 deals with an alternative way of claiming money, by way of restitution.

I. THE DISTINCTION BETWEEN RIGHTS AND REMEDIES

In some areas of law, there is a clear distinction between right and remedy. In the field of administrative law, for instance, it commonly happens that it can be shown that the defendant may have breached some duty imposed by the law or otherwise have acted illegally, yet the complainant cannot bring an action because he has no sufficient interest in the case (see *IRC v National Federation of Self-Employed and Small Businesses Ltd* [1982] AC 617). In contract law, this problem does not arise, at least in this form. If one party to a contract has committed a breach of it, the other party (or parties) will have a remedy in every case. Persons who are not party to the contract will (subject now to some important exceptions) not have a remedy if the contract is broken (this problem is examined in detail in Section 10), but any party will be entitled to at least nominal damages if the contract has been broken. In addition, the court may, in an appropriate case, grant a declaration that the other party's action, or threatened action, is in breach of contract.

A declaration or nominal damages may seem an insubstantial remedy, but frequently nothing more can be obtained unless the complaining party has suffered or is likely to suffer some loss as the result of the other party's breach. This follows from the nature of the remedies available for breach of contract. The first point is that, although it is common to speak of enforcing the contract, it is only in certain types of case that the court will actually compel the defaulting party to carry out his obligation. Before 1854, different remedies were available in respect of contracts in the common law courts and in Chancery. At common law, only money judgments could be recovered. If the defendant had simply failed to pay a sum of money due under the contract (eg the price of the goods sold to him), judgment could be given for the sum due, thus effectively enforcing the contract in a literal sense; if the default was of some other kind, the judgment would have to be for compensation, normally damages. The Court of Chancery would, in certain circumstances, order specific performance, that is, order the defendant to perform the contract on pain of being committed for contempt of court, or it would grant an injunction restraining him from actions that would be a breach of contract. These equitable remedies were seen as extraordinary, not generally available. For instance, the rule was developed that specific performance would not be granted unless for some reason damages at common law would not be an adequate remedy. Nowadays, specific performance and injunction can be awarded in any division of the High Court, but the distinction between common law and equitable remedies is maintained, and the latter remain restricted in their availability: as we shall see, specific performance is commonly granted for sales of land, because each piece of land is regarded as unique, but it is not usually available if the contract is for the sale of goods, because substitute goods can normally be obtained by a disappointed buyer. (There are also some restrictions on the action for the price, as we shall see.) Thus remedies may be divided into primary (those actually enforcing the primary obligations under the contract) and secondary (those leading to other relief as a substitute for performance).

Even when primary enforcement is concerned, it is relatively unusual for a party to have a substantial remedy unless he has suffered a loss. Thus he will not be able to get a common law judgment for payments due under the contract unless they were to be paid to him (see p 1138), and, save in exceptional circumstances, he will not be able to get specific performance unless he has suffered a loss that would not be adequately compensated by damages. We shall see that there are also other restrictions on the equitable remedies: for instance, specific performance will not usually be granted of a contract for personal services. The result may be that the wronged party who cannot show any particular loss flowing from the other's breach may have no effective remedy, despite a clear infringement of his rights. Thus if a university professor of economics were to depart two days before the beginning of term to take up a post with the World Bank in Washington DC, and the university could not show that his departure had not caused it to lose more than it saved in not having to pay his salary, it would at most get a declaration that his conduct was in breach, or nominal damages. That, at least, is the traditional position. Were the professor to make a large profit by his breach of contract (which is very likely if he taught in a university in the UK) and if the university could show that it had a legitimate interest in preventing him from working in the World Bank (doubtful), the university may be able to get an account of profits. This seems to follow from the recent decision of the House of Lords in *A-G v Blake* (p 750). (The courts have also recently recognised that damages may be awarded in some cases in which the loss is suffered not by the party to the contract who brings the action but by a third person: see p 1143 ff.)

Withholding performance and termination do not fit easily into the distinction between primary and secondary, although clearly the former is aimed at encouraging actual performance, whereas the latter involves giving up the right to actual performance. In theory, at least, neither is available as a matter of general law (as opposed to available under the express terms of the agreement) unless the default on account of which the complaining party is threatening withholding or termination is a critical one, or is likely to cause him serious loss. We shall see that in practice this is not always the case.

II. SELF-HELP AND JUDICIAL REMEDIES

It is also useful to distinguish between remedies that require the complainant to enlist the aid of a court and those that he can use on his own. Just as in tort you are permitted to use reasonable force to eject a trespasser from your land, so in contract there are some actions that can be taken without resort to litigation. Orders of specific performance, injunctions and judgments for sums due under the contract are judicial remedies, whereas withholding performance and termination may (if justified) be exercised as a form of self-help. Damages do not fall clearly into either category: if the claimant owes money to the other party under the contract, he may generally deduct the damages he claims from the money owed; if not, he will have to sue for damages that the other party refuses to pay.

III. OFF-THE-SHELF REMEDIES AND EXPRESSLY PLANNED REMEDIES

The remedies discussed so far are all ones made available by the general law of contract, and the general law also lays down the conditions under which they may be employed. Many contracting parties are content to rely on these standard remedies should a dispute arise, but in contracts of any sophistication, it is common to provide additional or different remedies by express agreement. Thus there may be express provision about the damages that may be recovered, either providing for the recovery of some item that might not be compensable at common law, or more commonly restricting the damages more narrowly than is done by the common law, by means of a limitation clause. Express planning is particularly common in relation to self-help remedies: as we shall see, contracts often make the remedies of withholding and termination more readily available than they would be at common law. There are a number of important remedies that are permitted only if the agreement expressly provides for them: for example, the forfeiture of money paid or the repossession of property under a contract of sale. One of the vital questions in this area is the extent to which the law permits the parties to alter the remedies available to them. We shall see that there are explicit rules controlling some of these remedies (this is particularly so of limitation clauses, and this topic will be kept for a separate detailed treatment in Section 8). Other expressly planned remedies may be permitted in theory, but in practice are treated with such hostility by the courts that it is difficult to employ them successfully.

CHAPTER TWENTY-ONE

WITHHOLDING PERFORMANCE AND TERMINATION FOR DEFAULT

In this chapter, we look at the two remedies of withholding performance (refusing to perform part or all of your contractual obligations until the other party has performed, or is ready to perform, some obligation of his) and termination for default (refusing to perform your further obligations at all, and refusing to accept further performance by the other party, on the grounds of his failure to perform some part of his obligations).

The two remedies are closely connected. Both depend on the notion that A may not be under any obligation to render his performance until B has done something or is ready to do it. Withholding performance depends on this alone. It is such a direct result of the terms of the contract that some commentators do not view it as a 'remedy' at all. As Lord Oliver put it in a case involving an employment contract:

The question to be asked . . . is not so much: has the employer a *right* to withhold from an employee who voluntarily absents himself from work wages for the period he is absent? but: is the employee entitled to sue for and recover from his employer wages in respect of a period during which he has made it perfectly clear he is not ready and willing to perform his own contractual obligations?

(*Miles v Wakefield Metropolitan District Council* [1987] 1 All ER 1089 at 1104) But in practical terms, withholding performance operates as a form of remedy by protecting the employer from having to perform and giving the employee an incentive to work.

Termination depends also on additional factors: A must show that his obligation to perform was conditional on B rendering his performance within a certain period of time, and that either the time has expired, or B has in advance repudiated his obligations. In this section, we shall refer to the former as 'default termination', and to the latter as termination for 'anticipatory repudiation'. (There is also the possibility that, by the time B defaults, A has already performed. A may still be able to terminate: see p 580.)

Although we treat withholding and termination as remedies, it is worth remembering that much of the law in this area is just a continuation of the process of gap-filling by interpretation and implication that we looked at in Section 4. In other words, the starting point is still: 'what does the contract provide?' The contract may state expressly that until B has done *x*, A need not do *y*, or that if B does not do *x* by a certain date A may terminate. What the parties have agreed will normally govern, although we shall see that on occasions, when what the parties seem to have agreed strikes the court as unreasonable, effect will only be given to it if the language is very clear.

In this chapter, we present the material in a way that will help you grasp the technical rules. After introducing the concept of conditions, we look at how it is determined in what order the parties are to perform. We then deal with whether A's obligation to perform is conditional on B doing everything the contract requires, or only on B performing the more important obligations, and, if the latter, the difficult question of determining which of B's obligations are the crucial ones. These points are all relevant to both withholding and termination. The law on when withholding and termination are permitted depends upon the concept of conditions in the contract. Thus cases on one topic are usually relevant to the other, and, because in practice litigation will not be resorted to until a fairly late stage, most of the cases are ones in which one party claims that he has justifiably terminated the contract. The chapter then concludes by looking at the rules on default termination and termination for anticipatory repudiation.

■ Treitel, 'Some Problems of Breach of Contract'
(1967) 30 MLR 139, 149–150

[J]ust what practical interest is at stake when a party seeks 'rescission' [termination] of a contract? A buyer who has undertaken to pay cash on delivery will obviously not want to pay for defective goods and be left to pursue his claim for damages. Rejection combines, for him, all the advantages of a specific remedy and self-help; it enables him to avoid the delays of litigation as well as the risk that the seller's credit may fail. If the sale is on credit, the buyer's interest in rejection is less strong, since the damages can be set off against the price. But even here an innocent party who wants to determine his precise liability without recourse to legal proceedings runs the risk of quantifying his damages wrongly; and he may also be prejudiced if some of the loss he suffers as a result of having to accept defective performance is regarded as too remote.

On the other hand, the party in breach may have equally strong interests in acceptance: for example if the market has fallen, if he has incurred expenses in making the defective performance, or if the result of that performance has been to enrich the other party. The first of these interests will be more fully discussed below; but at this stage it is worth stressing the distinction between the last two. The expense of making a defective tender (eg, at a distant place) may be considerable but may not enrich the other contracting party at all. It is obvious, also, that these two interests grow in importance the further performance has gone.

I. THE NOTION OF CONDITIONS

The idea that a party's obligation to perform might be conditional upon some event outside the control of the parties was introduced in Section 3 (p 278). Here, we are dealing with what are often called 'promissory' conditions.

■ *Trans Trust SPRL v Danubian Trading Co Ltd*
[1952] 1 All ER 970, Court of Appeal

On 10 September 1950, a Belgian company offered to A Co 1,000 tons of rolled steel, fob Antwerp, delivery in December, payment to be against an irrevocable and confirmed letter of credit. A Co, which was unable to produce the letter of credit itself, offered the steel to the sellers who in turn offered it to the buyers. On 20 September 1950, the buyers, subject to the requirements as to the provision of a letter of credit, offered the steel to an American company. Both the sellers and the buyers knew that neither of them was in a position to fulfil their contractual obligations unless the American company made the money available through a letter of credit. On 25 September, the American company accepted the buyers' offer, and on the same day, the buyers agreed with the sellers that they would purchase the steel, stating: 'A credit will be opened forthwith.' Thereupon the sellers gave a written order to A Co. The American company failed to open the credit, and, the buyers being unable to do so, the sellers claimed against the buyers for breach of contract and a declaration that the sellers were entitled to be indemnified against any damages payable by them to A Co. At all material times, the market value of the steel was higher than the contract price.

Denning LJ

This is another case concerned with the modern practice whereby a buyer agrees to provide a banker's confirmed credit in favour of the seller. This credit is an irrevocable promise by a banker to pay money to the seller in return for the shipping documents. One reason for this practice is because the seller wishes to be assured in advance, not only that the buyer is in earnest, but also that he, the seller, will get his money when he delivers the goods. Another reason is because the seller often has expenses to pay in connection with the goods and he wishes to use the credit to pay those expenses. He may, for instance, be himself a merchant, who is buying the goods from the growers or the manufacturers and has to pay for them before he can get delivery, and his own bank may only grant him facilities for the purpose if he has the backing of a letter of credit. The ability of the seller to carry out the transaction is, therefore, dependent on the buyer's providing the letter of credit, and for this reason the seller stipulates that the credit should be provided at a specified time well in advance of the time for delivery of the goods.

What is the legal position of such a stipulation? Sometimes it is a condition precedent to the formation of a contract, that is, it is a condition which must be fulfilled before any contract is concluded at all. In those cases the stipulation 'subject to the opening of a letter of credit' is rather like a stipulation 'subject to contract'. If no credit is provided, there is no contract between the parties. In other cases a contract is concluded and the stipulation for a credit is a condition which is an essential term of the contract. In those cases the provision of the credit is a condition precedent, not to the formation of a contract, but to the obligation of the seller to deliver the goods. If the buyer fails to provide the credit, the seller can treat himself as discharged from any further performance of the contract and can sue the buyer for damages for not providing the credit.

The first question is: What was the nature of the stipulation in this case? When the buyers sent their order, they stated in writing on Sept 25, 1950, that 'a credit will be opened forthwith'. It was suggested that the buyers were not making any firm promise on their own account, but were only passing on information which had been given to them by their American buyers. The judge did not accept that suggestion and I agree with him. The statement was a firm promise by the buyers by which they gave their personal assurance that a credit would be opened forthwith. At that time there were some discrepancies about gauges and dates of delivery which had to be cleared up, but these were all resolved at the meetings in Brussels, and there was then, as the judge found, a concluded contract by the sellers to sell, and the buyers to buy, the steel for December/ January delivery, and it was a part of that contract that the buyers would be personally responsible for seeing that a credit should be opened forthwith. Of those findings it is clear that the stipulation for a credit was not a condition precedent to the formation of any contract at all. It was a condition which was an essential term of a contract actually made. That condition was not fulfilled. The sellers extended the time for the credit, but it never came, not even after reasonable notice. The sellers were, therefore, discharged from any further performance on their side, and are entitled to claim damages.

Denning LJ went on to hold that, because the buyers knew that the sellers would not be able to obtain the goods unless the credit were opened, the sellers were entitled to damages for loss of profit. **Somervell** and **Romer LJJ** delivered concurring judgments.

Appeal allowed in part.

NOTES

1. Observe the distinction implicit in Denning's analysis between withholding perform-ance and termination. The sellers did not have to deliver until the credit was opened, and once the (extended) time for opening had expired, they were 'discharged from any fur-ther performance'—ie they were entitled to terminate the contract.

2. Denning contrasts the promissory condition found in this case with a 'condition prece-dent to the formation of a contract'. It will be remembered that, in fact, even non-promissory conditions, such as 'subject to satisfactory survey', are not usually construed as preventing the existence of a contract: both parties are bound, but the main obligations of the contract only come into play if the condition is fulfilled. See pp 281 ff.

II. CONDITIONS AND THE ORDER OF PERFORMANCE

■ *Kingston v Preston*

(1773) cited in 2 Doug KB at 689–691

The plaintiff agreed to serve the defendant for a year and a quarter in the defendant's business as silk-mercer, and the defendant agreed that, at the end of the period, he would convey the business and the stock in trade to the plaintiff and the defendant's nephew. The stock in trade was to be paid for over a period of time, and the plaintiff agreed to provide security for these payments. The plaintiff claimed that the defendant had failed to convey the business; the defendant pleaded that the plaintiff had failed to provide the promised security.

In delivering the judgment of the Court, Lord Mansfield expressed himself to the following effect: There are three kinds of covenants. 1. Such as are called mutual and independant, where either party may recover damages from the other, for the injury he may have received by a breach of the covenants in his favour, and where it is no excuse for the defendant, to allege a breach of the covenants on the part of the plaintiff. 2. There are covenants which are conditions and dependant, in which the performance of one depends on the prior performance of another, and, therefore, till this prior condition is performed, the other party is not liable to an action on his covenant. 3. There is also a third sort of covenants, which are mutual conditions to be performed at the same time; and, in these, if one party is ready, and offered, to perform his part, and the other neglected, or refused, to perform his, he who was ready, and offered, has fulfilled his engagement, and may maintain an action for the default of the other; though it is not certain that either is obliged to do the first act—His Lordship then proceeded to say, that the depen-dance, or independance, of covenants, was to be collected from the evident sense and meaning of the parties, and, that, however transposed they might be in the deed, their precedency must depend on the order of time in which the intent of the transaction requires their performance. That, in the case before the Court, it would be the greatest injustice if the plaintiff should prevail: the essence of the agreement was, that the defendant should not trust to the personal security of the plaintiff, but, before he delivered up his stock and business, should have good security for the payment of the money. The giving of such security, therefore, must necessarily be a condition precedent.—Judgment was accordingly given for the defendant, because the part to be performed by the plaintiff was clearly a condition precedent.

NOTES

1. Examples of Lord Mansfield's first category are relatively rare, at least where the basic obligations under the contract are concerned. However, under a lease, the tenant's obligation to pay the rent and the landlord's obligation to repair have been held to be independent, so that the tenant could not withhold the rent because of non-repair: *Taylor v Webb* [1937] 2 KB 283. Occasionally, unimportant terms of a contract are referred to as 'independent covenants', but this is a misnomer: see p 565.

2. An example of performances that the law treats as due simultaneously and as concurrently conditional on each other are delivery and payment in a sale of goods contract that does not expressly provide when the price is to be paid:

   Sale of Goods Act 1979

   Section 28

   Unless otherwise agreed, delivery of the goods and payment of the price are concurrent conditions, that is to say, the seller must be ready and willing to give possession of the goods to the buyer in exchange for the price and the buyer must be ready and willing to pay the price in exchange for possession of the goods.

   An example of how this section might work is provided by *Total Oil (Great Britain) Ltd v Thompson Garages (BigginHill) Ltd* [1972] 1 QB 318, in which the garage owner agreed to pay for petrol 'cash upon delivery'. The petrol company insisted on receiving a banker's draft before it would dispatch the petrol (which was to be 'delivered' at the filling station). This gave the garage owner the right to refuse to go on with the agreement. For a case in which the seller argued that he was not bound to deliver until the buyer provided a credit for the full price, see *W J Alan & Co Ltd v El Nasr Export and Import* Co (p 868).

3. The order in which the two performances are due, if not stated in the contract, seems to be determined in the light of common-sense considerations. If simultaneous exchange is feasible, they will be treated as due simultaneously; if one performance will take a period of time but the other will be more or less instantaneous, the former will be treated as due first—thus 'work first, payment later' (see Restatement 2d s 234). Why is there this preference for treating them as simultaneous?

4. Enabling A to say that he is not obliged to perform until B has done so clearly protects A. Does it have any other function? See the next reading.

5. When the agreement does not expressly state that A is to do *x* as a condition of B's having to perform, but the court construes the obligations in this way, it is common to call the condition a 'constructive' condition.

■ Patterson, 'Constructive Conditions in Contracts' (1942)

42 Col LR 903 at 917–920, 925–926

4. Order of time of performance. The order of the time of performance of the several promises has long been regarded as determining which promises are dependent and which are independent, and is the

subject of many of the rules relating to dependency. Obviously if A performs promptly his promise to convey land to B on July 1st, and B has promised to pay the price on August 1st, A will credit B for one month. Then if A does not convey on July 1st, B's action commenced on July 2nd may be maintained without B's having tendered the price before suing. Yet even this mechanical test of dependency is controlled and supplemented, it is submitted, by a principle of policy which favors the construction of concurrent conditions and thus minimizes the credit burden of the transaction...

Where one party's promise requires a substantial time for performance, some extension of credit is practically unavoidable. The rule laid down for all such promises, where the other party's performance does not require a substantial time, is that the latter's duty is conditional on performance by the former, the party whose performance requires time is to extend credit to the latter. This is not the only solution of the difficulty. The extension of credit might be reversed (as where a student pays tuition in advance)...[O]ne may ask, why should the party whose promised performance takes time be required to extend credit to the one whose performance does not? The typical case falling under this rule—of which it is a kind of extrapolation—is the contract to do work for money. The usual practice in the community to which the rule was applicable was to pay for the work after it was completed. This 'belief as to the practice of a community or a class' is empirically verified, but it does not settle the questions of justice or policy with which the law is concerned. The practice may be ascribed to the influence of employers as a dominant class, and to judicial inertia which allows an outmoded rule to continue unchanged. The dominance of employers as a class is not what it used to be, yet no demand has appeared to require that employees generally be paid their wages or salaries in advance. There may be sufficient reasons for the survival of the rule. Professor Williston suggests two: 1. The normally greater responsibility of the employer; and 2. The fact that the employee cannot be compelled to perform specifically.

The policy of the law, here as in the tendency to construct concurrent conditions, is to minimize credit risks. If employers usually present less credit risks than employees, the rule of construction effectuates this end. That colleges and theatres ordinarily require payment in advance for the services which they furnish merely exemplifies the operation of the principle. A further justification may be found in the belief that a moderate postponement of reward stimulates productivity of social goods; such a belief is operative as a part of the mores of a particular culture. This justification, like the second reason given by Professor Williston, must be limited in scope of application, if it is not to conflict with the prohibition of involuntary servitude: that is, it may become a too-effective means of coercing the employee to work. The rule which makes performance by the employee a condition precedent of the duty of payment by the employer and which thus places the credit risk and the credit strain on the employee has been mitigated in its severity by statutes requiring that wages be paid at short intervals (weekly or bi-weekly) to certain classes of employees (in the lower income brackets), by provisions making wage claims preferred in the case of bankruptcy of the employer and by a limited relief for unjust enrichment. The order-of-performance test of credit burdens is thus supplemented by custom and by policy.

6. *The coercive function of constructive conditions.* The construction of conditions of exchange not only protects a contracting party against impairment of his expectations and enhancement of his credit burden, but also gives him a method of coercing performance. The coercive effect on the employee was pointed out above. So, in *Kingston v Preston*, the refusal of the defendant to turn over his business was a more effective way of inducing the clerk to give security than would have been an action for damages. The constructive condition thus supplements the limited remedies for specific performance by a kind of legalized self-help. The promisor's privilege of refusing performance until a condition is fulfilled is a continuation of the coercive power which he had before he contracted, the power which any man has to refuse to relinquish his property or to perform his services unless paid or promised such return as he chooses to exact. This coercive power is preserved after the making of the contract in so far as is compatible with the terms of the bargain.

III. ENTIRE AND SEVERABLE OBLIGATIONS

■ *Cutter v Powell*
(1795) 6 Term Rep 320

To assumpsit for work and labour done by the intestate, the defendant pleaded the general issue. And at the trial at Lancaster the jury found a verdict for the plaintiff for 31/10s subject to the opinion of his Court on the following case.

The defendant being at Jamaica subscribed and delivered to T. Cutter the intestate a note, whereof the following is a copy; 'Ten days after the ship "Governor Parry" myself master, arrives at Liverpool, I promise to pay to Mr T. Cutter the sum of thirty guineas, provided he proceeds continues and does his duty as second mate in the said ship from hence to the port of Liverpool, Kingston, July 31 st, 1793'. The ship 'Governor Parry' sailed from Kingston on the 2d of August 1793, and arrived in the port of Liverpool on the 9th of October following. T. Cutter went on board the ship on the 31st of July, 1793, and sailed in her on the 2d day of August, and proceeded, continued and did his duty as second mate in her from Kingston until his death which happened on the 20th of September following, and before the ship's arrival in the port of Liverpool. The usual wages of a second mate of a ship on such a voyage, when shipped by the month out and home is four pounds per month: but when seamen are shipped by the run from Jamaica to England a gross sum is usually given. The usual length of a voyage from Jamaica to Liverpool is about eight weeks.

This was argued last term by J. Haywood for the plaintiff: but the Court desired the case to stand over, that inquiries might be made relative to the usage in the commercial world on these kinds of agreements. It now appeared that there was no fixed settled usage one way or the other: but several instances were mentioned as having happened within these two years, in some of which the merchants had paid the whole wages under circumstances similar to the present, and in others a proportionable part...

Lord Kenyon CJ

I should be extremely sorry that in the decision of this case we should determine against what had been the received opinion in the mercantile world on contracts of this kind because it is of great importance that the laws by which the contracts of so numerous and so useful a body of men as the sailors are supposed to be guided should not be overturned. Whether these kind of notes are much in use among the seamen we are not sufficiently informed: and the instances now stated to us from Liverpool are too recent to form any thing like usage. But it seems to me at present that the decision of this case may proceed on the particular words of this contract and the precise facts here stated, without touching marine contracts in general. That where the parties have come to an express contract none can be implied has prevailed so long as to be reduced to an axiom in the law. Here the defendant expressly promised to pay the intestate thirty guineas, provided he proceeded, continued and did his duty as second mate in the ship from Jamaica to Liverpool: and the accompanying circumstances disclosed in the case are that the common rate of wages is four pounds per month, when the party is paid in proportion to the time he serves: and that this voyage is generally performed in two months. Therefore if there had been no contract between these parties, all that the intestate could have recovered on a quantum meruit for the voyage would have been eight pounds; whereas here the defendant contracted to pay thirty guineas provided the mate continued to do his duty as mate during the whole voyage, in which case the latter would have received nearly four times as much as if he were paid for the number of months he served. He stipulated to receive the larger sum if the whole duty were performed, and nothing unless the whole of that duty were performed: it was a kind of insurance. On this particular contract my opinion is formed at present; at the same time I must say that if we were assured that these notes are in universal use and that the commercial world have received and acted upon them in a different sense, I should give up my own opinion.

Ashhurst J

We cannot collect that there is any custom prevailing among merchants on these contracts; and therefore we have nothing to guide us but the terms of the contract itself. This is a written contract, and it speaks for itself. And as it is entire and as the defendant's promise depends on a condition precedent to be performed by the other party, the condition must be performed before the other party is entitled to receive any thing under it. It has been argued however that the plaintiff may now recover on a quantum meruit: but she has no right to desert the agreement; for wherever there is an express contract the parties must be guided by it; and one party cannot relinquish or abide by it as it may suit his advantage. Here the intestate was by the terms of his contract to perform a given duty before he could call upon the defendant to pay him any thing; it was a condition precedent, without performing which the defendant is not liable. And that seems to me to conclude the question: the intestate did not perform the contract on his part; he was not indeed to blame for not doing it; but still as this was a condition precedent and as he did not perform it, his representative is not entitled to recover.

Grose and **Lawrence JJ** delivered concurring judgments.

NOTES

1. Constructive conditions are just as much 'standard terms' as the risk allocations discussed in the last section, and it is just as pertinent to ask, what would the parties have agreed if their minds had been directed to the question?

2. Cutter had apparently 'done his duty as second mate' until the time he died. Why was the full 30 guineas not due to his estate when the ship arrived at Liverpool?

3. Normally, a contract of employment will be treated as severable, so that the employee earns payment for the period served. It seems that, at common law, the contract would be severable into units corresponding to the intervals at which the employee was to be paid. Thus in *Taylor v Laird* (1856) 1 H & N 266 25 LJ Ex 329, the plaintiff was employed to command a steamer 'for an exploring and trading voyage up the river Niger . . . at the rate of £50 per month'. The plaintiff took the vessel up as far as Dagbo, but refused to go further and abandoned the command. It was held that this was not a contract for the entire voyage: the phrase 'per month' showed that he was entitled to be paid for each month he served. Pollock CB said that the parties could not have intended the plaintiff to have received no payment if the voyage had not been completed for reasons outside his control. See now Apportionment Act 1870 (below). Why was the contract in *Cutter v Powell* not treated as one under which Cutter earned so much a day or a month?

■ Apportionment Act 1870

Section 2

All rents, annuities, dividends, and other periodical payments in the nature of income . . . shall, like interest on money lent, be considered as accruing from day to day, and shall be apportionable in respect of time accordingly.

Section 5

The word annuities includes salaries and pensions.

NOTES

1.   Does this statute affect the decision in *Cutter v Powell*? Was there any 'periodical payment' in that case?

2.   *Cutter v Powell*, the contract was, in modern parlance, frustrated by Cutter's death. It seems that the defendant had received a benefit from Cutter's performance before he died. Why did the plaintiff not have a remedy in restitution (the *quantum meruit* referred to in the judgments)? For a similar refusal to award a *quantum meruit* in a case of breach, see below. If the facts were to recur today, would Cutter's estate recover anything under the Law Reform (Frustrated Contracts) Act 1943?

■ Sale of Goods Act 1979

Section 30

(1)   Where the seller delivers to the buyer a quantity of goods less than he contracted to sell, the buyer may reject them, but if the buyer accepts the goods so delivered he must pay for them at the contract rate.

(2)   Where the seller delivers to the buyer a quantity of goods larger than he contracted to sell, the buyer may accept the goods included in the contract and reject the rest, or he may reject the whole.

(2A)   A buyer who does not deal as consumer may not—

    (a)   where the seller delivers a quantity of goods less than he contracted to sell, reject the goods under subsection (1) above, or

    (b)   where the seller delivers a quantity of goods larger than he contracted to sell, reject the whole under subsection (2) above,

    if the shortfall or, as the case may be, excess is so slight that it would be unreasonable for him to do so.

(2B)   It is for the seller to show that a shortfall or excess fell within subsection (2A) above.

. . .

(3)   Where the seller delivers to the buyer a quantity of goods larger than he contracted to sell and the buyer accepts the whole of the goods so delivered he must pay for them at the contract rate.

(4)   (repealed).

(5)   This section is subject to any usage of trade, special agreement, or course of dealing between the parties.

Section 31

(1)   Unless otherwise agreed, the buyer of goods is not bound to accept delivery of them by instalments.

(2)   Where there is a contract for the sale of goods to be delivered by stated instalments, which are to be separately paid for, and the seller makes defective deliveries in respect of one or more instalments, or the buyer neglects or refuses to take delivery of or pay for one or more instalments, it is a question in each case depending on the terms of the contract and the circumstances of the case whether the breach of contract is a repudiation of the whole contract or whether it is a severable breach giving rise to a claim for compensation but not to a right to treat the whole contract as repudiated.

NOTES

1.   The effect of s 30 is that, unless the parties have agreed to delivery by instalments, a contract for the sale of goods is 'entire as to quantity', so that if the seller delivers too little or

too much the buyer need not perform its side. If the time for performance has not yet expired, the seller may make a fresh tender, and meanwhile, the buyer only has the right to withhold until a proper tender is made. If the time for performance has expired, the buyer may refuse any further tender and terminate the contract.

2.   Subsections 30(2A) and (2B) were added by the Sale and Supply of Goods Act 1994, s 4. Subsection 30 (4) was repealed by s 3(3) of the same Act; see now the new s 35A, below.

3.   In *Shipton Anderson & Cov Weil Bros* [1912] 1 KB 574, it was held that a firm that had agreed to buy 4,950 tons of wheat could not reject the goods when an extra 55 lbs were delivered. Subject to this *de minimis* rule, any breach of s 30(1) or (2) used to justify rejection. The aim of the new subs (2A) is to prevent non-consumer buyers rejecting when the discrepancy in quantity is more than trivial but still rejection is unreasonable: see p 598.

IV. EFFECT OF PARTIAL PERFORMANCE OF AN ENTIRE OBLIGATION

■ *Sumpter v Hedges*

[1898] 1 QB 673, Court of Appeal

(Note that a lump-sum building contract is normally construed as entire, so that no part of the contract price is due until completion.)

Appeal from the judgment of Bruce J at the trial before him without a jury.

The action was for work done and materials provided. The plaintiff, a builder, had contracted with the defendant to build upon the defendant's land two houses and stables for the sum of £565. The plaintiff did part of the work, amounting in value to about £333 and had received payment of part of the price. He then informed the defendant that he had no money, and could not go on with the work. The learned judge found that he had abandoned the contract. The defendant thereupon finished the buildings on his own account, using for that purpose certain building materials which the plaintiff had left on the ground. The judge gave judgment for the plaintiff for the value of the materials so used, but allowed him nothing in respect of the work which he had done upon the buildings.

Collins LJ

. . . I think the case is really concluded by the finding of the learned judge to the effect that the plaintiff had abandoned the contract. If the plaintiff had merely broken his contract in some way so as not to give the defendant the right to treat him as having abandoned the contract, and the defendant had then proceeded to finish the work himself, the plaintiff might perhaps have been entitled to sue on a quantum meruit on the ground that the defendant had taken the benefit of the work done. But that is not the present case. There are cases in which, though the plaintiff has abandoned the performance of a contract, it is possible for him to raise the inference of a new contract to pay for the work done on a quantum meruit from the defendant's having taken the benefit of that work, but, in order that that may be done, the circumstances must be such as to give an option to the defendant to take or not to take the benefit of the work done. It is only where the circumstances are such as to give that option that there is any evidence on which to ground the inference of a new contract. Where, as in the case of work done on land, the circumstances are such as to give the defendant no option whether he will take the benefit of the work or not, then one must look to other facts than the mere taking the benefit of the work in

order to ground the inference of a new contract. In this case I see no other facts on which such an inference can be founded. The mere fact that a defendant is in possession of what he cannot help keeping,
or even has done work upon it, affords no ground for such an inference. He is not bound to keep unfin-
ished a building which in an incomplete state would be a nuisance on his land. I am therefore of opinion that the plaintiff was not entitled to recover for the work which he had done.

A L Smith and **Chitty LJJ** delivered concurring judgments.

Appeal dismissed.

NOTES

1. The judgment for the cost of the materials was not appealed against. Why was the
   defendant liable for this? Goff and Jones, pp 441–442, argue that the defendant is liable
   for the value of the materials because he 'freely accepted' them (compare pp 42–43).

2. In *Sumpter v Hedges*, the builder had in fact received some payment (although he had no
   right to it), but the reasoning would be exactly the same if he had received nothing. You
   may have noticed exactly this result, and the same reasoning being used, in *Cutter v
   Powell* (p 556). To mitigate this harsh rule, the courts will try to find the contract severable (see *Appleby v Myers* (1867) LR 2 CP 651, 660), but in a lump-sum building contract
   this will normally be impossible, because there is no way of apportioning the price over
   the various items of work. (Some sophisticated building contracts do contain 'bills of
   quantities', which are lists of the items to be done, with unit prices inserted; these prices
   will not represent accurately the cost of doing each unit when the contract is only partly
   performed. They are intended primarily for valuing 'variations', eg additions to the work
   originally specified—see p 881—and may represent only the marginal cost of performing one additional unit.) Instead, the doctrine of 'substantial performance' has been
   developed.

■ *Hoenig v Isaacs*

[1952] 2 All ER 176, Court of Appeal

The defendant employed the plaintiff to decorate and furnish the defendant's flat for £750.
The work was finished bar some defects in a bookcase and a wardrobe, which would cost
about £55 to rectify, and the defendant moved into the flat, but he refused to pay the outstanding balance of the contract price.

Somervell LJ

...Each case turns on the construction of the contract. In *Cutter v Powell* the condition for the promissory note sued on was that the sailor should proceed to continue and do his duty as second mate in the
ship from Jamaica to the port of Liverpool. The sailor died before the ship reached Liverpool and it was
held his estate could not recover either on the contract or on a quantum meruit. It clearly decided that
his continuing as mate during the whole voyage was a condition precedent to payment. It did not decide
that if he had completed the main purpose of the contract, namely, serving as mate for the whole voyage, the defendant could have repudiated his liability by establishing that in the course of the voyage the
sailor had, possibly through inadvertence, failed on some occasion in his duty as mate whereby some
damage had been caused. ...

The learned official referee regarded *H Dakin & Co Ltd v Lee* laying down that the price must be paid
subject to set-off or counterclaim if there was a substantial compliance with the contract. I think on the

facts of this case where the work was finished in the ordinary sense, though in part defective, this is right. It expresses in a convenient epithet what is put from another angle in the Sale of Goods Act. 1893. The buyer cannot reject if he proves only the breach of a term collateral to the main purpose. I have, therefore, come to the conclusion that the first point of counsel for the defendant fails.

The learned official referee found that there was substantial compliance. Bearing in mind that there is an appeal on fact, was there evidence on which he could so find? The learned official referee having, as I hold, properly directed himself, this becomes, I think, a question of fact. The case on this point was, I think, near the border line, and if the finding had been the other way I do not think we could have interfered. Even if I had felt we could interfere, the defendant would be in a further difficulty. The contract included a number of chattels. If the defendant wished to repudiate his liability under the contract he should not, I think, have used those articles which he could have avoided using. On this view, though it is not necessary to decide it. I think he put himself in the same position as a buyer of goods who by accepting them elects to treat a breach of condition as a breach of warranty.

Denning LJ

This case raises the familiar question: Was entire performance a condition precedent to payment? That depends on the true construction of the contract. In this case the contract was made over a period of time and was partly oral and partly in writing, but I agree with the official referee that the essential terms were set down in the letter of Apr 25, 1950. It describes the work which was to be done and concludes with these words:

> 'The foregoing, complete, for the sum of £750 net. Terms of payment are net cash, as the work proceeds. and balance on completion.'

The question of law that was debated before us was whether the plaintiff was entitled in this action to sue for the £350 balance of the contract price as he had done. The defendant said that he was only entitled to sue on a quantum meruit. The defendant was anxious to insist on a quantum meruit, because he said that the contract price was unreasonably high. He wished, therefore, to reject that price altogether and simply to pay a reasonable price for all the work that was done. This would obviously mean an inquiry into the value of every item, including all the many items which were in compliance with the contract as well as the three which fell short of it. That is what the defendant wanted. The plaintiff resisted this course and refused to claim on a quantum meruit. He said that he was entitled to the balance of £350 less a deduction for the defects.

In determining this issue the first question is whether, on the true construction of the contract, entire performance was a condition precedent to payment. It was a lump sum contract, but that does not mean that entire performance was a condition precedent to payment. When a contract provides for a specific sum to be paid on completion of specified work, the courts lean against a construction of the contract which would deprive the contractor of any payment at all simply because there are some defects or omissions. The promise to complete the work is, therefore, construed as a term of the contract, but not as a condition. It is not every breach of that term which absolves the employer from his promise to pay the price, but only a breach which goes to the root of the contract, such as an abandonment of the work when it is only half done. Unless the breach does go to the root of the matter, the employer cannot resist payment of the price. He must pay it and bring a cross-claim for the defects and omissions, or, alternatively, set them up in diminution of the price. The measure is the amount which the work is worth less by reason of the defects and omissions, and is usually calculated by the cost of making them good: see *Mondel v Steel; H Dakin & Co Ltd v Lee* and the notes to *Cutter v Powell* in *Smith's Leading Cases*, 13th edn, vol 2, pp 19–21. It is, of course, always open to the parties by express words to make entire performance a condition precedent. A familiar instance is when the contract provides for progress payments to be made as the work proceeds, but for retention money to be held until completion. Then entire performance is usually a condition precedent to payment of the retention money, but not, of course, to the progress payments. The contractor is entitled to payment pro rata as the work proceeds, less a deduction for retention money. But he is not entitled to the retention money until the work is entirely finished, without defects or omission.... But... I think this contract should be regarded as an ordinary lump sum contract. It was substantially performed. The contractor is entitled, therefore, to the contract price, less a deduction for the defects.

Even if entire performance was a condition precedent, nevertheless the result would be the same, because I think the condition was waived...[The defendant] did not refuse to accept the work. On the contrary, he entered into possession of the flat and used the furniture as his own, including the defective items. That was a clear waiver of the condition precedent. Just as in a sale of goods the buyer who accepts the goods can no longer treat a breach of condition as giving a right to reject but only a right to damages, so also in a contract for work and labour an employer who takes the benefit of the work can no longer treat entire performance as a condition precedent, but only as a term giving rise to damages.

Romer LJ

...The position is, I think, in some respects analogous to a case where a man agrees to sell land and, before completion, finds that he is unable to make title to a small part of it which is of no great significance in relation to the whole. In such a case the vendor can substantially perform what he has agreed to do but cannot perform it wholly, and the Court of Chancery has never hesitated to grant specific performance at this instance against the purchaser subject to a proper and reasonable deduction being made in the purchase price. It would not, however, make such an order if it resulted in the purchaser getting something substantially less than or different from what he had bargained for.... I am, accordingly, of the opinion, as already indicated, that the learned official referee fell into no error of law and that this appeal fails. If, however, I had come to a different conclusion on the point which I have been considering I should, nevertheless, be inclined to the view (for the reasons stated by Denning LJ in his judgment) that the appeal must fail on the ground of the defendant's waiver.

Appeal dismissed.

NOTES

1.   Which is the better way of expressing the substantial performance rule: that the builder is entitled to the price once he has done almost all the work, or that he is entitled to it once he has done all the work, even though some of it is defective?

2.   Corbin, 'Conditions in the Law of Contract' (1919) 28 Yale LJ 739, 759 explains the doctrine of substantial performance thus:

> It is correct to say that substantial performance *of a condition* is sufficient; but it is frequently correct to say that absolutely exact and complete performance by the plaintiff as promised is not a condition precedent to the duty of the defendant. If substantial performance by the plaintiff was sufficient to charge the defendant, then such substantial performance was the only condition and the requirement has been exactly fulfilled. The question of the plaintiff's duty to pay damages for his own partial non-performance is a different question altogether. Substantial performance of A's promise may be sufficient to enable him to maintain action against B, and yet at the same time be insufficient to prevent B from having an action against A.

3.   Two members of the court considered that the defendant had waived any condition precedent. Given that the work was being done in the plaintiff's flat, is that consistent with *Sumpter v Hedges?* Would it be more accurate to say that he had waived the right to refuse payment for the furniture?

4.   Romer LJ refers to cases in which a vendor of land can obtain specific performance although he cannot make title to a small part of the land. An example is *Re Fawcett and Holmes' Contract* (1889) 42 ChD 150.

5. Denning LJ refers to a scheme of interim payments with retention money. The following is an example of such a scheme:

30.(3)(a) In respect of any Interim Certificate issued before the issue of the Certificate of Practical Completion the Employer may, subject to paragraph (c) of this sub-clause, retain a percentage (in these Conditions called 'the Retention Percentage') of the total value of the work, materials and goods referred to.... The Retention Percentage shall be 5 per cent. unless a lower rate shall be agreed between the parties and specified in the Appendix to these Conditions as the Retention Percentage....

(4)(b) On the issue of the Certificate of Practical Completion the Architect shall issue a certificate for one moiety of the total amounts then so retained and the Contractor shall, on presenting any such certificate to the Employer, be entitled to payment of the said moiety within 14 days from the presentation of that certificate.

(4)(c) On the expiration of the Defects Liability Period named in the Appendix to these Conditions, or on the issue of the Certificate of Completion of Making Good Defects, whichever is the later, the Architect shall issue a Certificate for the residue of the amounts then so retained and the Contractor shall, on presenting any such certificate to the Employer, be entitled to payment of the said residue within 14 days from the presentation of that certificate.

(Joint Contracts Tribunal Form of Building Contract, 1963)

6. In *Hoenig v Isaacs*, you can see a subplot emerging: it is not fair to allow the defendant to use some minor failure or imperfection as an excuse for not paying the price. Note, however, that the substantial performance rule only allows the builder to recover the price if the defects or shortcomings are slight. The employer doesn't have to pay if the work isn't substantially complete, even if a lot of it has been done. In *Bolton v Mahadeva* [1972] 1 WLR 1009, CA, the plaintiff agreed to install central heating in the defendant's house for a lump sum of £560. The system gave off insufficient and uneven heat, and also gave off fumes. The plaintiff refused to correct the defects, which could be put right for about £174. The defendant refused to pay anything, and the Court of Appeal held that the plaintiff was not entitled to recover, because there had been no substantial performance. Sachs LJ remarked (at 1015):

It is not merely that so very much of the work was shoddy, but it is the general ineffectiveness of it for its primary purpose that leads me to that conclusion.

7. The Law Commission, in its Report No 121, 'Pecuniary Restitution for Breach of Contract' (1983), criticised (at para 2.32) the result of cases such as *Bolton v Mahadeva*:

... [T]he mischief which we have identified is not that the parties can require complete performance before any counter-performance is due, but that under the present law they may, and usually will, be held to have done so merely by providing for postponement of payment. In our view the present law leads to a result which was not necessarily the one which the parties in all cases would have contemplated as flowing from their agreement solely by reason of the postponement of payment.

The Commission recommended that the law should be changed, so that a party who in breach of contract fails to complete an entire contract, but who by part-performance has conferred a net benefit on the innocent party, should be entitled to some payment, unless the contract expressly stipulated otherwise. However, Brian Davenport QC wrote a note of dissent:

Note of dissent
I have the misfortune to differ from my colleagues both as regards the principal policy conclusion reached in this report and as to the manner of its implementation. In almost all contracts of any

substance today under which one party promises to carry out certain work in return for a consideration to be given by the other, the contract will make provision for stage payments of one sort or another. The facts of modern economic life have demonstrated that payments on account while the work proceeds are a necessity. Both printed and specially prepared contracts will therefore, in almost every case, provide for such payments. Where a written contract does not provide for such payments, the reason may well be that the parties intended that payment would be due if, but only if, the contractor finished the work. The so-called mischief which the report is intended to correct is therefore likely only to exist in relation to small, informal contracts of which the normal example will be a contract between a householder and a jobbing builder to carry out a particular item of work. Experience has shown that it is all too common for such builders not to complete one job of work before moving on to the next. The effect of the report is to remove from the householder almost the only effective sanction he has against the builder not completing the job. In short, he is prevented from saying with any legal effect. 'Unless you come back and finish the job, I shan't pay you a penny'. In my view, the disadvantages in practice of the recommendations contained in the report outweigh the advantages to be gained from the search for theoretically perfect justice between the parties. If the report's recommendations are implemented, the jobbing builder can leave the site and, when the irate and exasperated householder finally brings the contract to an end, send in a bill for the work done up to the time when he abandoned the site. It will then be for the householder to dispute the amount and calculate his counter-claim for damages. To put the burden on the householder in this manner is, in my view, to put him in a disadvantageous position where he negotiates from a position of weakness. It must not be forgotten that it is the builder who has broken the contract, not the householder, and that the contract is one under which the parties agreed that payment would be by lump-sum only when the work was done. ....

It is understood that the recommendation in the Report has not been accepted. For criticism, see Burrows, pp 354–357.

V. CONDITIONS AND WARRANTIES

In all of the cases so far, the obligation that had to be performed as a condition of the other party's performance being due was clearly basic to the contract, and if there was not at least substantial performance, the result would be that the other party would not get the substance of what he contracted for. Clearly, not every non-performance of a contractual term would have this result. What if the obligation left unperformed was not so obviously basic? During the first half of the twentieth century, it became customary to deal with this problem by asking whether the term that had not been performed was a condition or merely a warranty. The distinction was explained by Fletcher Moulton LJ, in his dissenting judgment in *Wallis, Son & Wells v Pratt and Haynes* [1910] 2 KB 1003, in the following terms:

A party to a contract who has performed or is ready and willing to perform his obligations under that contract is entitled to the performance by the other contracting party of all the obligations which rest upon him. But from a very early period of our law it has been recognised that such obligations are not all of equal importance. There are some which go so directly to the substance of the contract, or, in other words, are so essential to its very nature, that their non-performance may fairly be considered by the other party as a substantial failure to perform the contract at all. On the other hand, there are other obligations which, though they must be performed, are not so vital that a failure to perform them goes to the substance of the contract. Both clauses are equally obligations under the contract, and the breach of any one of them entitles the other party to damages. But in the case of the former class he has the alternative of treating the contract as being completely broken by the non-performance, and (if he takes proper steps) he can refuse to perform any of the obligations resting upon himself and sue the other party for a total failure to perform the contract . . .

This usage has been followed in the codification of the law of the contract of sale in the Sale of Goods Act. . . .

Fletcher Moulton's judgment was approved by the House of Lords [1911] AC 394.

■ Sale of Goods Act 1979

Section 11 . . .

(2) Where a contract of sale is subject to a condition to be fulfilled by the seller, the buyer may waive the condition, or may elect to treat the breach of the condition as a breach of warranty and not as a ground for treating the contract as repudiated.

(3) Whether a stipulation in a contract of sale is a condition, the breach of which may give rise to a right to treat the contract as repudiated, or a warranty, the breach of which may give rise to a claim for damages but not to a right to reject the goods and treat the contract as repudiated, depends in each case on the construction of the contract; and a stipulation may be a condition, though called a warranty in the contract.

(4) Subject to s 35A below, where a contract of sale is not severable and the buyer has accepted the goods or part of them, the breach of a condition to be fulfilled by the seller can only be treated as a breach of warranty, and not as a ground for rejecting the goods and treating the contract as repudiated, unless there is an express or implied term of the contract to that effect.

NOTES

1. The terms 'condition' and 'warranty' can be confusing. Firstly (as noted on p 426), both have more general meanings: 'condition' is often used to mean just a term of a contract, as in the phrase 'conditions of contract', while 'warranty' is often used to denote a promise as to the quality of goods, as in the 'term or representation' cases (see p 323). Some of the promises were so crucial that they almost certainly were conditions in the technical sense, so that the buyer could refuse to accept goods that did not have the promised quality.

2. Secondly, as Reynolds, 'Warranty, condition and fundamental term' (1963) 79 LQR 534, 539, remarks:

The terminology [of 'condition' and 'warranty'] confuses . . . formation with performance: what is referred to as a condition is actually a promise the performance of which is a condition of the other party's liability. And, as Diplock LJ points out in the *Hong Kong Fir* case, it is the situation which ensues when one party fails to perform that entitles the other party to repudiate: whereas this terminology attracts attention away from that situation and focuses it upon the promise instead. In this respect it is misleading.

3. A further confusion can be caused by the not uncommon habit of referring to a warranty (in the technical sense) as an 'independent covenant'. What is meant is that a failure to perform the warranty does not justify the refusal to perform the rest of the contract. Thus if you order a new car, and one of the terms is that the seller is to fit the car with a radio, but the seller delivers the car without the radio, you would not be justified in refusing to accept the car. The obligation to fit the radio is probably only a warranty: you can get one fitted easily at some other garage, so damages will be adequate compensation. If

the word 'independent' is to be used at all, it might be better to say that the rest of the contract is independent of the warranty. In contrast, if the car turned out not to be new (it is a 'demonstrator', for instance), there is a breach of condition and you can refuse to accept the car: see *Andrews Bros Ltd v Singer & Co Ltd*, noted at **p 839**. Your obligation to accept the car is dependent on its being new.

A term may be a condition because the contract expressly says so. This is considered in detail below. Alternatively, a term may be a condition because statute so provides (eg Sale of Goods Act 1979, ss 13–15—see p 427, but note the qualifications referred to at pp 598 and 619 below, s 28—see p 554 or s 30—see p 558); or because the court construes it as one.

■ *Bentsen v Taylor, Sons & Co (No 2)*
[1893] 2 QB 274, Court of Appeal

A charterparty described the ship as 'now sailed or about to sail from a pitch pine port to the UK'. She did not in fact sail until over three weeks after the date of the charter. The charterers discovered what had occurred and entered into correspondence with the owner's brokers; ultimately, when the ship arrived, they refused to load.

Bowen LJ

...Of course it is often very difficult to decide as a matter of construction whether a representation which contains a promise, and which can only be explained on the ground that it is in itself a substantive part of the contract, amounts to a condition precedent, or is only a warranty. There is no way of deciding that question except by looking at the contract in the light of the surrounding circumstances, and then making up one's mind whether the intention of the parties, as gathered from the instrument itself, will best be carried out by treating the promise as a warranty sounding only in damages, or as a condition precedent by the failure to perform which the other party is relieved of his liability. In order to decide this question of construction, one of the first things you would look to is, to what extent the accuracy of the statement—the truth of what is promised—would be likely to affect the substance and foundation of the adventure which the contract is intended to carry out. There, again, it might be necessary to have recourse to the jury. In the case of a charterparty it may well be that such a test could only be applied after getting the jury to say what the effect of a breach of such a condition would be on the substance and foundation of the adventure: not the effect of the breach which has in fact taken place, but the effect likely to be produced on the foundation of the adventure by any such breach of that portion of the contract.

Applying this test, Bowen LJ held that the statement that the ship had sailed or was about to sail amounted to a condition precedent. He went on to hold, however, that the charterers had waived their right to terminate. **Lord Esher MR** and **Kay LJ** gave judgment to the same effect.

VI. A MORE FLEXIBLE APPROACH

Any failure to perform a condition will give the other party the right to refuse to perform. The only qualifications are the *de minimis* rule and certain exceptions recently introduced into the Sale of Goods Act (see pp 558 and 598). Before those exceptions came into force, a party might use a technical breach of the terms implied under the Act as an excuse for getting out of a contract even though the breach did it little or no harm. For example, in *Arcos Ltd v Ronaasen &*

Son (see p 429), the buyers terminated on the ground that the barrel staves delivered did not accord with the description under s 13. The staves were still perfectly good for the buyers' purpose and it seems the buyers' motivation to escape the contract was that the market had fallen and similar goods could now be obtained more cheaply. This example would probably now fall within the recent changes to the Sale of Goods Act, but the general rule remains that any breach of a condition entitles the innocent party to terminate the contract.

■ *Hong Kong Fir Shipping Co Ltd v Kawasaki Kisen Kaisha Ltd*
[1962] 1 All ER 474, Court of Appeal

A 24-month time charter provided that the vessel was to be delivered to the charterers at Liverpool, 'she being in every way fitted for ordinary cargo service'. The 'off-hire' clause provided that the charterers need not pay hire in respect of periods over 24 hours lost in carrying out repairs, and that such off-hire periods might, at the charterers' option, be added to the hire period. (The charter was on the Baltime 1939 form: see p 1224.) The vessel left for Newport News, to load a cargo of coal for carriage to Osaka. At the date of her delivery, the ship was unseaworthy because she had old engines that required careful supervision, whereas her engine-room staff was undermanned and inefficient. As a result, repairs had to be carried out on the way to Osaka, and after her arrival there, and it took a total of 18 weeks to make her seaworthy. This left a period of 17 months during which she could be available to the charterers. There had been a steep fall in freight rates since the date of the charter, and the charterers purported to terminate. Salmon J held that they had no right to do so, and they appealed.

Sellers LJ held that there had been only a breach of warranty.

Upjohn LJ

... Why is this apparently basic and underlying condition of seaworthiness not, in fact, treated as a condition? It is for the simple reason that the seaworthiness clause is breached by the slightest failure to be fitted 'in every way' for service. Thus, to take examples from the judgments in some of the cases I have mentioned above, if a nail is missing from one of the timbers of a wooden vessel, or if proper medical supplies or two anchors are not on board at the time of sailing, the owners are in breach of the seaworthiness stipulation. It is contrary to common sense to suppose that, in such circumstances, the parties contemplated that the charterer should at once be entitled to treat the contract as at an end for such trifling breaches. ...

... It is open to the parties to a contract to make it clear either expressly or by necessary implication that a particular stipulation is to be regarded as a condition which goes to the root of the contract, so that it is clear that the parties contemplate that *any* breach of it entitles the other party at once to treat the contract as at an end. That matter is to be determined as a question of the proper interpretation of the contract. Where ... on the true construction of the contract, the parties have not made a particular stipulation a condition, it would be unsound and misleading to conclude that, being a warranty, damages is a sufficient remedy.

In my judgment, the remedies open to the innocent party for breach of a stipulation which is not a condition strictly so called, depend entirely on the nature of the breach and its foreseeable consequences. Breaches of stipulation fall, naturally, into two classes. First, there is the case where the owner by his conduct indicates that he considers himself no longer bound to perform his part of the contract: in that case, of course, the charterer may accept the repudiation and treat the contract as at an end. The second class of case is, of course, the more usual one, and that is where, due to misfortune such as the perils of the sea, engine failures, incompetence of the crew and so on, the owner is unable to perform a particular stipulation precisely in accordance with the terms of the contract try he never so hard to remedy it. In that case, the question to be answered is, does the breach of the stipulation go so much to the root of the contract that it makes further commercial performance of the contract impossible, or, in other words, is the whole contract frustrated? If yea, the innocent party may treat the contract as at an end. If nay, his claim sounds in damages only.

If I have correctly stated the principles, then, as the stipulation as to seaworthiness is not a condition in the strict sense, the question to be answered is, did the initial unseaworthiness as found by the learned judge, from which finding there has been no appeal, go so much to the root of the contract that the charterers were then and there entitled to treat the charterparty as at an end? The only unseaworthiness alleged, serious though it was, was the insufficiency and incompetence of the crew, but that surely cannot be treated as going to the root of the contract for the parties must have contemplated that, in such an event, the crew could be changed and augmented. In my judgment, on this part of his case counsel for the charterers necessarily fails.

I turn, therefore, to his second point: Where there have been serious and repeated delays due to the inability of the owner to perform his part of the contract, is the charterer entitled to treat the contract as repudiated after a reasonable time, or can he do so only if delays are such as to amount to a frustration of the contract? Some of my earlier observations on the remedy available for breach of contract are relevant here, but I do not repeat them. I agree with the conclusions reached by the learned judge and by Sellers LJ . . . Accordingly, I agree that this appeal must be dismissed.

Diplock L J

. . . Every synallagmatic contract contains in it the seeds of the problem: in what event will a party be relieved of his undertaking to do that which he has agreed to do but has not yet done? The contract may itself expressly define some of these events, as in the cancellation clause in a charterparty, but, human prescience being limited, it seldom does so exhaustively and often fails to do so at all. In some classes of contracts, such as sale of goods, marine insurance, contracts of affreightment evidenced by bills of lading and those between parties to bills of exchange. Parliament has defined by statute some of the events not provided for expressly in individual contracts of that class; but, where an event occurs the occurrence of which neither the parties nor Parliament have expressly stated will discharge one of the parties from further performance of his undertakings, it is for the court to determine whether the event has this effect or not. The test whether an event has this effect or not has been stated in a number of metaphors all of which I think amount to the same thing: does the occurrence of the event deprive the party who has further undertakings still to perform of substantially the whole benefit which it was the intention of the parties as expressed in the contract that he should obtain as the consideration for performing those undertakings? This test is applicable whether or not the event occurs as a result of the default of one of the parties to the contract, but the consequences of the event are different in the two cases. Where the event occurs as a result of the default of one party, the party in default cannot rely on it as relieving himself of the performance of any further undertakings on his part and the innocent party, although entitled to, need not treat the event as relieving him of the performance of his own undertakings. This is only a specific application of the fundamental legal and moral rule that a man should not be allowed to take advantage of his own wrong. Where the event occurs as a result of the default of neither party, each is relieved of the further performance of his own undertakings, and their rights in respect of undertakings previously performed are now regulated by the Law Reform (Frustrated Contracts) Act, 1943.

This branch of the common law has reached its present stage by the normal process of historical growth, and the fallacy in counsel for the charterers' contention that a different test is applicable when the event occurs as a result of the default of one party from that applicable in cases of frustration where the event occurs as a result of the default of neither party arises, in my view, from a failure to view the cases in their historical context. The problem: in what event will a party to a contract be relieved of his undertaking to do that which he has agreed to do but has not yet done? has exercised the English courts for centuries, probably ever since assumpsit emerged as a form of action distinct from covenant and debt, and long before even the earliest cases which we have been invited to examine: but, until the rigour of the rule in *Paradine v Jane* was mitigated in the middle of the last century by the classic judgments of Blackburn J in *Taylor v Caldwell* and Bramwell B in *Jackson v Union Marine Insurance Co*, it was in general only events resulting from one party's failure to perform his contractual obligations which were regarded as capable of relieving the other party from continuing to perform that which he had undertaken to do. . . .

Once it is appreciated that it is the event and not the fact that the event is a result of a breach of contract which relieves the party not in default of further performance of his obligations, two consequences follow: (i) The test whether the event relied on has this consequence is the same whether the event is the result of the other party's breach of contract or not, as Devlin J pointed out in *Universal Cargo Carriers Corpn v Citati*. (ii) The question whether an event which is the result of the other party's breach of contract has this consequence cannot be answered by treating all contractual undertakings as falling into one of two separate categories: 'conditions', the breach of which gives rise to an event which relieves the party not in default of further performance of his obligations, and 'warranties', the breach of which does not give rise to such an event. Lawyers tend to speak of this classification as if it were comprehensive, partly for the historical reasons which I have already mentioned, and partly because Parliament itself adopted it in the Sale of Goods Act, 1893, as respects a number of implied terms in contracts for the sale of goods and has in that Act used the expressions 'condition' and 'warranty' in that meaning. But it is by no means true of contractual undertakings in general at common law.

No doubt there are many simple contractual undertakings, sometimes express, but more often because of their very simplicity ('It goes without saying') to be implied, of which it can be predicated that every breach of such an undertaking must give rise to an event which will deprive the party not in default of substantially the whole benefit which it was intended that he should obtain from the contract. And such a stipulation, unless the parties have agreed that breach of it shall not entitle the non-defaulting party to treat the contract as repudiated, is a 'condition'. So, too, there may be other simple contractual undertakings of which it can be predicated that *no* breach can give rise to an event which will deprive the party not in default of substantially the whole benefit which it was intended that he should obtain from the contract; and such a stipulation, unless the parties have agreed that breach of it shall entitle the non-defaulting party to treat the contract as repudiated, is a 'warranty'. There are, however, many contractual undertakings of a more complex character which cannot be categorised as being 'conditions' or 'warranties' if the late nineteenth century meaning adopted in the Sale of Goods Act, 1893, and used by Bowen LJ in *Bentsen v Taylor, Sons & Co*, be given to those terms. Of such undertakings, all that can be predicated is that some breaches will, and others will not, give rise to an event which will deprive the party not in default of substantially the whole benefit which it was intended that he should obtain from the contract; and the legal consequences of a breach of such an undertaking, unless provided for expressly in the contract, depend on the nature of the event to which the breach gives rise and do not follow automatically from a prior classification of the undertaking as a 'condition' or a 'warranty'. For instance, to take the example of Bramwell B in *Jackson v Union Marine Insurance Co*, by itself breach of an undertaking by a shipowner to sail with all possible despatch to a named port does not necessarily relieve the charterer of further performance of his obligation under the charterparty, but, if the breach is so prolonged that the contemplated voyage is frustrated, it does have this effect.

As my brethren have already pointed out, the shipowner's undertaking to tender a seaworthy ship has, as a result of numerous decisions as to what can amount to 'unseaworthiness', become one of the most complex of contractual undertakings. It embraces obligations with respect to every part of the hull and machinery, stores and equipment and the crew itself. It can be broken by the presence of trivial defects easily and rapidly remediable as well as by defects which must inevitably result in a total loss of the vessel. Consequently, the problem in this case is, in my view, neither solved nor soluble by debating whether the owners' express or implied undertaking to tender a seaworthy ship is a 'condition' or a 'warranty'. It is, like so many other contractual terms, an undertaking one breach of which may give rise to an event which relieves the charterer of further performance of his undertakings if he so elects, and another breach of which may not give rise to such an event but entitle him only to monetary compensation in the form of damages. It is, with all deference to counsel for the charterers' skilful argument, by no means surprising that, among the many hundreds of previous cases about the shipowner's undertaking to deliver a seaworthy ship, there is none where it was found profitable to discuss in the judgments the question whether that undertaking is a 'condition' or a 'warranty': for the true answer, as I have already indicated, is that it is neither, but one of that large class of contractual undertakings, one breach of which may have the same effect as that ascribed to a breach of 'condition' under the Sale of Goods Act, 1893, and a different breach of which may have only the same effect as that ascribed to a breach of 'warranty' under that Act. . . .

What the learned judge had to do in the present case as in any other case where one party to a contract relies on a breach by the other party as giving him a right to elect to rescind the contract, was to look at the events which had occurred as a result of the breach at the time at which the charterers purported to rescind the charterparty, and to decide whether the occurrence of those events deprived the charterers of substantially the whole benefit which it was the intention of the parties as expressed in the charterparty that the charterers should obtain from the further performance of their own contractual undertakings. One turns, therefore, to the contract, the Baltime 1939 Charter. Clause 13, the 'due diligence' clause, which exempts the shipowners from responsibility for delay or loss or damage to goods on board due to unseaworthiness unless such delay or loss or damage has been caused by want of due diligence of the owners in making the vessel seaworthy and fitted for the voyage, is in itself sufficient to show that the mere occurrence of the events that the vessel was in some respect unseaworthy when tendered or that such unseaworthiness had caused some delay in performance of the charterparty would not deprive the charterer of the whole benefit which it was the intention of the parties he should obtain from the performance of his obligations under the contract—for he undertakes to continue to perform his obligations notwithstanding the occurrence of such events if they fall short of frustration of the contract and even deprives himself of any remedy in damages unless such events are the consequence of want of due diligence on the part of the shipowner.

The question which the learned judge had to ask himself was, as he rightly decided, whether or not, at the date when the charterers purported to rescind the contract, namely June 6, 1957, or when the owners purported to accept such rescission, namely Aug 8, 1957, the delay which had already occurred as a result of the incompetence of the engine-room staff, and the delay which was likely to occur in repairing the engines of the vessel and the conduct of the owners by that date in taking steps to remedy these two matters, were, when taken together, such as to deprive the charterers of substantially the whole benefit which it was the intention of the parties they should obtain from further use of the vessel under the charterparty. In my view, in his judgment—on which I would not seek to improve—the learned judge took into account and gave due weight to all the relevant considerations and arrived at the right answer for the right reasons.

Appeal dismissed.

NOTES

1.   Diplock LJ seems to suggest that a term will be a condition only if the agreement so provides, or if 'it can be predicated that every breach of such an undertaking must give rise to an event which will deprive the party not in default of substantially the whole benefit . . .'. Upjohn LJ, in contrast, recognises that a term may be a condition by *implication*, without such serious consequences necessarily being entailed. The House of Lords has since held that the latter is the correct position: *Bunge v Tradax*, see p 576.

2.   The more flexible approach, of not classifying a term as a condition or a warranty but as an 'intermediate' or (for want of a better name) 'innominate' term, was applied to a sale of goods contract in *Cehave NV v Bremer Handelsgesellschaft mbH, The Hansa Nord* [1975] 3 All ER 739. Two contracts were made, each for 6, 000 tons of citrus pulp pellets

cif Rotterdam, on the Grain and Feed Trade Association (GAFTA) terms. Clause 7 provided that 'Shipment to be made in good condition'. The buyers paid the price, some £100,000, and obtained the shipping documents, but when the goods (which had been shipped as a single, undifferentiated cargo) were discharged at Rotterdam, it was found that part of the shipment had been damaged by overheating. The buyers rejected the whole shipment, and when the sellers refused to refund the price, the buyers applied to the court at Rotterdam, which ordered the shipment to be sold. The shipment was then bought for £30,000 by B, who sold it back to the buyers at the same price, and the buyers used it for their original purpose, making cattle feed. The dispute was referred to arbitration, and the umpire held that the buyers were not entitled to reject the goods, but on appeal to the Board of GAFTA, it was held that the buyers were entitled to reject on the grounds that (i) the goods, although merchantable in a commercial sense, were not merchantable within the meaning of the Sale of Goods Act, and (ii) the goods were not shipped in good condition. Mocatta J upheld the Board's findings. On the latter point, Mocatta J held that, under the Sale of Goods Act, terms in contracts for the sale of goods must be either conditions or warranties, and that, because a breach of the 'shipped in good condition' clause might have serious consequences, it must be a condition. The Court of Appeal allowed the sellers' appeal. It held that the goods were merchantable, because they were still fit for the purpose for which such goods are commonly sold, ie for making cattle food, even if they were only saleable at a reduced price (on the possible repercussions of this approach, see p 431). The Court went on to hold that the Sale of Goods Act did not exclude the rules of common law, under which the 'shipped in good condition' clause was not a condition. The Sale of Goods Act did not exclude the common law rules on termination and, as Roskill LJ put it: 'It is desirable that the same legal principles should apply to the law of contract as a whole and that different legal principles should not apply to different branches of that law.' The buyer's right to reject depended on the seriousness of the consequences of the breach, and on the facts rejection was not justified. Ormrod LJ said (at 766–767):

If this view is correct it is bound to have important repercussions on the way in which courts in future will approach the construction of stipulations in contracts for the sale of goods. It will no longer be necessary to place so much emphasis on the potential effects of a breach on the buyer, and to feel obliged, as Mocatta J did in this case, to construe a stipulation as a condition because in other cases or in other circumstances the buyer ought to be entitled to reject. Consequently, the court will be freer to regard stipulations, as a matter of construction, as warranties, if what might be called the 'back-up' rule of the common law is available to protect buyers who ought to be able to reject in proper circumstances. I doubt whether, strictly speaking, this involves the creation of a third category of stipulations; rather, it recognises another ground for holding that a buyer is entitled to reject, namely that, de facto, the consideration for his promise has been wholly destroyed.

The result may be summarised in this way. When a breach of contract has taken place the question arises: is the party who is not in breach entitled in law to treat the contract as repudiated or, in the case of a buyer, to reject the goods? The answer depends on the answers to a series of other questions. Adopting Upjohn LJ's judgment in the *Hong Kong Fir Shipping* case the first question is: does the contract expressly provided that in the event of the breach of the term in question the other party is entitled to terminate the contract or reject the goods? If the answer is No, the next question is: does the contract when correctly construed so provide? The relevant term, for example, may be described as a 'condition'. The question then arises whether this word is used as a code word for the phrase 'shall be entitled to repudiate the contract or reject the goods', or in some other sense as in *Wickman Machine Tool Sales Ltd v Schuler A G*. The next question is whether the breach of the relevant term creates a right to repudiate or reject. This may arise either from statute or as a result of judicial decision on particular contractual terms. For example, if the requirements of s 14(1) or (2) of the Sale of Goods Act 1893 are fulfilled, the buyer will be entitled to reject the goods, as a result of this section read with s 11(1). In fact, in all those sections of the 1893 Act which create implied conditions the word 'condition' is by definition a code word for 'breach of this term will entitle the buyer to reject the goods', subject to any other relevant provision of the Act. In other cases, the courts have decided that breach of some specific terms, such as, for example, an 'expected ready to load' stipulation, will ipso facto give rise to a right in the other party to repudiate the contract *(The Mihalis Angelos* per Lord Denning MR). In these two classes of case the consequences of the breach are irrelevant or, more accurately, are assumed to go to the root of the contract, and to justify repudiation. There remains the non-specific class where the events produced by the breach are such that it is reasonable to describe the breach as going to the root of the contract and so justifying repudiation.

If this approach is permissible in the present case I would unhesitatingly hold that the stipulation in cl 7 that the goods were to be shipped in good condition was not a condition, and that on the facts of this case the breach did not go to the root of the contract, and that, consequently, the buyers were not entitled to reject the goods.

If, on the contrary, I have to make an exclusive choice between condition and warranty I would categorise the relevant part of cl 7 as a warranty, mainly because I find it unrealistic to hold that parties who have expressly stipulated in cl 5 that terms as to quality shall be treated, in effect, as warranties, except in the special circumstances defined by the clause itself, should have intended the general stipulation as to condition of the goods on shipment to have any greater effect.

I would therefore allow the appeal, and hold that the buyers were not entitled to reject the goods but are entitled to such damages as may be appropriate.

3.   In contrast, in *Maredelanto Compania Naviera SA v Bergbau-Handel GmbH, The Mihalis Angelos* [1970] 3 All ER 125, a clause in a charterparty stating that the vessel was 'expected ready to load under this charter about 1 July 1965' was held to be a condition in the strict sense, so that the charterers could terminate the contract without having to prove that the breach had serious consequences. Megaw LJ said (at 138–139):

I reach that conclusion for four interrelated reasons. First, it tends towards certainty in the law. One of the essential elements of law is some measure of uniformity. One of the important elements of the law is predictability. At any rate in commercial law, there are obvious and substantial advantages in having, where possible, a firm and definite rule for a particular class of legal relationship, eg as here, the legal categorisation of a particular, definable type of contractual clause in common use. It is surely much better, both for shipowners and charterers (and, incidentally, for their advisers) when a contractual obligation of this nature is under consideration, and still more when they are faced with the necessity for an urgent decision as to the effects of a suspected breach of it, to be able to say categorically: 'If a breach is proved, then the charterer can put an end to the contract', rather than that they should be left to ponder whether or not the courts would be likely, in the particular case, when the evidence had been heard, to decide that in the particular circumstances the breach was or was not such as to go to the root of the contract. Where justice does not require greater flexibility, there is everything to be said for, and nothing against, a degree of rigidity in legal principle.

4.   Further cases on the question of whether a particular breach of contract justifies the innocent party in terminating the contract will be found in the next section. Note particularly the House of Lords decision in *Bunge Corpn v Tradax SA*, p 576.

5.   In both the *Hong Kong Fir* case and *The Hansa Nord*, the Court of Appeal held that there had been no breach of condition. This does not mean that the charterers' or buyers' obligations were unconditional. Their obligations were conditional upon the other party

performing in such a way that they would receive the substance of what they were contracting for, but were *not* conditional on absolute compliance with the seaworthiness or 'shipped in good condition' clauses. If the breaches had been sufficiently serious in effect, the charterers or buyers would still have been entitled to refuse to perform.

6. Terminology in this area is confused because differing terms are used to describe conditions and breaches that are sufficiently serious to justify the innocent party in terminating. In the *Suisse Atlantique* case, Lord Upjohn said ([1967] 1 AC 361 at 422):

> There was much discussion during the argument about the phrases 'fundamental breach' and 'breach of a fundamental term' and I think it is true that in some of the cases these terms have been used interchangeably; but in fact they are quite different. I believe that all of your Lordships are agreed and, indeed, it has not seriously been disputed before us that there is no magic in the words 'fundamental breach'; this expression is no more than a convenient shorthand expression for saying that a particular breach or breaches of contract by one party is or are such as to go to the root of the contract which entitles the other party to treat such breach or breaches as a repudiation of the whole contract. Whether such breach or breaches do constitute a fundamental breach depends on the construction of the contract and on all the facts and circumstances of the case. The innocent party may accept that breach or those breaches as a repudiation and treat the whole contract as at an end and sue for damages generally or he may at his option prefer to affirm the contract and treat it as continuing on foot in which case he can sue only for damages for breach or breaches of the particular stipulation or stipulations in the contract which has or have been broken.
>
> But the expression 'fundamental term' has a different meaning. A fundamental term of a contract is a stipulation which the parties have agreed either expressly or by necessary implication or which the general law regards as a condition which goes to the root of the contract so that *any breach* of that term may at once and without further reference to the facts and circumstances be regarded by the innocent party as a fundamental breach and thus is conferred on him the alternative remedies at his option that I have just mentioned.

7. Compare the *Hong Kong Fir* test ('does the breach deprive the innocent party of substantially the whole benefit of the contract?') to the doctrine of substantial performance. The two rules reflect similar ideas but isn't the emphasis different? It seems that defects or deficiencies in performance might prevent there being substantial performance even though they are not so serious as to deprive the innocent party of substantially the whole benefit of the contract. See p 596.

8. Note that if a party purports to terminate on an insufficient ground, it is normally permitted to justify its action later on some quite different ground, even if it was not aware of the other ground at the date of termination. In recent years, there has been an attempt to restrict this rule, but the exact limits (if any) that have been imposed on it are very unclear: see Treitel, pp 836–837.

VII. TIME STIPULATIONS

As we saw earlier, one party may be able to withhold his performance until the other is ready to perform or has done so, but in the absence of an anticipatory repudiation, he will not be entitled to terminate until the time for performance has expired (see the note on *Trans-Trust v Danubian Trading* on p 553). Meanwhile, the other party can perform. Thus in *Borrowman, Phillips & Co v Free and Hollis* (1878) 4 QBD 500, a seller who had tendered goods that did not conform to the contract, and which were rejected by the buyers, was permitted to retender within the contract period. For a recent case in which the assessment of damages depended on the same point, see *Berger & Co Inc v Gill & Duffus SA* [1984] AC 382.

Once the date set in the contract for performance has passed, the party who has unjustifiably failed to perform will normally be in breach and thus liable for damages even if he does later perform (for exceptional cases in which he may not be liable, see p 524). In addition, the other party may be able to terminate for default, but he will only be entitled to do this immediately if 'time was of the essence'.

1. Time of the essence

In ordinary commercial contracts for the sale of goods, the rule clearly is, that time is prima facie of the essence with respect to delivery.

(McCardie J in *Hartley v Hymans* [1920] 3 KB 475 at 484.)

2. Time not of the essence

■ Sale of Goods Act 1979

Section 10

(1) Unless a different intention appears from the terms of the contract, stipulations as to time of payment are not of the essence of a contract of sale.

For a case in which the parties had agreed expressly that time of payment should be of the essence, see p 605.

The time for performance of many obligations is not of the essence, unless the contract provides otherwise. Sometimes the reason is fairly obvious. For instance, if time for building work were of the essence, the employer would be able to terminate if, by the date for completion, the builder was a day behind and, under the rule in *Sumpter v Hedges* (p 559), the employer could avoid paying anything for what the builder had done.

If time is not of the essence, how long does the innocent party have to wait? In *Universal Cargo Carriers Corpn v Citati* [1957] 2 QB 401, the charterer had failed to provide a cargo within the lay days (the time permitted for loading—see Appendix), and the owners refused to keep the vessel at the charterer's disposal any longer. Devlin J held that time was not of the essence and that the owners could terminate only if the delay went to the root of the contract. What yardstick should be used to determine whether it went to the root? The arbitrator had held that the delay must have been for a reasonable time. Devlin J rejected this and held that the delay must 'frustrate' the charterparty. This was not frustration in the sense of the 'doctrine of frustration' considered in Section 4—it couldn't be a case of frustration in that sense because the delay was the charterer's fault—but in the older sense of defeating the object of the venture (compare Diplock's judgment in the *Hong Kong Fir* case, p 567). If the delay had become that serious, the owners could have terminated. (They could also have terminated before the delay had become that bad if it was clear that the charterer would not be able to load within a frustrating time. In the *Citati* case, Devlin explains this as depending on the doctrine of anticipatory repudiation: see pp 581 ff. Other explanations may be possible.)

At first sight, the distinction between a 'frustrating time' and a 'reasonable time' may seem semantic, but the point is that they involve different factors. 'Frustrating time' is determined by the effect on the innocent party: does the delay deprive him of substantially the whole benefit of the contract? 'Reasonable time' is governed by what remains to be done by the party in breach, how hard he has been pressed by the innocent party previously, and other such factors: see the judgment of Denning LJ in *Charles Rickards Ltd v Oppenheim* (p 859).

Since 1957, however, it seems that the law may have changed so that the innocent party need not wait so long. Once the date for performance has passed, he may serve notice on the other party to complete performance within a reasonable time; if the other fails to perform within this period, the innocent party may then terminate.

This had been the rule in contracts for the sale of land for a long time. The position was complicated because common law and equity took different views as to when time was of the essence. Originally, at common law, the time for the performance of both the vendor's and the purchaser's obligations was of the essence, but (with certain exceptions, for instance, if the contract *expressly* provided that time was to be of the essence) equity took a different view. If the innocent party purported to determine the contract, and to forfeit or recover a deposit, the court of equity could declare his action ineffective or stay it, and grant specific perform-ance to the party guilty of the delay. The equitable rule now prevails (Law of Property Act 1925, s 41, re enacting Judicature Act 1873, s 25(1)). Note that it was only termination of the contract, and the accompanying forfeiture or recovery of a deposit, that would be restrained: the party guilty of the delay would still be liable in damages to the other *(Raineri v Miles* [1981] AC 1050).

However, equity would not grant specific performance, or restrain termination by the innocent party, if the innocent party had 'made time of the essence' by serving a notice to complete within a reasonable time, and this notice had not been complied with (see *Stickney v Keeble* [1915] AC 386 and *Behdazi v Shaftesbury Hotels Ltd* [1992] Ch 1).

These rules appeared to depend upon the availability of specific performance, so that it did not seem that there was any general rule that time could be 'made' of the essence in contracts in which specific performance would not be granted. But *Halsbury's Laws of England*, 4th edn, Vol 9, para 481, had stated that there was a general rule:

The modern law, in the case of contracts of all types, may be summarised as follows. Time will not be considered to be of the essence unless: (1) the parties expressly stipulate that conditions as to time must be strictly complied with: or (2) the nature of the subject matter of the contract or the surrounding circumstances show that time should be considered to be of the essence: or (3) a party who has been subjected to unreasonable delay gives notice to the party in default making time of the essence.

This statement of the law has been accepted in dicta in two cases in the House of Lords. The first is *United Scientific Holdings Ltd v Burnley Borough Council* [1978] AC 904, in which the question was whether time was of the essence in a timetable of steps to be taken under a rent review clause in a lease. The House of Lords held that it was not, so that the landlords could still claim rent review despite the fact that they had allowed the prescribed time limits to expire. Viscount Dilhorne and Lord Simon explicitly approved the statement of law contained in the first two sections of the passage from *Halsbury's Laws of England*. Lord Fraser went fur-ther and approved the whole passage (at 958). He thus appears to accept that time can be made of the essence in any type of contract, irrespective of specific performance, and it may be that the same thought lay behind the rather delphic remarks of Lord Diplock (at 925) that 'the waters of the confluent streams of law and equity have surely mingled by now' (see Baker (1977) 93 LQR 529). Whether the owner in a case like *Citati* can now make time of the essence by serving the charterer with reasonable notice is not wholly clear. The second case is that which follows.

■ *Bunge Corpn v Tradax SA*

[1981] 2 All ER 513, Court of Appeal and House of Lords

Under a contract that incorporated GAFTA form 119, the buyers agreed to purchase from the sellers 15,000 tons of soya bean meal, 5 per cent more or less, for shipment from the USA. It was the practice in the trade for a string of contracts to be made in which the shipment contract was merely an intermediate contract made in the course of the passage of the goods from the supplier to the eventual receiver. The terms of the parties' contract required three shipments of 5,000 tons fob from an American port in the Gulf of Mexico nominated by the sellers. By agreement between the parties, one of the shipments was to be during June 1975. The buyers were to provide a vessel at the nominated port and, by virtue of cl 7 of form 119 as completed by the parties, they were required to 'give at least 15 consecutive days' notice' of the probable readiness of the vessel. If the goods were to be shipped during June, the buyers were therefore required to give notice of their vessel's readiness by 13 June. In fact, the buyers did not give notice until 17 June. The sellers claimed that the late notice was a breach of contract amounting to a repudiation and claimed damages from the buyers on the basis that by then the market price had fallen by over US$60 a ton. The dispute was referred to arbitration at which the sellers were awarded US$317, 500 damages. On appeal to the Commercial Court, the judge reversed that award on the ground that the term as to time when notice was required to be given was not a condition but an intermediate term, and the lateness of the notice did not amount to a breach of contract. The sellers appealed.

Megaw LJ

...I come to the second main issue: is the term of the contract which has been broken by the buyers a condition or an intermediate term? The sellers have, before us, made it clear that if the term is not a condition, but is an intermediate term, they will not seek to contend that they can discharge the burden of showing that they were entitled to treat the contract as having been repudiated by the buyers.

The contract is, by its express terms, governed by English law. That is the effect of c l25 of GAFTA 119.

It is an accepted principle of English law that in a mercantile contract for the sale of goods 'prima facie a stipulated time of delivery is of the essence'. This long-standing principle has recently been re-stated by Lord Diplock in *United Scientific Holdings Ltd v Burnley Borough Council*...

In the present case, then, there can be no doubt but that the obligation of the sellers to deliver the soya bean meal not later than 30th June 1975 was a condition of the contract. They had an obligation to tender the contractual quantity of the goods at the ship's rail so that they could be loaded in accordance with the contractual provision as to rate of loading, on or before that date. If they failed, in breach of contract, to carry out that obligation, and if the buyers thereupon were to treat the contract as having been wrongfully repudiated by the sellers, it would be no answer for the sellers to say that the buyers had not proved that they, the buyers, had suffered any loss or would suffer any loss, if loading were to take place on 1st July. It would be unreal to suggest that one day's lateness in delivery would necessarily be a matter of serious consequence to the buyers. The lateness might or might not have such consequences. But the buyers' right to treat the contract as repudiated, and to treat themselves as freed from the performance of any further contractual obligations which they would otherwise have been required to perform under the contact, does not depend on the buyers being able to prove any such thing....

In para 5 of the award the board of appeal, having said that the term means 'Buyers were to give at least 15 consecutive days' notice of probable readiness of vessel(s)', went on: 'Such a provision is customarily treated in the trade as being for the purpose of giving to sellers sufficient time to make necessary arrangements to get the goods to the port for loading on board the nominated vessel.' In other words, the parties have agreed, by acceptance of this term, that 15 days is the time which is reasonably required by the sellers for the purpose of this particular contract, to enable them to make the arrange-ments necessary for the fulfilment by them of their contractual duty to deliver the goods by the due time. It would, in my view, be impossible for a court to hold that that was not the parties' intention in agree-ing this term. There is no question here of the parties not being in an equal bargaining position. It would, in my opinion, be arrogant and unjustifiable for a court to substitute any view of its own for the view of the parties themselves as to what was a reasonable time for this purpose.

Unless there is some principle of law, or some authority binding on us, which leads necessarily to a contrary conclusion, it appears to me to follow that, just as the contractual time for delivery of the goods is a condition binding on the sellers, so that the contractual time by which the notice has to be given for the purpose of enabling the sellers to perform that condition should be regarded as a condition binding on the buyers. There is no more, and no less, reason to suppose that a breach of the time provision in the sellers' obligation will necessarily or probably lead to serious loss to the buyers than there is to suppose that a breach of the notice of readiness provision will necessarily or probably lead to serious loss to the sellers. . . .

I come back to the purpose of the notice of probable readiness term in the present contract. The com-mercial reasons why advance notice is required are, I think, obvious. The sellers have to nominate the loading port. Is loading going to be possible, and if possible convenient, at port A, or port B, or port C? Until the probable date of readiness is known, it may be impossible to answer those questions. Until they are answered, the sellers cannot perform their contractual duty of nominating the port. When the port is decided, arrangements have to be made to have the contract quantity (to be defined by the buyers by reference to '5% more or less') of the contract goods available when the vessel is ready. What is involved in making such arrangements? It may involve, or include, buying goods, arranging for them to be moved by road, rail or water from wherever they may be; for warehousing them or moving them from one warehouse to another. Of course, in any given case, some or all of these tasks may be simply achieved, or their achievement may be possible in less than 15 days, in order to have the goods ready for loading where and when the vessel is ready for loading. It obviously cannot be predicated that 14 days' notice, instead of 15 days', would necessarily and in all circumstances cause sellers serious difficulties in respect of a contract containing these terms. What can and should be accepted is that the parties have agreed that, for the purpose of this contract, the reasonable time required to enable the sellers to perform their contractual obligations as to delivery of the goods is 15 days' notice of the probable readiness of the vessel to load. . . .

Apart from [a] particular reason, relating to the extension of shipment clause, Parker J was of the opinion that the term could not be a condition because of what he regarded as being 'the principles established in the *Hong Kong Fir* case' . . . and *Cehave* NV *v Bremer Handelsgesellschaft mbH, The Hansa Nord*. In the latter case, Roskill LJ, while recognising that some terms of a contract of sale may be condi-tions, expressed the view that 'a court should not be over ready, unless required by statute or authority so to do, to construe a term in a contract as a "condition" . . . '

The passage in the *Hong Kong Fir* case, to which Parker J referred, was that where Diplock LJ said this . . . :

> 'No doubt there are many simple contractual undertakings, sometimes express, but more often because of their very simplicity ("It goes without saying") to be implied, of which it can be predicated that every breach of such an undertaking must give rise to an event which will deprive the party not in default of substantially the whole benefit which it was intended that he should obtain from the contract. And such a stipulation, unless the parties have agreed that breach of it shall not entitle the non-defaulting party to treat the contract as repudiated, is a "condition".'

If that statement is intended to be a definition of the requirements which must always be satisfied, in all types of contract and all types of clauses, in order that a term may qualify as a condition. I would very respectfully express the view that it is not a correct statement of the law. I am confirmed in the view that it was not so intended because of what was recently said by Lord Diplock in a passage . . . from his speech in *United Scientific Holdings Ltd v Burnley Borough Council* in relation to time being 'of the essence' in certain commercial contracts. . . .

In the light of what was said by their Lordships in that case, I think it can fairly be said that in mercantile contracts stipulations as to time not only may be, but usually are, to be treated as being 'of the essence of the contract', even though this is not expressly stated in the words of the contract. It would follow that in a mercantile contract it cannot be predicated that, for time to be of the essence, any and every breach of the term as to time must necessarily cause the innocent party to be deprived of substantially the whole of the benefit which it was intended that he should have. . . .

In my opinion in the term with which we are concerned the provision as to time is of the essence of the contract. The term is a condition.

It is, I believe, a factor which is not without weight in that conclusion that, at least, it tends towards certainty in the law . . . The parties, where time is of the essence, will at least know where they stand when the contractually agreed time has passed and the contract has been broken. They will not be forced to make critical decisions by trying to anticipate how serious, in the view of arbitrators or courts, in later years, the consequences of the breach will retrospectively be seen to have been, in the light, it may be, of hindsight.

I must, however, return to the *Hong Kong Fir* case . . . No one now doubts the correctness of that decision: that there are 'intermediate' terms, breach of which may or may not entitle the innocent party to treat himself as discharged from the further performance of his contractual obligation. No one now doubts that a term as to seaworthiness in a charterparty, in the absence of express provision to the opposite effect, is not a condition, but is an 'intermediate' term. The question arising on that case which I think we are compelled to examine in the present case is the test by which it falls to be decided whether a term is a condition.

I have previously quoted a passage from the judgment of Diplock LJ. In its literal sense, the words there used would mean that the test whether a term is a condition is whether *every* breach of such an undertaking *must* give rise to an event which will deprive the party not in default of *substantially the whole benefit which it was intended that he should obtain from the contract*. If this is a definition of the requirements which, in English law, must always be fulfilled before any contractual term (in the absence, of course, of express words) can achieve the legal status of a condition, then the term with which we are here concerned would not pass the test. The view which I have expressed that it is a condition would necessarily be wrong.

There are various reasons why I do not think that this was intended to be a literal, definitive and comprehensive statement of the requirements of a condition: and also, if it were, why, with great respect, I do not think that it represents the law as it stands today.

First, if it were intended to cover terms as to time in mercantile contracts, how could the requirements be said to be met in respect of stipulations in contracts of types in which, as Lord Diplock has recently said, time may be of the essence: for example, in respect of a stipulated time for delivery? It could never be said, as I see it, in any real sense, that *any* breach of such a stipulation *must necessarily cause the innocent party to be deprived of substantially all the benefit*.

Second, and following on what I have just said, I do not see how any contractual term, whether as to time or otherwise, could ever pass the test. Conditions would no longer exist in the English law of contract. For it is always possible to suggest hypothetically some minor breach or breaches of any contractual term which might, without undue use of the imagination, be wholly insufficient to produce serious effects for the innocent party, let alone the loss of substantially all the benefit.

Third, English law does recognise as conditions contractual terms which do not pass that test. For example, *Bowes v Shand* and, I think a substantial number of other cases which are binding, at least on this court.

Fourth, it is clear law, reaffirmed by the House of Lords since *Hong Kong Fir* was decided, that where there has been a breach of a condition the innocent party is entitled to elect whether or not to treat the contracts as repudiated. . . .

. . . How could this right of election be anything other than a legal fiction, a chimera, if the election can arise only in circumstances in which, as a result of the breach, an event has happened which will deprive the innocent party of substantially the whole benefit which it was intended that he should receive? This test, it is to be observed, is regarded *(Hong Kong Fir)* . . . as applying also where the term is an intermediate term, except that you then look to what has actually happened in order to see if the innocent party has lost substantially all the benefit. So, again, if the test be right, the former principle of English law that the innocent party has the right to elect is no longer anything but an empty shadow. For a right to elect to continue a contract, with the result that the innocent party will be bound to continue to perform his own contractual obligations, when he will, by definition, have lost substantially all his benefit under the contract, does not appear to me to make sense.

Fifth, the same considerations as I have set out in the previous paragraph apply if the test be that a breach of contract gives a right to the innocent party to treat it as a repudiation only if the events which in fact have flowed from the breach would, if they had come about otherwise than by a breach of contract, amount to frustration of the contract. . . .

I would allow the appeal and, subject to any questions of detail which may arise as to the form of the order, I would restore the decision of the board of appeal.

Browne LJ

I agree that this appeal should be allowed, for the reasons given by Megaw LJ, with which I entirely agree. . . .

Brightman LJ concurred.

The House of Lords affirmed the judgment of the Court of Appeal. **Lord Wilberforce** said:

. . . The fundamental fallacy of the appellants' argument lies in attempting to apply this analysis to a time clause such as the present in a mercantile contract, which is totally different in character. As to such a clause there is only one kind of breach possible, namely to be late, and the questions which have to be asked are: first, what importance have the parties expressly ascribed to this consequence? and, second, in the absence of expressed agreement, what consequences ought to be attached to it having regard to the contract as a whole?

The test suggested by the appellants was a different one. One must consider, they said, the breach actually committed and then decide whether that default would deprive the party not in default of substantially the whole benefit of the contract. They even invoked certain passages in the judgment of Diplock LJ in *Hong Kong Fir* to support it. One may observe in the first place that the introduction of a test of this kind would be commercially most undesirable. It would expose the parties, after a breach of one, two, three, seven and other numbers of days, to an argument whether this delay would have left time for the seller to provide the goods. It would make it, at the time, at least difficult, and sometimes impossible, for the supplier to know whether he could do so. It would fatally remove from a vital provision in the contract that certainty which is the most indispensable quality of mercantile contracts, and lead to a large increase in arbitrations. It would confine the seller, perhaps after arbitration and reference through the courts, to a remedy in damages which might be extremely difficult to quantify. These are all serious objections in practice. But I am clear that the submission is unacceptable in law. The judgment of Diplock LJ does not give any support and ought not to give any encouragement to any such proposition; for beyond doubt it recognises that it is open to the parties to agree that, as regards a particular obligation, any breach shall entitle the party not in default to treat the contract as repudiated. Indeed, if he were not doing so he would, in a passage which does not profess to be more than clarificatory, be discrediting a long and uniform series of cases, at least from *Bowes v Shand* onwards.

Lord Wilberforce also approved the paragraph from *Halsbury* extracted on p 575. Lords Fraser, Scarman and Lowry agreed with his speech. It is interesting to contrast this case with the House's attitude towards giving relief against forfeiture: see, pp 588 ff.

We saw earlier that if a party can cure a defective performance before the date set for performance, he can normally prevent the other from terminating. A parallel rule applies if time is not of the essence: the passing of the date for performance does not prevent the party in default from performing, or from curing an originally defective performance, providing that he can do so within a frustrating time (or, perhaps, within a reasonable time of being given notice to perform). Thus in *Stanton v Richardson* (1872) LR 7 CP 421; affd (1874) LR 9 CP 390, a ship chartered to carry a cargo of wet sugar was unseaworthy because her pumps could not cope with the liquid flowing from the sugar. The Court of Common Pleas held that the charterer was entitled to reject the ship at once, as the jury found that the defect could not be put right within a frustrating time. It did not decide the point, but it seems to follow that, if the defect *could* have been corrected within such a time, the charterer would at most have had an action for damages.

Stanton v Richardson again shows the distinction between withholding performance and termination: had the owner been able to adjust the pumps to make the ship suitable for the cargo, the charterer would not have been able to throw up the charter, but he would not have had to load the goods until the pumps had been put right.

Before leaving the question of time stipulations, it is perhaps worth reflecting for a moment on the *Hong Kong Fir* case. A ship is not seaworthy if it has any defect that a prudent shipowner would put right before allowing the ship to go to sea on the voyage and with the cargo in question (*McFadden v Blue Star Line* [1905] 1 KB 697 at 706). Can a charterer be expected to load his goods aboard a ship that is known to be unseaworthy at the time, even if the matter is a relatively trivial one? In the *Hong Kong Fir* case, the majority of the Court of Appeal seemed to say that seaworthiness itself is not a condition, which must mean that sometimes the charterer *will* have to load on to an unseaworthy ship. Perhaps a better analysis would be that seaworthiness *is* a condition in terms of *substance*, but that the owner does not have to make it seaworthy immediately—in other words, time is not of the essence. Thus, if the owner fails to make the ship seaworthy within a frustrating time, the charterer can refuse to load (if he has not done so) or can terminate the charter. See further Devlin, 'The Treatment of Breach of Contract' [1966] CLJ 192, 194–195.

Lastly, it should be remarked that we have presented the right of a party to withhold its performance, and ultimately to terminate the contract, as depending on the same idea: A does not have to perform her part of the contract if B has not performed a condition precedent, or if B is not ready and willing to perform a concurrent condition. Occasionally, however, B may commit a serious breach when A has already performed. For example, A might have contracted with B for B to advertise A's business on television and have paid B in advance. If B commits a very serious breach (eg by failing to show the advert), A can probably terminate the contract and recover the money she has paid. B's performance is not a condition precedent or a concurrent condition in the sense that until B has performed, or is willing to do so, A need not perform her side of the contract (the order of performance); here, A has already performed by paying B. But the substance of B's obligation is a condition in the sense that if B fails to perform it, A will have the right to terminate the contract. See Treitel (1990) LQR 185. The word 'condition' has thus become detached from its original meaning and indicates a term that is so important that, if it is not complied with, the other may terminate.

VIII. CONDITIONS IN UNILATERAL CONTRACTS AND OPTIONS

In *United Dominions Trust (Commercial) Ltd v Eagle Aircraft Services Ltd* [1968] 1 All ER 104, the Court of Appeal held that the 'flexible' approach is not applicable to conditions forming a unilateral contract: these are conditions in the strict sense, so that if they are not complied with exactly, the promisor need not perform his part of the bargain. In that case, Eagle had sold aircraft to UDT, who had let them on hire purchase to Orion Airways. A 'recourse' agreement between UDT and Eagle provided that, if for any reason the hire-purchase agreement was terminated before the full amount had been paid, Eagle would re purchase the aircraft from UDT when called upon to do so, at a price equal to the unpaid balance plus certain expenses. A compulsory winding-up order was made against Orion, and the aircraft were repossessed in December 1960, but UDT did not call upon Eagle to repurchase until the following May. The Court of Appeal held that it was an implied condition of the agreement that the call for repurchase must be made within a reasonable time of the repossession, and that as a reasonable time was three months, Eagle was no longer obliged to repurchase, whether or not it was prejudiced by the delay. Diplock LJ said (at 109) that two consequences followed from the fact that the contract was unilateral rather than bilateral:

The first is that there is no room for any inquiry whether any act done by the promisee in purported performance of a unilateral contract amounts to a breach of warranty or a breach of condition on his part, for he is under no obligation to do or to refrain from doing any act at all. The second is that, as respects the promisor, the initial inquiry is whether the event, which under the unilateral contract gives rise to obligations on the part of the promisor, has occurred. To that inquiry the answer can only be a simple 'Yes' or 'No'.

IX. ANTICIPATORY BREACH

■ *Hochster v De La Tour*
(1853) [1843–1860] All ER Rep 12

Lord Campbell CJ read the following judgment of the Court.—On this motion in arrest of judgment, the question arises, whether, if there be an agreement between A and B, whereby B engages to employ A on and from a future day for a given period of time, to travel with him into a foreign country as a courier and to start with him in that capacity on that day, A being to receive a monthly salary during the continuance of such service, B may, before the day, refuse to perform the agreement and break and renounce it so as to entitle A, before the day, to commence an action against B to recover damages for breach of the agreement, A having been ready and willing to perform it till it was broken and renounced by B.

The defendant's counsel very powerfully contended that, if the plaintiff was not contented to dissolve the contract and to abandon all remedy upon it, he was bound to remain ready and willing to perform it till the day when the actual employment as courier in the service of the defendant was to begin, and that there could be no breach of the agreement, before that day, to give a right of action. But it cannot be laid down as a universal rule that, where by agreement an act is to be done on a future day, no action can be brought for a breach of the agreement till the day for doing the act has arrived. If a man promises to marry a woman on a future day and before that day marries another woman, he is instantly liable to an action for breach of promise of marriage: *Short v Stone*. If a man contracts to execute a lease on and from a future day for a certain term, and, before that day, executes a lease to another for the same term, he may be immediately sued for breaking the contract: *Ford v Tiley*. So, if a man contracts to sell and deliver specific goods on a future day, and before the day he sells and delivers them to another, he is immediately liable to an action at the suit of the person with whom he first contracted to sell and deliver them: *Bowdell v Parsons*. One reason alleged in support of such an action is that the defendant has, before the day, rendered it impossible for the plaintiff to perform the contract at the day, but this does not necessarily follow, for, prior to the day fixed for doing the act, the first wife may have died, a surrender of the lease executed might be obtained, and the defendant might have re-purchased the goods so as to be in a situation to sell and deliver them to the plaintiff. Another reason may be that where there is a contract to do an act on a future day there is a relation constituted between the parties in the meantime by the contract, and that they impliedly promise that in the meantime neither will do any thing to the prejudice of the other inconsistent with that relation. As an example, a man and woman engaged to marry are affianced to one another during the period between the time of the engagement and the celebration of the marriage.

In the present case, of traveller and courier, from the day of the hiring till the day when the employment was to begin, the parties were engaged to each other, and it seems to be a breach of an implied contract if either of them renounces the engagement. This reasoning seems in accordance with the unanimous decision of the Exchequer Chamber in *Elderton v Emmens* which we have followed in subsequent cases in this court. The declaration in the present case, in alleging a breach, states a great deal more than a passing intention on the part of the defendant which he may repent of, and could only be proved by evidence that he had utterly renounced the contract or done some act which rendered it impossible for him to perform it. If the plaintiff has no remedy for breach of the contract unless he treats the contract as in force, and acts upon it down to June 1, 1852, it follows that, till then, he must enter into no employment which will interfere with his promise 'to start with the defendant on such travels on the day and year, and that he must then be properly equipped in all respects as a courier for a three months' tour on the continent of Europe.

But it is surely much more rational, and more for the benefit of both parties, that, after the renunciation of the agreement by the defendant, the plaintiff should be at liberty to consider himself absolved from any future performance of it, retaining his right to sue for any damage he has suffered from the breach of it. Thus, instead of remaining idle and laying out money in preparations which must be useless, he is at liberty to seek service under another employer, which would go in mitigation of the damages to which he would otherwise be entitled for a breach of the contract. It seems strange that the defendant, after renouncing the contract, and absolutely declaring that he will never act under it, should be permitted to object that faith is given to his assertion, and that an opportunity is not left to him of changing his mind. If the plaintiff is barred of any remedy by entering into an engagement inconsistent with starting as a courier with the defendant on June 1, he is prejudiced by putting faith in the defendant's assertion, and it would be more consonant with principle, if the defendant were precluded from saying that he had not broken the contract when he declared that he entirely renounced it.

Suppose that the defendant, at the time of his renunciation, had embarked on a voyage for Australia, so as to render it physically impossible for him to employ the plaintiff as a courier on the continent of Europe in the months of June, July and August, 1852. According to decided cases the action might have been brought before June 1, but the renunciation may have been founded on other facts, to be given in evidence, which would equally have rendered the defendant's performance of the contract impossible. The man who wrongfully renounces a contract into which he has deliberately entered cannot justly complain if he is immediately sued for a compensation in damages by the man whom he has injured: and it seems reasonable to allow an option to the injured party, either to sue immediately or to wait till the time when the act was to be done, still holding it as prospectively binding for the exercise of this option, which may be advantageous to the innocent party, and cannot be prejudicial to the wrongdoer.

An argument against the action before June 1 is urged from the difficulty of calculating the damages, but this argument is equally strong against an action before Sep 1, when the three months would expire. In either case, the jury in assessing the damages would be justified in looking to all that had happened, or was likely to happen, to increase or mitigate the loss of the plaintiff down to the day of trial.

We do not find any decision contrary to the view we are taking of this case....

If it should be held that, upon a contract to do an act on a future day, a renunciation of the contract by one party dispenses with a condition to be performed in the meantime by the other, there seems no reason for requiring that other to wait till the day arrives before seeking his remedy by action, and the only ground on which the condition can be dispensed with seems to be that the renunciation may be treated as a breach of the contract. Upon the whole, we think that the declaration in this case is sufficient. It gives us great satisfaction to reflect that, the question being on the record, our opinion may be reviewed in a court of error. In the meantime we must give judgment for the plaintiff.

Judgment for plaintiff.

NOTES

1. What did counsel for the defendant argue was the effect of the plaintiff's acceptance of the repudiation?

2. There will also be a repudiation if it is clear that the defendant will be unable to perform when the time comes: see *Citati*'s case.

3. The victim of an anticipatory repudiation may terminate the contract either by giving notice to the other party or by acting inconsistently with the continuance of the contract, provided that his actions are known to the repudiating party. In *Vitol SA v Norelf Ltd, The Santa Clara*, the buyer repudiated the contract. The seller did not respond but (as the buyer knew) resold the goods. Six months later, the seller started an arbitration claiming damages. The buyer argued that the seller had never accepted the repudiation. The arbitrator held that the repudiation had been accepted by the seller's inactivity and, at first instance, the buyer's appeal was rejected. Phillips J said ([1994] 4 All ER 109, 114–115):

The analogy with contractual offer and acceptance...cannot be applied precisely. Anticipatory repudiation comes in many forms and some have little similarity with a contractual offer. Acceptance of a repudiation comes closer to acceptance of a contractual offer, for what is required is words or conduct which makes it plain that the innocent party is responding to the repudiation by treating the contract as at an end. The position was clearly stated by Viscount Simon LC in a much cited statement in *Heyman v Darwins Ltd* [1942] AC 356 at 361:

'...the other party may rescind the contract, or (as it is sometimes expressed) "accept the repudiation", by so acting as to make plain that, in view of the wrongful action of the party who has repudiated, he claims to treat the contract as at an end, in which case he can sue at once for damages.'

I see no reason why acceptance of repudiation should not be effected by acts as opposed to by words. It may be more difficult by actions to indicate that one is responding to a repudiation by treating the contract as at an end, but in many circumstances there will be actions that the innocent party can take which will achieve this result. Nor can I see any reason why the act in question should not be one which, but for the fact that it is a response to a repudiation, would itself be a breach of contract. Mr Popplewell argued that in such circumstances the response of the innocent party will always be equivocal—it will not be apparent that the act is a response to the repudiation. He relied on the *Fercometal* case [see below] as an example of this. That was a case where the innocent party initially responded to the repudiation by affirming the contract. In such circumstances a subsequent breach by the innocent party of one of his own contractual obligations is unlikely to be or to be seen as a response to the repudiation. Where, however, the innocent party does not respond to a repudiation by affirmation, but proceeds to take action that is incompatible with his own continued performance of the contract, it may be quite clear that he is responding to the repudiation by treating the contract as at an end.

Can the innocent party demonstrate acceptance of a repudiation simply by failing further to perform his own contractual obligations? Again, Mr Popplewell submitted that he could not, and for the same reason inactivity is bound to be equivocal. Again, I cannot agree. It depends upon the circumstances. Failure to progress an arbitration is a good example of inertia that is likely to be equivocal. But in other types of contractual relationship where the parties are bound to perform specific acts in relation to one another, a failure to perform an act which a party is obliged to perform if the contract remains alive may be very significant. It is not difficult to envisage circumstances in which, if such conduct follows a renunciation, the obvious inference will be that the innocent party is responding to the repudiation by treating the contract as at an end.

I do not have to decide whether the failure on the part of Norelf to tender to Vitol a bill of lading, or any of the subsequent unspecified failures to perform the contract which were apparent to Vitol, gave clear indication to Vitol that, in view of Vitol's wrongful action, Norelf were treating the contract as at an end. That is a question of fact for the arbitrator. What I have to decide is whether, as a matter of law, mere failure to perform contractual obligations can ever constitute acceptance of an anticipatory repudiation by the other party. In my judgment, for the reasons that I have given, it can. It follows that this appeal must be dismissed.

The Court of Appeal disagreed ([1995] 3 All ER 971). Silence was equivocal and any equivocality was fatal to acceptance of a repudiation (cf p 211). As it was now too late for the seller to rely on its resale of the cargo as an acceptance, the appeal would be allowed.

However, the House of Lords disagreed with the Court of Appeal and restored the judgment of Phillips J [1996] 3 All ER 193.

In considering this case, it is crucial that the first decision was made by an arbitrator. In the law of arbitration, the decisions of the arbitrator on questions of fact cannot be challenged. There is a limited right of appeal on questions of law. So the only question was whether the arbitrator had asked himself the right legal question. The House of Lords thought he had. This could only be wrong if, as the Court of Appeal thought, silence was always equivocal. The House of Lords thought that silence was often equivocal but not always. As Lord Steyn said: 'Sometimes in the practical world of businessmen, an omission to act may be as pregnant with meaning as a positive declaration.'

4.   The victim of an anticipatory repudiation does not have to 'accept the repudiation' by terminating the contract: he or she can wait and see whether the repudiating party will perform when the time comes (see further pp 656 and 734). If, however, the contract is left in force, the fact that there has been a repudiation is for many purposes ignored. Thus, firstly, the victim must normally tender his performance as usual, and if he does not, he will himself be in breach of contract when the time comes, giving the party who repudiated the right to terminate. The only exception is if the repudiating party made it clear that it has no interest in receiving performance and the victim accordingly doesn't tender it, then the repudiating party would be estopped from complaining: *Fercometal SARL v Mediterranean Shipping Co SA* [1988] 2 All ER 742, HL.

5.   A second consequence of leaving the contract in force is that the repudiating party can take advantage of any subsequent circumstances that may arise to excuse him. In *Avery v Bowden* (1855) 5 E & B 714; affd 6 E & B 953, a ship was chartered to carry a cargo from Odessa. The master was told before the end of the lay days that no cargo was available,

but he remained in port and urged the charterers to perform. The contract was then frustrated by the outbreak of the Crimean War.

6. The test of whether a party has repudiated is whether there has been 'an intimation of an intention to abandon and altogether to refuse performance of the contract ... [or of] an intention no longer to be bound by the contract' (Lord Coleridge CJ in *Freeth v Burr* (1874) LR 9 CP 208 at 213). How is this to be applied if a party refuses to perform the contract but claims that this is because the terms of the contract allow him to do so in the circumstances? If a party terminates the contract alleging that some breach by the other party gives him the right to do so, but the court disagrees, the terminating party will himself normally be guilty of a wrongful repudiation and be liable to the other for damages: the *Hong Kong Fir* case is an example. Similarly if a party announces that he is going to perform in some way that the court decides is wholly inconsistent with the contract, even if his legal advisers have (wrongly) told him that what he plans is permissible, and he in fact wants to go on with his own version of the contract. Thus in *Federal Commerce and Navigation Ltd v Molena Alpha Inc, The Nanfri, The Benfri and The Lorfri* [1979] AC 757, the owners and the charterers were in dispute about some deductions the charterers were making from the hire payments. After taking legal advice, the owners announced that they were instructing the masters of the ships to issue bills of lading marked 'subject to lien for freight' instead of 'freight prepaid', and they refused to withdraw these instructions unless the disputed deductions from hire were paid. The issue of 'claused bills' would have very serious consequences for the charterers. The House of Lords held that ordering the masters to issue claused bills was a breach of contract, and that the owners' action amounted to a wrongful repudiation, even though the owners clearly wanted to continue with the charters, which were very profitable to them, and were simultaneously seeking resolution of the dispute about deductions through arbitration.

    In contrast, in *Woodar Investment Development Ltd v Wimpey Construction (UK) Ltd* [1980] 1 All ER 571, a contract for the sale of land provided that the purchasers (Wimpey) could rescind the contract if, prior to completion, a statutory authority 'shall have commenced' to acquire the property by compulsory purchase. In fact, at the date the contract was signed, the authority had already commenced compulsory-purchase proceedings in respect of part of the land. Meanwhile Wimpey wished to escape from the contract because land prices had fallen, and, after taking legal advice, it discussed the situation with Mr Cornwell of Woodar, the vendors. Wimpey proposed renegotiation, failing which it would serve notice of rescission under the clause; Mr Cornwell disputed Wimpey's right to do this and indicated that Woodar would take the matter to court. Wimpy then wrote purporting to rescind because of the authority's action, stating that 'the contract is now discharged'. Woodar did not accept this, and Mr Cornwell said the matter 'must now await the decision of the court' and 'I am sure you will abide by the result as I will'. Woodar then sought a declaration that the purchasers, Wimpey, were not entitled to rescind, and when Wimpey counterclaimed for a declaration that it had rescinded, Woodar brought a second action claiming that the purchasers had repudiated, that the repudiation was accepted and that they were entitled to damages. The majority of the House of Lords held that Wimpey had not repudiated the contract. Lord Wilberforce said:

    So far from repudiating the contract, Wimpey were relying on it and invoking one of its provisions, to which both parties had given their consent. And unless the invocation of that provision were totally abusive, or lacking in good faith, (neither of which is contended for), the fact that it has proved to be wrong in law cannot turn it into a repudiation. At the lowest, the notice of rescission was a neutral document consistent either with an intention to preserve, or with an intention to abandon, the contract, and I will deal with it on this basis, more favourable to Woodar. In order to decide which is correct Wimpey's conduct has to be examined. . . .

In my opinion . . . Wimpey are entitled to succeed on the repudiation issue, and I would only add that it would be a regrettable development of the law of contract to hold that a party who bona fide relies on an express stipulation in a contract in order to rescind or terminate a contract should, by that fact alone, be treated as having repudiated his contractual obligations if he turns out to be mistaken as to his rights. Repudiation is a drastic conclusion which should only be held to arise in clear cases of a refusal, in a matter going to the root of the contract, to perform contractual obligations. To uphold Woodar's contentions in this case would represent an undesirable [extension] of the doctrine.

Lord Scarman added:

. . . [T]he notice of rescission, which Wimpey gave, was not, in the circumstances which existed when it was given, one which Wimpey had any contractual right to give. But they honestly believed the contract did give them the right. When one examines the totality of their conduct and its impact on Mr Cornwell it is plain, as shown by my noble and learned friend Lord Wilberforce's analysis of the facts, that Wimpey, though claiming mistakenly to exercise a power given them by the contract to bring it to an end, were not evincing an intention not to be bound by the contract. On the contrary, they believed they were acting pursuant to the contract. And Mr Cornwell well understood the situation. As he put it in his final letter to Sir Godfrey Mitchell, the president of Wimpey: ' . . . all I need say now is that we will retire to our battle stations and it goes without saying I am sure that you will abide by the result as I will.' It never occurred to Mr Cornwell that Wimpey, if held not to have been entitled to give notice of rescission, would refuse to perform the contract. In fact, it would seem that he believed exactly the contrary. Such was the impact on him of Wimpey's conduct.

Woodar, in an effort to mitigate loss, had sold the land to a third party. Was this action itself a breach of contract? See Nicol and Rawlings (1980) 43 MLR 696.

In *Hochster v De La Tour*, the defendant had repudiated all his obligations. What if a party indicates that it is unwilling or unable to perform a part of the contract but will perform the rest? The test is the same as in cases of actual breach. In *Decro-Wall International SA v Practitioners in Marketing Ltd* [1971] 2 All ER 216, Buckley LJ said:

. . . To constitute repudiation, the threatened breach must be such as to deprive the injured party of a substantial part of the benefit to which he is entitled under the contract. The measure of the necessary degree of substantiality has been expressed in a variety of ways in the cases. It has been said that the breach must be of an essential term, or of a fundamental term of the contract, or that it must go to the root of the contract. Various tests have been suggested: see eg *Freeth v Burr* per Lord Coleridge CJ and Keating J; *Mersey Steel and Iron Co Ltd v Naylor, Benzon & Co* per the Earl of Selborne L C and per Lord Blackburn and Hong Kong Fir Shipping Co Ltd v Kawasaki Kisen Kaisha Ltd per Diplock LJ. I venture to put the test in my own words as follows: will the consequences of the breach be such that it would be unfair to the injured party to hold him to the contract and leave him to the remedy in damages as and when a breach or breaches may occur? If this would be so, then a repudiation has taken place.

In that case, the defendants, who had been appointed sole dealers in the UK for the plaintiffs, were short of working capital and were persistently slightly late in paying for goods received. This cost the plaintiffs a small amount in bank interest each month, but there was never any doubt that the payments would be made in the end. Even though this situation appeared likely to continue, it was not a repudiation of the contract. Time for payment was not a condition (see p 573) and the consequences of the late payments were not serious; they would be adequately compensated by recovering the extra interest.

As the *Decro-Wall* case suggests, the concept of anticipatory repudiation is very important in relation to contracts that are to be performed in stages or instalments. A breach relating to one stage may justify termination of the whole contract, but only if it amounts to a repudiation of the whole contract (Sale of Goods Act 1979, s 31(2), see p 558). In *Millar's Karri and Jarrah Co v Weddel, Turner & Co* (1908) 14 Com Cas 25, at 29, Bigham J said:

> Thus, if the breach is of such a kind, or takes place in such circumstances as reasonably to lead to the inference that similar breaches will be committed in relation to subsequent deliveries, the whole contract may there and then be regarded as repudiated and may be rescinded. If, for instance, a buyer fails to pay for one delivery in such circumstances as to lead to the inference that he will not be able to pay for subsequent deliveries; or if a seller delivers goods differing from the requirements of the contract, and does so in such circumstances as to lead to the inference that he cannot, or will not, deliver any other kind of goods in the future, the other contracting party will be under no obligation to wait to see what may happen: he can at once cancel the contract and rid himself of the difficulty.

In that case, the first of two deliveries was so defective that it justified termination. In contrast, in *Maple Flock Co Ltd v Universal Furniture Products (Wembley) Ltd* [1934] 1 KB 148, one delivery out of 20 was defective. Lord Hewart CJ, delivering the judgment of the Court of Appeal said (at 157):

> ... [T]he main tests to be considered in applying the sub-section to the present case are, first, the ratio quantitatively which the breach bears to the contract as a whole, and secondly the degree of probability or improbability that such a breach will be repeated. On the first point, the delivery complained of amounts to no more than $1\frac{1}{2}$ tons out of a contract for 100 tons. On the second point, our conclusion is that the chance of the breach being repeated is practically negligible.

Therefore the defective delivery did not justify termination.

In a contract for a large building or engineering project, the completion date is likely to be months or years after the start of the project. Supposing the contract said nothing about time except that the work was to be done by a certain date, what would the employer's rights be if the contractor: (i) failed to start work when expected; (ii) worked extremely slowly; (iii) did some work defectively at an early stage? A party may insert into the contract a clause intended to give it more extensive rights to withhold its performance or to terminate in such circumstances: see p 603.

Suppose that a party has considerable doubt whether the other will perform when the time comes: a seller, for instance, has heard that the buyer is having financial difficulties, or discovers that the buyer has not paid him for goods delivered under a separate contract, and is worried about delivering on credit. What can he do?

■ Sale of Goods Act 1979

Section 41

(1) Subject to this Act, the unpaid seller of goods who is in possession of them is entitled to retain possession of them until payment or tender of the price in the following cases:— ... (c) where the buyer becomes insolvent.

Suppose the problem is that he has to build a special machine for the buyer, which will have no value to anyone else if the buyer defaults, and the buyer has already failed to make an advance payment. How could you devise an agreement that would safeguard the seller? You may like to consider the following:

Terms of payment are usually net cash monthly account but we reserve the right at any time before delivery to enquire as to the customer's credit standing and to require cash before delivery if we see fit.

(PJ Hare Ltd; see also specimen conditions of sale, Appendix, cl 15.1) Do you think that English law should adopt the same approach as the UCC?

■ Uniform Commercial Code

2–609. Right to adequate assurance of performance

(1) A contract for sale imposes an obligation on each party that the other's expectation of receiving due performance will not be impaired. When reasonable grounds for insecurity arise with respect to the performance of either party the other may in writing demand adequate assurance of due performance and until he receives such assurance may if commercially reasonable suspend any performance for which he has not already received the agreed return.

(2) Between merchants the reasonableness of grounds for insecurity and the adequacy of any assurance offered shall be determined according to commercial standards.

(3) Acceptance of any improper delivery or payment does not prejudice the aggrieved party's right to demand adequate assurance of future performance.

(4) After receipt of a justified demand failure to provide within a reasonable time not exceeding thirty days such assurance of due performance as is adequate under the circumstances of the particular case is a repudiation of the contract.

Official comment

. . . 4. What constitutes 'adequate' assurance of due performance is subject to the same test of factual conditions. For example, where the buyer can make use of a defective delivery, a mere promise by a seller of good repute that he is giving the matter his attention and that the defect will not be repeated, is normally sufficient. Under the same circumstances, however, a similar statement by a known corner-cutter might well be considered insufficient without the posting of a guaranty or, if so demanded by the buyer, a speedy replacement of the delivery involved. By the same token where a delivery has defects, even though easily curable, which interfere with easy use by the buyer, no verbal assurance can be deemed adequate which is not accompanied by replacement, repair, money-allowance, or other commercially reasonable cure.

X. RELIEF AGAINST FORFEITURE

In certain cases, a party who has committed a default that would normally entitle the other party to terminate the contract and repossess property from the defaulter may be given a last chance to cure his default. This may be done by requiring a formal procedure before the property is recovered, or by giving the defaulter relief.

■ Consumer Credit Act 1974

Section 87: Need for default notice

(1) Service of a notice on the debtor or hirer in accordance with section 88 (a 'default notice') is necessary before the creditor or owner can become entitled, by reason of any breach by the debtor or hirer of a regulated agreement, —

  (a) to terminate the agreement, or

  (b) to demand earlier payment of any sum, or

  (c) to recover possession of any goods or land, or

  (d) to treat any right conferred on the debtor or hirer by the agreement as terminated, restricted or deferred, or

  (e) to enforce any security.

(2) Subsection (1) does not prevent the creditor from treating the right to draw upon any credit as restricted or deferred, and taking such steps as may be necessary to make the restriction or deferment effective. . . .

Section 88: Contents and effect of default notice

(1) The default notice must be in the prescribed form and specify—

  (a) the nature of the alleged breach;

  (b) if the breach is capable of remedy, what action is required to remedy it and the date before which that action is to be taken;

  (c) if the breach is not capable of remedy, the sum (if any) required to be paid as compensation for the breach, and the date before which it is to be paid.

(2) A date specified under subsection (1) must not be less than seven days after the date of service of the default notice, and the creditor or owner shall not take action such as is mentioned in section 87(1) before the date so specified or (if no requirement is made under subsection (1)) before those seven days have elapsed.

(3) The default notice must not treat as a breach failure to comply with a provision of the agreement which becomes operative only on breach of some other provision, but if the breach of that other provision is not duly remedied or compensation demanded under subsection (1) is not duly paid, or (where no requirement is made under subsection (1)) if the seven days mentioned in subsection (2) have elapsed, the creditor or owner may treat the failure as a breach and section 87(1) shall not apply to it.

(4) The default notice must contain information in the prescribed terms about the consequences of failure to comply with it.

(5) A default notice making a requirement under subsection (1) may include a provision for the taking of action such as is mentioned in section 87(1) at any time after the restriction imposed by subsection (2) will cease, together with a statement that the provision will be ineffective if the breach is duly remedied or the compensation duly paid.

Section 89: Compliance with default notice

If before the date specified for that purpose in the default notice the debtor or hirer takes the action specified under section 88(1)(b) or (c) the breach shall be treated as not having occurred.

Section 90: Retaking of protected hire-purchase etc. goods

(1) At any time when—

  (a) the debtor is in breach of a regulated hire-purchase or a regulated conditional sale agreement relating to goods, and

  (b) the debtor has paid to the creditor one-third or more of the total price of the goods, and

  (c) the property in the goods remains in the creditor.

the creditor is not entitled to recover possession of the goods from the debtor except on an order of the court. . . .

(7) Goods falling within this section are in this Act referred to as 'protected goods'.

Section 91: Consequences of breach of s 90

If goods are recovered by the creditor in contravention of section 90—

(a) the regulated agreement, if not previously terminated, shall terminate, and

(b) the debtor shall be released from all liability under the agreement, and shall be entitled to recover from the creditor all sums paid by the debtor under the agreement.

NOTE

See also s 129 (Time orders), on p 495. Compare the procedures governing the forfeiture of leases for non-payment of rent (governed by the Common Law Procedure Act 1852, ss 210–212) or other breaches of covenant (Law of Property Act 1925, s 146).

In addition to these statutory powers to grant relief, there is a more general equitable power to grant relief to a defaulter who stands to forfeit some proprietary or possessory interest but who is ready and able to cure his default. Nearly all of the cases involve contracts for the sale of land under which the price is payable in instalments and the purchaser is let into possession, with a provision for the termination of the agreement and the forfeiture of sums already paid in the event of a default. The defaulting purchaser must be ready and willing to pay the sums overdue with interest, and the vendor's costs; the court can then grant him specific performance, if the conveyance would be due when the payments in question are made, or restrain the vendor from terminating the contract. The purchaser need not be able to pay the whole sum due immediately, if he can do so within the time the court is prepared to allow: *Starside Properties Ltd v Mustapha* [1974] 2 All ER 567.

■ *Union Eagle Ltd v Golden Achievement Ltd*
[1997] 2 All ER 215

In this case, the parties entered into a written contract for the appellent to buy a flat in Hong Kong from the respondent for HK$ 4.2 m. The purchaser paid a 10 per cent deposit. The contract provided that completion was to take place before 5.00 pm on 30 September 1991, that time was of the essence in every respect of the contract and that, if the purchaser failed to comply with any of the terms and conditions of the contract, the deposit was absolutely forfeited 'as and for liquidated damages (and not a penalty)'. A messenger carrying cheques for the full balance of the price arrived ten minutes late at the office of the vendor's solicitor. The solicitor refused to accept the cheques, told the purchaser's solicitor that the contract would be rescinded and the deposit forfeited.

The purchaser commenced an action for specific performance, which failed before the Hong Kong High Court and the Hong Kong Court of Appeal. The purchaser appealed to the Privy Council, arguing that it was entitled to relief against forfeiture in respect of its equitable interest in the property. The Privy Council rejected the appeal.

Lord Hoffmann

This clears the way for the main point in the appeal. The boundaries of the equitable jurisdiction to relieve against contractual penalties and forfeitures are in some places imprecise. But their Lordships do not think that it is necessary in this case to draw them more exactly because they agree with Litton V-P that the facts lie well beyond the reach of the doctrine. The notion that the court's jurisdiction to grant relief is 'unlimited and unfettered' (per Lord Simon of Glaisdale in *Shiloh Spinners Ltd v Harding* [1973] 1 All ER 90 at 104, [1978] AC 692 at 726) was rejected as a 'beguiling heresy' by the House of Lords in *Scandinavian Trading Tanker Co AB v Flota Petrolera Ecuatoriana, The Scaptrade* [1983] 2 All ER 763 at 766, [1983] 2 AC 694 at 700). It is worth pausing to notice why it continues to beguile and why it is a heresy. It has the obvious merit of allowing the court to impose what it considers to be a fair solution in the individual case. The principle that equity will restrain the enforcement of legal rights when it would be unconscionable to insist upon them has an attractive breadth. But the reasons why the courts have rejected such generalisations are founded not merely upon authority (see Lord Radcliffe in *Campbell Discount Co Ltd v Bridge* [1962] 1 All ER 385 at 397, [1962] AC 600 at 626) but also upon practical considerations of business. These are, in summary, that in many forms of transaction it is of great importance that if something happens for which the contract has made express provision, the parties should know with certainty that the terms of the contract will be enforced. The existence of an undefined discretion to refuse to enforce the contract on the ground that this would be 'unconscionable' is sufficient to create uncertainty. Even if it is most unlikely that a discretion to grant relief will be exercised, its mere existence enables litigation to be employed as a negotiating tactic. The realities of commercial life are that this may cause injustice which cannot be fully compensated by the ultimate decision in the case. . . .

When a vendor exercises his right to rescind, he terminates the contract. The purchaser's loss of the right to specific performance may be said to amount to a forfeiture of the equitable interest which the contract gave him in the land. But this forfeiture is different in its nature from, for example, the vendor's right to retain a deposit or part-payment of the purchase price. So far as these retentions exceed a genuine pre-estimate of damage or a reasonable deposit they will constitute a penalty which can be said to be essentially to provide security for payment of the full price. No objectionable uncertainty is created by the existence of a restitutionary form of relief against forfeiture, which give the court a discretion to order repayment of all or part of the retained money. But the right to rescind the contract, though it involves termination of the purchaser's equitable interest, stands upon a rather different footing. Its purpose is, upon breach of an essential terms, to restore to the vendor his freedom to deal with his land as he pleases. In a rising market, such a right may be valuable but volatile. Their Lordships think that in such circumstances a vendor should be able to know with reasonable certainty whether he may resell the land or not.

NOTES

1.   Note that in this case the purchaser was not asking to recover the deposit but, no doubt for tactical reasons, going all out for specific performance of the contract to sell the flat. In English law at least, it is clear by virtue of s 49 of the Law of Property Act 1925 that the Court, on facts of this kind, would have jurisdiction to order a return of the deposit (see p 703).

2.   In denying that the Court had any jurisdiction to grant relief in circumstances of this kind, the Privy Council was refusing to follow two important decisions of the High Court of Australia in *Legione v Hately* (1983) 152 CLR 406 and *Stern v McArthur* (1988) 165 CLR 489. The decision has also been thought by some to be difficult to reconcile with the decision of the Court of Appeal in *Re Dagenham (Thames) Dock* Co (1873) 8 Ch App 1022. For further discussion, see Abedian and Furmston (1998) 12 JCL 189. It may be that, in *Tanwar Enterprises Pty Ltd v Cauchi* (2003) 217 CLR, the High Court of Australia retreated from *Legione v Hateley*, although not so far as to embrace *Union Eagle*.

In these cases, the question is whether relief can be given to a defaulter who is willing and able ultimately to cure his default. If he cannot do this, it is not completely clear what powers the courts have to grant relief from forfeiture of a deposit or of money paid on terms that it should be forfeited if he defaulted: see pp 703 ff.

It is also not clear whether relief may be given against forfeiture when the contract gives the innocent party a right to re-enter land sold. *In Jobson v Johnson* [1989] 1 All ER 621, a contract for the sale of shares in Southend United Football Club provided that, if the purchaser defaulted in paying instalments of the price, he would transfer a number of shares back to the vendor at a fixed price, which may have been less than their value. The Court of Appeal gave relief in the form of an order that if the shares were worth more than the instalments and the interest due, the shares should be sold and the plaintiff be paid only the instalments and interest. However, the clause seems to have been treated as a form of penalty clause for which similar relief is usual (see pp 689 ff).

The House of Lords has held that the jurisdiction to grant relief against forfeiture is confined to cases in which a proprietary or possessory right is to be forfeited. Thus a time-charterer of a ship who has failed to pay instalments of hire in time cannot invoke the jurisdiction to prevent the owner from withdrawing the ship under the 'withdrawal clause' (see Appendix): *Scandinavian Trading Tanker Co AB v Flota Petrolera Ecuatoriana, The Scaptrade* [1983] 2 All ER 763. See also *Sport International Bussum B V v Inter-Footwear Ltd* [1984] 2 All ER 321 and Harpum (1984) 100 LQR 369; contrast *BICC plc v Burndy Corpn* [1985] Ch 232. In *The Scaptrade*, the House of Lords (at [1983] 2 All ER 763, 768) also endorsed Robert Goff LJ's statement in the Court of Appeal:

Parties to such contracts should be capable of looking after themselves . . .

Lord Diplock's speech suggests that the power to grant relief depends upon the availability of specific performance, but relief has been given in contracts for the hire of a machine *(Barton, Thompson & Co Ltd v Stapling Machines Co* [1966] Ch 499) and for the hire purchase of vehicles *(Transag Haulage Ltd v Leyland Daf Finance plc* [1994] 2 BCLC 88, [1994] BCC 356, although it is doubtful whether either contract would have been specifically enforced (see Chapter 23). See also *On Demand Information plc v Michael Gerson (Finance) plc* [2002] UKHL 13, [2003] 1 AC 368. Lord Diplock's remarks were held not to prevent the granting of an injunction to restrain the owner from withdrawing the ship from a time charterparty in *Lauritzencool AB v Lady Navigation Inc* [2006] 1 All ER 860. For further discussion, see Smith, 'Relief against Forfeiture: a Restatement' [2001] Camb LJ 178.

XI. REPRISE: FLEXIBILITY OR CERTAINTY?

■ Priest, 'Breach and Remedy for the Tender of Non-conforming Goods' (1978)
91 Harv LR 960, 963, 965, 967–968

Once the contract is found to have been breached by a non-conforming tender, the law provides the buyer two possible remedies. He may call off the sale and return the goods to the seller, or he may keep the goods and seek damages for the non-conformity. The costs imposed by these two remedies can be classified into two categories. First, there are allocative costs—the transfer of real resources from one or both of the parties to the outside world. Freight and insurance for reshipment, administrative costs of resale, and fees for attorneys involved in dispute resolution fall into this category. Second are distributive costs, which consist of transfers of resources *between* the parties, as when one party recovers damages from the other. Ordinarily, the minimization of allocative costs will benefit the parties regardless of the distribution of costs between them. However, the distribution of costs will affect allocative costs because each party will strive to minimize his personal share of the joint costs, even if his effort increases joint costs. In fact, in any dispute over the interpretation of a contract, the parties will expend resources in negotiation or litigation, thereby reducing the joint value of the transaction. In the text that follows, the conditions for minimizing the allocative costs of a remedy are first analyzed apart from the effects of the distribution of costs. Then the causes and effects of the distribution of costs between the parties are analyzed separately. . . .

Although the comparison of the costs of rescission and damages appears complicated, it can be simplified. Parties wishing to maximize the *joint* value of the transaction will prefer return of the goods to damages whenever the goods have a greater value in the seller's hands than in the buyer's. The value of the goods in the seller's hands is their market value less the seller's costs of retrieval and resale. The value of the goods in the buyer's hands is the greater of (1) their market value less the buyer's costs of resale, or (2) their value to the buyer after adaptation less the costs of adapting them. If the parties seek to conserve costs, they might first compare the value of the defective goods to the buyer with the market value of the goods. Where the loss from the defect is less to the buyer than to the market, returning the goods is generally not the cheaper remedy. If, however, the value to the buyer of the defective goods is less than the market value, the parties would agree to return the goods to the seller if the seller's costs of resale were lower than the buyer's by an amount greater than the retrieval costs. If the buyer's business involves the sale of defective as well as conforming goods, the buyer's and the seller's costs of resale may be equivalent, so that retrieval costs tip the balance in favor of a damage remedy. However, if the buyer is a consumer or is engaged solely in manufacturing, the value of managerial time necessary to resell the defective goods may be substantial. Then the advantages of the original seller—superior information about potential customers for defective goods and a superior distribution system—may offset the costs of retrieval and make rescission the preferable remedy. . . .

Where the price of the goods declines after formation of the contract, the buyer has an incentive to conjure up defects or to exaggerate the materiality of real defects, and to demand rescission rather than damages, regardless of which remedy minimizes allocative costs. A similar incentive exists when the buyer realizes that he has chosen an unsuitable product. As long as the legal rules governing breach and remedy are sufficiently manipulable to offer the buyer a significant opportunity for distributional benefits, he will expend resources in negotiation or litigation in an attempt to gain them. Indeed, a rational buyer will spend nearly as much as the amount of the market price decline, discounted by his probability of prevailing in court.

Two conclusions may be drawn from this analysis. First, courts may reduce the parties' expenditures in attempts to gain distributional benefits by making legal rules certain in application. As legal rules became more certain, the probability of each party's manipulating them to his advantage decreases, and hence he is willing to spend less in such an effort. Second, the parties' expenditures in attempts to achieve private benefits sometimes may be greater than the savings achieved by choosing the remedy which otherwise would minimize allocative costs. For example, suppose that the market price of the goods has dropped $10 since contract formation, that the non-conformity in the goods is obviously trivial, that the buyer's and seller's resale costs are small and equal, and that the cost of shipment from buyer to seller is $4. If the buyer can rescind, the net cost to the parties is the $4 shipment cost, and the buyer avoids the market loss. If the buyer must accept damages, the net cost to the parties is just the cost of determining the buyer's damages, which is zero because the triviality of the defect is obvious. Thus damages are the more efficient remedy. However, if the legal rules for choosing the remedy are manipulable, in the case where the parties have equal probabilities of prevailing (50% each), the buyer may expend up to $5 on litigation attempting to avoid his market loss by rescission. And the *seller* may invest up to $5 in litigation trying to avoid bearing the loss which he thought he contracted away. In such a case, the joint expenditure on litigation may be $10, while the savings from avoiding reshipment is only $4. Thus the remedy of damages remains the more efficient, but its true value is never realized unless the legal rules are certain enough to discourage expensive legal disputes.

If the parties to a sale were to negotiate a remedy for a non-conforming tender explicitly, they probably would not limit themselves to an absolute choice between rescission and damages, but would structure a more flexible remedy which would preserve the allocation of risk implicit in a contract of sale at a fixed price. Where allocative costs can be minimized by rescission, the parties would maintain the distribution of risk by allowing the seller to repair the defective tender or to offset the decline in market price against the purchase price to be returned to the buyer. Either such remedy retains the cost advantages of the seller's resale or repair of the defective goods without disturbing the contractual allocation of risk. Similarly, where the goods prove unsuitable to the buyer despite the triviality of the defects, the allocation of risk can be maintained if the buyer reimburses the seller for retrieving and reselling the goods, as well as for depreciation. Even with such flexible remedies, however, there will still be the incentive of distributional benefits as long as the contract is not enforced with certainty. Moreover, the cost of uncertainty will exist whether these remedies are created by the parties or enforced by a court. Since the cost of uncertainty is inevitable and difficult to estimate, the flexibility of legal rules will always make it difficult to determine the most efficient remedy.

Although the courts now apply more flexible rules when dealing with constructive conditions, we have seen that sometimes the implied conditions under the Sale of Goods Act 1979 allowed a party to escape an unprofitable contract because of a relatively unimportant breach by the other party.

■ 'Sale and Supply of Goods' (Law Commission No 160, Cm 137, 1987)

2.26 A criticism of the classification of most of the implied terms in the Sale of Goods Act as 'conditions' is that it leads to inflexibility and to a danger that the obligation of the seller to supply goods of the appropriate quality will be watered down. If a defect is a minor one the court may be reluctant to allow rejection and so, under the present law, may be tempted to hold that there is no breach at all of the implied term as to quality.... [For example.]... in *Cehave* NV *v Bremer Handelsgesellschaft mbH* Lord Denning MR said that the implied condition was broken only if the defect was so serious that a commercial man would have thought that the buyer should be able to reject the goods. These cases illustrate the difficulties to which the rigid classification gives rise, and lower courts are bound by the precedents thus created. There has, moreover, been express criticism of the inflexibility of the present law as to compliance with description.

4.1.... The terms implied by sections 13 to 15 of the 1979 Act are capable of being broken in ways some of which may be very serious but some of which may be very slight. The classification of a term with such a flexible content as a 'condition' with the inflexible result that in all cases the buyer has the right to terminate the contract as well as claim damages can give rise to unfairness. On the one hand, the right to terminate a contract for a very slight breach which can easily be remedied may seem unjust on the seller whose loss might far exceed the cost of remedying the defect. On the other hand, the remedy of rejection is so powerful that it can be counterproductive. A court faced with a claim to reject which it considers thoroughly unreasonable may come to the conclusion that there was no breach of contract at all: the buyer cannot then even recover damages. What the court cannot do in the case of breach of condition is to award damages but at the same time decide that the breach was too slight to entitle the buyer to reject the goods. It is a case of 'rejectability or nothing'. Thus the strength of the buyer's remedy may actually work against his interests.

4.2 We considered in the Consultative Document whether the solution to this problem was to recommend the creation of a new term that goods would be free from all minor defects. Breach of this term would give rise only to a right to damages. We rejected that solution in the Consultative Document and consultation has confirmed us in that view. Such a term would be undesirable where the buyer was a consumer because it would weaken his bargaining position excessively, and for consumers and non-consumers alike there would be too much uncertainty about what was a 'minor defect'.

4.3 The question then asked by the Consultative Document was what the remedy should be when there was a breach of one of the statutory implied terms as to quality. Here, we suggested, there was a distinction to be drawn between the interests of the consumer and those of the non-consumer. . . .

4.4 . . . [T]he consumer is almost always buying goods for domestic use or consumption and not for the purpose of making a profit out of them; he will not usually be content with defective goods when he intended to buy perfect goods, even if the price were reduced or he were compensated in some way. If he wants to retain defective goods he can always keep them and claim damages. But should he ever be prevented from rejecting the goods and terminating the contract when this is what he wants to do? The consumer will not usually be in a position easily to dispose of defective goods and if he keeps them it may be difficult to quantify what his loss is in money terms, especially if the defect is only minor. The seller is also likely to be in a stronger bargaining position than the consumer buyer: the buyer may in practice have to drop his claim or accept less than his due. Given that the overwhelming majority of consumer disputes are not taken to court, or even to lawyers, the relative strength of the bargaining position of each party is, in our view, a factor of critical importance. Even if compensation were agreed, this would often still not be an adequate remedy for the consumer. What he wanted was goods of the proper quality at the full price, not defective goods at a lower price. It must be made as easy as possible for the consumer to get defective goods replaced by sound ones (if, as is so often the case, this is what he is prepared to agree to) or to get his money back (if this is what he insists on).

4.5 It seems to us that these considerations do not apply with the same force to most non-consumer transactions. Non-consumers who are in the business of dealing in goods are usually able to dispose of goods of different qualities through access to the appropriate markets. A breach of contract by the seller can usually be measured in monetary terms and then taken into account in calculating profits. The motive for rejection of goods may well differ between consumers and non-consumers. The consumer is unlikely to attempt to reject goods because of a fall in their market price. He rejects goods because he wants perfect goods, not defective ones. The non-consumer will also, of course, sometimes wish to reject goods for this reason. Not infrequently, however, the non-consumer who deals in goods uses their alleged non-conformity as his excuse for rejection: his real motive is that the market price of the goods has fallen. When prices fall it will be commercially advantageous to him to get rid of the expensive goods in his hands and perhaps then replace them with similar goods, bought at the lower price. The diminution in value caused by the quality defect may be trifling; the diminution caused by the fall in the market price may be immense. Is it just in those circumstances to allow the buyer to reject the goods and terminate the contract so as to cause the loss due to the change in the market to fall on the seller and not on himself?

4.6 Any distinction between the position of consumers and non-consumers may be objected to on the ground that it will be unfair to those near the borderline. We recognise and must accept that any definition of 'consumer' and 'non-consumer' is likely to give rise to some difficult borderline cases. We recognise that there are some powerful consumers who are in practice in a stronger bargaining position than their suppliers. There are also many non-consumers to whom the arguments in the preceding paragraph do not apply. Moreover, those arguments apply with special force to dealers in some types of goods only. They apply with little force, for example, to a retailer who makes his profit from a standard mark-up of goods sold at a standard price, and only slightly (if at all) to the non-consumer who buys goods in which he does not deal. An example of the latter is, perhaps, the small corner shop which buys an item of equipment such as a refrigerator for use in the shop. This type of non-consumer is probably in very much the same position as an individual consumer if the refrigerator proves to be defective. . . .

2. Policy for consumers

4.10 . . . It is, of course, very common in practice for a buyer and seller to agree that the goods should be repaired or replaced free of charge. Some might say that there are circumstances in which it would be unreasonable for the buyer to insist on rejecting the goods when the seller is prepared to replace them or remedy the [defect].

4.11 In the Consultative Document we used the word 'cure' to describe the remedy of repair or replacement. We said that this procedure should be encouraged and we put forward for discussion three possible schemes of remedies based upon the notion of 'cure'. Although the schemes differed in details, their essential feature was that in some instances a seller would have the right to 'cure' any defect but that if he did not do so the buyer could reject. The buyer would thus never have been required to keep defective goods but the seller could, if he wanted, have prevented rejection by correcting the defect or offering replacement goods. . . .

. . .

4.13 On consultation there was much support for our suggested scheme of 'cure'. However, two principal, and formidable, lines of objection emerged. First, it was suggested that the scheme was generally too adverse to consumers' interests because it gave the supplier a ground upon which he could argue that the buyer was not entitled to return defective goods and claim the price back. Secondly, we had recognised in the Consultative Document that the scheme left many questions unanswered. . . .

4.14 We have decided not to recommend a 'cure' scheme for consumer transactions, although not all of us are without regret on the matter. We are, in short, not sufficiently confident that such a scheme would be more beneficial to buyers and sellers generally than is the present law. . . .

We have reached the conclusion, therefore, that, for the consumer transaction, the regime which applies must be a simple one. Such is the present law. In legal theory the consumer has the absolute right to reject for any defect. True, he may seldom exercise that right, almost always being prepared to accept repair or replacement. However, if the seller is unreasonable it is against that legal background that the discussion takes place. Any legal ground upon which rejection might arguably be resisted, however weak such ground might be on the facts, gives the seller a potential weapon with which to undermine the position of the ordinary consumer. Sometimes, moreover, what the law is believed to be is more important than what it is. There should be no ambiguity or misunderstanding about the rights of the consumer buyer.

4.15 We have therefore decided to recommend the retention of the present law so far as concerns the consumer buyer's right to reject the goods and terminate the contract for breach of the statutory implied terms in sections 13 to 15 of the Sale of Goods Act. . . .

3. Policy for non-consumers

4.16 . . . So far as non-consumer buyers are concerned, however, our conclusions are different. The reasons of policy applicable to consumers do not apply to non-consumers. Such buyers cannot as a general rule be presumed to be in a weak bargaining position as against their sellers, and there is less objection to leaving them with non-conforming goods in their hands in an appropriate case, especially because they will still have a claim for damages (which in many cases will be fairly easy to quantify).

4.17 In the Consultative Document we discussed a number of possible ways of modifying the rights of the non-consumer buyer. Of these we provisionally rejected all but one, and those we rejected received little support on consultation. First, we rejected the idea that there should be a list of the circumstances in which rejection or (as the case may be) non-rejection would be permitted. The circumstances of sale transactions are so infinitely variable that any set of rules would both be extremely lengthy and yet incomplete. Secondly, we rejected any idea of a statutory right to 'cure', as we had provisionally proposed for consumers. Now that we are not recommending such a regime for consumers, the case for recommending it for non-consumers is even weaker than it was at the time we made our provisional recommendations. We do not wish to do anything to stop non-consumers from coming to their own agreement about 'curing' defects and, indeed, cure provisions (sometimes very detailed) are common in many types of commercial contract. The question, however, was whether there should be a statutory 'cure' regime in all cases and, for the reasons given in the Consultative Document, which were largely endorsed on consultation, we make no such recommendation. Thirdly, we rejected the idea that a non-consumer buyer should be entitled to reject goods only where damages would not be an adequate remedy. The effect of such a recommendation would be, we thought, that rejection would hardly ever be permissible; damages would in almost all cases be held to be an adequate remedy for a commercial buyer. Not only had there been no call for such a drastic change in the policy of the Act but we ourselves did not think such a change was desirable. Fourthly, we considered whether non-consumers should be entitled to reject only when the breach was very serious. For example, the test could have been taken from the *Hongkong Fir* case: was the breach so serious as to frustrate the contract? Such a test would in substance be a reversal of the present law for rejection would be permissible only in the most extreme cases. Notwithstanding that an express term relating to the quality of goods has been held by the Court of Appeal to carry these remedies, in the Consultative Document we expressed the provisional view that so severe a test was not appropriate for the statutory implied terms. This view has been confirmed on consultation and we do not recommend the major alteration of the law which would result from its adoption.

4.18 We did not think, therefore, that there was need for more than a slight change in the law. What was required was no more than a modification which would, in substance, prevent rejection in bad faith, where the breach was really so insignificant that, as a matter of justice, rejection should not be permitted. To introduce a general duty of good faith into the law relating to the sale of goods might perhaps be desirable but could not be justified by the particular problem which we had under examination. Moreover, if such a duty were to be introduced the question would also have to be asked whether the duty should not extend across the entire range of contract law.

4.19 The proposal we favoured in the Consultative Document aimed to preserve the present law as far as possible whilst lessening the risk of its abuse. Our provisional proposal was that in a non-consumer sale 'the buyer ought to be entitled to reject the goods for breach of any one of the terms implied by section 13 to 15 of the Sale of Goods Act unless the seller can show that the nature and consequences of the breach are so slight that rejection would be unreasonable'. In making this proposal we stressed that the buyer's motive in seeking to reject the goods and treat the contract as repudiated would not be relevant.

4.20 In the Consultative Document we said that we were concerned lest any such modification of the absolute right to reject defective goods should create undesirable uncertainty. Consultation has not affirmed this concern . . .

. . .

4.21 The *Law Commission's recommendations* apply to England and Wales. They are that for the non-consumer the statutory implied quality terms should remain as conditions but that the Act should provide that where the breach is so slight that it would be unreasonable for the buyer to reject the goods, the breach is not to be treated as a breach of condition but may be treated as a breach of warranty. The effect of this will be that the buyer will not be able to reject the goods but will only be able to claim damages. . . .

4.23 Both Commissions recognise that to introduce any modification of the absolute right to reject is to introduce a measure of uncertainty. As so often happens where reform of the law is concerned, a balance has to be struck. On the one hand is the benefit of certainty: on the other is the benefit of justice. We have concluded that the uncertainty will be more apparent than real and is a price worth paying. Parties will, of course, be able to provide, either expressly or by implication, that there shall be an absolute right to reject in any particular circumstances. Moreover, in the appropriate circumstances there will be no difficulty in inferring such an intention.

4.24 A particular example of such circumstances is that in many commercial situations it would be normal to infer an intention that any breach of a time clause, however slight, would justify rejection of the goods and termination of the contract. We do not expect our recommendations to have any effect on such time clauses. We have no doubt that it would continue to be the right to reject the goods and terminate the contract; and that when the contract was construed against its commercial matrix, a court would have no difficulty in so holding.

. . .

6.18 In the Consultative Document we raised three questions about [the rules contained in Sale of Goods Act 1979, s 30.]

6.19 *The first question* was whether the special regime of remedies which we proposed in the Consultative Document for breach of the implied terms contained in sections 13 to 15 of the 1979 Act should also apply to delivery of the wrong quantity of goods. Our provisional view was that it should not. We saw no obvious reason why the Act should not contain a number of specific and strict rules about delivery of the wrong quantity, which might differ in effect from the rules on breach of the implied terms.

6.20 We remain of this view. We think, however, that a refinement of our proposal for the restriction on the right to reject in non-consumer cases is desirable where a wrong quantity of goods is delivered to the buyer. Where a wrong quantity is delivered to the buyer he has at present the right to reject the *whole* of the goods; no matter how slight the shortfall or excess. Where there is an excess, he also has the right to reject the excess only. The Law Commission's *recommendation* for England and Wales is that the right to reject an excess should in all cases be preserved, but that where the non-consumer is delivered a wrong quantity of goods, and the shortfall or excess is so slight that it would be unreasonable to reject the *whole*, then he should be barred from so doing.

■ Sale and Supply of Goods Act 1994
Section 4

(1) After section 15 of the Sale of Goods Act 1979 there is inserted the following—

[*'Miscellaneous'*]

15 A (1) Where in the case of a contract of sale—
    (a) the buyer would, apart from this subsection, have the right to reject goods by reason of a breach on the part of the seller of a term implied by section 13, 14 or 15 above, but
    (b) the breach is so slight that it would be unreasonable for him to reject them,
    then, if the buyer does not deal as consumer, the breach is not to be treated as a breach of condition but may be treated as a breach of warranty.
(2) This section applies unless a contrary intention appears in, or is to be implied from, the contract.
(3) It is for the seller to show that a breach fell within subsection (1)(b) above.
(4) section does not apply to Scotland.'
(2) In section 30 of that Act (delivery of shortfall or excess) after subsection (2) there is inserted—[see above, p 554, subsections 2B and 2C].

NOTES

1.   Schedule 2 of the 1994 Act amends SGA s 61 to define 'dealing as consumer':

    (5A) References in this Act to dealing as consumer are to be construed in accordance with Part I of the Unfair Contract Terms Act 1977; and, for the purposes of this Act, it is for a seller claiming that the buyer does not deal as consumer to show that he does not.

2.   Similar restrictions to those in s 15A now apply to the rejection of goods under other contracts for the supply of goods or for hire of goods: Supply of Goods and Services Act 1982, ss 5A and 10A (inserted by Sale and Supply of Goods Act 1994, Sch 2.)

XII. AGREED RIGHTS OF TERMINATION

We have already noted that, in theory, the courts will enforce any express provision in the contract stating that, in certain circumstances, A may withhold performance or terminate if B doesn't do something. There is no difficulty if the obligation which B has to do is fundamental to the contract. But what if the obligation, or at least the failure to perform it, which has actually occurred, doesn't seem important?

■ *L Schuler AG v Wickman Machine Tools Sales Ltd*
[1973] 2 All ER 39, House of Lords

Wickman was appointed sole distributor of Schuler's panel presses in the UK for a period of four-and-a-half years. Clause 7(b) of the agreement provided that:

It shall be condition of this agreement that (i) [Wickman] shall send its representatives to visit [the six large UK motor manufacturers] at least once in every week for the purpose of soliciting orders for panel presses...

Clause 11(a) provided that either party might determine the agreement by notice in writing if:

(i) the other shall have committed a material breach of its obligations hereunder and shall have failed to remedy the same within sixty days of being required in writing so to do...

Wickman's representatives failed to make the weekly visit on a few occasions, and Schuler terminated the agreement immediately, claiming that Wickman was in breach of a condition under cl 7(b).

The dispute went to arbitration, and, on a case stated, Mocatta J held that Schuler's contention was correct, but the decision was reversed by the Court of Appeal. Schuler appealed.

Lord Reid

...I think it right first to consider the meaning of cl 11 because, if Wickman's contention with regard to this is right, then cl 7 must be construed in light of the provisions of cl 11. Clause 11 expressly provides that the agreement 'shall continue in force (unless previously determined as hereinafter provided) until' 31st December 1967. That appears to imply the corollary that the agreement shall not be determined before that date in any other way than as provided in cl 11. It is argued for Schuler that those words cannot have been intended to have that implication. In the first place Schuler say that anticipatory breach cannot be brought within the scope of cl 11 and the parties cannot have intended to exclude any remedy for an anticipatory breach. And, secondly, they say that cl 11 fails to provide any remedy for an irremediable breach however fundamental such breach might be.

There is much force in this criticism. But on any view the interrelation and consequences of the various provisions of this agreement are so ill-thought out that I am not disposed to discard the natural meaning of the words which I have quoted merely because giving to them their natural meaning implies that the draftsman has forgotten something which a better draftsman would have remembered. If the terms of cl 11 are wide enough to apply to breaches of cl 7 then I am inclined to hold that cl 7 must be read subject to the provisions of cl 11.

It appears to me that cl 11(a)(i) is intended to apply to all material breaches of the agreement which are capable of being remedied. The question then is what is meant in this context by the word 'remedy'. It could mean obviate or nullify the effect of a breach so that any damage already done is in some way made good. Or it could mean cure so that matters are put right for the future. I think that the latter is the more natural meaning. The word is commonly used in connection with diseases or ailments and they would normally be said to be remedied if they were cured although no cure can remove the past effect or result of the disease before the cure took place. And in general it can only be in a rare case that any remedy of something that has gone wrong in the performance of a continuing positive obligation will, in addition to putting it right for the future, remove or nullify damage already incurred before the remedy was applied. To restrict the meaning of remedy to cases where all damage past and future can be put right would leave hardly any scope at all for this clause. On the other hand, there are cases where it would seem a misuse of language to say that a breach can be remedied. For example, a breach of cl 14 by disclosure of confidential information could not be said to be remedied by a promise not to do it again.

So the question is whether a breach of Wickman's obligation under cl 7(b)(i) is capable of being remedied within the meaning of this agreement. On the other hand, failure to make one particular visit might have irremediable consequences, eg a valuable order might have been lost when making that visit would have obtained it. But looking at the position broadly I incline to the view that breaches of this obligation should be held to be capable of remedy within the meaning of cl 11. Each firm had to be visited more than 200 times. If one visit is missed I think that one would normally say that making arrangements to prevent a recurrence of that breach would remedy the breach. If that is right and if cl 11 is intended to have general application than cl 7 must be read so that a breach of cl 7(b)(i) does not give to Schuler a right to rescind but only to require the breach to be remedied within 60 days under cl 11(a)(i). I do not feel at all confident that this is the true view but I would adopt it unless the provisions of cl 7 point strongly in the opposite direction; so I turn to cl 7.

Clause 7 begins with the general requirement that Wickman shall 'use its best endeavours' to promote sales of Schuler products. Then there is in cl 7(b)(i) specification of those best endeavours with regard to panel presses, and in cl 12(b) a much more general statement of what Wickman must do with regard to other Schuler products. This intention to impose a stricter obligation with regard to panel presses is borne out by the use of the word 'condition' in cl 7(b). I cannot accept Wickman's argument that condition here merely means term. It must be intended to emphasise the importance of the obligations in sub-cll (b)(i) and (b)(ii). But what is the extent of that emphasis?

Schuler maintain that the word 'condition' has now acquired a precise legal meaning; that, particularly since the enactment of the Sale of Goods Act 1893, its recognised meaning in English law is a term of a contract any breach of which by one party gives to the other party an immediate right to rescind the whole contract. Undoubtedly the word is frequently used in that sense. There may, indeed, be some presumption that in a formal legal document it has that meaning. But it is frequently used with a less stringent meaning. One is familiar with printed 'conditions of sale' incorporated into a contract, and with the words 'for conditions see back' printed on a ticket. There it simply means that the 'conditions' are terms of the contract.

In the ordinary use of the English language 'condition' has many meanings, some of which have nothing to do with agreements. In connection with an agreement it may mean a pre-condition: something which must happen or be done before the agreement can take effect. Or it may mean some state of affairs which must continue to exist if the agreement is to remain in force. The legal meaning on which Schuler rely is, I think, one which would not occur to a layman; a condition in that sense is not something which has an automatic effect. It is a term the breach of which by one party gives to the other an option either to terminate the contract or to let the contract proceed and, if he so desires, sue for damages for the breach.

Sometimes a breach of a term gives that option to the aggrieved party because it is of a fundamental character going to the root of the contract, sometimes it gives that option because the parties have chosen to stipulate that it shall have that effect. Blackburn J said in *Bettini v Gye:* 'Parties may think some matter, apparently of very little importance, essential; and if they sufficiently express an intention to make the literal fulfilment of such a thing a condition precedent, it will be one.'

In the present case it is not contended that Wickman's failures to make visits amounted in themselves to fundamental breaches. What is contended is that the terms of cl 7 'sufficiently express an intention' to make any breach, however small, of the obligation to make visits a condition so that any such breach shall entitle Schuler to rescind the whole contract if they so desire.

Schuler maintain that the use of the word 'condition' is in itself enough to establish this intention. No doubt some words used by lawyers do have a rigid inflexible meaning. But we must remember that we are seeking to discover intention as disclosed by the contract as a whole. Use of the word 'condition' is an indication—even a strong indication—of such an intention but it is by no means conclusive. The fact that a particular construction leads to a very unreasonable result must be a relevant consideration. The more unreasonable the result the more unlikely it is that the parties can have intended it, and if they do intend it the more necessary it is that they shall make that intention abundantly clear.

Clause 7(b) requires that over a long period each of the six firms shall be visited every week by one or other of two named representatives. It makes no provision for Wickman being entitled to substitute others even on the death or retirement of one of the named representatives. Even if one could imply some right to do this, it makes no provision for both representatives being ill during a particular week. And it makes no provision for the possibility that one or other of the firms may tell Wickman that they cannot receive Wickman's representative during a particular week. So if the parties gave any thought to the matter at all they must have realised the probability that in a few cases out of the 1,400 required visits a visit as stipulated would be impossible. But if Schuler's contention is right failure to make even one visit entitles them to terminate the contract however blameless Wickman might be. This is so unreasonable that it must make me search for some other possible meaning of the contract. If none can be found then Wickman must suffer the consequences. But only if that is the only possible interpretation.

If I have to construe cl 7 standing by itself then I do find difficulty in reaching any other interpretation. But if cl 7 must be read with cl 11 the difficulty disappears. The word 'condition' would make any breach of cl 7(b), however excusable, a material breach. That would then entitle Schuler to give notice under cl 11(a)(i) requiring the breach to be remedied. There would be no point in giving such a notice if Wickman were clearly not in fault but if it were given Wickman would have no difficulty in shewing that the breach had been remedied. If Wickman were at fault then on receiving such a notice they would have to amend their system so that they could shew that the breach had been remedied. If they did not do that within the period of the notice then Schuler would be entitled to rescind.

In my view, that is a possible and reasonable construction of the contract and I would therefore adopt it. The contract is so obscure that I can have no confidence that this is its true meaning but for the reasons which I have given I think that it is the preferable construction. It follows that Schuler were not entitled to rescind the contract as they purported to do. So I would dismiss this appeal.

Lord Wilberforce

... Does cl 7(b) amount to a 'condition' or a 'term'? (to call it an important or material term adds, with all respect, nothing but some intellectual assuagement). My Lords, I am clear in my own mind that it is a condition, but your Lordships take the contrary view. On a matter of construction of a particular document, to develop the reasons for a minority opinion serves no purpose. I am all the more happy to refrain from so doing because the judgments of Mocatta J, Stephenson LJ, and indeed of Edmund Davies LJ on construction, give me complete satisfaction and I could in any case add little of value to their reasons. I would only add that, for my part, to call the clause arbitrary, capricious or fantastic, or to introduce as a test of its validity the ubiquitous reasonable man (I do not know whether he is English or German) is to assume, contrary to the evidence, that both parties to this contract adopted a standard of easygoing tolerance rather than one of aggressive, insistent punctuality and efficiency. This is not an assumption I am prepared to make, nor do I think myself entitled to impose the former standard on the parties if their words indicate, as they plainly do, the latter. I note finally, that the result of treating the clause, so careful and specific in its requirements, as a term is, in effect, to deprive the appellants of any remedy in respect of admitted and by no means minimal breaches. The arbitrator's finding that these breaches were not 'material' was not, in my opinion, justified in law in the face of the parties' own characterisation of them in their document: indeed the fact that he was able to do so, and so leave the appellants without remedy, argues strongly that the legal basis of his finding—that cl 7(b) was merely a term—is unsound.

I would allow this appeal.

Lords Morris of Borth-y-Gest, **Simon of Glaisdale** and **Kilbrandon** delivered speeches dismissing the appeal.

Appeal dismissed.

NOTES

1. If the purpose of visiting every week is to keep in close touch with every development at a potential purchaser's factory, how can a missed visit be 'remedied'?

2. Why was the result of treating cl 7(b) as a condition in the strict sense so unreasonable? Suppose Schulers had asked you to draft the contract, and had stressed that even though it might not be able to show that any particular visit missed had led to the loss of a sale (a point referred to by Mocatta J at first instance), it nonetheless wanted to be sure that Wickmans would not miss any; how would you have drafted the contract? (Of course, Wickmans might not have been prepared to sign your version, as Lord Kilbrandon remarked at 63.)

3. The House of Lords seems subsequently to have changed its attitude towards conditions in contracts, favouring certainty over a 'just' result on the facts of the case. Consider this statement by Lord Bridge in *Awilco A/S v Fulvia SpA di Navigazione, The Chikuma* [1981] 1 All ER 652 at 658–659:

    It has often been pointed out that shipowners and charterers bargain at arm's length. Neither class has such a preponderance of bargaining power as to be in a position to oppress the other. They should be in a position to look after themselves by contracting only on terms which are acceptable to them. Where, as here, they embody in their contracts common form clauses, it is, to my mind, of overriding importance that their meaning and legal effect should be certain and well understood. The ideal at which the courts should aim, in construing such clauses, is to produce a result such that in any given situation both parties seeking legal advice as to their rights and obligations can expect the same clear and confident answer from their advisers and neither will be tempted to embark on long and expensive litigation in the belief that victory depends on winning the sympathy of the court. This ideal may never be fully attainable, but we shall certainly never even approximate to it unless we strive to follow clear and consistent principles and steadfastly refuse to be blown off course by the supposed merits of individual cases.

    (See also *Bunge v Tradax*, above.) That is not to say that *Schuler v Wickman* would be decided differently today, but who knows..?

4. Suppose you decide that Schulers do need the right to terminate the contract for even a single visit missed and to recover any loss they suffer when they terminate. How could you draft a provision which would give them these rights? In *Total Gas Marketing Ltd v Arco British Ltd* [1998] 2 Lloyd's Rep 209, Lord Steyn said:

    The contractual language shows that the parties contemplated that *under the contract* a time would come when it was too late for the condition regarding an allocation agreement to be fulfilled, and that the contract would then be discharged. On the other hand, the construction put forward on behalf of the seller treats the words 'condition precedent', so far as it relates to the seller becoming party to an allocation agreement, as devoid of meaning. It is true, of course, that there is no provision setting out the consequences of the non-occurrence of this particular contingent condition. But, in regard to contingent conditions, it is not necessary for parties when stipulating for a condition precedent or a condition subsequent to spell out the consequences of non-occurrence of the condition: these are prima facie inherent in the use of such terms: compare the observation of Lord Wilberforce in *Wickman Machine Tool Sales Ltd v L Schuler AG* [1973] 2 Lloyd's Rep 53 at 65, col 2, [1974] AC 235 at 262G which is unaffected by the difference of opinion in *Wickman*. In this legal context an interpretation which gives *no* effect to the words 'condition precedent', so far as it applies to the allocation agreement, ought to be received with an initial sense of incredulity.

> The facts and decisions in this case are worth careful study as an example of how these problems are dealt with in practice.

Provisions which give one party the right to terminate because of a breach which would not normally justify it, or because of delays which would not normally amount to an anticipatory repudiation, are common.

■ Institution of Civil Engineers Conditions (7th edn)
cl 65(1)

Clause 65

Default of Contractor

(1) In the event that the Contractor

   (a) assigns or attempts to assign the Contract or any part thereof or any benefit or interest thereunder without the prior written consent of the Employer or

   (b) is in breach of Clause 4(1) or

   (c) (i) becomes bankrupt or presents his petition in bankruptcy or

      (ii) has a receiving order or administration order made against him or

      (iii) makes an arrangement with or an assignment in favour of his creditors or

      (iv) agrees to carry out the Contract under a committee of inspection of his creditors

      (v) (being a corporation) has a receiver or administrator appointed or goes into liquidation (other than a voluntary liquidation for the purposes of amalgamation or reconstruction) or

   (d) has an execution levied on his goods which is not stayed or discharged within 28 days

or if the Engineer certifies in writing to the Employer with a copy to the Contractor that in his opinion the Contractor

   (e) has abandoned the Contract without due cause or

   (f) without reasonable excuse has failed to commence the Works in accordance with Clause 41 or

   (g) has suspended the progress of the Works without due cause for 14 days after receiving from the Engineer written notice to proceed or

   (h) has failed to remove goods or materials from the Site or to pull down and replace work for 14 days after receiving from the Engineer written notice that the said goods material or work has been condemned and rejected by the Engineer or

   (j) despite previous warnings by the Engineer in writing is failing to proceed with the Works with due diligence or is otherwise persistently or fundamentally in breach of his obligations under the Contract

then the Employer may after giving 7 days notice in writing to the Contractor specifying the event relied on enter upon the Works and any other parts of the Site provided by the Employer and expel the Contractor therefrom without thereby avoiding the Contract or releasing the Contractor from any of his obligations or liabilities under the Contract.

Where a notice of termination is given pursuant to a certificate issued by the Engineer under this sub-clause it shall be given as soon as is reasonably possible after receipt of the certificate.

Provided that the Employer may extend the period of notice to give the Contractor an opportunity to remedy the situation.

NOTES

1. In what ways does this clause attempt to improve on the position of the employer at common law? To put the same question another way, would the employer be entitled to terminate the contract at common law in each of the situations listed in (a) to (j)?

2. Insolvency on the part of the contractor is not *itself* a ground for termination at common law; the liquidator could opt to perform the contract, and if it was one on which the contractor stood to make money, he would presumably do so.

In *Financings Ltd v Baldock* [1963] 2 QB 104, a hire-purchase agreement provided:

8. Should the hirer fail to pay the initial instalment . . . or any subsequent instalment . . . within ten days after the same shall have become due or if he shall die . . . the owner may . . . by written notice . . . forthwith and for all purposes terminate the hiring.

Clause 11 provided that if the agreement were terminated under cl 8, the hirer would pay to the owner 'such further sum as with the total amount of any instalments previously paid here-under will equal two-thirds of the total hiring cost'.

The hirer failed to pay the second and third instalments, and the owners gave notice of termination under cl 8 and repossessed the vehicle. Clause 11 was invalid as a penalty clause. (The rules on penalty clauses are explained in greater detail below (pp 689 ff), but in essence, if the parties agree on a sum that is to be paid as damages if one of them breaks the contract, the clause will be valid if it is a genuine pre-estimate of the loss that the breach is likely to cause ('liquidated damages'). If it exceeds this figure, the cl will be invalid as a 'penalty'. The reasons why clause 11 in the *Financings* contract was penal are explained on p 700. Therefore the owners claimed damages from the hirer for their full loss. The Court of Appeal held that they were entitled to the overdue instalments up to the date of repossession, but no more. The failure to pay one or two instalments on time would not justify termination of the contract under the general law (see p 574), and cl 8 merely conferred a right to terminate the agreement without making the failure to pay a breach of condition. If the hirer's failure to pay had amounted to a repudiation, as in *Overstone Ltd v Shipway* [1962] 1 All ER 52, CA, the hirer would have been liable in damages, but here the owners could only claim money due at the date of termination and any payments required under the termination clause itself (none in this case). On the effect of cl 8, Denning LJ said:

It seems to me that when an agreement of hiring is terminated by virtue of a power contained in it, and the owner retakes the vehicle, he can recover damages for any breach up to the date of termination but not for any breach thereafter, for the simple reason that there are no breaches thereafter. . . . That principle is implicit in what Salter J said as long ago as 1926 in *Elacy & Co Ltd, v Hyde*, an unreported case quoted by Jenkins LJ in *Cooden Engineering Co Ltd v Stanford*. Salter J took the very case

'where the hire is determined by the owner, because the hirer is in arrear with his payments. It is proved that this is a breach of this contract, and it is proved that that breach, apart from any termination of the hirer, would give the owner a right to damages against the hirer. But what would those damages be? They would be interest on the amount unpaid and nothing more. The fact that the hirer is in arrear with his payments will not entitle the owner to any damages for depreciation of these things. The reason that they have suffered is that they have secondhand goods put on their hands before they have received very much money in respect of them. That is not the result of the hirer's breach of contract, in being late in his payments, it is the result of their own election to determine the hiring. That passage is in my view good law: and Jenkins LJ seems to have accepted the reasoning in it as correct.'

Diplock LJ said:

...[The hirer] was clearly in breach of his obligation to pay two instalments on the due dates but, in the absence of any express provision to the contrary in the contract, these breaches of a contract of hire expressed to be for a duration of 24 months would not of themselves go to the root of the contract or evince an intention on the part of the hirer no longer to be bound by the contract. The owners' only remedy would have been to sue for the two instalments overdue and their measure of damages would have been the amount of these instalments, together with interest at the agreed rate of 10 per cent, per annum. They would also have continued to be liable to perform their own obligations under the contract, viz., to continue to hire the van to the hirer: for again, in the absence of express provision to the contrary, the non-payment of two instalments would not be an event which relieved the owners from their undertaking to do what they had agreed to do but had not yet done ...[P]arties to a contract may incorporate in it provisions which expressly define the events, whether or not they amount to breaches of contract, which are to have this result. But such a provision of itself may do no more than define an event which of itself, or at the option of one or other of the parties, brings the contract to an end and thus relieves both parties from their undertakings further to perform their obligations thereunder. Whether it does more than this and confers any other rights or remedies on either party on the termination of the contract, depends upon the true construction of the relevant provision. If it does not, then each party is left with such causes of action, if any, as had already accrued to him at the date that the contract came to an end, but acquires no fresh cause of action as a result of the termination.

In *Thomas Feather & Co (Bradford) Ltd v Keighley Corpn* (1953) 52 LGR 30, the same approach was taken to a clause in a building contract that gave the employer the right to determine the contract if the contractor subcontracted any of the work without consent. The contractor failed to obtain consent and the employer exercised its right to terminate. The employer then employed another contractor to finish the work at an extra cost of £21,000, but it was held that the employer could not recover this sum from the original contractor.

Thus merely giving Schulers the right to terminate if Wickmans miss a visit might leave Schulers with no right to damages. What if the clause, like the ICE cl 65(1) (above), goes on to state explicitly that full damages (or the equivalent of full damages) shall be recoverable? Or is there any other safe way of ensuring that the party will have a right both to terminate and to claim full damages, even though the breach would not normally be sufficiently serious to justify termination?

■ *Lombard North Central plc v Butterworth*
[1987] 1 All ER 267, Court of Appeal

The plaintiffs, a finance company, leased a computer to the defendant for a period of five years on payment of an initial sum of £584.05 and 19 subsequent quarterly instalments of the same amount. Clause *2(a)* of the hiring agreement made punctual payment of each instalment of the essence of the agreement and, under cl 5, failure to make due and punctual payment entitled the plaintiffs to terminate the agreement. By cl 6, the plaintiffs were entitled on termination to all arrears of instalments and all future instalments that would have fallen due had the agreement not been terminated, less a discount for accelerated payment. Although the defendant paid the first two instalments promptly, the next three were paid very belatedly, and on four occasions, payment made by direct debit was recalled by the bank. When the sixth instalment was six weeks overdue, the plaintiffs wrote to the defendant terminating the agreement. Subsequently, the plaintiffs recovered possession of the computer and sold it for only £172.88. The plaintiffs brought an action against the defendant claiming the amount of the unpaid sixth instalment and the 13 future instalments or, alternatively, damages for breach of contract. They then applied for and obtained summary judgment under RSC Ord 14 for damages to be assessed. In assessing the damages the master held that the defendant had, by his conduct, repudiated the contract and accordingly the plaintiffs were entitled to recover damages in respect of all future instalments less certain credits. The defendant appealed, contending that he ought not to be held liable for more than the amount due and unpaid at the date of termination.

Mustill LJ

... The Hiring agreement contained the following material provisions:

'THE LESSEE . . . AGREES . . .

2(a) to pay to the lessor: (i) punctually and without previous demand the rentals set out in Part 3 of the Schedule together with Value Added Tax thereon punctual payment of each which shall be of the essence of this Lease . . .

5. IN THE EVENT THAT *(a)* the Lessee shall (i) make default in the due and punctual payment of any of the rentals or of any sum of money payable to the Lessor hereunder or any part thereof . . . then upon the happening of such event . . . the Lessor's consent to the Lessee's possession of the Goods shall determine forthwith without any notice being given by the Lessor, and the Lessor may terminate this Lease either by notice in writing, or by taking possession of the Goods . . .

6. IN THE EVENT that the Lessor's consent to the Lessee's possession of the goods shall be determined under clause 5 hereof *(a)* the Lessee shall pay forthwith to the Lessor: (i) all arrears of rentals; and (ii) all further rentals which would but for the determination of the Lessor's consent to the Lessee's possession of the Goods have fallen due to the end of the fixed period of this Lease less a discount thereon for accelerated payment at the rate of 5 per cent per annum; and (iii) damages for any breach of this Lease and all expenses and costs incurred by the Lessor in retaking possession of the Goods and/or enforcing the Lessor's rights under this Lease together with such Value Added Tax as shall be legally payable thereon: *(b)* the Lessor shall be entitled to exercise any one or more of the rights and remedies provided for in clause 5 and sub clause *(a)* of this clause and the determination of the Lessor's consent to the Lessee's possession of the Goods shall not affect or prejudice such rights and remedies and the Lessee shall be and remain liable to perform all outstanding liabilities under this Lease notwithstanding that the Lessor may have taken possession of the Goods and/or exercised one or more of the rights and remedies of the Lessor; (c) any right or remedy to which the Lessor is or may become entitled under this Lease or in consequence of the Lessee's conduct may be enforced from time to time separately or concurrently with any other right or remedy given by this Lease or now or hereafter provided for or arising by operation of law so that such rights and remedies are not exclusive of the other or others of them but are cumulative' . . .

Three issues were canvassed before us. (1) Is cl 6 of the agreement to be disregarded, on the ground that it creates a penalty? (Strictly speaking, this issue does not arise, since the judgment was for damages to be assessed, but cl 6 was relied on by the plaintiffs before the master and in this court, without objection.) (2) Apart from cl *2(a)* of the agreement, was the master correct in holding that the conduct of the defendant amounted to a wrongful repudiation of the contract, and that the sum claimed was recoverable in damages? (3) Does the provision in cl *2(a)* of the agreement that time for payment of the instalments was of the essence have the effect of making the defendant's late payment of the out-standing instalments a repudiatory breach?

As to the first two issues, I need say only that I have had the advantage of reading in draft the judgment to be delivered by Nicholls LJ, and that I am in such entire agreement with his conclusions and reasons that it is unnecessary to add any observations of my own.

...

The reason why I am impelled to hold that the plaintiffs' contentions are well-founded can most conveniently be set out in a series of propositions. (1) Where a breach goes to the root of the contract, the injured party may elect to put an end to the contract. Thereupon both sides are relieved from those obligations which remain unperformed. (2) If he does so elect, the injured party is entitled to compensation for (a) any breaches which occurred before the contract was terminated and (b) the loss of his opportunity to receive performance of the promisor's outstanding obligations. (3) Certain categories of obligation, often called conditions, have the property that any breach of them is treated as going to the root of the contract. On the occurrence of any breach of condition, the injured party can elect to terminate and claim damages, whatever the gravity of the breach. (4) It is possible by express provision in the contract to make a term a condition, even if it would not be so in the absence of such a provision. (5) A stipulation that time is of the essence, in relation to a particular contractual term, denotes that timely performance is a condition of the contract. The consequence is that delay in performance is treated as going to the root of the contract, without regard to the magnitude of the breach. (6) It follows that where a promisor fails to give timely performance of an obligation in respect of which time is expressly stated to be of the essence, the injured party may elect to terminate and recover damages in respect of the promisor's outstanding obligations, without regard to the magnitude of the breach. (7) A term of the contract prescribing what damages are to be recoverable when a contract is terminated for a breach of condition is open to being struck down as a penalty, if it is not a genuine covenanted pre-estimate of the damage, in the same way as a clause which prescribes the measure for any other type of breach. No doubt the position is the same where the clause is ranked as a condition by virtue of an express provision in the contract. (8) A clause expressly assigning a particular obligation to the category of condition is not a clause which purports to fix the damages for breaches of the obligation, and is not subject to the law governing penalty clauses. (9) Thus, although in the present case cl 6 is to be struck down as a penalty, cl 2(a)(i) remains enforceable. The plaintiffs were entitled to terminate the contract independently of cl 5, and to recover damages for loss of the future instalments. This loss was correctly computed by the master.

These bare propositions call for comment. The first three are uncontroversial. The fourth was not, I believe, challenged before us, but I would in any event regard it as indisputable....

The fifth proposition is a matter of terminology, and has been more taken for granted than discussed. That making time of the essence is the same as making timely performance if condition was, however, expressly stated by Megaw and Browne LJJ in *Bunge Corp v Tradax SA* [above, p 438], and the same proposition is implicit in the leading speeches of Lord Wilberforce and Lord Roskill in the House of Lords.

The sixth proposition is a combination of the first five. There appears to be no direct authority for it, and it is right to say that most of the cases on the significance of time being of the essence have been concerned with the right of the injured party to be discharged, rather than the principles on which its damages are to be computed. Nevertheless, it is axiomatic that a person who establishes a breach of condition can terminate and claim damages for loss of the bargain, and I know of no authority which suggests that the position is any different where late performance is made into a breach of condition by a stipulation that time is of the essence.

I return to the propositions stated above. The seventh is uncontroversial, and I would add only the rider that when deciding on the penal nature of a clause which prescribes a measure of recovery for damages resulting from a termination founded on a breach of condition, the comparison should be with the common law measure, namely with the loss to the promises resulting from the loss of his bargain. If the contract permits him to treat the contract as repudiated, the fact that the breach is comparatively minor should in my view play no part in the equation.

I believe that the real controversy in the present case centres on the eighth proposition. I will repeat it. A clause expressly assigning a particular obligation to the category of condition is not a clause which purports to fix the damages for breach of the obligation, and is not subject to the law governing penalty clauses. I acknowledge, of course, that by promoting, term into the category where all breaches are ranked as breaches of condition, the parties indirectly bring about a situation where, for breaches which are relatively small, the injured party is enabled to recover damages as on the loss of the bargain, whereas without the stipulation his measure of recovery would be different. But I am unable to accept that this permits the court to strike down as a penalty the clause which brings about this promotion. To do so would be to reverse the current of more than 100 years' doctrine, which permits the parties to treat as a condition something which would not otherwise be so. I am not prepared to take this step.

For these reasons I conclude that the plaintiffs are entitled to retain the damages which the master has awarded. This is not a result which I view with much satisfaction, partly because the plaintiffs have achieved by one means a result which the law of penalties might have prevented them from achieving by another and partly because if the line of argument under cl 2 had been developed from the outset, the defendant might have found an answer based on waiver which the court is now precluded from assessing, for want of the necessary facts. Nevertheless, it is the answer to which, in my view, the authorities clearly point. Accordingly, I would dismiss the appeal.

Nicholls LJ

Shortly stated, the two issues raised on this appeal are whether the sums payable under cl 6 of the lease agreement constituted a penalty and, if so, whether the conduct of the hirer (the defendant) amounted to a repudiation of the agreement that was accepted by the owner (the plaintiffs).

The claim under cl 6

On the first issue, the criticism of cl 6 advanced on behalf of the defendant was confined to the absence of provision giving credit for the net amount of the price obtained by the plaintiffs on any resale of the goods effected by it after retaking possession. Argument in this court took place on the footing that the presence or absence of such a provision, which I shall call a 'resale price allowance', was crucial on the penalty point, counsel for the defendant putting forward the omission of such an allowance as the fundamental objection to the clause.

If this were right, and cl 6 would be unobjectionable if it included a resale price allowance, it could only be because cl 6, with the addition of a provision for such an allowance, would represent a genuine estimate of the loss likely to be suffered in this case by the plaintiffs. It is on this footing that the clause would be enforceable. In that event the sum of £6,869.97 claimed in the action with interest, would have been payable by the defendant (because in arriving at that sum the plaintiffs in fact gave credit for the net resale price of the computer, even though cl 6 did not require this). The sum of £6,869.97 is made up of one instalment in arrear (£585.05, plus £87.61 value added tax) and 13 future instalments (£7,592.65) less the net proceeds of sale (£172.85) and less also an allowance for accelerated receipt of the future instalments (£1,221.49). But, on the other hand, according to this argument advanced for the defendant, if cl 6 is struck down as a penalty because of the absence of a resale price allowance, the consequence in law is that nothing is recoverable by the plaintiffs except the one unpaid instalment (£585.05 plus value added tax) and interest thereon.

In my view these two alternative conclusions have only to be set beside each other for their mutual incompatibility to be evident. As Lord Denning pointed out in *Bridge v Campbell Discount Co Ltd*, when equity granted relief against a penalty it always required the recipient of its favours, as a condition of relief, to pay the damage which the other party had really sustained. If a genuine estimate of the damage really sustained by the plaintiffs here produces the sum of £6,869.97, how can the striking down of cl 6 as a penalty because of the omission of a resale price allowance somehow result in him recovering only £585.05?

As I see it, the answer to this question is to be found in the assumption underlying the argument of the defendant that cl 6 with the addition of a resale price allowance would not be a penalty. In my view, in the absence of a repudiatory breach that assumption is misconceived. The ratio of the decision of this court in *Financings Ltd v Baldock* [above, p 604] was that when an owner determines a hire-purchase agreement in exercise of a right so to do given him by the agreement, in the absence of repudiation he can recover damages for any breaches up to the date of termination but not thereafter, and a 'minimum payment' clause which purports to oblige the hirer to pay larger sums than this is unenforceable as a penalty.

This principle has since been applied in several decisions of this court, including *Brady v St Margaret's Trust Ltd, Charterhouse Credit Co Ltd v Tolly, United Dominions Trust (Commercial) Ltd v Ennis* and *Capital Finance Co Ltd v Donati*.

Of these I refer to one only, *Capital Finance Co Ltd v Donati*. There the court applied the principle in a hire-purchase case where on determination of one hiring, the owner having power to determine the hiring if the hirer made default in the punctual payment of any instalment, a minimum payment clause came into operation that was substantially similar to cl 6 save that, unlike cl 6, it did give credit to the hirer for any sum recovered on the sale of the Fiat car subject to that agreement. The sum expressed to be payable comprised the arrears of hire rent up to the date of termination, any expenses incurred by the owner in recovering possession of the car, and also the amount of the owner's loss on the transaction which was agreed as being the difference between the hire-purchase price and the total of (i) the net proceeds of sale of the car, (ii) the initial payment and the instalments paid by the hirer and (iii) a sum representing a reasonable proportion of the charges shown in the schedule applicable to that part of the hire-purchase price which the owner would by operation of the clause receive prematurely. Cairns LJ pointed out that while there was a difference of opinion in *Financings Ltd v Baldock* as to the proper measure of damages in a case of repudiation, all members of the court held that in the absence of repudiation the common law measure of damages was limited to the overdue instalments and interest thereon and that the provision for additional damages was a penalty clause. He said (I read from the transcript):

'The clause in the present case does differentiate between an early and a late breach by providing for the deduction of a reasonable proportion of the charges, but it makes no distinction between the most trivial breach (for example, delay of a few days in the payment of one instalment) and a repudiatory breach. It purports to assess 'the owners' loss on the transaction' and the method of assessment shows that what is meant is that the owners are to be recompensed for all the consequences of the hirer's breach and of their own election to determine the hiring. This could only be free from the element of penalty if the whole of this loss could be said to result from the breach, which would be contrary to the ratio decidendi of *Financings Ltd v Baldock.*'

In my view, applying the principle enunciated in *Financings Ltd v Baldock* to this case leads inescapably to the conclusion that in the absence of a repudiatory breach cl 6(a) is a penalty in so far as it purports to oblige the defendant, regardless of the seriousness or triviality of the breach which led to the plaintiffs terminating the agreement by retaking possession of the computer, to make a payment, albeit a discounted payment, in respect of rental instalments which had not accrued due prior to 20 December 1982.

From what I have said it will be apparent that I consider that, in the absence of a repudiatory breach, the outcome of this issue is not dependent on the inclusion or exclusion of a resale price allowance, and indeed the legal result would have been the same if cl 6 had contained a resale price allowance.

I consider below whether there was a repudiatory breach in this case, but for completeness I add here that it was accepted by counsel for the plaintiffs (and, in my view, rightly so) that it cl *6(a)* was unenforceable as a penalty, the provisions in cl *6(b)* would not assist the plaintiffs in this case.

Thus far I have reached my conclusion regarding repudiation without giving any weight or effect to the provision in cl 2*(a)* of the lease, that punctual payment of each rental instalment was of the essence of the lease.

I must now consider a further submission advanced by the plaintiffs that, time of payment having been made of the essence by this provision, it was open to the plaintiffs, once default in payment of any one instalment on the due date had occurred, to treat the agreement as having been repudiated by the defendant, and claim damages for loss of the whole transaction, even though in the absence of this provision such a default would not have had that consequence. On this, the question which arises is one of construction: on the true construction of the clause, did the 'time of the essence' provision have the effect submitted by the plaintiffs? In my view, the answer to that question is Yes. The provision in cl 2*(a)* has to be read and construed in conjunction with the other provisions in the agreement, including cll 5 and 6. So read, it is to be noted that failure to pay any instalment triggers a right for the plaintiffs to terminate the agreement by retaking possession of the goods (cl 5), with the expressed consequence that the defendant becomes liable to make payments which assume that the defendant is liable to make good to the plaintiffs the loss by them of the whole transaction (cl 6). Given that context, the 'time of the essence' provision seems to me to be intended to bring about the result that default in punctual payment is to be regarded (to use a once fashionable term) as a breach going to the root of the contract and, hence, as giving rise to the consequences in damages attendant on such a breach. I am unable to see what other purpose the 'time of the essence' provision in cl 2*(a)* can serve or was intended to serve or what other construction can fairly be ascribed to it.

If that construction of the agreement is correct then, as at present advised, it seems to me that the legal consequence is that the plaintiffs are entitled to claim damages for loss of the whole transaction. I have to say that I view the impact of that principle in this case with considerable dissatisfaction, for this reason. As already mentioned, the principle applied in *Financings Ltd v Baldock* was that when an owner determines a hire-purchase agreement in exercise of a power so to do given him by the agreement on non-payment of instalments, he can recover damages for any breaches up to the date of termination but (in the absence of repudiation) not thereafter. There is no practical difference between (1) an agreement containing such a power and (2) an agreement containing a provision to the effect that time for payment of each instalment is of the essence, so that any breach will go to the root of the contract. The difference between these two agreements is one of drafting form, and wholly without substance. Yet under an agreement drafted in the first form, the owner's damages claim arising on his exercise of the power of termination is confined to damages for breaches up to the date of termination, whereas under an agreement drafted in the second form the owner's damages claim, arising on his acceptance of an identical breach as a repudiation of the agreement, will extend to damages for loss of the whole transaction.

Nevertheless, as at present advised, I can see no escape from the conclusion that such is the present state of the law. This conclusion emasculates the decision in *Financings Ltd v Baldock*, for it means that a skilled draftsman can easily side-step the effect of that decision. Indeed, that is what has occurred here. . . .

For these reasons, I too would dismiss this appeal.

Lawton LJ

I have read in draft the judgments of Mustill and Nicholls LJJ: I agree and have nothing to add.

NOTES

1. In a case such as *Lombard*, what will the finance company consider that it has lost? If cl 6 had provided for the value of the goods repossessed to be taken into account, wouldn't the sum due under the clause have represented the difference between what the finance house had received and what it would have received had the contract been performed?

2. The decision seems to make avoidance of the rule in *Financings v Baldock* rather easy: all that is needed is to make time for payment 'of the essence'. It seems odd that if you state that, if the goods are repossessed, the lessee will pay the finance company's full loss (as defined in note 1), the clause is void as a penalty and the finance company can recover only the unpaid instalments, but that if you make time of the essence, the full amount is recoverable.

3. Should 'time of the essence' or 'condition precedent' clauses be subject to some control? If the agreement is one for consumer credit, the creditor's rights to terminate and repossess are to some extent limited by the Consumer Credit Act 1974 (see p 589), but these will not affect the finance company's right to its 'full loss' if ultimately the agreement is terminated. If the clause is in a consumer contract and has not been individually negotiated, it will now be subject to the Unfair Terms in Consumer Contracts Regulations (see Chapter 40). In a non-consumer contract, the only possibility seems to be that a 'condition precedent' clause might be caught by the Unfair Contract Terms Act 1977, s 3(2)(b)(ii), p 1009, but this is a 'long shot'.

4. Look again at ICE conditions cl 65. Suppose a contractor is employed to carry out engineering work on these terms and the employer relying on cl 65 terminates the contract for a breach that, at common law, would not be sufficiently serious to justify termination (eg not starting work on time, even though there will be plenty of opportunity to make up time later). The employer, after some inevitable delay, employs another contractor to do the work. In the light of the *Lombard* case, can the employer recover the extra cost plus compensation for delay from the original contractor? See (1988) 104 LQR 355.

5. The correctness of the *Financings* decision has been questioned by Opeskin (1990) 106 LQR 293. It is not easy to see why the loss that the finance company was seeking to recover was caused by its decision to terminate, rather than by the hirer's breach, when the agreement explicitly gave the finance company the right to terminate for such a breach. However, some have argued that full damages should not be recoverable even if the agreement expressly makes what would otherwise be a minor breach into a breach of condition (Treitel, p 854).

6. What is 'going on' in cases such as *Financings* and *Lombard?* Are the courts promoting efficiency by sometimes denying effect to the clauses permitting termination and recovery of the creditor's loss? might this be example of the courts trying to ensure cooperation between the parties by discouraging termination when they consider the breach was not serious? Compare Collins, p 66.

XIII. THE NATURE OF TERMINATION

■ *Photo Production Ltd v Securicor Transport Ltd*
[1980] 1 All ER 556, House of Lords

The facts of this case are set out on p 990. The issue was whether the termination of a contract prevents an exclusion clause applying to the event relied on as the ground for termination. As we shall see in Chapter 34, the Court of Appeal had held in a number of cases that, if the innocent party terminated the contract because of a fundamental breach by the other, that got rid of any exclusion or limitation clauses that would otherwise have governed the defaulter's liability. The argument seemed to be that because the contract had come to an end, the clauses had ceased to apply. The House of Lords had said, obiter, in the *Suisse Atlantique* case (see, p 987) that this doctrine was unsound as well as commercially inconvenient, but the Court of Appeal had continued to apply it. In the *Photo Production* case, the House of Lords decisively rejected it.

Lord Diplock

. . . A basic principle of the common law of contract, to which there are no exceptions that are relevant in the instant case, is that parties to a contract are free to determine for themselves what primary obligations they will accept. They may state these in express words in the contract itself, and, where they do, the statement is determinative; but in practice a commercial contract never states all the primary obligations of the parties in full; many are left to be incorporated by implication of law from the legal nature of the contract into which the parties are entering. But if the parties wish to reject or modify primary obligations which would otherwise be so incorporated, they are fully at liberty to do so by express words.

Leaving aside those comparatively rare cases in which the court is able to enforce a primary obligation by decreeing specific performance of it, breaches of primary obligations give rise to substituted secondary obligations on the part of the party in default, and, in some cases, may entitle the other party to be relieved from further performance of his own primary obligations. These secondary obligations of the contract breaker and any concomitant relief of the other party from his own primary obligations also arise by implication of law, generally common law, but sometimes statute, as in the case of codifying statutes passed at the turn of the century, notably the Sale of Goods Act 1893. The contract, however, is just as much the source of secondary obligations as it is of primary obligations; and like primary obligations that are implied by law secondary obligations too can be modified by agreement between the parties, although, for reasons to be mentioned later, they cannot, in my view, be totally excluded. In the instant case, the only secondary obligations and concomitant reliefs that are applicable arise by implication of the common law as modified by the express words of the contract.

Every failure to perform a primary obligation is a breach of contract. The secondary obligation on the part of the contract breaker to which it gives rise by implication of the common law is to pay monetary compensation to the other party for the loss sustained by him in consequence of the breach; but, with two exceptions, the primary obligations of both parties so far as they have not yet been fully performed remain unchanged. This secondary obligation to pay compensation (damages) for non-performance of primary obligations I will call the 'general secondary obligation'. It applies in the cases of the two exceptions as well.

The exceptions are: (1) where the event resulting from the failure by one party to perform a primary obligation has the effect of depriving the other party of substantially the whole benefit which it was the intention of the parties that he should obtain from the contract, the party not in default may elect to put an end to all primary obligations of both parties remaining unperformed (if the expression 'fundamental breach' is to be retained, it should, in the interests of clarity, be confined to this exception); (2) where the contracting parties have agreed, whether by express words or by implication of law, that *any* failure by one party to perform a particular primary obligation ('condition' in the nomenclature of the Sale of Goods Act 1893), irrespective of the gravity of the event that has in fact resulted from the breach, shall entitle the other party to elect to put an end to all primary obligations of both parties remaining unperformed (in the interests of clarity, the nomenclature of the Sale of Goods Act 1893, 'breach of condition', should be reserved for this exception).

Where such an election is made (a) there is substituted by implication of law for the primary obligations of the party in default which remain unperformed a secondary obligation to pay monetary compensation to the other party for the loss sustained by him in consequence of their non-performance in the future and (b) the unperformed primary obligations of that other party are discharged. This secondary obligation is additional to the general secondary obligation: I will call it 'the anticipatory secondary obligation'.

In cases falling within the first exception, fundamental breach, the anticipatory secondary obligation arises under contracts of all kinds by implication of the common law, except to the extent that it is excluded or modified by the express words of the contract. In cases falling within the second exception, breach of condition, the anticipatory secondary obligation generally arises under particular kinds of contracts by implication of statute law; though in the case of 'deviation' from the contract voyage under a contract of carriage of goods by sea it arises by implication of the common law. The anticipatory secondary obligation in these cases too can be excluded or modified by express words.

When there has been a fundamental breach or breach of condition, the coming to an end of the primary obligations of both parties to the contract at the election of the party not in default is often referred to as the 'determination' or 'rescission' of the contract or, as in the Sale of Goods Act 1893, 'treating the contract as repudiated'. The first two of these expressions, however, are misleading unless it is borne in mind that for the unperformed primary obligations of the party in default there are substituted by operation of law what I have called the secondary obligations.

The bringing to an end of all primary obligations under the contract may also leave the parties in a relationship, typically that of bailor and bailee, in which they owe to one another by operation of law fresh primary obligations of which the contract is not the source; but no such relationship is involved in the instant case.

I have left out of account in this analysis as irrelevant to the instant case an arbitration or choice of forum clause. This does not come into operation until a party to the contract claims that a primary obligation of the other party has not been performed; and its relationship to other obligations of which the contract is the source was dealt with by this House in *Heyman v Darwins Ltd.*

(For further extracts from this case, see p 990.)

NOTES

1. You may not find Diplock's explanation easy to follow, but the basic idea is simple enough. A contract contains 'primary obligations'—what each party is to do. When the innocent party terminates, the original obligation on the defaulting party is replaced by the ('secondary') obligation to pay damages—damages to compensate for any breaches that occurred before termination and to compensate for the fact that the defaulting party is now not going to perform the remainder of the contract ('anticipatory secondary obligation')—eg the cost of getting another contractor to finish the job. Just as the parties can agree what their primary obligations are, so they can fix their secondary obligations, eg by limiting the damages to so much. What they have agreed continues to govern their liability after termination, because it defines that liability.

2. Diplock says that, in cases of breach of condition, the anticipatory secondary obligation generally arises by implication of statute law. No doubt he was thinking of the implied conditions under the Sale of Goods Act, but it must be remembered that there are other examples of conditions at common law: see *Bunge v Tradax*, p 576.

3. Diplock refers to cases in which termination of the contract leaves the parties in a bailment relationship. A bailment occurs when one party is in possession of another party's goods, whether or not there is a contract between them (eg a finder is a bailee). The bailee owes the bailor various duties: see further p 1200.

4. The recent case of *Hurst v Bryk* [2000] 2 All ER 193, HL provides an interesting example of how the rules on termination apply to a partnership agreement. All of the partners except Hurst signed an agreement to dissolve the partnership. He refused to sign; instead he claimed that the others by signing had repudiated the partnership agreement and that

he accepted the repudiation. He then argued that the effect was that he no longer had to contribute to the rent of a building (in King Street), which the partnership had occupied and which it had not been possible to relet. The House of Lords held that he was still obliged to contribute to the rent because this was a liability which had been incurred while he was still a partner. Lord Millett, giving the only full speech in the House of Lords, said (at 198–199 and 204–205):

Mr Hurst . . . recognises that the contractual doctrine cannot affect his liability to third parties, but he claims that, as between himself and his fellow partners, he is discharged from all further performance of those obligations which he undertook by becoming a partner, and these include the obligation to contribute to the firm's losses.

The difficulty with this argument is that it does not accurately reflect the contractual doctrine. . . . [T]he acceptance by one party of a repudiatory breach of contract by the other operates to discharge *both* parties from further performance of their contractual obligations. If Mr Hurst is discharged from the obligation he owes his fellow partners to contribute to the assets available to the creditors, then his fellow partners are likewise discharged from the corresponding obligation they owe him. Since the creditors are unaffected, they can still recover judgment against the firm and execute against any of the partners separately. Mr Hurst's argument does not lead to the conclusion that he can walk away from the firm's liabilities and thereby reduce the security available to the creditors, but to the conclusion that the liability for the firm's debts must rest wherever the creditors choose to let it fall. The fact is that it is not enough for Mr Hurst to avoid his liability to contribute to the firm's assets to make up any shortfall; he needs an indemnity against his liability for the firm's debts. This can only be obtained by agreement or by rescinding the partnership contract ab initio. The contractual doctrine of repudiation is not sufficient.

It is no answer to say that, as the wronged party, Mr Hurst is entitled, as his fellow partners are not, to damages for the breach of contract which brought about the dissolution of the partnership. If he can show that he was thereby deprived of income which he has been unable to earn elsewhere, he is entitled to be compensated for his loss. But this cannot be measured by the contribution he must make to the accrued and continuing liabilities of the firm pending the completion of the winding up. His liability to contribute to these had accrued before any breach of the partnership agreement occurred and has in no sense been caused by his partners' breach of contract. He would have continued to be liable for the King Street rent if his partners had committed no breach of contract and the partnership had not been dissolved. To recover this head of damages he would have to show that the acquisition of King Street was a breach of the partnership deed, and he has not alleged this.

This is only another way of saying that, although both parties are discharged from further performance of their obligations, rights are not divested which have already been unconditionally acquired. Rights and obligations which arise by the partial execution of the contract continue unaffected. Mr Hurst's liability to contribute to the accrued and accruing liabilities of the firm, and his partners' rights of contribution, arise from the fact that the liabilities were incurred (or in the case of King Street assumed) by the firm when Mr Hurst was a partner. Once the firm had undertaken or assumed liability for the rent, each partner in the firm was entitled to have the liability taken into account in ascertaining his share of the firm's profits or losses both before and after dissolution, and that right was not lost merely because Mr Hurst's partners afterwards repudiated the contract and Mr Hurst accepted it.

Mr Hurst argues that the liability for rent is not unconditional, since it is consideration for the right to remain in possession. A tenant's liability for future rent is not a simple debt; its existence depends on counter-performance by the landlord: see *Re Park Air Services plc, Christopher Moran Holdings Ltd v Bairstow* [1999] 1 All ER 673, [1999] 2 WLR 396. The short answer to this is that Mr Hurst does not claim to be discharged from his liability to the landlord. He claims to be discharged from his liability to his fellow partners, and this is not conditional upon any future counter-performance by them.

This analysis can be tested by reference to the law of agency. Where an agent is in serious breach of his duty to his principal, the principal can refuse to pay commission and the agent loses his right to be indemnified *in respect of the transaction as to which the agent is in breach*. But the agent does not normally lose his rights to commission already earned and indemnity in respect of past transactions which were completed before the breach: see *Bowstead and Reynolds on Agency* (16th edn, 1996), art 62 and the cases there cited. . . .

The consequences when a contract is brought to an end by the acceptance by one party to it of a repudiatory breach of contract by the other party are well established. They were clearly stated by Dixon J in *McDonald v Dennys Lascelles Ltd* (1933) 48 CLR 457 at 476–477 where he said:

> 'When a party to a simple contract, upon breach by the other contracting party of a condition of the contract, elects to treat the contract as no longer binding on him, the contract is not rescinded as from the beginning. Both parties are discharged from the further performance of the contract, but rights are not divested or discharged which have already been unconditionally acquired. Rights and obligations which arise from the partial execution of the contract and causes of action which have accrued from its breach alike continue unaffected.'

This passage has been expressly approved by your Lordships' House: see *Johnson v Agnew* [1979] 1 All ER 883 at 892, [1980] AC 367 at 396 per Lord Wilberforce; and *Bank of Boston Connecticut v European Grain and Shipping Ltd, The Dominique* [1989] 1 All ER 545 at 549–550, [1989] AC 1056 at 1089, 1099 per Lord Brandon of Oakbrook.

The doctrine of accepted repudiation is of general application in the law of contract, and there is no reason why it should not apply to an agreement to enter into partnership or to the contractual obligations which the partners mutually undertake to observe after the partnership has come to an end. . . .

(Lord Millett expressed the view that acceptance of the repudiation, although it brought to an end the partnership contract, did not of itself end the partnership relationship. His principal reason was that this would be inconsistent with s 35(d) of the Partnership Act 1890, which gives the court a discretion as to whether or not to order a dissolution of the partnership; he argued that partners are subject to an equitable jurisdiction and, by entering the partnership, give up their right to bring about a dissolution by acceptance of a repudiatory breach. This view has been questioned: see Law Commission Consultation Paper No 159, Partnership Law (2000), para 6.29.)

XIV. LOSS OF THE RIGHT TO TERMINATE

■ *Allen v Robles*
[1969] 3 All ER 154, Court of Appeal

The defendant had a policy of motor insurance with the third party; the policy provided that the insured must notify any claim within five days, at the risk of forfeiture of the policy. The defendant drove negligently, injuring the plaintiff and damaging his property, but he failed to inform the third-party insurers for two months. The insurers were willing to indemnify the plaintiff for the personal injury, but not for the damage to his property, but they did not inform the defendant of this until over four months after they had been informed of the claim. Mocatta J held that the insurers had lost the right to repudiate their liability under the policy and held that they were liable to indemnify the defendant in full.

Fenton Atkinson LJ

. . . In dealing with this matter, the learned judge held that there had been a breach of the condition by the defendant and, that being so, the third party had the right to elect whether to repudiate liability to indemnify or whether to accept liability to indemnify; but he went on to hold that they had to make up their minds which they were going to do within a reasonable time, and, if they failed within a reasonable time to make up their minds one way or the other, they would thereby lose the right of election and would be compelled to accept liability to indemnify the defendant. He went on to hold that the delay until 29th November was of such a length of time that it was more than a reasonable time and that by that date they had lost their right to refuse to indemnify the defendant; and it is against that view of the law of the learned judge that this appeal is now brought.

Counsel for the third party has cited to us, in particular *Clough v London and North Western Rly Co* and, in particular, a passage set out in the judgment of the court. The law is there set out in this way, and it has been approved since and one finds it so stated in leading textbooks, such as *Chitty on Contract*. It is not necessary, I think, to set out the facts of the case in this judgment, but this is the passage:

> '. . . we agree with what seems to be the opinion of all the judges below, that if it can be shewn that the London Pianoforte Company have at any time after knowledge of the fraud, either by express words or by unequivocal acts, affirmed the contract, their election has been determined forever. But we differ from them in this, that we think the party defrauded may keep the question open so long as he does nothing to affirm the contract.'

In my view the position was this, that when the third party through their agents, their solicitors, discovered: (a) that there was a claim; and (b) that the defendant was in breach of his condition, they were in a position then either to elect by refusing to indemnify or to accept a liability to indemnify, or it was open to them to delay their decision, particularly in view of their letter of 10th August 1967, and mere lapse of time, in my view, on the facts of this case, would not lose them their right ultimately to decide to refuse to indemnify. The lapse of time would only operate against them if thereby there was prejudice to the defendant or if in some way rights of third parties intervened or if their delay was so long that the court felt able to say that the delay in itself was of such a length as to be evidence that they had in truth decided to accept liability. None of these possibilities arise here.

Phillimore and Danckwerts LJJ agreed.

Appeal allowed.

NOTES

1. A similar approach to the question was employed in *The Antaios* [1983] 3 All ER 777, CA; affirmed on other grounds [1984] 3 All ER 229, HL.

2. In *Peyman v Lanjani* [1985] Ch 457, the Court of Appeal held that there could be no affirmation unless the victim knew not only of the breach but also that it gave the right to terminate. However, if he gives the appearance of affirming and the other party acts on that apparent affirmation, the victim will be estopped by it irrespective of his knowledge. (Compare the *Hannah Blumenthal*, p 192.) In *The Kanchenjunga* [1990] 1 Lloyd's Rep 391, 399, Lord Goff said:

> Election is to be contrasted with equitable estoppel, a principle associated with the leading case of *Hughes v Metropolitan Railway* Co, [below, p 850]. Equitable estoppel occurs where a person, having legal rights against another, unequivocally represents (by words or conduct) that he does not

intend to enforce those legal rights; if in such circumstances the other party acts, or desists from acting, in reliance upon that representation, with the effect that it would be inequitable for the representor thereafter to enforce his legal rights inconsistently with his representation, he will to that extent be precluded from doing so.

There is an important similarity between the two principles, election and equitable estoppel, in that each requires an unequivocal representation, perhaps because each may involve a loss, permanent or temporary, of the relevant party's rights. But there are important differences as well. In the context of a contract, the principle of election applies when a state of affairs comes into existence in which one party becomes entitled to exercise a right, and has to choose whether to exercise the right or not. His election has generally to be an informed choice, made with knowledge of the facts giving rise to the right. His election once made is final; it is not dependent upon reliance on it by the other party. On the other hand, equitable estoppel requires an unequivocal representation by one party that he will not insist upon his legal rights against the other party, and such reliance by the representee as will render it inequitable for the representor to go back upon his representation. No question arises of any particular knowledge on the part of the representor, and the estoppel may be suspensory only. Furthermore, the representation itself is different in character in the two cases. The party making his election is communicating his choice whether or not to exercise a right which has become available to him. The party to an equitable estoppel is representing that he will not in future enforce his legal rights. His representation is therefore in the nature of a promise which, though unsupported by consideration, can have legal consequences; hence it is sometimes referred to as promissory estoppel.

On estoppel, see further p 864.

3.   Special rules about loss of the right to rescind apply to contracts for the sale of goods.

■ Sale of Goods Act 1979, ss 34 and 35 (as amended by Sale and Supply of Goods Act 1994, ss 2 and 3)

Section 34

Unless otherwise agreed, when the seller tenders delivery of goods to the buyer, he is bound on request to afford the buyer a reasonable opportunity of examining the goods for the purpose of ascertaining whether they are in conformity with the contract and, in the case of a contract for sale by sample, of comparing the bulk with the sample.

Section 35

(1) The buyer is deemed to have accepted the goods, subject to subsection (2) below—
   (a) when he intimates to the seller that he has accepted them, or
   (b) when the goods have been delivered to him and he does any act in relation to them which is inconsistent with the ownership of the seller.
(2) Where goods are delivered to the buyer, and he has not previously examined them, he is not deemed to have accepted them under subsection (1) above until he has had a reasonable opportunity of examining them for the purpose—
   (a) of ascertaining whether they are in conformity with the contract, and
   (b) in the case of a contract for sale by sample, of comparing the bulk with the sample.
(3) Where the buyer deals as consumer or (in Scotland) the contract of sale is a consumer contract, the buyer cannot lose his right to rely on subsection (2) above by agreement, waiver or otherwise.
(4) The buyer is also deemed to have accepted the goods when after the lapse of a reasonable time he retains the goods without intimating to the seller that he has rejected them.

(5) The questions that are material in determining for the purposes of subsection (4) above whether a reasonable time has elapsed include whether the buyer has had a reasonable opportunity of examining the goods for the purpose mentioned in subsection (2) above.

(6) The buyer is not by virtue of this section deemed to have accepted the goods merely because—

   (a) he asks for, or agrees to, their repair by or under an arrangement with the seller, or

   (b) the goods are delivered to another under a sub-sale or other disposition.

(7) Where the contract is for the sale of goods making one or more commercial units, a buyer accepting any goods included in a unit is deemed to have accepted **all** the goods making the unit; and in this subsection 'commercial unit' means a unit division of which would materially impair the value of the goods or the character of the unit.

Section 35A

(1) If the buyer—

   (a) has the right to reject the goods by reason of a breach on the part of the seller that affects some or all of them, but

   (b) accepts some of the goods, including, where there are any goods unaffected by the breach, all such goods,

he does not by accepting them lose his right to reject the rest.

(2) In the case of a buyer having the right to reject an instalment of goods, subsection (1) above applies as (1) if references to the goods were references to the goods comprised in the instalment.

(3) For the purposes of subsection (1) above, goods are affected by a breach if by reason of the breach they are not in conformity with the contract.

(4) This section applies unless a contrary intention appears in, or is to be implied from, the contract.

NOTES

1.   'Acceptance' under ss 34 and 35 is nothing to do with 'offer and acceptance': it deals with whether it is too late for the buyer to reject the goods.

2.   Until the 1994 Act, a buyer who intimated to the seller that he accepted the goods lost the right to reject even though he had not had a reasonable opportunity to examine the goods. The Law Commission was concerned that buyers might sign 'acceptance notes' when goods have been delivered without appreciating the consequences (Law Commission Report No 160, *Sale and Supply of Goods* (Cmnd 137, 1987), paras 5.20–5.25.) The new subs 35(1) and (2) are intended to enable buyers to have a reasonable chance to examine the goods before they lose the right to reject them, and in the case of consumer buyers to prevent them signing this right away.

3.   The intricacies of 'acts inconsistent with the ownership of the seller' can be left to books on sale of goods, but it was suggested that one such act was to ask for goods to be repaired. (It might also amount to affirmation: see p 363.) As the Law Commission said:

> If this be so, then buyers would be best advised *not* to allow the seller to try to put the goods right, but to insist on rejecting . . . we think that informal attempts at cure should be encouraged.

See now s 35(6) and *J & H Ritchie Ltd v Lloyd Ltd* [2007] UKHL 9, [2007] 2 All ER 353.

4.   The buyer also loses the right to reject by retaining the goods after a reasonable time without rejecting them (s 35(4)). In *Bernstein v Pamson Motors (Golders Green) Ltd*

[1987] 2 All ER 220, the engine of a new car had seized up after only 140 miles. It was held that the car was not merchantable, but that because the buyer had had the car for nearly a month, a reasonable time had elapsed under s 35 and he could no longer reject it. For much of the month, the buyer had been ill and unable to drive the car. Rougier J said (at 230):

...[W]hat is a reasonable time in the circumstances? And here the 1979 Act ceases to be helpful. By s 59 'a reasonable time' is defined as a question of fact, no more, as if it could be anything else.

The submission made on behalf of the defendants is that in the context of the sale of [a] new motor car a reasonable time must entail a reasonable time to inspect and try out the car *generally* rather than with an eye to any specific defect, and that to project the period further would be artificial and contrary to the general legal proposition that there should, whenever possible, be finality in commercial transactions. At first I regret to say this proposition got a hostile reception on the ground that a mere 140-odd miles, and some three weeks, part of which were occupied by illness, were not nearly enough to afford the plaintiff any opportunity of discovering this wholly latent defect.

However, it was pointed out, and in my view rightly, that the whole concept of discovery of any *particular* defect and subsequent affirmation of the contract was only material in contracts of hire purchase and that there was nothing in the Sale of Goods Act 1979 to justify any analogous approach. This distinction was clearly stated by Webster J in the recent case of *Laurelgates Ltd v Lombard North Central Ltd* (1983) 133 NLJ 720.

In effect, it was argued, the wording of s 35 of the 1979 Act creates its own implied affirmation, as it were, by stating merely that once a buyer has had the goods for a reasonable time, *not*, be it noted, related to the opportunity to discover any particular defect, he is deemed to have accepted them. I think that this submission is correct.

In my judgment, the nature of the particular defect, discovered ex post facto, and the speed with which it might have been discovered, are irrelevant to the concept of reasonable time in s 35 as drafted. That section seems to me to be directed solely to what is a reasonable practical interval in commercial terms between a buyer receiving the goods and his ability to send them back, taking into consideration from his point of view the nature of the goods and their function, and from the point of view of the seller the commercial desirability of being able to close his ledger reasonably soon after the transaction is complete. The complexity of the intended function of the goods is clearly of prime consideration here. What is a reasonable time in relation to a bicycle would hardly suffice for a nuclear submarine.

Turning to the facts of the present case one asks whether some three weeks and 140-odd miles constitute a reasonable time after taking delivery of a new motor car? I am bound to say that I think the answer is Yes...

It is understood that an appeal in the Bernstein case was settled at the doors of the court, so there may 'be a view' that it is incorrect. Subsequent decisions have allowed rejection after significantly longer periods: see *Rogers v Parish (Scarborough) Ltd* [1987] QB 933; *Clegg v Anderson* [2003] EWCA Civ 320, [2003] 2 Lloyd's Rep 32; compare *Jones v Gallagher* [2004] EWCA Civ 10.

5.   Do you think the result of *Bernstein* was fair? Bear in mind that, after the engine had been rebuilt, the car was 'as good as new'. Why would a consumer still want to reject it and, if he were permitted to do so, who would ultimately bear the cost (ie the difference between the original price and the resale value of the repaired car)? For discussion of whether consumers should have a long-term right to reject, see Law Commission No 160, paras 5.6–5.13.

XV. CONSUMER REMEDIES

For Consumers there have been profound changes as the result of EU Directive 1999/44/EC, which was implemented by Sale and Supply of Goods to Consumers Regulations 2002, SI 2002/3045. A consumer buyer who has received 'non-conforming' goods (i.e. where there has been a breach of an express term of the contract or of Sections 13–15 of the Sale of Goods Act 1979 (above, pp 427 ff)) is still entitled to reject the goods for breach of condition, subject to the rules on loss of the right to reject just described. As alternative, however, the consumer may seek repair or replacement of the goods under the new sections 48A–48E. If the consumer has justifiably demanded repair or replacement, he or she may be prevented from 'rescinding' (which seems to mean what we have referred to as 'terminating') the contract, or from demanding a reduction in price, unless the seller has failed to repair or replace the goods within a reasonable time and without significant inconvenience to the buyer. (Similar amendments have been made to Supply of Goods and Services Act 1982, see ss 11A–11F.)

■ **Sale of Goods Act 1979 (as amended by Sale and Supply of Goods to Consumers Regulations 2002, SI 2002/3045)**

Section 48A: Introductory

(1) This section applies if—
    (a) the buyer deals as consumer . . . and
    (b) the goods do not conform to the contract of sale at the time of delivery.
(2) If this section applies, the buyer has the right—
    (a) under and in accordance with section 48B below, to require the seller to repair or replace the goods, or
    (b) under and in accordance with section 48C below—
        (i) to require the seller to reduce the purchase price of the goods to the buyer by an appropriate amount, or
        (ii) to rescind the contract with regard to the goods in question.
    . . .

Section 48B: Repair or replacement of the goods

(1) If section 48A above applies, the buyer may require the seller—
    (a) to repair the goods, or
    (b) to replace the goods.
(2) If the buyer requires the seller to repair or replace the goods, the seller must—
    (a) repair or, as the case may be, replace the goods within a reasonable time but without causing significant inconvenience to the buyer;
    (b) bear any necessary costs incurred in doing so (including in particular the cost of any labour, materials or postage).
(3) The buyer must not require the seller to repair or, as the case may be, replace the goods if that remedy is—
    (a) impossible, or
    (b) disproportionate in comparison to the other of those remedies, or

(c) disproportionate in comparison to an appropriate reduction in the purchase price under paragraph (a), or rescission under paragraph (b), of section 48C(1) below.

(4) One remedy is disproportionate in comparison to the other if the one imposes costs on the seller which, in comparison to those imposed on him by the other, are unreasonable, taking into account—

    (a) the value which the goods would have if they conformed to the contract of sale,

    (b) the significance of the lack of conformity, and

    (c) whether the other remedy could be effected without significant inconvenience to the buyer.

(5) Any question as to what is a reasonable time or significant inconvenience is to be determined by reference to—

    (a) the nature of the goods, and

    (b) the purpose for which the goods were acquired.

Section 48C: Reduction of purchase price or rescission of contract

(1) If section 48A above applies, the buyer may—

    (a) require the seller to reduce the purchase price of the goods in question to the buyer by an appropriate amount, or

    (b) rescind the contract with regard to those goods,

if the condition in subsection (2) below is satisfied.

(2) The condition is that—

    (a) by virtue of section 48B(3) above the buyer may require neither repair nor replacement of the goods; or

    (b) the buyer has required the seller to repair or replace the goods, but the seller is in breach of the requirement of section 48B(2)(a) above to do so within a reasonable time and without significant inconvenience to the buyer.

    ...

Section 48E: Powers of the court

    ...

(2) On the application of the buyer the court may make an order requiring specific performance ... by the seller of any obligation imposed on him by virtue of section 48B above.

QUESTIONS

1. You employ a builder to build a wall in your garden for £1,000. You do not discuss the time of payment. After he has done half the work, the builder claims that he is entitled to be paid £500. Is he correct? If not, why not?

2. What is the difference between an entire obligation and a severable obligation? If one party fails to complete performance of an entire obligation, what is the effect?

3. If a party partially completes an entire obligation and in so doing confers a benefit on the other party, but the contract is then terminated because of the first party's default, need the benefited party pay anything for what it has received? If not, what is the justification for such a draconian rule?

4. What is the effect at common law if one party fails to perform a condition of the contract? What of a warranty? What is the effect if one party fails to perform a condition under the Sale of Goods Act 1979 (as amended)?

5.   What is the effect of a failure to perform an 'innominate term'? What factors led to the development of the innominate term approach? Do you think that development overall was a wise one or not?

6.   When may a party who has not received the substance of what she was promised go beyond refusing to perform her side of the contract until the other has performed, and terminate the contract? Is she entitled to terminate as soon as the date for performance has passed? Can she ever terminate before the date for performance has passed?

7.   How might a party who has the right to terminate a contract for the other's breach lose that right?

CHAPTER TWENTY-TWO

DAMAGES

I. THE BASIC MEASURE OF RECOVERY

The basic measure of damages for breach of contract was described in Chapter 2: so far as money can do it, the plaintiff is to be placed in the same situation as if the contract had been performed *(Robinson v Harman* (1848) 1 Exch 850 at 855). This is subject to two general qualifications: the mitigation rule, which provides that the plaintiff will not be allowed to recover for losses that might could have been avoided by taking reasonable steps, and the remoteness rule, under which the plaintiff will not recover for any unusual loss unless the possibility of such a loss occurring was contemplated by the parties when the contract was made. In *British Westinghouse Electric and Manufacturing Co Ltd v Underground Electric Rlys Co of London Ltd* [1912] AC 673, Viscount Haldane LC stated the general principles thus (at 688–689):

In order to come to a conclusion on the question as to damages thus raised, it is essential to bear in mind certain propositions which I think are well established. In some of the cases there are expressions as to the principles governing the measure of general damages which at first sight seem difficult to harmonise. The apparent discrepancies are, however, mainly due to the varying nature of the particular questions submitted for decision. The quantum of damage is a question of fact, and the only guidance which the law can give is to lay down general principles which afford at times but scanty assistance in dealing with particular cases. The judges who give guidance to juries in these cases have necessarily to look at their special character, and to mould for the purposes of different kinds of claim the expression of the general principles which apply to them, and this is apt to give rise to an appearance of ambiguity. Subject to these observations I think that there are certain broad principles, which are quite well settled. The first is that, as far as possible, he who has proved a breach of a bargain to supply what he contracted to get is to be placed, as far as money can do it, in as good a situation as if the contract had been performed. The fundamental basis is thus compensation for pecuniary loss naturally flowing from the breach; but this first principle is qualified by a second, which imposes on a plaintiff the duty of taking all reasonable steps to mitigate the loss consequent on the breach, and debars him from claiming in respect of any part of the damage which is due to his neglect to take such steps.

(This case is considered in detail p 660.)

In this introductory subsection, we will look briefly at how the rules of mitigation and remoteness affect the recovery of damages before considering in some detail the nature of the losses that are recoverable in contract. Remoteness and mitigation will be considered in more detail in subsections I and II.

■ Sale of Goods Act 1979

SELLER'S REMEDIES

...

Section 50

(1) Where the buyer wrongfully neglects or refuses to accept and pay for the goods, the seller may maintain an action against him for damages for non-acceptance.

(2) The measure of damages is the estimated loss directly and naturally resulting, in the ordinary course of events, from the buyer's breach of contract.

(3) Where there is an available market for the goods in question the measure of damages is prima facie to be ascertained by the difference between the contract price and the market or current price at the time or times when the goods ought to have been accepted or (if no time was fixed for acceptance) at the time of the refusal to accept.

BUYER'S REMEDIES

Section 51

(1) Where the seller wrongfully neglects or refuses to deliver the goods to the buyer, the buyer may maintain an action against the seller for damages for non-delivery.

(2) The measure of damages is the estimated loss directly and naturally resulting, in the ordinary course of events, from the seller's breach of contract.

(3) Where there is an available market for the goods in question the measure of damages is prima facie to be ascertained by the difference between the contract price and the market or current price of the goods at the time or times when they ought to have been delivered or (if no time was fixed) at the time of the refusal to deliver.

NOTES

1. There is 'an available market' if goods of the contract description can be readily bought or sold: see pp 666–670.

2. Why, when there is an available market for the goods, are the damages prima facie the difference between contract and market prices at the date for delivery? Do you see what is meant when it is said that the measures of damages set out in these subsections incorporate the principle of mitigation (eg *McGregor on Damages,* 17th ed, para 7–032)? If there is an available market, the claimant does not have to go into the market to buy/sell against the defendant. In many systems, a distinction is made between a 'concrete' measure, based on actual transactions in the market, and an 'abstract' measure, based on evidence of what the market price was at the relevant time, whether or not the claimant went into the market: Treitel, 'Remedies for Breach of Contract', pp 111–124. English law clearly proceeds on an abstract basis if there is an available market.

   Suppose A contracts to sell 100 tons of coffee beans to B for delivery on 1 February at £1,000 a ton. A does not deliver. The market price on 1 February is £ 1,050 a ton; on 2 February, £1,100 a ton; on 3 February, it is £1,000. In principle, on these facts, B can recover £50 a ton (there might be other facts that justify some further recovery). If B goes into the market on 2 February, she cannot recover £100 a ton because she could have mitigated by buying on 1 February (this assumes that she could, in practice, have bought on

1 February—probably true of a commodity market). However, it appears that if B takes a view of the market and does not buy until 3 February, she can still recover £50 a ton.

3. If there is no available market, the damages will be assessed according to the general principles. Thus if the seller fails to deliver and the buyer cannot obtain substitute goods in the market, the buyer may recover consequential losses that are suffered as a result— for instance, loss of profit from production or loss of profit on a resale. However, the loss must not be too remote: see the next case.

■ *Hadley v Baxendale*
(1854) 9 Exch 341, Exchequer

Where two parties have made a contract, which one of them has broken, the damages which the other party ought to receive in respect of such breach of contract should be such as may fairly and reasonably be considered either arising naturally, ie according to the usual course of things, from such breach of contract itself, or such as may reasonably be supposed to have been in the contemplation of both parties at the time they made the contract, as the probable result of the breach of it.—Where the plaintiffs, the owners of a flour mill, sent a broken iron shaft to an office of the defendants, who were common carriers, to be conveyed by them, and the defendants' clerk, who attended at the office, was told that the mill was stopped, that the shaft must be delivered immediately, and that a special entry, if necessary, must be made to hasten its delivery: and the delivery of the broken shaft to the consignee, to whom it had been sent by the plaintiffs as a pattern, by which to make a new shaft, was delayed for an unreasonable time; in consequence of which, the plaintiffs did not receive the new shaft for some days after the time they ought to have received it, and they were consequently unable to work their mill from want of the new shaft, and thereby incurred a loss of profits:—Held, that, under the circumstances, such loss could not be recovered in an action against the defendants as common carriers.

The judgment of the Court was now delivered by

Alderson B

We think that there ought to be a new trial in this case; but, in so doing, we deem it to be expedient and necessary to state explicitly the rule which the Judge, at the next trial, ought, in our opinion, to direct the jury to be governed by when they estimate the damages....

Now we think the proper rule in such a case as the present is this:—Where two parties have made a contract which one of them has broken, the damages which the other party ought to receive in respect of such breach of contract should be such as may fairly and reasonably be considered either arising naturally, ie, according to the usual course of things, from such breach of contract itself, or such as may reasonably be supposed to have been in the contemplation of both parties, at the time they made the contract, as the probable result of the breach of it. Now, if the special circumstances under which the contract was actually made were communicated by the plaintiffs to the defendants, and thus known to both parties, the damages resulting from the breach of such a contract, which they would reasonably contemplate, would be the amount of injury which would ordinarily follow from a breach of contract under these special circumstances so known and communicated. But, on the other hand, if these special circumstances were wholly unknown to the party breaking the contract, he, at the most, could only be supposed to have had in his contemplation the amount of injury which would arise generally, and in the great multitude of cases not affected by any special circumstances, from such a breach of contract. For, had the special circumstances been known, the parties might have specially provided for the breach of contract by special terms as to the damage in that case; and of this advantage it would be very unjust to deprive them. Now the above principles are those by which we think the jury ought to be guided in estimating the damages arising out of any breach of contract. Now, in the present case, if we are to apply the principles above laid down, we find that the only circumstances here communicated by the plaintiffs to the defendants at the time the contract was made, were, that the article to be carried was the broken shaft of a mill, and that the plaintiffs were the millers of that mill. But how do these circumstances shew reasonably that the profits of the mill must be stopped by an unreasonable delay in the delivery of the broken shaft by the carrier to the third person? Suppose the plaintiffs had another shaft in their possession put up or putting up at the time, and that they only wished to send back the broken shaft to the engineer who made it; it is clear that this would be quite consistent with the above circumstances, and yet the unreasonable delay in the delivery would have no effect upon the intermediate profits of the mill. Or, again, suppose that, at the time of the delivery to the carrier, the machinery of the mill had been in other respects defective, then, also, the same results would follow. Here it is true that the shaft was actually sent back to serve as a model for a new one, and that the want of a new one was the only cause of the stoppage of the mill, and that the loss of profits really arose from not sending down the new shaft in proper time, and that this arose from the delay in delivering the broken one to serve as a model. But it is obvious that, in the great multitude of cases of millers sending off broken shafts to third persons by a carrier under ordinary circumstances, such consequences would not, in all probability, have occurred; and these special circumstances were here never communicated by the plaintiffs to the defendants. It follows, therefore, that the loss of profits here cannot reasonably be considered such a consequence of the breach of contract as could have been fairly and reasonably contemplated by both the parties when they made this contract. For such loss would neither have flowed naturally from the breach of this contract in the great multitude of such cases occurring under ordinary circumstances, nor were the special circumstances, which, perhaps, would have made it a reasonable and natural consequence of such breach of contract, communicated to or known by the defendants. . . . There must therefore be a new trial . . .

NOTES

1. It has been held that the headnote states the facts wrongly: if the plaintiffs had told the defendants' clerk that the mill was stopped, they should have recovered. See *Victoria Laundry (Windsor) Ltd v Newman Industries Ltd* [1949] 2 KB 528, 537–538.

2. This case is considered in more detail p 644.

3. Subject to the rules of mitigation and remoteness, the innocent party can normally recover damages for all of the loss suffered as a result of the breach of contract. This will include any wasted expenditure, any expenditure reasonably incurred in mitigating loss and any loss of profit. In an appropriate case, the plaintiff will recover damages for all of these items. Thus in *Hydraulic Engineering Co Ltd v McHaffie, Goslett & Co* (1878) 4 QBD 670, the defendants had contracted to make a 'gun', which they knew was to form part of a 'gunpowder pile driver' that the plaintiffs had contracted to build for Justice. The defendants delivered late, which prevented the plaintiffs delivering the finished machine on time, and Justice refused to take it. The plaintiffs were permitted to recover the expenditure they had wasted in making other parts of the machine (which was 'useless except as old iron', having been built specially), the cost of painting it to preserve it and the reasonable net profit they would have made on the contract with Justice. For further consideration of these various heads of damage, see pp 628 ff.

■ **Fuller and Perdue, 'The Reliance Interest in Contract Damages'** (1936)
46 Yale LJ 52, 52–56

We are still all too willing to embrace the conceit that it is possible to manipulate legal concepts without the orientation which comes from the simple inquiry: toward what end is this activity directed? Nietzsche's observation, that the most common stupidity consists in forgetting what one is trying to do, retains a discomforting relevance to legal science.

In no field is this more true than in that of damages. In the assessment of damages the law tends to be conceived, not as a purposive ordering of human affairs, but as a kind of juristic mensuration. The language of the decisions sounds in terms not of command but of discovery. We *measure* the *extent* of the injury; we *determine* whether it was *caused* by the defendant's act; we *ascertain* whether the plaintiff has included the *same item* of damage twice in his complaint. One unfamiliar with the unstated premises which language of this sort conceals might almost be led to suppose that Rochester produces some ingenious instrument by which these calculations are accomplished.

. . . For example, one frequently finds the 'normal' rule of contract damages (which awards to the promisee the value of the expectancy, 'the lost profit') treated as a mere corollary of a more fundamental principle, that the purpose of granting damages is to make 'compensation' for injury. Yet in this case we 'compensate' the plaintiff by giving him something he never had. This seems on the face of things a queer kind of compensation. We can, to be sure, make the term 'compensation' seem appropriate by saying that the defendant's breach 'deprived' the plaintiff of the expectancy. But this is in essence only a metaphorical statement of the effect of the legal rule. In actuality the loss which the plaintiff suffers (deprivation of the expectancy) is not a datum of nature but the reflection of a normative order. It appears as a 'loss' only by reference to an unstated *ought.* Consequently, when the law gauges damages by the value of the promised performance it is not merely measuring a quantum, but is seeking an end, however vaguely conceived this end may be.

It is for this reason that it is impossible to separate the law of contract damages from the larger body of motives and policies which constitutes the general law of contracts. . . .

THE PURPOSES PURSUED IN AWARDING CONTRACT DAMAGES

It is convenient to distinguish three principal purposes which may be pursued in awarding contract damages. These purposes, and the situations in which they become appropriate, may be stated briefly as follows:

First, the plaintiff has in reliance on the promise of the defendant conferred some value on the defendant. The defendant fails to perform his promise. The court may force the defendant to disgorge the value he received from the plaintiff. The object here may be termed the prevention of gain by the defaulting promisor at the expense of the promisee; more briefly, the prevention of unjust enrichment. The interest protected may be called the *restitution interest.* For our present purposes it is quite immaterial how the suit in such a case be classified, whether as contractual or quasi-contractual, whether as a suit to enforce the contract or as a suit based upon a rescission of the contract. These questions relate to the superstructure of the law, not to the basic policies with which we are concerned.

Secondly, the plaintiff has in reliance on the promise of the defendant changed his position. For example, the buyer under a contract for the sale of land has incurred expense in the investigation of the seller's title, or has neglected the opportunity to enter other contracts. We may award damages to the plaintiff for the purpose of undoing the harm which his reliance on the defendant's promise has caused him. Our object is to put him in as good a position as he was in before the promise was made. The interest protected in this case may be called the *reliance interest.*

Thirdly, without insisting on reliance by the promisee or enrichment of the promisor, we may seek to give the promisee the value of the expectancy which the promise created. We may in a suit for specific performance actually compel the defendant to render the promised performance to the plaintiff, or, in a suit for damages, we may make the defendant pay the money value of this performance. Here our object is to put the plaintiff in as good a position as he would have occupied had the defendant performed his promise. The interest protected in this case we may call the *expectation interest.*

It will be observed that what we have called the *restitution interest* unites two elements: (1) reliance by the promisee, (2) a resultant gain to the promisor. It may for some purposes be necessary to separate these elements. In some cases a defaulting promisor may after his breach be left with an unjust gain which was not taken from the promisee (a third party furnished the consideration), or which was not the result of reliance by the promisee (the promisor violated a promise not to appropriate the promisee's goods). Even in those cases where the promisor's gain results from the promisee's reliance it may happen that damages will be assessed somewhat differently, depending on whether we take the promisor's gain or the promisee's loss as the standard of measurement. Generally, however, in the cases we shall be discussing, gain by the promisor will be accompanied by a corresponding and, so far as its legal measurement is concerned, identical loss to the promisee, so that for our purposes the most workable classification is one which presupposes in the restitution interest a correlation of promisor's gain and promisee's loss. If, as we shall assume, the gain involved in the restitution interest results from and is identical with the plaintiff's loss through reliance, then the restitution interest is merely a special case of the reliance interest; all of the cases coming under the restitution interest will be covered by the reliance interest, and the reliance interest will be broader than the restitution interest only to the extent that it includes cases where the plaintiff has relied on the defendant's promise without enriching the defendant.

It should not be supposed that the distinction here taken between the reliance and expectation interests coincides with that sometimes taken between 'losses caused' (damnum emergens) and 'gains prevented' (lucrum cessans). In the first place, though reliance ordinarily results in 'losses' of an affirmative nature (expenditures of labor and money) it is also true that opportunities for gain may be foregone in reliance on a promise. Hence the reliance interest must be interpreted as at least potentially covering 'gains prevented' as well as 'losses caused'. (Whether 'gains prevented' through reliance on a promise are properly compensable in damages is a question not here determined. Obviously, certain scruples concerning 'causality' and 'foreseeability' are suggested. It is enough for our present purpose to note that there is nothing in the definition of the reliance interest itself which would exclude items of this sort from consideration.) On the other hand, it is not possible to make the expectation interest entirely synonymous with 'gains prevented'. The disappointment of an expectancy often entails losses of a positive character.

(A further extract from this classic article will be found p 765.)

NOTES

1. You will recollect that earlier we drew a distinction between the losses that are recoverable in tort and those that are recoverable in contract. The former compensate the plaintiff for 'out-of-pocket' loss; the latter will give this plus loss of profit. Beware of assuming that tort damages cannot include compensation for 'loss of expectation'. A tortfeasor may have to compensate the victim for loss of expectation of life, or for loss of profit that the victim would have been able to make, for instance by using the property that the tortfeasor has destroyed. These expectations, however, were not created by the tortfeasor: they existed beforehand and were destroyed by him. A tort such as a negligent misrepresentation may engender expectations that the misrepresentation is true, but the victim may not recover damages for loss of this expectation. In contract, the expectations generated by the contract are protected. See pp 372 ff.

2. Later in the article, Fuller notes that sometimes in reliance on the contract the plaintiff will have passed up another opportunity to contract with someone else. Lost opportunity is compensable in tort—for instance, damages for personal injury will include damages for the loss of the opportunity to earn; in *East v Maurer* see (p 372), the damages for fraud included the profit the plaintiff might have made if she had bought some other business instead of the one she did buy as a result of the defendant's fraud. If the plaintiff would have made the same profit from the opportunity she passed over as she should have done on the contract itself, there will be no difference between expectation loss and reliance loss.

3. If you think about typical tort cases, you will see that Fuller's analysis is actually incomplete. If a plaintiff suffers personal injury or damage to property, she can recover for it whether the action is in tort or contract, but it seems odd to describe the injury as

'reliance' loss. Equally, she can recover expenses reasonably incurred in mitigating the loss (eg medical expenses or the cost of making a substitute transaction). These are not incurred in reliance on the contract either. We term them 'incidental' loss.

4.   It is only recently that the English courts have begun to adopt Fuller's terminology (see p 631). Often damages for breach of contract will be calculated by methods that seem to avoid splitting them up in this way. For instance, if a buyer fails to accept goods the seller has built for it and the seller resells the goods to someone else, the damages will normally be the difference between the original contract price and the resale price (cf Sale of Goods Act 1979, s 50(3), p 624). Nonetheless, Fuller's analysis is a useful way of sorting out what losses the plaintiff is compensated for. For instance, suppose that the contract price for the goods were £10,000 and the goods had cost the seller £9,000 to build (including overheads). If the price at which the seller manages to resell is £9,400 and it cost £100 to arrange the resale, the damages will be £700 (£10,000 + £100 − £9,400). It is clear that we are going beyond putting the plaintiff back into its pre-contractual position by reimbursing its out-of-pocket loss: we are giving damages for loss of expectation too.

5.   The English courts do not use a restitution measure in assessing contract *damages:* the traditional approach looks at what the plaintiff has lost, not what the defendant has gained (see pp 633 ff). Usually this benefits the plaintiff because its expenditure will be at least equal to and possibly higher than the gain to the defendant. However, the net effect is that the plaintiff recovers at least the value of any benefit conferred, plus any further wasted expenditure and loss of profit. The restitution measure is used by the courts when the plaintiff cannot claim damages (eg if there was no contract, p 39, or if the contract has been frustrated, see p 481). In addition, the victim of a breach of contract may sometimes opt to claim in restitution instead of claiming damages: see Chapter 24.

6.   In American law, the plaintiff is sometimes confined to claiming reliance loss even though the claim is for breach of contract: for instance, when the claim is based on the reliance principle stated in s 90 of the Restatement, although a recent study suggests that even in these cases the courts regularly award expectation damages (see p 171). In English law, the plaintiff is always entitled in theory to damages for loss of expectation if this can be proved. In practice, damages for breach of contract will not always include any expectation element. Firstly, the plaintiff will frequently be able to earn the same amount of profit on a substitute contract with someone else, and the mitigation rule will then rule out recovery of damages for loss of profit. (Some of the implications of this for contract theory are explored on p 771.) Secondly, the plaintiff may fail to prove that it lost any profit. An example is provided by *McRae v Commonwealth Disposals Commission* (the facts of this case are set out on p 500; it will be remembered that the High Court of Australia found that the Commission had sold McRae the wreck of an oil tanker, which the court held that it had promised was on the Jourmand Reef). McRae claimed loss of profit. This was disallowed on the ground that because the Commission had not promised to deliver a tanker of any specified size, nor any oil, the claim for loss of profit was too speculative, but it allowed McRae the wasted cost of equipping a salvage expedition.

■ ***Anglia Television Ltd v Reed***
[1971] 3 All ER 690, Court of Appeal

The plaintiff television company decided to make a film for television, and engaged the defendant, Robert Reed, to play the leading role. Later, Reed found himself unable to come to

England, and he repudiated the contract at the last moment. The plaintiffs could not obtain a suitable substitute, and they cancelled the film. They claimed for their wasted expenditure, part of which (hiring other members of the team) had been incurred before the contract with Reed had been made. The master held Reed liable for this part of the expenditure and he appealed.

Lord Denning MR

. . . It seems to me that a plaintiff in such a case as this has an election: he can either claim for his loss of profits; or for his wasted expenditure. But he must elect between them. He cannot claim both. If he has not suffered any loss of profits—or if he cannot prove what his profits would have been—he can claim in the alternative the expenditure which has been thrown away, that is, wasted, by reason of the breach. That is shown by *Cullinane v British 'Rema' Manufacturing Co Ltd.*

   If the plaintiff claims the wasted expenditure, he is not limited to the expenditure incurred *after* the contract was concluded. He can claim also the expenditure incurred *before* the contract, provided that it was such as would reasonably be in the contemplation of the parties as likely to be wasted if the contract was broken. Applying that principle here, it is plain that, when Mr Reed entered into this contract, he must have known perfectly well that much expenditure had already been incurred on director's fees and the like. He must have contemplated—or, at any rate, it is reasonably to be imputed to him—that if he broke his contract, all that expenditure would be wasted, whether or not it was incurred before or after the contract. He must pay damages for all the expenditure so wasted and thrown away. This view is supported by the recent decision of Brightman J in *Lloyd v Stanbury*. There was a contract for the sale of land. In anticipation of the contract—and before it was concluded—the purchaser went to much expense in moving a caravan to the site and in getting his furniture there. The seller afterwards entered into a contract to sell the land to the purchaser, but afterwards broke his contract. The land had not increased in value, so the purchaser could not claim for any loss of profit. But Brightman J held that he could recover the cost of moving the caravan and furniture, because it was 'within the contemplation of the parties when the contract was signed'. That decision is in accord with the correct principle, namely, that wasted expenditure can be recovered when it is wasted by reason of the defendant's breach of contract. It is true that, if the defendant had never entered into the contract, he would not be liable, and the expenditure would have been incurred by the plaintiff without redress; but the defendant having made his contract and broken it, it does not lie in his mouth to say he is not liable, when it was because of his breach that the expenditure has been wasted.

   I think the master was quite right and this appeal should be dismissed.

Phillimore LJ

I agree.

Megaw LJ

I also agree.

Appeal dismissed.

NOTES

1. Perhaps the plaintiffs did not claim lost profit because (except in the case in which a film is sold to other stations) it is very hard to show what profit is made on a film made for television: the company's earnings are derived from the advertising shown before, during and after the film.

2. *Cullinane v British 'Rema'* Manufacturing Co Ltd [1954] 1 QB 292 is cited for the proposition that the plaintiff cannot claim *both* wasted expenditure and lost profit. If gross

profit is meant, that must be correct, because if the contract had been performed the expenditure would have to have been paid for out of the gross profits, and to award both would be to give double recovery. If the proposition means that the plaintiff cannot recover the wasted expenditure and the net profit he would have earned at the end of the day had the contract been fulfilled, it seems inconsistent with principle as well as with the *Hydraulic Engineering* case (see p 626) in any event the court did not in fact decide that: see Macleod [1970] JBL 19.

3.   What if the plaintiff had made a 'bad bargain' in the sense that its out-of-pocket expenditure was greater than the amount it would have received if the contract had been performed?

■ *C & P Haulage (a firm) v Middleton*

[1983] 3 All ER 94, Court of Appeal

The appellant was given a licence to occupy premises on a renewable six-monthly basis, and he incurred expenditure in making the premises suitable for his work, even though it was expressly provided that fixtures put in by him were not to be removed at the end of the licence. He was wrongfully ejected from the premises by the licensor ten weeks before a six-months' term was up, but he obtained the local authority's permission to use his own garage instead, and continued to do this for more than ten weeks. He claimed the cost of the improvements effected by him to the premises, but the trial judge awarded him only nominal damages.

Ackner LJ

. . . The judge approached the case essentially on this basis, that the accepted principle in relation to the assessment of damages for breach of contract was to put the plaintiff in the same position, as far as one could, as he would have been in if the contract had been performed; and, in order to evaluate whether if the contract had been performed what was the nature, if any, of the damage that he should be entitled to claim, one had to look at the consequences of the breach of contract.

The consequences of this breach of contract were that, so far from the appellant suffering any damage as a result of being excluded from the premises ten weeks earlier than would lawfully have been the case, thanks to the tolerance of the planning authorities, he had in effect been saved the payment which was likely to be between £60 and £100 a week which he would have had to have paid for the use of the respondents' premises. He accordingly came to the conclusion that if he was to award the damages claimed he would be putting the appellant in a better position than would have been the case if the contract had been lawfully determined.

The case which was at the forefront of counsel for the appellant's submissions before the judge and before us as well is *Anglia Television Ltd v Reed* . . .

Lord Denning MR was not contemplating what has been referred to subsequently as the 'bad bargain' case, a case in which a plaintiff has entered into a loss-making contract or, I would include, an otherwise disadvantageous contract. He was considering a case where it would not be possible to establish any loss of profits because the situation could not be prophesied had the defendant complied with his contractual obligations. . . . [The appellant] is not claiming for the loss of his bargain, which would involve being put in the position that he would have been in if the contract has been performed. He is not asking to be put in that position. He is asking to be put in the position he would have been in if the contract had never been made at all. If the contract had never been made at all, then he would not have incurred these expenses, and that is the essential approach he adopts in mounting this claim; because, if the right approach is that he should be put in the position in which he would have been had the contract been performed, then it follows that he suffered no damage. He lost his entitlement to a further ten weeks of occupation after 5 October, and during that period he involved himself in no loss of profit, because he found other accommodation, and in no increased expense, in fact the contrary, because he returned immediately to his own garage, thereby saving whatever would have been the agreed figure which he would have to have paid the respondents. . . .

The case which I have found of assistance, and I am grateful to counsel for their research, is *Bowlay Logging Ltd v Domtar Ltd.* It is a case in the British Columbia Supreme Court. Berger J, in a very careful and detailed judgment, goes through various English and American authorities and refers to the leading textbook writers, and I will only quote a small part of his judgment. He refers to the work of Professor L L Fuller and William R Perdue Jr in 'The Reliance Interest in Contract Damages' (1936) 46 Yale LJ:

> 'We will not in a suit for reimbursement for losses incurred in reliance on a contract knowingly put the plaintiff in a better position than he would have occupied had the contract been fully performed.'

Berger J then refers to a case in 1949, *L Albert & Son v Armstrong Rubber* Co, in which Learned Hand CJ, speaking for the Circuit Court of Appeals, Second Circuit, 'held that on a claim for compensation for expenses in part performance the defendant was entitled to deduct whatever he could prove the plaintiff would have lost if the contract had been fully performed'.

What Berger J had to consider was this (at 105):

> 'The parties entered into a contract whereby the plaintiff would cut timber under the defendant's timber sale, and the defendant would be responsible for hauling the timber away from the site of the timber sale. The plaintiff claimed the defendant was in breach of the contract as the defendant had not supplied sufficient trucks to make the plaintiff's operation, which was losing money, viable, and claimed not for loss of profits but for compensation for expenditures. The defendant argued that the plaintiff's operation lost money not because of a lack of trucks but because of the plaintiff's inefficiency, and, further, that even if the defendant had breached the contract the plaintiff should not be awarded damages because its operation would have lost money in any case.'

This submission was clearly accepted because the plaintiff was awarded only nominal damages and Berger J said:

> 'The law of contract compensates a plaintiff for damages resulting from the defendant's breach; it does not compensate a plaintiff for damages resulting from his making a bad bargain. Where it can be seen that the plaintiff would have incurred a loss on the contract as a whole, the expenses he has incurred are losses flowing from entering into the contract, not losses flowing from the defendant's breach. In these circumstances, the true consequence of the defendant's breach is that the plaintiff is released from his obligation to complete the contract—or in other words, he is saved from incurring further losses. If the law of contract were to move from compensating for the consequences of breach to compensating for the consequences of entering into contracts, the law would run contrary to the normal expectations of the world of commerce. The burden of risk would be shifted from the plaintiff to the defendant. The defendant would become the insurer of the plaintiff's enterprise. Moreover, the amount of the damages would increase not in relation to the gravity or consequences of the breach but in relation to the inefficiency with which the plaintiff carried out the contract. The greater his expenses owing to inefficiency, the greater the damages. The fundamental principle upon which damages are measured under the law of contract is restitutio in integrum. The principle contended for here by the plaintiff would entail the award of damages not to compensate the plaintiff but to punish the defendant.'

It is urged here that the garage itself was merely an element in the appellant's business: it was not a profit-making entity on its own. Nevertheless, if as a result of being kept out of these premises the appellant had found no other premises to go to for a period of time, his claim would clearly have been a claim for such a loss of profit as he could establish his business suffered.

In my judgment, the approach of Berger J is the correct one. It is not the function of the courts where there is a breach of contract knowingly, as this would be the case, to put the plaintiff in a better financial position than if the contract had been properly performed. In this case the appellant, if he was right in his claim, would indeed be in a better position because, as I have already indicated, had the contract been lawfully determined, as it could have been in the middle of December, there would have been no question of his recovering these expenses. . . .

Fox LJ

. . . The present case seems to me to be quite different both from *Anglia Television Ltd v Reed* and from *Lloyd v Stanbury* in that, while it is true that the expenditure could in a sense be said to be wasted in consequence of the breach of contract, it was equally likely to be wasted if there had been no breach, because the respondents wanted to get the appellant out and could terminate the licence at quite short notice. A high risk of waste was from the very first inherent in the nature of the contract itself, breach or no breach. The reality of the matter is that the waste resulted from what was, on the appellant's side, a very unsatisfactory and dangerous bargain.

I agree with Ackner LJ that the appeal must be dismissed.

Appeal dismissed.

NOTES

1. The fact that the plaintiff suffered no net loss in this case seems to have flowed partly from the bad initial bargain (see Fox LJ) and partly from the favourable arrangements made subsequently (see Ackner LJ and below).

2. In CCC *Films (London) Ltd v Impact Quadrant Films Ltd* [1984] 3 All ER 298, Hutchison J held (i) that the plaintiff could claim reliance loss when he could not prove a profit even though the difficulty of proof was not caused by the defendant's breach, as it had been in *McRae's* case, and (ii) following a dictum of Learned Hand CJ in the *Albert* case, that it was for the defendant to prove that the plaintiff would not have recouped his expenditure even if the contract had been performed. See also *Commonwealth of Australia v Amann Aviation Pty Ltd* (1991) 174 CLR 64, High Court of Australia.

3. These cases seem to follow from the general principle that the plaintiff is entitled to damages only for the loss that the defendant's breach has caused.

4. Expectation has been used as a cap on reliance damages in proprietary estoppel cases also: see Gardner (1999) 115 LQR 438, 448–450.

■ *Surrey County Council v Bredero Homes Ltd*
[1993] 3 All ER 705, Court of Appeal

Two plaintiff councils were the respective registered freehold owners of two adjoining parcels of land totalling 12.33 acres in area, which had been acquired originally for road purposes. By 1980, the land was no longer required for those purposes and the councils, acting together, decided to offer the entire site for development as a housing estate. The councils subsequently accepted an offer by the defendant development company, which in the councils' view represented the best balance between the amount offered and development scheme submitted. By a contract in writing dated 28 November 1980, the councils agreed to sell the entire site to the defendant for £1.52m, subject to the defendant obtaining planning permission for the development of the site in accordance with the councils' development brief and the scheme for the development of the site. The defendant duly obtained the necessary planning permission, and by transfers dated 22 January 1981, the councils transferred the land to it. Under cl 2 of each transfer, the defendant covenanted with each council that it would carry out the development of the housing estate in accordance with the terms of the planning permission and the approved scheme. The defendant subsequently obtained fresh planning permission, which enabled it to build more houses on the site than the number specified in the approved scheme and it completed the development by building the extra houses without seeking any modification of the development covenants. The development was thus more profitable than that originally authorised. The councils, although aware of the breach of the covenants in the transfers, did not seek an injunction or specific performance to compel the defendant to develop the housing estate in accordance with the development covenants. However, after the defendant had disposed of all the houses on the estate, the councils brought proceedings against it for damages for breach of the covenants equal to the payment that might have been extracted from the defendant in return for agreed modifications to the covenants so as to authorise the more profitable development that had in fact been carried out. The defendant accepted that it was in breach of the covenants, but denied that the councils were entitled to recover anything more than nominal damages.

The trial judge agreed. The councils appealed.

Dillon L J

... The plaintiffs have merely sought damages which have been described as 'damages at common law', as opposed to 'damages in equity under Lord Cairns's Act' (the Chancery Amendment Act 1858). The plaintiffs accept that they have not suffered any damage at all of the nature of damage to adjoining property owned or occupied by them. What they claim as damages is essentially the profit made by the defendant by breaking the covenants and building 77 houses and not just 72—or, since the defendant wishes to be modest in its demands in putting forward a somewhat revolutionary development of the law of damages, such a part of the profit as would reflect the reasonable premium that the defendant should have paid them for contractual permission by way of relaxation of the covenants to build the 77 houses rather than 72.

Indeed, the plaintiffs say, and I have no reason to doubt, that their sole purpose in imposing the covenants at all—to commence and pursue the development to its completion in accordance with the first planning permission—was that the defendant would have to apply for and pay for a relaxation if it wanted to build anything more.

It is of course clear that had the contracts been worded otherwise there could have been provision for the payment by the defendant of an additional price of a specified amount or fixed by an appropriate formula for each extra house or bungalow, if they or their successors in title built more than 72 houses or bungalows on the land within a specified period, but that is not the contract that was made.

In putting forward the claim for damages with which we are concerned, the plaintiffs rely very strongly on the decision of Brightman J in *Wrotham Park Estate Co v Parkside Homes Ltd* [1974] 2 All ER 321, [1974] 1 WLR 798, to which I shall have to come.

The starting point, however, in my judgment is that the remedy at common law for a breach of contract is an award of damages and damages at common law are intended to compensate the victim for his loss, not to transfer to the victim, if he has suffered no loss, the benefit which the wrongdoer has gained by his breach of contract.... [The] innocent party is to be placed, so far as money can do so, in the same position as if the contract had been performed. That follows the wording of the statement of the rule of the common law by Parke B in *Robinson v Harman*. That rule has been referred to in argument in the present case as the 'conventional' rule.

Sir William Goodhart QC for the plaintiffs has pointed out that the conventional rule is not of universal application in that there are cases in which the plaintiff is awarded not what is required to place him in the same situation as if the contract had been performed, but what is required to recoup to him the expenditure which he has incurred which has been wasted because the contract has not been performed: see, for instance, *Wallington v Townsend* [1939] Ch 588 and *Anglia Television Ltd v Reed*.

The principle is still compensation for loss. The difference is merely that there are cases where the contract has so palpably not been performed at all that it would be unreal to assume that it had been performed and impossible to calculate damages on such an unreal assumption.

Every student is taught that the basis of assessing damages for breach of contract is the rule in *Hadley v Baxendale* [above, p 625], which is wholly concerned with the losses which can be compensated by damages. Such damages may, in an appropriate case, cover profit which the injured plaintiff has lost, but they do not cover an award to a plaintiff who has himself suffered no loss, of the profit which the defendant has gained for himself by his breach of contract.

In the field of tort there are areas where the law is different and the plaintiff can recover in respect of the defendant's gain. Thus in the field of trespass it is well established that if one person has, without leave of another, been using that other's land for his own purposes he ought to pay for such user. Thus even if he had done no actual harm to the land he was charged for the user of the land. This was applied originally in wayleave cases where a person had without authority used his neighbour's land for passage: see, for instance, *Phillips v Homfray, Fothergill v Phillips* (1871) LR 6 Ch App 770.

. . . [In] a case of detinue the defendant was ordered to pay a hire for chattels he had detained: see *Strand Electric and Engineering Co Ltd v Brisford Entertainments Ltd* [1952] 2 QB 246.

Those cases do not apply in the present case as the defendant has made no use of any property of either plaintiff.

The cases have been taken still further in some fields of tort, particularly concerned with intellectual property, where it is well established that the plaintiff can choose to have either damages or an account of profits made by the defendant by his wrongful acts: see, for instance, *Lever v Goodwin* (1887) 36 ChD 1 at 7, per Cotton LJ. This is in line with the long-established common law doctrine of waiving the tort.

The liability in the present case is solely in contract and not in tort.

I come then to the *Wrotham Park* case. In that case the predecessor in title of the plaintiffs had, in 1935, sold some land to a predecessor in title of the defendants, subject to a restrictive covenant restricting building to a particular layout. That covenant was duly registered under the Land Charges Act 1925. In 1971 the land was sold to the defendant, who had no actual knowledge of the restrictive covenant and proceeded to build 14 houses on the land in breach of the covenant. In early 1972 the plaintiffs, as successors in title to the benefit of the covenant, issued their writ against the defendant claiming an injunction to restrain building in breach of the covenant, and demolition of anything built in breach. The plaintiffs made no application for an interim injunction. By the time the action came on for trial in July 1973, the 14 houses had all been completed and sold to purchasers with the benefit of indemnity insurance policies. At the trial Brightman J held that the plaintiffs were indeed entitled to the benefit of the covenant and the defendant was bound by it.

For obvious reasons however—that he could not shut his eyes to the fact that the houses existed and it would be an unpardonable waste of much needed houses to direct that they be pulled down—he refused to grant a mandatory injunction. He commented that no damage of a financial nature had been done to the plaintiffs by the breach of the covenant and proceeded to consider what damages, if any, he should award under the jurisdiction which had originated under Lord Cairns's Act to award damages in substitution for an injunction.

It was submitted to him that the damages should be nil or purely nominal because the value of the Wrotham Park estate was not diminished by one farthing in consequence of the breach of covenant.

But Brightman J concluded that such a result would be of questionable fairness. He said ([1974] 2 All ER 321 at 339):

> 'If, for social and economic reasons, the court does not see fit in the exercise of its discretion, to order demolition of the 14 houses, is it just that the plaintiffs should receive no compensation and that the defendants should be left in undisturbed possession of the fruits of their wrongdoing?'

He then referred to the wayleave cases . . . and the other cases which I have mentioned where the same principle has been applied.

He concluded that the appropriate course was that the defendant should pay by way of damages the sum which the plaintiffs might hypothetically have been willing to pay—though actually they would never have been willing to relax the covenant to permit the defendant to do what it wanted to do on the land. He fixed that at a small percentage of the defendant's anticipated profit from building the 14 houses on the land.

The difficulty about the decision in the *Wrotham Park* case is that in *Johnson v Agnew* Lord Wilberforce, after citing certain decisions on the scope and basis of Lord Cairns's Act, which were not cited to Brightman J, stated in the clearest terms that on the balance of those authorities, and on principle, he found in the Act no warrant for the court awarding damages differently from common law damages (see [1979] 1 All ER 883 at 896, [1980] AC 367 at 400).

Sir William Goodhart submits that it follows from that analysis by Lord Wilberforce in *Johnson v Agnew* that the damages awarded by Brightman J in the *Wrotham Park* case were indeed damages assessed on recognised common law principles which should, so he says, be applied in the present case.

I doubt, however, whether that does follow from Lord Wilberforce's analysis in *Johnson v Agnew* . . .

Given that the established basis of an award of damages in contract is compensation for the plaintiff's loss, as indicated above, I have difficulty in seeing how Sir William Goodhart's suggested common law principle of awarding the plaintiff, who has suffered no loss, the gain which the defendant has made by the breach of contract, is intended to go. Is it to apply, for instance, to shipping contracts or contracts of employment or contracts for building works?

Sir William suggested, in his and Mr Weatherill's skeleton argument, that the conventional measure fails to do justice and a different measure should be applied where the following conditions are satisfied: (a) the breach is deliberate, in the sense that the defendant is deliberately doing an act which he knows or should know is plainly or arguably in breach of contract; (b) the defendant, as a result of the breach, has profited by making a gain or reducing a loss; (c) at the date of the breach it is clear or probable that damages under the conventional measure will either be nominal or much smaller than the profit to the defendant from the breach; and (d) if the profit results from the avoidance of expenditure, the expenditure would not have been economically wasteful or grossly disproportionate to the benefit which would have resulted from it.

He suggested in that paragraph in the skeleton argument that the underlying principle might be that the conventional measure of damages might be overridden 'in certain circumstances' by the rule that no one should benefit from his deliberate wrongdoing. In the course of his submissions Sir William limited his formulation and while retaining conditions (a), (b) and (c), substituted for condition (d) the following:

> 'Damages for loss of bargaining power can be awarded if—but only if—the party in breach could have been restrained by injunction from committing the breach of contract or compelled by specific performance to perform the contract. Where no such possibility existed, there was no bargaining power in reality and no right to damages for loss of it. Hence, damages for loss of bargaining power cannot be awarded where there is (for example) a contract for the sale of goods or (generally) a contract of employment.'

I find difficulty with that because in theory every time there is a breach of contract the injured party is deprived of his 'bargaining power' to negotiate for a financial consideration a variation of the contract which would enable the party who wants to depart from its terms to do what he wants to do. In addition it has been held in *Walford v Miles* [above, p 280] that an agreement to negotiate is not an animal known to the law and a duty to negotiate in good faith is unworkable in practice—and so I find it difficult to see why loss of bargaining or negotiating power should become an established factor in the assessment of damages for breach of contract.

Beyond that, since we are looking for the measure of damages at common law for breach of contract, apart from Lord Cairns's Act, I do not see why that should vary depending on whether the party in breach could or could not have been restrained by injunction from committing the breach or compelled by specific performance to perform the contract. Injunctions and specific performance were not remedies in the common law courts and were granted by the Court of Chancery, which, before Lord Cairns's Act, had no power to award damages, just because the common law remedy of damages was not an adequate remedy.

...I would dismiss the appeal.

Steyn LJ

I agree...Dillon L J has reviewed the relevant case law. It would not be a useful exercise for me to try to navigate through those much travelled waters again. Instead, it seems to me that it may possibly be useful to consider the question from the point of view of the application at first principles. An award of compensation for breach of contract serves to protect three separate interests. The starting principle is that the aggrieved party ought to be compensated for loss of his positive or expectation interests. In other words, the object is to put the aggrieved party in the same financial position as if the contract had been fully performed. But the law also protects the negative interest of the aggrieved party. If the aggrieved party is unable to establish the value of a loss of bargain he may seek compensation in respect of his reliance losses. The object of such an award is to compensate the aggrieved party for expenses incurred and losses suffered in reliance of the contract. These two complementary principles share one feature. Both are pure compensatory principles. If the aggrieved party has suffered no loss he is not entitled to be compensated by invoking these principles. The application of these principles to the present case would result in an award of nominal damages only.

There is, however, a third principle which protects the aggrieved party's restitutionary interest. The object of such an award is not to compensate the plaintiff for a loss, but to deprive the defendant of the benefit he gained by the breach of contract. The classic illustration is a claim for the return of goods sold and delivered where the buyer has repudiated his obligation to pay the price. It is not traditional to describe a claim for restitution following a breach of contract as damages. What matters is that a coherent law of obligations must inevitably extend its protection to cover certain restitutionary interests. How far that protection should extend is the essence of the problem before us. In my view *Wrotham Park Estate Co v Parkside Homes Ltd* is only defensible on the basis of the third or restitutionary principle (see *McGregor on Damages* (15th edn, 1988) para 18 and Professor P B H Birks *Civil Wrongs: A New World*, Butterworths Lectures [1990–1991] 55 at 71). The appellants' argument that the *Wrotham Park* case can be justified on the basis of a loss of bargaining opportunity is a fiction. The object of the award in the *Wrotham Park* case was not to compensate the plaintiff for financial injury, but to deprive the defendants of an unjustly acquired gain. Whilst it must be acknowledged that *Wrotham Park* represented a new development, it seems to me that it is based on a principle of legal theory, justice and sound policy. In the respondent's skeleton argument some doubt was cast, by way of alternative submission, on the correctness of the award of damages for breach of covenant in the *Wrotham Park* case. In my respectful view it was rightly decided and represents a useful development in our law. In *Tito v Waddell (No 2)* [see below, p 590] Megarry V-C interpreted the *Wrotham Park* case, and the decision in *Bracewell v Appleby* [1975] Ch 408, which followed *Wrotham Park*, as cases of the invasion of property rights. I respectfully agree. *Wrotham Park* is analogous to cases where a defendant has made use of the aggrieved party's property and thereby saved expenses: see *Penarth Dock Engineering Co Ltd v Pounds* [1963] 1 Lloyd's Rep 359. I readily accept that the word 'property' in this context must be interpreted in a wide sense. I would also not suggest that there is no scope for further development in this branch of the law.

But in the present case we are asked to extend the availability of restitutionary remedies for breach of contract considerably. I question the desirability of any such development. The acceptance of the appellants' primary or alternative submissions, as outlined by Dillon LJ, will have a wide-ranging impact on our commercial law. Even the alternative and narrower submission will, for example, cover charterparties and contracts of affreightment where the remedy of a negative injunction may be available. Moreover, so far as the narrower submission restricts the principle to cases where the remedies of specific performance and injunction would have been available, I must confess that that seems to me a bromide formula without any rationale in logic or common sense. Given a breach of contract, why should the availability of a restitutionary remedy, as a matter of legal entitlement, be dependent on the availability of the wholly different and discretionary remedies of injunctions specific to performance? If there is merit in the argument I cannot see any sense in restricting a compensatory remedy which serves to protect the restitutionary interests to cases where there would be separate remedies of specific performance or injunction, designed directly and indirectly to enforce payment, available.

For my part I would hold that if Sir William's wider proposition fails, the narrower one must equally fail. Both submissions hinge on the defendant's breach being deliberate. Sir William invoked the principle that a party is not entitled to take advantage of his own wrongdoing. Despite Sir William's disclaimer it seems to me that the acceptance of the propositions formulated by him will inevitably mean that the focus will be on the motive of the party who committed the breach of contract. That is contrary to the general approach of our law of contract and, in particular, to rules governing the assessment of damages. In my view there are also other policy reasons which militate against adopting either Sir William's primary or narrower submission. The introduction of restitutionary remedies to deprive cynical contract breakers of the fruits of their breaches of contract will lead to greater uncertainty in the assessment of damages in commercial and consumer disputes. It is of paramount importance that the way in which disputes are likely to be resolved by the courts must be readily predictable. Given the premise that the aggrieved party has suffered no loss, is such a dramatic extension of restitutionary remedies justified in order to confer a windfall in each case on the aggrieved party? I think not. In any event such a widespread availability of restitutionary remedies will have a tendency to discourage economic activity in relevant situations. In a range of cases such liability would fall on underwriters who have insured relevant liability risks. Inevitably underwriters would have to be compensated for the new species of potential claims. Insurance premiums would have to go up. That, too, is a consequence which militates against the proposed extension. The recognition of the proposed extension will in my view not serve the public interest. It is sound policy to guard against extending the protection of the law of obligations too widely. For these substantive and policy reasons I regard it as undesirable that the range of restitutionary remedies should be extended in the way in which we have been invited to do so.

The present case involves no breach of fiduciary obligations. It is a case of breach of contract. The principles governing expectation or reliance losses cannot be invoked. Given the fact of the breach of contract the only question is whether restitution is an appropriate remedy for this wrong. The case does not involve any invasion of the plaintiff property interests even in the broadest sense of that word, nor is it closely analogous to the *Wrotham Park* position. I would therefore rule that no restitutionary remedy is available and there is certainly no other remedy available.

I would dismiss the appeal.

Rose LJ

I agree. I also agree with the reasons given in both the previous judgments.

A feature which to my mind is capable of distinguishing the present case from *Wrotham Park Estate Co v Parkside Homes Ltd* [1974] 2 All ER 321, [1974] 1 WLR 798 is not just that damages were sought there in equity and here in contract at common law, but the different conduct of the respective plaintiffs in response to the breach of covenant.

In the *Wrotham Park* case the plaintiffs objected to building works in breach of covenant as soon as they learnt of them and, within a month, issued a writ seeking restraining and mandatory injunctions. They would not have granted any relaxation of the covenants even if this had been sought. From first to last they objected to what the defendants did.

In the present case, from first to last the plaintiffs have neither objected, nor wished to object, to what the defendants have done.

Appeal dismissed.

NOTES

1.   *Surrey County Council v Bredero Homes Ltd* appears to be the high-water mark of the orthodox view that the plaintiff can only recover in an action for breach of contract damages calculated on his own loss and not taking into account any profit made by the defendant. (It has always been recognised that there might be other types of claim in which the result was different, particularly if the defendant stands in a fiduciary position towards the plaintiff.)

     This decision provoked much academic comment, much of it hostile. Many commentators took the view that plaintiffs should sometimes be able to recover damages that took account of the profit made by the defendant as a result of the defendant's breach of contract although there was a striking lack of agreement as to what the relevant circumstances might be. A good survey of the literature can be found in Mitchell (1999) 15 JCL 133.

     The decision of the House of Lords in *A-G v Blake* [2000] 4 All ER 385 shows that indeed there are exceptional circumstances in which the award to the plaintiff should take account of the enrichment of the defendant. This is discussed more fully in Chapter 24.

     The general principle that the plaintiff can only recover for his own loss is subject to a further exception. Sometimes the plaintiff can recover where the loss is suffered by someone else. The difficult principles applicable here are discussed in Chapter 46.

2.   Punitive or exemplary damages may be awarded for a breach of contract that is also a tort, but not, it seems, for a mere breach of contract: *Perera v Vandiyar* [1953] 1 All ER 1109.

3.   Why is it that contract damages include compensation for 'expectation' losses as well as out-of-pocket loss? And why is the victim confined to recovering his loss, even if the breach has enabled the guilty party to make a greater profit—might that not actually encourage a party to break the contract if he do so profitably? Why not allow the victim to recover any profit the guilty party has made through breaking the contract—or, if it is feasible, grant the victim an order for specific performance?

■ Posner, *Economic Analysis of Law* (6th edn, 2002)
pp 118–122

§4.9 Fundamental Principles of Contract Damages

...

It makes a difference in deciding which remedy to grant whether the breach was opportunistic. If a promisor breaks his promise merely to take advantage of the vulnerability of the promisee in a setting (the normal contract setting) where performance is sequential rather than simultaneous, we might as well throw the book at the promisor....

Most breaches of contract, however, are not opportunistic. Many are involuntary; performance is impossible at a reasonable cost. Others are voluntary but (as we are about to see) efficient—which from an economic standpoint is the same case as that of an involuntary breach. These observations both explain the centrality of remedies to the law of contracts (can you see why?) and give point to Holmes's dictum that it is not the policy of the law to compel adherence to contracts but only to require each party to choose between performing in accordance with the contract and compensating the other party for any injury resulting from a failure to perform. This dictum, though overbroad, contains an important economic insight. In many cases it is uneconomical to induce completion of performance of a contract after it has been broken. I agree to purchase 100,000 widgets custom-ground for use as components in a machine that I manufacture. After I have taken delivery of 10,000, the market for my machine collapses.

I promptly notify my supplier that I am terminating the contract, and admit that my termination is a breach. When notified of the termination he has not yet begun the custom grinding of the other 90,000 widgets, but he informs me that he intends to complete his performance under the contract and bill me accordingly. The custom-ground widgets have no use other than in my machine, and a negligible scrap value. To give the supplier a remedy that induced him to complete the contract after the breach would waste resources. The law is alert to this danger and, under the doctrine of mitigation of damages, would not give the supplier damages for any costs he incurred in continuing production after notice of termination.

. . .

Now suppose that the widget contract is broken by the seller rather than the buyer. I really need those 100,000 custom-ground widgets for my machine but the supplier, after producing 50,000, is forced to suspend production because of a mechanical failure. Other suppliers are in a position to supply the remaining widgets that I need but I insist that the original supplier complete his performance of the contract. If the law compels completion (by ordering specific performance, a form of injunction), the supplier will have to make arrangements with other producers to complete his contract with me. Probably it will be more costly for him to procure an alternative supplier than for me to do so directly (after all, I know my own needs best); otherwise he would have done it voluntarily, to minimize his liability for the breach. To compel completion of the contract (or costly negotiations to discharge the promisor) would again result in a waste of resources, and again the law does not compel completion but confines the victim to simple damages.

. . .

In these examples the breach was committed only to avert a larger loss, but in some cases a party is tempted to break his contract simply because his profit from breach would exceed his profit from completion of the contract. If it would also exceed the expected profit to the other party from completion of the contract, and if damages are limited to the loss of that profit, there will be an incentive to commit a breach. But there should be; it is an efficient breach. Suppose I sign a contract to deliver 100,000 custom-ground widgets at 10¢ apiece to A for use in his boiler factory. After I have delivered 10,000, B comes to me, explains that he desperately needs 25,000 custom-ground widgets at once since otherwise he will be forced to close his pianola factory at great cost, and offers me 15¢ apiece form them. I sell him the widgets and as a result do not complete timely delivery to A, causing him to lose $1,000 in profits. Having obtained an additional profit of £1,250 on the sale to B, I am better off even after reimbursing A for his loss, and B is also better off. The breach is Pareto superior. True, had I refused to sell to B he could have gone to A and negotiated an assignment to him of part of A's contract with me. But this would have introduced an additional step, with additional transaction costs—and high ones, because it would be a bilateral-monopoly negotiation. On the other hand, litigation costs would be reduced.

. . .

The expectation measure of damages focuses on the gain that the victim of the breach anticipated from performance of the contract, the reliance measure on the victim's loss from the breach. If the victim "relied" by forgoing an equally profitable contract, the two measures merge. If not, the expectation measure may be a better approximation of the victim's real economic loss than the reliance measure, as well as produce better incentives. In long-run competitive equilibrium, the total revenues of the sellers in a market are just equal to their total costs; there is no 'profit' in an economic sense but merely reimbursement of the costs of capital, of entrepreneurial effort, and of other inputs, including the marketing efforts that led up to the contract. All these items of cost are excluded by the reliance measure of damages, which will tend, therefore, to understate the social costs of breach. Even if the breach occurs before the victim has begun to perform, the victim may have incurred costs (especially precontractual search costs). Suppose the victim has not, so that until performance begins the reliance cost is zero. If reliance costs were the exclusive measure of damages, it would follow that parties could walk away from their contracts whenever the contracts were still purely executory. Except in special situations, it is unclear what the social gain would be from such a 'cooling off' period and there may be a social loss as a result of uncertainty and the need to make additional transactions. Moreover, reliance costs incurred during the executory period are difficult to compute. Having signed a contract, a party will immediately begin to make plans both for performing the contract and for making whatever adjustments in the rest of his business are necessary to accommodate the new obligation. The costs of this planning, and the costs resulting from the change of plans when he finds out that the contract will not be performed, will be hard to estimate.

We should not suppose that the expectation measure is economically perfect. By giving the performing party a guaranteed profit, as it were, on what in the usual case will be a more or less risky venture—guaranteed, that is, should the other party break the contract—the expectation measure can induce overreliance by the performing party, just as any other form of business insurance will tend to induce the insured to relax his efforts to avoid the hazard insured against. . . .

■ **Cooter and Ulen,** *Law and Economics* (4th edn, 2003)
pp 261–265

C. Investment in Performance and Reliance

. . . Now we consider the incentive effects of several different remedies on two kinds of decisions (performance and reliance). . . .

1. Paradox of Compensation We begin by explaining the paradox of compensation in contracts. A contract imposes obligations on the promissory that are typically costly to perform. To perform or to increase the probability of performing, the promisor must invest. The promisor has an incentive to invest more on performing when liability for breach is higher. Conversely, the promisee can increase the value of performance by relying, but relying also increases the loss from breach. The promisee has an incentive to rely more when liability for breach is higher.

The following example illustrates the situation.

Example—The Waffle Shop: Yvonne owns a restaurant for economists that is called the Waffle Shop because of what it serves and whom it serves. Her business prospers so that she needs a larger facility. She enters into a contract with Xavier, a builder, who promises to construct the new restaurant for occupancy on September 1. Xavier knows that events could jeopardize completing the building on time, such as striking plumbers, recalcitrant city inspectors, or foul weather. He can reduce the probability of late completion by working overtime before the plumbers' contract expires, badgering the city inspectors, or accelerating work on the roof.

Yvonne anticipates a surge in business when she opens the new facility. To accommodate the surge in business, she needs to order more food that she can use in her old restaurant. She would like to order supplementary food for delivery on September 1 to assure continuous service, but she risks disposing of the supplementary food at a loss if the building is not completed on time.

Increasing the damages that Xavier must pay Yvonne for late completion of the building increases the incentives for Xavier to invest in performing and also increases the incentives for Yvonne to rely.

. . .

What level of damages gives efficient incentives to invest, so that the promisor does not over- or under-perform? For efficient incentives, the promisor must fully internalize the loss that the promisee suffers from breach. Perfect expectation damages cause the promisor to internalize the loss fully, as required for efficiency. Since perfect expectation damages are at least as great as perfect opportunity cost damages, the latter must often allow the promisor to externalize part of the cost of breach. Similarly, since perfect opportunity-cost damages are at least as great as perfect reliance damages, the latter must often allow the promisor to externalize even more of the cost of breach.

Turning to the promisee, what level of damages gives efficient incentives to rely, so that the promisee does not over- or under-rely? For efficient incentives, the promisee must fully internalize the loss from breach, which means that the promisee should receive no damages. As the measure of damages increases from reliance to opportunity-cost to expectation damages, the promisee externalizes an increasing fraction of the loss from breach. Perfect expectation damages cause the promisee to externalize 100% of the loss. Applied to contracts, the paradox of compensation is that, starting from perfect expectation damages, decreasing damages worsens the promisor's incentives and improves the promisee's incentives.

To illustrate the paradox of compensation, return to the example of Xavier and Yvonne. If Xavier is liable for the actual loss that late completion of the building causes, the Xavier fully internalizes Yvonne's benefits from timely completion. Consequently, he has efficient incentives to balance his cost of performing and the resulting benefit to Yvonne. Unfortunately, Xavier's liability distorts Yvonne's incentives. If Xavier is liable for the actual loss that late completion of the building causes, then Yvonne externalizes the cost of relying. In effect, Xavier will provide her with complete insurance against late completion. Consequently, she will have an incentive to act as if timely completion were certain and to order enough food for delivery on September 1.

. . .

Conversely, if Xavier is not liable for late completion, then Xavier externalizes the cost that late completion imposes on Yvonne, which gives inefficient incentives to Xavier and efficient incentives to Yvonne.

. . .

This paradox afflicts all areas of private law. You met the paradox of compensation in Chapter 4 when we discussed compensation for the taking of property by the state, and you will meet the paradox again in the next chapter when we consider compensation for accidents. In contract law, this paradox takes the following form. (1) In order for the promisor to internalize the benefits of precaution, he must fully compensate the promisee for breach. (2) In order for the promisee to internalize the costs of reliance, she must receive no compensation for breach. (3) In contract law, compensation paid by the promisor for breach equals compensation received by the promisee. (4) Therefore, contract law cannot internalize costs for the promisor and promisee as required for efficiency.

2. Contract Solutions to the Paradox of Compensation The paradox of compensation predicts that compensating the victims of breach will cause them to over-rely. The problem of over-reliance, however, is not so pervasive as this prediction suggests. Some contracts pose no problem of over-reliance because both parties want the promisee to rely as if performance were certain. Also, some contracts that pose a problem of over-reliance solve it by a variety of conceptual mechanisms. The paradox of compensation is the key to understanding these mechanisms. 'Why didn't the dog bark?' Great sleuths like Sherlock Holmes and Miss Marple sometimes crack a mystery by noticing that something did *not* happen. If over-reliance does *not* happen, then you should use the paradox of compensation to understand why.

Before discussing legal mechanisms to avoid the promisee's over-reliance, we will explain a general strategy for solving the paradox of compensation. Efficient incentives often require internalization of marginal costs, not internalization of total costs. *Sophisticated* damage measures cause the promisee to internalize the marginal costs of reliance, but not necessarily the total costs of reliance.

One way to achieve this goal is to base compensation on the promisee's hypothetical damages, not the promisee's actual damages. *Perfect hypothetical expectation damages* equal the gain that the promisee who relied optimally would have obtained from performance. Thus, perfect hypothetical expectation damages restore the promisee who relied optimally to the position that he would have enjoyed if the promise had been kept. Perfect hypothetical expectation damages, however, do not compensate for actual reliance. The promisee bears any increase in the promisee's losses caused by the promisee's actual reliance.

To illustrate, assume that breach causes the promisee who relies optimally to lose $100, and breach causes the promisee who over-relies to lose $125. Under these assumptions, perfect hypothetical expectation damages equal $100. If the court awards perfect hypothetical expectation damages, then the promisee who over-relies and suffers a loss of $125 from breach still receives $100 in damages from the court. The additional loss of $25 from over-reliance is internalized by the promisee. Thus the promisee internalizes the marginal cost of his actual reliance, as required for efficient incentives.

In the preceding case, the parties could give themselves efficient incentives by inserting a liquidation clause into their contract that stipulates damages of $100 for breach. If the parties fail to do so, the courts might decide to award perfect hypothetical expectation damages. Instead of approaching the problem directly, however, the courts might approach it indirectly through particular contract doctrines. We will explain the most famous such doctrine, called *foreseeability*.

Foreseeable reliance equals the amount that the promisor could reasonably expect the promisee to take in the circumstances. In contrast, unforeseeable reliance exceeds the amount that the promisor could reasonable expect the promise[e] to take in the circumstances. The foreseeability doctrine in common law compensates for foreseeable reliance and does not compensate for unforeseeable reliance. So, the foreseeability doctrine imposes a cap on damages for breach of contract. If "foreseeable" reliance equates with 'optimal' reliance, then the foreseeability doctrine caps damages at the level required for efficient incentives.

The famous case of *Hadley v. Baxendale* established the principle that over-reliance is unforeseeable, and, consequently, noncompensable. To summarize the facts of this case, Hadley owned a gristmill; the main shaft of the mill broke; and Hadley hired a shipping firm where Baxendale worked to transport the shaft for repair. The shipper did not deliver the shaft expeditiously. The damaged shaft was the only one in Hadley's mill, which remained closed awaiting return of the repaired shaft. After the tardy return of the repaired shaft, Hadley sued for breach of contract and asked for damages equal to his profits lost while his mill remained closed awaiting the return of the shaft. The defendant claimed that the measure of damages (if there was a breach) should be much less. The shipper assumed that Hadley, like most millers, kept a spare shaft. The shipper contended that Hadley did not inform him of the special urgency in getting the shaft repaired. The shipper prevailed in court on the damages issue, and the case subsequently stands for the principle that recovery for breach of contract is limited to the foreseeable damages.

We explained that the promisee has incentives for efficient reliance when damages are invariant with respect to reliance. The rule of *Hadley* is not the only way to produce this result. Liquidated damages are also invariant with respect to reliance. Stipulating an exact amount of damages in the contract is a common mechanism used to prevent over-reliance.

According to the doctrine of *Hadley*, a promisee who faces unforeseeable damages must inform the promisor in advance in order to recover damages fully. For this reason, the *Hadley* doctrine forces the exchange of information. Theorists have developed useful language to describe these facts. *Hadley* creates a 'penalty default rule' that is 'information-forcing.' [See Ayres & Gertner, Chapter 15, p 431 above.]

■ Shavell, *The New Palgrave Dictionary of Economics and Law* (1998)

A contract is said to be *complete* if the list of conditions on which the actions are based is exhaustive, that is, if the contract provides explicitly for all possible conditions. Otherwise, a contract will be referred to as *incomplete*. Typically, incomplete contracts do not include conditions which, were they easy to include, would allow both parties to be made better off in an expected sense. It should be noted that an incomplete contract may well not have literal gaps. For example, although a contract stating merely that a specified price is to be paid for a quantity of wheat that is to be delivered is incomplete (it does not mention many contingencies that might affect the buyer or the seller of wheat), the contract has no gaps, for it stipulates what the parties are to do (pay a price, deliver wheat) in all circumstances.

   . . .

Under the commonly employed *expectation measure*, damages equal the amount that compensates the victim of breach for his losses; these damages are often quite willingly paid by a party who commits a breach.

Why are damages not chosen to be so high as to guarantee performance? An important explanation is that parties do not always desire performance of the less-than-complete contracts that they write; it may not be Pareto efficient for there to be performance in circumstances for which the parties did not make provisions in their incomplete contract. . . . Higher damages than the expectation measure might induce performance when it is inefficient, and lower damages might induce breach when that is inefficient. Indeed, for this reason, the parties would often agree to choose the expectation measure over another measure of damages.

This understanding of damage measures as a device to induce the behaviour that the parties would have specified in more complete contracts sheds light on the notion, held by many legal commentators, that contract breach is immoral, as it constitutes the breaking of a promise. That belief is often incorrect, it is submitted, and might fairly be considered to be the opposite of the truth. The view that a contract breach is the breaking of a promise overlooks the point that the contract that is breached is generally an incomplete contract, and that the breach is what the parties *want* and would have specified in a complete contract. . . .

II. REMOTENESS OF DAMAGE

■ *Hadley v Baxendale*

(1854) 9 Exch 341 (see p 619)

NOTES

1.   What is the usual consequence of a few days' delay in delivering a broken millshaft?

2.   A good example of the way in which the remoteness rule operates is *Victoria Laundry (Windsor) Ltd v Newman Industries Ltd* [1949] 2 KB 528. The defendants, an engineering company, agreed to sell a boiler to the plaintiffs, who ran a laundry, not knowing that the plaintiffs intended to use the boiler to fulfil some highly lucrative government dyeing contracts. The boiler was damaged while it was being dismantled for transport to the plaintiffs, and it was delivered late. The plaintiffs claimed for loss of profit on the dyeing contracts. Streatfield J refused the plaintiffs any damages for loss of profits. In the Court of Appeal, Asquith LJ pointed out that the degree of knowledge about what losses are likely will vary from one context to another:

> A carrier commonly knows less than a seller about the purposes for which the buyer or consignee needs the goods or about 'other special circumstances' which may cause exceptional loss if due delivery is withheld.

Here, the defendants had not been told about the dyeing contracts and could not be expected to know about them, but it must have been obvious that, in all probability, the buyers wanted the boiler for immediate use in their laundering business. Asquith LJ said:

> . . . [I]n cases of breach of contract the aggrieved party is only entitled to recover such part of the loss actually resulting as was at the time of the contract reasonably foreseeable as liable to result from the breach. What was at that time reasonably foreseeable depends on the knowledge then possessed by the parties, or, at all events, by the party who later commits the breach. For this purpose, knowledge 'possessed' is of two kinds—one imputed, the other actual. Everyone, as a reasonable person, is taken to know the 'ordinary course of things' and consequently what loss is liable to result from a breach of that ordinary course. This is the subject-matter of the 'first rule' in *Hadley v Baxendale* but to this knowledge, which a contract-breaker is assumed to possess whether he actually possesses it or not, there may have to be added in a particular case knowledge which he actually possesses of special circumstances outside the 'ordinary course of things' of such a kind that a breach in those

special circumstances would be liable to cause more loss. Such a case attracts the operation of the 'second rule' so as to make additional loss also recoverable. In order to make the contract-breaker liable under either rule it is not necessary that he should actually have asked himself what loss is liable to result from a breach. As has often been pointed out, parties at the time of contracting contemplate, not the breach of the contract, but its performance. It suffices that, if he had considered the question, he would as a reasonable man have concluded that the loss in question was liable to result: see certain observations of Lord du Parcq in *Monarch Steamship Co, Ltd v A/B Karlshamns Oljefabriker.* Nor, finally, to make a particular loss recoverable, need it be proved that on a given state of knowledge the defendant could, as a reasonable man, foresee that a breach must necessarily result in that loss. It is enough if he could foresee it was likely so to result. It is enough, to borrow from the language of Lord du Parcq in the same case, if the loss (or some factor without which it would not have occurred) is a 'serious possibility' or a 'real danger'. For short, we have used the word 'liable' to result. Possibly the colloquialism 'on the cards' indicates the shade of meaning with some approach to accuracy.

Thus the defendants were not liable for loss of the dyeing contracts but should be liable for the amount of profit the plaintiffs would have made using the boiler for normal laundering. The fact that they actually would not have used it for this purpose but for the more profitable dyeing work did not prevent them recovering the normal profits. (See also *Cory v Thames Ironworks Co* (1868) LR 3 QB 181.)

■ **Posner, *Economic Analysis of Law*** (2nd edn, 1977)
pp 94–95

Foreseeability of damage

The economic rationale of contract damages is nicely illustrated by the famous rule of *Hadley v Baxendale* that the breaching party is liable only for the foreseeable consequences of the breach. Consider the following variant of the facts in that case. A commercial photographer purchases a roll of film to take pictures of the Himalayas for a magazine. The cost of development of the film by the manufacturer is included in the purchasing price. The photographer incurs heavy expenses (including the hire of an airplane) to complete the assignment. He mails the film to the manufacturer but it is mislaid in the developing room and never found.

Compare the incentive effects of allowing the photographer to recover his full losses and of limiting him to recovery of the price of the film. The first alternative creates little incentive to avoid similar losses in the future. The photographer will take no precautions, being indifferent as to successful completion of his assignment or receipt of adequate compensation for its failure. The manufacturer of the film will probably not take additional precautions either; the aggregate costs of such freak losses are probably too small to justify substantial efforts to prevent them. The second alternative, in contrast, should induce the photographer to take precautions that turn out to be at once inexpensive and effective: using two rolls of film or requesting special handling when he sends in the roll to be developed.

The general principle illustrated by this example is that where a risk of loss is known to only one party to the contract, the other party is not liable for the loss if it occurs. This principle induces the party with knowledge of the risk either to take any appropriate precautions himself or, if he believes that the other party might be the more efficient loss avoider, to disclose the risk to that party and pay him to assume it. In this way incentives are generated to deal with the risk in the most efficient fashion.

This principle is not applied, however, where what is unforeseeable is the other party's lost profit. Suppose I offer you $40,000 for a house that has a market value of $50,000, you accept the offer but later breach, and I sue you for $10,000, my lost profit. You would not be permitted to defend on the ground that you had no reason to think that the transaction was such a profitable one for me. Any other rule would make it difficult for a good bargainer to collect damages unless he made disclosures that would reduce the advantage of being a good bargainer—disclosures that would prevent the buyer from appropriating the gains from his efforts to identify a resource that was seriously undervalued in its present use. The *Hadley* principle is thus confined, and rightly so, to 'consequential' damages, ie damages unrelated to the profit from the contract.

The one case where application of the *Hadley* principle could produce an inefficient result in a setting of consequential damages is that of monopoly. If the film manufacturer in our variant of the facts of *Hadley* had a monopoly of film, he could use the information the photographer would have to disclose in order to shift the risk of loss to him to discriminate against the photographer in the price charged for the film more effectively than he otherwise could; the information would indicate that the photographer's demand for the film was far less elastic than that of the amateur photographers who comprise the great bulk of the manufacturer's customers (why would it indicate this?). This use of the information would discourage risk shifting in some cases where the manufacturer was in fact the superior risk bearer.

Thus the defendant is liable for unusual losses only if it knew of them or was warned of them by the plaintiff when the contract was made. At one time, it was said that the special circumstances 'must have been brought home . . . in such circumstances that the defendant impliedly undertook to bear any special loss referable to a breach': *British Columbia and Vancouver's Island Spar, Lumber and Sawmill Co Ltd v Nettleship* (1868) LR 3 CP 499 at 509. This has been rejected by the Court of Appeal: *GKN Centrax Gears Ltd v Matbro Ltd* [1976] 2 Lloyd's Rep 555. Should a mere notice to the defendant be sufficient to increase its liability?

■ Danzig, *'Hadley v Baxendale: a Study in the Industrialization of the Law'* (1975)
4 JLS 249, 279–283

Whether viewed as a simple 'notice' or a more exacting 'contemplation' requirement, however, this portion of the rule in *Hadley v Baxendale* runs counter to the tide of an industrializing economy. It was already somewhat out of date when expressed in the Exchequer opinion. For in *Hadley v Baxendale* the court spoke as though entrepreneurs were universally flexible enough and enterprises small enough for individuals to be able to serve 'notice' over the counter of specialized needs calling for unusual arrangements. But in mass-transaction situations a seller cannot plausibly engage in an individualized 'contemplation' of the consequences of breach and a subsequent tailoring of a transaction. In the course of his conversion of a family business into a modern industrial enterprise, Baxendale made Pickfords itself into an operation where the contemplation branch of the rule in *Hadley v Baxendale* was no longer viable. Even in the 1820's the Pickfords' operations were 'highly complex'.

'The bulk of Pickfords' traffic was of an intermediate kind, which came on to the main north-south route from east and west. This was directed to certain staging points, sorted, and thence dispatched to its destination. Cross-traffic of this kind was tricky to organize, and required very clear methods of procedure. According to Joseph Baxendale, then a senior partner in Pickfords, a cargo of 15 tons might involve up to 150 consignees and thus the same number of invoices.'

By 1865 the business had grown to the point where it left that contemporary chronicler of industry, Henry Mayhew, without words to 'convey . . . to the reader's mind a fair impression of the gigantic scale upon which the operations of the firm are conducted'. This was 'an enormous mercantile establishment with a huge staff of busy clerks, messengers and porters . . . It is divided into innumerable departments, the employees in each of which find it as much as they can comfortably do to master its details without troubling themselves about any other'.

A century later most enterprises fragment and standardize operations in just this way. This development—and the law's recognition of it—makes it self-evidently impossible to serve legally cognizable notice on, for example, an airline that a scheduled flight is of special importance or on the telephone company that uninterrupted service is particularly vital at a particular point in a firm's business cycle . . .

The inadequacies of the rule are masked by still more fundamental phenomena which render the case of very limited relevance to the present economy. At least in mass-transaction situations, the modern enterprise manager is not concerned with his corporation's liability as it arises from a particular transaction, but rather with liability when averaged over the full run of transactions of a given type. In the mass-production situation the run of these transactions will average his consequential-damages pay-out in a way far more predictable than a jury's guesses about the pay-out. In other words, for this type of entrepreneur—a type already emerging at the time of *Hadley v Baxendale*, and far more prevalent today—there is no need for the law to provide protection from the aberrational customer; his own market and self-insurance capacities are great enough to do the job . . .

It is only for small-volume sellers, those who deal in custom-made transactions or with a small number of customers—ie, for those transactions most like early nineteenth century commerce—that the rule invented in *Hadley v Baxendale* is arguably of commercial significance . . .

Even within this realm, however, it can be doubted that the rule much effects economic life. It is doubtful that it affects information flow at the time of the making of the contract, because by hypothesis the parties are not very accurate or self-conscious planners. A more sophisticated rationale for the rule in this context might focus on its effect on a seller not at the time of his entering a contract, but rather at the time of his deciding whether to voluntarily breach or to risk breaching. Only at that time and only where an option exists as to whether to breach or to increase the risk of breach, does it seem likely that a seller who has not opted for a limitation of liability clause will consult a lawyer, and consequently be affected by the legal rules. It can be argued that the societal gain from the rule in *Hadley v Baxendale* stems from its improvement of the seller's calculus about whether to breach in this situation.

To put this observation in context, consider the position of a truck owner, A, who has a contract to sell his truck to B, and assume that B would suffer a 'normal' net loss of $200 if the truck were not made available as scheduled. If C arrives on the scene and bids to preempt the truck for an urgent need, A can estimate the damages he will 'normally' owe B. He will presumably sell to C only if the new sale price will exceed the old sale price plus $200 in damages. If C is willing to buy for such a high price, it is to everybody's advantage to let him do so. C benefits because he values the truck more highly than he values the money he is paying for it; B benefits because he receives his expected profits by way of damages; A benefits because he makes more money, even after paying damages than he would have made had the truck not been sold to C. Society benefits because one party, C, has gained while no other party has lost. If B were in an abnormal situation and so expected to suffer greater damages than $200, the rule of *Hadley v Baxendale* would coerce him into signalling these higher damages, so that the proper damage calculation and subsequent truck allocation would be made. Thus, in theory, by facilitating an accurate calculus of breach, the rule optimizes resource allocation.

But if this is its modern rationale, it is apparent that considerable thought ought to be given to restructuring the rule. Resting the seller's liability on whether the type of damages incurred was 'normal' (or, in the UCC's words, whether it was a type of damage of which the seller had 'reason to know'), seems undesirable because it lets an all-or-nothing decision ride on an indicator about which many sellers cannot, at the time of breach, speculate with confidence. Further, if the recoverability of a type of damages is established, a seller may often have no reasonable basis for determining the magnitude of the damages involved. On this dimension—obviously critical to any calculus of the care warranted to avoid breach—the rule has nothing to say. Lastly, if the rule were truly finely geared to optimizing the allocation of resources, it would place its emphasis on the damage known to the seller at the time of breach, rather than at the time of contract, at least where the breach was voluntary. When the rule was framed stress had to be placed on communication at the time of the making of a contract because that was the only occasion on which information exchange could be coerced without fear of imposing enormous transaction costs. Now the telephone and vastly improved telegraphic facilities make it possible to mandate discussion at the time of breach. Would it be desirable to move the focus of the rule to this point? On this question, some empirical evidence would be desirable. Do the average transaction costs associated with information exchange at the time of the contract multiplied by the number of instances in which such information is exchanged exceed the average transaction costs of information exchange at the time of voluntary breach multiplied by the number of occasions when breach is seriously considered? If so, there is much to be said for a revision in the rule.

NOTES

1.   In *Kemp v Intasun Holidays Ltd* [1987] 2 FTLR 234, a case involving a package holiday contract, it was said that a merely casual remark about the plaintiff's medical condition should not fix the tour operator with additional liability. Shouldn't a deliberate notice suffice? Isn't it up to the company to create procedures by which special needs are taken into account—or bear the risk of not doing so?

2.   Danzig's article is a fascinating historical study of *Hadley v Baxendale* and deserves reading in full.

3.   Furmston rings up his local taxi driver and books a taxi to drive him to the airport at 7 am the next day. He tells the driver that it is most important, because he is flying to New York to sign a multimillion dollar contract. The taxi driver oversleeps, Furmston misses his flight and loses his deal. Is the driver liable? Would it, or should it, make any difference if the fare is fixed by law?

In *Koufos v C Czarnikow Ltd, The Heron II* [1969] 1 AC 350, the chartered ship deviated, with the result that it reached its destination nine days later than it would otherwise have done, and the market value of the cargo of sugar had fallen in the meantime. The House of Lords held that the shipowner was liable for this loss, which arose in the usual course of things, but stressed that, in an action for breach of contract, the mere fact that a loss is foreseeable is insufficient. Lord Reid said of the decision in *Hadley v Baxendale* (at 385–386):

I am satisfied that the court did not intend that every type of damage which was reasonably foreseeable by the parties when the contract was made should either be considered as arising naturally, ie, in the usual course of things, or be supposed to have been in the contemplation of the parties. Indeed the decision makes it clear that a type of damage which was plainly foreseeable as a real possibility but which would only occur in a small minority of cases cannot be regarded as arising in the usual course of things or be supposed to have been in the contemplation of the parties: the parties are not supposed to contemplate as grounds for the recovery of damage any types of loss or damage which, on the knowledge available to the defendant, would appear to him as only likely to occur in a small minority of cases.

In cases like *Hadley v Baxendale* or the present case it is not enough that in fact the plaintiff's loss was directly caused by the defendant's breach of contract. It clearly was so caused in both. The crucial question is whether, on the information available to the defendant when the contract was made, he should, or the reasonable man in his position would, have realised that such loss was sufficiently likely to result from the breach of contract to make it proper to hold that the loss flowed naturally from the breach or that loss of that kind should have been within his contemplation.

The modern rule in tort is quite different and it imposes a much wider liability. The defendant will be liable for any type of damage which is reasonably foreseeable as liable to happen even in the most unusual case, unless the risk is so small that a reasonable man would in the whole circumstances feel justified in neglecting it; and there is good reason for the difference. In contract, if one party wishes to protect himself against a risk which to the other party would appear unusual, he can direct the other party's attention to it before the contract is made, and I need not stop to consider in what circumstances the other party will then be held to have accepted responsibility in that event. In tort, however, there is no opportunity for the injured party to protect himself in that way, and the tortfeasor cannot reasonably complain if he has to pay for some very unusual but nevertheless foreseeable damage which results from his wrongdoing. I have no doubt that today a tortfeasor would be held liable for a type of damage as unlikely as was the stoppage of Hadley's Mill for lack of a crank shaft: to any one with the knowledge the carrier had that may have seemed unlikely, but the chance of it happening would have been seen to be far from negligible. But it does not at all follow that *Hadley v Baxendale* would today be differently decided.

If Asquith LJ in the *Victoria Laundry* case intended to go further than this, he was wrong; in particular, the use of the expression 'on the cards' was to be deprecated.

The House of Lords were insistent that, for a loss to be recoverable in contract, it must be more probable than is required in tort. Does Posner's analysis suggest why this might be so?

In *H Parsons (Livestock) Ltd v Uttley Ingham & Co Ltd* [1978] QB 791, the plaintiffs, who were pig farmers, bought a food storage hopper from the defendant manufacturers. When they were erecting the hopper, the defendants omitted to unseal a ventilator on top of the hopper; the ventilator could not be seen from the ground. The pignuts stored in the hopper became mouldy because of the lack of ventilation, and many of the pigs to which the nuts were fed died of a rare intestinal infection, E coli. The plaintiffs claimed for the loss of the pigs and lost sales. Swanwick J held that, at the time of the contract, neither the farmers nor the manufacturers would reasonably have contemplated as a serious possibility that feeding mouldy pignuts to the pigs would cause this illness in the pigs, but he held that this was irrelevant: the defendants had failed to supply a hopper that was reasonably fit for the purpose, some illness in the pigs was foreseeable and the defendants were liable for all the losses directly caused. The Court of Appeal upheld this decision, but on differing grounds. Lord Denning MR held that a distinction should be drawn in contract, as in tort, between physical damage and mere loss of profit. Loss of profit should be subject to *Hadley v Baxendale*, but physical damage should be recoverable even if it were only foreseeable as a slight possibility, and so the defendants should be liable. Scarman LJ, with whose reasoning Orr LJ agreed, said that the cases did not support this distinction. He considered that the difference between contract and tort was 'semantic, not substantial', but that, anyway, under either rule, it was not necessary that the degree of injury be contemplated. It was sufficient that some physical harm to the pigs would have been anticipated.

It is accepted that the extent of loss does not need to have been within the parties' contemplation provided the kind of loss was. Thus in *Balfour Beatty Construction (Scotland) Ltd v Scottish Power plc* 1993 SLT 1005, the plaintiffs had contracted for a continuous supply of power to enable them to make a 'continuous pour' of concrete to construct an aqueduct. The power was interrupted and they had to demolish what had been done and start again. This could not have been contemplated by the defendants but they were liable for the costs because they should have anticipated the necessity of some remedial work, such as cutting back the hardened concrete to form a joint with the new, and the difference was one of degree only. Similarly, in *Brown v KMR Services Ltd* [1995] 4 All ER 598, the plaintiff recovered for losses on the Lloyd's market even though the size and frequency of disasters that had hit the market was not foreseeable. However, the confusion in *Parsons v Uttley* may have been because the problem in that case was different to that in *Hadley v Baxendale*.

■ **Bishop, 'The Contract-Tort Boundary and the Economics of Insurance'** (1983)
12 JLS 241, 254–256, 259

[Bishop points out that the remoteness rule in tort prevents a negligent defendant from liability for losses that are 'events of very low probability'. He says that there is no clear economic rationale for the rule, but that there may be other justifications, such as that we simply think it unjust to a tortfeasor to make him pay for losses he could not have foreseen. He goes on to discuss the remoteness rule in contract:]

Lord Reid also used the expression 'not unlikely' as a test. Lord Reid gave as reason for the difference between tort and contract the fact that 'in contract, if one party wishes to protect himself against a risk which to the other party would appear unusual, he can direct the other party's attention to it before the contract is made.... But in tort there is no opportunity for the injured party to protect himself in that way....' Reid's view is widely, and correctly, regarded as the normal explanation for the difference. It has, however, ramifications so far not generally appreciated, which are pursued here.

The line of cases *Hadley v Baxendale*, *British Columbia Saw-Mill Co v Nettleship*, *Victoria Laundry*, and *Heron II* concerns a matter that is usually irrelevant in tort (at least as between strangers): the efficient transfer of information. The law of contract denies recovery to a plaintiff when four conditions are met:

1. The plaintiff possessed information unknown to the defendant.
2. The defendant, had he possessed that information, might have altered his behavior so as to make his breach less likely to occur.
3. The plaintiff could have conveyed the information to the defendant cheaply. (This condition is not mentioned in the cases, though it is clear that it is assumed by the courts to be fulfilled. Of course it is normally *not* fulfilled in tort.)
4. The plaintiff did not do so.

A good example of these rules in operation is the *Victoria Laundry* case. The defendant manufacturer of boilers contracted to supply them to the plaintiff laundry. In breach of contract the manufacturer delivered late. The laundry sought to recover damages for profit lost on an unusually lucrative dyeing contract. The court limited the plaintiff to such damages as would be normal in a case of this kind.

Less clear is *Heron II*. There the plaintiff charterer under a charterparty to transport sugar to a well known sugar market complained that the shipowner had in breach of contract delayed arrival in port by ten days. In the interim the price of sugar fell. The court held the shipowner liable for the loss. Lord Reid thought that the circumstances (that the charterer might well wish to sell on arrival) ought to have been so clear to the shipowner that the latter ought to have realized the risk without explicit warning. This case is near the line, with everything depending on the circumstances the parties were in. If the circumstances were clear, then to require an explicit warning of the obvious would be wasteful of resources (here labor and time).

I take no position on the doctrinal controversy about whether affirmative assumption of risk or merely notice of risk is needed to found liability. I doubt that it really matters very much. Sometimes merely receiving notice, particularly notice of strikingly unusual risks, will be tantamount to affirmative assumption and sometimes not. It is unlikely that a uniform general rule for such cases would be appropriate. It seems that courts treat this, sensibly I think, as depending on the facts of each case.

The central point here is that where the four conditions above are met, the value of the information to the defendant is greater than the cost to the plaintiff of conveying that information to him. To encourage such efficient transfers of information is the purpose of the contract remoteness rule of *Hadley v Baxendale*.

Note that the first limb of the rule in *Hadley* fits easily into this scheme. The normal case is one in which no information needs to be conveyed, since the defendant, knowing normal business conditions, already knows as much as the plaintiff. To require the plaintiff to inform the defendant of normal conditions would be inefficient, because the cost of transactions here, though low, is not zero. Any expenditure on information transfer is only wasted.

It might seem that there is a casus omissus. Consider the case where the consequence of the defendant's breach normally would be a certain loss but in fact is less. Then it seems the plaintiff has no incentive to transfer the information, even though the information would be valuable in that it would allow the defendant to spend less in essential reliance. Such transfer would be efficient: the marginal social value of expenditure on breach avoidance is lower and so less should be spent. But in fact there is no casus omissus. The plaintiff has sufficient incentive to inform the defendant, wholly without legal compulsion, if such information transfer is in fact cost justified. The reason is that the plaintiff can obtain a lower price for the defendant's performance if he informs the defendant of the limited damages for breach. The price is lower because such a contract is cheaper to perform than is a 'normal' contract. This incentive will induce parties to act efficiently in the case of unusually inexpensive breach as well as in the case of unusually expensive breach.

It should be clear that the function of remoteness in the *Hadley v Baxendale* line of contract cases is very different from the function of remoteness in tort. The tort measure of foreseeability seeks to define as too remote an event that no one would anticipate at all—one to which the ordinary observer would assign near zero probability. The contract measure of foreseeability will include as too remote many consequences which are merely unusual—ones that have quite substantial probabilities of occurring. The defining characteristics of an event that is too remote for the purposes of contract are those set out in conditions 1–4 above. These conditions have nothing to do with unforeseeability in the sense of very low probability. If this analysis is correct, it follows that Lord Scarman was wrong to suggest, as he did in *Parsons v Uttley*, that the differences between contract and tort remoteness are semantic only.

. . . [T]he desirability of the *Hadley* (contract) standard as opposed to the *Wagon Mound* (tort) standard for remoteness does *not* depend on any distinction between financial as against physical loss. Rather it depends on information asymmetry. That asymmetry was present in *Hadley*, *Victoria Laundry*, and *Heron II* and can be present in some physical loss cases. It happened not to be present in *Parsons v Uttley*. [NB. Swanwick J's finding that neither would reasonably have contemplated this illness.] We should not allow its absence to mislead us into a doctrine that allows potential victims to refrain from disclosing important information to potential injurers in cases where they have such information and could easily provide it.

NOTES

1.   A further problem over *Parsons v Uttley* is this: if it was foreseeable that some harm might come to the pigs through feeding them mouldy nuts, why were the farmers not contributorily negligent, or the cause of their own injury? See further p 656.

2.   *Hadley v Baxendale* and the other cases in this part assume that 'consequential losses' should be recoverable provided they were not too remote. For an argument to the contrary see p 706.

III. MITIGATION

1. Losses that could have been avoided by reasonable steps

We have already looked at the basic idea of mitigation (see p 623). To quote Viscount Haldane in the *British Westinghouse* case again:

I think that there are certain broad principles, which are quite well settled. The first is that, as far as possible, he who has proved a breach of a bargain to supply what he contracted to get is to be placed, as far as money can do it, in as good a situation as if the contract had been performed. The fundamental basis is thus compensation for pecuniary loss naturally flowing from the breach; but this first principle is qualified by a second, which imposes on a plaintiff the duty of taking all reasonable steps to mitigate the loss consequent on the breach, and debars him from claiming in respect of any part of the damage which is due to his neglect to take such steps. In the words of James LJ in *Dunkirk Colliery Co v Lever:*

> 'The person who has broken the contract is not to be exposed to additional cost by reason of the plaintiffs not having done what they ought to have done as reasonable men, and the plaintiffs not being under any obligation to do anything otherwise than in the ordinary course of business.'

As James LJ indicates, this second principle does not impose on the plaintiff an obligation to take any step which a reasonable and prudent man would not ordinarily take in the course of his business.

Thus if a seller fails to deliver, the buyer is normally expected to repurchase in the market in order to fill its commitments, and it will not recover any loss resulting from its failure to do so, such as loss of profit on a subsale. Thus, in practical terms, the innocent party is expected to act positively to reduce its own loss. But it need only do what is reasonable. For instance, it need not 'go hunting the globe' for snake, skins, which are not readily available *(Lesters Leather and Skin Co Ltd v Home and Overseas Brokers Ltd* (1948) 64 TLR 569). In the *British Westinghouse* case, the House of Lords said that the railway company could not have been required to instal the Parsons machines.

   This is consistent with the trend of mitigation decisions, which is not to expect the plaintiff to incur large expenditure or great risk. This approach has been criticised by MacIntosh and Frydenlund (1987) 37 University of Toronto LJ 113. They argue that the rules on mitigation should mimic the decisions that would have been made if the contracting parties were a single firm planning how to minimise the disruption caused by a breach. The managers would decide what investments to make by calculating the 'net present value' of each potential investment; each will involve different amounts of capital investment but may produce larger or smaller returns with different degrees of risk. An investment, which involves a considerable risk but a high rate of return, may thus have a greater net present value than a more normal investment with a lower rate of return. The damages should be assessed by the difference between the anticipated return (ie net present value) of the contract and that from the mitigation strategy (rather than the actual return on mitigation). If a mitigation strategy is risky but nonetheless offers a higher net present value, the victim of the breach should be expected to mitigate by opting for the riskier mitigation strategy. Among other conclusions, they say (at pp 147 and 157):

damages should be assessed as the difference between the NPV of the contract and the NPV of the mitigation strategy, both measured as of the date of breach, and without regard to the actual results of the mitigation or of the notional contract performance.

   . . . [This approach would involve] a reversal of the common law policy that the non-breacher need not take any considerable degree of risk in mitigating damages: the 'duty' to mitigate should extend to a risky strategy where it has the highest NPV of all available mitigation strategies.

   . . . Equally, it will reverse the common law rule that the plaintiff need not invest any non-trivial sum of money in the effort to mitigate: the duty to mitigate should extend to non-trivial investment where justified by the NPV of the mitigation strategy.

   . . .

   By comparison, the economic approach suggests that the rules should be structured so as to encourage the plaintiff to adopt his best mitigation strategy, whether or not this involves investment beyond that contemplated in the original contract (albeit, where an ex post rule is used, without taking inordinate risk). If purchasing the new machines was clearly the soundest decision that the plaintiff could have made (and this appears to have been the case) then this investment decision should be encompassed within the duty to mitigate.

They also note that mitigating by simply obtaining a substitute in the market may not have as great a net present value as other less usual strategies and should not necessarily be treated as a reasonable response.

Suppose that the victim takes what at the time seems a reasonable step to reduce his loss, but it turns out that some other method of mitigating would have been better? In *Gebrüder Metelmann GmbH & Cov NBR (London) Ltd* [1984] 1 Lloyd's Rep 614, this occurred, and the Court of Appeal allowed the victim's claim for the expenses of mitigating. Browne-Wilkinson LJ said (at 634):

Metelmann is entitled to be compensated for the additional damage flowing from the attempt to mitigate . . . If there are two methods of mitigating damage, both of which are practicable and reasonable in the circumstances known to the innocent party at the time the mitigating action is required, it is not possible to say that the innocent party acted unreasonably in selecting one of these methods just because, in the light of later events, it turns out that the loss would have been less had the other method been adopted.

The mitigation rule seems to have a clear economic rationale of encouraging the parties to avoid unnecessary waste. (For a full analysis, see Goetz and Scott (1983) *96* Virginia LR 967.) We shall see, however, that sometimes this rationale seems to be lost sight of.

■ *Payzu Ltd v Saunders*
[1918–19] All ER Rep 219, Court of Appeal

The defendant had agreed to sell the plaintiffs a quantity of silk on terms that permitted payment a month after delivery, but after some delays in payment she unjustifiably refused to make any further deliveries except for cash. The plaintiffs accepted this repudiation of the contract. The market price had risen considerably, and the plaintiffs were, in fact, unable to obtain the silk elsewhere. They claimed the difference between the contract price and the market price on the day they accepted the defendant's repudiation. McCardie J held that they had acted unreasonably in refusing the defendant's offer, and they could not recover more than they would have lost if they had accepted this offer.

Bankes LJ

. . . It is plain that the question what is reasonable for a person to do in mitigation of his damages cannot be a question of law, but must be one of fact in the circumstances of each particular case. There may be cases where as matter of fact it would be unreasonable to expect a plaintiff in view of the treatment he has received from the defendant to consider an offer made. If he had been rendering personal services and had been dismissed after being accused in presence of others of being a thief, and if after that his employer had offered to take him back into his service, most persons would think he would be justified in refusing the offer, and that it would be unreasonable to ask him in this way to mitigate the damages in an action of wrongful dismissal. But that is not to state a principle of law, but a conclusion of fact to be arrived at on a consideration of all the circumstances of the case. Counsel for the plaintiffs complained that the defendant had treated his clients so badly that it would be unreasonable to expect them to listen to any proposition that she might make. I do not agree. In my opinion each party to the contract was ready to accuse the other of conduct unworthy of a high commercial reputation, and there was nothing to justify the plaintiffs in refusing to consider the defendant's offer. I think the learned judge came to a right conclusion on the facts, and that the appeal must be dismissed.

Scrutton LJ and **Eve J** concurred.

NOTE

It is not clear whether the plaintiffs in this case were claiming the difference between the contract and market prices because, if the silk had been delivered, they would have been able to resell it at a profit, or whether they were claiming it as a surrogate for other forms of consequential loss (for instance, they had to break a contract to a sub-buyer when they could not obtain the silk, but they did not claim this as an item of loss because the subsale was not contemplated by the parties). But whatever the real loss was, did the plaintiffs' action make the defendant any worse off? Suppose the contract price was £x, and by the date the defendant's repudiation was accepted the market price was £x+y. If the plaintiffs had taken the silk offered for cash, the defendant would have received £x. If they bought in the market for £x+y, and were allowed to recover £y from the defendant, wouldn't the latter's financial position be just the same, because she could sell the original silk in the market at £x+y? So why refuse the plaintiffs' claim? See Bridge (1989) 105 LQR 398.

A question that is closely connected to mitigation is the date by which damages should be assessed.

In a case in which a seller of goods has failed to deliver, and there is an available market, the prima facie measure laid down in the Sale of Goods Act 1979, s 51(3) is the difference between the contract price and the market price at the date for delivery. When would it be appropriate to assess the damages by some later date? In *Johnson v Agnew* [1979] 1 All ER 883 at 896, Lord Wilberforce said:

The general principle for the assessment of damages is compensatory, ie that the innocent party is to be placed, so far as money can do so, in the same position as if the contract had been performed. Where the contract is one of sale, this principle normally leads to assessment of damages as at the date of the breach, a principle recognised and embodied in s 51 of the Sale of Goods Act 1893. But this is not an absolute rule; if to follow it would give rise to injustice, the court has power to fix such other date as may be appropriate in the circumstances.

In cases where a breach of a contract for sale has occurred, and the innocent party reasonably continues to try to have the contract completed, it would to me appear more logical and just rather than tie him to the date of the original breach, to assess damages as at the date when (otherwise than by his default) the contract is lost. Support for this approach is to be found in the cases.

In the cases and in the discussion in the books, the rule stated in Sale of Goods Act ss 50(3) and 51(3) have assumed perhaps disproportionate importance. If there is an available market, then the injured party can usually go into the market on the day of the breach, and this is the source of the so-called 'breach-date rule', that damages are assessed at the date of breach. In many (perhaps most) cases, there is no available market and we have to take account of events after breach. Typically, it is a case of what loss an injured party, behaving reasonably, has or would have) suffered.

Suppose that Eduardo, a highly successful football manager, makes a contract with Mudflats Rangers, a premiership club, to be its manager for five years at a salary of £3m a year. At the end of the first season, Rangers are relegated and Eduardo is dismissed. He clearly has an action for breach of contract, but he will not simply collect £12m. On any view, there will be a discount for getting all of the money at once and his tax position will have to be taken into account (see p 659) The biggest item will be his employment prospects. In practice, many football managers in this position get offers from other clubs, but the position may well take weeks, if not months, to become clear. In such a situation, it makes no sense to talk about assessment at the date of breach.

The date of assessment was an important issue in *Golden Strait Corp v Nippon Yusen Kubishika Kaisha, The Golden Victory* [2006] 1 All ER (Comm) 235.

In this case, the *Golden Victory* was the subject of a seven-year time charterparty. The charterers repudiated the charter on14 December 2001 and the owners accepted the repudiation as bringing the charter to an end on 17 December 2001. The earliest contractual date for redelivery would have been 6 December 2005. The owners had therefore, in a sense, lost four years. The evidence was that there was an available market, although the new charterparty would not have started until about 1 April 2002. The owners did not, in fact, relet the ship on a long charterparty but this was assumed not to matter.

The detailed calculation of the owner's loss was a matter for the arbitrator but the matter came before the courts on a question of principle. There was a provable 'difference' between the contract rate and the market rate, and the available substitute rate, but this produced a monthly figure. To convert it into damages, it had to be capitalised. This could not be done simply by multiplying the difference by 48: credit would have to be given for payment in a lump-sum form and allowance would have to be made for the fact that the ship would not have been working for every day of this 48 months, but would from time to time have been off-hire.

These difficulties were not reached because a more immediate difficulty lay in the way: the charterparty contained a provision that either the owner or the charterer could cancel if war broke out between any of a range of countries, including the USA and Iraq. Such a war broke out on 20 March 2003 and the charterers argued that damages should be calculated on the basis that they would have cancelled on this date and that the 'difference' should (roughly) be multiplied by 15 and not by 48. (The arbitrator heard evidence about the chances of war and held that, at 17 December 2001, a reasonably well-informed person would have considered war merely a possibility.)

The owners argued that damages should be assessed on the basis of what was known at 17 December 2001, but the arbitrator, Langley J and the Court of Appeal all disagreed and held that the calculation of damages should take account of the outbreak of war.

Lord Mance (sitting in the Court Appeal) said:

Mr Hamblen's submissions were, as always, presented with clarity and force, but I too have come to the conclusion that they must be rejected. As the judge observed, this charter always had inherent in it the uncertainty involved in the war clause. In many circumstances, this uncertainty could be disregarded— eg if damages were being assessed after the end of the original charter period and no relevant war had occurred, or if damages were being assessed during the original charter period on the basis that there was no significant prospect of any such war. In other circumstances, if damages were being assessed during the original charter period, account might have to be taken of the contingency (to use Lord Denning MR's word) or chance (to use Waller LJ's) that a war might occur, and consideration would then also have to be given to whether or not charterers would in that event probably cancel.

Certainty, finality and ease of settlement are of course important general considerations. But the element of uncertainty, resulting from the war clause, meant that the owners were never entitled to absolute confidence that the charter would run for its full seven-year period. They never had an asset which they could bank or sell on that basis. There is no reason why the transmutation of their claims to performance of the charter into claims for damages for non-performance of the charter should improve their position in this respect.

Further, as Mr Young submitted, the assessment of damages often depends on, or is informed by, subsequent events, and the claim for loss on the spot market from 17 December 2001 until 1 April 2002, the claim based on a substitute rate as from 1 April 2002 and the claim for loss of a profit share—which as I have said would surely depend on looking at actual market rates over the balance of the original charter—are all instances applicable in this case. The additional need to take into account the now known fact of the Second Gulf War is simply another instance.

In any event, I consider that this is a situation where any considerations of the type mentioned in the first sentence of [the second paragraph of this extract], above would have, so far as necessary, to yield to the greater importance of achieving an assessment of damages and compensation which more accurately reflects the actual loss which the owners can, at whatever is the date of assessment, now be seen to have suffered as a result of the charterers' repudiation.

The House of Lords [2007] UKHL 12, [2007] 3 All ER, I affirmed the decision, Lords Bingham and Walker dissenting.

At what date should damages be assessed in a case of anticipatory repudiation?

In *Kaines (UK) Ltd v Osterreichische Warenhandelsgesellschaft Austrowaren Gesellschaft mbH* [1993] 2 Lloyd's Rep 1, the sellers had repudiated a contract to supply oil in September. The buyers accepted the repudiation on 18 June when the price per barrel was $18.72. It then rose and fell slightly; on 25 June, it fell to $18.38, but it then rose until, by 29 June, it was at $19.23, when the buyers bought in a replacement supply for September. Steyn J held that in such a volatile market the buyers should have bought in on 18 or 19 June and fixed the damages accordingly. The Court of Appeal agreed. Bingham LJ said (at 10–11):

Given his factual conclusions, none of which can be effectively challenged, the learned Judge's approach was in my opinion correct. If a seller repudiates a contract before the time for performance arrives the buyer on existing authority is entitled to accept that anticipatory repudiation, treat the contract as at an end and claim damages. The basic measure of damages is such sum as will put the buyer in the same position as if the seller had duly performed the contract. The prima facie measure is, therefore, the difference between the contract price and the market price at the time of contractual performance. The seller is, however, only liable for such part of the buyer's loss as is properly to be regarded as caused by the seller's breach. If the buyer fails to take reasonable steps to mitigate his loss consequent on the seller's breach, he is debarred from claiming any part of the damage which is due to his neglect to take such steps. The seller's breach is not causative of that additional loss and therefore not recoverable. . . .

The Judge's conclusion that a reasonably prudent oil trader would have bought in a substitute cargo on June 19 in my opinion fixes the level of the plaintiffs' damages on the facts of this case irrespective of what the plaintiffs did or failed to do at the time. Had the market price risen steadily after June 19, their failure to buy could not have increased the damages payable by the defendants. Had the price fallen steadily after June 19, their failure to buy would not have reduced the damages.

There is no duty on the victim of an anticipatory repudiation to mitigate his damages if he does not wish to accept the repudiation. This rule was applied in *Shindler v Northern Raincoat Co Ltd* [1960] 2 All ER 239. If the victim were under a duty to mitigate before the date for performance, his choice whether to accept or ignore the repudiation would be fettered, which the courts have tried to avoid. But see further below.

2. Contributory negligence

Mitigation refers to actions that the victim took or might have taken *after* the breach to reduce his loss. What if the loss was caused partly by a breach and partly his own contemporaneous action? In the law of tort, such problems are dealt with by the doctrine of contributory negligence. At common law, contributory negligence was a complete defence, but since 1945, it has been a ground for reducing the plaintiff's damages.

Law Reform (Contributory Negligence) Act 1945

Section 1. Apportionment of liability in case of contributory negligence

(1) Where any person suffers damage as the result partly of his own fault and partly of the fault of any other person or persons, a claim in respect of that damage shall not be defeated by reason of the fault

of the person suffering the damage, but the damages recoverable in respect thereof shall be reduced to such extent as the court thinks just and equitable having regard to the claimant's share in the responsibility for the damage . . .

Section 4. Interpretation

The following expressions have the meanings hereby respectively assigned to them, that is to say—

'fault' means negligence, breach of statutory duty or other act or omission which gives rise to a liability in tort or would, apart from this Act, give rise to the defence of contributory negligence.

In relation to contract, there are two questions. The first is whether the Act applies so that the court has power to apportion liability. The second is, if the Act does not apply, does the contributory negligence operate to defeat the plaintiff's claim altogether?

In order to decide whether the Act applies, it is necessary to distinguish three situations:

(1) the defendant is in breach of a strict contractual duty;
(2) the defendant is in breach of a duty of care imposed by the contract. There is no corresponding duty in tort;
(3) the defendant is in breach of a contractual duty of care and a duty of care in tort;

It has been held that the Act applies to the third situation. In *Sayers v Harlow UDC* [1958] 2 All ER 342, the plaintiff found herself locked in a public lavatory. She attempted to climb out by standing on the toilet roll holder, which rotated, causing her to fall and suffer personal injury. The Court of Appeal applied the Act and reduced her damages. Apparently, the question of whether the Act applied to a breach of contract was not fully argued, but the Court of Appeal has recently confirmed that it does apply to this category of case: *Forsikringsaktieselskapet Vesta v Butcher* [1988] 2 All ER 43 (aff'd on other grounds [1989] 1 All ER 402). It was taken for granted that this was correct by the House of Lords in *Platform Home Loans Ltd v Oyston Shipways Ltd* [1998] 4 All ER 252, in which argument turned entirely on the mechanics of applying contributory negligence: see pp 385–386.

The Act does not apply to category (1) cases: *Barclays Bank plc v Fairclough Building Ltd* [1995] 1 All ER 289. This is because the defendant's conduct does not fall within the definition of 'fault' in s 4: 'negligence, breach of statutory duty or other act or omission giving rise to a liability in tort.' (The second limb of s 4, acts 'giving rise to the defence of contributory negligence', refers to the plaintiff's conduct.) It is irrelevant that the breach of the strict duty was in fact brought about by the defendant's negligence: Paull J in *Quinn v Burch Bros (Builders) Ltd* [1966] 2 QB 370 at 378–9; *Barclays* case at 305.

It seems probable that the Act does not apply to the second category of case either. This appears to have been the view of the Court of Appeal in the *Forsikrings* case. The Court adopted the view of the New Zealand equivalent of the Act taken by Pritchard J in *Rowe v Turner Hopkins and Partners* [1980] 2 NZLR 550, 555–556. Pritchard J had said:

. . . . [The] first limb of the definition is plainly directed to defining 'fault' as it relates to the conduct of the defendant—in other words, as it relates to the plaintiff's cause of action. This phrase is qualified by the expression 'which gives rise to a liability in tort'. It follows that no negligence, breach of statutory duty or other act or omission will bring [the section] into play unless it is one which gives rise to liability in tort. In other words, the Act applies only when the plaintiff's cause of action is in respect of some act or omission for which the defendant is liable in tort. Conceivably the defendant may be concurrently liable in contract—but that is immaterial . . . The second limb of the definition is concerned with and referable only to the conduct of the plaintiff.

Later cases have followed the same approach (eg *Gran Gelato*, above).

If the Act does not apply, it is not altogether clear whether the common law doctrine of contributory negligence (under which contributory negligence was a complete defence) may operate to defeat the plaintiff, but the courts reach the same result by treating the injury as being caused solely by the plaintiff's own fault. For example, in *Quinn v Burch Bros*, the defendants failed to provide the plaintiff plasterer with a stepladder, so he used a trestle, folded up and leant against the wall. He did not 'foot' the trestle, and it slipped, causing him injury. Paull J held that the injury was caused solely by his own action, and his decision was affirmed on appeal [1966] 2 QB 370 at 381. A recent House of Lords case contains dicta suggesting that this will apply unless the defendant has warranted that the plaintiff need not take the very precautions at issue: *Lambert v Lewis* [1982] AC 225.

Both *Quinn* and *Lambert* were cases in which the breach was clearly known to the plaintiff, who then acted carelessly. Suppose Beale takes his car to a garage, which fits a new master cylinder to the braking system, but without any fault on the garage's part the cylinder fitted is defective and the brakes fail, injuring Beale: would the garage escape liability if it could show that the reasonable driver would have realised from the fact that the brake pedal would go all the way to the floor that the system was defective? Wouldn't it make sense to give the courts power to apportion in such a case? The Law Commission has considered the question of contributory negligence in contract (*Contributory Negligence as a Defence in Contract*, Law Commission No 219 (1993). It concluded (Part IV):

4.1 The Commission's main recommendation is that apportionment of the plaintiff's damages on the ground of contributory negligence should be available in actions in contract where the defendant is in breach of an express or implied contractual duty to take reasonable care or exercise reasonable skill or both, but not where he is in breach of a contractual term which imposes a higher level of duty (which we refer to as 'strict').

Liability for breach of a strict contractual duty

4.2 We have rejected the possibility of apportionment where there is liability for breach of a strict contractual obligation for reasons both of principle and pragmatism. The reason of principle relates to a consideration of the position before the plaintiff is aware, or must be taken to be aware, of the defendant's breach of contract. If the defendant commits himself to a strict obligation regardless of fault, the plaintiff should be able to rely on him fulfilling his obligation and should not have to take precautions against the possibility that a breach might occur. This is the position under the present law and we consider that it would be wrong in principle to deviate from it. The rules on mitigation, although not a perfect substitute for apportionment, mean that the plaintiff is not entitled to act unreasonably once he is aware of his loss or of the defendant's breach.

4.3 An example of the type of situation we have in mind is that in *Lambert v Lewis*. There a farmer suffered loss when an accident occurred as the result of his use of a defective coupling supplied by the defendant. On the facts of the case his conduct was held to have broken the chain of causation as he had continued to use the coupling after he had become aware that it was damaged, without taking steps to have it repaired or to ascertain whether it was safe to use. However, the House of Lords indicated that if the accident had happened before the damage had become apparent to him he would have been able to recover damages for breach of warranty. In those circumstances he would 'have had a right to rely upon the dealers' warranty as excusing him from making his own examination of the coupling to see if it were safe.' We consider that this principle is correct. Where the plaintiff is a consumer, it is likely that the court would, in any event, find that it was reasonable, and not contributorily negligent, for him to rely on the defendant's warranty. However, this would not necessarily happen where the plaintiff is a professional or a commercial body. In the latter circumstances the court might well consider that he should have been aware of the risk that the goods supplied might be faulty and should have checked them before use.

...

4.5 Although the reason of principle relates only to a limited situation, for which provision could be made by careful legislative drafting, the comments of respondents to the consultation paper, have convinced us that apportionment in cases involving breach of a strict duty would be undesirable in practice. This is because, in order to apportion the plaintiff's damages, it would be necessary to consider the quality of the defendant's conduct, which is, at present, irrelevant. This would increase the number of issues which have to be determined, and would lead to undesirable complexity. The need to quantify the degree to which a defendant is to blame (for the purposes of calculating the appropriate reduction in the plaintiff's damages) in circumstances where his fault is irrelevant and difficult to assess would also create uncertainty.

4.6 We are opposed to any reform which would result in a substantial increase in uncertainty in contract, because this would make settlements more difficult to achieve, payments into court harder to assess, and trials longer and more expensive. This would not aid the efficient functioning of commerce and industry which requires that disputes be capable of quick resolution . . .

Liability for breach of a contractual duty of reasonable care

4.7 Where the plaintiff has suffered damage partly as the result of his own failure to take reasonable care for the protection of himself or his interests and partly as the result of the defendant's breach of a contractual duty to take reasonable care or exercise reasonable skill, we believe that it is correct in principle for his damages to be apportioned. As we stated in the consultation paper, there is a clear similarity in substance between an action for breach of a contractual duty of care and an action for breach of a tortious duty of reasonable care. Whether a duty of reasonable care is classified as tortious or contractual does not affect the content of that duty, and it is not, in our view, desirable that the availability of apportionment should depend upon how the duty is classified. Furthermore, where the defendant undertakes only a contractual duty of reasonable care, he has not (in contrast to the case where he has accepted a strict contractual obligation) guaranteed to produce a particular outcome. Thus it is unfair to assume that he has undertaken to compensate the plaintiff even where the plaintiff has contributed to his own loss. As seen above, the rules on causation, remoteness and mitigation do not provide an adequate substitute for apportionment and can be unfair to either defendant or plaintiff. This is because they either produce 'all or nothing' results, or do not have the flexibility of apportionment on the basis of what the court thinks just and equitable, given the agreed allocation of risks.

4.8 Nor do we consider that the introduction of apportionment on the ground of contributory negligence would result in the practical problems outlined in paragraphs 4.5 and 4.6, above. As explained in paragraphs 3.30–34, apportionment will not cause significant uncertainty where the defendant is in breach of a contractual duty of reasonable care.

3. Savings actually made

The plaintiff should not be awarded damages for more loss than he has suffered, and thus any savings that he has been able to make should be taken into account. Thus if the seller of a machine that is being custom-built for the buyer accepts a repudiation by the buyer and ceases work on the machine, he will not recover damages for the full contract price: any savings in labour and materials will be deducted, or he would be overcompensated. Similarly, if an employee is wrongfully dismissed, savings in tax should be taken into account. If the lost income was taxable, but the damages are not, damages should only be awarded for the net loss of income: *British Transport Commission v Gourley* [1956] AC 185. If the damages are also taxable, there appears to be some disagreement over how the tax should be taken into account. In *Parsons v BNM Laboratories Ltd* [1964] 1 QB 95, the Court of Appeal had expressed the view that neither amount of tax should be taken into account, thus achieving rough justice and saving a great deal of time. However, in *Shove v Downs Surgical plc* [1984] 1 All ER 7, Sheen J estimated the plaintiff's net loss of income after deduction of tax and then added an amount equivalent to the estimated tax. It appears that *Parsons* was not cited to Sheen J.

■ British Westinghouse Electric and Manufacturing Co Ltd v Underground Electric Railways Co of London Ltd

[1911–1913] All ER Rep 63, House of Lords

The appellants contracted to supply the respondents with turbines of a specified efficiency, but the machines supplied failed to meet the specification. The respondents used the machines for a time, but later replaced them with Parsons turbines. These were so much more efficient that the cost of installing and running them was less than the cost of running the Westinghouse machines would have been, even if the latter had performed as specified. In an arbitration, the appellants sought to recover the unpaid balance of the contract price; the respondents counterclaimed for the increased running costs of the appellants' machines during the period they were working and the cost of replacing them with the Parsons machines. The arbitrator allowed the first item of the counterclaim, and stated a special case for the opinion of the court on the second.

Viscount Haldane LC

... The arbitrator appears to me to have found clearly that the effect of the superiority of the Parsons' machines and efficiency in reducing working expenses was in point of fact such that all loss was extinguished and that actually the respondents made a profit by the course which they took. They were doubtless not bound to purchase machines of a greater kilowatt power than those originally contracted for, but they in fact took the wise course in the circumstances of doing so, with pecuniary advantage to themselves. They had, moreover, used the appellants' machines for several years, and had recovered compensation for the loss incurred by reason of these machines not being during these years up to the standard required by the contract. After that period the arbitrator found that it was reasonable and prudent to take the course which they actually did in purchasing the more powerful machines, and that all the remaining loss and damages was thereby wiped out.

[The Lord Chancellor then set out the general principles on which damages for breach of contract are assessed. He continued:]

... But when, in the course of his business, [the plaintiff] has taken action arising out of the transaction, which action has diminished his loss, the effect in actual diminution of the loss which he has suffered may be taken into account, even though there was no duty on him to act.

Staniforth v Lyall illustrates this rule. In that case the defendants had chartered a ship to New Zealand, where they were to load her, or by an agent there to give the plaintiff, the owner, notice that they abandoned the adventure, in which case they were to pay £500. The ship went to New Zealand, but found neither agent nor cargo there, and the captain chose to make a circuitous voyage home by way of Batavia. This voyage, after making every allowance for increased expense and loss of time, was more profitable than the original venture to New Zealand would have been. The Court of Common Pleas decided that the action was to be viewed as one for a breach of contract to put the cargo on board the plaintiff's vessel for which the plaintiff was entitled to recover all the damages which he had incurred, but that he was bound to bring into account, in ascertaining the damages arising from the breach, the advantages which had accrued to him because of the course which he had chosen to adopt. I think that this decision illustrates a principle which has been recognised in other cases that, provided the course taken to protect himself, by the plaintiff, in such an action was one which a reasonable and prudent person might in the ordinary conduct of business properly have taken, and in fact did take whether bound to or not, a jury or an arbitrator may properly look at the whole of the facts and ascertain the result in estimating the quantum of damage.

I think that the principle which applies here is that which makes it right for the jury or arbitrator to look at what actually happened, and to balance loss and gain. The transaction was not res inter alios acta, but one in which the person whose contract was broken took a reasonable and prudent course arising quite naturally out of the circumstances in which he was placed by the breach. Apart from the breach of contract, the lapse of time had rendered the appellants' machines obsolete, and men of business would be doing the only thing which they could properly do in replacing them with new and up-to-date machines. The arbitrator does not in his finding of fact lay any stress on the increase in kilowatt power of the new machines, and I think that the proper inference is that such increase was regarded by him as a natural and prudent course followed by those whose object was to avoid further loss, and that it formed part of a continuous dealing with the situation in which they found themselves, and was not an independent or disconnected transaction. For the reasons which I have given I think that the questions of law stated by the arbitrator in the Special Case have been wrongly answered by the courts below.

Lords Ashbourne, **Macnaghten** and **Atkinson** concurred.

Appeal allowed.

NOTES

1.   In *Harbutt's Plasticine Ltd v Wayne Tank and Pump Co Ltd* [1970] 1 QB 447, the plaintiffs' factory was burned down as a result of the defendants' breach of contract. The plaintiffs recovered the full cost of rebuilding, although this was greater than the value of the old factory. Widgery LJ said (at 472–473):

> I must now turn to the issues raised as to the measure of damage. The distinction between those cases in which the measure of damage is the cost of repair of the damaged article, and those in which it is the diminution in value of the article, is not clearly defined. In my opinion each case depends on its own facts, it being remembered, first, that the purpose of the award of damages is to restore the plaintiff to his position before the loss occurred, and secondly, that the plaintiff must act reasonably to mitigate his loss. If the article damaged is a motor car of popular make, the plaintiff cannot charge the defendant with the cost of repair when it is cheaper to buy a similar car on the market. On the other hand, if no substitute for the damaged article is available and no reasonable alternative can be provided, the plaintiff should be entitled to the cost of repair. It was clear in the present case that it was reasonable for the plaintiffs to rebuild their factory, because there was no other way in which they could carry on their business and retain their labour force. The plaintiffs rebuilt their factory to a substantially different design, and if this had involved expenditure beyond the cost of replacing the old, the difference might not have been recoverable, but there is no suggestion of this here. Nor do I accept that the plaintiffs must give credit under the heading of "betterment" for the fact that their new factory is modern in design and materials. To do so would be the equivalent of forcing the plaintiffs to invest their money in the modernising of their plant which might be highly inconvenient for them. Accordingly I agree with the sum allowed by the trial judge as the cost of replacement.

2.   This case has been overruled but on another point: see below. Widgery LJ's dictum was applied in *Bacon v Cooper (Metals) Ltd* [1982] 1 All ER 397, in which the defendant had supplied the wrong kind of scrap metal to the plaintiff and the metal broke the rotor arm of the plaintiff's fragmentiser. The plaintiff could not obtain a used rotor arm, so he bought a new one. Although rotor arms only last some seven years, and the broken one was three-and-a-quarter years old, Cantley J held that the plaintiff was entitled to the full cost of a new arm without giving credit for the fact that it would last longer: there was no certainty that the plaintiff would have bought a new rotor when the broken one wore out, because the fragmentiser itself might well be outmoded by then.

3.   Why were the defendants credited with the savings in the *British Westinghouse* case, but not with the increased value of the replacement in the other two cases? If Harbutts had planned to sell the factory in the foreseeable future, would the result have been different?

IV. QUANTIFICATION, MARKETS AND OTHER CONTRACTS

■ *Slater v Hoyle & Smith Ltd*

[1920] 2 KB 11, Court of Appeal

The sellers of 3,000 pieces of unbleached cotton cloth delivered 1,625 pieces, which were below the required quality, and the buyers, who had contracted to resell the goods, justifiably refused to accept further deliveries. In respect of the 1,375 pieces not delivered, the buyers claimed loss of profit on the subsale, but Greer J awarded them only nominal damages because the market price had fallen below the contract price. The 1,625 pieces they had passed to the sub-buyers with no reduction in price, but in respect of these Greer J awarded the difference in value between the goods as they should have been and as they were actually delivered. The sellers appealed.

Scrutton L J

... [T]he judge has refused to make the sellers pay the profits which the buyers might have made by supplying sound goods from this contract under their second sub-contract, but the sellers, though freed from liability for the higher price of the second sub-contract, desire to take advantage of the lower price of the first sub-contract. Can they do so? It is well settled that damages for non-delivery or delay in delivery of goods, where there is a market price, do not include damages for the loss of any particular contract unless that contract has been in contemplation of the parties to the original contract: *Horne v Midland Rly Co.* The value of the goods in the market independently of any circumstances peculiar to the plaintiff is to be taken: *Great Western Rly Co v Redmayne; Williams v Reynolds* per Blackburn J. If the plaintiff has a profitable contract to sell goods, and there is a market, he can supply himself with the goods by purchasing in the market; and he is then left without the goods he should have received under the original contract and has lost their market value. But suppose his sub-contract is at a price below instead of above the market price, so that, if he delivers goods under the sub-contract, he loses. Can his damages be limited by the amount he would have received on the sub-contract? On the above reasoning it would seem not. He could supply the sub-contract by buying in the market, and then should have goods delivered to him of a certain market value, which he has lost because they were not delivered. This has been decided in the case of non-delivery of goods by the Court of Appeal in *Rodocanachi v Milburn*, and by the House of Lords in *Williams v Agius* where *Rodocanachi v Milburn* was approved. ... A had not delivered coals which he had sold at 16s 3d a ton to W. At the time when they should have been delivered the market price was 23s 6d; but W had sold a similar quantity and description of coals at 19s; the question was whether A ought to pay 7s 3d a ton damages, or only 2s 9d a ton, being the amount W would have received if he had fulfilled his sub-contract. The House of Lords held the damages were 7s 3d a ton, approving *Rodocanachi v Milburn*, and Lord Dunedin held that the defaulting seller is neither mulct in damages for the extra profit the buyer would have got owing to a forward sale at over the market price, nor can he take benefit of the fact that the buyer has made a forward sale at under the market price. He put the case as a dilemma: 'The truth is that the respondents' argument leaves them in a dilemma. Either the sub-sale was of the identical article which was the subject of the principal sale or it was not. If it was not, it is absurd to suppose that a contract with a third party as to something else, just because it is the same kind of thing, can reduce the damages which the unsatisfied buyer is entitled to recover under the original contract. If, on the other hand, the sub-sale is of the selfsame thing or things as is or are the subject of the principal sale, then ex hypothesi the default of the seller in the original sale is going to bring about an enforced default on the part of the original buyer and subsequent seller. And how can it ever be known that the damages recoverable under that contract will be calculable in precisely the same way as in the original contract? All that will depend upon what the sub-buyer will be able to make out. The only safe plan is, therefore, in the original contract, to take the difference of market price as the measure of damages and to leave the sub-contract and the breach thereof to be worked out by those whom it directly concerns.'

Now apply these principles to the delivery of goods not sound but damaged. The only difference appears to be that in the case of non-delivery the buyer has not got the goods and has not paid their contract price: what he has lost is the difference between the market price of the goods and the contract price; he would have to pay to get them. If the goods are delivered damaged, he has got goods and has paid the contract price; what he has not got is sound goods, and his loss is therefore the difference between the market value of sound goods and the market value of these damaged goods. Again, sub-contracts do not come into account, for the buyer is under no obligation to use these goods for his sub-contract; he may buy in the market, and he will then be left with goods damaged to a certain extent at the then market price of such goods instead of sound goods at the then market price of sound goods. The difference between the two market prices should be the measure of damages. If the buyer delivers under the sub-contract the damaged goods and has to pay damages, these damages will not be the measure of damages. As Lord Dunedin says: 'How can it ever be known that the damages recoverable under that contract will be calculable in precisely the same way as in the original contract?' If these damages are greater than the difference in market price of sound and damaged goods, they will clearly not be recoverable. The result seems the same if they are less; it is res inter alios acta: 'circumstances peculiar to the plaintiff', which cannot affect his claim one way or the other. If the buyer is lucky enough, for reasons with which the seller has nothing to do, to get his goods through on the sub-contract without a claim against him, this on principle cannot affect his claim against the seller any more than the fact that he had to pay very large damages on his sub-contract would affect his original seller.

In support, however, of the proposition that the sellers could be relieved by what took place under the sub-contract, the case of *Wertheim v Chicoutimi Pulp Co* was relied on. This is a decision of Privy Council, and though not technically binding on us, is of course entitled to the greatest respect. It was a claim for delay in delivery. The contract was to deliver wood pulp in November, 1900, when the market price was 70s a ton. The pulp was delivered in July, 1901, when the market price was 42s 6d a ton; but the buyer had made a sub-contract for sale at 65s a ton. The Privy Council only gave the buyer 5s a ton damages. It is difficult to see how this fits in with the principles above stated. If the buyer had made a sub-contract at 30s a ton and only received that sum, it seems clear that the Privy Council would not have given him 40s but only 27s 6d a ton, for they would have said the seller had nothing to do with the sub-contract. If the buyer had made a forward contract at 80s, and lost it, the Privy Council would not have given him 37s 6d, but only 27s 6d: *Horne v Midland Rly Co;* again for the reason that the seller had no concern with matters peculiar to the buyer. The buyer was under no obligation to deliver the contract goods on the sub-contract. If he had bought other goods and used them for the sub-contract, he would have been left with goods delivered at a time when the market price was 42s 6d, instead of when it was 70s, and would have recovered 27s 6d. Lord Atkinson says that in the case of non-delivery the price at which the purchaser might in anticipation of delivery have resold the goods is properly treated, where no question of loss of profit arises, as an entirely irrelevant matter. It is always so treated, as I understand the law, unless the buyer can affect the seller with such notice of the sub-contract as makes him liable for loss by its non-fulfilment. But he goes on to say that the existence of a sub-contract shows that the real value of the goods is more than the market value and the loss he sustains must be measured by that price. I respectfully think that all the English decisions show that a plaintiff cannot measure the real value of what he has lost by reference to a contract peculiar to himself, for which the defendant is not responsible, and that his loss therefore is not measured by that price.

Wertheim v Chicoutimi Pulp Co was a case of delay in delivery and not, as the present, a case of delivery of inferior goods. I should myself have thought the principles applying to these two cases were the same as those applying to non-delivery, and that the Privy Council judgment was erroneous as departing from those principles. But at any rate it does not decide the case of delivery of inferior goods instead of sound goods, which appears to me the same as the case of non-delivery of any goods at all. It is true that on these principles the plaintiff may recover more than an indemnity. English law freqently gives him less than his real loss. The plaintiff in *Horne v Midland Rly Co*, a case of delay, certainly sustained a real loss greater than the amount he recovered. The plaintiff in *British Columbia Saw-Mill Co v Nettleship*, a case of non-delivery, certainly recovered much less than his real loss. He sometimes recovers more than his real loss. The plaintiffs in *Salford Corporation v Lever* recovered their real damage twice. The rules of English law do not always give exact indemnity, and in this case I think they do not.

For these reasons I think that Greer J was right in disregarding the fact that the buyers, for reasons we do not know, were able to deliver inferior goods under their sub-contract without having to pay damages, just as he would have been right in disregarding the fact if they had had to pay larger damages than the difference in market value.

In my view the appeal should be dismissed with costs.

Warrington and **Bankes LJJ** delivered concurring judgments.

Appeal dismissed.

NOTES

1. If the buyer has resold the goods to a sub-buyer at more than the market price, and the seller fails to deliver (or delivers late, with the result that the subsale is lost), Scrutton says that the buyer cannot recover more than the difference between the contract and market prices. Why not?

2. Sometimes the buyer will have resold the specific parcel of goods (eg 3,000 tons wheat *ex Challenger*). If so, he will not be able to buy a replacement in the market. Normally, however, the courts treat this case in the same way, holding that a resale of the specific parcel was not reasonably contemplated. For an exception in which the form of contract used contemplated resale of the specific cargo, and loss of profit on the resale was allowed, see *Re R & H Hall Ltd & WH Pim Jr & Co's Arbitration* (1928) 139 LT 50.

3. Scrutton continues that, if the resale is at *less* than the market price, it will still be ignored. What reason did Lord Dunedin give for this in *Williams Bros v E T Agius Ltd* [1914] AC 510? (Hint: think about the possible liability of the buyer to the sub-buyer.)

4. Scrutton then applies the same principles to a case of delivery of defective goods: damages are to be based on the difference between the market value the goods should have had, and their actual value. But if the buyer has resold the goods to a sub-buyer, who accepts them and does not claim on the buyer despite the defect, what justifies not reducing the buyer's damages accordingly? (Hint: could the buyer have made this 'advantageous' subsale anyway?)

5. The Court of Appeal refused to follow *Slater v Hoyle and Smith Ltd* in *Bence Graphics International Ltd v Fasson UK Ltd* [1997] 1 All ER 979. In this case, the defendants were suppliers of cast vinyl film and they supplied such film to the plaintiffs to the value of £564,328. The plaintiffs intended to use it, as the defendants knew, to manufacture decals, which were to be used in the shipping industry to identify bulk containers. It was a term of the contract that the film would survive in a good legible condition for at least five years. Unfortunately, the film degraded prematurely, so that many of the details became illegible but, by the time this became apparent, the plaintiffs had sold all but £22,000 worth of the film. It was accepted by the defendants that the plaintiffs were entitled to return this film to them and have a refund in full. The question was what damages the plaintiffs could recover.

The plainitffs argued that, at the time of delivery, the goods were in effect worthless since no one who had known the quality of the film would have bought it for its intended purpose. This was not effectively denied by the defendants but they argued that the plaintiffs had not in fact suffered any significant loss because very few of their sub-buyers had demanded a refund. The trial judge and Thorpe LJ in the Court of Appeal thought that the solution to the problem was simply to apply s 53(3). The majority of the Court of Appeal did not agree. In principle, they argued s 53(3) was simply a prima facie rule and subject to a more general rule set out in s 53(2). Of the judges in the majority, Otton LJ thought that it was possible to distinguish *Slater's* case, but Auld LJ thought that the latter case was not effectively distinguished, but that it was time to review it and that it should not be followed. He said:

In *Slater's* case all the members of the court were disinclined to extend the decision in *Wertheim's* case to a claim for breach of warranty of quality. Bankes LJ confined it in any event to a sub-sale of the identical goods, relying on reasoning of Lord Dunedin in the *Williams Bros* case [1914] AC 510 at 523, [1914–15] All ER Rep 97 at 101–102 about the difficulty of establishing damages based on the terms of a sub-sale in a non-delivery case (see [1920] 2 KB 11 at 15, [1918–19] All ER Rep 654 at 655–656). Warrington LJ appears to have been of the view—though he did not explain why—that s 53(3) of the Sale of Goods Act 1893 [corresponding to s 53(3) of the 1979 Act] was the right principle governing delivery of inferior goods to those provided for by the contract and that what the buyer did with the goods was irrelevant (see [1920] 2 KB 11 at 17–18, [1918–19] All ER Rep 654 at 656–657). Scrutton LJ expressed the view that the *Rodocanachi* principle as to non-delivery applied equally to delivery of inferior goods because if the buyer fulfils his sub-contract by buying in the market, he is left with the inferior goods at their market value against the market value of sound goods (see [1920] 2 KB 11 at 21–22, [1918–19] All ER Rep 654 at 658–659). Alternatively, if he applies the inferior goods to a sub-sale the damages he may have to pay to his buyer may be calculable differently from those in the contract with his seller. He acknowledged that, on this approach, the buyer may recover more than his true loss, but he cited examples of the same principle resulting in a recovery of less than the true loss.

With respect to the court of Appeal in that case, and to the authors of the supporting comments in *McGregor* para 774 and *Chitty* note 91 to para 41–300, it seems to me that they wrongly: (1) overlooked the basic rule in s 53(2) as to what would have been in the ordinary and natural contemplation of the parties in a commercial contract such as it was, namely, that the buyer could well be prejudiced in his onward dealing with the goods if they were defective; (2) disregarded the reasoning of the Privy Council in *Wertheim* as approved and restated by Lord Dunedin and Lord Atkinson in *Williams Bros v Ed T Agius Ltd*, that where there has been delivery in a mercantile contract and it can be seen what the buyer has done with the goods, it is possible and proper to measure his actual loss by reference to that outcome; (3) had too much regard to practicality at the expense of principle in relying on possible difficulties of establishing causation and of assessment where the goods sold have been subjected to some process or where the terms of the contract and sub-contract may for that or some other reason be different; and (4) were seemingly content to award a buyer more than the evidence clearly showed he had lost.

The position of the majority was vigorously criticised by Treitel at 113 LQR 189 and the leading judgment in *Slater* was delivered by Scrutton LJ, an acknowledged master of this area of the law. On the other hand, one can see why the Court of Appeal was reluctant to give the plaintiffs the best part of £500,000 for what was apparently a no-loss situation.

An interesting general discussion of the extent to that a buyer can recover in respect of defective goods which have been subsold when it has not paid damages to the sub-buyer is to be found in *Total Liban SA v Vitol Energy SA* [2000] 1 All ER 267.

6.   Other commentators agree that the *Wertheim* case is hard to fit with general principle (eg Treitel, pp 949–950). Assuming that the buyer had simply resold an equivalent quantity of goods to the sub-buyer, the subsale should be ignored because the buyer could have made this advantageous deal quite apart from the main sale. If, on the other hand, he had resold the exact same cargo of pulp before the breach occurred, he would not be able to resell it in the market but would have to supply it to the sub-buyer, and he might be liable to the sub-buyer for late delivery: again, the subsale price should be ignored for the reasons given by Lord Dunedin in *Williams v Agius*.

■ *W L Thompson v R Robinson (Gunmakers) Ltd*

[1955] 1 All ER 154

The defendants wrongfully repudiated a contract to buy a Standard Vanguard car from the plaintiff dealers. The plaintiffs returned the car to their suppliers, who did not seek compensation. The price of the cars was fixed by the manufacturer, and the dealers would have received a profit of £61 on the sale. The plaintiffs claimed this loss of profit. It was shown that locally there was a smaller demand for Standard Vanguards than there were cars available, although it was not shown that this was true nationally.

Upjohn J

... The plaintiffs say that the true measure of damages in those circumstances is no more, no less, than their loss of profit, £61. The defendants say: 'No, the loss is nominal, for you could have sold the car to another customer or you could do what, in fact, you did do, which was to get your suppliers to release you, and you have suffered no damage.'

The law is not really in doubt. It is set out in the Sale of Goods Act, 1893, s 50. That was declaratory of the existing law and the general principle which has been observed in all cases I take conveniently from the speech of Viscount Haldane LC, in *British Westinghouse Electric & Manufacturing Co Ltd v Underground Electric Rlys Co of London, Ltd*. Viscount Haldane LC said:

'Subject to these observations I think that there are certain broad principles which are quite well settled. The first is that, as far as possible, he who has proved a breach of a bargain to supply what he contracted to get is to be placed, as far as money can do it, in as good a situation as if the contract had been performed.'

That is the general rule.

Apart altogether from authority and statute, it would seem to me on the facts to be quite plain that the plaintiffs' loss in this case is the loss of their bargain. They have sold one Vanguard less than they otherwise would. The plaintiffs, as the defendants must have known, are in business as dealers in motor cars and make their profit in buying and selling motor cars, and what they have lost is their profit on the sale of this Vanguard. There is no authority exactly in point in this country, although it seems to me that the principle to be applied is a clear one. It is to be found in *Re Vic Mill, Ltd* in which the supplier was to supply certain machines which he had to make and they were to be made to the particular specification of the purchaser although they were of a type generally in common use. It was not, as the present case is, a sale by a motor dealer of a standardised product. The purchaser repudiated his order, and with a view to mitigating damages the supplier, on getting another order for somewhat similar machinery, very sensibly made such alterations as were necessary to the machinery that he had made for the original purchaser and sold the machinery so altered to the second purchaser. His costs of doing that were comparatively trivial. It was said by the supplier that the measure of his damages was the loss of his bargain; by the purchaser that the measure of damages was merely the cost of the conversion of the machinery for the second purchaser and his slight loss on the re-sale ... Buckley LJ put the matter succinctly in this way. ...

'As regards No 1, where the goods were manufactured, the respondents are, I think, entitled to both profits, because they were not bound to give the appellants the benefit of another order that the respondents had received. The respondents were left with these goods on their hands. They altered them and sold them to another buyer, but they could have made, and would otherwise, I suppose, have made, other goods for that buyer, and not employed these goods for that purpose. If they had done so, they would have made both profits.'

It seems to me that in principle that covers this case. True the motor car in question was not sold to another purchaser, but the plaintiffs did what was reasonable, they got out of their bargain with George Thompson, Ltd, but they sold one less Vanguard, and lost their profit on that transaction . . .

The main case, however, put by the defendants is this: they submit that s 50 of the Sale of Goods Act, 1893, applies, because they say there is an available market for the goods in question, and in that available market we know that the price of the Vanguard is fixed. It is fixed by the manufacturers. Therefore, they say the measure of damages must necessarily be little more than nominal. Had the plaintiffs kept the car and sold it to another at a later stage, no doubt they would have been entitled to the costs of storage in the meantime, possibly interest on their money laid out, and so on, but, as they in fact mitigated damages by getting out of the contract, damages are nil.

Counsel for the defendants said that the market now must be treated as a market or fair in a limited or technical sense. It is curious that there is a comparative absence of authority on the meaning of the phrase 'available market', because one would have thought there would have been many cases, but the researches of counsel have only disclosed one authority on s 50. It is *Dunkirk Colliery Co v Lever*, a decision of the Court of Appeal. The facts were far removed from the facts before me, and I do not think that I need recite them. It will be sufficient if I read an extract from the judgment of James LJ. He said (9 ChD at p 24):

'Under those circumstances the only thing that we can do is to send it back to the referee with an intimation that we are of opinion upon the facts (agreeing with the Master of the Rolls in that respect), that the facts do not warrant the application of the principle mentioned in the award, namely, that there was what may be properly called a market. What I understand by a market in such a case as this is, that when the defendant refused to take the three hundred tons the first week or the first month, the plaintiffs might have sent it in waggons somewhere else, where they could sell it, just as they sell corn on the Exchange, or cotton at Liverpool: that is to say, that there was a fair market where they could have found a purchaser either by themselves or through some agent at some particular place. That is my notion of the meaning of a market under those circumstances.'

If that be the right principle to apply, it was proved that there is nothing in the nature of a market like a Cotton Exchange or Baltic or Stock Exchange, or anything of the sort, for the sale of new motor cars. . . .

I think that . . . the decision of the Court of Appeal in *Dunkirk Colliery Co v Lever* is binding on me, and, therefore, unless one finds something in the nature of a market in the sense used by James LJ, s 50(3) has no further application. However, the point seems to me of somewhat academic interest in this case, because, if one gives to the word 'market' an extended meaning, in my view on the facts which I have to consider, a precisely similar result is reached.

Had the matter been res integra, I think I should have found that an 'available market' merely means that the situation in the particular trade in the particular area was such that the particular goods could freely be sold, and that there was a demand sufficient to absorb readily all the goods that were thrust on it, so that if a purchaser defaulted the goods in question could readily be disposed of. Indeed, such was the situation in the motor trade until very recently. It was, of course, notorious that dealers all over the country had long waiting lists for new motor cars. People put their names down and had to wait five or six years, and whenever a car was spared by the manufacturer from export it was snatched at. If any purchaser fell out, there were many waiting to take his place, and it was conceded that if those circumstances were still applicable to the Vanguard motor car, the claim for damages must necessarily have been purely nominal. But on the assumed facts, circumstances had changed in relation to Vanguard motor cars, and in March, 1954, there was not a demand in the East Riding which could readily absorb all the Vanguard motor cars available for sale. If a purchaser defaulted, that sale was lost and there was no means of readily disposing of the Vanguard contracted to be sold, so that there was not, even on the extended definition, an available market. But there is this further consideration: even if I accepted the defendants' broad argument that one must now look at the market as being the whole conspectus of trade, organisation and marketing, I have to remember that s 50 provides only a prima facie rule, and, if on investigation of the facts, one finds that it is unjust to apply that rule, in the light of the general principles mentioned above it is not to be applied. In this case, as I said in the earlier part of my judgment, it seems to me plain almost beyond argument that, in fact, the loss to the plaintiff is £61. Accordingly, however one interprets s 50, it seems to me on the facts that I have to consider one reaches the same result.

There will be judgment for the plaintiffs for £61 1s 9d, but the order must incorporate an undertaking by the plaintiffs to indemnify the defendants against their costs of this action. There must be a mutual set-off between the costs and the sum of £61.

Judgment for the plaintiffs.

NOTES

1. In *Charter v Sullivan* [1957] 2 QB 117, the buyer repudiated a contract to buy a Hillman Minx, which was then sold by the dealers to another customer. The dealers' manager admitted that they could sell all of the Hillman Minx cars they could get, and the Court of Appeal held that they were entitled to nominal damages only.

2. The situation in the *Thompson* case is often referred to as a problem of 'lost volume'. The dealer counts on receiving the mark-up on a certain number of sales to contribute to his fixed overheads and, at the end of the day, his profit. If because of the buyer's default the seller makes fewer sales than he otherwise would have done, he has lost the contribution from the lost sale.

■ *Lazenby Garages Ltd v Wright*
[1976] 2 All ER 770, Court of Appeal

Lord Denning MR

Mr Wright works on the land. On 19th February 1974 he went to the showrooms of motor dealers called Lazenby Garages Ltd. He saw some secondhand cars there. He agreed to buy a BMW 2002. He signed a contract to pay £1,670 for it. It was to be delivered to him on 1st March 1974. He went back home to his wife and told her about it. She persuaded him not to buy it. So next day he went back to the garage and said he would not have it after all. They kept it there offering it for resale. Two months later on 23rd April 1974 they resold it for £1,770, that is for £100 more than Mr Wright was going to pay.

Notwithstanding this advantageous resale, the garage sued Mr Wright for damages. They produced evidence that they had themselves bought the car secondhand on 14th February 1974, that is five days before Mr Wright had come in and agreed to buy it. They said that they had bought it for £1,325. He had agreed to buy it from them for £1,670, so they had lost £345 and they claimed that sum as damages.

In answer Mr Wright said: 'You haven't lost anything; you've sold it for a higher price'. The garage people said that they were dealers in secondhand cars; that they had had a number of cars of this sort of age and type, BMW 2002s; and that they had lost the sale of another car. They said that, if Mr Wright had taken this car, they would have been able to sell one of those other cars to the purchaser. So they had sold one car less and were entitled to profit accordingly.

The judge thought that they had not proved that they had sold one car less, but that there was a 50:50 chance that they would have sold an extra car. So he gave them damages for half the sum claimed. Instead of £345 he gave them £172.50.

Now there is an appeal to this court. The cases show that if there are a number of new cars, all exactly of the same kind, available for sale, and the dealers can prove that they sold one car less than they otherwise would have done, they would be entitled to damages amounting to their loss of profit on the one car: see the judgment of Upjohn J in *W L Thompson Ltd v Robinson (Gunmakers) Ltd*. The same has been held in the United States: *Torkomian v Russell* and *Stewart v Hansen;* in Canada, *Mason & Risch Ltd v Christner*, and in Australia, *Cameron v Campbell & Worthington*.

But it is entirely different in the case of a secondhand car. Each secondhand car is different from the next, even though it is the same make. The sales manager of the garage admitted in evidence that some secondhand cars, of the same make, even of the same year, may sell better than others of the same year. Some may sell quickly, others sluggishly. You simply cannot tell why. But they are all different.

In the circumstances the cases about new cars do not apply. We have simply to apply to s 50 of the Sale of Goods Act 1893. There is no 'available market' for secondhand cars. So its not sub-s (3) but sub-s (2). The measure of damages is the estimated loss directly and naturally resulting in the ordinary course of events from the buyer's breach of contract. That throws us back to the test of what could reasonably be expected to be in the contemplation of the parties as a natural consequence of the breach. The buyer in this case could not have contemplated that the dealer would sell one car less. At most he would contemplate that, if they resold this very car at a lower price, they would suffer by reason of that lower price and should recover the difference. But if they resold this very car at a higher price, they would suffer no loss. Seeing that these plaintiffs resold this car for £100 more than the sale to Mr Wright, they clearly suffered no damage at all.

In my opinion the appeal should be allowed and judgment entered for the defendant, Mr Wright.

Lawton LJ

In the course of argument counsel for the plaintiffs accepted that if a dealer was selling an article which is a unique article, for example if a secondhand car dealer was selling a vintage car, or if an antique dealer was selling a picture, then, if there were a repudiation by a buyer of a contract entered into, the damages would be the particular loss which was sustained on that transaction, and nothing more.

At the other end of the scale, the courts had to consider the principles accepted in a line of cases, of which the most recent one is probably *W L Thompson Ltd v Robinson (Gunmakers) Ltd*. As Lord Denning MR has pointed out, when the goods are not unique, but are mass-produced, different considerations may apply from those which apply when an article is unique.

The problem in this case is whether a secondhand car of the type with which we are concerned, namely a BMW 2002, petrol injected, was a unique article. The evidence from the plaintiffs' own sales manager shows that it was; he put the matter in this way: 'No one can say what makes a secondhand car sellable. It is the same with new cars. Cars vary as to date, mileage, sound of engine, wear and tear, upholstery etc.' Then, a few answers later, he said: 'In a secondhand showroom each car is different.' In other words, he was saying that secondhand cars are, from their very nature, unique. In those circumstances it seems to me that the *Thompson* type of case has no application to the circumstances of this particular case.

I agree that the appeal should be allowed.

Bridge LJ concurred.

NOTES

1. The trial judge recognised that, with second-hand cars, one cannot be sure that the second buyer would have bought another car if the car he actually bought was not available, having been sold to the defendant: but he thought there was a chance of it and therefore reduced the damages accordingly. Why was that inappropriate?

2.   The Court of Appeal described the car as 'unique', but it is very doubtful that it was 'unique' enough that a buyer of it could have obtained specific performance (see p 709).

3.   Even with new goods, lost-volume claims seem to be fairly rare. Why might this be? See 'Micro-economics and the Lost-Volume Seller' (1973) 24 Case W Res LR 712.

4.   It is clear that, in some circumstances, a plaintiff can recover damages for breach of contract that involve an assessment of the value of a loss of chance. For many years, the leading example was *Chaplin v Hicks* [1911] 2 KB 786. In this case, the plaintiff had been promised by the defendants that, if she attended for an audition, she would be considered for a place in the chorus line. In breach of contract, the defendant refused to consider the plaintiff when she attended. Obviously, the plaintiff was not bound to be chosen even if all had gone well, since there were 50 applicants for 12 places, but it was held that the jury's award of £100 damages should be upheld. The court did not, in this case, summon all of the possible applicants and seek to second-guess the defendant's judgement. It seems adequate to consider the value of success and apply a significant discount because of the real chance of not being chosen.

An important modern example is *Allied Maples Group v Simmons and Simmons* [1995] 4 All ER 907. In this case, the plaintiffs wished to expand their business by buying certain businesses and shop properties of another furnishing group and for this purpose engaged the services of the defendant solicitors. The defendants were held to have been negligent in that they had failed to warn the plaintiffs against the particular technique that was used for making the bid. In essence, the plaintiffs bought all of the shares in the target company and then sold off those properties that they did not require. The danger of this was that some of these properties had been subleased and this exposed the plaintiffs to financial risks where the sublessee had defaulted, which they had not taken into account when making the bid. The defendants argued that they were only liable if the plaintiffs could show that it was more likely than not that they would have avoided this trap if they had been properly advised. (In practice, this would be extremely difficult to establish without the cooperation, which could not normally be expected, of the target company and the target company's solicitors.) The Court of Appeal held that the plaintiffs had not had to go this far and it was sufficient to show that the plaintiffs would have had a substantial chance of negotiating a better deal if it had been properly advised.

In *Jackson v Royal Bank of Scotland* [2005] UKHL 3 [2005] 2 All ER 71, the claimants were importers of dog chews, which they sold to customers in the UK. Their principal customer was Economy Bag. Both the claimant and Economy Bag banked with the defendant. The sales were financed by transferable letters of credit issued by the bank. This meant that Economy Bag knew the identity of the claimant's supplier but not the size of the mark-up. In breach of contract, the bank sent to Economy Bag documents that revealed the extent of the mark-up and Economy Bag immediately terminated its relationship with the claimants.

It was clear that the bank was in breach of contract, but what was the extent of the claimants' loss? There was always a chance that Economy Bag would contact the supplier direct but it was less likely to bother so long as it did not realise the extent of the mark-up. The trial judge held that damages should be calculated on the basis that business would tail off over four years; the Court of Appeal held that it was better to hold that business would end within a year. The House of Lords preferred the trial judge's view. It was a better guess as to what was likely to happen.

(These cases, in most of which the chance was that, but for the wrong, a third party might have acted in a way that would have advantaged the claimant, must be distinguished from those (usually tort) cases in which the court is faced with evaluating whether or not an event occurred in the past. In the latter type of case, the claimant must prove his case on the balance of probabilities: *Hotson v East Berkshire Health Authority* [1987] AC 750; *Wilsher v Essex Health Authority* [1988] 1 All ER 871; *Gregg v Scott* [2005] UKHL 2 [2005] 4 All ER 812.)

V. PROBLEM CASES

1. Non-payment of money

The common law has developed two special rules about the non-payment of money, both of which are generally regarded as unsatisfactory. The first is that if the defendant's breach simply consists of a failure to pay money, the loss is normally to be measured in terms of the amount of money unpaid. (For a fuller discussion, see Ogus, *The Law of Damages*, pp 304–307.) A plaintiff might often plausibly argue that if the defendant had paid on time, he would have put the money to profitable use. A possible answer to this would be that the plaintiff might have used his own money, or have borrowed money, to achieve the same result. But firstly, this is often not the case, as is shown by *Trans-Trust SPRL v Danubian Trading* (see p 551): the plaintiff may have no other money and be unable to borrow. There, the Court of Appeal managed to sidestep the rule, by treating the failure to open the credit as being more than a mere failure to pay money. Secondly, whether the plaintiff planned to use the unpaid money in this way or simply to invest it, he will lose interest, and it is at this point that the second rule comes into play.

The second rule is that, as a general rule, debts do not carry interest, so that a debtor who pays late discharges his obligation by paying the sum originally due. This rule was treated as well settled by the House of Lords in *London, Chatham and Dover Rly Co v South Eastern Rly Co* [1893] AC 429, although without enthusiasm. With modern rates of interest and inflation, this rule is quite unfairly advantageous to debtors. It was cogently criticised by the Law Commission in its report on Interest in 1978 (Law Commission No 88, Cmnd 7229), which recommended legislation substantially designed to reverse it. The House of Lords, however, reaffirmed the rule in *President of India v La Pintada Cia Navegacion SA* [1984] 2 All ER 773. All of the members of the House thought that the rule was unsatisfactory, but they were unanimous that it must be reversed by statute and not by them. The principal reason for this cautious approach was that Parliament had considered the matter in 1982 (see below) and had not accepted the Law Commission's proposals in full (for a heart-rending account by the Lord Chancellor of his inability to move his cabinet colleagues further on the matter, see Hansard, 429 HL Official Report (5th series) cols 165–174, 6 April 1982).

This decision of the House of Lords makes it necessary to consider carefully the precise scope of the rule, and the qualifications upon it. The starting point must be the two rules mentioned: where there is a failure to pay money, only the amount due is recoverable, and the debtor may discharge his obligation by paying this amount without interest. To this, there are a number of exceptions, as follows.

(1) The parties may expressly agree that the debt shall carry interest. This is, of course, very common.

(2) The court may decide that the parties have implicitly agreed to pay interest: see *Minter v Welsh Health Technical Services Organization* (1980) 13 BLR 1.

(3) Under the Law Reform (Miscellaneous Provisions) Act 1934, s 3, the court was given a wide discretion to award interest on claims pursued to judgment. This applies to judgments on both debts and other damages claims. (In the event of claims for interest on damages, this may involve careful analysis of when the cause of action arose: see *Nykredit Mortgage Bank plc v Edward Erdman Group Ltd (No 2)* [1998] 1 All ER 305.) This statute suffered a grave defect, however, in that it only applied where the court delivered judgment. If the debtor paid the original sum in full even in the middle of the trial, he avoided having to pay interest. This rule was changed by the Administration of Justice Act 1982, s 15 (amending the Supreme Court Act 1981, s 35A): the court can now award interest so long as money was outstanding at the time proceedings were commenced. This still leaves it open to the debtor to escape liability for interest by paying the original sum just before proceedings are commenced, which may be several years after the debt was incurred. (It was the limited nature of this reform that persuaded the House of Lords that Parliament had not intended to make a more far-reaching change.)

(4) However, in certain circumstances it appears that, if the debtor knows when he makes the contract that the creditor is depending on receipt of the money for some particular purpose, and that the creditor has no other funds available, the debtor may be liable in damages for either the creditor's loss on the frustrated purpose (as in the *Trans-Trust* case), or, if the creditor does manage to borrow the money elsewhere, for the interest paid by the creditor. In *Wadsworth v Lydall* [1981] 2 All ER 401, the purchaser of land had agreed to pay £10,000 by a fixed date, knowing that the vendor was going to use the money to make a down payment on another piece of land. The purchaser paid only £7,200, and the vendor had to borrow the remaining £2,800 in order to make the down payment on time. The Court of Appeal held that the vendor could recover as part of his damages the interest he had had to pay on the £2,800. This case was expressly (and enthusiastically) approved by the House of Lords in the *President of India* case; it was treated as an application of the second rule in *Hadley v Baxendale*, that is, as dependent on the debtor's special knowledge of facts making the loss likely. Thus if the plaintiff can prove that he has suffered a particular loss as a result of the non-payment, and that the loss was within the contemplation of the parties, he may recover. The practical effect of the endorsement of *Wadsworth v Lydall* may be to take away from debtors some of the advantage conceded to them by the refusal to reverse the 'no interest' rule.

(5) A further statutory modification is made by the Late Payment of Commercial Debts (Interest) Act 1998. This Act goes further than any previous legislation to implement the Law Commission's general proposals as to interest by implying a term in the contract that 'statutory interest' will be payable on any 'qualifying debt'. The details of the Act are too complex to go into here but it should be noted that it only applies if both parties are acting in the course of a business and only to contracts under which one party is supplying goods or services.

2. Failure to make title to land—a problem no longer?

Until recently, there was an ancient and exceptional rule, confirmed by the House of Lords in *Bain v Fothergill* (1874) LR 7 HL 158, which provided that the vendor of land who, without any fault on his part, was unable to show good title was liable to the purchaser for the purchaser's costs in investigating title but not for the loss of bargain. It has been argued that this rule was a survivor from the days when no damages were awarded for loss of bargain (Atiyah, *Rise and Fall of Freedom of Contract*, 1979, p 203), but it is not at all clear that earlier law did refuse such damages in other types of contract (see Baker (1980) 43 MLR 467). Whatever its origin, the courts tended to limit the application of the rule in *Bain v Fothergill*. It did not apply when the vendor was unwilling to make proper efforts to make title *(Malhotra v Choudhury* [1980] Ch 52), nor did it apply to 'matters of conveyancing', an obscure phrase that seems to refer to obligations that are separate from the obligation to make title, for instance the obligation to deliver vacant possession (see *Wroth v Tyler* [1974] Ch 30). The rule was criticised as outmoded: see Sydenham, 'The Anomalous Rule in *Bain v Fothergill*' (1977) 41 Conv 341; Emery, 'In Defence of the rule in *Bain v Fothergill*' (1978) 42 Conv 338; Law Commission No 166, *Transfer of Land: The Rule in Bain v Fothergill* (Cm 192, 1987). It was abolished by Law of Property (Miscellaneous Provisions) Act 1989, s 3.

3. Non-pecuniary losses

In *Addis v Gramophone Co Ltd* [1909] AC 488, the plaintiff was employed as manager of the defendants' business in Calcutta. He could be dismissed on six months' notice. The defendants gave him six months' notice and, at the same time, appointed a successor, taking steps to prevent the plaintiff acting any longer as manager. A jury awarded the plaintiff £340 for loss of commissions and £600 for wrongful dismissal. The House of Lords allowed the first head, but not the second: the plaintiff could only recover his salary for the six months, and no more. Lord Loreburn said (at 491):

If there be a dismissal without notice the employer must pay an indemnity; but that indemnity cannot include compensation either for the injured feelings of the servant, . . .

For a long time, it was believed that there was a general rule that one could not recover damages for non-pecuniary losses in action for breach of contract. It is clear now that this is not always the case.

■ *Jarvis v Swans Tours Ltd*
[1973] 1 All ER 71, Court of Appeal

The plaintiff booked a winter sports holiday, which the defendants advertised in their brochure as 'a Houseparty in Morliap', with 'special resident host, . . . Welcome party . . . afternoon tea and cakes . . . Yodeller evening'. It was stated that ski-packs would be available, and added 'You will be in for a great time.' The house party consisted of 13 people for the first week and only the plaintiff for the second, during which week there was no representative at the hotel; there was no welcoming party; full-length skis were only available for two days; the cake for tea was only crisps and dry nutcake; the yodeller was a local man who sang a few songs in his working clothes. The plaintiff claimed damages for breach of a contract to provide the holiday promised. The trial judge awarded him £31.72, and he appealed.

Lord Denning MR
. . . What is the legal position? I think that the statements in the brochure were representations or warranties. The breaches of them give Mr Jarvis a right to damages. It is not necessary to decide whether they were representations or warranties; because, since the Misrepresentation Act 1967, there is a remedy in damages for misrepresentation as well as for breach of warranty.

The one question in the case is: what is the amount of damages? The judge seems to have taken the difference in value between what he paid for and what he got. He said that he intended to give 'the difference between the two values and no other damages' under any other head. He thought that Mr Jarvis had got half of what he paid for. So the judge gave him half the amount which he had paid, namely, £31.72. Mr Jarvis appeals to this court. He says that the damages ought to have been much more. . . .

What is the right way of assessing damages? It has often been said that on a breach of contract damages cannot be given for mental distress. Thus in *Hamlin v Great Northern Railway Co* Pollock CB said that damages cannot be given 'for the disappointment of mind occasioned by the breach of contract'. And in *Hobbs v London & South Western Railway Co* Mellor J said that—

' . . . for the mere inconvenience, such as annoyance and loss of temper, or vexation, or for being disappointed in a particular thing which you have set your mind upon, without real physical inconvenience resulting, you cannot recover damages.'

The courts in those days only allowed the plaintiff to recover damages if he suffered physical inconvenience, such as, having to walk five miles home, as in *Hobbs'* case; or to live in an overcrowded house: see *Bailey v Bullock*.

I think that those limitations are out of date. In a proper case damages for mental distress can be recovered in contract, just as damages for shock can be recovered in tort. One such case is a contract for a holiday, or any other contract to provide entertainment and enjoyment. If the contracting party breaks his contract, damages can be given for the disappointment, the distress, the upset and frustration caused by the breach. I know that it is difficult to assess in terms of money, but it is no more difficult than the assessment which the courts have to make every day in personal injury cases for loss of amenities. Take the present case. Mr Jarvis has only a fortnight's holiday in the year. He books it far ahead, and looks forward to it all that time. He ought to be compensated for the loss of it.

A good illustration was given by Edmund Davies LJ in the course of the argument. He put the case of a man who has taken a ticket for Glyndbourne. It is the only night on which he can get there. He hires a car to take him. The car does not turn up. His damages are not limited to the mere cost of the ticket. He is entitled to general damages for the disappointment he has suffered and the loss of the entertainment which he should have had. Here, Mr Jarvis's fortnight's winter holiday has been a grave disappointment. It is true that he was conveyed to Switzerland and back and had meals and bed in the hotel. But that is not what he went for. He went to enjoy himself with all the facilities which the defendants said he would have. He is entitled to damages for the lack of those facilities, and for his loss of enjoyment. . . . I think the damages in this case should be the sum of £125. I would allow the appeal accordingly.

Edmund Davies LJ and **Stephenson LJ** delivered concurring judgments.

Appeal allowed.

NOTES

1. Is Lord Denning's statement that it does not matter whether the damages are for breach of contract or for misrepresentation correct? Is the plaintiff recovering reliance loss or loss of expectation?

2. Some commentators referred to the damages in *Jarvis's* case as exemplary (eg Yates (1973) 36 MLR 535). Do you agree?

3. In *Heywood v Wellers* [1976] 1 All ER 300, the plaintiff employed the defendant solicitors to obtain an injunction to prevent a man molesting her. The solicitors were negligent in conducting the litigation, in particular in failing to bring the man before the court when he again molested the plaintiff, with the result that he molested her twice more. The

Court of Appeal held that she was entitled to damages for mental distress, which was the very thing that she was employing the solicitors to protect her from.

4.   In *Cox v Philips Industries Ltd* [1976] 1 WLR 638, the plaintiff suffered depression and ill health after his employer, in breach of contract, took away his responsibilities and gave him no work to do, although he was still paid his salary. In *Bliss v South East Thames Regional Health Authority*, (1983) Times, 13 December Farquharson J awarded the plaintiff orthopaedic surgeon damages for distress, frustration and vexation after the defendants had, in breach of contract, required him to submit to a medical examination by a psychiatrist and, when he refused, suspended him from duty; this part of the decision was reversed by the Court of Appeal [1985] IRLR 308 as contrary to *Addis v Gramophone Co*. *Cox's* case was overruled.

5.   In *Watts v Morrow* [1991] 4 All ER 937, the plaintiffs bought a house relying on a survey prepared by the defendant. The survey report had been prepared negligently and failed to reveal the need for major repairs. The trial judge included in the damages £8,000 for 'distress and inconvenience'. The Court of Appeal disallowed this. Bingham LJ said (at 959–960):

A contract-breaker is not in general liable for any distress, frustration, anxiety, displeasure, vexation, tension or aggravation which his breach of contract may cause to the innocent party. This rule is not, I think, founded on the assumption that such reactions are not foreseeable, which they surely are or may be, but on considerations of policy.

But the rule is not absolute. Where the very object of a contract is to provide pleasure, relaxation, peace of mind or freedom from molestation, damages will be awarded if the fruit of the contract is not provided or if the contrary result is procured instead. If the law did not cater for this exceptional category of case it would be defective. A contract to survey the condition of a house for a prospective purchaser does not, however, fall within this exceptional category.

In cases not falling within this exceptional category, damages are in my view recoverable for physical inconvenience and discomfort caused by the breach and mental suffering directly related to that inconvenience and discomfort. If those effects are foreseeably suffered during a period when defects are repaired I am prepared to accept that they sound in damages even though the cost of the repairs is not recoverable as such. But I also agree that awards should be restrained, and that the awards in this case far exceeded a reasonable award for the injury shown to have been suffered.

This part of the award was reduced to £1,500 for 'physical discomfort'.

6.   The leading case is now *Farley v Skinner* [2001] UKHL 49 [2001] 4 All ER 801.

The claimant was considering buying a large house in Sussex, which was not far from Gatwick Airport. He engaged the defendant to conduct a survey of the house and specifically asked him to report on aircraft noise. The defendant carelessly gave a reassuring answer. In fact, there were times at which noise was a serious problem, particularly at 6 o'clock in the morning, when holding patterns for Gatwick formed over the house. This was very distressing for the claimant because he liked to spend early morning in the garden.

The claimant did not discover about the noise until he had spent over £100,000 on improving the house. The trial judge held that the claimant had not paid any more for the house than would a reasonable purchaser who knew of the aircraft noise and so there was no financial loss. He awarded £10,000 for the claimant's distress. The Court of Appeal disagreed but the House of Lords restored the trial judge's holding.

Lord Scott:

It is time for me to turn to the present case and apply the principles expressed in the *Ruxley Electronics* case and *Watts v Morrow*. In my judgment, Mr Farley is entitled to be compensated for the 'real discomfort' that the judge found he suffered. He is so entitled on either of two alternative bases.

First, he was deprived of the contractual benefit to which he was entitled. He was entitled to information about the aircraft noise from Gatwick-bound aircraft that Mr Skinner, through negligence, had failed to supply him with. If Mr Farley had, in the event, decided not to purchase Riverside House, the value to him of the contractual benefit of which he had been deprived would have been nil. But he did buy the property. And he took his decision to do so without the advantage of being able to take into account the information to which he was contractually entitled. If he had had that information he would not have bought. So the information clearly would have had a value to him. Prima facie, in my opinion, he is entitled to be compensated accordingly.

In these circumstances, it seems to me, it is open to the court to adopt a *Ruxley Electronics* approach and place a value on the contractual benefit of which Mr Farley has been deprived. In deciding on the amount, the discomfort experienced by Mr Farley can, in my view, properly be taken into account. If he had had the aircraft noise information he would not have bought Riverside House and would not have had that discomfort.

Alternatively, Mr Farley can, in my opinion, claim compensation for the discomfort as consequential loss. Had it not been for the breach of contract, he would not have suffered the discomfort. It was caused by the breach of contract in a causa sine qua non sense. Was the discomfort a consequence that should reasonably have been contemplated by the parties at the time of contract as liable to result from the breach? In my opinion, it was. It was obviously within the reasonable contemplation of the parties that, deprived of the information about aircraft noise that he ought to have had, Mr Farley would make a decision to purchase that he would not otherwise have made. Having purchased, he would, having become aware of the noise, either sell, in which case at least the expenses of the resale would have been recoverable as damages, or he would keep the property and put up with the noise. In the latter event, it was within the reasonable contemplation of the parties that he would experience discomfort from the noise of the aircraft. And the discomfort was 'physical' in the sense that Bingham LJ in *Watts v Morrow* [1991] 4 All ER 937 at 960, [1991] 1 WLR 1421 at 1445 had in mind. In my opinion, the application of *Watts v Morrow* principles entitles Mr Farley to damages for discomfort caused by the aircraft noise.

I would add that if there had been an appreciable reduction in the market value of the property caused by the aircraft noise, Mr Farley could not have recovered both that difference in value and damages for discomfort. To allow both would allow double recovery for the same item.

Whether the approach to damages is on *Ruxley Electronics* lines, for deprivation of a contractual benefit, or on *Watts v Morrow* lines, for consequential damage within the applicable remoteness rules, the appropriate amount should, in my opinion, be modest. The degree of discomfort experienced by Mr Farley, although 'real', was not very great. I think £10,000 may have been on the high side. But in principle, in my opinion, the judge was right to award damages and I am not, in the circumstances, disposed to disagree with his figure.

7. In *Malik v Bank of Credit and Commerce International* [1997] 3 All ER 1, HL, the plaintiffs were middle managers employed by the defendant bank, which, unknown to them, was a massive fraud carried on to defraud customers and third parties. Eventually, the bank went into liquidation and the plaintiffs were made redundant. It was held that the bank had been in breach of implied terms as to trust and confidence, which should exist between employer and employee (see pp 455–456). This raised questions as to what damages the plaintiffs could recover for breach of these implied terms. The plaintiffs argued that their position in the employment market was seriously damaged because

they had once worked for the defendant bank. The House of Lords held that if this could be established on the facts in relation to particular plaintiffs, then the plaintiffs could recover damages for the loss of reputation that they would then have suffered and for the financial loss that flowed from that loss of reputation. Lord Steyn said:

THE AVAILABILITY OF THE REMEDY OF DAMAGES

In considering the availibility of the remedy of damages it is important to bear in mind that the employees claim damages for financial loss. That is the issue. It will be recalled that the Court of Appeal decided the case against the employees on the basis that there is a positive rule debarring the recovery of damages in contract for injury to an existing reputation, and that in truth the two employees were claiming damages for injury to their previously existing reputations. For this conclusion the Court of Appeal relied on three decided cases, namely *Addis v Gramophone Co Ltd* [1909] AC 488, [1908–10] All ER Rep 1, *Withers v General Theatre Corp Ltd* [1933] 2 KB 536, [1933] All ER Rep 385 and *O'Laoire v Jackel International Ltd (No 2)* [1991] I CR 718. It will be necessary to examine each of these authorities.

The true ratio decidendi of the House of Lords decision in *Addis v Gramophone Co Ltd* has long been debated. Some have understood it as authority for the proposition that an employee may not recover damages even for pecuniary loss caused by a breach of contract of the employer which damages the employment prospects of an employee. If *Addis's* case established such a rule it is an inroad on traditional principles of contract law. And any such restrictive rule has been criticised by distinguished writers: see Treitel *An Outline of the Law of Contract* (9th edn, 1995) p 893 and Burrows *Remedies for Torts and Breach of Contract* (2nd edn, 1994) pp 221–225. Moreover, it has been pointed out that *Addis's* case was decided in 1909 before the development of modern employment law, and long before the evolution of the implied mutual obligation of trust and confidence. Nevertheless, it is necessary to take a closer look at *Addis's* case so far as it affects the issues in this case. A company had dismissed an overseas manager in a harsh and oppressive manner. The House of Lords held that the employer was entitled to recover his direct pecuniary loss, such as loss of salary and commission. But the jury had been allowed to take into account the manner in which the employee had been dismissed and to reflect this in their award. The House of Lords, with Lord Collins dissenting, held that this was wrong. The headnote of the case states that in a case of wrongful dismissal the award of damages may not include compensation for the manner of his dismissal, for his injured feelings, or for the loss he may suffer from the fact that the dismissal of itself makes it more difficult to obtain fresh employment. Lord Collins was apparently alone in wanting time to consider the matter. The majority would apparently have dealt with with the matter summarily. And the majority did not find it necessary to analyse the matter in any depth. The speeches are not always easy to follow. Thus Lord Atkinson observed ([1909] AC 488 at 496, [1908–10] All ER Rep 1 at 5):

'I can conceive nothing more objectionable and embarrassing in litigation than trying in effect an action of libel or slander as a matter of aggravation in an action for illegal dismissal, the defendant being permitted, as he must in justice be permitted, to traverse the defamatory sense, rely on privilege, or raise every point which he could raise in an independent action brought for the alleged libel or slander itself.'

That is a misconception: ex hypothesi liability has been established and only the assessment of damages is at stake. Moreover, Lord Gorrell apparently arrived at his conclusion on the basis of ordinary principles of remoteness (see [1909] AC 488 at 501, [1908–10] All ER Rep 1 at 9). Depending on the facts those principles would not necessarily in all cases debar an award of damages for loss of employment prospects. I would accept, however, that Lord Loreburn LC and the other Law Lords in the majority apparently thought they were applying a special rule applicable to awards of damages for wrongful dismissal. It is, however, far from clear how far the ratio of *Addis's* case extends. It certainly enunciated the principle that an employee cannot recover exemplary or aggravated damages for wrongful dismissal. That is still sound law. The actual decision is only concerned with wrongful dismissal. It is therefore arguable that as a matter of precedent the ratio is so restricted. But it seems to me unrealistic not to acknowledge that *Addis's* case is authority for a wider principle. There is a common proposition in the speeches of the majority. That proposition is that damages for breach of contract may only be awarded for breach of contract, and not for loss caused by the manner of the breach. No Law Lord said that an employee may not recover financial loss for damage to his employment prospects caused by a breach of contract. And no Law Lord said that in breach of contract cases compensation for loss of reputation can never be awarded, or that it can only be awarded in cases falling in certain defined categories. *Addis's* case simply decided that the loss of reputation in that particular case could not be compensated because it was not caused by a breach of contract: see Nelson Enonchong 'Contract Damages for Injury to Reputation' (1996) 59 MLR 592 at 596. So analysed *Addis's* case does not bar the claims put forward in the present case.

Withers v General Theatre Corp Ltd [1933] KB 536, [1933] All ER Rep 385 may rule out a claim such as is under consideration in the present case. The case concerned an artist engaged to appear and perform at the London Palladium. The defendant refused to allow him to perform at the London Palladium. It was held to be a breach of contract. The Court of Appeal drew a distinction. It was held that the plaintiff was entitled to damages for the loss of reputation which the plaintiff would have acquired if the defendant had not committed the breach of contract. But the Court of Appeal held that the plaintiff was not entitled as a matter of law to damages to his existing reputation. Nothing in *Addis's* case supported this distinction. It is difficult as a matter of principle to justify it. A rule that damages can never be recovered in respect of loss of reputation caused by a breach of contract is also out of line with ordinary principles of contract law. Moreover, *Withers'* case is in conflict with *Marbe v George Edwardes (Daly's Theatre) Ltd* [1928] 1 KB 269, [1927] All ER Rep 253. In *Marbe's* case on similar facts the Court of Appeal came to the opposite conclusion: damages in respect of loss of an existing reputation was expressly held to be recoverable (see [1928] 1 KB 269 at 281, 288, 290, [1927] All ER Rep 253 at 259, 264, 266 per Bankes, Atkin and Lawrence LJJ). But in *Withers'* case Scrutton LJ erroneously considered that *Marbe's* case was inconsistent with the House of Lords decision in *Herbert Clayton & Jack Waller Ltd v Oliver* [1930] AC 209, [1930] All ER Rep 414. The latter case did not involve a claim for loss of existing reputation (see [1930] AC 209 at 214, [1930] All ER Rep 414 at 416). Moreover, as the headnote states, in *Herbert Clayton & Jack Waller Ltd v Oliver* [1930] AC 209 the House of Lords approved *Marbe's* case. The House of Lords did so expressly. The *Withers* decision was based on a misunderstanding. In any event, I am persuaded that the distinction drawn in *Withers*, and the rule applied, is contrary to the principle and unsound. In my judgment the decision in *Withers* was wrong on this point. Ordinary contract law principles govern.

O'Laoire v Jackel International Ltd (No 2) [1991] ICR 718 involved a claim by a dismissed employee for loss "due to the manner and nature of his dismissal". It was held that such a claim is excluded by *Addis's* case. But that does not affect the present case which is based not on the manner of a wrongful dismissal but on a breach of contract which is separate from and independent of the termination of the contract of employment.

For further proceedings, see [1999] 4 All ER 85.

8.　The law in this area is complicated by the existence of a statutory regime protecting employees in certain circumstances against unfair dismissal. This has led to three recent House of Lords decisions in *Johnson v Unisys* [2001] 2 All ER 801; *Eastwood v Magnox Electric plc* [2004] UKHL 35 [2004] 3 All ER 991; *Dunnachie v Kingston upon Hull City Council* [2004] UKHL 36 [2004] 3 All ER 1011, but this is not the place for a detailed examination.

9.　Rea, 'Non-pecuniary Loss and Breach of Contract' (1982) 11 J Legal Studies 35 argues that awarding full compensation for non-pecuniary losses in cases such as *Jarvis v Swan Tours* may overcompensate the plaintiff and thus be inefficient. His point is that, in many cases, what is lost is irreplaceable. If it were simply a question of deciding whether or not to take out insurance against a random event causing the same loss, the rational person would not insure or would do so at a lower level. If the supplier can influence the probability of a breach of contract leading to loss (as Swan clearly could) there is a conflict between the provision of optimal insurance for the buyer and providing an incentive for the supplier to take optimal precautions. Some liability must be imposed on defaulting suppliers or they will have inadequate incentives to take efficient precautions; the amount of liability need only be what is adequate to ensure that the proper precautions are taken, not the full non-pecuniary loss. Thus the damages should be somewhere between the optimal amount of insurance and the full non-pecuniary loss that was suffered. Full compensation should be given only when the breach was wilful (as is in fact the rule in some US jurisdictions).

4. Difference in value or cost of completion?

■ *Tito v Waddell (No 2)*

[1977] Ch 106 at 328

Only a small part of this long and complex case is presented here. Phosphate had been mined on Ocean Island under an agreement made in 1913 with the Banaban landowners. The agreement provided that the mining company (whose rights and obligations had now vested in the British Phosphate Commissioners) would return all worked-out lands to the owners, and would 'replant such lands— wherever possible—with coconuts and other food-bearing trees, both in the lands already worked out and in those to be worked out'. In 1942, the island had been occupied by the Japanese, who killed or deported most of the inhabitants and devastated the island. After the war, the surviving Banabans were resettled on the island of Rabi, some 1,500 miles away. This is a much larger island, unaffected by mining, whereas Ocean Island is five-sixths mined. The Banabans brought an action in which, inter alia, they claimed damages.

Megarry V-C

(a) BASIS. Mr Macdonald's primary contention was that the measure of damages was the cost of doing the work of replanting, limited to $A73,140 per acre. His secondary contention was that the measure of damages was a suitable proportion of the cost of replanting, to represent the sum which the British Phosphate Commissioners would have paid in order to be released from the obligation to replant. In a helpful summary of his submissions on this part of the case which he put in on Day 101, he worked out some figures on the assumption that the one third for which he had contended in argument was the suitable proportion. These contentions were, of course, made in relation to the extensive replanting obligations that he claimed and I have rejected; but in principle they must apply to the lesser obligation that I have held to exist.

Mr MacCrindle, on the other hand, contended that even if the action were not premature by reason of the failure of the resident commissioner to specify trees and shrubs, and was not barred on any other ground, the damages should be either nominal or minimal. His basic submission was that the proper measure of damages was not the cost of doing the work, but was the diminution in the market value of the land by reason of the work not having been done. Mr Macdonald's secondary contention, based on what British Phosphate Commissioners would have paid for being released from the obligation to replant, had not been put forward at that stage. But Mr Browne-Wilkinson met it on behalf of the British Phosphate Commissioners in his speech in reply; and he contended that this mode of assessment was inapplicable in cases such as this.

I shall take first the rival contentions of the cost of doing the work, and the diminution in the market value. The two approaches are exemplified *by Joyner v Weeks* and *Wigsell v School for Indigent Blind* respectively: both were cited to the House of Lords in *Conquest v Ebbetts*. In *Joyner v Weeks*, the action was by a landlord against the tenant, brought not during the term but at the end of it, for damages for breach of a covenant to keep the demised premises in repair, and to deliver them up in repair. The Court of Appeal held that the ordinary rule was that the damages recoverable were the cost of doing the repairs, and that there was nothing in the facts of the case which made that rule inapplicable . . .

Wigsell's case related to the purchase of 12 acres of land intended for a projected asylum. In the conveyance the purchasers covenanted with the vendor that they would keep their land enclosed on all sides which abutted on the vendor's land with a brick wall or an iron railing seven feet high. The conveyance also gave the vendor, his heirs and assigns a right of pre-emption if the purchasers did not require the land for a blind school or asylum, and desired within 10 years to sell all or any of it. Six years later the purchasers decided not to use any of the land for their projected asylum, and offered it back to the executors of the vendor, who had died in the meantime; but the offer was declined. No wall or fence had been erected, and the executors then sued the purchasers for damages for breach of covenant. The cost of erecting the wall or fence was far greater than the diminution in the value of the vendor's land by reason of the breach.

In delivering the judgment of a Queen's Bench Divisional Court, consisting of himself and Cave J, Field J said . . . that if the plaintiffs had really wished to have the wall built, they would have sued for specific performance; and if the court had thought damages an inadequate remedy, it could have ordered specific performance. Instead, the plaintiffs had elected to sue for damages. They would be under no obligation to spend the money on building the wall, and probably they would never think of such expenditure, which seemed to the court to be a simple waste of money. The effect of suing for damages was to entitle them to the amount of the difference between the state of the plaintiffs on the breach of the contract and what this would have been if the contract had been performed. . . .

Pausing there, it is clear that in some cases of a contract to do work to the plaintiff's land the measure of damages for breach is the reduction in value of the plaintiff's interest in the land, and in other cases it is the cost of doing the work. But which? . . .

For reasons that will appear, I do not think that the question falls to be determined by whether the plaintiff sues for damages or whether he sues for specific performance, even though *McGregor on Damages* appears to put the matter on this point, at any rate to a considerable extent: see at pp 493, 526. Plainly it may be important whether or not the plaintiff is claiming specific performance: but I do not think it can be decisive. Suppose that a recluse sells some of his land on terms that the purchaser will erect a high wall that will enclose most of the vendor's land: the wall is not built, and so the vendor builds a wall himself and then sues for damages. His land may be worth more on the market without the wall than with it, but I cannot see that either this or the fact that he is not suing for specific performance ought to debar him from obtaining damages equal to the cost of building the wall. Whether the wall to be taken for this purpose is the actual wall, if reasonable, or the contractual wall, I need not discuss. If, without erecting the wall, he sues merely for damages, but establishes that he will spend the money on erecting a wall, preferring to have nothing more to do with the faithless purchaser, I do not see why the result should not be the same.

Again, some contracts for alterations to buildings, or for their demolition, might not, if carried out, enhance the market value of the land, and sometimes would reduce it. The tastes and desires of the owner may be wholly out of step with the ideas of those who constitute the market; yet I cannot see why eccentricity of taste should debar him from obtaining substantial damages unless he sues for specific performance. Per contra, if the plaintiff has suffered little or no monetary loss in the reduction of value of his land, and he has no intention of applying any damages towards carrying out the work contracted for, or its equivalent, I cannot see why he should recover the cost of doing work which will never be done. It would be a mere pretence to say that this cost was a loss and so should be recoverable as damages.

In the absence of any clear authority on the matter before me, I think I must consider it as a matter of principle. I do this in relation to the breach of a contract to do work on the land of another, whether to build, repair, replant or anything else: and I put it very broadly. First, it is fundamental to all questions of damages that they are to compensate the plaintiff for his loss or injury by putting him as nearly as possible in the same position as he would have been in had he not suffered the wrong. The question is not one of making the defendant disgorge what he has saved by committing the wrong, but one of compensating the plaintiff. In the words of O'Connor LJ in *Murphy v Wexford County Council* [1921] 2 IR 230, 240:

'You are not to enrich the party aggrieved; you are not to impoverish him; you are, so far as money can, to leave him in the same position as before.'

Second, if the plaintiff has suffered monetary loss, as by a reduction in the value of his property by reason of the wrong, that is plainly a loss that he is entitled to be recouped. On the other hand, if the defendant has saved himself money, as by not doing what he has contracted to do, that does not of itself entitle the plaintiff to recover the savings as damages; for it by no means necessarily follows that what the defendant has saved the plaintiff has lost.

Third, if the plaintiff can establish that his loss consists of or includes the cost of doing work which in breach of contract the defendant has failed to do, then he can recover as damages a sum equivalent to that cost. It is for the plaintiff to establish this: the essential question is what his loss is.

Fourth, the plaintiff may establish that the cost of doing the work constitutes part or all of his loss in a variety of ways. The work may already have been done before he sues. Thus he may have had it done himself, as in *Jones v Herxheimer*. Alternatively, he may be able to establish that the work will be done. This, I think, must depend on all the circumstances, and not merely on whether he sues for specific performance. An action for specific performance is doubtless one way of manifesting a sufficient intention that the work shall be done: but there are others.

. . . [I]f the circumstances fail to indicate sufficiently that the work will be done, the court might accept an undertaking by the plaintiff to do the work; and this, as in the business tenancy cases, would surely 'compel fixity of intention'. Whatever the circumstances, if the plaintiff establishes that the contractual work has been or will be done, then in all normal circumstances it seems to me that he has shown that the cost of doing it is, or is part of, his loss, and is recoverable as damages. Even if it is open to question whether the plaintiff will do the work, the cost of doing it may afford a starting figure, though it should be scaled down according to the circumstances, the real question being that of the loss to the plaintiff: see *Smiley v Townshend* [1950] 2 KB 311, 322, per Denning LJ. In the words of Denning J in *Westminster (Duke) v Swinton* [1948] 1 KB 524, 534, 'The real question in each case is: What damage has the plaintiff really suffered from the breach?' In the end, the question seems to me to come down to a very short point. The cost is a loss if it is shown to be a loss.

There is a fifth point. In most cases there can be no certainty about the doing of work which has not yet been done. A lessee bound by covenant to his lessor to do the work may be released from his covenant, or may have his liability compounded on payment of less than the cost of doing that work, as was envisaged by Lord Herschell in *Conquest v Ebbetts* [1896] AC 490, 494. The local authority may decide not to enforce the statutory obligation, or the court may release a litigant from his undertaking. A plaintiff who had a firm and settled intention to do the work may later find that supervening events have weakened or destroyed his resolve.

I do not think that the plaintiffs' rights are affected by any such absence of certainty. . . .

I turn to Mr Macdonald's secondary contention, founded on a suitable proportion of the cost of replanting as representing what the British Phosphate Commissioners would have paid to be released from their obligation to replant. This contention did not emerge until very late in the proceedings. It was on Day *96* that Mr Macdonald first cited *Wrotham Park Estate Co Ltd v Parkside Homes Ltd* and *Bracewell v Appleby*, on which he relied. In the former case, houses had been built on land without the prior approval of the plaintiffs which a restrictive covenant made requisite. On the facts of the case a mandatory injunction to demolish the houses was refused, and damages in substitution therefore were held to be recoverable under the Act of 1858. Brightman J resolved the difficult question of the appropriate quantum of damages by holding that the plaintiffs should recover 5 per cent of the defendants' expected profit from their venture. In *Bracewell v Appleby*, Graham J applied the same principle where the right in question was not a consent under a restrictive covenant, but an easement of way.

I find great difficulty in seeing how these cases help Mr Macdonald. If the plaintiff has the right to prevent some act being done without his consent, and the defendant does the act without seeking that consent, the plaintiff has suffered a loss in that the defendant has taken without paying for it something for which the plaintiff could have required payment, namely, the right to do the act. The court therefore makes the defendant pay what he ought to have paid the plaintiff, for that is what the plaintiff has lost. The basis of computation is not, it will be observed, in any way directly related to wasted expenditure or other loss that the defendant is escaping by reason of an injunction being refused: it is the loss that the plaintiff has suffered by the defendant not having observed the obligation to obtain the plaintiff's consent. Where the obligation is contractual, that loss is the loss caused to the plaintiff by breach of contract.

In the present case, the loss caused to the plaintiffs by the British Phosphate Commissioners' failure to replant is the diminution in the value of their land resulting from that failure, or, if it is established that the land would be replanted, the cost of replanting. In the latter case, no doubt, the British Phosphate Commissioners might well have been willing to pay something to be released from their obligation to replant, though that something would probably be rather less than the total estimated cost of replanting. But the point is that not unless the British Phosphate Commissioners would be liable to replant or pay damages equal to the cost of replanting would there be any liability from which the British Phosphate Commissioners would seek release on the basis of paying a sum equal to the discounted cost of replanting. If Mr Macdonald establishes that liability, he does not need his less favourable secondary contention: if Mr Macdonald fails to establish that liability, there is no foundation on which to base his secondary contention. Of course, until it has been determined whether or not some burden exists, the person who would be subject to that burden may always be willing to pay something to be relieved of the risk: but I do not think that this can affect the measure of damages in the case which determines that the burden does exist. In any case, the two authorities in question seem to me to be a long way away from a case where the issue is not one of invading the property rights of another without consent, but of breach of a contract to replant his land.

(b) QUANTUM. I return, then, to Mr Macdonald's primary contention. Have the plaintiffs shown that the cost of replanting represents the loss to them caused by the failure to perform the replanting obligation? Only one answer to that question seems possible, and that is No. The plaintiffs own small scattered plots of land; there is nothing to establish that the owners of neighbouring plots of land, who are not parties to these proceedings, would procure the replanting of their plots rather than keep any damages for themselves or other purposes; the Banabans are now well established in Rabi, over 1,500 miles away; and there they have an island over 10 times the size and unaffected by mining, as contrasted with the much smaller Ocean Island with some five-sixths of it mined.

NOTE

Megarry V-C's approach was applied in *Radford v De Froberville* [1978] 1 All ER 33. In that case, the defendant had failed to perform a covenant to build a wall on her land along the boundary with the plaintiff's land, and had resold the land. Oliver J held that the plaintiff was entitled to the cost of building a wall on his side of the boundary, irrespective of whether it would increase the value of the property, and even though the plaintiff did not live on his property. It was sufficient that he had clearly established his intention to build the wall. It must also be reasonable to carry out the work.

For a further discussion of the economic issues, see Muris, 'Cost of Completion or Diminution in Market Value' (1983) 12 Journal of Legal Studies 379.

■ Harris, Ogus and Phillips, 'Contract Remedies and the Consumer Surplus' (1979)
95 LQR 581

In *Radford v De Froberville* the existence of the wall on the new boundary of his land was worth more to the plaintiff than the increase which the wall would make to the market value of the land; it was argued that he valued the particular architectural style and privacy it afforded more highly than would the average purchaser of the land. This is an example of what economists refer to as 'consumer surplus', the excess utility or subjective value obtained from a 'good' over and above the utility associated with its market price. The concept of consumer surplus is important in any attempt to measure consumer losses because, unlike firms, consumers make purchases for the pleasure or utility they confer; this utility has no necessary relationship with the price paid, and is of quite a different order from market prices or business profits. It is, of course, difficult to measure utility, but generally economists avoid the conceptual problem by measuring utility in terms of the maximum amount a consumer would pay for a particular purchase. For instance, if a purchaser can buy a plot of land for £1,000, when he would be prepared to pay up to £1,500 for it, the extra £500 represents his 'consumer surplus'. Without using this term, an intending bidder at an auction thinks in this way when he decides beforehand what is the maximum bid he is prepared to make: the difference between any lower price he pays and the higher price he is prepared to pay measures the consumer surplus expected at that time. Therefore willingness to pay, rather than market price, is the appropriate measure for estimating the value of a purchase, and the consumer surplus is the difference between this value and the market price.

Consumer surplus may arise from services as well as from the possession of land or goods. Thus, a holiday is generally worth more to the tourist than the price he has to pay for it, and the value to the family of wedding photographs exceeds their price. These illustrations show how individuals value performance of non-commercial contracts. However, consumer surplus has its analogue in commercial cases where profit rather than utility is the aim of the contract: the market price may underestimate the value of a good to the firm which buys it, and the surplus value above the market price will be represented by its contribution to profit-making. Lawyers are used to handling claims for loss of profits following the breach of a commercial contract. This article seeks to clarify the corresponding concept of the consumer surplus in the case of consumer contracts: both are relevant to the proper assessment of the expectation interest of the promisee.

... Within the framework of these remedies, there are various means whereby account may be taken of consumer surplus. First, the court has a discretionary power to force the promisor to perform (specific performance) (Section C). Secondly, it may indirectly achieve the same result by awarding the promisee such money as will enable him to employ a third party to perform (reinstatement damages) (Section D). Thirdly, either in exercise of its equitable jurisdiction to grant damages in lieu of specific relief (Section F), or in satisfaction of the plaintiff's common law right to damages upon a breach of contract (Section E), the court may attempt itelf to evaluate the consumer surplus by awarding a sum designed to compensate for that category of loss...

While, as will appear, the courts are in some situations prepared to adopt one of these remedies which does recognise the consumer surplus (though the recognition is rarely explicit), in many other situations they are not willing to do so, with the result that the plaintiff is, we would argue, under-compensated. This inhibition may lie in the common law's refusal to recognise consumer contracts as a separate category from commercial contracts: when claims for sums above the market price are made, judges have been accustomed to think only in terms of loss of profits or similar commercial interests and not in terms of loss of utility. Some categories of consumer contract have for long been recognised (eg landlord and tenant, hire purchase) but it is only more recently that the legislature has begun to recognise the need for general categories of consumer contracts in order to develop rules designed for such transactions. In some, typically civilian, systems, commercial and private contracts are separately categorised: the result, we believe, has been a greater readiness to compensate for the consumer surplus, either through specific relief or as reflected in an award of damages. A second inhibiting factor in the common law has been the fear that selection of one of the remedies may over-compensate the plaintiff or, as it is sometimes said, confer on him a 'windfall'. This would occur, for example, if an award of damages based on the cost of reinstatement in a case such as *Radford* were not actually spent on building the wall, but put to some other use. Thirdly, it can be objected that actual performance of the contractual undertaking would result in 'economic waste'. This may be the case, for example, where the cost of that performance would exceed the utility which the plaintiff expected to obtain on its completion. Thus, where premises are not built to specification, the plaintiff may (in preference to specific performance) be said to accept them in their present state and receive in compensation a small sum which is less than the cost of modifying them. The award of a sum which is in between the diminution in value and the cost of performance would increase the combined utilities of the parties.

C. Specific Performance

As regards the sale of chattels, the presumption that specific performance will not be available may be supplanted in the case of those which are 'unique', 'when there is, over and above the market value, that which has been called the *pretium affectionis*', and also, 'in the case of chattels which, though not unique, possess a special and peculiar value to the plaintiff'. This latter statement of principle could be interpreted in the light of the consumer surplus concept to mean that whenever, following the seller's failure to deliver a chattel, an award of damages would not enable the buyer to obtain a similar consumer surplus through a substitute purchase, the courts will be willing to grant specific performance. The reported cases show that specific performance has been ordered of contracts to buy a rare jewel, china vases, particular stones from Old Westminster Bridge, and an ornamental door designed by the famous architect Adam.

D. Substitute Performance: damages assessed as the cost of completion or reinstatement by a third party

One possible remedy is to secure what was promised by the indirect means of awarding damages to the promisee based on what it would cost him to obtain performance (or completion of performance) of the contractual undertaking by a third party. As with an order of specific performance, such a remedy would inevitably secure for the promisee any consumer surplus from which he would have benefited under performance of the contractual promise. The substitute or reinstatement approach has the added advantage of avoiding the problems of supervision which may arise under a specific performance order.

. . . [I]n some cases the court has to decide between two competing methods of assessing those damages: the measure based on the completion or reinstatement cost and that based on the difference between the market value of the defendant's performance in its defective or incomplete state and the market value of the performance if it had properly been completed. Again, although the matter is rarely made explicit, an intuitive perception of the consumer surplus problem is evident from the way in which the courts have selected as between these modes of compensation: they have tended to choose the alternative which they instinctively feel is closer to the plaintiff's 'real loss', *viz* the reinstatement measure when there is a substantial loss of consumer surplus, and the diminution in market value measure when there is no substantial loss of consumer surplus. This may be inferred from some of the reasons which have been offered for preferring the reinstatement measure. Thus it has been said that the plaintiff is entitled to the reasonable cost of having the remedial work done if in all the circumstances it is (or was) reasonable for him to insist on having the work done—and either (a) he has actually had the work done, or (b) he undertakes to have it done, or (c) he shows a 'sufficient intention' to have the work done if he receives damages on this basis. The implication of these requirements is that the court will have sufficient evidence from which it can assume that the plaintiff had an interest in performance which exceeded its market value. In the *Radford* case, it will be recalled, the plaintiff could show that the wall would fulfil 'a functional purpose', namely, 'that of enclosing and preserving the privacy of [his] land by a permanent boundary feature constructed in an acceptable architectural style'; and the judge was 'entirely satisfied that the plaintiff genuinely wants this work done and that he intends to expend any damages awarded on carrying it out'. In North America, the reinstatement measure has also been preferred where assessment of the difference in market value was too speculative and, perhaps more significantly, where there was no difference in market value between the performance as promised and that in fact executed, but where the difference is regarded by the plaintiff as of some importance: here the courts seem concerned to preserve some sanction for contract-breaking.

Conversely, the diminution measure has been preferred where the court suspects that the plaintiff does not really want the remedial work to be done but is merely hoping to inflate his damages award, or where it considers that the cost of the remedial work would be grossly and unfairly out of all proportion to the benefit to be obtained (thus amounting to economic waste). In so far as a court is correct in its estimation that the plaintiff's consumer surplus is not more than marginal, there can be no complaint with this approach, but to the extent that it is substituting its own ideas of what the plaintiff's utility *should* have been for what it was, the approach is clearly unsatisfactory. This may be amply demonstrated by the recent decision in *Tito v Waddell (No 2)* (the *Ocean Island* case) . . . .

Megarry V-C rejected the plaintiffs' claim not only to specific performance but also to damages based on the cost of reinstating the land. Instead, he applied the diminution measure, though, as he himself admitted, this was largely a matter of guesswork since there was no market for worked-out plots of land in Ocean Island. Refusal of the reinstatement measure (claimed to be A$73,140 per acre) was justified on the grounds that: (i) since the islanders were now established on another island some 1,500, miles away, they had not established that the cost of replanting represented the 'loss' suffered by them on breach and (ii) the Vice-Chancellor was not convinced that they intended to spend the damages on replanting the plots.

It is difficult, on the facts of the case, to accept the implication of this reasoning that the islanders (though now living elsewhere) did not have a substantial consumer surplus in the replanted land, but one can sympathise with the predicament of the judge who felt himself constrained by his interpretation of the law to make the choice between an award of damages based on the cost of reinstatement and one based on £75 an acre (his evaluation of the diminution loss). We shall argue below that in such circumstances awards of damages might properly be made somewhere between the two extremes. For the present, we must consider the consequences of the decision actually reached in the *Ocean Island* case.

In the first place, it should be clear that a large 'benefit' was thereby conferred on the British Phosphate Commissioners. Future increases in labour and other costs arising from replanting were clearly within the risks assumed by the Commissioners' predecessor when the original undertaking was given and escalation in these costs would have been balanced against expected increases in the value of the phosphate to be sold. The result of the judgment, however, is that the Commissioners have been allowed to enjoy all the benefits of the islanders' predecessors' obligations under the contracts, while avoiding the cost of their corresponding obligations to replant.

Secondly, a delicate question is raised as to the relationship between this decision and the doctrine of frustration. It is trite law that a party may be relieved of his contractual obligations only when supervening events have rendered performance impossible, or at least have robbed the contract of its original purpose. But the mere inflation of the costs of performance, even when unforeseeable, has never been a sufficient ground for invoking the doctrine of frustration. It seems anomalous that a result which the law refuses to reach via this doctrine can nevertheless be arrived at indirectly through the process of assessing damages.

The solution to the problem confronted in the *Ocean Island* case and in others where actual reinstatement is either impossible or the court regards its cost as grossly unreasonable in the light of the benefit to be obtained would be a principle by which the damages could be fixed *above* the difference in market values but *below* the cost of reinstatement. There are two ways in which the matter could be approached. The court might attempt to evaluate the plaintiff's loss of consumer surplus. The method of doing this will be considered below. The second alternative would not deal directly with the question of consumer surplus but would provide a justification for ignoring it. It would be to allocate the benefit which accrues to the promisor from the saving he has made in not performing his contractual obligation.

Hitherto, the courts seemed to have been concerned that the *promisee* should not make an undeserved 'profit' if damages are awarded on the reinstatement basis but the money is used for some other purpose. This assumes that the only question is whether the promisee 'deserves' to benefit from the 'windfall'; it fails to take into account that when there is a substantial difference between the diminution in market value and the cost of reinstatement, there may be a 'windfall' which must be 'awarded' to one party or the other. In the *Ocean Island* case, Megarry V-C in effect 'awarded' all the windfalls to the defendants, the contract-breakers, without (apparently) considering the possibility of dividing it between the parties. A fair allocation between the parties would strike a balance between their respective interests (following the analogies of unjust enrichment in the law on Restitution) and at the same time would provide the court with a justification for not attempting to compensate for the loss of the expected consumer surplus: the division of the windfall would be in lieu of such compensation, since it would often produce as damages a sum which exceeds the plaintiff's own valuation of his lost consumer surplus. . . .

E. Damages for Non-Pecuniary Loss

The common law systems have traditionally been hesitant to award non-pecuniary damages for breach of contract. This may again be attributed to the failure to distinguish between commercial and consumer contracts and to recognise that almost by definition the latter are concerned with the transfer to the promisee of a benefit to be enjoyed rather than a marketable good. But the absence of the award from the reported cases may also be explained by the fact that in most situations it is assumed that the promisee can avoid the loss by obtaining equivalent satisfaction from a substitute. In other words, the problem would arise only where such substitution was not available [as in *Jarvis v Swans Tours*]. . . .

F. Damages in lieu of specific performance (Lord Cairns' Act)

Under the Chancery Amendment Act 1858 (Lord Cairns' Act), a court of Equity was empowered to award damages in addition to, or in substitution for, specific performance where it had jurisdiction to grant such specific relief. This power still exists, and in certain respects equitable damages may be awarded in situations not recognised by common law; but the House of Lords has recently held that the Act does not provide for the assessment of damages on any new basis. However, the fact that equitable damages are granted *in lieu* of specific performance, with the consequent object of putting the plaintiff in the position he would have been in if specific relief had been ordered, suggests that to be an adequate substitute they should take account of the consumer surplus. It is difficult to find direct support for this proposition in the reported cases, but where equitable damages have been awarded in lieu of an injunction (a form of specific relief analogous to that of specific performance), they have been assessed at the 'proper and fair price' which the plaintiffs (albeit reluctantly) would have been willing to accept for the loss of an amenity attached to the beneficial use of property. (See *Bracewell v Appleby* [1975] Ch 408, 419–420.] This formulation may be related to the concept of consumer surplus: both are based on an individual's personal evaluation of an asset, although the courts evidently prefer to quantify this by reference to what the reasonable man in the plaintiff's position would have been prepared to accept.

G. Limits to Damages Awards: Mitigation and Remoteness

There are a number of doctrines in the law which limit the amount of damages which may be awarded for breach of contract . . . the mitigation principle can be applied to the additional value of the promise to the promisee, the consumer surplus. If a substitute which is reasonably available to the promisee would confer on him utility as great as that resulting from performance of the original contract, clearly there is no loss of consumer surplus. [Further] the loss must be such as to have been within the reasonable expectation of the parties as 'not unlikely' to arise on the breach of contract, as judged at the time of the making of the contract.

H. The Assessment of Damages for Loss of Consumer Surplus (Whether at Common Law or Equity)

Although economics can elucidate the concept of consumer surplus, it can offer little guidance on the methods by which a third party, such as a court, could assess in money the value of a lost consumer surplus....

The closest approach to the economist's concept of consumer surplus is found in cases where the plaintiff has been wrongfully deprived of an amenity attached to the beneficial use of land. Thus, where the defendant broke a covenant not to develop land for building purposes except in strict accordance with a plan approved by the plaintiffs, but the judge decided not to grant an injunction for the demolition of the houses erected in breach of the covenant, he concluded that 'a just substitute for a mandatory injunction would be in such a sum of money as might reasonably have been demanded by the plaintiffs from [the defendant] as a quid pro quo for relaxing the covenant.' [*Wrotham Park Estate Co Ltd v Parkside Homes Ltd* [1974] 1 WLR 798] In another case, which was concerned with the use of a right of way for a purpose not envisaged by the original grant, the court fixed the damages at the 'proper and fair price' which the plaintiffs, 'albeit reluctantly, would have been willing to accept for granting the more extensive right of way, *viz* 'as compensating them for loss of amenity and increased user.' [*Bracewell v Appleby*, above] In the case of the vendor's breach of a contract to sell a house to the defendant for the purpose of his own occupation, a convenient approach would be to fix a percentage of the agreed price as damages for loss of the purchaser's expected consumer surplus.

A second approach to the assessment of damages would be for the court to fix an arbitrary sum to provide some utility to replace that lost by the breach of contract. In personal injury cases, the injured person's own subjective valuation of his lost utility is ignored, and the courts have fixed arbitrary, conventional, sums to compensate for the loss of part of the body, for pain and suffering, or for reduction in the expectation of life....

J Formal Remedies and Informal Bargains

The [following] possibilities may provide satisfactory solutions to the consumer surplus problem:

(a) directly compelling performance of the contractual obligation by an order for specific performance or an injunction;

(b) indirectly compelling performance of the contractual obligation by awarding the promisee the cost of performance (or of completing performance) coupled with an undertaking that the damages will be spent for this purpose;

(c) awarding the promisee a sum of money by way of damages (at common law or in equity) which attempts to compensate him for the loss of consumer surplus....

A major problem with an order for specific performance (or an order for reinstatement damages linked with an undertaking to carry out the substance of the contract) is that the remedy may appear to be wasteful. The promisee may prefer to receive a sum of money which is less than the cost of performance, a solution which would also be to the promisor's advantage. This is most obviously the case when work carried out has not been to specification, but the cost of remedying it would be out of all proportion to the loss of consumer surplus. However, it is not to be assumed that in all cases an order for specific performance will in fact be executed or that such a failure thwarts the aims of the law. An order is not normally executed by the court of its own initiative: it is usually necessary for the party for whose benefit it is granted to return to court to complain of non-compliance and to seek execution, typically through the contempt process. Unless, therefore, there are considerations of public policy which render compliance essential, the promisee is entitled to waive or 'sell' his right to specific relief. He will, of course, ordinarily only be prepared to do so when he is offered a price high enough to compensate him for his expected loss from performance (which would include his consumer surplus); this loss will probably exceed the objective value of the benefit derived from performance (*viz* normally the market value). Viewed from this perspective, specific performance may be characterised as a formal declaration by the court that the promisee's interest in performance is absolute in the sense that he cannot be forced against his will to convert it into a monetary equivalent, but that at the same time it remains a negotiable asset in that he can, if he wishes, surrender it to the promisee for valuable consideration.

. . . Given a situation in which the plaintiff would prefer a monetary sum to performance, the question arises whether the appropriate amount should best be arrived at by the process of a compromise after a specific performance order or, rather, by limiting his remedy to damages. In the former case the parties themselves will be evaluating the consumer surplus; in the latter it will result from a judicial determination. The theoretical considerations which ought to be weighed when judging the merits of the two approaches include the following.

First, there is the problem of uncertainty. Even if the sum awarded or agreed upon will be the same, individuals generally prefer a more rather than less certain path in reaching the final result. The problem with an order for specific performance is that, unless the case falls within one of the well-known categories where the order is regularly made, there will be considerable uncertainty as to whether specific performance will be decreed (in contrast to the damages remedy to which the promisee is entitled as of right). . . .

A second problem concerns transaction costs, which include those expenses necessary to reaching the final solution. The damages solution may involve lower legal costs since there will not be a second stage of negotiations (as with the specific performance approach); on the other hand, the parties will incur the expense of collecting evidence relating to the loss.

A third factor relates to the bargaining position of the parties. The 'absolute' nature of the promisee's right, following a specific performance order, may lead to the problem of so-called 'hold-out': he may be tempted to extort from the promisor a sum which approaches as nearly as possible the cost of implementation, thereby exceeding the value he sets on his consumer surplus. In the situation where a settlement is reached on a damages claim, the parties will arrive at a compromise between two limits representing the estimate each has of the likely judicial award: to the extent that that award takes account of the consumer surplus, the bargaining limits should be located close to that figure, or in any event should not be weighted in favour of one party rather than the other. After a specific performance decree, however, the bargaining limits clearly favour the promisee: he will not be prepared to accept a sum less than his evolution of the consumer surplus. The upper limit will be the cost of performance and, if it be assumed that anything above the consumer's evaluation of the benefit will constitute overcompensation, then any bargain struck above the minimum will be subject to that criticism. The extent of overcompensation will depend on the relative bargaining strength of the two parties: the 'hold-out' strategy of the promisee may be tempered by the possibility of actual performance by the promisor *(ex hypothesi* not giving the promisee what he wants). Nevertheless some might regard the probability of overcompensation as an overwhelming objection to the specific performance approach, thus suggesting that the judge should only adopt such an approach when he estimates that the plaintiff's subjective valuation approaches the cost of performance. In any event the risk of overcompensation must be balanced against the risk of undercompensation which may result from the difficulty inherent in evaluating the consumer surplus. Indeed, from a perspective which has been described above, what is at stake is the amount of the windfall which the promisor receives from the court's decision that he will not be compelled to perform, and any 'overcompensation' received by the promisee may be regarded as his share in the 'windfall.'

■ **Posner, *Economic Analysis of Law*** (6th edn, 2003)
p 129

. . .

Moreover, a penalty clause discourages breach-averting modifications and renegotiations. Because contract liability is strict liability, a promisor may find himself in breach of his contract because he simply is unable, rather than merely unwilling, to carry out his promise yet has no defence of impossibility or *force majeure*. Very often in such a case the parties will agree to modify the contract, with appropriate compensation for the promisee. Modification is less likely when there is a penalty clause, because the clause raises the price that the promisee will demand for letting the promisor off the hook of the original contract. If a suit to enforce such a clause (assuming such clauses were enforceable) were very costly, the promisee would feel pressure to settle. But if enforcement is not costly (and why should it be if the clause specifies a sum certain as the damages for a breach?), the promisee may hold out for something very near the penalty and the promisor may decide he might as well let the promisee sue. As we shall see in Chapter 21, litigation may be very costly to the court system even when it is not to the parties—which is to say that parties are able to externalize some of the costs of their litigation. To limit the externality, courts may refuse to enforce contractual provisions that make litigation more likely, at least if there are no strongly offsetting efficiencies.

In *Ruxley Electronics and Construction Ltd v Forsyth* [1996] AC 344, [1995] 3 All ER 268, the defendant had contracted for a swimming pool 7ft 6in deep. In breach of contract, the finished pool was only 6ft deep and when the contractors sued for the price, the defendant counterclaimed for the cost of deepening it. This would have involved total reconstruction. The trial judge held that the depth was perfectly adequate for the off-the-side diving, which was all that was intended, and that it would be unreasonable to reconstruct the pool. The defendant was therefore only entitled to damages for any difference in value between a 6ft pool and a 7ft 6in one, plus £2,500 for loss of amenity. The Court of Appeal, by a majority, reversed this decision. The reasonableness of his desire to reconstruct the pool was irrelevant if that was the only way in which the defendant could get what he had contracted for (Staughton LJ), or reconstruction was not unreasonable (Mann LJ). The House of Lords restored the first instance judgment. If the object of the contract was to provide an amenity, the damages may include loss of amenity or (*per* Lord Mustill) 'consumer surplus'. But the cost of reconstruction should not be awarded if it would be disproportionate to the loss of amenity.

In *Ruxley*, the trial judge was sure the defendant would not actually reconstruct the pool even if the cost of doing so were awarded to him. Before the Court of Appeal, the defendant had offered an undertaking that he would carry out the work if he were awarded the cost of doing so as damages. The majority said that this was unnecessary: 'What the plaintiff intends to do, or does, with his damages is not material' (Mann LJ at 812). In the House of Lords, Lords Jauncey and Lloyd suggested that the defendant's intention was relevant to whether or not it would be reasonable to reconstruct the pool, but it was not conclusive. His undertaking could not create a loss that did not exist.

VI. AGREED DAMAGES, DEPOSITS AND FORFEITURES

I. Agreed damages

■ *Dunlop Pneumatic Tyre Co Ltd v New Garage and Motor Co Ltd*
[1915] AC 79, House of Lords

The appellants sold motor tyres, covers and tubes to the respondent dealers, who agreed, inter alia, not to sell or offer the goods to any private customers or to any cooperative society at less than the appellants' current list prices, nor to sell to any person whose supplies the appellants had decided to suspend, and to pay the sum of £5 per tyre by way of liquidated damages for every tyre cover or tube sold or offered in breach of the agreement. The respondents sold a tyre cover to a cooperative society at less than the list price, and the appellants claimed the agreed sum.

Lord Dunedin

. . . I shall content myself with stating succinctly the various propositions which I think are deducible from the decisions which rank as authoritative:—

1. Though the parties to a contract who use the words 'penalty' or 'liquidated damages' may prima facie be supposed to mean what they say, yet the expression used is not conclusive. The Court must find out whether the payment stipulated is in truth a penalty or liquidated damages. This doctrine may be said to be found passim in nearly every case.

2. The essence of a penalty is a payment of money stipulated as in terrorem of the offending party; the essence of liquidated damages is a genuine covenanted pre-estimate of damage (*Clydebank Engineering and Shipbuilding Co v Don Jose Ramos Yzquierdo y Castaneda*).

3. The question whether a sum stipulated is penalty or liquidated damages is a question of construction to be decided upon the terms and inherent circumstances of each particular contract, judged of as at the time of the making of the contract, not as at the time of the breach (*Public Works Commissioner v Hills* and *Webster v Bosanquet*).

4. To assist this task of construction various tests have been suggested, which if applicable to the case under consideration may prove helpful, or even conclusive. Such are:

   (a) It will be held to be penalty if the sum stipulated for is extravagant and unconscionable in amount in comparison with the greatest loss that could conceivably be proved to have followed from the breach. (Illustration given by Lord Halsbury in *Clydebank Case*.)

   (b) It will be held to be a penalty if the breach consists only in not paying a sum of money, and the sum stipulated is a sum greater than the sum which ought to have been paid *(Kemble v Farren)*. This though one of the most ancient instances is truly a corollary to the last test. Whether it had its historical origin in the doctrine of the common law that when A promised to pay B a sum of money on a certain day and did not do so, B could only recover the sum with, in certain cases, interest, but could never recover further damages for non-timeous payment, or whether it was a survival of the time when equity reformed unconscionable bargains merely because they were unconscionable—a subject which much exercised Jessel MR in *Wallis v Smith*—is probably more interesting than material.

   (c) There is a presumption (but no more) that it is penalty when 'a single lump sum is made payable by way of compensation, on the occurrence of one or more or all of several events, some of which may occasion serious and others but trifling damage' (Lord Watson in *Lord Elphinstone v Monkland Iron and Coal Co*).
   On the other hand:

   (d) It is no obstacle to the sum stipulated being a genuine pre-estimate of damages, that the consequences of the breach are such as to make precise pre-estimation almost an impossibility. On the contrary, that is just the situation when it is probable that pre-estimated damage was the true bargain between the parties (*Clydebank Case*, Lord Halsbury; *Webster v Bosanquet*, Lord Mersey).

Turning now to the facts of the case, it is evident that the damage apprehended by the appellants owing to the breaking of the agreement was an indirect and not a direct damage. So long as they got their price from the respondents for each article sold, it could not matter to them directly what the respondents did with it. Indirectly it did. Accordingly, the agreement is headed 'Price Maintenance Agreement', and the way in which the appellants would be damaged if prices were cut is clearly explained in evidence by Mr Baisley, and no successful attempt is made to controvert that evidence. But though damage as a whole from such a practice would be certain, yet damage from any one sale would be impossible to forecast. It is just, therefore, one of those cases where it seems quite reasonable for parties to contract that they should estimate that damage at a certain figure, and provided that figure is not extravagant there would seem no reason to suspect that it is not truly a bargain to assess damages, but rather a penalty to be held in terrorem.

The argument of the respondents was really based on two heads. They overpressed, in my judgment, the dictum of Lord Watson in *Lord Elphinstone's Case*, reading it as if he had said that the matter was conclusive, instead of saying, as he did, that it raised a presumption, and they relied strongly on the case of *Willson v Love*.

Now, in the first place, I have considerable doubt whether the stipulated payment here can fairly be said to deal with breaches, 'some of which'—I am quoting Lord Watson's words—'may occasion serious and others but trifling damage'. As a mere matter of construction, I doubt whether clause 5 applies to anything but sales below price. But I will assume that it does. None the less the mischief, as I have already pointed out, is an indirect mischief, and I see no data on which, as a matter of construction, I could settle in my own mind that the indirect damage from selling a cover would differ in magnitude from the indirect damage from selling a tube; or that the indirect damage from a cutting-price sale would differ from the indirect damage from supply at a full price to a hostile, because prohibited, agent. You cannot weigh such things in a chemical balance. The character of the agricultural land which was ruined by slag heaps in *Elphinstone's Case* was not all the same, but no objection was raised by Lord Watson to applying an overhead rate per acre, the sum not being in itself unconscionable.

I think *Elphinstone's Case*, or rather the dicta in it, do go this length, that if there are various breaches to which one indiscriminate sum to be paid in breach is applied, then the strength of the chain must be taken at its weakest link. If you can clearly see that the loss on one particular breach could never amount to the stipulated sum, then you may come to the conclusion that the sum is penalty. But further than this it does not go; so, for the reasons already stated, I do not think the present case forms an instance of what I have just expressed.

As regards *Willson's Case*, I do not think it material to consider whether it was well decided on the facts. For it was decided on the view of the facts that the manurial value of straw and of hay were known ascertainable quantities as at the time of the bargain, and radically different, so that the damage resulting from the want of one could never be the same as the damage resulting from the want of the other.

Lord Atkinson, **Lord Parker of Waddington** and **Lord Parmoor** delivered concurring judgments.

Appeal allowed.

NOTES

1. In *Willson v Love* [1896] 1 QB 626, 65 LJQB 474 (referred to in the *Dunlop* case), a lease of a farm provided that the lessees should not sell hay or straw off the premises during the last 12 months of the term, and that they should pay an additional rent of £3 for every ton of either so sold. Evidence was given that the manurial value of hay was over 15s per ton, but that of straw less than 5s per ton. The additional rent was held to be a penalty.

2. If the clause is a valid liquidated damages clause, the sum stipulated is recoverable upon the relevant breach, even though the actual loss is less or even nil. In *Clydebank Engineering and Shipbuilding Co v Castaneda* [1905] AC 6, 74 LJPC 1, HL, the sellers of four torpedo boats, which they had delivered late, argued that they should not have to pay liquidated damages to the buyers, the Spanish navy, on the ground that if the boats had been delivered in time, they would have shared the same fate as the rest of the Spanish navy, which had been sent to the bottom of the Atlantic by the American navy. The House of Lords rejected this argument as absurd.

3. Equally, if the clause is valid, it does not matter that the real loss suffered by the innocent party is greater than the stipulated sum: only the sum is recoverable. It is interesting to note that an agreed damages clause may be valid even though the sum is deliberately set at *less* than the estimated loss: *Cellulose Acetate Silk Co Ltd v Widnes Foundry (1925) Ltd* [1933] AC 20, 101 LJKB 694.

4. If the clause is invalid as a penalty, the innocent party may recover his actual loss, at least if it is less than the stipulated sum: see Hudson (1974) 90 LQR 31; Gordon 90 LQR 296; Hudson (1975) 91 LQR 25; Barton (1976) 92 LQR 20.

5. The penalty rules also apply to provisions that stipulate that, if a party breaks the contract, he must retransfer property to the seller: *Jobson v Johnson* (noted at **p 590**).

6. It is not clear whether it is permissible to stipulate for liquidated damages for a loss that might not be recoverable at common law, such as non-pecuniary loss. In *Robophone Facilities Ltd v Blank* [1966] 3 All ER 128 at 142–143, Diplock LJ suggested that a clause would be valid if it were a genuine pre-estimate of a loss that would not normally be recoverable because it was outside the ordinary course of things under the first limb of *Hadley v Baxendale*, but that was because the clause would put the other on notice of the amount of loss. However, *Lombard North Central plc v Butterworth* (see p 606) suggests a restrictive attitude towards losses that cannot normally be recovered.

■ Sweet, 'Liquidated Damages in California' (1972)
60 Calif LR 84, 86–89

A. Reasons for liquidated damages provisions

As the norm has changed from negotiated contract to adhesion contract, the reasons for employing liquidated damages clauses have changed, and accompanying this has been a change in judicial attitude toward enforcement. First, consider the use of liquidation clauses in the model of a negotiated contract. Both contracting parties often wish to control their risk exposure, and permitting them to do so encourages risk-taking. The performing party may also wish to avoid the feared irrationality of the judicial process in determining actual damages. He may also be fearful that the court will give insufficient consideration to legitimate excuses for nonperformance, that the court may be unduly sympathetic to plaintiff's claim that any loss he incurred should be paid for by the party whose nonperformance caused the loss, or that the court may consider contract breach an immoral act.

There are also reasons why the nonperforming party as well may wish to use a liquidated damages clause. Sometimes a breach will cause damage, but the amount of damages cannot be proven under damage rules. For example, in wartime procurement contracts it may be impossible to establish the damages caused by delayed or defective performance by the contractor. Without an enforceable clause purporting to liquidate damages, the nonperforming party may fear that the performing party will have insufficient incentive to perform if the latter realizes that damages he has caused are not sufficiently provable to be collected. Such a clause is a penalty in that its principal function is to coerce performance. Yet if it is reasonable—not disproportionate to actual, although unprovable, damages or to the contract price—it will be enforced. Without a liquidated damages clause there is also a danger the contractor may recover the full contract price despite a breach that caused some unprovable losses. Thus while the nonperforming party may be motivated principally by the penalty aspects of the clause, he may to a lesser degree be motivated by the desire to prevent what appears to him to be unjust enrichment.

Liquidated damages clauses may also be inserted to improve upon what the parties believe to be a deficiency in the litigation process: the cost and difficulty of judicially proving damages. Through a liquidation clause the parties attempt to use contract to settle the amount of damages involved and thus improve the normal rules of damages. Also, when the clause is phrased in such a way as to indicate that the breaching party will pay a specified amount if a particular breach occurs, troublesome problems involved in proving causation and foreseeability may be avoided. This was extremely helpful, for example, in wartime procurement contracts, where not only was it almost impossible to establish the amount of damages, but it was equally impossible to establish that delayed or defective performance by the contractor caused any particular loss and that the loss was reasonably foreseeable at the time the contract was made. Finally, the parties may feel that if they truly agree on damages in advance, it is unlikely that either would later dispute the amount of damages recoverable as the result of his breach.

In the adhesion contract situation there are some similarities in objectives; the desire to control the irrationality and expense of the litigation process and the need to know the extent of risk exposure are still involved. There are, however, obvious additional objectives of the stronger party. He can dictate the terms of the contract; if he is the performing party, he is likely to use the contract clause to limit his exposure almost to the vanishing point, and if he is the nonperforming party, he may try to use a penalty clause to coerce performance, or he may try to use a genuine liquidation clause to make vindication of his legal rights as convenient and inexpensive as possible. In the adhesion context, then, the stronger party may try to limit his own liability and to set an agreed amount that is sufficiently high to coerce performance. In the event performance is not rendered, the clause may obtain a settlement or win the case.

B. Judicial responses to liquidated damages provisions

Moving from the reasons why liquidated damages clauses are used by the parties, let us consider what motivates courts to uphold or reject these clauses. Some courts undoubtedly are persuaded by the argument that the parties have paid their money and taken their chances. Since the parties have assumed certain risks, courts often see no particular reason to relieve them from the risks they have taken. Treating the liquidated damages clauses as any other, such courts uphold the clauses to reward the party who has guessed best on the question of damages. Other courts enforce these clauses because they believe that protecting the reasonable expectations of the contracting parties encourages risk-taking and assists in planning. Still other courts look at the contract as a package and enforce the liquidation clause because they feel that the party attacking the clause has received benefits under the contract. This is especially likely when such a clause is directly related to the contract price. For example, in one important case, a gun manufacturer offered to supply guns at different prices depending upon when delivery had to be made. The government chose the quickest delivery at the highest price. Nonenforcement of the delay-damage liquidation clause in this case would have disturbed the package arrangement and created unjust enrichment.

Courts also enforce these clauses because they believe liquidated damages clauses help the courts achieve just results. Sometimes the computation of damages in litigation is no better than a guess; as long as the amount selected by the parties is within a reasonable range, the courts feel that enforcing the amount selected is likely to be as fair as any amount determined by the court. Furthermore, courts believe that if such agreements are enforced, at least in theory the use of such clauses should expand, resulting in fewer breaches, fewer law suits, fewer or easier trials, and in many cases, at least as just a result.

Finally, courts recognize that enforcement of these clauses can cure defects in the litigation process. For example, the requirements as to certainty may seem too restrictive. A court may enforce a liquidation clause to ensure that a party will get a just recovery that might otherwise be denied him because he cannot establish the loss with sufficient certainty.

Many purported liquidated damages clauses, however, are not enforced. The traditional rationale for nonenforcement is that courts will not aid in coercion, oppression, or unjust enrichment; courts seek only to compensate, and enforcement of penalty clauses is contrary to that purpose. Thus, enforcement of a clause not based upon an estimate of proper compensation would cause an unconscionable result.

Refusal to enforce these clauses may recognize the protection contracting parties need from their own unfortunate optimism and their failure to consider in advance the possibility that subsequent events may affect their performance.

NOTES

1.   How many of the advantages of liquidated damages would be lost if the party in breach were permitted to challenge the clause in the light of the actual loss, as the shipbuilders in the *Clydebank* case tried to do?

2.   It is often difficult to estimate the likely loss when drafting a liquidated damages clause. Firstly, the breach may occur in a variety of circumstances which will result in differing amounts of loss. Need the clause reflect all these possibilities? Secondly, with a non-profit-making project such as a road, what loss is suffered if the project is completed late? In *Philips Hong Kong Ltd v A-G of Hong Kong* (1993) 61 BLR 41 the plaintiffs were employed to design, supply and install a computerised supervisory system for a new road and tunnel. The contract set liquidated damages which would be payable if the plaintiffs failed to meet 'Key Dates' by which certain items had to be finished to enable other contractors to do their work unimpeded, and additional liquidated damages for failure to complete the whole project on time. The plaintiffs sought a declaration that the clauses were unenforceable as penalties. Lord Woolf, delivering the judgment of the Privy Council, said (at pp 54–55 and 58–61):

... [P]rovision for liquidated damages should enable the employer to know the extent to which he is protected in the event of the contractor failing to perform his obligations. ...

As for the contractor, by agreeing to a provision for liquidated damages, he is seeking to remove the uncertainty as to the extent of his liability under the contract if he is unable to comply with his contractual obligations ...

[The] court should not adopt an approach to provisions as to liquidated damages which could defeat their purpose.

Except possibly in the case of situations where one of the parties to the contract is able to dominate the other as to the choice of the terms of a contract, it will normally be insufficient to establish that a provision is objectionably penal to identify situations where the application of the provision could result in a larger sum being recovered by the injured party than his actual loss. Even in such situations so long as the sum payable in the event of non-compliance with the contract is not extravagant, having regard to the range of losses that it could reasonably be anticipated it would have to cover at the time the contract was made, it can still be a genuine pre-estimate of the loss that would be suffered and so a perfectly valid liquidated damage provision. The use in argument of unlikely illustrations should therefore not assist a party to defeat a provision as to liquidated damages ...

A difficulty can arise where the range of possible loss is broad. Where it should be obvious that, in relation to part of the range, the liquidated damages are totally out of proportion to certain of the losses which may be incurred, the failure to make special provision for those losses may result in the "liquidated damages" not being recoverable. ... However, the court has to be careful not to set too stringent a standard and bear in mind that what the parties have agreed should normally be upheld. Any other approach will lead to undesirable uncertainty especially in commercial contracts.

... [The] fact that two parties who should be well capable of protecting their respective commercial interests agreed the allegedly penal provision suggests that the formula for calculating liquidated damages is unlikely to be oppressive. ...

Here the Government in its evidence provides an explanation as to how the liquidated damages were calculated. So far as the missing of Key Dates was concerned, the amount of damages was calculated by applying a formula to what was anticipated would be the value of the interfacing contracts. (The actual value of the contracts was higher.) In the case of delay in completion of the whole of the Philips contract the calculation was partly based on a formula applied to the total value of the Philips contract in accordance with a manual of instructions for contracts of this nature which the Government had prepared. This was a perfectly sensible approach in a situation such as this where it would be obvious that substantial loss would be suffered in the event of delay but what that loss would be virtually impossible to calculate precisely in advance. In the case of a governmental body the nature of the loss it will suffer as the result of the delay in implementing its new road programme is especially difficult to evaluate. The Government reasonably adopted a formula which reflected the loss of return on the capital involved at a daily rate, to which were added figures for supervisory staff costs, the daily actual cost of making any alternative provision and a sum for fluctuations. Except for the "alternative provision", the appropriate figures were calculated by reference to the estimated final contract sum.

Nor was it an objection that the Government might recover twice if a Key Date was missed and as a result the project as a whole was finished late. The Key Date damages related to compensation payable to other contractors; the additional damages to loss of use of the project.

3.   In practice, liquidated damages for delay are commonly found coupled with an extension of time clause, giving the seller (or in a construction contract the contractor) the right to extra time if he is delayed by matters outside the control of either party (eg bad weather or industrial disputes) or by acts of the buyer or employer (eg ordering changes in the goods or work, or failing to make drawings available promptly). These clauses serve two functions. The more obvious one is to protect the contractor from liability for delay: without the clause his obligation to deliver or complete on time would be strict, save insofar as he was prevented from performing promptly by the other party. The second function is in just such cases of prevention. In a series of cases in the last century it was held that if a contractor is prevented from attaining the completion date by a breach by the employer or by compliance with some order of the employer, the latter cannot claim *any* liquidated damages, even for periods of delay that indubitably were the contractor's fault: see *Holme v Guppy* (1838) 3 M & W 387; *Dodd v Churton* [1897] 1 QB 562. The extension of time clause permits the completion date to be moved back, and thus operates to preserve the liquidated damages machinery.

■ 'Contracts between Businessmen' (1975)
2 Brit J Law & Society 45 at 55

It was only in the specifically negotiated contracts that liquidated damages clauses (clauses agreeing in advance the compensation payable for late delivery) were found. These clauses appear to be convenient ways both of encouraging timely performance and of avoiding disputes about compensation, and are commonly thought by lawyers to be attractive to the business community, but the criticisms made to us may explain why they are not more commonly used, particularly in standard conditions. Sellers clearly wished to avoid any liability for delay, but in most cases of negotiated sales they could not get away with excluding their liability altogether as they attempt to do in their 'back of order' conditions. They might therefore prefer a liquidated damages clause instead of full liability at common law. But this would not be the case if they thought that the customer was unlikely to press any claim for consequential loss, for instance because of a close relationship between the two firms, or was unlikely to be able to prove any loss, for instance because the project for which the goods were required was almost certain to be running late, or because the goods were required for a non-profit making purpose such as 'defence'.

Buyers might have been expected to favour liquidated damages just to avoid having to prove their losses. But again there were criticisms. Firstly, sellers would not usually accept liquidated damages clauses unless delays caused by *force majeure* were excepted, and *force majeure* clauses were so wide that the buyer would receive no compensation for much of the delay. Several buyers said that they preferred to preserve their common law rights even though they would not usually exercise them. Secondly, the administrative costs of enforcing liquidated damages clauses are relatively high because keeping track of delays and investigating the causes requires a lot of manpower.

Nor when a liquidated damages clause had been agreed did buyers seem very keen to make use of the remedy. We were told that often a negotiated settlement would be reached under which only part of the sum due would be paid. This seems to destroy one advantage of the device, and apparently another advantage was also sometimes thrown away: the buyer can normally 'set off' liquidated damages due against the price and pay only the balance, yet we were told of a buyer claiming liquidated damages long after paying the price in full. Our impression is that in the area of delay at least the main reason for liquidated damages was not to obtain compensation but to discipline the other party. One experienced officer told us that he favoured liquidated damages not because he wanted damages but because he wanted a realistic delivery date in the first place and to be told of any likely delay well in advance; in negotiated contracts he would ensure that the operation of the *force majeure* clause excusing the seller was conditioned on prompt notification of the excusable delay.

Thus in both negotiated and non-negotiated contract situations, late delivery seems to be regarded as primarily a commercial problem to be solved commercially rather than a legal problem susceptible to solution by the use of planning. Not surprisingly most buyers and sellers seemed to regard delivery dates as targets rather than firm promises.

Why are penalty clauses not enforceable?

■ Rea, 'Efficiency Implications of Penalties and Liquidated Damages' (1984)
13 JLS 147, at 147–161

Why should freely negotiated contract provisions that specify damages in the event of breach not be enforced? Posner has called this doctrine 'a major unexplained puzzle in the economic theory of the common law'. Previous economic explanations of the doctrine are not convincing...

The economic analysis of contracts suggests that damages for breach of contract serve two primary functions, assuming that there is no reliance. First, they provide an incentive for one party to take into account the losses suffered by the other when the former takes precautions against breach or decides whether deliberately to breach a contract. Second, the damages allocate risk between the two parties. The more risk-averse party can, in effect, buy some insurance from the less risk-averse party. The damages may be specified by the parties at the time of the contracting or determined by the courts at the time of breach. The economic literature on contract law usually assumes that the court provides the implicit terms of a contract, including the amount of damages, that the parties to the contract would have agreed to if contracting had been costless. By providing efficient implicit terms in contracts, courts reduce the costs of exchange. The perplexing aspect of the penalties-liquidated damages distinction is that there is a conflict between the apparent, but express, intention of the parties and the subsequent action of the courts...

IV. EX ANTE DETERMINATION OF DAMAGES

This section considers whether there are any circumstances in which the parties may wish to negotiate damages that exceed the actual loss. The basic principles of efficient damages can be illustrated with a simple model which I have discussed elsewhere. In that model a risk-neutral seller (the promisor) sells a product or service to a risk-averse buyer (the promisee). The product may fail to provide the anticipated service, imposing losses on the buyer. When the specific cause of breach, such as change in production cost, careless seller behavior, or a better offer by a third party, is not observable, the damage measure must be a compromise between the amount that will provide optimal insurance and the amount that will provide efficient seller breach or seller precautions against breach. If both the buyer and the seller are risk averse, the damages will also reflect risk sharing between the buyer and seller. The factors that influence the damage level are evaluated below, paying particular attention to the relationship between predetermined damages and the actual loss.

A. Risk Aversion

If the seller is risk neutral and the buyer is risk averse, it is beneficial to both parties for the seller to insure the buyer. The desired amount of insurance, ignoring incentives, will equal the actual loss when there are no nonpecuniary losses, as would be the case in a commercial setting. Damages in excess of full compensation would not appeal to a risk-averse buyer because he would face an unwanted variation in his income, depending on whether the product failed. He would not wish to pay a higher price for the product (to cover the added insurance cost) in order to increase risk.

If the buyer were risk preferring, a clause that specified damages in excess of losses would provide an opportunity to gamble . . .

It seems likely that the parties to most contracts are risk averse or at least risk neutral None of the commentators has pointed out a case in which gambling was the motivation for unreasonable damages, and it is unlikely that a preference for risk prevails in the commercial world.

Goetz and Scott argue that the court's unwillingness to compensate nonpecuniary losses following breach of contract has led courts to under-compensate victims of breach and has induced contracting parties to attempt to contract around the courts' rules. Goetz and Scott conclude that damage clauses calling for apparently excessive payments should be enforced in order to insure these losses. However, I have shown that it is usually irrational to insure such losses [see above, p 599]. The insurance decision involves transferring income from the state of the world in which the contract is not breached (a higher price will be paid for the contract) to the state of the world in which the contract is breached (damages will be received if breach occurs). If the loss is nonpecuniary, it is likely that the utility of the additional income in the breach state will fall short of the utility of the forgone income in the nonbreach state. Consequently nonpecuniary losses would not usually be fully compensated in an efficient contract. Therefore there will be few situations in which nonpecuniary losses provide an explanation for damages that are viewed as unreasonable by courts.

[Rea then considers the 'risk' of random higher offers from third parties and concludes that this does not explain stipulations for unreasonable damages either.]

B. Moral Hazard

Clarkson, Miller, and Muris (henceforth referred to as CMM) and Muris claim that economic efficiency requires that the courts not enforce damage clauses in situations in which the nonbreaching party can influence the probability of breach and will benefit from breach. Their argument does not explain why damages would deliberately be set in excess of losses. Moral hazard, which arises because the buyer's precautions cannot be unobserved, will be taken into account at the time of the bargain and will lead to a reduction in the predetermined damage level below the actual damages.

C. Imperfect Enforcement

Borrowing from the literature on enforcement of criminal laws, one can argue that damages should be punitive when the costs of detection or enforcement are such that breachers will be penalized with a probability less than one. For example, the breach may be costly to detect in franchise contracts. The franchisor is interested in maintaining quality of service, but it is costly to monitor continually the quality of all of the franchisees. Termination of the contract by the franchisor, imposing a substantial loss on the franchisee, may be an efficient method of encouraging quality. The same analysis would apply to termination-at-will employment contracts. Terminations of franchises and employment have not typically been challenged as penalties. It does not seem likely that breaches will go undetected in the kinds of cases which occur most frequently, such as delay in completion of a construction contract.

D. Penalties as a Signal

In many situations the promisor may know the probability of breach but the promisee may not. In the second edition of his text Posner points out that penalties promote efficient exchange by signaling a party's intention to honor his contracts. Although no one ever knows for sure that he will honor a contract, those who know that they are more likely to honor than others will find it less costly to agree to penalty clauses. If buyers cannot differentiate low risk from high risk sellers, a seller's acceptance of a penalty clause is a signal of a low probability of breach . . .

Even if signaling is the primary motive for damage clauses, there does not appear to be any reason a signal would involve a damage clause in excess of the actual loss. This can be demonstrated by considering a situation in which *(a)* there is only one type of customer with one type of loss. *(b)* there are numerous sellers who have different degrees of reliability, and (c) sellers can signal their reliability by offering guarantees or liquidated damages. If the damages equal the actual loss, the extent of reliability becomes irrelevant for the buyer. He will simply choose the lowest-cost seller offering full compensation in the event of breach. Sellers of less reliable products with the same manufacturing cost will not be able to compete in the market. The low-cost sellers, taking into account the buyers' losses, can drive the others out of the market without offering damages in excess of actual losses. . . .

In the next example consider a market in which buyers have different amounts of losses resulting from product failure. Sellers will offer different guarantees and degrees of reliability, depending on the type of buyer. An individual who expects to sustain a loss L . . . will purchase from the reliable seller, and those expecting only loss L_2 (less than L_1) will buy from the unreliable seller. Other sellers with higher costs for a given level of liquidated damages cannot survive in the market. Again, there is no reason a seller would signal reliability by offering damages in excess of the actual loss. Such a contract would always be inferior to a contract which compensates the buyer for his actual loss . . .

E. Probability of Breach Incorrectly Estimated

If the buyer overestimates the probability of breach or the seller underestimates the probability of breach, the buyer will find it desirable to buy more than full insurance. Cooter suggests that this leads to inefficiency. However, it is not necessarily true that both parties can be made better off by limiting damages to full compensation. A mandatory change in damages will lead to adjustments in precautions against breach which could make the parties worse off.

Misperception of risk explains why two parties might agree to penalty clauses, but it does not explain why courts refuse to enforce these clauses while at the same time underliquidated damages are enforced. Underliquidated damages would arise when the buyer underestimates the probability of breach and/or the seller overestimates the probability. Usually the buyer must assume that the seller has better information concerning the probability of breach and will be wise to specify that damages equal the actual loss.

F. Measurement Problems

When the buyer perceives that he will suffer a loss as a result of a breach of contract but realizes that the actual amount of the loss will be difficult to prove, he may wish to specify the damages at the time that the contract is signed. There is no incentive for him to overstate the loss because this would add to the contract price. At the same time he would not want to underestimate the loss because this would increase the risk that he would bear. After a breach, the victim has an incentive to exaggerate his loss, and the cost of negotiating a settlement or going to trial is high when losses cannot be easily measured. The expected sum of ex ante and ex post transaction costs may be reduced by predetermining damages, particularly if the probability of breach is high. The common law and the U.C.C. recognize the useful role of predetermined damages in situations in which losses are difficult to measure or prove, and courts have been inclined to enforce damage clauses in those situations.

G. Conclusion on Ex Ante Unreasonableness

The discussion in this section has indicated that the parties to a contract are unlikely to agree ex ante to damages that exceed the expected loss. It is rational to agree to excess damages when the optimal insurance amount exceeds full compensation, when only a fraction of the breaches can be detected, when the promisee is overly pessimistic, or when the promisor is overly optimistic. These circumstances are likely to be infrequent. On the other hand, predetermined damages may be set below the expected loss if the promisee wishes to bear some of the risk, if he can influence the probability of breach, if his losses are below average, or if he has non-pecuniary losses. Damages may also be set below the actual losses if the promisee underestimates the probability or size of loss or the promisor overestimates the probability of loss.

What can the court conclude in a situation in which damages are ex ante unreasonably large? There are at least four possible explanations for such a conclusion. First, the excess damages may have been optimal. In light of the discussion above this seems unlikely.

A second explanation for a finding of unreasonable damages is that the court made an incorrect evaluation of the loss. Although it is tempting to conclude that the existence of the clause is prima facie evidence of the court's mistake, much of the law rests on the assumption that courts can measure losses with a sufficient degree of accuracy to justify the court's intervention. The penalty doctrine implicitly recognizes the possibility of court error by tending to enforce damage clauses when the loss is difficult to evaluate. Furthermore, damages not ordinarily awarded, such as attorney's fees, are recognized as losses when a damage clause is evaluated.

A third explanation is that there has been a procedural deficiency in the formation of the contract. For example, one party may not have realized the implications of the damage clause. Such a situation is more likely to arise when one party is an unsophisticated customer than in a commercial setting.

A fourth explanation for excess damages is that the parties, although knowledgeable, made a mistake about the nature of the contract, the possible loss, the probability of loss, or the implications of the damage clause. It is argued below that the mistake is likely to be mutual.

The third and fourth explanations for excess damages seem the most reasonable. Consequently it might be efficient for courts to use unreasonable ex ante damages as evidence of unconscionability or mistake, given the difficulty of observing these two problems.

... Although the penalty doctrine addresses the substance of a contract, the existence of ex ante unreasonable clauses may be evidence of procedural unconscionability. Given the difficulty of detecting unconscionability, evidence of excessive damages may be a useful indicator of its existence.

REFERENCES

Chung, 'On the Social Optionality of Liquidated Damges Clauses: An Economic Analysis' (1992) 8 J Law, Econ & Organisation 280.

Clarkson, Muller and Muris, 'Liquidated Damages v Penalties: Sense or Nonsense?' [1978] Wisconsin LR 351.

Goetz and Scott, 'Liquidated Damages. Penalties and the Just Compensation Principle' (1977) 77 Col LR 554.

Muris, 'Opportunistic Behaviour and the Law of Contracts' (1981) 65 Minnesota LR 521.

Talley, 'Contract Renegotiation, Mechanism Design, and the Liquidated Damage Rule' (1994) 46 Stan L Rev 1195.

In the cases discussed so far, the sum alleged to be a penalty has been payable in the event of a breach of contract. It is quite common to provide for the payment of money on an event that is not a breach. It has usually been held that the penalty rules apply only when the event that triggers the obligation to pay is a breach of contract.

This distinction has been the basis of a number of hire-purchase cases. In a typical hire-purchase contract, the owner (the finance company) is entitled to bring the contract, to an end in a number of events, some of which involve breaches of contract (eg repudiation by the hirer) and some of which do not (the hirer's death or bankruptcy). In addition, the hirer is usually given an option to terminate the contract. Usually, the agreement provides for the same consequences in all of these cases: the hirer has to make further payments to bring the total paid up to a predetermined figure, often two-thirds of the total price. The Court of Appeal has consistently held that a hirer who breaks the contract by failing to pay an instalment can argue that the clause is penal, but that one who exercises his option to return the goods cannot.

The House of Lords was given the opportunity to decide the question in *Bridge v Campbell Discount Co Ltd* [1962] AC 600, but refused to do so in any helpful fashion. In that case, the hirer had written to the owner: 'I am very sorry but I will not be able to pay any more payments on the Bedford Dormobile.' In the Court of Appeal, this letter was treated as an exercise of the hirer's option to return the goods, and the minimum payment provision was held enforceable. The House of Lords (Viscount Simonds dissenting) held that the letter was not an exercise of the option but a repudiation, and had no difficulty in holding the clause penal, since, in Lord Radcliffe's words, 'it is a sliding scale of compensation, but a scale that slides in the wrong direction'. The shorter the time for which the hirer had kept the vehicle, the less the owners would lose through its depreciation, but the more the hirer would have to pay after termination.

This left it unnecessary to decide whether the Court of Appeal was right that the penalty rules did not apply if the hirer merely exercised the option. Viscount Simonds and Lord Morton thought they were; Lords Denning and Devlin, although for different reasons, thought they were wrong. Lord Radcliffe did not reach a definite view. However, the question came before the House again, although in a very different factual context, in *Export Credits Guarantee Department v Universal Oil Products Co* [1983] 2 All ER 205. The House of Lords held that a clause could not be a penalty if the sum was not payable on a breach of contract.

2. Advance payments, deposits and forfeitures

What is the position if the contract provides that one party will pay money to the other in advance, and after this payment has been made or has fallen due, the contract is justifiably terminated by one party because of the other party's breach?

(a) Advance payments by innocent party

If the money has been paid and the party *to whom it has been paid* is the party who has broken the contract, the party who has paid can recover the money, either in an action for damages or in an action for restitution (see Chapter 24). If the money is due but has not been paid by the innocent party, it will normally cease to be payable (although the innocent party might be liable in damages for any loss caused by the failure to pay promptly).

(b) Advance payments by party in breach

If *the party who has paid the money* is the party in breach, it is important to draw a distinction between payments on account, on the one hand, and deposits and money paid under provisions that state that in the event of default it is to be forfeited, on the other.

Payments on account

In contracts of sale, the usual rule is that advance payments on account may be recovered, although the seller can set off its actual loss: *Dies v British and International Mining and Finance Corpn Ltd* [1939] 1 KB 724. In *Hyundai Heavy Industries Co Ltd v Papadopoulos* [1980] 2 All ER 29, the House of Lords said that advance payments made in a shipbuilding contract could not be recovered. The distinction has been explained as follows. In a contract of sale, the seller's right to the money is conditional on the subsequent performance by delivery; in the shipbuilding case, the money was viewed as unconditional payment for the work already in progress (see *McDonald v Dennys Lascelles Ltd* (1933) 48 CLR 457, 476–478 and

Beatson (1981) 97 LQR 389). In *Rover International Ltd v Cannon Film Sales Ltd (No 3)* [1989] 3 All ER 423, Kerr LJ said (at 439–440):

The question is whether there was any consideration in the nature of part performance for which the instalment was payable, as in the *Hyundai Heavy Industries* case, or whether the instalment was payable in advance of any performance which was required from [the defaulting party].

He pointed out that in this context, as in the *Fibrosa* case (above), consideration refers to the promised performance, not the promise itself.

If the instalment is due but has not yet been paid at the date the contract is terminated, and if it had been paid it would be returnable under the rule just stated, it ceases to be payable (ibid).

■ *Stocznia Gdanska SA v Latvian Shipping Co*
[1998] 1 All ER 883, House of Lords

In this case, the plaintiff shipbuilders had entered into agreements for the design, building and delivery of six ships for the second defendant, a wholly owned subsidiary of the first defendant. The plaintiffs were a Polish company and the first defendants a Latvian company. The contracts were of a kind typically to be found in shipbuilding, requiring payment in instalments, the second instalment to be paid on the plaintiffs giving notice that 'the first and second section of the vessel's hull had been joined on the berth where the vessel is being constructed'. The contract contained a cl 5.05, which set out the remedies of the seller in the event of default by the purchaser. This read as follows (the numbering of the paragraphs is taken from the speech of Lord Goff and not from the original text of the draftsman):

[1] If the Purchaser defaults in the payment of any amount due to the Seller under sub-clauses (b) or (c) or (d) of Clause 5.02 for twenty-one (21) days after the date when such payment has fallen due the Seller shall be entitled to rescind the Contract.

[2] In the event of such rescission by the Seller of this Contract due to the Purchaser's default as provided for in this Clause, the Seller shall be entitled to retain and apply the instalments already paid by the Purchaser to the recovery of the Seller's loss and damage and at the same time the Seller shall have the full right and power either to complete or not to complete the Vessel and to sell the Vessel at a public or private sale on such terms and conditions as the Seller deems reasonable provided that the Seller is always obliged to mitigate all losses and damages due to any such Purchaser's default.

[3] The proceeds received by the Seller from the sale and the instalments already paid and retained shall be applied by the Seller as mentioned herinabove as follows:

[i] First, in payment of all reasonable costs and expenses of the sale of the Vessel.

[ii] Second, if the Vessel has been completed, in or towards satisfaction of the unpaid balance of the Contract Price, or if the Vessel has not been completed in or towards satisfaction of the unpaid amount of the cost incurred by the Seller prior to the date of sale on account of construction of the Vessel, including work, labour and materials which the Seller would have been entitled to receive if the vessel had been completed and delivered.

[iii] Third, the balance of the proceeds, if any, shall belong to the Purchaser and shall forthwith be paid over to the Purchaser by the Seller.

[4] In the event of the proceeds from the sale together with payments retained by the Seller being insufficient to pay the Seller, the Purchaser shall be liable for the deficiency and shall pay the same to the Seller upon its demand.

The plaintiffs were working simultaneously on two ships. The defendants came to realise that, although they wanted the ships, they could not afford to pay for them. There were attempts to negotiate a new contract, which came to nothing. The plaintiffs gave a keel laying notice in respect of ships 1 and 2. The defendants did not make the appropriate payment and the plaintiffs then gave notices under cl 5.05 bringing the contract to an end.

The plaintiffs then purported to give keel-laying notices in regards to ships 3 and 4, the keels being those in respect of which notices had in fact already been given in relation to ships 1 and 2. No payments were made and notices were given terminating contracts 3 and 4 under cl 5.05 and keel-laying notices were then given in respect of ships 5 and 6. The House of Lords had to sort out the results of this extraordinary series of events, a task made more complicated by a number of procedural mishaps that the case had incurred on its way through the lower courts. The central points of the House of Lords decision were:

1. clause 5.05, although complex, was not to be treated as an exhaustive statement of the plaintiffs' rights in the event of breach by the defendants. The general principle is that express statements of the parties' rights in a contract would not oust their common law basic rights unless very clear words were used;
2. as a matter of construction of the contracts, it was not possible to give keel-laying notices in respect of any given keel for more than one ship. Again, very clear words would be needed to produce this striking result. The speech of Lord Goff is particularly instructive as to the technique judges should use to solve this kind of question;
3. the plaintiffs did not have any rights under cl 5.05 against the defendants in respect of ships 3, 4, 5 and 6 since they had not given an effective keel-laying notice. However, the defendants had made it clear that they were not prepared to perform contracts 3, 4, 5 and 6 so the plaintiffs had their ordinary common law rights in respect of an anticipatory breach.

(The whole point of the plaintiffs' apparently strange tactics was, of course, to improve their position in respect of remedies. It is worth taking a few moments to work out how the plaintiffs would have been better off if their tactics had succeeded.)

For further proceedings, see *Stocznia Gdanska SA v Latvian Shipping Co (No 3)* [2002] EWCA Civ 889 [2002] 2 All ER (Comm) 768.

Deposits and money paid subject to forfeiture

A deposit is a sum paid in advance that the payee may keep if the payor defaults. The general rule appears to be that the payee can keep the whole of the deposit, even though it exceeds the loss he suffers as a result of the breach: *Howe v Smith* (1884) 27 Ch D 89. If the deposit is due but has not been paid, the innocent party may recover it. In *Damon Cia Naviera SA v Hapag-Lloyd International SA, The Blankenstein* [1985] 1 All ER 475, the contract provided for the payment of a deposit of 10 per cent, or $236,500, upon execution of a formal agreement. The buyers repudiated the contract before execution of the formal agreement and the Court of Appeal held, by a majority, that the sellers could recover damages of the same amount to compensate them for loss of the deposit. The seller's overall loss was a mere $60,000.

The rule that the money may be kept even though it exceeds the innocent party's loss seems to apply also to money paid under provisions for it to be forfeited in case of default: *Mayson v Clouet* [1924] AC 980. But while the courts continue to enforce deposits stringently (eg *The Blankenstein*—although it is, of course, possible that at the time the contract was made, a 10 per cent deposit was a pre-estimate of the seller's likely loss), the courts' treatment of forfeiture clauses has not been wholly consistent. They look very much like penalties paid in advance, and in *Public Works Comr v Hills* [1906] AC 368, the Privy Council granted a contractor in default relief against forfeiture of 'security deposits' given to the employer, ordering that the employer should return all but the actual amount of its loss. This case was cited with approval in *Jobson v Johnson* (noted at p 592) and was applied in the next case, below.

One of the most common cases of a deposit is the deposit (customarily 10 per cent of the price) paid by a purchaser of land when contracts are exchanged. It has recently been decided that, in such cases, the court has power to order a return of the deposit under the Law of Property Act 1925, s 49(2). This provides:

Where the court refuses to grant specific performance of the contract, or in any action for the return of a deposit, the court may, if it thinks fit, order the repayment of any deposit.

(See *Universal Corpn v Five Ways Properties Ltd* [1979] 1 All ER 552 and *Dimsdale Developments (South East) Ltd v De Haan* (1983) 47 P & CR 1.)

What is the position if the Law of Property Act 1925, s 49, does not apply?

See *Union Eagle Ltd v Golden Achievements Ltd* [1997] 2 All ER 215, discussed on p 590.

In *Luong Dinh Luu v Sovereign Development Pty Ltd* [2006] NSWCA 40, a contract for the sale of land provided for a 10 per cent deposit but the seller accepted a sum of about 1 per cent. There was a contractual provision for the payment of the balance if the seller defaulted. The New South Wales Court of Appeal held that this provision was penal.

■ Workers Trust and Merchant Bank Ltd v Dojap Investments Ltd

[1993] 2 All ER 370, Privy Council

A contract for the sale of land provided for a deposit of 25 per cent of the purchase price. The purchaser paid the deposit but then defaulted. It claimed relief against forfeiture of the deposit. The Court of Appeal in Jamaica granted relief to the extent that the deposit exceeded 10 per cent. Both parties appealed.

Lord Browne-Wilkinson

...In general, a contractual provision which requires one party in the event of his breach of the contract to pay or forfeit a sum of money to the other party is unlawful as being a penalty, unless such provision can be justified as being a payment of liquidated damages, being a genuine pre-estimate of the loss which the innocent party will incur by reason of the breach. One exception to this general rule is the provision for the payment of a deposit by the purchaser on a contract for the sale of land. Ancient law has established that the forfeiture of such a deposit (customarily 10% of the contract price) does not fall within the general rule and can be validly forfeited even though the amount of the deposit bears no reference to the anticipated loss to the vendor flowing from the breach of contract.

This exception is anomalous and at least one textbook writer has been surprised that the courts of equity ever countenanced it: see Farrand *Contract and Conveyancing* (4th edn, 1983) p 204. The special treatment afforded to such a deposit derives from the ancient custom of providing an earnest for the performance of a contract in the form of giving either some physical token of earnest (such as a ring) or earnest money. The history of the law of deposits can be traced to the Roman law of arra, and possibly further back still: see *Howe v Smith* (1884) 27 Ch D 89 at 101–102 per Fry LJ. Ever since the decision in *Howe v Smith* the nature of such a deposit has been settled in English law. Even in the absence of express contractual provision, it is an earnest for the performance of the contract: in the event of completion of the contract the deposit is applicable towards payment of the purchase price; in the event of the purchaser's failure to complete in accordance with the terms of the contract, the deposit is forfeit, equity having no power to relieve against such forfeiture.

However, the special treatment afforded to deposits is plainly capable of being abused if the parties to a contract, by attaching the label 'deposit' to any penalty, could escape the general rule which renders penalties unenforceable. ...

In the view of their Lordships . . . [it] is not possible for the parties to attach the incidents of a deposit to the payment of a sum of money unless such sum is reasonable as earnest money. The question therefore is whether or not the deposit of 25% in this case was reasonable as being in line with the traditional concept of earnest money or was in truth a penalty intended to act in terrorem.

The Chief Justice tested the question of 'reasonableness' by reference to the evidence before him that it was of common occurrence for banks in Jamaica selling property at auction to demand deposits of between 15% and 50%. He held that, since this was a common practice, it was reasonable. Like the Court of Appeal, their Lordships are unable to accept this reasoning. In order to be reasonable a true deposit must be objectively operating as 'earnest money' and not as a penalty. To allow the test of reasonableness to depend upon the practice of one class of vendor, which exercises considerable financial muscle, would be to allow them to evade the law against penalties by adopting practices of their own.

However, although their Lordships are satisfied that the practice of a limited class of vendors cannot determine the reasonableness of a deposit, it is more difficult to define what the test should be. Since a true deposit may take effect as a penalty, albeit one permitted by law, it is hard to draw a line between a reasonable, permissible amount of penalty and an unreasonable, impermissible penalty. In their Lordships' view the correct approach is to start from the position that, without logic but by long continued usage both in the United Kingdom and formerly in Jamaica, the customary deposit has been 10%. A vendor who seeks to obtain a larger amount by way of forfeitable deposit must show special circumstances which justify such a deposit.

. . .

Their Lordships agree with the Court of Appeal that [the evidence in this case] falls far short of showing that it was reasonable to stipulate for a forfeitable deposit of 25% of the purchase price or indeed any deposit in excess of 10%. . . .

The question therefore arises whether the court has jurisdiction to relieve against the express provision of the contract that the deposit of 25% was to be forfeited. Although there is no doubt that the court will not order the payment of a sum contracted for (but not yet paid) if satisfied that such sum is in reality a penalty, it was submitted that the court could not order, by way of relief, the repayment of sums already paid to the defendant in accordance with the terms of the contract which, on breach, the contract provided should be forfeit. The basis of this submission was the view expressed in a considered obiter dictum of Romer LJ in *Stockloser v Johnson* [1954] 1 QB 476 at 495–496.

In that case there was a contract for the sale of quarry machinery to the plaintiff, the purchase price to be paid by instalments. The contract provided that in the event of a default in payment of the instalments, the vendor could retake the machinery and all instalments of the price previously paid should be forfeit. Pursuant to the contract, the plaintiff took possession and used the machinery but defaulted in payment of an instalment. The defendant forfeited the instalments already paid. In the action, the plaintiff sought to recover the instalments, alleging that their forfeiture was a penalty. The Court of Appeal unanimously held that the forfeiture did not constitute a penalty on the facts of that case but went on to express conflicting views, obiter, as to whether, if the forfeiture had been a penalty, the court had jurisdiction to order repayment. Somervell and Denning LJJ expressed the view that there was such jurisdiction. Romer LJ held that there was no general right in equity to mend the parties' bargain and that, even where there was jurisdiction to relieve from forfeiture, that could only be exercised by allowing a late completion to a party who was in default in performance but willing and able to carry out the terms of the contract belatedly.

Their Lordships do not find it necessary to decide which of those two views is correct in a case where a party is seeking relief from forfeiture for breach of contract to pay a price by instalments, the party in default having been let into possession in the meantime. This is not such a case. In the view of their Lordships, since the 25%, deposit was not a true deposit by way of earnest, the provision for its forfeiture was a plain penalty. There is clear authority that in a case of a sum paid by one party to another under the contract as security for the performance of that contract, a provision for its forfeiture in the event of non-performance is a penalty from which the court will give relief by ordering repayment of the sum so paid, less any damage actually proved to have been suffered as a result of non-completion: *Public Works Comr v Hills* [1906] AC 368. Accordingly, there is jurisdiction in the court to order repayment of the 25% deposit.

The Court of Appeal took a middle course by ordering the repayment of 15% out of the 25% deposit, leaving the bank with its normal 10% deposit which it was entitled to forfeit. Their Lordships are unable to agree that this is the correct order. The bank has contracted for a deposit consisting of one globular sum, being 25% of the purchase price. If a deposit of 25% constitutes an unreasonable sum and is not therefore a true deposit, it must be repaid as a whole. The bank has never stipulated for a reasonable deposit of 10%: therefore it has no right to such a limited payment. If it cannot establish that the whole sum was truly a deposit, it has not contracted for a true deposit at all.

Appeal dismissed; cross-appeal allowed.

NOTES

1.   The Board left open the question raised in *Stockloser v Johnson* as to whether relief can be given against forfeiture of instalments of the price paid by a purchaser who has been let into possession of the property. Can you see any reason why this should not be subject to the same general rule? Conversely, can you see any reason why it *might* not be penal for the purchaser in such a case to lose the money it has paid?

2.   Are deposits that go beyond the customary 10 per cent subject to the rules on penalty clauses or are they subject to equitable relief against forfeiture, as suggested by Denning and Somervell LJJ in *Stockloser?* What difference might it make?

3.   What is the position if there is no customary amount for a deposit? Suppose a customer agrees to buy a new car from a dealer and pays a deposit of 10 per cent of the purchase price, the balance to be paid in cash on delivery of the new car. The customer repudiates the agreement—perhaps she loses her job, or is offered a new job with a company car provided—and the dealer resells the car for a similar price to another customer. Since the demand for this model exceeds the supply, the dealer does not suffer any reduction in the volume of its sales (see p 668) and its losses are much smaller than the deposit. Can the customer recover the deposit less the dealer's actual loss?

4.   It is possible to infer from Lord Browne-Wilkinson's speech that he thought the use of deposits not related to the payee's loss is permitted *only* in the case of sales of land and that all other deposits must be genuine pre-estimates. This was one of the provisional solutions put forward by the Law Commission in its Working Paper No 61, 'Penalty Clauses and Forfeiture of Monies Paid'; it does not represent the law as it is generally understood (eg Working Paper No 61, para 53).

5.   It seems strange enough that the innocent party is entitled to retain a deposit, or forfeit payments made, even though the effect is to penalise the party in breach; stranger still that the innocent party can recover damages as well if the loss he suffers exceeds the deposit: *Lock v Bell* [1931] 1 Ch 35. What justification is there for permitting the innocent party to retain it without enquiring whether or not it is a penalty? The only distinction between a deposit or forfeiture clause and a penalty clause seems to be that the party in breach has already parted with his money. The Law Commission, in its Working Paper No 61 provisionally concluded that the fact that a deposit is paid in advance is not sufficient to bring home to the payor that it may be lost if he defaults, and that deposits and clauses providing for the forfeiture of payments made should be subject to the penalty rules (paras 57–67).

VII. REPRISE: LIABILITY FOR CONSEQUENTIAL DAMAGES

Should the law routinely award consequential damages (subject to the remoteness and mitigation rules)? Epstein notes that parties frequently limit sellers' liability, either by 'underliquidating' agreed damages (see note 3 on p 692) or by limiting the seller's liability to repair or replacement of the goods (a form of exclusion clause). He makes this the basis of a more general argument.

■ **Epstein, 'Beyond Foreseeability: Consequential Damages in the Law of Contract'** (1989)
18 J Legal Studies 105, 108, 114–128, 120

Damage rules are no different from any other terms of a contract. They should be understood solely as default provisions subject to variation by contract. The operative rules should be chosen by the parties for their own purposes, not by the law for its purposes.

　. . .

CONSEQUENTIAL DAMAGES

With consequential damages, the superiority of the expectation measure of damages is far from self-evident. Whatever the abstract law of contract, many ordinary sales contracts contain warranty provisions that specify both the obligation of the supplier and the remedy in the event of breach. The provisions widely adopted across different industries stipulate for liquidated damages or call for the repair or replacement of damaged goods at the option of the seller. While the full expectation measure of damage may require the seller to bear the cost of delivery to the firm, contracts often leave that loss on the buyer, who likewise may receive no compensation for any interim loss of use. Often the warranty is voided where the product was damaged by excessive or impermissible use by the buyer. Most notably, all liability for personal injury or property damages is excluded. Without question, these warranties call for a risk-sharing arrangement, which leaves the buyer worse off when the seller honors the warranty in full than he, the buyer, would have been if the product had worked perfectly in the first place. Warranty restrictions similar to these led the New Jersey Court in *Henningsen v Bloomfield Motors, Inc* to invalidate these warranties as limitations on recovery for personal injury and to usher in the modern age of product liability law by imposing full tort liability for consequential damages.

Against this backdrop of express contractual provisions, there is ample reason to doubt that the expectation measure of damage of the classical common law maximizes the joint gains of the parties ex ante. If it did, we should expect to observe it frequently in practice, which is decidedly not the case. The failure to observe this standard in practice cannot easily be attributed to the systematic ignorance of buyers and sellers in all product markets, for someone must have the incentive to break the logjam if making the plaintiff whole on breach is the ideal contract measure of damages. The better approach, therefore, is to ask why it is that informed parties might not choose to use this damage measure. A closer inspection of the expectation measure of damages reveals some costs of its application.

First, under the orthodox view, the basic rule provides for full consequential damages, but (like the tort rules of contributory negligence it parallels) it then allows the defendant an affirmative defense, where the plaintiff is in breach of some condition precedent. The two halves of this rule thus raise two high-stakes issues (plaintiff's and defendant's breach) on which enormous liabilities can turn. As a general matter, the parties' investment in litigation increases with both the uncertainty of the outcome and the size of the stakes. Ex ante, the parties wish to avoid this cost, as it represents a deadweight loss to both sides. In addition, full consequential damages raise the real risk that the plaintiff, while in the better position to avoid the loss, will, in fact not take the right steps to do so. Any money that is spent on further loss reduction is his own, while the money that is saved is the defendant's. The temptation to maximize private gain results in the systematic externalization of losses: why should I spend my money to reduce his damages? The law recognizes this and imposes a duty of mitigation of damages to counter this all too-tenacious human tendency. But that duty is a very imprecise tool to use against so persistent a business practice, for defendant's monitoring of plaintiff conduct, whether under a misuse or a mitigation doctrine, is both costly and error prone. The expectation rules with affirmative defenses may not offer the best prospect of minimizing the total costs of contractual failure.

The weaknesses of the expectation damage system are thrown into high relief by comparing it with an alternative regime that gives fixed damages without making any provision for separate affirmative defenses. This system of damages could be superior for both parties because of the way in which it reduces the joint costs of litigation while preserving the incentives on both sides to perform as agreed. The plaintiff whose level of recovery is fixed in advance has a powerful incentive to mitigate his loss. Any rule of fixed damages, independent of subsequent events, makes him face the identical incentives of a single owner of all relevant inputs. Every dollar he spends in mitigation now results in a dollar's saving for himself from the reduction in consequential damages. He will therefore behave exactly as he would if he had been the sole and original author of his own harm. While one should not expect perfection in the delicate task of mitigation—the innocent party may be a complex firm with agency-cost problems of its own—clearly there is nothing that the legal rule could do to improve performance once it has eliminated this potential conflict of interest posed by any ad hoc mitigation rule. There is no need to build mitigation doctrines explicitly into legal rules in order to create the correct incentives to mitigate. Any fixed lump-sum damage award has just that effect, regardless of the level at which it is set.

The amount of the fixed damages is critical, however, in influencing the frequency of breach by the plaintiff. If damages were exceedingly high, the level of precautions taken would be low, given the fixed rate of return that the plaintiff could expect to receive. Similarly, the risk of fraudulent or dubious claims of seller's breach would increase as well. Where the seller is suing for the buyer's failure to accept goods or to pay for goods accepted, the question of seller's breach is relatively unimportant, so that all incentives can be directed toward the conduct of the single wrongdoer. Matters are far more complicated with lost profits, personal injury, and property damages, for here the possibility that both sides will be in breach is far more likely. Setting damages below actual loss is far more important in this context precisely because there is frequent need to restrain abuses by defendants and plaintiffs simultaneously.

Any effort to constrain misbehavior by the buyer invites misbehavior by the seller. But the critical question is the rate of substitution between buyer and seller incentives for breach. Here there are at least two reasons to think that the control of buyer's misconduct will often be the more important issue, pointing to a lower level of fixed damages. First, reputational constraints tend to operate far more powerfully upon institutional defendants than they do upon individual buyers. Major failures are perceived by the market, resulting in a loss of future sales that can best be avoided by maintaining product quality.

Second, it is important to note that even low damage awards can exert a considerable incentive on a defendant to perform his contracts. Consider the standard repair and replacement warranties set out above. Here defendant must lose from any individual transaction if required, say, to refund the consideration received or to make repairs while still having to bear other costs under the contract. In principle, the defendant will have no incentive to supply defective products so long as his breach costs him more than he gains. Even a low level of nonperformance is sufficient to remove all the profits that the defendant derives from other contracts that are performed successfully. The combination of reputational and financial losses helps keep the defendants in check.

The last point concerns administrative costs. Fixing these damages reduces the associated uncertainty and, therefore, the costs of administering the remedial provisions. Nonetheless, if there is any serious question whether the defendant was in breach, the costs of litigation will increase as the size of the damage award increases, even if damages are fixed. These administrative costs will become far larger if the level of damages is both large and uncertain and subject to reduction for plaintiff's misconduct and failure to mitigate. All in all, the optimal contracting strategy does not appear to call for the high conse-quential damages, subject to defense rules, that courts have tended to adopt. Less clearly, within the class of fixed damage awards, there is reason to expect these damages to be kept relatively limited, which is what the express contracts have typically provided....

COMMON CARRIERS

[This] argument helps explain the contractual provisions governing the liability of common carriers for lost profits attributable to the delayed shipment of goods. The expectation measure of damage calls forth the question of extensive litigation over both plaintiff's and defendant's conduct. In contrast, the use of a fixed tariff regardless of circumstances helps advance the joint interests of the parties. It gives the plaintiff the incentive to mitigate losses, while imposing on the defendant some financial incentives to perform as promised, which are doubtless augmented by the fear of reputational loss. The small level of damages awarded reduces the costs of both litigation and settlement....

NOTE

What assumptions does Epstein make about (a) the nature of the markets concerned, and (b) the characteristics of the buyers/consignors of goods? If the law has to adopt a single general default rule (ie consequential losses should, or should not, be recoverable), which rule would you favour? (You may like to return to this question after you have read Section 8.)

QUESTIONS

1.   What is the difference between the basic measure of damages in contract and the basic measure in tort? Construct an example that illustrates the difference.

2.   What is the so-called 'mitigation' rule?

3.   What is the remoteness rule? What justifications can be given for restricting the damages awarded in this way?

4.   In what circumstances will the courts award damages for non-pecuniary losses that were caused by a breach of contract?

5.   It has been argued that the combination of the mitigation and remoteness rules mean that the courts rarely award damages for full loss of expectation and that it would be more accurate to say that the normal measure of damages compensates the injured party for his proven, unavoidable losses, assessed by reference to comparable markets (see Collins, *Law of Contract*, 4th edn, 2003, p 418). Do you agree?

6.   What rules apply to clauses stating the damages to be paid by a party who has broken the contract?

7.   Are clauses providing for deposits or the forfeiture of money paid governed by the same rules or different ones? If the latter, what are the differences?

8.   A contract is terminated by one party because of the other's breach. The other party had made an advance payment. It was not paid as a deposit and there is no provision for for-feiture. When may the party in breach recover the money?

CHAPTER TWENTY-THREE

LITERAL ENFORCEMENT

I. SPECIFIC PERFORMANCE AND INJUNCTION

■ *Falcke v Gray*

(1859) 4 Drew 651

The defendant let her house to the plaintiff for six months, and gave him the option of purchasing at the end of the term certain articles of furniture at a valuation. Among the articles were what counsel described as 'a couple of large Oriental jars, with great ugly Chinese pictures upon them'. The valuer admitted that he was ignorant of the value of the vases, but a sum of £40 was eventually agreed on, although the defendant said in her evidence that she had been left the jars by a lady who had, she understood, been offered £100 for them by King George IV. The defendant was later offered £200 for the jars by a purchaser, to whom she had explained what had happened, and she accepted that offer. The plaintiff obtained an *ex parte* injunction against the defendant and the second purchaser, and then sought specific performance.

The Vice-Chancellor [Sir RT Kindersley]

The first ground of defence is that, this being a bill for the specific performance of a contract for the purchase of chattels, this Court will not interfere. But I am of opinion that the Court will not refuse to interfere simply because the contract relates to chattels, and that if there were no other objection the contract in this case is such a contract as the Court would specifically perform.

What is the difference in the view of the Court between realty and personalty in respect to the question whether the Court will interfere or not? Upon what principle does the Court decree specific performance of any contract whatever? Lord Redesdale in *Harnett v Yeilding* says: 'Whether Courts of Equity in their determinations on this subject have always considered what was the original foundation for decrees of this nature I very much doubt. I believe that from something of habit, decrees of this kind have been carried to an extent which has tended to injustice. Unquestionably the original foundation of these decrees was simply this, that damages at law would not give the party the compensation to which he was entitled; that is, would not put him in a situation as beneficial to him as if the agreement were specifically performed'. So that the principle on which a Court of Equity proceeds is this. A Court of law gives damages for the non-performance, but a Court of Equity says 'that is not sufficient—justice is not satisfied by that remedy'; and, therefore, a Court of Equity will decree specific performance because a mere compensation in damages is not a sufficient remedy and satisfaction for the loss of the performance of the contract.

Now why should that principle apply less to chattels? If in a contract for chattels damages will be a sufficient compensation, the party is left to that remedy. Thus if a contract is for the purchase of a certain quantity of coals, stock &c, this Court will not decree specific performance, because a person can go into the market and buy similar articles and get damages for any difference in the price of the articles in a Court of law. But if damages would not be a sufficient compensation, the principle, on which a Court of Equity decrees specific performance, is just as applicable to a contract for the sale and purchase of chattels, as to a contract for the sale and purchase of land.

In the present case the contract is for the purchase of articles of unusual beauty, rarity and distinction, so that damages would not be an adequate compensation for non-performance; and I am of opinion that a contract for articles of such a description is such a contract as this Court will enforce; and, in the absence of all other objection, I should have no hesitation in decreeing specific performance.

NOTES

1.   The purchaser's claim for specific performance was, in fact, denied in this case on the grounds that the consideration was inadequate, but there is some doubt whether the case is still supportable on this point: see Spry, *Equitable Remedies*, 4th edn, p 186–187.

2.   The second purchaser would be bound to hand over the jars if the plaintiff could get specific performance, since he took with notice of the plaintiff's claim. See further p 1205.

■ *Société des Industries Métallurgiques SA v Bronx Engineering Co Ltd*

[1975] 1 Lloyd's Rep 465, Court of Appeal

The sellers of a machine that they had built for the buyers alleged that the buyers had repudiated the contract, and advised them that it would be resold to a Canadian buyer. The buyers obtained an *ex parte* injunction restraining the sellers from removing the machine from the jurisdiction, but the judge refused to continue it until trial of the action. The Court of Appeal held that it would make an assumption that the buyers would succeed at trial in establishing a breach by the sellers: the question was thus whether specific performance would be granted at trial.

Lord Edmund Davies

...[T]he granting of such an injunction as is sought in the present case...is governed by s 52 of the Sale of Goods Act, 1893. That section enables the Court 'if it thinks fit' to order specific performance of a contract to deliver 'specific or ascertained goods'. For present purposes I understand the parties to accept that the machinery in question was 'ascertained goods' within the meaning of the section. But it is established law that such an order will not be made if damages would fully compensate the party wronged: *Whiteley Ltd v Hilt*. The crux of the present application accordingly, as I see it, is whether it is proper to draw the conclusion that damages would not or might well not duly compensate the plaintiffs if they establish a contractual breach by the defendants. That the subject-matter was not 'an ordinary article of commerce' is not open to doubt. That if they succeed the plaintiffs might well recover very substantial damages is certainly on the cards. But the defendants are not the only manufacturers of such machinery, and it lacks, in my judgment, the unique quality of such articles as that which was the subject-matter of the specific performance decree made in, for example, *Behnke v Bede Shipping Co Ltd*. That case is commonly cited in the textbooks as supporting the proposition that specific performance will be ordered of a contract for the sale of a ship, but merely to say that is to put the matter too broadly. It is of some importance to note that it was not just any ship, for, as Mr Justice Wright said...

'. . . in the present case there is evidence that the *City* was of peculiar and practically unique value to the plaintiff. She was a cheap vessel, being old, having been built in 1892, but her engines and boilers were practically new and such as to satisfy the German regulations, and hence the plaintiff could, as a German shipowner, have her at once put on the German register. A very experienced ship valuer has said that he knew of only one other comparable ship, but that could now have been sold. The plaintiff wants the ship for immediate use, and I do not think damages would be an adequate compensation.'

By way of contrast with that case, the real substance of the plaintiffs' claim here is that were they now obliged to go to another manufacturer, they would probably have to wait another 9–12 months before they could get delivery of such new machinery and that, by reason of that delay and other factors, they would stand to lose a substantial sum. There has been no suggestion of financial inability in the defendants to satisfy such a money judgment (whatever its dimensions) as might be awarded against them to cover all such items of damages as the plaintiffs could legitimately rely upon. While sympathizing with the dilemma in which the plaintiffs find themselves. I see nothing which removes this case from the ordinary run of cases arising out of commercial contracts where damages are claimed. Of course, if the plaintiffs are right, the delay that has arisen by reason of the assumed breach of the defendants will go to inflate their damages: the greater the delay the plaintiffs experience in getting such new machinery (despite their best efforts), the greater the potential liability of the defendants in the event of the plaintiffs' succeeding. But for my part I cannot see that, whatever be the balance of convenience of the parties to which reference has been made, the case is one which, on the authorities, justifies the defendants now being restrained from disposing of the machinery in question as they seek to do and claim they are entitled to do, the plaintiffs, on the other hand, meanwhile seeking to compel the defendants until the trial of the action in what must inevitably be the not very near future to maintain this machinery in store at an expense which runs into several thousand pounds a month. The defendants do undoubtedly run the risk of ultimately being mulcted in what may well be a most substantial sum, but that is a risk which they are seemingly prepared to take and, in my judgment, they must be left free to do so.

Lord Justice Buckley delivered a concurring judgment; **Lord Justice Ormrod** concurred.

Appeal dismissed.

NOTE

What distinction is there between this case and *Behnke v Bede?* Couldn't Behnke have had another ship fitted out so as to be registrable in Germany within a few months?

■ Sale of Goods Act 1979

Section 48A–48F (see p 620 above)

Section 52: Specific performance

(1) In any action for breach of contract to deliver specific or ascertained goods the court may, if it thinks fit, on the plaintiff's application, by its judgment or decree direct that the contract shall be performed specifically, without giving the defendant the option of retaining the goods on payment of damages.

(2) The plaintiff's application may be made at any time before judgment or decree.

(3) The judgment or decree may be unconditional, or on such terms and conditions as to damages, payment of the price and otherwise as seem just to the court.

(4) The provisions of this section shall be deemed to be supplementary to, and not in derogation of, the right of specific implement in Scotland.

■ *Sky Petroleum Ltd v VIP Petroleum Ltd*

[1974] 1 WLR 576

The defendants had agreed to sell the plaintiffs the latters' entire requirements of petrol and diesel fuel for the plaintiffs' filling stations, at fixed prices and with a minimum annual quantity being stipulated. During an oil crisis, when the plaintiffs had no prospect of finding an alternative source of supply, the defendants purported to terminate the contract on the ground that the plaintiffs had exceeded the credit provisions in the contract. The plaintiffs sought an interim injunction to restrain the defendants from withholding supplies.

Goulding J

... Now I come to the most serious hurdle in the way of the plaintiffs which is the well-known doctrine that the court refuses specific performance of a contract to sell and purchase chattels not specific or ascertained. That is a well-established and salutary rule, and I am entirely unconvinced by Mr Christie, for the plaintiffs, when he tells me that an injunction in the form sought by him would not be specific enforcement at all. The matter is one of substance and not of form, and it is, in my judgment, quite plain that I am, for the time being, specifically enforcing the contract if I grant an injunction. However, the ratio behind the rule is, as I believe, that under the ordinary contract for the sale of non-specific goods, damages are a sufficient remedy. That, to my mind, is lacking in the circumstances of the present case. The evidence suggests, and indeed it is common knowledge that the petroleum market is in an unusual state in which a would-be buyer cannot go out into the market and contract with another seller, possibly at some sacrifice as to price. Here, the defendants appear for practical purposes to be the plaintiffs' sole means of keeping their business going, and I am prepared so far to depart from the general rule as to try to preserve the position under the contract until a later date. I therefore propose to grant an injunction.

NOTES

1. Were the goods ascertained in this case? Suppose that the defendants had decided not to deliver petroleum to any buyer, but to stockpile it because they thought the price would rise. Could the plaintiffs have obtained an order of specific performance for the contract quantity?

2. The 'adequacy of damages test' is frequently applied when the plaintiff seeks an injunction, as well as when specific performance is sought. In *Evans Marshall & Co Ltd v Bertola SA* [1973] 1 WLR 349 at 379–380, Sachs LJ said:

    The standard question in relation to the grant of an injunction. 'Are damages an adequate remedy?', might perhaps, in the light of the authorities of recent years, be rewritten: 'Is it just, in all the circumstances, that a plaintiff should be confined to his remedy in damages?'

    The courts have repeatedly recognised that there can be claims under contracts in which, as here, it is unjust to confine a plaintiff to his damages for their breach. Great difficulty in estimating these damages is one factor that can be and has been taken into account. Another factor is the creation of certain areas of damage which cannot be taken into monetary account in a common law action for breach of contract: loss of goodwill and trade reputation are examples—see also, in another sphere, the judgment of Jenkins LJ in *Vine v National Dock Labour Board* which, albeit a dissenting judgment, was unanimously adopted in toto in the House of Lords. Generally, indeed, the grant of injunctions in contract cases stems from such factors.

    ...

    So far the question of adequacy of damages has been discussed on the footing that if judgment was recovered the sum awarded would be paid. But whenever the adequacy of damages falls to be considered in this class of case, there arises the further question—are the defendants good for the money?

3.   Although the *Sky Petroleum* case suggests a slightly more liberal attitude towards specific performance than earlier cases do, it is still the rule that a plaintiff will not get specific performance unless damages would not be an adequate remedy. Why?

■ Kronman, 'Specific Performance' (1978)
45 U Chicago LR 351, 357 363, 365–369

The most important common feature of these diverse cases on specific performance is the central role played by the idea of 'uniqueness'. If the 'subject matter of [a] contract is unique in character and cannot be duplicated' or if obtaining 'a substantial equivalent involves difficulty, delay, and inconvenience', a court will be more apt to compel specific performance. 'The fact that such a duplicate or equivalent cannot be so obtained does not necessarily show that money damages are not an adequate remedy, but is a fact that tends strongly in that direction'. Conversely, if the subject matter of a contract is such that 'its substantial equivalent for all practical purposes is readily obtainable from others than the defendant in exchange for a money payment, this fact will usually in the absence of other factors be sufficient to show that money damages are an adequate remedy for breach'. . . .

In common discourse 'unique' means without a substitute or equivalent. In the framework of conventional economic analysis, however, the concept of uniqueness is troublesome. . . .

[E]very good has substitutes, even if only very poor ones. Because all goods compete for consumer attention, a substantial change in the relative price of any good always affects the consumption of other goods. Economists are interested in determining how great a change in the price of one good is required to effect a change of given magnitude in the consumption of certain other goods. But these are really questions of degree, resting on the underlying assumption—fundamental to economic theory—that all goods are ultimately commensurable. If this assumption is accepted, the idea of a unique good loses meaning.

This point may be illustrated by a case that under present law would almost certainly be held to involve a unique good. Suppose that A contracts with Sotheby's to purchase the handwritten manuscript of Hobbes's *Leviathan.* If Sotheby's refuses to perform—perhaps because it has a more attractive offer from someone else—A will undoubtedly be disappointed. Yet no matter how strong his affection for Hobbes it is likely there are other things that would make A just as happy as getting the manuscript for the contract price. For example, A may be indifferent between purchasing the manuscript at the specified price and having twenty-five hours of violin lessons for the same amount. If so, then A will be fully compensated for the loss he suffers by Sotheby's breach upon receiving the difference between the cost of twenty-five hours' worth of violin lessons and the contract price. However, despite the fact that the manuscript has an economic substitute, a court would be likely to order specific performance of the contract (assuming Sotheby's still had the manuscript in its possession) on the ground that the subject matter of the contract is unique.

Pursuing the matter further it is not difficult to see why A's money damages remedy is likely to be inadequate and on the basis of this insight to develop an economic justification for the uniqueness test. Under a money damages rule, a court must calculate the amount Sotheby's is required to pay A to give A the benefit of his bargain. The amount necessary to fully compensate A is equal to the amount he requires to obtain an appropriate substitute. So in fixing the amount Sotheby's must pay A, the court must first determine what things A would regard as substitutes and then how much of any particular substitute would be required to compensate him for his loss.

In the hypothetical case, however it would be very difficult and expensive for a court to acquire the information necessary to make these determinations. Perhaps some information of this sort would be produced by the parties. For example, A could introduce evidence to establish a past pattern of consumption from which the court might draw an inference as to what would be a satisfactory substitute for the manuscript. Sotheby's could then attempt to rebut the evidence and establish some alternative theory of preferences and substitutes. But of course it would be time-consuming to produce information this way and any inference a court might draw on the basis of such information would be most uncertain.

Moreover this uncertainty cannot be avoided by simply looking to the selling price of other manuscripts or even the expected resale price of the Hobbes manuscript itself (unless, of course A is a professional dealer). It would be risky to infer the value A places on the Hobbes manuscript from the value placed on it by others and riskier still to infer it from the value others place on the manuscripts of, for example Harrington's *Oceana* or Locke's *Second Treatise*. If a court attempts to calculate A's money damages on the basis of such information there is a substantial probability that the award will miss the mark and be either under-or over-compensatory.

Of course if a court could accurately identify a substitute for the manuscript, it could disregard the fact that A may value the manuscript in excess of the price that he or anyone else has agreed to pay for it. But where it is difficult to identify a satisfactory substitute (as I assume it is here) the goal of compensation requires that an effort be made to determine the value the promisee places on the promisor's performance as distinct from what the promisee or anyone else, has offered to pay for it.

Although it is true in a certain sense that all goods compete in the market—that every good has substitutes—this is an empty truth. What matters in measuring money damages is the volume refinement and reliability of the available information about substitutes for the subject matter of the breached contract. When the relevant information is thin and unreliable there is a substantial risk that an award of money damages will either exceed or fall short of the promisee's actual loss. Of course this risk can always be reduced—but only at great cost when reliable information is difficult to obtain. Conversely when there is a great deal of consumer behavior generating abundant and highly dependable information about substitutes the risk of error in measuring the promisee's loss may be reduced at much smaller cost. In asserting that the subject matter of a particular contract is unique and has no established market value a court is really saying that it cannot obtain at reasonable cost enough information about substitutes to permit it to calculate an award of money damages without imposing an unacceptably high risk of undercompensation on the injured promisee. Conceived in this way the uniqueness test seems economically sound. . . .

The conclusion to be drawn from this analysis is a simple one. Whenever a court calculates money damages there is some risk that it will undercompensate the injured party. But the magnitude of this risk is inversely related to the completeness and reliability of the information on which the court bases its award. At one extreme where there is a well-developed market generating evidence of substitutability this risk is minimal. At the other extreme where there is no market or at most a few isolated transactions this risk is substantial. There is a point between these two extremes at which the risk becomes unacceptably large (or what amounts to the same thing, at which the risk can only be reduced by incurring unacceptable costs). This is the point separating those contracts that are specifically enforceable from those that are not—the point to which the uniqueness test obliquely refers . . .

A second, essentially economic, justification for the uniqueness test consists in showing that the test draws the line between specific performance and money damages in the way that most contracting parties would draw it were they free to make their own rules concerning remedies for breach and had they deliberated about the matter at the time of contracting. If this is true the uniqueness test promotes efficiency by reducing the costs of negotiating contracts. In general this way of thinking about the rules of contract law requires consideration of the *ex ante* interests of parties engaged in a hypothetical bargaining process struggling with a problem of rational choice under conditions of uncertainty. As I shall attempt to show in the next section an analysis based upon *ex ante* considerations does suggest, if only somewhat tentatively that contracting parties would be more likely to provide for specific performance where the subject matter of their contract is unique and for money damages where it is not. . .

When would the parties to a contract freely agree to a judicially enforceable provision giving the promisee an option to specifically enforce the other party's promise? Other things equal a promisee will always prefer to have such a provision included in the contract for it gives him an additional right which he would not otherwise possess. Other things equal, a promisor will always prefer a contract without such a provision—a contract in other words, which he may unilaterally breach on the condition that he make a subsequent compensatory payment to the promisee. Consequently a promisee intent upon writing a specific performance provision—a property rule—into the contract will have to pay to secure the promisor's consent. Similarly, a promisor must make a payment of some sort in order to exclude a provision for specific enforcement from the contract. If and only if the benefit which the promisee realizes from a specific performance provision exceeds the cost of the provision to the promisor will the provision be included in the final contract.

When the subject matter of a contrast is unique, the risk is greater that the promisee's money damage remedy will be under-compensatory. Since a right to compel specific performance reduces the risk, promisees—as a class—should be willing to pay more for a provision giving them a right of this sort when there is no developed market generating information about the value of the subject matter of their contract.

However, if a specific performance provision is likely to be more beneficial to a promisee when the subject matter of his contract is unique, it is also likely to be more costly to his promisor under the same circumstances. In the first place, a right in the promisee to compel specific performance increases the probability of costly negotiations for transfer of the promisee's contract rights. This of course always reinforces the promisor's preference for a money damages rule. However, a promisor is likely to regard this reason as especially compelling where the subject matter of his contract is unique, since the lack of information about substitutes will almost certainly make the parties' negotiations longer and more complicated and thus more costly.

Second, if the promisee is entitled to specifically enforce the promisor's obligation, the promisor who wishes to breach will have to make a release payment to the promisee and buy his way out of the contract. The amount of the release payment demanded by the promisee will be greater than what the promisor would have to pay the promisee under a money damages rule. This is so whether or not the subject matter of the contract is unique. But the difference between what the promisee would accept in exchange for a release and what he may be expected to receive under a court-administered money damages rule is likely to be larger where the subject matter of his contract is unique, because the risk that court-awarded damages will be undercompensatory is greater. For these two reasons, a specific performance provision will be more expensive to the promisor when the subject matter of his contract is unique.

Thus far, it would appear that the benefits to the promisee and the costs to the promisor of a specific performance provision are proportional; both are greater when the subject matter of the contract is unique. There is, however, an additional consideration influencing their *ex ante* deliberations that provides some basis for thinking that the parties to a contract will be more likely to provide for specific performance when the subject matter of their agreement is unique.

The cost of a specific performance provision to the promisor will be determined, in part, by his own estimate of the likelihood that he will want to breach the contract. If he fully intends to perform, and thinks breach unlikely, a promisor will be less hostile to a contract with a specific performance provision than he would otherwise be. One important factor influencing the promisor's thinking in this regard is the probability that he will receive a better offer for his goods or services in the interim between formation of the contract and performance. The higher the probability, the greater the likelihood he will want to breach. The probability of receiving an attractive alternative offer may be especially low where the subject matter of the contract is unique. In this case there is by definition no developed market, transactions are spotty at best, and therefore a promisor will often justifiably think it highly unlikely that he will receive any alternative offer (let alone a better one) for the promised goods or services. Indeed, where the subject matter of his contract is genuinely unique, a promisor may estimate the likelihood of a preferable alternative offer as close to zero, and thus be nearly indifferent as to what remedies the promisee will enjoy in the highly unlikely event of breach.

Although the promisor thinks breach highly improbable, the promisee may not. Despite the promisor's insistence that he intends to perform, the promisee may be skeptical. As long as he is anxious about the promisor's performance, the promisee will be concerned about the adequacy of his own remedies, and where the subject matter of his contract is unique he will likely have a decided preference for a contract that gives him the right to specifically enforce the other party's promise. Consequently, in the case of a contract for a unique good or service, the benefits the promisee derives from a specific performance provision are apt to outweigh its costs to the promisor, who, free of doubts about his own reliability, may regard the inclusion of such a provision as a relatively costless way of enticing the promisee to enter the contract on advantageous terms.

In the case of a contract for non-unique goods or services, by contrast, the existence of a developed market increases the likelihood that the promisor will receive alternative offers before he has performed the contract. The promisor will therefore be anxious to retain the freedom and flexibility enjoyed under a money damages rule.

Moreover, the promisor will be especially anxious in this case to avoid the additional transaction costs that would be incurred if he had to negotiate a voluntary transfer of the promisee's contract rights. Although these costs will tend to be smaller where the subject matter of the contract is not unique, they can never be less than some fixed minimum (the cost of contacting the promisee, notifying him of an intention to breach, obtaining a release statement of some sort, and so on). Where there is an established market in the goods or services involved, prices will ordinarily be grouped rather closely around a single point. The probability is therefore greater that any alternative offer the promisor does receive will not be sufficiently high to cover the cost of negotiating a release plus the amount he must pay the promisee for the release. Thus the likelihood increases that a promisor who has agreed to a specific performance provision will find himself in the undesirable position of having to decline an alternative offer that he would accept under a money damages rule. In some cases the alternative offer will cover the release payment but will be refused solely because the transaction costs of negotiating a transfer of the promisee's contract rights are prohibitively high. The promisor should therefore be willing to make a small payment to the promisee, perhaps in the form of a slightly reduced contract price, in order to exclude a specific performance provision and thus avoid these potential transaction costs. Because the transaction costs avoided by the promisor would not have benefited the promisee, the latter will be better off with the reduced contract price if he regards the risk of undercompensation under a money damages rule as minimal. The promisee will generally regard this risk as slight where there is a developed market generating information about suitable substitutes.

In sum, promisors and promisees will typically favor a money damages rule if the subject matter of their contract is not unique. When the contract is for unique goods or services, on the other hand, the benefit to the promisee of a specific performance provision is likely to be substantial and the promisor may well regard his own breach as only a remote possibility, so the opposite conclusion seems more plausible. There is thus some basis for believing the uniqueness test reflects the typical solution that contracting parties would arrange for themselves in light of their *ex ante* interests.

■ Schwartz, 'The Case for Specific Performance' (1979)
89 Yale LJ 271, 280–289

[Kronman argues that] in the unique goods case the parties would be expected to agree to a specific performance remedy; the promisee wants the remedy, whereas the promisor is indifferent. In the non-unique goods case, on the other hand, the parties would probably negotiate for a damage remedy, because damages would adequately protect the promisee, while the promisor would want to be free to accept more favorable offers.

Analysis of the equilibria in 'developed' and 'undeveloped markets' and their reactions to exogenous shocks suggests, however, that the promisors of unique goods care more about retaining the option of breach than do promisors of nonunique goods. Respecting equilibria, Professor Kronman equates an undeveloped market with a market in which unique goods are sold. This is misleading because unique goods markets often are well organized; the antique market provides an example. Such markets have two distinguishing features. First, they are usually characterized by greater price dispersion than obtains in the market equilibria for roughly fungible goods. In addition, sellers of unique goods face a lower 'rate of arrival' of potential buyers than do sellers of roughly fungible goods. These two phenomena are related; a high 'buyer arrival' rate implies extensive comparison shopping among firms, whereas the degree of price dispersion a market can sustain varies inversely with the amount of comparison shopping. Sellers of unique goods face a relatively low buyer arrival rate because each item they sell is highly differentiated; consequently, relatively few potential customers for such items exist. Also, search costs are comparatively higher for unique goods; locating them can be difficult, and the sellers often are geographically dispersed. Further, analyzing the quality of particular unique goods and comparing different goods usually are more time-consuming than searching for roughly fungible goods.

A promisor/seller in an 'undeveloped market'—a market in which unique goods are sold—thus faces a lower arrival rate of potential buyers together with the resultant higher degree of price dispersion than a promisor in a developed market. The promisor of unique goods consequently has grounds to believe that the offers he receives are to some extent random, and that later offers could be much higher than earlier ones. This promisor thus prefers damages to specific performance because the damages remedy preserves his freedom to breach.

This conclusion is reinforced by an examination of the differing reactions of 'developed' and 'undeveloped' markets to exogenous shocks. Exogenous shocks help to explain why promisors might receive better offers between the time they contract and the time they are supposed to render performance. This phenomenon needs explanation because a vendor of goods or services is generally assumed to sell to all of his purchasers on the same terms. Price discrimination is often unlawful and its costs in mass transactions exceed the gains it produces. Customers generally know whether a firm offers the same terms to all and are unlikely to make offers that exceed the going price. In addition, firms that negotiate contracts on an individual basis have a strong incentive not to breach, even if they receive better offers, in order to maintain goodwill. In what circumstances, then, will promisors receive and accept better offers?

The most frequent situation in which these circumstances arise is when there is an unexpected and dramatic increase in demand. The increase in demand will exert an upward pressure on prices. In the case of nonunique goods, this pressure is partially relieved by the ability of sellers to increase output. Unique goods, however, are in inelastic supply; only a few Rembrandts exist, and an increase in demand will not increase their number. In consequence, when buyers demand more of a unique item, the primary response of sellers is to increase the price; they can expand output only slightly, if at all.

The argument . . . can be clarified by a diagram.

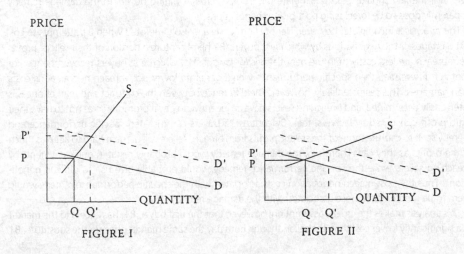

FIGURE I   FIGURE II

In both figures, an increase in demand is represented by a similar shift in the demand curve from D to D1. In Figure I, however, supply (S) is inelastic; no matter how great the shift in demand, little more of the good is supplied. Thus almost the full force of the demand shift is translated into the price increase. In Figure II, supply is elastic, so that output expands considerably and the price increase is more moderate.

Specific performance

Therefore, when demand unexpectedly increases, a promisor in a unique goods market could command higher prices than a promisor in a nonunique goods market. The seller of unique goods, when the contract is negotiated, thus has a strong incentive to preserve his freedom to breach. A seller of nonunique goods, by contrast, will probably have to compete with many other vendors for any new business that a demand increase generates, and the resultant price rise will be relatively modest. Thus he will care less about preserving his freedom to breach in response to demand shifts. In sum, if the promisor's preference for specific performance or damages is assumed to be determined solely by whether the performance at issue is unique, the promisor would not choose specific performance in situations in which the law now routinely grants it.

B. Post-breach negotiations

The second efficiency argument for restricting the availability of specific performance is that making specific performance freely available would generate higher post-breach negotiation costs than the damage remedy now generates. For example, suppose that a buyer (B1) contracts with seller (S) to buy a widget for $100. Prior to delivery, demand unexpectedly increases. The widget market is temporarily in disequilibrium as buyers make offers at different prices. While the market is in disequilibrium, a second buyer (B2) makes a contract with S to purchase the same widget for $130. Subsequently, the new equilibrium price for widgets is $115. If specific performance is available in this case. B1 is likely to demand it, in order to compel S to pay him some of the profit that S will make from breaching. B1 could, for example, insist on specific performance unless S pays him $20 ($15 in substitution damages plus a $5 premium). If S agrees, B1 can cover at $115, and be better off by $5 than he would have been under the damage remedy, which would have given him only the difference between the cover price and the contract price ($15). Whenever S's better offer is higher than the new market price, the seller has an incentive to breach, and the first buyer has an incentive to threaten specific performance in order to capture some of the seller's gains from breach.

The post-breach negotiations between S and B1 represent a 'dead-weight' efficiency loss; the negotiations serve only to redistribute wealth between S and B1, without generating additional social wealth. If society is indifferent as to whether sellers or buyers as a group profit from an increase in demand, the law should seek to eliminate this efficiency loss. Limiting buyers to the damage remedy apparently does so by foreclosing post-breach negotiations.

This analysis is incomplete, however. Negotiations costs are also generated when B1 attempts to collect damages. If the negotiations by which first buyers (B1 here) capture a portion of their sellers' profits from breach are less costly than the negotiations (or lawsuits) by which first buyers recover the market contract differential, then specific performance would generate lower post-breach negotiations costs than damages. This seems unlikely, however. The difference between the contract and market prices is often easily determined, and breaching sellers have an incentive to pay it promptly so as not to have their extra profit consumed by lawyers' fees. By contrast, if buyers can threaten specific performance and thereby seek to capture some of the sellers' profits from breach, sellers will bargain hard to keep as much of the profits as they can. Therefore, the damage remedy would probably result in quick payments by breaching sellers while the specific performance remedy would probably give rise to difficult negotiations. Thus the post-breach negotiation costs associated with the specific performance remedy would seem to be greater than those associated with the damage remedy.

This analysis makes the crucial assumption, however, that the first buyer, B1, has access to the market at a significantly lower cost than the seller; though both pay the same market price for the substitute, B1 is assumed to have much lower cover costs. If this assumption is false, specific performance would not give rise to post-breach negotiations. Consider the illustration again. Suppose that B1 can obtain specific performance, but that S can cover as conveniently as B1. If B1 insists on a conveyance, S would buy another widget in the market for $115 and deliver on his contracts with both B1 and B2. A total of three transactions would result: S-B1; S-B2; S2-S (S's purchase of a second widget). None of these transactions involves post-breach negotiations. Thus if sellers can cover conveniently, the specific performance remedy does not generate post-breach negotiation costs.

The issue, then, is whether sellers and buyers generally have similar cover costs. Analysis suggests that they do. Sellers as well as buyers have incentives to learn market conditions. Because sellers have to 'check the competition,' they will have a good knowledge of market prices and quality ranges. Also, when a buyer needs goods or services tailored to his own needs, he will be able to find such goods or services more cheaply than sellers in general could, for they would first have to ascertain the buyer's needs before going into the market. However, in situations in which the seller and the first buyer have already negotiated a contract, the seller is likely to have as much information about the buyer's needs as the buyer has. Moreover, in some markets, such as those for complex machines and services, sellers are likely to have a comparative advantage over buyers in evaluating the probable quality of performance and thus would have lower cover costs. Therefore, no basis exists for assuming that buyers generally have significantly lower cover costs than sellers. It follows that expanding the availability of specific performance would not generate higher post-breach negotiation costs than the damage remedy.

[A number of] serious objections may be made to this conclusion: (i) differential cover costs sometimes help induce breach, and their existence leads to higher post-breach negotiation costs under specific performance than under damages; (ii) in some cases, sellers cannot cover at all...

The first objection assumes that sellers breach partly because their cover costs are higher than those of their buyers; it then argues that when cover costs do diverge, allowing specific performance seemingly is less efficient than having damages be the sole remedy. Returning to the widget hypothetical, let Cb = the first buyer's (B1's) cover costs; Cs = the seller's cover costs. Assume that S has higher cover costs than B1, ie, $Cs > Cb$. If specific performance were available, B1 could threaten to obtain it, so as to force S to pay him part of the cover cost differential, $Cs-Cb$. If B1 made a credible threat, S would be better off negotiating than covering. Because only the availability of specific performance enables B1 to force this negotiation, one could argue that it is less efficient than having damages as the sole remedy.

This objection is incorrect, even if differential cover costs influence seller decisions to breach. A credible threat by B1 to seek specific performance would usually require preparing or initiating a lawsuit. This would entail costs of lost business time, lost goodwill and lawyer's fees, and these costs usually exceed any cover cost differential $(Cs - Cb)$ that may exist. This is because the magnitude of cover costs—and hence of the differential—are low in relation to legal costs. Locating and arranging for substitute transactions are routine, relatively inexpensive business activities. Since the legal and related costs necessary for a credible threat commonly exceed the cover cost differential, it would rarely pay buyers to threaten specific performance to capture part of this differential. Thus no post-breach negotiations would be engendered by any differences in the parties' cover costs.

The second objection to the conclusion that post-breach negotiation costs are no higher under specific performance than under damages follows from the fact that in some cases sellers cannot cover at all. In these cases, buyers can always compel post-breach negotiations by threatening specific performance. There are two situations in which a seller cannot cover: if he is a monopolist or if the goods are unique. In either event, the first buyer would also be unable to cover. If neither the seller nor the first buyer can cover, no reason exists to believe that there would be higher post-breach negotiation costs with specific performance than with damages. If specific performance were available, B1 and S would negotiate over B1's share of the profit that S's deal with B2 would generate, or B1 would insist on a conveyance from S and then sell to B2. If only the damages remedy is available, B1 would negotiate with S respecting his expected net gain from performance rather than over the contract market difference, because he could not purchase a substitute. This expected gain is often difficult to calculate, and easy for the buyer to exaggerate. There is no reason to believe the negotiations or litigation over this gain would be less costly than the negotiations over division of the profit that B2's offer creates, or the costs of a second conveyance between B1 and B2. Thus even when the seller cannot cover, specific perform-ance has not been shown to generate higher post-breach negotiation costs than damages. Moreover, when neither party can cover—the case under discussion—buyers have a right to specific performance under current law.

NOTE

Commenting on Schwartz's article, Muris [1982] Duke L J 1053 notes (at 1062–1066):

> Schwartz also asserts that even if cover costs do differ, post-breach negotiations will not occur. He argues that the buyer must make a credible threat before the seller will negotiate, that such a threat will usually require preparing or initiating a lawsuit, and that, because legal costs will usually exceed the differential in cover costs, credible threats will be rare. Although these factors will reduce the costs of specific performance, such costs will not be eliminated or even rendered trivial. Because the seller will be uncertain concerning the facts and the buyer's intentions, the seller cannot be positive that any buyer threat to seek specific performance is idle. A threat costs the buyer far less than a law-suit would, and the possibility of future breaches by sellers may encourage the buyer to expend con-siderable resources to demonstrate his willingness to seek the specific remedy. Even when the probability of the seller successfully 'calling the buyer's bluff' is high, resources will still be spent in the bluffing game that would not be spent under a damage rule. Further, the possibility of the buyer's threat being carried out may cause the seller to cover even if the buyer has lower cover costs. At min-imum, the possibility of specific performance increases uncertainty because its use will not be auto-matic. Increased uncertainty necessarily raises costs to those who prefer more certainty to less. . . . [E]ven when the market price is not obvious, in at least some of these cases, requiring specific per-formance is a more costly remedy than awarding damages. The non-breacher whose loss is less than the cost of correcting the defect in performance has incentive to bargain over specific performance to obtain part of the difference between the correction cost and his loss.
>
> The resources spent negotiating over specific performance or determining the market price are limited by the expected return on the 'investment' in negotiation. In the case of the market price, well-defined rules of law exist to guide the parties, setting reasonable lower and upper bounds that limit the return from the investment. In the case of specific performance, however, no such rules exist. The spread, therefore, is potentially as large as the cost of correcting the defects minus the dif-ference between the contract price of what was promised and the market price of what was deliv-ered (an amount equalling the non-breaching party's damage if subjective value is not relevant). Moreover, even with specific performance, the parties will probably spend some resources to esti-mate the market price and thereby find the lower boundary of a possible settlement. These resources will probably not be as great as they are when the market price is determined in court, but they need not be trivial. Therefore, the size of the amount the parties will bargain over if specific performance is allowed—the cost of correcting the defects minus the market-based damages—will sometimes exceed the amount in dispute if specific performance is not allowed.
>
> If specific performance is not allowed, the only dispute is between the upper and lower reasonable estimates for the market price. Thus, in some cases, allowing specific performance will give parties an incentive to spend more on deciding the amount of the 'bribe' that the breacher must pay than they would spend in determining the market price. Although in the aggregate parties may not always spend up to expected gains, the higher expected return from negotiating specific perform-ance creates a tendency to have higher expenditures in such cases. No empirical information exists on the frequency of the cases in which the disputed amount regarding the market price is less than the amount over which the parties will bargain with specific performance. Thus uncertainty, as well as the knowledge that even with specific performance parties will spend resources on estimating the

market price, places on a weak foundation the assertion that freely granting specific performance will not on balance raise costs compared to the current law.

■ Macneil, 'Efficient Breach of Contract: Circles in the Sky' (1982)
68 Vir LR 947, 957

Whether an expectation damages rule or a specific performance rule is more efficient depends entirely upon the relative transaction costs of operating under the rules. Where, as will most generally be the case, transaction costs under either rule will exceed gross efficiency gains made possible by scrapping one contract in favor of another, each rule is equally (in)efficient. Where both rules will permit substituting a more productive contract for a less productive contract, the difference in efficiency of the rules will be measured exactly by the difference in their respective transaction costs. Where one rule will permit substitution and the other will not, the difference in efficiency will be measured by the difference in respective transaction costs, but subject to an upper limit consisting of the hypothetical net efficiency gain under the rule with the lower transaction costs. None of the transaction costs can be deduced by use of the microeconomic model, but can only be determined inductively from empirical evidence.

■ Mahoney, 'Options Pricing and Contract Remedies' in *The New Palgrave Dictionary of Economics and the Law*
pp 715.

The theory of options valuation has found many uses outside the realm of finance. One of these is to illuminate the common law's preference for money damages over specific performance as the usual remedy for breach of contract, as shown by Mahoney (1995).

Justice Holmes (1897: 462) famously noted that a contractual undertaking is a promise either to perform or to pay damages. Under the common law, specific performance is an 'extraordinary' remedy, granted only when money damages would be inadequate to compensate the promisee for the lost value of the performance. We can therefore think of the promise as constituting the sale of the performance coupled with the purchase of an option to buy back the performance for a price equal to the damages awarded for breach. The option is valuable, and its value should be reflected as a decrease in the price that the promisee pays for the performance compared to an otherwise identical contract in which the remedy would be specific performance. Consideration of the option value embedded in a contract for which the remedy will be money damages shows why specific performance is not the preferred remedy.

For the sake of simplicity, consider a bilateral executory contract in which Seller agrees to sell a marketable good to Buyer for a fixed price on a defined date in the future. At the time of contracting, Seller's cost of performance (that is, the cost of making or acquiring the good and of foregoing a spot sale at the time of performance) is unknown, but we will assume that the parties agree as to its probability distribution. The same is true of the value of that performance to Buyer, but for expositional clarity we can consider that value as fixed and focus only on the variability in Seller's cost. When the time for performance arrives, depending on the realized cost of performance, performance may be inefficient—i.e., it may cost more than the value of the good to Buyer.

A specific-performance remedy and a money-damages remedy are two different ways of allocating the value that can be created by rescinding the contract if the cost of performance exceeds its value to Buyer. If Seller may breach and pay money damages, the amount of those damages under the standard expectationary measure will be the value of the good to Buyer less the unpaid portion of the contract price. Seller will therefore capture the full gain from termination, which is the cost of performance to Seller less the (smaller) value of that performance to Buyer. On the other hand, if Buyer is entitled to specific performance, Buyer has the right to demand performance regardless of its cost to Seller. When termination is efficient, by definition Seller would be willing to pay more to be released from that obligation than Buyer would be willing to pay for the good. Excluding transaction costs, therefore, Seller will offer, and Buyer will accept, a sum greater than expectational damages but less than Seller's full cost of performance to be released from the contract. Thus Buyer will obtain some or all of the value of termination.

Consider a simple example. In period 1, Buyer agrees to pay $100 for a good that Seller will manufacture and deliver in period 2. In the first state, Seller's cost of performance is $60 and in the second it is $120. The value of the good to Buyer is $110 in both states. In the high-cost state, performance is inefficient in the sense defined above, and a money-damages remedy permits Seller to escape performance by paying Buyer $10 (the difference between the value of the performance to Buyer and the contract price). A specific-performance remedy entitles Buyer to insist on performance in either state. In the high-cost state, Buyer's insistence on performance will provide it with a $10 net benefit at a net cost to Seller of $20. Both parties will be better off if Seller pays Buyer some amount greater than $10 but less than $20 to terminate the contract. This suggests that seller will again escape performance, but at a higher price than was true under a money-damages regime.

So long as the rule is clear, the parties are identically informed and risk-neutral, and transaction costs low, the parties should be indifferent between the two remedies. In either case, as the Coase theorem (see Coase 1960) suggests, Seller will perform when it is efficient to do so and won't when it is not. As in the above example, the rule will affect the distribution of the gain from termination when termination is efficient, but this also will not matter, because the parties can agree to a contract price that reflects the additional value of the contract to Buyer when the remedy is specific performance.

This is where the theory of option valuation steps in. Option pricing techniques can be used to calculate the difference in value between a contractual obligation coupled with a money-damages remedy and the identical obligation coupled with a specific-performance remedy. The difference is the value of a call option on the performance, with the damages award as the strike price. More importantly, the option approach helps to show why the choice of remedy *does* matter in many situations.

In effect, the money-damages 'option' enables Seller to hedge his exposure from the contract. Seller is, in financial parlance, 'short' the performance—that is to say, Seller is obligated to deliver the performance at a future date. By holding an option to purchase the performance, Seller caps the potential loss from his short position. A risk-averse Seller would be better off holding the short position coupled with a fairly priced option than holding the short position alone. In financial markets, we see traders take short positions without hedging, because those traders are engaged in speculation; they are attempting to profit from what they perceive to be their insight into the future returns on a financial asset. In markets for products and services, we would imagine that most people in Seller's position hope to profit from their ability to provide the product or service efficiently, rather than their ability to forecast the returns on that product or service. We therefore frequently observe hedging in such markets, and indeed we would expect most people in Seller's position to desire the hedge that money damages provides.

The analysis is similar from Buyer's perspective. Buyer's likely objective is to acquire the good or service for use in Buyer's business or for consumption. If Buyer holds a 'long' position in the performance without writing (that is, selling) an option to Seller, Buyer is speculating on Seller's cost of performance, and in doing so is giving up cash-in-hand in the amount of the option value. Buyer would presumably rarely wish to do this, so long as money damages are an adequate substitute for performance (see Craswell 1988; Schwartz 1990).

The option analysis supplements the conventional way of thinking about the choice between money damages and specific performance, which focuses on the transaction costs associated with each (see Kronman 1978; Schwartz 1979). Money-damages awards are thought to be systematically undercompensatory. Indeed, standard doctrine regarding the calculation of money damages fails to provide compensation for some of the costs incurred by a promisee in the event of breach. Courts award damages only to the extent that they are reasonably certain, and no compensation is given for some of the incidental costs that accompany a contract breach (such as legal fees). Money damages are therefore an imperfect substitute for performance. Specific performance may solve that problem, but it introduces another imperfection. When performance would be inefficient, specific performance requires negoti-ation of an appropriate payment from Seller to Buyer in lieu of performance. Bargaining is costly, and there is always the possibility that Seller and Buyer will fail to reach agreement even though it is clearly the efficient thing to do. As described in detail by Bishop (1985), the relative magnitudes of these imperfections vary with the context, and so too will the preferred remedy.

The transaction-costs argument, while correct, provides only limited help in making sense of what courts do. In all but the most extreme cases, the relative magnitudes of the transaction costs associated with money damages and specific performance are not obvious. In most circumstances, it is difficult to argue persuasively that the imperfections noted above are very significant, and harder still to argue that one or the other clearly dominates.

The options approach, by contrast, explains in a reasonably straightforward way both the strong general preference for money damages and the most important exceptions. The most prominent excep-tion to the money-damages rule involves contracts to sell a 'unique' good. In such cases, courts award specific performance on the grounds that money damages would be insufficient, and commentators have generally explained the result by noting that money damages would not adequately protect the subjective value that Buyer sees in the good. Note that the reference to 'subjective value' suggests that Buyer's purpose in entering into the contract is more analogous to that of the unhedged speculator in financial markets than to the hedged producer or user of a commodity in markets for goods. This becomes even more plausible when we look at the sorts of goods at stake in the classic specific-performance cases. Specific performance is routinely granted in cases involving 'unique' goods. The paradigmatic unique good, and the one most often at issue, is real estate. . . . Other cases have involved works of art (see *Falcke v Gray*), race horses. . . and shares of stock with a limited public market. . . . each of these cases shares important characteristics with financial markets. It is likely that the motivation for the contract is Seller's and Buyer's differing beliefs about the future value of the good. The good in ques-tion is pre-existing, that is, Seller is not manufacturing the good for Buyer. Thus opportunity costs are the most relevant component of Seller's cost of performance, and Seller's estimate of those costs may rise prior to performance if Seller concludes that it has underestimated the future returns on the asset. Should Seller then breach, Buyer may be unable to take advantage of his insights into the future value of the good unless those returns have already materialized at the time of suit. In short, Buyer and Seller are in a position very closely analogous to the speculative buyer and seller of a financial asset (except that the efficiency of financial markets makes it much more likely that information about future returns will be promptly reflected in market prices), and a specific performance remedy is merely a means of permitting them to hold unhedged positions.

. . .

There will, of course, be cases in which the parties have idiosyncratic reasons for preferring an over-compensatory remedy. For example, both parties may recognize that Seller is much better informed about the distribution of the cost of performance than Buyer. Seller could agree to an overcompensatory remedy as a means of signalling credibly to Buyer that Seller believes that the cost of performance has a low variance. Expressed in option terms, Seller may be unwilling to pay the cost of the money-damages option because Seller believes that the variance of the underlying asset is low, and accordingly the value of the option is low. When this occurs, and the situation is not one in which specific performance is otherwise likely, we would expect to see the parties agree to liquidated damages, which can mimic the risk-shifting effects of specific performance (see Polinsky 1983). The same is true if the parties have some reason to believe that a court is particularly likely to award insufficient damages in their situation. The options perspective therefore supplements the arguments that have been made in favour of the pre-sumptive enforceability of liquidated damages clauses.

The considerations as set out in these articles were very relevant to the decision of the House of Lords in *Cooperative Insurance Society Ltd v Argyll Stores (Holdings) Ltd* [1998] AC 1, [1997] 3 All ER 297.

In this case, the plaintiffs were the developers of a shopping centre and they had secured the defendants, a leading supermarket chain, as tenants of the one of the major stores within the shopping centre. (In such developments, it is very important to have attractive tenants in the major stores so as to persuade other tenants to take tenancies in the belief that the public will be attracted in large numbers to a development with such tenants.)

In such a situation, the developer will be anxious to secure, so far as possible, that the attractive tenants will not move out. In the present case, the defendants had not only taken a 35-year lease, but had expressly covenanted that they would operate the leased land as a super-market and that they would window dress the shop to an appropriate standard.

After some 15 years, the defendants decided that they did not wish to continue to run this particular supermarket and they stripped the supermarket out and left without any notice to the plaintiffs. This was clearly a breach of contract. In principle, the plaintiffs could have sued for damages and could have recovered, as part of the damages, compensation for the effect on the operation of the shopping centre caused by the defendants' departure. On the other hand, the process of computing this loss would be extremely difficult since it would be very difficult to establish what the behaviour of the other tenants would be over the next twenty years as a result of the departure of the defendants.

The majority of the Court of Appeal thought it appropriate in the circumstances therefore to order specific performance. The House of Lords unanimously reversed this decision. Lord Hoffmann said:

It is true that the defendant has, by his own breach of contract, put himself in such an unfortunate position. But the purpose of the law of contract is not to punish wrongdoing but to satisfy the expectations of the party entitled to performance. A remedy which enables him to secure, in money terms, more than the specific performance due to him is unjust. From a wider perspective, it cannot be in the public interest for the courts to require someone to carry on business at a loss if there is any plaus-ible alternative by which the other party can be given compensation. It is not only a waste of resources but yokes the parties together in a continuing hostile relationship. The order for specific performance prolongs the battle. If the defendant is ordered to run a business, its conduct becomes the subject of a flow of complaints, solicitors' letters and affidavits. This is wasteful for both parties and the legal system. An award of damages, on the other hand, brings the litigation to an end. The defendant pays damages, the forensic link between them is severed, they go their separate ways and the wounds of conflict can heal.

In practice, in a case of this kind, whatever the courts may order, it was very unlikely that the defendant would actually stay in position as a tenant for the next twenty years. It was much more likely that the tenants would negotiate with the plaintiffs and, at a price, buy themselves out. However, in such negotiations, the position of the plaintiffs would be much stronger if they were holding an order for specific performance and therefore they could expect to recover a much bigger sum from the defendants as the price of letting them go.

In addition to the 'adequacy of damages' rule, there are a number of other restrictions on the availability of specific performance. It is convenient to take the first two together, since they seem to be interconnected. The first is that, traditionally, an order of specific perform-ance would not be granted of a contract that was to be carried out over a period of time. Thus in *Ryan v Mutual Tontine Westminster Chambers Association* [1893] 1 Ch 116, the court refused to order specific performance of a contract to provide portering service for a flat. The usual explanation is that the court has no way of supervising performance. The second is that specific performance will not be granted of a contract involving personal services.

■ *C H Giles Co v Morris*

[1972] 1 WLR 307

The contract was for, among other things, the reorganisation of a company and the sale of certain of its shares to the plaintiff company. Clause 2 provided that the vendors would procure the appointment of Mr Giles as managing director of a company (Invincible) for five years.

Megarry J

...What I have to consider is whether the presence in the agreement of clause 2(f), providing for Mr Giles to enter into a service agreement with Invincible in the form of the draft annexed to the contract, prevents the court from decreeing specific performance of the entire agreement, including that subclause. It will be observed that there is no question of the plaintiff seeking to enforce any order of the court which will compel any of the defendants to carry out, either as employer or employee, any personal services. The order made is an order to procure 'the execution by the company of the engrossment' of the service agreement. The question is whether such an order falls within the principle that the court will not decree specific performance of a contract for personal services.

On the face of it the answer must be No. There is no question of the execution of the decree requiring constant superintendence by the court of a continuous series of acts such as arose in *Ryan v Mutual Tontine Westminster Chambers Association*, a case that was mentioned but not cited during argument. All that the decree requires in this respect is the procuring of a single act, namely, the execution of the service agreement. When that has been done, the question of any breach of the service agreement and any remedies for that breach is one between Invincible and Mr Giles and not between Invincible and the plaintiff. Invincible, too, is a party neither to the contract nor to the action.

The distinction between an order to perform a contract for services and an order to procure the execution of such a contract seems to me to be sound both in principle and on authority. I do not think that the mere fact that the contract to be made is one of which the court would not decree specific performance is a ground for refusing to decree that the contract be entered into. During the argument Mr Harman cited *Fry on Specific Performance*, 6th edn (1921), pp 50, 51, in support of the proposition that the court will not order specific performance of a contract of hiring and service. This, however, is not the whole of the story: and if one turns on to pp 388 to 390 one finds *Ryan's* case cited, together with certain other cases. To one of the latter, *Wilson v West Hartlepool Railway Co*, I drew the attention of counsel towards the conclusion of Mr Neill's argument.

...Knight Bruce L J said...:

'I agree that there may be and have been cases in which it may well be and has been held that there may, under a bill for specific performance of a contract, be a decree against a defendant to execute a deed containing covenants on his part to do acts of which, from their nature, specific performance could not directly be enforced. But the present I think not a case of that description.'

As Turner LJ held not only that the agreement did contemplate the execution of a further deed, but also that the execution of such a deed should be specifically enforced, I think it is clear that both members of the court took the view that specific performance may be decreed of an agreement to execute an instrument even if the obligations under that instrument would not be specifically enforced. It is true that the ground on which specific performance was resisted in that case was not that the further instrument related to acts of personal service but that it was too indefinite in its obligations, requiring a contracting party to use a particular railway 'in preference to all others', 'whenever reasonably practicable', and 'for the longest distance it is reasonably capable of use'. However, in this context I can see no sensible distinction between this objection to specific performance and an objection based on the performance of personal services; and I do not think that the judgments support any such distinction.

That is not the only authority to this effect. Thus there is *Granville v Betts* of which *Fry* says, at p 389. 'The real contract here which the court enforces is a contract to execute the deed'; and see *Stocker v Wedderburn*. So too in *Wilson v Wilson* Lord St Leonards said:

> 'it does not at all follow, because the court of equity compels the appellant in this case to enter into a covenant that he will not, by the force of ecclesiastical censures, compel restitution of his conjugal rights, that the court would enjoin him from breaking that covenant which he has entered into; the court, I apprehend, would leave him to answer any action that might be brought for damages upon the covenant.'

Indeed, were the rule otherwise, I do not see why a lessor could not resist specific performance of a contract to grant a lease if that lease contained any term of which specific performance would not be granted, such a provision like that in *Ryan's* case for the services of a porter, or for repairs; yet he cannot: see *Paxton v Newton.*

There is a further consideration. The obligation to enter into a service agreement is merely one part of a contract which deals with many other matters; and that obligation is the only part of that complex which is said not to be specifically enforceable. Now there is authority for saying that the mere presence in a contract of one provision which, by itself, would not be specifically enforceable (because, for example, it requires the performance of personal services) does not prevent the contract as a whole from being specifically enforced. This is so even if the obligation to perform personal services could be enforced only, for instance, by ordering sequestration: see *Fortescue v Lostwithiel and Fowey Railway Co; Fry on Specific Performance* 6th edn (1921), p 53. In such cases, the contract must be regarded as a whole, and the court may refuse to let the disadvantages and difficulties of specifically enforcing the obligation to perform personal services outweigh the suitability of the rest of the contract for specific performance, and the desirability of the contract as a whole being enforced. After all, pacta sunt servanda.

One day, perhaps, the courts will look again at the so-called rule that contracts for personal services or involving the continuous performance of services will not be specifically enforced. Such a rule is plainly not absolute and without exception, nor do I think that it can be based on any narrow consideration such as difficulties of constant superintendence by the court. Mandatory injunctions are by no means unknown, and there is normally no question of the court having to send its officers to supervise the performance of the order of the court. Prohibitory injunctions are common, and again there is no direct supervision by the court. Performance of each type of injunction is normally secured by the realisation of the person enjoined that he is liable to be punished for contempt if evidence of his disobedience to the order is put before the court; and if the injunction is prohibitory, actual committal will usually so long as it continues, make disobedience impossible. If instead the order is for specific performance of a contract for personal services, a similar machinery of enforcement could be employed, again without there being any question of supervision by any officer of the court. The reasons why the court is reluctant to decree specific performance of a contract for personal services (and I would regard it as a strong reluctance rather than a rule) are, I think, more complex and more firmly bottomed on human nature. If a singer contracts to sing, there could be no doubt be proceedings for committal if, ordered to sing, the singer remained obstinately dumb. But if instead the singer sang flat, or sharp, or too fast, or too slowly, or too loudly, or too quietly, or resorted to a dozen of the manifestations of temperament traditionally associated with some singers, the threat of committal would reveal itself as a most unsatisfactory weapon: for who could say whether the imperfections of performance were natural or self-induced? To make an order with such possibilities of evasion would be vain; and so the order will not be made. However, not all contracts of personal service or for the continuous performance of services are as dependent as this on matters of opinion and judgment, nor do all such contracts involve the same degree of the daily impact of person upon person. In general, no doubt, the inconvenience and mischief of decreeing specific performance of most of such contracts will greatly outweigh the advantages, and specific performance will be refused. But I do not think that it should be assumed that as soon as any element of personal service or continuous services can be discerned in a contract the court will, without more, refuse specific performance. Of course, a requirement for the continuous performance of services has the disadvantage that repeated breaches may engender repeated applications to the court for enforcement. But so may many injunctions; and the prospects of repetition, although an important consideration, ought not to be allowed to negative a right. As is so often the case in equity, the matter is one of the balance of advantage and disadvantage in relation to the particular obligations in question: and the fact that the balance will usually lie on one side does not turn this probability into a rule. The present case, of course, is a fortiori, since the contract of which specific performance has been decreed requires not the performance of personal services or any continuous series of acts, but merely procuring the execution of an agreement which contains a provision for such services or acts.

It follows that in my judgment the agreement is specifically enforceable, the consent order was properly made, and the advice given by junior counsel that there was no defence to the action on this score was sound advice. In those circumstances. I can see no defence to the plaintiff's motion to enforce the order.

NOTE

In *Posner v Scott-Lewis* [1986] 3 All ER 513, Mervyn Davies J, relying on what Megarry had said, granted specific performance of a term in a contract that required the defendant to appoint a porter. He said (at 521):

> Whether or not an order for specific performance should be made seems to me to depend on the following considerations: (a) is there a sufficient definition of what has to be done in order to comply with the order of the court; (b) will enforcing compliance involve superintendence by the court to an unacceptable degree; and (c) what are the respective prejudices or hardships that will be suffered by the parties if the order is made or not made?
>
> As to (a), one may in this case sufficiently define what has to be done by the defendants by ordering the defendants, within say two months, to employ a porter to be resident at Danes Court for the purpose of carrying out the cl 3(11) duties. It is to be borne in mind that there is still a vacant flat available for a resident porter. As to (b), I do not see that such an order will occasion any protracted superintendence by the court. If the defendants without good cause fail to comply with the order in due time, then the plaintiffs can take appropriate enforcement proceedings against the defendants. As to (c), I see no hardship or prejudice resulting to the defendants from the order. They will simply be performing what they have promised to do and what has been carried out by the lessors over the past 20 years.

While this case is certainly not an abandonment of the 'supervision' rule, it does suggest some relaxation of it. In fact, at least one exception to the rule has been recognised for a long time. In *Wolverhampton Corpn v Emmons* [1901] 1 KB 515 at 524–525, Romer J stated it thus:

> There is no doubt that as a general rule the Court will not enforce specific performance of a building contract, but an exception from the rule has been recognised. It has, I think, for some time been held that, in order to bring himself within that exception, a plaintiff must establish three things. The first is that the building work, of which he seeks to enforce the performance, is defined by the contract; that is to say, that the particulars of the work are so far definitely ascertained that the Court can sufficiently see what is the exact nature of the work of which it is asked to order the performance. The second is that the plaintiff has a substantial interest in having the contract performed, which is of such a nature that he cannot adequately be compensated for breach of the contract by damages. The third is that the defendant has by the contract obtained possession of land on which the work is contracted to be done.

In *Carpenters Estates Ltd v Davies* [1940] Ch 160, Farwell J held that the defendant need not have acquired the land under the contract in question. In that case, a vendor of land had undertaken to do work on adjacent land she retained. Why is specific performance available because the work is to be done on the defendant's land? It appears that, even if the work is to be done on the defendant's land, an order will not be made unless damages would be inadequate for other reasons as well. What sort of damages could be awarded in such circumstances?

There has also been some relaxation of the rule that contracts for personal services will not be specifically enforced. As we shall see shortly, there is a 'companion' rule that the court will not grant an injunction that would amount to ordering specific performance of an employment contract. However, in *Hill v CA Parsons Ltd* [1972] Ch 305, the Court of Appeal issued an injunction to restrain an employer from dismissing an employee wrongfully. Both parties wished the relationship to continue, but union pressure caused the employer to threaten dismissal of the employee shortly before he was due to retire and shortly before the coming into force of the Industrial Relations Act 1971, which would have given the employee some protection. It was subsequently emphasised that the case was exceptional: see *Chappell v Times Newspapers Ltd* [1975] 1 WLR 482 at 501,503,506; but an injunction was issued in *Powell v Brent London Borough Council* [1987] IRLR 466. The plaintiff applied for promotion to the post of principal benefits officer. After interviews, she was told that she had been selected and she reported to her new place of employment. It was then alleged that the selection procedure had not complied with the borough's equal opportunity code of practice and she was instructed to return to her previous post. She refused. Although the borough strongly opposed her continuing in her job, it was stated that her superiors had complete confidence in her and that her return would cause no friction with those with whom she would be working. The Court of Appeal granted an interlocutory injunction. Ralph Gibson LJ stated (at 473):

For my part on this issue I have reached the conclusion that the decision of Mr Justice Knox cannot stand. I have reached that conclusion with hesitation because it seems to me essentially unlikely for a plaintiff to be able to satisfy the court that, despite strenuous opposition by her employers to her continuing in her job, nevertheless there subsists the necessary confidence between her and her employers to justify the making of an injunction. The fact of the opposition is likely in my view to be a true indication of the absence of confidence, but as I said at the outset I think this is a most unusual case.

First I must state the principle which must, I think, guide our decision. It is clear to me that part of the basis of the general rule against specific performance of contracts of service is that mutual confidence is normally a necessary condition for the satisfactory working of a contract of service. If one party refuses to allow the relationship to continue the mutual confidence is almost certainly missing. Mr Justice Knox referred to the judgment of Lord Justice Geoffrey Lane (as he then was) in *Chappell v Times Newspapers Ltd* [1975] IRLR 90 at p 95.

For my part I am not able to derive much assistance from the words 'complete confidence' for the purposes of this case. I prefer to state what I think the applicable principle to be in this way. Having regard to the decision in *Hill v Parsons* and to the long-standing general rule of practice to which *Hill v Parsons* was an exception, the court will not by injunction require an employer to let a servant continue in his employment, when the employer has sought to terminate that employment and to prevent the servant carrying out his work under the contract, unless it is clear on the evidence not only that it is otherwise just to make such a requirement but also that there exists sufficient confidence on the part of the employer in the servant's ability and other necessary attributes for it to be reasonable to make the order. Sufficiency of confidence must be judged by reference to the circumstances of the case, including the nature of the work, the people with whom the work must be done and the likely effect upon the employer and the employer's operations if the employer is required by injunction to suffer the plaintiff to continue in the work.

In *Robb v London Borough of Hammersmith and Fulham* [1991] IRLR 72, Morland J issued an injunction to restrain the defendants from dismissing the plaintiff without completing the disciplinary proceedings that they had started but then aborted. Although the defendants had lost confidence and trust in the plaintiff, the test was not this but whether the order would be workable. There was nothing unworkable about restraining dismissal while the proceedings were completed, which would give the plaintiff the chance to ventilate his case and justify himself at the hearing.

Would it be fair to say that the 'contract for personal service rule' was developed in the context of employment by individuals or small organisations and is not necessarily appropriate to employment within a very large organisation? How many unusual cases must there be before the exception becomes a rule?

Specific performance, which is a discretionary remedy, may also be refused on other equitable grounds, such as hardship to the defendant. For a recent case involving hardship, see *Patel v Ali* [1984] Ch 283, in which the vendor of a house had, since the sale, become disabled and heavily dependent for help on neighbours whom she would lose if she had to move. Goulding J refused to grant specific performance, leaving the purchasers to their remedy in damages. Other grounds on which specific performance may be refused are delay ('laches') and mistake (not amounting to a mistake preventing the formation of a contract) on the part of the defendant (see p 290).

The court may also refuse to grant specific performance of an obligation that is due to be performed before the plaintiff's own performance, if, when the time comes for the plaintiff to perform, specific performance will not be available against him. The point seems to be that it might be unfair to force the defendant to go to the expense of performing, only to find that later the plaintiff will not do so, and in addition is perhaps unable to pay any damages: the defendant might have preferred not to perform and to pay damages, which at that stage will be lower, because the plaintiff has not had to perform. The rule is often called the 'mutuality rule', but this name can be misleading, because it is not the case that specific performance will never be granted to a plaintiff against whom it could not be ordered. If the plaintiff has already performed, it is immaterial that an order could not have been made against him: *Price v Strange* [1978] Ch 337. Even if the plaintiff has not performed, and it will not be possible to order him to do so when the time comes, the problem may be solved by taking security from the plaintiff: see *Langen & Wind Ltd v Bell* [1972] Ch 685.

■ *Warner Bros Pictures Inc v Nelson*
[1937] 1 KB 209

The defendant, the film star Bette Davis, entered into a contract with the plaintiffs on 27 December 1934 for 52 weeks, extendable at the plaintiffs' option until 1942, to render her exclusive services as a motion picture and/or legitimate stage actress to the plaintiffs, and to perform solely and exclusively for them. In June 1936, the defendant, in admitted breach of contract, refused to be further bound, came to England and entered into a contract to act in a film for another company.

The plaintiffs sought an injunction to restrain the defendant 'from rendering without the written consent of the plaintiffs . . . any services for or in any motion picture or stage production or productions of any person, firm or corporation other than the plaintiffs'.

Branson J

. . . It is conceded that our Courts will not enforce a positive covenant of personal service; and specific performance of the positive covenants by the defendant to serve the plaintiffs is not asked in the present case. The practice of the Court of Chancery in relation to the enforcement of negative covenants is stated on the highest authority by Lord Cairns in the House of Lords in *Doherty v Allman*. His Lordship says: 'My Lords, if there had been a negative covenant, I apprehend, according to well-settled practice, a Court of Equity would have had no discretion to exercise. If parties, for valuable consideration, with their eyes open, contract that a particular thing shall not be done, all that a Court of Equity has to do is to say, by way of injunction, that which the parties have already said by way of covenant, that the thing shall not be done; and in such case the injunction does nothing more than give the sanction of the process of the Court to that which already is the contract between the parties. It is not then a question of the balance of convenience or inconvenience, or of the amount of damage or of injury—it is the specific performance, by the Court, of that negative bargain which the parties have made, with their eyes open, between themselves.'

That was not a case of a contract of personal service; but the same principle had already been applied to such a contract by Lord St Leonards in *Lumley v Wagner.* The Lord Chancellor used the following language: 'Wherever this Court has not proper jurisdiction to enforce specific performance, it operates to bind men's consciences, as far as they can be bound, to a true and literal performance of their agreements; and it will not suffer them to depart from their contracts at their pleasure, leaving the party with whom they have contracted to the mere chance of any damages which a jury may give. The exercise of the jurisdiction has, I believe, had a wholesome tendency towards the maintenance of that good faith which exists in this country to a much greater degree perhaps than in any other; and although the jurisdiction is not to be extended, yet a Judge would desert his duty who did not act up to what his predecessors have handed down as the rule for his guidance in the administration of such an equity.'

The defendant, having broken her positive undertakings in the contract without any cause or excuse which she was prepared to support in the witness-box, contends that she cannot be enjoined from breaking the negative covenants also. The mere fact that a covenant which the Court would not enforce, if expressed in positive form, is expressed in the negative instead, will not induce the Court to enforce it.

. . . The Court will attend to the substance and not to the form of the covenant. Nor will the Court, true to the principle that specific performance of a contract of personal service will never be ordered, grant an injunction in the case of such a contract to enforce negative covenants if the effect of so doing would be to drive the defendant either to starvation or to specific performance of the positive covenants: see *Whitwood Chemical Co v Hardman* . . . but this is subject to a further consideration. An injunction is a discretionary remedy, and the Court in granting it may limit it to what the Court considers reasonable in all the circumstances of the case.

This appears from the judgment of the Court of Appeal in *William Robinson & Co, Ltd v Heuer.* The particular covenant in that case is set out at p 452 and provides that 'Heuer shall not during this engagement, without the previous consent in writing of the said W. Robinson & Co. Ltd', and so forth, 'carry on or be engaged either directly or indirectly, as principal, agent, servant, or otherwise, in any trade, business, or calling, either relating to goods of any description sold or manufactured by the said W. Robinson & Co. Ltd. . . or in any other business whatsoever'.

. . . [T]he Court there proceeded to sever the covenants and to grant an injunction, not to restrain the defendant from carrying on any other business whatsoever, but framed so as to give what was felt to be a reasonable protection to the plaintiffs and no more. The plaintiffs waived an option which they possessed to extend the period of service for an extra five years, and the injunction then was granted for the remaining period of unextended time.

It is said that this case is no longer the law, but that *Attwood v Lamont* has decided that no such severance is permissible. I do not agree. *Attwood v Lamont* was a case where the covenants were held void as in restraint of trade. There is all the difference in the world between declining to make an illegal covenant good by neglecting that which makes it contrary to law and exercising a discretion as to how far the Court will enforce a valid convenant by injunction. The latter was done in the Court of Appeal in *William Robinson & Co v Heuer*, the former in *Attwood v Lamont*.

The case before me is, therefore, one in which it would be proper to grant an injunction unless to do so would in the circumstances be tantamount to ordering the defendant to perform her contract or remain idle or unless damages would be the more appropriate remedy.

With regard to the first of these considerations, it would, of course, be impossible to grant an injunction covering all the negative covenants in the contract. That would, indeed, force the defendant to perform her contract or remain idle; but this objection is removed by the restricted form in which the injunction is sought. It is confined to forbidding the defendant, without the consent of the plaintiffs, to render any services for or in any motion picture or stage production for any one other than the plaintiffs.

It was also urged that the difference between what the defendant can earn as a film artiste and what she might expect to earn by any other form of activity is so great that she will in effect be driven to perform her contract. That is not the criterion adopted in any of the decided cases. The defendant is stated to be a person of intelligence, capacity and means, and no evidence was adduced to show that, if enjoined from doing the specified acts otherwise than for the plaintiffs, she will not be able to employ herself both usefully and remuneratively in other spheres of activity, though not as remuneratively as in her special line. She will not be driven, although she may be tempted, to perform the contract, and the fact that she may be so tempted is no objection to the grant of an injunction.

With regard to the question whether damages is not the more appropriate remedy, I have the uncontradicted evidence of the plaintiffs as to the difficulty of estimating the damages which they may suffer from the breach by the defendant of her contract. I think it is not inappropriate to refer to the fact that, in the contract between the parties, in clause 22, there is a formal admission by the defendant that her services, being 'of a special, unique, extraordinary and intellectual character' gives them a particular value 'the loss of which cannot be reasonably or adequately compensated in damages' and that a breach may 'cost the producer great and irreparable injury and damage', and the artiste expressly agrees that the producer shall be entitled to the remedy of injunction. Of course, parties cannot contract themselves out of the law; but it assists, at all events, on the question of evidence as to the applicability of an injunction in the present case, to find the parties formally recognizing that in cases of this kind injunction is a more appropriate remedy than damages.

Furthermore, in the case of *Grimston v Cuningham*, which was also a case in which a theatrical manager was attempting to enforce against an actor a negative stipulation against going elsewhere, Wills J granted an injunction, and used the following language: 'This is an agreement of a kind which is pre-eminently subject to the interference of the Court by injunction, for in cases of this nature it very often happens that the injury suffered in consequence of the breach of the agreement would be out of all proportion to any pecuniary damages which could be proved or assessed by a jury. The circumstance affords a strong reason in favour of exercising the discretion of the Court by granting an injunction'.

I think that that applies to the present case also, and that an injunction should be granted in regard to the specified services.

Then comes the question as to the period for which the injunction should operate. The period of the contract, now that the plaintiffs have undertaken not as from October 16, 1936, to exercise the rights of suspension conferred upon them by clause 23 thereof, will, if they exercise their options to prolong it, extend to about May, 1942. As I read the judgment of the Court of Appeal in *Robinson v Heuer* the Court should make the period such as to give reasonable protection and no more to the plaintiffs against the ill effects to them of the defendant's breach of contract. The evidence as to that was perhaps necessarily somewhat vague. The main difficulty that the plaintiffs apprehend is that the defendant might appear in other films whilst the films already made by them and not yet shown are in the market for sale or hire and thus depreciate their value. I think that if the injunction is in force during the continuance of the contract or for three years from now, whichever period is the shorter, that will substantially meet the case.

NOTES

1. For all practical purposes, didn't this amount to ordering Bette Davis to work for Warner Bros? Compare *Page One Records Ltd v Britton* [1968] 1 WLR 157 at 167.

2. The quotation from *Doherty v Allman* (1878) 3 App Cas 709 seems to suggest that adequacy of damages is irrelevant if there is an express negative stipulation. Why should

this be? In practice, adequacy of damages is often taken into account even when there is a negative stipulation, eg *Decro-Wall International SA v Practitioners in Marketing Ltd* [1971] 2 All ER 216.

3.　It appears that, in contracts for employment, an injunction will not be granted merely to restrain the employee from working for another employer unless there is an express negative covenant: *Whitwood Chemical Co v Hardman* [1891] 2 Ch 416. This does not apply to other contracts: the court may restrain the defendant from some act implicitly inconsistent with his contractual obligations. In *Bower v Bantam Investments Ltd* [1972] 1 WLR 1120 at 1124–1125, Goff J said:

Where a positive contract is in substance negative the court may grant an injunction: see *Metropolitan Electric Supply Co Ltd v Ginder.* It will be observed there that the substance was indeed negative as there was no contract to take the supply of electricity. Buckley J (referring to the decision of Fry J in *Donnell v Bennett)* said:

'He says this at the beginning of his judgment, after reading or referring to the passage in Lord Selborne's judgment to which I have referred: "that the court ought to look at what is the nature of the contract between the parties; that if the contract as a whole is the subject of equitable jurisdiction, then an injunction may be granted in support of the contract, whether it contain or does not contain a negative stipulation." I think this is such a contract, because it appears to me that the contract for this present purpose is not one for the supply by the plaintiffs to the defendant of electricity—he is not bound to take any. The contract really is a contract, the whole of which is in substance the negative part of it, that he will take the whole from them, involving that he will not take any from anybody else. I therefore think that the fact that the contract is affirmative in form and not negative in form is no ground for refusing an injunction.'

[Moreover] . . . it is clear that in some cases the court will grant an injunction restraining a breach of a negative provision which is part of a positive contract, and moreover, of a contract which is not capable of specific performance: see *Wolverhampton and Walsall Railway Co v London and North-Western Railway Co* and *Catt v Tourle*, particularly per Giffard LJ.

Further, except probably in cases of contracts of personal service and, I think, fiduciary agency as to which special considerations apply, it is not necessary in my judgment to found an express negative covenant; an implied one will suffice: see the interlocutory observation of Buckley J in *Metropolitan Electric Supply Co Ltd v Ginder*, and, as to the requirement of an express covenant in the particular cases mentioned, see the judgment at p 807.

However, in my view, to found a claim for relief by way of injunction it is necessary to point to something specific which a defendant has by implication agreed not to do. The mere fact that his conduct or proposed conduct is inconsistent with his obligations under the contract is not sufficient, although, of course, if he does so act, that may well be in itself a breach of contract giving rise to an immediate right to damages as in *Stirling v Maitland.* This, in my judgment, follows from the basic principle that an injunction will never be granted unless it is clear and certain exactly what a defendant may not do.

II. ACTION FOR SUMS DUE UNDER THE CONTRACT

In contrast to the restrictive attitude towards specific performance, a defendant who has failed to pay money will routinely be forced to pay.

■ Sale of Goods Act 1979

Section 49: Action for price

(1) Where, under a contract of sale, the property in the goods has passed to the buyer and he wrongfully neglects or refuses to pay for the goods according to the terms of the contract, the seller may maintain an action against him for the price of the goods.

(2) Where, under a contract of sale, the price is payable on a day certain irrespective of delivery and the buyer wrongfully neglects or refuses to pay such price, the seller may maintain an action for the price, although the property in the goods has not passed and the goods have not been appropriated to the contract.

NOTES

1. Thus if the seller has delivered goods to the buyer and the buyer has failed to pay for them, the seller's remedy is to sue for the price. (Note that there are procedural advantages in suing for a 'liquidated' sum rather than 'unliquidated' damages, because you can apply for summary judgment.)

2. Note that the seller's right is only a personal one against the buyer. Under the general law, once the property has passed and the goods have been delivered to the buyer, the seller cannot exercise any right against the goods themselves (such as seizing them). If the buyer is insolvent, a personal right against it may be of little value, so sellers often attempt to preserve a right to repossess the goods. A common way of doing this is by a 'reservation of title' or 'Romalpa' clause. The simplest form of clause is a provision that the goods will remain the seller's property until paid for. See *Aluminium Industrie Vaassen B V v Romalpa Aluminium Ltd* [1976] 2 All ER 552 (the first case on such a clause), *Clough Mill Ltd v Martin* [1984] 3 All ER 982 (which explains how a simple clause operates) and *Armour v Thyssen* [1991] 2 AC 339.

3. Under a contract for the sale of goods, it is quite common for the property in the goods to pass before delivery: in the case of specific goods that are in a state ready to be delivered, the normal presumption (under s 17 and s 18 r 1) is that the property passes at the time the contract is made. In such a case, what is the practical effect of allowing a seller to sue a defaulting buyer for the price, rather than having to accept the buyer's repudiation and sue for damages? Is the outcome always a sensible one, given that the buyer may have no use for the goods? See Atiyah, *Sale of Goods*, 10th edn, 485–486.

4. However, if the buyer repudiates *before* the property has passed to him, the seller cannot pass it to him and recover the price. For instance, if a seller under a cif contract (one under which the seller's obligation is not actually to deliver the goods to the buyer, but to ship them to a named port and to deliver to the buyer the shipping documents, namely a bill of lading, an invoice and an insurance policy covering the voyage: see below) has reserved the right of disposal of the goods by providing that he will deliver the documents only against cash, it seems he cannot hold the documents for the repudiating buyer and sue for the price: *Colley v Overseas Exporters* [1921] 3 KB 302. Contrast this with the outcome of the next case.

■ *White & Carter (Councils) Ltd v McGregor*

[1961] 3 All ER 1178, House of Lords

The appellants made litter bins, on which they placed advertisements, and supplied them to local authorities. The respondent's sales manager entered a contract for the respondent's business to be so advertised for three years. The same day, the respondent repudiated the agreement, but the appellants made the advertisements and displayed them throughout the three-year period. They sued the respondent for the payments due under the contract.

Lord Reid

... The general rule cannot be in doubt. It was settled in Scotland at least as early as 1848 and it has been authoritatively stated time and again in both Scotland and England. If one party to a contract repudiates it in the sense of making it clear to the other party that he refuses or will refuse to carry out his part of the contract, the other party, the innocent party, has an option. He may accept that repudiation and sue for damages for breach of contract whether or not the time for performance has come; or he may if he chooses disregard or refuse to accept it and then the contract remains in full effect.

... I need not refer to the numerous authorities. They are not disputed by the respondent but he points out that in all of them the party who refused to accept the repudiation had no active duties under the contract. The innocent party's option is generally said to be to *wait* until the date of performance and then to claim damages estimated as at that date. There is no case in which it is said that he may, in face of the repudiation, go on and incur useless expense in performing the contract and then claim the contract price. The option, it is argued, is merely as to the date as at which damages are to be assessed. Developing this argument, the respondent points out that in most cases the innocent party cannot complete the contract himself without the other party doing, allowing or accepting something, and that it is purely fortuitous that the appellants can do so in this case. In most cases by refusing co-operation the party in breach can compel the innocent party to restrict his claim to damages. Then it was said that even where the innocent party can complete the contract without such co-operation it is against the public interest that he should be allowed to do so. An example was developed in argument. A company might engage an expert to go abroad and prepare an elaborate report and then repudiate the contract before anything was done. To allow such an expert then to waste thousands of pounds in preparing the report cannot be right if a much smaller sum of damages would give him full compensation for his loss. It would merely enable the expert to extort a settlement giving him far more than reasonable compensation.

The respondent founds on the decision of the First Division in *Langford & Co Ltd v Dutch*. There an advertising contractor agreed to exhibit a film for a year. Four days after this agreement was made the advertiser repudiated it but, as in the present case, the contractor refused to accept the repudiation and proceeded to exhibit the film and sue for the contract price. The sheriff-substitute dismissed the action as irrelevant and his decision was affirmed on appeal. In the course of a short opinion the Lord President (Lord Cooper) said:

'... The pursuers could not force the defender to accept a year's advertisement which she did not want, though they could of course claim damages for her breach of contract. On the averments the only reasonable and proper course, which the pursuers should have adopted, would have been to treat the defender as having repudiated the contract and as being on that account liable in damages, the measure of which we are, of course, not in a position to discuss.'

The Lord President cited no authority and I am in doubt what principle he had in mind....

... We must now decide whether that case was rightly decided. In my judgment it was not. It could only be supported on one or other of two grounds. It might be said that, because in most case the circumstances are such that an innocent party is unable to complete the contract and earn the contract price without the assent or co-operation of the other party, therefore in cases where he can do so he should not be allowed to do so. I can see no justification for that.

The other ground would be that there is some general equitable principle or element of public policy which requires this limitation of the contractual rights of the innocent party. It may well be that, if it can be shown that a person has no legitimate interest, financial or otherwise, in performing the contract rather than claiming damages, he ought not to be allowed to saddle the other party with an additional burden with no benefit to himself. If a party has no interest to enforce a stipulation he cannot in general enforce it: so it might be said that if a party has no interest to insist on a particular remedy he ought not to be allowed to insist on it. And, just as a party is not allowed to enforce a penalty, so he ought not to be allowed to penalise the other party by taking one course when another is equally advantageous to him. If I may revert to the example which I gave of a company engaging an expert to prepare an elaborate report and then repudiating before anything was done, it might be that the company could show that the expert had no substantial or legitimate interest in carrying out the work rather than accepting damages: I would think that the de minimis principle would apply in determining whether his interest was substantial and that he might have a legitimate interest other than an immediate financial interest. But if the expert had no such interest then that might be regarded as a proper case for the exercise of the general equitable jurisdiction of the court. But that is not this case. Here the respondent did not set out to prove that the appellants had no legitimate interest in completing the contract and claiming the contract price rather than claiming damages, there is nothing in the findings of fact to support such a case, and it seems improbable that any such case could have been proved. It is, in my judgment, impossible to say that the appellants should be deprived of their right to claim the contract price merely because the benefit to them as against claiming damages and reletting their advertising space might be small in comparison with the loss to the respondent: that is the most that could be said in favour of the respondent. Parliament has on many occasions relieved parties from certain kinds of improvident or oppressive contracts, but the common law can only do that in very limited circumstances. Accordingly, I am unable to avoid the conclusion that this appeal must be allowed and the case remitted so that decree can be pronounced as craved in the initial writ.

Lord Morton of Henryton [dissenting]

... It is well established that repudiation by one party does not put an end to a contract. The other party can say 'I hold you to your contract, which still remains in force'. What, then, is his remedy if the repudiating party persists in his repudiation and refuses to carry out his part of the contract? The contract has been broken. The innocent party is entitled to be compensated by damages for any loss which he has suffered by reason of the breach, and in a limited class of cases the court will decree specific implement. The law of Scotland provides no other remedy for a breach of contract, and there is no reported case which decides that the innocent party may act as the appellants have acted. The present case is one in which specific implement could not be decreed, since the only obligation of the respondent under the contract was to pay a sum of money for services to be rendered by the appellants. Yet the appellants are claiming a kind of inverted specific implement of the contract. They first insist on performing their part of the contract, against the will of the other party, and then claim that he must perform his part and pay the contract price for unwanted services. In my opinion, my Lords, the appellants' only remedy was damages, and they were bound to take steps to minimise their loss, according to a well-established rule of law. Far from doing this, having incurred no expense at the date of the repudiation, they made no attempt to procure another advertiser, but deliberately went on to incur expense and perform unwanted services with the intention of creating a money debt which did not exist at the date of the repudiation.

Lord Keith of Avonholm also delivered a dissenting judgment.

Lord Hodson

... It is settled as a fundamental rule of the law of contract that repudiation by one of the parties to a contract does not itself discharge it. See the speech of Viscount Simon LC in *Heyman v Darwins, Ltd* citing with approval the following sentence from a judgment of Scrutton LJ in *Golding v London & Edinburgh Insurance Co, Ltd:*

> 'I have never been able to understand what effect repudiation by one party has unless the other party accepts [the repudiation].'

In *Howard v Pickford Tool Co, Ltd* Asquith LJ said: 'An unaccepted repudiation is a thing writ in water and of no value to anybody: it confers no legal rights of any sort or kind'. These are English cases but that the law of Scotland is the same is, I think, clear from the authorities, of which I need only refer to one, namely, *Howie v Anderson* where language to the same effect is to be found in the opinions of the Lord President and Lord Moncrieff.

It follows that, if, as here, there was no acceptance, the contract remains alive for the benefit of both parties and the party who has repudiated can change his mind but it does not follow that the party at the receiving end of the proffered repudiation is bound to accept it before the time for performance and is left to his remedy in damages for breach.

Counsel for the respondent did not seek to dispute the general proposition of law to which I have referred but sought to argue that if at the date of performance by the innocent party the guilty party maintains his refusal to accept performance and the innocent party does not accept the repudiation, although the contract still survives, it does not survive so far as the right of the innocent party to perform it is concerned but survives only for the purpose of enforcing remedies open to him by way of damages or specific implement. This produces an impossible result; if the innocent party is deprived of some of his rights it involves putting an end to the contract except in cases, unlike this, where, in the exercise of the court's discretion, the remedy of specific implement is available.

The true position is that the contract survives and does so not only where specific implement is available. When the assistance of the court is not required the innocent party can choose whether he will accept repudiation and sue for damages for anticipatory breach or await the date of performance by the guilty party. Then, if there is failure in performance, his rights are preserved.

It may be unfortunate that the appellants have saddled themselves with an unwanted contract causing an apparent waste of time and money. No doubt this aspect impressed the Court of Session but there is no equity which can assist the respondent. It is trite that equity will not rewrite an improvident contract where there is no disability on either side. There is no duty laid on a party to a subsisting contract to vary it at the behest of the other party so as to deprive himself of the benefit given to him by the contract. To hold otherwise would be to introduce a novel equitable doctrine that a party was not to be held to his contract unless the court in a given instance thought it reasonable so to do. In this case it would make an action for debt a claim for a discretionary remedy. This would introduce an uncertainty into the field of contract which appears to be unsupported by authority either in English or Scottish law save for the one case on which the Court of Session founded its opinion and which must, in my judgment, be taken to have been wrongly decided.

Lord Tucker agreed with the reasoning of Lord Hodson.

Appeal allowed.

NOTES

1.   Lord Reid points out that, in many cases, the innocent party will not be able to carry out his performance without the cooperation of the repudiating party. This was considered further by Megarry J in *Hounslow London Borough Council v Twickenham Garden Developments Ltd* [1970] 3 All ER 326. Considering the application of the *White & Carter* case to a building contract, the judge said:

> ... Quite apart from questions of active co-operation, cases where one party is lawfully in possession of property of the other seem to me to raise issues not before the House of Lords in the *White* case.

Suppose that A, who owns a large and valuable painting, contracts with B, a picture restorer, to restore it over a period of three months. Before the work is begun. A receives a handsome offer from C to purchase the picture, subject to immediate delivery of the picture in its unrestored state, C having grave suspicions of B's competence. If the work of restoration is to be done in A's house, he can effectually exclude B by refusing to admit him to the house; without A's "co-operation" to this extent B cannot perform his contract. But what if the picture stands in A's locked barn, the key of which he has lent to B so that he may come and go freely, or if the picture has been removed to B's premises? Can B insist in these cases in performing his contract, even though this makes it impossible for A to accept C's offer? In the case of the barn, A's co-operation may perhaps be said to be requisite to the extent of not barring B's path to the barn or putting another lock on the door; but if the picture is on B's premises, no active co-operation by A is needed. Nevertheless, the picture is A's property, and I find it difficult to believe that Lord Reid intended to restrict the concept of "co-operation" to active co-operation. In the *White* case, no co-operation by the proprietor, either active or passive, was required; the contract could be performed by the agent wholly without reference to the proprietor or his property. The case was far removed from that of a property owner being forced to stand impotently aside while a perhaps ill-advised contract is executed on property of his which he has delivered into the possession of the other party, and is powerless to retrieve.

Accordingly, I do not think that the *White* case has any application to the case before me.

In the Canadian case of *Finelli v Dee* [1968] 1 OR 676, 76 DLR(2d) 393, a homeowner repudiated a contract to have his driveway surfaced. The builder entered and did the work without notice while the owner was away. It was held that the builder could not recover the price: without deciding whether the builder's licence to enter the land had been revoked, the court held that he was not entitled to do the work without giving notice.

2.   A wrongfully dismissed employee cannot keep himself available for work and recover his wages. (There were, at one time, indications that a doctrine of 'constructive service', as it was called, might develop, but the idea was ultimately rejected: see Freedland, *Contract of Employment*, 1976, p 294.) How would you explain the different outcome?

3.   Lord Reid also suggests that the innocent party may not be able to carry out the contract and recover the price after a repudiation if he has no substantial or legitimate interest in doing so. Did the other members of the House accept this?

4.   What is the distinction between the example given of the expert going abroad and preparing his report and the facts of the *White & Carter* case? A possible difference, although not one stated in any of the judgments, is that the pursuers in *White & Carter* could not have relet the space to any other client—they were 'lost-volume sellers'. See Diamond (1978) 11 Melbourne ULR 573 at 575–576.

The legitimate interest point has remained controversial. In *Attica Sea Carriers Corpn v Ferrostaal Poseidon Bulk Reederei GmbH, The Puerto Buitrago* [1976] 1 Lloyd's Rep 250, it appears to have been accepted by all of the members of the Court of Appeal, but it is not clear that the principle formed part of the *ratio* of the case. The charterers of a ship by demise (a form of charter under which the charterer takes over the management of the ship) were obliged to return her at the end of the charter in as good condition as when she was delivered to them. In the event, the repairs would have cost more than the ship would have been worth even when repaired, so the charterers returned her unrepaired, admitting liability for damages. It was held that the owners could not have the ship repaired and meanwhile continue to charge the charterers hire. The principal ground for the decision was that the obligation to repair was not a condition precedent to the right to redeliver. However, the court added that the owners would also fail for other reasons: the redelivery was in any event effective, notwithstanding the fact that the vessel had not been repaired; the charter could not continue without the charterers' cooperation; and, finally, the owners had no legitimate interest in claiming the hire rather than in taking the ship back and claiming damages.

The legitimate interest point seems also to have been accepted by Kerr J in *The Odenfeld* [1978] 2 Lloyd's Rep 357 (at 374), although only as applicable:

... in extreme cases, viz, where damages would be an adequate remedy and where an election to keep the contract alive would be wholly unreasonable

... Kerr J held that the innocent party in that case, the owners under a time charter, did have a legitimate interest in continuing with the contract, because it would be difficult to find other employment for the ship, termination of the charter would put them into breach of other contracts and the damages would be hard to assess.

■ *Clea Shipping Corpn v Bulk Oil International Ltd, The Alaskan Trader*
[1984] 1 All ER 129

By a time charter dated 19 October 1979, the owners chartered a vessel to the charterers for a period of approximately 24 months. After the vessel had been in service for nearly a year, the vessel suffered a serious engine breakdown and it became apparent that the repairs would take several months. The charterers then indicated that they had no further use for the vessel but the owners nevertheless went ahead with the repairs at a cost of £800,000. The repairs were completed on 7 April 1981. The owners then informed the charterers that the vessel was once again at their disposal, but the charterers declined to give the master of the vessel any orders because they regarded the charterparty as having come to an end. The owners refused to treat the charterers' conduct as a repudiation of the charterparty and maintained the vessel at anchor with a full crew ready to sail until the time charter expired in December 1981. Hire was paid throughout the period from 7 April until December 1981, first under a letter of credit opened in favour of the owners and thereafter by the charterers themselves without prejudice. When the charterparty came to an end, the question of whether the charterers could recover the hire paid for the period from April to December 1981 was referred to arbitration. The charterers contended that the owners ought to have accepted the charterers' conduct as a repudiation of the charterparty and confined their claim to damages. The owners contended that, in the case of repudiation, the innocent party had an unfettered right to elect whether to accept or refuse the repudiation, and accordingly, they were entitled to keep the vessel at the disposal of the charterers throughout the period and to retain the hire. The arbitrator found that the owners had no legitimate interest in pursuing their claim for hire rather than a claim for damages. He held that the owners ought to have accepted the charterers' repudiation by midnight on 8 April 1981, with a view to mitigating their damage and, accordingly, that the charterers were entitled to recover the hire, while remaining liable for damages. The owners appealed.

Lloyd J

... [The arbitrator said:]

'I am satisfied that this commercial absurdity is not justified by a proper interpretation of the decided cases. I consider that the analogy of a contract between Master and servant applies more closely to a timecharter than the analogy of a simple debt. The Owner supplies the vessel and crew; the Charterer supplies fuel oil, pays disbursements and gives orders. The Charterers were also able to satisfy me that at that stage the Owners had no legitimate interest in pursuing their claim for hire rather than a claim for damages. In these respects the present case differs materially from the case of *White & Carter v McGregor*, and is more closely analogous to the case of *The Puerto Buitrago*, where the judgments of Lord Denning MR and Lord Orr are particularly in point.'

It seems to me that the arbitrator is here distinguishing clearly between the two observations or limitations on the general principle to which Lord Reid had drawn attention in his speech. He is saying that a time charter is more analogous to a contract between master and servant than a simple debt, ie that it is a contract which calls for co-operation between both parties. He is also saying ('The charterers were *also* able to satisfy me. . . ') that the owners had no legitimate interest in pursuing their claim for hire as distinct from damages. I will take the legitimate interest point first.

In addition to arguing that what Lord Reid had said about legitimate interest was only a quotation from counsel, and in any event obiter, arguments with which I have already dealt, counsel for the owners, submitted that Lord Reid was, quite simply, wrong. It seems to me that it would be difficult for me to take that view in the light of what was said by all three members of the Court of Appeal in *The Puerto Buitrago*. Whether one takes Lord Reid's language, which was adopted by Orr and Browne LJJ in *The Puerto Buitrago*, or Lord Denning MR's language in that case ('in all reason'), or Kerr J's language in *The Odenfeld* ('wholly unreasonable. . . quite unrealistic, unreasonable and untenable'), there comes a point at which the court will cease, on general equitable principles, to allow the innocent party to enforce his contract according to its strict legal terms. How one defines that point is obviously a matter of some difficulty, for it involves drawing a line between conduct which is merely unreasonable (see per Lord Reid in *White & Carter v McGregor*, criticising the Lord President in *Langford & Co Ltd v Dutch*) and conduct which is *wholly* unreasonable (see per Kerr J in *The Odenfeld*). . . But however difficult it may be to define the point, that there *is* such a point seems to me to have been accepted both by the Court of Appeal in *The Puerto Buitrago* and by Kerr J in *The Odenfeld*.

I appreciate that the House of Lords has recently re-emphasised the importance of certainty in commercial contracts, when holding that there is no equitable jurisdiction to relieve against the consequences of the withdrawal clause in a time charter: see *Scandinavian Trading Tanker Co AB v Flota Petrolera Ecuatoriana, The Scaptrade*. I appreciate, too, that the importance of certainty was one of the main reasons urged by Lord Hodson in *White & Carter v McGregor* in upholding the innocent party's unfettered right to elect. But, for reasons already mentioned, it seems to me that this court is bound to hold that there *is some* fetter, if only in extreme cases; and for want of a better way of describing that fetter, it is safest for this court to use the language of Lord Reid, which, as I have already said, was adopted by a majority of the Court of Appeal in *The Puerto Buitrago*.

. . . Counsel for the owners argued that the finding must be wrong in law. The arbitrator must have misunderstood what was said by Lord Reid, or applied the wrong test. But I could only accept that submission if the conclusion reached by the arbitrator was one which no reasonable arbitrator could have reached applying the right test. I cannot take that view. Indeed I can well understand why the arbitrator reached the conclusion he did. It is of course quite unnecessary for me to say whether I would have reached the same conclusion on the facts myself; nor by saying even that, do I mean to imply that I would have reached a different conclusion. It was the arbitrator who heard the evidence over many days, not me. It was for him to decide.

Counsel for the owners then turned to the further reasons given by the arbitrator which I have mentioned earlier in this judgment. But counsel was unable to extract any error of law or any mistake in approach. The arbitrator analysed in detail the main grounds on which it could be said that the owners were justified in continuing to claim hire, rather than damages, namely the requirements of the bank, the difficulty in assessing damages and the difficulty in obtaining alternative employment. These are all matters which were considered by Kerr J in *The Odenfeld*. For example, on the question of damages the arbitrator said:

'I did not accept that the assessment of damages in fact presented any special difficulty, or that the poor prospects of obtaining alternative employment would preclude the Owners from obtaining substantial damages. It was a matter of evidence.'

On the difficulty of assessing damages therefore, as on the other matters, the arbitrator reached, as he was entitled, a different view on the facts than did Kerr J in *The Odenfeld*. I cannot begin to say that he was wrong in law. . . .

I turn last to the alternative ground on which the arbitrator based his decision, that this was a contract which called for co-operation between the parties, and therefore fell within Lord Reid's first limitation. Counsel for the charterers argued that a time charter is a contract for services, to be performed by the owners through the master and crew, and through the use of their vessel. As a contract for services, it is, as Lord Diplock pointed out in *The Scaptrade*—

'the very prototype of a contract of which before the fusion of law and equity a court would never grant specific performance. . . '

As in any other contract for services the owners earn their remuneration by performing the services required. If they are wrongfully prevented from performing any services, then, as in any other contract for services, the only remedy lies in damages. The fact that the owners' remuneration in this case, called hire, is payable in advance makes no difference. Counsel for the owners, on the other hand, argued that the owners earned their hire simply by holding the vessel and the services of their master and crew at the charterers' disposal. He concedes that in the case of master and servant, where the master has wrongfully dismissed the servant, the servant cannot earn remuneration by holding himself at the disposal of his master. He is confined to his remedy in damages. But counsel for the owners submits that a time charter is different. In view of my decision on the legitimate interest point, it is unnecessary for me to decide between these rival arguments, or to explore the nature of a time charter contract any further. All I will say is that, at first blush, there seemed much to be said for the argument of counsel for the charterers. I say no more, because in *The Odenfeld* Kerr J found a similar argument unimpressive.

For the reasons I have given I would dismiss the owners' appeal and uphold the award.

Appeal dismissed. Leave to appeal granted.

NOTES

1.   What do you think constitutes a 'legitimate interest'? In *The Odenfeld*, Kerr J held that the owners were justified in carrying on with the charter because they would otherwise have to break other contracts under which they had assigned the hire. In *The Alaskan Trader*, the owners had assigned the hire payments to the bank to which the ship was mortgaged. In view of the difficulty of reletting the ship, might they be forgiven for feeling they had a legitimate interest in claiming the hire?

2.   The behaviour of the parties in this case seems clearly inefficient, in that if the ship could have been relet, both parties could have been better off. Why do you think that they did not bargain their way to a solution under which the ship was relet, and the charterers paid the owners a sum somewhere between the full hire under the original charter and the amount payable as damages (viz the difference between the charter rate and the rate at which the ship was relet)? Does the extract from Priest, 'Breach and Remedy for the Tender of Non-conforming Goods' (see p 592) suggest any reason?

QUESTIONS

1. Explain the basic rules governing specific performance.

2. It is sometimes claimed that the courts are becoming more liberal in their use of specific performance. What evidence do you see of that?

3. Why is specific performance not the normal remedy for breach of contract in cases in which it is possible for the defendant to perform the contract? Should specific performance be given more readily?

4. A party who has completed performance of its side of the contract will be able to claim the price due from the other party (indeed that will usually be its only remedy). If, before it has completed its performance, it is told by the other that the performance is no longer wanted, and the case is not one in which specific performance would be granted, what can it do:

   (i) in a case in which it cannot perform without the other party's cooperation;
        or

   (ii) in a case in which it could do so?

   Can you invent an example of each kind of case?

CHAPTER TWENTY-FOUR

RESTITUTIONARY REMEDIES

The victim of a breach of contract who has justifiably terminated because of it may, instead of claiming damages, opt to claim in restitution for the return of any money paid or for the value of services rendered to the party in breach. This is sometimes referred to as reversing 'unjust enrichment by subtraction' (eg Burrows, p 480) because the defendant has received a benefit at the plaintiff's expense. A second possibility is that, as we saw earlier (p 639), the plaintiff might seek restitution of the gain the defendant made, over and above any loss to the plaintiff, through breaking the contract ('unjust enrichment by wrongdoing').

I. UNJUST ENRICHMENT BY SUBTRACTION

Money paid may be recovered provided that there has been a total failure of consideration—ie the party in breach did not perform at all or the victim has justifiably rejected the performance. See the *Fibrosa* case, noted at p 481.

■ *Whincup v Hughes*
(1871) LR 6 CP 78

The plaintiff apprenticed his son to a watchmaker and jeweller for the term of six years, paying to the master a premium of £25. The master duly instructed the apprentice for a year, and then died. The plaintiff sought, in an action against the master's executrix for money had and received, to recover the whole or some part of the premium, on the ground of failure of consideration.

Bovill CJ

This is an action brought to recover a part of the premium paid upon the execution of an apprenticeship deed, on the ground of failure of consideration. The general rule of law is, that where a contract has been in part performed no part of the money paid under such contract can be recovered back. There may be some cases of partial performance which form exceptions to this rule, as, for instance, if there were a contract to deliver ten sacks of wheat and six only were delivered, the price of the remaining four might be recovered back. But there the consideration is clearly severable.

... The contract having been in part performed, it would seem that the general rule must apply unless the consideration be in its nature apportionable. I am at a loss to see on what principle such apportionment could be made. It could not properly be made with reference to the proportion which the period during which the apprentice was instructed bears to the whole term. In the early part of the term the teaching would be most onerous, and the services of the apprentice of little value: as time went on his services would probably be worth more, and he would require less teaching.

NOTES

1. *Whincup v Hughes* was a case of what is now termed frustration, but at common law, the same rules of restitution applied to contracts discharged by frustration and terminated for breach (see also p 481).

2. The plaintiff can only use a restitutionary remedy instead of damages if the contract has been terminated (see Burrows, pp 250–251).

3. Why bring a restitutionary claim when you could sue for damages? In *Ebrahim Dawood Ltd v Heath (Est 1927) Ltd* [1961] 2 Lloyd's Rep 512, McNair J held that a buyer who had justifiably rejected part of a consignment of steel sheets for which he had paid in advance was entitled to recover a proportionate part of the money. The seller had argued that the buyer's only remedy was to claim damages, but McNair J pointed out that the result would be:

    ... that if—let us take the figure in this case—the market price at the time of the delivery conformed to £70 against the contract price of £73 10s, there would be recovered on this argument only £70 per ton and not £73 10s per ton, leaving a profit of £3 10s in the pockets of the seller

    Another reason why the innocent party may prefer to recover the price paid than to sue for damages is that an action for a liquidated sum is, generally speaking, quicker and cheaper to bring than a claim for damages.

4. The requirement that the failure of consideration be total has been criticised (eg Burrows, pp 323–324). In Working Paper No 65, *Pecuniary Restitution on Breach of Contract*, the Law Commission had provisionally proposed extending the right to recover money paid to cases of partial failure of consideration. In the ensuing report (No 121, 1983), Part III, the proposal was dropped. Perhaps because the requirement of total failure seems to have no very obvious purpose, the courts have been rather lenient in applying it. In *Ebrahim Dawood*, a restitutionary remedy was given even though the buyer had received some of the steel; the price (£73 10s per ton) was apportionable and the court said there was a failure of consideration in relation to the steel not delivered. In *Rover International Ltd v Cannon Film Sales Ltd (No 3)* [1989] 3 All ER 423, the Court of Appeal held that there had been a total failure of consideration even though the films had been received by Rover, on the ground that they had bargained to get a profit from the films and this had been prevented. (For criticism of this, see Burrows, pp 330–331.)

    If the innocent party has performed work before he terminates the contract he may, as an alternative to damages, claim a *quantum meruit* for the value of the work done. The best known example is probably *Planché v Colburn* (1831) 8 Bing 14. The plaintiff had been employed to write, for a fee, a book on armour for a series to be called 'The Juvenile Library'. After he had written several chapters, the defendant cancelled the series. The plaintiff justifiably refused the defendant's offer to publish the work separately and terminated the contract. He recovered the value of his wasted work from the publisher, even though it does not appear that he had delivered any of the manuscript before the publisher repudiated the contract.

■ *Slowey v Lodder*

(1900) 20 NZLR 321

The plaintiff was wrongly prevented by the defendants from completing a construction contract. At first instance, Edwards J had held that the measure of damages for breach of contract and on a *quantum meruit* was the same. In the Court of Appeal:

Williams J

. . . Is, then, the plaintiff entitled to recover on a *quantum meruit?* and, if so, on what principle ought the amount which he can recover to be fixed? The law is stated by Mr J W Smith, in the notes to *Cutter v Powell* in *Smith's Leading Cases*, as follows:

> 'It is submitted that it is an invariably true proposition that, wherever one of the parties to a special contract not under seal has in an unqualified manner refused to perform his side of the contract, or has disabled himself from performing it by his own act, the other party has thereupon a right to elect to rescind it, and may, on doing so, immediately sue on a *quantum meruit* for anything which he had done under it before the rescission.'

Mr Smith's notes to the leading cases are classical: they are cited in every text-book, and references to them appear frequently in the judgments of the Courts in England. The doctrine above laid down has been universally recognised. . . .

That a plaintiff in a case like the present can recover on a *quantum meruit* is fully recognised in the case of *Appleby v Myers*. . . .

But it is contended that the result must be the same whether a plaintiff sues upon the special contract or upon a *quantum meruit*. If the result must be the same, how can it profit a plaintiff to have—what he certainly has—an alternative remedy? If, however, the principle on which a plaintiff becomes entitled to sue on a *quantum meruit* is considered but for a moment, it is obvious that the amount he can recover must be estimated in a different way from the amount he could recover if he sued for a breach of the special contract. If the plaintiff sues on the contract, treating it as still open, he is entitled, and the defendant is entitled, to place before the jury what the result would have been if the plaintiff had been allowed to complete the contract. If the plaintiff can show that by the action of the defendant he has been prevented from making in the future a large profit, he is entitled to recover for the loss of that profit. So, if the defendant can show that, taking the ultimate result of the contract, the plaintiff has been deprived of no profit, and has possibly been saved from loss, then, though the breach by the defendant may have been wrongful, the damages would properly be nominal. But a *quantum meruit* is different. The right to sue on it rests on this: that the defendant has done something which is equivalent to an abandonment of the contract on his part. Then the right arises for the plaintiff to say. 'You have abandoned the contract. So be it: let the contract be rescinded. But you have in your hands the fruits of my labour: pay me for the work I have done and the materials I have supplied.' . . .

The judgment of the Court of Appeal, including specifically this point, was affirmed by the Privy Council: [1904] AC 442, at 453.

NOTES

1. Just as where a plaintiff wishes to recover money paid, it seems obviously advantageous for the plaintiff who was working under a losing contract to claim a *quantum meruit* rather than damages. In *Boomer v Muir* 24 P 2d 570 (California, 1933), a contractor who built part of a dam before justifiably terminating the contract was held to be entitled to recover on a *quantum meruit* more than the contract price that would have been payable had he finished the work. Do you think that is right? See Burrows, pp 341–343.

2.   Can you see any reason why a contractor, who stood to make a normal profit if he had been allowed to complete the work, might prefer to claim on a *quantum meruit* rather than claim damages?

3.   Even in cases that are less extreme than *Boomer v Muir*, it seems that the result of allowing the plaintiff to recover the money he has paid, or to recover the value of the services he has rendered, may be to allow him to escape a bad bargain. If he is allowed to recover all that he has paid out or spent, he may come out better off than if the contract had been performed. This is just what the courts have refused to allow when the plaintiff is claiming reliance loss (see p 629). Do you see any justification for allowing it when the plaintiff is claiming restitution?

4.   Under the law at present, a party who has performed work cannot claim its value if the contract was terminated because of *his* breach.

5.   *Planché v Colburn* (above) is regarded as a difficult case by restitution lawyers, because the plaintiff was permitted to recover on a *quantum meruit* even though it does not appear that he had ever delivered any of the manuscript of the book to the defendant. Thus how can the defendant have been enriched? Birks (eg in *Essays on the Law of Restitution*, Burrows (ed), pp 140–141) argues that perhaps it can be justified on the assumptions that (i) the defendant 'had commissioned not merely the book but the work of researching and writing the book', and (ii) that the defendant cannot make the 'subjective devaluation' argument (see p 42) that the work was of no value to him when he prevented the plaintiff from finishing the book. Most restitution lawyers seem to prefer to see the case as not one of restitution at all but of a kind of damages for wasted effort (cf p 629): see Birks, on p 140, and Burrows, p 17 and 343. The case was decided in 1831, at a time when the modern law on how damages should be calculated had not even started to develop. It is clear that today on identical facts an author could sue for damages for breach of contract. What is not clear is to what extent a damages action and a *quantum meruit* would (or should) produce different figures.

II. UNJUST ENRICHMENT BY WRONGDOING

As mentioned earlier (p 639), in certain circumstances, for instance when the party in breach owes a fiduciary duty to the innocent party, the latter may bring an action in restitution and recover the profit the defendant has made through breaking the contract. It has been argued that this remedy should be more widely available. See Jones, 'Recovery of Benefits Gained by Breach of Contract' (1983) 99 LQR 443; Birks, 'Restitutionary Remedies for Breach of Contract' [1987] LMCLQ 421.

In the third edition of this work, we said that the prospect of restitutionary damages being available for a breach of contract that involves neither wrongful use of the plaintiff's property nor a breach of fiduciary duty seems slim after the decision in *Surrey County Council v Bredero* (see p 631). We asked whether this was a satisfactory state of affairs. In [1989] 48 CLJ 302, 319–321, Jackman wrote:

Why, then, has the law taken such an absolute stance against regarding breach of contract as a restitution-yielding wrong? The answer may lie in the nature of the pecuniary remedies already available for breach of contract. The aim of compensatory damages in contract is to place the innocent party 'so far as money can do it . . . in the same situation . . . as if the contract had been performed,' which typically involves compensating the plaintiff for the gains which he expected to receive from the performance of the other party's obligations. Atiyah has argued that, contrary to this orthodoxy, contractual expectations are relatively unworthy of legal protection, for 'a disappointed expectation is a psychological rather than a pecuniary injury, and the law is generally sparing in its willingness to award compensation for injuries or losses which are neither physical nor pecuniary' [*Essays in Contract* (1986) pp 34–35]. This argument, however, does not conclude the matter. It may be that any personal harm caused by disappointed expectations is a weak ground for protecting those expectations, but there remains the problem of institutional harm. On this basis, expectation damages may be seen as aimed at preserving the integrity and stability of contractual obligations, by making good the underlying promises. As Raz [(1982) 95 Harvard LR 916, 937] argues:

> ' "Harm" includes institutional harm. Preventing the erosion or debasement of the practice of undertaking voluntary obligations is therefore a fit object for the law to pursue.'

Herein lies an asymmetry, though not an anomaly, in the availability of restitution for wrongs. The analysis of proprietary torts and relationships of trust and confidence suggests a simple dichotomy whereby restitutionary remedies are directed against institutional harm, whereas compensatory remedies operate to redress personal harm. But the rationale for awarding compensation for lost expectations in contract is to give contracts sufficient institutional protection to maintain that degree of stability which is essential to any practice of promise-making. Hence, the compensatory remedy provides protection from institutional harm, without the intervention of restitution.

English law, at present, is content to leave the matter there. The common law does not take a censorious attitude to breach of contract, consistently with the view that a party to a contract, unlike a fiduciary, operates at arm's length and holds his powers for his own benefit. He is thus free to change his mind about the wisdom of a particular contract which he has entered into and, in the absence of specific performance or an injunction, then on payment of compensation for the other party's reliance or lost expectations, he may deploy his resources more profitably elsewhere. Once expectation damages are awarded, the argument might run, there is no institutional harm left to be redressed.

Elsewhere in this topic, however, the availability of particular measures of restitutionary relief indicates that the flatness and moral bluntness of a rule based solely on the nature of the facilitative institution may need to be supplemented by the infusion of a hierarchy of moral fault, although this has not been achieved systematically in our law. In the same way, the person who makes 'deliberate recourse to breach of contract for the sake of making a gain' threatens the integrity of contracts in a way which might demand additional institutional protection, in the form of an account of profits in equity. The availability of such a remedy would then enable the court to consider the full range of features of each case, particularly the moral quality of the breach, which should, but cannot at present, influence the measure of pecuniary relief.

After the *Bredero* case, Birks (1993) 109 LQR 518, 519 was more forthright:

The Court of Appeal's rejection of this claim, especially in the more absolute form followed by Dillon LJ, raises some worrying questions about the capacity of our law of contract to deal with certain kinds of breach. Suppose that a great hospital contracts out certain of its cleaning needs, specifying rigorous standards in the interests of hygiene and hence of safety. Knowing the dangers but hoping for the best, the successful firm decides to take a 20 per cent excess profit by ignoring those standards. After, say, two years, the hospital discovers what is going on. In the meantime the firm has been lucky. Its gamble has paid off, in the sense that no deaths or other bad consequences can actually be attributed to its substandard performance. It pays nominal damages. Again, suppose that a celebrity offers employees good terms of employment but in every case, from gardener to personal assistant, exacts the same promise not to make money by selling stories to the media. The gardener turns out to have broken this promise by selling a series of articles about his work and his employer's horticultural preferences. Again, nominal damages. The real cause for concern in these cases is not the inadequacy of the remedy in the particular case but the general tendency of that inadequacy to encourage the kind of calculation made by Bredero. The law is deficient when a legitimate interest cannot be safe-guarded against such opportunism.

Could allowing the plaintiff to recover the profit the defendant has made through breach be justified in terms of economic efficiency? If restitutionary recovery were permitted, what behaviour would you expect from a party who is presented with the opportunity to make a greater profit if he can avoid performing the existing contract?

■ Friedmann, 'The Efficient Breach Fallacy' (1989)

18 Journal of Legal Studies 1, 1–2, 4–6

'The only universal consequence of a legally binding promise is that the law makes the promisor pay damages if the promised event does not come to pass. In every case it leaves him free from interference until the time for fulfillment has gone by, and therefore free to break his contract if he chooses.'

So wrote Oliver Wendell Holmes in his seminal discussion of contract remedies in *The Common Law*. That position, while widely discussed, is not acceptable as a normative (nor, as will be shown, as a positive) account of the question of contract remedies. Stated in a phrase, the weakness of Holmes's approach lies in its conclusion that the remedy provides a perfect substitute for the right, when in truth the purpose of the remedy is to vindicate that right, not to replace it. Holmes's analysis mistakenly converts the remedy into a kind of indulgence that the wrongdoer is unilaterally always entitled to purchase. As with any unifying ideal, Holmes's proposition is difficult to confine to the contract cases to which it was originally applied. Why not generalize the proposition so that every person has an 'option' to transgress another's rights and to violate the law, so long as he is willing to suffer the consequences? The legal system could thus be viewed only as establishing a set of prices, some high and some low, which then act as the only constraints to induce lawful conduct.

The modern theory of 'efficient breach' is a variation and systematic extension of Holmes's outlook on contractual remedy. It assumes that role because of the dominance that it gives to the expectation measure of damages in cases of contract breach: the promisor is allowed to breach at will so long as he leaves the promisee as well off after breach as he would have been had the promise been performed, while any additional gain is retained by the contract breaker. . . .

The essence of the theory is 'efficiency.' The 'right' to break a contract is not predicated on the nature of the contractual right, its relative 'weakness,' or its status as merely in personam, as opposed to the hardier rights in rem. Rather it is on the ground that the breach is supposed to lead to a better use of resources. The theory, therefore, is, in principle, equally applicable to property rights, where it leads to the adoption of a theory of 'efficient theft' or 'efficient conversion.' To see the point, observe how this account of efficiency plays out in two cases. In the first, A promises to sell a machine to B for $10,000 but then turns around and sells it instead to C for $18,000. In the second, B owns a machine for which he has paid $10,000, which A takes and sells to C for $18,000.

To keep matters simple, assume that B values the machine at exactly $12,000 in both cases. If the wilful contract breach is justified in the first case, then the wilful conversion is justified in the second. In the first, B gets $2,000 in expectation damages and is released from paying the $10,000 purchase price. In the second, B obtains damages for conversion equal to $12,000 because he has already paid the $10,000 purchase price to his seller. The two cases thus look identical even though they derive from distinct substantive fields.

No doubt in the contract situation, A may negotiate with B a release from his contractual obligation. But this, in Posner's view, would lead to additional transaction costs. It is, therefore, preferable to permit the 'efficient breach.' But the property example is indistinguishable on this ground, for in the second, A, when he takes the machine from B, avoids the transaction cost of having to purchase it from him. The similarity between the two situations (breach of contract and conversion) becomes more striking if the converter did not wrongfully deprive the owner of his possession. Thus, suppose that A is a bailee who keeps B's goods. C offers A for the goods an amount that exceeds their value to B. A can negotiate with B for the purchase of the goods and, if he is successful, sell them to C at a profit. The cost of this transaction could be saved, just as in the contract example, if A were allowed to sell the goods to C, while limiting his liability to B's expectation-like damages. Nevertheless, the better rule, which has been universally adopted by Anglo-American law, is that the plaintiff is entitled to recover in restitution the proceeds of the sale from the defendant who converted the plaintiff's property and sold it to a third party. Efficient breach theory does not provide an explanation why the promisee in a contract of sale should not be accorded similar rights.

There are, of course, refinements. Where the promisor is a merchant engaged in selling these types of goods, he may be in a better position to find a buyer willing to pay a higher price for them, so that his transaction costs may be somewhat lower. This, however, is not necessarily the case, and in any event it does not justify the breach. Again, the situation can be compared to conversion. The fact that A, for example, is a car dealer who is likely to know that C is an excellent buyer for B's car does not justify him to take B's car from his driveway in order to sell it to C. Nor if B's car has been left with A for repairs can A sell it to C.

The real issue in both the conversion and the breach situation is who should benefit from C's willingness to pay a high price for the goods owned by B (the conversion example) or promised to him (the breach example). In principle, there should be in both situations only one transaction; in my view, it should be between C and B (the owner or the promisee). If A promised to sell a piece of property to B for $10,000 and C is willing to have it for $18,000, he should negotiate its purchase from B. A is simply not entitled to sell to C something he has promised to return or transfer to B, and A is therefore not the right party to negotiate with. Consequently, if C negotiates such a purchase, he may be exposed to liability toward B, the promisee. Similarly, with a bailment, C must negotiate with B (the owner) and not with the bailee. Hence, the question of additional transaction costs does not arise.

It is, of course, conceivable that a person (in the above example, A) would like to take advantage of a potential transaction between two other parties (B and C). In some instances this can legitimately be done. A may know that C is the best buyer for B's property (or for the property promised to B), while B and C are unaware of each other. A may buy the property from B and sell it to C, or he may reach an agreement (with B or C or with both) for the payment of a commission. If this is done, the inevitable result would be that the transfer from B to C would involve two or more transactions (and, arguably, additional transaction costs). This course of dealing is not objectionable. What is, however, objectionable is an attempt by A to obtain through the commission of a wrong (breach of contract or a tort such as conversion) the benefit of a transaction that should have been concluded between B and C....

NOTES

1.   O'Dair [1993] Current Legal Problems 113 argues that the courts should award restitutionary damages when the parties would have stipulated for this explicitly had their contract been negotiated in sufficient detail. He argues that the parties would do this when, for some reason, the normal measure of damages would not give adequate compensation if the contract were to be broken (cf the justifications for liquidated damages, p 605). He points out, however, that, frequently, to include a clause providing for one party to pay restitutionary damages if it broke the contract would result in the other having to pay a higher price. This would be pointless when expectation damages would be adequate compensation, because the liability to pay restitutionary damages would remove any incentive for the first party to commit an efficient breach, since the gain would all have to be paid to the other party. He continues (at 130–133):

Those familiar with the economic analysis of contract law will know that there is or at least seems to be an answer to the charge that by removing the incentive to breach restitutionary damages will lead to a waste of resources. It is that the seller of goods in a case like [the one put by Friedmann] should not miss the opportunity for profitable resale. The solution is rather to negotiate for a release from the obligation to deliver . . . the result will be a sharing of the profits to be made from non perform-ance. The problem however is that such negotiations are likely to be extremely difficult and costly. If I wish to buy a second hand car, it is relatively easy to investigate the state of the market for second hand cars and thus to gain some idea of what is a fair price to pay. Not so if a promisor is seeking to purchase a release from an obligation to perform. Release is available from only one seller and pur-chaseable by only one buyer, this being what economists term a situation of bilateral monopoly. As a consequence, there is plenty of scope for brinkmanship with each party threatening not to make a mutually beneficial arrangement unless granted a higher share of the profit. The costs and difficul-ties of negotiating under conditions of bilateral monopoly are in themselves a good reason for the parties to a complete contingent contract not to adopt a remedial scheme which makes such nego-tiations inevitable. Professor Schwartz has objected that expectation damages are open to the same objection since following a breach of contract for which such damages are specified as the remedy the parties will have to negotiate a settlement of the compensatory damages claim in order to avoid the costly disaster of litigation. However, the objection seems unsound since the difficulty is com-pounded in the case of negotiations for a release. There the parties must agree not only on the promisee's losses but also on the division of the gains to be made from non performance.

There are two powerful objections to [my argument] which must be considered. The first is that I may be said to have assumed wrongly that the parties to a complete contract have only two possible options when it comes to dealing with the profits of breach: ie that they must be awarded in their entirety either to the promisor or to the promisee. Why should the parties not agree on a division of the profits? . . . The buyer would have to pay an increased price for such an arrangement, therefore it would be a gamble and the law should therefore presume that the parties would have agreed to split the profits of non performance only if it is prepared to view the buyer as being willing if asked to gamble slightly higher contractual consideration for the chance of a share in the profits of resale. In technical terms such an arrangement would make sense only in a contract where the promisee is less risk averse than the promisor, an attitude to risk which is highly unlikely to be present in contracts for the sale of goods. [Consideration of the second objection omitted]

2.   The Law Commission considered the question of restitutionary damages in its Consultation Paper No 132, *Aggravated, Exemplary and Restitutionary Damages* (1993). It said:

7.18 . . .

5. In the case of breach of contract several arguments have been made against the general avail-ability of restitutionary awards. First, many breaches of contract are made for commercial reasons and it is difficult to draw the line between 'innocent' breach for which there would be only com-pensation and 'cynical' breach in which there would also be the option of restitution in the way sug-gested by some commentators. This would lead to greater uncertainty in the assessment of damages in commercial and consumer disputes. Secondly, in seeking restitution the plaintiff might be evading the requirements of the mitigation rule. Thirdly, a restitutionary award is in reality a monetized form of specific performance but not all contracts are specifically enforceable. Fourthly, there may be dif-ficulties of attribution. The making of a profit in excess of that which the plaintiff might have made had the contract been performed may require skill and initiative which should not be taken from the defendant save in exceptional cases.

PROVISIONAL CONCLUSION

7.19 We do not believe that the only function of the civil law should be to compensate and it is our provisional view that restitutionary awards are *prima facie* justified if certain conditions are satisfied. Although the case in favour of restitutionary awards would be strengthened if exemplary damages were abolished, we do not consider that it depends on such abolition.

7.20 Subject to the views of consultees, our provisional view is that for there to be a restitutionary award the following conditions must be satisfied. First, there must have been either interference with

a proprietary right or an analogous right (such as confidentiality and the rights enjoyed by the beneficiary of a fiduciary relationship) or deliberate wrongdoing which could have been restrained by
injunction. Secondly, the gains made by the defendant must be attributable to the interest
infringed . . .

7.21 In the case of breach of contract we incline to the view that the distinction that appears to be
drawn between specifically enforceable contracts and contracts between fiduciaries where a restitutionary award may be made, and other contracts where the gain to a defendant from breach is irrelevant, reflects an appropriate balance of the respective interests of the parties.

■ *A-G v Blake*
[2000] 4 All ER 385

The predictions made in the third edition and referred to above were falsified by the decision
of the House of Lords in this extraordinary case.

George Blake was, for many years, employed by the British Secret Intelligence Service and
had signed a contract of employment with them that contained, amongst other things, a provision for lifelong confidentiality. Unknown to the British Secret Service, he was also
employed by the KGB and, in 1961, this was discovered and he was charged and convicted with
five offences, receiving a sentence of 42 years, an exceptionally long sentence by English standards, indicating the trial judge's disapproval of his conduct. In 1965, he managed to escape
from prison and made his way to Moscow, where he has been ever since. He made a contract
with the publisher Jonathan Cape Ltd to publish his autobiography. Under the terms of this
contract, he was entitled to an advance on royalties of £150,000 and appears to have actually
received £60,000. In practice, whatever the legal position, this money could not in fact be
recovered from Blake who was safely in Moscow but the Crown was anxious to prevent him
receiving the balance or even perhaps to secure it for itself.

At first instance, the Crown argued that Blake was a fiduciary. If this was so, the Crown
would clearly have been entitled to the money because fiduciaries can be forced to disgorge
the profits they have made by breach of their fiduciary duties. However, Scott V-C held that
Blake was no longer a fiduciary since he had not been employed by the Crown for many years
and the information revealed in the book was all long since in the public domain. This finding was not challenged in the later proceedings.

Before the Court of Appeal, the Crown put forward a completely different argument based
on public law grounds, seeking an extension of the undoubted public law capacity of the
Attorney General to seek an injunction in support of the control of criminal activity.
Undoubtedly, this represented an extension of what had previously been thought to be the law
but the Court of Appeal was willing to take this step. At the time of the hearing before the
Court of Appeal, it appeared likely that that would be the end of the matter since Blake was not
represented and the Crown would not appeal because it had been successful. However, a public interest group succeeded in getting leave from the House of Lords to appeal and an argument was put to the House of Lords *pro bono* that this extension of the Attorney General's
function was misconceived. The House of Lords unanimously accepted this view.

This might perhaps have been the end of the matter but for the fact that, in the Court of
Appeal, the Court had also discussed the question of restitutionary damages. Technically, in
view of its decision on the public law point, this was probably obiter but the discussion was
extensive. The Court of Appeal held that, although normally a party could only recover the
loss that it had itself suffered, there were exceptional cases in which a party might recover

damages that forced the other party to disgorge the profits that it had improperly made in breaking the contract. One such possibility that clearly did not arise on the facts of Blake was the so-called case of skimped performance, discussed by Birks, in which the defendant deliberately sets out to make a profit by delivering a shoddy performance, gambling that the performance will not be detected and that the plaintiff will not suffer any loss. The second possibility was that which the Court of Appeal thought occurred on the facts of the *Blake* case, that is, one in which the defendant does 'the very thing the person has contracted not to do'.

The House of Lords required the parties to argue fully this damages question. It is clear that they found the account given by the Court of Appeal unsatisfactory but they came clearly to the conclusion that there were exceptional circumstances in which the contract breaker should be compelled to disgorge, although they disliked the use of the expression 'restitutionary damages'.

Lord Nicholls delivered the principal judgment and said:

My conclusion is that there seems to be no reason, *in principle*, why the court must in all circumstances rule out an account of profits as a remedy for breach of contract. I prefer to avoid the unhappy expression 'restitutionary damages'. Remedies are the law's response to a wrong (or, more precisely, to a cause of action). When, exceptionally, a just response to a breach of contract so requires, the court should be able to grant the discretionary remedy of requiring a defendant to account to the plaintiff for the benefits he has received from his breach of contract. In the same way as a plaintiff's interest in performance of a contract may render it just and equitable for the court to make an order for specific performance or grant an injunction, so the plaintiff's interest in performance may make it just and equitable that the defendant should retain no benefit from his breach of contract.

The state of the authorities encourages me to reach this conclusion, rather than the reverse. The law recognises that damages are not always a sufficient remedy for breach of contract. This is the foundation of the court's jurisdiction to grant the remedies of specific performance and injunction. Even when awarding damages, the law does not adhere slavishly to the concept of compensation for financially measurable loss. When the circumstances require, damages are measured by reference to the benefit obtained by the wrongdoer. This applies to interference with property rights. Recently, the like approach has been adopted to breach of contract. Further, in certain circumstances an account of profits is ordered in preference to an award of damages. Sometimes the injured party is given the choice: either compensatory damages or an account of the wrongdoer's profits. Breach of confidence is an instance of this. If confidential information is wrongfully divulged in breach of a non-disclosure agreement, it would be nothing short of sophistry to say that an account of profits may be ordered in respect of the equitable wrong but not in respect of the breach of contract which governs the relationship between the parties. With the established authorities going thus far, I consider it would be only a modest step for the law to recognise openly that, exceptionally, an account of profits may be the most appropriate remedy for breach of contract. It is not as though this step would contradict some recognised principle applied consistently throughout the law to the grant or withholding of the remedy of an account of profits. No such principle is discernible.

The main argument against the availability of an account of profits as a remedy for breach of contract is that the circumstances where this remedy may be granted will be uncertain. This will have an unsettling effect on commercial contracts where certainty is important. I do not think these fears are well founded. I see no reason why, *in practice*, the availability of the remedy of an account of profits need disturb settled expectations in the commercial or consumer world. An account of profits will be appropriate only in exceptional circumstances. Normally the remedies of damages, specific performance and injunction, coupled with the characterisation of some contractual obligations as fiduciary, will provide an adequate response to a breach of contract. It will be only in exceptional cases, where those remedies are inadequate, that any question of accounting for profits will arise. No fixed rules can be prescribed. The court will have regard to all the circumstances, including the subject matter of the contract, the purpose of the contractual provision which has been breached, the circumstances in which the breach occurred, the consequences of the breach and the circumstances in which relief is being sought. A useful general guide, although not exhaustive, is whether the plaintiff had a legitimate interest in preventing the defendant's profit-making activity and, hence, in depriving him of his profit.

It would be difficult, and unwise, to attempt to be more specific. In the Court of Appeal Lord Woolf MR suggested there are at least two situations in which justice requires the award of restitutionary damages where compensatory damages would be inadequate (see [1998] 1 All ER 833 at 845–846, [1998] Ch 439 at 458). Lord Woolf MR was not there addressing the question of when an account of profits, in the conventional sense, should be available. But I should add that, so far as an account of profits is concerned, the suggested categorisation would not assist. The first suggested category was the case of 'skimped' performance, where the defendant fails to provide the full extent of services he has contracted to provide. He should be liable to pay back the amount of expenditure he saved by the breach. This is a much discussed problem. But a part refund of the price agreed for services would not fall within the scope of an account of profits as ordinarily understood. Nor does an account of profits seem to be needed in this context. The resolution of the problem of cases of skimped performance, where the plaintiff does not get what was agreed, may best be found elsewhere. If a shopkeeper supplies inferior and cheaper goods than those ordered and paid for, he has to refund the difference in price. That would be the outcome of a claim for damages for breach of contract. That would be so irrespective of whether the goods in fact served the intended purpose. There must be scope for a similar approach, without any straining of principle, in cases where the defendant provided inferior and cheaper services than those contracted for.

The second suggested category was where the defendant has obtained his profit by doing the very thing he contracted not to do. This category is defined too widely to assist. The category is apt to embrace all express negative obligations. But something more is required than mere breach of such an obligation before an account of profits will be the appropriate remedy.

The present case is exceptional. The context is employment as a member of the security and intelligence services. Secret information is the lifeblood of these services. In the 1950s Blake deliberately committed repeated breaches of his undertaking not to divulge official information gained as a result of his employment. He caused untold and immeasurable damage to the public interest he had committed himself to serve. In 1990 he published his autobiography, a further breach of his express undertaking. By this time the information disclosed was no longer confidential. In the ordinary course of commercial dealings the disclosure of non-confidential information might be regarded as venial. In the present case disclosure was also a criminal offence under the Official Secrets Acts, even though the information was no longer confidential. Section 1 of the 1989 Act draws a distinction in this regard between members of the security and intelligence services and other Crown servants. Under s 1(3) a person who is or has been a Crown servant is guilty of an offence if without lawful authority he makes 'a damaging disclosure' of information relating to security or intelligence. The offence is drawn more widely in the case of a present or past member of the security and intelligence services. Such a person is guilty of an offence if without lawful authority he discloses 'any information' relating to security or intelligence which is or has been in his possession by virtue of his position as a member of those services. This distinction was approved in Parliament after debate when the legislation was being enacted.

In considering what would be a just response to a breach of Blake's undertaking the court has to take these considerations into account. The undertaking, if not a fiduciary obligation, was closely akin to a fiduciary obligation, where an account of profits is a standard remedy in the event of breach. Had the information which Blake has now disclosed still been confidential, an account of profits would have been ordered, almost as a matter of course. In the special circumstances of the intelligence services, the same conclusion should follow even though the information is no longer confidential. That would be a just response to the breach. I am reinforced in this view by noting that most of the profits from the book derive indirectly from the extremely serious and damaging breaches of the same undertaking committed by Blake in the 1950s. As already mentioned, but for his notoriety as an infamous spy his autobiography would not have commanded royalties of the magnitude Jonathan Cape Ltd agreed to pay.

Lord Hobhouse dissented. He said:

I cannot join your Lordships in that conclusion. I have two primary difficulties. The first is the facts of the present case. The speech of my noble and learned friend explores what is the 'just response' to the defendant's conduct. The 'just response' visualised in the present case is, however it is formulated, that Blake should be punished and deprived of any fruits of conduct connected with his former criminal and reprehensible conduct. The Crown have made no secret of this. It is not a commercial claim in support of any commercial interest. It is a claim relating to past criminal conduct. The way it was put by the Court of Appeal was:

'The ordinary member of the public would be shocked if the position was that the courts were power-less to prevent [Blake] profiting from his criminal conduct.' (See [1998] 1 All ER 833 at 851, [1998] Ch 439 at 464.)

The answer given by my noble and learned friend does not reflect the essentially punitive nature of the claim and seeks to apply principles of law which are only appropriate where commercial or proprietary interests are involved. Blake has made a financial gain but he has not done so at the expense of the Crown or making use of any property of or commercial interest of the Crown either in law or equity.

My second difficulty is that the reasoning of my noble and learned friend depends upon the conclusion that there is some gap in the existing state of the law which requires to be filled by a new remedy. He accepts that the term 'restitutionary damages' is unsatisfactory but, with respect, does not fully examine why this is so, drawing the necessary conclusions.

NOTE

The facts of *A-G v Blake* were so special and the reasoning of Lord Nicholls so wide that it is likely to take many years and many cases to work out its full implications.

The most significant case so far is *Experience Hendrix LLC v PPX Enterprises Inc* [2003] EWCA Civ 323 [2003] 1 All ER (Comm) 830. This case arose out of a compromise agreement, which itself sought to resolve a dispute arising out of recordings made by the late Jimi Hendrix. This agreement entitled the first defendants to license various masters of recordings. In breach of contract, they licensed other masters. It was clearly assumed that this created profit for the defendants but did not cause loss to the claimants. The Court of Appeal refused to order an account of profits but did give the claimants damages, calculated on the basis of a reasonable payment for use of the material.

Do you think this case would have been decided the same way before *Blake*? Have a look at *Wrotham Park Estate Co Ltd v Parkside Homes Ltd* [1974] 1 WLR 798.

SECTION SIX

CONTRACT THEORY

CHAPTER TWENTY-FIVE

WHY ARE PROMISES BINDING?

If you have worked through most of the material in Chapters 1–24, you will have studied enough contract law that in this and the following chapters in Section 6 we can turn to various theoretical issues. Some of these relate to material already covered; others, particularly those in Chapter 30, anticipate material yet to come. You may read that chapter as an introduction to the material or return to the chapter later.

Contract theory is concerned with a number of distinct but related questions. One is why we regard promises as *morally* binding; another, why our legal system treats some promises at least as *legally* binding; a third, whether the central principle of contract law is really the enforcement of promises, or whether this is merely the incidental result of rules that are primarily aimed at liability on some other basis, such as compensation of reliance.

The first question is primarily one of moral philosophy. It has been argued plausibly that philosophical discussion has been impoverished by a failure to refer to the vast body of legal materials illustrating the difficulties in the view that promises are 'usually binding'. Whatever the answer to the first question, most legal systems, and certainly English law, do not enforce all promises that are morally binding.

We start with a piece that provides a good summary of the literature up to 1933, and follow with a number of pieces that represent current viewpoints and reflect current controversies. Space precludes anything but a very small selection of readings on contract theory, with notes simply providing references for further reading.

The title of this section refers to 'contract theory' in the general sense of theoretical writings about contract. Stephen Smith, in *Contract Theory*, 2003, uses 'contract theory' in a more limited sense: interpretations of contract law that attempt to reveal an intelligible order in contract law. For instance, his notion of contract theory is limited to contract *law*, as opposed to, for example, the empirical studies of contract behaviour from which there are extracts in Chapters 5 and 27. It is limited to *contract* law, as opposed to the laws of tort or of unjust enrichment, even though the latter may impinge on contracts (Smith at pp 7–11). Further, his is a general theory that purports to explain the basic concepts of contractual obligation, as opposed to certain aspects of it (such as limitations on freedom of contract derived from concerns about fairness—see Chapter 30). This chapter and the next, on economic analysis, do contain extracts from works on contract theory that fall within Smith's definition.

Smith also points out (at pp 42–47) that contract theory has to ask two questions that need to be kept distinct. The first is an analytic question: 'What are the essential characteristics of a contractual obligation?' The second question is a normative question: 'Why give legal force to contractual obligations?'

... general theories should be classified according to how they answer two questions: an analytic question about the nature of contract law and a normative question about the justification for contract law.

With respect to the analytic question, a further distinction was drawn between: promissory theories, which regard contractual obligations as promises or another kind of self-imposed obligation; reliance theories, which regard contractual obligations as obligations to ensure that those whom you induce to rely are not made worse off; and transfer theories, which regard contractual obligations as obligations to respect rights transferred between parties. A further distinction was also drawn with respect to answers to the normative question. In this case the distinction is between: utilitarian theories, which justify contract law on the basis that it promotes utility (broadly defined), and rights-based theories, which justify contract law on the ground that it gives legal force to individual rights. Significantly, it was argued that while the analytic and normative questions are related, particular examples of general theories may (and in practice do) defend different combinations of answers to these questions (e.g., rights-based promissory theories, utilitarian promissory theories, rights-based transfer theories, and so on).... (Smith, *Contract Theory*, 2003, p 52)

We shall see that there are competing theories. Some, such as the 'will theory' (see p 759) or Fried's theory, put forward in his *Contract as Promise* (see p 778), stress the binding nature of the defendant's promise; others, the fact that the claimant has relied on the defendants. Smith offers criteria by which to evaluate competing theories:

... An interpretive theory is a theory that helps us to better understand the law by illuminating the significance of, and connections between, its different parts. As such, interpretive theories are linked to, but different than, historical, prescriptive, and descriptive theories. Interpretive theories are assessed according to: (1) how well they fit the rules and decisions that make up contract law, (2) how coherent they are, and (3) how well they explain the way that legal actors themselves explain what they are doing. The third criterion can be subdivided into two parts: (1) how well does the theory explain law's claims to authority (the claim that law is a legitimate or morally justified authority), and (2) how well does the theory explain law's claim to transparency (the claim that legal reasoning is meaningful)?

A further distinction was drawn between weak, moderate, and strong versions of what is required to explain the above claims to authority and transparency. The weak versions hold that any explanation is sufficient, even if it shows legal actors to be insincere in their claims. The strong versions hold that a good explanation of the law will show that the law's claims to authority and transparency are actually true, that is, that the law is actually morally justified and that the reasons alleged to motivate decision-making actually do motivate decision-making. Finally, the moderate—and, I argued, most persuasive—versions state that a good explanation must show that the law's claim to authority and claim to transparency must be thought to be true (even if they are not in fact true). This can be done either by advancing a functionalist explanation or, more plausibly, by advancing an interpretation that shows legal actors to have been mistaken. To fit within the latter approach, an interpretation of the law must propose a normative justification for the law that is recognizably 'moral' (in order to make sense of law's claim to authority) and must explain the law in terms that are recognizably 'legal' (in order to make sense of the law's claim to transparency). (Smith, *Contract Theory*, p 36)

After you have read the extracts in this book, you may like to read Smith's text to see how he evaluates the different theories against his criteria. We do not include extracts of what Smith calls 'transfer theory' (eg Benson, 'Contract', in Patterson (ed), *A Companion to the Philosophy of Law and Legal Theory*, 1996; Benson, 'The Unity of Contract Law' in Benson (ed), *The Theory of Contract Law*, 2001) in this chapter. Smith gives convincing reasons for regarding this type of theory as having weak explanatory power: *Contract Theory*, pp 97–102.

■ Cohen, 'The Basis of Contract' (1933)

46 Harv LR 553, 571–589, 591–592

III. THE JUSTIFICATION OF CONTRACT LAW

A. The sanctity of promises

Contract law is commonly supposed to enforce promises. Why should promises be enforced?

The simplest answer is that of the intuitionists, namely, that promises are sacred *per se*, that there is something inherently despicable about not keeping a promise, and that a properly organized society should not tolerate this. This may also be said to be the common man's theory.

... If, then, we find ourselves in a state of society in which men are, as a matter of fact, repelled by the breaking of promises and feel that such practice should be discouraged or minimized, that is a primary fact which the law must not ignore.

But while this intuitionist theory contains an element of truth, it is clearly inadequate. No legal system does or can attempt to enforce all promises. Not even the canon law held all promises to be sacred. And when we come to draw a distinction between those promises which should be and those which should not be enforced, the intuitionist theory, that all promises should be kept, gives us no light or guiding principle.

Similar to the intuitionist theory is the view of Kantians like Reinach that the duty to keep one's promise is one without which rational society would be impossible. There can be no doubt that from an empirical or historical point of view, the ability to rely on the promises of others adds to the confidence necessary for social intercourse and enterprise. But as an absolute proposition this is untenable. The actual world, which assuredly is among the possible ones, is not one in which all promises are kept, and there are many people—not necessarily diplomats—who prefer a world in which they and others occasionally depart from the truth and go back on some promise. It is indeed very doubtful whether there are many who would prefer to live in an entirely rigid world in which one would be obliged to keep *all* one's promises instead of the present more viable system, in which a vaguely fair proportion is sufficient. Many of us indeed would shudder at the idea of being bound by every promise, no matter how foolish, without any chance of letting increased wisdom undo past foolishness. Certainly, some freedom to change one's mind is necessary for free intercourse between those who lack omniscience.

For this reason we cannot accept Dean Pound's theory that all promises in the course of business should be enforced. He seems to me undoubtedly right in his insistence that promises constitute modern wealth and that their enforcement is thus a necessity of maintaining wealth as a basis of civilization. My bank's promise to pay the checks drawn to my account not only constitutes my wealth but puts it into a more manageable form than that of my personal possession of certain goods or even gold. Still, business men as a whole do not wish the law to enforce every promise. Many business transactions, such as those on a stock or produce exchange, could not be carried on unless we could rely on a mere verbal agreement or hasty memorandum. But other transactions, like those of real estate, are more complicated and would become too risky if we were bound by every chance promise that escapes us. Negotiations would be checked by such fear. In such cases men do not want to be bound until the final stage, when some formality like the signing of papers gives one the feeling of security, of having taken proper precautions. The issue obviously depends upon such factors as the relative simplicity of a given transaction, the speed with which it must be concluded, and the availability of necessary information....

B. The will theory of contract

According to the classical view, the law of contract gives expression to and protects the will of the parties, for the will is something inherently worthy of respect. Hence such authorities as Savigny, Windshield, Pothier, Planiol, Pollock, Salmond, and Langdell hold that the first essential of a contract is the agreement of wills, or the meeting of minds.

The metaphysical difficulties of this view have often been pointed out. Minds or wills are not in themselves existing things that we can look at and recognize. We are restricted in our earthly experience to the observation of the changes or actions of more or less animated bodies in time and space; and disembodied minds or wills are beyond the scope and reach of earthly law. But while this objection has become familiar, it has not been very effective. The force of the old ideas, embodied in the traditional language, has not always been overcome even by those who like Langdell and Salmond profess to recognize the fictional element in the will theory.

Another line of objection can be found in the incompatibility of the classical theory with the consequences that the law attaches to an offer. Suppose that I offer to buy certain goods from A at a given price, and, following his refusal, give him a week's time to reconsider it. If I change my mind the next day but fail to notify him, a contractual obligation will none the less arise if five days later he notifies me that he has accepted my terms. Here obviously there is never a moment of time when the two parties are actually in agreement or of one mind. Yet no one denies that the resulting rights and duties are identical with those called contractual. It does not help the classical theory to say that I am under a legal duty to notify A (the offeree) and that if I fail to perform this duty in the proper way, the law will treat my change of mind as a nullity, *as if it* had never happened. The phrase italicized indicates that we are moving in the realm of fiction (or better, rights and duties imposed by law) and not in the realm of fact. No one denies that the contractual obligation should attach in this case; but there is in point of fact no actual agreement or meeting of minds. The latter, then, is not always necessary for a legal contract.

The logical inconsistency of the classical theory is not cured if we say that the law protects not the will but the expression or declaration of the will. Suppose that in the case mentioned I make a solemn declaration of the revocation of my offer, or write a letter but fail to communicate it. The law, in refusing to give effect to my declared revocation, is not protecting my expressed will, but is enforcing a duty on me in the interest of the general security of business transactions.

A more important objection to the theory that every contract expresses the consensus or agreed wills of the two parties is the fact that most litigation in this field arises precisely because of the advent of conditions that the two parties did not foresee when they entered into the transaction. Litigation usually reveals the absence of genuine agreement between the parties *ab initio*. If both parties had foreseen the difficulty, provision would have been made for it in the beginning when the contract was drawn up. . . .

The obvious limitations of the will theory of contract have caused a reaction that takes the form of positivism of behaviorism: Away with the whole notion of will!—the only realities are specific acts to which the law attaches certain consequences, that is, if you do something by word of mouth, by writing, or by any other act that someone else takes as a promise, then the latter can, under certain conditions, bring an action. In its extreme form, this appears in what Dean Pound calls the state of strict law, which, like everything called primitive, is always with us. A developed system of law, however, must draw some distinction between voluntary and involuntary acts. Mr Justice Holmes thinks that even a dog discriminates between one who stumbles over him and one who kicks him. The whole of the modern law of contract, it may be argued, thus does and should respond to the need of greater or finer discrimination in regard to the intentional character of acts. The law of error, duress, and fraud in contract would be unintelligible apart from such distinction.

C. The injurious-reliance theory

Though this seems the favorite theory today, it has not as yet been adequately formulated, and many of those who subscribe to it fall back on the will theory when they come to discuss special topics in the law of contract. The essence of the theory, however, is clear enough. Contractual liability arises (or should arise) only where (1) someone makes a promise explicitly in words or implicitly by some act, (2) someone else relies on it, and (3) suffers some loss thereby.

This theory appeals to the general moral feeling that not only ought promises to be kept, but that anyone innocently injured by relying on them is entitled to have the loss 'made good' by the one who thus caused it. If, as Schopenhauer has maintained, the sense of wrong is the ultimate human source of the law, then to base the obligations of the promise on the injury of the one who has relied on it, is to appeal to something really fundamental.

This theory also appeals to modern legal theorists because it seems to be entirely objective and social. It does not ask the court to examine the intention of the promisor. Instead, the court is asked to consider whether what the defendant has said or done is such that reasonable people generally do rely on it under the circumstances. The resulting loss can be directly proved and, to some extent, even measured. In emphasizing the element of injury resulting from the breach, the whole question of contract is integrated in the larger realm of obligations, and this tends to put our issues in the right perspective and to correct the misleading artificial distinctions between breach of contract and other civil wrongs or torts.

Nevertheless, this theory is not entirely consistent with existing law, nor does it give an altogether satisfactory account of what the law should do.

Contractual obligation is not coextensive with injurious reliance because (1) there are instances of both injury and reliance for which there is no contractual obligation, and (2) there are cases of such obligation where there is no reliance or injury.

(1) Clearly, not all cases of injury resulting from reliance on the word or act of another are actionable, and the theory before us offers no clue as to what distinguishes those which are. There is, first, the whole class of instances of definite financial injury caused by reliance on an explicit promise made in social relations, such as dinner parties and the like. . . .

Even clearer are those cases where someone advertises goods for sale or a position to be filled, and, when I come, tells me that he has changed his mind. . . .

(2) In formal contracts, such as promises under seal, stipulation in court, and the like, it is clearly not necessary for the promisee to prove reliance and injury. . . . To be sure, where the law recognizes no loss, only nominal damages are usually awarded. But the fact that the plaintiff receives judgment is of practical, as well as of theoretic, importance. Clearly, the law favors the carrying-out of promises even in cases where there is no actual reliance or actual loss from nonperformance.

(3) Finally, the recovery that the law allows to the injured promisee is not determined by what he lost in relying on the promise, but rather by what he would have gained if the promise had been kept. There are obviously many cases where the injured party is substantially no worse after the breach than if the contract had never been made. He has thus not been in fact injured. And yet he may recover heavy damages if he would have gained heavily by the performance of the contract. The policy of the law, then, is not merely to redress injuries but also to protect certain kinds of expectation by making men live up to certain promises.

There can be no question about the soundness of the injurious-reliance theory in accounting for a dominant phase of the law of contract, and the foregoing difficulties may thus seem petty. But they do call attention to fundamental obscurities in the very idea of 'reliance' as well as in the criteria of 'injury'. The injurious-reliance theory, like others, calls attention to a necessary element but does not give an adequate account of the whole of the law of contract. Its merits become clearer when its claims are properly limited.

D. The equivalent theory

Popular sentiment generally favors the enforcement of those promises which involve some *quid pro quo*. It is generally considered unfair that after A has given something of value or rendered B some service, B should fail to render anything in return. Even if what A did was by way of gift, B owes him gratitude and should express it in some appropriate way. And if, in addition, B has promised to pay A for the value of services received, the moral sense of the community condemns B's failure to do so as even more unfair. The demand for justice behind the law is but an elaboration of such feelings of what is fair and unfair.

The equivalent theory of contract has the advantage of being supported by this popular sentiment. This sentiment also explains the primacy of *real* contracts.

While a legal theory must not ignore common sense, it must also go beyond it. For common sense, while generally sound at its core, is almost always vague and inadequate. Common sentiment, for instance, demands an equivalent. But what things are equivalent? It is easy to answer this in regard to goods or services that have a standard market value. But how shall we measure things that are dissimilar in nature, or in a market where monopolistic or other factors prevent a fair or just price? Modern law therefore professes to abandon the effort of more primitive systems to enforce material fairness within the contract. The parties to the contract must themselves determine what is fair. Thereby, however, the law loses a good deal of support in the moral sense of the community. . . .

. . . Consideration is in effect a formality, like an oath, the affixing of a seal, or a stipulation in court.

E. Formalism in contract

The recognition of the formal character of consideration may help us to appreciate the historical myopia of those who speak of seal as 'importing' consideration. Promises under seal were binding (because of the formality) long before the doctrine of consideration was ever heard of. The history of forms and ceremonies in the law of contract offers an illuminating chapter in human psychology or anthropology. We are apt to dismiss the early Roman ceremonies of *mancipatio, nexum*, and *sponsio*, the Anglo-Saxon *wed* and *borh*, or the Frankish ceremonies of *arramitio, wadiatio*, and of the *fesruca*, as peculiar to primitive society. But reflection shows that our modern practices of shaking hands to close a bargain, signing papers, and protesting a note are, like the taking of an oath on assuming office, not only designed to make evidence secure, but are in large part also expressions of the fundamental human need for formality and ceremony, to make sharp distinctions where otherwise lines of demarcation would not be so clearly apprehended.

Ceremonies are the channels that the stream of social life creates by its ceaseless flow through the sands of human circumstances. Psychologically, they are habits; socially, they are customary ways of doing things; and ethically, they have what Jellinek has called the normative power of the actual, that is, they control what we do by creating a standard of respectability or a pattern to which we feel bound to conform. . . .

F. Contract and the distribution of risks

Mr Justice Holmes has suggested that a legal promise may be viewed as a wager: I assure you of a certain event (which may or may not be within my control) and I pay in case of failure.

This view has not found much favor. . . .

Nevertheless, when taken in a wider sense in connection with Mr Justice Holmes's general philosophy concerning the risk in all human affairs, his theory is illuminating and important.

All human transactions are directed to a future that is never free from elements of uncertainty. Every one of our ventures, therefore, involves the taking of a risk. When I board a train to go home I am betting my life that I will get to my destination. Now a contract or agreement may be viewed as an agreement for the distribution or anticipated gains or losses. If I agree to sell certain goods or services I expect that I shall be paid in good United States money and that with this money I shall be able to acquire certain other goods. I do not generally take into account the possibility that the purchasing power of the American dollar may be radically reduced when I receive my pay. That contingency is generally not thought of or else deemed too remote, yet certain bondholders do think of it and specify payment in gold of a certain standard. Now the human power to foresee all the consequences of an agreement is limited, even if we suppose that the two parties understand each other's meaning to begin with. Disputes or disagreements are therefore bound to come up; and the law of contract may thus be viewed as an attempt to determine the rights and duties of the two parties under circumstances that were not anticipated exactly in the same way by the two contracting parties, or at any rate were not expressly provided for in an unambiguous way. One can therefore say that the court's adjudication supplements the original contract as a method of distributing gains and losses.

From this point of view, we may look upon the law of contract as a number of rules according to which courts distribute gains and losses according to the equities of such cases; and the pretense that the result follows exclusively from the agreement of the two parties is fictional. Just as the process of interpreting a statute is really a process of subsidiary legislation, so is the interpretation of a contract really a method of supplementing the original agreement by such provisions as are necessary to determine the point at issue.

If we view the law of contract as directed to strengthening the security of transactions by enabling men to rely more fully on promises, we see only one phase of its actual workings. The other phase is the determination of the rights of the contracting parties as to contingencies that they have not foreseen, and for which they have not provided. In this latter respect the law of contract is a way of enforcing some kind of distributive justice within the legal system. And technical doctrines of contract may thus be viewed as a set of rules that will systematize decisions in this field and thus give lawyers and their clients some guidance in the problem of anticipating future decisions. Thus, for instance, if the question arises as to who should suffer a loss caused by the destruction of goods in transit, the technical doctrine of when title passes enables us to deal with the problem more definitely. In any case, the essential problem of the law of contract is the problem of distribution of risks. The other phase, namely, the assurance that what the parties have actually agreed on will be fulfilled, is a limiting principle.

IV. CONTRACT AND SOVEREIGNTY

... This task of formulating a comprehensive theory of contract, that shall do justice to its many sources and various phases, is one that I shall not undertake here. But I wish to emphasize certain considerations that supplement the theories discussed so far.

The cardinal error of the traditional individualistic theories of contract is their way of speaking as if the law does nothing but put into effect what the contracting parties originally agreed on. The best that can be said for this is that it may sometimes be true. But even if that were more generally the case, we should still have to attach more importance to the factor of enforcement than the prevailing theories do. The fact, then, that in the general run of transactions people do not resort to actual litigation, is certainly in part due to the fact that they know in a general way what will be the outcome of that process. The law of contract, then, through judges, sheriffs, or marshals puts the sovereign power of the state at the disposal of one party to be exercised over the other party. It thus grants a limited sovereignty to the former.

From this point of view the law of contract may be viewed as a subsidiary branch of public law, as a body of rules according to which the sovereign power of the state will be exercised as between the parties to a more or less voluntary transaction.

The first rules of public law, generally called constitutional law, regulate the conduct of the chief state officials by indicating the scope of their powers. Within this scope legislatures use their discretion or wisdom to enact certain statutes; and judges, by following precedents, elaborate certain rules as to when and how the power of the state shall be exercised. Among these rules we have the laws of partnership, leases, agreements for services, contracts of surety or insurances, and the like. Now, just as the rules of constitutional law are general and leave blanks to be filled in by the legislature, courts, and administrative officials (whose rules and habitual practices are law to those over whom they have authority), so do the rules of contracts allow men to formulate for themselves, within the prescribed limits, certain rights and duties governing certain transactions between them; and when the parties have thus formulated their agreements, the latter become a part of the law of the land, just as much as do treaties between our nation and others, compacts between states, contracts between a state or division thereof and a private corporation, or the grant of a pension to the widow of a former president. ...

If, then, the law of contract confers sovereignty on one party over another (by putting the state's forces at the disposal of the former), the question naturally arises: For what purposes and under what circumstances shall that power be conferred? Adherents of the classical theory have recognized that legal enforcement serves to protect and encourage transactions that require credit or reliance on the promises of others. But we also need care that the power of the state be not used for unconscionable purposes, such as helping those who exploit the dire need or weakness of their fellows. Usury laws have recognized that he who is under economic necessity is not really free. To put no restrictions on the freedom to contract would logically lead not to a maximum of individual liberty but to contracts of slavery, into which, experience shows, men will 'voluntarily' enter under economic pressure—a pressure that is largely conditioned by the laws of property. Regulations, therefore, involving some restrictions on the freedom to contract are as necessary to real liberty as traffic restrictions are necessary to assure real freedom in the general use of our highways. . . .

We may thus view the law of contract not only as a branch of public law but also as having a function somewhat parallel to that of the criminal law. Both serve to standardize conduct by penalizing departures from the legal norm. Not only by decrees of specific performance or by awards of damages, but also by treating certain contracts as void or voidable and thus withholding its support from those who do not conform to its prescribed forms, does the law of contract in fact impose penalties. Thus even when certain practices like gambling, illicit sex relations, or agreements in restraint of trade are not criminal offences, the law regards them with sufficient disfavor to refuse them the protection of its enforcing machinery.

The function of the law of contract in promoting the standardization of transactions is at all times an important one. . . .

There is no inherent reason for rejecting the view that the roots of the law of contract are many rather than one. Agreements and promises are enforced to enable people to rely on them as a rule and thus make the path of enterprise more secure; but in this connection the law must also go beyond the original intention of the parties to settle controversies as to the distribution of gains and losses that the parties did not anticipate in the same way. Some recognition must always be given to the will or intention of those who made the contract, but the law must always have regard for the *general* effects of classes of transactions, and it cannot free men from the necessity of acting at their peril when they do not know the consequences that the law will attach to their acts—and this needs to be emphasized in any attempt to formulate a rational theory. The law is a going concern and like all social institutions is governed by habit. It therefore will continue to enforce promises and agreements, for no better reason than they have been enforced and there is no sufficient countervailing consideration to force or justify a break with the established habit that has become the basis of social expectancies. Legal and other habits are not always deliberately formed to serve a definite purpose. Certain forms or ceremonies arise under special circumstances but continue to appeal to us through the principle of economy of effort: it is generally easier to use the existing forms than to break with them and adopt new ones. Of course old forms may become inconvenient or positive hindrances. They are then whittled away by pious fiction or violently changed by revolutionary legislation. In general, however, the ancient truth that men are creatures of habit will put us on guard against the vain assumption that we can get rid of formalism in the law of contract or anywhere else. We may flatter ourselves on getting rid of seal or other ancient binding ceremony. But we must remember that these forms seemed as naturally obligatory to our fathers as the signing of papers or the administering of oaths seems to us today.

In arguing for their indispensability we may recognize that not all forms are perfectly congenial or responsive to the need of the life that pulses through them. And as men become more enlightened they become more ready to discard, as well as employ, diverse instruments or vessels. Wisdom is not attained either by blind acceptance or blind rejection. We need a discriminating evaluation of what exists and what is possible; and this is something to which we can apply Spinoza's dictum: All things excellent are as difficult as they are rare.

NOTES

1.   The views of Holmes referred to will be found in *The Common Law*, 1882, pp 297–303. They are further discussed by Buckland, 'The Nature of Contractual Obligation' (1944) 8 CLJ 247.

2.   The reliance theory was developed further in the classic piece that follows.

■ Fuller and Perdue, 'The Reliance Interest on Contract Damages' (1936)
46 Yale LJ 52, 56–65

(An extract from the first few pages of this article will be found on pp 626–628. In that extract, the authors distinguish the 'restitution', 'reliance' and 'expectation' interests. The present extract is a continuation.)

It is obvious that the three 'interests' we have distinguished do not present equal claims to judicial intervention. It may be assumed that ordinary standards of justice would regard the need for judicial intervention as decreasing in the order in which we have listed the three interests. The 'restitution interest,' involving a combination of unjust impoverishment with unjust gain, presents the strongest case for relief. If, following Aristotle, we regard the purpose of justice as the maintenance of an equilibrium of goods among members of society, the restitution interest presents twice as strong a claim to judicial intervention as the reliance interest, since if A not only causes B to lose one unit but appropriates that unit to himself, the resulting discrepancy between A and B is not one unit but two.

On the other hand, the promisee who has actually relied on the promise, even though he may not thereby have enriched the promisor, certainly presents a more pressing case for relief than the promisee who merely demands satisfaction for his disappointment in not getting what was promised him. In passing iron compensation for change of position to compensation for loss of expectancy we pass, to use Aristotle's terms again, from the realm of corrective justice to that of distributive justice. The law no longer seeks merely to heal a disturbed status quo, but to bring into being a new situation. It ceases to act defensively or restoratively, and assumes a more active role. With the transition, the justification for legal relief loses its self-evident quality. It is as a matter of fact no easy thing to explain why the normal rule of contract recovery should be that which measures damages by the value of the promised performance. Since this 'normal rule' throws its shadow across our whole subject it will be necessary to examine the possible reasons for its existence. It may be said parenthetically that the discussion which follows, though directed primarily to the normal measure of recovery where damages are sought, also has relevance to the more general question, why should a promise which has not been relied on ever be enforced at all, whether by a decree of specific performance or by an award of damages?

Why should the law ever protect the expectation interest?

Perhaps the most obvious answer to this question is one which we may label 'psychological'. This answer would run something as follows: The breach of a promise arouses in the promisee a sense of injury. This feeling is not confined to cases where the promisee has relied on the promise. Whether or not he has actually changed his position because of the promise, the promise has formed an attitude of expectancy such that a breach of the promise causes him to feel that he has been 'deprived' of something which was 'his'. Since this sentiment is a relatively uniform one, the law has no occasion to go back of it. It accepts it as a datum and builds its rule about it.

The difficulty with this expectation is that the law does in fact go back of the sense of injury which the breach of a promise engenders. No legal system attempts to invest with juristic sanction all promises. Some rule or combination of rules effects a sifting out for enforcement of those promises deemed important enough to society to justify the law's concern with them. Whatever the principles which control this sifting out process may be, they are not convertible into terms of the degree of resentment which the breach of a particular kind of promise arouses. Therefore, though it may be assumed that the impulse to assuage disappointment is one shared by those who make and influence the law, this impulse can hardly be regarded as the key which solves the whole problem of the protection accorded by the law to the expectation interest.

A second possible explanation for the rule protecting the expectancy may be found in the much-discussed 'will theory' of contract law. This theory views the contracting parties as exercising, so to speak, a legislative power, so that the legal enforcement of a contract becomes merely an implementing by the state of a kind of private law already established by the parties. If A has made, in proper form, a promise to pay B one thousand dollars, we compel A to pay this sum simply because the rule or *lex* set up by the parties calls for this payment. *Uti lingua nun cupassit, ita jus esto.*

It is not necessary to discuss here the contribution which the will theory is capable of making to a philosophy of contract law. Certainly some borrowings from the theory are discernible in most attempts to rationalize the bases of contract liability. It is enough to note here that while the will theory undoubtedly has some bearing on the problem of contract damages, it cannot be regarded as dictating in all cases a recovery of the expectancy. If a contract represents a kind of private law, it is a law which usually says nothing at all about what shall be done when it is violated. . . .

A third and more promising solution of our difficulty lies in an economic or institutional approach. The essence of a credit economy lies in the fact that it tends to eliminate the distinction between present and future (promised) goods. Expectations of future values become, for purposes of trade, present values. In a society in which credit has become a significant and pervasive institution, it is inevitable that the expectancy created by an enforceable promise should be regarded as a kind of property, and breach of the promise as an injury to that property. In such a society the breach of a promise works an 'actual' diminution of the promisee's assets—'actual' in the sense that it would be so appraised according to modes of thought which enter into the very fiber of our economic system. That the promisee had not 'used' the property which the promise represents (had not relied on the promise) is as immaterial as the question whether the plaintiff in trespass *quare clausum fregit* was using his property at the time it was encroached upon. The analogy to ordinary forms of property goes further, for even in a suit for trespass the recovery is reduced accordingly. Ordinary property differs from a contract right chiefly in the fact that it lies within the power of more persons to work a direct injury to the expectancy it represents. It is generally only the promisor or some one working through or upon him who is able to injure the contract expectancy in a direct enough manner to make expedient legal intervention.

The most obvious objection which can be made to the economic or institutional explanation is that it involves a *petitio principii*. A promise has present value, why? Because the law enforces it. 'The expectancy', regarded as a present value, is not the cause of legal intervention but the consequence of it. This objection may be reinforced by a reference to legal history. Promises were enforced long before there was anything corresponding to a general system of 'credit', and recovery was from the beginning measured by the value of the promised performance, the 'agreed price'. It may therefore be argued that the 'credit system' when it finally emerged was itself in large part built on the foundations of a juristic development which preceded it.

The view just suggested asserts the primacy of law over economics; it sees law not as the creature but as the creator of social institutions. The shift of emphasis thus implied suggests the possibility of a fourth explanation for the law's protection of the unrelied-on expectancy, which we may call *juristic*. This explanation would seek a justification for the normal rule of recovery in some policy consciously pursued by courts and other lawmakers. It would assume that courts have protected the expectation interest because they have considered it wise to do so, not through a blind acquiescence in habitual ways of thinking and feeling, or through an equally blind deference to the individual will. Approaching a problem from this point of view, we are forced to find not a mere explanation for the rule in the form of some sentimental, volitional, or institutional datum, but articulate reasons for its existence.

What reasons can be advanced? In the first place, even if our interest were confined to protecting promisees against an out-of-pocket loss, it would still be possible to justify the rule granting the value of the expectancy, both as a cure for, and as a prophylaxis against, losses of this sort.

It is a cure for these losses in the sense that it offers the measure of recovery most likely to reimburse the plaintiff for the (often very numerous and very difficult to prove) individual acts and forbearances which make up his total reliance on the contract. If we take into account 'gains prevented' by reliance, that is, losses involved in foregoing the opportunity to enter other contracts, the notion that the rule protecting the expectancy is adopted as the most effective means of compensating for detrimental reliance seems not at all far-fetched. Physicians with an extensive practice often charge their patients the full office call fee for broken appointments. Such a charge looks on the face of things like a claim to the promised fee; it seems to be based on the 'expectation interest'. Yet the physician making the charge will quite justifiably regard it as compensation for the loss of the opportunity to gain a similar fee from a different patient. This foregoing of other opportunities is involved to some extent in entering most contracts, and the impossibility of subjecting this type of reliance to any kind of measurement may justify a categorical rule granting the value of the expectancy as the most effective way of compensating for such losses.

But, as we have suggested, the rule measuring damages by the expectancy may also be regarded as a prophylaxis against the losses resulting from detrimental reliance. Whatever tends to discourage breach of contract tends to prevent the losses occasioned through reliance. Since the expectation interest furnishes a more easily administered measure of recovery than the reliance interest, it will in practice offer a more effective sanction against contract breach. It is therefore possible to view the rule measuring damages by the expectancy in a quasi-criminal aspect, its purpose being not so much to compensate the promisee as to penalize breach of promise by the promisor. The rule enforcing the unrelied-on promise finds the same justification, on this theory, as an ordinance which fines a man for driving through a stop-light when no other vehicle is in sight.

In seeking justification for the rule granting the value of the expectancy there is no need, however, to restrict ourselves by the assumption, hitherto made, that the rule can only be intended to cure or prevent the losses caused by reliance. A justification can be developed from a less negative point of view. It may be said that there is not only a policy in favor of preventing and undoing the harms resulting from reliance, but also a policy in favor of promoting and facilitating reliance on business agreements. As in the case of the stop-light ordinance we are interested not only in preventing collisions but in speeding traffic. Agreements can accomplish little, either for their makers or for society, unless they are made the basis for action. When business agreements are not only made but are also acted on, the division of labor is facilitated, goods find their way to the places where they are most needed, and economic activity is generally stimulated. These advantages would be threatened by any rule which limited legal protection to the reliance interest. Such a rule would in practice tend to discourage reliance. The difficulties in proving reliance and subjecting it to pecuniary measurement are such that the business man knowing, or sensing, that these obstacles stood in the way of judicial relief would hesitate to rely on a promise in any case where the legal sanction was of significance to him. To encourage reliance we must therefore dispense with its proof. For this reason it has been found wise to make recovery on a promise independent of reliance, both in the sense that in some cases the promise is enforced though not relied on (as in the bilateral business agreement) and in the sense that recovery is not limited to the detriment incurred in reliance.

The jurisitic explanation in its final form is then twofold. It rests the protection accorded the expectancy on (1) the need for curing and preventing the harms occasioned by reliance, and (2) on the need for facilitating reliance on business agreements. From this spelling out of a possible juristic explanation, it is clear that there is no incompatibility between it and the economic or institutional explanation. They view the same phenomenon from two different aspects. The essence of both of them lies in the word 'credit'. The economic explanation views credit from its institutional side; the juristic explanation views it from its rational side. The economic view sees credit as an accepted way of living; the juristic view invites us to explore the considerations of utility which underlie this way of living, and the part which conscious human direction has played in bringing it into being.

The way in which these two points of view supplement one another becomes clearer when we examine separately the economic implications of the two aspects of the juristic explanation. If we rest the legal argument for measuring damages by the expectancy on the ground that this procedure offers the most satisfactory means of compensating the plaintiff for the loss of other opportunities to contract, it is clear that the force of the argument will depend entirely upon the existing economic environment. It would be most forceful in a hypothetical society in which all value were available on the market and where all markets were 'perfect' in the economic sense. In such a society there would be no difference between the reliance interest and the expectation interest. The plaintiff's loss in foregoing to enter another contract would be identical with the expectation value of the contract he did make. The argument that granting the value of the expectancy merely compensates for that loss, loses force to the extent that actual conditions depart from those of such a hypothetical society. These observations make it clear why the development of open markets for goods tends to carry in its wake the view that a contract claim is a kind of property.... He who by entering one contract passes by the opportunity to accomplish the same end elsewhere will not be inclined to regard contract breach lightly or as a mere matter of private morality. The consciousness of what is foregone reinforces the notion that the contract creates a 'right' and that the contract claim is itself a species of property.

If, on the other hand, we found the juristic explanation on the desire to promote reliance on contracts, it is not difficult again to trace a correspondence between the legal view and the actual conditions of economic life. In general our courts and our economic institutions attribute special significance to the same types of promises. The bilateral business agreement is, generally speaking, the only type of informal contract our courts are willing to enforce without proof that reliance has occurred—simply for the sake of facilitating reliance. This is, by no accident, precisely the kind of contract (the 'exchange', 'bargain', 'trade', 'deal') which furnishes the indispensable and pervasive framework for the 'unmanaged' portions of our economic activity.

The inference is therefore justified that the ends of the law of contracts and those of our economic system show an essential correspondence. One may explain this either on the ground that the law (mere superstructure and ideology) reflects inertly the conditions of economic life, or on the ground that economic activity has fitted itself into the rational framework of the law. Neither explanation would be true. In fact we are dealing with a situation in which law and society have interacted. The law measures damages by the expectancy *in part* because society views the expectancy as a present value; society views the expectancy as a present value *in part* because the law (for reasons more or less consciously articulated) gives protection to the expectancy.

The combined juristic and economic explanation which has just been developed may seem vulnerable to one serious objection. This lies in the fact that the 'normal' rule, which measures damages by the expectancy, has been frequently applied to promises of a type having no conceivable relation to 'the credit system', the division of labor, or the organization of economic activity....

Is the application of the 'normal' rule of damages to non-bargain promises then an unanswerable refutation of the explanation which we have attempted of the rule? We think not. In the first place, it is obviously possible that the courts have, through force of habit, given a broader application to the rule than a philosophic inquiry into its possible bases would justify. In the second place, it is by no means clear, from the decisions at any rate, that the rule of recovery in the case of these 'non-bargain' promises *is* necessarily that which measures damages by the expectancy.

NOTES

1. Fuller and Perdue continue by examining various aspects of the reliance interest. In particular, they draw a distinction between reliance, which takes the form of money wasted preparing to perform (which they term 'essential reliance'), and expenditure, which was not required by the contract but which the plaintiff incurred in the expectation that the contract would be fulfilled and which was wasted when the contract was broken ('incidental reliance'): see 46 Yale LJ 78.

2. They also discuss the question of whether a plaintiff should be able to recover more by seeking reliance damages than he would by claiming for loss of expectation, and conclude that this should not be permitted. On this, see p 631.

3.   They end the first part of their article by pointing out that the recovery of essential reliance loss was barely recognised by the (First) Restatement of Contracts, and the recovery of incidental reliance was not recognised at all. In a second part to their article (46 Yale LJ 373), they start by describing a number of situations in which the courts do not give damages for loss of expectation even in bargain situations (eg if the lost profit cannot be proved with certainty, cf p 629). They then examine a series of situations in which the contract is further and further away from being a commercial bargain, arguing that the further away it is, the stronger the tendency to limit recovery to reliance losses. In particular, in cases that would fall under Restatement s 90, they argue that courts have frequently given no more than compensation for reliance loss. They conclude that it would be better if the possibility of awarding reliance damages were openly recognised, because when full expectation damages do not seem appropriate, some courts may deny any recovery at all.

4.   Fuller's article is evaluated by, among others, Rakoff [1991] Wisconsin LR 203, Macaulay [1991] Wisconsin LR 247 and Craswell, 'Against Fuller and Perdue' (2000) 67 University of Chicago LR 99, who argues that the analysis is neither useful nor much used (see below).

5.   We saw earlier (p 171 and see further p 807) that recent work has challenged the common assumption that the courts responded to Fuller's call and awarded only reliance damages in s 90 cases.

6.   Fuller's analysis cannot be applied directly to English law, which, as we have seen, does not openly enforce gratuitous promises merely because they have been relied on, and under which damages for breach of contract are almost always said to be damages for loss of expectation. But Atiyah has questioned whether the classical model of the voluntarily assumed and bargained-for obligation, protected by the award of expectation damages, really represents English law accurately.

■ Craswell, 'Against Fuller and Perdue' (2000)
67 U Chi Law Rev 99

...More fundamentally, whenever different amounts of damages would be optimal for each of the different incentives to be optimized, the measure that is optimal when all of the relevant incentives are considered will often be some hybrid or intermediate number. For example, if the potential breacher's incentives to perform or to take appropriate precautions would be optimized by full expectation damages, but if the nonbreacher's attitude toward risk leads him to prefer less than full insurance, the measure that best accommodates both of those goals will normally be more than would be chosen if insurance were the only relevant goal, but less than what would be chosen if precautions alone were relevant. Once this has been recognized, it is not too far-fetched to say that the measure of damages that is truly optimal—optimal, that is, when all of the relevant factors have been considered—could lie anywhere on the real number line.

...

2. Diversity within the reliance cases
To begin with, not all of the cases awarding 'reliance damages' are necessarily pursuing the same goal, or are even awarding the same measure of damages. Fuller and Perdue defined reliance damages as the amount needed to put the promisee in the position he would have occupied if the promise had never been made. This would normally include the value of any opportunities the promisor could have taken

had he not instead relied on the promise now at issue. For example, if the promisee turns down one high-paying job because he has been promised a higher-paying job somewhere else, and if the latter promise is then broken, the promisee's reliance interest should include the value of the job that he would have accepted had it not been for the promise that was later broken.

However, as Michael Kelly has shown, courts often exclude those opportunities from their measure of reliance damages, meaning that they award less than Fuller and Purdue's definition of the reliance interest. . . .

A similar point can be made about the cases that award reliance damages in an effort to apportion losses, if the contract has become unenforceable through some contingency that was not the fault of either party. An award of reliance damages (when that measure is less than expectation damages) is one way to split the losses, by giving the plaintiff less than he would have received had the contract been performed, but more than he would get if he were denied recovery entirely. But there are other ratios into which the losses could be divided—for example, both parties' lost profits could be added together and divided by two, so that each party bore exactly half of the combined losses from the misfortune. Alternatively the combined losses could be divided in proportion to the parties' relative fault. . . .

In short, even when courts do use the reliance remedy to reduce the promisee's recovery, it is not clear that they are always reducing it to the same level. Fuller and Purdue's classification, which speaks of only a single reliance 'interest', tends to obscure these differences among the various reliance cases. While the total number of such cases may not be large enough to count this as a severe drawback, it does add to the disadvantages of that classification scheme.

. . . There are, of course, many doctrines that courts can invoke to reduce a promisee's recovery even while awarding expectation damages. For example, elements of expectation damages can be disallowed if they were not reasonably foreseeable by the promisor, or if they could have been avoided by reasonable mitigation, or if their amount cannot be proven with reasonable certainty. There are also categorical rules that exclude certain elements—for example, the exclusion of attorneys' fees and other costs of litigation, or the exclusion of compensation for emotional distress (except when physical injury results, or when the contract could be expected to have particular emotional significance).

. . .

In short, once we stop focusing on Fuller and Perdue's three 'interests', we can see a wide range of sub-expectation levels to which a promisee's recovery might be reduced, and a wide range of legal doctrines that might effect such a reduction. Given this range of possibilities, the question of whether any particular reduction should be classified as protecting the reliance 'interest' or the expectation "interest" seems to me one of the least interesting questions to ask about the award. In this way, too, Fuller and Perdue's categories obscure much more than they clarify.

. . .

IV. Beyond Fuller and Perdue?

The question, then, is what should replace that classification. . . .

In short, the classification that I propose has three parts: (1) remedies above expectation, (2) remedies that approximate expectation, and (3) remedies below expectation. The middle category, remedies that approximate the expectation interest, is essentially the same as Fuller and Perdue's (and the traditional category that preceded them), so I cannot claim any improvement in that regard. But the first category— encompassing remedies above the expectation interest—is clearly an advance over Fuller and Perdue, since they saw the expectation interest as the largest possible remedy (except in the unusual case of a losing contract, where expectation might be exceeded by reliance and restitution). As a result, Fuller and Perdue's three categories do not help us talk about the many other remedies that exceed, and often intentionally exceed, the expectation interest. At the same time, my third category (remedies that aim below the expectation interest) should also be viewed as an advance over Fuller and Perdue. While Fuller and Perdue provided two categories for remedies that fall below the expectation interest—restitution and reliance—my third category is even broader, to reflect the many other sub-expectation remedies besides these two.

■ Atiyah, 'Promises, Obligations and The Law of Contract' in *Essays on Contract* (1986)
pp 19–31, 33–41

... To what extent is it true to say that contractual liabilities arise from agreement or promises or depend on the voluntary assumption of obligation? I want to begin by suggesting that the power of the classical model here derives largely from its stress on the executory contract. If two parties do exchange promises to carry out some performance at a future date, and if, immediately on the exchange of promises, a binding legal obligation comes at once into existence, then it seems inexorably to follow that the obligation is created by the agreement, by the intention of the parties. If they have done nothing to implement the agreement, if no actions have followed the exchange of promises, then manifestly the legal obligation cannot arise from anything except the exchange of promises. Thus far the classical model appears to be impregnable. But closer examination suggests that the area of impregnability is really rather small.

The first point to note is that wholly executory contracts are rarer, more ephemeral in practice, and somewhat less binding than the classical model of Contract would suggest. In the classical model ... the executory transaction lies at the very heart of Contract. It is precisely because the classical model largely defines Contract in terms of executory transactions that it necessarily locates the source of contractual liability in what the parties intend rather than in what they do. But large numbers of contracts are regularly made in which the making and the performance, or at least part performance, are simultaneous or practically simultaneous events. Consider such simple transactions as the boarding of a bus, or a purchase of goods in a supermarket, or a loan of money. Is it really sensible to characterise these transactions as agreements or exchanges of promises? Is it meaningful or useful to claim that a person who boards a bus is promising to pay his fare? If so, would it not be just as meaningful to say that when he descends from the bus and crosses the road he promises to cross with all due care for the safety of other road users? I do not, of course, deny that all these transactions involve some element of voluntary conduct. People do not generally board buses, buy goods in a supermarket, or borrow money in their sleep. But they involve much else besides voluntary conduct. They usually involve the rendering of some benefit, or actions of detrimental reliance, or both. A person who is carried by a bus from point A to point B after voluntarily boarding the bus can normally be presumed to have derived some benefit from the arrangements. Does his liability to pay his fare have nothing to do with this element of benefit?

Consider next the possibility of detrimental reliance by the promisee. Is it not manifest that a person who has actually worsened his position by reliance on a promise has a more powerful case for redress than one who has not worsened his position by reliance on the promise at all? ...

... [I]n morality and in law the rendering of benefits and actions of detriment reliance can give rise to obligations even where there was no promise at all. The law of restitution is almost entirely concerned with situations in which one party is entitled to recompense for a benefit received by another from him, or at his expense even though the latter made no promise to pay for it. ...

And so far I have said nothing about one of the most obvious bodies of legal doctrine which is not easy to reconcile with the theory that contractual and promissory obligations rest on voluntary obligation. I refer, of course, to the so-called 'objective-test' theory of contractual liability. Every law student is taught from his earliest days that contractual intent is not really what it seems; actual subjective intent is normally irrelevant. It is the appearance, the manifestation of intent that matters. Whenever a person is held bound by a promise or a contract contrary to his actual intent or understanding, it is plain that the liability is based not on some notion of a voluntary assumption of obligation, but on something else. And most frequently it will be found that that something else is the element of reasonable reliance. One party relies on a reasonable construction of an offer, or he accepts an offer, reasonably thinking it is still open when the offeror has revoked it but failed to communicate his revocation. All this is standard stuff but I suggest that cases of this type have for too long been regarded as of marginal importance only, as not affecting the fundamental basis and theory of liability. In a simple world of simple promises and contracts this might have been an acceptable perspective. But the arrival of written contracts and above all the standard printed form has surely rendered this approach much less defensible. A party who signs an elaborate printed document is almost invariably held bound by it not because of anything he intended; he is bound in the teeth of his intention and understandings except in some very exceptional cases of fraud or the like. The truth is he is bound not so much because of what he intends but because of what he does. Like the man who is bound to pay his fare because he boards a bus, the man who signs a written contract is liable because of what he does rather than what he intends. And he is liable because of what he does for the good reason that other parties are likely to rely upon what he does in ways which are reasonable and even necessary by the standards of our society.

What I suggest then, is that whatever benefits are obtained, wherever acts of reasonable reliance take place, obligations may arise, both morally and in law.... Now I want next to suggest that these cases of benefits received or of action in reliance, are more common than is suggested by our conventional image of the legal world. In conventional contract theory, the paradigm of contract is the executory arrangement. Executory contract theory has totally subsumed liabilities and obligations which arise from the receipt of benefits or from acts of reasonable reliance. But in practice, the wholly executory transaction is nothing like such a paradigm as it appears in the books. I have already said something of the difficulties involved in the very concept of a paradigm in this context, but the most cursory look at the world and at the law will reveal that many types of transactions do not fit the model of the wholly executory arrangement at all. Vast numbers of transactions are not in any real sense binding prior to something being *done* by one or both of the parties. This may partly reflect the fact that lawyers have traditionally implied promises very easily from transactions, and that in consequence today there are many situations in which the lawyer would assert that an executory arrangement involves implied mutual promises while the parties themselves might very well deny that they promised anything at all. The language of consumer transactions, in particular, is not couched in terms of promises. People 'book' holidays, or air reservations, they 'order' goods, they 'accept' estimates, and so on. Even in business circles this sort of terminology is more common than the express language of promises and undertakings. Whether language of this kind is treated as creating an obligation is traditionally thought of as depending upon whether the language is tantamount to being promissory. But it is at least arguable that in many cases of this nature the reality is otherwise. Frequently, both in law and in moral discourse we appear to determine whether there should be an obligation first, and then decide how the language should be constructed afterwards. And it follows that the existence or non-existence of the obligation is then being decided independently of the existence of any promise....

Now I must repeat that I am not arguing that consent, promise, intention, voluntary conduct, are irrelevant to the creation of obligations even where an element of reciprocal benefit is present, or some act of reasonable reliance has taken place. In the first place, where liability arises out of conduct rather than from the voluntary assumption of an obligation, the conduct itself is usually of a voluntary character. Even if liability on a part-executed arrangement can properly be said to the benefit-based rather than promise-based, a man is normally entitled to choose what benefits he will accept— normally, though by no means invariably. Similarly, with reliance-based liability; it is normally open to a person to warn others that they are not to rely upon him, but must trust to their own judgment. Obviously this raises difficulty where a person wants to have his cake and eat it, where he wants to influence others to behave in a certain manner but wants also to disclaim responsibility for their doing so. There is little doubt that in such circumstances the trend is towards insisting on the imposition of responsibility. The striking down of exemption clauses and disclaimers of liability are evidence of the unacceptability of these attempts to have things both ways. This trend may reflect the increased emphasis on reliance and the declining stress on free choice.

But secondly, and much more important, I would argue that even where obligations can be said to be primarily benefit-based or reliance-based, explicit promises may have a valuable role to play. I referred earlier to the conventional wisdom of English common lawyers which some decades ago suggested that the only rational function of the doctrine of consideration was to serve as evidence of the seriousness of a promise. I now want to suggest that the truth lies more closely in the precise converse of this assertion. Where obligations arise out of the rendering of benefits or from acts of reasonable reliance, the presence of an explicit promise may, I suggest, serve valuable evidentiary purposes. Consider the simple example of a loan of money which I referred to earlier as an illustration of a liability which could not, without distortion, be viewed as purely promissory. The presence of an explicit promise may nevertheless serve valuable evidentiary purposes. First, it helps to avoid doubt about the nature of the transaction. The possibility of a gift is ruled out by the express promise to repay. Then it helps clarify who the parties to the transaction may be, for the handing of money by A to B may create a loan from X to Y where A and B are acting as agents or in a transaction of any complexity. An explicit promise may resolve any ambiguities about such matters. Then again an explicit promise may help settle many minor or ancillary terms, and it is worth reflecting on how and why this is the case. Suppose, for example, that the borrower promises to repay the loan with interest at a specified rate. In the sort of society we live in, it can be taken for granted that a loan should normally carry some rate of interest, and in the absence of an agreed rate, the fixing of the rate would fall to the court in the last resort. What would the court do? The court would, of course, endeavour to fix on a just or reasonable rate of interest having regard to all the circumstances. Here again, therefore, the explicit promise to pay a specified rate does not seem to create the obligation, which would exist anyhow, but to give it precision. And the reason why it gives it precision is, surely, that it functions very like a conclusive admission. If the court is to search for a fair and reasonable rate of interest, the rate which the borrower has agreed to pay is good evidence that that is in fact the fair and reasonable rate. Good evidence, but not, at least not always, conclusive evidence. For if the agreed rate of interest is extortionate, or if it has been obtained by fraud or misrepresentation the promise to pay will not bind.

There are, indeed, some cases in which the evidentiary value of promises has already been distinctly recognised by the courts. Naturally enough, given the classical model of Contract, these cases concern situations in which an independent legal obligation already exists. For example, where a person promises to pay for valuable services previously rendered to him—the so-called past consideration cases—the promise may be treated as evidence of the value of those services. And again, where services are rendered in pursuance of a contract which turns out to be invalid for some technical reason, the value of the services may nevertheless be recovered and the contract can be treated as evidence of that value.

It may, of course, be said that these cases are no illustration of the general nature of contractual liability, but on the contrary serve to illustrate the difference between contractual and other forms of liability. For (it may be urged) the whole point of contractual liability is to permit parties to determine conclusively their own obligations. The promise creates the liability, and does not merely evidence it. In non-contractual cases, *per contra*, the duty is in the first instance created by the law; and the promise cannot be treated as creating the obligation. But I suggest that this analysis is the result of treating the executory contract as the paradigm of contract, the heritage of the classical law which I have already criticised. In the part-executed transaction, as I have argued, it is in fact frequently the case that there would be a liability even apart from any express or implied promise. Promises are not a necessary condition of the existence of a liability or the creation of an obligation. The performance by one party of acts which are beneficial to the other, the rendering of services to another, for instance, would normally be thought of as creating some sort of obligation even in the absence of a promise. Similarly, acts of reasonable reliance would often create liability in tort, or by way of trust, or other equitable obligation, even where there is no express or implied promise. Indeed, did not the whole law of trusts arise because property was entrusted to other hands, usually no doubt because of some understanding that the trustee would behave in a certain fashion? In circumstances of this kind, therefore, where obligations would normally be thought of as arising from what has been done, rather than from what has been said, there seems to me no difficulty in regarding promises as having primarily an evidentiary role.

Treating explicit promises as prima-facie evidence, and as strong prima-facie evidence of the fairness of a transaction, of the appropriate price to be paid for goods and services, is an indispensable tool of efficient administration in a free market society. For any other rule would leave it open to a dissatisfied party to any and every transaction to appeal to a judge to upset an agreed price and fix a new one. But, it may be urged, the law does not treat promises as only prima-facie evidence of the fairness of a transaction, or of the terms which should bind the parties; in most circumstances, a promise is treated as conclusive of these matters. If I am right in thinking that the role of the promise is thus limited it is incumbent on me to explain why promises are normally treated as conclusive of most of these questions, and this task I attempt in Essay 5. Here I will content myself with pointing out that promises are never treated as wholly conclusive in law. All promises and contracts are defeasible in *some* circumstances. A promise or agreement extorted by violence is no evidence of the fairness of a transaction, and is there-fore naturally set aside by the courts. Promises given as a result of certain types of mistake may likewise be set aside. Alternatively, the courts may uphold the validity of the exchange but adjust the obligations of the parties (for example by implying appropriate terms) so as to ensure, so far as possible, that the exchange is a fair or reasonable one, despite the disparity between the literal obligations assumed by the parties. But the *extent* of the indefeasibility of a promise, the *extent* to which it is to be treated as a con-clusive admission of the fairness and reasonableness of the terms of an exchange, is a much less simple proposition. The extent to which the courts and the law are prepared to go in treating promises as defeasible, or merely as prima-facie rather than conclusive evidence of the fairness of an exchange, is obviously something determined by the degree of paternalism which commends itself to the society and the judiciary in question. A society which believes in allowing the skilful and knowledgeable to reap the rewards of their skill and knowledge is likely to have a higher regard for the sanctity of promises than a society which wishes to protect the weak and foolish from the skilful and knowledgeable. As we shall see, this point is a good deal more important in the case of executory transactions.

Now as we know, in modern law, all this is different. A plaintiff is unquestionably entitled to expecta-tion damages for breach of an executory contract, without any actual consideration passing. There is no need to show any actual benefit, any detrimental reliance. The modern law is squared with the doctrine of consideration by saying that the mere promises constitute consideration for each other. That indeed was what judges had been saying since the time of Elizabeth I, but it has not generally been perceived what an enormous difference has come over the practical import of this formula. For in the reign of Elizabeth I, a promise was good consideration for a promise precisely because both promises had to be performed. In our modern law, a plaintiff's promise is good consideration for the defendant's promise even though the plaintiff is discharged from performing his promise by the defendant's breach. It is only since these rules grew up, therefore, that liability on the wholly executory contract has truly become promise-based, rather than benefit or reliance-based.

But although this form of liability must be treated as promise-based, we are entitled to ask how extensive it is in relation to the rest of the law, and whether it deserves to occupy the central role in Contract and even in promissory theory that it occupies today. It is, I think, worth observing that wholly executory contracts are generally nothing like as binding in practice as legal theory might suggest. Consumers and even business men often expect to be able to cancel executory agreements with the minimum of penalty, paying perhaps only for actual expenses laid out in reliance on the promise. And such reliance expenditures would by definition, not exist if the arrangement were still wholly executory. And even in strict law, it must be stressed that the expectations protected by executory contracts are limited. They are not generally expectations of performance but expectations of profit. Where there is no difference in the market price of the goods or services which are the subject of the contract, and the market price of comparable goods or services, the contract may in law be broken with impunity. In practice this must comprise a high proportion of cases in which executory arrangements are broken. Then again, the binding force of wholly executory contracts is normally of an ephemeral nature. Executory contracts do not normally remain executory for very long. Even if made well before the time for performance, the whole purpose of making them is frequently to enable the parties to make preliminary arrangements in confident reliance on reciprocal performance. Thus action in reliance is likely to follow hard on the heels of the making of most executory contracts, and it is only in the rare cases where cancellation is sought very soon after making the contract, or where, despite the lapse of some longer period of time no action in reliance has been commenced, that the source of the obligation has to be rested in the promise alone. Whatever the paradigm of actual Contract may be, there can be no doubt that the paradigm of *a breach of contract* is not the breach of a wholly executory contracts. And this surely reflects the intention of most parties who enter into executory contracts. The primary purpose of making such a contract is usually to agree upon the terms which are to regulate a contemplated exchange, when and if it is carried through; it is surely—in most instances—a subordinate and less obvious purpose that the contract binds both parties to see that the exchange is indeed carried through.

. . . The modern, and perhaps even, by now, the traditional legal view would probably be that promises and executory contracts give rise to reasonable expectations and that it is the function of the law to protect reasonable expectations. But this is itself a somewhat circular justification. We all have a large number of expectations, many of which are perfectly reasonable, but only a few of them are protected by the law. Besides, the reasonableness of an expectation is itself something which turns largely upon whether it is in fact protected. If the law did not protect expectations arising from a wholly executory arrangement, then it would be less reasonable to entertain such expectations, or at any rate to entertain them as entitlements. . . .

Then again, the explanation appears to prove too much. For reasonable expectations may arise from assertions or representations of fact as much as from promises. Yet the law seldom or never protects such expectations unless and until they have been acted upon. If we can, as I think we should, conceptually equate the idea of action in reliance on representations with the notion of detrimental reliance as a consideration in the case of promises, then we must recognise that representations can only give rise to a contractual-type obligation in the case of a part-executed transaction. And this remains true even in the extreme case of fraud. No matter what expectations are thereby generated a person who tells a downright and deliberate falsehood is not subject to legal obligations unless and until someone suffers loss through acting upon it. Indeed, even when it is acted upon, it is widely thought that the measure of any consequent liability is fixed by the extent of the reliance losses and not by the expectations generated. This, at least, is said to be the measure of damages in tort for fraud, although it is certainly not the measure in cases classified as warranty or estoppel. It is, perhaps, possible that the explanation for this otherwise puzzling distinction between the law's treatment of promises and assertions lies in the too ready acceptance of the idea that words or conduct are in practice easily classifiable as the one or the other. Perhaps the reality is that in more cases than lawyers are willing to admit, words or conduct are classified as promises or assertions precisely because in the particular circumstances the expectations aroused are, or are not, felt worthy of protection. But if this is the case, then it is clear that we cannot defend the protection of bare expectations by pointing to the fact that they derived from a promise. . . .

The second possible argument for upholding executory contracts is the argument from principle. Executory contracts are made so that the parties can rely upon each other and take the necessary preliminary steps to performance. The whole point of such contracts is that they invite reliance. Therefore, it may be urged, *even if there has in fact been no reliance yet*, it is desirable that the principle of upholding the sanctity of contracts should be maintained. Supporters of this argument, however, must explain why a shift in the onus of proof would not meet the case. . . .

The third possible argument in support of the executory contract concerns the case where the contract is a deliberate exercise in risk allocation. Where the primary purpose of a contract is to shift a risk of some future possibility from one party to another, and where, in particular, the risk is thereby shifted to a party who in a commercial sense is better able to take the risk, or to take avoiding action against the risk eventuating, there appears to be a strong economic case for the executory contract. I believe that this argument lies at the heart of the historical development of the binding executory contract in English law, but it is imperative to note the limits upon its application. It is very far from being true that all contracts, even all executory contracts, are exercises in risk allocation. Frequently, it is the interpretation of the law which converts a simple postponed exchange into a risk-allocation exercise, rather than any deliberate intent of the parties. . . . It is also far from being always the case that the purpose of an executory contract is to shift a risk to a party whose business it is to handle such risks and who can, therefore, be assumed to be generally more efficient at handling them . . .

...I must now observe that if the primary justification for the enforcement of executory contracts is that they are risk-allocation devices, then it follows that the enforcement of such contracts raises profoundly value-laden questions. The justification for the executory contract becomes, in effect, an economic justification, an argument for greater economic efficiency. The purpose of enforcing such contracts is that of facilitating the use of greater skill, intelligence, foresight, knowledge and perhaps even resources by those who possess these advantages. To the extent that the law refuses to recognise the binding force of executory transactions in order to protect the weak, the foolish, the improvident or those who lack bargaining power, it must necessarily weaken the incentives and indeed the power of those not suffering these disadvantages...

...The economic arguments for the binding executory contract, like those in favour of the institution of property itself, involve a tendency to a perpetuation of existing inequalities. To strike down, or limit the binding force of executory contracts in order to protect some people from their own folly or ignorance is, by contrast, a redistributive device, and like all such devices must impose costs as well as benefits.

The fourth argument, which I have left to the last, for the binding executory contract is the moral argument. It is simple and appealing to argue that promises are morally obligatory, and that this remains the case whether they have been paid for, or relied upon or not. But as the case for the morally binding nature of promises is examined more closely, it bears a curious resemblance to the case for the binding nature of legal contracts rather than offering an independent reason in support of the law. One of the most commonly adduced reasons for arguing that promises are morally binding is that they have a tendency to be relied upon. We then find it being argued that, if that is the only justification, it is a somewhat circular one. For if, promises were not binding, they might not be relied upon. And again, it is argued that if the tendency to rely on promises is the source of their binding character, what of the case where reliance is distinctly disproved?...

...[W]hen all is said, I do not find the moral contribution to the problem to be a very satisfying one. For moralists and philosophers, like the lawyers themselves, have not generally perceived the need to separate off the wholly executory arrangement for independent justification. Virtually all discussion of the source of contractual and promissory obligation, in law and in morality, has failed to draw the all important distinction between promises and contracts which rest purely in intention, and promises and contracts which depend partly on action. Surely, nobody can doubt that morally speaking promises are more strongly binding where payment has already been received, or where there is a clear and significant act in reliance which would worsen the position of the promisee if the promise were not performed. And just as I have suggested that, in the law of part executed contracts, explicit promises may play a useful evidentiary role, so it may be suggested that promises themselves are frequently of an evidentiary character. The purpose of a promise, far from being, as is so often assumed, to create some wholly independent source of an obligation, is frequently to bolster up an already existing duty. Promises help to clarify, to qualify, to give precision to moral obligations, many of which already exist or would arise anyhow from the performance of acts which are contemplated or invited by the promise. The promise which is given without *any* independent reason for it is a peculiarity, just as the wholly executory contract is a legal peculiarity. Is it pure coincidence that the phrase, a 'gratuitous promise' means both promise without payment and a promise without reason? Could it then be that the refusal of English law to recognise the binding force of executory gratuitous promises is not the peculiarity, the idiosyncrasy it has so long been thought to be? Might it not be that the real oddity lies in the belief that a bare promise creates a moral obligation and should create a legal obligation, without any inquiry into the reason for which the promise was given, or the effect that the promise has had?

These arguments, of course, require much greater development than they can be given here; but enough has been said to show that, if they stand up to further examination, they should suffice to dethrone the executory contract from the central place which it occupies in contract theory. The consequences of this would be to require some drastic redrawing of the lines of the conceptual structure of contractual and promissory obligation. In the first place, the distinction between contract and restitution would surely come crashing to the ground...

A similar fate may well await the distinction between contract and tort when once the executory contract is removed from the central place in the law of obligations. I have already suggested that our nineteenth-century heritage has led us to place undue emphasis on the extent to which contractual obligations depend upon intentions and the voluntary assumption of liability. But is it not equally true that, perhaps by way of reaction, tort theory has swung too far in the opposite direction? In their reaction away from contract, lawyers and judges have tended to stress the positive nature of tortious liability. Tort duties are imposed by law, not assumed by the parties. They are the reflection of society's standards of fairness and reasonableness and not the result of deliberate submission to a mutual binding arrangement, and so on. I want to suggest that all this has tended to draw far too sharp a line between contract and tort.

NOTES

1. These views underlie much of Atiyah's *Rise and Fall of Freedom of Contract*, 1979. They are developed further in his *Promises, Morals and Law*, 1981. An instructive review of the first book from a historical viewpoint will be found in Baker (1980) 43 MLR 467; the second is usefully reviewed in Raz (1982) 95 Harvard LR 916 and Simpson (1982) 98 LQR 470.

2. Do you agree with Atiyah's analysis? Does he put too much emphasis on 'marginal' cases and not pay enough attention to cases involving commercial contracts? Aren't most of these conscious attempts to allocate a variety of risks?

3. Atiyah's views, which were first published in (1978) 94 LQR 413, have not gone unchallenged: see Raz (1982) 95 Harvard LR 916; Birks [1983] Current Legal Problems 141; Burrows (1983) 99 LQR 216. Atiyah replies to his critics in *Essays in Contract*, pp 43–56.

4. The view that contractual liability has become almost indistinguishable from liability in tort and restitution was expressed even more forcibly by Gilmore in *The Death of Contract*, 1974. Gilmore argued that classical contract law was the artificial creation of academics (Christopher Columbus Langdell of Harvard, who produced the first casebook on contracts, got most of the blame). Gilmore concluded (at 87–88 and 90):

Speaking descriptively, we might say that what is happening is that 'contract' is being reabsorbed into the mainstream of 'tort'. Until the general theory of contract was hurriedly run up late in the nineteenth century, tort had always been our residual category of civil liability. As the contract rules dissolve, it is becoming so again. It should be pointed out that the theory of tort into which contract is being reabsorbed is itself a much more expansive theory of liability than was the theory of tort from which contract was artificially separated a hundred years ago.

We have had more than one occasion to notice the insistence of the classical theorists on the sharp differentiation between contract and tort—the refusal to admit any liability in 'contract' until the formal requisites of offer, acceptance and consideration had been satisfied, the dogma that only 'bargained-for' detriment or benefit could count as consideration, and notably, the limitations on damage recovery. Classical contract theory might well be described as an attempt to stake out an enclave within the general domain of tort. The dykes which were set up to protect the enclave have, it is clear enough, been crumbling at a progressively rapid rate. With the growth of the ideas of quasi-contract and unjust enrichment, classical consideration theory was breached on the benefit side. With the growth of the promissory estoppel idea, it was breached on the detriment side. We are fast approaching the point where, to prevent unjust enrichment, any benefit received by a defendant must be paid for unless it was clearly meant as a gift; where any detriment reasonably incurred by a plaintiff in reliance on a defendant's assurances must be recompensed. When that point is reached, there is really no longer any viable distinction between liability in contract and liability in tort. . . .

I have occasionally suggested to my students that a desirable reform in legal education would be to merge the first-year course in Contracts and Torts into a single course which we could call Contorts. Perhaps the same suggestion would be a good one when the time comes for the third round of Restatements.

5.   Partly as a response to Atiyah and Gilmore, Fried in 1981 attempted to justify contract law in terms of what he called the 'promise principle'. A short extract from his work follows.

■ Fried, 'Contract as Promise: A Theory of Contractual Obligations' (1981) pp 14–21, 69–73

THE MORAL OBLIGATION OF PROMISE

Once I have invoked the institution of promising, why exactly is it wrong for me then to break my promise?

My argument so far does not answer that question. The institution of promising is a way for me to bind myself to another so that the other may expect a future performance, and binding myself in this way is something that I may want to be able to do. But this by itself does not show that I am morally obligated to perform my promise at a later time if to do so proves inconvenient or costly. That there should be a system of currency also increases my options and is useful to me, but this does not show why I should not use counterfeit money if I can get away with it. In just the same way the usefulness of promising in general does not show why I should not take advantage of it in a particular case and yet fail to keep my promise. That the convention would cease to function in the long run, would cease to provide benefits if everyone felt free to violate it, is hardly an answer to the question of why I should keep a particular promise on a particular occasion.

David Lewis has shown that a convention that it would be in each person's interest to observe if everyone else observed it will be established and maintained without any special mechanisms of commitment or enforcement. Starting with simple conventions (for example that if a telephone conversation is disconnected, the person who initiated the call is the one who calls back) Lewis extends his argument to the case of language. Now promising is different, since (unlike language, where it is overwhelmingly in the interest of all that everyone comply with linguistic conventions, even when language is used to deceive) it will often be in the interest of the promisor *not* to conform to the convention when it comes time to render his performance. Therefore individual self-interest is not enough to sustain the convention, and some additional ground is needed to keep it from unraveling. There are two principal candidates: external sanctions and moral obligation.

David Hume sought to combine these two by proposing that the external sanction of public opprobrium, of loss of reputation for honesty, which society attaches to promise-breaking, is internalized, becomes instinctual, and accounts for the sense of the moral obligation of promise. Though Hume offers a possible anthropological or psychological account of how people feel about promises, his is not a satisfactory *moral* argument. Assume that I can get away with breaking my promise (the promisee is dead), and I am now asking why I should keep it anyway in the face of some personal inconvenience. Hume's account of obligation is more like an argument *against* my keeping the promise, for it tells me how any feelings of obligation that I may harbor have come to lodge in my psyche and thus is the first step toward ridding me of such inconvenient prejudices.

Considerations of self-interest cannot supply the moral basis of my obligation to keep a promise. By an analogous argument neither can considerations of utility. For however sincerely and impartially I may apply the utilitarian injunction to consider at each step how I might increase the sum of happiness or utility in the world, it will allow me to break my promise whenever the balance of advantage (including, of course, my own advantage) tips in that direction. The possible damage to the institution of promising is only one factor in the calculation. Other factors are the alternative good I might do by breaking my promise, whether and by how many people the breach might be discovered, what the actual effect on confidence of such a breach would be. There is no a priori reason for believing that an individual's calculations will come out in favor of keeping the promise always, sometimes, or most of the time.

Rule-utilitarianism seeks to offer a way out of this conundrum. The individual's moral obligation is determined not by what the best action at a particular moment would be, but by the rule it would be best for him to follow. It has, I believe, been demonstrated that this position is incoherent: Either rule-utilitarianism requires that rules be followed in a particular case even where the result would not be best all things considered, and so the utilitarian aspect of rule-utilitarianism is abandoned; or the obligation to follow the rule is so qualified as to collapse into act-utilitarianism after all. There is, however, a version of rule-utilitarianism that makes a great deal of sense. In this version the utilitarian does not instruct us what our individual moral obligations are but rather instructs legislators what the best rules are. If legislation is our focus, then the contradictions of rule-utilitarianism do not arise, since we are instructing those whose decisions can *only* take the form of issuing rules. From that perspective there is obvious utility to rules establishing and enforcing promissory obligations. Since I am concerned now with the question of individual obligation, that is, moral obligation, this legislative perspective on the argument is not available to me.

The obligation to keep a promise is grounded not in arguments of utility but in respect for individual autonomy and in trust. Autonomy and trust are grounds for the institution of promising as well, but the argument for *individual* obligation is not the same. Individual obligation is only a step away, but the step must be taken. An individual is morally bound to keep his promises because he has intentionally invoked a convention whose function it is to give grounds—moral grounds—for another to expect the promised performance. To renege is to abuse a confidence he was free to invite or not, and which he intentionally did invite. To abuse that confidence now is like (but only *like*) lying: the abuse of a shared social institution that is intended to invoke the bonds of trust. A liar and a promise-breaker each *use* another person. In both speech and promising there is an invitation to the other to trust, to make himself vulnerable; the liar and the promise-breaker then abuse that trust. The obligation to keep a promise is thus similar to but more constraining than the obligation to tell the truth. To avoid lying you need only believe in the truth of what you say when you say it, but a promise binds into the future, well past the moment when the promise is made. There will, of course, be great social utility to a general regime of trust and confidence in promises and truthfulness. But this just shows that a regime of mutual respect allows men and women to accomplish what in a jungle of restrained self-interest could not be accomplished. If this advantage is to be firmly established, there must exist a ground for mutual confidence deeper than and independent of the social utility it permits.

The utilitarian counting the advantages affirms the general importance of enforcing *contracts*. The moralist of duty, however, sees *promising* as a device that free, moral individuals have fashioned on the premise of mutual trust, and which gathers its moral force from that premise. The moralist of duty thus posits a general obligation to keep promises, of which the obligation of contract will be only a special case—that special case in which certain promises have attained legal as well as moral force. But since a contract is first of all a promise, the contract must be kept because a promise must be kept.

To summarize: There exists a convention that defines the practice of promising and its entailments. This convention provides a way that a person may create expectations in others. By virtue of the basic Kantian principles of trust and respect, it is wrong to invoke that convention in order to make a promise, and then to break it.

. . .

WHAT A PROMISE IS WORTH

If I make a promise to you, I should do as I promise; and if I fail to keep my promise, it is fair that I should be made to hand over the equivalent of the promised performance. In contract doctrine this proposition appears as the expectation measure of damages for breach. The expectation standard gives the victim of a breach no more or less than he would have had had there been no breach—in other words, he gets the benefit of his bargain. Two alternative measures of damage, reliance and restitution, express the different notions that if a person has relied on a promise and been hurt, that hurt must be made good; and that if a contract-breaker has obtained goods or services, he must be made to pay a fair (just?) price for them. Consider three cases:

> II-A. I enter your antique shop on a quiet afternoon and agree in writing to buy an expensive chest I see there, the price being about three times what you paid for it a short time ago. When I get home I repent of my decision, and within half an hour of my visit—before any other customer has come to your store—I telephone to say I no longer want the chest.
>
> II-B. Same as above, except in the meantime you have waxed and polished the chest and had your delivery van bring it to my door.
>
> II-C. Same as above, except I have the use of the chest for six months, while your shop is closed for renovations.

To require me to pay for the chest in case II-A (or, if you resell it, to pay any profit you lost, including lost business volume) is to give you your expectation, the benefit of your bargain. In II-B if all I must compensate is your effort I am reimbursing your reliance, and in II-C to force me to pay a fair price for the use I have had of the chest is to focus on making me pay for, restore, an actual benefit I have received.

The assault on the classical conception of contract, the concept I call contract as promise, has centered on the connection—taken as canonical for some hundred years— between contract law and expectation damages. To focus the attack on this connection is indeed strategic. As the critics recognize and as I have just stated, to the extent that contract is grounded in promise, it seems natural to measure relief by the expectation, that is, by the promise itself. If that link can be threatened, then contract itself may be grounded elsewhere than in promise, elsewhere than in the will of the parties.

The insistence on reliance or benefit is related to disputes about the nature of promising. As I have argued, reliance on a promise cannot alone explain its force: There is reliance because a promise is binding, and not the other way around. But if a person is bound by his promise and not by the harm the promisee may have suffered in reliance on it, then what he is bound to is just its performance. Put simply, I am bound to do what I promised you I would do—or I am bound to put you in as good a position as if I had done so. To bind me to do no more than to reimburse your reliance is to excuse me to that extent from the obligation I undertook. If your reliance is less than your expectation (in case II-A there is no reliance), then to that extent a reliance standard excuses me from the very obligation I undertook and so weakens the force of an obligation I chose to assume. Since by hypothesis I chose to assume the obligation in its stronger form (that is, to render the performance promised), the reliance rule indeed precludes me from incurring the very obligation I chose to undertake at the time of promising. The most compelling of the arguments for resisting this conclusion and for urging that we settle for reliance is the sense that it is sometimes harsh and ungenerous to insist on the full measure of expectancy. (This is part of Atiyah's thrust when he designates the expectation standard as an aspect of the rigid Victorian promissory morality.) The harshness comes about because in the event the promisor finds the obligation he assumed too burdensome.

This distress may be analyzed into three forms: (1) The promisor regrets having to pay for what he has bought (which may only have been the satisfaction of promising a gift or the thrill of buying a lottery ticket or stock option), though he would readily do the same thing again. I take it that this kind of regret merits no sympathy at all. Indeed if we gave in to it we would frustrate the promisor's ability to engage in his own continuing projects and so the promisor's plea is, strictly speaking, self-contradictory. (2) The promisor regrets his promise because he was mistaken about the nature of the burdens he was assuming—the purchaser in case II-A thought he would find the money for the antique but in fact his savings are depleted, or perhaps the chest is not as old nor as valuable as he had imagined, or his house has burned down and he no longer needs it. All of these regrets are based on mistaken assumptions about the facts as they are or as they turn out to be. As we shall see..., the doctrines of mistake, frustration, and impossibility provide grounds for mitigating the effect of the promise principle without at all undermining it.

Finally there is the most troublesome ground of regret: (3) The promisor made no mistake about the facts or probabilities at all, but now that it has come time to perform he no longer values the promise as highly as when he made it. He regrets the promise because he regrets the value judgment that led him to make it. He concludes that the purchase of an expensive antique is an extravagance. Compassion may lead a promisee to release an obligation in such a case, but he releases as an act of generosity, not as a duty, and certainly not because the promisor's repentance destroys the force of the original obligation. The intuitive reason for holding fast is that such repentence should be the promisor's own responsibility, not one he can shift onto others. It seems too easy a way of getting out of one's obligations. Yet our intuition does not depend on suspicions of insincerity alone. Rather we feel that holding people to their obligations is a way of taking them seriously and thus of giving the concept of sincerity itself serious content. Taking this intuition to a more abstract level, I would say that respect for others as free and rational requires taking seriously their capacity to determine their own values. I invoke again the distinction between the right and the good. The right defines the concept of the self as choosing its own conception of the good. Others must respect our capacity as free and rational persons to choose our own good, and that respect means allowing persons to take responsibility for the good they choose. And, of course, that choosing self is not an instantaneous self but one extended in time, so that to respect those determinations of the self is to respect their persistence over time. If we decline to take seriously the assumption of an obligation because we do not take seriously the promisor's prior conception of the good that led him to assume it, to that extent we do not take him seriously as a person. We infantilize him, as we do quite properly when we release the very young from the consequences of their choices

Since contracts invoke and are invoked by promises, it is not surprising that the law came to impose on the promises it recognized the same incidents as morality demands. The connection between contract and the expectation principle is so palpable that there is reason to doubt that its legal recognition is a relatively recent invention. It is true that over the last two centuries citizens in the liberal democracies have become increasingly free to dispose of their talents, labor, and property as seems best to them. The freedom to bind oneself contractually to a future disposition is an important and striking example of this freedom (the freedom to make testamentary dispositions or to make whatever present use of one's effort or goods one desires are other examples), because in a promise one is taking responsibility not only for one's present self but for one's future self. But this does not argue that the promise principle itself is a novelty—surely Cicero's, Pufendorf's and Grotius's discussions of it show that it is not—but only that its use has expanded greatly over the years.

...

FILLING THE GAPS

It would be irrational to ignore the gaps in contracts, to refuse to fill them. It would be irrational not to recognize contractual accidents and to refuse to make adjustments when they occur. The gaps cannot be filled, the adjustments cannot be governed, by the promise principle. We have already encountered the two competing residuary principles of civil obligation that take over when promise gives out: the tort principle to compensate for harm done, and the restitution principle for benefits conferred.

Unfortunately in many cases both parties are harmed, neither is at fault, neither benefits. The half-built house is destroyed by an earthquake. The half-built machine is rendered useless by government regulation. The program printed for the canceled yacht race is of no interest to anyone. In such situations a distinct third principle for apportioning loss and gain comes into play: the principle of sharing.

NOTES

1. Fried's book was reviewed by Atiyah in (1981) 95 Harvard LR 509. Atiyah was not persuaded. He argues, for instance, that Fried's account of damages pays insufficient

attention to mitigation, which means that what the party who breaks his promise has to pay is often much less than he promised. A more fundamental criticism is that Fried has to admit that a considerable number of contract doctrines, such as common mistake and frustration, cannot be justified in terms of the promise principle; other principles are being brought in. Atiyah says this 'calls into question how often judicial decisions in contractual disputes can be attributed to the promise principle' (at 516).

2. In contrast, Smith (*Contract Theory*, 2003) does not see these doctrines as fatal to promissory theory; they present implicit limitations in the promise (at p 66). He concludes that, at an analytical level, promissory theory provides a better 'fit', and on the normative question is less open to moral objections, than reliance theory. He also finds that rights-based analysis is more convincing than the utilitarian 'efficiency arguments' because the latter fail to meet his 'transparency' criterion (at pp 132–136). You may like to return to Smith's argument when you have read the next chapter.

3. Raz, in his review of Atiyah, *Promises, Morals and Law*, in (1982) 95 Harvard LR 915, 933ff, puts forward a third theory, which he claims is more consistent with the principle that the only proper purpose for imposing legal obligations on individuals is to prevent harm (p 934).

The purpose of contract law *should* be not to enforce promises but to protect both the practice of undertaking voluntary obligations and the individuals who rely on that practice... One protects the practice of undertaking voluntary obligations by preventing its erosion—by making good any harm caused by its use or abuse. (p 933)

Thus the law should support social practices. However, it goes beyond that by invalidating contracts that the lawmaker regards as unacceptable, even if that view is not necessarily shared by the community (eg contracts that are racist), and also by preventing people from taking advantage of the practice by making it appear that they have agreed to obligations when they have not (eg the 'objective test'; see p 935). Raz points to two main differences between his position and that of those who see the law's function as protecting promises. Firstly, his theory explains why the law protects voluntary obligations that are not promises but which result from voluntary actions to which the law attaches an obligation (such as the obligation to pay customs duty on goods that the defendant chooses to import; see p 936). Secondly, it explains why the law may not always protect the practice by enforcing the obligation. Sometimes, a lesser measure, such as compensation for reliance, will suffice (p 937); at other times, enforcement of promises is justified as a means of protecting the practice of undertaking voluntary obligations from erosion, although not as an end in itself (p 938).

4. Kimel, *From Promise to Contract: Towards a Liberal Theory of Contract*, 2005, draws a distinction between the value of promises and that of contracts. He argues, at pp 65 and 78, that:

... whereas promises are normally made in the framework of some on-going personal relationship, with the cases of promises between strangers accounted for as the exception, in the case of contract the opposite is true: the practice is designed, first and foremost, to facilitate co-operation or mutual reliance between strangers, while making do with the kind of trust that is likely to obtain between strangers (so that the invocation of the practice in the context of personal relations can sometimes be utterly inappropriate)...

...[The value of] the legal practice of contract... consists in the very framework contracts provide for doing certain things with others not only outside the context of already-existing relationships, but also without a commitment to the future prospect of such relationships, without being required to know much or form opinions about the personal attributes of others, and without having to allow others to know much and form opinions about oneself. It is, if you like, the value of personal detachment.

5.   Eisenberg, 'The Theory of Contracts' in Benson (ed), *The Theory of Contract Law*, 2001, p 206, rejects the idea that any 'single-value theory' (such as that promises should be kept) can generate complete and desirable rules of contract law. He argues for what he terms a multi-value theory of contracts. He writes (at p 261):

... [T]he law should not simply require that all promises be performed. Instead, the law should effectuate the objectives of parties to a promissory transaction if, but only if, appropriate conditions are satisfied, and subject to appropriate constraints. The issue then is, what additional moral or policy elements, beyond the moral obligation to keep a promise, should make a given type of promise enforceable, assuming that all other appropriate conditions (such as capacity) are satisfied and that no special constraints apply. I will briefly describe these three such considerations.

To begin with, the law should enforce types of promises whose enforcement will enhance social welfare. The major type of promise that should be enforceable on social-welfare grounds consists of bargain promises, including promises that are in aid of or ancillary to bargains. Bargains serve social welfare, both because they increase wealth by trade and because they facilitate private economic planning by allowing actors to allocate risks and to coordinate economic activity through the acquisition of control over inputs and outputs. Enforcing bargain promises furthers the welfare purposes that such promises serve.

Next, the law should enforce types of promises whose breach tends to cause significant harm to the promisee—in particular, promises that have been relied upon, so that the promisee is worse off than he would have been if the promise had not been made. The principle here is one of liability for significant harm caused by an actor's fault. The promisor is at fault for having made a promise and then breaking it, and that fault caused a loss to the promisee, because the promise induced the promisee to incur costs that he would not otherwise have incurred, on the reasonable assumption that the promise would be kept.

The law should also enforce promises that are made to compensate a promisee, *B*, who has previously conferred a benefit for which the promisor, *A*, is morally but not legally obliged to compensate *B*, as where *B* has rescued *A* from danger at some cost to himself. Presumably, in such cases *A* is not legally obliged to compensate *B* only because it is deemed desirable to protect actors against liability for benefits that they might have declined to accept and pay for if they had been given the choice, and because of the severe difficulty in many such cases of measuring the value of the benefit to *A*. A later promise to make compensation invariably removes the first obstacle and normally removes the second. Such a promise should therefore be enforceable.

These three considerations—social welfare, significant harm, and a moral obligation to make compensation—are not exhaustive. . . .

CHAPTER TWENTY-SIX

ECONOMIC ANALYSIS OF CONTRACT LAW

■ **Kronman and Posner, *The Economics of Contract Law*** (see p 73)

The law-and-economics literature, of which Kronman and Posner, *The Economics of Contract Law* (see p 73) contains many extracts, represents a rather different viewpoint. Atiyah certainly does not accept all of its assumptions (see his *Essays on Contract*, chapter 7). We find economic analysis useful because it seems to provide insights into the way in which the rules of law may affect the behaviour of contracting parties. We are very aware, however, that it begs a number of very important questions. We have chosen two short extracts from a scathing (and typically amusing) review of the first edition of Posner's *Economic Analysis of Law* by Arthur Leff to illustrate just two of the problems.

■ **Leff, 'Economic Analysis of Law: Some Realism about Nominalism'** (1974)
60 Virginia LR 451, 456–458 and 478–479

To follow this initially attractive development in legal criticism (for purposes both of admiration and scorn), one will have to master the critical early moves. The first and most basic is 'the assumption that man is a rational maximizer of his ends in life . . .' As Posner points out, this assumption 'is no stronger than that most people in most affairs of life are guided by what they conceive to be their self-interest and that they choose means reasonably (not perfectly) designed to promote it.' In connection with this assumption, several 'fundamental economic concepts' emerge. 'The first is that of the inverse relation between price charged and quantity demanded.' The second is the economist's definition of cost, 'the price that the resources consumed in making (and selling) the seller's product would command in their next best use—the alternative price.'

> 'The third basic concept, which is also derived from reflection on how self-interested people react to a change in their surroundings, is the tendency of resources to gravitate toward their highest valued uses if exchange is permitted. . . . By a process of voluntary exchange, resources are shifted to those uses in which the value to the consumer, as measured by the consumer's willingness to pay, is highest. When resources are being used where their value is greatest, we may say that they are being employed efficiently.'

Now it must immediately be noted, and never forgotten, that these basic propositions are really not empirical propositions at all. They are all generated by 'reflection' on an 'assumption' about choice under scarcity and rational maximization. While Posner states that 'there is abundant evidence that theories derived from those assumptions have considerable power in predicting how people in fact behave,' he cites none. And it is in fact unnecessary to cite any, for the propositions are not empirically falsifiable at all.

> 'Efficiency is a technical term: it means exploiting economic resources in such a way that human satisfaction *as measured by aggregate consumer willingness to pay* for goods and services is maximized. Value too is defined by willingness to pay.'

In other words, since people are rationally self-interested, what they do shows what they value, and their willingness to pay for what they value is proof of their rational self-interest. Nothing merely empirical could get in the way of such a structure because it is definitional. That is why the assumptions can predict how people behave: in *these* terms there is no other way they can behave. If, for instance, a society dentist raises his prices and thereby increases his gross volume of business, it is no violation of the principle of inverse relation between price and quantity. It only proves that the buyers now perceive that they are buying something else which they now value more highly, 'society dentistry,' say, rather than 'mere' dentistry. And if circularity isn't sufficient, the weak version of the rational maximization formula ('most people in most affairs of life ... choose means reasonably (not perfectly) designed. ...') has the effect of chewing up and spitting out any discordant empirical data anyway. Any puzzling observation fed into that kind of definition will always be able to find a 'most,' or a 'reasonably,' way out.

Thus what people do is good, and its goodness can be determined by looking at what it is they do. In place of the more arbitrary normative 'goods' of Formalism, *and* in place of the more complicated empirical 'goods' of Realism, stands the simple definitionally circular 'value' of Posner's book. If human desire itself becomes normative (in the sense that it cannot be criticized), and if human desire is made definitionally identical with certain human acts, then those human acts are also beyond criticism in normative or efficiency terms; everyone is doing as best he can exactly what he set out to do which, by definition, is 'good' for him. In those terms, it is not at all surprising that economic analyses have 'considerable power in predicting how people in fact behave.'

> 'Despite the use of terms like "value" and "efficiency," economics cannot tell us how society should be managed. Efficiency is a technical term: it means exploiting economic resources in such a way that human satisfaction as measured by aggregate consumer willingness to pay for goods and services is maximized. Value too is defined by willingness to pay. Willingness to pay is in turn a function of the existing distribution of income and wealth in the society. Were income and wealth distributed in a different pattern, the pattern of demands might also be different and efficiency would require a different deployment of our economic resources. The economist cannot tell us whether the existing distribution of income and wealth is just, although he may be able to tell us something about the costs of altering it as well as about the distributive consequences of various policies. Nor can he tell us whether, assuming the existing distribution is just, consumer satisfaction should be the dominant value of society. The economist's competence in a discussion of the legal system is limited to predicting the effect of legal rules and arrangements on value and efficiency, in their strict technical sense, and on the existing distribution of income and wealth.'

In such a system whatever is, is. If you do not 'buy' something, you are *unwilling* to do so. There is no place for the word or concept 'unable'. Thus, in this system, there is nothing which is coerced. For instance, let us say that a starving man approaches a loaf of bread held by an armed baker. Another potential buyer is there. The baker institutes an auction: he wants cash only (having too great doubts about the starveling's health to be interested in granting credit). The poor man gropes in his pockets and comes up with a dollar. The other bidder immediately takes out $1.01 and makes off with the bread. Now under Posner's definitional system we must say that the 'value' of the bread was no more than a dollar to the poor man because he was 'unwilling' to pay more than that. An observer not bound within that particular definitional structure might find it somehow much more illuminating to characterize the poor man's failure as being the result of being unable to pay more than a dollar. But one cannot, consistent with Posner's system, say any such thing. One's actual power is irrelevant.

CHAPTER TWENTY-SEVEN

THE IMPACT OF THE EMPIRICAL STUDIES

Earlier, we looked at a variety of empirical studies of the law of contract (eg, Beale & Dugdale, pp 81 and 223; Macaulay, pp 117 and 389; Lewis, p 250). In the next piece, Macaulay asks how pp 117 and 389 we should look at contract law in the light of these studies.

■ **Macaulay, 'Elegant Models, Empirical Pictures, and the Complexities of Contract'** (1977)

11 Law & Society Review 507, 508–509, 511–515, 519, 520–521, 523

The group of studies about contract practices is interesting largely because many who write about contract law or who advocate social reforms using that body of law argue *as if they* were unaware of what these studies show. The problem arises from confusing what we can call a classical model of a contract system with an empirical picture of the relationship between law and the contract process. A rough sketch of the classical model of the contract process in western capitalist societies would stress its formal and normative aspects. Formally, it assumes that the rules of contract law will be invoked by parties and applied by courts; normatively, it holds that they ought to be.

This classical model starts with the assumption that entrepreneurs need to plan and deal with risk. They do so by carefully drafting contracts, which they understand and agree to. In order to increase the chance that the contract will be performed and expectations honored, the legal system defines when a contract is made, stands ready to interpret the language used by the parties and to fill any gaps in that language by applying norms reflecting the customs of the commercial community and, importantly, offers remedies that either induce performance or compensate for non-performance. Disputes are avoided by asking a lawyer to predict what a court would do, or settled through adjudication. The more predictable the outcome of this process, the better contract law can facilitate the planning and settlement process that is essential to a market society. . . .

The studies as a whole show that the *empirical* picture of the contract process in capitalist societies differs sharply from the classical model. Planning for the risk of nonperformance often is none too careful, and disputes are seldom resolved by litigation or even by applying the norms of contract law outside of litigation. The classical model of the contract process may fit one-shot transactions, such as those sometimes found in financing and real estate, but the reality of modern business, particularly manufacturing, generally involves long-term continuing relationships. My colleague, David Trubek (1975), has argued that economic actors will employ the litigation process to settle disputes only to the extent that (1) the present value of continuing relationships is low, and (2) the anticipated return from the litigation process is relatively high. The classical model of the contract process thus operates only in a special and limited case where these conditions are met. Max Weber's theories about the role of contract law in the development of capitalism rest on a model of economic relations in which the typical dispute occurs between firms operating in what we would call a perfectly competitive market. In such conditions continuing relations have no economic value, and no actor has economic power over another.

All of this raises an interesting question barely mentioned by any of the authors of this group of studies: what functions might a classical picture of the contract process serve if it is not an adequate description of what happens? If one shows that business people in all societies compromise differences rather than invoke contract norms to seek victories, rely on a network of contacts, and seek to avoid being dependent on other firms, one must still explain the existence of a widely held, if often implicit, picture of the contract process that varies so markedly from reality. A major conclusion to be drawn from these studies is that we should give further thought to the functions of the classical model. All that can be done here is to offer a very sketchy explanation.

The most obvious explanation for the persistence of the classical model would be that scholars and reformers are unaware that the contract process described in the law books seldom affects behavior very directly. Yet, for many, it is an unwillingness to listen rather than unfamiliarity. Some actively resist considering the implications of empirical findings, dismissing them grandly as mere counting. Ignorance can be but a partial explanation.

Another explanation for the persistence of the classical model of the contract process may be that it is partially accurate. The classical picture may be just an overgeneralization from a biased sample. There *are* appellate opinions—the basic data about law for most legal scholars in the United States—that concern contracts. People will litigate and bring appeals when the potential benefits are thought to outweigh the costs. Occasionally, it is necessary to vindicate rights even at the cost of a valuable long-term relationship.... [It] is sometimes critically important to vindicate a right. For example, large corporations do sue each other about patent licenses, and they will sometimes litigate the question of which organization is to be saddled with a multimillion dollar loss. However, they are not likely to litigate and pursue appeals merely for the principle of the matter or for entertainment. In Aubert's terms (1963), they are quick to transform a conflict of value into a conflict of interest if that will look better on the profit and loss statement. When they look to contract norms, it is often to help ward off large potential losses for which they could be held liable if they had not placed them elsewhere by contract. Large corporations often dump these losses on organizations lacking the economic power to refuse to accept the risk. Some contemporary cases appear to stem from situations where one party, who has made a bad deal, is scrambling for a loophole, a tactic that is likely to be extremely damaging to a long-term relationship because it violates expectations that the other party views as justified. As a result, a large organization that plans on continuing in business is hesitant to assert technical defenses unless absolutely necessary, and is likely to do so only when its economic power so outweighs that of its adversary that it can ignore the reaction of the latter.

Other cases before the courts involve relationships already shattered, where contract is used for scavenger purposes to salvage something from the wreckage. For example, large organizations can be involved in bankruptcy proceedings or the cancellations of franchises. However, franchise cases often involve a weaker party suing a stronger corporation, and the weaker is likely to discover that freedom of contract is freedom for large organizations to avoid any contractual duties. Large organizations seldom need legal rights against weaker parties because they get what they want by command; the documents they draft assure that they are not significantly hampered by contractual duties owed to the weaker parties. Courts generally have refused to intervene on the side of the weaker party, and modern franchise protection statutes have been only partially successful in altering this balance of power.

However, the bulk of modern contract litigation usually involves something far less exalted than multimillion dollar deals that have soured. Edmundo Fuenzalida, in his study of the activity of the courts in Chile (1973, 1974), found that as the nation became more urban and industrialized, and as the population grew, commercial litigation in the ordinary civil courts did not rise at the same rate. After an initial increase roughly paralleling demographic and economic change, the demands on the courts reached a plateau and then began to decline. Moreover, the composition of these demands changed from cases involving the adjudication of rights to those involving only the enforcement of obligations that were fairly clear. In short, there was a shift from adjudication to a bureaucratic role for the courts as part of a debt collection process—they rubber-stamped claims and made them legal. And there is evidence that this shift in functions is not peculiarly Chilean (see Toharia, 1971; Friedman and Percival, 1976). Marc Galanter reviewed data about who uses courts in the United States and for what purposes, and found much the same pattern. Organizations seldom sue other organizations about anything. Galanter tells us: 'We cannot escape the conclusion that in gross the courts in the United States are forums which are used by organizations to extract from and discipline individuals' (1975: 360). Beale and Dugdale, examining British practices, note that 'if a serious bad debt problem did arise it was quite likely that a solution would be sought through legal procedures. . . . It is probably also relevant that the debt action, being for a liquidated (preascertained sum), is relatively simple and cheap. Resort to the courts seemed far rarer in cases where there was any difficult question of fact, such as a performance dispute' (1975: 51).

In summary, loopholes, salvage operations, the bureaucratic process of debt collection, and evasions of responsibility seem to account for a large proportion of contract activity found in the real world of the courts. Yet these are not the topics likely to excite most contract scholars. Large important business organizations seldom are involved in these cases. Perhaps that is why they are not well represented in the model of the contract process held and disseminated by prominent legal scholars from all parts of the world. Perhaps it is necessary to ignore the fact that these kinds of cases predominate in order to give sufficient attention to the interesting situations that are the bulwarks of the remarkable intellectual creation that is contract law. Arguably, empirical research that challenges this elegant creation is mere counting, and scholars and intellectuals do not find the mundane task of describing the real world as delightful as polishing and fine-tuning the formal model. Frequency, of course, is not the only test of importance. But economically important contract cases that adjudicate rights are too rare to serve as a solid foundation for the classical model.

Of course, contract norms and the possibility of contract litigation can play important roles that are not clearly reflected in court records and appellate opinions. One such role is that of weaponry in the process of dispute settlement. The threat of litigation can be invoked without carrying the case to a conclusion in the courts. Contract here forms the foundation for strategic maneuvers in the game of negotiated settlement. Courts may be involved only marginally: filing a complaint, or even merely writing a letter on an attorney's letterhead, may be enough to provoke serious negotiation. In other situations, settlement comes only after a trial, one or more appeals, and perhaps an order for further trials.

. . .

Although it would be hard to prove, the contract litigation process may also exert an indirect influence on the behavior of the managers of industrial enterprises even where they devote little thought to it. Those making bargains may tacitly rely on the law to fill gaps and provide sanctions, in order to avoid the costs of negotiating about unlikely contingencies or of constructing elaborate systems of security to insure performance. Contract law may crystallize business customs and provide a normative vocabulary, affecting expectations about what is fair . . .

The contract litigation process may also maintain a vague sense of threat that keeps everyone reasonably reliable (see Llewellyn, 1931: 725 n 47). For this process to operate, it is not necessary that business managers understand contract norms and the realities of the litigation process. Perhaps all that is needed is a sense that breach may entail disagreeable legal problems. . . .

Finally, the classical model of contract may serve as one of many ways to legitimate the accepted ideology of a society and that ideology, in turn, may serve to legitimate contract norms and their application through the litigation process. Though sociological theory suggests that law and the legal system serve a legitimating function, it is difficult to identify all the links in the chain of events by which a statute or a decision might affect the attitudes of people who are not legal professionals.

No sociological theorist has devoted much attention to the symbolic role of contract doctrine. However, one could argue that in most societies people, as a result of their socialization and experiences, will have some opinion about the obligation to perform promises. The legal system, as but one of many influences in this socialization, declares that contracts generally ought to be performed. It also offers remedies that purport to compensate those injured by nonperformance, thereby emphasizing the importance of compliance with the norm of performance. Lawmakers claim to speak in the name of the society as a whole, and to do so on the basis of principles such as election by a majority of the voters, selection by the revolution, the revelation of God's will, or the like. As a result, citizens may tend to identify what is legal with what is good and right. . . . Insofar as they know or think they know something about the nature of contract law, this knowledge may affect their beliefs. And their attitudes may affect their behavior.

Actually, there is little empirical evidence to support theories of symbolic legitimation through law. Indeed, a number of studies indicate that most people know very little about the content of most legal norms (see Friedman and Macaulay, 1977: 607–8). As a result, the symbolic impact of law, if it has any, usually must be achieved by indirect and subtle means. This is not to say that theories about symbolic legitimation are wrong; only that they must be far more specific about the circumstances under which laws as symbols influence attitudes.

Whatever its functions for the larger society, the classical model of contract may serve the needs of law professors with a professional interest in contract and those appellate judges who are interested in doctrinal development . . .

Other factors may also contribute to the persistence of the classical model of contract. Lawyers probably have some interest in mystification as a means of status-preservation. They may believe that the illusion of certainty and predictability facilitates business planning and ensures the performance of obligations, and they may be correct to some degree. But it is clear that legal scholars risk serious error if they refuse to recognize that we have found, in a variety of societies, that the application of contract norms through litigation, or even through buying legal advice, is extremely costly and seldom pays. Scholars must also deal with the fact that few nonlawyers know much about the content of the formal norms or the realities of litigation. Any serious and satisfactory view of contract must acknowledge that much, if not most, significant economic behavior takes place almost untouched by contract norms or litigation. Indeed, Lawrence Friedman reminds us that in the mid-1950s,

> 'the law of contract remained alive, not, however, as the organic law of the state's economic system—a kind of constitution for business transactions—but as one among many. It was the system of rules applicable to marginal, novel, as yet unregulated, residual, and peripheral business and quasi-business transactions, transactions which might, in exceptional cases, call for problem-solving and dispute-settling. "Contract" stepped in where no other body of law and no agency of law other than the court was appropriate or available [1965: 193]'.

REFERENCES [SELECTED]

Aubert, Vilhelm (1963) 'Competition and Dissensus: Two Types of Conflict and of Conflict Resolution,' 7 *Journal of Conflict Resolution* 26.

Beale, Hugh and Tony Dugdale (1975) [above, p 79].

Friedman, Lawrence M (1965) *Contract Law in America*. Madison: University of Wisconsin Press.

Friedman, Lawrence M and Stewart Macaulay (1977) *Law and the Behavioral Sciences* (2d ed). Indianapolis: Bobbs-Merrill.

Friedman, Lawrence M and Robert V Percival (1976) 'A Tale of Two Courts: Litigation in Alameda and San Benito Counties,' 10 *Law & Society Review* 267.

Fuenzalida, Edmundo (1973, 1974) *Fluctuaciones de la Demanda por Justicia en Función del Cambio Social I & II*. Santiago: Instituto de Docencia e Investigación Jurídicas.

Galanter, Marc (1974) 'Why the "Haves" Come Out Ahead: Speculations on the Limits of Legal Change,' 9 *Law & Society Review* 95.

——(1975) 'Afterword: Explaining Litigation,' 9 *Law & Society Review* 347.

LLEWELLYN, Karl N (1931) 'What Price Contract? An Essay in Perspective,' 40 *Yale Law Journal* 704.

TOHARIA CORTES, José Juan (1971) *Cambio Social y Vida Jurídica en España, 1900–1970*. Ph.D. Dissertation, Facultad de Derecho, Universidad Complutense de Madrid, summarized and translated as *Social Life and Legal Activity in Spain, 1900–1970*. Translated by C Lynch. New Haven: Yale Law School Program in Law and Modernization.

TRUBEK, David M (1975) 'Notes on the Comparative Study of Processes of Handling Disputes between Economic Enterprises.' Paper presented at the United States-Hungarian Conference on Contract Law and the Problems of Large Scale Economic Enterprise, New York (August).

WEBER, Max (1954) *Max Weber on Law in Economy and Society*. Translated by M Rheinstein and E Shils. Cambridge, Mass.: Harvard University Press.

NOTES

1.   It seems that in the United Kingdom, contract law may play a greater role in solving contractual disputes than in the USA, at least in commercial contracts in volatile markets: see, for instance, many of the cases in previous chapters that have arisen from commodity and charter markets. See further p 894.

2.   For an interesting overview, including consideration of historical material and an account of how Macaulay came to begin his empirical work, see Hedley, 'The "Needs of Commercial Litigants" in Nineteenth and Twentieth Century Contract Law' (1997) 19 J Legal History 85.

3.   A very useful discussion of the implications of some of the empirical studies will be found in Collins, *Regulating Contracts*, 1999, especially chapters 6 and 7.

CHAPTER TWENTY-EIGHT

CRITICAL APPROACHES TO CONTRACT

■ **Kennedy, 'Form and Substance in Private Law Adjudication'** (1976)
89 Harvard LR 1685, 1685, 1687 91, 1698–1700, 1713–18, 1738–40 (see p 49)

One of the ideas underlying the 'classical' law of contract (see the extract from Atiyah's 'Rise and Fall of Freedom of Contract' on p 47) was that parties were free to assume or decline contractual obligations without interference from the state: in other words, that there was a 'private sphere' of autonomy in which there was little public intervention. The next extract challenges this assumption in particular.

■ **Dalton, 'An Essay in the Deconstruction of Contract Doctrine'** (1985)
94 Yale LJ 997, 1000–1001, 1015–1019

INTRODUCTION

Law, like every other cultural institution, is a place where we tell one another stories about our relationships with ourselves, one another, and authority. In this, law is no different from the *Boston Globe*, the CBS evening news, *Mother Jones*, or a law school faculty meeting. When we tell one another stories, we use languages and themes that different pieces of the culture make available to us, and that limit the stories we can tell. Since our stories influence how we imagine, as well as how we describe, our relationships, our stories also limit who we can be.

In this Article, by examining the rules of contract law as applied by judges and elaborated by commentators, I ask whether we can begin to understand the particular limits law stories impose on the twin projects of self-definition and self-understanding. Can we, in other words, expose the way law shapes all stories into particular patterns of telling, favors certain stories and disfavors others, or even makes it impossible to tell certain kinds of stories?

The stories told by contract doctrine are preoccupied with what must be central issues in any human endeavor of our time and place. One set of questions concerns power: What separates me from others and connects me to them? What is the threat and the promise to me of other individuals? Can I enjoy the promise without succumbing to the threat? Am I able to create protective barriers that will not at the same time prevent me from sharing the pleasures of community? What is the role of the state in regulating my relations with others? The other set of questions concerns knowledge: How can I know what others see, what they intend? On what basis can I share my understanding of the world with others? Is there a reality separate from my grasp of it? Is communication possible? These central questions of power and knowledge devolve from the split between self and other, subject and object, which structures our experience of the world. This Article examines precisely how this split structures our contract doctrine; how doctrine devotes its energies to describing, policing, and disguising the divide.

A. The project described

In this Article, I give an account of selected portions of contract doctrine and the themes and problems that permeate them. I demonstrate how our preoccupation with questions of power and knowledge is mirrored in doctrinal structures that depend on the dualities of public and private, objective and subjective, form and substance. I suggest that it is these problems of power and knowledge, these doctrinal structures, which contribute to the inconsistency and substantial indeterminacy of contract doctrine.

In elaborating doctrinal dichotomies, I suggest that contract doctrine consistently favors one pole of each duality: Contract law describes itself as more private than public, interpretation as more about objective than subjective understanding, consideration as more about form than about substance. And I suggest further that while the method of hierarchy in duality allows our doctrinal rhetoric to avoid the underlying problems of power and knowledge, it is an avoidance that is also a confession: The problems are only displaced, not overcome. This displacement is both diachronic and synchronic: The problems are frequently presented as having been then and not now, and equally frequently presented as being there and not here. To answer the strategy of displacement, my account necessarily deals with historical moments in the development of doctrine, as well as with doctrine in its current state. My claim is that the problems are now as well as then, here as well as there.

I begin the Article with a discussion of the public-private distinction in contract law, as reflected in the law's treatment of the implied contract. The implied-in-law contract or quasi-contract is traditionally considered an exceptional supplement to the body of contract doctrine; its reliance on social norms to create a public obligation is traditionally viewed as a deviation from contract doctrine's focus on the facilitation of private intent. But I demonstrate that the same factors that lead judges to impose quasi-contractual obligations influence both the 'finding' of obligations implied-in-fact and the interpretation of express contracts. In this sense all contracts are public. The courts' creation of categories of contract of varying degrees of privateness is therefore only a strategy of displacing and containing, not resolving, the public threat to the private world of contract.

. . .

. . . We need first to understand more concretely how doctrinal inconsistency necessarily undermines the force of any conventional legal argument, and how opposing arguments can be made with equal force. We need also to understand how legal argumentation disguises its own inherent indeterminacy and continues to appear a viable way of talking and persuading. We need, finally, to understand how legal argumentation is used, knowingly or unknowingly, to perpetuate a world view that imposes itself upon constituencies that it simultaneously leaves essentially without power or resources.

In addressing the way legal doctrine is unable to provide determinate answers to particular disputes while continuing to claim an authority based on its capacity to do so, I have drawn on another critical tradition, described loosely as post-structuralism. In particular, I have benefited from the 'deconstructive' textual strategies developed by Jacques Derrida, and from the input of colleagues who are incorporating various of these techniques into their own work [Eg Frug (1984) 97 Harvard LR 1276].

Derrida affirms the role of conceptual duality in the discourse of philosophers since the eighteenth century, and observes that all discourse tends to favor one pole of any duality over the other, creating a hierarchical relationship between the poles. The disfavored pole he calls the dangerous supplement, 'dangerous' because of its undermining potential, its role in revealing to us that things are not, after all, what they seem.

Taking as his starting point that philosophy as a discipline depends on a capacity for objective reason and transparent communication, Derrida is concerned to expose the sleight of hand by which philosophers convince their readership that language can represent an objective reality, and serve as a transparent medium of thought. He would restore us to a world in which we would be not only without a false confidence in either the power of objective reason or the possibility of transparent communication, but also without a sense of false constraint. I believe Derrida's strategies are singularly apt for the analysis of a legal order that has, like the philosophy he critiques, founded its authority on objectivity, and that presumes access to individual intentions and understandings.

...

D. Implications

It is distressingly common to interpret the kind of analysis I undertake in this Article as an attack on doctrine, as a claim that doctrinal talk is somehow 'meaningless.' I hope to show that such interpretations are misperceptions. At the most practical level, my analysis suggests that the advocate's task is precisely as traditionally imagined, a job requiring a most sophisticated sense both of the array of available argument and of the limits of legal discourse. At the level of theory, my account suggests that doctrine is redolent with meaning, that it incorporates debates about commitments and concerns central to our society. However, the usefulness of those debates is unfortunately limited by their stylized distance from the core issues they represent. Debate on these core issues is further limited by doctrine's pretense that it can resolve these issues rather than simply articulate them in a fashion that would allow a decisionmaker to make a considered choice in the case before her.

To expose the limitations of doctrine—to reveal the poverty of legal discourse, its dependence on only a few types of feint and parry, eminently graspable—is one of the major goals of this piece. That done, it becomes possible systematically to surface the core issues underlying contractual disputes, by decoding the doctrinal formulations.

My analysis, which supports the idea that judicial decisionmaking is indeterminate, is rendered vulnerable by our experience of being able to speculate successfully about how at least some cases will come out. One response is that our ability to speculate has less to do with the determinacy of doctrine than with our sensitivity to cultural values and understandings as they impinge on and are created by our decisionmakers. This implies that while 'doctrine-as-rule-system' is indeterminate, 'doctrine-in-application' is after all determinate, needing just that infusion of (determinate) cultural value and understanding to make it so. But if doctrinal indeterminacy is produced, as I have suggested, by the *same* dualities that structure the rest of our life and thought, that affect the very development of our cultural values and understandings, then indeterminacy must exist at *all* these levels. Our seeming ability nonetheless to understand and to predict (in a historically contingent fashion) the particular links that decisionmakers create between particular arguments, and the particular fact situations decisionmakers construct from the testimony submitted to them, requires us to search for other explanations. The devaluing of doctrine clears the ground for this further work.

I. PUBLIC AND PRIVATE

The opposing ideas of public and private have traditionally dominated discourse about contract doctrine. The underlying notion has been that to the extent contract doctrine is 'private,' or controlled by the parties, it guarantees individual autonomy or freedom; to the extent it is 'public,' or controlled by the state, it infringes individual autonomy.

Since at least the mid-nineteenth century, the discourse of contract doctrine has tried to portray contract as essentially private and free. At all times, nonetheless, traditional doctrine has uneasily recognized a public aspect of contract, viewing certain state interests as legitimate limitations on individual freedom. But this public aspect has traditionally been assigned a strictly supplemental role; indeed, a major concern of contract doctrine has been to suppress 'publicness' by a series of doctrinal moves.

The public aspect of contract doctrine is suppressed differently in each area of that doctrine, and in each historical period. The method of suppression is generally either an artificial *conflation* of public and private, in which the public is represented as private, or an artificial *separation* of public from private, which distracts attention from the public element of the protected 'private' arena by focusing attention on the demarcated (and limited) 'public' arena.

The current mainstream treatment of quasi-contracts and implied contracts illustrates doctrine's techniques of separation and conflation. The prevailing position, represented by the *Second Restatement*, but also by cases and commentary from the 1850's to the present, is that quasi-contracts are not contracts at all, but constitute instead an exceptional imposition of obligation by the state in order to prevent unjust enrichment. An artificially sharp line of demarcation is therefore presented as separating quasi-contracts from implied-in-fact contracts, and public from private. But this position obscures the fact that the finding of contractual implication is guided in the so-called 'private' sphere by the same considerations that dictate the imposition of quasi-contract. Any inquiry into a party's intent must confront the problem of knowledge—our ultimate inability to gain access to the subjective intent underlying any particular agreement. The indicia or manifestations of intent, discussed in detail in Part II, serve as substitutes for subjective intent. But in relying on this objective evidence, we move from the realm of the private to that of the public. Calling implied contracts based on party intention 'private,' and thereby ignoring the extent to which their content is shaped by external norms, conflates public with private.

Hertzog v Hertzog [29 Pa 465], decided by the Pennsylvania Supreme Court in 1857, is reputedly the first American case to distinguish the quasi-contract from the implied-in-fact contract. The themes and method of analysis present in *Hertzog* still reverberate in the treatment of implied contract found in the *Second Restatement* and in modern case law.

In *Hertzog*, an adult son lived and worked with his father until his father's death, at which point the son sued the estate for compensation for services rendered. The trial judge instructed the jury that John Hertzog could recover only if an employment contract existed between father and son. Two witnesses gave testimony that could be interpreted as evidence of such an agreement: One Stamm testified that he 'heard the old man say he would pay John for the labour he had done,' while one Roderick swore that the father 'said he intended to make John safe.' The jury found for John, and the defendant appealed, successfully.

Pennsylvania Supreme Court Justice Lowrie begins the opinion by distinguishing express, implied-in-fact, and implied-in-law contracts. In advancing this categorization, Lowrie particularly criticized Blackstone for failing to distinguish the implied-in-fact from the implied-in-law contract.

Blackstone had suggested that '[i]mplied [contracts] are such as reason and justice dictate; and which, therefore, the law presumes that every man undertakes to perform.' Lowrie, true to his advanced under-standing of the implications of the will theory of contract, observes, 'There is some looseness of thought in supposing that reason and justice ever dictate any contracts between parties, or impose such upon them. All true contracts grow out of the intentions of the parties to transactions, and are dictated only by their mutual and accordant wills.' The only 'contracts' that reason and justice dictate, according to Lowrie, are '*constructive* contracts' in which the contract is 'mere fiction', a form adopted solely to enforce a duty independent of intention. 'In one,' says Lowrie, 'the duty defines the contract; in the other, the contract defines the duty.'

Lowrie offers this definition of quasi-contract:

> [W]henever, not our variant notions of reason and justice, but the common sense and common justice of the country, and therefore the common law or statute law, impose upon any one a duty, irrespective of contract, and allow it to be enforced by a contract remedy, [this is] a case of [quasi-] contract.

For Justice Lowrie, quasi-contract, unlike contract proper, reflects public norms. Public norms, however, require legitimation and Lowrie offers two types—one positivist, the other dependent on natural law. The norms are 'positively' binding because they are part of the body of common law or statute recognized as authoritative. They are 'naturally' binding because they reflect 'common sense and common justice.' While Lowrie distinguishes these public obligations from obligations based on con-sent, he invokes consent to legitimize public norms: Consent underlies his distinction between '*variant* notions of reason and justice' and '*common* sense and *common* justice.'

Lowrie avoids the need to devote more time and attention in *Hertzog* to quasi-contract by stating that '[i]n the present case there is no pretence of a constructive contract, but only of a proper one, either express or implied.' The focus of the opinion, then, is on whether John Hertzog can demonstrate the existence of a contract by words spoken or by an account of the relationship and circumstances.

As to the express contract, Lowrie explicitly uses the parties' relationship and their circumstances to 'frame' the words spoken in such a way that they become words of 'non-contract' instead of contract:

> 'The court told the jury that a contract of hiring might be inferred from the evidence of Stamm and Roderick. Yet these witnesses add nothing to the facts already recited, except that the father told them, shortly before his death, that he intended to pay his son for his work. This is no making of a contract or admission of one; but rather the contrary. It admits that the son deserved some reward from his father, but not that he had contract for any.'

The father-son relationship clearly influences Lowrie's conclusion. *Hertzog* thus illustrates that words of intentions are inconclusive until they are shaped by a judicial reading of the context in which they are uttered. Even the paradigmatically self-sufficient 'express' contract, in which 'the terms of the agreement are openly uttered and avowed at the time of the making,' is invaded by 'publicness' in its interpretation and enforcement.

In regard to the implied-in-fact contract, Lowrie says that '[t]he law ordinarily presumes or implies a contract whenever this is necessary to account for other relations found to have existed between the parties.' In *Hertzog*, Lowrie's willingness to find an employment contract will therefore turn on whether the parties are related: He assumes that strangers assist one another only on the expectation of reward, whereas precisely the opposite is true of employment between intimates.

Lowrie thus bases his conclusion that no implied contract exists almost entirely upon 'the customs of society' and commonly accepted notions about human nature in general and family relationships in particular. But his reliance on result customs and commonalities hopelessly undermines his distinction between contracts implied-in-fact and quasi-contracts. Lowrie's treatment of the absence of a contract proper could just as easily be read as an account of the absence of a quasi-contract. Plainly he has decided that common sense and common justice demand a finding that no contract exists here. The advantage of his contractual analysis is that it permits public considerations to be introduced as if they were private, without the elaborate scrutiny of their source and justification that a quasi-contractual analysis would require.

Lowrie's concluding ruminations about the jury's finding for the son ironically illustrate his obliviousness to the 'publicness' of his analysis:

> 'The difficulty in trying causes of this kind of arises from juries supposing that, because they have the decision of the cause therefore they may decide according to general principles of honesty and fairness without reference to the law of the case. But this is a despotic power, and is lodged with no portion of this government.
>
> Their verdict may, in fact, declare what is honest between the parties, and yet it may be a mere usurpation of power, and thus be an effort to correct one evil by a greater one. Citizens have a right to form connexions on their own terms and to be judged accordingly. When parties claim by contract, the contract proved must be the rule by which their rights are to be decided. To judge them by any other rule is to interfere with the liberty of the citizens.'

This moralizing might be more convincing if the judge had not just exercised, in the guise of fact-finding, the type of state power he now labels 'despotic.'

In resolving this dispute, then, Lowrie proves incapable of sustaining the distinction between public and private on which he places so much emphasis. He asserts that the intrusion of the state into the relationships of private individuals is generally undesirable. He suggests that in extreme circumstances such intrusion can be justified, provided we impose only those obligations grounded both in community standards and in positive promulgation. In normal circumstances, however, contract law is purely about the intentions of the parties. Disciplined and rational judges, aware of the limitations of their authority, are better equipped to discern these intentions than undisciplined and irrational juries who confuse their sense of what is fair and honest with what the parties had in mind. But when it comes to deciding the case, Lowrie uses standards that were neither explicitly adopted by the parties nor promulgated by the state. In determining that the relationship between the parties was not contractual, he invokes common understandings about the context of the agreement to transform words of agreement into evidence of non-contract. In so doing he avoids the problem of power by appearing to endorse the parties' own choice that their relationship be without legal consequence, and avoids the problem of knowledge by presenting his own normative interpretation of the situation as nothing more than a transparent reading of the parties' intentions.

NOTES

1.   Dalton's article explores a number of examples of the contradictory tendencies and potential indeterminacy in contract law. The tension she identifies between power and knowledge is one that we have encountered before, even if not expressed in this way. Take the objective principle (p 192 above). Classical contract law conceives of contractual liability as depending on voluntary assent, not on a rule imposed by the state. But neither the court nor the other party can know for certain what was in the promisor's mind, so it must be judged objectively. This not only means that a party may incur liabilities that she did not intend, but also that she is made liable according to a 'public' standard: that of how her words and actions would be understood by the reasonable person.

2.   What other examples have you seen of the general run of contract cases 'favouring one pole of [a] duality over the other'? Have you seen examples of what, after Derrida, Dalton calls the 'dangerous supplement', taking over as suddenly the disfavoured pole becomes favoured? Before you answer, you may find it helpful to read the next extract, because the authors use as an example a case that we have come across before. They also outline some of the judicial techniques by which these changes are achieved, and the implication of the claim that law is 'indeterminate'.

■ Drahos and Parker, 'Critical Contract Law in Australia' (1990)
3 JCL 30, 38–49

...Dalton...argues that judges draw on a series of devices, 'a few types of feint and parry'. These devices keep some distance between form and substance and tend to prioritise form. To foreshadow our own argument slightly, we can say that these techniques have operated as conventions about how lawyers should reason and they have allowed a degree of determinate application of otherwise indeterminate rules. Thus, it might not be readily apparent to an outsider (a first year law student for example) when a particular situation is correctly analysed as giving rise to an action in promissory estoppel rather than contract. In order to make that judgment, we will argue, the outsider cannot rely on some statement of the rule, but must in addition develop a sense for the conventions about applying the rule. Our extraction from Dalton suggests there are four kinds of techniques claimed, although she nowhere lists them clearly.

Privileging

Drawing on Derrida, Dalton argues that one half of a duality is regularly favoured or privileged. So, for example, form is normally privileged over substance, writing over oral words, words over silence and signature over non-signature.

Displacing

Essentially, this is hiving off uncomfortable parts of doctrine which liberalism does not wish to abandon altogether. For example, quasi-contract in traditional contract courses and texts is somehow a presence lurking at the margins, mysteriously invoked from time to time in circumstances where the analytical scheme of contract law seems to produce the opposite result. Hiving off an area of obvious public intervention seems to protect the apparently private law of contract from contamination.

Rhetoric

Rhetoric as a technique for handling dichotomies is the use of language games to mystify or cloud what is going on. An obvious example is the ritual of claiming that one is enforcing intention when the reasonable man in the objective test is just an anthropomorphic male representation of justice dispensed by the courts. The language of intention is rhetoric that 'reprivatises' the result to ease liberalism's concerns about public intervention.

Duty creation

As we have seen, legal liberalism tends (according to CLS) to privilege action over inaction, commission over omission and words over silence, in the sense that it sees more justification for public intervention in the privileged half of each duality. On the other hand, this can be inconvenient when a court wishes to create liability from inaction (the dangerous supplement to action) as it might wish to do when altruism appeals more than individualism. One technique is to create a duty, pretend it was anterior to the facts, and then enforce it. The duty might be created openly, for example by calling an existing relationship fiduciary, perhaps by discovering that an equity has been raised on the particular 'facts' or, less directly, through concepts of constructive notice of the other's understanding.

When taken individually, many of the arguments in 'An Essay in the Deconstruction of Contract Law' could be accepted to some degree by scholars with quite different outlooks. After all, the very division between the courts of common law and equity is often presented as a reflection of competing views on morality and the role of public intervention. It is hardly revolutionary to suggest therefore that doctrine should embody impulses which are in some tension with each other. More controversial, however, may be the views of some CLS exponents, such as Dalton, who hold that law is fundamentally indeterminate so that doctrine does not constrain the outcome of any particular dispute.

THE INDETERMINACY THESIS

The indeterminacy thesis, which has been controversial since the days of the American Legal Realists, hardly sits easily alongside a post-structuralism claiming regular preference for one pole. If one knows which side of a duality the liberal legal mind tends to favour, how can law be so unpredictable?

What has been described as the strong indeterminacy thesis—the view that legal doctrine is never able to provide a determinate answer with respect to a given fact situation—is unnecessarily ambitious. Whilst we concede that law permits a far greater range of plausible outcomes than formalistic scholarship would suggest, it can nevertheless be distinguished from purely political or moral argumentation through the conventions that prevail about the way that it is to be used. These conventions might be fragile, specific to a particular community of rule-users and lacking in logical compulsion. They certainly require regular renewal by rule-users. But when they exist they exist.

To give an example, take the history of modern negligence liability. The conclusion of the majority of the House of Lords in *Donoghue v Stevenson* that a manufacturer was liable in negligence to an end-user of his product was a conclusion of law which could have been reached at least in the second half of the 19th century. The concepts central to modern negligence such as the standard of the reasonable man and the duty of care were then available in legal materials and had been available in embryonic form for some time. Why then did the rule not emerge until the 1930s? Fleming's answer to the comparatively late development of negligence is the familiar one. The restriction on a manufacturer's liability in the 19th century was a product of values and social policies which sought, among other things, the development of a strong industry through limiting individual responsibility for harmful action. So, like more radical scholars, Fleming thinks the answer lies in the ideology of the period.

The problem with this answer is that it does not explain how the possibility of using concepts such as reasonableness and duty of care, with all their inherent indeterminacies, to construct a different outcome were regularly screened out by the judiciary as part of their internal way of engaging in legal reasoning. Surely a fuller explanation is that the reasoning conventions of the time, informed no doubt by prevailing ideologies such as the limited role for the public sphere to enter into the private, did not allow the rules to be operated in certain ways. One notable deviant was the Master of the Rolls in 1883.

In *Heaven v Pender* Brett MR attempted to use inductive logic to extract a general principle of negligence liability from the existing case law. His brethren expressly dissented from this part of the judgment but not, we argue, because they specifically thought through all the consequences that such a principle might entail for industry, nor because they could fault the logic, but because in a more diffuse way it offended against their view of the world and sense of how law should be used. Brett MR was literally not reasoning conventionally.

Our argument, then, is that conventions help to fix the application of rules and determine their scope of application. They may not always be articulated, they may not be readily apparent to outsiders or inexperienced rule users and they may be internal to a particular community much smaller than 'a legal system' but they provide some standardisation of outcome for so long as they exist. None of this need threaten the kind of approach that Dalton adopts; indeed it makes it more credible. It rescues her from the paradox which she noted herself. It suggests that conventions about rule use are the reason why one pole might be more regularly chosen whilst simultaneously leaving room for the occasional invocation of dangerous supplements.

We should now draw together some of the strands of the argument before taking it further. The immediate focus of the paper is to examine claims about a turning point in Australian contract law. Whilst such claims are plausible we wish to remain sceptical about them, if only because they are easy to make. We have turned to critical legal studies in the search for a theory about the underlying structure of classical contract law so that we have a benchmark against which to measure alleged change. This has provided us with an analysis of contradictions and choices within contract doctrine stemming from more fundamental antinomies within liberal thought. Having cleared away an impediment to the credibility of the CLS position (namely, the tension between deconstructionism and its formulation of the indeterminacy thesis) we can turn to a case which is said to be part of some sea-change and examine whether different choices are being made and different reasoning conventions invoked. If they are, then one has the makings of a phenomenon which, if repeated sufficiently often and widely, truly does mark a departure.

DECONSTRUCTING *WALTONS STORES v MAHER*

The basic deconstructive steps would be something like these. First, try to determine the reading of the story that dominated the case and speculate on other plausible readings. This might alert us to how the 'facts' have been constructed and give us a preliminary view of which pole of a duality is being favoured. Second, examine directly the duality and determine which pole is favoured. Third, consider the techniques by which the duality has been operationalised. If the normally favoured pole has been taken then relatively little might need to be said. Existing doctrine, which already embodies the techniques, will simply have been invoked. If, however, the dangerous supplement is resorted to then the techniques may well be evident. This is particularly so in a final court of appeal where there may be a stronger convention about giving justifications and where signals need to be sent out about the scope of the relevant convention for this rule in the future: in effect, how doctrine is to be reconstructed.

Reading the text

Can we ... expose the way law shapes all stories into particular patterns of telling, favours certain stories and disfavours others, or even makes it impossible to tell certain kinds of stories?

It seems to us that there were at least three readings of the story in *Waltons Stores* which could somehow have been processed through existing doctrinal categories. The first, which we might call the classical reading, goes something like this.

The Mahers owned some land. Waltons Stores were interested in opening a store on it. Negotiations took place for the Mahers to knock down existing premises, build new ones and lease them to Waltons. Waltons were in a hurry and wanted the building erected in unusually quick time. The Mahers were happy to do it because they wanted the rental income. They were not acting out of love for Waltons Stores. They retained a solicitor to look after their interests. They assumed that contracts would be exchanged and on completion a lease would be executed. They further assumed that no liability arose either way until exchange. It was standard market-place behaviour.

The Mahers started on the work without exchanging contracts. Because they were worried about going too far they instructed their solicitors to push Waltons. There were still some proposed amendments to the lease to be dealt with. Waltons' solicitors said they had oral agreement from their clients and wrote to the Mahers' solicitors saying that they believed agreement to the amendments was forthcoming and they would let them know tomorrow if they were not. That was the last that the Mahers or their solicitors heard from Waltons' solicitors for two months when the latter announced Waltons' withdrawal.

In the meantime, the Mahers' solicitors had sent their clients' signed part of the contract to Waltons' solicitors describing it 'by way of exchange', the traditional phrase but clearly inappropriate here. At no stage did they chase up the Waltons' solicitors for the return part of the contract but they wrote to the Mahers warning them they would lose the deal if the building was not completed on time. The Mahers took this as advice to get on with it.

Then things really went off the rails. Waltons had a change of heart about taking the lease (for reasons unconnected with the land). They ascertained from their solicitors that they were still free to withdraw and instructed them to go slow. The solicitors therefore made no response to the Mahers' solicitor.

During this period the Mahers had been busily constructing the new premises. Some of Waltons' staff and also their property consultant knew about this. When Waltons withdrew from the proposed transaction they left the Mahers in an exposed position with the work 40 per cent completed. Under cross-examination, Mr Maher admitted that he knew there was no contract when he commenced the work.

Read in this light, the conclusion on classical principles is that the Mahers took the risk of Waltons withdrawing. They hoped to gain the rental income. In a market system, some risks do not pay off and the loss lies where it falls. If they had thought they were secure then they might examine the advice they received from their solicitors to see whether an action in negligence lies. Failing that, the market system is there to weed out those who do not take sufficient precautions. The market requires clear moments of responsibility. Hence, signature and writing are privileged over words, conduct and silence.

To be clear, we are not saying that this did happen. The post-structuralist endeavour denies that one can separate the events from the interpretation of them. Rather we are saying that this is a plausible reading of the information that has made its way through to a law report. Had the story been presented like this then the conclusion of no liability would have been much easier to arrive at. A year or so earlier, the Privy Council had constructed such a story in *A-G of Hong Kong v Humphreys Estates* and decided just that.

Alternatively, what we might call an estoppel in pais reading could have been adopted. It would have involved a David and Goliath depiction, certainly in terms of the litigants and perhaps also their respective solicitors. It would have dwelt on a departure from standard conveyancing procedure (the prospective lessee preparing the draft lease) which might have confused the actors. It would have discounted some of the answers that David gave to Goliath's counsel in cross-examination because counsel himself confused lessor and lessee in his questioning. It would have suggested that Goliath was trying to have it both ways by leaving the options of withdrawal or continuation open as long as possible. Goliath's solicitor would also have come under some adverse comment.

This reading would suggest that the market will be converted into a power order if large organisations can practice deception (albeit by silence). The public must intervene in order to protect the integrity of the private sphere in the *long* term. Waltons would have been precluded from denying that they already had a binding agreement with the Mahers, albeit not an agreement crystallised by exchanging pieces of paper.

A third reading might be called the promissory estoppel reading. It differs from the second reading only in the interpretation placed on Mr Maher's answers. In cross-examination he is taken to have admitted that he knew there had been no exchange of contracts when he commenced work but as believing that exchange was a formality. This rules out estoppel in pais because that only precludes departure from an assumed present state of affairs. Mr Maher's acknowledgment that exchange was a formality shows his belief as to the future. Hence, if the Mahers are to have a remedy it cannot be through contract or estoppel in pais. It must be in promissory estoppel. The conduct of Waltons has to be read as a promise to the Mahers that a contract would come about.

In the result, no judge took the first reading. The second was essentially taken by Kearney J at first instance and by the New South Wales Court of Appeal. It was the preferred reading of Deane J and (apparently) Gaudron J in the High Court. The remainder of the court took the third reading.

The choice of poles

The classical reading would have pushed the reader in the direction of the normally favoured pole of form. As we have seen, liberal principles on state intervention into private association suggest that some minimum formal sign is required. In truth, as Dalton shows, this is an impossibility without supplementation either by subjective intention or objective value. Here, the parties had agreed that the formal sign indicating that one must grant and the other must take the lease was to be the exchange of pieces of paper which were to be identical, mutatis mutandis. The parties had not complied with the form they had chosen so, prima facie, there should be no intervention by the state.

Instead, the High Court chose a reading that pushed it in the direction of the dangerous supplement of substance. The substance of this association was that Waltons' behaviour was interpreted as an unconscionable use of the market system. A clear example of this is at the beginning of Deane J's judgment:

> 'In so far as the substantive merits are concerned, the Mahers have them all: Waltons deliberately failed to speak or to warn in circumstances where, as Priestley JA commented in the Court of Appeal, "simple standards of honesty and fair dealing required [it] to make known to [the Mahers] that the assumption they were acting on was mistaken".'

It is interesting to note at this stage that the High Court is using the very words that Dalton adopts to describe this dichotomy. The Mahers thought that exchange was a mere formality and they have the substantive merits.

The techniques

We turn now to the manner in which the substance pole was put into operation. It was done in such a way as to preserve as much of the previous scheme as possible and to prevent the duality from obviously falling in on itself. One of the paradoxical features of judicial innovation is that in creating what is potentially dramatic change it must simultaneously legitimate the innovation by reference to previous doctrine. In simpler terms the particular piece of innovation cannot be seen to sweep away too much. The way this is achieved in *Waltons Stores* is by tampering with the established convention surrounding the techniques we have identified whilst retaining doctrinal language. The use of the techniques might be described as the reconstruction of doctrine after the judges themselves had taken it apart.

Privileging. Because Waltons Stores is a case where the normally privileged choices were not made then naturally we see little of this technique in action. Nevertheless there are revealing comments about how privileging has operated in the past and some suggestions as to how it might operate under the new conditions.

There is now recognition that consideration and estoppel can swallow each other up and that consideration has been privileged in the past. This was largely through the use in Anglo-Australian law of promissory estoppel as a defensive equity only, as a shield not a sword. Thus, for example, Mason CJ and Wilson J note that there 'has been for many years a reluctance to allow promissory estoppel to become the vehicle for the positive enforcement of a representation by a party that he would do something in the future'. They note on the same page that enforcing promises in the absence of a pre-existing relationship would 'outflank the principles of the law of contract'. Yet they also impliedly admit, by referring to academic opinion, that it would actually have been more logical that promissory estoppel should have been a sword only.

Despite these acknowledgments, the invocation of substance here is presented in such a way as to make it seem exceptional and to make form and consideration still the first port of call. Privilege is thereby reasserted although in a way that is no more convincing than what went before. Unconscionability, said to be the basis of promissory estoppel, is purportedly confined by the justices. Mere reliance on a voluntary promise does not by itself make it unconscionable for the promisor to breach it. That would completely undercut consideration. But the justices are vague when it comes to suggesting what the 'extra' requirements must be to make a breach unconscionable.

The second requirement, that the promisor knows of the promisee's detriment, is also capable of manipulation. To begin with, there is the issue of what amounts to detriment....

The critical legal scholar who accepts the view that conventions can operate to cure indeterminacy might say of these limits on unconscionability that they will be effective for so long as a community of rule users deploys them in the appropriate way. Just as the 'shield not sword' doctrine could be demonstrated to be illogical, so can the confined version of unconscionability.

Displacement. In Daltons' scheme much displacement is simply a corollary to privileging something else. An example in the case is how the justices deal with silence. Basically, liberalism is reluctant to attribute consequences to silence. If it is to do so then the occasion must be hived off; placed in the category of 'for emergency use only'. Thus, for example, Brennan J says that silence 'will support an equitable estoppel only if it would be inequitable thereafter to assert a legal relationship different from the one which, to the knowledge of the silent party, the other party assumed or expected'. So inaction, the dangerous supplement to action, can only be used to avoid inequity.

Working on the assumption that judges usually want to avoid what they regard as inequity, this seems like saying that judges can invoke silence when they want to. The additional requirement of knowledge by the silent party evaporates as soon as constructive knowledge is admitted.

Rhetoric. The distinction drawn by the justices between contract and the new model estoppel seems to us to be the finest rhetoric. Brennan J, for example, is adamant that contract and estoppel are about different things. Contract is there to enforce expectations and estoppel to avoid detriment....

Duty creation. We mentioned earlier that duty creation is a useful technique to legitimate invocation of dangerous supplements such as inaction or silence. The issue arises head on here because of Waltons Stores' failure to warn the Mahers of their possible change of mind. It also arises because of Waltons' solicitor's failure to return the Mahers' contract and perhaps to disabuse the Mahers' solicitor of his mistake.

...

There seems also to be some kind of duty-creation going on regarding Waltons' solicitor. Brennan J and Deane J, asserted that retention of the Mahers' signed part contract was only justified for so long as Waltons intended to go through with the transaction. It seems to us that the solicitors may honestly have taken the conventional position in the legal profession that one does not run into ethical difficulties about failing to disclose a client's change of heart until one is asked about it. The mere fact that someone decides to send one a contract does not, ordinarily, impose any obligation to do anything about it, or even acknowledge receipt. Given that no argument about detinue was presented, it is difficult to see why there was any obligation to return the document.

CONCLUSION

... Our analysis of *Waltons Stores v Maher* would suggest that the case is consistent with the making of fundamentally different conventions for handling the conflicts between self and other; partly because of the way the story was read, partly because issues of substance were addressed and partly because those issues were dealt with by direct resort to dangerous supplements rather than manipulation of favoured poles. On the other hand, the techniques used to reconstruct doctrine make us cautious. What seem to us to be arbitrary spacers inserted between the categories of contract and equitable estoppel and the devices used to justify the outcome indicate a continuing willingness to bring a particular story face to face with the language of moral evaluation.

Naturally we have only examined one case. This was partly because of the space required to explain and justify the method but partly also because the remaining case law said to form part of the turning point falls far short of the data set we would require anyway. It is quite possible that conventions will arise to limit considerably the impact of *Waltons Stores*. Put simply, judges will tend not to read the stories in the way that the High Court did here. They will just not use promissory estoppel as a sword very often. Techniques might arise to give a veneer of logic to this in a similar way to ones still being advanced in England and Wales for not having it as a sword at all. What we might see, therefore, is a limited adjustment in the use of dualities but nothing that indicates a major change in lawyers' visions of the world. The critical legal studies position should be that nothing is inevitable or determined, whether by precedent or the forces of economics or morality (this indeed is the principal reason for the CLS rejection of Marxism) but it can be changed when its basis in thought is made clear.

Conscious as we are that, despite some iconoclasm, we have reached a rather modest conclusion, it is appropriate to end by touching on the practical importance of these matters for lawyers of different kinds. First, there is the question of training. Early in a lawyer's training she learns a method of reading a law report which seems to be an efficient use of time; that is to scan the key facts, extract the legal issues, pick out the ones relevant to the task in hand and see how they were dealt with on those key facts. This, in some elusive way, helps her to make progress on another set of 'facts' which confronts her.

CLS does not go so far as to claim this to be fundamentally misguided but it suggests a fuller reading method which comes nearer to the core issues in the case. Once one traverses the stylised distance of doctrinal language and reaches those core issues one might understand better the conventions which, as we said earlier, are not otherwise readily apparent to inexperienced rule users. This remains a spartan claim at present but if there is anything in the notion that legal reasoning is a series of specific conventions which reduce the indeterminacy of legal rules then a new reading technique which appreciates this may lead to a better understanding of how the conventions are deployed. If this is so then it is possible that one becomes a better predictor of the use of conventions and accordingly of outcomes.

This leads to the second practical justification for this method: the business of prediction. It seems likely that any move away from the kind of formalism we defined earlier will result in a loss of predictability, if only because the move will signify less regular use of particular poles. Nevertheless some predictability might still be tapped from a system if its apparently new workings are understood.

NOTE

For further reading, see Unger, *The Critical Legal Studies Movement*, 1986, especially chapter 3.

Some writers have claimed that a major role of contract law is to legitimate existing power relations within society. Whether or not you agree (and see Macaulay, p 784), it is a view worth considering.

■ Gabel and Feinman, 'Contract Law as Ideology' in Kairys (ed), *The Politics of Law*
chapter 8

The recent use of right-wing forces in the United States has been brought about in large part through the shaping and manipulation of collective fantasies. Among the most powerful of these fantasies is a resurgence of what one might call the utopian imagery of freedom of contract...

For this resurgent ideology to enjoy a temporary measure of success, it makes no difference that it is based upon a lie. The truth is that those of us living in the United States today cannot actually achieve our desire for increased personal power, for freedom, and for genuine social connection and equality so long as we are trapped within ubiquitous hierarchies that leave us feeling powerless, alienated from one another, and stupefied by the routines of everyday activities...

A principal vehicle for the transmission of such ideological imagery has been and continues to be 'the law.' In order to understand the present and historical function of the legal system, and of contract law as a part of this system, one must grasp the relationship between the utopian images transmitted through legal ideas and the socioeconomic context that these ideas serve to justify. In this essay, we provide a brief introduction to a method for understanding this ideological power of law by tracing the relationship between the history of contract law and the development of capitalism over the last two hundred years.

CONTRACT LAW IN THE EIGHTEENTH CENTURY

Eighteenth-century contract law would be barely recognizable to the modern lawyer. The vision of eighteenth-century contract law was not the enforcement of private agreements but the implementation of customary practices and traditional norms. Indeed, in his *Commentaries on the Law of England*, written in the 1760s, Sir William Blackstone did not consider contracts to be a separate body of law at all.

In part, contracts was that portion of the law of property concerning the transfer of title to specific things from one person to another—the process by which 'my horse' became 'your horse.' . . .

In all types of contracts cases, the substantive fairness of the agreement or relation was subject to scrutiny by a lay jury applying community standards of justice. If a physician sued for his fee or a seller of goods for her price, the jury could decide that even an amount agreed to by the parties was excessive and inequitable, and so award a smaller sum instead.

Thus, eighteenth-century contract law was hostile to commercial enterprise. The traditional image of the world presented by contract law regarded the enforcement of market transactions as often illegitimate, so a seller could never be guaranteed the price he or she had bargained for, and liability might be imposed in the absence of agreement when required by popular notions of fairness. Such a system could exist because the development of a system of production founded upon universal competition in national and world markets had not yet fully emerged, and the political world-view that justified the relatively static property relations of traditional, precapitalist society had not yet been entirely overturned.

Between the latter part of the eighteenth century and the middle of the nineteenth century, both the economic and political foundations of eighteenth-century contract law were, in Marx's phrase, 'burst asunder.' In this period the system of economic and social relations known as free-market capitalism achieved a full development . . .

CONTRACT LAW IN THE NINETEENTH CENTURY

In the nineteenth century, the key changes in society were its split into capital-owning and nonowning classes, and the dissolution of traditional patterns of social relations . . .

The social meaning of work, property, and community were increasingly fragmented as socio economic processes based on competition and individual self-interest reorganized the social universe . . .

How could people have been persuaded or forced to accept such massive disruptions in their lives? One vehicle of persuasion was the law of contracts, which generated a new ideological imagery that sought to give legitimacy to the new order. To speak of 'ideological imagery' is to imply that there is a reality behind the image that is concealed and even denied by the image. The reality was the new system of oppressive and alienating economic and social relations. Contract law denied the nature of the system by creating an imagery that made the oppression and alienation appear to be the consequences of what the people themselves desired.

Denial and legitimation were accomplished by representing reality in ideal terms, as if things were the way they were because the people wished them to be so. This representation was not the product of conspiratorial manipulation by power-mad lawyers and judges. Instead, the legal elites tended to identify with the structure of the social and economic order because of what they perceived to be their privileged position within it, and they expressed the legitimacy of that structure when arguing and deciding cases in their professional roles. During this period important members of the bench and bar associated themselves emotionally and intellectually with the capitalist transformation and became imbued with the 'logic' of the new system. In arguing and deciding cases, they fit the situation presented within that logic to resolve the conflict represented by the dispute at issue. Those resolutions tended to legitimate the basic social relations, no matter how unjust, oppressive and alienating they actually were. In the process of resolving many cases, legal concepts were built up that embodied the new social relations. The result was a system of contract law that appeared to shape economic affairs according to normative principles but that was, in fact, only a recast form of the underlying socioeconomic relations.

The legitimating image of classical contract law in the nineteenth century was the ideal of free competition as the consequence of wholly voluntary interactions among many private persons, all of whom were in their nature free and equal to one another. From one point of view this was simple truth, for the practical meaning of the market system was that people conceived of as interchangeable productive units ('equality') had unfettered mobility ('freedom') in the market. From another point of view, however, this was denial and apology. It did not take account of the practical limitations on market freedom and equality arising from class position or unequal distribution of wealth. It also ignored other meanings of freedom and equality having to do with the realization of human spirit and potential through work and community. The legitimation of the free market was achieved by seizing upon a narrow economic notion of freedom and equality, and fusing it in the public mind with the genuine meaning . . .

The results in [some nineteenth century] cases may seem unfair or irrational today, but to the judges of the time they were neither. The courts could not easily have intervened to protect a party or to remedy unfairness without violating the ideological image that the source of social obligation rests only upon the bargain that the parties themselves have evinced, not upon the community's version of justice. This imagery, drawn as it was from the exigencies of competitive exchange, served to deny the oppressive character of the market and the lack of real personal liberty experienced by people in their private and work lives. Most important, it served to deny that there was a system at all that was coercively shaping and constricting the social world, because the imagery made it appear that this world was simply the perpetual realization of an infinite number of free choices made by an infinite number of voluntary actors.

CONTRACT LAW IN THE TWENTIETH CENTURY

Today judges applying contemporary contract law would probably reach different results in these cases . . .

Contemporary contract law views these cases differently not because twentieth-century judges are wiser or smarter than their nineteenth-century counterparts, or because a new and more equitable style of legal reasoning has somehow sprung into being through a progressive maturation of the judicial mind. The old rules disintegrated for the same reason they were conceived: there has been a transformation of social and economic life that has brought about a parallel transformation in the ideological imagery required to justify it.

The transformation from the nineteenth-century to the twentieth-century forms of American capitalism was the consequence of a variety of factors that can only be summarized here: competition among businesses produced ever larger concentrations of capital within fewer and fewer companies; workers organized in response to their collective dependence on these emerging monopolies and challenged in a revolutionary way the myths of freedom and equality: exploitation of the Third World, advancing technology, and efficient organization of production facilitated the partial assimilation of the American labor movement, allowing for the payment of higher wages while deflecting more radical labor demands: this increase in the level of wages, the use of part of the economic surplus for unemployment insurance. Social Security, and other types of welfare benefits, and the greater psychological control of consumer purchases through the mass media helped to alleviate the system's persistent tendency toward underconsumption. The basic requirement for understanding contemporary contract law is to look at the socioeconomic system thus produced and to observe its transformation, through the medium of law, into an imaginary construct that attempts to secure the system's appearance of legitimacy.

The essential characteristic of contemporary capitalism is the substitution of integration and coordination in the economy for the unbridled competition of the free market. Coordination is accomplished first by monopolistic corporations that are vertically and horizontally integrated (meaning there are but a few 'horizontal' corporations at the top of the major industries that own the capital that controls 'vertically' production and distribution in each industry); and second, by a massive involvement of the state in regulating and stabilizing the system. In place of the unrestricted mobility of productive units that characterized the operation of the market in the nineteenth century, we now have integration, coordination, and cooperation to above all maintain systemic stability through an ever more pervasive and efficient administration.

A brief look at the dominant American industry, the automobile industry, will illustrate. The industry is composed of three giant companies and one smaller firm, which account for three fourths of the vehicles sold annually. The firms are vertically integrated in fact. . . .

The rise of the coordinated economy has created a major problem for the law— how to transform the ideology of 'freedom and equality' and its adjunct, 'freedom of contract,' into a new image that might retain the legitimating power of the older images while modifying them to conform more closely to the actual organization of daily life in the era of monopoly capitalism. The strategy for solving this problem has been to transform contract law into a relatively uniform code for business transactions that is predominantly defined not by the individualist principle of unregulated free competition but by the more collective principle of competition regulated by trade custom. Since most 'trades' (whatever nostalgia for a bygone era that term may evoke) are actually integrated production networks subject to supervision by dominant firms, the modern law of contracts is able to retain the legitimating features of private agreement while effectuating the regulatory and stabilizing component that is a central principle of the contemporary economy . . .

[S]ometimes consumers and other parties with little economic power can be protected from the more outrageous excesses of economic predators. In sum, people are conceived to be partners in a moral community where equity and the balancing of interests according to standards of fair dealing have supplanted the primitive era, when every moral tie was dissolved in 'the icy waters of egotistical calculation.' And the state as passive enforcer of private transactions has become the state as active enforcer of the newly conceived notion of the general welfare.

CONCLUSION

. . . This is a very different explanation of the role of contract law from liberal or leftist instrumental analyses, which suggest that particular rules of law or particular results 'helped' capitalists by providing a framework for legal enforcement of market activity. Instrumental analyses of contract law confuse the role of direct force with the role of law in the development of sociohistorical processes. Social processes like 'free-market capitalism' do not get 'enforced' by 'laws.' Rather, these processes are accepted through social conditioning, through the collective internalization of practical norms that have their foundation in concrete socioeconomic reality. Since these norms are alienating and oppressive, the process of collective conditioning requires the constant threat of force and the occasional use of it. For example, if you fail to perform your part of a bargain, it *may* be the case that a sheriff with a gun will attach your bank account to pay the aggrieved party his or her damages. The occasional deployment of direct force serves to maintain the status quo as well as to get people to accept its legitimacy.

The law' does not enforce anything, however, because the law is nothing but ideas and the images they signify. Its purpose is to justify practical norms (and in so doing to help constitute them by contributing to the collective conditioning process). One important way that this justification process occurs is through judicial opinions. Judicial opinions 'work' as ideology by a rhetorical process in which oppressive practical norms are encoded as 'general rules' with ideological content; these 'rules' then serve as the basis for a logic ('legal reasoning') that supposedly determines the outcome of the lawsuit. The key social function of the opinion, however, is not to be found in the outcome and the use of state power which may follow from it, but in the rhetorical structure of the opinion itself, in the legitimation of the practical norm that occurs through the application of it in the form of a 'legal rule.' That enforcement of bargains was much more likely to occur under nineteenth-century contract law than under eighteenth-century law is, of course true; but this does not mean that the function of nineteenth-century contract law was to 'enforce bargains.' The reverse expresses the truth more accurately—that the enforcement of bargains functioned to permit the elaboration of contract law as legitimating ideology.

The central point to understand from this is that contract law today constitutes an elaborate attempt to conceal what is going on in the world....

Most of the time the socioeconomic system operates without any need for law as such because people at every level have been imbued with its inevitability and necessity. When the system breaks down and conflicts arise, a legal case comes into being. This is the 'moment' of legal ideology, the moment at which lawyers and judges in *their* narrow, functional roles seek to justify the normal functioning of the system by resolving the conflict through an idealized way of thinking about it.

But this also can be the moment for struggle against the narrow limits imposed in law on genuine values such as freedom, equality, moral community, and good faith. By questioning whether the legal system helps or hinders the actual realization of those values in a meaningful sense in everyday life, the critical approach permits us to expose the illegitimacy of the system and to explore the possibility of a different order of things.

CHAPTER TWENTY-NINE

DEVELOPING THE RELATIONAL CONTRACT NOTION

■ **Macneil, 'Relational Contract Theory as Sociology'** (1987)

143 Journal of Institutional and Theoretical Economics 272, 274–276 (see p 63)

Macneil's theory is normally considered to have its greatest impact in relation to long-term relations. This is considered in Chapter 33. However, at least one writer has argued that Macneil's theory has radical implications for the very way in which we conceive of liability.

■ **Feinman, 'The Last Promissory Estoppel Article'** (1992)

61 Fordham LR 303, 303–308, 311–316

INTRODUCTION

The doctrine of promissory estoppel, currently embodied in section 90 of the *Restatement (Second) of Contracts*, has been the focus of some of the most important and interesting debates in contract law in this century. Many scholars have added to our understanding of the subject (as well as adding lustre to their scholarly reputations) by writing about the doctrine. Lon Fuller was the first, writing one of the greatest of all law review articles, *The* Reliance Interest *in Contract Damages.* Some fifty-five volumes of the *Yale Law Journal* later, in the last article published before his death, Edward Yorio and his colleague Steve Thel have brought us full circle in a careful article that challenges some of the received wisdom about section 90 that developed from Fuller's work. [(1991) 101 Yale LJ 111, referred to above, p 179.]

I THE OBJECTIVE OF PROMISSORY ESTOPPEL AND ITS ROLE TODAY

The original objective of promissory estoppel was to provide a substitute for consideration in certain cases involving promises that were not bargained for. Defining this as the doctrine's 'objective,' of course, does not mean that judges and scholars consciously designed it to fill a perceived gap in the case law. Instead, the doctrine evolved through the common law process as a device that helped avoid results that were perceived to be unjust in particular kinds of cases. These cases mostly involved gratuitous, non-commercial promises: charitable subscriptions, gift promises between relatives, and marriage settlements.

The accumulation of cases like these forced the drafters of the *Restatement of Contracts* to include section 90 on reliance as an alternative to section 75 on bargain consideration. In the view of Yorio and

Thel, although reliance was the 'binding thread of principle' in the cases on which section 90 was based, protecting the promisee's unbargained-for reliance was not the ultimate objective of the section. The key element of the doctrine for Samuel Williston, the *Restatement's* Reporter, was the promise, not the reliance. Reliance was only one of the factors that indicated that the promise was of sufficient quality so that it ought to be enforced. The other elements in section 90 (whether the reliance was foreseeable, whether it was of a definite and substantial character, and whether it actually was induced by the promise) would determine the appropriate scope of the doctrine.

. . .

The focus of contract scholars shifted away from the promissory core of section 90 largely as a result of Fuller and Perdue's analysis of contract interests in their 1936 article . . . .

The central thesis of Yorio and Thel's article is that the courts have not followed the scholars in moving from an analysis like Williston's, which focuses on the promise, to an analysis like Fuller's, which focuses on reliance. Based on an extensive survey of classic and recent cases, Yorio and Thel conclude that '[j]udges actually enforce promises rather than protect reliance in section 90 cases,' judges use the doctrine to discriminate between promises that are likely to be serious manifestations of intent and those that are not, and judges apply ordinary contract remedies in enforcing promises under section 90, rather than remedies limited 'as justice requires.'

If Yorio and Thel are correct about what the courts are doing, then several doctrinal consequences follow. First, determining whether a promise is enforceable under section 90 is very much like determining whether any other promise is enforceable. The presence or absence of reliance and the character of that reliance are factors to be considered but are not in themselves determinative. Second, expectation damages—or specific performance in an appropriate case—are the normal measure of recovery in a section 90 case; damages are restricted to reliance recovery only in cases in which the expectation measure is not available for some special reason.

There are two levels of dispute over the role of section 90. The first level, which is the immediate concern of Yorio and Thel's article, is about the accurate characterization of the state of the law, if we take 'the law' to be what the courts typically do. Yorio and Thel believe the courts are essentially enforcing promises. The *Restatement (Second)*—to the extent that it attempts to reflect the current state of the law as well as the 'better rule'—and the scholars allied with it think that the courts are protecting reliance. The second level of dispute is prescriptive. Because Yorio and Thel explicitly disclaim a prescriptive view of their subject, the advocates for this second level must be Williston and his few heirs, who argue that promissory estoppel ought to focus on promises more than on reliance. The line of thinking from Fuller through the *Restatement (Second)*, on the other hand, advances a reliance-based view of the doctrine.

. . .

However, there is an even more important connection to be made here. I suggest that the different descriptive and prescriptive positions are much more alike than they seem. All of these views proceed from the same general understanding of neoclassical contract law. The problem is that that understanding so distorts our analysis and has been so highly contested that it retains little integrity. Therefore, I propose that we ought to employ an alternate frame of analysis for the section 90 problem and for contract generally. That alternative is relational contract theory, and its adoption would lead to the abandonment of promissory estoppel. I focus on the section 90 problem and on Yorio and Thel's article because they are the occasion for this essay, but the analysis applies to the whole of contract law.

. . .

The idea of limited responsibility, although modified by recent developments . . . still plays a central role in contract law. The classical ideal of contract was the total absence of liability unless it was assumed by bargained-for promise, and then liability would be imposed only to the extent that it had been assumed. In neoclassical law, liability can arise from something less than an explicit assumption of it and it may be shaped by background assumptions, such as trade usage and the relational liabilities imposed on certain types of activity (such as an implied warranty imposed on a merchant seller). Nevertheless, as the debate about promissory estoppel illustrates, the initial step in any contract action is to search for 'the promise,' without which liability will not be imposed.

...

II THE RELATIONAL APPROACH

I propose that contract law should...embrace a truly relational analysis. This relational approach would constitute revolutionary science, rather than a further attempt to refine the normal science of neoclassical law. As particularly relevant to promissory estoppel, this move would replace the neoclassical elements of a focus on promise and a baseline of limited liability with the ideas that relationships are both different from, and more common than, discrete transactions. Furthermore, relationships necessarily involve obligations; the only questions are what kinds of obligations different relationships involve and which of those obligations should be translated into legal obligations.

The prescriptive basis of relational theory is more complex. The relational approach is most appropriately viewed as a framework for analysis and argument, rather than a concrete set of principles that lead to fixed results. Nevertheless, the relational approach embodies a set of values that differ from those expressed in neoclassical law. Ian Macneil the originator of relational contract theory, has explored the historical and ahistorical dimensions of neoclassical and relational values. [See above, p 61 and below, p 762.] Here I want to emphasize...a difference between relational theory and neoclassical law.

...

The difference in the values of neoclassical and relational contract lies in the baseline approach to obligation. Neoclassical contract emphasizes the autonomy of individuals from each other, and the limited liability that that autonomy necessitates. Relational contract, in contrast, emphasizes the interdependence of individuals in social and economic relationships. Because its paradigmatic unit of inquiry is the extensive relation rather than the discrete transaction, relational contract focuses on the necessity and desirability of trust, mutual responsibility, and connection among people. Not all of these bonds should be legally enforceable, but beginning analysis by recognizing them is likely to produce a broader set of legal obligations.

Relational analysis entails several steps. The first step responds to the neoclassical focus on discrete transactions by describing the range of types of exchange interactions that occur, from the wholly discrete to the wholly relational. There are three paradigmatic cases: a discrete transaction, a discrete transaction which takes place within a system of relationships, and a complex relation. The second step is to develop and apply the norms relevant to the understanding and evaluation of the transaction or relation. These norms include both norms generated internally by the parties and external social norms. The norms differ depending on the type of case under scrutiny. In a discrete transaction, for example, implementing planning and effectuating consent are particularly important, while contractual solidarity and flexibility are more important in an ongoing relation. The third step is to decide whether and how the norms can be effectively implemented through rules of legal obligation. For example, while contractual solidarity may be important in preserving relations, in some situations to impose a legal standard of solidarity might create disharmony instead.

The application of a full relational approach can be quite complex, so I only suggest some of the ways in which this approach could contribute to the reevaluation of promissory estoppel. This is not to suggest that the relational approach provides rules of easy application to classes of cases. It may turn out to be true that in using a relational approach we would conclude that, for example, many charitable subscriptions should be enforceable, as should many promises by employers to employees, whereas family promises would not. But those results are the product of complex analysis in individual situations, rather than *Restatement*-like rules.

Begin with cases near the discrete end of the discrete-relational continuum. Section 90 doctrine deals reasonably well with these cases as it stands, although the scholarly dispute about exactly how it does so indicates that it could be clarified. Absent the kind of obligation that accompanies relational characteristics, the issue in these cases is the extent to which the parties' words and conduct indicate substantial planning and understanding of the significance of the consequences of the words and conduct (i.e. consent). In discrete cases, it may be reasonable to require evidence of this planning through a degree of specificity in the statement and a definite and substantial act of reliance. Where an employer offers a job to a prospective employee and encourages her to quit her job in reliance on the offer, for example, there is sufficient evidence of planning and consent to impose liability.

...

Consider next the cases involving promises, representations, and assurances made by an employer to an employee during the course of employment. These cases often involve promises to pay bonuses or pension benefits or promises regarding the duration of employment, or even promises to keep a plant open. Scholars take different approaches to these cases, variously emphasizing the 'implicit bargain' or the 'public policy' involved, the economic nature of the setting, or the status of the parties. All of these are helpful, but none of them is complete. To say, for example...that these promises ought to be enforceable because they are in furtherance of economic activity does little to help us distinguish which of these statements constitute a promise. The advantages of relational analysis here are to direct our attention to the extensive, responsibility-creating nature of the employment relationship, to provide a vocabulary for analyzing its elements, and to emphasize the care with which the legal system must intervene.

Finally, consider *Hoffman v Red Owl Stores, Inc*, probably the most famous of all section 90 cases. The decision always has been problematic. As Yorio and Thel note,

> '[t]he court may have found a promise, however, because it saw no other basis on which to hold for Hoffman, shoehorning the facts into Section 90 in order to afford Hoffman some relief for what the trial judge apparently regarded as (negligent) misrepresentation by *Red Owl's* agent.'

Hoffman can hardly be understood on the basis of promissory estoppel doctrine. As Barnett and Becker suggest [(1987) 15 Hofstra LR 443; see also above, p 260], it may be better understood as a tort case involving negligent misrepresentation of a peculiar kind. It can be best understood, though, as a relational case. The relational analysis would proceed at two levels; it would examine the interactions between the parties, which extended over several years, involved many different issues, and were conducted by several agents of Red Owl, and would then look at the broader setting in which franchisors and their agents employ a variety of techniques to procure franchises. That kind of analysis, not constrained by notions of promise or reliance, would provide a better understanding of how courts treat such cases and how they should do so. It might well provide a contested understanding; we could argue about the appropriate scope of liability of franchisors for the acts of their agents in particular settings, but at least the argument would proceed from a fuller understanding of the case, and one that is more attuned to the responsibilities that arise from relationships.

CONCLUSION

Is it likely that we will soon stop talking in terms of promissory estoppel and of the neoclassical framework of which it is a part? Perhaps not, as the weight of tradition is very great. There is, however, a growing recognition that the framework is ailing, if not moribund. The repeated attempts by neoclassical scholars to redescribe, reclassify, and reconceptualize section 90 cases seems to me to be a recognition of difficulty. Furthermore, over the last few years the increased significance in contract scholarship of law and economics, rational choice theory, rights theories, relational theory, empirical studies of contract, critical legal studies, and feminist theory as competitors of neoclassical contract are further symptoms of illness. The prescription, it seems to me, is to stop addressing old questions—by debating whether the core of section 90 is promise or reliance, for example—and address the more fundamental issue of what kind of framework we should have, for that will determine the questions we should ask.

NOTES

1. To what extent does English or Australian law recognise that there may be liability without a promise? Consider *Crabb v Arun DC* (see p 155); *Walton Stores v Maher* (p 158); *Smith v Eric Bush* (p 1021).

2. The extent to which English law recognises the 'relational context' of contracts is explored in a valuable piece by Campbell and Collins, 'Discovering the Implicit Dimensions of Contracts' in Campbell, Collins and Wightman (eds), *Implicit Dimensions of Contract*, 2003, pp 25–49. They summarise their argument thus (at pp 26–27):

> ...[T]he classical law of contract does not exclude implicit dimensions of contracts from its reasoning altogether. References to implicit dimensions can be inserted by a variety of devices: such as rules that invalidate consent on grounds of misrepresentation and undue influence, the technique of supplementing express terms by implied terms and rules such as mitigation that determine the quantification of damages as a remedy. Our argument, therefore, is not that the classical law could not recognise implicit dimensions of contractual relationships, but rather that its techniques for instantiating these implicit dimensions frequently proved inadequate. The framework of the classical analysis always commences with the assumption that legal reasoning need not incorporate reference to implicit dimensions. As the reasoning proceeds, however, exceptions and qualifications creep in to subvert the exclusive emphasis on the explicit, discrete contractual relationship through references to its social context and the implicit understandings generated by that context. But these insertions of implicit dimensions must always be marginalised or minimised by the classical legal doctrine, for they represent 'dangerous supplements' to classical reasoning, in the sense that an acknowledgement of the pertinence of implicit dimensions threatens the collapse of an analysis that holds itself out as being an instrument of explicit, rational choices. In other words, to be fully operational and to achieve closure in legal reasoning, the manipulation of the classical rules frequently requires reference to the implicit dimensions of contractual relationships, yet these references always threaten to undermine the integrity of the classical discourse.

3. Some of the implications of the choice between more 'formal' and more 'relational' approaches to solving contract disputes are explored in Macaulay, 'The Real and the Paper Deal: Empirical Pictures of Relationships, Complexity and the Urge for Transparent Simple Rules', in Campbell, Collins and Wightman (eds), *Implicit Dimensions of Contract*, 2003, pp 51–102.

4. In the USA, there have been many calls for a return to a more formal approach (often dubbed 'neo-formalism'), in particular for business-to-business contracts: eg Schwartz and Scott, 'Contract Theory and the Limits of Contract Law' (2003) 113 Yale LJ 541; Scott, 'The Death of Contract *Law*' (2004) Uni Tor LJ 369. To some extent, this seems to be a reaction against decisions that apply doctrines such as unconscionability (see Chapter 37) to business-to-business contracts in a way that has not been done by the English courts.

5. Bernstein has studied customs and practices in a number of industries in the USA. She has concluded that, in many cases, it would be very difficult to incorporate trade understandings into contracts because there is little agreement on what the customs actually are: in particular, many terms and practices are understood differently in different parts of the country. She argues that these 'weak' customs do play an important role in commercial relationships, as what she terms 'relationship-preserving norms': seeing whether a new contracting partner will adhere to them is a useful way of establishing

whether the partner is reliable. However, she argues that when the relationship breaks down—'end-game disputes'—the parties do not want any dispute to be decided by these customs but rather by the letter of the contract (see Bernstein, 'The Questionable Empirical Basis of Article 2's Incorporations Strategy' (1996) 66 Uni Chi LR 710, and 'Private Commercial Law in the Cotton Industry: Creating Cooperation through Rules, Norms and Institutions' (2001) 99 Mich LR 1724). See, however, Charny, 'The New Formalism in Contract' (1996) 66 Uni Chi LR 842, asking why the formal written agreement is more appropriate to 'end-game' disputes than an 'all things considered' approach.

CHAPTER THIRTY

FAIRNESS AND DISTRIBUTIVE JUSTICE

This chapter contains readings that look forward to the material that is to follow, particularly in Section 8. You may read it as an introduction to that material, or you may prefer to leave it until you have covered that section.

Section 8 is primarily concerned with the various ways in which the law explicitly tries to control contracts for fairness. As we will see, this comprises two distinguishable elements. One is procedural fairness: was the means by which the contract was made a fair one? If there was fraud, duress (eg a threat of some illegitimate action against the party unless she signed) or something similar, the courts will often give relief. But they may refuse relief unless the party also shows that the contract that resulted was unfair in substance (eg in some cases of undue influence, the plaintiff must show that the transaction was 'manifestly disadvantageous', or at least 'called for explanation': see p 912). In fact, most of the doctrines described in Section 8 seem to require a combination of procedural and substantive unfairness. On procedural and substantive fairness, see further pp 901 and 945.

Will a contract ever be set aside on the ground that it is substantively unfair even though the party who gains the advantage seems to have done nothing wrong except to charge a high price (or, if he is the buyer, to offer a low one)? The doctrine of adequacy of consideration (p 122) suggests that a contract will be enforceable despite inadequacy of consideration unless there is also some procedural unfairness in addition.

There are some writers who consider that it is not the proper role of contract to do more than ensure fair procedure: see the next two extracts. The first deals with the proper scope of policing of contracts for fairness or 'unconscionability'. (On unconscionability, see further Chapter 37.) The second argues that the law of contracts should not aim to make contracts distributionally fairer.

■ Epstein, 'Unconscionability: A Critical Reappraisal' (1975)
18 J Law & Econ 293, 293–294, 306–308, 315

The classical conception of contract at common law had as its first premise the belief that private agreements should be enforced in accordance with their terms. That premise of course was subject to important qualifications. Promises procured by fraud, duress, or undue influence were not generally enforced by the courts; and the same was true with certain exceptions of promises made by infants and incompetents. Again, agreements that had as their object illegal ends were usually not enforced, as, for example, in cases of bribes of public officials or contracts to kill third persons. Yet even after these exceptions are taken into account, there was still one ground on which the initial premise could not be challenged: the terms of private agreements could not be set aside because the court found them to be harsh, unconscionable, or unjust. The reasonableness of the terms of a private agreement was the business of the parties to that agreement. True, there were numerous cases in which the language of the contract stood in need of judicial interpretation, but once that task was done there was no place for a court to impose upon the parties its own views about their rights and duties. 'Public policy' was an 'unruly horse', to be mounted only in exceptional cases and then only with care.

This general regime of freedom of contract can be defended from two points of view. One defense is utilitarian. So long as the tort law protects the interests of strangers to the agreement, its enforcement will tend to maximize the welfare of the parties to it, and therefore the good of the society as a whole. The alternative defense is on libertarian grounds. One of the first functions of the law is to guarantee to individuals a sphere of influence in which they will be able to operate, without having to justify themselves to the state or to third parties: if one individual is entitled to do within the confines of the tort law what he pleases with what he owns, then two individuals who operate with those same constraints should have the same right with respect to their mutual affairs against the rest of the world.

Whatever its merits, however, it is fair to say that this traditional view of the law of contract has been in general retreat in recent years. That decline is reflected in part in the cool reception given to doctrines of laissez-faire, its economic counterpart, since the late nineteenth century, or at least since the New Deal. The total 'hands off' policy with respect to economic matters is regarded as incorrect in most political discussions almost as a matter of course and the same view is taken, moreover, toward a more subtle form of laissez-faire that views all government interference in economic matters as an evil until shown to be good. Instead, the opposite point of view is increasingly urged: market solutions—those which presuppose a regime of freedom of contract—are sure to be inadequate, and the only question worth debating concerns the appropriate form of public intervention. That attitude has, moreover, worked its way (as these things usually happen) into the fabric of the legal system, for today, more than ever, courts are willing to set aside the provisions of private agreements.

One of the major conceptual tools used by courts in their assault upon private agreements has been the doctrine of unconscionability. That doctrine has a place in contract law, but it is not the one usually assigned it by its advocates. The doctrine should not, in my view, allow courts to act as roving commissions to set aside those agreements whose substantive terms they find objectionable. . . .

[As an example of what he regards as misguided interference, Epstein refers to 'add-on' clauses. This is a reference to the leading US unconscionability case, *Williams v Walker-Thomas Furniture Co* 121 US App DC 315, 350 F 2d 445 (1965). In this case, a woman known by the seller to be completely dependent on social security payments was sold a stereo on credit under a form of contract containing an 'add-on' clause. This permitted the seller, in the event of her default, to repossess any goods it had sold to her previously and on which a balance was outstanding, and further permitted the seller to pro-rate any payment across each debt, so that a balance would remain outstanding on each item until all were paid for. At the date of the contract, the buyer had paid off all but $164 on previous purchases totalling $1,800. When she defaulted, the seller claimed to repossess all the previously sold items—beds, furniture, a washing machine and even a pair of oven gloves—as well as the stereo. The US Court of Appeals held that the add-on clause might be unconscionable and unenforceable at common law, and remanded the case for the question to be determined.]

a. 'Add-on' clauses

One sort of clause that has come under both judicial and statutory scrutiny is the so-called 'add-on' clause used in consumer credit sales. These clauses govern the security interest taken back by the seller, and, in one common form, provide that all previous goods purchased by the buyer from the seller will secure the debts incurred with the current purchase. The security agreement also provides that each payment made with respect to any of the items purchased would be applied against all outstanding balances, allowing the seller in effect to retain his security interest in all the goods sold until the debts with respect to all items are discharged. A single default on a single payment could trigger the plaintiff's right to repossess all the goods subject to the comprehensive security arrangement.

Although agreements of this kind can, and have, been attacked on unconscionability grounds, they make good sense in the cases to which they apply. One of the major risks to the seller of personal property is that the goods sold will lose value, be it through use or abuse, more rapidly than the purchase price is paid off. The buyer can, and quite often does, have a 'negative' equity in the goods. The seller, therefore, who takes back a security interest only in the goods sold, runs the real risk that repossession of the single item sold will still leave him with a loss on the transaction as a whole, taking into account the costs of interest and collection. One way to handle this problem is to require the purchaser of the goods to make a larger cash down payment, but that, of course, is something which many buyers, particularly those of limited means, do not want to do. Another alternative is for the buyer to provide the seller with additional collateral; yet here the best collateral is doubtless in goods sold by the seller to the buyer. Other goods already in the possession of the buyer may be of uncertain value, and they may well be subject to prior liens. Again, they may be of a sort that the seller cannot conveniently resell in the ordinary course of his business. Even if the goods are suitable collateral for the loan, it could take a good deal of time and effort for the seller to determine that fact. The 'add-on' clause allows both parties to benefit from the reduction in costs in the setting up of a security arrangement.

The case for the add-on clauses is strengthened, moreover, when we note its legal effects. As between the buyer and seller the clause allows the seller to collect on his unpaid debt without having to avail himself of the awkward procedures established for unsecured creditors. The clause assures the seller that the value he has furnished the buyer will, if need be, first be used to satisfy his own claims and not those of third parties. The only disadvantage to the buyer therefore is that he will not be able to use the goods purchased to obtain some economic benefit in a subsequent transaction. But it is difficult in a commercial context to see why a seller should not be paid before his buyer or third parties are able to use the goods he furnished for their own satisfaction.

The sense of these clauses, regardless of the particular form which they take, is demonstrated anew, moreover, once we realize that they operate within one very strong constraint, often imposed by statute, which restricts the creditor in a secured transaction to the recovery of principal, interest and costs in cases of default by the buyer. Within the framework of these limitations, the add-on clause can do no harm at all, for it only makes it more certain that the seller will be able to collect that to which on any view he is entitled.

CONCLUSION

In this paper I have sought to defend against modern attacks the principle of freedom of contract which was central to the classical common law. Properly understood, that position does not require a court to enforce every contract brought before it. It does, however, demand that the reasons invoked for not enforcing the contract be of one of two sorts. Either there must be proof of some defect in the process of contract formation (be it duress, fraud or undue influence); or there must be, but only within narrow limits, some incompetence of the party against whom the agreement is to be enforced. The doctrine of unconscionability is important in both these respects because it can, if wisely applied, allow the courts to police these two types of problems, and thereby improve the general administration of the contract law. Yet when the doctrine of unconscionability is used in its substantive dimension, be it in a commercial or consumer context, it serves only to undercut the private right of contract in a manner that is apt to do more social harm than good. The result of the analysis is the same even if we view the question of unconscionability from the lofty perspective of public policy. '[I]f there is one thing which more than another public policy requires, it is that men of full age and competent understanding shall have the utmost liberty of contracting, and that their contracts when entered into freely and voluntarily shall be held sacred and shall be enforced by Courts of justice' [Jessel MR in *Printing and Numerical Registering Co v Sampson*].

■ Nozick, 'Anarchy State and Utopia'

pp 151, 153, 155–164

I. The entitlement theory

If the world were wholly just, the following inductive definition would exhaustively cover the subject of justice in holdings.

1. A person who acquires a holding in accordance with the principle of justice in acquisition is entitled to that holding.
2. A person who acquires a holding in accordance with the principle of justice in transfer, from someone else entitled to the holding, is entitled to the holding.
3. No one is entitled to a holding except by (repeated) applications of 1 and 2.

The complete principle of distributive justice would say simply that a distribution is just if everyone is entitled to the holdings they possess under the distribution.

A distribution is just if it arises from another just distribution by legitimate means. The legitimate means of moving from one distribution to another are specified by the principle of justice in transfer. The legitimate first 'moves' are specified by the principle of justice in acquisition. Whatever arises from a just situation by just steps is itself just. The means of change specified by the principle of justice in transfer preserve justice ...

...The general outlines of the entitlement theory illuminate the nature and defects of other conceptions of distributive justice. The entitlement theory of justice in distribution is *historical;* whether a distribution is just depends upon how it came about.

...

II. Patterning

...[To better understand the precise character of the entitlement principles of justice] we shall distinguish them from another subclass of the historical principles. Consider, as an example, the principle of distribution according to moral merit. This principle requires that total distributive shares vary directly with moral merit; no person should have a greater share than anyone whose moral merit is greater. (If moral merit could be not merely ordered but measured on an interval or ratio scale, stronger principles could be formulated.) Or consider the principle that results by substituting 'usefulness to society' for 'moral merit' in the previous principle. Or instead of 'distribute according to moral merit,' or 'distribute according to usefulness to society,' we might consider 'distribute according to the weighted sum of moral merit, usefulness to society, and need,' with the weights of the different dimensions equal. Let us call a principle of distribution *patterned* if it specifies that a distribution is to vary along with some natural dimension, weighted sum of natural dimensions, or lexicographic ordering of natural dimensions. And let us say a distribution is patterned if it accords with some patterned principle....

Almost every suggested principle of distributive justice is patterned: to each according to his moral merit, or needs, or marginal product, or how hard he tries, or the weighted sum of the foregoing, and so on. The principle of entitlement we have sketched is *not* patterned. There is no one natural dimension or weighted sum or combination of a small number of natural dimensions that yields the distributions generated in accordance with the principle of entitlement. The set of holdings that results when some persons receive their marginal products, others win at gambling, others receive a share of their mate's income, others receive gifts from foundations, others receive interest on loans, others receive gifts from admirers, others receive returns on investment, others make for themselves much of what they have, others find things, and so on, will not be patterned.... Though the resulting set of holdings will be unpatterned, it will not be incomprehensible, for it can be seen as arising from the operation of a small number of principles. These principles specify how an initial distribution may arise (the principle of acquisition of holdings) and how distributions may be transformed into others (the principle of transfer of holdings). The process whereby the set of holdings is generated will be intelligible, though the set of holdings itself that results from this process will be unpatterned....

To think that the task of a theory of distributive justice is to fill in the blank in 'to each according to his—' is to be predisposed to search for a pattern; and the separate treatment of 'from each according to his—' treats production and distribution as two separate and independent issues. On an entitlement view these are *not* two separate questions. Whoever makes something, having bought or contracted for all other held resources used in the process (transferring some of his holdings for these cooperating factors), is entitled to it. The situation is *not* one of something's getting made, and there being an open question of who is to get it. Things come into the world already attached to people having entitlements over them. From the point of view of the historical entitlement conception of justice in holdings, those who start afresh to complete 'to each according to his—' treat objects as if they appeared from nowhere, out of nothing. A complete theory of justice might cover this limit case as well, perhaps here is a use for the usual conceptions of distributive justice.

So entrenched are maxims of the usual form that perhaps we should present the entitlement conception as a competitor. Ignoring acquisition and rectification, we might say:

> 'From each according to what he chooses to do, to each according to what he makes for himself (perhaps with the contracted aid of others) and what others choose to do for him and choose to give him of what they've been given previously (under this maxim) and haven't yet expended or transferred.'

This, the discerning reader will have noticed, has its defects as a slogan. So as a summary and great simplification (and not as a maxim with any independent meaning) we have:

> *From each as they choose, to each as they are chosen.*

III. How liberty upsets patterns

It is not clear how those holding alternative conceptions of distributive justice can reject the entitlement conception of justice in holdings. For suppose a distribution favored by one of these nonentitlement conceptions is realized. Let us suppose it is your favorite one and let us call this distribution D1; perhaps everyone has an equal share, perhaps shares vary in accordance with some dimension you treasure. Now suppose that Wilt Chamberlain is greatly in demand by basketball teams, being a great gate attraction. (Also suppose contracts run only for a year, with players being free agents.) He signs the following sort of contract with a team: In each home game, twenty-five cents from the price of each ticket of admission goes to him. (We ignore the question of whether he is 'gouging' the owners, letting them look out for themselves.) The season starts, and people cheerfully attend his team's games; they buy their tickets, each time dropping a separate twenty-five cents of their admission price into a special box with Chamberlain's name on it. They are excited about seeing him play; it is worth the total admission price to them. Let us suppose that in one season one million persons attend his home games, and Wilt Chamberlain winds up with $250,000, a much larger sum than the average income and larger even than anyone else has. Is he entitled to this income? Is this new distribution D2, unjust? If so, why? There is *no* question about whether each of the people was entitled to the control over the resources they held in D1; because that was the distribution (your favorite) that (for the purposes of argument) we assumed was acceptable. Each of these persons *chose* to give twenty-five cents of their money to Chamberlain. They could have spent it on going to the movies, or on candy bars, or on copies of Dissent magazine, or of Monthly Review. But they all, at least one million of them, converged on giving it to Wilt Chamberlain in exchange for watching him play basketball. If D1, was a just distribution, and people voluntarily moved from it to D2, transferring parts of their shares they were given under D1 (what was it for if not to do something with?), isn't D2 also just? If the people were entitled to dispose of the resources to which they were entitled (under D1), didn't this include their being entitled to give it to, or exchange it with, Wilt Chamberlain? Can anyone else complain on grounds of justice? Each other person already has his legitimate share under D1. Under D1, there is nothing that anyone has that anyone else has a claim of justice against. After someone transfers something to Wilt Chamberlain, third parties *still* have their legitimate shares; *their* shares are not changed. By what process could such a transfer among two persons give rise to a legitimate claim of distributive justice on a portion of what was transferred, by a third party who had no claim of justice on any holding of the others *before* the transfer? To cut off objections irrelevant here, we might imagine the exchanges occurring in a socialist society, after hours. After playing whatever basketball he does in his daily work, or doing whatever other daily work he does, Wilt Chamberlain decides to put in *overtime* to earn additional money. (First his work quota is set; he works time over that.) Or imagine it is a skilled juggler people like to see, who puts on shows after hours.

Why might someone work overtime in a society in which it is assumed their needs are satisfied? Perhaps because they care about things other than needs. I like to write in books that I read, and to have easy access to books for browsing at odd hours. It would be very pleasant and convenient to have the resources of Widener Library in my back yard. No society, I assume, will provide such resources close to each person who would like them as part of his regular allotment (under D1). Thus, persons either must do without some extra things that they want, or be allowed to do something extra to get some of these things. On what basis could the inequalities that would eventuate be forbidden? Notice also that small factories would spring up in a socialist society, unless forbidden. I melt down some of my personal possessions (under D1) and build a machine out of the material. I offer you, and others, a philosophy lecture once a week in exchange for your cranking the handle on my machine, whose products I exchange for yet other things, and so on. (The raw materials used by the machine are given to me by others who possess them under D1, in exchange for hearing lectures.) Each person might participate to gain things over and above their allotment under D1. Some persons even might want to leave their job in socialist industry and work full time in this private sector. I shall say something more about these issues in the next chapter. Here I wish merely to note how private property even in means of production would occur in a socialist society that did not forbid people to use as they wished some of the resources they are given under the socialist distribution D1. The socialist society would have to forbid capitalist acts between consenting adults.

The general point illustrated by the Wilt Chamberlain example and the example of the entrepreneur in a socialist society is that no end-state principle or distributional patterned principle of justice can be continuously realized without continuous interference with people's lives. Any favored pattern would be transformed into one unfavored by the principle, by people choosing to act in various ways; for example, by people exchanging goods and services with other people, or giving things to other people, things the transferrers are entitled to under the favored distributional pattern. To maintain a pattern one must either continually interfere to stop people from transferring resources as they wish to, or continually (or periodically) interfere to take from some persons resources that others for some reason chose to transfer to them. (But if some time limit is to be set on how long people may keep resources others voluntarily transfer to them, why let them keep these resources for *any* period of time? Why not have immediate confiscation?) It might be objected that all persons voluntarily will choose to refrain from actions which would upset the pattern. This presupposes unrealistically (1) that all will most want to maintain the pattern (are those who don't, to be 'reeducated' or forced to undergo 'self-criticism'?), (2) that each can gather enough information about his own actions and the ongoing activities of others to discover which of his actions will upset the pattern, and (3) that diverse and far-flung persons can coordinate their actions to dovetail into the pattern. Compare the manner in which the market is neutral among persons' desires, as it reflects and transmits widely scattered information via prices, and coordinates persons' activities.

. . . Any distributional pattern with any egalitarian component is overturnable by the voluntary actions of individual persons over time; as is every patterned condition with sufficient content so as actually to have been proposed as presenting the central core of distributive justice. . . .

Other writers take rather different views, arguing either for an expanded notion of unconscionability, which would treat departure from the market price as inefficient and therefore not to be upheld, or arguing for the setting aside of any contract that departs from the market price as unjust, unless there is some other factor to explain it.

■ Eisenberg 'The Bargain Principle and its Limits' (1982)
95 Harvard LR 741, 742–750, 754, 778, 780–782, 784, 790–800

The subject of this Article is the bargain principle and its limits. By bargain, I mean an exchange in which each party views the performance that he undertakes as the price of the performance undertaken by the other. Although parties may barter bargained-for performances without making any promises, contract law is concerned with those bargains that involve a present promise to render a future preformance—that is, that involve an exchange over time. By the bargain principle, I mean the common law rule that, in the absence of a traditional defense relating to the quality of consent (such as duress, incapacity, misrepresentation, or mutual mistake), the courts will enforce a bargain according to its terms, with the object of putting a bargain-promisee in as good a position as if the bargain had been performed. . . .

I. THE BARGAIN PRINCIPLE

Since the law does not enforce promises as such, a legal analysis of bargain promises must start with the question whether such promises should be enforceable at all. In considering this question, it is easiest to begin with those bargains in which one party's performance is both due and rendered before the other's, so that the bargain has become a half-completed or credit transaction. For convenience, I shall generally call the unperformed promise a half-completed-bargain promise: the party who has already rendered performance the plaintiff; and the party who has bargained for that performance the defendant.

. . .

The hard question, therefore, is not *whether* half-completed-bargain promises should be legally enforced, but the *extent* to which such promises should be enforced. Three broad possibilities serve as starting points. Such a promise may be enforced: (1) to the extent of the plaintiff's cost, including his opportunity cost (the reliance measure); (2) to the extent of the value conferred upon the defendant (the restitution measure); or (3) to the extent of the value to the plaintiff of the promised performance—that is, the amount required to put the plaintiff in as good a position as if the contract had been performed (the expectation measure). Often these three measures coincide. But what if they do not? Suppose, in particular, that the defendant resists all but restitutionary damages, on the ground that the terms of the bargain were unfair, in the sense that the value of the performance he promised to render exceeded the value he was to receive in exchange.

Generally speaking, the answer of the common law has been to invoke what I have called the bargain principle, which is commonly expressed by such catchphrases as 'courts do not inquire into the adequacy of consideration' or 'mere inadequacy of consideration will not void a contract.' When stated in this way, the principle appears to be substantive, but in large part it is a rule about remedies. What it means is that damages for unexcused breach of a bargain promise should invariably be measured by the value the promised performance would have had to the plaintiff, rather than, and regardless of, the cost or value of the performance for which the defendant's promise was exchanged—a formulation that can be expressed by the concept that a bargain promise should be enforced to its full extent.

If this principle were to be rigorously applied, bargain promises could never be reviewed for fairness of terms. A number of arguments can be made, on the bases of fairness and economic efficiency, that the principle should be so applied, at least in the context of a half-completed bargain.

First. The idea of reviewing a bargain for fairness of terms implies that an objective value can be placed upon a bargained-for performance. It can be argued, however, that objective value of a bargained-for performance is not a meaningful concept, because the value of such a performance is that which the parties assign to it. A related argument is that a party who has received a bargained-for performance cannot legitimately object to paying a price that reflects is value to him, and his agreement shows that he valued the performance at least as high as the promised price.

Second. If *A* has rendered a bargained-for performance to *B*, we know that *A* was willing to render that performance to *B* for the agreed-upon price. We cannot know whether *A* would have rendered that performance to *B* for any lesser price. It can therefore be argued that, having rendered the performance, *A* cannot legitimately be required to accept any lesser price. Such a requirement would unfairly convert *A* from a voluntary to an involuntary actor, because had he known in advance that the price would be reduced, he might not have contracted and performed.

Third. The extent to which private actors are willing to engage in credit transactions (that is, bargains involving exchanges over time) and make plans on the basis of those transactions depends partly on the probability that bargain promises will be kept. It can therefore be argued that failure to enforce bargain promises to their full extent would subvert efficiency by diminishing the willingness of private actors to enter into and plan upon the basis of credit transactions.

Fourth. The contract price is normally the most efficient price, in the economist sense of that term, because permitting the price of a commodity to be determined by the interaction of buyers and sellers will normally move the commodity to its highest-valued uses, as expressed by the amounts competing buyers are willing to pay, and will best allocate the factors necessary for the commodity's production.

These arguments find their fullest justification in what might be called the exemplary case for application of the bargain principle—that is, a half-completed bargain in a perfectly competitive market. . . . in the exemplary case the bargain principle is supported by considerations of both fairness and efficiency. Indeed, the bargain principle may well have been formulated on the premise that real cases did not materially differ from the exemplary case. In practice, however, such differences frequently arise, and the balance of this Article considers the strength of the bargain principle when the assumptions of the exemplary case are relaxed. Part II shows that if the assumption of a perfectly competitive market is relaxed, the stage is set for invoking limits on the bargain principle based on the quality of the underlying bargain. . . .

II. THE PRINCIPLE OF UNCONSCIONABILITY

Each of the arguments supporting the bargain principle has considerable force, even outside the context of the exemplary case. Each, however, overstates its claim when it is extended beyond that case. The argument that objective value is neither a meaningful nor an appropriate concept can be countered by observing that the law often measures objective value in bargains that are not made in a perfectly competitive market. For example, off-market contracts between a beneficiary and his trustee or between a fiduciary and his corporation are customarily subject to review for objective fairness. If the mechanism by which a contract price was generated is inferior, in a normative way, to some other mechanism available to a court—such as measurement based on market price, cost, or benefit conferred—then resort to the other mechanism may well be in order. This point also helps answer the related argument that a promisor who has received a bargained-for performance cannot legitimately object to paying a price that reflects the value he placed on the performance. A promisee is not necessarily entitled to capture a surplus representing the excess of the promisor's subjective value over a price set in an objectively desirable manner.

The argument that revising a bargained-for price may unfairly convert a party who has rendered a bargained-for performance into an involuntary actor can be countered by a similar objection. If the price was not set by a mechanism that is regarded as fair, such as a competitive market, it may not be unfair or undesirable to revise it judicially. Many rules of law induce some form of involuntary behavior.

The argument based on the need to facilitate credit transactions and private planning depends for its weight on the strength of the policy behind facilitation, which in turn depends in part on the quality of the market in which the contract is made. In any event, not all types of credit transactions are necessarily to be encouraged, not all bargains involve planning, and in some transactions occurring off competitive markets a party might not be deterred from contracting by the prospect of a reduction in price.

The argument based on the efficiency of contract price is fully effective only to the extent that the relevant market does not materially differ from a perfectly competitive market. In fact, however, many contracts are made in markets that are highly imperfect.

In short, while the arguments supporting the bargain principle are weighty and suggest that limits on the principle should be imposed cautiously, they are not conclusive.

...

It is not the purpose of Part II to exhaust the concept of unconscionability. Quite the contrary: a basic thesis of this Article is that unconscionability is a paradigmatic concept that can never be exhaustively described. It is, however, a major purpose of Part II to suggest a methodology by which specific unconscionability norms should be developed. Accordingly, the norms described in this Part are important not only in themselves, but also as demonstrations of that methodology. Three general propositions underlie the methodology, and should be stated at the outset: (1) Since the bargain principle rests on arguments of fairness and efficiency, it is appropriate to develop and apply a specific unconscionability norm whenever a class of cases can be identified in which neither fairness nor efficiency support the bargain principle's application. (2) The development and application of specific unconscionability norms is closely related to the manner in which the relevant market deviates from a perfectly competitive market. (3) The distinction between procedural and substantive unconscionability is too rigid to provide significant help in either the development or the application of such norms.

[In sections A-C, Eisenberg considers cases of distress (ie in which the buyer is in desperate need), transactional incapacity (eg inability to understand) and unfair persuasion. Generally, the apparent bargain in such cases should not be enforced.]

D. Price-ignorance

One condition of a perfectly competitive market is a homogeneous marketplace in which cost-free information concerning price is readily available. When this condition is not satisfied and marketplaces are differentiated, the price of a homogeneous commodity in a given marketplace may be strikingly higher than the price at which the commodity is normally sold. For example, the *New York Times* recently reported as follows on a group of Manhattan stores, most of them clustered on Fifth Avenue, which apparently specialize in one-shot sales, often to tourists:

> '[S]uch shops . . . [offer] $40 radios for $80, $30 calculators for $95 and ivory and jade collectibles, so-called, at similarly inflated prices, according to cases cited by the New York City Department of Consumer Affairs.'

...

Caveat emptor might be viewed as justified in its day if we assume that when this doctrine prevailed, buyers had little or no confidence in sellers and therefore had no expectation of quality beyond such expectations as arose from their own search. In a modern economy, however, buyers place confidence in merchant-sellers regarding a great variety of product attributes, and most merchants work hard to engender and maintain that confidence. So too with price. At one time, perhaps, buyers viewed every sale transaction as an occasion for haggling and had no expectations concerning price beyond those engendered by their own search. Today, however, haggling is the exception, not the rule, and it seems clear that in most consumer marketplaces the quotation of a price, like other statements made by a seller, is understood to convey information. This information, in turn, raises certain expectations and implicitly gives rise to certain representations. In particular, it would conform to modern understanding to adopt a rule that a merchant who offers a homogeneous commodity at a fixed price impliedly represents that the price is not strikingly disproportionate to that at which the commodity is normally sold in readily accessible marketplaces, giving due weight to the merchant's relevant advantages, reputation, and normal price variations.

Under such a rule, however, whether the seller knew or had reason to know that the price quotation was strikingly disproportionate would be irrelevant. The rule would therefore not be based on a concept of fault, and accordingly would go beyond the concept of unconscionability. For now, it is not necessary to go that far. Instead, it suffices to adopt the fault-based doctrine that it is unconscionable for a merchant to exploit a consumer's price-igorance by offering a homogeneous commodity at a price he knows or has reason to know is strikingly disproportionate in the stated manner. Application of the bargain principle to such cases is unsupported by either of that principle's two major props. Fairness does not support application of the principle, since the promisee has violated conventional morality by making a kind of misrepresentation and by exploiting the promisor's ignorance of a body of cheaply acquired and readily available knowledge (as opposed to knowledge that is generated by the promisee's own skill and diligence). Efficiency considerations are at worst neutral: since the commodity is by hypothesis selling at a much lower price in comparable marketplaces, it hardly seems likely that the higher price is required to move the commodity to its highest-valued uses or to allocate properly the factors necessary for its production. Indeed, it is arguable that by reducing wasteful search, a prohibition on exploitation of price-ignorance would lead to greater efficiency than would enforcing the bargain to its full extent. A consumer who knows that the law prohibits a merchant from charging a price for a homogeneous commodity that the merchant knows or should know strikingly exceeds the prevailing price in comparable marketplaces can make a more or less informed decision on whether the likelihood of finding a moderately lower price justifies the cost of searching for such a price. In contrast, a consumer who knows that the law does not prohibit such behavior may feel constrained to search several marketplaces for every purchase, lest he be exploited in the first marketplace.

Thus far, no assumption has been made concerning the seller's profits. Is the argument affected if the seller's profits are not above normal? To explore this issue, let us return to door-to-door sales at prices very much higher than those charged for comparable goods at conventional retail outlets, which I shall refer to hereinafter as high-price door-to-door selling. Assume, for purposes of argument, that high-price door-to-door sellers do not earn above-normal profits. In that case, they are recovering their costs but not much more and their high prices must therefore reflect high costs. This in turn raises two issues. First, can prices be deemed unconscionable if the seller is only covering its costs, including a fair return? Second, if a high-cost seller is making only normal profits, can it not be inferred that the costs are translated into consumer benefits? The two issues are intimately connected, since if the seller's costs are completely translated into consumer benefits, its price can hardly be deemed unconscionable.

To address these issues, consider two possible models of high-price door-to-door selling. Under one model, prices are high because these sellers offer nonprice benefits that consumers value to the extent of the difference between the contract price and the normal retail price. In particular, these sellers may bring to a buyer's attention information the buyer did not previously have—for example, that a certain type of product exists. Under this model the sellers' high prices are justified since the consumer is paying for both a commodity a special service.

The second model is much less flattering. Under this model, high-price door-to-door firms are not selling information, but searching out and exploiting price-ignorant buyers. . . .

. . . [If], as seems likely, the second model describes high-price door-to-door sales better than the first, the fact that such sellers earn only normal returns becomes irrelevant. In terms of fairness, conduct may be exploitive even if it does not produce above-normal returns. In terms of efficiency, profits are normal only because the seller incurs the socially wasteful cost of searching out and intercepting the price-ignorant. Even if the seller's prices do provide only a fair return on investment, the investment is not one that the law should promote by enforcing a recovery that reimburses those unproductive costs.

A doctrine prohibiting the exploitation of price-ignorance is sufficiently justified by the principle of unconscionability.

[In Part III, which is omitted for reasons of space, Eisenberg considers the case of the executory bargain and concludes that, in some cases—particularly those involving breaches by consumers of contracts for standard items—the normal loss of bargain damages are too generous.]

CONCLUSION

. . .

Until recently, courts have tended either to apply the bargain principle to cases raising such problems, despite the difficulties this application presents, or to deal with these difficulties in covert and unsystematic ways. Over the past thirty years, however, a new paradigmatic principle—unconscionability—has emerged. This principle explains and justifies the limits that should be placed upon the bargain principle on the basis of the quality of a bargain.

Looking backward, the new paradigm enables us to reconstruct prior theory and phenomena by providing a general explanation for a wide variety of contract concepts that heretofore seemed distinct. So, for example, duress may now be seen as simply a special case of the exploitation of distress; undue influence may now be seen as simply a special case of unfair persuasion; and the prohibition against exploiting palpable unilateral mistake may now be seen as a specific norm of unconscionability. Similarly, the apparent anomaly of review for fairness in courts of equity and admiralty can be explained by the new paradigm, while guidelines can now be set for that review; and the doctrine of general incapacity might be reformulated to apply only when exploitation is present.

Looking forward, the paradigm must be articulated and extended through the development of more specific norms to guide the resolution of specific cases, provide affirmative relief to exploited parties, and channel the discretion of administrators and legislators. In accomplishing this task, it now appears that the distinction between procedural and substantive unconscionability, which may have served a useful purpose at an earlier stage, does not provide much help once the relatively obvious norms of uncon-scionability, such as unfair surprise, have been articulated. For example, it is both difficult and unpro-ductive to classify as exclusively either 'substantive' or 'procedural' the problems posed by the extraction of an unduly high price from a person who is in distress, lacks transactional capacity, or is price-ignorant. Development of more specific norms must instead proceed by the identification of classes of cases in which neither fairness nor efficiency supports the application of the bargain principle—an effort that can be guided in part by the reconstruction and extension of existing contract doctrines.

■ Gordley, 'Equality in Exchange' (1981)

60 California LR 1587, 1588–90, 1600, 1612–1610, 1622–1625

I. THE MEANING OF EQUALITY IN EXCHANGE

A The Aristotelian theory

Pre-nineteenth-century jurists and philosophers developed the doctrine of equality in exchange by drawing upon two different authorities. One was a theory of exchange proposed by Aristotle in his *Nichomachean Ethics*, the other was a Roman text in the *Corpus iuris civilis* of Justinian, which provided a legal remedy for those who sold land at less than half its just price. Before the Aristotelian theory was even known in Europe, the Roman text had been extended beyond sales of land to provide a general-ized remedy for any large disparity in the values exchanged, that is, for what the medieval jurists termed *laesio enormis*. Eventually, the Aristotelian theory was used to explain why this remedy was given. The remedy provided for *laesio enormis* will be discussed later in this Article. Our initial concern will be with the Aristotelian theory and the criticisms directed against it.

In the Fifth Book of the *Nichomachean Ethics*, Aristotle presents three ideas in quick succession. One is the distinction between distributive and commutative justice. The second is a principle that some jurists still say underlies the law of unjust enrichments that no one should be enriched at another's expense. The third is the distinction between contract or tort. Most lawyers still encounter all three ideas, although they do not think of them as closely related. For Aristotle, however, each idea followed logically on the heels of the other.

Distributive justice, according to Aristotle, 'is manifested in distributions of honor or money or other things that fall to be divided among those who have a share in the constitution.' Commutative justice 'plays a rectifying part in transactions between man and man.' Distributive justice follows a geometrical proportion. Each citizen receives a share of whatever there is to be divided. It is the mathematics of divid-ing a pie. Aristotle noted that there is no one correct principle for determining the share each person should receive. Rather, a particular society will adopt a principle consistent with its political regime. Democracies favor the principle that each citizen should receive an equal share. Aristocracies tend to divide goods according to 'excellence.' Even an illegitimate regime will have a characteristic principle. In an oligarchy, which Aristotle regarded as the corruption of an aristocracy, goods are divided according to the principle that 'them that has, gets': the mere possession of wealth and power is recognized as a claim to receive them.

Commutative justice, in contrast, follows an arithmetic proportion. It is concerned not with sharing resources, but with preserving each citizen's share. Therefore, the party who has lost resources to another has a claim for the amount necessary to restore his original position. It is the mathematics of addition and subtraction, of balancing accounts.

To paraphrase Aristotle only slightly, commutative justice operates on the principle that no one should gain by another's loss. This principle later made its way into Roman law in a famous passage of the *Corpus iuris:* 'By nature it is equitable that no one should be made richer by another's loss or injury'. The text eventually played a major role in developing the modern law of unjust enrichment. According to modern scholars, if the principle stated in this text was not taken directly from Aristotle, it was taken from a pool of classical ideas to which he had been a prime contributor.

Nevertheless, what Aristotle had in mind when he spoke of commutative justice was not unjust enrichment in the modern sense, but rather contract and tort. He distinguished two kinds of commutative justice: the 'voluntary,' which includes 'such transactions as sale, purchase, loan for consumption, pledging, loan for use, depositing, letting,' and the 'involuntary,' which includes such 'clandestine' acts as 'theft' and 'adultery' and such 'violent' acts as 'assault, imprisonment, murder, robbery with violence, mutilation, abuse, insult.' This distinction may be the linear ancestor of the one we draw between contract and tort. Our distinction ultimately derives from the Roman jurist Gaius, who divided obligations into the two classes, *contractus* and *delictus.* Some modern scholars believe that Gaius took the distinction from Aristotle. Before Gaius, other Roman jurists had discussed what we would call particular contracts and torts without drawing the general distinction.

Thus, for Aristotle, contract and tort were two different kinds of commutative justice, both subject to the principle that no one should become richer at another's expense. In tort, this principle requires that a person who has deprived another of his resources must compensate him by the amount necessary to restore his initial position. In contract, the principle requires that parties exchange performances of equal value. Aristotle's interpreters sometimes expressed this idea by saying that the exchange should impose the same burden on each of the parties.

. . .

b. Equality and the market price. One can see how the market price would preserve equality if the market price always returned the seller his costs, as the earlier writers thought it would normally or eventually, or as modern economists think it does in a long term equilibrium. In that event, an exchange would not make the seller any richer in purchasing power. Similarly, in a certain sense, the buyer would be made no poorer. He would have paid only the amount needed to produce the commodity. Moreoever, if prices were stable, he could always resell what he had purchased for precisely the amount he had paid for it (less the amount it had physically depreciated or the amount he had consumed). In these circumstances a party demanding a higher or lower price would be in the odd moral position of asking that another party transfer wealth to him.

Precisely because the market price would preserve an equality in purchasing power if it returned the seller his costs, it is hard to see how that price could preserve equality even when it returned the seller a greater or lesser amount, as the earlier writers knew it sometimes would. Some modern scholars have tried to get around the problem by assuming that the earlier writers equated the just price with the cost of production. More recent scholars are less willing to evade the problem. . . .

Whatever the earlier writers may have had in mind, the entire argument just sketched can be restated more precisely and more persuasively in terms of modern economics. Suppose it is true, as the reader was asked to grant earlier, that redistributions of wealth should be avoided, at least when they are not part of a program of redistribution set up by someone authorized to do so. Suppose next that the economy were actually in the long-run equilibrium state hypothesized by economists: prices would never change and producers would always recover their costs. In that event, contracts at the market price would not change the wealth of the parties in the sense of the purchasing power that each of them commands. Under these conditions, it is hard to see why a contract should be enforced at any other price than the market price since any such contract would change the distribution of purchasing power. And were we living in such a world where plane fares never rose or fell, and where peaches sold year in and year out for the same price, we would not easily be persuaded to regard a contract at a different price as anything other than an unjustified gain for one party and an unjustified loss for the other.

Does it matter then that we live in a world where prices do fluctuate? Suppose now that people know in advance that prices fluctuate, but not in which direction or by how much. If markets behave as economists say they do, the market price will discount for the risk. The price on one day will accurately reflect the odds that the price may be different on the next. If so, then, even though a seller may sometimes sell high, or a buyer may find himself richer for having bought when he did, their contracts will still be equal in the actuarial sense described earlier. As in the case of a fair bet, at the time a contract is made, one cannot say that it enriches either party at the other's expense, although it will have that effect in the future.

Presumably, a society wishing to avoid redistributions of wealth would prefer that contracts be equal in outcome and not merely actuarially. Such a society would therefore prevent price fluctuations entirely by freezing prices if it could do so without fear of causing greater evils. But the result, according to economists, would be to waste goods that would accumulate unsold or to ration goods among buyers according to some arbitrary principle such as the place they hold in line. To avoid these consequences, a society might compromise by allowing prices to fluctuate, thereby settling for an actuarial equality rather than a perfect equality in outcome. Nevertheless, there would still be no reason for enforcing contracts not made at the market price. If the market accurately discounts for the risk of price fluctuations, contracts at any other price will not be equal even in the actuarial sense. They will give one party an expected gain and the other an expected loss. Even if the market does not perfectly discount the risk, the market price will still be the best evidence of the actuarially fair price. The market price depends on the judgment of many buyers and sellers as to what future prices will be. In contrast, a contract price deviating from the market price was determined by only two parties, one of whom was acting under circumstances of ignorance or necessity that prevented him from taking advantage of the market.

Next, suppose that there are some risks that are not discounted in the market price because they are wholly unforeseen. It is admittedly rather difficult to distinguish this case from the last since the most unlikely events can be foreseen at some degree of probability. Still, suppose there are such risks and that because of them contracts at the market price are sometimes unequal even in the actuarial sense. The society must then ask itself again whether to tolerate the inequality to avoid greater evils or whether to remedy the inequality by freezing prices. If prices remain unfrozen, the society will have decided to accept the market price, whatever its inequalities, so that the market can clear. But there will still be no reason for enforcing contracts at other than the market price. Such contracts tend to cause further inequalities that there is no need to tolerate. Even if they do not—if, by happenstance, a seller who would otherwise suffer a loss due to wholly unforeseen risks meets a buyer who through ignorance or necessity can be prevailed upon to pay more than any other buyer is being charged—the contract still should not be enforced. If sellers generally are required to suffer a loss so that the market may clear, it would seem odd to exempt a particular seller simply because he happens to find some ignorant or necessitous person to make the sacrifice for him.

This line of argument parallels one recently advanced by Professor Eisenberg in defense of the American doctrine of unconscionability. Eisenberg asks what reasons a society might have for enforcing a contract at one price rather than another. He concludes that enforcement will find its 'strongest justification' when contracts are made at the market price and the economy is in a 'steady state.' Under these conditions, the price will be efficient, the same for all buyers and sellers, and sufficient to return the producer his costs. Nevertheless, if prices fluctuate so that producers do not always recover their costs, there will still be compelling reasons for enforcing contracts at the market price: that price will still be the same for all buyers and sellers, and it will still be the efficient price. Eisenberg then examines a range of situations, such as those involving distress and monopoly, in which contracts are made at other than a competitive market price; in each instance the reasons for enforcing them are less compelling or absent.

A difference between Eisenberg's argument and mine is our reason for believing that ideally the market price should return the seller his costs. Eisenberg argues that 'a promisee should usually be entitled, at a minimum, to recover an amount equal to his costs. . . . ' I have argued that a price that covers costs is both an ideal minimum and an ideal maximum because at that price the wealth of the parties remains constant. Consequently, my argument is open to an objection to which Eisenberg's is less vulnerable. At a price that covers costs, the 'wealth' of the parties remains the same only in the sense that the purchasing power of the assets they hold does not change. The personal satisfaction or benefit that they derive from the assets they hold obviously does change since the parties would not exchange unless each expected to derive more benefit from what he receives. In this sense, the 'wealth' of each party increases, and perhaps by different amounts. Thus, one might object that my argument ignores the change in wealth that must occur in any exchange. It ignores a basic problem that has concerned a great many writers: how the mutual benefits of exchange are to be divided.

[Gordley considers this and concludes that] . . . to the extent it is a problem at all, the problem of dividing the benefits of exchange is one of distributive justice rather than commutative justice. Even one who thought these benefits should be divided would have to do it by assigning citizens a certain amount of purchasing power, allowing them to trade, and then readjusting their shares of purchasing power until they approximated his ideal. The system of exchange itself should merely avoid random redistributions of purchasing power.

This issue has been discussed at length because it is central to the argument that an exchange can be unfair. If the seller had some moral or equitable claim to the benefits that exchange confers on the buyer, no exchange would be unfair as long as the buyer knew what he was receiving and what he was giving up in turn, since all such exchanges were presumably of some benefit to the buyer. The seller, however, has no such claim. Therefore, he should not be permitted to take a portion of this benefit even if the ignorance or necessity of the buyer permits him to dictate a price that does so. The earlier authors expressed this idea by saying that the seller could not increase the price because of the 'singular utility or necessity of the buyer.' Otherwise, they observed, one could charge the poor a higher price than the rich since the goods that enable the former to survive may be unimportant to the latter.

One of the nineteenth-century arguments can therefore be answered: the argument that one cannot speak of equality in exchange since value at the market price is irrelevant and value to the parties subjective and not discoverable without a psychological investigation into their motives. We have seen that the market price is not irrelevant to a society interested in avoiding purposeless or random redistributions of purchasing power. If prices were stable, contracts at the market price would return the seller his costs and purchasing power would not be redistributed. If prices are unstable, contracts at the market price may not be equal in outcome, but they still may be either equal in the actuarial sense or equal to the extent possible if worse evils are to be avoided. And if a society decides that such evils are more tolerable than the inequalities caused by exchange at the market price, the remedy is for public authorities to intervene and set a more equal price at which everyone must trade. In contrast, the personal value or benefit each party derives from the exchange is relevant only in that each party must receive such a benefit if they are to exchange advantageously. Neither can claim that the other party should share that benefit with him.

2. The second argument reconsidered: private autonomy in the law of contracts

[A] second nineteenth-century argument can now be answered more easily. According to this argument, the general principles of contract law bind the parties to what they have agreed. A court that interferes is ousting party autonomy by making itself judge of the wisdom or profitability of the bargain; moreover, if contracts are to be binding, the fact that the bargain was unwise or unprofitable cannot be a ground for relief.

This argument requires us to consider the role of party autonomy in contract formation. One very important role was mentioned earlier. Each party agrees to exchange because he believes he will receive something of greater value to him than what he is to give in return. Therefore, the exchange will benefit each party, at least in his own eyes, by comparison with no exchange at all. The decision by each party that the exchange will do so is a minimum condition for the exchange to occur; however, it is not the only decision that each party may need to make. A party must also decide whether he can receive a better deal by dickering, waiting, or going elsewhere. However advantageous an exchange may be in comparison with no exchange at all it will still be less advantageous than an exchange on better terms.

The nineteenth-century argument fails to distinguish between these two types of decisions. The argument applies with full force only to decisions of the first kind. As long as a party knows what he will receive and what he will give up, it is indeed his business to decide whether the one is worth more to him than the other. The 'wisdom' of the decision, whether he is buying dinner dishes or data processing equipment, depends on his aspirations and his circumstances, which will differ from one buyer to the next. He is in a unique position and, perhaps, the best position to judge. In any case, it is hard to imagine a law of contracts that does not, as a general principle, leave the 'wisdom' of that decision to the parties.

The decision as to whether the price offered is the best available is quite different. It is a decision that all potential buyers and sellers face whatever their aspirations and circumstances. A decision to buy bananas for more when they can be obtained for less will be unwise no matter who is buying them. Moreover, to decide wisely, one must know, not only about one's own needs, but about what others will do: what a particular party will offer if one dickers, what others will offer if one shops around, or what they will offer someday if one waits. Since these matters do not turn on the aspirations and circumstances of a particular party, they are not matters that he is uniquely qualified or perhaps even particularly well qualified to judge. Fortunately, this second decision is made for the parties whenever a definite market price is known to all and available to all. If so, dickering or bargaining over the price is pointless since only the market price will be acceptable to both parties. There is no point in shopping around since both parties know the price that other parties are offering. The only way either party could obtain a better price is by waiting for the market price to change. In the hypothetical world imagined earlier in which market prices never changed, even this alternative would not be open to them. The only real decision each party would have to make is a decision of the first type: whether what he receives at this price is worth more to him than what he gives. A party's autonomy to make this decision would be complete; his autonomy to make the second decision would be virtually nonexistent. If a party wishes to contract at all, there is only one price he can 'choose,' and he need not deliberate to find out what it is.

In the real world of fluctuating prices, there is the alternative of waiting for a better price. The existence of a definite market price, however, protects buyers and sellers against misjudging whether to wait. If the market accurately discounts the risk of price fluctuations, a party will not gain or lose in the actuarial sense, whether or not he waits. The contract will be no more unwise than any other contract that involves a fair gamble. Even if the market does not accurately discount the risk, it at least reflects the cumulative judgment of all buyers and sellers. Whether he waits or not, a party will have acted no more 'unwisely' than many others. In short, as long as there is a definite market price available to all, the parties hardly have the opportunity to exercise their judgment unwisely.

It is a mistake, then, to think that because it is up to each party whether to contract at a given price, it is therefore up to each party to decide at what price he will contract. . . .

The difficulty with the nineteenth-century argument, then, is that it does not distinguish between different kinds of autonomy which the law should value differently. The parties' decision to exchange or not at a given price ensures that any exchange they make will be beneficial in their eyes. In contrast, their ability to determine the price at which they exchange serves a useful purpose only in the imperfect markets described, and there the purpose is to encourage the parties to contract at the market price. In a more perfect market with a definite price, the parties would always exchange at that price, absent ignorance or necessity, unless one party wished to change the distribution of wealth in the other's favor by making him a gift. Where there is ignorance or necessity, a party may be induced to make what amounts to a gift even though he does not wish to change the distribution of wealth. Such an exercise of party autonomy has no value; nor is it even autonomous in the sense that decisions to give or to exchange at the market price are autonomous. It is not true, then, that there is only one kind of party autonomy that the law must always respect by holding the parties to what they agreed.

These two different types of autonomy were distinguished implicitly and automatically by Aristotle's definition of exchange. What was 'voluntary' about the 'voluntary' kind of commutative justice was not that the parties determined the price at which they would exchange. Rather, it was that the parties determined whether to exchange at the price that commutative justice required.

Eventually, the Aristotelian definition of exchange, and with it the implicit distinction between these two kinds of party autonomy, was grafted onto the Roman law of contracts. The Romans had never worked out the implications of Aristotle's definition. Instead, their contract law remained for the most part a law of particular contracts, each with its own particular rules. For example, they had a set of rules for lease, for partnership or *societas*, for gift or *donatio*, and for gratuitous contracts of loan, bailment, and agency known as *mutuum, commodatum, depositum*, and *mandatum*. They classified these contracts, not according to whether they fit the Aristotelian definition of voluntary commutative justice, but according to the way in which they became binding under Roman law. Sale, lease, partnership, and gratuitous agency, for example, were all classed as contracts *consensu* since they became binding on consent; gratuitous loans and bailments were contracts *re* since they were only binding when the object loaned or bailed was actually delivered.

In the thirteenth century, when translations of the *Ethics* first became available in the West, an effort began to apply the Aristotelian definition to Roman contract law. Philosophers and theologians such as Thomas Aquinas distinguished between exchanges based on commutative justice and gratuitous arrangements based on the Aristotelian virtue of 'liberality,' which leads a person to make gifts. They then tried to place the Roman contracts in one category or the other. By the fourteenth century, this enterprise seems to have influenced leading jurists as well. An example is the formulation of the doctrine of *causa*, which identified two reasons for giving an agreement legal recognition: because it was made to receive something in return, or because it was made out of 'liberality.' By the sixteenth and seventeenth centuries, jurists were developing systems to classify the Roman contracts according to the type of *causa* for which they were made.

An example is the system of Hugo Grotius. He defines a contract as a kind of act advantageous to another. Such acts could be either gratuitous or reciprocal. Gratuitous acts could be purely gratuitous, like the Roman *donatio*, or they could involve an obligation on the part of the person benefited, like the Roman contracts of gratuitous bailment or agency. Reciprocal acts could be exchanges like sale or lease, or poolings of interests like *societas* or partnership. In either case, they required equality. In an exchange, the things traded had to be equal in value; in a partnership, the share each partner took out had to be equal to the share he put in. As Professor Watson has noted, Grotius' system was a most un-Roman way to distinguish among the Roman contracts.

Although Grotius' scheme differed in important respects from those of other jurists, a common feature of such systems was the distinction between those contracts in which something was sought in return, and which therefore required equality, and those in which some benefit was liberally conferred. Once this distinction was drawn, the distinction between the two types of party autonomy described earlier followed implicitly. If an exchange requires equality, then the parties to an exchange are free to decide whether to contract at a fair price, but they are not free to decide at what price they will contract. At any price other than the market price, the contract enriches one party at the expense of the other, a result that is not permissible unless the disadvantaged party actually intends, not merely to exchange, but to make a gift. As Grotius observed: 'Nor is it enough for anyone to say that what a party has promised beyond equality should be regarded as a gift. For such is not the intention of the contracting parties, and should not be presumed to be, unless it appear.'

These earlier ways of defining contract are very different from those that became popular with the rise of the 'will theories' of the nineteenth century. These earlier definitions start by identifying the goals that contracts are supposed to enable the parties to accomplish. The sorts of private autonomy that the law will respect then follow from these goals. In contrast, nineteenth-century definitions of contract tend to begin with the idea of autonomy itself. Germans typically defined contract by speaking of 'mani-festations of will.' Frenchmen such as Demolombe explained that 'consent is the contract itself.' Americans and Englishmen defined contract in terms of promise, will, or consent. The nineteenth-century innovation was not the idea that the parties must consent in order to be bound. Continental jurists such as Grotius had been saying for centuries that contracts are formed by promises or expressions of will, just as Aristotle had said that exchange must be 'voluntary.' The innovation, as Simpson has pointed out, was to regard consent as a sort of *Grundnorm* from which the basic rules of contract law should be derived. The business of contract law was to see whether an agreement had been made and, if so, to enforce it according to its terms, subject to whatever extra requirements the law might impose.

Once that step was taken, any requirement that the parties must contract at a certain price or on certain terms seemed to be both an interference with the freedom of contract and a violation of the general principles of contract law. The reason was that freedom of contract and the general principles of contract law were now defined without reference to the goals that contract law was to enable the parties to pursue. We can now see some reasons why that was not a sensible way to look at either con-tract law or party autonomy.

First, unless enforcement of promises is considered an end in itself, one must ask to what end they are being enforced. To ask that question is to ask, as the earlier jurists did, about the kind of arrangement the parties are making and the purpose which that arrangement serves in society. If mutually beneficial exchanges serve a useful purpose and random redistributions of wealth do not, then the society should enforce transactions that enable the parties to do the one and not the other.

Furthermore, if one does define party autonomy or freedom of contract *in vacuo*, one cannot even claim to be better protecting party autonomy. Enforcing a contract at other than the market price protects the freedom of one party to profit from the ignorance or necessity of the other, but sacrifices the freedom the other party would enjoy in a normal well-functioning market. Contract law cannot protect freedom in the abstract; rather, it must determine what kind of freedom it will protect. To do so, it must ask what goals each party should be free to pursue. If there are reasons why a party should be free to exchange but should not be free to redistribute wealth in his own favor, then the law should insist that he exchange without redistributing. To put it another way, exchange should require equality. *Ut dicit Aristoteles*.

...

NOTE

The three views put forward by Nozick, Eisenberg and Gordley are considered by Collins [1992] Current Legal Problems 67. The question of whether and why the law should refuse to enforce contracts that are substantively unfair is considered by Smith. He argues that the 'most persuasive reason ... is that contracts at non-normal prices may disrupt planning and hence our ability to lead self-directed, autonomous lives'.

■ **Smith, 'In Defence of Substantive Unfairness'** (1996)
112 LQR 138, 145, 149–152

Contract law is, in Hart's terminology, a power-conferring legal doctrine. [Hart, *The Concept of Law* (1961) at pp 27–38.] Like the law regarding wills, trusts and marriages, its underlying justification is that it helps people do things they could not do otherwise or not do as easily. Thus it is the good of con-tracting, rather than the wrong of contract breaking, that is the foundation of contract law. This view of contract law has important implications for the role of the courts in assessing contractual validity. In particular, it means that refusing to enforce a procedurally valid contract does not condone infringements of individual liberty. It is merely a refusal to *help* the parties to do certain things.

The advocate of substantive fairness must still explain why substantively unfair contracts are bad. The enforcement of contracts is presumably a good thing generally, so some reason for non-enforcement must be provided. But the reason need not be along the lines that one of the parties coerced, defrauded, or manipulated the other party (though these are good reasons). All that needs to be shown, broadly speaking, is that a substantively unfair contract is not the sort of contract the law should promote. This is an easier standard to meet than the wrongfulness standard used in duress, fraud and so on. The difference is the same as the difference between deciding what sorts of activities the state should prohibit, or at least deter, and deciding what sorts of activities the state should subsidise. We may be uncertain, for example, whether prostitution should be prohibited, yet be reasonably confident that brothels should not be subsidised. Contract law—which is funded from tax revenue—subsidises certain sorts of activities.

. . .

Autonomy and basic needs

One reason for not enforcing a contract is that it does not support a valuable or worthwhile activity. The rules regarding so-called immoral or illegal contracts, such as contracts to sell babies and contracts of self-enslavement, are most naturally defended (insofar as they can be defended) on this basis. The problem with substantively unfair contracts is different. A substantively unfair contract may support a perfectly worthwhile endeavour. Yet there is a connection between substantive fairness and 'non-valuable' contracts. The underlying justification for not enforcing non-valuable contracts is that the state should only lend a hand to endeavours that help individuals to achieve well-being and thus to realize fulfilling lives. Worthless activities, even if freely chosen, do not contribute to well-being. [See Raz, *The Morality of Freedom* (1986), Chap. 14.] Contract prices can affect contracting parties' abilities to achieve fulfilling lives. One explanation of how this can happen draws on the importance, for well-being, of leading an autonomous, self-directed, life and, more specifically, on the importance of having a threshold level of material wealth. It is not necessary to be rich to lead an autonomous life, but it is necessary to have one's basic physical needs met. Individuals whose every choice is dictated by the need to survive cannot lead autonomous lives. They are unable to direct their lives in any meaningful sense. A contract at abnormal prices can leave a contracting party in this position. If the magnitude of the deviation is severe enough, the wealth of the losing party may be reduced to less than the threshold level.

The problem with contracts that leave contracting parties in poverty is significant and helps to explain why some contracts at abnormal prices appear so repugnant. But, again, it is not a problem of substantive unfairness. Contracts which leave a party in poverty are like contracts of self-enslavement. They are bad, but they are not unfair (or at least only coincidentally unfair). Fairness is a relational concept: if someone has been treated unfairly, someone else has been treated differently. Yet in explaining why a contract that leaves someone in poverty is bad the situation of the other party to the contract is irrelevant. All we need to know is that one party has been left destitute. The same is true of contracts of self-enslavement: all we need to know to condemn such contracts is that someone has been made a slave. Thus, while some unfair contracts may be objectionable because they leave one of the parties in a state of poverty, the substantive unfairness of such contracts is not the reason for the objection.

Autonomy and planning

The final reason for caring about contract prices is also founded on the importance, for achieving well-being, of living an autonomous life. More specifically, it is founded on the importance of being able to plan and control one's life. It is here, I suggest, that the key to understanding the value and meaning of substantive fairness is found. The problem with substantively unfair contracts is that they make it more difficult to direct our lives.

An autonomous life, in the sense I use this phrase, requires more than freedom from coercion. Autonomy is fundamentally a matter of being able to direct one's life: we lead autonomous lives, broadly speaking, when we direct our lives to a significant degree. Autonomous individuals need not live their lives according to rigid patterns, but they must have a reasonable ability to shape and plan their lives. Contract law helps us to lead autonomous lives by helping us do this autonomously. It increases our options and lets us decide what goals to pursue. The enforcement of contracts at abnormal prices, however, can make it more difficult to lead an autonomous life. Contracts at abnormal prices upset the material foundations upon which plans and aspirations are built. Rich or poor, we plan and shape our lives upon assumptions and expectations about our purchasing power. Contracts at abnormal prices upset plans and, more generally, individuals' abilities to control and direct their lives.

A concern for the way that shifts in purchasing power can upset planning is found in many other features of our legal system. The most obvious—and important—example is 'the rule of law'. The requirement that laws be clear, stable, prospective and so on protects the ability of individuals to plan their lives. It is the importance of planning that explains why tax laws, for example, should meet this requirement no matter how justifiable they are in substance. A contract at an abnormal price is similar to an unannounced change in tax policy. It shifts purchasing power, leaving the losing party worse-off than before the contract, and thereby making it more difficult for that party to achieve an autonomous, that is, self-directed, life. This is true regardless of the justice of the prior distribution of resources. Of course it is not possible or desirable to protect individuals from all uncertainty. But avoidable, undesired, uncertainty should not be promoted by the law.

The 'planning' justification supports a normal price standard for assessing contracts. Plans are built upon normal prices. To be sure, courts could ensure that plans were never upset by imposing fixed prices for all goods. This solution is undesirable because contracting parties are normally better able than courts to set prices at mutually attractive levels. Setting fixed prices would make contracting far less appealing, thus limiting the good that contracting can achieve.

The importance of planning and the relation between shifts in purchasing power and planning explain why courts should be concerned about contracts at abnormal prices. But these considerations do not apply equally to all contracts at abnormal prices. First, not all abnormal price contracts upset planning. In particular, contracts where either (1) the losing party was making a gift, (2) the losing party did not care about price, or (3) the losing party was mistaken as to the nature and hence value of the good he or she was selling (for example, not realising that the painting offered was a Rembrandt) do not upset the losing party's ability to plan. In the first and third situation the losing party's expectations were not upset and in the second case the losing party had no expectations. Such contracts should therefore be enforced...

The next extract in this chapter argues that, although libertarian writers argue for limited controls over the kinds of control over contracting behaviour that the law should impose (eg, that interference should be limited to fraud or duress), there is no logical stopping place.

■ Kronman, 'Contract Law and Distributive Justice' (1980)
89 Yale LJ 472, 477–483

But when is an agreement voluntary? For a libertarian, committed to the notion that all voluntary agreements must be enforced, the widest view of voluntariness is almost surely unacceptable. Suppose that I sign a contract to sell my house for $5,000 after being physically threatened by the buyer. It is possible to characterize my agreements as voluntary in one sense: after considering the alternatives, I have concluded that my self-interest is best served by signing and have deliberately implemented a perfectly rational decision by doing precisely that. Described in this general way, my agreement to sell appears in the same light that it would if, for example, I had not been threatened but signed the contract because I thought $5,000 a good price for the house. Under this description, however, my act of signing will be involuntary only if it is not motivated by a decision of any sort at all on my part. Such would be the case, for example, if the purchaser forcibly grabbed my hand and guided it over the document himself, or commanded me to sign the contract while I was in an hypnotic state.

There is, of course, nothing logically absurd about drawing the line between voluntary and involuntary agreements at this point, but I doubt most libertarians would wish to do so. Among other things, defining voluntariness in this way conflicts with deeply entrenched notions of moral responsibility. In assessing the voluntariness of an agreement, it is not enough merely to determine that the agreement was motivated by a deliberate decision of some sort; we also want to know something about the circumstances under which it was given. But if this is true, the problem of drawing a line between agreements that are voluntary and agreements that are not—a problem the libertarian must confront if the idea of voluntary exchange is to have any meaning at all—can be understood as the problem of specifying the conditions that must be present before we will consider an agreement to have been voluntarily concluded. Put differently, unless the libertarian is prepared to accept a very broad concept of voluntariness, which equates voluntary agreement with rational choice, he must specify the various circumstances under which even a deliberately given, rational agreement will be held to have been coerced.

B. Advantage-Taking

Whenever a promisor complains that his agreement was coerced and therefore ought not to be enforced, he should be understood as claiming that the agreement was given under circumstances that rendered it involuntary. In making an argument of this sort, a promisor may point to many different circumstances or conditions: he may say, for example that his agreement was involuntary because he lacked the mental and emotional capacities required to appreciate its consequences; or a promisor may claim that he was threatened or deceived by the other party, or that his agreement was given at a time he was hard-pressed for cash and therefore had no choice but to accept the terms proposed by the promisee; or a promisor may assert that his agreement was involuntary because he, unlike the other party, was ignorant of certain facts which, if known at the time of contracting, would have led him to make a different agreement or no agreement at all; or he may say that the other party had a monopoly of some scarce resource—the only water hole or the best cow or the strongest shoulders in town—a monopoly which enabled him to dictate terms of sale to the promisor, making their agreement what is sometimes called a 'contract of adhesion.'

In some of these cases, the circumstances allegedly making the promisor's agreement involuntary is an incapacity of the promisor himself—his insanity, youth, ignorance or impecuniousness. In others, the involuntariness of the promisor's agreement is attributable to an act by the other party—a fraudulent deception or threat of physical harm. Finally, in some cases, it is the other party's monopolization of a scarce resource and the market power he enjoys as a result which (it is claimed) renders the promisor's agreement involuntary. In each case, however, the promisor is asserting that his agreement, although deliberately given, lacked voluntariness because of the circumstances under which it was made—circumstances that in one way or another restricted his range of alternatives to a point where the promisor's choice could be said to be free in name only.

The problem, of course, is to determine when the circumstances under which an agreement is given deprive it of its voluntariness in this sense. In my view, this problem is equivalent to another—the problem of determining which of the many forms of advantage-taking possible in exchange relationships are compatible with the libertarian conception of individual freedom. The latter way of stating the problem may appear to raise new and distinct issues but in fact it does not. In each of the hypothetical cases considered above, the promisee enjoys an advantage of some sort which he has attempted to exploit for his own benefit. The advantage may consist in his superior information, intellect, or judgment, in the monopoly he enjoys with regard to a particular resource, or in his possession of a powerful instrument of violence or a gift for deception. In each of these cases, the fundamental question is whether the promisee should be permitted to exploit his advantage to the detriment of the other party, or whether permitting him to do so will deprive the other party of the freedom that is necessary, from a libertarian point of view, to make his promise truly involuntary and therefore binding.

The term 'advantage-taking' is often used in a pejorative fashion, to refer to conduct we find morally objectionable or think the law should disallow. I mean the term to be understood in a broader sense, however, as including even those methods of gain the law allows and morality accepts (or perhaps even approves). In this broad sense, there is advantage-taking in every contractual exchange. Indeed, in mutually advantageous exchanges, there is advantage-taking by both parties. Suppose I have a cow you want, and you have a horse I want, and we agree to exchange our animals. The fact that you want my cow gives me an advantage I can exploit by insisting that you give me your horse in return. Your ownership of the horse gives you a symmetrical advantage over me. Each of us exploits the advantage we possess and—in this transaction at least—are both made better off as a result. This might seem to make my broad conception of advantage-taking empty or trivial. There is, however, an important reason for using the term in the unconventionally broad way that I do. By using the term to refer to *all* types of advantage-taking—those we tolerate as well as those we do not—attention is focused more sharply on the need to explain why the illicit methods of gain for which we normally reserve the term are thought to be objectionable.

In order to give meaningful content to the idea of voluntary exchange, a libertarian theory of contract law must provide an explanation of precisely this sort. However, although some principle or rule is needed as a basis for deciding which forms of advantage-taking should be allowed and which should not be, it is unclear what this principle or rule might be. Suppose, for example, that my neighbor threatens to shoot me unless I agree to buy his house. If there is one thing which must be treated as a condition for voluntary exchange, it is the absence of direct physical compulsion of the sort involved in this first case. But suppose that instead of threatening me with physical harm, the seller merely lies to me about the house—he tells me, for example, that water pipes inaccessibly buried beneath the basement are copper when in fact he knows them to be made of iron, an inferior material. Ought such advantage-taking be allowed? While it is possible to justify advantage-taking of this sort on the grounds that only physical coercion should be disallowed, there is no good reason for making *this* distinction the decisive one. Moreover, even if one fastens on the physical nature of the advantage-taking act, explicit misrepresentation can be characterized by saying that the misrepresentation is communicated by soundwaves which stimulate an auditory response in the listener which in turn provokes a neural change that causes him to sign the contract. This may be fanciful, but it suggests that with enough imagination any form of advantage-taking can be characterized as a physical intrusion, and the question of when such a characterization is appropriate cannot be answered by simply repeating that it is the physical nature of the act which makes it objectionable.

At this point, many will be tempted to acknowledge explicit misrepresentation as an illegitimate form of advantage-taking, but insist that the line be drawn there—limiting the conditions necessary for voluntary exchange to two (absense of physical coercion and fraud). Suppose, however, that the seller makes no threats and tells no lies, but does say things that, although true, are meant to encourage me to draw a false conclusion about the condition of the house and to inspect the premises less carefully than I might otherwise. (The seller tells me, for example, that the house has been inspected by an exterminator from the Acme Termite Company every six months for the last ten years, which is true, but neglects to inform me that during his last visit the exterminator discovered a termite infestation which the seller has failed to cure.) But telling me only certain things about the house, and not others, the seller intends to throw me off the track and thereby take advantage of my ignorance and naiveté. The same is true if he tells me nothing at all, but simply fails to reveal a defect he knows I am unaware of—a case of pure nondisclosure.

Should this last form of advantage-taking be allowed? At this point, undoubtedly, many will be inclined to say I have only myself to blame for drawing an incorrect inference from the seller's truthful representations and for failing to take precautionary measures such as having the house inspected by an expert. But why is this a good reason for holding me to my bargain here, but not in the previous cases as well? I can, for example, protect myself against the risk that I will be forced to sign a contract at gunpoint by hiring a bodyguard to accompany me wherever I go; and I can protect myself against the danger of explicit misrepresentation by requiring the other party to take a lie detector test or, more simply, by insisting that he warrant the house to be free of pests or any other possible defect that happens to concern me. Why isn't my failure to protect myself in these cases a good reason for enforcing the agreement I have made?

In attempting to sort out these various forms of advantage-taking, a number of distinctions suggest themselves—for example, the distinction between physical and non-physical advantage-taking, or between those forms of advantage-taking that can be prevented by the victim and those that cannot. None, however, provides a principled basis for determining which forms of advantage-taking ought to be allowed. Each can be interpreted in different ways, yielding different results, and the distinctions themselves provide no guidance in deciding which of the competing interpretations is the right one. An independent principle of some sort is required to detemine the scope and relevance of these distinctions, and consequently it is that principle, whatever it might be, rather than the distinctions themselves that explains why we ought to allow some forms of advantage-taking but not others.

[Kronman goes on to discuss a principle he terms 'Paretianism'. He states (p 488):]

Paretianism permits only those forms of advantage-taking that work to the benefit of all concerned, a requirement rooted in the conviction that every person has an equal right not to have his own welfare reduced for the sole purpose of increasing someone else's.

[This would, for instance, justify a rule allowing a buyer not to disclose the fact that there is oil under the seller's land, since the effect would be to lower oil prices generally, which would also benefit sellers as a class.

He then discusses the use of contract law as a means of redistributing wealth. He concludes (at pp 510–511):]

If one believes it is morally acceptable for the state to forcibly redistribute wealth from one group to another, the only question that remains is how the redistribution should be accomplished. I have described two methods of redistributing wealth, taxation and the regulatory control of private transactions, and have argued that the choice between them ought to be made on the basis of contextual considerations that are likely to vary from one situation to the next.

Both methods may be more or less neutral in effect and both are costly to administer. Each necessarily imposes limitations on individual liberty and, on occasion, has incentive effects that make its adoption irrational. These are considerations we must always keep in view in choosing between the two methods, but they do not invariably dictate the same choice: instead, they are likely to suggest that sometimes one method, sometimes the other, most often, perhaps, a mix of the two, is the best way of achieving whatever distributional goal we have set for ourselves. I have attempted to show (admittedly, in a casual way) that a blanket preference for taxation is unwarranted, and that contractual regulation will on occasion be the least intrusive and most efficient way of redistributing wealth to those who have a legitimate claim to a larger share of society's resources. If I am right in thinking this is so, distributive considerations should be permitted to influence our choice of contract rules, as circumstances dictate, and should not be flatly excluded from the domain of private exchange for what are alleged to be principled reasons.

I would like to conclude by returning briefly to the problem of liberty and fairness. I have argued that distributive fairness can only be achieved, by taxation or contractual regulation, at some sacrifice in individual liberty. This claim reflects what I believe is the core of truth in Nozick's assertion that the implementation of any patterned conception of justice is bound to require interference in people's lives. As I have suggested, however, the conflict between these values is not itself a reason for abandoning liberalism and embracing libertarianism, nor is it a reason for endorsing a non-distributive conception of contract law. But the conflict does present any liberal theory with a central and difficult challenge—the challenge of elaborating a reasoned basis for reconciling the claims of liberty and fairness, without abandoning either. The measure of success achieved by a liberal theory of society will depend, in large part, upon the extent to which it is able to avoid arbitrariness at just this point.

NOTE

Kronman's theory is criticised by Kramer and Simmonds [1996] CLJ 358.

Some writers argue that the pursuit of 'freedom of contract' leaves so much room for manoeuvre that it is 'incoherent'.

■ **Kennedy, 'Distributive and Paternalist Motives in Contract and Tort Law'** (1982)
41 Maryland LR 563, 580–583

3. *The Critique of Freedom of Contract as Incoherent and Therefore Incapable of Determining Outcomes*—The real problem with freedom of contract is that neither its principles, nor its principles supplemented by common moral understanding, nor its principles supplemented by historical practice, are definite enough to tell the decision maker what to do when asked to change or even just to elaborate the existing law of agreements. This is not to say the principles or the actual elaborated body of law have *no* meaning and no influence. Of course they have both. But of course there are also gaps, conflicts, and ambiguities, and in an area like that of the law of agreements the parties themselves will often have a motive for drafting themselves into these areas of uncertainty.

Confronted with a choice, the decision maker will have available two sets of stereotypical policy arguments. One 'altruist' set of arguments suggests that he should resolve the gap, conflict, or ambiguity by requiring a party who injures the other to pay compensation, and also that he should allow a liberal law of excuse when the injuring party claims to be somehow not really responsible. The other 'individualist' set of arguments emphasizes that the injured party should have looked out for himself, rather than demanding that the other renounce freedom of action, and that the party seeking excuse should have avoided binding himself to obligations he couldn't fulfill.

The arguments on each side take different forms—some are utilitarian, others appeal to rights or fairness, still others work by evoking stylized images of the social world, or by appealing to common moral sentiments, like self-sacrifice and self-reliance. Because the arguments are symmetrical, few in number, and repeated endlessly in different legal contexts, the legally sophisticated decision maker is unlikely to see them as *in themselves* powerful determinants of his own views about proper outcomes.

The experience of gaps, conflicts, and ambiguities within the institution of freedom of contract, and of the availability of two rhetorical modes for arguing about proper resolution of such situations, puts in question the whole structure of rules. Our decision maker has the power to modify the law of agreements as well as to specify it where there is doubt. The same problem of being 'unmoored' that exists when all agree the case is one of first impression exists as well whenever someone asks him to look at a *settled* rule as open to question and objection. There will be arguments in favor of changing the status quo in the direction of more altruism, and others in favor of restricting the range of duty to give actors more freedom. The system as a whole is radically undetermined, at least when viewed as the product of a rational decision process rather than of the brute facts of economic or social or political power.

We have seen already that through the constitutive exceptions for fraud, duress, incapacity and 'no intent to be bound,' the law of freedom of contract claimed to resolve basic issues of distribution and paternalism. Yet these constitutive exceptions refer ultimately to the abstract notion of voluntariness or freedom, which is among the most manipulable and internally contradictory in the legal repertoire. The historical treatment of the issues has produced a mass of conflicting precedents and ambiguous pseudo-resolutions. The flow of social and technological development means that new cases arise regularly, and the new cases may be very important in a practical way even if they seem to be about mere details of the law. It follows that even if he accepts without question that he should put into effect the distributive and paternalist outcome mandated by freedom of contract, the decision maker cannot do so, because the mandate is just too vague.

For example, without doing violence to the notion of voluntariness as it has been worked out in the law, the decision maker could adopt a hard-nosed, self-reliant, individualist posture that shrinks the defenses of fraud and duress almost to nothing. At the other extreme, he could require the slightly stronger or slightly better-informed party to give away all his advantage if he doesn't want to see the agreement invalidated when he tries to enforce it later. If we cut back the rules far enough, we would arrive at something like the state of nature—legalized theft. If we extended them far enough, we would jeopardize the enforceability of the whole range of bargains that define a mixed capitalist economy (capital/labor, business/consumer, and small/large business deals). In either extreme case, we would have departed from freedom of contract—the concept has some meaning and imposes some loose limits. But staying well within those limits, the decision maker's choices in the definition of voluntariness can have substantial distributive effect.

Take the case of fraud. When two parties are bargaining over the distribution of a transaction surplus, information is a crucial element of power, particularly information about the real properties of the commodity in question or about market circumstances affecting its value to others than the two involved. Suppose you know, but the buyer does not know, that the war has ended so that the value of your merchandise is almost certain to fall precipitously as peacetime trade is restored. Do you have to tell the other about the peace treaty? If so, you'll make less from the deal, and he'll make more, than if you could keep silent. Suppose the other party asks you outright if you have any news. Can you keep silent? Evade? Can you put out an advertisement quoting the war-time price 'because of current conditions,' when you know those conditions have ceased to exist?

One way to understand this issue is in terms of the extent of private property in information. As we push the law of fraud from caveat emptor to liability for concealment, then to liability for negligent failure to disclose, to liability for non-negligent failure to disclose and finally to a duty to generate the information as well as to share it, we are 'socializing' a resource. The result will be to reduce the bargaining power of one party vis-à-vis the other, and to change the distribution of transaction surplus between them. This will be the case whether or not the market is competitive. When we make sellers, for example, reveal information detrimental to their position, we reduce the demand for the product at any given price. As a result of having the new information, some people won't transact at all. Those who do transact will pay less now that they know more. All buyers regard themselves as better off with the information than they would be without it. Their new knowledge brings about a price reduction that directly reduces the welfare of sellers.

The decision maker might resolve issues of this kind without reference to the distributive consequences. He could try to determine, for example, the intrinsic fairness or morality of withholding information, without looking at the division of transaction surplus between the parties. Or he could do an analysis of property rights in information based on a theory of the 'original position' rather than on concern about the particular parties before him. There would be nothing irrational about such an approach. And it would be no more and no less consistent with freedom of contract than to undertake a careful analysis in terms of distributive objectives each time a rule came up for consideration. The demise of freedom of contract as a powerful, operative determinant of legal outcomes does not require the decision maker to embrace distributive motives. It merely permits him to do so without appearing to violate a basic institutional arrangement. The supposedly basic arrangement no longer tells him what to do one way or another.

This development has rendered obsolete the old debate between those who adored and those who abhorred the 'strict logic' of free contract. The social or collective principle that the opponents put forward as an alternative to contract turns out to have been well established *within* contract from the very beginning. It is possible, for example, to argue on the most technical grounds for strict scrutiny of the voluntariness of consumer agreements, and for compulsory terms and set prices wherever voluntariness is in doubt. If one takes this approach seriously, there is little of the reformers' program that can't be restated as the implementation of freedom of contract, rather than its displacement by a new regime.

NOTE

Distributional questions involve looking at the fairness of the contract as a whole. We will see that 'fairness' doctrines of general contract law sometimes do this (eg undue influence, Chapter 35, and the various doctrines that seem to be used against other forms of possible unconscionability (Chapter 36). Other rules affect only particular types of harsh clause, leaving the consideration unregulated. This is true of the rules against unfair exclusion clauses (Chapter 39) and unfair terms in consumer contracts (Chapter 40). Thus it has been pointed out by Collins (*Law of Contract*, 4th edn, 2003, p 284) that the latter type of rules cannot clearly be tied to distributional aims. There are, however, some contracts that are regulated as a whole by statute: for instance, if both the terms and rent of a tenancy are controlled to protect the tenant. On such controls, see Chapter 41, and on the justification of such distributional aims, the extract from Kronman, 'Paternalism and the law of contracts' on p 1061.

CHAPTER THIRTY-ONE

TRANSFORMATION THESIS

In Chapter 3, we saw that Collins claims that contract law has undergone a transformation (see p 66). What are the values that underlie the new conception of the social market for which he argues?

■ **Collins, *The Law of Contract*** (4th edn, 2003)
pp 30–35

...Another way in which to make the same point is to interpret the modern law of contract as not regarding the market merely as a source of preference satisfaction, but as an opportunity to augment and contribute to the sense of 'meaning' of a person's life. The purchase of a house, for example, although certainly sharing a dimension of preference satisfaction, will often mean so much more to an individual, for it offers security, a home and a base from which the rest of life may be organized. Similarly, the entry into a contract of employment will often mean more than simply the opportunity to earn cash for purchasing goods; it marks the entry into a career, the acquisition of status, and an opportunity to gain dignity and respect. To understand the realm of the market order merely in terms of preference satisfaction, as the sophisticated economic models tend to do, seriously misunderstands the significance of many market transactions.

When contracts have these qualities—of contributing in important ways to the sense of meaning in a person's life—the modern law of contract responds by securing that person's reasonable expectations. The concept of the social market appreciates how the market must be channeled and controlled to preserve its quality as an opportunity for individual aspiration. To perform this function so that the law can reflect in its standards the different satisfactions which may be derived from economic transactions, the unity of the law of contract must be sacrificed. Each type of transaction must be governed by its own distinctive standards, which seek to preserve and enhance the opportunities afforded by that type of transaction for the establishment of meaning.

(a) Unjustifiable domination

One derivation from this more complex notion of liberty or autonomy concerns the power relations developed through contractual relations. Under the principles of the justice of exchange, with its idol of freedom of contract, the potentialities of ownership and knowledge can be realized into oppressive forms of domination to the extent that lawyers can devise complex organizational structures in the form of exchange relations. The main constraint upon the facility for domination lies in the limits of one's ability to persuade others to bind themselves by way of contract. But here the discipline of economic necessity operates to provide compelling inducements to contract. Since the principal source of wealth lies in the market in the form of wages and profits, few can afford to stay aloof. Consequently, the law of contract lies at the intersection of the market and state power, and it uses the coercion of the latter to reinforce the discipline of the former.

One response to this risk of domination through contract is to limit freedom of contract to prevent persons from making such binding commitments. In some instances contractual rights will be superseded by a statutory framework of rights. For example, under English law an employee is granted a statutory right to challenge unfair dismissal from employment, which circumscribes the power of management to coerce the worker, and this right cannot normally be given up by contractual agreement. Although these rules still permit the individual to choose his occupation unfettered by law, they ensure that any choice will not be one which in effect establishes an unjustifiable level of subordination. In other instances mandatory terms shape the reciprocal obligations of the parties. Indeed, with little exaggeration, we can say that in most standard types of contracts made by ordinary persons, apart from the price, the parties have little choice over the terms of the agreement. The law adopts a number of model contracts, such as in purchases, loans, employment and leases, and describes a pattern for these economic relations which is imposed by a set of compulsory terms. For example, the seller of goods to a consumer must guarantee their satisfactory quality and fitness for their normal purpose, and any attempt to limit or qualify this guarantee in the terms of the contract will be void. Although businesses still enjoy a greater measure of freedom when contracting amongst themselves, even here the courts have powers to control unreasonable terms inserted in standard form contracts, and through interpretation of the terms of the contracts the courts may more subtly ensure conformity with unarticulated model agreements.

Another way in which to counter domination through contracts is to introduce a more substantive conception of equality. Although an ordinary consumer and a large business such as a retail chain store enjoy the formal equality to own property and enter bargains, it is clear that a business can often call upon much greater technical knowledge and legal expertise in order to secure favourable transactions. These disparities become particularly noticeable in complex transactions, as where the consumer requires a credit arrangement or a loan in order to complete the purchase, or when the item purchases involves complex technology as in the case of a car or electrical goods. But disparities appear in even a simple purchase of a can of beans at the supermarket, where the business is likely to have a much better understanding of the quality of the goods and the exact contents of the tin, which may include, besides the beans, various sauces, preservatives, colourings and so forth. The modern law recognizes these differentials in knowledge and expertise by introducing measures of consumer protection, and in so doing drops the presumption that citizens enter the market on equal terms. The credit arrangement must follow a prescribed explanatory form and cannot be extortionate; the seller of the car or electrical appliance must guarantee its quality, and the manufacturer will be liable for any injury caused to the purchaser; and the contents of the can of beans must be clearly labeled. The modern law replaces the commitment to formal equality by a recognition that each person enters the market from a different situation, and that to ignore those differences in knowledge, expertise, needs and command over resources is not to treat people equally but to treat unlike cases alike.

Behind these responses to unjustifiable domination lies a perception that the traditional separation between public and private spheres has become inadequate. Under the classical law, problems of power and domination were regarded as problems presented exclusively by the state. The role of public law was to combat state power by subjecting government bodies to controls over the exercise of discretionary power. Once it is recognised that similar problems of power arise in the context of contractual relations, especially those contracts which establish organizations such as firms, trade unions and trade associations, the case for extending controls over discretionary power to such private relations becomes pressing. We therefore discover the courts and the legislature inserting rules into such organizations which require them to follow fair procedures, to exercise discretion rationally and for lawful purposes, and to respect the rights of individuals. In other words, concepts and values formerly present exclusively in public law are applied to market relations where the contracts establish the potential for domination.

(b) Fairness of the exchange

A second derivation from this complex notion of liberty concerns the fairness of the price of exchanges. Although the modern law tolerates considerable disparity of prices, for this divergence reflects the different values which people choose to place on opportunities, it is sceptical about choices which amount to contracts setting a price significantly above or below comparable market prices or under which most of the reciprocal promises seem illusory. Such a choice does not amount to a worthwhile exploration of market opportunities, unless, of course, it signifies than an outright gift was intended. Statutes give the courts the power to revise or invalidate unfair transactions, either explicitly as in the case of extortionate credit bargains, or indirectly by monitoring whether the quality of the goods supplied lives up to the expected standard in the light of the price paid for them. The statutory power to invalidate unreasonable exemption clauses which limit or exclude liability for defective performance also contributes to equivalence in exchange, for it is no longer possible for one party to reduce drastically his or her obligations without a commensurate reduction in the price paid. Under the judge-made common law the courts deploy a battery of legal doctrines which tend to ensure an equivalence in exchange. When the circumstances surrounding the formation of contract signify the possibility of pressure or exploitation of a necessitous position or person's weak understanding of business, the court will rely upon the unfairness of the terms of the contract, judged by reference to other similar market transactions and the degree of disadvantage to the weaker party, in order to impugn the validity of the contract under the doctrines of duress and undue influence. These developments in the law of contract signify an abandonment of the presumption of fairness in exchanges.

(c) Co-operation

A third derivation from this complex notion of liberty concerns the relation between the individual and others. The underlying image of the individual in the ideals of the justice of exchange was one who was antagonistic towards others and who entered transactions solely for the sake of his or her own interests. Indeed, from this perspective it is hard to find adequate justification for the enforcement of contracts against the will of the individual in the absence of clear economic harm to others. If, however, one regards the law of contract as offering an opportunity for entering into binding long-term commitments with others, an opportunity which augments the freedom of the individual, precise calculations of self-interest at every stage in the transaction should not be permitted to subvert the value of the institution of contracts. Indeed, the law must impose certain duties of co-operation in the formation and performance of contracts, which reflect the need to secure reliable and worthwhile opportunities for market exchanges. These duties both expand and articulate the reciprocal duties implicit in a contractual relation.

Furthermore, this new interpretation of the relation between the individual and others introduces two kinds of limitations on the freedom to choose whether or not to enter a contract. In the first place, this freedom has been curtailed in order to ensure better equality of opportunity in the market. For this purpose, sex and race discrimination legislation deters refusals to enter contracts on the grounds of sex, marital status, race, nationality and other motives which display a lack of respect for the equality of others. In *Quinn v Williams Furniture Ltd*, a married woman agreed to purchase a three-piece suite of furniture, paid a deposit, and then requested a loan arrangement for the balance of the price. The shop assistant said that the loan could not be made without her husband signing a collateral personal guarantee for the loan as well. The Court of Appeal decided that, since a similar guarantee from a spouse would not have been demanded by the shop in the case of a loan to a married man, this conduct constituted unlawful sex discrimination.

In the second place, the choice of whether or not to undertake an obligation, although still a characteristic of contractual obligations, has in practice been significantly diminished by the expansion of alternative grounds for the imposition of obligations. The law of tort, for instance, implies a duty of care between manufacturers and ultimate consumers regardless of their choice. This liability for negligence may extend to many kinds of relations of economic dependence, which, although not established by agreement between the parties, nevertheless are regarded as entailing an obligation to take care. For example, the decision in *White v Jones* illustrates how a solicitor who negligently fails to draft a Will with the consequence that the testator's intentions are frustrated, will be held liable to the intended beneficiaries to the extent of their expected inheritance. Although the solicitor never entered a contract with these beneficiaries, he or she nevertheless owes them a similar duty to take care as that established in the contractual relation with the testator. The precise ambit of such tortious duties of care between parties who have not made agreements or bargains remains controversial, but the possibility of liability in tort in order to protect economic interests represents a major invasion of the freedom of individuals from obligations without their consent.

4. Conclusion—a regulatory perspective

The above discussion claims that the modern themes in the law of contract which I have identified as constituting a transformation in the market order may be derived from a sophisticated version of liberalism which relies upon a perfectionist conception of liberty or autonomy. It suggests that the modern law of contract should be understood by an examination of themes such as restrictions on the scope of contracts, mandatory terms, fairness, co-operation and imposed duties of care and responsibility. The details of this interpretation will be elaborated in the course of the book. But it is important to repeat that this transformation in values is masked at all times by the persistence of traditional legal categories and the differentiation of large fields of contractual practices, such as consumer purchases and employment, from mainstream discussions of the law of contract. Nor should I be understood as claiming that the modern values were completely unknown to the classical law of contract. No doubt courts in the nineteenth century occasionally found a way to permit a person to escape from an improvident bargain, to deter unco-operative or opportunistic behaviour that undermined the economic value of the transaction to the other party, or to give relief from an oppressive power relation established by contract. My point is rather that the modern values infuse the law at every point, encouraging the courts to evolve doctrines in new directions and providing the basis for a considerable body of regulatory intervention by legislatures.

This perspective on the law of contract can perhaps be given sharper focus by contrasting a traditional private law view with a modern regulatory perspective. Under the traditional private law view, which infused discussions of the classical law of contract, the law provided a facility for individuals to enter into voluntary binding commitments. The private ordering of individuals was respected and supported by legal enforcement of their agreements. In this modern perspective, however, the function of the law of contract is to regulate markets, market practices and the social practices of making contracts with a view to controlling the types of relationships established through contracts and their distributive consequences. This regulation of markets still pays considerable respect to private ordering, for the continuing strength of the law of contract is that it attaches great significance to the self-regulation of the parties established by their contractual agreement. Indeed, the law can contribute to the success of self-regulation by improving the operation of competitive markets and by steering contractual relations in ways that are likely to help to maximise the joint wealth of the parties. But this power of self-regulation is limited in most common transactions with a view to steering the outcomes of these transactions in ways that the values of the modern law wish to support.

C. Contextual legal reasoning

The second element of the transformation of the law of contract concerns the method of legal reasoning. Of course the basic elements of legal reasoning have remained constant. The courts follow precedent, apply statutes and distinguish cases on their facts. Nevertheless, there has been a shift in the scope of reasoning and the complexity of the system of classification. The scope becomes broader as the courts acknowledge the relevance of a greater diversity of considerations. The system of classification becomes complex as different types of contractual relation receive differentiated treatment. In short, the formalism and unity of the classical law is replaced by contextual legal reasoning.

CHANGING THE BARGAIN

CHAPTER THIRTY-TWO

RESCISSION, VARIATION, WAIVER AND PROMISSORY ESTOPPEL

I. THE SETTING

It is not surprising to find that, with any contract running over a period of time, it is quite common for the parties to agree on some adjustment to the contract terms. Many contracts, particularly longer term contracts, contain elaborate clauses providing for adjustment, and we shall look at some of these in the next chapter. However, we have seen already that a great deal of contracting takes place with a minimal degree of planning for future contingencies, even quite likely contingencies.

Look again at Macaulay, 'Non-Contractual Relations in Business' (see p 389). Some at least of the lack of planning is due to the difficulty of foreseeing in advance what problems may arise and what will be the most appropriate solutions; some is because the cost of agreeing mechanisms of adjustment does not seem worth incurring when the likelihood of the contingency is low. The latter would explain why adjustment mechanisms are much more common in longer term contracts: see Chapter 33.

As we saw in Section 4, a great deal of contract law is concerned with where the losses caused by such unplanned-for contingencies should fall. In some cases, the parties will simply rely on the general law to settle their dispute. At a guess, however, it is equally or more common for a solution to be reached by an ad hoc ageement, and it is with these that this section is primarily concerned.

Adjusting for such contingencies is not the only reason why a contract may be renegotiated, however. An agreement running over a period of time may give a party the scope for 'opportunism', by taking advantage of the other's circumstances to threaten a breach of contract unless the deal is renegotiated in his favour. Frequently, the opportunity for such extortion arises from the operation of the contract itself. Even if the parties met on an equal footing originally, when the time for performance draws near, one party may be heavily dependent on the other: he may face serious losses if he does not get the other's performance and has nowhere that he can readily obtain a substitute. The old case of *Stilk v Myrick* (see p 110) suggests the possibilities graphically, although it may be that the master's promise in that case was entirely voluntary (for an American case in which the crew reached the fishing grounds and then refused to go on fishing unless their pay was increased, see *Alaska Packers' Association v Domenico*, discussed on p 859).

In the case in which the contract is adjusted to deal with an unplanned-for contingency, the reasons for upholding or not upholding the contract modification clearly differ markedly from those in the extortion case. Until fairly recently, however, it has not been clear that English law would treat the two cases differently.

II. BASIC CONCEPTS

The traditional approach of English law was that, for a renegotiation to be effective to change the contract terms in such a way that neither party could go back on the new agreement, there had to be all of the elements that would be required if a fresh binding contract were being made—in other words, offer and acceptance, intention to create legal relations and consideration, or a deed under seal. If these elements were present, the change was irrevocable; if they were not, it was of no effect. For the reasons suggested, this approach was too rigid to work satisfactorily, and there has been considerable departure from the traditional position. Some of this involves paying lip service to the traditional rules but apparently distorting them; some, the development of an alternative basis on which a promised change in the contract terms may become binding, through waiver or (what some think is indistinguishable) promissory estoppel. These developments lead to more changes in the contract terms becoming irrevocably binding, because neither a deed nor consideration for the promised change may be required. At the same time, however, it has been found that the traditional doctrine upholds changes that should not be enforced, and the doctrine of economic duress has developed to cope with this.

The starting point of any enquiry into whether the terms of a contract have effectively been changed remains: did the parties agree on the alleged change, and was their agreement made by deed or supported by consideration? If yes, it will be binding unless it can be upset on the ground of economic duress or any of the other grounds upon which contracts generally may be invalidated. If there was no consideration, the inquiry shifts to waiver or promissory estoppel.

'Changes' in the contract may be divided into three types:

(1) *rescission*, under which each party releases the other from liability to perform his outstanding obligations under the contract. Sometimes rescission involves each party returning benefits received under the contract, but an agreement simply to release outstanding obligations on each side will also operate as a rescission: in this case, it is sometimes called 'abandonment'. Rescission or abandonment requires agreement and consideration or a deed. It may be followed immediately by the making of a new contract ('rescission and replacement');

(2) *variation*, under which the parties agree that the terms of the contract will be changed. To be fully effective, a variation requires agreement and consideration just like a fresh contract, and if these are present, the variation cannot be withdrawn unilaterally by either party. It is sometimes said that an effective variation produces a permanent change in the contract terms, but this can be misleading, because sometimes the agreement is that the changed terms shall apply for a limited period only;

(3) *waiver*, in contrast, is where one party states or indicates by his conduct that he will not exercise some remedy available to him under the contract, or will not insist on his full contractual rights, without there being any consideration for his promise. A purported variation that fails for want of consideration may also be treated as a waiver. As we shall see, even on the traditional view, a waiver might have some interim effect, but it will not

normally lead to an irrevocable loss of rights by the waiving party, because the waiver might be withdrawn. The doctrinal development referred to above has taken the form of limiting the circumstances in which withdrawal is permissible.

III. DISCHARGE OR VARIATION BY CONTRACT

1. Was there agreement?

■ *The Hannah Blumenthal*

[1983] 1 All ER 34, House of Lords (see p 192)

NOTE

In *Allied Marine Transport Ltd v Vale do Rio Navegacao SA, The Leonidas D* [1983] 3 All ER 737 (see p 194), a dispute under a charterparty was referred to arbitration, but thereafter nothing happened for five-and-a-half years. At 741, Mustill J summarised the effect of the decision in *The Hannah Blumenthal* thus:

Principles
Without going in great detail into matters which have already been thoroughly explored in previous cases, including those already cited, and Birkett v James, I believe that the relevant principles can now be summarised as follows.

(1) An arbitration agreement creates mutual promises to submit to arbitration all disputes falling within the stated category, and to abide by the award of the arbitrator in respect of disputes actually referred to him.

(2) On the happening of three successive events, viz (a) the making by one party of a claim falling within the arbitration agreement and (b) the invoking of the arbitration agreement in respect of the dispute raised by that claim and (c) the appointment of an arbitrator in respect of the dispute, there comes into existence a series of mutual contractual relationships between the parties inter se, and between each party and the arbitrator. I will for convenience refer to the group of relationships between the parties as 'the reference'.

(3) As with any other bilateral contractual relationship, both the arbitration agreement and the reference are capable of discharge by consent.

(4) The reference may be terminated by consent, leaving the arbitration agreement intact.

(5) A consent to discharge the reference may be inferred from prolonged inactivity on both sides.

(6) Discharge by consent inferred from inactivity may take place in two situations: (i) where each party conducts himself so as to evince to the other party an intention to treat the reference as ended; (ii) where the conduct of B is such as to lead A reasonably to believe that B intends to treat the reference as ended, and A alters his position in reliance on that belief. This second way of procuring a consensual discharge of the reference represents the important addition to the law brought about by the speeches in the House of Lords in The Hannah Blumenthal to which I have already referred.

(7) In neither of these two situations is it material to examine the actual subjective belief and intention of B.

(8) In situation (i), since the test is objective, it is necessary to look only at the conduct of each party actually brought to the notice of the other. But in situation (ii) the court must investigate the state of A's mind at the relevant time. The oral evidence of A will be admissible on this question. So also will be evidence of his actions at the time, even if these were not brought to the attention of B.

In *The Leonidas D*, the question was whether the parties had abandoned merely the reference to arbitration, or had abandoned the whole claim. Mustill J held that the charterers, by commencing arbitration but then totally stopping, tacitly represented that they did not intend to pursue the claim, and the owners, whose response (with one exception, which the judge held was neutral) had been 'a complete blank', had accepted the tacit offer of abandonment. The Court of Appeal disagreed: they thought that mere silence is equivocal and neither offer and acceptance, nor any representation, could be inferred from it.

The view that silence is always equivocal is difficult to reconcile with the *Hannah Blumenthal* or with the later decision of the House of Lords in *Vitol SA v Norelf Ltd, The Santa Clara* [1996] 3 All ER 193, in which Lord Steyn said 'sometimes in the practical world of businessmen, an omission to act may be as pregnant with meaning as a positive declaration'.

2. The meaning of the agreement

■ *Bank of Credit and Commerce International SA
(in liquidation) v Ali*
[2001] 1 All ER 961

In 1990, the appellant bank made the respondent redundant. There were negotiations between the parties as to the terms on which the respondent would be made redundant. It was agreed that he would receive his full notice entitlement, the statutory redundancy payment (plus accrued holiday pay) and an *ex gratia* payment. In addition, the respondent was offered an additional month's gross salary if he was willing to sign an ACAS form acknowledging that the payment he would receive was the full and final settlement. In due course, following a short interview with an ACAS official, the respondent signed a form, which said:

The Applicant (Mr Naeem) agrees to accept the terms set out in the documents attached in full and final settlement of all or any claims whether under statute, Common Law or in Equity of whatsoever nature that exist or may exist and, in particular, all or any claims rights or applications of whatsoever nature that the Applicant has or may have or has made or could make in or to the Industrial Tribunal, except the Applicant's rights under the Respondent's [the bank's] pension scheme.

In July 1991, an application was made that the bank be wound up. It then became clear that the bank had, in fact, been insolvent for some years and that it was being operated as a giant fraud. In *Malik v Bank of Credit and Commerce International SA* [1998] AC 20, [1997] 3 All ER 1, the House of Lords held that plaintiffs, ex-employees who were entitled to sue the bank for breach of contract, were entitled to recover so-called 'stigma' damages, that is damages that reflected their difficulty in finding alternative employment because of the possibility that future employers would refuse to employ them because they had once worked for BCCI.

The respondent, the plaintiff in the present action, sought to claim such damages on his own account. BCCI argued that any such claim was barred by the terms of the release that the respondent had signed on leaving its employment. It was accepted that in 1990 it would have been very difficult for either party to perceive the decision of the House of Lords in 1997, which in any view had represented significant developments over the previous law. It was also accepted that the respondents had no knowledge of the corrupt way in which the bank had been operated but, obviously, the bank must have known this itself. Lightman J held that the release was effective to bar the respondent's claim: [1999] 2 All ER 1005. This decision was reversed by the Court of Appeal but the three members of the Court of Appeal gave significantly different reasons for their view. Sir Richard Scott V-C took the view that the words used were not sufficiently clear as to exclude a potential claim for stigma damages. Chadwick and Buxton LJJ disagreed. They thought that as a matter of construction, the words were clear, but they thought the release was not binding on the respondent either (*per* Chadwick LJ) because the release involved a situation in which the person benefiting from the release knew a fact that gave rise to a claim, deliberately concealed those facts from the other party in circumstances under which he knows or believes that the other party cannot discover them for himself, or (*per* Buxton LJ), on the basis that there was a general principle that equity would not permit general words in a release to debar a party using them from asserting claims that arise from circumstances of which the party had no knowledge and that they had not contemplated.

The bank appealed to the House of Lords. The House of Lords, by a majority, affirmed the decision of the Court of Appeal but not on the same grounds.

Lord Bingham of Cornhill

I consider first the proper construction of this release. In construing this provision, as any other contractual provision, the object of the court is to give effect to what the contracting parties intended. To ascertain the intention of the parties the court reads the terms of the contract as a whole, giving the words used their natural and ordinary meaning in the context of the agreement, the parties' relationship and all the relevant facts surrounding the transaction so far as known to the parties. To ascertain the parties' intentions the court does not of course inquire into the parties' subjective states of mind but makes an objective judgment based on the materials already identified. The general principles summarised by Lord Hoffmann in *Investors Compensation Scheme Ltd v West Bromwich Building Society, Investors Compensation Scheme Ltd v Hopkin & Sons (a firm), Alford v West Bromwich Building Society, Armitage v West Bromwich Building Society* [1998] 1 All ER 98 at 114–115, [1998] 1 WLR 896 at 912–913 apply in a case such as this.

A party may, at any rate in a compromise agreement supported by valuable consideration, agree to release claims or rights of which he is unaware and of which he could not be aware, even claims which could not on the facts known to the parties have been imagined, if appropriate language is used to make plain that that is his intention. This proposition was asserted by Lord Keeper Henley in *Salkeld v Vernon* (1758) 1 Eden 64, 28 ER 608, in a passage quoted in [11] below. It was endorsed by the high court of Australia in *Grant v John Grant & Sons Pty Ltd* (1954) 91 CLR 112 at 129.

But a long and in my view salutary line of authority shows that, in the absence of clear language, the court will be very slow to infer that a party intended to surrender rights and claims of which he was unaware and could not have been aware.

So I turn to consider the agreement made between the bank and Mr Naeem. His employment was terminated on grounds of genuine redundancy. The agreement provided for payment in full of salary in lieu of notice and redundancy pay. It took account of matters such as holiday pay and season ticket loans. It plainly covered the ordinary incidents of the employer-employee relationship. But the liquidators contend that it cannot have been limited to such incidents or to claims which might be made to an industrial tribunal: otherwise the reference to 'all or any claims whether under statute, Common Law or in Equity of whatsoever nature that exist or may exist' would lack any field of potential reference. This is a compelling submission which has, understandably, found favour with the courts below and with my noble and learned friend Lord Hoffmann. But the liquidators accept that the language of the clause is subject to some implied limitations: where ex-employees have had deposits with the bank, the liquidators have not (very properly) sought to resist claims for repayment in reliance on the general release. Such claims, they say, fall outside the clause because they do not relate to the employer-employee relationship. That would be true, if employees were entirely free to make whatever banking arrangements they chose. But acceptance of these claims involves acceptance that the clause does not mean all it might be thought to say. What of a latent claim for industrial disease or personal injury caused to the employee by the negligence of the employer but unknown to both parties? Mr Jeans QC for the liquidators, in the course of an admirable argument, recognised the difficulty of submitting that such a claim would be precluded by the provision, even though it would relate to the employer-employee relationship. I would not myself infer that the parties intended to provide for the release of such a claim. The same would in my view be true if, unknown to the employee, the bank had libelled him as an employee. The clause cannot be read literally.

What, then, of the claim for stigma damages which lies at the heart of this appeal? The bank, through its senior employee, is fixed with knowledge of the bank's insolvency and nefarious practices, although it seems unlikely that those negotiating with the employees were alert to these facts, very carefully concealed from the world. Mr Naeem had no such knowledge. Neither the bank, even when fixed with such knowledge, nor Mr Naeem could realistically have supposed that such a claim lay within the realm of practical possibility. On a fair construction of this document I cannot conclude that the parties intended to provide for the release of rights and the surrender of claims which they could never have had in contemplation at all. If the parties had sought to achieve so extravagant a result they should in my opinion have used language which left no room for doubt and which might at least have alerted Mr Naeem to the true effect of what (on that hypothesis) he was agreeing.

Lord Hoffmann dissented

I agree with my noble and learned friend that the first issue raises an ordinary question of construction. What would a reasonable person have understood the parties to mean by using the language of the document against all the background which would reasonably have been available to them at the time? But I regret that I cannot agree with his answer. It appears to me to give too little weight to the actual language and background and to rely unduly upon the expressions of judges used in other cases dealing with different documents.

The language of the document is very wide. The impression it conveys is that the draftsman meant business. He has gone to some trouble to avoid leaving anything out. He uses traditional style: pairs of words like 'full and final settlement', 'all or any claims', 'that exist or may exist' and phrases like 'whether under statute, Common law or in Equity' and 'of whatsoever nature'. Admittedly, he could have gone further. *Tudor Grange Holdings Ltd v Citibank NA* [1991] 4 All ER 1 at 5, [1992] Ch 53 at 57 contains an even more elaborate release and I have seen American documents in which the release covers an entire page. But most people in this country would regard this as overkill. The modern English tradition, while still erring on the side of caution, is to avoid the grosser excesses of verbiage and trust to the judges to use common sense to get the message. I think that this tendency should be encouraged. So I think that anyone who was simply reading the document without preconceptions would accept that the draftsman was not leaving deliberate gaps. It does not however, follow that the language was to be read completely literally. There may be limitations in scope to be inferred from the background, limitations from context which the draftsman may have thought too obvious to mention. But that is a different matter from saying that he did not use enough words.

I am therefore in complete agreement with Chadwick LJ on both the construction of the document and the principles which determine whether or not BCCI may rely upon it. Where I respectfully part company from him is on the application of the law to the facts. In my opinion, there are no grounds for holding that in July 1990 BCCI knew that Mr Naeem had or might have a claim for stigma against the bank of which he himself was unaware. The representative of the bank who negotiated the agreement was also unaware of the central fraud, but I shall for present purposes assume that the knowledge of the higher management should be attributed to BCCI. The bank would therefore have known that it had been continuously in breach of its implied obligation of trust and confidence. But that breach had not caused any damage to Mr Naeem in the past and there was nothing to suggest that, now that he was leaving the bank, it would give rise to a claim in the future. The bank was going to go on trading from Abu Dhabi and did not contemplate an imminent disclosure of the fraud which might affect Mr Naeem's prospects of re-employment. And even if BCCI knew or ought to have known that such might be the case, any lawyer whom it consulted in 1990 would have advised that such consequences were too remote to form the subject matter of a claim. It was not until *Malik v Bank of Credit and Commerce International SA (in liq), Mahmud v Bank of Credit and Commerce International SA (in liq)* [1997] 3 All

ER 1, [1998] AC 20 that it would have occurred to anyone. So the concealment of the central fraud was extremely reprehensible conduct in relation to the depositors and the public at large, but there was no reason to think it in any way relevant to the bank's dealings with Mr Naeem in 1990. Accordingly I do not think that a case of suppressio veri has been made out.

NOTE

If the solution to this case is the construction of the release, what would the release have to have said in order for the result to be different?

3. Rescission and replacement or variation?

There are a number of cases on the question of whether the parties intended to rescind the existing contract and replace it with a new one, or to vary the existing contract. Some involve the Statute of Frauds. Under this, a contract that was unenforceable unless evidenced in writing could equally not effectively be varied unless the variation was also evidenced in writing; it could, however, be rescinded by a purely oral agreement. If the parties orally agreed to some alteration in the original contract, should the oral agreement be treated as an ineffective attempt to vary the contract, or should it be treated as a rescission of it, so that the parties end up with no contract? An example of this problem is *Morris v Baron & Co* [1918] AC 1. A similar problem arose in *United Dominions Corpn (Jamaica) Ltd v Shoucair* [1969] 1 AC 340. The Moneylending Law of Jamaica provided that no contract for repayment of money lent and no security given was enforceable unless a memorandum in writing, containing all the terms of the contract, was signed by the borrower before the money was lent or the security given. The appellants had lent the respondent £55,000 on a mortgage, and later had written raising the interest on the loan from 9 per cent to 11 per cent. The respondent wrote acknowledging this, but later he defaulted, and the question was whether the original mortgage remained enforceable. The Privy Council adopted the approach used by the House of Lords in *Morris v Baron & Co*. Lord Devlin said (at 348):

... the view adopted by the House of Lords ... is based on the intentions of the parties. They cannot have that which presumably they wanted, that is, the old agreement as amended; so the court has to make up its mind which comes nearer to their intention—to leave them with an unamended agreement or without any agreement at all ... If the new agreement reveals an intention to rescind the old, the old goes; and if it does not, the old agreement remains in force and unamended.

It was held that the original mortgage remained in force.

An interesting analysis of whether a complex series of agreements amounted to variations or new contracts can be found in *Compagnie Noga D'Importation et D'Exportation Sa v Abacha* [2003] EWCA Civ 1100 [2003] 2 All ER (Comm) 915.

4. Was there consideration?

There have been evident changes during the last hundred years in what will be recognised as consideration for a promise to change the terms of a contract. These changes do not make it easier to state the present law.

■ *Foakes v Beer*

(1884) [1881–5] All ER Rep 106, House of Lords

The respondent brought an action against the appellant and obtained judgment for a specific sum. Later, the parties made a written agreement by which they agreed that, in consideration of the appellant paying part of the sum due on signing the agreement and the remainder by equal half-yearly instalments, the respondent undertook not to take any proceedings on the judgment. The appellant paid all the instalments, so that the respondent had been paid the principal sum, but after the payment of the last instalment, the respondent claimed interest from the date of the judgment. The House of Lords were divided on whether the agreement made amounted to a promise to forgo interest, but held that, in any event, such a promise would be unenforceable.

The Earl of Selborne LC

...But the question remains whether the agreement is capable of being legally enforced. Not being under seal, it cannot be legally enforced against the respondent unless she received consideration for it from the appellant, or unless, though without consideration, it operates by way of accord and satisfaction, so as to extinguish the claim for interest. What is the consideration? On the face of the agreement none is expressed except a present payment of £500 on account and in part of the larger debt then due and payable by law under the judgment. The appellant did not contract to pay the future instalments of £150 each at the times therein mentioned; much less did he give any new security in the shape of negotiable paper, or in any other form The promise de futuro was only that of the respondent, that, if the half-yearly payments of £150 each were regularly paid, she would 'take no proceedings whatever on the judgment'. No doubt, if the appellant had been under no antecedent obligation to pay the whole debt, his fulfilment of the condition might have imported some consideration on his part for that promise. But he was under that antecedent obligation; and payment at those deferred dates, by the forbearance and indulgence of the creditor, of the residue of the principal debt and costs could not, in my opinion, be a consideration for the relinquishment of interest and discharge of the judgment unless the payment of the £500 at the time of signing the agreement was such a consideration.

As to accord and satisfaction, in point of fact there could be no complete satisfaction so long as any future instalment remained payable; and I do not see how any new payments on account could operate in law as a satisfaction ad interim conditionally upon other payments being afterwards duly made, unless there was a consideration sufficient to support the agreement while still unexecuted. Nor was anything in fact done by the respondent in this case, on the receipt of the last payment, which could be tantamount to an acquittance, if the agreement did not previously bind her. The question, therefore, is nakedly raised by this appeal whether your Lordships are now prepared, not only to overrule as contrary to law the doctrine stated by Sir Edward Coke to have been laid down by all the judges of the Common Pleas in *Pinnel's Case* in 1602, and repeated in his note to Littleton, s 344...., but to treat a prospective agreement, not under seal for satisfaction of a debt by a series of payments on account to a total amount less than the whole debt, as binding in law, provided those payments are regularly made, the case not being one of a composition with a common debtor agreed to inter se by several creditors...

The distinction between the effect of a deed under seal and that of an agreement by parol, or by writing not under seal, may seem arbitrary, but is established in our law; nor is it really unreasonable or practically inconvenient that the law should require particular solemnities to give to a gratuitous contract the force of a binding obligation. If the question be, as in the actual state of the law I think it is, whether consideration is or is not given in a case of this kind by the debtor who pays down part of the debt presently due from him, for a promise by the creditor to relinquish, after certain further payments on account, the residue of the debt, I cannot say that I think consideration is given, in the sense in which I have always understood that word as used in our law. It might be, and indeed I think it would be, an improvement in our law, if a release or acquittance of the whole debt on payment of any sum which the creditor might be content to receive by way of accord and satisfaction, though less than the whole, were held to be generally binding, though not under seal; nor should I be unwilling to see equal force given to a prospective agreement like the present, in writing, though not under seal; but I think it impossible, without refinements which practically alter the sense of the word, to treat such a release or acquittance as supported by any new consideration proceeding from the debtor.

All the authorities subsequent to *Cumber v Wane* which were relied upon by the appellant, such as *Sibree v Tripp, Curlewis v Clark*, and *Goddard v O'Brien*, have proceeded upon the distinction that, by giving negotiable paper or otherwise, there had been some new consideration for a new agreement, distinct from mere money payments in or towards discharge of the original liability. I think it unnecessary to go through those cases, or to examine the particular grounds upon which each of them was decided. There are no such facts in the case now before your Lordships. What is called 'any benefit, or even any legal possibility of benefit', in Mr Smith's notes to *Cumber v Wane* (1 Smith, LC, 8th edn, 366) is not, as I conceive, that sort of benefit which a creditor may derive from getting payment of part of the money due to him from a debtor who might otherwise keep him at arm's length, or possibly become insolvent, but is some independent benefit, actual or contingent, of a kind which in law might be a good and valuable consideration for any other sort of agreement not under seal. My conclusion is that the order appealed from should be affirmed and the appeal dismissed with costs and I so move your Lordships.

Lord Blackburn

. . . I think, therefore, that it is necessary to consider the ground on which the Court of Appeal based their judgment, and to say whether the agreement can be enforced. I construe it as accepting and taking £500 in satisfaction of the whole £2,090 19s, subject to the condition that, unless the balance of the principal debt was paid by the instalments, the whole might be enforced with interest. If instead of £500 in money it had been a horse valued at £500, or a promissory note for £500, the authorities are that it would have been a good satisfaction, but it is said to be otherwise as it was money. This is a question, I think, of difficulty. Lord Coke says (Co Litt 212 b):

'Where the condition is for payment of £20, the obligor or feoffor cannot at the time appointed pay a lesser sum in satisfaction of the whole, because it is apparent that a lesser sum of money cannot be a satisfaction of a greater. . . . If the obligor or feoffor pay a lesser sum, either before the day or at another place than is limited by the conditions, and the obligee or feofee receiveth it, this is a good satisfaction.'

For this he cites *Pinnel's Case*. That was an action on a bond for £16, conditional for the payment of £8 10s on Nov 11, 1600. Plea, that defendant, at plaintiff's request, before the said day, to wit, on Oct 1, paid to the plaintiff £5 2s 2d, which the plaintiff accepted in full satisfaction of the £8 10s. The plaintiff had judgment for the insufficient pleading. But, though this was so, Lord Coke reports that it was resolved by the whole Court of Common Pleas,

'that payment of a lesser sum on the day in satisfaction of a greater cannot be any satisfaction for the whole, because it appears to the judges that by no possibility a lesser sum can be a satisfaction to the plaintiff for a greater sum; but the gift of a horse, a hawk, or a robe, etc, in satisfaction is good, for it shall be intended that a horse, hawk, or robe might be more beneficial to the plaintiff than the money in respect of some circumstance, or otherwise the plaintiff would not have accepted of it in satisfaction. But when the whole sum is due, by no intendment the acceptance of a parcel can be a satisfaction to the plaintiff; but in the case at Bar it was resolved that the payment and acceptance of parcel before the day in satisfaction of the whole would be a good satisfaction in regard of circumstance of time; for peradventure parcel or it before the day would be more beneficial to him than the whole at the day, and the value of the satisfaction is not material; so if I am bound in £20 to pay you £10 at Westminster, and you request me to pay £5 at the day at York, and you will accept it in full satisfaction for the whole £10, it is a good satisfaction for the whole, for the expenses to pay it at York is sufficient satisfaction.'

There are two things here resolved. First, that where a matter paid and accepted in satisfaction of a debt certain might by any possibility be more beneficial to the creditor than his debt, the court will not inquire into the adequacy of the consideration. If the creditor, without any fraud, accepted it in satisfaction when it was not a sufficient satisfaction, it was his own fault; and that payment before the day might be more beneficial, and consequently that the plea was in substance good; and this must have been decided in the case. There is a second point stated to have been resolved, namely.

'that payment of a lesser sum on the day cannot be any satisfaction of the whole, because it appears to the judges that by no possibility a lesser sum can be a satisfaction to the plaintiff for a greater sum.'

This was certainly not necessary for the decision of the case; but, though the resolution of the Court of Common Pleas was only a dictum, it seems to me clear that Lord Coke deliberately adopted the dictum, and the great weight of this authority makes it necessary to be cautious before saying that what he deliberately adopted as law was a mistake, and though I cannot find that in any subsequent case this dictum has been made the ground of the decision, except in *Fitch v Sutton*, as to which I shall make some remarks later, and in *Down v Hatcher*, as to which Parke, B, in *Cooper v Parker* said, 'Whenever the question may arise as to whether *Down v Hatcher* is good law, I should have a great deal to say against it', yet there certainly are cases in which great judges have treated the dictum in *Pinnel's Case* as good law.

For instance, in *Sibree v Tripp*, Parke B, says (15 M & W at p 33):

'it is clear that if the claim be a liquidated and ascertained sum, payment of part cannot be satisfaction of the whole, although it may, under certain circumstances, be evidence of a gift of the remainder.'

Alderson, B, in the same case says (ibid at pp 37, 38):

'It is undoubtedly true that payment of a portion of a liquidated demand, in the same manner as the whole liquidated demand ought to be paid, is payment only in part, because it is not one bargain but two, viz., payment of part, and an agreement without consideration to give up the residue. The courts might very well have held the contrary, and have left the matter to the agreement of the parties, but undoubtedly the law is so settled.'

After such strong expressions of opinion, I doubt much whether any judge sitting in a court of first instance would be justified in treating the question as open. But, as this has very seldom, if at all, been the ground of the decision, even in a court of first instance, and certainly never been the ground of a decision in the Court of Exchequer Chamber, still less in this House, I did think it open to your Lordships' House to re-consider this question. Notwithstanding the very high authority of Lord Coke, I think it is not the fact that to accept prompt payment of a part only of a liquidated demand can never be more beneficial than to insist on payment of the whole. And if it be not the fact, it cannot be apparent to the judges. . . .

What principally weighs with me in thinking that Lord Coke made a mistake of fact is my conviction that all men of business, whether merchants or tradesmen, do every day recognise and act on the ground that prompt payment of a part of their demand may be more beneficial to them than it would be to insist on their rights and enforce payment of the whole. Even where the debtor is perfectly solvent, and sure to pay at last, this often is so. Where the credit of the debtor is doubtful it must be more so. I had persuaded myself that there was no such long-continued action on this dictum as to render it improper in this House to re-consider the question. I had written my reasons for so thinking; but, as they were not satisfactory to the other noble and learned Lords who heard the case, I do not now repeat them nor persist in them. I assent to the judgment proposed, though it is not that which I had originally thought proper.

Lords Watson and **Fitzgerald** delivered concurring judgments.

Appeal dismissed

NOTES

1. 'Accord and satisfaction' refers to an agreement to accept a lesser sum and payment of it. But there is no 'satisfaction' unless payment of the sum amounts to consideration. See Treitel, pp 100 and 125. In *Ferguson v Davies* [1997] 1 All ER 315, the plaintiff brought proceedings in the county court claiming £486.50. The defendant sent the plaintiff a cheque for £150 saying that it was sent in full settlement. The plaintiff cashed the cheque and continued the action for the balance. The defendant also completed a county court form admitting that he owed £150 and had paid this. The county court judge held that, by cashing the cheque, the plaintiff had accepted it in full settlement but the Court of Appeal disagreed. It seems that the result would have been diferent if the defendant had agreed that he owed £150 and had sent £160 in full settlement.

2. Thus a promise to accept part-payment in satisfaction of the debt—ie to release the debtor from the rest of the debt if he pays part of the sum due— was not binding under *Foakes v Beer* for want of consideration. There is a close parallel to *Stilk & Myrick* (see p 110).

3. A agrees to sell a widget to B for £100. Before delivery or payment, the parties agree to cancel the contract. Is there consideration?

4. A agrees to sell a widget to B for £100, payment to be made within 30 days of delivery. After delivery but before payment, they agree that the contract should be cancelled if B returns the widget, which he does. Is there consideration?

5. A agrees to sell a 'standard' widget to B for £100. Before delivery, they agree that A will fit the widget with an extra gadget and B will pay £110. Is there consideration?

6. A agrees to sell a widget to B for delivery in six months' time, at £100 plus the percentage change recorded in the index of retail prices between the dates of contract and delivery. A week later, they agree to change the price to a fixed price of £105. Is there consideration?

7. A agrees to sell a 'standard' widget to B for £100. Before delivery, they agree that A will supply the widget fitted with a gadget at no extra charge. Is there consideration?

8. A agrees to sell B a basic model car for £6,000. Before delivery, A agrees to supply a 'super deluxe' model at no extra charge. Is this an ineffective variation of the existing contract, or is the original contract rescinded and replaced by a new one?

9. How sensible is it to require consideration in a case such as *Foakes v Beer*? Why was Lord Blackburn so hesitant in following *Pinnel's Case*? In Chapter 6, we examined the factors that might underlie the consideration when a fresh contract is being made; how many of them apply when an existing contract is being changed?

■ Fuller, 'Consideration and Form' (1941)
41 Col LR 799, 821

... [I]f we look at the problem now under discussion from the standpoint of the cautionary function of form it will be apparent that there is a difference between releasing a claim and creating a claim by a promise. The release of a claim, even if made orally, carries with it normally a sense of deprivation which is lacking in the case of a promise. Where words have this effect, where they tend to produce a psychological wrench on the speaker, they satisfy the desideratum of inducing deliberation as well as a writing or a seal.

As Lord Blackburn's judgment suggests, the rule in *Foakes v Beer* is commercially inconvenient (see further p 857) and a number of exceptions to the rule in *Foakes v Beer* have grown up. One, that there would be consideration if the creditor accepted a cheque or negotiable instrument for less than the amount of the debt, is discussed further in *D & C Builders Ltd v Rees* (see p 856). A second is that if the holder of a bill of exchange or promissory note (see p 1197), at or after its maturity, writes unconditionally renouncing his rights against any person liable on it, the latter is discharged (Bills of Exchange Act 1882, s 62). A third is referred to by the Lord Chancellor in his judgment: if a debtor enters a composition agreement with his creditors, whereby he agrees to pay each of them a proportion of what is due, no creditor can later turn round and sue the debtor for the balance of the debt (*Goods v Cheesman* (1831) 2 B & Ad 328). It is hard to see that there is any consideration in this case if there is none when a single creditor agrees to accept part-payment in full satisfaction. A fourth exception is that if the creditor agrees to accept payment from a third party in discharge of the debt, he cannot sue the debtor for the balance. This was applied in *Hirachand Punamchand v Temple* [1911] 2 KB 330. Lieutenant Temple had given the plaintiffs a promissory note in exchange for money lent. His father offered them a draft for a lesser amount in full satisfaction, and they accepted it. The Court of Appeal held that they could not recover the balance from Lieutenant Temple. Three separate explanations seem to be given: (1) the promissory note became extinct, just as if the creditor had renounced it; (2) there was a binding contract between the creditor and the father that the creditor would not sue the son, and it would be an abuse of the process of the court to permit the creditor to sue (compare *Snelling v John G Snelling Ltd*, p 1178); (3) it would be fraud on the father to bring an action for the debt. The last resort at least looks pretty fictitious: it is not normally fraud to change your mind and break your promise.

See also *Stilk v Myrick* (p 110).

■ *Williams v Roffey Bros & Nicholls (Contractors) Ltd*

(see p 111)

NOTES

1. It seems that *Foakes v Beer* was not cited in *Williams v Roffey Bros*. In *Re Selectmove Ltd* [1995] 2 All ER 531 (noted by Peel (1994) 110 LQR 353), it was held that the court was bound by *Foakes v Beer* and could not apply *Williams v Roffey Bros* to a promise to release part of a debt. But if the House of Lords had adopted the same approach as the majority of the Court of Appeal in *Williams v Roffey Bros*, do you think Mrs Beer would have been bound by her promise? Would you need to know any extra facts in order to decide? See also *Re C (a debtor)* (1994) Times, 11 May, and Carter, Phang and Poole (1995) 8 JCL 248.

2. Whatever the present state of the 'existing contractual duty' rule, the cases that follow were decided on the basis that a promise to release part of a debt if the debtor pays the rest is made without consideration, unless one of the exceptions noted above applies.

■ *D & C Builders Ltd v Rees* [1966]

2 QB 617, Court of Appeal

The plaintiffs were a two-man firm of jobbing builders, who had done work on the defendant's premises. The account for this came to some £732, of which the defendant had paid only

£250. The plaintiffs were facing bankruptcy if they were not paid the balance, but the defendant's wife, who was acting for him, refused to pay more than £300, alleging that the workmanship was bad. Because of their financial straits, which the defendant's wife allegedly knew about, the plaintiffs reluctantly accepted a cheque for £300, marked 'in completion of account'. They later brought an action for the balance. On a preliminary issue of whether there was a binding settlement, the trial judge held that there was not, and the defendant appealed.

Danckwerts LJ

... *Foakes v Beer*, applying the decision in *Pinnel's Case* settled definitely the rule of law that payment of a lesser sum than the amount of a debt due cannot be a satisfaction of the debt, unless there is some benefit to the creditor added so that there is an accord and satisfaction.

In *Foakes v Beer*, Lord Selborne, while approving *Cumber v Wane*, did not overrule the cases which appear to differ from *Cumber v Wane*, saying:

> 'All the authorities subsequent to *Cumber v Wane*, which were relied upon by the appellant at your Lordships' Bar (such as *Sibree v Tripp*, *Curlewis v Clark* and *Goddard v O'Brien*) have proceeded upon the distinction, that, by giving negotiable paper or otherwise there had been some new consideration for a new agreement, distinct from mere money payments in or towards discharge of the original liability.'

Lord Selborne was distinguishing those cases before the House.

But the giving of a cheque of the debtor for a smaller amount than the sum due is very different from 'the gift of a horse, hawk, or robe, etc' mentioned in *Pinnel's Case*. I accept that the cheque of some other person than the debtor, in appropriate circumstances, may be the basis of an accord and satisfaction, but I cannot see how in the year 1965 the debtor's own cheque for a smaller sum can be better than payment of the whole amount of the debt in cash. The cheque is only conditional payment, it may be difficult to cash, or it may be returned by the bank with the letters 'RD' [Refer to Drawer] upon it, unpaid. I think that *Goddard v O'Brien*, either was wrongly decided or should not be followed in the circumstances of today.

I agree also that, in the circumstances of the present case, there was no true accord. The Rees really behaved very badly. They knew of the plaintiffs' financial difficulties and used their awkward situation to intimidate them. The plaintiffs did not wish to accept the sum of £300 in discharge of the debt of £482, but were desperate to get some money. It would appear also that the defendant and his wife misled the plaintiffs as to their own financial position. Rees, in his evidence, said: 'In June (1964) I could have paid £700 odd. I could have settled the whole bill'. There is no evidence that by August, or even by November, their financial situation had deteriorated so that they could not pay the £482.

In my view the county court judge was right in applying the rule in *Foakes v Beer*, and I would dismiss the appeal.

Winn LJ delivered a concurring judgment.

Appeal dismissed.

(Lord Denning decided this case on a different ground: extracts from his judgment follow on p 867).

■ Posner, 'Gratuitous Promises in Economics and Law' (1977)
6 JLS 411, at 421–424

(NB Posner is discussing US law, which is different to English law in this area, but the economic ideas are still relevant.)

E. Contract modification

Often it is possible for a party to make a binding promise, unsupported by any fresh consideration, to modify a term of an existing contract. For example, the payor in a construction contract might agree to pay a higher price to a builder who had encountered unexpected soil conditions. The motives for such promises are various: to gain a reputation for 'fair dealing' (really risk sharing), to avoid driving the promisee into bankruptcy (which might prevent his completing performance or raise the cost of his doing so), or even to be altruistic (the contingency giving rise to modification may have dramatically altered the relative wealth position of the parties). In any event, the stakes are often substantial in such cases, while the increment in utility to the promisor may also be substantial because of the length of time over which optimal performance may extend.

Consider the example of the house purchaser who promises the builder a higher than contract price because the builder has encountered some unexpected difficulty which may make it impossible to complete the contract at the agreed price. If the purchaser merely declares his intention of paying the builder a higher price, but is free to renege, the builder may decide not to complete performance but instead to take his chances in bankruptcy court. Yet the promisor dare not pay him the extra price in advance in exchange for the builder's promise to continue, for if the contractor is financially shaky for other reasons, the prepayment may end up in the hands of a trustee in bankruptcy, with the purchaser relegated to the status of an unsecured creditor. This is a clear case where the enforcement of a promise not supported by fresh consideration enhances the welfare of the promisor.

The facts of a real case upholding enforceability of such a promise, *Goebel v Linn*, are rather similar to those of the last example. The defendants were brewers who had a contract with the plaintiff in the case, an ice company, to supply them with ice at a price not to exceed $2 a ton. An unusually mild winter ruined the local ice 'crop' and the ice company informed the defendants that it would not continue to supply them with ice at the contract price. The defendants had a large stock of beer on hand that would spoil without refrigeration, and therefore agreed to pay the ice company $3.50 to continue the supply of ice under the contract. The defendants later repudiated the agreement and the ice company sued. In upholding the plaintiff's claim, the court observed that the defendants

> 'chose for reasons which they must have deemed sufficient at the time to submit to the company's demand and pay the increased price rather than rely upon their strict rights under the existing contract.... Suppose, for example, the defendants had satisfied themselves that the ice company under the very extraordinary circumstances of the entire failure of the local crop of ice must be ruined if their existing contracts were to be insisted upon, and must be utterly unable to respond in damages; it is plain that then, whether they chose to rely upon their contract or not, it could have been of little or no value to them. Unexpected and extraordinary circumstances had rendered the contract worthless; and they must make a new arrangement, or, in insisting on holding the ice company to the existing contract, they would ruin the ice company and thereby at the same time ruin themselves.'

The result in this case has been criticized on the ground that it exposes promisees to extortion. In economic terms, the making of a contract may confer on the seller a monopoly vis-à-vis the buyer which the seller can exploit by threatening to terminate the contract unless the buyer agrees to pay a higher price than originally agreed upon. The court in *Goebel* was aware of this danger but found that the ice company's claim was not extortionate in this case. This raises the question, however, whether extortion can be given a meaningful definition in the modification setting. To answer this question, it is helpful to distinguish three situations in which modification might be sought:

1. Nothing has changed since the contract was made, but the promisor, realizing that the remedies for breach of contract would not fully compensate the promisee, gives the promisee the unhappy choice of either paying the promisor more to complete the contract or pursuing his legal remedies.
2. Something has changed since the contract signing: the promisee has given up alternative sources of supply or otherwise increased his dependence on the promisor. If modification is permitted the promisor can extract a monopoly rent from the promisee.

3. Something has changed since the contract signing: an unexpected event which, as in *Goebel v Linn*, prevents the (willing) promisor from completing the promised performance without a modification of the contract.

The third case is the clearest for allowing modification. The inability of a willing promisor to complete performance removes the factor of strategic behavior that is present in cases one and two. No exploitation of a monopoly position or of the inadequacy of contractual remedies is involved in allowing modification in the third case. The first case might also seem one where modification should be allowed, on the basis of Holmes's 'bad man' theory of contract law which has close affinities with the economic approach. The legal obligation of a promisor is to perform or pay damages. If the promisee wants more—wants in effect specific performance—he must pay extra for it. That is all that *seems* to be involved in the first case but if we pause to ask why the promisee in the first case would ever agree to pay extra, we shall see that the first case is in reality a version of the second, the monopoly case. If the promisee in the first case has equally good alternative sources of supply, or at least no worse than he had when he made the original contract, he will have no incentive to pay a premium above the contract price for the promisor to perform as agreed; he will allow the promisor to breach and turn elsewhere. He will pay the premium only if his dependence on the promisor has increased since the signing of the contract, ie, only if the contract gave the promisor a monopoly position vis-à-vis the promisee.

Alaska Packers' Ass'n v Domenico was such a case. The plaintiffs (technically 'libelants') hired out as sailors and fishermen to the defendant (appellant), but soon after beginning work stopped and threatened to quit [without any legally valid reason] unless their wages were raised above the agreed amount. Defendant's agent agreed to pay the higher wage demanded but defendant later reneged. The court refused to enforce the modified contract, noting that

'the libelants agreed in writing, for a certain stated compensation, to render their services to the appellant in remote waters where the season for conducting fishing operations is extremely short, and in which enterprise the appellant had a large amount of money invested; and, after having entered upon the discharge of their contract, and at a time when it was impossible for the appellant to secure other men in their places, the libelants, without any valid cause, absolutely refused to continue the services they were under contract to perform unless the appellant would consent to pay them more money.'

This seems a clear case where the motive for the modification was simply to exploit a monopoly position conferred on the promisors by the circumstances of the contract. It might seem that the promisee would have been in even worse shape if the men had quit as they threatened to do. However, since their only motive for threatening to quit was to extract a higher wage, there was probably little danger of their actually quitting. The danger would have been truly negligible had they known that they could not extract an enforceable commitment to pay them a higher wage.

The court in *Alaska Packers'* criticized the earlier result in *Goebel v Linn*, yet the cases are readily distinguishable, with the help of economic analysis. In *Goebel*, without a modification the promisor might well have terminated the contract, so the modification conferred a real benefit on the promisee. But in *Alaska Packers'* the likelihood of termination was much less since the threat to terminate was not a response to external conditions genuinely impairing the promisor's ability to honor the contract but merely a strategic ploy designed to exploit a monopoly position. A firm rule of nonenforceability in such cases solves the monopoly problem and thereby facilitates the making of contractual arrangements in which the promisee will be dependent on the good faith of the promisor.

One can relate this distinction back to the basic theme of this paper by noting that one effect of enforcing the kind of modification attempted in the *Alaska Packers'* case would be to reduce the benefits of contracting to people in the same situation as the plaintiffs in that case. Seamen thereafter could not expect to be promised a high wage in exchange for agreeing to work for a stated period at that wage, since the employer would know that the seamen were not obliged to honor their promise but could at any time 'hold him up' for a higher wage. In a different form, this is the same problem as that of the man who derives little value from promising a future gift because the promise is not binding on him.

An intermediate case between the involuntary threat to terminate *(Goebel v Linn)* and the monopolistic *(Alaska Packers' Ass'n v Domenico)* is that of a promisor who threatens to terminate only because a third party has offered him a higher price for his goods. Because the higher price is a genuine opportunity cost of continued compliance with the contract, the promisor should be allowed to terminate subject only to his obligation to make good the promisee's loss from the breach, and hence he should be allowed to negotiate with the promisee over a modification that will compensate the promisor for the lost opportunity. This was the result in *Schwartzreich v Bauman-Basch, Inc.*

In the cases presented so far, the problem has been whether there was any consideration for the creditor's promise to accept less than was due in full satisfaction, and it is clear that, in some of the cases at least, the requirement of consideration operated to protect the creditor from extortion. Needless to say, the presence of consideration does not indicate the absence of extortion by the debtor. True, a debtor bent on extortion may not commonly make any concession to the creditor in return—but what if he does, perhaps because he is advised to do so? It is to deal with this problem that the doctrine of economic duress has been developed. We will consider it in Section 8.

As Posner suggests, however, there are situations in which it makes perfectly good sense to enforce the creditor's promise even though it was made without consideration (although on p 873 it is argued that it may not be sensible to enforce modifications as readily as Posner suggests). One situation that might seem worthy is if the debtor acts in reliance on the creditor's promise, as in the case of *Jorden v Money*, at which we looked in Chapter 6 (see p 149). There, the debtor pleaded estoppel, but the plea failed because the creditor had not made any representation of fact, only a promise. You will remember that Atiyah has argued that, in the nineteenth century, an otherwise gratuitous promise that had been relied on would be treated as having been made for good consideration, and that Money only failed because the resulting contract was unenforceable under the Statue of Frauds (see p 144). Whether this thesis is correct or not, the modern law appears to be that the act must have been expressly or impliedly requested by the promisor for it to constitute consideration: *Combe v Combe* (see p 152).

You will also remember that, in the *High Trees* case, Denning J suggested a new principle that would make a gratuitous promise binding if it was intended to be and was acted on. *Combe* held that this could not create new obligations where none had existed before, but left open the possibility that the principle might apply to gratuitous promises to give up existing contractual or other rights. It is to this that we now turn. One of the sources from which Denning derived his doctrine was a line of cases on waiver.

IV. WAIVER

An example of waiver is provided by *Hickman v Haynes* (1875) LR 10 CP 598. The buyer of a quantity of iron under a written contract (at that time, the contract had to be evidenced in writing because the goods were worth more than £10: see p 144) *orally* requested the seller to defer delivery, which the seller did, but after protracted delays on the buyer's part, the seller brought an action for non-delivery. The buyer argued that he was not liable because there had only been an ineffective oral variation of the original contract, and the seller had not tendered delivery at the proper time, but the court, not surprisingly, rejected this. The buyer had asked for extra time, and could not complain that the seller had not delivered on the original date; the seller's damages should be assessed by the date at which the seller terminated the contract.

■ *Charles Rickards Ltd v Oppenheim*

[1950] 1 All ER 420, Court of Appeal

The defendant had agreed to buy a Rolls-Royce chassis, which was to be fitted with a coach-built body and delivered to him by 20 March 1948. The car was not delivered on time (which would give the buyer the right to terminate the contract: see p 574), but the defendant pressed for delivery. On 29 June, the defendant gave notice that, if the car was not delivered within four weeks, he would not accept it. The car was ready in October, and the defendant refused to take it.

Denning LJ

... It is clear on the findings of the judge that there was an initial stipulation making time of the essence of the contract between the plaintiffs and the defendant, namely, that it was to be completed 'in six, or, at the most, seven months'. Counsel for the plaintiffs did not seek to disturb that finding—indeed, he could not successfully have done so—but he said that that stipulation was waived. His argument was that, the stipulated time having been waived, the time became at large, and that thereupon the plaintiffs' only obligation was to deliver within a reasonable time. He said that, in accordance with well-known authorities, 'a reasonable time' meant a reasonable time in the circumstances as they actually existed, ie, that the plaintiffs would not exceed a reasonable time if they were prevented from delivering by causes outside their control, such as strikes or the impossibility of getting parts, and so forth, and that, on the evidence in this case, it could not be said that a reasonable time was in that sense exceeded. He cited the well-known words of Lord Watson in *Hick v Raymond and Reid* to support the view that in this case, on the evidence, a reasonable time had not been exceeded. If this had been originally a contract without any stipulation in regard to time, and, therefore, with only the implication of reasonable time, it may be that the plaintiffs could have said that they had fulfilled the contract, but, in my opinion, the case is very different when there was an initial contract, making time of the essence, of 'six or, at the most, seven months'. I agree that that initial time was waived by reason of the requests for delivery which the defendant made after March, 1948, and that, if delivery had been tendered in compliance with those requests, the defendant could not have refused to accept. Supposing, for instance, delivery had been tendered in April, May, or June, 1948, the defendant would have had no answer. It would be true that the plaintiffs could not aver and prove that they were ready and willing to deliver in accordance with the original contract. They would have had, in effect, to rely on the waiver almost as a cause of action. At one time there would have been theoretical difficulties about their doing that. It would be said that there was no consideration, or, if the contract was for the sale of goods, that there was nothing in writing to support the variation. *Plevins v Downing*, coupled with what was said in *Beseler, Waechter Glover & Co v South Derwent Coal Co Ltd* gave rise to a good deal of difficulty on that score, but all those difficulties are swept away now. If the defendant, as he did, led the plaintiffs to believe that he would not insist on the stipulation as to time, and that, if they carried out the work, he would accept it, and they did it, he could not afterwards set up the stipulation in regard to time against them. Whether it be called waiver or forbearance on his part, or an agreed variation or substituted performance, does not matter. It is a kind of estoppel. By his conduct he made a promise not to insist on his strict legal rights. That promise was intended to be binding, intended to be acted on, and was, in fact, acted on. He cannot afterwards go back on it. That, I think, follows from *Panoutsos v Raymond Hadley Corpn of New York*, a decision of this court, and it was also anticipated in *Bruner v Moore*. It is a particular application of the principle which I endeavoured to state in *Central London Property Trust, Ltd v High Trees House, Ltd*.

Therefore, if the matter stopped there, the plaintiffs could have said that, notwithstanding that more than seven months had elapsed, the defendant was bound to accept, but the matter does not stop there, because delivery was not given in compliance with the requests of the defendant. Time and time again the defendant pressed for delivery, time and time again he was assured that he would have early delivery, but he never got satisfaction, and eventually at the end of June he gave notice saying that, unless the car was delivered by July 25, he would not accept it. The question thus arises whether he was entitled to give such a notice, making time of the essence, and that is the question which counsel for the plaintiffs has argued before us. He agrees that, if this is a contract for the sale of goods, the defendant could give such a notice. He accepted the statement of McCardie, J in *Hartley v Hymans*, as accurately stating the law in regard to the sale of goods, but he said that that statement did not apply to contracts for work and labour. He said that no notice making time of the essence could be given in regard to contracts for work and labour. The judge thought that the contract was one for the sale of goods, but, in my view, it is unnecessary to determine whether it was a contract for the sale of goods or a contract for work and labour, because, whichever it was, the defendant was entitled to give a notice bringing the matter to a head. It would be most unreasonable if, having been lenient and having waived the initial expressed time, he should thereby have prevented himself from ever thereafter insisting on reasonably quick delivery. In my judgment, he was entitled to give a reasonable notice making time of the essence of the matter. Adequate protection to the suppliers is given by the requirement that the notice should be reasonable.

The next question, therefore, is: Was this a reasonable notice? Counsel for the plaintiffs argued that it was not. He said that a reasonable notice must give sufficient time for the work then outstanding to be completed, and that, on the evidence in this case, four weeks was not a reasonable time because it would, and did, in fact, require three and a half months to complete it. In my opinion, however, the words of Lord Parker of Waddington in *Stickney v Keeble* apply to such a case as the present, just as much as they do to a contract for the sale of land. Lord Parker said . . . :

'In considering whether the time so limited is a reasonable time the court will consider all the circumstances of the case. No doubt what remains to be done at the date of the notice is of importance, but it is by no means the only relevant fact. The fact that the purchaser has continually been pressing for completion, or has before given similar notices which he has waived, or that it is specially important to him to obtain early completion, are equally relevant facts . . . '

To that statement I would add, in the present case, the fact that the original contract made time of the essence. In this case, not only did the defendant press continually for delivery, not only was he given promises of speedy delivery, but, on the very day before he gave the notice, he was told by the sub-contractors' manager, who was in charge of the work, that it would be ready within two weeks. He than gave a four weeks' notice. The judge found that it was a reasonable notice and, in my judgment, there is no ground on which this court could in any way differ from that finding. The reasonableness of the notice must, of course, be judged at the time at which it is given. It cannot be held to be a bad notice because, after it is given, the suppliers find themselves in unanticipated difficulties in making delivery.

The notice of June 29, 1948, was, therefore, a perfectly good notice so as to make time of the essence of the contract.

Singleton LJ delivered a concurring judgment; **Bucknill LJ** concurred.

Appeal dismissed.

NOTES

1.   Although Denning LJ cites *High Trees* (see p 150), the decision in the *Charles Rickards* case does not depend on that case: it follows dicta in *Panoutsos v Raymond Hadley Corpn* [1917] 2 KB 473.

2.   If the car had been delivered on 1 April, the buyer would have had to accept it: *Panoutsos.*

3.   Did the buyer waive his *right* to prompt delivery, or only his *remedy* of termination? If he had received and accepted the car on 1 April, could he have recovered damages for late delivery?

■ *Hughes v Metropolitan Rly Co*

(1877) 2 App Cas 439, House of Lords

Under a lease, the tenant was obliged to repair the premises. The landlord was entitled to give the tenant six months' notice to carry out any repairs and, if the tenant failed to do the repairs within that time, to forfeit the lease. The landlord served a notice, but the tenant commenced negotiations to sell the lease to the landlord, stating that in the meantime it would not commence the repairs. The negotiations broke down, and when, a few days later, the six months expired, the landlord claimed that the lease was forfeited. The Court of Appeal, reversing the court below, held that the plaintiff's action of ejectment should be stayed.

Lord Cairns LC

... It was not argued at your Lordship's Bar, and it could not be argued, that there was any right of a Court of Equity, or any practice of a Court of Equity, to give relief in cases of this kind, by way of mercy, or by way merely of saving property from forfeiture, but it is the first principle upon which all Courts of Equity proceed, that if parties who have entered into definite and distinct terms involving certain legal results—certain penalties or legal forfeiture—afterwards by their own act or with their own consent enter upon a course of negotiation which has the effect of leading one of the parties to suppose that the strict rights arising under the contract will not be enforced, or will be kept in suspense, or held in abeyance, the person who otherwise might have enforced those rights will not be allowed to enforce them where it would be inequitable having regard to the dealings which have thus taken place between the parties. My Lords, I repeat that I attribute to the Appellant no intention here to take advantage of, to lay a trap for, or to lull into false security those with whom he was dealing; but it appears to me that both parties by entering upon the negotiation which they entered upon, made it an inequitable thing that the exact period of six months dating from the month of October should afterwards be measured out as against the Respondents as the period during which the repairs must be executed.

I therefore propose to your Lordships that the decree which is appealed against should be affirmed, and the present appeal dismissed with costs.

Lord Selborne

... I think the consequence is that which Lord Justice Baggallay derives from it. He says that the circumstances 'were of a character to lead the company to consider that the notice to repair was at any rate suspended for some period of time', at least until the 31st of December. What is the meaning, in the view of a Court of Equity, of suspending a notice to repair? Manifestly that during that time the notice is not to be operative. What is the reasonable result of that in the circumstances of this case? Why, when the notice is to become operative, the same will be a reasonable time for the execution of the repairs which would have been a reasonable time if the notice had been given at that period, that is, six months from at least the 31st of December, 1874.

Lords Blackburn and **O'Hagan** delivered concurring judgments; **Lord Gordon** concurred.

Appeal dismissed.

NOTES

1. Do you see any inconsistency between this decision and either *Jorden v Money* or *Foakes v Beer*? Did the landlord lose his right to have the repairs done? Or was his right to forfeit the lease simply suspended until the tenant had been given a further six months?

2.   Is Lord Cairns' statement of 'the first principle upon which all courts of equity proceed' *ratio*, in the sense of being no broader than was necessary for the decision?

3.   Under this principle, would a landlord ever lose its rights for ever? In *Birmingham and District Land Co v London and North Western Rly Co* (1888) 40 ChD 268, a building lease was determinable if the tenant had not built on the land by 30 November 1885. As a railway bill affecting the land was pending, the landlord told the tenant to put off building, and the land had not been built on when the railway later acquired the land subject to the lease. Its argument that the tenant had lost his interest in the land through non-building was rejected. Lord Justices Cotton and Lindley simply applied Lord Cairns' statement. Bowen LJ said:

> Now, it was suggested by Mr Clare that that proposition only applied to cases where penal rights in the nature of fortfeiture, or analogous to those of forfeiture, were sought to be enforced. I entirely fail to see any such possible distinction. The principle has nothing to do with forfeiture. It is a principle which lies outside forfeiture, and everything connected with forfeiture, as will be seen in a moment of reflection. It was applied in *Hughes v Metropolitan Railway Company* in a case in which equity could not relieve against forfeiture upon the mere ground that it was a forfeiture, but could interfere only because there had been something in the nature of acquiescence, or negotiations between the parties, which made it inequitable to allow the forfeiture to be enforced. The truth is that the proposition is wider than cases of forfeiture. It seems to me to amount to this, that if persons who have contractual rights against others induce by their conduct those against whom they have such rights to believe that such rights will either not be enforced or will be kept in suspense or abeyance for some particular time, those persons will not be allowed by a Court of Equity to enforce the rights until such time has elapsed, without all events placing the parties in the same position as they were before. That is the principle to be applied. I will not say it is not a principle that was recognised by Courts of Law as well as of Equity. It is not necessary to consider how far it was always a principle of common law. Applying that principle to the facts here, I think nobody can come to any but one conclusion, viz, that Mr Boulton (and the railway company took subject to his liabilities) had induced the Plaintiff company reasonably to believe that time would not run against them as regards the building agreements, and that he would not enforce his rights as regards time for building, until a reasonable period had elapsed after they should have received notice from him. As soon as the railway company served notice to treat the reasonable time it seems to me necessarily began to run.

What did he mean by saying that the proposition is wider than cases of forfeiture?

■ *Central London Property Trust Ltd v High Trees House Ltd*
(see p 150)

NOTES

1.   Is the obiter dictum that the rent was reduced to £1,250 during the war (ie that the landlord could not recover the rent that he had agreed to forgo during the war years) consistent with *Foakes v Beer*?

2.   Do the *Hughes* and *Birmingham* cases support the dictum? What was being waived in those cases? In *High Trees*?

■ *Combe v Combe*

(see p 152)

NOTES

1. Is this case saying that the *High Trees* principle cannot be used by a plaintiff? Suppose the landlord company had threatened to evict the tenant company during the war on the ground that the full rent had not been paid: could the tenant have obtained an injunction to prevent it? If so, when can the *High Trees* principle be relied on? (See the argument of the sellers in *The Post Chaser*, noted on p 872, that the buyers' failure to live up to its representation entitled the sellers to damages. This argument failed for other reasons.)

2. Thus it seems that if an employer promises to let a builder off some of the work the builder had promised to do, without reducing the price, the doctrine of promissory estoppel might apply, but not if the employer promises to pay the builder 10 per cent extra for completing the original work. In *Williams v Roffey Bros* (see p 111), it was not argued that promissory estoppel applied, but Russell LJ said:

    I would have welcomed the development of argument, if it could have been properly raised in this court, on the basis that there was here an estoppel and that the defendants, in the circumstances prevailing, were precluded from raising the defence that their promise to pay the extra £10,300 was not binding.

    In contrast, Glidewell LJ said:

    ... the application of the doctrine of promissory estoppel to facts such as those of the present case has not yet been fully developed: see eg the judgment of Lloyd J in *The Proodos* C [1981] 3 All ER 189 at 191.

    But see the decision in *Re Selectmove Ltd*.

In *Tool Metal Manufacturing Co Ltd v Tungsten Electric Co Ltd* [1955] 2 All ER 657, HL, TMMC had granted TECO a licence to deal with patented hard metal alloys. The licence commenced in 1937 and was to continue until 1947, subject to termination by either party on six months' notice. TECO was to pay a royalty on any similar material it used not supplied by TMMC, and by cl 5, it was also to pay 'compensation' if the amount of such material used by it in any month exceeded a named quota. The compensation was to be at 30 per cent of the net value of the excess material. During the war, TMMC voluntarily agreed in the national interest to forgo compensation and accept a flat royalty of 10 per cent, it being contemplated that some new agreement, possibly not including compensation, should be entered after the war. No compensation was paid after the end of 1939. In 1944, TMMC submitted a draft agreement with a compensation provision to TECO, which rejected it; in 1945, TECO brought an action against TMMC for fraud and breach of contract, alleging that it had been agreed that no compensation should be payable after 1939. In March 1945, TMMC counterclaimed for compensation from June 1945, although not for the period 1940-May 1945.

The Court of Appeal held, affirming on this point the judgment of Devlin J (1952) 69 RPC 108, that there was no contract to end compensation, only a temporary arrangement to suspend its payment pending a new agreement. This arrangement could not be terminated without reasonable notice and (allowing the appeal on this point) reasonable notice had not been given: the presentation of the draft agreement was not sufficient. Somervell LJ dropped the hint that nine months might be sufficient notice, and accordingly, TMMC commenced another action claiming compensation as from 1 January 1947, relying on the delivery of the counterclaim in the first action as reasonable notice.

In the second action, the House of Lords held that the delivery of the counterclaim was sufficient notice to enable TMMC to claim compensation payments once more. The decision was confined, however, to that point: because of the principle of *res judicata*, it was not open to the House to reopen the first decision of the Court of Appeal, even if it thought the decision had been wrong. Lord Tucker said (at 674):

...the parties to the present action are estopped from disputing the correctness of the decision of the Court of Appeal in the first action to the effect that circumstances existed which gave rise to the application of the equitable principle in *Hughes v Metropolitan Rly Co* and that no sufficient intimation to terminate the period of suspension of payment had been given prior to the counterclaim in that action, but it would be wrong, in my opinion, if the view were to prevail that your Lordships in the present case are tacitly accepting the correctness of that decision.

Further discussion will be found in Gordon [1963] CLJ 222; Wilson [1965] CLJ 93.

■ *E A Ajayi v R T Briscoe (Nigeria) Ltd*

[1964] 3 All ER 556, Privy Council

The owners had let some lorries on hire purchase to the defendant, who had experienced difficulty in getting them serviced. The owners consented (in a letter dated 22 July) to the defendant 'withholding instalments due [on the lorries] as long as they are withdrawn from active service'. The owners later sued to recover the instalments due, and on appeal, the defendant pleaded promissory estoppel. The Privy Council held that this did not defeat the owners' claim, because the defendant had not proved that the lorries remained unavailable for use after they had been repaired.

Lord Hodson

...The hire-purchaser's final contention was that having altered his position in the manner indicated the owners never gave notice that the period of suspension was at an end before issuing their summons and that accordingly the lorries never having been returned or made available for service he was entitled to rely on the equitable defence as defined by Bowen LJ in the *Birmingham and District Land Co* case. Alternatively he went further and contended on the authority of the cases of *Central London Property Trust, Ltd v High Trees House, Ltd* and *Combe v Combe* that the promise given by the letter of 22 July was irrevocable unless the lorries were made available for service and that, since this never happened, the owners cannot enforce their claim.

Their lordships are of opinion that the principle of law as defined by Bowen LJ has been confirmed by the House of Lords in the case of the *Tool Metal Manufacturing Co, Ltd v Tungsten Electric Co, Ltd*, where the authorities were reviewed, and no encouragement was given to the view that the principle was capable of extension so as to create rights in the promisee for which he had given no consideration. The principle, which has been described as quasi estoppel and perhaps more aptly as promissory estoppel, is that when one party to a contract in the absence of fresh consideration agrees not to enforce his rights an equity will be raised in favour of the other party. This equity is, however, subject to the qualification (a) that the other party has altered his position, (b) that the promisor can resile from his promise on giving reasonable notice, which need not be a formal notice, giving the promisee a reasonable opportunity of resuming his position, (c) the promise only becomes final and irrevocable if the promisee cannot resume his position.

. . . It would not be just to the owners to remit the matter either for a new trial or for a decision to be given at this late stage on facts which have not been expressly found. Their lordships agree with the Federal Supreme Court in thinking that an application to that end should be rejected, especially as the defence sought to be raised is of a suspensory or delaying nature and not of itself decisive to defeat the owners' claim for all time.

Lord Morris of Borth-y-Gest and **Lord Guest** concurred.

Appeal dismissed.

NOTES

1. What does 'resile from his promise' mean? Can the creditor ultimately get all that was originally due to him?
2. In this case, the promise made by the creditor was only that the debtor could *defer* paying some instalments, not that he need not make them at all. Thus it is not clear that either the language used or the decisions support Denning's principle as stated in *High Trees*.

■ *D & C Builders Ltd v Rees*

(For the facts and the judgments of the majority, see p 847)

Lord Denning MR concurred in holding that the cheque had been accepted only as conditional payment, and continued:

. . . in point of law payment of a lesser sum, whether by cash or by cheque, is no discharge of a greater sum.

This doctrine of the common law has come under heavy fire . . . The harshness of the common law has been relieved . . . [he quoted Lord Cairns in *Hughes v Metropolitan Rly Co* and continued:]

It is worth noticing that the principle may be applied, not only so as to suspend strict legal rights, but also so as to preclude the enforcement of them . . .

In applying this principle, however, we must note the qualification: The creditor is only barred from his legal rights when it would be *inequitable* for him to insist upon them. Where there has been a *true accord*, under which the creditor voluntarily agrees to accept a lesser sum in satisfaction, and the debtor *acts upon* that accord by paying the lesser sum and the creditor accepts it, then it is inequitable for the creditor afterwards to insist on the balance. But he is not bound unless there has been truly an accord between them.

In the present case, on the facts as found by the judge, it seems to me that there was no true accord. The debtor's wife held the creditor to ransom. . . .

In my opinion there is no reason in law or equity why the creditor should not enforce the full amount of the debt due to him. I would, therefore, dismiss this appeal.

NOTES

1. To what extent is the rule put forward in this judgment different from that Denning suggested in *High Trees* itself?
2. Is Denning correct to say that the earlier decisions cover precluding the creditor from ever enforcing his rights?
3. *D & C Builders Ltd v Rees* may be described as a case of economic duress (see p 905), although at the time of the decision the English courts had not yet recognised the concept. See, however, Cheshire and Fifoot, *Law of Contract*, 8th edn, 1972, p 283.

■ *W J Alan & Co Ltd v El Nasr Export and Import Co*

[1972] 2 All ER 127, Court of Appeal

The sellers made two contracts for the sale of coffee to the buyers, shipment in the first to be in September/October, and in the second, October/ November, at 262 Kenyan shillings per cwt. Payment was to be by confirmed irrevocable letter of credit in Kenyan shillings. The credit opened was not in accordance with the contract, in that it was opened in sterling, which was then at parity with Kenyan currency, and was valid only until 5 October. Nonetheless, the sellers drew on the credit for the shipment under the first contract, and for another shipment of part of the second contract quantity, and negotiated for the credit to be extended to cover shipment of the remainder in November. The second shipment was made on 16 November, and the sellers prepared an invoice made out in sterling. Before they had presented this to the bank, sterling was devalued on 18 November. The sellers presented the invoice and were paid in sterling, but they claimed the difference between what they were paid and the original contract price for the quantity of the last shipment in Kenyan shillings, which had not been devalued.

Lord Denning MR

...

Variation or waiver

All that I have said so far relates to a 'conforming' letter of credit; that is, one which is in accordance with the stipulations in the contract of sale. But in many cases—and our present case is one—the letter of credit does not conform. Then negotiations may take place as a result of which the letter of credit is modified so as to be satisfactory to the seller. Alternatively, the seller may be content to accept the letter of credit as satisfactory, as it is, without modification. Once this happens, then the letter of credit is to be regarded as if it were a conforming letter of credit. It will rank accordingly as conditional payment.

There are two cases on this subject. One is *Panoutsos v Raymond Hadley Corpn of New York*, but the facts are only to be found fully set out in Commercial Cases. The other is *Enrico Furst & Co v W E Fischer Ltd*. In each of those cases the letter of credit did not conform to the contract of sale. In each case the non-conformity was in that it was not a confirmed credit. But the sellers took no objection to the letter of credit on that score. On the contrary, they asked for the letter of credit to be extended; and it was extended. In each case the seller sought afterwards to cancel the contract on the ground that the letter of credit was not in conformity with the contract. In each case the court held that they could not do so.

What is the true basis of those decisions? Is it a variation of the original contract or a waiver of the strict rights thereunder or a promissory estoppel precluding the seller from insisting on his strict rights or what else? In *Enrico Furst* Diplock J said it was a 'classic case of waiver'. I agree with him. It is an instance of the general principle which was first enunciated by Lord Cairns LC in *Hughes v Metropolitan Railway Co*, and rescued from oblivion by *Central London Property Trust Ltd v High Trees House Ltd*. The principle is much wider than waiver itself; but waiver is a good instance of its application. The principle of waiver is simply this: if one party, by his conduct, leads another to believe that the strict rights arising under the contract will not be insisted on, intending that the other should act on that belief, and he does act on it, then the first party will not afterwards be allowed to insist on the strict legal rights when it would be inequitable for him to do so: see *Plasticmoda Societa Per Azioni v Davidsons (Manchester) Ltd*. There may be no consideration moving from him who benefits by the waiver. There may be no detriment to him by acting on it. There may be nothing in writing. Nevertheless, the one who waives his strict rights cannot afterwards insist on them. His strict rights are at any rate suspended so long as the waiver lasts. He may on occasion be able to revert to his strict legal rights for the future by giving reasonable notice in that behalf, or otherwise making it plain by his conduct that he will thereafter insist on them: see *Tool Metal Manufacturing Co Ltd v Tungsten Electric Co Ltd*. But there are cases where no withdrawal is possible. It may be too late to withdraw; or it cannot be done without injustice to the other party. In that event he is bound by his waiver. He will not be allowed to revert to his strict legal rights. He can only enforce them subject to the waiver he has made.

Instances of these principles are ready to hand in contracts for the sale of goods. A seller may, by his conduct, lead the buyer to believe that he is not insisting on the stipulated time for exercising an option: see *Bruner v Moore*. A buyer may, by requesting delivery, lead the seller to believe that he is not insisting on the contractual time for delivery: see *Charles Rickards Ltd v Oppenheim*. A seller may, by his conduct, lead the buyer to believe that he will not insist on a confirmed letter of credit: see *Plasticmoda*, but will accept an unconfirmed one instead: see *Panoutsos v Raymond Hadley Corpn of New York and Enrico Furst v Fischer*. A seller may accept a less sum for his goods than the contracted price, thus inducing him to believe that he will not enforce payment of the balance: see *Central London Property Trust Ltd v High Trees House Ltd and D & C Builders Ltd v Rees*. In none of these cases does the party who acts on the belief suffer any detriment. It is not a detriment, but a benefit to him, to have an extension of time or to pay less, or as the case may be. Nevertheless, he has conducted his affairs on the basis that he has that benefit and it would not be equitable now to deprive him of it.

The judge rejected this doctrine because, he said, 'there is no evidence of the [buyers] having acted to their detriment'. I know that it has been suggested in some quarters that there must be detriment. But I can find no support for it in the authorities cited by the judge. The nearest approach to it is the statement of Viscount Simonds in the *Tool Metal* case that the other must have been led 'to alter his position', which was adopted by Lord Hodson in *Emmanuel Ayodeji Ajayi v R T Briscoe (Nigeria) Ltd*. But that only means that he must have been led to act differently from what he otherwise would have done. And, if you study the cases in which the doctrine has been applied, you will see that all that is required is that the one should have 'acted on the belief induced by the other party'. That is how Lord Cohen put it in the *Tool Metal* case, and is how I would put it myself.

The judge also rejected the doctrine because of something which was said in the recent case of *Woodhouse v Nigerian Produce Marketing Co Ltd* about estoppel; but no question of waiver arose there; no question of letters of credit; or anything of that kind. It has no application here and neither counsel relied in any way on it before us.

Conclusion

Applying the principle here, it seems to me that the sellers, by their conduct, waived the right to have payment by means of a letter of credit in Kenyan currency and accepted instead a letter of credit in sterling. It was, when given, conditional payment; with the result that, on being duly honoured (as it was) the payment was no longer conditional. It became absolute, and dated back to the time when the letter of credit was given and acted on. The sellers have, therefore, received payment of the price and cannot recover more.

Megaw LJ

...The first issue is whether in the original contract, the contract of 13 July 1967, the money of account was initially Kenyan currency or sterling. To my mind, Orr J was right, for the reasons given by him, in holding that when that contract was made the money of account was Kenyan. The fact that it was expressed in a form which was appropriate for Kenyan currency and was not appropriate for sterling must outweigh, and far outweigh, the various indications relied on by the buyers as pointing to sterling. However, in my judgment the currency of account was subsequently varied from Kenyan currency to sterling. That being so, the sellers have been paid the full amount to which they are entitled and they have no valid claim against the buyers.

The contract of sale contained its own express provision for payment, which I have already quoted in full. I repeat the essential words: 'Payment: by confirmed, irrevocable letter of credit...' There is nothing else in the contract, at least in its express terms, which adds to, subtracts from, or qualifies that contractual provision as to payment of the price. It was the buyers' obligation to procure that a bank should offer to the sellers its confirmation of an irrevocable credit which would provide for payment of the contract price as specified in the contract of sale, against delivery to the bank of the proper documents.

The offer made by the confirming bank, as I have already said, did not comply, in several respects, with what the sellers were entitled to require. However, the only non-conforming aspect of the offer which I regard as relevant for the purposes of this appeal is the term of the offer in respect of currency. That, in my view, is not only relevant, it is vital. The confirming bank's offer, made to the sellers with the knowledge of, and on the instructions of, the buyers, was an offer which involved sterling, not merely as the currency of payment, but as the currency of account, in respect of that transaction. The sellers accepted the conforming bank's offer, including its terms as to currency, by submitting invoices and drafts with the form and contents which I have already described.

As I see it, the necessary consequence of that offer and acceptance of a sterling credit is that the original term of the contract of sale as to the money of account was varied from Kenyan currency to sterling. The payment, and the sole payment, stipulated by the contract of sale was by the letter of credit. The buyers, through the confirming bank, had opened a letter of credit which did not conform, because it provided sterling as the money of account. The sellers accepted that offer by making use of the credit to receive payment for a part of the contractual goods. By that acceptance, as the sellers must be deemed to have known, not only did the confirming bank become irrevocably bound by the terms of the offer (and by no other terms), but so also did the buyers become bound. Not only did they incur legal obligations as a result of the sellers' acceptance— for example, an obligation to indemnify the bank—but also the buyers could not thereafter have turned round and said to the sellers (for example, if Kenyan currency had been devalued against sterling) that the bank would thereafter pay less for the contractual goods than the promised sterling payment of £262 per ton. If the buyers could not revert unilaterally to the original currency of account, once they had offered a variation which had been accepted by conduct, neither could the sellers so revert. The contract had been varied in that respect.

The sellers, however, contend that they were, indeed, entitled to make use of the non-conforming letter of credit offered to them, without impairing their rights for the future under the original terms of the contract, if and when they chose to revert. They seek to rely on the analogy of a sale of goods contract where the goods are deliverable by instalments, and one instalment falls short of the prescribed quality. The buyer is not obliged, even if in law he could do so, to treat the contract as repudiated. He is not, it is said, even obliged to complain. But he is in no way precluded from insisting that for future instalments of the goods the seller shall conform with the precise terms of the contract as to quality. That is not, in my opinion, a true analogy. The relevant transaction here is not one of instalments. It is a once-for-all transaction. It is the establishment of a credit which is to cover the whole of the payment for the whole of the contract. Once it has been accepted by the sellers, the bank is committed, and is committed in accordance with its accepted terms, and no other terms. Once the credit is established and accepted it is unalterable, except with the consent of all the parties concerned, all of whose legal rights and liabilities have necessarily been affected by the establishment of the credit. Hence the sellers cannot escape from the consequences of the acceptance of the offered credit by any argument that their apparent acceptance involved merely a temporary acquiescence which they could revoke or abandon at will, or on giving notice. It was an acceptance which, once made, related to the totality of the letter of credit transaction; and the letter of credit transaction was, by the contract of sale, the one and only contractual provision for payment. When the letter of credit was accepted as a transaction in sterling as the currency of account, the price under the sale of contract could not remain as Kenyan currency.

For the buyers it was submitted further that, if there were not here a variation of the contract, there was at least a waiver, which the sellers could not, or did not properly revoke. I do not propose to go into that submission at any length. On analysis, it covers much the same field as the question of variation. In my view, if there were no variation, the buyers would still be entitled to succeed on the ground of waiver. The relevant principle is, in my opinion, that which was stated by Lord Cairns LC in *Hughes v Metropolitan Railway Co.* The acceptance by the sellers of the sterling credit was, as I have said, a once-for-all acceptance. It was not a concession for a specified period of time or one which the sellers could operate as long as they chose and thereafter unilaterally abrogate; any more than the buyers would have been entitled to alter the terms of the credit or to have demanded a refund from the sellers if, after this credit had been partly used, the relative values of the currencies had changed in the opposite way. . . .

Stephenson LJ

I agree that this appeal succeeds on the second point of variation or waiver for reasons which I shall state in my own words, although they add little or nothing to what Lord Denning MR and Megaw LJ have already said.

The currency of account fixed by the contract of sale was clearly Kenya shillings and not sterling. I agree with the judge in attaching importance to the use of the abbreviation 'Shs', recognised as denoting Kenya shillings by the schedule to the Central Bank of Kenya Act 1966. It stamps Kenya on the contract as the money of account almost as 'schillings' would stamp Austria on it. Unlike the judge, I also attach importance to the presumption created by s 21 of the same Act, which does not seem to me to have been displaced by the agreement between buyers and sellers.

The letter of credit varied the currency of account in the events that happened from Kenya shillings to pounds sterling . . .

By not objecting to the non-conforming letter of credit, by obtaining payment on it in sterling from the bank and by extending it the sellers clearly accepted and agreed to it and were treated as having done so not only by the bank but by the buyers, who may be presumed (although there was no evidence about it) to have paid charges and incurred liabilities such as a liability to indemnify the bank. The sellers never indicated any reservations about the change from Kenya shillings to pounds sterling or asked for any adjustment, probably for the simple reason that they considered sterling as good as Kenya shillings if not better. When after devaluation of sterling they invoiced the balance of the goods against part payment of the balance of the price and claimed the difference created by devaluation from the buyers, they were attempting to assert a liability which, whether by variation or waiver, they had allowed the buyers to alter.

I agree also with the views expressed by Lord Denning MR on the first point that this confirmed irrevocable letter of credit operated as a conditional payment of the price which, when honoured, discharged the buyers' debt to the sellers. And I agree further that this would in the ordinary way be the effect of such a letter of credit being issued and accepted by the seller in performance of a contract of sale which does not stipulate expressly or impliedly that its issue and acceptance should have different effect. But on the second point I would leave open the question whether the action of the other party induced by the party who 'waives' his contractual rights can be any alteration to his opposition, as Lord Denning MR has said, or must, as the judge thought, be an alteration to his detriment, or for the worse, in some sense. In this case the buyers did, I think, contrary to the judge's view, act to their detriment on the sellers' waiver, if that is what it was, and the contract was varied for good consideration, which may be another way of saying the same thing; so that I need not, and do not, express a concluded opinion on that controversial question.

Appeal allowed.

NOTES

1. The majority said there was a binding variation in this case, but they did not elaborate on what constituted the consideration for the sellers' promise to accept sterling. What was the consideration?

2. Does the Court of Appeal accept the *High Trees* principle as good law? With what qualifications, if any?

3. Was there any detrimental reliance on the representation in *Hughes* or *Birmingham?* See the definition of detrimental reliance given by Dixon J in *Grundt's* case, p 148. What would the tenants in *Hughes* or *Birmingham* have done if the landlords had not made the representations they did? If the landlords were now allowed to enforce their original

rights, would the tenants be in the same position as before the representations had not been made, or worse off? What about in *High Trees*?

4.   In *Société Italo-Belge pour le Commerce et l'Industrie S A v Palm and Vegetable Oils (Malaysia) Sdn Bhd, The Post Chaser* [1982] 1 All ER 19, the sellers of a quantity of palm oil were obliged to make a declaration of which ship was carrying the oil. They made the declaration out of time, but the buyers made no protest: instead, they requested the sellers to hand the shipping documents to sub-buyers. However, when two days later the sub-buyers rejected the documents, the buyers in turn rejected them the same day, and the sellers were forced to sell the oil elsewhere at a loss. The sellers did not argue that the buyers, by taking the documents, had elected to accept them in performance (cf p 616); they accepted that the buyers' rejection was effective. But they argued that the buyers had represented that they would not exercise their right of rejection and that doing so later was a breach of contract for which the sellers were entitled to damages. Robert Goff J said (at 26–27):

I approach the matter as follows. The fundamental principle is that stated by Lord Cairns LC, viz that the representor will not be allowed to enforce his rights "where it would be inequitable having regard to the dealings which have thus taken place between the parties." To establish such inequity, it is not necessary to show detriment; indeed, the representee may have benefited from the representation, and yet it may be inequitable, at least without reasonable notice, for the representor to enforce his legal rights. Take the facts of *Central London Property Trust Ltd v High Trees House Ltd*, the case in which Denning J breathed new life into the doctrine of equitable estoppel. The representation was by a lessor to the effect that he would be content to accept a reduced rent. In such a case, although the lessee has benefited from the reduction in rent, it may well be inequitable for the lessor to insist on his legal right to the unpaid rent, because the lessee has conducted his affairs on the basis that he would only have to pay rent at the lower rate; and a court might well think it right to conclude that only after reasonable notice could the lessor return to charging rent at the higher rate specified in the lease. Furthermore it would be open to the court, in any particular case, to infer from the circumstances of the case that the representee must have conducted his affairs in such a way that it would be inequitable for the representor to enforce his rights, or to do so without reasonable notice. But it does not follow that in every case in which the representee has acted, or failed to act, in reliance on the representation, it will be inequitable for the representor to enforce his rights for the nature of the action, or inaction, may be insufficient to give rise to the equity, in which event a necessary requirement stated by Lord Cairns LC for the application of the doctrine would not have been fulfilled.

This, in my judgment, is the principle which I have to apply in the present case. Here, all that happened was that the sellers, through Kievit, presented the documents on the same day as the buyers made their representation; and within two days the documents were rejected. Now on these simple facts, although it is plain that the sellers did actively rely on the buyers' representation, and did conduct their affairs in reliance on it, by presenting the documents, I cannot see anything which would render it inequitable for the buyers thereafter to enforce their legal right to reject the documents. In particular, having regard to the very short time which elapsed between the date of the representation and the date of presentation of the documents on the one hand and the date of rejection on the other hand, I cannot see that, in the absence of any evidence that the sellers' position had been prejudiced by reason of their action in reliance on the representation, it is possible to infer that they suffered any such prejudice. In these circumstances, a necessary element for the application of the doctrine of equitable estoppel is lacking; and I decide this point in favour of the buyers.

5.   *Should* the debtor have to prove detrimental reliance? Sometimes detrimental reliance seems the factor that justifies holding the creditor to his or her promise (compare *Jorden v Money*, p 149), but not always. If the concession is properly viewed as an attempt by the

parties to deal with a situation that was not provided for in the original contract, it should be regarded as an extension of the original agreement—the original contract did not provide for all eventualities; now one of the gaps has been filled in by the parties themselves. The original agreement was enforceable as soon as made, without either party having to rely to his detriment on it: why shouldn't the same be true of the supplementary agreement?

6. It may be hard for the debtor to show exactly how it has relied on the promise to its detriment when 'it has conducted its affairs on the basis that it would only have to pay rent at the lower rate', as Robert Goff J put it. Is the point that detriment is presumed after a significant period of time has elapsed? (Compare Fuller's argument about proving reliance, pp 765–767.)

7. *Woodhouse A C Israel Cocoa Ltd S A v Nigerian Produce Marketing Co Ltd* [1972] AC 741 was another case involving the devaluation of sterling, but here, the House of Lords held that the sellers could claim the sterling equivalent of the original contract price, which had been expressed in Nigerian pounds: the sellers had said that 'payment may be made in pounds sterling in London or in £N in Lagos', but that was a statement only that they would accept *payment* in sterling of the sterling equivalent of the price calculated in Nigerian pounds. Even if the statement was ambiguous, to found a promissory estoppel, there had to be a clear and unequivocal representation. Lord Hailsham said:

> Counsel for the appellants was asked whether he knew of any case in which an ambiguous statement had ever formed the basis of a purely promissory estoppel, as contended for here, as distinct from estoppel of a more familiar type based on factual misrepresentation. He candidly replied that he did not. I do not find this surprising, since it would really be an astonishing thing if, in the case of a genuine misunderstanding as to the meaning of an offer, the offeree could obtain by means of the doctrine of promissory estoppel something that he must fail to obtain under the conventional law of contract. I share the feeling of incredulity expressed by Lord Denning MR in the course of his judgment when he said:
>
> > 'If the judge be right, it leads to this extraordinary consequence: a letter which is not sufficient to *vary* a contract is, nevertheless, sufficient to work an *estoppel*, which will have the same effect as a *variation*'.
>
> There seem to me to be so many and such conclusive reasons for dismissing this appeal that it may be thought a work of supererogation to add yet another. But basically I feel convinced that there was never here any real room for the doctrine of estoppel at all. If the exchange letter was not variation, I believe it was nothing. The appellants asked for a variation in the mode of discharge of a contract of sale. If the proposal meant what they claimed, and was accepted and acted on, I venture to think that the respondents would have been bound by their acceptance at least until they gave reasonable notice to terminate, and I imagine that a modern court would have found no difficulty in discovering consideration for such a promise. Businessmen know their own business best even when they appear to grant an indulgence, and in the present case I do not think that there would have been insuperable difficulty in spelling out consideration from the earlier correspondence. If, however, the two letters were insufficiently unambiguous and precise to form the basis, if accepted, for a variation in the contract I do not think their combined effect is sufficiently unambiguous or precise to form the basis of an estoppel which would produce the result of reducing the purchase price by no less than 14 per cent against a vendor who had never consciously agreed to the proposition.
>
> I desire to add that the time may soon come when the whole sequence of cases based on promissory estoppel since the war, beginning with *Central London Property Trust Ltd v High Trees House Ltd*, may need to be reviewed and reduced to a coherent body of doctrine by the courts. I do not mean to say

that any are to be regarded with suspicion. But, as is common with an expanding doctrine, they do raise problems of coherent exposition which have never been systematically explored. However this may be, we are not in a position to carry out this exploration here and in the present proceedings. It is sufficient to say here that, for the reasons I have given above, I would dismiss this appeal with costs.

8.   It is interesting to contrast this insistence that a clear promise (or at least an unambiguous representation) is needed for promissory estoppel with the cases on *proprietary* estoppel, in which something less clear seems to suffice: see p 163.

9.   Could an explanation be that, in promissory estoppel, the promise itself may be taken to have affected the promisor's right to revert to the original state of affairs, unless any reliance by the promisee is disproved (as in *The Post Chaser*), but that a proprietary estoppel only comes into play when it is shown that the other party has acted to its detriment on the representation, so that for proprietary estoppel the courts are less insistent that the representation be a clear one?

In *Brikom Investments Ltd v Carr* [1979] 2 All ER 753, the landlords of four blocks of flats offered to sell 99-year leases to their sitting tenants. At the time, the roofs of each block were in need of repair and the landlords made oral representations to the tenants that the landlords would repair the roofs at their own expense. The leases, which were subsequently signed, provided that the tenants would contribute to maintenance expenses incurred by the landlords. The landlords had the roofs repaired and then claimed contributions from the tenants (in some cases, the assignees of the original tenants who had been given the assurances), who refused to pay. The Court of Appeal upheld the judgment of the county court that the landlords' claim should be dismissed. All three members of the court agreed that the landlord's assurance amounted to a collateral contract with each tenant. The assignees were also protected because, after the first day in the county court, the original tenants who had assigned their leases had also assigned the benefits of any collateral contract to their successors.

However, the main ground on which Lord Denning MR rested his judgment was that both the original tenants and their assignees could rely on promissory estoppel. Roskill LJ refused to decide the case on promissory estoppel but held that, in addition to the collateral contract, both original tenants and assignees were protected by what he described as 'a plain waiver by the landlords of their right to claim the cost of these repairs from these tenants'. He said:

I do not rest my decision on any question of promissory estoppel; and I do not think it necessary on the facts of this case to investigate the jurisprudential basis of that doctrine in order to arrive at which I conceive to be the right decision. It is necessary to do no more than to apply that which was said by the House of Lords and especially by Lord Cairns LC in *Hughes v Metropolitan Railway Co.*
Spencer Bower on Estoppel [3rd edn, 1977, pp 383, para 349]...I would respectfully add to that that it would be wrong to extend the doctrine of promissory estoppel, whatever its precise limits at the present day, to the extent of abolishing in this back-handed way the doctrine of consideration...
It seems to me in the present case that counsel for the tenants' argument (in so far as it rests on promissory estoppel) involves taking that doctrine a great deal further than it has hitherto been taken.
...

I think it necessary to go no further than what Lord Cairns LC said in *Hughes v Metropolitan Railway Co* where the matter was put not as one of promissory estoppel but as a matter of contract law or equity (call it which you will):
   [Roskill LJ quoted an extract from the judgment of Lord Cairns (see above, pp 741–742) and continued:]
For my own part, I would respectfully prefer to regard that as an illustration of contractual variation of strict contractual rights. But it could equally well be put as an illustration of equity relieving from the consequences of strict adherence to the letter of the lease.

But, whichever is the right way of putting it, ever since *Hughes v Metropolitan Railway Co*, through a long line of cases of which there are many examples in the books, one finds that where parties have made a contract which provides one thing and where, by a subsequent course of dealing, the parties have worked that contract out in such a way that one party leads the other to believe that the strict rights under that contract will not be adhered to, the courts will not allow that party who has led the other to think the strict rights will not be adhered to, suddenly to seek to enforce those strict rights against him. That seems to me to be precisely what the landlords are trying to do here.

Cumming-Bruce LJ agreed that the appeal should be dismissed for the reasons given by Roskill LJ. Do you agree that, on the facts, this case was governed by *Hughes v Metropolitan Railway* Co? In *Hughes*, the landlord was ultimately entitled to have the repairs done or to forfeit the lease if the tenant did not do them. In *Brikom*, could the landlords ever recover the cost of the repairs from the tenants? If not, doesn't that suggest that Roskill LJ is actually applying not the older principle of waiver but the newer principle of promissory estoppel?

■ **Aivazian, Trebllcock and Penny, 'The Law of Contract Modifications: The Uncertain Quest for a Benchmark of Enforceability'** (1984)
22 Osgoode Hall LJ 173, at 187–205

We assume a rather prosaic objective for the law on modifications: minimizing transaction costs, and proceed to develop an economic framework that attempts to identify the variables that must be taken into account in formulating legal rules that advance this objective.

We shall follow Posner and initially distinguish two alternative sets of cases in which contract modifications might be sought. In one set of cases there are no changes in the underlying economic conditions governing the initial contract except that the promisee has acquired some monopoly power *ex post* and exploits this power by forcing higher returns than provided for in the initial contract. Posner argues for the non-enforcement of contract modifications in such cases. The second set of cases is characterized by changes in the underlying economic conditions, or the emergence of new information about the underlying economic conditions governing the contract which prevent or inhibit the promisee from completing the promised performance without a modification of the contract. Posner argues that modification is justified in such cases because without that ability mutually advantageous exchanges may be precluded. . . .

Consider now the first set of cases. For these cases *ex post* contract modification is a zero sum game. What one party gains the other loses—in other words there is, by assumption, no room for co-operative recontracting. Assume an economic environment characterized by zero transaction costs, rational expectations and complete information about all contingencies. Assume also that the contract is initially drawn up under perfectly competitive conditions. We will argue that in such an environment whether the law enforces contract modifications is irrelevant from a resource perspective and has no bearing on the economic welfare of the contracting parties. All that is required is that the law be *unambiguous*.

Suppose the law does enforce contract modifications. Then the terms of the initial contract will reflect the optimal future *(ex post)* strategy of the promisee. Suppose the promisor initially enters into the contract recognizing that the promisee's optimal future strategy will be to force higher returns through contract modifications. Since the law will enforce such modifications, the initial contract terms will be adjusted to reflect these future payoffs to the promisee. Potential extortionary monopoly rents will thus be fully impounded—given perfect competition and rational expectations—into *ex ante* contract terms. As long as the promisee's optimal *ex post* strategy (whether opportunistic or not) is unique, it will be fully reflected in the initial contract in this rational expectations environment.

Suppose, on the other hand, that the law does *not* enforce contract modifications. Then the initial contractual terms will be adjusted so that the return to the promisee, under the contract, will exceed his return in the previous case by a margin which exactly corresponds to the present value of the extortionary monopoly rents that would have accrued to the promisee if contract modifications were allowed and the promisee's optimal *ex post* strategy was to act opportunistically. . . .

However, if there are positive transactions costs, then the choice of legal regime may have a significant influence on resource allocation. Initial analysis suggests that a law which unambiguously disallows contract modifications will generally be more efficient. Such a law economizes on the transaction costs that would otherwise be incurred in a regime that allowed contract modification. These costs not only include the direct costs associated with contract modifications (contract renegotiations take time and absorb other resources), but also those associated with various contractual and institutional arrangements designed to forestall opportunistic behaviour. These latter costs include those of writing, monitoring and enforcing detailed contractual provisions to penalize or constrain opportunism, as well as the costs of the resources expended by the promisee (for example bonding costs) to convince the promisor that he will not behave opportunistically. It is in the promisee's interest to incur such costs (which limit his potential opportunism) in a regime that allows contract modifications to induce an optimal initial level of mutually advantageous contracts. However, such costs engender a reduction in the initial exchange opportunity since the exchange process is more costly. . . .

In short, in cases where contract modifications occur purely and simply as a result of changes in the strategic circumstances of the contracting parties, the enforcement or non-enforcement of modified contracts in a zero transaction costs environment with complete information about future contingencies and rational expectations will have no bearing on resource allocation or economic welfare. In an environment with positive transaction costs or incomplete information, a law which disallows contract modifications will economize on transaction costs and maximize the gains from contractual agreements. Hence, efficiency considerations dictate that contract modifications in this context be non-enforceable.

The second set of cases in which contract modifications may be sought (supervening changes in the economic environment of the contract) are those in which modifications can represent mutually advantageous positive-sum games . . .

If recontracting between the parties in a particular *ex post* state of nature is mutually advantageous, then it will occur, leading to an optimal restructuring of contractual terms. These considerations suggest that contract modifications are necessary for the attainment of Pareto efficiency and should be allowed by law in this second set of cases. However, as we will see, such a conclusion is premature since there are additional considerations that bear on the problem . . .

Where the contract has specifically assigned certain risks, the presumption should be that they have been assigned to the superior (that is, most efficient) risk bearer and, moreover, that he has been adequately compensated for bearing them, thus removing any distributional objections to leaving him to bear the costs. Where the contract is not explicit about the allocation of a given risk, it seems a reasonable presumptive rule of interpretation to assume that the parties intended for it to be borne by the superior risk bearer and that it has simply been impounded in the categoric terms of the contract. In either case, the party bearing such risks should not be permitted to subsequently reallocate them to the other party by contract modification, taking advantage of limitations in the relief available to the party on breach in order to induce the modification.

If the law allows contract modifications, it imposes at least part of the risk of adverse outcomes on the promisor. To the extent that the promisee can modify risks by his activities, and there is imperfect monitoring of his activities by the promisor, a moral hazard problem will arise. The promisee will have incentives to increase his risk exposure (relative to the case where he fully bears the risks) over time by devoting fewer resources to risk prevention than is optimal and increasing the probability of occurrence of adverse states (for example, bankruptcy) in which contract modifications may be necessary. Thus, the enforcement of contract modifications may generate inappropriate incentives over time that affect the probabilities of alternative outcomes or states of nature. Inappropriate incentives are created not only for the immediate contracting parties but, even more importantly, for future contracting parties in similar circumstances. . . .

In effect, we view enforceable modifications as a substitute for the doctrine of frustration: contracting parties, facing the occurrence of some intervening event that substantially affects the cost of performance may, under some circumstances, rearrange their contractual rights and obligations either through invocation of the assistance of the courts pursuant to the doctrine of frustration or through private recontracting. In other cases, while the underlying factual circumstances of the contract may not have changed, new information about those circumstances may have been uncovered. The parties may have contracted on the basis of incomplete or inaccurate information about the underlying factual environment of the contract. This situation is the domain of the doctrine of mistake. The economic considerations bearing on permissible rearrangements by virtue of contract modifications, the doctrine of frustration, or the doctrine of mistake would seem to be similar. . . .

However, in applying this approach both to frustration and modification cases, several problems must be acknowledged. First, the contract may not clearly assign given risks and an objective inquiry into who is the superior risk bearer may sometimes be indeterminate (for example, one party may have superior ability to appraise the probability of a particular event occurring, but the other party may have superior ability to appraise the magnitude of the costs entailed if it does). . . .

Another problem may arise in cases where it may be feasible to identify clearly the superior risk bearer but the risk in question is very remote . . . if the risk is remote enough, that is, carries a very low probability, the effects of assigning it to one party or the other may have little effect on contractual behaviour because the *expected* (that is, *ex ante*) costs to whoever bears the risk are so small as to warrant very little, if anything, in the way of efficient precautionary responses.

Taking these two problematic cases together—(a) indeterminacy in the identification of the superior risk bearer, and (b) highly remote risks—it can be argued that these are the transactional domains where contractual modifications should be permitted. In both cases, permitting modifications enables the party to whom a modification is proposed to capture some of the static gains from recontracting by avoiding losses he may well sustain in the event of a breach. Losses in dynamic efficiency associated with a rule that permits subsequent reassignment of initially efficiently assigned risks are likely to be small, in the first case because we cannot determine with confidence what is an efficient allocation of risks, and in the second case because while this can be determined, disturbing the efficient allocation of risks will have little impact on the long-run behaviour of contracting parties at large while enabling the static gains for the immediate parties from recontracting, which may be significant, to be realized.

Permitting modifications in these two classes of cases, in effect, permits a flexible form of risk sharing by the contracting partners. Assuming the parties to be risk averse and the risk in question one that neither can readily control or insure against, contract modification may reduce the variance in possible contractual outcomes for the parties and thus be Pareto efficient. A countervailing consideration is, of course, that the promisor now is exposed to the risk of strategic behaviour by the promisee designed to exploit or manipulate these two exceptions and to the adjudication costs attendant on courts attempting to apply rules that do not supply knife-edged sharpness in the characterization of situations as falling within or outside given rules or exceptions thereto . . .

Posner endorses the result in *[Goebel v Linn]* case on the basis of his distinction between modifications entered into where there has been a change in underlying circumstances and those where there has not. However, our emphasis on efficient risk allocation suggests a more cautious approach to evaluating the correctness of this decision. If mild winters were one of the occupational hazards of running an ice business during the era in question, the ice company would seem clearly to be the superior risk bearer, both in terms of risk reduction (for example, making different inventory or stand-by sub-contractual arrangements) and in terms of risk insurance (that is, being better able to appraise the impact of climatic variations on the supply of ice and adjusting the initial contractual fixed price accordingly). Only where the winter in question was quite out of the ordinary so that the gains from recontracting were likely to outweigh the long-run costs of moral hazard problems associated with permitting recontracting in these circumstances, could one support the decision. Otherwise, permitting recontracting is inefficient.

NOTES

1.   Posner is now on the bench. In *Selmer Co v Blakeslee-Midwest Co* 704 F 2d 924 (USCA 7th Cir, 1983), he had to decide a case in which the facts resembled *D&C Builders v Rees* (see p 856) save that the amount due was in dispute. Judge Posner held that an agreement to accept only part of what was claimed was binding, even though the party accepting the

settlement was in 'financial distress', when the distress was not due to the other party's conduct.

2.   Judge Posner was also involved in a very interesting case on the question of the need for reliance on a waiver: *Wisconsin Knife Works v National Metal Crafters* 781 F 2d 1280 (USCA 7th Cir, 1986). Uniform Commercial Code, s 2–209 removes the requirement of consideration for an agreement to modify a contract, but allows the parties to agree that modifications will be binding only if they are in writing.

UCC § 2–209

(1) An agreement modifying a contract within this Article needs no consideration to be binding.

(2) A signed agreement which excludes modification or rescission except by a signed writing cannot be otherwise modified or rescinded, but except as between merchants such a requirement on a form supplied by the merchant must be separately signed by the other party.

(3) The requirements of the statute of frauds section of this Article (Section 2–201) must be satisfied if the contract as modified is within its provisions.

(4) Although an attempt at modification or rescission does not satisfy the requirements of subsection (2) or (3) it can operate as a waiver.

(5) A party who has made a waiver affecting an executory portion of the contract may retract the waiver by reasonable notification received by the other party that strict performance will be required of any term waived, unless the retraction would be unjust in view of a material change of position in reliance on the waiver.

In the contract in question, there was a requirement that any modification be in writing, but there had been an oral agreement to change the terms. Posner, for the majority, argued that an oral agreement should be enforceable as a waiver if the party who stood to benefit from the waiver had relied on it, and could not be withdrawn. He said (at 1286 ff):

...the framers of the Uniform Commercial Code, as part and parcel of rejecting the requirement of consideration for modifications...must have believed that the protection which the doctrines of duress and bad faith give against extortionate modifications might need reinforcement—if not from a requirement of consideration, which had proved ineffective, then from a grant of power to include a clause requiring modifications to be in writing and signed. An equally important point is that with consideration no longer required for modification, it was natural to give the parties some means of providing a substitute for the cautionary and evidentiary function that the requirement of consideration provides; and the means chosen was to allow them to exclude oral modifications.

If section 2–209(4), which as we said provides that an attempted modification which does not comply with subsection (2) can nevertheless operate as a "waiver," is interpreted so broadly that *any* oral modification is effective as a waiver notwithstanding section 2–209(2), both provisions become superfluous and we are back in the common law—only with not even a requirement of consideration to reduce the likelihood of fabricated or unintended oral modifications....

...A conceivable but unsatisfactory way around this result is to distinguish between a modification that substitutes a new term for an old, and a waiver, which merely removes an old term. On this interpretation National Metal Crafters could not enforce an oral term of the allegedly modified contract but could be excused from one of the written terms. This would take care of a case such as *Alaska Packers*, where seamen attempted to enforce a contract modification that raised their wages, but would not take care of the functionally identical case where seamen sought to collect the agreed-on wages without doing the agreed-on work. Whether the party claiming modification is seeking to impose an onerous new term on the other party or to wriggle out of an onerous term that the original contract imposed on it is a distinction without a difference....

The path of reconciliation with subsection (4) is found by attending to the precise wording of (4). It does not say that an attempted modification "is" a waiver; it says that "it can operate as a waiver." It

does not say in what circumstances it can operate as a waiver; but if an attempted modification is effective as a waiver only if there is reliance, then both sections 2–209(2) and 2–209(4) can be given effect. Reliance, if reasonably induced and reasonable in extent, is a common substitute for consideration in making a promise legally enforceable, in part because it adds something in the way of credibility to the mere say-so of one party. The main purpose of forbidding oral modifications is to prevent the promisor from fabricating a modification that will let him escape his obligations under the contract; and the danger of successful fabrication is less if the promisor has actually incurred a cost, has relied. There is of course a danger of bootstrapping—of incurring a cost in order to make the case for a modification. But it is a risky course and is therefore less likely to be attempted than merely testifying to a conversation; it makes one put one's money where one's mouth is.
[The majority said the case should be remanded for determination of whether there had been reliance.]

Easterbrook, Circuit Judge, dissented, holding that this was not a permissible reading of the statute: an oral waiver could be withdrawn. He said (at 1292):

The majority makes reliance an ingredient of waiver not because the structure of the UCC demands this reading, but because it believes that otherwise the UCC would not deal adequately with the threat of opportunistic conduct. The drafters of the UCC chose to deal with opportunism not through a strict reading of waiver, however, but through a statutory requirement of commercial good faith. See 2–103 and comment 2 to 2–209. The modification-only-in-writing clause has nothing to do with opportunism. A person who has his contracting partner over a barrel, and therefore is able to obtain a concession, can get the concession in writing. The writing will be the least of his worries. In almost all of the famous cases of modification the parties reduced the new agreement to writing.

A useful survey of the field of waiver and promissory estoppel will be found in Dugdale and Yates 'Variation, Waiver and Estoppel—a Reappraisal' (1976) 39 MLR 680.

QUESTIONS

1. According to the traditional doctrine, what had to be shown to prove that a contract had been (i) rescinded or (ii) varied? What was the effect of a valid variation?

2. A creditor knows that a debtor who owes him £1,000 is unable to pay him in full. He promises that, if the debtor pays £500, he will release the debtor from the rest. Is the creditor's promise made for good consideration? Are there any circumstances in which the creditor's promise *will* be regarded as having been given for good consideration?

3. An employer knows that a building contractor will be unable to finish the contract work unless the employer pays him 10 per cent extra, so he promises to pay this amount. Is this promise supported by consideration?

4. If your answer to question 2 was that the promise is normally not supported by consideration, but your answer to question 3 was that it sometimes will be, do you think there is any justification for treating one promise as being made for good consideration but not the other?

5. Describe the principal features of the doctrine of promisory estoppel.

6. To what extent is this doctrine a departure from the older doctrine of waiver? What was being 'given up' by the party who made the waiver in those cases? When could the waiver be withdrawn and when could it not?

7.   To what extent has the doctrine expounded by Denning in *High Trees* and the subsequent cases in this chapter been accepted by the courts?

8.   Is there now any practical difference between the circumstances in which a promise to release a debt, or not to enforce some other contractual right, on the one hand, and a promise to pay extra, or to perform some other action at no extra cost, on the other, will be treated as binding?

9.   *Should* the law enforce a promise to pay, extra, or to give up an existing contractual right, which is given freely, even if there is no consideration? Should the promisee have to show that he has relied on the promise to his detriment? Or at all?

10.   Are the development of promissory estoppel and the recent changes to consideration doctrine in this context examples of 'consumer-welfarism', or could they equally well be justified in terms of supporting the market (see Adams & Brownsword, above, and the readings on pp 857 and 875)?

CHAPTER THIRTY-THREE

ADJUSTMENTS IN LONGER TERM CONTRACTS

Many contracts are designed to run over a period of time, and it may be difficult to predict in advance how such matters as the costs of performing or the parties' needs may change during the period. It is very common for the parties to attempt to build a degree of flexibility into the agreement by the use of various types of clause. An obvious example is a price fluctuation clause, under which the price to be paid will vary as certain costs involved in performing (eg the cost of labour or materials) change. Another is a clause allowing one party to change what is to be done by the other.

■ ICE Conditions of Contract (7th edn)

cll 51–52

ALTERATIONS, ADDITIONS AND OMISSIONS

51.(1) *Ordered variations.* The Engineer
- (a) shall order any variation to any part of the Works that is in his opinion necessary for the completion of the Works and
- (b) may order any variation that for any other reason shall in his opinion be desirable for the completion and/or improved functioning of the Works. Such variations may include additions omissions substitutions alterations changes in quality form character kind position dimension level or line and changes in any specified sequence method or timing of construction required by the Contract and may be ordered during the Defects Correction Period.

(2) *Ordered variations to be in writing.* All variations shall be ordered in writing but the provisions of clause 2(6) in respect of oral instructions shall apply.

(3) *Variation not to affect Contract.* No variation ordered in accordance with sub-clauses (1) and (2) of this Clause shall in any way vitiate or invalidate the Contract but the value (if any) of all such variations shall be taken into account in ascertaining the amount of the Contract Price except to the extent that such variation is necessitated by the Contractor's default.

(4) *Changes in quantities.* No order in writing shall be required for increase or decrease in the quantity of any work where such increase or decrease is not the result of an order given under this clause but is the result of the quantities exceeding or being less than those stated in the Bill of Quantities.

52.(1) *Valuation of ordered variations.* If requested by the Engineer the Contractor shall submit his quotation for any proposed variation and his estimate of any consequential delay. Wherever possible the value and delay consequences (if any) of each variation shall be agreed before the order is issued or before work starts.

(2) Where a request is not made or agreement is not reached under sub-clause (1) the valuation of variations ordered by the Engineer in accordance with Clause 51 shall be ascertained as follows.

  (a) As soon as possible after receipt of the variation the Contractor shall submit to the Engineer
    (i) his quotation for any extra or substituted works necessitated by the variation having due regard to any rates or prices included in the Contract and
    (ii) his estimate of any delay occasioned thereby and
    (iii) his estimate of the cost of any such delay
  (b) Within 14 days of receiving the said submission the Engineer shall
    (i) accept those submissions or
    (ii) negotiate with the Contractor thereon.
  (c) Upon reaching agreement with the Contractor the Contract Price shall be amended accordingly.

(3) Failing agreement between the Engineer and the Contractor under either sub-clause (1) or (2) the value of variations ordered by the Engineer in accordance with Clause 51 shall be ascertained by the Engineer in accordance with the following principles and be notified to the Contractor.

  (a) Where work is of similar character and carried out under similar conditions to work priced in the Bill of Quantities it shall be valued at such rates and prices contained therein as may be applicable.
  (b) Where work is not of a similar character or is not carried out under similar conditions or is ordered during the Defects Correction Period the rates and prices in the Bill of Quantities shall be used as the basis for valuation so far as may be reasonable failing which a fair valuation shall be made.

(4) *Engineer to fix rates.* If in the opinion of the Engineer or the Contractor any rate or price contained in the Contract for any item of work (not being the subject of any variation) is by reason of any variation rendered unreasonable or inapplicable either the Engineer shall give to the Contractor or the Contractor shall give to the Engineer notice before the varied work is commenced or as soon thereafter as is reasonable in all the circumstances that such rate or price should be increased or decreased and the Engineer shall fix such rate or price as in the circumstances he shall think reasonable and proper and shall so notify the Contractor.

(5) *Daywork.* The Engineer may if in his opinion it is necessary or desirable order in writing that any additional or substituted work shall be carried out on a daywork basis in accordance with the provisions of Clause 56(4).

NOTES

1.   Why insert a clause of this type rather than agree changes in the specification as and when necessary? Can you see why it would be unwise for the employer to count on persuading the original contractor to do the extra work, or to get in someone else to do it if he cannot reach agreement?

2.   Note that the power to order variations under cl 51 is expressly limited: the variation must 'in his opinion be desirable for the satisfactory completion and functioning of the Works'. Ordering that an item be omitted simply to save money is probably outside the engineer's powers. Of course, he might try to persuade the contractor to consent to such an omission, but the contractor would be within his rights to refuse to consent unless he was given compensation. A variation that is outside the scope of cl 51 will equally be outside the scope of the valuation mechanisms of cl 52, unless the contractor is prepared to waive his rights and treat it in all respects as a proper variation.

3. Even more broadly phrased variation clauses may be subject to implicit limitations. In *Carr v JA Berriman Pty Ltd* (1953) 27 ALJ 273, the defendant had contracted to erect a factory for the plaintiff; the variation clause provided: 'The Architect may in his absolute discretion and from time to time issue . . . written instructions or written directions . . . in regard to the . . . omission . . . of any work . . .' The contract provided for the free issue of steel by the plaintiff and its fabrication by the defendant to the architect's instructions. The High Court of Australia held that the architect was not entitled to award a contract for the fabrication of the steel to another company. Fullagar J said: 'The words quoted . . . do not . . . authorize him to say that particular items so included shall be carried out not by the builder with whom the contract is made but by some other builder or contractor. The words used do not, in their natural meaning, extend so far, and a power in the architect to hand over at will any part of the contract to another contractor would be a most unreasonable power, which very clear words would be required to confer.' (Compare the cases on the interpretation of exclusion clauses in the next section.)

4. A converse problem arose in *Sir Lindsay Parkinson & Co Ltd v Comrs of Works and Public Buildings* [1949] 2 KB 632. The contract (as subsequently varied by deed) contemplated work costing some £5m in the first instance. It provided that the contractor could be ordered to carry out any extras, but that in no circumstances might the contractor's profit (which was estimated as a percentage of the cost) be less than £150,000 or exceed £300,000. A note in the bill of quantities stated: 'It is probable that further work to the value of approximately £500,000 will be ordered . . .' The extra work ordered took the cost to £6.5m and the contractor claimed that it was entitled to additional profit. The Court of Appeal allowed the claim, because the extra work was outside the scope of the contract.

5. The decisions in *Carr* and *Lindsay Parkinson* may be viewed as the courts controlling 'opportunism' on the part of contracting parties who are attempting to exploit the terms of the contract. See further Muris, 'Opportunistic Behaviour and the Law of Contracts' (1981) 65 Minnesota LR 521.

6. Note also that, in some circumstances, the engineer may be under an *obligation* to order a variation: he *'shall* order any variation . . . that may in his opinion be necessary'. If, for instance, a design error makes the original specification impossible to reach, the employer will be in breach of contract if the engineer does not issue a variation order to deal with the problem. The same result was reached in *Holland, Hannen & Cubitts (Northern) Ltd v Welsh Health Technical Services Organization* (1981) 18 BLR 80, even though the variation clause (under the JCT form, 1963 edn) said nothing expressly about any duty to issue a variation order.

The ICE conditions also exhibit another characteristic often found in contracts designed to last over a period of time: decisions as to what is to be done, and how the consequent costs are to be allocated, are left to a third party, in this case, the engineer. He or she is not a party to the contract, and although employed by the employer, he or she is frequently expected to act in an independent manner in administering the contract—for instance, in deciding whether it is necessary to order a variation, or whether a price contained in the bill of quantities is applicable to the work ordered. In fact, the engineer's decisions are not final, because if either party is dissatisfied it may seek arbitration, but clearly there is less likely to be dissatisfaction over an 'independent' decision than one taken by the employer unilaterally, and in addition, most matters can only be arbitrated after completion of the contract.

In what can again be viewed as a move against opportunism, the courts attempt to ensure that the engineer (or the architect, who is given a parallel role under many building contracts) does act impartially. If the engineer allows himself or herself to be unduly influenced by the employer, or simply only has regard to one side's (typically the employer's) interests, he or she is disqualified. This means that sums that would normally be due to the contractor if the engineer has so certified may be recovered without the engineer's certificate: *Hickman & Co v Roberts* [1913] AC 229. In *Perini Corpn v Commonwealth of Australia* (1969) 12 BLR 82, it was held that the engineer's failure to act impartially put the *employer* into breach of contract, so that the contractor could recover damages for the increased cost it incurred after the engineer failed to grant extensions of time and the contractor speeded up work.

In recent years, a considerable amount of theoretical work has been done on long-term contractual and other relationships, particularly by Macneil. A summary of Macneil's theory of relational contracting will be found at pp 65 ff. It will be remembered that he highlights the contrast between discrete exchanges, in which nothing before the contract and nothing after it is relevant, and relational exchanges, particularly those designed to take a period of time— although he argues that all exchanges are to some extent relational in that the social matrix in which they take place gives rise to understandings and expectations (see notes on p 66).

A particular difference between discrete contracts and relational exchanges, which are to take place over a period of time, is the extent to which the parties' rights and obligations can be fixed at the outset—or, as Macneil puts it, 'presentiated'.

■ Macneil, 'Restatement (Second) of Contracts and Presentiation' (1974)
60 Virginia LR 589, 589–596

To presentiate: 'to make or render present in place or time; to cause to be perceived or realized as present.' Presentiation is only a manner in which a person perceives the future's effect on the present; but it depends upon events outside the individual psyche, events viewed as determining the future. Presentiation is thus a recognition that the course of the future is bound by present events, *and* that by those events the future has for many purposes been brought effectively into the present.

Although we are surrounded by this phenomenon, its name was described as rare even forty years ago. Thus it is not surprising that the term was never employed in a traditional contract theory implicitly requiring total presentiation of each contract relation at the time of its formation through offer and acceptance.

A remark made by Anthony Quinn while playing an Eskimo in *The Savage Innocents* (1961) illustrates further the concept of presentiation. One of the two white men with Quinn had fallen through the ice in the midst of a raging blizzard, and Quinn and the other had quickly pulled him out of the water. The victim was freezing to death in spite of the efforts of his friend to slap circulation through his body. Watching the frantic efforts, Quinn said, 'Your friend is dead.' It was a perfectly sensible statement even though the doomed man was still breathing, his heart still beating, and his limbs still moving. All the events had occurred which would cause his death, and there was not the slightest chance of avoiding that event.

Because presentiation depends upon recognition of the binding of the future, anything preventing either binding of the future or recognition of that binding frustrates presentiation. Such an impediment is the existence of choice. To the extent that people have choice and we do not know how they will exercise it, the future remains unbound, and cannot be presentiated.

TRADITIONAL CONTRACT LAW AND PRESENTIATION

Several generations ago the German legal scholar, Kohler, said, 'It is the province of the law of obligations to draw the future into the present.' This is precisely what traditional contract law was designed to do, by adding legal sanctions to the bindingness of mutual assent. This aspect of traditional contract law, most highly developed in this country by Williston, was a truly ingenious intellectual creation. Primarily through manipulations of the notion of consent, traditional contract theory created a legal structure which in theory attempted to presentiate not just part of the relation between contracting parties, but virutally all of it. When a subjective meeting of the minds became too narrow a concept upon which to base complete presentiation, the contract structure shifted to an objective theory of contracts, reinforced by such doctrines as the parol evidence rule. Unfortunately, sometimes consent, even objective consent, was too vague in commitment or content to serve as a basis for total presentiation. The relation created by such vague consent was excluded from the realm of contract altogether, leaving the parties with only the legal reinforcement they might find in the law of quasi-contract or torts. Since this was often undesirable, the designers of the structure went to great lengths to infer consent to such things as reasonable times or prices, or to imply conditions and other terms. Faced with inevitable problems of mistakes, impossibility, or other frustration of original goals, the theory utilized implied conditions in an attempt to preserve the facade of initial presentiation by mutual assent. When consent was stretched as far as it reasonably could be or, some would say, farther, then the gap-filling Corpus Juris Contractus took over directly, exemplified by Williston's analysis of impossibility . . .

No one was ever so naive as to believe that contract law could indeed achieve total presentiation, but there are some kinds of contracts where close approximations may be possible. Complete presentiation is most likely to lead to useful outcomes in contracts properly described as discrete transactions. These are contracts of short duration, with limited personal interactions, and with precise party measurements of easily measured objects of exchange, for example money and grain. They are transactions requiring a minimum of future cooperative behavior between the parties and not requiring a sharing of benefits or burdens. They bind the two parties tightly and precisely. The parties view such transactions as deals free of entangling strings, and they certainly expect no altruism. The parties see virtually everything connected with such transactions as clearly defined and presentiated. If trouble is anticipated at all, it is anticipated only if someone or something turns out unexpectably badly. The epitome of discrete contract transactions: two strangers come into town from opposite directions, one walking and one riding a horse. The walker offers to buy the horse, and after brief dickering a deal is struck in which delivery of the horse is to be made at sundown upon the handing over of $10. The two strangers expect to have nothing to do with each other between now and sundown, they expect never to see each other again thereafter, and each has as much feeling for the other as has a Viking trading with a Saxon.

A high degree of presentiation is possible in truly discrete transactions, because it is possible to approach complete mutual planning and to do so at one point in time. This completeness and unity of planning creates a situation where it is reasonable for the parties to bind themselves to stick rigorously by the planning. That in turn permits the application of the legal reinforcing structure of traditional contract law. Because of the close connection of traditional contract law with discrete transactions, it is appropriate to refer to it as transactional contract law.

RELATIONAL CONTRACTS AND PRESENTIATION

Few economic exchanges occur entirely in the discrete transactional pattern. Virtually all economic exchange takes place in circumstances characterized by one or more of the following: The relations are of significant duration (for example, franchising). Close whole person relations form an integral aspect of the relation (employment). The object of exchange typically includes both easily measured quantities (wages) and quantities not easily measured (the projection of personality by an airline stewardess). Many individuals with individual and collective poles of interest are involved in the relation (industrial relations). Future cooperative behavior is anticipated (the players and management of the Oakland Raiders). The benefits and burdens of the relation are to be shared rather than divided and allocated (a law partnership). The bindingness of the relation is limited (again a law partnership in which in theory each member is free to quit almost at will). The entangling strings of friendship, reputation, interdependence, morality, and altruistic desires are integral parts of the relation (a theatrical agent and his clients). Trouble is expected as a matter of course (a collective bargaining agreement). Finally the participants never intend or expect to see the whole future of the relation as presentiated at any single time, but view the relation as an ongoing integration of behavior which will grow and vary with events in a largely unforeseeable future (a marriage; a family business).

In circumstances such as the foregoing each exchange no longer stands alone as in the discrete transaction, but is part of a relational web. Since most actual exchanges are at least partially relational, most contracts could be called relational. It is, however, more useful to think of transactional and relational characteristics as creating a spectrum ranging from such extremes as the highly transactional horse selling epitome to the highly relational nuclear family or commune. As one moves towards the relational end of this spectrum presentation plays a relatively smaller role, since increasing aspects of the relation must be left to future determination. This fact poses problems for contract law.

■ Macneil 'Contracts Adjustment of Long-Term Economic Relations under Classical, Neo-Classical and Relational Contract Law' (1978)
72 Northwestern University LR 854, 859–870, 873–874, 901

Adjustment and Termination of Economic Relations in a System of Discrete Transactions

An economic and legal system dominated by discrete transactions deals with the conflict between various needs for stability and needs for flexibility in ways described below. (The treatment following deals both with present exchanges of existing goods and with forward contracts where exchange is projected into the future. But the latter are assumed to be of a fairly discrete nature, eg, a contract for 100 tons of iron at a fixed price, delivery in one month.)

Planning Flexibility into Economic Relations—Within itself, a discrete transaction is rigid, there being no intention to achieve internal flexibility. Planning for flexibility must, therefore, be achieved outside the confines of the transaction. Consider, for example, a nineteenth century manufacturer of stoves who needs iron to be cast into stove parts but does not know how many stoves he can sell. The required flexibility has to be achieved, in a pattern of discrete transactions, by keeping each iron purchase contract small in amount, thereby permitting adjustments of quantity up or down each time a contract is entered. Thus, the needed flexibility comes from the opportunity to enter or to refrain from entering the market for iron. This market is external to the transaction rather than within it. The epitome of this kind of flexibility is the purchasing of needs for immediate delivery, rather than using any kind of a forward contract for future delivery. Such flexibility is reduced by use of forward contracts; the larger and longer they are, the greater is the reduction.

Dealing with Conflict between Specific Planning and Needs to Adapt to Change Arising Thereafter— Only rarely in a discrete transaction will the items contracted for become useless before the forward contract is performed or become of such lessened value that the buyer either will not want them or will want them in greatly changed form. To put this another way, only rarely will there be *within* the transaction a serious conflict between specific planning and changed needs. To return to the stove manufacturer as an example, seldom will the demand for iron stoves drop so much that the manufacturer comes to regret that he contracted for as much iron as he did.

The discrete transaction technique does not, however, produce a paradise of stability for economic activity; the conflict between specific planning and the need to adapt to change arising thereafter still remains. In those relatively rare cases of difficulties arising while the contract remains unperformed, the conflict exists but is resolved entirely in favor of the specific planning and against the party desiring flexibility.

Preserving Relations When Conflicts Arise—Where the mode of operation is a series of discrete transactions, no significant relations exist to be preserved when conflicts arise. Inside the discrete transaction all that remains is a dispute. Outside the discrete transaction no relation (other than legal rights arising out of the dispute) exists to be preserved. Thus, all that remains is a dispute to be settled or otherwise resolved. The existence of the market that the discrete transactional system presupposes eliminates the necessity for economic relations between the firms to continue in spite of the disputes. That market, rather than continued relations between these particular parties, will supply their future needs . . .

Classical Contract Law and Discrete Transactions

Any contract law system necessarily must implement certain norms. It must permit and encourage participation in exchange, promote reciprocity, reinforce role patterns appropriate to particular kinds of exchange relations, provide limited freedom for exercise of choice, effectuate planning, and harmonize the internal and external matrixes of particular contracts. A contract law system reinforcing discrete contract transactions, however, must add two further goals: enhancing discreteness and enhancing presentation . . .

A classical contract law system implements these two norms in a number of ways. To implement discreteness, classical law initially treats as irrelevant the identity of the parties to the transaction. Second, it transactionizes or commodifies as much as possible the subject matter of contracts, eg, it turns employment into a short-term commodity by interpreting employment contracts without express terms of duration as terminable at will. Third, it limits strictly the sources to be considered in establishing the substantive content of the transaction. For example, formal communication (eg, writings) controls informal communication (eg, oral statements); linguistic communication controls nonlinguistic communication; and communicated circumstances (to the limited extent that any circumstances outside of 'agreements' are taken into account at all) control noncommunicated circumstances (eg, status). Fourth, only limited contract remedies are available, so that should the initial presentiation fail to materialize because of nonperformance, the consequences are relatively predictable from the beginning and are not open-ended, as they would be, for example, if damages for unforeseeable or psychic losses were allowed. Fifth, classical contract law draws clear lines between being in and not being in a transaction; eg, rigorous and precise rules of offer and acceptance prevail with no half-way houses where only some contract interests are protected or where losses are shared. Finally, the introduction of third parties into the relation is discouraged since multiple poles of interest tend to create discreteness-destroying relations.

Since discreteness enhances the possibility and likelihood of presentiation, all of the foregoing implementations of discreteness by the classical law also tend to enhance presentiation. Other classical law techniques, however, are even more precisely focused on presentiation. The first of these is the equation of the legal effect of a transaction with the promises creating it. This characteristic of classical contract law is commonly explained in terms of freedom of contract, providing maximum scope to the exercise of choice. Nevertheless, a vital consequence of the use of the technique is presentiation of the transaction. Closely related to the first technique is the second: supplying a precise, predictable body of law to deal with all aspects of the transaction not encompassed by the promises. In theory, if not practice, this enables the parties to know exactly what the future holds, no matter what happens to disrupt performance. Finally, stress on expectation remedies, whether specific performance or damages measured by the value of performance, tends to bring the future into the present, since all risks, including market risks, are thereby transferred at the time the 'deal is made.' . . .

VARIATIONS FROM THE DISCRETE TRANSACTION: NEOCLASSICAL CONTRACT LAW

The discrete transaction is at one end of a spectrum, at the other end of which are contractual relations. Were we to push far in the direction of contractual relations, we would come to the firm itself, since a firm is, in significant ways, nothing more than a very complex bundle of contractual relations. It is not my intention at this point to push that far, but rather to confine consideration of adjustment and termination of long-term economic relations to those where it is clear that the contractual relations are *between* firms rather than *within* a firm. They are, even in traditional terms, contracts. Again, this section will be organized around variations of the questions appearing in the introduction.

Planning Flexibility into Long-Term Contractual Relations and the Neoclassical Response

Two common characteristics of long-term contracts are the existence of gaps in their planning and the presence of a range of processes and techniques used by contract planners to create flexibility in lieu of either leaving gaps or trying to plan rigidly. Prior to exploring the legal response to such planning, an examination of the major types of planning for flexibility used in modern American contracts is in order.

Standards—The use of a standard uncontrolled by either of the parties to plan the contractual relation is very common. One important example is the provision in many collective bargaining agreements for adjustments of wages to reflect fluctuations in the Consumer Price Index...

Direct Third-Party Determination of Performance—The role of the architect under form construction contracts of the American Institute of Architects (AIA) provides a good example of direct third-party determination of the performace. The architect is responsible for determining many aspects of the performance relation, including everything from 'general administration' of the contract and making final decisions 'in matters relating to artistic effect' to approving the contractor's selection of a superintendent....

A particularly important and increasingly used technique for third-party determination of performance content is arbitration. Arbitration is best known for its utilization in resolving 'rights disputes,'—disputes about existing rights, usually growing out of existing contracts and always substantially defined and narrowed by law at the time the arbitration takes place. Planning for the arbitration or rights disputes is an important aspect of risk planning. But arbitration is also used for filling gaps in performance planning, eg, in industrial relations where the inability of management and labor to negotiate on their own the performance terms of a collective bargaining agreement is known as an 'interest dispute.' Collective bargaining agreements are not, however, the only agreements that leave open issues relating to future performance and provide for their arbitration: For example, certain joint ventures among design professionals may leave important aspects open to arbitration to provide necessary flexibility.

Interest disputes and hence their arbitration are inherently more open-ended than rights disputes...

One-Party Control of Terms—Rather than use external standards or independent third parties, the contract may provide that one of the parties to the contract will define, directly or indirectly, parts of the relation...

Agreement to Agree—A flexible technique used more often than one might initially expect is an 'agreement to agree.'...

...

Conflict between Specific Planning and Needs for Flexibility

The Neoclassical Response As a general proposition in American neoclassical contract law, specific planning in contractual relations governs in spite of changes in circumstances making such planning undesirable to one of the parties. The same principle of freedom of contract leading to this result permits the parties, however, to adjust their relations by subsequent agreement. A description of these processes and some of the legal considerations follows.

Adjustments of existing contractual relations occur in numerous ways. Performance itself is a kind of adjustment from original planning. Even meticulous performance of the most explicit planning transforms figments of the imagination, however precise, into a new, and therefore different, reality. A set of blueprints and specifications, however detailed, and a newly built house simply are not the same. Less explicit planning is changed even more by performance. For example, the vaguely articulated duties of a secretary are made concrete by his or her actual performance of a day's work. Perhaps this is merely a way of saying that planning is inherently filled with gaps, and that performance fills the gaps, thereby altering the relations as originally planned.

Events outside the performance of the parties also may effect adjustments in contractual relationships. The five dollars per hour promised an employee for his work in 1977 is not the same when paid in November 1977 as it was when promised at the beginning of the year; inflation and other economic developments have seen to that. More or less drastic changes in outside circumstances constantly effect contractual adjustments, however firmly the parties may appear to be holding to their original course.

Nonperformance by one of the parties without the consent of the other also alters contractual relations, although in a way different from performance. This is true no matter how many powers are available to the other party to redress the situation.

Another kind of adjustment occurring in any contractual relation is that based either on mutual agreement or on unilateral concession by one of the parties of a planned right beneficial to him. These alterations, additions, subtractions, terminations, and other changes from original planning may take place at any time during any contractual relation. This is vividly illustrated by various processes of collective bargaining, including periodic renegotiation of the 'whole' contract.

When disputes arise out of contractual relations after adjustment by mutual assent or concession, does the original planning or the adjusted planning govern? . . .

[Macneil goes on to consider the law's response when there is a need to change the on-going relationship but 'the conflict levels in exchange processes . . . exceed the resolution capacity of bargaining and other exchange processes' (p 891). He argues that the law has not developed a coherent response, but refers to the 'interest arbitration' (or mediation) often employed to resolve industrial disputes as one device used in relational contracting.]

Somewhere along the line of increasing duration and complexity, trying to force changes into a pattern of original consent becomes both too difficult and too unrewarding to justify the effort, and the contractual relation escapes the bounds of the neoclassical system. That system is replaced by very different adjustment processes of an ongoing-administrative kind in which discreteness and presentiation become merely two of the factors of decision, not the theoretical touchstones. Moreover, the substantive relation of change to the status quo has now altered from what happens in some kind of a market external to the contract to what can be achieved through the political and social processes of the relation, internal and external. This includes internal and external dispute-resolution structures. At this point, the relation has become a minisociety with a vast array of norms beyond the norms centred on exchange and its immediate processes.

NOTES

1. A range of papers evaluating Macneil's work, given at a symposium in his honour, is published in (2000) 94 Northwestern University LR 735–1098.

2. It has been pointed out that to view Macneil's work as solely, or even primarily, about 'relational' as opposed to 'discrete' contracts is a distortion, because the 'common contract norms' (see the extract on p 63) are also a vital part of his theory: see Vincent-Jones, 'The Reception of Ian Macneil's Work on Contract in the UK' in Campbell (ed), *The Relational Theory of Contract: Selected Works of Ian Macneil*, 2001, pp 69–73. We have already seen work that applies Macneil's theory more generally (p 807). Nonetheless, we find the distinction between relational and discrete contracts a useful one to consider in the context of long-term arrangements.

■ Williamson, 'Contract Analysis: The Transaction Cost Approach' in Burrows and Veljanovski, *The Economic Approach to Law* (1981)
pp 41–46, 50–54

My transaction cost approach follows Commons by making the transaction the basic unit of analysis. Also, like Commons, I am interested in the design of institutions, legal and otherwise, that serve to promote the renewal or continuity of exchange relations. I follow Coase by regarding the firm as an important alternative to the market for governing economic activity, and I share Hayek's views on the limits of human agents and on the importance of organizing transactions in such a way as to realize more assuredly the productive values embedded in idiosyncratic human and physical assets. To be sure, legal rules and market processes remain important under this extended view of contract, but informal procedures and nonmarket organization also perform important governance functions. Moreover, and crucially to the exercise, *governance structures are matched with transactional attributes in a discriminating way* under the transaction cost approach to contracting set out here . . .

A three-way classification of contracts

Although there is a widespread agreement that the discrete-transaction paradigm—'sharp in by clear agreement; sharp out by clear performance' (Macneil, 1974, p 738)—has served both law and economics well, there is increasing awareness that many contractual relations are not of this well-defined kind. A deeper understanding of the nature of contract has emerged as the legal-rule emphasis associated with the study of discrete contracting has given way to a more general concern with the contractual purposes to be served.

Ian Macneil, in a series of thoughtful and wide-ranging essays on contract, usefully distinguishes between discrete and relational transactions *(see* Macneil, 1976; 1978). He further supplies twelve different 'concepts' with respect to which these differ. Serious problems of recognition and application are posed by such a rich classificatory apparatus. More useful for my purposes is the three-way classification of contracts that Macneil offers in a more recent article, where classical, neoclassical and relational categories of contract law are recognized.

Classical contract law

As Macneil (1978) observes, any system of contract law has the purpose of facilitating exchange. What is distinctive about classical contract law is that it attempts to do this by enhancing discreteness and intensifying 'presentiation' (ibid, p 862), where the presentiation has reference to efforts to 'make or render present in place or time; to cause to be perceived or realized as present'. The economic counterpart to complete presentiation is contingent-claims contracting, which entails comprehensive contracting in which all relevant future contingencies pertaining to the supply of a good or service are described and discounted with respect to both likelihood and futurity.

Classical contract law endeavours to implement discreteness and presentiation in several ways. For one thing, the identity of the parties to a transaction is treated as irrelevant. In this respect it corresponds exactly with the 'ideal' market transaction in economics. Secondly, the nature of the agreement is carefully delimited and the more formal features govern when formal (for example, written) and informal (for example, oral) terms are contested. Thirdly, remedies are narrowly prescribed such that, 'should the initial presentiation fail to materialize because of nonperformance, the consequences are relatively predictable from the beginning and are not open-ended'. Additionally, third-party participation is discouraged (Macneil, 1978, p 864). The emphasis, thus, is on legal rules, formal documents and self-liquidating transactions.

Neoclassical contract law

Not every transaction fits comfortably into the classical contracting scheme. In particular, long-term contracts executed under conditions of uncertainty are ones for which complete presentiation is apt to be prohibitively costly if not impossible. Problems of several kinds arise. First, not all future contingencies for which adaptations are required can be anticipated at the outset. Secondly, the appropriate adaptations will not be evident for many contingencies until the circumstances materialize. Thirdly, except where changes in states of the world are unambiguous, hard contracting between autonomous parties may well give rise to vertical disputes when state-contingent claims are made. In a world in which (at least some) parties are inclined to be opportunistic, whose representations are to be believed?

Faced with the prospective breakdown of classical contracting in these circumstances, three options are available. One would be to forgo such transactions altogether. A second would be to remove these transactions from the market and organize them internally: adaptive, sequential decision making would then be implemented under common ownership and with the assistance of hierarchical incentive and control systems. Third, a different contracting relation that preserves trading but provides for additional governance structure might be devised. This last choice brings us to what Macneil refers to as neoclassical contracting.

As Macneil observes, 'two common characteristics of long-term contracts are the existence of gaps in their planning and the presence of a range of processes and techniques used by contract planners to create flexibility in lieu of either leaving gaps or trying to plan rigidly.' (ibid, p 865). Third-party assistance in resolving disputes and evaluating performance often has advantages over litigation in serving these functions of flexibility and gap filling . . .

A recognition that the world is complex, that agreements are incomplete and that some contracts will never be reached unless both parties have confidence in the settlement machinery thus characterizes neoclassical contract law...

Relational contracting

The pressures to sustain continuing relations 'have led to the spin-off of many subject areas from the classical, and later the neoclassical contract law system, eg, much of corporate law and collective bargaining' (Macneil, 1978, p 885). Thus, progressively increasing the 'duration and complexity' of contract has resulted in the displacement of even neoclassical adjustment processes by adjustment processes of a more thoroughly transaction-specific, ongoing-administrative kind (ibid, p 901). The fiction of discreteness is fully displaced as the relation takes on the properties of 'a minisociety with a vast array of norms beyond those centred on the exchange and its immediate processes' (ibid). By contrast with the neoclassical system, in which the reference point for effecting adaptations remains the original agreement, the reference point under a truly relational approach is the 'entire relation as it has developed ... [through] time. This may or may not include an "original agreement"; and if it does, may or may not result in great deference being given to it'. (ibid, p 890).

TRANSACTION COST ECONOMICS

Macneil's three-way discussion of contracts discloses that contracts are a good deal more varied and complex than is commonly realized. It furthermore suggests that governance structures—the institutional matrix within which transactions are negotiated and executed— vary with the nature of the transaction. But the critical dimensions of contract are not expressly identified, and the purposes of governance are not stated. The harmonizing of interests that would otherwise give [way] to antagonistic subgoal pursuits appears to be an important governance function but this is not explicit in his discussion...

Behavioural assumptions

Bounded rationality and opportunism are the central behavioural assumptions upon which the transaction cost approach is based. Bounded rationality, which should not be confused with irrationality, refers to a condition in which human agents are 'intendedly rational, but only *limitedly* so' (Simon, 1961)...

Opportunism extends the usual motivational assumption of self-interest to make allowance for self-interest with guile. Thus, whereas bounded rationality suggests decision-making less complex than the usual assumption of hyperrationality, opportunism suggests calculating behaviour that is more sophisticated than the usual assumption of simple self-interest. Opportunism refers to 'making false or empty, that is, self-disbelieved threats or promises' (Goffman, 1969), cutting corners for undisclosed personal advantage, covering-up tracks and the like.

Dimensionalizing

The puzzle of vertical integration is that under conventional assumptions it is an anomaly; if the costs of operating competitive markets are zero, 'as is usually assumed in our theoretical analysis' ... why integrate? Coase, in his 1937 paper (p 336), took exception to the usual assumption and argued that vertical integration permitted the firm to economize on the 'cost of negotiating and concluding' many separate intermediate product market contracts by substituting a flexible employment agreement. Inasmuch, however, as the factors that were responsible for differential transaction costs in the intermediate product market were not identified, the argument lacked testable implications. Why not use a flexible employment agreement to organize all transactions rather than just some? Until such time as the transaction cost argument was able to explain the organization of transactions in a discriminating way, it remained rather tautological.... Coase's observation (1972, p 63), some twenty-five years later, that his 1937 article was 'much cited and little used' is presumably explained by the failure to operationalize the issues over that interval.

. . . [T]he critical dimensions for describing transactions, and hence for assigning some to markets and others to internal organization, are:

(1) uncertainty;
(2) the frequency with which transactions recur;
(3) the degree to which durable transaction-specific investments are required to realize least-cost supply.

The main governance modes to which transactions need to be matched are:

(1) markets (with varying degrees of adjudicatory support);
(2) internal organization;
(3) an intermediate form of bilateral exchange referred to as 'obligational market contracting'.

Transactions for which internal organization is well-suited are those that involve recurrent exchange in the face of a nontrivial degree of uncertainty and for which transaction-specific investments are incurred. Since internal organization requires the development of a specialized governance structure, the cost of which must be amortized across the transactions organized thereunder, it is rarely economical to organize infrequent (or occasional) transactions internally. Likewise, transactions for which uncertainty is low require little adaptation and hence little governance. Unspecialized market structures commonly work well for these. It should not be inferred, however, that markets function poorly wherever high frequency or great uncertainty, either individually or in combination, appear. On the contrary, except when *transaction-specific investments* are involved, neither frequency nor uncertainty, individually or in combination, would justify the creation of internal organization (with its associated transaction-specific governance structure).

Considering the importance that I attach to transaction-specific investments, some explication is needed. The crucial issue is the degree to which durable, nonmarketable expenses are incurred. Items that are unspecialized among users pose few hazards, since buyers in these circumstances can easily turn to alternative sources, and suppliers can sell output intended for one buyer to other buyers without difficulty. Nonmarketability problems arise when the *specific identity* of the parties has important cost-bearing consequences. Transactions of this kind will be referred to as idiosyncratic.

Occasionally the identity of the parties is important from the outset, as when a buyer induces a supplier to invest in specialized physical capital of a transaction-specific kind. Inasmuch as the value of this capital in other uses is, by definition, much smaller than the specialized use for which it has been intended, the supplier is effectively 'locked into' the transaction to a significant degree. This is symmetrical, moreover, in that the buyer cannot turn to alternative sources of supply and obtain the item on favourable terms, since the cost of supply from unspecialized capital is presumably great. The buyer is thus committed to the transaction as well.

Ordinarily, however, there is more to idiosyncratic exchange than specialized physical capital. Human-capital investments that are transaction-specific commonly occur as well. Specialized training and learning-by-doing economies in production operations are illustrations. Except when these investments are transferable to alternative suppliers at low cost, which is rare, the benefits of the set-up costs can be realized only so long as the relationship between the buyer and seller of the intermediate product is maintained . . .

Governance structures

Three broad types of governance structures will be considered: non-transaction-specific, semi-specific, and highly specific. The market is the classic nonspecific governance structure within which 'faceless buyers and sellers . . . meet . . . for an instant to exchange standardized goods at equilibrium prices'. . . . By contrast, highly specific structures are tailored to the special needs of the transaction. Identity here clearly matters. Semi-specific structures, naturally, fall in between. Several propositions are suggested immediately.

(1) Highly standardized transactions are not apt to require a specialized governance structure.

(2) Only recurrent transactions will support a highly specialized governance structure.

(3) Although occasional transactions of a nonstandardized kind will not support a transaction-specific governance structure, they require special attention nonetheless.

In terms of Macneil's three-way classification of contract, classical contracting presumably applies to all standardized transactions (whatever the frequency), relational contracting develops for transactions of a recurring and nonstandardized kind and neoclassical contracting is needed for occasional, nonstandardized transactions.

Market governance: classical contracting

Market governance is the main governance structure for nonspecific transactions of both occasional and recurrent contracting. . . .

The assumptions of the discrete-contracting paradigm are rather well satisfied for transactions where markets serve as a main governance mode. Thus the specific identity of the parties is of negligible importance, substantive content is determined by reference to formal terms of the contract and legal rules. Market alternatives are mainly what protect each party against opportunism by his opposite . . .

Trilateral governance: neoclassical contracting

. . . The interests of the principals in sustaining the relations are especially great for highly idiosyncratic transactions.

Market relief is thus unsatisfactory. Often the set-up costs of a transaction-specific governance structure cannot be recovered for occasional transactions. Given the limits of classical contract law for sustaining these transactions on the one hand, and the prohibitive cost of transaction-specific (bilateral) governance on the other, an intermediate institutional form is evidently needed.

Neoclassical contract law has many of the sought-after qualities. Thus rather than resort immediately to strict reliance on litigation—with its transaction-rupturing features—*third-party assistance* (arbitration) in resolving disputes and evaluating performance is employed instead. (Thus use of the architect as a relatively independent expert to determine the content of form construction contracts is an example; Macneil, 1978, p 866.). . .

Transaction-specific governance: relational contracting

. . . [1.] *Bilateral governance: obligational contracting.* Highly idiosyncratic transactions are ones where the human and physical assets required for production are extensively specialized, so there are no obvious scale economies to be realized through interfirm trading that the buyer (or seller) is unable to realize himself through vertical integration . . . .

. . . Inasmuch as the interests of the parties will commonly be at variance when adaptation proposals (originated by either party) are made, a dilemma is evidently posed.

On the one hand, both parties have an incentive to sustain the relationship rather than to permit it to unravel, the object being to avoid the sacrifice of valued transaction-specific economies. On the other hand, each party appropriates a separate profit stream and cannot be expected to accede readily to any proposal to adapt the contract. What is needed, evidently, is some way for delaring admissible dimensions for adjustment such that flexibility is provided under terms in which both parties have confidence. This can be accomplished partly by, first, recognizing that the hazards of opportunism vary with the type of adaptation proposed and, secondly, restricting adjustments to those where the hazards are least. But the spirit within which adaptations are effected is equally important.

Quantity adjustments have much better incentive-compatibility properties than do price adjustments. For one thing, price adjustments have an unfortunate zero-sum quality, whereas proposals to increase, decrease or delay delivery do not. . . .

[2] *Unified governance: internal organization.* Incentives for trading weaken as transactions become progressively more idiosyncratic. The reason is that as the specialized human and physical assets become more specialized to a single use, and hence less transferable to other uses, economies of scale can be as fully realized by the buyer as by an outside supplier. The choice of organizing mode then turns on

which mode has superior adaptive properties...vertical integration will invariably appear in these circumstances....

Many of the references in the above have been omitted. Those remaining are as follows:

COASE, R. H. (1937), The nature of the firm, *Economica NS*, 4,336–405, repr. in *Readings in Price Theory* (1952). (G. J. Stigler and K. E. Bouldings, eds), Homewood, Ill: Richard D. Irwin Inc.

COASE, R. H. (1972), Industrial organization: a proposal for research, in *Policy Issues and Research Opportunities in Industrial Organization*, 59–73, (V. R. Fuchs, ed), New York: National Bureau of Economic Research.

COMMONS, J. R. (1934), Institutional Economics, Madison: University of Wisconsin Press.

GOFFMANN, I. (1969) *Strategic Interaction*, Philadelphia: University of Pennsylvania Press.

GOLDBERG, V. P. (1976), Toward an expanded theory of contract, *Journal of Economic Issues*, 10,45–61.

HAYEK, F. (1945), The use of knowledge in society, *American Economic Review* 35,519–530.

MACNEIL I. R. (1974), The many futures of contract, *Southern California Law Review*, 47,691–816.

MACNEIL I. R. (1978), Contracts: adjustment of long-term economic relations under classical, neo-classical and relational contract law, *Northwestern University Law Review*, 72, no 6, 854–905.

SIMON, H. A. (1961), *Administrative Behaviour*, 2nd ed, p xxiv, New York: The Macmillan Company.

NOTES

1. We find Williamson's analysis to be useful for a number of purposes. One is to explain why businesses may choose particular forms of organisation to satisfy their needs—buying in the market, internal production or, as an intermediate step, long-term contracting with another business.

2. Another is to explain some of the features found in long-term contracts, eg clauses allowing one party to determine the terms or provisions for a third party to settle a dispute.

3. Thirdly, Williamson's analysis helps to explain how firms such as those surveyed by Macaulay (see p 389) or Beale and Dugdale (p 81) seemed able to maintain such effective long-term relations with each other without the need for either formal dispute resolution or even detailed contract planning. In many cases, the exchanges involved—eg the purchase of specially made parts—entailed 'transaction-specific' investments (eg the seller would have to make special jigs and acquire special knowledge of the buyer's needs in order to produce the parts). This, as Williamson explains, tends to lock the parties into the relationship. The seller will not recoup the investment if the relationship breaks down, while the seller will find it expensive to turn to other buyers. So quite apart from the law, there is a strong incentive to maintain the commercial relationship.

4. On the face of it, English law does not provide mechanisms for adjusting even long-term contracts; if the parties want these, they must agree them explicitly. The clauses may be quite precise (eg price-indexation clauses or the variations clauses considered earlier) or quite general. See, for example, the 'hardship' clause, which fell to be interpreted in *Superior Overseas Development Corpn v British Gas Corpn* [1982] 1 Lloyd's Rep 262:

   (a) If at any time or from time to time during the contract period there has been any substantial change in the economic circumstances relating to this Agreement and (notwithstanding the effect of the other relieving or adjusting provisions of this Agreement) either party feels that such change is causing it to suffer substantial economic hardship then the parties shall (at the request of either of them) meet together to consider what (if any) adjustments in the prices...are justified in the circumstances in fairness to the parties to offset or alleviate the said hardship caused by the change.

(b) If the parties shall not within 90 days after any such request have reached agreement on the adjustments (if any) in the said prices . . . the matter may forthwith be referred by either party for determination by experts . . .

(c) The experts shall determine what (if any) adjustment in the said prices . . . shall be made . . . and any revised prices or any change in the price revision mechanism so determined by such experts shall take effect 6 months after the date on which the request for the review was first made.

■ Collins, *Law of Contract* (4th edn, 2003)

pp 362–363

The right to terminate not only provides an incentive to perform the contract, but also it can give the parties an incentive to renegotiate the terms of a contract in the light of changed circumstances and unplanned contingencies. The long-term business interests of the parties may dictate a renegotiation rather than the conclusion of business relations. For instance, in *Staffordshire Area Health Authority v South Staffordshire Waterworks Co*, these two government agencies, a water supplier and a hospital, made a long-term contract for the supply of water at a fixed price. After more than 60 years had passed, the price was plainly unrealistic due to inflation. Although the terms provided that the contract was to be binding 'at all times hereafter', the English Court of Appeal implied a term permitting the supplier to terminate the contract upon reasonable notice. The effect of the implied term was to force the hospital authority back to the bargaining table to renegotiate the cost of water supplies up to a more economic price.

The difficult question is whether a right to terminate the contract best serves the purpose of encouraging co-operation in the form of renegotiation to handle unexpected contingencies. An alternative consists in permitting the courts to revise contracts in the manner of judicial revision to secure fairness considered in Chapter 13. Were the courts to possess such a power, there would be an incentive to renegotiate the contract on terms comparable to those likely to be imposed by the court. This approach has the advantage over the right to terminate the contract in that neither party is given the option to walk away from the contract altogether, which avoids the possibility of opportunism in the light of changed circumstances. As we have seen, English law does not grant the courts an express power to revise contracts, although techniques of construction can achieve comparable results in some cases. In the USA, some courts have experimented with judicial revision, most famously in *Aluminium Co of America v Essex Group*. Under a 16-year contract with an option to renew for an additional five years, the claimant company ('ALCOA') agreed to convert alumina supplied by Essex into molten aluminium. The contract contained detailed provisions designed to raise the price in line with the wholesale price index, but this index failed to account for the sharp rise in the cost of energy to ALCOA, so the contract because increasingly unprofitable to them. The Federal District Court declared that the contract had gone awry because of a mistake in formulating the pricing mechanism to account for inflation. So the court set aside the contract and imposed a new pricing formula. The parties subsequently renegotiated the contract in the light of this judicial revision of the contract.

The UNIDROIT Principles of International Commercial Contracts provide in Article 6 Section 2 for hardship as follows:

■ UNIDROIT Principles of International Commercial Contracts

Section 2: Hardship

Article 6.2.1

(Contract to be observed)

Where the performance of a contract becomes more onerous for one of the parties, that party is nevertheless bound to perform its obligations subject to the following provisions on hardship.

COMMENT

1. Binding character of the contract the general rule

The purpose of this article is to make it clear that as a consequence of the general principle of the binding character of the contract... performance must be rendered as long as it is possible and regardless of the burden it may impose on the performing party. In other words, even if a party experiences heavy losses instead of the expected profits or the performance has become meaningless for that party the terms of the contract must nevertheless be respected.

Illustration

In January 1990 A, a forwarding agent, enters into a two-year shipping contract with B, a carrier. Under the contract B is bound to ship certain goods from Hamburg to New York at a fixed price, on a monthly basis throughout the two-year period. Alleging a substantial increase in the price of fuel in the aftermath of the 1990 Gulf crisis, B requests a five per cent increase in the rate for August 1990. B is not entitled to such an increase because B bears the risk of its performance becoming more onerous.

2. Change in circumstances relevant only in exceptional cases

The principle of the binding character of the contract is not however an absolute one. When supervening circumstances are such that they lead to a fundamental alteration of the equilibrium of the contract, they create an exceptional situation referred to in these Principles as 'hardship' and dealt with in the following articles of this section.

The phenomenon of hardship has been acknowledged by various legal systems under the Guise of other concepts such as frustration of purpose, *Wegfall der Geschäftesgrundlage, imprévision, eccessiva onerosità sopravvenuta*, etc. the term 'hardship' was chosen because it is widely known in international trade practice as confirmed by the inclusion in many international contracts of so-called 'hardship clauses'.

Article 6.2.2

(Definition of hardship)

There is hardship where the occurrence of events fundamentally alters the equilibrium of the contract either because the cost of a party's performance has increased or because the value of the performance a party receives has diminished, and

- (a) the events occur or become known to the disadvantaged party after the conclusion of the contract;
- (b) the events could not reasonably have been taken into account by the disadvantaged party at the time of the conclusion of the contract;
- (c) the events are beyond the control of the disadvantaged party; and
- (d) the risk of the events was not assumed by the disadvantaged party.

COMMENT

1. Hardship defined

This article defines hardship as a situation where the occurrence of events fundamentally alters the equilibrium of the contract, provided that those events meet the requirements which are laid down in subparas. (a) to (d).

2. Fundamental alteration of equilibrium of the contract

Since the general principle is that a change in circumstances does not affect the obligation to perform (see Art. 6.2.1), it follows that hardship may not be invoked unless the alteration of the equilibrium of the contract is fundamental. Whether an alteration is 'fundamental' in a given case will of course depend upon the circumstances. If, however, the performances are capable of precise measurement in monetary terms, an alteration amounting to 50% or more of the cost or the value of the performance is likely to amount to a 'fundamental' alteration.

Illustration

1. In September 1989 A, a dealer in electronic goods situated in the former German Democratic Republic, purchases stocks from B, situated in country X, also a former socialist country. The goods are to be delivered by B in December 1990. In November 1990, A informs B that the goods are no longer of any use to it, claiming that after the unification of the German Democratic Republic and the Federal Republic of Germany there is no longer any market for such goods imported from country X. Unless the circumstances indicate otherwise, A is entitled to invoke hardship.

a. Increase in cost of performance

In practice a fundamental alteration in the equilibrium of the contract may manifest itself in two different but related ways. The first is characterised by a substantial increase in the cost for one party of performing its obligation. This party will normally be the one who is to perform the non-monetary obligation. The substantial increase in the cost may, for instance, be due to a dramatic rise in the price of the raw materials necessary for the production of the goods or the rendering of the services, or to the introduction of new safety regulations requiring far more expensive production procedures.

b. Decrease in value of the performance received by one party

The second manifestation of hardship is characterised by a substantial decrease in the value of the performance received by one party, including cases where the performance no longer has any value at all for the receiving party. The performance may be that either of a monetary or of a non-monetary obligation. The substantial decrease in the value or the total loss of any value of the performance may be due either to drastic changes in market conditions (e.g. the effect of a dramatic increase in inflation on a contractually agreed price) or the frustration of the purpose for which the performance was required (e.g. the effect of a prohibition to build on a plot of land acquired for building purposes or the effect of an export embargo on goods acquired with a view to their subsequent export).

. . .

Sometimes the change in circumstances is gradual, but the final result of those gradual changes may constitute a case of hardship. If the change began before the contract was concluded, hardship will not arise unless the pace of change increases dramatically during the life of the contract . . .

. . .

5. Hardship normally relevant to long-term contracts

Although this article does not expressly exclude the possibility of hardship being invoked in respect of other kinds of contracts, hardship will normally be of relevance to long-term contracts, i.e. those where the performance of at least one party extends over a certain period of time.

. . .

7. Hardship and contract practice

The definition of hardship in this article is necessarily of a rather general character. International commercial contracts often contain much more precise and elaborate provisions in this regard. The parties may therefore find it appropriate to adapt the content of this article so as to take account of the particular features of the specific transaction.

Article 6.2.3

(Effects of hardship)

(1) In case of hardship the disadvantaged party is entitled to request renegotiations. The request shall be made without undue delay and shall indicate the grounds on which it is based.

(2) The request for renegotiation does not in itself entitle the disadvantaged party to withhold performance.

(3) Upon failure to reach agreement within a reasonable time either party may resort to the court.

(4) If the court finds hardship it may, if reasonable,
    (a) terminate the contract at a date and on terms to be fixed, or
    (b) adapt the contract with a view to restoring its equilibrium.

NOTES

1.   The UNIDROIT Principles are the result of a study taken for 20 years by contract lawyers from all over the world, both from common law and civil law countries. The Principles are not intended to be the subject of an international convention leading to legislation in individual countries but will have operation by virtue either of the parties to an international commercial contract adopting the Principles rather than the national law of some country or by international commercial arbitrators who have power under their arbitration agreement to apply general principles of international commercial law using these Principles as a source of such law.

2.   In formulating Art 6 s 2, the Working Group had very much in mind that many international commercial contracts do contain provisions about hardship and the text might be regarded as representing best practice in contracts of this kind. Note that it is regarded as sensible and appropriate to require the parties to renegotiate as the primary remedy.

3.   The UNIDROIT Principles also contain a provision about force majeure (Article 7.1.7). There is some measure of overlap between the force majeure and hardship provisions. See p 493.

4.   See also Bell, 'The Effect of Changes in Circumstances on Long-Term Contracts' Harris and Tallon (eds), in *Contract Law Today*, 1989, pp 195ff.

POLICING THE BARGAIN

CHAPTER THIRTY-FOUR

DURESS

We suggested in the Introduction (see Chapter 3) that many rules of contract law are, to a greater or lesser extent, concerned with ensuring the fairness of contracts. (For a fuller account, see Atiyah, *Essays on Contract*, 1986, chapter 11.) In this section, we will look at various rules that are openly concerned with fairness: firstly, in relation to contracts in general, and then in relation to standard-form contracts and exemption clauses. There are a number of distinct (although sometimes overlapping) doctrines in this area, and as we look at each, it is important to ask a number of questions. In what way is the contract supposedly unfair? Does the unfairness lie in the way in which the contract was made, ie 'procedural unfairness'? Or does it lie in the terms of the resulting contract: 'substantive unfairness'? Or is there a combination of the two? (The distinction between procedural and substantive unfairness is adopted from a famous article by Leff in (1967) 115 UPa LR 485 on s 2–302 of the UCC (see p 958), and has now found its way into English case law: see pp 945–946.) If substantive unfairness is involved, what precisely is wrong: is one party being overcharged or underpaid, or is something else wrong? If relief is given, what form does it take?

■ *Barton v Armstrong*

[1975] 2 All ER 465, Privy Council

B, the managing director of a company, executed on its behalf a deed by which the company agreed to pay $140,000 to A, its chairman, and to buy A's shares from him for $180,000, in order to get him off the board of the company. He did this at least partly for commercial reasons, but the trial judge also found that A had threatened to have B killed if he did not make the arrangements. B later tried to have the deed set aside for duress, but the Court of Appeal of New South Wales, affirming the decision at first instance, held that the onus was on B to show that he would not have signed the deed but for the threats, and he had failed to discharge that onus. B appealed.

Lord Cross

... Their Lordships turn now to consider the question of law which provoked a difference of opinion in the Court of Appeal Division. It is hardly surprising that there is no direct authority on the point, for if A threatens B with death if he does not execute some document and B, who takes A's threats seriously, executes the document it can be only in the most unusual circumstances that there can be any doubt whether the threats operated to induce him to execute the document. But this is a most unusual case and the findings of fact made below do undoubtedly raise the question whether it was necessary for Barton in order to obtain relief to establish that he would not have executed the deed in question but for the threats. In answering this question in favour of Barton Jacobs JA relied both on a number of old common law authorities on the subject of 'duress' and also—by way of analogy—on later decisions in equity with regard to the avoidance of deeds on the ground of fraud. Their Lordships do not think that the common law authorities are of any real assistance for it seems most unlikely that the authors of the statements relied on had the sort of problem which has arisen here in mind at all. On the other hand they think that the conclusion to which Jacobs JA came was right and that it is supported by the equity decisions. The scope of common law duress was very limited and at a comparatively early date equity began to grant relief in cases where the disposition in question had been procured by the exercise of pressure which the Chancellor considered to be illegitimate—although it did not amount to common law duress. There was a parallel development in the field of dispositions induced by fraud. At common law the only remedy available to the man defrauded was an action for deceit but equity in the same period in which it was building up the doctrine of 'undue influence' came to entertain proceedings to set aside dispositions which had been obtained by fraud: see Holdworth's History of English Law [vol V, pp 328–329]. There is an obvious analogy between setting aside a disposition for duress or undue influence and setting it aside for fraud. In each case—to quote the words of Holmes J in *Fairbanks v Snow*—'the party has been subjected to an improper motive for action'. Again the similarity of the effect in law of metus and dolus in connection with dispositions of property is noted by Stair in his *Institutions of the Law of Scotland*. Had Armstrong made a fraudulent misrepresentation to Barton for the purpose of inducing him to execute the deed of 17th January 1967 the answer to the problem which has arisen would have been clear. If it were established that Barton did not allow the representation to affect his judgment then he could not make it a ground for relief even though the representation was designed and known by Barton to be designed to affect his judgment. If on the other hand Barton relied on the misrepresentation Armstrong could not have defeated his claim to relief by showing that there were other more weighty causes which contributed to his decision to execute the deed, for in this field the court does not allow an examination into the relative importance of contributory causes. 'Once make out that there has been anything like deception, and no contract resting in any degree on that foundation can stand' (per Lord Cranworth LJ in *Reynell v Sprye*; see also the other cases referred to in Cheshire and Fifoot's Law of Contract). Their Lordships think that the same rule should apply in cases of duress and that if Armstrong's threats were 'a' reason for Barton's executing the deed he is entitled to relief even though he might well have entered into the contract if Armstrong had uttered no threats to induce him to do so. . . . The proper inference to be drawn from the facts found is, their Lordships think, that though it may be that Barton would have executed the documents even if Armstrong had made no threats and exerted no unlawful pressure to induce him to do so the threats and unlawful pressure in fact contributed to his decision to sign the documents and to recommend their execution by Landmark and the other parties to them. It may be, of course, that Barton's fear of Armstrong had evaporated before he issued his writ in this action but Armstrong—understandably enough—expressly disclaimed reliance on the defence of delay on Barton's part in repudiating the deed.

In the result therefore the appeal should be allowed and a declaration made that the deeds in question were executed by Barton under duress and are void so far as concerns him. . . .

Lord Wilberforce and Lord Simon of Glaisdale

. . . The action is one to set aside an apparently complete and valid agreement on the ground of duress. The basis of the plaintiff's claim is, thus, that though there was apparent consent there was no true consent to the agreement: that the agreement was not voluntary.

This involves consideration of what the law regards as voluntary, or its opposite; for in life, including the life of commerce and finance, many acts are done under pressure, sometimes overwhelming pressure, so that one can say that the actor had no choice but to act. Absence of choice in this sense does not negate consent in law; for this the pressure must be one of a kind which the law does not regard as legitimate. Thus, out of the various means by which consent may be obtained—advice, persuasion, influence, inducement, representation, commercial pressure—the law has come to select some which it will not accept as a reason for voluntary action: fraud, abuse of relation of confidence, undue influence, duress or coercion. In this the law, under the influence of equity, has developed from the old common law conception of duress—threat to life and limb—and it has arrived at the modern generalisation expressed by Holmes J—'subjected to an improper motive for action' *(Fairbanks v Snow)*.

In an action such as the present, then, the first step required of the plaintiff is to show that some illegitimate means of persuasion was used. That there were threats to Barton's life was found by the judge, though he did not accept Barton's evidence in important respects. We shall return to this point in detail later.

The next necessary step would be to establish the relationship between the illegitimate means used and the action taken. For the purposes of the present case (reserving our opinion as to cases which may arise in other contexts) we are prepared to accept, as the formula most favourable to Barton, the test proposed by the majority, namely that the illegitimate means used was *a* reason (not *the* reason, nor the *predominant* reason nor the *clinching* reason) why the complainant acted as he did. We are also prepared to accept that a decisive answer is not obtainable by asking the question whether the contract would have been made even if there had been no threats because, even if the answer to this question is affirmative, that does not prove that the contract was not made because of the threats.

Assuming therefore that what has to be decided is whether the illegitimate means used was a reason why the complainant acted as he did, it follows that his reason for acting must (unless the case is one of automatism which this is not) be a conscious reason so that the complainant can give evidence of it: 'I acted because I was forced'. If his evidence is honest and accepted, that will normally conclude the issue. If, moreover, he gives evidence, it is necessary for the court to evaluate his evidence by testing it against his credibility and his actions.

In this case Barton gave evidence—his was, for practical purposes, the only evidence supporting his case. The judge rejected it in important respects and accepted it in others. The issues as to Barton's motivations were issues purely of fact (that motivation is a question of fact hardly needs authority, but see *Cox v Smail* per Cussen J); the findings as to motivation were largely, if not entirely, findings as to credibility. It would be difficult to find matters more peculiarly than these within the field of the trial judge who saw both contestants in the box, and who dealt carefully and at length with the credibility, or lack of credibility, of each of them. . . .

The judge's findings were also accepted, after careful examination by Taylor A-JA: ' . . . the conclusion', he finds, 'that Barton entered into this agreement because he wanted to and from commercial motives only is, I think, undoubtedly correct'.

The appeal cannot succeed unless these most explicit findings are overturned. We consider that no basis exists for doing so.

NOTES

1. Barton had the deed set aside: in other words, duress is a ground on which an executed contract may be set aside. Equally, a 'gift' made under duress may be set aside.

2. Although Lord Cross refers to the deeds as 'void', it seems that a contract made under duress to the person is voidable. Cross also refers to 'setting aside' the contract, as for fraud, and the dissenting speeches seem to treat duress as making the contract voidable. In cases of economic duress, it has been held that the contract is voidable and that the right to have it set aside may be lost through affirmation or delay: see p 905.

3. Presumably the contract would equally be voidable if the threat were to destroy or damage the plaintiff's property wantonly: see *The Siboen and The Sibotre* (p 905).

As we suggested in the last section, it has been recognised that there may be other forms of duress besides threats of physical injury or damage. As early as the eighteenth century, relief was given when a payment was made in order to avert a wrongful seizure or detention of the plaintiff's goods. Recent cases recognise that relief may also be given when the threat is to break a contract in circumstances that will cause the party threatened severe economic loss.

But these new categories of duress raise new problems. Why shouldn't the victim refuse to pay up, and sue in damages for any loss the threatening party causes him by carrying out the threat? What if the other party is acting in the honest belief that he is entitled to detain the plaintiff's goods, or to refuse to perform his contract? What if the plaintiff is not much influenced by the threat, and agrees to pay up primarily because he does not want the bother of contesting the claim? These points are taken up in the materials that follow.

■ *Maskell v Horner*

[1915] 3 KB 106, Court of Appeal

The plaintiff was a dealer in produce who carried on business near Spitalfields market. The defendant, the owner of the market, demanded tolls from him, and when the plaintiff refused, seized the plaintiff's goods. Thereafter, the plaintiff paid the tolls, always under protest, for some 12 years; whenever he challenged the defendant's right to the tolls, seizure or threatened seizure followed. After it had been decided in another case that the tolls were unlawful, the plaintiff sought to recover the money.

Lord Reading CJ

. . . [T]he plaintiff asserts that he paid the money not voluntarily but under the pressure of actual or threatened seizure of his goods, and that he is therefore entitled to recover it as money had and received. If the facts proved support this assertion the plaintiff would, in my opinion, be entitled to succeed in this action.

If a person with knowledge of the facts pays money, which he is not in law bound to pay, and in circumstances implying that he is paying it voluntarily to close the transaction, he cannot recover it. Such a payment is in law like a gift, and the transaction cannot be reopened. If a person pays money, which he is not bound to pay, under the compulsion of urgent and pressing necessity or of seizure, actual or threatened, of his goods he can recover it as money had and received. The money is paid not under duress in the strict sense of the term, as that implies duress of person, but under the pressure of seizure or detention of goods which is analogous to that of duress. Payment under such pressure establishes that the payment is not made voluntarily to close the transaction (per Lord Abinger CB and per Parke B in *Atlee v Backhouse*). The payment is made for the purpose of averting a threatened evil and is made not with the intention of giving up a right but under immediate necessity and with the intention of preserving the right to dispute the legality of the demand (per Tindal CJ in *Valpy v Manley*). There are numerous instances in the books of successful claims in this form of action to recover money paid to relieve goods from seizure. Other familiar instances are cases such as *Parker v Great Western Rly* Co, where the money was paid to the railway company under protest in order to induce them to carry goods which they were refusing to carry except at rates in excess of those they were legally entitled to demand. These payments were made throughout a period of twelve months, always accompanied by the assertion that they were made under protest, and it was held that the plaintiffs were entitled to recover the excess payments as money had and received, on the ground that the payments were made under the compulsion of urgent and pressing necessity.

Pickford and **Buckley LJ** delivered concurring judgments.

Appeal allowed.

NOTE

Is saying that the payment is recoverable unless it was made 'voluntarily to close the transaction' the same as saying that relief will be given unless the party threatened was not influenced by the threat at all (cf *Barton v Armstrong*), or does the party threatened have to show something more—for example, that the threat was overwhelming? This point seems not to be resolved in the cases that follow: see further pp 906–907.

■ *North Ocean Shipping Co v Hyundai Construction Co, The Atlantic Baron*
[1978] 3 All ER 1170

Shipbuilders agreed to build a tanker for the owners at a price that was fixed (except in certain events, which did not occur). The price was payable in five instalments, and the builders opened a 'reverse' letter of credit to secure repayment of the instalments in the event of their default. After the first instalment had been paid, the dollar was devalued and the builders threatened not to deliver unless the remaining instalments were increased by 10 per cent. The owners were advised that there was no legal basis for the claim, but were anxious that they might lose a favourable charter they had arranged for the vessel to Shell, and in a telex dated 28 June 1973, they agreed to pay the extra 10 per cent 'to maintain an amicable relationship and without prejudice to our rights'. They requested the builders to increase the reverse letter of credit by a corresponding percentage. The builders did this and delivered the tanker; the owners paid the final instalment, and took delivery, without protest. Some eight months later, the owners claimed the return of the 10 per cent extra; it was suggested that they did not seek its return earlier because they were concerned that delivery of a sister ship also being built for them might be affected, but the arbitrators found that this fear was groundless. Mocatta J held that preserving 'amicable relations' could not amount to consideration (see above), but that there was no obligation on the builders to increase the letter of credit if the price were increased, and doing so was consideration for the promise to pay the extra 10 per cent.

Mocatta J

... Having reached the conclusion that there was consideration for the agreement made on 28th and 29th June 1973 I must next consider whether even if that agreement, varying the terms of the original shipbuilding contract of 10th April 1972, was made under a threat to break that original contract and the various increased instalments were made consequentially under the varied agreement, the increased sums can be recovered as money had and received. Counsel for the owners submitted that they could be, provided they were involuntary payments and not made, albeit perhaps with some grumbling, to close the transaction.

Certainly this is the well-established position if payments are made, for example, to avoid the wrongful seizure of goods where there is no prior agreement to make such payments. The best known English case to this effect is probably *Maskell v Horner* ...

There has been considerable discussion in the books whether, if an agreement is made under duress of goods to pay a sum of money and there is some consideration for the agreement, the excess sum can be recovered. The authority for this suggested distinction is *Skeate v Beale*. It was there said by Lord Denman CJ that an agreement was not void because it was made under duress of goods, the distinction between that case and the cases of money paid to recover goods wrongfully seized being said to be obvious in that the agreement was not compulsorily but voluntarily entered into. In the slightly later case of *Wakefield v Newborn*, Lord Denman CJ referred to cases such as *Skeate v Beale* as 'that class where the parties have come to a voluntary settlement of their concerns, and have chosen to pay what is found due'. Kerr J in *The Siboen and The Sibotre*, gave strong expression to the view that the suggested distinction based on *Skeate v Beale* would not be observed today. He said, though obiter, that *Skeate v Beale* would not justify a decision that—

'if, for instance, I should be compelled to sign a lease or some other contract for a nominal but legally sufficient consideration under an imminent threat of having my house burnt down or a valuable picture slashed, though without any threat of physical violence to anyone, I do not think the law would uphold the agreement'.

I was referred to a number of cases decided overseas: *Nixon v Furphy, Knutson v Bourkes Syndicate* and *Re Hooper and Grass' Contract*, all of which have a similarity to *Close v Phipps*. Perhaps their greatest importance, however, is the quotation in the first mentioned from the judgment of Isaacs J in *Smith v William Charlick Ltd*, where he said:

'It is conceded that the only ground on which the promise to repay could be implied is "compulsion". The payment is said by the respondent not to have been "voluntary" but "forced" from it within the contemplation of the law ... "Compulsion" in relation to a payment of which refund is sought, and whether it is also variously called "coercion", "extortion", "exaction" or "force", includes every species of duress or conduct analogous to duress, actual or threatened, exacted by or on behalf of the payee and applied to the person or the property or any right of the person who pays ... Such compulsion is a legal wrong, and the law provides a remedy by raising a fictional promise to repay'.

These cases do not, however, expressly deal with the position arising when the threat or compulsion results in a new or varied contract. This was, or something very like it, however, the position in T *A Sundell & Sons Pty Ltd v Emm Yannoulatos (Overseas) Pty Ltd*. In that case the plaintiff had originally entered into a contract to buy from the defendant a quantity of galvanised iron at £100 15s a ton and had established a letter of credit in favour of the defendant seller accordingly. The iron was to come from France and some months after the contract had been entered into the seller said that an increase in price of probably £27 was inevitable and requested that the letter of credit be increased, otherwise the plaintiff would not get his iron. Eventually the buyer on 17th April sent the seller a fresh order for the same quantity of iron at £140 per ton, but asking the seller to acknowledge that the buyer should have the right to contend that the original contract required the seller to supply the iron at £109 15s a ton. The buyer amended and increased his letter of credit accordingly, but the seller in acknowledging the buyer's letter did not accept the terms laid down in it. Eventually the iron arrived before the argument had been resolved and full use was made of the increased letter of credit.

The buyer thereafter sued to recover the excess he had paid through the increased letter of credit as having been paid under 'practical compulsion'. The first point taken in answer to this was that the original contract was varied or superseded by a new contract made on 17th April and that accordingly the buyer was obliged thereunder to pay. This argument failed since the court found there was no consideration for the provision of the increased letter of credit. The second point argued was that a payment could not be said to have been made under 'practical compulsion' where a threat was made by the payee to withhold from the payer a contractual right as distinct from a right of possession of property, a statutory right or some proprietary right. This it was argued would be to break new ground and would be contrary to what was said by Lord Sumner in *Sinclair v Brougham* against extending the action for money had and received. These arguments were rejected by the court who cited the passage from the judgment of Isaacs J, set out above emphasising by italics the words 'or any right' of the person paying under compulsion. It would seem, therefore, that the Australian courts would be prepared to allow the recovery of excess money paid, even under a new contract, as the result of a threat to break an earlier contract, since the threat or compulsion would be applied to the original contractual right of the party subject to the compulsion or economic duress. This also seems to be the view in the United States, where this was one of the grounds of decision in *King Construction Company v Smith Electric Co*. This view also accords with what was said in *D C & Builders Ltd v Rees* per Lord Denning MR: 'No person can insist on a settlement procured by intimidation.'

Before proceeding further it may be useful to summarise the conclusions I have so far reached. First, I do not take the view that the recovery of money paid under duress other than to the person is necessarily limited to duress to goods falling within one of the categories hitherto established by the English cases. I would respectfully follow and adopt the broad statement of principle laid down by Isaacs J cited earlier and frequently quoted and applied in the Australian cases. Secondly, from this it follows that the compulsion may take the form of 'economic duress' if the necessary facts are proved. A threat to break a contract may amount to such 'economic duress'. Thirdly, if there has been such a form of duress leading to a contract for consideration. I think that contract is a voidable one which can be avoided and the excess money paid under it recovered.

I think the facts found in this case do establish that the agreement to increase the price by ten per cent reached at the end of June 1973 was caused by what may be called 'economic duress'. The yard were adamant in insisting on the increased price without having any legal justification for so doing and the owners realised that the yard would not accept anything other than an unqualified agreement to the increase. The owners might have claimed damages in arbitration against the yard with all the inherent unavoidable uncertainties of litigation, but in view of the position of the owners vis-à-vis their relations with Shell it would be unreasonable to hold that this is the course they should have taken: see *Astley v Reynolds*. The owners made a very reasonable offer of arbitration coupled with security for any award in the yard's favour that might be made, but this was refused. They then made their agreement, which can truly I think be said to have been made under compulsion, by the telex of 28th June without prejudice to their rights. I do not consider the yard's ignorance of the Shell charter material. It may well be that had they known of it they would have been even more exigent.

If I am right in the conclusion reached with some doubt earlier that there was consideration for the ten per cent increase agreement reached at the end of June 1973 and if it be right to regard this as having been reached under a kind of duress in the form of economic pressure, then what is said in *Chitty on Contracts*, to which both counsel referred me, is relevant, namely that a contract entered into under duress is voidable and not void—

> 'that a person who has entered into the contract may either affirm or avoid such contract after the duress has ceased; and if he has so voluntarily acted under it with a full knowledge of all the circumstances, he may be held bound on the ground of ratification, or if, after escaping from the duress, he takes no steps to set aside the transaction, he may be found to have affirmed it.'

On appeal in *Ormes v Beadel* and in Kerr J's case there was on the facts action which was held to amount to affirmation or acquiescence in the form of taking part in an arbitration pursuant to the impugned agreement. There is nothing comparable to such action here.

On the other hand, the findings of fact in the special case present difficulties whether one is proceeding on the basis of a voidable agreement reached at the end of June 1973 or whether such agreement was void for want of consideration, and it were necessary in consequence to establish that the payments were made involuntarily and not with the intention of closing the transaction.

I have already stated that no protest of any kind was made by the owners after their telex of 28th June 1973, before their claim in this arbitration on 30th July 1975, which was shortly after, in July of that year, the Atlantic Baroness, a sister ship of the Atlantic Baron, had been tendered, though, as I understand it, she was not accepted and arbitration proceedings in regard to her are in consequence taking place. There was therefore a delay between 27th November 1974, when the Atlantic Baron was delivered and 30th July 1975, before the owners put forward their claim.

The owners were, therefore, free from the duress on 27th November 1974 and took no action by way of protest or otherwise between their important telex of 28th June 1973 and their formal claim for the return of the excess ten per cent paid of 30th July 1975, when they nominated their arbitrator. One cannot dismiss this delay as of no significance, though I would not consider it conclusive by itself. I do not attach any special importance to the lack of protest made at the time of the assignment, since the documents made no reference to the increased ten per cent. However by the time the Atlantic Baron was due for delivery in November 1974 market conditions had changed radically, as is found in the special case and the owners must have been aware of this. The special case finds, as stated earlier, that the owners did not believe that if they made any protest in the protocol of delivery and acceptance the yard would have refused to deliver the vessel or the Atlantic Baroness and had no reason so to believe. Counsel for the owners naturally stressed that in the rather carefully expressed findings in the special case, there is no finding that if at the time of the final payments the owners had withheld payment of the additional ten per cent, the yard would not have delivered the vessel. However, after careful consideration, I have come to the conclusion that the important points here are that (i) since there was no danger at this time in registering a protest, (ii) the final payments were made without any qualification, and (iii) were followed by a delay until 31st July 1975 before the owners put forward their claim, the correct inference to draw, taking an objective view of the facts, is that the action and inaction of the owners can only be regarded as an affirmation of the variation in June 1973 of the terms of the original contract by the agreement to pay the additional ten per cent. In reaching this conclusion I have not, of course, overlooked the findings in the special case [that the owners never intended to affirm the agreement for extra payments] but I do not think that an intention on the part of the owners not to affirm the agreement for the extra payments, not indicated to the yard, can avail them in view of their overt acts. As was said in *Deacon v Transport Regulation Board* in considering whether a payment was made voluntarily or not: 'No secret mental reservation of the doer is material. The question is—what would his conduct indicate to a reasonable man as his mental state'. I think this test is equally applicable to the decision this court has to make whether a voidable contract has been affirmed or not and I have applied this test in reaching the conclusion I have just expressed.

I think I should add very shortly that having considered the many authorities cited, even if I had come to a different conclusion on the issue about consideration, I would have come to the same decision adverse to the owners on the question whether the payments were made voluntarily in the sense of being made to close the transaction.

I accordingly answer the question of law in the negative with the consequences set out in the award.

Judgment for the yard.

■ *Pao On v Lau Yiu Long*

[1980] AC 614, Privy Council

(For the facts of this case, see p 126.)

Lord Scarman

... The American Law Institute in its *Restatement of the Law, Contracts*, Chapter 3, section 84(d), has declared that performance (or promise of performance) of a contractual duty owed to a third person is sufficient consideration. This view (which accords with the statement of our law in *New Zealand Shipping Co Ltd v A M Satterthwaite & Co Ltd*) appears to be generally accepted but only in cases where there is no suggestion of unfair economic pressure exerted to induce the making of what *Corbin on Contracts* calls 'the return promise'.

Their Lordships' knowledge of this developing branch of American law is necessarily limited. In their judgment it would be carrying audacity to the point of foolhardiness for them to attempt to extract from the American case law a principle to provide an answer to the question now under consideration. That question, their Lordships repeat is whether, in a case where duress is not established, public policy may nevertheless invalidate the consideration if there has been a threat to repudiate a pre-existing contractual obligation or an unfair use of a dominating bargaining position. Their Lordships' conclusion is that where businessmen are negotiating at arm's length it is unnecessary for the achievement of justice, and unhelpful in the development of the law, to invoke such a rule of public policy. It would also create unacceptable anomaly. It is unnecessary because justice requires that men, who have negotiated at arm's length, be held to their bargains unless it can be shown that their consent was vitiated by fraud, mistake or duress. If a promise is induced by coercion of a man's will, the doctrine of duress suffices to do justice. The party coerced, if he chooses and acts in time, can avoid the contract. If there is no coercion, there can be no reason for avoiding the contract where there is shown to be a real consideration which is otherwise legal.

Such a rule of public policy as is now being considered would be unhelpful because it would render the law uncertain. It would become a question of fact and degree to determine in each case whether there had been, short of duress, an unfair use of a strong bargaining position. It would create anomaly because, if public policy invalidates the consideration, the effect is to make the contract void. But unless the facts are such as to support a plea of 'non est factum', which is not suggested in this case, duress does no more than confer upon the victim the opportunity, if taken in time, to avoid the contract. It would be strange if conduct less than duress could render a contract void, whereas duress does no more than render a contract voidable. Indeed, it is the defendant's case in this appeal that such an anomaly is the correct result. Their case is that the plaintiffs, having lost by cancellation the safeguard of the subsidiary agreement, are without the safeguard of the guarantee because its consideration is contrary to public policy, and that they are debarred from restoration to their position under the subsidiary agreement because the guarantee is void, not voidable. The logical consequence of Mr Leggatt's submission is that the safeguard which all were at all times agreed the plaintiffs should have—the safeguard against fall in value of the shares—has been lost by the application of a rule of public policy. The law is not, in their Lordships' judgment, reduced to countenancing such stark injustice: nor is it necessary, when one bears in mind the protection offered otherwise by the law to one who contracts in ignorance of what he is doing or under duress. Accordingly, the submission that the additional consideration established by the extrinsic evidence is invalid on the ground of public policy is rejected.

The third question

Duress, whatever form it takes, is a coercion of the will so as to vitiate consent. Their Lordships agree with the observation of Kerr J in *Occidental Worldwide Investment Corporation v Skibs A/S Avanti* ... that in a contractual situation commercial pressure is not enough. There must be present some factor 'which could in law be regarded as a coercion of his will so as to vitiate his consent'. This conception is in line with what was said in this Board's decision in *Barton v Armstrong* by Lord Wilberforce and Lord Simon of Glaisdale—observations with which the majority judgment appears to be in agreement. In determining whether there was a coercion of will such that there was no true consent, it is material to inquire whether the person alleged to have been coerced did or did not protest; whether, at the time he was allegedly coerced into making the contract, he did or did not have an alternative course open to him such as an adequate legal remedy; whether he was independently advised; and whether after entering the contract he took steps to avoid it. All these matters are, as was recognised in *Maskell v Horner*, relevant in determining whether he acted voluntarily or not.

In the present case there is unanimity amongst the judges below that there was no coercion of the first defendant's will. In the Court of Appeal the trial judge's finding (already quoted) that the first defendant considered the matter thoroughly, chose to avoid litigation, and formed the opinion that the risk in giving the guarantee was more apparent than real was upheld. In short, there was commercial pressure, but no coercion. Even if this Board was disposed, which it is not, to take a different view, it would not substitute its opinion for that of the judges below on this question of fact.

It is, therefore, unnecessary for the Board to embark upon an inquiry into the question whether English law recognises a category of duress known as 'economic duress'. But, since the question has been fully argued in this appeal, their Lordships will indicate very briefly the view which they have formed. At common law money paid under economic compulsion could be recovered in an action for money had and received: *Astley v Reynolds*. The compulsion had to be such that the party was deprived of 'his freedom of exercising his will' (see p 916). It is doubtful, however, whether at common law any duress other than duress to the person sufficed to render a contract voidable: see *Blackstone's Commentaries*. Book 1, 12th edn pp 130–131 and *Skeate v Beale*. American law (*Williston on Contracts*, 3rd edn) now recognises that a contract may be avoided on the ground of economic duress. The commercial pressure alleged to constitute such duress must, however, be such that the victim must have entered the contract against his will, must have had no alternative course open to him and must have been confronted with coercive acts by the party exerting the pressure: *Williston on Contracts*, 3rd edn, vol 13 (1970), section 1603. American judges pay great attention to such evidential matters as the effectiveness of the alternative remedy available, the fact or absence of protest, the availability of independence advice, the benefit received, and the speed with which the victim has sought to avoid the contract. Recently two English judges have recognised that commercial pressure may constitute duress the pressure of which can render a contract voidable: Kerr J in *Occidental Worldwide Investment Corporation v Skibs A/S Avanti* and Mocatta J in *North Ocean Shipping Co Ltd v Hyundai Construction Co Ltd*. Both stressed that the pressure must be such that the victim's consent to the contract was not a voluntary act on his part. In their Lordships' view, there is nothing contrary to principle in recognising economic duress as a factor which may render a contract voidable, provided always that the basis of such recognition is that it must amount to a coercion of will, which vitiates consent. It must be shown that the payment made or the contract entered into was not a voluntary act.

Appeal allowed.

NOTE

Lord Scarman speaks of 'coercion of the will so as to vitiate consent'. Is this either an accurate description of the victim's state of mind when duress operates or an adequate explanation of why a contract may be voidable for duress? Compare the words of Lord Wilberforce in *Barton v Armstrong* (above) to what was said in *Lynch v DPP for Northern Ireland* [1975] 1 All ER 913, at 926a–c, 938h:

Lord Wilberforce

... [D]uress in the English law of contract ... deflects, without destroying, the will of one of the contracting parties. There is still an intention on his part to contract in the apparently consensual terms; but there is coactus volui [ie intention as the result of coercion—eds] on his side. The contrast is with non est factum. The contract procured by duress is therefore not void: it is voidable—at the discretion of the party subject to duress.

Lord Simon of Glaisdale

... At the present time, whatever the ultimate analysis in jurisprudence may be, the best opinion, as reflected in decisions of judges and in writers, seems to be that duress per minas [by threats—eds] is something which is superimposed on the other ingredients which by themselves would make up an offence, ie on the act and intention. 'Coactus volui' sums up the combination: the victim completes the act and knows that he is doing so; but the addition of the element of duress prevents the law from treating what he has done as a crime. One may note—and the comparison is satisfactory—that an analogous result is achieved in a civil law context: duress does not destroy the will, for example, to enter into a contract, but prevents the law from accepting what has happened as a contract valid in law (see the Privy Council case of *Barton v Armstrong* and the judgments in the Supreme Court of New South Wales).

On this, see the debate: Atiyah 98 LQR 197; Tiplady *99* LQR 188; Atiyah *99* LQR 353.

■ *Universe Tankships Inc of Monrovia v International Transport Workers' Federation*
[1982] 2 All ER 67, House of Lords

The plaintiffs' ship was blacked by the defendant union ('ITF'). To secure its release, the plaintiffs inter alia paid the sum of $6,480 to ITF's welfare fund. They later sought to recover this sum. ITF admitted that it had been paid under economic duress, but argued that the threat had been made in connection with a trade dispute and that it was therefore protected by the immunity against actions in tort conferred by the Trade Union and Labour Relations Act 1974, s 13.

Lord Diplock

... My Lords, I turn to the second ground on which repayment of the $6,480 is claimed, which I will call the duress point. It is not disputed that the circumstances in which the ITF demanded that the shipowners should enter into the special agreement and the typescript agreement and should pay the moneys of which the latter documents acknowledge receipt amounted to economic duress on the shipowners; that is to say, it is conceded that the financial consequences to the shipowners of the Universe Sentinel continuing to be rendered off hire under her time charter to Texaco, while the blacking continued, were so catastrophic as to amount to a coercion of the shipowners' will which vitiated their consent to those agreements and to the payments made by them to the ITF. This concession makes it unnecessary for your Lordships to use the instant appeal as the occasion for a general consideration of the developing law of economic duress as a ground for treating contracts as voidable and obtaining restitution of money paid under economic duress as money had and received to the plaintiffs' use. That economic duress may constitute a ground for such redress was recognised, albeit obiter, by the Privy Council in *Pao On v Lau Yiu*. The Board in that case referred with approval to two judgments at first instance in the Commercial Court which recognised that commercial pressure may constitute duress: one by Kerr J in *The Siboen and The Sibotre, Occidental Worldwide Investment Corp v Skibs A/S Avanti*; the other by Mocatta J in *North Ocean Shipping Co Ltd v Hyundai Construction Co Ltd, The Atlantic Baron*, which traces the development of this branch of the law from its origin in the eighteenth and early nineteenth century cases.

It is, however, in my view crucial to the decision of the instant appeal to identify the rationale of this development of the common law. It is not that the party seeking to avoid the contract which he has entered into with another party, or to recover money that he has paid to another party in response to a demand, did not know the nature or the precise terms of the contract at the time when he entered into it or did not understand the purpose for which the payment was demanded. The rationale is that his apparent consent was induced by pressure exercised on him by that other party which the law does not regard as legitimate, with the consequence that the consent is treated in law as revocable unless approbated either expressly or by implication after the illegitimate pressure has ceased to operate on his mind. It is rationale similar to that which underlies the avoidability of contracts entered into and the recovery of money exacted under colour of office, or under undue influence or in consequence of threats of physical duress.

Commercial pressure, in some degree, exists wherever one party to a commercial transaction is in a stronger bargaining position than the other party. It is not, however, in my view, necessary, nor would it be appropriate in the instant appeal, to enter into the general question of the kinds of circumstances, if any, in which commercial pressure, even though it amounts to a coercion of the will of a party in the weaker bargaining position, may be treated as legitimate and, accordingly, as not giving rise to any legal right of redress. In the instant appeal the economic duress complained of was exercised in the field of industrial relations to which very special considerations apply. ...

Lord Scarman

... Before turning to this issue, it is necessary to state, albeit very briefly, my view as to the nature of the modern law of duress.

It is, I think, already established law that economic pressure can in law amount to duress; and that duress, if proved, not only renders voidable a transaction into which a person has entered under its compulsion but is actionable as a tort, if it causes damage or loss: see *Barton v Armstrong* and *Pao On v Lau Yiu*. The authorities on which these two cases were based reveal two elements in the wrong of duress: (1) pressure amounting to compulsion of the will of the victim; and (2) the illegitimacy of the pressure exerted. There must be pressure, the practical effect of which is compulsion or the absence of choice. Compulsion is variously described in the authorities as coercion or the vitiation of consent. The classic case of duress is, however, not the lack of will to submit but the victim's intentional submission arising from the realisation that there is no other practical choice open to him. This is the thread of principle which links the early law of duress (threat to life or limb) with later developments when the law came also to recognise as duress first the threat to property and now the threat to a man's business or trade. The development is well traced in Goff and Jones *The Law of Restitution* (2nd edn, 1978) ch 9.

The absence of choice can be proved in various ways, eg by protest, by the absence of independent advice, or by a declaration of intention to go to law to recover the money paid or the property transferred; see *Maskell v Horner*. But none of these evidential matters goes to the essence of duress. The victim's silence will not assist the bully, if the lack of any practicable choice but to submit is proved. The present case is an excellent illustration. There was no protest at the time, but only a determination to do whatever was needed as rapidly as possible to release the ship. Yet nobody challenges the judge's finding that the owners acted under compulsion. He put it thus:

> 'It was a matter of the most urgent commercial necessity that the plaintiffs should regain the use of their vessel. They were advised that their prospects of obtaining an injunction were minimal, the vessel would not have been released unless the payment was made, and they sought recovery of the money with sufficient speed once the duress had terminated.'

The real issue in the appeal is, therefore, as to the second element in the wrong duress: was the pressure applied by the ITF in the circumstances of this case one which the law recognises as legitimate? For, as Lord Wilberforce and Lord Simon in *Barton v Armstrong* said: '... the pressure must be one of a kind which the law does not regard as legitimate'.

As Lord Wilberforce and Lord Simon remarked, in life, including life in commerce and finance, many acts are done 'under pressure, sometimes overwhelming pressure'; but they are not necessarily done under duress. That depends on whether the circumstances are such that the law regards the pressure as legitimate.

In determining what is legitimate two matters may have to be considered. The first is as to the nature of the pressure. In many cases this will be decisive, though not in every case. And so the second question may have to be considered, namely, the nature of the demand which the pressure is applied to support.

The origin of the doctrine of duress in threats to life or limb, or to property, suggests strongly that the law regards the threat of unlawful action as illegitimate, whatever the demand. Duress can, of course, exist even if the threat is one of lawful action; whether it does so depends on the nature of the demand. Blackmail is often a demand supported by a threat to do what is lawful, eg to report criminal conduct to the police. In many cases, therefore, what [one] has to justify is not the threat, but the demand ...' (see *Thorne v Motor Trade Association*, per Lord Atkin).

The present is a case in which the nature of the demand determines whether the pressure threatened or applied, ie the blacking, was lawful or unlawful. If it was unlawful, it is conceded that the owner acted under duress and can recover. If it was lawful, it is conceded that there was no duress and the sum sought by the owners is irrecoverable. The lawfulness or otherwise of the demand depends on whether it was an act done in contemplation or furtherance of a trade dispute. If it was, it would not be actionable in tort: s 13(1) of the Act. Although no question of tortious liability arises in this case and s 13(1) is not, therefore, directly in point, it is not possible, in my view, to say of acts which are protected by statute from suit in tort that they nevertheless can amount to duress. Parliament having enacted that such acts are not actionable in tort, it would be inconsistent with legislative policy to say that, when the remedy sought is not damages for tort but recovery of money paid, they become unlawful.

In order to determine whether the making of the demand was an act done in contemplation or furtherance of a trade dispute, it is necessary to refer to s 29 which sets out the statutory meaning of 'trade dispute'. . . .

By a majority, the House held that the payment was recoverable because it was not 'connected with ... the terms and conditions of employment' of the crew members so as to constitute a 'trade dispute' within s 29(1) of the Act.

NOTE

In *B & S Contracts and Design Ltd v Victor Green Publications Ltd* [1984] ICR 419, the plaintiffs had contracted to erect an exhibition stand for the defendants at Olympia. The plaintiffs' workmen went on strike and the plaintiffs informed the defendants that the contract would be cancelled unless the latter agreed to contribute £4,500 towards paying the workmen's claims. If the stands were not erected, the defendants faced serious losses and claims from exhibitors to whom they had let space, so they paid up, but the Court of Appeal held that the promise had been made when the plaintiffs had the defendants 'over a barrel' and the defendants could deduct the £4,500 they had paid from the final sum due. A promise to pay an additional charge was also held to be ineffective because made under economic duress in *Atlas Express Ltd v Kafco (Importers and Distributors) Ltd* [1989] 1 All ER 641.

If the 'vitiation of consent' test is not to be used, the critical factors seem to be, as Lord Scarman puts it in the *Universe Tankships* case, the degree of compulsion and the legitimacy of the threat. It is not wholly clear how these are to be applied. A number of questions may be asked.

(i)   In *Pao On*, Lord Scarman said that 'the victim must have had no alternative open to him'. Presumably, if the victim did have an alternative, he was not compelled to enter the contract. (In *The Atlantic Baron*, why did the judge consider that refusing to pay extra and suing for damages for late delivery if the contract was broken was not a realistic alternative for the buyers?)

(ii) The 'degree of compulsion' seems to ask how serious was the threat for the victim. What is required is not wholly clear. For example, is it enough that a threat to break the contract was made and that this influenced the victim's decision to make the promise he is now trying to avoid? Or must the pressure have been more overbearing than that? In *Occidental Worldwide Investment Corpn v Skibs A/S Avanti, The Siboen and The Sibotre* [1976] 1 Lloyd's Rep 293, at 334–336, Kerr J was prepared to assume that English law recognises economic duress: he considered that this was an alternative ground for the decision in *D & C Builders v Rees* (see p 856)—'there was no true accord'. However, he rejected as much too wide counsel's proposition that the defence is made out 'whenever one party to a contract threatens to commit a breach of it and the other party agrees to vary or cancel the contract under this threat because it has no effective legal remedy in respect of the threatened breach and has in this sense been compelled to agree'. The compulsion must deprive the promisor of *animus contrahendi*, and on the facts, the promisor was 'acting under great pressure, but only commercial pressure, and not under anything which in law could be regarded as a coercion of his will so as to vitiate his consent'. In the *B & S Contracts* case, Griffiths LJ said [1984] ICR at 425:

> . . . it is certainly not on every occasion when one of the parties unwillingly agrees to a variation that the law would consider that he had acted by reason of duress.

(iii) 'The pressure must be illegitimate.' Does this mean that not every threat of a breach of contract is illegitimate? If not every threat of breach of contract is illegitimate, which threats are legitimate and which are not?

(iv) One way of distinguishing the legitimate from the illegitimate is to ask whether the threatening party was acting in bad faith; see Birks, *Introduction to the Law of Restitution*, 1985, p 183.

(v)   Might the threat be legitimate or illegitimate according to why the party was threatening to break the contract—for example, simply to get a higher price or because he would be genuinely unable to perform unless the contract were changed? Was there a threat or merely a warning that the party would not be able to perform because of a pressure 'applied by circumstances to himself'? See Birks (above) and Halson (1991) 110 LQR 649.

(vi) Could the fairness of the agreement be relevant? It is noticeable that, in the *Pao On* case, the Laus realised at the time that the initial agreement was very favourable to them, much more so than the arrangement originally contemplated, so that in a sense the second agreement was merely correcting a mistake made by Pao On in negotiating the first. (Compare also the requirement in cases of undue influence that the agreement must be not readily explicable by the parties' relationship before relief will be given: see p 932.)

(vii) Lord Scarman accepts that, occasionally, there may be duress, although the threat made is to do something that is not itself unlawful; he gives the example of blackmail. In *CTN Cash and Carry Ltd v Gallaher Ltd* [1994] 4 All ER 714, the parties were in dispute as to whether the plaintiffs were liable to pay for a consignment of cigarettes that had been delivered to the wrong warehouse and, before the defendants had arranged for them to be transferred to the right one, had been stolen. The defendants believed in good faith that the plaintiffs were liable to pay for the cigarettes because the risk had passed to them, and they threatened to withdraw the plaintiffs' credit facilities for future dealings (as they were entitled to do for any reason) if the plaintiffs did not pay. The withdrawal of credit would have been very serious for the plaintiffs and they paid for the goods, but when later it was determined that the goods had not been at their risk, they claimed the money back on the basis of duress. The Court of Appeal upheld the first instance decision that there had been no duress. Steyn LJ said (at 719):

> We are being asked to extend the categories of duress of which the law will take cognisance. That is not necessarily objectionable, but it seems to me that an extension capable of covering the present case, involving "lawful act duress" in a commercial context in pursuit of a bona fide claim, would be a radical one with far-reaching implications. It would introduce a substantial and undesirable element of uncertainty in the commercial bargaining process. Moreover, it will often enable bona fide settled accounts to be reopened when parties to commercial dealings fall out. The aim of our commercial law ought to be to encourage fair dealing between parties. But it is a mistake for the law to set its sights too highly when the critical inquiry is not whether the conduct is lawful but whether it is morally or socially unacceptable. That is the inquiry in which we are engaged. In my view there are policy considerations which militate against ruling that the defendants obtained payment of the disputed invoice by duress.
>
> Outside the field of protected relationships, and in a purely commercial context, it might be a relatively rare case in which 'lawful act duress' can be established. And it might be particularly difficult to establish duress if the defendant bona fide considered that his demand was valid. In this complex and changing branch of the law I deliberately refrain from saying 'never'. But as the law stands, I am satisfied that the defendants' conduct in this case did not amount to duress.
>
> It is an unattractive result, inasmuch as the defendants are allowed to retain a sum which at the trial they became aware was not in truth due to them. But in my view the law compels the result.

(For a discussion of points (iii)–(vi) see Burrows, pp 230–234.)

At this stage, you may find it useful to refer back to Posner, 'Gratuitous Promises in Economics and Law' (p 854), and you may like to compare Uniform Commercial Code s 2–209.

■ Uniform Commercial Code, s 2–209

2–209. Modification, Rescission and Waiver

(1) An agreement modifying a contract within this Article needs no consideration to be binding.

. . .

Official Comment

... 2 ... modifications ... must meet the test of good faith imposed by this Act. The effective use of bad faith to escape performance on the original contract terms is barred, and the extortion of a 'modification' without legitimate commercial reason is ineffective as a violation of the duty of good faith ... good faith ... may in some situations require an objectively demonstrable reason for seeking a modification. But such matters as a market shift which makes performance come to involve a loss may provide such a reason even though there is no such unforeseen difficulty as would make out a legal excuse from performance.

NOTE

If the UCC test were applicable to *D & C Builders v Rees*, would the outcome change? What about *The Atlantic Baron*?

One author has argued that the law should develop two defences, one under which the contract was made as the result of the plaintiff's wrongdoing, the other based on the defendant's lack of consent.

■ Smith, *'Contracting Under Pressure: A Theory of Duress'* [1997]
Cambridge LJ 343, 371–373

By way of a summary description of the main features of the account of duress developed in this article, the questions that a court should ask in the most complex variant of a pressure case, a contractual modification case, will be described briefly. The first question is whether the plaintiff is barred from enforcing the modification because it was obtained as a result of his wrongdoing. In assessing wrongdoing in a modification context, the wrong, if there has been a wrong, is almost always a threat to breach the original contract. If the court establishes that the plaintiff made a threat to breach (and not merely a warning, request, or offer), the next question is whether that threat was operative in the sense that it was a necessary element of a set of actual conditions sufficient for the occurrence of the result. An affirmative answer means that the plaintiff is precluded from enforcing the contract by virtue of the wrongdoing principle. If the answer is negative, or if the plaintiff did not make a threat, then the wrongdoing principle does not apply. This will often be the conclusion reached in modification cases, since modifications are frequently the consequence of the plaintiff's impending bankruptcy or the defendant's wish to maintain a good reputation.

If operative wrongdoing is not established, the court must then consider whether the contract should be invalidated because the defendant's consent was impaired. The defendant is unlikely to be able to establish that his consent was impaired by a wrongful threat because, if the case has gone this far, either no wrongful threat was made or that threat was not operative in the weak sense required under the wrongdoing principle. Only if the defendant can show that there was a risk of non-performance (say because of the plaintiff's impending bankruptcy) and that this risk placed him in a necessitous situation, in the sense that he would suffer an unavoidable loss if the contract was not performed, is a plea of impaired consent possible. Such facts can often be established in modification cases, the parties being in a bilateral monopoly from which neither can exit without incurring losses. If a lack of options is made out, then the defendant must further prove that the lack of options was operative in his decision to renegotiate. The existence of the required but-for causation will typically turn upon the fairness of the contract terms: if the terms are unfair, causation normally is established. Finally, if the contract is invalid, the plaintiff may have a claim for restitution of benefits conferred or for reliance-based losses.

The contractual modification example illustrates the main themes of this article: that pressure cases typically raise two concerns, one for wrongdoing and the other for autonomy and that, while these concerns often overlap and require courts to ask similar questions (Was there a threat to harm? Was the threat operative?) the overlap is not perfect and the questions not identical. In particular, the scope of the concerns diverge where the reason a contracting party was under pressure was not because the other party acted wrongly, in other words, in necessity cases.

That English courts have thus far not distinguished clearly between wrongdoing and lack of consent in pressure cases is understandable. In many pressure cases it is clear that the contract should be invalidated, but less clear whether the reason for invalidity is wrongdoing or lack of consent or both wrongdoing and lack of consent. The distinctions between, for example, wrongful and non-wrongful threats, non-wrongful threats and wrongly exerting pressure other than by threats, and [different tests of] causation, can be difficult to apply. Second, some of the questions relevant to establishing no consent (e.g. Did the defendant have a non-bad alternative to contracting? Was the contract price fair?) are questions that courts traditionally and for good reasons have been cautious to address. Third, failing to identify the precise reason a contract is invalid has little consequence as far as contract law is concerned so long as it clear, as it often will be, that the contract is invalid.

The main consequence of the failure to distinguish wrongdoing from lack of consent is the underdevelopment of the latter defence. This underdevelopment may be significant when considering possible restitutionary claims following a finding of contractual invalidity since the amount of relief awarded may depend in part on whether or not the enriched party acted wrongly. More importantly, at least from the perspective of contract law, the failure to develop a coherent defence of no consent has resulted in the failure to develop a defence of duress by necessity. A sophisticated approach to pressure cases must therefore distinguish clearly between wrongdoing and lack of consent and, a related matter, take seriously the meaning and value of consent.

CHAPTER THIRTY-FIVE

UNDUE PRESSURE AND UNDUE INFLUENCE

An executory or executed contract or gift would also be set aside in equity in certain circumstances. Following the judgment of Cotton LJ in *Allcard v Skinner* (1887) 36 Ch D 145, 171, it is customary to divide the cases into two broad classes:

First where the court has been satisfied that the gift was the result of influence expressly used by the donee for the purpose; second, where the relations between the donor and donee have at or shortly before the execution of the gift been such as to raise a presumption that the donee had influence over the donor.

An example of the first class is *Williams v Bayley* (1866) LR 1 HL 200. The respondent's son had given the appellants promissory notes on which he had forged his father's indorsement. The father, threatened by the appellants with criminal prosecution of his son, agreed to make an equitable mortgage in favour of the appellants in exchange for the return of the notes. The House of Lords upheld cancellation of the agreement. At the time, threats of criminal prosecution were thought to be outside the scope of duress at common law; perhaps this case might now be reclassified as one of duress. A modern example of 'actual' undue influence is *Bank of Credit & Commerce International SA v Aboody* [1992] 4 All ER 955, in which a wife signed a document creating a charge over the family home in favour of the bank to secure the borrowing of her husband's company. There was evidence that the husband had bullied her: she was under pressure and had signed to get some peace. (The charge was not set aside because the transaction was not 'manifestly disadvantageous' to the wife, but the case has been overruled on this point: see p 922.)

It has become common to subdivide undue influence into categories referred to in *BCCI v Aboody* and adopted by Lord Browne-Wilkinson in *Barclays Bank plc v O'Brien* [1993] 4 All ER 417 (for the facts of this case, see p 923). He said (at 423):

A person who has been induced to enter into a transaction by the undue influence of another (the wrongdoer) is entitled to set that transaction aside as against the wrongdoer. Such undue influence is either actual or presumed. In *Bank of Credit and Commerce International SA v Aboody* (1988) [1992] 4 All ER 955 at 964 the Court of Appeal helpfully adopted the following classification.

Class 1: actual undue influence. In these cases it is necessary for the claimant to prove affirmatively that the wrongdoer exerted undue influence on the complainant to enter into the particular transaction which is impugned.

Class 2: presumed undue influence. In these cases the complainant only has to show, in the first instance, that there was a relationship of trust and confidence between the complainant and the wrongdoer of such a nature that it is fair to presume that the wrongdoer abused that relationship in procuring the complainant to enter into the impugned transaction. In class 2 cases therefore there is no need to produce evidence that actual undue influence was exerted in relation to the particular transaction impugned: once a confidential relationship has been proved, the burden then shifts to the wrongdoer to prove that the complainant entered into the impugned transaction freely, for example by showing that the complainant had independent advice. Such a confidential relationship can be established in two ways, viz:

Class 2A. Certain relationships (for example solicitor and client, medical advisor and patient) as a matter of law raise the presumption that undue influence has been exercised.

Class 2B. Even if there is no relationship falling within class 2A, if the complainant proves the de facto existence of a relationship under which the complainant generally reposed trust and confidence in the wrongdoer, the existence of such relationship raises the presumption of undue influence. In a class 2B case therefore, in the absence of evidence disproving undue influence, the complainant will succeed in setting aside the impugned transaction merely by proof that the complainant reposed trust and confidence in the wrongdoer without having to prove that the wrongdoer exerted actual undue influence or otherwise abused such trust and confidence in relation to the particular transaction impugned.

■ *Lloyds Bank Ltd v Bundy*
[1974] 3 All ER 757, Court of Appeal

The plaintiff was an elderly farmer who was not well versed in business affairs. His son had formed a plant hire company, which was in financial difficulties, and the plaintiff had already given a guarantee and a charge for £7,500 over his farmhouse, which was his only asset, to secure the company's debts to the bank at which father, son and the company had their accounts. At that time, the plaintiff had consulted his solicitor, who had advised him that this was the most he should commit to the son's business. The company's affairs got worse, and the assistant bank manager and the son went to see the plaintiff. The assistant manager told him that the bank could only continue to support the company if the plaintiff increased the guarantee and charge to £11,000; although he realised that the plaintiff was relying on him for advice, and that the house was his only asset, the assistant manager did not explain the company's position in full. The plaintiff signed the form of guarantee and charge. Later, the bank proceeded to enforce the charge and brought an action for possession of the house.

Sir Eric Sachs

... whilst disclaiming any intention of seeking to catalogue the elements of such a special relationship, it is perhaps of a little assistance to note some of those which have in the past frequently been found to exist where the court had been led to decide that this relationship existed as between adults of sound mind. Such cases tend to arise where someone relies on the guidance or advice of another, where the other is aware of that reliance and where the person on whom reliance is placed obtains, or may well obtain, a benefit from the transaction or has some other interest in it being concluded. In addition, there must, of course, be shown to exist a vital element which in this judgment will for convenience be referred to as confidentiality. It is this element which is so impossible to define and which is a matter for the judgment of the court on the facts of any particular case.

Confidentially, a relatively little used word, is being here adopted, albeit with some hesitation, to avoid the possible confusion that can arise through referring to 'confidence'. Reliance on advice can in many circumstances be said to import that type of confidence which only results in a common law duty to take care—a duty which may co-exist with but is not coterminous with that of fiduciary care. 'Confidentiality' is intended to convey that extra quality in the relevant confidence that is implicit in the phrase 'confidential relationship'....

It was inevitably conceded on behalf of the bank that the relevant relationship can arise as between banker and customer. Equally, it was inevitably conceded on behalf of the defendant that in the normal course of transactions by which a customer guarantees a third party's obligations, the relationship does not arise. The onus of proof lies on the customer who alleges that in any individual case the line has been crossed and the relationship has arisen . . .

It is . . . to be emphasised that as regards the second class the exercise of the court's jurisdiction to set aside the relevant transaction does *not* depend on proof of one party being 'able to dominate the other as though a puppet' (to use the words again adopted by the learned county court judge when testing whether the defence was established) nor any wrongful intention on the part of the person who gains a benefit from it, but on the concept that once the special relationship has been shown to exist, no benefit can be retained from the transaction unless it has been positively established that the duty of fiduciary care has been entirely fulfilled. To this second class. however, the learned judge never averted and plainly never directed his mind.

. . . [Once] the existence of a special relationship has been established, then any possible use of the relevant influence is, irrespective of the intentions of the persons possessing it, regarded in relation to the transaction under consideration as an abuse—unless and until the duty of fiduciary care has been shown to be fulfilled or the transaction is shown to be truly for the benefit of the person influenced. This approach is a matter of public policy.

One further point on which potential confusion emerged in the course of the helpful addresses of counsel stemmed from submissions to the effect that Mr Head, the assistant bank manager, should be cleared of all blame in the matter. When one has to deal with claims of breach of either common law or fiduciary care, it is not unusual to find that counsel for a big corporation tends to try and focus the attention of the court on the responsibility of the employee who deals with the particular matter rather than on that of the corporation as an entity. What we are concerned with in the present case is whether the element of confidentiality has been established as against the bank; Mr Head's part in the affair is but one link in a chain of events. Moreover, when it comes to a question of the relevant knowledge which will have to be discussed later in this judgment, it is the knowledge of the bank and not merely the personal knowledge of Mr Head that has to be examined.

Having discussed the nature of the issues to which the learned county court judge should have directed his mind, it is now convenient to turn to the evidence relating to the first of them—whether the special relationship has here been shown to exist at the material time . . .

The situation was thus one which to any reasonably sensible person, who gave it but a moment's thought, cried aloud the defendant's need for careful independent advice. Over and above the need any man has for counsel when asked to risk his last penny on even an apparently reasonable project, was the need here for informed advice as to whether there was any real chance of the company's affairs becoming viable if the documents were signed. If not, there arose questions such as, what is the use of taking the risk of becoming penniless without benefiting anyone but the bank; is it not better both for you and your son that you, at any rate, should still have some money when the crash comes; and should not the bank at least bind itself to hold its hand for some given period? The answers to such questions could only be given in the light of a worthwhile appraisement of the company's affairs—without which the defendant could not come to an *informed judgment* as to the wisdom of what he was doing.

No such advice to get an independent opinion was given; on the contrary, Mr Head chose to give his own views on the company's affairs and to take this course, though he had at trial to admit: 'I did not explain the company's affairs very fully. I had only just taken over'. (Another answer that escaped entry in the learned judge's original notes.)

On the above recited facts, the breach of the duty to take fiduciary care is manifest . . . [Once] the relevant duty is established, it is contrary to public policy that benefit of the transaction be retained by the person under the duty unless he positively shows that the duty of fiduciary care has been fulfilled; there is normally no room for debate on the issue as to what would have happened had the care been taken. . . .

There remains to mention that counsel for the bank, whilst conceding that the relevant special relationship could arise as between banker and customer, urged in somewhat doom-laden terms that a decision taken against the bank on the facts of this particular case would seriously affect banking practice. With all respect to that submission, it seems necessary to point out that nothing in this judgment affects the duties of a bank in the normal case where it is obtaining a guarantee, and in accordance with standard practice explains to the person about to sign its legal effect and the sums involved. When, however, a bank, as in this case, goes further and advises on more general matters germane to the wisdom of the transaction, that indicates that it may—not necessarily must—be crossing the line into the area of confidentiality so that the court may then have to examine all the facts, including, of course, the history leading up to the transaction, to ascertain whether or not that line has, as here, been crossed. It would indeed be rather odd if a bank which vis-à-vis a customer attained special relationship in some ways akin to that of a 'man of affairs'—something which can be a matter of pride and enhance his local reputation—should not where a conflict of interest has arisen as between itself and the person advised be under the resulting duty now under discussion. Once, as was inevitably conceded, it is possible for a bank to be under that duty, it is, as in the present case, simply a question for 'meticulous examination' of the particular facts to see whether that duty has arisen. On the special facts here it did arise and it has been broken.

The appeal should be allowed.

Cairns LJ concurred.

(The judgment of Lord Denning MR will be considered on p 954.)

In contrast to *Lloyds Bank v Bundy*, in *National Westminster Bank plc v Morgan* [1983] 3 All ER 85, Court of Appeal; [1985] 1 All ER 821, House of Lords, it was held by the House of Lords, reversing the Court of Appeal, that there was no confidential relationship between the wife and the manager of the bank to which she charged the matrimonial home in order to refinance the husband's business debts. Although the manager had come to the house to get her to sign a charge and she had had no independent advice, the House upheld the trial judge's finding that the relationship never went 'beyond the normal business relationship of banker and customer'. Thus no presumption could arise. In that case, there was also disagreement between the Court of Appeal and the House of Lords over a separate point: in order to raise the presumption of undue influence, was it necessary just to show the existence of a confidential relationship, or must the transaction also be obviously a disadvantageous one for the wife to enter? On the facts, the transaction was not manifestly disadvantageous, because without the refinancing, the wife was threatened with loss of the home to a mortgagee to whom the husband also owed money. The Court of Appeal held that manifest disadvantage was not a necessary ingredient. Dunn LJ said ([1983] 3 All ER 85, 90):

Slade LJ posed the case in argument of a solicitor who bought his client's house at a full and fair valuation. No doubt the relationship of confidence would exist, and there would be a presumption of undue influence. Only if the solicitor could show that the client had formed an independent and informed judgment could the transaction be upheld, and the mere fact that the price was fair would not be enough to discharge this. There might be all sorts of reasons, apart from the price, why the client did not want to sell his house.

It is true that in all the reported cases of undue influence to which we were referred the transactions were disadvantageous to the person influenced, otherwise they would not have sought to set them aside . . . it is a matter of public policy which requires that once the relationship of confidence is established, then any possible use of the influence is regarded as an abuse.

But the House of Lords disagreed. Lord Scarman, delivering the only full speech, said ([1985] 1 All ER 821, 827–829):

Like Dunn LJ, I know of no reported authority where the transaction set aside was not to the manifest disadvantage of the person influenced. It would not always be a gift: it can be a 'hard and inequitable' agreement *(Ormes v Beadel)*; or a transaction 'immoderate and irrational' *(Bank of Montreal v Stuart)* or 'unconscionable in that it was a sale at an undervalue *(Poosathurai v Kannappa Chettiar)*. Whatever the legal character of the transaction, the authorities show that it must constitute a disadvantage sufficiently serious to require evidence to rebut the presumption that in the circumstances of the relationship between the parties it was procured by the exercise of undue influence. In my judgment, therefore, the Court of Appeal erred in law in holding that the presumption of undue influence can arise from the evidence of the relationship of the parties without also evidence that the transaction itself was wrongful in that it constituted an advantage taken of the person subjected to the influence which, failing proof to the contrary, was explicable only on the basis that undue influence had been exercised to procure it.

The principle justifying the court in setting aside a transaction for undue influence can now be seen to have been established by Lindley LJ in *Allcard v Skinner*. It is not a vague 'public policy' but specifically the victimisation of one party by the other. It was stated by Lindley LJ in a famous passage:

'The principle must be examined. What then is the principle? Is it that it is right and expedient to save persons from the consequences of their own folly? or is it that it is right and expedient to save them from being victimised by other people? In my opinion the doctrine of undue influence is founded upon the second of these two principles. Courts of equity have never set aside gifts on the ground of the folly, imprudence, or want of foresight on the part of donors. The courts have always repudiated any such jurisdiction. *Huguenin v Baseley* is itself a clear authority to this effect. It would obviously be to encourage folly, recklessness, extravagance and vice if persons could get back property which they foolishly made away with, whether by giving it to charitable institutions or by bestowing it on less worthy objects. On the other hand, to protect people from being forced, tricked or misled in any way by others into parting with their property is one of the most legitimate objects of all laws; and the equitable doctrine of undue influence has grown out of and been developed by the necessity of grappling with insidious forms of spiritual tyranny and with the infinite varieties of fraud.'

In *Poosathurai v Kannappa Chettiar* (1919) LR 47 Ind App 1, 3 Lord Shaw, after indicating that there was no difference upon the subject of undue influence between the Indian Contract Act 1872 and English law quoted the Indian statutory provision, section 16(3):

'Where a person who is in a position to dominate the will of another enters into a contract with him, and the transaction appears on the face of it, or on the evidence, to be unconscionable, the burden of proving that such contract was not induced by undue influence shall lie upon the person in the position to dominate the will of the other.'

He proceeded (at p 4) to state the principle in a passage of critical importance, which, since, so far as I am aware, the case is not reported elsewhere, I think it helpful to quote in full.

'It must be established that the person in a position of domination has used that position to obtain unfair advantage for himself, and so to cause injury to the person relying upon his authority or aid. Where the relation of influence, as above set forth, has been established, and the second thing is also made clear, namely, that the bargain is with the "influencer", and in itself unconscionable, then the person in a position to use his dominating power has the burden thrown upon him, and it is a heavy burden, of establishing affirmatively that no domination was practised so as to bring about the transaction, but that the grantor of the deed was scrupulously kept separately advised in the independence of a free agent. These general propositions are mentioned because, if laid alongside of the facts of the present case, then it appears that one vital element—perhaps not sufficiently relied on in the court below, and yet essential to the plaintiff's case—is wanting. It is not proved as a fact in the present case that the bargain of sale come to was unconscionable in itself or constituted an advantage unfair to the plaintiff; it is, in short, not established as a matter of fact that the sale was for undervalue.'

The wrongfulness of the transaction must, therefore, be shown: it must be one in which an unfair advantage has been taken of another. The doctrine is not limited to transactions of gift.

In *BCCI v Aboody* (see p 917), the Court of Appeal held that, as a result of the decision in *National Westminster Bank v Morgan*, manifest disadvantage must be shown even in cases of actual undue influence. Slade L J pointed out, however, that in the example of the sale of a house by a client to a solicitor given in *Morgan's* case, the transaction might be set aside even if the full market price had been paid under a separate principle known as 'abuse of confidence'. This applies between solicitor and client and principal and agent (see [1992] 4 All ER 971–973). But the decision in the House of Lords, *CIBC Mortgages plc v Pitt* [1993] 4 All ER 433, overruled *BCCI v Aboody* on the need for manifest disadvantage in cases of actual undue influence and cast some doubt on *Morgan* itself on this point. Lord Browne-Wilkinson said (at 438–440):

My Lords, I am unable to agree with the Court of Appeal decision in *BCCI v Aboody*. I have no doubt that the decision in *Morgan* does not extend to cases of actual undue influence. Despite two references in Lord Scarman's speech to cases of actual undue influence, as I read his speech he was primarily concerned to establish that disadvantage had to be shown, not as a constituent element of the cause of action for undue influence, but in order to raise a presumption of undue influence within class 2. That was the only subject matter before the House of Lords in *Morgan* and the passage I have already cited was directed solely to that point. With the exception of a passing reference to *Ormes v Beadel* (1860) 2 Giff 166, 66 ER 70 all the cases referred to by Lord Scarman were cases of presumed undue influence. In the circumstances, I do not think that this House can have been intending to lay down any general principle applicable to all claims of undue influence, whether actual or presumed.

Whatever the merits of requiring a complainant to show manifest disadvantage in order to raise a class 2 presumption of undue influence, in my judgment there is no logic in imposing such a requirement where actual undue influence has been exercised and proved. Actual undue influence is a species of fraud. Like any other victim of fraud, a person who has been induced by undue influence to carry out a transaction which he did not freely and knowingly enter into is entitled to have that transaction set aside as of right. No case decided before *Morgan* was cited (nor am I aware of any) in which a transaction proved to have been obtained by actual undue influence has been upheld nor is there any case in which a court has even considered whether the transaction was, or was not, advantageous. A man guilty of fraud is no more entitled to argue that the transaction was beneficial to the person defrauded than is a man who has procured a transaction by misrepresentation. The effect of the wrongdoer's conduct is to prevent the wronged party from bringing a free will and properly informed mind to bear on the proposed transaction which accordingly must be set aside in equity as a matter of justice.

I therefore hold that a claimant who proves actual undue influence is not under the further burden of proving that the transaction induced by undue influence was manifestly disadvantageous: he is entitled as of right to have it set aside.

I should add that the exact limits of the decision in *Morgan* may have to be considered in the future. The difficulty is to establish the relationship between the law as laid down in *Morgan* and the long stand-ing principle laid down in the abuse of confidence cases, viz the law requires those in a fiduciary position who enter into transactions with those to whom they owe fiduciary duties to establish affirmatively that the transaction was a fair one: see for example *Demarara Bauxite Co Ltd v Hubbard* [1923] AC 673, *Moodie v Cox* [1917] 2 Ch 71, and the discussion in *BCCI v Aboody* [1992] 4 All ER 955 at 971–973. The abuse of confidence principle is founded on considerations of general public policy, viz that in order to protect those to whom fiduciaries owe duties *as a class* from exploitation by fiduciaries *as a class*, the law imposes a heavy duty on fiduciaries to show the righteousness of the transactions they enter into with those to whom they owe such duties. This principle is in sharp contrast with the view of this House in

Morgan that in cases of presumed undue influence (a) the law is not based on considerations of public policy and (b) that it is for the claimant to prove that the transaction was disadvantageous rather than for the fiduciary to prove that it was not disadvantageous. Unfortunately, the attention of this House in *Morgan* was not drawn to the abuse of confidence cases and therefore the interaction between the two principles (if indeed they are two separate principles) remains obscure: see also 48 MLR 579 and *Wright v Carter* [1903] 1 Ch 27.

Several of the cases we have considered have involved a recurrent problem: a person agrees to charge their property, or their matrimonial home, to a bank in order to secure the business debts of their spouse, but does so as the result of duress, misrepresentation or undue influence by the spouse. Is the bank able to enforce the charge? The rule is that the bank is not affected by the improper action of the spouse unless either it had notice of it when it took the charge, or the spouse was acting as agent for the bank. In the latter case, the bank is treated as having knowledge. In a number of cases, it was held that the bank had 'left it to the spouse' (or other relation) to obtain the signature on the charge, so that the spouse or relation was acting as the bank's agent: see *Avon Finance Co Ltd v Bridger* [1985] 2 All ER 281; *Coldunnell v Gallon* [1986] QB 1184. In *Barclays Bank plc v O'Brien*, this approach was described in the Court of Appeal as artificial, and relief was given on the basis of a 'special equity' in favour of wives derived from the case of *Turnbull v Duval* [1902] AC 429, PC.

■ *Barclays Bank plc v O'Brien*

[1993] 4 All ER 417, House of Lords

Lord Browne-Wilkinson

Mr and Mrs O'Brien were husband and wife. The matrimonial home, 151 Farnham Lane, Slough, was in their joint names subject to a mortgage of approximately £25,000 to a building society. Mr O'Brien was a chartered accountant and had an interest in a company, Heathrow Fabrications Ltd. The company's bank account was at the Woolwich branch of Barclays Bank. In the first three months of 1987 the company frequently exceeded its overdraft facility of £40,000 and a number of its cheques were dishonoured on presentation. In discussions in April 1981 between Mr O'Brien and the manager of the Woolwich branch, Mr Tucker, Mr O'Brien told Mr Tucker that he was remortgaging the matrimonial home: Mr Tucker made a note that Mrs O'Brien might be a problem. The overdraft limit was raised at that stage to £60,000 for one month. Even though no additional security was provided, by 15 June 1987 the company's overdraft had risen to £98,000 and its cheques were again being dishonoured.

On 22 June 1987 Mr O'Brien and Mr Tucker agreed (1) that the company's overdraft limit would be raised to £135,000 reducing to £120,000 after three weeks, (2) that Mr O'Brien would guarantee the company's indebtedness and (3) that Mr O'Brien's liability would be secured by a second charge on the matrimonial home.

The necessary security documents were prepared by the bank. They consisted of an unlimited guarantee by Mr O'Brien of the company's liability and a legal charge by both Mr and Mrs O'Brien of the matrimonial home to secure any liability of Mr O'Brien to the bank. Mr Tucker arranged for the documents, together with a side letter, to be sent to the Burnham branch of the bank for execution by Mr and Mrs O'Brien. In a covering memorandum Mr Tucker requested the Burnham branch to advise the O'Briens as to the current level of the facilities afforded to the bank (£107,000) and the projected increase to £135,000. The Burnham branch was also asked to ensure that the O'Briens were 'fully aware of the nature of the documentation to be signed and advised that if they are in any doubt they should contact their solicitors before signing'.

Unfortunately the Burnham branch did not follow Mr Tucker's instructions. On 1 July Mr O'Brien alone signed the guarantee and legal charge at the Burnham branch, the document simply being produced for signature and witnessed by a clerk. On the following day Mrs O'Brien went to the branch with her husband. There were produced for signature by Mrs O'Brien the legal charge on the matrimonial home together with a side letter, which reads:

'We hereby agree acknowledge and confirm as follows: . . . (3) That you recommended that we should obtain independent legal advice before signing this letter.'

In fact the Burnham branch gave Mrs O'Brien no explanation of the effect of the documents. No one suggested that she should take independent legal advice. She did not read the documents or the side letter. She simply signed the legal charge and side letter and her signature was witnessed by the clerk. She was not given a copy of the guarantee.

The company did not prosper and by October 1987 its indebtedness to the bank was over £154,000. In November 1987 demand was made against Mr O'Brien under his guarantee. When the demand was not met possession proceedings under the legal charge were brought by the bank against Mr and Mrs O'Brien. Mrs O'Brien seeks to defend these proceedings by alleging that she was induced to execute the legal charge on the matrimonial home by the undue influence of Mr O'Brien and by his misrepresentation. The trial judge, Judge Marder QC, and the Court of Appeal rejected the claim based on undue influence: on the appeal to this House the claim based on undue influence is not pursued. However, the judge did find that Mr O'Brien had falsely represented to Mrs O'Brien that the charge was to secure only £60,000 and that even this liability would be released in a short time when the house was remortgaged. On those findings of fact the trial judge granted an order for possession against Mrs O'Brien holding that the bank could not be held responsible for the misrepresentation made by Mr O'Brien.

The decision of the Court of Appeal

The Court of Appeal (Purchas, Butler-Sloss and Scott LJJ) reversed his decision. The leading judgment in the Court of Appeal was given by Scott LJ, who found that there were two lines of authority. One line would afford no special protection to married women: the rights of the creditor bank could only be adversely affected by the wrongful acts of the principal debtor, the husband, in procuring the surety's liability if the principal debtor was acting as the agent of the creditor in procuring the surety to join or the creditor had knowledge of the relevant facts. I will call this theory 'the agency theory'. The other line of authority (which I will call 'the special equity theory) detected by Scott L J considers that equity affords special protection to a protected class of surety, viz those where the relationship between the debtor and the surety is such that influence by the debtor over the surety and reliance by the surety on the debtor are natural features of the relationship. In cases where a surety is one of this protected class, the surety obligation is unenforceable by the creditor bank if (1) the relationship between the debtor and the surety was known to the creditor, (2) the surety's consent was obtained by undue influence or by misrepresentation or without 'an adequate understanding of the nature and effect of the transaction' and (3) the creditor had failed to take reasonable steps to ensure that the surety had given a true and informed consent to the transaction. The Court of Appeal preferred the special equity principle. They held that the legal charge on the O'Briens' matrimonial home was not enforceable by the bank against Mrs O'Brien save to the extent of the £60,000 which she had thought she was agreeing to secure.

Policy considerations

The large number of cases of this type coming before the courts in recent years reflects the rapid changes in social attitudes and the distribution of wealth which have recently occurred. Wealth is now more widely spread. Moreover a high proportion of privately owned wealth is invested in the matrimonial home. Because of the recognition by society of the equality of the sexes, the majority of matrimonial homes are now in the joint names of both spouses. Therefore in order to raise finance for the business enterprises of one or other of the spouses, the jointly owned home has become a main source of security. The provision of such security requires the consent of both spouses.

In parallel with these financial developments, society's recognition of the equality of the sexes has led to a rejection of the concept that the wife is subservient to the husband in the management of the family's finances. A number of the authorities reflect an unwillingness in the court to perpetuate law based on this outmoded concept. Yet, as Scott LJ in the Court of Appeal rightly points out, although the concept of the ignorant wife leaving all financial decisions to the husband is outmoded, the practice does not yet coincide with the ideal (see [1992] 4 All ER 983 at 1008, [1993] QB 109 at 139). In a substantial proportion of marriages it is still the husband who has the business experience and the wife is willing to follow his advice without bringing a truly independent mind and will to bear on financial decisions. The number of recent cases in this field shows that in practice many wives are still subjected to, and yield to, undue influence by their husbands. Such wives can reasonably look to the law for some protection when their husbands have abused the trust and confidence reposed in them.

On the other hand, it is important to keep a sense of balance in approaching these cases. It is easy to allow sympathy for the wife who is threatened with the loss of her home at the suit of a rich bank to obscure an important public interest, viz the need to ensure that the wealth currently tied up in the matrimonial home does not become economically sterile. If the rights secured to wives by the law render vulnerable loans granted on the security of matrimonial homes, institutions will be unwilling to accept such security, thereby reducing the flow of loan capital to business enterprises. It is therefore essential that a law designed to protect the vulnerable does not render the matrimonial home unacceptable as security to financial institutions.

With these policy considerations in mind I turn to consider the existing state of the law.... [Lord Browne-Wilkinson then set out the various categories of undue influence: see pp 917–918.]

As to dispositions by a wife in favour of her husband, the law for long remained in an unsettled state. In the nineteenth century some judges took the view that the relationship was such that it fell into class 2A, ie as a matter of law undue influence by the husband over the wife was presumed. It was not until the decisions in *Howes v Bishop* [1909] 2 KB 390 and *Bank of Montreal v Stuart* [1911] AC 120 that it was finally determined that the relationship of husband and wife did not as a matter of law raise a presumption of undue influence within class 2A. It is to be noted therefore that when *Turnbull v Duval* was decided in 1902 the question whether there was a class 2A presumption of undue influence as between husband and wife was still unresolved.

An invalidating tendency?

Although there is no class 2A presumption of undue influence as between husband and wife, it should be emphasised that in any particular case a wife may well be able to demonstrate that de facto she did leave decisions on financial affairs to her husband thereby bringing herself within class 2B. ie that the relationship between husband and wife in the particular case was such that the wife reposed confidence and trust in her husband in relation to their financial affairs and therefore undue influence is to be presumed. Thus, in those cases which still occur where the wife relies in all financial matters on her husband and simply does what he suggests, a presumption of undue influence within class 2B can be established solely from the proof of such trust and confidence without proof of actual undue influence.

In the appeal in *CIBC Mortgages plc v Pitt* [1993] 4 All ER 433 (judgment in which is to be given immediately after that in the present appeal) Mr Price QC for the wife argued that in the case of transactions between husband and wife there was an 'invalidating tendency', ie although there was no class 2A presumption of undue influence, the courts were more ready to find that a husband had exercised undue influence over his wife than in other cases. Scott LJ in the present case also referred to the law treating married women 'more tenderly' than others. This approach is based on dicta in early authorities. . . .

In my judgment this special tenderness of treatment afforded to wives by the courts is properly attributable to two factors. First, many cases may well fall into the class 2B category of undue influence because the wife demonstrates that she placed trust and confidence in her husband in relation to her financial affairs and therefore raises a presumption of undue influence. Second, the sexual and emotional ties between the parties provide a ready weapon for undue influence: a wife's true wishes can easily be overborne because of her fear of destroying or damaging the wider relationship between her and her husband if she opposes his wishes.

For myself, I accept that the risk of undue influence affecting a voluntary disposition by a wife in favour of a husband is greater than in the ordinary run of cases where no sexual or emotional ties affect the free exercise of the individual's will.

Undue influence, misrepresentation and third parties

Up to this point I have been considering the right of a claimant wife to set aside a transaction as against the wrongdoing husband when the transaction has been procured by his undue influence. But in surety cases the decisive question is whether the claimant wife can set aside the transaction, not against the wrongdoing husband, but against the creditor bank. Of course, if the wrongdoing husband is acting as agent for the creditor bank in obtaining the surety from the wife, the creditor will be fixed with the wrong-doing of its own agent and the surety contract can be set aside as against the creditor. Apart from this, if the creditor bank has notice, actual or constructive, of the undue influence exercised by the husband (and consequentially of the wife's equity to set aside the transaction) the creditor will take subject to that equity and the wife can set aside the transaction against the creditor (albeit a purchaser for value) as well as against the husband: see *Bainbrigge v Browne* (1881) 18 Ch D 188 and *BCCI v Aboody*. Similarly, in cases such as the present where the wife has been induced to enter into the transaction by the husband's mis-representation, her equity to set aside the transaction will be enforceable against the creditor if either the husband was acting as the creditor's agent or the creditor had actual or constructive notice.

[Lord Browne-Wilkinson then considered *Turnbull v Duval* and concluded that it was not a sound decision.] ... [In] my view it is the proper application of the doctrine of notice which provides the key to finding a principled basis for the law.

... [the] present law is built on the unsure foundations of *Turnbull v Duval*. Like most law founded on obscure and possibly mistaken foundations it has developed in an artificial way, giving rise to artificial distinctions and conflicting decisions. In my judgment your Lordships should seek to restate the law in a form which is principled, reflects the current requirements of society and provides as much certainty as possible.

Conclusions

(a) Wives. My starting point is to clarify the basis of the law. Should wives (and perhaps others) be accorded special rights in relation to surety transactions by the recognition of a special equity applicable only to such persons engaged in such transactions? Or should they enjoy only the same protection as they would enjoy in relation to their other dealings? In my judgment, the special equity theory should be rejected. First, I can find no basis in principle for affording special protection to a limited class in relation to one type of transaction only. Second, to require the creditor to prove knowledge and understanding by the wife in all cases is to reintroduce by the back door either a presumption of undue influence of class 2A (which has been decisively rejected) or the Romilly heresy (which has long been treated as bad law). Third, although Scott LJ found that there were two lines of cases one of which supported the special equity theory, on analysis although many decisions are not inconsistent with that theory the only two cases which support it are *Yerkey v Jones* and the decision of the Court of Appeal in the present case. Finally, it is not necessary to have recourse to a special equity theory for the proper protection of the legitimate interests of wives as I will seek to show.

In my judgment, if the doctrine of notice is properly applied, there is no need for the introduction of a special equity in these types of cases. A wife who has been induced to stand as a surety for her hus-band's debts by his undue influence, misrepresentation or some other legal wrong has an equity as against him to set aside that transaction. Under the ordinary principles of equity, her right to set aside that transaction will be enforceable against third parties (eg against a creditor) if either the husband was acting as the third party's agent or the third party had actual or constructive notice of the facts giving rise to her equity. Although there may be cases where, without artificiality, it can properly be held that the husband was acting as the agent of the creditor in procuring the wife to stand as surety, such cases will be of very rare occurrence. The key to the problem is to identify the circumstances in which the creditor will be taken to have had notice of the wife's equity to set aside the transaction.

The doctrine of notice lies at the heart of equity. Given that there are two innocent parties, each enjoying rights, the earlier right prevails against the later right if the acquirer of the later right knows of the earlier right (actual notice) or would have discovered it had he taken proper steps (constructive notice). In particular, if the party asserting that he takes free of the earlier rights of another knows of certain facts which put him on inquiry as to the possible existence of the rights of that other and he fails to make such inquiry or take such other steps as are reasonable to verify whether such earlier right does or does not exist, he will have constructive notice of the earlier right and take subject to it. Therefore where a wife has agreed to stand surety for her husband's debts as a result of undue influence or misrepresentation, the creditor will take subject to the wife's equity to set aside the transaction if the circumstances are such as to put the creditor on inquiry as to the circumstances in which she agreed to stand surety.

It is at this stage that, in my view, the 'invalidating tendency' or the law's 'tender treatment' of married women, becomes relevant. As I have said above in dealing with undue influence, this tenderness of the law towards married women is due to the fact that, even today, many wives repose confidence and trust in their husbands in relation to their financial affairs. This tenderness of the law is reflected by the fact that voluntary dispositions by the wife in favour of her husband are more likely to be set aside than other dispositions by her: a wife is more likely to establish presumed undue influence of class 2B by her husband than by others because, in practice, many wives do repose in their husbands trust and confidence in relation to their financial affairs. Moreover the informality of business dealings between spouses raises a substantial risk that the husband has not accurately stated to the wife the nature of the liability she is undertaking, ie he has misrepresented the position, albeit negligently.

Therefore, in my judgment a creditor is put on inquiry when a wife offers to stand surety for her husband's debts by the combination of two factors: (a) the transaction is on its face not to the financial advantage of the wife; and (b) there is a substantial risk in transactions of that kind that, in procuring the wife to act as surety, the husband has committed a legal or equitable wrong that entitles the wife to set aside the transaction.

It follows that, unless the creditor who is put on inquiry takes reasonable steps to satisfy himself that the wife's agreement to stand surety has been properly obtained, the creditor will have constructive notice of the wife's rights.

What, then are the reasonable steps which the creditor should take to ensure that it does not have constructive notice of the wife's rights, if any? Normally the reasonable steps necessary to avoid being fixed with constructive notice consist of making inquiry of the person who may have the earlier right (ie the wife) to see if whether such right is asserted. It is plainly impossible to require of banks and other financial institutions that they should inquire of one spouse whether he or she has been unduly influenced or misled by the other. But in my judgment the creditor, in order to avoid being fixed with constructive notice, can reasonably be expected to take steps to bring home to the wife the risk she is running by standing as surety and to advise her to take independent advice. As to past transactions, it will depend on the facts of each case whether the steps taken by the creditor satisfy this test. However for the future in my judgment a creditor will have satisfied these requirements if it insists that the wife attend a private meeting (in the absence of the husband) with a representative of the creditor at which she is told of the extent of her liability as surety, warned of the risk she is running and urged to take independent legal advice. If these steps are taken in my judgment the creditor will have taken such reasonable steps as are necessary to preclude a subsequent claim that it had constructive notice of the wife's rights. I should make it clear that I have been considering the ordinary case where the creditor knows only that the wife is to stand surety for her husband's debts. I would not exclude exceptional cases where a creditor has knowledge of further facts which render the presence of undue influence not only possible but probable. In such cases, the creditor to be safe will have to insist that the wife is separately advised.

. . .

If the law is established as I have suggested, it will hold the balance fairly between on the one hand the vulnerability of the wife who relies implicitly on her husband and, on the other hand, the practical problems of financial institutions asked to accept a secured or unsecured surety obligation from the wife for her husband's debts. In the context of suretyship, the wife will not have any right to disown her obligations just because subsequently she proves that she did not fully understand the transaction: she will, as in all other areas of her affairs, be bound by her obligations unless her husband has, by misrepresentation, undue influence or other wrong, committed an actionable wrong against her. In the normal case, a financial institution will be able to lend with confidence in reliance on the wife's surety obligation provided that it warns her (in the absence of the husband) of the amount of her potential liability and of the risk of standing surety and advises her to take independent advice.

Mr Jarvis QC for the bank urged that this is to impose too heavy a burden on financial institutions. I am not impressed by this submission. . . . the Code of Banking Practice (adopted by banks and building societies in March 1992) provides in para 12.1 as follows:

'Banks and building societies will advise private individuals proposing to give them a guarantee or other security for another person's liabilities that: (i) by giving the guarantee or third party security he or she might become liable instead of or as well as that other person; (ii) he or she should seek independent legal advice before entering into the guarantee or third party security. Guarantees and other third party security forms will contain a clear and prominent notice to the above effect.'

'Thus good banking practice (which applies to all guarantees, not only those given by a wife) largely accords with what I consider the law should require when a wife is offered as surety. The only further substantial step required by law beyond that good practice is that the position should be explained by the bank to the wife in a personal interview. I regard this as being essential because a number of the decided cases show that written warnings are often not read and are sometimes intercepted by the husband. It does not seem to me that the requirement of a personal interview imposes such an additional administrative burden as to render the bank's position unworkable.

(b) Other persons. I have hitherto dealt only with the position where a wife stands surety for her husband's debts. But in my judgment the same principles are applicable to all other cases where there is an emotional relationship between cohabitees. The 'tenderness' shown by the law to married women is not based on the marriage ceremony but reflects the underlying risk of one cohabitee exploiting the emotional involvement and trust of the other. Now that unmarried cohabitation, whether heterosexual or homosexual, is widespread in our society, the law should recognise this. Legal wives are not the only group which are now exposed to the emotional pressure of cohabitation. Therefore if, but only if, the creditor is aware that the surety is cohabiting with the principal debtor, in my judgment the same principles should apply to them as apply to husband and wife.

In addition to the cases of cohabitees, the decision of the Court of Appeal in *Avon Finance Co Ltd v Bridger* [1985] 2 All ER 281 shows (rightly in my view) that other relationships can give rise to a similar result. In that case a son, by means of misrepresentation, persuaded his elderly parents to stand surety for his debts. The surety obligation was held to be unenforceable by the creditor inter alia because to the bank's knowledge the parents trusted the son in their financial dealings. In my judgment that case was rightly decided: in a case where the creditor is aware that the surety reposes trust and confidence in the principal debtor in relation to his financial affairs, the creditor is put on inquiry in just the same way as it is in relation to husband and wife.

. . .

The decision of this case

Applying those principles to this case, to the knowledge of the bank Mr and Mrs O'Brien were man and wife. . . .

Unfortunately Mr Tucker's instructions were not followed and to the knowledge of the bank (through the clerk at the Burnham branch) Mrs O'Brien signed the documents without any warning of the risks or any recommendation to take legal advice. In the circumstances the bank (having failed to take reasonable steps) is fixed with constructive notice of the wrongful misrepresentation made by Mr O'Brien to Mrs O'Brien. Mrs O'Brien is therefore entitled as against the bank to set aside the legal charge on the matrimonial home securing her husband's liability to the bank.

For these reasons I would dismiss the appeal with costs.

The other members of the House agreed.

Appeal dismissed.

NOTES

1. It is the combination of a relationship that makes undue influence a risk and a transaction that is not to the wife's apparent benefit which should put the bank on notice. In *CIBC Mortgages plc v Pitt* [1993] 4 All ER 433, in which judgment was given immediately after that in *O'Brien's* case, the mortgage loan application signed by the husband and wife was a joint one stating that the purpose was to pay off an existing mortgage and buy a holiday home. In fact, the husband wanted money to invest in the stock market, and when the market crashed, he could not keep up the repayments. Although he had used undue influence to obtain the wife's signature, the bank was not put on notice of it; as Lord Browne-Wilkinson put it (at 441):

    So far as the plaintiff was aware, the transaction consisted of a joint loan to the husband and wife to finance the discharge of an existing mortgage on 26 Alexander Avenue and, as to the balance, to be applied in buying a holiday home. The loan was advanced to both husband and wife jointly. There was nothing to indicate to the plaintiff that this was anything other than a normal advance to a husband and wife for their joint benefit.

2. The decision in *O'Brien* is a significant step towards protecting spouses and others, but for a note questioning how far it can offer real protection from what has come to be called 'sexually transmitted debt', see Fehlberg, *Sexually Transmitted Debt*, 1997.

3. The decision of the House of Lords in *O'Brien* was followed by extensive litigation. Many cases reached the Court of Appeal and eventually eight decisions were taken together to the House of Lords in *Royal Bank of Scotland v Etridge (No 2)* [2001] UKHL 44 [2001] 4 All ER 449.

    Lord Bingham:

    The transactions which give rise to these appeals are commonplace but of great social and economic importance. It is important that a wife (or anyone in a like position) should not charge her interest in the matrimonial home to secure the borrowing of her husband (or anyone in a like position) without fully understanding the nature and effect of the proposed transaction and that the decision is hers, to agree or not to agree. It is important that lenders should feel able to advance money, in run-of-the-mill cases with no abnormal features, on the security of the wife's interest in the matrimonial home in reasonable confidence that, if appropriate procedures have been followed in obtaining the security, it will be enforceable if the need for enforcement arises. The law must afford both parties a measure of protection. It cannot prescribe a code which will be proof against error, misunderstanding or mishap. But it can indicate minimum requirements which, if met, will reduce the risk of error, misunderstanding or mishap to an acceptable level. The paramount need in this important field is that these minimum requirements should be clear, simple and practically operable.

    My Lords, in my respectful opinion these minimum requirements are clearly identified in the opinions of my noble and learned friends Lord Nicholls of Birkenhead and Lord Scott of Foscote. If these requirements are met the risk that a wife has been misled by her husband as to the facts of a proposed transaction should be eliminated or virtually so. The risk that a wife has been overborne or coerced by her husband will not be eliminated but will be reduced to a level which makes it proper for the lender to proceed. While the opinions of Lord Nicholls and Lord Scott show some difference of expression and approach, I do not myself discern any significant difference of legal principle applicable to these cases, and I agree with both opinions. But if I am wrong and such differences exist, it is plain that the opinion of Lord Nicholls commands the unqualified support of all members of the House.

Lord Nicholls:

The issues raised by these appeals make it necessary to go back to first principles. Undue influence is one of the grounds of relief developed by the courts of equity as a court of conscience. The objective is to ensure that the influence of one person over another is not abused. In everyday life people constantly seek to influence the decisions of others. They seek to persuade those with whom they are dealing to enter into transactions, whether great or small. The law has set limits to the means properly employable for this purpose. To this end the common law developed a principle of duress. Originally this was narrow in its scope, restricted to the more blatant forms of physical coercion, such as personal violence.

Here, as elsewhere in the law, equity supplemented the common law. Equity extended the reach of the law to other unacceptable forms of persuasion. The law will investigate the manner in which the intention to enter into the transaction was secured: 'how the intention was produced', in the oft repeated words of Lord Eldon LC, from as long ago as 1807 (*Huguenin v Baseley* (1807) 14 Ves Jun 273 at 300, [1803–13] All ER Rep 1 at 13). If the intention was produced by an unacceptable means, the law will not permit the transaction to stand. The means used is regarded as an exercise of improper or 'undue' influence, and hence unacceptable, whenever the consent thus procured ought not fairly to be treated as the expression of a person's free will. It is impossible to be more precise or definitive. The circumstances in which one person acquires influence over another, and the manner in which influence may be exercised, vary too widely to permit of any more specific criterion.

Equity identified broadly two forms of unacceptable conduct. The first comprises overt acts of improper pressure or coercion such as unlawful threats. Today there is much overlap with the principle of duress as this principle has subsequently developed. The second form arises out of a relationship between two persons where one has acquired over another a measure of influence, or ascendancy, of which the ascendant person then takes unfair advantage. An example from the nineteenth century, when much of this law developed, is a case where an impoverished father prevailed upon his inexperienced children to charge their reversionary interests under their parents' marriage settlement with payment of his mortgage debts (see *Bainbrigge v Browne* (1881) 18 Ch D 188).

In cases of this latter nature the influence one person has over another provides scope for misuse without any specific overt acts of persuasion. The relationship between two individuals may be such that, without more, one of them is disposed to agree a course of action proposed by the other. Typically this occurs when one person places trust in another to look after his affairs and interests, and the latter betrays this trust by preferring his own interests. He abuses the influence he has acquired. In *Allcard v Skinner* (1887) 36 Ch D 145, [1886–90] All ER Rep 90, a case well known to every law student, Lindley LJ ((1887) 36 Ch D 145 at 181, [1886–90] All ER Rep 90 at 98) described this class of cases as those in which it was the duty of one party to advise the other or to manage his property for him. In *Zamet v Hyman* [1961] 3 All ER 933 at 936, [1961] 1 WLR 1442 at 1444–1445 Lord Evershed MR referred to relationships where one party owed the other an obligation of candour and protection.

The law has long recognised the need to prevent abuse of influence in these 'relationship' cases despite the absence of evidence of overt acts of persuasive conduct. The types of relationship, such as parent and child, in which this principle falls to be applied cannot be listed exhaustively. Relationships are infinitely various. Sir Guenter Treitel QC has rightly noted that the question is whether one party has reposed sufficient trust and confidence in the other, rather than whether the relationship between the parties belongs to a particular type (see Treitel, *The Law of Contract* (10th edn, 1999) pp 380–381). For example, the relation of banker and customer will not normally meet this criterion, but exceptionally it may (see *National Westminster Bank plc v Morgan* [1985] 1 All ER 821 at 829–831, [1985] AC 686 at 707–709).

Even this test is not comprehensive. The principle is not confined to cases of abuse of trust and confidence. It also includes, for instance, cases where a vulnerable person has been exploited. Indeed, there is no single touchstone for determining whether the principle is applicable. Several expressions have been used in an endeavour to encapsulate the essence: trust and confidence, reliance, dependence or vulnerability on the one hand and ascendancy, domination or control on the other. None of these descriptions is perfect. None is all embracing. Each has its proper place.

. . .

Generations of equity lawyers have conventionally described this situation as one in which a presumption of undue influence arises. This use of the term 'presumption' is descriptive of a shift in the evidential onus on a question of fact. When a plaintiff succeeds by this route he does so because he has succeeded in establishing a case of undue influence. The court has drawn appropriate infer- ences of fact upon a balanced consideration of the whole of the evidence at the end of a trial in which the burden of proof rested upon the plaintiff. The use, in the course of the trial, of the foren- sic tool of a shift in the evidential burden of proof should not be permitted to obscure the overall position. These cases are the equitable counterpart of common law cases where the principle of res ipsa loquitur is invoked. There is a rebuttable evidential presumption of undue influence.

The availability of this forensic tool in cases founded on abuse of influence arising from the parties' relationship has led to this type of case sometimes being labelled 'presumed undue influence'. This is by way of contrast with cases involving actual pressure or the like, which are labelled 'actual undue influence' (see *Bank of Credit and Commerce International SA v Aboody* [1992] 4 All ER 955 at 964, [1990] 1 QB 923 at 953, and *Royal Bank of Scotland Plc v Etridge (No 2)* [1998] 4 All ER 705 at 711–712 (paras 5–7)). This usage can be a little confusing. In many cases where a plaintiff has claimed that the defendant abused the influence he acquired in a relationship of trust and confi- dence the plaintiff has succeeded by recourse to the rebuttable evidential presumption. But this need not be so. Such a plaintiff may succeed even where this presumption is not available to him; for instance, where the impugned transaction was not one which called for an explanation.

The evidential presumption discussed above is to be distinguished sharply from a different form of presumption which arises in some cases. The law has adopted a sternly protective attitude towards certain types of relationship in which one party acquires influence over another who is vulnerable and dependent and where, moreover, substantial gifts by the influenced or vulnerable person are not normally to be expected. Examples of relationships within this special class are parent and child, guardian and ward, trustee and beneficiary, solicitor and client, and medical advisor and patient. In these cases the law presumes, irrebuttably, that one party had influence over the other. The com- plainant need not prove he actually reposed trust and confidence in the other party. It is sufficient for him to prove the existence of the type of relationship.

It is now well established that husband and wife is not one of the relationships to which this latter principle applies. In *Yerkey v Jones* (1939) 63 CLR 649 at 675 Dixon J explained the reason. The Court of Chancery was not blind to the opportunities of obtaining and unfairly using influence over a wife which a husband often possesses. But there is nothing unusual or strange in a wife, from motives of affection or for other reasons, conferring substantial financial benefits on her husband. Although there is no presumption, the court will nevertheless note, as a matter of fact, the oppor- tunities for abuse which flow from a wife's confidence in her husband. The court will take this into account with all the other evidence in the case. Where there is evidence that a husband has taken unfair advantage of his influence over his wife, or her confidence in him, 'it is not difficult for the wife to establish her title to relief' (see *Re Lloyds Bank Ltd, Bomze v Bomze* [1931] 1 Ch 289 at 302, per Maugham J).

Independent advice

Proof that the complainant received advice from a third party before entering into the impugned transaction is one of the matters a court takes into account when weighing all the evidence. The weight, or importance, to be attached to such advice depends on all the circumstances. In the normal course, advice from a solicitor or other outside advisor can be expected to bring home to a complainant a proper understanding of what he or she is about to do. But a person may understand fully the implications of a proposed transaction, for instance, a substantial gift, and yet still be acting under the undue influence of another. Proof of outside advice does not, of itself, necessarily show that the subsequent completion of the transaction was free from the exercise of undue influence. Whether it will be proper to infer that outside advice had an emancipating effect, so that the transaction was not brought about by the exercise of undue influence, is a question of fact to be decided having regard to all the evidence in the case.

MANIFEST DISADVANTAGE

As already noted, there are two prerequisites to the evidential shift in the burden of proof from the complainant to the other party. First, that the complainant reposed trust and confidence in the other party, or the other party acquired ascendancy over the complainant. Second, that the transaction is not readily explicable by the relationship of the parties.

Lindley LJ summarised this second prerequisite in the leading authority of *Allcard v Skinner* (1887) 36 Ch D 145, [1886–90] All ER Rep 90, where the donor parted with almost all her property. Lindley LJ pointed out that where a gift of a small amount is made to a person standing in a confidential relationship to the donor, some proof of the exercise of the influence of the donee must be given. The mere existence of the influence is not enough. He continued:

> 'But if the gift is so large as not to be reasonably accounted for on the ground of friendship, relationship, charity, or other ordinary motives on which ordinary men act, the burden is upon the donee to support the gift.'

In *Bank of Montreal v Stuart* [1911] AC 120 at 137 Lord Macnaghten used the phrase 'immoderate and irrational' to describe this concept.

The need for this second prerequisite has recently been questioned: see Nourse LJ in *Barclays Bank plc v Coleman* [2000] 1 All ER 385 at 397–399, [2001] QB 20 at 30–32, one of the cases under appeal before your Lordships' House. Mr Sher QC invited your Lordships to depart from the decision of the House on this point in *Morgan*'s case.

My Lords, this is not an invitation I would accept. The second prerequisite, as expressed by Lindley LJ, is good sense. It is a necessary limitation upon the width of the first prerequisite. It would be absurd for the law to presume that every gift by a child to a parent, or every transaction between a client and his solicitor or between a patient and his doctor, was brought about by undue influence unless the contrary is affirmatively proved. Such a presumption would be too far-reaching. The law would out of touch with everyday life if the presumption were to apply to every Christmas or birthday gift by a child to a parent, or to an agreement whereby a client or patient agrees to be responsible for the reasonable fees of his legal or medical advisor. The law would be rightly open to ridicule, for transactions such as these are unexceptionable. They do not suggest that something may be amiss. So something more is needed before the law reverses the burden of proof, something which calls for an explanation. When that something more is present, the greater the disadvantage to the vulnerable person, the more cogent must be the explanation before the presumption will be regarded as rebutted.

> . . .

Which, then, is the correct approach to adopt in deciding whether a transaction is disadvantageous to the wife: the narrow approach, or the wider approach? The answer is neither. The answer lies in discarding a label which gives rise to this sort of ambiguity. The better approach is to adhere more directly to the test outlined by Lindley LJ in *Allcard v Skinner*, and adopted by Lord Scarman in *Morgan*'s case, in the passages I have cited.

I return to husband and wife cases. I do not think that, *in the ordinary course*, a guarantee of the character I have mentioned is to be regarded as a transaction which, failing proof to the contrary, is explicable only on the basis that it has been procured by the exercise of undue influence by the husband. Wives frequently enter into such transactions. There are good and sufficient reasons why they are willing to do so, despite the risks involved for them and their families. They may be enthusiastic. They may not. They may be less optimistic than their husbands about the prospects of the husbands' businesses. They may be anxious, perhaps exceedingly so. But this is a far cry from saying that such transactions as a class are to be regarded as prima facie evidence of the exercise of undue influence by husbands.

...

The problem considered in *Barclays Bank plc v O'Brien* [1993] 4 All ER 417, [1994] 1 AC 180 and raised by the present appeals is of comparatively recent origin. It arises out of the substantial growth in home ownership over the last 30 or 40 years and, as part of that development, the great increase in the number of homes owned jointly by husbands and wives. More than two-thirds of householders in the United Kingdom now own their own homes. For most home-owning couples, their homes are their most valuable asset. They must surely be free, if they so wish, to use this asset as a means of raising money, whether for the purpose of the husband's business or for any other purpose. Their home is their property. The law should not restrict them in the use they may make of it. Bank finance is in fact by far the most important source of external capital for small businesses with fewer than ten employees. These businesses comprise about 95% of all businesses in the country, responsible for nearly one-third of all employment. Finance raised by second mortgages on the principal's home is a significant source of capital for the start-up of small businesses.

If the freedom of home-owners to make economic use of their homes is not to be frustrated, a bank must be able to have confidence that a wife's signature of the necessary guarantee and charge will be as binding upon her as is the signature of anyone else on documents which he or she may sign. Otherwise banks will not be willing to lend money on the security of a jointly owned house or flat.

At the same time, the high degree of trust and confidence and emotional interdependence which normally characterises a marriage relationship provides scope for abuse. One party may take advantage of the other's vulnerability. Unhappily, such abuse does occur. Further, it is all too easy for a husband, anxious or even desperate for bank finance, to misstate the position in some particular or to mislead the wife, wittingly or unwittingly, in some other way. The law would be seriously defective if it did not recognise these realities.

...

These novelties do not point to the conclusion that the decision of this House in *O'Brien*'s case is leading the law astray. Lord Browne-Wilkinson ([1993] 4 All ER 417 at 430, [1994] 1 AC 180 at 197) acknowledged he might be extending the law. Some development was sorely needed. The law had to find a way of giving wives a reasonable measure of protection, without adding unreasonably to the expense involved in entering into guarantee transactions of the type under consideration. The protection had to extend also to any misrepresentations made by a husband to his wife. In a situation where there is a substantial risk the husband may exercise his influence improperly regarding the provision of security for his business debts, there is an increased risk that explanations of the transaction given by him to his wife may be misleadingly incomplete or even inaccurate.

The route selected in *O'Brien*'s case ought not to have an unsettling effect on established principles of contract. *O'Brien*'s case concerned suretyship transactions. These are tripartite transactions. They involve the debtor as well as the creditor and the guarantor. The guarantor enters into the transaction at the request of the debtor. The guarantor assumes obligations. On the face of the transaction the guarantor usually receives no benefit in return, unless the guarantee is being given on a commercial basis. Leaving aside cases where the relationship between the surety and the debtor is commercial, a guarantee transaction is one-sided so far as the guarantor is concerned. The creditor knows this. Thus the decision in *O'Brien*'s case is directed at a class of contracts which has special features of its own. That said, I must at a later stage in this speech return to the question of the wider implications of the *O'Brien* decision.

...

The practice of the banks involved in the present cases, and it seems reasonable to assume this is the practice of banks generally, is not to have a private meeting with the wife. Nor do the banks themselves take any other steps to bring home to the wife the risk she is running. This has continued to be the practice since the decision in *O'Brien*'s case. Banks consider they would stand to lose more than they would gain by holding a private meeting with the wife. They are, apparently, unwilling to assume the responsibility of advising the wife at such a meeting. Instead, the banking practice remains, as before, that in general the bank requires a wife to seek legal advice. The bank seeks written confirmation from a solicitor that he has explained the nature and effect of the documents to the wife.

Many of the difficulties which have arisen in the present cases stem from serious deficiencies, or alleged deficiencies, in the quality of the legal advice given to the wives. I say 'alleged', because three of the appeals before your Lordships' House have not proceeded beyond the interlocutory stage. The banks successfully applied for summary judgment. In these cases the wife's allegations, made in affidavit form, have not been tested by cross-examination. On behalf of the wives it has been submitted that under the current practice the legal advice is often perfunctory in the extreme and, further, that everyone, including the banks, knows this. Independent legal advice is a fiction. The system is a charade. In practice it provides little or no protection for a wife who is under a misapprehension about the risks involved or who is being coerced into signing. She may not even know the present state of her husband's indebtedness.

My Lords, it is plainly neither desirable nor practicable that banks should be required to attempt to discover for themselves whether a wife's consent is being procured by the exercise of undue influence of her husband. This is not a step the banks should be expected to take. Nor, further, is it desirable or practicable that banks should be expected to insist on confirmation from a solicitor that the solicitor has satisfied himself that the wife's consent has not been procured by undue influence. As already noted, the circumstances in which banks are put on inquiry are extremely wide. They embrace every case where a wife is entering into a suretyship transaction in respect of her husband's debts. Many, if not most, wives would be understandably outraged by having to respond to the sort of questioning which would be appropriate before a responsible solicitor could give such a confirmation. In any event, solicitors are not equipped to carry out such an exercise in any really worthwhile way, and they will usually lack the necessary materials. Moreover, the legal costs involved, which would inevitably fall on the husband who is seeking financial assistance from the bank, would be substantial. To require such an intrusive, inconclusive and expensive exercise in every case would be an altogether disproportionate response to the need to protect those cases, presumably a small minority, where a wife is being wronged.

...

When an instruction to this effect is forthcoming, the content of the advice required from a solicitor before giving the confirmation sought by the bank will, inevitably, depend upon the circumstances of the case. Typically, the advice a solicitor can be expected to give should cover the following matters as the core minimum. (1) He will need to explain the nature of the documents and the practical consequences these will have for the wife if she signs them. She could lose her home if her husband's business does not prosper. Her home may be her only substantial asset, as well as the family's home. She could be made bankrupt. (2) He will need to point out the seriousness of the risks involved. The wife should be told the purpose of the proposed new facility, the amount and principal terms of the new facility, and that the bank might increase the amount of the facility, or change its terms, or grant a new facility, without reference to her. She should be told the amount of her liability under her guarantee. The solicitor should discuss the wife's financial means, including her understanding of the value of the property being charged. The solicitor should discuss whether the wife or her husband has any other assets out of which repayment could be made if the husband's business should fail. These matters are relevant to the seriousness of the risks involved. (3) The solicitor will need to state clearly that the wife has a choice. The decision is hers and hers alone. Explanation of the choice facing the wife will call for some discussion of the present financial position, including the amount of the husband's present indebtedness, and the amount of his current overdraft facility. (4) The solicitor should check whether the wife wishes to proceed. She should be asked whether she is content that the solicitor should write to the bank confirming he has explained to her the nature of the documents and the practical implications they may have for her, or whether, for instance, she would prefer him to negotiate with the bank on the terms of the transaction. Matters for negotiation could include the sequence in which the various securities will be called upon or a specific or lower limit to her liabilities. The solicitor should not give any confirmation to the bank without the wife's authority.

The solicitor's discussion with the wife should take place at a face-to-face meeting, in the absence of the husband. It goes without saying that the solicitor's explanations should be couched in suitably non-technical language. It also goes without saying that the solicitor's task is an important one. It is not a formality.

...

Before turning to the particular cases I must make a general comment on the *O'Brien* principle. As noted by Professor Peter Birks QC, the decision in *O'Brien*'s case has to be seen as the progenitor of a wider principle (see 'The Burden on the Bank', in *Restitution and Banking Law*, ed Rose (1998) p 195). This calls for explanation. In *O'Brien*'s case the House was concerned with formulating a fair and practical solution to problems occurring when a creditor obtains a security from a guarantor whose sexual relationship with the debtor gives rise to a heightened risk of undue influence. But the law does not regard sexual relationships as standing in some special category of their own so far as undue influence is concerned. Sexual relationships are no more than one type of relationship in which an individual may acquire influence over another individual. The *O'Brien* decision cannot sensibly be regarded as confined to sexual relationships, although these are likely to be its main field of application at present. What is appropriate for sexual relationships ought, in principle, to be appropriate also for other relationships where trust and confidence are likely to exist.

The courts have already recognised this. Further application, or development, of the *O'Brien* principle has already taken place. In *Credit Lyonnais Bank Nederland NV v Burch* [1997] 1 All ER 144 the same principle was applied where the relationship was employer and employee. Miss Burch was a junior employee in a company. She was neither a shareholder nor a director. She provided security to the bank for the company's overdraft. She entered into a guarantee of unlimited amount, and gave the bank a second charge over her flat. Nourse LJ (at 146) said the relationship 'may broadly be said to fall under [*O'Brien*'s case]'. The Court of Appeal held that the bank was put on inquiry. It knew the facts from which the existence of a relationship of trust and confidence between Miss Burch and Mr Pelosi, the owner of the company, could be inferred.

The crucially important question raised by this wider application of the *O'Brien* principle concerns the circumstances which will put a bank on inquiry. A bank is put on inquiry whenever a wife stands as surety for her husband's debts. It is sufficient that the bank knows of the husband/wife relationship. That bare fact is enough. The bank must then take reasonable steps to bring home to the wife the risks involved. What, then, of other relationships where there is an increased risk of undue influence, such as parent and child? Is it enough that the bank knows of the relationship? For reasons already discussed in relation to husbands and wives, a bank cannot be expected to probe the emotional relationship between two individuals, whoever they may be. Nor is it desirable that a bank should attempt this. Take the case where a father puts forward his daughter as a surety for his business overdraft. A bank should not be called upon to evaluate highly personal matters such as the degree of trust and confidence existing between the father and his daughter, with the bank put on inquiry in one case and not in another. As with wives, so with daughters, whether a bank is put on inquiry should not depend on the degree of trust and confidence the particular daughter places in her father in relation to financial matters. Moreover, as with wives, so with other relationships, the test of what puts a bank on inquiry should be simple, clear and easy to apply in widely varying circumstances. This suggests that, in the case of a father and daughter, knowledge by the bank of the relationship of father and daughter should suffice to put the bank on inquiry. When the bank knows of the relationship, it must then take reasonable steps to ensure the daughter knows what she is letting herself into.

The relationship of parent and child is one of the relationships where the law irrebuttably presumes the existence of trust and confidence. Rightly, this has already been rejected as the boundary of the *O'Brien* principle. *O'Brien's* case was a husband/wife case. The responsibilities of creditors were enunciated in a case where the law makes no presumption of the existence of trust and confidence.

But the law cannot stop at this point, with banks on inquiry only in cases where the debtor and guarantor have a sexual relationship or the relationship is one where the law presumes the existence of trust and confidence. That would be an arbitrary boundary, and the law has already moved beyond this, in the decision in the *Credit Lyonnais* case. As noted earlier, the reality of life is that relationships in which undue influence can be exercised are infinitely various. They cannot be exhaustively defined. Nor is it possible to produce a comprehensive list of relationships where there is a substantial risk of the exercise of undue influence, all others being excluded from the ambit of the *O'Brien* principle. Human affairs do not lend themselves to categorisations of this sort. The older generation of a family may exercise undue influence over a younger member, as in parent/child cases such as *Bainbrigge v Browne (1881)* 18 Ch D 188 and *Powell v Powell* [1900] 1 Ch 243. Sometimes it is the other way round, as with a nephew and his elderly aunt in *Inche Noriah v Shaik Allie Bin Omar* [1929] AC 127, [1928] All ER Rep 189. An employer may take advantage of his employee, as in the *Credit Lyonnais* case. But it may be the other way round, with an employee taking advantage of her employer, as happened with the secretary/companion and her elderly employer in *Re Craig (decd)* [1970] 2 All ER 390, [1971] Ch 95. The list could go on.

These considerations point forcibly to the conclusion that there is no rational cut-off point, with certain types of relationship being susceptible to the *O'Brien* principle and others not. Further, if a bank is not to be required to evaluate the extent to which its customer has influence over a proposed guarantor, the only practical way forward is to regard banks as 'put on inquiry' in every case where the relationship between the surety and the debtor is non-commercial. The creditor must always take reasonable steps to bring home to the individual guarantor the risks he is running by standing as surety. As a measure of protection, this is valuable. But, in all conscience, it is a modest burden for banks and other lenders. It is no more than is reasonably to be expected of a creditor who is taking a guarantee from an individual. If the bank or other creditor does not take these steps, it is deemed to have notice of any claim the guarantor may have that the transaction was procured by undue influence or misrepresentation on the part of the debtor.

Different considerations apply where the relationship between the debtor and guarantor is commercial, as where a guarantor is being paid a fee, or a company is guaranteeing the debts of another company in the same group. Those engaged in business can be regarded as capable of looking after themselves and understanding the risks involved in the giving of guarantees.

By the decisions of this House in *O'Brien's* case and the Court of Appeal in the *Credit Lyonnais* case, English law has taken its first strides in the development of some such general principle. It is a workable principle. It is also simple, coherent and eminently desirable. I venture to think this is the way the law is moving, and should continue to move. Equity, it is said, is not past the age of child-bearing. In the present context the equitable concept of being 'put on inquiry' is the parent of a principle of general application, a principle which imposes no more than a modest obligation on banks and other creditors. The existence of this obligation in all non-commercial cases does not go beyond the reasonable requirements of the present times. In future, banks and other creditors should regulate their affairs accordingly.

4.   The speeches in this complex case, although long, repay careful study. It is clear that the House of Lords wished to give guidance to banks as to what to do. It is very desirable that

banks understand this because otherwise they will not make such loans or will charge more for them. Effectively, explanation by the bank is abandoned in favour of the bank taking steps to encourage or require the provision of independent advice.

The principles are not confined to wives, who are simply the typical case. Note, in particular, the approval of *Crédit Lyonnais Bank Nederland NV v Burch*. In the *Etridge* case Lord Nicholls said the principles apply whenever the relationship between the debtor and the surety is non-commercial (see p 936 above).

CHAPTER THIRTY-SIX

UNCONSCIONABLE BARGAINS

This chapter deals with an apparent ragbag of cases, which all involve further interference with freedom of contract. Some of the cases are old and, some lawyers may think, obsolete, but they may be adaptable to modern-day conditions. Moreover, it has been suggested that there is an important general principle underlying them all. We shall return to that question and, if there is such a principle, what its content might be, in Chapter 37.

I. MORTGAGES

The classical common law forms of lending on the security of land involved a conveyance of the land to the lender with a contractual provision that the land might be redeemed by the repayment of capital and interest. Typically, the contractual date of redemption would be relatively soon after the loan, eg six months. Equity early held that if the transaction was in substance a mortgage, the borrower (mortgagor) still had an equitable right to redeem after the contractual date had passed: see, for example, *Howard v Harris* (1683) 1 Vern 190; *Spurgeon v Collier* (1758) 1 Eden 55; *Jennings v Ward* (1705) 2 Vern 520. The reason given for this was that the lender (mortgagee) was adequately protected if he recovered the money lent in full plus interest at the agreed rate, and he should not make a profit beyond this by retaining land worth more. This was no doubt based on an unarticulated assumption that borrowers, as a class, often needed protection from lenders, and reinforced by the fact that at the time that the doctrine was first developed, there were statutory limits (since abolished) on the rates of interest that lenders could charge.

From this beginning, the doctrine gradually developed a number of subrules. The question was to be treated as one of substance, so that what was essentially a mortgage could not be dressed up as a conveyance (compare the quite different treatment of hire purchase, which is essentially a chattel mortgage dressed up as a contract of hire); a transaction that was essentially a mortgage could not be made irredeemable; and a condition rendering redemption illusory or limiting it was invalid: *Fairclough v Swan Brewery* [1912] AC 565; *Salt v Marquess of Northampton* [1892] AC 1. Even an option to the mortgagee to purchase the land was held invalid in *Samuel v Jarrah Timber and Wood Paving Corpn Ltd* [1904] AC 323.

Although these rules undoubtedly had roots in considerations of unconscionability, by the early nineteenth century, they were being applied even where borrowers and lenders were bargaining on equal terms and at arm's length: see, for example, *Bradley v Carritt* [1903] AC 253, in which the holder of shares in a tea company mortgaged the shares to a tea broker and agreed to use his best endeavours to see that the mortgagee should have the sale of all of the company's tea, and if the tea was sold through another broker, to pay compensation for the loss of commission. After the mortgagor had redeemed, the tea company changed its broker. The House of Lords held (Lords Lindley and Shand dissenting) that this stipulation was not enforceable because it had some tendency to discourage the mortgagor from disposing of the shares, and was thus an indirect fetter on the right of redemption.

This decision was effectively overruled by *Kreglinger v New Patagonia Meat and Cold Storage Co Ltd* [1914] AC 25, which reached a different result on indistinguishable facts. There, a firm of wool brokers lent money to a firm of meat preservers under a contract including a provision that the borrowers would, for five years, sell all their sheepskins to the lenders, provided the latter were willing to pay the best price offered by anyone else. Lord Parker said:

... there is now no rule in equity which precludes a mortgagee, whether the mortgage be made upon the occasion of a loan or otherwise, from stipulating for any collateral advantage, provided such collateral advantage is not either (1) unfair and unconscionable, or (2) in the nature of a penalty clogging the equity of redemption, or (3) inconsistent with or repugnant to the contractual and equitable right to redeem.

The clause was upheld. Similarly, in *Knightsbridge Estates Trust Ltd v Byrne* [1939] Ch 441 at 457, Sir Wilfred Greene MR said:

Equity may give relief against contractual terms in a mortgage transaction if they are oppressive or unconscionable ... But equity does not reform mortgage transactions because they are unreasonable.

The same distinction between unreasonableness and unconscionability was drawn in *Multiservice Bookbinding Ltd v Marden* [1979] Ch 84. The lender had stipulated for interest at 2 per cent above (English) bank rate, and also for both the amount of capital to be repaid and the sums due by way of interest to be linked to the movement of the Swiss franc against the pound. Browne-Wilkinson J held that there was no significant inequality of bargaining power as between the borrower and the lender; that it was unreasonable to stipulate for interest at English rates when the capital value was tied to the Swiss franc, since English interest rates reflected in part the current English rate of inflation; but that the transaction was not unconscionable and should be upheld.

II. POOR AND IGNORANT PERSONS AND EXPECTANT HEIRS

In the eighteenth century, the Court of Chancery seems regularly to have set aside contracts and dispositions that were unfair, at least if there was gross inadequacy of consideration and some overreaching (see Atiyah, *Rise and Fall of Freedom of Contract*, 1979, pp 169–174). One category of cases involved purchases of property at undervalue from poor and ignorant persons: perhaps the best-known example is *Evans v Llewellin* (1787) 1 Cox Eq Cas 333. There, a man of very modest means was unexpectedly told that he had inherited a share in his sister's estate, and his brother-in-law, who claimed that the sister had not intended the share to go to the plaintiff, offered to buy it from him for 200 guineas. The plaintiff accepted this offer without having time for reflection or to obtain advice. The share was worth much more and the Master of the Rolls set the transaction aside.

Some of the categories of cases, for instance that of sailors who were persuaded to give up their shares in prize money for much smaller amounts of ready cash, seem to have fallen into disuse early, but others survived well into the nineteenth century. In particular, there are many cases involving expectant heirs, who either parted with their reversions at much less than their true value, or who borrowed money at exorbitant rates of interest, to be repaid when they came into their inheritances. Such persons were felt to be particularly at risk from unscrupulous money lenders, because they would not care to risk revealing their circumstances to their families by seeking advice from family advisers. In *Earl of Aylesford v Morris* (1873) 8 Ch App 484 at 491, the Lord Chancellor said:

The result of the decisions is that where a purchase is made from a poor and ignorant man at a considerable undervalue, the vendor having no independent advice, a Court of Equity will set aside the transaction.

This will be done even in the case of property in possession, and a *fortiori* if the interest be reversionary.

The circumstances of poverty and ignorance of the vendor, and absence of independent advice, throw upon the purchaser, when the transaction is impeached the onus of proving, in Lord *Selborne's* words, that the purchase was 'fair, just, and reasonable'.

■ *Fry v Lane*
(1888) 40 Ch D 312

The plaintiffs, two brothers who were a plumber's assistant and a laundryman, sold their reversionary interests at considerably below the true value, receiving advice only from an inexperienced solicitor who was also acting for the purchaser.

Kay J

...I reserved judgment that I might more carefully consider the facts of the case, and the law which is applicable to them since the passing of the statute 31 Vict c 4.

Long before the passing of that Act it was settled that the Court of Chancery would relieve against a sale of or other dealing with a remainder or reversion at an undervalue on that ground alone, and this even where the remainderman was of mature age and accustomed to business: *Wiseman v Beake; Berkley–Freeman v Bishop; Davis v Duke of Marlborough; Earl of Portmore v Taylor; Boothby v Boothby; Foster v Roberts; Beynon v Cook*. In such cases it was held that the onus lay upon the purchaser to shew that he had given the 'fair' value as it was called in *Earl of Aldborough v Trye*, or 'the market value': *Talbot v Staniforth*.

By the 31 Vict c 4, reciting that it was expedient to amend the law as administered in Courts of Equity with respect to sales of reversions, it was enacted (by sect 1) that 'no purchase, made *bonâ fide* and without fraud or unfair dealing, of any reversionary interest in real or personal estate shall hereafter be opened or set aside merely on the ground of undervalue', and by sect 2 the word 'purchase' in the Act is to include 'every kind of contract, conveyance, or assignment, under or by which any beneficial interest in any kind of property may be acquired'. This Act came into operation on the 1st day of January, 1868.

It is obvious that the words 'merely on the ground of undervalue' do not include the case of an undervalue so gross as to amount of itself to evidence of fraud, and in *Earl of Aylesford v Morris* Lord Selborne said that this Act 'leaves undervalue still a material element in cases in which it is not the sole equitable ground for relief. These changes of the law have in no degree whatever altered the *onus probandi* in those cases, which, according to the language of Lord Hardwicke, raise "from the circumstances or conditions of the parties contracting—weakness on one side, usury on the other, or extortion, or advantage taken of that weakness"—a presumption of fraud'. 'Fraud,' says Lord Selborne, 'does not here mean deceit or circumvention; it means an unconscientious use of the power arising out of these circumstances and conditions; and when the relative position of the parties is such as *primá facie* to raise this presumption, the transaction cannot stand unless the person claiming the benefit of it is able to repel the presumption by contrary evidence, proving it to have been in point of fact fair, just, and reasonable.'

The most common case for the inference of a Court of Equity is that of an expectant heir, reversioner, or remainderman who is just of age, his youth being treated as an important circumstance. Another analogous case is where the vendor is a poor man with imperfect education, as in *Evans v Llewellin; Haygarth v Wearing*. . . .

Sale set aside.

■ *Cresswell v Potter*
(1978) 1 WLR 255n

The wife left the husband. Later, she conveyed to him her half-share in the matrimonial home, in exchange for being released from her liability under the mortgage. The property was worth considerably more than the amount of the mortgage. The husband later sold the property and the wife claimed a half-share in the proceeds of sale.

Megarry J

. . . [Kay J in *Fry v Lane*] laid down three requirements. What has to be considered is, first, whether the plaintiff is poor and ignorant; second, whether the sale was at a considerable undervalue; and third, whether the vendor had independent advice. I am not, of course, suggesting that these are the only circumstances which will suffice; thus there may be circumstances of oppression or abuse of confidence which will invoke the aid of equity. But in the present case only these three requirements are in point. Abuse of confidence, though pleaded, is no longer relied on; and no circumstances of oppression or other matters are alleged. I must therefore consider whether the three requirements laid down in *Fry v Lane* are satisfied.

I think that the plaintiff may fairly be described as falling within whatever is the modern equivalent of 'poor and ignorant'. Eighty years ago, when *Fry v Lane* was decided, social conditions were very different from those which exist today. I do not, however, think that the principle has changed, even though the euphemisms of the 20th century may require the word 'poor' to be replaced by 'a member of the lower income group' or the like, and the word 'ignorant' by 'less highly educated'. The plaintiff has been a van driver for a tobacconist, and is a Post Office telephonist. The evidence of her means is slender. The defendant told me that the plaintiff probably had a little saved, but not much, and there was evidence that her earnings were about the same as the defendant's, and that these were those of a carpenter. The plaintiff also has a legal aid certificate.

In those circumstances I think the plaintiff may properly be described as 'poor' in the sense used in *Fry v Lane*, where it was applied to a laundryman who, in 1888, was earning £1 a week. In this context, as in others, I do not think that 'poverty' is confined to destitution. Further, although no doubt it requires considerable alertness and skill to be a good telephonist, I think that a telephonist can properly be described as 'ignorant' in the context of property transactions in general and the execution of conveyancing documents in particular. I have seen and heard the plaintiff giving evidence, and I have reached the conclusion that she satisfies the requirements of the first head.

The second question is whether the sale was at a 'considerable undervalue'.

[The judge held that the plaintiff was getting 'virtually nothing' from the agreement.]

As for independent advice, from first to last there is no suggestion that the plaintiff had any. The defendant, his solicitor and the inquiry agent stood on one side: on the other the plaintiff stood alone. This was, of course, a conveyancing transaction, and English land law is notoriously complex. I am certainly not saying that other transactions, such as hire-purchase agreements, are free from all difficulty. But the authorities put before me on setting aside dealings at an undervalue all seem to relate to conveyancing transactions, and one may wonder whether the principle is confined to such transactions, and, if so, why? I doubt whether the principle is restricted in this way: and it may be that the explanation is that it is in conveyancing matters that, by long usage, it is regarded as usual, and, indeed, virtually essential, for the parties to have the services of a solicitor. The absence of the aid of a solicitor is thus, as it seems to me, of especial significance if a conveyancing matter is involved. The more usual it is to have a solicitor, the more striking will be his absence, and the more closely will the courts scrutinise what was done.

Mr Balcombe points out that the plaintiff was not bereft of possible legal assistance; for on or before July 28, 1959, when she was having difficulty in getting some furniture and effects from Slate Hall, she consulted a Colchester firm of solicitors, who wrote a letter dated July 28, 1959, that produced the required result. If she wanted legal advice, he said, this shows that she knew how to get it. However, what matters, I think, is not whether she could have obtained proper advice but whether in fact she had it; and she did not. Nobody, of course, can be compelled to obtain independent advice: but I do not think that someone who seeks to uphold what is, to him, an advantageous conveyancing transaction can do so merely by saying that the other party could have obtained independent advice, unless something has been done to bring to the notice of that other party the true nature of the transaction and the need for advice.

At the end of the day, my conclusion is that this transaction cannot stand. In my judgment the plaintiff has made out her case, and so it is for the defendant to prove that the transaction was 'fair, just, and reasonable'. This he has not done.

Accordingly, it seems to me that this action ought to succeed, and subject to discussion of the terms of the appropriate order, I so hold.

Order accordingly.

NOTES

1. *Cresswell v Potter* was considered in *Backhouse v Backhouse* [1978] 1 All ER 1158. In *Watkin v Watson-Smith* (1986) Times, 3 July, Hirst J held that 'a desire for a quick sale' could be substituted for 'poverty' and 'old age with its accompanying diminution of physical and mental capacity' for 'ignorance'. He set aside a contract for the sale of land at less than its true value.

2. Suppose a client asks you to act for her in the purchase of a house, and she tells you that the vendor is acting on his own behalf and has not had the house valued. What would you advise?

3. How do these cases differ from those of undue influence?

4. It seems that a contract will not be set aside for unconscionability unless there was some form of conscious advantage-taking: see *Hart v O'Connor*, below, and *Boustany v Pigott* [1993] NPC 75.

5. Although there have been few recent cases in England applying the unconscionable bargain doctrine, there have been a fair number in Canada (eg *Morrison v Coast Finance Ltd (1965)* 55 DLR (2d) 710 (British Columbia)) and in Australia. In *Commercial Bank of Australia Ltd v Amadio* (1983) 151 CLR 447, Vincenzo Amadio was the managing director of Amadio Builders, a company that banked with the Commercial Bank of Australia. The company appeared to be successful and Vincenzo's parents appear to have been very proud of their son's success. Mr and Mrs Amadio were Italian immigrants to Australia, who apparently only had a limited knowledge of written English.

In fact, the company's business was in serious financial difficulties and the company was heavily overdrawn with the bank. The bank manager cooperated with Vincenzo in maintaining the appearance of prosperity by honouring selected cheques that were issued on the company's account. The bank only agreed to continue the account if it was given a mortgage over property owned by Vincenzo's parents. The parents agreed to this and the mortgage was executed at their home in the presence of the bank manager. The mortgage, in fact, secured all borrowings by the company from the bank, although Vincenzo told his parents that the guarantee was for six months and had an upper limit of $50,000. Soon afterwards, the company went into liquidation owing the bank nearly $240,000.

Cases of this kind have usually been approached in England through the doctrine of undue influence. However, in *Amadio*, the majority of the High Court of Australia set the transaction aside on the grounds that it was unconscionable. Deane J said:

The jurisdiction of courts of equity to relieve against unconscionable dealing developed from the jurisdiction which the Court of Chancery assumed, at a very early period, to set aside transactions in which expectant heirs had dealt with their expectations without being adequately protected against the pressure put upon them by their poverty . . . The jurisdiction is [now] established as extending generally to circumstances in which (i) a party to a transaction was under a special disability in dealing with the other party with the consequences that there was an absence of any reasonable degree of equality between them and (ii) that disability was sufficiently evident to the stronger party to make it prima facie unfair or 'unconscientious' that he procure, or accept, the weaker party's assent to the impugned transaction in the circumstances in which he procured or accepted it. Where such circumstances are shown to have existed, an onus is cast upon the stronger party to show that the transaction was fair, just and reasonable . . .

The equitable principles relating to relief against unconscionable dealing and the principles relating to undue influence are closely related. The two doctrines are, however, distinct. Undue influence, like common law duress, looks to the quality of the consent or assent of the weaker party . . . Unconscionable dealing looks to the conduct of the stronger party in attempting to enforce, or retain the benefit of, a dealing with a person under a special disability in circumstances where it is not consistent with equity or good conscience that he should do so. The adverse circumstances which may constitute a special disability for the purposes of the principles relating to relief against unconscionable dealing may take a wide variety of forms and are not susceptible to being comprehensively catalogued. In *Blomley v Ryan* (1956) 99 CLR 362, 405, Fullagar J listed some examples of such disability: 'poverty or need of any kind, sickness, age, sex, infirmity of body or mind, drunkenness, illiteracy or lack of education, lack of assistance or explanation where assistance or explanation is necessary'. As Fullagar J remarked, the common characteristic of such adverse circumstances 'seems to be that they have the effect of placing one party at a serious disadvantage vis-à-vis the other'.

In most cases where equity courts have granted relief against unconscionable dealing, there has been an inadequacy of consideration moving from the stronger party. It is not, however, essential that that should be so . . . Notwithstanding that adequate consideration may have moved from the stronger party, a transaction may be unfair, unreasonable and unjust from the view point of the party under the disability . . .

It is apparent that Mr and Mrs Amadio, viewed together, were the weaker party to the transaction between themselves and the bank. Their weakness may be likened to that of the defendant in *Blomley v Ryan* (above) of whom McTiernan J said (at p 392):

'His weakness was of the kind spoken of by Lord Hardwicke [in *Earl of Chesterfield v Jansen* (1751) 2 Ves Sen, 125, at pp 155–156 (28 E R 82, at p 100)] in defining the fraud characterised as taking surreptitious advantage of the weakness, ignorance or necessity of another. The essence of such weakness is that the party is unable to judge for himself.'

That weakness constituted a special disability of Mr and Mrs Amadio in their dealing with the bank of the type necessary to enliven the equitable principles relating to relief against unconscionable dealing. Put more precisely, the result of the combination of their age, their limited grasp of written English, the circumstances in which the bank presented the document to them for their signature and, most importantly, their lack of knowledge and understanding of the contents of the document was that, to adapt the words of Fullagar J quoted above, they lacked assistance and advice where assistance and advice were plainly necessary if there were to be any reasonable degree of equality between themselves and the bank.

The next question is whether the special disability of Mr and Mrs Amadio was sufficiently evident to the bank to make it prima facie unfair or 'unconscientious' of the bank to procure their execution of the document of guarantee and mortgagee in the circumstances in which that execution was procured. In procuring it, the bank acted through Mr Virgo: his actions were the actions of the bank and his knowledge was the knowledge of the bank. His evidence indicates that he was not unacquainted with the personal circumstances of Mr and Mrs Amadio and their reliance on Vincenzo whom he described as the 'dominant member of the family'. He was aware of the inability of Amadio Builders to pay its debts as they fell due and must also have been aware of the potential consequences to Mr and Mrs Amadio of the unlimited guarantee in the document which he tendered to them for their immediate execution.

Do you think that an English court would set aside such a transaction on the basis of (i) unconscionable bargain or (ii) undue influence?

In *Crédit Lyonnais v Burch* [1997] 1 All ER 144, the bank had accepted a guarantee by way of charge for a business's debts from the junior employee, Miss Burch. It was clearly not in her interests to give the charge, which constituted a grave risk to her. The charge was set aside on the ground that the bank had constructive notice of undue influence by Miss Burch's employer, but Nourse LJ said (at 151):

...[I]t must, I think, have been very well arguable that Miss Burch could, directly against the bank, have had the legal charge set aside as an unconscionable bargain. Equity's jurisdiction to relieve against such transactions, although more rarely exercised in modern times, is at least as venerable as its jurisdiction to relieve aginst those procured by undue influence. In *Fry v Lane, Re Fry, Whittet v Bush* (1889) 40 Ch D 312 at 322, [1886–90] All ER Rep 1084 at 1089, where sales of reversionary interests at considerable undervalues by poor and ignorant persons were set aside, Kay J, having reviewed the earlier authorities, said:

'The result of the decisions is that where a purchase is made from a poor and ignorant man at a considerable undervalue, the vendor having no independent advice, a Court of Equity will set aside the transaction. This will be done even in the case of property in possession, and *a fortiori* if the interest be reversionary. The circumstances of poverty and ignorance of the vendor, and absence of independent advice, throw upon the purchaser, when the treansaction is impeached, the onus of proving, in Lord Selborne's words, that the purchase was "fair, just and reasonable".'

Lord Selborne LC's words will be found in *Earl of Aylesford v Morris* (1873) 8 Ch App 484 at 491, [1861–73] All ER Rep 300 at 303. The decision of Megarry J in *Cresswell v Potter* [1978] 1 WLR 255n at 257 where he suggested that the modern equivalent of 'poor and ignorant' might be 'a member of the lower income group ... less highly educated', demonstrates that the jurisdiction is in good heart and capable of adaptation to different transactions entered into in changing circumstances. See also the interesting judgment of Balcombe J in *Backhouse v Backhouse* [1978] 1 All ER 1158 at 1165–6, [1978] 1 WLR 243 at 250–252, where he suggested that these cases may come under the general heading which Lord Denning MR referred to in *Lloyds Bank Ltd v Bundy* [1975] QB 326 at 339, [1974] 3 All ER 757 at 765 as "inequality of bargaining power;'.

Millett LJ seemed to agree that unconscionability would be relevant if there had been 'some impropriety' on the part of the bank (at 153).

In contrast, in *Portman Building Society v Dusangh* [2000] 2 All ER (Comm) 221, a father borrowed on mortgage from the plaintiffs some 75 per cent of the value of his house so as to fund a loan to his son who was planning to buy a supermarket. The father was 72 years old, retired, and illiterate and poorly spoken in English. The father, the son and the building society were represented by the same solicitor. The supermarket failed and the building society sought to enforce the mortgage against the father who argued that the transaction was unconscionable. No fraud or undue influence by the son on the father was alleged, and the son, unlike Vincent Amadio, was not in financial difficulties at the time of the transaction, which was held not to be unconscionable.

III. THE INSANE

■ Sale of Goods Act 1979

Section 3: Capacity to buy and sell

(2) Where necessaries are sold and delivered to a minor or to a person who by reason of mental incapacity or drunkenness is incompetent to contract, he must pay a reasonable price for them.

NOTE

This liability is probably restitutionary rather than contractual.

■ *Hart v O'Connor*
[1985] 2 All ER 880, PC

In 1977, the appellant entered into an agreement to buy farmland in New Zealand, which was the subject matter of a testamentary settlement. The agreement was expressed to be made between the appellant and J, the then sole trustee of the trust estate. The initiative for the sale came from the trust's solicitor and members of the testator's family. All of the terms of the agreement were drawn up by the trust's solicitor, including provision for valuation of the property and the nomination of a valuer. The trust's solicitor sent the agreement to the appellant's solicitor's for approval and took it to J for signature. Unknown to the appellant, J was of unsound mind when he signed the agreement. In May 1980, the respondents, the then trustees and beneficiaries of the estate, applied to set aside the agreement on the ground that J was of unsound mind when he entered into it and the contract was unfair to him. The valuer nominated by the trust's solicitor had valued the land at $180,000 as at 1 September 1977, whereas the respondent trustees' valuer later valued the land at $197,000 as at that date. The trial judge held that, although J's unsoundness of mind was not apparent, his unsoundness of mind coupled with the unfairness of the contract that resulted because of the parties' consequent inequality of bargaining position made the contract unenforceable. However, the judge gave judgment for the appellant on the ground that the respondents had been guilty of laches. The New Zealand Court of Appeal allowed an appeal by the respondents. The appellant appealed to the Privy Council.

Lord Brightman

. . . The action came to trial before Cook J and occupied 14 days. The judge delivered a reserved judgment, dismissing the action. He first considered Jack's capacity to contract, and found on a balance of probabilities that Jack did not have contractual ability to enter into the agreement, and would not have had a proper understanding of the matters for decision even if (contrary to the judge's view) they had been adequately explained to him. He then considered the circumstances in which a contract made by a person who lacked mental capacity was liable to be set aside. The traditional view in English law was that it must be proved that the other contracting party knew of or ought to have appreciated such incapacity. Otherwise the contract stood, assuming it was not voidable on equitable principles as an unconscionable bargain. But in *Archer v Cutler* [1980] 1 NZLR 386 it had been decided that a contract made by a person of insufficient mental capacity was voidable at his option not only if the other party knew of or ought to have appreciated his unsoundness of mind, but also if the contract 'was unfair to the person of unsound mind'. *Archer v Cutler*, to which their Lordships will have to refer in detail later, was accepted by both sides and by the judge as a correct statement of the law, and there was no argument on it; in a court of first instance this was almost inevitable . . .

[In *Archer v Cutler* the judge] found that the vendor was suffering from advanced senile dementia at the time of the agreement which rendered her incapable of understanding the bargain, but that the purchaser was unaware of this. The agreement represented a sale at a substantial undervalue. It was held that contractual incapacity was established; that a contract entered into by a person of unsound mind was voidable at that person's option if the other party knew of the incapacity or, whether or not he knew, if the contract was 'unfair' to the person of unsound mind; and that the contract was unfair, the indicia of unfairness being (i) a price significantly below the true value, (ii) the absence of independent legal advice for the vendor and (iii) the difference in bargaining positions resulting from disparity in their respective mental capacities.

If a contract is stigmatised as 'unfair', it may be unfair in one of two ways. It may be unfair by reason of the unfair manner in which it was brought into existence; a contract induced by undue influence is unfair in this sense. It will be convenient to call this 'procedural unfairness'. It may also, in some contexts, be described (accurately or inaccurately) as 'unfair' by reason of the fact that the terms of the contract are more favourable to one party than to the other. In order to distinguish this 'unfairness' from procedural unfairness, it will be convenient to call it 'contractual imbalance'. The two concepts may overlap. Contractual imbalance may be so extreme as to raise a presumption of procedural unfairness, such as undue influence or some other form of victimisation. Equity will relieve a party from a contract which he has been induced to make as a result of victimisation. Equity will not relieve a party from a contract on the ground only that there is contractual imbalance not amounting to unconscionable dealing. Of the three indicia of unfairness relied on by the judge in *Archer v Cutler* (assuming unfairness to have existed) the first was contractual imbalance and the second and third were procedural unfairness.

[Lord Brightman reviewed the cases relied on in *Archer v Cutler* and *McLaughlin v Daily Telegraph Newspaper Co Ltd*, and continued:]

In the opinion of their Lordships it is perfectly plain that historically a court of equity did not restrain a suit at law on the ground of 'unfairness' unless the conscience of the plaintiff was in some way affected. This might be because of actual fraud (which the courts of common law would equally have remedied) or constructive fraud, ie conduct which falls below the standards demanded by equity, traditionally considered under its more common manifestations of undue influence, abuse of confidence, unconscionable bargains and frauds on a power (*cf Snell's Principles of Equity* (27th edn, 1973) p 545 ff). An unconscionable bargain in this context would be a bargain of an improvident character made by a poor or ignorant person acting without independent advice which cannot be shown to be a fair and reasonable transaction. 'Fraud' in its equitable context does not mean, or is not confined to, deceit: 'it means an unconscientious use of the power arising out of [the] circumstances and conditions [of the contracting parties]': see *Earl of Aylesford v Morris* (1873) 8 Ch App 484 at 490–491, [1861–731] All ER Rep 300 at 303. It is victimisation, which can consist either of the active extortion of a benefit or the passive acceptance of a benefit in unconscionable circumstances.

Their Lordships have not been referred to any authority that a court of equity would restrain a suit at law where there was no victimisation, no taking advantage of another's weakness, and the sole allegation was contractual imbalance with no undertones of constructive fraud. It seems to their Lordships quite illogical to suppose that the courts of common law would have held that a person of unsound mind, whose affliction was not apparent, was nevertheless free of his bargain if a contractual imbalance could be demonstrated which would have been of no avail to him in equity. Nor do their Lordships see a sufficient foundation in the authorities brought to their attention to support any such proposition.

[Lord Brightman then discussed the Australian case of *Tremills v Benyon* and quoted Hodges J (18 VLR 607, at 622–623):]

> 'There the word "fairly" could not, I think, be referring to a perfect equality of the consideration given by each party to the contract. Again, a little further on, the Vice-Chancellor quotes with approval the following passage from *Story (Equity Jurisprudence* 227):—"The ground upon which courts of equity now interfere to set aside the contracts and other acts, however solemn, of persons who are idiots, lunatics, and otherwise *non compotes mentis*, is fraud." The Vice-Chancellor could not quote, with approval, Story's opinion that the ground on which courts of equity set aside these contracts is *fraud*, if he was deciding that inequality of consideration was a sufficient ground for setting aside such contracts. Again, the Vice-Chancellor a little further on again quotes with approval Story's view (*Equity Jurisprudence* 228) that "If a purchase is made without any knowledge of the incapacity, *and no advantage has been taken*, courts of equity will not interfere to set aside the contract etc." Here again the Vice Chancellor shows that what invalidates these contracts is not mere inequality of consideration, but the taking of an advantage. If an advantage is taken, the contract is not "fair".'

This case appears to their Lordships to be directly contrary to the proposition adopted in *Archer v Cutler*, because it plainly recognises that a contract with an unsuspected lunatic will not be set aside short of equitable fraud.

In the opinion of their Lordships, to accept the proposition enunciated in *Archer v Cutler* that a contract with a person ostensibly sane but actually of unsound mind can be set aside because it is 'unfair' to the person of unsound mind in the sense of contractual imbalance is unsupported by authority, is illogical and would distinguish the law of New Zealand from the law of Australia, as exemplified in *McLaughlin's* case and *Tremills's* case, for no good reason, as well as from the law of England from which the law of Australia and New Zealand and other 'common law' countries has stemmed. In so saying their Lordships differ with profound respect from the contrary view so strongly expressed by the New Zealand courts.

To sum the matter up, in the opinion of their Lordships, the validity of a contract entered into by a lunatic who is ostensibly sane is to be judged by the same standards as a contract by a person of sound mind, and is not voidable by the lunatic or his representative by reason of 'unfairness' unless such unfairness amounts to equitable fraud which would have enabled the complaining party to avoid the contract even if he had been sane.

Their Lordships turn finally to issue (c), whether the respondent trustees are entitled to have the contract set aside as an 'unconscionable bargain'. This issue must also be answered in the negative, because the appellant was guilty of no unconscionable conduct. Indeed, as is conceded, he acted with complete innocence throughout. He was unaware of Jack's unsoundness of mind. Jack was ostensibly advised by his own solicitor. The appellant had no means of knowing or cause to suspect that Jack was not in receipt of and acting in accordance with the most full and careful advice. The terms of the bargain were the terms proposed by Jack's solicitor, not terms imposed by the appellant or his solicitor. There was no equitable fraud, no victimisation, no taking advantage, no overreaching or other description of unconscionable doings which might have justified the intervention of equity to restrain an action by the appellant at law. The respondent trustees have in the opinion of their Lordships failed to make out any case for denying to the appellant the benefit of a bargain which struck with complete propriety on his side. For these reasons their Lordships have tendered to Her Majesty their humble advice that the appeal should be allowed.

NOTE

If, during the course of negotiating a contract, you make a statement of fact that later is found to be untrue, the other party may (subject to the court's discretion under Misrepresentation Act 1967, s 2(2)) rescind the contract, even though your statement was made not only honestly but with reasonable grounds for believing it to be true.

> Even assuming that moral fraud must be shewn in order to set aside a contract, you have it where a man, having obtained a beneficial contract by a statement which he now knows to be false, insists upon keeping that contract. (Jessel MR in *Redgrave v Hurd*: see p 355.)

If, on the other hand, you manage to buy a piece of land on very advantageous terms and subsequently you discover that you were dealing with an insane person, or a 'poor and ignorant' person, you can keep the land. Why is there moral fraud in one case but not the other? The philosophies underlying *Hart v O'Connor*, on one hand, and *Redgrave v Hurd*, on the other, seem very different.

IV. SALVAGE AGREEMENTS

We saw in Chapter 34 that the doctrine of duress applies only in cases in which the victim has received an 'illegitimate threat'. What if, without the fault of either party, one party finds himself in a dire situation and the other party takes advantage of that to extract a harsh bargain? In Admiralty, this problem arose in relation to salvage agreements; relief would be granted.

■ The Port Caledonia and The Anna [1903]
P 184

Two large laden sailing vessels were sheltering in Holyhead Harbour from a south-westerly gale, when the master of one of them, finding that his vessel had dragged down into dangerous proximity to the other, signalled for a tug. In response to the signal, a tug came up, but her master demanded '£1000 or no rope'. The master of the vessel, which had dragged her anchors, after some demur agreed to pay the sum named, and was towed back to his original berth. An action was brought by the owners, master, and crew of the tug against both vessels, their cargoes and freights upon the agreement in the one case, and for a salvage award in the other.

Bucknill J

... With the £1000 agreement on one side, and that which I think was the value of the services on the other, I have to ask myself whether the bargain that was made was so inequitable, so unjust, and so unreasonable that the Court cannot allow it to stand?

The first question to consider is, What was the position of the two persons who made the agreement? The position was this. One man was in a position to insist upon his terms, and the other man had to put up with it. He could not help himself. He says in his letter to his owners: 'He demanded £1000 to take me away. I offered him £100, or to leave it to the owners; but he would not agree, so I agreed to give £1000 rather than foul the *Anna*. He appreciated the possibility of fouling the *Anna* if the weather had remained bad, and if the wind had remained in the SW, neither of which things happened. So he found himself obliged to give way to a person who would not move him, and who would have allowed him and the *Anna* to drift towards the rocks, and who would, I think, have seen them go there without putting a hawser on board unless he got a promise of £1000.

I have expressed my opinion about the matter. This opinion is shared by the Elder Brethren, and I hold that this agreement cannot be allowed to stand, and I set it aside.

I hope that those who perform such grand services in tugs from time to time, in worse weather than this, and, in peril of their own lives, save property around the coast, will note that this Court will keep a firm hand over them if they attempt to do what has been done in this case.

This was an inequitable, extortionate, and unreasonable agreement, and I think that the services rendered will be well rewarded by the sum of £200, and with county court costs.

Bucknill J held that the second vessel, *The Anna*, was not in danger and need not contribute.

NOTE

This appears to be a special rule of admiralty law without a general common law equivalent but see p 956.

V. CONSUMER CREDIT

■ Consumer Credit Act 1974, ss 67, 68

Section 67: Cancellable agreements

A regulated agreement may be cancelled by the debtor or hirer in accordance with this Part if the antecedent negotiations included oral representations made when in the presence of the debtor or hirer by an individual acting as, or on behalf of, the negotiator, unless—

(a) the agreement is secured on land, or is a restricted-use credit agreement to finance the purchase of land or is an agreement for a bridging loan in connection with the purchase of land, or

(b) the unexecuted agreement is signed by the debtor or hirer at premises at which any of the following is carrying on any business (whether on a permanent or temporary basis)—

 (i) the creditor or owner;

 (ii) any party to a linked transaction (other than the debtor or hirer or a relative of his);

 (iii) the negotiator in any antecedent negotiations.

Section 68: Cooling-off period

The debtor or hirer may serve notice of cancellation of a cancellable agreement between his signing of the unexecuted agreement and—

(a) the end of the fifth day following the day on which he received a copy under section 63(2) or a notice under section 64(1)(b), or

(b) if (by virtue of regulations made under section 64(4)) section 64(1)(b) does not apply, the end of the fourteenth day following the day on which he signed the unexecuted agreement.

NOTES

1. These provisions apply however good a price the consumer was offered. Why?
2. Why are the provisions limited to sales away from business premises?

3. Why is this right of cancellation limited to transactions involving credit? Do you see any parallel between this and the cases in subsections I, II and III above?

4. You will find an explanation and critique of ss 67 and 68 in Cranston, *Consumers and the Law*, 2nd edn, pp 192–193.

5. Needless to say, these and other rights given by the Consumer Credit Act will not be of much avail to consumers if they are unaware of their rights. Look at the specimen contract in the Appendix. Section 60 of the Act provides:

(1) The Secretary of State shall make regulations as to the form and content of documents embodying regulated agreements, and the regulations shall contain such provisions as appear to him appropriate with a view to ensuring that the debtor or hirer is made aware of—

(a) The rights and duties conferred or imposed on him by the agreement,

(b) the amount and rate of the total charge for credit (in the case of a consumer credit agreement),

(c) the protection and remedies available to him under this Act, and

(d) any other matters which, in the opinion of the Secretary of State, it is desirable for him to know about in connection with the agreement.

(2) Regulations under subsection (1) may in particular—

(a) require specified information to be included in the prescribed manner in documents, and other specified material to be excluded.

(b) contain requirements to ensure that specified information is clearly brought to the attention of the debtor or hirer, and that one part of a document is not given insufficient or excessive prominence compared with another.

■ Consumer Credit Act 1974, as amended by Consumer Credit Act 2006

Section 140A (inserted by CCA 2006 s 19): Unfair relationships between creditors and debtors

(1) The court may make an order under section 140B in connection with a credit agreement if it determines that the relationship between the creditor and the debtor arising out of the agreement (or the agreement taken with any related agreement) is unfair to the debtor because of one or more of the following—

(a) any of the terms of the agreement or of any related agreement;

(b) the way in which the creditor has exercised or enforced any of his rights under the agreement or any related agreement;

(c) any other thing done (or not done) by, or on behalf of, the creditor (either before or after the making of the agreement or any related agreement).

(2) In deciding whether to make a determination under this section the court shall have regard to all matters it thinks relevant (including matters relating to the creditor and matters relating to the debtor).

...

Section 140B (inserted by CCA 2006 s 20): Powers of court in relation to unfair relationships

(1) An order under this section in connection with a credit agreement may do one or more of the following—

(a) require the creditor, or any associate or former associate of his, to repay (in whole or in part) any sum paid by the debtor or by a surety by virtue of the agreement or any related agreement (whether paid to the creditor, the associate or the former associate or to any other person);

(b) require the creditor, or any associate or former associate of his, to do or not to do (or to cease doing) anything specified in the order in connection with the agreement or any related agreement;

(c) reduce or discharge any sum payable by the debtor or by a surety by virtue of the agreement or any related agreement;

(d) direct the return to a surety of any property provided by him for the purposes of a security;

(e) otherwise set aside (in whole or in part) any duty imposed on the debtor or on a surety by virtue of the agreement or any related agreement;

(f) alter the terms of the agreement or of any related agreement;

(g) direct accounts to be taken, or (in Scotland) an accounting to be made, between any persons.

. . .

(9) If, in any such proceedings, the debtor or a surety alleges that the relationship between the creditor and the debtor is unfair to the debtor, it is for the creditor to prove to the contrary.

NOTES

1. These sections replace sections 137–140 of the 1974 Act, which dealt with 'extortionate credit bargains'.

2. A loan at 48 per cent interest, but made at short notice and on little security, has been held not to be extortionate because of the risk to the lender: *Ketley Ltd v Scott* [1981] ICR 241.

VI. MINORS

The law of minors', or infants', contracts is very complicated, and space precludes a full consideration of it. Nonetheless, a simplified outline provides a useful comparison to the rules governing the relief that may be given to adult contracting parties.

The general rule is that a minor cannot set aside a contract once he has performed it, but he is not bound to perform his obligations while they remain executory. He can enforce the other party's obligations against him.

To this general rule that the minor is not bound, there are a number of exceptions:

(1) if he is supplied with goods or services that are 'necessaries' for him or (if he is married) his family, he must pay a reasonable sum for them. What is necessary is to be determined by the minor's actual needs at the time, and his position in life, but after one or two rather extravagant decisions by juries of tradesmen (for instance, that wild ducks and champagne were 'necessaries' to an undergraduate), it was established that it must first be decided as a matter of law whether the goods or services are capable of being necessaries, before the minor's actual needs are considered;

(2) a minor is also bound to perform contracts of service, apprenticeship and the like, provided the contract taken as a whole is for his benefit;

(3) there are four types of contract that are binding on a minor but which he can repudiate either during his minority or within a reasonable time after it. These are: agreements to buy or sell land, or to take or grant a lease of land; marriage settlements made by him; contracts whereby a minor incurs liability for calls on shares in a company; and partnerships.

These rules raise a number of interesting questions of policy.

(1) A minor is supplied on credit with goods that are 'necessaries' for him. He is liable for their reasonable value, not the contract price. Why?

(2) A minor buys and pays the contract price for something of which he had no need (wild ducks and champagne, say). The minor cannot recover the price he has paid, or even the amount by which the contract price exceeded the fair value of the goods (unless, perhaps, he can bring himself within the class of poor and ignorant persons. This may not be as fanciful as it sounds: in *Fry v Lane*, expectant heirs and poor and ignorant persons are treated as a single category.) If he obtains the same goods on credit and eats them, he need pay nothing, not even the price of a regular meal. Why?

(3) A minor is not bound by a contract for non-necesssaries or that is not for his benefit, but he can enforce it against the other party. Why?

(4) A minor enters a training contract that is, taken as a whole, for his benefit. He is probably bound even though he has not yet started the training. Why?

VII. RESTRAINT OF TRADE

The doctrine of restraint of trade, which may render a contract wholly or partly void as contrary to public policy, is treated in detail in Section 9. For present purposes, it is enough to note that many of the cases do seem to involve protecting an economically weaker party—in particular, an employee—against harsh clauses. In *Schroeder Music Publishing Co Ltd v Macaulay* [1974] 3 All ER 616, at 623, Lord Diplock said:

It is, in my view, salutory to acknowledge that in refusing to enforce provisions of a contract whereby one party agrees for the benefit of the other party to exploit or to refrain from exploiting his own earning-power, the public policy which the court is implementing is not some 19th century economic theory about the benefit to the general public of freedom of trade, but the protection of those whose bargaining power is weak against being forced by those whose bargaining power is stronger to enter into bargains that are unconscionable. Under the influence of Bentham and of laissez-faire the courts in the 19th century abandoned the practice of applying the public policy against unconscionable bargains to contracts generally, as they had formerly done to any contract considered to be usurious; but the policy survived in its application to penalty clauses and to relief against forfeiture and also to the special category of contracts in restraint of trade. If one looks at the reasoning of 19th century judges in cases about contracts in restraint of trade one finds lip service paid to current economic theories but if one looks at what they said in the light of what they did, one finds that they struck down a bargain if they thought it was unconscionable as between the parties to it, and upheld it if they thought that it was not.

So I would hold that the question to be answered as respects a contract in restraint of trade of the kind with which this appeal is concerned is: was the bargain fair? The test of fairness is, no doubt, whether the restrictions are both reasonably necessary for the protection of the legitimate interests of the promisee and commensurate with the benefits secured to the promisor under the contract. For the purpose of this test all the provisions of the contract must be taken into consideration.

(Further extracts from this case will be found later.)

If Lord Diplock's statement was intended to describe every case of restraint of trade in which one party agrees to refrain from exploiting his earning power, it is too broad: there are cases of the seller of a business agreeing not to compete with the buyer, or the owner of a business agreeing to sell certain products only, where there is no question of the restraint being unreasonable *as between the parties.* It is struck down because it is inimical to the *public interest* (see Chapter 44). However, Lord Diplock's statement seems to fit the majority of cases of employees who have accepted restraints on their activities during or, more usually, after their employment. (The other categories Lord Diplock mentions, penalty clauses and relief from forfeiture, were dealt with earlier: see pp 689 and 588 respectively.)

CHAPTER THIRTY-SEVEN

A GENERAL PRINCIPLE?

I. IS THERE A GENERAL PRINCIPLE?

■ *Lloyds Bank Ltd v Bundy*
[1974] (See p 918)

Lord Denning MR
The general rule

Now let me say at once that in the vast majority of cases a customer who signs a bank guarantee or a charge cannot get out of it. No bargain will be upset which is the result of the ordinary interplay of forces. There are many hard cases which are caught by this rule. Take the case of a poor man who is homeless. He agrees to pay a high rent to a landlord just to get a roof over his head. The common law will not interfere. It is left to Parliament. Next take the case of a borrower in urgent need of money. He borrows it from the bank at high interest and it is guaranteed by a friend. The guarantor gives his bond and gets nothing in return. The common law will not interfere. Parliament has intervened to prevent moneylenders charging excessive interest. But it has never interfered with banks.

Yet there are exceptions to this general rule. There are cases in our books in which the courts will set aside a contract, or a transfer of property, when the parties have not met on equal terms—when the one is so strong in bargaining power and the other so weak—that, as a matter of common fairness, it is not right that the strong should be allowed to push the weak to the wall. Hitherto those exceptional cases have been treated each as a separate category in itself. But I think the time has come when we should seek to find a principle to unite them. I put on one side contracts or transactions which are voidable for fraud or misrepresentation or mistake. All those are governed by settled principles. I go only to those where there has been inequality of bargaining power, such as to merit the intervention of the court.

The categories

The first category is that of 'duress of goods'. A typical case is when a man is in a strong bargaining position by being in possession of the goods of another by virtue of a legal right, such as by way of pawn or pledge or taken in distress. The owner is in a weak position because he is in urgent need of the goods. The stronger demands of the weaker more than is justly due: and he pays it in order to get the goods. Such a transaction is voidable. He can recover the excess: see *Astley v Reynolds* and *Green v Duckett*. To which may be added the cases of 'colore oficii', where a man is in a strong bargaining position by virtue of his official position or public profession. He relies upon it so as to gain from the weaker—who is urgently in need—more than is justly due: see Pigot's case cited by Lord Kenyon C J in *Cartwright v Rowley; Parker v Bristol and Exeter Railway Co* and *Steel v Williams*. In such cases the stronger may make his claim in good faith honestly believing that he is entitled to make his demand. He may not be guilty of any fraud or misrepresentation. The inequality of bargaining power—the strength of the one versus the urgent need of the other—renders the transaction voidable and the money paid to be recovered back: see *Maskell v Horner*.

The second category is that of the 'unconscionable transaction'. A man is so placed as to be in need of special care and protection and yet his weakness is exploited by another far stronger than himself so as to get his property at a gross undervalue. The typical case is that of the 'expectant heir'. But it applies to all cases where a man comes into property, or is expected to come into it—and then being in urgent need—another gives him ready cash for it, greatly below its true worth, and so gets the property transferred to him: see *Evans v Llewellin*. Even though there be no evidence of fraud or misrepresentation, nevertheless the transaction will be set aside: see *Fry v Lane*, where Kay J said:

'The result of the decisions is that where a purchase is made from a poor and ignorant man at a considerable undervalue, *the vendor having no independent advice*, a court of equity will set aside the transaction.'

This second category is said to extend to all cases where an unfair advantage has been gained by an unconscientious use of power by a stronger party against a weaker: see the cases cited in *Halsbury's Laws of England*, 3rd edn, vol 17 (1956), p 682 and, in Canada, *Morrison v Coast Finance Ltd* and *Knupp v Bell*.

The third category is that of 'undue influence' usually so called. These are divided into two classes as stated by Cotton LJ in *Allcard v Skinner*. The first are those where the stronger has been guilty of some fraud or wrongful act—expressly so as to gain some gift or advantage from the weaker. The second are those where the stronger has not been guilty of any wrongful act, but has, through the relationship which existed between him and the weaker, gained some gift or advantage for himself. Sometimes the relationship is such as to raise a presumption of undue influence, such as parent over child, solicitor over client, doctor over patient, spiritual adviser over follower. At other times a relationship of confidence must be proved to exist. But to all of them the general principle obtains which was stated by Lord Chelmsford LC in *Tate v Williamson*:

'Wherever two persons stand in such a relation that, while it continues, confidence is necessarily reposed by one, and the influence which naturally grows out of that confidence is possessed by the other, and this confidence is abused, or the influence is exerted to obtain an advantage at the expense of the confiding party, the person so availing himself of his position will not be permitted to retain the advantage, although the transaction could not have been impeached if no such confidential relation had existed.'

Such a case was *Tufton v Sperni*.

The fourth category is that of 'undue pressure'. The most apposite of that is *Williams v Bayley*, where a son forged his father's name to a promissory note and, by means of it, raised money from the bank of which they were both customers. The bank said to the father, in effect: 'Take your choice—give us security for your son's debt. If you do take that on yourself, then it will all go smoothly: if you do not, we shall be bound to exercise pressure.' Thereupon the father charged his property to the bank with payment of the note. The House of Lords held that the charge was invalid because of undue pressure exerted by the bank. Lord Westbury said,

'A contract to give security for the debt of another, which is a contract without consideration, is above all things, a contract that should be based upon the free and voluntary agency of the individual who enters into it.'

Other instances of undue pressure are where one party stipulates for an unfair advantage to which the other has no option but to submit. As where an employer—the stronger party—has employed a builder—the weaker party—to do work for him. When the builder asked for payment of sums properly due (so as to pay his workmen) the employer refused to pay unless he was given some added advantage. Stuart V-C said: 'Where an agreement, hard and inequitable in itself, has been exacted under circumstances of pressure on the part of the person who exacts it, this court will set it aside'; see *Ormes v Beadel* and *D Builders Ltd v Rees*.

The fifth category is that of salvage agreements. When a vessel is in danger of sinking and seeks help, the rescuer is in a strong bargaining position. The vessel in distress is in urgent need. The parties cannot be truly said to be on equal terms. The Court of Admiralty have always recognised that fact. The 'fundamental rule' is

'if the parties have made an agreement, the court will enforce it, unless it be manifestly unfair and unjust; but if it be manifestly unfair and unjust, the court will disregard it and decree what is fair and just.'

See *Akerblom v Price, per* Brett LJ, applied in a striking case *The Port Caledonia and The Anna*, when the rescuer refused to help with a rope unless he was paid £1,000.

The general principles

Gathering all together, I would suggest that through all these instances there runs a single thread. They rest on 'inequality of bargaining power'. By virtue of it, the English law gives relief to one who, without independent advice, enters into a contract upon terms which are very unfair or transfers property for a consideration which is grossly inadequate, when his bargaining power is grievously impaired by reason of his own needs or desires, or by his own ignorance or infirmity, coupled with undue influences or pressures brought to bear on him by or for the benefit of the other. When I used the word 'undue' I do not mean to suggest that the principle depends on proof of any wrongdoing. The one who stipulates for an unfair advantage may be moved solely by his own self-interest, unconscious of the distress he is bringing to the other. I have also avoided any reference to the will of the one being 'dominated' or 'overcome' by the other. One who is in extreme need may knowingly consent to a most improvident bargain, solely to relieve the straits in which he finds himself. Again, I do not mean to suggest that every transaction is saved by independent advice. But the absence of it may be fatal. With these explanations, I hope this principle will be found to reconcile the cases. Applying it to the present case, I would notice these points:

(1) The consideration moving from the bank was grossly inadequate. The son's company was in serious difficulty. The overdraft was at its limit of £10,000. The bank considered that its existing security was insufficient. In order to get further security, it asked the father to charge the house—his sole asset—to the uttermost. It was worth £10,000. The charge was for £11,000. That was for the benefit of the bank. But not at all for the benefit of the father, or indeed for the company. The bank did not promise to continue the overdraft or to increase it. On the contrary, it required the overdraft to be reduced. All that the company gained was a short respite from impending doom.

(2) The relationship between the bank and the father was one of trust and confidence. The bank knew that the father relied on it implicitly to advise him about the transaction. The father trusted the bank. This gave the bank much influence on the father. Yet the bank failed in that trust. It allowed the father to charge the house to his ruin.

(3) The relationship between the father and the son was one where the father's natural affection had much influence on him. He would naturally desire to accede to his son's request. He trusted his son.

(4) There was a conflict of interest between the bank and the father. Yet the bank did not realise it. Nor did it suggest that the father should get independent advice. If the father had gone to his solicitor—or to any man of business—there is no doubt that any one of them would say: 'You must not enter into this transaction. You are giving up your house, your sole remaining asset, for no benefit to you. The company is in such a parlous state that you must not do it.'

These considerations seem to me to bring this case within the principles I have stated. But, in case that principle is wrong, I would also say that the case falls within the category of undue influence of the second class stated by Cotton LJ in *Allcard v Skinner*. I have no doubt that the assistant bank manager acted in the utmost good faith and was straightforward and genuine. Indeed the father said so. But beyond doubt he was acting in the interests of the bank—to get further security for a bad debt. There was such a relationship of trust and confidence between them that the bank ought not to have swept up his sole remaining asset into its hands—for nothing—without his having independent advice. I would therefore allow this appeal.

Sir Eric Sachs

As regards the wider areas covered in masterly survey in the judgment of Lord Denning MR, but not raised arguendo, I do not venture to express an opinion—though having some sympathy with the views that the courts should be able to give relief to a party who has been subject to undue pressure as defined in the concluding passage of his judgment on that point.

NOTES

1.   It appears unlikely that any general principle will be recognised in English law in the near future. In *National Westminster Bank plc v Morgan* (see p 920) Lord Scarman said ([1985] 1 All ER 821 at 830):

Lord Denning MR believed that the doctrine of undue influence could be subsumed under a general principle that English courts will grant relief where there has been "inequality of bargaining power".... He deliberately avoided reference to the will of one party being dominated or overcome by another. The majority of the court did not follow him; they based their decision on the orthodox view of the doctrine as expounded in *Allcard v Skinner.* This opinion of the Master of the Rolls, there-fore, was not the ground of the court's decision, which has to be found in the view of the majority, for whom Sir Eric Sachs delivered the leading judgment.

Nor has counsel for the respondent sought to rely on Lord Denning's general principle: and, in my view, he was right not to do so. The doctrine of undue influence has been sufficiently developed not to need the support of a principle which by its formulation in the language of the law of contract is not appropriate to cover transactions of gift where there is no bargain. The fact of an unequal bar-gain will, of course, be a relevant feature in some cases of undue influence. But it can never become an appropriate basis of principle of an equitable doctrine which is concerned with transactions "not to be reasonably accounted for on the ground of friendship, relationship, charity, or other ordinary motives on which ordinary men act" (Lindley LJ in *Allcard v Skinner*). And even in the field of contract I question whether there is any need in the modern law to erect a general principle of relief against inequality of bargaining power. Parliament has undertaken the task (and it is essentially a legislative task) of enacting such restrictions on freedom of contract as are in its judgment necessary to relieve against the mischief: for example, the hire-purchase and consumer protection legislation, of which the Supply of Goods (Implied Terms) Act 1973, Consumer Credit Act 1974. Consumer Safety Act 1978, Supply of Goods and Services Act 1982 and Insurance Companies Act 1982 are examples. I doubt whether the courts should assume the burden of formulating further restrictions.

2.   In *Burmah Oil Co Ltd v Governor of the Bank of England* (1981) (noted 125 Sol Jo 528), Burmah's main asset was a large shareholding in British Petroleum (BP). The quoted Stock Exchange price of BP shares fell, causing Burmah grave financial embarrassment, because its own borrowings were structured in such a way as to be dependent on higher BP shares. Burmah approached the Bank of England for help. The Bank consulted the government. The government would probably not have wanted to see Burmah go into liquidation, or to see its BP shares fall into foreign hands. The Bank bought the BP shares. In due course, the quoted price of BP shares rose very considerably, and Burmah brought an action claiming to set aside the transaction on the ground that the Bank had taken unfair advantage of inequality of bargaining power between the parties. Walton J was clearly sceptical as to whether Denning's judgment in *Lloyd's Bank Ltd v Bundy* rep-resented English law, but held that in any case the facts did not come within the prin-ciple. Burmah was at all times advised by expert lawyers and merchant bankers, and could not have obtained a better price for its shares elsewhere (to sell such a large block of shares on the Stock Exchange at one time would depress the price dramatically, so a sale

to a single buyer was very desirable, but it was not proved that there was any other buyer in field). The Bank's terms were tough, but not unconscionably so, given that Burmah's difficulties were largely of its own making and that public money was being provided for the rescue of Burmah and its shareholders. Nor was Burmah in a gravely unequal bargaining position, since although in financial difficulties, it could see that the Bank and the government would not wish to see a large company collapse, and were thus under pressure to come up with a rescue package.

Suppose the Bank had intimated informally that it would give generous terms, and on the strength of that, Burmah had given up other offers, but when it was too late to revive these other offers, the Bank had reduced its offer to below the level of the other offers. Should Burmah be able to avoid the agreement, or part of it? On what terms? Is 'inequality of bargaining power' a useful concept to help decide this sort of case, or do you need such concepts as good faith bargaining and misrepresentation?

3.   Academic commentators have not all been so dismissive. For instance, Waddams, 'Unconscionability in Contracts' (1976) 39 MLR 369 also suggests that there is a single principle running through the cases mentioned, and calls for the recognition of a general principle.

4.   Denning's general principle has been accepted by a number of courts in Canada (see Enman, 'Doctrines of Unconscionability in England, Canada and the Commonwealth' (1987) 16 Anglo-Am LR 191).

5.   A more general doctrine has been adopted in many of the US states. Uniform Commercial Code s 2–302 provides:

Unconscionable contract or clause

(1) If the court as a matter of law finds the contract or any clause of the contract to have been unconscionable at the time it was made the court may refuse to enforce the contract, or it may enforce the remainder of the contract without the unconscionable clause, or it may so limit the application of any unconscionable clause as to avoid any unconscionable result.

Article 2 of the UCC applies only to 'transactions in goods', but some courts have applied an analogous doctrine to other contracts, and Restatement 2d s 208 adopts a similar provision for application to any contract. The 'unconscionability' doctrine is used both in cases of traditional exploitation (eg *Laters v Min Ltd* 412 Mass 64, 587 NE 2d 231 (1992), and against unfair clauses in standard-form contracts.

II. POSSIBLE ADVANTAGES OF A GENERAL DOCTRINE

Is English law defective in not recognising any general doctrine of unconscionability? Firstly, are there any agreements that are manifestly 'unfair' in some sense but which the courts cannot strike down under any of the existing doctrines? Slayton, 'The Unequal Bargain Doctrine' (1976) 22 McGill LJ 94, at 106, says:

How does the unequal bargain doctrine differ from that of undue influence? The traditional view is that the latter applies either when undue influence resulting in a contract that would not otherwise have been made can be proved as a fact, or when a confidential relationship exists leading to a duty of fiduciary care and giving rise to a presumption of undue influence which is not rebutted. In my opinion, under the unequal bargain doctrine as set forth by Lord Denning (1) no confidential relationship or duty of fiduciary care is necessary, and (2) undue influence need not be proved as a fact, but will be presumed when bargaining power is impaired and the terms are very unfair or consideration grossly inadequate. If this is so, then clearly a new doctrine of momentous scope has been introduced into the law of contract.

Secondly, might a general doctrine be given a sufficiently coherent content that it would be a workable tool, with criteria that would give an answer in each case without an unacceptable degree of uncertainty? Take Lord Denning MR's formulation in *Lloyds Bank Ltd v Bundy* (see p 956) and test it against the existing categories. He seems to envisage the following criteria:

(1) the terms of the contract must be very unfair or the consideration inadequate;
(2) the bargaining power of the party must have been impaired by necessity, ignorance, or infirmity;
(3) the other party, or someone else on his behalf, must have used undue pressure or influence. This need not be conscious, but the pressure must emanate from him, not from a general situation like a housing shortage;
(4) independent advice will not always save a transaction but its absence is usually fatal.

How do these fit the five categories of case on which Denning relied? The other ones we have looked at? Other instances of 'unfair contracts' that you can envisage?

■ Trebilcock, 'Economic Criteria of Unconscionability', in Reiter and Swan (eds), Studies in Contract Law
pp 390–396, 404–408

In fashioning economically defensible criteria of unconscionability, it is submitted that two criteria are central. First, if the market in which the transaction occurs is *structurally impaired*, this may provide grounds for judicial intervention by way of preventing the enforcement of such a transaction. Secondly, even in cases where the transaction in question is entered into in a structurally sound market, the market may be *informationally-impaired*, thus rendering the transaction suspect. It is proposed to examine each of these two concepts in turn.

(b) Structurally impaired markets

What is contemplated here is the case of a market which is so structurally impaired as to preclude the behaviour of one or other of the parties to a contract being effectively disciplined in his behaviour towards the other party by market (competitive) forces. Two subsets of circumstances can be identified in this respect. First, there is the case of what might be called situational (or 'spot') monopolies where special circumstances have arisen giving one contracting party abnormal market power with respect to the other, albeit perhaps not in relation to other parties in the same market. The second is what might be called market-wide monopolies where it is claimed that one contracting party is the victim of abnormal market power possessed by the other and obtaining, on a relatively pervasive and durable basis, throughout the whole of the market in question.

(i) Situational monopolies
This class of case is approximately coterminous with those circumstances often considered as falling under the doctrine of duress. . . .

   As the scope of the doctrine of duress has moved from the narrow case of physical threats to less clearly specified cases of 'economic duress', it has become more important to define precisely what it is that will constitute unacceptable forms of coercion. The failure to articulate the essence of the concept of duress in meaningful economic terms has led courts to rely on a variety of dubiously useful criteria. For example, in the *Occidental* case, the emphasis on whether the coercion had vitiated the consent of the party pleading duress seems unhelpful. In any operational sense, clearly consent has been forthcoming to the transaction. Indeed, even in the physical threat cases, the consent of the party threatened is entirely real. To attach significance to the absence of a protest by a party to an allegedly coerced argeement, as was also suggested in *Occidental*, again seems of doubtful soundness if it was clear that a protest would be futile. Yet again, to talk of these transactions as 'one-sided' is also unhelpful, because even in the extreme example of a contract induced by physical threat, there are substantial mutual advantages to the transaction. Finally, to attach redemptive significance to the presence of independent advice in a situation where it is acknowledged that the presence of independent advice does 'nothing to expand the choices open' to the party alleging duress seems again mistaken.

It is submitted that the relevant test in all of the so-called duress cases is whether the conduct of the party against whom the doctrine is pleaded was as to remove from, or to take advantage of the absence of, effective access by the other party to a workably competitive range of alternative choices. For example, in the salvage cases, what may be objectionable about the terms exacted by a tug owner from the owner or captain of a sinking ship is that the latter faces no realistic alternative suppliers of the demanded service. Similarly, in cases where one contracting party threatens to suspend performance unless the other party agrees to a variation in the contract. Here, again, the latter may face a form of situational monopoly if the nature of the contract and the stage of performance is such that he cannot readily obtain an alternative supplier to complete the contract, (and is unlikely to obtain full compensation through a damages award). While, as will be argued later in this study, a judicial doctrine of unconscionability can play only a very limited role in redressing distributional imbalances in the marketplace, it is possible that in particular circumstances the fact of poverty may create situational monopolies which other parties can exploit. For example, in *D and C Builders Ltd v Rees*. . . .

The extension of the doctrine of duress to any form of monopolistic threat would seem a promising and defensible line of development for the doctrine to take. Beyond rationalizing all the various classes of cases hitherto subsumed under the doctrine of duress, a doctrine so functionally defined has the advantage of posing a relatively realistic inquiry for the courts to embark upon. In cases of situational monopolies, the circumstances directly surrounding the particular transaction between the two parties in question will generally yield reliable inferences as to the extent of the monopoly power possessed by one in relation to the other. This is in sharp and significant contrast to the problems posed in cases of market-wide monopolies, discussed below. On the other hand, several cautions need to be added.

First, despite the monopoly that exists in these cases some of these transactions may be value maximizing; what has happened is that the monopolist has taken all or almost all the consumer surplus in rents (eg, in the salvage cases). Thus, these transactions may not be so much allocatively inefficient as distributively 'unfair'. What makes them distributively unfair cannot avoid a value judgment, although economic analysis might suggest some caution in intervention where excessive profits merely signal a transition to a new equilibrium or where excessively blunt intervention may eliminate incentives to supply the product or service in question. Second, in a number of the standard duress cases, the circumstances are more accurately characterized, economically, not as simple monopolies but as bilateral monopolies. For example, even in the salvage cases, depending on the circumstances, it may be the case that both the owners of the tug and the vessel in distress each possess abnormal market power in relation to the other. That is to say, the tug owner may be the only supplier of salvage services readily accessible to the distressed vessel, but in turn, the distressed vessel may be the only one readily available demander of the tug's services. As economic theorizing has shown, in bilateral monopoly situations the outcomes of the resulting bargaining processes are somewhat indeterminate in terms of a competitive market benchmark. The implications of this for a judicial doctrine of unconscionability is that it will sometimes be difficult to determine whether resulting contracts are optimal in any relevant economic sense. However, apart from 'fairness' considerations, one potential advantage of a properly fashioned intervention here is that the social waste (inefficiency) that is often generated by strategic behaviour in bilateral monopoly situations might be reduced. Thus, for example, excessive investments in bargaining activities, as in the recent Amoco Cadiz incident where protracted salvage negotiations led to the foundering of an oil tanker, might be discouraged.

(ii) Market-wide monopolies

Here, the case differs from situational monopolies because of the difficulty facing a court in making reliable determinations of abnormal market power simply by looking at the relationship and interactions between the two parties to a contested contract. Claims of abuse of market power can only be validated by extensive inquiry into the structure of the entire market in which the transaction has taken place. The difficulties facing a court in this context are well illustrated by the decision of the House of Lords in *Macaulay v Schroeder Publishing Co Ltd. . . .* [For details of this case and Trebilcock's comments on it, see p 965 ff.]

It is submitted that the difficulties exemplified in the decision in *Macaulay v Schroeder Publishing Co* suggest extreme caution on the part of courts in withholding contract enforcement on the grounds of inequality of bargaining power involving alleged abuses of market-wide monopoly power. First, inferences of such monopolies are frequently likely to be drawn incorrectly by the courts. Secondly, even where correctly drawn, the courts do not have at their disposal the remedial instruments required to foreclose all second-order, substitution, effects.

(c) Informationally impaired markets

In this context, it is proposed to examine three classes of situations where a party to a contract may have entered into it with imperfect information; first, the case where that party lacks a normal capacity for processing information; second, the case where one party to a contract possesses material information which has not been disposed to the other party to the contract prior to formation; third, the case of standard form contracts containing clauses which have not been read, or understood by the parties to such contracts. . . . As was suggested earlier in this essay, current rules bearing on contractual invalidity, such as those relating to contractual capacity, involve arbitrary boundary lines which make them at the same time both over and under inclusive. To take the case of rules of incapacity governing infants' contracts, it is clear that some infants who are able to take advantage of these rules to avoid contract performance have as much information-processing capacity as many adults who would be held bound on the same contracts. Conversely, there are some adults who are likely to be afflicted by the same lack of information-processing capacity as is exhibited by less mature infants. Setting aside the problems associated with the over inclusive nature of current rules on capacity and instead focusing on their under inclusive character, it is useful to 'decompose' the concept of infancy into some set of physiological characteristics which might then be extrapolated into a set of guidelines for the courts in applying the doctrine of unconscionability to transactions involving adults. . . .

More difficult issues are posed by cases where the source of the impaired information-processing capacity cannot be so precisely identified. For example, in door-to-door sale transactions, where a party is induced to buy something that, on mature reflection, he does not really want or has agreed to pay an excessive price for, or in the dance studio type situation, where a party is induced to sign up for many more dancing lessons than, on mature reflection, were really wanted, the argument can be made that in these situations psychological vulnerabilities are particularly amenable to exploitation, although care is called for in not casting the doctrine in so expansive a form that it loses all focus and rigour. Obviously, if the courts are to avoid a pervasively interventionist role in the market-place as second guessers of people's bargains and if the costs of error and uncertainty that would be engendered by such a role are to be contained, there should be some costs to non-excusable incompetence in participating in market transactions, and thus, conversely, appropriate incentives to develop some threshold level of competence.

The doctrine of unconscionability, as it applies to the foregoing cases of impaired ability to process information, seems to be playing a very useful and defensible role. The scope of the inquiry posed for the courts by the doctrine in this context seems a relatively manageable one, given that typically the courts need only to examine the circumstances immediately surrounding the particular transaction in question, the characteristics of the parties, and the nature of the relationship between them. They are not called on to embark upon extensive inquiries into conditions generally in the relevant market beyond establishing, where possible, a market norm against which the values exchanged in the transaction in question can be measured.

However, it is important that the doctrine be seen as a constrained tool of intervention and not the basis for unfettered judicial second-guessing of market participants. The constraints that ought to be particularly noted are: first, the courts, wisely, have generally insisted on a conjunction of a substantial divergence between the consideration received by the party seeking relief and the consideration available from elsewhere in the market and some quite specifically identifiable source of impairment in the information-processing powers of the party seeking relief which prevented him from capturing the benefits of those market alternatives. This constraint on the doctrine, of course, differentiates it from rules on the incapacity of infants where an infant may avoid a contract for non-necessaries even if the consideration which he has received under it comports entirely with relevant market norms. Second, even where this conjunction of circumstances is present, it should probably be treated as doing no more than raising a strong presumption of unconscionability which the other party to the transaction should be at liberty to attempt to rebut. This is particularly important in family-type transactions where what to an outsider might seem a grossly inadequate consideration passing from one party to another may be explained by eg donative intentions or the provision of non-market type services such as eg, companionship. Third, to the extent that the party seeking relief is not able to identify any precise source of impairment to his information-processing capabilities, to that extent the court should insist on more rigorous proof of the market norm against which the applicant seeks to have the inadequacy of consideration provided under the impinged transaction measured. Thus…the court might wish to insist, first, on a very substantial disparity between the consideration obtained under the contract and the consideration otherwise available in the market and, second, on very rigorous proof as to the existence and availability to the plaintiff of these market alternatives. Fourth, it is axiomatic that if a person who would otherwise be entitled to relief under the criteria outlined above nevertheless has the advantage of independent legal or similar advice, the presence of an agent with presumably normal information-processing capabilities fully answers any claim for relief by the applicant.

(Further extracts from Trebilcock will be found in the sections on standard-form contracts and exemption clauses, p 968 and on illegality, p 1116.)

NOTES

1.   Trebilcock characterises the typical duress case as a 'situational monopoly'. How would you describe Denning's case of the poor man who is homeless and has to pay a high rent? Should contract law intervene to upset the bargain in the latter case?

2.   Cases of minors' contracts and contracts with insane persons fit into Trebilcock's second category of 'informationally impaired markets'. We shall see another very important example of this with standard-form contracts: see Chapter 38.

3.   How would you apply Trebilcock's analysis to undue influence?

4.   Do you think English law should introduce a broad doctrine of unconscionability?

5.   Capper (1998) 114 LQR 479 argues for a broader use of unconscionability to include, for instance, undue influence cases.

QUESTIONS

1.   What does a party who wants to avoid a contract on the ground of duress to the person have to prove?

2. Why is the 'vitiation of consent' test so much criticised? What test is now preferred and why?

3. What will constitute economic duress? In particular, what is the relevance of the following factors:
    (i)   whether the victim had an legal remedy that it might have sought?
    (ii)   whether it had an alternative course of action of another kind?
    (iii) the degree to which its decision to make the promise that it seeks to avoid was influenced by other factors besides the wrongful threat?
    (iv)   whether the action threatened would be a legal wrong in itself?
    (v)   whether the party making the threat acted in good or bad faith?
    (vi)   whether what the threatening party was promised was, in the light of the transaction as a whole, fair or unfair?
    (vii) whether the victim had legal advice?
    (viii) whether the victim protested?
    (ix)   whether the victim took immediate steps to avoid the contract once the threat had ceased?

4. For the purposes of undue influence, when will a confidential relationship be assumed? If the case is not one in which there is an automatic presumption, what has to be shown in order to establish a confidential relationship?

5. If a confidential relationship is presumed or shown to exist, when will the presumption of undue influence arise? How may it be rebutted?

6. What sort of thing might constitute actual undue influence?

7. In what circumstances will a contract between A and B be voidable because of undue influence, duress or misrepresentation by a third person, C?

8. In English law, what must be shown before a transaction may be set aside as an unconscionable bargain? To what extent does the Australian *Amadio* case go beyond English law?

9. A householder is told by a jobbing builder that her roof needs repairs, which is true. She accepts his offer to do the work, which he carries out satisfactorily. She then discovers that the price she has agreed to pay is about three times the normal rate for the job. Can she obtain any relief if (i) she is to pay by instalments; (ii) she had agreed to pay a lump sum in cash?

10. *Should* the law give relief in such a case? What arguments can be made for or against doing so?

11. Do you think that it was a shame or a good thing that the courts did not accept Lord Denning's suggested general doctrine of inequality of bargaining power? What arguments may be made on either side?

CHAPTER THIRTY-EIGHT

STANDARD-FORM CONTRACTS

■ Kessler, 'Contracts of Adhesion—Some Thoughts about Freedom of Contract' (1943)
Col LR 629, at 631–632

The development of large scale enterprise with its mass production and mass distribution made a new type of contract inevitable—the standardized mass contract. A standardized contract, once its contents have been formulated by a business firm, is used in every bargain dealing with the same product or service. The individuality of the parties which so frequently gave color to the old type contract has disappeared. The stereotyped contract of today reflects the impersonality of the market. It has reached its greatest perfection in the different types of contracts used on the various exchanges. Once the usefulness of these contracts was discovered and perfected in the transportation, insurance, and banking business, their use spread into all other fields of large scale enterprise, into international as well as national trade, and into labor relations. It is to be noted that uniformity of terms of contracts typically recurring in a business enterprise is an important factor in the exact calculation of risks. Risks which are difficult to calculate can be excluded altogether. Unforeseeable contingencies affecting performance, such as strikes, fire, and transportation difficulties can be taken care of. The standard clauses in insurance policies are the most striking illustrations of successful attempts on the part of business enterprises to select and control risks assumed under a contract. The insurance business probably deserves credit also for having first realized the full importance of the so-called 'juridical risk', the danger that a court or jury may be swayed by 'irrational factors', to decide against a powerful defendant. Ingenious clauses have been the result. Once their practical utility was proven, they were made use of in other lines of business. It is highly probable that the desire to avoid juridical risks has been a motivating factor in the widespread use of warranty clauses in the machine industry limiting the common law remedies of the buyer to breach of an implied warranty of quality and particularly excluding his right to claim damages. The same is true for arbitration clauses in international trade. Standardized contracts have thus become an important means of excluding or controlling the 'irrational factor' in litigation. In this respect they are a true reflection of the spirit of our time with its hostility to irrational factors in the judicial process, and they belong in the same category as codifications and restatements.

In so far as the reduction of costs of production and distribution thus achieved is reflected in reduced prices, society as a whole ultimately benefits from the use of standard contracts. And there can be no doubt that this has been the case to a considerable extent. The use of standard contracts has, however, another aspect which has become increasingly important. Standard contracts are typically used by enterprises with strong bargaining power. The weaker party, in need of the goods or services, is frequently not in a position to shop around for better terms, either because the author of the standard contract has a monopoly (natural or artificial) or because all competitors use the same clauses. His contractual intention is but a subjection more or less voluntary to terms dictated by the stronger party, terms whose consequences are often understood only in a vague way, if at all. Thus, standardized contracts are frequently contracts of adhesion; they are *à prendre ou à laisser*. Not infrequently the weaker party to a prospective contract even agrees in advance not to retract his offer while the offeree reserves for himself the power to accept or refuse, or he submits to terms or change of terms which will be communicated to him later. To be sure, the latter type of clauses regularly provide for a power to disaffirm, but as a practical matter they are acquiesced in frequently, thus becoming part of the 'living law'. Lastly, standardized contracts have also been used to control and regulate the distribution of goods from producer all the way down to the ultimate consumer. They have become one of the many devices to build up and strengthen industrial empires.

NOTE

It has been said that Kessler's analysis represents what has been termed the 'exploitation theory' of standardised contracts (see Priest (1981) 80 Yale L J 1267, at 1299–1302. An extreme statement of the exploitation theory will be found in Kahn-Freund, Introduction to Renner, *The Institutions of Private Law*, 1949, pp 38–39). We shall see later (pp 968 ff) that there is good reason to doubt whether the exploitation analysis is an accurate description of the effects of the use of standard-form contracts by business concerns. However, this approach has been very influential among academics and the judiciary both in England and the USA.

■ *A Schroeder Music Publishing Co Ltd v Macaulay* [1974]
3 All ER 616, House of Lords

Lord Diplock

. . . Standard forms of contracts are of two kinds. The first, of very ancient origin, are those which set out the terms on which mercantile transactions of common occurrence are to be carried out. Examples are bills of lading, charterparties, policies of insurance, contracts of sale in the commodity markets. The standard clauses in these contracts have been settled over the years by negotiation by representatives of the commercial interests involved and have been widely adopted because experience has shown that they facilitate the conduct of trade. Contracts of these kinds affect not only the actual parties to them but also others who may have a commercial interest in the transactions to which they relate, as buyers or sellers, charterers or shipowners, insurers or bankers. If fairness or reasonableness were relevant to their enforceability the fact that they are widely used by parties whose bargaining power is fairly matched would raise a strong presumption that their terms are fair and reasonable.

The same presumption, however, does not apply to the other kind of standard form of contract. This is of comparatively modern origin. It is the result of the concentration of particular kinds of business in relatively few hands. The ticket cases in the 19th century provide what are probably the first examples. The terms of this kind of standard form of contract have not been the subject of negotiation between the parties to it, or approved by any organisation representing the interests of the weaker party. They have been dictated by the party whose bargaining power, either exercised alone or in conjunction with others providing similar goods of services, enables him to say: 'If you want these goods or services at all, these are the only terms on which they are obtainable. Take it or leave it.'

To be in a position to adopt this attitude towards a party desirous of entering into a contract to obtain goods or services provides a classic instance of superior bargaining power.

Thus it seems that standard-form contracts are a mixed blessing. They enable business to save costs but they may enable one party to dictate terms to the other. As a result, the weaker party may find that she has to agree to clauses that she considers unfair. These may include clauses that define what the other party has to do in unacceptably narrow ways (eg 'exceptions' in an insurance policy), that allow the other party to increase the price, that allow it to terminate the contract at its convenience without compensation, that require a large pre payment that will be forfeited if she cancels the contract, and so on (for further examples, see p 1040).

Is the 'take or leave it' nature of the standard-form contract the only problem? Until recently, the debate in the United Kingdom has been largely about one particular kind of clause often contained in standard-form contracts: exclusion (or exemption) clauses. The law that has been developed around these clauses will be considered in the next chapter, but at this stage, you may find it useful to read the following extract from Law Commission Report No 69, because the points it makes apply to many types of clause found in standard-form contracts.

■ **'Second Report on Exemption Clauses in Contracts' (No 69) (Law Commission)** (1975)
paras 11, 146

THE CASE FOR CONTROL

11. It is clear that exemption clauses are much used both in dealings with private individuals and in purely commercial transactions. We are in no doubt that in many cases they operate against the public interest and that the prevailing judicial attitude of suspicion, or indeed of hostility, to such clauses is well founded. All too often they are introduced in ways which result in the party affected by them remaining ignorant of their presence or import until it is too late. That party, even if he knows of the exemption clause, will often be unable to appreciate what he may lose by accepting it. In any case, he may not have sufficient bargaining strength to refuse to accept it. The result is that the risk; of carelessness or of fail-ure to achieve satisfactory standards of performance is thrown on to the party who is not responsible for it or who is unable to guard against it. Moreover, by excluding liability for such carelessness or failure the economic pressures to maintain high standards of performance are reduced. There is no doubt that the misuse of these clauses is objectionable. Some are unjustified. Others, however may operate fairly or unfairly, efficiently or inefficiently depending on the circumstances: for example, the cost and practica-bility of insurance may be factors in determining how liability should be apportioned between two con-tracting parties. The problem of devising satisfactory methods of controlling the use of these clauses, and indeed of identifying some of them, has proved both difficult and complicated.

146. . . . We do not propose to define exemption clauses in general terms: we regard this expression not as a legal term of art but as a convenient label for a number of provisions which may be mischievous in broadly the same way. Their mischief is that they deprive or may deprive the person against whom they may be involved either of certain specific rights which social policy requires that he should have (for example the right of a buyer in a consumer sale to be supplied with goods of merchantable quality, the right of a person to whom a service has be supplied to a reasonable standard of care and skill on the part of the supplier) or of rights which the promisee reasonably believed that the promisor had conferred upon him.

NOTES

1.   These passages seem to identify three distinct problems with exclusion clauses. Firstly, the party affected may remain 'ignorant of their presence or import until it is too late'. The commentary to UCC s 2–302 (above) terms this 'unfair surprise'. Sometimes, refer-ences to 'inequality of bargaining power' seem to refer to this problem: it might be bet-ter to call it 'inequality of information' or 'inequality of bargaining sophistication'. Compare the extracts from Trebilcock, pp 959–962 and pp 968–973.

2. Secondly, the party 'may not have sufficient bargaining strength to refuse to accept it'. This is lack of bargaining power in a different and more accurate sense—the party does not have enough influence to get the terms changed. It seems to be this to which Lord Diplock was referring (see p 965), although below we shall question whether he was right to attribute the problem to 'the concentration of particular kinds of business in relatively few hands' (see p 968).

3. Thirdly, the clauses may deprive the party 'of certain specific rights which social policy requires that he should have'. As you read the pages that follow, you may like to ponder on what rights fall into this category, and on how this statement is to be reconciled with the notion of freedom of contract.

Although English law first developed controls over exclusion clauses (see the next chapter), it has long been recognised that other types of term found in standard-form contracts can also operate harshly and may equally need to be controlled. We have already seen examples of statutory controls over clauses permitting termination and repossession of property in consumer credit agreements (see p 589). We have also seen that there are some controls at common law, such as the rules on penalty clauses and deposits, although these rules are not limited to standard-form contracts or even to cases of inequality of bargaining power. Now, as the result of the EC Directive on Unfair Terms in Consumer Contracts, there are controls over any unfair term that is contained in a consumer contract and which has not been individually negotiated (see Chapter 40). As we shall see, there is a substantial overlap between the Regulations implementing this Directive and the statutory controls over exclusion clauses introduced by the Unfair Contract Terms Act 1977.

Why are harsh clauses (whether exclusion clauses or clauses of other types) a particular problem in standard-form contracts?

Some commentators seem to deny that there is a problem at all.

If one seller offers unattractive terms to a purchaser, a competing seller, desiring to obtain the sale for himself, will offer more attractive terms. The process should continue until the terms are optimal from the purchaser's standpoint. Thus, the purchaser who is offered a printed contract on a take-it-or-leave-it basis does have a real choice: he can refuse to sign, knowing that if better terms are possible another seller will offer them to him. (Posner, *Economic Analysis of Law*, 2nd edn, p 85)

■ Goldberg, 'Institutional Change and the Quasi-Invisible Hand' (1974)
17 J Law and Economics 461, 483–486

...[Turn to] the problem of the standard form contract. The truncated self-interest model treats the problem by assuming it away. If people voluntarily enter into contracts it is because it is in their best interest to do so. If the terms of one producer are unsatisfactory, the customer will shop around for others; if information on contract terms were costlessly available (and could be analyzed costlessly) he would continue shopping until he received precisely the desired combination of price, quantity, and other contract terms. This, implicitly, is how economists have handled the problem. Additional sophistication occasionally creeps in by the recognition of costs of attaining, processing, and evaluating information; the consumer then would engage in such information processing to the point at which the expected marginal benefits of the additional information are equated to the marginal costs of its acquisition.

Suppose, however, that rather than view the standard form contract as a voluntary agreement, we view it instead as private legislation; the legislature in effect delegates the lawmaking process to private parties. The previous analysis suggests the bias that this 'legislation' might have. We will first stipulate that we are interested here only in the 'hidden' terms of the contract—those beside the basic price and quantity terms. While such terms could be tailor-made for each contract, there are substantial economies to be gained by spreading the costs of producing (and analyzing the impact of) these terms over a large number of contracts. The firm, which regularly enters into the same type of transactions, will be able to achieve these economies (either by itself or by purchasing the service from specialists—lawyers); the consumer, generally, will not. The standard form contract therefore will be legislation produced in an arena which rewards the resources held by one party—the firm. The result, in Llewellyn's words 'has seemed even in such highly competitive spheres as installment sales, residence leases, investments, and commercial banking to be . . . [the] accumulation of seller-protective instead of customer-protective clauses.'

We might expect competition in the market to constrain the firm's power in this arena. After all, the firm makes its price in this arena too, and if the industry is reasonably competitive we would expect that this competition would shield the price taker from the firm's power. Why will not competition among producers protect the contract term taker as well? The answer is twofold. On the one hand the cost of acquiring and processing information on contract terms is much greater than for price; unless the firm intentionally makes the particular term an important selling point—as is sometimes the case with the length or inclusiveness of the warranty—few, if any, customers will perceive the existence of variations in terms. Any movement toward contractual equilibrium due to the aggressive bargain-seeking of a few customers will be slow indeed due to both (1) the fewness of customers who will find it worthwhile to pay the costs of acquiring information, and (2) the ease with which a producer can 'contract term discriminate'— renegotiate the terms for the few aggressive customers while keeping the high information barrier for other customers virtually intact. The second answer is that the 'aggressive bargain-seeking customer' is usually just a minor figure in the equilibrating process. More important, in general, is the role of new entry (or exit) of producers. If the firms in an industry are making profits because they have written standardized contract terms that are very favorable to them, they will attract new entrants into the industry. The entry will continue until excess profits are bid away. The benefits to the firms of the standardized terms will be capitalized into the firms' value. Thus, while competition between producers will in the long run yield zero profits, the firm will be able to attain a capital gain (or prevent a capital loss) by choosing the appropriate standard contract terms.

This does not necessarily mean, however, that the industry as a whole will be better off or that the industry's gains will come at the expense of the consumer. It might well be that the equilibrium terms arrived at are optimal for both producers and consumers, but there is no reason to presume this to be true. Consider, for example, the following scenario. Assume a competitive insurance industry with minimal government intervention. Firms in the industry compete by lowering their price and then compensate for this by decreasing the coverage (in as hidden a way as possible) with other firms being forced to cut also in order to remain competitive. A sort of 'Gresham's Law' of bad policies driving out good would ensue. Both the quality of insurance contracts and the total sales of the industry are likely to fall.

This is not the end of the story. Both producers and consumers will have incentives to search for methods for improving upon this result. Ignoring solutions relying on an active government . . . a number of solutions might arise. Brand names and advertising might be used as indicators of product quality in general (including the terms of the contract); consumers might take price as an indicator of quality; or private producers of information might appear. While such private market solutions will, to some extent, ameliorate the Gresham's Law problem considered in the previous paragraph, there is no reason to believe that the market will negate the standard form contract problem.

■ Trebilcock, 'An Economic Approach to Unconscionability' in Reiter and Swan (eds), *Studies in Contract Law*
pp 398–400, 412–421

While recognizing that the assumptions underlying [Lord Diplock's] analysis of the use of standard form contracts have enjoyed considerable academic currency, it is submitted that they are fallacious. First, the proposition that the use of consumer standard-form contracts is the result of the concentration of market power is entirely without factual foundation. The reason why such contracts are used is exactly the same as for their use in the commercial context, that is to 'facilitate the conduct of trade', or in economic terms, to reduce transaction costs. If an agreement had to be negotiated and drafted from scratch every time a relatively standard transaction was entered into the costs of transacting for all parties involved would escalate dramatically. Moreover, it is a matter of common observation that standard forms are used (for this reason) in countless contexts where no significant degree of market concentration exists. Dry-cleaners have standard form dry-cleaning agreements, hotels standard registration forms, credit-grantors standard financing agreements, insurance companies standard life, fire, and automobile insurance policies, real estate agents standard sale and purchase agreements, landlords standard leases, restaurants set menu and price lists, and, for that matter, department and grocery stores set product ranges and price terms. The fact that in these cases a supplier's products are offered on a take-it-or-leave-it basis is evidence not of market power but of a recognition that neither producer nor consumer interests are served by incurring the costs involved in negotiating separately every transaction. Moreover, even the presence of dickering between parties, standing alone, is ambiguous as between the presence or absence of competition. Dickering may, for example, be merely a reflection of attempts by a monopolist to price discriminate among consumers by ascertaining and exploiting different demand elasticities. The use of standard forms is a totally spurious proxy for the existence of market power. The real measure of market power is not whether a supplier presents his terms on a take-it-or-leave-it basis but whether the consumer, if he decides to 'leave it' has available to him a workably competitive range of alternative sources of supply. Whether this is or is not so simply cannot be derived intuitively from the fact that a particular supplier is offering non-negotiable standard-form terms. It is a matter for independent inquiry. If the market is workably competitive, any supplier offering uncompetitive standard-form terms will have to reformulate his total package of price and non-price terms to prevent consumers (at least consumers at the margin, which are the decisive consideration in such a market) from switching their business to other competitors.

It is, of course, true that general use of common standard-form contracts throughout an industry may, on occasion, be evidence of cartelization. But here one must be discriminating. If a reasonable choice of different packages of price and non-price terms is available in the market, albeit all through the medium of different standard-form contracts, then obviously the allegation of a 'fix' will not stand up. Even where all contracts are the same, in perfectly competitive markets where the product is homogeneous, commonality of terms is what one would expect to find (for example, the wheat market). Every supplier simply 'takes' his price and probably other terms from the market and is powerless to vary them. In a perfectly competitive market, with many sellers and many buyers each supplying or demanding too insignificant a share of total market output to influence terms, all participants, sellers and buyers, are necessarily confronted with a take-it-or-leave-it proposition. Thus uniformity of terms, standing alone, is ambiguous as between the presence or absence of competition. . . .

(iii) Information problems with standard form contracts

Courts and commentators alike have commonly taken the view of standard form contracts that the party who draws them up has a disproportionate bargaining power in terms of his ability to impose terms involuntarily on the other party. To use Lord Reid's language in *Suisse Atlantique*, 'the consumer has not time to read [standard form clauses], and if he did read them, he would probably not understand them. And if he did understand and object to any of them, he would generally be told he could take it or leave it'. Assuming for the purposes of argument that Lord Reid correctly describes the typical bargaining process entailed when a consumer enters into a contract with a supplier on standard form terms, does it follow that the supplier has an unconstrained ability to impose uncompensated risks unilaterally on an uninformed consumer? We have already examined the market structure argument in this respect, and rejected it. However, the issue remains whether information imperfections afflicting a consumer in this context are such as to lead to unconscionable contractual outcomes even in structurally sound markets. The disclaimer clause/fundamental breach cases are the classic example of the courts attempting to struggle with the answer to this question. A number of difficult conceptual issues are raised by the question of the abuse of bargaining power through differential information about the content of stand-ard form contracts.

First, even in cases where Lord Reid's theorem is factually accurate, it does not follow that the sup-plier has unconstrained bargaining power to impose any terms that he wishes on a consumer. One of the most important determinants of whether contract terms in such circumstances might be consid-ered fair, in the sense of having been effectively disciplined by market forces, is whether at the *margin* of the market, there are *enough* consumers who are sensitive to the content of these clauses to bring effective pressure to bear on suppliers to modify them in an acceptable way. Non-economists often overlook the importance of marginal analysis in this context. For example, if only 10 per cent of the buyers of insurance policies or dry-cleaning services studied all terms scrupulously before contracting and were influenced in their choice of policy by their evaluation of the so-called fine print clauses, and if no supplier of insurance or dry-cleaning services was able to 'term discriminate' between these con-sumers and other consumers in the market, there would be strong competitive pressures on each sup-plier to adjust the terms of his contracts so as to avoid losing this potential business. Perhaps more important than the impact of marginal consumers on the initial formulation of standard form contract terms is their impact on the subsequent enforcement of these terms. For example, no matter how dra-conian the exculpatory clauses in insurance polices or dry-cleaning contracts, few, if any, suppliers in either market will be able to survive the market reactions likely to be engendered by a supplier treat-ing these clauses as defining the limits of his required performance. A dry cleaner who loses or ruins half the suits that are brought in for cleaning is likely to find little long-term solace in exculpatory clauses on his dry-cleaning tickets (even if enforceable).

A recognition of the importance of the marginal consumer confronts a court with intractable factual issues pertaining to how 'thick' the margin of sophisticated consumers is in the relevant market and how well a supplier is able to discriminate in favour of those consumers and against the inframarginal con-sumers. Both issues are difficult. As in the case of market-wide monopolies, the first issue requires evi-dence and analysis of conditions prevailing throughout the market in question. The question of whether discrimination is occurring on a non-cost justified basis is one of the most notoriously difficult issues in the whole of anti-trust law. A supplier, in deciding whether to avail himself of terms in a contract which excuse sub-normal performance will have to reckon with a potential consumer reaction that treats this as tantamount to contractual non-performance. This may take the form of threats to initiate legal pro-ceedings, threats to withdraw future business, or threats to undermine the supplier's credibility with other potential customers. It is primarily consumers who cannot make credible threats of these kinds, and who can be identified and thus discriminated against by suppliers at economic cost, who are most vulnerable to overreaching through standard form contracts.

In the light of these factors, it can be appreciated that the courts face a real problem in looking at the fairness of a standard form contract in the context of some particular transaction and assuming that sim-ply because the particular consumer had not studied, understood, or negotiated about, the terms, the supplier was free of effective constraints on the terms included in the transaction or, as importantly, on the performance called for thereunder. Again, the ability of the court to weigh these kinds of market-wide considerations may be very limited.

Second, even if a court were to decide that a particular market was functioning imperfectly because of information breakdowns in that market, the appropriate remedial response on the part of the courts is by no means clear. One line of attack on fine-print clauses in standard form contracts, based on per-ceived aberrations in the bargaining process, derives from the so-called Coase theorem. This theorem asserts that, in a world of zero transaction costs, irrespective of the legal allocation of risks, the mutual interests of the parties will tend to lead them to bargain their way to the most efficient allocation of risks, that is, the risk allocation that maximizes the joint value of their respective resources, in which state, in a Pareto optimal sense, both parties are better off. If, on the other hand, transaction costs are significant, at least in relation to the stakes involved, allocative efficiency may not be achieved through voluntary exchange, and liability rules may be justified which attempt to stimulate the market outcomes that would have occurred had frictionless exchange been possible.

The Coase theorem does not permit of a straightforward application to the standard-form contractual setting, for, unlike many tort cases where *a priori* bargaining over allocation is impossible, in standard-form contracts some voluntary interaction, by definition, occurs. One implication from this is that in those areas of a transaction where bargaining does typically occur, one might often expect to find adjustments made which are designed to offset any legal allocations of risks in areas of the transaction where information and transaction costs arguably prevent negotiation. Thus, importantly, in this context, the general balance of advantage between the parties may not be significantly affected by the law's intervention.

From broadly these premises, Goldberg has argued that in the case of standard-form insurance policies, the costs to the consumer of obtaining, processing, and evaluating information about the implications of 'hidden', subsidiary clauses in such contracts will tend to direct competitive forces, even in workably competitive markets, away from the subject-matter of these clauses and towards broader price-quantity comparisons. The result of such a process may be harsh-term-low-price policies, whereas many consumers, in the absence of information and transaction costs, may have preferred an easier-term-higher-price combination. Thus, bargaining processes are distorted. This may be so, Goldberg argues, even though the industry is making no supra-competitive profits. Therefore the argument goes, the industry would be made no worse off, and many consumers might be made better off, by liability rules designed to produce the mix of terms that would have been reached by the parties in a world without information or transaction costs. Unlike rules designed to improve the quality of available information discussed below, these rules would take information markets as given and simply regulate the substantive contents of contracts.

There are several difficulties with Goldberg's argument. First, even assuming that information and transaction costs relative to the stakes involved in matters dealt with in subsidiary terms (for example, the termination and assignment provisions in *Macaulay*) are as high as Goldberg asserts, how does one determine whether more or fewer consumers will be advantaged under a legal reallocation of risks which produces an easier-term-high-price contract and displaces previous harsher-term-lower-price combinations, given that on Goldberg's hypothesis, information costs are such that consumers' true preferences can never be revealed?

If the answer to this is that in fact one must look for some kind of revealed preference on the part of the general body of affected consumers, say in the form of transactions which reallocate offered risks which a minority of consumers are left bearing (unwittingly), then one is conceding that transaction costs are not generally so high as to prevent voluntary reallocation of risks, and firms in the industry will have an incentive to reflect the generally preferred combination of terms in adjustments to their standard-form contracts, thus avoiding needless transaction costs.

A further factor unaccounted for in Goldberg's analysis, as in that of other critics of standard-form contracts who point to the absence of subjective consumer consent to all contractual terms, is the price that most consumers attach to uncertainty. Making the usual assumption that most consumers are risk-averse, consumers who sign contracts containing clauses which have been drafted by the other party with his advantage obviously in mind and which they do not understand will reflect their aversion to the assumption of undetermined, but intuitively adverse, risk allocations by discounting the consideration they are prepared to offer for entering into such contracts.

Finally, if courts were to impose liability rules on parties to standard form contracts on Goldberg's rationale, then *ex post ad hoc* judicial interventions cannot fairly take the form simply of invalidating 'harsh' clauses. In addition, other clauses will have to be reworked to compensate the supplier for the expanded package of contractual benefits which he is now providing to the consumer. In effect, this form of judicial policing of standard-form contracts should strictly involve reformulating whole contracts. If substantive intervention is to occur, this may argue for general, *ex ante*, legislative intervention where 'harsh' terms are invalidated and the market is permitted to take care of consequential adjustments to other terms.

Even if the preferred policy response is not outright prohibition or replacement of certain terms, but rather conditional prohibition in the sense that terms are only prohibited if they fail to meet some test of comprehensibility (rules against unfair surprise), another difficult set of issues must be faced. Even if one were to assume that some of the more common categories of standard form contracts, eg conditional sales contracts, insurance contracts, were all printed in large print and written in English that anybody with a grade 6 education and modest intelligence could read, it is not clear that this would prove an effective response to the information problem in many cases. Intuitively, one suspects many consumers would continue not to read most of these kinds of contracts in any detail before signing them. When one asks why, many consumers probably rely in part on the constraints imposed by other consumers at the margin (ie, they let the market shop for them). More importantly, they are probably recognizing that the information problem they often face is not figuring out what particular clauses mean in the sense of how they are allocating certain risks, but instead the problem of relating that information in a meaning-ful way to their personal circumstances. For example, in the case of an insurance policy which allocates risks in different ways between myself and my insurance company, I may understand perfectly how the pol-icy allocates those risks, but what I may have difficulty in assessing is how likely it is that certain risks may materialize, and if they do, what kinds of costs are likely to be entailed. Thus, how likely is it, as a matter of probability, that my house will catch on fire, and if it does, how much damage is likely to be done? If there are exemptions for earthquakes. Acts of God, fires caused in certain ways, certain classes of property, etc. my problem lies in assessing whether my personal circumstances at any given time during the currency of the policy will fall within one of these clauses and what costs will be entailed for me if it does. This is not information which can be conveyed by the policy, or at least not easily, and as between the insurance com-pany and myself, this may be information to which I have superior access (no matter how difficult), relative to the insurance company (which may in part explain why coverage for certain kinds of risks is excluded). Moreover, even if all clauses in all insurance policies were clearly written, I would face a formidable task in comparing alternative offerings, which involves figuring out a net worth for the various policies given dif-ferent patterns of coverage and exemption. Again, it is difficult to see how improving the clarity or con-spicuousness of what are at present fine print clauses can address this problem. In other words, it is one thing to acquire relevant information: it may be quite another thing to process it effectively. . . .

III Distributive considerations in the application of the doctrine of unconscionability

In the course of this essay, circumstances have been identified where lack of endowments might well lead to circumstances which justify intervention by the courts to prevent contract enforcement. For example, it was pointed out that poverty may in some cases be conducive to the creation of situational monopolies. Secondly, poverty as it manifests itself in illiteracy, lack of education, or lack of experience with market activity may provide grounds for intervention on the grounds of impaired information-processing ability. However, outside limited cases of this kind, this essay has not suggested distributive considerations as a major underpinning for a judicial doctrine of unconscionability. It is important to elaborate on why this view has been taken.

First, while it is clear that poor people often will be compelled, eg, to enter into consumer credit trans-actions at very high rates of interest, or to rent accommodation of very low quality, it is not at all clear that this apparently differential treatment of poor people in the marketplace is in any way attributable to objectionable behaviour on the part of the suppliers who deal with them. Even though the demand on the part of poor people for necessities of life may be highly inelastic, ie, unresponsive to price, given their resources, it does not follow from that fact alone that they will be exploited. Exploitation will only occur, in the sense of a charging of supra-competitive prices etc, if there are restrictions on supply in the relevant markets. Studies of low-income markets disclose with remarkable consistency that the rates of return earned by merchants in these markets are entirely normal. Thus, however objectionable the dis-tributive outcomes from these markets, the source of the problem does not lie with the supply side of the market but instead with the simple fact of lack of endowments and the implications this carries for successful participation in market activity. Moreover, the objectionable conditions are not amenable to abatement by judicial intervention which prevents contract enforcement. As again many studies of low-income markets have shown, this simply produces substitution effects, with resources being moved away from low income consumers in such markets. For example, consumer credit will be withdrawn from low income consumers if constraints are imposed on the interest rates that can be charged or collection remedies that can be invoked. Rental accommodation is withdrawn from such markets if rent controls are imposed at below competitive levels. Thus, acknowledging both that suppliers in such markets are not the source of the problem, and judicial intervention in contract enforcement will not alleviate the problem and indeed will often aggravate it, it is submitted that the doctrine of unconscionability should not be given a significant realm of application in this context.

Beyond the conventional poverty context, there is a question of whether despite no clear evidence of a structurally or informationally impaired market, and no clear evidence of a substantial divergence between a party's returns from a contract and returns otherwise available from similar transactions in the market. . . . it might still be plausible to conclude, in the case of a particular transaction, that the values exchanged are so disproportionate to each other that in some sense the bargain is distributively 'unfair'.

As Left has pointed out, the concept of substantive unfairness in the sense of a judicially perceived non-equivalence in the values exchanged by contracting parties, poses real conceptual difficulties following a determination of (1) no abnormal market power and (2) no aberrations in the process of contract formation. Almost by definition, the outcome of such a process cannot be unfair.

NOTES

1. For an explanation of the Coase theorem, see p 78.

2. Goldberg argues that customers will tend to shop in terms of price alone. Why? What information-processing problems are customers likely to face?

3. What is the result of these information problems? Are customers being exploited in terms of monopoly pricing? If not, are the contracts that are made not efficient?

4. Both the Law Commission (see p 966) and Lord Reid (see pp 989–990) make the point that even a consumer who is aware of the clause in question may have no choice but to accept it or do without the goods or service. In the light of the analysis presented, is this surprising? To produce a 'one-off' contract for him would often be very expensive—so much so, that he will seldom be prepared to pay the extra cost. On the other hand, as Schwartz, 'Seller Unequal Bargaining Power and the Judicial Process' (1974) 49 Ind LJ 367, at 370–371, remarks:

   Although it may be difficult to establish whether an individual buyer could or could not have affected a particular term, it is generally true that most buyers will be able to avoid any one term, if they concentrate their entire resources on doing so.

5. Even if the supplier using standard terms is a monopolist, there is no particular reason to think that the terms on which he will offer goods or services will be harsher, except that he will charge more for them: see Schwartz, ibid, pp 380–381.

6. Goldberg argues that suppliers cut costs by putting more and more risks onto the customers via the harsh standard terms. Are there any constraints on how far suppliers will go in this? What constraints?

7. Trebilcock suggests that it only needs a margin of customers to shop around for there to be pressure on suppliers to offer better terms to all. Thus even if there were no negotiations over the clause between the individual parties, it does not follow that the apparently harsh clause is, in fact, inefficient. It is possible that the contract represents the balance between risk and price that the 'active margin' of customers prefers. The question must be whether there is a 'thick enough' margin of aware customers to have had any impact.

8. It seems unlikely that a court will have any direct evidence about the 'thickness of the margin'. How might a court try to work this out? Is it relevant whether the clause has ever been the subject of negotiation between, say, suppliers and purchasers' trade or consumer associations? Whether the clause is one that relates to a well-known risk? Whether it is obvious in the documents and easy to understand?

9. Trebilcock distinguishes the question of whether the clause is included in the initial contract from whether it is relied on later by the supplier. (His example is bizarre: a dry cleaner that ruined half the suits would go out of business clause or no clause. What is important is whether when something does go wrong, the supplier 'stands on its rights'.) As he points out, there is much greater scope for discrimination between customers here. As we shall see, the courts have sometimes been harsh on suppliers who discriminate in this way (see pp 1014 ff).

CHAPTER THIRTY-NINE

EXCLUSION CLAUSES

The problem with standard-form contracts is that they may contain apparently unfair terms. In particular, they frequently contain exclusion or limitation clauses, clauses that exclude some right which one of the parties would otherwise have had under the common law, or reduce the remedies available to him. Both the courts and the legislature in England have been particularly concerned with such clauses, and in this chapter, we shall examine the rules that have been developed.

Many types of exclusion (or 'exemption') and limitation clauses are found. Here are some examples.

(1) *Limiting the compensation for a breach of contract*: '... provided always that our total liability for loss, damage or injury shall not exceed the total value of the contract.' *(Harbutt's Plasticine Ltd v Wayne Tank and Pump Co Ltd* [1970] 1 QB 447, noted on pp 661 and 990)

(2) *Limiting the remedies available*: 'Whatever the difference of the shipment may be in value from the grade, type or description specified ... such question shall not ... entitle the buyers to reject the delivery or any part thereof.' *(J Aron & Co Inc v Comptoir Wegimont* [1921] 3 KB 435)

(3) *Limiting the time during which a remedy is available*: 'The goods delivered shall be deemed to be in all respects in accordance with the contract ... unless the sellers shall within 14 days after the arrival of the goods ... receive notice ...' *(Beck & Co v Szymanowski* [1924] AC 43)

(4) *Imposing a condition on the remedy*: '... limited to making good at its factory any part or parts thereof which shall ... be returned to it with transportation charges prepaid.'

(5) *Excluding normal rules of evidence*: '... the Final Certificate ... shall constitute conclusive evidence for all purposes and in any proceedings whatsoever ... that the contractor has completed the design of the works and completed the works ... in all respects in accordance with the contract.' (I Chem E conditions of contract for process plant, 1st edn)

(6) *Excluding express or implied terms*: 'No condition or warranty that the vehicle is roadworthy or as to its age, condition or fitness for any purpose is given by the owner or implied herein.' *(Karsales (Harrow) Ltd v Wallis* [1956] 2 All ER 866; see p 985)

(7) *Giving one party a broad discretion over the manner or the substance of performance*: 'Steamers, sailing dates, rates and itineraries are subject to change without notice.' *(Anglo-Continental Holidays Ltd v Typaldos Lines (London) Ltd* [1967] 2 Lloyd's Rep 61; see further p 1009)

Further examples will be found in the cases that follow.

As with contract law generally, there is not a great deal of empirical evidence on the use of exclusion clauses. Yates conducted a small survey in Bristol and Manchester on the use of clauses in contracts between commercial organisations and in consumer contracts: see Yates, *Exclusion Clauses in Contracts*, 2nd edn, pp 24–30. See also Livermore [1986] JBL 90.

You will find that the courts tend to be hostile to exclusion clauses and frequently find a means to avoid having to give effect to them. Possible reasons for this hostility were explored in the last chapter.

The cases that follow are ones applying the common law rules about exemption clauses. We will then, in subsection II, look at the statutory controls that have been brought in to supplement the common law. The cases in subsection I mostly involve applying strict construction to the wording of the clause. They demonstrate the courts' hostility, in that some of the constructions seem rather strained, but because this common law 'control' over exemption clauses is an indirect one, the court frequently avoids having to articulate the reasons for its hostility. It is not always clear on what ground the hostility is based. As you read each case, you should ask yourself: what is the purpose of this clause? Is it objectionable or acceptable? Why? Is it objectionable in *any* circumstances, or only in the circumstances of this case? To take up some of the points made in the extracts from the Law Commission Report, is the problem that the party affected did not know of the clause? That he would not have understood it to have the effect contended for? That he could not have obtained what he wanted without the clause? Or that the clause deprives him of some specific right that 'social policy requires that he should have'? What would have been the effect on the contract as a whole if one party had insisted on the clause being deleted? If the court by one means or another refuses to give effect to the clause, what will be the effect on similar contracts in the future?

The theme of how the controls over exemption clauses can be reconciled with freedom of contract is one that will recur often. It is important not only at the theoretical level but also at the technical one. How far can the parties make their own contract, rather than having to select one of a number of standardised 'contract types', each with its own 'central obligations' that cannot necessarily be altered?

At the technical level, the debate usually appears in this form: should an exclusion or limitation clause be treated as a kind of defensive mechanism that operates to restrict 'normal liability' and which may be 'disallowed' in certain circumstances, or should it be treated as defining what is being undertaken in the first place, so that it should be given equal weight to the other terms of the contract?

It has been argued that an exclusion clause merely defines what is being undertaken and should be given equal weight to the other terms of the contract: see Coote, *Exception Clauses*, 1964, especially chapters 1 and 8 and Lord Diplock's speech in the *Photo Productions* case (see p 611). On occasion, particularly when the clause concerned is unobjectionable, the courts have approached the matter this way, saying that the clause is part of the definition of what is to be done and should be given full effect (for examples, see p 981 note 5 and p 983 note 5). More usually, the courts have tended not to take this approach, but to view exclusion clauses as defensive and to be given second place to the positive obligations under the contract. Thus exclusion clauses are usually interpreted narrowly, so as to leave the positive obligations as far as possible unaffected. The main statute, the Unfair Contract Terms Act 1977 (UCTA), takes the same line: in certain situations, exclusion clauses are invalidated, leaving the parties subject to the 'normal liability'.

As the extract from the Law Commission report suggests, there are often very good reasons for doing this, but on occasion, this approach might result in the contract becoming rather different to what either party envisaged. A farmer who has sold a horse as 'warranted sound except for hunting' might have just cause for complaint if, as the result of judicial or statutory intervention, she were made liable for providing a hunter, just as an insurance company that had insured a car against damage 'except when used for rallying or motor sport' would if it were made to pay out for damage incurred during a race. We shall see instances of the courts recognising this and switching their approach, so that the clause is regarded as a part of the definition of what was being undertaken (see eg below). The extent to which the UCTA leaves the parties free to define their own responsibilities is not wholly clear (see p 999). As we shall see in chapter 40, the same difficulty occurs under the Directive on Unfair Terms in Consumer Contracts.

In the sections that follow, it is assumed that the exclusion clause has been incorporated into the contract, for instance, by forming part of a signed written contract, or by reasonable notice: see pp 332–344.

I. THE COMMON LAW APPROACH TO EXCLUSION CLAUSES: INTERPRETATION

An exclusion clause will always be construed narrowly, against the party who put it forward (*contra proferentem*; see also **p 1027**). In addition to cases applying this general approach, we shall look at a number that employ specific 'rules of construction', or, more properly, interpretative devices, to limit the application of the clause.

An example of the general *contra proferentem* rule being applied is *Andrews Bros (Bournemouth) Ltd v Singer & Co Ltd* [1934] 1 KB 17. In that case, the plaintiffs were appointed by the defendants as dealers for 'new Singer cars'. They contracted to buy a number of such cars under an agreement that provided, inter alia, that 'all conditions, warranties and liabilities implied by statute, common law or otherwise are excluded'. The defendants delivered a car, which was not strictly a 'new' car, because it had already been driven a considerable mileage to be shown to another customer. The Court of Appeal held that the defendants could not rely on the clause, which dealt only with implied terms, since the obligation to deliver a new car was an *express* term.

In *Beck & Co v Szymanowski & Co* [1924] AC 43, cl 5 of a contract for the sale of reels of sewing cotton provided that the goods delivered should be deemed to be in all respects in accordance with the contract unless the sellers were notified within 14 days of delivery. After 18 months, the buyers complained that, on average, each reel contained only 188 yards of cotton instead of the stipulated 200. The House of Lords held that the sellers were not protected by cl 5, which referred to 'goods delivered', whereas the buyers were complaining that a portion of the goods had not been delivered.

A particular application of the *contra proferentem* approach is found in a group of cases involving the question of whether the clause covers negligence. In *White v John Warwick & Co Ltd* [1953] 2 All ER 1021, the plaintiff hired a bicycle from the defendants. Clause 11 of the Agreement provided:

Nothing in this agreement shall render the owners liable for any personal injuries . . .

The plaintiff was thrown from the bicycle and injured when the saddle tilted as he was riding it. The Court of Appeal held that the defendants were liable for negligence: cl 11 excluded their strict liability in contract, but they were also under a duty in tort to take reasonable care, and cl 11 did not cover that.

■ *Hollier v Rambler Motors (AMC) Ltd*

[1972]1 All ER 399, Court of Appeal

The plaintiff took his car to a garage for repairs, as he had done on several previous occasions. Normally he signed a form, which provided:

The company is not responsible for damage caused by fire to customers' cars on the premises.

On the occasion in question, he did not sign the form. His car was damaged in a fire caused by the negligence of the garage. The court held that the form was not incorporated into the contract by a previous course of dealing (see p 340).

Salmon LJ

... That really disposes of this appeal, but in case I am wrong on the view that I have formed, without any hesitation I may say, that the course of dealing did not import the so-called exclusion clause, I think I should deal with the point as to whether or not the words on the bottom of the form, had they been incorporated in the contract, would have excluded the defendants' liability to compensate the plaintiff for damage to the plaintiff's car by a fire which had been caused by the defendant's own negligence. It is well settled that a clause excluding liability for negligence should make its meaning plain on its face to any ordinarily literate and sensible person. The easiest way of doing that, of course, is to state expressly that the garage, tradesman or merchant, as the case may be, will not be responsible for any damage caused by his own negligence. No doubt merchants, tradesmen, garage proprietors and the like are a little shy of writing in an exclusion clause quite so bluntly as that. Clearly it would not tend to attract customers, and might even put many off. I am not saying that an exclusion clause cannot be effective to exclude negligence unless it does so expressly, but in order for the clause to be effective the language should be so plain that it clearly bears that meaning. I do not think that defendants should be allowed to shelter behind language which might lull the customer into a false sense of security by letting him think—unless perhaps he happens to be a lawyer—that he would have redress against the person with whom he was dealing for any damage which he, the customer, might suffer by the negligence of that person.

The principles stated by Scrutton LJ with his usual clarity in *Rutter v Palmer*:

> 'For the present purposes a rougher test will serve. In construing an exemption clause certain general rules may be applied: First the defendant is not exempted from liability for the negligence of his servants unless adequate words are used: secondly, the liability of the defendant apart from the exempting words must be ascertained; then the particular clause in question must be considered; and if the only liability of the party pleading the exemption is a liability for negligence, the clause will more readily operate to exempt him.'

Scrutton LJ was far too great a lawyer, and had far too much robust common sense, if I may be permitted to say so, to put it higher than that 'if the only liability of the party pleading the exemption is a liability for negligence, the clause will more readily operate to exempt him.' He does not say that 'if the only liability of the party pleading the exemption is a liability for negligence, the clause will necessarily exempt him'. After all, there are many cases in the books dealing with exemption clauses, and in every case it comes down to a question of construing the alleged exemption clause which is then before the court. It seems to me that in *Rutter v Palmer*, although the word 'negligence' was never used in the exemption clause, the exemption clause would have conveyed to any ordinary, literate and sensible person that the garage in that case was inserting a clause in the contract which excluded their liability for the negligence of their drivers. The clause being considered in that case—and it was without doubt incorporated in the contract—was: 'Customers' cars are driven by your staff at customers' sole risk ...' Any ordinary man knows that when a car is damaged it is not infrequently damaged because the driver has driven it negligently. He also knows, I suppose, that if he sends it to a garage and a driver in the employ of the garage takes the car on the road for some purpose in connection with the work which the customer had entrusted the garage to do, the garage could not conceivably be liable for the car being damaged in an accident unless the driver was at fault. It follows that no sensible man could have thought that the words in that case had any meaning except that the garage would not be liable for the negligence of their own drivers. That is a typical case where, on the construction of the clause in question, the meaning for which the defendant was there contending was the obvious meaning of the clause.

The next case to which I wish to refer is the well-known case of *Alderslade v Hendon Laundry Ltd*. In that case articles were sent by the plaintiff to the defendants' laundry to be washed, and they were lost. In an action by the plaintiff against the defendants for damages, the defendants relied on the following condition to limit their liability: 'The maximum amount allowed for lost or damaged article is 20 times the charge made for laundering'. Again, this was a case where negligence was not expressly excluded. The question was: what do the words mean? I have no doubt that they would mean to the ordinary housewife who was sending her washing to the laundry that, if the goods were lost or damaged in the course of being washed through the negligence of the laundry, the laundry would not be liable for more than 20 times the charge made for the laundering. I say that for this reason. It is, I think, obvious that when a laundry loses or damages goods it is almost invariably because there has been some neglect or default on the part of the laundry. It is said that thieves break in and steal, and the goods (in that case handkerchiefs) might have been stolen by thieves. That of course is possible, but I should hardly think that a laundry would be a great allurement to burglars. It is a little far-fetched to think of burglars breaking into a laundry to steal the washing when there are banks, jewellers, post offices, factories, offices and homes likely to contain money and articles far more attractive to burglars. I think that the ordinary sensible housewife, or indeed anyone else who sends washing to the laundry, reading that clause must have appreciated that almost always when goods are lost or damaged it is because of the laundry's negligence, and, therefore, this clause could apply only to limit the liability of the laundry, when they were in fault or negligent.

But counsel for the defendants has drawn our attention to the words used by Lord Greene MR in delivering the leading judgment in this court, and he contends that Lord Greene MR was in fact making a considerable extension to the law as laid down by Scrutton LJ in *Rutter v Palmer*. For this proposition he relies on the following passage in Lord Greene MR's judgment.

> 'The effect of those authorities can I think be stated as follows: where the head of damage in respect of which limitation of liability is sought to be imposed by such a clause is one which rests on negligence and nothing else, the clause must be construed as extending to that head of damage, because if it were not so construed it would lack subject-matter.'

If one takes that word 'must' au pied de la lettre that passage does support counsel for the defendants' contention. However, we are not here construing a statute, but a passage in an unreserved judgment of the Master of the Rolls, who was clearly intending no more than to restate the effect of the authorities as they then stood. It is to be observed that MacKinnon LJ, who gave the other judgment in this court, relied on the rule or principle which he said was very admirably stated by Scrutton LJ in *Rutter v Palmer*. He said:

> 'Applying that principle to the facts of this case, I think that this clause does avail to protect the proprietor of the laundry in respect of liability for negligence, which must be assumed to be the cause of these handkerchiefs having disappeared.'

And clearly it did, for the reasons that I have already given. I do not think that Lord Greene MR was intending to extend the law in the sense for which counsel for the defendants contends. If it were so extended, it would make the law entirely artificial by ignoring that rules of construction are merely our guides and not our masters; in the end you are driven back to construing the clause in question to see what it means. Applying the principles laid down by Scrutton LJ, they lead to the result at which the court arrived at in *Alderslade v Hendon Laundry Ltd*. In my judgment these principles lead to a very different result in the present case. The words are: 'The Company is not responsible for damage caused by fire to customer's cars on the premises'. What would that mean to any ordinary literate and sensible car owner? I do not suppose that any such, unless he is a trained lawyer, has an intimate or, indeed, any knowledge of the liability of bailees in law. If you asked the ordinary man or woman: 'Supposing you send your car to the garage to be repaired, and there is a fire, would you suppose that the garage would be liable?', I should be surprised if many of them did not answer, quite wrongly, 'Of course they are liable if there is a fire'. Others might be more cautious and say, 'Well, I had better ask my solicitor', or, 'I do not know. I suppose they may well be liable'. That is the crucial difference, to my mind, between this case and *Alderslade v Hendon Laundry Ltd* and *Rutter v Palmer*. In those two cases, any ordinary man or woman reading the conditions would have known that all that was being excluded was the negligence of the laundry, in the one case, and the garage, in the other. But here I think the ordinary man or woman would be equally surprised and horrified to learn that if the garage was so negligent that a fire was caused which damaged their car, they would be without remedy because of the words in the condition. I can quite understand that the ordinary man or woman would consider that, because of these words, the mere fact that there was a fire would not make the garage liable. Fires can occur from a large variety of causes, only one of which is negligence on the part of the occupier of the premises, and that is by no means the most frequent cause. The ordinary man would I think say to himself: 'Well, what they are telling me is that if there is a fire due to any cause other than their own negligence they are not responsible for it'. To my mind, if the defendants were seeking to exclude their responsibility for a fire caused by their own negligence, they ought to have done so in far plainer language than the language here used. In my view, the words of the condition would be understood as being meant to be a warning to the customer that if a fire does occur at the garage which damages the car, and is not caused by the negligence of the garage owner, then the garage owner is not responsible for damage.

Stamp LJ and **Latey J** delivered concurring judgments.

Appeal allowed.

NOTE

This case did not escape criticism when it was decided (see Barendt (1972) 35 MLR 644), and it *might* not be decided the same way today on the construction point: as we shall see (p 982), the House of Lords has subsequently deplored strained construction, which is not so necessary now that the courts have power to hold a clause unreasonable under the Unfair Contract Terms Act 1977 (hereafter UCTA). However, the general approach of reading the clause as it might appear to the intelligent layman is attractive—indeed, UCTA itself seems to take this approach in one section (see p 1009) and it is arguable that some of the other cases on construction rest on a similar basis (eg the 'main purpose' rule, see p 981).

■ *J Evans & Son (Portsmouth) Ltd v Andrea Merzario Ltd*
[1976] 2 All ER 930, Court of Appeal

(For additional facts, see p 185.) The defendants had orally promised to arrange that the container holding the plaintiff's goods would be stored below decks. The contract was held to be partly oral and partly on the standard conditions of the forwarding trade, which exempted the defendants from liability for loss or damage to the goods unless it occurred while the goods were in their actual custody and by reason of their wilful neglect or default. Clause 4 provided:

Subject to express instructions in writing given by the customer, the Company reserves to itself complete freedom in respect of the means, route and procedure to be followed in the handling and transportation of goods.

Roskill LJ

... It is suggested that even so these exemption clauses apply. I ventured to ask counsel for the defendants what the position would have been if when the defendants' first quotation had come along there had been stamped on the face of that quotation: 'No containers to be shipped on deck'; and this container had then been shipped on deck. He bravely said that the exemption clauses would still have applied. With great respect, I think that is an impossible argument. In the words which Devlin J used in *Firestone Tyre & Rubber Co Ltd v Vokins & Co Ltd*, and approved by Lord Denning MR in *Mendelssohn v Normand Ltd*, the defendants' promise that the container would be shipped on deck would be wholly illusory.

... It is a question of construction. Interpreting the contract as I find it to have been, I feel driven to the conclusion that none of these exemption clauses can be applied, because one has to treat the promise that no container would be shipped on deck as overriding any question of exempting condition. Otherwise, as I have already said, the promise would be illusory.

NOTES

1. Could the principle invoked by Roskill LJ be used if the clauses had merely been inconsistent with some term that would normally be *implied* into the contract, or would the implied term have to be read as qualified by the express provision? See pp 412–413.

2. Could the principle have been used if the only clause had said 'in the event of the goods being carried on deck, whether through our carelessness or otherwise, our liability for loss or damage to the goods shall be limited to $500 per container'?

3. Roskill LJ treats both clauses as exemption clauses. Is that strictly correct in the case of cl 4? See p 1009.

4. This case involves two express terms of the contract, which are inconsistent with each other. The court treats the positive oral promise (to load the container below decks) as overriding the printed clause. Are there any circumstances in which it would be more appropriate to treat the printed clauses as paramount? *(Hint:* what if the court thinks that the oral promise was not meant as a legal commitment, which was the effect of the judgment at first instance: see p 185; see also the parol evidence 'rule', pp 349 ff.)

5. What if two printed clauses, one positive and one an exception clause, are inconsistent with each other? At least when the contract is between businesses, the courts have on occasion applied the exception clause even though it has the effect of depriving the other clause of any meaning: eg *Istros, SS (Owner) v F W Dahlstroem & Co* [1931] 1 KB 247 (see p 976 and pp 998–999). However, as we suggested earlier (see p 977), the courts more usually 'prefer' the positive obligation. Examples will follow.

■ *Glynn v Margetson & Co*

[1893] AC 351, House of Lords

The plaintiff shipped oranges at Malaga for carriage to Liverpool under a printed bill of lading, which stated that the ship should have 'liberty to proceed to and stay at any port or ports in any station in the Mediterranean, Levant, Black Sea, or Adriatic, or on the coasts of Africa, Spain, Portugal, France, Great Britain or Ireland, for the purposes of delivering coals, cargo or passengers, or for any other purpose whatsoever'. The ship left Malaga and proceeded to a port 350 miles further away from Liverpool to pick up a cargo. Because of the delay, the oranges arrived at Liverpool damaged.

Lord Herschell LC

... My Lords, the main object and intent, as I have said, of this charterparty is the carriage of oranges from Malaga to Liverpool. That is the matter with which the shipper is concerned, and it seems to me that it would be to defeat what is the manifest object and intention of such a contract to hold that it was entered into with a power to the shipowner to proceed anywhere that he pleased, to trade in any manner that he pleased, and to arrive at the port at which the oranges were to be delivered when he pleased.

Then is there any rule of law which compels the construction contended for? I think there is not. Where general words are used in a printed form which are obviously intended to apply, so far as they are applicable, to the circumstances of a particular contract, which particular contract is to be embodied in or introduced into that printed form, I think you are justified in looking at the main object and intent of the contract and in limiting the general words used, having in view that object and intent. Therefore, it seems to me that the construction contended for would be an unreasonable one, and there is no difficulty in construing this clause to apply to a liberty in the performance of the stipulated voyage to call at a particular port or ports in the course of the voyage. That port or those ports would differ according to what the stipulated voyage was, inasmuch as at the time when this document was framed the parties who framed it did not know what the particular voyage would be, and intended it to be equally used whatever that voyage is. The ports a visit to which would be justified under this contract would, no doubt, differ according to the particular voyage stipulated for between the shipper and the shipowner; but it must, in my view, be a liberty consistent with the main object of the contract—a liberty only to proceed to and stay at the ports which are in the course of the voyage. ...

I move your Lordships that this appeal be dismissed with costs.

Lord Halsbury

... My Lords, I am entirely of the same opinion. It seems to me that in construing this document, which is a contract of carriage between the parties, one must in the first instance look at the whole of the instrument and not at one part of it only. Looking at the whole of the instrument, and seeing what one must regard, for a reason which I will give in a moment, as its main purpose, one must reject words, indeed the whole provisions, if they are inconsistent with what one assumes to be the main purpose of the contract. The main purpose of the contract was to take on board at one port and to deliver at another port a perishable cargo. ...

My Lords, I also concur with my noble and learned friend on the woolsack that the particular words which give the liberty are to be construed to refer to a liberty to deliver in the course of a voyage which has been agreed upon between the parties. ...

Lords Macnaghten and **Shand** concurred.

Appeal dismissed.

NOTES

1. Would the decision have been the same if the cargo had not been perishable?

2. Why view the contract as essentially one to carry a perishable cargo, rather than essentially one to have the cargo carried to Liverpool by tramp steamer (ie a ship that 'tramps' from port to port in search of cargo)? Do you suppose the decision would have been different if it wasn't apparent that the goods were perishable and the carrier hadn't known that they were?

3. Do you think the decision would have been the same if the liberty to deviate clause had not been part of a standard printed form, but part of a contract specially typed up after negotiation?

4. Note that the contract itself makes no reference to any obligation to go directly to the port of discharge. The court is striking out the clause as inconsistent with the *implicit*

main purpose of the contract: ie the court implies a term (with a perishable cargo, an essential implied term) that the ship will go direct and then strikes the clause down as inconsistent with the implied term.

5.   How does the court decide whether a clause is inconsistent with the main purpose, and therefore to be rejected, and when it is merely a qualification to or definition of what is being undertaken by the carrier? In *GH Renton & Co Ltd v Palmyra Trading Corpn of Panama* [1957] AC 149, timber was shipped under bills of lading from Canada to London and Hull 'or as near thereunto as the vessel may safely get . . . '. By cl 14(c) of the bills, it was provided that, in the event of strikes preventing discharge at the named port, 'the master may discharge the cargo at . . . any other safe and convenient port'. Clause 14(f) stated: "The discharge of any cargo under the provisions of this clause shall be deemed due fulfilment of the contract.' London and Hull were closed by strikes and the cargo was discharged at Hamburg; the carrier refused to accept responsibility for not arranging for it to be forwarded to England. It was argued that the clause deeming delivery at Hamburg to be due fulfilment of the contract was inconsistent with the main purpose of the contract, but the House of Lords rejected the argument for reasons given by Jenkins LJ in the Court of Appeal:

It seems to me that there is a material difference between a deviation clause purporting to enable the shipowners to delay indefinitely the performance of the contract voyage simply because they choose to do so, and provisions such as those contained in clause 14(c) and (f) in the present case, which are applicable and operative only in the event of the occurrence of certain specified emergencies. The distinction is between a power given to one of the parties which, if construed literally, would in effect enable that party to nullify the contract at will, and a special provision stating what the rights and obligations of the parties are to be in the event of obstacles beyond the control of either arising to prevent or impede the performance of the contract in accordance with its primary terms.

The House of Lords discussed the *Renton* case in *Jindal Iron and Steel Co Ltd v Islamic Solidarity Co Jordan Inc* [2005] 1 All ER 175 and decided not to reconsider it.

■ *Gibaud v Great Eastern Rly Co*
[1921] 2 KB 426, Court of Appeal

The plaintiff left his bicycle at one of the defendants' stations, and received in return a ticket containing the usual provision limiting liability unless the value of the goods was declared to be in excess of £5. The bicycle was not put in the cloakroom but left in the booking hall, from where it was stolen.

Scrutton LJ

. . . [It was argued] that the appellant was not bound by the conditions relieving the company from liability, because the company had not kept the bicycle in the place in which they had contracted to keep it. The principle is well known, and perhaps *Lilley v Doubleday* is the best illustration, that if you undertake to do a thing in a certain way, or to keep a thing in a certain place, with certain conditions protecting it, and have broken the contract by not doing the thing contracted for in the way contracted for, or not keeping the article in the place in which you have contracted to keep it, you cannot rely on the conditions which were only intended to protect you if you carried out the contract in the way in which you had contracted to do it. In *Lilley v Doubleday* the defendant had contracted to warehouse certain goods at the main warehouse. He warehoused part of them at another place and, without negligence on his part, they were lost from the other place. It was held that though he would have been protected if the good had been lost without negligence from the place where he contracted to keep them, he lost that protection when he warehoused them in a place where he had not contracted to keep them. *Lilley v Doubleday* and *Davis v Garrett* were approved by this Court in *James Morrison & Co v Shaw, Savill, & Albion Co.*

Having stated this principle, Scrutton LJ went on to hold that it did not apply to the facts of the case, since the contract should be treated as one to receive the bicycle, not one to keep it in the cloakroom.

Lord Sterndale MR and **Younger LJ** concurred.

NOTE

The interpretative device Scrutton LJ describes is often called the 'four corners rule', or 'quasi deviation'. Be careful not to confuse it with deviation proper: the four corners rule is one of construction only, unlike deviation proper (see pp 986 ff). Both seem to be confined to contracts of bailment.

■ *Pinnock Bros v Lewis & Peat Ltd*
[1923] 1 KB 690

The plaintiffs bought from the defendants East African copra cake, which they resold to B, who resold to dealers, who resold to a farmer who used it for feeding cattle. The cake was so contaminated with castor beans as to be poisonous, and the cattle became ill. Each buyer sued his seller, and in the action by the plaintiffs, the defendants relied on an exclusion clause.

Roche J

... The next defence raised was based on the clause of the contract which provides that the goods are not warranted free from defect rendering same unmerchantable which would not be apparent on reasonable examination, any statute or rule or law to the contrary notwithstanding. In my view, where a substance quite different from that contracted for has been delivered, that clause has no application, as such a difference of substance cannot be said to constitute a defect. It was said for the defendants that the admixture of castor beans and copra cake was so common that the presence of the castor beans could not be regarded as otherwise than a 'defect'. Upon the acts I am against this contention, and I hold that the delivery in this case could not be properly described as copra cake at all. That is sufficient to dispose of the defendants' contention, and it is therefore unnecessary to decide whether if there was a defect it was latent. If it were necessary to decide the point I should hold that the defect was not latent, for, in my opinion, that word is only applicable to such a defect as is not discoverable by the exercise of reasonable care. I think this defect, if it could be so called, could have been discovered by the exercise of reasonable care.

Judgment for the plaintiffs.

NOTE

This device is sometimes called the 'total non-performance rule', and sometimes (for reasons that will emerge later), 'breach of fundamental term'. You will find another application of it in *Karsales (Harrow) Ltd v Wallis* (below). More recently, the House of Lords warned against taking the device too far, and refused to apply it in a case in which the seed supplied produced not cabbages as it should have done, but only little floppy green plants: a clause limiting the suppliers' liability for consequential loss arising from the use of the seeds was still applicable, because seeds had been supplied, even if the seeds were commercially valueless. However, the device itself was not said to be wrong, and presumably it would have prevented the sellers relying on the clause if what had been supplied turned out to be little chips of wood or sand. See *George Mitchell Ltd v Finney Lock Seeds Ltd* (see p 1014).

From the cases you have read, how many different interpretative devices can you identify? (You may like to check your answer against Coote [1970] CLJ 221, at 238.)

The cases you have read so far were decided on the basis of construction of the contract, ie wording of the clause. In a series of cases in the 1950s and early 1960s, however, some judges went beyond the construction approach and held that a party who had committed a 'fundamental breach' or 'breach of a fundamental term' could not rely on an exclusion clause, no matter how widely it was worded. See Denning LJ's judgment in the next case.

■ *Karsales (Harrow) Ltd v Wallis*
[1956] 1 WLR 936, Court of Appeal

A man named Stinton offered a Buick car to Wallis, the defendant. Wallis wished to buy it, but could only afford to do so on credit. Stinton was not a dealer and could not arrange hire purchase directly, so he sold the car to Karsales, who sold it to a finance company who let it on hire purchase to Wallis. Stinton retained possession of the car throughout, but when he delivered it to Wallis, the cylinder head had been removed, the valves in the engine had been burnt out, two of the pistons had been broken, the tyres had been damaged and the radio removed. The car was towed to Wallis' premises late at night. Wallis refused to accept the car and got Stinton to take it away. The finance company got Karsales to take over the hire-purchase agreement, and Karsales sued Wallis for arrears. Karsales relied on cl 3(g):

No condition or warranty that the vehicle is roadworthy, or as to its age, condition or fitness for any purpose is given by the owner or implied herein.

The county court judge gave judgment for the plaintiffs.

Denning LJ

... The law about exempting clauses has been much developed in recent years, at any rate about printed exempting clauses, which so often pass unread. Notwithstanding earlier cases which might suggest the contrary, it is now settled that exempting clauses of this kind, no matter how widely they are expressed, only avail the party when he is carrying out his contract in its essential respects. He is not allowed to use them as a cover for misconduct or indifference or to enable him to turn a blind eye to his obligations. They do not avail him when he is guilty of a breach which goes to the root of the contract. The thing to do is to look at the contract apart from the exempting clauses and see what are the terms, express or implied, which impose an obligation on the party. If he has been guilty of a breach of those obligations in a respect which goes to the very root of the contract, he cannot rely on the exempting clauses. I would refer in this regard to what was said by Roche J in the 'copra cake' case *(Pinnock Brothers v Lewis & Peat Ltd)* and the judgments of Devlin J in *Alexander v Railway Executive* and *Smeaton Hanscomb & Co Ltd v Sassoon I Setty, Son & Co (No 1)* and the recent case in this court of J *Spurling Ltd v Bradshaw* and the cases there mentioned. The principle is sometimes said to be that the party cannot rely on an exempting clause when he delivers something 'different in kind' from that contracted for, or has broken a 'fundamental term' or a 'fundamental contractual obligation', but these are, I think, all comprehended by the general principle that a breach which goes to the root of the contract disentitles the party from relying on the exempting clause. In the present case the lender was in breach of the implied obligation that I have mentioned. When the defendant inspected the car before signing the application form, the car was in excellent condition and would go: whereas the car which was subsequently delivered to him was no doubt the same car, but it was in a deplorable state and would not go. That breach went, I think, to the root of the contract and disentitles the lender from relying on the exempting clause.

Birkett LJ

... The defendant said: 'The original Buick car is the car I had seen before and which I would like to have.' Clearly it was the duty of the finance company in those circumstances, having regard to the history, to supply to the defendant a 'car', in the ordinary sense of that term, and not something that needed towing, because in the true meaning of words a car that would not go was not a car at all; and on the evidence before the county court judge that was the kind of article which was supplied.

Parker LJ

... [H]owever extensive the exception clause may be, it has no application if there has been a breach of a fundamental term. We were referred to a number of cases, the most recent of which, I think, is that decided by Devlin J, *Smeaton Hanscomb & Co Ltd v Sassoon I Setty, Son & Co (No 1)*, in which Devlin J said:

> 'It is no doubt, a principle of construction that exceptions are to be construed as not being applicable for the protection of those for whose benefit they are inserted if the beneficiary has committed a breach of a fundamental term of the contract; ... I do not think that what is a fundamental term has ever been closely defined. It must be something, I think, narrower than a condition of the contract, for it would be limiting the exceptions too much to say that they applied only to breaches of warranty. It is, I think, something which underlies the whole contract so that, if it is not complied with, the performance becomes something totally different from that which the contract contemplates.'

Applying that to the facts of this case it seems to me that the vehicle delivered in effect is not properly described (as the agreement describes it) as a motor vehicle, 'Buick', giving the chassis and engine number. By that I am not saying that every defect in a car which renders it for the moment unusable on the road amounts to a breach of a fundamental term; but where, as here, a vehicle is delivered incapable of self-propulsion except after a complete overhaul and in the condition referred to by my Lord, it seems to me that it is abundantly clear that there was a breach of a fundamental term and that, accordingly, the exceptions in clause 3(g) do not apply.

I think the same result is achieved by saying, in effect, that what was delivered was not what was contracted for ... *Andrews Brothers (Bournemouth) Ltd v Singer & Co Ltd* might well have been decided on the basis that there had been a breach of a fundamental term. In that case the contract was for the sale of new Singer cars, and again there was an elaborate exception clause. Scrutton LJ in that case held that, there being an express term that what was sold was a new Singer car, and there having been a breach of that express term, the exception clauses dealing with implied conditions and warranties had no application.

Appeal allowed.

NOTE

Did the Lord Justices decide the case on the same or different grounds?

Because the new doctrine did not depend on the wording, or construction, of the contract, it became known as the 'substantive doctrine'. It was derived from a series of cases on carriage of goods by sea, the 'deviation' cases, in which it was held that a carrier who departed from the agreed route lost the benefit of the exception clauses in his contract. The carrier thus became liable to pay for any subsequent loss of or damage to the goods, unless he could show either that the loss must have occurred even if he had stayed on course, or that the owner of the goods had, with full knowledge of the deviation, affirmed the contract. The loss might be quite unconnected with the deviation: in *Joseph Thorley Ltd v Orchis Steamship Co Ltd* [1907] 1 KB 660, the ship had deviated but had returned to its original route without incident; the goods were damaged while being unloaded. Nonetheless it was held that the deviation prevented the normal exceptions applying to any subsequent loss, and the carrier was liable. The best explanation of this strict rule rests on the carrier's status as a bailee who has exceeded his authority (see Coote, *Exception Clauses*, chapter 6), but in *Hain Steamship Co v Tate & Lyle Ltd* [1936] 2 All ER 597, the House of Lords explained it in terms of deviation being a breach of condition entitling the owner to put an end to the contract, with the result that the exception clauses were no longer in force when the loss occurred. This ignored the point that, normally, a contract remains in force, despite a breach of condition, until the innocent party elects to terminate it (see p 611), whereas in most of the deviation cases, the owner did not know of the deviation, and thus could not have elected to terminate, until after the loss occurred.

Once the deviation rule had been explained as resting on the general law of contract, it was then applied to contracts generally. Further, it was quietly forgotten that the deviation cases depended on there being a deviation, depriving the carrier of his protective clauses, *prior* to the loss complained of: the two were elided and the rule produced that if one party committed a very serious, or 'fundamental', breach of contract, the other could terminate the contract and the first party was automatically prevented from relying on any exclusion or limitation of liability clause, whatever the clause said (see further, Coote, chapter 8).

One of the difficulties was that this is not consistent with the general principle that termination of a contract does not 'wipe it out' as if it had never been (see p 611). The innocent party is entitled to refuse to perform its side of the contract, but the clauses of the contract may continue to apply (unless as a matter of construction they were only to apply up until any termination: see the *Suisse Atlantique* case.) For example, it is well settled that an arbitration clause may apply after termination: *Heyman v Darwins Ltd* [1942] AC 356.

In addition there was doubt as to what constituted a fundamental breach or breach of fundamental term. One definition was given by Devlin J in *Smeaton Hanscomb & Co Ltd v Sassoon I Setty, Son & Co* [1953] 1 WLR 1468, at 1470 (quoted by Parker LJ in *Karsales*, above). It is reminiscent of the 'total non-performance' cases we looked at earlier. However, it is not easy to see the difference between a breach making the performance totally different and a breach 'depriving the innocent party of the substance of what he contracted for', ie a breach of condition (although it must be admitted that not all breaches of the implied conditions under SGA seem to have a very serious effect: see pp 566–567). Certainly, in some cases, breach of condition and fundamental breach seem to have been treated as interchangeable: eg J *Spurling Ltd v Bradshaw* [1956] 2 All ER 121.

The matter was first discussed in the House of Lords in *Suisse Atlantique Société d'Armement Maritime SA v NV Rotterdamsche Kolen Centrale* [1967] 1 AC 361. However, what was said about fundamental breach was strictly obiter. The facts were that, in December 1956, the respondents agreed to charter a ship from the appellants for coal-carrying voyages from the USA to Europe, 'for a total of two years consecutive voyages'. (Thus the owners would be paid according to the freight earned, so that it was in their interest that the ship should make as many voyages as possible.) The charter provided lay time and fixed demurrage at $1,000 per day (for an explanation of these terms, see p 1234). Between October 1957 and the end of the charter, the ship made eight round trips. The owners claimed that if loading and discharging had been carried out within the lay time, a further six voyages could have been made, and they claimed damages for the lost freight. The charterers contended that their liability was limited to the demurrage. (At one point, the owners were minded to terminate the charter, but in fact, they allowed it to continue under a 'without prejudice' agreement.)

The owners failed before Mocatta J and the Court of Appeal. In the House of Lords, they raised for the first time the argument that the charterers had committed a fundamental breach and could not rely on the demurrage clause. The House of Lords held that no fundamental breach had been committed, and in any event, a demurrage clause was a form of liquidated damages, not an exclusion clause. The House went on to express its view on the 'substantive doctrine' of fundamental breach.

The House appeared to be unanimous that there was no rule that an exclusion clause could not nullify or limit liability for even a fundamental breach. There was no authority for such a rule in the older cases. It is simply a matter of construction and, provided the clause is worded clearly enough, even liability for a fundamental breach may be excluded. Many of the decisions made on the basis of the 'substantive' doctrine could be justified as a matter of construction of the clause.

Lord Wilberforce was perhaps a little guarded on whether it is *all* a matter of construction; he seems to recognise that when the breach is so serious that it amounts to total non-performance of the contract (see above), it may be hard to limit liability and still have anything left of the contract. He said:

> ... Next for consideration is the argument based on 'fundamental breach' or, which is presumably the same thing, a breach going to the root of the contract'. These expressions are used in the cases to denote two quite different things, namely, (i) a performance totally different from that which the contract contemplates, (ii) a breach of contract more serious than one which would entitle the other party merely to damages and which (at least) would entitle him to refuse performance or further performance under the contract.

Both of these situations have long been familiar in the English law of contract; and it will have to be considered whether the conception of 'fundamental breach' extends beyond them. What is certain is that to use the expression without distinguishing to which of these, or to what other, situations it refers is to invite confusion.

The importance of the difference between these meanings lies in this, that they relate to two separate questions which may arise in relation to any contract. These are (as to (i)) whether an 'exceptions' clause contained in the contract applies as regards a particular breach and (as to (ii)) whether one party is entitled to elect to refuse further performance.

The appellants, in their submission that exceptions clauses do not apply to 'fundamental breaches' or 'repudiations' confuse these two questions. There is in fact no necessary coincidence between the two kinds of (so-called fundamental) breach. For, though it may be true generally, if the contract contains a wide exceptions clause, that a breach sufficiently serious to take the case outside that clause, will also give the other party the right to refuse further performance, it is not the case, necessarily, that a breach of the latter character has the former consequence. An act which, apart from the exceptions clause, might be a breach sufficiently serious to justify refusal of further performance, may be reduced in effect, or made not a breach at all, by the terms of the clause.

The present case is concerned with the application of what may be said (with what justice will be later considered) to be an exceptions clause to a possible type of 'fundamental breach'. I treat the words 'exceptions clause' as covering broadly such clauses in a contract as profess to exclude or limit, either quantitatively or as to the time within which action must be taken, the right of the injured party to bring an action for damages. Such a clause must, ex hypothesi, reflect the contemplation of the parties that a breach of contract, or what apart from the clause would be a breach of contract, may be committed, otherwise the clause would not be there; but the question remains open in any case whether there is a limit to the type of breach which they have in mind. One may safely say that the parties cannot, in a contract, have contemplated that the clause should have so wide an ambit as in effect to deprive one party's stipulations of all contractual force: to do so would be to reduce the contract to a mere declaration of intent. To this extent it may be correct to say that there is a rule of law against the application of an exceptions clause to a particular type of breach. But short of this it must be a question of contractual intention whether a particular breach is covered or not and the courts are entitled to insist, as they do, that the more radical the breach the clearer must the language be if it is to be covered. ...

The conception, therefore, of 'fundamental breach' as one which, through ascertainment of the parties' contractual intention, falls outside an exceptions clause is well recognised and comprehensible. Is there any need, or authority, in relation to exceptions clauses, for extension of it beyond this? In my opinion there is not. The principle that the contractual intention is to be ascertained—not just grammatically from words used, but by consideration of those words in relation to commercial purpose (or other purpose according to the type of contract)—is surely flexible enough, and though it may be the case that adhesion contracts give rise to particular difficulties in ascertaining or attributing a contractual intent, which may require a special solution, those difficulties need not be imported into the general law of contract nor be permitted to deform it.

The only new category of 'fundamental breach' which in this context I understand to have been suggested is one of 'deliberate' breaches. ... The 'deliberate' character of a breach cannot, in my opinion, of itself give to a breach of contract a 'fundamental' character, in either sense of that word. Some deliberate breaches there may be of a minor character which can appropriately be sanctioned by damages: some may be, on construction, within an exceptions clause (for example, a deliberate delay for one day in loading). This is not to say the 'deliberateness' may not be a relevant factor: depending on what the party in breach 'deliberately' intended to do, it may be possible to say that the parties never contemplated that such a breach would be excused or limited: and a deliberate breach may give rise to a right for the innocent party to refuse further performance because it indicates the other party's attitude towards future performance. All these arguments fit without difficulty into the general principle: to create a special rule for deliberate acts is unnecessary and may lead astray.

For Lord Upjohn's view of the difference between 'fundamental breach' and 'breach of fundamental term', see p 573.

In addition, members of the House clearly had doubts about the wisdom of the rule. These were clearly articulated by Lord Reid:

> ... In my view no such [substantive] rule of law ought to be adopted. I do not take that view merely because any such rule is new or because it goes beyond what can be done by developing or adapting existing principles. Courts have often introduced new rules when, in their view, they were required by public policy. In former times when Parliament seldom amended the common law, that could hardly have been avoided. And there are recent examples although, for reasons which I gave in *Shaw v Director of Public Prosecutions*, I think that this power ought now to be used sparingly. But my main reason is that this rule would not be a satisfactory solution of the problem which undoubtedly exists.
>
> Exemption clauses differ greatly in many respects. Probably the most objectionable are found in the complex standard conditions which are now so common. In the ordinary way the customer has no time to read them, and if he did read them he would probably not understand them. And if he did understand and object to any of them, he would generally be told he could take it or leave it. And if he then went to another supplier the result would be the same. Freedom to contract must surely imply some choice or room for bargaining.

At the other extreme is the case where parties are bargaining on terms of equality and a stringent exemption clause is accepted for a quid pro quo or other good reason. But this rule appears to treat all cases alike. There is no indication in the recent cases that the courts are to consider whether the exemption is fair in all the circumstances or is harsh and unconscionable or whether it was freely agreed by the customer. And it does not seem to me to be satisfactory that the decision must always go one way if, e.g. defects in a car or other goods are just sufficient to make the breach of contract a fundamental breach, but must always go the other way if the defects fall just short of that. This is a complex problem which intimately affects millions of people and it appears to me that its solution should be left to Parliament. If your Lordships reject this new rule there will certainly be a need for urgent legislative action but that is not beyond reasonable expectation. . . .

However, the judgments of Lords Reid and Upjohn, while apparently denying the existence of a substantive doctrine, contained passages that could be interpreted as suggesting that, had the contract in the *Suisse Atlantique* case not been affirmed but terminated, the exemption clauses would have ceased to apply. (One of the passages is reproduced on p 979.) It is possible that at this point their Lordships actually had in mind not exclusion clauses in general, but the demurrage clause involved in the case. A demurrage clause will not apply once the shipowner has terminated by 'sailing away', since it is only designed to apply to delays while the ship is under the charterers' control. These dicta were seized upon by the Court of Appeal in *Harbutt's Plasticine Ltd v Wayne Tank and Pump Co Ltd* [1970] 1 QB 447 as showing that the substantive rule still applied if the contract had been terminated. Lord Denning MR summarised his view thus:

Before leaving this part of the case, I would just like to say what, in my opinion, is the result of the *Suisse Atlantique* case. It affirms the long line of cases in this court that when one party has been guilty of a fundamental breach of the contract, that is, a breach which goes to the very root of it, and the other side accepts it, so that the contract comes to an end . . . then the guilty party cannot rely on an exception or limitation clause to escape from his liability for the breach.

If the innocent party, on getting to know of the breach, does not accept it, but keeps the contract in being . . . then it is a matter of construction whether the guilty party can rely on the exception or limitation clause . . .

This approach was followed in a number of other cases, and one case, *Wathes (Western) Ltd v Austins (Menswear) Ltd* [1976] 1 Lloyd's Rep 14, has been interpreted as applying the substantive doctrine even when the contract had been affirmed after the breach (see 98 LQR 172).

■ *Photo Productions Ltd v Securicor Transport Ltd*

[1980] 1 All ER 556, House of Lords

Lord Wilberforce

My Lords, this appeal arises from the destruction by fire of a factory owned by the respondents ('Photo Productions') involving loss and damage agreed to amount to £615,000. The question is whether the appellants ('Securicor') are liable to the respondents for this sum.

Securicor are a company which provides security services. In 1968 they entered into a contract with Photo Productions by which for a charge of £8 15s 0d (old currency) per week it agreed to 'provide their Night Patrol Service whereby four visits per night shall be made seven nights per week and two visits shall be made during the afternoon of Saturday and four visits shall be made during the day of Sunday'. The contract incorporated printed standard conditions which, in some circumstances, might exclude or limit Securicor's liability. The questions in this appeal are (i) whether these conditions can be invoked at all in the events which happened and (ii) if so, whether either the exclusion provision, or a provision limiting liability, can be applied on the facts. The trial judge (MacKenna J) decided these issues in favour of Securicor. The Court of Appeal decided issue (i) in Photo Productions' favour invoking the doctrine of fundamental breach. Waller LJ in addition would have decided for Photo Productions on issue (ii).

What happened was that on a Sunday night the duty employee of Securicor was one Musgrove. It was not suggested that he was unsuitable for the job or that Securicor were negligent in employing him. He visited the factory at the correct time, but when inside he deliberately started a fire by throwing a match onto some cartons. The fire got out of control and a large part of the premises was burnt down. Though what he did was deliberate, it was not established that he intended to destroy the factory. The judge's finding was in these words:

> 'Whether Musgrove intended to light only a small fire (which was the very least he meant to do) or whether he intended to cause much more serious damage, and, in either case, what was the reason for his act, are mysteries I am unable to solve.'

This, and it is important to bear in mind when considering the judgments in the Court of Appeal, falls short of a finding that Musgrove deliberately burnt or intended to burn Photo Productions' factory.

The condition on which Securicor relies reads, relevantly, as follows:

> 'Under no circumstances shall the Company [Securicor] be responsible for any injurious act or default by any employee of the Company unless such act or default could have been foreseen and avoided by the exercise of due diligence on the part of the Company as his employer; nor, in any event, shall the Company be held responsible for: (a) Any loss suffered by the customer through burglary, theft, fire or any other cause, except insofar as such loss is solely attributable to the negligence of the Company's employees acting within the course of their employment . . . '

There are further provisions limiting to stated amounts the liability of Securicor on which it relies in the alternative if held not to be totally exempt.

It is first necessary to decide on the correct approach to a case such as this where it is sought to invoke an exception or limitation clause in the contract. The approach of Lord Denning MR in the Court of Appeal was to consider first whether the breach was 'fundamental'. If so, he said, the court itself deprives the party of the benefit of an exemption or limitation clause. Shaw and Waller LJJ substantially followed him in this argument.

Lord Denning MR in this was following the earlier decision of the Court of Appeal, and in particular his own judgment in *Harbutt's Plasticine Ltd v Wayne Tank and Pump Co Ltd*. . . .

My Lords, whatever the intrinsic merit of this doctrine, as to which I shall have something to say later, it is clear to me that so far from following this House's decision in the *Suisse Atlantique* case it is directly opposed to it and that the whole purpose and tenor of the *Suisse Atlantique* case was to repudiate it. The lengthy, and perhaps I may say sometimes indigestible speeches of their Lordships, are correctly summarised in the headnote—

> '(3) That the question whether an exceptions clause was applicable where there was a fundamental breach of contract was one of the true construction of the contract.'

That there was any rule of law by which exception clauses are eliminated, or deprived of effect, regardless of their terms, was clearly not the view of Viscount Dilhorne, Lord Hodson or myself. The passages invoked for the contrary view of a rule of law consist only of short extracts from two of the speeches, on any view a minority. But the case for the doctrine does not even go so far as that. Lord Reid, in my respectful opinion, and I recognise that I may not be the best judge of this matter, in his speech read as a whole, cannot be claimed as a supporter of a rule of law.

. . . His conclusion is stated thus: 'In my view no such rule of law ought to be adopted', adding that there is room for legislative reform.

My Lords, in the light of this, the passage from the *Suisse Atlantique* case cited by Lord Denning MR has to be considered. For convenience I restate it:

'If fundamental breach is established, the next question is what effect, if any, that has on the applicability of other terms of the contract. This question has often arisen with regard to clauses excluding liability, in whole or in part, of the party in breach. I do not think that there is generally much difficulty where the innocent party has elected to treat the breach as a repudiation, bring the contract to an end and sue for damages. Then the whole contract has ceased to exist including the exclusion clause, and I do not see how that clause can then be used to exclude an action for loss which will be suffered by the innocent party after it has ceased to exist, such as loss of the profit which would have accrued if the contract had run its full term.'

It is with the utmost reluctance that, not forgetting the 'beams' that may exist elsewhere. I have to detect here a mote of ambiguity or perhaps even of inconsistency. What is referred to is 'loss which will be suffered by the innocent party after [the contract] has ceased to exist' and I venture to think that all that is being said, rather elliptically, relates only to what is to happen in the future, and is not a proposition as to the immediate consequences caused by the breach; if it were, that would be inconsistent with the full and reasoned discussion which follows.

It is only because of Lord Reid's great authority in the law that I have found it necessary to embark on what in the end may be superfluous analysis. For I am convinced that, with the possible exception of Lord Upjohn whose critical passage, when read in full, is somewhat ambiguous, their Lordships, fairly read, can only be taken to have rejected those suggestions for a rule of law which had appeared in the Court of Appeal and to have firmly stated the question is one of construction, not merely of course of the exclusion clause alone, but of the whole contract.

Much has been written about the *Suisse Atlantique* case. Each speech has been subjected to various degrees of analysis and criticism, much of it constructive. Speaking for myself I am conscious of imperfections of terminology, though sometimes in good company. But I do not think that I should be conducing to the clarity of the law by adding to what was already too ample a discussion a further analysis which in turn would have to be interpreted. I have no second thoughts as to the main proposition that the question whether, and to what extent, an exclusion clause is to be applied to a fundamental breach, or a breach of a fundamental term, or indeed to any breach of contract, is a matter of construction of the contract. Many difficult questions arise and will continue to arise in the infinitely varied situations in which contracts come to be breached: by repudiatory breaches, accepted or not, anticipatory breaches, by breaches of conditions or of various terms and whether by negligent, or deliberate, action, or otherwise. But there are ample resources in the normal rules of contract law for dealing with these without the superimposition of a judicially invented rule of law. I am content to leave the matter there with some supplementary observations.

1. The doctrine of 'fundamental breach' in spite of its imperfections and doubtful parentage has served a useful purpose. There were a large number of problems, productive of injustice, in which it was worse than unsatisfactory to leave excepting clauses to operate. Lord Reid referred to these in the *Suisse Atlantique* case, pointing out at the same time that the doctrine of fundamental breach was a dubious specific. But since then Parliament has taken a hand: it has passed the Unfair Contract Terms Act 1977. This Act applies to consumer contracts and those based on standard terms and enables exception clauses to be applied with regard to what is just and reasonable. It is significant that Parliament refrained from legislating over the whole field of contract. After this Act, in commercial matters generally, when the parties are not of unequal bargaining power, and when risks are normally borne by insurance, not only is the case for judicial intervention undemonstrated, but there is everything to be said, and this seems to have been Parliament's intention, for leaving the parties free to apportion the risks as they think fit and for respecting their decisions.

At the stage of negotiation as to the consequences of a breach, there is everything to be said for allowing the parties to estimate their respective claims according to the contractual provisions they have themselves made, rather than for facing them with a legal complex so uncertain as the doctrine of fundamental breach must be. What, for example, would have been the position of Photo Productions' factory if instead of being destroyed it had been damaged, slightly or moderately or severely? At what point does the doctrine (with what logical justification I have not understood) decide, ex post facto, that the breach was (factually) fundamental before going on to ask whether legally it is to be regarded as fundamental? How is the date of 'termination' to be fixed? Is it the date of the incident causing the damage, or the date of the innocent party's election, or some other date? All these difficulties arise from the doctrine and are left unsolved by it.

At the judicial stage there is still more to be said for leaving cases to be decided straight-forwardly on what the parties have bargained for rather than on analysis, which becomes progressively more refined, of decisions in other cases leading to inevitable appeals. The learned judge was able to decide this case on normal principles of contractual law with minimal citation of authority. I am sure that most commercial judges have wished to be able to do the same (cf *The Angelia, Trade and Transport Inc v Iino Kaiun Kaisha Ltd*, per Kerr J). In my opinion they can and should.

2. *Harbutt's Plasticine Ltd v Wayne Tank and Pump Co Ltd* must clearly be overruled. It would be enough to put that on its radical inconsistency with the *Suisse Atlantique* case. But even if the matter were res integra I would find the decision to be based on unsatisfactory reasoning as to the 'termination' of the contract and the effect of 'termination' on the plaintiffs' claim for damage. I have, indeed, been unable to understand how the doctrine can be reconciled with the well accepted principle of law, stated by the highest modern authority, that when in the context of a breach of contract one speaks of 'termination' what is meant is no more than that the innocent party or, in some cases, both parties are excused from further performance. Damages, in such cases, are then claimed under the contract, so what reason in principle can there be for disregarding what the contract itself says about damages, whether it 'liquidates' them, or limits them, or excludes them? These difficulties arise in part from uncertain or inconsistent terminology. A vast number of expressions are used to describe situations where a breach has been committed by one party of such a character as to entitle the other party to refuse further performance: discharge, rescission, termination, the contract is at an end, or dead, or displaced; clauses cannot survive, or simply go. I have come to think that some of these difficulties can be avoided; in particular the use of 'rescission', even if distinguished from rescission ab initio, as an equivalent for discharge, though justifiable in some contexts *(see Johnson v Agnew)* may lead to confusion in others. To plead for complete uniformity may be to cry for the moon. But what can and ought to be avoided is to make use of these confusions in order to produce concealed and unreasoned legal innovation: to pass, for example, from saying that a party, victim of a breach of contract, is entitled to refuse further performance, to saying that he may treat the contract as at an end, or as rescinded, and to draw from this the proposition, which is not analytical but one of policy, that all or (arbitrarily) some of the clauses of the contract lose, automatically, their force, regardless of intention.

If this process is discontinued the way is free to use such words as 'discharge' or 'termination' consistently with principles as stated by modern authority which *Harbutt's* case disregards. I venture with apology to relate the classic pages. In *Heyman v Darwins Ltd* Lord Porter said:

> 'To say that the contract is rescinded or has come to an end or has ceased to exist may in individual cases convey the truth with sufficient accuracy, but the fuller expression that the injured party is thereby absolved from future performance of his obligations under the contract is a more exact description of the position. Strictly speaking, to say that, upon acceptance of the renunciation of a contract, the contract is rescinded is incorrect. In such a case the injured party may accept the renunciation as a breach going to the root of the whole of the consideration. By that acceptance he is discharged from further performance and may bring an action for damages, but the contract itself is not rescinded.'

Similarly Lord Macmillan; see also *Boston Deep Sea Fishing and Ice Co Ltd v Ansell* per Bowen LJ. In *Moschi v Lep Air Services Ltd* my noble and learned friend Lord Diplock drew a distinction (relevant for that case) between primary obligations under a contract, which on 'rescission' generally come to an end, and secondary obligations which may then arise. Among the latter he included an obligation to pay compensation, ie damages. And he stated in terms that this latter obligation 'is just as much an obligation arising from the contract as are the primary obligations that it replaces'. My noble and learned friend has developed this line of thought in an enlightening manner in his opinion which I have now had the benefit of reading.

These passages I believe to state correctly the modern law of contract in the relevant respects; they demonstrate that the whole foundation of *Harbutt's* case is unsound. A fortiori, in addition to *Harbutt's* case there must be overruled *Wathes (Western) Ltd v Austins (Menswear) Ltd* which sought to apply the doctrine of fundamental breach to a case where, by election of the innocent party, the contract had not been terminated, an impossible acrobatic, yet necessarily engendered by the doctrine. Similarly, *Charterhouse Credit Co Ltd v Tolly* must be overruled, though the result might have been reached on construction of the contract.

3. I must add to this, by way of exception to the decision not to 'gloss' the *Suisse Atlantique*, a brief observation on the deviation cases, since some reliance has been placed on them, particularly on the decision of this House in *Hain Steamship Co Ltd v Tate & Lyle Ltd* (so earlier than the *Suisse Atlantique*) in the support of the *Harbutt* doctrine. I suggested in the *Suisse Atlantique* that these cases can be regarded as proceeding on normal principles applicable to the law of contract generally, viz that it is a matter of the parties' intentions whether and to what extent clauses in shipping contracts can be applied after a deviation, ie a departure from the contractually agreed voyage or adventure. It may be preferable that they should be considered as a body of authority sui generis with special rules derived from historical and commercial reasons. What on either view they cannot do is to lay down different rules as to contracts generally from those later stated by this House in *Heyman v Darwins Ltd*.

4. It is not necessary to review fully the numerous cases in which the doctrine of fundamental breach has been applied or discussed. Many of these have now been superseded by the Unfair Contract Terms Act 1977. Others, as decisions, may be justified as depending on the construction of the contract (cf *Levison v Patent Steam Carpet Cleaning Co Ltd*) in the light of well-known principles such as that stated in *Alderslade v Hendon Laundry Ltd*.

In this situation the present case has to be decided. As a preliminary, the nature of the contract has to be understood. Securicor undertook to provide a service of periodical visits for a very modest charge which works out at 26p per visit. It did not agree to provide equipment. It would have no knowledge of the value of Photo Productions' factory; that, and the efficacy of their fire precautions, would be known to Photo Productions. In these circumstances nobody could consider it unreasonable that as between these two equal parties the risk assumed by Securicor should be a modest one, and that Photo Productions should carry the substantial risk of damage or destruction.

The duty of Securicor was, as stated, to provide a service. There must be implied an obligation to use care in selecting their patrolmen, to take care of the keys and, I would think, to operate the service with due and proper regard to the safety and security of the premises. The breach of duty committed by Securicor lay in a failure to discharge this latter obligation. Alternatively it could be put on a vicarious responsibility for the wrongful act of Musgrove, viz starting a fire on the premises; Securicor would be responsible for this on the principle stated in *Morris v C W Martin & Sons Ltd*. This being the breach, does condition 1 apply? It is drafted in strong terms, 'Under no circumstances, any injurious act or default by an employee'. These words have to be approached with the aid of the cardinal rules of construction that they must be read contra proferentem and that in order to escape from the consequences of one's own wrongdoing, or that of one's servant, clear words are necessary. I think that these words are clear. Photo Productions in fact relied on them for an argument that since they exempted from negligence they must be taken as not exempting from the consequence of deliberate acts. But this is a perversion of the rule that if a clause can cover something other than negligence it will not be applied to negligence. Whether, in addition to negligence, it covers other, eg deliberate, acts, remains a matter of construction requiring, of course, clear words. I am of opinion that it does and, being free to construe and apply the clause, I must hold that liability is excluded. On this part of the case I agree with the judge and adopt his reasons for judgment. I would allow the appeal.

Lords Diplock, Salmon, Keith and **Scarman** also delivered judgments in favour of the appellants. Extracts from Lord Diplock's judgment will be found on pp 611–612.

Appeal allowed.

NOTE

In *Ailsa Craig Fishing Co Ltd v Malvern Fishing Co Ltd* [1983] 1 All ER 101, the appellants were the owners of a fishing boat, which sank in Aberdeen harbour. At the time, the respondents, Securicor, were required by contract with a fishing boat owners' association of which the appellants were members to provide a security service in the harbour, and specifically for the appellants' vessel. There was a clause in that contract limiting the respondents' liability to £1,000. The appellants argued that the clause should not avail the respondents because they had totally failed to provide any security cover at all, but the House of Lords held that their liability was still limited to £1,000. Lord Wilberforce said (at 102–103):

... one must not strive to create ambiguities by strained construction, as I think the appellants have striven to do. The relevant words must be given, if possible, their natural, plain meaning. Clauses of limitation are not regarded by the courts with the same hostility as clauses of exclusion; this is because they must be related to other contractual terms, in particular to the risks to which the defending party may be exposed, the remuneration which he receives and possibly also the opportunity of the other party to insure.

In *Darlington Futures Ltd v Delco Australia Pty Ltd* (1986) 161 CLR 500, the High Court of Australia disagreed with the view that there was a different principle to be applied in the construction of exemption clauses on the one hand and limitation clauses on the other. The Court remarked (at 510):

[A] limitation clause may be so severe in its operation as to make its effect virtually indistinguishable from that of an exclusion clause.

II. STATUTORY CONTROLS

Until 1977, the statutory controls over the use of exemption clauses, although going back as far as the Canals and Railways Act of 1854, were piecemeal: only certain types of clause were controlled, either by allowing them only if reasonable (under the 1854 Act, limitations of liability had to be reasonable) or by making them of no effect (for example, exclusions of liability for death or personal injury of passengers in a public service vehicle, under the Road Traffic Act 1960). In 1973, the Supply of Goods (Implied Terms) Act controlled the exclusion or restriction of liability for breach of terms implied under the SGA: these provisions were then incorporated into the Unfair Contract Terms Act 1977 (s 6). This Act does not, as we shall see, touch every exemption clause in every type of contract, but it does impose fairly sweeping controls. The Act is complicated. It seems easiest to take the sections not in the order in which they appear in the Act, but grouped according to their subject matter, starting with the sections derived from the 1973 Act. However, it will help to give first a broad overview of the provisions:

- s 1–Definitions of 'negligence' and of 'business liability';
- s 2–Negligence liability;

- s 3–Clauses in consumer contracts and 'written standard terms of business';
- s 4–Indemnity clauses;
- s 5–Clauses in 'guarantees' of consumer goods;
- s 6–Description and quality in sale and HP contracts;
- s 7–Description and quality in other supply of goods contracts;
- s 8–Misrepresentation (see p 386);
- s 9–Effect of breach;
- s 10–Secondary contracts;
- s 11–Definitions of unreasonableness;
- s 12–Definition of 'dealing as consumer';
- s 13–Varieties of exemption clause;
- s 14–Definitions.

Some types of clause are made ineffective in all circumstances; others may be effective if they are reasonable.

As we go through the Act (hereafter referred to as UCTA, as before), we can ask questions at two levels: firstly, at the technical level, on the exact effect of the UCTA, and secondly, at the policy level–why is this type of clause controlled or banned?

You should remember that, so far as consumer contracts are concerned, there may well be an overlap between UCTA and the Unfair Terms in Consumer Contracts Regulations (UTCCR) (see Chapter 40). In many cases, the consumer's position will be stronger under UCTA, since under the Regulations no clauses are *always* ineffective. Where, under UCTA, the clause is subject to the reasonableness test, the relative advantage is less clear (see pp 1035 ff).

1. Obligations as to correspondence with description, quality, etc in supply of goods: ss 6(2), (3); 7(1), (2), (3)

Section 6

(2) As against a person dealing as a consumer, liability for breach of the obligations arising from—
  (a) section 13, 14 or 15 of the 1979 Act (seller's implied undertakings as to conformity of goods with description or sample or as to their quality or fitness for a particular purpose);
  (b) section 9, 10 or 11 of the 1973 Act (the corresponding things in relation to hire-purchase), cannot be excluded or restricted by reference to any contract term.
(3) As against a person dealing otherwise than as consumer, the liability specified in subsection (2) above can be excluded or restricted by reference to a contract term, but only in so far as the term satisfies the requirement of reasonableness.

Section 7

(1) Where the possession or ownership of goods passes under or in pursuance of a contract not governed by the law of sale of goods or hire-purchase, subsections (2) to
(4) below apply as regards the effect (if any) to be given to contract terms excluding or restricting liability for breach of obligation arising by implication of law from the nature of the contract.
(2) As against a person dealing as consumer, liability in respect of the goods' correspondence with description or sample, or their quality or fitness for any particular purpose, cannot be excluded or restricted by reference to any such term.
(3) As against a person dealing otherwise than as consumer, that liability can be excluded or restricted by reference to such a term, but only in so far as the term satisfies the requirement of reasonableness.

NOTES

1. Section 6 replaces the corresponding provisions of the 1973 Act. Section 7 is new, and covers the supply of goods under contracts of hire, work and materials (such as a building contract or a contract to repair a car) and exchange (or barter).

2. Both sections draw a crucial distinction between consumer and non-consumer contracts. The definition of 'dealing as a consumer' is in s 12.

   Section 12
   (1) A party to a contract deals as consumer' in relation to another party if—
      (a) he neither makes the contract in the course of a business nor holds himself out as doing so; and
      (b) the other party does make the contract in the course of a business; and
      (c) in the case of a contract governed by the law of sale of goods or hire-purchase, or by section 7 of this Athe goods passing under or in pursuance of the contract are of a type ordinarily supplied for private use or consumption.
   (2) But on a sale by auction or by competitive tender the buyer is not in any circumstances to be regarded as dealing as consumer.
   (3) Subject to this, it is for those claiming that a party does not deal as consumer to show that he does not.

   Suppose Furmston buys a minibus, without revealing to the dealer that he is not buying it for business but to transport his family. Is he dealing as a consumer? Suppose Beale goes to a cash-and-carry to buy a large tub of honey for his children, and presents a trade card to obtain a discount. Is he dealing as a consumer?

3. It has been held that a contract may be a consumer sale even though the buyer is a business. In *R & B Customs Brokers Co Ltd v United Dominions Trust Ltd* [1988] 1 All ER 847, the plaintiffs bought from the defendant finance company a car supplied to it by a motor dealer. The plaintiff, a private company, bought the car for the personal and business use of its directors. It had done the same two or three times before. The conditional sale contract between the plaintiff and defendant excluded any implied conditions as to the condition or quality of the car or to its fitness for purpose. The car leaked. The Court of Appeal held that there was a breach of s 14(3), unless that section was excluded by the terms of the contract, and that the plaintiff company was dealing as a consumer, so that the obligations under s 14(3) could not be excluded. The court reached this surprising conclusion by applying the same test as is used to decide whether a false description has been applied in the course of a business under the Trade Description Act 1968: if the transaction is only incidental to the business activity, rather than integral to it, it is not done 'in the course of a business' unless a degree of regularity is established, which had not been shown on the facts.

   Whether this is a sensible outcome may, with respect, be doubted. It is true that many small businesses have no more influence in the market, and are no more sophisticated as bargainers, than private consumers, but the Court of Appeal's approach means that any occasional and 'incidental' purchase by a business of goods 'of a type ordinarily supplied for private use or consumption' will be a consumer sale, however large and sophisticated the buyer. The buyer might also have considerable bargaining power that it could use to obtain better terms, because while it will only count as a consumer if it makes occasional purchases of the type of goods in question, there is nothing to prevent it being a very large customer of the seller for other purchases. (Compare the definition of consumer under the UTCCR, below). The decision of the Court of Appeal in *R&B Customs Brokers Co Ltd v United Dominions Trust Ltd* is not easy to reconcile with the later decision of the Court of Appeal in *Stevenson v Rogers* [1999] 1 All ER 613. In this case, the defendant was a fisherman who, in 1988, sold his fishing boat to the plaintiff. The plaintiff sought to bring an action on the implied term contained in s 14(2) of the Sale of Goods Act 1979. The defendant argued that although he was in business as a fisherman, he was not in the business of selling ships and that therefore the sale was not a business sale. The Court of Appeal rejected this argument. It distinguished the *R&B Customs* case on the grounds that although both cases involved the meaning of the word 'business', the word was contained in different statutes and therefore did not necessarily have the same meaning. This is technically true but a careful reading of both cases suggests doubt as to whether they can both be correctly decided (and see the reservations about the *R&B Customs* case expressed by Potter LJ at 625).

·Suppose that the seller in *Stevenson v Rogers* had sold to a buyer which was a small company constituted like that in the *R&B Customs* case. Should such a transaction be treated as a business-to-business transaction or as a business-to-consumer transaction?

4.   Section 6(4) provides:

(4) The liabilities referred to in this section are not only the business liabilities defined by section 1(3), but include those arising under any contract of sale of goods or hire-purchase agreement.

Thus, although broadly speaking UCTA affects only business liability, in this case, a clause in a private sale might be affected. Note, however, that by s 12, such a sale could not be a consumer sale, so a reasonableness test under s 6(3) would apply; only attempts to exclude liability for correspondence with description or sample (and title: see next note) would be affected, because the implied terms as to merchantability and fitness for purpose apply only to sales made in the course of a business. Of course, a private seller may give *express* undertakings on these matters, but s 6 does not prevent him excluding or restricting his liability in respect of express undertakings.

5.   Under s 6(1), the implied obligations as to title cannot be excluded in any contract of sale or hire purchase, whether consumer or non-consumer. Under s 7(3A) and (4), the prohibition on the exclusion of the implied obligations as to title in other contracts is not absolute but is subject to the reasonableness test.

6.   What counts as an exclusion or restriction of liability for breach of the relevant obligation? Section 13 provides:

(1) To the extent that this Part of this Act prevents the exclusion or restriction of any liability it also prevents—
   (a) making the liability or its enforcement subject to restrictive or onerous conditions;
   (b) excluding or restricting any right or remedy in respect of the liability, or subjecting a person to any prejudice in consequence of his pursuing any such right or remedy;
   (c) excluding or restricting rules of evidence or procedure;
   and (to that extent) sections 2 and 5 to 7 also prevent excluding or restricting liability by reference to terms and notices which exclude or restrict the relevant obligation or duty.
(2) But an agreement in writing to submit present or future differences to arbitration is not to be treated under this Part of this Act as excluding or restricting any liability.

You have already seen examples of (a), (b) and (c): see the specimen clauses on p 975 numbers (4), (2) and (5) respectively. The last part of s 13(1) is intended to deal with the argument we noted earlier (p 976) that a possible effect of an exclusion clause is to define the duties under the contract rather than to act as a partial or total defence. For instance, if a contract of sale contains a clause that states that the seller will not be liable for any defect rendering the goods unmerchantable beyond the cost of repairing or replacing the goods, there is obviously still an obligation on the seller to deliver goods of merchantable quality, but its liability for breach is restricted. If, on the other hand, the clause states that there is no implied undertaking as to merchantability, it might be argued that the clause is not 'excluding or restricting' liability for breach of s 14 because there is no liability under s 14 to exclude, s 13(1) brings this clause within the scope of the Act. However, it has been argued forcefully that s 13 is actually draconian in effect, in that it may prevent the parties defining the type of transaction that they wish to enter. Suppose Beale, acting in the course of a business, wants to sell Bishop, a consumer, an old machine that Beale has never used and about which he knows nothing, without taking any responsibility for its quality. Bishop agrees to a sale on this basis at a suitably reduced price. If they express their agreement by using the clause just given as an example, is it caught by s 6(2)? Perhaps the operation of s 6(2) can be avoided by saying that, quite apart from the clause, there would in the circumstances be no obligation as to merchantability, and s 6(2) is to be confined to the case in which there would be an obligation *but for the clause in question.* See Yates, *Exclusion Clauses in Contracts,* 2nd edn, p 78; Macdonald, *Exemption Clauses and Unfair Terms,* 2nd edn, 2006, pp 103–108, who argues for an 'expectations' test.

7. Why is the exclusion or restriction of these obligations totally banned in consumer contracts? You may like to read the extract that follows with some of the following questions and points in mind: how common was it for retail sellers and others dealing with consumers to exclude this type of liability? If it was common, why, and how serious a matter was it? Even if it is right to prevent the total *exclusion* of these obligations, does it make sense to prevent the retailer excluding *any* of the liability, even for consequential loss? Suppose a defective appliance causes a fire: the retailer may have no idea of what is likely to be damaged, while the consumer may already have insurance on the property damaged.

■ 'First Report on Exemption Clauses in Contracts' (No 24)
(Law Commission) (1969)

68. On the strength of the evidence which they had collected, the Molony Committee declared themselves compelled to view the practice of contracting out as a general threat to consumer interest, in the sense that 'heavy and irrecoverable loss may fall upon the consumer who is unlucky enough to get a defective article.' ... [The Working Party] found an overriding argument in favour of prohibiting 'contracting out'. The mischief was that this practice enabled well-organised commerce 'consistently to impose unfair terms on the consumer and to deny him what the law means him to have'. On the whole, the consumer did not even know how he was being treated; but where he was alive to the position, he found it difficult and sometimes impossible to avoid submitting to the terms of business universally adopted, because he had no bargaining power of sufficient weight. This being the essence of the case for intervention in support of the consuming public, the Molony Committee endorsed the soundness of the case and accepted the need to ban 'contracting out'. ...

69. The evidence collected by the Working Party showed that contracting out of the statutory conditions and warranties has continued to be a source of dissatisfaction to consumers. Representatives of the consumer interest have suggested that for the most part the situation has not changed in its essentials during the years which have elapsed since the Molony Committee's inquiry, although it is conceded that there has been a measure of improvement. In the motor vehicle trade contracting out, though still

widespread, no longer appears to be 'universal'. Similarly, it has been said that in respect of electrical and mechanical appliances there has been a less 'general' tendency to introduce sweeping exemption clauses. In some cases it would seem that improvements have flowed from the pressure both of the Consumer Council and of other associations and groups representing consumers combined with the work of trade associations and the lead given by certain traders.

. . .

73. Before reaching the conclusion that the Molony Committee's proposal for a general ban on exemption clauses in sales to private consumers was justified and entitled to support, the Working Party considered and rejected a number of other possible solutions. One suggestion was that there should be certain exceptions to the ban on contracting out—for instance, that the exclusion of consequential damage should be permissible, at least in certain specified classes of sale. This was rejected not only because of the difficulty of defining the exceptions, but also because it was felt that as between the retailer and private consumer the burden of liability under the implied conditions and warranties should fall upon the retailer. Secondly, it was argued that assuming that there was merit in the suggestion that the law should cater for exceptional cases, the only realistic alternative to an unqualified ban was a general test for reasonableness exercisable by the courts on the model of section 3 of the Misrepresentation Act 1967; but this solution was also rejected, on the ground that it would import an element of uncertainty into sales to private consumers whereas certainty and simplicity were of predominant importance in that area of commerce.

. . .

79. . . . [I]t is clear to us that there is widespread public misunderstanding and uncertainty about the purchaser's legal rights against the retailer where the manufacturer's 'guarantee' is offered and accepted. It is our view that legislation, in addition to providing a remedy against effective and oppressive contracting out can perform the important function of clarifying the legal position of the private consumer. Whatever rights a buyer may have against the manufacturer, and they may be valuable rights, it may be the local retailer rather than the distant (possibly overseas) manufacturer with whom the buyer can most conveniently discuss a complaint and perhaps come to terms, or, in the last resort, litigate his claim. In our view the rights of the private consumer against his seller under the statutory conditions and warranties should be expressly and clearly maintained and safeguarded by the law.

NOTES

1. In what sense are exclusion clauses even in a consumer contract 'unfair'? Do they indicate that consumers are being exploited in the sense that they are being overcharged for what they are receiving? As Trebilcock (above) points out, standard-form contracts with exclusion clauses are not only used in trades in which there is a monopoly or even a high concentration; if Goldberg's explanation of their prevalence is correct, they represent 'value of money', in the sense that they are used by businesses as a way of reducing costs to keep prices down to a competitive level. It is rather that the clauses are not necessarily the terms on which the consumer would have liked to do business had he or she the choice.

2. 'On the whole, the consumer did not even know how he was being treated.' In what sense is this unfair? Suppose a consumer buys a used car from a dealer and, shortly afterwards, the engine blows up. He then discovers that the contract he signed excludes any liability on the part of the dealer. Assuming the clause to be valid, how would it be unfair? How would the consumer have acted had he or she known the clause was there? Even if the consumer would not have been able to go to another dealer who offered better terms, there are a number of possibilities.

    (a) He might have had the car checked by an independent mechanic before buying it.
    (b) He might have taken out 'extended warranty cover' (a form of insurance).

(c) He might have refused to pay so much for the car, or if the seller would not reduce the price, have bought a cheaper one, so as to give himself some cash in hand to meet repair bills.

(d) He might have decided to buy a newer, more reliable, car.

(e) He might have decided not to buy a car at all.

(f) He might have gone ahead anyway (he may not mind taking this kind of risk).

Leaving case (f) aside, is the unfairness in the clause that it was unexpected, and in reliance on there being some kind of warranty protecting him, the consumer has failed to take steps that would have safeguarded his position at least in part? What if he had assumed that there was no warranty even though he hadn't read the contract?

3.   If this were the full extent of the problem, would it be necessary to do more than require that the clause be obvious and immediately comprehensible to the ordinary consumer? Apparently, there is more to it: 'where he was alive to the position, he found it difficult and sometimes impossible to avoid submitting to the terms of business universally adopted, because he had no bargaining power of sufficient weight.' Suppose that Furmston, a consumer at least dimly aware of the legal position, tries to buy a lawn-mower from Beale Ltd. Beale offers him a contract containing exclusion clauses, and when Furmston replies that he would prefer to have more generous terms (even if that means paying more), Beale tells Furmston to take it or leave it. Unless Furmston is a very large customer for lawnmowers, this seems a likely outcome: he has no bargaining power of sufficient weight. But what do we mean by bargaining power in this context? It is not a case of the crafty exploiting the poor and ignorant (cf *Evans v Llewellin*, p 939), nor of improper persuasion or pressure (compare Chapters 34 and 35). Nor does it seem to be a case of Beale taking advantage of Furmston's necessity when there is no one else to whom Furmston can turn; there is no suggestion that Beale is a monopolist, and anyway a lawnmower is hardly a necessity: Furmston can always get a flock of sheep or junior lecturers to do the job instead. Moreover, is it really likely that Furmston couldn't get bet-ter terms *however* much he was prepared to pay? (Look again at the extract from Schwartz, on p 973 note 4.) We suggested (on pp 972–973) that the explanation is a great deal less sinister: it is simply too costly to produce and administer a special set of terms for the odd small customer if the vast majority are apparently content with the terms usually offered. It is no more sinister than finding that Beale won't at any reasonable price produce a custom-built mower. Remember Henry Ford and the Model T, available in any colour so long as it's black. But it may be that only the Furmstons of this world ever ask Beale for better terms because no one else is alive to the problem until too late, and actually everyone would be happier paying slightly more for improved terms *if only they understood*. Is the total ban on excluding merchantability obligations trying to pre-vent this kind of inefficiency?

4.   What if there is a substantial number of customers who ask for something better? Look again at Trebilcock (p 968). Isn't it very likely that gradually the contractual offerings will improve? Is this perhaps an explanation of the improvement noted by the Law Commission since the time of the Molony report? In other words, as the Consumers Association and others gradually educated consumers into shopping not only in terms of price, the problem might have gone away.

5.   Assuming there were no protective legislation, but that there were a sizeable margin of fully informed shoppers in the relevant market, what kind of terms might one expect to find? Would there be no exclusion clauses at all, so that sellers remained fully responsible

for any foreseeable loss resulting from the goods not being merchantable, or would there still be some restrictions because both parties found that a more efficient method of dealing with the problem? Priest, 'A Theory of the Product Warranty' (1981) 90 Yale L J 1297 develops a theory that helps to explain the content of manufacturers' warranties of products. A commentator, Whitford, summarises the theory thus:

Professor Priest's "investment theory" predicts that warranties will contain the same terms that they would contain in a nearly perfect market. According to his investment theory, there are two principal determinants of warranty content in such a market.

First, if the losses from product defects are avoidable through appropriate actions, the warranty will allocate the loss to the party who can avoid it at least cost. Sometimes losses are best avoided through preventive investments—by the manufacturer through investments in product design or quality control, or by the consumer through investments in a search for the product best adapted to the intended use and investments in proper care and maintenance of the product after purchase. In other instances, losses are best avoided through the repair of a malfunctioning product, and either the manufacturer or the consumer can be the least-cost repairer. Whatever the cheapest method of loss avoidance, the investment theory predicts that warranty terms will allocate losses to induce efficient loss avoidance by the efficient loss avoider.

If losses from product defects are not totally avoidable, then the second determinant of warranty content under the investment theory is the effectiveness of the manufacturer as an insurer against losses. For example, if the risk of loss from product defects varies greatly among consumers, due to important differences in the circumstances of each consumer, Priest believes that the manufacturer is a relatively poor insurer because it usually cannot segregate consumers into risk classes as cheaply and effectively as alternative insurers. In these circumstances, the investment theory predicts that manufacturers will limit warranty coverage to those risks that virtually all consumers share, forcing consumers that face greater risks to self-insure or to obtain alternative insurance. Thus, low risk consumers will not pay for more insurance than their circumstances require. Warranties are likely to exclude consequential damages on this basis, for example, if the potential magnitude of consequential damages varies dramatically among consumers.

Whitford is doubtful about the explanatory power of the theory: see 91 Yale L J 1372. But see also Priest's reply, 91 Yale L J 1386.

Priest is describing the position between manufacturer and consumer, but probably similar factors would apply between retail seller and consumer. In the light of his analysis, how sensible is it to impose a total ban on *any* restriction of liability for non-merchantability in a consumer sale? What sort of effects is such a ban likely to have on (a) product quality and (b) the number of consumers who can afford to buy the goods? Why did the Law Commission recommend a total ban?

We can measure the feelings of manufacturers and consumers about warranties by the behaviour of the market. Twenty years ago, car manufacturers routinely warrantied their cars for one year but now some manufacturers routinely offer a three-year warranty. This suggests that such companies have high confidence in the quality of their product, so that they do not expect to pay out unacceptable amounts on honouring the warranty, and also that some customers at least like to buy cars with a three-year warranty. We can see a slightly different development in the case of such things as washing machines and television sets. Here, the traditional one-year warranty continues, but retailers often offer extended warranties for up to five years. Commentators tend to argue that extended warranties are unduly expensive and the customer would be better off not buying the warranty but waiting for the washing machine or television to break down, and that, on average, the cost of the payout would be less than the cost of the warranty. The popularity of the warranties suggests, however, that risk aversion is strongly developed in this area.

6. The Molony Committee found an overriding argument in favour of a prohibition on contracting out, that the latter enabled commerce to deny the consumer 'what the law means him to have'. What assumptions lie beneath this phrase? Simply that the consumer's rights should not be reduced without his informed consent, or that even informed individuals should *not be allowed* to accept certain risks? If so, why not? Good old paternalism? See further p 1061.

7. Even if a clause is legally ineffective, it may mislead the consumer into thinking he has no rights. Under the Fair Trading Act 1973, now replaced by Enterprise Act 2002, delegated legislation may be made to prohibit 'consumer trade practices', including the terms and conditions used in contracts and the manner of their communication, which inequitably affect the economic interests of consumers. The Consumer Transactions (Restrictions on Statements) Order 1976 (SI 1976/1813, as amended by SI 1978/127) makes it a criminal offence to include in a consumer contract of sale an exclusion clause that would be automatically void under UCTA s 6.

2. Manufacturers' guarantee of consumer goods: s 5

Section 5

(1) In the case of goods of a type ordinarily supplied for private use or consumption, where loss or damage—
  (a) arises from the goods proving defective while in consumer use; and
  (b) results from the negligence of a person concerned in the manufacture or distribution of the goods,
liability for the loss or damage cannot be excluded or restricted by reference to any contract term or notice contained in or operating by reference to a guarantee of the goods.

(2) For these purposes—
  (a) goods are to be regarded as 'in consumer use' when a person is using them, or has them in his possession for use, otherwise than exclusively for the purposes of a business; and
  (b) anything in writing is a guarantee if it contains or purports to contain some promise or assurance (however worded or presented) that defects will be made good by complete or partial replacement, or by repair, monetary compensation or otherwise.

(3) This section does not apply as between the parties to a contract under or in pursuance of which possession or ownership of the goods passed.

NOTES

1. Beale, a travelling salesman, buys a car primarily for business but he occasionally uses it for private purposes at weekends. While he is on a business trip, he has an accident caused by negligence in manufacture. The manufacturers' guarantee purports to exclude the manufacturers' liability in tort. Is the exclusion effective?

2. Bishop buys a toaster from a retailer for private use. In the box with the toaster was a guarantee card, which stated that in consideration of the purchaser of the toaster waiving all other rights against the manufacturer, the manufacturer would repair or replace any faulty machine within 12 months of purchase. Bishop fills in a tear-off acceptance slip and sends it off. Ten months later, the toaster breaks down. The retailer has gone out of business. The manufacturer has been taken over since Bishop returned the slip and

refuses to honour the guarantee. Can Bishop recover the cost of having the toaster repaired elsewhere by suing on the guarantee?

3.   Can Bishop recover the cost of repair from the manufacturer *in tort?* See *Murphy v Brentwood District Council* (p 33). Could a manufacturer who advertised a product as having a year's manufacturer's guarantee be heard to argue that the purchaser did not rely on the manufacturer to produce a non-defective article?

4.   The purpose of s 5(3) is simply to prevent an overlap between s 5 and ss 6 and 7.

5.   What policy underlies preventing manufacturers excluding *any* type of tort liability in this manner? Is the guarantee likely to be misleading? You may like to consider the following extract from Law Commission, Second Report on Exemption Clauses (No *69)* (1975), para 100:

> In our view, the buyer in a consumer sale who accepts such a guarantee is just as much in need of protection against the manufacturer as he is when dealing with the immediate seller. The guarantee is attractive because it offers him a cheap and simple alternative to an action for damages against the seller if the goods are defective. At the time when the buyer accepts it he may not contemplate the possibility of suffering personal injury or damage to his property because the goods are defective or dangerous and, even if he does, he is not in a position to evaluate the relevant advantages of the guarantee on the one hand and the common law remedies on the other. It is obvious that cases can arise in which he will have abandoned rights far more valuable than those he has gained. Such an exemption clause is a potential trap and we think it should be made void.

6.   In the US case of *Collins v Uniroyal Inc* 64 NJ 260, 315 A 2d 16 (1974), a tyre manufacturer gave a guarantee against *any* blowout, including those caused not by any defect in the tyre but by 'road hazards'. It excluded any liability for consequential loss under the guarantee. A purchaser suffered personal injury when a road hazard caused a blowout and the manufacturer was held liable, the court saying that the exclusion was 'unconscionable'. Would the exclusion be valid under UCTA? Do you think the result is a sensible one? See Epstein, 18 J Law & Econ 293.

3. Liability for negligence: ss 1 (1) and (3), 2(1)–(3)

Section 1

(1) For the purposes of this Part of this Act, 'negligence' means the breach—

   (a) of any obligation, arising from the express or implied terms of a contract, to take reasonable care or exercise reasonable skill in the performance of the contract;

   (b) of any common law duty to take reasonable care or exercise reasonable skill (but not any stricter duty);

   (c) of the common duty of care imposed by the Occupiers' Liability Act 1957 or the Occupiers' Liability Act (Northern Ireland) 1957.

   . . .

(3) In the case of both contract and tort, sections 2 to 7 apply (except where the contrary is stated in section 6(4)) only to business liability, that is liability for breach of obligations or duties arising—

   (a) from things done or to be done by a person in the course of a business (whether his own business or another's); or

   (b) from the occupation of premises used for business purposes of the occupier; and references to liability are to be read accordingly but liability of an occupier of premises for breach of an obligation or duty towards a person obtaining access to the premises for recreational or educational purposes, being liability for loss or damage suffered by reason of the dangerous state of the premises, is not a business liability of the occupier unless granting that person such access for the purposes concerned falls within the business purposes of the occupier.

Section 2

(1) A person cannot by reference to any contract term or to a notice given to persons generally or to particular persons exclude or restrict his liability for death or personal injury resulting from negligence.

(2) In the case of other loss or damage, a person cannot so exclude or restrict his liability for negligence except in so far as the term or notice satisfies the requirement of reasonableness.

(3) Where a contract term or notice purports to exclude or restrict liability for negligence a person's agreement to or awareness of it is not of itself to be taken as indicating his voluntary acceptance of any risk.

NOTES

1. The obligation to deliver goods on time under a contract of sale is normally a strict one. In a contract with Beale, Furmston excludes any liability for consequential loss caused by late delivery. He delivers late because he carelessly sends the goods to Bishop. Is the exclusion clause subject to s 2(2)?

2. What counts as a business? There is a partial definition in s 14:

   'business' includes a profession and the activities of any government department or local or public authority.

   Is a charity shop a business within the Act? A university? A student union? The organising committee of the annual church fete? What criteria should be applied to determine the question?

3. Any form of clause that has the effect of excluding the 'business' liability of one party to the other for negligence will fall within s 2. In *Phillips Products Ltd v Hyland* [1987] 2 All ER 620, the plaintiffs had hired a JCB and driver (Mr Hyland) from Hamstead. The contract was on the CPA conditions of hire (for the current version, see Appendix). Clause 8 provided that drivers should:

   for all purposes in connection with their employment in the working of the plant be regarded as the servants or agents of the Hirer who alone shall be responsible for all claims arising in connection with the operation of such plant by the said drivers or operators.

   Hyland negligently damaged the plaintiff's building. Hamstead argued that, as the result of this clause, it was not vicariously liable for Hyland and that the clause was one that 'transferred' liability, not one that excluded or restricted it. The Court of Appeal held that the clause was caught by s 2(2); if the clause were enforced, the effect would be 'to negative a common law liability in tort which would otherwise admittedly fall on the plant-owner'. Furthermore, cl 8 fell within s 13(1). (The court went on to hold that the clause was unreasonable: see p 1018. On the question of whether this clause always operates to exclude liability, see p 1010.)

4. As s 1 makes clear, s 2 applies also to purely tortious liability, so that liability for death or personal injury caused in the course of a business can no longer be excluded by notices, etc (cf *Ashdown v Samuel Williams & Sons Ltd* [1957] 1 QB 409.) Until recently, there was some doubt whether a disclaimer of liability for the accuracy of a statement, as in *Hedley Byrne v Heller* (see p 28) is within s 2(2): again, the argument is that the disclaimer

prevents the liability ever arising, rather than excluding it (cf p 995). In *Smith v Eric S Bush* [1989] 2 All ER 514, the House of Lords rejected this argument: the effect of s 13(1) was to subject the disclaimer to s 2(2). (On the issue of reasonableness in this case, see p 1021.)

5.   Why are exclusions of liability for negligence subject to such stringent control? Consider the following from Law Commission Report No 69:

54 ... It may be said that to permit a person who owes such a duty to contract out of liability for the breach of it is tantamount to giving him a licence to behave carelessly. This, it may be said, is ... socially inexpedient because it tends to reduce standards of care and competence. ...

56 ... [T]he effect on the interests of those it is intended to protect of imposing a complete ban on exemptions from liability for negligence ... would be to make a person supplying services in the course of his business the insurer of the person to whom a service is supplied (whether the latter is acting in the course of a business or not) against loss or damage due to the negligence of the supplier. There is nothing inherently unreasonable about that, so long as it is the most economical way of providing cover for the customer. Our Working Party were advised, however, by the insurance experts, whose valuable assistance we have already acknowledged in our joint document, that there are many cases in which it is more economical for the person to whom the service is supplied to effect a separate insurance. In one way or the other, it is said, the customer must always pay for the insurance cover in the form either of an extra charge or of insurance premiums. If that cover is provided by the supplier, he will either insure his liability with an insurance company or, as some very large undertakings do, act as his own insurer. In either event the cost of insurance will normally be added to the supplier's charges to his customer. If it costs more for the supplier than for the customer to cover the risk of loss or damage, it would pay the customer to agree that the supplier should not be liable, to effect his own insurance and to pay a lower charge for the service. We are told that it is in fact generally cheaper for the customer to insure, at any rate for part of the risk, especially in those cases where he knows, and the supplier cannot know, the limit up to which the insurance is required; in such cases the supplier is very likely to over-insure because he will feel that he has to insure up to the maximum of each claim.

For similar reasons, the Law Commission did not recommend a total ban on exclusion or restriction of liability for negligently caused personal injury, but bans in specific cases, including car parks and 'movement by mechanical device', where (para 88) one party is weak in bargaining power and he places a high degree of reliance for his personal safety on the other's lack of negligence. The total ban was inserted in Parliament.

6.   Is it true that exclusions of liability for negligence reduce the pressure on the party whose liability is excluded to take optimal precautions? Consider the following extract from Schwartz, 'Private Law Treatment of Defective Products in Sales Situations' (1970) 49 Ind LJ 8, at 21–22:

The goal of improving product quality has been a part of sales law since at least 1829, when Chief Justice Best explained a decision to impose an implied warranty of fitness on a copper manufacturer as compelled by the court's duty "... to make it the interest of manufacturers and those who sell, to furnish the best article that can be supplied". *[Jones v Bright* (1829) 5 Bing 533.] In recent years the goal has been rephrased to provide that courts should hold liable the party who can best (ie, more cheaply) reduce the costs of defects. No matter how the goal is phrased, however, it is misguided in bargaining situations, where courts can only achieve what economists refer to as optimality: that level of consumer sovereignty where no buyer can be made better off by further market transactions without making another buyer worse off.

Imposing risks on a party will not, of itself, cause that party to do things differently if risks could be completely shifted, for then change is pointless. Risks, however, cannot be completely shifted.

Should a seller raise prices by the risk's value he will lose sales. Sellers must therefore decide whether the loss of profit from raising the price by R is greater or less than the loss caused by avoiding or ameliorating that risk. For example, let P be the price, exclusive of risk costs, and R the risk cost. If the seller disclaims, thereby shifting R to buyers, buyers face a cost of P + R; if the seller does not disclaim, and instead charges R's value for bearing it, buyers again face a cost of P + R. Whether sellers will avoid risks is determined by whether P + R <gt> P + A(s); that is, whether avoidance cost is cheaper than risk cost. Sellers therefore face the same incentive to avoid defects whether they disclaim or not, for in either case buyers will perceive the total cost as P + R, and thus force sellers to compare risk and avoidance costs.

The point is that when buyers can correctly value the risk, nothing is to be gained by shifting that risk to sellers. When buyers cannot value the risk, a shift will not necessarily yield improved products. Assume, for example, that the seller disclaims, that A(s) is $8, R is $5, and that many buyers perceive R as $9. Such buyers will be responding to artificially high prices; hence they will purchase less, thereby possibly inducing the seller to avoid defects. If a court bans the disclaimer, the seller (who presumably can value R) will raise price by $5 rather than avoid defects. If this is done, those buyers who overvalued R will perceive a cost reduction of $4, with the result that purchases will increase and there will be more defective products than before judicial intervention. By the same token, when buyers undervalue risks, sellers who disclaim feel artificially low pressure to do things differently. In that case, banning the disclaimer will then force a price of P <+> R or P <+> A(s), either of which will be perceived by buyers who have undervalued R as higher than the costs they previously faced. Matters will then be better since less will be bought, and what is bought may be better made.

Suppose a person thinking of taking a ride on a big dipper is confronted with a choice: he can ride on one for £1.00 but entirely at his own risk, or on another one, the owner of which does not disclaim liability, for £1.25. What information would he need in order to decide which ride to take? How often will a private person have the necessary information when the risk is one of death or personal injury? Is he more likely to have the information if the risk is of damage to his property?

7. Even if your answer to the last question was 'hardly ever', does society have any legitimate interest in preventing a person who is aware of what he or she is doing from accepting an exclusion of a business's liability for death or personal injury? Is the problem perhaps what economists call an 'externality', ie the parties do not bear the full cost of their actions because part of the loss is borne willy-nilly by someone else?

4. Other clauses in consumer or standard-form contracts: s 3

Section 3

(1) This section applies as between contracting parties where one of them deals as consumer or on the other's written standard terms of business.

(2) As against the party, the other cannot by reference to any contract term—

    (a) when himself in breach of contract, exclude or restrict any liability of his in respect of the breach; or

    (b) claim to be entitled—

        (i) to render a contractual performance substantially different from that which was reasonably expected of him, or

        (ii) in respect of the whole or any part of his contractual obligation, to render no performance at all,

except in so far as (in any of the cases mentioned above in this subsection) the contract term satisfies the requirement of reasonableness.

NOTES

1.   'Written standard terms of business' is not defined. Presumably it includes the printed terms on a purchase order or a sales form used by a business buying from or selling to another, if the form was devised by the company concerned. But would it include the following?

    (i)   A set of terms regularly used by a firm, but drafted by a trade association (eg the Road Haulage Association conditions of carriage),

    (ii)   A set of conditions drawn up by a body representing both sides of an industry (eg the Joint Contracts Tribunal form of building contract),

    (iii)   A term in a contract for the sale of a machine, if the contract was negotiated clause by clause, but the clause in question was adopted without amendment from a 'precedent contract' that the seller always uses in such negotiations and often gets adopted at least in part. In *Chester Grosvenor Hotel v Alfred McAlpine Management Ltd* (1991) 56 BLR 115, Judge Stannard said (at 133):

> I accept that where a party invariably contracts in the same written terms without material variation, those terms will become its 'standard form contract' or 'written standard terms of business'. However, it does not follow that because terms are not employed invariably, or without material variation, they cannot be standard terms. If this were not so the statute would be emasculated, since it could be excluded by showing that, although the same terms had been employed without modification on a multitude of occasions, and were employed on the occasion in question, previously on one or more isolated occasions they had been modified or not employed at all. In my judgment the question is one of fact and degree. What are alleged to be standard terms may be used so infrequently in comparison with other terms that they cannot realistically be regarded as standard, or on any particular occasion may be so added to or mutilated that they must be regarded as having lost their essential identity. What is required for terms to be standard is that they should be regarded by the party which advances them as its standard terms and that it should habitually contract in those terms. If it contracts also in other terms, it must be determined in any given case, and as a matter of fact, whether this has occurred so frequently that the terms in question cannot be regarded as standard, and if on any occasion a party has substantially modified its prepared terms, it is a question of fact whether those terms have been so altered that they must be regarded as not having been employed on that occasion.

In *St Albans City and District Council v International Computers Ltd* [1996] 4 All ER 481, the plaintiff local authority entered into a contract with the defendant company for the supply of a computer system to be used in administering its collection of the community charge. The software was defective so that the council overestimated the population by which the charge was payable and therefore set the charge at a rate which meant that, in fact, it recovered significantly less than it needed to do. The defendants argued that the contract was not on their standard conditions of business because the contract had been preceded by negotiations. This argument was rejected by the Court of Appeal because the result of the negotiations was that the defendant's conditions were accepted substantially unamended.

(iv) A clause in a standard purchase order under which one of the other terms, the payment clause for example, has been altered for this contract only.

2.   Section 13 does not apply to s 3. Instead, if a term operates by defining the initial obligation rather than by excluding a liability, s 3(2)(b) comes into play. Law Commission No 69, paras 141 and 143, explain the problem thus:

> 141. One category ... comprises those provisions which exclude or restrict the exercise of a right or remedy or any liability arising out of the breach of any obligation, express or implied, in the contract.

Here the danger of injustice is aggravated by the fact that the promisee will normally assess the value of the contract on the assumption that it will be performed; he may not pay much attention to the provisions for dealing with the consequences of breach. In our view there is a clear case for imposing some degree of control on clauses of this sort, even when the obligations to which they relate can be ascertained only by reference to the express terms of an agreement between the parties. . . .

Other 'exemption clauses'

143. There is another and less easily distinguishable class of provisions. These differ from provisions of the category described at paragraph 141 above in that they are expressed not as excluding or restricting liability for the breach of subsisting obligations but as preventing the obligations to which they relate from arising or as providing that such obligations are to arise only in restricted or qualified form.

. . . [T]he mischief we wish to control . . . is the likelihood (in the light of the surrounding circumstances including the way in which the contract is expressed) that the promisee might reasonably have misunderstood the extent of the promisor's obligation.

3.   Suppose a package holiday contract contains a clause permitting the holiday company to substitute another hotel, or another hotel in another resort, for the one named in the booking form (compare *Anglo-Continental Holidays Ltd v Typaldos*, above). How should the court trying to apply s 3(2)(b)(i) ascertain what was reasonably expected? Surely not by the standards of that odious reasonable man, who no doubt reads the small print on everything from his cornflakes packet in the morning to his Horlicks tin at night and suspects the worst at every turn: this would make the section virtually toothless. By the standard of the person who never reads anything he signs? Or by the standard of the person who knows what the contract says but expects the clauses to be applied fairly in the circumstances? If the last, is s 3(2)(b)(i) anything more than a statutory enactment of the main purpose rule?

4.   Section 3(2)(b)(ii) is clearly designed to prevent partial or total cancellation. But how is it to be applied? There is no reference to the customer's reasonable expectations here. And if the company reserves the right to cancel the holiday in certain circumstances that have arisen, are they 'rendering no performance at all' 'in respect of . . . their contractual obligation'? Surely their contractual obligation to perform has now ended. To make sense of the subsection, it must be interpreted as meaning: what *would* be the contractual obligation if it were not for the clause in question? But if that is the case, isn't the subsection extremely far-reaching? Wouldn't it catch, for instance, any clause making some performance by the other party an express condition when it wouldn't normally be so, eg 'time of payment in this contract for sale of goods to be of the essence' (see *Lombard North Central v Butterworth*, p 605)? Such a clause allows a party to refuse to perform (and to terminate the contract) when, without the clause, he would have to continue performance.

5. Misrepresentation

See the Misrepresentation Act 1967, s 3, as amended by UCTA s 8, on p 386.

6. Indemnity clauses

Section 4

(1) A person dealing as a consumer cannot by reference to any contract term be made to indemnify another persons (whether a party to the contract or not) in respect of liability that may be incurred

by the other for negligence or breach of contract, except in so far as the contract term satisfies the requirement of reasonableness.

(2) This section applies whether the liability in question—

    (a) is directly that of the person to be indemnified or is incurred by him vicariously;

    (b) is to the person dealing as consumer or to someone else.

NOTES

1.   It is not uncommon for a contract to provide that party A must indemnify party B against any liability B may incur to third parties. For instance, construction work that B is to carry out for A might interfere with a third party's property rights and it seems only right that A should bear the ultimate cost of this. Sometimes A will have to indemnify B against B's liability to a third party caused by B's negligence, or which results from some action that was a breach by B of its contract with A. This may be a perfectly sensible arrangement if A carries insurance and B does not. However, such clauses can expose parties to unexpected or unwanted risks and this section, which was inserted in the draft bill in Parliament, will protect consumers.

2.   An indemnity clause that operates in the ways just described is not, strictly speaking, an exemption clause: it transfers liability rather than excluding it. However, if A had to indemnify B against its liability *to A* for negligence or breach of contract, the clause would operate as an exclusion and would fall under s 2, just like the transfer of liability clause in the *Hyland* case (see p 1005). It is interesting to contrast *Hyland* with *Thompson v Lohan (Plant Hire) Ltd* [1987] 2 All ER 631. This case involved the same clause (cl 8) of the CPA conditions, but here the question was whether the owner or the hirer was liable to a third party who had been injured by the negligence of the driver. It was held that the clause was not in this situation 'excluding or restricting' liability for negligence and thus was not within s 2; it was operating as a transfer of liability clause and, as it was not a consumer contract, was not caught by UCTA at all.

7. The reasonableness test

There are, in fact, three separate reasonableness tests under the Act. The first is general: s 11(1), (3) and (5).

Section 11

(1) In relation to a contract term, the requirement of reasonableness for the purposes of this Part of this Act, section 3 of the Misrepresentation Act 1967 and section 3 of the Misrepresentation Act (Northern Ireland) 1967 is that the term shall have been a fair and reasonable one to be included having regard to the circumstances which were, or ought reasonably to have been, known to or in the contemplation of the parties when the contract was made.

    . . .

(3) In relation to a notice (not being a notice having contractual effect), the requirement of reasonableness under this Act is that it should be fair and reasonable to allow reliance on it, having regard to all the circumstances obtaining when the liability arose or (but for the notice) would have arisen.

    . . .

(5) It is for those claiming that a contract term or notice satisfies the requirement of reasonableness to show that it does.

The second applies to clauses limiting the amount of compensation recoverable:

Section 11

(4) Where by reference to a contract term or notice a person seeks to restrict liability to a specified sum of money, and the question arises (under this or any other Act) whether the term or notice satisfies the requirement of reasonableness, regard shall be had in particular (but without prejudice to subsection (2) above in the case of contract terms) to—

  (a) the resources which he could expect to be available to him for the purpose of meeting the liability should it arise; and

  (b) how far it was open to him to cover himself by insurance.

The third applies only to clauses caught by ss 6(3) and 7(3) and (4): s 11(2) and Sch 2.

Section 11

(2) In determining for the purposes of section 6 or 7 above whether a contract term satisfies the requirement of reasonableness, regard shall be had in particular to the matters specified in Schedule 2 to this Act; but this subsection does not prevent the court or arbitrator from holding, in accordance with any rule of law, that a term which purports to exclude or restrict any relevant liability is not a term of the contract.

  . . .

Schedule 2: 'Guidelines' for application of reasonableness test

The matters to which regard is to be had in particular for the purposes of sections 6(3), 7(3) and (4), . . . are any of the following which appear to be relevant—

  (a) the strength of the bargaining positions of the parties relative to each other, taking into account (among other things) alternative means by which the customer's requirements could have been met;

  (b) whether the customer received an inducement to agree to the term, or in accepting it had an opportunity of entering into a similar contract with other persons, but without having to accept a similar term;

  (c) whether the customer knew or ought reasonably to have known of the existence and extent of the term (having regard, among other things, to any custom of the trade and any previous course of dealing between the parties);

  (d) where the term excludes or restricts any relevant liability if some condition is not complied with, whether it was reasonable at the time of the contract to expect that compliance with that condition would be practicable;

  (e) whether the goods were manufactured, processed or adapted to the special order of the customer.

NOTES

1. Under s 11(1), reasonableness of the clause is to be judged at the time the contract was made. Under the Supply of Goods (Implied Terms) Act 1973, the test had been whether:

   . . . it is shown that it would not be fair or reasonable to allow reliance on the term.

   What difference does this change make? What if a clause that seemed reasonable at the outset actually turns out to operate harshly? What if the business includes an exclusion clause that is wider than is reasonable but it would have been perfectly reasonable to exclude or limit liability for the loss that actually occurred? (See also the *George Mitchell* case, p 1014.) In practice, it seems doubtful whether a court will ever ignore what has actually happened.

2.   Can the court 'save' a clause that is unreasonably wide in order to apply it to a situation
      in which it would have been reasonable to exclude or limit liability? In *Stewart Gill Ltd v
      Horatio Myer & Co Ltd* [1992] 2 All ER 257, a clause in a contract for the supply and
      installation of an overhead conveyor provided in cl 12.4 that 'the Customer shall not be
      entitled to withhold payment of any amount due to the Company under the Contract by
      reason of any payment credit set-off counter-claim allegation of incorrect or defective
      goods or for any other reason whatsoever which the Customer may allege excuses him
      from performing his obligations hereunder'. The customer resisted paying alleging
      breaches of contract. It was held that the whole clause was unenforceable because it
      would prevent the customer setting off a payment already made and would extend to a
      defence of fraud, neither of which would be reasonable. Stuart Smith LJ said (at
      262–263):

> In my judgment it is the term as a whole that has to be reasonable and not merely some part of it.
> Throughout the Act the expression used is 'by reference to any contract term', 'the [contract] term
> satisfies the requirement of reasonableness' (see ss 3 and 7). And in s 11(1) the reasonableness test
> is laid down as:
>
> > 'In relation to a contract term, the requirement for reasonableness . . . is that the term shall have
> > been a fair and reasonable one to be included having regard to the circumstances which were, or
> > ought reasonably to have been, known to or in the contemplation of the parties when the con-
> > tract was made.'
>
> Although the question of reasonableness is primarily one for the court when the contract term is
> challenged, it seems to me that the parties must also be in a position to judge this at the time the
> contract is made. If this is so, I find it difficult to see how such an appreciation can be made if the cus-
> tomer has to guess whether some, and if so which, part of the term will alone be relied upon. Section
> 11(2) of the Act requires the court which is determining the question of reasonableness for the pur-
> pose of ss 6 and 7 to have regard in particular to the matters specified in Sch 2. Although Sch 2 does
> not apply in the present case, the considerations there set out are usually regarded as being of gen-
> eral application to the question of reasonableness. Two paragraphs of these guidelines would in my
> judgment be unworkable unless the whole term is being considered.
>   Paragraph *(b)* provides:
>
> > 'whether the customer received an inducement to agree to the term, or in accepting it had an
> > opportunity of entering into a similar contract with other persons, but without having to accept
> > a similar term.'
>
> If there was an inducement, it would I think be quite impossible in most cases to say that it related
> only to the words which the party seeking to establish reasonableness relies upon as opposed to
> those he wishes to delete. It is equally unreal to suppose that the customer could divine which part
> the vendor will ultimately seek to rely upon so as to decide whether other persons are willing to con-
> tract without the term.
>   Paragraph (c) provides:
>
> > 'whether the customer knew or ought reasonably to have known of the existence and extent of
> > the term (having regard, among other things, to any custom of the trade and any previous course
> > of dealing between the parties).'
>
> In my judgment the customer would be most unlikely ever to know the extent of the term if the
> vendor is entitled, when it is questioned as to reasonableness, to rely on only part of it.
>   These examples in my judgment support the construction of the word 'term' as being the whole
> term or clause as drafted, and not merely that part of it which may eventually be taken to be relevant
> to the case in point.

Nor does it appear to me to be consistent with the policy and purpose of the Act to permit a contractor to impose a contractual term, which taken as a whole is completely unreasonable, to put a blue pencil through the most offensive parts and say that what is left is reasonable and sufficient to exclude or restrict his liability in a manner relied upon.

Perhaps a reasonable part of a clause may survive if the clause is clearly separable into reasonable and unreasonable bits, each of which can stand alone. (This may explain why some contracts contain overlapping clauses, each one wider than the last!)

3. Section 11(5) puts the burden of proving reasonableness on the party trying to rely on the clause. This also seems to be a change from the earlier statute. It has been argued that even before this, there had been a shift in the courts' attitude: the *Photo Productions* case (see p 990) had been in favour of allowing businesses to determine their contract terms freely, but the cases on the 1973 Act had appeared to apply the opposite presumption. See Adams and Brownsword, 'The Unfair Contract Terms Act: A Decade of Discretion' (1988) 104 LQR 94.

4. Although the guidelines in Sch 2 apply only to clauses caught by ss 6 and 7, the courts consider them, or at least the same factors, in other cases: eg *Rees Hough Ltd v Redland Reinforced Plastics Ltd* (1984) 27 BLR 136; *Phillips v Hyland* (see p 1018).

5. What do the guidelines mean and how should they be applied?
   (a) What does the 'strength of the bargaining positions of the parties' refer to?
   (b) If Goldberg's analysis that harsh terms are a way of reducing producers' costs, so that they can offer lower prices (see p 953) is correct, don't most customers in effect 'receive an inducement to agree to the term' in the form of a lower price? Or is (b) referring to the customer who accepts the clause as part of a special deal?
   (c) Knowledge of the 'existence and extent' of the term seems to cover the questions of whether the customer knows of the clause and understands its meaning. What about the problems of seeing how it may affect him or her (see the 'big dipper' example on p 1007)?
   (d) For an example of the operation of (d) see *RW Green Ltd v Cade Bros Farm*, see p 1015.
   (e) What difference might it make that the goods were a 'special order'?

In *Levison v Patent Steam Carpet Cleaning Co Ltd* [1978] QB 69, the plaintiffs sent a Chinese carpet worth £900 to the defendants for cleaning and signed a form stating that the maximum value of the carpet was deemed to be £40 and that 'all merchandise is expressly accepted at owner's risk'. The form recommended that owners should insure their goods. The defendants never returned the carpet and were unable to explain its disappearance. The Court of Appeal held that the plaintiffs were entitled to recover the full value of the carpet: the majority held that the words were not clear enough to exclude liability for fundamental breach, and that, in the circumstances, the burden of proving that the loss was not due to a fundamental breach was on the defendants. Lord Denning held the clause did apply, but was void at common law because it was unreasonable. This is a heretical view of the law that cannot have survived the *Photo Productions* case (**p 976**), but his view that the clause was unreasonable is puzzling. The carpet was already insured; if the owner had been asked whether he wished to have this form of contract, or one with full liability but a higher charge, which do you think he would have chosen?

■ *George Mitchell (Chesterhall) Ltd v Finney Lock Seeds Ltd*

[1983] 1 All ER 108, Court of Appeal; [1983] 2 All ER 737, House of Lords

The defendant seed merchants agreed in December 1973 to supply the plaintiff farmers with 30lbs of Dutch winter cabbage seed for £192. An invoice that accompanied the seed when it was delivered, and which was treated as forming part of the contract, contained a clause purporting to limit liability if the seed sold were defective to replacing the seed or refunding the price. It went on to exclude 'all liability for any loss or damage arising from the use of any seeds or plants supplied by us and for any consequential loss or damage arising out of such use . . . or for any other loss or damage whatsoever'.

The plaintiffs planted some 63 acres with the seed, but the seed was of the wrong kind and also unmerchantable, and the crop was a total failure. The plaintiffs claimed compensation of some £63,000 for loss of production.

In the Court of Appeal, the majority held that, as a matter of construction, the clause did not apply: it was not clear enough to protect the sellers from the consequences of their own negligence, and (*per* Oliver LJ) it did not apply when the sellers had delivered something wholly different in kind from what had been ordered. Lord Denning thought the clause did apply. However, all three judges agreed that, in any event, the clause was invalid under the Supply of Goods (Implied Terms) Act 1973 (by the date of judgment incorporated into SGA 1979 as s 55) because it was unreasonable.

Kerr LJ

. . . However, even if [the decision on construction] be wrong, I would unhesitatingly also decide this case in favour of the plaintiffs on the ground that it would not be fair or reasonable to allow the defendants to rely on this clause, by applying s 55(4) and (5) in Sch 1 to the Sale of Goods Act 1979. In this regard the balance of fairness and reasonableness appears to me to be overwhelmingly on the side of the plaintiffs, and I will only mention some of the most material facts in this connection.

The plaintiffs have suffered a loss of some £61,000 in terms of money; and in terms of time and labour the productivity of over 60 acres has been wasted for over a year. There was nothing whatever which the plaintiffs could have done to avoid this. As between them and the defendants all the fault lay admittedly on the side of the defendants. Further, farmers do not, and cannot be expected to, insure against this kind of disaster; but suppliers of seeds can. We were referred to a 'Wrong Variety of Seed Indemnity Insurance Scheme', set up under the auspices of the United Kingdom Agricultural Supply Trade Association Ltd (UKASTA), which provides an annual cover of £20,000. Although this particular scheme stipulates the exercise of due diligence on the part of the supplier, I am not persuaded that liability for rare events of this kind cannot be adequately insured against. Nor am I persuaded that the cost of such cover would add significantly to the cost of the seed. Further, although the present exemption clause has been in existence for many decades, the evidence shows that it was never negotiated. In effect, it was simply imposed by the suppliers, and no seed can in practice be bought otherwise than subject to its terms. To limit the suppliers' liability to the price of the seed in all cases, as against the magnitude of the losses which farmers can incur in rare disasters of this kind, appears to me to be a grossly disproportionate and unreasonable allocation of the respective risks. Furthermore, the evidence clearly shows that the clause is not relied on 'to the letter' in practice, and that neither the suppliers nor the farmers expect it to be applied literally. Its existence merely provides a basis for the negotiation of mutually acceptable settlements. Thus, we were told that there had been some inconclusive negotiations in the present case, though no figures were mentioned. However, these negotiations do not matter, since the defendants are now seeking to uphold the clause to the letter. It is on this basis that we have to decide whether reliance on the clause would be fair or reasonable, and in my view the answer is clearly that it would not be.

Furthermore, to my mind there is another, overriding, consideration. It seems to me that this new legislation, the modified version of s 55 of the Sale of Goods Act 1979 and the Unfair Contract Terms Act 1977, was designed for exempting provisions whose meaning is clear. Thus, one of the matters to be taken into account in judging fairness and reasonableness (under s 55(5)(c)) is 'whether the buyer knew or ought reasonably to have known of the ... extent of the term ... '. But we have several days of argument about the meaning and effect of the present clause, and it is already clear to what extent opinions may differ about it. I do not think that this is the kind of situation for which this legislation was designed. It was designed for exempting provisions whose meaning is plain. Thus, if the present clause had been headed, for instance, 'Supply of wrong or unmerchantable seed, whether by negligence or otherwise', the defendants' case in relation to fairness and reasonableness would to that extent be strengthened. The effect of the parties' bargain would then be plain. But businessmen do not choose to make plain the meaning of the 'small print' which they use, and often do not themselves know what it really means. In that event they must take the consequences of the uncertainty which their 'small print' has created; and uncertainty involves unfairness to the other side. Perhaps the effect of this new legislation will bring about a welcome change in this respect. But so long as the meaning and effect of such provisions remains shrouded in obscurity unless and until determined by the courts (and to many minds even thereafter), I think that the courts should hold that reliance on such provisions would in any event be unfair and unreasonable.

Finally, I must briefly refer to *R W Green Ltd v Cade Bros Farm* on which counsel strongly relied on behalf of the defendants. In that case, seed potatoes had been sold subject to the standard form of conditions of the National Association of Seed Potato Merchants. These included a time limit for claims, and they also limited the supplier's liability to refunding the contract price. The potatoes were suffering from a virus which was undetectable by either party. Griffiths J held that the exempting provision protected the sellers and that it was neither unfair nor unreasonable for them to rely on it. In the latter regard he used language suggesting that he was merely exercising a discretion, but I do not think that this was his intention. As stated by this court in *Conemsco Ltd v Contrapol Ltd*, a determination under s 55 or under the Unfair Contract Terms Act 1977 constitutes a decision, of mixed fact and law, and not merely the exercise of a discretion. But that case was very different from the present. In particular, no blame attached to either party, and the standard condition had been negotiated within the trade. There was also no basis for argument about its meaning and effect. Further, there was evidence that the buyers could have purchased seed certified by inspectors from the Ministry of Agriculture at a small extra charge, whereas it was accepted on behalf of the defendants in the present case that there was nothing equivalent which the plaintiffs could have done. I therefore do not think that that case assists the defendants here in any way.

In the House of Lords, there was unanimous agreement that the clause as a matter of construction did cover the loss. Given that the clause was only one of limitation and not a total exclusion, there was no reason why it should not cover the sellers' negligence; the clauses applied to seeds 'sold' and 'supplied', which these had been, even if they were not the correct variety of seed. However, the House agreed that the clause was unreasonable.

Lord Bridge

... My Lords, it seems to me, with all due deference, that the judgments of the trial judge and of Oliver LJ on the common law issue come dangerously near to reintroducing by the back door the doctrine of 'fundamental breach' which this House in the *Photo Production* case had so forcibly evicted by the front. The judge discusses what I may call the 'peas and beans' or 'chalk and cheese' cases, ie those in which it has been held that exemption clauses do not apply where there has been a contract to sell one thing, eg a motor car, and the seller has supplied quite another thing, eg a bicycle. I hasten to add that the judge can in no way be criticised for adopting this approach since counsel appearing for the appellants at the trial had conceded 'that, if what had been delivered had been beetroot seed or carrot seed, he would not be able to rely on the clause'. Different counsel appeared for the appellants in the Court of Appeal, where that concession was withdrawn.

In my opinion, this is not a 'peas and beans' case at all. The relevant condition applies to 'seeds'. Clause I refers to 'seeds sold' and 'seeds agreed to be sold'. Clause 2 refers to 'seeds supplied'. As I have pointed out, Oliver LJ concentrated his attention on the phrase 'seeds agreed to be sold'. I can see no justification, with respect, for allowing this phrase alone to dictate the interpretation of the relevant condition, still less for treating cl 2 as 'merely a supplement' to cl 1. Clause 2 is perfectly clear and unambiguous. The reference to 'seeds agreed to be sold' as well as to 'seeds sold' in cl 1 reflects the same dichotomy as the definition of 'sale' in the Sale of Goods Act 1979 as including a bargain and sale as well as a sale and delivery. The defective seeds in this case were seeds sold and delivered, just as clearly as they were seeds supplied, by the appellants to the respondents. The relevant condition, read as a whole, unambiguously limits the appellants' liability to replacement of the seeds or refund of the price. It is only possible to read an ambiguity into it by the process of strained construction which was deprecated by Lord Diplock in the *Photo Production* case . . . and by Lord Wilberforce in the *Ailsa Craig* case [1983] 1 All ER 101 at 102.

In holding that the relevant condition was ineffective to limit the appellants' liability for a breach of contract caused by their negligence, Kerr LJ applied the principles stated by Lord Morton giving the judgment of the Privy Council in *Canada Steamship Lines Ltd v R.* Kerr LJ stated correctly that this case was also referred to by Lord Fraser in the *Ailsa Craig* case. He omitted, however, to notice that, as appears from the passage from Lord Fraser's speech which I have already cited, the whole point of Lord Fraser's reference was to express his opinion that the very strict principles laid down in the *Canada Steamship Lines* case as applicable to exclusion and indemnity clauses cannot be applied in their full rigour to limitation clauses. Lord Wilberforce's speech contains a passage to the like effect, and Lord Elwyn-Jones, Lord Salmon and Lord Lowry agreed with both speeches. Having once reached a conclusion in the instant case that the relevant condition unambiguously limited the appellants' liability, I know of no principle of construction which can properly be applied to confine the effect of the limitation to breaches of contract arising without negligence on the part of the appellants. In agreement with Lord Denning MR, I would decide the common law issue in the appellants' favour.

. . . The statutory issue . . . turns on the words in s 55(4) 'to the extent that it is shown that it would not be fair or reasonable to allow reliance on 'this restriction of the appellants' liabilities, having regard to the matters referred to in subs (5).

This is the first time your Lordships' House has had to consider a modern statutory provision giving the court power to override contractual terms excluding or restricting liability, which depends on the court's view of what is 'fair and reasonable'. The particular provision of the modified s 55 of the 1979 Act which applies in the instant case is of limited and diminishing importance. But the several provisions of the Unfair Contract Terms Act 1977 which depend on 'the requirement of reasonableness', defined in s 11 by reference to what is 'fair and reasonable', albeit in a different context, are likely to come before the courts with increasing frequency. It may, therefore, be appropriate to consider how an original decision what is 'fair and reasonable' made in the application of any of these provisions should be approached by an appellate court. It would not be accurate to describe such a decision as an exercise of discretion. But a decision under any of the provisions referred to will have this in common with the exercise of a discretion, that, in having regard to the various matters to which the modified s 55(5) of the 1979 Act, or s 11 of the 1977 Act direct attention, the court must entertain a whole range of considerations, put them in the scales on one side or the other and decide at the end of the day on which side the balance comes down. There will sometimes be room for a legitimate difference of judicial opinions as to what the answer should be, where it will be impossible to say that one view is demonstrably wrong and the other demonstrably right. It must follow, in my view, that, when asked to review such a decision on appeal, the appellate court should treat the original decision with the utmost respect and refrain from interference with it unless satisfied that it proceeded on some erroneous principle or was plainly and obviously wrong.

Turning back to the modified s 55 of the 1979 Act, it is common ground that the onus was on the respondents to show that it would not be fair or reasonable to allow the appellants to rely on the relevant condition as limiting their liability. It was argued for the appellants that the court must have regard to the circumstances as at the date of the contract, not after the breach. The basis of the argument was that this was the effect of s 11 of the 1977 Act and that it would be wrong to construe the modified s 55 of the Act as having a different effect. Assuming the premise is correct, the conclusion does not follow. The provisions of the 1977 Act cannot be considered in construing the prior enactments now embodied in the modified s 55 of the 1979 Act. But, in any event, the language of sub-ss (4) and (5) of that section is clear and unambiguous. The question whether it is fair or reasonable to allow reliance on a term excluding or limiting liability for a breach of contract can only arise after the breach. The nature of the breach and the circumstances in which it occurred cannot possibly be excluded from 'all the circumstances of the case' to which regard must be had.

The only other question of construction debated in the course of the argument was the meaning to be attached to the words 'to the extent that' in sub-s (4) and, in particular, whether they permit the court to hold that it would be fair and reasonable to allow partial reliance on a limitation clause and, for example, to decide in the instant case that the respondents should recover, say, half their consequential damage. I incline to the view that, in their context, the words are equivalent to 'in so far as' or 'in circumstances in which' and do not permit the kind of judgment of Solomon illustrated by the example.

But for the purpose of deciding this appeal I find it unnecessary to express a concluded view on this question.

My Lords, at long last I turn to the application of the statutory language to the circumstances of the case. Of the particular matters to which attention is directed by paras (a) to (e) of s 55(5), only those in paras (a) to (c) are relevant. As to para (c), the respondents admittedly knew of the relevant condition (they had dealt with the appellants for many years) and, if they had read it, particularly cl 2, they would, I think, as laymen rather than lawyers, have had no difficulty in understanding what it said. This and the magnitude of the damages claimed in proportion to the price of the seeds sold are factors which weigh in the scales in the appellants' favour.

The question of relative bargaining strength under para (a) and of the opportunity to buy seeds without a limitation of the seedsman's liability under para (b) were interrelated. The evidence was that a similar limitation of liability was universally embodied in the terms of trade between seedsmen and farmers and had been so for very many years. The limitation had never been negotiated between representative bodies but, on the other hand, had not been the subject of any protest by the National Farmers' Union. These factors, if considered in isolation, might have been equivocal. The decisive factor however, appears from the evidence of four witnesses called for the appellants, two independent seedsmen, the chairman of the appellant company, and a director of a sister company (both being wholly-owned subsidiaries of the same parent). They said that it had always been their practice, unsuccessfully attempted in the instant case, to negotiate settlements of farmers' claims for damages in excess of the price of the seeds if they thought that the claims were 'genuine' and 'justified'. This evidence indicated a clear recognition by seedsmen in general, and the appellants in particular, that reliance on the limitation of liability imposed by the relevant condition would not be fair or reasonable.

Two further factors, if more were needed, weigh the scales in favour of the respondents. The supply of autumn, instead of winter, cabbage seed was due to the negligence of the appellants' sister company. Irrespective of its quality, the autumn variety supplied could not, according to the appellants' own evidence, be grown commercially in East Lothian. Finally, as the trial judge found, seedsmen could insure against the risk of crop failure caused by supply of the wrong variety of seeds without materially increasing the price of seeds.

My Lords, even if I felt doubts about the statutory issue, I should not, for the reasons explained earlier, think it right to interfere with the unanimous original decision of that issue by the Court of Appeal. As it is, I feel no such doubts. If I were making the original decision, I should conclude without hesitation that it would not be fair or reasonable to allow the appellants to rely on the contractual limitation of their liability.

I would dismiss the appeal.

■ *Phillips Products Ltd v Hyland* [1987]
2 All ER 620, Court of Appeal

The plaintiffs hired an excavator and driver from the second defendants, the plant owner. The contract, by cl 8, provided that drivers 'supplied by the owner … shall for all purposes in connection with their employment in the working of the plant be regarded as the servants or agents of the hirer who alone shall be responsible for all claims arising in connection with the operation of the plant by the … drivers'. The driver negligently drove the excavator into collision with, and damaged, the plaintiffs' building. On the plaintiffs' claim for damages for negligence against the driver and the second defendants, the judge, giving judgment for the plaintiffs, held that cl 8 did not satisfy 'the requirement of reasonableness' in s 2(2) of the Unfair Contract Terms Act 1977 and, accordingly, the second defendants were precluded from relying on the clause as exempting them from liability for negligence.
(On the question of whether s 2(2) applied to cl 8, see p 1005.)

Slade LJ

… As the judge pointed out, all the relevant circumstances were known to both parties at that time. The task which he therefore set himself was to examine all the relevant circumstances and then ask himself whether, on the balance of probabilities, he was satisfied that clause 8, in so far as it purported to exclude Hamstead's liability for Mr Hyland's negligence, was a fair and reasonable term. As to these matters, his conclusions as set out in his judgment were:

'What then were the relevant circumstances? Firstly, the second defendants carried on the business of hiring out plant and operators. In contrast the first defendants were steel stockholders, and as such had no occasion to hire plant except on the odd occasions when they had building work to be done at their premises. There had been apparently only three such occasions: one in 1979, one in July 1980 when the drainage trench was dug and the final occasion when the damage was done in August 1980.

Secondly, the hire was to be for a very short period. It was arranged at very short notice. There was no occasion for the plaintiffs to address their mind to all the details of the hiring agreement, nor did they do so. The inclusion of condition 8 arose because it appeared in the second defendants' printed conditions. It was not the product of any discussion or agreement between the parties.

Thirdly, there was little if any opportunity for the plaintiffs to arrange insurance cover for risks arising from the first defendant's negligence. In so far as the first defendant was to be regarded as the plaintiffs' servant it might have been an easy matter to ensure that the plaintiffs' insurance policies were extended, if necessary, to cover his activities in relation to third party claims. Any businessman customarily insures against such claims. He does not usually insure against damage caused to his own property by his own employees' negligence. Thus to arrange insurance cover for the first defendant would have required time and a special and unusual arrangement with the plaintiffs' insurers.

Fourthly, the plaintiffs played no part in the selection of the first defendant as the operator of the JCB. They had to accept whoever the second defendant sent to drive the machine. Further, although they undoubtedly would have had to, and would have had the right to, tell the JCB operator what job he was required to do, from their previous experience they knew they would be unable in any way to control the way in which the first defendant did the job that he was given. They would not have had the knowledge to exercise such control. All the expertise lay with the first defendant. I do not think condition 8 could possibly be construed as giving control of the manner of operation of the JCB to the plaintiffs. Indeed in the event the first defendant made it perfectly plain to Mr Pritchard, the plaintiffs' builder, that he would brook no interference in the way he operated his machine.

Those being the surrounding circumstances, was it fair and reasonable that the hire contract should include a condition which relieved the second defendants of all responsibility for damage caused, not to the property of a third party but to the plaintiff's own property, by the negligence of the second defendants' own operators? This was for the plaintiffs in a very real sense a 'take it or leave it' situation. They needed a JCB for a simple job at short notice. In dealing with the second defendants they had the choice of taking a JCB operator under a contract containing some 43 written conditions or not taking the JCB at all. The question for me is not a general question whether *any* contract of hire of the JCB could fairly and reasonably exclude such liability, but a much more limited question as to whether *this* contract of hire entered into in these circumstances fairly and reasonably included such an exemption.

I have come to the conclusion that the second defendants have failed to satisfy me that condition 8 was in this respect a fair and reasonable term.'

In approaching the judge's reasons and conclusions on this issue, four points have, in our judgment, to be borne in mind. First, as the judge himself clearly appreciated, the question for the court is not a general question whether or not clause 8 is valid or invalid in the case of any and every contract of hire entered into between a hirer and a plant owner who uses the relevant C.P.A. conditions. The question was and is whether the exclusion of Hamstead's liability for negligence satisfied the requirement of reasonableness imposed by the Act, in relation to *this particular contract.*

Secondly, we have to bear in mind that the relevant circumstances, which were or should have been known to or contemplated by the parties, are those which existed when the contract was made. Section 11 (1) is specific on that point. Hence, evidence as to what happened during the performance of the contract must, at best, be treated with great caution. As we have indicated, such evidence was adduced at the trial, apparently without objection. At best, it could probably be used to show, by evidence of conduct and absence of objection to that conduct, what the attitude of the parties would have been in that respect, what they would have contemplated, at the time when they made the contract.

Thirdly, the burden of proof falling upon the owner under section 11(5) of the Act is, in our judgment, of great significance in this case in the light, or rather in the obscurity, of the evidence and the absence of evidence on issues which were, or might have been, relevant on the issue of reasonableness. One particular example is the matter of insurance. The insurance position of all the parties was canvassed to some extent in oral evidence at the trial, but such evidence seems to us to have been singularly imprecise and inconclusive.

Finally, by way of approach to the issue of reasonableness, it is necessary to bear in mind, and strive to comply with, the clear and stern injunction issued to appellate courts by Lord Bridge of Harwich in his speech, concurred in by the other members of the House of Lords in *George Mitchell (Chesterhall) Ltd v Finney Lock Seeds Ltd* [see above]

In the context of issue (iii), criticism has been made by Mr Thompson of some parts of the judge's reasoning. It is said that in some respects he misunderstood or mis-recollected the evidence. Some of the evidence was indeed confused and not easy to follow. It is, in some passages, difficult to be confident what was really meant. It may be that the judge placed more stress than we would think right on the lack of opportunity of Mr Phillips to study and understand the conditions, and in particular clause 8. But this is the very sort of point to which Lord Bridge referred in saying that there is room for a legitimate difference of judicial opinion.

Against this, there is to be set the fact, as it appeared at the trial, that the general conditions with their 43 clauses were adopted by and used by all the members of the trade association to which Hamstead belonged. (Counsel has told us that there is other material which might alter the picture, but we cannot go beyond the evidence which was in fact before the judge.) Thus, we think he was justified in saying that in dealing with Hamstead this was for Phillips in a very real sense a 'take it or leave it situation.' As he said, they needed a JCB for a simple job at short notice and, in dealing with Hamstead, had the choice of taking a JCB operator under the general conditions or not taking the JCB at all. Even if Mr Phillips had understood and had been worried by the effect of clause 8 before he arranged for the conclusion of the earlier contracts or before he authorised Mr Pritchard to conclude the contract in August 1980 now in question, it is reasonable to assume, on the evidence as it stood, that he would not have thought that there was much that he could do about it, except to take the conditions offered.

It is fair to say that we were told that various changes had been made, including the alterations to some of the general conditions since the coming into force of the Act and that the position today might be very different. But Mr Thompson necessarily and realistically accepts that we have to deal, as the judge had to deal, with the contractual terms as they were and with the facts as to the relevant considerations as they were given in evidence at the trial: not as the terms are now or as the relevant facts might have appeared to be if further evidence had been given.

As appears from the passage which we have cited, other matters which influenced the judge in his decision on unreasonableness, and which we think were clearly relevant factors to be weighed in the balance, were that the hirers could play no part in the selection of the operator who was to do the work. Nor did the general conditions contain any warranty by Hamstead as to his fitness or competence for the job. Furthermore, despite the words in clause 8, 'he shall be under the direction and control of the hirer,' we think it reasonable to infer that the parties, when they made the contract, would have assumed that the operator would be the expert in the management of this machine and that he would not, and could not be expected to, take any instructions from anyone representing the hirers as to the manner in which he would operate the machine to do the job, once the extent and nature of the job had been defined to him by the hirers; in short they would tell him what to do but not how to do it. If such evidence is admissible, which we do not find it necessary to decide, this inference would be strongly supported by the evidence of what actually happened on the site before the accident occurred.

It may be that in several respects this is a very special case on its facts, its evidence and its paucity of evidence. But on these facts and on the available evidence, we are wholly unpersuaded that the judge proceeded upon some erroneous principle or was plainly and obviously wrong in his conclusion that Hamstead had not discharged the burden upon them of showing that clause 8 satisfied the requirement of reasonableness in the context of this particular contract of hire. It is important therefore that our conclusion on the particular facts of this case should not be treated as a binding precedent in other cases where similar clauses fall to be considered but the evidence of the surrounding circumstances may be very different. Issue (iii) accordingly has to be answered 'No' and we dismiss this appeal.

Appeal dismissed with costs.

It is not easy to draw general conclusions from these two cases about when a clause will be treated as fair and reasonable. The reluctance to interfere with first-instance decisions makes the task of predicting harder. There are now a great many cases about the meaning of unreasonableness under UCTA (see Macdonald, *Exemption Clauses and Unfair Terms*, 2nd edn, 2006, pp 161–186. With such a flexible test, it would be a great surprise if it were mechanically applied in a rigid way, particularly because there are a wide range of situations and of possibly relevant factors. What follows are no more than tentative pointers and suggestions.

(1) In *George Mitchell*, Bridge treats the facts that the clause was known to the farmers and easy to understand as in its favour. Compare *The Zinnia* [1984] 2 Lloyd's Rep 211, in which Staughton J commented (at 222):

I would have been tempted to hold that all the conditions are unfair and unreasonable for two reasons: first, they are in such small print that one can barely read them; secondly, the draughtsmanship is so convoluted and prolix that one almost needs an LL.B. to understand them. However, neither of those arguments was advanced before me, so I say no more about them.

However, it is clear that the fact that a clause is known and understood will not necessarily make it reasonable—in other words, the courts are concerned to do more than prevent unfair surprise.

(2) It is not surprising to find the courts reluctant to allow the exclusion of liability for negligence. As we saw earlier (see p 395), it will normally be efficient to place liability on the least cost avoider. (Schwartz's argument that excluding liability will not lessen the incentive to perform carefully, noted on p 1006, operates only under the very restrictive assumption that information costs are near zero—ie that the buyer can easily get the relevant information. As the note hints, this will seldom be the case.)

(3) Equally, insurance or other mechanisms by which the parties can protect themselves from loss are also crucial. In *Smith v Eric S Bush* [1989] 2 All ER 514, the question was whether it was reasonable for a surveyor, employed by a building society to inspect and value a house, to disclaim responsibility to the purchaser to whom the report would be passed and who was paying a fee to the building society to have the valuation made. The House of Lords held that it was not. Lord Griffiths said (at 531–532):

I believe that it is impossible to draw up an exhaustive list of the factors that must be taken into account when a judge is faced with this very difficult decision. Nevertheless, the following matters should, in my view, always be considered.

(1) Were the parties of equal bargaining power? If the court is dealing with a one-off situation between parties of equal bargaining power the requirement of reasonableness would be more easily discharged than in a case such as the present where the disclaimer is imposed on the purchaser who has no effective power to object.

(2) In the case of advice, would it have been reasonably practicable to obtain the advice from an alternative source taking into account considerations of costs and time? In the present case it is urged on behalf of the surveyor that it would have been easy for the purchaser to have obtained his own report on the condition of the house, to which the purchaser replies that he would then be required to pay twice for the same advice and that people buying at the bottom end of the market, many of whom will be young first-time buyers, are likely to be under considerable financial pressure without the money to go paying twice for the same service.

(3) How difficult is the task being undertaken for which liability is being excluded? When a very difficult or dangerous undertaking is involved there may be a high risk of failure which would certainly be a pointer towards the reasonableness of excluding liability as a condition of doing the work. A valuation, on the other hand, should present no difficulty if the work is undertaken with reasonable skill and care. It is only defects which are observable by a careful visual examination that have to be taken into account and I cannot see that it places any unreasonable burden on the valuer to require him to accept responsibility for the fairly elementary degree of skill and care involved in observing, following up and reporting on such defects. Surely it is work at the lower end of the surveyor's field of professional expertise.

(4) What are the practical consequences of the decision on the question of reasonableness? This must involve the sums of money potentially at stake and the ability of the parties to bear the loss involved, which, in its turn, raises the question of insurance. There was once a time when it was considered improper even to mention the possible existence of insurance cover in a lawsuit. But those days are long past. Everyone knows that all prudent, professional men carry insurance, and the availability and cost of insurance must be a relevant factor when considering which of two parties should be required to bear the risk of a loss. We are dealing in this case with a loss which will be limited to the value of a modest house and against which it can be expected that the surveyor will be insured. Bearing the loss will be unlikely to cause significant hardship if it has to be borne by the surveyor but it is, on the other hand, quite possible that it will be a financial catastrophe for the purchaser who may be left with a valueless house and no money to buy another. If the law in these circumstances denies the surveyor the right to exclude his liability, it may result in a few more claims but I do not think so poorly of the surveyors' profession as to believe that the floodgates will be opened. There may be some increase in surveyors' insurance premiums which will be passed on to the public, but I cannot think that it will be anything approaching the figures involved in the difference between the Abbey National's offer of a valuation

without liability and a valuation with liability discussed in the speech of my noble and learned friend Lord Templeman. The result of denying a surveyor, in the circumstances of this case, the right to exclude liability will result in distributing the risk of his negligence among all house purchasers through an increase in his fees to cover insurance, rather than allowing the whole of the risk to fall on the one unfortunate purchaser.

I would not, however, wish it to be thought that I would consider it unreasonable for professional men in all circumstances to seek to exclude or limit their liability for negligence. Sometimes breathtaking sums of money may turn on professional advice against which it would be impossible for the adviser to obtain adequate insurance cover and which would ruin him if he were to be held personally liable. In these circumstances it may indeed by reasonable to give the advice on a basis of no liability or possibly of liability limited to the extent of the adviser's insurance cover.

In addition to the foregoing four factors, which will always have to be considered, there is in this case the additional feature that the surveyor is only employed in the first place because the purchaser wishes to buy the house and the purchaser in fact provides or contributes to the surveyor's fees. No one has argued that if the purchaser had employed and paid the surveyor himself, it would have been reasonable for the surveyor to exclude liability for negligence, and the present situation is not far removed from that of a direct contract between the surveyor and the purchaser. The evaluation of the foregoing matters leads me to the clear conclusion that it would not be fair and reasonable for the surveyor to be permitted to exclude liability in the circumstances of this case. I would therefore dismiss this appeal.

It must, however, be remembered that this is a decision in respect of a dwelling house of modest value in which it is widely recognised by surveyors that purchasers are in fact relying on their care and skill. It will obviously be of general application in broadly similar circumstances. But I expressly reserve my position of valuations of quite different types of property for mortgage purposes, such as industrial property, large blocks of flats or very expensive houses. In such cases it may well be that the general expectation of the behaviour of the purchaser is quite different. With very large sums of money at stake prudence would seem to demand that the purchaser obtain his own structural survey to guide him in his purchase and, in such circumstances with very much larger sums of money at stake, it may be reasonable for the surveyors valuing on behalf of those who are providing the finance either to exclude or limit their liability to the purchaser.

> It is usually assumed that it is easier to persuade the court that a limitation on liability is reasonable than that an exclusion is reasonable. This would be in line with the distinction drawn in common law (see p 995). However, in *St Albans City and District Council v International Computers Ltd* [1996] 4 All ER 481, the defendant's standard conditions of business limited its liability in the circumstances that applied to £100,000. This limitation was held by the Court of Appeal to be unreasonable. In the circumstances of the case, the defendant's potential liability was far in excess of £100,000 and it was insured for a much large sum. (Note that s 11(4) did not apply on the facts of this case.)

(4) As Lord Griffiths makes clear, the courts will sometimes assume that the parties are the best judges of their own interests. What is not clear is the extent to which the circumstances of the individual contract will be looked at. In *Hyland*, Slade stressed that the court was concerned with the particular contract, but suppose that most firms that use plant hire are, in fact, already insured against damage to buildings? (This is not purely hypothetical. Probably most plant is hired for work on building sites where the building work done already will be insured by either contractor or employer.) Should a contract that is suitable for the majority of contracting parties be held unreasonable because it wasn't reasonable for the individual plaintiff?

(5) If the terms aren't what the plaintiff wants, why not ask for a change? One factor that seems to recur in the cases is whether the individual would have been able to bargain for

better terms. How likely is it that a single individual will be able to do this? What if there is a trade association that could bargain on behalf of its members?

(6) Sometimes a firm can be persuaded to make a concession on terms. In *The Zinnia* [1984] 2 Lloyd's Rep 211, 222–223, Staughton J said:

The point which was most discussed was the strength of the bargaining positions of the parties relative to each other. This I find to have been, in broad terms, equal. The owners could and apparently did, obtain tenders from a number of other yards. The defendants did from time to time relax some of their standard terms at the request of a particular customer, but that had only happened in the past at the request of customers with more economic power than the present owners. They had never in the past relaxed the exclusion in cl 8(9) of economic loss, or modified cl 8 otherwise than by extending the period of guarantee. But they have never been asked to do so. I do not find that surprising. Commercial men negotiating a contract for the future are not too concerned about the small print if they can secure a guarantee clause which seems to them satisfactory. It is only after a breach has occurred that they may take a different view.

In February, 1980, when this contract was made, the defendants were very busy. They would have been reluctant to make any concession. At other times, when they were short of work, they would have been much more ready to do so. In the circumstances of this case, I do not think that I can take that factor into account or at any rate give it much weight. It can scarcely have been the intention of Parliament that a clause in a ship repairer's standard terms would be fair and reasonable one week—when the yard had no work and was willing to make concessions if asked—but unfair and unreasonable the following week, when the yard was busy. Relative bargaining power must surely be judged by somewhat broader considerations.

Do you think this is correct? If the plaintiffs had the chance to get better terms but did not try to do so, what does that suggest?

(7) In the *George Mitchell* case, the farmers' trade association had never negotiated the clause. What does that suggest? Was Bridge correct to regard the absence of negotiation as 'equivocal'?

(8) It may happen that an unreasonable clause is never taken up in negotiations because it very seldom causes trouble. This may have been the case in *Walker v Boyle* [1982] 1 All ER 634. This case arose out of a contract for the purchase of a house. Before the contract is concluded, it is normal for the purchaser's solicitors to address a number of enquiries to the vendor. In this case, the vendor was asked if she knew of any disputes regarding the boundaries of the property. She allowed her husband to manage her business affairs, and he replied that he knew of no such disputes. In fact, there was a serious boundary dispute with a neighbour but the husband was so convinced that his view of it was correct that he honestly thought there was no dispute. In due course, contracts were exchanged on the National Conditions of Sale (19th edn). Condition 17(1) provided that 'no error, misstatement or omission in any preliminary answer shall annul the sale'. When the purchaser discovered the dispute, he brought an action seeking rescission and the return of his deposit. It was argued that Condition 17(1) was unreasonable and of no effect by virtue of the Misrepresentation Act 1967, s 3. Dillon J said:

... I do not regard condition 17 as satisfying that requirement [of reasonableness] in the circumstances of this case. Another way of putting it is that Mrs Boyle has not shown that it does satisfy that requirement.

It has been submitted by counsel for Mrs Boyle that as there were solicitors acting for both parties, it would be a very strong thing to say that any term of the contract which resulted is not a fair and reasonable one in the circumstances. That argument would have great force, no doubt, if the solicitors had specifically directed their minds to the problem and had evolved the clause which was under attack. In fact, however, neither solicitor directed his mind to condition 17, and they have both told me, and they are men of not inconsiderable experience as conveyancing solicitors, that they have never come across a case where any question under condition 17 has arisen. It was submitted that it was the duty of the purchaser's solicitor to advise his client, Mr Walker, of the implications of condition 17 and of the other terms of the contract which Mr Walker was going to enter into, and he must be taken to have discharged that duty and satisfied himself and Mr Walker that the terms were reasonable. It is, of course, the duty of a solicitor to advise his client about any abnormal or unusual term in a contract, but I think it is perfectly normal and proper for a solicitor to use standard forms of conditions of sale such as the National Conditions of Sale. I do not think he is called on to go through the small print of those somewhat lengthy conditions with a tooth-comb every time he is advising a purchaser or to draw the purchaser's attention to every problem which on a careful reading of the conditions might in some circumstance or other conceivably arise. I cannot believe that purchasers of house property throughout the land would be overjoyed at having such lengthy explanations of the National Conditions of Sale ritually foisted on them.

It has also been submitted by counsel for Mrs Boyle that the court should be very slow to hold that a common-form clause like condition 17 is not fair and reasonable. Of course it is true that there are common-form clauses which have been evolved by negotiation between trade associations, associations of merchants or associations of growers or trade unions or other such bodies concerned to protect the rights of their members, which can be regarded as representing what consensus in the trade regards as fair and reasonable. Again, the National Conditions of Sale are not the product of negotiation between such bodies and it is plain from the conditions I have cited in the *Nottingham Patent Brick and Tile Co* case and Clauson J's case of *Charles Hunt Ltd v Palmer* that what now appears in condition 17 has come down through the ages despite very drastic limitations imposed on it by the courts. I do not think it can be said that its precarious survival until 1977 entitles it to the automatic accolade of fairness and reasonableness.

> Dillon J ordered the vendor to return the purchaser's deposit. Is it ever reasonable to exclude liability for the inaccuracy of information to which you have already access but the other party does not? For a rather inconclusive discussion on this point, see *Howard Marine and Dredging Co Ltd v A Ogden & Sons (Excavations) Ltd* [1978] QB 574.
>
> (9) Even if there is no association representing the customers, does it follow that the business is completely unconstrained in putting into the contract whatever clauses it likes? Go back to Trebilcock's analysis (on p 968). How can the court distinguish between a clause that is inefficiently harsh and one that (whatever this plaintiff knew or thought about it) represents the balance between risk and price that the 'informed margin' of consumers prefer? Consider this account of *Woodman v Photo Trade Processing Ltd* by Lawson (1981) 131 NLJ 933 at 935:

A reel of film had been given to the defendants for processing. The subject matter was a wedding. Most of the snaps were lost and the defendants pleaded reliance on this clause: 'All photographic materials are accepted on the basis that their value does not exceed the cost of the material itself. Responsibility is limited to the replacement of the films. No liability will be accepted consequential or otherwise, however caused'. Judge Clarke examined both the *Schroeder* and *Levison* cases and turned also to the very important House of Lords' decision in *Peek v North Staffordshire Rly Co* (1863) 10 HLCas 473 at 493. This case arose from the terms of the Railway and Canal Traffic Act 1854, which permitted transport undertakings to limit their liability providing they used clauses which were 'just and reasonable'. The clause in issue excluded all liability for loss or damage to fragile goods unless these were declared and insured according to their value. By six to five, the House ruled against this clause: it excluded liability for mistake as well as negligence; the railway had a monopoly which in effect forced the customer to take the company's terms; insurance was available, but only at a rate which could be properly described as 'exorbitant'. The conclusion is irresistible that the same The view taken by Judge Clarke was that, having regard to the three cases put before him, the exclusion clause was unreasonable. But before he was prepared to come to a final decision, he felt obliged to consider whether there were alternative means by which the customer's needs could have been met. The judge had recognised that this factor, which appears in the guidelines, contained in Schedule 2 to the Act, was necessarily only to be applied, according to the strict wording of the Act, to contracts for the sale, supply or disposition of goods. Judge Clarke fairly rationalised its application to the case in hand, which involved a contract of services, on the ground that the matters contained in the Schedule were such matters as would usually be taken into account in differing categories of case as well.

The crucial point was that the Code of Practice for the Photographic Industry, as agreed with the Office of Fair Trading, clearly recognised the possibility of a two-tier system of trade: the lower tier would be the present way of trade, with full exclusion of liability; the other possibility would be a more expensive service, but with the processors accepting a greater degree of liability. Such an approach, the judge concluded, was not 'only reasonable but practicable'. For that reason, the defendants, upon whom the burden lay, failed to persuade him that the clause 'satisfies the statutory test of reasonableness'.

> Was the clause in this case obscure, or well known and easy to understand? If there were any significant number of consumers who wanted a more expensive service on 'lower risk' terms, why wasn't one already on offer? (Note: a bit of 'Saturday afternoon empiricism' in Leamington by one of your editors suggests that a choice of level of service is now readily available—perhaps as the result of the Code of Practice and this decision. What isn't known is how many people opt for the more expensive service . . .)

(10) The main ground for the decision in the *George Mitchell* case seems to have been that the seed company in practice often did pay compensation. Why did this make a difference? Was there an element of unfair surprise in that the seed company did not waive its defence under the clause and pay up? Why would the seed company ever pay up after putting this clause into the contract? If it were shown that it only ever did so for old-established customers, and the plaintiff were not one of these, would reliance on the clause be unreasonable?

(11) A less charitable explanation for inserting harsh clauses but paying up sometimes anyway is that the company is quite prepared to pay in any 'genuine case' (in which the farmer has taken all the correct steps?) but the company wants to decide which is a genuine case and which not itself, rather than leave it to judicial decision or arbitration: see Beale & Dugdale 2 Brit J Law & Society 45, at 57.

(12) Would the outcome of cases such as *George Mitchell* be different now that it is the reasonableness of including the clause, not of relying on it, that is the test (see note 1 on p 1011)? Adams and Brownsword 104 LQR 94, 100, 108–109 argue that this might change the result, but wouldn't it be unreasonable to include a clause that gives the company power to decide?

We mentioned earlier (see p 958) that, in the USA, unfair clauses may be attacked under the unconscionability doctrine of UCC s 2–302, even if the clause meets the additional requirement of s 2–316 that a disclaimer be 'conspicuous'. For example, in *A & M Produce Co v FMC Corpn* 135 Cal App 3d 473 (Court of Appeals of California, 4th District, 1982), a farming company decided to grow tomatoes for the first time and needed to buy a weight-sizing machine. The owner of A & M, Abbati, ordered a machine from FMC relying on various statements made by FMC about the machine's speed of operation; the back of the order form contained clauses excluding any 'warranties' and disclaiming responsibility for any consequential losses. The machine did not perform as stated and the crop was lost. The trial court held that the disclaimers were uncon-scionable and the Court of Appeals upheld the decision. Wiener J said:

The Uniform Commercial Code does not attempt to precisely define what is or is not 'unconscionable.' Nevertheless, '[unconscionability] has generally been recognized to include an absence of meaningful choice on the part of one of the parties together with contract terms which are unreasonably favorable to the other party.' (*Williams v Walker–Thomas Furniture Company* (DC Cir 1965) 350 F 2d 445, 449.) Phrased another way, unconscionability has both a 'procedural' and a 'substantive' element.

The procedural element focuses on two factors: 'oppression' and 'surprise.' 'Oppression' arises from an inequality of bargaining power which results in no real negotiation and 'an absence of meaningful choice.' (*Williams v Walker–Thomas Furniture Company*, supra,) ... 'Surprise' involves the extent to which the supposedly agreed-upon terms of the bargain are hidden in a prolix printed form drafted by the party seeking to enforce the disputed terms. ... Characteristically, the form contract is drafted by the party with the superior bargaining position. (See Calamari and Perillo, Contracts (2d ed 1977) §9–40, p 325.)

Of course the mere fact that a contract term is not read or understood by the nondrafting party or that the drafting party occupies a superior bargaining position will not authorize a court to refuse to enforce the contract. Although an argument can be made that contract terms not actively negotiated between the parties fall outside the 'circle of assent' which constitutes the actual agreement, commercial practi-calities dictate that unbargained-for terms only be denied enforcement where they are also substantively unreasonable. (Ellinghaus (1969) 78 Yale LJ 757 at pp 766–767) No precise definition of substantive unconscionability can be proffered. Cases have talked in terms of 'overly harsh' or 'one-sided' results ... One commentator has pointed out, however, that' ... unconscionability turns not only on a "one-sided" result, but also on an absence of "justification" for it.' (Eddy (1977) 65 Cal L Rev 28, at p 45), which is only to say that

substantive unconscionability must be evaluated as of the time the contract was made. (See U Com Code, §2–302.) The most detailed and specific commentaries observe that a contract is largely an allo-cation of risks between the parties, and therefore that a contractual term is substantively suspect if it reallocates the risks of the bargain in an objectively unreasonable or unexpected manner. (Murray, Unconscionability: Unconscionability (1969) 31 U Pitt L Rev 1, 12–23.) But not all unreasonable risk reallocations are unconscionable; rather, enforceability of the clause is tied to the procedural aspects of unconscionability such that the greater the unfair surprise or inequality of bargaining power, the less unreasonable the risk reallocation which will be tolerated. (See Spanogle, (1969) 117 U Pa L Rev 931 at pp 950, 968.)

Turning first to the procedural aspects of unconscionability, we note at the outset that this contract arises in a commercial context between an enormous diversified corporation (FMC) and a relatively small but experienced farming company (A & M). Generally, '... courts have not been solicitous of business-men in the name of unconscionability.' (White and Summers, *Uniform Commercial Code*). This is prob-ably because courts view businessmen as possessed of a greater degree of commercial understanding and substantially more economic muscle than the ordinary consumer. Hence, a businessman usually has a more difficult time establishing procedural unconscionability in the sense of either 'unfair surprise' or 'unequal bargaining power.'

Nevertheless, generalizations are always subject to exceptions and categorization is rarely an adequate substitute for analysis. With increasing frequency, courts have begun to recognize that experienced but legally unsophisticated businessmen may be unfairly surprised by unconscionable contract terms, and that even large business entities may have relatively little bargaining power, depend-ing on the identity of the other contracting party and the commercial circumstances surrounding the agreement. This recognition rests on the conviction that the social benefits associated with freedom of contract are severely skewed where it appears that had the party actually been aware of the term to which he 'agreed' or had he any real choice in the matter, he would never have assented to inclusion of the term.

Both aspects of procedural unconscionability appear to be present on the facts of this case. Although the printing used on the warranty disclaimer was conspicuous, the terms of the consequential damage exclusion are not particularly apparent, being only slightly larger than most of the other contract text. Both provisions appear in the middle of the back page of a long preprinted form contract which was only casually shown to Abatti. It was never suggested to him, either verbally or in writing, that he read the back of the form. Abatti testified he never read the reverse side terms. There was thus sufficient evidence before the trial court to conclude that Abatti was in fact surprised by the warranty disclaimer and the consequential damage exclusion. How 'unfair' his surprise was is subject to some dispute. He certainly had the opportunity to read the back of the contract or to seek the advice of a lawyer. Yet as a factual matter, given the complexity of the terms and FMC's failure to direct his attention to them, Abatti's omission may not be totally unreasonable. In this regard, the comments of the Indiana Supreme Court in *Weaver v American Oil Company*, supra, 276 NE 2d 144 (Indiana, 1972) at pages 147–148 are apposite: 'The burden should be on the party submitting [a standard contract] in printed form to show that the other party had knowledge of any unusual or unconscionable terms contained therein. The principle should be the same as that applicable to implied warranties, namely that a package of goods sold to a purchaser is fit for the purposes intended and contains no harmful materials other than that represented.' Here, FMC made no attempt to provide A & M with the requisite knowledge of the disclaimer or the exclusion. In fact, one suspects that the length, complexity and obtuseness of most form contracts may be due at least in part of the seller's preference that the buyer will be dissuaded from reading that to which he is supposedly agreeing. This process almost inevitably results in a one-sided 'contract.'

Even if we ignore any suggestion of unfair surprise, there is ample evidence of unequal bargaining power here and a lack of any real negotiation over the terms of the contract. Although it was conceded that A & M was a large-scale farming enterprise by Imperial Valley standards, employing 5 persons on a regular basis and up to 50 seasonal employees at harvest time, and that Abatti was farming some 8,000 acres in 1974, FMC Corporation is in an entirely different category. The 1974 gross sales of the Agriculture Machinery Division alone amounted to $40 million. More importantly, the terms on the FMC form contract were standard. FMC salesmen were not authorized to negotiate any of the terms appearing on the reverse side of the preprinted contract. Although FMC contends that in some special instances, individual contracts are negotiated, A & M was never made aware of that option. The sum total of these circumstances leads to the conclusion that this contract was a 'bargain' only in the most general sense of the word.

...

Although the procedural aspects of unconscionability are present in this case, we suspect the substantive unconscionability of the disclaimer and exclusion provisions contributed equally to the trial court's ultimate conclusion. As to the disclaimer of warranties, the facts of this case support the trial court's conclusion that such disclaimer was commercially unreasonable. The warranty allegedly breached by FMC went to the basic performance characteristics of the product. In attempting to disclaim this and all other warranties, FMC was in essence guarantying nothing about what the product would do. Since a product's performance forms the fundamental basis for a sales contract, it is patently unreasonable to assume that a buyer would purchase a standardized mass-produced product from an industry seller without any enforceable performance standards. From a social perspective, risk of loss is most appropriately borne by the party best able to prevent its occurrence. ... Rarely would the buyer be in a better position than the manufacturer-seller to evaluate the performance characteristics of a machine.

In this case, moreover, the evidence establishes that A & M had no previous experience with weight-sizing machines and was forced to rely on the expertise of FMC in recommending the necessary equipment. FMC was abundantly aware of this fact. The jury here necessarily found that FMC either expressly or impliedly guaranteed a performance level which the machine was unable to meet. Especially where an inexperienced buyer is concerned, the seller's performance representations are absolutely necessary to allow the buyer to make an intelligent choice among the competitive options available. A seller's attempt, through the use of a disclaimer, to prevent the buyer from reasonably relying on such representations calls into question the commercial reasonableness of the agreement and may well be substantively unconscionable. The trial court's conclusion to that effect is amply supported by the record before us.

[The majority of case references have been omitted.]

■ Beale, 'Unfair Contracts in Britain and Europe' [1989]
CLP 197, 201–209, 212

Lord Reid [see pp 989–990] is pointing to two distinct forms of imbalance. The first is an imbalance in information: because the customer does not know about the clause or does not understand its implications, he is likely to be taken unfairly by surprise. At a guess—and in the present state of empirical knowledge it can only be a guess—this kind of problem with harsh contract terms is much the most common. There must be many occasions when, if the clauses of the contract were to be applied literally, the customer would have far fewer rights, or would be exposed to much greater risks, than she expected; and, if only she had known, she would have taken steps to safeguard her position. . . .

   This suggests when it has to be decided whether or not a clause is 'fair and reasonable' under the Unfair Contract Terms Act the first question should be, did the customer know of it and understand the risk? In some cases I would go so far as to say that the customer should either be given a full explanation or the other party should ensure that the customer actually gets legal advice: I am thinking of such one-sided and ill-understood agreements as guarantees given to banks. Normally, however, we would not be justified in requiring such individualised treatment: we are dealing with mass transactions and the whole point of the standard form is to avoid the need for individual negotiations. It should suffice that the clause is conspicuous and in language that is readily comprehensible, not just to the lawyer but to the customer who is likely to be affected by it—it might sometimes not be unreasonable to require that the clause be repeated in minority languages. There is an obvious parallel between what I am suggesting and the so-called 'ticket cases' on whether a clause in a ticket or notice is incorporated into the contract; but I am suggesting not just that reasonable notice be given of the existence of the clause, as required by the ticket cases, but also of its content and meaning.

   Of course the regulations made under the Consumer Credit Act 1974 already require this sort of thing for consumer credit agreements, and so do Codes of Practice promoted by the Office of Fair Trading. . . .

   The second problem that Lord Reid identifies is that the customer who knows of the clause and objects to it may be powerless to get it changed and unable to find another supplier who will offer better terms. Lord Reid, like others before and since, seems to find this sinister. To repeat, he says: 'Freedom to contract must surely imply some choice or room for bargaining.' This suggests that what is unfair is that the individual cannot co-determine the terms. It is at this point that, respectfully, I part company with Lord Reid. I agree that preserving the individual's right to self-determination is important, but there are competing values; and in my view, in this area we have already as a society chosen that a competing value should prevail. It is universally recognised that the advantage of standard forms is that they enable mass contracting to be carried out economically, and at the same time enable businesses to estimate their risks and costs more accurately—so generating savings which, if the market is price-competitive, can be passed on to the customer. The standard form contract is just part of the system of mass production which enables more and more people to obtain goods and services they might not otherwise be able to afford. The benefits of all this are far from being distributed equally or fairly, but there is no prospect of going back to individually negotiated contracts.

   In today's world it is unrealistic to expect the individual customer to be able to co-determine the terms of the offer. It will simply be too expensive to negotiate each contract and to administer a mass of contracts each on slightly different terms. The latter point in particular gets some support from the empirical evidence. Certainly the occasional change will be made to catch a customer who might otherwise go elsewhere, but such a case is likely to be the exception not the general practice.

This does not mean that no one can exert any influence over the terms offered. Again to repeat the economists' argument, the business is constrained by the forces of competition. First there may be overt competition to offer, for example, better warranties for cars. But even if there is no overt competition, and the majority of customers remain ignorant of, and so apparently indifferent to, the small print, it only requires a certain percentage or margin of customers to complain about the terms on offer, and to try to shop around for something better, to create pressure on the supplier to offer less harsh terms in the hope of capturing the business of these marginal customers. Since it is expensive and difficult to treat different customers differently, the process is likely to result in better terms being offered to everyone. I am not sure that this thesis has been tested empirically either, but it seems consistent with our experience in this country, where as consumer awareness has grown the terms on offer have slowly improved. But in this process it is the run of customers who induce the change; the individual cannot expect special treatment unless either it is a very important customer in terms of the volume of business it will bring to the supplier, or it is prepared to pay very heavily for the luxury of special terms.

If we can't expect freedom to negotiate on an individual basis, when are clauses which do not come as a surprise and which are counter-balanced by a lower price nonetheless unfair?

It seems to me that when we are talking about a known and understood clause which the customer cannot get changed, the real reasons for saying that it may be unfair rest on one of two . . . grounds. One is that we feel that there are, as a matter of social policy, certain obligations which suppliers should not be able to escape and, correspondingly, certain rights of which the customer should not be deprived. The German Standard Business Terms Act of 1976 makes this assumption explicit. Art 9 provides that terms in standard terms of business shall be void if they put the other party at an unreasonable disadvantage, and then states that unreasonable disadvantage is presumed if the clause is incompatible with the fundamental idea behind the legal rule from which it deviates. But it takes only a moment's reflection to see that our own Unfair Contract Terms Act, and before it the doctrine of fundamental breach, depend on the same notion: exclusion clauses do not normally define the primary obligations of the parties, rather they act somehow as defences to the normal liability, and one may not be able to rely on them at all, or only if one can justify them.

I am quite happy to accept that some prohibitions on exclusion clauses can be justified on this reasoning—the ban on exclusions of liability for death or personal injury caused by negligence, for example. I am more concerned with clauses which, by general consensus, may be fair in at least some circumstances, for instance because the customer can insure more cheaply. I would repeat the question raised by Professor Hellner [(1981) 1 Oxford JLS 13, 26]: why do we assume that the rule provided by the general law should be the benchmark? To take a single instance, should sellers who deliver late always be liable for the consequential losses suffered by the buyer? The empirical evidence, though of course it is very scanty, suggests that this may not be what business people expect; and I begin to doubt whether there is anything 'naturally right' about the seller having to take this responsibility when we find that in Swedish law, compensation for consequential loss caused by delay is not normally granted.

The other explanation is the one which I find much more persuasive. This is to say that the clause is unfair if, although it is compensated by a lower price, it exposes the customer to an unacceptable degree of risk. But what is unacceptable? Brownsword has recently suggested that to judge the fairness of contracts we should use a test derived from Rawls: are the terms

> 'such that they could be accepted by rational agents who, without knowing on which side of the transaction they might stand, had to imagine themselves as parties to the transaction?' [Liberalism and the law of contract, in Bellamy, *Liberalism and Recent Social and Legal Philosophy* (1989)]

Brownsword argues that contracts which fail this test should not be upheld unless the losing party was consciously engaged in risk-taking. If we assume that most people are normally risk-averse, this test may work where there is exploitation of the traditional value-for-money sense. But I do not think we can use the Rawls test for harsh terms which are off-set by a lower price. If we ask whether the other party would have been prepared to enter the transaction on the same terms, we shall not get any conclusive answer.

It depends upon the individual's preferences, on how averse she is to taking risks, on how serious the loss would be compared to her overall wealth.

What I think we are really saying is that a known and understood risk is nonetheless unacceptable when, not only was this customer reluctant to take it, but so would most customers be. We have moved, perhaps almost without noticing it, from controlling unfairness to promoting better, more efficient contract terms, giving the customer the rights she would have preferred and would have been prepared to pay the direct cost of, but did not get because of the costs involved in getting the standard form changed.

We now have an obvious difficulty. If we cannot assume that the general law necessarily provides the 'right' answer, and if we are dealing with questions of customer preference, how is customer preference to be determined? For the reasons already given, we cannot rely on the fact that this individual customer was dissatisfied but could not secure anything better. It is not even conclusive that there appears never to have been any negotiation over the clause, even if there is some body, a trade association for instance, with whom the suppliers might have been expected to negotiate. First, the absence of negotiation or any change in the clause over time may mean that there is no margin of aware customers to bring pressure for change: but equally it might indicate that, though there are enough aware customers, the clause is acceptable to them. Secondly, if the marginal customers were dissatisfied, the supplier may have made the change unilaterally, without negotiation—it would be in its own interests to do so. As Lord Bridge remarked in the *George Mitchell* case, the absence of negotiation is 'equivocal.'

What I believe we can do is to look to see whether it is likely that there is a sufficient margin of customers who are aware of the impact of the clause to exert pressure on the supplier should the terms offered not be what the customers want. The more prominent the clause, the more readily comprehensible it is, the easier it is to understand the risks it entails, and the greater the perceived probability of the risk, the more likely that customers will know enough and will bother to complain if they do not find what they want. In consumer contracts, at least, one might take into account whether the contract is one that is likely to be entered by those articulate middle-class persons who seem so ready to complain. So again, conspicuousness and intelligibility come to the fore, but this time in a different role, as creating at least a mild presumption that the clause is acceptable. Again as Lord Bridge said in the seed case, where the farmers had known of the clause, the fact that even as laymen they would have had no difficulty in understanding it was a factor in the clause's favour.

If on the facts this presumption cannot be made, we then have to fall back on the normal criteria for determining whether an allocation of risk is efficient [see above, p 354]. If the clause is one excluding or limiting liability for some event which the supplier could more easily prevent than the customer, would there still be adequate incentives for the supplier to take precautions if the clause were upheld? Which party is in the better position to effect insurance or to carry the risk? How serious is the loss and what is the relative wealth of the parties? But it follows from what I said earlier that these questions should not be asked in relation to the particular customer concerned, but in relation to the run of customers. To go back to *Phillips Products Ltd v Hyland*, the trial judge seems to have thought that it would be hard for Phillips to arrange insurance cover at short notice. I wonder whether Phillips was typical of Hyland's customers, at least many of whom may have been civil engineering or building contractors—the CPA conditions are approved by the Federation of Civil Engineering Contractors. Contractors are often required by the contracts under which they are employed to carry insurance against damage to property, including the works which they are constructing. Thus many of Hyland's customers may already have had insurance cover. But the Court of Appeal stressed that the question was not whether the clause was fair in other contracts on these conditions, but 'in relation to *this particular contract.*' I believe this approach may be mistaken.

I am not suggesting that individual circumstances should always be disregarded: for some purposes they are critical. Take guidelines (a) and (b) in Schedule 2 of the Unfair Contract Terms Act: the court is to take into account the strength of the bargaining positions, whether the customer could have entered a similar contract with other persons but without a similar term, and so on. While the absence of bargaining power or of choice should not necessarily count against a clause, if the customer was important enough to have bargaining power or lucky enough to have choice but did not exercise it, that is a factor *in favour* of the clause. The individual circumstances are relevant in determining whether the clause was genuinely unacceptable to the plaintiff when the contract was made.

Unfortunately the authorities are again against me. In *Stag Line Ltd v Tyne Shiprepair Group Ltd* Staughton J was faced with a clause in a ship-repairing contract. He said that he did not think that the reasonableness of the clause should depend on whether or not the yard had plenty of business at the date the contract was made. I would respectfully submit that on some occasions just that would make all the difference, because while concessions are more likely to be made on price, it is certainly not unknown for a business to alter its standard terms as a special concession to get a valued customer when things are slack, and the owners might have asked for a change to the clause if they were particularly concerned about it.

Thus I submit that the individual circumstances should be taken into account as negativing any unreasonableness; but that normally the question should be whether the clause is a fair one for the normal run of contracts rather than for the individual customer.

I end with a reflection and a question. I have been suggesting that a clause should be considered fair if it does not cause unfair surprise and if it represents a balance of risk against price that is acceptable to the margin of aware consumers. I have even suggested ways in which we might increase the flow of information to improve the efficiency of the market. This is fine if the market is homogeneous, in the sense that the vast majority of customers want the same balance of price and risk. But do they? I have said that every individual cannot expect personalised treatment, but I would be worried if there were a substantial majority of customers who have significantly different needs and desires from the 'market makers,' the active margin. If the groups are clearly distinct, one might expect the market to produce, as it were, two tiers, one set of terms for those who want the minimum risk even if it costs more and another for those who are not so bothered about risk but would prefer lower prices. But I am not sure that it is always realistic to assume either homogeneity or that a choice will be provided. We know that the elderly, the infirm, the disabled and perhaps the less well-off, sometimes have very different needs to the middle aged and middle class like myself. What to me may be a minor inconvenience—no washing machine or cooker for a couple of days—may be a disaster to someone less privileged. It is just these groups who are likely to be less mobile, so that they are less able to shop around, and perhaps less articulate or forceful in their demands. I believe that this may even be a problem in non-consumer contracts, where larger businesses might have different needs to the small firm, but it is most obvious in the consumer context.

What worries me is that it may be the articulate, pushy middle class that makes the market, and minority interests may be pushed aside. Do we need a watchdog to ensure that minority interests are safeguarded, and for this purpose how do we determine which minority interests are large enough to justify special protection?

NOTE

For an argument that individual needs and preferences should be taken into greater account, see Wilhelmsson, *Critical Legal Studies in Private Law*, 1992, pp 72ff.

8. Exclusions from the Act

Although the Act is of general application, a number of contracts are specifically excluded from it. A full list will be found in Cheshire, Fifoot and Furmston, pp 232–234 or Treitel, pp 264–267. Perhaps the most important exclusions are:

(1) contracts relating to the creation, transfer or termination of interests in land;

(2) contracts of insurance;

(3) contracts of charterparty or carriage of goods by sea (except for personal injury liability and as against consumers);
(4) international supply contracts;
(5) contracts in which English law is the proper law of the contract only by choice of the parties.

See s 31; s 1(2) and Sch 1; ss 26 and 27.

9. Evasion by secondary contract

Section 10

A person is not bound by any contract term prejudicing or taking away rights of his which arise under, or in connection with the performance of, another contract, so far as those rights extend to the enforcement of another's liability which this Part of this Act prevents that other from excluding.

In *Tudor Grange Holdings Ltd v Citibank NA* [1991] 4 All ER 1, it was held that s 10 does not apply to a contract to settle a dispute that has arisen under an earlier contract; s 10 was designed to prevent evasion of the provisions of the Act by use of another contract. Sir Nicholas Browne-Wilkinson V-C (at 13) said s 10 would apply when A agrees with B that A will not exercise his rights under another contract between A and C, and the Act would invalidate a clause excluding those rights in the contract between A and C. He suggested that s 10 does not apply when the parties to both contracts are the same. This, with respect, may be doubted. If, for example, a distributorship contract between a car manufacturer and one of its dealers were to state that the dealer would not bring any claim in respect of any defect in cars to be delivered under separate contracts of sale, s 10 would seem to apply to prevent the manufacturer using the distributorship contract to restrict its liability in a way that would be subject to s 6 if the clause were in the contracts of sale.

10. Other statutory controls over exemption clauses

There are a number of enactments controlling the use of exemption clauses in specific types of contract: a notable example is the Carriage of Goods by Sea Act 1971, which adopts the Hague-Visby Rules. This prevents shipowners excluding certain types of liability towards owners of goods, but explicitly permits the use of other exceptions. The subject is too complex for treatment here: a simple account can be found in Payne and Ivamy, *Carriage of Goods by Sea*, 13th edn, pp 193–210. See also p 1058.

Other examples are as follow.

■ Defective Premises Act 1972

Section 1

(1) A person taking on work for or in connection with the provision of a dwelling (whether the dwelling is provided by the erection or by the conversion or enlargement of a building) owes a duty—
(a) if the dwelling is provided to the order of any person, to that person; and
(b) without prejudice to paragraph (a) above, to every person who acquires an interest (whether legal or equitable) in the dwelling;

to see that the work which he takes on is done in a workmanlike or, as the case may be, professional manner, with proper materials and so that as regards that work the dwelling will be fit for habitation when completed.

Section 6

...

(3) Any term of an agreement which purports to exclude or restrict, or has the effect of excluding or restricting, the operation of any of the provisions of this Act, or any liability arising by virtue of any such provision, shall be void.

■ Consumer Protection Act 1987

Section 7

The liability of a person by virtue of this Part to a person who has suffered damage caused wholly or partly by a defect in a product, or to a dependant or relative of such a person, shall not be limited or excluded by any contract term, by any notice or by any other provision.

QUESTIONS

1. What may be objectionable about exclusion or limitation of liability clauses contained in standard-form contracts? To what extent do the objections apply (i) to similar clauses in contracts that have been drawn up for the particular transaction or (ii) to similar clauses in standard-form contracts that are in regular use between businesses?

2. From the cases you have read, how many interpretative devices ('rules of construction') can you identify?

3. Taking each device in turn, try to create a problem that involves a situation in which there is a clause in the contract that, at first sight, might appear to protect one party but actually does not do so because of the interpretative device you are dealing with (and preferably which is not covered by any of the other rules, although this is not always easy.) In other words, pretend you are setting an exam problem to see if students can apply the rule!

4. Your client wants to be protected from liability when its employees have been negligent but does not want the word 'negligence' to appear in the clause in case it is off-putting to customers. Draft a suitable clause (don't worry about UCTA).

5. Your client is a company which warehouses goods. Although it normally tells the customer where the goods will be stored, goods sometimes have to be moved or are sometimes stored in the wrong place by mistake. Wherever the goods are, the client does not wish to be liable for loss, damage or destruction of the goods by any means. Draft a suitable clause.

6. Your client is a tramp-steaming company that does not wish to have to send its ships by direct routes to anywhere, even if some shipper is foolish enough to have shipped a perishable cargo that may be rotten by the time it arrives if the most direct route is not taken. Draft a suitable clause—if you can!

7. Your client is a business which sells old bangers; it cannot take any responsibility for the condition of them—and some of them don't go at all. Draft a suitable clause.

8. What was the difference between the 'substantive' doctrine of fundamental breach and the construction approach? What was objectionable about the substantive doctrine?

9. Ace Ltd makes pickup trucks that are sold to both businesses and private purchasers. It makes some sales direct to customers and some through independent distributors, who buy the pickups from Ace and resell them to customers. When Ace sells, whether to a customer or to a distributor, it issues the following warranty as part of the contract:

   > This vehicle is warranted free from defects in manufacture to the extent that Ace Ltd undertake to replace any defective part within the first twelve months or 10,000 miles, whichever occurs earlier, but shall be under no further liability. This warranty shall be in lieu of the purchaser's rights at common law or under statute.

   Ace instructs its distributors to include the same warranty in their sales contracts.

   Suppose that customers bring claims for goods that are damaged when their pickups break down because of defects in manufacture, and for the cost of hiring replacement vehicles while their own are being repaired. Where the pickups were sold by distributors, the distributors have indicated that, if they are liable to the customers, they will attempt to reclaim the sums paid out from Ace.

   Which sections of UCTA 1977 might apply to the clause in the various contracts?

10. The partners of Suem, Grabbit & Runn, Solicitors, decide that it would add the final touch to their new client waiting room to install a machine for making cappuccinos. Their secretary, Andy, orders a Froth Model 30 in brown from Jason's, a mail order company. He is told over the telephone that orders are taken on the basis that, if the precise goods are not available, the nearest equivalent will be sent and that, in any event, goods can be returned within 14 days of delivery and the money will be refunded in full. Jason's finds it does not have the correct model in brown but has one in white, which it sends. Andy is away when it arrives and, because the partners are too busy, the package is not opened until 21 days after delivery. The partners do not want a white machine because it does not fit in with the muted decor of the room but Jason's refuses to take it back. Which sections of UCTA, if any, might apply?

11. How is the reasonableness of a clause to be judged under s 11? If a clause is unreasonably broad but parts of it are reasonable and might stand on their own, can the clause be upheld in part?

12. List the factors that in the cases you have read, have been taken into account in deciding whether or not clauses are reasonable. How many of the factors are referred to in s 11 or Sch 2 of UCTA?

13. What kinds of clause and what types of contract are exempt from UCTA?

CHAPTER FORTY

UNFAIR TERMS IN CONSUMER CONTRACTS

In 1993, the EC Council of Ministers adopted a Directive on Unfair Terms in Consumer Contracts (Council Directive 93/13/EEC of 5 April 1993, OJ L95/29), which member States were supposed to implement by 31 December 1994. The legal basis used was that of Art 100A of the Treaty of Rome, empowering the adoption of measures aimed at completion of the internal market. Thus the recitals speak of distortion of competition arising from the fact that the laws on member States differ, and claim that consumers' ignorance of the law of member States other than their own may deter them from direct transactions for the purchase of goods or services in another member State. There are also references to the two Community programmes for a consumer protection and information policy.

The Directive is at once both wider and narrower than the Unfair Contract Terms Act. It is wider in that it applies to any unfair term in any consumer contract: so, for example, a clause allowing a seller to increase its price before delivery or providing for the forfeiture of a deposit on breach by the consumer might be caught. There is no exemption for insurance contracts. It is narrower in applying only to consumer contracts (and, as we shall see, a company is never a consumer under the Directive), and only to terms that are not individually negotiated. However, the Directive does not prevent member States giving consumers more extensive protection than the Directive requires (Art 8).

The Directive does not make any terms automatically invalid (in 'Eurospeak', it does not contain a 'blacklist'), although earlier drafts, had done so (for earlier drafts, see OJ 1990 C243/2 and OJ C73/7). It uses a test of unfairness that may differ from the reasonableness test under the Unfair Contract Terms Act 1977, s 11 (see further below).

Article 7 provides for procedures to prevent the continued use of unfair terms. There is no equivalent in the Unfair Contract Terms Act and the Directive seems to require more extensive powers and different procedures from those given to the Director-General of Fair Trading by the Fair Trading Act 1973 (see below).

In the United Kingdom, the government decided on implementation by statutory instrument under the European Communities Act 1972, leaving the existing Unfair Contract Terms Act 1977 untouched. The overlap that results was criticised (eg Reynolds (1994) 110 LQR 3) but the Department of Trade and Industry (*Implementation of the EC Directive on Unfair Terms in Consumer Contracts (93/13/EEC): A Further Consultation Document*) took the view that it was not possible to align the Act and the Directive by providing common tests of fairness or equating fairness and reasonableness. A subsequent Report by the Law Commissions (*Unfair Terms in Contracts*, LC No 292, 2005) recommended unifying the legimes but at present that a consumer may be able to challenge some clauses under either UCTA or the Regulations on Unfair Terms.

In 1999, the 1994 Regulations were replaced by the Unfair Terms in Consumer Contracts Regulations 1999, which came into force on 1 October 1999.

The explanatory note issued with the Regulations does not appear to explain all of the changes made by the 1999 version of the Regulations, but generally, the aim of the changes seems to have been to bring the wording of the Regulations even closer to that of the Directive, so as to minimise the risk that the UK would be held not to have implemented the Directive correctly. In particular, it appears, although the matter is not wholly clear, that the 1999 Regulations are capable of applying to contracts for the sale of land, which was not the case with the 1994 version. Compare, for this purpose, the definition of seller and supplier in the 1994 version with that in the 1999 version. It seems probable that the Directive was meant to apply to contracts for the sale of land. This is a good deal clearer in the French version of the Directive than in the English version. The European Court of Justice assumed that the Directive applied to a contract for the purchase of a building in *Freiburger Kommunalauten Gmbh Baugesellschaft & Co KG v Hofstetter* Case C-237/02 [2004] CMLR 13, and the Court of Appeal applied the Regulations in the context of the responsibility of local authorities to homeless persons under s 193 of Housing Act 1996 in *London Borough of Newham v Khatun* [2004] 3 WLR 417.

There are also a number of other linguistic changes. Matters are not necessarily dealt with in the same numbered Regulation in the two versions. Anyone who has mastered the 1994 version would find the 1999 version rather confusing. Fortunately, most readers of this passage will not be in this position and will be reading the Regulations for the first time.

■ The Unfair Terms in Consumer Contract Regulations 1999, SI 1999/2083 (as amended by SI 2001/1186)

The Regulations provide for the first time that a qualifying body named in Schedule 1 (statutory regulators, trading standards departments and Consumers' Association) may also apply for an injunction to prevent the continued use of an unfair contract term provided it has notified the Director General of its intention at least 14 days before the application is made (unless the Director General consents to a shorter period) (regulation 12). A qualifying body named in Part One of Schedule 1 (public bodies) shall be under a duty to consider a complaint if it has told the Director General that it will do so (regulation 11).

The Regulations provide a new power for the Director General and the public qualifying bodies to require traders to produce copies of their standard contracts, and give information about their use, in order to facilitate investigation of complaints and ensure compliance with undertakings or court orders (regulation 13).

. . .

Citation and commencement

1. These Regulations may be cited as the Unfair Terms in Consumer Contracts Regulations 1999 and shall come into force on 1st October 1999.

Revocation

2. The Unfair Terms in Consumer Contracts Regulations 1994 are hereby revoked.

Interpretation

3.-(1) In these Regulations-
    'the Community' means the European Community;
        'consumer' means any natural person who, in contracts covered by these Regulations,
        is acting for purposes which are outside his trade, business or profession; 'court' in relation
    to England and Wales and Northern Ireland means a county court or

the High Court, and in relation to Scotland, the Sheriff or the Court of Session; 'Director' means the Director General of Fair Trading;

'EEA Agreement' means the Agreement on the European Economic Area signed at Oporto on 2nd May 1992 as adjusted by the protocol signed at Brussels on 17th March 1993:

'Member State' means a State which is a contracting party to the EEA Agreement:

'notified' means notified in writing:

'qualifying body' means a person specified in Schedule 1;

'seller or supplier' means any natural or legal person who, in contracts covered by these Regulations, is acting for purposes relating to his trade, business or profession, whether publicly owned or privately owned:

'unfair terms' means the contractual terms referred to in regulation 5.

(2) In the application of these Regulations to Scotland for references to an 'injunction' or an 'interim injunction' there shall be substituted references to an 'interdict' or 'interim interdict' respectively.

Terms to which these Regulations apply

4.-(1) These Regulations apply in relation to unfair terms in contracts concluded between a seller or a supplier and a consumer.

(2) These Regulations do not apply to contractual terms which reflect-

(a) mandatory statutory or regulatory provisions (including such provisions under the law of any Member State or in Community legislation having effect in the United Kingdom without further enactment):

(b) the provisions or principles of international conventions to which the Member States or the Community are party.

Unfair terms

5.-(1) A contractual term which has not been individually negotiated shall be regarded as unfair if, contrary to the requirement of good faith, it causes a significant imbalance in the parties' rights and obligations arising under the contract, to the detriment of the consumer.

(2) A term shall always be regarded as not having been individually negotiated where it has been drafted in advance and the consumer has therefore not been able to influence the substance of the term.

(3) Notwithstanding that a specific term or certain aspects of it in a contract has been individually negotiated, these Regulations shall apply to the rest of a contract if an overall assessment of it indicates that it is a pre-formulated standard contract.

(4) It shall be for any seller or supplier who claims that a term was individually negotiated to show that it was.

(5) Schedule 2 to these Regulations contains an indicative and non-exhaustive list of the terms which may be regarded as unfair.

Assessment of unfair terms

6.-(1) Without prejudice to regulation 12, the unfairness of a contractual term shall be assessed, taking into account the nature of the goods or services for which the contract was concluded and by referring, at the time of conclusion of the contract, to all the circumstances attending the conclusion of the contract and to all the other terms of the contract or of another contract on which it is dependent.

(2) In so far as it is in plain intelligible language, the assessment of fairness of a term shall not relate-

(a) to the definition of the main subject matter of the contract, or

(b) to the adequacy of the price or remuneration, as against the goods or services supplied in exchange.

Written contracts

7.-(1) A seller or supplier shall ensure that any written term of a contract is expressed in plain, intelligible language.

(2) If there is doubt about the meaning of a written term, the interpretation which is most favourable to the consumer shall prevail but this rule shall not apply in proceedings brought under regulation 12.

Effect of unfair term

8.-(1) An unfair term in a contract concluded with a consumer by a seller or supplier shall not be binding on the consumer.

(2) The contract shall continue to bind the parties if it is capable of continuing in existence without the unfair term.

Choice of law clauses

9. These Regulations shall apply notwithstanding any contract term which applies or purports to apply the law of a non-Member State, if the contract has a close connection with the territory of the Member States.

Complaints-consideration by Director

10.-(1) It shall be the duty of the Director to consider any complaint made to him that any contract term drawn up for general use is unfair, unless-

(a) the complaint appears to the Director to be frivolous or vexatious; or

(b) a qualifying body has notified the Director that it agrees to consider the complaint.

(2) The Director shall give reasons for his decision to apply or not to apply, as the case may be, for an injunction under regulation 12 in relation to any complaint which these Regulations require him to consider.

(3) In deciding whether or not to apply for an injunction in respect of a term which the Director considers to be unfair, he may, if he considers it appropriate to do so, have regard to any undertakings given to him by or on behalf of any person as to the continued use of such a term in contracts concluded with consumers.

Complaints-consideration by qualifying bodies

11. If a qualifying body specified in Part One of Schedule 1 notifies the Director that it agrees to consider a complaint that any contract term drawn up for general use is unfair, it shall be under a duty to consider that complaint.

(2) Regulation 10(2) and (3) shall apply to a qualifying body which is under a duty to consider a complaint as they apply to the Director.

Injunctions to prevent continued use of unfair terms

12.-(1) The Director or, subject to paragraph (2), any qualifying body may apply for an injunction (including an interim injunction) against any person appearing to the Director or that body to be using, or recommending use of, an unfair term drawn up for general use in contracts concluded with consumers.

(2) A qualifying body may apply for an injunction only where-

(a) it has notified the Director of its intention to apply at least fourteen days before the date on which the application was made, beginning with the date on which the notification was given: or

(b) the Director consents to the application being made within a shorter period.

(3) The court on an application under this regulation may grant an injunction on such terms as it thinks fit.

(4) An injunction may relate not only to use of a particular contract term drawn up for general use but to any similar term, or a term having like effect, used or recommended for use by any person.

Powers of the Director and qualifying bodies to obtain documents and information

13.-(1) The Director may exercise the power conferred by this regulation for the purpose of-

    (a) facilitating his consideration of a complaint that a contract term drawn up for general use is unfair; or

    (b) ascertaining whether a person has complied with an undertaking or court order as to the continued use, or recommendation for use, of a term in contracts concluded with consumers.

(2) A qualifying body specified in Part One of Schedule 1 may exercise the power conferred by this regulation for the purpose of-

    (a) facilitating its consideration of a complaint that a contract term drawn up for general use is unfair, or

    (b) ascertaining whether a person has complied with-

        (i) an undertaking given to it or to the court following an application by that body, or

        (ii) a court order made on an application by that body,

        as to the continued use, or recommendation for use, of a term in contracts concluded with consumers.

(3) The Director may require any person to supply to him, and a qualifying body specified in Part One of Schedule 1 may require any person to supply to it-

    (a) a copy of any document which that person has used or recommended for use at the time the notice referred to in paragraph (4) below is given, as a pre-formulated standard contract in dealings with consumers:

    (b) information about the use, or recommendation for use, by that person of that document or any other such document in dealings with consumers.

(4) The power conferred by this regulation is to be exercised by a notice in writing which may-

    (a) specify the way in which and the time within which it is to be complied with: and (b) be varied or revoked by a subsequent notice.

(5) Nothing in this regulation compels a person to supply any document or information which he would be entitled to refuse to produce or give in civil proceedings before the court.

(6) If a person makes default in complying with a notice under this regulation, the court may, on the application of the Director or of the qualifying body, make such order as the court thinks fit for requiring the default to be made good, and any such order may provide that all the costs or expenses of and incidental to the application shall be borne by the person in default or by any officers of a company or other association who are responsible for its default.

Notification of undertakings and orders to Director

14. A qualifying body shall notify the Director-

    (a) of any undertaking given to it by or on behalf of any person as to the continued use of a term which that body considers to be unfair in contracts concluded with consumers:

    (b) of the outcome of any application made by it under regulation 12, and of the terms of any undertaking given to, or order made by, the court;

    (c) of the outcome of any application made by it to enforce a previous order of the court.

Publication, information and advice

15.-(1) The Director shall arrange for the publication in such form and manner as he considers appropriate, of-

    (a) details of any undertaking or order notified to him under regulation 14;

(b) details of any undertaking given to him by or on behalf of any person as to the continued use of a term which the Director considers to be unfair in contracts concluded with consumers;

(c) details of any application made by him under regulation 12, and of the terms of any undertaking given to, or order made by, the court;

(d) details of any application made by the Director to enforce a previous order of the court.

(2) The Director shall inform any person on request whether a particular term to which these Regulations apply has been-

(a) the subject of an undertaking given to the Director or notified to him by a qualifying body; or

(b) the subject of an order of the court made upon application by him or notified to him by a qualifying body; and shall give that person details of the undertaking or a copy of the order, as the case may be, together with a copy of any amendments which the person giving the undertaking has agreed to make to the term in question.

(3) The Director may arrange for the dissemination in such form and manner as he considers appropriate of such information and advice concerning the operation of these Regulations as may appear to him to be expedient to give to the public and to all persons likely to be affected by these Regulations.

...

SCHEDULE 1: QUALIFYING BODIES (Regulation 3)

PART ONE

1. The Information Commissioner.
2. The Gas and Electricity Markets Authority.
3. The Director General of Electricity Supply for Northern Ireland.
4. The Director General of Gas for Northern Ireland.
5. The Office of Communications.
6. The Director General of Water Services.
7. The Office of Rail Regulation.
8. Every weights and measures authority in Great Britain.
9. The Department of Enterprise, Trade and Investment in Northern Ireland.
10. The Financial Services Authority.

PART TWO

11. Consumers' Association.

SCHEDULE 2: INDICATIVE AND NON-EXHAUSTIVE LIST OF TERMS WHICH MAY BE REGARDED AS UNFAIR (Regulation 5(5))

1. Terms which have the object or effect of-

(a) excluding or limiting the legal liability of a seller or supplier in the event of the death of a consumer or personal injury to the latter resulting from an act or omission of that seller or supplier;

(b) inappropriately excluding or limiting the legal rights of the consumer vis-à-vis the seller or supplier or another party in the event of total or partial non-performance or inadequate performance by the seller or supplier of any of the contractual obligations, including the option of offsetting a debt owed to the seller or supplier against any claim which the consumer may have against him;

(c) making an agreement binding on the consumer whereas provision of services by the seller or supplier is subject to a condition whose realisation depends on his own will alone;

(d) permitting the seller or supplier to retain sums paid by the consumer where the latter decides not to conclude or perform the contract, without providing for the consumer to receive compensation of an equivalent amount from the seller or supplier where the latter is the party cancelling the contract;

(e)   requiring any consumer who fails to fulfil his obligation to pay a disproportionately high sum in compensation;

(f)   authorising the seller or supplier to dissolve the contract on a discretionary basis where the same facility is not granted to the consumer, or permitting the seller or supplier to retain the sums paid for services not yet supplied by him where it is the seller or supplier himself who dissolves the contract;

(g)   enabling the seller or supplier to terminate a contract of indeterminate duration without reasonable notice except where there are serious grounds for doing so;

(h)   automatically extending a contract of fixed duration where the consumer does not indicate otherwise, when the deadline fixed for the consumer to express his desire not to extend the contract is unreasonably early;

(i)   irrevocably binding the consumer to terms with which he had no real opportunity of becoming acquainted before the conclusion of the contract;

(j)   enabling the seller or supplier to alter the terms of the contract unilaterally without a valid reason which is specified in the contract;

(k)   enabling the seller or supplier to alter unilaterally without a valid reason any characteristics of the product or service to be provided;

(l)   providing for the price of goods to be determined at the time of delivery or allowing a seller of goods or supplier of services to increase their price without in both cases giving the consumer the corresponding right to cancel the contract if the final price is too high in relation to the price agreed when the contract was concluded;

(m)   giving the seller or supplier the right to determine whether the goods or services supplied are in conformity with the contract, or giving him the exclusive right to interpret any term of the contract;

(n)   limiting the seller's or supplier's obligation to respect commitments undertaking by his agents or making his commitments subject to compliance with a particular formality;

(o)   obliging the consumer to fulfil all his obligations where the seller or supplier does not perform his;

(p)   giving the seller or supplier the possibility of transferring his rights and obligations under the contract, where this may serve to reduce the guarantees for the consumer, without the latter's agreement;

(q)   excluding or hindering the consumer's right to take legal action or exercise any other legal remedy, particularly by requiring the consumer to take disputes exclusively to arbitration not covered by legal provisions, unduly restricting the evidence available to him or imposing on him a burden of proof which, according to the applicable law, should lie with another party to the contract.

2. Scope of paragraphs 1(g), (j) and (l)

(a)   Paragraph 1(g) is without hindrance to terms by which a supplier of financial services reserves the right to terminate unilaterally a contract of indeterminate duration without notice where there is a valid reason, provided that the supplier is required to inform the other contracting party or parties thereof immediately.

(b)   Paragraph 1(j) is without hindrance to terms under which a supplier of financial services reserves the right to alter the rate of interest payable by the consumer or due to the latter, or the amount of other charges for financial services without notice where there is a valid reason, provided that the supplier is required to inform the other contracting party or parties thereof at the earliest opportunity and that the latter are free to dissolve the contract immediately.

Paragraph 1(j) is also without hindrance to terms under which a seller or supplier reserves the right to alter unilaterally the conditions of a contract of indeterminate duration, provided that he is required to inform the consumer with reasonable notice and that the consumer is free to dissolve the contract.

(c) Paragraphs 1(g), (j) and (l) do not apply to:
-transactions in transferable securities, financial instruments and other products or services where the price is linked to fluctuations in a stock exchange quotation or index or a financial market rate that the seller or supplier does not control;—contracts for the purchase or sale of foreign currency, traveller's cheques or international money orders denominated in foreign currency;

(d) Paragraph 1(l) is without hindrance to price indexation clauses, where lawful, provided that the method by which prices vary is explicitly described.

NOTES

1. What terms are subject to the Regulations? Firstly, note the way in which consumer is defined in reg 2(1). How does this differ from the definition in UCTA, s 12 (see, p 997)?

2. Secondly, the Regulations apply only to terms that have 'not been individually negotiated'. Is this the same as the 'written standard terms of business' of UCTA, s 3 (see p 1007)? One obvious difference is that the Regulations will apply to oral clauses (eg terms that are stated to you when you order goods or services over the telephone). But are there other differences? See regs 5(2) and 5(3). Article 3(2) of the Directive states:

A term shall always be regarded as not individually negotiated where it has been drafted in advance and the consumer has therefore not been able to influence the substance of the term...

Note the burden of proof, reg 5(4).

3. Can the price charged to the consumer be unfair under the Regulations? Regulation 6(2) seems to exempt the price from control 'in so far as [such a term] is in plain, intelligible language'. When can the court hold a price to be unfair under the Regulations? And what will be the effect? (On the latter, see note 11.)

4. Regulation 6(2) also exempts definitions of the main subject matter of the contract, subject to the same proviso. What does this mean? The regulation simply repeats Art 4(2) of the Directive, but the 19th recital adds:

...whereas it follows, *inter alia*, that in insurance contracts, the terms which clearly define or circumscribe the insured risk and the insurer's liability shall not be subject to such assessment since these are taken into account in calculating the premium paid by the customer.

The recitals of a Directive may be used to interpret it (*Marleasing SA v La Comercial Internacional de Alimentación SA*, Case C-106/89 [1990] ECR I-4135) and would almost certainly be used to interpret the Regulations under *Pepper (Inspector of Taxes) v Hart* [1993] 1 All ER 42. If the recital is taken literally, almost any clause in an insurance contract defining the risk (as opposed to, eg, laying down procedures for claims) might be exempt, because it will arguably affect the premium. Suppose a holiday insurance contract contains a clause in the 'small print' stating that the holidaymaker is not insured against the theft of any item that he leaves unattended. Is the clause caught by the Regulations? Does it depend on the wording of the clause, or can its position be taken into account?

5. What is the effect of of reg 7, first clause? Is it merely a preamble to the second clause about the *contra proferentem* rule, or does it impose a separate obligation to use plain, intelligible language? (Something may be clear and unambiguous to a lawyer without being plain and intelligible to a consumer!) If you think it imposes a separate obligation on suppliers to make their terms intelligible, what is the sanction for not doing so? (The Directive, Art 5, suffered from the same lack of clarity!)

6. The test of unfairness used in reg 5(1) is copied straight from the Directive, Art 3(1). This, in turn, seems to be derived from the test used by the German AGB–Gesetz (Standard Form Contracts Act) of 1976. How it will be interpreted in this country is very far from clear. A number of suggestions may be made.

7. One is that the 'significant imbalance' does not appear to refer to the consumer being overcharged. Although recital 19 states that 'the price/quality ratio may... be taken into account in assessing the fairness of other terms', to confine the unfairness to cases of imbalance between the price and what the consumer is to receive would be inconsistent with the exemption of the price term under reg 6(2). Rather, the imbalance must be understood in a broader sense, that the disadvantage caused by the term to the consumer is not matched by the advantage to the other party (eg if the seller or supplier could easily insure against the risk but the consumer cannot).

8. The 1994 Regulations contained in the second Schedule guidance as to the meaning of good faith. This guidance is not replicated in the 1999 Regulations although the original language was taken from recital 16 of the Directive. A judge could properly have regard to the language of the Directives in interpreting good faith and it is perhaps worth therefore setting out here what was set out in the second Schedule to the 1994 Regulations:

SCHEDULE 2. ASSESSMENT OF GOOD FAITH (Regulation 4(3))
In making an assessment of good faith, regard shall be had in particular to–
(a) the strength of the bargaining positions of the parties;
(b) whether the consumer had an inducement to agree to the term;
(c) whether the goods or services were sold or supplied to the special order of the consumer; and
(d) the extent to which the seller or supplier has dealt fairly and equitably with the consumer.

Obviously, this language is reminiscent of some parts of the definition of reasonableness under the Unfair Contract Terms Act. It may be doubted in any case whether it is an exhaustive statement of what good faith amounts to. In particular, it must be a serious question whether there were not some terms so detrimental to the consumer that even if the seller or supplier makes them crystal clear and takes adequate steps to bring them to the attention of the consumer, they will be valid.

9. Schedule 2 contains a list of terms that may be regarded as unfair. Note that they are not automatically unfair: this is not a blacklist but only a 'grey list'. There is not even a presumption that such terms are unfair: cf UCTA

10. The fairness of the term is to be judged by the circumstances at the time the contract was made: cf UCTA s 11(1) (on p 1010).

11. Under reg 8, it seems that the normal consequence of a term being held unfair is the same as when an exclusion clause is held to be invalid under UCTA: the contract is treated as if the clause were not there. Thus a contract that unfairly gives the seller the right to increase the price will be treated as a fixed-price contract. But what if the clause is essential to the contract, eg it is the only clause that indicates how the price is to be calculated?

12. The Director-General's power under reg 8 of the 1994 Regulations to obtain an injunction to prevent the continued use of an unfair term was new. Although under the Fair Trading Act 1973, Pt III the Director-General had power to act against traders who persist in a course of conduct that is detrimental or unfair to consumers, the latter was defined in terms of breaches of either the civil or the criminal law, so that it did not cover the use of even blacklisted terms unless an order prohibiting their use had been made under Pt II (see p 1003). (The procedures had a number of other serious defects and the

Director-General had called for major improvements (*Trading Malpractices*, 1990). These would extend his powers to deal with both 'Deceptive and misleading practices' and 'Unconscionable practices'.)

The powers given to the Director-General under the 1994 Regulations and continued under the 1999 Regulations are of great importance. In practice, the Director-General is much better equipped than the consumer to persuade trading bodies to change their practice in relation to contractual terms. The DTI issues regular bulletins setting out the substance of negotiations it has had with sellers and suppliers. In the vast majority of cases, the Department has been able to persuade sellers and suppliers to change their practices. The ambit of activities that have been subject to this review is very wide, including the letting of rooms in halls of residence by universities!

13. The first case in which the powers of the Director-General came before the courts because the trader has not accepted the Director-General's advice is *Director-General of Fair Trading v First National Bank plc* [2001] UKHL 52 [2002] AC 481 [2002] 1 All ER 97.

In this case, the clause that was objected to was a clause in the defendant bank's standard conditions for consumer finance, which provided in the event of default by the borrower that

interest on the amount which becomes payable shall be charged in accordance with Condition 4, at the rate stated in paragraph D overleaf (subject to variation) until payment after as well as before any judgment (such obligation to be independent of and not to merge with the judgment).

If this clause were valid, its effect would be to prevent the obligation to pay interest merging into the judgment so as to ensure that interest continued to accrue at the contractual rate rather than at the (usually lower) rate on judgment debts.

The Director-General commenced proceedings against the bank, seeking to restrain the bank, from including terms having this general effect. The bank raised two points. First, it was argued that the relevant clause did not fall to be considered for fairness at all since it was part of the core obligation that was excluded from review by the Regulations. The second argument was that the clause was, in any event, fair. The trial judge, the Court of Appeal and the House of Lords all held that the clause was within the area of review. This unanimity did not extend to whether the clause was fair. The Court of Appeal held that it was unfair. The Court attached great importance to the unpleasant surprise suffered by the debtor, who did not realise that the contractual rate of interest was still running at its (normally) higher rate. The House of Lords, reinstating the trial judge's finding, did not agree. On the assumption that the interest rate was initially fair, it would not become unfair because of the judgment.

14. The procedure for the Director-General to attempt to get an assurance from the seller or supplier not to use the term in future is parallel to that under the Fair Trading Act 1973, Pt III. Germany has a similar procedure, but at the behest of the consumer organisations empowered to act under the Law on Standard Contracts. They can obtain a written assurance from the business and take proceedings if the assurance is broken. This has proved extremely important and effective. See Micklitz, (1989) 41 Rev int droit comparé 101; Hondius, *Unfair Terms in Consumer Contracts*, Molengraaf Institute for Private Law, 1987, p 184.

15. The biggest change made by the 1999 Regulations was to extend the powers of the Director-General to the bodies set out in the First Schedule. Clearly, this widens the scope of the possible protectors of the consumer interest dramatically. It is worth pointing out especially that the Consumers' Association, which is a wholly non-governmental body, is amongst those bodies that have received this power.

16. The Law Commissions have recommended that the UTCCR and the Unfair Contract Terms Act 1977 be replaced by a single regime, to avoid the confusion caused by overlapping provisions and differing concepts and terminology. The regime would apply to terms of consumer contracts, other than 'core terms', whether or not the terms had been negotiated. They also recommended that protection similar to that currently afforded to consumers should be extended to small businesses. See *Unfair Terms in Contracts* (Law Com No 292, Scot Law Com No 199, 2005). The Government has accepted the Report in principle, subject to further evaluation.

■ Collins, 'Good Faith in European Contract Law' (1994)
14 Oxford J Legal Studies 229, 234–238

2 The scope of European contract law

My interpretation of the logic of harmonization qualified by the principle of subsidiarity indicates that limits on the scope of European contract law can be maintained. But these limits depend upon the purpose of the legal regulation itself. If one views the general law of contract as much more than a basic tool to support market exchanges, but rather a complex regulatory code designed to channel, encourage, and shape market transactions, then it becomes difficult to resist the case for uniformity or at least approximation of contract law. The medicinal properties of the carbolic smoke ball seem destined to become as legally irrelevant as the errant snail in the ginger beer bottle.

Yet the political conversations of the EC do not proceed so far. They focus on harmonization of the ground rules governing consumer contracts, and exclude commercial transactions between businesses. The organs of the EC have produced a number of reasons for this limited province for harmonization of contract law. This reasoning, which appears in many official documents, and most recently provides the substance or the Preamble for the Unfair Terms in Consumer Contracts Directive, combines the intricate sentence structure of French with the optimism of government statistics. It offers four reasons for confining harmonization to consumer contracts, none of which bear close inspection.

The Preamble claims first of all that the divergencies between the laws applicable to consumer contracts are greater than those applicable between businesses.[1] This establishes a greater risk of distortions of competition in consumer contracts, so they should receive priority in the push towards harmonization. It is true that consumer contracts have been subjected to specific regulation in most Member States and that this regulation diverges in technique, but it also has to be observed that the objectives of this regulation have been very similar. In contrast, commercial contracts have generally been left to regulation by ordinary private law, which preserves the fundamental divergences of concepts and techniques of national private law systems. The subtleties of the law governing conditions and warranties, for instance, must compel any foreign trader to seek legal advice before entering a commercial contract governed by English law.[2] The premise on which consumer contracts are awarded priority, namely that the laws of Member States diverge more substantially in this context, is therefore suspect. The truth of the matter, I suspect, is more subtle. Given the existence of extensive national regulation of consumer contracts already, there is far less political resistance to regulation by the EC. Re-regulation may create a fog of regulatory complexity, but it impinges far less on ideals of freedom of contract than regulation of virgin terrain, for it can be presented as approximation of regulatory economic laws rather than imposed harmonization of private law.

Secondly, in the Preamble the EC claims that there is a greater risk of market failure in the market for contract terms where consumers are involved.[3] But the Preamble stresses the market failure arising from ignorance of the applicable law in different Member States, and ignores the other crucial source of market failure: the extensive use of standard form contracts containing unread or incomprehensible small print, perhaps in a foreign language.[4] When we bring this second source of market failure into the picture, we must suspect that businesses also frequently overlook or fail to comprehend the small print proffered in standard form contracts, which similarly undermines competition for contract terms. The market failure analysis thus pushes towards regulation of all standard form contracts, not merely consumer contracts.

Thirdly, given the declared original and persisting purposes of the EC to improve the standard of living of its citizens by bringing them the benefits of a larger, more competitive, trading area, the Preamble suggests that this purpose is furthered by consumer protection against unfair contract terms.[5] Whilst it can be accepted that establishing a market which supplies high quality goods and services at competitive prices improves the standard of living, it is far from clear that consumer protection measures are as crucial in that respect as wider regulation of quality in contracts. Given that many goods and services pass through a chain of supply between businesses, and given that businesses are likely to have greater resources which enable them to insist upon conformity to contract standards of quality, then guarantees of quality granted to businesses will probably achieve the aim of establishing a marketplace containing high quality goods and services more effectively.[6] For example, if the retailer of cameras or jewellery in Athens can insist upon a high standard of quality from the distributor or manufacturer, then this is more likely to ensure that poor cameras or standard jewellery are not put on the market than simply giving guarantees of quality from the retailer to the tourist.

Finally, the Preamble argues that the consumer will not receive the benefit of price reductions forced by more competition if traders are reluctant to enter foreign markets, and in so far as this reluctance might be prompted by uncertainties with respect to their legal responsibilities, then harmonization of the legal rules will remove this deterrent.[7] But traders entering foreign markets are less likely to deal with consumers directly than with local businesses, so this argument for harmonization again pushes regulation towards control over business contracts, as has happened, for instance, in the case of public procurement through competitive contract tendering.

The shakiness of the factual assumptions and reasoning behind the EC focus on consumer contracts both alerts us to the possibility of an expansion of the province of EC contract law, and leads us to look for more contingent political explanations of the scope of the Directive. Such explanations may take the form that a consumerist movement has percolated into the organs of the EC, particularly the Commission, so that while the professed objectives of this regulation are couched in terms of improving the competitiveness of the single market and expanding consumer choice, the real agenda for many participants has been consumer protection as an end in itself.

3 Consumers' Economic Interests

Once attention is confined to consumer contracts, then we must address the question of what measures of harmonization are likely to promote best the economic interests of consumers? Here we encounter the sharp division of opinion between free marketeers and the advocates of consumer rights.

Some argue that the interests of consumers are best served by free competition. Legal regulation should be confined to instances of demonstrable market failure, where free competition does not exist in practice. This policy supports such measures as providing greater amounts of intelligible information to consumers and discouraging false and misleading information. It can also justify control over pressurized sales techniques, such as the harassment by doorstep sales representatives, for these practices prevent informed choice by consumers.

Others argue that consumers should be entitled to rights protecting their interests against unscrupulous and negligent traders. Indeed, in 1975 the Council declared that Community law should respect five basic rights of consumers:

(a) the right to protection of health and safety,
(b) the right to protection of economic interests,
(c) the right of redress,
(d) the right to information and education,
(e) the right of representation.[8]

This policy could even go as far as implementing a principle that consumers should receive good value for money and fulfilment of legitimate expectation. In short, an adequate protection of consumer rights may entail a mandatory requirement of fairness in consumer contracts.

Despite the rhetorical support for the policy of consumer rights, the emerging pattern of EC regulation of consumer contracts reveals a succession of victories for the free marketeers. The Misleading Advertising Directive 1984 fits squarely into a policy of remedying market failure, for it seeks to deter acts which distort competition between businesses by purveying false information to consumers when such conduct harms the economic interests of consumers.[9] Similarly, the justification for regulating doorstep sales in the Directive on Contracts negotiated away from Business Premises of 1985 was that the consumer in such situations is unable to make an informed judgment about alternative market opportunities because of the elements of surprise and pressure, so that these contracts are often coloured by market failure.[10] Concerns about market failure also determine the thrust of the Directive on Consumer Credit.[11] Its emphasis is upon the provision of clear information to consumers who seek credit arrangements, such as the insistence in Article 3 on the use of the annual percentage rate as the means of indicating the cost of credit, and the provision to the consumer of a full statement of the terms in writing mandated by Article 4. There is nothing in the Directive about the fairness of the credit terms. As Reich observes, 'Consumer rights have, it seems, been overridden by consumer choice'.[12]

This outcome should come as no surprise. Given that the justification for harmonization depends upon a policy of enhancing the competitiveness of the single market, arguments for regulation based upon market failure dovetail neatly into the central policy of completing the internal market. In contrast, arguments in support of consumer rights must always propose the elimination of competition between contract terms, so they run against the grain of the justification for harmonization.[13] There is another pragmatic reason for the success of the free marketeers. Since their proposals for regulation will inevitably encompass a narrower range of topics by being confined to demonstrated instances of market failure, it will be much easier to gather unanimous support for a compulsory law. The ambitious programmes of consumer rights inevitably raise a host of objections based upon the different traditions and methods of the laws of Member States, so that agreement on a precise form of words for a set of measures will prove elusive.

Perhaps most important of all for the predominance of the policy of consumer choice over consumer rights is the difference between legislative procedures introduced by Article 100A of the amended Treaty of Rome. If a Directive can be presented as a contribution to the removal of obstacles from the free movement of persons, goods and services, then it may be adopted under the qualified majority voting procedure (as opposed to the normal requirement of unanimity) designed to expedite the completion of the internal market. The Maastricht Treaty amendment to Article 129A of the Treaty of Rome explicitly confirms this bifurcation of procedures for consumer protection measures. These considerations tip the scale in favour of free marketeers even without taking into account the political disposition of the governments of some Member States.

The history of the EC Directive on Unfair Terms in Consumer Contracts reveals the struggle between these two interpretations of the economic interests of consumers. Even at a late stage in the negotiations, the draft Directive proposed by the Commission envisaged the introduction of a general principle against substantive unfairness in consumer contracts.[14] It invalidated terms in standard form consumer contracts which caused 'the performance of the contract to be significantly different from what the consumer could legitimately expect', or which caused 'the performance of the contract to be unduly detrimental to the consumer'.[15] But in the battle between the advocates of consumer rights and the supporters of free competition, eventually the latter emerged victorious in the Council of Ministers. The fairness of the transaction in the sense of the price paid for the goods or services should not be subjected to review or control. This is the meaning of the obscure Article 4(2):

> Assessment of the unfair nature of the terms shall relate neither to the definition of the main subject-matter of the contract nor to the adequacy of the price and remuneration, on the one hand, as against the services or goods supplied in exchange, on the other, insofar as these terms are in plain intelligible language.

The final reservation in this provision is significant. The Directive does not require consumer contracts to be substantively fair, but it does require them to be clear. Clarity is essential for effective market competition between terms. What matters primarily for EC contract law is consumer choice, not consumer rights.

[1] Recitals 6 and 7.

[2] We should also note the added risk that the legal advice may turn out to be false when dealing with the subtleties of the common law, as in *Schuler (L) AG v Wickman Machine Tool Sales Ltd* [1974] AC 235.

[3] Recitals 9 and 11. This point was also stressed in the EC Commission's original proposal for the Directive COM (90) 322—SYN 285, 14 September 1990, OJ C 243, 28 September 1990, 2, reprinted in House of Lords Select Committee on the European Communities, Session 1991–2, 6th Report, *Unfair Contract Terms*, III Paper 28 (London) 36.

[4] This was an earlier justification for the Directive: European Commission, *A New Impetus for Customer Protection Policy* (Luxembourg, 1985) para 30. The market failure analysis is given formal explanation in V Goldberg, 'Institutional Change and the Quasi-Invisible Hand' (1974) 17 *Journal of Law & Economics* 461 [see above, p 830].

[5] Recitals 12 and 13, referring back to earlier statements of the rationale for consumer protection by the EC, such as OJ C 92 of 25 April 1975, 1, and OJ C 133 of 3 June 1981, 1.

[6] The EC Economic and Social Committee Report, 24 April 1991, criticized the Directive on the ground, particularly with its failure to protect small businesses: reprinted in House of Lords Select Committee on the European Communities, Session 1991–2, 6th Report, *Unfair Contract Terms*, HI. Paper 28 (London), 62, paras 2.3.3–4.

[7] Recital 11.

[8] OJ C 92 of 25 April 1975, 1.

[9] Directive 84 450, OJ L 1984 250/17, implemented by the Control of Misleading Advertisement Regulations, SI 1988 No 915.

[10] Directive 85 577, OJ L 1985 372/31, implemented by the Consumer Protection (Cancellation of Contracts Concluded away from Business Premises) Regulations 1987, SI 1987 No 2117.

[11] Directive 87/102, OJ L 1987 42/48, as amended by 90/88, OJ L 1990 61/14.

[12] N Reich, 'Protection of Consumers' Economic Interests by the EC' (1992) 14 *Sydney L Rev* 23, 25. Similar emphasis upon consumer choice is displayed in other relevant Directives: 90/314, OJ L 1990 ISS59 (package travel); 92/96, OJ L1992 360/1 Art 31 (life insurance). It follows that proposed legislation which adopts a consumer rights policy finds itself stalled: eg Proposal for Council Directive on the Liability of Suppliers of Services, 9 November 1990, OJ C 12/8, 18.1.91.

[13] Wetherill, '1992 and Consumer Law: Can Free Trade be Reconciled with Effective Protections?' 1988 6 *Trading Law* 175.

[14] OJ C 73, 24.3.92, 7.

[15] Id Articles 3 and 4.

Earlier we saw arguments that considered whether English law already recognises a general duty of good faith (pp 271 ff) or whether it should do so (p 283). The assumption appears to be that the doctrine would apply in English law rather as it does in, say, German law. Now we have seen that, in the context of the Unfair Terms in Consumer Contracts Regulations, good faith to some extent already forms part of English law. Will it mean that our law on unfair terms will become closer to the German model on which the Unfair Terms Directive seems to have been based? One writer argues that the concept will not simply be transplanted; rather it will act as an 'irritant' in the English legal system, which may react to the notion of good faith in a very different way to the German legal system. The article extracted below is complex and repays study in full but the extract should give an idea of the thrust of the arguments.

■ **Teubner, 'Legal Irritants: Good Faith in British Law or How Unifying Law Ends Up in New Divergences'** (1998)
61 Modern LR 11, 11–12, 19–21, 23–30

Legal transplant: a misleading metaphor

Some academic commentators have expressed deep worries: 'Good faith could well work practical mis-chief if ruthlessly implanted in our system of law.' [M.G. Bridge, 'Does Anglo-Canadian Contract Law Need a Doctrine of Good Faith?'] Others have welcomed good faith as a healthy infusion of communi-tarian values, hoping that it will cure the ills of contractual formalism and interact productively with other substantive elements in British contract law. The whole debate is shaped by the powerful metaphor of the 'legal transplant'. Will good faith, once transplanted, be rejected by an immune reaction of the *corpus iuris britannicum?* Or will it function as a successful transplant interacting productively with other elements in the legal organism?

Repulsion or interaction? In my view, this is a false dichotomy because the underlying metaphor of legal transplants, suggestive as it is, is in itself misleading. I think 'legal irritant' expresses things better than 'legal transplant'.... '[T]ransplant' creates the wrong impression that after a difficult surgical oper-ation the transferred material will remain identical with itself playing its old role in the new organism. Accordingly, it comes down to the narrow alternative: repulsion or integration. However, when a foreign rule is imposed on a domestic culture, I submit, something else is happening. It is not transplanted into another organism, rather it works as a fundamental irritation which triggers a whole series of new and unexpected events. It irritates, of course, the minds and emotions of tradition-bound lawyers; but in a deeper sense,—and this is the core of my thesis—it irritates law's 'binding arrangements'. It is an outside noise which creates wild perturbations in the interplay of discourses within these arrangements and forces them to reconstruct internally not only their own rules but to reconstruct from scratch the alien element itself....

Thus, the question is not so much if British contract doctrine will reject or integrate good faith. Rather it is what kind of transformations of meaning will the term undergo, how will its role differ, once it is reconstructed anew under British law? My guess is that this is not only a matter of reconstructing it from a common law as opposed to a civil law perspective. There is also the crucial difference of 'production regimes'. The imperatives of a specific Anglo-American economic culture as against a specific Continental one will bring about an even more fundamental reconstruction of good faith under the new conditions. This is why I think that in spite of all benign intentions towards an 'Ever Closer Union', attempts at unifying European contract law will result in new cleavages....

[The] famous *bona fides* principle is clearly one of the unique expressions of continental legal culture. The specific way in which continental lawyers deal with such a 'general clause' is abstract, open-ended, principle-oriented, but at the same time strongly systematised and dogmatised. This is clearly at odds with the more rule-oriented, technical, concrete, but loosely systematised British style of legal reasoning, especially when it comes to the interpretation of statutes. Does then the inclusion of such a broad prin-ciple in a British statute also imply that British lawyers are now supposed to 'concretise' this general clause in the continental way? Will British judges now 'derive' their decisions from this abstract and vague principle moving from the abstract to the concrete via different and carefully distinguished steps of concretisation? Will they reconstruct good faith in a series of abstract well-defined doctrinal con-structs, translate it into a system of conditional programmes, apply to it the obscurities of teleological reasoning, and indulge in pseudo-historical interpretation of the motives why good faith had been incorporated into the Euro-Directive? From my impressions of British contract law I would guess that good faith will never be 'transplanted' this way. But it will 'irritate' British legal culture considerably. Under the permanent influence of continental noise this culture is indeed undergoing considerable change and is developing a new order of principle-oriented statutory interpretation which is, however, remarkably different from its continental counterpart. New dissonances from harmonisation!

Under present conditions it is inconceivable that British good faith will be the same as *Treu und Glauben* German style which has been developed in a rather special historical and cultural constellation. *Treu und Glauben* has been the revolutionising instrument by which the formalistic civil code of 1900 has been 'materialised' and adapted to the convulsions of Germany's history in the 20th century. During this time German legal culture developed an intimate 'symbiotic relationship' between the new powers that the national constitution and the civil code had given to the judiciary and the old powers invested in the authorities of pandectic legal scholarship. The result of this unique type of episode linkage was that the highly ambivalent and open-ended good faith principle which was originally supposed to flexibly counteract on an ad hoc basis the rigidities of formal law, was actually propelled into an incredible degree of conceptual systematisation and abstract dogmatisation. . . .

In Britain, it may well be that 'good faith' (together with 'legitimate expectation', 'proportionality' and other continental general clauses) will trigger deep, long-term changes from highly formal rule-focused decision-making in contract law toward a more discretionary principle-based judicial reasoning. [See Jonathan Levitsky, 'The Europeanization of the British Legal Style' (1994) 42 *American journal of Comparative Law* 347, 368–378.] But it will probably move into a direction quite different from German-style dogmatisation. Given the distinctive British mode of episode linkages, good faith will be developed rather in forms of judicial activism similar to those other common law countries have adopted, combining close fact-oriented case analysis with loosely arranged arguments from broad principles and policies. British lawyers will avoid the recourse to elaborate intermediate structures, dogmatic constructs, juridical theories and conceptual systematisation which is so close to the heart of German law. The predictable result will be a judicial doctrine of good faith that is much more 'situational' in character. [For such a situational approach to good faith, see Todd Rakoff, 'The Implied Terms of Contracts: Of "Default Rules" and "Situation Sense"' in J. Beatson and D. Friedmann (eds), *Good Faith and Fault in Contract Law* (Oxford: Clarendon, 1995) 191–228 201ff.] . . .

English law will develop on a analogical basis new rules coming out of a close analysis of the factual situations involved. And principles will enter the scene which will not be translated into strictly conceptualised and systematised doctrines, but rather appear as loosely organised ad hoc arguments that do not deny their political-ethical origin.

Tying law to social fragments

. . . Historically, *bona fides* had been contract law's recourse to social morality. Whenever the application of strict formal contract rules led to morally unacceptable results, *bona fides* was invoked to counteract the formalism of contract law doctrine with a substantive social morality. Contracts were performed in good faith when the participants behaved in accordance with accepted standards of moral behaviour.

Under contemporary conditions of moral pluralisation and social fragmentation, good faith cannot play this role any more. There have been attempts to take into account these historical changes and to replace recourse to morality by recourse to the 'purpose' of the legal institutions involved. Contracts are performed in good faith when the participants are responsive to the policy of the rules, the *telos* of their rights, the *idées directrices* of the institutions, the elements of 'ordre public', the values of the political constitution law within private arrangements. This new policy-oriented interpretation of good faith which gained high prominence in this century, especially in the debate about institutional *abus des droits*, reflected indeed the more selective nature of law's social ties. It concentrated them on the policies of institutionalised politics. But in a sense it privileged the political ties of law, neglecting ties to other discourses.

Formal contractual obligations are not only linked to substantive policy requirements and the *ordre public* of institutionalised politics, they are equally exposed to substantive demands of other social institutions. Markets and organisations, the professions, the health sector, social security, family, culture, religion — they all impose certain requirements on the 'private' contractual relation. . . . Good faith complements contractual duties with social expectations stemming from those various fields. Due to its high degree of indeterminacy, the general clause of good faith is particularly suited to link contracts selectively to their unstable social environments with constantly shifting and conflicting requirements.

It is this selective and fractured linkage of good faith to highly diverse social environments that will be responsible for newly emerging cleavages. If, under European law, good faith is transferred from the Continent to British law and if it is supposed to play also in the new context its role of linking contracts to a variety of different discourses, then it is bound to produce results at great variance with continental legal orders. Good faith will reproduce in legal form larger differences of the national cultures involved, and it will do so, paradoxically, because it was meant to make their laws more uniform. . . .

Divergent production regimes

. . .

More specifically, the following characteristics of the German production regime find their structural correlates in an extensive series of good faith obligations which have been developed by the courts.

(1) German corporate governance and corporate finance tend to favour long-term financing of firms. Private law supports this by good faith obligations which the participant owners, companies and banks, owe to each other. Under the umbrella of good faith, not only partners of a business association are under a general duty of mutual loyalty; German law acknowledges a far-reaching obligation upon the owners of capital and other constituencies of the firm to further actively the long-term 'company interest' as opposed to their partial self-interest. An extensive system of duties of disclosure and provision of information has been developed in the relation between bank and company.

(2) Industrial relations within the firm and in the industry are highly cooperative relations in which labour unions play an important part. As a corollary of employees' high autonomy, the courts have developed extensive good faith duties of loyalty toward the organisation which mitigate the risk of moral hazard inherent in their autonomous position. In turn the law gives them a protected status within the firm. There are equally extensive legal duties of responsibility and care of managers toward the employees.

(3) Inter-company relations tend to be cooperative networks with relational long-term contracting, horizontally within markets as well as vertically between different suppliers, producers and distributors. Under the good faith clause, courts have imposed duties of cooperation which are geared toward the common purpose of the contract. In relational contracts they have developed the general duty *ex lege* to renegotiate contractual terms if a new situation arises. And one of the most important judicial innovations has been to re-introduce the old *clausula rebus sic stantibus* which the Civil Code had excluded. Judges take the freedom to rewrite contractual terms in case of supervening events.

(4) Business associations and large firms coordinate markets via technical standard setting, business standard contracting and dispute resolution. In support of this self-coordination of industries, courts have recognised and reconstructed multilateral firm relations well beyond the wording of bilateral contracts. However, their most important contribution to associational market coordination was to acknowledge standard terms as binding and to regulate them by taking certain interests, particularly that of the consumer, into account.

(5) Business associations negotiate technical and business standards with government. Other non-economic interest groups, such as consumer associations and ecological movements, favour a 'neo-corporatist' culture of mediating economic transactions with their outside world, with political, social and ecological concerns. The courts can build on such a body of negotiated *ordre public* and reconstruct good faith standards on its basis to counteract excessive economic transactions.

An implantation of this 'living law' into the British soil simply would not find its roots in a corresponding economic culture. The British economic culture, together with United States, Ireland, Canada, New Zealand, make up a group of relatively unregulated Liberal Market Economies (LME). In contrast to continental Business-Coordinated Economies (CME), organised business is weak and plays rather a limited role in coordinating the institutional framework. Instead, a rather unmediated interplay of market forces on the one side and external governmental regulation on the other takes place. Government, regulatory agencies, quasi-public bodies and the legal system play the major role in rule-setting with the rules typically taking a low-discretionary form. How would good faith duties of cooperation, information, renegotiation, contractual adaptation 'fit' into a production regime that is characterised by the following traits?

(1) financial systems which impose relatively short-term horizons on companies, but at the same time allow high risk-taking.

(2) industrial relations systems in deregulated labour markets which discourage effective employee representation within companies—hence weak unions, but which facilitate unilateral control by top management;

(3) inter-company systems which impose strong competition requirements and hence limits on possible cooperation between companies.

(4) a coordination between the economic sector and other sectors of society which is either left to market forces or is exclusively assigned to governmental regulation, in contrast to neo-corporatist style of intermediation which is typical of continental production regimes.

The difference between the production regimes is striking. The British economic culture does not appear to be a fertile ground on which continental *bona fide* would blossom. Thus, the 'legal transplant' approach would lead us to expect repulsion, not interaction. The good faith clause will remain an exotic exception in the British landscape. Alternatively, what is the narrative that emerges from the irritant metaphor?

Co-evolving trajectories

. . .

A binding arrangement, tying law to a social discourse, does not develop in one single historical trajectory but in two separate and qualitatively different evolutionary paths of the two sides which are re-connected via co-evolution. Their legal side takes part in the evolutionary logics of law while the social side obeys a different logic of development. Their changes however interact insofar as due to their close structural coupling they permanently perturb each other and provoke change on the other side.

Now it becomes clear why the transferred rule can only serve as an irritation, and never as a transplantation, if a transfer of legal rules is supposed to change a binding arrangement between law and another social discourse. It irritates a co-evolutionary process of separate trajectories. On the legal side of the binding institution, the rule will be recontextualised in the new network of legal distinctions and it may still be recognisable as the original legal rule even if its legal interpretation changes. But on the social side, something very different will take place. The legal impulse, if it is recognised at all, will create perturbations in the other social system and will trigger there some changes governed by the internal logics of this world of meaning. It will be reconstructed in the different language of the social system involved, reformulated in its codes and programmes, which in turn leads to a new series of events. This social change in its turn will work back as an irritation to the legal side of the institution thus creating a circular co-evolutionary dynamic that comes to a preliminary equilibrium only once both the legal and the social discourse will have evolved relatively stable eigenvalues in their respective sphere. This shows how improbable it is that a legal rule will be successfully transplanted in a binding arrangement of a different legal context. If it is not rejected outright, either it destroys the binding arrangement or it will result in a dynamics of mutual irritations that alter its identity fundamentally.

And good faith?—It will not even be an irritant to the British production regime if it presents itself as a bundle of legal duties of mandatory cooperation, German style, imposed on the parties to a contract. The British regime would react with cool indifference. However,—and this is my concluding thesis—good faith will become a strong irritant to the market-driven production regime in Britain if the new context transforms good faith from a facilitative rule into a prohibitive rule. Instead of facilitating autonomy, trust and cooperation, its effect would be to outlaw certain excesses of economic action.

Good faith would become a quasi-constitutional constraint on two central elements of the production regime: a constraint on strong hierarchies of private government and a constraint on certain expansionist tendencies of competitive processes.

The continental production regime to which *Treu und Glauben* responded, as we said, was characterised by high autonomy and high trust relations within the market and within the organisations. They carry specific risks and dangers which were mitigated by an elaborate system of legal cooperation duties. The risks and dangers that the British production regime carry are not problems of high autonomy and high trust, but rather the opposite. This production regime is governed by the risks of 'financial Fordism' where low-cost standardised production requires detailed work regulation and frequent personnel change, by the dangers of project organisations that manage complex tasks by a strong managerial prerogative, by the steep hierarchy within economic organisation, and asymmetric relations between powerful companies and their dependent satellites. The role of the good faith principle cannot conceivably be to transform these tightly coordinated organisations into cooperative arrangements. Rather, the task for contract law would be to define quasi-constitutional rights and to protect them against encroachments of private government, to set low-discretionary rules that draw clearly-defined legal limits to quasi-administrative discretion. The good faith principle would have to develop into judicial constraints on arbitrary decisions of private government. As opposed to activating the communitarian traditions of 'duties' of trustful cooperation, the judiciary would have to activate the tradition of constitutional 'rights' which have historically been invoked against governmental authority, and reinforce them in the private law context.

There is a second re-interpretation of good faith which seems equally relevant in the new production regime. It takes into account the fundamental difference between associational coordination and market-driven coordination in standard setting — in the broad sense of technical, intra-organisational, and contractual standards. While on the continent the judiciary frequently refers to neo-corporatist processes of standardisation where negotiations between associations result in a certain mediation of social and political interests with market results, standard setting in Britain is basically driven by market processes. Thus, according to its production regime, British law tends to invalidate standard terms when business associations have been involved unilaterally in imposing uniform standard terms over the whole market. In *George Mitchell (Chesterhall) Ltd* v *Finney Lock Seeds Ltd* the court saw it as an invalidating factor that 'a similar limitation of liability was universally embodied in the terms of trade between seedsmen and farmers and had been so for many years'. Under the British production regime, business associations are not supposed to play a decisive role in the formulation of standard contracts. The courts see it as a market failure when business associations produce uniform standard contracts which exclude competition between diverse contractual regimes. This is in striking contrast to the German situation where business associations play a crucial role in the unilateral standardisation of business conditions. As a consequence, under German good faith rules it does not make a difference whether the standard contracts had been formulated by one enterprise or by business associations for the whole market.

Under the British production regime, it is exceptional for standard terms to be bilaterally negotiated by the relevant interest associations to which the courts could then refer as a fair compromise. Standardisation is more or less exclusively left to market mechanisms. In such a situation, it would be disastrous if the judiciary understood good faith as an incorporation of spontaneously developed standards into private law. The law would simply sanction the standard-eroding effects of market-competition and would effectively rule out non-economic political and cultural aspects of standardisation. In such a situation, the role of the judiciary becomes much closer to that of an external political regulatory agency which sets firm boundaries to market dynamics when they work against the fundamental requirements of other social spheres. In conjunction with government, regulatory agencies and quasi-public organisations, the judiciary of the British production regime needs to set its own external standards to economic action without having recourse to social norms that have been preformulated in inter-associational negotiations.

Thus, the procedural dimension of good faith is profoundly influenced by the difference of production regimes. If good faith means among other things that one party has to take the other party's legitimate interest into account, and in the case of consumer contracts that standardised contracts must reflect the consumer interest, then the central question is what kind of procedures are effectively working to satisfy this requirement. This is, to be sure, a more demanding procedural requirement of good faith than the usual question of absence of pressure and deception. Under an association-driven production regime the courts have to monitor whether the negotiations between different associations and regulatory agencies fulfil the procedural requirement of an adequate and effective representation of consumer interests in the process of standardisation. Their corrective action would primarily consist in changing the rules of the game and re-defining the property rights of the collective actors involved. Under a market-driven production regime, the courts will have to take a more active approach in order to make sure that standardised contracts fulfil the procedural requirements of good faith. . . .

QUESTIONS

1.   To what kinds of contract do the Regulations apply?

2.   What types of clause commonly found in consumer contracts are not caught by UCTA or any of the other statutes, but are likely to be caught by the Regulations?

3.   What is the test of whether or not a clause is unfair? How do you think this will differ, if at all, from the test of reasonableness under UCTA?

4.   If you travel to another EC member State and enter a consumer contract there, you will probably find your contract is subject to the law of that member State. Supposing that State has done the minimum required by the Directive to protect consumers from unfair exemption and other clauses: how well can you count on being protected compared to the protection you have at home under UCTA and other statutes?

5.   In what ways is enforcement of the Unfair Terms in Consumer Contracts Regulations handled differently from enforcement of the Unfair Contract Terms Act?

CHAPTER FORTY-ONE

REGULATED CONTRACTS

The account of contract law given in this book has been largely abstract, that is, concerned with rules that are true of contracts whatever their subject matter. In this, it has followed the prevalent Anglo-American pattern of the last hundred years. Discussions of particular contracts have commonly been found in other books—on sale, hire purchase, labour law, insurance and so on. This reflects the prevalent view of English lawyers that we have a law of contract rather than of contracts.

One of the consequences of this approach is to exclude from the general law of contract much of the (statutory) regulation of individual contracts on the basis that what applies only to a special contract is not of general interest. The process of regulation has, however, been carried very far and indeed some commentators have doubted whether this leaves much of general contract law left. This view seems to us an exaggeration but it is worthwhile to look briefly at some examples of regulation, which we classify according to the rationale for adopting regulation. The list that follows is not exhaustive and no doubt in some cases the examples overlap two or more categories.

I. 'NECESSITIES' IN SHORT SUPPLY

In ordinary circumstances, market exchange mediated by contract operates to provide necessities such as food. Prices are dictated by supply and demand, so that a poor potato crop will lead to higher potato prices. There is nowadays considerable interference with pure market forces but this tends to take the form of encouraging farmers to produce more food than customers will buy at market prices (hence butter mountains and wine lakes). In times of famine and war, governments have, for millennia, tried to hold down the prices of staple foods such as corn, although this has often led simply to the development of black markets. One of the most interesting examples of regulation in this field is rented housing, which has been the subject of legislation in England since 1915. The statutory regime is complex, largely as a result of the need to control attempts by landlords to evade the scheme, for example, by demanding the payment of 'premiums' before letting tenants into possession (see *Kiriri Cotton Ltd v Dewani*, p 1092). Under the original scheme, rents were frozen. Under the scheme that operated until the coming into force of the Housing Act 1988 (and which still applies to many tenancies), rents were held to a 'fair' level but it was assumed that this would often (usually) be below the level that would be fixed by the market. The rationale for intervention is that landlords will be unfairly enriched and tenants unduly impoverished by payment of the difference between 'market' rents and 'fair' rents. The operation of the scheme has been the subject of extensive economic and political debate. There is no doubt that, since 1915, the amount of rented accommodation provided by private landlords has diminished greatly; the critical question is whether this has been caused by the scheme. It can be plausibly argued that landlords as a class will not build houses for rent or continue to rent out houses they already own unless the return is commensurate with that to be expected from other forms of investment. If this is true, regulation may operate in the long run to diminish the supply, thereby exacerbating the problem that it is designed to solve. (Of course, all is not so simple, because in the long run, demand is also not constant and governments have adopted other policies, such as tax relief on mortgages which encourage customers for accommodation to move if possible from renting houses to buying them.) The Housing Act 1988 introduces changes that attempt to ensure that market rents are reflected in the rents set. Whether it will result in an increased supply of rented accommodation remains to be seen.

II. INTRACTABLE PROBLEMS OF INADEQUATE INFORMATION

Economists sometimes divide goods into 'search goods' and 'experience goods'. When a potential customer has poor information about the former, he searches for it until satisfied. But for some goods, search will not do, because there is no good way to get information before buying. So here the customer commonly must 'experience' the goods in order to inform himself. Such a practice works satisfactorily enough as a basis for choosing between one brand of instant coffee and another, but it is hardly satisfactory if the consumer is to make a once-in-a-lifetime purchase. He may often be able to use other people's experience, since reputation will often be the key. In many fields, a firm's reputation for good work is one of its most valuable assets, which it will not depreciate by cheating customers because the short-term gain is small compared with the long-term loss. But this does not help if no reputation can be built up.

A classic example is the supply of passages to emigrants from Europe to America in the nineteenth century.

■ **'Atiyah, The Rise and Fall of Freedom of Contract'**
pp 337–338

The Passenger Acts

...Between 1803 and 1860 a large number of emigrants from England, and more especially, Ireland, took their lives in their hands and boarded an emigrant passenger vessel, usually at Liverpool. In the 1840s as a result of failure of the Irish potato crop, the numbers rose hugely, and between 1844 and 1852 some one and a half million persons sought to cross the Atlantic in search of a better life. Most of the emigrants were very poor, many had worked for months to save up the fare—little as it was—many were illiterate, and nearly all were imposed upon. The conditions on these ships were, at the beginning of the century, appalling. The emigrants were crammed into the ships, sometimes with barely room to stand up, let alone lie down, there were no sanitary facilities of any kind, no privacy, no segregation of the sexes, and no food was provided: the passengers were expected to bring their own. When it ran out, as it might do if the voyage was prolonged, they either starved or bought supplies from the ship's master at enormously inflated prices. Disease was rife, and many ships arrived in America or Canada with rotting corpses littering the decks.

The facts first came to light almost by accident, in 1803, when a Select Committee inquiring into the Scottish highlands was fed a great deal of information about the emigrant trade. They were told, for example, of a ship in which three-fifths of the passengers had died, and thirty corpses were found when it arrived. The reaction was instantaneous. A Bill was hastily drafted and passed without a single voice being raised against it. But the Act did more credit to the heart than to the head of its sponsors. It threw away, indeed, any notion of freedom of contract and constituted what Professor MacDonagh has called a revolutionary breach of this principle. But as I have previously pointed out, in 1803 the principle had barely been formulated, for the equitable jurisdiction at that time provided many forms of redress for poor and ignorant contracting parties who were imposed upon by others. In any event the Act did not work. It was too burdensome on the shipowners, and if it had been enforced, the cost of a passage on an emigrant ship would have been priced beyond the reach of the passengers.

We have also seen how in 1826–7 a Parliamentary Select Committee suddenly woke up to the fact that the Act represented an infringement of the important principle of freedom of contact and secured its repeal and how, almost immediately, new revelations about the appalling conditions in the trade led to more legislation. In 1828 a new Act was passed, more modest in its requirements, and this time, though (it seems) largely by accident, the Act was enforced. This came about because the draftsman of the Act, A. C. Buchanan, was appointed Agent-General for Emigration to Canada; in that capacity he took it on himself to prosecute for breaches of the Act and to present annual reports on his efforts to Parliament. An amending Act of 1835 required the shipowners to pay 1s. per day detention money to passengers waiting for their vessel in Liverpool. This Act also required the ships to carry 'sufficient' medicines for the voyage and to post up price lists for the food on sale to the passengers. As usual it was enforcement which remained the principal problem. The Acts conferred all manner of contractual rights on the passengers, but once aboard the ships there was nothing that anyone could do to enforce his rights. Complaints were often made at the other end, but the survivors were generally only too eager to disembark and get away as fast as they could. It was unthinkable for any of them to wait around at the place of disembarkation in order to bring a civil action for damages. Sir James Stephen, Under-Secretary in the Colonial Office, commented somewhat fatalistically, that 'These Irishmen are not the first, nor will they be the last, to make the discovery that a man may starve and yet have the best right of action that a special pleader could wish for'. But this fatalism did not satisfy everybody, and demands for more rigorous enforcement by the Government were frequent. By 1836–40 even the political economists had quite abandoned their opposition to the legislation and were as keen as anyone to suggest tightening-up of the requirements. A Report on the Acts in 1842 paid lip service to the principle of *laissez-faire*, arguing that Acts of Parliament could not 'supply the want of proper discretion in individuals', but generally speaking these cautionary words had little effect.

An important Act was drafted and carried in 1842, based on the detailed proposals of the new emigration officers. This Act was quite destructive of what remained of freedom of contract. It required a written contract in a prescribed form to be given to the passengers, it required the licensing of brokers and agents, compulsory provision of food for the passengers both on board, and even prior to embarkation, from the day appointed for departure. The Act was drafted with a view to its enforceability and it was enforced. The new Commissioner for Emigration was given power to sue the shipowners in the name, and on behalf of, the passengers, and for some years after the Act was passed the Commissioner was recovering some £1,500 annually on their behalf.

The same reasoning has led many countries to undertake extensive regulation of their tourist industries.

Even when information does spread about goods or services, it may spread slowly and unevenly. Much consumer protection legislation arises from this problem and the belief that ordinary contract principles alone will not lead to results that maximise consumer welfare.

Similar problems confront the customer who seeks professional services. It is difficult for a non-lawyer to discover which lawyers are competent to undertake which (if any) kinds of work. In many countries, this leads to state-imposed minimum standards. In England, the tradition of professional self-regulation has been very strong.

III. PROBLEMS WITH TRANSACTIONS COSTS

Negotiating contracts takes time and therefore costs money. We have seen that one of the responses to this has been the development of standard-form contracts, one of the advantages of which is that contract making can be delegated to relatively low-level staff who have no authority other than to use the standard form. Similar considerations enter into the thinking of governments and are one of the reasons for the development of special mandatory regimes for certain kinds of international transaction, particularly international carriage. The best example of this is the Hague Rules, enacted into English law by the Carriage of Goods by Sea Act 1924 (now replaced by the Hague–Visby Rules, enacted by the Carriage of Goods by Sea Act 1971). These rules, which form the background to a number of cases in this book (see eg *The Eurymedon*, p 1145), provide a mandatory regime for carriage of goods by sea under a bill of lading and have been enacted into law by nearly all countries. This means that there will be a very high degree of similarity between all bills of lading, which greatly facilitates dealing with them. Similar developments have followed in relation to international carriage of goods by rail and by road.

It would be an oversimplification to regard the Hague Rules simply in this light; they also represent a compromise between the interests of shipowners and shippers, in that they achieve a set of terms that was apparently seldom achieved by negotiation previously. A person or company sending goods under a bill of lading would normally find it uneconomic to pay the amount that a shipping line would demand to alter its standard terms in his favour— he might well be prepared to pay the extra cost of better standard terms if they were shared by all other shippers too, but he would not pay the cost of arranging a special one-off deal (compare note 4 on p 973). This might be true of a considerable number of shippers, and although their aggregate dissatisfaction with the terms offered would have some influence on the shipping lines, there might not be enough shippers aware of the problem to bring about a change (see p 970). Thus high transactions costs seem to have prevented an efficient solution until the adoption of the Hague Rules. This analysis seems to be confirmed by the fact that the Rules do not apply to charterparties: a charter is a larger contract and charterers would find it cost-effective to negotiate over the terms.

IV. VULNERABILITY TO EXPLOITATION IN LONG-TERM RELATIONSHIPS

It is often the case that parties enjoy roughly equal bargaining power at the time the contract is entered into, but that once the contract is on foot, the balance of advantage changes sharply. The classic example is a contract of employment. The individual employee commonly has more options open to him before, than after, taking the contract of employment. Often the employee will develop skills that are job-specific and make him less attractive to other employers; often the decision to accept the post will involve forgoing alternative kinds of training and experience. Further, the central place that work plays in most people's lives will mean that employer and employee view termination of the contract in quite a different light.

In the last twenty years, regulation of the contract of employment has been extensive. Particularly interesting has been the introduction of the notion of 'unfair dismissal', that is, a dismissal that is not wrongful within the terms of the contract of employment but nevertheless contravenes acceptable norms and entitles the employee thereby dismissed to compensation.

V. PRIVATE ENFORCEMENT COSTS ARE TOO HIGH

Private enforcement of contracts is likely to be effective only if the value of the sum sued for exceeds the likely cost of the action to the plaintiff. This will not be the case if there are many victims of contractual misperformance, each of whom suffers a small loss. This is the normal position at the shoddy end of the retail trade and led to the passing of the Fair Trading Act 1973 Part II, under which the Director-General of Fair Trading was given wide powers in respect of 'unfair' consumer trade practices. He could also take steps against persistent contract breakers.

Part II of the Fair Trading has been repealed and replaced by Part 8 of the Enterprise Act 2002. This enables the Office of Fair Trading and other 'enforcers' to act against businesses that commit 'domestic' or 'community' infringements—the latter being breaches of the requirements of listed Directives.

■ Enterprise Act 2002

Section 211 Domestic infringements

(1) In this Part a domestic infringement is an act or omission which—
   (a) is done or made by a person in the course of a business,
   (b) falls within subsection (2), and
   (c) harms the collective interests of consumers in the United Kingdom.
(2) An act or omission falls within this subsection if it is of a description specified by the Secretary of State by order and consists of any of the following—
   (a) a contravention of an enactment which imposes a duty, prohibition or restriction enforceable by criminal proceedings;
   (b) an act done of omission made in breach of contract;
   (c) an act done or omission made in breach of a non-contractual duty owed to a person by virtue of an enactment or rule of law and enforceable by civil proceedings;
   (d) an act or omission in respect of which an enactment provides for a remedy or sanction enforceable by civil proceedings;
   (e) an act done or omission made by a person supplying or seeking to supply goods or services as a result of which an agreement or security relating to the supply is void or unenforceable to any extent;
   (f) an act or omission by which a person supplying or seeking to supply goods or services purports or attempts to exercise a right or remedy relating to the supply in circumstances

where the exercise of the right or remedy is restricted or excluded under or by virtue of an enactment;

(g) an act or omission by which a person supplying or seeking to supply goods or services purports or attempts to avoid (to any extent) liability relating to the supply in circumstances where such avoidance is restricted or prevented under an enactment.

. . .

(5) References to an enactment include references to subordinate legislation (within the meaning of the Interpretation Act 1978 (c. 30)).

(6) The power to make on order under this section must be exercised by statutory instrument . . .

Subsequently the European Council and Parliament have adopted a Directive which requires Member States to provide mechanisms to prevent 'unfair commercial practices'. The Government has announced that regulations to implement the Directive will come into force in April 2008. The Directive 'is without prejudice to contract law and, in particular, to the rules on the validity, formation or effect of a contract' (art 3(2)) but it is likely to have a significant effect on the practices of some businesses.

Directive concerning unfair business-to-consumer commercial practices in the internal market of 11 May 2005, 2005/29/EC

Article 5

Prohibition of unfair commercial practices

1. Unfair commercial practices shall be prohibited.
2. A commercial practice shall be unfair if:
   (a) it is contrary to the requirements of professional diligence, and
   (b) it materially distorts or is likely to materially distort the economic behaviour with regard to the product of the average consumer whom it reaches or to whom it is addressed, or of the average member of the group when a commercial practice is directed to a particular group of consumers.
3. Commercial practices which are likely to materially distort the economic behaviour only of a clearly identifiable group of consumers who are particularly vulnerable to the practice or the underlying product because of their mental or physical infirmity, age or credulity in a way which the trader could reasonably be expected to foresee, shall be assessed from the perspective of the average member of that group. This is without prejudice to the common and legitimate advertising practice of making exaggerated statements or statements which are not meant to be taken literally.
4. In particular, commercial practices shall be unfair which:
   (a) are misleading as set out in Articles 6 and 7, or
   (b) are aggressive as set out in Articles 8 and 9.
5. Annex 1 contains the list of those commercial practices which shall in all circumstances be regarded as unfair. The same single list shall apply in all Member States and may only be modified by revision of this Directive.

Section 1
Misleading commercial practices

Article 6

Misleading actions

1. A commercial practice shall be regarded as misleading if it contains false information and is therefore untruthful or in any way, including overall presentation, deceives or is likely to deceive the average consumer, even if the information is factually correct, in relation to one or more of the following elements, and in either case causes or is likely to cause him to take a transactional decision that he would not have taken otherwise: . . .

2. A commercial practice shall also be regarded as misleading if, in its factual context, taking account of all its features and circumstances, it causes or is likely to cause the average consumer to take a transactional decision that he would not have taken otherwise …

Article 7

Misleading omissions

1. A commercial practice shall be regarded as misleading if, in its factual context, taking account of all its features and circumstances and the limitations of the communication medium, it omits material information that the average consumer needs, according to the context, to take an informed transactional decision and thereby causes or is likely to cause the average consumer to take a transactional decision that he would not have taken otherwise.

…

Section 2
Aggressive commercial practices
Article 8
Aggressive commercial practices

A commercial practice shall be regarded as aggressive if, in its factual context, taking account of all its features and circumstances, by harassment, coercion, including the use of physical force, or undue influence, it significantly impairs or is likely to significantly impair the average consumer's freedom of choice or conduct with regard to the product and thereby causes him or is likely to cause him to take a transactional decision that he would not have taken otherwise.

…

VI. MONOPOLIES, OLIGOPOLIES AND ANTI-COMPETITIVE ARRANGEMENTS

Regulation through the common law rules on restraint of trade is discussed in Chapter 44. Since the war, these rules have been buttressed by a complex statutory regime operating through the Restrictive Practices Court, the Monopolies and Mergers Commission and the European Commission.

VII. PATERNALISM

■ **Kronman, 'Paternalism and the Law of Contracts'** (1983)
92 Yale LJ 763–766, 771–779, 786–787, 797–798

In general, any legal rule that prohibits an action on the ground that it would be contrary to the actor's own welfare is paternalistic. The prohibition against suicide, the requirement that motorcyclists wear helmets, laws that restrict the use of drugs or make education compulsory are all examples of legal paternalism. In this Article, I shall be concerned with one branch of this wide and heterogeneous family of legal rules—those that may properly be regarded as belonging to the law of contracts because the liberty they restrict is the liberty to bind oneself by making a legally enforceable promise.

One (relatively new) example of the kind of restriction I have in mind is the rule invalidating any provision in a residential lease that purports to waive the tenant's right to withhold rent if the property fails to meet certain minimum standards of habitability. Even if a tenant believes that a waiver of this sort would be in his own interest and voluntarily agrees to include it in the lease, the law protects him by refusing to enforce his waiver. The invalidity of contracts of peonage or self-enslavement, of agreements purporting to waive the promisor's right to obtain a divorce or sue for relief under the bankruptcy laws, of provisions conferring on either party a right to specifically enforce their agreement (where no right of this sort exists as a matter of law); the voidability of most contracts made by infants: and the nonwaiveable 'cooling-off' period imposed by law in many consumer transactions all also have, at least in part, a paternalistic objective. Unquestionably, some of these limitations on the enforceability of private agreements also seek to protect the moral and economic interests of third parties and, to this extent, have a nonpaternalistic objective as well. One central purpose of each, however, is to protect the promisor himself by limiting his power to do what the law judges to be against his own interests; this is paternalism, and there is more of it in our law of contracts than one might suspect....

I. Economic Efficiency and Distributive Justice

In many jurisdictions, a nondisclaimable warranty of habitability is now applied, as a matter of law, in every lease of residential property. Because the warranty is nondisclaimable, any agreement a tenant makes to waive its benefits will be unenforceable. It is sometimes said that if tenants were given the power to waive the warranty of habitability they might be tricked or forced into doing so—to their own disadvantage—and that the warranty has been made nondisclaimable in order to protect tenants from themselves.

To the extent the rule barring free waiver of the warranty of habitability is acknowledged to have a paternalistic aim, its justification is a mixed one, turning in part on considerations of efficiency and in part on a conception of distributive justice.

The attack on contracts of adhesion rests upon an unstated conception of distributive fairness; though often overlooked, it is this conception that gives the attack its appeal. Many contracts are contracts of adhesion in the general sense that one party is able to dictate terms to the other, but this alone does not make an agreement objectionable. Suppose, for example that my neighbor owns a painting I happen to covet. I offer him $5000 for it. He responds. '$10,000 and no warranties regarding its authenticity. Take it or leave it.' Clearly, the fact that I lack bargaining power and must adhere to the terms he proposes does not by itself justify a judicial or legislative effort to tip the balance in my favor. The imbalance in this case which stems from the fact that he owns the painting and I do not, is unobjectionable because we do not care how control over the painting is distributed.

We feel differently about the distribution of control over society's available housing stock, and inequalities of bargaining power in this context therefore seem a more appropriate target for judicial or legislative attack. The distribution of housing matters more to us than the distribution of paintings: Only the first is likely to seem important from the standpoint of most theories of distributive justice. Those contracts of adhesion that disturb us do so, then, because they reflect an underlying distribution of power or resources that offends our conception of distributive fairness; when distributive concerns are weak or nonexistent, contracts of adhesion are less troubling and the concept of adhesion itself loses meaning.

It is therefore misleading to describe the nondisclaimable warranty of habitability as simply a device for correcting an imbalance in bargaining power. More accurately, it is an instrument of redistribution that seeks to shift control over housing from one group (landlords) to another (tenants) in a way that furthers the widely shared goal of insuring everyone shelter of at least a minimally decent sort. To achieve this goal, the warranty must be made nondisclaimable, for if it is not, tenants—poor tenants in particular—will routinely be required to waive their rights to habitable premises, thereby restoring whatever distributional inequities exist at the outset....

[Kronman considers and rejects one objection.]

A second objection to using the nondisclaimable warranty of habitability as an instrument of distributive justice has greater force. Even if landlords are barred from disclaiming responsiblity for the habitability of property they rent, as long as they are not similarly prevented from altering other aspects of their contractual relationship with their tenants, they can easily pass along—in the form of an increased rent charge—whatever additional insurance or compliance costs they incur as a result of their expanded warranty liability. To the extent this is true, the tenant must pay for the increased protection the warranty gives him—whether he wants it or not. Landlords, one could argue, are likely to be unaffected by a nondisclaimable warranty of habitability, since they will not bear its cost; by contrast, tenants will have to purchase a form of compulsory insurance and can only be made worse off as a result.

There are two ways of meeting this criticism. The first is to deny the unstated premise on which it rests—that the rule in question must be evaluated from the standpoint of the tenants' own preferences. Even if the costs of complying with the warranty are fully passed along, this only means that some tenants will have to pay for protection they do not want, and this is objectionable only in case the wishes of the tenants themselves should be controlling. But there may be nothing wrong with forcing tenants, including poor tenants, to spend their money on better housing (or more exactly, on insurance against the risk of inadequate housing). We recognize the legitimacy of compulsory insurance in other areas; social security is one example, and the inalienable right to a discharge in bankruptcy is another. Whether we should also recognize it in the area of housing will depend upon the relative importance we attach to this good and our confidence that poor tenants will not discount too sharply the value of housing insurance.

Second, even if we evaluate the warranty of habitability on the basis of what tenants actually want, the pass-along argument sketched above is less persuasive than its initial formulation suggests. The extent to which landlords are able to pass along the increased costs of a nondisclaimable warranty of habitability will depend upon characteristics of the rental market that are contingent and variable and cannot be determined in an a priori fashion. Under certain empirically possible conditions, landlords will be able to pass along only a small portion of these costs and will have to absorb the rest; moreover, if alternative uses of the property are economically unattractive, the added cost to landlords of a nondisclaimable warranty of habitability may cause the number of available rental units to decline only slightly, if at all. When these conditions are satisfied, tenants will receive the benefit of the warranty for less than its full cost and will not be hurt through disinvestment in the rental market. In the limiting case, tenants will get something for nothing, and, short of that, they may get it for less than what they would be willing to pay. If so, they are clearly better off, from their own point of view, under a legal regime that makes the warranty of habitability nondisclaimable.

II. Personal Integrity

The nondisclaimable warranty of habitability seems best explained by considerations of economic efficiency and distributive justice. There are, however, many paternalistic restrictions in our law of contracts that cannot be wholly, or most convincingly, explained on these same grounds. One important example is the varied group of restrictions intended to prevent an individual from contracting away too large a part of his personal liberty. ... Even the prohibition against peonage or self-enslavement as well entrenched as it is, permits a variety of employment relationships that exhibit many of the same characteristics. In short, the limits each of these 'absolute' prohibitions imposes on contractual freedom may be approached in varying degrees; the result is a gray zone of increasing restrictiveness, rather than a bright line crisply demarcating the permissible from the impermissible. Still, one wonders, why are there any restrictions at all?

The first step in answering this question is to clarify the meaning of self-enslavement. Every executory contract limits the freedom of the parties by creating an enforceable obligation, on both sides, to perform or pay damages: Once an individual has made a contractually binding commitment, his alternatives are limited to these two (assuming the other party is not himself in breach). The distinguishing mark of a contract of self-enslavement is that it purports to take away the latter alternative. From a legal point of view, it is not the length of service that makes a contract of employment self-enslaving, nor is it the nature of the services to be performed; even a contract of short duration that calls for the performance of routine and unobjectionable tasks is a contract of self-enslavement and therefore legally unenforceable if it bars the employee from substituting money damages for his promised performance. The law will not permit an employee to contract away his right to 'depersonalize' a relationship by paying damages in the event he chooses to breach. Whatever its other terms, an employment contract is enslaving if it gives the employer a right to compel specific performance of the agreement.

An antenuptial agreement waiving the right to sue for divorce can be described as a contract of self-enslavement in just this sense. The parties to a marital contract have considerable freedom to define in advance the nature and extent of their financial responsibilities in the event of a divorce or separation, but neither can give the other the power to compel specific performance by waiving the right to terminate the relationship through divorce. Here, as in the employment context, the right to substitute damages for the actual performance of the contract is inalienable, and any agreement purporting to forfeit this entitlement is invalid as a matter of law.

III. Judgment and Moral Imagination

In addition to the two forms of paternalism I have described, it is possible to distinguish a third. The restrictions that compose this third group include some that are paternalistic in the most literal sense; I have in mind various limitations on the enforcement of promises made by children and other incompetent persons. These restrictions all differ in one important respect from those I have characterized as prohibitions against self-enslavement. The latter bar certain agreements without qualification: Under no circumstances will the law recognize the validity of a promise to become the slave of another or to abstain from bringing a divorce action against one's spouse. Agreements of this sort are prohibited because of their content; it makes no difference whether they have been entered into impulsively and without consideration of the consequences, or after careful deliberation. By contrast, the class of restrictions I now wish to consider—exemplified by the rule that a child's contracts will generally not be enforced against him—seems primarily concerned with defects in the promisor's reasoning process.

Restrictions belonging to this third class characteristically prohibit the enforcement of agreements only for a time, often referred to as a 'cooling-off' period, after which the restraint is lifted. The imposition of a mandatory cooling-off period insures that the promisor has an opportunity to reflect on his commitment and to withdraw from the contract if he wishes. A temporary suspension of the promisor's contractual powers reduces the likelihood of an overly hasty decision and thus helps counteract what I have described as a defect in his reasoning process; its purpose is to prevent the promisor from binding himself too quickly or while his judgment is impaired. Unlike the prohibition against self-enslavement, however, the imposition of a cooling-off period does not by itself guarantee (or forbid) any particular substantive result...

Conclusion

Our legal system restricts contractual freedom in many ways and for many reasons. Some of these restrictions are paternalistic: Their purpose is to prevent people from harming themselves through their own ill-considered or disadvantageous promises. The paternalistic rules in our law of contracts do not derive, however, from a single principle, nor is there any one idea that best explains them all. In this Article, I have described three different forms of paternalism and have attempted to clarify the philosophical presuppositions that underlie each. I have argued that only the first, the nondisclaimable warranty, can be defended persuasively in economic terms. All three may be justified on moral grounds; in each case, however, the justification turns upon a different principle or ideal: distributive fairness, self-respect, and the value of judgment or moral imagination. The concept of paternalism conceals too much philosophical variety to be useful by itself; it wrongly suggests that all paternalistic restrictions address a single problem and must be justified by a single principle, or not at all.

VIII. HUMAN RIGHTS

The passing of the Human Rights Act 1998 has introduced the possibility that contract rights may be affected by the Act. This was illustrated by *Wilson v First County Trust* [2003] UKHL 40 [2003] 4 All ER 97.

In this case, Mrs Wilson borrowed £5,000 from FCT and the transaction was secured against her BMW 318. She failed to repay the loan, but it appeared that the transaction was invalid because the fee of £250 that she had been charged had been wrongly described in the paperwork as part of the loan, thereby falling foul of the provisions of the Consumer Credit Act 1974. In the Court of Appeal and the House of Lords, it was accepted that the effect of this was that Mrs Wilson got her car back, kept the money and did not have to repay the loan. This was thought by the Court of Appeal to infringe the human rights of FCT. The House of Lords disagreed, but principally because most of the key facts had taken place before the Act had come into force. It is far from clear what the House would have decided if all of the key facts had taken place after the Act was fully in force.

ILLEGALITY

CHAPTER FORTY-TWO

CONTRACTS CONTRARY TO PUBLIC POLICY

The rules in this section are significantly different from those in other sections of the book. The contract is alleged to be defective but this defect is not internal to the contract (absence of consent, fraud, duress, etc) but external, that is, enforcement of the contract will infringe some policy quite independent of the agreement of the parties. Suppose a Mafia boss hires a hit man to kill another Mafia boss for $10,000. This has, in a sense, all of the ingredients we look for in a binding contract (agreement, exchange, adequate certainty as to what is to be done and paid) and it is unlikely that there will be inequality of bargaining power because there is no doubt a well-developed and competitive market for contracts of this kind. (Is it significant that, in films, such an arrangement is always described as 'contract'?) The refusal of courts to enforce such transactions clearly proceeds from general policy considerations that, in England, are usually referred to as 'public policy'.

It is worth noting that 'public policy' is not the same as 'policy'. The doctrine of 'public policy' was recognised at a time when judges seldom overtly recognised that their decisions were based on policy considerations. The 'policy' considerations relevant to contract law in general have been explained in Section One and are concerned with the question of why agreements should be enforced (eg protection of reasonable expectations). 'Public policy' is concerned with special situations in which there are compelling reasons for departing from these general considerations.

Not all of the cases in this section fit into this pattern of infringing some interest external to the parties. We saw earlier (p 952) that some of the restraint of trade cases, with which we will deal in Chapter 44, are best explained as attempts to protect a party with weak bargaining power. We deal with them in this section because the legal mechanism used to 'regulate' the contract, the doctrine of public policy, is the same as that used when the contract would adversely affect third parties.

What sort of factor is liable to make a contract illegal as being contrary to public policy? The public policy seems to be derived from two sources. One is the rest of the law: a contract may be illegal because it involves something that is independently unlawful, such as a crime or a tort. The other is the courts' own initiative. There are some contracts that are considered to be so inimical to the interest of the public (or sometimes, as explained in the previous paragraph, to the interest of one of the parties) that they should not be enforced.

In fact, it is very difficult to maintain this distinction, because even when some crime or tort is involved, the question of whether the contract is rendered unenforceable is nearly always a question of public policy for the courts. Very occasionally, statute explicitly makes some contract illegal and unenforceable (for examples, see Treitel, pp 487–488). More usually, it is simply some action taken in the course of the contract that is illegal and the court has to decide whether that should affect the contract in addition to creating criminal or tortious liability.

■ Furmston, 'The Analysis of Illegal Contracts' (1966)
16 U of Toronto LJ 267

The purpose of this paper is to show that the question of whether a contract is illegal is one of considerable complexity which demands precise analysis. The conventional emphasis on stating the various social and economic interests which are protected by this branch of the law has obscured the fact that even when it is agreed on all hands that these interests should be protected, their protection may not necessarily demand the invalidation of a given contract. We may illustrate our point for the moment by a very simple case. There is no doubt that the law has a strong policy against murder but this does not necessarily mean that an agreement to commit murder and a contract to sell a gun, which is to be used to commit murder, should be treated in the same way. It may well be that the latter contract is illegal but it is abundantly clear that the two situations do not of necessity demand the same solution. In practice, of course, no one would suggest that the two situations were identical but the normal method of stating the rule obscures the distinction. It is important therefore to consider not merely the various interests involved but also the various ways in which they may be involved with a contractual situation.

We will see that the consequences of the contract involving some illegality vary widely. For instance, if the whole purpose of it is to commit a crime, as in the example of the hit man, neither party will be able to enforce the contract; whereas some illegal act accidentally committed during the course of performance, such as a taxi breaking the speed limit, may have no effect on the contractual liability at all.

■ *Goodinson v Goodinson*
[1954] 2 QB 118, Court of Appeal

Somervell LJ

...In *Bennett v Bennett*, it was pointed out that there are two kinds of illegality of differing effect. The first is where the illegality is criminal, or contra bonos mores, and in those cases, which I will not attempt to enumerate or further classify, such a provision, if an ingredient in a contract, will invalidate the whole, although there may be many other provisions in it. There is a second kind of illegality which has no such taint; the other terms in the contract stand if the illegal portion can be severed, the illegal portion being a provision which the court, on grounds of public policy, will not enforce. The simplest and most common example of the latter class of illegality is a contract for the sale of a business which contains a provision restricting the vendor from competing in or engaging in trade for certain period or within a certain area. There are many cases in the books where, without in any way impugning the contract of sale, some provision restricting competition has been regarded as in restraint of trade and contrary to public policy. There are many cases where not only has the main contract to purchase been left standing but part of the clause restricting competition has been allowed to stand.

Birkett and **Romer LJJ** delivered concurring judgments.

NOTE

The cases seem to establish that illegal contracts fall into at least two groups. It may be that more than two groups are required but no case has yet arisen to test this point.

Although the consequences of a contract involving an illegal act or something contrary to public policy vary from situation to situation, it should not be thought that this is because the courts have a simple discretion to do what they think fit. The outcome may be the result of statutory interpretation or of the rules that apply to that class of case. On the other hand, the courts often have some leeway in deciding how to classify the facts and will no doubt decide with a view to the result that the classification will produce.

It should be noted that the most draconian rules on illegal contracts are likely to have only a limited deterrent effect, because they will only come into play if the case comes to court. It is true that if a case that, on the facts pleaded, raises some question of illegality does reach court, the court does not have to wait for the issue to be raised by the parties. It may consider the point of its own motion. It should not do so, however, unless the contract is clearly illegal or the whole of the relevant facts are before it. It should not refuse to enforce a contract, for instance, merely because there is some suggestion that it may be an unreasonable restraint of trade: *North-Western Salt Co Ltd v Electrolytic Alkali Co Ltd* [1914] AC 461.

What is more serious is that, in many cases, the parties have every incentive to avoid litigation. For instance, a cartel agreement between manufacturers to limit output and keep up prices may be clearly detrimental to the public, but the more successful it is, the less likely the parties are to bring it to court. Meanwhile, third parties who are being injured may not have a remedy unless the contract involves a crime or tort committed against them.

■ *A-G of Commonwealth of Australia v Adelaide Steamship Co Ltd*
[1913] AC 781, PC

Lord Parker of Waddington

. . . It is only necessary to add that no contract was ever an offence at common law merely because it was in restraint of trade. The parties to such a contract, even if unenforceable, were always at liberty to act on it in the manner agreed. Similarly combinations, not amounting to contracts, in restraint of trade were never unlawful at common law. To make any such contract or combination unlawful it must amount to a criminal conspiracy, and the essence of a criminal conspiracy is a contract or combination to do something unlawful, or something lawful by unlawful means. The right of the individual to carry on his trade or business in the manner he considers best in his own interests involves the right of combining with others in a common course of action, provided such common course of action is undertaken with a single view to the interests of the combining parties and not with a view to injure others (the *Mogul Steamship (Case)*).

NOTE

Although this statement is undoubtedly orthodox, it produced results that are not wholly satisfactory. The more effective a combination is in damaging a third party's interests, the less likely the members of it are to bring it before the court. In the *Mogul Steamship* case [1892] AC 25, the defendants, who were members of a shipping association, made arrangements amongst themselves designed to drive the plaintiffs, a shipping company which was not a member of the association, out of the China trade. They gave rebates to shippers who dealt exclusively with them and forbade their agents to have any dealings with the plaintiffs. As a consequence, the plaintiffs were ruined. As between the defendants, these arrangements were very likely in restraint of trade but the House of Lords held that they were not actionable by the plaintiffs.

It is clear enough that many illegal contracts must be happily performed by the parties with damage both to other parties and to the public interest. There are signs that, in certain cases, relief may be given to third parties.

■ *Eastham v Newcastle United Football Club Ltd*
[1964] Ch 413

The plaintiff had a contract with the first defendants. He wished to play for another club. Under the then rules of the Football Association and the Football League, a retain and transfer system operated, which Wilberforce J held an unreasonable restraint of trade. The plaintiff sought a declaration against the club, the Football Association and the Football League. He had no contract with either the association or the league.

Wilberforce J

...[I]s it open to an employee to bring an action for a declaration that the contract between the employers is in restraint of trade? To my mind it would seem unjust if this were not so. The employees are just as much affected and, indeed, aimed at by the employers' agreement as the employers themselves. Their liberty of action in seeking employment is threatened just as much as the liberty of the employers to give them employment, and their liberty to seek employment is considered by the law to be an important public interest. Is the defence of that interest to be left exclusively in the hands of the employers themselves, who have set up the ring against the employees and who have (as here) shown every intention of maintaining it as long as they can; left to the chance that one day there may be a blackleg among the employers who will challenge it? In my judgment to grant a remedy by way of declaration to the persons whose interests are vitally affected would be well within the spirit and intent of the rule as to declaratory judgments...

If I am right so far, then the court has jurisdiction to grant a declatory judgment, not only against the employer who is in contractual relationship with the employee, but also against the association of employers whose rules or regulations place an unjustifiable restraint on his liberty of employment. A case where the employee is himself contractually bound by the employers' rules (as the employee is here, by virtue of registration and the terms of his contract) is a fortiori to the case last mentioned.

NOTE

In this case, the plaintiff was simply granted a declaration that the retain-and-transfer system was in restraint of trade. The declaration did not actually require the defendants to do anything but the Football Association and the Football League did substantially alter the transfer system as a result. In *Nagle v Feilden* (see p 1074), the Court of Appeal thought it not unarguable that the plaintiff might obtain an injunction against the stewards of the Jockey Club. The Jockey Club avoided further litigation by giving Mrs Nagle a licence. It is not clear whether these cases would help a plaintiff in a case such as the *Mogul Steamship* case. Declarations do not *order* anyone to do anything; bodies like the Football Association and the Jockey Club are unlikely in practice to ignore a public statement by a judge as to what the law is, but this is not true of all commercial companies.

I. THE HEADS OF PUBLIC POLICY

What are the grounds on which a contract may be held illegal as against public policy? We have already mentioned that the fact that the contract somehow involves the commission of a crime or tort *may* lead to its illegality. This is a complex topic with which we deal in the next chapter. Of the other grounds of public policy, by far the most frequently litigated and well developed is that the contract is in restraint of trade, and that is dealt with in detail in Chapter 44. For reasons of space, the other heads of public policy will not be covered in detail. They are summarized as follows.

(1) *Contracts involving or tending to promote sexual immorality*: eg *Pearce v Brooks* (1866) LR 1 Exch 213 (coachbuilders could not recover the hire payable for a 'curiously constructed' brougham, which they knew that the defendant, a prostitute, intended to use to attract customers).

(2) *Contracts tending to undermine marriage*: *Fender v St John-Mildmay* [1938] AC 1 is a leading case, although there the contract was upheld (the defendant had promised to marry the plaintiff while he was already married but after a decree nisi of divorce from his earlier marriage had been granted. In two earlier cases, promises to marry after the death of one's existing spouse had been held illegal. In all of the cases, actual performance was legal; the argument was that the existence of the contract might tend to encourage conduct of which the law would disapprove. In *Fender's* case, this tendency was considered by the majority of the House of Lords to be insubstantial).

Since 'marriages are made in Heaven', is it contrary to public policy to recruit spouses for a fee? There are many seventeenth- and eighteenth-century cases to that effect. In many (but not all) of them, the agreement was disreputable, eg to kidnap an heiress. In the only modern case, *Hermann v Charlesworth* [1905] 2 KB 123, these cases were applied to a matrimonial agency. It may be doubted whether there is any serious danger to the public good in the activities of such organisations.

(3) *Contracts that tend adversely to affect the conduct of foreign affairs*: there are many cases, particularly from the First World War, of 'trading with the enemy', a rather technical part of the law, perhaps unlikely to be of much interest in the future. A more relevant example is *Foster v Driscoll* [1929] 1 KB 470. The Court of Appeal held that an agreement to smuggle whisky into the USA during Prohibition was illegal.

(4) *Contracts to pervert the course of justice*: obviously, agreements to pay a juror for a perverse verdict or a witness to tell lies fall within this principle. Less obviously, the principle has been held to prohibit agreements to abandon the prosecution of most (although not all) crimes. The modern law turns on the construction of s 5 of the Criminal Law Act 1967: see Buckley (1974) 3 Anglo-American LR 472.

A related, although less serious, head is agreements to oust the jurisdiction of the courts. So, for instance, a club or trade association cannot make itself the final arbiter of the application of its own rules. Traditionally, this reasoning was applied to arbitration agreements, which made the decision of the arbitrator final, even though such agreements are common in many countries: *Czarnikow v Roth, Schmidt & Co* [1922] 2 KB 478. In effect, the parties were permitted to make the decision of the arbitrator final on questions of fact but not on questions of law. The Arbitration Act 1979 gave the parties a qualified power to make the arbitrator's decision final, even on questions of law. The principal reason for the change was the desire to preserve the importance of London as a centre for international arbitration (see above). See now the Arbitration Act 1996, s 69.

(5) *Contracts tending to encourage corruption in public life*: selling honours is an obvious example (see *Parkinson v College of Ambulance Ltd* [1925] 2 KB 1). The murkier borderlines of this principle—how, for instance, it might apply to some of the activities of lobbyists of MPs and central and local government officials—have not been much explored in the English courts.

(6) *Agreements to defraud the Revenue*: these may be no more than a specific example of contracts to defraud but they are usually treated as a special class. A regrettably common example is an agreement to pay an increased salary and to call the increase 'expenses'. Such an arrangement makes not only the 'expenses' but also the basic salary irrecoverable: *Miller v Karlinski* (1945) 62 TLR 85.

(7) *Contracts to conceal information that ought to be revealed*: there are many situations in which a party ought to keep information confidential because he has contracted to do so or because he has acquired it in circumstances that impose a duty of confidence. However, where the duty is based on contract and would cover information which, in the public interest, ought to be revealed, the contract may be illegal: eg *Neville v Dominion of Canada News Co Ltd* [1915] 3 KB 556 (agreement that newspaper, which purported to give readers advice on investment schemes, would not comment on the plaintiff's scheme held illegal).

(8) *Contracts tending to promote religious, sexual or racial discrimination*: eg *Nagle v Feilden* [1966] 2 QB 633 (Court of Appeal refused to strike out claim for a declaration that Jockey Club's practice of refusing licences to women trainers was illegal).

■ *Janson v Driefontein Consolidated Mines Ltd*

[1902] AC 484, House of Lords

Lord Halsbury LC

...I do not think that the phrase 'against public policy' is one which in a Court of law explains itself. It does not leave at large to each tribunal to find that a particular contract is against public policy....

But I do not think the law of England does leave the matter so much at large as seems to be assumed. In treating various branches of the law learned persons have analyzed the sources of the law, and have sometimes expressed their opinion that such and such a provision is bad because it is contrary to public policy; but I deny that any Court can invent a new head of public policy; so a contract for marriage brokerage, the creation of perpetuity, a contract in restraint of trade, a gaming or wagering contract, or, what is relevant here, the assisting of the King's enemies, are all undoubtedly unlawful things; and you may say that it is because they are contrary to public policy they are unlawful; but it is because these things have been either enacted or assumed to be by the common law unlawful, and not because a judge or Court have a right to declare that such and such things are in his or their view contrary to public policy. Of course, in the application of the principles here insisted on, it is inevitable that the particular case must be decided by a judge; he must find the facts, and he must decide whether the facts so found do or do not come within the principles which I have endeavoured to describe— that is, a principle of public policy, recognised by the law, which the suggested contract is infringing, or is supposed to infringe.

■ Lord Radcliffe, *The Law and its Compass*

pp 46–52, 54–55

One curious product of this judicial suspicion of 'public policy' is the theory that its heads have now been finally determined. The list, is closed: and though it is a judge's duty, if very cautiously, to give effect to the old rules when facts cry out for it, nothing can permit an extension of the conception to cover new situations and new categories (see, for instance, this question discussed in *Fender v Mildmay*).

[In *Janson v Driefontein*, Lord Halsbury, the Lord Chancellor of the day, made a statement which, psychologically, is of great interest.]

... [N]ot only does it make the definite assumption that one branch, at any rate, of the common law had become a completely closed system, not admitting of development, somewhere before the year 1902, but also it expresses very forcibly the idea that the principles of the common law somehow succeeded in establishing themselves by their own force and not because at some date or dates this or that judge or combination of judges took upon themselves to recognize as law what had not hitherto had that recognition. Practically, I doubt whether it will matter very much whether judges do or do not regard themselves as at liberty to 'invent' new heads of public policy. To some extent it is a question of words. Heads of this kind are inevitably a categorization after the event. The instances come first and the classification follows. I should think that there are by now enough instances covering a wide enough conspectus of human conduct to provide all the principles that may be needed to keep the doctrine in working order for those who may think it right to use it in the future.

In *Fender v St John-Mildmay* [1938] AC 1 Lord Atkin said:

In [*Janson v Driefontein*] Lord Halsbury indeed appeared to decide that the categories of public policy are closed, and that the principle could not be invoked anew unless the case could be brought within some principle of public policy already recognized by the law. I do not find, however, that this view received the express assent of the other members of the House; and it seems to me, with respect, too rigid. On the other hand, it fortifies the serious warning illustrated by the passages cited above that the doctrine should only be invoked in clear cases in which the harm to the public is substantially incontestable, and does not depend upon the idiosyncratic inferences of a few judicial minds. I think that this should be regarded as the true guide. In popular language, following the wise aphorism of Sir George Jessel [cited above p 60], the contract should be given the benefit of the doubt.

NOTE

The controversy about whether the heads of public policy are closed is, as Lord Radcliffe observes, rather strange. If judges change law at all, it would seem that principles that directly and explicitly reflect current society values must be more and not less prone to change than ordinary rules, many of which are (relatively) value-free.

It is worth observing the following.

(1) Although there are many statements in the reports that echo Lord Halsbury, it is very difficult to find a case in which a judge thought a transaction contrary to public policy but was deterred from so holding by the absence of an available head. In *Lancashire County Council v Municipal Mutual Insurance Ltd* [1996] 3 All ER 545, the question was raised as to whether a contract to insure oneself against having to pay exemplary damages was contrary to public policy, as has been held in some of the US states. The question was discussed on the merits and answered in the negative. No one seems to have thought that the question could be resolved simply by denying the possibility of creating new heads.

(2) It is clear that existing heads of public policy may be closed down as a result of changes in society values. Contrast *Cowan v Milbourn* (1867) LR 2 Exch 230 and *Bowman v Secular Society* [1917] AC 406. In the former of these cases, it is asserted that Christianity is part of the law of England and that therefore a contract to let a room for a meeting to promote atheism was contrary to public policy. Fifty years later, this view was regarded as clearly unarguable.

(3) Changing social mores and new technology are bound to combine to present courts with questions that Lord Halsbury would not have dreamed of. Californian courts have had to consider whether surrogacy arrangements are contrary to public policy.

■ *Johnson v Calvert*

851 P 2d 776 (Cal SC 1993)

Panelli J

...In this case we address several of the legal questions raised by recent advances in reproductive technology .When, pursuant to a surrogacy agreement, a zygote formed of the gametes of a husband and wife is implanted in the uterus of another woman, who carries the resulting fetus to term and gives birth to a child not genetically related to her, who is the child's 'natural mother' under California law? Does a determination that the wife is the child's natural mother work a deprivation of the gestating woman's constitutional rights?And is such an agreement barred by any public policy of this state?

We conclude that the husband and wife are the child's natural parents, and that this result does not offend the state or federal Constitution or public policy.

FACTS

Mark and Crispina Calvert are a married couple who desired to have a child. Crispina was forced to undergo a hysterectomy in 1984. Her ovaries remained capable of producing eggs, however, and the couple eventually considered surrogacy. In 1989 Anna Johnson heard about Crispina's plight from a co-worker and offered to serve as a surrogate for the Calverts.

On January 15, 1990, Mark, Crispina, and Anna signed a contract providing that an embryo created by the sperm of Mark and the egg of Crispina would be implanted in Anna and the child born would be taken into Mark and Crispina's home 'as their child'. Anna agreed she would relinquish 'all parental rights' to the child in favour of Mark and Crispina. In return, Mark and Crispina would pay Anna $10,000 in a series of instalments, the last to be paid six weeks after the child's birth. Mark and Crispina were also to pay for a $200,000 life assurance policy on Anna's life.

The zygote was implanted on January 19, 1990. Less than a month later, an ultrasound test confirmed Anna was pregnant.

Unfortunately, relations deteriorated between the two sides. Mark learned that Anna had not disclosed she had suffered several stillbirths and miscarriages. Anna felt Mark and Crispina did not do enough to obtain the required insurance policy. She also felt abandoned during an onset of premature labour in June.

In July 1990, Anna sent Mark and Crispina a letter demanding the balance of the payments due her or else she would refuse to give up the child. The following month, Mark and Crispina responded with a lawsuit, seeking a declaration they were the legal parents of the unborn child. Anna filed her own action to be declared the mother of the child, and the two cases were eventually consolidated....

The child was born on September 19, 1990 and blood samples were obtained from both Anna and the child for analysis. The blood test results excluded Anna as the genetic mother. The parties agreed to a court order providing that the child would remain with Mark and Crispina on a temporary basis with visits by Anna.

At trial in October 1990, the parties stipulated that Mark and Crispina were the child's genetic parents. After hearing evidence and arguments, the trial court ruled that Mark and Crispina were the child's 'genetic, biological and natural' father and mother, that Anna had no 'parental' rights to the child, and the surrogacy contact was legal and enforceable against Anna's claims. The court also terminated the order allowing visitation. Anna appealed from the trial court's judgement. The Court of Appeal for the Fourth District, Division Three, affirmed. We granted review.

[Panelli J discussed the meaning of maternity under the Uniform Parentage Act of California and concluded that:]

[A]lthough the Act recognizes both genetic consanguinity and giving birth as a means of establishing a mother and child relationship, when the two means do not coincide in one woman, she who intended to procreate the child—that is, she who intended to bring about the birth of a child that she intended to raise as her own—is the natural mother under Californian law....

Anna urges that surrogacy contracts violate several social policies. Relying on her contention that she is the child's legal, natural mother, she cites the public policy embodied in Penal Code Section 273, prohibiting the payment for consent to adoption of a child. She argues further that the policies underlying the adoption laws of this state are violated by the surrogacy contract because it in effect constitutes a prebirth waiver of her parental rights.

We disagree. Gestational surrogacy differs in crucial respects from adoption and so is not subject to the adoption statutes. The parties voluntarily agreed to participate in in vitro fertilization and related medical procedures before the child was conceived; at the time when Anna entered into the contract, therefore, she was not vulnerable to financial inducements to part with her own expected offspring. As discussed above, Anna was not the genetic mother of the child. The payments to Anna under the contract were meant to compensate her for her services in gestating the fetus and undergoing labour, rather than for giving up 'parental' rights to the child. Payments were due both during the pregnancy and after the child's birth...

It has been suggested that gestation surrogacy may run afoul of prohibitions on involuntary servitude.... We see no potential for that evil in the contract at issue here, and extrinsic evidence of coercion or duress is utterly lacking. We note that although at one point the contract purports to give Mark and Crispina the sole right to determine whether to abort the pregnancy, at another point it acknowledges: 'All parties understand that a pregnant woman has the absolute right to abort or not abort any fetus she is carrying. Any promise to the contrary is unenforceable.' We therefore need not determine the validity of a surrogacy contract purporting to deprive the gestator of her freedom to terminate pregnancy.

Finally, Anna and some commentators have expressed concern that surrogacy contracts tend to exploit or dehumanize women, especially women of lower economic status. Anna's objections centre around the psychological harm she asserts may result from the gestator's relinquishing the child to whom she has given birth. Some have also cautioned that the practice of surrogacy may encourage society to view children as commodities, subject to trade at their parents' will.

We are all too aware that the proper forum for resolution of this issue is The Legislature, where empirical data, largely lacking from this record, can be studied and rules of general applicability developed. However, in light of our responsibility to decide this case, we have considered as best we can its possible consequences.

We are unpersuaded that gestational surrogacy arrangements are so likely to cause the untoward results Anna cites as to demand their invalidation on public policy grounds. Although common sense suggests that women of lesser means serve as surrogate mothers more often than do wealthy women, there has been no proof that surrogacy contracts exploit poor women to any greater degree than economic necessity in general exploits them by inducing them to accept lower-paid or otherwise undesirable employment. We are likewise unpersuaded by the claim that surrogacy will foster the attitude that children are mere commodities; no evidence is offered to support it. The limited data available seem to reflect an absence of significant adverse effects of surrogacy on all participants.

The argument that a woman cannot knowingly and intelligently agree to gestate and deliver a baby for intending parents carries overtones of the reasoning that for centuries prevented women from attaining equal economic rights and professional status under the law. To resurrect this view is both to foreclose a personal and economic choice on the part of the surrogate mother, and to deny intending parents what may be their only means of procreating a child of their own genetic stock. Certainly in the present case it cannot seriously be argued that Anna, a licensed vocational nurse who had done well in school and who had previously borne a child, lacked the intellectual wherewithal or life experience necessary to make an informed decision to enter into the surrogacy contract...

Lucas CJ and **Mosk, Arabian and George JJ** concurred with Panelli J; **Kennard J** dissented.

II. POLICY ISSUES

In a broad sense, to say that a contract is illegal indicates that the court disapproves of it. It is surprisingly difficult to offer a more sophisticated analysis because neither judges nor commentators have often gone further than this. One factor must be to discourage the making of such contracts. It would be fanciful to suppose that the Mafia boss and his contract killer will be influenced by the study of the law on illegal contracts, although there is a (perhaps apocryphal) eighteenth-century *Highwayman's* case in which the plaintiff sued his partner 'for an account of trading together on Newmarket Heath'. Both plaintiff and defendant were hanged! However, there are cases in which rational men who knew the law would be less likely to make a contract because they knew it would not be enforced. A good example is *Brown Jenkinson & Co Ltd v Percy Dalton (London) Ltd* (see p 1080).

Another factor is the desire to avoid besmirching the reputation of the court by appearing to involve it in unseemly transactions (see further below). So, although enforcement or non-enforcement is very unlikely to affect the volume of prostitution, it is rational to say that courts are not provided by taxpayers in order for prostitutes to sue their clients.

Where the contract is wholly executory, the court will want to encourage the parties not to perform it. The policy consideration may be different if the contract has been partly performed and one party is seeking not to enforce it but to recover money or property that he has transferred (see p 1094).

Then, there is the question of whether a party who has contracted in excusable ignorance of the illegality should be affected. We shall see that in many, if not most, cases, the courts have contrived to give innocent parties a remedy.

The object of the statute or other rule infringed should be considered. It may be designed to protect one of the parties, and here it may well be right to allow that party some remedy but not the other.

It has also been pointed out that the object of the statute should be looked at each time. For instance, quite a number of the cases involve regulations imposed in times of shortages of goods and labour; presumably where the resources will end up as a result of the decision should also be a factor (see Treitel in *Crime, Proof and Punishment: Essays in Memory of Sir Rupert Cross*, 1981, pp 93–104).

CHAPTER FORTY-THREE

CONTRACTS INVOLVING THE COMMISSION OF A CRIME OR A TORT

As suggested earlier, contracts that somehow involve the commission of an unlawful act will be affected in different ways according to the circumstances. The unlawful act may have no effect at all on contractual liability. Many of the rules apply also to other contracts that are contrary to public policy.

I. CONTRACTS REQUIRING THE DELIBERATE COMMISSION OF A CRIME OR A TORT

■ *Scott v Brown, Doering, McNab & Co*

[1892] 2 QB 724, Court of Appeal

The plaintiff agreed with the defendant stockbrokers that they would buy shares on the Stock Exchange with a view to inducing the public to believe that there was a real market in the shares. The plaintiff alleged that the defendants, instead of buying shares, had transferred their own shares to him and sought return of his money. The defendants alleged that the contract was illegal. (The plaintiff was arguing that the defendants had not kept their deal. In effect, the defendants admitted this, but argued (successfully) that the deal was illegal. The real reason for the dispute was that if the defendants unloaded their own shares on the plaintiff, there would be no dealings on the Stock Exchange and therefore no upward pressure on the price. Dealings on the Stock Exchange are public and therefore affect the behaviour of other members of the Exchange.)

Lindley LJ

...[T]he correspondence put in evidence by the plaintiff in support of the claim he made at the trial shews conclusively that the sole object of the plaintiff in ordering shares to be bought for him at a premium was to impose upon and to deceive the public by leading the public to suppose that there were buyers of such shares at a premium on the Stock Exchange, when in fact there were none but himself. The plaintiff's purchase was an actual purchase, not a sham purchase; that is true, but it is also true that the sole object of the purchase was to cheat and mislead the public. Under these circumstances, the plaintiff must look elsewhere than to a court of justice for such assistance as he may require against the persons he employed to assist him in his fraud, if the claim to such assistance is based on his illegal contract. Any rights which he may have irrespective of his illegal contract will, of course, be recognised and enforced. But his illegal contract confers no rights on him:see *Pearce v Brooks*. The illegal purpose of the plaintiff distinguishes this case from *Wetherell v Jones*, and others of a similar kind. I am quite aware that what the plaintiff has done is very commonly done; it is done every day. But this is immaterial. Picking pockets and various forms of cheating are common enough, and are nevertheless illegal. The plaintiff was not entitled to judgment in the Court below, and he has no right to a new trial.

Lopes and **A L Smith LJJ** delivered judgments to the same effect.

NOTES

1.   The conduct that the parties had agreed on here was directly contrary to public policy. If successful in inducing members of the public to buy shares for more than they were worth, it would have been both a crime and a tort.

2.   In *Brown, Jenkinson & Co Ltd v Percy Dalton (London) Ltd* [1957] 2 QB 621, the defendants wished to ship orange juice to Hamburg. The plaintiffs, as agents for the shipowners, told the defendants that they would have to 'clause' the bill of lading (that is note on the bill that the goods were not in good order and condition). It is inconvenient for shippers to have to deal with such claused bills and the defendants asked the shipowners to issue a clean bill, promising in return to indemnify them against the consequences. The shipowners issued a clean bill, knowing that the goods were, in fact, in poor condition. On arrival in Hamburg, the barrels of orange juice were leaking and the shipowners had to make good the loss. They sued on the indemnity but were met by the defence that the indemnity contract was illegal because it involved the issue of a bill of lading that the shipowners knew to be false, with the intention that it be relied on, and that this amounted to the tort of deceit. The Court of Appeal (Evershed MR dissenting) upheld this defence.

3.   The effect in both *Scott v Brown Doering* and *Brown Jenkinson* was to deny the plaintiff any remedy on the contract, whether to enforce it or to recover money.

4.   The parties' conduct in both cases was deliberate with full knowledge of the relevant facts. It is usually irrelevant that the parties did not know the law and therefore did not realise that what they were agreeing on was a crime or tort.

5.   What if they did not know the facts that made the conduct wrongful? At common law, there will normally be no criminal liability without *mens rea* but statutory offences may be committed without any criminal intent. The fact that a contract necessarily involves the unintentional commission of a crime does not always make it illegal: see next subsection. Equally, some torts may be committed through deliberate actions but without knowing the facts that make the conduct tortious: eg a printer might agree to publish material that he did not know was defamatory. Such a case is also treated differently: see p 1086.

6.   All of the cases of deliberate crimes seem to involve fairly serious crimes. It is not at all clear that an agreement that calls for the commission of some minor statutory crime (eg a contract to deliver goods by a certain time, which the parties know can only be carried out by parking in a prohibited zone) would be affected at all by the illegality.

II. CONTRACTS INVOLVING OTHER UNLAWFUL ACTS

1. An outline of the rules

■ *St John Shipping Corpn v Joseph Rank Ltd*

[1957] 1 QB 267

The defendants chartered the plaintiff's ship to carry grain from the USA to the UK. During the voyage, the ship was overloaded in contravention of the Merchant Shipping (Safety and Load Line Conventions) Act 1932. On arrival in the UK, the master was convicted and fined the maximum fine of £1,200. The defendants paid part of the freight but withheld a sum equivalent to the extra freight earned by the overloading. They argued that the plaintiffs could not recover the freight because they had illegally performed the charterparty.

Devlin J

. . . It is a misfortune for the defendants that the legal weapon which they are wielding is so much more potent than it need be to achieve their purpose. Believing, rightly or wrongly, that the plaintiffs have deliberately committed a serious infraction of the Act and one which has placed their property in jeopardy, the defendants wish to do no more than to take the profit out of the plaintiff's dealing. But the principle which they invoke for this purpose cares not at all for the element of deliberation or for the gravity of the infraction, and does not adjust the penalty to the profits unjustifiably earned. The defendants cannot succeed unless they claim the right to retain the whole freight and to keep it whether the offence was accidental or deliberate, serious or trivial. The application of this principle to a case such as this is bound to lead to startling results. Mr Wilmers does not seek to avert his gaze from the wide consequences. A shipowner who accidentally overloads by a fraction of an inch will not be able to recover from any of the shippers or consignees a penny of the freight . . . . Carriers by land are in no better position; again Mr Wilmers does not shrink from saying that the owner of a lorry could not recover against the consignees the cost of goods transported in it if in the course of the journey it was driven a mile an hour over its permitted speed. If this is really the law, it is very unenterprising of cargo owners and consignees to wait until a criminal conviction has been secured before denying their liabilities. A service of trained observers on all our main roads would soon pay for itself. An effective patrol of the high seas would probably prove too expensive, but the maintenance of a corps of vigilantes in all principal ports would be well worth while when one considers that the smallest infringement of the statute or a regulation made thereunder would relieve all the cargo owners on the ship from all liability for freight.

Of course, as Mr Wilmers says, one must not be deterred from enunciating the correct principle of law because it may have startling or even calamitous results. But I confess I approach the investigation of a legal proposition which has results of this character with a prejudice in favour of the idea that there may be a flaw in the argument somewhere.

. . .

. . . There are two general principles. The first is that a contract which is entered into with the object of committing an illegal act is unenforceable. The application of this principle depends upon proof of the intent, at the time the contract was made, to break the law; if the intent is mutual the contract is not enforceable at all, and, if unilateral, it is unenforceable at the suit of the party who is proved to have it. This principle is not involved here. Whether or not the overloading was deliberate when it was done, there is no proof that it was contemplated when the contract of carriage was made. The second principle is that the court will not enforce a contract which is expressly or impliedly prohibited by statute. If the contract is of this class it does not matter what the intent of the parties is; if the statute prohibits the contract, it is unenforceable whether the parties meant to break the law or not. A significant distinction between the two classes is this. In the former class you have only to look and see what acts the statute prohibits; it does not matter whether or not it prohibits a contract; if a contract is deliberately made to do a prohibited act, that contract will be unenforceable. In the latter class, you have to consider not what acts the statute prohibits, but what contracts it prohibits; but you are not concerned at all with the intent of the parties; if the parties enter into a prohibited contract, that contract is unenforceable . . .

Two questions are involved. The first—and the one which hitherto has usually settled the matter—is: does the statute mean to prohibit contracts at all? But if this be answered in the affirmative, then one must ask: does this contract belong to the class which the statute intends to prohibit? For example, a person is forbidden by statute from using an unlicensed vehicle on the highway. If one asks oneself whether there is in such an enactment an implied prohibition of all contracts for the use of unlicensed vehicles, the answer may well be that there is, and that contracts of hire would be unenforceable. But if one asks oneself whether there is an implied prohibition of contracts for the carriage of goods by unlicensed vehicles or for the repairing of unlicensed vehicles or for the garaging of unlicensed vehicles, the answer may well be different. The answer might be that collateral contracts of this sort are not within the ambit of the statute.

On Mr Wilmers's third point I take the law from the dictum in *Beresford v Royal Insurance Co Ltd* [below] that was adopted and applied by Lord Atkin:'no system of jurisprudence can with reason include amongst the rights which it enforces rights directly resulting to the person asserting them from the crime of that person.' I observe in the first place that in the Court of Appeal in the same case Lord Wright doubted whether this principle applied to all statutory offences. His doubt was referred to by Denning LJ in *Marles v Philip Trant & Sons,* . . . The distinction is much to the point here. The Act of 1932 imposes a penalty which is itself designed to deprive the offender of the benefits of his crime. It would be a curious thing if the operation could be performed twice— once by the criminal law and then again by the civil. It would be curious, too, if in a case in which the magistrates had thought fit to impose only a nominal fine, their decision could, in effect, be overridden in civil action. But the question whether the rule applies to statutory offences is an important one which I do not wish to decide in the present case. The dicta of Lord Wright and Denning LJ suggest that there are cases where its application would be morally unjustifiable; but it is not clear that they go as far as saying that the application would not be justified in law. I prefer, therefore, to deal with Mr Wilmers's submission in another way.

The rights which cannot be enforced must be those 'directly resulting' from the crime. That means, I think, that for a right to money or to property to be unenforceable the property or money must be identifiable as something to which, but for the crime, the plaintiff would have had no right or title. That cannot be said in this case. The amount of the profit which the plaintiffs made from the crime, that is to say, the amount of freight which, but for the overloading, they could not have earned on this voyage, was, as I have said, £2,295. The quantity of cargo consigned to the defendants was approximately 35 per cent of the whole and, therefore, even if it were permissible to treat the benefit as being divisible pro rata over the whole of the cargo, the amount embodied in the claim against the defendants would not be more than 35 per cent of £2,300. That would not justify the withholding of £2,000 . . .

The fact is that in this type of case no claim or part of a claim for freight can be clearly identified as being the excess illegally earned.

Judgment for the plaintiffs.

NOTE

Thus, according to Devlin, there seems to be a three-stage test:

(i)   did the statute mean that the contract was expressly or impliedly forbidden?

(ii)   did either party intend, when the contract was made, to perform it illegally?

(iii) is the plaintiff claiming some benefit that is the direct result of an illegal act on his part?

In fact, we shall see that Devlin's analysis is incomplete. There are some cases in which a party who had made a perfectly legal contract, and who had no intention of performing in it an illegal manner, in fact did commit some illegal act in the course of performing it and is thereby disabled from enforcing the contract, although not falling within (iii).

2. Is the contract expressly or impliedly forbidden by statute?

■ *Re Mahmoud and Ispahani*

[1921] 2 KB 716, CA

By delegated legislation, licences were necessary for either the sale or purchase of linseed oil. The plaintiff sold linseed oil to the defendant. The plaintiff had a licence. Before entering into the contract, he asked the defendant whether he had a licence and the defendant said he had. He had not. The defendant later refused to accept delivery and, on being sued for damages for non-acceptance, argued that the contract was illegal.

Atkin LJ

...It is admitted that the Order of the Food Controller, made under the Defence of the Realm Regulations, has the effect of a statute, and the contention is that by that Order the contract in this case was prohibited. When the Court has to deal with the question whether a particular contract or class of contract is prohibited by statute, it may find an express prohibition in the statute, or it may have to infer the prohibition from the fact that the statute imposes a penalty upon the person entering into that class of contract. In the latter case one has to examine very carefully the precise terms of the statute imposing the penalty upon the individual. One may find that the statute imposes a penalty upon an individual, and yet does not prohibit the contract if it is made with a party who is innocent of the offence which is created by the statute. I prefer not to deal with the question of contracts forbidden by the common law as being contrary to public policy, because, despite the great authority of Parke B, I think a question might be raised whether or not it is right to say that those contracts are prohibited by the common law. The right view may be that the common law refuses to enforce them. I think a different set of circumstances may arise in respect of such contracts as those, but here it appears to me to be plain that this particular contract was expressly prohibited by the terms of the Order which imposes the necessity of a compliance with the licence.

Bankes and **Scrutton LJJ** delivered judgments to the same effect.

Judgment for the defendant.

NOTES

1. What was the purpose behind the statute? How might the court best further that purpose?

2. What remedy was the plaintiff seeking? Do you think the court would have denied a remedy if he had delivered the oil and was now seeking to recover payment? Compare p 1087.

■ *Archbolds (Freightage) Ltd v S Spanglett Ltd* [1961]

1 QB 374, CA

The defendants owned a number of vans with C licences, entitling them to carry their own goods by road but not to carry the goods of others. They entered into a contract with the plaintiffs, who believed the defendants had A licences, which would have entitled them to carry other people's goods for reward, to carry whisky from London to Leeds. The whisky was stolen in transit owing to the negligence of the defendants' driver. On a claim for damages for loss of the whisky, the defendants pleaded that the contract was illegal.

Pearce LJ

. . . If a contract is expressly or by necessary implication forbidden by statute, or if it is ex facie illegal, or if both parties know that though ex facie legal it can only be performed by illegality or is intended to be performed illegally, the law will not help the plaintiffs in any way that is a direct or indirect enforcement of rights under the contract. And for this purpose both parties are presumed to know the law.

The first question, therefore, is whether this contract of carriage was forbidden by statute. The two cases on which the defendants mainly rely are *In re an Arbitration between Mahmoud and Ispahani* and *J Dennis & Co Ltd v Munn*. In both those cases the plaintiffs were unable to enforce their rights under contracts forbidden by statute. In the former case the statutory order said: 'a person shall not . . . buy or sell . . . [certain] articles . . . except under and in accordance with the terms of a licence.' In the latter case the statutory regulation provided: 'subject to the provisions of this regulation . . . the execution .. of any operation specified . . . shall be unlawful except in so far as authorised.' In neither case could the plaintiff bring his contract within the exception that alone would have made its subject-matter lawful, namely, by showing the existence of a licence. Therefore, the core of both contracts was the mischief expressly forbidden by the statutory order and the statutory regulation respectively.

In *Mahmoud's* case the object of the order was to prevent (except under licence) a person buying and a person selling, and both parties were liable to penalties. A contract of sale between those persons was therefore expressly forbidden. In *Dennis's* case the object of the regulation was to prevent (except under licence) owners from performing builders operations, and builders from carrying out the work for them. Both parties were liable to penalties and a contract between these persons for carrying out an unlawful operation would be forbidden by implication.

The case before us is somewhat different. The carriage of the plaintiffs' whisky was not as such prohibited; the statute merely regulated the means by which carriers should carry goods. Therefore this contract was not expressly forbidden by the statute.

Was it then forbidden by implication? The Road and Rail Traffic Act, 1933, section 1, says: 'no person shall use a goods vehicle on a road for the carriage of goods . . . except under licence', and provides that such use shall be an offence. Did the statute thereby intend to forbid by implication all contracts whose performance must on all the facts (whether known or not) result in a contravention of that section?

The object of the Road and Rail Traffic Act 1933, was not (in this connection) to interfere with the owner of goods or his facilities for transport, but to control those who provided the transport, with a view to promoting its efficiency. Transport of goods was not made illegal but the various licence holders were prohibited from encroaching on one another's territory, the intention of the Act being to provide an orderly and comprehensive service. Penalties were provided for those licence holders who went outside the bounds of their allotted spheres. These penalties apply to those using the vehicle but not to the goods owner. Though the latter could be convicted of aiding and abetting any breach, the restrictions were not aimed at him. Thus a contract of carriage was, in the sense used by Devlin J, 'collateral', and it was not impliedly forbidden by the statute.

This view is supported by common sense and convenience. If the other view were held it would have far-reaching effects. For instance, if a carrier induces me (who am in fact ignorant of any illegality) to entrust goods to him and negligently destroys them, he would only have to show that (though unknown to me) his licence had expired, or did not properly cover the transportation, or that he was uninsured, and I should then be without a remedy against him. Or, again, if I ride in a taxicab and the driver leaves me stranded in some deserted spot, he would only have to show that he was (though unknown to me) unlicensed or uninsured, and I should be without remedy. This appears to me to be an undesirable extension of the implications of a statute.

Sellers and **Devlin LJJ** delivered concurring judgments.

NOTES

1. What factors led the court to hold that the contract was not impliedly prohibited?

2. The result of the *Mahmoud* case was that neither party could enforce the contract. This is not convenient if the statute was intended to protect one of the parties, and in such a case, the court will lean in favour of holding that, even if the statute makes it an offence for one party to make the contract, it does not impliedly forbid its performance, so that it can be enforced. Alternatively, the court may construe the statute as not preventing the party for whose protection it was intended from enforcing the contract. Thus in *Nash v Halifax Building Society* [1979] 2 All ER 19, the society was forbidden by s 32 of Building Societies Act 1962 from advancing money on a property subject to a prior mortgage to some other lender; Browne-Wilkinson J held that this was intended to protect those people who were interested in the society (whether members or outside creditors) and that the society could therefore recover the money advanced and enforce its security.

3. Sometimes, however, the words of the statute are too clear for the court to be able to uphold the contract even though the outcome is unfair and inconvenient. For example, Insurance Companies Act 1974 ss 2 and 83(4) forbid the 'business of effecting and carrying out of contracts of insurance' without authorisation. In *Bedford Insurance Co Ltd v Instituto de Resseguros do Brasil* [1985] QB 966, Parker J held that this rendered insurance policies made without authorisation void. This was approved, obiter, by the Court of Appeal in *Phoenix General Insurance Co of Greece SA v Administratia Asigurarilor de Stat* [1987] 2 All ER 152. Kerr LJ said (at 176):

The problem is therefore to determine whether or not the 1974 Act prohibits contracts of insurance by necessary implication, since it undoubtedly does not do so expressly. In that context it seems to me that the position can be summarised as follows.

(i) Where a statute prohibits both parties from concluding or performing a contract when both or either of them have no authority to do so, the contract is impliedly prohibited: see *Mahmoud and Ispahani's* case and its analysis by Pearce LJ in the *Archbolds* case with which Devlin LJ agreed.

(ii) But where a statute merely prohibits one party from entering into a contract without authority and/or imposes a penalty on him if he does so (ie a unilateral prohibition) it does not follow that the contract itself is impliedly prohibited so as to render it illegal and void. Whether or not the statute has this effect depends on considerations of public policy in the light of the mischief which the statute is designed to prevent, its language, scope and purpose, the consequences for the innocent party, and any other relevant considerations. The statutes considered in *Cope v Rowlands* and *Cornelius v Philips* fell on one side of the line; the Food Act 1984 would clearly fall on the other.

(iii) The Insurance Companies Act 1974 only imposes a unilateral prohibition on unauthorised insurers. If this were merely to prohibit them from carrying on 'the business of effecting contracts of insurance' of a class for which they have no authority, then it would clearly be open to the court to hold that considerations of public policy preclude the implication that such contracts are prohibited and void. But unfortunately the unilateral prohibition is not limited to the business of 'effecting contracts of insurance' but extends to the business of 'carrying out contracts of insurance'. This is a form of statutory prohibition, albeit only unilateral, which is not covered by any authority. However, in the same way as Parker J in the *Bedford* case, I can see no convincing escape from the conclusion that this extension of the prohibition has the unfortunate effect that contracts made without authorisation are prohibited by necessary implication and therefore void. Since the statute prohibits the insurer from carrying out the contract (of which the most obvious example is paying claims), how can the insured require the insurer to do an act which is expressly forbidden by statute? And how can a court enforce a contract against an unauthorised insurer when Parliament has expressly prohibited him from carrying it out? In that situation there is simply no room for the introduction of considerations of public policy. As Parker J said in the *Bedford* case:

> '...once it is concluded that on its true construction the Act prohibited both contract and performance, that is the public policy'.

(iv) It follows that, however reluctantly, I feel bound to agree with the analysis of Parker J in the *Bedford* case and his conclusion that contracts of insurance made by unauthorised insurers are prohibited by the 1974 Act in the sense that they are illegal and void, and therefore unenforceable. In particular, I agree with the following passages which led him to this conclusion:

> 'The express prohibition is on the carrying on of insurance business of a relevant class, but, as I have already mentioned, the definition in the case of each class begins 'the effecting and carrying out of contracts of insurance'. What therefore is prohibited is the carrying on of the business of effecting and performing contracts of insurance of various descriptions in the absence of an authorisation. It is thus both the contracts themselves and the performance of them at which the statute is directed.'

The result was later reversed by statute: Financial Services Act 1986 s 132.

4.   There may be cases in which, although the statute does not expressly or impliedly prohibit the making of the contract, a contract that necessarily involves the breach of the statute is invalid because it is a contract to commit a crime. So a contract to carry goods to a destination within a time limit, which could be achieved only by breaking the speed limit, might be illegal as being an inducement to commit a crime.

3. Contracts intended to be performed in an illegal way

In *Archbolds v Spanglett* (see p 1083), the plaintiffs were innocent because they did not know the defendants were not properly licensed. Suppose the goods had been delivered safely but the plaintiffs had refused to pay the carriage charges? Compare the *St John Shipping* case (p 1081).

If the plaintiffs had known when they made the contract that the defendants would carry the goods in an unlicensed vehicle, would they have been able to recover the value of the stolen goods? If not, why not?

Both the *Archbold* and the *StJohn Shipping* cases involved statutory crimes, but the same rule appears to apply to torts. Thus in *Clay v Yates* (1856) 1 H & N 73, a printer printed a book before discovering that the dedication to it was libellous. He refused to print the dedication but it was held that he could recover for the work done already (see Treitel, pp 432–433).

The rule that a party who did not intend to perform a contract illegally can enforce it, but one who did, cannot, applies also to some other heads of illegality (eg contracts that promote sexual immorality).

4. Contracts that are performed in an illegal manner

Alternatively, one party may, in the course of performing the contract, infringe some statute. So a carrier may break the speed limit without having agreed in advance to do so. In practice, illegal performance of this kind is likely to be much more common than prior agreement to perform illegally. This distinction is important for a number of reasons.

(a)   Illegal performance alone should not affect the rights of the other party. So if, in *Archbolds v Spanglett*, all that happened was that the carrier chose to carry the goods in an unlicensed vehicle, that would be no defence to the goods owner's complaint that the carrier had negligently lost the goods.

(b) Illegal performance will not *necessarily* defeat the claim of the party who has performed illegally. This is the point of *St John Shipping Co v Rank* and of the next case.

■ *Marles v Philip Trant & Sons Ltd (No 2)*

[1954] 1 QB 29, CA

The defendants, seed merchants, bought from a farmer, Mackinnon, wheat, described as spring wheat called Fylgia, and resold part of it to the plaintiffs under the same description. The wheat was not spring wheat and the plaintiffs successfully claimed damages from the defendants. The defendants sought to claim over against Mackinnon. He set up the defence that, in delivering the wheat to the plaintiffs, the defendants had failed to supply the statement required by the Seeds Act 1920 and therefore their performance of that contract was illegal.

Denning LJ

The first question which arises in this case is: what is the legal effect of the omission to supply the particulars prescribed under the Seeds Act? The trial judge has held that it turned the contract with the farmer, so far as the seed merchant was concerned, into an illegal contract. The judge so held on the authority of *Anderson Ltd v Daniel* and *B & B Viennese Fashions v Losane*, and there are indeed some observations in those cases which warrant him taking that view. But I do not think that they are correct. There can be no doubt that the contract between the seed merchants and the farmer was not unlawful when it was made. If the farmer had repudiated it before the time for delivery arrived, the seed merchants could certainly have sued him for damages. Nor was the contract rendered unlawful simply because the seed was delivered without the prescribed particulars. If it were unlawful, the farmer himself could not have sued upon it as he has done. The truth is that it was not the contract itself which was unlawful, but only the performance of it. The seed merchants performed it in an illegal way in that they omitted to furnish the prescribed particulars. That renders the contract unenforceable by them, but it does not render the contract illegal. Atkin LJ expressed the position with his usual accuracy in *Anderson Ltd v Daniel* when he said simply that the contract was unenforceable. I do not think that the law has ever countenanced the idea that a transaction, lawful when done, can be rendered unlawful by the doctrine of relation back: see *Elliot v Boynton* . . .

Once rid of the notion that the contract with the farmer was itself illegal, the question becomes: what is the effect of the admitted illegality in performance? It certainly prevents the seed merchants from suing the farmer for the price, but does it prevent them suing their supplier for damages? I think not. There was nothing unlawful in the contract between the seed merchants and their supplier, neither in the formation of it, nor in the performance of it. The seed merchants must therefore be entitled to damages for the breach of it. So far so good, but the difficulty comes when they seek to prove their damages. They want to be indemnified for the damages which they have been ordered to pay to the farmer. To prove those damages, they have to prove the contract with the farmer, and the circumstances under which the damages were awarded. It is said that once they begin to rely on their deliveries to the farmer, they seek aid from their own illegality; and that that is a thing which they are not allowed to do. The maxim is invoked: ex turpi causa non oritur actio. That maxim must not, however, be carried too far . . . they are entitled to recover . . . .

Singleton LJ delivered a concurring judgment. **Hodson LJ** dissented.

Appeal allowed.

NOTES

1.   Was the contract between the seed merchants and the plaintiffs in this case expressly or impliedly forbidden when it was made?

2.   Did the seed merchants intend to perform the contract with the plaintiffs in an illegal manner? If you cannot answer this question, what additional facts would you need to know in order to answer it?

3.   Note that Denning says that the seed merchants could not have enforced the contract against the plaintiffs because of the illegal act they had committed in performing it. However, they were still able to enforce their contract against the farmer: this was not 'tainted' by the illegality.

There are other suggestions that a party who did not know at the time the contract was made that it was to be performed in an illegal way may be debarred from a remedy if he 'participated' in the illegal act. In *Ashmore Benson Pease & Co Ltd v AV Dawson Ltd* [1973] 2 All ER 856, the plaintiffs made a contract with the defendant, a small haulage company, to carry two 25-ton tube banks to a port for shipment at £55 a trip. The defendants sent articulated lorries to collect the load. These could not legally be used to carry it. The plaintiffs' transport manager and assistant watched the lorries being loaded. One of the lorries toppled during the journey and the load was damaged. There was evidence that the transport manager knew that it was illegal to carry that load on that vehicle. The Court of Appeal held that the plaintiffs' action for damages to the tube bank failed because they had 'participated' in the illegal performance. Obviously, the contract's illegal performance disabled the defendant from enforcing it, but what might it mean that the plaintiffs 'participated' in the illegal performance? Much turns on the effect that the evidence has on the court in a case of this kind. For instance, the court may have thought that the plaintiffs knew or ought to have known that there were special rules about carrying 25-ton tube banks and that it was not likely that a small carrier such as the defendant would have the right equipment.

III. BENEFITS FROM DELIBERATE ILLEGAL ACTS

■ *Beresford v Royal Insurance Co Ltd*
[1938] AC 586, HL

Major Rowlandson had made a contract of life insurance with the defendants. On its true construction, the policy covered death brought about by suicide provided it took place more than two years after the policy. Major Rowlandson committed suicide more than two years after taking out the policy. His executors brought an action on the policy.

Lord Atkin

...My Lords, I entertain no doubt that on the true construction of this contract the insurance company have agreed with the assured to pay to his executors or assigns on his death the sum assured if he dies by his own hand whether sane or insane after the expiration of one year from the commencement of the assurance. The express protection limited to one year, and the clause as to the policy being indisputable subject to that limited exception seem to make this conclusion inevitable. The respondents' counsel appeared shocked that it should be considered that a reputable company could have intended to make such a contract: but the meaning is clear: and one may assume from what one knows of tariff conditions that it is a usual clause. There is no doubt therefore that on the proper construction of this contract the insurance company promised Major Rowlandson that if he in full possession of his senses intentionally killed himself they would pay his executors or assigns the sum assured.

...I think that the principle is that a man is not to be allowed to have recourse to a Court of Justice to claim a benefit from his crime whether under a contract or a gift. No doubt the rule pays regard to the fact that to hold otherwise would in some cases offer an inducement to crime or remove a restraint to crime, and that its effect is to act as a deterrent to crime. But apart from these considerations the absolute rule is that the Courts will not recognize a benefit accruing to a criminal from his crime.

The application of this principle to the present case is not difficult. Deliberate suicide, felo de se, is and always has been regarded in English law as a crime, though by the very nature of it the offender escapes personal punishment... The remaining question is whether the principle applies where the criminal is dead and his personal representative is seeking to recover a benefit which only takes shape after his death. It must be remembered that the money becomes due, if at all, under an agreement made by the deceased during his life for the express purpose of benefiting his estate after his death. During his life he had power of complete testamentary disposition over it. I cannot think the principle of public policy to be so narrow as not to include the increase of the criminal's estate amongst the benefits which he is deprived of by his crime. His executor or administrator claims as his representative, and, as his representative, falls under the same ban.

Anxiety is naturally aroused by the thought that this principle may be invoked so as to destroy the security given to lenders and others by policies of life insurance which are in daily use for that purpose. The question does not directly arise, and I do not think that anything said in this case can be authoritative. But I consider myself free to say that I cannot see that there is any objection to an assignee for value before the suicide enforcing a policy which contains an express promise to pay upon sane suicide, at any rate so far as the payment is to extend to the actual interest of the assignee. It is plain that a lender may himself insure the life of the borrower against sane suicide; and the assignee of the policy is in a similar position so far as public policy is concerned.

...It was suggested to us that so far as the doctrine was applied to contracts it would have the effect of making the whole contract illegal. I think that the simple answer is that this is a contract to pay on an event which may happen from many causes, one only of which involves a crime by the assured. The cause is severable and the contract, apart from the criminal cause, is perfectly valid.

Lord Macmillan delivered a judgment to the same effect and **Lords Thankerton** and **Russell** concurred.

NOTES

1. The rules about illegal performance overlap with but are distinct from the general doctrine that a person should not benefit from his own crime. So Major Rowlandson in *Beresford v Royal Insurance* did not perform the contract of life insurance illegally by committing suicide but he did fall foul of the benefit of a crime rule, because suicide was then a crime. It is strongly arguable that, because suicide is no longer a crime, the result would be different today. See Salmon LJ in *Gray v Barr* (p 1091).

2. Normally, a person in Major Rowlandson's position would be able to surrender the policy, that is, to bring it to an end and receive a cash payment reflecting the premiums paid and interest thereon. Most insurance companies will also lend eg 90 per cent of the current surrender value. Major Rowlandson could not take advantage of these possibilities because he had already borrowed up to the limit. This makes the practical effect of the decision less harsh. It also explains why the insurance company took the illegality point. In practice, companies would usually pay up in such cases.

3.   The possibility that an initially valid contract of insurance may not be enforceable against the insurance company presents particular problems if the policy is one of liability insurance, as the next three cases show.

In *Tinline v White Cross Insurance Association Ltd* [1921] 3 KB 327, the insured took out a third-party liability policy in respect of his motor car. While driving the car too fast, he knocked down three people, injuring two and killing one, and was convicted of manslaughter. He was sued for damages and sought a declaration that he was entitled to be indemnified by the defendants. Bailhache J held that it was not against public policy to allow recovery on such facts. He pointed out that virtually all motor accidents involving negligence must involve some breach of the criminal law by the negligent driver, so that to hold that any crime prevented the insured claiming on the policy would have made the policy nugatory. (Note that third-party insurance was not yet mandatory at the date of this case.)

■ *Hardy v Motor Insurers' Bureau*

[1964] 2 QB 745, CA

The plaintiff, a security officer at a large metal works, sought to stop the driver of a van bearing a stolen road fund licence. While the plaintiff was holding onto the van, the driver drove off at speed and the plaintiff was seriously injured. The plaintiff brought an action for personal injuries. The driver was not insured but, under an agreement with the Minister of Transport, the MIB indemnifies the victims of uninsured drivers in all cases in which the insurance company of an insured driver would be obliged to do so. The MIB argued that a contract to indemnify a driver against the consequences of criminal driving was contrary to public policy.

Lord Denning MR

... The policy of insurance which a motorist is required by statute to take out must cover any liability which may be incurred by him arising out of the use of the vehicle by him. It must, Ithink, be wide enough to cover, in general terms, any use by him of the vehicle, be it an innocent use or a criminal use, or be it a murderous use or a playful use. A policy so taken out by him is good altogether according to its terms. Of course, if the motorist intended from the beginning to make a criminal use of the vehicle—intended to run down people with it or to drive it recklessly and dangerously—and the insurers knew that that was his intention, the policy would be bad in its inception. No one can stipulate for iniquity. But that is never the intention with which such a policy is taken out. At any rate no insurer is ever party to it. So the policy is good in its inception. The question only arises when the motorist afterwards makes a criminal use of the vehicle. The consequences are then these:if the motorist is guilty of a crime involving a wicked and deliberate intent, and he is made to pay damages to an injured person, he is not himself entitled to recover on the policy. But if he does not pay the damages, then the injured third party can recover against the insurers under section 207 of the Road Traffic Act, 1960; for it is a liability which the motorist, under the statute, was required to cover. The injured third party is not affected by the disability which attached to the motorist himself.

So here the liability of Philips to Hardy was a liability which Philips was required to cover by a policy of insurance, even though it arose out of his wilful and culpable criminal act. If Philips had been insured, he himself would be disabled from recovering from the insurers. But the injured third party would not be disabled from recovering from them. Seeing that he was not insured, the Motor Insurers'Bureau must treat the case as if he were. They must pay the injured third party, even though Philips was guilty of felony. I would therefore dismiss the appeal.

Pearson and **Diplock LJJ** delivered concurring judgments.

■ *Gray v Barr*

[1971] 2 QB 554, CA

The defendant went with a loaded shotgun to the farm of the plaintiff's husband to look for his wife, who had been having an affair with Mr Gray. Mrs Barr was not there but the defendant did not accept Mr Gray's statement to this effect, and in a scuffle, the shotgun went off and Mr Gray was killed. Mr Barr was subsequently acquitted by a jury of manslaughter. Mrs Gray brought an action under the Fatal Accident Acts and Mr Barr claimed an indemnity from his insurers who argued, inter alia, that recovery would be against public policy.

Geoffrey Lane J held that Mr Barr's claim was barred by public policy. Mr Barr appealed.

Salmon LJ

... It is well settled that if a man commits murder or committed felo de se in the days when suicide was still a crime, neither he nor his personal representatives could be entitled to reap any financial benefit from such an act: *In the Estate of Crippen: Beresford v Royal Insurance Co Ltd.* This was because the law recognised that, in the public interest, such acts should be deterred and moreover that it would shock the public conscience if a man could use the courts to enforce a money claim either under a contract or a will by reason of his having committed such acts.

Crimes of violence, particularly when committed with loaded guns, are amongst the worse curses of this age. It is very much in the public interest that they should be deterred. A man, covered by a 'hearth and home' policy such as the present, walks into a bank with a loaded gun. He intends only to frighten and not to shoot the cashier. He slips and accidentally shoots a customer standing by the counter. It would be strange indeed if he could enforce the policy in respect of his liability to that customer. Once you threaten violence with a loaded gun and it goes off it is so easy to plead accident. Evidently it is very difficult for the prosecution to prove the contrary. Although public policy is rightly regarded as an unruly steed which should be cautiously ridden, I am confident that public policy undoubtedly requires that no one who threatens unlawful violence with a loaded gun should be allowed to enforce a claim for indemnity against any liability he may incur as a result of having so acted. I do not intend to lay down any wider proposition. In particular, I am not deciding that a man who has committed manslaughter would, in any circumstances, be prevented from enforcing a contract of indemnity in respect of any liability he may have incurred for causing death or from inheriting under a will or upon the intestacy of anyone whom he has killed. Manslaughter is a crime which varies infinitely in its seriousness.

I. The cases of *Tinline* [above] and James in which it was held that persons convicted of manslaughter for reckless and drunken driving could nevertheless recover indemnity from their insurers, were doubted in *Haseldine v Hosken* but approved by this court in *Marles v Philip Trant & Sons Ltd.* It seems now to be settled law that a motorist can rely on his policy of insurance to indemnify him in respect of his liability for any injuries which he has caused otherwise than on purpose: *Hardy v Motor Insurers' Bureau.* These road traffic cases may be sui generis. In any event, although motor cars have sometimes been called lethal weapons, these cases are not in my view akin to the cases in which injuries are caused in the course of unlawfully threatening a man with a loaded gun. Public policy is not static. Even if the crime of suicide had not been abolished by statute, it may be that today *Beresford's* case would have been differently decided. In any event, threatening violence with a loaded gun would, I am sure, now be generally regarded as much more shocking and necessary to be deterred than what the unfortunate Major Rowlandson did in *Beresford's* case. I am confident that, in any civilised society, public policy requires that anyone who inflicts injuries in the course of such an act shall not be allowed to use the courts of justice for the purpose of enforcing any contract of indemnity in respect of his liability in damages for causing injury by accident.

Lord Denning MR and **Philimore LJ** delivered judgments to the same effect.

Appeal dismissed.

■ **Shand, 'Underblinkering the Unruly Horse'** [1972A]
CLJ 144, 164

Let us take *Gray v Barr*. Applying the Diplock test, the gravity of Mr Barr's anti-social act was certainly considerable; but there the weighing of the insurers' side of the scales ends. The encouragement of similar anti-social acts, despite the frequent references to deterrence, would in reality be non-existent. Nor would considerations of punishing Mr Barr or abating public outrage be relevant, for in all probability it would not be he who would benefit from the indemnity, but the plaintiffs. On the other side of the scale, the social harm which would be caused by refusal of indemnity, both in the specific case and generally, would be enormous; for not only would the innocent dependants of the deceased be deprived of redress, but the business efficacy of indemnity in cases of this kind, would be undermined. Having received Mr Barr's premiums over the years, all that remained to the insurers was to cover the loss arising from the accident. It is submitted with some confidence that if such broader considerations of public policy were admitted, the result in *Gray v Barr* would be reversed.

NOTE

Do you agree with this criticism?

IV. SUMMARY SO FAR

(1) Contracts to commit serious crimes or torts deliberately are unenforceable by either party.
(2) Contracts that can only be performed by some other unlawful act, or in the course of performing which, some unlawful act is committed, may be expressly or impliedly forbidden by statute.
(3) In other cases, parties who intended to perform in an illegal way when the contract was made will be unable to enforce it.
(4) Parties who commit illegal acts in the course of performance are sometimes disabled from enforcing the contract, but more usually, the court takes the view that this would not further the aim of the statute (as in the *St John Shipping* case).
(5) Parties may be unable to claim benefits under the contract if their entitlement is the direct result of their own illegal act.
(6) A party who acted 'innocently', not intending to perform in an illegal way, will often be able to enforce the contract as usual.

So what of parties who are innocent but fall within case (2)? See the next subsection.

V. COLLATERAL CONTRACTS

■ ***Strongman (1945) Ltd v Sincock*** [1955]
2 QB 525, CA

Denning LJ

The plaintiffs, Strongman (1945) Ltd, are builders in the county of Cornwall. Two practical men, Mr George and Mr Williams Nicholls, are directors of the company. The defendant, Mr Sincock, is an architect. The builders claim against the architect for building work which they have done for him. The architect admits that the work was done, but he says that the plaintiffs are not entitled to be paid because it was all done illegally.

The architect has no merits at all. In addition to being an architect he was the owner of some buildings in Cornwall, and he employed the builders to convert these buildings into modern dwellings. One was at Penpol, and the other at Greatwood, Mylor. The work done was of the value of £6,359. Licences were obtained for only £2,150. The architect says that the builders cannot recover anything above the licensed figure because it was unlawful. It comes ill from him to say this, when on his own admission he sold these converted dwellings altogether for a sum of £10,650. He said in evidence: 'If I paid the plaintiffs for the work they have done, I should have been left with a very handsome profit.' Not only does he wish to keep that profit, but he also wishes to avoid payment of some £4,000 to the plaintiffs on the ground that it was an unlawful contract. But if the defence is good in law, effect must be given to it.

Let me say first that the builders cannot sue here on the contract to do the work, which was done in 1948 and 1949. At that time it was unlawful under Defence Regulation 56A for the work to be done without a proper licence. Licences were only in force to the amount of £2,150. When work was done to the value of over £6,000 the builders and the architect were all guilty of an offence for which they might have been prosecuted. Under many decisions in this court it has been held that a builder doing work without a licence cannot recover under the contract.

The builders seek to overcome this objection by saying that there was a warranty, or (putting it more accurately) a promise by the architect that he would get supplementary licences, or that if he failed to get them he would stop the work. The builders say that on the faith of that promise they did the work, and as the promise was broken they can recover damages in respect of it. . . .

The second question is whether the builders can recover in law on this collateral promise. The promise itself was not illegal, but it is said that damages cannot be recovered for the breach of it. It is said that, if damages could be recovered, it would be an easy way of getting round the law about illegality. This does not alarm me at all. It is, of course, a settled principle that a man cannot recover for the consequences of his own unlawful act, but this has always been confined to cases where the doer of the act knows it to be unlawful or is himself in some way morally culpable. . . . I think the law is that, although a man may have been guilty of an offence which is absolutely prohibited so that he is answerable in a criminal court, nevertheless if he has been led to commit that offence by the representation or by the promise of another, then in those circumstances he can recover damages for fraud if there is fraud, or for breach of promise or warranty if he prove such to have been given, provided always that he himself has not been guilty of culpable negligence on his part disabling him from that remedy.

Mr Dingle Foot referred us to the observations of this court in *In Re Mahmoud and Ispahani*. On a consideration of that case it seems to me that the court only decided that no action lay upon the contract for the purchase of goods. They did not decide whether there was an action for fraud or breach of promise or warranty: and I do not think that their observations were intended to express any view on the matter.

Birkett and **Romer LJJ** agreed.

NOTES

1. This was a case of statutory illegality to which the principle of 'innocence' apparently does not apply (see p 1081).

2. Do you think this case is distinguishable from *Re Mahmoud and Ispahani* (see p 1083)?

3. Once the work had been done, was anything to be gained by refusing to allow the builder to recover?

4. What was the consideration for the architect's promise?

5. See Wedderburn, 'Collateral Contracts' [1959] CLJ 58 at 73–4.

VI. RECOVERY OF PAYMENTS OR PROPERTY

The starting point for what follows is that even if neither of the parties can enforce an illegal contract, the contract is not totally ineffective. For instance, it has been held that property may pass under it from one party to the other just as if it were not illegal, and the seller cannot simply take the goods back. In *Sajan Singh v Sardara Ali* [1960] AC 167, under regulations made in Malaya in 1945, permits were necessary for the use of motor vehicles for the carriage of goods. Government policy was to restrict the issue of permits to those who had had them before the war. The plaintiff, who had not had a permit before the war, bought a lorry from the defendant who had. The plaintiff paid for the lorry, took possession of it and operated it for the carriage of goods, but under a licence that had been issued to the defendant. If the authorities had been told of this arrangement, they would not have issued a permit in relation to the lorry.

In 1956, the defendant removed the lorry from the plaintiff's premises without his consent and refused to return it. The plaintiff sued for its return or its value. The Privy Council held that he was entitled to succeed. The transaction between plaintiff and defendant had been fully carried out and was effective to transfer ownership to the plaintiff. This result has been criticised and it should be noted that the result in the case can be justified on the simpler ground that whoever was the owner of the lorry, the plaintiff was in possession of it and that his possession should be protected. Even if the defendant were still the owner, the court should not allow him to resort to self-help in this way. If this were not so, the lorry could have been seized not only by the defendant but by anyone else in the world. The problem is clearly more difficult if the plaintiff has never been in possession and relies on ownership only.

It does not follow that the buyer would be able to recover the goods from the seller only because the property had passed to the buyer, even though the goods have not been delivered. That would be tantamount to enforcing the contract of the sale. But it has been held that the buyer of goods under an illegal contract of sale has the right to sue a third party who wrongfully interferes with the goods (eg by converting them), even though the buyer never had possession of them because they were delivered straight to the third party: *Belvoir Finance Co Ltd v Stapleton* [1971] 1 QB 210. It was reasoned that if the buyer had no action, no one else could sue the third party.

Thus a party who has transferred property under an illegal contract cannot simply get it back. The same applies to money that has been paid over: it now belongs to the other party. No action will be given on the contract, and usually no action in restitution will be allowed either. As it is often put, '*in pari delicto potior est conditio defendentis*'—'when the parties are equally guilty, the defendant is in the stronger position'.

However, the parties may not be equally guilty. Firstly, of course, an innocent party may be able to enforce the contract anyway (see above), but aside from this, the courts also recognise that a party who is technically guilty should sometimes be allowed to recover from the other party. The next two subsections consider these cases.

1. Weaker parties

■ *Kiriri Cotton Co Ltd v Dewani*

[1960] AC 192, PC

The appellant company let a flat in Kampala, Uganda to the respondent for a term of seven years and one day, and received from him a premium of Shs 10,000. To take premiums was contrary to the terms of the Uganda Rent Restriction Ordinance, although neither party thought they were doing anything illegal. The Ordinance made no provision for the recovery of illegal premiums (unlike the corresponding English legislation). The respondent, having gone into occupation, brought an action to recover the premium. The High Court of Uganda gave judgment for the respondent.

The Court of Appeal for Eastern Africa affirmed the decision. The appellant appealed to Her Majesty in Council.

Lord Denning

...Their Lordships desire to point out at once that neither party thought they were doing anything illegal. The lease was for more than seven years and it was thought that, on a lease for that length of time, there was nothing wrong in asking for a premium or receiving it.

This was an easy mistake to make...

Nevertheless, no matter whether the mistake was excusable or inexcusable, or the premium fair or extortionate, the fact remains that the landlord received a premium contrary to the provisions of the Ordinance: and the question is whether the tenant can recover it back—remembering always that there is nothing in the Uganda Ordinance, comparable to the English Acts, enabling a premium to be recovered back...

It is clear that in the present case the illegal transaction was fully executed and carried out. The money was paid. The lease was granted. It was and still is vested in the plaintiff. In order to recover the premium, therefore, the plaintiff must show that he was not in pari delicto with the defendant. That was, indeed, the way he put his claim in the pleadings.

...

The issue thus becomes: Was the plaintiff in pari delicto with the defendant? Mr Elwyn Jones, for the appellant, said they were both in pari delicto. The payment was, he said, made voluntarily, under no mistake of fact, and without any extortion, oppression or imposition, and could not be recovered back. True, it was paid under a mistake of law, but that was a mistake common to them both. They were both equally supposed to know the law. They both equally mistook it and were thus in pari delicto. In support of this argument the appellant referred to such well-known cases as *Harse v Pearl Life Assurance Co; William Whiteley Ltd v The King; Evanson v Crooks;* and particularly to *Sharp Brothers & Knight v Chang.*

Their Lordships cannot accept this argument. It is not correct to say that everyone is presumed to know the law. The true proposition is that no man can excuse himself from doing his duty by saying that he did not know the law on the matter. Ignorantia juris neminem excusat. Nor is it correct to say that money paid under a mistake of law can never be recovered back. The true proposition is that money paid under a mistake of law, by itself and without more, cannot be recovered back. James LJ pointed that out in *Rogers v Ingham.* If there is something more in addition to a mistake of law—if there is something in the defendant's conduct which shows that, of the two of them, he is the one primarily responsible for the mistake— then it may be recovered back. Thus, if as between the two of them the duty of observing the law is placed on the shoulders of the one rather than the other—it being imposed on him specially for the protection of the other—then they are not in pari delicto and the money can be recovered back: see *Browning v Morris,* by Lord Mansfield. Likewise, if the responsibility for the mistake lies more on the one than the other—because he has misled the other when he ought to know better—then again they are not in pari delicto and the money can be recovered back; see *Harse v Pearl Life Assurance Co,* by Romer LJ...

Appeal dismissed.

2. The *locus poenitentiae*

Even where the parties are *in pari delicto*, a plaintiff may succeed in recovering his property if he 'repents' before things have gone too far. How far is too far? In *Taylor v Bowers* (1876) 1 QBD 291, Mellish J said:

If money is paid or goods delivered for an illegal purpose, the person who had so paid the money or delivered the goods may recover them back before the illegal purpose is carried out; but if he waits till the illegal purpose is carried out, or if he seeks to enforce the illegal transaction, in neither case can he maintain an action; the law will not allow that to be done.

■ *Kearley v Thomson*

(1890) 24 QBD 742, CA

Fry LJ

... The facts are shortly these:—A petition in bankruptcy was presented by one Baynes against Clarke, and a receiving order was made. The defendants were the solicitors acting for the petitioning creditor. That being the condition of things, the plaintiff, who appears to have been a friend of Clarke, intervened, and on October 6, 1887, Messrs Thomson & Ward, the defendants wrote this letter to the plaintiff Kearley:—'Re Clarke. At the request of Mr Kearley we have received from him the sum of 20*l* on account of our costs herein, and he is to pay us before twelve tomorrow a further sum of 20*l*; and in consideration of this sum of 40*l* we waive all our claim for costs, and undertake not to appear at the bankrupt's public examination, nor to oppose his order of discharge. 'That was signed by the defendants. On the following day, it appears that the second sum of 20*l* was paid, and a receipt was given by the defendants in these terms:—'7th October, 1887. Re Clarke. Received of Mr Kearley the further sum of 20*l*, mentioned in our receipt of yesterday.' On the same October 7 the public examination of the bankrupt took place, and, in accordance with the stipulation in the letter of the 6th, at that public examination the defendants did not appear.

The tendency of such a bargain as that entered into between the plaintiff and the defendants is obviously to pervert the course of justice. Although the defendants were under no obligation to appear, they certainly were under an obligation not to contract themselves out of the opportunity of appearing...

As a general rule, where the plaintiff cannot get at the money which he seeks to recover without shewing the illegal contract, he cannot succeed. In such a case the usual rule is *potior est conditio possidentis*. There is another general rule which may be thus stated, that where there is a voluntary payment of money it cannot be recovered back. It follows in the present case that the plaintiff who paid the 40l cannot recover it back without shewing the contract upon which it was paid, and when he shews that he shews an illegal contract. The general rule applicable to such a case is laid down in the very elaborate judgment in *Collins v Blantern* ... To that general rule there are undoubtedly several exceptions, or apparent exceptions. One of these is the case of oppressor and oppressed, in which case usually the oppressed party may recover the money back from the oppressor. In that class of cases the *delictum* is not par, and therefore the maxim does not apply. Again, there are other illegalities which arise where a statute has been intended to protect a class of persons, and the person seeking to recover is a member of the protected class. Instances of that description are familiar in the case of contracts void for usury under the old statutes, and other instances are to be found in the books under other statutes, which are, I believe, now repealed, such as those directed against lottery keepers. In these cases of oppressor and oppressed, or of a class protected by statute, the one may recover from the other, notwithstanding that both have been parties to the illegal contract.

There is suggested to us a third exception, which is relied on in the present case, and the authority for which is to be found in the judgment of the Court of Appeal in the case of *Taylor v Bowers*. In that case Mellish, LJ, in delivering judgment, says at p 300: 'If money is paid, or goods delivered for an illegal purpose, the person who has so paid the money or delivered the goods may recover them back before the illegal purpose is carried out.' It is remarkable that this proposition is, as I believe, to be found in no earlier case than *Taylor v Bowers*, which occurred in 1867, and, notwithstanding the very high authority of the learned judge who expressed the law in the terms which I have read. I cannot help saying for myself that I think the extent of the application of that principle, and even the principle itself, may, at some time hereafter, require consideration, if not in this Court, yet in a higher tribunal: and I am glad to find that in expressing that view I have the entire concurrence of the Lord Chief Justice. But even assuming the exceptions to exist, does it apply to the present case? What is the condition of things if the illegal purpose has been carried into effect in a material part, but remains unperformed in another material part? As I have already pointed out in the present case, the contract was that the defendants should not appear at the public examination of the bankrupt or at the application for an order of discharge. It was performed as regards the first; but the other application has not yet been made. Can it be contended that, if the illegal contract has been partly carried into effect and partly remains unperformed, the money can still be recovered? In my judgment it cannot be so contended with success. Let me put an illustration of the doctrine contended for, which was that partial performance did not prevent the recovery of the money. Suppose a payment of 100l by A to B on a contract that the latter shall murder C and D. He has murdered C, but not D. Can the money be recovered back? In my opinion it cannot be. I think that case illustrates and determines the present one.

I hold, therefore, that where there has been a partial carrying into effect of an illegal purpose in a substantial manner, it is impossible, though there remains something not performed, that the money paid under that illegal contract can be recovered back.

Lord Coleridge CJ agreed.

In *Alexander v Rayson* [1936] 1 KB 169, the defendant agreed to let a flat in Piccadilly from the plaintiff for a rent of £1,200 a year. The contract was embodied in two documents: one, a lease with some services for £450 a year, and the other, an agreement to provide services for £750 a year. The services in the second agreement were much the same as in the first, with the addition of the provision of a fridge. The plaintiff intended to show only the first document to the rating authorities in the hope of getting the rateable value of the premises reduced. This scheme was unsuccessful because the fraud was detected. The contract was held illegal as intending to defraud the Revenue (this is not without difficulties; see 16 U of Toronto LJ at 286–8: the reasoning in this part of the article was cited and applied by Field J in *21st Century Logistic Solutions Ltd v Madysen Ltd* [2004] 2 Lloyd's Rep 92). The Court of Appeal further held that once the plaintiff's illegal purpose had been revealed and frustrated, it was too late for him to repent.

■ **Grodecki, *'In Pari Delicto'*** (1955)
71 LQR 254, 265–270

1. *The dignity of the court*

In many judgments there is present a feeling that the court must not be humiliated by an enquiry into base and shameful bargains. Such feeling is amply warranted if these involve gross moral turpitude. But, as Story has points out, 'there may be, on the part of the court itself, a necessity of supporting the public interests or public policy, in many cases, however reprehensible the acts of the parties may be.' This explanation alone cannot justify the maxim *in pari delicto*. The oft-stated proposition that the courts 'will not assist an illegal transaction in any respect' is far from self-evident if what is sought is not enforcement of an illegal contract but quasi-contractual recovery of money paid or property delivered under it . . . .

2. *Morality*

The maxim is sometimes regarded as expressing a moral principle; and the plaintiff deprived of his remedy because he is a willing party to a bargain involving moral turpitude. The dictates of an objective moral order prevent the court from entertaining his claim. In other words, he is unworthy of help . . .

It would seem that the morality embodied in the maxim *in pari delicto*, as applied by the courts, is of a dubious kind. This may be shown in several ways. Relief is denied to a claimant who is unaware of the illegality of the transactions to which he is a party and who is thus morally innocent. On the other hand, the maxim directly benefits the defendant who, as often as not, is more guilty and the initiator of the scheme. It protects his possession of money, goods or land to which, apart from the unlawful and void contract, he has no right whatsoever. It thus allows him to reap the fruits of his own turpitude whilst the punishment of the plaintiff is often out of all proportion to his wrong. Furthermore, if the maxim were truly based on a moral principle, one would expect less attention paid to the accident of one party being the plaintiff and the other the defendant. Instead, details of procedure obscure ethical considerations. In all these cases, if realities are faced, it is the defendant who resorts to the illegality to secure for himself an unjust benefit rather than the plaintiff who merely claims his own property. Again, the 'moral' approach would lead the court to distinguish between the party who intends to make a gain out of the illegality and the party who is merely concerned to avoid a loss. This, however, is not the case . . . The court, therefore, does not inquire into the morality of the parties' conduct since the *delictum*. Finally, if accurate apportionment of blame between the parties were possible it would be called for on moral grounds. In fact, the plaintiff is penalised without any investigation into real culpability.

The maximum *in pari delicto* cannot thus be explained and justified by reference to ethics. It is, indeed, amoral . . . From a moral point of view the best solution might well be confiscation of the money paid or property delivered under an unlawful contract. St Thomas Aquinas advocated this solution:'the giver deserves to lose what he gave, wherefore restitution should not be made to him; and, since the receiver acted against the law in receiving, he must not retain the price but must use it for some pious object.'.

. . .

3. *Public policy*

The third reason sometimes given to explain the application of the maxim is respect for public policy. The following passage from Lord Mansfield's judgment in *Holman v Johnson* may be regarded as the *locus classicus:* 'The objection that a contract is immoral or illegal as between plaintiff and defendant sounds at all times ill in the mouth of the defendant. It is not for his sake, however, that the objection is ever allowed; but it is founded in general principles of policy, which the defendant has the advantage of, contrary to the real justice, as between him and the plaintiff, by accident, if I may so say.'

The doctrine of public policy is invoked in support of the maxim in many cases. Why precisely the public interest is thereby promoted is, however, seldom explained. It may only be assumed that what the courts have in mind is, apart from the punitive, the deterrent and preventive effect of the maxim. Refusal of action leaves the parties at the discretion of one another, with sole reliance upon personal honour. Unlawful transactions become risky and precarious and are thus discouraged. This is by far the most pertinent argument in favour of the maxim *in pari delicto*. The plaintiff's claims are sacrificed in the general interest, but as he is *ex hypothesi* a delinquent the court is not under any obligation to redress his grievance.

Unfortunately, however, just as it came to be assumed that the grant of recovery must be immoral, so it came to be overlooked that in some cases it might have a stronger deterrent effect than its denial. The maxim is directed against the plaintiff, restitution against the defendant. A system under which, in the court's discretion, recovery may be given or refused, whichever happens to further the ends of the law most effectively, would seem to have the best of both worlds. The illegal agreements are rendered even more precarious and the parties still remain at each other's mercy. The hope that the court may exercise its discretion in his favour will often induce the plaintiff to abandon the unlawful bargain before it is fully performed. Moreover, the person to whom money is paid or property delivered is never secure in his possession of them. The merits of restitution as a weapon of social policy are particularly obvious where, as in cases of marriage brokage and evasion of currency regulations, the defendant is conducting an organised unlawful business. It is essential that he, in particular, should be discouraged. His enterprise constitutes a serious social menace and he will always be cunning enough to entice new clients. The value of restitution as a deterrent is recognised by the Rent Restriction Acts in allowing a tenant to recover illegal premiums paid to the landlord . . .

. . . [M]orality and public interest dictated the application of the maxim *in pari delicto*. The truth of this assumption was never questioned.

3. Proprietary claims

It is sometimes said that a plaintiff may succeed in recovering property if he can show that he has a right to possession without having to 'reveal' the illegality. This is misleading because, if the plaintiff does not reveal it, the defendant certainly will if it suits his purpose. The crucial point is that if a plaintiff can formulate a claim, the legal reasoning oh which is wholly independent of the illegal contract, he will succeed. The classic example is a lease of Blackacre by A to B for five years, A knowing that B intends to use Blackacre as a brothel. A cannot sue B for the rent nor can he turn B out for non-payment of the rent. He can, however, turn B out after five years. This is because, after five years, he is simply enforcing his rights as a freeholder, which do not depend on the validity or invalidity of the lease.

■ *Taylor v Chester*
(1869) LR 4 QB 309

Mellor J

In this case the plaintiff declared on the bailment on the half of a 50l Bank of England note, to the defendant, to be redelivered on request, alleging a refusal by the defendant to redeliver such half-note. The second count was in detinue for the same half-note [.]

The defendant, after traversing the delivery and detention of the note, and to the second count denying that it was the property of the plaintiff, pleaded separately and specifically to both counts, in effect, that the half-note in question had been deposited by the plaintiff with the defendant by way of pledge, to secure the repayment of money due and money then advanced by the defendant to the plaintiff and then due.

The plaintiff joined issue on the defendant's pleas, and also replied specially that the alleged debt or sum, in respect of which the defendant justified the non-delivery and detention of the half-note, was for wine and suppers, supplied by the defendant in a brothel and disorderly house kept by the defendant, for the purpose of being consumed there by the plaintiff and divers prostitutes in a debauch there, to incite them to riotous, disorderly, and immoral conduct, and for money knowingly lent for the purpose of being expended in riot and debauchery and immoral conduct...

The true test for determining whether or not the plaintiff and the defendant were in pari delicto, is by considering whether the plaintiff could make out his case otherwise than through the medium and by the aid of the illegal transaction to which he was himself a party: *Simpson v Bloss*... The plaintiff, no doubt, was the owner of the note, but he pledged it by way of security for the price of meat and drink provided for, and money advanced to, him by the defendant. Had the case rested there, and no pleading raised the question of illegality, a valid pledge would have been created, and a special property conferred upon the defendant in the half-note, and the plaintiff could only have recovered by showing payment or a tender of the amount due. In order to get rid of the defence arising from the plea, which set up an existing pledge of the half-note, the plaintiff had recourse to the special replication, in which he was obliged to set forth the immoral and illegal character of the contract upon which the half-note had been deposited. It was, therefore, impossible for him to recover except through the medium and by the aid of an illegal transaction to which he was himself a party. Under such circumstances, the maxim 'in pari delicto potior est conditio possidentis', clearly applies, and is decisive of the case.

■ *Bowmakers Ltd v Barnet Instruments Ltd*
[1945] KB 65, CA

The plaintiffs let machine tools to the defendants under three hire-purchase agreements, each of which was illegal as contravening statutory instruments. The defendants resold the tools that were the subject of the first and third agreements and refused to pay the hire on the second. The plaintiffs sued for conversion.

Du Parcq LJ

... The question, then, is whether in the circumstances the plaintiffs are without a remedy. So far as their claim in conversion is concerned, they are not relying on the hiring agreements at all. On the contrary, they are willing to admit for this purpose that they cannot rely on them. They simply say that the machines were their property, and this, we think, cannot be denied. We understand Mr Gallop to concede that the property had passed from Smith to the plaintiffs, and still remained in the plaintiffs at the date of the conversion. At any rate, we have no doubt that this is the legal result of the transaction and we find support for this view in the dicta of Parke B in *Scarfe v Morgan*.

Why then should not the plaintiffs have what is their own? No question of the defendants' rights arises. They do not, and cannot pretend to have any legal right to possession of the goods at the date of the conversion. Their counsel has to rely, not on any alleged right of theirs, but on the requirements of public policy ... Prima facie, a man is entitled to his own property, and it is not a general principle of our law (as was suggested) that when one man's goods have got into another's possession in consequence of some unlawful dealings between them, the true owner can never be allowed to recover those goods by an action. The necessity of such a principle to the interests and advancement of public policy is certainly not obvious. The suggestion that it exists is not, in our opinion supported by authority ...

In our opinion, a man's right to possess his own chattels will as a general rule be enforced against one who, without any claim of right, is detaining them, or has converted them to his own use, even though it may appear either from the pleadings, or in the course of the trial, that the chattels in question came into the defendant's possession by reason of an illegal contract between himself and the plaintiff, provided that the plaintiff does not seek, and is not forced, either to found his claim on the illegal contract or to plead its illegality in order to support his claim.

NOTE

By reselling the machines subject to the first and third agreements, the defendant had performed an act fundamentally inconsistent with the bailment. This normally results in the bailee's right to possession coming to an end. But in relation to the second agreement, the defendant had merely failed to pay the hire. As we have seen, this does not, under the general law, bring the contract to an automatic end; if it amounts to a repudiation, it may give the owner the right to terminate.

■ Hamson, 'Illegal Contracts and Limited Interests' (1949)
10 CLJ 249, 258–259

The question in *Bowmakers' Case* is 'when can a bailor recover from the bailee under an illegal bailment the chattel bailed or its value?' The simplest answer would no doubt have been to treat an illegal bailment as a bailment at will and to permit the bailor always to recover the chattel upon mere demand. This answer had however been rejected in *Taylor v Chester* despite Herschell's argument; and the court in *Bowmaker's Case* accepts that decision as correct. The bailee accordingly still acquires, by virtue of the illegal bailment, some interest or property in the chattel other than one defeasible merely on demand. In *Bowmaker's Case*, however, the court goes on to hold that the bailor can recover the chattel bailed under an illegal hire purchase contract even though the only wrongful act by the bailee, in one of the instances, was his mere continuance in possession after demand made for the return of the chattel upon his failure to pay some instalments of the hire reserved by the bailment. Those instalments could not, by reason of the illegality, be recovered directly by action against the bailee. The difficulty is that the court, while declaring, as indeed it was bound to, that 'no claim founded on an illegal contract will be enforced' and that 'no technical meaning must be ascribed to the words "founded on an illegal contract"', nevertheless appears to come very close, under cover of an action in tort, to enforcing the terms of the illegal bailment against the defendants.

It is suggested that, despite the court's laudable desire to avoid technicalities, the question who is to keep a chattel which has been the subject of an illegal contract will continue to be decided with the aid of very abstruse technicalities; that the established principle that delivery or conveyance under an illegal contract effects a valid transfer of property or of an interest in property is itself no mean technicality and forms the basis of rules which are therefore likely to have a technical bias; and that in *Bowmakers' Case* perhaps the court applied the technicalities with less consideration than they merited, and with results which both to the technician and to the layman are somewhat startling.

It is further suggested that, if *Bowmakers' Case* is rightly decided, there is now no objection to the lessor also recovering possession of premises demised under an illegal lease upon non-payment of the rent reserved, even if the lease has been executed under seal, provided it contain the normal provision for determination upon non-payment. Before *Bowmakers' Case* the balance of authority was against such a recovery during the period of the term.

■ Coote, 'Another Look at *Bowmakers*' (1972)
35 MLR 38, 42–44

[T]here is no longer anything particularly cynical about the rule stated in the *Bowmakers* case. On the contrary, it makes good sense. Nor is recovery by the owner merely the unmeritorious result of an accident of pleading. What the *Bowmakers* rule means is that he will obtain restitution if his claim is based on rights which belong to him independently of the illegal contract. He will not recover if he has, before suit, effectively transferred his rights away under an executed illegal contract. This, it may be added, is substantially the effect of a dictum by Watermeyer JA of the South African Appellate Division in *Jajbhay v Cassim*, which for many years has appeared in successive editions Cheshire and Fifoot on *The Law of Contract*. According to that learned judge:

> '...the Court will not assist a party to recover what he has paid or transferred to defendant in terms of the illegal contract, save in exceptional circumstances, but there is no need to go further and deprive him of his rights which he has not transferred to defendant.'

On this line of reasoning, or something like it, the *Bowmakers* decision has been accepted by many commentators to be correct, so far as agreements 1 and 3 are concerned. The plaintiffs were able to plead their ownership and there was no reason for them to rely in any way on the illegal hire-purchase agreements in order to establish their immediate right to restitution. The explanation offered by the commentators for this latter point was that the defendants' act of selling the tools had automatically revested in the plaintiffs a right to immediate possession. Because of a similarly automatic revesting, the argument runs, the plaintiffs could equally have recovered possession once the term of the bailment contract had expired by effluxion of time. They might even have done so upon default in payment of hire, if the contract had contained a clause which terminated the bailment automatically for non-payment. By the same token, a lessor would be able to recover his land on the expiry of the term of an illegal lease.

...But these arguments...do not, the critics say, cover the circumstances of the second hire-purchase agreement, for in that case there had been no conversion of the tools, and therefore no automatic termination of the bailment. The defendants had failed to comply with a demand for the return of the tools, but the plaintiffs, to show that they were entitled to make the demand, would have been driven back onto the cesser provisions of the contract. To enable them to recover in those circumstances would be to recognise and enforce a right of termination given them by the illegal contract. Such enforcement would be contrary to the *ex turpi causa* rule.

The fact that this line of reasoning leaves unexplained the Court of Appeal's decision on the second agreement is not its only disadvantage. It rests the court's decision in respect of agreements 1 and 3 on the quite fortuitous circumstance that a conversion of bailed goods, while it apparently does not automatically terminate the bailment contract, does revest an immediate right to possession in the bailor. Not only was this a factor not adverted to by du Parcq LJ when he delivered the judgment of the court; it also has the effect of confining the decision substantially to bailment contracts, since there seems to be no equivalent automatic revesting under the law governing leases. It also seems to exclude the possibility of recovery on repudiatory breach generally, since termination in such cases is ordinarily not automatic but depends on an election by the injured party.

Despite the weight of opinion to the contrary, it is submitted that there do exist at least two ways in which both aspects of the *Bowmakers* decision can be justified. The first finds its basis in the dictum of Watermeyer JA in *Jajbhay v Cassim* which has already been referred to, and in the line of South African cases which derive from it. The other involves a direct application of the principle which the Court of Appeal itself purported to apply in the *Bowmakers* case.

This question of whether the plaintiff can succeed in asserting property rights without relying on the illegal transaction was considered by the House of Lords in the following case.

■ *Tinsley v Milligan*
[1993] 3 All ER 65, HL

In this case, T and M, who were lovers, jointly purchased a house that was, however, registered in the name of T as the sole legal owner. The reason for this was to make it easier for M make false claims to the Department of Social Security for benefits. This was done for several years and the income was shared between the parties, although it did not form a very substantial part of their joint income, which was mainly derived from using the house as a lodging house. In due course, M revealed the fraud to the Department of Social Security and settled matters with them.

Later, T and M quarrelled and T moved out. T brought an action claiming possession of the house and asserting ownership of it. M counterclaimed for an order for sale and a declaration of the house as held by T in trust for the parties in equal shares. T argued that M was barred from denying T's ownership of the house because the arrangement had only been made in order to facilitate the fraud on the Department of Social Security and was therefore tainted by illegality.

The Court of Appeal, following a number of recent earlier Court of Appeal decisions, held that the Court had a flexible jurisdiction, which could balance the illegality against the consequences of denying the claim, and concluded that, in the circumstances, to deny M an equal share of the house would be a disproportionate penalty. The House of Lords were unanimous in agreeing that the Court of Appeal's views were wrong.

However, the House of Lords itself was divided as to what the correct answer was. The view of the majority, Lord Browne-Wilkinson, Lord Jauncey and Lord Lowry, was that the question should be settled by applying the technical rules of equity about resulting trusts and presumptions of advancement. These rules may be roughly summarised by saying that there is a presumption that husbands make gifts to wives (the presumption of advancement) but a presumption that wives do not make gifts to husbands and that non-married people do not make substantial gifts to each other (the presumption of resulting trust). It follows that, if there is a presumption of resulting trust and a house is bought with A's money in B's name or with A and B's money in B's name, there will normally be a presumption that B holds that part of the purchase price, which comes from A, on resulting trust for A unless the relationship between A and B is such as to give rise to a presumption of advancement. It followed that, in the present case, since M had contributed a half-share of the purchase price, T held half of the property on resulting trust for M. M could reach this position simply on the basis of contribution to the purchase price and did not therefore have to rely on any illegal transaction. On this analysis, indeed, it is T who is seeking to rely on the illegal transaction and is not allowed to do so. Of course, in an ordinary transaction, the presumptions both of resulting trust and advancement would be rebuttable but the point of the present case is that whoever has to rebut the relevant presumption would be prevented from doing so because it would have involved revealing the illegality to which both parties had been party.

Lord Goff and Lord Keith dissented. They thought that the governing principle was that if A puts property in the name of B intending to conceal his (A's) interest in the property for a fraudulent or illegal purpose, neither law nor equity will allow A to recover the property, and equity will not assist him in asserting an equitable interest in it. This principle applies whether the transaction takes the form of a transfer of property by A to B, or the purchase by A of property in the name of B.

The reasoning of the House of Lords was mildly criticised and then distinguished by the Court of Appeal in *Tribe v Tribe* [1995] 4 All ER 236. The plaintiff owned 459 shares out of 500 in a family company and was the tenant of two leasehold properties, which were occupied by the company as licensee. In 1987, the landlords served schedules of dilapidation on the plaintiff, requiring him to repair, and his solicitor advised him that he was facing the possibility of large payments. In order to put assets outside the reach of the landlords, the plaintiff transferred the shares to his son. The documentation said that the transfer was for a consideration of £78,030 but it was never intended that this sum would be paid.

In fact, the scheme proved unnecessary because one of the landlords accepted a surrender of the lease and the other sold the reversion. When the plaintiff asked his son for the shares back, the son refused on the ground that there was a presumption of advancement in his favour and that his father would have to rely on the illegality.

The Court of Appeal rejected this reasoning on the ground that the illegality had never been carried into effect and that therefore the *locus poenitentiae* applied (see p 1095).

In 1999, the Law Commission produced a very full Working Paper entitled 'Illegal Transactions: The Effect of Illegality on Contracts and Trusts'. It took the position that the existing rules were unduly complex and uncertain. Its provisional view, on which it asked for comments, was that the existing rules should be replaced by a discretion. The flavour of the Commission's current thinking can perhaps be captured by quoting paras 9.8, 9.9 and 9.10 of the 'Summary' of the questions it was posing to consultees.

9.8 Do consultees agree with our provisional view that (a) a court should have a discretion to decide whether illegality should act as a defence to the recognition of contractually transferred or created property rights where the formation, purpose or performance of the contract involves the commission of a legal wrong (other than the mere breach of the contract in question) or is otherwise contrary to public policy; but (b) that illegality should not invalidate a disposition of property to a third party purchaser for value without notice of the illegality? (Paragraph 7.26)

Structuring the discretion

9.9 Do consultees agree with our provisional view that the proposed discretion should be structured so that the court should be required to take into account specific factors in reaching its decision; and that those factors should be: (1) the seriousness of the illegality involved; (2) the knowledge and intention of the plaintiff; (3) whether denying relief will act as a deterrent; (4) whether denying relief will further the purpose of the rule which renders the contract illegal; and (5) whether denying relief is proportionate to the illegality involved? We also ask consultees whether there are any other factors which they consider the courts should take into account in exercising the discretion. If consultees do not agree with our provisional view, we would ask them to explain why not. (Paragraph 7.43)

The starting point of the discretion

9.10 Do consultees consider that the starting point of the provisionally proposed discretion should be:

    (a) that illegality will act as a defence unless the court declares otherwise;

    (b) that the plaintiff's claim will be allowed unless the court decides that because of the involvement of illegality it would not be in the public interest to allow the claim;

    (c) one which varies according to whether the claim is for contractual enforcement; restitution pursuant to a contract which has failed for illegality; or the recognition of contractually transferred or created property rights; or

    (d) that a claim by a party who has neither carried out nor intends to carry out the illegality will be allowed, unless the court declares otherwise; but a claim by a party who has carried out or intends to carry out the illegality will be refused, unless the court declares otherwise?

Alternatively we ask consultees whether they consider that it would be preferable that no starting point should be expressed. (Paragraph 7.57)

VII. SEVERANCE

In many cases in which a contract is illegal because it involves some unlawful act, the whole contract is rendered invalid because the illegality affects the substance of the contract. If the illegality relates only to a part of it, the position is less clear. Sometimes it is treated as infecting the whole thing. Thus in *Miller v Karlinski* (1945) 62 TLR 85, a provision in a contract of employment was aimed at defrauding the Revenue (see p 1074) and this rendered the whole contract invalid. Sometimes, however, the court will treat the illegal part as severable, leaving the rest of the contract enforceable. This is particularly common with contracts that are in restraint of trade, and severance will be discussed in some detail in the next section. It can also be done with contracts involving unlawful acts if the illegal part can readily be separated out. Thus in *Ailion v Spiekermann* [1976] Ch 158, the vendor of a leasehold interest committed an offence by demanding a premium from the purchasers. The latter were permitted to recover the premium yet could still enforce the rest of the agreement.

CHAPTER FORTY-FOUR

CONTRACTS IN RESTRAINT OF TRADE

As we shall see, the law handles contracts in restraint of trade in a number of ways that are different to the main body of illegal contracts. One is that although competition is usually desirable, it is not a value which in all circumstances outweighs all others. At least since the early eighteenth century, the law has recognised that some contracts in restraint of trade are acceptable. Many of the cases are concerned therefore with striking a balance.

■ *Nordenfelt v Maxim Nordenfelt*

[1894] AC 535, HL

Lord Macnaghten

My Lords, the appellant, Thorsten Nordenfelt, a Swedish gentleman of much intelligence, as his able address to your Lordships proved, and of great skill in certain branches of mechanical science, had established in England and Sweden a valuable business in connection with the manufacture of quick-firing guns. His customers were comparatively few in number, but his trade was world-wide in extent. He had upon his books almost every monarch and almost every State of any note in the habitable globe. In 1886 Mr Nordenfelt sold his business to a limited company which was formed for the purpose of purchasing it. At the same time and as part of the same transaction he entered into a restrictive covenant with the purchasers intended to protect the business in their hands. In 1888 the purchasers transferred their business to the respondents, a limited company established with the object of combining the Nordenfelt business with a similar business founded by a Mr Maxim. The transfer was made with the concurrence of Mr Nordenfelt. Without his concurrence and co-operation it is plain that it would not have been made at all. On the occasion of the transfer, and as part of the arrangement, Mr Nordenfelt entered into a restrictive covenant with the respondents. This covenant was in some respects wider, in others less wide, than the covenant with the original purchasers. But it was in lieu of, and in substitution for, that covenant, which of course would have been kept alive if Mr Nordenfelt had declined to come into the new arrangement.

In these circumstances I think that the Court of Appeal were right in regarding the covenant which Mr Nordenfelt entered into with the respondents as a covenant made upon the occasion of the sale of his business, and as depending for its validity upon the principles and considerations applicable to such a case.

The stipulation was that Mr Nordenfelt should not, during the term of twenty-five years from the date of the incorporation of the company, if the company should so long continue to carry on business, 'engage except on behalf of the company either directly or indirectly in the trade or business of a manufacturer of guns, gun-mountings or carriages, gunpowder explosives or ammunition'—so far the covenant has been held good; then come the words, 'or in any business competing or liable to compete in any way with that for the time being carried on by the company'. A proviso was added to the effect that such restriction should not apply to explosives other than gunpowder, or to subaqueous or submarine boats or torpedoes, or castings or forgings of steel or iron, or alloys of iron or of copper. The latter part of the covenant, which extends to all competing businesses, may be disregarded. In view of the manifold objects of the company, as set out in their memorandum of association, it was held by the Court of Appeal to be void; and there is no appeal from that part of the decision. The proviso also,I think, may be put aside. It is one of the circumstances to be taken into consideration as bearing upon the question of the reasonableness of the agreement; but it is not, I think, essential to the validity of this covenant ...

In the age of Queen Elizabeth restraints of trade, whatever they were, general or partial were thought to be contrary to public policy, and therefore void *(Colgate v Bacheler)*. In time, however, it was found that a rule so rigid and far-reaching must seriously interfere with transactions of every-day occurrence. Traders could hardly venture to let their shops out of their own hands; the purchaser of a business was at the mercy of the seller; every apprentice was a possible rival. So the rule was relaxed. It was relaxed as far as the exigencies of trade for the time being required, gradually and not without difficulty, until it came to be recognised that all partial restraints might be good, though it was thought that general restraints, that is, restraints of general application extending throughout the kingdom, must be bad. Why was the relaxation supposed to be thus limited? Simply because nobody imagined in those days that a general restraint could be reasonable, not because there was any inherent or essential distinction between the two cases....

The true view at present time I think, is this: The public have an interest in every person's carrying on his trade freely:so has the individual. All interference with individual liberty of action in trading, and all restraints of trade of themselves, if there is nothing more, are contrary to public policy, and therefore void. That is the general rule. But there are exceptions:restraints of trade and interference with individual liberty of action may be justified by the special circumstances of a particular case. It is a sufficient justification, and indeed it is the only justification, if the restriction is reasonable— reasonable, that is, in reference to the interests of the parties concerned and reasonable in reference to the interests of the public, so framed and so guarded as to afford adequate protection to the party in whose favour it is imposed, while at the same time it is in no way injurious to the public. That, I think, is the fair result of all the authorities.

...I think the restraint in the present case is reasonable in every point of view ...

Lord Herschell LC, Lord Watson, Lord Ashbourne and **Lord Morris** also delivered judgments in favour of dismissing the appeal.

Appeal dismissed.

NOTES

1. Although all the members of the Court of Appeal and the House of Lords reached the same conclusion in this case, they did so for a variety of different reasons. Lord Macnaghten's statement has come to be treated as the authoritative starting point of the modern law.

2. It is usually accepted that there are a number of recognised categories of covenant that are in restraint of trade (see further p 1111). This case illustrates one of the major categories, restraints imposed on competition by the seller of a business.

3. Once it is established (by previous authority or otherwise, see pp 1111 ff) that a covenant is in restraint of trade, the covenant will be unenforceable unless it is shown to be reasonable. Thus the burden of proof will be on the buyer of the business.

4. In order to show that a covenant is reasonable, it is usually said that the party seeking to enforce it must show two things: first, that he has some legally recognised interest to protect, and second, that the covenant is no wider than is reasonably necessary to protect the interest.

5. What legitimate interest does the buyer of a business have in preventing the seller from competing in the future? Is it to the seller's advantage to be able to make a covenant not to compete? (*Hint:* how much would you get for the goodwill of your business if you couldn't be stopped from opening up a new, competing business next door next week?)

6. In *Nordenfelt*, why do you think that there was no appeal from the Court of Appeal's decision that the part of the covenant undertaking not to engage 'in any business competing or liable to compete in any way with that for the time being carried on by the company' was invalid? For a further example of a covenant invalid because it covered something the seller didn't sell, see *Vancouver Malt and Sake Brewing Co Ltd v Vancouver Breweries Ltd* [1934] AC 181.

7. Even if the buyer has a legitimate interest to protect, the covenant must be reasonable, eg in area and duration. In practice, this overlaps with the legitimate interest question. If Nordenfelt's business had been only in Europe, it could have been said either that a worldwide covenant was unreasonably broad or that the company had no legitimate interest in preventing him competing outside Europe.

■ *Mason v Provident Clothing & Supply Co Ltd*
[1913] AC 724, HL

Lord Moulton

... The law as to covenants in restraint of trade was so carefully and authoritatively formulated in this House in the *Nordenfelt Case* that I do not think it necessary to discuss the numerous authorities cited in the course of the argument in order to ascertain what is the critical question which the Court ought to put to itself in such a case as this. It is as follows: Are the restrictions which the covenant imposes upon the freedom of action of the servant after he has left the service of the master greater than are reasonably necessary for the protection of the master in his business? ...

The nature of the employment of the appellant in this business was solely to obtain members and collect their instalments. A small district in London was assigned to him, which he canvassed and in which he collected the payments due, and outside that small district he had no duties. His employment was therefore that of a local canvasser and debt collector, and nothing more.

Such being the nature of the employment, it would be reasonable for the employer to protect himself against the danger of his former servant canvassing or collecting for a rival firm in the district in which he had been employed. If he were permitted to do so before the expiry of a reasonably long interval he would be in a position to give to his new employer all the advantages of that personal knowledge of the inhabitants of the locality, and more especially of his former customers, which he had acquired in the service of the respondents and at their expense. Against such a contingency the master might reasonably protect himself, but I can see no further or other protection which he could reasonably demand. If the servant is employed by a rival firm in some district which neither includes that in which he formerly worked for the respondents, nor is immediately adjoining thereto, there is no personal knowledge which he has acquired in his former master's service which can be used to that master's prejudice ....

These, then, being the limits of the protection which the master might reasonably insist on. I turn to the covenant in order to see whether it exceeds these limits .... [I]t prohibits the appellant from entering into a similar employment within 25 miles of [London] for a period of three years ... such an area is very far greater than could be reasonably required for the protection of his former employers.

It was suggested in the argument that even if the covenant was, as a whole, too wide, the Court might enforce restrictions which it might consider reasonable (even though they were not expressed in the covenant), provided they were within its ambit. My Lords, I do not doubt that the Court may, and in some cases will, enforce a part of a covenant in restraint of trade, even though taken as a whole the covenant exceeds what is reasonable. But, in my opinion, that ought only to be done in cases where the part so enforceable is clearly severable, and even so only in cases where the excess is of trivial importance, or merely technical, and not a part of the main purport and substance of the clause. It would in my opinion be pessimi exempli if, when an employer had exacted a covenant deliberately framed in unreasonably wide terms, the Courts were to come to his assistance and, by applying their ingenuity and knowledge of the law, carve out of this void covenant the maximum of what he might validly have required. It must be remembered that the real sanction at the back of these covenants is the terror and expense of litigation, in which the servant is usually at a great disadvantage, in view of the longer purse of his master. It is sad to think that in this present case this appellant, whose employment is a comparatively humble one, should have had to go through four Courts before he could free himself from such unreasonable restraints as this covenant imposes, and the hardship imposed by the exaction of unreasonable covenants by employers would be greatly increased if they could continue the practice with the expectation that, having exposed the servant to the anxiety and expense of litigation, the Court would in the end enable them to obtain everything which they could have obtained by acting reasonably. It is evident that those who drafted this covenant aimed at making it a penal rather than a protective covenant, and that they hoped by means of it to paralyse the earning capacities of the man if and when he left their service, and were not thinking of what would be a reasonable protection to their business, and having so acted they must take the consequences.

Viscount Haldane LC and **Lords Dunedin** and **Shaw of Dunfermline** delivered judgments to the same effect.

Appeal allowed.

NOTES

1. This is an example of a second major category: covenants by employees not to compete after the end of their employment.

2. In Lord Macnaghten's analysis, a valid covenant has to be reasonable both as between the parties and in the public interest. In practice, the vast majority of the cases have been decided on the issue of reasonableness as between the parties. This is another example of the unusual nature of the restraint of trade doctrine since reasonableness as between the parties is an internal and not an external matter. As the remarks of Lord Moulton above show, these cases can be regarded as early examples of inequality of bargaining power (see also p 950).

3. In *Mason's* case, the employer had a protectable interest in his connection with his customers but the covenant was much too wide. Similarly, an employer may be entitled to protect trade secrets.

■ *Herbert Morris Ltd v Saxelby*

[1916] 1 AC 688, HL

The plaintiffs were the leading manufacturers of hoisting machinery in the UK. The defendant had been employed by them since leaving school. After several years he was given a contract as an engineer for two years, certain and thereafter subject to four months' notice on either side. As part of this agreement, he covenanted:

that he would not during a period of seven years from his ceasing to be employed by the company, either in the United Kingdom of Great Britain or Ireland, carry on either as principal, agent, servant, or otherwise, alone or jointly or in connection with any other person, firm, or company, or be concerned or assist directly or indirectly, whether for reward or otherwise, in the sale or manufacture of pulley blocks, hand overhead runways, electric overhead runways, or hand overhead travelling cranes…

Lord Parker

… [F]or a restraint to be reasonable in the interests of the parties it must afford *no more than* adequate protection to the party in whose favour it is imposed. So conceived the test appears to me to be valid both as regards the covenantor and covenantee, for though in one sense no doubt it is contrary to the interests of the covenantor to subject himself to any restraint, still it may be for his advantage to be able so to subject himself in cases where, if he could not do so, he would lose other advantages, such as the possibility of obtaining the best terms on the sale of an existing business or the possibility of obtaining employment or training under competent employers. As long as the restraint to which he subjects himself is no wider than is required for the adequate protection of the person in whose favour it is created, it is in his interest to be able to bind himself for the sake of the indirect advantages he may obtain by so doing. It was at one time thought that, in order to ascertain whether a restraint were reasonable in the interests of the covenantor, the Court ought to weigh the advantages accruing to the covenantor under the contract against the disadvantages imposed upon him by the restraint, but any such process has long since been rejected as impracticable. The Court no longer considers the adequacy of the consideration in any particular case. If it be reasonable that a covenantee should, for his own protection, ask for a restraint, it is in my opinion equally reasonable that the covenantor should be able to subject himself to this restraint. The test of reasonableness is the same in both cases.

My Lords, it appears to me that Lord Macnaghten's statement of the law requires amplification in another respect. If the restraint is to secure no more than 'adequate protection' to the party in whose favour it is imposed, it becomes necessary to consider in each particular case what it is for which and what it is against which protection is required. Otherwise it would be impossible to pass any opinion on the adequacy of the protection…. I cannot find any case in which a covenant against competition by a servant or apprentice has, as such, ever been upheld by the Court. Wherever such covenants have been upheld it has been on the ground, not that the servant or apprentice would, by reason of his employment or training, obtain the skill and knowledge necessary to equip him as a possible competitor in the trade, but that he might obtain such personal knowledge of and influence over the customers of his employer, or such an acquaintance with his employer's trade secrets as would enable him, if competition were allowed, to take advantage of his employer's trade connection or utilize information confidentially obtained.

An attempt was, however, made in argument to justify the restraint on the ground that it was no more than adequate for the protection of the plaintiffs' trade connection and trade secrets. I am of opinion that this attempt completely failed. With regard to the plaintiffs' connection, there is little or no evidence that the defendant ever came into personal contact with the plaintiffs' customers. For a period, it is true, he was manager of the London branch of the plaintiffs' business, and for another period sales manager at Loughborough. With the exception of these periods he was employed entirely in the engineering department. Had the restraint been confined to London and Loughborough and a reasonable area round each of these centres, it might possibly have been supported as reasonably necessary to protect the plaintiffs' connection, but a restraint extending over the United Kingdom was obviously too wide in this respect.

With regard to trade secrets, I am not satisfied that the defendant was entrusted with any trade secret in the proper sense of the word at all. Mr Walter boldly argued that the expression trade secrets ought to be extended so as to include everything which Mr Morris claimed to be peculiar to the plaintiffs' method of carrying on their business.

I will assume that the matters referred to by Mr Walter are in fact peculiar to the plaintiffs' business, though I can hardly regard Mr Morris's uncorroborated evidence as very satisfactory proof that the practices in question were unknown to other firms. Still, the manner in which Sargant J dealt with this part of the case appears to me to be unanswerable. Though the defendant had access to the E charts, the L sheets, the drawings of special machines, the costs index, and other documents, all of which may be considered confidential, these documents were far too detailed for the defendant to carry away the contents thereof in his head. All that he could carry away was the general method and character of the scheme of organization practised by the plaintiff company. Such scheme and method can hardly be regarded as a trade secret. The same applies to the plaintiff company's system of standardizing mechanical apparatus capable of being used in more than one class of machine. The nearest approach that I can find in the evidence to anything in the nature of a trade secret is the mention of certain formulae, said to be based on the plaintiffs' experience, and to be more trustworthy than Molesworth's formulae for similar purposes.

Lords Atkinson, Shaw and **Sumner** delivered judgments to the same effect.

Appeal dismissed.

Another category is restrictive trading agreements and the like. In *McEllistrim v Ballymacelligot Co-operative Agricultural and Dairy Society Ltd* [1919] AC 548, the plaintiff was a member of the defendant society, which carried on the business of manufacturing butter and cheese from milk supplied by some of its members. The society bound itself to take all milk produced by members' cows within a defined area and members agreed not to sell milk to any other creamery or to anyone who sold milk or manufactured butter for sale. Under the rules, it was effectively impossible for a member to leave without the consent of the committee. The House of Lords held (Lord Parmoor dissenting) that this feature, combined with the restriction of the selling of milk, was wider than reasonably necessary for the protection of the society.

As a means of promoting competition, the common law rules on restraint of trade suffered from two defects. Firstly, the question would normally only come before the courts if one of the parties was dissatisfied. Clearly, the more cosy a cartel, the less the incentive for the parties to fall out amongst themselves (see p 1071). Secondly, the courts in practice seemed to attach more weight to reasonableness between the parties than to the public interest (this latter defect has, in fact, been less apparent in more recent cases: see the next case). The result has been the adoption of statutory regimes, operating partly through a special court, the Restrictive Practices Court, and partly through a standing commission, the Monopolies and Mergers Commission. These statutory developments overlap and coexist with the common law. English competition law has recently undergone a major change. The Restrictive Practices Court has disappeared and the Monopolies and Mergers Commission replaced by the Competition Commission. In addition, competition law is one of the most important parts of the law of the European Communities (for further details on all of this, see Whish, *Competition Law*, 5th edn, 2003; Jones and Sufrin, *EC Competition Law*, 2nd edn, 2004).

If a case does not fall within one of the recognised categories of restraint of trade, how is it to be determined whether the doctrine applies, so that the covenant must be shown to be reasonable before it can be enforced? This question arose with 'solus agreements'. These are agreements between petrol companies and garage owners, whereby in exchange for finance, which is often secured by a mortgage on the premises, the garage owner agrees to buy all of its petrol from the petrol company, to keep open at all reasonable times and to extract similar undertakings from anyone to whom it sells the garage. The precedents were confused. It had often (but not always) been assumed that simple 'exclusive dealing contracts' were valid (see Treitel pp 468–469), while restrictive covenants imposed on buyers of land preventing them from using the land for various trades had always been enforced without question.

■ *Esso Petroleum Co Ltd v Harper's Garage (Stourport) Ltd*
[1968] AC 269, HL

The appellants had entered into agreements with the respondents in relation to two filling stations owned by the respondents. Under the agreements, the respondents agreed to buy all of their requirements of motor fuels from the appellants at their current list prices. One agreement was to last for four years five months and the other for 21 years. The respondents wished to shift to another brand of petrol and the appellants sought an injunction to restrain them from doing so.

Lord Reid

. . . The main argument submitted for the appellant on this matter was that restraint of trade means a personal restraint and does not apply to a restraint on the use of a particular piece of land. Otherwise, it was said, every covenant running with the land which prevents its use for all or some trading purposes would be a covenant in restraint of trade and therefore unenforceable unless it could be shown to be reasonable and for the protection of some legitimate interest. It was said that the present agreement only prevents the sale of petrol from other suppliers on the site of the Mustow Green Garage:It leaves the respondents free to trade anywhere else in any way they choose. But in many cases a trader trading at a particular place does not have the resources to enable him to begin trading elsewhere as well, and if he did he might find it difficult to find another suitable garage for sale or to get planning permission to open a new filling station on another site. As the whole doctrine of restraint of trade is based on public policy its application ought to depend less on legal niceties or theoretical possibilities than on the practical effect of a restraint in hampering that freedom which it is the policy of the law to protect.

It is true that it would be an innovation to hold that ordinary negative covenants preventing the use of a particular site for trading of all kinds or of a particular kind are within the scope of the doctrine of restraint of trade. I do not think they are. Restraint of trade appears to me to imply that a man contracts to give up some freedom which otherwise he would have had. A person buying or leasing land had no previous right to be there at all, let alone to trade there, and when he takes possession of that land subject to a negative restrictive covenant he gives up no right or freedom which he previously had . . . .

In my view this agreement is within the scope of the doctrine of restraint of trade as it had been developed in English law. Not only have the respondents agreed negatively not to sell other petrol but they have agreed positively to keep this garage open for the sale of the appellants' petrol at all reasonable hours throughout the period of the tie. It was argued that this was merely regulating the respondent's trading and rather promoting than restraining his trade. But regulating a person's existing trade may be a greater restraint than prohibiting him from engaging in a new trade. And a contract to take one's whole supply from one source may be much more hampering than a contract to sell one's whole output to one buyer. I would not attempt to define the dividing line between contracts which are and contracts which are not in restraint of trade, but in my view this contract must be held to be in restraint of trade. So it is necessary to consider whether its provisions can be justified . . . .

Where two experienced traders are bargaining on equal terms and one has agreed to a restraint for reasons which seem good to him the court is in grave danger of stultifying itself if it says that it knows that trader's interest better than he does himself. But there may well be cases where, although the party to be restrained has deliberately accepted the main terms of the contract, he has been at a disadvantage as regards other terms: for example where a set of conditions has been incorporated which has not been the subject of negotiation—there the court may have greater freedom to hold them unreasonable.

. . . .

What were the appellants' legitimate interests must depend largely on what was the state of affairs in their business and with regard to the distribution and sale of petrol generally. And those are questions of fact to be answered by evidence or common knowledge. In the present case restraint of trade was not pleaded originally and the appellants only received notice that it was to be raised a fortnight before the trial. They may have been wise in not seeking a postponement of the trial when the pleadings were amended. But the result has been that the evidence on this matter is scanty. I think however that it is legitimate to supplement it from the considerable body of reported cases regarding solus agreements and from the facts found in the Report of the Monopolies Commission of July, 1965.

When petrol rationing came to an end in 1950 the large producers began to make agreements, now known as solus agreements, with garage owners under which the garage owner, in return for certain advantages agreed to sell only the petrol of the producer with whom he made the agreement. Within a short time three-quarters of the filling stations in this country were tied in that way and by the dates of the agreements in this case over 90 per cent had agreed to ties. It appears that the garage owners were not at a disadvantage in bargaining with the large producing companies as there was intense competition between these companies to obtain these ties. So we can assume that both the garage owners and the companies thought that such ties were to their advantage. And it is not said in this case that all ties are either against the public interest or against the interests of the parties. The respondents' case is that the ties with which we are concerned are for too long periods.

The advantage to the garage owner is that he gets a rebate on the wholesale price of the petrol which he buys and also may get other benefits or financial assistance. The main advantages for the producing company appear to be that distribution is made easier and more economical and that it is assured of a steady outlet for its petrol over a period. As regards distribution, it appears that there were some 35,000 filling stations in this country at the relevant time, of which about a fifth were tied to the appellants. So they only have to distribute to some 7,000 filling stations instead of to a very much larger number if most filling stations sold several brands of petrol. But the main reason why the producing companies want ties for five years and more, instead of ties for one or two years only, seems to be that they can organise their business better if on the average only one-fifth or less of their ties come to an end in any one year. The appellants make a point of the fact that they have invested some £200 millions in refineries and other plant and that they could not have done that unless they could foresee a steady and assured level of sales of their petrol. Most of their ties appear to have been made for periods of between five and 20 years. But we have no evidence as to the precise additional advantage which they derive from a five-year tie as compared with a two-year tie or from a 20-year tie as compared with a five-year tie.

The Court of Appeal held that these ties were for unreasonably long periods. They thought that, if for any reason the respondents ceased to sell the appellants' petrol, the appellants could have found other suitable outlets in the neighbourhood within two or three years. I do not think that this is the right test. In the first place there was no evidence about this and I do not think that it would be practicable to apply this test in practice. It might happen that when the respondents ceased to sell their petrol, the appellants would find such an alternative outlet in a very short time. But, looking to the fact that well over 90 per cent of existing filling stations are tied and that there may be great difficulty in opening a new filling station, it might take a very long time to find an alternative. Any estimate of how long it might take to find suitable alternatives for the respondents' filling stations could be little better than guesswork.

I do not think that the appellants' interest can be regarded so narrowly. They are not so much concerned with any particular outlet as with maintaining a stable system of distribution throughout the country so as to enable their business to be run efficiently and economically. In my view there is sufficient material to justify a decision that ties of less than five years were insufficient, in the circumstances of the trade when these agreements were made, to afford adequate protection to the appellants' legitimate interests . . . . A tie for 21 years stretches far beyond any period for which developments are reasonably foreseeable. Restrictions on the garage owner which might seem tolerable and reasonable in reasonably foreseeable conditions might come to have a very different effect in quite different conditions: the public interest comes in here more strongly.

Lord Wilberforce

. . . The doctrine of restraint of trade (a convenient, if imprecise, expression which I continue to use) is one which has throughout the history of its subject-matter been expressed with considerable generality, if not ambiguity. The best-known general formulations, those of Lord Macnaghten in *Nordenfelt* and Lord Parker of Waddington in *Adelaide*, adapted and used by Diplock LJ in the Court of Appeal in the *Petrofina* case, speak generally of all restraints of trade without any attempt at a definition. Often we find the words 'restraint of trade'in a single passage used indifferently to denote, on the one hand, in a broad popular sense, any contract which limits the free exercise of trade or business, and, on the other hand, as a term of art covering those contracts which are regarded as offending a rule of public policy. Often, in reported cases, we find that instead of segregating two questions, (i) whether the contract is in restraint of trade, (ii) whether, if so, it is 'reasonable', the courts have fused the two by asking whether the contract is in 'undue restraint of trade' or by a compound finding that it is not satisfied that this contract is really in restraint of trade at all but, if it is, it is reasonable. A well-known text book describes contracts in restraint of trade as those which 'unreasonably restrict' the rights of a person to carry on his trade or profession. There is no need to regret these tendencies: indeed, to do so, when consideration of this subject has passed through such notable minds from Lord Macclesfield onwards, would indicate a failure to understand its nature. The common law has often (if sometimes unconsciously) thrived on ambiguity and it would be mistaken, even if it were possible, to try to crystallise the rules of this, or any, aspect of public policy into neat propositions. The doctrine of restraint of trade is one to be applied to factual situations with a broad and flexible rule of reason . . . .

This does not mean that the question whether a given agreement is in restraint of trade, in either sense of these words, is nothing more than a question of fact to be individually decided in each case. It is not to be supposed, or encouraged, that a bare allegation that a contract limits a trader's freedom of action exposes a party suing on it to the burden of justification. There will always be certain general categories of contracts as to which it can be said, with some degree of certainty, that the 'doctrine' does or does not apply to them. Positively, there are likely to be certain sensitive areas as to which the law will require in every case the test of reasonableness to be passed: such an area has long been and still is that of contracts between employer and employee as regards the period after the employment has ceased. Negatively, and it is this that concerns us here, there will be types of contract as to which the law should be prepared to say with some confidence that they do not enter into the field of restraint of trade at all.

How, then, can such contracts be defined or at least identified? No exhaustive test can be stated— probably no precise non-exhaustive test. But the development of the law does seem to show that judges have been able to dispense from the necessity of justification under a public policy test of reasonableness such contracts or provisions of contracts as, under contemporary conditions may be found to have passed into the accepted and normal currency of commercial or contractual or conveyancing relations. That such contracts have done so may be taken to show with at least strong prima force that, moulded under the pressures of negotiation, competition and public opinion, they have assumed a form which satisfies the test of public policy as understood by the courts at the time, or, regarding the matter from the point of view of the trade, that the trade in question has assumed such a form that for its health or expansion it requires a degree of regulation. Absolute exemption for restriction or regulation is never obtained: circumstances, social or economic, may have altered, since they obtained acceptance, in such a way as to call for a fresh examination: there may be some exorbitance or special feature in the individual contract which takes it out of the accepted category:but the court must be persuaded of this before it calls upon the relevant party to justify a contract of this kind.

Some such limitation upon the meaning in legal practice of 'restraints of trade' must surely have been present in to the minds of Lord Macnaghten and Lord Parker. They cannot have meant to say that any contract which in whatever way restricts a man's liberty to trade was (either historically under the common law, or at the time of which they were speaking) prima facie unenforceable and must be shown to be reasonable. They must have been well aware that areas existed, and always had existed in which limitations of this liberty were not only defensible, but were not seriously open to the charge of restraining trade. Their language, they would surely have said, must be interpreted in relation to commercial practice and common sense.

Lords Morris, Hodson and **Pearce** agreed that the shorter agreement was valid but the longer one void.

NOTES

1. The argument in this case was concerned with two separate issues. Firstly, was the agreement within the category of restraint of trade? Secondly, if it was, was it reasonable? The positive answer to the first question exemplifies the broader view that has recently been taken on this question. It will be seen that, although Lord Reid and Lord Wilberforce answered the first question in the same way, they proposed substantially different tests for arriving at the answer. Lord Morris and Lord Hodson agreed with Lord Reid but his test is open to serious criticism, in particular because it is formalistic and easy to evade (Heydon, *The Restraint of Trade Doctrine*, 1971, pp 55–73). Subsequent cases leave the question obscure—*Cleveland Petroleum Co Ltd v Dartstone Ltd* [1969] 1 All ER 201; *Amoco Australia Pty Ltd v Rocca Bros Motor Engineering Co Pty Ltd* [1975] AC 561, PC; *Alec Lobb (Garages) Ltd v Total Oil (GB) Ltd* [1985] 1 All ER 303, CA—but see the next case.

2. In the *Esso* case, the House of Lords attached considerable weight to the public interest question. On this question, they relied significantly on a contemporary report of the Monopolies Commission (1965 HC 24), which stated:

> 379.... [We] consider that the solus system for petrol, as such, has led to some reduction in suppliers' costs which has exerted a downward pressure on prices, has had some beneficial effect in producing improvements in petrol stations, does not restrict the motorist's choice of petrol and does not, in practice lead to the setting up of excessive numbers of petrol stations. It follows from this that we think it perfectly possible to have a system of solus trading in petrol which does not operate against the public interest. In arriving at this preliminary conclusion we have left out of account a number of features of the system as now practised in this country. These are features which are capable of being altered or eliminated without destroying the basis of solus trading. It remains for us to consider whether any of these features should be altered or eliminated, or in other words whether the solus arrangements, as they exist at present, operate or may be expected to operate against the public interest in any particular respects. Broadly the questions which arise in this connection are concerned with the effects upon the public interest of:
>   (i) the length of term of solus agreements:
>   (ii) the terms and conditions of the loans which are made by petrol suppliers to retailers:
>   (iii) the provisions of agreements concerned with the supply of petrol equipment by petrol suppliers:
>   (iv) the provisions under which petrol retailers accept restrictions on their trade in other petroleum goods, in particular lubricants:
>   (v) the degree of control which is, or may be, exercised by the petrol suppliers over the general conduct of their exclusive retailers' businesses, including trade in tyres, batteries and accessories:
>   (vi) provisions which restrict the retailer in relation to the sale of his premises, including option clauses and undertakings to obtain the purchaser's acceptance of the exclusive obligations:
>   (vii) the acquisition and ownership of retail premises by petrol suppliers and the terms upon which these premises are let to tenants:
>   (viii) arrangements at motorway petrol stations.

It is worth emphasising that it is difficult for a court trying a restraint of trade case to ensure that all of the relevant commercial and economic information is before it. The Monopolies Commission and its successors are in a much better position in this respect.

■ *A Schroeder Music Publishing Co Ltd v Macaulay*

[1974] 3 All ER 616, HL

The respondent, an unknown songwriter of 21, entered into an agreement with the appellants, music publishers, for his exclusive services. He gave the appellants the copyright of all compositions during the term of the contract (five years), which was extendable for a further five years if royalties exceeded £5,000. The agreement was terminable by the publishers on one month's notice but not by the respondent. It was assignable by the publishers but not, without the publishers' consent, by the respondent. The publishers accepted no obligation to publish any of the songs.

The respondent sought a declaration that the contract was contrary to public policy. This was granted by Plowman J and the Court of Appeal. On appeal to the House of Lords:

Lord Reid

. . . The public interest requires in the interests both of the public and of the individual that everyone should be free so far as practicable to earn a livelihood and to give to the public the fruits of his particular abilities. The main question to be considered is whether and how far the operation of the terms of this agreement is likely to conflict with this objective. The respondent is bound to assign to the appellant during a long period the fruits of his musical talent. But what are the appellants bound to do with those fruits? Under the contract nothing. If they do use the songs which the respondent composes they must pay in terms of the contract. But they need not do so. As has been said they may put them in a drawer and leave them there . . . .

It was argued that there must be read into this agreement an obligation on the publisher to act in good faith. I take that to mean that he would be in breach of contract if by reason of some oblique or malicious motive he refrained from publishing work which he would otherwise have published. I very much doubt this but even if it were so it would make little difference. Such a case would seldom occur and then would be difficult to prove.

I agree with the appellants' argument to this extent. I do not think that a publisher could reasonably be expected to enter into any positive commitment to publish future work by an unknown composer. Possibly there might be some general undertaking to use his best endeavours to promote the composer's work. But that would probably have to be in such general terms as to be of little use to the composer.

But if no satisfactory positive undertaking by the publisher can be devised, it appears to me to be an unreasonable restraint to tie the composer for this period of years so that his work will be sterilised and he can earn nothing from his abilities as a composer if the publisher chooses not to publish. If there had been in clause 9 any provision entitling the composer to terminate the agreement in such an event the case might have had a very different appearance, but as the agreement stands not only is the composer tied but he cannot recover the copyright of work which the publisher refuses to publish.

It was strenuously argued that the agreement is in standard form, that it has stood the test of time, and that there is no indication that it ever causes injustice. Reference was made to passages in the speeches of Lord Pearce and Lord Wilberforce in the Esso case with which I wholly agree. Lord Pearce said:

> 'It is important that the court, in weighing the question of reasonableness, should give full weight to commercial practices and to the generality of contracts made freely by parties bargaining on equal terms.'

Later Lord Wilberforce said:

> 'The development of the law does seem to show, however, that judges have been able to dispense from the necessity of justification under a public policy test of reasonableness such contracts or provisions of contracts as, under contemporary conditions, may be found to have passed into the accepted and normal currency of commercial or contractual or conveyancing relations. That such

contracts have done so may be taken to show with at least strong prima force that, moulded under the pressures of negotiation, competition and public opinion, they have assumed a form which satisfies the test of public policy as understood by the courts at the time, or, regarding the matter from the point of view of the trade, that the trade in question has assumed such a form that for its health or expansion it requires a degree of regulation.'

But those passages refer to contracts 'made freely by parties bargaining on equal terms'or 'moulded under the pressures of negotiation, competition and public opinion'. I do not find from any evidence in this case, nor does it seem probable, that this form of contract made between a publisher and an unknown composer has been moulded by any pressure of negotiation. Indeed, it appears that established composers who can bargain on equal terms can and do make their own contracts.

Any contract by which a person engages to give his exclusive services to another for a period necessarily involves extensive restriction during that period of the common law right to exercise any lawful activity he chooses in such manner as he thinks best. Normally the doctrine of restraint of trade has no application to such restrictions:they require no justification. But if contractual restrictions appear to be unnecessary or to be reasonably capable of enforcement in an oppressive manner, then they must be justified before they can be enforced.

In the present case the respondent assigned to the appellants 'the full copyright for the whole world'in every musical composition 'composed created or conceived'by him alone or in collaboration with any other person during a period of five or it might be ten years. He received no payment (apart from an initial £50) unless his work was published and the appellants need not publish unless they chose to do so. And if they did not publish he had no right to terminate the agreement or to have any copyrights re-assigned to him. I need not consider whether in any circumstances it would be possible to justify such a one-sided agreement. It is sufficient to say that such evidence as there is falls far short of justification. It must therefore follow that the agreement so far as unperformed is unenforceable.

I would dismiss this appeal.

Viscount Dilhorne, Lord Diplock, Lord Kilbrandon and **Lord Simon** concurred.

Appeal dismissed.

(For extracts from Lord Diplock's judgment, see pp 952.)

■ Trebilcock, 'An Economic Approach to Unconscionability'in Reiter and Swan (eds), *Studies in Contract Law*
pp 399–404

NB. Trebilcock treats *Schroeder v Macaulay* as establishing a general doctrine of inequality of bargaining power. Your editors do not accept this, but Trebilcock's comments are illuminating.
   For other extracts from this piece, see pp 952 and 965.

It is clear that the music publishing industry does not conform to all the criteria of a perfectly competitive market, given that the products (that is, the service packages)offered by different suppliers to composers are presumably widely differentiated. Because each package may possess a degree of uniqueness, each supplier may have a small measure of ability to adjust price and output combinations in relation to his differentiated product. But, provided that a substantial measure of substitutability is possible between one supplier's product and those of others, the market is as workably competitive as most real-world markets are likely to be. Moreover, as experience in the anti-trust context has demonstrated, an industry whose products are widely differentiated will almost never be able to sustain a stable cartel, as the possibilities for cheating on agreed price and output restrictions are extensive and largely unpoliceable. This difficulty in the way of effective cartelization is, of course, compounded if the industry comprises many firms and entry barriers are low, both features of the music publishing industry, as we shall see.

The suggestion by Lord Diplock, that consumer standard-form contracts are explicable only on the basis that they are dictated by a party whose bargaining power, either exercised alone (monopolization) or in conjunction with others (cartelization), enables him to adopt the position that these are the only terms on which the product is obtainable, simply does not stand up as a matter of *a priori* analysis. This is not to suggest that monopolization or cartelization may not in fact have been present in *Macaulay*. But not a shred of relevant evidence was adduced on this issue.

In contrast, in the landmark U.S. case on manufacturers' products liability, *Henningsen v Bloomfield Motors Inc*, where the New Jersey Supreme Court struck down as unconscionable certain restrictive provisions in Chrysler's new car warranty, the court relied heavily on the fact that the 'Big Three' automobile manufacturers controlled 93.5 percent of passenger-car production in 1958 and that the warranty was a uniform warranty promulgated by the Automobile Manufacturers Association comprising all the major automobile manufacturers, including Chrysler. Thus the existence of substantial and demonstrated market power and proof of explicit cartelization in relation to warranty terms provided a defensible basis for judicial intervention. The court said:'The gross inequality of bargaining position occupied by the consumer in the automobile industry is thus apparent. There is no competition among car makers in the area of the express warranty. Where can the car buyer go to negotiate for better protection?' The court in *Macaulay* was in a position to say none of these things. Indeed, had it chosen to examine data on the structure and performance of the music industry (which it did not), it is unlikely that it could have defended contractual invalidation on a monopolization or cartelization rationale. Before looking at this data, one or two preliminary observations are in order.

First, even if market concentration exists, there will be the intractable problem highlighted in many anti-trust cases, of determining whether, and to what extent, it has produced anti-competitive effects. Relative long-run industry profit rates are sometimes considered an alternative, or additional, indicator of non-competitive behaviour, and may be equally relevant in a case such as *Macaulay*. However, for a variety of reasons, neither the market concentration test, the profit rate test, nor related tests, can be readily applied in practice to yield reliable predictions of non-competitive behaviour. Whether in ordinary civil litigation between private parties there will normally be sufficient economic incentive for parties to invest in the complex task of producing reliable economic evidence on the issue of abuse of market power raises further problems.

Secondly, the corporate structure of the defendants in *Macaulay* made it presumptively implausible that they had monopoly power or were playing a dominant firm role in the industry. The defendants were a wholly owned subsidiary of a U.S. parent company, whose sole shareholders and directors were a husband and wife. They were also the sole directors of the defendant subsidiary.

As to aggregate data on the United Kingdom music industry, unfortunately the British Census of Production does not disaggregate the numbers of firms or concentration data for either the music-publishing industry or the record-manufacturing industry.However, to cite suggestive figures, Billboard's 1975–76 International Buyer's Guide lists 428 United Kingdom music publishers (after consolidating affiliates). While the defendants in *Macaulay* appear to have been only in the music-publishing business significant integration between music publishing and record manufacturing has occurred, so that figures on record manufacturers are also worth citing. Billboard lists 276 United Kingdom record and tape manufacturers/distributors/importers (after consolidating affiliates and multiple labels) and 54 independent record producers. These numbers appear to suggest a dynamic and highly competitive music industry, probably comprising more competing firms than several of the industries cited in Lord Diplock's first category.

Because experience has shown that industry type tends to generate similar industry structures across industrialized economics, patterns in the United States music industry are worth brief mention. In 1965, an executive of a United States music publishing house, in a description of the industry, said that there are 'thousands' of music-publishing firms in the United States, one of the reasons being that they can be started up with very little capital:many attorneys know that often the only space required is a file drawer in their office and a telephone answering service. The industry was described as highly volatile, with a large annual turnover of firms. Billboard's 1975–76 International Buyer's Guide lists 1,466 United States music publishers (after consolidating affiliates), 1,027 record manufacturers (after consolidating affili-ates and multiple labels), and 404 independent record producers.

It is important that the potential breadth of the decision in *Macaulay* be fully appreciated. Treating standard forms as being merely symptomatic of what Lord Diplock found ultimately objectionable in this case, that is, the exercise of abnormal market-power, the decision, in its broadest construction, appears to be enunciating the rule that any exercise of abnormal market-power, whatever its transactional form, is *prima facie* reviewable by the courts in a civil action.

The intent of the doctrine of inequality of bargaining power, at least as it emerges from *Macaulay*, is clearly to redistribute contractual incidents between contracting parties, for example, to make it less costly for songwriters to secure publishers' services and more costly for publishers to provide them, in other words to adjust the relative values exchanged. What will be its effect?

This is most easily considered by taking two polar market models:a perfectly competitive market and a monopolized market. By assumption, in a perfectly competitive market both for the final product and for intermediate inputs, no excess profits are being made (that is, no profits beyond a reasonable return on capital), so that any reduction in industry profits will also induce a reduction in output and thus intermediate inputs (for example, the work of unknown songwriters). The response of firms in such a market to a cost-increasing rule (for example, all contracts terminate on non-publication) will be offset this cost increase with an appropriate reduction in the prices they are willing to pay for songwriters' ser-vices as a factor input in the production of music or records. In the music-publishing industry, the most obvious way of reducing the price paid for songwriters' services is for firms to cut their royalty rates. Alternatively, or in addition, because of the reduced prospect now of returns on successful composers' efforts (because of greater ease of contractual termination) publishers in their turn will presumably find it no longer rational to make the same investment in promoting unknown songwriters. Probably they will 'carry' high risks for shorter periods before setting them adrift. If this is what unknown songwriters were really demanding, why had not some publishers in the market already found it in their interests to meet that demand? If, going further than regulating termination provisions, royalty rates were also frozen at their previous level by an additional rule, firms would then reduce their demand for this class of writer, perhaps partly substituting the services of more established songwriters by paying them more to produce more, or the services of 'unknown' songwriters from other jurisdictions. Indeed, at the limit, music publishers may demand that composers compensate them directly for their promotional efforts on a composer's behalf, thus inducing a composer (rather than a publisher), in effect, to make an invest-ment in human capital by securing at his own expense the services of an agent (a common arrangement in other contexts). In other words, any attempt to regulate the full wage (that is, the normal wage plus other, non-explicit, 'wage' terms of the contract which regulate returns to the recipient) payable to unknown songwriters will operate like a minimum wage law, perhaps benefiting some writers whose services continue to be retained, and prejudicing others whose services are displaced by substitution away from them and towards other factors of production. The lesson of economics, in this context, is that legal liability rules are unlikely to be able to affect the broad balance of advantage between buyers and sellers.

If the market for the final products of songwriters' service is monopolized, the analysis changes little. A single music-publisher acting as a monopolist in the sale of a songwriter's output is also likely to respond to a cost-increasing rule (for example, termination on non-publication) by reducing royalties or 'carry' periods. He has limited ability (depending on the price elasticity of demand and supply for his product) to pass on increased costs to consumers of the final product, and thus has an incentive to min-imize costs similar to firms in a competitive industry. Even assuming supra-competitive profits, further rules which proscribe reductions in royalty rates or other contract variations (that is, increase the full wage to songwriters) will generate similar economic incentives to those facing firms in a competitive industry to make substitutions of other factors. Even the relatively enlightened decision in *Henningsen* fails to address the likely response of automobile manufacturers (assuming monopoly power) to imposed warranty terms of greater stringency than those previously prevailing and whether consumers end up any further ahead in the light of that response.

Only in the situation where a music publisher is acting as a monosonist (that is, sole buyer) of song-writers'factor-inputs in the production of the final products being marketed by the publisher could rules imposing an increase in the full wage payable to songwriters avoid displacement effects. But problems of identifying such a factor market and of determining the magnitude of an imposed wage increase which is possible without creating displacement effects are acute.

In short, to attempt comprehensive wage rate regulation and control over employment of factors by judicial fiat in an industry like the music publishing industry, with many firms and substantial product differentiation, would make the acknowledged problems of public-utility regulation look easy. But anything short of this is like squeezing putty.

It is submitted that the difficulties exemplified in the decision in *Macaulay v Schroeder Publishing Co* suggest extreme caution on the part of courts in withholding contract enforcement on the grounds of inequality of bargaining power involving alleged abuses of market-wide monopoly power. First, inferences of such monopolies are frequently likely to be drawn incorrectly by the courts. Secondly, even where correctly drawn, the courts do not have at their disposal the remedial instruments required to foreclose all second-order, substitution, effects.

The doctrine of restraint of trade has been applied not only to new types of contract but also to other forms of restriction. In *Pharmaceutical Society of Great Britain v Dickinson* [1970] AC 403, the appellant society was the professional body of registered pharmacists. The society had a code of practice that laid down guidance on professional conduct. The society was concerned about the increased selling of non-pharmaceutical goods in chemists' shops and proposed a new ethical rule, which was approved by a majority of those attending a specially convened meeting of members. This rule would limit the range of goods that could be sold in existing pharmacies and require new pharmacies to be in physically distinct premises. The respondent, a member, brought an action for a declaration that the motion was ultra vires and contrary to public policy. The Society made no attempt to justify the rule but argued that the restraint of trade doctrine did not apply to rules of professional conduct. The House of Lords rejected the argument and declared the rule invalid. (On restraint of trade generally, see Trebilcock, *The Common Law Doctrine of Restraint of Trade*).

A covenant that is in restraint of trade and which has not been shown to be reasonable is void. What is the effect on the rest of the contract? If the covenant forms the major part of the contract, the whole contract will be void. If, as more usually happens, the covenant is a subsidiary part, the covenant is void but the rest of the contract is unaffected.

In *Bennett v Bennett* [1952] 1 KB 249, CA, a case involving a wife's covenant not to apply to the court for maintenance, Denning LJ said:

. . . In solving this problem a useful analogy may be drawn from covenants in unreasonable restraint of trade. Such covenants offend public policy, just as the covenants of a wife not to apply to the courts may do. They are not 'illegal', in the sense that a contract to do a prohibited or immoral act is illegal. They are 'unenforceable', in the sense that a contract within the Statute of Frauds is unenforceable for want of writing. These covenants lie somewhere in between. They are invalid and unenforceable. The law does not punish them. It simply takes no notice of them. They are void, not illegal. That is how they were described by the full Court of Exchequer Chamber in *Price v Green*, and by the Court of Appeal in *Evans & Co v Heathcote*.

The presence of a void covenant of the kind does not render the deed totally ineffective. That has been well shown by Professor Cheshire and Mr Fifoot in their book on Contracts, 2nd ed, pp 242–3. The party who is entitled to the benefit of the void covenant, or rather who would have been entitled to the benefit of it if it had been valid, can sue upon the other covenants of the deed which are in his favour; and he can even sue upon the void covenant, if he can sever the good from the bad *(Goldsoll v Goldman)*, even to the extent of getting full liquidated damages for a breach of the good part: *Price v Green.* So also the other party, that is, the party who gave the void covenant and is not bound by its restraints, can himself sue upon the covenants in his favour, save only when his void covenant forms the whole, or substantially the whole, consideration for the deed. If the void covenant goes only to part of the consideration, so that it can be ignored and yet leave the rest of the deed a reasonable arrangement between the parties, then the deed stands and can be enforced in every respect save in regard to the void covenant. That seems to me to be the explanation of *Bishop v Kitchen, Kearney v Whitehaven Colliery Co* and *Czarnikow v Roth, Schmidt & Co.*

A second question concerns the internal reformation of an invalid provision. Suppose a covenantee in a restraint of trade case could have enforced a reasonable restraint but the actual restraint is wider than reasonable. Will the court sever the unreasonable from the reasonable? In *Mason v Provident Clothing* (see p 1106), it will be remembered that the court refused to rewrite the covenant to make it reasonable. What if the covenant could be made reasonable by simply striking out parts of it 'with a blue pencil', as is the phrase? (The expression 'blue pencil' was first used by Kipling in the 1890s to refer to the activities of a censor simply striking out material that was objectionable. The censor did not, of course, rewrite material. The authors would be grateful to any reader who can explain why the pencil was blue.)

■ *Goldsoll v Goldman*
[1915] 1 Ch 292, CA

Lord Cozens-Hardy MR

This is an appeal from Neville J. and the question is whether a covenant entered into between Goldsoll and Goldman is unreasonable as it stands, and, if it is, whether it is severable, so that it may be good in part and bad in part. The plaintiffs are carrying on the business of dealers in imitation jewellery. They do not carry on business in real jewellery, and I say this although some of the articles they deal in are made of real gold in which Tecla pearls are set and occasionally the pearls are set in small diamonds. Substantially the business is in imitation jewellery. In 1912 Goldman was carrying on a business in competition with Goldsoll, and the agreement in question was entered into with the object of putting an end to the competition. There was ample consideration for the agreement, and by the clause of the deed which we have to consider Goldman covenanted with Goldsoll that he would not for a period of ten years (which was reduced by a subsequent agreement to two years) 'either solely or jointly with or as agent or employee for any person or company directly or indirectly carry on or be interested in the business of a vendor of or dealer in real or imitation jewellery in the county of London, England, Scotland, Ireland, Wales, or any part of the United Kingdom of Great Britain and Ireland and the Isle of Man or in France, the United States of America, Russia or Spain, or within twenty-five miles of Potsdamerstrasse, Berlin, or St Stefans Kirche, Vienna.' Notwithstanding this covenant Goldman has, according to the finding of the learned judge, been assisting and rendering services to a confederate who is carrying on a business identical to that of the plaintiffs in the same street. It is perfectly clear that there has been a breach of the covenant; but that is not conclusive of the case, for what we have to consider is whether the covenant he has broken can be treated as good either in whole or in part, and can be enforced. On the question of the space covered by the covenant Neville J has held, and I entirely agree with him, that it is unnecessarily large in so far as it is intended to cover not merely the United Kingdom and the Isle of Man but also the foreign countries mentioned in the covenant. he has also held, and his decision is consistent with a long series of authorities, that the covenant can be severed as regards the space covered by it. It is clear that part of the covenant dealing with the area is reasonable, and the learned judge has limited the injunction he has granted to 'the county of London, England, Scotland, Ireland, Wales, or any part of the United Kingdom of Great Britain and Ireland and the Isle of Man.' That such a covenant is severable in this respect has been decided by authorities nearly 200 years old. No objection is taken or could be taken with regard to the limit of time, but the further difficulty has been raised that, while the business of the plaintiffs was, as I said, a business in imitation jewellery, the covenant is against carrying on or being interested in 'the business of a vendor of or dealer in real or imitation jewellery'. It is admitted that the business of a dealer in real jewellery is not the same as that of a dealer in imitation jewellery. There are many shopkeepers who would be insulted if they were asked whether they sold imitation jewellery. That being so, it is difficult to support the whole of this provision, for the covenant must be limited to what is reasonably necessary for the protection of the covenantee's business. Then comes the question whether the doctrine of severability is applicable to this part of the covenant. In my opinion it is, and the covenant is good in so far as it operates to restrain the covenantor from carrying on business in imitation jewellery.

Swinfen Eady and **Kennedy LJJ** delivered concurring judgments.

Appeal dismissed.

■ *Attwood v Lamont*
[1920] 3 KB 571, CA

Younger LJ

...[T]he position appears to be that the respondent is the owner of a considerable business at Kidderminster, described in the agreement in question as a business of drapers, tailors and general outfitters. The business is, I presume for convenience, divided into different departments all under the same roof, customers going from one to another, and many customers dealing in all departments. The agreement into which the appellant entered, a printed form which all managers of departments are required to sign with modifications of salary and detail appropriate to the individual case, is indorsed as 'An agreement not to trade in opposition with a radius of 10 miles of Regent House, Kidderminster', and contains a recital 'that the assistant', the appellant, 'has requested the employers to employ him as an assistant in their business at Kidderminster at an annual salary commencing at 208/ and two and a half per cent commission on turnover above 1000/ in tailoring department and the employers are only willing to do so upon his entering into the agreement not to trade in opposition with him which is hereinafter expressed' and witnesses 'that in consideration of the employers employing him in the capacity and the salary aforesaid...he will not at any time thereafter...carry on or be in any way directly or indirectly concerned in any of the following trades or businesses, that is to say, the trade or business of a tailor, dressmaker, general draper, milliner, hatter, haberdasher, gentlemen's ladies' or children's outfitter at any place, within a radius of 10 miles of the employers' place of business at Regent House, Kidderminster, aforesaid.' The agreement is expressed to be and is, in my opinion, nothing more than an agreement not to trade in opposition with the employers in any part of their business. It will be broken if the appellant not only carries on but is directly or indirectly concerned in any of the specified businesses; and the period of restriction is to cover the whole life of the appellant, although the employment was itself an employment only for a month certain...

...That evidence confirms me in the conclusion which I should have drawn from the case generally, that it is the appellant's known personal skill as a cutter which attracts to him the customers to whom he attended when with the respondent, and except that they made his acquaintance when he was in the respondent's service, it was not his position there, but it is his own skill which leads them to desire to have the continued benefit of his services, now that he is in business for himself. The question accordingly is whether in these circumstances, and in view of the principles applicable to them enunciated by the House of Lords, this covenant has any validity. In my opinion, as I have already said, it has none. It was apparently strongly urged in the Divisional Court that the covenant was valid as it stands. The learned judges there held that extending to businesses with which the appellant had had no connection when in the respondent's employment it was manifestly too wide, and they so held.

But the learned judges held also that they were entitled to sever the covenant by limiting it to the business of a tailor, and this they did.

Now I agree with the Master of the Rolls that this was not a case in which upon any principle this severance was permissible. The learned judges of the Divisional Court. I think, took the view that such severance always was permissible when it could be effectively accomplished by the action of a blue pencil. I do not agree. The doctrine of severance has not, I think, gone further than to make it permissible in a case where the covenant is not really a single covenant but is in effect a combination of several distinct covenants. In that case and where the severance can be carried out without the addition or alteration of a word, it is permissible. But in that case only.

Now, here, I think, there is in truth but one covenant for the protection of the respondent's entire business, and not several covenants for the protection of his several businesses. The respondent is, on the evidence, not carrying on several businesses but one business, and, in my opinion, this covenant must stand or fall in its unaltered form.

But, further, I am of opinion that even if this were not so this case is not one in which any severance, even if otherwise technically permissible, ought to be made. In my view the necessary effect of the application of the principle on which *Mason's Case* and *Morris v Saxelby* have both been decided has been to render obsolete the cases in which the Courts have severed these restrictive covenants when acting on the view that being prima facie valid it was their duty to bind the covenantee to them as far as was permissible.

Lord Sterndale MR delivered a judgment to the same effect. **Atkin LJ** concurred.

Appeal allowed.

NOTES

1.   What is the distinction between these two cases?

2.   For further discussion, see Marsh 'The Severance of Illegality in Contract' (1948) 64 LQR 230 and 347.

QUESTIONS

1.   Discuss the rules as to the severance of invalid from valid clauses in contracts.

2.   'As the whole doctrine of restraint of trade is based on public policy its application ought to depend less on legal niceties or theoretical possibilities than on the practical effect of a restraint in hampering that freedom which it is the policy of the law to protect.' (Lord Reid)

      How successful has the common law been in developing techniques to attain this end?

3.   One month ago, S bought a commercial vehicle at an auction. By the Auction Regulations 1976, 'No person shall on his own behalf or on behalf of any other person buy or sell a motor vehicle at an auction sale other than one covered by a licence issued in accordance with these regulations'. No such licence had been issued for the auction. S hired the vehicle to G for six months and directed the auctioneer to let G collect the vehicle. S knew that G intended to use it to transport loads that transport regulations would not permit him to carry on it. G collected the vehicle, but has now discovered that

the local police are suspicious of his operations and are checking consignments carried by him. G refuses to pay S or to return the vehicle. Advise S.

4. C is the owner of Blackacre. He sells it to the D Petrol Company Ltd and takes a leaseback for 99 years. It is a term of the lease that for the period of the lease C shall only sell D's petrol on Blackacre. Six months after signing of the lease, C starts to sell E Ltd's petrol on the site. Advise D Ltd.

5. Suppose that on 1 February this year an Order was made under statutory authority requiring a deposit of 25 per cent in certain hire-purchase contracts, and a maximum period of two years. On 2 February, Electrical Appliances Ltd entered into a contract with Jones under which Jones took a washing machine on hire purchase, paying a deposit of 15 per cent and the balance by instalments over three years. In May, Jones ceased to pay his instalments and refused to return the machine. Advise Electrical Appliances Ltd on the two following separate assumptions:
   (a) both parties acted in ignorance of the fact that the Order, which undoubtedly applies to the machine in question, had been made;
   (b) the Order applies to new machines only; the manager of Electrical Appliances Ltd told Jones—untruthfully—that the machine was second-hand.

6. In 1945, A took out a policy of life insurance with the B Life Insurance Co Ltd. The policy provided for payment of yearly premiums over a period of 30 years. On 1 March 1992, A committed suicide while sane. Advise the estate of A.

7. Because of the low price of its shares on the Stock Exchange, the directors of the C Co Ltd fear a takeover bid from the D Co Ltd. So as to raise the price of the shares and reduce the chances of a successful bid, they decided to buy shares themselves. They each pay £10,000 to X, the managing director, who buys shares on the market in his own name. X refuses to account for the shares or the money. Advise the directors.

8. G is a cut-price trader, who habitually omits to disclose part of his cash income to HMRC. He offers goods to J, who knows this. J agrees to pay £3,000 for goods, and after taking delivery, offers a cheque. G refuses the cheque and demands cash. J refuses to pay. Advise G.

9. A visits the offices of Express Transportation Services in Exeter at 9.30 am on Monday morning. After negotiations, an agreement is reached at 10.00 am that a goods lorry belonging to Express Transportation Services will carry a cargo of coal to Newcastle on Tyne, which is approximately 360 miles from Exeter, delivery to be by 9.00 pm on Monday. All lorries belonging to Express Transportation Services have a maximum speed of 30 mph under the Road Traffic Act 1960, Sch 1. The coal is safely delivered on time but A refuses to pay. Advise Express Transportation Services.

10. A agrees to pay B £500 for B's car and information about trade secrets of B's employer C. B does not deliver the car or provide the information. Advise A.

INTERMEDIARIES, THIRD PARTIES AND ASSIGNMENT

CHAPTER FORTY-FIVE

AGENCY

This section examines the problems that arise in contract law when more than two parties are involved in the making of a contract, or the contract affects more than the immediate parties to it. These cases involve not only contract law but also its relationship to the law of tort and the law of property, and the various rules must be considered together if the functioning of the law is to be understood properly.

We have already seen many contracts that involve agents. The vast majority of contracts are made by agents, at least on one side, because, of course, a company can only contract through agents. A complete study of the law of agency is too complex to be covered adequately in a basic contract course. This chapter will merely introduce four fundamental points: the legal effect of the normal situation where a properly authorised agent makes a contract explicitly on behalf of his principal; the types of authority; the consequences of lack of authority; and the doctrine of the undisclosed principal.

I. INTERMEDIARY OR PARTY?

When a properly authorised agent makes a contract on behalf of his principal, the normal position is that the agent can neither sue nor be sued on the contract, which is between the principal and the third party. However, it is not always clear whether a person was contracting as agent or on his own behalf, or both simultaneously. In *The Swan* [1968] 1 Lloyd's Rep 5, the defendant J D Rodger owned the fishing vessel *Swan*, which he hired to J D Rodger Ltd. The two plaintiffs had carried out repairs to *Swan* on instructions, some of which were oral and some on company notepaper signed 'J D Rodger, Director'. The plaintiffs sent their accounts to the company, which was unable to pay them. Brandon J said that whether J D Rodger was liable as well as the company depended on the intentions of the parties, to be gathered from the words of the agreement and the circumstances. He continued:

Where such words are not used but the person is merely stated to be an agent, or the word 'agent' is just added after his signature, the result is uncertain, because it is not clear whether the word is used as a qualification or merely as a description: see *Gadd v Houghton and another*, per Lord Justice James; and *Universal Steam Navigation Company, Ltd v James McKelvie & Co*, per Lord Sumner. In general it would seem that in such a case the person does not avoid personal liability, although there may be exceptions to this general rule depending on the other terms of the contract or the surrounding circumstances.

Brandon J held that this case was near the borderline, but that Rodger was personally liable:

> [W]hen a person who is known or correctly assumed to be the owner of a boat, has discussions with a repairing company's manager about repairs to her, it is natural for the manager to assume that, if an order for the repairs is placed, that person will accept personal liability for them as such owner unless he makes the contrary clear beyond doubt.

In contrast, see *The Santa Carina* [1977] 1 Lloyd's Rep 478, CA.

In *The Swan*, the result was that both the company and the defendant were liable. Where more than one party is liable on one side of a contract, the liabilities can be of various types, and if the contract makes no express provision, the court will have to construe it to decide which was 'intended'. If there are really two separate debts, so that the creditor is entitled to be paid in full by both, the liability is called 'several'. Clearly, that was not the situation in *The Swan*. If the creditor is only entitled to a single payment, the liability may be 'joint' or 'joint and several'. Joint liability involves a number of technical rules: in particular, all of the parties jointly liable must be joined in any action, and on the death of one joint party, his liability passes to the other(s). It might be sensible to construe some contracts as having this effect, for instance, when the joint debtors were co-trustees, but liability will more often be construed as joint and several, so that the creditor is entitled to payment once only but the technical rules of joint liability do not apply. The court may also have to decide whether the two parties on one side of the contract were *entitled* severally, jointly or jointly and severally: thus had the repairs to *Swan* been carried out defectively or late, the court might have had to decide whether Rodger and the company were each entitled to damages for their separate losses, or, if only one set of damages were payable, whether they were payable to them jointly or jointly and severally. It seems likely that Rodger and the company were liable and entitled jointly and severally; it would be inconvenient, for instance, if the company could not be sued or sue without joining Rodger as co-defendant or co-plaintiff.

Sometimes it will be clear that one party is an agent but unclear on whose behalf he acts. So many insurance contracts are arranged through intermediaries but it is often unclear for which side the intermediary acts. This can be very important. For instance, is information disclosed by the insured to the intermediary to be treated as revealed to the insurer?

The parties may agreee expressly or impliedly that an agent shall act for both sides (agreement would usually be necessary because an agent for one side cannot properly accept payment from the other). A common example is a standard mortgage under which the same solicitors often act for both lender and borrower. Where everything goes smoothly, this probably saves money, but if things go wrong, the lender will often argue that the solicitors ought to have alerted them to suspicious behaviour by the borrower. See, for example, *Mortgage Express Ltd v Bowerman & Partners* [1996] 2 All ER 836 and see *Hilton v Barker, Booth and Eastwood* [2005] UKHL8, [2005] 1 All ER 651, above, p 530.

II. TYPES OF AUTHORITY

It is usually said that there are four types of authority: express, implied, ostensible (or apparent) and usual. Express authority needs no comment. Implied authority is authority to do all that is reasonable incidental to achieving what was expressly authorised, or authority by custom: in either case, it may be expressly negatived or limited by the principal. Ostensible authority is a form of estoppel: if the principal, by words or conduct, indicates that a person has authority to act on his behalf, and the third party contracts with the agent on that basis, the principal is estopped from denying the agent's authority even if, in fact, the agent was unauthorised. Usual authority applies only where there is an 'undiscovered principal' and will be dealt with in sub section IV.

■ *Waugh v H B Clifford and Sons Ltd*
[1982] 1 All ER 1095, CA

The buyers of two houses brought an action against the builders claiming damages. Negotiations took place between the parties' solicitors over a compromise under which the builders would repurchase the houses at their current value (disregarding the alleged defects), that value to be fixed by an independent valuer. The builders' solicitors informed their clients of this proposal and stated that they would appoint a valuer unless they received contrary instructions. The builders telephoned instructions not to proceed, but the instructions did not reach the relevant partner until after he had agreed to proceed with the compromise, which the builders then claimed was not binding on them. The buyers obtained specific performance of the repurchase agreement and the builders appealed.

Brightman LJ

... The law thus became well established that the solicitor or counsel retained in an action has an *implied* authority as between himself and his client to compromise the suit without reference to the client, provided that the compromise does not involve matter 'collateral to the action'; and *ostensible* authority, as between himself and the opposing litigant, to compromise the suit without actual proof of authority, subject to the same limitations; and the court could not have ordered by way of judgment in the action: for example, the return of the piano in *Prestwich v Poley*, the withdrawal of the imputations in *Matthews v Munster* and the highly complicated terms of the compromise in *Little v Spreadbury*.

In none of the cases cited to us has there been any debate on the question whether the implied authority of the advocate or solicitor as between himself and his client is necessarily as extensive as the ostensible authority of the advocate or solicitor vis-à-vis the opposing litigant. The possibility of a difference seems to have been adverted to by Byles J in *Prestwich v Poley.* In my judgment there is every reason to draw a distinction.

Suppose that a defamation action is on foot; that terms of compromise are discussed; and that the defendant's solicitor writes to the plaintiff's solicitor offering to compromise at a figure of £100,000, which the plaintiff desires to accept. It would in my view by officious on the part of the plaintiff's solicitor to demand to be satisfied as to the authority of the defendant's solicitor to make the offer. It is perfectly clear that the defendant's solicitor has *ostensible* authority to compromise on behalf of his client, notwithstanding the large sum involved. It is not incumbent on the plaintiff to seek the signature of the defendant, if an individual, or the seal of the defendant if a corporation, or the signature of a director.

But it does not follow that the defendant's solicitor would have *implied* authority to agree damages on that scale without the agreement of his client. In the light of the solicitor's knowledge of his client's cash position it might be quite unreasonable and indeed grossly negligent for the solicitor to commit his client to such a burden without first inquiring if it were acceptable. But that does not affect the *ostensible* authority of the solicitor to compromise, so as to place the plaintiff at risk if he fails to satisfy himself that the defendant's solicitor has sought the agreement of his client. Such a limitation on the ostensible authority of the solicitor would be unworkable. How is the opposing litigant to estimate on which side of the line a particular case falls?

It follows in my view that a solicitor (or counsel) may in a particular case have ostensible authority vis-à-vis the opposing litigant where he has no implied authority vis-à-vis his client. I see no objection to that. All that the opposing litigant need ask himself when testing the ostensible authority of the solicitor or counsel, is the question whether the compromise contains matter 'collateral to the suit'. The magnitude of the compromise, or the burden which its terms impose on the other party, is irrelevant. But much more than that question may need to be asked by a solicitor when deciding whether he can safely compromise without reference to his client.

If I am right so far, all that has to be considered in the present appeal, which concerns *ostensible* and not *implied* authority, is whether the repurchase of the allegedly defective dwelling houses is properly to be described as matter collateral to the action. For the buyers and their solicitors had no notice of any limitation imposed by the builders on the *ostensible* authority of the builders' solicitors . . . .

I think it would be regrettable if this court were to place too restrictive a limitation on the *ostensible* authority of solicitors and counsel to bind their clients to a compromise. I do not think we should decide that matter is 'collateral' to the action unless it really involves extraneous subject matter . . . .

I can see no difference, except in degree and in the importance of the subject matter, between this case and the case of the sale of an imperfect chattel. In an action for damages by the purchase of a defective chattel, it would be within the *ostensible* authority of the vendor's solicitor to agree terms of compromise involving the handing back of the defective chattel in exchange for the price paid. So it was within the *ostensible* authority of the solicitor in the present case to agree terms of compromise which involved the handing back of the defective houses in return for a price reflecting their current value in proper condition . . . .

I wish to emphasise that I am not saying that the terms of the compromise in the present case would have been within the *implied* authority of the builders' solicitors . . . . I would dismiss the appeal.

Cumming Bruce and **Ackner LJJ** agreed.

Appeal dismissed.

NOTE

Brightman LJ contrasts the ostensible authority of the solicitors as between themselves and the buyers with their implied authority as between themselves and the client. What does the latter mean? To put the same question another way, would the builders have any claim against the solicitors, and if so, why?

An act performed by an agent who did not have authority at the time may be ratified later by the principal, with retroactive effect: thus if, in the meanwhile, the third party has repudiated or broken the contract, the principal has an action against him. On the other hand, it has been held that at common law a principal that was not in existence at the time the agent made the contract cannot subsequently ratify, so that a newly incorporated company cannot ratify prior contracts made by its promoters: *Kelner v Baxter* (1866) LR 2 CP 174. (The contract will take effect as one between the third party and the promoter: Companies Act 1985, s 36C.) Also, the principal cannot ratify if, at the time of purported ratification, it could not validly have made the contract itself: thus a principal cannot ratify a contract of insurance after the loss has occurred (*Grover & Grover Ltd v Mathews* [1910] 2 KB 401); for an exception, see the Marine Insurance Act 1906, s 86. For a further restriction, see pp 1161–1162.

III. THE UNAUTHORISED AGENT

■ *Yonge v Toynbee*

[1910] 1 KB 215, CA

The defendant instructed solicitors to conduct his defence in an action by the plaintiff. Subsequently, the defendant was certified as being of unsound mind but the solicitors did not know this; they entered an appearance on his behalf and took various subsequent steps. When the plaintiff was informed of the certification, she successfully applied for the appearance and subsequent steps to be struck out, and she also applied for an order that the defendant's solicitors should pay her costs to date on the ground that the solicitors had acted without authority. This the master refused and the judge in chambers affirmed the refusal.

Buckley LJ

... The interesting and important question in this case is as to the extent to which the principle of *Smout v Ilbery* remains good law after the decision in *Collen v Wright*. I understand *Smout v Ilbery* to hold that ... where [the agent] originally had authority, but that authority has ceased without his having knowledge, or means of knowledge, that it has ceased he is not liable ... I can see no distinction in principle between the case where the agent never had authority and the case where the agent originally had authority, but that authority has ceased without his knowledge or means of knowledge. In the latter case as much as in the former proposition, I think, is true that without any mala fides he has at the moment of acting represented that he had an authority which in fact he had not. In my opinion he is then liable on an implied contract that he had authority, whether there was fraud or not. That this is the true principle is, I think, shewn by passages which I will quote from judgments in three which I have selected out of the numerous cases upon this subject. In *Collen v Wright* Willes J in giving the judgment of the Court uses the following language: 'I am of opinion that a person who induces another to contract with him, as the agent of a third party, by an unqualified assertion of his being authorized to act as such agent, is answerable to the person who so contracts for any damages which he may sustain by reason of the assertion of authority being untrue. . . . The fact that the professed agent honestly thinks that he has authority affects the moral character of his act; but his moral innocence, so far as the person whom he has induced to contract, in no way aids such person or alleviates the inconvenience and damage which he sustains. The obligation arising in such a case is well expressed by saying that a person professing to contract as agent for another, impliedly, if not expressly, undertakes to or promises the person who enters into such contract, upon the faith of the professed agent being duly authorized, that the authority which he professes to have does in point of fact exist.' This language is equally applicable to each of the two classes of cases to which I have referred. The language is not, in my opinion, consistent with maintaining that which *Smout v Ilbery* had laid down as the true principle, that there must be some wrong or omission of right on the part of the agent in order to make him liable. The question is not as to his honesty or bona fides. His liability arises from an implied undertaking or promise made by him that the authority which he professes to have does in point of fact exist. I can see no difference of principle between the case in which the authority never existed at all and the case in which the authority once existed and has ceased to exist ....

This implied contract may, of course, be excluded by the facts of the particular case. If, for instance, the agent proved that at the relevant time he told the party with whom he was contracting that he did not know whether the warrant of attorney under which he was acting was genuine or not, and would not warrant its validity, or that his principal was abroad and he did not know whether he was still living, there will have been no representation upon which the implied contract will arise. This may have been the ratio decided in *Smout v Ilbery* as expressed in the passage 'The continuance of the life of the principal was, under these circumstances, a fact equally within the knowledge of both contracting parties'; and this seems to be the ground upon which *Story on Agency*, s 265a, approves the decision. The husband had left England for China in May, 1839, a time in the history of the world when communication was not what it is now, and the Court seems to have decided upon the ground that the butcher who supplied the goods knew that the facts were such that the wife did not, because she could not, take upon herself to affirm that he was alive. If so, there was no implied contract.

For these reasons I think that the appellant is entitled to succeed and to have an order against the solicitors for damages, and the measure of damage is, no doubt, the amount of the plaintiff's costs thrown away in the action. The appeal, therefore, should be allowed with costs here and below.

Swinfen Eady J delivered judgment to the same effect and **Vaughan Williams LJ** concurred.

Appeal allowed.

NOTES

1.   The agent who is made liable on an implied warranty of authority is not liable as if he were principal: he is liable for the loss of rights against the principal. This was explained by Brett MR in *Re National Coffee Palace Co, ex p Panmure* (1883) 24 Ch D 367, at 371–372, thus:

> . . . It has been held that when a person in error assumes that he has authority to make a contract for a principal when he is not really his principal, by assuming that he had authority to bind the principal, he warrants that he had that authority which he represented himself to have. The contract in respect of which damages are claimed is not the contract which the principal would have made, but only a contract to the extent of the warranty. That is shewn clearly by *Collen v Wright*. He contracts that he had authority to bind the principal whereas he had no such authority . . . . the measure of damages [is] what the plaintiff actually lost by losing the particular contract which was to have been made by the alleged principal if the defendant had had the authority he professed to have; in other words, what the plaintiff would have gained by the contract which the defendant warranted should be made. If that be the measure of damages, it does not depend upon the amount which would have been awarded to him in an action against the alleged principal if the contract had been broken by him; that may not be the same amount as what the plaintiff has actually lost. We may test it in this way. If the action were brought against the principal because he had broken the contract, the amount actually recovered would be quite different if he were solvent than if he were insolvent; if he were solvent the plaintiff would recover the whole loss, if he were insolvent he might not recover a shilling.

2.   Atiyah, *Essays on Contract*, 1986, pp 209–210, comments:

> It is sometimes argued that cases of implied warranty are not 'really' contractual at all; such cases are in fact actions for misrepresentation and would have been brought in tort if the law of torts had been more willing to recognize liability for misrepresentation at an earlier date. There is a germ of truth in this inasmuch as the 'promise' in many actions of this kind is plainly a fiction; the desired result is to impose liability on the agent and this is done by implying a promise. But the explanation is nevertheless not wholly acceptable. For one thing, the liability of the agent is strict; he is liable as for a warranty, and not merely for negligence. Secondly, the measure of damages awarded in these cases is plainly the measure appropriate to contract and not tort; for instance, the plaintiff can recover for loss of his profit in the *Collen v Wright* situation. I now think that these two rules (certainly the second) are mistaken deductions from the assumption that the case of action ought to be treated as contractual, rather than as tortious, but all this goes to show how expansive the concept of contract is, and what uses it has been put to. If contract can be usefully used to enforce a tortious liability, then it is not surprising if difficulty is found in squeezing all contracts into the concept of bargain.

IV. THE UNDISCLOSED PRINCIPAL

There is nothing to stop an agent contracting explicitly on someone else's behalf without naming his principal. The third party may not be worried about who the principal is, and if it does concern him, he can, of course, refuse to contract without the identity of the principal being revealed. What, however, if the agent appears to contract in his own name but is, in fact, acting on behalf of an 'undisclosed' principal? Under a doctrine that common lawyers usually regard as anomalous, the principal can both sue and be sued on the contract, unless to permit this would be inconsistent with the express terms of the contract or the contract involves some personal element. Thus in *Said v Butt* [1920] 3 KB 497, the plaintiff wished to attend the opening night of a play but knew that the management would refuse an application for a ticket made in his own name because he had made serious and unfounded allegations against members of the theatre staff. He therefore arranged for a friend to buy the ticket without disclosing that it was for the plaintiff. The plaintiff was refused admission to the theatre on the orders of the defendant, the managing director, and the plaintiff claimed damages from him for maliciously procuring a breach of a contract between the plaintiff and the theatre. McCardie J held that the contract for a ticket to the first night was one involving a personal element and that, as the theatre would not have contracted with the plaintiff directly, he could not claim to be an undisclosed principal and could not claim that any breach of contract between him and the theatre had been caused. (Compare *Dyster v Randall & Sons* [1926] Ch 932.)

■ *Keighley, Maxsted & Co v Durant*

[1900–3] All ER Rep 40, HL

The following statement of facts is taken from the opinion of **Lord Brampton:**

The appellants, Keighley, Maxsted & Co, were corn merchants at Hull, and one Wright was their manager and agent. Durant, the respondent, was a corn merchant in London, trading as Bryan, Durant & Co, and one Roberts was a corn merchant at Wakefield. On the morning of May 11, 1898, Roberts received from Durant's brokers a telegram containing an offer from Durant of 500 tons of new white Karachi wheat at 46s per quarter and 500 tons of red wheat at 45s per quarter. Later on the same morning Roberts had an interview with Wright, and told him of Durant's offer, and they agreed that, if Roberts could get the wheat at 45s 3d for the white and 44s 3d for the red, Roberts and Keighleys would become the purchasers on joint account. Roberts, however, was unable to get the wheat at those prices; the proposal, therefore, for a purchase on joint account came to nothing. Between 3 and 4 pm on the same day, Roberts, without any further communication with or authority from Keighleys, and apparently purely on his own separate and sole account, by an interchange of telegrams with Durant's brokers, concluded a contract for the purchase by him, in his own name, from Durant of the whole of the wheat, at 45s 6d for the white and 44s 6d for the red. On the following day, May 12, Roberts met Wright casually at the Manchester Corn Market, and told him that he had bought the wheat at 3d a quarter more than the price they had settled on the previous day. Wright replied he had given too much, but he thought the wheat was worth it, and told him to take it. Roberts did so, but failing to fulfil his contract with Durant the latter sold it at a loss to recover which this action was commenced by Durant against Roberts and Keighley, Maxsted & Co jointly, upon the suggestion of Roberts that this purchase had been made on joint account. Day J, gave judgment for Keighley, Maxsted & Co, on the ground that they were not parties to the contract, and no subsequent ratification by them could make them liable to sue or be sued upon it, but his judgment was reversed by the Court of Appeal, and Keighley, Maxsted & Co now appealed to the House of Lords.

Lord Macnaghten

…As a general rule, only persons who are parties to a contract acting either by themselves or by an authorised agent can sue or be sued on the contract. A stranger cannot enforce the contract, nor can it be enforced against a stranger. That is the rule; but there are exceptions. The most remarkable exception, I think, results from the doctrine of ratification as established in English law. The doctrine is thus stated by Tindal, CJ, in *Wilson v Tumman*:

> 'That an act done, for another, by a person, not assuming to act for himself, but for such other person, though without precedent authority whatever, becomes the act of the principal, if subsequently ratified by him, is the known and well-established rule of law. In that case the principal is bound by the Act, whether it be for his detriment or his advantage, and whether it be founded on a tort or on a contract to the same effect as by, and with all the consequences which follow from, the same act done by his previous authority.'

And so by a wholesome and convenient fiction a person ratifying the act of another who without authority has made a contract openly and avowedly on his behalf, is deemed to be, though in fact he was not, a party to the contract. Does the fiction cover the case of a person who makes no avowal at all, but assumes to act for himself and for no one else? If Tindal CJ's statement of the law is accurate, it would seem to exclude the case of a person who may intend to act for another, but at the same time keeps his intentions locked up in his own breast; for it cannot be said that a person who so conducts himself does assume to act for anybody but himself.

But ought the doctrine of ratification to be extended to such a case? On principle I should say certainly not. It is, I think, a well-established principle in English law that civil obligations are not to be created by or founded upon undisclosed intentions That is a very old principle. Lord Blackburn, enforcing it in *Brogden v Metropolitan Rail* Co, traces it back to the *Year Books* of Edward IV (17 Edw 4, 2 Term Pasc) and to a quaint judgment of Brian CJ, a great authority in those days, who said:

> 'It is common learning that the thought of a man is not triable, for the Devil has not knowledge of man's thoughts.'

Sir E. Fry quotes the same observation in his work on *Specific Performance* (3rd Edn), s 282. It is, I think, a sound maxim—at least, in its legal aspect—and, in my opinion, it is not to be put aside or disregarded merely because it may be that in a case like the present no injustice might be done to the actual parties to the contract by giving effect to the undisclosed intentions of a would-be agent.

... [I]t seems to me to be conclusive against the argument for the respondent, that if his reasoning were sound it would be in his power, on an averment of what was passing in his own mind, to make the contract afterwards, either one for himself only, as in fact it was, or one affecting or binding on another as a contracting party, even although he had no authority for this. The result would be to give one of two contracting parties in his opinion, merely from what was passing in his own mind, and not disclosed, the power of saying that the contract was his alone, or a contract in which others were bound to him. That I think he certainly cannot do in any case where he had no authority when he made the contract to bind anyone but himself....

Lord Davey

... [T]he rule which permits an undisclosed principal to sue and be sued on a contract to which he is not a party, though well settled, is itself an anomaly, and to extend it to the case of a person who accepts the benefit of an undisclosed intention of a party to the contract would, in my opinion, be adding another anomaly to the law, and not correcting an anomaly.

The other members of the House delivered judgments to similar effect.

Appeal allowed.

■ *Watteau v Fenwick*

[1893] 1 QB 346

Lord Coleridge CJ

The judgment which I am about to read has been written by my brother Wills, and I entirely concur in it.

Wills J

The plaintiff sues the defendants for the price of cigars supplied to the Victoria Hotel, Stockton-upon-Tees. The house was kept, not by the defendants, but by a person named Humble, whose name was over the door. The plaintiff gave credit to Humble, and to him alone, and had never heard of the defendants. The business, however, was really the defendants', and they had put Humble into it to manage it for them, and had forbidden him to buy cigars on credit. The cigars, however, were such as would usually be supplied to and dealt in at such an establishment. The learned county court judge held that the defendants were liable. I am of opinion that he was right.

There seems to be less of direct authority on the subject than one would expect. But I think that the Lord Chief Justice during the argument laid down the correct principle, viz, once it is established that the defendant was the real principal, the ordinary doctrine as to principal and agent applies—that the principal is liable for all the acts of the agent which are within the authority usually confided to an agent of that character, notwithstanding limitations, as between the principal and the agent, put upon that authority. It is said that it is only so where there has been a holding out of authority—which cannot be said of a case where the person supplying the goods knew nothing of the existence of a principal. But I do not think so. Otherwise, in every case of undisclosed principle, or at least in every case where the fact of there being a principal was undisclosed, the secret limitation of authority would prevail and defeat the action of the person dealing with the agent and then discovering that he was an agent and had a principal.

But in the case of a dormant partner it is clear law that no limitation of authority as between the dormant and active partner will avail the dormant partner as to things within the ordinary authority of a partner. The law of partnerships is, on such a question, nothing but a branch of the general law of principal and agent, and it appears to me to be undisputed and conclusive on the point now under discussion.

The principle laid down by the Lord Chief Justice, and acted upon by the learned county court judge, appears to be identical with that enunciated in the judgments of Cockburn CJ, and Mellor J, in *Edmunds v Bushell*, the circumstances of which case, though not identical with those of the present, come very near to them. There was no holding out, as the plaintiff knew nothing of the defendant. I appreciate the distinction drawn by Mr Finlay in his argument, but the principle laid down in the judgments referred to, if correct, abundantly covers the present case. I cannot find that any doubt has ever been expressed that it is correct, and I think it is right, and that very mischievous consequences would often result if that principle were not upheld.

In my opinion this appeal ought to be dismissed with costs.

Appeal dismissed.

NOTE

Is it consistent with the approach in the *Keighley* case to make an undisclosed principal liable for something he had not actually authorised (indeed, had forbidden), when *ex hypothesi* the plaintiff knew nothing of him at the time he contracted with the agent? The correctness of this case has often been doubted, but it remains the law: see Treitel, p 723.

A third party who thought that he was dealing with the agent personally might be seriously prejudiced if he found that the agent was acting for an undisclosed principal with whom the third party would not have dealt—for instance, because he distrusted him or doubted his credit—and had no rights against the agent personally. For this reason, the case of the undisclosed principal is subject to another exceptional rule—the third party can elect to hold the agent liable rather than the principal, and the agent may sue on the contract in turn. As to what constitutes election, see *Clarkson Booker Ltd v Andjel* [1964] 2 QB 775.

CHAPTER FORTY-SIX

PRIVITY AND THE BENEFIT OF A CONTRACT BETWEEN OTHERS

We now turn to the question of the extent to which a person who is not a party to a contract can gain rights under it (the benefit) or be adversely affected by it (the burden). This chapter looks at the question of benefits under the original contract and Chapter 47 at the subsequent passing of benefits by assignment. Chapters 48 and 49 then look at questions of burdens.

WARNING. The law discussed in this chapter has been subjected to major change by the Contract (Rights of Third Parties) Act 1999. However, the Act has not abolished the doctrine of privity of contract but rather created a new and larger exception to it. The Act is discussed in detail at the end of the chapter but you need to keep its existence in mind as you read through the chapter.

The cases to be considered fall into two groups. The first group (subsections I to VII) raise the question of how a contract between A and B under which A promises to confer a benefit on C can be enforced. It would clearly be inefficient if neither B nor C could enforce the contract against A, because this would allow A to break a deliberate bargain with impunity, but which of them should be able to enforce A's promise, and how? The second group of cases (subsection VIII) involve a rather different problem: to what extent can a contract, which purports to be solely between A and B, and not to mention C, but which is to C's advantage, be enforced by him?

I. THE BASIC RULE

■ *Dunlop Pneumatic Tyre Co Ltd v Selfridge & Co Ltd*
[1915] AC 847, HL

The plaintiffs had sold some of their tyres to Dew & Co, on terms that Dews would not resell them at less than the plaintiffs' list prices and that, if they resold them to trade buyers, they would extract a similar undertaking from the trade buyers. Dews resold the tyres to Selfridge, who agreed to observe the restrictions and to pay to Dunlops £5 for each tyre sold in breach of the agreement. Selfridge supplied tyres to two of their customers at below the list price, and Dunlops sought to recover two sums of £5 each as liquidated damages.

Viscount Haldane LC

...My Lords, in the law of England, certain principles are fundamental. One is that only a person who is a party to a contract can sue on it. Our law knows nothing of a jus quaesitum tertio arising by way of contract. Such a right may be conferred by way of property, as, for example, under a trust, but it cannot be conferred on a stranger to a contract as a right to enforce the contract in personam. A second principle is that if a person with whom a contract not under seal has been made is to be able to enforce it consideration must have been given by him to the promisor or to some other person at the promisor's request. These two principles are not recognized in the same fashion by the jurisprudence of certain Continental countries or of Scotland, but here they are well established. A third proposition is that a principal not named in the contract may sue upon it if the promisee really contracted as his agent. But again, in order to entitle him so to sue, he must have given consideration either personally or through the promisee, acting as his agent in giving it.

My Lords, in the case before us, I am of opinion that the consideration, the allowance of what was in reality part of the discount to which Messrs Dew, the promisees, were entitled as between themselves and the appellants, was to be given by Messrs Dew on their own account, and was not in substance, any more than in form, an allowance made by the appellants. The case for the appellants is that they permitted and enabled Messrs Dew, with the knowledge and by the desire of the respondents, to sell to the latter on the terms of the contract of January 2, 1912. But it appears to me that even if this is so the answer is conclusive. Messrs Dew sold to the respondents goods which they had a title to obtain from the appellants independently of this contract. The consideration by way of discount under the contract of January 2 was to come wholly out of Messrs Dew's pocket, and neither directly nor indirectly out of that of the appellants. If the appellants enabled them to sell to the respondents on the terms they did, this was not done as any part of the terms of the contract sued on.

No doubt it was provided as part of these terms that the appellants should acquire certain rights, but these rights appear on the face of the contract as jura quaesita tertio, which the appellants could not enforce. Moreover, even if this difficulty can be got over by regarding the appellants as the principals of Messrs Dew in stipulating for the rights in question, the only consideration disclosed by the contract is one given by Messrs Dew, not as their agents, but as principals acting on their own account.

The conclusion to which I have come on the point as to the consideration renders it unnecessary to decide the further question as to whether the appellants can claim that a bargain was made in this contract by Messrs Dew as their agents; a bargain which, apart from the point as to consideration, they could therefore enforce. If it were necessary to express an opinion of this further question, a difficulty as to the position of Messrs Dew would have to be considered. Two contracts—one by a man on his own account as principal, and another by the same man as agent—may be validly comprised in the same piece of paper. But they must be two contracts, and not one as here. I do not think that a man can treat one and the same contract as made by him in two capacities. He cannot be regarded as contracting for himself and for uno flatu.

My Lords, the form of the contract which we have to interpret leaves the appellants in this dilemma, that, if they say that Messrs Dew contracted on their behalf, they gave no consideration, and if they say they gave consideration in the shape of a permission to the respondents to buy, they must set up further stipulations, which are neither to be found in the contract sued upon nor are germane to it, but are really inconsistent with its structure. That contract has been reduced to writing, and it is in the writing that we must look for the whole of the terms made between the parties. These terms cannot, in my opinion consistently with the settled principles of English law, be construed as giving to the appellants any enforceable rights as against the respondents.

I think that the judgment of the Court of Appeal was right, and I move that the appeal be dismissed with costs.

Lord Dunedin

My Lords, I confess that this case is to my mind apt to nip any budding affection which one might have had for the doctrine of consideration. For the effect of that doctrine in the present case is to make it possible for a person to snap his fingers at a bargain deliberately made, a bargain not in itself unfair, and which the person seeking to enforce it has a legitimate interest to enforce.

Notwithstanding these considerations I cannot say that I have ever had any doubt that the judgment of the Court of Appeal was right.

[Lord Dunedin referred to Pollock's definition of consideration, above.]

. . . [S]peaking for myself, I should have no difficulty in the circumstances of this case in holding it proved that the agreement was truly made by Dew as agent for Dunlop, or in other words that Dunlop was the undisclosed principal, and as such can sue on the agreement. None the less, in order to enforce it he must show consideration, as above defined, moving from Dunlop to Selfridge.

In the circumstances, how can he do so? The agreement in question is not an agreement for sale. It is only collateral to an agreement for sale; but that agreement for sale is an agreement entirely between Dew and Selfridge. The tyres, the property in which upon the bargain is transferred to Selfridge, were the property of Dew, not of Dunlop, for Dew under his agreement with Dunlop held these tyres as proprietor, and not as agent. What then did Dunlop do, or forbear to do, in a question with Selfridge? The answer must be, nothing.

To my mind, this ends the case. That there are methods of framing a contract which will cause persons in the position of Selfridge to become bound I do not doubt. But that has not been done in this instance; and as Dunlop's advisers must have known of the law of consideration, it is their affair that they have not so drawn the contract.

I think the appeal should be dismissed.

Lords Atkinson, **Parker**, **Sumner** and **Parmoor** also thought the appeal should be dismissed for similar reasons.

Appeal dismissed.

NOTES

1.   The doctrine of privity appears to have become firmly established in the case of *Tweddle v Atkinson* (1861) 1 B & S 393, 30 LJQB 265. In consideration of the intended marriage between his daughter and the plaintiff, Guy made a contract with the plaintiff's father whereby each promised to pay the plaintiff a sum of money. Guy failed to pay and the plaintiff sued his executors. The action was dismissed on the ground that the plaintiff was a stranger to the consideration.

2.   It is much disputed whether the doctrine of privity is made up of two rules, as Viscount Haldane seems to suggest, or one, namely that only someone who is party to a bargain can enforce it: see Furmston, 23 MLR 383–384. It is not clear that it makes any practical difference, nor, in the opinion of some of your editors, that there is any real difference between the two viewpoints: one may 'not be party' to a bargain either because he does not assent to it even though he provides something that could be labelled consideration, or because although he assents, he does not provide consideration—or, of course, for both reasons at once. In the *Dunlop* case, it seems the lack of consideration was a crucial factor: the House of Lords was not convinced that Dews was acting as agents for Dunlops, but said that even if it was (which would make Dunlops 'a party' in the sense of assenting), its claim would fail for want of consideration.

3. Lord Dunedin said he did not doubt that Dunlops could have framed the agreement so as to bind Selfridge. How do you think this might have been done? You may like to return to this question when you have read the rest of the chapter.

4. Could Dews have forced Selfridge to pay the £5 per tyre to Dunlops?

■ *Beswick v Beswick*
[1968] AC 58, HL

Lord Reid

My Lords, before 1962 the respondent's deceased husband carried on business as a coal merchant. By agreement of March 14, 1962, he assigned to his nephew, the appellant, the assets of the business and the appellant undertook first to pay to him £6 10s per week for the remainder of his life and then to pay to the respondent an annuity of £5 per week in the event of her husband's death. The husband died in November, 1963. Thereupon, the appellant made one payment of £5 to the respondent but he refused to make any further payment to her. The respondent now sues for £175 arrears of the annuity and for an order for specific performance of the continuing obligation to pay the annuity. The Vice-Chancellor of the County Palatine of Lancaster decided against the respondent but the Court of Appeal reversed this decision and, besides ordering payment of the arrears, ordered the appellant to pay to the respondent for the remainder of her life an annuity of £5 per week in accordance with the agreement.

It so happens that the respondent is administratrix of the estate of her deceased husband and she sues both in that capacity and in her personal capacity. So it is necessary to consider her rights in each capacity.

For clarity I think it best to begin by considering a simple case where, in consideration of a sale by A to B, B agrees to pay the price of £1,000 to a third party X. Then the first question appears to me to be whether the parties intended that X should receive the money simply as A's nominee so that he would hold the money for behoof of A and be accountable to him for it, or whether the parties intended that X should receive the money for his own behoof and be entitled to keep it. That appears to me to be a question of construction of the agreement read in light of all the circumstances which were known to the parties. There have been several decisions involving this question. I am not sure that any conflicts with the view which I have expressed: but if any does, for example, *In re Engelbach's Estate*, I would not agree with it. I think that *In re Schebsman* was rightly decided and that the reasoning of Uthwatt J and the Court of Appeal supports what I have just said. In the present case I think it clear that the parties to the agreement intended that the respondent should receive the weekly sums of £5 in her own behoof and should not be accountable to her deceased husband's estate for them. Indeed the contrary was not argued.

Reverting to my simple example the next question appears to me to be: Where the intention was that X should keep the £1,000 as his own, what is the nature of B's obligation and who is entitled to enforce it? It was not argued that the law of England regards B's obligation as a nullity, and I have not observed in any of the authorities any suggestion that it would be a nullity. There may have been a time when the existence of a right depended on whether there was any means of enforcing it, but today the law would be sadly deficient if one found that, although there is a right, the law provides no means for enforcing it. So this obligation of B must be enforceable either by X or by A. I shall leave aside for the moment the question whether section 56(1) of the Law of Property Act 1925, has any application to such a case, and consider the position at common law.

Lord Denning's view, expressed in this case not for the first time, is that X could enforce this obligation. But the view more commonly held in recent times has been that such a contract confers no right on X and that X could not sue for the £1,000. Leading counsel for the respondent based his case on other grounds, and as I agree that the respondent succeeds on other grounds, this would not be an appropriate case in which to solve this question. It is true that a strong Law Revision Committee recommended so long ago as 1937 (Cmd 5449):

'That where a contract by its express terms purports to confer a benefit directly on a third party it shall be enforceable by the third party in his own name . . . ' (p 31).

And, if one had to contemplate a further long period of Parliamentary procrastination, this House might find it necessary to deal with this matter. But if legislation is probably at an early date I would not deal with it in a case where that is not essential. So for the purposes of this case I shall proceed on the footing that the commonly accepted view is right.

What then is A's position? I assume that A has not made himself a trustee for X, because it was not argued in this appeal that any trust had been created. So, if X has no right, A can at any time grant a discharge to B or make some new contract with B. If there were a trust the position would be different. X would have an equitable right and A would be entitled and, indeed, bound to recover the money and account for it to X. And A would have no right to grant a discharge to B. If there is no trust and A wishes to enforce the obligation, how does he set about it? He cannot sue B for the £1,000 because under the contract the money is not payable to him, and, if the contract were performed according to its terms, he would never have any right to get the money. So he must seek to make B pay X.

The argument for the appellant is that A's only remedy is to sue B for damages for B's breach of contract in failing to pay the £1,000 to X. Then the appellant says that A can only recover nominal damages of 40s because the fact that X has not received the money will generally cause no loss to A: he admits that there may be cases where A would suffer damage if X did not receive the money but says that the present is not such a case.

Applying what I have said to the circumstances of the present case, the respondent in her personal capacity has no right to sue, but she has a right as administratrix of her husband's estate to require the appellant to perform his obligation under the agreement. He has refused to do so and he maintains that the respondent's only right is to sue him for damages for breach of his contract. If that were so, I shall assume that he is right in maintaining that the administratrix could then only recover nominal damages because his breach of contract has caused no loss to the estate of her deceased husband.

If that were the only remedy available the result would be grossly unjust. It would mean that the appellant keeps the business which he bought and for which he has only paid a small part of the price which he agreed to pay. He would avoid paying the rest of the price, the annuity to the respondent, by paying a mere 40s damages.

. . . The respondent's second argument is that she is entitled in her capacity of administratrix of her deceased husband's estate to enforce the provision of the agreement for the benefit of herself in her personal capacity, and that a proper way of enforcing that provision is to order specific performance. That would produce a just result, and, unless there is some technical objection, I am of opinion that specific performance ought to be ordered. For the reasons given by your Lordships I would reject the arguments submitted for the appellant that specific performance is not a possible remedy in this case.

Lord Pearce

My Lords, if the annuity had been payable to a third party in the lifetime of Beswick senior and there had been default, he could have sued in respect of the breach. His administratrix is now entitled to stand in his shoes and to sue in respect of the breach which has occurred since his death.

It is argued that the estate can only recover nominal damages and that no other remedy is open, either to the estate or to the personal plaintiff. Such a result would be wholly repugnant to justice and commonsense. And if the argument were right it would show a very serious defect in the law.

In the first place, I do not accept the view that damages must be nominal. Lush LJ in *Lloyd's v Harper* said:

'Then the next question which, no doubt, is a very important and substantial one, is, that Lloyd's, having sustained no damage themselves, could not recover for the losses sustained by third parties by reason of the default of Robert Henry Harper an underwriter. That, to my mind, is a startling and alarming doctrine, and a novelty, because I consider it to be an established rule of law that where a contract is made with A for the benefit of B, A can sue on the contract for the benefit of B, and recover all that B could have recovered if the contract had been made with B himself.'

(See also *Drimmie v Davies*.) I agree with the comment of Windeyer J in the case of *Coulls v Bagot's Executor and Trustee Co Ltd* in the High Court of Australia that the words of Lush LJ cannot be accepted without qualification and regardless of context and also with his statement:

'I can see no reason why in such cases the damages which A would suffer upon B's breach of his contract to pay C $500 would be merely nominal: I think that in accordance with the ordinary rules for the assessment of damages for breach of contract they could be substantial. They would not necessarily be $500, they could I think be less or more.'

In the present case I think that the damages, if assessed, must be substantial. It is not necessary, however, to consider the amount of damages more closely since this is a case in which, as the Court of Appeal rightly decided, the more appropriate remedy is that of specific performance.

The administratrix is entitled, if she so prefers, to enforce the agreement rather than accept its repudiation, and specific performance is more convenient than action for arrears of payment followed by separate actions as each sum falls due. Moreover, damages for breach would be a less appropriate remedy since the parties to the agreement were intending an annuity for a widow; and a lump sum of damages does not accord with this. And if (contrary to my view) the argument that a derisory sum of damages is all that can be obtained be right, the remedy of damages in this case is manifestly useless.

The present case presents all the features which led the equity courts to apply their remedy of specific performance. The contract was for the sale of a business. The defendant could on his part clearly have obtained specific performance of it if Beswick senior or his administratrix had defaulted. Mutuality is a ground in favour of specific performance.

Moreover, the defendant on his side has received the whole benefit of the contract and it is a matter of conscience for the court to see that he now performs his part of it. Kay J said in *Hart v Hart*:

'...when an agreement for valuable consideration...has been partially performed, the court ought to do its utmost to carry out that agreement by a decree for specific performance.'

What, then, is the obstacle to granting specific performance?

It is argued that since the widow personally had no rights which she personally could enforce the court will not make an order which will have the effect of enforcing those rights. I can find no principle to this effect. The condition as to payment of an annuity to the widow personally was valid. The estate (though not the widow personally) can enforce it. Why should the estate be barred from exercising its full contractual rights merely because in doing so it secures justice for the widow who, by a mechanical defect of out law, is unable to assert her own rights? Such a principle would be repugnant to justice and fulfil no other object than that of aiding the wrongdoer. I can find no ground on which such a principle should exist.

Lords Upjohn, Hodson and **Guest** agreed that, in her capacity as administratrix, Mrs Beswick was entitled to specific performance.

Appeal dismissed.

NOTES

1. The extract above omits the second point of the decision, which was that the doctrine of privity of contract was not overturned by the Law of Property Act 1925, s 56(1). The effect of that section is dealt with on pp 1151–1153.

2. *Beswick v Beswick* reaffirms that a person who is not a party to a contract cannot enforce it. Who is a party to a contract? Would Mrs Beswick have been able to claim the money

in her own name if, for instance, she had signed the agreement? The answer seems to depend on a number of factors. Firstly, she certainly could not claim unless she could show that the agreement was intended to give her a right to the money, rather than merely giving the nephew authority to pay her in discharge of his obligations. The fact of her signature would not be conclusive on this point. In *Coulls v Bagot's Executor and Trustee Co Ltd* (1967) 119 CLR 460, an agreement for royalties for quarrying provided:

I authorize the . . . Company to pay all money connected with this agreement to my wife, Doris Sophia Coulls and myself, Arthur Leopold Coulls as joint tenants (or tenants in common?) (the one which goes to the living partner) [sic].

It was signed by Mrs Coulls as well as her husband. However, the majority of the High Court of Australia held that this was merely a mandate to pay in this manner and was revoked by the husband's death, so that the royalties belonged to his estate. One of the reasons was that the husband said he 'authorised' payment to her, which was incompatible with her having a right. In *Beswick*, however, it was clear that it was intended that Mrs Beswick should have a right to the money: see the judgment of Lord Reid.

Secondly, however, it is doubtful whether the act of signing (even explicitly signing 'as a party') would make Mrs Beswick privy to the contract if (as was the case) she provided no consideration. It is possible that if the nephew had promised his uncle and aunt *jointly*, she might have an enforceable right. A different majority in *Coulls'* case said that the court would not enquire which of the joint promisees had provided the consideration. Thus Barwick CJ said:

In such a case it cannot lie in the mouth of A, in my opinion, to question whether the consideration which he received for his promise moved from both B and C, or as between themselves, only from one of them.

Support for this in English law may be found in a dictum of Lord Atkin in *McEvoy v Belfast Banking Co Ltd* [1935] AC 24. A customer had deposited funds in the joint names of himself and his infant son, and after his death, the money had been taken by his executors. Some time after his majority, the son claimed the money from the bank. His claim failed for another reason but Atkin said:

The suggestion is that where A deposits a sum of money with his bank in the names of A and B, payable to A or B, if B comes to the bank with the deposit receipt he has no right to demand the money from the bank or to sue them if his demand is refused. . . . I have myself no doubt that in such a case B can sue the bank. The contract on the face of it purports to be made with A and B, and I think with them jointly and severally. A purports to make the contract on behalf of B as well as himself and the consideration supports such a contract. If A has actual authority from B to make such a contract, B is a party to the contract ab initio. If he has not actual authority then subject to the ordinary principles of ratification B can ratify the contract purporting to have been made on his behalf and his ratification relates back to the original formation of the contract.

It has been pointed out, however, that these dicta confuse two questions: the promise of consideration and the performance of the promise. It does not matter which of the two actually furnished the consideration, but it is crucial to know whether the joint promisees were both undertaking (in a bilateral contract) to provide it or see that it was provided by the other. If one of two apparently joint promisees was not so undertaking, he or she was not a party to the bargain and should have no enforceable right (Coote [1978] CLJ 301). This seems theoretically correct, but it is, of course, inconsistent with Lord Atkin's dictum at least, because the son had provided no consideration.

Thus it remains uncertain whether Mrs Beswick could have sued on the agreement in her own name even if she had signed it as a joint promisee.

3. How could the sale have been arranged so as to give Mrs Beswick an indisputable right to the £5 per week?

4. Why was the administratrix granted specific performance? Was it to avoid the need for an action every time the nephew failed to pay an instalment? Or because the estate was losing nothing? Or because the estate was losing nothing *and* the nephew would otherwise escape paying the full price for what he had received? Do you think specific performance would have been granted if old Mr Beswick had died before the business had been transferred to the nephew?

II. DAMAGES ON BEHALF OF ANOTHER

In *Jackson v Horizon Holidays Ltd* [1975] 3 All ER 92, the plaintiff booked a package holiday for himself and his family. The accommodation and facilities provided were not in accordance with the contract, and the plaintiff claimed damages in respect of the loss of the holiday for himself, his wife and his children. The defendants admitted liability but appealed against the trial judge's awards of £1,100 damages. The Court of Appeal dismissed the appeal. Lord Denning MR said that the father had made the contract for the benefit of his wife and children and could recover damages for their loss as well as his own; he relied on the dictum of Lush LJ in *Lloyd's v Harper* quoted by Lord Pearce in *Beswick v Beswick*, see p 1140. James LJ said that the father had contracted for a family holiday and had not received one. Orr LJ gave no reasons. In *Woodar Investment Development Ltd v Wimpey Construction (UK) Ltd* [1980] 1 All ER 571, the main question was whether the purchasers had wrongfully repudiated the contract. The House of Lords held that they had not (see p 589). One point that was discussed in argument was, if the purchasers had wrongfully repudiated, what the measure of damages would be, since under the contract £150,000 of the purchase price was to be paid not to the vendors but to Transworld Trade Ltd, a Hong Kong company not directly connected with the vendors. The Court of Appeal had awarded the vendors damages to be held on behalf of Transworld. Given the decision in the House of Lords that the purchases had not repudiated, the question of damages did not arise, but the Lords disagreed with the approach of the Court of Appeal, while remarking that the law was not satisfactory. Lord Wilberforce said (at 576–577):

1. The majority of the Court of Appeal followed, in the case of Goff LJ with expressed reluctance, its previous decision in *Jackson v Horizon Holidays Ltd*. I am not prepared to dissent from the actual decision in that case. It may be supported either as a broad decision on the measure of damages (per James LJ) or possibly as an example of a type of contract, examples of which are persons contracting for family holidays, ordering meals in restaurants for a party, hiring a taxi for a group, calling for special treatment. As I suggested in *New Zealand Shipping Co Ltd v A M Satterthwaite & Co Ltd*, there are many situations of daily life which do not fit neatly into conceptual analysis, but which require some flexibility in the law of contract. *Jackson's* case may well be one.

I cannot agree with the basis on which Lord Denning MR put his decision in that case. The extract on which he relied from the judgment of Lush LJ in *Lloyd's v Harper* was part of a passage in which Lush LJ was stating as an 'established rule of law' that an agent (sc an insurance broker) may sue on a contract made by him on behalf of the principal (sc the assured) if the contract gives him such a right, and is no authority for the proposition required in *Jackson's* case, still less for the proposition, required here, that, if Woodar made a contract for a sum of money to be paid to Transworld, Woodar can, without showing that it has itself suffered loss or that Woodar was agent or trustee for Transworld, sue for damages for non-payment of that sum. That would certainly not be an established rule of law, nor was it quoted as such authority by Lord Pearce in *Beswick v Beswick*.

2. Assuming *that Jackson's* case was correctly decided (as above), it does not carry the present case, where the factual situation is quite different. I respectfully think therefore that the Court of Appeal need not, and should not have followed it.

3. Whether in a situation such as the present, viz where it is not shown that Woodar was agent or trustee for Transworld, or that Woodar itself sustained any loss, Woodar can recover any damages at all, or any but nominal damages, against Wimpey, and on what principle, is, in my opinion, a question of great doubt and difficulty; no doubt open in this House, but one on which I prefer to reserve my opinion.

There are a number of exceptional commercial cases in which a party may recover damages on behalf of others as well as himself and must pay them over to the others. Thus a consignor of goods may insure them for their full value, and recover this if the goods are lost, even though he has only a limited interest in the goods (*Hepburn v A Tomlinson (Hauliers) Ltd* [1966] AC 451; see also *Albacruz (Cargo Owners) v Albazero (owners), The Albazero* [1977] AC 774, referred to below). A bailee may recover for damage to the bailor's goods even though he is not himself liable to the bailor for the damage. Under the doctrine of subrogation, an insured who has suffered a loss through the tort of a third party but who has been paid by his insurer may still recover from the tortfeasor; he is accountable to the insurer for the proceeds.

■ ***Linden Gardens Trust Ltd v Lenesta Sludge Disposals Ltd and St Martins Property Corp Ltd v Sir Robert McAlpine & Sons Ltd***
[1993] 3 All ER 417, HL

These two cases, which were heard together, each involved contracts made on the JCT standard form of building contract. The first was for the removal of asbestos, the second for work on a 'podium deck'. In each case, the property on which the work was to be done had been assigned by the original employer to new owners, referred to here as 'Linden Gardens' and 'Investments'. The original employers also purported to assign the benefit of the building contracts but cl 17 of the JCT contract prohibited assignment of the contract by either employer or contractor without the consent of the other, which had not been obtained in either case. The House of Lords held that this prohibition rendered the purported assignment of the building contracts ineffective, which prevented the new owners from suing for alleged breaches of the contracts. That disposed of the first action, but in the second action, the original employers, 'Corporation', had been joined as co-plaintiffs. The Court of Appeal held that Corporation could recover substantial damages even though it no longer owned the property.

Lord Griffiths

. . . McAlpines have successfully resisted Corporation's claim to have assigned the benefit of the contract to Investments. It follows that throughout the performance of the contract McAlpines owed to Corporation a contractual duty to build the podium deck of sound materials and with all reasonable skill and care. Upon the assumption that McAlpines broke this contractual duty the normal measure of damages in such circumstances is the cost of remedying the defect in the building: see *East Ham BC v Bernard Sunley & Sons Ltd* [1965] 3 All ER 619, [1966] AC 406. If the cost of remedying the defect in the podium deck was £800,000 Corporation would in my opinion be entitled to recover that sum from McAlpines.

It is however submitted that two factors prevent this normal and just result of McAlpines' breach of contract. The first ground upon which McAlpines resist the claim is that Corporation had transferred their building lease to Investments before the podium deck was built and thus had no proprietary interest in the property when the breach occurred. The second is that for financial reasons beneficial to Corporation and Investment, Investment reimbursed Corporation for the money that they paid for the repairs to the podium deck.

In my view neither of these considerations provide McAlpines with a defence to Corporation's claim. I cannot accept that in a contract of this nature, namely for work, labour and the supply of materials, the recovery of more than nominal damages for breach of contract is dependent upon the plaintiff having a proprietary interest in the subject matter of the contract at the date of breach. In everyday life contracts for work and labour are constantly being placed by those who have no proprietary interest in the subject matter of the contract. To take a common example, the matrimonial home is owned by the wife and the couple's remaining assets are owned by the husband and he is the sole earner. The house requires a new roof and the husband places a contract with a builder to carry out the work. The husband is not acting as agent for his wife, he makes the contract as principal because only he can pay for it. The builder fails to replace the roof properly and the husband has to call in and pay another builder to complete the work. Is it to be said that the husband has suffered no damage because he does not own the property? Such a result would in my view be absurd and the answer is that the husband has suffered loss because he did not receive the bargain for which he had contracted with the first builder and the measure of damages in the cost of securing the performance of that bargain by completing the roof repairs properly by the second builder. To put this simple example closer to the facts of this appeal—at the time the husband employs the builder he owns the house but just after the builder starts work the couple are advised to divide their assets so the husband transfers the house to his wife. This is no concern of the builder whose bargain is with the husband. If the roof turns out to be defective the husband can recover from the builder the cost of putting it right and thus obtain the benefit of the bargain that the builder had promised to deliver. It was suggested in argument that the answer to the example I have given is that the husband could assign the benefit of the contract to the wife. But what if, as in this case, the builder has a clause in the contract forbidding assignment without his consent and refuses to give consent as McAlpines have done? It is then said that neither husband nor wife can recover damages; this seems to me to be so unjust a result that the law cannot tolerate it.

The principal authority relied upon by McAlpines in support of the proposition that the contracting party suffers no loss if they did not have a proprietary interest in the property at the time of the breach was *The Albazero, Albacruz (cargo owners) v Albazero owners* [1976] 3 All ER 129, [1977] AC 774. The situation in that case was however wholly different from the present. *The Albazero* was not concerned with money being paid to enable the bargain, ie the contract of carriage, to be fulfilled. The damages sought in *The Albazero* were claimed for the loss of the cargo, and as at the date of the breach the property in the cargo was vested in another with a right to sue it is readily understandable that the law should deny to the original party to the contract a right to recover damages for a loss of cargo which had caused him no financial loss. In cases such as the present the person who places the contract has suffered financial loss because he has to spend money to give him the benefit of the bargain which the defendant had promised but failed to deliver. I therefore cannot accept that it is a condition of recovery in such cases that the plaintiff has a proprietary right in the subject matter of the contract at the date of breach.

The second ground upon which the recovery of damages is resisted is that Investments in fact reimbursed Corporation for the money they spent on the repairs. But here again in my view who actually pays for the repairs is no concern of the defendant who broke the contract. The court will of course wish to be satisfied that the repairs have been or are likely to be carried out but if they are carried out the cost of doing them must fall upon the defendant who broke his contract. Authority for this is to be found in *Jones v Stroud DC* [1988] 1 All ER 5, [1986] 1 WLR 1141.

There are many cases where a tortfeasor's liability has been temporarily discharged by payment by a third party on behalf of the plaintiff. A very common example occurs in personal injury cases where the cost of medical treatment is borne by a relative; but that has never been seen as a reason why that sum should not ultimately be paid by the defendant if he is found liable for the injuries. The law regards who actually paid for the work necessary as a result of the defendant's breach of contract is a matter which is raised inter alios acta so far as the defendant is concerned.

It will be seen that my reasons for holding that Corporation can recover damages are essentially those canvassed in the speech of Lord Browne-Wilkinson in the introduction to that part of his speech dealing with Corporation's claim for damages. Whilst I always welcome and find the views of academic writers most helpful, I am prepared even without the benefit of their views to adopt the direct route to the award of damages to Corporation.

Lord Browne-Wilkinson

. . . McAlpines accept that, since the attempted assignment by Corporation of its rights under the contract to Investments was ineffective, Corporation has retained those rights and is entitled to judgment against McAlpines for any breach of contract. But, McAlpines submit, Corporation is only entitled to nominal damages. Corporation has suffered no loss: it had parted with its interest in the property (and therefore with the works when completed) before any breach of the building contract; moreover Corporation received full value for that interest on its disposal to Investments. Therefore, it is said, neither of the plaintiffs has any right to substantial damages: Investments has incurred damage (being the cost of rectifying the faulty work) but has no cause of action; Corporation has a cause of action but has suffered no loss. If this is right, in the words of Lord Keith of Kinkel in *GUS Property Management Ltd v Littlewoods Mail Order Stores Ltd* 1982 SC (HL) 157 at 177, 'the claim to damages would disappear . . . into some legal black hole, so that the wrongdoer escaped scot-free'.

The Court of Appeal was able to avoid this result by reason of the continuing liability on Corporation to indemnify Investments against the cost of remedying the defects. [His Lordship rejected it is on the basis that this was too remote a consequence of Corporation's failure to obtain McAlpine's consent to assignment.]

It is therefore necessary to consider Mr Fernyhough's principal argument in some detail. He starts from the well known proposition that the measure of damages is generally 'that sum of money which will put the party who has been injured, or who has suffered, in the same position he would have been in if he had not sustained the wrong for which he is now getting his compensation or reparation': per Lord Blackburn in *Livingstone v Rawyards Coal Co* (1880) 5 App Case 25 at 39. Since, before the date of any breach of contract by McAlpines, Corporation had disposed of all its interest in the property on which the building works were carried out, Corporation has suffered no loss. Corporation received the full value of the property from Investments. The measure of damages for defective performance of a building contract is the diminution in value of the plaintiff's property, which diminution is usually properly reflected by the cost of carrying out the repairs necessary to effect reinstatement: *East Ham BC v Bernard Sunley & Sons Ltd* [1965] 3 All ER 619, [1966] AC 406. Since at the date of breach Corporation did not own the property, Corporation suffered no loss by any diminution in its value nor could Corporation carry out any works of reinstatement. Therefore, it is said, Corporation has suffered no loss.

Mr Fernyhough accepted that central to his argument is the fact that *at the date of breach* Corporation no longer owned the property . . . In support of the proposition that only nominal damages are recoverable by a plaintiff who has parted with ownership of the property at the date of breach, Mr Fernyhough . . . relied on two cases concerned with breach of contract for the carriage of goods, *The Albazero* [1977] AC 774 and *Obestain Inc v National Mineral Development Corp Ltd, The Sanix Ace* [1987] 1 Lloyd's Rep 465.

This is a formidable, if unmeritorious, argument since it is apparently soundly based on principle and is supported by authority. In *The Albazero* the plaintiffs chartered the defendant's vessel for the carriage of oil. The carriage was covered by a bill of lading which names the plaintiffs as consignees. In the course of the voyage the vessel and cargo became a total loss. However, on the day before that loss, the plaintiffs endorsed the bill of lading to a third party: the property in the goods and the right to sue the defendants were thereby vested in the third party. The plaintiffs , although having no property in the goods at the date of breach of the contract of carriage, sued the defendants for the full value of the goods. This House held that the plaintiffs were not entitled to substantial damages. Lord Diplock treated the general rule as being clear: a party who has no property in the goods at the date of breach has suffered no loss. However, he recognised that there were exceptions to this general rule and I will consider those exceptions later.

Notwithstanding the apparent logic of Mr Fernyhough's submission, I have considerable doubts whether it is correct. A contract for the supply of goods or of work, labour and materials (a supply contract) is not the same as a contract for the carriage of goods. A breach of a supply contract involves a failure to provide the very goods or services which the defendant had contracted to supply and for which the plaintiff has paid or agreed to pay. If the breach is discovered before payment of the contract price, the price is abated by the cost of making good the defects: see, as to the sale of goods, *Mondel v Steel* (1841) 8 M & W 858 and the Sale of Goods Act 1979, s 53(1), as to building contracts, *Mondern Engineering (Bristol) Ltd v Gilbert-Ash (Northern) Ltd* [1974] AC 689. Mr Fernyhough accepted that this right to abatement of the price does not depend on ownership by the plaintiff of the goods and it would be odd if the plaintiff's rights arising from breach varied according to whether the breach was discovered before or after the payment of the price. No such similar principle of abatement applies to freight charges; the freight charges have to be paid in full leaving the consignor to bring a separate action for damages for breach of the contract of carriage: *Colonial Bank v European Grain and Shipping Ltd, the Dominique* [1989] AC 1056 at 1067–1068.

In contracts for the sale of goods, the purchaser is entitled to damages for delivery of defective goods assessed by reference to the difference between the contract price and the market price of the defective goods, irrespective of whether he has managed to sell on the goods to a third party without loss: *Slater v Hoyle & Smith Ltd* [above p 579] All ER Rep 654; see also as to non-delivery *Williams Bros v E T Agius Ltd* [1914] AC 510. In those cases the judgments contained no consideration of the person in whom the property in the goods was vested although it appears that some of the sub-contracts had been made prior to the breach of contract.

If the law were to be established that damages for breach of a supply contract were not quantifiable by reference to the beneficial ownership of goods or enjoyment of the services contracted for but by reference to the difference in value between that which was contracted for and that which is in fact supplied, it might also provide a satisfactory answer to the problems raised where a man contracts and pays for a supply to others, eg a man contracts with a restaurant for a meal for himself and his guests or with a travel company for a holiday for his family. It is apparently established that, if a defective meal or holiday is supplied, the contracting party can recover damages not only for his own bad meal or unhappy holiday but also for that of his guests or family: see *Jackson v Horizon Holidays Ltd* as explained in *Woodar Investment Development Ltd v Wimpey Construction.*

There is therefore much to be said for drawing a distinction between cases where the ownership of goods or property is relevant to prove that the plaintiff has suffered loss through the breach of a contract other than a contract to supply those goods or property and the measure of damages in a supply contract where the contractual obligation itself requires the provision of those goods or services. I am reluctant to express a concluded view on this point since it may have profound effects on commercial contracts which effects were not fully explored in argument. In my view the point merits exposure to academic consideration before it is decided by this House. Nor do I find it necessary to decide the point since, on any view, the facts of this case bring it within the class of exceptions to the general rule to which Lord Diplock referred in *The Albazero*. In *The Albazero* [1976] 3 All ER 129 at 136–7 Lord Diplock said:

> 'Nevertheless, although it is exceptional at common law that a plaintiff in an action for breach of contract, though he himself has not suffered any loss, should be entitled to recover damages on behalf of some third person who is not a party to the action for a loss which that third person has sustained, the notion that there may be circumstances in which he is entitled to do so was not entirely unfamiliar to the common law . . . ' [Lord Diplock referred to the cases of bailment and insurance, above].

In addition, the decision in *The Albazero* itself established a further exception. This House was concerned with the status of a long-established principle based on the decision in *Dunlop v Lambert* (1839) 6 Cl & F 600, 7 ER 824 that a consignor of goods who had parted with the property in the goods before the date of breach could even so recover substantial damages for the failure to deliver the goods. Lord Diplock identified the rationale of that rule as being—

'The only way in which I find it possible to rationalise the rule in *Dunlop v Lambert* so that it may fit into the pattern of the English law is to treat it as an application of the principle, accepted also in relation to policies of insurance on goods, that in a commercial contract concerning goods where it is in the contemplation of the parties that the proprietary interests in the goods may be transferred from one owner to another after the contract has been entered into and before the breach which causes loss or damage to the goods, an original party to the contract, if such be the intention of them both, is to be treated in law as having entered into the contract for the benefit of all persons who have or may acquire an interest in the goods before they are lost or damaged, and is entitled to recover by way of damages for breach of contract the actual loss sustained by those for whose benefit the contract is entered into.' (See [1977] AC 774 at 847.)

In *The Albazero* it was held that the principle in *Dunlop v Lambert* no longer applied to goods consigned under a bill of lading because both the property in the goods and the cause of action for breach of the contract of carriage passes to the consignee or indorsee by reason of the consignment or indorsement; therefore, since the consignee or indorsee will in any event be entitled to enforce the contract direct there is no ground on which one can impute to the parties an intention that the consignor is entering into the contract for the benefit of others who will acquire the property in the goods but no right of action for breach of contract.

However, this House was careful to limit its decision to cases of carriage by sea under a bill of lading, leaving in force the principle in *Dunlop v Lambert* in relation to other contracts for the carriage of goods where such automatic assignment of the rights of action for breach does not take place . . . .

In my judgment the present case falls within the rationale of the exceptions to the general rule that a plaintiff can only recover damages for his own loss. The contract was for a large development of property which, to the knowledge of both Corporation and McAlpines, was going to be occupied, and possibly purchased, by third parties and not by Corporation itself. Therefore it could be foreseen that damage caused by a breach would cause loss to a later owner and not merely to the original contracting party, Corporation. As in contracts for the carriage of goods by land, there would be no automatic vesting in the occupier or owners of the property for the time being who sustained the loss of any right of suit against McAlpines. On the contrary, McAlpines had specifically contracted that the rights of action under the building contract could *not* without McAlpines' consent be transferred to third parties who became owners or occupiers and might suffer loss. In such a case, it seems to me proper, as in the case of the carriage of goods by land, to treat the parties as having entered into the contract on the footing that Corporation would be entitled to enforce contractual rights for the benefit of those who suffered from defective performance but who, under the terms of the contract, could not acquire any right to hold McAlpines liable for breach. It is truly a case in which the rule provides 'a remedy where no other would be available to a person sustaining loss which under a rational legal system ought to be compensated by the person who has caused it'.

Mr Fernyhough submitted that it would be wrong to distort the law in order to meet what he described as being an exceptional case. He said that this was a one-off or exceptional case since the development was sold before any breach of contract had occurred and there was an express contractual prohibition on assignment. He submitted that to give Corporation a right to substantial damages in this case would produce chaos when applied to other cases where the contractors have entered into direct warranties with the ultimate purchasers of the individual parts of a development. I am not impressed by these submissions. I am far from satisfied that this is a one-off or exceptional case. We are concerned with standard forms of building contracts which prohibit the assignment of the benefit of building contracts to the ultimate purchasers. In the prolonged period of recession in the property market which this country has experienced many developments have had to be sold off before completion, thereby producing the risk that the ownership of the property may have become divided from the right to sue on the building contract at a date before any breach occurs. As to the warranties given by contractors to subsequent purchasers, they will not, in my judgment, give rise to difficulty. If, pursuant to the terms of the original building contract, the contractors have undertaken liability to the ultimate purchasers to remedy defects appearing after they acquired the property, it is manifest the case will not fall within the rationale of *Dunlop v Lambert*. If the ultimate purchaser is given a direct cause of action against the contractor (as is the consignee or indorsee under a bill of lading) the case falls outside the rational of the rule. The original building owner will not be entitled to recover damages for loss suffered by others who can themselves sue for such loss. I would therefore hold that Corporation is entitled to substantial damages for any breach of McAlpines of the building contract....

Lords Keith, **Bridge** and **Ackner** agreed with **Lord Browne-Wilkinson**'s reasoning; **Lords Keith** and **Bridge** expressed sympathy with **Lord Griffiths**'s approach but preferred to base their decision on the narrower ground.

Appeal and cross-appeal in St Martin's case dismissed.

NOTES

1. In *Darlington Borough Council v Wiltshier Northern Ltd* [1995] 1 WLR 68, the question arose as to what damages can be recovered by an assignee of a building contract that *does* permit assignment, if a breach is shown. It was conceded that the assignee cannot recover more than the assignor could—but how much would the assignor be able to recover? The Court of Appeal held that the principle applied in *Linden Gardens* was not confined to cases in which there was a prohibition on assignment and so the assignee can recover substantial damages under the *Dunlop v Lambert* principle. Alternatively, Dillon and Waite LJ considered that, on the facts, the original employers were constructive trustees (on trusts, see p 1150). Steyn LJ relied in the alternative on the principle set out by Lord Griffiths, although in Steyn LJ's view, one qualification of that principle was needed: it was irrelevant whether or not the work would be carried out (see p 689).

2. Were Lord Griffiths' principle to be adopted generally, it would enable a plaintiff who has made a contract for the benefit of a third party (seemingly whether or not the defendant knew that a third party was involved or not) to recover the cost of providing the benefit that the defendant has failed to provide, or the loss directly caused by the defendant's failure (eg the loss of enjoyment suffered by other members of the party when the hotel or meal is not up to scratch). What, however, if the party is supplied with food that is not fit for human consumption and the other members suffer personal injury? Or suppose a builder who has promised to repair the roof on a third party's property does an inadequate job, with the result that the third party's property is damaged? The hotel or builder may be liable in tort, but it is possible that there was no negligence on its part, eg if ingredients or materials used were unforeseeably defective. These losses seem to be outside Lord Griffiths' principle. As Lord Griffiths points out, losses such as the damage to the cargo in *The Albazero* are different to the amount of money necessary 'to enable the bargain, ie the contract of carriage, to be fulfilled'.

■ *Panatown v McAlpine Construction Ltd*
[2000] 4 All ER 97

In 1989, the claimant had entered into a contract as employer with the defendant as main contractor to build an office building and a car park in Cambridge on the 1981 JCT design & build contract. Panatown was a member of the UNEX group of companies, of which UNEX

Corp Ltd was the parent company. The site in Cambridge belonged to another member of the group, UNEX Investment Properties Ltd (UIPL). The decision that Panatown should be the employer under the building contract was apparently based on perfectly proper tax considerations. In due course, it was alleged that there had been major flaws in the building work done by McAlpine and Panatown brought an action for damages, but there was one major difference between the facts of the present case and those in *Linden Gardens Trust Ltd v Lenesta Sludge Disposals Ltd*, above. This was that, at the same time as venturing into the building contract, McAlpine had entered into a duty of care deed with UIPL under which that company acquired a direct remedy against McAlpine in respect of any failure by McAlpine to exercise reasonable skill, care and attention in respect of any matter within the scope of McAlpine's responsibilities under the building contract. This deed was expressly assignable by UIPL to its successors in title (although this is not explained, it was apparently assumed by the members of the UNEX group that Panatown could recover more if they could recover under the building contract than UIPL could recover under the duty of care deed). Lord Goff and Lord Millett thought that the duty of care deed made no difference and that Panatown should be able to recover in full the damages suffered by its sister company against McAlpine. They regarded the duty of care deed as of little relevance, since they assumed its commercial purpose would be to be able to offer a remedy in respect of defective work to anyone who bought the building from UIPL (it is not completely clear from the report, but it looks as if the building was being put up as a speculative office development and not for use by any member of the UNEX Group). The majority, Lord Clyde, Lord Jauncey and Lord Browne-Wilkinson, disagreed. They thought the duty of care deed was a decisive factor. They explained the earlier decision in *Linden Gardens* (in which, of course, Lord Browne-Wilkinson delivered the leading judgment) on what may be called the 'black hole' theory of liability. This is that the law abhors situations in which one party has a claim but has suffered no loss and another party has suffered loss but has no claim. In this situation, it will often be desirable for the party with the claim to be able to recover the loss suffered by the party that has suffered loss and to account for it. There is no need for such a device if the party who has suffered a loss has a claim even if, for some reason or other, it may be somewhat less satisfactory.

NOTE

This is clearly a very important decision. All of the judgments, which are unfortunately rather long, would repay careful study. Note that this case is not affected by the 1999 Act because Panatown was undoubtedly a party to the contract and the parties had deliberately chosen a mechanism for contracting so that the other members of the UNEX Group were not parties.

III. QUALIFICATIONS TO THE PRIVITY RULE

1. Trusts

If property is given to a person in trust for another, the beneficiary is treated as equitable owner of the property. It is the duty of the trustee to take all necessary steps to safeguard the property, including taking action against any third party who is under an obligation to the trust. If he fails to do so, not only can the beneficiary sue the trustee; he can bring an action against the third party, joining the trustee as co-plaintiff if the latter consents and as co-defendant if he does not. In addition to property or money, a chose in action may constitute the 'trust property', and thus it is possible for one contracting party to hold the other's promise on trust for a third party, so giving the third party the right to enforce the promise in the name of the promisee. If in every contract containing a promise for the benefit of a third party, the promise were treated as being held on trust for the third party by the promisee, the doctrine of privity would be circumvented. There were signs in the nineteenth and early twentieth centuries that the courts might take this approach, and it appears to have been sanctioned by the House of Lords in *Les Affréteurs Réunis SA v Leopold Walford (London) Ltd* [1919] AC 801. In that case, a shipowner promised a charterer that he would pay a commission to the broker who had negotiated the charter, and it was held that the charterer held this promise on trust for the broker so that the latter could enforce it. However, the tide of judicial opinion seems to have swung against the implication of trusts in order to overcome the privity doctrine: a trust may be created if the intention to do so is clearly expressed, but one will not be implied. A typical example of this more recent attitude is to be found in the last reported case in which the 'trust device' seems to have been seriously argued: *Green v Russell* [1959] 2 QB 226. An architect had taken out an insurance policy covering accidents sustained by his employees, one of whom died in a fire at the office. In the course of an action by the deceased's mother under the Fatal Accidents Act, it became necessary to decide whether the deceased had had an enforceable right to the insurance monies, which had been paid to the deceased's personal representatives.

The Court of Appeal held that he did not, with the result that the payments did not fall to be deducted from the damages in tort. Romer LJ said:

> The suggestion that Russell assumed the position and obligations of a trustee was based primarily on the recital to the policy . . . An intention to provide benefits for someone else, and to pay for them, does not in itself give rise to a trusteeship; and yet that is all that emerges from the recital. Nor does the judge's finding that the existence of the policy was known to the employees in such a manner as to create in them a reasonable expectation of benefit affect the matter. There was nothing to prevent Russell at any time, had he chosen to do so, from surrendering the policy and receiving back a proportionate part of the premium which he had paid. Nor was he under any obligation to pay the renewal premiums each year. The truth is that the benefits payable in pursuance of the policy were sums which the company would become contractually liable to Russell to pay if the insured risks matured; and as Lord Greene MR said in *In Re Schebsman*, to which the judge referred: 'It is not legitimate to import into the contract the idea of a trust when the parties have given no indication that such was their intention. To interpret this contract as creating a trust would, in my judgment, be to disregard the dividing line between the case of a trust and the simple case of a contract made between two persons for the benefit of a third.'

Note that there was no suggestion that the money paid to the personal representatives should be repaid, or paid to the employer. The fact that the third party cannot enforce the promise that was intended to benefit him does not mean that the promisor does not discharge his contractual obligation by paying him, although it will mean that, for the purposes of assessing damages, the payment was gratuitous, and similarly for tax purposes: *Re Schebsman* [1944] Ch 83.

Thus it is probable that the 'implied trust' device will no longer be accepted by the courts as a means of overcoming the doctrine of privity. However, the exceptional cases already noted, in which a party with a limited interest in goods is permitted to insure them on behalf of others interested, recover the full value and hold the excess for the other parties, are still recognised as good law, even though they are sometimes thought of as involving a trust of the insurance policy (see the explanation of Pearson LJ in *A Tomlinson (Hauliers) Ltd v Hepburn* [1966] 1 QB 21 of 57; in the House of Lords, Lord Reid gave a different explanation based on the special position of a bailee of goods, [1966] AC 451 at 470–471).

2. Statutory exceptions

It must be clear by now that the doctrine of privity can have inconvenient effects, especially in insurance contracts, under which it is very common for the policy to provide for coverage of loss or liability of someone other than the insured, or for money to be paid to someone else. In a number of situations, statute now gives the beneficiary a direct right of action.

■ *Married Women's Property Act 1882, s 11*

A policy of assurance effected by any man on his own life and expressed to be for the benefit of his wife, or of his children, or of his wife and children, or any of them, or by any woman on her own life, and expressed to be for the benefit of her husband, or of her children, or of her husband and children, or any of them, shall create a trust in favour of the objects therein named, and the moneys payable under any such policy shall not, so long as any object of the trust remains unperformed, form part of the estate of the insured, or be subject to his or her debts.

■ *Marine Insurance Act 1906, s 14(2)*

A mortgagee, consignee, or other person having an interest in the subject-matter insured may insure on behalf and for the benefit of other persons interested as well as for his own benefit.

■ *Road Traffic Act 1988, s 148(7)*

Notwithstanding anything in any enactment, a person issuing a policy of insurance under section 145 of this Act shall be liable to indemnify the persons or classes of persons specified in the policy in respect of any liability which the policy purports to cover in the case of those persons or classes of persons.

■ *Defective Premises Act 1972, s 1(1)*

A person taking on work for or in connection with the provision of a dwelling (whether the dwelling is provided by the erection or by the conversion or enlargement of a building) owes a duty—

  (a) if the dwelling is provided to the order of any person, to that person; and
  (b) without prejudice to paragraph (a) above, to every person who acquires an interest (whether legal or equitable) in the dwelling;

to see that the work he takes on is done in a workman-like or, as the case may be, professional manner, with proper materials and so that as regards that work the dwelling will be fit for habitation when completed.

■ *Law of Property Act 1925, ss 47(1), 56(1), 205(1)*

Section 47(1)

Where after the date of any contract for sale or exchange of property, money becomes payable under any policy of insurance maintained by the vendor in respect of any damage to or destruction of property included in the contract, the money shall, on completion of the contract, be held or receivable by the vendor on behalf of the purchaser and paid by the vendor to the purchaser on completion of the sale or exchange, or so soon thereafter as the same shall be received by the vendor.

Section 56(1)

A person may take an immediate or other interest in land or other property, or the benefit of any condition, right of entry, covenant or agreement over or respecting land or other property, although he may not be named as a party to the conveyance or other instrument.

Section 205(1)

In this Act unless the context otherwise requires, the following expressions have the meaning hereby assigned to them respectively, that is to say . . . (xx) Property includes any thing in action, and any interest in real or personal property.

Note

In *Beswick v Beswick*, the majority of the Court of Appeal (Lord Denning MR, Danckwerts LJ and Salmon LJ leaving the question open) held that Mrs Beswick was entitled to enforce the contract in her own right by virtue of s 56 ([1966] Ch 538, following dicta of Denning in *Drive Yourself Hire Co (London) Ltd v Strutt* and *Smith and Snipes Hall Farm Ltd v River Douglas Catchment Board*). The argument was that s 56 provides that a person not named as a party can take the benefit of an agreement respecting property and that, by virtue of s 205, 'property' includes a chose in action such as a debt. Thus it was said that the doctrine of privity of contract had been abolished by statute. The House of Lords were unanimous in holding that s 56 does not have this effect and that Mrs Beswick had no remedy in her own name. It was agreed that the context required that the definition of property given in s 205 should not apply to s 56, but the exact scope of s 56 (fortunately not now of concern to mere contract lawyers) was left unclear. See Treitel, pp 669–671; *Amsprop Trading Ltd v Harris Distribution Ltd* [1997] 2 All ER 990.

IV. NEGATIVE BENEFITS, OR VICARIOUS IMMUNITY

■ *Elder, Dempster & Co v Paterson, Zochonis & Co Ltd*
[1924] AC 522, HL

The respondents shipped some casks of palm oil under a bill of lading contract, on board a vessel that had been chartered by the appellants from her owners. Normally, when goods are shipped under a bill of lading contract in a chartered ship, the contract will be between the shipper and the owners (see below), and the bill of lading will be issued by the owners or on their behalf. However, in this case, it was the charterers (who operated a fleet of their own vessels and had chartered this ship to supplement it) who issued the bill of lading in their own name, so that the contract was between the appellants, the charterers, and the respondents, the shippers. The casks were damaged when bags of palm kernels were stowed on top of them. The House of Lords held that the loss was caused not by the ship being unseaworthy but by bad stowage. The result was that the appellants, the charterers, were concededly protected from liability by an exception clause in the bill of lading. The second question the House had to decide was whether the owners, whose servants had actually carried out the stowage, were also protected by the clause.

Viscount Cave

... There remains a further question, which arises between the shippers and the shipowners, the Griffiths Lewis Steam Navigation Company. It is contended on behalf of the respondents that, assuming their loss to be due to bad stowage on the part of the master of the ship, the owners are not protected by the conditions of the bill of lading, to which they were not parties, and are accordingly liable in tort for the master's negligence. In support of this contention the respondents rely on such cases as *Martin v Great Indian Peninsula Rly Co; Hayn v Culliford;* and *Meux v Great Eastern Rly Co.* I do not think that this argument should prevail. It was stipulated in the bills of lading that 'the shipowners' should not be liable for any damage arising from other goods by stowage or contract with the goods shipped under the bills of lading; and it appears to me that this was intended to be a stipulation on behalf of all the persons interested in the ship, that is to say, charterers and owners alike. It may be that the owners were not directly parties to the contract; but they took possession of the goods (as Scrutton LJ says) on behalf of and as the agents of the charterers, and so can claim the same protection as their principals.

Viscount Finlay

... [T]he act complained of was done in the course of the stowage under the bill of lading, and ... the bill of lading provided that the owners are not to be liable for bad stowage. If the act complained of had been an independent tort unconnected with the performance of the contract evidenced by the bill of lading, the case would have been different. But when the act is done in the course of rendering the very services provided for in the bill of lading, the limitation on liability therein contained must attach, whatever the form of the action and whether owner or charterer be sued. It would be absurd that the owner of the goods could get rid of the protective clauses of the bill of lading, in respect of all stowage, by suing the owner of the ship in tort. The Court of Appeal were, in my opinion, right in rejecting this contention, which would lead to results so extraordinary as those referred to by Scrutton LJ, in his judgment.

... It may be, that in the circumstances of this case the obligations to be inferred from the reception of the cargo for carriage to the United Kingdom amount to a bailment upon terms, which include the exceptions and limitations of liability stipulated in the known and contemplated form of bill of lading. It may be, that the vessel being placed in the Elder, Dempster & Co's line, the capital signs the bill of lading and takes possession of the cargo only as agent for the charterers, though the time charter recognizes the ship's possessory lien for hire. The former I regard as the preferable view, but, be this as it may, I cannot find here any such bald bailment with unrestricted liability, or such tortious handling entirely independent of contract, as would be necessary to support the contention.

Lord Dunedin delivered a concurring judgment; **Lord Carson** concurred.

Order of the Court of Appeal reversed.

■ *Scruttons Ltd v Midland Silicones Ltd*
[1962] AC 446, HL

The respondents were consignees and, at the material time, owners of a drum of chemicals bought on terms cif London and consigned to them from America by ship under a bill of lading (dated 26 March 1957) signed on behalf of the shipowners. The bill of lading incorporated s 4(5) of the US Carriage of Goods by Sea Act 1936, which in the circumstances limited the liability of the shipowners (as carriers) for loss or damage to the goods to $500. The bill provided that 'carrier' included 'the ship ... her owner, operator and demise character, and also any ... person to the extent bound by this bill of lading, whether acting as carrier or bailee'. Section 1(a) of the Act of 1936 (incorporated into the bill of lading) provided that the term 'carrier' included the owner or character who entered into a contract of carriage with a shipper.

For some years past, the shipowners had employed the appellant stevedores to discharge their vessels at the port of London and deliver goods to consignees, and the contract (dated in 1952) between the shipowners and the stevedores stated that the stevedores would be responsible for any negligence of themselves or their servants, but should have 'such protection as is afforded by the terms . . . or the bills of lading'. The consignees did not know of the contract of 1952. The stevedores, when handling the drum at the port of London in the course of their duties regarding unloading and delivery, negligently dropped it causing damage amounting to £593 12s 2d. In an action by the consignees against the stevedores for the sum as damages, the stevedores admitted negligence but contended that they were entitled to limit their liability to $500 (or £179 1s) by virtue of the contract of carriage (evidenced by the bill of lading) between the shipowners and the consignees on the ground of the decision in *Elder, Dempster & Co v Paterson, Zochonis & Co*, or because the shipowners contracted as agents for the stevedores or because there was an implied contract, independent of the bill of lading, between the consignees and the stevedores that the stevedores should have the benefit of the provision limiting liability in the contract of carriage.

Lord Reid

. . . We were informed that questions of the kind frequently arise and that this action had been brought as a test case.

In considering the various arguments for the appellants, I think it is necessary to have in mind certain established principles of the English law of contract. Although I may regret it, I find it impossible to deny the existence of the general rule that a stranger to a contract cannot in a question with either of the contracting parties take advantage of provisions of the contract, even where it is clear from the contract that some provision in it was intended to benefit him. That rule appears to have been crystallised a century ago in *Tweedle v Atkinson* and finally established in this House in *Dunlop Pneumatic Tyre Co Ltd v Selfridge & Co Ltd*. There are, it is true, certain well-established exceptions to that rule—though I am not sure that they are really exceptions and do not arise from other principles. But none of these in any way touches the present case.

The actual words used by Lord Haldene in the *Dunlop* case were made the basis of an argument that, although a stranger to a contract may not be able to sue for any benefit under it, he can rely on the contract as a defence if one of the parties to it sues him in breach of his contractual obligation—that he can use the contract as a shield though not as a sword. I can find no justification for that. If the other contracting party can prevent the breach of contract well and good, but if he cannot I do not see how the stranger can. As was said in *Tweedle v Atkinson*, the stranger cannot 'take advantage' from the contract.

It may be that in a roundabout way the stranger could be protected. If A, wishing to protect X, gives to X an enforceable indemnity, and contracts with B that B will not sue X, informing B of the indemnity, and then B does sue X in breach of his contract with A, it may be that A can recover from B as damages the sum which he has to pay X under the indemnity, X having had to pay it to B. But there is nothing remotely resembling that in the present case.

The appellants in this case seek to get round this rule in three different ways. In the first place, they say that the decision in *Elder, Dempster & Co Ltd v Paterson, Zochonis & Co Ltd* establishes an exception to the rule sufficiently wide to cover the present case. I shall later return to consider this case. Secondly, they say that through the agency of the carrier they were brought into contractual relation with the shipper and that they can now found on that against the consignees, the respondents. And thirdly, they say that there should be inferred from the facts an implied contract, independent of the bill of lading, between them and the respondents. It was not argued that they had not committed a tort in damaging the respondents' goods.

I can see a possibility of success of the agency argument if (first) the bill of lading makes it clear that the stevedore is intended to be protected by the provisions in it which limit liability, (secondly) the bill of lading makes it clear that the carrier, in addition to contracting for these provisions on his own behalf, is also contracting as agent for the stevedores that these provisions should apply to the stevedore, (thirdly) the carrier has authority from the stevedore to do that, or perhaps later ratification by the stevedore would suffice, and (fourthly) that any difficulties about consideration moving from the stevedore were overcome. And then to affect the consignee it would be necessary to show that the provisions of the Bills of Lading Act, 1855, apply.

But again there is nothing of that kind in the present case. I agree with your Lordships that 'carrier' in the bill of lading does not include stevedore, and if that is so I can find nothing in the bill of lading which states or even implies that the parties to it intended the limitation of liability to extend to stevedores. Even if it could be said that reasonable men in the shoes of these parties would have agreed that the stevedores should have this benefit, that would not be enough to make this an implied term of the contract. And even if one could spell out of the bill of lading an intention to benefit the stevedore, there is certainly nothing to indicate that the carrier was contracting as agent for the stevedore in addition to contracting on his own behalf. So it appears to me that the agency argument must fail.

And the implied contract argument seems to me to be equally unsound. From the stevedores' angle, they are employed by the carrier to deal with the goods in the ship. They can assume that the carrier is acting properly in employing them and they need not know whom the goods belong to. There was in their contract with the carrier a provision that they should be protected, but that could not by itself bind the consignee. They might assume that the carrier would obtain protection for them against the consignee and feel aggrieved when they found that the carrier did not or could not do that. But a provision in the contract between them and the carrier is irrelevant in a question between them and the consignee. Then from the consignee's angle they would know that stevedores would be employed to handle their goods, but if they read the bill of lading they would find nothing to show that the shippers had agreed to limit the liability of the stevedores. There is nothing to show that they ever thought about this or that if they had they would have agreed or ought as reasonable men to have agreed to this benefit to the stevedores. I can find no basis in this for implying a contract between them and the stevedores. It cannot be said that such a contract was in any way necessary for business efficiency.

So this case depends on the proper interpretation of the *Elder, Dempster* case. What was there decided is clear enough. The ship was under time charter, the bill of lading made by the shippers and the charterers provided for the exemption from liability in the event which happened and this exemption was held to ensure to the benefit of the shipowners who were not parties to the bill of lading but whose servant the master caused damage to the shippers' goods by his negligence. The decision is binding on us but I agree that the decision by itself will not avail the present appellants because the facts of this case are very different from those in the *Elder, Dempster* case. For the appellants to succeed it would be necessary to find from the speeches in this House a ratio decidendi which would cover this case and then to follow that ratio decidendi.

I would certainly not lightly disregard or depart from any ratio decidendi of this House. But there are at least three classes of case where I think we are entitled to question or limit it: first, where it is obscure, secondly, where the decision itself is out of line with other authorities or established principles, and thirdly, where it is much wider than was necessary for the decision so that it becomes a question of how far it is proper to distinguish the earlier decision. The first two of these grounds appear to me to apply to the present case.

It can hardly be denied that the ratio decidendi of the *Elder, Dempster* decision is very obscure ... [The House of Lords] must all have thought that they were merely applying an established principle to the facts of the particular case.

But when I look for such a principle I cannot find it, and the extensive and able arguments of counsel in this case have failed to discover it.... [Scrutton LJ in the Court of Appeal, in the *Elder, Dempster* case] was saying in terms that servants and 'agents' can take advantage of contracts made by their master or 'principal'. I would not dissent from a proposition that something of that kind ought to be the law if that was plainly the intention of the contract, and it may well be that this matter is worthy of consideration by those whose function it is to consider amending the law. But it seems to me much too late to do that judicially.

In such circumstances I do not think that it is my duty to pursue the unrewarding task of seeking to extract a ratio decidendi from what was said in this House in *Elder, Dempster*. Nor is it my duty to seek to rationalise the decision by determining in any other way just how far the scope of the decision should extend. I must treat the decision as an anomalous and unexplained exemption to the general principle that a stranger cannot rely for his protection on provisions in a contract to which he is not a party. The decision of this House is authoritative in cases of which the circumstances are not reasonably distinguishable from those which gave rise to the decision. The circumstances in the present case are clearly distinguishable in several respects. Therefore I must decide this case on the established principles of the law of England apart from that decision, and on that basis I have no doubt this appeal must be dismissed.

[**Viscount Simonds** delivered a speech to the same effect, adding: . . .] In the course of this opinion I have already borrowed freely, without acknowledgement, from the judgment of the late Fullager J in *Wilson v Darling Island Stevedoring and Lighterage Co Ltd*. . . . I will quote a passage from it which expresses my own view of *Elder, Dempster*. After referring to a passage in *Carver on the Law of Carriage of Goods by Sea*, 9th ed, at p 294, that learned judge said: 'In my opinion what the *Elder, Dempster* case decided, and all that it decided, is that in such a case, the master having signed the bill of lading, the proper inference is that the shipowner, when he receives the goods into his possession, receives them on the terms of the bill of lading. The same inference might perhaps be drawn in some cases even if the charterer himself signed the bill of lading, but it is unnecessary to consider any such question.' This appears to me to be the only possible generalisation, or if your Lordships think 'rationalisation' an appropriate word, the only possible rationalisation of *Elder, Dempster*, and it is a far cry from the circumstances to which it is sought to apply that decision in the present case . . . .

Lord Keith of Avonholm and **Lord Morris of Borth-y-Gest** delivered concurring judgments; **Lord Denning** dissented.

Appeal dismissed.

NOTES

1.　The notion of 'vicarious immunity' does, however, have some force. The point has been made that, in some situations, it must be that a servant or agent of a contracting party has the same immunity in tort as is enjoyed by his employer or principal, even if he is not mentioned in the agreement that gives the latter the immunity. Thus if a patient in a private hospital were to sign an agreement consenting to surgery, and the surgery were properly carried out by either an employee of the hospital or an independent contractor, it is inconceivable that the patient could sue the surgeon for battery: see Coote, *Exception Clauses*, pp 129–130. Similarly, it has been held that an agent who deals with the property of an estate with the consent of the executor does not become an *executor de son tort*: *Sykes v Sykes* (1870) LR 5 CP 113. Presumably, it must now be taken that this principle may protect the stevedore from liability in trespass for simply handling the consignee's goods but does not protect him from liability for negligent damage. But see further below.

2.　On the point that, in *Elder Dempster*, the shipowner received the goods on the terms of the bill of lading, see further p 1202.

■ *New Zealand Shipping Co Ltd v A M Satterthwaite & Co Ltd (The Eurymedon)*

[1974] 1 All ER 1015, PC

Cargo was shipped on board a vessel at Liverpool by the consignor for transhipment to the plaintiff as consignee in New Zealand, pursuant to a bill of lading issued by agents for the carrier. Clause 1 of the bill of lading (see p 1221) conferred certain exemptions and immunities on the carrier. The clause further provided:

It is hereby expressly agreed that no servant or agent of the Carrier (including every independent contractor from time to time employed by the Carrier) shall in any circumstances whatsoever be under any liability whatsoever to the Shipper, Consignee or Owner of the goods or to any holder of this Bill of Lading for any loss or damage or delay of whatsoever kind arising or resulting directly or indirectly from any act neglect or default on his party while acting in the course of or in connection with his employment and, without prejudice to the generality of the foregoing provisions in this Clause, every exemption, limitation, condition and liberty herein contained and every right, exemption from liability, defence and immunity of whatsoever nature applicable to the Carrier or to which the Carrier is entitled hereunder shall also be available and shall extend to protect every such servant or agent of the Carrier acting as aforesaid and for the purpose of all the foregoing provisions of this Clause the Carrier is or shall be deemed to be acting as agent or trustee on behalf of and for the benefit of all persons who are or might be his servants or agents from time to time (including independent contractors as aforesaid) and all such persons shall to this extent be or be deemed to be parties to the contract in or evidenced by this Bill of Lading.

The defendant company acted as stevedore for the carrier in New Zealand, being employed as an independent contractor. After the plaintiff had become the holder of the bill of lading, the cargo was damaged as a result of the defendant's negligence during unloading. The plaintiff brought an action against the defendant claiming that the defendant could not escape liability by virtue of the exceptions and immunities conferred on it under the terms of cl 1 of the bill of lading, since it was not a party to the contract.

Lord Wilberforce

[Lord Wilberforce, delivering the judgment of the majority, quoted the part of Lord Reid's speech in the *Midland Silicones* case in which Lord Reid stated the prerequisites for success of the 'agency' argument and continued:]

The question in this appeal is whether the contract satisfies these propositions.

Clause 1 of the bill of lading, whatever the defects in its drafting, is clear in its relevant terms. The carrier, on his own account, stipulates for certain exemptions and immunities: among these is that conferred by art III(6) of the Hague Rules which discharges the carrier from all liability for loss or damage unless suit is brought within one year after delivery. In addition to these stipulations on his own account, the carrier as agent for, inter alios, independent contractors stipulates for the same exemptions.

Much was made of the fact that the carrier also contracts as agent for numerous other persons: the relevance of this argument is not apparent. It cannot be disputed that among such independent contractors, for whom, as agent, the carrier contracted, is the appellant company which habitually acts as stevedore in New Zealand by arrangement with the carrier and which is, moreover, the parent company of the carrier. The carrier was, indisputably, authorised by the stevedore to contract as its agent for the purposes of cl 1. All of this is quite straightforward and was accepted by all of the learned judges in New Zealand. The only question was, and is, the fourth question presented by Lord Reid, namely that of consideration.

It was on this point that the Court of Appeal differed from Beattie J, holding that it had not been shown that any consideration for the shipper's promise as to exemption moved from the promisee, ie, the stevedore.

[Lord Wilberforce held that the terms of the bill of lading amounted to an offer by the shipper to the stevedore, made through the agency of the carrier, that if the stevedore unloaded the goods it should have the benefit of the exemption clause. This part of Lord Wilberforce's judgment is reproduced on p 108. Lord Wilberforce continued:]

But whether one describes the shipper' promise to exempt as an offer to be accepted by performance or as a promise in exchange for an act seems in the present context to be a matter of semantics. The words of Bowen LJ in *Carlill v Carbolic Smoke Ball Co*: 'why should not an offer by made to all the world which is to ripen into a contract with anybody who comes forward and performs the condition?' seem to bridge both conceptions: he certainly seems to draw no distinction between and offer which matures into a contract when accepted and a promise which matures into a contract after performance, and, though in some special contexts (such as in connection with the right to withdraw) some further refinement may be needed, either analysis may be equally valid. On the main point in the appeal, their Lordships are in substantial agreement with Beattie J.

The following other points require mention:

1. In their Lordships' opinion, consideration may quite well be provided by the stevedore, as suggested, even though (or if) it was already under an obligation to discharge their carrier. (There is no direct evidence of the existence or nature of this obligation, but their Lordships are prepared to assume it.) An agreement to do an act which the promisor is under an existing obligation to a third party to do, may quite well amount to valid consideration and does so in the present case: the promisee obtains the benefit of a direct obligation which he can enforce. This proposition is illustrated and supported by *Scotson v Pegg* ... which their Lordships consider to be good law.

2. The consignee is entitled to the benefit of, and is bound by, the stipulations in the bill of lading by his acceptance of it and request for delivery of the goods thereunder. This is shown by *Brandt v Liverpool, Brazil and River Plate Steam Navigation Co Ltd*, and a line of earlier cases. The Bills of Lading Act 1855, section 1 (in New Zealand the Mercantile Law Act 1908, section 13) gives partial statutory recognition to this rule, but, where the statute does not apply, as it may well not do in this case, the previously established law remains effective.

3. The stevedore submitted, in the alternative, an argument that, quite apart from contract, exemptions from, or limitation of, liability in tort may be conferred by mere consent of the part of the party who may be injured. As their Lordships consider that the stevedore ought to succeed in contract, they prefer to express no opinion upon this argument: to evaluate it requires elaborate discussion.

4. A clause very similar to the present was given effect by a United States District court in *Carle & Montanari Inc v American Export Isbrandtsen Lines Inc.* The carrier in that case contracted, in an exemption clause, as agent, for, inter alios, all stevedores and other independent contractors, and although it is no doubt true that the law in the United States is more liberal than ours as regards third party contractors, their Lordships see no reason why the law of the Commonwealth should be more restrictive and technical as regards agency contracts. Commercial considerations should have the same force on both sides of the Pacific.

In the opinion of their Lordships, to give the stevedore the benefit of the exemptions and limitations contained in the bill of lading is to give effect to the clear intentions of a commercial document, and can be given within existing principles. They see no reason to strain the law or the facts in order to defeat these intentions. It should not be overlooked that the effect of denying validity to the clause would be to encourage actions against servants, agents and independent contractors in order to get round exemptions (which are almost invariably and often compulsorily) accepted by shippers against carriers, the existence, and presumed efficacy, of which is reflected in the rates of freight. They see no attraction in this consequence.

Their Lordships will humbly advise Her Majesty that the appeal be allowed and the judgment of Beattie J restored. The consignee must pay the costs of the appeal and in the Court of Appeal.

Viscount Dilhorne and **Lord Simon** dissented. They rejected the theory adopted by the majority, on the grounds that the bill of lading purported to be a bilateral agreement with the stevedores and not an offer of unilateral contract, and that, as a bilateral contract, it failed for want of consideration: the stevedores were not promising the consignee that they would unload the goods. In effect, they held that a document drafted by a skilled lawyer (the clause is known to have been drafted by Lord Roskill while at the Bar) should be treated at face value.

On the alternative argument for the stevedores (referred to as their fourth proposition, but mentioned by Lord Wilberforce (above) in his point 3), on which the majority had declined to express an opinion, Lord Simon said:

It is really sufficient to dispose of this proposition in the circumstances of the instant case to say that, were it correct, all five of Lord Reid's conditions, which were common ground between the parties, would be entirely irrelevant: *Midland Silicones* should have been decided the other way.

Furthermore, in my opinion, the stevedore's fourth proposition is inconsistent with both the reasoning and the actual decision in *Cosgrove v Horsfall*. It was argued for the stevedore in *Midland Silicones* that *Cosgrove's* case was wrongly decided; but the decision in *Midland Silicones* was inconsistent with that contention (cf Lord Denning, dissenting). In *Cosgrove's* case, the plaintiff, an employee of a transport company, was travelling in one of their omnibuses on a free pass, when a collision occurred with another of the company's omnibuses, causing the plaintiff injuries. One of the conditions to which the grant of the free pass was subject was that neither the company nor their servants were to be liable to the holder of the pass for personal injury however caused. The plaintiff sued the driver of his omnibus and recovered damages. The defendant's appeal to the Court of Appeal was dismissed, on the ground that the defendant was not a party to the contract between the plaintiff and the company, the condition of exemption from liability not having been imposed by the company as agent for the defendant. On the stevedore's fourth proposition (unlike the first three) agency is quite irrelevant; moreover, the stevedore's fourth proposition, if valid, merely needs rephrasing to fit the facts of *Cosgrove v Horsfall* so that the defendant should have succeeded.

Counsel relied for the stevedore's fourth proposition on the cases where a licence is coupled with a disclaimer of liability and on *Hedley Byrne & Co Ltd v Heller & Partners Ltd*. In all these cases, however, the right or service extended was gratuitous; and obviously any person making a gift can delimit its extent. The cases give no ground, in my opinion, for any such general principle of law as is implicit in the stevedore's fourth proposition, which, if valid, would seem to provide a revolutionary short cut to a jus quaesitum tertio.

Since I cannot accept the stevedore's fourth proposition, it is unnecessary to discuss the fine and difficult distinctions which counsel sought to draw between this proposition and the doctrine of volenti non fit injuria.

NOTES

1. Suppose the stevedores are employed to unload goods that are being carried under a bill of lading containing the same clause as in the *New Zealand Shipping* case, but they damage the goods before they have started to unload them—eg while unloading other goods belonging to a different party but which are stowed on top of the damaged goods? See *Raymond Burke Motors Ltd v Mersey Docks and Harbour Board Co* [1986] 1 Lloyd's Rep 155.

2. Coote [1981] CLJ 13 asks why it is necessary to establish agency if, as the Privy Council held, the bill of lading contains an offer of a unilateral contract. Might the answer be that the stevedore will not necessarily receive the bill of lading before commencing unloading?

3. What if the stevedores were not only not in the same group of companies as the carrier but had not even been employed by the carriers before the occasion on which the loss or damage occurred? In *Port Jackson Stevedoring Pty Ltd v Salmond & Spraggon Pty (Australia) Ltd, The New York Star* [1980] 3 All ER 257, a case also involving stevedores in the same group as the carriers, the Privy Council emphasised the general principle underlying the earlier decision, Lord Wilberforce saying (at 261):

    Although, in each case, there will be room for evidence as to the precise relationship of carrier and stevedore and as to the practice at the relevant port, the decision does not support, and their

Lordships would not encourage, a search for fine distinctions which would diminish the general applicability, in the light of established commercial practice, of the principle...

4.   There have been two further Privy Council decisions, in each of which the judgment has been delivered by Lord Goff. The first was *The Pioneer Container* [1994] 2 All ER 250. The second case was *The Mahkutai* [1996] 3 All ER 502, which contains a masterly summary of the development of this subject. In this case, there was an action by cargo owners against shipowners in respect of a cargo of plywood, which was brought in the courts of Hong Kong. The bill of lading had not been issued by the shipowners but by time charterers. It contained both the Himalaya clause and also a clause purporting to give exclusive jurisdiction to the courts of Indonesia. Lord Goff pointed out that, in the last twenty years, judicial opinion had swung strongly away from the attitude in *Scruttons v Midland Silicones* because the cargo owner should not be too easily able to sidestep an agreed regime for the carriage of goods, which would inevitably be insured. Lord Goff said:

...there can be no doubt of the commercial need of some such principle as this...[and] it is legitimate to wonder whether that development is yet complete...the time may well come when, in an appropriate case, it will fall to be considered whether the courts should take what may legitimately be perceived to be the final, and perhaps inevitable, step in this development and recognise in these cases a fully-fledged exception to the doctrine of privity of contract, thus escaping from all the technicalities with which courts are now faced in English law.

In *The Mahkutai*, the real dispute was not so much about the limitation of liability clause but about the exclusive jurisdiction clause. Lord Goff thought that although there were very strong policy considerations for uniform application of the agreed allocation of risk of damage to the goods, these considerations were much weaker in relation to jurisdiction. An exclusive jurisdiction clause, which might be appropriate between time charterer and cargo owner, is not necessarily appropriate between shipowner and cargo owner.

5.   In *Southern Water Authority v Carey* [1985] 2 All ER 1077, the plaintiffs employed a contractor to design and build a sewage works. Subsequently, the contractor employed subcontractors to carry out the works. Clause 30 of the main contract, which was on the Institute of Mechanical Engineers/ Institute of Electrical Engineers form, limited the contractor's liability to making good defects that appeared within 12 months of completion and stated:

(iv) The Contractor's liability under this clause shall be in lieu of any condition of warranty implied by law as to the quality or fitness for any particular purpose of any portion of the Works taken over...and save as in this clause expressed neither the Contractor nor his Sub-contractors, servants or agents shall be liable, whether in contract, tort or otherwise in respect of defects in or damage to such portion, or for any injury, damage or loss of whatsoever kind attributable to such defects or damage. For the purposes of this sub-clause the Contractor contracts on his own behalf and on behalf of and as trustee for his Sub-Contractors, servants and agents.

The plaintiff alleged that the works failed because of negligence on the part of the third and fourth defendants, who were subcontractors. A number of issues were tried as preliminary issues, including whether the third and fourth defendants were protected from liability to the plaintiff in tort by the clause in the main contract. Judge David Smout QC referred to Lord Reid's discussion of the 'agency' argument in the *Midland Silicones* case (see pp 1155–1156) and accepted that the clause was intended to protect the subcontractors and that the contract made it clear that, for this purpose, the contractor was acting as agent for the subcontractors. Nor was there any difficulty over consideration. However, there was no evidence that the third and fourth defendants had authorised the contractors to do this, and they could not ratify what had been done afterwards. This was because of a well-established rule that ratification of an act is not possible unless the principal was capable of being ascertained at the time when the act was done. The subcontractors were only selected after the main contract had been signed. Thus the clause did not protect the third and fourth defendants from liability in tort. This suggests a major weakness in the 'agency device' as a way of conferring immunity on subcontractors, stevedores and the like: it won't work if, at the time of the main contract, you haven't decided who they are going to be.

6.   However, Judge Smout went on to hold that the existence of the ineffective clause was sufficient to protect the subcontractors from being liable in tort in the first place: see p 1167.

V. PRIVITY OF CONTRACT AND LIABILITY IN TORT

The relationship between contractual and tortious liability needs careful consideration. Firstly, there is the question raised in the introductory section of the book (Chapter 2): when can a party who has broken a contract be liable in tort to a person who is not a party to the contract? Secondly, there is the question touched on in the last subsection: will the terms of a contract to which the defendant is a party but the plaintiff is not ever affect the defendant's potential liability in tort to the plaintiff?

Before you read further, we suggest you look again at the extracts from *Donoghue v Stevenson, Hedley Byrne v Heller, Caparo v Dickman* and *Murphy v Brentwood District Council*, and the notes that accompany them (pp 28–39).

1. Tort as a substitute for contract

It may be helpful to think of two examples of situations in which a party who cannot sue in contract because of the privity doctrine may wish to sue in tort. One is the case of a customer who has bought goods from a retailer and who has discovered that the goods are defective because of defect in manufacture or design—but who cannot proceed against the retailer, either because she cannot prove which retailer supplied the goods (as in *Lexmead v Lewis* [1982] AC 225) or because the retailer has gone out of business. The other is the employer under a building contract who finds that a subcontractor employed by the contractor has done defective work—but cannot pursue the contractor, perhaps because it has already reached a final settlement of all claims against the contractor before this defect appeared (as probably occurred in the next case), or because the contractor has now gone out of business.

Can the customer or the employer recover the cost of buying replacement goods or the cost of having the defective work redone from the manufacturer or subcontractor under the *Donoghue v Stevenson* principle? (If you are in doubt, look again at *Murphy v Brentwood District Council*.)

■ *Junior Books Ltd v Veitchi Co Ltd*

[1983] 1 AC 520, [1982] 3 All ER 201, HL

The respondents, the owners, engaged a building company to build a factory for them under a form of building contract that required the builders to employ for certain tasks subcontractors 'nominated' by the owners. The owners nominated the appellant subcontractors to lay a special concrete floor in the main production area and the appellants duly entered a subcontract with the builders. There was no contract between the owners and the nominated subcontractors. Two years after the floor had been laid, it developed cracks, and rather than have perpetual maintenance to keep the floor usable, the owners wanted to have it replaced, which they alleged would be cheaper. They brought an action against the subcontractors, alleging that the subcontractors had laid the floor negligently and claiming the cost of replacing the floor, and the economic loss that would result from closing the factory and moving the machinery out of it while the work was done. The subcontractors replied that, because there was no allegation that the floor was dangerous, the owners' claim disclosed no cause of action. The Lord Ordinary and, on appeal, the Court of Session, rejected this contention, and held that the owners were entitled to proceed with their action. The subcontractors appealed.

Lord Roskill

...[In] *Anns v Merton London Borough council*, Lord Wilberforce...said: 'the position has now been reached that in order to establish that a duty of care arises in a particular situation, it is not necessary to bring the facts of that situation within those of previous situations in which a duty of care has been held to exist. Rather the question has to be approached in two stages. First one has to ask whether, as between the alleged wrongdoer and the person who has suffered damage there is a sufficient relationship of proximity or neighbourhood such that, in the reasonable contemplation of the former, carelessness on his part may be likely to cause damage to the latter—in which case a prima facie duty of care arises. Secondly, if the first question is answered affirmatively, it is necessary to consider whether there are any considerations which ought to negative, or to reduce or limit the scope of the duty or the class of person to whom it is owed or the damages to which a breach of it may give rise: ...'

Applying those statements of general principle as your Lordships have been enjoined to do both by Lord Reid and by Lord Wilberforce rather than to ask whether the particular situation which has arisen does or does not resemble some earlier and different situation where a duty of care has been held or has not been held to exist, I look for the reasons why, it being conceded that the appellants owed a duty of care to others not to construct the flooring so that those others were in peril of suffering loss or damage to their persons or their property, the duty of care should not be equally owed to the respondents. The appellants, though not in direct contractual relationship with the respondents, were as nominated subcontractors in almost as close a commercial relationship with the respondents as it is possible to envisage short of privity of contract. Why then should the appellants not be under a duty to the respondents not to expose the respondents to a possible liability to financial loss for repairing the flooring should it prove that the flooring had been negligently constructed? It is conceded that if the flooring had been so badly constructed that to avoid imminent danger the respondents had expended money upon renewing it the respondents could have recovered the cost of so doing. It seems curious that, if the appellants' work had been so bad that to avoid imminent danger expenditure had been incurred, the respondents could recover that expenditure, but that if the work was less badly done so that remedial work could be postponed they cannot do so. Yet this is seemingly the result of the appellants' contentions...

Turning back to the present appeal I therefore ask first whether there was the requisite degree of proximity so as to give rise to the relevant duty of care relied on by the respondents. I regard the following facts as of crucial importance in requiring an affirmative answer to that question. (1) The appellants were nominated sub-contractors. (2) The appellants were specialists in flooring. (3) The appellants knew what products were required by the respondents and their main contractors and specialised in the production of those products. (4) The appellants alone were responsible for the composition and construction of the flooring. (5) The respondents relied upon the appellants' skill and experience. (6) The appellants as nominated sub-contractors must have known that the respondents relied upon their skill and experience. (7) The relationship between the parties was as close as it could be short of actual privity of contract. (8) The appellants must be taken to have known that if they did the work negligently (as it must be assumed that they did) the resulting defects would at some time require remedying by the respondents expending money upon the remedial measures as a consequence of which the respondents would suffer financial or economic loss.

My Lords, reverting to Lord Devlin's speech in *Hedley Byrne & Co Ltd v Heller & Partners Ltd*, it seems to me that all the conditions existed which give rise to the relevant duty of care owed by the appellants to the respondents.

I then turn to Lord Wilberforce's second proposition. On the facts I have just stated, I see nothing whatsoever to restrict the duty of care arising from the proximity of which I have spoken. During the argument it was asked what the position would be in a case where there was a relevant exclusion clause in the main contract. My Lords, that question does not arise for decision in the instant appeal, but in principle I would venture the view that such a clause according to the manner in which it was worded might in some circumstances limit the duty of care just as in the *Hedley Byrne* case the plaintiffs were ultimately defeated by the defendants' disclaimer of responsibility. But in the present case the only suggested reason for limiting the damage (ex hypothesi economic or financial only) recoverable for the breach of the duty of care just enunciated is that hitherto the law has not allowed such recovery and therefore ought not in the future to do so. My Lords, with all respect to those who find this a sufficient answer, I do not. I think this is the next logical step forward in the development of this branch of the law. I see no reason why what was called during the argument 'damage to the pocket' simpliciter should be disallowed when 'damage to the pocket' coupled with physical damage has hitherto always been allowed. I do not think that this development, if development it be, will lead to untoward consequences. The concept of proximity must always involve, at least in most cases, some degree of reliance—I have already mentioned the words 'skill' and 'judgment' in the speech of Lord Morris of Borth-y-Gest in *Hedley Byrne* [1964] AC 465 at 503. These words seem to me to be an echo, be it conscious or unconscious, of the language of section 14(1) of the Sale of Goods Act 1893. My Lords, though the analogy is not exact, I do not find it unhelpful for I think the concept of proximity of which I have spoken and the reasoning of Lord Devlin in the *Hedley Byrne* case involve factual considerations not unlike those involved in a claim under section 14(1); and as between an ultimate purchaser and a manufacturer would not easily be found to exist in the ordinary everyday transaction of purchasing chattels when it is obvious that in truth the real reliance was upon the immediate vendor and not upon the manufacturer ...

Lords Fraser and **Russell** agreed; **Lord Keith** delivered a separate concurring judgment and **Lord Brandon** dissented.

Appeal dismissed.

NOTES

1. In the normal case, what will be the method of recovery from a nominated subcontractor who does defective work? As we saw earlier, the fact that a contractor is permitted to delegate work does not relieve him of responsibility if the work is not done properly, and the same is true even if he is required by the contract to delegate the work to a subcontractor nominated by the employer, at least if he had the right to object to the nominee but did not do so (see below). Thus the employer will be able to recover his loss from the contractor, and the contractor will be able to recover the same amount, plus any

other expense to which he was put, from the subcontractor. You may remember that this was the outcome of the *IBA* case (see p 186): the difficulty there was that the defect was one of design, which the contractor argued it was not responsible for, but the House of Lords held that it had expressly undertaken responsibility for design in its tender. Why did the employer not sue the contractor in the *Junior Books* case? What is the practical effect of allowing him to bypass privity by suing in tort? Is it rather similar to allowing the employer to come in as an undisclosed principal? (On the last point, see p 1194.)

2.   Apart from practical problems such as the contractor's insolvency, there may be legal reasons why, if the subcontractor defaults, the employer cannot sue 'down the chain of contracts' to recover its loss and might therefore wish to sue the subcontractor in tort— if that were possible. In certain circumstances, the contractor may not be responsible for what has occurred. One example we saw earlier: in *Gloucestershire County Council v Richardson* (see p 442), it was held that the contractor was not responsible for the quality of materials supplied by a nominated supplier. Although a subsequent change in the forms of contract used means that this particular problem is unlikely to recur, there may be others, particularly when a nominated subcontract is terminated for default by the subcontractor (this is often referred to as the subcontractor 'dropping out'). It is apparently the law that if a nominated subcontractor drops out, and getting the work completed by another subcontractor costs more than the original subcontract price, the contractor (in the absence of provisions to the contrary) is not liable to the employer for this amount. In *North West Metropolitan Regional Hospital Board v T A Bickerton & Son Ltd* [1970] 1 All ER 1039, [1970] 1 WLR 607, HL, which involved a building contract under the JCT form, a nominated subcontractor went into liquidation and the liquidator refused to carry out the subcontract, which was then terminated. The employer asked the main contractor to complete the subcontract work, which it did under protest. It was held by the House of Lords that the main contractor was entitled to the reasonable value of the work he thus had to do, not only the price agreed in the original subcontract. The reason given was that the main contractor was not even entitled, let alone bound, to do the nominated subcontract work: it was the duty of the employer to renominate. The practical effect of this decision is extraordinary. The extra cost of getting the work completed falls on the employer, who cannot recover it from the contractor, while the subcontractor gets away scot-free, because the only person with whom he has a contract, the main contractor, cannot sue him for this loss since he is not suffering it. Many forms of contract that envisage the use of nominated subcontractors now have express provisions to deal with this problem.

3.   When a nominated subcontractor drops out, there is also likely to be a serious problem of delay while a replacement is found. Whether the contractor is responsible for this in the absence of an express provision is a matter of considerable doubt after the House of Lords decision in *Percy Bilton Ltd v Greater London Council* [1982] 2 All ER 623.

4   *Junior Books* represents a high-water mark, and in several subsequent cases, broad hints were given that it was wrongly decided. For example, in *D & F Estates Ltd v Church Comrs for England* [1989] AC 177, Lord Bridge remarked that it 'is so far dependent upon the unique, albeit contractual relationship between the pursuer and the defender . . . that the decision cannot be regarded as laying down any principle of general application in the law of tort'.

5.   What was the principle underlying *Junior Books*? Lord Roskill seems to suggest an analogy with *Hedley Byrne v Heller*. If liability under *Junior Books* depends on a 'special

relationship', what are the elements of such a relationship? Would you expect the courts to find a special relationship between an employer and a subcontractor selected by the *contractor* (cf *Muirhead v Industrial Tank Specialities Ltd* [1985] 3 All ER 705)? Or between a *contractor* and a supplier nominated by the employer (*Simaan General Contracting Co v Pilkington Glass Ltd* [1988] 1 All ER 791)? If your answer is 'no', then it may be that some of the criticism of *Junior Books* resulted from attempts to apply it to inappropriate facts. More recently, it seems to have been accepted by the House of Lords as an application of the *Hedley Byrne* principle (see *Murphy v Brentwood District Council*, p 33).

6. Why is a consumer who has bought goods that are worthless because of a defect caused by negligence in design or manufacture not able to sue the manufacturer? Lord Roskill clearly thinks that this is out of the question but, with respect, his reasoning is not convincing. Certainly, sometimes a consumer does rely exclusively on the retailer (eg when she buys 'own brand' goods), but what if she buys goods carrying the manufacturer's brand name, without consulting the retailer about which brand to buy? Can you see any *other* reason why there is probably no special relationship sufficient to create liability in such a case? (*Hint:* compare *Caparo v Dickman*, p 30.)

7. The Department of Trade and Industry has canvassed making the manufacturer jointly and severally liable with the retailer for the satisfactory quality of consumer goods (*Consumer Guarantees: A Consultation Document*, 1992). The same theme has been taken up by the European Commission in a paper that canvasses views on requiring member States to impose minimum 'guarantees' for consumer goods (*Green Paper on Guarantees for Consumer Goods and After-sales Services*, COM (93) 509 of 15 November 1993).

8. The courts have been reluctant to allow plaintiffs to recover purely economic loss in tort, even if otherwise the case might seem to involve a 'special relationship', when the parties already have a contract with each other—eg a contract that might (but did not) deal with the matter. In *Greater Nottingham Co-operative Society Ltd v Cementation Piling and Foundations Ltd* [1988] 2 All ER 971, the facts were indistinguishable *from Junior Books* except that the employer and the nominated subcontractor had actually entered into a direct contract with one another (in addition to the normal contracts each had with the main contractor). This 'collateral' contract required the subcontractor to exercise reasonable care and skill in the design of the subcontract works and the selection of materials. The subcontractors caused delay to the project through carrying out their work negligently, a point on which the collateral contract said nothing. The Court of Appeal held that, if there was a contract between the parties, it was to be assumed that the parties had defined in it whether and in what circumstances they would be liable to each other for economic loss. As liability for delay was not provided for, there was no liability in tort.

9. Even if a subcontractor is liable to an employer in tort under *Junior Books*, the employer's recovery may be less full than it would be if there were a contract between them. Suppose the facts had been these: the subcontractors had been selected because the price at which they offered to do the work (say £50,000) was £25,000 less than any of the other tenders. The subcontractors started work only to discover that they had seriously underestimated the work, tried to cut corners to save money and consequently laid the floor with defects that reasonable care and skill would have prevented. If the owners can get the floor relaid for £85,000, and their other losses will amount to £10,000, how much do you think they

would recover in a tort action against the subcontractors? One possible answer is £95,000, but is this the amount by which they are out of pocket by reason of their reliance on the subcontractors? If they had employed another subcontractor, they would have had to pay him an extra £25,000: should this be taken into account, so that they recover only £70,000? If they recover the full £95,000, they seem to be compensated for losing the 'profit' they were making on the original subcontract, and while that is wholly proper in an action for breach of contract, is it the correct measure of damages in tort? It would be the equivalent of allowing Miss Donoghue's friend to recover the normal price of a bottle of ginger beer, although she had paid Minchella less than that price because he was offering a 'special' that week (see p 39).

10. Lord Roskill raises the problem of whether a clause in the contract between the employer and contractor should have any bearing on the liability in tort of a subcontractor. It is to this that we now turn.

2. Contract as restricting liability in tort

You will remember that, in *Hedley Byrne v Heller*, it was held that there was no liability for negligent misstatement because the defendants had given the information with a disclaimer of responsibility. This negated a special relationship. We have seen that if the facts otherwise strongly suggest a special relationship, and the disclaimer seems unreasonable, the courts may hold that there is a special relationship and that the disclaimer is ineffective under the Unfair Contract Terms Act 1977 (*Smith v Eric S Bush*, see pp 1006 and 1021). In less compelling circumstances, a disclaimer or exclusion clause may negate liability. In *Southern Water v Carey* (see p 1161), the subcontractor's liability was purportedly excluded by the contract between employer and contractor. It was held that this negated any duty of care under the *Junior Books* principle. Judge Smout said ([1985] 2 All ER 1077, 1085):

In *Junior Books Ltd v Veitchi Co Ltd* Lord Roskill cited the passage from Lord Wilberforce's speech in *Anns v Merton London Borough* to which I have referred and with the agreement of Lord Fraser and Lord Russell expressed the majority view of the House of Lords in his approval of Lord Wilberforce's proposition. Significantly, Lord Roskill added this:

'During the argument it was asked what the position would be in a case where there was a relevant exclusion clause in the main contract. My Lords, that question does not arise for decision in the instant appeal, but in principle I would venture the view that such a clause according to the manner in which it was worded might in some circumstances limit the duty of care just as in the *Hedley Byrne* case [1963] 2 All ER 575, [1964] AC 465 the plaintiffs were ultimately defeated by the defendants' disclaimer of responsibility.'

The case has now arisen where there is such a limitation that is directly in point. While the terms of cl 30(vi) may, if literally interpreted, exceed the bounds of common sense the intent is clear, namely that the sub-contractor whose works have been so completed as to be the subject of a valid taking-over certificate should be protected in respect of those works from any liability in tort to the plaintiffs. As the plaintiffs' predecessor did so choose to limit the scope of the sub-contractors' liability, I see no reason why such limitation should not be honoured.

Similar concerns seem to underlie the decision of the House of Lords in *The Aliakmon* [1986] AC 785. A cargo of steel was damaged by the negligence of the carriers while it was at the risk of the buyers but remained the property of the sellers. Because the buyers found themselves unable to pay for the steel, the contract was varied so that the steel remained the seller's property even after delivery. This meant that the buyers could not sue under the Bills of Lading Act (see Appendix) and so they brought an action against the carriers in tort. It was held that their loss was purely economic and that they could not recover. One concern appears to have been that the carriers' liability is limited by various exceptions permitted by the Hague Rules in the bill of lading (see Appendix). The House of Lords could not see how liability in tort to the buyers could be qualified by these exceptions, so to impose liability would be to allow the buyer to avoid them.

What if the damage caused is not economic loss but physical?

■ *Norwich City Council v Harvey*
[1989] 1 All ER 1180, CA

The plaintiff building owners entered into a contract for the extension of a swimming pool complex under a contract in the JCT standard form of local authority building contract (1963 edition, revised in 1977), cl 20[C] of which provided that 'The existing structures . . . owned by him or for which he is responsible and the Works . . . shall be at the sole risk of the Employer [ie the building owners] as regards loss or damage by fire . . . and the Employer shall maintain adequate insurance against those risks'. The contractor subcontracted certain roofing work to the defendant subcontractors, one of whose employees, while using a blowtorch, set fire to both the existing buildings and the new extension. The building owners brought an action against the subcontractors and their employee claiming damages for negligence. The trial judge dismissed the action and the building owners appealed to the Court of Appeal.

May LJ

. . . The judge held that there was no privity of contract between the employer and the sub-contractors, and also that there was no question of the main contractor acting either as the agent or trustee for the sub-contractors (see his Honour Judge David Smout QC in *Southern Water Authority v Carey*). The judge further declined to act on any analogy with the bailment cases where, as in *Leigh & Sillavan Ltd v Aliakmon Shipping Co Ltd, The Aliakmon*, the contractual exemption is in the defendant sub-bailee's contract with the bailee. Having considered a number of recent authorities relating to the existence and extent of a duty of care he concluded:

> 'The matter must be approached as one of principle: is the duty owed by the defendant to the plain-tiff qualified by the plaintiff's contract with the main contractor, or to put it more broadly, by the plaintiffs propounding a scheme whereby they accepted the risk of damage by fire and other perils to their own property—existing structures and contents—and some property which does not belong to them—unfixed materials and goods, the value of which has not been included in any certificate—while requiring the contractor to indemnify them against liabilities arising from the omission or default of both the contractor and of any sub-contractor; then requiring the contractor to insure and to cause any sub-contractor to insure against the liabilities included in the indemnity? I am left in no doubt that the duty in tort owed by the sub-contractor to the employer is so qualified. This appears to me to follow from the passage to which I have referred in *Peabody v Parkinson*, and to be consist-ent with the approach, albeit on different facts in *Scottish Housing v Wimpey* and *Mark Rowlands v Berni Inns* . . . Each case must turn both on its own facts, and on the authority of *Peabody v Parkinson*, what is just and reasonable.'

I trust I do no injustice to the plaintiffs' argument in this appeal if I put it shortly in this way. There is no dispute between the employer and the main contractor that the former accepted the risk of fire dam-age: *see James Archdale & Co Ltd v Comservices Ltd* and *Scottish Special Housing Association v Wimpey*

Construction UK Ltd. However cl 20[C] does not give rise to any obligation on the employer to indemnify the sub-contractor. That clause is primarily concerned to see that the works were completed. It was intended to operate only for the mutual benefit of the employer and the main contractor. If the judge and the sub-contractors are right, the latter obtain protection which the rules of privity do not provide. Undoubtedly the sub-contractors owed duties of care in respect of damage by fire to other persons and in respect of other property (for instance the lawful visitor, employees of the employer or other buildings outside the site); in those circumstances it is impracticable juridically to draw a sensible line between the plaintiffs on the one hand and others on the other to whom a duty of care was owed. The employer had no effective control over the terms on which the relevant sub-contract was let and no direct contractual control over either the sub-contractors or any employee of theirs.

In addition, the plaintiffs pointed to the position of the first defendant, the sub-contractors' employee. Ex hypothesi he was careless and, even if his employers are held to have owed no duty to the building employers, on what grounds can it be said that the employee himself owed no such duty? In my opinion, however, this particular point does take the matter very much further. If in principle the sub-contractors owed no specific duty to the building owners in respect of damage by fire, then neither in my opinion can any of their employees have done so.

In reply the defendants contended that the judge was right to hold that in all the circumstances there was no duty of care on the sub-contractors in this case.

The law relevant to the question whether or not a duty of care arises in given circumstances has been considered by the House of Lords and the Privy Council in a number of recent decisions. For present purposes one can start with the dictum from the speech of Lord Wilberforce in *Anns v Merton London Borough* [see above] . . .

In *Yuen Kun-yeu v A-G of Hong Kong*, the question arose whether the Commissioner of Deposit-taking Companies owed any duty to persons who deposited moneys with a company which he had registered to take reasonable care to ensure that the company's affairs were not being conducted fraudulently, speculatively or to the detriment of its depositors. The opinion of the Privy Council was delivered by Lord Keith. He quoted the familiar passage to which I have already referred from the speech of Lord Wilberforce in *Anns'* case and after referring to other cases in which the passage had been treated with some reservation, he said:

'Their Lordships venture to think that the two-stage test formulated by Lord Wilberforce for determining the existence of a duty of care in negligence has been elevated to a degree of importance greater than its merits, and greater perhaps than its author intended.'

He then went on to express the approval of their Lordships of the view favoured by Gibbs CJ in the High Court of Australia in *Sutherland Shire Council v Heyman* that Lord Wilberforce meant the expression 'proximity of neighbourhood' to be a composite one importing the whole concept of necessary relationship between the plaintiff and the defendant described by Lord Atkin in *Donoghue v Stevenson*. Lord Keith pointed out that although the foreseeability of harm is a necessary ingredient of such a relationship, it is not the only one and, having quoted from passages from the speech of Lord Atkin in *Donoghue v Stevenson*, he said:

'Lord Atkin clearly had in contemplation that all the circumstances of the case, not only the foreseeability of harm, were appropriate to be taken into account in determining whether a duty of care arose.'

Subsequently he expressed the opinion that the second stage of Lord Wilberforce's test in *Anns v Merton London Borough* was one which would rarely have to be applied. It can arise only in a limited category of cases where, notwithstanding that a case of negligence is made out on a proximity basis, public policy requires that there should be no liability.

In my opinion the present state of the law on the question whether or not a duty of care exists is that, save where there is already authority that in the circumstances there is such a duty, it will only exist in novel situations where not only is there foreseeability of harm, but also such a close and direct relation between the parties concerned, not confined to mere physical proximity, to the extent contemplated by Lord Atkin in his speech in *Donoghue v Stevenson*. Further, a court should also have regard to what it considers just and reasonable in all the circumstances and facts of the case.

In the instant case it is clear that as between the employer and the main contractor the former accepted the risk of damage by fire to its premises arising out of and in the course of the building works. Further, although there was no privity between the employer and the sub-contractor, it is equally clear from the documents passing between the main contractors and the sub-contractors to which I have already referred that the sub-contractors contracted on a like basis. In *Scottish Special Housing Association v Wimpey Construction UK Ltd* the House of Lords had to consider whether, as between the employer and main contractors under a contract in precisely the same terms as those of the instant case, it was in truth intended that the employer should bear the whole risk of damage by fire, even fire caused by the contractor's negligence. The position of sub-contractors was not strictly in issue in the *Scottish Housing* case, which I cannot think the House did not appreciate, but having considered the terms of cll 18, 19 and 20[C] of the same standard form as was used in the instant case Lord Keith, in a speech with which the remainder of their Lordships agreed, said:

> 'I have found it impossible to resist the conclusion that it is intended that the employer shall bear the whole risk of damage by fire, including fire caused by the negligence of the contractor or that of sub-contractors.'

As Lord Keith went on to point out, a similar conclusion was arrived at by the Court of Appeal in England in *James Archdale & Co Ltd v Comservices Ltd*, on the construction of similarly but not identically worded corresponding clauses in a predecessor of the standard form used in the *Scottish Housing* and instant cases. Again the issue only arose in the earlier case as between employer and main contractor, but approaching the question on the basis of what is just and reasonable I do not think that the mere fact that there is no strict privity between the employer and the sub-contractor should prevent the latter from relying on the clear basis on which all the parties contracted in relation to damage to the employer's building caused by fire, even when due to the negligence of the contractors or sub-contractors.

Croom Johnson and **Glidewell L JJ** agreed.

Appeal dismissed.

NOTES

1.   Is burning down someone else's building with a blowlamp a 'novel situation'?

2.   Is the real point that the courts are unwilling to allow tort to be used, even in cases of physical harm, when that would seem to upset the 'contractual' allocation of risks?

■ *Marc Rich & Co AG v Bishop Rock Marine Co Ltd*

[1995] 3 All ER 307, HL

Early in 1986, the vessel Nicholas H loaded bulk cargoes of lead and zinc concentrate at Callao in Peru and Antofagasta in Chile for carriage to Italy and the Black Sea. Two weeks or so after embarking on this voyage, the vessel anchored of San Juan, Puerto Rico, having reported to the US coastguard a crack in her hull. The vessel was inspected at anchor by a surveyor acting on behalf of her classification society, Nippon Kaiji Kyokai (NKK), after which she entered San Juan harbour where, according to her owners, some repairs were effected. The surveyor then recommended that the vessel continued on the intended voyage, but that the repairs carried out at San Juan be further examined and dealt with at the earliest opportunity after discharge of the cargo, before loading any further cargo and not later than 30 May 1986.

The vessel sailed from San Juan on 2 March 1986. The next day she reported that the welding of the temporary repairs had cracked, and despite attempted repairs at sea, she sank a few days later. The cargo was totally lost.

The cargo owners brought proceedings against the shipowners, the head charterers of the vessel and the classification society. The proceedings against the charterers were not pursued. Those against the shipowners were settled by a payment to the claimants of a proportion of the claim. The proceedings against the classification society were pursued, for the balance of the claim.

The claim against the classification society was in tort, namely an allegation that the society owed a duty to the plaintiffs as cargo owners to take reasonable care over the class surveys carried out and the recommendations given in and off San Juan so as not to expose the cargo to risk of damage or loss, that the society (through its surveyor) was in breach of this duty and that in consequence the cargo was lost.

The case came before the Commercial Court by way of a preliminary issue, which in its final form was in the following terms:

Whether on the facts pleaded in the Points of Claim NKK owed any duty of care to Rich [the first plaintiffs] capable of giving rise to a liability in damages. (See [1992] 2 Lloyd's Rep 481 at 483.)

For the purposes of this issue and the appeal, the parties accepted that all of the plaintiffs had a sufficient proprietary interest in the cargo at the relevant time to give them title to sue if they establish that NKK owed them a duty of care, that the damage suffered by the plaintiffs was physical damage to their goods, that it was foreseeable that lack of care by NKK was likely to expose the plaintiffs' cargo to danger or physical damage, and that, although the events took place abroad, there were no conflict of laws problems about the need for 'double actionability' of the alleged claim in tort. In addition, the parties agreed that, for the purposes of the issue, the relevant facts pleaded in the points of claim were assumed to be proved.

Proceeding upon this basis, Hirst J held that NKK did owe a duty of care to the first plaintiffs capable of giving rise to a liability in damages. The Court of Appeal reversed this decision and the cargo owners appealed.

Lord Steyn

...

The requirements in physical damage cases

Counsel for the cargo owners submitted that in cases of physical damage to property in which the plaintiff has a proprietary or possessory interest the only requirement is proof of reasonable foreseeability. But since the decision in *Home Office v Dorset Yacht Co Ltd* it has been settled law that the elements of foreseeability and proximity as well as considerations of fairness, justice and reasonableness are relevant to all cases whatever the nature of the harm sustained by the plaintiff.

The factors pointing towards the existence of a duty of care

Not surprisingly, there are substantial factors pointing in favour and against the recognition of a duty of care. [Lord Steyn recited various factors in favour of a duty and continued:]

Other material factors

It is now necessary to examine a number of other factors in order to put the case in its right perspective, and to consider whether some of those factors militate against the recognition of a duty of care....

(a) Direct physical loss?

Counsel for the cargo owners argued that the present case involved the infliction of *direct* physical loss. At first glance the issue of directness may seem a matter of terminology rather than substance. In truth it is a material factor. The law more readily attaches the consequences of actionable negligence to directly inflicted physical loss than to indirectly inflicted physical loss. For example, if the NKK surveyor had carelessly dropped a lighted cigarette into a cargo hold known to contain a combustible cargo, thereby causing an explosion and the loss of the vessel and cargo, the assertion that the classification society was in breach of a duty of care might have been a strong one. That would be a paradigm case of directly inflicted physical loss. In the present case the shipowner was primarily responsible for the vessel sailing in a seaworthy condition. The role of the NKK was a subsidiary one. In my view the carelessness of the NKK surveyor did not involve the direct infliction of physical damage in the relevant sense. That by no means concludes the answer to the general question. But it does introduce the right perspective on one aspect of this case.

(b) Reliance

It is possible to visualise direct exchanges between cargo owners and a classification society, in the context of a survey on behalf of owners of a vessel laden with cargo, which might give rise to an assumption of responsibility in the sense explained by Lord Goff in *Henderson v Merrett Syndicates Ltd* . . . In the present case there was no contact whatever between the cargo owners and the classification society. Moreover, as Saville L J pointed out, in this case it is not even suggested that the cargo owners were aware that NKK had been brought in to survey the vessel: see [1994] 3 All ER 686 at 697. The cargo owners simply relied on the owners of the vessel to keep the vessel seaworthy and to look after the cargo. Saville L J and Balcombe LJ regarded this feature as sufficient to demonstrate that the necessary element of proximity was absent: see [1994] 3 AllER 686 at 697 and 704. I would approach the matter differently. In my view this feature is not necessarily decisive but it also contributes to placing the claim in the correct perspective.

(c) The bill of lading contracts

The first and principal ground of the decision of Saville LJ was the impact of the terms of the bill of lading contracts. He said ([1994] 3 AllER 686 at 695–696):

> 'The Hague Rules (and their successor the Hague-Visby Rules (which are scheduled to the Carriage of Goods by Sea Act 1971)) form an internationally recognised code adjusting the rights and duties existing between shipowners and those shipping goods under bills of lading. As Donaldson MR said in *Leigh &Sillavan Ltd v Aliakmon Shipping Co Ltd, The Aliakmon* [1985] 2 All ER 44 at 54 the rules create an intricate blend of responsibilities and liabilities, rights and immunities, limitations on the amount of damages recoverable, time bars, evidential provisions, indemnities and liberties, all in relation to the carriage of goods under bills of lading. The proposition advanced by Mr Gross would add an identical or virtually identical duty owed by the classification society to that owed by the shipowners, but without any of these balancing factors, which are internationally recognised and accepted. I do not regard that as a just, fair or reasonable proposition.'

Saville LJ ended this part of his judgment by explicitly stating ([1994] 3 AllER 686 at 697):

> 'The question is not whether the classification society is covered by the rules, but whether in all the circumstances it is just, fair and reasonable to require them to shoulder a duty which by the rules primarily lies on the shipowners, without the benefits of those rules or other international conventions.'

That question Saville L J (and, by adoption, Balcombe L J) answered in the negative. And Mann L J was in substantial agreement on this point.

It was the principal task of counsel for the cargo owners to try to dismantle the reasoning of Saville LJ. He pointed out that Saville LJ apparently assumed that the limitation of the claim of cargo owners against the shipowners arose under the Hague Rules. In truth the limitation arose by reason of tonnage limitation as already explained. This is not a point of substance. Tonnage limitation is a part of the international code which governs the claims under consideration. It is as relevant as any limitation under the Hague Rules . . .

The dealings between shipowners and cargo owners are based on a contractual structure, the Hague Rules, and tonnage limitation, on which the insurance of international trade depends: see Dr Malcolm

Clarke 'Misdelivery and Time Bars' [1990] LMCLQ 314. Underlying it is the system of double or overlapping insurance of cargo. Cargo owners take out direct insurance in respect of the cargo. Shipowners take out liability risks insurance in respect of breaches of their duties of care in respect of the cargo. The insurance system is structured on the basis that the potential liability of shipowners to cargo owners is limited under the Hague Rules and by virtue of tonnage limitation provisions. And insurance premiums payable by owners obviously reflect such limitations on the shipowners exposure...

Counsel for the cargo owners said that classification societies already carry liability risks insurance. That is no doubt right since classification societies do not have a blanket immunity from all tortious liability. On the other hand, if a duty of care is held to exist in this case, the potential exposure of classification societies to claims by cargo owners will be large. That greater exposure is likely to lead to an increase in the cost to classification societies of obtaining appropriate liability risks insurance. Given their role in maritime trade classification societies are likely to seek to pass on the higher cost to owners. Moreover, it is readily predicable that classification societies will require owners to give appropriate indemnities. Ultimately, shipowners will pay.

The result of a recognition of a duty of care in this case will be to enable cargo owners, or rather their insurers, to disturb the balance created by the Hague Rules and Hague-Visby Rules as well as by tonnage limitation provisions, by enabling cargo owners to recover in tort against a peripheral party to the prejudice of the protection of shipowners under the existing system. For these reasons I would hold that the international trade system tends to militate against the recognition of the claim in tort put forward by the cargo owners against the classification society.

(d) The contract between the classification society and shipowners

Mr Aikens QC, who appears for NKK, argued that the contract between the shipowners and the classification society must be a factor against the recognition of the suggested duty of care. He referred to *Pacific Associates Inc v Baxter* [1989] 2 All ER 159. That was a case where the Court of Appeal held that the network of contracts between a building owner, the head contractor, subcontractors and even suppliers militated against imposing duties in tort on peripheral parties. In the present case the classification society was not involved in such a web of contracts.

(e) The position and role of NKK

The fact that a defendant acts for the collective welfare is a matter to be taken into consideration when considering whether it is fair, just and reasonable to impose a duty of care:...

(f) Policy factors

Counsel for the cargo owners argued that a decision that a duty of care existed in this case would not involve wide ranging exposure for NKK and other classification societies to claims in tort. That is an unrealistic position. If a duty is recognised in this case there is no reason why it should not extend to annual surveys, docking surveys, intermediate surveys, special surveys, boiler surveys, and so forth. And the scale of NKK's potential liability is shown by the fact that NKK conducted an average of 14,500 surveys per year over the last five years.

At present the system of settling cargo claims against shipowners is a relatively simple one. The claims are settled between the two sets of insurers. If the claims are not settled, they are resolved in arbitration or court proceedings. If a duty is held to exist in this case as between the classification society and cargo owners, classification societies would become potential defendants in many cases. An extra layer of insurance would become involved. The settlement process would inevitably become more complicated and expensive. Arbitration proceedings and court proceedings would often involve an additional party. And often similar issues would have to be canvassed in separate proceedings since the classification societies would not be bound by arbitration clauses in the contracts of carriage. If such a duty is recognised, there is a risk that classification societies might be unwilling from time to time to survey the very vessels which most urgently require independent examination. It will also divert men and resources from the prime function of classification societies, namely to save life and ships at sea. These factors are, by themselves, far from decisive. But in an overall assessment of the case they merit consideration.

Is the imposition of a duty of care fair, just and reasonable?

Like Mann LJ in the Court of Appeal ([1994] 3 All ER 686 at 701), I am willing to assume (without deciding) that there was a sufficient degree of proximity in this case to fulfil that requirement for the existence of a duty of care. The critical question is therefore whether it would be fair, just and reasonable to impose such a duty. For my part I am satisfied that the factors and arguments advanced on behalf of cargo owners are decisively outweighed by the cumulative effect, if a duty is recognised, of the matters discussed in paras (c), (e) and (f), ie the outflanking of the bargain between shipowners and cargo owners, the negative effect on the public role of NKK and the other considerations of policy.

Assumption of responsibility

Given that the cargo owners were not even aware of NKK's examination of the ship, and that the cargo owners simply relied on the undertakings of the shipowners, it is in my view impossible to force the present set of facts into even the most expansive view of the doctrine of voluntary assumption of responsibility.

Conclusion

For the reasons already given I would dismiss the appeal.

Lords Keith, **Jauncey** and **Browne-Wilkinson** agreed; **Lord Lloyd** dissented.

Appeal dismissed.

NOTES

1. If the classification society is not liable because, inter alia, that would allow the cargo owners to avoid tonnage limitations and other exemptions, why is the same not true in the case of stevedores? It was assumed that they were liable in *Midland Silicones* (see p 1154) and the *New Zealand Shipping* case (p 1157). The first case can be distinguished on the ground that the clause did not purport to protect the stevedores, but the clause in the second case did. Of course, in those two cases, the damage was caused directly by the stevedores, but is that a sufficient distinction between their situation and that of the classification society?

2. The argument that immunity could be conferred by 'mere consent' (cf the fourth proposition put by the stevedores in *New Zealand Shipping*, on p 1159) could not work in this case, but might it succeed in a case in which the defendant *was* known to the plaintiff? See Furmston 23 MLR 373.

It is not safe at present to rely on a clause in the main contract by which a party accepts the risk of damage as sufficient to negate the tortious liability of subcontractors or employees. We have also seen that the 'agency device' is not a totally sure one. Can you think of any other way in which to protect the third party from the liability? Read again Lord Reid's speech in the *Midland Silicones* case (see particularly p 1155) and consider the possibilities raised by the next case.

VI. CIRCLES OF INDEMNITY

■ *Gore v Van der Lann*

[1967] 1 All ER 360, CA

The Liverpool Corporation issued, in 1963, a 'free pass' on the corporation's buses to the plaintiff, who was about 79 years of age and in receipt of a retirement pension; she made and

signed a written application whereby 'in consideration of my being granted a free pass...
I undertake and agree that the use of such pass by me shall be subject to the conditions
overleaf.' These conditions included 'The pass is issued and accepted on the understanding
that it merely constitutes and grants a licence to the holder to travel on the [corporation's]
buses, with and subject to the conditions that neither the [corporation] nor any of [its]
servants or agents responsible for driving, management, control or working of their bus
system are to be liable to the holder... for loss of life, injury... or other loss or damage to
property however caused'. The pass itself bore a statement that it was 'issued subject to the
conditions of grant set out in the written form of application... and upon the express condition that the [corporation] and [its] servants shall be under no liability, either contractual or
otherwise, to the pass-holder when boarding, alighting from or being carried on [the corporation's] vehicles'. Subsequently, a bus that the plaintiff was boarding moved off, and she fell
and was injured. She brought an action for damages against the conductor (who was
employed by the corporation), alleging that the accident was due to his negligence in causing
the bus to move off while she was boarding. The corporation intervened in the action, asking
the court to stay the proceedings, under proviso (b) to s 41 of the Supreme Court of Judicature
(Consolidation) Act 1925, on the ground that the plaintiff was bound by the condition in her
pass that its servant, the conductor, should not be liable to her.

Wilmer LJ

...On behalf of the plaintiff it has been contended that the effect of the plaintiff's application and its
acceptance by the corporation was to constitute 'a contract for the conveyance of a passenger in a
public service vehicle', which is rendered void by s 151 of the Road Traffic Act 1960. That section
provides as follows:

> 'A contract for the conveyance of a passenger in a public service vehicle shall, so far as it purports to
> negative or restrict the liability of a person in respect of a claim which may be made against him in
> respect of the death of, or bodily injury to, the passenger while being carried in, entering or alight-
> ing from the vehicle, or purports to impose any conditions with respect to the enforcement of any
> such liability, be void.'

If this contention is well founded it is obvious that, assuming negligence on the part of the defendant, it
effectively demolishes any possible defence to the plaintiff's claim, not only by the defendant but also by
the corporation itself. In the circumstances it is tempting to ask why the plaintiff's advisers have seen fit
to adopt the tortuous procedure of suing the defendant when there would have been an equally good
claim against the corporation. Be that as it may, however, it is plain that if the plaintiff's contention be
well founded, the corporation can have no possible ground for seeking to interfere with the prosecution
of the present action against the defendant.

In reply to this contention counsel for the corporation relied on the decision of Lord Goddard CJ and
of Lord Greene MR, in this court in *Wilkie v London Passenger Transport Board*, as authority for the
proposition that the issue by a transport authority of a free pass subject to conditions does not constitute a contract between the holder and the authority, but amounts to no more than the grant of a
revocable licence with the condition that, while it is being enjoyed, certain consequences are to follow.

[Wilmer LJ read part of Lord Greene MR's judgment in *Wilkie's* case, including the following:]

> 'It is clearly nothing but a licence subject to conditions, a very common form of licence, eg, a licence
> to a neighbour to walk over a field, providing he does not go with a dog. You cannot spell such a
> thing as being a contract: "I will let you go across my field in consideration of you, as a contracting
> party, agreeing not to take your dog." In other words, looking at this document shortly and sensibly,
> it contains no intention to contract.'

[Wilmer LJ continued:]

Wilkie's case, being a decision of this court, is binding on us unless it is distinguishable. I have found the question one of no little difficulty, but I have come to the conclusion, not without some hesitation, that the present case is to be distinguished. The circumstances surrounding the issue of the free pass in the present case were quite different from those in which the pass in *Wilkie's* case was issued. There the pass was issued to an employee of the board as a matter of course as one of the privileges attaching to his employment. There was certainly nothing contractual about it; there was, as Lord Greene said, no contractual animus. In the present case, on the other hand, the pass was issued, not to an employee, but to a stranger, and only in response to a written application. By the terms of the application which she signed the plaintiff specifically undertook and agreed that the use of the pass should be subject to the conditions. The very wording of that which the plaintiff signed was couched in the language of contract. It appears to me that all the elements of contract were present. By signing and submitting her application, the plaintiff, as I see it, was accepting the offer of the corporation to carry her free on its buses subject to the conditions specified. Each party gave good consideration by accepting a detriment in return for the advantages gained. Unlike *Wilkie's* case, the facts of the present case do in my judgment reveal a contractual animus. This conclusion is, of course, fatal to the corporation's application. If, as I think, there was a contract, it is clearly rendered void by s 151 of the Road Traffic Act 1960. There can, therefore, be no obstacle in the way of the plaintiff prosecuting an action for negligence, whether against the corporation or against its employee. The corporation can have no possible ground for seeking to interfere with the plaintiff's right to prosecute her action.

That is sufficient to dispose of the appeal; but I think it right to add that, even if I had thought that the issue of the free pass amounted to no more than the grant of a licence subject to conditions, I should still have arrived at the same conclusion so far as this application is concerned. It is true that the conditions accepted by the plaintiff when she accepted the offer of a free pass included a provision that the employees of the corporation were not to be liable to her for any injury or loss; but I cannot construe this provision as a promise by the plaintiff not to institute proceedings against an employee. If the corporation desired such a promise from the holder of a free pass, it could have said so in clear and unambiguous terms. In my judgment the conditions are to be construed strictly against the corporation which put them forward. It is not enough to say that a promise not to sue the employee is to be implied. At the best for the corporation, the condition relied on is ambiguous, and any ambiguity must be resolved in favour of the plaintiff.

In these circumstances the corporation has not satisfied me that it has any justification for interfering with the plaintiff's prima facie right at common law to bring proceedings against the defendant whom she accuses of negligence. On this ground also I am of opinion that the judge came to the right conclusion, and that the appeal should be dismissed.

Since preparing this judgment I have had the advantage of reading the judgment of Harman LJ. I should desire to express my concurrence with his view that, since it has not been shown that there was any contract between the corporation and the defendant rendering the corporation liable in law to indemnify the defendant, there is no ground on which the corporation could be held to have an interest entitling it to relief under s 41 of the Act of 1925. On this ground, also, in addition to those which I have already set out, I am satisfied that the corporation's application was rightly dismissed.

Harman LJ (read by Salmon LJ)

...This question, therefore, is whether before the Supreme Court of Judicature Act, 1873 the corporation would have been entitled to apply to restrain the action. This would have been done by a bill in Chancery. The ground stated is that the prosecution of the action would be a fraud on the corporation, and the fraud alleged apparently is that, if the action succeeded and damages were obtained against the conductor, the corporation would in some way be liable to indemnify him. It is here in my judgment that the case breaks down, for I do not see how the corporation could be liable in law for what would be a tort of its servant....

There is no suggestion in the instant case that there is any contract between the corporation and the defendant making the corporation liable for the torts of the latter, and in its absence I cannot see that the corporation is liable at law and, if not, I think that the corporation has no interest which would entitle it to relief under the section. This seems to me to be in accordance with the opinion expressed in the passage which I have read.

In these circumstances I am of opinion that the judge below was right in refusing the corporation's application. I do not think that the question of the applicability of s 151 of the Road Traffic Act 1960 arises. I therefore propose to express no opinion on the difficult question whether the free pass constituted a contract between the plaintiff and the corporation, or whether it was merely a licence subject to a condition having no contractual effect.

Salmon LJ

I agree with both the judgments which have been delivered.

For my part I have little doubt but that there was a contract between the plaintiff and the Liverpool Corporation. The plaintiff signed an application for a pass on one of the corporation's printed forms, the very language of which is calculated to impress on an applicant that she is entering into a legally binding agreement with the corporation.

> 'In consideration of my being granted a free pass for use on the buses of Liverpool Corporation, I undertake and agree that the use of such pass by me shall be subject to the conditions overleaf.'

... Even had there been no contract in the present case, I would have come to the clear conclusion that the corporation must fail. For the corporation to obtain the relief which it claims, it would be necessary for it to show (as Harman LJ points out) that, before the Supreme Court of Judicature Act 1873, it would have been entitled to apply to the court in Chancery to restrain the plaintiff from bringing her action against the defendant. In order to succeed, the corporation would have had to establish that the action was a fraud on the corporation either (i) because the plaintiff had agreed with the corporation for good consideration not to bring such an action, or (ii) because of some other good reason. As to (i) this presupposes a contractual promise by the plaintiff not to sue the corporation's servant. I do not think that any such promise can be implied. Even if it could, it would mean that there was a contract between the plaintiff and the defendant which, in so far as it purported to negative or restrict the plaintiff's right to sue, would be void under s 151 of the Road Traffic Act 1960. As to (ii), the only other reason for holding that the plaintiff's action could be a fraud on the corporation would be that the corporation would in law be obliged to indemnify its servant, the defendant, against his liability to the plaintiff in negligence. Clearly there is no such legal obligation on the corporation. I appreciate that the corporation would not wish to leave the defendant personally to bear the burden of this action, and moreover that it might face trouble with his trade union if it did so; but this is not, in my view, sufficient to stigmatise the plaintiff's action against the defendant as a fraud on the corporation.

For these reasons I agree that the appeal must be dismissed.

Appeal dismissed.

NOTES

1. In order to succeed, would an intervening party have to show *either* that the plaintiff had promised him not to sue the defendant *or* that he was liable to indemnify the defendant, or must he show both?

2. If you wished to draft a clause that *would* prevent a third party being sued, how would you go about it in the light of this case? Consider the following, which is from the warranty clause of a 'precedent' sales contract for aircraft:

   (f) the rights expressly conferred upon the Purchaser by paragraphs (a) and (b) of this Condition are accepted by the Purchaser in place of all other warranties or conditions as to quality or fitness express or implied by law or otherwise and Westland shall not be liable to the Purchaser in contract or for negligence or otherwise in respect of any injury loss damage or expenses which directly or indirectly is caused by or arises out of either:

(i)   any defect in or failure of or unsuitability of any Contract Item or of any component or part replaced repaired or supplied by Westland in pursuance of this Contract; or

(ii) any advice instruction service training or work given rendered or done by Westland or any employee or agent of Westland in pursuance of or for the purpose of this Contract.

It is agreed that in the event of the above provision relieving Westland from the unlimited consequences of negligence being rendered ineffective by legislation or by the decision of any Court of competent jurisdiction, the remainder of this paragraph (f) shall remain in full force and effect.

(g) The Purchaser agrees to indemnify Westland against all claims against Westland for which Westland may be liable made by persons in the employment of the Purchaser liability for which would have been excluded by this Condition if such claim had been made by the Purchaser.

(h) In the event of a claim being made by the Purchaser or any person in the employment of the Purchaser against any servant of Westland liability for which would have been excluded by this Condition if such claim had been by the Purchaser against Westland, Westland shall be entitled (if such servant of Westland be liable therefor) to indemnify such servant as aforesaid in respect of such claim and the Purchaser will repay to Westland any sum paid by Westland by reason of such indemnity.

(This clause may be varied in negotiations, particularly in domestic sales.)

3.   In *Beswick v Beswick*, specific performance was *ordered* because the estate was suffering no loss from the breach. In *Gore*, a stay was *refused* because the corporation was suffering no loss of a kind recognised by law. Does that strike you as curious?

4.   In *Snelling v John G Snelling Ltd* [1973] QB 87, the plaintiff and the second and third defendants were brothers and all directors of the defendant company. The company was financed by substantial loans from all three brothers. As part of an arrangement to borrow money from a finance company, the three brothers made an arrangement between themselves not to seek repayment of their loans during the currency of the loan from the finance company, and that if, during this period, any of them should voluntarily resign his directorship, he should forfeit the money owing to him. The defendant company was not a party to this agreement between the brothers. Later, the plaintiff resigned his directorship and sued the company for repayment of his loan. The other two brothers sought to be joined as defendants and counterclaimed for a declaration that the plaintiff had forfeited the money. Ormrod J held that the defendant brothers were entitled to have his action stayed because it was a breach of the plaintiff's contract with them: unlike *Gore's* case, there was a clearly implicit undertaking by the plaintiff not to sue the company. As all the parties were before the court and the reality was that the plaintiff's action failed, it should be dismissed. Whether the defendant brothers would have been liable to the company or the lender if the plaintiff had been permitted to recover does not appear to have been discussed.

VII. REFORM

In many situations, the doctrine of privity has been abrogated by statute; in cases of exception clauses, it has added a clause (admittedly a complicated one) to contracts; even in the case of positive benefits, such as the £5 per week in *Beswick v Beswick*, it is relatively easy to avoid the doctrine by careful contract planning. If Mr and Mrs Beswick had gone to a competent solicitor, he could, for instance, have advised that Mr Beswick should sell half his business to his wife for £10 and that they should then jointly sell the business to the nephew. There would then have been no doubt that the wife would contract just as effectively as her husband. It looks as if the Beswicks may have gone to a solicitor to help them with drafting the contract but that he had forgotten about the doctrine of privity of contract. In general, the doctrine does not very often raise problems with people who have had access to competent lawyers but, of course, many people make contract without access to lawyers at all.

For years, the rule has been criticised in textbooks and law review articles and, in more recent years, increasingly by judges. Lord Scarman said in *Woodar Investment Development Ltd v Wimpey Construction (UK) Ltd* (see p 1143) at 591:

I wish to add nothing to what your Lordships have already said about the authorities which the Court of Appeal cited as leading to the conclusion that Woodar is entitled to substantial damages for Wimpey's failure to pay Transworld. I agree that they do not support the conclusion. But I regret that this House has not yet found the opportunity to reconsider the two rules which effectually prevent A or C recovering that which B, for value, has agreed to provide.

First, the jus quaesitum tertio. I respectfully agree with Lord Reid [in *Beswick v Beswick*] that the denial by English law of a jus quaesitum tertio calls for reconsideration.... *Beswick v Beswick* was decided in 1967. It is now 1979; but nothing has been done. If the opportunity arises, I hope the House will reconsider *Tweddle v Atkinson* and the other cases which stand guard over this unjust rule.

Certainly the crude proposition for which Wimpey contends, namely that the state of English law is such that neither C for whom the benefit was intended nor A who contracted for it can recover it if the contract is terminated by B's refusal to perform, calls for review, and now, not 40 years on.

Lord Keith associated himself with these observations.

In *Darlington Borough Council v Wiltshier Northern Ltd* (above), Steyn LJ said:

The case for recognising a contract for the benefit of a third party is simple and straightforward. The autonomy of the will of the parties should be respected. The law of contract should give effect to the reasonable expectations of contracting parties. Principle certainly requires that a burden should not be imposed on a third party without his consent. But there is no doctrinal, logical or polict reason why the law should deny effectiveness to a contract for the benefit of a third party where that is the expressed intention of the parties. Moreover, often the parties, and particularly third parties, organise their affairs on the faith of the contract. They rely on the contract. It is therefore unjust to deny effectiveness to such a contract. I will not struggle further with the point since nobody seriously asserts the contrary...

A more debatable question was whether the change should be made by the courts or by legislative action.

As long ago as 1937, the Law Revision Committee (sixth Interim Report (Cmd 5449)), section D, recommended that:

Where a contract by its express terms purports to confer a benefit directly on a third party it shall be enforceable by the third party in his own name subject to any defences that would have been valid between the contracting parties.

Unless the contract otherwise provides it may be cancelled by the mutual consent of the contracting parties before the third party has adopted it either expressly or by conduct.

The subsequent fate of this proposal has been described by Beatson [1992] CLP 1.

Meanwhile, there have been significant developments at common law in both Australia and Canada.

In *Trident General Insurance Co Ltd v McNiece Bros Pty Ltd* (1988) 165 CLR 107, Blue Circle Cement Ltd had entered into a contract of insurance with Trident. Subsequently, McNiece became the principal contractor for construction work that was being carried out at Blue Circle's plant. The policy that had been issued covered, amongst other things, liability to members of the public for accidents occurring during this construction work and the policy defined the assured in addition to Blue Circle as all its contractors and subcontractors. A worker was seriously injured at the site and recovered a judgment against McNiece. McNiece claimed to be entitled to indemnity against this liability from Trident but Trident denied liability.

Five of the seven members of the High Court of Australia held that McNiece were entitled to be indemnified under the policy. Mason CJ and Wilson J were in favour at least of creating an exception to a privity of contract so as to enable the beneficiary of an insurance policy such as this to take advantage of it. Their reasoning suggested they would be willing to go significantly further and to view with equanimity a rule that said that a third party could enforce a contract under which the parties had a contractual intention to benefit a third party. Toohey J's judgment goes in a similar direction, though perhaps less far. Deane J would have been willing to hold for McNiece by using the trust exception (although this gave rise to procedural problems because McNiece had not alleged a trust in its claim and had been refused leave by the New South Wales Court of Appeal to amend its pleadings so as to allege a trust). Gaudron J held for McNiece on the basis of principles of unjust enrichment. Brennan and Dawson JJ dissented. Mason CJ and Wilson J said:

Should it be a sufficient foundation for the existence of a third party entitlement to sue on the contract that there is a contractual intention to benefit a third party? Or, should an intention that the third party should be able to sue on the contract be required? Under s 48 of the *Insurance Contracts Act* 1984 (Cth) and in the United States an intention to benefit a third party alone is necessary and that seems to be the position in Western Australia. But in Queensland (*Property Law Act* 1974 (Qld) ss 55(1), 55(6)(c)(ii)) and in New Zealand (*Contracts Privity Act* 1982 (NZ) ss4, 8) an intention that the third party should be able to sue is required. This requirement again seems to have its origin in the recommendations of the English Law Revision Committee. As the contracting parties are unlikely to turn their attention to the enforcement by the third party, the ascertainment of this intention may well be fraught with similar problems to those that have surrounded the trust concept.

The variety of these responses to the problems arising from contracts to benefit a third party indicate the range of the policy choices to be made and that there is room for debate about them. A simple departure from the traditional rules would lead to third party enforceability of such a contract, subject to the preservation of a contracting party's right to rescind or vary, in the absence of reliance by the third party to his detriment, and to the availability in an action by the third party of defences against a contracting party. The adoption of this course would represent less of a departure from the traditional exposition of the law that other legislative choices which have been made. Moreover, as we have seen, the traditional rules, which were adopted here as a consequence of their development in the United Kingdom, have been the subject of much criticism and of legislative erosion in the field of insurance contracts. Regardless of the layers of sediment which may have accumulated, we consider that it is the responsibility of this court to reconsider in appropriate cases common law rules which operate unsatisfactorily and unjustly. The fact that there have been recent legislative developments in the relevant field is not a reason for continuing to insist on the application of an unjust rule as it stood before its alteration by the *Insurance Contracts Act* 1984 (Cth).

In the ultimate analysis the limited question we have to decide is whether the old rules apply to a policy of insurance. The injustice which would flow from such a result arises not only from its failure to give effect to the expressed intention of the person who takes out the insurance but also from the common intention of the parties and the circumstance that others, aware of the existence of the policy, will order their affairs accordingly. We doubt that the doctrine of estoppel provides an adequate protection of the legitimate expectations of such persons and, even if it does, the rights of persons under a policy of insurance should not be made to depend on the vagaries of such an intricate doctrine. In the nature of things the likelihood of some degree of reliance on the part of the third party in the case of a benefit to be provided for him under an insurance policy is so tangible that the common law rule should be shaped with that likelihood in mind.

This argument has even greater force when it is applied to an insurance against liabilities which is expressed to cover the insured and its subcontractors. It stands to reason that many subcontractors will assume that such an insurance is an effective indemnity in their favour and that they will refrain from making their own arrangements for insurance on that footing. That, it seems, is what happened in the present case. But why should the respondent's rights depend entirely on its ability to make out a case of estoppel?

In the circumstances, notwithstanding the caution with which the court ordinarily will review earlier authorities and the operation of long-established principle, we conclude that the principled development of the law requires that it be recognised that McNiece was entitled to succeed in the action.

For the foregoing reasons, we would dismiss the appeal.

In *London Drugs Ltd v Kuehne & Nagel International Ltd* (1992) 97 DLR (4th) 261, London Drugs delivered a transformer weighing some 7,500 lbs to Kuehne & Nagel for storage on Kuehne & Nagel's standard terms. These terms included a provision as to liability:

Sec 11

(a) The responsibility of a warehouseman in the absence of written provisions is the reasonable care and diligence required by the law.

(b) The warehouseman's liability on any one package is limited to $40 unless the holder has declared in writing a valuation in excess of $40 and paid the additional charge specified to cover warehouse liability.

London Drugs did not declare that the transformer was worth more than $40 nor did it pay any extra charge. Two employees at Kuehne & Nagel were instructed to load the transformer onto a truck to delivery to London Drugs. They attempted to do this by lifting with two forklift vehicles. The safe practice would have been to lift using overhead equipment attached to brackets fixed to the transformer. As a result of their attempt to use the forklift trucks, the transformer toppled over and was damaged to an amount in excess of $30,000. London Drugs sued both Kuehne & Nagel and the employees.

At first instance, the liability of Kuehne & Nagel was limited to $40, but the employees were held liable for the full value of the damage to the transformer. By a majority, the British Columbia Court of Appeal reduced the award against the employees to $40.

London Drugs appealed to the Supreme Court of Canada, arguing that the doctrine of privity of contract prevented the employees relying on the provision in Kuehne & Nagel's standard conditions. The Supreme Court of Canada rejected the appeal. Iacobucci J delivered the majority opinion, in which he said:

For my part, I prefer to deal head-on with the doctrine of privity and to relax its ambit in the circumstances of this case. Some may argue that the same result can (and should) be reached by using a number of approaches which are seemingly less drastic and/or allegedly more theoretically sound, such as the one advanced in the Court of Appeal by McEachern CJBC and Wallace JA, or the 'no duty' approach advocated by my colleague, La Forest J, and authors such as B Reiter, 'Contracts, Torts, Relations and Reliance', in B Reiter and J Swan, editors *Studies in Contract Law* (Toronto: Butterworths, 1980) at p 235, or the doctrine of 'vicarious immunity' allegedly adopted by the House of Lords in *Elder, Dempster and Co v Paterson, Zochonis & Co*.

In my view the respondents were third party beneficiaries to the limitation of liability clause found in the contract of storage between their employer and the appellant and, in view of the circumstances involved, may benefit directly from this clause notwithstanding that they are not a signing party to the contract. I recognize that such a conclusion collides with privity of contract in its strictest sense; however, for reasons that follow, I believe that this court is presented with an appropriate factual opportunity in which to reconsider the scope of this doctrine and decide whether its application in cases such as the one at bar should be limited or modified. It is my opinion that commercial reality and common sense require that it should.

Many have noted that an application of the doctrine so as to prevent a third party from relying on a limitation of liability clause which was intended to benefit him or her frustrates sound commercial practice and justice. It does not respect allocations and assumptions of risk made by the parties to the contract and it ignores the practical modification to the contract by circumventing its provisions and the express or implied intention of the parties. In addition, it is inconsistent with the reasonable expectations of all the parties to the transaction, including the third party beneficiary who is made to support the entire burden of liability. The doctrine has also been criticised for creating uncertainty in the law. While most commentators welcome, at least in principle, the various judicial exceptions to privity of contract, concerns about the predictability of their use have been raised. Moreover, it is said, in cases where the recognized exceptions do not appear to apply, the underlying concerns of commercial reality and justice still militate for the recognition of a third party beneficiary right.

For a further development by the Canadian Supreme Court, see *Fraser River Pile & Dredge Ltd v Can-Dive Services Ltd* (1999) 176 DLR (4th) 257.

In the USA, many states have abandoned the doctrine of privity, following the famous case of *Lawrence v Fox* 20 NY 268 (Court of Appeals, New York, 1859). Restatement 2d now provides:

§302. Intended and incidental beneficiaries

(1) Unless otherwise agreed between promisor and promisee, a beneficiary of a promise is an intended beneficiary if recognition of a right to performance in the beneficiary is appropriate to effectuate the intention of the parties and either

  (a) the performance of the promise will satisfy an obligation of the promisee to pay money to the beneficiary; or

  (b) the circumstances indicate that the promisee intends to give the beneficiary the benefit of the promised performance.

(2) An incidental beneficiary is a beneficiary who is not an intended beneficiary.

§304. Creation of duty to beneficiary

A promise in a contract creates a duty in the promisor to any intended beneficiary to perform the promise, and the intended beneficiary may enforce the duty.

§307. Remedy of specific performance

Where specific performance is otherwise an appropriate remedy, either the promisee or the beneficiary may maintain a suit for specific enforcement of a duty owed to an intended beneficiary.

§311. Variation of a duty to a beneficiary

(1) Discharge or modification of a duty to an intended beneficiary by conduct of the promisee or by a subsequent agreement between promisor and promisee is ineffective if a term of the promise creating the duty so provides.

(2) In the absence of such a term, the promisor and promisee retain power to discharge or modify the duty by subsequent agreement.

(3) Such a power terminates when the beneficiary, before he receives notification of the discharge or modification materially changes his position in justifiable reliance on the promise or brings suit on it or manifests assent to it at the request of the promisor or promisee.

(4) If promisee receives consideration for an attempted discharge or modification of the promisor's duty which is ineffective against the beneficiary, the beneficiary can assert a right to the consideration so received. The promisor's duty is discharged to the extent of the amount received by the beneficiary.

§315. Effect of a promise of incidental benefit

An incidental beneficiary acquires by virtue of the promise no right against the promisor or the promisee.

It will be observed that the Restatement 2d does not confer a right of action on every third party who will benefit from the promised performance, even if he is explicitly referred to in the contract. The decision whether he is an intended beneficiary is often very difficult and courts have reached different conclusions on very similar facts. See Farnsworth, *Contracts*, s 10(3).

The Law Commission recommended that English law should take the path of statutory change and this course has been adopted.

■ *Law Commission Consultation Paper No 121, 'Privity of Contract: Contracts for the Benefit of Third Parties'*
paras 4.1–4.6, 5.8–5.14, 6.2–6.12, 6.14–6.15

THE CASE FOR REFORM

...[The] case for reform...rests on a number of considerations. First, the fact that the rule prevents effect being given to the intentions of the contracting parties has caused difficulties in practice. Secondly, the rule has led to unnecessary complexity and uncertainty in the law in view of the number of common law and statutory exceptions to it. The technical hurdles which must be overcome if one is to circumvent the rule by drafting also lead to uncertainty since it will often be possible to raise plausible arguments that some requirement has not been satisfied. This uncertainty is commercially inconvenient and may lead to inefficient duplication of insurance cover. The combination of the denial of rights to the third party and the rule that the promisee when suing can only recover for his own loss, and not that of another, may also lead to injustice. Finally, the justifications of the rule are unconvincing.

...

1. An overall assessment of the rule

4.3 The case for the third party rule rests on a number of factors:-

    (i) Although English law does not as a general rule permit the creation of contractual rights in third parties it does not prohibit the achievement of the same result in practice, providing that the appropriate drafting is used.

    (ii) Contracts are personal transactions whose ambit only extends to the contracting parties.

    (iii) It is undesirable for the promisor to be liable to two actions from both the promisee and the third party.

    (iv) It is unjust that a person could be treated as a party to a contract for the purpose of suing upon it when he could not be sued.

    (v) Since a contract is of its nature a bargain, a third party cannot sue because he has not provided any consideration, ie he is getting something for nothing. If a promisee must furnish consideration, it would appear anomalous that a gratuitous third party beneficiary could be in a better position than a gratuitous promisee.

    (vi) f third parties could enforce contracts made for their benefit, the rights of contracting parties to rescind or vary such contracts would be affected.

    (vii) The third party rule imposes to limit on the potential liability of a contracting party to a wide range of possible third party plaintiffs.

4.4 We do not regard any of the explanations outlined in paragraph 4.3 as convincing justifications of the rule.

    (i) Whereas situations exist where properly advised parties can draft around the third party rule, the reality is that laymen left to themselves may understandably fail to do so. Indeed, the rule has caused problems even where the parties have taken legal advice, or have taken steps to draft around the third party rule.

(ii) To say that third parties cannot sue because contracts are a personal affair between the contracting parties is simply a deduction from a proposition which itself requires justification. One such justification is the notion that contracts need an element of consent which is provided by making an offer or accepting one, and thus not consented, he should not obtain any contractual rights. However, presumably the purpose of requiring consent is the protection of personal autonomy. Allowing third parties to enforce contracts made for their benefit will not undermine this autonomy as only the question of giving third parties benefits (and not that of imposing burdens) is in issue. Furthermore, when both parties have agreed to benefit a third party, allowing the third party an enforceable claim gives effect to their intention and promotes the idea of agreement. Indeed, wider community interests in security of transactions are undermined when a bargain is disregarded.

(iii) The argument that the promisor could be faced with actions from both the promisee and the third party can be addressed in several ways. One answer is that there is only one promise which can give rise to only one cause of action. Once the promise is enforced, it is extinguished and the promisor will no longer be liable.

(iv) As for the argument that it is unfair that a person should be able to sue when he cannot be sued, this should not in fact be an impediment to enforceability since unilateral contracts in which only one person is obliged to perform are enforceable. Furthermore, even if the third party is immune from reciprocal suit by the promisor, the promisor's interests are protected by having a claim against the promisee.

(v) To say that a third party cannot sue because he is not a party to a bargain is to confuse two issues. Whereas the third party rule relates to the question who may enforce a contract, the doctrine of consideration decides which promises may be enforced. Where consideration has been furnished, albeit by the promisee and not the third party, there is a bargain and the promisor's promise has been 'paid for' albeit not by the third party. This explains the apparent anomaly that the gratuitous third party has rights which the gratuitous promisee does not have. The gratuitous third party has rights under a valid contract, whereas in the case of the gratuitous promisee there is, *ex hypothesi*, no valid contract.

(vi) &

(vii) It is true that reform of the third party rule might prejudice the rights of the contracting parties to vary or rescind the contract, and would expose the promisor to a wider range of possible third party plaintiffs. These are issues which must be considered, but which do not necessarily preclude reform. It is possible to have a reform which respects the rights of the contracting parties even though third parties are given enforceable rights. Similarly, a sufficiently circumscribed test of who is a third party beneficiary will prevent a flood of litigation.

4.5 Although the development of English contract law has been pragmatic and not the outcome of one particular theory, it appears that the third party rule is not a necessary part of any of the supposed theoretical foundations of contractual liability.

(a) According to the 'will' theory of contract, liability is based on a person's intention, will or promise, such that the law of contract is designed to give effect to the intentions of the parties, regardless of any element of benefit or detrimental reliance. It would not appear that the will theory requires the third party rule, particularly where it is the manifest intention of both parties that a third party should have enforceable rights.

(b) According to the 'bargain' theory of contract, the courts only enforce agreements where there has been an exchange of, or a promise to exchange, value. However, even where the third party is not a party to the bargain, and yet where value has been exchanged between the parties on the basis that the third party is to have enforceable rights, the bargain may be defeated if the third party does not in fact have such rights.

(c) Whether or not the law of contract has as its main purpose the protection of expectations reasonably created, or the protection of reliance reasonably incurred, it would not appear that the third party rule is required. A contract made between A and B for the benefit of C may create a reasonable expectation in C that it will be performed. Likewise, C may act in reliance on this. On either theory, C should have a legal right to enforce performance.

4.6 In many commercial situations there exists a complex pattern of relationships, from which it may be difficult to discern the traditional requirements of offer, acceptance and consideration. In these situations, paradigm examples of which are building and carriage contracts considered below, it may be contrary to the commercial reality of the situation to preclude a third party, who is in a continuing relationship with the parties to a contract, from enforcing rights under it which are given for his benefit. It has been suggested that within a 'network' of linked commercial contracts, that is to say a group of contracts which have collectively as their object the attainment of a common underlying purpose, the doctrine should have no application. [Adams and Brownsword, above, p 1020.]

...

2. Test of enforceable benefit

5.8 This is the central issue involved in reform of the third party rule. It is an issue on which there is no consensus among the various jurisdictions which we have examined. There are several options, including the following:

(i) A third party may enforce a contract which expressly in its terms purports to confer a benefit directly on him. [See section 11(2) of the Western Australia Property Law Act 1969.]
(ii) A third party may enforce a contract in which the parties intend that he should receive the benefit of the promised performance, regardless of whether they intend him to have an enforceable right of action.
(iii) A third party may enforce a contract in which the parties intend that he should receive the benefit of the promised performance and also intend to create a legal obligation enforceable by him. [See the law in Queensland, New Zealand and Scotland: Appendix, paras 4, 9 & 22. We will refer to this as the 'dual intention' test.]
(iv) A third party may enforce a contract where to do so would effectuate the intentions of the parties and either the performance of the promise satisfies a monetary obligation of the promisee to him or it is the intention of the promisee to confer a gift on him. [See sections 302 & 304 of the Restatement (Second) of Contracts: Appendix, para 16.]
(v) A third party may enforce a contract on which he justifiably and reasonably relies, regardless of the intentions of the parties.
(vi) A third party may enforce a contract which actually confers a benefit on him, regardless of the purpose of the contract or the intentions of the parties.

5.9 We think that the options of allowing a third party to sue on any contract which happens to confer a benefit on him or on which he justifiably and reasonably relied would be unacceptably wide. They raise the possibility of an unacceptable volume of litigation and leave promisors open to liability to a potentially intermediate class of third parties. The option of allowing a third party to sue on a contract which expressly in its terms purports to benefit him would not cater for those contracts under which the parties intend to confer an enforceable benefit on him but have not spelled this out expressly. Likewise, we do not think it sufficient that the contracting parties intend that the third party should receive the benefit of the promised performance: again, for the reasons that the parties' intentions could be defeated and an unacceptably large number of potential plaintiffs created. For instance, in the example discussed earlier of a building company contracting with a highway authority for the construction of a new road, the road may be intended for the benefit of all road-users, or even for an identified number of users (such as the residents of a private estate). However, it is a different issue whether individual road-users should have a right of action on the agreement in the event of delay in construction.

5.10 We provisionally recommend that a third party should be able to enforce a contract in which the parties intend that he should receive the benefit of the promised performance and also intend to create a legal obligation enforceable by him. From this it follows that the creation of a right in a third party should not be inferred from the mere fact that he will derive benefit from performance of the contract. Equally, a third party should not be allowed to sue on any contract which is simply made for his benefit or which merely happens to benefit him or on which he has happened to rely.

5.11 The basic principle on which our proposal rests is to allow a remedy to the third party when to do so would give effect to the intentions of the contracting parties. Intention should not necessarily be associated with motive. If A, in buying property from B, promises to pay the purchase price to C, A's motive or purpose in making the promise may be simply to comply with the proposed bargain. Likewise, the reason why B extracted the promise may have been to make a gift to a close friend or to fulfil a duty to a sworn enemy. Whether or not a contract is intended to create a legal obligation enforceable by the third party is to be derived from the terms of the contract and the surrounding circumstances.

5.12 Furthermore, it is the objectively determined intentions of the parties which matter rather than their private thoughts. Parties to the contract may frequently omit provisions from their contract, whilst relying on prior dealing, trade customs or other shared beliefs. We provisionally recommend that reform should enable consideration of the circumstances surrounding the making of the contract when deducing the parties' intentions.

5.13 Although we provisionally recommend the dual intention test, we are aware of the criticisms of it.

(i) Where the contract is silent or ambiguous on the question of enforcement by a third party, the ascertainment of a contractual intention may be difficult.

(ii) Concentration on the intention of the parties has been argued to be a substitute for the real enquiry, which should be on the third party's actual reliance and the needs of the market in which the parties operate. Where a third party becomes involved, generally by reliance on the contract, a court may be unduly restricted if it only has regard to the intent of the contracting parties.

5.14 However, we do not regard these criticisms as convincing. First, the problem of detecting an unexpressed intention is a familiar one for courts as is the idea of giving effect to the intentions of the parties. We do not think that ascertainment of the parties' intentions in a three party situation poses any more difficulties than in a two-party situation. Indeed, even if such ascertainment is difficult, this does not of itself point in favour of a later rule which may not reflect the intentions of the contracting parties. Secondly, we have already stated why we think that it would be unacceptable if a third party could sue on any contract on which he justifiably and reasonably relied.

…

6.2 Of the various options for reform which we have examined, it is our provisional recommendation that reform should be by way of a detailed legislative scheme.

C. The main issues

1. Test of enforceable benefit

6.3 We provisionally recommend that a third party should be able to enforce a contract in which the parties intend that he should receive the benefit of the promised performance and also intend to create a legal obligation enforceable by him.

6.4 We provisionally recommend that reform should enable consideration of the circumstances surrounding the making of the contract when deducing the parties' intentions.

2. Range of benefits

6.5 We provisionally recommend that rights created against a contracting party should be governed by the contract and be valid only to the extent that it is valid, and may be conditional upon the other contracting party performing his obligations under it.

6.6 We provisionally recommend that rights which may be created in favour of a third party extend (a) to the right to receive the promised performance from the promisor where this is an appropriate remedy and also to the right to pursue any remedies for delayed or defective performance, and (b) to the right to rely on any provisions in the contract restricting or excluding the third party's liability to a contracting party as if the third party were a party to the contract.

3. Designation of third party

6.7 We invite views on whether there should have to be a particular form of designation: whether express designation (eg the third party's name) or implied designation, including a description of the type of employment (eg stevedores) or class of employment (eg sub-contractor) or type of interest (eg consignee).

4. Ascertainability and existence of third party

6.8 We provisionally recommend that rights may be created in a third party even though he is not in existence or ascertained at the time the contract is made.

. . .

5. Defences and joinder

6.10 We provisionally recommend that the rights of the third party against the promisor should be subject to the promisor's defences, set-offs and counterclaims which would have been available to the promisor in an action by the promisee. We invite views on whether, in the case of a set-off or counterclaim, a promisor may only rely on matters arising from the contract in which the promise is contained or may also set up against the third party defences arising out of other relations between promisor and promisee

6.11 We invite views on whether there should be a requirement that the promisee, as well as the promisor, be a party to the litigation when a third party sues to enforce a contract made for his benefit.

6. Variation and cancellation

6.12 We invite views on (i) whether (in the absence of an agreement between the contracting parties and the third party) acceptance, adoption or material reliance should be required before modification is prevented; (ii) whether such adoption, acceptance or material reliance should be known to the parties (or at least the promisee) or be such that the promisee could reasonably have anticipated it; (iii) whether modification should be permitted where the contract allows it either expressly or impliedly regardless of adoption, acceptance or material reliance or at least where the third party knows (or should reasonably have been aware) that the contract permits modification even though he subsequently adopts, accepts or materially relies on the contract.

. . .

8. Can the promisee sue in addition to the third party?

6.14 We provisionally recommend that the promisor's duty to perform is owed both the third party and the contractual promisee, but in so far as he makes performance to or is released from performance by the third party he discharges his duty under the contract and all remedies against him for any breach of the contract are available to the third party and may be pursued by him in preference to the contractual promisee.

6.15 We invite views on what should be the position where the promisor has made performance to the promisee and then the third party seeks to enforce the contract.

. . .

■ *Contracts (Rights of Third Parties) Act 1999*

Right of third party to enforce contractual term.

1. —(1) Subject to the provisions of this Act, a person who is not a party to a contract (a 'third party') may in his own right enforce a term of the contract if-
(a) the contract expressly provides that he may, or
(b) subject to subsection (2), the term purports to confer a benefit on him.

(2) Subsection (1)(b) does not apply if on a proper construction of the contract it appears that the parties did not intend the term to be enforceable by the third party.

(3) The third party must be expressly identified in the contract by name, as a member of a class or as answering a particular description but need not be in existence when the contract is entered into.

(4) This section does not confer a right on a third party to enforce a term of a contract otherwise than subject to and in accordance with any other relevant terms of the contract.

(5) For the purpose of exercising his right to enforce a term of the contract, there shall be available to the third party any remedy that would have been available to him in an action for breach of contract if he had been a party to the contract (and the rules relating to damages, injunctions, specific performance and other relief shall apply accordingly).

(6) Where a term of a contract excludes or limits liability in relation to any matter references in this Act to the third party enforcing the term shall be construed as references to his availing himself of the exclusion or limitation.

(7) In this Act, in relation to a term of a contract which is enforceable by a third party-

'the promisor' means the party to the contract against whom the term is enforceable by the third party, and

'the promisee' means the party to the contract by whom the term is enforceable against the promisor.

Variation and rescission of contract.

2. —(1) Subject to the provisions of this section, where a third party has a right under section 1 to enforce a term of the contract, the parties to the contract may not, by agreement, rescind the contract, or vary it in such a way as to extinguish or alter his entitlement under that right, without his consent if-

(a) the third party has communicated his assent to the term to the promisor,

(b) the promisor is aware that the third party has relied on the term, or

(c) the promisor can reasonably be expected to have foreseen that the third party would rely on the term and the third party has in fact relied on it.

(2) The assent referred to in subsection (1)(a)-

(a) may be by words or conduct, and

(b) if sent to the promisor by post or other means, shall not be regarded as communicated to the promisor until received by him.

(3) Subsection (1) is subject to any express term of the contract under which-

(a) the parties to the contract may by agreement rescind or vary the contract without the consent of the third party, or

(b) the consent of the third party is required in circumstances specified in the contract instead of those set out in subsection (1)(a) to (c).

(4) Where the consent of a third party is required under subsection (1) or (3), the court or arbitral tribunal may, on the application of the parties to the contract, dispense with his consent if satisfied-

(a) that his consent cannot be obtained because his whereabouts cannot reasonably be ascertained, or

(b) that he is mentally incapable of giving his consent.

(5) The court or arbitral tribunal may, on the application of the parties to a contract, dispense with any consent that may be required under subsection (1)(c) if satisfied that it cannot reasonably be ascertained whether or not the third party has in fact relied on the term.

(6) If the court or arbitral tribunal dispenses with a third party's consent, it may impose such conditions as it thinks fit, including a condition requiring the payment of compensation to the third party.

(7) The jurisdiction conferred on the court by subsections (4) to (6) is exercisable by both the High Court and a county court.

Defences etc. available to promisor.

3. —(1) Subsections (2) to (5) apply where, in reliance on section 1, proceedings for the enforcement of a term of a contract are brought by a third party.

(2) The promisor shall have available to him by way of defence or set-off any matter that-

(a) arises from or in connection with the contract and is relevant to the term, and

(b) would have been available to him by way of defence or set-off if the proceedings had been brought by the promisee.

(3) The promisor shall also have available to him by way of defence or set-off any matter if-

(a) an express term of the contract provides for it to be available to him in proceedings brought by the third party, and

(b) it would have been available to him by way of defence or set-off if the proceedings had been brought by the promisee.

(4) The promisor shall also have available to him-

(a) by way of defence or set-off any matter, and

(b) by way of counterclaim any matter not arising from the contract,

that would have been available to him by way of defence or set-off or, as the case may be, by way of counterclaim against the third party if the third party had been a party to the contract.

(5) Subsections (2) and (4) are subject to any express term of the contract as to the matters that are not to be available to the promisor by way of defence, set-off or counterclaim.

(6) Where in any proceedings brought against him a third party seeks in reliance on section 1 to enforce a term of a contract (including, in particular, a term purporting to exclude or limit liability), he may not do so if he could not have done so (whether by reason of any particular circumstances relating to him or otherwise) had he been a party to the contract.

Enforcement of contract by promisee.

4. Section 1 does not affect any right of the promisee to enforce any term of the contract.

Protection of promisor from double liability.

5. Where under section 1 a term of a contract is enforceable by a third party, and the promisee has recovered from the promisor a sum in respect of-

(a) the third party's loss in respect of the term, or

(b) the expense to the promisee of making good to the third party the default of the promisor,

then, in any proceedings brought in reliance on that section by the third party, the court or arbitral tribunal shall reduce any award to the third party to such extent as it thinks appropriate to take account of the sum recovered by the promisee.

Exceptions.

6.   (1) Section 1 confers no rights on a third party in the case of a contract on a bill of exchange, promissory note or other negotiable instrument.

(2) Section 1 confers no rights on a third party in the case of any contract binding on a company and its members under section 14 of the Companies Act 1985.

(3) Section 1 confers no right on a third party to enforce-

(a) any term of a contract of employment against an employee,

(b) any term of a worker's contract against a worker (including a home worker), or

(c) any term of a relevant contract against an agency worker.

(4) In subsection (3)-

(a) 'contract of employment', 'employee', 'worker's contract', and 'worker' have the meaning given by section 54 of the National Minimum Wage Act 1998.

(b) 'home worker' has the meaning given by section 35(2) of that Act,

(c) 'agency worker' has the same meaning as in section 34(1) of that Act, and

(d) 'relevant contract' means a contract entered into, in a case where section 34 of that Act applies, by the agency worker as respects work falling within subsection (1)(a) of that section.

(5) Section 1 confers no rights on a third party in the case of-

(a) a contract for the carriage of goods by sea, or

(b) a contract for the carriage of goods by rail or road, or for the carriage of cargo by air, which is subject to the rules of the appropriate international transport convention, except that a third party may in reliance on that section avail himself of an exclusion or limitation of liability in such a contract.

(6) In subsection (5) 'contract for the carriage of goods by sea' means a contract of carriage-

(a) contained in or evidenced by a bill of lading, sea waybill or a corresponding electronic transaction, or

(b) under or for the purposes of which there is given an undertaking which is contained in a ship's delivery order or a corresponding electronic transaction.

(7) For the purposes of subsection (6)-

(a) 'bill of lading', 'sea waybill' and 'ship's delivery order' have the same meaning as in the Carriage of Goods by Sea Act 1992, and

(b) a corresponding electronic transaction is a transaction within section 1(5) of that Act which corresponds to the issue, indorsement, delivery or transfer of a bill of lading, sea waybill or ship's delivery order.

(8) In subsection (5) 'the appropriate international transport convention' means-

(a) in relation to a contract for the carriage of goods by rail, the Convention which has the force of law in the United Kingdom under section 1 of the International Transport Conventions Act 1983,

(b) in relation to a contract for the carriage of goods by road, the Convention which has the force of law in the United Kingdom under section 1 of the Carriage of Goods by Road Act 1965, and

(c) in relation to a contract for the carriage of cargo by air-

(i) the Convention which has the force of law in the United Kingdom under section 1 of the Carriage by Air Act 1961, or

(ii) the Convention which has the force of law under section 1 of the Carriage by Air (Supplementary Provisions) Act 1962, or

(iii) either of the amended Conventions set out in Part B of Schedule 2 or 3 to the Carriage by Air Acts (Application of Provisions) Order 1967.

Supplementary provisions relating to third party.

7. —(1) Section 1 does not affect any right or remedy of a third party that exists or is available apart from this Act.

(2) Section 2(2) of the Unfair Contract Terms Act 1977 (restriction on exclusion etc. of liability for negligence) shall not apply where the negligence consists of the breach of an obligation arising from a term of a contract and the person seeking to enforce it is a third party acting in reliance on section 1.

(3) In sections 5 and 8 of the Limitation Act 1980 the references to an action founded on a simple contract and an action upon a specialty shall respectively include references to an action brought in reliance on section 1 relating to a simple contract and an action brought in reliance on that section relating to a specialty.

(4) A third party shall not, by virtue of section 1(5) or 3(4) or (6), be treated as a party to the contract for the purposes of any other Act (or any instrument made under any other Act).

Arbitration provisions.

8.—(1)Where-

(a) a right under section 1 to enforce a term ('the substantive term') is subject to a term providing for the submission of disputes to arbitration ('the arbitration agreement'), and

(b) the arbitration agreement is an agreement in writing for the purposes of Part I of the Arbitration Act 1996,

the third party shall be treated for the purposes of that Act as a party to the arbitration agreement as regards disputes between himself and the promisor relating to the enforcement of the substantive term by the third party.

(2) Where-

    (a) a third party has a right under section 1 to enforce a term providing for one or more descriptions of dispute between the third party and the promisor to be submitted to arbitration ('the arbitration agreement'),

    (b) the arbitration agreement is an agreement in writing for the purposes of Part I of the Arbitration Act 1996, and

    (c) the third party does not fall to be treated under subsection (1) as a party to the arbitration agreement,

the third party shall, if he exercises the right, be treated for the purposes of that Act as a party to the arbitration agreement in relation to the matter with respect to which the right is exercised, and be treated as having been so immediately before the exercise of the right.

Northern Ireland.

9. —(1) In its application to Northern Ireland, this Act has effect with the modifications specified in subsections (2) and (3).

(2) In section 6(2), for 'section 14 of the Companies Act 1985' there is substituted 'Article 25 of the Companies (Northern Ireland) Order 1986'.

(3) In section 7, for subsection (3) there is substituted-

'(3) In Articles 4(a) and 15 of the Limitation (Northern Ireland) Order 1989, the references to an action founded on a simple contract and an action upon an instrument under seal shall respectively include references to an action brought in reliance on section 1 relating to a simple contract and an action brought in reliance on that section relating to a contract under seal.'

(4) In the Law Reform (Husband and Wife) (Northern Ireland) Act 1964, the following provisions are hereby repealed-

    (a) section 5, and

    (b) in section 6, in subsection (1)(a), the words 'in the case of section 4' and 'and in the case of section 5 the contracting party' and, in subsection (3), the words 'or section 5'.

Short title, commencement and extent.

10. —(1) This Act may be cited as the Contracts (Rights of Third Parties) Act 1999.

(2) This Act comes into force on the day on which it is passed but, subject to subsection (3), does not apply in relation to a contract entered into before the end of the period of six months beginning with that day.

(3) The restriction in subsection (2) does not apply in relation to a contract which-

    (a) is entered into on or after the day on which this Act is passed, and

    (b) expressly provides for the application of this Act.

(4) This act extends as follows-

    (a) section 9 extends to Northern Ireland only;

    (b) the remaining provisions extend to England and Wales and Northern Ireland only.

NOTES

1.   There is a theoretical question whether the Act has abolished the privity rule or simply created a very large exception to it. On the whole, it appears usual to talk of it creating a large

exception but, in a sense, this depends on exactly what the rule was. What was peculiar about the English rule was that the parties could not confer rights to a third party even if they wanted to. Virtually all legal systems appear to have a rule that contracts normally only create rights and duties between the parties because normally the parties are only thinking in terms of creating rights and duties between themselves. This rule has not, of course, been abolished but it was not this rule that distinguished English law from most other systems.

2.   Once it was decided to abolish the rule, it became clear that the rule had very few defenders, except within the construction industry, in which a good many lawyers turned out to be anxious to preserve the existing arrangements under which there were networks of contracts and one only has rights against the other parties to the particular contract to which one is a party. (But there is nothing in the Act that prevents parties continuing to offer this kind of system if that is what they want to do.)

In Ontario, a similar Law Commission report proposed, in effect, a one-line statute simply saying that the privity rule is abolished and leaving the courts to work out the practical implications of this. Such an approach has a good many attractions because it would enable the courts practically to work out the best solutions over a period of time in the light of the real facts in real cases, which is what the common law is good at. However, it would have been a very unusual English statute that took this bold approach. The 1937 proposal (see p 1179) had the great advantage of simplicity. The parties would know exactly where they stood and parties with competent lawyers would have no problems. However, it is very unusual in English contract law to distinguish between what is expressly agreed and what is impliedly agreed. It is clear that the parties may expressly say that they intend to confer a benefit on a third party and in a well-drafted contract that is what should normally happen. Equally, the parties may expressly say that they do not intend to confer a benefit on a third party and the most obvious immediate impact of the Act has been the proliferation of clauses in contracts saying exactly this.

3.   The critical question, therefore, is when an intention to benefit a third party is to be implied. The test of intention used is different to the 'double intention test' provisionally proposed in the Consultation Paper (para 6.3, see p 1186). When the intention is not express (s 1(1)(a)), the answer is to be found in a combination of s 1(1)(b); 1(2) and 1(3). Professor Andrew Burrows, who was the Law Commissioner most closely connected with the proposals as they were going through the Law Commission and through Parliament, has described this as creating a rebuttable presumption. Undoubtedly, there will be differences of opinion as to whether, in particular cases, the court should hold that the third party does acquire rights. You may like to consider whether you think T would be able to enforce the contract in each of the following cases.

(1)   Professor A makes a contract with the University of Utopia under which he agrees to give 40 one-hour lectures comparing the Utopian and Ruritanian laws of contract. Professor A only appears for 20 lectures and does not mention Ruritanian law in the lectures. T, a student who has failed the examination in this course, is aggrieved.

(2)   A takes out a policy of insurance on the family car, which is regularly driven by his wife, his two daughters and himself. The contract provides that the insurance company will cover anyone driving the car with A's consent. A's wife, T, has an accident while driving the car.

(3)   A sells his business to B on the terms that B will pay A £1,000 a month for the rest of his life and will pay A's wife, T, £500 a month if A predeceases her. A dies. B refuses to pay T anything.

(4) A married man with children but no grandchildren makes a contract with the XYZ insurance company under which A pays £10 a month to the insurance company and it promises to pay £10,000 to each of his grandchildren on his death.

(5) T, the International World University, wishes to build a new law library. For legitimate tax reasons, the contract for the erection of the library is made by Denning Ltd, a company wholly owned by the University, although the contractor well knows that, when completed, the library will be occupied and used by T. The building has been badly done and it will cost US $5,000,000 to complete it satisfactorily.

(6) A goes to an expensive furrier and selects and buys a coat. He tells the assistant (truthfully) that he is buying it for his wife T. By the side of the coat is a prominent card saying 'It looks like mink, it feels like mink but is guaranteed man made'. A gives the coat to his wife. In fact, owing to a mistake by the store, the coat is a real mink coat and T is ostracised by her friends.

(7) A buys a new car, which is the subject of warranties both by the manufacturer and by the dealer. After he has had the car a month without any problems, he allows his wife, T, to drive it. Without warning, the brakes fail and T is seriously injured.

(8) A hospital buys blood from a blood centre, which pays members of the public to supply blood. The blood is used by the hospital to give a transfusion to T but it turns out to be infected with HIV.

(9) A instructs his lawyer, X, to prepare a will, the main effect of which will be to divide his property equally between his wife and his sister, T. By gross professional incompetence, X prepares a will that is invalid. The effect is that A dies intestate and, under the relevant succession law, all of his property goes to his wife.

(10) A, a company with a large factory, makes a contract with a company operating the local sewage system. Under the contract, A is entitled to discharge its waste into the sewer but undertakes not to discharge certain types of waste. In breach of this undertaking, A discharges waste that blocks the sewer and causes damage to T, another user of the sewer.

4.   Reported cases involving the Act have been slow to appear. The first is *Nisshin Shipping Co v Cleaves & Co* [2003] EWHC 2602 [2004] 1 All ER (Comm) 481. A contract between shipowners and charterers contained a provision for payment of commission to brokers who had negotiated the charterparty but were not parties to it. Colman J held that the brokers were entitled to commission by virtue of the Act. This was a straightforward decision because these were essentially the facts of *Les Affreteurs Reunis v Leopold Walford (London) Ltd* (discussed on p 1151). The Act was also applied in *The Laemthong Glory (No 2)* [2005] EWCA Civ 519, [2005] 1 Lloyd's Rep 632.

5.   *Variation and cancellation*

One might take the view that, once the contract is made, the rights of the third parties are inviolate. Alternatively, one might take the view that it is open to the promisor and promisee to revoke the rights of the third party at any time. The Act does not take either of these extreme positions. It takes an intermediate position, as set out in s 2. Note that it is quite likely that, in practice, the promisor and promisee may want expressly to provide for their ability to change. This is very common in the Continental countries, where this possibility has been in existence for many years. For instance, one might make a contract with an insurance company under which the proceeds of life insurance were to be paid to a named person but reserving the right to change the person who is to receive the benefits. In practice, this might well be reserved to one party because it is unlikely that the insurance company will care to whom the money is paid, as long as this is clearly defined.

6.   *Defences*

Have a look at s 3. Suppose A takes out life insurance with the B insurance company under which he agrees to pay premiums for 20 years, in return for the insurance company promising to pay £50,000 to T on A's death. If A never pays anything, it is obvious that the insurance company will have no liability to T. Suppose A pays for ten years and then stops. What do you think the answer should be then?

Note that this section does not only apply to the defences but applies to set-off as well. Suppose A, a wine merchant, agrees to deliver 20 cases of champagne to B and B agrees to pay the price to C. Suppose also that A owes B money in respect of a previous transaction. It would follow that B only has to pay to C the balance between the two transactions. The exact width of this principle depends on the complexities of the law of set-off, which are well outside the scope of this book.

7.   *Exemption clauses and third parties*

Note that this is dealt with by s 1(6). Do you think this subsection would reverse the decision of the House of Lords in *Scruttons v Midland Silicones* (see above)?

8.   *Existing exceptions*

Note s 7(1), which means that all the existing exceptions continue in existence.

VIII. AGENCY AND PRIVITY

Two types of qualification to the basic privity rule need to be considered. One is that the benefits of a contract may *subsequently* be transferred: this is dealt with in the next chapter. The qualifications dealt with here relate to initial entitlement to sue.

The rules relating to agents acting for disclosed principals do not, in theory, conflict at all with the doctrine of privity, although they do offer a method of escape from its consequences, provided that the third party whom it is wished to benefit can be said to be providing consideration. The doctrine of the undisclosed principal does seem to infringe on the doctrine of privity: the principal may sue the third party even though the latter had no idea that he was contracting with anyone but the agent. Of course, the third party may equally hold the principal responsible, but a notion of being able to take the benefits if one is made to take the burdens does not explain the rule: the principal can sue the third party even though the latter has not attempted to enforce the contract against the principal. It seems better to regard the doctrine of the undisclosed principal as a straightforward exception to the doctrine of privity.

What, however, is the practical point behind allowing the undisclosed principal to sue the third party, rather than confining his rights to those he had against the agent and allowing only the agent to sue the third party? The original rationale, or at least the effect, seems to have been to allow a person for whom a middleman had been selling goods on credit to recover the price directly from the purchaser if the middleman were to become insolvent. Equally, because any money paid to the middleman by the purchaser would be the principal's, the latter could recover it from the middleman's trustee in bankruptcy (see Stoljar, *The Law of Agency*, 1961, pp 204–211).

CHAPTER FORTY-SEVEN

SUBSEQUENT ASSIGNMENT OF THE BENEFIT OF A CONTRACT

I. ASSIGNMENT

Like agency, assignment is a complex subject that cannot be treated in full here. Instead, enough of the doctrine will be summarised to enable the reader to understand the cases that follow.

At common law, a debt or other contractual right could not be assigned without the assent of the debtor unless it was a debt due on a negotiable instrument (see pp 1197–1198). It was only possible to transfer contractual rights with the consent of the debtor, either by making a tripartite agreement called a 'novation' between the creditor, the debtor and the new creditor (in strict theory, this extinguishes the old contract and substitutes a new one), or by getting the debtor to tell the new creditor that he will pay him, which apparently gives the new creditor the right to recover from the debtor (*Shamia v Joory* [1958] 1 QB 448, [1958] 1 All ER 111).

However, equity recognised assignment: if notice was given to the debtor, he became liable to pay the assignee and could no longer discharge his obligation by paying the assignor. However, unless the right assigned were a purely equitable one, the assignor had to be joined in any action by the assignee. Among the reasons were the historical procedural ones that equity did not enforce legal choses in action, so the action had to be brought in the assignor's name even if equity would compel him to cooperate, and that if the assignee could enforce the debt in equity, the debtor might be subjected to a second action by the assignor in the then separate common law courts.

The Judicature Act 1873, s 25(6) provided for legal assignment: since there was now only one system of courts, the old procedural difficulties were gone. Section 25(6) was replaced by the Law of Property Act 1925, s 136(1), which reads:

Section 136

(1) Any absolute assignment by writing under the hand of the assignor (not purporting to be by way of charge only) of any debt or other legal thing in action, of which express notice in writing has been given to the debtor, trustee or other person from whom the assignor would have been entitled to claim such

debt or thing in action, is effectual in law (subject to equities having priority over the right of the assignee) to pass and transfer from the date of such notice—

(a) the legal right to such debt or thing in action;

(b) all legal and other remedies for the same; and

(c) the power to give a good discharge for the same without the concurrence of the assignor:

Provided that, if the debtor, trustee or other person liable in respect of such debt or thing in action has notice—

(a) that the assignment is disputed by the assignor or any person claiming under him;

or

(b) of any other opposing or conflicting claims to such debt or thing in action; he may, if he thinks fit, either call upon the persons making claim thereto to interplead concerning the same, or pay the debt or other thing in action into court under the provisions of the Trustee Act, 1925.

It will be noted that, for there to be an effective legal assignment, notice must have been given in writing to the debtor, the assignment must be in writing signed by the assignor and the assignment must be absolute. If an assignment of a legal chose in action fails to met the second or third requirement, it may still be effective, but only as an equitable assignment, with the result that the assignee may have to join the assignor in the action. In these cases, there are good substantive reasons for joining the assignor. If the assignment is not written, he may wish to dispute that he made any assignment (compare the evidentiary functions of the seal and consideration, p 133). If the assignment is not absolute but conditional (for instance, a debt is assigned as security for a loan until such time as the loan is repaid to the assignee), the court will not be able to determine whom the debtor should pay without having the assignor before the court as well as the assignee, so that the state of accounts between the two of them can be determined. This is an important safeguard for the debtor, who might otherwise pay the wrong party and have to pay all over again. In contrast, there can be an absolute assignment even if it is provided that, at some future time, when a loan is repaid for instance, the debt shall be reassigned; the reassignment will require a fresh notice to the debtor, so the latter will be in no doubt about whom he should pay. For different reasons, the assignment of part of a debt is treated as not absolute: here, the problem is that the debtor might want to dispute the existence of a debt and if the assignor and assignee could each recover his part in separate actions, the debtor would have to defend himself twice over.

An equitable chose may be assigned under the statute, or if it is not absolute, in equity; at all events, the assignment must be in writing because this is required of any disposition of an equitable interest (Law of Property Act 1925, s 53(1)(c)).

Not every contractual right can be assigned. Thus if the contract provides that a particular right (eg the contractor's right to money under a building contract) may not be assigned at all, or not without the employer's consent and consent is not obtained, any purported assignment is simply ineffective (*Helstan Securities Ltd v Hertfordshire County Council* [1978] 3 All ER 262; *Linden Gardens Trust Ltd v Lenesta Sludge Disposals Ltd*, see p 1144). Needless to say, the result may be to put the assignor into breach of contract with the assignee. Equally, contracts with a 'personal' element may not be assigned: see, for example, *Cooper v Micklefield Coal and Lime Co Ltd* (1912) 107 LT 457. However, an assignment of a contractual right the assignment of which is forbidden or if the right is personal and not assignable may be effective as a declaration of trust: *Don King Productions Inc v Warren* [1999] 2 All ER 218.

Note that an assignee takes 'subject to equities': ie the debtor can use any defence that he could have used against the assignor against the assignee. This is explored in Chapter 49.

II. NEGOTIABLE INSTRUMENTS

■ **Lawson and Rudden,** *Law of Property (2nd edn, 1982)*
pp 26–32

(ii) Negotiable instruments The best-known negotiable instruments are the bill of exchange, the promissory note, and the cheque. For the law of property the essential feature of a bill of exchange is that it represents, in physical form, the debt which the buyer owes and the seller owns, and the latter may deal with it just as he may his own books or motorcar. Indeed a negotiable instrument is even more suitable to commence than either of those things. The quality of *negotiability* means that anyone taking the instrument in good faith and for value obtains a good title despite any defect in the title of the transferor. Thus if, in good faith, you buy my books or car from someone who has stolen them from me you must return then to me and are left—for what it may be worth—to an action against the thief. But a thief can pass to an innocent purchaser a good title to a negotiable instrument.

A simple form of bill of exchange, used nowadays in overseas trade, occurs when goods are sold but are still on their way to the buyer. He will get the documents of title described below. But if the seller does not get the cash at once he will take a bill from the buyer which he can then use as if it were cash.

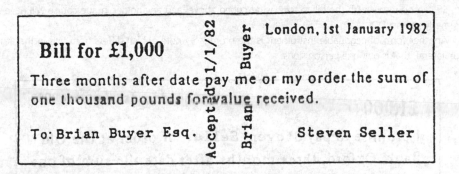

Bill for £1,000

Accepted 1/1/82

Brian Buyer

London, 1st January 1982

Three months after date pay me or my order the sum of one thousand pounds for value received.

To: Brian Buyer Esq.   Steven Seller

The buyer signs the bill for acceptance, gives it to the seller, and has three months in which to find the money. In the hands of the seller, however, the bill of exchange is an immediately realizable asset. He can endorse it, by writing his name on the back, and transfer it by delivery to anyone he chooses. It can then be passed from hand to hand, the holder being entitled to be paid by Brian Buyer when the three months expires and the bill matures. Assuming that the buyer is solvent, and that there are no particular risks in the transaction, Steven Seller will usually endorse and transfer the bill to a bank. The process is known as 'discounting' because the bank will give him for it an amount based on that sum of money which, invested then, would produce £1,000 on the date the bill matures. Thus, during the three months, the claim represented by the bill is an asset which is growing in value; and we shall see later that, in relation to land, the concept of the 'estate' is used to express in legal terms the vital factor of *time* which determines present values.

The bill can then, on endorsement, pass from hand to hand—from that bank to another, or to a customer. Any holder in due course, that is to say anyone who has physical control of the bill at maturity and has bought in good faith, is entitled to be paid the £1,000 by Brian Buyer, even if it had been stolen on its way to him or even if the buyer had a good defence against the seller, because, for instance, the goods never arrived. In other words any transfer of the bill to a purchaser in good faith is a transfer of the right to receive £1,000 from Brian Buyer.

The example just given is of the very simplest type of bill of exchange. Historically, however, the bill evolved to deal with a rather more sophisticated situation. Suppose that when Brian Buyer contracted to buy goods from Steven Seller he was already owed £1,000 by David Debtor. One way to resolve matters would be for DD to send bullion, notes, or coin to BB, and for him then to send them on to SS—a process both expensive and risky. A much cheaper and safer method, especially if DD and SS live in the same place, is for BB to order DD to pay the money to SS. But for DD to be liable directly to SS he must *accept* this order, and so the bill would look like this:

```
                                              London, 1st January 1982
  Bill for £1,000

  Three months after date pay Steven Seller or order
  the sum of one thousand pounds for value received.

  To: David Debtor Esq.            Brian Buyer
```
(marginal annotation: Accepted 3/1/82 David Debtor)

SS can now deal with the bill exactly as described above, and any holder in due course will have a remedy against DD.

Another form of negotiable instrument is the promissory note, which differs from bills in that it is unilateral, that is only one person signs.

```
  £1,000                          London, 1st January 1982

  I promise to pay Steven Seller or order at the Old
  Bank, Oxford, three months after date the sum of one
  thousand pounds for value received.

                                        Brian Buyer
```

Most people have in their pockets at some time or another examples in the shape of Bank of England notes. The result is rather interesting: a private-law obligation under which, to use the above example, BB owes SS £1,000 is performed by payment—that is, by handing over banknotes which themselves bear a promise to pay. This obligation, however, is strictly one of public law and the nature of money will be briefly discussed later.

The same rules as to negotiability apply to the cheque, which is defined by statute as 'a bill of exchange, drawn on a banker, payable on demand'. This definition is likely to confuse the beginner. Admittedly a cheque looks like a bill of exchange.

```
                                    1st January 1982
                          Old Bank Ltd.,
                          High Street, Oxford

         Pay  Steven Seller          or order

         one thousand pounds/00      £1000.00

                          Brian Buyer
```

As however, the bank never accepts the order by signing the cheque it is never directly liable to the payee. When the cheque is presented it should, of course, meet it—for the cheque is a bill of exchange *payable on demand*. This obligation, however, is only to the drawer, BB, and arises out of the bank's contract with him; so that if he has neither credit balance nor overdraft facilities the bank need not pay. In fact a cheque is more like a promissory note, that is a promise by the drawer that his bank will pay.

CHAPTER FORTY-EIGHT

PRIVITY AND BURDENS

The converse of the rule that you cannot sue on a contract to which you are not a party is that you cannot normally have your rights diminished by a contract to which you are not a party. There are, however, qualifications to this rule, too.

I. UNDISCLOSED PRINCIPALS

Look again at *Watteau v Fenwick* (p 1134). It was only when the manager failed to pay for the cigars that the plaintiffs discovered the existence of the principal behind him, but nonetheless the principal was made liable. What is the practical effect of such a decision?

II. BAILMENT

■ *KH Enterprise (cargo owners) v Pioneer Container (owners), The Pioneer Container*
[1994] 2 All ER 250, PC

The plaintiffs contracted with freight carriers for the carriage of the plaintiffs' goods by container from Taiwan to Hong Kong, either as a complete voyage or as part of through carriage to other ports. The carriers issued the plaintiffs with bills of lading, which provided that the carrier was entitled to subcontract 'on any terms' the whole or any part of the handling, storage or carriage of the goods. The carriers subcontracted the carriage to the defendant shipowners, who issued two feeder bills of lading acknowledging receipt of the plaintiffs' containers for shipment. The feeder bills of lading incorporated an exclusive jurisdiction clause (cl 26), which provided that the bills of lading were governed by Chinese law and that any claim or other dispute arising under the 'bill of lading contract' was to be determined in Taiwan unless the carrier otherwise agreed. The vessel on which the plaintiffs' containers were being shipped from Taiwan to Hong Kong sank, with the loss of all cargo, following a collision with another vessel during the voyage. The plaintiffs commenced proceedings in Hong Kong by the issue of a writ *in rem* against a sister ship of the vessel, claiming damages for the loss of their cargo. The shipowners applied to have the proceedings stayed on the grounds that the plaintiffs had, by cl 26 of the bills of lading, agreed that any claim or other dispute thereunder should be determined in Taiwan, or alternatively, that in all the circumstances the courts of Taiwan were the natural and appropriate forum for the trial of the action.

The plaintiffs appealed to the Privy Council, contending, inter alia, that cl 26 was not binding on them because there was no contractual relationship between them and the shipowners.

Lord Goff, delivering the judgment of the Board, held on the authority of the case of *Gilchrist Watt & Sanderson Pty Ltd v York Products Pty Ltd* [1970] 3 All ER 825 that where a bailee sub-bailed goods with the authority of the owner the relationship between the owner of the goods and the sub-bailee was that of bailor and bailee. He continued:

But the question then arises whether, as against the owners (here the two groups of plaintiffs), the sub bailees (here the shipowners) can invoke any of the terms on which the goods were sub-bailed to them, and in particular the exclusive jurisdiction clause (cl 26).

In *Morris v C W Martin & Sons Ltd* [1965] 2 All ER 725 at 733, [1966] 1 QB 716 at 729 Lord Denning MR expressed his opinion on this point in clear terms, though on the facts of the case his opinion was obiter. He said:

'The answer to the problem lies, I think, in this: the owner is bound by the conditions if he has expressly or impliedly consented to the bailee making a sub-bailment containing those conditions, but not otherwise.'

His expression of opinion on this point has proved to be attractive to a number of judges. In *Morris v C W Martin & Son* [1966] 1 QB 716 at 741 itself, Salmon LJ expressed himself to be strongly attracted by it: see also *Cia Portorafti Commerciale SA v Ultramar Panama Inc, The Captain Gregos (No 2)* [1990] 2 Lloyd's Rep 395 at 405 per Bingham LJ (delivering the judgment of the court). Furthermore, on this point Lord Denning MR's statement of the law was applied by Steyn J in *Singer Co (UK) Ltd v Tees and Hartlepool Port Authority* [1988] 2 Lloyd's Rep 164. It was not however followed by Donaldson J in *Johnson Matthey & Co Ltd v Constantine Terminals Ltd* [1976] 2 Lloyd's Rep 215, a decision to which their Lordships will revert at a later stage.

In order to decide whether, like Steyn J, to accept the principle so stated by Lord Denning MR, it is necessary to consider the relevance of the concept of 'consent' in this context. It must be assumed that, on the facts of the case, no direct contractual relationship has been created between the owner and the sub-bailee, the only contract created by the sub-bailment being that between the bailee and the sub-bailee. Even so, if the effect of the sub-bailment is that the sub-bailee voluntarily receives into his custody the goods of the owner and so assumes towards the owner the responsibility of a bailee, then to the extent that the terms of the sub-bailment are consented to by the owner, it can properly be said that the owner has authorised the bailee so to regulate the duties of the sub-bailee in respect of the goods entrusted to him, not only towards the bailee but also towards the owner....

Such a conclusion, finding its origin in the law of bailment rather than the law of contract, does not depend for its efficacy either on the doctrine of privity of contract or on the doctrine of consideration. That this may be so appears from the decision of the House of Lords in *Elder Dempster & Co Ltd v Paterson Zochonis & Co Ltd* [above]. In that case, shippers of cargo on a chartered ship brought an action against the shipowners for damage caused to the cargo by bad stowage, for which the shipowners were responsible. It is crucial to observe that the cargo was shipped under charterers' bills of lading, so that the contract of carriage contained in or evidenced by the bills of lading was between the shippers and the charterers. The shipowners nevertheless sought to rely, as against the shippers, upon an exception in the bill of lading which protected the charterers from liability for damage due to bad stowage. It was held that the shipowners were entitled to do so, the preferred reason upon which the House so held (see *Midland Silicones Ltd v Scruttons Ltd* [above p 996] per Viscount Simonds, following the opinion of Fullagar J in *Wilson v Darling Island Stevedoring and Lighterage Co Ltd* (1955) 95 CLR 43 at 78) being found in the speech of Lord Sumner where he said ([1924] AC 522 at 564, [1924] All ER Rep 135 at 155):

'... in the circumstances of this case the obligations to be inferred from the reception of the cargo for carriage to the United Kingdom amount to a bailment upon terms, which include the exceptions and limitations of liability stipulated in the known and contemplated form of bill of lading.'

Of course, there was in that case a bailment by the shippers direct to the shipowners, so that it was not necessary to have recourse to the concept of sub-bailment. Even so, notwithstanding the absence of any contract between the shippers and the shipowners, the shipowners' obligations as bailees were effectively subject to the terms upon which the shipowners implicitly received the goods into their possession. Their Lordships do not imagine that a different conclusion would have been reached in the *Elder Dempster* case if the shippers had delivered the goods, not directly to the ship, but into the possession of agents of the charterers who had, in their turn, loaded the goods on board; because in such circumstances, by parity of reasoning, the shippers may be held to have impliedly consented that the sub-bailment to the shipowners should be on terms which included the exemption from liability for bad stowage.

The Johnson Matthey case

At this stage, their Lordships turn to the decision of Donaldson J in *Johnson Matthey & Co Ltd v Constantine Terminals Ltd* [1976] 2 Lloyd's Rep 215. In that case, the plaintiffs sought to hold sub-bailees of their goods liable to them as bailees; and the sub-bailees in their turn sought to rely, as against the plaintiffs, on certain clauses in the contract of sub-bailment. Donaldson J cited the relevant passage from the judgment of Lord Denning MR in *Morris v C W Martin & Sons Ltd* [1966] 1 QB 716 at 729 and held that, on the facts of the case, the plaintiffs had consented to a sub-bailment on the conditions of Constantine Terminals, the sub-bailees. It was however his opinion that the consent of the plaintiffs was not relevant in the case before him. He nevertheless held that the sub-bailees were entitled to rely on the clauses in question. He said ([1976] 2 Lloyd's Rep 215 at 222):

> 'But the plaintiffs cannot prove the bailment upon which, in my judgment, they must rely, without referring to terms upon which the silver was received by Constantine Terminals from International Express. These terms establish (a) that Constantine Terminals were bailees for reward but also (b) that the implied duties of such a bailee were qualified by exceptions. And, despite [counsel's] vigorous argument to the contrary, I really do not see how the plaintiffs can rely upon one part of the contract while ignoring the other. Consent seems to me to be relevant only between the bailor and head bailee. If the sub-bailment is on terms to which the bailor consented, he has no cause of action against the head bailee. If it was not, the sub-bailee is still protected, but if the bailor is damnified by the terms of the sub-bailment he has a cause of action against the head bailee.'

The reasoning of Donaldson J (if correct) is, of course, highly relevant to the present case, since it leads to the conclusion that, if (as here) the plaintiffs seek to hold the shipowners liable as bailees, they will ipso facto be bound by the terms of the sub-bailment under which the shipowners received the goods into their possession, including cl 26 (the exclusive jurisdiction clause). However their Lordships are, with respect, unable to accept this reasoning which (related, as it was, to an authorised sub-bailment) is, in their opinion, inconsistent with the decision of the Court of Appeal in *Morris v C W Martin & Son* (by which Donaldson J was bound) and also with the decision of the Privy Council in *Gilchrist Watt & Sanderson Pty Ltd v York Products Pty Ltd* [1970] 3 All ER 825, [1970] 1 WLR 1262. Both these decisions proceeded on the basis that the voluntary taking by a sub-bailee of the owner's goods into his custody of itself results in his owing to the owner the duties of a bailee—as Diplock LJ put it in *Morris v Martin* [1966] 1 QB716 at 731, it brings into existence 'the relationship of bailor and bailee by sub-bailment'. It is therefore from these facts that the owner can prove the bailment upon which he relies when he proceeds directly against the sub-bailee. He does not for this purpose have to rely upon the contract of sub-bailment as between the bailee and the sub-bailee. Moreover, the reasoning of Donaldson J leads to the conclusion that the owner who holds an authorised sub-bailee responsible to him as bailee of his goods has to accept all the terms of the contract of sub-bailment, apparently without limit; indeed logically it leads to the further conclusion that a sub-bailee under an unauthorised sub-bailment which he knew to be unauthorised would likewise be able to invoke all such terms against the owner who sought to hold him responsible as bailee. Their Lordships do not find these conclusions attractive. Furthermore, in their opinion, the approach of Donaldson J cannot be rescued by resort to the doctrine of ratification; for if, as the authorities demonstrate, the owner is able to hold the sub-bailee responsible to him as bailee without reliance on the contract of sub-bailment, it cannot be said that his so doing amounts to ratification of the terms of that contract if unauthorised by him.

In addition, the conclusion of Donaldson J that consent is relevant only between the owner and the bailee is inconsistent with the reasoning of Lord Denning MR in *Morris v C W Martin & Son* when he expressed the opinion that the bailor is bound by the terms of the sub-bailment to which he has consented but not otherwise. Their Lordships have already expressed their agreement with the approach of Lord Denning MR on this point. Indeed, as they see it, once it is recognised that the sub-bailee, by voluntarily taking the owner's goods into his custody, ipso facto becomes the bailee of those goods vis-à-vis the owner, it must follow that the owner's rights against the sub-bailee will only be subject to terms of the sub-bailment if he has consented to them, ie if he has authorised the bailee to entrust the goods to the sub-bailee on those terms. Such consent may, as Lord Denning MR pointed out, be express or implied; and in this context the sub-bailee may also be able to invoke, where appropriate, the principle of ostensible authority.

In truth, at the root of this question lies a doctrinal dispute of a fundamental nature, which is epitomised in the question—is it a prerequisite of a bailment that the bailor should have consented to the bailee's possession of the goods? An affirmative answer to this question (which is the answer given by Bell *Modern Law of Personal Property in England and Ireland* (1989) pp 88–89) leads to the conclusion that, if the owner seeks to hold a sub-bailee responsible to him as bailee, he has to accept all the terms of the sub-bailment, warts and all; for either he will have consented to the sub-bailment on those terms or, if not, he will (by holding the sub-bailee liable to him as bailee) be held to have ratified all the terms of the sub-bailment. A negative answer to the question is however supported by other writers, notably by *Palmer's Bailment* pp 31 ff, where Professor Palmer cites a number of examples of bailment without the consent of the owner, and by Professor Tay in her article 'The essence of bailment' (1966) 5 Syd LR 239. On this approach, a person who voluntarily takes another person's goods into his custody holds them as bailee of that person (the owner); and he can only invoke, for example, terms of a sub-bailment under which he received the goods from an intermediate bailee as qualifying or otherwise affecting his responsibility to the owner if the owner consented to them. It is the later approach which, as their Lordships have explained, has been adopted by English law and, with English law, the law of Hong Kong.

Their Lordships wish to add that this conclusion, which flows from the decisions in *Morris v C W Martin & Son* and the *Gilchrist Watt* case, produces a result which in their opinion is both principled and just. They incline to the opinion that a sub-bailee can only be said for these purposes to have voluntarily taken into his possession the goods of another if he has sufficient notice that a person other than the bailee is interested in the goods so that it can properly be said that (in addition to his duties to the bailee) he has, by taking the goods into his custody, assumed towards that other person the responsibility for the goods which is characteristic of a bailee. This they believe to be the underlying principle. Moreover, their Lordships do not consider this principle to impose obligations on the sub-bailee which are onerous or unfair, once it is recognised that he can invoke against the owner terms of the sub-bailment which the owner has actually (expressly or impliedly) or even ostensibly authorised. In the last resort the sub-bailee may, if necessary and appropriate, be able to invoke against the bailee the principle of warranty of authority.

Lord Goff went on to hold that, on the facts, the plaintiffs had contracted with the freight carriers that they were entitled to sub-contract the carriage 'on any terms', which was wide enough to be express consent to the application of an exclusive jurisdiction clause to the sub-bailment, since an exclusive jurisdiction clause was not so unusual or unreasonable as to be excluded from the wide consent given by the plaintiffs.

Appeal dismissed.

NOTES

1. What is the practical difference between the approach taken by the Privy Council in *The Pioneer Container* and that of Donaldson J in the *Johnson Matthey* case?

2. Lord Goff says that the principle adopted is fair and just. The sub-bailee might agree to take the goods only on terms that limited its liability, but then find that the original bailee/sub-bailor did not have the owner's authority to sub-bail the goods on limited liability terms, so that the sub-bailee's liability to the owner is not limited after all. How does Lord Goff answer that point?

3. In *Scruttons Ltd v Midland Silicones Ltd* (see p 1154), Lord Denning pointed out that the stevedores had been employed by the carriers on terms under which they should 'have such protection as is afforded by the terms, conditions and exceptions of the bill of lading'. As he considered (unlike the majority) that the stevedores *were* intended to be protected by the clauses in the bill, Lord Denning held that this was a second reason why they should not be liable for more than $500. This seems to go even further than *the Johnson Matthey* case did. The point is not discussed in the other judgments.

III. TORT

In *Lumley v Gye* (1853) 2 E & B 216, the plaintiff had engaged Joanna Wagner to sing at the Queen's Theatre for the season, with a stipulation that she should not sing elsewhere during that period without his written consent. The defendant, who knew of this contract, persuaded Miss Wagner to sing for him at Covent Garden instead. The plaintiff obtained an injunction against Miss Wagner (referred to on p 730), whereupon she left the country; he then claimed damages from the defendant, and succeeded on the ground that the defendant had committed a tort by 'maliciously' (ie intentionally) procuring a breach of the plaintiff's contract with Miss Wagner.

A more recent application of the tort of intentionally inducing a breach of contract is *British Motor Trade Association v Salvadori* [1949] Ch 556. The purchaser of a new car had covenanted with the plaintiffs that he would not resell it within one year without first offering it to them. He sold it to the defendant without first offering it to the plaintiffs. The defendant had notice of the covenant and was held liable to the plaintiffs.

IV. PROPERTY

Obviously, a contract may result in a transfer of property rights that must be respected by third parties. In some circumstances, what starts off as an agreement may also create what the law recognises as property rights, which will then affect third parties. Thus the covenants contained in a lease will bind and entitle successors in title to both landlord and tenant, and under the rule in *Tulk v Moxhay* (1848) 2 Ph 774, the owner of a piece of land may accept a restrictive covenant that will bind his successors in title to the successors in title of the covenantee, provided the latter retain land capable of benefiting from enforcement of the covenant. Outside the realm of real property, however, the law has been most reluctant to recognise parallel 'proprietary' rights. Thus it has been held that an agreement by a buyer of goods that neither he nor any successor in title would sell them at below a price set by the original seller does not create a covenant running with the goods, even when the restriction was clearly marked on the goods: *Taddy & Co v Sterious & Co* [1904] 1 Ch 354, followed by the Court of Appeal in *McGruther v Pitcher* [1904] 2 Ch 306. Some of the reasons for this reluctance appear from the judgment of Brougham LC in *Keppell v Bailey* (1834) 2 My & K 517, in which it was held that an agreement by a quarry owner to carry all of his stone on the Trevil Railroad was not binding on the quarry owner's successors in title. Lord Brougham said (at 534–538):

... But it must not therefore be supposed that incidents of a novel kind can be devised and attached to property at the fancy or caprice of any owner. It is clearly inconvenient both to the science of the law and to the public weal that such a latitude should be given. There can be no harm in allowing the fullest latitude to men in binding themselves and their representatives, that is, their assets real and personal, to answer in damages for breach of their obligations. This tends to no mischief, and is a reasonable liberty to bestow; but great detriment would arise and much confusion of rights if parties were allowed to invent new modes of holding and enjoying real property, and to impress upon their lands and tenements a peculiar character, which should follow them into all hands, however remote. Every close, every messuage, might thus be held in a several fashion; and it would hardly be possible to know what rights the acquisition of any parcel conferred, or what obligations it imposed.

In one class of case, a subsequent purchaser of a chattel or even a chose in action may be affected by an earlier contract to which he was not a party: that is, if the original contract is specifically enforceable and the subsequent purchaser took with actual or constructive notice of it. This point arose in *Swiss Bank Corpn v Lloyds Bank Ltd* [1979] Ch 548, [1979] 2 All ER 853. It was argued that a borrower (IFT), who had used the loan to acquire securities (the FIBI securities), was under a contractual obligation to the lender to repay the loan out of the proceedings of the securities, and that this was a specifically enforceable obligation that would affect the defendants, to whom the securities had been charged. Browne-Wilkinson J said:

As I have indicated, Mr Scott's first contention is that the plaintiff has at all times had a right specifically enforceable against IFT requiring IFT to employ the FIBI securities in the manner specified in the Bank of England conditions, which right confers a property interest enforceable against Lloyds as subsequent equitable chargee....

Turning now to the legal effect of such a contract, I propose first to set out my understanding of the equitable principles which are involved and to consider how in principle the position should stand as between the plaintiff and Lloyds.

Historically the courts of equity acted in personam. Whether equity was supplementing the common law by giving additional remedies or correcting the common law by imposing a different legal result, the courts of equity intervened by directing the defendant personally to do, or refrain from doing, a specific act. In deciding whether or not to intervene, the courts of equity required first, that the plaintiff should have some enforceable right and, secondly, that the conscience of the defendant was affected in some way so as to make the failure of the defendant to give effect to the plaintiff's rights contrary to justice.

The rights which the plaintiff asserted were normally either contractual rights or rights under a trust. In the realm of contracts equity supplemented the common law by ordering the party in default to perform the contract—instead of merely paying damages. In the realm of trusts equity ordered the legal owner of property, the trustee, specifically to carry out the trust which he had accepted. In matters involving property equity intervened by ordering that the defendant do deal with the property in question in a specific manner, whether the plaintiff's rights were founded in contract or trust.

But, although the basis of the equity jurisdiction was and still is founded on an order in personam, the courts of equity evolved the doctrine that, in the eyes of equity, that which ought to have been done is to be treated as having been done. Thus under a specifically enforceable contract for the sale of land, the purchaser is treated in equity as the owner of the property whether or not an order for specific performance has been made. Again, in the law of trusts the beneficiary is treated as immediately entitled to his interest in the trust property whether or not an order for the execution of the trust has been made against the trustee. In this way the plaintiff's rights, although founded upon the ability of the court to make an order in personam against the other contracting party or the trustee, become an interest in the property itself, an equitable interest. Once the position is reached that an order for specific performance could have been made against the legal owner if the matter had been brought before the court, thereafter the legal owner holds the property shorn of those rights in the property which the courts of equity would decree belong to another.

Once an equitable interest in property is established, thereafter any third party taking that property from the original contracting party or the original trustee only takes it, in the eyes of equity shorn of, or subject to, the equitable interest. But as the right and the remedy is equitable only, the courts of equity would not enforce the equitable interest against the third party unless it was inequitable for him not to give effect to the prior equitable interest. It is on this ground that a subsequent purchaser for value of a legal interest without notice takes free of prior equitable interests.

Therefore, in my judgment, on principle, if as between the plaintiff and IFT there was a contractual obligation to service and repay the loan out of the FIBI securities and that was a specifically enforceable obligation, the plaintiff has an equitable interest in those securities, and Lloyds, as subsequent equitable chargee, took the FIBI securities subject to the prior equitable interest of the plaintiff.

He went on to hold that there was such an obligation, but on this point he was reversed by the Court of Appeal and the House of Lords agreed: [1982] AC 584. However, Lord Wilberforce said (at 613) that he did not doubt the correctness of the principles of law stated by the judge.

Even if there is no specifically enforceable right that can be enforced against a subsequent purchaser, it has occasionally been suggested that equity will intervene to protect the rights of a party to the original contract. In *De Mattos v Gibson* (1858) 4 De G & J 276, on appeal, 28 LJ Ch 498, it was held by the Lord Justices of Appeal that a charterer of a vessel was entitled to an injunction to prevent a subsequent mortgagee of her using her inconsistently with the charter. Knight Bruce LJ expressed himself in terms very reminiscent of *Tulk v Moxhay*:

Reason and justice seem to prescribe that, at least as a general rule, where a man, by gift or purchase, acquires property from another, with knowledge of a previous contract, lawfully and for valuable consideration made by him with a third person, to use and employ the property for a particular purpose in a specified manner, the acquirer shall not, to the material damage of the third person, in opposition to the contract and inconsistently with it, use and employ the property in a manner not allowable to the giver or seller.

The Lord Chancellor also considered that the charterer might be entitled to an injunction (although he refused one for other reasons) but it is not clear on what basis he thought the charterer entitled. In *Lord Strathcona Steamship Co Ltd v Dominion Coal Co Ltd* [1926] AC 108, 95 LJPC 71, the Privy Council applied Knight Bruce's dictum and restrained a purchaser of a ship from using her inconsistently with a charter made by a previous owner and of which the purchaser knew when he bought the vessel. This decision has been much criticised as contrary to principle, and in *Port Line Ltd v Ben Line Steamers Ltd* [1958] 2 QB 146, Diplock J refused to follow it. He pointed out however (at 165) that the decision in *De Mattos v Gibson* could have been reached on the basis of *Lumley v Gye* (indeed, he thought that the Lord Chancellor had decided the case on this basis); the same explanation has been given of the *Lord Strathcona* case (see *Swiss Bank Corpn v Lloyds Bank Ltd* [1979] Ch 548, at 574, reversed without reference to this point: [1982] AC 584). The difference is significant: procuring a breach of contract is a tort of intention, so that the defendant will not be liable unless he knew of the contract, whereas under *Tulk v Moxhay*, the defendant will be bound unless he was a good faith purchaser without notice, which might be only constructive.

CHAPTER FORTY-NINE

ASSIGNMENT AND THE BURDEN OF A CONTRACT

It is frequently stated that whereas the benefit of a contract can be assigned, the burden cannot. This is quite true, in that the assignor cannot assign away his liability. It does not mean, however, that the assignee will always be able to insist on the debtor performing without having to worry about whether the debtor is receiving the performance he was due from the assignor. Firstly, as we saw in the previous chapter, an assignee takes subject to equities. Thus the debtor can use against him any defence that would have been available against the assignor, including defences that do not arise until after the assignment provided they arise out of the same contract. The result is that while he still has to look to the assignor to perform his part of the bargain, the debtor may be able to refuse to perform his part unless the assignor has done his-or the assignee will do it for him.

A practical example may make this clearer. In building and engineering contracts, it is common to provide that if the contract is terminated by the employer because of a serious breach or insolvency on the part of the contractor, the contractor will assign any subcontracts to the employer. The intention is to enable the employer to get the project finished using the original subcontractors. The result of the assignment will be that the employer is owed the duty to perform the subcontract work, but it is the contractor who is obliged to pay the subcontractor. Suppose the contractor has not paid for work already done, and will not pay for future work: does the subcontractor have to perform and sue the contractor? If, as is normally the case, the subcontractor has the right to be paid as work progresses, he would ultimately be entitled to refuse to do any more until he is paid, and he can use this as a defence against the employer. The employer must therefore see that the subcontractor is paid.

If the subcontractor has been paid for the work that he has done at the date of termination, he may have to continue working without being sure of payment until such time as he is entitled not only to be paid for the future work, but is entitled to *refuse to do any more until he has been paid for what he has done*. At this stage, he can effectively insist that the employer pay him, even though it is the dismissed contractor who is theoretically liable to him. It will obviously be easier for the subcontractor to demand payment if he has a clause in his subcontract entitling him to suspend work after payment is overdue by a fairly short time, as it will be remembered that, in the absence of express provision to the contrary, payment is not treated as a condition of the obligation to do further work (see *Mersey Steel and Iron Co v Naylor, Benzon & Co* (1884) 9 App Cas 434, and on p 586.)

Thus even when it is just a question of ensuring payment for future work, the subcontractor may find it far from easy to ensure that he is paid; when he has not been paid for what he has done at the date of termination and the contractor is insolvent, he may find it next to impossible under the regime apparently envisaged by the standard forms. The terms of the original contract are that payments ultimately destined for the subcontractor be paid to the contractor, who should then pay them on; at least as regards payments due before the main contract was terminated, the contractor's liquidator can demand that the payment still be made to the contractor. If the employer pays the subcontractor directly, he will have to pay the same sum again to the contractor; if he does not pay, the subcontractor will have to prove in the insolvency and is unlikely to recover anything. Some forms confer a power on the employer to pay unpaid subcontractors directly, but as the result of the House of Lords decision in *British Eagle International Airlines Ltd v Compagnie Nationale Air France* [1975] 2 All ER 390, such a clause may well be invalid as against the insolvent creditor as an attempt to alter the statutory priorities of creditors on insolvency. In practice, the employer may have to enter a novation with contractor and subcontractor and agree to shoulder the full burden of paying the subcontractor.

There seems to be a second way in which an assignee may become liable to the burdens of the contract assigned to him (although without releasing the assignor). This is under what Megarry V-C in *Tito v Waddell (No 2)*. [1977] Ch 106 called 'the pure principle of benefit and burden'. In that long and complicated case about Ocean Island, which had been strip-mined of its guano (see p 679), one of the questions that arose was whether the British Phosphate Commissioners, to whom the mining licences had been assigned, were under any obligation to replant the island in accordance with the agreement. The judge held that they were. He said (at 302–303):

> . . . If the initial transaction has created benefits and burdens which, on its true construction, are distinct, the question whether a person who is not an original party can take one without the other will prima facie depend upon the circumstances in which he comes into the transaction. If, for instance, all that is assigned to him is the benefit of a contract, and the assignor, who is a party to the contract, undertakes to continue to discharge the burdens of it, it would be remarkable if it were to be held that the assignee could not take the benefit without assuming the burden. The circumstances show that the assignee was intended to take only the benefit, and that the burden was intended to be borne in the same way as it had been borne previously.
>
> On the other hand, if the assignee takes as a purported assignee of the whole contract from a company which is on the point of going into liquidation, he undertaking to discharge all the burdens and to indemnify the company, then, unless the benefit and burden principle is to be rejected in its entirety, I would have thought that the circumstances showed that he was not intended to take the benefit without also assuming the burdens, and that the result would accord with the intention, vis-à-vis not only the company but also the persons entitled to enforce those burdens. No doubt the terms of any relevant document would be of major importance: but I would regard the matter as one which has to be determined from the surrounding circumstances as a whole.

This doctrine seems distinct from that discussed in the previous paragraph: it does not seem to be based on the debtors' duty to perform being conditional on receiving what they had been promised by the assignors-the debtors in the case (the land owners) had no outstanding duties.

SPECIMEN CONTRACTS

The notes that follow each form are not intended to be exhaustive. They point out some of the distinctive clauses of each type of contract, particularly clauses that have been involved in cases considered earlier in the book.

■ Standard-form buyer's order

NOTES ON STANDARD-FORM BUYER'S ORDER

1. The boxes on the face of the form are for items that will be expressly agreed on each occasion: items, prices, delivery dates, etc. The back contains a set of standard terms.

2. Some of the 'back of the order' conditions seem broadly similar to the rules that would apply even without an express agreement: for example, at common law, the buyer would have the right to terminate if the goods were not delivered on time (see p 574). Clause 8 confirms this right, although it also purports to give a right of partial termination. A clause that merely restates the general law is nonetheless useful. Firstly, the other party may be far less unhappy about the buyer exercising its rights if the buyer can point to a provision for this in the contract documents. Secondly, the clause may show that the buyer does not accept the seller's terms, which will usually be very different (see next specimen). Even if the contract ends up being made on the seller's terms, the fact that the buyer has stated its term gives it a starting point from which to negotiate (see pp 223–225).

3. The buyer tries to ensure that its terms will prevail over any put forward by the seller: see cl 2. It is very doubtful if this clause will have any effect if the seller, as seems frequently to happen, purports to accept the order using a standard acknowledgment form, which states its own, different, terms. Then, the contract will usually be made on the last set of terms sent (see p 228). However, the buyer tries to get the seller to accept the buyer's terms by providing a duplicate form (referred to at the foot of the face of the order form), which the seller should sign and return if it wants to accept the order. If the seller does this, the contract will be on the buyer's terms (p 225).

4. Clause 2 has another aim: to exclude from the contract any statement that is not recorded in it (a 'merger' clause: see p 349). It also tries to exclude any remedy for misrepresentation if the seller has been given incorrect information (cf p 386).

5. Some of the terms differ significantly from what would apply in the absence of express agreement. For instance, in the absence of an express clause, the buyer would have to pay

STANDARD FORM SALES QUOTATION

Westland Helicopters Limited
Westland Works,
Yeovil, Somerset,
England BA20 2YB

Telephone 01935 75222
Fax 01935 702131/702132
Telex 46277 WHL YEO G

Messrs.	In the event of a query please contact:
	Ext:
	Supplier	Buyer	Inspection Requirements

| Contract | Terms |

This duplicate must be signed and returned to Westland Helicopters Ltd., as acknowledgment of order/amendment.

(No Amendment of this acknowledgement will be accepted either expressly or tacitly nor shall acceptance of the goods comprised in the order be construed as acceptance of any such purported amendment.)

We acknowledge receipt of the Purchase Order/Amendment of which this duplicate is a copy and which is hereby accepted in accordance with and subject to the conditions appearing in the Purchase Order/Amendment.

Dated ....19....   ....

(for and on behalf of) Supplier

A Member of the Westland Group plc   Registered Office: Westland Works, Yeovil, England BA20 2YB   Registered number 604352 England   VAT No. GB 100 3286 30 712

online resource centre
www.oxfordtextbooks.co.uk/orc/beale5e

Visit the **online resource centre** to view a full-size version of this document if you would like to read it in more detail.

CONDITIONS OF PURCHASE (Ref. WHL/PUR/001)

1. **DEFINITIONS**
Within these conditions the following definitions shall apply:
"WHL" shall mean Westland Helicopters Limited, Registered Office, Westland Works, Yeovil, Somerset BA20 2YB.
"Supplier" shall mean the contracting party on whom the Order is placed.
"Supplies" shall mean all goods and services to be supplied under the Order.
"Order" shall mean the authorised Purchase Order placed by WHL upon the Supplier for goods and services, including the conditions detailed herein and any subsequent authorised amendment thereto.

2. **APPLICABLE CONDITIONS**
These Conditions and the Order shall constitute the entire agreement between the parties and shall supersede any prior communications or representations between the parties, including any Conditions of Sale issued by the Supplier.

3. **OFFICIAL ORDER**
No Supplier will be accepted or paid for unless supplied in accordance with the Order. The Supplier shall reference the order number on all correspondence entered into. Within 14 days of the Order being issued, the Supplier shall sign and return the Order Acknowledgement. Failure to comply will result in the Order being deemed as accepted.

4. **AMENDMENTS**
No variation to the Order will be recognised by WHL, unless presented in writing and duly authorised by the buyer named overleaf.

5. **SPECIFICATION**
All Supplies under this Order shall conform where applicable with the quantity, quality, standard and specification stated in the Order, shall be fit for the purpose required by WHL, and free from any defect whether actual or latent.

6. **PACKAGING**
All Supplies under the Order shall be securely and adequately packed, and the packaging marked with WHL's Order number. All packaging shall be non-chargeable and non-returnable, unless otherwise agreed in writing by WHL, whereupon it may be returned at the Supplier's risk and expense.

7. **CERTIFICATES OF CONFORMITY / RELEASE NOTES**
(a) Where stated in the Inspection Requirements overleaf, one copy of a numbered Certificate of Conformity / Release Certificate detailing order number, part number, description, serial number and quantities delivered, shall accompany each consignment of Supplies delivered.
(b) Where applicable, the Supplier, if a stockist, shall provide one copy of the Certificate of Conformity / Release Certificate from the manufacturer of the Supplies and one copy of the Supplier's own release document.

8. **DELIVERY**
(a) Delivery shall be strictly in accordance with the instructions detailed on the Order, and shall be at the risk of the Supplier.
Deliveries unless otherwise stated shall be to the WHL Receiving Wharf during the following times:
Monday to Thursday - 7.30 a.m. to 12.00 noon
- 12.45 p.m. to 4.30 p.m.
Friday - 7.30 a.m. to 12.30 p.m.
(b) If, for whatever reason, delivery is not effected in accordance with the Order, then WHL may, without prejudice to any other right or remedy, wholly or partly terminate the Order without incurring liability to the Supplier.
(c) Title in the Supplies shall pass to WHL on delivery. Such passing of title shall not constitute acceptance of the Supplies.
(d) In the event of WHL being unable to accept deliveries, for whatever reason, WHL shall have the right to suspend, wholly or in part, deliveries under the Order.

9. **INSPECTION AND REJECTION**
(a) Pre-delivery inspection requirements shall be in accordance with the provisions on the face of the Order.
(b) WHL shall have the right to reject at any time any Supplies that are not in accordance with the Order, specification or fit for the reasons. Rejected Supplies returned shall be at the Supplier's risk and expense. Any Supplies rejected shall be deemed as having not been delivered.

10. **PRICE**
Prices shall be as stated on the face of the Order and unless agreed otherwise shall be exclusive of VAT, customs duties and taxes. No alterations will be accepted unless by prior written agreement with the buyer named overleaf.

11. **INVOICES AND PAYMENT**
(a) Invoices quoting the order number, Certificate of Conformity / Release Certificate number (where applicable), part numbers, description and quantities of Supplies delivered shall be forwarded at the time of despatch to WHL Financial Accounts Department, Box 101, Westland Helicopters Limited, Westland Works, Yeovil, Somerset, BA20 2YB. Failure to detail any of the above information may result in a delay in payment by WHL.
(b) Payment will normally be made in the month following the month in which the Supplies in accordance with the Order, and a correct invoice, are received.

12. **INDEMNITY**
In respect of the Order the Supplier hereby agrees to indemnify and hold harmless WHL against all claims, damages, liabilities and costs whatsoever resulting from:
(a) any damage, loss, death or injury caused by any act, negligence or omission of the Supplier or any of its sub-contractors.
(b) any alleged or actual infringement of any patent, registered design, trademark or copyright in existence or pending at the date of the Order, relating to the Supplies.

13. **WHL FURNISHED EQUIPMENT**
(a) Any free issue material, drawings, documents, samples, jigs, tools or patterns supplied by WHL, or manufactured for WHL, by the Supplier in connection with the Order:
(i) shall be adequately insured by the Supplier.
(ii) shall be clearly marked as the property of WHL.
(iii) shall be maintained in a reasonable condition (fair wear and tear excepted) at the Supplier's premises and entirely at the risk of the Supplier.
(v) shall not be copied or communicated to any other party or used for any work other than that detailed on this Order, without the express written consent of WHL.
(vi) shall, where applicable, be clearly marked with the tooling number as issued by WHL, from the 673 Tooling Register.
(b) WHL shall at all times have property in any scrap resulting from free issue material, and the sole discretion as to its disposal.
(c) WHL may at any time request the return of WHL furnished equipment at the risk and expense of the Supplier.

14. **DESIGN RIGHTS**
Where any work in pursuance of the Order includes design to be performed by the Supplier, then all rights in such design shall be vested in WHL and such design shall not be used except for the purpose of the Order, nor copied or communicated to any other party without WHL's express written consent. All drawings and other documents delineating or recording such shall likewise be WHL property and shall be formally returned or requested by WHL immediately upon completion of the Order.

15. **UK GOVERNMENT CONTRACT CONDITIONS**
In the event that it is indicated on the face of the Order that Supplies are required for a Government Contract then the Order shall be subject to such conditions detailed in the latest issue of the "Standard Conditions of Government Contracts for Stores Purchases" (Form GC/STORES/1) and any other such Government conditions as specified on the face of the Order.

16. **WORK ON SITE**
The Supplier accepts that if any work in pursuance of the Order is carried out by or on behalf of the Supplier in WHL's works, then it shall be subject to Westland Group Plc General Conditions of Work on Site, copies available on request.

17. **ASSIGNMENT**
(a) The Supplier hereby agrees that no work in pursuance of the Order shall be assigned without the prior written agreement of WHL.
(b) When certain operations or processes are to be undertaken by a second stage sub-contractor, the Supplier must ensure that the second stage sub-contractor is WHL approved prior to placement of each Order.

18. **CONFIDENTIALITY**
All information associated with the Order shall be treated as strictly confidential between WHL and the Supplier.

19. **PARTIAL INVALIDITY AND WAIVER**
Any provision of the Order subsequently found to be invalid shall not in any way affect the validity or enforceability of the remainder of the Order. Any failure by either party to enforce any provision of the Order shall not be construed as a waiver of that or any other provision.

20. **NOTICES**
Any Notice or other communication entered into shall be in writing, and addressed to the buyer named overleaf.

21. **TERMINATION**
(a) For Convenience
WHL shall have the right to terminate the Order in whole or in part, at any time, by serving on the Supplier written notice of termination. Upon receipt of such notice of termination all terminated work shall be discontinued and WHL shall pay to the Supplier such sum as is fair and reasonable in respect of any direct loss sustained by the Supplier by reason solely of such termination and the Supplier agrees to accept such sum in full and final satisfaction of all claims arising out of such termination.
In the event of termination of the Order, the Supplier shall use its best endeavours to mitigate the loss arising from such termination.
In no case shall the amount payable by WHL for the terminated work exceed the price which would have been payable if the work had been completed. WHL reserve the right to recover any part completed work, including any relevant jigs, tools, fixtures or documentation.
(b) For Default
WHL shall notify the Supplier of any breach or default of these conditions. If the Supplier is unable to remedy such breach or default within a period of 30 days from the notice being given, then WHL reserve the right to terminate the Order in whole or in part without incurring liability to the Supplier.
(c) For Insolvency
In the event that the Supplier becomes insolvent then WHL reserves the right to suspend or terminate the Order without incurring liability to the Supplier.

22. **APPLICABLE LAW**
This Agreement and any Order shall be subject to and interpreted in accordance with the Laws of England and the Supplier hereby submits to the jurisdiction of the English Courts.

online resource centre
www.oxfordtextbooks.co.uk/orc/beale5e

Visit the **online resource centre** to view a full-size version of this document if you would like to read it in more detail.

on delivery, whereas cl 11(b) provides for payment within the month following the month in which the goods and an invoice is received.

6.   Clause 8(d) is also very different to the general law: normally, a buyer has no right to suspend deliveries at its convenience.

7.   In other cases, the differences may appear greater than they really are. For example, a buyer cannot normally cancel an order without the seller's consent merely because that is convenient for the buyer (compare cl 21). However, the buyer can always simply refuse to perform the contract, and in practice, the seller's only remedies will usually be to terminate the contract and claim damages (see Chapter 23). Because under cl 21, WHL undertakes to pay compensation for direct losses suffered by the seller as the result of termination, the actual outcome may not be so different.

quotation

WAE
LIMITED

WESLAKE AEROMARINE ENGINES LIMITED
YEOVIL SOMERSET ENGLAND BA20 2YD

wq № 00065

Telephone Yeovil (Code 0935) 75181
Telex 46132
Fax (0935) 27600
our ref
your ref   date

To :

We have pleasure in submitting below our quotation as requested by your

This quotation is valid for   days only from this date and is subject to the conditions below and overleaf

item no.	qty	part number	description	£ decimal	per	£ decimal

V.A.T. The price quoted does not include any allowance for the extent to which the goods or services provided by us will be subject to Value Added Tax. Accordingly, to the extent that the goods or services are charged with tax, the price will be increased by the gross amount of the tax chargeable thereon.

carriage

delivery   for WESLAKE AEROMARINE ENGINES LIMITED

special conditions

Registered office: Westland Works, Yeovil, Somerset, England. Reg. no. 925550 England.

NW.6/18

online resource centre
www.oxfordtextbooks.co.uk/orc/beale5e

Visit the **online resource centre** to view a full-size version of this document if you would like to read it in more detail.

CONDITIONS OF SALE OF WESLAKE AEROMARINE ENGINES LIMITED ("WAE")

IMPORTANT: CONDITIONS 7, 13 AND 14 PROVIDE THAT CERTAIN RISKS ARE TO BE BORNE BY THE BUYER AND MAY AFFECT THE BUYER'S INSURANCE ARRANGEMENTS

1. **DEFINITIONS**: "the contract" means the agreement between WAE and the Customer for the supply of goods; "the Buyer" means the purchaser of the goods; "the goods" means the subject-matter of the contract and includes services; "the price" means the price of the goods and any other payment to be made by the Buyer to WAE hereunder.

2. **GENERAL**: The contract is entered into and all quotations are given subject to these conditions which may only be varied or waived by written agreement between WAE and the Buyer. No contract shall be made until WAE has accepted in writing an order placed by the Buyer. If these conditions differ from the terms of any offer made or order placed by the Buyer any subsequent communication by WAE constitutes a counter-offer and not acceptance of such terms. Any quotation is not an offer and may be varied or withdrawn without notice.

3. **DECRIPTIONS**: All photographs, drawings, descriptions and details in WAE catalogues, price lists and other documents are only indicative of a type of product and do not constitute warranties, conditions or representations. No report, representation, advice, communication or statement made by a representative of WAE shall be binding on WAE unless expressly contained herein. WAE reserves the right to incorporate improvements in the general development of its products and make and charge for mandatory modifications to the goods.

4. **PRICE**:
   - 4.1 Unless otherwise agreed in writing, all prices quoted are net ex-works unpacked and apply only in relation to the total quantities and dates and rates of delivery quoted. All prices are subject to the addition of all other costs duties and taxes (including where applicable Value Added Tax at the rate ruling at the relevant tax point).
   - 4.2 The invoiced amount may be adjusted to take account of increases in:
     - costs of components or equipment not manufactured by WAE, raw materials, wages, general commodities, freight or insurance;
     - rates of currency exchange, duties, import duties, taxes or surcharges, or improvements or mandatory modifications made under Clause 3 above.

5. **PAYMENT**: Unless otherwise agreed in writing, all payments shall be made in full without deduction or withholding whether or not required by law in cash in pounds sterling within 30 days of date of invoice and free of setoff, or counterclaim. Failure by the Buyer to make payment in accordance with the terms agreed shall, without prejudice to any other remedies WAE may have, render the Buyer liable to pay interest upon the total sums outstanding calculated at the rate of 3% above National Westminster Bank PLC base rate from time to time in force calculated from the date of delivery, such interest accruing on a daily basis and being payable on demand. Time for payment is of the essence of the contract.

6. **DELIVERY**:
   - 6.1 Unless otherwise agreed and stated on the face hereof, all deliveries shall be made ex-WAE Works, and shall be deemed to have been effected when WAE shall have notified the Buyer the goods are ready for collection.
   - 6.2 Any periods quoted for delivery or despatch are estimates only and WAE shall not be liable for failure to meet such periods (whether due to WAE's negligence or otherwise) nor shall the Buyer be entitled to reject any consignment of the goods or to treat the contract as repudiated in the event of any such failure.
   - 6.3 Delivery of the goods to a carrier for transmission to the Buyer or the prior delivery of the goods to the stipulated place of delivery shall constitute delivery to the Buyer and the risk therein shall upon such delivery pass to the Buyer. Section 32(2) and (3) of the Sale of Goods Act 1979 shall not apply.
   - 6.4 WAE shall be entitled to make partial deliveries or deliveries by instalments and these conditions shall apply to each partial delivery.
   - 6.5 Where the goods are ready for delivery but cannot be delivered for any reason beyond the control of WAE or through the fault or delay of the Buyer, WAE shall be entitled to make a reasonable charge in respect of storage and insurance of the goods.

7. **PROPERTY AND RISK**:
   - 7.1 Property in the goods shall remain in WAE until it has received payment in full for the goods. Risk in the goods shall pass to the Buyer on delivery.
   - 7.2 While property in the goods remains in WAE, WAE shall have the right, without prejudice to the obligation of the Buyer to purchase the goods, to re-take possession of the goods (and for that purpose to go upon any premises occupied by the Buyer). If so required by WAE the Buyer shall insure mark and store the goods identifying them as the property of WAE.
   - 7.3 WAE shall have the right to maintain an action for the price notwithstanding that property in the goods may not have passed to the Buyer.

8. **TRANSIT**: Claims for damages to goods occurring in transit or for shortage in delivery of goods received from carriers will be considered by WAE only if the carriers and WAE receive written notification of such damage or shortage within three days of arrival or in the event of loss of goods in transit within 21 days of the date of consignment. Where delivery is taken of goods without being checked they will be deemed to have been accepted unless the carrier's delivery book is signed "Not Examined".

9. **INSPECTIONS**:
   - 9.1 Unless otherwise agreed in writing, WAE will carry out such tests and inspection as it usually carries out on such goods. Any additional tests or inspections required by the Buyer will be at his expense.
   - 9.2 The goods shall be manufactured and released in accordance with the relevant requirements of such public or responsible body or bodies in the United Kingdom to whose jurisdiction, control or regulation the goods may from time to time be subject and in addition such of the goods as are manufactured by WAE shall be inspected and released by WAE under its own system of inspection as approved by any such body as above and such inspection and release shall constitute acceptance of all the goods.

10. **INTELLECTUAL PROPERTY RIGHTS ("IPR")**:
    - 10.1 The Buyer shall indemnify WAE against any claim alleging infringement of trade marks, trade names, patents, copyrights, registered designs or any other IPR which arises as a result of WAE's compliance with the Buyer's specifications, designs and instructions.
    - 10.2 (i) The Buyer shall notify WAE forthwith of any claim that the sale or use of the goods infringes any IPR and give authority, information and every reasonable assistance to WAE for the defence of any such claim and shall not itself admit, handle, deal with or compromise any such claim except with the written consent of WAE;
      (ii) The Buyer shall comply with all instructions of WAE and all legislation in relation to the sale and use of the goods. WAE may without liability cancel or suspend any deliveries or manufacture of any of the goods which have become the subject of a claim by a third party alleging infringement of any IPR.
    - 10.3 The contract does not grant the Buyer or any other third party any licence, express or implied, under any IPR of WAE for the goods or any product, process, design or machine of which the goods form part, nor does the sale of the goods or supply of supporting information imply the goods do not infringe a third party's intellectual property right.

11. **COPYRIGHT**: Copyright in the goods and copyright and property in all drawings, descriptions, specifications and other documents supplied by WAE to the Buyer shall remain in WAE.

12. **WARRANTY**:
    - 12.1 WAE will at its option either replace or repair or issue credit for the price to the Buyer for any goods found to be defective by sole reason of faulty materials or poor workmanship (fair wear and tear excluded) within 50 hours of use or 6 months from the date of delivery (whichever shall first expire) provided that:
      (i) WAE is notified in writing within 7 days of the discovery of any such defects by the Buyer and the defective goods are returned to WAE, transportation charges being prepaid by the Buyer;
      (ii) examination by WAE of such goods shall establish to its satisfaction that such defects exist and have not been caused by misuse, neglect, improper installation or repair, alteration or accident, inadequate storage;
      (iii) this warranty shall not extend to any products or parts thereof not manufactured by WAE. In the case of products not manufactured by WAE, WAE will so far as possible pass to the Buyer the benefit of any warranty or guarantee to WAE by the manufacturers.
    - 12.2 In the case of a consumer transaction as defined in the Consumer Transactions (Restrictions on Statements) Order 1976 (as amended) this condition shall not affect the statutory rights of the Buyer.

13. **EXCLUSION OF LIABILITY**
    - 13.1 SAVE AS EXPRESSLY PROVIDED IN CONDITION 12 ABOVE WAE SHALL BE UNDER NO LIABILITY (INCLUDING LIABILITY FOR ANY INDIRECT OR CONSEQUENTIAL LOSS OR DAMAGE) OF WHATSOEVER KIND HOWSOEVER CAUSED WHETHER OR NOT DUE TO THE NEGLIGENCE OR WILFUL DEFAULT OF WAE OR ITS SERVANTS OR AGENTS ARISING OUT OF OR IN CONNECTION WITH THE GOODS. ALL CONDITIONS, WARRANTIES OR OTHER TERMS EXPRESS, IMPLIED, STATUTORY OR OTHERWISE ARE HEREBY EXCLUDED.
    - 13.2 IF PARAGRAPH 13.1 ABOVE IS HELD TO BE WHOLLY OR PARTLY INEFFECTIVE IN RELATION TO ANY CLAIM THE BUYER SHALL NOT BE ENTITLED TO REJECT THE GOODS AND ANY DAMAGES RECOVERED BY THE BUYER SHALL BE LIMITED TO THE PRICE OR, IF LOWER, TO THE REASONABLE COST OF REMEDYING THE BREACH OF DUTY, PROVIDED THAT WAE SHALL FIRST BE AFFORDED THE OPPORTUNITY TO CARRY OUT SUCH REMEDIAL WORK ITSELF.
    - 13.3 Except where the contract is an international supply contract within section 26 of the Unfair Contract Terms Act 1977 ("the Act") nothing contained in this condition shall exclude or restrict:-
      (i) any liability of WAE for death or personal injury (as defined in the Act) resulting from negligence (as defined in the Act).
      (ii) any liability of WAE for breach of the implied undertakings as to title contained in section 12 of the Sale of Goods Act 1979; and
      (iii) where the Buyer deals as a consumer within the meaning of the Act, any liability of WAE for breach of its implied undertakings as to conformity of the goods with description or sample or as to their quality or fitness for a particular purpose contained in sections 13, 14 and 15 of the Sale of Goods Act 1979.

14. **FORCE MAJEURE**:
    - 14.1 WAE shall not be liable for delay in performance or for non-performance in whole or in part of its obligations under the contract directly or indirectly resulting from causes beyond control either of WAE or of WAE's suppliers including, but not limited by reference to, acts of God, acts of the Buyer or a third party, hostilities, embargoes, sabotage, civil disturbance, government regulations, strikes, lock-outs or other industrial action, illness, flood, fire, impact, explosion, adverse weather, delay in delivery to WAE or WAE's suppliers or shortage of any services, products or materials.
    - 14.2 In any such event WAE may without liability vary the terms of the contract including, but not limited to, extending the time for performing the contract. If the contract is frustrated or so cancelled WAE shall be entitled to such reasonable remuneration as it may specify.

15. **BREACH AND FINANCIAL CONDITIONS**:
    - 15.1 If any of the Buyer's obligations to WAE under any agreement are not fulfilled or if the Buyer's financial condition at any time does not in WAE's unfettered judgement justify continuance of the contract on the terms of payment specified, WAE may, without prejudice to any other rights it may have, forthwith re-possess the goods or by notice in writing cancel any outstanding order or suspend any deliveries of or work on any of the goods unless the Buyer makes such payment for any of the goods ordered as WAE may require.
    - 15.2 In addition to any rights of lien to which WAE may by law be entitled, while any amount remains due to it from the Buyer, WAE shall be entitled to a general lien for such amount on all property of the Buyer in WAE's possession (whether paid for by the Buyer or not).

16. **HEALTH & SAFETY AT WORK ETC. ACT 1974**:
    - 16.1 If the goods are articles for use at work within the meaning of the Health & Safety at Work etc. Act 1974 the Buyer hereby agrees that it is responsible for taking all necessary steps to ensure that the goods are safe and without risks to health when properly used including:-
      (i) regularly and properly testing, inspecting and maintaining, properly installing, storing and housing the goods,
      (ii) disseminating adequate detailed information regarding their safe and proper use to the persons using the goods, and ensuring that the goods are adequately manned, and the Buyer's order for the goods shall be deemed to be its written undertaking therefor pursuant to the said Act.

17. **USE**: The Buyer shall comply with all instructions of WAE and all legislation in relation to the use, processing, storage and sale of the goods.

18. **BUYER'S PROPERTY**: Any property of the Buyer received by WAE whether for incorporation in goods of WAE or for repair or otherwise will be held by WAE at the Buyer's risk as regards loss or damage howsoever arising.

19. **PROPER LAW AND JURISDICTION**: The contract shall be governed by and construed in accordance with English law and the Courts of England shall have non-exclusive jurisdiction to hear all disputes arising in connection with the contract.

20. **CONFIDENTIALITY**: Any information or data given in confidence or any confidential drawings or other general commercial intelligence which may be received by the Buyer or any representative of the Buyer shall not be divulged to any third party and may be used by the Buyer only in connection with the goods supplied hereunder and not in any other connection whatsoever. In the event that the Buyer or any such representative so divulges any such data drawings information or intelligence to the detriment of WAE, the Buyer shall indemnify WAE in full against all costs, expenses damage or loss directly or indirectly occasioned thereby.

21. **EXPORTS**: In the case of export contracts the following additional conditions shall apply:
    - 21.1 It is hereby declared and agreed that the Uniform Laws on International Sales Act 1967 and any statutory modification or enactment thereof shall not apply.
    - 21.2 WAE shall not be taken as indemnifying the Buyer or as being liable for IPR infringement where the goods are sold or used outside UK or their usual function.

online resource centre
www.oxfordtextbooks.co.uk/orc/beale5e

Visit the **online resource centre** to view a full-size version of this document if you would like to read it in more detail.

NOTES ON STANDARD-FORM SALES QUOTATION

1. This form, which is used by another company in the same group as the one whose purchase order is reproduced above, shows the differences between what companies are likely to seek when they are buying and what they want when they are selling. A simple illustration is cl 4, allowing price increases: there is no equivalent in the buyer's order.

2. Similarly, cl 5 gives the seller a right to interest on late payments (cf p 671) and makes time for payment 'of the essence' (ie gives the seller the right to terminate the contract if the buyer is late in paying), which is not the position under the general law: see p 574.

3. Clause 2 states that no order will become binding until accepted by WAE; this quotation is not an offer.

4. The same clause attempts to ensure that these conditions will apply to the exclusion of any standard conditions used by the buyer—even, it seems to say, if WAE does not reply using an acknowledgment restating its own conditions but simply sends a letter accepting the offer!

5. Clause 3 seeks to prevent WAE being liable if any descriptions in its publicity or information given by its representatives are inaccurate. Compare pp 387 and 996.

6. The contract contains a number of clauses that would limit the buyer's rights if the goods are defective: cl 5 prevents the buyer making deductions from or setting off losses against the price, while cl 13 limits WAE's liability in several ways. Note the way in which cl 13.2 attempts to provide a separate protection, which might survive even if cl 13.1 is held to be invalid under the Unfair Contract Terms Act 1977: see p 1012.

7. Clause 6.2 purports to exclude WAE's liability for late delivery, by stating that the delivery time quoted is an estimate only. On whether this form of clause is within the Unfair Contract Terms Act 1977, see p 1009.

8. Clause 14 excludes the seller from liability for delays cause by factors outside its control ('force majeure'; cf p 469) and, if the contract is frustrated, purports to enable it to claim whatever remuneration it thinks is reasonable (cf pp 481 ff).

9. There seem to be more differences between the conditions stated in this form and the general law than between the general law and the purchase order form reproduced earlier. One reason for this is that the general law seems more favourable to the buyer than to the seller.

■ *Conditions for the hiring of plant*

MODEL CONDITIONS FOR THE HIRING OF PLANT (WITH EFFECT FROM JULY 2001)
These conditions are not to be used for consumer contracts

1. DEFINITIONS

(a) The **"Owner"** is the Company, firm or person letting the plant on hire and includes their successors, assigns or personal representatives.

(b) The **"Hirer"** is the Company, firm, person, Corporation or public authority taking the owner's plant on hire and includes their successors or personal representatives.

(c) **"Plant"** covers all classes of plant, machinery, vehicles, equipment and accessories therefor, which the Owner agrees to hire to the Hirer.

(d) A **"day"** shall be 8 hours or if the day is a Friday it shall be 7 hours, unless otherwise specified in the Contract.

(e) A **"working week"** covers the period from starting time on Monday to finishing time on Friday.

(f) The **"hire period"** shall commence from the time when the plant leaves the Owner's depot or place where last employed and shall continue until the plant is received back at the Owner's named depot or other agreed location.

(g) A **"Consumer Contract"** is a contract entered into with a person acting in his own capacity and not for or on behalf of any business or trade entity.

2. EXTENT OF CONTRACT

No conditions other than specifically set forth in the Offer and Acceptance and herein shall be deemed to be incorporated in or to form part of the Contract or shall otherwise govern the relationship between the Owner and the Hirer in relation to the hire of any particular plant pursuant to the Offer and Acceptance. The Contract does not create any right enforceable by or purport to confer any benefit on any person not a party to it except that a person who is a successor to or an assignee of the rights of the Owner is deemed to become a party to the Contract after the date of succession or assignment (as the case may be).

3. ACCEPTANCE OF PLANT

Acceptance of the plant on site implies acceptance of all terms and conditions herein unless otherwise agreed in writing.

4. UNLOADING AND LOADING

The Hirer shall be responsible for the unobstructed access and, unless otherwise agreed in writing, for unloading and loading of the plant at the site, and any personnel supplied by the Owner for such unloading and/or loading shall be deemed to be under the direction and control of the Hirer. Such personnel shall for all purposes in connection with their employment in the unloading and/or loading of the plant be regarded as the servants or agents of the Hirer (but without prejudice to any of the provisions of Clause 13) who alone shall be responsible for all claims arising in connection with unloading and or loading of the plant by, or with the assistance of, such personnel.

5. DELIVERY IN GOOD ORDER AND MAINTENANCE: INSPECTION REPORTS

(a) Unless notification in writing to the contrary is received by the Owner from the Hirer in the case of plant supplied with an operator within four working days, and in the case of plant supplied without an operator within three working days, of the plant being delivered to the site, the plant shall be deemed to be in good order, save for either an inherent fault or a fault not ascertainable by reasonable examination, in accordance with terms of the Contract and to the Hirer's satisfaction, provided that where plant requires to be erected on site, the periods above stated shall be calculated from the date of completed erection of plant. The Hirer shall be responsible for its safe keeping, use in a workmanlike manner within the manufacturer's rated capacity and return on the completion of the hire in equal good order (fair wear and tear excepted).

(b) The Hirer shall when hiring plant without Owner's operator or driver take all reasonable steps to keep himself acquainted with the state and condition of the plant. If such plant is continued at work or in use in an unsafe and unsatisfactory state or environment, the Hirer shall be solely responsible for any damage, loss or accidents whether

directly or indirectly arising therefrom.

(c) The current Inspection Report required under the relevant legislation, or a copy thereof, shall be supplied by the Owner if requested by the Hirer and returned on completion of hire.

6. SERVICING AND INSPECTION

The Hirer shall at all reasonable times allow the Owner, his Agents or his Insurers to have access to the plant to inspect, test, adjust, repair or replace the same. So far as reasonably possible, such work will be carried out at times to suit the convenience of the Hirer.

7. TIMBER MATS OR EQUIVALENT

(a) If the ground (including any private access road or track) is soft or unsuitable for the plant to work on, travel, or be transported over without timbers or equivalents the Hirer shall supply and lay suitable timbers or equivalents in a suitable position for the plant to travel over, work on, or be transported over, including for the purpose of delivery and collection.

(b) Where the hire is for lifting equipment, any sound timber or other material supplied by the Owner for use with outriggers/stabilisers is provided solely to assist the Hirer and expressly not to relieve him of his legal, regulatory or contractual obligations to ensure adequate stability of the lifting equipment under the imposed loading.

8. HANDLING OF PLANT

When a driver or operator or any person is supplied by the Owner with the plant, the Owner shall supply a person competent in operating the plant or for such purpose for which the person is supplied and such person shall be under the direction and control of the Hirer. Such drivers or operators or persons shall for all purposes in connection with their employment in the working of the plant be regarded as the servants or agents of the Hirer (but without prejudice to any of the provisions of Clause 13) who also shall be responsible for all claims arising in connection with the operation of the plant by the said drivers/operators/persons. The Hirer shall not allow any other person to operate such plant without the Owner's previous consent to be confirmed in writing.

9. BREAKDOWN, REPAIRS AND ADJUSTMENT

(a) When the plant is hired without the Owner's driver or operator any breakdown or the unsatisfactory working of any part of the plant must be notified immediately to the Owner. Any claim for breakdown time will only be considered from the time and date of notification.

(b) Full allowance for the hire charges and for the reasonable cost of repairs that have been authorised by the Owner will be made to the Hirer for any stoppage due to breakdown of plant caused by the development of either an inherent fault or a fault not ascertainable by reasonable examination or fair wear and tear and for all stoppages for normal running repairs in accordance with the terms of the Contract.

(c) The Hirer shall not, except for the changing of any tyre and repair of punctures, repair the plant without the written authority of the Owner. The changing of any tyre and repair of punctures are however the responsibility of the Hirer who should arrange for them to be changed/repaired without awaiting authorisation from the Owner. The Hirer is responsible for all costs incurred in the changing or replacement of any tyre and the repair of any puncture.

(d) The Hirer shall be responsible for all expense involved arising from any breakdown and all loss or damage incurred by the Owner due to the Hirer's negligence, misdirection or misuse of the plant, whether by the Hirer or his servants, and for the payment of hire at the idle time rate as defined in Clause 25 during the period the plant is necessarily idle due to such breakdown, loss or damage. The Hirer is responsible for the cost of spares and/or repairs due to theft, loss or vandalism of the plant. The Owner will be responsible for the cost of repairs, inclusive of the cost of spares, to the plant involved in breakdown from all other causes.

Copyright CPA

online resource centre
www.oxfordtextbooks.co.uk/orc/beale5e

Visit the **online resource centre** to view a full-size version of this document if you would like to read it in more detail.

10. OTHER STOPPAGES

No claims will be admitted (other than those allowed for under "Breakdown" or for "Idle Time", as herein provided), for stoppages through causes outside the Owner's control, including bad weather or ground conditions nor shall the Owner be responsible for the cost or expense of recovering any plant from soft ground.

11. LOSS OF OTHER PLANT DUE TO BREAKDOWN

Each item of plant specified in the Contract is hired as a separate unit and the breakdown or stoppage of one or more units or vehicles (whether the property of the Owner or otherwise) through any cause whatsoever, shall not entitle the Hirer to compensation or allowance for the loss of working time by any other unit or units of plant working in conjunction therewith, provided that where two or more items of plant are expressly hired together as a unit, such items shall be deemed a unit for the purpose of breakdown.

12. LIMITATION OF LIABILITY

Except for liability on the part of the Owner which is expressly provided for in the Contract (including these Clauses):

(a) the Owner shall have no liability or responsibility for any loss or damage of whatever nature due to or arising through any cause beyond his reasonable control;

(b) the Owner shall have no liability or responsibility, whether by way of indemnity or by reason of any breach of the Contract, breach of statutory duty or misrepresentation or by reason of the commission of any tort (Including but not limited to negligence) in connection with the hire, for any of the Hirer's loss of profit, loss of use of the plant or any other asset or facility, loss of production or productivity, loss of contracts with any third party, liabilities of whatever nature to any third party, and/or any other financial or economic loss or indirect or consequential loss or damage of whatever nature; and

(c) whenever the Contract (including these Clauses) provides that any allowance is to be made against hire charges, such allowance shall be the Hirer's sole and exclusive remedy in respect of the circumstances giving rise to the allowance, and such remedy shall be limited to the amount of hire charges which would otherwise be or become due if the allowance in question had not been made.

13. HIRER'S RESPONSIBILITY FOR LOSS AND DAMAGE

(a) For the avoidance of doubt it is hereby declared and agreed that nothing in this Clause affects the operation of Clauses 4, 5, 8 and 9 of this Agreement.

(b) During the continuance of the hire period the Hirer shall subject to the provisions referred to in sub paragraph (a) make good to the Owner all loss of or damage to the plant from whatever cause the same may arise, fair wear and tear excepted, and except as provided in Clause 9 herein, and shall also fully and completely indemnify the Owner in respect of all claims by any person whatsoever for injury to person or property caused by or in connection with or arising out of the storage, transit, transport, unloading, loading or use of the plant during the continuance of the hire period, and in respect of all costs and charges in connection therewith whether arising under statute or common law In the event of loss of or damage to the plant, hire charges shall be continued at Idle time rates as defined in Clause 25 until settlement has been effected.

(c) Notwithstanding the above the Hirer shall not be responsible for damage, loss or injury due to or arising:

(i) prior to delivery of any plant to the site (or, where the site is not immediately adjacent to a highway maintainable at the public expense, prior to its leaving such highway) where the plant is in transit by transport of the Owner or as otherwise arranged by the Owner,

(ii) during the erection and/or dismantling of any plant where such plant requires to be completely erected/dismantled on site, always provided that such erection/dismantling is under the exclusive control of the Owner or his Agent,

(iii) after the plant has been removed from the site and is in transit on a highway maintainable at the public expense (or where the site is not immediately adjacent to a highway maintainable at the public expense after it has joined such highway) to the Owner by transport of the Owner or as otherwise arranged by the Owner,

(iv) where plant is travelling to or from a site on a highway maintainable at the public expense (or, where the site is not immediately adjacent to a highway maintainable at the public expense, prior to its leaving or after its joining such highway) under its own power with a driver supplied by the Owner.

14. NOTICE OF ACCIDENTS

If the plant is involved in any accident resulting in injury to persons or damage to property, immediate notice must be given to the Owner by telephone and confirmed in writing to the Owner's office. In relation to any claim in respect of which the Hirer is not bound fully to indemnify the Owner, no admission, offer, promise of payment or indemnity shall be made by the Hirer without the Owner's consent in writing.

15. RE-HIRING ETC.

The plant or any part thereof shall not be re-hired, sub-let, or lent to any third party without the written permission of the Owner.

16. CHANGE OF SITE

The plant shall not be moved from the site to which it was delivered or consigned without the written permission of the Owner.

17. RETURN OF PLANT FOR REPAIRS

If during the hire period the Owner decides that urgent repairs to the plant are necessary he may arrange for such repairs to be carried out on site or at any location of his nomination. In that event the Owner shall be obliged to replace the plant with similar plant if available, the Owner (but without prejudice to any of the provisions of Clauses 9 and/or 13) paying all transport charges involved. In the event of the Owner being unable to replace the plant he shall be entitled to determine the Contract forthwith (but without prejudice to any of the provisions of Clauses 9 and/or 13) by giving written notice to the Hirer. If such determination occurs:

(a) within three months from the commencement of hire, the Owner (but without prejudice to any of the provisions of Clauses 9 and/or 13) shall pay all transport charges involved, or,

(b) more than three months from the commencement of hire, the Owner (but without prejudice to any of the provisions of Clauses 9 and/or 13) shall be liable only for the cost of reloading and return transport.

18. BASIS OF CHARGING

(a) The Hirer shall render to the Owner for each week an accurate statement of the number of hours the plant has worked each day. Where the plant is accompanied by the Owner's driver or operator, the Hirer shall sign the employee's Time Record Sheets. The signature of the Hirer's representative shall bind the Hirer to accept the hours shown on the Time Record Sheets.

(b) Full allowance will be made for breakdown periods resulting from mechanical or electrical faults or absence of driver or operator supplied by the Owner except where breakdown is due to acts or omissions of third parties and/or the Hirer's misuse, misdirection or negligence, subject however to the provisions of Clause 8 of this Agreement.

(c) Breakdown time in respect of such periods shall be allowed for not more than 8 hours Monday to Thursday and not more than 7 hours on Friday less the actual hours worked.

(d) Plant shall be hired out either:

(i) for a stated minimum number of hours per day or per week or,

(ii) without any qualification as to minimum hours. Odd days at the beginning and at the end of the hire period shall be charged pro rata.

(e) Stoppages due to changing of tyres and repairs to punctures will be chargeable as working time up to a maximum of 2 hours for any one stoppage and any excess will be charged for at the appropriate idle time rates.

(f) In the case of plant which requires to be dismantled for the purpose of transportation, if the Owner agrees to a modification of the hire charge for the period required for assembling on site and dismantling upon completion of hire, such modification of the hire charge and the period for which it shall apply shall be stated on the Hire Contract

19. PLANT HIRED ON A DAILY BASIS WITHOUT QUALIFICATION AS TO HOURS

The full daily rate will be charged on a daily basis irrespective of the hours worked except in the case of breakdown for which the Owner is responsible, when the actual hours worked will be charged pro rata of the average working day. No hire charge shall be made for Saturday and/or Sunday unless the plant is actually worked.

20. PLANT HIRED BY THE WEEK OR MONTH WITHOUT QUALIFICATION AS TO HOURS

The weekly or monthly rate shall be charged irrespective of the number of hours worked, except in the case of breakdown for which the Owner is responsible when an allowance pro rata of the agreed weekly rate or pro rata of the agreed monthly rate will be made for each full working day broken down calculated to the nearest half working day.

21. PLANT HIRED BY THE WEEK OR THE HOUR FOR A MINIMUM OF 39 HOURS PER WEEK

If no breakdown occurs, the full hire for the minimum period in the Contract will be charged and an additional pro rata charge will be made for hours worked in excess of such minimum period. Allowance will be made for breakdowns up to 8 hours except on Fridays when the allowance will be up to 7 hours providing always that where the actual hours worked are in excess of the minimum period less breakdown time, the actual hours worked shall be chargeable. Idle time for this purpose shall be treated as actual working time. The minimum week of 39 hours shall be reduced by 8 hours Monday to Thursday and 7 hours Friday for each day's statutory holiday occurring in such week, provided that the plant does not work on the holiday.

online resource centre

www.oxfordtextbooks.co.uk/orc/beale5e

Visit the **online resource centre** to view a full-size version of this document if you would like to read it in more detail.

22. "ALL-IN" RATES

Where "All-In" rates are charged by agreement the minimum period shall be as defined in the Contract and in accordance with the hire rates and terms contained therein, subject to the provisions of Clause 26.

23. COMMENCEMENT AND TERMINATION OF HIRE (TRANSPORT OF PLANT)

(a) The hire period shall commence from the time when the plant leaves the Owner's depot or place where last employed and shall continue until the plant is received back at the Owner's named depot or other agreed location but an allowance shall be made of not more than one day's hire charge each way for travelling time. If the plant be used on day of travelling, full hire rates shall be paid for the period of use on that day. If more than one day be properly and unavoidably occupied in transporting the plant, a hire charge at idle time rates shall be payable for such extra time, provided that where plant is hired for a total period of less than one week, the full hire rate shall be paid from the date of despatch to the date of return to the Owner's named depot or other agreed location.

(b) An allowance of not more than one day's travelling time shall be allowed when the plant is travelling to a site other than that specified in the Contract provided that:
　(i) consent to such transfer has been given by the Owner under Clause 16, and,
　(ii) the plant is moved by means other than under its own power, and,
　(iii) the plant shall have been on the site specified in the Contract or on any other site to which consent to transfer has been given under Clause 16 for a period of at least 14 days.

24. NOTICE OF TERMINATION OF CONTRACT

Where the period of hire is indeterminate or having been defined becomes indeterminate the Contract shall be determinable by seven days notice in writing given by either party to the other except in cases where the plant has been lost or damaged. Notwithstanding that the Owner may have agreed to accept less than 7 days notice of termination, the Hirer's obligations under Clause 13 shall continue until the plant is returned to the Owner in accordance with Clause 31 or until the Owner has collected the plant within the 7 days following the acceptance of short notice. Oral notice given by the Hirer to the Owner's driver or operator shall not be deemed to constitute compliance with the provisions of this Clause.

25. IDLE TIME

When the plant is prevented by prolonged inclement weather from working for a complete week, the charge shall be two thirds of the hire rate or such other idle time rate as is stated in the Offer. If the plant works for any time during the guaranteed hire period then the whole of that guaranteed minimum period shall be charged as working time. In any case no period less than one day shall be reckoned as idle time save for as provided for in clause 18(e). Where an "All-In" rate is charged, idle time is charged on the machine element only. Full rate will be charged for the operator.

26. WAGES AND OTHER CHARGEABLE ITEMS RELATING TO DRIVERS AND OPERATORS OF PLANT

All chargeable items shall be paid by the Hirer at the rates contracted save that any subsequent increases before and/or during the hire period arising from awards under any wage agreements and/or from increases in the employer's statutory contribution shall be charged as additions at cost by the Owner and shall be admitted and paid by the Hirer.

27. TRAVELLING TIME AND FARES

Travelling time and fares for drivers, operators and any person supplied by the Owner, similar expenses incurred at the beginning and end of the hire period and where appropriate return fare of the driver, operator and any person supplied by the Owner to his home will be chargeable at cost. No charge shall be made by the Owner for any such expenses incurred by other employees of the Owner for the purpose of relieving, repair or maintenance of plant, unless necessitated by the Hirer's negligence, misdirection or misuse of the plant.

28. FUEL, OIL AND GREASE

Fuel, oil and grease shall, when supplied by the Owner, be charged at net cost or an agreed estimate of net cost, and when supplied by the Hirer, shall be of a grade or type specified by the Owner.

29. SHARPENING OF DRILLS/STEELS ETC.

The cost of re-sharpening shall be borne by the Hirer.

30. OWNER'S NAME PLATES

The Hirer shall not remove, deface or cover up the Owner's name plate or mark on the plant indicating that it is his property.

31. TRANSPORT

The Hirer shall pay the cost of and if required by the Owner, arrange transport of, the plant from the Owner's depot or other agreed location to the site and return to named depot or other agreed location on completion of the hire period.

32. GOVERNMENT REGULATIONS

The Hirer will be responsible for compliance with relevant regulations issued by the Government or Local Authorities, including regulations under the Factories Acts, Health and Safety at Work Act etc and observance of the Road Traffic Acts should they apply, including the cost of Road Fund Licences and any insurances made necessary thereby, save that if and during such time as the plant is travelling, whether for full or part journey from Owner to site and site to Owner under its own power with a driver supplied by the Owner, the Owner and not the Hirer shall be responsible as aforesaid.

33. PROTECTION OF OWNER'S RIGHTS

(a) The Hirer shall not re-hire, sell, mortgage, charge, pledge, part with possession of or otherwise deal with the plant except as provided under Clause 15 and shall protect the same against distress, execution or seizure and shall indemnify the Owner against all losses, damage, costs, charges and expenses arising as a direct result of any failure to observe and perform this condition except in the event of Government requisition.

(b) If the Hirer make default in punctual payment of any sum due to the Owner for hire of plant or other charges or shall fail to observe and perform the terms and conditions of this Contract, or if the Hirer shall suffer any distress or execution to be levied against him or make or propose to make any arrangement with his creditors or becomes insolvent within the meaning of Section 113 of the Housing Grants, Construction and Regeneration Act 1996 or any amendment or re-enactment thereof for the time being in force; or shall do or cause to be done or permit or suffer any act or thing whereby the Owner's rights in the plant may be prejudiced or put into jeopardy, this Contract may forthwith be determined by notice from the Owner to the Hirer (notwithstanding that the Owner may have waived some previous default or matter of the same or a like nature). The Contract shall thereupon be deemed determined by reason of the Hirer's breach and it shall be lawful for the Owner to retake possession of the said plant and for that purpose enter into or upon any premises where the same may be and the determination of the hiring under this Condition shall not affect the right of the Owner to recover from the Hirer any monies due to the Owner under the Contract or any of the Owner's rights and remedies. In particular, without limitation, the Owner shall be entitled to claim the hire charges outstanding as at the date of determination of the hire under this clause, return transport charges under clause 31, and damages for the Hirer's actual or deemed breach of the Contract under this Clause.

34. CHANGES IN NORMAL WORKING WEEK

The foregoing provisions have been framed upon the basis of the Hirer working a 5-day week of 39 hours; it is hereby agreed that in the event of:
(a) there being any change in the normal weekly hours in the industry in which the Hirer is engaged or,
(b) the Contract being made with reference to a 5 day week of other than 39 hours.

Clauses 1(d) and (e), 18(c) and (d), 20 and (in regard to breakdown allowance and reduction for statutory holidays) 21 shall be deemed to be modified conformably and in the event of an alteration in the normal weekly working hours in the said industry the "Hire Rates and Terms" of plant hired for a minimum weekly or daily period shall be varied pro rata.

35. DISPUTE RESOLUTION

(a) If the original site is in England or Wales, the proper law of the Contract shall be English law. If the original site is in Scotland, the Contract shall in all respects be construed and operated as a Scottish contract, and shall be interpreted in accordance with Scots law. If the original site is in Northern Ireland, the proper law of the Contract shall be Northern Ireland law.

(b) The Scheme for Construction Contracts contained in the Scheme for Construction Contracts (England and Wales) Regulations 1998, or any amendment or re-enactment thereof for the time being in force, shall apply to the Contract. The person (if any) specified in the Contract to act as adjudicator may be named in the Offer. The specified nominating body to select adjudicators shall be the Construction Plant Hire Association acting by its President or Chief Executive for the time being. In paragraph 21 of the Scheme "this paragraph" shall be deleted and "paragraph 20" substituted.

(c) The Owner and the Hirer shall comply forthwith with any decision of the adjudicator; and shall submit to summary judgment and enforcement (and/or, under Scots law, shall consent to a motion for summary decree and submit to enforcement) in respect of all such decisions; in each case, without any defence, set-off, counterclaim, abatement or deduction. Where, under Scots law, the Owner, the Hirer, or the adjudicator, wishes to register a decision of the adjudicator for execution in the Books of Council and Session, any other party shall, on being requested to do so, forthwith consent to such registration by subscribing the decision before a witness.

online resource centre
www.oxfordtextbooks.co.uk/orc/beale5e

Visit the **online resource centre** to view a full-size version of this document if you would like to read it in more detail.

NOTES ON CONDITIONS FOR THE HIRING OF PLANT

1. This form of contract reflects the normal pattern in straightforward contracts of hire, that the owner is responsible for providing a machine that works at the beginning of the hire period (see cl 5) and for keeping the machine working: if the machine breaks down, the hirer is given an allowance for the time lost (cl 9(b) and cl 19–21). Note, however, that the hirer may be responsible for notifying the owner of breakdowns (cl 9(a)) and, except for punctures, may not effect repairs himself without permission (cl 9(c)). Moreover, the owner may not be responsible for consequential losses of time, etc, cause by the breakdown (cl 12).

2. If the owner finds it necessary to remove the plant for repairs, and he cannot provide a replacement, he may determine the contract (cl 17).

3. The hirer is responsible for damage to the plant, unless the damage was caused by an initial defect, a breakdown for which the owner is responsible or an incompetent driver supplied by the owner (cl 13(b), as qualified by cl 5, 8, 9, and 13(a)). The hirer is also responsible for most cases of loss or injury caused to third parties, promising that if the owner is made liable to the third party, the hirer will indemnify the owner (cl 8 and 13(b)).

4. If the contract is not for a fixed period of time, either party may determine it on seven days' notice (cl 24). The owner also has the right to terminate the contract if the hirer defaults in paying, commits any breach or becomes insolvent (cl 33(b)).

5. For cases involving similar terms, see pp 340, 1010 and 1018.

■ *Bill of lading*

NOTES ON BILL OF LADING

1.   A very large proportion of the world's shipping contracts are aranged in London and are subject to English law. This makes law a considerable 'export industry', and explains why so many of the reported contract cases involve shipping contracts of various types.

2.   A 'bill of lading' is a contract made between a person who ships goods by sea and (usually—see note 13) the owner of the vessel on which the goods are shipped.

3.   The bill of lading itself serves three functions. Firstly, it contains the terms of the contract (although occasionally the shipper and carrier will have agreed different terms to those in the bill, which is only issued after the goods have been shipped: in that case, it is the terms agreed that will apply, and therefore it is often said that the bill is only evidence of the terms).

4.   Secondly, the bill acts as a receipt for the goods, showing the quantity shipped, their apparent condition when shipped and any leading (identifying) marks. Note the headings to be filled in on the face of the bill, and the first clause also on the fact (starting 'SHIPPED . . . '). If the bill states that the goods were shipped in good order and condition, this may 'estop' the ship owner from claiming that they had been damaged befoer loading: see p 148.

5.   Thirdly, the bill operates as a document of title: the shipper can transfer his ownership of the goods while they are afloat by indorsing the bill of lading to the transferee. (Note that the bill reproduced is simply the copy retained by the master of the ship, and is stamped 'not negotiable', so that it does not act as a document of title. The other copies of the bill will not bear these words.) The bill may be taken to the order of the consignee (see the second box on the face), or to the order of the shipper himself.

6.   When the bill is indorsed to the consignee or buyer, the latter acquires the right to sue the carrier on this bill of lading contract. This is the effect of the Carriage of Goods by Sea Act 1992, s 2. The consignee or buyer will also become liable on the bill of lading contract by taking or demanding delivery of the goods (s 3). Thus the buyer can sue the shipowner if the goods are damaged, and is liable to pay the freight of it has not been paid already. As between the shipowner and the indorsee of the bill, the terms of the bill are the contract: any different arrangement made betwen the shipowner and the original shipper is irrelevant.

7.   It is common for the bill of lading to be indorsed to a bank by way of pledge— in other words, as security for a loan, rather as you might pledge your watch to a pawnbroker. A common example of the bill being pledged to a bank occurs when the buyer pays via a documentary credit in favour of the seller: see p 121. In this case, the bank has the normal rights of a bill of lading holder under s 2, but under s 3, the bank will become liable in the bill of lading contract only if it takes or demands delivery or makes a claim against the carrier under the contract of carriage.

8.   All bill of lading contracts for goods being shipped from the UK are subject to the Hague-Visby Rules, by virtue of the Carriage of Goods by Sea Act 1992, s 1(3): these rules are referred to in cl 1 on the back of the bill. The rules, and their predecessors, the Hague Rules, are part of the international convention designed to strike a fair balance between shippers and carriers, by, on the one hand, limiting the carrier's liability for loss or

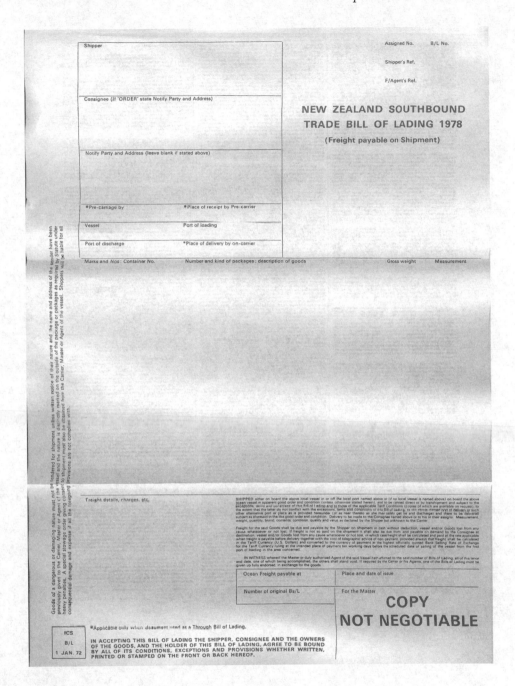

Visit the **online resource centre** to view a full-size version of this document if you would like to read it in more detail.

1. It is mutually agreed that this Bill of Lading shall have effect subject to the provisions of the International Convention relating to Bills of Lading dated Brussels 25th August, 1924 (hereinafter called the Hague Rules) except where legislation giving effect to the Hague Rules as amended by the Protocol signed at Brussels 23rd February, 1968 (hereinafter called the Hague Visby Rules) is compulsorily applicable, in which case this Bill of Lading shall have effect subject to the provisions of such legislation. Neither the Hague Rules nor the Hague Visby Rules shall apply to this Contract where the goods carried hereunder consist of live animals or cargo which by this Contract is stated as being carried on deck and is so carried. Nothing herein contained shall be deemed to be a surrender by the Carrier of any of his rights or immunities or an increase of any of his responsibilities or liabilities under the provisions of the said legislation or Rules (as the case may be) and the said provisions shall not (unless and to the extent that they are by law compulsorily applicable) apply to that portion of the contract evidenced by this Bill of Lading which relates to forwarding under Clause 4 hereof. If anything herein contained be inconsistent with or repugnant to the said provisions, it shall, to the extent of such inconsistency or repugnance and no further, be null and void.

Nothing herein contained shall prevent the Carrier from claiming in the Courts of any Country the benefit of, or derogate in any way from, any statutory protection or limitation of liability afforded to Shipowner or Carrier by the laws of such Country or by the laws of the Country in which the goods were shipped. In this Bill of Lading "the vessel" means any vessel carrying the goods other than one by which the goods are forwarded under Clause 4.

It is hereby expressly agreed that no servant or agent of the Carrier (including every independent contractor from time to time employed by the Carrier) shall in any circumstances whatsoever be under any liability whatsoever to the Shipper, Consignee or Owner of the goods or to any holder of this Bill of Lading for any loss, damage or delay of whatsoever kind arising or resulting directly or indirectly from any act, neglect or default on his part while acting in the course of or in connection with his employment and, without prejudice to the generality of the foregoing provisions in this Clause, every exemption, limitation, condition and liberty herein contained and every right, exemption from liability, defence and immunity of whatsoever nature applicable to the Carrier or to which the Carrier is entitled hereunder shall also be available and shall extend to protect every such servant or agent of the Carrier acting as aforesaid and for the purpose of all the foregoing provisions of this Clause the Carrier is or shall be deemed to be acting as agent or trustee on behalf of and for the benefit of all persons who are or might be his servants or agents from time to time (including independent contractors as aforesaid) and all such persons shall to this extent be or be deemed to be parties to the contract in or evidenced by this Bill of Lading.

2. (*a*) Neither the Carrier, his agents, servants nor the vessel shall be liable for any loss, detention or damage of or to the goods or any part thereof howsoever caused prior to loading on or subsequent to discharge from the ocean vessel even though such loss, detention or damage be caused by the negligence of the Carrier, his agents or servants or other persons for whom the Carrier is responsible, or by the unseaworthiness or unfitness of any ship, craft or conveyance at the time the goods or any part thereof are placed therein or at any time thereafter, and even though the goods or any part thereof are in the custody of the Carrier, his agents or servants as warehousemen or otherwise howsoever, and the goods or any part thereof prior to loading or subsequent to discharge as aforesaid are at the sole risk of the Owner of the goods.

(*b*) (i) In respect of goods which in this Bill of Lading are stated as being carried on deck and are so carried, the Carrier, whether in his capacity as Carrier or otherwise, shall not be liable for any loss, damage or delay whatsoever and wheresoever arising, and even though caused by the negligence of the Carrier, his agents or servants, or by the unseaworthiness or unfitness at any time of the vessel or of any ship, craft, conveyance or place.

(ii) Livestock are kept and carried at the sole risk of the owner thereof and the Carrier shall be under no liability for any injury, death, illness or delay whatsoever and wheresoever arising and even though caused or contributed to by the act, neglect or default of the Carrier, or by unseaworthiness or unfitness of any vessel, craft, conveyance or place existing at any time. In the event of any livestock being likely, in the sole discretion of the Master, to be dangerous or injurious to the lives or health of any other livestock or of any person on board, such livestock may upon the Master's order be destroyed and thrown overboard without liability to the Carrier. The owner of the livestock shall indemnify the Carrier against the cost of providing forage required for any period during which the carriage or custody of the livestock is delayed for any reason whatsoever, and for the cost of all veterinary service on the voyage.

The Carrier shall not be responsible for injury, death, illness, destruction or delay of or to the livestock arising directly or indirectly from compliance with quarantine regulations or the regulations, orders or directions of any Authority of any country, and in the event of quarantine or the intervention of any such Authority the livestock may be discharged into any depot hulk or sanitary or other vessel or craft or place as required for the prompt despatch of the vessel. If any Authority refuses to allow the vessel transit through waters controlled by that Authority the livestock may, on the Master's orders, be killed and thrown overboard in order to secure the vessel's passage through those waters and without any liability attaching to the Carrier. All expenses whatsoever and wheresoever incurred in complying with any of the said regulations, orders or directions or in destruction of the livestock shall be borne by the owner of the livestock.

3. (*a*) The vessel is at liberty to proceed by any route, to proceed to, return to and stay at any port or ports whatsoever (including the loading port) in any order in or out of the route or in a contrary direction to or beyond the port of discharge once or oftener for taking on board bunkers or supplies or loading or discharging cargo or embarking or disembarking passengers whether in connection with the present or prior or subsequent voyage, or for any other purpose whatsoever, and after arrival at the port of discharge herein provided to leave such port and with the like liberties as aforesaid to return to and discharge the said cargo at such port. The exercise of any liberty in this clause shall form part of the agreed voyage.

(*b*) The vessel may sail with or without pilots and may adjust compasses and make trial trips with or without cargo on board and may tow and be towed and tow and assist vessels or aircraft in all situations, and may put into and remain at or delay sailing from any port or ports for repairing or dry-docking with or without cargo on board or for any other purpose whatsoever should circumstances in the opinion of the Carrier, Master or Agents render this desirable all as part of the agreed voyage.

(*c*) The Carrier may carry the goods to or from the vessel in any ship, craft or land conveyance, and the Carrier shall not be liable for any loss of or damage or delay to the goods while in such ship, craft or land conveyance, even though caused by negligence of the Carrier, his agents or servants or by the unseaworthiness or unfitness of any such ship, craft or land conveyance or otherwise howsoever.

(*d*) The goods or part thereof may be carried by the named or other vessels, whether belonging to the Line or others, and should circumstances in the opinion of the Carrier, Master or Agent render transhipment desirable or expedient may be transhipped at any port or ports, place or places whatsoever, and while in course of transhipment may be placed or stored in craft or ashore and may be re-shipped or forwarded or returned by land and/or water and/or air at Carrier's option and expense, all as part of the contract voyage and all the provisions of this Bill of Lading shall continue to apply.

(*e*) If the voyage to or entering of the port of discharge or if the ship or cargo operations thereat or if the departure therefrom shall be or shall at any time appear likely to be prohibited or prevented or delayed by any of the following matters or events (whether existing or anticipated) : ice ; weather ; blockade ; interdict ; quarantine ; strikes, lock-outs or labour troubles (whether the Carrier or his servants or agents are or are likely to be parties thereto or not) ; civil commotions ; riot ; or any other disturbances ; epidemic ; fever or other illness ; congestion ; obstruction ; or any other cause whatsoever beyond the Carrier's control ; or shall be considered by the Carrier, Master or Agents (whose decision shall be absolute and binding on all parties) to be unsafe or likely to prejudice the interests of the vessel (including her future engagements) or her cargo whether by delay or otherwise howsoever ; then the goods may at the Carrier's option be landed or put into lighters there or at such other port or place as the Carrier, Master or Agents shall in his or their absolute discretion select and there discharged, or they may be carried back in the same vessel to the country of shipment and either discharged there or returned (subject to the foregoing options if any of the foregoing events shall recur) to the port of discharge and there discharged all as part of the agreed voyage, and until the goods are discharged as aforesaid all the provisions of this Bill of Lading shall continue to apply. In the case of a strike or lock-out (whether the Carrier, his agents or servants are parties thereto or not) at an intermediate port on either the original voyage or return voyage from the country of shipment preventing the sailing of the vessel when ready to proceed to the port of discharge, the Carrier may discharge the goods at the intermediate port. The Carrier is hereby expressly permitted to discharge at any such port whether intermediate or otherwise as aforesaid notwithstanding that such discharge would delay, defeat or frustrate in whole or in part the object for which the goods were shipped. In any case where discharge is effected under provision of this clause the Carrier's responsibility shall cease on such discharge the goods being thereafter at the risk of the Owner of the goods, and such discharge shall, notwithstanding anything contained in this Bill of Lading, constitute due delivery of the goods under this Bill of Lading, and the Holder of the Bill of Lading the Owner of the goods and the Consignee shall be jointly and severally liable for all charges and expenses incurred in consequence of such discharge, the Carrier, Master and Agents acting solely as agents of the Consignee and/or Owner of the goods after completion of discharge. The Carrier will so far as practicable give immediate notice of such discharge to the Consignee of the goods, if known, but shall incur no liability for failure so to do.

(*f*) The vessel may carry cargo of all kinds, dangerous or otherwise. The Carrier may stow the goods in poop, forecastle, deckhouse, shelter deck, passenger space, bunker space or any other covered in space, and unless stated as being carried on deck such goods shall be deemed for all purposes (including general average) to be stowed under deck. The goods may also be stowed by the Carrier or his agents or servants in containers ; and containers whether stowed as aforesaid or received fully stowed from the Shippers may be carried on or under deck without notice to the Shipper, and, if they are so carried, the Hague Rules as incorporated herein shall be applicable notwithstanding carriage on or under deck, and the goods and/or containers shall contribute to general average, whether carried on or under deck.

(*g*) In the event of the imminence or existence of any of the following :—War between any nations, hostilities, war-like operations, rebellion or civil war ; prohibition, restriction or control by any Government of intercourse, commercial or otherwise, with any country from at or to which the vessel normally proceeds or calls ; control or direction by any Government or other Authority of the use or movements of the vessel or the insulated or other space in the vessel ; the Carrier and /or his Agents and /or the Master, if he or they consider there to be any risk that the vessel or her Master, Officers, Crew, Passengers or any of them or cargo or any part thereof could be subject to loss, damage, injury, detention or delay in consequence of the said war, hostilities, war-like operations, rebellion, civil war, prohibition, restriction, control or direction, may at any time before or after the commencement of the voyage, alter or vary or depart from the proposed or advertised or agreed or customary route or voyage (including the right to omit ports or places not directly affected by any of the matters aforesaid) and /or delay or detain the vessel and /or discharge the cargo (for delivery or storage or transhipment) at or off any port or ports, place or places without being liable for any loss or damage whatsoever directly or indirectly sustained by the Owner of the goods. If and when the goods are so discharged at such port or ports, place or places they shall be landed or put into craft or vessels at the expense and risk of the Owner of the goods and the Carrier's responsibility shall cease on discharge, the Carrier, Master or Agents giving notice of such discharge to the Consignee of the goods so far as he is known. The vessel, in addition to any liberties expressed or implied herein, shall have liberty to comply with any orders or directions as to departure, arrival, route, voyage, ports of call, delay, detention, discharge (for delivery or storage or transhipment) or otherwise howsoever, given by any Government or any Department thereof, or any person acting or purporting to act with the authority of any Government or of any Department thereof, or by any Committee or person having under the terms of the War Risks Insurance on the vessel the right to give such orders or directions, and if by reason of or in compliance with any such orders or directions or by reason of the exercise by the Carrier of any other liberty mentioned in this Clause anything is done or is not done the same shall be within this contract. Discharge under any liberty mentioned in this clause shall, notwithstanding anything contained in this Bill of Lading constitute due delivery of the goods under this Bill of Lading and the Owner and /or Consignee of the goods shall bear and pay all charges and expenses resulting from such discharge, and the full freight stipulated herein, if not prepaid, shall on such discharge become immediately due and payable by the Owner and/or Consignee of the goods, and if freight has been prepaid the Carrier shall be entitled to retain the same. The vessel is free to carry contraband, explosives, munitions or war-like stores, and may sail armed or unarmed.

4. If this Bill of Lading provides for the goods to be transhipped at a port or place in New Zealand or Fiji and to be forwarded thence, the Carrier shall be under no obligation himself to deliver the goods at the port or place of delivery, but on arrival of the vessel at the named port of transhipment or at such other port or place which the Carrier may elect as the port or place of transhipment the Carrier shall at his own expense (unless otherwise herein provided for) discharge and tranship or land or store the goods (either ashore or afloat) at such port or place and with all reasonable despatch forward them by sea or inland waterways or by land or by air by any route to the port or place of delivery. The Carrier has the right to forward in lots or parts. On discharge from the vessel at such port or place of transhipment the Carrier's responsibility shall cease, and neither he nor the vessel shall be liable in any circumstances for any loss or detention of or damage to the goods howsoever caused occurring after such discharge. In respect of the on-carriage of goods from such port or place of transhipment to the port or place of delivery, and of the storage, transport and transhipment of the goods while not on board the vessel, the Carrier acts as forwarding agent only, making a contract for such storage, transport, transhipment and on-carriage on the terms and subject to the provisions of the contract in use by the person or on-carrier with whom such contract is made and not making any declaration of value unless expressly instructed by the Shipper, and paying the expenses of such operations but incurring no responsibility as carrier or custodian of the goods or otherwise for any loss, damage or detention howsoever caused ; in respect of such on-carriage, the goods shall be subject to all the liberties (including the liberty to carry the goods on deck), conditions and exceptions of the on-carrier conveying them beyond the port or place of transhipment, and the Shipper will have the benefit of any obligations of any such on-carrier (by sea and/or inland waterways and/or land and/or air) or of any warehouseman, lighterman or others under their respective contracts with the on-Carrier. If for any cause whatsoever the goods shall be delayed at the port or place of transhipment beyond the period which would elapse before transhipment in normal circumstances, the storage and other charges upon the goods after the expiration of the normal period shall be borne by the Consignee or Owner of the goods.

5. The freight payable as herein has been calculated and based upon the description and particulars of the goods declared by the Shipper to the Carrier. The Carrier shall be entitled to re-weigh or re-measure any goods, and freight shall be paid on the excess weight or measurement (if any) so ascertained. The expense incident to re-weighing or re-measuring shall be borne by the Carrier if the weights or measurements as furnished by the Shipper are found to be correct, but otherwise such expenses shall be borne and paid by the Owner or Consignee of the goods. If the description or (in cases where the value has been stated) the value of the goods has been mis-stated by the Shipper, double the amount of such freight shall be paid as liquidated damages by the Shipper, Consignee and/or Owner of the goods as would have been charged if the goods had been accurately described and valued, and a certificate signed by the Carrier or his Agents shall be conclusive evidence of the amount that would have been so charged.

6. The Carrier or any person to whom the Carrier has sub-contracted the Carriage or any person authorised by the Carrier shall be entitled, but under no obligation, to open any Container or package at any time and to inspect the Goods.

7. The Shipper, Consignee and/or Owner of the goods shall bear and pay the cost of labour and material for mending, bailing, bagging, packing, cooperage and repairs to and renewals of packages, boxes, crates, wrappers, bales, bags or barrels resulting from insufficiency of packing or from excepted perils.

8. The Carrier shall have a lien over the goods, and the right to sell the same by public auction or otherwise for all freight, primage, charges (including additional freight or double freight and/or expenses under Clause 5 payable on corrected weight or measurement), demurrage, damages for detention, and for all payments made and liabilities incurred in respect of charges, expenditure, damages (including damage to the vessel or other cargo), costs and expenses (including the costs and expenses of exercising such lien and of such sale), and for the interest (if any) payable which under this Bill of Lading are to be borne and paid by the Shipper, Consignee or Endorsee of the Bill of Lading, or Receiver of the goods. If on a sale of the goods the proceeds fail to cover the amount for which the Carrier has a lien on the goods and the costs and expenses of exercising such lien and of the sale, the Carrier shall be entitled to recover the difference from the Shipper, Consignee and/or the Owner of the goods.

9. (*a*) Delivery of the goods shall be taken immediately the vessel is ready to discharge, berthed or not berthed, and continuously as fast as vessel can deliver, and the Carrier shall be at liberty to discharge continuously day and night, Sundays and holidays included, on to quay or into craft, all extra expense to be for account of the Consignee, the Owner of the goods and the Holder of the Bill of Lading jointly and severally. The Carrier shall be under no liability to notify the Consignee or any other party of the arrival of the goods, notwithstanding any custom of the port to the contrary or any written request in this Bill of Lading or otherwise. If the Consignee, the Owner of the goods or the Holder of the Bill of Lading requires delivery before or after usual hours he shall pay on demand any extra expense incurred.

(*b*) If delivery is not taken as aforesaid the Shipper, the Consignee, the Owner of the goods and the Holder of the Bill of Lading shall be jointly and severally liable to pay the Carrier, by way of liquidated damages, a sum calculated at the rate of 40 U.S. cents per gross register ton of the vessel's tonnage for each day or part of a day during which there is delay in taking delivery and such damages shall be due daily and payable on demand. Also the Carrier may at his option and at the expense of the goods discharge all or any part of the goods and/or sort and/or stack and/or store them in shed, store or craft or land conveyance, subject to the Carrier's liens and to the provisions of Clause 2 hereof, and without prejudice to the Carrier's right to the said damages for any periods prior to such discharge. The Carrier in addition to his other rights under this paragraph, may shift, re-stow, land and re-ship any goods which in the opinion of the Carrier are delaying the prompt discharge of other goods and the expense of so doing and of labour standing by on ship and/or quay and any other expenses incurred by the Carrier during the period of delay in the reception of any goods shall be due and payable on demand by the Consignee, the Owner of the goods and the Holder of the Bill of Lading jointly and severally and the Carrier's decision regarding the amount of such expenses shall be conclusive.

(*c*) The current landing, overside and/or reception charges, including lighterage if any and also the current charges for sorting and stacking cargo on wharf or in shed, shall be for account of the goods notwithstanding any custom of the port to the contrary. The Shipper, the Consignee, the Owners of the goods and the Holder of the Bill of Lading shall jointly and severally indemnify the Carrier against all loss, liability or expense caused owing to Customs, Consular or other regulations not being complied with, or to Customs permit and/or other necessary papers not being lodged within twenty four hours after vessel's entry at the Customs or when required, or to importation of the goods being prohibited, and the Carrier shall be at liberty to return the goods to the port of shipment, or to discharge them at any other port and such discharge shall constitute due delivery under this Bill of Lading, and in either case at the expense of the Shipper, the Consignee, the Owner of the goods and the Holder of the Bill of Lading, who shall be liable jointly and severally for all charges, freights and forwarding expenses thereon, and the Carrier shall have a lien on the goods for all such loss, liability, expense, charges, freights and forwarding expenses.

10. The Carrier and his Agents shall have the right of nominating the berth or berths for loading and discharging at all ports and places whatsoever, any custom to the contrary notwithstanding.

11. The Carrier will not be accountable for goods of any description in respect of any one package or unit for an amount beyond the sum stipulated in the provisions of the said legislation or Rules (as the case may be) referred to in Clause 1 hereof, unless the value thereof shall have been stated in writing both on the Broker's Order, which must be obtained before shipment, and on the Shipping Note presented on shipment, and extra freight agreed upon and paid, and Bills of Lading signed with a declaration of the nature and value of the goods appearing thereon. When the value is declared and extra freight agreed as aforesaid, the carrier's liability shall not exceed such value, or *pro rata* on that basis in the event of partial loss or damage.

12. In the event of the Carrier being liable for damage to or loss of any goods carried by the vessel, all claims in respect of such loss or damage shall be deemed to be waived unless notice of claim is made in writing to the Carrier or his Agents at the final port of discharge of the goods in respect of which the claim is made within seven days after such goods were or should have been discharged from the vessel.

13. In the event of accident, danger, damage, or disaster, before or after the commencement of the voyage, resulting from any cause whatsoever, whether due to negligence or not, for which, or for the consequence of which, the Carrier is not responsible, by Statute, contract, or otherwise, the goods, Shipper, Consignee, or Owner of the goods shall contribute with the Carrier in general average to the payment of any sacrifices, losses, or expenses of a general average nature that may be made or incurred, and shall pay salvage and special charges incurred in respect of the goods.

If a salving ship is owned or operated by the Carrier, salvage shall be paid for as fully as if the said salving ship or ships belonged to strangers. Such deposit as the Carrier or his agents may deem sufficient to cover the estimated contribution of the goods and any salvage and special charges thereon shall, if required, be made by the goods, Shippers, Consignees or Owners of the goods to the carrier before delivery. General average shall be adjusted according to York-Antwerp Rules, 1974. Adjustments shall be prepared at such port as shall be selected by the Carrier.

14. If the vessel comes into collision with another ship as a result of the negligence of the other ship and any act, neglect or default of the master, mariner, pilot or the servants of the Carrier in the navigation or in the management of the vessel, the Owner of the goods carried hereunder will indemnify the Carrier against all loss or liability to the other or non-carrying ship or her Owners in so far as such loss or liability represent loss of, or damage to or any claim whatsoever of the Owner of the said goods, paid or payable by the other or non-carrying ship or her Owners to the Owner of the said goods and set off, recouped or recovered by the other or non-carrying ship or her Owners as part of their claim against the carrying vessel or Carrier. The foregoing provisions shall also apply where the Owners, Operators or those in charge of any ship or ships or objects other than, or in addition to, the colliding ships or objects are at fault in respect to a collision or contact.

15. If the vessel is not owned by or chartered by demise to the Company or Line by whom this Bill of Lading is issued (as may be the case notwithstanding anything that appears to the contrary) this Bill of Lading shall take effect only as a contract with the Owner or Demise Charterer as the case may be as Principal made through the agency of the said Company or Line who act as Agents only and shall be under no personal liability whatsoever in respect thereof.

16. The contract evidenced by this Bill of Lading shall be governed by the law of England.

online resource centre
www.oxfordtextbooks.co.uk/orc/beale5e

Visit the **online resource centre** to view a full-size version of this document if you would like to read it in more detail.

damage to the goods (cl 11) and, on the other, controlling the 'exceptions' from liability that the carrier is allowed to insert into the bill. Examples of exceptions will be found in cl 2: these particular clauses relate to deck cargo and livestock, to which the rules do not apply. An account of the background to the Hague Rules will be found on p 1058.

9. The bill also purports to limit the liability of contractors ('stevedores' and others) employed by the carrier in discharging his contractual obligations: see cl 1 on the back. These independent contractors are not parties to the contract between shipper and carrier, and the attempt to protect them has given rise to great legal difficulty: see the cases on pp 1153 ff.

10. The carrier is at common law obliged to proceed directly to the port of destination by the normal route. Clause 3(a) permits the ship to deviate from this route: for the interpretation of this clause, see p 981.

11. The carrier is also obliged to deliver the goods at the port of destination. The first clause on the face and cl 3(e) permit discharge elsewhere in certain circumstances (see p 983).

12. The bill contemplates the freight (the price of the carriage) being paid either in advance by the shipper or by the consignee at the destination (see second clause on face). In the latter event, cl 8 gives the carrier a lien over the goods (ie the right to retain them until the freight is paid) and a power to sell them.

13. Occasionally, goods will be carried for a shipper in a ship that is under charter to another person. Usually, the shipper's contract will still be with the owner of the ship, unless the charterer has taken over complete control of the ship and its crew under what is called a 'demise' charter. Clause 15 expressly states that this is how the bill of lading contract is to take effect.

■ *BALTIME 1939 time charter*

1. Shipbroker	BIMCO UNIFORM TIME-CHARTER (AS REVISED 2001) CODE NAME: "BALTIME 1939" PART I
3. Owners/Place of business	2. Place and Date of Charter
	4. Charterers/Place of business
5. Vessel's Name	6. GT/NT
7. Class	8. Indicated brake horse power (bhp)
9. Total tons d.w. (abt.) on summer freeboard	10. Cubic feet grain/bale capacity
11. Permanent bunkers (abt.)	12. Speed capability in knots (abt.) on a consumption in tons (abt.) of
13. Present position	14. Period of hire (Cl. 1)
15. Port of delivery (Cl. 1)	16. Time of delivery (Cl. 1)
17. (a) Trade limits (Cl. 2)	
(b) Cargo exclusions specially agreed	
18. Bunkers on re-delivery (state min. and max. quantity)(Cl. 5)	19. Charter hire (Cl. 6)
20. Hire payment (state currency, method and place of payment; also beneficiary and bank account) (Cl. 6)	
21. Place or range of re-delivery (Cl. 7)	22. Cancelling date (Cl. 21)
23. Dispute resolution (state 22(A), 22(B) or 22(C); if 22(C) agreed Place of Arbitration must be stated) (Cl. 22)	24. Brokerage commission and to whom payable (Cl. 24)
25. Numbers of additional clauses covering special provisions, if agreed	

Left margin (vertical text): Issued 1909; Amended 1911; 1912; 1920; 1920; 1939; 1950; 1974; and 2001

It is mutually agreed that this Contract shall be performed subject to the conditions contained in this Charter which shall include PART I as well as PART II. In the event of a conflict of conditions, the provisions of PART I shall prevail over those of PART II to the extent of such conflict.

Signature (Owners)	Signature (Charterers)

@ online resource centre
www.oxfordtextbooks.co.uk/orc/beale5e

Visit the **online resource centre** to view a full-size version of this document if you would like to read it in more detail.

PART II
"BALTIME 1939" Uniform Time-Charter (as revised 2001)

It is agreed between the party mentioned in Box 3 as Owners 1
of the Vessel named in Box 5 of the gross/net tonnage 2
indicated in Box 6, classed as stated in Box 7 and of indicated 3
brake horse power (bhp) as stated in Box 8, carrying about 4
the number of tons deadweight indicated in Box 9 on 5
summer freeboard inclusive of bunkers, stores and 6
provisions, having as per builder's plan a cubic-feet grain/ 7
bale capacity as stated in Box 10, exclusive of permanent 8
bunkers, which contain about the number of tons stated in 9
Box 11, and fully loaded capable of steaming about the 10
number of knots indicated in Box 12 in good weather and 11
smooth water on a consumption of about the number of 12
tons fuel oil stated in Box 12, now in position as stated in 13
Box 13 and the party mentioned as Charterers in Box 4, as 14
follows: 15

1. Period/Port of Delivery/Time of Delivery 16
The Owners let, and the Charterers hire the Vessel for a 17
period of the number of calendar months indicated in 18
Box 14 from the time (not a Sunday or a legal Holiday 19
unless taken over) the Vessel is delivered and placed at 20
the disposal of the Charterers between 9 a.m. and 6 21
p.m., or between 9 a.m. and 2 p.m. if on Saturday, at the 22
port stated in Box 15 in such available berth where she 23
can safely lie always afloat, as the Charterers may direct, 24
the Vessel being in every way fitted for ordinary cargo 25
service. The Vessel shall be delivered at the time 26
indicated in Box 16. 27

2. Trade 28
The Vessel shall be employed in lawful trades for the 29
carriage of lawful merchandise only between safe ports 30
or places where the Vessel can safely lie always afloat 31
within the limits stated in Box 17. No live stock nor 32
injurious, inflammable or dangerous goods (such as 33
acids, explosives, calcium carbide, ferro silicon, 34
naphtha, motor spirit, tar, or any of their products) shall 35
be shipped. 36

3. Owners' Obligations 37
The Owners shall provide and pay for all provisions and 38
wages, for insurance of the Vessel, for all deck and 39
engine-room stores and maintain her in a thoroughly 40
efficient state in hull and machinery during service. The 41
Owners shall provide winchmen from the crew to 42
operate the Vessel's cargo handling gear, unless the 43
crew's employment conditions or local union or port 44
regulations prohibit this, in which case qualified shore- 45
winchmen shall be provided and paid for by the 46
Charterers. 47

4. Charterers' Obligations 48
The Charterers shall provide and pay for all fuel oil, port 49
charges, pilotages (whether compulsory or not), canal 50
steersmen, boatage, lights, tug-assistance, consular 51
charges (except those pertaining to the Master, officers 52
and crew), canal, dock and other dues and charges, 53
including any foreign general municipality or state taxes, 54
also all dock, harbour and tonnage dues at the ports of 55
delivery and re-delivery (unless incurred through cargo 56
carried before delivery or after re-delivery), agencies, 57
commissions, also shall arrange and pay for loading, 58
trimming, stowing (including dunnage and shifting 59
boards, excepting any already on board), unloading, 60
weighing, tallying and delivery of cargoes, surveys on 61
hatches, meals supplied to officials and men in their 62
service and all other charges and expenses whatsoever 63
including detention and expenses through quarantine 64
(including cost of fumigation and disinfection). All ropes, 65
slings and special runners actually used for loading 66

and discharging and any special gear, including special 67
ropes and chains required by the custom of the port for 68
mooring shall be for the Charterers' account. The Vessel 69
shall be fitted with winches, derricks, wheels and or- 70
dinary runners capable of handling lifts up to 2 tons. 71

5. Bunkers 72
The Charterers at port of delivery and the Owners at port 73
of re-delivery shall take over and pay for all fuel oil 74
remaining in the Vessel's bunkers at current price at the 75
respective ports. The Vessel shall be re-delivered with 76
not less than the number of tons and not exceeding the 77
number of tons of fuel oil in the Vessel's bunkers stated 78
in Box 18. 79

6. Hire 80
The Charterers shall pay as hire the rate stated in Box 81
19 per 30 days, commencing in accordance with Clause 82
1 until her re-delivery to the Owners. 83
Payment of hire shall be made in cash, in the currency 84
stated in Box 20, without discount, every 30 days, in 85
advance, and in the manner prescribed in Box 20. In 86
default of payment the Owners shall have the right of 87
withdrawing the Vessel from the service of the Charterers, 88
without noting any protest and without interference by 89
any court or any other formality whatsoever and without 90
prejudice to any claim the Owners may otherwise have 91
on the Charterers under the Charter. 92

7. Re-delivery 93
The Vessel shall be re-delivered on the expiration of the 94
Charter in the same good order as when delivered to 95
the Charterers (fair wear and tear excepted) at an ice- 96
free port in the Charterers' option at the place or within 97
the range stated in Box 21, between 9 a.m. and 6 p.m., 98
and 9 a.m. and 2 p.m. on Saturday, but the day of re- 99
delivery shall not be a Sunday or legal Holiday. 100
The Charterers shall give the Owners not less than ten 101
days' notice at which port and on about which day the 102
Vessel will be re-delivered. Should the Vessel be ordered 103
on a voyage by which the Charter period will be exceeded 104
the Charterers shall have the use of the Vessel to enable 105
them to complete the voyage, provided it could be 106
reasonably calculated that the voyage would allow 107
redelivery about the time fixed for the termination of the 108
Charter, but for any time exceeding the termination date 109
the Charterers shall pay the market rate if higher than 110
the rate stipulated herein. 111

8. Cargo Space 112
The whole reach and burthen of the Vessel, including 113
lawful deck-capacity shall be at the Charterers' disposal, 114
reserving proper and sufficient space for the Vessel's 115
Master, officers, crew, tackle, apparel, furniture, 116
provisions and stores. 117

9. Master 118
The Master shall prosecute all voyages with the utmost 119
despatch and shall render customary assistance with 120
the Vessel's crew. The Master shall be under the orders 121
of the Charterers as regards employment, agency, or 122
other arrangements. The Charterers shall indemnify the 123
Owners against all consequences or liabilities arising 124
from the Master, officers or Agents signing Bills of Lading 125
or other documents or otherwise complying with such 126
orders, as well as from any irregularity in the Vessel's 127
papers or for overcarrying goods. The Owners shall not 128
be responsible for shortage, mixture, marks, nor for 129
number of pieces or packages, nor for damage to or 130
claims on cargo caused by bad stowage or otherwise. If 131

online resource centre
www.oxfordtextbooks.co.uk/orc/beale5e

Visit the **online resource centre** to view a full-size version of this document if you
would like to read it in more detail.

PART II
"BALTIME 1939" Uniform Time-Charter (as revised 2001)

the Charterers have reason to be dissatisfied with the 132
conduct of the Master or any officer, the Owners, on 133
receiving particulars of the complaint, promptly to 134
investigate the matter, and, if necessary and practicable, 135
to make a change in the appointments. 136

10. Directions and Logs 137
The Charterers shall furnish the Master with all 138
instructions and sailing directions and the Master shall 139
keep full and correct logs accessible to the Charterers 140
or their Agents. 141

11. Suspension of Hire etc. 142
(A) In the event of drydocking or other necessary 143
measures to maintain the efficiency of the Vessel, 144
deficiency of men or Owners' stores, breakdown of 145
machinery, damage to hull or other accident, either 146
hindering or preventing the working of the Vessel and 147
continuing for more than twenty-four consecutive hours, 148
no hire shall be paid in respect of any time lost thereby 149
during the period in which the Vessel is unable to perform 150
the service immediately required. Any hire paid in 151
advance shall be adjusted accordingly. 152
(B) In the event of the Vessel being driven into port or to 153
anchorage through stress of weather, trading to shallow 154
harbours or to rivers or ports with bars or suffering an 155
accident to her cargo, any detention of the Vessel and/or 156
expenses resulting from such detention shall be for the 157
Charterers' account even if such detention and/or 158
expenses, or the cause by reason of which either is 159
incurred, be due to, or be contributed to by, the 160
negligence of the Owners' servants. 161

12. Responsibility and Exemption 162
The Owners only shall be responsible for delay in 163
delivery of the Vessel or for delay during the currency of 164
the Charter and for loss or damage to goods onboard, if 165
such delay or loss has been caused by want of due 166
diligence on the part of the Owners or their Manager in 167
making the Vessel seaworthy and fitted for the voyage 168
or any other personal act or omission or default of the 169
Owners or their Manager. The Owners shall not be 170
responsible in any other case nor for damage or delay 171
whatsoever and howsoever caused even if caused by 172
the neglect or default of their servants. The Owners shall 173
not be liable for loss or damage arising or resulting 174
from strikes, lock-outs or stoppage or restraint of labour 175
(including the Master, officers or crew) whether partial 176
or general. The Charterers shall be responsible for loss 177
or damage caused to the Vessel or to the Owners by 178
goods being loaded contrary to the terms of the Charter 179
or by improper or careless bunkering or loading, stowing 180
or discharging of goods or any other improper or 181
negligent act on their part or that of their servants. 182

13. Advances 183
The Charterers or their Agents shall advance to the 184
Master, if required, necessary funds for ordinary 185
disbursements for the Vessel's account at any port 186
charging only interest at 6 per cent. p.a., such advances 187
shall be deducted from hire. 188

14. Excluded Ports 189
The Vessel shall not be ordered to nor bound to enter: 190
(A) any place where fever or epidemics are prevalent or 191
to which the Master, officers and crew by law are not 192
bound to follow the Vessel; 193
(B) any ice-bound place or any place where lights, 194
lightships, marks and buoys are or are likely to be 195
withdrawn by reason of ice on the Vessel's arrival or 196
where there is risk that ordinarily the Vessel will not be 197

able on account of ice to reach the place or to get out 198
after having completed loading or discharging. The 199
Vessel shall not be obliged to force ice. If on account of 200
ice the Master considers it dangerous to remain at the 201
loading or discharging place for fear of the Vessel being 202
frozen in and/or damaged, he has liberty to sail to a 203
convenient open place and await the Charterers' fresh 204
instructions. Unforeseen detention through any of above 205
causes shall be for the Charterers' account. 206

15. Loss of Vessel 207
Should the Vessel be lost or missing, hire shall cease 208
from the date when she was lost. If the date of loss 209
cannot be ascertained half hire shall be paid from the 210
date the Vessel was last reported until the calculated 211
date of arrival at the destination. Any hire paid in advance 212
shall be adjusted accordingly. 213

16. Overtime 214
The Vessel shall work day and night if required. The 215
Charterers shall refund the Owners their outlays for all 216
overtime paid to officers and crew according to the hours 217
and rates stated in the Vessel's articles. 218

17. Lien 219
The Owners shall have a lien upon all cargoes and 220
sub-freights belonging to the Time-Charterers and any 221
Bill of Lading freight for all claims under this Charter, 222
and the Charterers shall have a lien on the Vessel for all 223
moneys paid in advance and not earned. 224

18. Salvage 225
All salvage and assistance to other vessels shall be for 226
the Owners' and the Charterers' equal benefit after 227
deducting the Master's, officers' and crew's proportion 228
and all legal and other expenses including hire paid 229
under the charter for time lost in the salvage, also repairs 230
of damage and fuel oil consumed. The Charterers shall 231
be bound by all measures taken by the Owners in order 232
to secure payment of salvage and to fix its amount. 233

19. Sublet 234
The Charterers shall have the option of subletting the 235
Vessel, giving due notice to the Owners, but the original 236
Charterers shall always remain responsible to the 237
Owners for due performance of the Charter. 238

20. War ("Conwartime 1993") 239
(A) For the purpose of this Clause, the words: 240
(i) "Owners" shall include the shipowners, bareboat 241
charterers, disponent owners, managers or other 242
operators who are charged with the management of the 243
Vessel, and the Master; and 244
(ii) "War Risks" shall include any war (whether actual or 245
threatened), act of war, civil war, hostilities, revolution, 246
rebellion, civil commotion, warlike operations, the laying 247
of mines (whether actual or reported), acts of piracy, 248
acts of terrorists, acts of hostility or malicious damage, 249
blockades (whether imposed against all vessels or 250
imposed selectively against vessels of certain flags or 251
ownership, or against certain cargoes or crews or 252
otherwise howsoever), by any person, body, terrorist or 253
political group, or the Government of any state 254
whatsoever, which, in the reasonable judgement of the 255
Master and/or the Owners, may be dangerous or are 256
likely to be or to become dangerous to the Vessel, her 257
cargo, crew or other persons on board the Vessel. 258
(B) The Vessel, unless the written consent of the Owners 259
be first obtained, shall not be ordered to or required to 260
continue to or through, any port, place, area or zone 261
(whether of land or sea), or any waterway or canal, where 262

online resource centre
www.oxfordtextbooks.co.uk/orc/beale5e

Visit the **online resource centre** to view a full-size version of this document if you
would like to read it in more detail.

PART II
"BALTIME 1939" Uniform Time-Charter (as revised 2001)

it appears that the Vessel, her cargo, crew or other 263
persons on board the Vessel, in the reasonable 264
judgement of the Master and/or the Owners, may be, or 265
are likely to be, exposed to War Risks. Should the Vessel 266
be within any such place as aforesaid, which only 267
becomes dangerous, or is likely to be or to become 268
dangerous, after her entry into it, she shall be at liberty 269
to leave it. 270
(C) The Vessel shall not be required to load contraband 271
cargo, or to pass through any blockade, whether such 272
blockade be imposed on all vessels, or is imposed 273
selectively in any way whatsoever against vessels of 274
certain flags or ownership, or against certain cargoes 275
or crews or otherwise howsoever, or to proceed to an 276
area where she shall be subject, or is likely to be subject 277
to a belligerent's right of search and/or confiscation. 278
(D) (i) The Owners may effect war risks insurance in 279
respect of the Hull and Machinery of the Vessel and their 280
other interests (including, but not limited to, loss of 281
earnings and detention, the crew and their Protection 282
and Indemnity Risks), and the premiums and/or calls 283
therefor shall be for their account. 284
(ii) If the Underwriters of such insurance should require 285
payment of premiums and/or calls because, pursuant 286
to the Charterers' orders, the Vessel is within, or is due 287
to enter and remain within, any area or areas which are 288
specified by such Underwriters as being subject to 289
additional premiums because of War Risks, then such 290
premiums and/or calls shall be reimbursed by the 291
Charterers to the Owners at the same time as the next 292
payment of hire is due. 293
(E) If the Owners become liable under the terms of 294
employment to pay to the crew any bonus or additional 295
wages in respect of sailing into an area which is 296
dangerous in the manner defined by the said terms, 297
then such bonus or additional wages shall be re- 298
imbursed to the Owners by the Charterers at the same 299
time as the next payment of hire is due. 300
(F) The Vessel shall have liberty:- 301
(i) to comply with all orders, directions, recom- 302
mendations or advice as to departure, arrival, routes, 303
sailing in convoy, ports of call, stoppages, destinations, 304
discharge of cargo, delivery, or in any other way 305
whatsoever, which are given by the Government of the 306
Nation under whose flag the Vessel sails, or other 307
Government to whose laws the Owners are subject, or 308
any other Government, body or group whatsoever acting 309
with the power to compel compliance with their orders 310
or directions; 311
(ii) to comply with the order, directions or recom- 312
mendations of any war risks underwriters who have the 313
authority to give the same under the terms of the war 314
risks insurance; 315
(iii) to comply with the terms of any resolution of the 316
Security Council of the United Nations, any directives of 317
the European Community, the effective orders of any 318
other Supranational body which has the right to issue 319
and give the same, and with national laws aimed at 320
enforcing the same to which the Owners are subject, 321
and to obey the orders and directions of those who are 322
charged with their enforcement; 323
(iv) to divert and discharge at any other port any cargo or 324
part thereof which may render the Vessel liable to 325
confiscation as a contraband carrier; 326
(v) to divert and call at any other port to change the crew 327
or any part thereof or other persons on board the Vessel 328
when there is reason to believe that they may be subject 329
to internment, imprisonment or other sanctions. 330
(G) If in accordance with their rights under the foregoing 331
provisions of this Clause, the Owners shall refuse to 332
proceed to the loading or discharging ports, or any one 333

or more of them, they shall immediately inform the 334
Charterers. No cargo shall be discharged at any 335
alternative port without first giving the Charterers notice 336
of the Owners' intention to do so and requesting them 337
to nominate a safe port for such discharge. Failing such 338
nomination by the Charterers within 48 hours of the 339
receipt of such notice and request, the Owners may 340
discharge the cargo at any safe port of their own choice. 341
(H) If in compliance with any of the provisions of sub- 342
clauses (B) to (G) of this Clause anything is done or not 343
done, such shall not be deemed a deviation, but shall 344
be considered as due fulfilment of this Charter. 345

21. Cancelling 346
Should the Vessel not be delivered by the date indicated 347
in Box 22, the Charterers shall have the option of 348
cancelling. If the Vessel cannot be delivered by the 349
cancelling date, the Charterers, if required, shall declare 350
within 48 hours after receiving notice thereof whether 351
they cancel or will take delivery of the Vessel. 352

22. Dispute Resolution 353
*) **(A)** This Charter shall be governed by and construed in 354
accordance with English law and any dispute arising 355
out of or in connection with this Charter shall be referred 356
to arbitration in London in accordance with the Arbitration 357
Act 1996 or any statutory modification or re-enactment 358
thereof save to the extent necessary to give effect to the 359
provisions of this Clause. 360
The arbitration shall be conducted in accordance with 361
the London Maritime Arbitrators Association (LMAA) 362
Terms current at the time when the arbitration 363
proceedings are commenced. 364
The reference shall be to three arbitrators. A party 365
wishing to refer a dispute to arbitration shall appoint its 366
arbitrator and send notice of such appointment in writing 367
to the other party requiring the other party to appoint its 368
own arbitrator within 14 calendar days of that notice and 369
stating that it will appoint its arbitrator as sole arbitrator 370
unless the other party appoints its own arbitrator and 371
gives notice that it has done so within the 14 days 372
specified. If the other party does not appoint its own 373
arbitrator and give notice that it has done so within the 374
14 days specified, the party referring a dispute to 375
arbitration may, without the requirement of any further 376
prior notice to the other party, appoint its arbitrator as 377
sole arbitrator and shall advise the other party 378
accordingly. The award of a sole arbitrator shall be 379
binding on both parties as if he had been appointed by 380
agreement. 381
Nothing herein shall prevent the parties agreeing in 382
writing to vary these provisions to provide for the 383
appointment of a sole arbitrator. 384
In cases where neither the claim nor any counterclaim 385
exceeds the sum of US$50,000 (or such other sum as 386
the parties may agree) the arbitration shall be conducted 387
in accordance with the LMAA Small Claims Procedure 388
current at the time when the arbitration proceedings are 389
commenced. 390
*) **(B)** This Charter shall be governed by and construed in 391
accordance with Title 9 of the United States Code and 392
the Maritime Law of the United States and any dispute 393
arising out of or in connection with this Contract shall 394
be referred to three persons at New York, one to be 395
appointed by each of the parties hereto, and the third by 396
the two so chosen; their decision or that of any two of 397
them shall be final, and for the purposes of enforcing 398
any award, judgement may be entered on an award by 399
any court of competent jurisdiction. The proceedings 400
shall be conducted in accordance with the rules of the 401
Society of Maritime Arbitrators, Inc. 402

online resource centre
www.oxfordtextbooks.co.uk/orc/beale5e

Visit the **online resource centre** to view a full-size version of this document if you would like to read it in more detail.

PART II
"BALTIME 1939" Uniform Time-Charter (as revised 2001)

In cases where neither the claim nor any counterclaim 403
exceeds the sum of US$50,000 (or such other sum as 404
the parties may agree) the arbitration shall be conducted 405
in accordance with the Shortened Arbitration Procedure 406
of the Society of Maritime Arbitrators, Inc. current at the 407
time when the arbitration proceedings are commenced. 408

*) **(C)** This Charter shall be governed by and construed in 409
accordance with the laws of the place mutually agreed 410
by the parties and any dispute arising out of or in 411
connection with this Charter shall be referred to 412
arbitration at a mutually agreed place, subject to the 413
procedures applicable there. 414

(D) Notwithstanding (A), (B) or (C) above, the parties 415
may agree at any time to refer to mediation any difference 416
and/or dispute arising out of or in connection with this 417
Charter. 418

In the case of a dispute in respect of which arbitration 419
has been commenced under (A), (B) or (C) above, the 420
following shall apply:- 421

(i) Either party may at any time and from time to time 422
elect to refer the dispute or part of the dispute to 423
mediation by service on the other party of a written notice 424
(the "Mediation Notice") calling on the other party to agree 425
to mediation. 426

(ii) The other party shall thereupon within 14 calendar 427
days of receipt of the Mediation Notice confirm that they 428
agree to mediation, in which case the parties shall 429
thereafter agree a mediator within a further 14 calendar 430
days, failing which on the application of either party a 431
mediator will be appointed promptly by the Arbitration 432
Tribunal ("the Tribunal") or such person as the Tribunal 433
may designate for that purpose. The mediation shall 434
be conducted in such place and in accordance with such 435
procedure and on such terms as the parties may agree 436
or, in the event of disagreement, as may be set by the 437
mediator. 438

(iii) If the other party does not agree to mediate, that fact 439
may be brought to the attention of the Tribunal and may 440
be taken into account by the Tribunal when allocating 441
the costs of the arbitration as between the parties. 442

(iv) The mediation shall not affect the right of either party 443
to seek such relief or take such steps as it considers 444

necessary to protect its interest. 445

(v) Either party may advise the Tribunal that they have 446
agreed to mediation. The arbitration procedure shall 447
continue during the conduct of the mediation but the 448
Tribunal may take the mediation timetable into account 449
when setting the timetable for steps in the arbitration. 450

(vi) Unless otherwise agreed or specified in the 451
mediation terms, each party shall bear its own costs 452
incurred in the mediation and the parties shall share 453
equally the mediator's costs and expenses. 454

(vii) The mediation process shall be without prejudice 455
and confidential and no information or documents 456
disclosed during it shall be revealed to the Tribunal 457
except to the extent that they are disclosable under the 458
law and procedure governing the arbitration. 459

*(Note: The parties should be aware that the mediation 460
process may not necessarily interrupt time limits.)* 461

(E) If Box 23 in Part I is not appropriately filled in, sub- 462
clause (A) of this Clause shall apply. Sub-clause (D) 463
shall apply in all cases. 464

*) *(A), (B) and (C) are alternatives; indicate alternative 465
agreed in Box 23.* 466

23. General Average 467
General Average shall be settled according to York/ 468
Antwerp Rules, 1994 and any subsequent modification 469
thereof. Hire shall not contribute to General Average. 470

24. Commission 471
The Owners shall pay a commission at the rate stated 472
in Box 24 to the party mentioned in Box 24 on any hire 473
paid under the Charter, but in no case less than is 474
necessary to cover the actual expenses of the Brokers 475
and a reasonable fee for their work. If the full hire is not 476
paid owing to breach of Charter by either of the parties 477
the party liable therefor shall indemnify the Brokers 478
against their loss of commission. Should the parties 479
agree to cancel the Charter, the Owners shall indemnify 480
the Brokers against any loss of commission but in such 481
case the commission not to exceed the brokerage on 482
one year's hire. 483

online resource centre
www.oxfordtextbooks.co.uk/orc/beale5e

Visit the **online resource centre** to view a full-size version of this document if you would like to read it in more detail.

NOTES TO BALTIME 1939 TIME CHARTER

1. A time charter is a contract by which the charterer obtains the services of a ship and its crew for a specified period of time (see face, box 14). He can then use the ship to carry cargo that is not excluded (see box 17(b) and cl 2 on back) between any safe ports within the trading limits (see box 17(a) and cll 2 and 14).

2. The feature that distinguishes a time charter from a voyage charter (see next specimen) is that the owner is paid hire on a time basis (usually monthly or semi-monthly) by the charterer: see box 20 and cl 6. The different payment bases will have effects on the risk of delay, for example, by congestion of the ports of loading and unloading (look at notes on voyage charterparties). Note particularly the second part of cl 6 allowing the owner to 'withdraw' the vessel in default of payment (and see above). The charterer does not have to pay for the ship if it is unavailable because it needs repairs, etc: see cl 11 (the 'off-hire' clause, see above).

3. The vessel is to be delivered at a specified port at a specified time (see boxes 15 and 16). If the vessel is not delivered within an agreed time after this date, the charterer may cancel the charter: see box 22 and cl 21.

4. At the end of the charter, the ship must be redelivered. In practice, it may be difficult for the charter to ensure that the last voyage ends on the last day of the charter. This is a fertile source of disputes. The charterparty may contain provisions designed to deal with this problem (see cl 7 and p 738).

■ *GENCON voyage charter*

1. Shipbroker	RECOMMENDED THE BALTIC AND INTERNATIONAL MARITIME COUNCIL UNIFORM GENERAL CHARTER (AS REVISED 1922, 1976 and 1994) (To be used for trades for which no specially approved form is in force) CODE NAME: "GENCON" Part I
	2. Place and date
3. Owners/Place of business (Cl. 1)	4. Charterers/Place of business (Cl. 1)
5. Vessel's name (Cl. 1)	6. GT/NT (Cl. 1)
7. DWT all told on summer load line in metric tons (abt.) (Cl. 1)	8. Present position (Cl. 1)
9. Expected ready to load (abt.) (Cl. 1)	
10. Loading port or place (Cl. 1)	11. Discharging port or place (Cl. 1)
12. Cargo (also state quantity and margin in Owners' option, if agreed; if full and complete cargo not agreed state "part cargo") (Cl. 1)	
13. Freight rate (also state whether freight prepaid or payable on delivery) (Cl. 4)	14. Freight payment (state currency and method of payment; also beneficiary and bank account) (Cl. 4)
15. State if vessel's cargo handling gear shall not be used (Cl. 5)	16. Laytime (if separate laytime for load. and disch. is agreed, fill in a) and b). If total laytime for load. and disch., fill in c) only) (Cl. 6)
17. Shippers/Place of business (Cl. 6)	a) Laytime for loading
18. Agents (loading) (Cl. 6)	b) Laytime for discharging
19. Agents (discharging) (Cl. 6)	c) Total laytime for loading and discharging
20. Demurrage rate and manner payable (loading and discharging) (Cl. 7)	21. Cancelling date (Cl. 9)
	22. General Average to be adjusted at (Cl. 12)
23. Freight Tax (state if for the Owners' account) (Cl. 13 (c))	24. Brokerage commission and to whom payable (Cl. 15)
25. Law and Arbitration (state 19 (a), 19 (b) or 19 (c) of Cl. 19; if 19 (c) agreed also state Place of Arbitration) (if not filled in 19 (a) shall apply) (Cl. 19)	
(a) State maximum amount for small claims/shortened arbitration (Cl. 19)	26. Additional clauses covering special provisions, if agreed

Copyright, published by The Baltic and International Maritime Council (BIMCO), Copenhagen

It is mutually agreed that this Contract shall be performed subject to the conditions contained in this Charter Party which shall include Part I as well as Part II. In the event of a conflict of conditions, the provisions of Part I shall prevail over those of Part II to the extent of such conflict.

Signature (Owners)	Signature (Charterers)

Printed by The BIMCO Charter Party Editor

online resource centre
www.oxfordtextbooks.co.uk/orc/beale5e

Visit the **online resource centre** to view a full-size version of this document if you would like to read it in more detail.

PART II
"Gencon" Charter (As Revised 1922, 1976 and 1994)

1. It is agreed between the party mentioned in Box 3 as the Owners of the Vessel 1
named in Box 5, of the GT/NT indicated in Box 6 and carrying about the number 2
of metric tons of deadweight capacity all told on summer loadline stated in Box 3
7, now in position as stated in Box 8 and expected ready to load under this 4
Charter Party about the date indicated in Box 9, and the party mentioned as the 5
Charterers in Box 4 that: 6

The said Vessel shall, as soon as her prior commitments have been completed, 7
proceed to the loading port(s) or place(s) stated in Box 10 or so near thereto as 8
she may safely get and lie always afloat, and there load a full and complete 9
cargo (if shipment of deck cargo agreed same to be at the Charterers' risk and 10
responsibility) as stated in Box 12, which the Charterers bind themselves to 11
ship, and being so loaded the Vessel shall proceed to the discharging port(s) or 12
place(s) stated in Box 11 as ordered on signing Bills of Lading, or so near 13
thereto as she may safely get and lie always afloat, and there deliver the cargo. 14

2. Owners' Responsibility Clause 15
The Owners are to be responsible for loss of or damage to the goods or for 16
delay in delivery of the goods only in case the loss, damage or delay has been 17
caused by personal want of due diligence on the part of the Owners or their 18
Manager to make the Vessel in all respects seaworthy and to secure that she is 19
properly manned, equipped and supplied, or by the personal act or default of 20
the Owners or their Manager. 21
And the Owners are not responsible for loss, damage or delay arising from any 22
other cause whatsoever, even from the neglect or default of the Master or crew 23
or some other person employed by the Owners on board or ashore for whose 24
acts they would, but for this Clause, be responsible, or from unseaworthiness of 25
the Vessel on loading or commencement of the voyage or at any time 26
whatsoever. 27

3. Deviation Clause 28
The Vessel has liberty to call at any port or ports in any order, for any purpose, 29
to sail without pilots, to tow and/or assist Vessels in all situations, and also to 30
deviate for the purpose of saving life and/or property. 31

4. Payment of Freight 32
(a) The freight at the rate stated in Box 13 shall be paid in cash calculated on the 33
intaken quantity of cargo. 34
(b) *Prepaid.* If according to Box 13 freight is to be paid on shipment, it shall be 35
deemed earned and non-returnable, Vessel and/or cargo lost or not lost. 36
Neither the Owners nor their agents shall be required to sign or endorse bills of 37
lading showing freight prepaid unless the freight due to the Owners has 38
actually been paid. 39
(c) *On delivery.* If according to Box 13 freight, or part thereof, is payable at 40
destination it shall not be deemed earned until the cargo is thus delivered. 41
Notwithstanding the provisions under (a), if freight or part thereof is payable on 42
delivery of the cargo the Charterers shall have the option of paying the freight 43
on delivered weight/quantity provided such option is declared before breaking 44
bulk and the weight/quantity can be ascertained by official weighing machine, 45
joint draft survey or tally. 46
Cash for Vessel's ordinary disbursements at the port of loading to be advanced 47
by the Charterers, if required, at highest current rate of exchange, subject to 48
two (2) per cent to cover insurance and other expenses. 49

5. Loading/Discharging 50
(a) Costs/Risks 51
The cargo shall be brought into the holds, loaded, stowed and/or trimmed, 52
tallied, lashed and/or secured and taken from the holds and discharged by the 53
Charterers, free of any risk, liability and expense whatsoever to the Owners. 54
The Charterers shall provide and lay all dunnage material as required for the 55
proper stowage and protection of the cargo on board, the Owners allowing the 56
use of all dunnage available on board. The Charterers shall be responsible for 57
and pay the cost of removing their dunnage after discharge of the cargo under 58
this Charter Party and time to count until dunnage has been removed. 59
(b) Cargo Handling Gear 60
Unless the Vessel is gearless or unless it has been agreed between the parties 61
that the Vessel's gear shall not be used and stated as such in Box 15, the 62
Owners shall throughout the duration of loading/discharging give free use of 63
the Vessel's cargo handling gear and of sufficient motive power to operate all 64
such cargo handling gear. All such equipment to be in good working order. 65
Unless caused by negligence of the stevedores, time lost by breakdown of the 66
Vessel's cargo handling gear or motive power - pro rata the total number of 67
cranes/winches required at that time for the loading/discharging of cargo 68
under this Charter Party - shall not count as laytime or time on demurrage. 69
On request the Owners shall provide free of charge cranemen/winchmen from 70
the crew to operate the Vessel's cargo handling gear, unless local regulations 71
prohibit this, in which latter event shore labourers shall be for the account of the 72
Charterers. Cranemen/winchmen shall be under the Charterers' risk and 73
responsibility and as stevedores to be deemed as their servants but shall 74

always work under the supervision of the Master. 75
(c) Stevedore Damage 76
The Charterers shall be responsible for damage (beyond ordinary wear and 77
tear) to any part of the Vessel caused by Stevedores. Such damage shall be 78
notified as soon as reasonably possible by the Master to the Charterers or their 79
agents and to their Stevedores, failing which the Charterers shall not be held 80
responsible. The Master shall endeavour to obtain the Stevedores' written 81
acknowledgement of liability. 82
The Charterers are obliged to repair any stevedore damage prior to completion 83
of the voyage, but must repair stevedore damage affecting the Vessel's 84
seaworthiness or class before the Vessel sails from the port where such 85
damage was caused or found. All additional expenses incurred shall be for the 86
account of the Charterers and any time lost shall be for the account of and shall 87
be paid to the Owners by the Charterers at the demurrage rate. 88

6. Laytime 89
(a) Separate laytime for loading and discharging 90
The cargo shall be loaded within the number of running days/hours as 91
indicated in Box 16, weather permitting, Sundays and holidays excepted, 92
unless used, in which event time used shall count. 93
The cargo shall be discharged within the number of running days/hours as 94
indicated in Box 16, weather permitting, Sundays and holidays excepted, 95
unless used, in which event time used shall count. 96
* *(b) Total laytime for loading and discharging* 97
The cargo shall be loaded and discharged within the number of total running 98
days/hours as indicated in Box 16, weather permitting, Sundays and holidays 99
excepted, unless used, in which event time used shall count. 100
(c) Commencement of laytime (loading and discharging) 101
Laytime for loading and discharging shall commence at 13.00 hours, if notice of 102
readiness is given up to and including 12.00 hours, and at 06.00 hours next 103
working day if notice given during office hours after 12.00 hours. Notice of 104
readiness at loading port to be given to the Shippers named in Box 17 or if not 105
named, to the Charterers or their agents named in Box 18. Notice of readiness 106
at the discharging port to be given to the Receivers or, if not known, to the 107
Charterers or their agents named in Box 19. 108
If the loading/discharging berth is not available on the Vessel's arrival at or off 109
the port of loading/discharging, the Vessel shall be entitled to give notice of 110
readiness within ordinary office hours on arrival there, whether in free pratique 111
or not, whether customs cleared or not. Laytime or time on demurrage shall 112
then count as if she were in berth and in all respects ready for loading/ 113
discharging provided that the Master warrants that she is in fact ready in all 114
respects. Time used in moving from the place of waiting to the loading/ 115
discharging berth shall not count as laytime. 116
If, after inspection, the Vessel is found not to be ready in all respects to load/ 117
discharge time lost after the discovery thereof until the Vessel is again ready to 118
load/discharge shall not count as laytime. 119
Time used before commencement of laytime shall count. 120
* *Indicate alternative (a) or (b) as agreed, in Box 16.* 121

7. Demurrage 122
Demurrage at the loading and discharging port is payable by the Charterers at 123
the rate stated in Box 20 in the manner stated in Box 20 per day or pro rata for 124
any part of a day. Demurrage shall fall due day by day and shall be payable 125
upon receipt of the Owners' invoice. 126
In the event the demurrage is not paid in accordance with the above, the 127
Owners shall give the Charterers 96 running hours written notice to rectify the 128
failure. If the demurrage is not paid at the expiration of this time limit and if the 129
vessel is in or at the loading port, the Owners are entitled at any time to 130
terminate the Charter Party and claim damages for any losses caused thereby. 131

8. Lien Clause 132
The Owners shall have a lien on the cargo and on all sub-freights payable in 133
respect of the cargo, for freight, deadfreight, demurrage, claims for damages 134
and for all other amounts due under this Charter Party including costs of 135
recovering same. 136

9. Cancelling Clause 137
(a) Should the Vessel not be ready to load (whether in berth or not) on the 138
cancelling date indicated in Box 21, the Charterers shall have the option of 139
cancelling this Charter Party. 140
(b) Should the Owners anticipate that, despite the exercise of due diligence, 141
the Vessel will not be ready to load by the cancelling date, they shall notify the 142
Charterers thereof without delay stating the expected date of the Vessel's 143
readiness to load and asking whether the Charterers will exercise their option 144
of cancelling the Charter Party, or agree to a new cancelling date. 145
Such option must be declared by the Charterers within 48 running hours after 146
the receipt of the Owners' notice. If the Charterers do not exercise their option 147
of cancelling, then this Charter Party shall be deemed to be amended such that 148

This computer generated form is printed by authority of BIMCO. Any insertion or deletion to the form must be clearly visible. In event of any modification being made to the preprinted text of this document, which is not clearly visible, the original BIMCO approved document shall apply. BIMCO assume no responsibility for any loss or damage caused as a result of discrepancies between the original BIMCO document and this document.

online resource centre
www.oxfordtextbooks.co.uk/orc/beale5e

Visit the **online resource centre** to view a full-size version of this document if you would like to read it in more detail.

PART II
"Gencon" Charter (As Revised 1922, 1976 and 1994)

the seventh day after the new readiness date stated in the Owners' notification 149
to the Charterers shall be the new cancelling date. 150
The provisions of sub-clause (b) of this Clause shall operate only once, and in 151
case of the Vessel's further delay, the Charterers shall have the option of 152
cancelling the Charter Party as per sub-clause (a) of this Clause. 153

10. Bills of Lading 154
Bills of Lading shall be presented and signed by the Master as per the 155
"Congenbill" Bill of Lading form, Edition 1994, without prejudice to this Charter 156
Party, or by the Owners' agents provided written authority has been given by 157
Owners to the agents, a copy of which is to be furnished to the Charterers. The 158
Charterers shall indemnify the Owners against all consequences or liabilities 159
that may arise from the signing of bills of lading as presented to the extent that 160
the terms or contents of such bills of lading impose or result in the imposition of 161
more onerous liabilities upon the Owners than those assumed by the Owners 162
under this Charter Party. 163

11. Both-to-Blame Collision Clause 164
If the Vessel comes into collision with another vessel as a result of the 165
negligence of the other vessel and any act, neglect or default of the Master, 166
Mariner, Pilot or the servants of the Owners in the navigation or in the 167
management of the Vessel, the owners of the cargo carried hereunder will 168
indemnify the Owners against all loss or liability to the other or non-carrying 169
vessel or her owners in so far as such loss or liability represents loss of, or 170
damage to, or any claim whatsoever of the owners of said cargo, paid or 171
payable by the other or non-carrying vessel or her owners to the owners of said 172
cargo and set-off, recouped or recovered by the other or non-carrying vessel 173
or her owners as part of their claim against the carrying Vessel or the Owners. 174
The foregoing provisions shall also apply where the owners, operators or those 175
in charge of any vessel or vessels or objects other than, or in addition to, the 176
colliding vessels or objects are at fault in respect of a collision or contact. 177

12. General Average and New Jason Clause 178
General Average shall be adjusted in London unless otherwise agreed in Box 179
22 according to York-Antwerp Rules 1994 and any subsequent modification 180
thereof. Proprietors of cargo to pay the cargo's share in the general expenses 181
even if same have been necessitated through neglect or default of the Owners' 182
servants (see Clause 2). 183
If General Average is to be adjusted in accordance with the law and practice of 184
the United States of America, the following Clause shall apply: "In the event of 185
accident, danger, damage or disaster before or after the commencement of the 186
voyage, resulting from any cause whatsoever, whether due to negligence or 187
not, for which, or for the consequence of which, the Owners are not 188
responsible, by statute, contract or otherwise, the cargo shippers, consignees 189
or the owners of the cargo shall contribute with the Owners in General Average 190
to the payment of any sacrifices, losses or expenses of a General Average 191
nature that may be made or incurred and shall pay salvage and special charges 192
incurred in respect of the cargo. If a salving vessel is owned or operated by the 193
Owners, salvage shall be paid for as fully as if the said salving vessel or vessels 194
belonged to strangers. Such deposit as the Owners, or their agents, may deem 195
sufficient to cover the estimated contribution of the goods and any salvage and 196
special charges thereon shall, if required, be made by the cargo, shippers, 197
consignees or owners of the goods to the Owners before delivery.". 198

13. Taxes and Dues Clause 199
(a) *On Vessel* -The Owners shall pay all dues, charges and taxes customarily 200
levied on the Vessel, howsoever the amount thereof may be assessed. 201
(b) *On cargo* -The Charterers shall pay all dues, charges, duties and taxes 202
customarily levied on the cargo, howsoever the amount thereof may be 203
assessed. 204
(c) *On freight* -Unless otherwise agreed in Box 23, taxes levied on the freight 205
shall be for the Charterers' account. 206

14. Agency 207
In every case the Owners shall appoint their own Agent both at the port of 208
loading and the port of discharge. 209

15. Brokerage 210
A brokerage commission at the rate stated in Box 24 on the freight, dead-freight 211
and demurrage earned is due to the party mentioned in Box 24. 212
In case of non-execution 1/3 of the brokerage on the estimated amount of 213
freight to be paid by the party responsible for such non-execution to the 214
Brokers as indemnity for the latter's expenses and work. In case of more 215
voyages the amount of indemnity to be agreed. 216

16. General Strike Clause 217
(a) If there is a strike or lock-out affecting or preventing the actual loading of the 218
cargo, or any part of it, when the Vessel is ready to proceed from her last port or 219

at any time during the voyage to the port or ports of loading or after her arrival 220
there, the Master or the Owners may ask the Charterers to declare, that they 221
agree to reckon the laydays as if there were no strike or lock-out. Unless the 222
Charterers have given such declaration in writing (by telegram, if necessary) 223
within 24 hours, the Owners shall have the option of cancelling this Charter 224
Party. If part cargo has already been loaded, the Owners must proceed with 225
same, (freight payable on loaded quantity only) having liberty to complete with 226
other cargo on the way for their own account. 227
(b) If there is a strike or lock-out affecting or preventing the actual discharging 228
of the cargo on or after the Vessel's arrival at or off port of discharge and same 229
has not been settled within 48 hours, the Charterers shall have the option of 230
keeping the Vessel waiting until such strike or lock-out is at an end against 231
paying half demurrage after expiration of the time provided for discharging 232
until the strike or lock-out terminates and thereafter full demurrage shall be 233
payable until the completion of discharging, or if ordering the Vessel to a safe 234
port where she can safely discharge without risk of being detained by strike or 235
lock-out. Such orders to be given within 48 hours after the Master or the 236
Owners have given notice to the Charterers of the strike or lock-out affecting 237
the discharge. On delivery of the cargo at such port, all conditions of this 238
Charter Party and of the Bill of Lading shall apply and the Vessel shall receive 239
the same freight as if she had discharged at the original port of destination, 240
except that if the distance to the substituted port exceeds 100 nautical miles, 241
the freight on the cargo delivered at the substituted port to be increased in 242
proportion. 243
(c) Except for the obligations described above, neither the Charterers nor the 244
Owners shall be responsible for the consequences of any strikes or lock-outs 245
preventing or affecting the actual loading or discharging of the cargo. 246

17. War Risks ("Voywar 1993") 247
(1)   For the purpose of this Clause, the words: 248
(a) The "Owners" shall include the shipowners, bareboat charterers, 249
disponent owners, managers or other operators who are charged with the 250
management of the Vessel, and the Master; and 251
(b) "War Risks" shall include any war (whether actual or threatened), act of 252
war, civil war, hostilities, revolution, rebellion, civil commotion, warlike 253
operations, the laying of mines (whether actual or reported), acts of piracy, 254
acts of terrorists, acts of hostility or malicious damage, blockades 255
(whether imposed against all Vessels or imposed selectively against 256
Vessels of certain flags or ownership, or against certain cargoes or crews 257
or otherwise howsoever), by any person, body, terrorist or political group, 258
or the Government of any state whatsoever, which, in the reasonable 259
judgement of the Master and/or the Owners, may be dangerous or are 260
likely to be or to become dangerous to the Vessel, her cargo, crew or other 261
persons on board the Vessel. 262
(2)   If at any time before the Vessel commences loading, it appears that, in the 263
reasonable judgement of the Master and/or the Owners, performance of 264
the Contract of Carriage, or any part of it, may expose, or is likely to expose, 265
the Vessel, her cargo, crew or other persons on board the Vessel to War 266
Risks, the Owners may give notice to the Charterers cancelling this 267
Contract of Carriage, or may refuse to perform such part of it as may 268
expose, or may be likely to expose, the Vessel, her cargo, crew or other 269
persons on board the Vessel to War Risks; provided always that if this 270
Contract of Carriage provides that loading or discharging is to take place 271
within a range of ports, and at the port or ports nominated by the Charterers 272
the Vessel, her cargo, crew, or other persons onboard the Vessel may be 273
exposed, or may be likely to be exposed, to War Risks, the Owners shall 274
first require the Charterers to nominate any other safe port which lies 275
within the range for loading or discharging, and may only cancel this 276
Contract of Carriage if the Charterers shall not have nominated such safe 277
port or ports within 48 hours of receipt of notice of such requirement. 278
(3)   The Owners shall not be required to continue to load cargo for any voyage, 279
or to sign Bills of Lading for any port or place, or to proceed or continue on 280
any voyage, or on any part thereof, or to proceed through any canal or 281
waterway, or to proceed to or remain at any port or place whatsoever, 282
where it appears, either after the loading of the cargo commences, or at any 283
stage of the voyage thereafter before the discharge of the cargo is 284
completed, that, in the reasonable judgement of the Master and/or the 285
Owners, the Vessel, her cargo (or any part thereof), crew or other persons 286
on board the Vessel (or any one or more of them) may be, or are likely to be, 287
exposed to War Risks. If it should so appear, the Owners may by notice 288
request the Charterers to nominate a safe port for the discharge of the 289
cargo or any part thereof, and if within 48 hours of the receipt of such 290
notice, the Charterers shall not have nominated such a port, the Owners 291
may discharge the cargo at any safe port of their choice (including the port 292
of loading) in complete fulfilment of the Contract of Carriage. The Owners 293
shall be entitled to recover from the Charterers the extra expenses of such 294
discharge and, if the discharge takes place at any port other than the 295
loading port, to receive the full freight as though the cargo had been 296

online resource centre
www.oxfordtextbooks.co.uk/orc/beale5e

Visit the **online resource centre** to view a full-size version of this document if you would like to read it in more detail.

PART II
"Gencon" Charter (As Revised 1922, 1976 and 1994)

carried to the discharging port and if the extra distance exceeds 100 miles, 297
to additional freight which shall be the same percentage of the freight 298
contracted for as the percentage which the extra distance represents to 299
the distance of the normal and customary route, the Owners having a lien 300
on the cargo for such expenses and freight. 301

(4) If at any stage of the voyage after the loading of the cargo commences, it 302
appears that, in the reasonable judgement of the Master and/or the 303
Owners, the Vessel, her cargo, crew or other persons on board the Vessel 304
may be, or are likely to be, exposed to War Risks on any part of the route 305
(including any canal or waterway) which is normally and customarily used 306
in a voyage of the nature contracted for, and there is another longer route 307
to the discharging port, the Owners shall give notice to the Charterers that 308
this route will be taken. In this event the Owners shall be entitled, if the total 309
extra distance exceeds 100 miles, to additional freight which shall be the 310
same percentage of the freight contracted for as the percentage which the 311
extra distance represents to the distance of the normal and customary 312
route. 313

(5) The Vessel shall have liberty:- 314
(a) to comply with all orders, directions, recommendations or advice as to 315
departure, arrival, routes, sailing in convoy, ports of call, stoppages, 316
destinations, discharge of cargo, delivery or in any way whatsoever which 317
are given by the Government of the Nation under whose flag the Vessel 318
sails, or other Government to whose laws the Owners are subject, or any 319
other Government which so requires, or any body or group acting with the 320
power to compel compliance with their orders or directions; 321
(b) to comply with the orders, directions or recommendations of any war 322
risks underwriters who have the authority to give the same under the terms 323
of the war risks insurance; 324
(c) to comply with the terms of any resolution of the Security Council of the 325
United Nations, any directives of the European Community, the effective 326
orders of any other Supranational body which has the right to issue and 327
give the same, and with national laws aimed at enforcing the same to which 328
the Owners are subject, and to obey the orders and directions of those who 329
are charged with their enforcement; 330
(d) to discharge at any other port any cargo or part thereof which may 331
render the Vessel liable to confiscation as a contraband carrier; 332
(e) to call at any other port to change the crew or any part thereof or other 333
persons on board the Vessel when there is reason to believe that they may 334
be subject to internment, imprisonment or other sanctions; 335
(f) where cargo has not been loaded or has been discharged by the 336
Owners under any provisions of this Clause, to load other cargo for the 337
Owners' own benefit and carry it to any other port or ports whatsoever, 338
whether backwards or forwards or in a contrary direction to the ordinary or 339
customary route. 340
(6) If in compliance with any of the provisions of sub-clauses (2) to (5) of this 341
Clause anything is done or not done, such shall not be deemed to be a 342
deviation, but shall be considered as due fulfilment of the Contract of 343
Carriage. 344

18. General Ice Clause 345
Port of loading 346
(a) In the event of the loading port being inaccessible by reason of ice when the 347
Vessel is ready to proceed from her last port or at any time during the voyage or 348
on the Vessel's arrival or in case frost sets in after the Vessel's arrival, the 349
Master for fear of being frozen in is at liberty to leave without cargo, and this 350
Charter Party shall be null and void. 351
(b) If during loading the Master, for fear of the Vessel being frozen in, deems it 352
advisable to leave, he has liberty to do so with what cargo he has on board and 353
to proceed to any other port or ports with option of completing cargo for the 354
Owners' benefit for any port or ports including port of discharge. Any part 355
cargo thus loaded under this Charter Party to be forwarded to destination at the 356
Vessel's expense but against payment of freight, provided that no extra 357
expenses be thereby caused to the Charterers, freight being paid on quantity 358
delivered (in proportion if lumpsum), all other conditions as per this Charter 359
Party. 360
(c) In case of more than one loading port, and if one or more of the ports are 361
closed by ice, the Master or the Owners to be at liberty either to load the part 362
cargo at the open port and fill up elsewhere for their own account as under 363
section (b) or to declare the Charter Party null and void unless the Charterers 364
agree to load full cargo at the open port. 365

Port of discharge 366
(a) Should ice prevent the Vessel from reaching port of discharge the 367
Charterers shall have the option of keeping the Vessel waiting until the re- 368
opening of navigation and paying demurrage or of ordering the Vessel to a safe 369
and immediately accessible port where she can safely discharge without risk of 370
detention by ice. Such orders to be given within 48 hours after the Master or the 371
Owners have given notice to the Charterers of the impossibility of reaching the 372

of destination. 373
(b) If during discharging the Master for fear of the Vessel being frozen in deems 374
it advisable to leave, he has liberty to do so with what cargo he has on board and 375
to proceed to the nearest accessible port where she can safely discharge. 376
(c) On delivery of the cargo at such port, all conditions of the Bill of Lading shall 377
apply and the Vessel shall receive the same freight as if she had discharged at 378
the original port of destination, except that if the distance of the substituted port 379
exceeds 100 nautical miles, the freight on the cargo delivered at the substituted 380
port to be increased in proportion. 381

19. Law and Arbitration 382
* (a) This Charter Party shall be governed by and construed in accordance with 383
English law and any dispute arising out of this Charter Party shall be referred to 384
arbitration in London in accordance with the Arbitration Acts 1950 and 1979 or 385
any statutory modification or re-enactment thereof for the time being in force. 386
Unless the parties agree upon a sole arbitrator, one arbitrator shall be 387
appointed by each party and the arbitrators so appointed shall appoint a third 388
arbitrator, the decision of the three-man tribunal thus constituted or any two of 389
them, shall be final. On the receipt by one party of the nomination in writing of 390
the other party's arbitrator, that party shall appoint their arbitrator within 391
fourteen days, failing which the decision of the single arbitrator appointed shall 392
be final. 393
For disputes where the total amount claimed by either party does not exceed 394
the amount stated in Box 25** the arbitration shall be conducted in accordance 395
with the Small Claims Procedure of the London Maritime Arbitrators 396
Association. 397
* (b) This Charter Party shall be governed by and construed in accordance with 398
Title 9 of the United States Code and the Maritime Law of the United States and 399
should any dispute arise out of this Charter Party, the matter in dispute shall be 400
referred to three persons at New York, one to be appointed by each of the 401
parties hereto, and the third by the two so chosen; their decision or that of any 402
two of them shall be final, and for purpose of enforcing any award, this 403
agreement may be made a rule of the Court. The proceedings shall be 404
conducted in accordance with the rules of the Society of Maritime Arbitrators, 405
Inc.. 406
For disputes where the total amount claimed by either party does not exceed 407
the amount stated in Box 25** the arbitration shall be conducted in accordance 408
with the Shortened Arbitration Procedure of the Society of Maritime Arbitrators, 409
Inc., 410
* (c) Any dispute arising out of this Charter Party shall be referred to arbitration at 411
the place indicated in Box 25, subject to the procedures applicable there. The 412
laws of the place indicated in Box 25 shall govern this Charter Party. 413
(d) If Box 25 in Part 1 is not filled in, sub-clause (a) of this Clause shall apply. 414
* (a), (b) and (c) are alternatives; indicate alternative agreed in Box 25. 415
** Where no figure is supplied in Box 25 in Part 1, this provision only shall be void but 416
the other provisions of this Clause shall have full force and remain in effect. 417

online resource centre
www.oxfordtextbooks.co.uk/orc/beale5e

Visit the **online resource centre** to view a full-size version of this document if you
would like to read it in more detail.

NOTES TO GENCON VOYAGE CHARTER

1.   A voyage charter is a contract between a shipowner and the charterer to carry a stated cargo (see box 12: the charterer may be given an option as to the cargo) from the loading port (box 10) to the port of discharge (box 11).

2.   The distinguishing feature of a voyage charter is that the owner is paid freight on the quantity of cargo carried rather than on a time basis. This payment basis is reflected in a number of other clauses in the contract.

3.   Firstly, the charterer agrees to load a full and complete cargo (see cl 1). If he loads less than this, so that the freight is less than it might have been, the charterer will be liable for the difference in damages, often called 'dead freight'.

4.   Secondly, the shipowner will obviously be concerned to make as many voyages as possible, and to have the ship kept in port loading and discharging for as short a time as he can. The charter therefore allows a fixed number of days, the 'lay time' or 'lay days', for these operations (box 15 and cl 6). The lay days start running once the ship has arrived and the charterer has been notified, and if (because of congestion in the port or because of some order given by the charterer) the ship is kept in port for longer than the lay days, the charterer has to pay liquidated damages, called 'demurrage' (see box 20 and cl 7). For a case involving the demurrage clause, see p 987.

5.   Instead of a straightforward time or voyage charter, the parties may adopt a hybrid form. So a ship may be chartered on a time basis but the trading limits be fixed, so that the ship can only be used between a small number of ports, eg Rotterdam and the US Gulf ports. Alternatively, sometimes the charter is for a whole series of consecutive voyages between the two ports. In the *Suisse Atlantique* case (see p 987), the charter was for as many consecutive voyages as could be performed within two years. This looks rather like a time charter, but the shipowner is being paid on a freight, not a time, basis, so it is still a form of voyage charter, and the allocation of risks of delays in port is the same as for other voyage charters.

6.   The shipowner can seldom undertake that the ship will be ready to load the cargo by a fixed date; instead, the charter states the current position of the ship (box 8) and the date at which the ship is 'expected ready to load' (box 9), and gives the charterer a right to cancel if the ship is not ready by an agreed date thereafter (box 21 and cl 9). for the operation of these clauses, see p 572.

■ *Fob sales contract*

Effective 1st January 2006

Gafta No.119

Copyright

THE GRAIN AND FEED TRADE ASSOCIATION

GENERAL CONTRACT FOR FEEDINGSTUFFS IN BAGS OR BULK
FOB TERMS

* *delete/specify as applicable*   Date..

1   SELLERS ....
2
3   INTERVENING AS BROKERS...
4
5   BUYERS...
6   have this day entered into a contract on the following terms and conditions.
7
8   **1.   GOODS-** ....
9   If in bags, in new and/or second-hand bags of suitable strength to withstand ordinary wear and tear to port of destination. Bags of each
10   mark shall be of uniform weight and shall be properly marked. If in bulk, Buyers may call for up to 10% in stowage bags, such bags to
11   be taken and paid for as goods and any cutting to be paid for by Buyers. Buyers have the option of calling for an additional quantity to
12   be shipped in bags, in which case they will be responsible for providing the extra bags and any additional costs incurred, but shall not be
13   required to pay for the extra bags as goods.
14
15 **2.   QUANTITY** ....5% more or less at Buyers' option.
16   In the event of the quantity contracted being a full and complete cargo and/or cargoes the margin of contract quantity shall be 10% more
17   or less, any excess or deficiency over 5% shall be settled at the FOB price on date of last bill of lading; value shall be fixed by arbitration
18   unless mutually agreed. In the event of more than one delivery being made each delivery shall be considered a separate contract, but the
19   margin on the mean quantity sold shall not be affected thereby. Each mark/parcel shall stand as a separate delivery.
20
21 **3.   PRICE-** at ....
22   * per tonne of 1000 kilograms   }
23   } gross weight, delivered Free on Board Buyers' vessel at ....
24   * per ton of 1016 kilograms or 2240 lbs. }
25
26 **4.   BROKERAGE** ....per tonne, to be paid by Sellers on the mean contract quantity, goods lost or not lost,
27   contract fulfilled or not fulfilled unless such non-fulfilment is due to the cancellation of the contract under the terms of the
28   Prohibition or Force Majeure Clause. Brokerage shall be due on the day shipping documents are exchanged, or if the goods are not
29   delivered then the brokerage shall be due on the 30th consecutive day after the last day for delivery.
30
31 **5.   QUALITY-** ....
32
33   *Official .... certificate of inspection, at time of loading into the ocean carrying vessel, shall be final as to quality.
34
35   Warranted to contain not less than ....
36   % of oil and protein combined and not more than 2.50% of sand and/or silica. Should the whole, or any portion, not turn out equal to
37   warranty, the goods must be taken at an allowance to be agreed or settled by arbitration as provided for below, except that for any
38   deficiency of oil and protein there shall be allowances to Buyers at the following rates, viz.: 1% of the contract price for each of the
39   first 3 units of deficiency under the warranted percentage; 2% of the contract price for the 4th and 5th units and 3% of the contract
40   price for each unit in excess of 5 and proportionately for any fraction thereof. When the combined content of oil and protein is
41   warranted within a margin (as for example 40%/42%) no allowance shall be made if the analysis ascertained as herein provided be
42   not below the minimum, but if the analysis results below the minimum warranted the allowance for deficiency shall be computed
43   from the mean of the warranted content. For any excess of sand and/or silica there shall be an allowance of 1% of the contract price
44   for each unit of excess and proportionately for any fraction thereof. Should the goods contain over 5% of sand and/or silica the
45   Buyers shall be entitled to reject the goods, in which case the contract shall be null and void, for such quantity rejected. For the
46   purpose of sampling and analysis each mark/parcel shall stand as a separate shipment. The right of rejection provided by this Clause
47   shall be limited to the mark/parcel or marks/parcels found to be defective.
48
49   **Condition.** Delivery shall be made in good condition.
50 **6.   PERIOD OF DELIVERY**
51
52   **Delivery during** .... at Buyers' call.
53

119/1

online resource centre
www.oxfordtextbooks.co.uk/orc/beale5e

Visit the **online resource centre** to view a full-size version of this document if you
would like to read it in more detail.

54   **Nomination of Vessel-** Buyers shall serve not less than ....consecutive day's notice of the name and
55   probable readiness date of the vessel and the estimated tonnage required. Buyers have the right to substitute the nominated vessel,
56   but in any event the original delivery period and any extension shall not be affected thereby. Provided the vessel is presented at the
57   loading port in readiness to load within the delivery period, Sellers shall if necessary complete loading after the delivery period and
58   carrying charges shall not apply. In case of re-sales a provisional notice shall be passed on without delay, where possible, by
59   telephone and confirmed on the same day in accordance with the Notices Clause.
60
61   **7.**   **SHIPMENT AND CLASSIFICATION-** Shipment by first class mechanically self-propelled vessel(s) suitable for the carriage of the
62   contract goods, classed in accordance with the Institute Classification Clause of the International Underwriting Association in force
63   at the time of shipment, excluding tankers and vessels which are either classified in Lloyd's Register or described in Lloyd's
64   Shipping Index as "Ore/Oil" vessels.
65
66   **8.**   **LOADING -** Vessel(s) to load in accordance with the custom of the port of loading unless otherwise stipulated. Bill of lading shall be
67   considered proof of delivery in the absence of evidence to the contrary.
68
69   **9.**   **EXTENSION OF DELIVERY-** The contract period of delivery shall be extended by an additional period of not more than 30
70   consecutive days, provided that Buyers serve notice claiming extension not later than the next business day following the last day of the
71   delivery period. In this event Sellers shall carry the goods for Buyers' account and all charges for storage, interest, insurance and other
72   such normal carrying expenses shall be for Buyers' account, unless the vessel presents in readiness to load within the contractual delivery
73   period.
74   Any differences in export duties, taxes, levies etc, between those applying during the original delivery period and those applying during
75   the period of extension, shall be for the account of Buyers. If required by Buyers, Sellers shall produce evidence of the amounts paid. In
76   such cases the Duties, Taxes, Levies Clause shall not apply.
77   Should Buyers fail to present a vessel in readiness to load under the extension period, Sellers shall have the option of declaring Buyers to
78   be in default, or shall be entitled to demand payment at the contract price plus such charges as stated above, less current FOB charges,
79   against warehouse warrants and the tender of such warehouse warrants shall be considered complete delivery of the contract on the part
80   of Sellers.
81
82   **10.** **ICE -** ....
83
84   **11.** **PAYMENT-**
85   (a) By cash in .... against the
86
87   following shipping documents ....
88
89   (b) No clerical error in the documents shall entitle the Buyers to reject them or delay payment, but Sellers shall be responsible for all loss
90   or expense caused to Buyers by reason of such error, and Sellers shall on request of Buyers furnish an approved guarantee in respect
91   thereto.
92
93   (c) Amounts payable under this contract shall be settled without delay. If not so settled, either party may notify the other that a dispute has
94   arisen and serve a notice stating his intention to refer the dispute to arbitration in accordance with the Arbitration Rules.
95
96   (d) **Interest** – If there has been unreasonable delay in any payment, interest appropriate to the currency involved shall be charged. If such
97   charge is not mutually agreed, a dispute shall be deemed to exist which shall be settled by arbitration. Otherwise interest shall be payable
98   only where specifically provided in the terms of the contract or by an award of arbitration. The terms of this clause do not override the
99   parties' contractual obligation under sub-clause (a).
100
101 **12.** **EXPORT LICENCE** - if required, to be obtained by Sellers.
102
103 **13.** **DUTIES, TAXES, LEVIES, ETC.-** All export duties, taxes, levies, etc., present or future, in country of origin, or of the territory where
104   the port or ports of shipment named herein is/are situate, shall be for Sellers' account.
105
106 **14.** **INSURANCE-** Marine and war risk insurance including strikes, riots, civil commotions and mine risks to be effected by Buyers with
107   first class underwriters and/or approved companies. Buyers shall supply Sellers with confirmation thereof at least 5 consecutive days
108   prior to expected readiness of vessel(s). If Buyers fail to provide such confirmation, Sellers shall have the right to place such insurance
109   at Buyers' risk and expense.
110
111 **15.** **WEIGHING-** the terms and conditions of GAFTA Weighing Rules No.123 are deemed to be incorporated into this contract. Final
112   at time and place of loading, as per GAFTA registered superintendent certificate at Sellers' choice and expense. Buyers have the
113   right to attend at loading.
114
115 **16.** **SAMPLING, ANALYSIS AND CERTIFICATE OF ANALYSIS-** the terms and conditions of GAFTA Sampling Rules No. 124,
116   are deemed to be incorporated into this contract. Samples shall be taken at time and place of loading. The parties shall appoint
117   superintendents, for the purposes of supervision and sampling of the goods, from the GAFTA Register of Superintendents. Unless
118   otherwise agreed, analysts shall be appointed from the GAFTA Register of Analysts
119
120 **17.** **PROHIBITION-** In case of prohibition of export, blockade or hostilities or in case of any executive or legislative act done by or on

online resource centre
www.oxfordtextbooks.co.uk/orc/beale5e

Visit the **online resource centre** to view a full-size version of this document if you
would like to read it in more detail.

121 behalf of the government of the country of origin or of the territory where the port or ports of shipment named herein is/are situate,
122 restricting export, whether partially or otherwise, any such restriction shall be deemed by both parties to apply to this contract and to the
123 extent of such total or partial restriction to prevent fulfilment whether by shipment or by any other means whatsoever and to that extent
124 this contract or any unfulfilled portion thereof shall be cancelled. Sellers shall advise Buyers without delay with the reasons therefor and,
125 if required, Sellers must produce proof to justify the cancellation.
126

127 **18. LOADING STRIKES-**
128 (a) Should delivery of the goods or any part thereof be prevented at any time during the last 28 days of guaranteed time of delivery or at
129 any time during guaranteed contract period if such be less than 28 days, by reason of riots, strikes or lock-outs at port(s) of loading or
130 elsewhere preventing the forwarding of the goods to such port(s), then Sellers shall be entitled at the resumption of work after
131 termination of such riots, strikes or lock-outs to as much time, not exceeding 28 days, for delivery from such port(s) as was left for
132 delivery under the contract prior to the outbreak of the riots, strikes or lock-outs, and in the event of the time left for delivery under the
133 contract being 14 days or less, a minimum extension of 14 days shall be allowed.
134

135 (b) In the event of further riots, strikes or lock-outs occurring during the time by which the guaranteed time of delivery has been
136 extended by reason of the operation of the provisions of paragraph (a), the additional extension shall be limited to the actual duration of
137 such further riots, strikes or lock-outs. In case of non-delivery under the above circumstances the date of default shall be similarly
138 deferred.
139

140 (c) If delay in delivery is likely to occur for any of the above reasons, Sellers shall serve notice on their Buyers within 7 consecutive
141 days of the occurrence, or not less than 21 consecutive days before the commencement of the contract period, whichever is later, if they
142 intend to claim an extension for delivery, such notice shall limit the port(s) for delivery after expiry of contract period to those for which
143 an extension is claimed.
144

145 (d) If required by Buyers, Sellers must provide documentary evidence to establish any claim for extension under this clause.
146

147 **19. FORCE MAJEURE - ** ....
148

149 **20. CIRCLE-** Where Sellers re-purchase from their Buyers or from any subsequent Buyer the same goods or part thereof, a circle shall be
150 considered to exist as regards the particular goods so re-purchased, and the provisions of the Default Clause shall not apply. (For the
151 purpose of this clause the same goods shall mean goods of the same description, from the same country of origin, of the same quality,
152 and, where applicable, of the same analysis warranty, for delivery from the same port(s) of loading during the same period of delivery).
153 Different currencies shall not invalidate the circle.
154

155 Subject to the terms of the Prohibition Clause in the contract, if the circle is established before the goods are delivered, or if the goods are
156 not delivered invoices based on the mean contract quantity, or if the goods have been delivered invoices based on the delivered quantity,
157 shall be settled by all Buyers and their Sellers in the circle by payment by all Buyers to their Sellers of the excess of the Sellers' invoice
158 amount over the lowest invoice amount in the circle. Payment shall be due not later than 15 consecutive days after the last day for
159 delivery, or, should the circle not be ascertained before the expiry of this time, then payment shall be due not later than 15 consecutive
160 days after the circle is ascertained.
161

162 Where the circle includes contract expressed in different currencies the lowest invoice amount shall be replaced by the market price on
163 the first day for contractual delivery and invoices shall be settled between each Buyer and his Seller in the circle by payment of the
164 differences between the market price and the relative contract price in the currency of the contract.
165

166 All Sellers and Buyers shall give every assistance to ascertain the circle and when a circle shall have been ascertained in accordance with
167 this clause same shall be binding on all parties to the circle. As between Buyers and Sellers in the circle, the non presentation of
168 documents by Sellers to their Buyers shall not be considered a breach of contract. Should any party in the circle prior to the due date of
169 payment commit any act comprehended in the Insolvency Clause of this contract, settlement by all parties in the circle shall be
170 calculated at the closing out price as provided for in the Insolvency Clause, which shall be taken as a basis for settlement, instead of the
171 lowest invoice amount in the circle. In this event respective Buyers shall make payment to their Sellers or respective Sellers shall make
172 payment to their Buyers of the difference between the closing out price and the contract price.
173

174 **21. NOTICES-** All notices required to be served on the parties pursuant to this contract shall be communicated rapidly in legible form.
175 Methods of rapid communication for the purposes of this clause are defined and mutually recognised as: - either telex, or letter if
176 delivered by hand on the date of writing, or telefax, or E-mail, or other electronic means, always subject to the proviso that if receipt
177 of any notice is contested, the burden of proof of transmission shall be on the sender who shall, in the case of a dispute, establish, to
178 the satisfaction of the arbitrator(s) or board of appeal appointed pursuant to the Arbitration Clause, that the notice was actually
179 transmitted to the addressee. For the purpose of serving notices in a string, any notice received after 1600 hours on a business day
180 shall be deemed to have been received on the business day following. In case of resales/repurchases all notices shall be served
181 without delay by sellers on their respective buyers or vice versa. A notice to the Brokers or Agent shall be deemed a notice under
182 this contract.
183

184 **22. NON-BUSINESS DAYS-** Saturdays, Sundays and the officially recognised and/or legal holidays of the respective countries and any
185 days, which GAFTA may declare as non-business days for specific purposes, shall be non-business days. Should the time limit for doing
186 any act or serving any notice expire on a non-business day, the time so limited shall be extended until the first business day thereafter.
187 The period of delivery shall not be affected by this clause.

119/3

online resource centre
www.oxfordtextbooks.co.uk/orc/beale5e

Visit the **online resource centre** to view a full-size version of this document if you would like to read it in more detail.

188
189 **23.** **DEFAULT-** In default of fulfilment of contract by either party, the following provisions shall apply: -
190 (a) The party other than the defaulter shall, at their discretion have the right, after serving notice on the defaulter, to sell or purchase, as
191 the case may be, against the defaulter, and such sale or purchase shall establish the default price.
192
193 (b) If either party be dissatisfied with such default price or if the right at (a) above is not exercised and damages cannot be mutually
194 agreed, then the assessment of damages shall be settled by arbitration.
195
196 (c) The damages payable shall be based on, but not limited to, the difference between the contract price and either the default price
197 established under (a) above or upon the actual or estimated value of the goods, on the date of default, established under (b) above.
198
199 (d) In all cases the damages shall, in addition, include any proven additional expenses which would directly and naturally result in the
200 ordinary course of events from the defaulter's breach of contract, but shall in no case include loss of profit on any sub-contracts made by
201 the party defaulted against or others unless the arbitrator(s) or board of appeal, having regard to special circumstances, shall in his/their
202 sole and absolute discretion think fit.
203
204 (e) Damages, if any, shall be computed on the quantity called for if any but, if no such quantity has been declared then on the mean
205 contract quantity, and any option available to either party shall be deemed to have been exercised accordingly in favour of the mean
206 contract quantity.
207
208 **24.** **INSOLVENCY-** If before the fulfilment of this contract, either party shall suspend payments, notify any of the creditors that he is unable
209 to meet debts or that he has suspended or that he is about to suspend payments of his debts, convene, call or hold a meeting of creditors,
210 propose a voluntary arrangement, have an administration order made, have a winding up order made, have a receiver or manager
211 appointed, convene, call or hold a meeting to go into liquidation (other than for re-construction or amalgamation) become subject to an
212 Interim Order under Section 252 of the Insolvency Act 1986, or have a Bankruptcy Petition presented against him (any of which acts
213 being hereinafter called an "Act of Insolvency") then the party committing such Act of Insolvency shall forthwith serve a notice of the
214 occurrence of such Act of Insolvency on the other party to the contract and upon proof (by either the other party to the contract or the
215 Receiver, Administrator, Liquidator or other person representing the party committing the Act of Insolvency) that such notice was thus
216 served within 2 business days of the occurrence of the Act of Insolvency, the contract shall be closed out at the market price ruling on the
217 business day following the serving of the notice. If such notice has not been served, then the other party, on learning of the occurrence of
218 the Act of Insolvency, shall have the option of declaring the contract closed out at either the market price on the first business day after
219 the date when such party first learnt of the occurrence of the Act of Insolvency or at the market price ruling on the first business day after
220 the date when the Act of Insolvency occurred. In all cases the other party to the contract shall have the option of ascertaining the
221 settlement price on the closing out of the contract by re-purchase or re-sale, and the difference between the contract price and the
222 re-purchase or re-sale price shall be the amount payable or receivable under this contract.
223
224 **25.** **DOMICILE-**This contract shall be deemed to have been made in England and to be performed in England, notwithstanding any
225 contrary provision, and this contract shall be construed and take effect in accordance with the laws of England. Except for the
226 purpose of enforcing any award made in pursuance of the Arbitration Clause of this contract, the Courts of England shall have
227 exclusive jurisdiction to determine any application for ancillary relief, (save for obtaining security only for the claim or counter-
228 claim), the exercise of the powers of the Court in relation to the arbitration proceedings and any dispute other than a dispute which
229 shall fall within the jurisdiction of arbitrators or board of appeal of the Association pursuant to the Arbitration Clause of this
230 contract. For the purpose of any legal proceedings each party shall be deemed to be ordinarily resident or carrying on business at the
231 offices of The Grain and Feed Trade Association, (GAFTA), England, and any party residing or carrying on business in Scotland
232 shall be held to have prorogated jurisdiction against himself to the English Courts or if in Northern Ireland to have submitted to the
233 jurisdiction and to be bound by the decision of the English Courts. The service of proceedings upon any such party by leaving the
234 same at the offices of The Grain and Feed Trade Association, together with the posting of a copy of such proceedings to his address
235 outside England, shall be deemed good service, any rule of law or equity to the contrary notwithstanding.
236
237 **26.** **ARBITRATION-**
238 (a) Any and all disputes arising out of or under this contract or any claim regarding the interpretation or execution of this contract
239 shall be determined by arbitration in accordance with the GAFTA Arbitration Rules, No 125, in the edition current at the date of this
240 contract, such Rules are incorporated into and form part of this Contract and both parties hereto shall be deemed to be fully
241 cognisant of and to have expressly agreed to the application of such Rules.
242
243 (b) Neither party hereto, nor any persons claiming under either of them shall bring any action or other legal proceedings against the
244 other in respect of any such dispute, or claim until such dispute or claim shall first have been heard and determined by the
245 arbitrator(s) or a board of appeal, as the case may be, in accordance with the Arbitration Rules and it is expressly agreed and
246 declared that the obtaining of an award from the arbitrator(s) or board of appeal, as the case may be, shall be a condition precedent
247 to the right of either party hereto or of any persons claiming under either of them to bring any action or other legal proceedings
248 against the other of them in respect of any such dispute or claim.
249
250 (c) Nothing contained under this Arbitration Clause shall prevent the parties from seeking to obtain security in respect of their claim
251 or counterclaim via legal proceedings in any jurisdiction, provided such legal proceedings shall be limited to applying for and/or
252 obtaining security for a claim or counterclaim, it being understood and agreed that the substantive merits of any dispute or claim
253 shall be determined solely by arbitration in accordance with the GAFTA Arbitration Rules, No 125.
254

119/4

online resource centre
www.oxfordtextbooks.co.uk/orc/beale5e

Visit the **online resource centre** to view a full-size version of this document if you
would like to read it in more detail.

255   **27. INTERNATIONAL CONVENTIONS-**
256   The following shall not apply to this contract: -
257
258   (a) The Uniform Law on Sales and the Uniform Law on Formation to which effect is given by the Uniform Laws on International Sales
259   Act 1967;
260
261   (b) The United Nations Convention on Contracts for the International Sale of Goods of 1980; and
262
263   (c) The United Nations Convention on Prescription (Limitation) in the International Sale of Goods of 1974 and the amending Protocol of
264   1980.
265
266   (d) Incoterms
267
268   (e) Unless the contract contains any statement expressly to the contrary, a person who is not a party to this contract has no right
269   under the Contract (Rights of Third Parties) Act 1999 to enforce any term of it.

Sellers...   Buyers...

Printed in England and issued by
GAFTA
(THE GRAIN AND FEED TRADE ASSOCIATION)
GAFTA HOUSE, 6 CHAPEL PLACE, RIVINGTON ST, LONDON EC2A 3SH

119/5

online resource centre
www.oxfordtextbooks.co.uk/orc/beale5e

Visit the **online resource centre** to view a full-size version of this document if you
would like to read it in more detail.

NOTES ON FOB SALES CONTRACT

1.   The two most common types of international sale of goods contract are the fob (free on board) and the cif (cost, insurance and freight) contracts. Under a classic fob contract, the seller's obligation is to deliver the goods by having them loaded onto a ship nominated by the buyer, which is responsible for arranging the contract of carriage. (This might be under a bill of lading or a charter of the whole ship.)

2.   The description of the goods is entered in cl 1 and the quantity in cl 2. Note that the quantity is flexible at the buyer's option, to enable the buyer to arrange economical use of the available shipping space.

3.   The port at which the goods are to be loaded is entered in the second blank in cl 3. Sometimes the form is amended so that the goods are to be loaded at one of several ports that are near each other, eg 'one US Gulf port' and the seller is given the right to choose which one later on.

4.   Under cl 6, the buyer has to tender the vessel ready to load within certain dates. The seller must be given an agreed number of days' notice of the date at which the ship is expected to be ready, and, if the contract quantity is too large for one ship so that the buyer will have to nominate several, of the estimated tonnage that will be required for each. If the seller is to choose the port of loading (see note 3), it may have to select one within a set number of days of receiving the notice of expected readiness. (For a case involving Form 119 amended in this way, see p 576.)

5.   Under some fob contracts, the seller agrees to arrange shipment to a particular destination and insurance; if so, this will be arranged as an extra on top of the fob price.

6.   Under a cif contract, many of the clauses will be similar, but the seller's fundamental delivery obligation is different: it is to have the goods on board a ship bound for a named port (the goods are often already afloat by the time the contract is made), properly insured and with the freight paid. The cif price includes insurance and freight. If, as sometimes is agreed, the freight is only payable on arrival, the buyer may deduct what it has to pay from the cif price. The seller must ship the goods, or have had them shipped already between stated dates.

7.   After shipment under a cif contract, the seller will present the shipping documents (an invoice for the goods, a bill of lading or a ship's delivery order and the insurance policy) to the buyer, or if payment is to be by documentary credit (see p 121), to the bank at which the credit has been opened, and will be paid the contract price.

8.   Even if the goods are totally lost before the documents have been presented, the buyer must 'take up' the documents and pay the price; it will have to claim on the insurance policy or sue the carrier. Provided that the buyer has received a bill of lading or a 'ship's delivery order' (an order by which the carrier undertakes to deliver to the person named in the order), it will have a contractual right of action against the carrier: see p 1220. If it has accepted some other document, such as a 'seller's delivery order' (which is merely an order issued by the seller to the carrier to deliver to the buyer), there may be severe problems about recovering form the carrier: see *The Aliakmon* [1986] AC 785, in which it was held that the buyer has no action in tort if the goods had not become its property when they were destroyed. Even though the goods are at the buyer's risk, its loss is purely economic.

■ *Hire-purchase agreement*

Agreement no _____

HIRE-PURCHASE AGREEMENT REGULATED BY THE CONSUMER CREDIT ACT 1974
Between us (the Owner) and you (the Customer), on the terms set out below and over the page.

Name (the Owner)	
Address	Postcode
Name (the Customer)	
Address	Postcode

KEY FINANCIAL INFORMATION

1 Amount of Credit (3-4)	£	Term	months
2 Total Amount Payable (3+8)	£	APR	%

Total Amount Payable (less Deposit) is payable by:
a first instalment (incl Document Fee, if charged) of: £
followed by _____ instalments, each in the sum of: £
followed by a final instalment
(incl Option to Purchase Fee, if payable) in the sum of: £

Each instalment is due and payable on the same day of each consecutive month commencing one month from the date of this Agreement or, if a date is inserted opposite, on that date.

OTHER FINANCIAL INFORMATION

Description of the goods	Cash price (incl VAT)
	£
	£
	£
	£
3 Total Cash Price (incl VAT)	£
4 Deposit *Cash/debit card/credit card/cheque £	£
Trade-in £	
5 Interest	£	Interest is charged at an equivalent rate of ___ % p.a. on the Amount of Credit, calculated and applied at the date, and for the Term, of this Agreement
6 Document Fee	£	
7 Option to Purchase Fee	£	
8 Total Charge For Credit (5+6+7)	£	

KEY INFORMATION

Charges
We may charge you default interest in accordance with clause 9 over the page .We may also require payment of our reasonable charges for (a) sending arrears letters, reminders or documents to which you are not entitled; (b) tracing you if you move address without notifying us; (c) finding the goods if they are not at the address given by you; or (d) cheques, standing orders or direct debits which are dishonoured, stopped or not paid by you. Where known at the date of this agreement, our costs for the above are, ___ for (a) ___, for (b) ___, for (c) ___ and for (d) ___ and otherwise as notified to you. See also clause 9 (b) - costs for enforcing this agreement.

Amount payable on early settlement under s94 Consumer Credit Act 1974
You can settle this agreement at any time by paying off the amount you owe, which may be reduced by a rebate. Appearing below are examples indicating the amount payable if you wanted to settle on the date when a ¼, ½ or ¾ of the term (shown in periods of months) has passed or, on the first repayment date after each of these dates.

months	months	months
£	£	£

The examples are illustrative only and are based on the assumption that all instalments are up to date. No account has been taken of any variation to this agreement.
IMPORTANT-READ THIS CAREFULLY TO FIND OUT ABOUT YOUR RIGHTS
The Consumer Credit Act 1974 lays down certain requirements for your protection which should have been complied with when this agreement was made. If they were not, we cannot enforce this agreement without getting a court order.
The Act also gives you a number of rights You can settle this agreement at any time by giving notice in writing and paying off the amount you owe under the agreement which may be reduced by a rebate. Examples indicating the amount you might have to pay appear in the agreement.
If you would like to know more about your rights under the Act, contact either your local Trading Standards Department or your nearest Citizens' Advice Bureau.
MISSING PAYMENTS
Missing payments could have severe consequences and make obtaining credit more difficult.

* Delete nature of deposit where inapplicable

KEY INFORMATION (cont)

TERMINATION: YOUR RIGHTS
You have a right to end this agreement. To do so, you should write to the person you make your payments to. They will then be entitled to the return of the goods and to half the total amount payable under this agreement, that is £ _____ .If you have already paid at least this amount plus any overdue instalments and have taken reasonable care of the goods, you will not have to pay any more.
REPOSSESSION: YOUR RIGHTS
If you do not keep your side of this agreement but you have paid at least one third of the total amount payable under this agreement, that is £ _____ we may not take back the goods against your wishes unless we get a court order. (In Scotland, we may need to get a court order at any time.) If we do take the goods without your consent or a court order, you have the right to get back any money you have paid under this agreement.

YOUR RIGHT TO CANCEL
Once you have signed this agreement, you will have a short time in which you can cancel it .We will send you exact details of how and when you can do this.

This is a Hire-Purchase Agreement regulated by the Consumer Credit Act 1974. Sign it only if you want to be legally bound by its terms.
Signature(s)
of Customer(s)
Date(s) of signature(s)
The goods will not become your property until you have made all the payments. You must not sell them before then.

Before you sign this Agreement please read the following:
• This Agreement is entered into on the understanding that you are over the age of 18 and the information you have provided is true and accurate.
• Read the column to the left first, then this column and then the terms over the page.
• Note clause 11 over the page
• If you settle this Agreement early as set out in the section headed **Key Information** opposite you will own the goods. However, if you terminate this Agreement and make the payment set out above under the heading **Termination: Your Rights**, you will have to return the goods to the Owners.

CUSTOMER'S CONTACT DETAILS

Tel	Fax
E-mail	

OWNER'S CONTACT DETAILS AND SIGNATURE

Correspondence address	
Regt'd in	Reg No
Tel	VAT No

HPC 04/06 Original

Signed _____ for and on behalf of the Owner
Date_____ which is the date of this Agreement

🔒 IMPORTANT: USE OF YOUR INFORMATION Please read "Use of Your Information" over the page before you sign as by signing you are agreeing to this use and disclosure of your information. We may:
• send you information about our products and services and those of other businesses;
• pass your details to other selected businesses and to anyone who introduced you to us, to send you information about their products and services.
To stop us doing this, write to us or tick this box ☐
To stop us or other businesses contacting you by telephone to offer you other products or services, write to us or tick this box ☐
If you are willing to be contacted by email, automated calling system or personal fax, tick this box ☐

Information held about you by credit reference agencies may be linked to records relating to any person with whom you are linked financially. Please read "Use of Associated Records" over the page before you sign.

online resource centre
www.oxfordtextbooks.co.uk/orc/beale5e

Visit the **online resource centre** to view a full-size version of this document if you would like to read it in more detail.

TERMS OF AGREEMENT

1 Payment by you
a) You must pay the Deposit (if any) shown over the page when, or before, you sign this agreement.
b) You agree to pay us the Total Amount Payable (less any Deposit paid) as shown over the page, for the hire of the goods, by the instalments and at the times shown over the page. Any Option to Purchase Fee, included in the final instalment, need only be paid if you want to become the owner of the goods, as set out in Clause 7.
c) It is essential that you make all payments in full and on time. If you pay by post, you will be responsible for any payment lost in the post.

2 Selling or disposing of the goods
You must keep the goods safely at your address shown over the page. You may not sell or dispose of the goods or transfer your rights under this agreement. You may only part with the goods to have them repaired. You may not use the goods as security for your outstanding debts or responsibilities. If the goods are a motor vehicle, you must keep it at your address shown over the page when it is not in use.

3 Caring for the goods
a) You must keep the goods in good working order and condition at your expense. You are responsible for all loss of, or damage to, the goods even if caused by events beyond your control. However, you are not responsible for loss or damage due to fair wear and tear.
b) You must not let a repairer, or any other person to whom you owe money, keep the goods as a result of your not paying the money you owe.
c) You must make sure that any tests or inspections needed by law or by the insurers are carried out.
d) Unless we have given you permission in writing, you may not make any alterations or additions to the goods (including fixing a personalised or non-original number plate). Any alterations or additions made without our permission will become our property.
e) You must allow our representative to inspect and test the goods at all reasonable times.

4 Change of address
You must let us know, in writing, within seven days about any change of your address.

5 Inspection
You must allow us or our representative to inspect and test the goods at all reasonable times.

6 Insuring the goods
At all times, you must insure the goods and keep them insured under a fully comprehensive policy with a reputable insurer at your own expense. You must tell us and your insurer about any loss or damage to the goods within 48 hours of the loss or damage happening, and whether you or anybody else will be making a claim under the policy. You agree to hold in trust for us any insurance money you receive. You authorise us to:
• negotiate and settle any claim with your insurer; and
• receive any money from your insurer under the policy. You may not withdraw this authority, and you agree to accept any settlement we may reach with the insurer. You must pay us any outstanding balance under this agreement. Unless any of the events referred to in clause 10 happens, this agreement will continue even if the goods are lost or damaged.
If you enter into this agreement for business purposes, you must get adequate insurance cover for employer's liability, liability to third parties and liability for negligence and loss, damage or injury arising out of you using and possessing the goods.

7 Ownership of the goods
We hire the goods to you for The term shown over the page. (subject to clause 10)
You will become the owner of the goods only when you have paid us all the instalments shown over the page, together with all other amounts you owe us under this agreement and you exercise the option to purchase by paying the Option to Purchase Fee shown over the page or, if none is shown, by notifying us in writing of your decision to retain the goods. Until then your rights are only those of a hirer.

8 Your right to end the agreement
You may end this agreement by taking the steps set out in the notice 'Termination: your rights' shown over the page. You must then (at your own expense) return the goods to us and, in the case of a motor vehicle, the registration document, tax disc and MOT test certificate. You must also pay us any further amount mentioned in the notice.

9 Default interest and other enforcement rights
a) If you fail to pay us any amount you owe under this agreement by the date it is due, we may charge you interest on that amount until you pay it. We will charge interest for each day you still owe the payment, at the rate shown in the section 'Other Financial Information' over the page. We can charge this interest even after we have received a court judgment against you.
b) You agree to pay us any charges or costs shown in 'Key Information' over the page which may become payable by you, including our reasonable legal costs for enforcing this agreement.

10 Our right to end the agreement
10.1 We will assume that you refuse to comply with the terms and conditions of this agreement, and we will be entitled to end this agreement after giving you a 'default notice', if:

a) you break any of clauses 1, 2 or 6 of this agreement;
b) you provided false information to enter into this agreement;
c) the goods are destroyed or treated as a total loss under any insurance claim;
d) you are a business and you stop trading, or you are a partnership and the partnership is ended or court action has begun to end it;
e) you have done something which would allow any of your belongings, property, income or savings to be legally removed to pay off any of your debts; or
f) any of the following happens:
• A statutory demand (that is, a written demand for paying a debt of at least £750, which, if not paid in full, may result in bankruptcy proceedings being brought against you) is not paid for 21 days, or any steps are taken by you or anyone else to declare you bankrupt.
• You take steps to enter into any arrangement or debt management plan with your creditors.
• A bailiff or other officer controls or seizes the goods or any of your goods following a court order.
• The landlord of the premises where the goods are situated threatens, or takes steps, to seize or in any other way control the goods or any of your goods.
10.2 If we end this agreement you will no longer be in possession of the goods with our consent, we may take back the goods from you and you must pay us:
a) all payments you still owe us;
b) the balance of the Total Amount Payable; less
• any rebate (reduction) of charges you may be entitled to and;
• any money we receive from selling the goods after we have taken off the costs of recovery, insurance and storage.
However, your rights in the notice 'Repossession: your rights' over the page apply.

11 Exclusion
a) If you are dealing as a consumer, as described in the Unfair Contract Terms Act 1977, nothing in this agreement will take away your rights under the Supply of Goods (Implied Terms) Act 1973.
b) In all other cases:
• you must inspect the goods and use your own skill and judgement to decide whether the goods are of satisfactory quality and fit for their intended purpose; and
• we will not be responsible for the quality of the goods or whether they are fit for their intended purpose, or whether they match any description or specification.

12 General conditions
a) 'Goods' means the goods described over the page and includes any replacements, renewals and additions we or any insurers have agreed to.
b) References to any Act or regulation includes any amendments to that Act or regulation.
c) If at any time we allow you to do something which is against any of the terms and conditions of this agreement, this will not prevent us from insisting that you strictly follow the terms and conditions at any later time.
d) If two or more of you have signed this agreement as the Customer, you are liable jointly and severally, that is together as well as separately under this agreement. This means that either of you can be held fully responsible for the responsibilities of the Customer under this agreement.
e) We may transfer our rights and responsibilities under this agreement to another person. This will not take away any of your rights or responsibilities under this agreement. You may not transfer any of your rights or responsibilities under this agreement to another person.
f) A notice or document under this agreement may be given or served by delivery, post or facsimile: (i) on you at your address stated in this agreement or your last known address; (ii) on us at our address stated in this agreement or other address notified by us to you. A notice or document sent by first-class post shall be taken to have been received 48 hours after posting.
g) English law will apply to this agreement. If you entered into this agreement in Scotland, words that are not in current use in Scotland will have their nearest equivalent meanings.

13 When this agreement comes into force
This agreement will only come into force when we or our authorised representative have signed it.

14 Rights of other people
Nothing in this agreement will give any person, other than you or us (or anyone who takes over from us or any person we have transferred our rights to under this agreement), any rights under this agreement.

online resource centre
www.oxfordtextbooks.co.uk/orc/beale5e

Visit the **online resource centre** to view a full-size version of this document if you would like to read it in more detail.

NOTES ON HIRE-PURCHASE AGREEMENT

1.   Buying goods on hire purchase (HP) normally involves three parties. The retailer or dealer from whom the customer wishes to obtain the goods sells them to a finance company, which becomes the 'owner'. This company then hires the goods out to the customer, who is often referred to as the 'hirer'. The customer agrees to pay the price of the goods and the credit charges (cl 1). When he has made all the payments, the ownership of the goods passes to him; until then, it remains with the owners as, in effect, 'security' (cl 7). The point of making the contract one of hire, rather than a 'conditional sale' with the passing of property deferred until the price has been paid, was originally to evade the rule that a buyer of goods who is given possession of them has the power to sell the goods to a third party, who will get good title to the goods, even though the first buyer had not yet become owner. In respect of conditional sales to consumers, the rule has in any event been reversed by statute.

2.   The distorted nature of an HP agreement is reflected in the imposition on the customer of the obligation to repair the goods (cl 3): compare the simple contract of hire, p 1216).

3.   If the customer defaults, the owner is entitled to terminate the agreement and repossess the goods (cl 10). The customer will have to pay the costs of so doing (cl 9(b)). Note, however, the statutory restriction on the owner's right of repossession once the customer has paid one third of the price (see the notice headed 'REPOSSESSION: YOUR RIGHTS' on the face of the agreement).

4.   The customer may also opt to terminate the agreement at any time (cl 8), but if he does so, he must return the goods and may have to make his payments up to half the amounts of the price (see the notice headed 'TERMINATION: YOUR RIGHTS').

5.   This form is designed for use if the agreement is signed by the customer away from the business premises of the dealer or finance company—on his own doorstep, for instance. In such circumstances, the customer may have a 'cooling-off period' during which he may cancel the agreement (see p 949). This is referred to in the boxes at the foot of the page.

■ *Guarantee and indemnity*

IC
10/01
Guarantee and Indemnity *subject to the Consumer Credit Act 1974*
Relating to a regulated consumer credit agreement.

Original – White
Copy – Pink

Agreement No. _____

To _____
(Full Name of Creditor)   Co Reg. No. _____
of _____
(Postal address)   ('the Creditor')
Telephone _____   Fax _____

I, _____   Title _____
(Full names of Indemnifier)   (Mr, Mrs, Miss, Ms etc.)
of _____
(Postal address)

_____ Post Code _____ ('the Indemnifier')

request you, the Creditor (which expression shall include your successors and assigns), to enter into the agreement briefly described below ('the Agreement') with:

_____

of _____ ('the debtor')

and, in consideration of your doing so, irrevocably agree as follows:
1 I will pay to you the Creditor, on demand, any amount which is due and payable and unpaid to you by the debtor under the Agreement;
2 I will indemnify you against all loss, damages, claims, costs and expenses incurred by you as a result of your entering into the Agreement, whether arising out of a breach by the debtor or otherwise, as if I had entered into it as the debtor;
3 If you relax or do not enforce the Agreement, this guarantee and indemnity or any other security, it will not affect your rights against me under this guarantee and indemnity;
4 A judgment against the debtor given in connection with the Agreement shall also bind me;
5 Any notice to me may be sent to or delivered at my address

Description of the Agreement

stated above, any other address of which I may notify you in writing or my address last known to you;
6 You may transfer this guarantee and indemnity and/or any or all of your rights under it to any other person provided that this does not affect my obligations under this guarantee and indemnity or my rights, including my rights under the Consumer Credit Act 1974;
7 If this guarantee and indemnity is signed on behalf of any person, references to 'I/me' shall be construed accordingly. This guarantee and indemnity will not be affected by my death (but shall be binding upon my Personal Representatives), nor by any change in the composition of the debtor or the Indemnifier.

Type of Contract _____
(Insert Hire Purchase, Credit Sale, Loan or as appropriate)
Total Amount Payable/Credit Limit £ _____
(Delete inapplicable item)

Description of Goods _____
(If applicable)
Registration Number _____
(If a motor vehicle)

IMPORTANT - YOU SHOULD READ THIS CAREFULLY
YOUR RIGHTS

The Consumer Credit Act 1974 covers this guarantee and indemnity and lays down certain requirements for your protection. If they are not carried out, the creditor cannot enforce the guarantee and indemnity against you without a court order.

Until the agreement between the creditor and the debtor has been made, you can change your mind about giving the guarantee and indemnity. If you wish to withdraw, you must give WRITTEN notice to the creditor which must reach him BEFORE the main agreement is made. Once it has been made you can no longer change your mind.

Under this guarantee and indemnity YOU MAY HAVE TO PAY INSTEAD of the debtor and fulfil any other obligations under the guarantee and indemnity. (But you cannot be made to pay more than he could have been made to pay unless he is under 18). However, if the debtor fails to keep to his side of the agreement, the creditor must send him a default notice (and a copy to you) giving him a chance to put things right before any claim is made on you.

If you would like to know more about your rights under the Act, you should contact either your local Trading Standards Department or your nearest Citizens' Advice Bureau.

IMPORTANT USE OF YOUR INFORMATION
You have a right to know how we will use your personal information. It is important that you read the **"Use of Your Information"** Notice (overleaf) **before** you sign since by signing you are agreeing to this use and disclosure of your information. We may:
● send you useful information about ours and other businesses products and services;
● pass your details to other selected businesses and to anyone who introduced you to us, to send you information about their products and services;
You may at any time stop us doing so. **To stop us, tick this box ☐ or write to us.**
We and other businesses may contact you by telephone or e-mail to offer you other products and services. **To stop us, tick this box ☐ or write to us.**
If you are willing to be contacted by automated calling system or personal fax, tick this box ☐
Information held about you by Credit Reference Agencies may be linked to records relating to any person with whom you are linked financially. Read the **"Use of Associated Records"** **before** you sign.

Acknowledgement by You
(1) By entering into this guarantee and indemnity you might become liable instead of or as well as the debtor. You acknowledge that you should seek independent legal advice before signing.
(2) You acknowledge that you have received a copy of this guarantee and indemnity.

Witness to Indemnifier's Signature

Signature _____

Name _____
Block letters please
Address _____

_____

Notes:
(1) Provision is made on the back of this form for completion of the Indemnifier's details if required.
(2) Where there is more than one indemnifier, a separate form

This is a guarantee and indemnity subject to the Consumer Credit Act 1974. If the debtor fails to keep to his agreement with the creditor, YOU MAY HAVE TO PAY INSTEAD and fulfil any other obligations under the guarantee and indemnity. Sign only if you want to be legally bound by its terms.

Signature(s)* of
Indemnifier(s) _____

Date of Indemnifier's
Signature

online resource centre
www.oxfordtextbooks.co.uk/orc/beale5e

Visit the **online resource centre** to view a full-size version of this document if you would like to read it in more detail.

IC
10/01

USE OF YOUR INFORMATION:
In considering whether to enter into this Agreement, we will search your record at Credit Reference Agencies. They will add, to their record about you, details of our search and your request and this will be seen by other organisations that make searches. This and other information about you and those with whom you are linked financially may be used to make credit decisions about you and other members of your household. We may use a credit scoring or other automated decision making system.
We will also add to your record with the Credit Reference Agencies details of your Agreement with us, any payments you make under it and any default or failure to keep to its terms. These records will be shared with other organisations and may be used and searched by us and them to:
● consider applications for credit and credit related services, such as insurance, for you and any associated person;
● trace debtors, recover debts, prevent or detect money laundering and fraud, and to manage your account(s).
It is important that you provide us with accurate information. We may check your details with fraud prevention agencies and if you provide false or inaccurate information or we suspect fraud, this information may be recorded.
Fraud prevention agency records will be shared with other organisations to help make decisions on credit, motor, household, life and other insurance proposals and claims, for you and members of your household.
We will use personal information about you which we acquire in connection with any application you make to us, or any Agreement you enter into with us, to manage your Agreement and for statistical or market research purposes.
Please telephone or write to us at the telephone number / address stated overleaf if you want to have details of the Credit Reference Agencies or any other agencies from whom we obtain, and to whom we pass, information about you. You have a legal right to these details. You have a right to receive a copy of the information we hold about you if you apply to us in writing. A fee may be payable.

USE OF ASSOCIATED RECORDS
We may before entering into this Agreement search records at Credit Reference Agencies which may be linked to records relating to your spouse/partner or other persons with whom you are linked financially and other members of your household. For the purposes of your request to enter into this Agreement or the Agreement itself you may be treated as financially linked and you will be assessed with reference to "associated records".

Where any search or application is completed or agreement entered into and signed by joint parties, you both consent to us recording details at Credit Reference Agencies. As a result an "association" will be created which will link your financial records and your associates information may be taken into account when a future search is made by us or another lender unless you file a 'disassociation' at the credit reference agencies.

Particulars of the Indemnifier (for creditor's use only)

Full Names of Indemnifier _____ Date of Birth _____

Home address _____

_____

Description of premises (house, flat, etc) _____

Occupied as   ☐ Owner   ☐ Tenant (Furnished)   ☐ Tenant (Unfurnished)

How long occupied _____ Married/Single _____ No. of dependants _____

Phone No. – Home _____ Work _____

Business or Occupation _____

Business Address or Name and Address of Employers _____

_____ How long
_____ so engaged _____

Bankers (state branch) _____

Building Society (state branch) _____

Particulars of two current or previous credit transactions:
Company Name _____

Account No. _____

Company Name _____

Account No. _____

online resource centre
www.oxfordtextbooks.co.uk/orc/beale5e

Visit the **online resource centre** to view a full-size version of this document if you would like to read it in more detail.

NOTES ON GUARANTEE AND INDEMNITY

1. This specimen is for a guarantee of specific obligation, in this example under a regulated consumer credit agreement (for example, the buyer's obligation under a conditional sale agreement).

2. Note the opening words emphasising that the guarantee is given in exchange for the finance company ('the Creditor') entering the consumer credit agreement with the buyer. If the guarantee were not given in exchange for this or some other consideration (for instance, if the guarantee were only asked for and obtained *after* the agreement had been made, and before there had been any default or any question of giving any extra time to pay or other concession to the buyer), the guarantee would be unenforceable for want of consideration (see p 126).

3. The probable intention of the words used is not to put the finance company under any obligation *to the guarantor* to enter the main agreement with the buyer. Guarantees of consumer debts at least are more usually in the form, 'you agree that *if we* lend money to the debtor, you will guarantee repayment'.

4. This form contains not only a guarantee but also an indemnity—a device that is very similar but subject to a number of different rules. One of the differences is that a guarantor is not liable if, for some reason, the debtor is not liable (eg because the debtor is under the age of 18: see p 951), but a promise to indemnify is independent and will be enforceable even if the creditor has no enforceable rights under the main contract: see Treitel, p 181.

5. The purpose of the third paragraph is to avoid the effect of the common law rule that the granting of any concession by the creditor (the finance company) to the debtor (the buyer) releases the guarantor.

■ **The Carbolic Smoke Ball Company's advertisement (see** *Carlill v Carbolic Smoke Ball Co Ltd,* pp 14 and 215**).**

CARLILL V. CARBOLIC SMOKE BALL CO. (1893)

online resource centre
www.oxfordtextbooks.co.uk/orc/beale5e

Visit the **online resource centre** to view a full-size version of this document if you would like to read it in more detail.

INDEX

Abandonment of contract
offer and acceptance 193, 194, 212
Acceptance
in bilateral contracts 204–15
communication of 211–15
by conduct 208–11
by correspondence 215
duration of power of 214–15
by exercise of dominion 213
notification to offeror 221
by performance 221
postal communications 230–40
by silence 213
in unilateral contracts 215–20
by words 204–8
see also Offer and acceptance
Accord and satisfaction
meaning 855
Adams, John 57–63, 72
'Add-on' clauses
consumer credit sales 814–15
Adhesion, contracts of
and freedom of contract 964–5
Advantage-taking, and distributive justice 832–5
physical and non-physical 834
Advertisements
and contractual liability 15, 19
offer or preliminary negotiations 199–202
specimen contracts 1247
and tenders 247
Affreightment contracts
damages 635
Agent
authority of 1128–30
intermediary or party 1127–8
and privity of contract 1194
unauthorised 1130–2
and undisclosed principal 1132–5
Agreements
cancellable 949
and contract law 6–7
existence of 847–8
'farm-in' 486
'fly on the wall' theory 309
fraudulent 1074

meaning 848–51
oral, express terms 323–44
re-opening of, and extortionate credit bargains 951
reaching *see* Offer and acceptance
rival theory 308–9
'swap' 508
ultra vires 508
Aivazian, A. 875–9
Altruism
ideal of 49, 52–3
and individualism 53, 54
Anticipatory breach
and withholding performance 581–8
Aquinas, Thomas 828
Arbitration
privity of contract 1190–1
in United Kingdom 89
Aristotelian theory
equality in exchange 823–4, 828
Assignment
benefit of a contract, subsequent 1195–6
burden of a contract 1207–8
Assumpsit, action of
consideration doctrine 8
frustration of contracts 482
Atiyah, P. S.
on consideration 165–9
on contract law and political thought 8
on contractual liability 129, 135
on functions of contract law 47–9, 55
on Passenger Acts 1056–8
on promises 139, 771–7
and written contracts 347–8
Auctions
preliminary negotiations or offer 202–4
Australia
contract law in 85
critical approach 796–802
frustration of contract 496–7
Autonomy 829–31
and basic needs 830

and planning 830–1
private, in contract law 826–9
value 71–2
Ayres, I. 431–7

Back of order conditions
offer and acceptance 224, 225
Bad faith principle
consumer-welfarism 59
Bailment 1198–9
defined 427
and privity of contract 1200–4
termination of contracts 613
Baltime 1939 time charter 567
specimen contracts 1224–9
Bankers
commercial credits of 121–2
Bargains
enforceable, and unenforceable gift promises 129
executory 130
and gratuitous promises 129–39
impossibility 460
inequality of bargaining power 956
informal, and formal remedies 687–8
principle of bargain 819–20
unconscionable *see*
Unconscionable bargains
Battle of the Forms
formalism 60
offer and acceptance 226
restitutionary liability 266
Beale, Hugh 81–5
Better-loss-bearer principle
consumer-welfarism 59
Bid bonds
tenders 243, 251
Bilateral contracts
acceptance in 204–15
communication of 211–5
by conduct 208–11
by words 204–8
and consideration doctrine 98
definitions 23
or unilateral contracts 221–2
and specific performance 721

Bilateral governance
  relational contracting 893
Bill of lading contracts
  definition of 'bill of lading'
    1220
  interpretation 402
  privity of contract 1154–7
    and liability in tort 1172–3
  specimen contracts 1220–2
  tort, contract restricting
    liability in 1172–3
  see also **Vessels, contracts
    relating to**
Bills of exchange 1197–9
Bona fides **principle**
  good faith 1049, 1050
Braucher, Robert 143
Breach of contract
  advance payments by party in
    breach 700–1
  anticipatory 581–8
  and contractual relationships
    25
  damages for 504
  efficiency 721
  'efficient breach fallacy' 747–50
  'fundamental' breach/'breach
    of fundamental term'
    573, 984, 985, 988–94
  incorrect estimation 698
  performance, withholding
    551, 571
  probability of, incorrectly
    estimated 698
  problems 551
  supply 1147
  and warranties 19
Brownsword, Roger
  on functions of contract law 53
  on ideologies of contract law
    57–63, 72
  and offer 254–6
  on statutory controls 1029
  on work done and steps taken
    prior to agreement of
    contract 283–7
Building contracts 530–1
  assignment of subcontracts
    1207
  builders, liability of 36
  building labour and materials,
    going rates 265
  complex structure theory
    34–5, 37
  councils, liability of 31, 35, 36
  damages, on behalf of another
    1147

defective construction 26–7,
    31, 32–4
  quality standard, implied
    terms 440–3
  health or safety, imminent
    danger to 35–6
  interim payments, with
    retention money 563
  latent defects 34, 441
  modification 858
  penalty clauses 111
  'rise-and-fall' clauses 404
  standard nature of 403
  subcontractors, liability of 26,
    32–3, 1164–5
Burden of a contract
  and assignment 1207–8
Burden of proof
  restraint of trade 1106
  unfair terms 1042
Burrows, Andrew 1192
Business efficacy
  implied terms, in contracts
    417, 418
Businesses
  contracts between
    businessmen 81–5
  definition of 'business' 1005
  non-contractual relations
    389–92
  statements by, assumed to be
    contractual 19
  transactions not in ordinary
    course of business, and
    need for contracts 391

Cancellation
  frustration of contract 469
  privity of contract 1187
  unconscionable bargains 949
Cargo claims, settling 1170–4
  see also **Vessels, contracts
    relating to**
Carriage of goods
  exclusion clauses 1032
Cautionary function
  legal formalities 133
Caveat emptor **doctrine**
  disclosure 533
  and price-ignorance 821
Chain transactions
  exchange of contracts 242
Channeling function
  legal formalities 133
Chattels
  complex 34
  defective 33–4

enforcement 709–10
  specific performance 684
Cheques
  as negotiable instruments
    1198–9
Choice of law clauses
  unfair terms 1038
Civil Justice Review (1986)
  on contract work 84
Civil law
  and common law 9
  and frustration of contracts
    474
  and good faith principle 338
  and mistake 499
Classical contract law
  discrete transactions 4–5, 887
  empirical work 786
  functions of contract law 63
  market governance 893
  market place, rule of 47, 48
  transaction cost approach 890
**CLS (Critical Legal Studies)
    movement** 53, 798
**CME (continental
    Business-Coordinated
    Economies)** 1051
Co-operation
  transformation thesis 840–1
'Coactus volui'
  duress 910
Cohen, Morris R. 759–63
Collateral contracts
  illegal contracts 1092–3
Collins, Hugh
  on functions of contract law
    66–8, 72
  on implied terms 457
  on judicial revision 526–7
  on long-term contracts 895
  on transformation thesis
    836–9
Comfort letter
  concept 17
Commercial credits
  irrevocable 121–2
**Commission on European
    Contract Law** 9
Common carrier
  liability of 708
Common law
  bargain principle 819
  and civil law 9
  damages assessment 687
  exclusion clauses 976
    interpretation 977–95
  implied terms 413–25

manufacturers' liability 34
misrepresentation, rescission
    for 355, 356
mutual or common mistake
    514–6
and private agreements 813
Common mistake
alternative mode of expressing
    result of 506
cancellation agreement,
    invalidation for 504
common law 514–6
non-discharge of contract 499
unilateral mistake
    distinguished 534,
    537–8
Common understanding
oral contracts 340–1
Communication
of acceptance 211–5
    postal 230–40
telex communications 236
Commutative justice
and distributive justice 824
Company law
and nature of contract law 4
Compensation
reliance damages 637
res judicata principle 866
see also **Damages**
Competition Commission
Monopolies and Mergers
    Commission replaced by
    1110
Complex structure theory 34–5,
    37
Conditions
breach, and termination of
    contract 567
concurrent, delivery and
    payment as 554
constructive, in contracts
    554–5, 557, 594
hiring of plant, specimen
    contract 1216–19
by implication 570
legal meaning 600
notion 551–3
in options 581
and order of performance
    553–5
precedent to contract
    formation 553
precedent to payment 561
'promissory' 551–3
in unilateral contracts 581
and warranties 564–6

Conduct
acceptance by 208–11
Conflicts of interest
offer and acceptance 191
Consequential loss
and rescission 369–70
Consideration
absence of, and mistake 509
act done in reliance on
    promise as 165–70
    frontier between promissory
    estoppel and unilateral
    contracts 166–9
adequacy issues 122–3
and assumpsit, action of 8
'benefit' and 'detriment' 99, 102
cars, contracts to build and sell
    American contract law, and
    blanket orders 118–9
    blanket order system 117–8
    reform movement, absence
    of 119
definitions 97–9
estoppel
    promissory, and unilateral
    contracts (frontier
    between) 166–9
    as substitute for 148–64
exchange 123–9
existence of 851
'existing duty' cases 115
and form 855–6
formal requirements 143–6
gratuitous promises *see*
    Gratuitous promises
implied terms
    services, contracts for 447
inadequate, and specific
    performance 708
irrevocable commercial credits
    121–2
lack of, and gifts 23
marriage 123–5
moral obligation 139–43
non-bargain promises, reliance
    on 146–73
    estoppel, as substitute for
    consideration 148–64
    promissory estoppel and
    unilateral contracts,
    frontier between 166–9
or conditional gift 123–6
past
    and exchange 126–9
    legal relations, intention to
    create 187
    moral obligation 140–1

promisee, moving from 115
reliance, recognition 170–3
requirement contracts 116–21
services, contracts for 447
substantial performance rule
    562
sufficient 99–123
    compromise of a claim
    102–5
    intangible returns 100–2
    performance of contractual
    duty owed to promisor
    109–15
    performance of duty
    imposed by contract,
    with third party 107–9
    performance of duty
    imposed by law 105–7
total failure of 427, 482, 743
Consideration in Contracts: A
    Fundamental Restatement
    (Atiyah) 165–9
Constancy principle
consumer-welfarism 59
Constitutional law
contract and sovereignty 763
Construction contracts *see*
    Building contracts
Construction, discharge of
    contract by 521–8
currency depreciation 522–3
fairness 526–7
judicial revision 526–7
Construing of contracts *see*
    Interpretation
Consumer credit
'add-on' clauses 814–5
cancellable agreements 949
cooling-off period 949
extortionate credit bargains
    950–1
    re-opening of agreements
    951
forfeiture, relief against 588–92
and hire purchase 493–4
unconscionable bargains
    949–51
Consumer Ombudsmen
and hardship relief 495
Consumer protection
consumer-welfarism 58
exclusion clauses 1033
inertia selling 210
offer and acceptance 202
product liability 26
remedies for consumers 91
statutory controls 1033

Consumer surplus
and contract remedies 683–8
loss of, damages assessment
687
Consumer-welfarism
advertisements and displays of
goods 202
functions of contract law 57,
58–9
Consumers
withholding of performance,
policy 595–6
and non-consumers 596–8
Contingencies
and adjustment to contract
terms 845
Contra proferentum **rule**
exclusion clauses 977
unfair terms 1042
Contract
assignment of benefit,
subsequent 1195–6
contractual liability 13–24
definitions 828–9
at grass roots 55–7
law of *see* **Contract law**
liability in tort and contract
37–8
performance of duty imposed
by, with third party
107–9
promise, as 778–83
and proprietory estoppel 163,
164
public policy, contrary to
1069–78
relationships equivalent to
29, 45
and restitution 39–45
and risk distribution 762–3
and sovereignty 763–4
theory of *see* **Contract theory**
and tort 24–39
implied terms 422
preliminary contracts 277
recoverable losses 628
remoteness of damage
650–1
as substitute for contract
1162–7
see also **Contracts**
Contract law
approaches to 10–11
Australia 85
critical approaches
796–802
and businesses 389–92

classical
and discrete transactions *see*
**Discrete contracts/
transactions**
market governance 893
transaction cost approach 890
and criminal law 764
critical approaches 791–806
Australia 796–802
displacement 796, 801
duty creation 797, 801
indeterminacy thesis 796,
797–8
poles, choice of 800
privileging 796, 800
rhetoric 797, 801
Waltons Stores v Maher,
deconstructing 798–801
definitions 3
development of, and
contemporary political
thought 8
dispute resolution 6, 7
distributive and paternalist
motives 835–6
and distributive justice *see*
Distributive justice
as dynamic body of rules 8–10
economic analysis 11, 73–80,
784–5
economic principles 394–6
empirical work 11, 81–93
impact 786–90
and exchanges 4, 7
fixed rules, emphasis on 47
functions 5–8, 46–72, 764
historical perspective
eighteenth century 803
nineteenth century 803–4
twentieth century 804–5
as ideology 802–6
judicial decisions *see* Judicial
decisions; Judicial
ideologies
justification of 759–63
libertarian theory 833
motives, distributive and
paternalistic 835–6
neoclassical
and discrete transactions *see*
Discrete contracts
and flexibility in long-term
contractual relations
887–9
transaction cost approach
890
trilateral governance 893

private autonomy in 826–9
promises and obligations
771–78
purposes 6
relevance 4
Roman 828
scope 3–5
traditional, and longer-term
contracts 884–5
see also **Contract; Contracts**
Contract terms *see* **Terms of
contracts**
Contract theory
bargain theory 1184
deconstructive analysis
791–96
doctrine-as-rule/doctrine-
in-application system 793
equivalent theory 761–62
injurious-reliance theory
760–1
public/private aspects of
doctrine 793–6
separation and conflation
793–4
utilitarian and rights-based
theory 758
will theory 758, 759–60, 766
and privity 1184
Contracts
abandonment 193, 194, 212
belief as to non-existence 22
bilateral *see* **Bilateral contracts**
c&f 500
collateral 1092–3
'complete contingent' 459
crime, requiring deliberate
commission of 1079–80
discharge of *see* **Discharge of
contracts**
discrete *see* **Discrete contracts**
employment *see* **Employment
contracts**
equilibrium, fundamental
alteration 896–7
exclusive/non-exclusive 116,
120
illegal 1070–1
implied 42
law of 5
see also **Contract law**
longer-term *see* **Long-term
contracts**
modification 858–60
motor vehicle 117–9
preliminary 271–80
quasi-contracts 793–4

regulated *see* **Regulated contracts**
relational *see* **Relational contracts**
requirement 116–21
secondary, evasion of exclusion clauses by 1032
specimens 1209–47
three-way classification of 890–1
uberrimae fidei 530–1
unfair, United Kingdom and Europe 1028–31
unilateral
  acceptance in 215–20
  and promissory estoppel 166–9
unlawful acts, involving *see* **Unlawful acts**
work done and steps taken, prior to agreement 281–7
see also **Contract; Contract law; Contract theory**
Contractual relationships
and breach of contract 25
Contributory negligence
apportionment of liability 375, 656–7
breach of strict contractual duty 658–9
interpretation 657–9
The Control of Contract Power (Reiter) 54–7
Cooling-off period
consumer credit agreements 949
Coote, B. 1101–2
Cooter, Robert 535–8, 641–43
Corpus iuris civilis (**Justinian**) 823, 824
Correspondence
acceptance by 215
preliminary negotiations or offer 195–8
'subject to contract' 240
Corruption in public life
contracts encouraging 1073
Course of dealing
oral contracts 339–40
Courts
dispute resolution 88–90
and misrepresentation, rescission for 370–1
and property recovery 1097
workloads 84–5

Covenants
independent
  unimportant contract terms as 554
  warranties 565–6
restraint of trade 1106
void, and effectiveness of deed 1119–20
Craswell, Richard 769–70
Crime
contracts requiring deliberate commission of 1079–80
Criminal law
and contract law 764
mens rea 1080
Critical Legal Studies movement 53, 798
Custom
implied terms 411–2

Dalton, C. 791–6
Damages 813–37
adequacy test 712–13, 724
advance payments
  by innocent party 700
  by party in breach 700–1
agreed 688–9, 689–700
  'contracts between businessmen' 695–6
  liquidated damages 691–5
assessment
  as at completion cost 684–6
  loss of consumer surplus 687
  reinstatement by third party 684–6
on behalf of another, and privity 1143–50
breach of warranty 426
common carrier, liability of 708
consequential, liability for 706–8
for deceit 372–77
difference in value or completion cost 679–89
  substitute performance 684–6
ex ante determination 696–9
  imperfect enforcement 697
  measurement problems 698
  moral hazard 697
  penalties as signal 697–8
  probability of breach incorrectly estimated 698

risk aversion 697
unreasonableness 698–9
expectation
  fundamental principles of damages 640
  weaknesses of system 707
false statements 543
forfeiture, deposits and money paid subject to 702–3
formal remedies, and informal bargains 687–8
fraudulent misrepresentation 504
fundamental principles 639–41
hypothetical expectation 642
and innocent misrepresentation 542
investment in performance, and reliance 641–63
land, failure to make title to 672–3
limits to awards, mitigation and remoteness 686
liquidated
  judicial responses to provisions 693–5
  reasons for 692–3
'loss volume', problem of 668
misrepresentation
  availability 370–2
  measure of damages 372–86
  statutory damages 379–88
mitigation
  avoidable losses 651–6
  breach of strict contractual duty 658–9
  contributory negligence 656–9
  limits to damages awards 686
  savings actually made 659–61
nominal 547, 632
non-payment of money 671–2
non-pecuniary losses 673–9, 686
  availability of damages remedy 677–8
'normal' rule 627
oral agreements 331–2
paradox of compensation 641–2
  contract solutions to 642–3
payments on account 700–1
penalties, efficiency implications 696

Damages (*cont.*)
  problem cases
    land, failure to make title to
      672–3
    non-payment of money
      671–2
    non-pecuniary losses
      673–9
  promises, failure to perform
    23
  purposes pursued in awarding
    625–6
  quantification, markets and
    other contracts 662–71
  quantum meruit claims 743,
    744, 745
  recovery, basic measure of
    623–44
  reliance interest 626–9
  remoteness of damage 644–51
    contract-tort boundary
      650–1
    foreseeability of damage
      645–6
    limits to damages awards 686
  and restitution 743
  restitution interest 627
  restitutionary 43
  seller's and buyer's remedies
    624
  sophisticated measures 642
  and specific performance 290,
    684
    in lieu of 686
  substitute performance 684–6
  see also **Losses**
Danzig, Richard 646–9
De minimis **rule**
  and non-performance 566
Deceit
  damages for 372–7
Deeds
  effectiveness of, and void
    covenants 1119–20
  promises 23
    gift promise, enforceability
      of 130
    under seal 137–8
  statutory provisions 132
Default notice
  termination of contracts 589
'Default' rules, sale or supply of
  goods contracts
  contract law 457
  efficient defaults, normative
    appeal 435–6
    degree of efficiency 436–7

and 'immutable' rules 432
  penalty defaults 433–5
  tailored and untailored
    defaults 432
  zero-quantity default 433
Delayed payments
  social force majeure 494
Delivery of goods
  destruction of goods prior to
    462–3
  late 40
  and payment of price, as
    concurrent conditions
    554
  strict obligation 1005
  time and place, implied terms
    439–40
Demand
  elasticity of 77
Demurrer
  definitions 103
Deposits
  customary accounts, lack of
    705
  and forfeiture, money paid
    subject to 702–3
Derrida, Jacques
  deconstructive strategies of
    792–3
Development risk defence
  negligence 26
Discharge of contract
  by construction 521–8
  by frustration *see* **Frustration**
    of contract
  or variation 847–60
Disclosure 529–43
  dishonesty, failure to disclose
    539–40
  duty of
    general 532–43
    statutory 532
  inaccurate and inadequate
    information 541
  information wrongfully
    obtained 531–2
  statutory duties 532
  uberrimae fidei contracts
    530–1
  undue influence 530
  see also **Information**
Discrete contracts/transactions
  adjustment and termination of
    economic relations
    886–7
  characteristics 64
  classical contract law 887

and neoclassical contract law
    887–8
  and relational contracts 4–5
Discrimination
  contracts promoting 1074
Displacing
  and critical contract law 796,
    801
Dispute resolution
  and contract law 6, 7
  modern trends 88–90
Distributive justice
  and commutative justice 824
  and contract law 831–5
    advantage-taking 832–4
  and economic efficiency
    1062–3
  entitlement theory 816
  fairness 69, 70, 813–37
  motives, distributive and
    paternalistic 835–6
  patterning 816–7
    and liberty 817–8
  price-ignorance 821–2
  transformation thesis 69–70
  unconscionability 813–5,
    972–3
Division of labour
  and contract law 65
Domination
  unjustifiable 838–9
'Double intention test'
  privity of contract 1192
Dugdale, Tony 81–5
Duress 901–16
  coercion of will 908
  and consideration doctrine
    105
  'degree of compulsion' 911
  economic 111, 112, 846, 907,
    909
  and functions of contract law
    56
  of goods 954
  illegitimate threat suffered by
    victim 948
  'lawful act' 914
  modern law 911–12
  restitutionary liability 42
  unfairness, procedural vs
    substantive 901
  Uniform Commercial Code
    914–15
  'vitiation of contract' test 913
Duty creation
  and critical contract law
    797, 801

Duty of care
and disclosure obligations 540
existence of 1171
foreseeability of damage 32
imposition of as fair, just and
reasonable 1174
and negligence 24
neighbour principle 24, 27
privity of contract, and
liability in tort 1171
proximity considerations 31,
32, 36
reasonable, liability for breach
659
as standard 50
warning, failure to give 331

Economic analysis
conflicts, preserving economic
relations 886–7
efficiency 75, 79
exchange, instantaneous/
non-instantaneous 74
externalities 76
flexibility, planning into
economic relations 886
information 78
marginal cost 79
market price 79
monopolies 79, 80
see also **Monopolies**
opportunities foregone 75
and profit 76
remedies, effect 76
resources, use of 75–6
second best, economics of 78
transaction costs 77
utility principle 75
Economic principles
contract law in general 394–5
economics of impossibility
395–6
Economic relations
longer-term contracts 886–9
Efficiency
allocative, and disclosure
obligations 534
breach of contract 721
economic, and distributive
justice 1062–3
'efficient breach fallacy' 747–50
reliance, efficient level of 214
and wealth 75, 79
Egotism
and individualism 51, 52
Eisenberg, Melvin A. 819–23,
825–6

Ellinghaus, M. P. 85
Empirical studies 11, 81–93
impact 786–90
Employment contracts 449–54
contract as authoritative
source of rules 452–3
development 450–2
exchanges, discrete and
relational 5
exploitation, vulnerability to
1058–9
express and implied terms
452–3
and frustration of contracts
467
injunctions 732
judicial attitudes 455
modern law, characteristics
452
and nature of contract law 4
obedience, duty of 453–4
redundancy law 454
as 'relational' contracts 455
responsibilities of employers,
implied terms 422
severable nature 557
status and contract 450–2
subcontractors, liability of 26,
32–3
substance of contract 453–4
terms of collective agreement
183
unfair dismissal law 453
withholding of performance
550
Enforcement 732–40
actions for sums due 732–40
advice prior to purchase 19,
30
blanket orders, and American
contract law 118–9
gap-filling, by interpretation
392
gratuitous promises 137–8
imperfect, ex ante damages
determination 697
offer and acceptance 225
post-breach negotiations
718–20
private costs, excessive nature
1059–61
privity of contract 1189
specific performance
and injunctions 709–32
Entitlement theory
distributive justice 816
Epstein, Richard A. 706–8

Equality
transformation thesis 69, 839
Equality in exchange
Aristotelian theory 823–4, 828
and market price 824–6
meaning 823–6
Equity
and estoppel 156
misrepresentation, rescission
for 355
and notice, doctrine of 926,
927
and unconscionable conduct
161
Equivalent theory
promises, binding nature of
761–2
Error doctrine
Roman law 500
Estoppel
consideration, as substitute for
148–64
equitable 872
ostensible authority as
1128
promissory
and equity 156
non-bargain promises,
reliance on 160, 161
objective and current role
807–9
and proprietory 874
relational approach 809–10
and unilateral contracts
166–9
work done prior to contract
agreement 282
proprietory
and contract 163
and equity 156, 164
and promissory 874
reliance damages 633
traditional doctrine 148, 149
European contract law
consumers' economic interests
1046–9
scope 1045
Evidentiary function
legal formalities 133
Ex post rule
damages mitigation 652
Exchange
competitive, and market
place 58
consideration or conditional
gift 123–6
costs of 74–5

Exchange (*cont.*)
creation of relationships
390–2
discrete and relational
exchanges 4–5
equality in, meaning 823–6
fairness of 839–40
instantaneous/non-
instantaneous 74
and nature of contract law 4, 7
past consideration 126–9
of resources 6
risk factors 77
voluntary, and freedom of
contract 73, 74
Exchange of contracts
non-bargain promises, reliance
on 159
offer and acceptance 240–2
Exchange relationships
interpretation 390–2
Exclusion clauses
carriage of goods by sea 1032
common law rules 976
consumer protection 1033
evasion by secondary contract
1032
examples 975
exclusions from Unfair
Contract Terms Act 1977
1031–2
goods, obligations as to
996–1003
implied terms, sale of goods
413
indemnity clauses 1009–10
interpretation 977–95
Law Commission on 966–7,
976, 999–1000, 1006
manufacturers' guarantees,
consumer goods 1003–4
misrepresentation 1009
negligence, liability for
1004–7
privity rule qualifications
1152–3
reasonableness 1010–31
guidelines for application of
test 1011
unfair contracts, United
Kingdom and Europe
1028–31
standard form contracts 1007–9
see also **Standard form
contracts**
statutory controls 995–1033
sale of goods 996–1003

Exemption clauses *see* **Exclusion
clauses**
Expectation interest
damages 627
protection 765–9
Expectations
mistaken 303–9
Exploitation principle
consumer-welfarism 59
Externalities
economic analysis of contract
law 76
Extortionate credit bargains
950–1
re-opening of agreements 951

Fact
statements of 19, 323
misrepresentation 359
Fairness 765–9
bargain principle 819
construction, discharge of
contract by 526–7
consumer-welfarism 58
distributive justice 69, 70,
813–37
of exchange 839–40
fair dealing principle
48, 59
fair trading, private
enforcement costs
1059–60
transformation thesis 839–40
see also **Unfairness**
Fault concept
and price-ignorance 821
Feinman, Jay 802–6, 807–12
Ferguson, Robert B. 88–90
Feveroles
defined 406
Flessner, Axel 9
Fob sales contract
specimen contracts 1235–40
Force majeure
and liquidated damages 695,
696
social, and hardship relief
493–5
Foreign affairs
contracts adversely affecting
1073
Foreseeability of damage
duty of care 32
remoteness of damage 645–6
Foreseen events
and frustration of contracts
479–81

Forfeiture
deposits and money paid
subject to 702–3
relief against, withholding
performance 588–92
Forgeries
and implied terms 430
Form, dimensions of 50
Formal realizability
and rules 50, 51
Formalism
judicial ideologies 59, 60
and market-individualism 62
promises, binding nature of
762
and realism 57
and rule-book 60
Fraud
liability in 38
Freedom of contract
and adhesion, contracts of
964–5
defence 814
and domination 839
functions of contract law 47
individualist ideology 58
justice of exchange 68, 70
and voluntary exchange 73, 74
Fried, Charles 135, 758, 778–9
Front-end loading
tenders 247
Frustration of contract 459–98
automatic nature of 466, 467
cancellation 469
effect 481–92
assessment of just sum 490–1
defendant's benefit,
identification 488
recovery principle 486–7
statutory claims 487–91
foreseen events 479–81
gap-filling, by interpretation
392, 393
hardship relief 493–7
Australia 496–7
force majeure, social 493–5
hire purchase and consumer
credit 493–4
interest on delayed
payments 494
registration of delayed
payments 494
impossibility doctrine,
contract law 459–63
juristic basis 463–7
origination in *Taylor v
Caldwell* case 463

purpose, frustration by 473–9
quantum meruit claims 463
recovery principle 486–7
restitutionary liability 42
risk born by one party 467–73
risk-sharing/diversification
    justification 459–63
self-induced 503
statutory claims 487–91
UNIDROIT Principles of
    International Commercial
    Contracts 493
and unjust enrichment 743
Fuller, Lon
on consideration 133–35, 139,
    143, 855–6
Craswell on 769–70
on damages 626–9, 765–9
Furmston, M. P 1070

Gabel, Peter 802–6
Gaius (Roman jurist) 824
GENCON voyage charter
specimen contracts 1230–34
General principles
categories 954–6
existence of 954–8
possible advantages of general
    doctrine 958–62
structurally impaired markets
    959–61
Germany
production regimes 1051–2
Gerntner, R. 431–7
Gibson, Ralph 18
Gifts
conditional, or consideration
    123–6
informal, and executory
    promises 130
lack of consideration 23
setting aside, and duress 903
Gilmore 56
Goldberg, Victor P. 967–8, 971,
    973
Goldwyn, Samuel 143
Good faith principle
adoption by English law 9–10,
    1049–54
and bills of exchange 1197
and *bona fides* principle 1049,
    1050
and consideration doctrine
    120–1
and nature of contract law 4
and oral agreements 338
and preliminary contracts 276

as standard 50
'visceral justice' 287
work done prior to contract
    agreement 283, 284
see also **Bad faith principle**
Goods
available market 624
delivery *see* **Delivery of goods**
description, sale by 427
destruction prior to delivery
    462–3
duress of 954
exclusion clauses 996–1003
manufacturers' guarantees
    1003–4
Molony Committee on 999,
    1000, 1003
non-conforming, breach and
    remedy for tender 594–6
quality or fitness 428
sale or supply *see* **Sale of goods**
sample, sale by 428–29
title, implied terms as to
    426–7
unsolicited 211
Gordley, James 823–9
Governance
bilateral 893
market 893
transaction-specific 893–4
trilateral 893
Grass roots
contract at 55–7
Gratuitous promises
and bargains 129–39
economics of 136–7
legal formalities, functions
    performed by 133–35
optimal rules for enforcing
    137–8
Grodecki, J. K. 1097–8
Grotius, Hugo 828–9
Guarantees
manufacturers', of consumer
    goods 1003–4
by National House Building
    Council 27
recommendation by a
    minority as to 145–6
specimen contracts 1244–6
and tenders 243, 251
wives, given by 928

Hamson, C. J. 1100–1
Hardship
and contract practice 897
defined 896

effects 897–8
longer-term contracts,
    normally relevant to 897
relief *see* **Hardship relief,**
    frustration of contract
UNIDROIT Principles of
    International
    Commercial Contracts
    895
Hardship relief, frustration of
    contract
delayed payments 494
force majeure, social 493–5
hire purchase and consumer
    credit 493–4
UNIDROIT Principles of
    International Commercial
    Contracts 493
Harris, Donald 683–8
Hire-purchase agreements
communication of acceptance
    211
frustration of contract 493–4
implied terms 425
penalty rules 699
specimen contracts 1241–3
uncertainty 261–2
Holders in due course
and bills of exchange 1197
Holmes, Oliver Wendell 9
Honour, selling of
contracts encouraging 1073
Horwitz, Morton
on contract law 8
Human rights issues
regulated contracts 1065
Hume, David 778

ICE conditions of contract
    881–4
Identity
mistakes as to 309–18
Ideology
contract law as 802–6
judicial *see* **Judicial ideologies**
Illegal contracts
collateral contracts 1092–3
contract expressly or implicitly
    forbidden by statute
    1083–6
deliberate acts, benefits from
    1088–1192
and limited interests 1100–1
outline of rules 1081–3
payments or property,
    recovery of 1094–1104
dignity of court 1097

Illegal contracts (*cont.*)
    locus poenitentiae 1095–6,
      1103
    morality 1097–8
    weaker parties 1094–5
  proprietary claims
    1099–1104, 1100–1
  public policy, contrary to
    1069, 1070–1, 1098
  restitutionary liability 42, 44
  severance 1104
  three-stage test 1082–3
  unlawful acts, involving
    contract expressly or
      implicitly forbidden by
      statute 1083–6
    contracts intended to be
      performed in illegal way
      1086
    contracts performed in
      illegal manner 1086–7
    outline of rules 1081–3
    three-stage test 1082–3
Implied terms
  alteration
    quality of goods 437
  categories 418–20
  common law 413–25
  custom 411–2
  employment contracts 452–3
  exclusion of 413
  and express terms, employment
    contracts 452–3
  functions 437–9
  gap-filling, by interpretation
    393
  insurance provision 420
  justification for 456–7
  'officious bystander' test 418,
    419
  property cases 415–20
  re-definition 437–9
  sale of goods contracts 425–46
    'default' rules 431–7
    delivery 439–40
    description, sale by 427
    'immutable' rules 432
    quality or fitness 428, 437,
      440–6
    sample, sale by 428–9
    title 426–7
  services, contracts for 446–9
    care and skill 447
    consideration 447
    contracts concerned 446–7
    time for performance 447
  statute 412–3

strict necessity standard
    424–5
Impossibility
  destruction of goods before
    delivery 462–3
  economics of 395–6
  frustration of contract 459–63
    frustration of purpose 474
  and interpretation 393–7
In pari delicto
  recovery of payments or
    property 1097–8
Incompleteness 263–71
  damages 641
  default rule theory 432
  property law 268–70
  reasons for 432
  sale of goods contracts 263, 268
Indemnity
  circles of 1174–8
Indemnity clauses
  exclusion clauses 1009–10
Independent advice
  and undue influence 931–2
Indeterminacy thesis
  and critical contract law 796,
    797–8
Individualism
  and altruism 53, 54
  ideal of 49, 51–2
  see also **Market-individualism**
Individualistic ideology
  and market-individualism 58
Industrialization
  and *Hadley v Baxindale*
    principle 646–9
Information
  asymmetry 651
  contracts to conceal 1074
  'deliberately acquired' 534
  disclosure *see* **Disclosure**
  economic analysis 78
  inaccurate
    and disclosure 541
    misrepresentation 354–88
  inadequate 542, 1056–8
    Passenger Acts 1056–7
  incorrect, reliance on 38
  mixed 538
  productive and redistributive
    536–8
  public and private 535
  standard form contracts,
    problems with 969–72
  structurally impaired markets
    961–2
  wrongly obtained 531–2

Informational advantage
  principle
  consumer-welfarism 59
Injunctions
  employment contracts 732
  and licences 21
  and specific performance
    709–32
  unfair terms, prevention of
    continued use 1038–9
Injurious-reliance theory
  justification of contract law
    760–1
Inland Revenue
  agreements to defraud 1074
Insurance
  and contract-law boundary
    650–1
  contracts *uberrimae fidei* 530
  delayed payment of premiums
    494
  implied terms 420
  marine 531
Intentions of parties
  and advertisements 19
  consumer sales, implied terms
    413
  legal relations, creation
    175–87
  oral agreements 323
Interest
  delayed payments 494
Interpretation 396–7
  businesses and contract law
    389–92
  contributory negligence
    657–9
  economic principles
    impossibility, economics of
      395–6
  exclusion clauses 977–95
  express terms of contract,
    application 397–410
  gap-filling by 389–410
    'discharge solution' 393
    promises 781
    uncertainty 259
    withholding performance
      550
    'would have wanted'
      approach 432
  and implication 424
  literalism 400, 401
  'preferred supplier status',
    meaning 407
  risk aversion 396–97
  subsequent conduct 410

vague/ambiguous terms 403
whole contract, necessary to
read 401
Irrevocable commercial credits
and consideration doctrine
121–2

Jessel, Sir George 47, 54, 357
Judicial decisions
changing nature of judges'
perceptions 19–20
general judicial ideologies
59–61
and specimen contracts,
limitations of examining
11
underlying policy 7
Judicial ideologies
formalism 60
general 59–61
ideological field 61–2
realism 60–1
Judicial review
and arbitration 89–90
Justice of exchange 68–70
freedom of contract 68, 70

Kennedy, Duncan 49–53, 54,
791, 835–6
Kessler, Friedrich 964–5
Kötz, Hein 9
Kronman, Anthony T.
on distributive justice 831–35
economic analysis by 73–80,
81
on regulated contracts
1061–4
on specific performance 713–16

Laissez faire
control 66
and freedom of contract 47, 49
Law Commission
on consumer goods 999–1000,
1004
Conveyancing Standing
Committee, on
disclosure 541
on deeds 130
on deposits 705
on exemption clauses 966–7,
976, 999–1000, 1006
on parol evidence rule 350
on partial performance 563
on past consideration 140
on privity of contract 1183–7
on restitutionary damages
749–50

on sale and supply of goods,
implied terms 437–9
on termination for default
596–600
Law Reform Committee
First Report (1952) 146
on misrepresentation 368
on reliance 170
Law Revision Committee
on past consideration 187
Sixth Interim Report 144–5,
187, 1179
Seventh Interim Report 485
Lawrence, M. 86–8
Lawson, F. H. 1197–9
Leff, Arthur Alan 784–5
Legal formalities
functions performed by 133–5
**Legal relations, intention to
create** 175–87
circumstances of case 177
hazards of everyday life 179
lifts, liability to pay for
179–80
matrimonial home 176–7
'officious bystander' test 180
and promises 182
Licences
and contractual liability 21
Literalism
and frustration of contracts 466
interpretation of contracts
400, 401
'Litigation explosion'
current trends 84
Llewellyn, Karl 85
Lloyd's Reports
and empirical work 83
**LME (Liberal Market
Economies)** 1052
Local authorities
liability for defective
construction 31, 35, 36
Lockout agreements
preliminary contracts 272,
273, 275
Locus poenitentiae
contracts involving
commission of crime or
tort 1095–8, 1103
Long-term contracts
alterations, additions and
omissions 881–2
economic relations,
adjustment and
termination 886–9
hardship normally relevant
to 897

ICE conditions of contract
881–4
neoclassical contract law
discrete transactions,
variation from 887
flexible approach 887–9
specific planning, and need
for flexibility 888–9
presentation
and relational contracts
885–6
and traditional contract law
884–5
relational contracting 66
termination rights 895
traditional contract law and
presentation 884–5
transaction cost approach
889–94
behavioural assumptions 891
classical and neoclassical
contract law 890
dimensionalizing 891–2
governance structures
892–4
relational contracting 891
three-way classification of
contracts 890–1
Losses
avoidable, and mitigation of
damages 651–6
chance, loss of 276
consequential 369–70, 651
direct physical 1168–70,
1171–2
economic 27, 29, 31, 34, 35
expectation 628, 639
incidental 629
non-pecuniary 673–9, 686
of opportunity 375
'out-of-pocket' 628, 639, 766
profit 630–1
recoverable in tort and
contract, distinction 628
and restitution 43
termination rights 617–21
see also **Damages**

Macaulay, Stewart
on empirical work 81, 82, 83,
786–9
on interpretation 389–92
Macneil, Ian 4, 807
on enforcement 721
on functions of contract law
63–5
on long-term contracts 884–6,
886–9

Mahoney, Paul G. 721–4
Mailbox rule
  acceptance by correspondence
    215
Marginal cost
  defined 79
Maritime Arbitrators'
    Association
  dispute resolution 89
Market governance
  classical contract law 893
Market ideology 58
Market-individualism
  advertisements and displays of
    goods 202
  and consumer-welfarism 61
  and formalism 62
  functions of contract law 57–8
  and realism 62
  static 254
    static and dynamic
      contrasted 255–6
Market order
  autonomy, value of 71, 72
  functions of contract law 66–8
Market place, rule of
  functions of contract law 47, 48
Market principles
  society organized on 54–5
Markets
  informationally-impaired
    961–2
  structurally impaired 959–61
Marriage
  contracts undermining 1073
Marriage consideration
  and exchange 123–5
Matrimonial home
  legal relations, intention to
    create 176–7
  and undue influence 923–37
    policy considerations
      924–5
Mayhew, Henry 646
Mentally disordered persons
  necessaries, supply to 44
  unconscionable bargains
    945–8
Micro-economics 11
Minors
  unconscionable bargains
    951–2
Misrepresentation
  damages for
    availability 370–2
    measure of 372–86
    statutory 377–86

exclusion clauses 1009
fraudulent 319, 356
and inaccurate information
  354–88
innocent
  materiality 357
  and rescission 518, 542
  and statements as terms of
    contract 325
liability, attempts to exclude or
  restrict 386–7
negligent 370, 371
negligent misstatements *see*
  Negligent misstatements
non est factum 318
oral agreements 323
rescission for 346, 355–63
  bars to 363–68
  and consequential loss
    369–70
  court discretion 368–9
  limits to 363–9
  and third parties 357–8, 926
  and undue influence 926
  voidable contracts 42
Mistakes
  actual agreements 302
  actual knowledge of 293
  common *see* **Common**
    mistake
  common law 514–16
  construction technique
    513–4, 517
  and disclosure obligations
    533–5
  equitable 517
  expectation 303–9, 499–520
  identity, as to 309–18
  information as antidote to
    534
  law, applying to facts 516–7
  mutual *see* **Common mistake**
  non est factum 318–20
  quantum meruit claims 509
  rectification 296–301
  restitutionary liability 42
  as to terms 289–96
  unilateral 504, 536–8
    common distinguished
      534, 537–8
  see also **Void contracts;**
    Voidable contracts
Misunderstanding
  as to terms 301–3
Molony Committee
  on consumer goods 999, 1000,
    1003

Money
  forfeiture, paid subject to
    702–3
  non-payment 671–2
Monopolies
  and contract law 10
  marginal cost 79–80
  market-wide 961
  regulated contracts 1061
  situational 959–61
Monopolies and Mergers
    Commission
  and restraint of trade 1110
Moral hazard
  damages, ex ante
    determination 697
  information asymmetries 460
Moral obligation
  consideration 139–43
  contractual liability 21
  of promises 778–9
Morality
  recovery of payments or
    property 1097–8
Mortgages
  unconscionable bargains
    938–9
Motor vehicles
  contracts to build and sell
    117–9
Mutual mistakes *see* **Common**
    mistake

Napier, B. W. 449–54
National Consumer Council
  on litigation rates 90
'Necessities'
  regulated contracts 1055–6
Negation by circumstances
  oral contracts 342–4
Negative benefits
  privity of contract 1153–62
Negligence
  careless statements 25, 27–8
  development risk defence 26
  and duty of care 24
  exclusion clauses 1004–7
  indeterminancy thesis 797
  physical injury caused by 27
  by professionals 30, 31
  and special relationship
    between parties
      36, 38
  statutory definition 1004
Negligent misstatement
  damages 371
  tort, liability in 28, 29, 31

Negotiable instruments
  bills of exchange as 1197–8
  cheques as 1198–9
  promissory notes as 100–1,
    1198
Negotiations
  post-breach 718–20
Neighbour principle
  and duty of care 24, 27
Neo-formalism
  and relational contracts 811
Neoclassical contract law
  discrete transactions 887
  flexibility in long-term
    contractual relations
    887–8
  and functions of contract
    law 63
  longer-term contracts,
    planning flexibility into
    887–8
  planning and flexibility needs,
    conflict 888–9
  and relational approach 809
  transaction cost approach 890
  trilateral governance 893
Nichomachean Ethics (Aristotle)
  823
Nominalism
  and economic analysis 784–5
Non est factum
  duress 909
  mistakes 318–20
Non-performance of contract
  anticipatory breach 581–8
  breach of contract 551
    anticipatory 581–8
    see also **Breach of contract**
  conditions
    notion 551–3
    in options 581
    and order of performance
     553–5
    in unilateral contracts 581
    and warranties 564–6
  consumers, policy for 595–6
  flexible approach 566–73
    or certainty 592–8
  forfeiture, relief against
    588–92
  goods
    non-conforming, breach
     and remedy for tender
     592–4
    sale and supply of 594–5
  non-consumers, policy for
    596–8

obligations
  entire and severable
    556–9
  entire, partial performance
    559–64
  time stipulations 573–80
    time not of essence
     574–80
    time of essence 574, 609,
     610
  'total non-performance rule'
    984, 987
  see also **Performance**
Norms
  and quasi-contracts 794
Northern Ireland
  Privity of contract 1191
Nozick, Robert 816–8
Nuisance
  and consideration doctrine
    105

Objective principle
  offer and acceptance 192–5
Obligations
  contractus and *delictus* 824
  entire and severable 556–9
  partial performance, effect
    559–64
  primary and secondary 612–13
  and promises 771–0
Offer and acceptance 191–257
  advertisements and displays of
    goods 199–202
  auctions 202–4
  choice by offeree 221
  correspondence 195–8
  exchange of contracts 240–2
  finding an offer 214
  and freedom of contract 47
  notification to offeror 221
  objective principle 192–5
  offers to public, contracts
    distinguished 15
  preliminary negotiations or
    offer 195–204
    advertisements and displays
     of goods 199–202
    auctions 202–4
    correspondence 195–8
  proposals 222–30
  tenders 242–57
    market-individualism
     255–6
  Uniform Commercial Code
    228
  see also **Acceptance**

Offer or preliminary negotiations
  advertisements and displays of
    goods 199–202
  auctions 202–4
  correspondence 195–8
'Officious bystander' test
  implied terms 418, 419
  legal relations, intention to
    create 180
Ogus, Anthony 681–6
Oligopolies
  regulated contracts 1061
Opinion
  statements of 323
    misrepresentation 359
Opportunities forgone
  and cost 75
Options
  conditions in 581
  pricing and contract remedies
    721–4
Oral agreements
  damages 331–2
  enforceability 143
  incorporation of written terms
    into
    common understanding
     340–1
    course of dealing 339–40
    negation by circumstances
     342–4
    reasonable notice 332–9
    tickets, as mere receipts
     334, 335
  intentions of parties 323
  and interpretation 399
  misrepresentation 323
  promises
    matter promised 328–32
    'puffs' distinguished 323
  statements of fact and opinion
    323
  warranties 329–30

Paretianism
  defined 834
Parol evidence rule 349–53
  applicable contracts 350
  and interpretation 399
  'merger' or 'integration' clauses
    349
  rectification 352
Parties
  identity of 1141–2
  intentions of *see* **Intentions of**
    parties
  repudiation by one 734–8

Parties (*cont.*)
  risk born by one party 467–73
  special relationship between,
    and liability in tort 36, 38
  third *see* Third parties
Partner-freedom principle
  individualist ideology 58
Paternalism
  consumer-welfarism 59
  economic efficiency, and
    distributive justice
    1062–3
  judgment and moral
    imagination 1064
  personal integrity 1063–4
  in regulated contracts
    1061–4
Patterning
  distributive justice 816–7
  and liberty 817–8
Patterson, E. 554–5
Penalty clauses
  building contracts 111
  damages 692
  and damages, ex ante
    determination 697–8
  efficiency implications 696
Penalty clauses
  forfeiture, relief against 592
Penalty defaults
  sale of goods contracts,
    implied terms 433–5
Penny, Michael 875–9
Perdue, William R. 626–9,
    765–9
  Craswell on 769–70
Performance
  acceptance by 221
  of contractual duty owed to
    promisor 109–15
  direct determination of, by
    third parties 888
  of duty imposed by contract,
    with third party 107–9
  of duty imposed by law 105–7
  effect where offer invites either
    performance or promise
    221–2
  by offeree, where offer invites
    either performance or
    promise 221
  order of, and conditions
    553–5
  partial, of entire obligation
    559–64
  specific *see* Specific performance
  substitute 684–6

time stipulations 573–80
  'frustrating'
    time/'reasonable' time
    574–5
  services, contracts for 447
  time not of essence 574–80
  time of essence 574, 609, 610
withholding
  breach of contract 551
  certainty or flexibility
    592–8
  conditions *see* Conditions
  entire and severable
    obligations 556–59
  flexible approach 566–73
  forfeiture, relief against
    588–92
  and gap-filling 550
  partial performance of
    entire obligation, effect
    559–64
  rights and remedies 548
  time stipulations 447,
    573–80
  unilateral contracts 581
  see also Non-performance of
    contract
Perverting course of justice
  public policy, contracts
    contrary to 1073
Phillips, Jennifer 683–8
Physical injury
  liability in tort and contract
    37–8
  and negligence 27
Planning
  and autonomy 830–1
  creation of exchange
    relationships 390
  and empirical work 82
  flexibility needs, conflict with
    888–9
  remedies 549
  standardized 391
Plant, hiring of
  specimen contracts 1216–19
Polanyi, Karl 55
Policy statements
  in shops 18–9
Pollock, Frederick 99, 173
Poor and ignorant persons
  unconscionable bargains
    939–45, 952
Posner, Richard A.
  on economics of contract law
    73–80, 81, 393–7, 639–40,
    645–9, 688–9

  on gratuitous promises 136–9,
    140–1, 142–3, 857–60
  on implied terms 393–7, 456
  on penalties 697
  on risk aversion 396–7, 460
Pothier, Robert-Joseph 9
Pound, Dean 759
Preliminary contracts 271–80
  binding force 278
  lockout agreements 272, 273,
    275
  restitutionary liability 41
  statements of claim 273, 274
Preliminary negotiations, or
    offer
  advertisements and displays of
    goods 199–202
  auctions 202–4
  correspondence 195–8
Premises
  defective construction 26–7,
    31, 32–4
  quality standards, implied
    terms 440–3
  statutory controls 1032–3
  liability of builders 36
Pretium affectionis
  defined 684
Price
  action for 733
  and delivery, as concurrent
    conditions 554
  door-to-door sales 822
  and equality 824–6
  open 270
  options pricing and contract
    remedies 721–4
  price-ignorance 821–2
  reasonableness 435
  and Roman law 259
Priest, George 592–4
Private law adjudication
  and critique of contract
    law 791
  functions of contract
    law 49–53
Privileging
  and critical contract law 796,
    800
Privity of contract 1136–94
  and agency 1194
  arbitration provisions 1190–1
  basic rule 1136–43
  beneficiaries 1182–3
  and burdens 1200–6
  damages on behalf of another
    1143–50

defences and joinder 1187
'double intention test' 1192
double liability, protection
    from 1189
enforceable benefit, test of
    1185–6
enforcement of contract by
    promissee 1189
incidental benefit, effect of
    promise 1183
indemnity, circles of 1174–8
Law Commission on reform
    1183–7
legislative changes 26
and liability in tort 1204
    contract restricting liability
        1167–74
    tort as substitute for
        contract 1162–7
negative benefits or vicarious
    immunity 1153–62
and negligence 25
Northern Ireland 1191
promissee, action by 1187
and property 1204–6
qualifications to rule
    statutory exceptions
        1152–3
    trusts 1150–1
range of benefits 1186–7
reform 1178–94
    beneficiaries 1182–3
    incidental benefit, effect of
        promise 1183
    specific performance
        1182
specific performance 1182
third parties 1187
United States 1182
variation and rescission of
    contract 1188

Product liability
consumer protection 26
dangerous products 31
defective products 27
    and dangerous products
        32, 33–4
manufacturers' liability 36

Profit
and cost 76
loss of, in damages claims
    630–1

Promises
absence of express words 17,
    18
act done in reliance on, as
    consideration 165–70

frontier between
    promissory estoppel and
    unilateral contracts 166–9
binding nature of 757–83
    morally and legally binding
        757
contract as 778–83
and contractual liability 13–4
in deeds 23
enforceability 8
extension of credit for
    performance 555
family and social
    arrangements 99–100
fresh, and fresh contracts 140
gratuitous
    economics of 136–7
    legal formalities, functions
        performed by 133–5
    optimal rules for enforcing
        137–8
inaccurate information treated
    as 542
incidental benefit 1183
informal gifts 130
legal commitments, not
    intended as 16
and legal relations, intention to
    create 182
moral obligation of 778–9
non-bargain, reliance on
    146–73
    estoppel, as substitute for
        consideration 148–64
    promissory estoppel and
        unilateral contracts
        (frontier between) 166–9
non-contractual 161
and obligations 771–8
oral agreements 328–32
petitio principii 766
'puffs' distinguished 14–5,
    16, 323
sanctity of 759
and statements of fact 150
unilateral 153
value 779–81

Promissory estoppel
and equity 156
non-bargain promises, reliance
    on 160, 161
objective and current role
    807–9
and proprietary estoppel 874
relational approach 809–10
and unilateral contracts,
    frontier 166–9

factual difficulty of defining
    frontier 167–8
policy arguments for
    maintaining frontier
    167–8
unnecessary nature of
    frontier 168–9
work done prior to contract
    agreement 282

Promissory notes
as negotiable instruments
    100–1, 1198

Property
damage to
    liability in tort and contract
        37–8
    liability in tort, limiting
        1171
deterioration, and rescission
    367–8
implied terms, in contracts
    415–20
incompleteness of law 268–70
privity of contract 1204–6
recovery of 1094–1104
    dignity of court 1097
    locus poenitentiae 1095–6,
        1103
    morality 1097–8
    public policy 1098
    statutory protection 36
    weaker parties 1094–5

Proportionality principle
consumer-welfarism 59

Proprietary claims
illegal contracts and limited
    interests 1100–1
recovery of payments or
    property 1099–1104

Proprietary estoppel
and contract 163, 164
and equity 156
and promissory estoppel 872
reliance damages 631

Proximity
and duty of care 31, 32, 36

Public policy
contracts contrary to 1069–78
    corruption in public life
        1073
    discrimination, promoting
        1074
    foreign affairs, contracts
        adversely affecting 1073
    honours, selling of 1073
    information, concealing
        1074

Public policy (*cont.*)
 marriage, contracts
  undermining 1073
 perverting course of justice
  1073
 restraint of trade 1072
 Revenue, agreements
  defrauding 1074
 sexual immorality, contracts
  involving 1073
 heads of 1072–7
 'policy'/policy issues 1069,
  1078
 recovery of payments or
  property 1098
 sexual immorality, contracts
  involving 1073
'Puffs'
 promises distinguished 14–5,
  16, 323
Purpose
 frustration by 473–9

Quality
 defects of 33–4
***Quantum meruit* claims**
 damages, alternative to 743,
  744, 745
 expectation mistakes 509
 frustration of contract 463
 restitution and contract 39
 restitutionary or contractual
  liability 42
 unilateral contracts,
  acceptance in 219
 withholding of performance
  558
 work done prior to contract
  agreement 281
Quasi-contracts 793–4
 restitutionary liability 41
 see also **Restitution**

Ramsay, Iain 91
Realism
 judicial ideologies 57, 60–1
 and market-individualism 62
Reasonable notice
 oral contracts 332–9
Reasonableness
 consumer-welfarism 58
 exclusion clauses 1010–31
 guidelines for application of
  test 1011
 prices 435
 private agreements, terms 814
 restraint of trade 1107, 1114

 as standard 50
 unfair contracts, United
  Kingdom and Europe
  1028–31
Reciprocity
 and behavioural patterns 66
Recovery
 basic measure, for damages
  623–44
 of payments or property
  locus poenitentiae 1095–8,
   1103
  weaker parties 1094–95
 principle of, frustration of
  contracts 486–7
Rectification
 communication mistakes
  296–301
 parol evidence rule 352
Regulated contracts 1055–65
 anti-competitive arrangements
  1061
 economic efficiency, and
  distributive justice
  1062–3
 human rights issues 1065
 inadequate information
  1056–8
  Passenger Acts 1056–7
 judgment and moral
  imagination 1064
 long-term relationships,
  vulnerability to
  exploitation 1058–9
 monopolies 1061
 'necessities', in short supply
  1055–6
 oligopolies 1061
 paternalism 1061–4
 personal integrity 1063–5
 private enforcement costs,
  excessive nature
  1059–61
 transaction costs, problems
  1058
Reiter, Barry J. 54–7
Relational contracts 807–12
 characteristics 64
 employment contract as
  example of 455
 long-term relationships 66
 neo-formalism 811
 and presentation 885–6
 promissory estoppel
  objective and current role
   807–9
  relational approach 809–10

 sociology, relational contract
  theory as 63–5, 807
 transaction-specific
  governance 893–4
Reliance
 and contract damages 765
 and damages 626–29, 641–3
 detrimental 872
 diversity within reliance cases
  769–70
 efficient level of 214
 essential 768
 incidental 768
 privity of contract, and
  liability in tort 1172
 recognition 170–3
 tort, contract restricting
  liability in 1172
Reliance interest
 damages 627
Remedies
 blanket orders, and American
  contract law 119
 and consumer surplus 683–8
  loss of, damages assessment
   687
 consumers 91
 damages *see* **Damages**
 expressly planned 549
 formal, and informal bargains
  687–8
 judicial, and self-help 549
 and likelihood of default 76
 off-the-shelf 549
 restitutionary
  'efficient breach fallacy'
   747–50
  unjust enrichment 742–53
 and rights 547–8
 self-help 549
 specific performance *see*
  Specific performance
Repudiation of contracts
 action for sums due 734–8
 anticipatory breach 581–8,
  656
Requirement contracts
 cars, contracts to build and sell
  117–9
 consideration 116–21
***Res judicata* principle**
 and compensation payments
  866
Rescission
 concept 846
 and consequential loss
  369–70

limits to
  bars to rescission 363–8
  court discretion 368–9
  for misrepresentation 346,
      355–63
  innocent 542
  or variation 851
  third party rights 1188
Reservation of title clauses
  action for sums due 733
Responsibility for fault principle
  consumer-welfarism 59
Restitution
  absence of defence condition
      41, 44
  benefit of defendant condition
      41, 42, 43
  and contract 39–45
  and damages 743
  and frustration of contracts 481
  illegal contracts 42, 44
  and reliance interest 765
  subjective devaluation
      argument 42
  unjust enrichment
    by subtraction 742–5
    by wrongdoing 745–53
  unjust enrichment condition
      44
  see also Quasi contracts
Restitution interest
  damages 627–8
Restraint of trade 1105–23
  'blue pencil' provisions 1120
  covenant in
    categories of covenants
      1106
    reasonableness 1107
    recognised categories of
      1106
    void 1119–20
  'exclusive dealing contracts'
      1111
  public interest 1114
  public policy, contrary to
      1072
  reasonableness 1107, 1114
  recognised categories of
      covenant 1106
  'solus agreements' 1110
  unconscionability, economic
      approach 1116–20
  unconscionable bargains
      952–3
  unreasonable 1117
  void covenants, and effectiveness
      of deed 1119–20

Restrictive Practices Court
  and restraint of trade 1108
Revocable commercial credits
  and consideration doctrine
      121–2
Rhetoric
  and critical contract law 797, 801
Rights
  and remedies 547–8
  termination 598–611
Risk
  born by one party 467–73
  distribution of 762–3
  frustration of contract
      459–63, 467–73
  juridical 964
  risk-sharing/diversification
      justification
      impossibility 459–63
Risk aversion
  damages, ex ante
      determination 697
  interpretation 396–7
'Romalpa' clauses
  action for sums due 733
Roman law
  application in English law 474
  and contract law 9
  error, doctrine of 500
  price 259
Rosenfeld, Andrew 393–7, 460
Rudden, B. 1197–9
Rules
  contract as authoritative
      source of 452–3
  contract as dynamic body of
      8–10
  critique of argument for 50–1
  fixed, of contract law 47
  and formal realizability 50, 51
  versus formalities 50
  jurisprudence 50–4
  and standards 50, 53
  unlawful acts 1081–83
  wrongful behaviour, designed
      to deter 50

Sale of goods
  action for price 733
  anticipatory breach 587–8
  auctions 202
  capacity to buy and sell,
      mentally disordered
      persons 945
  contract for
    'default' rules 431–7
    description and quality of

goods 427–39
  implied terms 425–46
  quality or fitness of goods
      428
  sample, sale by 428–9
  title, implied terms as to
      426–7
damages 624
'dealing as a customer', defined
    997
'default' rules *see* 'Default'
    rules, sale or supply of
    goods contracts
delivery *see* Delivery of goods
  by description 427, 429–30
  door-to-door sales 822
  efficient defaults
    amount of efficiency 436–7
    normative appeal 435–6
  exclusion clauses 996–1003
  FOB sales contract 1235–40
  'immutable' rules 432
  implied terms 425–46
    alteration, as to quality 437
    'default' rules 431–7
    delivery 439–40
    description and quality of
        goods 427–39
    quality or fitness 428, 437,
        440–6
    title 426–27
  incompleteness 263, 268
  inertia selling 210
  non-performance 594–5
  price
    action for 733
    and equality 824–6
    price-ignorance 820–2
  quality or fitness
    alteration of implied terms
        437
    implied terms 428
    merchantable quality 430
    standard of liability 440–6
    suitable for purpose 430–1
    unfair contract terms 443
  by sample 428–9
  specific performance 711
  uncertainty or incompleteness
      258
  void contracts 501, 502
Salvage agreements
  unconscionable bargains
      948–9
Sanctity of contract
  individualist ideology 58
Schwartz, Alan 716–21

Seal
promises under 137–8
Second best
economics of 78
Self-interest
economic analysis of contract
law 75
and individualism 51
Services, contracts for
implied terms 446–9
care and skill 447
consideration 447
contracts concerned 446–7
time for performance 447
Severance
illegal contracts 1104
Sexual immorality
public policy, contracts
contrary to 1073
Shand, J. 1092
Sharing and sacrifice
altruism ideal 52
Shavell, Steven M. 643–4
Ships, contracts relating to *see*
Vessels, contracts
relating to
Shops
displays of goods in, and offers
201
policy statements in 18–9
Signature, effect
written contracts 345–8
Silence
acceptance by 213
Smith, Stephen Alexander
829–31, 915–16
Solidarity
and behavioural patterns 66
Sovereignty
and contract 763–4
Specific performance
'arrival rate' 717
case for 716–21
and damages 290, 684, 686
'developed' and 'undeveloped'
markets 717
as discretionary remedy 729
and inadequate consideration
710
and injunctions 709–32
personal services contracts
728, 729
post-breach negotiations
718–20
privity of contract 1182
sale of goods 711
uniqueness test 714, 715

Spencer, J. R. 346–7
Spirit of Roman Law (von
Ihering) 50
Spouses
and undue influence 926–8
Standard form contracts 964–74
adhesion, contracts of 964–5
buyer's order 1209–12
control, case for 966, 966–7
exclusion clauses 1007–9
see also **Exclusion clauses**
'exploitation theory' 965
information problems 969–72
institutional change 967–8
sales quotations, specimen
1213–5
specimens 1209–12
take-it-or-leave it basis 969
unconscionability
distributive considerations
972–3
economic approach
968–74
and unconscionable conduct
968–73
unfair terms in 975
Standards
and rules 50, 53
Statements of fact
interpretation 19
and promises 150
terms, representations and
puffs 323
Statements of opinion 323
Structurally impaired markets
informationally-impaired
961–2
market-wide monopolies 961
situational monopolies 959–61
Subcontractors
assignment of subcontracts
1207
liability of 26, 32–33, 1164–5
Substantial performance
doctrine
and partial performance, effect
560, 562, 563
Substitute performance
damages assessment 684–6
Subtraction
unjust enrichment by 742–5
Sykes, Allen 459–60

Tenders
bid bonds 243, 251
front-end loading 247
market-individualism 255–6

non-conforming goods 592–4
offer and acceptance 242–57
open procedure 247
restricted procedure 247
Term-freedom principle
individualist ideology 58
Termination of contracts 594–8
anticipatory breach 581–8
and breach of condition 567
by construction 521–8
default notice 589
by frustration *see* **Frustration**
of contract
insolvency of contractor 603
loss of rights 615–9
nature 611–5
repudiation for anticipatory
breach 581–8, 656
rights agreed 598–611
longer-term contracts 895
rights and remedies 548
see also **Performance:**
withholding
Terms
adjustment to
concepts 846–7
contingencies 845
discharge or variation
847–60
longer-term contracts *see*
Long-term contracts
see also **Discharge of**
contract; Variation of
contract
innominate,
conditions/warranties
distinguished 570–1
mistakes as to 289–96
misunderstanding as to 301–3
in oral agreements 323–44
private agreements 812
Teubner, Gunther 1049–50
Third parties
contracts with, performance
of duty imposed by
107–9
direct determination of
performance 888
and exemption clauses 1194
and misrepresentation 357–8,
926
privity of contract 1187, 1190
reinstatement by, damages
assessment 684–6
rights
arbitration provisions
1190–1

defences available to
promisor 1189
double liability, protection
from 1189
enforcement by promisee
1189
enforcement of contractual
term 1187–8
exceptions 1189–90
variation and cancellation
1193
variation and rescission of
contract 1188
and undue influence 926
Time orders
and hardship relief 495–6
Tort
complex structure theory
34–5, 37
and contract 24–39
implied terms 422
preliminary contracts 277
recoverable losses 628
remoteness of damage
650–1
as substitute for tort
1162–7
contract restricting liability
bill of lading contracts
1172–3
reliance 1172
contract restricting liability in
1167–74
contracts requiring deliberate
commission of 1079–80
dangerous products 31, 33–4
defective premises 26–27,
32–4
direct physical loss 1171–2
distributive and paternalist
motives 835–6
duty of care
existence of 1171
foreseeability of damage 32
imposition of as fair, just
and reasonable 1174
neighbour principle 24, 27
proximity considerations
31, 32, 36
and foreseeability of damage
648–9
fraud, liability in 38
health or safety, imminent
danger to 35–6
liability in contract and tort
37–8
losses recoverable in 628

motives, distributive and
paternalistic 835–6
negligent misstatements 28,
29, 31
physical damage cases 1171
and privity 1162–74, 1204
remoteness rule 650
responsibility, assumption of
1174
as substitute for contract
1162–7
see also **Dispute resolution**
Transaction cost approach
behavioural assumptions 891
classical contract law 890
dimensionalizing 891–2
examples 77
governance structures 892–4
incompleteness 432
longer-term contracts 889–94
neoclassical contract law 890
regulated contracts 1058
relational contracting 891
and specific performance 723
three-way classification of
contracts 890–1
Transaction-specific governance
relational contracting 893–4
Transformation thesis 838–41
co-operation 840–1
contextual legal reasoning 841
fairness of exchange 839–40
functions of contract law
68–72
regulatory perspective 841
unjustifiable domination
838–9
Trebilcock, Michael J.
on general doctrine 959–62
on restraint of trade 1116–20
on standard-form contracts
968–73
on statutory controls 1001
on waiver 875–9
Treitel, G. H. 551
Trilateral governance
neoclassical contract law 893
Trusts
privity rule qualifications
1150–1

Uberimmae fidei **contracts**
construction, discharge of
contract by 530–1
UCC *see* **Uniform Commercial
Code**
Ulen, Thomas 535–38, 641–3

Uncertainty 259–63
consensus ad idem 261
fair specification standards
260, 261
hire purchase agreements
261–62
inflation 523
meaningless clauses and clauses
yet to be agreed 263
Unconscionability
critical reappraisal 813–5
distributive considerations
972–3
economic approach 968–74
restraint of trade 1116–20
informationally-impaired
markets 961–2
and misrepresentation 356
principle of 820–1
restitutionary liability 42
transactions 955
Unconscionable bargains
consumer credit
cancellable agreements 949
cooling-off period 949
extortionate credit bargains
950–1
see also **Consumer credit**
minors 951–2
mortgages 938–9
poor and ignorant persons,
and expectant heirs
939–45, 952
restraint of trade 952–3
salvage agreements 948–9
striking out of 338
Undisclosed principal
and agency 1132–5
Undue influence
'abuse of confidence' 922
actual 917, 922
classes of 955
disclosure 532
general principles 955, 957
and independent advice
931–2
manifest disadvantage 932
and matrimonial home 923–37
policy considerations
924–5
misrepresentation, and third
parties 926
notice, doctrine of 926, 927
presumed 916–8
restitutionary liability 42
and undue pressure 917–37
wives 926–8, 929

Undue pressure
examples 955
Unenforceable contracts
and requirement contracts
116
restitutionary liability 45
see also **Illegal contracts; Void
contracts; Voidable
contracts**
Unfair terms
assessment 1037
written contracts 1038
burden of proof 1042
choice of law clauses 1038
co-evolving trajectories
1052–4
in consumer contracts
1035–54
choice of law clauses 1038
complaints-consideration
1038
European contract law
1045–9
good faith principle
1049–54
Regulations 1036–45
definitions 1037
Director, powers of 1039
divergent production regimes
1051–2
effect 1038
European contract law
consumers' economic
interests 1046–9
scope 1045
good faith, assessment 1043
injunctions to prevent
continued use 1038–9
legal transplant metaphor
1049
list of terms possibly regarded
as unfair 1040–1106
powers to obtain documents
and information 1039–40
'significant imbalance' 1043
standard form contracts 975
written contracts 1038
see also **Exclusion clauses**
Unfairness 829–31, 1247
and contractual imbalance
946
duress 901
oral agreements 338
substantive 829–31
versus procedural 901
test of, in consumer contracts
1043

unfair contracts, United
Kingdom and Europe
1027–31
see also **Fairness**
**UNIDROIT Principles of
International
Commercial Contracts**
binding nature of contract
896
change in circumstances,
relevance only
exceptional cases 896
and contract law 9
frustration of contract 493
hardship 895
offer and acceptance 229
Unified governance
relational contracting 893–4
Uniform Commercial Code
assurance of performance,
right to 588
contract modifications 878
default rule theory 433, 435
duress 914–5
incompleteness 270–1
offer and acceptance 228
**Uniform Customs and Practice
for Documentary
Credits**
and irrevocable commercial
credits 121
Unilateral contracts
acceptance in 215–20
conditions in, and withholding
of performance 581
and consideration doctrine 98
definitions 23
offer and acceptance 218
and promissory estoppel,
frontier 166–9
factual difficulty of defining
frontier 167
policy arguments for
maintaining frontier
167–8
unnecessary nature of
frontier 168–9
Unitary theory
and nature of contract law 5
United Kingdom
British Standards Institution
447
disclosure law 532
good faith principle, adoption
by British law 9–10,
1049–54
labour law 449–54

Roman law, application in
English law 474
United States
disclosure law 532
interpretation of contracts
403
neo-formalism 811
privity doctrine 1182
reliance loss, claiming 629
Wisconsin Supreme Court 85,
86–8
Unjust enrichment
consumer-welfarism 59
and frustration of contract
743
frustration of contract, effect
487, 491
restitutionary liability 41, 44
as standard 50
by subtraction 742–5
by wrongdoing 745–53
Unlawful acts
contract expressly or implicitly
forbidden by statute
1083–6
contracts intended to be
performed in illegal way
1086
contracts performed in illegal
manner 1086–7
deliberate, benefits from
1088–1192
outline of rules 1081–3
three-stage test 1082–3
Utility
and wealth 75

Vagueness of contracts
and liability 15
Variation of contract
concept 846
ICE conditions of contract
881
or discharge 847–60
or rescission and replacement
851
or waiver 868–9
and privity of contract 1188
third party rights 1188
Vertical integration
and long-term contracts 891
Vessels, contracts relating to
action for sums due 740
Baltime 1939 time charter
567, 1224–9
classification societies
1170–4

contract with shipowners
1173
damages 637
mitigation 655
dispute resolution 89
foreseen events 479–81
Hague-Visby Rules 1058,
1172, 1220
interpretation of contracts
401, 405
'off-hire' clauses 567
policy considerations 1173
salvage agreements 948–9
seaworthiness clauses 573, 580
and termination of contracts,
waiver of 566
see also **Bill of lading contracts**
Vicarious immunity
force of 1157
privity of contract 1153–62
'Vitiation of contract' test
duress 913

Void contracts
frustration 518
mistake 392, 499, 507, 513
sale of goods contracts 501,
502
Voidable contracts
and duress 903
and fraud 367
and mistake 392, 511
restitutionary liability 42
Von Ihering, Rudolph 50

Waiver 860–79
concept 846
or variation 868–9
Warranties
absence of express words 17, 18
breach of 426
collateral 27, 329–30
and conditions 564–6
legal meaning 19
oral agreements 324, 329–30

Wilhelmsson, Thomas 493–6
Will theory of contract 758,
759–60, 766
and privity 1184
Williamson, Oliver E.
889–95
Wives
and undue influence 926–8,
929
Words
acceptance by 204–8
'Would have wanted' approach
implied terms 432
Written contracts
compulsory, when 143–4
contents
parol evidence rule 349–53
signature, effect of 345–8
evidence of 144
unfair terms 1038
Wrongful behaviour
deterrence 50